AMERICAN WRITERS

AMERICAN WRITERS

JAY PARINI
Editor

SUPPLEMENT XXII

CHARLES SCRIBNER'S SONS
A part of Gale, Cengage Learning

Detroit • New York • San Francisco • New Haven, Conn • Waterville, Maine • London

American Writers Supplement XXII

Editor in Chief: Jay Parini

Project Editor: Lisa Kumar

Permissions: Leitha Etheridge-Sims

Composition and Electronic Capture: Gary Leach

Manufacturing: Cynde Lentz

Publisher: Jim Draper

Product Manager: Philip J. Virta

LIBRARY OF CONGRESS CATALOGING-IN-PUBLICATION DATA

American writers: a collection of literary biographies / Leonard Unger, editor in chief.
p. cm.
The 4-vol. main set consists of 97 of the pamphlets originally published as the University of Minnesota pamphlets on American writers; some have been rev. and updated. The supplements cover writers not included in the original series.
Supplement 2, has editor in chief, A. Walton Litz; Retrospective suppl. 1, c1998, was edited by A. Walton Litz & Molly Weigel; Suppl. 5–7 have as editor-in-chief, Jay Parini.
Includes bibliographies and index.
Contents: v. 1. Henry Adams to T.S. Eliot — v. 2. Ralph Waldo Emerson to Carson McCullers — v. 3. Archibald MacLeish to George Santayana — v. 4. Isaac Bashevis Singer to Richard Wright — Supplement\[s\]: 1, pt. 1. Jane Addams to Sidney Lanier. 1, pt. 2. Vachel Lindsay to Elinor Wylie. 2, pt. 1. W.H. Auden to O. Henry. 2, pt. 2. Robinson Jeffers to Yvor Winters. — 4, pt. 1. Maya Angelou to Linda Hogan. 4, pt. 2. Susan Howe to Gore Vidal — Suppl. 5. Russell Banks to Charles Wright — Suppl. 6. Don DeLillo to W. D. Snodgrass — Suppl. 7. Julia Alvarez to Tobias Wolff — Suppl. 8. T.C. Boyle to August Wilson. — Suppl. 11 Toni Cade Bambara to Richard Yates.
ISBN 978-0-684-31596-6
1. American literature—History and criticism. 2. American literature—Bio-bibliography. 3. Authors, American—Biography. I. Unger, Leonard. II. Litz, A. Walton. III. Weigel, Molly. IV. Parini, Jay. V. University of Minnesota pamphlets on American writers.

PS129 .A55
810'.9
\[B\] 73-001759

ISBN-13: 978-1-4144-8024-4
ISBN-10: 1-4144-8024-5

Charles Scribner's Sons an imprint of Gale, Cengage Learning
27500 Drake Rd.
Farmington Hills, MI, 48331-3535

Printed in Mexico
1 2 3 4 5 6 7 15 14 13 12 11

Acknowledgments

Acknowledgment is gratefully made to those publishers and individuals who permitted the use of the following material in copyright. Every effort has been made to secure permission to reprint copyrighted material.

ARNA BONTEMPS. From *Anyplace But Here.* Hill and Wang, 1966. Copyright © 1945, 1966 by Arna Bontemps and Jack Conroy. Reproduced by permission. / From *Personals.* Paul Breman, 1973. © Arna Bontemps 1963. Reproduced by permission. / From *Personals.* Paul Breman, 1973. © Arna Bontemps 1963. Reproduced by permission of Harold Ober Associates Incorporated. / "Youth" from *The Collected Poems of Langston Hughes* by Langston Hughes, edited by Arnold Rampersad with David Rooessel, Associate Editor, copyright © 1994 by the Estate of Langston Hughes. Used by permission of Alfred A. Knopf, a division of Random House, Inc. and by permission of Harold Ober Associates.

AGNES BOULTON. From "Letter to Peggy Conklin" 1958. Reproduced by permission from the Estate of Agnes Boulton. / King, William Davies. From *Another Part of a Long Story: Literary Traces of Eugene O'Neill and Agnes Boulton.* The University of Michigan Press, 2010. Reproduced by permission of the University of Michigan Press.

KEVIN BROCKMEIER. From *Publishers Weekly.* Pwxyz, 2002. Copyright 2002 Reed Business Information. Reproduced from Publishers Weekly, published by the PWxyz, LLC, by permission. / O'Malley, Anne. From *Booklist.* American Library Association, 2002. Copyright 2002 American Library Association. Reproduced by permission. / E. Knight, Elaine. From *School Library Journal.* 2002. Copyright 2002 Reed Business Information. Reproduced by permission. / Brockmeier, Kevin. From *The Truth About Celia.* Vintage, 2003. Copyright © 2003 by Kevin Brockmeier. Reproduced by permission. / Brockmeier, Kevin . From *The Brief History of the Dead.* Pantheon Books, 2006. Copyright © 2006 by Kevin Brockmeier. Reproduced by permission. / Gevers, Nick. From *Locus: The Magazine of the Science Fiction and Fantasy Field.* Locus Publicatons, 2006. Reproduced by permission. / From *Kirkus Reviews. 2008. Copyright © 2008 Kirkus Media. All rights reserved. Reproduced by permission. / Cheney, Matthew. From Real Unreal: Best American Fantasy Volume 3.* Underwood Press, 2010. Copyright © Underland Press 2010. Reproduced by permission. / Brockmeier, Kevin . From *Real Unreal: Best American Fantasy Volume 3.* Underwood Press, 2010. Copyright © Underland Press 2010. Reproduced by permission.

MICHELLE CLIFF. Palmer Adisa, Opal. From *African American Review.* 1994. © 1994 Opal Palmer Adisa. Reproduced by permission.

LARRY HEINEMANN. Heinemann, Larry. From *Paco's Story.* Vintage Books, 2005. Copyright © 1986, 2005 by Larry Heinemann. Reproduced by permission. / Heinemann, Larry. From *Black Virgin Mountain.* Vintage Books, 2006. Copyright © 2005 by Larry Heinemann. Reproduced by permission.

MINA LOY. "English Rose," "Exodus," "Love Songs to Joannes," "Parturition," "Three Moments in Paris." From *The Last Lunar Baedeker.* The Jargon Society, 1982. Works of Mina Loy copyright © 1996 by the Estate of Mina Loy. Introduction and edition copyright © 1996 by Roger L. Conover. Reprinted by permission of Farrar, Straus and Giroux, LLC.

ACKNOWLEDGMENTS

CAROLINE MILLER. Lewis, Sinclair. From *Lamb in His Bosom.* Harper's, 1933. Reproduced by permission. / MacAfee, Helen. From *Saturday Review of Literature.* Book Review Digest, 1933. Reproduced by permission. / Kronenberger, Louis. From *New York Times Book Review.* 1933. Reproduced by permission. / unknown. From Time. Time Inc., 1933. Reproduced by permission. / Bates Penland, Nell. From *The Atlanta Journal.* October 15, 1933 © 1933 The Atlanta Journal. All rights reserved. Used by permission and protected by the Copyright Laws of the United States. The printing, copying, redistribution, or retransmission of this Content without express written permission is prohibited. / Hansen, Harry. From *New York Herald-Tribune.* 1934. Reproduced by permission. / Selby, John. From *Savannah Morning News.* 1934. Reprinted with permission of the Associated Press. / Stallings, H.A. From *Waycross Journal Herald.* 1934. Reproduced by permission. / Sibley, Celestine. From *The Atlanta Journal-Constitution.* July 15, 1992 © 1992 The Atlanta Journal-Constitution. All rights reserved. Used by permission and protected by the Copyright Laws of the United States. The printing, copying, redistribution, or retransmission of this Content without express written permission is prohibited. / Fox-Genovese, Elizabeth. From *Lamb in His Bosom.* Peachtreee Publisher's, 1993. © 1933, 1960 by Caroline Miller. Reproduced by permission.

HOWARD FRANK MOSHER. LeClair, Thomas. From *Commonweal,* 1977. Reproduced by permission of Commonweal Foundation. / Lehmann-Haupt, Christopher. From *The New York Times,* October 26, 1989. Copyright © 1989 The New York Times. All rights reserved. Used by permission and protected by the Copyright Laws of the United States. The printing, copying, redistribution, or retransmission of this Content without express written permission is prohibited. / Delbanco, Nicholas. From *Writers and Their Craft: Short Stories & Essays on the Narrative.* Wayne State University Press, 1991. Reproduced by permission. / M. Miller, John. From *Deer Camp: Last Light in the Northeast Kingdom.* MIT Press, 1992. © 1992 John M. Miller. Reproduced by permission. / Stegner, Wallace. From *Where the Blue Bird Sings to the Lemonade Springs.* Random House, 1992. Copyright © 1992 by Wallace Stegner. Reproduced by permission. / Hayford, James. From *Notes Left Behind: Last and Selected Poems.* Oriole Books, 1997. © by Helen Hayford. Reproduced by permission. / McNamee, Thomas. From *The New York Times.* 1997. Reproduced by permission. / B. Marlowe, Kimberly. From *New York Times.* 1999. Copyright 1999 The New York Times Company. Reprinted with permission. / Anonymous. From *Virginia Quarterly Review.* Copyright 2003 University of Virginia Reproduced by permission of the publisher. / Hinckley, David. From *New York Daily News.* 2004. Reproduced by permission. / McMichael, Barbara Lloyd. From *The Seattle Times,* July 20, 2007. Reproduced by permission of the author. / DeSilva, Bruce. From *Pittsburgh Tribune-Review.* Copyright 2011 Associated Press. All rights reserved. Reproduced by permission.

ALICE NOTLEY. From *Grave of Light: New and Selected Poems 1970-2005.* Wesleyan University Press, 2005. Copyright © 2005 by Alice Notley. All rights reserved. Reproduced by permission. / From *165 Meeting House Lane.* C Press Publications, 1971. Reproduced by permission. / From *For Frank O'Hara's Birthday.* Street Editions, 1976. Copyright © Alice Notley 1975. Reproduced by permission. / From *A Diamond Necklace.* Frontward Books, 1977. Copyright © Alice Notley 1977. Reproduced by permission. / From *When I Was Alive.* Vehicle Additions, 1980. Copyright © Alice Notley 1980. Reproduced by permission. / From *How Spring Comes.* Toothpaste Press, 1981. Copyright © 1981 by Alice Notley. Reproduced by permission. / From *Sorrento.* Sherwood Press, 1984. Copyright 1984 by Alice Notley. All rights reserved. Reproduced by permission. / From *Margaret & Dusty.* Coffee House Press, 1985. Copyright © 1985 by Alice Notley. All rights reserved. Reproduced by permission. / From *From a Work in Progress.* Dia Art Foundation, 1988. Copyright 1988 Alice Notley. Reproduced by permission. / From *Homer's Art.* Glover Publishing, 1990. © Copyright 1990 by Alice Notley. Reproduced by permission. / From

ACKNOWLEDGMENTS

Close to me & Closer (The Language of Heaven) and Desamere. O Books, 1995. Reproduced by permission. / From *The Descent of Alette.* Penguin Books, 1996. Copyright © Alice Notley, 1992. All rights reserved. Used by permission of Penguin Group (USA) Inc. / From *Mysteries of Small Houses.* Penguin Books, 1998. Copyright © Alice Notley, 1998. All rights reserved. Used by permission of Penguin Group (USA) Inc. / From *Disobedience.* Penguin Books, 2001. Copyright Alice Notley, 2001. All rights reserved. Used by permission of Penguin Group (USA) Inc. / From *From the Beginning.* Owl Press, 2004. Reproduced by permission. / From *Coming After: Essays on Poetry.* University of Michigan Press, 2005. Reproduced by permission of the author. / From *Alma or The Dead Women.* Granary Books, 2006. Copyright © 2006 by Alice Notley. Reproduced by permission. / From *In the Pines.* Penguin Poets, 2007. Copyright Alice Notley, 2007. All rights reserved. Used by permission of Penguin Group (USA) Inc. / Joel Brouwer, "A State of Disobedience," *New York Times Sunday Book Review,* October 14, 2007. Reproduced by permission.

ANNE RIVERS SIDDONS. White, Dana. From *Making of Modern Atlanta.* WPBA-TV, 1991-93. Reproduced by permission from Public Broadcasting Atlanta. / From *The Auburn Plainsman.* 1956. Reproduced by permission. / Rivers Siddons, Anne. From *The Auburn Plainsman.* October 18, 1957. Reproduced by permission. / Copyright "Habersham, West Wesley, Tuxedo and All That" © 1964 by Anne Rivers Siddons. "Habersham, West Wesley, Tuxedo and All That" first appeared in *Atlanta,* Atlanta Chamber of Commerce, v. 4, no. 1 (May 1964). / Peterson, George. From *Creative Loafing Atlanta.* 1987. Reproduced by permission. / Rivers Siddons, Anne. From *Peachtree Road.* HarperTorch, 1988. Copyright © 1988 by Anne Rivers Siddons. Reproduced by permission. / M. Drennen, Eileen. From *Atlanta Journal-Constitution.* August 20, 1989 © 1989 The Atlanta Journal-Constitution. All rights reserved. Used by permission and protected by the Copyright Laws of the United States. The printing, copying, redistribution, or retransmission of this Content without express written permission is prohibited. / Rivers Siddons, Anne. From *Downtown.* HarperTorch, 1994. Copyright © 1994 by Anne Rivers Siddons. Reproduced by permission. / Copyright "Removing The Rose-Colored Glasses" © 2001 by Anne Rivers Siddons "Removing The Rose-Colored Glasses" first appeared in *Atlanta Magazine*, v.41, no. 1, (May 2001).

LEE SIEGEL. Bursey, Jeff. From *A Myth of One's Won: Henry Miller and Lee Siegel.* Reproduced by permission of the author. / Siegel, Lee. From *Letter to Henry Miller.* Reproduced by permission of the author. / LeClair, Tom. "Love and Other Games of Chance from *Book, March-April 2003. Copyright © 2003 West Egg Communications LLC. Used with permission from Sterling Publishing Co., Inc. / Seaman, Donna. From Booklist.* American Library Association, 2005. Copyright © 2005 by the American Library Association. Reproduced by permission. / J. Burns, Stephen. From *Electronic Book Review.* creativecommons.org, 2006. Reproduced by permission.

GENEVIEVE TAGGARD. Marburg, Anita. From *Genevieve Taggard As I Knew Her.* Unpublished, unknown. Reproduced by permission. / Wood, Harrison. From *Memoir: Notes on Genevieve Taggard as a Teacher.* Unpublished, unknown. Reproduced by permission. / Flint, Helen. From *Memoirs: Genevieve Taggard: Mt. Holyoke 1929-1931.* Unpublished, unknown. Reproduced by permission. / Genevieve Taggard, "To The Natural World: at 37," *To The Natural World,* 1980. Copyright © 1980 by Marcia D. Liles. Reproduced by permission of Judith Benét Richardson. / *The Nation,* February 28, 1923. Reproduced by permission. / Taggard, Genevieve. From *Words for the Chisel.* Alfred A. Knopf, 1926. Copyright © 1926 by Alfred A. Knopf, Inc. Reproduced by permission of Judith Benét Richardson. / *The Nation-*,April 28, 1926. Reproduced by permission. / Genevieve Taggard, "Last Words," *Overland Monthly and Out West Magazine,* Dec, 1927. Reproduced by permission of Judith Benét Richardson. / Taggard, Genevieve. From *Traveling Standing Still: Poems 1928-1938.* Alfred A. Knopf, 1928. Reproduced by permission of Ju-

ACKNOWLEDGMENTS

dith Benét Richardson. / *The Nation,* June 25, 1930. Reproduced by permission. / *The Nation,* August 20, 1930. Reproduced by permission. / Taggard, Genevieve. From *Not Mine to Finish: Poems, 1928-1934.* Harper & Brothers, 1934. Copyright © 1934 by Harper & Brothers. All rights reserved. Reproduced by permission of Judith Benét Richardson. / Taggard, Genevieve. From *Calling Western Union.* Harper & Brothers Publishers, 1936. Reprinted with the permission of Scribner, a Division of Simon & Schuster, Inc., from *Scribner's Magazine,* October 1934. Copyright © 1934 by Charles Scribner's Sons; copyright renewed 1962 by Charles Scribner's Sons. All rights reserved. / From *Calling Western Union.* Harper & Brothers, 1936. Copyright 1936 by Harper & Brothers. Reproduced by permission of Judith Benét Richardson. / From *Collected Poems, 1918-1938.* Harper & Brothers, 1938. Reproduced by permission of Judith Benét Richardson. / Taggard, Genevieve. From *Long View.* Harper & Brothers, 1942. Copyright © 1938, 1939, 1940, 1941, 1942 by Genevieve Taggard. All rights reserved. Reproduced by permission of Judith Benét Richardson. / From *Long View.* Harper & Brothers, 1942. Copyright 1938, 1939, 1940, 1941, 1942 by Genevieve Taggard. All rights reserved. Reproduced by permission. / From *Slow Music.* Harper & Brothers, 1946. Reproduced by permission of Judith Benét Richardson. / *California Poetry Folios,* v. IV, 1947. Reproduced by permission. / From *Origin Hawaii.* Donald Angus, 1947. Copyright 1947 by Genevieve Taggard. Reproduced by permission of Judith Benét Richardson. / Wilson, Edumund. From *The Shores of Light: A Literary Chronicle of the Twenties and Thirties.* Farrar, Straus and Young, 1952. Reproduced by permission. / Genevieve Taggard, "To the Powers of Darkness," *To The Natural World,* 1980. Copyright © 1980 by Marcia D. Liles. Reproduced by permission of Judith Benét Richardson. / Perloff, Marjorie. From *symploke. 2000. Reproduced by permission.*

LAURA INGALLS WILDER. Anne T. Eaton, "The New Books for Younger Readers - The Long Winter," *The New York Times,* January 26, 1941. Copyright © The New York Times. Reproduced by permission.

List of Subjects

Introduction *xi*

List of Contributors *xiii*

ARNA BONTEMPS 1
Kathleen Pfeiffer

AGNES BOULTON 17
W. D. King

WILLIAM BRADFORD 33
Paul Johnston

KEVIN BROCKMEIER 49
F. Brett Cox

MICHELLE CLIFF 65
Jennifer Hirt

PATRICIA HAMPL 81
Angela Garcia

LARRY HEINEMANN 103
Lea M. Williams

ELISABETH SANXAY HOLDING 119
Elaine Roth

EDWARD P. JONES 139
Joseph Dewey

MINA LOY 155
Caleb Puckett

CLARENCE MAJOR 171
Nancy Bunge

CAROLINE MILLER 187
Emily Wright

HOWARD FRANK MOSHER 203
Ann McKinstry Micou

ALICE NOTLEY 223
Karin Gottshall

ANNE RIVERS SIDDONS 239
Margaret T. McGehee

LEE SIEGEL 255
Stephen J. Burn

GENEVIEVE TAGGARD 271
Robert Niemi

LAURA INGALLS WILDER 289
Susan Carol Hauser

Cumulative Index *305*

Introduction

Mark Twain once wrote to a friend: "Creed and opinion change with time, and their symbols perish; but Literature and its temples are sacred to all creeds and inviolate." That is, literature has something important to tell us about the nature of life, and this information doesn't change. This is true of the classics—poems, novels, plays, and other texts that have achieved a solid position in the historical imagination—and fresh works that have both resonance and resilience. Our hope is that, in this fresh volume of critical and biographical essays on a range of American writers, we deal with work that will last, with material that is, as Twain said, "inviolate," as the writers of the work have aimed high.

In this twentieth-second volume of *American Writers,* we offer articles on writers from a wide variety of genres; they are all well-known figures who have aspired to the kind of quality that Twain mentions above, yet none of them has yet been featured in this series. Readers who wish to look more thoroughly into the work of these writers will find many things here to attract and sustain them: biographical and historical context, close readings of texts, and supplementary material designed to enhance the reading of the individual subject and his or her work.

This series itself has its origins in a series of critical and biographical monographs that appeared between 1959 and 1972. The *Minnesota Pamphlets on American Writers* achieved fame in their time; they were incisively written and informative, treating ninety-seven American writers in a format and style that attracted a devoted following of readers. The series proved invaluable to a generation of students and teachers, who could depend on these reliable and interesting critiques of major figures. The idea of reprinting these essays occurred to Charles Scribner, Jr. (1921-1995). The series appeared in four volumes entitled *American Writers: A Collection of Literary Biographies* (1974).

Since then, twenty-one supplements have appeared, treating hundreds of well-known and less known American writers: poets, novelists, playwrights, screenwriters, essayists, and autobiographers, even a handful of literary critics who have managed to create texts that somebody might want to read in future years. The idea has been consistent with the original series: to provide informative essays aimed at the general reader. These essays often rise to a high level of craft and critical vision, but they are meant to introduce a body of work of some importance in the history of American literature, and to provide a sense of the scope and nature of the career under review. Each article puts the author at hand in the context of his or her time.

Supplement twenty-two treats a range of authors from the past and present. William Bradford—a major memoirist from the seventeenth century—has for whatever reason been overlooked thus far, and it is good that we can at last include an essay on him in this volume. Most of the writers included here are from the twentieth century, with the exception Larua Ingalls Wilder, author of the famous Little House series, who was born in 1867, while Agnes Boulton, Elisabeth Sanxay Holding, Mina Loy, and Genevieve Taggard were born in the nineteenth century but did their writing in the twentieth. Clarence Major, Edward P. Jones, Howard Frank Mosher, Caroline Miller, Larry Heinemann, and Michelle Cliff belong to the twentieth century—indeed, Cliff, Jones, Mosher, and Siddons are still at work, producing new work on a regular basis.

INTRODUCTION

While each of these writers has been written about in journals and newspapers, few of them—William Bradford would be an exception—have had the kind of sustained critical attention they deserve, and we hope to provide a beginning here, as the work certainly deserves close reading and rereading.

As always in this series, we insisted that each critical and biographical essay should be accessible to the non-specialist reader or beginning student; that is, we did not invite or encourage the kind of critical jargon that is so prevalent in the criticism in our time. One could argue that the creation of culture involves the continuous reassessment of major texts, and my belief is that this collection of articles performs a useful service, offering intelligent introductions to American writers who have found a readership because of the high quality of their work, their attempts to aim high, sticking to the high ideals mentioned by Mark Twain above.

—JAY PARINI

Contributors

Nancy Bunge. Nancy Bunge, a professor at Michigan State University, has held senior Fulbright lectureships at the University of Vienna, the University of Ghent, the Free University of Brussels and the University of Siegen. She is the interviewer and editor of *Finding the Words: Conversations with Writers Who Teach* and *Master Class: Lessons from Leading Writers;* the editor of *Conversations with Clarence Major* and *Woman in the Wilderness: Letters of Harriet Wood Wheeler, Missionary Wife, 1832-1892;* and the author of *Nathaniel Hawthorne: A Study of the Short Fiction.* CLARENCE MAJOR

Stephen J. Burn. Stephen J. Burn is the author of *Jonathan Franzen at the End of Postmodernism* (2008), *David Foster Wallace's Infinite Jest: A Reader's Guide* (2003), editor of *Conversations with David Foster Wallace* (2011), and co-editor of *Intersections: Essays on Richard Powers* (2008). His work has appeared in *Modern Fiction Studies, Contemporary Literature,* the *Paris Review,* the *New York Times Book Review,* the *Times Literary Supplement,* and other journals. He is an Associate Professor at Northern Michigan University. LEE SIEGEL

F. Brett Cox. F. Brett Cox is Associate Professor of English at Norwich University. He is co-editor, with Andy Duncan, of *Crossroads: Tales of the Southern Literary Fantastic* (Tor, 2004) and is a member of the Board of Directors for the Shirley Jackson Award. His fiction, esssays, and reviews have appeared in numerous publications, including the *North Carolina Literary Review, Postscripts, New England Quarterly, Science Fiction Studies, The Robert Frost Encyclopedia,* and *The Cultural Influences of William Gibson, the "Father" of Cyberpunk Science Fiction: Critical and Interpretive Essays.* KEVIN BROCKMEIER

Joseph Dewey. Joseph Dewey is Associate Professor of Modern American Literature and Culture at the University of Pittsburgh. He published *In a Dark Time: The Apocalyptic Temper in the American Novel of the Nuclear Age; Understanding Richard Powers; Grief and Nothing: A Reading of Don DeLillo;* and *Novels from Reagan's America: A New Realism.* He has edited or co-edited casebooks on the short fiction of Henry James, J. D. Salinger's *The Catcher in the Rye,* and DeLillo's *Underworld.* EDWARD P. JONES

Angela Garcia. Angela Garcia teaches English Language Development at Linn-Benton Community College and in the public school system in Corvallis, Oregon. She received degrees in English from the University of California, Davis and University of California, Berkeley, where she specialized in the study and writing of poetry. PATRICIA HAMPL

Karin Gottshall. Karin Gottshall is the author of the book *Crocus* (Fordham University Press, 2007), and the chapbook *Flood Letters* (Argos Books, 2011). Her poems and reviews have appeared in the *Gettysburg Review, Harvard Review,* and *Shenandoah.* Gottshall teaches poetry writing at Middlebury College. ALICE NOTLEY

Susan Carol Hauser. Susan Carol Hauser is an essayist, poet and natural history writer. Her books include *My Kind of River: Seeking Passage on the Mississippi; Outside After Dark: New & Selected Poems;* and *Sugaring: A Maple Syrup Memoir, with Instructions.* She is the recipient of a 2010 McKnight Artist Fellowship, Loft Award in Poetry, two Minnesota Book

Awards and other honors. She has been a commentator on National Public Radio and Minnesota Public Radio and her freelance writing has appeared in regional and national magazines. She has a Master of Fine Arts degree in poetry from Bowling Green State University, Ohio and is an Emerita Professor of English at Bemidji State University. LAURA INGALLS WILDER

Jennifer Hirt. Jennifer Hirt is the author of the memoir *Under Glass: The Girl With a Thousand Christmas Trees.* Her creative writing has won a Pushcart Prize and the Drake University Emerging Writer Prize. She teaches at Pennsylvania State University at Harrisburg. MICHELLE CLIFF

Paul Johnston. Paul Johnston is an associate professor of English at the State University of New York College at Plattsburgh, where he teaches courses in colonial and nineteenth-century American literature. He has published articles on Benjamin Franklin, Jonathan Edwards, Henry Wadsworth Longfellow and the Fireside Poets, and Susan and James Fenimore Cooper. He is currently writing a study of Catholicism in nineteenth-century American literature. WILLIAM BRADFORD

W. D. King. William Davies King is Professor of Theater at the University of California, Santa Barbara. His *Collections of Nothing* (Chicago, 2008) was named as one of the top 100 books of 2008 by Amazon.com. In addition to his writings about Agnes Boulton, he is the author of *Henry Irving's "Waterloo": Theatrical Engagements with Late-Victorian Culture and History* (California, 1993; winner of the 1993 Joe A. Callaway Prize) and *Writing Wrongs: The Work of Wallace Shawn* (Temple, 1997). AGNES BOULTON

Margaret T. McGehee. Dr. Margaret T. McGehee is assistant professor of English at Presbyterian College, in Clinton, SC, where she also directs the Southern Studies program. Dr. McGehee received her Ph.D. in American Studies from Emory University and her M.A. in Southern Studies from the University of Mississippi. Her published work has appeared in *Southern Spaces, Cinema Journal,* and the *Journal of East Tennessee History.* ANNE RIVERS SIDDONS

Ann McKinstry Micou. Ann McKinstry Micou has a bachelor's degree, Phi Beta Kappa, from Mills College in Oakland, California and a master's degree from The New School in New York City. She is the author of a trilogy of reference books: *A Guide to Fiction Set in Vermont* (2005); *A Guide to Fiction Set in Vermont for Children & Young Adults* (2008); and *Fiction Set in Vermont 3* (2009). She is currently a freelance writer and editor in Upper Montclair, New Jersey. HOWARD FRANK MOSHER

Robert Niemi. Robert Niemi teaches American literature, film, and American Studies at St. Michael's College, Colchester, Vermont, and is the author of four books and numerous essays on a wide range of American culture topics. GENEVIEVE TAGGARD

Kathleen Pfeiffer. Kathleen Pfeiffer, Ph.D. is associate professor of English at Oakland University in Rochester, Michigan, where she teaches courses in American literature, African American literature and American Studies. Her book, *Brother Mine: The Correspondence of Jean Toomer and Waldo Frank,* was published in 2010 by the University of Illinois Press. She has edited and written the introductions to the re-issues of two Harlem Renaissance novels, Carl Van Vechten's *Nigger Heaven* (2000) and Waldo Frank's *Holiday* (2003), both also published by the University of Illinois Press. Her book, *Race Passing and American Individualism,* was published by the University of Massachusetts Press in 2003. ARNA BONTEMPS

Caleb Puckett. Caleb Puckett is an Assistant Professor at Emporia State University, where he works as a Reference and Instruction Librarian. Puckett is also a poet, short story writer and editor for *Nimrod International Journal.* MINA LOY

CONTRIBUTORS

Elaine Roth. Elaine Roth is Associate Professor of Film Studies and Chair of the English Department at Indiana University, South Bend. Co-editor of *Motherhood Misconceived: Representing the Maternal in U.S. Films* (SUNY Press, 2009), she has also published articles in Feminist Media Studies, The Quarterly Review of Film and Video, and *Genders.* She is currently pursuing a project on international auteurs during a Fulbright Senior Lectureship at the Universidad Complutense in Madrid, Spain. ELISABETH SANXAY HOLDING

Lea M. Williams. Lea M. Williams is an associate professor of English at Norwich University. Her research and teaching interests include the literature of war, memoirs and autobiography, and gender studies. She is currently working on a project that investigates the intersections of gender and memory in women's twentieth-century writings about war and its aftermath. LARRY HEINEMANN

Emily Wright. Emily Wright is McLean Professor of English and dean of the School of Arts & Humanities at Methodist University in Fayetteville, North Carolina, where she directs Methodist University's Southern Writers Symposium. She has written a number of papers and articles on southern women writers and on the role that the South has played in the national imagination. CAROLINE MILLER

AMERICAN WRITERS

ARNA BONTEMPS

(1902—1973)

Kathleen Pfeiffer

MEMORIALIZED POSTHUMOUSLY BY the poet and critic Sterling Brown as "a sober, austere, melancholy, meditative, meticulous Christian gentleman" (p. 95), Arna Bontemps has been perhaps one of the most frequently overlooked and underrated writers of the twentieth century. His contributions to fiction, poetry, and literary criticism alone would characterize him as an important literary force; these writings pale, however, in comparison to his distinguished contributions to the canon of children's and young adult literature. As the children's and young adult genre has finally been getting its long overdue recognition by literary critics, Arna Bontemps too has begun to receive the acknowledgment he so richly deserves. In particular, he created a critical mass of fiction and nonfiction texts that speak specifically and directly to African American youth; impressively, he managed to appeal to white readers and publishers at the same time.

BIOGRAPHY

Arna Bontemps was the first child of Paul Bismark and Maria Carolina Pembrooke Bontemps, born October 13, 1902, at home in Alexandria, Louisiana. A Creole in Cajun country, Bontemps came into the world during a time of inhospitable race relations. Named Arnaud Wendell, he was soon known as Arna, which would be the name he claimed throughout his life. His parents were descendants of Louisiana freedmen. Both were literate and skilled: Paul, raised Roman Catholic, was trained as a brick mason, and Maria, a Methodist schoolteacher, was also an accomplished dressmaker. Maria was remembered by her son as having had her own literary and artistic inclinations. Jack Conroy, a close friend of the writer, reports that Bontemps' family name—French for "good times"—traces to an antebellum slave owner who had been a comedian calling himself "Mr. Good Times" (p. 55). Whether this etymology is true or apocryphal, the family found itself in difficult times when, after the birth of Arna's sister Ruby Sarah in 1905, race relations in Alexandria continued to deteriorate. A climate of racial intolerance and violence led Paul and Maria Bontemps to leave Louisiana so that they could seek better opportunities for their children in the West.

Along with Arna's maternal grandfather, Joseph Pembrooke, Paul Bontemps traveled to California where Bontemps selected a home in the Watts section of Los Angeles, an integrated neighborhood that was already home to some of the family's Louisiana friends and relatives. Preferring a more rural location, Joseph Pembrooke established a farm on the Alameda Highway, in the Furlough Track area outside the city. In April 1906 Arna, his sister, and his mother traveled across country to join their father on the West Coast. Though the conditions of their integrated neighborhood were racially far friendlier than they had left behind in segregated Louisiana, when Bontemps entered kindergarten he was the only African American student in the class; this racial isolation would continue throughout his schooling.

In California the family converted to the Seventh-Day Adventist faith; Arna's father, while working hard to support his family financially, also completed the course of study that led him to become the first African American Adventist minister in the area. The family group shifted, however, when Joseph Pembrooke died within a year of their move West. Sarah Pembrooke, Arna's maternal grandmother, took her husband home to Louisiana for burial; upon her return,

the entire Bontemps family moved out to the Pembrooke farm on Alameda Highway, where Arna spent many happy childhood days. Eventually other family members migrated west from Louisiana, including Sarah Pembrooke's alcoholic younger brother Joseph Ward, Arna's beloved and admired "Uncle Buddy." Despite his father's disapproval of Buddy's down-home manner (indeed, perhaps rebelliously encouraged by it), young Arna grew deeply attached to his uncle and absorbed the older man's folkways: Buddy spoke in colloquialisms, freely used the word "nigger," and brought Louisiana food, culture, and stories with him to California. Bontemps' own parents had studiously avoided southern speech and Negro dialect, and Uncle Buddy reminded young Arna of the cultural heritage that he had left behind in Louisiana. Indeed, his uncle was so important to Bontemps' imagination that he would later develop his first novel, *God Sends Sunday* (1931), around a character based on Buddy.

Bontemps lost his mother to pulmonary tuberculosis shortly before his twelfth birthday, and in the process, young Arna also lost a compassionate advocate who would defend him against his father's rigid expectations. Following his mother's death, Bontemps became an avid reader, through which he cultivated the lifelong interest in African American history and culture that would define his professional accomplishments. As he later recalled,

> I was seeking a recognizable reflection of myself and my world in the collections of books available to a boy reader going on twelve. What I found was of cold comfort, to say the least. Nothing more inspiring than Our Little Ethiopian Cousin was on the shelves ... [which was] not what I needed or expected. He was not me, and his world was not mine. The Our of the title did not include me.
>
> (quoted in Jones, p. 45)

In 1917 Bontemps' father became supervisor of a Los Angeles Seventh Day-Adventist school; that same year, he enrolled the fifteen-year-old Arna in the San Fernando Academy, an Adventist boarding school, where Arna was the youngest student and one of the very few blacks. In a line that has been often quoted by writers examining Bontemps' sense of race pride, his father advised Arna, "Now don't go up there acting colored" (quoted in Jones, p. 47). At San Fernando, Arna began to write poetry. Father and son soon clashed over Arna's desire to earn a living as a writer, and though the young man entered Pacific Union College in Napa County, California (another Adventist school), under the auspices of a premed degree that his father insisted upon, he soon changed his major to English. Completing his bachelor of arts degree in three years, Bontemps graduated in May 1923. He took a job at the Los Angeles post office, where he met and befriended the writer Wallace Thurman. A year later, Bontemps' first poem, "Hope," was accepted for publication in the *Crisis,* and in July 1924, on Thurman's advice, Bontemps moved to Harlem.

Upon his arrival in New York, Bontemps took a teaching job at the Harlem Academy, an Adventist school. He met his future wife, Alberta Johnson, the year he arrived, when she was a sixteen-year-old student at the academy. She shared his faith. Adventists shun alcohol, tobacco, and secular songs; they maintain strict moral standards and practice vegetarianism; moreover, as the church's name implies, a heavy emphasis is placed on observing the Saturday (Seventh-Day) Sabbath. Later in life, Bontemps attempted to explain the Adventist faith to a fellow writer who was trying to understand the sect. "Boiled down then," he wrote, "the SDA hope is that Christ will literally return to the earth in 'this generation' to redeem the godly. The rest is preparation for that event.... Hence their extensive health program, their system of schools, their many publishing houses and books defining the good life" (quoted in Jones, p. 123).

Bontemps' strong religious faith would provide private spiritual nourishment throughout his life, though he frequently clashed with church authorities. Nevertheless, the disciplined religious practices of Bontemps' Adventist beliefs likely circumscribed his involvement in Harlem's nightlife during his time there. Thus, while he was active in the Harlem Renaissance's literary culture, Bontemps' name is rarely associated with

Harlem's rent parties, cabarets, nightclubs, or other notoriously intemperate cultural events.

In Harlem he continued to write poetry, and his efforts were amply rewarded. His poem "Golgotha Is a Mountain" was awarded *Opportunity* magazine's Alexander Pushkin Poetry Prize in 1926; his poem "The Return" won the same prize a year later; also in 1927, the *Crisis* awarded its first Poetry Prize to Bontemps' poem "Nocturne at Bethesda." Later in life, Bontemps looked back on this summer with affection:

> And what a year for a colored boy to be leaving home for the first time! Twenty-one, sixteen months out of college, full of golden hopes and romantic dreams, I had come all the way from Los Angeles to find the job I wanted, to hear the music of my taste, to see serious plays and, God willing, to be come a writer.
>
> (Preface to *Personals,* p. 4)

Bontemps also quickly established friendships with Countee Cullen and Langston Hughes; these connections would not only provide lifelong affection and mutual support for each man, they also led to extraordinarily rich literary collaborations.

Bontemps married Alberta Johnson on August 26, 1926, when he was twenty-three and she eighteen. The two would raise six children together—Joan, Paul, Poppy, Camille, Constance, and Alex—born during the course of the first nineteen years of their marriage. Langston Hughes later noted how the family shaped Arna's interaction in Harlem during the heady, vivacious years that have since become known as the Harlem Renaissance. "All the writers wondered who [Alberta] was and what she looked like," Hughes writes in *The Big Sea.*

> He never brought her with him to any of the parties, so she remained the mystery of the New Negro Renaissance. But I went with him once to his apartment to meet her, and found her a shy and charming girl, holding a golden baby on her lap. A year or two later there was another golden baby. And every time I went away to Haiti or Mexico or Europe and came back there would be a new golden baby, each prettier than the last—so that was why the literati never saw Mrs. Bontemps.
>
> (p. 248)

While his wife and children provided tremendous love and emotional sustenance for Bontemps, the financial demands of such a large family soon became a defining characteristic of his professional life. Few of Bontemps' contemporaries bore the familial and financial responsibilities he did, and his remarkable productivity is in part explained by these pressures. Neither teaching nor marriage interfered with Bontemps' literary ambition, however, and in the late 1920s he began writing "a first novel with autobiographical overtones about a sensitive black boy in a nostalgic setting" ("The Awakening: A Memoir," p. 25). By the time the novel was completed, however, the stock market had crashed, and publishers showed no interest in such fiction. Bontemps persevered, this time undertaking a new, more marketable subject. This effort met with success; in 1931, Harcourt, Brace published his first novel, *God Sends Sunday*, the story of a black jockey's rise and fall. Although the novel contained inherent deference to W. E. B. Du Bois, the distinguished elder writer was critical of Bontemps' work, objecting to its depiction of the low-life scenes of a gambling culture. Bontemps' father, Paul, likewise viewed the novel harshly, taking a dim view of the secular themes that, in the conservative minister's view, failed to provide its audience with appropriate moral guidance. To many Adventists, Bontemps' greatest crime was the blasphemy of using God's name in his novel's title.

Despite encouraging reviews, the reading public had little money for books, and the novel failed to sell. The Depression also took its toll on the Harlem Academy, and the school ceased operations following the 1930–1931 academic year. Bontemps and many of his fellow faculty members secured teaching positions at the Oakwood College in Huntsville, Alabama, an Adventist junior college that had been in operation since 1896. The relocation to the South, with its stifling summers and cold, damp winters, presented the family with considerable social challenges that rivaled even Alabama's inhospitable weather. The tense racial climate of the Jim Crow South—particularly during the Scottsboro trials, which were unfolding in nearby Decatur—and the social

conservatism that viewed the writing life with judgmental bemusement left Bontemps feeling artistically isolated. He would later refer to these as "three horrifying years" (*Black Thunder,* p. xxi). Moreover, Bontemps' close friendship with Langston Hughes was known to the Adventist authorities in Alabama, and many of them frowned upon both the friendship and Hughes himself. The politically and socially conservative Adventist establishment looked askance at Hughes, who had become increasingly outspoken about his radical politics in the late 1920s and early 1930s. As a result, when Hughes visited his friend in Alabama during the holiday season of 1931, it led to some trouble for Bontemps. The tension this friendship created is perhaps best illustrated in the demand placed on Bontemps by the white head of Oakwood College that he disavow the radical politics of his friends. As Bontemps recalled, "I could do it, he demanded publicly, by burning most of the books in my small library, a number of which were trash in his estimation anyway, the rest, race-conscious and provocative" (*Black Thunder,* p. xxviii). That Bontemps refused to do this only exacerbated the tension of his position at Oakwood.

During these years, Bontemps collaborated by mail with Hughes on a children's book, *Popo and Fifina: Children of Haiti,* which was published in 1932. As the novel documents the everyday lives of these peasant children, it treats their daily interactions as grand adventures. It was very well received, and Bontemps was encouraged to continue writing single-authored children's fiction: *You Can't Pet a Possum* was published in 1934 by Morrow, and *Bubber Goes to Heaven* was written at this time as well, although it was not published until 1998. Notwithstanding his evident success in writing, publishing, and finding an audience within several literary modes—a particularly noteworthy accomplishment given the economic hardship of the times—Bontemps' literary skill failed to secure his position at Oakwood College. To the contrary, as he began work on what would be his next book, the highly regarded historical novel *Black Thunder,* Bontemps felt again the tensions between Huntsville's conservative culture and his own creative life. Antagonism toward his work emerged in full force and led church authorities to question his habit of borrowing library books by mail. In the introduction to *Black Thunder,* Bontemps recalls the "quaint hostilities":

> Wasn't there a whole room of books in the school where I worked—perhaps as many as a thousand? How many books could a man read in one lifetime anyway? We laughed together at the questions, but I realized they were not satisfied with my joking answers.... At the end of the following term we drove to California, sold our car, and settled down in Watts in the hope that what we had received for the car would buy food till I could write my book.
>
> (pp. xxvii–xxviii)

The trip across the country for a black family (consisting at the time of Arna, Alberta, two small children, and a baby) in 1934, traveling with all of their possessions, proved challenging, demanding, and exhausting. Nor did their arrival in California afford much relief or comfort, as they stayed with Bontemps' father—the entire family cramped into the single extra bedroom of his home in Los Angeles. "Not having space for my typewriter," Bontemps later admitted, "I wrote the book in longhand on the top of a folded-down sewing machine" (*Black Thunder,* p. xxii).

Bontemps continued to write children's literature even as he was working on *Black Thunder*. One of these stories, "Dang Little Squirt," appeared in *New Challenge* in May 1935, providing both income and encouragement. Beacon's advance check for *Black Thunder* gave the young family the economic means to leave California, and in late spring of 1935 they moved to Chicago. There, while living, somewhat nervously, on the city's violent South Side, Bontemps served as the principal of the Shiloh Academy through the spring of the 1937–1938 academic year. Because Shiloh was also an Adventist school, and because Bontemps' literary activities increased, rather than diminished, upon his arrival in Chicago, he despaired to learn that church authorities in the urban northern city maintained as hostile an attitude of judgment toward his literary ambition as had those in the rural South. A confrontation with church authorities led to his departure from the school; this was

the last employment Bontemps would ever hold with an Adventist-affiliated establishment. Bontemps accepted his first secular job: a position as an editorial supervisor with the Federal Writer's Project, a division of the Illinois Works Progress Administration (WPA). Bontemps met Jack Conroy while working in Chicago; the friendship soon became a source of creative productivity for both men as they began collaborating on a number of writing projects. Working together, Conroy and Bontemps published three children's books over the next decade—*The Fast Sooner Hound* (1946); *Slappy Hooper, the Wonderful Sign Painter* (1946); and *Sam Patch, the High, Wide & Handsome Jumper* (1951)—and a nonfiction text, *They Seek a City* (1945), a history of the African American Great Migration.

Bontemps' work at the WPA differed dramatically from his previous jobs. Notwithstanding the vagaries of his professional life, Bontemps' creative life continued unabated: Houghton Mifflin published his next single-authored book, a children's novel titled *Sad-Faced Boy,* in 1937. In 1938 Bontemps won a fellowship from the Julian Rosenwald Fund; his proposal sought funding to travel and research in the Caribbean, an experience that would prove invaluable in developing his understanding of black culture. *Drums at Dusk* was the 1939 novel of purpose that resulted, and it drew heavily on his Caribbean experience. Yet in startling contrast to *Drums,* Bontemps' next publication was a ghostwritten "autobiography" of W. C. Handy, titled *Father of the Blues* and published by Macmillan in 1941. Also in 1941, Harper published *Golden Slippers: An Anthology of Negro Poetry for Young Readers*; this was but the first of many successful anthologies by which Bontemps would establish his literary and cultural significance.

Upon arriving in Chicago, Bontemps had undertaken graduate study at the University of Chicago; though his initial goal was to earn a Ph.D. in English, he was only able to take courses intermittently over the next few years. In 1942 he reapplied to the Graduate School of Library Science, a degree that he would complete the following year. His graduate study was aided by Rosenwald funding (he also won an additional Rosenwald fellowship in 1942 to pursue research on "the Negro in Illinois"), and he wrote a master's thesis examining the James Weldon Johnson Memorial Collection of Arts and Letters at Yale University (a version of this was published in the Yale Library *Gazette* in October 1943; another version was published in the *Library Quarterly* the following year).

Having earned the master of library science degree, Bontemps moved his family to Nashville, where he accepted a position as Fisk University's head librarian in 1943. The job at Fisk—which he would hold for more than two decades—provided him with the financial security, professional importance, and personal satisfaction that would allow him to develop as a writer and an intellectual to his fullest potential. His library work not only provided inspiration and material for his fiction, it also complemented his goals as a writer. For example, one of his first major acquisitions as head librarian at Fisk was the George Gershwin Memorial Collection of Music and Musical Literature, which had been established by the white writer Carl Van Vechten. During the heady Harlem days of the 1920s, Van Vechten had been a major force in bringing young black writers to the attention of his friend, the publisher Alfred A. Knopf; like Bontemps, Van Vechten had been a longtime friend of Langston Hughes. Bontemps' own friendship with the aging Van Vechten had been cultivated in the early 1940s by mail, as the elder man had solicited contributions from the writer's personal papers to add to the James Weldon Johnson Collection, which was a pet project that Van Vechten had undertaken shortly after Johnson's untimely death. (Bontemps' master's thesis had also been a valuable resource to the collection.) As Van Vechten worked on compiling both the James Weldon Johnson and George Gershwin collections, he grew particularly fond of the racial tricksterism behind the two collections. Thus, Van Vechten purposely donated the James Weldon Johnson Collection of black literary materials to Yale, the white institution, and the George Gershwin Collection, documenting the work of a white composer, to Fisk, the black institution.

Work on the James Weldon Johnson Collection in particular proved to be a demanding and exhausting undertaking, one to which Van Vechten dedicated untold hours of labor; yet today it stands as one of the nation's most important collections of African American literature, and Arna Bontemps' participation was central to the endeavor. Indeed, the pedagogical impulse behind virtually all of Bontemps' writing is mirrored in his efforts as head librarian to promote awareness of black history and culture. He helped shape Fisk's collection at a pivotal moment in the library's history. Having acquired a significant collection of African American archives and materials at its founding, Fisk also benefited from a collection of resources established by Arthur Schomburg in the early 1930s. Under Bontemps' leadership, the library expanded these holdings: he acquired the papers of the Harlem Renaissance writers Jean Toomer, Charles S. Johnson, and Countee Cullen, among others. While some of these acquisitions developed out of his close friendships with the writers involved, one significant collection, the Charles Chesnutt papers, resulted from the sheer skill of Bontemps' personal diplomacy.

Since 1933 Bontemps had been working on and off with his friend Countee Cullen by mail, collaborating on a dramatic musical version of *God Sends Sunday*. The theatrical production was titled *St. Louis Woman* and included a musical score written by Harold Arlen and Johnny Mercer; the song "Come Rain or Come Shine" was the most successful of the hits that emerged from the play. Its premiere, on March 30, 1946, at the Martin Beck Theater on New York's West Forty-fifth Street, opened to mixed reviews, and the show closed after a month. Undeterred, Bontemps kept writing, and his productivity at this time continued unabated. He cultivated proficiency in a variety of genres during these years: *We Have Tomorrow,* a collection of biographical profiles of black professionals, appeared in 1945, followed by a biography of Frederick Douglass and one of George Washington Carver that was successful enough to be expanded and revised for reissue; he also developed a historical text, *Story of the Negro* (1948), and another history, *100 Years of Negro Freedom* (1961). For juvenile audiences Bontemps wrote *Chariot in the Sky: A Story of the Jubilee Singers* (1951), *Lonesome Boy* (1955), and a book profiling *Famous Negro Athletes* (1964).

In addition to his writing, Bontemps' years at Fisk were distinguished by his professional generosity: he taught, mentored, lectured, and wrote. He formed numerous fond attachments, particularly with students. He undertook service to professional organizations like the American Library Association and to racially conscientious organizations like the American Society for African Culture. He traveled extensively, lectured regularly, and attended a writer's retreat at Yaddo. He collected numerous prizes and awards throughout his life: poetry prizes at *Crisis* and *Opportunity* magazines, two Rosenwald Fellowships, two Guggenheim Fellowships for creative writing, and the Jane Addams Children's Book Award, among others. When he tried to retire from his position as head librarian in 1964, the university's administration appealed to him to stay on as acting head librarian and director of university relations, and he reluctantly agreed to the duties. In 1966, however, he was offered the position of associate professor of American literature at the Chicago Circle campus of the University of Illinois, and he accepted. After a year, he was promoted to full professor of English, but when he suffered a stroke in the winter of 1968, he and Alberta returned to Nashville so that he could rest and recover.

Following the death of his cherished friend Langston Hughes in 1967, Bontemps was named together with George Bass as coexecutor of the Hughes estate, a massive and complex responsibility. In 1969, he accepted a position at Yale University, where he was named curator of the James Weldon Johnson Collection. Years later the writer and scholar Houston Baker recalled his interactions with Bontemps at Yale: "The man was simply a very deep and very cool well of learning," Baker wrote, "and he shared his bounty with superb generosity" (p. 7). Bontemps remained at Yale until 1971 and then returned to Nashville, where his wife preferred that they spend their sunset years. Fisk welcomed him back

with the title of writer in residence and the opportunity to teach creative writing. Bontemps's many accomplishments continued to earn recognition: he was named an honorary doctor of humane letters at Morgan State University in Baltimore in 1969 as well as at Berea College in Kentucky in 1973. He continued to write and publish books in a variety of genres, including the children's story *Mr. Kelso's Lion* (1970); biographies of Frederick Douglass (1971) and Booker T. Washington (1972); *Personals,* a collection of his own poetry (1973); and a collection of adult short stories, *The Old South: "A Summer Tragedy" and Other Stories* (1973).

While at Yale, Bontemps taught a graduate seminar in the Harlem Renaissance. During this time in America the combined cultural forces propelling the Black Power movement, the Black Arts movement, and the civil rights movement led to increased scholarly interest in Afro-American literature, as it was then sometimes called. The early 1970s saw the birth of academic programs dedicated exclusively to the study of black art, literature, and culture; a renewed interest in the Harlem Renaissance naturally followed. As one of the few remaining living members of the New Negro Renaissance, Arna Bontemps found himself, during his later years, in a welcome position of influence. He had long sought occasions to promote the Harlem Renaissance's artistic legacy: in 1960, he wrote an introduction to the reissue of James Weldon Johnson's groundbreaking modernist novel *The Autobiography of an Ex-Colored Man*; in 1962 he lectured on the Harlem Renaissance as part of the Jackman Memorial Lectures, organized by Langston Hughes in New York (his remarks were later published in an issue of *Phylon*); and throughout the 1960s he published literary criticism on Harlem writers as well as reminiscences of his years as a "New Negro."

In January 1972 Bontemps sat for an interview with L. M. Collins of Fisk University. In the resulting typescript, "Arna Bontemps Talks About the Renaissance," the elder writer shared memories and anecdotes about the writers who were his friends in the 1920s and beyond. He admits that without the supportive community provided by Harlem's writers and artists, he "would never have become a first-rate writer." And he meditates on the larger meaning for him personally of those Harlem Renaissance years:

> I, as anyone in the same position, in defining soul and seeking a philosophical base for writing in the years after those golden days, have had to ask myself: Was that time really special. about which I am yet sentimental,—just the bloom of youth that had been lost or something else more essential, more enduring?
>
> (p. 219)

Culminating this activity was the volume of essays he edited titled *The Harlem Renaissance Remembered* (1972). Dedicated to Charles S. Johnson and Alain Locke, two of the movement's prominent leaders, the collection includes historical analysis of the era, literary criticism, and a memoir by Bontemps; it is illustrated with photographs of Bontemps, Langston Hughes, Countee Cullen, Zora Neale Hurston, and others. In his memoir, the opening essay of the collection, Bontemps cites Countee Cullen's poetry as the triggering force for the "upsurge of Negro creativity in the 1920's" ("The Awakening: A Memoir," p. 1). Bontemps' overview of the Harlem Renaissance and its cultural evolution pays particular attention to those individuals who crossed his own path: when Marcus Garvey came to speak in Los Angeles in the year before Bontemps headed out for Harlem, the young man "was not prepared for [Garvey's] oddly lyrical style" (p. 8); it made a great impact on him, as on many. Both the individual memoir and the larger collection itself served to establish the Harlem Renaissance as a movement with significant cultural and literary significance; Bontemps' book laid the groundwork for future studies of the era, studies that continue to be produced in the twenty-first century.

The sudden heart attack that took Bontemps's life on June 4, 1973, occurred at the wake of a friend. *Jet* magazine's obituary reported that Bontemps was reading the rosary of sorrows for Clara Perry at her home in Nashville when he collapsed. Alberta Bontemps, however, reported to Bontemps' biographer that her husband had been walking across the front yard to greet Dr. Perry,

the widower, and his brother when he collapsed. In addition to his wife, Alberta, Bontemps was survived by his six children, ten grandchildren, and his sister Ruby. Funeral services at Fisk University's Memorial Chapel on June 7 preceded his interment in Greenwood Cemetery in Nashville. Several other memorials and tributes followed: in Christ Chapel at New York City's Riverside Church on June 20, 1973; at the Summer Institute in Directed Research at Jackson State College in Jackson, Mississippi, on July 18, 1973; and a Fisk University tribute on January 27, 1974. In 1988 the Arna Bontemps Foundation established the Arna Bontemps African American Museum in Alexandria, Louisiana. Bontemps's childhood home, which has been placed on the National Register of Historic Places, houses the museum.

POETRY

Bontemps' writing career began with poetry: he found recognition and publication in the 1920s at *Opportunity* and the *Crisis* magazines, two important outlets through which Harlem Renaissance writers found a voice. His early poems are his most frequently anthologized, particularly "Golgotha Is a Mountain" (1926) and "The Return" (1927), both winners of the Alexander Pushkin Award for Poetry sponsored by *Opportunity,* and "Nocturne at Bethesda" (1927), which won first prize in the poetry contest sponsored by the *Crisis*. Looking back on Bontemps' career as a poet, Sterling Brown concluded in 1973:

> His poetry is as unlike mine as poetry could be, but I still admire it for diction, cadence, thought and tone: it has meditativeness, Christianity, forgiveness but still shrewd awareness, as in "A Hand Is on the Gate," [which contains] sad but sympathetic qualities.... At its best Arna's poetry established that, for most men, freedom is a necessity, but that winning it against powerful forces without the race and within the race is no easy thing.
>
> (p. 96)

Brown's impressions can be illustrated in "The Return," which laments a broken romance through lyric language:

> once more, you and I, and above the hurting sound
> of these comes back the throbbing of remembered
> rain,
> treasured rain falling on dark ground.
>
> (*Personals,* p. 12)

Yet the poet also integrates racial consciousness through the judicious evocation of the jungle imagery through which Harlem Renaissance writers often celebrated their cultural heritage. In this poem, "Darkness brings the jungle to our room," where the "throb of muffled drums" and memories "retained from those lost nights our fathers slept / in huts" form the backdrop to the "night of love." Images that also pervaded writings by Langston Hughes and Countee Cullen appear here, such as "the young spice trees" and the "jungle tapestries" against which we hear "the muffled drum-beats throb." This poem successfully combines the imagery of racial pride with more traditional elements of lyric love poetry.

Much of Bontemps' early poetry employs images of strength and racial pride, as in "The Day-Breakers," which was included in Alain Locke's seminal anthology *The New Negro* (1925). In "The Day-Breakers," the poet speaks of communal ambition and determination, noting that "We are not come to wage a strife" but insisting in the end that "we" seek "the rising sun." The sense of optimism that informed his young pieces endured as a central facet of his poetic vision. Late in his life, Bontemps assembled his poetry in the volume *Personals*. Though published by Paul Breman in 1963, many of the poems that comprise *Personals* were written earlier in his life. Reissued as part of Breman's selective "Heritage" series, the collection stands as a testament to Bontemps' continued importance as a poet.

NOVELS AND SHORT STORIES

Bontemps' initial foray as a professional writer was serious adult fiction; it was in this genre that he sought to earn an income and an audience, despite considerable obstacles to both. His novels and stories paid respectful attention to their African American protagonists, depicting these

people and their struggles as dignified and honorable. His first novel, *God Sends Sunday,* was published in 1931. Set in the late nineteenth century, the bildungsroman traces the fortunes and tragedies that befall one Li'l Augie, a black jockey who bears a striking resemblance to Bontemps' beloved Uncle Buddy. The twinned themes of luck and chance run throughout the novel, most notably foregrounded in the culture of gambling and horseracing by which Augie's life is defined. Paradoxically, in Bontemps' own life, fate interrupted the book's success. "No doubt the greatest irony surrounding *Sunday*'s publication," writes his biographer Kirkland Jones, "is that as the novel was coming off the press, its author lost his 'Uncle Buddy.' Buddy, who had received an autographed copy of the work, went out celebrating, and returning home on foot, was hit and killed by a car" (p. 73).

Yet the novel also pays homage to W. E. B. Du Bois, whose celebration of black racial identity in *The Souls of Black Folk* declared that "the Negro is a sort of seventh son, born with a veil, and gifted with second sight" (p. 5). Evoking the mystic tradition, "Little Augie believed in conjure and 'signs,' " Bontemps writes, early in *God Sends Sunday*. "Having been born with a caul over his face, he was endowed (he believed) with clairvoyant powers" (p. 10). While the evocation of folk tradition and conjuring situates Augie's narrative within the African American cultural heritage, the novel also grapples with the larger (American) epistemological conflict between fate and self-determination. As the critic Lisa Abney notes, "Bontemps ... does not leave Augie's destiny as the driving force in the text; the author brings the issue of free will into the novel. In many ways, Augie's choices lead to a self-fulfilling prophecy, for his decisions are often motivated by his quest for wholeness" (p. 88).

In the same year that *God Sends Sunday* was published, Bontemps won the *Opportunity* literary prize for "A Summer Tragedy," a story that he remained proud of throughout his life. It traces the final afternoon in the life of Jeff and Jennie Patton, a loving couple of elderly black sharecroppers, as they embark upon what soon becomes clear is their final journey. Solitary in their old age, the loving couple (Jeff addresses Jennie as "baby" throughout the story) have lost their five grown children in two years and can no longer care for themselves or each other. Jeff's flashes of fear as he prepares for the trip serve to foreground the tragic ending in which they run their rattletrap Ford into a roaring river. Such moments are juxtaposed, however, against the formal deliberation of their departure, as they dress in their best clothes with careful attention to detail. Poignant and haunting, the tale has been frequently anthologized.

Published in 1936 by the Beacon Press, Bontemps' historical novel *Black Thunder* received excellent reviews upon its release and it remains an important and highly regarded work today. Using court records from the actual case, Bontemps develops a fictionalized account of the 1800 slave revolt near Richmond, Virginia, that came to be known as the Gabriel Insurrection. The novel depicts slavery in a realistic fashion, noting the tensions between literate and illiterate characters, while still honoring the cultural value of the black vernacular tradition. While the novel is peopled with a range of characters (slave and free, black and white, young and old), its central force is Gabriel Prosser, author of the putative rebellion. "Don't you want to be free?" the characters repeatedly ask themselves and each other, and the question resonated as much for the era in which Bontemps wrote the novel as that in which he set it. "*Black Thunder* reflects its author's growing ambivalence concerning religion, which in his recent experience had opposed his art and humiliated him," writes Arnold Rampersad in his introduction to the novel's 1992 edition.

> It expresses his deepening respect for radicalism, and his growing outrage at how blacks were treated from time immemorial in the United States. It also shows his related concern with the proper assertion of sexuality, as Bontemps wrestled with the consequences of growing up in a repressive, puritanical religion.
>
> (p. xiii)

Bontemps' 1939 historical novel, *Drums at Dusk*, reflected his Rosenwald Fellowship–funded research in Haiti. Situated during the Haitian

revolution of 1791, the echoes of the French Revolution's bloody massacre still linger in the memory of Bontemps' fictional white French slave owners. Though the novel is more interested in the everyday life of Saint-Domingue's people than in the details of political rebellion, Toussaint L'Ouverture appears as a minor character in the novel. Like Bontemps' other adult fiction, *Drums at Dusk* is characterized by both a seriousness of purpose and a commitment to aesthetic expression manifested in lyric language and eloquent, poetic descriptions. Late in his life, Bontemps expressed disappointment that his novels failed to find an audience large and consistent enough to support his continued attention to that genre and approach. "I began to suspect that it was fruitless," he lamented, "for a Negro in the United States to address serious writing to my generation" (*Black Thunder,* 1992, p. xxiv).

COLLABORATIONS

Bontemps successfully collaborated with two dear lifelong friends, an accomplishment that not only speaks to his admirable aesthetic and generic range but also suggests his equanimity as coauthor and coeditor. Many of these collaborations involved children's literature and as such reflected a deep political commitment. As the critic Katherine Capshaw Smith has argued,

> Bontemps believed children's morals to be malleable, and he thought literature the best means to influence the child's ethical development toward social change. Bontemps also argued for the gravity of writing for children, depicting his turn away from adult novels as a plunge into more serious social literature.
>
> (p. 237)

Popo and Fifina, coauthored with Langston Hughes in 1932, was developed largely through correspondence by mail. Written in lyric language reflecting its two authors' accomplishments in poetry, the book celebrates the Haitian children's black heritage. Proud, lively, obedient, and inquisitive, Popo and Fifina personify a promising future; Bontemps and Hughes deliberately eschew the caricatures through which blackness is often described. The plot itself is nothing spectacular: the story follows the two children and their family as they move from their home in the mountains to live in a village at the shore. But the book's distinctive celebration of the children's blackness as a source of beauty is what gives the story its aesthetic richness. The children's Papa Jean, the opening pages announce, is "a big powerful man ... and there was a happy bounce in his step." Their Mamma Anna was "a strong woman with high glossy cheek bones" (p. 2). The book is filled with happiness and jubilation that belie the characters' impoverished condition. To be sure, *Popo and Fifina* is quite clear about the economic challenges facing the family; yet the difficulty of their material conditions has little impact on their fortitude. Of the collaboration, Bontemps later wrote, with characteristically self-effacing good humor, "He had the story and I had the children, so my publisher thought it might work" (*Black Thunder,* 1992, p. xxviii). Bontemps also collaborated successfully with Hughes on several anthologies, discussed below.

When Bontemps met Jack Conroy in 1938, he befriended a children's author with whom he would share a lifelong camaraderie and a very successful collaboration. Joining his efforts with Conroy's like-minded talent, Bontemps was able to develop a vision for children's literature as a genre with political as well as aesthetic resonance. The stories produced by Bontemps and Conroy contain two distinctive characteristics: they all combine some element of the oral storytelling tradition, and they all feature white characters. In her study "From *Little Black Sambo* to *Popo and Fifina*: Arna Bontemps and the Creation of African-American Children's Literature," Violet J. Harris speculates about the reasons for this choice (it may have been publisher's demands, self-confidence, or perhaps simply an exercise of a writer's prerogative). Her excellent, detailed analysis underscores the extraordinary range of Bontemps' skills, interpersonal and literary.

Bontemps' first collaborative effort with Jack Conroy, *The Fast Sooner Hound,* was published the same year and was a best seller. Originating in an assortment of "industrial tall tales" that

Conroy had collected as part of a Federal Writers Project study on "The Negro in Illinois," the tale describes a wager between two railroad men—the "Boomer fireman," who keeps the coal fire stoked on the steam locomotives, and the "Roadmaster," who oversees the operation of the trains—about whether the fireman's Sooner hound can outrun the Cannon Ball, the fastest train around. In the tale's denouement, the Sooner hound not only keeps up with the speeding train, he is able to both run alongside the train and urinate on the fire that results from the Roadmaster's running the train too fast. "The original tale might be considered a little too robustious both in language and situation for kiddies," Conroy later recalled, "and Arna helped in gentling it a bit (but not much!)" (p. 55).

In 1945 Bontemps and Conroy published *They Seek a City*. Documenting the African American Great Migration from the South to northern cities during the early decades of the century, the book later seemed unfinished to the writers. As Bontemps wrote, "We soon realized that we were dealing with currents that were still running vigorously and that we could not tell when or where they would crest. To that extent, our book was premature" (Preface to *Anyplace but Here,* p. vi). Conroy agreed, recalling that each man kept "a file on likely additional material" in the intervening years—adding, significantly, "and there was plenty of it!" (*Memories,* p. 55). Thus, the two revised the work, and in 1966 a revised and enlarged version appeared, titled *Anyplace but Here*. That same year, the two published a children's book titled *Slappy Hooper, the Wonderful Sign Painter*. Also adapted from one of Conroy's collection of industrial tall tales, the story follows Slappy, whose adventures emerge from him being too good at what he does: because his signs are too realistic, chaos ensues. Their final collaboration, *Sam Patch, the High, Wide & Handsome Jumper,* was published in 1951. As Conroy recalled, the story "was based on an actual person, a crazy boy who during the Jacksonian period achieved fame by his daring leaps. Arna and I injected some conflict by introducing a Westerner of the ring-tailed roarer breed, a chest-thumping braggart, who competed with modest Yankee Sam in a jumping contest and lost" (*Memories,* p. 55).

ANTHOLOGIES

Golden Slippers, Bontemps' first poetry anthology, was distinguished by the excellent range, variety, eloquence, and aesthetic accomplishment of its contributors. Appealing specifically to black children and teenagers, *Golden Slippers* sought to expand the cultural work begun in Bontemps' children's novels by demonstrating, with example after magnificent example, the richness of the African American literary tradition. It was published in 1941 and was an extraordinary accomplishment for its time.

Bontemps' next anthology, in collaboration with Langston Hughes, was *The Poetry of the Negro, 1746–1949,* published in 1949; it reflects both men's desire to shape a more encompassing curriculum. The anthology's implicit argument—that black American poets have a distinguished tradition of aesthetic accomplishment dating back to the eighteenth century—is evident in the broad strokes of its inclusiveness. James Weldon Johnson had offered readers the first anthology of black verse, *The Book of American Negro Poetry,* in 1922, and the Bontemps-Hughes collaboration expands and develops Johnson's efforts. The table of contents shows Negro poetry to be a large tent, housing the likes of Jupiter Hammon, George Moses Horton, Frances E. W. Harper, and Paul Laurence Dunbar. Though critical response to the anthology was generally positive, some reviewers took issue with the absence of spirituals; others were unimpressed by the section documenting "Tributary Poems by Non-Negroes." Critics objected again when Hughes and Bontemps revised the collection later in life to include poetry published through 1970. The absence of explicitly political poets like Nikki Giovanni suggested to some readers that the volume sought to reinforce a particular aesthetic ideology.

Published in 1958, *The Book of Negro Folklore,* also a Bontemps and Langston Hughes collaboration, was the first comprehensive anthology of black American folk tales. Bontemps

wrote the book's introduction. Tracing back to antebellum days, the large (over six hundred pages) illustrated volume includes a variety of raw, anonymously authored tales: many of these have been transcribed for accuracy, not edited for eloquence. A literary mind is evident in the headings by which the volume's contents are organized, however. Though some sections are announced with straightforward descriptors (such as "Animal Tales," "Animal Rhymes," "Ballads," "Blues," and "Work Songs"), other section titles betray a poetic impulse. "Sometimes in the Mind," "God, Man, and the Devil," and "Do You Call That a Preacher?" are a few such examples. The contents are exhaustive: folk music includes gospel, blues, spirituals, and work songs; folk tales include animal stories and rhymes, slave narratives, ghost stories, magical tales, and superstitions; religious tales include preacher stories, sermons, and prayers; and modern folklore includes Harlem slang, city jive, jazz tales, and street cries. Some critical essays are included as well: Julia Peterkin explains black burial societies; Sterling Brown discusses spirituals; and Zora Neale Hurston tells about High John de Conquerer. This anthology implicitly testifies to the richness and diversity of the African American cultural heritage; it has been a staple in college anthropology courses for many years.

CHILDREN'S AND YOUNG ADULT LITERATURE

While his first coauthored children's book, *Popo and Fifina,* allowed Bontemps to integrate his love for writing with his love for his family, in his first single-authored children's book, *You Can't Pet a Possum,* he successfully incorporated his love for black culture into the mix. The story of an eight-year-old boy from Alabama named Shine Boy and his dog Butch, published in 1934, remains a distinctive contribution to the canons of both African American and children's literature. *Possum* not only employs black colloquial speech in a racially sensitive and authentic manner, it simplifies the speech patterns of its black characters so as to make them accessible to younger readers. Focusing on the rhythms of dialect, Bontemps drew out the natural poetry in African America's speech habits, offering a linguistic model in which both his own children and his readers at large could take pride.

Following the adventures of three Alabama farm boys as they hop a train to visit their uncle in Harlem, the novel *Sad-Faced Boy* (1937) traces some of African America's central historical themes: the Great Migration, the conflict between farm and city life, the search for identity. Laura Gray-Rosendale has argued that "Bontemps has yet to receive adequate attention for the complicated rhetorical tactics" in books like *Sad-Faced Boy*, a novel that is, in her view, "quite discursively complex" (p. 149). By deploying Slumber, Rags, and Willie as trickster figures who both appeal to and subvert a white audience's expectations, Bontemps satirizes city life and celebrates the rural folk as racially and culturally authentic.

Bontemps undertook a new genre for young readers, biography, during a time when his family life was active and he was in the midst of extraordinary professional productivity. *We Have Tomorrow,* a collection of profiles of twelve successful African Americans, appeared in 1945. Appealing more to an adolescent than a juvenile audience, the book featured a range of personalities, including the commercial artist E. Simms Campbell, the diplomat and political scientist Ralph Bunche, and the pianist Hazel Scott. Creative as well as didactic, each profile contains a distinctive title (the distinguished milliner Mildred E. Blount, for instance, is "A Girl Who Liked Hats") thereby conveying an implicit thesis about the black community's range of professions, talents, and paths to success. The book's title comes from Langston Hughes's poem "Youth" and underscores the book's optimistic tone: "We have tomorrow / Bright before us / Like a flame" (*Collected Poems*, p. 39).

Story of the Negro, published in 1948, continues and expands Bontemps' efforts to present young readers with the cultural and historical legacy of the Negro people. Tracing the legacy of African Americans throughout civilization, the book includes a chronology that traces "Negro history" alongside "world history," thereby offering an alternative interpretation of

America itself. "Bontemps spotlights a second approach in texts contending with black identity and its relationship to America," notes Katherine Capshaw Smith, "an exchange between the categories that allows black identity to take its place on the terrain of American history" (p. 167). Bontemps' own comments about *Story of the Negro* make clear that his motivation in writing was both personal and ideological. When the idea of this book was first proposed, he explained,

> I had some trouble thinking of it as a juvenile.... in this regard, all I can say now is that it consists mainly of things I learned after I left school that I wish I had known much earlier.... These things that I would like to have known as a schoolboy and as a college student in the integrated schools of California ... when we were given the small fragments of ... uncomplimentary information about Negro Americans.
>
> (quoted in Jones, pp. 134–135)

The popularity of the text led to its being revised and reissued in 1955. It was a runner-up for the Newbery Medal in 1949 and won the Jane Addams Children's Book Award in 1956.

Because Bontemps tended to juggle several projects simultaneously, the overlap and intersection of his personal and professional lives led to a richness and diversity of approach. For example, his library work in cultivating the collection of Negroana at Fisk made him particularly aware of the fertile tradition of slave narratives. This led to several related books, beginning with a biography of George Washington Carver, published in 1950 and then revised and reissued as *The Story of George Washington Carver* in 1954. This book not only extended the ideological and pedagogical work of Bontemps' other children's and young adult literature but also sought to cultivate national interest in African American culture. As Violet Harris notes, the work Bontemps produced specifically for a young audience "represents the acceptance of African American children's literature among White publishers and readers and the continued expansion of the literature for African American children" (p. 548). By showing how Carver's story is inextricably interwoven in the larger narrative of American life, Bontemps emphasizes the unique and precious value of Negro culture. Bontemps also published *Frederick Douglass: Slave, Fighter, Freeman* in 1959. Addressed to a young audience, the biography's originality lies in its focus on Douglass' childhood and youth.

The diversity of Bontemps' perspective (in terms of genre, audience, approach, and execution) is also evident in *Chariot in the Sky* (1951), an ambitious and historically resonant account of the renowned Fisk Jubilee Singers. Bontemps' biographer points out that *Chariots* "represented the fulfillment of one of Arna's long-held dreams.... for he had been fascinated with the singers who gave to the world Negro spirituals and to the South its foremost liberal arts college for African Americans" (Jones, p. 125). Opening in the antebellum South, the novel follows the extraordinary transformation of a talented young singer named Caleb; born into slavery but freed after the Civil War, Caleb grows into full, independent selfhood, not only through hard work but also through the support and guidance of the music program at Fisk University. Alain Locke dismissed the effort cruelly, claiming that the retelling of the Jubilee Singers' origins has "sparse justification" and arguing condescendingly that a "more mature interpretation of the social background of Reconstruction would have been both useful and enhancing" (p. 12). Regardless of Locke's reservations in 1951, the book was reissued in 2002 by Oxford University Press in a volume that includes a foreword by David Levering Lewis; the renewed interest and evident audience suggests that the novel is, in fact, of lasting value.

Lonesome Boy (1955), a book that has been characterized as Bontemps' masterpiece, originated as a short story for adults. The children's editors at Houghton Mifflin, where it was published, initially had some reservations about the story; in Bontemps' words, "they couldn't dig it" (quoted in Jones, p. 132). Nevertheless, the tale of a boy named Bubber and his silver trumpet has endured. Written in two days, the bildungsroman contains some resonant autobiographical overtones. For example, Bontemps' own father had, like Bubber, played trombone in Claiborne Williams' jazz band in the years before he settled

down to become a brick mason. In responding to Langston Hughes's complimentary comments about the book, Bontemps wrote quite directly about his attachment to it. "This is the book I *enjoyed* writing," he explained, "perhaps because I did it impulsively for myself, while editors hounded me for my misdeeds and threatened me if I did not deliver manuscripts I had contracted for. So I closed the door for two days and had myself a time" (*Arna Bontemps–Llangston Hughes Letters, 1925–1967*p. 319).

Bubber, the lonesome title character, finds solace in his trumpet; but this source of comfort and self-expression drives a wedge between the boy and his grandfather, who views the horn as a source of "devilment." Without his grandfather's understanding, Bubber leaves one night for New Orleans, where he achieves instant success. He becomes disoriented, however, and his self-absorption alienates Bubber from himself: "he scarcely knew himself in a mirror. He scarcely knew day from night" (p. 10). Rather than providing a source of nourishing self-expression, Bubber's music takes him instead into the marketplace where it is commodified and exploited. "But he went to so many places to play his trumpet," the story explains, "he forgot where he had been and he got into the habit of not paying much attention" (p. 13). One night, Bubber is summoned to play at a dazzling ball (the reader is led to believe that this is the Devil's ball), and he becomes so enchanted by the frenzy of his own music that the scene passes by him "like a dream" (p. 21), leaving Bubber to awaken, solitary, up in a tree. Upon returning home to his grandfather, Bubber learns that the older man had had a similar experience in his own youth, and that his warning to Bubber sought to prevent him from ending up at "the devil's ball" himself.

Critics have celebrated the sophisticated rhetorical, cultural, and aesthetic maneuvers in the story. Katherine Capshaw Smith, for example, notes how "Bontemps clearly links Bubber's loss of self with enslavement" (p. 268). Smith persuasively connects the story's denouement to the legacy of the Harlem Renaissance, where black artistic development found itself hostage to a white audience. "Through Grandpa's aesthetic statement and Bubber's experience with the faceless white patrons at the devil's ball," she explains, "Bontemps comments on the bondage of Harlem Renaissance writers to images of themselves as solitary artists and to a confining patronage system" (p. 269). Joseph A. Alvarez offers a broader argument, suggesting that "a careful look at Bontemps's work shows the lonesome boy theme appearing over several years and in different forms" (p. 23). In Alvarez's reading of Bontemps' oeuvre, the lonesome boy personifies the alienation felt by the writer himself when, throughout his youth and school life, he found no images of black people or African American cultural heritage. Thus, "a powerful and deeply felt sense of injustice and an equally heartfelt nostalgic longing" (pp. 24–25) lie behind Bubber. "We ... see Bontemps's recognition that all students suffer when schools socialize students in a monocultural context," Alvarez asserts. "He set about remedying that no-longer-acceptable situation through his own literary production" (p. 25). This compelling argument illuminates the generally unacknowledged but powerfully active political impulse behind Bontemps' children's and young adult fiction. Bontemps himself admitted, later in life, that publishers' resistance to his serious fiction frustrated his efforts as a writer, "and I began to consider the alternative of trying to reach young readers not yet hardened or grown insensitive to man's inhumanity to man, as it is called" (*Black Thunder,* 1992, p. xxiv).

Selected Bibliography

WORKS OF ARNA BONTEMPS

Novels, Stories, and Poetry

God Sends Sunday. New York: Harcourt, Brace, 1931.

With Langston Hughes. *Popo and Fifina: Children of Haiti*. New York: Macmillan, 1932.

You Can't Pet a Possum. New York: Morrow, 1934.

Black Thunder. New York: Macmillan, 1936; Boston: Beacon Press, 1992.

Sad-Faced Boy. Boston: Houghton Mifflin, 1937.

Drums at Dusk. New York: Macmillan, 1939; London: Harrap, 1940.

With Jack Conroy. *The Fast Sooner Hound*. Boston: Houghton Mifflin, 1942.

With Jack Conroy. *Slappy Hooper, the Wonderful Sign Painter*. Boston: Houghton Mifflin, 1946.

Chariot in the Sky: A Story of the Jubilee Singers. Philadelphia: Winston, 1951; Oxford and New York: Oxford University Press, 2002.

With Jack Conroy. *Sam Patch, the High, Wide & Handsome Jumper*. Boston: Houghton Mifflin, 1951.

Lonesome Boy. Boston: Houghton Mifflin, 1955.

Personals. London: Breman, 1963.

Mr. Kelso's Lion. Philadelphia: Lippincott, 1970.

The Old South: "A Summer Tragedy" and Other Stories of the Thirties. New York: Dodd, Mead, 1973.

Bubber Goes to Heaven. New York: Oxford University Press, 1998.

NONFICTION

With Jack Conroy. *They Seek a City*. Garden City, N.Y.: Doubleday, 1945. Revised and enlarged as *Anyplace but Here,* New York: Hill & Wang, 1966.

We Have Tomorrow. Boston: Houghton Mifflin, 1945.

Story of the Negro. New York: Knopf, 1948; 2nd ed., enl., 1955.

George Washington Carver. Evanston, Ill: Row, Peterson, 1950. Rev. as *The Story of George Washington Carver,* New York: Grossett & Dunlap, 1954.

Frederick Douglass: Slave, Fighter, Freeman. New York: Knopf, 1959.

100 Years of Negro Freedom. New York: Dodd, Mead, 1961.

Famous Negro Athletes. New York: Dodd, Mead, 1964.

With Langston Hughes. *I Too Sing America*. Dortmund, Germany: Verlag Lambert Lensing, 1964.

Free at Last: The Life of Frederick Douglass. New York: Dodd, Mead, 1971.

Young Booker: Booker T. Washington's Early Days. New York: Dodd, Mead, 1972.

EDITED VOLUMES

Father of the Blues: An Autobiography of W. C. Handy. New York and London: Harper, 1941.

Golden Slippers: An Anthology of Negro Poetry for Young Readers. New York & London: Harper, 1941.

With Langston Hughes. *The Poetry of the Negro, 1746–1949*. Garden City, N.Y.: Doubleday, 1949. Rev. and enl. as *The Poetry of the Negro, 1746–1970,* 1970.

With Langston Hughes. *The Book of Negro Folklore*. New York: Dodd, Mead, 1958.

The Harlem Renaissance Remembered: Essays. Edited by Bontemps. New York: Dodd, Mead, 1972.

American Negro Poetry. New York: Hill & Wang, 1963. Rev. ed., 1974.

OTHER WORKS

With Countee Cullen. *St. Louis Woman*. New York, Martin Beck Theater, March 30, 1946. (A version of this play, *Free and Easy,* ran in Amsterdam in 1959 and in Paris in 1960.)

"The Awakening: A Memoir." In *The Harlem Renaissance Remembered: Essays*. Edited by Bontemps. New York: Dodd, Mead, 1972.

Arna Bontemps–Langston Hughes Letters, 1925–1967. Edited by Charles Harold Nichols. New York: Dodd, Mead, 1980.

PAPERS

Three separate library collections house the papers of Arna Bontemps. The Arna Bontemps Collection residing in the Special Collections Research Center at the Syracuse University Library is by far the largest, and includes correspondence as well as manuscripts of plays, stories, songs and speeches. Additional correspondence and writings are also included in the James Weldon Johnson Collection in the Yale Collection of American Literature, Beinecke Rare Book and Manuscript Library. The Arna Bontemps Collection that is housed in the Special Collections and Archives at Fisk University reflects Bontemps's career as Fisk's librarian, and includes correspondence, library materials, committee and organizational items, newspaper clippings, and photographs.

CRITICAL AND BIOGRAPHICAL STUDIES

Abney, Lisa. "Dualism and the Quest for Wholeness in Arna Bontemps's *God Sends Sunday*." In *Upon Further Review: Sports in American Literature*. Edited by Michael Cocchiarale and Scott Emmert. Westport, Conn.: Greenwood Press, 2004. Pp. 87–95.

Alvarez, Joseph A. "The Lonesome Boy Theme as Emblem for Arna Bontemps's Children's Literature." *African American Review* 32, no. 1:23–31 (spring 1998).

Baker, Houston. "Arna Bontemps." *Black World,* September 1973, pp. 4–9.

Brown, Sterling. "Arna Bontemps: Co-Worker, Comrade." *Black World,* September 1973, pp. 91–97.

Conroy, Jack. "Memories of Arna Bontemps: Friend and Collaborator." *Negro American Literature Forum* 10, no. 2:53–57 (summer 1976).

Du Bois, W. E. B. *The Souls of Black Folk*. New York: Penguin, 1989.

Flamming, Douglas. "A Westerner in Search of 'Negroness': Region and Race in the Writing of Arna Bontemps." In *Over the Edge: Remapping the American West*. Edited by Valerie J. Matsumoto and Blake Allmendinger.

Berkeley and Los Angeles: University of California Press, 1999. Pp. 85–106.

Fleming, Robert E. *James Weldon Johnson and Arna Wendell Bontemps: A Reference Guide.* Boston: G. K. Hall, 1978.

Gray-Rosendale, Laura. "Geographies of Resistance: Rhetorics of Race and Mobility in Arna Bontemps' *Sad-Faced Boy* (1937)." In *Alternative Rhetorics: Challenges to the Rhetorical Tradition.* Edited by Laura Gray-Rosendale and Sibylle Gruber. Albany: State University of New York Press, 2001. Pp. 149–165.

Harris, Violet J. "From *Little Black Sambo* to *Popo and Fifina*: Arna Bontemps and the Creation of African-American Children's Literature." *Lion and the Unicorn* 14, no. 1:108–127 (June 1990).

———. "African American Children's Literature: The First One Hundred Years." *Journal of Negro Education* 59, no. 4:540–555 (autumn 1990).

Hughes, Langston. *The Big Sea.* New York: Knopf, 1945.

———. *The Collected Poems of Langston Hughes.* New York: Vintage, 1994.

Jones, Kirkland C. *Renaissance Man from Louisiana: A Biography of Arna Wendell Bontemps.* Westport, Conn.: Greenwood Press, 1992.

Locke, Alain. "The High Price of Integration: A Review of the Literature of the Negro for 1951." *Phylon* 13, no. 1:7–18 (1952).

Rampersad, Arnold. Introduction to *Black Thunder.* New York: Boston: Beacon Press, 1992.

Smith, Katherine Capshaw. *Children's Literature of the Harlem Renaissance.* Bloomington: Indiana University Press, 2004.

INTERVIEWS

"Arna Bontemps Talks About the Renaissance." In *The Harlem Renaissance Generation: An Anthology.* Vol. 1. Compiled and edited by L. M. Collins. Typescript. Fisk University Library, Nashville, Tenn., 1972. Pp. 207–219.

James, Charles. "On the Legacy of the Harlem Renaissance: A Conversation with Arna Bontemps and Aaron Douglas." *Obsidian* 4, no. 1:32–53 (1978).

AGNES BOULTON

(1892—1968)

W. D. King

THE *NEW YORK Times* obituary of Agnes Boulton, late in November of 1968, is an act of battery. The second wife of Eugene O'Neill, dead at the age of seventy-five (actually seventy-six), faces scorn and divorce again, only this time the decree comes from the paper of record. With a whip of the wrist, the obituary tells her story as one of literary and emotional failure. We hear of tumult and tempest in the decade of her marriage (1918–1929) to the iconic father of American drama, while she is said to have disdained the theater. Her early work disappears under the smear of "pulp," and no mention is made of her praised 1944 novel, *The Road Is Before Us*. The only words of hers quoted come from the memoir she wrote late in her life, which celebrated a marriage that did not endure to a writer she could not fathom. The *Times* insists on naming her with the name of a third husband from whom it says she was separated, though in fact she had divorced him several years earlier. It assaults her motherhood, her housekeeping, her diet. The photograph shows her downcast and corpselike, and no wonder. It is an untidy grave dug here for a woman who wrote virtually every day of her adult life and who articulated much of what words can mean—or not—for a woman in the twentieth century.

The anonymous obituarist was only following a trend set at the time of Boulton's divorce of O'Neill, in 1929, immediately after which he married the actress Carlotta Monterey. The latter soon settled into the conviction that Boulton was a wicked and deceitful woman who had never been worthy to be in the same room with O'Neill, much less married to him and mother to his children, Shane and Oona. O'Neill, who was then at the peak of his prosperity, used all his leverage to limit Boulton's stake in the settlement. Furthermore, the terms of the divorce specified severe penalties should she write about him or the marriage, whether it be fiction or nonfiction. Relations between Boulton and O'Neill (backed by his new wife) only deteriorated from then on.

But then O'Neill died in 1953, releasing her from the restriction, and Boulton published her memoir in 1958, at just the time when the first wave of biographers were seeking sources on O'Neill. Every biographer knows that the work begins with gaining access and rights, and Carlotta O'Neill held rights to O'Neill's archive. Associates of O'Neill had long noted what a fierce control she exerted, almost from the beginning of her relationship with him in 1926, three years before the completion of the divorce. After his death, the widow, who was also the executor, controlled the story of his life. To the extent that Boulton was a part of the story of O'Neill's life, Carlotta controlled her story, too, to put it mildly. The *Times* obituary is indicative.

So, perhaps it is time to look again at the life and career of Agnes Boulton, putting aside Carlotta and Gene, and assessing her in her own right. That would seem to accord with certain principles of literary criticism, but unfortunately it would largely miss what is important about this writer (and perhaps most writers), which is how her words work in contingency. Few would argue that her early writings—short stories, novelettes, dramatic sketches—deserve special praise as lasting works of literature, but they are well worth reading as windows on the values and practices of an author at a fascinating moment of change in the literary marketplace. Most of the writings from her middle period (and there were a lot) have been lost—never finished, never published, it's hard to say why. Her one novel, *The Road Is Before Us,* is worthy of another look

in terms of how novelists were depicting American subjectivity at a moment of awakening existentialism, but it is no forgotten masterpiece, though it is forgotten. Her book belongs on page two or three of a lengthy purgatorial list.

The same cannot be said of the outstanding product of her career, *Part of a Long Story: Eugene O'Neill as a Young Man in Love,* which is indeed a forgotten masterpiece. Her writing about the most self-reflexive writer in American drama had the effect of carrying her narration into an extraordinary category within memoir, unsettling many of the master narratives of modernism and American literary history. However, one might well ask whether this means that her book must be read as a correlative of his status as a modernist innovator and iconic figure of twentieth-century American culture.

The singular perspective she brings to this story—and it is her story, as well as his—suggests that, yes, her work must be read as correlative and that, nevertheless, or for that reason, it should be seen as distinctive and important. While O'Neill's work demonstrates a driven psychological development toward a self characterized by autonomy and mastery, in line with Freudian models, Boulton's work demonstrates a development in line with a relational model, as developed in the 1980s by Jean Baker Miller and others associated with the Stone Center at Wellesley College. This group challenged the idea that human beings pass through phases of relationship (in childhood) only in order to achieve independence and self-determination in adulthood. The Freudian model and its derivatives tended to view women as deficient or undeveloped because they often seemed to persist in relational modes throughout childhood and adolescence and into adulthood. Was this because they lacked clear boundaries or were too emotional or were lacking? The researchers at the Stone Center argued that, instead, women might follow a different course of development from men, one that always operated with "self-in-relation," even in adulthood. Rather than looking at the relational as a failed version of autonomy, they saw the autonomous self as a version or mode of the relational.

This theory of development ran parallel to and in some ways was initiated by Carol Gilligan's important *In a Different Voice* (1982), which argued that women might operate with a moral structure fundamentally different from that of men. Since men had largely defined the terms of ethical thinking, Gilligan argued that an effort should be made to hear the "different voice" of women on morality. This work, along with the Stone Center's, helped inspire a generation of feminist thinking about women's self-expression.

It is fruitful to interpret Boulton's writing using these terms and thus to see her work ironically in contrast to the solitary genius model of the expressive self in O'Neill's writing. The plays he wrote while married to Boulton, especially during the later years of the marriage, epitomize the contrast. He created towering, domineering, visionary plays in which he constructs the self resisting submersion in the modern muddle. As an author, he embodied the man who would not be co-opted or subjected, and in some ways he also played the role of the man who would not be married and would not be a father. Even before she knew O'Neill, Boulton was testing the postulate of marriage to such a man in her writing, and *Part of a Long Story* is an astonishing, though unfinished, report on the test. Thus, without at all implying that her work is secondary or derivative of O'Neill's, her literary career might best be understood in terms of phases: before, during, and after O'Neill.

A FAMILY TRADITION: LOOKING BEYOND THE SURFACE

Agnes Ruby Boulton was born in London, September 19, 1892, an American child. Her parents had gone to England for an extended stay with relatives, but they were residents of Philadelphia. Her father, Edward W. Boulton, was a painter, one of the foremost students of Thomas Eakins at the Pennsylvania Academy of the Fine Arts during the 1880s. Those were difficult years for Eakins, who was taking "life study" beyond where it usually went in an era when sentimental and idealized representations matched the genteel view of life. Eakins insisted

that the artist should begin with the anatomical, the naked being, in and within the skin. He insisted on fully unclothed models and reportedly, on certain occasions, offered his own nudity to study. He also experimented with photography of the nude model and plaster casting of body parts, including those of corpses, to take the study of physical form to a new level of actuality.

Much of this offended the sensibilities of the Academy's board of directors, and Eakins was asked to resign in 1886. Some of his students, including Edward Boulton, formed the Art Students' League of Philadelphia, retaining Eakins as their teacher. Late in the 1880s Agnes Boulton's mother, Cecil Williams, began to pose as a model in the League's classes. It is not known exactly when she married Edward Boulton or why they decided to travel to England, but Agnes was born during that journey. Soon after their return, they moved to West Point Pleasant, New Jersey, to an area near the Manasquan River, which Eakins and Boulton had painted during the 1880s. The Eakins background is important to consider because Agnes admired her mother as a "free soul," an emancipated woman, who read widely and unconventionally in search of wisdom, and she admired her father for his gentle spirit and his ability to look beyond the surface of things in his art. A liberated address of the real characterized much of Boulton's early writing, indeed her whole career, if you consider that she was also always trying to sell her words for cash.

EARLY STORIES: BREEZY AND SNAPPY

Much of Boulton's schooling was in Philadelphia, where the Boultons and Williams had family, but before she finished high school she published her first short story, "The Pink Dress," in the *New York Evening Telegram.* Venues for new fiction were just beginning to crest during those years, in newspapers, journals, and magazines, from slick to pulp. After a brief exploratory period she began publishing stories regularly in *Young's Magazine,* which was, in terms of paper quality and literary merit, between a slick and a pulp.

Young's was named for Courtland Young, who founded it in 1899. It flourished not because its writers were outstanding but because virtually every magazine prospered in that burgeoning era, attaining circulation numbers enviable even now. The top of the market—magazines like *Munsey's* and *Cosmopolitan*—attained staggeringly high numbers and did much to shape the market for popular storytelling before radio drama came along. *Young's* was in the middle of the pack, seeking to pay as little as possible for material from lesser-known writers in order to gain the maximum effect on circulation, mainly seeking women readers. The newsstand price, not advertisements, paid most of the bills. By the 1910s Young had picked up on new trends in popular culture, and to some extent he pioneered a trend toward stories that were "snappy," "breezy," "live wire," which meant they expressed modern and relatively liberated attitudes about male-female relations, including sex, though carefully guarded against smuttiness.

In 1915 Young started another monthly magazine, *Breezy Stories,* which continued this trend, and Boulton was a frequent contributor. In the 1920s this magazine got only "saucier," with more and more erotic cover art, apparently now aimed at a male readership, but during the 1910s these magazines would have appealed to an urbane, unembarrassed, but not necessarily libertine readership, perhaps evenly balanced among men and women. Boulton mostly wrote short stories for these magazines, at about a penny a word, but occasionally she wrote a novelette (around fifteen thousand words) or a dramatic sketch (using dramatic dialogue or monologue and minimal scene description to tell a story, but not intended for performance). Her pieces almost uniformly dealt with the complexities of premarital and marital relationships, usually told from the female point of view. Her stories are realistic in that some end more or less happily, with no sudden miracle having occurred, while others end sadly, with no cosmic tragedy having been recognized. Men can be treacherous, but so can women. Working women scheme for release from drudgery and convention, but men also know the burdens of respectability.

Is there a trace of Eakins in these stories, a willingness to visualize human life in terms of its

blood and guts, the subdermal nakedness of the human condition? A few of her stories might suggest that degree of artistic scrutiny, and they all tend toward frankness, but mostly her stories seem to be alert to market expectations and the curiosity of a wide range of readers who were then being flooded with fiction. Desire wells in her heroines, but they turn sharply from hedonism. Bills must be paid, and that generally leads them to men who function within the middle class. Such men can be deceptive, and it's crucial that a woman should learn to work that way, too, ideally a step ahead. A certain amount of sex will sell, but the selling of sex must be punished.

Boulton had three younger sisters, and they all faced the challenge of how to establish freedom in their lives without independent means. Though both mother and father had ties to prosperous relatives, they had chosen to live an outsider existence. He sold a painting from time to time, and she occasionally worked in a pajama factory and rolled her own cigarettes. She was defiant enough to become a "life model" in the name of art. She also studied Buddhism, read Yeats and Synge, and her father was in the circle of Lady Wilde. The four daughters found their own separate paths into adulthood, each eventually marrying, but all defying convention to some degree.

Boulton published a story called "Sisters" in *Breezy Stories* in November 1916, at which point she was twenty-four and had published approximately fifteen stories. One of her sisters was an artist, another wanted to become a lawyer, and the third won a motorcycle at the age of twenty and taught herself how to ride it. The story speaks to the choices made by self-determining women of that era, and one can imagine Boulton and her sisters considering such choices. In the story, Iris had hoped to make a living selling short stories, with little success, but she is tall and fascinating and finds work as an artist's model and eventually as a chorus girl, hoping to move up as an actress. Her sister, Daphne, is small and shy and works as a stenographer in a real estate office. She also does the housework in the modest apartment they share. Daphne worries about the growing hardness and cynicism in her sister, which she interprets as a failure of true feeling.

A rich man, Arthur, takes an interest in Iris, but Daphne expresses doubts about Arthur's intentions, even directly to Arthur. Realizing that she challenges his integrity, Arthur takes peculiar pleasure in praising Iris in front of Daphne, though it is clear he does not intend to marry Iris and instead just wishes to needle Daphne, who has seen through his empty seduction of Iris. By this point, Iris has grown haughty with self-confidence, largely due to Arthur's show of admiration, to the degree that she believes Arthur to be a stepping-stone to better things. Meanwhile, though, Daphne has discovered that Arthur has made his money in real estate, and he recognizes that Daphne knows his business, excels at housework, and suits him fine. At just the point when Iris believes he is about to propose marriage to her, he instead proposes to Daphne, whom he has seen as the good-hearted one all along. The story ends happily for Iris, too, because now she will get the good part for which she recently auditioned, because she will be sister to the wife of Arthur, and he will presumably give her the connections she needs to succeed. Happy ending for all, thanks to Art.

Cinderella, with her homespun values, does not always triumph in Boulton's stories, as she does in this one, but the important thing to note is that Boulton does not reserve contempt for the choices made by the older sister. Iris has seen that there is a significant advantage to playing her attractiveness for all it is worth, which is a lot more than stenographic skills. She is not deluded by romantic notions, understanding that her initial wish to marry Arthur was not to be confused with love. It was a strategic move to advance her worldly power, and in the end she will get the part she desires, which is, in part, disentanglement from housework and the drudgery of commonplace affections. Daphne holds closer to conventional values, but it is her self-sufficiency, more than anything else, that attracts Arthur.

In her stories, Boulton frequently chooses characters who are looking for the fast track and

willing to play the game, aggressively, in order to attain independence. Between 1917 and 1919 she wrote a set of six monologue pieces featuring Hazel and Hermione, hard-boiled chorus girls who daily cope with the clamoring desires of men, especially men of means and profiteers, who presume to hold sway over them. They know to play defensively with that type, and to steal advantage when possible. They are advanced versions of Iris, more hardened by bad breaks, but they navigate well the difficult waters of independence, using the solid currency of the desirous male as fuel.

Boulton never had any notion of becoming an actress, but stories were, for her, a way of performing on the edge, at or beyond the line of what most would consider proper. She could engage the desires of her audience, male and female, with a glimpse of extramarital flirtation, carelessly revealed flesh, the huff and puff of dating and dancing and a woman alone with a man in an uptown apartment. There was a steady demand for that sort of experience, in easy prose, in the mid-1910s. Iris was right to think that she might earn a living by channeling her liberated imagination into prose, but she never sold a story. After receiving several rejections, she became convinced that her manuscripts were being returned unread. So she took the best story she had written directly to the publisher one day, brashly delivering it to him face to face. He absolutely refused to read the story while she waited, and the next day she received a rejection. So, on she went to other means of selling, using her body to gain advantage.

Boulton's fate was different. Her stories sold. In *Part of a Long Story,* she recalls Bob Davis, the editor of *Cavalier* as well as several other magazines owned by Frank Munsey, calling her in about a story she had submitted, called "Lanigan—Lineman." He asked, "Young lady, where did *you* learn about linemen?" She could only answer that one day, when she was walking home from high school, she had heard a wolf call from the top of a pole, and the lineman had offered, "You for me when *you* develop!" which made her think (p. 24). Boulton did develop and learned to answer that sort of call to the point that by 1916 she was earning a solid living by her typewriter.

She experienced the perils of such a career as well as the pleasures. The most important editor she dealt with during these years, who receives no mention in the pages of her memoir, was Courtland Young, the editor of *Young's* and *Breezy Stories,* a married man. From him she received title to a dairy farm at Cornwall Bridge, Connecticut, roughly coinciding with the time she gave birth to Barbara Burton in 1915. A story was concocted to say that Burton, the father, was a "war correspondent" who died in Belgium during the Great War. Needless to say, no trace of him has been found. He is a fiction to conceal the fact that the girl was an illegitimate child, and the editor was the father, who paid for the issue in real estate. So, a career as a writer had its hazards. With the help of her family, Boulton tried to make a go of the Connecticut dairy farm, but that life also proved challenging, as she told a newspaper reporter: "At first, you know, every time I got a check for a story I'd buy another cow. I thought that was investing the money. Now, whenever I can, I put the cows into a short story. That's the only way I can invest them so they will earn their keep, unless we get more for milk" (quoted in King, *Another Part of a Long Story*, p. 37).

Whether or not they feature dairy products, Boulton's stories nearly always address the matter of earning a living, and as a species of realism they could be understood as stories of earning life. In her concentration on the lives of women, especially women engaged in the struggle for power and independence, though often in concert with men in relationship, she could be seen as in line with early feminist writing, though with no explicit program. Not a single one of her characters would identify themselves as feminist, yet they all know the struggle.

MARRIAGE: WELDED TO O'NEILL

When her daughter was about two, in the fall of 1917, she left the farm for New York City in

order to look for factory work, "some sort of place where one sat with other girls and occupied oneself with a monotonous job, doing it over and over, requiring, once one had learned it, no more than the constant surface attention of one's mind." A friend had told her that there was "a strange, barren spirit among the girls, something that in some way, at some time, people should know about" (*Part of a Long Story,* p. 14). She would take a night shift and write during the day. But instead she ran into Eugene O'Neill that day of her arrival, and that evening he walked her back to her hotel and declared, "I want to spend every night of my life from now on with *you.* I mean this. *Every night of my life*" (p. 21). Within six months, on April 12, 1918, they were married.

O'Neill was, at the time, a promising writer of one-act plays, best known for some hard-bitten sketches of working men at sea. He was central to a group of bohemian radicals who were trying to push the American theater into the modern world of ideas, working outside the commercial "showshop" of Broadway. He had been writing plays for about four years at that point and had earned virtually nothing, except for respect from these idealistic amateurs. His income was a weekly allowance from his father. He was at an emotional low point, having come to the end of his affair with Louise Bryant, the wife of John Reed, and was drinking heavily. Suddenly there was Agnes, who might have suggested to him, if only indirectly, that he might feel better about himself if he started to earn some money for his unmistakable genius. He already had the idea for his full-length play, his first for Broadway, *Beyond the Horizon,* but it tells a story not unlike those Boulton had been telling, set on a farm in New England. O'Neill worked on it through the first two years of their marriage until it was finally produced in 1920 and won the Pulitzer Prize. He dedicated the play to her, and she often referred to it as "our play."

Other works from the early years of their marriage show her influence on him, and his influence on her stories can also be seen. Less than a year after they met, she wrote "The Letter," published in October 1918 in *Snappy Stories.* Here she captures the dismal atmosphere of a marriage not unlike the one O'Neill portrayed in *Before Breakfast* (1916), in which O'Neill, by way of monologue, gives a glimpse of the deep trough of despair into which an impoverished couple have fallen, until in the end the alcoholic husband kills himself. In Boulton's story, the wife, Anna, has seen her husband succumb to drink and drugs and the influence of a prostitute. She declares that, even so, she remains loyal. But that night, when she is asleep, he discovers that she has received a letter. Believing her to be unfaithful, he beats her with a poker, leaving her most likely dead. Only then does he discover that the letter is in fact a pattern for a baby's dress. It's hard to see what is "snappy" about this story except that it confronts such up-to-date issues as drug addiction. What's clear is that she got the idea from O'Neill that her stories should confront the harsh realities of life, where life gives way to tragedy, not just ironic twists on the struggle to earn life.

In "A Decent Woman," published in *Snappy Stories* in June 1919, she writes again of a woman named Anna, but this time the character is middle-aged and embittered about some sort of betrayal of her marriage that occurred eight years earlier. She has never forgiven her husband for his indecency, preferring instead to see him suffer, but oddly her punishment of him and the fact that he deserves punishment constitutes an attachment to him, something she clings to, even though it gives her no true satisfaction. Therefore, when he tells her that he is leaving her for another woman, she considers a desperate strategy to punish him: suicide. But that would be to abandon her moral advantage, her decency, so instead she must live on in misery.

This story anticipates and perhaps influenced O'Neill's *Diff'rent,* which he wrote the following year, a naturalistic study of a doomed couple that has frequently been read as an antifeminist work since it seems to blame the woman for blind intolerance of the human fallibility of men. For anyone who insists on reading a naturalistic study of an individual case as a general statement on the human condition, it would also be possible to interpret Boulton's story as antifeminist. She prefers to show her female character caught in a

neurotic bind, acting irrationally in response to self-destructive impulses. O'Neill instead rationalizes the dysfunction in the relationship, seeing the breakdown of the relationship in terms of a failure of ideals. Neither story needs to be read as a general statement about men and women.

Both Boulton and O'Neill followed the example of August Strindberg, especially his set of short stories, *Married,* which had been published in the United States in 1913, featuring the notoriously misogynistic Swedish writer's disastrous depictions of modern marriage. O'Neill was reading these stores as early as 1915, while Boulton was, perhaps, directed to them by O'Neill after 1917. Her earlier stories reflect doubts about the possibility of an equitable and happy marriage, but the stories written after she met O'Neill seem even more pessimistic, ironically, since she was, by her own testimony, delighted to be married to O'Neill.

She was ready to move beyond pulp, though, and took a first step by publishing two stories in the *Smart Set,* which was edited by H. L. Mencken and George Jean Nathan. Their magazine was known as a "clever" magazine, which meant that it favored a sharp, cynical attitude toward everything, especially conventional values but also unconventional values. Nathan had taken a strong interest in O'Neill's playwriting, and Mencken saw promise in Boulton, though at one point he had to reject a story she had submitted because he feared the Comstockers (guardians of public morality) would be on his head if he were to publish it. The two she published, "The Snob" and "The Hater of Mediocrity," featured unappealing portraits of pretentious men and the women who must cope with them. The misanthropy of these stories far outstrips anything she had written before.

In a 1922 story called "Fixin' Road" in *Holland's Magazine,* a glossy monthly, she takes another look back at a world centered around a capable and self-defining woman, in fact a Connecticut dairy farmer who "*loved* her cows" and is single-mindedly determined to keep her failing farm. She relies on her daughter, who has caught the eye of a confident young man of the neighborhood, an alliance that to the mother represents a threat. She has had a dispute with the young man over a cow and uses that to spoil the relationship, which triggers the daughter's anger: "What other girl has a mother like you ... a mother that looks and acts like a man?" (p. 8). Ultimately the mother realizes the tragic emptiness of the life she imposes on her daughter, and so she stands back to allow the "road" to go through: marriage. Meanwhile, "the heavy fertile earth beneath her plow" will be where she nurtures her independence (p. 9). By the time this story was published, Boulton's mother and father were living in rural Connecticut, caring for her daughter Barbara, who saw her mother only now and then.

Marriage to O'Neill proved challenging, though his fortunes quickly improved after the success of *Beyond the Horizon* in 1920. They were then living mostly in a renovated life-saving station outside Provincetown, which his parents had given to them as a wedding present. Royalties flowed from a stream of plays he now had little trouble in selling, though several flopped. They lived a comfortable life, broken by periods of his drinking and ill health, scenes of brutality, episodes of mourning (at the death of his father, his mother, his brother, and her father), and the insistent presence of their son, Shane, born in November 1919, followed by Oona in 1925. From Provincetown, they moved to a large house in Ridgefield, Connecticut, and soon after, they were looking at property in Bermuda, first for rental, later for sale, always in search of that space they could define as home.

Her published writing ceased almost entirely during these years, but she reportedly drafted a novel (said to have been thrown into the fire by O'Neill in a moment of particular hostility) and finished two full-length plays, which circulated among producers and survive in typescript. For these plays she took a pseudonym for the first time in her life, perhaps suggesting some feeling that as a playwright she might be imposing on his name, but they are awkward dramas, affecting a jaunty modernity, perhaps influenced by Frank Wedekind's writings, which she admired, and stood little chance even in the overheated Broadway market of the 1920s.

Boulton's impact on the theater of the day is more evident in her influence on the aesthetic of O'Neill's writing and the way she was depicted in his plays. Study of the development of *Anna Christie* from its previous versions shows him recentering the play on the female protagonist, and the plot more and more resembles a Boulton short story. The play was a commercial success and did much to elevate their lives into comfort, but the reviewers who noted the happy ending as a significant departure from previous O'Neill plays triggered his fury enough that he (and she) wrote angry letters to the critics. *Welded,* which failed at the box office and with the critics, openly depicted the O'Neill-Boulton marriage as a creative/destructive partnership in Strindbergian terms. O'Neill seems to have intuited that the relational mode, which he had absorbed from Boulton, did not serve his self-image, which was that of an autonomous, above-the-crowd, solitary genius, and his plays from the later years of the marriage are exercises in high aspiration—or overreach—each more audacious than the last. These plays put female characters in the background, up until the culminating play of this period of experimentation, *Strange Interlude,* which, over four-and-a-half hours, in nine acts, again puts a female character at the center. Nina Leeds has been read as a composite character, partly based on Boulton and partly on Carlotta Monterey, while others have read her as an avatar of O'Neill.

He called it his "woman play," but Nina is a character caught in a series of endless inadequate substitutions for a lost man, literally a lover who died young but figuratively an unattainable autonomy or even (after all, the play does reflect O'Neill's reading of Freud) a phallus. She has her more exultant moments, when she sees herself as the junction of masculine needs, as in act 6, when we hear the following inner monologue: "My three men! ... I feel their desires converge in me! ... to form one complete beautiful male desire which I absorb ... and am whole ... they dissolve in me, their life is my life ... I am pregnant with the three! ... husband! ... lover! ... father! ... and the fourth man! ... little man! ... little Gordon ... he is mine too! ... that makes it perfect!" (O'Neill, *Complete Plays,* vol. 2, p. 756). In this sense, she is a figure of connectedness, but only as defined by men. The "strange interlude" of the title is an image of the present moment, held in tension between the introjected past (the Oedipal origins of current dissatisfaction and neurosis) and the projected future (the fantasized fulfillment). Boulton occupied that present for O'Neill, as an increasingly estranged composite of a mother who betrayed him and a lover who could not give him transcendence. Boulton enjoyed feeling herself in a lattice of desires or connections (husband, lover, father, little man), but not, egotistically, as a central self. Nina comes to the end of the play in a state of tragic emptiness because her self has been frustrated or exhausted, not expressed. Boulton came to *Strange Interlude* as a woman who bridged the gap between O'Neill's failed mother and his romanticized fulfillment in Carlotta Monterey, and she too experienced the moment as one of frustration and exhaustion. Even as he was reaching beyond her, she was becoming bored and fed up with him.

Then, he was gone for good and using all the leverage of a good lawyer to limit her position in the divorce. The financial terms he offered were unfavorable, but worse were the terms of the divorce, which explained how she could be punished if she were to write about the marriage, in fiction or nonfiction, during his lifetime. Her story was put in brackets right then, and she only rarely broke free of that container until his death. The characters in her early stories would have understood that her self-sufficiency could only be bought by self-denial; that is one of the bargains a woman might have to strike in life. In a statement given to reporters at the time when the impending divorce was announced, Boulton said:

> I had attempted the experiment of giving an artist-husband the freedom he said was necessary for his dramatic success. Perhaps from the standpoint of dramatic art and the American theatre, my decision may be a success; matrimonially, it has proved a failure. This illusion of freedom—so long maintained by the male sex, particularly by the artistic male—is very much an illusion. Now I know that

> the only way to give a man the freedom he wants is to open the door to captivity.
>
> (quoted in King, pp. 190–191)

That degree of cynicism comes out of an extreme moment, but soon she would have to discover that her freedom as a divorced woman was even more limited than when she was an unwed mother before meeting O'Neill.

AFTER O'NEILL: THE ROAD BEFORE HER

At first, Boulton felt confident that she could reinvest the sheer energy she had put into the marriage in stories that would connect to the popular market of readers, whom she had "divorced" when she isolated herself with O'Neill, but by then the magazine market had changed. "Snappy" stories had hardened into titillation or "hard-boiled dicks" or facetious parodies. On her train ride to the dude ranch outside of Reno, where she had to reside for three months before she could get a Nevada divorce, Boulton cooked up plots for a couple of stories, one of which she published in *Liberty*. "En Route" is an outrageous story of con men and schemers, and by the end we know that the main character, who is going to Nevada for a divorce, is as much a schemer as anyone. You can tell that the story comes from one part anger, one part self-hatred, and one part revenge fantasy, but it's all a cheap thrill, with nothing of Eakins in it.

Radio had eaten into the easy market for "realism." Horace Liveright expressed interest in a book she projected, a series of fictional portraits of New England women, which had potential to draw deeply on the experienced life, but Liveright's life was unraveling at that moment—with divorce, drink, bankruptcy—and the book never came about. The manuscript of one story survives. It begins in the neighborhood of the dairy farm Boulton had owned in the 1920s. Sarah is a vigorous woman of forty-three who takes joy in her life, but the weakness and selfishness of men, also enough self-pity to set her drinking, put her life on a downward slide till at the end she is running a low boardinghouse for railroad men.

By the time of the divorce, Boulton herself was coping with a drinking problem. She was living again in the antiquated family house in New Jersey, renting the Bermuda house to help pay the bills in the early years of the Depression. She was raising three children and trying to make ends meet, helped by a lover/handyman, James Delaney, a former newspaperman who now aimed to write a novel. A posthumous inventory of her manuscripts made by her daughter Barbara shows that she was writing steadily through the 1930s—stories, novels, screenplays, some of it in collaboration with Delaney—but all of that has apparently been lost. Her 1931 diary shows her chastising herself for periods of inactivity. She is happiest when she can see daily progress on projects like a story called "The Philosopher's Night." At the end of the year, she resolves to finish a novel in the coming year, sell six stories, read twenty volumes of history, learn a foreign language, and get out of debt, all without gaining any weight ("No tummy!").

In the late 1930s she broke up with Delaney and took an apartment in Greenwich Village, and in 1940 she transferred Oona, then fifteen, to the exclusive Brearley School in Manhattan. Oona's best friends were Gloria Vanderbilt and Carol Marcus (later Saroyan, later Matthau), the legendary *Trio* about whom Aram Saroyan wrote a group portrait in 1985. By the early 1940s O'Neill had already nearly written off Shane as a lost cause, but he still had hopes for Oona—that is, until she began drawing the attention of columnists at places like the Stork Club, where she was elected Number One Debutante. In 1943 she and Boulton traveled to Hollywood, where Oona, in her first screen test, drew the attention of Charlie Chaplin. They were married not long afterward, with Oona having just turned eighteen and Chaplin a year younger than her father, fifty-four. O'Neill would not tolerate this marriage and disowned her at once. The alliance gave Boulton access to a different circle of people, including other writers, but she was reportedly living in a Los Angeles trailer park because of wartime housing restrictions.

In 1944 Lippincott published Boulton's novel *The Road Is Before Us,* which she had reportedly

been working on since the late 1930s. The novel recounts a five-day car journey from New Jersey to Florida. The car is owned by T. E. Edgrin, a newspaperman, who has lately received the news that his sister Ann has died from an abortion in Florida. He feels compelled to find the man who had gotten her pregnant, and ... he's not sure what. To cover the expenses of the long drive, he has lined up several passengers, including an elderly couple, Mr. and Mrs. Rawl, who are making their annual excursion to spend the winter with friends in Florida, and a black woman, Addie Brown, who is heading for seasonal employment down south where her intended husband has gone to work. Unfortunately, both Addie and her fiancé need to finalize divorces from their absent spouses before they can marry, and they lack the money to do so. All four of these characters are of modest means and limited imagination. Their worlds are small, and they are inexperienced in the world, but during this prolonged car ride they have much time to ruminate, and the dislocation from familiar space and the inevitable interaction with each other force them out of the usual narrow tracks of thinking about their lives. The novel might be said to consist of a minute examination of the dislocations and adjustments in the experience of these characters.

Two catastrophic events occur, and they help T.E. frame the story he is trying to comprehend, of his sister's death. On the third night, in transit, Mr. Rawl, an old man, dies in his sleep. He does not wake up, and Mrs. Rawl faces the difficulty of grieving among people who barely know her husband. She also has to deal with the practical question of what one does in this situation, with little money, no family or friends. How will she get the body to Florida? Then, the next evening, deep in the South, Addie, who can't help but think herself cursed by this turn of events, has a miscarriage, secretly. The emotional investment she has in this baby cannot be shared, and in fact she must conceal, by herself, all traces of the delivery and bear the pain in solitude.

Meanwhile, that same evening, T.E. goes on a wild excursion that brings him to the lowdown heart of the South. There, after careening through several scenes of gutbucket country nightlife, he encounters a tall black woman who had studied sculpture in Paris, who tells him she has returned to the South "to get back to where the seen and the unseen are one" (p. 196). That resonates with T.E., as this journey is aimed at reconnecting with his sister, and their father was an artist. (The initials T.E., by which this character is known, are those of Thomas Eakins.) He had been tormented by ideas that he must fulfill some heroic role in answer to the wrongs of the world, but the journey has the effect of helping him to realize that life is mostly not laid out in melodramatic form, and it is better for him to come to terms with the reality rather than some narrative construct. The journey has clarified his relation to life and death. It has also been a comprehending of the deep American themes, and now he can return home with a clarified sense of purpose. The masculine impulse to revenge has transformed through the displaced, multiple encounters with mortality, isolation, and segregation into a wish to reintegrate.

Oona and Charlie threw a glamorous party in Hollywood to celebrate the publication of *The Road Is Before Us*. This must have been a proud moment for Boulton, since the reviews, in the *New Yorker, New York Times,* and other important publications were encouraging. They made no reference to her association with O'Neill or Chaplin. She had published a serious novel, with hints of Erskine Caldwell, Willa Cather, and Thomas Wolfe, but an original creation. However, we know this was also a difficult moment for her. Shane had never found a way of life for himself and was made to feel shame by his Nobel Prize–winning father. He began drinking and taking heroin during the war years, when he worked as a merchant seaman under dangerous conditions. He married in 1944, at just about the time when his mother's book was coming out. He had not seen his father in nearly five years when his wife gave birth to Eugene O'Neill III in 1945. The infant suddenly died before it was three months old. O'Neill tended to blame the Boulton line for this calamity, as he did Oona's early marriage and what seemed to him an unfair dependency on his wealth and fame.

Those circumstances changed in 1947 when Boulton accepted a lump sum in place of any future alimony and then married Morris Kaufman, a fisherman and would-be screenwriter. They collaborated on several projects, now lost, while living in California, later in New Jersey. In the early 1950s they made several trips to Mexico (where her father had gone to paint as a young man), remaining there for months at a time. It was on her return from one of these excursions that she read in the newspaper of the death of O'Neill in Boston on November 23, 1953.

Carlotta Monterey O'Neill had maintained such a wall of privacy around her husband's life that no one was invited to the funeral, and she was soon engaged in the task of memorializing him as a literary immortal and shaping his legacy in a way that had nothing to do with family. She overrode O'Neill's expressed wishes and permitted the publication and production of his posthumous play, *Long Day's Journey into Night,* in 1956. This crowning masterpiece of his career, which won the Pulitzer Prize, the Tony Award for Best Play, and other awards, opened such a profound new way of reading the life story of O'Neill that it immediately generated a fascination with his biography.

MEMOIR: ONLY PART OF A LONGER STORY

Carlotta O'Neill had much leverage on how the story would be told, but Boulton also had her part to tell. Seizing her opportunity, Boulton began writing a memoir in 1957, and it was published in 1958 as *Part of a Long Story: Eugene O'Neill as a Young Man in Love*. She had resisted the attachment of that subtitle, but the publisher, Doubleday, insisted on it for marketing purposes. It only appears on the book jacket. Her wish was to tell this story as part of *her* long story. In her life she had known many interesting people, and foremost among them was O'Neill, but he was there because she had married him. Of course, she knew that her own importance in this story rested almost entirely on how well she could tell about him, while O'Neill's importance could stand on its own—and sell a book or two. Being the daughter of a painter and a female iconoclast, the husband of a playwright, the mother-in-law of a comic genius, as well as whatever else, would mean little if she could not realize fully her sensibility in the midst of these others. She had not developed into an autonomous self, at least not literarily. Instead, she had remained a self-in-relation, but this book could realize that model of self in an unprecedented way. To a friend, Peggy Conklin, she wrote that she "wanted to have others share the experience of a (woman?) in her relationship to life, to a husband, to the world as it is even now, because told as honestly as possible, I knew that in sharing, they would feel a kinship with all this—a sense perhaps of wonder at how basically similar in all of us life is" (letter to Peggy Conklin, August 29, 1958; the parenthesis is Boulton's). Here she articulates the relational self with the aesthetic of Eakins.

She started with the aim of writing one volume, but by the time she got to the birth of Shane, she had written a sufficiently long book, one that concluded well and happily, with O'Neill coming to terms with marriage and fatherhood. However, she knew that ending to be misleading. The marriage would not last, and the fatherhood grossly failed. As such, it might sell, but it would not get at the subdermal anatomy, the real story. She projected a second volume, which would have taken the story through the next phase of her life and presumably to some form of completion. It is difficult to imagine a book that never came to be, but we do have some evidence.

Her outline says that the second volume would have begun with a section called "Three Deaths," which would have addressed the successive deaths of O'Neill's father, mother, and brother (1920–1923). Then would have come a section called "A Wind Is Rising," which would contain a series of nine short chapters of five thousand words each, about the length of a *Breezy Stories* piece, and with titles evocative of such tales, such as "Dilemma of the Dance Hall." The last of these, toward which the "wind" presumably rises, was to be called "Full Fathom Five (1927 Spithead)," which might be taken to mean that it would lead up to the tempest of the divorce. However, that implies that the "com-

plete" story would be the story of her marriage to O'Neill, which is, again, the book that the publisher wished to sell. Several of the reviewers of the first volume thought the book skewed all too much to Boulton rather than O'Neill, and it seems as if the second volume might have done the same. The marriage unraveled late in 1927, which is the latest date in the outline, but Boulton was in New York as the new year began, still trying to determine what was really happening. The end came shortly afterward, in February 1928, when O'Neill left for Europe with Carlotta, and the divorce became final in 1929. Nevertheless, she associates this final chapter with 1927, using Ariel's line.

It might be more accurate to think of this endpoint as a reference to her father's death in the spring of 1927. Ariel's line in *The Tempest* is, after all, "Full fathom five thy father lies." If Boulton's father can be taken as a link to Eakins, then the loss of him might be seen as a crisis, when she lost her great example of how an artist might look beyond the seen to the unseen. To a degree, she had initially seen O'Neill as a superb substitute for that example. He had amazed Boulton (and the world), in plays like *Moon of the Caribbees* and *Beyond the Horizon,* with his ability to look beneath the surface of common humanity. This is an aesthetic to which he returned in his late plays, so that he could say, of *The Iceman Cometh,* "there are moments in it that suddenly strip the soul of a man stark naked, not in cruelty or moral superiority, but with an understanding compassion which sees him as a victim of the ironies of life and of himself" (quoted in Sheaffer, *O'Neill: Son and Artist,* p. 504). Boulton saw that degree of penetration as a worthy ideal of art and a dramatic variation on what Eakins was doing with paint. However, she came to feel that O'Neill had lost his footing during the period of his marriage. She felt he had spent too much time engaged in the shifty world of Broadway production, and he had lost a sense of how to use his art to bring a reader or audience member to a close study of what is, and beyond, into the anatomy.

The end of the marriage left her, like Prospero, marooned on an island (Bermuda) because of the betrayal of a loved one, needing to raise a daughter (actually two daughters and a son), using whatever magic she could raise. The "sea-change / Into something rich and strange," which would come of her lost father, might have been a transmutation from the woman who would serve as the pedestal to O'Neill's autonomous self to a woman who would try to return to the self-in-relation. Ultimately she found a Ferdinand for her Miranda (Oona), though she found no perfect release for her Caliban (Shane). Toward the end of her life, she pulled her book from the sea, at least the first part, to tell what any story, by its limited magic, can tell, which is part of a long story. By the publisher's tag line, and by the world's insistence, it came to seem that her story was just a footnote to his. If she had managed to complete the second volume, then perhaps her placement of the work in relation, not in deferral, would have become clear. Some portion of the manuscript was reportedly taken to Switzerland by Oona following her mother's death, and perhaps it will someday come to light, but for the time being we are left with just the first volume, which is an extraordinary book in itself.

The book begins with Boulton's arrival in New York from that failing Connecticut dairy farm. She encounters the dark-eyed playwright who declares his wish to spend every night of his life with her. It's a memorable scene of love at first sight, but already the next day he is elusive, then openly insulting of her. He has cultivated a niche for himself in the Village, consorting with male artists and writers but also some working-class heroes and the members of a street gang. It is a tough world, men among men, but at the moment he identifies with it more than the world of men among women, which brings the risk of betrayal. Other women abjectly populate his hard-drinking days and nights, some real, some phantasmic, and Boulton blurs into that company. His dramatic imagination might be fertile, but he is willing to be cruel, even abusive, to assert his independence, and the closer one becomes to him, the more one should stand back. His identification with male society comes to a bitter climax with the discovery of the suicidal overdose of a man he counted as a close friend, and he

leaves New York and the circle of self-defining artists and writers to spend the winter in isolation with Boulton in Provincetown.

They both thrived in the raw beauty of life on the outer banks, and he especially. A snow-bound winter in Provincetown, with no access to alcohol, only a fireplace and a human body for warmth and distraction, fed their passion and their creativity. She wrote a story a month in those days, or more, and he was searching for a way to convert the seriousness and amateur vitality of his one-act plays into a full evening of professional theater. He needed help in converting his hard work and strong ideas into success, or at least self-sufficiency, and she needed help in converting her success and self-sufficiency into something real and deep, something like the art of Eakins. The memoir makes this collaboration, which might sound like a dry exercise in editing, into a vivid account of literary fusion, and Boulton's prose attests to the result—a perfect marriage long after the divorce.

Probably during that first year, she wrote a short story that did not get published, but which survives in manuscript. "On the Wharf" tells of a young woman, a writer, still unproven, who comes to an isolated town like Provincetown on a gamble that there, by the sea, she might learn to write with enough success to avoid the alternative, a working-class life. Next door, she encounters a young man, a painter named Teddy (Boulton's father's name), who is on the verge of acknowledging his failure as an artist. The young woman, who similarly doubts her own talent, persuades the young man to help her with a story she has written, her effort to write "a *real* story." The young man suggests changes, but then she, sensing his capacity to carry her story beyond the ordinary, gives it to him. His rewriting is so inspired that it immediately wins the favor of a famous novelist who is in the area, and so his genius is on the way to being recognized. She will be by his side.

Boulton's portrayal of the first few months in the book suggests no such sudden deferral. His genius was plain from the start, and her pace of publication continued just as strong. Eventually, when her pregnancy became evident a year and a half after their first meeting, she became distracted from writing. By then, she had gotten to know his self-destructive brother, Jamie, and his mother and father, the whole cast of characters from *Long Day's Journey into Night*. The book contains the most vivid portrayal of O'Neill's family outside of that play, and Jamie, in particular, can be seen as the ghost in life, who both attracts and repels Gene. It takes time for Agnes, the narrator, to know this mysterious man in her life, even when she is married to him. He contains within himself a paradox of creation and destruction.

The book ends with a birth wail and Gene's proud naming of his newborn son, "Shane the Loud." During the years she was writing the book, Boulton was dealing with how that "gene" developed into the Shane who was a tragically beset drug addict, a father of five children, who had never learned to overcome the absence of his own father. Boulton could see in her son a "victim of the ironies of life and himself," and she knew that that tragedy lay beneath the surface of the story she was telling in *Part of a Long Story*. Shane was a man destined for suicide, which Boulton did not live to know but which she might have intuited in a child born of a father so dead as a relational self. The loudness of Shane, bursting forth at the end of this part of a long story, could be seen as a metaphor of the incarnation of Boulton's story in the publication of her book. In that writing, she returned to the aesthetic of her buried father—and Thomas Eakins, sunk full fathom five—and the "different voice" that had been denied, to draw forth this book of the feminine self, loud and clear.

The happy ending of the book is a hopeful vision—not that the child was born of the father but that a father was born of the child. Could it be that the brilliantly autonomous self of O'Neill might evolve into a self-in-relation? Father? Son? Husband? Lover? Friend? *Part of a Long Story* takes the reader to quite a different strange interlude from the one conceived by O'Neill. The man is the one who is seen to be isolated here, barely able to make contact except through his rarefied art. He requires solitude to write. He mistrusts actors and audiences. Children should

withdraw. Requiring an absence of the other in his life, he asks for self-denial from his wife. But then, by artfully choosing to close the first volume at the birth of Shane, she created the illusion for the reader that he had come to a turning point, acknowledging the presence and selfhood of mother and newborn son.

That ending would prove a dream, as the second volume of her *Part of a Long Story* would have shown. The marriage would worsen through the 1920s until it could no longer be tolerated. O'Neill's late plays, which he wrote a decade later, all seem efforts to remediate that failure. They show human beings desperately attempting to put the self in relation, but mostly thwarted by tragic circumstance. *Long Day's Journey into Night* shows how especially difficult it is for a woman, especially the mother, to find herself in relation to any O'Neill, including herself. *Part of a Long Story* can be read as Boulton's counterpart and reply to that play. Dead fathers come to life in those works, and women have the last word.

Ariel, invisible, the captive spirit of the island, is the one who sings to Ferdinand of his (or her?) father lying "full fathom five," offering the hope that loss, even the death of a father, might change into something rich and strange. However, it is conceivable that Boulton, in choosing the title "Full Fathom Five" for the last chapter of the projected second volume, was alluding to Sylvia Plath's poem of that title, written in 1958. Plath conceives her dearly missed father, who died when she was eight, as a submerged sea god, at one with the flows of tidal rhythm.

When she first came to know O'Neill, Boulton thought of him too as a creature of the sea, and they lived on the beach in those early years, but he moved away from the sea and away from her. Signs of Ted Hughes's betrayal of Plath triggered her Electra complex in this and other poems, notably "Daddy," leading her to draw from her dead father a sense of how "murderous" her life had become.

In 1958 (and 1927), Boulton had experienced a parallel series of losses, of father and husband. Upon O'Neill's death in 1953, Boulton wrote a poem, never published, that contains the following Plathian lines (reconstructed by this writer from a problematic manuscript):

> I do not think that what was really you
> would suddenly dissolve into the ether's blue.
> No, all at once that part of you that must have been just you
> rolled, wrapped together, down some slope, into a world that's new.
> You rolled, & landed on a dune, that ended by the sea.
> Your garb was thick green sea-weed,
> dried, like kelp, from neck to knee.
> You wet it, & got free.
>
> (quoted in King, pp. 210–211)

The awkward grammar of the opening line of this excerpt—the present tense of "do not think," tied to the imperfect past of "what was really you"—expresses the "murderous" aspect of her living on. Plath seems inclined to trade "this thick air" for death in the watery medium of the father. Boulton took a different approach to survival. O'Neill's "wet" escape from her and from life might have left her gasping with anger. Instead, she reconnected with her "long story," in part. Instead of taking in the "thick air," she stopped eating. She melted into thin heir, as Prospero might have punned. Boulton's final years were spent amid a landscape of the hoarded past in a house that was falling down, with dozens of cats wandering through. But she was eating less and less, preferring her Parliaments and whisky. She loved to know she was a mother and grandmother, visited often, someone married and married again and again, someone who knew other people and could write stories about them and to them, someone-in-relation. That's how she got free.

Selected Bibliography

WORKS OF AGNES BOULTON

FICTION

"The Pink Dress." *New York Evening Telegram,* May 14, 1910.

"Sisters." *Breezy Stories* 3, no. 2:65–74 (November 1916).

"The Letter." *Snappy Stories: A Magazine of Entertaining Fiction,* October 4, 1918, pp. 27–31.

"A Decent Woman." *Snappy Stories: A Magazine of Entertaining Fiction,* June 18, 1919, pp. 85–94.

"On the Wharf." Typescript [1919?].

"The Hater of Mediocrity." *Smart Set* 62, no. 3:119–124 (July 1920).

"The Snob." *Smart Set* 65, no. 2:83–98 (June 1921).

"Fixin' Road." *Holland's Magazine* 41, no. 8:7–9, 30 (August 1922).

"A New England Woman." Typescript [1928]. Liveright Collection, Van Pelt Library, University of Pennsylvania.

"En Route: The Story of a Game of Guile." *Liberty,* February 22, 1930, pp. 47–56.

The Road Is Before Us. Philadelphia: J. B. Lippincott, 1944.

"Poem by Agnes, written just after she heard of O'Neill's death" [1953]. Transcribed, probably by Louis Sheaffer. Louis Sheaffer–Eugene O'Neill Collection, Linda Lear Center for Special Collections & Archives, Connecticut College.

"The Guilty One." (As Elinor Rand.) In *The Unknown O'Neill: Unpublished or Unfamiliar Writings of Eugene O'Neill.* Edited by Travis Bogard. New Haven, Conn.: Yale University Press, 1988.

Selected Stories of Agnes Boulton. Edited by William Davies King. Online (http://www.eoneill.com/library/abstories/contents.htm).

MEMOIR, CORRESPONDENCE, AND MANUSCRIPTS

Letter to Peggy Conklin, August 29, 1958. Louis Sheaffer–Eugene O'Neill Collection, Linda Lear Center for Special Collections & Archives, Connecticut College.

Part of a Long Story: Eugene O'Neill as a Young Man in Love. Garden City, N.Y.: Doubleday, 1958. Restored edition, edited and introduced by William Davies King. Jefferson, N.C.: McFarland, 2011.

"A Wind Is Rising": The Correspondence of Agnes Boulton and Eugene O'Neill. Edited by William Davies King. Madison, N.J.: Fairleigh Dickinson University Press, 2000.

PAPERS

Boulton's papers are collected in the Louis Sheaffer-Eugene O'Neill Collection, Linda Lear Center for Special Collections, Charles E. Shain Library, Connecticut College; the Harvard Theatre Collection, Houghton Library, Harvard University; and the Yale Collection of American Literature, Beinecke Rare Book and Manuscript Library, Yale University

OTHER SOURCES

Dowling, Robert M. *Critical Companion to Eugene O'Neill: A Literary Reference to His Life and Work.* 2 vols. New York: Facts on File, 2009.

Gelb, Arthur, and Barbara Gelb. *O'Neill.* New York: Harper, 1962.

Gilligan, Carol. *In a Different Voice: Psychological Theory and Women's Development.* Cambridge, Mass.: Harvard University Press, 1982.

Jordan, Judith V., Alexandra G. Kaplan, Jean Baker Miller et al. *Women's Growth in Connection: Writings from the Stone Center.* New York: Guilford Press, 1991.

King, William Davies. *Another Part of a Long Story: Literary Traces of Eugene O'Neill and Agnes Boulton.* Ann Arbor: University of Michigan Press, 2010.

Miller, Jean Baker. *Toward a New Psychology of Women.* 2nd ed. Boston: Beacon Press, 1987.

"Mrs. Agnes Kaufman, 75, Dies; Eugene O'Neill's Second Wife." *New York Times,* November 26, 1968.

O'Neill. Eugene. *Complete Plays.* Vol. 1:*1913–1920.* Vol. 2: *1920–1931.* Vol. 3: *1932–1943.* New York: Library of America, 1988.

Plath, Sylvia. *The Colossus & Other Poems.* New York: Vintage Books, 1968.

Ranald, Margaret Loftus. *The Eugene O'Neill Companion.* Westport, Conn.: Greenwood Press, 1984.

Saroyan, Aram. *Trio: Oona Chaplin, Carol Matthau, Gloria Vanderbilt; Portrait of an Intimate Friendship.* New York: Linden Press, 1985.

Scovell, Jane. *Oona: Living in the Shadows; A Biography of Oona O'Neill Chaplin.* New York: Warner Books, 1998.

Sheaffer, Louis. *O'Neill: Son and Playwright.* Boston: Little, Brown, 1968.

———. *O'Neill: Son and Artist.* Boston: Little, Brown, 1973.

WILLIAM BRADFORD

(1590—1657)

Paul Johnston

When the lost manuscript of William Bradford's *Of Plymouth Plantation* was discovered in London in 1855 and published in America the following year, the ground had already been well prepared for the reception of his history of the Pilgrim colony at Plymouth as a foundational document of both American culture and American literature. Forefather's Day, honoring the Pilgrim colonists, had been celebrated first in New England and then by New England Societies throughout the new American nation annually since 1769. These celebrations featured speakers who emphasized—drawing on early colonial historians who had themselves had access to Bradford's manuscript before its disappearance during the American Revolutionary War—the role of the Pilgrims in establishing the quintessential character of American society: independent, industrious, Protestant, democratic, heroic. Nineteenth-century historians, most notably George Bancroft in his popular ten-volume *History of the United States* (1834–1874), codified this view and took it into America's sitting rooms and schoolhouses. Historical novels, poems, and plays had added their own takes. The Pilgrims, the *Mayflower,* Plymouth Rock—all these had become ingrained in the American consciousness when *Of Plymouth Plantation* was simultaneously published in 1856 by the Massachusetts Historical Society and by Little, Brown & Company, some two hundred years after its author had finished his work.

WILLIAM BRADFORD AND THE PILGRIMS

William Bradford was born on March 19, 1590, in northern rural England, in the village of Austerfield in Yorkshire. Its population of 130 was scarcely larger than the population of Plymouth would be the first winter the Pilgrims spent there. From an early age Bradford read the Bible, a penchant only made possible by the Protestant Reformation and the vernacular translations of the Bible it produced. At age sixteen he became a member, apart from his family, of a newly formed Congregational Church in the nearby village of Scrooby. Congregationalists took the congregation to be the only legitimate organizational basis for a Christian church and thus rejected the official Church of England, with its hierarchies of priests and bishops, as just a continuation of the corrupt Catholic Church the Protestant Reformation was meant to replace. The Scrooby church, like other Congregational churches, would be led only by elders chosen from the congregation. It would select its own pastor, or do without if no satisfactory man could be found. It was organized by a group who had been meeting at the house of William Brewster for prayer and discussion, part of the movement called Puritanism by its detractors, for its perceived intention of purifying the Anglican Church of the idolatrous and ornate accretions that it retained after its separation from the Roman Catholic Church.

Puritanism, even within the official church, was widespread in northern England and somewhat tolerated, largely because the official church, headed by the English monarch, was more concerned with Catholic reemergence in England than with the challenge to authority represented by the other end of the religious spectrum. But in 1605 King James I ordered that Puritans in the north be treated the same as Catholics, and charges of nonconformity with the Church of England were brought against five Anglican ministers in the area of Scrooby. Four were dismissed from their parishes by the archbishop

of York, and three of these were excommunicated. When a new archbishop of York came into office, he turned his attention to those Puritans who sought to worship separately from the official church, including those at Scrooby. A warrant was issued for the arrest of Brewster, who disappeared rather than face the charge. Other Separatists were arrested, however, and were punished with fines or banishment. Thus in 1608, when William Bradford was eighteen years old, the Scrooby congregation decided to emigrate to Holland, where they would be free to practice their religion as they pleased. After many trials and difficulties and separations, in groups large and small, they arrived in Amsterdam in the spring of that year.

They remained in Amsterdam for only a year before removing to the smaller industrial city of Leiden. Economic hardship in Amsterdam partly explains this move, but the chief motive was the desire to escape religious divisions that quickly grew between them and other English Separatists in Amsterdam. In Leiden their number grew to about four hundred, unmolested by the tolerant Dutch society and undisturbed by any further divisions among themselves. But Leiden was not an unmixed blessing. Coming from a rural agricultural society, the group's members had now to find their way in an urban society where they found themselves at the economic and social bottom. Through hard work and thrift—Bradford, for example, became a weaver in the city's substantial textile industry—many achieved some modest success but little material ease, however much they enjoyed, in Bradford's words, "peace and ... spiritual comfort" (*Of Plymouth Plantation,* p. 17). By 1617 discussion grew up among them about finding yet another place to settle, leading to the departure of a small group—fewer than a hundred—from Holland in 1620, bound for the "vast and unpeopled" land of America (p. 25).

They left Holland in a small ship named the *Speedwell,* sailing first to England to take on supplies and more passengers, both fellow Separatists and "strangers" placed among them by their financial backers, to be divided between the *Speedwell* and a second, larger vessel, the *Mayflower*. Owing to delays by their emissaries in England in arranging matters there, the Leiden group did not arrive in England until the end of July. They were further delayed by the necessity of repairing the *Speedwell,* which sprang a leak soon after the two ships set out together for America, and did not get out into the open ocean until late August. Once again, though, the *Speedwell* sprang a leak, forcing a return to the English port at Plymouth, where the *Speedwell* was given up and the passengers and provisions combined aboard the *Mayflower*. Finally, on September 6, far behind schedule and with many of their provisions already consumed and morale low from the weeks already spent onboard, the *Mayflower* and her passengers set sail.

Early in *Of Plymouth Plantation,* Bradford identifies his companions as "pilgrims," and so are they known to the world today, the Pilgrims who founded America. But Bradford did not use the term in reference to their pilgrimage to America, or to an earthly pilgrimage at all. When they departed Leiden for the coastal city of Delfshaven, from whence they were to sail for England, Bradford writes that they were leaving "a goodly and pleasant city which had been their resting place near twelve years." "But they knew they were pilgrims," Bradford continues, "and looked not much on those things, but lift up their eyes to the heavens, their dearest country, and quieted their spirits" (p. 47). That is, they were not pilgrims on a journey from England (or Holland) to America, but rather pilgrims in this world on their way to heaven.

The *Mayflower*'s crossing of the stormy Atlantic took two months, during which early fall turned to early winter. Land was at last sighted on November 9, and the *Mayflower* dropped anchor on the lee shore of Cape Cod two days later, on November 11. They were far to the northeast of their intended destination, the mouth of the Hudson River. But winter was already upon them, and there they would have to stay and make the best of it. By the following summer only about half of the 102 who had sailed from England would still be alive. Among those who died was John Carver, who had been chosen by the group upon their arrival as their first

governor. As his successor the group chose Bradford. He was then just thirty-one years old. Thereafter he would be chosen as governor each year until his death thirty-five years later, with the exception of five years when, at his own request, to give himself some rest, he was chosen only assistant governor. His last year as governor was 1656. He died the next year, on May 9, 1657.

COMPOSITION AND SCOPE OF PLYMOUTH PLANTATION

Bradford began writing *Of Plymouth Plantation* in 1630 and continued working on it off and on for the next twenty years. Though its second half is a year-by-year account of the colony, it is not a diary or journal. Rather it is a history reconstructed by Bradford from his memory, augmented by letters written and received, many of which are included in the narrative. Though it seems likely he drew on other aids—even a diary or journal—no other materials have been discovered.

Of Plymouth Plantation is divided into two books. After an introductory chapter in which Bradford situates their story in the religious history of England, the First Book covers in nine chapters the history of the Pilgrims over a period of twelve years, beginning with their emigration from England to Holland in 1608 and ending with their settlement on the Plymouth site on December 25, 1620. These chapters are told as a continuous narrative. They cover the years the Pilgrims spent in Holland, the reasons for their decision to leave Holland to go to America, the complex business relationships they entered into in order to finance their voyage, their departure from Holland, their crossing of the Atlantic on the *Mayflower,* their arrival at Cape Cod in November, and their search for a suitable place to settle. These chapters present a story of great difficulties and great determination, demonstrating the strength of character that later generations of Americans have wished to claim as their own.

The Second Book continues this story of difficulties and determination, beginning with the Pilgrims' first winter, during which time half of their small number died. The colony survives, however, through the heroic efforts of the few who did not fall ill. The chapters that follow chronicle the colonists' complex relations with the native people they encounter, their progress in both security and prosperity, their conflicts with both their business partners in London and other wayfarers from England, the gradual peopling of New England, and the eventual passing of the original Pilgrims and their ideals. Throughout, Bradford's focus is on the Pilgrims themselves, even as much larger settlements are established throughout New England. These chapters sometimes make for difficult reading, as Bradford shifts from one focus to another, at the expense of continuity or coherence. Passages of interest to the general reader become lost among detailed passages of interest primarily to historians.

The establishment, growth, and eventual decline of the original small colony gives *Of Plymouth Plantation* a general, if undeclared, arc. Nevertheless, it cannot be considered a finished work. Its final chapter, covering the year 1646, is the book's shortest, and is followed in the manuscript by blank pages titled "*Anno* 1647" and "*Anno* 1648." And then nothing more. No summation. No reflection. There follows only a list in Bradford's hand of the names of the hundred passengers who crossed on the *Mayflower,* together with his comments on what had become of them and their descendants through 1650, when thirty of the fifty survivors of the first winter were still alive. Entries added by two other hands update the record through 1698, the year before the last survivor died.

SAINTS AND SATAN: THE PILGRIMS' WORLDVIEW

The historian Samuel Eliot Morison, whose 1952 edition of *Of Plymouth Plantation* remains both the most accessible and the best edition for general readers, advises the modern reader not to begin reading *Of Plymouth Plantation* at the beginning. Rather, he recommends, "begin with Chapter iv 'Showing the Reasons and Causes of

Their Removal' and read at least through the eloquent and moving Chapter ix" (p. x). Yet while it's true that the early chapters are difficult, particularly for readers not familiar with the history of the Protestant Reformation in England, these chapters are essential for understanding not just the Pilgrims but the society that has taken them as its forefathers. Chapter 1 in particular provides the context Bradford thought necessary for understanding what follows. Perhaps more importantly, chapter 1 enables the reader to see aspects of the Pilgrims' thought that continue to be influential in America today, aspects that are sometimes at odds with America's conscious understanding of its heritage.

Bradford begins by declaring his intention to begin "at the very root and rise" of the settlement of Plymouth Plantation (p. 3). His history begins in the reign of Queen Mary I, daughter of Henry VIII, almost seventy years before the Pilgrims sailed to America. Mary ascended to the throne in 1553, following the six-year reign of her young half-brother Edward VI and the nine-day reign of Lady Jane Grey. Mary had the support of the English people, who rejected the rule of her distant cousin Jane, but many feared that she would attempt to restore the Catholic Church as the official church of England. Throughout her youth Mary had persisted in her Catholic faith despite the excommunication of her father in 1533 and the Act of Supremacy in 1534, which created the Church of England under the authority of the English sovereign. The people's fears were justified when in 1555 Parliament bowed to Mary's wishes and restored the authority of the Catholic Church in England. There followed three years of persecution of English Protestants, chronicled in John Fox's *Acts and Monuments of These Latter and Perilous Days* (1563), commonly known as the *Book of Martyrs*. Burnings at the stake and other atrocities earned Mary the epithet "Bloody Mary."

Though Fox's *Book of Martyrs* occupied an important place in the imagination of all English Puritans, including the Pilgrims, Bradford only briefly alludes to the "fiery flames" and "cruel tragedies" of Mary's reign (p. 5). His main focus is on the errors and heresies that resulted in contentions and schisms among Protestant believers themselves following the death of Mary and the restoration of the Church of England. Such errors and divisions were nothing new, Bradford notes. Satan had used such stratagems against true Christianity since the earliest days of the Church, leading to the "vile ceremonies" and "gross darkness of popery" (pp. 4, 3) that the Protestant Reformation should have done away with, but which still persisted in the Church of England. The role of Satan is central to Bradford's view of history: for Bradford and his fellow Pilgrims, all the "wars and oppositions" that had challenged true Christianity from the beginning down to the present time were the work of Satan, as Satan is "loath his kingdom should go down, the truth [of Christianity] prevail and the churches of God revert to their ancient purity and recover their primitive order, liberty and beauty" (p. 3). Thus the struggle to restore Christianity to its ancient purity was still ongoing in England, despite the breaking away of the Church of England from "the darkness of popery." But if the chief embodiment of Satan's will was the pope and the Catholic Church, many of Catholicism's "vile ceremonies" and nonbiblical hierarchical structure remained in the Church of England. It was hardly a reformed church such as those that had sprung up in northern Europe. The king had merely substituted his own authority for that of the pope, retaining beneath him the hierarchy of priests and bishops and archbishops. To those zealous for true reform, too little had changed.

Though those who wished to get rid of these ceremonies and this hierarchical structure and thus purify Christianity became popularly known as Puritans, they did not refer to themselves in this way. In chapter 1, Bradford refers rather to those committed to a true Christian church as "the Saints." These are not the saints of the Catholic Church, but those, including himself and his fellow Pilgrims as well as other Puritans in England, who were determined to restore to the churches of God "their primitive order, liberty and beauty." The world, in other words, was a world of struggle between us and them, God's chosen people and the forces of Satan.

The disposition of the Pilgrims to see themselves in an us/them world was only one consequence of their belief in themselves as God's chosen people. A second is their identification of themselves with the Israelites of the Old Testament. At important junctures of their story, the Pilgrims gather strength and resolve by reminding themselves of this identity. Thus at the beginning of chapter 7, when the Pilgrims have made their decision to leave Holland for America and have provided themselves with a ship for that purpose, they observe a day of solemn humility. Their pastor, John Robinson, preaches to them on a text from the Old Testament Book of Ezra. Ezra is the leader who leads the Israelites out of Babylon to Jerusalem following the Babylonian Exile. Ezra emphasizes to the Israelites that they are a community bound to the God of Israel, the God of their fathers, a community that must keep itself separate from others not chosen by God. In chapter 4, "Showing the Reasons and Causes of Their Removal," Bradford cites as one of the chief reasons for their decision to leave Holland for America their concern that their children would lose their community identity and take on instead the ways and practices of the people of Holland, just as many among the Israelites failed to keep themselves aloof from the Canaanites and other foreign peoples they found themselves among, drawing a sharp rebuke from Ezra. It is to the efforts of Ezra at this time that the Jewish people owed the preservation of their identity as God's chosen people. A similar effort now, Robinson preached, was necessary to preserve the Pilgrims departing for America as God's chosen people.

It was thus concern for the cohesion of their community, rather than a desire for religious freedom, that led the Pilgrims to leave Holland for America. Their reason for leaving England, to be sure, was their desire for religious freedom, which they did not enjoy in England. They found religious freedom in Holland, however. In chapter 3, Bradford extols the "comfortable condition" they enjoyed in Holland, particularly after they left Amsterdam for Leiden:

> Being thus settled (after many difficulties) they continued many years in a comfortable condition, enjoying much sweet and delightful society and spiritual comfort together in the ways of God, under the able ministry and prudent government of Mr. John Robinson [their pastor] and Mr. William Brewster [their Elder].... So as they grew in knowledge and other gifts and graces of the Spirit of God, and lived together in peace and love and holiness and many came unto them from divers parts of England, so as they grew a great congregation.
>
> (pp. 17–18)

Bradford takes pains, because of the false reports of adversaries back in England, to deny that the Pilgrims were in any way forced to leave Holland as they had felt themselves forced to leave England. (He notes in passing that "heathen historians" made similar false reports "of Moses and the Israelites when they went out of Egypt.") Rather they left of "their own free choice and motion" to found a more homogenous and sustainable religious community (p. 19).

ADVERSITY AND PERSEVERANCE

If the Pilgrims had been strong merely in their religious beliefs it is unlikely that they could have found their way to America from Holland, much less survived after they arrived. Qualities other than faith were necessary as well. Their voyage and colony needed financing for the hiring of a ship and for the supplies necessary both to get them across the ocean and to sustain them until they could provide for themselves in their new home. Once the Pilgrims settled on English North America as their destination, a relationship with the Virginia Company that held the king's charter for colonization had to be worked out. Chapters 5 and 6 deal with these business matters in some detail, involving negotiations with both the Virginia Company and the "Adventurers," the venture capitalists who would fund their enterprise with the expectation of financial profit. These matters are of more interest to the historian than the general reader, but some sense of them is necessary for a full appreciation of the determination and perseverance of the Pilgrims.

Of far greater interest are the physical difficulties the Pilgrims encountered and surmounted. Indeed, this part of their story is the

basis for much of the later admiration Americans have felt toward them. When not yet halfway across the Atlantic, they encountered fierce storms that strained the *Mayflower* to the point that the mariners hired to take them across debated turning back. Though they finally decided to forge ahead, the storms made progress impossible for days at a time. The crossing eventually took sixty-five days, two months at sea in often miserable conditions—crowded, cold, wet, unsteady, and uncertain. And when they finally arrived, it was not early fall, as they had planned, but mid-November, cold and bleak. They were off course and low on supplies, with no known harbor where they might moor the *Mayflower* and come ashore.

At this point, Bradford interrupts his narrative to reflect, in *Of Plymouth Plantation*'s finest passage, on what the Pilgrims had undergone to get to the new world and what faced them when they arrived:

> But here I cannot but stay and make a pause, and stand half amazed at this poor people's present condition; and so I think will the reader, too, when he well considers the same. Being thus passed the vast ocean, and a sea of troubles before in their preparation ... they had now no friends to welcome them nor inns to entertain or refresh their weatherbeaten bodies; no houses or much less towns to repair to, to seek for succour.... And for the season it was winter, and they that know the winters of that country know them to be sharp and violent, and subject to cruel and fierce storms, dangerous to travel to known places, much more to search an unknown coast. Besides, what could they see but a hideous and desolate wilderness, full of wild beasts and wild men—and what multitudes there might be of them they knew not....
>
> What could now sustain them but the Spirit of God and His grace? May not and ought not the children of these fathers rightly say: "Our fathers were Englishmen which came over this great ocean, and were ready to perish in this wilderness; but they cried unto the Lord, and He heard their voice.... Let them therefore praise the Lord, because He is good: and His mercies endure forever."
>
> (pp. 61–63)

Another six weeks of exploration took place before a suitable harbor with ground for a settlement nearby was found. It was not until December 25, nearly four months since setting sail from England, that they were able to come ashore and begin work on their first building.

These months of hardship and trial, difficult as they were, proved to be only the prelude to a much more difficult time to come as they struggled to survive the winter. In Bradford's words, the Pilgrims were not only exposed to the cold without adequate shelter or food, they were also afflicted with "scurvy and other diseases" (p. 77). Of the hundred who had made the crossing, only six or seven, including Myles Standish and their elder, William Brewster, were untouched. These toiled heroically through the winter; without regard for their own health they "fetched them [the sick] wood, made them fires, dressed them meat, made their beds, washed their loathsome clothes, clothed and unclothed them" (p. 77). Because of these heroic efforts, half the company survived. But half did not. Among the fifty-two dead come spring were fourteen heads of families and eleven of the eighteen wives who accompanied their husbands, including Rose Standish. Sadly, the first to die had been Dorothy Bradford, William Bradford's wife, whose death took place shortly after the arrival of the *Mayflower*, before the Pilgrims even came ashore. Those who died were buried not in a cemetery but in the field that was planted with corn the first spring, to disguise their true number from the Indians.

THE LAND THEY FOUND

In the minds of both Americans and Europeans, no word more distinguishes American nature from European nature than "wilderness." By the time of the European migration to America, nature in Europe had been completely wrought over by man. Even its forests were tended to, including the royal forests of England. But not the nature we find in William Bradford's passage reflecting on the plight of the Pilgrims quoted above, when they first arrived in New England. "Besides, what could they see but a hideous and desolate wilderness, full of wild beasts and wild men" (p. 62). And again, they "were Englishmen which came over this great ocean, and were ready

to perish in this wilderness; but they cried unto the Lord, and He heard their voice and looked on their adversity" (p. 63).

But did the Pilgrims actually find a wilderness when they arrived in New England? Arriving in November, they undoubtedly found a landscape bleak enough to discourage the stoutest hearts. They certainly did not find the countryside of the rural England they had left behind so many years ago. But neither did they find simply forests untouched by the hands of man. The site they chose to settle, Bradford relates, was cleared land, cornfields that had been planted by the Indians. True, there were no pastures for domestic animals, as the Indians had no cattle or sheep to graze. But the Indians had modified the forest a great deal, burning the undergrowth twice a year to encourage an abundance of deer and other game, upon which they depended for food and skins. The Pilgrims enjoyed this bounty, taking waterfowl, wild turkey, and deer to augment the crops they grew the first summer in the fields already cleared when they arrived, leading Bradford to declare at the end of their first year that they "had all things in good plenty" (p. 90).

The word "wilderness" does not in fact often appear in the second, larger half of *Of Plymouth Plantation,* Bradford's year-by-year chronicle of the Pilgrims' life in New England. Its appearance at the culmination of the First Book derives not from the look of the land that lay before the Pilgrims, however grim their situation, but from the Old Testament, from the story of the Jews the Pilgrims so identified with. "Wilderness" appears in the Old Testament of the Pilgrims' Geneva Bible over 250 times, a hundred times in the Pentateuch, twenty-two times in the Psalms, forty-five times in the prophets Isaiah and Jeremiah. (In contrast, it appears only seven times in the entire works of Shakespeare, written in the years between the translation of the Geneva Bible and the arrival of the Pilgrims in New England.) That the term has stuck, that Americans still think of their land's original nature as "wilderness," is a testament to the degree to which the Pilgrims' identification with God's chosen people has been absorbed into American consciousness.

The land of New England was not wilderness but rather an occupied landscape transformed by its inhabitants in ways that supported their culture; nevertheless the land would undergo a transformation in response to the new European culture that would come to dominate it. The Indians were transformers of the land, but they had neither edge tools nor domestic animals. These two possessions of the Europeans would both enable and require much more widespread forest clearing than the Indians had practiced. Though the Pilgrims had had to rely on corn from the Indians their first two years—they had begun by appropriating baskets of corn they found where the Indians had fled their approach even before they disembarked—the balance soon turned the other way. Corn became the primary good the Pilgrims traded for fur, simultaneously depleting native animals and depriving them of their habitat. The year 1624 saw the arrival of cattle at Plymouth—three heifers and a bull, a small number that would multiply rapidly with the arrival of greater numbers of immigrants in the years to come. Though pigs could root in the forests for acorns and beechnuts, cattle could not, and the forests would soon yield to the fields of corn and grasses needed to support them. The abundance of wildlife, upon which the Indians depended and which they had cultivated, would become the stuff of memory.

THE PEOPLE THEY FOUND

Most Americans who went through American elementary school know the story of the first Thanksgiving, briefly described in chapter 7, at which the Pilgrims feasted for three days on venison, turkey, and Indian corn. They were joined by the local Indians whom they had invited, and to whom they owed, at least in part, their abundance, as the Indians had shown them how to plant and fertilize the unfamiliar Indian corn. It is not just a picture of plenty following hardship, of reward won through faith and hard work; it is also a picture of amity between the Pilgrim Fathers and the native people into whose land they had moved. While celebrated by some, this picture has come to be questioned by others

who see it as inconsistent not only with subsequent white-Indian history but also with the attitudes and later history of the Pilgrims themselves. The attitudes and history present in *Of Plymouth Plantation* regarding the native people cannot be simply characterized, however, whether by admirers of the Pilgrims or by their critics.

Bradford's first reference to the native people comes in chapter 4, when he relates the deliberations of the Pilgrims as to where they would go from Holland:

> The place they had thoughts on was some of those vast and unpeopled countries of America, which are fruitful and fit for habitation, being devoid of all civil inhabitants, where there are only savage and brutish men which range up and down, little otherwise than the wild beasts of the same.
>
> (p. 25)

This characterization, though written much later when Bradford had the experience to know differently, nevertheless captures the mindset of the Pilgrims before they came to America. They wished to start a new society where none existed, and thus of necessity pictured those already living there as "little otherwise than the wild beasts." When a few sentences later Bradford presents the objections some had to going to America, his focus changes to the reputed cruelty of the Indians, as reported in the printed narratives of Europeans who had been to America and returned. The Indians become "savage people, who are cruel, barbarous, and most treacherous" (p. 26). But little in Bradford's subsequent narrative bears out this negative view.

When Bradford makes his "pause" at the end of chapter 9, he speaks for the final time of the Indians as his framework demands, rather than as his actual experience showed them to be. Bradford writes that the Indians were "wild men," "savage barbarians ... readier to fill their sides full of arrows than otherwise" (p. 62). This characterization is justified in Bradford's eyes by the "first encounter" recounted a few pages later, in chapter 10. The first glimpse the Pilgrims have of actual Indians comes at the beginning of the chapter, when the first group to go ashore from the *Mayflower* comes upon five or six native men, accompanied by a dog, walking on the beach. These flee at the sight of the Pilgrims, who follow their tracks into the woods, where they lose the trail. Eventually, though, they come upon land cleared by the Indians, an Indian graveyard, and hastily buried corn, to which the Pilgrims help themselves. Three weeks later a second party exchanges shot for arrows when they are attacked in the early morning by a party of Indians. No Englishman is struck, though Bradford reports that "sundry of their coats, which hung up in the barricade, were shot through and through" (p. 70). Whether it was the Indians' intention to "fill their sides full of arrows" or simply to scare them back to their ship, having once lost corn to them, Bradford does not consider.

In the Second Book, actual acquaintance shows the Indians not to be the "wild men" of the Pilgrims' precontact imagination but a people with their own social order and customs, modifiers of the land and tillers of the soil, as their fields and graveyards had already suggested. For the first few months of the Plymouth settlement they remained shadowy figures, "skulking about" but keeping their distance (p. 79). In mid-March, however, an Indian approached them who spoke English. This was Samoset. A native of the coast of what is now the state of Maine, Samoset had learned English from the English fishermen who regularly plied the plentiful fishing grounds there. From Samoset the Pilgrims learned of the people nearest their settlement, "of their names, number and strength, of their situation and distance from this place, and who was chief amongst them" (p. 79). The people were the Wampanoags, and their chief, or sachem, was Massasoit.

Samoset arranged a meeting between the Pilgrims and Massasoit and his people. The two peoples agreed to the terms by which they should live as neighbors, terms that stipulated not only peace and mutual protection against injury and theft but also mutual aid in war. These terms were kept between the Plymouth people and the Wampanoags as long as Massasoit lived, providing the basis not only for mutual security but for the trade that eventually enabled Plymouth not only to survive, but thrive.

Accompanying Massasoit at this meeting was another English-speaking Indian, Squanto. Unlike Samoset, Squanto was a native of the area; indeed, he was the only survivor of the Patuxet people who had occupied the site of Plymouth before the arrival of the Pilgrims and who had succumbed, like so many other native people, to the infectious diseases brought by the Europeans who had come to New England to fish, explore, and attempt settlements before the arrival of the Pilgrims. Also unlike Samoset, Squanto remained among the Pilgrims, interpreting for them and teaching them how to survive—"how to set their corn, where to take fish, and to procure other commodities" (p. 81). He also guided them "to unknown places for their profit," in other words, to places where they might meet natives of other tribes for trade.

But the First Book's negative stereotype of the Indians is not entirely replaced by the amity in the Second Book. The Pilgrims' positive relationship with the Wampanoags was based largely on mutual self-interest, which had to be continually managed as conflicts arose among the Indians themselves. It also was based on the relatively weak position of the Plymouth colony, which did not present much of a threat to the Wampanoag culture. Other Europeans had come to the coast of New England, primarily to fish, and though these sometimes harmed the Indians, provoking some violence, and though they also brought the diseases that devastated the native populations, the former did not encroach on native territory and the latter was not recognized by either side fully for what it was. Thus the Wampanoags would have seen little to fear in the Pilgrims. Other native groups, though—the Narragansett, Pequot, and Massachusetts tribes—divided themselves between trading with the Pilgrims and resenting the shifts in power their trading and alliances brought about. And as the numbers of Europeans began to increase dramatically in the coming years, accompanied by larger demands for land, these other Indian tribes took an even less friendly stance.

These trends culminated in the Pequot War. As Bradford records, the Pequots saw even better than the English themselves where things were heading. Bradford recounts the "pernicious arguments" the Pequots used to try to woo the Narragansetts, their traditional enemies, from the English side to theirs, telling them that "the English were strangers and began to overspread their country, and would deprive them thereof in time, if they were suffered to grow and increase. And if the Narragansetts did assist the English to subdue them [i.e., the Pequots], they did but make way for their own overthrow" (p. 294). The Narragansetts were not persuaded by the Pequots, however, and in 1637 joined with the English in a night attack on the Pequot's chief fort at the mouth of the Mystic River, in response to an earlier attack by the Pequots on English settlers in Connecticut. With the Pequots surrounded, the English set fire to their houses, giving them the choice of burning to death or presenting themselves to their swords. "Thereby," Bradford writes, "more were burnt to death than was otherwise slain.... those that scaped the fire were slain with the sword, some hewed to pieces, others run through with their rapiers, so as they were quickly dispatched and very few escaped" (p. 296). The Narragansetts did not directly take part in the killing, according to Bradford, but mocked the Pequots as they died. In all, Bradford estimates, four hundred were killed. "It was a fearful sight," Bradford concludes, "to see them thus frying in the fire and the streams of blood quenching the same, and horrible was the stink and scent thereof; but the victory seemed a sweet sacrifice, and they gave the praise thereof to God, who had wrought so wonderfully for them, thus to enclose their enemies in their hands and give them so speedy a victory over so proud and insulting an enemy" (p. 296).

This is the last of the Pequots in Bradford's narrative, a picture not of mutual amity but rather of war against an enemy once again perceived as little other than savages. But it is not the last of the Narragansetts. The next-to-last chapter of *Of Plymouth Plantation*, for the year 1645, brings to its conclusion the story of the Narragansetts and the English. As the war predicted by the Pequots between the English and the Narragansetts approaches, the English present an overwhelming show of force that convinces the Narragansetts to

agree to a treaty of peace. Among other particulars, this treaty gave to the English final say on any disposition the Narragansetts might wish to make of their land.

A RELIGIOUS COMMUNITY

Though many aspects of mainstream American religious practice can be found in the Pilgrims, there are also aspects of their beliefs and practices that set them apart from mainstream American religious practice today, or that persist in ways that are not always recognized. To begin with, the Pilgrims were not ecumenical. They were fiercely anti-Catholic, as were all English Puritans. A letter from one who stayed behind in Holland, included by Bradford in *Of Plymouth Plantation,* declares flatly that "the Pope is Antichrist" (p. 355). They were also resolute in their opposition to the Church of England. The Church of England remained too much like the Catholic Church, even though it had broken with Rome. Its hierarchy, canons, and ceremonies were "popish trash," and its corruption was so bad that "sin hath been countenanced; ignorance, profaneness and atheism increased, and the papists encouraged to hope again for a day" (p. 7).

Among the sins countenanced by the Church of England were those elements of "Merrie Olde England" which tended to profane pursuits—the festivals, pageants, and games that were linked to the Catholic/Anglican liturgical calendar, such as Christmas. The Puritans, on the other hand, did not celebrate, or even acknowledge, Christmas. Thus, though the First Book of *Of Plymouth Plantation* concludes with the statement that the colonists on "the 25th day [of December] began to erect the first house for common use to receive them and their goods" (p. 72), Bradford makes no comment on the date. It is just another day. When December 25th came round again, there were young men come among the Pilgrims who expected to observe Christmas as they were accustomed to in England. Bradford recounts:

> On the day called Christmas Day, the Governor [i.e. Bradford himself] called them out to work as was used. But the most of this new company excused themselves and said it went against their consciences to work on that day. So the Governor told them that if they made it a matter of conscience, he would spare them till they were better informed; so he led away the rest and left them. But when they came home at noon from their work, he found them in the street at play, openly; some pitching the bar, and some at stool-ball and such like sports. So he went to them and took away their implements and told them that was against his conscience, that they should play and others work. If they made the keeping of it [i.e., Christmas] matter of devotion, let them keep to their houses; but there should be no gaming or reveling in the streets.
>
> (p. 97)

Bradford calls this a matter "rather of mirth than of weight," and it shows a restraint in Bradford that contrasts with the severity often associated with the Puritans, a severity more characteristic of the much larger contingent of Puritans who a few years later founded the city of Boston. Nevertheless, the celebration of Christmas in the Old English way was suppressed. "Since [that] time," Bradford concludes, "nothing hath been attempted that way, at least openly" (p. 97).

Those sacraments of the Catholic Church that were similarly seen as unbiblical were likewise rejected. This included the sacrament of marriage. Thus Bradford writes in chapter 12:

> May 12 was the first marriage in this place which, according the laudable custom of the Low Countries [Holland], in which they had lived, was thought most requisite to be performed by the magistrate, as being a civil thing, upon which many questions about inheritances do depend, with other things most proper to their [i.e., the civil authorities'] cognizance and most consonant to the Scriptures (Ruth iv) and nowhere found in the Gospel to be laid on the ministers as a part of their office.
>
> (p. 86)

This rejection of many of the Catholic sacraments included rejection of the priesthood invested with the power to administer them. Ministers chosen by the congregation took the place of priests appointed by papal authority. The function of the minister was principally that of a teacher, and in the absence of a suitable minister a Congregational church such as that of the Pilgrims could continue to function with only the leadership of an unordained elder. Such was the situation of

the Pilgrims at Plymouth, whose minister—John Robinson—stayed behind in Holland, leaving the leadership of the church to the elder William Brewster. During the years it took for the Pilgrims to find a suitable minister, neither baptisms nor the sharing of the Eucharist—the two sacraments the Puritans retained—took place at Plymouth. Their religious life was not a life of ceremony but a life of moral principles and moral rectitude, which required no minister.

SOCIAL AND ECONOMIC ORDER I: THE MAYFLOWER COMPACT

The Second Book of *Of Plymouth Plantation* opens with the writing and signing of the document that has come to be known as the Mayflower Compact. It is occasioned, Bradford explains, by the declarations of some of the "strangers" among the *Mayflower*'s passengers—that is, colonists accompanying the Pilgrims but not of their religious community—that once ashore they will go their own way and pursue their own interests ungoverned by any leaders. To avoid this threat to the success of the community before it had even gotten a foothold in America, a compact was drawn up to "combine" its signers into "a Civil Body Politic" with the power to "enact, constitute, and frame such just and equal Laws, Ordinances, Acts, Constitutions and Offices... as shall be most meet for the general good of the Colony" (p. 76).

While this document is often celebrated as the beginning of self-rule in America, of greater importance to the subsequent history both of the Plymouth colony and American society is the phrase "general good." Throughout *Of Plymouth Plantation,* Bradford distinguishes between the General Body (often shortened to the General) and the Particulars. The General was that community of Pilgrims who had come as a body to America and had equal stakes in the success of the colony. Their roots were in the Leiden church they had left behind, and their hopes were for a godly community that would eventually take in those they had left behind. Furthermore, the General shared equally in the debt to the London Adventurers who had put up the capital that financed their voyage. The Particulars, by contrast, had no stake in the community beyond what was necessary to enable them, so they hoped, to achieve their own wealth and prosperity.

The number of Particulars at Plymouth increased over time, and Bradford, both as governor and author, saw them as a threat to the community he envisioned and strove for. In this, Bradford shared the vision of Reverend Robinson, the pastor and spiritual leader they had left behind in Holland. In Robinson's farewell letter to the Pilgrims, he wrote of the importance of subordinating individualism to the common good of the group: "Let every man repress in himself and the whole body in each person, as so many rebels against the common good, all private respects of men's selves, not sorting with the general conveniency" (pp. 369–370). But though this was the Pilgrims' goal, they soon found that compromises between individual self-interest and the general good were necessary. Most famously, in chapter 14, Bradford tells of the means taken to increase the colony's supply of corn in the spring of 1623, at a time when rations were still short despite two years of planting and harvesting. "At length," Bradford writes, "after much debate of things, the Governor (with the advice of the chiefest among them), gave way that they should set corn every man for his own particular, and in that regard trust to themselves; in all other things to go on in the general way as before" (p. 120). This resort to self-interest in working the fields had positive results. When the harvest came the following fall, Bradford continues, "instead of famine God now gave them plenty" (p. 132).

But self-interest did not then become the rule at Plymouth. Dedication to the general good remained uppermost in the minds of the Pilgrims, enabling their survival. When one of the London Adventurers, Thomas Weston, decided to go his own way and sent over colonists of his own, intending them to settle near the Pilgrims for mutual aid, he sent only men, eventually numbering over sixty. These men held the Plymouth colony in contempt for having women, children, and frail old men among them. But without order and discipline, and without a commitment to the general good among them, each being on his own

particular, they soon came into difficult straits, some in desperation becoming servants to the Indians in exchange for food, others succumbing to starvation, and they soon gave up and left to join the fishermen to the east and so find their way back to England.

As time went on, self-interest began to be exercised in other ways as well, to the disadvantage of the colony and the displeasure of Bradford and his peers. The most egregious example was Isaac Allerton, himself one of the Pilgrims, who traveled back and forth between Plymouth and London on the colony's business. Allerton began to engage in business for himself as well, bringing back goods from England that he sold for profit both within the colony and to others settling throughout New England, which the others at Plymouth, Bradford writes, "considering their common course, they began to dislike" (p. 211). This was in 1628. Nevertheless, the Pilgrims continued to put their trust in Allerton, though giving him precise instructions as to what he was to bring back from his next trip. Allerton, though agreeing, nevertheless ignored their instructions and over the next two years so entangled his own ventures with that of the colony that when he finally separated himself from Plymouth to go into competition with them in the fur trade that was Plymouth's only hope of resolving their debt, the Plymouth colony found itself in debt not for hundreds of pounds to the London Adventurers, as they had been, but for "many thousands" (p. 243).

But Allerton was the exception among the first generation, or "Old Comers." The others carried on the work of hunting and fishing, building and making, carrying and trading, not for individual profit but for the general good. When a new deal with the London Adventurers was struck in 1627 and later when the debt was finally paid off in 1641, new divisions of land were made so that none came out ahead of the others, though legally some among them, Bradford included, could have taken more land in recompense for their agreeing to take on more of the risk. The community, in turn, when the land was made over to the entire body of the freemen of Plymouth in 1641, "recognized [the Old Comers'] generosity in [their] renunciation of special privilege" (p. 429) by reserving three tracts of land out of the whole for their particular use. Even these lands were largely freely transferred to still newer settlers in the years to come. Much of our admiration for the Pilgrims comes from this spirit, not the spirit of enlightened self-interest but a spirit of enlightened selflessness.

SOCIAL AND ECONOMIC ORDER II: THOMAS MORTON OF MERRY-MOUNT

Other small settlements arose near the Pilgrims in the half-dozen years following the settlement at Plymouth, most proving to be good neighbors. One that did not, however, was only eight miles from Plymouth, first called Mount Wollaston, after its leader, Captain Wollaston, but called Merry-Mount after Wollaston departed for Virginia, leaving behind mostly men who had come to America as indentured servants. This new name was instituted by a one-time lawyer among them named Thomas Morton, who convinced the servants to sever their ties with Wollaston rather than follow him to Virginia only to be sold again. Morton could not have been more different from the Pilgrims, a contrast utilized two hundred years later by Nathaniel Hawthorne in his story "The May-Pole of Merry Mount." Embodying the spirit of the Old England the Pilgrims had hoped to leave behind, Merry-Mount proved a thorn in the side not just of Plymouth but of the other English settlements as well.

After the servants threw in their lot with Morton, Bradford relates, "they fell to great licentiousness and led a dissolute life, pouring out themselves into all profaneness" (p. 205). What they got through trade with the Indians they consumed in drinking and dancing, erecting a maypole in the Old English way as the center of their revels. They invited the Indians, including Indian women, to join them in this revelry, "dancing and frisking together like so many fairies, or furies rather; and worse practices" (p. 205). Morton's relationship with the native people was in all ways quite different from that of the Pilgrims; he treated them as companions rather

than as others to be reckoned with, just as he did those who had been indentured servants, and mingled with them as such. He went so far as to trade guns, powder, and shot with them, as the French and Dutch did, and thus gained an advantage over the Pilgrims in the fur trade, which the Pilgrims depended on to discharge their debt to the London Adventurers. For the Indians, guns, which would increase their success in hunting, were more attractive than the corn the Pilgrims offered.

The existence of Merry-Mount thus threatened both the safety and the economic survival of the other English settlements, as well as threatening their social order. (The Pilgrims could keep no servants, Bradford ruefully notes.) Twice they visited Merry-Mount: the first time, led by John Endecott of Salem, to cut down the maypole; the second, led by Miles Standish of Plymouth, to arrest Morton and send him back to England. (The latter visit is described by Morton himself in his *New English Canaan*; as one might expect, his satiric telling, in which the Puritans are led by "Captain Shrimp," differs considerably from Bradford's, as does Morton's account of the New England landscape, the native people, and the Puritans themselves.) Morton avoided imprisonment, despite the charges made against him by the Puritans, and returned to New England. His influence was much diminished, however, and he continued to be only an irritant to the Puritans, rather than the threat they had earlier perceived him to be, until finally, in old age, he faded into the woods he loved.

DISPERSION AND DECLINE

The settlement that brought the greatest changes to the Plymouth colony and to New England in general began in 1629, with the arrival of 350 Puritan settlers in the area of Massachusetts Bay. By the end of the 1630s their number would increase into the thousands, far overshadowing the Pilgrims at Plymouth. Though Bradford originally welcomed them as fellow believers, the transformation of New England engendered by this great migration would eventually bring about the end of Bradford's long-held hopes for his community.

Bradford and the other original leaders of the Plymouth colony had from the beginning hoped for a tight-knit community focused on their small congregational church. But this community never fully materialized. Many left behind in Holland—in particular, Reverend Robinson—never joined them. Just as vexingly, forces within Plymouth colony—whether the strangers among them or the inevitable tendency toward expansion and dispersion—also pressed toward division. The rapid growth of the Bay Colony, then, perhaps only hastened the inevitable. In chapter 23, for the year 1633, Bradford already notes the economic effect on his fellow Pilgrims of the rapid population growth around Massachusetts Bay. A great market opened up for corn and cattle, which the Pilgrims were in a position to supply, but only by greatly expanding their own farms. Their focus thus turned from the general good to individual wealth: "And no man now thought he could live except he had cattle and a great deal of ground to keep them, all striving to increase their stocks. By which means they were scattered all over [Plymouth] Bay quickly and the town [Plymouth] in which they lived compactly till now was left very thin and in a short time almost desolate" (p. 253).

Worse, in Bradford's view, was the division this dispersion brought to the church itself. As farmsteads grew up farther and farther from town, those who removed to them declared that the distance to church grew too great and so sued to have their own church across the Plymouth Bay at Duxbury. "And so they were dismissed," Bradford relates, "though very unwillingly" (p. 253). Others soon followed suit and were likewise reluctantly granted permission to separate when the only alternative was to "live in continual opposition and contention" (p. 253). As Plymouth thus was being emptied, it was suggested in 1644 that the entire settlement move to a place more favorable to growth. Though the majority agreed to move, the place chosen—about fifty miles away—seemed too great a move to some, and so the community was split yet again. "And this I fear will be the ruin of New England," Bradford laments, "at least of the churches of God there,

and will provoke the Lord's displeasure against them" (p. 254).

Prosperity and dispersion were not the only factors undermining Bradford's hopes. Chapter 32—for the year 1642—is almost entirely despairing. Plymouth's business relationship with what was left of the London Adventurers comes to its conclusion without much satisfaction for any involved. Letters come from the Bay Colony inquiring what should be done regarding those religious dissenters who had been forced from Massachusetts—Anne Bradstreet and Roger Williams, among others—but who had gone no farther than Rhode Island and Connecticut, and thus still bedeviled the Puritan goal of a religiously pure New England. The Pilgrims, to their credit, were less concerned with this than was the much larger Bay Colony, where religious persecution was much more prevalent. The fur trade was waning, turning the colonists more and more to agriculture, bringing them into more and more conflict with the Indians. But Bradford is most concerned with another developing problem: the growth of "wickedness" among them, not just the murders addressed in earlier chapters but also drunkenness and "uncleanness," that is, sexual transgressions of one sort or another, whether "incontinency between persons unmarried," adultery, sodomy, bestiality, or even the rape of two young girls. Such transgressions, Bradford declares, were "much witnessed against ... narrowly looked into ... and severely punished" (p. 316). The execution according to the law of Leviticus of one unfortunate young man for having sexual relations with farm animals—"a very sad spectacle" (p. 320)—is described at some length.

What can explain such behavior among them, Bradford asks, especially when "it was religious men that began the work and they came for religion's sake?" (p. 321). Bradford suggests that it was inevitable that ungodly persons would be among the godly, whether those who came as servants to the religious people or those who were brought simply to fill up the ships of unscrupulous traders. Finally, Bradford again refers to the parallels between the Pilgrims and the Jews who came out of Egypt, who had among them those who simply came along to benefit from the better outward life that God's people inevitably enjoy. But whatever the reason, the religious community of God's people Bradford hoped for was not to be.

The final chapters of *Of Plymouth Plantation* are thus written more in resignation than in triumph. The death of William Brewster, the elder in whose home in rural England the Scrooby church had begun, and the departure of Edward Winslow, the longtime emissary of the Pilgrims in the affairs with England, form the final chapters. Bradford's last two chapters are left unwritten.

THE PILGRIMS AND AMERICA TODAY

In 1646, the year of Bradford's last chapter, John Winthrop of Boston, the governor of the neighboring Bay Colony, recorded in his journal that Plymouth "was now almost deserted" (vol. 2, p. 272). The subsequent history of Massachusetts would be the history of Boston and those who came out of that much larger emigration. Yet Bostonians themselves, as well as their fellow citizens of Massachusetts and New England and eventually, the United States of America, gave pride of place to the small group at Plymouth. What can Americans, more than 350 years later, make of this choice? Bradford, when he first learned of the newcomers at Boston, reflected on his own small community's importance as forerunners in this larger development:

> Thus out of small beginnings greater things have been produced by His hand that made all things of nothing, and gives being to all things that are; and, as one small candle may light a thousand, so the light here kindled hath shone unto many, yea in some sort to our whole nation; let the glorious name of Jehovah have all the praise.
>
> (p. 236)

Unquestionably, the Pilgrims' light has shone unto many, even unto a whole nation. How much this is so because of who the Pilgrims were and what they did, and how much because of who Americans have since said they were and said they did, cannot be untangled. They were a godly people who believed themselves to be God's people in a way that Thomas Morton at Merry-

Mount, for instance, did not consider himself to be. And so many Americans since have thought of themselves as a special people chosen by God, in constant struggle with those who oppose their ways. Yet at the same time the America of today can be said to resemble Merry-Mount more than Plymouth. The tension between the general good of the community and the economic interests of the individual so prevalent at Plymouth continues in American society today, with similar results. All of our attempts to follow our best instincts, whether in relationship to the land or those different from us or in our business and social lives, meet with the same human shortcomings that finally overwhelmed Bradford's modestly small utopian vision. Courage and perseverance over adversity are followed by complication, compromise, and decline. *Of Plymouth Plantation* finally gives us the opportunity not simply to immerse ourselves in myths of origins, but to contemplate how those myths correspond to reality, whether the reality of early America or the reality of America today. The answers are more complicated than we often recognize.

Selected Bibliography

WORKS OF WILLIAM BRADFORD

History of Plymouth Plantation.... Edited by Charles Deane. Boston: Massachusetts Historical Society and Little, Brown, 1856. Republished as *Of Plymouth Plantation, 1620–1647.* Edited by Samuel Eliot Morison. New York: Knopf, 1952. (The Morison edition remains the standard for both the scholar and the general reader. Its introduction contains both a history of the manuscript, including its incorporations into other texts, and an account of all important prior editions.)

"Governor Bradford's Letter Book." *Collections of the Massachusetts Historical Society,* first series 3:27–76 (1794).

A Dialogue; or, Third Conference Between Some Young Men Born in New England, and Some Ancient Men Which Came Out of Holland and Old England: Concerning the Church and the Government Thereof. Edited by Charles Deane. Boston: J. Wilson, 1870.

RELATED SOURCES

Morton, Thomas. *New English Canaan.* Amsterdam: Jacob Frederick Stam, 1637. (An account of New England and the Plymouth colony written by its nemesis. Morton's account, particularly of his own arrest, should be compared with Bradford's account in *Of Plymouth Plantation.*)

Winthrop, John. *Winthrop's Journal, "History of New England," 1630–1649.* 2 vols. Edited by James Kendall Hosmer. New York: Scribners, 1908.

Young, Alexander. *Chronicles of the Pilgrim Fathers of the Colony of Plymouth, from 1602–1625.* Boston: Little, Brown, 1841. (Contains both the First Book of *Of Plymouth Plantation* and "Bradford's and Winslow's Journal," commonly known as "Mourt's Relation." For the provenance of these texts, see Morison.)

MANUSCRIPTS

Bradford's manuscript of *Of Plymouth Plantation* is held in the Massachusetts State Library in Boston, Massachusetts.

CRITICAL AND BIOGRAPHICAL STUDIES

Abrams, Ann Uhry. *The Pilgrims and Pocahontas: Rival American Myths of American Origin.* Boulder, Colo.: Westview Press, 1999.

Arber, Edward, ed. *The Story of the Pilgrim Fathers, 1606–1623 A.D.* Boston: Houghton Mifflin, 1897.

Bunker, Nick. *Making Haste from Babylon: The Mayflower Pilgrims and Their World: A New History.* New York: Knopf, 2010.

Franklin, Wayne. *Discoverers, Explorers, Settlers: The Diligent Writers of Early America.* Chicago: University of Chicago Press, 1979.

Howard, Alan B. "Art and History in William Bradford's *Of Plymouth Plantation.*" *William and Mary Quarterly,* 3rd series 28:237–266 (1971).

Morison, Samuel Eliot. "William Bradford." In *Dictionary of American Biography.* Vol. 2. New York: Scribners, 1929.

Pafford, John M. *How Firm a Foundation: William Bradford and Plymouth.* Bowie, Md.: Heritage Books, 2002.

Parini, Jay. "Of Plymouth Plantation." In his *Promised Land: Thirteen Books That Changed America.* New York: Doubleday, 2008.

Philbrick, Nathan. *Mayflower: A Story of Courage, Community, and War.* New York: Viking, 2006.

Salisbury, Neal. *Manitou and Providence: Indians, Europeans, and the Making of New England, 1500–1643.* New York: Oxford University Press, 1982.

Schmidt, Gary D. *William Bradford: Plymouth's Faithful Pilgrim.* Grand Rapids, Mich.: Eerdmans Books, 1999.

Seelye, John. *Memory's Nation: The Place of Plymouth Rock.* Chapel Hill: University of North Carolina Press, 1998.

Smith, Bradford. *Bradford of Plymouth.* Philadelphia: Lippincott, 1951.

Westbrook, Perry D. *William Bradford.* Boston: Twayne, 1978.

KEVIN BROCKMEIER

(1972—)

F. Brett Cox

ONE OF THE most intriguing developments in contemporary American fiction is the gradual eradication of the barriers of literary genres. From the rise of so-called pulp magazines in the early 1900s through most of the remainder of the twentieth century, publishing categories became more firmly entrenched, as did the attitudes of both authors and readers. Mysteries, westerns, and, most of all, the literatures of the fantastic—science fiction, fantasy, horror—were set aside as popular entertainments that were, almost by definition, artistically inferior to the "mainstream" of realist fiction. With a handful of exceptions (Ray Bradbury, Kurt Vonnegut Jr.), to be identified as a genre writer was to forgo the approval of literary critics and scholars, while a writer of "literary fiction" was highly unlikely to be caught exploring the territories of science fiction or fantasy.

By the early twenty-first century, however, the genre-mainstream dichotomy, while not disappearing altogether, had been significantly weakened. Modern genre writers such as Ursula K. Le Guin and William Gibson were recognized as authors of significant literary and cultural influence, while two of the most distinctive (and eccentric) genre writers of the twentieth century, Philip K. Dick and H. P. Lovecraft, were canonized with volumes in the prestigious Library of America series. Most significantly, a number of writers who rose to prominence in the 1990s and since seemed increasingly unconcerned with genre distinctions. Writers such as Jonathan Lethem, Karen Joy Fowler, and Neal Stephenson emerged from the science fiction genre to produce award-winning and best-selling literary fiction, while a new generation of mainstream literary writers such as Michael Chabon, Aimee Bender, George Saunders, Daniel Wallace, and Ron Moody, as well as more established figures such as Richard Powers and Steven Millhauser, increasingly viewed the themes and tropes of genre fiction not as markers of artistic inferiority but as simply more tools in the workbox of fiction. Literary border crossings became more and more common. Lethem's *Motherless Brooklyn* (1999), a detective novel, won the National Book Critics Circle Award. Chabon, after winning a Pulitzer Prize for a novel about comic book writers, *The Amazing Adventures of Kavalier & Clay* (2000), won the World Science Fiction Convention's Hugo Award for an "alternate history" novel, *The Yiddish Policemen's Union* (2007). Saunders received both a MacArthur "genius grant" and a World Fantasy Award for his short fiction. And one of the most revered of modern American novelists, Cormac McCarthy, won a Pulitzer Prize for *The Road* (2006), a novel set in a postapocalyptic future.

Among American writers under forty, Kevin Brockmeier is perhaps the most visible example of this blurring of genre distinctions. A graduate of the Iowa Writers' Workshop, one of the most distinguished graduate creative writing programs in the country, Brockmeier publishes regularly in elite magazines and journals such as the *New Yorker, Granta,* and *Georgia Review*. However, his two novels and two children's books are all explicitly stories of the fantastic, as are most of the short stories in his two collections. Like his contemporary George Saunders, he has received honors from all directions, winning the O. Henry Award for short fiction and being a finalist for the Science Fiction Writers of America Nebula Award (the latter for a short story originally published in the *New Yorker*).

Appropriately, Brockmeier served as editor for the 2010 volume of *Best American Fantasy,* a

series of anthologies designed to showcase works of fantastic fiction across the entire range of contemporary American literature. In his preface to the volume, the series editor Matthew Cheney notes that Brockmeier, "equally comfortable" in "the worlds of genre and non-genre writing" while "reveal[ing] the complexities (and absurdities!) of such a dichotomy," is "a writer who represents everything we hoped *Best American Fantasy* could champion" (p. xi). In his own introduction, Brockmeier addresses the deep tradition of the fantastic in world literature—from works of Homer, Dante, Shakespeare, and Poe to those of late-twentieth-century fantasists such as Jorge Luis Borges, Gabriel García Márquez, and Salman Rushdie—and observes that "some of this literature presents itself as a violation of the ordinary, some as merely an augmentation of it" (p. xiii). He goes on to acknowledge that this "conjunction of the real with the unreal, of the complications of human feeling with the whimsies and dreamlike visitations of fantasy, is an inescapable feature of my aesthetic" (p. xiv). These two statements might serve as an epigraph to any consideration of Brockmeier's fiction. Even when he is working in a realist mode, the worlds of his characters are, on one level or another, augmented and sometimes outright violated by an unanticipated intervention, be it from a specific individual or the forces of the world at large. And when Brockmeier turns to the fantastic, human feeling is not only complicated by, but also inextricable from, the "whimsies" and "visitations" of fantasy. Brockmeier's active and enthusiastic embrace of the modes of the literary fantastic, combined with a strikingly rich, lyrical approach to language and a willingness to experiment with narrative form, has earned him critical comparisons not only to writers such as Millhauser and Bradbury but also to such major twentieth-century writers as Borges and Italo Calvino.

LIFE

The online *Encyclopedia of Arkansas History and Culture* states that Kevin John Brockmeier was born on December 6, 1972, in Hialeah, Florida, to Jack Brockmeier, an insurance agent, and Sally Brockmeier, a legal secretary. In 1976 the family moved to Arkansas after Brockmeier's father was reassigned to an office in Little Rock. Brockmeier was a precocious child who "spoke in full sentences by the age of two and was writing mysteries by age eight." In a 2006 interview, Brockmeier noted that "when I look back over the reading I actually did as a child, I realize that it was mostly made up of comic books, along with works of fantasy and science fiction and mysteries and film novelizations and various paraliterary genres like joke books and catalogs of do-it-yourself science experiments" ("Kevin Brockmeier Interview," *Earth Goat*). As a student at the Parkview Arts and Science Magnet High School, Brockmeier actively participated in speech and theater events before graduating with honors in 1991. In 1995 he received a B.A. degree from Southwest Missouri State University, where he constructed "an interdisciplinary major in creative writing, philosophy, and theater" (*Encyclopedia of Arkansas History and Culture*). During his college years, he drifted away from theater and toward writing, a move that solidified during a postgraduate year in Ireland.

Upon his return to the United States, Brockmeier was admitted to the Iowa Writers' Workshop, where he studied with Frank Conroy and Marilynne Robinson and received an M.F.A. in 1997. That same year saw the appearance of Brockmeier's short story "A Day in the Life of Half of Rumpelstiltskin" in *Writing on the Edge,* which marked the beginning of his career as a fiction writer. Since then, he has been a full-time writer and has also taught creative writing at the University of Arkansas–Little Rock and the Iowa Writers' Workshop. He continues to live in Little Rock.

THINGS THAT FALL FROM THE SKY

Brockmeier's first published book, *Things That Fall from the Sky* (2002), is a collection of eleven short stories, six previously published and five original to the book. Although several of the stories in the book operate in a realist mode, even

the most down-to-earth of them offer protagonists whose worlds have been, in the words of Brockmeier's previously quoted introduction, violated or augmented by unusual people, or events, or both. The book opens with "These Hands," the story of Lewis Winters, a writer of fairy tales who supplements his income by hiring out as a nanny. When he takes a job with Lisa and Thomas Mitchell to look after their daughter Caroline, he finds that, in his daily care for the child, he develops an overpowering love for her that comes to dominate and even define his life: "My love for Caroline is the lens through which I see the world, and the world through that lens is a place whose existence addresses my own" (p. 14). His relationship with Caroline comes to an unhappy end, not because of anything he does related to the child but because of an unexpectedly intimate (but nonsexual) moment as he awkwardly comforts Caroline's mother when she breaks down after telling Lewis that she has lost her job. Dismissed by the father and permanently separated from Caroline, Lewis chooses not to force the issue and walks away, a decision he regards as "one of the most truly contemptible acts of his life. If he had been a good man, he would have found a way, no matter the resistance, to tell her good-bye" (p. 40).

"These Hands" is the longest story in the collection and, from its opening paragraph, sets the tone for much of what follows: "The protagonist of this story is named Lewis Winters. He is also its narrator, and he is also me. He is thirty-four years old.... He writes fairy tales. This is not one of them" (pp. 3–4). Although there are no overtly fantastic elements in the story, its realism is suffused with a degree of otherworldliness. Lewis' work as a nanny is the most settled of occupations, yet he is also a writer of fairy tales; his competent execution of the daily, ordinary tasks of a babysitter is grounded in a love whose fierce purity is extraordinary. But even the reality of that love may be questioned, as Lewis declares early on that he has never read Nabokov (whose *Lolita* remains the most famous fictional account of a man's erotic obsession with a young girl) but later on states, "Number of lies I've told you about my behavior toward Caroline: 0; about fairy tales: 0; about Nabokov: 1" (p. 33). This conflation of the real and the not-quite-real is reinforced by the story's structure, which alternates between a third-person narrative that charts the actual course of events between Lewis and the Marshall family and first-person ruminations on memory, dream, and the degree to which a person is defined by, and arguably exists because of, both. After declaring that "Memories and dreams are the two most potent methods by which the mind investigates itself" (p. 41), Lewis concludes his story with a vivid childhood memory of a lost balloon and a dream of escape with Caroline: "We'll watch the far white stars and the soaring red airplanes, ask *Which is the more beautiful? Which is the more true?* and in finding our answers, we will find what we believe in" (p. 42).

The collection's remaining realist stories continue the approach of "These Hands" in their depiction of a recognizable world touched by the unexpected. In the title story, Katherine, a librarian of late middle age, feels little connection with her job, is estranged to varying degrees from her grown sons, and begins to doubt her own knowledge of the world and of herself: "My sense of what it takes to live with other people is slowly drifting away.... More and more I think as I grow older that I live in this world and know nothing about it" (p. 52). However, repeated encounters with an elderly library patron named Woodrow, who interrogates the laws of gravity by dropping books on the floor and urges upon Katherine a chronicle of unexplained phenomena titled *Things That Fall from the Sky,* lead her to both a new attitude and a new relationship. The narrator of "Apples" recalls "the fall of my thirteenth year ... when all the important events in my life seemed to cluster together like bees" (p. 68). Both his first kiss and the revelation of his parents' separation occur against the backdrop of the unlikely accidental death of one of his teachers. "Space" finds a widower turning to the vastness of the night sky and the image of light thrown endlessly into outer space to provide both context and comfort to himself and his teenage son as they cope with the death of his wife. And in an interesting strategic reversal from the collection's

earlier stories, "The House at the End of the World" is a fantastic scenario invaded by reality: a father cares for his daughter in the wilderness after both survive "the collapse of civilization" (p. 193), only to have the child's mother show up and reveal that the father had kidnapped his own daughter and that civilization, however in decline, still very much exists.

While the realist stories in *Things That Fall from the Sky* are expertly crafted, with "These Hands" particularly noteworthy for its ambitious and thoughtfully intricate narrative, the collection's forays into the fantastic display the author's talent and ambition more memorably as they move beyond the well-made, thoroughly workshopped short story and point more directly toward what Brockmeier accomplishes in his later work. "A Day in the Life of Half of Rumpelstiltskin" considers what happens next to the character who, at the end of the Brothers Grimm fairy tale, literally tears himself in half. The half that has remained in the recognizably real world keeps a carefully ordered itinerary, as documented by the story's section headings: "12:15 p.m. He eats lunch in the park.... 2:30 p.m. He delivers a speech to a local women's auxiliary organization" (pp. 89, 93). Half of Rumpelstiltskin copes, and even prospers, but not without acute knowledge of his own catastrophe: "you can change in such a way as to never again be complete ... sometimes what's missing isn't somebody else" (pp. 99–100).

"Small Degrees" and "The Light Through the Window" also draw on the classic fairy tale, in tone if not in specific content. In the former, a man who, as a child, was dismissed by his parents as "a fool" (p. 119) grows up to be a skilled typesetter and designer whose ultimate goal is to design a unique typeface that will "render his heart into letters and signs" (p. 121). He does so, but at the cost of his marriage, and when the completion of his task triggers a vision that leads to a clear realization of what he has lost, he abandons his achievement to reunite with his wife. Similarly, the third-generation high-rise window cleaner in "The Light Through the Window" is led while on the job to visions of his family's past that connect him more fully with both his heritage and himself. "The Jesus Stories" adopts the language of the scientific report and reference book to tell of an isolated society that, upon being converted to Christianity, determines that "it is our duty as Christians to tell *every possible story* of the life of Jesus," so that when "the final story has been told ... Jesus will descend from the heavens and the Kingdom of God will be upon us" (p. 140). The fantasy of "The Passenger" draws on the science fiction trope of the enclosed universe—a multigenerational vessel whose inhabitants do not know, or at least are not certain, that a world exists outside their immediate environment. The narrator of the story was born, lives, and presumably will die with the other passengers on a never-ending flight of a commercial airliner, an environment within which standing on solid ground is literally the stuff of dreams. As in "These Hands," however, the dream is not merely fantasy or escape but a kind of definition: "It is difficult to overestimate the potential in infinity, the depth of any single thought. We die into our vision of forever. Falling, never landing, we believe our eternity into existence" (p. 178).

The remaining story, "The Ceiling," is at once the collection's most extreme and most successful story of a fantastic interruption of recognizable reality. As the narrator celebrates his son's seventh birthday with family and friends, he looks up at the moon and notices that "against its blank white surface was a square of perfect darkness" (p. 103). Over the next months, the object grows larger and begins to descend. It appears in the daytime, altering the nature of sunlight; birds and insects gradually disappear, and scientists offer no explanation. Yet the narrator's life—and the lives of those around him—continues, made up of events both mundane (getting a haircut) and exceptional (discovering that his wife is having an affair). By the end of the story, the object now known as "the ceiling" has descended fully, taking out trees and buildings, and when it is "no higher than a coffee table" (p. 116) the narrator, lying on the ground beside his wife, squeezes her hand and waits for her to return the gesture: "I could wait the whole life of the world for such a thing, until the earth

and the sky met and locked and the distance between them closed forever" (p. 117).

In "The Ceiling," Brockmeier clearly grasps what the science fiction writers he read as a child instinctively understood: the metaphoric power of the fantastic as literal event, as the narrator's world collapses both figuratively (his marriage) and literally (the descent of the ceiling). Where Brockmeier differs from more traditional genre writers is in his insistence on maintaining extraordinarily close focus on his characters and their immediate environment and concerns, a focus that can exclude broader concerns of plot and setting. Although the descent of the ceiling is, presumably, a worldwide phenomenon, we are given no word of situations and responses elsewhere; significantly, the only direct reference to outside response comes not from a newscast but from a "member of a local guerrilla theater troupe ... delivering a recitation from beneath a streetlamp ... as if into a camera" (p. 107). In Brockmeier's vision, the apocalypse is local and, ultimately, individual.

Things That Fall from the Sky received generally favorable reviews, with several of its stories being individually honored. Writing in the *New York Times,* Hillary Frey found the title story "excessively tidy" but praised most of the others, especially "These Hands" and "The House at the End of the World," and compared Brockmeier favorably to Steven Millhauser. James Klise found the title story "genuinely moving" and the entire book "outstanding," while *Kirkus Reviews* declared the book "a promising first collection, showcasing a new writer's significant powers of invention." The *New Yorker* praised Brockmeier for avoiding sentimentality and for his high level of craft: "Brockmeier investigates our capacity for wonder with the fastidious precision of a clockmaker, and the result is exacting and perfectly strange." "Apples" was a runner-up for the *Chicago Tribune's* Nelson Algren Award for short fiction, "A Day in the Life of Half of Rumpelstiltskin" received the Italo Calvino Short Fiction Award, and both "These Hands" and "The Ceiling" were recognized by the O. Henry Awards, with "The Ceiling" winning first prize.

THE TRUTH ABOUT CELIA

Brockmeier's first novel, *The Truth About Celia*, published in 2003, is a strikingly ambitious and complex narrative that proceeds from a simple, appalling premise. On March 15, 1997, seven-year-old Celia, daughter of Christopher and Janet Brooks, is playing outside of her house in the town of Springfield when she mysteriously disappears. Neither the police nor anyone else can explain her disappearance, and her parents never see her again. The town's outpouring of sympathy and support is sincere but cannot last; eventually, Christopher and Janet become The Couple Whose Daughter Went Missing, as much a landmark as the antebellum house in which they live. Their marriage does not survive their loss: Janet has an affair with the policeman who leads the search for their missing daughter, the couple eventually separate, and by the end of the novel, Christopher is alone in the old house with his memories of Celia.

Such a scenario would seem to lead inevitably in one of two directions: a sensationalized exploration, at once sentimental and prurient, of the innocent child and the evil force that claimed her; or a grim account of the parents' grief as it turns to emptiness. Brockmeier chooses a strikingly different path. *The Truth About Celia* contains two title pages, one credited to Kevin Brockmeier, the other credited to Christopher Brooks. The "About the Author" note on the book's final page identifies Brooks as "the author of several highly acclaimed works of fantasy and science fiction, including ... the bestselling Gates of Horn and Ivory Trilogy.... *The Truth About Celia* is his first book-length work of fiction since 1997." "A Note from the Author" at the front of the book, credited to Brooks, declares, "The stories in these pages were written after the disappearance of my daughter.... They are a mixture of fact and speculation.... I think I believed that by writing them I could rescue or resurrect my daughter, that the fact might reconstruct her as she used to be and the speculation might call her back from wherever she is today."

What follows are eight stories in which "Brooks" assesses the catastrophe of Celia's disappearance from different times—before, dur-

ing, and after the event—and different points of view, and in at least two cases, with narratives that on the surface appear to have nothing to do with the event itself. "March 19, 1997" offers a brief but intensely focused account of the day and hour of Celia's disappearance from her father's point of view. "Faces, and How They Look from Behind" employs multiple perspectives as it surveys assorted residents of Springfield, including Christopher and Janet, on the day of a memorial service held four years after Celia's disappearance. "The Green Children" appears to separate completely from the main narrative in its retelling of the appearance of two children with green skin in the British town of Woolpit in the twelfth century (an incident that may or may not have actually happened but was reported in a contemporary account by William of Newburgh [p. 55]). "As the Deck Tilted into the Ocean" returns to the main narrative and Janet's point of view as, in the immediate aftermath of Celia's disappearance, she tries to lose herself in moviegoing, only to break down and literally deface the movie screen when confronted with a film about parents whose child has gone missing. "The Ghost of Travis Worley" is narrated in the first person by an apparently adult Celia who, resident in some undefined Other Place, remembers the events of her childhood, including the moments before, but not after, her disappearance, as she is led away by a neighborhood child known to everyone simply as "Kid" (p. 110). "Appearance, Disappearance, Levitation, Transformation, and the Divided Woman" marks another apparent departure from the main narrative as a single mother named Stephanie arranges for her son, Micah, to take magic lessons from a less-than-expert magician who nonetheless becomes a fixture in their lives, to the point of having Micah assist as his mother participates in a potentially dangerous stage stunt. "The Telephone" returns to Christopher's point of view as he tells of receiving calls from Celia over a toy telephone that promise, but do not deliver, a reunion with his daughter. In the book's final section, "Love Is a Chain, Hope Is a Weed," it is seven years since Celia's disappearance, and Christopher lives alone in their house, seemingly resigned to the loss of his daughter and his wife (who by this point has abandoned her affair and moved away altogether) but also holding out the possibility of something wholly different: "Why had he imagined that life must always end in death, and never in anything else? He is not nearly at the end" (p. 216).

On the one hand, *The Truth About Celia* bears the mark of a natural short-story writer coming to terms with a novel by piecing together disparate stories into a more-or-less continuous narrative. However, Brockmeier's playing to his strengths in this fashion yields a novel that is both strikingly intricate and, ultimately, fully coherent. By keeping careful track of a large cast of supporting characters, several of whom appear multiple times in the various stories—Tommy Taulbee, a local teacher; Enid Embry, a widow who believes sincerely in UFOs and expresses her support to Christopher and Janet through covered-dish meals; Kristen Lanzetta, Celia's best friend; Kimson Perry, the policeman who becomes Janet's lover—Brockmeier provides a consistent context for Christopher's diverse attempts to write a narrative that provides some kind of explanation and closure, for himself if for no one else.

The explanations are there for the attentive reader, even within the stories that seem wholly removed from the main narrative. In "The Green Children," the female child who survives identifies herself as "Seel-ya" (p. 76); in "Appearance, Disappearance ... ," we are told that the adult Stephanie "remembered nothing at all of her life before the age of seven, when she woke in her bedroom from what her parents told her was a high fever.... she sometimes wondered about those missing years and whether part of her hadn't gone missing as well, some small shape inside her no bigger than a girl" (p. 139). (In a 2007 interview, Brockmeier cites numerous other details in the story to support his unequivocal declaration that "Stephanie is Celia" [McMyne].) Joined with the disembodied communications of "The Telephone" and the briefly but clearly identified supernatural presence in "The Ghost of Travis Worley"—the "Kid" who leads Celia away, who in 1997 wears a brace on his leg because of a disease Celia has

never heard of called polio and who, as revealed in the book's final section, died in 1925—these disparate storylines offer the possibility of an outcome that, while far from a happy ending for Christopher, is still something other than tragic.

What even the attentive reader will not find is a definite, unitary truth about Celia, or a definite answer to the question, what happened to her? Brockmeier has said of his first novel that "almost all the stories ... rely on a different set of ground rules" and that Christopher Brooks, in losing his daughter, is "devastated" but also "in some way introduced to himself" (McMyne). *The Truth About Celia* by Christopher Brooks may be the consoling fantasy of a grieving father, but *The Truth About Celia* by Kevin Brockmeier is, at the end, a story of survival.

The Truth About Celia received wide critical acclaim when it appeared. Many reviewers had particular praise for Brockmeier's elegant prose. The *New York Times Book Review* suggested that the novel's "unvarying gracefulness takes some of the bite out of the sadness," but more typically, the *San Francisco Chronicle* hailed the work as "beautifully styled" and "heartbreaking." *Publishers Weekly* and others compared the novel favorably to Alice Sebold's best seller *The Lovely Bones*. And in a noteworthy tribute to Brockmeier's confident presentation of fantasy elements, "The Green Children" was included as a stand-alone short story in the 2004 volume of the anthology series *Year's Best Fantasy and Horror*.

CITY OF NAMES *AND* GROOVES: A KIND OF MYSTERY

In the same years that Brockmeier published his first short fiction collection and second novel, he also published two books for young readers ("young" being defined by the publishers of both books as ages eight to twelve): *City of Names* (2002) and *Grooves: A Kind of Mystery* (2006). Both stories are set in the imaginary town of North Mellwood; consistent with Brockmeier's adult fiction, both deal with fantastic events impacting the lives of ordinary people. However, the books have different characters, and each story stands independent of the other.

City of Names is narrated by ten-year-old Howie Quackenbush, a fifth-grader at Larry Boone Elementary School whose mother is pregnant—a topic of some interest to Howie, but not quite as much as a book he obtains through his school book club. Having ordered *101 Pickle Jokes,* he receives instead the *Secret Guide to North Mellwood,* a book that reveals that "every place in North Mellwood has two names—a false name and a true name" (p. 16). There are also five "portals" located throughout the city, and anyone who goes to one of the portals, knocks three times, and says the true name of any location in the town will be instantly transported there and can return the same way. After quickly determining that this system works, Howie lets his best friend, Kevin Bugg, in on the secret, and then Casey Robinson, a girl he has had "sort of a crush on" since he was six (p. 30).

Howie at first uses the portal located on the school grounds solely to enjoy the exhilaration of instant transport while impressing his friends and luxuriating in a secret well kept. However, his gradual discovery of the other portals leads to other discoveries: the older boy who has been bullying him has problems of his own; Howie's Aunt Margie knows about the portals and has been using them for years; Larry Boone, the Revolutionary War hero after whom Howie's school is named, maintains his existence in an underground "White Room," from where he has been monitoring Howie and friends' activities. The most striking discovery is the Hall of Babies, where Howie meets his yet-to-be-born sister and learns that she, like the locations of North Mellwood, has a true name—information he manages to convey to his parents when his sister is born shortly after his return.

Early on in *City of Names,* Howie declares, "Every night I go to sleep happy" (p. 7), and it is obvious throughout the narrative that Howie is a boy who is not facing a great deal of difficulty in his life. His discovery of the portals provides new knowledge and insight but, with the exception of the school bully, does not solve any problems because, fundamentally, there are no

problems to be solved. Travel through the portals takes some getting used to, and the journeys to the White Room and the Hall of Babies are marked by obstacles, but there is never any sense of real danger. The one time a potentially dangerous situation arises—when Howie and Casey, in front of a single portal, say two different true names at once and become disembodied—it is more disorienting than threatening. While this relative lack of dramatic stakes arguably results in a corresponding lack of narrative tension, it does afford Brockmeier the opportunity to focus closely on his characters and continue to explore, even in a story aimed at ten-year-olds, his recurrent theme of how we define ourselves, how we know who we are. But while the characters of Brockmeier's adult stories know themselves through memories and dreams filtered through often catastrophic loss, the children of *City of Names* increase their self-awareness through the pleasures of secret knowledge that leads to fundamental truth, truth that has the potential to move everyone forward, even the adults. When Howie convinces his parents that his new sister's true name is Marie, "it seemed like they were remembering something. And then, after a second, it seemed like they were discovering something" (p. 137).

In *Grooves: A Kind of Mystery,* the underlying thematic concerns are the same, but the immediate stakes are higher. The narrator, Dwayne Ruggles, is an eighth-grader who, orphaned as an infant, lives with his irascible grandfather, who owns a secondhand goods shop that contains as much junk as collectibles. Nonetheless, Dwayne leads an ordinary kid's life, hanging out with best friend, Kevin Applebab, who shares Dwayne's passion for comic books. Everything changes the day Dwayne applies a classroom experiment in acoustics at home. When he runs a needle connected to a paper loudspeaker over the grooves in a pair of his jeans, he discovers a hidden message: "Please. You must help us. He's stealing the light from our eyes" (p. 46). With the help of friend Kevin and Emily Holmes, the fearless younger sister of Dwayne's favorite childhood babysitter, he discovers that local industrialist Howard Thigpen is behind a sinister plot to increase his own personal and economic power by literally stealing the spark of light from the eyes of other people. After a couple of initial failures, the three friends finally manage to gain entry to the secret domain within the Thigpen Corporation Factory Complex that houses the "Spark Transplantation Machine" (p. 150), where they discover the worker who sent the message and, despite being captured and threatened by Thigpen, ultimately defeat him.

As the above summary suggests, *Grooves* is a much more conventionally action-filled children's adventure than *City of Names,* with clearly defined heroes and villains and juvenile protagonists who are periodically in actual physical danger. However, the livelier plot also makes room for a wider range of more developed characters, especially among the adults: Mr. Fred, the science teacher whose experiment leads to Dwayne's discovery of the message and who shares Dwayne's love of comics; Shimerman, Dwayne's grandfather's environmentalist assistant; and Thigpen himself, who values money not for the things it can buy but for the power it gives him over other people. Like *City of Names, Grooves* ends happily, and, like the children of the earlier novel, Dwayne and his friends are better off for the knowledge they have gained. But the very existence of a Howard Thigpen, of a world where some have appalling and undeserved power over others, raises the possibility of threat and loss, the actuality of which permeates Brockmeier's adult fiction.

Although generally admired for their cleverness and readability, Brockmeier's books for young readers have not received the same widespread critical enthusiasm as his adult fiction. Anne O'Malley, writing in *Booklist,* considered *City of Names* "a clever, enjoyable read with a likeable hero," but *Publishers Weekly* found that "while the [book's] contrivances are clever, the author fails to use them to exciting or meaningful effect," and the *School Library Journal* concluded, "While the premise has potential, the author doesn't carry it off successfully." *Booklist* found the premise of *Grooves* "silly" but concluded it was "a compulsively readable story

with charmingly eccentric characters," while the *Kirkus* review service found the book "has enough internal logic (of a daft sort) to hold together," and the *School Library Journal* declared, "Kids will laugh their way through the ridiculous situations.... The novel is a hoot." Nonetheless, Brockmeier has remained committed to writing for young readers as well as adults. In a 2007 interview, he said that he was inspired to write for children as a result of his college experience working at a nursery school and that, while writing *City of Names,* he discovered "certain things—modes of storytelling, incidents from my own life, understandings and misunderstandings of language—that I could make better use of when I was writing for children than I could when I was writing for adults." In the same interview, he expressed a desire to alternate between writing books for adults and books for children (McMyne).

THE BRIEF HISTORY OF THE DEAD

Brockmeier's second novel, *The Brief History of the Dead* (2006), marks his most overt use of the materials of genre fiction, a move clearly signaled in the novel's opening lines: "When the blind man arrived in the city, he claimed that he had traveled across a desert of burning sand. First he had died, he said, and then—*snap!*—the desert" (p. 3). The man quickly discovers that he has arrived at a "city of the dead, 'not heaven' and 'not hell' " (p. 7), but rather a kind of limbo where the dead exist in a comfortable urban landscape, complete with coffee shops and a daily newspaper. None of the dead are certain exactly how the city functions or what their ultimate destination is, but there is general belief that the dead inhabit the city only as long as someone remains in the actual world who knew and remembers them: "When the last person who had actually known them died, they would pass over into whatever came next" (p. 7). However, the city has begun to "empty out" (p. 13), and the publisher of the city's newspaper, Luka Sims, notes that most of the recently arrived identify themselves as victims of an epidemic. By chapter's end, the city appears deserted, and the blind man fears he may be the only one left.

In the second chapter, the scene shifts to an Antarctic research station whose three inhabitants, Michael Puckett, Robert Joyce, and Laura Byrd, have lost communication with the outside world because of an antenna malfunction and are on the verge of running out of supplies. Complicating the situation is the fact that they are neither highly trained scientists nor experts on the region. The station is under the control of the Coca-Cola corporation, they are there "to explore methods of converting polar ice for use in the manufacture of soft drinks," and there is some controversy as to whether their base is a legitimate research station or "a publicity exercise" (p. 20). After concluding that nobody will be arriving with supplies, the two men head for another research outpost which, they hope, will have workable communications. Weeks pass, and the men do not return. Faced with failing electricity and left with less than a month's worth of supplies, Laura is forced to leave the outpost and journey toward the other research station alone if she hopes to survive.

The remaining chapters alternate between an account of Laura's journey across the Antarctic wilderness and vignettes of life in the City of the Dead. In the former, Laura reaches the other station only to discover the bodies of its inhabitants and news of the worldwide plague—the "Blinks," so called because of its initial symptom of severe eye irritation—that has reached Antarctica and left her, almost certainly, the last person alive on earth. Meanwhile, in the City of the Dead, it becomes apparent that the only inhabitants who remain do so because they are, however casually, people whom Laura has known and of whom she has some memory.

As Laura continues her doomed journey to try to find some means to communicate with the outside world, the inhabitants of the City all enact their individual stories, some positive (the newspaper publisher Sims, who had had a brief affair with Laura, forms a rewarding relationship with another woman), some not (the paranoid and profane Lindell, a Coca-Cola executive through whom we learn that it was his company's

soft drink that served as a vector for the plague). By the time Laura reaches her destination—a penguin rookery where, according to a journal left by her companions, there might be a workable radio—she has contracted the Blinks and begins to succumb to the Antarctic cold. In the final two chapters, Laura undergoes an extraordinary metamorphosis and transition that may or may not take her to the City whose few remaining inhabitants, without Laura's memories to sustain them, watch the City constrict and disappear, block by block, building by building, leaving them to "wait for that power that would pull them like a chain into whatever came next" (p. 252).

The Laura chapters of *The Brief History of the Dead* offer the most sustained linear narrative to be found in Brockmeier's work, a narrative that draws freely on the traditions and strategies of science fiction in its attention to the material reality of the future in which the story takes place: the technology of the base camp and the sledge that enables Laura to survive as long as she does; the changes in global climate and global politics that cause the Antarctic to be given over to corporate exploitation. In their detailed descriptions of the physical progress and hazards of Laura's journey (including a harrowing fall into a crevasse), the chapters are also strongly informed by the tradition of polar exploration narratives, both factual and fictional. In a note at the end of the book, Brockmeier acknowledges his use of "Apsley Cherry-Garrard's unparalleled memoir of Antarctic exploration, *The Worst Journey in the World*" (p. 253), while the more sensational (and hallucinatory) aspects of Laura's journey recall such classic fiction as Edgar Allan Poe's "The Narrative of Arthur Gordon Pym" and H. P. Lovecraft's "At the Mountains of Madness." The City chapters have more of the feel of Brockmeier's short fiction in their close focus on the characters' inner lives and how those lives are defined in terms of personal memory. As in *The Truth About Celia,* Brockmeier juggles a relatively large cast of characters with considerable skill, gradually, subtly revealing the connections among them, and their connections with Laura: in one scene in the City, two unnamed men are having an argument whose content and context eventually reveals them to be Laura's companions Puckett and Joyce, who, when their time came, crossed over with the rest of the dead.

However, Brockmeier has not simply jammed together a collection of lyrical musings with a near-future adventure story. As Laura's journey becomes more and more difficult, she turns increasingly inward, looking to her own memories, at first as a means of escape from the dire situation she faces: "in the same way that the tent was a refuge from the weather, [her memory of] the park was a refuge from the present, a shelter she could rest inside while the cold and wind went rushing and swirling around her" (p. 171). Eventually, however, her memories become a means of holding on to her own sense of self: "those skeletonized images from her early childhood that sometimes flashed into her mind when her thoughts began to drift, disconnected from anything that might put them into context" (p. 196). By the end of the novel, both story lines are rhetorically and thematically consistent, with each other and with Brockmeier's earlier work. If those earlier stories suggested that we are defined by what we remember and dream, this novel proposes that we are also defined by the memories and dreams of others.

In its deliberate and urgent conflation of the traditions of genre science fiction with the concerns of "literary" fiction, *The Brief History of the Dead* is arguably Brockmeier's most audacious book, a novel that runs the risk of alienating readers from both audiences. Those who come to the novel from the perspective of the mainstream character study might be uninterested in the novel's careful exposition of technology and politics, while readers from a genre tradition might feel that the author sacrificed narrative momentum for thematic complexity. The novelist Patrick McGrath, writing in the *New York Times,* condemned the book's "tedious digressions and flashbacks," while *Booklist* thought it "uneven." However, the overall critical response to Brockmeier's second novel was strongly positive, typified by the *San Francisco Chronicle*'s praise of its "warm wit and generous heart" and *Library Journal*'s verdict that the novel is "beautifully

written and brilliantly realized." Notably, reviews from within the science fiction genre were very positive. The novelist Charles de Lint, writing in the *Magazine of Fantasy and Science Fiction,* praised the novel's "fascinating concepts," "captivating group of individuals," and "elegant and luminous" prose style (p. 33), while the editor and critic Nick Gevers, writing in *Locus,* celebrated its "brilliant character sketches" and declared the book "metaphysical horror fiction of exceptional quality" (p. 27). The first chapter, when published under the novel's title as a standalone short story in the *New Yorker,* was a finalist for the Science Fiction and Fantasy Writers of America Nebula Award, and the novel itself received the PEN USA Award for fiction.

THE VIEW FROM THE SEVENTH LAYER

Brockmeier's sixth book and second short story collection, *The View from the Seventh Layer* (2008), finds the author returning to, expanding upon, and refining the themes and motifs of his previous books, including (in at least one case) his books for children. The collection clearly signals his continuing emphasis on the fantastic by framing nine short stories with four very short "fables," none longer than eight pages. Each of three fables is followed by three stories, with the fourth fable concluding the book. "A Fable Ending in the Sound of a Thousand Parakeets" tells of a man who cannot speak who lives in a city "where everyone had the gift of song" (p. 3). He devotes his life to maintaining a houseful of parakeets, birds which, upon the man's death, "reproduced all the sounds of [his] daily life.... It sounded for all the world like a symphony" (p. 10). "A Fable with a Photograph of a Glass Mobile on the Wall" tells of a skilled cabinetmaker who, upon achieving unexpected fame, is offered a commission that forces him to live in someone else's home for four months, where he gains unexpected and enriching knowledge of a boy whose spirit permeates the home, even though the boy himself is alive and well elsewhere. "A Fable Containing a Reflection the Size of a Match Head in Its Pupil" tells of a land whose inhabitants cannot look each other in the eye in order to avoid having "the spark of life" contained in one's eyes "consumed, if not devoured in a single swallow, then eaten away a piece at a time" (p. 201), and of what happens when, inevitably, two people in love look into each other's eyes anyway. And in "A Fable with Slips of White Paper Spilling from the Pockets," Brockmeier recalls Nikolai Gogol's classic story "The Overcoat," as a man who buys a thrift-store coat discovers in its pockets slips of paper containing people's prayers and further discovers that, while the coat is in his possession, he has the power to grant these prayers. In their elegant use of the once-upon-a-time rhetoric of the fairy tale, all four fables recall "Small Degrees" and "The Light Through the Window" from *Things That Fall from the Sky*, while the conceit of "A Fable Containing a Reflection" hearkens back to the fantasy element of *Grooves*.

The remaining nine stories once again find Brockmeier moving freely between fantastic and realist modes, bringing the concerns and strategies of one mode to the other. "The Lives of the Philosophers" is a realist story about graduate student Jacob's conflicted attitudes toward pending fatherhood, and the disastrous results for his marriage when he makes up his mind on the issue too late. It is also a story of the search for transcendent understanding as Jacob tries to gain insight into the moments when Thomas Aquinas and Friedrich Nietzsche, "polar opposites in their roles as icons and thinkers," both experienced "revelations" that left them unwilling to continue their philosophical writings (p. 49). Faced with a major crisis of his own, Jacob realizes that the philosophers "were given a glimpse of the future" and "observed the brutality in whose service their ideas would be employed" (p. 59), leading him to conclude that "there is no change machine.... The past is irreparable and so is the future" (p. 60). In "The Year of Silence," the residents of a nameless city experience random moments of silence that lead to a campaign to abolish all background noise. After a period of universal silence "plain and rich and deep ... infinitely delicate, yet strangely irresistible" (p. 70), the people of the city allow ordinary noise to return, only to realize that "the episodes of silence and

the episodes of clamor resembled communications taking the form of Morse code" (p. 73), a message, reports a police cryptographer, "whose meaning was explicit ... but whose import he could not fathom" (p. 78).

Several of the stories in the collection find Brockmeier exploring more traditional narrative approaches. "Father John Melby and the Ghost of Amy Elizabeth" is perhaps the closest Brockmeier has come to a conventional ghost story, as a priest discovers that his unexpected transition from being "a feeble speaker" (p. 88) to delivering powerful and compelling sermons is linked to the supernatural presence of a young woman who "failed to love anyone" (p. 99) and so remains trapped on earth. To escape, she must "hand [her]self over to somebody ... who will accept [her] willingly" (p. 105); when the devout priest refuses, his new power from the pulpit disappears, and he is forced to acknowledge that "he had been damned by the purity of his devotion" (p. 109). "Home Videos," narrated by an associate producer of a TV reality show whose job, and life, are changed forever as he traces the origin of a series of distinctive videos submitted anonymously to his show, detours into situation comedy. "The Air Is Full of Little Holes" is fiction based on fact as Brockmeier draws on the story of Sharbat Gula, a refugee from Afghanistan who, as a young girl in the 1980s, was the subject of a cover photograph for *National Geographic* (*Contemporary Authors Online*). The only previously unpublished story in the collection, it is a rare instance of a Brockmeier short story that is not set either in the contemporary United States or in a wholly fantastic landscape—although the arrival and, years later, return of an American photographer into the strictly demarcated environment of the young woman who narrates the story is, arguably, for her as fantastic an intervention as anything to be found in Brockmeier's fiction.

Having paid tribute to Gogol in "A Fable of Slips," Brockmeier steps all the way into parody as he rewrites Anton Chekhov's "The Lady with the Pet Dog" while indulging his own enthusiasm for genre science fiction in "The Lady with the Pet Tribble," wherein "James," a love-'em-and-leave-'em starship captain, falls unexpectedly in love while on shore leave on an alien planet. The skill Brockmeier displayed in his adult novels for planting clues for the attentive reader serves him well as he carefully, but never directly, references the original *Star Trek* television series, from the title pet (an alien creature from one of the original series' most famous, and most overtly comic, episodes) to a final pun on the name of one of Captain James T. Kirk's most trusted crewmen: Pavel Chekov. "The Lady with the Pet Tribble" is, fundamentally, an elaborate joke, but it also may be Brockmeier's most direct assertion of his refusal to accept boundaries between realist and fantastic fiction. While any given episode of *Star Trek* ends, if not always on a positive note, then on a note of firm resolution, Brockmeier's story is ultimately more faithful to Anton Chekhov than to Gene Roddenberry, as its conclusion echoes the uncertainty of Chekhov's original story. "James" may have acknowledged his newfound love, and he may be a better and deeper person for it, but "he understood that a long time of difficulty lay before them and their troubles were only beginning" (p. 199).

The book's literal centerpiece, and also its longest and most formally audacious story, is "The Human Soul as a Rube Goldberg Device: A Choose-Your-Own-Adventure-Story," a second-person account of an ordinary morning in the life of an ordinary person. The title is literal. The story is structured in the manner of a children's "choose-your-own-adventure" book; every two pages, "you" are presented with an either-or choice that will send "you" in one of two different directions: "If you decide to do a little grocery shopping, turn to page 156. If you decide to clean the bathroom mirror, turn to page 170" (p. 127). However, unlike the children's books that lead to alternative outcomes, every possible path through the story eventually leads to an instruction to turn to page 146, where "you" collapse and die of a heart attack. A grim outcome, but not a meaningless one, as explained in the one section of the story that cannot be connected to from any other point: "You have a pet theory ... that life itself is a kind of Rube Goldberg device, an extremely complicated machine designed to carry out the extremely simple task of constructing

your soul.... finally, with your dying breath, you emerge from the mouth of the machine and roll to a stop ... burnished now with the markings you will carry with you through an eternity" (pp. 124–125).

In keeping with the careful arrangement of the stories, Brockmeier frames his collection with its two most striking examples of fantastic versus realist stories. "The View from the Seventh Layer" surveys the life of Olivia, a young woman who lives on an island where she works as an assistant for a wealthy widow and, during tourist season, at a stand, owned by her father, where she sells maps, "umbrellas, candy, and prophylactics" (p. 12). It is a comfortable yet ordinary life, with one extraordinary aspect: five years earlier, "the Entity had taken Olivia into the sky" (p. 13), arriving from "the seventh layer of space," where "the past was indistinguishable from the present, so nothing was ever truly lost, and nothing was ever truly irreparable" (p. 24). (It is worth noting that the realist story that follows this one, "The Lives of the Philosophers," concludes with exactly the opposite assertion: "The past is irreparable and so is the future" [p. 60].) Against this backdrop, and in a manner that recalls the City sections of *A Brief History of the Dead,* Olivia attempts to make sense of her life not through her ordinary daily activities but through deep memories of her past and through her ongoing efforts to understand others in terms of the books they read. ("People who read Ann Rice believe that tragedy is romantic. People who read Salman Rushdie use their scruples like a blade: the humane ones use them for opening, the cruel ones use them for wounding" [p. 22].) Mainly, though, she waits for "the day when the Entity would come back for her ... and the two of them would set out from the island together, driven through the layers of space by a radiant dream of the way things could be" (p. 38). The story never states conclusively if the Entity is reality or delusion, and it scarcely matters. What is inescapably real is the sad situation of a young woman for whom nothing is really wrong but nothing is really right, either, and whose sense of self is grounded not in memories or other people but in a desire for a means of escape that may or may not ever arrive.

A more straightforward but equally affecting portrait of a young woman's attempt to come to terms with her world is "Andrea Is Changing Her Name," in which we follow the title character through childhood and adolescence to an adulthood that is, unsurprisingly, nothing she expected. It is not a story with any fantastic elements, or any plot to speak of. It is a story held together by a tour de force use of point of view, as we gradually realize that the story is not a third-person narrative from Andrea's perspective but a first-person account by a high school friend who knows Andrea better than she knows herself because he is "the boy ... who loved that girl, after all" (p. 259). Although Brockmeier has written many stories about love, this is perhaps his only work that is truly a love story, and it is one of his best.

The View from the Seventh Layer was greeted with the same level of critical acclaim as Brockmeier's other adult books, with most reviewers now immediately recognizing the author as a specialist in the literature of the fantastic. *Kirkus* found the book "the work of a consummate stylist whose chosen limits are the source of his quirky fiction's truest strengths," while *Library Journal* declared it "an ambitious collection ... a feast of reader's delights." David Abrams, writing for the online *Barnes & Noble Review,* praised the book for "brisk, lucid writing of the highest caliber," the *Los Angeles Times* praised the "clarity and beautiful subtlety" of Brockmeier's writing, and the *Arkansas Times* pronounced Brockmeier "perhaps the country's leading fabulist."

Having published six books in seven years, and with *The Illumination,* a new novel for adults, appearing in early 2011, Kevin Brockmeier has proved not only one of the most innovative and acclaimed of younger American fiction writers but also one of the most prolific. And perhaps more than any of his peers, he has shown that, as he stated in his 2006 *Earth Goat* interview, to "navigate the tension between the realistic and the fantastic largely by failing to recognize it" is not only a viable strategy but one that can lead to

considerable success. Readers should not be surprised, and indeed may hope, to see more writers freely crossing the various borders of literature by ignoring them.

Selected Bibliography

WORKS BY KEVIN BROCKMEIER

Novels

The Truth About Celia. New York: Pantheon, 2003.

The Brief History of the Dead. New York: Pantheon, 2006.

The Illumination. New York: Pantheon, 2011.

Short Story Collections

Things That Fall from the Sky. New York: Pantheon, 2002.

The View from the Seventh Layer. New York: Pantheon, 2008.

Novels for Children

City of Names. New York: Viking, 2002.

Grooves: A Kind of Mystery. New York: Katherine Tegen, 2006.

Uncollected Stories

"The Brief History of the Dead." *New Yorker,* September 8, 2003 (http://www.newyorker.com/archive/2003/09/08/030908fi_fiction).

"The Untimely Death of the Federation of Saint Kitts and Nevis." *Lifted Brow* 6, 2010 (http://www.theliftedbrow.com/?page_id=554).

Nonfiction

"The Last Words." *New York Times Magazine,* July 27, 2008 (http://www.nytimes.com/2008/07/27/magazine/27lives-t.html?scp=2&sq=%22The%20View%20from%20the%20Seventh%20Layer%22&st=cse).

Introduction to *Real Unreal: Best American Fantasy, Volume 3*. Volume editor, Kevin Brockmeier; series editor, Matthew Cheney. Portland, Ore.: Underland, 2010. Pp. xiii–xvi.

"Ten Great Novels of the Apocalypse." Future Issue. *Oxford American* 70:130–132 (August 2010).

CRITICAL AND BIOGRAPHICAL STUDIES

Cheney, Matthew. Preface to *Real Unreal: Best American Fantasy, Volume 3*. Volume editor, Kevin Brockmeier; series editor, Matthew Cheney. Portland, Ore.: Underwood Press, 2010. Pp. xi–xii.

"Kevin Brockmeier." *Contemporary Authors Online*. Gale, 2010.

"Kevin John Brockmeier (1972–)." In *The Encyclopedia of Arkansas History and Culture* (http://encyclopediaofarkansas.net/encyclopedia/entry-detail.aspx?entryID=3722).

Windling, Terri. "Have Pen, Will Travel: The Fiction of Kevin Brockmeier and Kelly Link." Interstitial Arts Foundation (http://www.interstitialarts.org/what/featuredBrockmeierLink1.html).

REVIEWS

Abrams, David. *"The View from the Seventh Layer." Barnes & Noble Review,* March 17, 2008 (http://bnreview.barnesandnoble.com/t5/In-Brief/The-View-from-the-Seventh-Layer/ba-p/336).

Berry, Michael. "Keep Those Ears away from Cell Phones." *San Francisco Chronicle*, February 19, 2006 (http://www.sfgate.com/cgi-bin/article.cgi?f=/c/a/2006/02/19/RVGHKH6NGJ1.DTL; review of *The Brief History of the Dead.*)

"Books Briefly Noted." *New Yorker,* June 17, 2002. (Review of *Things That Fall from the Sky.*)

"The Brief History of the Dead." Publishers Weekly, December 19, 2005, p. 38.

"Brockmeier, Kevin: *The Brief History of the Dead." Kirkus Reviews,* December 1, 2005, p. 1243.

"Brockmeier, Kevin: *Grooves: A Kind of Mystery." Kirkus Reviews,* January 15, 2006, p. 82.

"Brockmeier, Kevin: *The View from the Seventh Layer." Kirkus Reviews,* February 15, 2008.

Carton, Debbie. "Brockmeier, Kevin. *Grooves: A Kind of Mystery." Booklist,* February 1, 2006, p. 47.

"*City of Names* (Children's Books)." *Kirkus Reviews,* May 1, 2002, p. 649.

"*City of Names* (Fiction)." *Publishers Weekly,* May 27, 2002, p. 60.

de Lint, Charles. "Books to Look For." *Magazine of Fantasy and Science Fiction,* April 2006, pp. 32–35. (Review of *The Brief History of the Dead.*)

Frey, Hillary. "Lift Up Your Eyes." *New York Times Book Review,* April 14, 2002, p. 18. (Review of *Things That Fall from the Sky.*)

Fristoe, Travis. "Brockmeier, Kevin. *The View from the Seventh Layer." Library Journal,* April 15, 2008, p. 79.

Gevers, Nick. "*Locus* Looks at Books." *Locus: The Magazine of the Science Fiction and Fantasy Field,* February 2006, pp. 25, 27, 71–72. (Review of *The Brief History of the Dead.*)

Hoffert, Barbara. "Brockmeier, Kevin. *The Brief History of the Dead." Library Journal,* February 15, 2006, p. 106.

Klise, James. "*Things That Fall from the Sky.* (General Fiction)." *Booklist,* February 15, 2002, p. 990.

Larman, Alex. "End of the World as We Know It." *New Statesman,* March 27, 2006, p. 54. (Review of *The Brief History of the Dead.*)

McGrath, Patrick. "Welcome to Limbo." *New York Times Book Review,* March 5, 2006, p. 15. (Review of *The Brief History of the Dead.*)

O'Malley, Anne. "Brockmeier, Kevin. *City of Names.*" *Booklist,* June 1, 2002, p. 1720.

Owchar, Nick. "Book of Beasts." *Los Angeles Times,* April 27, 2008 (http://www.latimes.com/features/la-bkw-owchar23apr27,0,55343,full.story; review of *The View from the Seventh Layer.*)

"The View from On High: Kevin Brockmeier's Latest Short Story Collection Is His Best." *Arkansas Times,* March 6, 2008 (http://www.arktimes.com/arkansas/the-view-from-on-high/Content?oid=862839; review of *The View from the Seventh Layer.*)

"The View from the Seventh Layer." Publishers Weekly, January 14, 2008, p. 38.

Wiegan, David. "Novelist Kevin Brockmeier's Story of a Missing Child Is a Heartbreaking Meditation on Time, Loss, and Perception." *San Francisco Chronicle,* July 12, 2003 (http://www.sfgate.com/cgi-bin/article.cgi?f=/c/a/2003/07/12/DD198237.DTL&ao=all; review of *The Truth About Celia.*)

INTERVIEWS

Cowles, Gregory. "Stray Questions for: Kevin Brockmeier." *Paper Cuts: A Blog About Books,* November 13, 2009 (http://papercuts.blogs.nytimes.com/2009/11/13/stray-questions-for-kevin-brockmeier/).

"Kevin Brockmeier Interview." *Earth Goat,* April 3, 2006 (http://earthgoat.blogspot.com/2006/04/kevin-brockmeier-interview.html).

McMyne, Mary. "Turning Inward: A Conversation with Kevin Brockmeier." *Del Sol Literary Dialogues* (http://www.webdelsol.com/Literary_Dialogues/interview-wds-brockmeier.htm).

"Powell's Q&A: Kevin Brockmeier." Powell's Books (http://www.powells.com/ink/brockmeier.html).

Rudd, Alyson. "Interview with Kevin Brockmeier." *Sunday Times* (London), February 17, 2007 (http://entertainment.timesonline.co.uk/tol/arts_and_entertainment/books/books_group/article1394807.ece).

Simmons, Matthew. "An Interview with: Kevin Brockmeier." *Hobart: Another Literary Journal,* January 2007 (http://www.hobartpulp.com/website/january/brockmeier.html).

MICHELLE CLIFF

(1946—)

Jen Hirt

To READ THE work of the Jamaican American feminist writer Michelle Cliff is to get a glimpse behind the stagecraft of colonialism, patriarchal societies, imperialism, and the ideologies of language. Big ideas, yes, but Cliff brings them all to the literary table and into the mainstream with her powerful prose poetry and memorable fiction. Whether she is writing about the real-life abolitionist Mary Ellen Pleasant or the fictional heroine Clare Savage, or reflecting on her own young adulthood during the turbulent 1960s, Cliff holds nothing back when it comes to revealing oppression and resistance. Her favorite topics include feminism and lesbianism, convoluted racial identities, and postcolonial island life on Jamaica, as well as revolutionary moments in American history.

Cliff commented in a 1993 interview with Meryl F. Schwartz:

> The most exciting writing that's going on right now is being done, for the most part, by people of color or Third World peoples.... We're able to be freer, more experimental because we're not faithful to Western forms as much as white, Western writers are. We have a different sense of time and space, and we have more access to a dream life.... That's a very prejudiced point of view, but that's how I see it.
>
> (pp. 617–618)

That energy has carried Cliff through one scholarly book, three works of nonfiction prose poetry, and seven works of fiction. Her writing has been published in magazines and journals ranging from *Callaloo* to *Southwest Review* to the *American Voice*, and she has made an appearance in the *Best American Short Stories* series. Not only an accomplished writer of original works, she has translated the Spanish poetry of Federico García Lorca, Alfonsina Storni, and Pier Paolo Pasolini, and she writes book reviews for *Ms.* and the *Village Voice*. The longtime partner of the poet Adrienne Rich, she has traveled in (and subverted) literary circles since her days as an editor at *Sinister Wisdom* magazine.

Her work is not always easy to read; she favors mixing mainstream English with the patois or Creole dialects of her native Jamaica, and her earliest novel actually featured a patois glossary. As her literary critics have observed, her work often references the heroes and heroines of Jamaican and African legends in ways that are fascinating yet sometimes foreign to a wider audience. At the same time, she has lived much of her life in the United States and has written extensively on the underrepresented elements of American history. Thus she brings her own style to historical fiction, sometimes infusing it with the mythmaking, oral-storytelling style of island life. Critics have likened her to Toni Morrison and Jamaica Kinkaid, and labels for her works range from postcolonial to postmodern to political, yet the Michelle Cliff writing style stands alone with its unique voice, vibrant characters, and sharp insights into race, culture, gender, and equality.

CAREER AND MAJOR WORKS

Michelle Cliff was born on November 2, 1946, in Kingston, Jamaica, to a white father and a black mother. Her light skin was immediately noted, and in her essay "If I Could Write This in Fire, I Would Write This in Fire," from her nonfiction prose poem book *The Land of Look Behind* (1985), Cliff describes it this way:

> There was land. My grandparents' farm. And there was color.
>
> (My family was called *red*. A term which signified a degree of whiteness. "We's just a flock of red

> people," a cousin of mine said once.) In the hierarchy of the shades I was considered among the lightest. The countrywomen who visited my grandmother commented on my "tall" hair—meaning long. Wavy, not curly.
>
> (p. 59)

Cliff has said in interviews that her parents were descended from both slaves and slave owners, and that in Jamaica, people of her skin color were also called "local whites." In an interview with Opal Palmer Adisa, Cliff described her family's racial situation as "strange and very schizophrenic" (p. 275).

During her childhood her parents sought jobs in New York City, leaving Cliff and her siblings with relatives in Jamaica. When Cliff was three years old the family reunited in New York City, then returned to Jamaica in 1956. From age eleven to age fourteen, Cliff attended the Saint Andrews High School for Girls in Kingston. Her family eventually lived permanently in America, only visiting Jamaica on vacation. Cliff became a naturalized U.S. citizen. However, in *The Land of Look Behind* she asserts that "it is Jamaica that forms my writing for the most part, and which has formed for the most part, myself" (p. 12).

She attended college in America, graduating with an A.B. in European history from Wagner College in Staten Island, New York, in 1969. She attended graduate school at the Warburg Institute, University of London, where in 1974 she earned a master of philosophy in comparative historical studies of the Renaissance. Her dissertation explored the Italian Renaissance passion for highbrow parlor games among the intellectual elite.

Her career as a writer and editor has been wide ranging. In 1969–1970 she was a reporter and researcher for *Life*. From 1970 to 1979 she held editorial positions at the publishing house W. W. Norton. Her first creative work, the prose poetry book *Claiming an Identity They Taught Me to Despise,* was published in 1980 by Persephone Press. From 1981 to 1983 Cliff coedited, with Adrienne Rich, *Sinister Wisdom* magazine, which billed itself as a multicultural publication featuring works by lesbians. Throughout the 1980s Cliff was on the editorial board of *Signs: A Journal of Women and Culture in Society.*

In 1982 Cliff won two fellowships that launched her creative writing career. First, she won a fellowship from the National Endowment for the Arts (NEA), which provided financial support for her writing. Second, she earned a fellowship at the MacDowell Colony in New Hampshire, where she had six weeks to write her first novel, *Abeng,* which would be published in 1984. The success of her early writing earned her more opportunities in 1984: a fellowship through the Massachusetts Artists' Foundation and yet another residency at a writer's colony, this time at Yaddo in upstate New York. Two more books followed in the 1980s: *The Land of Look Behind* (1985) and the critically acclaimed novel *No Telephone to Heaven* (1987), a sequel to *Abeng.* In 1988 she won a Fulbright scholarship to New Zealand, and in 1989 she won a second NEA fellowship, this time in fiction.

Literary circles have claimed her variously as a Jamaican writer, a feminist writer, a lesbian writer, and a postcolonial writer. One debate hinges on whether she is best labeled an African American writer or a postmodern writer. Suzanne Bost argues that those who categorize Cliff as a postmodern novelist have ignored the fact that Cliff's style has more in common with biracial and African American writing than it does with postmodernism. Bost notes that "shifting, multivalent subjectivity and fluctuating signs of difference" originated in "biracial artistic expression" long before those techniques garnered fame in postmodernism (p. 674). In response to whether or not she sees herself as a Caribbean woman writer, Cliff said in a 1991 interview with Judith Raikin in the *Kenyon Review* that "I don't think of myself that way at all. This is going to sound so self-pitying, and self-involved, but I feel that in almost every group I'm an outsider" (p. 60). In her 1993 interview with Meryl Schwartz, Cliff categorized herself as a political novelist (p. 597).

Regardless of what the critics were positing, Cliff continued through the 1990s to write fiction that explored racial identity and sexual identity through nonlinear storytelling. She published the linked short-story collection *Bodies of Water* in

1990, the historical novel *Free Enterprise* in 1993, and *The Store of a Million Items* (short stories) in 1998. Since the turn of the millennium, she has published the nonfiction book *If I Could Write This in Fire* (2008), new and collected short stories in *Everything Is Now* (2009), and the novel *Into the Interior* (2010).

Cliff has taught at many colleges and universities as she has juggled writing, fellowships, residencies, and other obligations. She started in 1974 in New York City, at the New School for Social Research, where she taught until 1976. Brief appointments (sometimes yearly, sometimes just a semester) found her at the University of Massachusetts at Amherst in 1980, Hampshire College in 1980–1981, and at Norwich University in Vermont in 1983–1984. In the mid-1980s she moved west to California. Her teaching there started at the Martin Luther King Jr. Public Library, where she taught creative writing and history. Meanwhile she picked up other positions: Vista College in 1985, San Jose State University in 1986, University of California–Santa Cruz in 1987, and four years at Stanford University, from 1987 to 1991. Heading back east, she served during spring semesters (starting in 1990) as Allan K. Smith Professor of English Language and Literature at Trinity College in Hartford, Connecticut. In the late 1990s and early 2000s, Cliff stepped away from teaching to focus on translations, reviews, and her own creative writing. She lives in Santa Cruz, California.

NONFICTION: DEFENDING AND CLAIMING IDENTITY

Although Cliff is known primarily as a fiction writer, looking first at her nonfiction is instructive because much of her fiction is autobiographical. It is important to note that she did not write traditional nonfiction, such as memoir or autobiography. Instead, she wrote slim books that fluctuate between prose and poetry. Two of her three prose poem nonfiction books were written and published before most of her well-known fiction.

Cliff's first major publishing project was as editor of the book *The Winner Names the Age,* a 1978 collection of writings by Lillian Smith. Smith was a white Southern woman, born into a well-off family in 1897. But by the time she was eighteen, Smith was giving speeches and writing editorials and essays on radical topics: racial equality, gender equality, and communal understanding between cultures. She had become a social reformer. In *The Winner Names the Age,* Cliff organizes Smith's challenges to the status quo into three categories: politics of the South; expanding the politics of the South into the larger arena of America's human condition; and the role of women's identity and equal rights.

Cliff followed the weighty and academic Smith collection with her own creative work, the prose poetry book *Claiming an Identity They Taught Me to Despise,* in 1980. It is written in a fragmented style (a mix of paragraphs, stanzas, one-line fragments, diary entries, and quotes from luminaries such as Audre Lorde, Oscar Wilde, and Virginia Woolf). In the *Kenyon Review* interview, Cliff commented on the context in which she wrote this first book. "I was writing it while I had a nine-to-five job, and so it's written in a very jerky form, with a lot of starting and stopping" (p. 70). Yet the tone of these fragments is far from disjointed or staccato. Rather, it is hypnotic, as Cliff pulls the reader into her onslaught of memories about growing up as a light-skinned Jamaican woman, torn between the formal education of British colonialism, the island routines of her Caribbean family, and the milieus of New York City and London.

The book begins with the section "Passing," where a young narrator whom we can assume is Cliff presents a series of observations having to do with camouflage, silence, and the self. The term "passing" refers to a situation in which a person's appearance (skin color, hair type, facial features) and behavior (word use, mannerisms, customs) can be associated with more than one ethnicity, and the person can consciously choose to "pass" or "get by" as a member of the dominant society. For example, Cliff tells an anecdote about going to a West Indian potluck at her church in New York City. There, she and her mother watch a white woman spit out a piece of green banana after she tries a bite of the West

Indian dish Cliff's mother has brought. Cliff writes, "My mother sees this. She says nothing. / Passing demands quiet. And from that quiet—silence" (p. 6).

Marian Aguiar, in her article "Decolonizing the Tongue: Reading Speech and Aphasia in the Work of Michelle Cliff," writes that, from a psychological standpoint, the instances of silence speak to Cliff's realization that if her dark-skinned mother represents Africa, and if the mother chooses to remain quiet in certain situations, then "language is a false knowing where a filial body of knowledge should be" (p. 103). Aguiar also comments that when Cliff writes about silence or aphasia (loss of words), "Cliff attempts to become the simulacrum for the lost 'whole' language of her Afro-Caribbean mother" (p. 103).

In the section "Women's Work," Cliff plays with language by creating her own compound words to describe the women she is seeing and studying. For example, she has passages about scrubwomen, slavewomen, blackwomen, fisherwomen, and trackwomen (who were laying railroad tracks during wartime). The section ends with snippets from female myth and legend and reality, such as the American spy Ethel Rosenberg comforting a prostitute in prison. The final scene is set on an isolated country road, with men catcalling from their truck as Cliff attempts to leave in her car. She fears they will rape her, so she makes a quick exit, ending with the realization that "There's a need for rage in this work" (p. 42).

The section that bears the same title as the book is a sobering look at how mainstream America approaches "The Other." In the 1950s, Cliff was in the third grade. She recounts how a teacher asked who, among the students, was not born in the United States. "I stood up and mumbled, 'Jamaica,' and became the focus of their scrutiny. I filled their silence with rapid lies" (p. 43). The section moves on to excerpts and analysis of two books famous for their dealings with Creole women in a white society: Charlotte Bronte's *Jane Eyre* and Jean Rhys's *Wide Sargasso Sea,* both of which tell the story of the madwoman in the attic, but from different viewpoints. Cliff juxtaposes these references with two definitions of the word "pinion." It can refer to the wing of a bird, or it can refer to the act of clipping the wing so the bird cannot fly. Adding one more layer, Cliff cites the eleventh edition of the *Encyclopaedia Britannica,* which claims that "Creole" can be used to describe horses just as it describes people. These layers of observation coalesce to show us the viewpoint from the outside.

In *The Land of Look Behind* (1985), Cliff comments directly on her motives and goals in *Claiming an Identity They Taught Me to Despise* as well as her frustration over living a fragmented life. On the topic of why she was choosing to write in a combination of prose and poetry, she observes in the preface that these books are "halfway between poetry and prose, as I am halfway between Africa and England, patriot and expatriate, white and Black" (p. 16).

The Land of Look Behind begins with the preface "A Journey into Speech," a straightforward defense of her decision to use both proper English (which she refers to as the King's English) and patois, or the dialect of native people that outsiders often consider to be crude or uneducated. Cliff explains that "to write as a complete Caribbean woman, or man for that matter," she has to speak "in the *patois* forbidden us" (p. 14).

The best-known writing in the book is the centerpiece essay, "If I Could Write This in Fire, I Would Write This in Fire," which Cliff was inspired to write after reading *Our Sister Killjoy; or, Reflections from a Black-Eyed Squint* by Ama Ato Aidoo, a writer from Ghana. Cliff saw how Aidoo wrote in short spurts of language as a way to show her rage about being a "been-to"—a colonized person who visits the motherland but can never be a part of it and can only say he or she has "been to" it. In the essay Cliff writes, "After reading Aidoo I knew I wanted to tell exactly how things were, what had been done, to us and by us, without muddying the issue with conventional beauty, avoiding becoming trapped in the grace of language for its own sake, which is always seductive" (pp. 15–16).

Thus, when Cliff writes about the sports at her English-run grammar school, she chooses an abrupt, almost spitting style: the school's teams were "named for Joan of Arc, Edith Cavell, Florence Nightingale, Jane Austen. Four white heroines. Two martyrs. One saint. Two nurses. (None of us knew then that there were Black women with Nightingale at Scutari.) One novelist. Three involved in whitemen's wars. Two dead in whitemen's wars. *Pride and Prejudice*" (p. 62).

The essay also recounts her childhood friendship with Zoe, a darker-skinned Jamaican. As an adult, Cliff returns to the island and is startled to see the different paths their lives have taken. Zoe remains poor in Jamaica; she has a child and an abusive husband. Cliff reflects with a mix of guilt and relief that "I can come and go. And I leave. To complete my education in London" (p. 64).

The essay concludes with a list of grievances as the college-educated Cliff begins to realize the calamities of slavery and colonization. She relates incidents from the history of slavery, but she leaves out the precise historical context and often writes the stories in present tense, which makes the stories seem as though they are still happening (and from Cliff's perspective, they still are). For example: "A pregnant woman is to be whipped—they dig a hole to accommodate her belly and place her face down on the ground. Many of us become light-skinned very fast," she writes, adding, "Our mothers' rapes were the thing unspoken" (pp. 65–66). She explores a memory about how she and her dark-skinned cousin, Henry, were refused service at a bar, and yet when they relocate to a gay bar, the cousin ridicules the gay white waiters. Cliff tells the story with a double consciousness: as a writer, she is clearly furious at the instances of racism, but as a shy young lady out with a cousin, she writes, "I have a hard time realizing that I am angry with Henry" (p. 69). Instead, she deflects her anger and blurts out to him, "Jesus Christ, I hate the fucking English" (p. 68), a moment that students reading Cliff sometimes criticize as reverse racism. However, Lindsay Pentolfe Aegerter argues that Cliff is not racist, maintaining that Cliff's writing is a "sophisticated postcolonial analysis of the processes and consequences of colonization" (p. 899). Furthermore, Aegerter emphasizes that much of the anger in Cliff's essay is "directed at herself, at those Jamaicans who, like her, either literally or metaphorically became as 'light-skinned' as possible" (p. 900).

"If I Could Write This in Fire, I Would Write This in Fire" continued on from its 1985 publication to become the book *If I Could Write This in Fire,* published in 2008. That book contains the title essay and a revision of "A Journey into Speech," the preface of *The Land of Look Behind,* as well as one poem and five essays that document Cliff's keen eye for attitudes about subcultures and hegemony. In "Sites of Memory," she writes, "I gaze the gaze of reverse anthropologist" (p. 57), which is a good summary of her commentary on subjects from American diners to ignorant students to international conferences on postcolonialism.

EARLY FICTION: MEET CLARE SAVAGE

Cliff's first two novels, *Abeng* (1984) and *No Telephone to Heaven* (1987) are well known for the protagonist Clare Savage, a light-skinned Jamaican whose personal struggles symbolize postcolonial struggles. The title *Abeng* refers to the African word for the conch shell, which served two purposes historically: first, it was used to call slaves to work; and second, the Maroon militias of Jamaica used it to pass secret messages.

Abeng introduces readers to twelve-year-old Clare, whose father, Boy, is considered white, and whose mother, Kitty, is considered a red Jamaican from the countryside. Set in 1958, the novel traces Clare's coming-of-age awareness about her convoluted identities, which mostly have to do with Jamaica's own convoluted identity as an island that was forced into colonization by Britain, severely damaged by the slave trade, then abruptly cast aside when Britain ended its slave trade in 1834. The Savages are middle-class, urban, and employ a black servant. Clare goes to a reputable school, learns the King's English, and memorizes the British rulers. Yet Clare also learns the alarming truth about her ancestors. Her white great-great-grandfather (one

of the vanguard of British colonizers in Jamaica) burned his slaves to death rather than let them go free. And she learns about the obeah (tribal magic) of the Africans and island natives from whom she might be descended, including the legend of Nanny, a female warrior who fought the colonizers with spells, amulets, and otherworldly powers.

The structure and style of *Abeng* is notable. Like *Claiming an Identity* it is written in fragments, and instead of staying in the year 1958 it uses an omniscient point of view to jump between historical moments in order to make thematic connections. In the article "Race, Privilege, and the Politics of (Re)Writing History: An Analysis of the Novels of Michelle Cliff," Belinda Edmondson observes that Cliff "mixes genres of narrative—historical, autobiographical, myth—to achieve a dialectical representation of the West Indian experience" (p. 182).

For example, in the beginning, we learn that the Savages are preparing for church, and it sounds as if Clare will be our narrator. But the point of view steps outside of Clare and heads into a comparison of the two churches the family attends. The father's preferred church offers an English minister, Presbyterian hymns, a British harpsichord, and a Scottish choir leader. In contrast, the congregation of the mother's church is almost entirely black women, descended from slaves, who embrace the minister's fire-and-brimstone sermons, often speaking in tongues or bursting into convulsions or song.

The next section introduces the reader to a Jamaican creation story that also speaks to what has happened under colonization. "In the beginning, there had been two sisters—Nanny and Sekesu. Nanny fled slavery. Sekesu remained a slave. Some said this was the difference between the sisters. It was believed that all island children were descended from one or the other. All island people were first cousins" (p. 18). Nanny proves to be a powerful warrior and an ethical leader. That she is a myth makes no difference. Thus Clare's dilemma is framed: Will she focus her allegiance on British history (her white blood) or on island folklore (her black blood)?

Identity becomes even more mixed for Clare as she spends a summer in the country with Miss Mattie, her maternal grandmother. The grandmother arranges for Clare to have a permanent playmate, the dark-skinned Zoe, whose family lives on Miss Mattie's land. Suzanne Bost notes the intertextuality of the Zoe character: biracial works by nineteenth-century writers such as Elizabeth Livermore and Dion Boucicault featured a mulatto character named Zoe, who was treated with a sense of pity for her mixed blood. Bost explains that in *Abeng,* "Clare and Zoe present different sides of the Zoe/mulatta narrative: light and dark, privileged and outcast. Their differences invoke both the positive and the negative aspects of the literary biracial experience, presenting two sides of the same story" (p. 682).

The section of *Abeng* dealing with that summer is all about privilege, as Clare learns about Zoe (considered to be lower class) and also her male cousins, who, by virtue of being male, outrank Clare and thus get to witness the slaughter of a hog and then eat its genitals. Meanwhile, Clare is reading *The Diary of Anne Frank:* both the book and the girl who wrote it amaze her and fill her with questions about fate and God. She poses these questions to her father (Boy Savage), but he cannot answer them in a way that satisfies her. She also reads *I Am Alive,* by Kitty Hart, a woman who survived Auschwitz (and who shares the same first name as Clare's mother, as well as the name of the imaginary friend to whom Anne Frank wrote). But she is hesitant to think about the women too much. "Had she done so, she would have probably concluded that they had done something which made their fates just. For that is what she had been taught. She was a colonized child, and she lived within certain parameters—which clouded her judgment" (pp. 76–77). Sidonie Smith, writing in "Memory, Narrative, and the Discourses of Identity in *Abeng* and *No Telephone to Heaven,*" notes the importance of *The Diary of Anne Frank*: since the diary inspires Clare to ask questions about equality, race, and religion, "she glimpses the inadequacies of Boy's explanations, as well as those of the teachers at her school. She glimpses, that is, the inadequacy of official history" (p. 49).

The end of the book deals with a horrible mistake that Clare has made. One summer morning, she steals Miss Mattie's rifle and intends to kill a wild hog with it. Zoe comes along but eventually talks Clare out of the hog hunt (which is masculine), and instead the two girls go swimming naked (which is feminine). When a strange man approaches, Clare fires a warning shot but accidentally shoots and kills Miss Mattie's bull, Old Joe, instead. The omniscient narrator wonders if Clare's parents will blame each other's race for the girl's bad behavior, but the parents don't want to talk about it and simply ship her off to a white family friend (who lives in town) for the remainder of the summer. "She had stepped out of line, no matter what, in a society in which the lines were unerringly drawn. She had been caught in rebellion. She was a girl. No one was impressed with her" (p. 150). While in town, Clare visits the white woman's supposedly "mad" sister, but Clare learns that the sister had to give up a mixed-race baby many years ago and has been haunted by the decision ever since. Clare dreams of fighting Zoe (which can be psychoanalyzed as the light skin metaphorically battling the dark skin), then wakes up to her menstrual period beginning, and the novel ends. The reader is left with the awareness that not only is Clare becoming a woman, she is becoming an intellectual who will analyze her roles in society. Bost notes that the events at the end challenge "not only Jamaican standards of 'woman's work' but [overturn] the literary tradition in which Zoe, the biracial woman, had to assume white standards of domestic morality in order to gain literary visibility" (p. 682).

No Telephone to Heaven (1987) was the highly successful sequel to *Abeng*. Clare Savage returns as the main character, but now she is thirty-six years old, and she is a revolutionary leading rural Jamaican militants who call themselves "No Telephone to Heaven," after the mysterious slogan painted on the truck they buy from an old man who had once transported poor women to church.

The novel is a flashback-style recounting of the cultural forces that shaped Clare Savage into a leader of militants. In the present-day time of the novel, Clare is riding in the No Telephone to Heaven truck, taking her army deep into the countryside, handing out food as they go. As she rides, she thinks about her past, and each section of the novel reveals formative moments. Readers are also introduced to the pivotal character named Harry/Harriet, a gay Jamaican man who cross-dresses as a woman. Through the years that span the narrative, Harry/Harriet speaks to Clare (in letters and in face-to-face reunions) about the courage of retaking Jamaican identity and the necessity of being true to one's sexual orientation.

The memories that Clare cycles through as she rides in the truck with comrades are vivid, and Cliff uses a variety of narrative voices to tell the stories. One chapter speaks of class warfare: a lower-class Jamaican gardener named Christopher massacres his upper-class Jamaican employers, a family of four. And he murders the other servant, too, even though she is of the same class as he is. Clare knew the son who was murdered, and the reader learns later that she had slept with him at a party the last night of his life. The reader also learns that Christopher grew up in the most poverty-stricken region of Jamaica and was denied a stable family life. He is not arrested for the murders, and he shows up later in the novel as a key character.

Another chapter skips to an earlier time when Clare was a young girl and the Savage family moved to America. Told from the point of view of Clare's father, Boy, it recounts instances of American racism and discrimination, and it lays the foundation for light-skinned Clare's ability to pass (assimilate) in American and European cultures, an ability she then feels guilty about as an adult. She loses contact with her family after her mother dies of a brain hemorrhage. Boy marries an Italian American, and Clare's little sister becomes a homeless junkie somewhere in New York City.

The memories of Clare's college years in London address the topics of poverty, loneliness, and more varieties of discrimination. For example, when she is able to attain legal residency, someone comments, "Then again, you're not like our other Jamaicans, are you" (p. 117). When she enrolls in the University of London, she is told

she should pursue African studies, but instead she is interested in the classics. She excels, and "people admired her mind and implied her good fortune in escaping the brain damage common to creoles" (p. 117). Clare slowly becomes aware that no matter what she does, she is constantly compared to others in the lowest, most derogatory ways.

A Jamaican reunion with Harry/Harriet plants in her the seeds of revolution. Drinking at a bar, the two play a trick on naive white tourists by calling themselves Prince Badnigga and Princess Cunnilinga. But Harry/Harriet is not just a prankster who flaunts all the taboos of sexuality. He sees a grander potential in Clare, and he says, "Come home. I'll be here. Come back to us, once your studies are finished. Could help bring us into the present" (p. 127). He adds, "Jamaica's children have to work to make her change. It will be worthwhile ... believe me" (p. 127). Later, after Clare has quit college in the 1970s, traveled around Europe, encountered the stories of Pocahontas and Jane Eyre, failed at friendships and heterosexual love and even suffered a miscarriage, she receives a letter from Harry/Harriet. He tells her disturbing news from Jamaica—167 old women have died in a fire. The tragic news shifts Clare's self-obsessed (and self-pitying) thinking, as indicated by a two-page chapter of the novel titled "Magnanimous Warrior!" It reads as an obeah-inspired call to action:

> She writes in her own blood across the drumhead. Obeah-woman. Myal-woman. She can cure. She can kill. She can give jobs. She is foy-eyed. The bearer of second sight. Mother who goes forth emitting flames from her eyes. Nose. Mouth. Ears. Vulva. Anus. She bites the evildoers that they become full of sores. She treats cholera with bitterbush. She burns the canefields. She is River Mother. Sky Mother. Old Hige. The Moon. Old Suck.
>
> (pp. 163–164)

Clare returns to Jamaica but is quickly waylaid by an infection stemming from the miscarriage. She wakes in a hospital where Harry/Harriet is working as a nurse, and he/she has embraced the "she" side. "Harriet live and Harry be no more," she tells Clare (p. 168). As a course of recovery, Harriet takes Clare to visit Clare's grandmother's homestead. Clare reconnects with the land and her ancestry but soon sees that the Jamaicans are suffering under poverty and deprivation. Necessities such as sugar and fuel are limited and expensive, and in one instance, people steal an iguana from the zoo and eat it. Harriet shares Clare's horror at the depraved conditions. So Harriet introduces Clare to an unnamed female leader of the resistance, and Clare earns her seat on the No Telephone to Heaven truck.

At the end of the novel, set in the 1980s, the truck has reached its destination, which is a field where movie producers are shooting a film about Nanny and Cudjoe, two players in Jamaican myth who are about to encounter Sasabonsam, a forest monster. It turns out that Sasabonsam is being played by the lower-class Jamaican Christopher, who murdered the family earlier in the novel. Since the murders, Christopher has avoided capture as a peculiar homeless man known as De Watchman.

It appears that Clare and the militants are going to sabotage the film set. But as Christopher/De Watchman takes his cue to roar like a monster, his roars become otherworldly and unending, as if he is the real Sasabonsam. Spooked, the film crew retreats to their trailers, and military helicopters appear unexpectedly, shooting Christopher/De Watchman and some of the militants hidden nearby. Clare and her comrades fall: "Some returned the fire—but were no match for the invaders. Some could not—surprise and sadness held them still" (p. 208). The novel ends with twenty-one lines of sound, such as "Coo, cu, cu coo / coo, cu, cu, coo / piju, piju, piju" (p. 208). From Clare we learn "She remembered language. / Then it was gone" (p. 208), a sentence that purposefully contains a poetry-inspired blank space in the middle of it. Day breaks and we are to assume that Clare and her followers are dead.

Critical response to *No Telephone to Heaven* has been prolific and varied. Critics have been analyzing the novel for over two decades since its publication, often in comparison to other seminal works with feminist-Caribbean or African American themes, such as writings by Jean Rhys, Audre Lorde, Toni Morrison, and Jamaica Kincaid.

Maria Helena Lima, writing in *Ariel,* identifies the strong allegorical elements of the novel. The militants represent the real-life People's National Party, and Harry/Harriet's letter about the 167 elderly women who died references the fatalities of an actual fire at the Kingston Almshouse. The various grandmothers in the story symbolize Nanny, the female warrior of Jamaican legend. Furthermore, Lima argues that the allegory expands when "Cliff posits Clare's urge to return to the island in essentialist terms, representing her homeland, the landscape of her identity, as female" (p. 38).

The unique title and strange ending of the novel have not gone unnoticed. The title "suggests radical disillusionment in a postcolonial novel with epic features," writes Mary Lou Emery in her article "Refiguring the Postcolonial Imagination: Tropes of Visuality in Writing by Rhys, Kincaid, and Cliff" (p. 272). Emery analyzes the tragedy at the end, acknowledging that "many readers find it difficult to distinguish between narrative descriptions of the film scene and those of 'real' attack" (p. 273). She points out that "when the film-as-film, with its false images, can no longer be separated from the 'real' narrative action, the rebels' power diminishes, and their reconceptualized identities and newly imagined community are lost" (p. 273). In other words, the ending is a commentary on postcolonial struggles not only with politics but with the popular visual conception of Jamaica, which was being ransacked by cinema profiteers.

Ramchandran Sethuraman also comments on the title and the conclusion in his article "Evidence-cum-Witness: Subaltern History, Violence, and the (De)formation of Nation in Michelle Cliff's *No Telephone to Heaven.*" Sethuraman writes that "The truck emblazoned with the phrase 'No Telephone to Heaven' is a prophetic embodiment of the way the revolutionaries will be excluded from the nation-state, as subalterns generally are from the socializing ends of the novel" (p. 252). Like many people who were surprised by the ending, Sethuram wonders "why the insurgency that ought to be aimed against the neocolonial government is instead planned against a joint film company from Britain and the United States" (p. 274). In an analysis similar to Emery's, he concludes that the ending, although unexpected, successfully "strikes at the heart of the violence of visual culture" (p. 274).

When it comes to the structure of the novel (shifting viewpoints, allegory, myth, current events, realism, dreams, and a range of dialects), critics debate exactly what to call it. Is it a bildungsroman? A postcolonial critique? A postmodern experiment? Maureen Moynagh argues in "The Ethical Turn in Postcolonial Theory and Narrative: Michelle Cliff's *No Telephone to Heaven*" that we should "read the tension between realism and other genres in Cliff's novel as a marker of its imbrication in a contradictory ethicopolitical space that we might call the postnational" (p. 116). In contrast, Constance S. Richards posits it as a classic postcolonial narrative because of "the important role of Black liberation discourse in identity formation, while at the same time [complicating] the binary discourses of race (black/white) and colonialism (colonizer/colonized) with questions of gender, sexuality, and color privilege" (p. 22).

Finally, homosexuality and the he/she character of Harry/Harriet has been a focus of critical attention. Writing in *Callaloo,* Nada Elia contends that reading through the lens of queer theory is the best way to read *No Telephone to Heaven.* She writes that a queer theory reading "allows for the ultimate move beyond divisive paradigms" and "the dominant discourse," which fail "to accommodate multiplicity" (p. 353). She makes the point that "Harry/Harriet displays the greatest insight into the political hierarchies of the island and is the one character with the power of self-definition, of choice" (p. 353). She also explains how Harry/Harriet knows how to pass as heterosexual when the situation warrants it, just as Clare knows how to pass as white when necessary. Analyzing the characters via queer theory, Elia realizes that "such passing ... is alienating and disempowering. On the other hand, Harry/Harriet's passing allows her/him to live her/his life in the most fulfilling and productive ways possible. It is guerrilla camouflage" (p. 358). In her 1993 interview with *Contemporary Literature,* Cliff commented that "the most

complete character in *No Telephone to Heaven* is Harry/Harriet. And I did that purposely because Jamaica is such a repellently homophobic society, so I wanted to have a gay hero/heroine" (p. 601).

Many critics have categorized Cliff's fiction as autobiographical, which makes sense given that parts of Clare Savage's life (her light-skinned status, her move to America, her college years in London and Europe) parallel Cliff's life. But Cliff herself argues that her fiction should not be read as strictly autobiographical. In her essay "Sites of Memory" from *If I Could Write This in Fire,* she explains how frustrated she was with presenters at a conference on identity: "They read my fiction—and other Caribbean fictions—as autobiography, diluting and undermining the politics of the narrative. They want to reduce the collective to the individual" (pp. 57–58).

REFINING TECHNIQUE: SHORT STORIES

After *No Telephone to Heaven*, Cliff wrote two more novels, but she also published a fascinating array of short stories in three separate collections. It is useful to look at her short stories before contemplating the more recent novels.

Her first short story collection was *Bodies of Water,* published in 1990. This was followed by *The Store of a Million Items* in 1998. The 2009 collection *Everything Is Now* reprints both of the earlier collections in their entirety and contains fourteen new stories.

Several of the ten stories in *Bodies of Water* stand out for their commentaries on power, authority, history, and resistance. The opening story, "Columba," first appeared in the *American Voice*. A young girl (the first-person narrator) goes to live with her aunt, the aunt's Cuban lover, and their servant, a Jamaican boy named Columba. She befriends Columba, and in the countryside of Kingston they discover an abandoned car inhabited by a colony of doves, which they find exhilarating and beautiful. However, the Cuban lover also finds the doves and orders Columba to slaughter them and freeze them for a future meal.

"A Hanged Man" is based on two historical details, which are explained in a brief prologue. The first is about the slave-whipping houses found on American plantations. The second is the legend of Peg-leg Joe, an abolitionist who led slaves to freedom. The story takes us into the scene of a slave owner who has hung himself in his own whipping house; meanwhile, a female slave has escaped on her own, and she takes comfort in spotting the shoe and peg tracks of Peg-leg Joe's path, which she knows she can follow to freedom.

Another story grounded in the details of a real person is "A Woman Who Plays Trumpet Is Deported," which was inspired by the actual events surrounding Valaida Snow, an accomplished trumpet player who was captured by Nazi troops. Cliff starts the story pre-Holocaust and imagines Snow's struggles as a black female musician in Europe—the crowd always asks her to sing instead of playing the trumpet. In 1942 she gets caught up in the Holocaust and is shipped to a concentration camp. Waiting in the line that splits into two lines (one to the gas chambers, one to the camp), Snow clutches her trumpet. Guards notice her and ask her questions about Beethoven and Telemann. The story ends on the image of Jews leaving their belongings in huge piles, with Snow keenly aware of all eyes on her prized trumpet. However, readers know from the explanation at the beginning of the story that Snow will survive the concentration camp, and we are left with the sense that her knowledge of music saved her life.

Cliff has a keen eye for evocative private narratives within the larger narrative of history. She also works in a number of movie references, films that the characters admire and attempt to incorporate into their own lives. In "Columba" she refers to the 1941 classic *The Lady Eve* and movie stars such as Marilyn Monroe, Tony Curtis, and John Wayne. Characters in "The Ferry" mention the movies *Splendor in the Grass, Shall We Dance, Outward Bound,* and *Rebel Without a Cause.* In Opal Palmer Adisa's 1994 interview with Cliff, Adisa asked about the references to movies. Cliff responded, "My writing is very visual. And I find movies coming into it a lot, using movies as an idea, and the effects of movies. Growing up in Jamaica movies were one of the

only contacts with the outside world for many people" (p. 274).

Discussing the stories "Burning Bush" and "Screen Memory," Suzanne Bost notes the "reconceptualization of racial constitution" (p. 684). Both stories are about biracial woman. In "Burning Bush" the biracial woman purposefully paints part of her skin white so she can make a sideshow living as the checkerboard-skinned "Girl from Martinique." In "Screen Memory" a biracial girl takes piano lessons from her black grandmother. When the girl makes mistakes, the grandmother reminds her, " 'Hastiness, carelessness, will never lead you to any real feeling, or,' she pauses, 'any lasting accomplishment. You have to go deep inside yourself—to the best part' " (p. 92). The girl concludes that the "best part" of herself is the black part. Commenting on both stories, Bost writes, "Cliff does subvert the conventional narrative in which black is the threatening color" (p. 685). However, Bost goes on to argue that "Cliff is never fully celebratory of biracialism, and her readers are unable to forget that racial mixture often began (and begins) with rape" (p. 685).

Cliff's next collection, *The Store of a Million Items* (1998), contains eleven short stories. This writing marks a shift into more solidified narratives; gone are the fragmented insights and the shifting (sometimes unidentified) points of view. What emerges in this collection are troubled characters making peculiar decisions in neighborhoods that often contain residents of mixed identities.

The lead story, "Transactions," was originally published in *Tri-Quarterly* and went on to be included in *Best American Short Stories 1997.* One of her finest short stories, it is about a traveling salesman who is "in love with American things" (p. 4). He encounters a blond, blue-eyed, German-Jamaican girl, age three or so, on the roadside somewhere in Jamaica. He seeks out her mother in an impoverished dwelling nearby and pays the mother twenty dollars for the girl because he suddenly wants her for his own, and he and his Jamaican wife are childless The girl is covered with sores, so he takes her to a spring water bath famous for its healing properties. However, she hates the bath and bites his cheek. The man starts to doubt his transaction, and he worries that his wife will refuse the girl. So instead of going home, they spend the night in a room in a boardinghouse near the bath. In the morning, the girl is gone.

Among the goods the salesman is delivering to country stores in Jamaica are magazines from America, and the American proprietress of the boardinghouse, glancing at a magazine, notices the real-life story of Emmett Till, a fourteen-year-old African American boy from Chicago who was murdered by white men in Mississippi in 1955 after he allegedly whistled at a white man's wife. Till's family allowed photos to be published of his open-casket funeral, which showed mutilation. The proprietess is so upset by the photos from her homeland that she burns all the copies of the magazine rather than sell them.

The infamous photos of Emmett Till are referenced in two other stories in this collection, "Contagious Melancholia" and the title story. The reference has its most profound impact in "The Store of a Million Items," a story about how youngsters in a Jamaican town adore a variety shop that always has new and exciting toys, like fancy yo-yos. This story is also set in 1955, and the children are learning in their history classes about the hard life in places like the USSR. But they have also heard about the recent murder of Till and the hard life of a being a minority in America. None of their schoolteachers address the murder—or the American civil rights movement. The narrator of the story notes, "On August 28, 1955, Emmett Till's body was dredged from the River Pearl. But teachers weren't responsible for telling us things that happened in the summer" (p. 44). The story contrasts themes of idle oblivion (the wonders of the toy store) and violence, underlining the way children know what is going on in the adult world even if adults don't tell them.

The last four stories in *The Store of a Million Items* touch more on the topics of feminism and lesbianism than racism, and some of the settings shift from Jamaica to America. In "Art History," a young lesbian couple house-sits in New York City for a socialite art historian who has an estranged son and intriguing neighbors. The

neighbors refer to the lesbian couple as lovers before the narrator can even admit it to herself. The story is a meditation on the ways we love (and don't love) our families and ourselves.

In "Rubicon," a closeted lesbian leaves her daughter downstairs at the Rubicon Bar while she engages a woman upstairs. This is a regular Thursday occurrence, and the mother always says, "Don't tell your father I brought you here" (p. 95). The young girl always agrees to keep the secret. The story ends on this awareness from the daughter's perspective: "As long as this remains ritual, as long as whatever happens upstairs does not come downstairs, everything will be as it is and has been. Ritual contains" (p. 101).

In "Apache Tears," we see Cliff's first story not set in Jamaica or New York City; instead, this one is set in a small, odd town near Los Angeles. It is the story of a museum filled with possessions of the dead. The female curator likes to dress in dead people's clothes and tell the visitors about the clothing. In the final story, "A Public Woman," death comes full circle as a coroner and a male investigator enter the bedroom of a murdered prostitute. They take stock of the items in her room and make hasty judgments. For example, they find her diary, and the investigator says, "Never heard of a whore keeping a diary" (p. 112). The men are reluctant to do the detective work necessary to find the killer because "the trouble with the murder of a whore ... is that the number of suspects grows according to the popularity of the whore" (p. 114). The details of the woman's possessions (and her detailed diary) elicit sympathy with the murdered prostitute while the callous assumptions of the coroner and the investigator grate on the reader's moral sensibilities.

Cliff's next book of short stories, *Everything Is Now,* was published by the University of Minnesota Press in 2009; it features fourteen new stories and the twenty-one stories from the two earlier collections. It also contains a helpful first-publication history of her major short stories, which range from "Columba" in the spring 1988 issue of the *American Voice* to one of the new stories, "Crocodilopolis," in the July 2004 issue of *Bloom.* For first-time readers of Cliff, *Everything Is Now* serves as a fine introduction.

The new stories in the collection return to Cliff's familiar themes (sexuality, exclusion, feminism, history), but they are marked by a more composed tone and less raw anger. In "Then as Now," a woman is at a concert, listening to a pianist she first heard years ago. A man near her in the audience is correcting medical illustrations for the galley of a book. One of the illustrations is of a woman's reproductive anatomy. The main character then remembers a harrowing abortion from years ago, which she had had to endure without anesthetic. The abortion doctor had asked her to play a record to cover up suspicious noise during the procedure. Cliff's advanced writing skill is evident in the piece, with its present concert and its remembered concert, its present doctor and the remembered doctor, all linked by the narrator.

Other stories also include mature characters noticing the strange world around them. In "Crocodilopolis," set in 1905, a British woman travels to Cairo and then Crocodilopolis, an ancient oasis, with her brother, her friend, and an Egyptian servant. The woman envies the servant and her practical clothing (linen, loose) and gets nostalgic for a female lover she has left behind and can tell no one about because of the taboo against lesbianism. The story ends with lines from Sappho. Elsewhere in the collection, the story "Ecce Homo" too quotes Sappho and recounts the tragic love story of a black American linguist who finds himself working for the U.S. embassy in Fascist Italy as World War II begins to consume Europe. He falls in love with an Italian man. They are captured and sent to a concentration camp, but they escape and live in the woods during the war until a group of black American troops finds them and gets them to a way station. The Italian is kept as a prisoner of war; the linguist is sent back to America. The Italian hangs himself and the linguist goes mad. Many of Cliff's characters in these short stories

walk the line between madness and sanity in cultures that do not fully accept them.

LATER NOVELS: HISTORICAL AND MODERN

If *No Telephone to Heaven* is Cliff's best-known novel, *Free Enterprise* (1993) is a close second. It is a historical novel that introduces readers to Mary Ellen Pleasant, a real-life and lesser-known abolitionist who helped with John Brown's failed raid at Harpers Ferry in 1859.

Pleasant is accompanied by a host of secondary characters. Some are real, some are fictional. The narrative rotates through the viewpoints of all of them, so it is important to know who they are before tackling the events of the novel. Annie Christmas is a masculine-looking Jamaican woman who has fled the island and found herself in America. Rachel is the storytelling leper who befriends Annie. Alice Hooper is the wealthy white abolitionist who invites Mary Ellen Pleasant to an unveiling of the famous real-life painting "Slavers Throwing Overboard the Dead and Dying, Typhoon Coming On," by J. M. W. Turner. Marian "Clover" Adams, a real-life Civil War photographer, is Alice's cousin. Captain Parsons is Mary Ellen Pleasant's father, and Quasheba is her mother. The real-life sculptor Augustus Saint-Gaudens and the real-life Civil War sergeant Lewis Douglass (son of Frederick Douglass) appear near the end of the book in a series of letters. It's a complicated cast with complicated relations, but Cliff handles the rotating narratives with an accomplished style and just enough historical events to keep the reader grounded.

The novel starts in 1920, with an aged Annie Christmas reflecting on the tumultuous abolitionist days of the nineteenth century. She remembers learning the various antislavery viewpoints popular before the Civil War. Should there be an armed revolution? Should the slaves be freed through peaceful diplomatic means? She recalls going to hear Frances Ellen Watkins' 1858 presentation of a paper titled "The Education and Elevation of the Colored Race." Watkins argued that the "Talented Tenth" of African Americans were the best hopes for leadership. Annie finds herself concerned that Watkins would disregard ninety percent of African Americans, so she speaks out at the presentation, arguing that all African Americans are exceptional. Readers then learn that the wealthy black hotel owner, Mary Ellen Pleasant, who has been watching and listening in the back row, sees promise in the young Annie Christmas. They make each other's acquaintance, and the two of them eventually work in secret to help get weapons and funding to the revolutionaries who might help John Brown.

The novel then shifts to time frames after the 1859 raid at Harpers Ferry. Annie has retreated from the abolitionist movement (we find out why later) and spends her days helping out at a leper colony in the South. Details emerge about conspiracy theories surrounding the disease, which affects Africans more than Caucasians. Annie serves as a sounding board for the many accomplished storytellers in the colony, including the young woman Rachel, who has a rare form of internal leprosy.

Letters appear in part 3 of the novel as Mary tries to reestablish contact with Annie fifteen years after Harpers Ferry. Mary shares her observations on racism in America, including much meditation on Turner's painting of slaves drowning, which haunts her.

Around the middle of the book, Mary finally begins to express (in a letter to Annie) her disbelief that John Brown's name has received all the attention, and Cliff emphasizes the feminist take on the situation. Mary writes to Annie that

> I get very fed up with everyone referring to our enterprise as "John Brown's Raid on Harper's Ferry." I get very fed up with the engraving in history books.... I do not want fame, truly, or ownership of history, for that matter, but the official version is a cheat.
>
> But then, what's to be done? The winner names the age. Renaissance, Enlightenment, Age of Reason.
>
> But then again, even when we are winners—not of ages, my dear, of certain moments—our victories are not recorded, not really.
>
> (p. 137)

More letters appear in part 4, which begins in 1881, sixteen years after the end of the Civil

War. The sculptor Augustus Saint-Gaudens is communicating with a range of people who want to be involved in Saint-Gaudens' monument honoring the Fifty-fourth Massachusetts Regiment (a colored or Negro regiment, as it was called at the time). Clover becomes involved because she has prewar portraits of a similar regiment, which include her brother Ned, the leader. However, Saint-Gaudens eventually reveals that he decided not to use Clover's photos and claims he mailed them back, but neither Clover nor Ned ever sees them again. Clover sinks into depression.

The end of the book takes us to 1920, with Annie being visited by her old friend Rachel from the leper colony. The two women talk and tie up the plot points: Clover has committed suicide; the Turner painting now hangs in a museum; and Annie reveals that she had to murder white women to escape from the debacle in the wake of Harpers Ferry. Mary narrowly escaped capture (John Brown had a note from her in his pocket, but authorities famously misread her initials), retreated to San Francisco, and successfully advocated for civil rights until her death. Annie and Rachel raise a toast of cognac to their heroine and add a fascinating level of legend to the 1906 earthquake in San Francisco: it's said that the spirit of Mary Ellen Pleasant caused the quake, a rumor supported by the observation that the real-life eucalyptus trees Pleasant planted were not harmed (and are today denoted with a historical marker).

The concluding chapter is a lyrical and present-tense scene with Mary in a rented boat, heading out to sea, admiring the seagulls. The narrative has a moment of flash-forward to the wording on Mary's tombstone: "She was a friend of John Brown" (p. 213).

Free Enterprise received warm reviews in mainstream magazines such as *Elle* and *Essence,* given that it was turning the spotlight on female characters often relegated to the sidelines of history. Some critics compared it to Toni Morrison's *Beloved,* and in her interview with Opal Palmer Adisa, Cliff said, "I don't think I could have written this novel if [Morrison] hadn't written *Beloved.* Her imagining of that period, of slavery and its aftermath, opened up my imagination with regard to the rewriting of history, revising the history we've all been taught" (p. 280).

In that same interview (one year after the release of *Free Enterprise*), Adisa asked Cliff if she was a feminist. Cliff responded, "I consider myself a feminist in the way I choose to define feminism. That is, a world view which focuses on the experiences of women. It doesn't mean excluding men. I have real problems with that idea" (p. 278). She went on to explain that she wants to focus on both the oppression of women as well as the resistance of women. Adisa asked what Cliff wants readers to take from *Free Enterprise.* Cliff responded, "I've always been struck by the misrepresentation of history and have tried to correct received version of history, especially the history of resistance. It seems to me that if one does not know that one's people have resisted, then it makes resistance difficult" (p. 280).

Suzanne Bost praises Cliff's skill as a writer of historical fiction in *Free Enterprise:* "Looking backward, Cliff juxtaposes history and fiction, amplifying some events and decentering others" (p. 686). Bost also notes Cliff's unique position to be a writer of a book such as *Free Enterprise:* "Biracial writers such as Cliff have access to multiple spheres of reference ... that are as yet unrecognized by most Americans" (p. 686).

Another pair of critics, Ewart Skinner and Nicole Waller, presented a paper at the 1996 symposium "Postcolonialism and Autobiography" arguing that the African legend of Gang Gang Sara, a witch who wants to return to Africa but cannot, "provides a blueprint" for *Free Enterprise* (p. 99). "It is through old myths that Cliff, herself a university professor well ensconced in the world of academia, seems to weave historical accounts that are most compelling to the artist's writing voice" (p. 99). Metaphorically, the entire novel represents "the failed flight of the Africans" (p. 107), be it John Brown's failed raid, the scourge of leprosy, or Mary Ellen Pleasant's failure to get an accurate chapter in the history books.

Like Cliff's other novels, *Into the Interior,* published in 2010, deals with the long-range

consequences of colonialism. A nameless female narrator tells us, from a first-person point of view, of her childhood in Jamaica and her young adulthood in England. Cliff returns to her earlier, fractured style of writing, often just an abrupt list of evocative images and allusions from art and literature: "Trade winds bring sick, and color. Red moonlight. Boiling Sea. Hurricanes pose as tempest. Crusoe loses his way, swims in Friday's footprint" (p. 3). But in a completely new structure, the novel also contains footnotes. For example, the characters encounter graffiti, and the footnote tells us that the graffiti is actually a poem by the Afrikaner poet Ingrid Jonker. The footnote continues across two pages in order to tell us about Jonker's life and suicide (pp. 40–41).

Into the Interior works on many accomplished levels: into the physical interior of an island and a childhood; into the interior of England and its colonizing assumptions; and into the interior of language, as expressed by the footnotes, which seek to convey more than the main text can possibly hold. It exemplifies the struggles that Cliff has always faced: who are we, really, and how were we shaped (and misshapen) by our cultures and languages? Although Cliff has often stood in the shadow of peers such as Toni Morrison, her extensive work and her wide-ranging approach to colonialism, feminism, racism, and sexual identity make her a notable American writer, one who finds intriguing narratives in our shared (but obscured) histories.

Selected Bibliography

WORKS OF MICHELLE CLIFF

Prose Poetry

Claiming an Identity They Taught Me to Despise. Waterton, Mass.: Persephone Press, 1980.

The Land of Look Behind: Prose and Poetry. Ithaca, N.Y.: Firebrand Books, 1985. (Reprints six pieces from *Claiming an Identity.*)

If I Could Write This in Fire. Minneapolis: University of Minnesota Press, 2008.

Novels

Abeng. Trumansburg, N.Y.: Crossing Press, 1984; New York: Plume/Penguin, 1995. (Usually considered a prequel to *No Telephone to Heaven.*)

No Telephone to Heaven. New York: Dutton, 1987; New York: Plume/Penguin, 1996. (Features the main character of Clare Savage, who first appeared in *Abeng.*)

Free Enterprise. New York: Dutton, 1993; New York: Plume/Penguin, 1994. Reissued, San Francisco: City Lights Books, 2004.

Into the Interior. Minneapolis: University of Minnesota Press, 2010.

Short Stories

Bodies of Water. New York: Dutton, 1990; New York: Plume/Penguin, 1995.

The Store of a Million Items. Boston: Houghton Mifflin, 1998.

Everything Is Now: New and Collected Stories. Minneapolis: University of Minnesota Press, 2009.

Other Works

The Winner Names the Age: A Collection of Works by Lillian Smith. New York: Norton, 1978. (Edited by Cliff.)

"Sister/Outsider: Some Thoughts on Simone Weil." In *Between Women: Biographers, Novelists, Critics, Teachers, and Artists Write About Their Work on Women*. Edited by Carol Ascher, Louise DeSalvo, and Sara Ruddick. Boston: Beacon Press, 1984.

"Clare Savage of Crossroads Character." In *Caribbean Women Writers: Essays From the First International Conference*. Edited by Selwyn R. Cudjoe. Wellesley, Mass.: Calaloux, 1990. Pp. 263–268.

"Caliban's Daughter: The Tempest and the Teapot." *Frontiers* 12, no. 2:36–51 (1991).

"History as Fiction, Fiction as History." *Ploughshares* 20, nos. 2–3:196–202 (1994).

CRITICAL AND BIOGRAPHICAL STUDIES

Adjarian, M. M. "White Skin, Black Masks: Michelle Cliff and the Allegory of the Dream Deferred." In her *Allegories of Desire: Body, Nation, and Empire in Modern Caribbean Literature by Women*. London: Praeger, 2004. Pp.15–49.

Aegerter, Lindsay Pentolfe. "Michelle Cliff and the Paradox of Privilege." *College English* 59, no. 8:898–915 (December 1997).

Aguiar, Marian. "Decolonizing the Tongue: Reading Speech

and Aphasia in the Work of Michelle Cliff." *Literature and Psychology* 47, nos. 1–2:94–108 (2001).

Bost, Suzanne. "Fluidity Without Postmodernism: Michelle Cliff and the 'Tragic Mulatta' Tradition." *African American Review* 32, no. 4:673–689 (winter 1998).

Edmondson, Belinda. "Race, Privilege, and the Politics of (Re)Writing History: An Analysis of the Novels of Michelle Cliff." *Callaloo* 16, no. 1: 180–191 (winter 1993).

Elia, Nada. "'A Man Who Wants To Be a Woman': Queerness as/and Healing Practices in Michelle Cliff's *No Telephone to Heaven*." *Callaloo* 23, no. 1:352–365 (winter 2000).

Emery, Mary Lou. "Refiguring the Postcolonial Imagination: Tropes of Visuality in Writing by Rhys, Kincaid, and Cliff." *Tulsa Studies in Women's Literature* 16, no. 2:259–280 (autumn 1997).

Floyd-Thomas, Stacey M., and Laura Gillman. "Subverting Forced Identities, Violent Acts, and the Narrativity of Race: A Diasporic Analysis of Black Women's Radical Subjectivity in Three Novel Acts." *Journal of Black Studies* 32, no. 5: 528–556 (May 2002).

Hornung, Alfred, and Ernstpeter Ruhe, eds. *Postcolonialism & Autobiography.* Amsterdam and Atlanta, Ga.: Rodopi, 1998. (Manuscripts presented at the "Postcolonialism & Autobiography" symposium held June 19–22, 1996, in Würzburg, Germany.)

Johnson, Erica L. "Ghostwriting Transnational Histories in Michelle Cliff's *Free Enterprise*." *Meridians* 9, no. 1:114–159 (fall 2008).

Lima, Maria Helena. "Revolutionary Developments: Michelle Cliff's *No Telephone to Heaven*." *Ariel* 24, no. 1:35–56 (January 1993).

Moynagh, Maureen. "The Ethical Turn in Postcolonial Theory and Narrative: Michelle Cliff's *No Telephone to Heaven*." *Ariel* 30, no. 4: 109–133 (October 1999).

Richards, Constance S. "Nationalism and Development of Identity in Postcolonial Fiction: Zoë Wicomb and Michelle Cliff." *Research in African Literatures* 36, no. 1:20–33 (spring 2005).

Robinson-Walcott, Kim. "Claiming an Identity We Thought They Despised: Contemporary White West Indian Writers and Their Negotiation of Race." *Small Axe* 7, no. 2:93–110 (September 2003).

Sethuraman, Ramchandran. "Evidence-cum-Witness: Subaltern History, Violence, and the (De)formation of Nation in Michelle Cliff's *No Telephone to Heaven*." *Modern Fiction Studies* 43, no. 1:249–287 (spring 1997).

Skinner, Ewart C., and Nicole Waller. "Auto-bio-historiography: Gang Gang Sara's Shadow in Michelle Cliff's *Free Enterprise*." In *Postcolonialism & Autobiography.* Edited by Alfred Hornung and Ernstpeter Ruhe. Amsterdam and Atlanta, Ga.: Rodopi, 1998.

Smith, Sidonie. "Memory, Narrative, and the Discourses of Identity in *Abeng* and *No Telephone to Heaven*." In *Postcolonialism & Autobiography*. Edited by Alfred Hornung and Ernstpeter Ruhe. Amsterdam and Atlanta, Ga.: Rodopi, 1998.

Toland-Dix, Shirley. "Re-negotiating Racial Identity: The Challenge of Migration and Return in Michelle Cliff's *No Telephone to Heaven*." *Studies in the Literary Imagination* 37, no. 2: 37–52 (fall 2004).

INTERVIEWS

Adisa, Opal Palmer. "Journey into Speech—A Writing Between Two Worlds: An Interview with Michelle Cliff." *African American Review* 28, no. 2:273–281 (summer 1994).

Raikin, Judith. "The Art of History: An Interview with Michelle Cliff." *Kenyon Review* 15, no. 1:57–71 (winter 1993).

Schwartz, Meryl F. "An Interview with Michelle Cliff." *Contemporary Literature* 34, no. 4:595–619 (winter 1993).

PATRICIA HAMPL

(1946—)

Angela Garcia

MEMOIR, CRITICS AGREE, is the signature genre of the age. And Patricia Hampl may stand, as the *Los Angeles Times* has dubbed her, as its queen. In a 2009 lecture titled "Sacrament of Self: Catholic Roots of Contemporary Memoir" at Fairfield University in Connecticut, Hampl pronounced this form the voice of the twenty-first century (Healy, *Fairfield Mirror*). An acclaimed memoirist for three decades, Hampl has deeply examined the spiritual and historical truths touching her generation; as an essayist and teacher, her observations on the nature and power of the "first-person singular" have enriched critical understanding of the memoir form itself.

Of all the literary forms, the once-submerged memoir is the genre that has most remarkably transformed the world's publishing marketplace in the late twentieth and early twenty-first century. Its growth in the United States has eclipsed that of any other form. Readers, in turn, have responded with gusto to the variety of literature it has spawned, whether tell-alls or blogs. As evidenced from its pervasive online guises, the memoir's versatile and fiery popularity continues to be indisputable.

Within contemporary culture, forms as diverse as opinion page columns and histories have blended elements of memoir into their narratives, with authors seemingly more and more eager to incorporate the first person. In interviews, Hampl has stated her belief in the first-person singular as the American (literary) birthright, and has cited Herman Melville's *Moby-Dick,* Mark Twain's *Huckleberry Finn,* and F. Scott Fitzgerald's *The Great Gatsby* as classic, even quintessential, American works made possible only with the intimate "I." Stylistically, and ironically, Hampl has claimed, the personal voice translates most readily into universal experience for American readers.

Perhaps because of the nation's culture of independence, the American reader is uniquely poised to trust the personal "I." Walt Whitman and Emily Dickinson employ poetic examples of this technique, Whitman most lavishly illustrating the democratic, individual impulse we have come to see as particularly American in such works as "Song of Myself". Hampl's interest in this voice extends to a course she teaches titled "First Person Singular" at the University of Minnesota, where she has worked as a professor since 1979.

As a form, the memoir is engaged in a twofold purpose: to express the stories at once above and below the surface. In documenting its consciousness of events, Hampl has stated, the story of the thought becomes as significant as the recording of the events themselves. The narrative events may even take second place to the meditation implicit in the narration. In terms of this lyric consciousness inherent in the memoir, the author has said she admires the deep engagement with language, and the musicality of language, even—or especially—if that engagement evinces an intense struggle with the language itself. According to Hampl, it is this signal lyricism that allows a memoir to tell a story but also, simultaneously, to *think about* that same story. She particularly delights in exploring this intersection between narration and meditation through her prose.

But these essay-like tendencies, this genre-bending or -blurring within the memoir, can pose its own challenges and confusions. As Hampl and her coeditor Elaine Tyler May define the newness and risks of the phenomenon in their introduction to the essay collection *Tell Me True: Memoir, History, and Writing a Life* (2008), "The

equation has changed ... when the personal story claims the authority of nonfiction while clinging to the gripping suspense and charms of fiction" (p. 5). And so questions arise of whether the narrator is reliable, of truth versus fact, or of what may be invented in contrast to what may not. But the form soldiers on, a specimen of living language being shaped on a daily basis. And whether expressed online, in newspaper or magazine columns, or between the covers of history or biography best sellers, memoir is everywhere, continuing to revitalize language and to raise deep questions of truth and authenticity.

While Hampl's star has shone less brightly, or risen more slowly, than those of some of the wildly popular American memoirists who have become household names since the 1990s, she has contributed a consistently dignified sensibility through the powerful prose of her four memoirs. Equally importantly, her rigorous essays on the memoir and the nature of memory in literature have bolstered the form, adding to its legitimacy and authority.

CAREER

Born March 12, 1946, Hampl grew up in post–World War II provincial St. Paul, Minnesota, with parents Stanley and Mary, who well remembered the Depression and lived by its modest strictures. In classic American literature, St. Paul occupies sacred ground. The town represents the indelible brand of the Midwest made famous by the author who left St. Paul, F. Scott Fitzgerald. In parallel fashion, his timeless characters Jay Gatsby and Nick Carraway undertake the same migration eastward to better things in *The Great Gatsby,* fleeing that quaint region of innocence for a world of lurid experience, at dubious cost to themselves and their own integrity. Although the transplant Gatsby meets a tragic fate, Carraway vows to the reader to return to the Midwest and family at the end, a type of normalcy.

Hampl grew up not far from Fitzgerald's home. Daughter of a first-generation Czech father, a florist, and an Irish American mother who toiled mainly as a library file clerk, the writer basked in the Sunday dinners and extended familial love of her mostly Czech clan. She shows, ultimately, affection for the parochial spirit of the town and, along with it, her staunchly middle-class but nonetheless comforted and cosseted youth. Hampl extends her affection to architectural features of the town such as the mansions on the hill, its cathedral, and even the Schlitz brewery sign that flashed on and off in her youth, before the freeways intervened in the late 1960s and easy access was gained to Minneapolis. Cultural fixtures such as the Czech community hall are also fondly noted in her writings.

The author's seminal work, *A Romantic Education* (1981), took a literary risk in constructing a collage of observations on her St. Paul girlhood, particularly her grandmother; meditations on beauty; and travel writing in cold war Prague. The bold amalgamation has been called a classic of the memoir genre and revived the form for a generation of American writers, while setting a precedent for the blending of genres.

The writer's Catholic faith, stemming from her time in Catholic school, has also strongly shaped her work, as when her spiritual searching takes her to Assisi, Italy, in *Virgin Time: In Search of the Contemplative Life* (1992). She has written extensively of the indelible impression left by the school, from the singing of the nuns to the angle of light within the classrooms, and of the feeling of security the old building and tradition evoked in her.

At the same time, she paints her hunger for Whitman's passion during her coming-of-age in the 1960s. It was a time, she says, of extreme, even grotesque discomfiture with the American national identity. Guilt, confusion, betrayal, and alienation colluded to push her and other young men and women of the era to seek answers in the face of death and destruction perpetrated by the American military abroad in Vietnam. Contemporary poets formed the bulk of her reading, and though she read Emily Dickinson as well as Whitman, she soon chose the Father over the Mother, enticed by Whitman's "gorgeously optimistic voice" and "prophetic gleam" (*A Romantic Education,* p. 46). She read his essays,

his prose on democracy and the character of the American people, for its "good news" while her contemporaries Robert Bly, Galway Kinnell, Denise Levertov, and others kept Hampl's eyes simultaneously fixed on the "moral pulse" of the late 1960s and early 1970s (p. 46). Vietnam meant, in part, arguing with family.

The memoirist has described herself as a wide-eyed provincial when she entered the University of Minnesota in nearby Minneapolis. In this bastion of midwestern liberalism, where only a few years earlier a fellow Minnesotan, Robert Zimmerman, had changed his name to Bob Dylan and begun to develop his own burning first-person voice, Hampl became engaged in the politically charged, questioning culture of the time. An English major, she took a course with John Berryman and wrote for the college newspaper, the *Minnesota Daily;* her first article was on Sylvia Plath, whose death bewildered her. She also worked on the *Ivory Tower,* a student magazine edited by Garrison Keillor, whose long-running radio show *Prairie Home Companion,* launched in 1974 out of St. Paul, would provide an affectionate take on the Lutheran version of wholesomeness, neighborliness, modesty, and moderation of Hampl's home state.

After graduating in 1968, Hampl entered the prestigious Writers' Workshop at the University of Iowa, earning her M.F.A. in 1970. She has since explained that at the time, there was no alternative—one wrote either fiction or poetry; creative nonfiction did not exist as a valid literary choice of study. Since the memoir form lacked authenticity and authority in 1970, it was not yet recognized as a viable genre for graduate students. At least two decades would pass before nonfiction would provide that third option so popular in American M.F.A. programs today.

Instead, the author began her career as a lyric poet, and has attested to the lyric elements of tightness and rhapsody that have remained vital elements in her prose. As she worked in odd jobs as a sales clerk and telephone operator, and held more regular employment with Minnesota Public Radio, she continued to write. Journalism was one field that invited the newly graduated author. Hampl served as the first editor of *Minnesota Monthly,* then a cultural magazine, from 1973 to 1975. From 1975 to 1979 she worked as a freelance writer and editor.

She first broke into publishing through her poetic craft, which she had honed in graduate school. Her two poetry collections were titled *Woman Before an Aquarium* (1978) and *Resort and Other Poems* (1983). Gradually, Hampl has claimed, she felt she needed a greater narrative space or canvas and turned to prose—mainly nonfiction but also including a number of short stories over the years, one of which, "The Bill Collector's Vacation," earned a Pushcart Prize in 1999. However, Hampl specializes in and is most esteemed for her works of literary nonfiction, including memoir, essays, autobiography, and travelogue or travel writing. Indeed, her books combining travelogue with honest, searching meditations have offered a prototype for much subsequent American memoir and nonfiction writing. Works such as *Eat Pray Love* by Elizabeth Gilbert utilize the travelogue as a frame for the spiritual search for the self.

Hampl pioneered this cross-genre approach in *A Romantic Education,* which won the Houghton Mifflin Literary Fellowship Award and pursued Hampl's Czech heritage (on her father's side) both at home in St. Paul and during a trip abroad to Prague. Here, as in later books, her prose crisscrosses the always porous borders between these genres. And consequently, the genres bend and stretch to accommodate introspection as well as anecdote, public as well as personal history—and always memory. The prose in *A Romantic Education* possesses the fluidity, the lyric spirit and quality of graceful meditation, that has distinguished her writing throughout her career.

Hampl's second travelogue, *Virgin Time: In Search of the Contemplative Life* (1992), returned to Europe, this time spanning Assisi, Lourdes, and finally, back in the States, the Lost Coast of California in its search for the sacred. Referencing the American mystic Thomas Merton, Hampl addresses the popularity of Eastern traditions, Zen and meditation particularly, in the practices of former Catholics. As for herself, however, she prefers to go deeper into the practice in which

she was reared. Therefore she immerses herself, temporarily in each instance, in the life of a Carmelite nun, a pilgrim to Lourdes, and finally, a participant in a retreat at a small Cistercian monastery.

As an essayist, Hampl has explored similar preoccupations. In her essay collection *I Could Tell You Stories: Sojourns in the Land of Memory* (1999), she provides original, powerful explorations of Catholic writers such as St. Augustine and Edith Stein, a convert from Judaism. Another essay pays homage to F. Scott Fitzgerald's vision of St. Paul and the Midwest, in which Hampl acknowledges its dismal status in the American (especially expatriate) literary pantheon as the place that the writer most desires to leave behind. This book garnered high praise for its meticulous and illuminating analyses of memory and imagination in such lives as Stein's, as well as in the writings of Walt Whitman, Czeslaw Miłosz, and Sylvia Plath.

In 2008 Hampl and her coeditor Elaine Tyler May published *Tell Me True,* a book that continues to enlarge upon the contemplation of form, taking a meta-cognitive look at the style of the modern memoir and what it allows and entails, including the mind's responses, interpretations, and inquiries. Her own essay contribution to the book, "You're History," takes a fresh view of her own career and the writing choices she made along the way. Drama, humor, and empathy prove key elements of her graceful, condensed prose as she documents her writer's journey.

At the same time, the prose's meditative quality—and her careful consideration of all the nuances of the spiritual life, in an age when many contemporary writers shy away from this—afford the language a timelessness and discretion. Hampl maintains a tone more sincere and decidedly less ironic than many other popular memoirists. As she states in "You're History," even when writing about her family background, she tends to seek out something bigger than herself—something she claims for the memoirist in general; an approach to writing that is not self-absorbed but, on the contrary, in search of the world. This is the quest for soul, rather than self (*Shooting Star* interview). And the seeker in the reader responds. In her 2009 Fairfield University lecture, she likened the reflection inherent in the autobiographical essay to the work that goes on in the Catholic confessional, the holy sacrament of confession. The author refers to this form in Catholic terms, pronouncing the memoir—as a confessional piece of literature—the most sacramental of genres, as it both reveals consciousness and seeks the soul (Healy, *Fairfield Mirror*).

Sixteen years after the publication of *A Romantic Education,* the sacramental duty continued with *The Florist's Daughter* (2007), a memoir that takes on the challenging theme of a family's ordinariness: middling, middle-class humility with all the decent gestures it embodies. Indeed, with this book her writing comes full circle, and Hampl recognizes that to write about the lost world of St. Paul and her modest middle-class family qualifies as history as well. There too, from the seemingly flattest and most prosaic place of all, springs life, springs culture. And from her gentle tribute to her very decent mother and father, who would stay together in spite of their opposing sensibilities, emerges a deep compassion in the prose. They prove an emblem of the era. As her parents age and she becomes their caregiver, the challenges the grown daughter faces strike a chord with many readers.

In turning to family, Hampl's fluid language manages to capture the evasive presences of her father and mother, both as middle-aged parents and in the difficult throes of aging. Although, as the writer avows, she has no abuse or violence to confess—so prevalent in published memoirs of the last few decades—the narration does not shy away from problematic parts of her parents' personalities, their complexities. Through the details and motifs—often repeated key quotations—the reader glimpses the stories and psyches behind the middle-class, mild-mannered lives. By the end of the book, the daughter's visits to her ever-strong mother in the nursing home are all the more poignant for the intimacy stitched patiently by the narration.

Hampl's literary accomplishments have met with wide recognition. In 1990 she was named a MacArthur Fellow, and the National Endowment for the Arts has awarded her two grants, one for

prose and one for poetry. She was awarded a Guggenheim Foundation Fellowship in 1976. She has published in newspapers and literary magazines throughout her career, including numerous reviews in the *New York Times*. Other awards and fellowships include the Bush Foundation Fellowship (1979), the McKnight Distinguished University Professorship (1995), and a Fulbright scholarship (1995). *The Florist's Daughter,* which the *New York Times* called her strongest nonfiction to date, won the 2008 Minnesota Book Award for Memoir and Creative Nonfiction.

If, as Hampl has wryly noted, St. Paul has a reputation as a place writers want to leave, she nevertheless forged an independent path and ultimately decided to stay in her hometown, where she has been a professor in the Department of English and Creative Writing Program at the University of Minnesota–Twin Cities for more than three decades; she is currently Regents Professor at the university, its highest teaching honor. The author is also a permanent member of the Prague Summer Writing Program and a founding member of the Loft Literary Center in Minneapolis.

Through the years Hampl has received honorary doctorates from the College of St. Catherine, University of St. Thomas, and Luther College. The writer continues to lecture at universities on her memoirs and to present her work on such stages as the Fitzgerald Theater in St. Paul. Hampl's current project is *The Art of the Wasted Day,* a meditation on leisure and Michel Montaigne's essay form.

SISTERS AT SCHOOL: AT HOME IN CATHOLICISM

Reflections on St. Paul and her Catholic school, elemental to her Czech-Irish upbringing, adorn several of Hampl's books. She describes the feeling of security among the nuns at the school, the implicit encouragement toward observation and imagination, toward the soul's music: "Pondering was the highest vocation.... It was the essence of aloofness.... The life lived within these red brick walls was so clearly *something,* in distinction to the random snarl of existence littering life in general, life *out there*" (*Virgin Time,* pp. 62, 64). She remarks that

> even [the] light seemed contemplative.... Perhaps the light streaming into our classrooms was the opposite of a passion subdued; it was light slowed to a voluptuous stretch.... The place was dedicated, perhaps unconsciously, to the imagination. We were left to daydream.... The whole place was an injunction to metaphor, to the endless noticing of detail that is rendered into transformation.
>
> (p. 65)

Hampl spoke to Margot Patterson of the *National Catholic Reporter* about her Catholicism. She said that although she did not go to church for a span of twenty years, from about college age until her mid-thirties, she was finally drawn back to the faith by virtue of Franciscan monasteries such as the Poor Clare order in Minnesota. She has been a regular churchgoer since then, grateful for the sense of wonder that faith has increased in her. Hampl says she had to learn to recognize that the Church could be imperfect, and accept this. (There is no record of her response to the priest abuse crisis.) Patterson notes, in turn, that the author's unabashedly Catholic writing, evident in all her memoirs, is rare in this secular, material-driven age.

Hampl claims that hers is a naturally Catholic language when she writes, a distinctly Catholic sensibility, and that atheism now seems barren to her. However, as in many Eastern traditions, her writing seeks to dissolve the artificial division between the secular and the sacred, so prominent in the West and in Western faiths, and to see the everyday, most ordinary act as divine. One vivid example, in *The Florist's Daughter,* is the meticulously crystallized lilacs she makes as her mother is slowly dying; this is a task she faces with purpose, as something holy, sacred or wondrous. Later her mother happily partakes of the sugared flowers.

Monasticism continues to be a draw for the author, who admires the spirit of silence and prayer, especially the chanting or singing of psalms traditional in Benedictine and Franciscan practice. In the essay "A Week in the Word," Hampl reveals herself as one who has attended numerous retreats, including several Vipassana

Buddhist retreats, which incorporate silence in sitting and walking meditation. One to two weeks at a time, she goes in order to immerse herself as fully as individually possible in the life of prayer. Both types of retreats, she writes, serve to focus her attention onto the present moment.

This hermitage, which she characterizes as her niche of cultural memory for the week, is called Logos; hence, the name of the essay. It overlooks Big Sur, California. The nomenclature seems marvelously apt; as a writer, Hampl treats the word as holy.

POETRY COLLECTIONS

Hampl has spoken often of the great influence of Walt Whitman's poetry and essays on her writing sensibility, from his freedom of voice—his plainness in addressing the reader—to his vision of an ideal America. Her own first poetry collection, *Woman Before an Aquarium,* published in 1978, also explores the ordinary interactions of daily life in lyric form. Its title poem seizes upon the image of a woman's face from an Henri Matisse painting of the same name and, through the metaphor of a mermaid trapped on the rocks merely combing her golden hair, iterates a (female) fear of passivity—of dreaming of swimming but never actually swimming. This tension between the object viewed and the object taking purposeful action is revisited in her later work *Blue Arabesque.*

In her second poetry volume, *Resort and Other Poems* (1983), the speaker captures the small but dramatic moments of daily life in precise images; sometimes the lyrics work to discover the truths underlying people's interactions, and other times they record her own questionings, musings, or longings in order to see beyond the surface. In her interview with Patterson, she characterizes her own writing, including prose, as thematically focused on her longings.

"Resort," the ambitious title poem written after weeks spent at a modest lake resort on Lake Superior's North Shore, emerges as a long, bold set of sections that begin with the narrator announcing her own noticing. In a nod to Whitman, the poem draws attention to its creator's thinking process as well as to the images and details sharply noticed. The speaker engages in a two-way conversation with the self to proclaim the factotum of place and then the purpose of her stay; the speaker asserts that a love affair ended badly, and that is why she is there.

The long lines and use of first person, as well as a directness of tone, continue to evoke the easy, democratic, and specifically American currents of Whitman's poetry. The speaker continues to quiz herself about whether she would ever kill herself, among other questions. She begins to intertwine memories of her St. Paul past with the resort's present.

An intermittent pattern of rose images that arises as metaphor seems to stem from the speaker's relationship with the florist father, and the poem leads back to him. The final section ends with verve, first with a lavish but graceful description of the night sky, and then, most interestingly, with what prefigures the later memoirist and essayist self: remembrances of the parent. Musings on her father's staunchly pragmatic character, and its consequent collision with his artist daughter's ideals, include a recalled and extended mental plea with him to see more than what is there in front of him. But this is not a man of imagination.

So what feels safe for the daughter, to adorn or ornament truth, does not make sense for her father. Although he is an artist and creates beauty in his own right, every day, as a florist, this is a father who plainly—though poignantly for his daughter—refuses to see rain as ballerinas. And so, while the gulf is not bridged, he too remains true to himself and his own pragmatic world.

Finally, what engulfs the poem are lyric passages on the nature that surrounds the speaker. In simple but elegant diction, the poem captures flowers and berries, insects and webs, until September swings in with its slinking fog and first frosts, marking the end of resort days. The poem's central metaphor elegantly concentrates from the rose into the rosehip, what the summer leaves behind it. Indeed, the poem suggests, this rosehip carries something useful (a nod to the father), nothing less than something that is

awaited; purpose; memory; hidden mystery; silent or subverted intent; root emotion; truth; and rapture. This Keatsian return to a marriage of truth and beauty becomes the motif of several of Hampl's works of nonfiction.

The poem is not always successful in its mix of styles and voices, and its large scope is difficult to manage. Sometimes the flashes between past and present, or its metaphors (the rose figures intermittently but prominently, like a chorus) falter. However, near the end of the poem the lyric sounds a convincing note, and the various styles stream and echo together more harmoniously, in counterbalance. The deep humanity behind the long poem grows evident as the poet renders that persistent searching for resolution into the consoling language of lyricism.

In 1995 Hampl edited a collection of sacred poetry from all three Western religious traditions titled *Burning Bright: An Anthology of Sacred Poetry*. She arranges the pieces—Christian, Judaic, Muslim—to follow the rhythms of the day. The poems selected include works by poets as diverse as the Persian mystic Rumi and Emily Dickinson.

THE CZECH GRANDMOTHER AND A PRAGUE AWAKENING

A Romantic Education (1981), which crosses between travel writing and memoir, is a work that critics have heralded in retrospect as having revived the memoir as an American genre at that juncture, when memoirs had not yet crowded library or bookstore shelves. The book migrates from a meditation on family and place—centering on Hampl's so seemingly foreign Czech grandmother and so markedly intimate St. Paul—to a meditation on beauty in its myriad forms, then fans out to Prague, which exhibits its own broken beauty. Looking back at her book, Hampl has identified the two diverse strands of her journey: an immigration story, documenting the homeland of her Czech grandmother, and an examination of the historical and sociological context of cold war Prague, a Prague which stood, in 1975, behind the Iron Curtain.

The grandmother who eventually inspires the germinal excursion to the homeland is presented by Hampl in all her earthy peasant glory: "Food was the potent center of my grandmother's life" (p. 70). She cooks and dances; she does not trust her granddaughter's books and reading, in fact whipping a novel from her hand to bring her back to daily living. She presides over a large garden that she harvests to make Sunday dinners with all the meat and potatoes or dumplings, beer, and cakes and coffee the extended family can desire. The grandmother is the matriarch always commanding the others to eat more, her home her own fiefdom. The grandfather is a pale shadow beside this powerhouse of nurturance, hardly speaking or smiling in Hampl's memory.

Meanwhile, the grandmother imprints herself on her granddaughter. While she may not know the English word "science" (to her granddaughter's shame and horror) and works as a house cleaner in the wealthy mansions of St. Paul, her skin is beautiful, and she cries sentimentally at photos of Golden Praha (Prague). An elegant Aunt Lillian and bothersome brother emerge as peripheral characters. The Irish side is all but absent in this volume, except in glimpses of Hampl's mother, but the fierce love of grandmother and mother for their offspring is clear.

The garden merits a section unto itself, as a fantastical place for a young girl, where the vegetables are forever ripe for canning, rhubarb and beets spring eternally ruby red, and old-fashioned roses grow thick and wild. Dandelion wine is fashioned from the dark riches of the garden as well. As Hampl attests, it is no accident that her handsome father's job is to bring beauty to the world as a florist, nurturing and arranging flowers for the people of St. Paul. Hampl's evocation is primal, a world of darkness and raw smells.

Beauty's power floats from the sensory profusion of the garden and grandmother, food and church, and the hushed and mysterious Catholic school, St. Luke's—fond memories of the people and experiences that for Hampl constitute links to the old world, the traditional world of custom. Hampl traces her grandmother from her primal place in her family to her disappearance into the nursing home her family hated, indicating a

bedridden and garden-shorn collapse of that family structure.

In another meditation on beauty Hampl offers a feminist analysis of how beauty holds young women captive through popular magazines. But the meat of her story lies in anecdote: the Catholic schoolgirl everyone branded as ugly (although, Hampl the schoolgirl marvels, she doesn't *know* she is ugly), resurrected in the St. Paul newspapers a few years later as a Paris model, her thinness and high cheekbones turned suddenly glamorous.

The memoirist readily admits the midwestern writer's disdain for the Midwest, once he has moved on to New York City or Paris. Of course he turns up his nose at the place, Hampl suggests; this is part of the natural writer's progress. St. Paul reveals itself as vaguely "old money," and Hampl alludes to F. Scott Fitzgerald's *The Great Gatsby* when, as an adult, she takes up lodging at what turns out to be the servant's quarters of one of the city's mansions. More pervasive in the imagery of her St. Paul is the tireless "Schlitz" sign, the letters lighting themselves up in red, one at a time like dominos, then blinking together—Hampl's midwestern answer to Gatsby's green light at the end of the dock, and one she recollects with fondness.

It is quite a leap from memories of her grandmother's garden in St. Paul and meditations on beauty to an exegesis of Prague, a smoke-filled land an ocean away, but the connections become clear as Hampl hints at the difficulty for the American artist to be nourished on beauty because of a primal or psychic loss of culture: "The ghost of a lost, smudged Europe and its culture, and the ghost of the undefiled American continent: these, to me, are the two spooks of our immigrant heritage," she writes. "We are aware that our presence on the continent has made it less beautiful.... We have not been able to use our past, more specifically our folk heritage, as other cultures have" (p. 121). And so, framed thusly, Hampl's journey becomes another instance of a quest for the soul.

In traveling to Prague, Hampl propels herself toward the culture that formed the grandmother she saw in America as feudal, even peasant, a cook and gardener but certainly without any background of book learning. At the same time, this is a chance for a young woman to transgress borders and to see her own country, America, from a new perspective, given the established, intellectual, and bleak European culture with which she is then able to contrast it.

Hampl undertakes her journey in 1975, seven years after the Prague Spring, a thaw of communism in Eastern Europe during which liberalization and reforms in Czechoslovakia attempted to loosen the Soviet Union's grip on the nation. However, these reforms were quashed in a Soviet invasion. (It would be fourteen years until the final fall of the Communist regime, when the Velvet Revolution returned Czechoslovakia to democracy under populist pressure.) At the time of Hampl's visit, the nation's history bestows upon the city a grim cold war "black-leather-jacket glamour," its hopes cruelly broken (p. 310).

When Hampl visits her grandmother's homeland, its otherness fascinates her; she falls in love precisely with the crumbled dignity of the capital. Unlike other American tourists, she refuses to embark on a quest to discover the roots of her family in the country's small towns. Instead, she focuses on living in and learning about Prague, in her catalogue of the aesthetic. In an era of dingy shops and restaurants and few American tourists, with Czechoslovakians obsessed with American freedom and American jeans, Hampl is helped along by guides such as a native poet friend and begins to discover that the Kafkaesque is everywhere.

While often rhapsodizing on the smoky depths of her temporarily adopted city, its cathedrals and museums—the whole medieval cityscape more intact and preserved than that of any other European city at that time, she avers—Hampl also concedes the grayness of reality: the restriction of liberties, the limited access to goods and services, the fear never far from the surface.

Essentially, she seeks the culture that America seems so basely to lack. In this she follows in the footsteps of the Lost Generation—among them, H.D. (Hilda Doolittle), who wrote autobiographically from London—and Henry Miller, who later transformed his experiences in Paris.

Indeed, Hampl places herself historically in juxtaposition to America's foreign war at that time, Vietnam, noting that the week she arrived in May 1975 was the week the American troops left Saigon after fifteen years. She turns to Prague after suffering the "long anguish" of many young Americans over Vietnam and seeks to cleanse her soul somewhat in the small country of her ancestry, a victim nation rather than a perpetrator (p. 310).

Although the nation's mystery and opaqueness remain romantic to her—for example, her friends Zdenka and Jaromil, both suspicious, each warn her vaguely about the other—she continues to confront the Kafkaesque long waits of everyday people for basic foods and supplies, a larger living space, or simple services or repairs, plumbing and electrical. As an American, she has the privilege of observing without undergoing the citizens' sufferings. Sometimes, however, she plays the bamboozled Westerner, a telling role; one acquaintance manipulates Hampl into donating money for a Czech friend out of charity and pressures her into buying things for her.

Indeed, both Franz Kafka and Rainer Maria Rilke are ghosts the writer turns to again and again, particularly Kafka, as both writers hail from Prague. While Rilke is presented as a poet for his birthplace to be proud of, Kafka, with his tragic irony, seems to pervade Hampl's observations of daily life, a patron saint of this country's seemingly bitter, signature trait. A Czech poet who is her guide laughs humorlessly, repeating Kafka's name, as he shows her the worn streets inappropriately named after this or that official. Hampl says that she returns home a more ironic individual.

With Kafka, her friend Jaromil suggests, "only the details count" (p. 279), and lead to tragedy of Sisyphean proportions: recurrent, never-ending, senseless, and unredeemable. This is a mystery Hampl senses and evokes in the ruin-filled city. Rilke himself escaped from his hometown of Prague to Germany, then Paris, and at the end to Switzerland.

But the magical American passport remains at the ready, the memoirist admits. So while another friend, Anna, shakes with terror at the prospect of being found without her identification card late at night by a young Czech soldier, the American can hug and hold her, try to comfort her, once inside the door. But the narrow escape is not hers, and the grim consequences of the Iron Curtain lie forever beyond her imagination, an imagination that can only grapple to parallel Theresienstadt, the Czechoslovakian concentration camp, with My Lai—the analogy emblematic of her youthful generation's still raw American outrage regarding the horrors of Vietnam:

> Still, I often feel *wrong* to be approaching this history as I am—I who have been untouched by this kind of suffering. I go cold at the thought that silence *is* the only response, as so many of the real witnesses have said....
>
> Why such timidity? It comes, I think, from the peculiar relation the "untouched," such as myself, must have to the Holocaust. It remains the central episode of our history, the horror against which all other atrocities are measured, even previous ones, and by which innocence is gauged. My relation to it is not one of personal or even national guilt (as, say, a young German might feel). Mine is the confusion, the search, of someone unmarked. *Nothing bad has ever happened to me*. Nothing impersonally cruel or ruinous—and that is an odd, protected history or nonhistory to have in this century. I can only proceed, assuming that to be untouched has some significance in the presence of the deeply touched life of this city.
>
> (p. 252)

The narrator's search for culture, and cultural memory, is a search for deep history as well. She feels that she has not suffered, as the people around her so clearly have; thus the American observations are tinged with a moral unease and self-consciousness, with Hampl essentially marveling at her own naïveté even as she meticulously details the stark lives of others. In this she follows the great American literary tradition of the innocent abroad, as Mark Twain and Henry James had sketched. As an American she finds herself the privileged deliverer of jeans (a Czech obsession) and cigarettes, living with the Czech assumption that she is wealthy—which, comparatively, she is—and submerged in the intellectual, artistic, and political education that had evaded her in midwestern, Catholic, middle-class,

sheltered America. Indeed, the May 1945 exodus of Nazi troops is so recent for the grand city that she often sees framed photos propped on its street corners, where parents (she realizes suddenly, with awe, that they are still alive, having outlived their young children) have placed flowers on memorials for their dead offspring.

While Kafka and Rilke recoiled from Prague, and found it difficult to view the city with objective distance of fondness, Hampl readily admits in her afterword, written ten years later in 1991 for a commemorative edition, that

> I was entranced. Even as I acknowledged its misery, I accepted utterly its national anguish—required it, even. As a young American aggrieved by the Vietnam War ... I wasn't ... looking for history, but for that more dangerous elixir: purity. How sentimental it was possible to be, contemplating Prague's weird isolation in the center of Europe, its gray beauty, its moral presence, as I stood in the Kampa under a flowering chestnut tree, the flimsy white blossoms stained with red falling all around me, as I stared down at the dark Vltava, the cool blue of my American passport snug in the zippered pocket of my backpack.
>
> (p. 311)

THE CONTEMPLATIVE TRADITION

In an era of Western intellectual atheism and agnosticism, Hampl again swam against the tide—choosing the daunting challenge of exploring the Western mystical tradition in *Virgin Time: In Search of the Contemplative Life* (1992). Part travelogue through Italy, Spain, and California and part wonder, examination, and questioning, this mixed-genre work revisits her earlier memoir's sense of a ceremonial quest or hunt—or in Christian terms, Jesus' disappearance into the desert to receive wisdom. Like Augustine, the memoir's style, although contemplative, is always tempered with the prosaic. The earthbound narrator weaves in dialogues and records of interviews (for example, with a Detroit-born nun transplanted to a Carmelite monastery in Italy) amid the journeys, and probes the loveliness of the nature that surrounds her.

This religious searching becomes a pilgrimage; in an interview with Maureen Abood, Hampl emphasizes the humility that is required in such a journey. *Virgin Time* predates, and sets a template for, such immensely popular narrative quests as *Eat, Pray, Love* by Elizabeth Gilbert. However, Hampl grounds herself in the Western tradition rather than voyaging to yogic discovery in India or to love in Thailand. Married, without children, Hampl duly records brief phone calls to her husband, who waits supportively at home as she carves out space for her soul-seeking.

Titled perhaps less evocatively in its translation of the phrase than in the original language, near the end of her exploration Hampl defines *temps vierge* with a quotation from Thomas Merton, the American mystic writer:

> The contemplative life must provide an area, a space of liberty, of silence, in which possibilities are allowed to surface and new choices—beyond routine choice—become manifest. It should create a new experience of time, not as stopgap stillness, but as *"temps vierge"*—not a blank to be filled or an untouched space to be conquered and violated, but a space which can enjoy its own potentialities and hopes—and its own presence to itself. One's *own* time. But not dominated by one's own ego ... open to others—*compassionate* time, rooted in the sense of common illusion and in criticism of it.
>
> (pp. 224–225)

Initiating her tour in Italy, Hampl's tour group of British cohorts, with their frequent hounding of her as the sole American of the group, soon drop away. But solitude is bliss. Aptly, the narrator is reborn when she ventures out alone, essentially taking part in a joyful soul cleansing at an ancient Carmelite monastery where the nuns welcome travelers. Here the readers are educated regarding the various orders and ways of Franciscans and nuns, their Renaissance traditions that have abided for centuries. However, the writer maintains an easy intimacy and humor in depicting those who have been called into religious vocations, and her prose emphasizes their humanity.

The precepts followed by the Carmelite order in Assisi require that they provide shelter for those who ask for it, and so Hampl receives a plain windowed room, which she treasures, and follows the calls to Mass and to prayer. The world recedes—what is distilled comes into finer focus—and this is what she is seeking, to know

what matters: what lies beyond the words to the prayer, the contemplation. She finds herself drawn toward the stray shards of memory that float up from her St. Paul girlhood. Time becomes amorphous for Hampl: "I was elsewhere. I was long gone" (p. 107).

Throughout her travels, stays, and retreats Hampl manages to convey the affability and humor of the Franciscan monks and of the nuns that she encounters—their irreverence—and helps to extend the reader's empathy toward these very religious vocations and the choices they imply. Rather than mock, as some contemporary memoirists do their Catholic beginnings and the adults who represent the system, she honors their calling to forsake material things and even friends and family, beginning with the radical tales of St. Francis, "a joyous mystic who *needed* to suffer the great pain of his age, because not to suffer ... was not to live" (p. 121). For these dedicated members of the various orders, each defined by its individual spirit, the work is to pray and to find God. As Hampl observes:

> They *liked* poverty, not as a condition, but as a dynamic process.... Finally, however, the Church was just a place, not life itself. Life was prayer. And that was to be found in every second of every minute of all the days of their lives.... *The life of the gaze*—that's what they were after, a way of life that trained attention beyond the physical, beyond will and desire. Such a life made possible the concentration that was the real point of their vow of poverty. (p. 147)

Peace and solitude, praise and prayer recur as the motifs of life in the cloister or along the pilgrimage. The conventional sense of time deserting her, Hampl continues to angle her own writer's gaze on the seemingly small things: snatches of conversation, interactions witnessed. As in *A Romantic Education,* sometimes these anecdotes prove more memorable in their imagery or recorded dialogue than any spiritual thought; as metaphors, they are meant to embody spiritual thinking, even spiritual teachings about what is truly important.

One such incident takes place in Lourdes, where Hampl sees an extraordinarily handsome and vibrant man with his wife in the hotel restaurant; she slowly notices the inability of his arms to function, then his wife feeding him, and then his smallness in a wheelchair. And yet the obvious gestures of love and affection between them are what holds her gaze. While her pilgrimage is thronged with the expected individuals suffering and looking for solace and healing from that suffering, Hampl—with her snapshot mind—zooms in on this couple's love made manifest in spite of all the striving and processions and hopeful seeking; this love, she suggests, is what stands and abides above all. And this is what the narrator keeps close to her heart from her solitary visit there.

As she finds herself surrounded by the throngs of people and the chanting of the Rosary, the revelation for Hampl is that her awe is directed toward the communal moment, which is in itself divine, spiritual. What Scripture exposes, she learns, is "the fact that we are a People," and that in itself is holy (p. 179).

Later, on the remote California coast, Hampl enters into sessions of meditative silence with her fellow seekers. At the monastery called Rosethorn amid the redwoods, the retreat's silences and its concomitant work of gardening—weeding and harvesting—nourish and focus her spirit. Hampl, consistently unsentimental and sober in her narration, also observes that in the background is the noise of clear-cutting. The nuns have lost their fight against the logging company, but as the Sisters observe, the loggers are also human.

At the end of the day, as the secular and sacred merge in the imagery and metaphor of these three places, Hampl does not detail her own spiritual beliefs among her observations; however, in a statement, the author describes herself as aiming for paganism but reaching pantheism. Although *Virgin Time* is presented as a spiritual search, critics have taken issue with her avoidance of larger questions of faith. Paul Elie noted this omission in *Commonweal:*

> *Virgin Time* is distinguished by ardor, candor, and elegant prose. No saint, Hampl nevertheless keeps good notes. But in her willingness to sidestep the real questions of faith, even as faithful Christians sponsor her own spiritual growth, she leaves one

feeling that she is little different from the pilgrims she stands apart from—a tourist regarding the holy places as settings for her portraits, going on pilgrimage mainly to confirm the impressions that she brought with her from home.

ESSAYS ON THE POWER OF MEMORY IN POETRY AND MEMOIR

Hampl's most intellectually rigorous and engaging examinations of other writers are collected in *I Could Tell You Stories: Sojourns in the Land of Memory* (1999). This work emerges as landmark creative nonfiction, especially in its meditations on the art of memoir. Its essays, particularly effective in their focus and discipline, take on weighty literary subjects—among them Walt Whitman and St. Augustine, Czeslaw Miłosz and Sylvia Plath—and argue their points cogently. This literary examination of memory as integral and powerful in the writer's art won critical accolades for its contemplation of this psychological force and its role in our lives.

If Fitzgerald is the grandfather-exile that haunts Hampl's St. Paul with his incessant yearning for something more, the green light to come, Whitman provided radical sustenance and lyrical guidance during the writer's self-described immersion in the protest culture against the Vietnam War.

In acknowledging her own move from poetry to prose, Hampl mentions the attractiveness of Whitman's role as a prose stylist as well as poet; it gives him greater authority and accessibility, even charm. In his prose Hampl finds the innocence of the "pure idea," America shimmering in its "refracted identity" (p. 49). Looking back, Hampl observes the complexities in his language that her younger self missed, or simply refused to recognize in that difficult period. In *Leaves of Grass* she notes a leaning toward privacy in spite of the public language and, in the missives from his poetic self to the reader's own, the ringing advice for the reader to go and do his or her own work likewise.

"What She Couldn't Tell" and "Czeslaw Miłosz and Memory" read as two very divergent accounts of Eastern Europeans, one an anonymous immigrant woman—Mrs. Beranek, Hampl's tutor in the Czech language—and the other a world-famous poet, essayist, and memoirist who also sought refuge in the United States. But both grapple with the heritage of terror-filled memory. The marked difference is that while Mrs. Beranek seems to have sought to hide in the States because of her husband's mysterious, never-revealed war crimes, Miłosz seeks exile as a Polish poet.

Nevertheless, Hampl wishes to demonstrate something of the heavy weight of remembrance and to emphasize its public, impersonal dimension during the cold war era; despite the differences, theirs is a shared remembrance, quite possibly unimaginable for the American reader: "Seen in this light, the work of memory becomes politically dynamic, and personal testimony approaches danger, for its purpose becomes not only elegy but survival.... Memory, for a small nation ... *is* the nation" (p. 84). James Joyce made the same claim about Ireland and its long memory in his work.

Appropriately, this leads into the next subject in the collection, Edith Stein, a nun and writer who literally smuggled her testimony perilously through World War II Germany. The piece reads like a short biography. In a fascinating retelling of the little-known Stein, who converted to Catholicism from Judaism, Hampl reinforces the spiritual ideals and reverence toward faith that reverberate through most of her nonfiction. She traces this woman pilgrim and memoirist from childhood, then teenage atheism, through baptism into the Catholic Church (after reading the autobiography of St. Teresa of Avila). Having earned a doctorate with a brilliant dissertation, Stein—also a gifted linguist—teaches literature and history as a Catholic college professor until the Nazi decree against Jewish teachers in 1933 ends her career. Stein enters a Carmelite monastery in Cologne, Germany, and the accompanying full-time employment in prayer and contemplative life.

Hampl notes that Stein seeks, as a mystic in her contemplation, ultimately oneness with God and with the suffering in the world. Perhaps her most lasting legacy is her stunning integrity and

courage in the face of the encroaching Nazis in Germany. Hampl draws attention to Stein's sense of sacrifice. The superiors try to protect her by moving her (and her sister, who had also converted) to a sanctuary in Holland. The tone turns more desperate. Throughout this period Stein works on her autobiography, but it is never completed.

In 1941, although in hiding, Stein is discovered by the Nazis who—despite the outcry of the church—ship all Jews who converted to Catholicism to a transfer camp and then to Auschwitz. Stein understands the sacrifice when the soldiers arrive, saying that she and her sister would go for (the good of) their people, and then, from the train, tells a witness she would never see her home again, understanding that she was to be killed.

Citing the Greek root of the word "martyr" meaning "to witness," Hampl points out a related Sanskrit root, *smar,* meaning "to remember" (p. 127). Stein, then, offers her written memory of her own Jewish family, in all its humanity, in the face of racial hatred.

However, on one point, the author notes, Stein remains silent: the circumstances of her conversion. How this occurred, and what event or contemplation exactly spurred the dramatic decision of her conversion, remains a mystery Stein refuses to divulge. Hampl seems to honor this reticence, and indeed has held up reticence as an admirable element in memoir writing.

The essayist's choice of Edith Stein's life as a subject for her writing is telling. She depicts the woman, in all of her complexity, as the Catholic Church views her—essentially, as a hero. Through Hampl's telling of a little-known life, the reader too grows to admire Stein's unwavering faith, commitment, and integrity, and the humility in her greatness. The Catholic Church canonized Edith Stein in 1998.

Hampl's placement of the Sylvia Plath essay directly after this story is an effective one, reinforcing the passion, authority, and integrity of Plath's vision, poetics, and even her final act. In offering an interpretation of the poetry at the end of Plath's life, Hampl interestingly uses Simone Weil's ideas of the "decreation" or "affliction" of self.

Such affliction changes the rules into paradox: death as rebirth, loss as freedom. The fevered ambition of the young poet leads ultimately to the metaphorical scorching, in Weil's sense of the term, of the self—born of extreme psychological, psychic, and social degradation, felt as utter anguish. The autobiographical lyric voice, according to Hampl, which tends to inflate the self's experience, then transforms into an impersonal "post-autobiographical" voice—in Plath's case, the otherworldly, ultra-authoritative voice of the *Ariel* poems, with their tone beyond any everyday feeling, distilled to an "urgency of utterance" (p. 149). Hampl links the mythical language of these grim but undeniably powerful poems to the mythic figure that the self has become:

> Poetry's essence is not to show or to tell as we say of fiction, but to reveal. This means the poet is not really in control, great as that illusion may sometimes be, especially in highly formal poetry. The illusion is great in Sylvia Plath's poems. Her form is meticulous, her imagination refined, severe, her vision at the extreme edge of the sayable.
>
> (p. 153)

Hampl notices in the lyrics the agonizing weight of "effort and impotence and exhaustion" that crown them (p. 158). At the same time, she emphasizes the spiritual drive, beyond pieties, from variations on death toward redemption and rebirth—as gleaned from Plath's (unpublished) original ordering of the collection, which was designed to end on the word "spring."

In the essay "The Invention of Autobiography," Hampl focuses on the *Confessions* of St. Augustine, setting the stage in his fourth-century sociohistorical place as a Catholic bishop in a Mediterranean seaport. She reminds us of Augustine's late-life baptism and his age (forty-three) at writing this plea addressed to God. As soul-searching as any modern writer, Augustine's *confessio* is his "life quest for God" and "can never be finished" (p. 178). His is the intimate language of renewal. And in the quest for memory's intelligence, its mystery, its limitless depths, he seeks to "meet [him]self" (p. 169), or find his soul.

The struggling uncertainty that pervades the tone of Augustine's work, Hampl argues, keeps the language passionate and alive; these qualities are what lend the classic its raw power. The dynamic process of questioning, not the act of converting, rule his book, which serves as both urgent plea and meditation. A man of faith, he nevertheless longs for meaning.

As Hampl follows Augustine to the end of his life, she depicts him in a cell with the Psalms of David he had asked to have hung on the walls, "praying his way out of this world, merged at last into the Word" (p. 183). Or, one could say, merged into poetry.

Training her eye more broadly toward literary form, Hampl examines the ever-more-popular genre of memoir in "Memory and Imagination" and "The Need to Say It." Hampl describes the form as nearer to lyric poetry rather than prose: "Strangely enough, contemporary memoir, all the rage today as it practically shoves the novel off the book review pages, has its roots not in fiction which it appears to mimic and tease, but in poetry. The chaotic lyric impulse, not the smooth drive of plot, is the engine of memory.... Shards glinting in the dust" (p. 224). Franz Kafka and Rainer Maria Rilke, she suggests, also claimed that memory and not experience rule the imagination.

As a memoirist, Hampl recognizes the transformation that is implicit in transcribing one's version of events but also the authority or power that writers gain by shaping their world this way. This, she states, stands as a primary purpose or motivation in writing a memoir. To control meaning and memory, according to the author, is to control history and, ultimately, reality.

Writing candidly, Hampl honors the shards and fragments of images—the mostly unacknowledged messiness—that become the details that drive the memoir forward. She emphasizes the active, not static, nature of the potent detail in capturing a moment. These details or moments satisfy both writer and reader as they grasp what little can be had of the truth of the often fragmented pieces of experience.

The past's radiance, whether beautiful or terrible, is what draws Hampl to choose the memoir form for her writing. "To write one's life is to live it twice, and the second living is both spiritual and historical, for a memoir reaches deep ... as it seeks its narrative form and ... grasps the life-of-the-times as no political analysis can" (p. 37). Just as Hampl evokes middle-class 1950s St. Paul in her prose, popular memoirs have evoked the desperate poverty of the slums of Limerick, Ireland—as in Frank McCourt's *Angela's Ashes* (1996)—or bohemian New York City in the 1960s in Patti Smith's *Just Kids* (2010).

To lie, she acknowledges, may be part and parcel of the process of remembering and recording. Hampl addresses the fact of falsification or invention within memoir writing (hence, the alliance of memory with imagination) in the quest for a greater truth: writing not about what one knows but to find out what one knows. In "Other People's Secrets" she offers anecdotes of friends, and even her mother, who feel cautious (will the memoirist use this conversation in her writing?) or angry and betrayed when they find themselves within the author's pages.

Nevertheless, the urge to commemorate, whether righteous or misguided, remains the memoirist's spur and all that they see and hear their domain. Hampl confesses herself to be continually surprised by other people's fury at finding themselves in her writing, where "imagination take[s] on the lost life, even a whole world, bringing it to the only place it can live again, reviving it in the pools and freshets of language" (p. 225).

And so the spiritual theme resurges, as Hampl hints at how language can serve to revive a lost past: death and rebirth once more. Perhaps the best example of this in Hampl's own writing is the memoir of her St. Paul girlhood, *The Florist's Daughter,* which conveys and reimagines her parents' old age, infirmity, and finally their quiet, middle-class and dignified deaths.

MEMOIR WRITING AS CULTURAL SHIFT

Another timely inquiry into the memoir form emerges in *Tell Me True: Memoir, History, and Writing a Life* (2008), a volume in which Hampl

and her coeditor, the historian Elaine Tyler May, have gathered fourteen original essays by memoirists and historians. As popular nonfiction, even blogs, swing from third-person omniscient to first person narrator, or "facts to voice" (p. 4), this volume provides an important record of this cultural shift.

The editors' introduction suggests that the memoir raises new questions about how the reader can successfully distinguish between fact and fiction, truth or invention. These questions of authority and authenticity have touched a whole host of works and have perhaps been raised in the press most vocally concerning such memoirs as James Frey's *A Million Little Pieces* (2003). Historians have also been called into question for their factual integrity, or their use of sources. Whatever the subject, the editors observe that writers are struggling through a mélange of genres that can no longer boast the comfort of solid borders, pure separation. What is at stake? "Nothing less ... than the search for our individual and shared truth" (p. 6). The testimonials in this volume represent the dynamic and complex process of locating meaning.

Significantly, the introduction names *The Autobiography of Malcolm X* (1965) as the most influential and important autobiographical work of the twentieth century: "a personal story, but one properly read as history, taught as history" (p. 5). The editors also cite the Holocaust's and Gulag's "vast bibliography of memoirs" (p. 5) and memoirs springing from the women's movement, which coined the statement "The personal is political." Hampl and May contend that history no longer reads as formal and impersonal. Even the novel's territory has been encroached upon by the memoir.

In today's literary culture, historians, journalists, poets, and fiction writers can all be memoirists, according to the editors. For example, Helen Epstein, in her essay "Coming to Memoir as a Journalist," details her journey as a writer who in 1976 finally convinced her editors at the *New York Times Magazine* to assign her an article about the children of Holocaust survivors. The piece struck such a chord that she turned it into a book, *Children of the Holocaust.* Based on "extensive research and in-depth interviews" but serving the collective function of healing, it braided "personal narrative, oral history and reportage because the concept of intergenerational psychic trauma was then new ... and I felt obliged to produce more persuasive evidence than my own experience" (p. 52). This book, which was widely translated, helped create an "international second-generation community" (p. 52).

Hampl's own essay within the anthology, "You're History," revisits her trip to Prague in the 1970s and tells the story of that journey in retrospect. Initially the prose conveys the workings of the writer's mind in the process of working out a biography on her grandmother, questioning her limited sources, shelving the project, then returning to it via a commemoration. From the broken images she shapes a rhapsody of sorts.

Candidly, Hampl also brings the reader to her work from the point of view of daughter, saying that she wrote *The Florist's Daughter* out of her "raw urgency to evoke that lost world as, finally, [her] mother was being lost to [her]" (p. 143). She finds that modesty, personal and familial, can stand as the actual subject in her book. Although the writer did not traverse the globe as with several of her previous works, this was also history, "history from the inside"; "my bit of truth, put ... forward on the great heap of history" (p. 144). Not war or political death or exile, but the ordinary happiness afforded by modesty. This, though fragile and lost time and time again, she claims, is what we are striving for after all.

A GREENHOUSE GIRLHOOD

With *The Florist's Daughter* (2007) Hampl blends elegy and history and returns to those themes that have reverberated through most, if not all, of her earlier works. Here the persistent shrapnel of memory that had crept through her consciousness, even at a Carmelite cloister in Assisi, are held up and examined at all angles, in the light of memory. Nostalgia? Perhaps. But Hampl defends the notion of nostalgia as sweet, a yearning for community, one's place and kin. The graceful, lucid prose is comfortable in the

intimate knowledge of its subject, the family, or Hampl's people.

While St. Paul is evoked as more than a backdrop or setting, rather almost as a character in the novel (its ice skating, its mid-May lilac-heavy air, the greenhouse where she played), the subjects the author pursues and paints are her parents. Even she herself, as the daughter, is peripheral to the ebb and flow of the adults' dramatic action. Her work stands essentially as a tribute to both parents.

In order to return to these fragments of memory and reimagine them, Hampl employs a frame, the singular convention of writing her mother's obituary with one hand as she holds her dying mother's hand with the other, an approach predictably disdained by the nurses. As she scrawls the ostensible obit, which presumably becomes the volume held in the reader's hand, she dips into asides to the reader:

> It's time to look at the picture. Not a photograph. Later we'll look at more photographs, the way every family does, making much of frozen moments, the icons of ancestry, the dead laughing right in your face, or just staring that noncommittal historical gaze. And before this is over I'll have to pick a photograph of Leo the Lion [Hampl's nickname for her mother] for her obit in the *Pioneer Press*. I have one in mind. But that can wait.
>
> (p. 68)

For her mother, as for Hampl, words are everything.

The memoir dwells equally, however, on the devotion and moral strength of the father. When *The Florist's Daughter* names, and indeed radiates, the traditional midwestern values of modesty, tolerance, and prudence, it best conveys these through Stanislaus Rudolf, the Czech father, spotlighting his careful dedication to his florist business, his fortitude as apparent in his love of the icy Minnesota winter, and his hard work. This is a man who sees and believes the best in everyone around him, even when he gets burned. While his sought-after arrangements decorate the mansions of St. Paul, he remains the service provider, handsome as a film star yet humble. The society ladies, the rich, love him—cooing "Oh *Stan!*" at his handiwork but remaining a step above and beyond—even as he mingles and interacts easily with them (p. 35).

Her stubbornly innocent father, always believing the best in people, not really ambitious beyond his station, neither criticizes nor judges this crowd, even when they are delinquent on their accounts. In multiple instances Hampl demonstrates to the reader his fatalism, a trait that alternately maddens and bemuses his daughter, a passivity that she sees as the gist of his character to the end of his life. Her attitude, in turn, is not one of impatience but, echoing her father's spirit, one of wonder and bewilderment at his eternal lack of anger, his eternal forgiveness of people who, he believes, can't be changed.

A fair employer and a decent man, Stan treats his workers well. The one business venture he undertakes late in life, the risky buyout of a legendary florist business in town, goes sour. And her father, tellingly, is left holding the bag, not angry, never in a temper, but shaking his head in disbelief at the foibles of men less honorable than himself.

His belief in beauty, the odd-numbered stalks he has a flair for displaying, he passes down to his daughter. Hampl links his Christmas garlands to Catholic teachings, as the "*outward and visible sign* ... of an *inward and spiritual grace*" (p. 79). He brings quietude in his flower arranging.

Hampl elegantly inscribes her father's artistic bent: "He waited all his life for the chairwomen of the world to admit that beauty had rules, was a unity and not a bunch of random gestures, and that elegance was a matter of classic, indisputable forms" (p. 78). Her Czech father, in one sense, represents the aesthetic, artistic power in the family. He also retains the moral power.

His goal for his daughter is to keep her innocent and wholesome, just as he works to keep himself "one of the strenuously innocent" (p. 149). His marriage too remains faithful and honorable, for he is nothing if not consistent, even when he lets slip to his daughter that he thought—hoped—he would soon be left alone. In her parents' twilight years, he only acknowledges that her mother used to be so sweet, and now has, perplexedly, turned out to be "quite a handful" (p. 167). Hampl later learns from an old

bleached blond Czech flame (in sharp contrast to his "mixed" marriage to the Irish American Mary) that he had said to her, "You're the one I should have married" (p. 184). In light of his steady-as-a-rock character, this comes as a shocking revelation, one that Hampl refuses to interpret or analyze. She lets the incident stand without comment. As it turns out, Stan's heart disease advances and he dies first; his wife outlives him after all, and he never receives the respite he dared imagine.

Stan is not a book reader, never one to show interest in his culture, although his own mother becomes central to Hampl's childhood. Stan's signature trait of wonder is reserved for daily life.

The mother's role, on the other hand, is to pass the literary torch, the gift of language. She is the history devourer and storyteller, passing on the details of the party to her daughter the morning after by elaborating at length on the choice details or telling snatches of dialogue—always from the perspective of the outsider peering in, Hampl makes clear, never pretending to be one of the ritzy crowd. Meanwhile the daughter listens rapt at the kitchen counter as her mother fills in the scene, painting it lovingly with words. It turns out that Mary, the library clerk, was a frustrated author herself. She always wanted to write books, she informs her daughter near the end of her life. Ultimately, the narrator comes to realize, she owes a greater debt to her mother than to her father for the artistic bent she has inherited, the drive to create and express in words.

The mother-daughter relationship is curious: storyteller and audience, the mother generally the cynical, knowing one with the Celtic grudge against England fortified by her reading of histories. Later, the mother builds a virtual shrine to her daughter in the spare room over the years, overflowing with clippings and saved papers extolling her daughter's accomplishments. Hampl gradually takes over the role as both parents' caregiver, chauffeur to medical appointments, companion; her brother, occasionally mentioned in anecdotes from her childhood, now lives on the West Coast and reappears only sporadically within the memoir.

A heavy smoker and drinker all her life, Irish Mary also bares her dark side, as when she proclaims, fallen on the sidewalk, that she wishes she were dead. She survives grand mal seizures, the suffering of a mastectomy, botched cataract surgery that leaves her half-blind (and still trying to read), a broken knee (twice), and more medical complications. At the end she lies with wet breathing, the death rattle, in the nursing home.

Hampl offers the portrait of her mother as imperfect and human. Through memories, she is able to paint a portrait of Mary as a person with affection and spite, pride and anger and frustration. This discerning woman who described the St. Paul soirees succeeds in passing the greatest narrative sensibility, a gift, to her writer daughter.

Stylistically, the grown daughter-writer remains a vibrant narrative presence in the novel, not disappearing into the story as with most memoir voices. As she describes key scenes, her commentary weaves in and out, but as a separate voice looking back in retrospect, rather than caught up in the present (and present-tense) action. The effect is not intrusive, but the reader stands aware of the distinction between past and present, regularly reminded that the unfolding events are indeed memories recalled in serenity.

At the same time, choice dialogue—as in Mary's cri de coeur, "*I wish I were dead*" (p. 161)—drive the narrative, words Hampl replays like a detective investigating a particularly mysterious incident, or perhaps more appropriately, like a poet, seeking the evanescent truth of their now-vanquished spirits. The telling detail also brings the reader more deeply into this exploration; her father, when cheated by his business partner and others, makes a fist in his pocket. Refusing to blame, point fingers, or file a lawsuit, he characteristically represses his fury. "The good, the true, the beautiful," Hampl writes. "Our father" (p. 196). At his death, she murmurs her thanks—a self-described innocent, wholesome, good daughter.

When he arranges his flowers, she says that he "didn't arrange them. It was himself he arranged, standing at the ready, sharp knife moving over his materials lightly, surely, like a Japanese

ink brush" (p. 82). As Hampl has delineated herself as a lover of metaphor, this may be extended to herself in her practice of the art of the memoir, as indeed it would apply to any memoirist's experience in recording and thus shaping, rewriting past events. In choosing and arranging words and incidents, linked to but seemingly outside of herself, Hampl suggests, she is writing herself.

OTHER MUSES: DVORAK AND MATISSE

In *Spillville* (1987), the writer delves into the world of classical music. Hampl reimagines a real-life visit that occurred when the composer Antonin Dvořák visited small-town Iowa. In her fiction, she faithfully captures the 1893 midwestern landscape and speculates on the town's reception of this temporarily immigrant composer, who suddenly finds himself in the New World context as a church organist in tiny Spillville, Iowa.

This is a place where nature and musical aesthetics blend. The process of artistic discovery and inspiration shapes the biographical for Hampl, who has long professed that her art features much hunting and gathering. Dvořák, relishing the fields and hills that surround the town, decides to include birdsong in his active collection of sounds for his *American Quartet* and endeavors to record the native calls precisely as he listens. In the end, the composer's treks through the nineteenth-century countryside, as depicted and enhanced by the powerful engravings of Hampl's fellow Minnesotan Steven Sorman, are infused with a passionate intensity through Hampl's spiritually touched prose.

Nearly twenty years later, Hampl turns to the visual arts in *Blue Arabesque: A Search for the Sublime* (2006). This is actually a return to familiar ground, as art and architecture have long served as a wellspring for much of her nonfiction. Interweaving historical and interpretive analyses, the work examines aesthetic process and inspiration but also the feminine form as rendered by the hand of Henri Matisse, an artist who has greatly inspired Hampl's work for the whole of her writing career.

Critics have noted the author's obsession with the aesthetic and her personal canonization of the writers and artists who most affect and influence her. In her nonfiction quest for the sublime, she easily and deliberately confounds the Catholic and the secular—attributing holy significance to a painting, for example, as something touched and transmitted by the sacred beyond—and links her pilgrimages and relics to an artist's places and objects. In so doing, Hampl conveys the highest regard and, truly, worship for the high art she treasures.

With Matisse the author is finally able to equate the aesthetic and the religious in a literal sense, for his culminating masterpiece was his design of a chapel near Nice, France. Her entire foray into Matisse's art is spurred by the same painting that inspired her first book of poems. Indeed, the title poem of Hampl's initial collection of lyric poetry, *Woman Before an Aquarium* (1978), marks a similar exploration of the tension inherent in the feminine: between creator and creation, stasis and action, perception and reception.

The poem subsumes the reader in its eerie tone; amid its half-submerged setting, the goldfish move their mouths futilely but are unable to speak. Likewise in the poem, the subject of the painting wants more than to sit weightily on her cushions; she wants to be a mermaid, but more than combing her hair, she wishes to swim. Ultimately, the commentator on the scene, who is the narrative voice in the poem and the viewer of Matisse's figure, finds herself equally afraid, equally mindful of her goal.

The fear may lie in the danger of the living woman narrator merging into or becoming the painted woman, wordless as the fish swimming round and round in the fishbowl that the narrator, ironically, had insisted upon buying. The tragedy lies in powerlessness—not possessing the magic of the enchantress but rather enduring the stasis of the mermaid eternally stranded on the rocks, who combs and combs her hair and thinks only of when she can finally dive off and swim. This Lorelei is not perilous except to herself; the implication is that to be merely viewed is a terrifying fate.

Since this literary debut, Hampl has often described her own artistic process as the cadging of images or snapshots in time. Remarkably, a full thirty-four years later, she returns to the first love and—on the surface, at least—the first theme of her literary career, which inspired her title poem. *Blue Arabesque* crisscrosses East and West in its investigation of Matisse's artistic genius. But like most of Hampl's published works, it does much more, taking in its long gaze the artist's process, inspiration, and the feminine form as rendered by the master's hand. The tension between objectification and purposeful action remains a central motif of the work.

In *Blue Arabesque,* Matisse's genius represents the grail for the essayist, and her role is to pay homage. Hampl argues that by devoting himself to configuring the "self" of the odalisque, reproducing again and again the languid female figure draped and lounging (popularly exemplified by Edouard Manet's 1863 *Olympia*), Matisse tracks "the larger mystery of creation" (p. 28). It remains to Hampl, then, to trace the odalisque as well. And so the narrator takes her magnifying glass to the canvases and stories of Matisse's working habits and relationships with his models to find the sense or sensibility behind the masks of blank, impassive artist and poser. The essayist has license to paint her own word-filled canvas.

On her quest, Hampl tracks Matisse to Nice and divulges the personalities behind several of his models, transformed as they were on canvas to "these ripe fruits" (p. 56) upon divans that the narrator says she loves and collects on picture postcards as her own miniature gallery. Again, she gives names—the French Henriette, the Italian Zita—and at least some personality to the models, as she detects in Zita's expression a note of worry. But the feminist view remains necessarily complex, speculative and ambiguous, drawing from the writer's imaginative wells to ascribe equal status to the model, or at least to pull Matisse temporarily from the pedestal of Grand Master: "Or is it—and I give over to this thought—that she feels a surprising empathy that perhaps only a model could feel. It is an abashed look ... a brief solidarity that he has been reduced, as she is daily, to a pose" (p. 59).

Aesthetically, Hampl suggests that she is drawn to Matisse for his sense of decoration and ornament, and she links this magnetic lure again to her father, ascribing her sense of kinship with the paintings to her upbringing bathed in the greenhouse activity of arrangements and flourishes, "where the cut flowers waited in tubs ... beauty for its own sake, for the show of it" (pp. 77–78). She goes on to suggest that the decorative arts harbor an appeal that transcends class, something that Matisse, with his working-class roots, would approve:

> Matisse stood like a lightning rod between the sumptuous aesthetic of the rich that demanded the fabrics of Bohain and the proud craft of the laborers of the muddy town who provided the objects that, alone, connected the two worlds. Beauty was business; it was food and shelter. In such a hierarchical world, a world in which beauty ... provides the very bread on the table, poverty cannot be untouched by the glories it is consigned to create. It seems Matisse never forgot that the hunger of the poor is, as the old union hymn has it, for bread—and roses.
>
> (p. 80)

Hampl travels briefly to the Middle East and to Turkey and records her experience of a Turkish bath, then heads for the Côte d'Azur to rediscover the light that Matisse loved. In researching the housemaid or night nurse/models Matisse employed late in life, Lydia Delectorskaya and Monique Bourgeois, she notably rewrites the odalisque to place the figure in a more active position than the static, passive manner depicted by the paintings. Even in their leisure, *especially* in their leisure, the women in the paintings, she offers, meditate upon or take in the colors, patterns, and forms dancing around them. And, it is implied, in their deep perceiving—like the poet or writer, any artist—they essentially create or transform what they see, as Matisse did. These lives or sensibilities are more than echoes of their painter's.

Indeed, the models go on to live their own lives after they pose for the great artist. Lydia Delectorskaya reportedly commits suicide in old age, and Monique Bourgeois leaves immediately after her sessions to take a new name: Soeur Jacques-Marie. After posing for four canvases,

Matisse's final model, fascinatingly, rejects her role and enters a cloister, where Hampl encounters her on a trip to France. This is the chapel Matisse designs and paints, a culmination of his life's work, infused by the mystery, peace, and lavish colors he seeks: another instance of the divinity of detail. In the author's search, the figure viewed has the last word, or at least the last definitive action in her relinquishment of self and devotion to the Catholic divine, as Hampl imagines her rising boldly from her divan to pursue her own life's work.

Throughout her works, Hampl notes the essential images and conversations and records her thought processes. As she has stated in interviews, the memoir is as much a story of a thought as a story of the events that take place. As a form, it shares with the essay the license to meander and muse, question and scrutinize as it goes. In this vision, then, for Hampl, the wonderings and wanderings have led her once again to the heart of the matter: art and the sacred sharing space in their mutual quest for truth and beauty.

Selected Bibliography

WORKS OF PATRICIA HAMPL

POETRY

Woman Before an Aquarium. Pittsburgh, Pa.: University of Pittsburgh Press, 1978.

Resort and Other Poems. Boston: Houghton Mifflin, 1983.

LITERARY NONFICTION

A Romantic Education. New York: Houghton Mifflin, 1981. Second paperback ed., Boston: Houghton Mifflin, 1992.

Spillville. Engravings by Steven Sorman. Minneapolis: Milkweed Editions, 1987.

Virgin Time: In Search of the Contemplative Life. New York: Farrar, Straus and Giroux, 1992.

I Could Tell You Stories: Sojourns in the Land of Memory. New York: Norton, 1999.

Blue Arabesque: A Search for the Sublime. Orlando, Fla.: Harcourt, 2006.

The Florist's Daughter: A Memoir. Orlando, Fla.: Harcourt, 2007.

ESSAYS, REVIEWS, AND ARTICLES

"The Lax Habits of the Free Imagination." *New York Times Book Review,* March 5, 1989, p. 1.

"Trying to Get God's Attention." *New York Times Book Review,* May 15, 1994, p. 26.

"The Whole Anne Frank." *New York Times Book Review,* March 5, 1995, p. 1.

"A Mississippi Sojourn: Two Weeks on River Time." *New York Times,* May 14, 1995.

"A Week in the Word." *Image* 9, spring 1998 (http://imagejournal.org/page/journal/articles/issue-19/hampl-essays).

"Celebration: Montreal." *New York Times,* September 29, 2002.

"Comeback for Capek." *New York Times Book Review,* December 22, 2002, p. 12.

"Whistling in the Dark: The Katherine Mansfield Notebooks." *New York Times Book Review,* March 16, 2003, p. 12.

"The Dark Heart of Description." In *Best American Essays 2009.* Edited by Mary Oliver. Boston: Mariner Books, 2009.

EDITED ANTHOLOGIES

Burning Bright: An Anthology of Sacred Poetry. New York: Ballantine, 1995.

With Dave Page. *The St. Paul Stories of F. Scott Fitzgerald*. St. Paul, Minn.: Borealis Books, 2004.

With Elaine Tyler May. *Tell Me True: Memoir, History, and Writing a Life*. St. Paul, Minn.: Borealis Books, 2008.

CRITICAL AND BIOGRAPHICAL STUDIES

Elie, Paul. *"Virgin Time: In Search of the Contemplative Life." Commonweal,* November 6, 1992, p. 27.

Harrison, Katherine. "Hammered by Art." *New York Times Book Review,* October 29, 2006, p. 16. (Review of *Blue Arabesque.*)

Healy, Meghan. "Author Patricia Hampl Speaks About Catholic Roots of the Memoir." *Fairfield Mirror,* November 3, 2009 (http://fairfieldmirror.com/2009/11/03/author-patricia-hampl-speaks-about-catholic-roots-of-the-memoir/).

"Patricia Hampl." *Contemporary Authors Online,* Gale, 2010.

Reynolds, Susan Salter. "Patricia Hampl Remembers Some More." *Los Angeles Times,* October 2, 2007 (http://articles.latimes.com/2007/oct/02/entertainment/et-book2; review of *The Florist's Daughter*).

Trussoni, Danielle. "The Hopelessness of Escape." *New York Times Book Review,* October 7, 2007, p. 16. (Review of *The Florist's Daughter.*)

PATRICIA HAMPL

INTERVIEWS

Abood, Maureen. "In Memory of Me: An Interview with Patricia Hampl." *U.S. Catholic,* September 2006.

Kehe, Patricia. "Patricia Hampl: A True Daughter of the Midwest." *Christian Science Monitor,* October 16, 2007, p. 13.

Lanpher, Katherine. "Patricia Hampl: Barnes & Noble Studio" (http://media.barnesandnoble.com/?fr_story=ad0a2236cbc988a3f96494b351278706cb672b2b&rf=sitemap).

Patterson, Margot. "Pilgrim Soul." *National Catholic Reporter,* January 11, 2008 (http://natcath.org/NCR_Online/archives2/2008a/011108/011108z.html).

Rehm, Diane. "Patricia Hampl: *The Florist's Daughter.*" National Public Radio, November 27, 2007.

Shea, Peter. "Patricia Hampl: The Bat of Minerva." University of Minnesota English Department, winter 2009 (http://english.umn.edu/faculty/videoInterviews.html 2009).

"*Shooting Star* Interviews Patricia Hampl." December 28, 2010 (http://www.shootingstaronline.org/2010/12/shootingstar-interviews-patricia-hampl.html).

LARRY HEINEMANN

(1944—)

Lea M. Williams

"TORQUE," THE TITLE of the third chapter of Larry Heinemann's debut novel, *Close Quarters* (1977), points to the energy and purpose of Heinemann's writing. Edward Frederick Palm, discussing Heinemann's novel in his dissertation, "American Heart of Darkness: The Moral Vision of Five Novels of the Vietnam War" (1983), defines the term as "the twisting or warping force exerted by the war on moral character" (p. 83). In fact, torque and its destructive consequences constitute a recurring motif in much of Larry Heinemann's work. Three of his four published long works are about the Vietnam War and its aftermath, and in them Heinemann's aggressive prose applies relentless pressure, creating haunting images of violence that force the reader to contend with the darkness of the war and its terrible consequences.

It is no exaggeration to say that the Vietnam War made Larry Curtiss Heinemann a writer. He was born on January 18, 1944, to Dorothy and John Heinemann in Chicago. Heinemann's father was a bus driver, and his mother ran a babysitting service. According to Heinemann's statements in interviews and in his memoir, *Black Virgin Mountain* (2005), his family was dominated by his father's temper, which at times manifested itself in brutal beatings of his sons. There was nothing in his home life that would have encouraged him or his three brothers—Heinemann is the second born—to become readers or creative individuals. School was a hardship, probably because of undiagnosed learning disabilities, providing no intellectual stimulation. Nevertheless Heinemann attended community college in the Chicago area, eventually receiving his associate's degree in 1966.

Heinemann's life underwent massive upheaval when he and his brother Richard were drafted in 1966. They attended basic training together at Fort Polk before Heinemann went on to advanced infantry training at Fort Knox, where he was assigned to an armored cavalry reconnaissance unit. He was shipped to Vietnam in March 1967 where he, much like the main character of his first novel, drove an armored personnel carrier. He later served in the area around Black Virgin Mountain, a significant landmark in his 2005 memoir. Upon his discharge from the army in 1968 he returned to the Chicago area, where he married Edie Smith, with whom he has two children, Sarah Catherine and Preston John. Heinemann also returned to college, earning a bachelor's degree in English from Columbia College in 1971. Heinemann's postwar years were marked by the disintegration of his family: in 1970 Heinemann's elder brother John left the family, never to be heard from again. In 1982 his youngest brother, Philip, who served as a marine in Vietnam, abandoned his wife and children without any warning. In 1992 Richard committed suicide. In the midst of this upheaval, Heinemann began writing about Vietnam, establishing a reputation as one of the important writers of the war. As a result of his work, Heinemann has received many prestigious awards, including the National Book Award in 1987 for *Paco's Story* (1986), and Guggenheim and Fulbright Fellowships. Though Heinemann has traveled to the former Soviet Union, China, and Vietnam, often as part of a group of invited writers of the Vietnam War, he has lived much of his life in Chicago, a city he highlights in his third novel, *Cooler by the Lake* (1992). As of 2011, Heinemann was on the faculty of Texas A&M University, where he was a visiting writer in residence and was working on a murder mystery.

LARRY HEINEMANN

CLOSE QUARTERS

Heinemann's debut novel, *Close Quarters*, was generously reviewed in July 1977 by Richard Lingeman in the *New York Times* ("Inside the Meat Grinder"). Lingeman described Heinemann's language as "obscene poetry," praising it for communicating the "physicality" of the Vietnam War while faulting the novel for its "awkward" and at times "excessive" prose. Despite this criticism, Lingeman situated *Close Quarters* in the growing body of literature emerging in the wake of the Vietnam War, comparing Heinemann's work to texts written by Philip Caputo and Ron Kovic, and established Heinemann's novel as an integral part of the fledgling canon of literature about the Vietnam War.

In an early scholarly study, Palm is less effusive in his praise; he describes the novel as "seriously marred by overwriting and an excess of sentiment" (p. 74). This assessment is one with which most contemporary readers, viewing the novel thirty years after its initial publication, would probably agree. While *Close Quarters* was important when published in the 1970s because it helped to legitimize the Vietnam War as a literary topic, it possesses many characteristics typical of first novels: its prose is overly dramatic, its characters are underdeveloped, and its themes are belabored.

For example, Philip Dosier, the first-person protagonist of *Close Quarters,* is a man typical to many novels about the initiation into soldiering. He arrives in Vietnam a complete innocent who has to learn the "ugly deadly music"—the title of the first chapter of the book—of the war (p. 3). In Dosier's case, his education consists of becoming part of an armored personnel carrier unit. Upon his arrival, fresh from Fort Knox, he observes the return of the reconnaissance platoon and is "astonished" by the men's "easy obscenities and shit laughs" (pp. 3, 4). He "shudder[s]" in an initial response to the "squeaks," "scratching noises," and "grindings" of the track vehicles (p. 4), which make a music to which Dosier will all too quickly become accustomed. These dirty, exhausted men are of course intended to serve as models for what Dosier will eventually become over the course of the novel: war hardened, indifferent, violent, and intensely cynical.

In addition to becoming familiar with the sounds of the vehicles that Dosier will ride for much of his time in Vietnam, he also has to learn the vocabulary unique to this environment. Heinemann recognizes that the reader too needs this lesson and provides an appendix in which he defines many of the slang terms and acronyms and explains the weapons commonly used in the novel. With this tool, the reader acquires a vicarious education via Dosier's experiences.

Dosier, now the FNG (fucking new guy) of the platoon, will experience a series of "firsts"—first time getting high, first patrol, first firefight, first kill, first time with a prostitute—that will forever strip him of his innocence, thereby conducting him into a world of experience from which he can never return. Dosier's guardian in this unknown terrain is Cross, the driver of Dosier's assigned track vehicle, the seven-three. On Dosier's first night Cross introduces him to the intimate camaraderie of the track by sharing beer, food, and "smoke"—slang for marijuana—with him. During this gathering, Dosier exposes his naïveté by revealing he has never smoked marijuana and asking, "Outside the wire. In the field. What's it like?" (p. 18). Cross has been anticipating such a question and gleefully gives Dosier more than a page-long response in which he spews forth his hatred for all of Vietnam: "There ain't one, not one square inch of muck within five or six thousand miles of here that I would fight anybody for, except what I'm standing on.... I never met a squint-eye that I would call anything but gook.... Gooks don't know how ta do shit. Can't get the hang a blackjack, don't even know how to plant somethin' simple-ass, like corn" (p. 19).

Cross's plain speech has many lessons for Dosier. First, Dosier learns what would become a commonly expressed point of view in writings about the Vietnam War: soldiers are there only to survive. The political and ideological reasons for which they were sent to Vietnam have no bearing on their daily lives on the ground. Their mission is to leave Vietnam, a country they hate because

of its poverty and unfamiliar language and culture, alive after one year. Nothing, except the welfare of their fellow soldiers, is worth risking their lives. Cross's speech emphasizes that it is nearly impossible to discern who is supportive of American troops and that he is indifferent to which Vietnamese, for whom he has no intention of giving his life, are his allies. As far as he is concerned, the Vietnamese lack human characteristics and do not merit any consideration except when they are present as obstacles that must be overcome, or when they provide services that Cross and the other soldiers want.

The soldiers buy beer, cigarettes, and drugs from the Vietnamese who always follow the Americans around in hopes of making a sale. Additionally, Vietnamese women are, predictably enough, valued by the men because they provide sexual services. Cross introduces Dosier to "Claymore Face, the greatest piece of ass this side of the Saigon River" (p. 35). Claymore Face, aptly named after the antipersonnel mines often employed by the Americans, is extremely ugly, yet prized because "she puts out like crazy" (p. 35). Dosier is not tempted by her wares on his virgin visit but sits sipping a warm beer while Cross and Rayburn, a track mechanic, take turns having sex with her. Their visit to Claymore Face is unauthorized; when they return in the track to the base, they are confronted by Sergeant Trobridge, the track commander, described earlier as "on the chunky side with a flabby face and thick wetted lips" (p. 13). This effeminizing description emphasizes the contempt that all of the men feel for Trobridge and that Dosier is meant to emulate.

While Trobridge is despised because of his unmanly "smallish waist" and "wide fleshy hips," in Heinemann's oeuvre all incarnations of authority are the recipients of harsh criticism, whether they be commissioned or noncommissioned officers (p. 13). When Cross points Dosier to Lieutenant Greer, he tells him he cannot miss him because "he's the dude with silver spoon in his mouth" (pp. 7–8). Staff Sergeant Surtees is treated with particular derision by Cross and, later, Dosier. Surtees is described as "the only man, other than the Lieutenant, wearing a shirt, the sleeves rolled in precise folds with all his insignia and rank patches" (p. 10). Surtees' insistence on following garrison protocols in the field, where the other men are dressed only in vests, separates him in a negative fashion from the rest of the soldiers and singles him out as an object of ridicule.

While Surtees is despised because of his status as a "lifer"—Heinemann defines the term in his glossary as "slang for any career military personnel. Always derogatory" (p. 344)—he is also hated because Cross and Atevo, the gunner on Dosier's track, hold him responsible for calling in a helicopter too late to save their friend Murphy, who consequently bled to death. Although the men, according to their views, have good reason to hate the by-the-book staff sergeant, their hatred is expressed in overtly racist terms. Cross calls him a "spook" and threatens to break "his nappy fucken head" (p. 20). When Quinn, a soldier who becomes Dosier's guide and best friend after Cross's departure, says goodbye to Surtees he gives him a present as a final insult and tells him to "shove it up yer fat nigger ass," after which everyone present bursts into laughter (p. 10). While the hatred for Surtees emerges in large part because of his alignment with military authority, the same kind of vitriol Cross articulates about the Vietnamese is aimed at Surtees, emphasizing that the intimate camaraderie shared by Dosier, Cross, Atevo, Quinn, and others, all of whom are white and lower class, allows for no racial difference.

The clashes between white and African American soldiers frequently involve Quinn, who says about Surtees that he is going to "toss him out a fucken plane or some shit over Harlem an' let the niggers in coon heaven stomp him for an ass-kissing whitey" (p. 159). Dosier observes neutrally that "Quinn ... was laying it out for Surtees that there was going to be a lynching" (p. 160). While the men never carry out the threats against Surtees, they do in a sense "lynch" Lavery, an African American "tunnel rat" ("a soldier who crawled into tunnels to search, usually armed with a flashlight and a .45 semiautomatic pistol," p. 347). Quinn, in a drunken state, waves his bowie knife around and challenges the men to

fight. The only one to step up is Lavery, who does so with his M-16 with the safety off. The men quickly intervene, taking Lavery's weapon away but leaving it loaded because "undeniable proof was needed" (p. 168). By the time Surtees charges in, Quinn's bowie knife is put away and all of the "white dudes" in the tent back Quinn's assertion that Lavery pulled his weapon on Quinn and that Quinn only acted to defend himself (p. 168). With no remorse, Dosier later reports that Lavery would serve 120 days in an army prison for something he never did.

Dosier successfully makes his way in this environment in part because of the acceptance his race earns for him. His belonging is solidified as he experiences events that season and harden him, including his first firefight. He reacts violently to the aftermath of the stress and fear of the encounter. He observes, "My arms shake, my fingers open and close just to feel the muscles work against the earth. I am soaked to the skin and fiery hot. There is something jammed in my throat. I feel as though I will have to puke or choke on it" (p. 45). Atevo soon appears, soothing Dosier and telling him, "get your shit together" (p. 46). Dosier is brought back to his senses only to find out that they have been fighting their allies, South Vietnamese soldiers, because they had wandered off course owing to an error on Trobridge's part. While the fight with friendly forces is no less dangerous—three ARVN (Army of the Republic of South Vietnam) soldiers are killed and fifteen injured—than a fight with the real enemy, Dosier's baptism by fire is undercut by the absurdity of the whole encounter. Not only does he learn what it is like to be under fire, he learns that the war is experienced by those fighting it, at least among the ranks, as an endeavor without a clear-cut purpose. To the men, it is all the same whether they have been fighting ARVN or North Vietnamese soldiers. In fact, Mac, a soldier who accompanies Dosier on his first ambush, brags, "I fucken told ya I got them three little mothers with the first burst. They was crouched down by that bush there, an' me an' ma E-deuce swung around right then and there an' blew their shit a-way" (p. 51). Dosier says nothing in response to Mac's bragging, but he takes a cup of coffee back to his tent where he "felt very small and lonely" (p. 52). It is unclear if his decision to leave is prompted by some objection to Mac's pride, to the letdown of the firefight, or to some combination of the two.

The moment of calm isolation permits Dosier a rare opportunity for reflection. His thoughts turn to home as he recalls childhood snowball fights with his two brothers and making angels that "were white and as deep as the snow" (p. 52). The innocence of these activities forms an obvious point of contrast to the environment Dosier now inhabits. He questions his reasons for being in Vietnam, asking himself, "What in the world am I doing here? My parents raised me on 'Thou-shalt-nots' and willow switches and John Wayne (even before he became a verb), the Iwo Jima bronze and First and Second Samuel, and always, always the word was 'You do what I tell you to do' " (p. 53). The obedience to authority drilled into him by his parents resulted in his becoming "a true son of the empire, trusting enough to buy that sorry myth of having to pay my dues—and so hauled off by the ears to sit on this cot and struggle around these woods, taking the cure" (p. 53). Of course, there are no clear answers to what he is doing there, and soon enough Dosier stops asking questions, living only in the moment as he waits for his "cure" to end.

His initiation speeds up as he experiences more "firsts." The prospect of seeing his first "Charlie" (enemy soldier) excites him, but what he sees is disappointing: a severely injured "boyish" looking man who cannot respond to any of their questions (p. 61). When the man will not stop moaning, the medic, Stepik, gives him an overdose of morphine. Dosier remarks, "I could feel my stomach go numb" in a shocked response to the murder (p. 63). Cross, once again intent on educating Dosier to their real purpose, tells him, "it was a gook.... Listen, I took a chance for Murphy, I'll take a chance for Atevo, and I'll take a chance for you, but don't ask me to take a chance for gooks. Dosier, look: the only thing more fucked up than being here, is getting killed here. Savvy?" (p. 63). Dosier says nothing else; he only glances at Stepnik, sitting with "his forty-five in his lap and his aid bag over his shoulder"

as the men leave the next morning (p. 64). Nothing more is said about the event by either men; clearly Stepnik's indifference to Vietnamese life has reached the point that he can kill without compunction or any need for justification.

As demonstrated in the next short chapter, "Moon of Atevo," Dosier absorbs Cross's lesson. Dosier is with Atevo on an ambush when they suddenly come under fire. Dosier attacks an enemy soldier, telling himself as he is on top of the man with a knife ready, "All I have to do is bring the knife down, drop it straight into his chest ... It would be like slicing twine" (p. 73). Rather than using his bayonet, he chooses to strangle the man: "Lift. Push. Squeeze. Like working a tool smooth" (p. 73). Dosier's rage at the enemy turns out to be justified when he finds out shortly after that Atevo has been killed. Dosier, having demonstrated that he has the capacity for ruthlessness deemed a necessity by Cross, is now fully initiated into the realm of experience by having killed a man at such close quarters.

The killing brings changes in Dosier. He begins taking a painkiller, Darvon, in large quantities and asks Cross if he can train to drive the track vehicles as a method of ensuring that he will not be sent on any more ambushes. Cross agrees and fulfills his commitment to training him before he is sent home. Shortly after Cross's departure, Quinn becomes Dosier's new guide and companion. Quinn is much admired by Dosier and the others because "he knew maps, compass, recon, S & D [search and destroy], ambush, and maintenance inside and out" (p. 95). Other aspects of Quinn's personality that Dosier admires include his ability to take large quantities of drugs, his indifference to all forms of authority, and his capacity for cruelty. Dosier finds much hilarity in Quinn's tormenting of a Vietnamese child in front of whom he dangles C rations as the child runs behind the track for half a mile. At the same time, Quinn throws fifty-caliber cartridges at the child's head before finally releasing the rations to him.

Dosier is more than capable of all kinds of cruel actions himself at this point. When he and the other men are guarding a woman whose hut is discovered to be "a VC hooch" they destroy her well, prompting her to say, "Fucken GI" (p. 108). Dosier's ire is then aroused and he tells her, "Well, clap your slanted eyes on this" as he proceeds to shoot her water buffalo (p. 108). Heinemann takes an entire page to describe the felling of the animal, communicating in excruciating detail the effects of the rounds on the animal as it repeatedly attempts to regain its footing. The Vietnamese owner collapses, "weeping and rocking" as the men take pictures of her, the slaughtered water buffalo, and the hut and then proceed to steal items from her home to keep as souvenirs (p. 110). Contemplating the destruction that he has helped to inflict, Dosier reflects, "And it all came on a whim. She was gook. The hooch was gook. The buff was a gook buff. But it always came with that hard-faced, uncaring, eye-aching whim; like hands squeezing down on hands.... Slowly, slowly, so slow it is only glimpsed in time-lapse, those two or three scraps of good and real and soft things left of you are sucked down into a small hard pea" (p. 110). Dosier has become all impulse when it comes to his interactions with the Vietnamese. Just as he strangled the man on impulse during the attack in which Atevo was killed, preferring to feel the man's life fade away beneath his own hands, he has again reacted, allowing the full force of his anger to be unleashed on those powerless to do anything to him. The result, evidenced by the brief moment of reflection narrated above, is that whatever goodness that may have existed in him is slowly being transformed into something like hard pieces of twisted metal because of the torque being exerted on him by the war.

The last remnants of his humanity are soon obliterated when, once again, he becomes enraged and reacts to the force of his own anger. This time he is furious that he has been shot at shortly after a mine explosion, which killed an engineer. In the aftermath of the violence, a boy of perhaps thirteen or fourteen, with an injury to his shoulder, emerges with an old man from a bunker. Dosier is supposed to guard the boy, yet he is overcome by such a strong desire to kill him that he finally shoots "the top of his head off" (p. 219). The other soldiers serve as false witnesses, as they

did against Lavery, and swear to a colonel that the boy had made a grab for Dosier's rifle. The colonel, though clearly skeptical about the story, is not interested in pursuing the matter, and Dosier gets away with the killing without any further commentary.

Dosier's wish to humiliate and injure extends to times outside of combat as well. In another atrocious scene, Dosier forces Claymore Face to perform oral sex on him and six other soldiers twice, threatening her with his forty-five when she hesitates. She does as she is told, fearfully looking at their weapons as she services soldier after soldier. While Dosier has become the kind of man who sees no problem with threatening to kill a woman if she does not provide a sexual service, a "fucking new guy" who witnesses the scene tries to tell "Sergeant Corso and the El-tee and some other dudes in the platoon, but nobody paid any attention to him until Stepik finally told him not to be such a fucking Boy Scout" (p. 261). Clearly this soldier protests because he is new to the war and has not lost his ethics as he is sure to do, according to Heinemann, when the war grinds him down. Dosier, by contrast, simply reports laconically that "after that Claymore Face didn't come around much, and nobody much cared" (p. 261).

This encounter with Claymore Face is just one of the problematic depictions of Dosier's interactions with women. In *Close Quarters* women are objectified, whether they are Asian prostitutes or Dosier's American sweetheart. When Dosier goes on leave to Tokyo he stays at the Perfect Room Hotel, a place he has chosen because he believes he will be able to find sex at a price he can afford for his entire leave. He imagines that any kind of woman can be had; indeed, in the hotel bar he finds Susie, a prostitute for whom Dosier "would pay ... cash" but with whom he wants intimacy rather than just a quick sexual experience (p. 183). In Heinemann's vision, prostitutes such as Susie can find pleasure and fulfillment while selling themselves to American soldiers. The entire chapter, "The Perfect Room," presents this male fantasy as fact as Dosier is bathed and made love to by Susie. At one point he contrasts the experience with having sex with Claymore Face, which he describes as "fucking a fat man's fist" (p. 192). Apparently Susie is a prostitute of a different kind, one who is intent on satisfying Dosier's every sexual need and is also interested in being a good companion to him as they eat at restaurants and go to the movies and theater.

Being with Susie causes Dosier to recall another idealized woman: Jennie, his girlfriend attending college back home. He reminisces about Jennie, who "liked farming because it was clean and honest work; who was just the right height in bare feet to dance with, and loved to polka most of all" (p. 185). Jennie represents a clean past when the most morally questionable actions Dosier took included having sex with Jennie in his car. While Jennie's parents clearly did not feel such activities were innocent, they seem so compared to the terrible things Dosier is doing in Vietnam.

Jennie is not only a refuge from the violence of the war, one he can escape to in memory at will when he is Vietnam; she serves in the same role once Dosier physically returns to Chicago after his tour is completed. He feels estranged from his family, not because they do not warmly welcome him but because he feels he "would always be a boy in that house" (p. 307). The only person with whom he connects is his brother Eddie, who is blind from wounds he received in Vietnam; they have an understanding based on their shared knowledge of combat. Dosier, then, is eager to leave his family to find comfort in Jennie, living in Kentucky, and the final chapter of the novel, "Climbing Down," documents how, in a clichéd section of the book, the love of a good woman helps a man to recover from his traumatic past. In fact, as soon as he sees Jennie ascending a staircase in the Brown Hotel in Louisville, Dosier asserts that "it all fell away—Quinn and the platoon and whatever was left.... I was suddenly tired and felt my shoulders go limp" (pp. 316–317).

While in reality Dosier is not magically cured of his Vietnam experience, he is well on his way to recovery thanks to Jennie's welcoming soft touch. When he moves into the apartment Jennie has found for him, he "shoved the door shut and

... was home" (p. 319). Once he finds this safe haven where Jennie is available to him to satisfy his sexual and emotional needs, he eventually confides in her all that he experienced. When he cannot sleep, and even sex does not help, he talks the night away, telling her about "the powerful madness that settles over a person when he stares at a corpse for hours" (p. 322). Heinemann says virtually nothing about Jennie's response or about the kinds of questions she might have asked. It is clear that her purpose is to serve as a kind of blankness on which he can compose all of the ugliness and horror of Vietnam.

Jennie is a particularly important source of comfort for Dosier when he receives a letter from a soldier with whom he served in Vietnam telling him that Quinn died. He breaks down, weeping uncontrollably as he storms, "I was in a rage. People would die. At that moment I could have destroyed whole cities, whole civilizations, whole fucking races of people. If Quinn can't make it back, none of us can" (p. 329). Of course, Quinn suspected he would not survive the war. One night in Vietnam when he and Dosier are drunk he shows him a newspaper photograph of five men in their Army uniforms. The caption explains that they completed basic training together, and Quinn relates that the five of them—Quinn is one of the men in the photo—were from the same town and went to high school together. Three of the others have been killed in action in Vietnam, and Dosier observes, looking at the photo, "I've been in the bushes long enough to know that Teleck, just by the look of him, ain't long for this world" (p. 162). Quinn ends up sobbing, mourning his lost buddies but also crying because he has "this glimmer of an inkling that he's dead as he sits here" (p. 162). Quinn thus mourns for himself, for what he knows will probably happen to him in Vietnam. Interestingly, he does not die in combat but in a vehicle accident, hardly the death expected of one who was renowned for his fighting abilities and risk-taking in battle.

The novel ends with Dosier at Quinn's grave a year and a half after Quinn's burial, reminiscing about all he experienced with him. Everything he remembers about Quinn highlights his violent personality brought to the fore any time someone questioned him, gave him an order he did not want to follow, or teased him. As he remembers, Dosier is possessed by a "sad and bitter feeling" (p. 335), one he attempts to resolve by "making fists and letting go" while saying the last words of the novel: "Goddamn you, Quinn" (p. 336). While Quinn's death is obviously meant to be a key event for Dosier, it is difficult for the reader to invest any emotion in the moment. Quinn is never presented as anything but violent, and perhaps even psychotic. If Heinemann wishes to demonstrate what war does to a man through the character of Quinn, he is ultimately unsuccessful because there is nothing in the novel that supports the claim that Quinn ever was something different. Heinemann obviously intends to demonstrate what happens when a man hears the "ugly deadly music" of the Vietnam War, but Dosier is so mechanically sketched that his lack of warmth and humanity make it nearly impossible to invest in his alteration. As a result of not investing in Dosier, the reader never fully connects to the larger picture of the war drawn in the novel. While *Close Quarters* might be an important contribution to the literature of the Vietnam War published in the 1970s, it is not a novel that stands out among the many high-quality works about the war published over the next three decades. Heinemann's second novel, *Paco's Story,* published in 1986, however, is an exceptional work that tells a disturbing story of return from Vietnam.

PACO'S STORY

Heinemann's second novel earned him a great deal of critical praise and scrutiny, including the National Book Award in 1987. The award, essentially an endorsement from American literary circles of Heinemann's talent, caused considerable upset. The reviewer Michiko Kakutani's *New York Times* article titled "Did 'Paco's Story' Deserve Its Award?" answers its own question by arguing that *Paco's Story,* though "a well-crafted, often admirable novel," lacks the maturity of the book most critics anticipated would win the award: Toni Morrison's *Beloved.* What it does share with *Beloved* is that both novels use ghosts

in pivotal ways. Heinemann added a foreword to the 2005 Vintage edition of *Paco's Story* explaining that the novel is, in keeping with "many rich examples in both American and Vietnamese fiction," a "ghost story" (p. xii). The reader eventually realizes the main narrator of the novel is in fact a dead man, or more specifically, the collective voice of the men who died in the attack on Fire Base Harriette in Vietnam, from which Paco emerges as the sole survivor. Heinemann offers further guidance to the reader, explaining that this narrator is addressing his story to "James," not an actual character or person; rather, "the 'James' comes from the custom of street folks engaging total strangers by calling them 'Jim' or 'Jack' " (p. xii).

By having a ghost recount the story of Paco's wounding, survival, and postwar existence to an imaginary listener, Heinemann highlights the artificiality of narrative. The narrator opens the novel by describing "the first clean fact," also the title of the first chapter, which is that "this ain't no war story" (p. 3). According to the narrator, "some people ... do not want to hear about Alpha Company—us grunts—busting jungle" (p. 5). Notwithstanding this perceived objection to his topic, the narrator proceeds to recount how he and everyone but Paco, including many Vietnamese, were killed in an attack that caused them to "disappear ... like sand dunes in a stiff and steady offshore ocean breeze" (p. 16). Paco is left for two days in the ruins of Fire Base Harriette until a medic from Bravo Company finds him, covered with blood and bugs, among the wreckage. At this point, in what becomes a common pattern of shifting narratives in the novel, the narrator recounts how the medic will tell the story of Paco's discovery "in Weiss's Saloon, over and over again" (p. 20) for many years to come. The medic's life is upended by his discovery of Paco, and his attempts to tell the story repeatedly do nothing to help him recover from the experience: he drinks himself into a stupor night after night after the war, proclaiming that "he could have made something of himself. 'Would have been a goddamn *good* doctor, hear?' he will tell you, James.... 'Except for this one guy, this *geek*,' the guy not dead, but should have been" (p. 33). Paco's second chance at life, then, becomes the source of the medic's own undoing.

What happens to Paco, the miraculous survivor? In the sarcastically titled third chapter, "The Thanks of a Grateful Nation," Paco is on a bus that stops at the town of Boone. The driver, who has pegged him as a GI "three-quarters stoned on some newfangled junk" (p. 36), leaves Paco at a garage to hitchhike his way into the center of the town. Although Paco is not high on the kinds of drugs the driver imagines, Paco is indeed sluggish and sleepy from the medications he takes to help him contend with the "glowing, suffocating uncomfortability that is more or less the permanent condition of his waking life" (p. 36). His injuries from the attack at Fire Base Harriette have left him walking with a pronounced limp and a cane, a sight that attracts questions from strangers who want to know what happened to him. For example, the young mechanic who drives Paco into town asks him what happened after being rescued from the fire base—Paco has revealed the bare bones of the story—and Paco responds, "They had me so zonked out on morphine I don't much remember" (p. 45). The narrator informs us, however, that "Paco remembers all right, and vividly" (p. 45). What Paco remembers is weeks spent in hospitals in Vietnam and Japan, where he is known as the amazing survivor of Alpha Company, gazed at incredulously by medical and military staff alike because the very fact that he is still breathing defies all logic.

In Boone, Paco is once again a spectacle, now because he is a stranger in a small town and because his injuries attract attention and speculation. Paco reluctantly submits to the visual probing of others when the mechanic takes him into Rita's, the local bar. Paco is an unwilling recipient of the hospitality the mechanic shows him, steeling himself to endure the social interaction and advice he receives about leaving town until he can make his escape to wander the streets, looking for a business that will hire him. Paco is out of money and is essentially stranded in Boone, where he encounters strangers from whom he hopes to receive hospitality in the form of gainful employment. Paco's first few forays

into the businesses that line Boone's main street do not yield the desired results. His visit to a small store called Mr. Elliot's Goods causes Mr. Elliot, a Russian immigrant who often converses with his long dead wife, to lapse into a confused reverie about his desertion from the "Czar's army ... in 1917" (p. 73). Unbeknownst to Paco, Mr. Elliot has returned to his own violence-strewn past. When he looks up he asks Paco in which war he received his wounds, angering Paco because yet another person has asked this question, "as if not one word of the fucking thing had ever made the papers" (p. 75). In Mr. Elliot's case he may not know where Vietnam is, but he also is stuck in his own deteriorating mind, reflecting on events that seem more real to him than the present moment.

As Paco makes the circuit of the town, visiting the barbershop, laundry, drugstore, auto parts store, and insurance agency, he has little luck. Work is scarce in this rundown town and Paco is met with skepticism, resentment, and even fear at times. During this section of the novel Heinemann alternates narrative perspectives, allowing the reader to witness the miscommunication between Paco and the townspeople as they misjudge one another. Paco finally finds a warmer welcome when he wanders into the Texas Lunch, a local restaurant—Heinemann first used the name the "Texas Lunch" in *Close Quarters* when Dosier mentions it as one of the places he passes as he walks around Springfield, Kentucky—with his last bit of money in hand. The reader knows Paco will have better luck in this establishment because Ernest Monroe, the owner, "fully recognizes Paco's 1,000-meter stare" (p. 95). Monroe's capacity for understanding comes from the fact that he is "a Guadalcanal Marine who went ashore at Iwo Jima" (p. 125). Monroe gives Paco a job and recommends that he stay at the Geronimo Hotel across the street.

The rest of the novel takes place in the narrow confines of the restaurant and the hotel. Heinemann details the rhythm of Paco's work, spending pages explaining his system for washing the endless dishes in a routine that offers Paco a way of structuring his days. Paco needs the routine of the work, the lack of surprises, because so much of his energy is consumed with managing his pain, which by the end of the day drives him to take his medication and collapse. Despite the innocuous nature of the setting and the work, Paco cannot escape remembering the war. Once a week when he cleans out the grease traps Paco is reminded of "that day and a half he spent by himself at Fire Base Harriette—it is the stink, the stench of many well-rotted human corpses—[that] always sends him home Saturdays looking for a drink" (p. 116). The ghost narrator makes it clear that "Paco is made to dream and remember, and we make it happen in this way ... we bestir and descend. We hover around him like an aura" (p. 137). The impetus for the haunting of Paco is a key question. Though Paco never asks, "Why me?—the dumbest, dipstick question only the most ignorant fucking new guy would ever bother to ask" (p. 136), it is "the ghosts, the dead ... who ask, Why him?" (p. 137). Filled with resentment at Paco's survival, the dead visit him, disrupting his sleep and plaguing him with disturbing and terrifying dreams of various kinds.

While the dead watch Paco, Paco begins to watch Cathy, the niece of the owners of the Geronimo Hotel. Her room is visible from where Paco takes his smoke break, sitting "in the full light of the doorway" of the Texas Lunch (p. 146). He believes that she does not know he is watching her moving around in various states of undress; however, one evening he "sits in his trancelike stupor in the deepest darkness beyond the doorway light next to the garbage dumpster" (p. 147), and his new position allows him to observe Cathy as she pulls up a chair and looks over at the restaurant, clearly waiting for Paco to emerge so she can pretend to not know that he is watching her. While the reader has assumed she is simply the object of Paco's voyeuristic gaze, the narrator tells us that "for weeks now, James, Cathy would turn off all the lights in her apartment, pull a bentwood chair ... to the middle of the room, and sit, slouching just so—tranquil and patient.... And she would watch Paco work" (p. 147). Paco "feels the excitement of his blood rushing through his body—and for a moment the pain in his back is gone" as he realizes that he has been watched (p. 148). He decides to com-

municate his knowledge to Cathy. He lights his cigarette from the darkness of the alley, "looking straight up at her, James, with eyes as clear as ice" (p. 148), shocking Cathy into moving her chair back and slinking out of the room.

The parameters of the game with Cathy subsequently change. She now listens for the sound of Paco returning from work, for the "black hickory cane on the asphalt" (p. 166). She then appears at the door to her room in the hotel, seemingly naked, where she peers down at Paco in the entranceway, daring him to ascend the stairs and get to her door before she ducks inside. The prize, if he could ever make the trip before she disappears, would be entering the room and having sex with her. His damaged body ensures that he will never be fast enough to make the trip and possess Cathy; instead, he must settle for the frustrating experience of having vicarious sex with her. One night when she is not at the door to tease him, he hears her having sex with her boyfriend and "is furiously jealous [at] Marty-boy's clean haircut and the undulating smoothness of his back (not a mark on the son-of-a-bitch, James)" (p. 172). Paco is frustrated with desire, not only for Cathy but for the restoration of his physical wholeness, a feeling the narrator explains as a desire "to fuck away all that pain and redeem his body" (p. 173). Paco has to settle for fantasy since the desired reality is so far outside his grasp. He thus imagines bursting into the room and tearing Marty off Cathy, to finish the job for him.

Paco's sexual fantasies lead him to remember suddenly a scene from Vietnam. He recalls the forearm of Gallagher, a buddy killed at Fire Base Harriette, covered with a "red-and-black dragon"—"a goddamned work of art, everyone said, a regular fucking masterpiece" (p. 174). The tattoo in turn leads him to remember the rape of a Vietnamese woman. Though Paco resists his mind's return to the past, his body "winc[ing] and squirm[ing]," "he cannot choose but [to] remember" (p. 174). He recalls Gallagher's rage that this VC woman had ambushed a platoon, killing two men, the night before. To satiate his fury, Gallagher takes the woman by the hair to a hut to rape her; a group of men including Paco and the narrator join him, lining up to take their turns. The narrator takes great pains to explain that if the woman had been a male soldier instead they "would have punched on him, then killed him right then and there and left him for dead" (p. 177). The soldier, however, is not a man, and her feminine identity means, to the American men, that she needs to be sexually humiliated before being killed. Paco is specifically involved as the narrator tells us how he helped to tie the woman's hands behind her back and how he could feel "her whole body pucker down" as he raped her (p. 180). After he and the other men have exhausted themselves raping her, Gallagher takes her outside and executes her by shooting her in the forehead.

Though the rape of the Vietnamese woman obviously happened years before, during the war, it is significant that the event is remembered by Paco, and narrated by the ghost, in the final thirty pages of the novel. In fact, this violent event is the climatic event of *Paco's Story;* it causes the narrator and other men to realize that it "was a moment of evil, that we would never live the same" (p. 184). It is of course also crucial that Paco unwillingly remembers this event right after he has fantasized about breaking into Cathy's apartment and raping her—though in his male fantasy she is a willing participant as he imagines "that she whimpers grotesquely, encircling him at once with her arms and legs, holding him to her like warm covers" (p. 173). However, Paco soon has to face the reality that Cathy would most assuredly not, despite her pleasure in teasing and tantalizing Paco, have welcomed him into her bed when he breaks into her bedroom and reads her diary.

The night after his recollection of the Vietnamese woman's rape and murder, he enters his room and is certain that someone has been in it. He, in turn, decides that he is going to break into Cathy's room. He is "preoccupied about what he's going to find in Cathy's apartment" all day at work, though it is unclear to the reader what Paco hopes to find (p. 188). It becomes apparent that, since his decision to break in comes on the heels of his thoughts about raping women, it is not an object or knowledge that Paco wishes to

discover; rather, what is exciting to him is the very act of transgressing prohibited feminine space.

The description of Paco's preparations for entering Cathy's room makes his excitement palpable. Paco is no longer the disabled vet walking with a cane that everyone can hear minutes before they actually see him; instead, he is the stealthy soldier again, "the company booby-trap man" (p. 190). Once he stands in her room, he falls into "an ambush trance" and "a grim shiver of anticipation ripples through his feet and fingers" (p. 197). While he will not literally rape Cathy, he does invade her space, looking at and touching her things, and then reads her diary, which he has found hidden under her mattress. He settles down with a glass of water and makes himself comfortable as he pages through entries going back a year. He eventually comes to the section in which she describes learning that "there is a good-looking guy working at the Texas Lunch" (p. 202). Cathy makes sporadic entries about Paco, sometimes referring to his good looks or imagining having sex with him, until he eventually reads one in which she details his movements, including his after-work routine when he would come home, remove his clothes, and take pills and perhaps drink cheap alcohol. She also describes his scars, which "look like purple and brown and white swirls, deep, and pinched together here and there like the heavy stitches of a quilt" (pp. 204–205).

Paco is aroused by reading her diary, especially the sections in which she talks about her sexual activities, and looking at her bras, but his excitement is soon quashed when he reads more recent sections in which she depicts Paco as a crazy drunk who stumbles around and talks to himself, both when he's awake and when he's asleep. She no longer sees him as attractive but as a "creep" that even her uncle, the owner of the hotel, believes is "best got rid of" (p. 206). As Cathy coldly portrays Paco as repellent and unstable, the narrator's voice breaks in to explain why Paco behaves the way he does. For example, when Cathy complains about Paco crying out in his sleep, the narrator tells us he is "dreaming of executions" (p. 206). The ghost narrator can humanize and explain the grief and pain that keep Paco in agony even when he is supposed to be enjoying the oblivion of sleep.

Reading these descriptions, Paco is forced to see himself as the world sees him, and the portrait is unflattering at best. The final devastating assessment comes in the form of one of Cathy's dreams. In it, Cathy imagines Paco in her room, the two of them kissing each other and "eager to get into bed" (p. 208). Once there, however, Cathy cannot "bring [her]self to touch him" (p. 208). The dream turns into a nightmare as, after Paco has climaxed, he stays on top of her and begins "to peel the scars off as if they were a mask" (p. 208). He then begins the process of transferring his scars to Cathy's body, causing her to "burn" (p. 208). Paco lays the scars from his back across her "breasts and belly—tingling and burning" and then entwines them "around [her] head, like a skull cap" (p. 208). She wakes from this nightmare disgusted. Paco's reaction is immediate: he "feels as if he's met his wraith" (p. 209). He stops reading, puts the room in order, packs his things, and hitchhikes to the Texaco station. He tells himself, "Whatever it is I want, it ain't in this town; thinking, Man, you ain't just a brick in the fucking wall, you're just a piece of meat on the slab" (p. 209). His solution is to take the bus west because "there's less bullshit the farther west you go" (p. 210). His solution to his current alienation is a familiar one for men in American literature: moving west to find a new identity and new opportunities. The promise of this move, however, is undercut by the final image of the novel. Paco does not go west on a horse, or even in an automobile, but via the drabbest and most uninspiring of American forms of transportation: the bus, which "[coasts] down the long incline of the entrance ramp ... and is soon gone" (p. 210). With that last sentence, Paco leaves Boone, a place where he has lived so lightly that he can pack up in minutes, only taking the time to leave Ernest a quick note of thanks for employing him; otherwise, Paco has neither put down roots nor formed friendships. He arrived alone and maintained his loner status throughout his sojourn.

Paco's disconnection from Boone and its citizens is in part explained by his exceptional status. He is a veteran of an unpopular war that people prefer to not think about at all, yet his wounded body speaks for that experience, giving out just enough information to invite queries from strangers, thus bringing the war and the reality of what it does to the soldiers into the foreground. Paco's exceptionalism is furthered by the fact that he is the lone survivor of the attack on Fire Base Harriette, yet his survival apparently has no larger meaning. He is not destined to do great things with his second chance at life; he simply drifts along, trying to contend with the permanent pain of the war he carries in his body and mind. When outsiders like Cathy look at him they see only disfigurement and difference, things that set Paco apart and make him a grotesque figure. Heinemann uses the alienated relationship between the returning veteran and the civilian population to make a pointed statement about the ludicrous nature of fighting wars in which the people for whom they are supposedly fought have no interest. Paco survives the destruction of the war only to return to something ultimately much more damaging: indifference.

COOLER BY THE LAKE

Heinemann's third novel, *Cooler by the Lake,* published in 1992, is a radical departure from his first two works. With it he leaves the subject of Vietnam far behind, focusing instead on territory familiar to him since his childhood: Chicago. The novel employs a narrative technique used to much greater effect in *Paco's Story,* where the narrator often goes on conversational tangents that give the novel an improvisational, informal feel, though this time the narrator is not a ghost but one who possesses detailed knowledge of Chicago streets and history. The knowledge is shared as the narrator tells the story of Maximilian Nutmeg, "a mildly incompetent, mostly harmless petty crook, [who was] always hustling for money" (p. 3). Nutmeg's need for cash to support his extended, and unconventional, family leads him to streets where he tells tall tales to strangers in an effort to extract a few dollars from them. His penchant for storytelling and gross exaggeration makes him wildly successful. On one of these escapades he finds a wallet, and much of the novel is devoted to his comic misadventures as he, a thief and a man of little integrity, attempts to locate its rightful owner.

The plot seems primarily to be an excuse for Heinemann to showcase his grasp of Chicago lore, which he inserts into the narrative by way of frequent parenthetical digressions citing the origin of a city street or landmark. The technique becomes belabored as the lightweight story of Nutmeg's attempts to return the wallet with eight hundred dollars in it (demonstrating that he still has ethics, even if he lies to people on a regular basis to make money) gets bogged down by these side notes that at times last for pages. In the end, Nutmeg proves he has his own set of ethics when he does return the wallet, thus ensuring a positive outcome for him and the extended cast of characters in his family. The novel's most compelling aspect is the portrait of Chicago over several decades; otherwise, as Tim Sandlin noted in his *New York Times* review, it is "a highly entertaining circus act that brings us a few laughs ... then moves on down the road."

BLACK VIRGIN MOUNTAIN

Heinemann's 2005 volume of nonfiction returns to a familiar topic, the Vietnam War, but it does so in a new genre, a mix of memoir and travel narrative. *Black Virgin Mountain* documents Heinemann's changing attitudes toward Vietnam and the Vietnamese, attitudes that developed in part because of trips he made to Vietnam in 1990, 1992, 1997, and 2003, which he describes in some detail in the book. This is the first major work in which Heinemann details his war experiences in a first-person narrative, in which he also contemplates how his memory of those experiences has been tempered over the years.

The memoir's first chapter, "Several Facts," begins with a description of when, with whom, and where he served during the Vietnam War. The same angry tone that marks Heinemann's fictional works about Vietnam is present as he

details how he was drafted at twenty-two, stressing that "no one told us we could hightail it to Canada. No one told us we could declare ourselves conscientious objectors and opt for alternative service" (p. 3). He and his younger brother Richard accepted their draft notices and went to Fort Polk for basic training before being separated, Richard to go to Fort Sill, Oklahoma, and Heinemann to Fort Knox "to join the armored cavalry" (p. 7). Heinemann describes his training and induction into army life with rage-soaked prose, highlighting as he does in *Close Quarters* and *Paco's Story* the stupidity of military authority from the lowest-ranking noncommissioned officers to "professional patriots" like James (Jim) Webb (p. 161). Webb, a former marine and secretary of the navy (and, since 2007, a U.S. senator from Virginia), is the author of *Fields of Fire,* a 1978 novel based on his experiences serving in Vietnam, a novel Heinemann could not finish reading because "the story itself [was] so cliché ridden" (p. 163). Heinemann spends pages documenting his accidental meeting with Webb in Hanoi, claiming that Webb made an "irritated gesture—a sort of shivering all over as if his bowels were trying to move a watermelon" when he found out that Heinemann was traveling around Vietnam via train (p. 164). Heinemann also shares his view of General William Westmoreland, about whom he says, "His participation in the Johnson administration's program of extraordinary lies ... will always be his special shame" (pp. 67–68). When Heinemann is airing his longstanding grudges rather than focusing on analyzing his complicated relationship with Vietnam, the memoir suffers from a lack of focus and momentum.

When he is talking about Vietnam itself, whether when he was there in 1967–1968 or during one of his later trips, *Black Virgin Mountain* is more powerful. For example, Heinemann describes his amnesia regarding his flight as a draftee to Tan Son Nhut Air Base in March 1967, which he explains as a symptom of his numbness, "as if I were already dead—distracted; numb—to everything, including memory" (p. 99). Heinemann does recall many events during the twelve months he served in Vietnam and the blackness that settled on him after he returned to the United States, where he "felt joyless and old, physically and spiritually exhausted, mean and grateful and uncommonly sad" (p. 35). His reaction to these feelings of confusion and unease was to talk endlessly about the war: "I could not shut up about what I had seen, what I had done, and what I had become" (p. 37). What he had become, according to his own account, was "not simply a witness, but an integral, even dedicated, party to a very wrong thing" (p. 37). Heinemann never gets into specific actions he took; rather, he describes events in broad details, yet it is evident that the memoir is an attempt to reckon with his participation in the war as one among millions and as an individual soldier who took actions that he regrets later in life. In addition, Heinemann discusses other sources of sorrow in his life, including the fact that by 1999, Heinemann's parents and brothers were either dead or missing. When reflecting on his personal losses Heinemann points to the silence that reigned in his house: his mother never talked about what it was like dealing with her youngest son, Philip, while he recovered from wounds he received while serving in the Marine Corps in Vietnam, and Philip never spoke about the war though it "brought forth a violent rage ... that became a permanent fixture of his persona" (p. 51).

Though Heinemann clearly points to the long-reaching effects of the war, he is quick to tell the reader on several occasions that his return trips to Vietnam "are not 'guilt trips.' And I don't go to Vietnam to 'heal' myself with one of those good, cleansing New Age crying jags. No, 'healing' is too dicey a business to be settled with a couple weeks' vacation" (p. 118). As he nears the emotional climax of the memoir, the trip to the top of Nui Ba Den—Black Virgin Mountain—Heinemann reiterates that he does not visit Vietnam to heal or "to 'see' the war, but to be rid of it" (p. 238). Ridding himself of the war means transforming Vietnam from the place where he found the evil in himself into a location he can call home. This alteration takes place when he is on top of the mountain where he can see his "war-year of soul-deadening dread ... every place I ever camped; laagered, humped an

ambush" (p. 227). Standing on the mountain, he describes the memoir's final revelation: "the clear sense rises in me, bursting on me in a rush of honest revelation; and how odd a sensation. I'm home, I say to myself; I have arrived home; *this* place is home" (p. 243). Heinemann's transcendent moment comes suddenly and unexpectedly at the end of a memoir that has been defiant in its wish to reject all displays of emotion except anger and frustration. It is unclear what has allowed Heinemann to transfer these strong negative emotions into a peacefulness that the word "home" implies. In the structure of the memoir the final revelation is unconvincing because there is no context for it, though perhaps in reality that moment on top of the Black Virgin Mountain did give Heinemann the ability to accept the place Vietnam has in his life story. Heinemann told Tobey C. Herzog in his book *Writing Vietnam, Writing Life: Caputo, Heinemann, O'Brien, Butler,* that "this [the interview with Herzog] will be the last time I sit down with anyone and talk about these things. I've finally worn myself out talking about it—the war, I mean" (p. 45). It remains to be seen whether Heinemann will uphold the promise of these lines and whether he will be able to build his literary reputation without the Vietnam War as his subject.

Selected Bibliography

WORKS OF LARRY HEINEMANN

Novels

Close Quarters. New York: Farrar, Straus and Giroux, 1977. New York: Vintage Contemporaries–Random, 2005.

Paco's Story. New York: Farrar, Straus and Giroux, 1986. New York: Vintage Contemporaries-Random, 2005.

Cooler by the Lake. New York: Farrar, Straus and Giroux, 1992. New York: Penguin, 1992.

Nonfiction/Memoir

Black Virgin Mountain: A Return to Vietnam. New York: Doubleday, 2005. New York: Vintage-Random, 2006.

"Prologue: Vietnam After All These Years." In *The United States and Viet Nam from War to Peace: Papers from an Interdisciplinary Conference on Reconciliation*. December 2–4, 1993, University of Notre Dame. Edited by Robert M. Slabey. Jefferson, N.C.: McFarland, 1996. Pp. 9–15.

CRITICAL STUDIES

Anisfield, Nancy. "After the Apocalypse: Narrative Movement in Larry Heinemann's *Paco's Story*." In *America Rediscovered: Critical Essays on Literature and Film of the Vietnam War*. Edited by Owen W. Gilman Jr. and Lorrie Smith. New York: Garland, 1990. Pp. 275–281.

Bonn, Maria S. "A Different World: The Vietnam Veteran Novel Come Home." In *Fourteen Landing Zones: Approaches to Vietnam War Literature*. Edited by Philip K. Jason. Iowa City: University of Iowa Press, 1991. Pp. 1–14.

Boulting, David. "Veterans, Vietcong, and Others: Enemies and Empathies in Larry Heinemann's *Paco's Story*." In *The New Order of War*. Edited by Bob Brecher. Amsterdam: Rodopi, 2010. Pp. 111–130.

Campbell, James. "Coming Home: Difference and Reconciliation in Narratives of Return to 'the World.' " In *The United States and Viet Nam from War to Peace: Papers from an Interdisciplinary Conference on Reconciliation*. December 2–4, 1993, University of Notre Dame. Edited by Robert M. Slabey. Jefferson, N.C.: McFarland, 1996. Pp. 198–207.

Connolly, Donna M. "The Face of the (Other) Enemy: Aspects of the Feminine in Vietnam War Novels." Ph.D. dissertation, University of Notre Dame, 1991.

Cronin, Cornelius A. "Historical Background to Larry Heinemann's *Close Quarters*." *Critique* 24, no. 2:119–130 (winter 1983).

Durham, Marilyn. "Narrative Strategies in Recent Vietnam War Fiction." In *America Rediscovered: Critical Essays on Literature and Film of the Vietnam War*. Edited by Owen W. Gilman Jr. and Lorrie Smith. New York: Garland, 1990. Pp. 100–108.

Everett, Graham. "The American National Character and the Novelization of Vietnam." Ph.D. dissertation, State University of New York at Stony Brook, 1994.

Ferguson, Lisa Dawn. "Men, Women, and Masculinity in Vietnam War Literature: A Study of Major Works by Larry Heinemann and Tim O'Brien." Ph.D. dissertation, University of Alabama, 2005.

Grieff, Louis K. "In the Name of the Brother: Larry Heinemann's *Paco's Story* and Male America." *Critique* 41, no. 4:381–389 (summer 2000).

Hantke, Steffan H. "The Uses of the Fantastic and the Deferment of Closure in American Literature on the Vietnam War." *Rocky Mountain Review of Language and Literature* 55, no. 1:63–82 (spring 2001).

Jason, Philip K. "Sexism and Racism in Vietnam War Fiction." *Mosaic* 23, no. 3:125–137 (summer 1990).

Jeffords, Susan. "Tattoos, Scars, Diaries, and Writing Masculinity." In *The Vietnam War and American Culture.* Edited by John Carlos Rowe and Rick Berg. New York: Columbia University Press, 1991. Pp. 208–225.

Kennedy, Leslie Carol. "Ghosts Through the Looking Glass: The Vietnam War and Its Narrative Representation in the Novels of Heinemann, Herr, O'Brien, and Wright." Ph.D. dissertation, Texas A&M University, 1995.

Morris, Gregory L. "Telling War Stories: Larry Heinemann's *Paco's Story* and the Serio-Comic Tradition." *Critique* 36, no. 1: 58–68 (fall 1994).

Myers, Thomas. "Dispatches from Ghost Country: The Vietnam Veteran in Recent American Fiction." *Genre* 21, no. 4:409–428 (winter 1988).

Palm, Edward Frederick. "American Heart of Darkness: The Moral Vision of Five Novels of the Vietnam War." Ph.D. dissertation, University of Pennsylvania, 1983.

Scott, Grant F. "*Paco's Story* and the Ethics of Violence." *Critique* 36, no. 1:69–80 (fall 1994).

Slabey, Robert M. "Heinemann's *Paco's Story.*" *Explicator* 52, no. 3:187–189 (spring 1994).

Smith, Lorrie. "Back Against the Wall: Anti-Feminist Backlash in Vietnam War Literature." *Vietnam Generation* 1, nos. 3–4:115–126 (1989).

Stovall, Connie. "Larry Heinemann: An Annotated Guide to Selected Sources." *Collection Building* 29, no. 2:50–54 (January 2010).

Vickroy, Laurie. "Elusive Redemptions: Trauma, Gender, and Violence in *Bastard Out of Carolina* and *Paco's Story.*" *Journal of Evolutionary Psychology* 22, nos. 1–2:37–44 (March 2001).

REVIEWS

Benfey, Christopher. "Finding Peace at the Sink." *New York Times,* November 8, 1987, p. A19. (Review of *Paco's Story.*)

Hedges, Chris. "All Grunts Together." *New York Times Book Review,* August 28, 2005, p. 20. (Review of *Black Virgin Mountain.*)

Kakutani, Michiko. "Did 'Paco's Story' Deserve Its Award?" *New York Times,* November 16, 1987, p. C15.

Lingeman, Richard R. "Inside the Meat Grinder." *New York Times,* July 18, 1977, p. L25. (Review of *Close Quarters.*)

Sandlin, Tim. "Maximilian Nutmeg Does the Right Thing." *New York Times Book Review,* June 14, 1992, p. 27. (Review of *Cooler by the Lake.*)

INTERVIEWS

Herzog, Tobey C. "Conversation with Larry Heinemann." In his *Writing Vietnam, Writing Life: Caputo, Heinemann, O'Brien, Butler.* Iowa City: University of Iowa Press, 2008. Pp. 45–87.

Jacobsen, Kurt. "Larry Heinemann in Conversation with Kurt Jacobsen." *Logos* 2, no. 1:141–160 (winter 2003).

Schroeder, Eric James. "An Interview with Larry Heinemann: 'Novels Are More Polite Than a Simple Fuck You. ' " *Writing on the Edge* 2, no. 2:31–47 (spring 1991).

Schuette-Hoffman, Allison. "A Conversation with Larry Heinemann: February 9, 2006." *Willow Springs* (http://willowsprings.ewu.edu/interviews/heinemann.php).

Silesky, Barry. "Larry Heinemann: A Conversation." *Another Chicago Magazine* 25:179–196 (spring 1993).

ELISABETH SANXAY HOLDING

(1889—1955)

Elaine Roth

ELISABETH SANXAY HOLDING wrote twenty-four novels, one children's book, and many short stories over the course of a long career. Her first six novels depicted young women making their way in the world, in the tradition of British nineteenth-century novels of manners such as those by the Brontës. In 1929, however, Holding branched out into the suspense novels that were to become her trademark and for which she became fairly well known in her time; her subsequent eighteen novels were all in this genre. Several commentators, such as Peter Schwed and Gregory Shepard, have linked this transition to the fall of the stock market in 1929; both Schwed and Shepard have noted the increased revenue that genre books were capable of generating.

Raised in wealth, Elisabeth Sanxay was born in Brooklyn on June 8, 1889. She attended private schools and then married a British diplomat, George E. Holding, when she was twenty-four. With her husband, she traveled throughout South America and the Caribbean, locations she would later use as settings for her novels. The couple had two daughters, Skeffington and Antonia. Antonia married Peter Schwed, himself an author as well as a publisher at Simon & Schuster. Schwed became executor of Holding's estate after her death and was instrumental in Ace Books reprinting a number of Holding's novels in the 1960s, as well as the reprinting of *The Blank Wall* and *The Innocent Mrs. Duff* by Academy Chicago in the 1990s. Schwed has since died, but the crusade to bring Holding's work back in print has been taken up by Gregory Shepard, a publisher at Stark House Books, which reprinted a number of her novels in the first decade of the twenty-first century.

While providing financial stability, Holding's transition to the suspense genre also extended her literary range by allowing her to delve into the world of men: roughly half her suspense novels have male protagonists. In addition, this genre facilitated Holding's investigation of a topic that clearly fascinated her: guilt and its repercussions. The shifting nature of guilt lends itself well to the genre of suspense, in which suspicion circulates and characters' motivations remain unclear until the end. In Holding's considerations of guilt, she frequently complicates who deserves punishment as well as who should determine criminals' fates. Throughout her novels, Holding concludes that only those intimately involved can truly understand and judge the nature of crime. Often, of course, those intimately involved are themselves implicated in criminal acts, if they are not outright criminals. Yet Holding frequently depicts such characters operating according to a code of ethics that she privileges over sanctioned legal practice.

Other masters of the suspense genre, such as Raymond Chandler and Alfred Hitchcock, appreciated her work. In a published collection of his letters, Chandler said of Holding: "For my money she's the top suspense writer of them all" (quoted in Schwed, p. ii). In 1959 Hitchcock selected *The Blank Wall* as one of the twenty stories in his anthology *My Favorites in Suspense*. Holding further may have had a lasting effect on popular literature in an indirect way, in that the protagonist of her novel *The Virgin Huntress* (1951) seems to anticipate the infamous protagonist of Patricia Highsmith's *The Talented Mr. Ripley* (1955), who debuted just four years later. In

her own right, Holding is probably best known for her novel *The Blank Wall* (1947), which was twice adapted as a film: *The Reckless Moment* (1949), with James Mason; and *The Deep End* (2001), starring Tilda Swinton.

Holding's novels, as exemplified by *The Blank Wall,* generally follow a scenario whereby an average, law-abiding citizen is thrust into a situation far more criminal and complex than he or she has previously encountered. In Holding's hands, this scenario is often further complicated by the fact that the protagonist is a woman who must simultaneously struggle against gendered social conventions. In *The Blank Wall,* the protagonist is Lucia, a mother of three struggling to make ends meet while her husband serves in World War II. Holding is particularly adept at conveying the sense of being overwhelmed by larger circumstances beyond the protagonist's control, while brilliantly depicting the other concerns that compete with the criminal plot. Lucia, for instance, must continue to maintain her household—preparing meals and cleaning up after her family—while negotiating with blackmailers.

Holding accomplishes some of her most impressive feats of storytelling when she constructs initially sympathetic narrators that readers eventually identify as pathologically unreliable; she adopts this strategy to great effect in *The Death Wish* (1934), *The Unfinished Crime* (1935), and *The Innocent Mrs. Duff* (1946). Holding also shifts perspective effectively throughout her novels, from male to female, youth to adult. In an unusual play with perspective, Holding moved between two points of view in *Who's Afraid?* (1940): that of Susie Alban, a young professional traveling with four male strangers, and one of the four men, who is out to kill her. The reader is unclear until quite late in the novel which of the four men is the would-be murderer.

ANGELICA *(1921)*

Holding's first three novels were named after young women. *Angelica*, the last of these three, was dedicated to Holding's husband, George; they had been married eight years at the time. *Angelica* follows the travails of the eponymous heroine, a teenage inner-city factory worker who wants to better her social standing. Hired for her pluck, Angelica takes on a strange assignment whereby she is meant to act as an upper-middle-class companion to a woman who has lost a child. Although this ruse is not sustainable, Angelica remains in the household in an intermediate position between servant and family member. Over the course of the novel, the young unmarried head of the household takes on Angelica as a project, seeking to better a member of the lower classes, but eventually falls in love with her. Meanwhile, however, Angelica is swept into a romance with his older brother, a manipulative would-be artist and the husband of the grieving woman Angelica was originally hired to console. Although the premise that introduces Angelica into the family is barely plausible, the class dynamics that ensue afterward, and the workings of the household, are fascinating through Holding's lens.

Most notable is the depiction of the older brother, a brooding, volatile patriarch who strongly resembles precursors such as Rochester in *Jane Eyre* (1847) or St. Elmo, in Augusta Jane Evans' popular 1866 novel of the same name. The redemption of a wealthy, mysterious older man by a younger woman of no social standing is a familiar narrative, from Samuel Richardson's *Pamela* (1740) to Daphne du Maurier's *Rebecca* (1938). *Angelica* departs significantly from these predecessors, however, in that the handsome rake is ultimately unsalvageable. Whether because of Angelica's truly impoverished class standing—she has no education or religious belief with which to save him—or Holding's conviction that human nature is essentially immutable—some people are trustworthy and some simply are not—the novel segues from the standard tale of an attractive ingenue's journey through the marriage plot to a fascinating portrait of a dysfunctional but intense relationship between Angelica and her married lover. In another significant departure, Holding refuses to demonize Angelica's lover's wife; instead, this character remains a sympathetic ally to Angelica, even after she is aware of Angelica's relationship with her husband.

The novel ends with Angelica having risen in class status, as co-owner of an elite women's clothing store, but at the expense of her affectionate ties with her nuclear family and two broken love affairs. Meanwhile, her illegitimate son, conceived with the older brother, is being raised by his wife. Rather than ending on a pessimistic note, however, the novel resolves into a testament to the resilience of civilians, primarily women, like Angelica, carrying on the home front, a theme Holding returned to in her most famous novel, *The Blank Wall.*

THE UNLIT LAMP *(1922)*

Like *Angelica, The Unlit Lamp,* Holding's next novel, is a domestic novel of manners deeply attuned to the dynamics of social class. The novel follows a family for several generations; we begin with a young couple at the end of the nineteenth century and return after they have been married, unhappily, for twenty years and are facing the marriage of one of their daughters to a man originally of the working class. Once that class difference has been negotiated, the primary narrative conflict for the second half of the novel becomes the tension between the former member of the working class and his mother-in-law. He believes in a radical commitment to social change, whereas she values the quiet suppression of all passions. Yet each holds the other in high esteem, and both are profoundly frustrated by the character they have in common, his wife and her daughter.

The novel closes on a more depressed note than *Angelica;* it is also a deeply ironic ending. The working-class character decides to abandon his investment in challenging the conventions of social class and instead use his mother-in-law's humility and politeness as a model. Meanwhile, however, the mother-in-law has grown disgusted with her life, convinced that she has wasted her youthful potential and become a shadow of her earlier, more vibrant self; the novel's title refers to her latent desire, which is never kindled. The son-in-law announces his conversion to her mode of subdued living just as she resolves to abandon it forever. While she allows him to convince her that her behavior is worthwhile and dignified, the novel nonetheless quietly questions that capitulation with its melancholy tone, particularly at the end.

MIASMA *(1929)*

Holding's writing clearly undergoes a major shift in 1929, the year of the stock market crash. Her six previous books were domestic novels featuring female protagonists; the subsequent eighteen books are suspense novels divided almost equally between male and female perspectives. *Miasma* signals this shift in genre as well as the gender of the protagonist by following the career of young Dr. Dennison, who hopes to earn enough to marry his fiancée. Because his medical practice is floundering, he is susceptible to the overture of an established doctor, who invites Dennison to serve as an apprentice while living in the older doctor's large home. The older doctor turns out to be a practitioner of euthanasia, administered through powerful drugs, a theme Holding returns to throughout her career. Meanwhile, Dennison, wooed by the wealth of the household, and soon unable to buy his way out, becomes involved in a series of strange events, from patients receiving lethal doses of drugs to addicts plotting to kill their unfaithful husbands.

Holding's first foray into the suspense genre establishes several themes to which she returned over the seventeen novels that follow *Miasma.* One subject Holding enjoys exploring is the brutal nature of the official justice system, here embodied by Dennison's fiancée, whose father is a district attorney. Although Holding expresses admiration for members of the police force, in particular Lieutenant Levy, who plays a role in several later novels, her work repeatedly asserts that the larger truth of criminal events lies beyond the purview of the legal system. Instead, Holding suggests that only those wholly involved can comprehend and respond appropriately to illegal circumstances. In *Miasma,* for instance, the established doctor truly believes that his practice of euthanasia has benefited his patients, including forcing a homicidal drug addict to overdose

rather than murder her husband. Although Holding does not allow the doctor to continue his practices (he commits suicide rather than face apprehension at the end of the novel), she also does not present the official arm of the law—Dennison's young, righteous, and outraged fiancée—in flattering terms. Meanwhile, Dennison, who has become enamored of the doctor's nurse, Hilda Napier, fears the scrutiny of the law because he worries that Napier will be implicated.

The ending institutes one of Holding's narrative patterns, closure that tacitly implies the formation of a couple but refrains from depicting it. Repeatedly in Holding's work, couples are drawn together seemingly without noticing it themselves. The circumstances that allow them to unite are set in motion by the final events of the plot, after which the novel ends without representing, and occasionally without even explicitly suggesting, their union. In *Miasma,* at the close of the novel Dennison's fiancée announces that she no longer loves him. The stage is thus set for Dennison and Napier to become a couple (as well as the doctor's divorcée sister and the husband—now widower—of the drug addict). The last line implies that Dennison will pursue Napier, but the novel stops there.

Miasma also features several sequences in which Dennison is drugged, a phenomenon Holding returns to in her later work. Her description of these interludes is vividly rendered and sympathetic to the intoxicated Dennison, who experiences the highs and lows of some kind of opiate narcotic, perhaps laudanum or heroin. These moments presumably account for the title of the novel, as Dennison becomes increasingly mired in a household that first confuses him and then results in him taking leave of his senses.

Another recurring theme established in *Miasma* is that of the working-class or middle-class character down on his luck, who is vulnerable to the plots of upper-class people who offer sustenance but at a dangerous exchange. Particularly during the Depression, such a depiction, which at once admires the comforts of class privilege and condemns the upper-class as criminals, must have been appealing. Even as Dennison becomes convinced that the doctor he has become indebted to is involved in unethical practices, Dennison nonetheless cannot help appreciating the doctor's comfortable, even decadent, lifestyle: the luxury car, the delicious meals, the attractive rooms, the nice clothing: "He thought of dinner, eaten with heavy silver, from fine china, the woodfire in the library; Mrs. Lewis in evening dress, all the charm, the dignity of that life. And he clung to it, with all his heart" (p. 202). The novel renders palpable the allure of such wealth, which in turn makes Dennison's descent into moral ambiguity comprehensible, especially to a strapped Depression audience.

DARK POWER *(1930)*

The novel Holding wrote next pursues the subject of class inequities again, but with a female protagonist, Diana Leonard, an assistant to a fabulously wealthy woman who flies off on a honeymoon as the book begins, forgetting to pay Diana or provide her with a letter of reference. (Her absent-minded employer is named Angelina, echoing Angelica, an earlier character, and perhaps also Holding's own daughter Antonia.) Left to her own devices, Diana accepts an unexpected invitation from an estranged uncle to take up residence with him and serve as an apprentice. Once again, strange medical practices are being performed in the house, this time by Diana's aunt, who is training mentally handicapped children according to her own bizarre belief system. An Ayn Rand–type eugenicist who proclaims that "the world is largely peopled by idiots" (p. 176), the aunt eventually compels one of her charges to commit suicide by jumping off the roof. In an attempt to convince Diana to kill herself as well, the aunt argues, "There's nothing ahead of you but a lifetime of poorly paid work" (p. 268). On top of these outrages, the family is keeping an elderly patriarch on the grounds against his will in the hope that they can convince him to make them his heirs before he dies.

Diana is more vulnerable than Dennison, if less seduced by her circumstances (which are also more austere than Dennison's). Penniless, without employment, she quickly recognizes that she is entirely trapped; she has no access to the

postal service and the house is in a remote location with no working telephone. Although she is plucky and resolute in her attempts to escape, she quickly comes to rely upon one of Angelina's dashing male friends, James Fennel, who has followed her out to the remote house. Fennel avoids calling the police because he fears that Diana has become involved in the nefarious goings-on in the house and would be implicated in an investigation of her family. Ultimately, both Fennel and Diana need to be rescued by Angelina, who finally shows up and resolves everything with her wealth. Fennel is revealed at this point to be Angelina's brother; his marriage proposal in the final pages serves to save Diana once and for all.

THE DEATH WISH *(1934)*

In *The Death Wish,* Holding introduces her first pathologically unreliable narrator, a device she returns to in *The Unfinished Crime* and *The Innocent Mrs. Duff. The Death Wish* begins with an unhappy protagonist, Shawe Delancey, whose bad marriage is mirrored by his friend's similarly miserable union. Delancey's friend has fallen in love with a beautiful young neighbor and has decided to kill his wife.

The novel then switches perspectives and follows Hugh Acheson, a handsome, wealthy bachelor—somewhat reminiscent of Fennel, in *Dark Power*—who has been invited to visit friends as a prospect for the young neighbor. When Delancey's friend follows through on his threat and murders his wife, Acheson suspects that something criminal has transpired and begins to investigate the case.

The novel switches back and forth between the perspective of Delancey, who himself decides to murder his own wife, both for her money and to escape his marriage, and the perspective of Acheson, who feels increasing contempt for both Delancey and his friend. In addition, Acheson himself has fallen in love with the young neighbor, or at least has begun to admire her to the extent that he proposes to her as a way to divert public attention from her affair with a married man being charged with the murder of his wife. As Delancey begins feverishly plotting—and drinking—the novel tips toward Acheson's point of view as well as a few passages from other characters' perspectives. By the end, Delancey's voice has receded almost entirely and the novel remains wholly with Acheson. The young neighbor rejects Acheson's marriage proposal, preferring instead to dedicate herself to the memory of Delancey's married friend, who has killed himself rather than stand trial for the death of his wife, since the trial would implicate his lover, the young neighbor. Acheson's crusade to discover what happened to Delancey's wife, who does indeed die, reveals that she perished in a car accident and not at Delancey's hand, although Delancey blames himself for wishing her dead; meanwhile, other characters reproach Acheson for his quest to implicate people for the deaths of the two wives. The novel ends on an extremely unstable, downbeat note, with a rejected proposal and a perspective that has shifted entirely away from the original protagonist.

The strangely unresolved ending of *The Death Wish* raises the question of whether wishing someone dead is as bad as actually committing the crime—and goes on to conclude that it is not. Acheson doggedly pursues first Delancey's friend and then Delancey, but his quest for official justice slackens in the face of Delancey's confession that he suffers terrible guilt for plotting to kill his wife, even without following through. Ultimately Holding rewards Delancey with the only whisper of a happy ending that the novel offers, the possibility of his relationship with Helen Phillips, a single woman who has been staying at the Delancey house.

THE UNFINISHED CRIME *(1935)*

The Unfinished Crime extends this consideration of guilt with an even more unreliable and much less sympathetic narrator. Like *Death Wish, The Unfinished Crime* begins with a male protagonist who initially seems normal enough but is soon proven to be homicidal; at some point in each novel, readers realize that they are receiving distorted information, muddled by a deeply

unstable perspective. *The Unfinished Crime* concerns Andrew Branscombe, a controlling bachelor who lives with his younger sister and has fallen for an older, single mother whom he believes is a divorcée. When his love interest's former husband reappears, however, and it turns out that there was never actually a divorce, Branscombe, in a fit of impotent rage, brutally murders him. Branscombe then spends the rest of the novel in an increasing state of agitation and guilt, a situation exacerbated by his negotiations with Jerry, a drifter con artist who witnessed the crime. It is later revealed that the ex-husband has survived being attacked, a plot device used in several of Holding's novels. (For example, in *Dark Power,* Diana fears that Fennel is dead after being assaulted and left in the woods, and in *A Strange Crime in Bermuda,* a character is drugged and hidden in a closet for several days, while characters fear that he has been murdered.) Meanwhile, Branscombe is being blackmailed by Jerry, and several characters investigate the whereabouts of the husband, including a young man in love with Branscombe's sister. Branscombe cannot abide this suitor, an utterly reliable, devoted neighbor bent on liberating Branscombe's sister from her domineering brother.

In *The Unfinished Crime,* Branscombe's perfidy is revealed by the end of chapter 3, when he commits the violent act that he believes results in the former husband's death. The novel also features passages from the perspectives of several other characters, including Branscombe's sister, her suitor, Jerry, the blackmailer, and a young woman, Blanche, that the former husband had taken up with. Branscombe's brutal treatment of Blanche, whom he fears can implicate him in the former husband's disappearance, reveals his malevolent nature to the rest of the characters. Over the course of the novel, Branscombe becomes increasingly enmeshed in a series of deceptions and misdeeds in order to cover his original crime; he impersonates people, forges letters, and builds a massive network of lies. While his ruthless quest for control is despicable, he maintains a remarkable ability to lie his way out of tricky situations. Branscombe's amorality, self-centeredness, and quick wits anticipate Monty Duchesne, the protagonist of *The Virgin Huntress,* who in turn seems to provide a model for Patricia Highsmith's Tom Ripley.

Even at the close of the novel, when Branscombe has lured Blanche to a lonely barn so that Jerry can kill her, only to discover that the former husband is still alive, Branscombe manages to talk himself into the clear. However, he becomes overwhelmed with emotion, not with guilt but with frustration at his inability to contain events. Branscombe further recognizes that his sister plans to marry her suitor and will soon leave him. Feeling abandoned and full of self-pity, he kills himself.

The novel is more an intimate portrait of a control freak than the excursions into guilt that Holding usually pursues. In fact, the career criminal, Jerry, suffers far more guilt than Branscombe, as passages from Jerry's perspective reveal. In an ending typical of Holding, the gesture toward a happy ending occurs offstage and after the grim close of the novel, in that Branscombe's sister presumably weds the suitable beau to whom her brother had objected.

THE STRANGE CRIME IN BERMUDA *(1937)*

Holding's next novel is much more straightforward in terms of perspective. We remain almost exclusively with the protagonist, Hamish Grier, a young man who travels to Bermuda at the request of a friend, Hector Malloy, who disappears the moment Hamish arrives. Because Bermuda is an island, it is quickly verified that Malloy has not left its perimeter and must still be somewhere on it. Hamish does not understand Malloy's circumstances, or the motivation for his invitation, or the country of Bermuda itself; as a result, he, like the reader, struggles to fathom the increasingly disturbing events that surround him. Holding generates suspense by maintaining a single point of view—Hamish's—that is confused, away from home, and out of sorts, an effect that transfers the disorientation he suffers onto the reader.

Holding lived for some time in Bermuda because of her husband's work, and she depicts

the country's customs as mysterious but alluring, with local servants woven into the fabric of middle-class families' lives and references to Caribbean religion, which is portrayed as a form of magic. Malloy is married to a mysterious dark "foreign" woman, Faquita, born in the United States but raised in Argentina; after their move to Bermuda, Faquita employed a local woman, Leah, who claims to have special powers passed down to her through her family.

Eventually it is revealed that when Malloy decided to leave Faquita, she responded by giving him a "potion" that incapacitated him and hiding him in her wardrobe. Leah then cast a spell on her husband, Sam, after he threatened to give Hamish information about Malloy's whereabouts. Faquita and Leah also poison the household butler when he raises his own suspicions about these events. Finally, Faquita smothers a neighbor, a little old lady who has become involved in the case. Faquita is characterized as being capable of these criminal acts because she lacks a conscience as well as an understanding of the distinction between life and death, a misunderstanding attributed to the Caribbean location; the novel vaguely invokes the voodoo religion to explain Faquita's confusion.

Meanwhile, Hamish works to solve the mystery of his friend's disappearance with the help of Stephanie, Malloy's young, attractive, and blond neighbor. Her fairness is particularly significant in this novel, given that the population of Bermuda is otherwise depicted as "dark." Hamish resists complying with the police for fear of implicating Stephanie, who is suspected of having had an affair with Malloy. This is revealed as a false charge, and the novel ends with the exposure of Faquita's crimes, her subsequent suicide, Malloy's recovery, and the possibility of Stephanie and Hamish marrying.

WHO'S AFRAID? *(1940)*

In terms of narrative strategy, *Who's Afraid?* is dramatically different from *Strange Crime* in that a shifting perspective is key to the novel's suspense. *Who's Afraid?* follows young Susie Alban, a new saleswoman for Gateways, a correspondence course that teaches women charm. Unbeknownst to Susie, her employer's ne'er-do-well nephew had been passed over for this job and resents Susie for getting it; he first attempts to ruin her business prospects and then plots to kill her. This character remains a mystery to both the reader and Susie; as the novel opens, Susie is staying with three fellow male travelers at a bed-and-breakfast run by a fourth man. The novel switches between chapters in Susie's perspective and chapters from the perspective of one of the four men—the one trying to kill her.

The juxtaposition of the two perspectives begins almost comically: the first chapter ends with Susie relishing the adventure of traveling, thinking to herself, "The open road, and meeting new people. This is the life!" (p. 11). The next line, which begins the second chapter, is: "I'll have to get rid of this girl, one of the four men in the car was thinking" (p. 11). The unscrupulous nephew is thwarted in eliminating Susie because she is surrounded by the three other men. Meanwhile, Holding maintains each of the four male characters as potential suspects. In addition, Susie is attracted to the younger two of the four men. The two perspectives finally combine late in the novel, after Susie has been kidnapped by the man who is revealed to be the nefarious nephew. The novel ends with an extended shootout in the woods during a rainy night. Along the way, it turns out that Susie has been aided by the oldest of the three travelers, who has commissioned a detective to follow and protect her, and the second of the younger two travelers, who not only has fallen in love with Susie and vowed to defend her, but also, in the final pages of the novel, is revealed as the heir to millions.

Unfolding within a twenty-four-hour period, the play of perspective is a tour de force. In particular, Holding once again effectively voices the self-pitying, egotistic perspective of the killer, who is convinced that he is the victim of poor treatment, even as he murders and attempts to murder other characters. Like Branscombe in *The Unfinished Crime,* the killer remains unceasingly self-righteous, believing deeply in the validity of his motives and actions. Maintaining four charac-

ters as suspects for so long takes a certain toll on Susie's discernment; Holding is clearly torn between presenting Susie as a fresh young employee, unsophisticated and gullible, while also wanting to reward her for her desire for adventure and her determination to be brave. The novel, written during World War II, includes a moment in which the older of the four men muses admiringly about Susie: "I've met so many young people lately," he says, "who wanted to be safe ... I don't think you're very much interested in being safe" (p. 94). While Susie cheerfully responds that this may be because she's "stupid," both the older man and Holding appreciate Susie's pluck and spirit in taking to the road for her profession, and then later in capably defending herself. Primarily, however, the novel is an achievement in terms of perspective.

THE GIRL WHO HAD TO DIE *(1940)*

With *The Girl Who Had to Die,* Holding begins a series of novels set on cruise ships, including *Hostess to Murder* and *Lady Killer*. *The Girl* is striking in its candor about sexuality, a topic Holding does not otherwise broach until late in her career, in the 1950s. Told from the perspective of John Killian, the novel focuses on the aftermath of the escapades of an extremely attractive nineteen-year-old grifter, Jocelyn Frey, who has ensnared a series of men. Killian is initially torn between Jocelyn's instability and her beauty. After she apparently throws herself off the ship as a result of his rejection, he eventually capitulates to her in a fit of pity and guilt. After their reconciliation, Holding subtly indicates that Killian has consummated his relationship with Jocelyn and now feels compelled to marry her—despite the fact that Jocelyn continues to insist that Killian tried to kill her by pushing her off the boat.

As it turns out, this has been a pattern of Jocelyn's for some time: she manipulates men by claiming to have been mistreated by them. While underage, she engaged in a relationship with a much older man, Luther Bell, and subsequently blackmailed him for money by claiming to have been ruined by him; she later manipulated a doctor into giving her drugs by claiming that he made her an addict. Finally, it turns out that she is already married to the cruise ship's purser, although seeking divorce. After the ship lands, Jocelyn, Killian, the purser, and the purser's new girlfriend all head to the Bell family estate, most of the party unaware of Jocelyn's extortionist relationship with the Bells.

Although the novel begins with Killian already distressed about his relationship with Jocelyn and hoping to extricate himself, it nonetheless manages to deliver each new unsavory revelation about Jocelyn as a surprise. Killian is further suspicious of the wealth that the Bells enjoy and to which Jocelyn aspires. In these uncertain, confusing circumstances, Killian soldiers on, resisting Jocelyn and the Bells alike.

In the end, Mrs. Bell, like Killian new to her husband's social class, begs Killian to take Jocelyn away, strongly insinuating that he should kill her; she is just one in a string of characters who have wished Jocelyn dead, a sentiment that Jocelyn uses to justify her feeling of victimization. Killian is aghast at Mrs. Bell's suggestion, but soon finds himself on a small boat with only a crazed captain and Jocelyn, who confesses to committing a murder. Her motivation was to eliminate a witness to Killian's supposed attempted murder of Jocelyn earlier on the ship. Jocelyn is so wholly fixated on the man she loves that she is willing to commit terrible crimes; she also seems entirely ready to accept the notion that he too is inclined to criminal behavior. Although Holding returns to similarly ruthless and benighted characters in later novels, such as Virginia in *Net of Cobwebs* (1945) or Norma in *Too Many Bottles* (1950), Jocelyn is a particularly disturbed figure and a formidable adversary.

Killian navigates a relentless barrage of confusing motivations and poor logic, wondering, for instance, how Jocelyn gets away with her exaggerated claim that he has murdered her, given that she is still alive. Finally, horrified by her amorality, Killian jumps from the boat onto its dinghy; when Jocelyn follows him, Killian dives into the water and swims to shore, after which the boat drifts into an incoming squall.

Killian has thus inadvertently carried out Mrs. Bell's instructions and made good on Jocelyn's initial claim that he tried to kill her. In a typical Holding ending, the novel quietly paves the way for Killian to take up with the Bells' daughter, Harriet, although that relationship is never explicitly referenced.

SPEAK OF THE DEVIL / HOSTESS TO MURDER *(1941)*

Hostess to Murder, an abridged version of *Speak of the Devil,* follows Miss Karen Peterson, one of the more mature and capable of Holding's female protagonists. Multilingual—she speaks Swedish, Spanish, German, and English—Miss Peterson carries a gun and muses upon her many previous adventures. Recruited during a cruise to serve as the hostess of a hotel on the imaginary Caribbean island of Riquezas, Miss Peterson first withstands a powerful tropical storm and then the mysterious deaths of several hotel guests. As in *The Strange Crime in Bermuda,* voodoo and zombies are invoked in this island drama, although in the end everyone has died of more common causes (at least in Holding's world), such as poison. The final climax of the novel relies upon Miss Peterson's knowledge of Swedish and Spanish and involves a gun struggle between two men, one bound and slowly dying of thirst.

Once again, a character presumed dead is revealed to be alive, this time the chief antagonist. Once again, characters are poisoned, resulting in drug-induced sequences. And once again, Miss Peterson resists telling the police everything she knows, torn by her trust in her employer, the owner of the hotel, Don Carlos Fernandez, even as she suspects him of ruthlessness if not outright criminal acts. Ultimately Fernandez is proven trustworthy, and Miss Peterson's impulse not to confide in the police is justified. An innovation of this novel is an entertaining sequence in which Miss Peterson helps a young woman successfully navigate the legal system by encouraging her to dye her hair blond, returning it to its natural color. The makeover is successful and the woman is judged less harshly as a result of her more flattering locks.

Hostess ends without the formation of a couple. Miss Peterson receives repeated overtures from Fernandez, but although she pronounces him "magnificent!" at the close of the novel, she remains uninterested in marrying him. Meanwhile, the members of the other possible couple, a young man fleeing a murder he believes he has committed (in fact, the presumed victim is still alive) and an aspiring pianist avidly seeking publicity, have become estranged from one another.

LADY KILLER *(1942)*

Like *The Girl Who Had to Die* and *Hostess to Murder, Lady Killer* takes place on a cruise ship. The novel follows Honey, a former model who has recently married Mr. Stapleton, a wealthy older man, and is discovering that she has made a bad match. Querulous and paranoid, Mr. Stapleton tyrannizes his young wife, constantly suspecting her of infidelity and betrayal. Honey, who married Stapleton not for love but money, had hoped to enjoy at least a pleasant marriage but is recognizing that this will be impossible with Stapleton. In Honey, Holding seems to punish more severely than usual the impulse of those down on their luck to be seduced by the luxury promised by wealth.

Nonetheless, almost immediately upon embarking on the cruise, Honey becomes aware of Michael, a good-looking young man who also turns out to be wealthy. Meanwhile, Honey becomes convinced that the husband of another couple on the ship is plotting to murder his wife. The wife herself turns out to be a plotting murderer, too, and the novel ends with the couple departing together in a hydroplane, each hoping to kill the other. Along the way, the hypochondriacal Stapleton has died of a heart attack, a victim of overmedication. The novel closes with the possibility of Honey and Michael uniting at some point in the future, but in the meantime, the two stand unbetrothed, in the ruins of other relationships—Honey's disastrous first marriage and the lethal union of the couple bent on killing one another.

THE OLD BATTLE-AX *(1943)*

The Old Battle-Ax is one of Holding's few novels to explicitly reference World War II. Written when Holding herself was fifty-two, the protagonist, Mrs. Herriott, who is fifty, undergoes a wonderful metamorphosis over the course of the narrative. A character who has settled into her ways and is making do in a quiet, refined way, although her fortunes have fallen, Mrs. Herriott rises to circumstances admirably when a series of strange events befalls her. Transformed by the end of the novel, she reenters the world as a vigorous and contemporary force with competing romantic prospects. Mrs. Herriott's reemergence draws upon several themes dear to Holding: the pluck of regular people in extraordinary circumstances, a notion probably underwritten by the impact of World War II; and the resourcefulness of people having to make do or do without.

At a time when people were fleeing Europe, Mrs. Herriott receives a letter from her sister, Madge, who has been living in France, stating that she is returning to live with Mrs. Herriott. When Mrs. Herriott goes to meet the boat, from which injured Jewish men are being removed on stretchers, she is appalled by Madge, whom she finds "rakish and tawdry" (p. 16). Madge has been twice married and widowed, the second time to a Frenchman, and is now keen on marrying a man named Ramon. Shortly after arriving and drinking herself into a stupor, Madge leaves Mrs. Herriott's house and is found dead outside on the sidewalk.

The drama begins here, in that Mrs. Herriott is so scandalized by the sight of her sister, in bright makeup with her garters exposed, that she declares the body is a stranger's. Because almost no one else has met the sister, Mrs. Herriott's testimony is accepted. Meanwhile, she maintains that her sister has taken to her bed and cannot be disturbed. It is a desperate, irrational lie that Mrs. Herriott believes will be exposed at any minute, but to her amazement, even those who know otherwise play along, and the lie perpetuates itself. Mrs. Herriott's chauffeur conspires with Mrs. Herriott's niece, who begins to impersonate Madge to the police. The young niece, previously shy and withdrawn, relishes the opportunity to play a harridan. It is eventually revealed that the chauffeur has taken up the lie because Mrs. Herriott's sister confessed to him that she is not in fact Mrs. Herriott's sister, but an imposter attempting to gain access to Mrs. Herriott's sister's money.

The imposter has also given the chauffeur a large sum of money, which Mrs. Herriott and the niece use to flee the investigation. The two head into New York City, where they undergo makeovers: the niece convinces Mrs. Herriott to purchase contemporary clothing, and Mrs. Herriott educates her niece in the culture of ritzy hotels as the niece throws herself into playing her glamorous and dashing role.

At one point, Mrs. Herriott's chauffeur, his wife, and her teenage brother, together with Mrs. Herriott, her niece, and Ramon, the young Cuban who was betrothed to her sister, all end up at the beach together. Everyone dons swimsuits and desire circulates freely: the chauffeur is attracted to the niece, the chauffeur's wife wears a daring two-piece suit, Ramon also covets the niece, and Mrs. Herriott is revealed as a champion swimmer. Mrs. Herriott is suddenly caught up in the lives of young people, and, reanimated, newly recognizes the extent of her own strength. The interlude ends with the death of the chauffeur under mysterious circumstances, after which Mrs. Herriott takes a stiff drink and then requests morphine, resulting in one of the drug-induced sequences at which Holding excels.

The police once again play a peripheral if consistent role in the novel. In one gripping scene, Mrs. Herriott faces off against Sergeant Tucker as the two spar about the terms of class, gender, and power:

> "Don't!" she said. "Please don't talk in that horrible way ..."
>
> "I apologize," he said coldly. "If I haven't got the right expressions and—phraseologies, you got to remember I never went to college."
>
> "I never went to college, either," said Mrs. Herriott.
>
> "My schooling ended when I was eighteen years of age," said Sergeant Tucker.

> "*Mine* ended when I was *seventeen,*" said Mrs. Herriott.
>
> They looked squarely at each other.
>
> (p. 129)

Even formerly privileged women like Mrs. Herriott would have been denied access to higher education at this time, an omission that Mrs. Herriott wields against the police officer. According to her logic, she is justified in being simultaneously vulnerable and tough because of her gender; it has both protected and limited her, and she vigorously mobilizes both aspects against the policeman in this exchange.

The novel ends with a dramatic action sequence in which it is revealed that the maid's young brother is responsible for killing both the woman masquerading as Mrs. Herriott's sister and the chauffeur, whom the boy believed was abandoning his sister. The boy attempts to strangle Mrs. Herriott, who has a gun but refuses to use it against a child. At this suspenseful climax, Ramon's mother storms in and saves the day. In the denouement, Mrs. Herriott's true sister turns out to be alive in Europe and planning to return at a later date. Meanwhile, Mrs. Herriott, with a new wardrobe and improved figure, having lost weight during her ordeals, is taken up by Ramon's mother, who invites her to Cuba and tactfully points out what readers have already noticed: that Ramon is in love with Mrs. Herriott's niece, and also that Mrs. Herriott herself has two suitors, her lawyer and her clergyman. The novel thus ends with Holding's trademark promise of romance to come. The primary pleasure of *The Old Battle-Ax* is the revelation of Mrs. Herriott, who earlier seems to have quietly relinquished her claim to romance and even activity, as a force to be reckoned with.

NET OF COBWEBS *(1945)*

Holding's first postwar novel, *Net of Cobwebs* invokes the aftermath of war by featuring a damaged protagonist, Malcolm Drake, recovering from trauma sustained during a battle at sea and vulnerable to those around him. Reliant upon some kind of tranquilizer, Malcolm has been secretly stockpiling the drug, in part to consider suicide but also because he is addicted. Malcolm has returned to convalesce in his brother's household, which is filled with a bevy of unhelpful well-wishers, all of whom inhibit him and make him feel self-conscious: these include his brother's wife, Helene; her sister, Virginia, who has fallen in love with Malcolm; the girls' judgmental Aunt Evie; and the intrusive Dr. Lurie, himself in love with Virginia and therefore hostile to Malcolm. As in *The Strange Crime in Bermuda,* the most seemingly helpless, passive, and domestic character in the novel, Virginia, whose name suggests her youth and lack of experience, turns out to be the most dangerous. According to the logic of the novel, Malcolm is being smothered by (primarily) female solicitousness. The narrative hilariously contrasts his cynicism to the unsolicited advice with which he is constantly bombarded. (For example, Dr. Lurie advises Malcolm that "it's a very bad, a dangerous thing, to withdraw into yourself," to which Malcolm responds, "If I knew how to do it ... I'd be doing it now" [p. 199]).

Emboldened by his interest in a slightly older widow, Mrs. Kingscrown, Malcolm aggressively encourages irritating Aunt Evie to have a drink; he mixes her a tiny amount of alcohol, after which she immediately drops dead. When it turns out that she has left him a large amount in her will, Malcolm comes under increasing suspicion; thus, the irritant haunts him even after her death. However, the real threat is Virginia. As in *The Strange Crime in Bermuda,* this young, naive woman is dangerous not because she is clever or sophisticated but because she is simplemindedly and ruthlessly fixated on a particular version of events. She has concocted an elaborate scheme to ensnare Malcolm, wholly convinced that her actions are justified, even as she poisons people with Malcolm's barbiturates. Because her plot makes sense only from her deranged perspective, it is difficult for any of the other characters, or indeed the reader, to figure out what is going on. The novel pits the worldly-wise—widows, shell-shocked veterans—against the naive—Virginia—to suggest that those who believe them-

selves innocent may in fact be the most treacherous.

Malcolm's interior monologue throughout the novel is ribald; a former seaman, he covets his brother's maid, is bored by the polite conversation of the two sisters, and relishes his interactions with Mrs. Kingscrown, who, as the former wife of a seaman, seems comfortable with male companionship. After his pills are stolen by Virginia as part of her scheme, Malcolm stops taking the drugs. While he seems to begin self-medicating with alcohol instead, the novel suggests that drinking with Mrs. Kingscrown represents a healthier, more social and socially sanctioned form of intoxication, and that Malcolm is on the road to recovery.

THE INNOCENT MRS. DUFF *(1946)*

In her next two novels, *The Innocent Mrs. Duff* and *The Blank Wall,* Holding reached the high point of her career. *The Innocent Mrs. Duff* is a marvelous descent into the subjectivity of a deeply flawed character, in which Holding manages to express the skewed perspective of her protagonist while simultaneously signaling reality to her readers. The novel follows Jacob Duff, a man susceptible to self-delusion. Although it takes a while for readers to recognize that they are receiving a distorted version of Duff's world, Holding in fact indicates it in the first line of the novel, where Duff is surprised and outraged to discover that he has gained weight. Shortly after this revelation, Duff directs his irritation at his wife, Reggie. Because the reader receives no information from the wife's perspective, initially it is easy enough to believe that she plagues Duff. A younger second wife, Reggie worked previously as a model, like Honey in *Lady Killer*; Duff is embarrassed by her working-class ways, a theme Holding introduced in *The Unlit Lamp.* In addition, because of Reggie's beauty and former profession, Duff, like Honey's husband, suspects her of infidelity. This paranoia increases when one of Duff's neighbors mentions that Duff's handsome chauffeur, Nolan, is the talk of the middle-class matrons in the neighborhood. Rejecting Reggie, Duff mourns the death of his first wife, Helen.

Not until we receive a counter-narrative from Duff's beloved, no-nonsense Aunt Lou does it become apparent that Duff's vision is flawed. Aunt Lou declares, fairly early in the novel, that Duff never cared for his first wife, either; she then follows up this revelation by noting that she doesn't think Duff will ever be able to be happily married.

Increasingly fueled by alcohol and regularly experiencing a "feeling, now growing familiar, of dread and confusion" (p. 67), Duff goes to great lengths to set up Reggie and Nolan, his chauffeur, but neither is interested in the other and Duff's plot fails. Afterward, Nolan accuses Duff of attempting to frame him and Duff fires Nolan in a panic. Duff is incensed when a neighbor later comes over to defend Nolan's honor, and when the neighbor strikes Duff, he responds by killing the man, in full view of Reggie. After Duff has disposed of the body, Lieutenant Levy becomes involved in the case. This novel marks Levy's debut in Holding's work; he goes on to appear in three of Holding's next four novels. Solemn and grim, dogged and resolute, misread as slow but unerring in his perceptions, Levy suggests Holding's admiration for the careful work of police investigation. Alongside Holding's investment in the ethics of criminals, Levy represents the conscience and competence of the police force. In narrative terms, he is a formidable opponent.

Meanwhile, Nolan, unaware that Duff has committed a murder, returns to work for him, and the two men begin to plot together. Duff believes that Nolan is helping him trap Reggie, whereas Nolan is actually luring Duff into taking revenge on an old enemy with a crime that will lead to Duff's arrest, not Nolan's. In the end, under Levy's scrutiny, Reggie proves herself utterly devoted to Duff, including lying to the police to protect him. Duff, however, confesses to the neighbor's death, and Levy promises to hunt down Nolan, who has strangled his enemy and attempted to frame Duff for the crime.

At the novel's close, Duff, in an alcohol-induced state of despondency, commits suicide

after being arrested by Levy. This act flummoxes the sensible police detective, who cannot understand Duff's motivation, given his wealth, resources, social standing, and beautiful, dedicated young wife. The only conclusion Levy can come to invokes one of Holding's chief concerns, as well as providing the final line of the novel: "He must have been guilty as hell" (p. 199).

THE BLANK WALL *(1947) AND ITS FILM ADAPTATIONS*

The Blank Wall is probably Holding's most famous novel; it has been adapted twice for the cinema, once as *The Reckless Moment* (1949) and again as *The Deep End* (2001). A masterful depiction of domestic travails at the end of World War II, when even the middle and upper-middle classes were feeling the impact of the war, the novel follows Lucia Holley, whose husband is away at war. As a result, she has assumed charge of a household, somewhere in Long Island or along the Connecticut coast, that includes her teenage daughter, a younger son, and her father. Lucia and her maid, Sibyl, scrimp and save in order to keep the household afloat. Meanwhile, Lucia's daughter, Bee, has been carrying on an affair with an older, disreputable man. Lucia successfully breaks up the relationship by offering to pay the man off, but when he returns to their house, Lucia's father engages in a nighttime argument with him and pushes him off a dock, where he falls to his death, unbeknownst to her father. Lucia discovers the body in the morning and disposes of it in an attempt to protect her daughter and father.

It turns out that Bee's lover was a petty criminal who had hoped to blackmail the family with amorous letters she had written him. Once he goes missing, these letters rise in value because of her family's desperation to conceal the connection between Bee and a dead criminal. A thug, Martin Donnelly, soon arrives at Lucia's home to extract money in exchange for the letters. However, during their interactions, Donnelly and Lucia become complicit in maintaining appearances. Donnelly is willing to pretend to be a friend of family so that he can gain access to Lucia's home, while Lucia plays along so that no one will suspect the truth. As Lucia negotiates with Donnelly and attempts to raise the blackmail money, she is simultaneously required to run the household, which formerly absorbed all her energy. Meanwhile, Bee's lover's body has been discovered on the island where Lucia deposited it and Lieutenant Levy is put on the case—always bad news for an anxious person on the wrong side of the law.

As Donnelly and Lucia conspire in discreet locations, Donnelly grows enamored of her, attracted by her commitment to her family and her devotion to her children. He first refuses his share of the blackmail and then begins bringing black market gifts to the household. He hires someone to do the family's laundry and bestows an entire ham upon them, a meal they cannot afford with ration tickets alone. While Lucia appreciates Donnelly's support, she suspects his motives and is further self-conscious about the gifts, attempting to hide the expensive ham from neighbors. Meanwhile, her children react with horror as she flouts social conventions to meet Donnelly repeatedly. Lucia's husband is never a presence in the narrative; although she regularly writes him letters, she dares not convey the gravity of the situation in which she finds herself. Furthermore, both Lucia and Donnelly are described as good looking. Given these factors, Lucia and Donnelly emerge as the primary couple of the novel.

The growing connection between Lucia and Donnelly, with its romantic possibility, is one of the book's most compelling aspects. In bringing together characters from different class backgrounds with motivations almost entirely at odds with one another, Holding creates a fascinating combination of opposition, attraction, and mutual appreciation. Both are skilled and powerful in their own ways, but while Donnelly, as a career criminal, might be expected to be tough and resourceful, the revelation of Lucia's unexpected strength, as she fights to defend her family, is fascinating. An accomplished swimmer, Lucia is apparently strong enough to drag a grown man's corpse into a small motorboat and then dispose of it on an isolated island. Later, she proves

herself a talented liar, using her status as a middle-class mother to great effect.

Increasingly cognizant of her own ruthlessness, Lucia begins to recognize that Donnelly is completely trustworthy; she comes to rely on his strength as well as hers. Meanwhile, they grow more intimate; he calls her "dear," and "darlin' "; she calls him "Marty"; they drink together. When Lieutenant Levy learns of their relationship, he insinuates to Lucia that they must be lovers.

Finally, Donnelly's boss shows up; he threatens Lucia, at which point Donnelly kills him in her defense, after which he, Lucia, and eventually also Sibyl help dispose of the body. Lucia and Donnelly part ways, but shortly afterward Lucia is cornered by Levy into calling Donnelly and asking him to return to the house. She agrees, only because she believes that Donnelly has left the country. However, although he never receives her phone call, Donnelly comes back to Lucia's house of his own volition, on a romantic mission to return the jewels she pawned to cover the ransom. Learning of her betrayal, Donnelly sacrifices himself by confessing to the murder of not only his crime boss but also Bee's lover. In doing so, he ties himself forever to Lucia and her family, having claimed responsibility for an act committed by her father. He further demonstrates the intensity of his conscience in that he feels great remorse for having killed his partner in crime, an act he easily could have gotten away with. The sympathy the audience is encouraged to feel for Donnelly helps justify Lucia's own reluctant admiration for him. In Donnelly, Holding's belief in the possibility of ethical criminals is most fully realized.

Just two years after the publication of *The Blank Wall,* the novel was adapted for cinema as *The Reckless Moment* (1949). In the film version, Lucia's husband is away because he is involved in postwar efforts to rebuild Europe. Because he is a businessman rather than a soldier, his absence feels more like abandonment than service to country. Directed by Max Ophüls, the film features his characteristically mobile camera, moving fluidly through domestic space or tracking Lucia (played by Joan Bennett) as she walks along the beach. Filmed in black and white, the film includes several sequences with atmospheric shadows that indicate the dangerous world that Lucia enters when she meets with Martin. James Mason plays the role of Martin, Lucia's adversary cum romantic interest, with aplomb; his accent suggests the dangerous "foreignness" that Martin represents. Furthermore, the star's brooding handsomeness helps underwrite the attraction between the two main characters. Together, they quickly resemble a couple, with Martin seamlessly stepping in to play the role of father of the household: he helps her son repair the family car and gives her father tips on the horse races, without the father understanding that the bets are fixed.

The film characterizes Lucia's toughness by making her a smoker well before she faces the threat of blackmail, after which she smokes even more. Meanwhile, Martin worries about her habit; he buys her a cigarette holder with a filter and includes it with the rest of her groceries in an attempt to protect her health. His gift, however, goes unrecognized; neither Lucia nor her maid understands where the item came from and Lucia asks the maid to return it to the store.

In the end, after murdering his boss and hiding the body in the trunk of his car, Martin drives away injured but has an accident shortly afterward. Lucia, who has been following him, comes upon the scene first. The car has rolled, and Martin hangs trapped upside down. In a close-up of the two, Martin instructs Lucia to retrieve her daughter's letters from the car. To do so, Lucia, sobbing, must put her head very close to Martin's; the close-up shot resembles an upside-down kiss. Martin ends this moment of intimacy, however, by sacrificing himself for Lucia and her family: he insists that she leave, and when the police arrive, in the moments before he dies, he confesses to the murder of Lucia's daughter's lover.

In the novel, Lucia and Martin come together as a couple; in the film, this formation is all the more obvious, given James Mason's appeal and soulful expressions, and the fact that Lucia's husband never appears onscreen and is almost never referred to. The working-class criminal's self-sacrifice in order to maintain the integrity of

the middle-class family is even more poignant, given the power of the screen connection between Lucia and Martin.

In remaking the novel over fifty years later, the question must have been: What infraction could terrorize a middle-class family into agreeing to pay blackmail? Simply having a sexually active daughter would no longer ruin a family in the twenty-first century, even if her lover were a sleazy criminal. Instead, in *The Deep End* (2001), the answer was to make the oldest child of the family a boy engaged in a homosexual relationship. The family has a long-standing connection to the military; the father is away on a navy ship. However, even the context of a possibly repressive, homophobic atmosphere does not convey the same threat to middle-class propriety that the daughter's transgression fifty years ago would have.

Nonetheless, Tilda Swinton is impressive in her role as a stay-at-home mother, this time with three children, one quite small; this additional, younger child is perhaps meant to explain why the protagonist, named Margaret in this version, does not work outside the home and therefore has no access to income when the blackmailer arrives. The blackmailer is played by Goran Visnjic, who, like James Mason, has an accent (Visnjic is Croatian), to indicate the foreign threat he poses. Visnjic's career was at its peak at the time, as a result of his role as Dr. Luka Kovac on the television show *ER,* a popular emergency room drama. The film overtly references this role in that the blackmailer, named Alek Spera in this version, insinuates himself into Margaret's home by tending to her father-in-law when he has a heart attack. In the midst of negotiating with Margaret, Alek springs into action and performs CPR, saving the father-in-law's life.

Alek and Margaret make a handsome couple. Visnjic is dashing and Swinton is simultaneously vulnerable and resourceful, in a sinewy way. Again, the rightful husband remains entirely offscreen; in addition, because the father and his role in the military are the source of the homophobia driving Margaret's panic to protect her son, viewers are subtly encouraged to dislike the offscreen father. In contrast, the handsome Alek attempts to help Margaret and finally rescues her after she is physically attacked—a twenty-first-century addition—by Alek's criminal boss.

The remake adapts both the novel and the film, drawing elements from the two texts in this third version. For instance, the remake uses the first film's ending, so that Alek drives away with a broken arm but then wrecks the car. Margaret comes upon the crash and the two engage in a moment of intimacy very similar to the first film; the remake features an extreme close-up of their juxtaposed mouths while Margaret reaches to salvage the evidence—this time a videotape—from the car. Once again, Alek insists that Margaret leave the scene to protect herself and her family, then dies.

MISS KELLY *(1947)*

In the midst of writing about criminals, Holding also penned an illustrated children's book about a cat, an animal that makes many appearances in her novels. In this story, animals are able to speak to each other, and some special animals, like Miss Kelly, are able to understand and speak English. When a tiger escapes from the zoo and threatens the family Miss Kelly lives with, she must reveal her talent in order to communicate with the tiger and protect the family she lives with, or her Humans, as she calls them.

Holding draws upon many themes from her suspense novels in this book. For instance, the notion of guilt is once again explored: Is the tiger wrong for wanting to kill and eat Humans? Can he transcend his essential nature? Similarly, the previously domesticated cat suddenly thrown into negotiations with a wild animal strongly echoes the plot of *The Blank Wall,* with the cat playing the middle-class matron with hidden talents and the tiger playing the criminal who is ultimately too large and scary to remain unnoticed in a middle-class neighborhood but does have a raw appeal.

In the children's book, Holding is able to create a third space that allows the connection between characters from different worlds to continue permanently. Miss Kelly transitions from house cat into translator at the local zoo,

where both worlds, domestic and feral, can intersect. She helps the animals express their needs to the zoo curator and educates them in understanding English. In exchange, the zookeeper teaches her to read. Most importantly, she gets to maintain her relationship with the tiger, of whom she states: "He's so intelligent and so honorable and so eager to learn. I can't leave him" (p. 119). Written the same year as *The Blank Wall, Miss Kelly* allows Holding to resolve the earlier novel's central narrative conflict in a different, more satisfying way. If Lucia must abandon, even betray Martin, in *Miss Kelly,* Holding creates a version in which a domestic cat can live forever with her regal, devoted, only somewhat dangerous wild tiger, and further enjoy a rewarding, productive job. *Miss Kelly*'s coy dedication—"To the Tiger who was my First Playmate"—may explain the energy Holding brings to the potential relationship in *The Blank Wall.* This teasing reference raises the question of whether the Tiger was Holding's husband or an earlier companion. In any case, the children's novel—her only one—provides her with the freedom to realize a fantasy version of a permanent union between these characters. It is one of the few truly happy endings Holding ever scripted.

TOO MANY BOTTLES *(1950)*

In *Too Many Bottles,* Holding returns to adult material and plays so dramatically with narrative that she presciently invokes a postmodern style yet to dominate the literary arena. The protagonist, James Brophy, is another husband stuck in a bad marriage, this time to Lulu, who is both his wife and patron. Like *The Death Wish,* the husband is financially dependent on his wife, who, again as in *Death Wish,* is clinging, demanding, and an unsuccessful social climber resentful of her inability to climb higher. In addition, she is addicted to prescription medicine, an accidental overdose of which kills her in the first act. However, unlike *Death Wish,* the protagonist is sympathetic and insouciant in the face of these domestic difficulties.

Most significantly, Brophy is a writer of pulp fiction, the closest Holding ever came to referring to her own occupation. Throughout the novel, he is constantly riffing in an interior monologue, devising plots to mystery novels. Like Malcolm in *Net of Cobwebs,* Brophy lives in a household dominated by women, in this case his wife and her sister Norma, another apparently helpful but also helpless, completely domestic female character. Yet again, this figure proves to be ruthlessly driven to enact her own version of events, which involves marrying Brophy.

It is Brophy who accidentally overdoses Lulu during a cocktail party, leading to her death. This happens while he is mentally rearranging the narrative of a piece of fiction he plans to write in which a cocktail party is disrupted by a murder. As he considers a woman at the party whom he finds attractive, Biddy Hamilton, he ponders how to include her in his story, revising the plot and struggling to move beyond genre conventions: "The girl in my Party story could be her type, more or less, thought Brophy, sitting on the arm of a chair and watching her. She's been avoiding the man the hostess wants, but she loves him. Why has she been running away from him? Because she thinks he's guilty of—something? No. That's the pulp touch. It's got to be more psychological" (p. 152).

The plot grows increasingly bizarre, including a humorous, nightmarish sequence in which Norma throws repeated funerals for her sister, basically bankrupting Brophy, who has no money of his own. Brophy learns upon Lulu's death that she has in fact been supporting them all on alimony from her first husband, while promising that Brophy will eventually repay him. Throughout the criminal investigation that ensues, Brophy is increasingly hell-bent on finishing his story because he needs the money; at the same time, he feels self-conscious about having been a kept man and ambivalent about his job. His story in fact becomes woven into the narrative of the novel, in that Norma finds a draft, reads it, and becomes convinced that he killed her sister. Brophy's anxiety about the finances associated

with professional writing, scripted by an author who earned good money by doing so but came from a social class in which writing pulp fiction would have been looked down upon, provides a telling insight into Holding's possibly ambivalent relationship to her own profession.

Once again, in this later novel competent and bold characters prevail, while naive homebodies like Norma turn out to be dangerous. In contrast, Biddy makes outrageously cheeky statements for the early 1950s during her interrogation by Lieutenant Levy, who reappears in this novel. In recounting the exchange, she tells Brophy:

> "[Lieutenant Levy] asked me, right out, Is Brophy your lover? and I said no, unfortunately."
>
> "You said—what?"
>
> "You heard me," said Biddy.
>
> (p. 229)

The novel ends with the possibility of Brophy and Biddy eventually forming a couple, although in typical Holding style, offscreen.

THE VIRGIN HUNTRESS *(1951)*

Holding's penultimate novel, *The Virgin Huntress,* introduces Montford Duchesne, a character who is remarkably similar to the protagonist of five of Patricia Highsmith's novels, Tom Ripley. Given that Ripley debuted just four years later, in 1955, that Holding was widely read at the time, and that the authors wrote in the same genre, one can't help wondering whether Duchesne served as an inspiration for Ripley. Certainly many aspects of the novel bear similarities.

With both Duchesne and Ripley we follow the misadventures of a self-centered liar and thief wholly convinced of his own, if not innocence, then justification in committing the series of crimes he perpetrates. Each battles terrible self-loathing and feels his social persona is a facade that barely conceals his unremitting unease with himself and others. While Duchesne is handsome, Ripley is cunning and clever; both men use these traits to their advantage. Highsmith gives Tom a family background that may explain to some extent his resulting socio-pathology, in that he was orphaned at a young age and brought up by a cruel aunt. Holding either provides no explanation for Duchesne's immorality, or perhaps suggests that his "Latin" roots—his mother is Venezuelan—"explain" his bad behavior. Both Holding and Highsmith create outrageous but entertaining narrators who proceed blithely along, feeling entitled to carry out increasingly violent misdeeds. Along the way, they encounter the occasional suspicious character; Ripley proves capable of evading such figures, but Duchesne is pursued doggedly by a young woman whom he dubs a virgin huntress. In the end, she succeeds in bringing him down.

Holding addresses sexuality much more explicitly in this novel than in any of her others, and much more so than in any of Highsmith's novels, which suggest that Tom is either asexual or a repressed homosexual; in either case, his sexuality remains at bay throughout the five-novel series. In contrast, Duchesne's libido draws him to a series of vulnerable young women, but he is nervous about being trapped in a relationship by any of them. After he impregnates one of the women, he drugs her and flees the premises, not knowing what happens afterward; because she never knows his true name, he is not pursued for the crime, even after she dies from his overdose. When he circles back to try to cover his tracks, he is confronted by the victim's sister, who does not believe the official verdict that her sister committed suicide. Holding goes to some lengths to keep the reader sympathetic to Duchesne for as long as possible, in part by delaying information, such as drugging his pregnant girlfriend. However, when he cold-bloodedly strangles the girlfriend's sister, he is revealed as a monster. Shortly afterward, the young woman investigating him calls the police, and as he is going to be arrested, he throws himself out the window to his death.

Like *The Death Wish, The Unfinished Crime,* and *The Innocent Mrs. Duff, The Virgin Huntress* plays out within the interiority of a character that the reader increasingly recognizes as unhinged. Delancey, of *The Death Wish,* is the most

salvageable. Although the novel abandons his perspective for the close of the narrative, he is allowed to survive and even given a hint of a happy ending. In his case, the novel suggests that his wife's unpleasantness justifies his bad behavior. In contrast, like the protagonists of *The Unfinished Crime* and *The Innocent Mrs. Duff,* Duchesne commits suicide at the end.

WIDOW'S MITE *(1952)*

In Holding's final novel, maturity is once again rewarded. Told from the perspective of Tilly MacDonald, a widow with a five-year-old son named Robert, the novel follows a series of events that commence when Robert claims that he has been menaced in the woods by a boy who poisons animals. Tilly depends upon the intermittent generosity of her tyrannical cousin, who is herself poisoned almost immediately after Robert's announcement. When increasingly frightening events befall Robert, Tilly grows to rely on her cousin's friend, Osborne. Although Holding makes some effort to cast doubt upon Osborne, readers quickly suspect that he is another in a series of reliable men worthy of the protagonist's trust. Lieutenant Levy also reappears in this novel, to keep everyone on their toes.

The novel flirts with the possibility that Robert has accidentally poisoned Tilly's cousin. Although he is quickly exonerated, suspicion then falls upon another child, the teenage son of Tilly's cousin, the older boy who has been tormenting Robert and killing woodland creatures. Eventually the murderer is revealed to be a woman friend of the cousin's who has descended into drug addiction. However, she involves Tilly in the murder, in that Tilly unwittingly administers the lethal dose that kills her cousin. This inadvertent act is echoed toward the end of the novel, when Robert poisons his beloved nanny by mistake with cyanide that has been hidden in the sugar bowl of a child's tea set.

Despite the uneasiness about guilt that circulates throughout this novel, it ends, unusually for Holding, with a kiss, albeit not a romantic one. Nonetheless, when Osborne encourages Tilly not to be morbid and then kisses her on the temple in the closing lines of the novel, the somewhat optimistic, somewhat intimate moment is the closest Holding comes in her twenty-five novels to the possibility of a romantic relationship (outside of her children's book). It provides a hopeful final note at the end of a long and significant career.

Holding did more than earn a living by writing novels. She also expanded the terms of the suspense genre for future writers, perhaps particularly women genre writers like Patricia Highsmith. Reading her work chronologically, it makes sense that the very elements that destabilize Holding's early domestic novels serve her well in the suspense genre, such as characters who struggle mightily against social conventions rather than succumbing to them. Angelica's refusal in a 1921 domestic novel to wed the rich man who loves her, the prescribed fate for a female protagonist, thoroughly undermines the expectations of that genre, but it resonates thrillingly in a 1947 suspense novel in Lucia, the housewife drawn despite herself to a mobster. Holding developed a range of characters that challenged the notion of middle-class complacency and suggested instead the restless energy of otherwise mainstream U.S. life. Especially during the two world wars and in their aftermath, Holding recognized the resourcefulness that otherwise normal, law-abiding people are capable of when they run up against the propriety of social norms and the law. That these characters are often women, occasionally themselves surprised at the emergence of their own power, allows Holding to further expand the suspense genre. Relishing figures that are energetic, vibrant, and daring, Holding quietly pushed against not only the conventions of the genre of the suspense novel but also against the social conventions of the U.S. middle class. Her own restless energy, which generated twenty-five books, lives on in her novels and their film adaptations.

Selected Bibliography

WORKS OF ELISABETH SANXAY HOLDING

DOMESTIC NOVELS

Invincible Minnie. New York: George H. Doran, 1920.

Rosaleen Among the Artists. New York: George H. Doran, 1921.

Angelica. New York: George H. Doran, 1921. Reprinted, LaVergne, Tenn.: Kessinger, 2010.

The Unlit Lamp. New York: Dutton, 1922. Reprinted, LaVergne, Tenn.: Kessinger, 2010.

The Shoals of Honour. New York: Dutton, 1926.

The Silk Purse. New York: Dutton, 1928.

SUSPENSE NOVELS

Miasma. New York: Dutton, 1929. Reprinted, Eureka, Calif.: Stark House Press, 2003.

Dark Power. New York: Vanguard Press, 1930. Reprinted, Eureka, Calif.: Stark House Press, 2008.

The Death Wish. New York: Dodd, Mead, 1934. Reprinted, Eureka, Calif.: Stark House Press, 2004.

The Unfinished Crime. New York: Dodd, Mead, 1935.

The Strange Crime in Bermuda. New York: Dodd, Mead, 1937. Reprinted, Eureka, Calif.: Stark House Press, 2005.

The Obstinate Murderer. New York: Dodd, Mead, 1938. Also published as *No Harm Intended,* London: Lane, 1938.

Who's Afraid? New York: Duell, Sloan and Pearce, 1940. Reprinted, New York: Ace Books, 1953. Also published as *Trial by Murder,* New York: Novel Selections, 1940.

The Girl Who Had to Die. New York: Dodd, Mead. 1940. Reprinted, New York: Ace Books, 1947.

Speak of the Devil. New York: Duell, Sloan and Pearce, 1941. Abridged version, *Hostess to Murder,* New York: Novel Selections, 1941.

Kill-Joy. New York: Duell, Sloan and Pearce, 1942. Also published as *Murder Is a Kill-Joy,* New York: Dell, 1946.

Lady Killer. Duell, Sloan and Pearce, 1942. Reprinted, Eureka, Calif.: Stark House Press, 2003.

The Old Battle-Ax. New York: Simon & Schuster, 1943. Reprinted, Eureka, Calif.: Stark House Press, 2008.

Net of Cobwebs. New York: Simon & Schuster, 1945. Reprinted, Eureka, Calif.: Stark House Press, 2004.

The Innocent Mrs. Duff. New York: Simon & Schuster, 1946. Reprinted, Chicago: Academy Chicago, 1991.

The Blank Wall. New York: Simon & Schuster, 1947. Reprinted, Chicago: Academy Chicago, 1991.

Too Many Bottles. New York, Simon & Schuster, 1950. Reprinted, Eureka, Calif.: Stark House Press, 2005. Also published as *The Party Was the Pay-Off,* New York: Mercury, 1951.

The Virgin Huntress. New York: Simon & Schuster, 1951.

Widow's Mite. New York: Simon & Schuster, 1952.

OTHER WORKS

Miss Kelly. New York: Morrow, 1947. (Children's book.)

"The Matador." *Munsey's Magazine,* June 1923. Reprinted, Eureka, Calif.: Stark House Press, 2008.

CRITICAL AND BIOGRAPHICAL STUDIES

Kelleher, Ed. "Going Off the Deep End: Directors McGehee and Siegel Create a Domestic Film Noir." *Film Journal International* 104, no. 8:12–14 (August 2001).

Schwed, Peter. Introduction to *The Blank Wall.* Chicago: Academy Chicago, 1991.

Scruggs, Charles. "The Depth of the Deep End: The Noir Motif in *The Reckless Moment* and *The Deep End.*" *Mosaic* 37, no. 1:17–32 (March 2004).

Shepard, Gregory. Introduction to *The Strange Crime in Bermuda and Too Many Bottles.* Eureka, Calif.: Stark House Press, 2005.

Wood, Robin. "Plunging Off *The Deep End* into *The Reckless Moment.*" *CineAction* 59:14–19 (2002).

FILMS BASED ON THE WORK OF ELISABETH SANXAY HOLDING

The Reckless Moment. Directed by Max Ophüls. Screenplay by Henry Garson and Robert Soderberg. Columbia Pictures, 1949.

The Deep End. Direction and screenplay by Scott McGehee and David Siegel. Twentieth Century Fox, 2001.

EDWARD P. JONES

(1950—)

Joseph Dewey

THE VOLUMES THAT line the ornate hand-carved oak bookcase in the parlor of John Skiffington, the sheriff of Manchester County in *The Known World,* Edward P. Jones's Pulitzer Prize–winning novel set in pre–Civil War Virginia, reflect (by Skiffington's own admission) more the reading habits of his wife. Skiffington, we are told, is not much of a reader. Indeed, save for the Bible (actually just the story of the long-suffering Job), Skiffington admits a fondness for only one volume in the huge collection, Washington Irving's *Sketch Book,* a beautiful red leatherbound second edition he had presented to his wife to celebrate their engagement twenty years earlier. The sheriff is particularly partial to "Rip Van Winkle"; he never tires of reading to his guests the tale of the mountain man and his twenty-year absence after encountering strange little Dutchmen drinking lager and playing nine-pins in the cloud-shrouded Catskills.

It is at first glance the sort of throwaway detail that Jones so relishes in his meticulous recreation of antebellum Virginia—after all, Irving's celebrated best seller is period appropriate and thus helps render the verisimilitude that animates Jones's panoramic novel and coaxes the reader into the verbal suction of his historic recreation. But the introduction of "Rip Van Winkle" may actually reveal something of the fictive sensibility of Jones himself. Not to put extraordinary interpretive weight on a minor detail in a four-hundred-plus-page novel, but the elements of Irving's tale triangulate Jones's own larger thematic interests. There is first the extravagant fantasy of Rip's winsome disappearance, quaffing a mysterious elixir that affords him a twenty-year escape from the dreary reality of his impoverished day-to-day existence, his rundown farm, his needful children, and supremely his joyless wife. Then there is the frame: Rip's narrative is told by Diedrich Knickerbocker, a smirking historian-raconteur who swears that the most marvelous elements of Rip's story are, in fact, true, making Rip's narrative at once history and a parody of history, history that foregrounds the spacious grasp of the imagination and questions the viability of fact. And there is a third element, the easily ignored reality of Dame Van Winkle herself, determined in the two-decade absence of her slacker husband to shoulder, with Job-like grit, the responsibilities of family and farm.

In an accomplished if slender body of work—two collections of interrelated stories and a novel—Jones has tested each element: the desperate, grateful retreat into refuge-shelters against an oppressive reality (Rip); the tricky work of constructing viable histories, how a culture seeks the elaborate refuge of invented narratives to make sense of raw and often brutal events (Diedrich Knickerbocker); and ultimately the affirmation of virtues that refuse to sparkle, the determination to engage the work of marriage, family, and community (Dame Van Winkle). These are the signature themes of a man raised amid the harrowing hopelessness of inner-city poverty; whose earliest recollections were of happy retreat into the welcoming coziness of comic books and television; and who first tapped the power of fiction not in its ability to incite social or political reform or to define an African American self—despite being an African American teenager growing up during the bloody street birth of the civil rights movement and living in the capital of a divided nation, in the epicenter of political turmoil, race riots, and assassinations—but rather its ability to conjure coaxing faux-realities, tender escapes. As Jones told the

interviewer Lawrence P. Jackson, when he was seventeen he was reading James Jones's best seller *From Here to Eternity* when he came upon a scene that describes Private Pruitt playing his saxophone, a textual moment conjured so carefully that Pruitt seemed inescapably immediate, an emotional empathy that for a slender stunning moment liberated the teenage Jones from his grim tenement world. That, Jones intuited, was the worth of fiction. Indeed, when Jones himself published for the first time, nearly a decade later, that short story would not bear the autobiographical impress typical of first-time writers. Rather it would measure the reach of his imagination, the depth of his escape: Jones, who at that time had never been married and whose parents had separated before he was three, projected himself into an entirely imagined dilemma, the story of a long-suffering woman who waits patiently with a Christmas present for a philandering boyfriend.

Taken together, Jones's three works cooperate into a kind of trilogy that maps a hesitant, but determined movement outward; the narrative arc of Jones's three works reveals a writer coming to terms with the problematic consolations of the imagination and the need to violate the self through commitment to family, love, and community. In his first work, the gloomy stories gathered in *Lost in the City* (1992), characters withdraw in desperate gestures of retreat, overwhelmed, like Rip, by the implication of vulnerability and the brutality of contingency and uninterested in the logic of responsibility. In his second work, *The Known World* (2003), Jones tackles the curious logic of withdrawal by satirizing, like the gamester historian Diedrich Knickerbocker, the most privileged refuge-shelter of them all, the sacrosanct edifice of history through which an anxious culture collectively pretends a raw, ugly event is actually coherent and patterned. And in Jones's third work, the magnificent stories of *All Aunt Hagar's Children* (2006), his beleaguered Job-like characters are determined now, like Dame Van Winkle, to accept the decidedly unglamorous responsibility of making relationships work, sustaining the dynamic of family, and ultimately confronting sickness and mortality itself.

BIOGRAPHY

The materials of Jones's life story had little direct impact in his fictions, nor is there a triggering traumatic event that determined young Edward would write. Rather the difficult conditions of his childhood made him into a kind of Rip, shaped his fascination with the suasive escape of invented worlds, the bunker-logic of the imagination. Edward Paul Jones was born on October 5, 1950, in Washington, D.C. He grew up in abject poverty in the rundown neighborhoods that ironically surround the elegant monuments of the National Mall. Jones had little memory of his father, a Jamaican immigrant who abandoned the family before Jones was three, even as the family dealt with the difficulties of Edward's younger brother, Joseph, born with severe retardation. Jeanette, Jones's heroic mother, a woman who could neither read nor write, was determined to raise her family on her own against the constant pressure of foster care; she worked long hours as a restaurant dishwasher and hotel chambermaid. During his adolescence, Edward and his sister, Eunice, were moved constantly (Joseph had been committed to the care of a group home outside the city)—eighteen different addresses in eighteen years as Jeanette resolutely negotiated relentless bill collectors and unsympathetic landlords. The constant relocations made friendships difficult for Edward, and early on he turned to the refuge of schoolwork. He excelled in the classroom. Although Baptist, his mother dreamed of a private Catholic education for her perspicacious son, but the money was never there and Jones attended public school.

When he was not gratefully immersed in his schoolwork, Edward happily slipped into the inviting fantasies of comic books, particularly Batman. Or he would watch TV, enthralled by the flickering images on the little black-and-white televisions of friends who could afford such luxuries. Or when he could afford it, he would spend long afternoons in the cavernous refuge of movie theaters. But it was ultimately novels, made-up people doing made-up things, which offered the shy teenager his amplest and sturdiest refuge. What recollections Jones offers of his childhood center not on ugly confrontations with

bigotry (he seldom ventured beyond his neighborhood) but rather on the difficult prison of poverty and the tonic liberation of reading, his imagination unfettered. Book fed and word fat, Jones would be the first in his family to attend college: a chance encounter with a Catholic missionary at his high school encouraged Jones to apply for a scholarship to study literature at the College of the Holy Cross, a small, prestigious Catholic university in distant Massachusetts. Escaping the claustrophobic environs of Washington, he came to embrace fiction as a calling. Tested by the rigors of a Jesuitical education, Jones ironically abandoned belief in God—the more he studied fiction, particularly the modernists, most notably James Joyce, the more he was convinced that the writer was a sufficient deity, fashioning intricate private universes of clear design where causality worked, where events followed reassuring logic.

After graduating in 1972, Jones returned to Washington to assume custodial care of his mother, who had suffered a series of debilitating strokes and was in the early stages of lung cancer. He worked odd jobs but found refuge in writing stories; he would write in longhand at a folding table late into the night. In January 1975 Jeanette died. Her death spiraled Jones into a profound depression. Finding Washington too painful, he sought refuge in Philadelphia, living there for five months, for a time in homeless shelters. But in what was becoming a pattern—the shuttling between harsh reality and the grateful retreat into invented worlds—Jones continued to write. His sister had subscribed to *Essence,* then as now a magazine targeted at young black women that dispensed advice on relationships and fashion but also featured stories. Jones, convinced his stories were better than what he read, sent along one of his efforts, "Harvest," the story of the woman entangled in a damaging relationship. The story, which would be Jones's first publication, appeared in November, 1975.

In early 1976 he returned to Washington, determined to resume his life. He landed a secretarial job at *Science* magazine, cataloguing research papers submitted to the journal for publication. It was this very sort of clerical work, soul-numbing and mindlessly repetitive, that encouraged Jones to return to writing fiction, which he did at night in a sparsely furnished apartment he seldom left. As he would later tell an interviewer, "If you're in your home, your apartment, and the rent is paid up, and there's [no] reason for the landlord to knock on your door, then you're okay. But once you leave your apartment ... then you can't predict anything. It's not your world; you can't control it" (Rucker). In fall 1979, on a whim, he enrolled in an evening creative writing class advertised at nearby George Washington University. There he met James Alan McPherson, the iconic short story writer who had just become the first African American to win the Pulitzer Prize. McPherson found Jones engaging and encouraged him to apply to the MFA program at the University of Virginia, where McPherson was on the faculty. Jones did just that. He quickly fell in love with the environment at Charlottesville. In addition to honing his craft, he read widely and leisurely, most notably the entire Bible. An atheist, he intuited its real consolation was not its message of faith or its promise of salvation but rather the satisfying sturdiness of its intricate narrative, the rococo architecture of the Christian story from creation to apocalypse.

Completing his degree in 1981, determined now to pursue writing, Jones returned to Washington and promptly accepted another dead-end secretarial job—at *Tax Notes* in Arlington, where for the next eighteen years he dutifully gathered, collated, and summarized news articles on insurance and tax laws. But like Nathaniel Hawthorne's Surveyor or Herman Melville's sub-sub-librarian, and Irving's Diedrich Knickerbocker, Jones relished the freedom from such stultifying routine he found in the restless energy of his imagination. By night, he wrote stories. Over more than a decade of patient reworking, the stories gradually took shape. Each drew on Jones's familiarity with Washington but through the experiences of characters whose poignant struggles bore little resemblance to his own upbringing. These cheerless stories were ironically the sheer exuberance of an imagination at full throttle. After publishing several in small, prestigious journals, Jones selected fourteen of

them and shaped them into what became *Lost in the City* (1992). The book was greeted with extravagant praise and Jones (although in his early forties) as a major new find, winning the PEN-Hemingway Foundation Award for best first work of fiction and short-listed for the National Book Award.

Although now an established writer, Jones changed little of his lifestyle. He continued to work at *Tax Notes*. His apartment was still a monkish refuge—little furniture, few accessories, indeed without a bed (he slept on a pallet). He had no car, in fact, no driver's license. He watched television sparingly—mostly courtroom reality shows (he didn't have cable and didn't own a VCR). Although now in demand for readings and interviews, Jones resisted; he published nothing for more than a decade, slipping gratefully free of the burden of celebrity. Yet he was writing, sort of—conjuring in his imagination an epical period story based on an odd fact he had learned at Holy Cross: in the South in the years leading up to the Civil War, freed blacks, coming into their own property, had owned slaves. With deliberate extravagance and daring scale, Jones imagined such a plantation. Conceiving of intricate backstories for dozens of characters—free and slave—and conjuring in his mind the feel of a fictitious northern Virginia county circa 1855, Jones relished the giddy energy of such formidable brooding, never drafting any of it into writing and never attending to what he disdained as the distractions of library research. After a decade, in 2001, intuiting that the time had come to write down the story, Jones began a flurry of what became a kind of elaborate dictation, taking down in narrative shape the stories that had germinated in his imagination for years. As he was fond of telling myriad interviewers much later, he simply wanted to create a world. When, two weeks into the process, *Tax Notes* laid him off, like Hawthorne's Surveyor who finds himself wonderfully liberated from the onerous employment at the Custom-House and free now to hunker by his fireplace and give play to his imagination, Jones happily completed the five-hundred-plus-page manuscript in a furious three weeks.

The 2003 publication of *The Known World* was a landmark event. Critics lauded the book's gorgeous prose line, its sweeping cinematic feel, its intertwined plotlines, its leisurely care in developing scores of named characters, its meticulous re-creation of the feel of antebellum Virginia, but primarily its heroic revelation of a much-neglected aspect of African American history. When the book won the National Book Critics Circle Award and then the Pulitzer and then the Lannan Literary Award, some African American critics dismissed the awards (and the book for that matter) for appeasing white America's conscience by focusing on what was historically a very small number of black slave owners. But, read in connection with *Lost in the City,* the novel was less an indictment of blacks or whites, less a narrative driven by any social or political agenda, and more a luminous and deftly realized audacity, historic realism less interested in replaying incendiary arguments about the immorality of slavery and more in exploring, much like Diedrich Knickerbocker, the problematic boundary between fact and fiction, between history and story. But the novel, widely regarded as a book about race, created buzz, and Jones adjusted to the realities (and responsibilities) of a wide readership. His sophomore effort had positioned him as a promising writer of the first degree (although he was past fifty); his works were now read at universities and explicated in literary journals. He was in the rarified atmosphere of public scrutiny. Being awarded in 2004 one of the genius grants from the MacArthur Foundation (worth $500,000 over five years) cemented Jones's position as an influential cultural figure. The sedentary office clerk, comfortable in his cubicle and in his bare apartment, began an awkward negotiation outward. He embarked, reluctantly at first, on reading tours, accepted invitations for interviews, and even agreed to conduct what became immensely popular workshops in the Washington area on the dynamics of creative writing.

Although conjecturing about the premise for any writer's work is precarious, that movement outward is evident in Jones's decision to revisit his earlier collection of stories and significantly

alter that earlier collection's troubling claustrophobic feel. Indeed, *All Aunt Hagar's Children* (2006) modeled each of its fourteen stories after stories in *Lost in the City*—minor characters from the earlier collection now became the primary characters—save that now Jones's characters come to understand, much as Jones himself had in the wake of his critical success, the complex responsibility of accepting the vulnerabilities and the struggles implicit in the beauty and mayhem of the everyday. It is surely one of the keener ironies that shortly after the collection's publication Jones's sister, the last of his family, would be hit by a car and killed in the streets of New York City. It was a difficult adjustment for Jones, suddenly compelled to do what his own characters had done, live fully without retreat. Soon after the death of his sister, Jones completed his own trajectory outward, teaching creative writing part time on the faculty of George Washington University, where thirty years earlier a retiring young bespectacled office clerk had, on a whim, taken a night class in fiction writing. In 2010 Jones accepted a full-time position in the department.

It is not to impose a too-neat reading on Jones's complex trilogy of works to suggest that the boy with the fondness for comic books and television shows and long afternoons in movie theaters, the boy who grew up rootless, impoverished, and friendless, and who sought the consolation of made-up people in made-up worlds, became not surprisingly a writer who would trace in his own fiction the difficult (and inevitable) trajectory outward from the safe confines of the imagination, a writer coming to terms with the limits of the imagination and the difficult joy in embracing the real.

LOST IN THE CITY: *JONES'S CENTRIPETAL NARRATIVES*

In "The Girl Who Raised Pigeons," the poignant opening story in Jones's first collection, Betsy Ann Morgan lives with her father in a low-rent apartment building near the Capitol. After her mother died from a brain tumor the night Betsy was born, her father dedicated himself to his daughter, helped by his sister-in-law, whose spoiled son is Betsy Ann's closest friend, an asthmatic who seldom leaves their apartment. Betsy Ann particularly loves her cousin's miniature train set, a "marvelous and complete world" (p. 17) with a lovingly detailed tiny town with tiny trees and hand-carved people. Now eleven and lonely despite (or perhaps because of) her father's doting presence, Betsy Ann pesters her father to allow her to keep pigeons on the rooftop of their building. Although he has misgivings, the father agrees. Despite the fickle nature of pigeons, within months the child has established her coop; her pigeons, more than a dozen, fly the city but return each evening to the safety of the massive wooden roost. For her part, Betsy Ann comes to love the time she spends up on the rooftop—she loves their forlorn cooing and the soft give of their feathers. To protect his daughter, the father faithfully checks the coop each morning for any dead birds. But Betsy Ann herself is growing up, and one day her friends convince her after school to participate in an ill-advised attempt to steal candy from a neighborhood drugstore. She is caught, and the store owner, a longtime friend of the father's, remands her to her father. After meting out his punishment, however, the father keeps even closer surveillance on Betsy Ann, determined to protect her from the pernicious temptations of the world. Then, one morning in his routine check of the coop, he is stunned to find more than a dozen of the birds dead, their bloody bodies shredded by the razor-sharp teeth of the apartment's rats. Only two of the birds survive. Betsy Ann is inconsolable. The coop is dismantled for firewood. Weeks later, one of the surviving birds returns to the empty rooftop. Betsy Ann catches sight of the pigeon but only watches it take flight, never, we presume, to return, its refuge gone.

That story could serve as a thematic template for Jones's early fictions—the heroic if futile determination to withdraw from a brutal and dangerous world. Like a matryoshka doll, the story closes in on itself; its narrative momentum is relentlessly centripetal with successive layers of enfolding claustrophobic imagery. Like Dublin in Joyce's *Dubliners,* Washington, D.C., func-

tions not as a setting but as the collection's antagonist. If Joyce used Dublin's drab brown neighborhoods with their tight gridlock of narrow streets to create a forbidding sense of paralysis and futility, Jones uses Washington to create a sense of a world riven by routine brutalities, compelled by the ugly urgencies of the basest instincts and by the graceless logic of mortality; a world subject to the grim intrusion of chance; a world that casually disappoints and inevitably frustrates, where the simplest gestures of the heart and the slenderest dreams are exposed as cruel ironies. In the grim observation of one of the characters, "When the world pisses on you, it then spits on you to finish the job" (p. 78). Characters fear venturing into the city, dread getting lost in its forbidding immensity. In "A New Man," when the teenage daughter of Woodrow Cunningham, a maintenance man and church deacon, runs away from home (one of the collection's many gestures of flight that turns disastrous), months after her disappearance Cunningham's wife tacks up a giant map of Washington to help direct their search—and Rita glumly admits, "I didn't know the city was this big" (p. 211).

These, then, are manifestly the retreat-fictions of a painfully shy cubicle clerk who, despite holding an MFA from the University of Virginia, for nearly twenty years collated news articles on tax laws and by night behind the locked door of his apartment gave free rein to his imagination. Not surprisingly, within Jones's vision, the most heroic characters (and, inevitably, the most tragic) counter the threat of the real world by deliberately abandoning the imperative to engage it, exiling themselves into grateful isolation like Rip loping off into the Catskill foothills. Again and again, characters reject the fearsome imperative of restlessness and settle into the stability of contained environments, willingly retreat into cloistered worlds. Most often these refuges are real and immediate: gardens, apartments, jail cells, neighborhood churches, corner markets, classrooms, public libraries, museums, hospital wards; sometimes the shelters are more symbolic landscapes, aesthetic refuges such as music or books, letters and photographs. These characters are anxious, their lives in studied surrender, a part but apart. Like Rip, they move gratefully into protective environments that are reassuring assertions of order, artificial zones of design. Inevitably, however, Jones concedes that each shelter, each gesture of withdrawal, each construct must give way; the world overwhelms, its toxic absurdities, its pressing brutalities finally too much.

Consider "The Night Rhonda Ferguson Was Killed," Jones's bleak coming-of-age story about a group of girlfriends set in the late 1950s in Jones's alma mater, Cardozo High. It is an unsettling world where students are inchoately hostile, hormonally driven, indifferent to their education; they skip classes and smoke, they steal and drink. They must contend with the hard realities of unwanted pregnancies, abusive boyfriends, and broken families. Rhonda Ferguson is no exception: although only sixteen, she already has a child out of wedlock. But she is gifted with a singing voice that has already secured her a promising recording contract and the possibility of pop music stardom. It is pop music that creates a powerfully persuasive, entirely symbolic landscape wherein these troubled kids retreat, there to embrace the cozy ideal of innocent love and easy happiness. In the car on the way back from a drunken party where one of the girls had been attacked by a boy, her friends sing, without evident irony, the Shirelles' syrupy "Will You Love Me Tomorrow." Surrounded by a harsh environment where love is only about glandular gratification, an exertion of violence and domination, the girls retreat into the protective refuge of pop music with its reassuring affirmation of love's magic. Of course, like the pigeon coop, the fragile shelter of pop music cannot be sustained—when they get home, the girls are told that Rhonda's estranged boyfriend has shot and killed her. In shock, unable to sleep, one of the girls sings the Shirelles' song quietly to herself all night long, retreating to its comforting shelter, "her voice pushing back everything she did not yet understand" (p. 54).

It is the signal strategy that Jones's characters pursue against a world that presses in. In "The

Store," for instance, when a neighborhood grocery shop owner accidentally hits a girl playing in the streets with her car and the girl dies, she recoils and abandons her shop, her refuge forever lost to her. In "The Sunday Following Mother's Day," Maddie Williams spends years interred in public libraries perusing newspaper articles and court transcripts attempting to construct some understanding of why her father had stabbed her mother to death when she was four. She begins to receive long letters from her father in jail, letters that never talk about the killing, and when he is released she agrees to meet him. It ends disastrously, and by day's end Maddie deeply regrets how her father's intrusion had upended her refuge-routine, what would have been another ordinary Sunday. In "Young Lions," when a street thug moves his mother into a commodious apartment paid for by his drug money, the mother hangs on to a single item of furniture, a glass-topped coffee table in which are pressed the photographs of her family long ago, even as that family is being destroyed by the violence of the drug business (in a dispute over money, her son shoots to death the son of her best friend). In the title story, Lydia Walsh, a successful if unhappy career woman addicted to cocaine and casual sex (shelters of their own), is shattered by the intrusive ring of the phone. She is told that her mother has just died in a nearby hospital after a lingering fight with breast cancer. Lydia is shaken. She gathers herself sufficiently to call for a cab, but before leaving her current lover asleep in her bed, she does several lines of cocaine. That cab ride turns into a desperate dodge—she tells the cabdriver to just drive, to get lost in the city. As the cab wanders through her old neighborhood, in a tearful epiphany she comes to realize what Jones's characters here each perceive: the shabby pointlessness of love itself.

As the collection unfolds, retreat becomes increasingly inaccessible, precarious. It is fitting then that in the closing story Jones suspends his character uneasily in a terrifying limbo, unable to retreat and unwilling to engage. Marie Delaveaux Wilson, a headstrong eighty-six-year-old retiree, blind in one eye, must visit the Social Security office annually to butt heads with indifferent bureaucrats to confirm she is alive and to keep her checks coming. Appropriate for the summa figure in Jones's centripetal narratives, Marie seldom leaves her apartment (she "had learned that life was all chaos and painful uncertainty.... Offer a crust of bread to a sick bird and you often drew back a bloody finger" [p. 230]). When she does venture out, she carries an intimidating seven-inch knife that she had serrated herself with a neighbor's saw because years earlier she had been robbed on the street. At this year's visit, Marie is made to wait for hours. After years of patiently enduring such indifferent treatment, she snaps: when an office girl, filing her nails, flippantly tells her to go back to her seat, Marie slaps her with all her might.

The action haunts her. She immediately retreats to her locked apartment, certain that the agency will cut off her checks or have her arrested (she tries futilely to reach out, to call the girl to apologize). The next morning there is a knock at the door—Marie freezes. But it is a student from nearby Howard University gathering materials for a folklore class project who asks her to make tapes, to record her own recollections. She reluctantly agrees. Over the next several weeks, the two tape long sessions as Marie recollects her long life. We hear an excerpt about her arrival in Washington decades earlier, how, on a train trip to a job opportunity in Baltimore, she had been left accidentally at the station in Washington and had decided to stay. It is itself a familiar conundrum among Jones's characters, bravely attempting to engage the world but made vulnerable by the hard toss of bad luck. As Marie makes her last tape, she receives a letter summoning her to the Social Security office—she does not know whether it is the usual meeting or whether they will arrest her. She is paralyzed. When the student, his project finished, returns the tapes to her, she just packs them away. "She knew that however long she lived, she would not ever again listen to them, for in the end, despite all that was on the tapes, she could not stand the sound of her own voice" (p. 243). It is the nadir of Jones's harrowingly centripetal collection—a character, on the thresh-

old of death, left alone, afraid to venture outside and denied even the slender comfort of her own voice, her own story.

THE KNOWN WORLD: *JONES'S THRESHOLD NARRATIVE*

It is difficult for contemporary American readers, black or white, to approach *The Known World* dispassionately. It is, after all, a slave narrative, a genre of fiction set in the turbulent and often violent world of Southern plantations in the foment leading up to the Civil War, a controversial genre of historical fiction that, as Valerie Smith suggests, has long compelled American readers to confront the thorniest moral issue in nearly four centuries of the American experience. But Jones upends conventions of the genre and conceptions about the peculiar institution: not all slave owners, he reminds us, were white. His is a provocative, even incendiary premise, Jones deforming the assumptions of one of the defining narratives in American history, the familiar dynamic of mercenary Southern white master and exploited African slave. Although a novel with such generous plotting defies summarizing, the narrative centers on Henry Townsend, himself born a slave, his freedom purchased by his father (who had earlier purchased his own freedom as well as his wife's) but not before young Henry, as the houseboy of a magnanimous white, had come to see the natural order and economic necessity of slavery. By 1855, now thirty-one years old, Townsend controls a thriving fifty-acre plantation in northern Virginia and owns more than thirty slaves, despite grave objections from both his parents. Although neither cruel nor sadistic, Townsend understands the need to control and direct his slaves, and he metes out measured punishment to keep the plantation working. In shedding light on the reality of black slave owners, *The Known World,* like all landmark works of historic realism, would presumably intend to provoke its culture to reflect on its very identity and on wider moral questions about the nature of good and evil, right and wrong, innocence and culpability. And Jones certainly could have written such a historic novel, one conventionally researched and conventionally told.

But despite the period feel of *The Known World,* despite its seductive textures, its luxurious detailing, its stately prose line, its leisurely pace, its convincing verisimilitude, this is hardly a work of historic realism. Jones's ambition reaches beyond the genre. This is both a story about *slavery* and a *story* about slavery. Jones's earlier collection helps define his larger interest—specifically, the imperative to interrogate the premise of history itself as an expression of the tension between engagement and withdrawal, confrontation and anxiety. "[The novel] is skeptical about history as a discipline, and constantly highlights the artifice and limitations of historical studies" (Ryan, p. 193). Like Irving's gamester historian, Jones investigates the very concept of realism, tests the legitimacy of history itself, challenges us to acknowledge that history is a reassuring escape, a sheltering narrative a culture tells itself; historians constellate the hard collision of raw events, impose order after the fact, and in doing so rescue events from the welter of confusion and provide an anxious culture with heroes and villains, cause and effect, foreshadowing and fate, providence and inevitability, the suasive feel of design and coherence, and even the reassuring logic of irony, all those splendidly coaxing illusions that we need in an absurd world that otherwise regularly ambushes us with shivery jolts of surprise. History shelters us. As a culture, we relish that gesture of retreat, never wanting to acknowledge the flimsy made-ness of our history narrative, how an accidental conspiracy of historians across decades, even centuries, gathers hard data and, ironically, conjures from such facts an elegant and convincing fiction, the cozy once-upon-a-time construct that we call history. Within the tidy parameters of its historic record, a nation's most brutal events, its most sinister mayhem, and even the catastrophic handiwork of blind chance all yield coaxing fractal patterns of causality, even inevitability.

Jones is clearly not content to merely conjure antebellum Virginia and seduce us into the narrative spell of historic realism. He conjures,

certainly—but by Jones's own admission, we know the story percolated in his imagination for years, imaginative foreplay unconcerned by the pedantic tedium and dreary responsibilities of research. Accordingly, Jones disturbs the spell by fashioning a series of wider narrative frames that mark *The Known World* as another box of nested narratives, counternarratives, and asides. We cannot relax into the historic narrative—we are made jarringly aware that we are reading a fashioned thing, at once a splendid example of old school historic realism and a subversive parody of it. Jones keeps shattering the narrative spell. If we get the requisite symbols, conflict, characters, and suspense of historic realism, we also are introduced to a coterie of later historians and researchers, some more than a century later, who are attempting themselves to write the history of Manchester County. There is Anderson Frazier, an earnest Canadian journalist who some thirty years after the Civil War is authoring a series of respected historic pamphlets on different aspects of the war. He is intrigued by the concept of black slave owners and seeks eyewitness testimony from surviving ex-slaves. Even as he interviews a neighbor of the Townsends, a black schoolteacher named Fern Elston who was herself a slave owner, Fern distorts, deliberately obfuscates her recollections. Later, we are told of an earnest college professor, Roberta Murphy, who in 1979 is gathering data about pre–Civil War Manchester County for one of those dreary academic monographs Jones cannot resist mocking: this academic finds fascinating not the looming threat of civil war but rather the birth in the county of five two-headed chickens, two of which could dance to harmonica music. Of course, the omniscient narrator concedes that the data about Manchester County from three successive pre–Civil War censuses had been gathered by careless bureaucrats and was uniformly unreliable. And we are later told that many of the nineteenth-century records of the county were lost in a massive fire in 1912, which raises issues of reliability until, of course, we realize Manchester County itself is a conjure. Furthermore, Jones regularly disturbs his "historic" fiction with supernatural moments, deadpan descriptions of ghosts or inexplicable apparitions, extended dreams, post-death experiences, moments of evident paranormality that play havoc with the premise of historic realism. We also get the intrusive artificiality of Jones's flash-forwards, the narrative at times lurching years, sometimes decades, ahead in a character's life, with heavy-handed obviousness and unapologetic abruptness, often without even a paragraph break. Even Jones's florescence of narrative lines—dozens of fascinating episodes introduced and then abandoned—challenges the unidirectional premise of linear history, the novel composed less of smoothly transitioned scenes and more of engaging tableaux that recall the structure of Hawthorne's *The Scarlet Letter,* another apparent work of historic realism that in fact is far more interested in testing the limits and reach of the fancy. And, as if to make evident the made-ness of the novel, Jones uses lengthy chapter headings that parody those of the grand serial novels of nineteenth-century historic realism.

The Known World then delegitimizes realism itself, unsettles the convenient assumption that history is reliable. As such the novel is a kind of threshold narrative for Jones, a midway stage in the development of his wider aesthetic sensibility. In testing history itself as our grandest and most convincing refuge, Jones edges beyond his earlier constrictive volume in which anxious characters withdraw, finding the real world inhospitable. In his burlesque of historic realism, Jones begins freeing his own narrative sensibility from the claustrophobic submission to the logic of retreat. Jones upends the expectation of the American slavery narrative—here, blacks own slaves—to emancipate the reader from the simplifications that are necessarily a culture's history and to affirm, in turn, what history cannot brook: uncertainty and unreliability.

This, then, is a novel about systems—the Townsend plantation, slavery, and ultimately narrative itself—giving way, what Carolyn Vellenga Berman terms the "destruction of an idyll" (p. 3). Indeed, if a narrative as diffuse as Jones's can be said to have a plot, it is the rapid deterioration of the Townsend plantation in the wake of Henry's death (he dies on page 10). Tellingly, Townsend's

favorite read is John Milton's *Paradise Lost*. After Townsend's death, his plantation is first plagued by a rash of runaways. Then, although married with a child, Moses, Townsend's overseer, schemes to take over direction of the lucrative plantation by becoming the lover of Townsend's widow (an ironic Moses, hardly interested in leading his people to freedom). Townsend's father, who had paid for his freedom years earlier and even carries papers that testify to that, is kidnapped by a roving band of slave trackers and is sold back into slavery, where, although legally a free man, he is shot and killed while trying to escape from his new owners. When it is clear that Townsend's widow will not accept Moses as anything but a lover, Moses impulsively runs. Desperate to avoid slave trackers, he hides in the home of Townsend's mother, who in turn is shot accidentally in a standoff with the sheriff, who in turn is shot dead by his own deputy, who stumbles on what he assumes is a large cache of money in the woman's bedroom (it is not) and is determined to steal it. The Townsend plantation, once a tidy and efficient refuge, a clear and organized system, gives way to a wonderland world of chaos, contingency, violence, and greed. Law and order, right and wrong, collapse; slave and free are rendered meaningless and all assumed absolutes subverted as bald chance plays havoc on events and renders logic ironic. It is a descent into raw event, the very world that haunted the residents of Washington in Jones's early stories.

This dilemma is suggested by three artistic constructions introduced into the novel. The first is a massive woodcut map of the New World (weighing more than thirty pounds) that hangs in Sheriff Skiffington's office. The itinerant Russian who sold the ugly thing to Skiffington made the dubious claim that it was the first map to use the word "America." More than three hundred years old, it is of course as a map quite useless; although titled "The Known World," the "realistic" map is long outdated. The other two artistic constructions are the creative works of Alice Night, an eccentric slave from the Townsend plantation (she was kicked in the head by a mule as a child). In 1861 Alice, a runaway, finds celebrity as a folk artist in wartime Washington. Had she appeared in Jones's earlier collection, Alice would have been a heroic presence, brutalized by events but finding solace and affirmation in retreating into lavishly executed aesthetic refuges. But something troubles now. Alice has on display in a swanky Washington hotel two enormous wall hangings of Manchester County, each of them part tapestry, part painting, and part clay figurines. The first is a stunning depiction, from the distant perspective of God, of the county itself: the land, farmhouses, barns, roads, even the cemetery. The other creation is of the Townsend plantation, meticulously re-created with cabins and barns, chickens and horses, but most gloriously with people; indeed every single person from the plantation is recorded, their faces lifted up in generous glow of affirmation (even in the cemetery, the dead have risen)—ironic given what we know of the plantation life. Although Susan Donaldson and Katherine Clay Bassard see Alice's tapestries as redemptive, these cool expressions of the imagination recall the disturbing imagery from the nested narratives of *Lost in the City:* they are decidedly two-dimensional, sterile, symbolic refuges, contained, artificial, both failing (as Jones's own novel, indeed as history itself does) to capture the paradoxical complexities of the antebellum South.

Uneasy with history, ambivalent about the imagination (in short, all shelters closed), Jones turns outward. No character better exemplifies this nascent centrifugal impulse than the slender presence of the slave Stamford. Ironically, when we first meet Stamford, he embodies the centripetal impulse, escaping harsh realities into pleasant nullity. Stamford, in his early forties, scours the plantation for young women, believing that such sexual excess with "young stuff" keeps him young. His is a life of casual morality and carefree promiscuity—within Jones's larger argument, a life in perfect retreat, using sex as a refuge from the harsh realities of his dead-end life as a slave. But it does not work. When Stamford tries to fall asleep, he struggles with the fear that he will die in chains. More poignantly, he tries to remember even his parents' names—slave traders had split up the family

when he was only five. Troubled, he eases himself into his imagination, comforting himself with the illusion that he has parents waiting for him somewhere. His is a psyche nested with strategies for escape. When Stamford is beaten nearly to death after he accosts a field hand having lunch with a girl he had designated as his next conquest, that beating occasions a simplistic (and predictable) response: recovering from his injuries, he begins to consider his own mortality, his selfishness, his life of mindless pleasures. In short, he confronts the real, and like other Jones characters before him, he cannot handle its implications. He turns sullen, bitter. He escapes, into drink.

The turning point comes, however, when Stamford offers to gather blueberries for a young girl he barely knows who is determined to pick berries despite a rapidly approaching storm. It is hardly a generous gesture—Stamford hopes a chance lightning strike will end his misery and that this gesture might afford him "a nothing stool way off in the corner of heaven that nobody cared about" (p. 201). When Stamford is out in the open field, a freakish lightning strike splits an oak tree, in turn killing dozens of crows. As Stamford contemplates the perfectly preserved carcasses, he talks to each, lovingly stroking their feathers (recalling young Betsy Ann and her pigeons). He is unexpectedly showered by bits of dull green eggshells and yolks from the crows' nests overhead, suggesting his own rapidly approaching rebirth. He rubs the yolks all over the dead birds and, in one of those moments in which Jones audaciously suspends the imperative of realism, the ground opens up and swallows the carcasses. Stamford sucks on one of the blueberries, relishes its tang. Then Stamford sees a cabin hurtling down from the sky. It lands, its door opens, and he is greeted by the young girl who had asked for the berries, her mouth now sticky with berry juice. It is a jolting vision rich with imagery that suggests the sweetness of the immediate, the possibility of rebirth, and the magic within the tawdry limits of the real.

In that moment, as in a parable, Stamford experiences a kind of jolting epiphany that Jones refuses to cut with irony. Stamford's heart opens up to the logic of selflessness, a spiritual redemption centered on his sudden conviction that the world needs to be cared for. He changes his name to Stamford Crow Blueberry to commemorate the tectonic moment. Now he soars into authentic engagement. We are told in a flash-forward that after the war Stamford will go to Richmond and there open an orphanage for black children. His heroic efforts to rescue the abandoned children amid the rubble of Richmond are amply rewarded: over decades of selfless charity work, helping generations of street kids, kids who watched their parents die, victims of crime, child abuse, poverty, he establishes a reputation for compassion such that, nearly a century after the war, the city government approves renaming one of the longest streets in the city after Stamford. He embraces the difficult immediate and, unlike other Jones characters, does not end up cowering behind locked doors, anxious, angry, victimized, brutalized, suicidal, or addicted to drugs or alcohol. It is, for Jones, an emancipation proclamation of a different sort—a character liberated into the harsh exhilaration of the unknown now.

Stamford's redemption parable signals an important evolution for Jones, one confirmed by the novel's decidedly muted ending. If *Lost in the City* closes with the boarded-up narrative of Marie Delaveaux Wilson, *The Known World* ends on a far more uplifting note. It is 1861. Moses, the scheming overseer who, caught escaping, had been hobbled (the tendon in his foot sliced, thus making flight virtually impossible), now lives by himself on the plantation (as part of his scheme to marry Townsend's widow, he had arranged for his wife and son to run north with Alice). Now crippled, when he returns from the fields, he can barely bring himself to move from his pallet by the fire. But he is tended by slave children, a quiet routine of care that includes bringing him his meals every evening. And we are told—in Jones's final flash-forward—that Moses would be tended for years until his death, a striking affirmation of simple compassion, a routine of (extra)ordinary caring that celebrates what Jones's characters have so often sought to escape and what a culture skirts in embracing the pleasing simplications of history: the pressing respon-

sibilities and terrifying vulnerability of life in the known world.

ALL AUNT HAGAR'S CHILDREN: *JONES'S CENTRIFUGAL NARRATIVES*

The biblical figure of Hagar provides an appropriate guiding spirit for Jones's triumphant late-career centrifugal imperative. In Genesis, Hagar is the beautiful Egyptian servant to Sarah, the wife of Abraham. When it is clear that Sarah cannot bear Abraham children, it is Hagar who becomes Abraham's surrogate wife, giving birth to Ishmael. But when, after divine intervention, Sarah conceives, Abraham exiles Hagar and Ishmael, his own family. In a harrowing journey, the two innocents wander in the desert wastes of Beersheba and nearly die, saved only by the intervention of God. As slaves came to know the stories of Christianity, they found in Hagar a fitting model for their own condition: a noble people, exiled from their homeland, punished for no reason, doomed to wander far from their roots in a brutal and unfamiliar world, forever essentially and necessarily a people in unforgiving exile. Of course, there is little about the heroic Hagar that would have intrigued the younger Jones—hers is a woeful tale that neither encourages the comfort of isolation nor celebrates the energy of the imagination. A woman and her son negotiate the vicissitudes of a strange, harsh land, pitched about by chance and misfortune, accepting the reality of their vulnerability and nevertheless refusing to abandon hope.

Returning to the short story after nearly fifteen years, Jones completes the centripetal strategy he tested in *The Known World*. He revisits his first collection (the stories match the first collection sequentially, each story developing a character from the previous collection), determined to create not so much a sequel as a counternarrative. As such, *All Aunt Hagar's Children* is his emancipation text, his characters finally freed of the suffocating boundaries of self-imposed retreats. Stories in this collection are richer, longer, broader, more energetic, with restless plotlines that move across decades and range well beyond the tight gridlock of Washington streets that provided the confining setting for the earlier collection. Indeed, each of the stories centers on Washington residents who were part of the diaspora, the early-twentieth-century migration of millions of southern blacks looking for economic opportunity in the North. That journey-spirit compels the collection. Characters decide, in story after story, to engage the world, to move outward to experience the bruising, chaotic, splendid, unpredictable now.

The first story, "In the Blink of God's Eye," can serve as a kind of template. It is the backstory of the shopkeeper who sold Betsy Ann her pigeons in the opening story in *Lost in the City*. It is 1901. Ruth Patterson is newly arrived in Washington from Virginia. One night she is disturbed by an odd sound in her backyard. Terrified by stories she has heard of roaming wolves in the Washington area, she nevertheless goes out into her yard, armed with a pistol and knife (the first of many such movements outward). What she finds, however, is a bundle twisting on the low branches of an apple tree—it is, she discovers, an abandoned newborn (as readers of the earlier collection, we know the infant will grow up to be the shopkeeper). Ruth accepts the burden of responsibility: she is determined to make a home for the abandoned infant. Her husband, Aubry, comes to resent the attention she pays to the foundling. They quarrel, they separate, and, like Rip, the husband flees. He returns to Virginia. But after much soul-searching, Aubry returns to Washington—on horseback, in the gray shimmer of a hard winter snow—ready to navigate the uncertain now. "His heart was pained," the story closes, "and it was pain enough to overwhelm a city of men" (p. 30) It is a most difficult close that affirms what stories in Jones's earlier collection routinely dismissed or feared: the strategy of the longanimous Dame Van Winkle, the unglamorous strategy of engagement.

In story after story, the claustrophobic feel of Jones's earlier fictions gives way to breathtaking risk. Restless characters move outward into uncertain, potentially brutal realities. They reject the pretense of control and the contentment of refuge; they accept pain, sorrow, anger, disappointment; and supremely they test compassion,

accept the intrusive logic of caring. Jones himself forsakes the comfortable tidiness of the all-knowing author-ity shaping events into satisfying narrative—we are left again and again on the threshold of characters' decisions, left with open ends, in a most problematic (and richly satisfying) uncertainty. In "Resurrecting Methuselah," for instance, Anita Channing is a working mom with a decidedly unfaithful husband stationed overseas in the military. Her daughter, Bethany, attends a small Catholic school where her teacher is a born-again zealot eager to push the Catholic agenda of the arduous pilgrimage to the afterlife. In his classroom, he hangs a poster extolling the Old Testament figure Methuselah, who in exchange for an ascetic life of strict devotion (a sort of joyless anti-life in full retreat from living) was given the (mixed) blessing of centuries of longevity. In addition to the routine trials of single parenting, Anita is dealing with the shocking diagnosis her husband has just received: he has breast cancer and faces an uncertain future after a mastectomy. But Anita does not surrender. In the closing scene, she embraces the now. As she drives her sick daughter home from school, she feels with epiphanic joy that one day, she and her daughter will drive about the city, will venture into neighborhoods they do not know, relishing the chance to get lost in a pulsing city that beckons them to such explorations. As Anita declares without irony, "What time could be better than today?" (p. 73). It is an ending that defies the simplification of happy or sad. We have the essential dynamic of Jones's new fictional sensibility: characters buffeted by chance, compelled to confront the hard reality of mortality, blindsided by bad luck, and, given the chance to live passively within a protective shelter or charmed escape (in this case, Catholic Christianity), rejecting it, character and reader left suspended in the richness of possibility.

There is Caesar Matthews ("Old Boys, Old Girls"), a hardened street thug who in the earlier collection is responsible for shooting a childhood friend over drug money, now released from jail. He moves into an apartment building where he meets an ex-girlfriend, now a junkie and a prostitute. When one night after work he finds her dead, naked, and in a grotesque position in her bed, he is moved to spend the entire night bathing her body and then cleaning her apartment. It is an unforced act of kindness. He then departs to greet the dawn; he allows the toss of a quarter, bright as it flips in the morning sun, to determine which street he will take. As Daniel Torday concludes in his painstaking analysis of the story, that gesture is Caesar's embrace of his own destiny. Or there is the nameless narrator in the title story, a burned-out Korean War veteran who embodies Jones's earlier centripetal impulse: he avoids complications (he is literally hiding from an ex-girlfriend), regularly drinks himself into numbness, and dreams of escaping to Alaska to hunt gold. To bring solace to a grieving mother, he gets caught up in solving the death some two years earlier of a family friend, a notorious drug dealer who had mistreated his wife. He as well is sorting through the implications of witnessing the death of a woman, a rabbi's wife, who had collapsed as she and Caesar were exiting a streetcar and died in his arms. She had whispered to him in Yiddish, "*Listen, children, remember, precious ones, what you're learning here*" (p. 131)—itself a powerful imperative to engage the immediate. He will ultimately abandon the idea of running away to Alaska, and as the story ends, he is cradling the photo of the dead woman even as he relishes the sight of schoolgirls dressed in vivid colors walking down the sidewalk. And there is Noah Robinson ("Adam Robinson Acquires Grandparents and a Little Sister"), a retired school janitor, whose quiet life (he raises exquisite Japanese bonsai trees at a time, he acknowledges, when the trees in Washington are dying) is upended when he and his wife of forty-five years become guardians of Adam, their six-year old grandson, after their son, Adam's father, dies from drug addiction. It is not easy; Noah and his wife had planned an active retirement of travel. But during a Sunday worship service, Noah impulsively pulls close the troubled child and feels himself "go light as a blossom in the wind" (p. 270). There is Roxanne Stapleton, who on her way to see Sam Cooke in concert suddenly goes blind on a city bus. Doctors are flummoxed by her condition, but she refuses self-pity

or bitterness (even after her boyfriend cheats on her with her best friend). In the closing scene, savoring her morning coffee, she sits listening to the snow falling, and in her mind's eye reaching through the vastness of space itself, expanding, widening her heart to a generous richness that includes even the least of God's children ("Blindsided"). These are sumptuous stories of reaching out, of engagement, stories that console, even inspire without the simplistics of unearned optimism. The endings are troubled and troubling, open-ended; we are sure only that characters are capable of accepting the risk of compassion.

The closing story is perhaps Jones's most pointed indication of his own evolution from the charms of retreat. Indeed, Jones told the *Washington Post* that "Tapestry" is a "kind of summoning up" of his fiction (Rucker). Much about Anne Perry suggests Jones's earlier characters: she is a tapestry artist, her opulent work consuming years of meticulous effort, a consummate artist whose most accomplished work is a half-finished tableau of her rural Mississippi in a fierce winter storm, the pure product of her fervid imagination. With thin prospects for marriage partners in her Mississippi town—really two—a jaded Anne freely imagines her life married to one of them, an ornate divertissement that goes on for nearly six pages and includes the courtship, the wedding, the children, and ultimately their deaths. True to Jones's new imperative, however, imaginative retreat will not do. At a picnic, Anne chances to meet a cousin's friend, George Carter, a railroad porter visiting from distant Washington, D.C. We watch the slow, stumbling ignition of their love in some of the most fetching and sweetly romantic scenes in Jones's fiction.

After they marry some two years later, they head to Washington aboard George's train. As the train moves through Tennessee, Anne unthinkingly ventures beyond the blacks-only cars to talk to her husband only to see George humiliated by his white boss for a minor infraction in the whites-only dining car. But Anne is stunned when, in turn, George upbraids her for being in the wrong car. Reeling, humiliated, Anne returns to her seat and does what Jones's earlier characters routinely did—"she ... began to encase herself so that everything around her disappeared" (p. 392). She retreats into the private consolation of her imagination, closes her eyes and imagines she abandons this new marriage and returns home to Mississippi. It becomes as intricately designed a fantasy as the tapestries she weaves, going on for pages as her imagination meticulously conjures her long walk home from the train station. Then, the reverie is shattered: George comes back to her car and offers an awkward apology. ("Take my pology. I couldn't mean anything more" [p. 397]). He then falls asleep on her shoulder, but in his sleep he speaks in a troubled whisper, even as he grinds his teeth, "*I'll clean every barn before I sleep, master. No need for that thing. No need for that again. I'll do it. I told yall I'd do it all*" (p. 398). Here, in channeling the lost voice of centuries of dead slaves, George reminds Anne of the hard reality they will face in the North, the pressing weight of racism, the living presence of what history narratives cool into convenient stories with tidy lessons. Suddenly, in the hush dark of the railroad car, Anne hears from other sleeping riders the voices of slaves, restless ghosts, part of the very living history whose impact she will feel keenly in the days and years ahead. Yet it is then that she resolves not to run—she will stay with her imperfect husband in that imperfect and difficult world. We close the collection as the train pulls into Washington, Anne whispering into the "darkness and confusion," "Mama, I'm a long way from home" (p. 399). Jones's voiceover tells us what Anne cannot know, that her decision to risk engagement will bring its own bounteous reward: she will die nearly seventy years later, the mother of nine children, twenty-four grandchildren, and twelve great-grandchildren, her long life a rich and complex tapestry, Jones's sumptuous centrifugal impulse now complete.

Although Jones is very much a vigorous presence with the promise of new work, "Tapestry" could stand as a fitting capstone to a rich body of work in which he has moved from characters willingly revoking the imperative to engage life to characters who move heroically to accept the puzzling beauty of risk. Jones cannot offer the grand solutions or incendiary visions of social

and political activists. He cannot cauterize the deep wounds of racism, he cannot alleviate poverty. A nerdy kid who surrendered happily to the invitatory pull of comic books and movies, who would be for twenty years a nondescript cubicle fixture inventing worlds to relieve the frustrations and loneliness of such a life, Jones in his full comes to reject the logic of retreat that paradoxically had sustained him across forty years. Ultimately, Jones perceives what generations of readers of Washington Irving's fabulous tale too easily miss, the modest, understated heroism of the long-suffering who stay, the unspectacular life of routine indignities and occasional reward. That, finally, is the reassurance, at once modest and magnanimous, that Jones whispers to us in the darkness and the confusion that we all share, all of us a long way from home.

Selected Bibliography

WORKS OF EDWARD P. JONES

Lost in the City. New York: Morrow, 1992. New York: Amistad, 2005.

The Known World. New York: Amistad, 2003, 2004.

All Aunt Hagar's Children. New York: Amistad, 2006.

CRITICAL STUDIES AND REVIEWS

Bassard, Katherine Clay. "Imagining Other Worlds: Race, Gender, and the 'Power Line' in Edward P. Jones's *The Known World*." *African American Review* 42, nos. 3–4:407–419 (fall–winter 2008).

Berman, Carolyn Vellenga. "The Known World in World Literature: Bahktin, Glissant, and Edward P. Jones." *Novel* 42, no. 2:231–237 (summer 2009).

Donaldson, Susan V. "Telling Forgotten Stories of Slavery in the Postmodern South." *Southern Literary Journal* 60, no. 2:267–283 (spring 2008).

Mason, Wyatt. "Ballad for Americans: The Stories of Edward P. Jones." *Harper's,* September 2006, pp. 87–92 (http://www.harpers.org/archive/2006/09/0081200).

Ryan, Tim A. "Mapping the Unrepresentable: Slavery Fiction in the New Millennium." In his *Calls and Responses: The American Novel of Slavery Since "Gone with the Wind."* Baton Rouge: Louisiana State University Press, 2008. Pp. 185–208.

Saunders, James Robert. "A World of Irony in the Fiction of Edward P. Jones." *Hollins Critic* 44, no. 3:1–10 (2007).

Smith, Valerie. "Neo-Slave Narratives." In *The Cambridge Companion to the African American Slave Narrative.* Edited by Audrey Fisch. Cambridge, U.K.: Cambridge University Press, 2007. Pp. 168–185.

Torday, Daniel. "Young Boys and Old Lions: Fatalism in the Stories of Edward P. Jones." *Literary Imagination* 11, no. 3:349–369 (2009).

INTERVIEWS

Elam, Angela. "To Make a Story: An Interview with Edward P. Jones." *New Letters* 74, no. 1:121–135 (2007–2008).

Graham, Maryemma. "An Interview with Edward P. Jones." *African American Review* 42, nos. 3–4:421–438 (fall–winter 2008).

Jackson, Lawrence P. "An Interview with Edward P. Jones." *African American Review* 34, no. 1:95–103 (spring 2000).

Rucker, Neely. "The Known World of Edward P. Jones." *Washington Post,* November 15, 2009 (http://www.washingtonpost.com/wp-dyn/content/article/2009/11/06/AR2009110603404.html).

MINA LOY

(1882—1966)

Caleb Puckett

MINA LOY IS at once one of the most challenging, fascinating, and widely overlooked figures of modernist poetics. Except for brief resurgences in interest among experimental poetry aficionados and scholars in the 1960s and 1990s, Loy's innovative work remains widely ignored by the poetry establishment when one compares it with that of her celebrated contemporaries, including T. S. Eliot, William Carlos Williams, Gertrude Stein, and Marianne Moore. Although, as Roger L. Conover writes, "it was once common ... to assume that Mina Loy's name belonged next to those who are now part of the Pantheon," official verse culture still balks at giving proper recognition to this exceptional poet (p. 251). Nonetheless, a study of Loy's life and work makes it clear that she has made a matchless contribution to modernism and continues to provoke and encourage new trajectories in verse, particularly within avant-garde circles. Indeed, contemporary poets such as Lisa Robertson, C. A. Conrad, and Andrei Codrescu continue to engage with and respond to Loy, thus assuring that her iconoclastic vision and audacious approach to poetics will remain relevant in the foreseeable future.

A DAUGHTER DIVIDED: 1882–1901

Mina Loy was born Mina Gertrude Löwy in London, England, on December 27, 1882. According to Loy's reflections on her middle-class Victorian childhood, she was an inquisitive, independent-minded, and creative girl whose parents discouraged her from making any choices that might set her at variance with the strict social norms of the era. Loy also grew up in a household where her identification with a particular class, religion, and nationality was constantly called into question because of her parents' divergent backgrounds and differing approaches to rearing their precocious child. Loy's mother, Julia, was a devout English Protestant and self-conscious traditionalist who closely monitored the impression her daughter made in polite society and worked hard to quell her desire to become an artist because of the profession's undesirable associations. Julia Löwy even went so far as to lock away books she deemed unsuitable for her daughter, search her room for contraband literature, and obliterate her artwork in a bid for absolute control. Loy's father, Sigmund, was a Hungarian Jew and successful, self-made businessman who initially tended to tolerate Loy's artistic aspirations and indulge certain aspects of her unconventional behavior. As an amateur painter and social outsider, it appears that Sigmund Löwy empathized with Loy and subsequently became her champion when she began lobbying for a chance to receive an education by attending art school.

The cultural, intellectual, and spiritual fissures between Julia and Sigmund Löwy became more irreparable over time, which greatly affected Loy's sense of stability and bid for self-definition. To complicate matters, Loy felt that her mother viewed her as "alien" and she came to believe that her father found her "untrustworthy and potentially traitorous" (Pozorski, p. 48). Nonetheless, Loy clearly favored her father, despite his increasing conservatism and misgivings regarding her opinions and choices. Loy chose to primarily identify with his artistic sensibility, Jewish heritage, and status as an underdog at the expense of the socially expedient, ladylike, Anglo-Saxon qualities her mother foisted upon her with stifling insistence. In fact, over time, Loy regarded the latter qualities as abhorrent and entirely antithetical to the pluralism, dynamism,

and freedom that defined her conception of modern life. Carolyn Burke writes that Loy came to consider "her mother's tyrannizing as the domestic version of imperial rule: just as Britannia had taken for granted her right to govern the uncivilized people over whom she held sway, so her mother believed it her duty to encourage the repression of her daughter" and obscure the seeming blight of a mixed-race family with "unfailing attention to external forms" (pp. 17, 19). Loy would later excoriate her mother's failings in the poem "Anglo-Mongrels and the Rose" (1923–1925). In the piece, Loy characterizes her mother as English Rose, writing:

Rose of arrested impulses
self-pruned
of the primordial attributes
a tepid heart inhibiting
with tactful terrorism
the Blossom Populous
to mystic incest with its ancestry
...
Conservative Rose
storage
of the British Empire-made pot-pourri
of dry dead men making a sweetened smell
among a shriveled collectivity

(*The Last Lunar Baedeker,* 2.14–20, 2.31–35)

Given these contentions with her mother, Loy desperately sought some reprieve from her rule and thus redoubled her efforts to receive permission to enroll in art school.

After winning over her father, Loy was allowed to enroll at St. John's Wood School in 1897. While at the school, Loy learned the basics of composition, began to formulate her own theories about art's purpose and prospects, found her first influences in the poetry and paintings of the Pre-Raphaelites Dante Gabriel Rossetti and Edward Burne-Jones, who were responsible for the young lady's first "ideal of artistic purity," and won a school prize for one of her Burne-Jones-inspired paintings. Julia Löwy, however, continued to rail against her daughter's seemingly corrupted ambitions and destroyed a nude portrait that she had made of the chained heroine from Greek mythology, Andromeda (Burke, pp. 41–42). Loy's miseries at home increased, and she found life at the old-fashioned school uninspiring. By 1899 the atmosphere in the Löwy household was charged with unrelenting animosity—much of which seemed related to Loy's ambitions—so her parents allowed her to enroll in the Women's Academy in Munich with the requirement that she remain closely supervised by a Bavarian baron and baroness lest she be lured into compromising territory while away from home. Curiously, however, her parents would have less to fear with regard to the ideas and people Loy encountered in art school than they would with the seemingly respectable baron and baroness themselves, both of whom attempted to shape the comely young lady into a "femme fatale" and present her as a young "courtesan" to a succession of young men so that they might procure some additional income (Burke, pp. 57–61). A bemused but steadfast Loy resisted their uncomfortable overtures and avoided scandal by focusing on her schooling and freely crafting a unique image for herself among the less insidious poseurs and eccentrics of Munich.

During those years in Munich, Loy began to deliberately destroy the oppressive external forms of her Victorian background with art and usher in newer, more suitable modes of seeing and living that would grant her the autonomy to reinvent herself and enjoy self-fulfillment. The polarities in the Löwy household certainly caused Loy to view her upbringing with a marked degree of ambivalence and irony, for these very polarities fostered the bewilderment, alienation, imagination, and self-determination that complicated her personal life but also drove her work as an artist into its sharpest exploratory focus. Over time, these tensions would energize and inform Loy's push for a radically inventive, hybridized form of poetics and provide subjects for many of her poems. In fact, some of Loy's finest pieces, such as "Anglo-Mongrels and the Rose," are audacious renderings of these familial conflicts in terms of racial, gender, and national politics. The concept of race, of course, would remain an ever-present and essential component of Loy's bid for reinvention. Loy considered race to be one of the "chief impediments to evolutionary progress,"

for she believed that "cross-breeding between those of different races produces a unique level of self-awareness in the consciousness of the 'mongrel' offspring, self-knowledge that lays bare the fictional nature of race as a category" (Vetter, pp. 48–49). In this respect, Loy would spend her most productive years as a poet articulating her "struggle with racial consciousness and the problem of representing identity" (Pozorski, p. 44).

EMBATTLED WOMAN AND EMERGING ARTIST: 1901–1915

Loy journeyed back to London in 1901 to study with the renowned painter Augustus John, all the more determined to find artistic and personal self-fulfillment after her experiences in Munich. However, Loy soon determined that the constant conflict and dreariness at home were unsuitable to her growing aspirations and newfound perspective. Loy's yearning for "the possibilities for experience, for becoming" would not be easily satisfied (Kouidis, *Mina Loy,* p. 40). By 1903 the restive young artist was on the move again, this time to attend art school at the Académie Colarossi in Paris. Among the students Loy fell in with at school was an ostentatious painter and self-styled genius who came from a distinguished but impoverished British family, Stephen Haweis. Despite Haweis' affectedness and air of superiority, Loy found the young man captivating, for she viewed his behavior as an expression of individualism and self-confidence. For his part, Haweis was physically attracted to Loy, who has been aptly described as "tall and willowy, a glamorous creature with chiseled features and a razor-sharp wit" (Barnet, p. 18). Haweis was also drawn to Loy because of her ability to support him financially with the allowance she received from her parents. Indeed, Haweis quickly came to rely on Loy for support while he tried to establish a name for himself as an artist. Caught up in bouts of mutual infatuation, Loy and Haweis began to flirt with the idea of marriage despite the fact that neither free spirit appeared particularly interested in committing to one another in any deep or abiding way. Indeed, as Loy indicated later in life, their eventual decision to marry was more a matter of parental appeasement and preserving their relative independence than one of love (Blackburn and Vas Dias interview, pp. 240–241). Of course, after Loy was, by her own account, drugged and seduced by Haweis, only to discover a month later that she was pregnant, there was no question that the hesitant couple must wed as soon as possible if they wished to avoid a scandal (Barnet, p. 20).

Haweis and Loy were married under duress in Paris in 1903, and in 1904 a twenty-one-year-old Loy gave birth to a girl, whom she named Oda. Despite—or perhaps because of—their union, husband and wife appeared more concerned with satisfying their own egos than achieving harmony. Both Haweis and Loy felt that they had effectively compromised their status as individuals through the marriage: Haweis had married an unjustifiably aloof woman who was unworthy of his vaunted family name, and Loy had married a sexually inadequate man whom she saw as less attractive, gifted, and prosperous than herself (Burke, pp. 88–89). During this time, however, the struggling couple threw themselves into various artistic projects and started to find success. Haweis received recognition as a photographer of Auguste Rodin's sculptures and hobnobbed with notable artists, including Colette and George Moore. Loy also busied herself with painting and generated some definite interest in her own talent. Her work was soon exhibited at the innovative Salon d'Automne, alongside works by luminaries such as Rodin and Henri Matisse. Even with some measure of success, however, the couple was still financially strained, and Loy remained unsatisfied and restless in both her artistic life and her personal life. In 1905 their infant daughter Oda died of meningitis, and the couple's relationship degenerated still further; they engaged in wounding extramarital affairs and briefly separated. Loy sought a divorce from Haweis, but she kept up the pretence of their marriage in order to secure income from her parents (Burke, pp. 101–102). The couple concluded that a move might improve their ever more miserable lot in life, so they set off for Florence, Italy, in 1906.

Burke describes the Florence that Loy and Haweis entered as a land full of bohemian expatriates where "eccentricity was admired" and "one might do anything, provided one was not commonplace" (pp. 105, 108). Given Haweis' predilection toward flamboyance and Loy's decidedly unconventional outlook, Florence would eventually prove to be an excellent match for Haweis' social and artistic aspirations, and it would give Loy her first association with those people who would inform and support her newest endeavor: poetry. However, those first few years in Florence were not without their share of difficulties. Loy remained isolated from Haweis' Florentine associates on the whole; she felt weary and at odds with the interminable tea times and joyless social calls her husband had thrown himself into as a means of creating interest in his work (Burke, p. 106). The most acute problem of all, though, was her relationship with Haweis. Regardless of their efforts to repair their relationship, including the hopeful birth of another daughter, Joella, in 1907 and a son, Giles, in 1909, the couple seemed incapable of any real reconciliation. Fortunately, Loy's life did start to improve in 1910, if only because she discovered ways to reinvigorate and foster her once waning faith in social, artistic, and personal progress. Loy had been studying the influential French philosopher Henri Bergson and found that his theories regarding direct experience, consciousness, and the revelatory power of intuition suited her own evolving ideas. Loy had also fully converted to Christian Science as a means to cope with her poor health and to help heal Joella's polio (Kouidis, *Mina Loy,* p. 7). Her involvement with this new religion, which had been founded by the theologian and feminist Mary Baker Eddy in 1866, appeared to be anything but casual, for she treasured the joining of mysticism with scientific thought and thoroughly embraced the promises for autonomous self-improvement it held for all serious practitioners. As Suzanne Zelazo explains, "Drawing from these two theorists, Loy cultivated an understanding of human consciousness as an ever-evolving flux, and she advocated the need to forge aesthetic modes of representing that dynamism" (p. 55). According to Richard Cook, these influences would, in great part, prompt Loy's lifelong exploration of the "thematic of will and its relationship to spiritually heightened senses" in her poetry and paintings (p. 458).

During this time, Loy befriended a number of expatriates who helped renew her artistic fervor and reorient her creative focus. Among the most important persons Loy befriended was the American heiress, salon hostess, and art patron Mabel Dodge. Dodge consistently assembled lively groupings of notable artists and colorful exiles at her villa near Florence. At Dodge's salon, Loy met her future editor, Carl Van Vechten, and one of the most radical writers of the day, Gertrude Stein. Loy and Stein formed an immediate and lasting connection with one another. As a collector of avant-garde paintings, including early pieces by Pablo Picasso, Stein recognized Loy's talent as a painter and appreciated Loy's uncommon beauty, wit, and receptiveness to experimental writing. Loy's open-mindedness in this respect prompted Stein to introduce the young painter to theories and approaches that would directly lead to Loy taking up writing. Loy, for her part, appears to have found something of a mentor and advocate in Stein. Indeed, Loy was so taken with Stein's literary advances and companionship that she would write a poem about Stein, defend her work against unfavorable criticism, and lecture on her seventeen years later. As Burke writes, Loy saw Stein's "attempts to place the individual temperament within the overlapping contexts of personal and social history" as particularly exciting and felt that "she might do the same with her own background" (p. 130). Given Loy's conflicted sense of identity and restless desire for self-determination, Stein's revolutionarily syncretic writing was nothing short of revelatory for the young artist. Indeed, as Zelazo notes, Loy's "integrationist tendencies" as person were directly translated into her work as a poet and visual artist, both in terms of her subject matter and formal experimentation (p. 48). This viewpoint and approach would reach a zenith with her eventual move to one of the most mongrelized cities in the world, New York.

Despite the relative comfort Loy had come to enjoy in the company of Stein and other friends, her domestic life was far from peaceful. Loy had to oversee the well-being of her children and maintain a facade of respectability so that she might secure the allowance that kept the family relatively secure while Haweis flitted about Italy in order to promote his artistic wares. Looking back on this time, Loy sarcastically remarked that she did indeed attempt to make her relationship with Haweis work by "trying to look as though [she] liked—accepted him—respected him" (Blackburn and Vas Dias interview, p. 241). Loy's tolerance of Haweis' careless behavior reached a critical point in 1912 when he engaged in yet another affair. Rather than being heartbroken by the infidelity, Loy saw an opportunity for escape and volunteered to hand over Haweis to his covetous mistress. Haweis, though, felt no compunction about ending what he viewed as a capricious affair, and he showed no desire to grant Loy her freedom even though he had plans to leave her alone in Florence so that he might seek his fame and fortune alone in Tahiti and Australia (Burke, pp. 136–141). Of course, given the social and legal climate of the times, Loy had little choice but to remain married to her inconstant and now absconding husband until she could find some viable means of supporting herself. Loy would condemn Haweis' attitude and behavior in "Parturition" (1914) and "Anglo-Mongrels and the Rose," among other poems, while using her newfound feminist beliefs and natural inventiveness to tirelessly combat the limitations such men attempted to impose on women.

After Haweis' departure in 1913, Loy filed for divorce and decided that she would travel to New York to pursue work as a clothing designer. In order to gain the money necessary for passage, she began renting out her husband's studio. This decision would prove fateful, for through her American lodger and new friend, Frances Simpson Stevens, she became involved with an artistic movement that fundamentally altered her perspective on identity, the woman question, and art: Italian futurism. The aim of futurism as it was articulated by its most vocal leader, F. T. Marinetti, was to cast off the fusty and stultifying elements of European culture in order to embrace the vigor of a new age through politically charged art. Among their many ambitions, the futurists were interested in radicalizing the fine arts, eliminating age-old sexual taboos, celebrating technology, promoting nationalism, and advocating the purportedly hygienic affects of war.

Arrogant, extreme, and blustery, Marinetti was a divisive figure and a difficult person, even for those predisposed to appreciate his ideas and theatrics. However, this provocative speaker and would-be leader of men ultimately won over Loy, who by now had dismissed her husband as little more than an anemic poseur. Andrea Barnet explains that "for all his posturing, his infuriating hubris, there was an energy in Marinetti she found magnetizing" (p. 23). Perhaps most importantly, though, he "encouraged her to take her life and her work more seriously" (p. 24). After years of tedium and misery, Loy doubtless felt that Marinetti's antics, charisma, and praise were too much to resist, for they became lovers. However, their relationship was far from exclusive, for Loy also found Marinetti's chief rival among the futurists, Giovanni Papini, irresistibly intriguing. It seems that Loy saw the homely Papini as more subtle, discerning, and mysterious than his riotous and dashing adversary (Burke, pp. 154–155). Loy soon vacillated between these two intimates and agents of change, all the while adopting or recasting those futurist ideas that would seem to support her aesthetic aims and empower her. Loy even went so far as to boldly articulate her engagement with the movement in the piece "Aphorisms on Futurism," which was published in Alfred Stieglitz's *Camera Work* in 1914 alongside writing by Gertrude Stein.

Loy obviously found much to like in futurism, yet she was not without some wariness with regard to several of its dominant assumptions and most audacious proclamations. In fact, Loy started to feel disenfranchised with the movement, especially once it began to divide into factions, the most dominant of which had unabashed fascist objectives. Scholarship surrounding Loy's exact position within the spectrum of futurist thought has certainly proved thorny, for it is rife

with seemingly irreconcilable contradictions. While Loy admired the grand, uncompromising spirit of the movement, she showed a marked aversion to the militancy and fascism it promoted. However, the most salient conflicts Loy experienced with futurism were with its gender and racial politics. Loy's commitment to feminism, for one, had certainly deepened during her time with Marinetti. In fact, it was during this period that she composed her "Feminist Manifesto" (1914). The manifesto, which affords a curious glimpse into Loy's evolving philosophy, has been accurately characterized as a striking but unstable amalgamation of feminist, futurist, and Victorian thought that seeks to free women from a passive acquiescence to genteel respectability so that they can pursue self-respecting actions that might solidify their personal and social autonomy (Walter, p. 666).

As an instigator of revolutionary ideas and supporter of Loy's work, Marinetti had been instrumental in her approach to this document; however, as a misogynist whose manifesto zealously expressed a desire to "demolish ... feminism" and declared "contempt for woman," Marinetti's designs clearly ran counter to Loy's vision. Race was also a point of contention, for as Aimee L. Pozorski writes, "As a feminist and daughter of a Jewish tailor, Loy continuously struggled with the conflict between the value futurists represented for rethinking language and the racism their language embodied" (p. 45). Certainly the xenophobic leanings in futurism's militant agenda necessarily undermined the aspirations of this self-identified mongrel who showed such disdain for the similarly bigoted views of her mother and tended to assign great value to her father's otherness. Ultimately, though, Loy found the movement's views far too restrictive for her ambitions and the actions advocated by Marinetti unconscionably destructive in light of her quest for constructive social change and personal fulfillment.

Amid the artistic and personal upheavals Loy had been experiencing, World War I began in the summer of 1914. Loy soon began working in an Italian war hospital and urgently resolved to leave the tumult of Europe as soon as possible. While working in the hospital, Loy wrote one of her best early poems, "Parturition," which Carl Van Vechten helped her publish in the little magazine *Trend*. Throughout "Parturition," Loy focuses on her experience during the birth of Oda, while caustically criticizing Haweis' absence and affair during that time. The poem contrasts the pettiness, selfishness, and unnatural remoteness of Haweis to Loy's own serious commitment to childbirth, pointing to the ugly inequities inherent in marriage. The piece is darkly confessional, exuding anguish, alienation, and contempt through Loy's exacting use of diction, prosody, and white space. Loy writes:

> I am the centre
> Of a circle of pain
> Exceeding its boundaries in every direction
> ...
> Locate an irritation without
> It is within
> Within
> It is without.
> ...
> The conception Brute
> Why?
> The irresponsibility of the male
> Leaves woman her superior Inferiority.
>
> (*The Last Lunar Baedeker,* 1–3, 11–14, 36–39)

According to Alex Goody, Loy takes a futurist approach to the poem as a means to develop a "linguistic enactment of childbirth" that powerfully communicates the "disjunctions, extremities and realisations of parturition" (p. 47). Indeed, the tautly rendered series of declarations that comprise the piece create a confrontational tone entirely in keeping with the strident futurist aesthetic. While Loy doubtless composed the piece under the influence of futurism's call for sexual frankness, political activism, and dynamic expression, she asserts herself in a style all her own and disregards the sexist dictates of a movement that would negate a feminine perspective on the failings of patriarchal authority. Paul Peppis maintains that the poem "not only promotes women as sexual beings, cultural producers, and philosophical theorists, but also challenges defensive assertions by leading male modernists" (p. 572). In "Parturition," Loy confronts the self-

satisfied men who would dominate her life through her use of unflattering characterization and the development of her theme; however, as Marjorie Perloff explains, even Loy's formal choices in the poem run in critical opposition to the rules of composition as they are laid out in Marinetti's "Technical Manifesto of Futurist Literature," thereby signaling yet another form of dissent (p. 137).

At the age of thirty-two Loy became weary of her volatile existence and began to dissolve her ever more uncomfortable personal ties to Marinetti and Papini, both of whom by now appeared interested in competing with one another at the expense of all else. Loy, too, was radically departing from acceptable taste in most quarters of conventional society by speaking in a forceful female voice and detailing the misery produced by a socially expedient but altogether loveless union. The sharply ironic, confrontational narrator of the piece makes no attempt to appease polite readers of the era. In fact, as Virginia M. Kouidis maintains, Loy's mission during this phase was both "attacking her Victorian heritage which calculated the marriage value of women according to their purity and ignorance, and imprisoned their spiritual vitality" and "fighting the failure of literature to treat life honestly" ("Rediscovering," p. 170). Loy's unorthodox and unabashed treatment of these issues showed further intensification in several poems she published in 1915, including "Virgins Plus Curtains Minus Dots" (1915) and, perhaps most impressively, in her groundbreaking sequence "Love Songs" (1915), which would later be expanded, revised, and renamed "Love Songs to Joannes" (1917). The infamous first stanza of "Love Songs," with its wry, pseudo-scientific deromanticization of coitus, shocked many readers:

Spawn of Fantasies
Sitting the appraisable
Pig Cupid
His rosy snout
Rooting erotic garbage
"Once upon a time"
Pulls a weed
White star topped
Among wild oats
Sown in mucous-membrane

(*The Last Lunar Baedeker,* 1.1–10)

Besides mocking the chauvinistic attitude of the futurists, Loy targets the debilitating romantic pretenses of Papini, the "Pig Cupid," and goes so far as to question the efficacy of coupling altogether. While Loy undoubtedly makes daring stylistic strides and confidently exhibits her satirical abilities in the poem, it also conveys a vision of frustration, isolation, and fragility. As Kouidis explains, "The juxtaposition of heterogeneous images forms a collage of biological, romantic, religious, and cosmological fragments, as well as past, present and future times, to depict the disintegration of an ordered, purposeful existence" ("Rediscovering," p. 181). In this respect, the poem asserts that breaking from the strictures of conventional romance has little abiding value unless one is willing to replace self-aggrandizing behavior with a spirit of generosity.

The style and content of "Love Songs" immediately turned Loy into a polarizing figure, even among the seemingly forward-thinking followers and practitioners of the avant-garde. The American poet Amy Lowell refused to submit any future work to the magazine *Others* because the editors had published Loy's poetry, and Haweis accused his wife of writing lascivious and amateurish poetry that brought disgrace on them both (Burke, pp. 191–193). Suffice it to say, Loy was beginning to make a name—however notorious—for herself as an uncompromising poet, particularly in America, where all of her controversial writing was now being placed under the direction of Dodge and Van Vechten. Alfred Kreymborg, who founded and edited *Others,* writes of the reception of "Love Songs" in the States:

> In an unsophisticated land, such sophistry, clinical frankness, sardonic conclusions, wedded to a madly elliptical style scornful of the regulation grammar, syntax and punctuation (E. E. Cummings), horrified our gentry and drove our critics into furious despair. The nudity of emotion and thought roused the worst disturbance, and the utter nonchalance in revealing the secrets of sex was denounced as nothing less

> than lewd. It took a strong digestive apparatus to read Mina Loy.
>
> (pp. 488–489)

Kouidis concurs with Kreymborg, noting that "later readers were to understand her unconventionality as proto-Surrealist; but when her poetry first appeared, its free-verse presentation of human absurdity and sexual and psychic frustration confused and shocked traditionalists" (*Mina Loy,* p. 15). With her reputation as a taboo-shattering poet now preceding her, Loy made arrangements to leave for New York in 1916. Loy chose to leave her children in Florence under the care of the headmistress of the English School, Miss Penrose, presumably in order to lessen their exposure to instability and so that she might pursue her business and artistic ventures unencumbered. Loy boarded a ship for New York on October 15, caught somewhere between the guilt of leaving her children and the hope that she would enjoy self-determination, security, and recognition in America (Burke, pp. 193–194).

LIBERATED WOMAN AND NOTORIOUS ARTIST: 1916–1923

As Loy's ship pulled into New York, the careworn poet was awestruck by the dazzling architecture of the city and inspired by the innovative spirit and remarkable vitality it communicated. As Burke writes, New York at the time "was the embodiment of the new, the site where the twentieth century was being unveiled," and Loy imagined it as a "vortex of energy, an urban parade, an artistic and intellectual community, and a refuge for those who, for diverse reasons, were outcasts of Europe" (p. 212). Loy saw a world ahead of her where mongrels were not outcasts and the prospect of reinvention and autonomy were possible—a place less bound by the cultural restrictions she experienced in London, Paris, and Florence. Loy would later communicate her impression of her newly adopted land, writing:

> It was inevitable that the renaissance of poetry should proceed out of America, where latterly a thousand languages have been born, and each one, for purposes of communication at least, English—English enriched and variegated with the grammatical structure and voice-inflection of many races, in novel alloy with the time-is-money idiom of the United States, discovered by the newspaper cartoonists.
>
> (*The Lost Lunar Baedeker,* p. 158)

Upon her arrival in the city Loy wasted no time reconnecting with her friend and former boarder Frances Simpson Stevens. Stevens proved immensely helpful to Loy from the start, helping her to find an apartment and establishing her as a social fixture at Walter and Louise Arensberg's apartment, which served as the American equivalent to the artistic salons she frequented back in Europe (Burke, p. 213). The Arensbergs were enthusiastic art collectors and played host to a diverse band of artists, poets, eccentrics, and expatriates, including Marcel Duchamp, Francis Picabia, Wallace Stevens, and William Carlos Williams. Loy was a success with this group, owing in part to the fact that some of its key members were familiar with her work and modernist credentials. As in her student days, Loy also succeeded because of her intelligence and attractiveness. Conover writes that Loy was "full of sauce and style: opinionated, even intransigent, yet full of grace and wit ... engaging and distant, like the moon" (p. 253). Among the friendships and association Loy fostered, Duchamp was one of the first people she found herself drawn to at the Arensbergs' salon.

Duchamp had recently caused an uproar and gained renown in international art circles with his exhibit at the 1913 Armory Show, which included his most famous work, *Nude Descending a Staircase,* and he was subsequently at the height of his confidence as an artistic provocateur and avant-garde celebrity. Many bohemians in Greenwich Village regarded Duchamp as the epitome of urbanity and artistic iconoclasm, while others, including French-speaking expatriates such as Loy, found him to be an amusing and roguish ally (Barnet, p. 36). Loy certainly appreciated Duchamp's company and benefited from his Dadaist theories and techniques, which she soon started to incorporate into her own designs, paintings, and poetry. Dada's flagrant disdain for the status quo, emphasis on intuition,

and frequent use of disruptive satire certainly appealed to Loy, as she had been exploring each of those areas to some degree for the better part of a decade. Loy also found the movement's use of collage and found objects suitable for her own emerging aesthetic, and she would continue to deepen her engagement with both approaches to expression well into the twilight of her career. While Loy was enthralled with the creativity and entertained by the decadence surrounding her, she did not indulge in affairs with Duchamp or any other member of the Arensbergs' circle. One reason for her reserve may be attributed to the tumultuous relationships she had just concluded with Marinetti and Papini. However, perhaps the greatest reason for her reserve was that she did not wish to compromise her bid for divorce, for Haweis' indiscreet and irresponsible actions over the past years had placed her in a position of power, and their divorce appeared imminent (Burke, p. 220).

Once Loy had established important connections in New York, she became involved in a flurry of artistic enterprises. Loy acted as leading lady in Kreymborg's play *Lima Beans,* exhibited her art at the Society of Independent Artists alongside pieces such as Duchamp's *Fountain,* gave poetry readings with Williams and others, and published pieces in Duchamp's short-lived magazine *The Blind Man*. Loy also started a lampshade business, which was both an extension of her involvement with the arts and one of the few ways she could hope to establish economic security on her own terms, but she quickly discovered that it was extremely difficult to make a profit from the enterprise (Dunn, pp. 444, 447). Nonetheless, Loy's open-mindedness and consistent involvement with the arts had helped her to become integrated into the culture around her in short order. In fact, Loy was such a part of the Greenwich Village scene that she became the very symbol of the bohemian "new woman," according to the reporter who in 1917 wrote a feature piece on her for the *Sun* titled "Mina Loy, Painter, Poet and Playwright, Doesn't Try to Express Her Personality by Wearing Odd Looking Draperies—Her Clothes Suggest the Smartest Shops, but Her Poems Would Have Puzzled Grandma."

Loy also completed and published "Love Songs to Joannes" during this immensely productive period of her life. Far from reining in her radicalism, Loy boldly asserted her feminist beliefs and made great formal leaps with "Love Songs." The publication of the controversial sequence proved to be a literary coup for Loy, as the poem comprised an entire issue of *Others* and became the subject of much lively discussion among the literati of New York. Peter Quartermain explains that the poem "attacks romanticized sexuality as one of the principle means of subjecting women" and "explores the damaging myth which creates not love but powerless contempt" (p. 76). Indeed, the narrator relentlessly swoops down on "Pig Cupid" and snatches away the most degrading portions of their experience, only to reassemble and expose the ugliest bits and pieces for all to see.

> We might have coupled
> In the bed-ridden monopoly of a moment
> Or broken flesh with one another
> At the profane communion table
> Where wine is spilled on promiscuous lips
>
> We might have given birth to a butterfly
> With the daily news
> Printed in blood on its wings
>
> (*The Last Lunar Baedeker,* 3.1–8)

Jeffrey Twitchell-Waas argues that the poem "is Loy's most audacious assault on language and the genre of the romantic lyric.... In this assault she not only manages to ironically dismantle the genre's sentimentality, its privileging of emotional dependency, but transforms it into a tentative exploration of new possibilities of relations between the sexes" (p. 127). If Loy still had doubts regarding her skill as a poet and ability to attract notice, they must have been lessened considerably with the reception of "Songs to Joannes."

Loy gained further control over her personal life during this period, as she was granted her much-anticipated divorce from Haweis and received custody of her children in 1917. Her newfound freedom and association with Dada

also came together to produce an unexpected result: she was introduced to her future husband, Arthur Cravan (aka Fabien Lloyd), at the Independent's exhibit and began seeing him regularly thereafter at the Arensbergs'. Cravan was a Swiss poet, boxer, instigator, raconteur, wanderer, and exemplar of Dadaist absurdity and revolt who claimed, among other things, to be an American and the nephew of Oscar Wilde. Barnet notes that with his striking physique, love of self-promotion, and pursuit of public outrages, Cravan had created an infamous reputation for himself before he even arrived in New York (p. 37). Despite the vibrant aura surrounding Cravan, Loy initially found him to be little more than a drunken, muscle-bound boor. However, despite her misgivings and warnings from her friends, Loy's found herself becoming increasingly attracted to Cravan, whose sensitivity appeared much more acute than she had first imagined and whose body suggested a level of protection and sexual fulfillment she had failed to experience with Haweis and her former lovers (Burke, pp. 239–242). The skeptic and ironist behind "Songs to Joannes" had cautiously but resolutely discovered in Cravan a clever and gifted man worthy of her esteem. Perhaps most of all, though, she had found a man who could reinvigorate her spiritually, someone with whom she could freely share her desires and, in turn, receive acceptance rather than ridicule and betrayal. Looking back on her short-lived but passionate relationship with Cravan, Loy repeatedly stressed her singular connection with him. In her 1965 interview with Paul Blackburn and Robert Vas Dias, Loy maintained that she was the only person who had the ability to communicate with Cravan in earnest and affirmed that he was the only person to fully understand her.

In an effort to evade service in World War I, Cravan began tramping all over North America, eventually choosing to sail to Mexico so that he could travel to Argentina to wait out the war in relative safety and comfort. Back in New York, Loy was confronted with her father's death, a growing patriotic antipathy toward radicals and foreigners, and the unsettling absence of Cravan. Despite her ties to New York, lack of sufficient income, and fears regarding the Mexican Revolution, Loy could not bear to be separated from Cravan and decided to follow him to Mexico. On January 25, 1918, Loy and Cravan were married in a civil ceremony in Mexico City. Loy was delighted with the union, but the trying circumstances of their existence in Mexico soon began to poison her joy. Among the difficulties the couple faced, Loy had to nurse Cravan through a prolonged illness, live in a squalid quarter of the city, and skip meals so they might make what little money they had last until they could find some means of support (Burke, pp. 258–259). This time would mark Loy's first real experience with the ravages of destitution, but it would not be her last.

Once Cravan recovered, he began coaching boxing and participating in matches in order to generate some income; however, Cravan earned little from the ad hoc, sloppy, and altogether damaging slug-outs he threw himself into across Mexico. With what money they had, a pregnant Loy and battered but confident Cravan decided to purchase a rundown but seemingly seaworthy boat so that they could sail to Argentina, where the cost of living was said to be cheaper (Burke, pp. 261–265). Loy was to secure passage on a hospital ship and the inexperienced Cravan was to sail their boat to Argentina. Regardless of the questionable viability of their plan, the beleaguered couple now had some prospect for relief in sight. As a precautionary measure, Cravan began putting the boat through its paces as Loy watched from the shore, but it appears that Cravan ran into difficulties along the way. The ship sailed on and eventually vanished, leaving an uncomprehending and panicked Loy searching for some sign of Cravan from the beach. A week went by without any sign of Cravan, and a desperate and penniless Loy had no choice but take the last boat out with the hope that she would reunite with him somewhere in South America (Barnet, p. 44). Loy nervously waited for Cravan in Argentina for months before breaking down and requesting funds from her disapproving mother so that she might sail back to England. Undaunted, Loy would continue searching for Cravan, but she would never find him,

nor would she ever know the exact circumstances behind his disappearance and ultimate fate.

Loy's next few years were marked by trouble, heartbreak, and restlessness. Loy gave birth to Cravan's daughter, Fabienne, in London on April 5, 1919, had the child baptized in Geneva, Switzerland, traveled to Florence to reunite with Giles and Joella, and left her children once again so that she might return to New York to search for Cravan. Upon her return to New York in 1920, Loy discovered that many of her friends and associates had left or were leaving, the editors of the *Little Review* were facing obscenity charges for publishing *Ulysses,* and America had entered into Prohibition. For all intents and purposes, the heady and seemingly unrestricted atmosphere she had become accustomed to before the war had begun to dissipate, but Loy still found ready friendships with William Carlos Williams and Djuna Barnes to help ease her back into the city. Loy soon busied herself by seeking news regarding Cravan and publishing book reviews and poems. One poem in particular, "Ineffectual Marriage" (1917–1920), brought her attention, as it was included in Ezra Pound's *Instigations* (1920). Taking his cue from Loy's penchant for exactitude and irony, as well as the strong undercurrent of melancholia in the poem, Pound praised the piece and made a claim for it as an exemplary instance of "logopoeia ... a dance of intelligence among words ... the utterance of clever people in despair" (p. 234). The despair Pound detected in Loy was quickly intensified in 1921 when she found out that Haweis had sold their house in Florence and kidnapped Giles while he was at it. Apparently Haweis felt that the house was his alone and assumed it was his right to take Giles with him to the Caribbean, despite the fact that he did not have custody of the boy (Burke, p. 304). Loy immediately left for Florence, hoping that she might somehow stabilize her rapidly degenerating personal life.

Once Loy had returned to Florence and collected Joella and Fabienne, she set off for Vienna in order to recuperate from the disquiet that had been silently gnawing at her for years. Loy met Sigmund Freud during this time of respite and persuaded him to sit for a portrait. According to Burke, Loy valued the revealing conversations she shared with the psychoanalyst, and he found the poet's writing to be remarkably "analytic." Ever restless, though, Loy soon left Vienna for Berlin, but not before installing her children in Potsdam and enrolling Joella in Isadora Duncan's dance school (p. 313). On the whole, Loy's brief tenure in Berlin was fairly unremarkable, except for publishing a few poems in the *Dial* and securing a publisher for a collection she had been working on—*Lunar Baedecker* (1923). Loy soon became dissatisfied with Berlin and decided to revisit Paris, where she would work on her manuscript, cross paths with her old friends Duchamp, Barnes, and Stein, and be introduced to an entirely new group of writers who gravitated around Sylvia Beach's bookshop.

A POETICS OF SELF: 1923–1936

The forty-year-old Loy discovered that Paris had changed considerably from her last extended residency there almost twenty years ago. Paris was swarming with disillusioned expatriates, and the Jazz Age was at its raucous height. Loy arrived to a city full of skeptical, adventurous, and creative men and women, including groundbreaking writers such as James Joyce, Ford Madox Ford, Ernest Hemingway, and members of the Lost Generation. The environment was rife with change and unmistakably modern in tone. Tragedy, however, would quickly follow Loy's reintroduction to Paris. Loy, who had not told Haweis of her move and who had not kept in touch with her estranged son, received a delayed letter informing her that Giles was ill with cancer, which was followed by yet another delayed letter informing her that he had died from the disease (Burke, p. 327). Loy must have taken an extraordinarily stoical approach to the death of Giles, for there is little to no indication that she ever gave vent to her grief, other than in oblique references in some of her poems. In fact, it appears that Loy's only means of dealing with those years of subjugation, loss, and insecurity was to socialize and throw herself into creative enterprises. Of the social connections that supported her enterprises, Peggy Guggenheim's backing of Loy's new lampshade business helped alleviate her

financial woes, and Robert McAlmon's decision to publish *Lunar Baedecker* secured her reputation as an astonishingly original poet.

Despite some negative reviews, *Lunar Baedecker* was received with great enthusiasm among those members of the intelligentsia with an eye toward the advancement of poetry. The poet and critic Edwin Muir reviewed the book twice, remarking that it captured the right mixture of mysticism and disdain for crass materiality necessary for modern poetics (Burke, p. 337). Kouidis observes that throughout the *Lunar Baedeker*, Loy focuses on this dichotomy through two central emblematic figures: the artist, "who alone among humanity possesses the vision for intuiting the essence of life's chaos and the skill to shape his intuitions into form—the divine principle"; and the bum, "emblem of timid or failed vision, who seeks transcendence or worldly care in false Elysiums and Nirvanas" (*Mina Loy,* p. 109). These two figures would consistently appear in Loy's visual art and poetry until her death, suggesting that she continued to struggle with the essential question of the artist's ability to surpass the trappings of a socially prescribed identity.

Loy would examine this concern on a grand scale and push her formal innovations to new extremes with what may be regarded as one her most important poems, "Anglo-Mongrels and the Rose." The poem would also effectively serve as Loy's most powerful autobiographical work, for it treats many of the aspirations, disappointments, suffering, and contempt she had experienced from childhood to her mid-forties. Sections of "Anglo-Mongrels and the Rose" appeared in McAlmon's *Contact Collection of Contemporary Writers* and the *Little Review,* but the pieces of this long poem were not published together at the time, thereby delaying its full impact. Taken as a whole, the poem involves an allegorical cast of characters based on people who had been, for better or worse, instrumental in Loy's life: her mother, portrayed as English Rose; her father, portrayed as Exodus; Haweis, portrayed as Esau Penfold; Cravan, portrayed as Colossus; and Loy herself, portrayed as Ova. Helen Jaskoski summarizes the themes and approach to the poem nicely, noting that in it Loy addresses "the function of the artist as seer and maker, the Outsider as a touchstone of integrity and authenticity, and the nature of identity—sexual, social and psychic" in a fashion that "suggests a Modernist verse novel" (pp. 349–350). Whether one takes the poem as an expression of Loy's hopelessly fragmented identity, as Pozorksi suggests, or as an argument that mongrelization can ultimately free a person from the restrictions of conventional identification, as Lara Vetter suggests, it is doubtlessly a caustic, densely layered social satire directly informed by Loy's dissension from the rank-and-file expectations of those who were once closest to her (pp. 46–47, 58).

Part 1 of the poem does well to illustrate Loy's approach to these topics and her larger project of a poetics of self. Loy examines the destructive relationship between her imperializing mother, Rose, and her imperialized father, Exodus, critiquing the artistic, cultural, and spiritual concessions the latter has made in order to appease the demands of the former. Loy at once empathizes with her father and admonishes him, aligning his difficulties with her own but taking him to task for ultimately failing his daughter and himself. Indeed, as Melita Schaum observes, "Like the poet, Exodus is a character out of synchronization with his world.... His attempted escape from the restrictions of culture and parentage seems liberating, but proves illusionary" (p. 266). Exodus, moreover, becomes a Judas figure whose desire for money and prestige eventually prompts him to indulge in falsehoods and betrayals that compromise his character and permanently taint his relationship with his daughter (pp. 265–270). Loy writes:

He paints
He feels his pulse

The spiritual tentacles of vanity
That each puts out towards the culture
of his epoch knowing not how to find
and finding not contact he has repealed
to fumble among his guts

...

The parasite attaches to the English Rose
at a guinea a visit

...

Exodus knows
no longer father
or brother
or God of the Jews
it is his to choose
finance or
romance of the rose

(*The Last Lunar Baedeker* 1.340–341, 1.352–353, 1.394–400)

If the poem may be said to have a heroic figure—one who, unlike the weak Exodus and even weaker Esau, has the strength to resist the lures of self-negating conformity—it would be Colossus. Even Colossus, though, is not without his share of debilitating flaws. As with her past objections to futurism, Loy refuses to fully endorse the mighty Colossus and the ostensibly liberating movement he represents: Dadaism. Kouidis explains that, in Loy's estimation, even this newest and most promising of movements ultimately leads to social, artistic, and spiritual dead ends. She writes: "Colossus represents the art-for-art's-sake defiance of convention carried to the destructive extreme of Dada. Loy sympathizes with the Dada trend in twentieth-century art, especially its encouragement of experiment; but Dada's nihilistic current runs counter to her constructive quest" (*Mina Loy,* p. 118).

Although Loy achieved a personal breakthrough and gained favorable notice for *Lunar Baedecker* and "Anglo-Mongrels and the Rose," her productivity and impact as a poet lessened over the next several years. In fact, it appears as if Loy lost much of her interest in writing and in the prospect of capitalizing on her recent breakthrough, for she even started to disregard solicitations for her poetry. Regrettably, Loy would never again match the sheer innovation and visceral impact of *Lunar Baedecker* and "Anglo-Mongrels and the Rose," and her reputation as a poet would eventually rest on that single book and those few scattered pieces of poetry produced in the early 1920s.

Rather than dedicating herself to writing, Loy spent much of the remainder of the era socializing with Stein, Barnes, and the rest of the ever-revolving cast of expatriates in Paris. Barnes was so keen on their renewed friendship that she immortalized Loy as the character Patience Scalpel in *Ladies Almanack* (1928). Loy also busied herself creating and exhibiting her visual art and designs and managing her increasingly successful lampshade business, which Joella helped her to run. In 1927 Loy even enjoyed the privilege of consenting to Joella's marriage with Julien Levy, a New York art dealer and early champion of surrealism who happened to be visiting Paris, but not without having first generated quite a bit of sexual tension with the young man herself (Burke, p. 346). From all indications, Loy did quite well with her lampshade business, for she consistently sold her art nouveau–inspired work in England and America and had examples of her pieces featured in the magazine *Arts and Decoration* (Burke, p. 365). Loy had managed to establish herself as an independent businesswoman, but it seems that she was unhappy with workaday realities and the commercial nature of her work, which appeared to set her at odds with her fundamental beliefs regarding purity in art. Loy chose to sell her lampshade business, and in 1931 she became an art agent for Julien Levy. Around this time, Loy also started an autobiographical novel, *Insel* (1991), that like so much of her writing was inspired by a love affair: in this case a relationship with the German surrealist painter Richard Oelze. Their short-lived, ill-fated affair would prove emotionally damaging to Loy, who by now was showing definite signs of withdrawing from the companionship of others. Their personal conflict was only exacerbated by the fear of Nazi and Fascist threats that had begun to pervade Paris. With the failure of love and onset of war, Loy once again orchestrated an escape: she set her eyes on that familiar land of mongrels across the pond, America.

A WOMAN OBSCURED AND AN ARTIST REDISCOVERED: 1936–1966

An impoverished and heartsick Loy returned to New York in 1936. She immediately reunited with her family, first living with Joella and Julien Levy and then sharing residences with Fabienne. However, the reunion was far from joyful or even comfortable for all involved. As Burke relates,

Loy appeared to be quite a changed woman in the eyes of her estranged daughters, for she had visibly aged, lost her spirited manner, and appeared entirely beaten by the difficult circumstances of her life. Despite finding some solace by working with Julien and creating designs, Loy was distracted, miserable, and seemingly goaded into constant irritation by her poverty and perceived failures. Other than writing on occasion and working on her visual art, Loy appears to have undergone some radical changes, particularly with regard to her once adventuresome, outgoing personality. She now quarreled with her daughters on a regular basis and tended to avoid anyone associated with her past. On the whole, Loy seemed ready to resign from any sustained contact with the outside world and willfully cultivated obscurity by resisting overtures from friends and admirers for both companionship and new work. By the early 1940s, Loy relegated most of her social contact to the artist Joseph Cornell. Cornell was an avant-garde sculptor, Christian Scientist, and soft-spoken hermit with a mystical bent—a perfect match for Loy.

Regardless of Loy's withdrawal from society, she had developed a love for her adopted country over the years and found ready identification with it. It seems that the world traveler had indeed found a country to call home, for she became a naturalized citizen of the United States in 1946. By the late 1940s, Loy once again faced the prospect of moving, as a recently divorced Joella and a newly single Fabienne decided to move to Aspen, Colorado, with their partners. Although Loy was encouraged to accompany them, she elected to stay in New York and settled into a communal house in the Bowery. The Bowery, which by then was widely referred to as "Skid Row," was a notorious haven for many of the homeless, ill, and outcast members of New York society. Ever the outsider, Loy felt at home in her new environment and showed a brief resurgence in creativity, writing new poems, such as "Hot Cross Bum," and creating Cornell-inflected assemblages inspired by her experiences and observations in the Bowery. As with her poetry from the 1920s, her visual art from the 1950s frequently addressed and employed "urban detritus and the abject" as a means to explore the role of mongrelization in modern society (Goody, p. 177). Loy used an array of found objects she encountered in the streets, meshing the actual with allegorical in pieces such as *Communal Cot* (1950) and *Christ on a Clothesline* (1955–1959). Zelazo writes that ideologically Loy's "democratic use of materials provocatively dissolved barriers of class and consciousness" and gave "possession to the dispossessed" (p. 65).

In 1953 Loy reluctantly left the Bowery for Aspen at the insistence of her daughters. Loy was now in her seventies, and her isolation and poor health all but necessitated the move. While it was evident that Loy's productivity and influence as a poet and visual artist had been waning for decades, she was nonetheless contacted by the publisher Jonathan Williams regarding the publication of a revised and expanded version of *Lunar Baedecker*. In 1958 *Lunar Baedeker and Time-Tables* appeared as part of the Jargon Society series, falling in between new works by the literary pioneers Henry Miller and Charles Olson. The book was introduced by her old friend William Carlos Williams and included further introductions by members of a new generation of admirers—Kenneth Rexroth and Denise Levertov. During this time Cornell and Duchamp also arranged a one-woman show for Loy in New York. Loy assemblages gained a considerable degree of favorable attention, for she won a Copley Foundation Award for her artwork. While the publication of *Lunar Baedeker and Time-Tables* and the exhibition of her assemblages did not bring about great gains in terms of financial rewards or newfound fame, this renewed interest among aficionados did provide Loy with a sense of validation.

Loy's health continued to worsen, but she appeared committed to maintaining some vestige of her hard-won independence. According to Burke, she had become exceedingly frail, forgetful, and obsessive by the early 1960s, leading her daughters to determine that she required regular supervision. Shortly thereafter, Loy was hospitalized and spent time recovering in a nursing home, all the while exhibiting flashes of her well-known wit and irascibility between bouts of listlessness.

Despite her illness and troubling loss of lucidity, Loy consented to an interview with Paul Blackburn and Robert Vas Dias in 1965. The interview serves as a succinct encapsulation of Loy's life and works, for in it she reads some of her best poems and discusses many of the significant people and events that shaped her singular life. Loy stresses two threads of discussion in the interview: the seemingly ephemeral nature of her career as a poet and her uncommon bond with Cravan. In terms of her writing, Loy displays a puckish pride in some of her better-known poems; however, she also holds no great hopes that her body of work will transcend the moment. Whether one views this as bitter self-recrimination or uncommon humility, Loy understood that she had been remiss in creating and promoting her poetry. In terms of her relationship with Cravan, it is clear that her loss was much more deeply felt and lasting than she ever let on during those restless years she spent traveling throughout the Americas and Europe. Taken as a whole, the interview has the feel of a confession—an opening up of that seemingly impenetrable character she had cultivated for so long. This opening up extended to her children, from whom she had been estranged for so much of her life and who had cared for her during the last thirty years of her life. She is said to have reached out to Joella in particular shortly before her death from pneumonia on September 25, 1966, at the age of eighty-three (Burke, p. 440).

LOY'S LITERARY AFTERLIFE

For some critics and readers, Loy's subtleties, mongrelizations, ironies, and apparent contradictions are still problematic, for they defy the easy paraphrasing and comforting sense of categorization that helps many poets attain canonical status. Loy, too, had a hand in obscuring her contribution to the art, owing in part to her restless travel, ever-shifting identity, unapologetic courting of controversy, relatively small output, and eventual withdrawal from society. Nonetheless, it is evident that the work Loy did produce as a poet is exceptionally vital, especially if one recognizes it as a radical antecedent to postmodern identity poetics. Kouidis contends that while Loy's forward-looking experimentation and integrity have proven particularly important to poetry, her greatest contribution to the art was developing a language that effectively "shatters the clichés of experience" ("Rediscovering," p. 186). Given that experience has become increasingly mediated, formulaic, and commodified, as evidenced by the ubiquity of so-called lifestyle products, television reality shows, and other contemporary phenomena that would oversimplify our notions of identity and fix our potentiality, Loy's piquant vision and counter-poetics will doubtlessly continue to resonate with readers.

Selected Bibliography

WORKS OF MINA LOY

Poetry and Prose

Lunar Baedecker. Dijon, France: Contact, 1923.

Lunar Baedeker and Time-Tables. Highlands, N.C.: Jonathan Williams, 1958.

The Last Lunar Baedeker. Edited by Roger L. Conover. Highlands, N.C.: Jargon Society, 1982. (Note: All quotes from Loy's poetry have been taken from the Jargon Society edition.)

The Last Lunar Baedeker. Edited by Roger L. Conover. Manchester, U.K.: Carcanet, 1985.

The Lost Lunar Baedeker: Poems of Mina Loy. Edited by Roger L. Conover. New York: Farrar, Straus and Giroux, 1997.

Insel. Edited by Elizabeth Arnold. Santa Rosa, Calif.: Black Sparrow, 1991.

Papers

Mina Loy Papers. Yale Collection of American Literature, Beinecke Rare Book and Manuscript Library, New Haven, Conn.

CRITICAL AND BIOGRAPHICAL STUDIES

Barnet, Andrea. *All-Night Party: The Women of Bohemian Greenwich Village and Harlem, 1913–1930.* Chapel Hill, N.C.: Algonquin Books, 2004.

Blackburn, Paul, and Robert Vas Dias. Interview with Mina

Loy. In *Mina Loy: Woman and Poet*. Edited by Maeera Shreiber and Keith Tuma. Orono, Maine: National Poetry Foundation, 1998. Pp. 205–243.

Burke, Carolyn. *Becoming Modern: The Life of Mina Loy*. New York: Farrar, Straus and Giroux, 1996.

Conover, Roger. "(Re)Introducing Mina Loy." In *Mina Loy: Woman and Poet*. Edited by Maeera Shreiber and Keith Tuma. Orono, Maine: National Poetry Foundation, 1998. Pp. 245–259.

Cook, Richard. "The 'Infinitarian' and Her 'Macro-Cosmic Presence.' " In *Mina Loy: Woman and Poet*. Edited by Maeera Shreiber and Keith Tuma. Orono, Maine: National Poetry Foundation, 1998. Pp. 457–465.

Dunn, Susan E. "Mina Loy, Fashion, and the Avant-Garde." In *Mina Loy: Woman and Poet*. Edited by Maeera Shreiber and Keith Tuma. Orono, Maine: National Poetry Foundation, 1998. Pp. 443–455.

Goody, Alex. *Modernist Articulations: A Cultural Study of Djuna Barnes, Mina Loy, and Gertrude Stein*. London: Palgrave MacMillan, 2007.

Januzzi, Marisa. "Dada Through the Looking Glass; or, Mina Loy's Objective." In *Women in Dada: Essays on Sex, Gender, and Identity*. Edited by Naomi Sawelson-Gorse. Cambridge, Mass.: Massachusetts Institute of Technology, 1998. Pp. 579–649.

Jaskoski, Helen. "Mina Loy: Outsider Artist." *Journal of Modern Literature* 18, no. 4:349–368 (fall 1993).

Kouidis, Virgina M. *Mina Loy: American Modernist Poet*. Baton Rouge: Louisiana State University Press, 1980.

———. "Rediscovering Our Sources: The Poetry of Mina Loy." *Boundary 2* 8, no. 3:167–188 (spring 1980).

Kreymborg, Alfred. *Our Singing Strength: An Outline of American Poetry (1620–1930)*. New York: Coward-McCann, 1929.

Peppis, Paul. "Rewriting Sex: Mina Loy, Marie Stopes, and Sexology." *Modernism/Modernity* 9, no. 4:561–569 (November 2002).

Perloff, Marjorie. "English as a 'Second' Language: Mina Loy's 'Anglo-Mongrels and the Rose.' " In *Mina Loy: Woman and Poet*. Edited by Maeera Shreiber and Keith Tuma. Orono, Maine: National Poetry Foundation, 1998. Pp. 131–148.

Pound, Ezra. *Instigations of Ezra Pound*. New York: Boni & Liveright, 1920.

Pozorski, Aimee L. "Eugenicist Mistress and Ethnic Mother: Mina Loy and Futurism, 1913–1917." *MELUS* 30, no. 3:41–69 (fall 2005).

Quartermain, Peter. " 'The Tattle of Tongueplay': Mina Loy's *Love Songs*." In *Mina Loy: Woman and Poet*. Edited by Maeera Shreiber and Keith Tuma. Orono, Maine: National Poetry Foundation, 1998. Pp. 75–85.

Ress, Lisa. "From Futurism to Feminism: The Poetry of Mina Loy." *Poetry Criticism 16*. Edited by Margaret Haerens and Christine Slovey. Detroit: Gale, 1997.

Schaum, Melita. " 'Moon-flowers out of Muck': Mina Loy and the Female Autobiographical Epic." *Massachusetts Studies in English* 10, no. 4:254–276 (1986).

Shreiber, Maeera, and Keith Tuma, eds. *Mina Loy: Woman and Poet*. Orono, Maine: National Poetry Foundation, 1998.

Twitchell-Waas, Jeffrey. " 'Little Lusts and Lucidities': Reading Mina Loy's *Love Songs*." In *Mina Loy: Woman and Poet*. Edited by Maeera Shreiber and Keith Tuma. Orono, Maine: National Poetry Foundation, 1998. Pp. 111–128.

Vetter, Lara. "Theories of Spiritual Evolution, Christian Science, and the 'Cosmopolitan Jew': Mina Loy and American Identity." *Journal of Modern Literature* 31, no. 1:47–63 (fall 2007).

Walter, Christina. "Getting Impersonal: Mina Loy's Body Politics from 'Feminist Manifesto' to *Insel*." *Modern Fiction Studies* 55, no. 4:663–692 (winter 2009).

Zelazo, Suzanne. " 'Altered Observation of Modern Eyes': Mina Loy's Collages and Multisensual Aesthetics." *Senses and Society* 4, no. 1:47–73 (2009).

CLARENCE MAJOR

(1936—)

Nancy Bunge

Clarence Major was born December 31, 1936, to Clarence Major and Inez Huff in Atlanta, Georgia. His biography of his mother, *Come By Here* (2002), based on years of taped conversations with her and presented in her own voice, explains how shortly after the birth of his sister, Serena, his mother began trying to escape his father, finally succeeding by moving to Chicago and leaving her children with her parents in Lexington, Georgia. There Clarence completed farm tasks like gathering eggs from chickens and chopping wood; these years left him with an intimate knowledge of nature that he still savors, but he missed his mother. When she did appear in Georgia, he hesitated to speak to her and asked his grandmother if his mother was white because of her light skin. His mother, then, seemed mysterious to him from the start.

After an aunt severely beat Clarence for coming home with a dog, his mother brought her children to Chicago, and there his sense of his mother's otherness persisted, for he learned that his mother's employer could not see him and his sister because she worked as a white woman. As soon as his mother could make good money as a black woman, she resumed her racial identity full time; but before that, she needed the extra money she made passing as white to support her children.

Clarence Major and his mother both suggest that he felt angry with her for leaving him and his sister behind in Georgia, but at the same time, his mother's decision reveals her determination to live as fully as possible. A girl from a small town in Georgia where everyone knew her biological father was a local white man, not the black Papa who raised her and whom she adored, she found her way to Atlanta and into marriage with a glamorous older man. When that didn't work out she moved to Chicago, made enough money to raise two children by sometimes passing as white, married and divorced again, started her own dry-cleaning business, and eventually bought a house that provided a center for her children and grandchildren.

Inez Huff well understood the obstructions that racism placed in her way, but she refused to let them stop her from making the most of her life. Instead, she followed Papa's instructions to go after her dreams. Passing as white did not impede this process of self-realization: a friend who also passed advised her that she would escape notice if she acted like herself. She became so accomplished at passing that she sometimes lost track of when she was doing it and would return to venues she had enjoyed as a white woman with obviously black friends only to be denied entrance. Thus Clarence Major's mother learned, and undoubtedly taught him, an indelible lesson in both the power and the absurdity of racism. Simultaneously, she showed him that a determined person could do just about anything.

Clarence responded by adopting Leonardo da Vinci as his role model because, like his mother, and with her help, he discovered that he had a multitude of interests and abilities. Before he started school, he drew a picture of an apple, which his mother proudly showed around. After he started school, his teacher pointed out to his mother that while all the other children drew cars with two wheels, Clarence's car had four; the teacher saw this as a sign of originality and ability, which his mother sought to nourish. When she moved to Chicago, Inez Huff thought that her son would enjoy the Art Institute of Chicago, as he did. A large Van Gogh exhibit there especially impressed him, and this painter, who also loved reading and writing, has served as an

enduring model for Major. He seized the chance to study painting with Gus Nall and to attend the Art Institute on a James Nelson Raymond fellowship awarded to high school students.

He also loved words. Before he could write, he recited a poem his mother had written in church and identifies that as the moment he understood that human beings can produce literature. Although he wrote from a young age, he felt compelled to hide it because he knew that an author, especially one who wrote poetry, would attract suspicion and perhaps even bullying from peers. Nevertheless, one day he wandered around the schoolyard bravely writing down whatever he saw. While engaging in this exercise, he encountered a girl who interested him. His explanation to her of his activities constituted their last conversation. Still, he kept writing, and worked in multiple genres from the start: poetry, fiction, essays, and eventually even a collection of African American slang.

Although his mother did her best to encourage his development as a painter and writer, she also tried to get her son to acknowledge limits, telling him, for example, that aspiring to horse ownership did not make sense in Chicago. He apparently used his imagination to transcend that obstacle, writing his first novel about a horse; convinced it would make a wonderful screenplay, he sent it off to Hollywood. He remains grateful for the gentle rejection letter he got in response from William Self, because it provided a soft lesson in the central role that getting turned down plays in a writer's life.

His mother's deep knowledge of racism's destructive power as well as its senselessness helps explain why Clarence Major has repeatedly attempted to correct willful ignorance of black culture's strengths. His collection *The New Black Poetry* (1969) is the first of several books and anthologies he has produced celebrating African American writing. His *Dictionary of Afro-American Slang* (1971) and the more recent expanded version, *Juba to Jive* (1994), reveal the richness of black speech. At the same time, however, he has steadfastly maintained that speaking of a "black aesthetic" makes little sense and could impede the autonomy of African American writers and artists by encouraging programmatic art. Moreover, seeing authors and artists as "black authors" or "black artists" encourages shutting them off into a subgroup instead of admitting that they, like people of every other race, strive to realize the universality at the heart of all great literature and art.

Major himself has spent his career exploring a multitude of artistic options, moving easily not only from one literary genre to another but also between writing and painting. His voracious reading presented him with many options from a young age, a habit he sustained through his peripatetic years as a young writer, which included a stint in the air force and earning a living as a steelworker in Omaha, Nebraska. He came to believe that living in the Midwest stifled him creatively, so he moved to New York City in 1966. There he found himself in the middle of a stimulating group of writers and artists including Ishmael Reed, June Jordan, Allen Ginsberg, Grace Paley, and Alice Walker and heard spectacular jazz played by the likes of John Coltrane and Miles Davis. He also started teaching, and in due course earned a Ph.D. in fine arts and literature from Union Graduate Institute and University/Vermont College. He discovered not only that he could teach and keep his own work in motion but also that interaction with students mollified the loneliness of the artistic life. As a result he has taught almost as continuously as he has written and painted at a variety of institutions including Brooklyn College, Queens College, Sarah Lawrence College, Howard University, the University of Washington, the University of Colorado at Boulder, the University of Nice, and, finally, the University of California at Davis, from which he retired in 2007. He also has traveled widely, to Yugoslavia, the Netherlands, Italy, Greece, France, England, Germany, Poland, and Algeria, and has lived in Nice, Paris, and Venice. Clarence Major so loves learning and challenging himself that his work would have enormous complexity even if he had spent his life in a single room writing and painting, but all these experiences have undoubtedly enriched a body of work impossible to characterize without simplifying it.

CLARENCE MAJOR

ALL-NIGHT VISITORS

Not surprisingly, the publisher of his first novel, *All-Night Visitors* (1969), asked Major to tone down its complexity. Because he wanted the book to appear in print, Major acceded to the publisher's demands, but still, given his view that art reflects and reinforces people's shared humanity, he must have found it somewhat dismaying when the novel appeared in a form that convinced many critics it primarily celebrated black male sexuality. Major understood that the revisions diminished his novel, as did his partner at the time, who left him because she thought he was selling out. As the years passed, he longed to publish the original manuscript. In 1998 Northeastern University Press did just that, making it easy to understand his desire to get the original version of the novel into print.

In both renditions, the protagonist, Eli Bolton, likes sex, and both novels offer vivid, expressionistic descriptions of his sexual experiences. At the start of both books, Eli himself describes his sexual obsession as an evasion, but the original version makes clear that through all this sexual activity he seeks to escape the disconnection from others and from life established during his childhood. His mother regretted ever having him and put him in an orphanage where his "caretakers" treated their charges cruelly; the boys responded by relating to each other in the same manner. The novel offers a particularly vivid description of a scene in which a bully forces another orphan to slice open a dog with a knife. Not surprisingly, Eli emerged from these experiences detached. His time in Vietnam assaulted whatever ability to care about and connect with others his early experiences left whole, for there, he helplessly watched the rape of a Vietnamese girl, a memory that recurs throughout the novel. The sections on Eli's childhood and Vietnam experiences all but disappear in the version of the novel first published by Olympia Press.

Moreover, the sequence of Eli's relationships in the original version suggests that he moves toward genuine connection. The absurdity of his sexual adventuring becomes clear in a dreamlike chapter in the unexpurgated novel when he and his current girlfriend, Cathy, get into a cab with no idea where they want to go. Apparently undeterred by the fact that she has no destination, Cathy argues so ferociously with the cabdriver about the pervasiveness of superstition in Manhattan that Eli struggles to keep peace between them. Eli's next relationship, with Eunice, seems richer than any of his earlier ones in that the two of them do something besides have sex: they share an interest in art. Most of the chapters about Eunice disappear in the first published version, and the one that survives appears near the start of the book. Such changes meant that the first printed version provided neither an underlying explanation for Eli's fascination with sex nor any character development. A chapter linking Eli's sexual escapades to myth, suggesting that he struggles through sex to reach some larger meaning, also was cut when the novel first appeared.

At the end of both published versions, Eli takes in a Puerto Rican woman and her children. In the original manuscript this makes sense because he has achieved self-awareness and some ability to relate to a woman as a human being; in the shortened version, however, the development comes from nowhere, as does his feeling so alive after turning his apartment over to her that he stands in the street just looking at his surroundings until dawn.

The reviews that praised the Olympia Press version have validity: the writing in both books powerfully evokes the inner life. But Major wrote a much more thoughtful and complex book than the one that initially appeared. Having it cut must have been especially frustrating for Major since he had worked hard to create *All-Night Visitors* from the strongest sections of three failed novels. Still, any reader misled by the simplified version of his first published novel into categorizing Clarence Major as an author gifted in writing only about sex would find that notion shattered by the rich variety of books and paintings that appeared between 1969 and 1973. During these four years, Major explored a variety of processes and interests so seriously and well that his experiments found their way into print or into exhibits. In 1969, the year *All-Night Visitors* appeared,

Major published *The New Black Poetry,* a collection of poems by African Americans. The following year his *Dictionary of Afro-American Slang* appeared along with a collection of his poetry, *Swallow the Lake,* which makes it clear that unlike Eli Bolton, Clarence Major cares deeply about people he sees on the streets, the women he becomes involved with, his children, racism, and America. Two more books of poetry, *Private Line* and *Symptoms and Madness* appeared in 1971; another, *The Cotton Club,* in 1972. These poems share density, music, and complexity and cover a wide range of topics, moving from anger to delight, from politics to the deeply personal. In 1973 *NO* was published; Major wrote this novel spontaneously on a long roll of paper he set up on a spool. As a painter, he produced enough good work for a one-person show in the library at Sarah Lawrence College.

REFLEX AND BONE STRUCTURE

Critics often group together Major's next three novels, *Reflex and Bone Structure* (1975), *Emergency Exit* (1979), and *My Amputations* (1986), because their lack of traditional plot and the way they repeatedly call attention to their own artificiality marks them as clearly experimental. That the Fiction Collective, an organization of writers devoted to producing and supporting innovative work, published all three certifies them as iconoclastic. Major's earlier poetry collection *The Syncopated Cakewalk* (1974) anticipates this direction in his fiction, for many of these poems, such as "Words into Words Won't Go," rely heavily on wordplay, while others, such as "The Expanded Composition," call attention to his role as poet manipulating what happens in the poem.

When composing *Reflex and Bone Structure,* Major sat down to write every day as though starting afresh and let the writing take him away. Major has said that the resulting fragmented structure reflects his own lack of center at the time he wrote it. But he also avoids a traditional plot sequence in order to signal the novel's distance from realism. The narrator, also sometimes a protagonist, makes no attempt to disguise his influence over events; indeed, he brags that as an author he has access to private documents forbidden to others. He underlines his freedom by moving his characters seemingly at random from place to place and event to event, explaining that "I keep them all moving going coming around, even when they don't care" (p. 7). They are buried in the desert as saints, sail from Casablanca for Miami, perform in an off-Broadway play in 1965, and ride cable cars in Squaw Valley, with no explanation. To emphasize the book's disjointed nature visually, Major surrounded sections of text with white blocks. In producing this kind of digressive work, he sees himself operating in the tradition of Herman Melville.

The narrator also complains to the reader about his struggles with his three characters: Dale, Cora Hull, and Canada. He has the most trouble connecting with Dale, so he sends Dale out of state when he can't stand dealing with him any more. He loses himself so completely in Cora that he gets caught in her self-absorption and loses track of other important elements of his novel. He does not get that involved with Canada but respects him. At the same time that the author asserts his control of these characters, he clearly cannot control them. He describes Cora as a tree, suggesting that she has her own direction and destiny that he can follow and record but cannot shape.

To further emphasize the work's artificiality, famous people appear in it with abandon: Cary Grant, Adolf Hitler, Grant Wood, Isadora Duncan, and the band Jefferson Airplane all play roles in Major's novel. From time to time the narrator stresses the importance of language in shaping the reality of a novel, for instance explaining about Cora's lovers that "none of them were aware of being words themselves suspended in space on a page" (p. 75). The wildly imaginative life taking place in *Reflex and Bone Structure* contrasts with the deadening ways people more typically entertain themselves: the book alludes to these and portrays the negative influences of scandal papers, empty TV shows, and junk food.

Toward the end of the first half of the novel, the narrator occasionally explains himself directly, claiming that the novel can be anything it wants because he lets it have its own life. Major

has said that he wanted this novel to resemble a dream; it has the absurd movement and suggestive content of a dream, and the narrator says he hopes he will wake up and discover he has dreamed the whole thing. At the beginning of part 2, the narrator explains that he writes from a dimension of himself that knows more than he does; in other words, he hopes that *Reflex and Bone Structure* accesses the unconscious that reveals itself in dreams. He also says that he learns a great deal from imagining himself into the perspectives of his characters, in part because the characters' natures all reflect his own. For instance, he guesses that Dale's shallowness results from his own inability to accept a part of himself. When he grows tired of the novel, he kills Dale and Cora and breaks the phone in half when Canada calls him.

Major has explained that he felt fragmented himself when he wrote the book and that it seemed important to put this honest rendition of his state of mind on the page. But for him, composing *Reflex and Bone Structure* was no game: he believes profoundly in writing as an artifice that displays perceptions of and reactions to reality rather than reality itself. Along with the challenges it presents to the reader, *Reflex and Bone Structure* offers many delights, among them frequent opportunities to laugh out loud.

EMERGENCY EXIT

Emergency Exit (1979) shares obvious characteristics with *Reflex and Bone Structure,* including an episodic structure and frequent allusions to the importance of language and to the artifice involved in making art. Indeed, the narrator responds to someone who calls modern experimental writing a "gimmick" by pointing out that language is itself a gimmick in that it does not mirror reality but offers a symbol of it. At times the narrator overtly ridicules fictional clichés, asserting, for instance, that it is time for a flashback and then identifying it with a large arrow. The book also includes mock documents such as lists of names from the Inlet, Connecticut, telephone directory and a completely realistic photograph of Clarence Major appearing to flee from a group of standing cows. But *Emergency Exit* also concerns itself with relationships between men and women. It opens with an explanation of the importance assigned to women in earlier cultures because of women's ability to give birth and the determined and largely successful attempt of men to control women, turning the blood at the center of women's power into a symbol of evil. In a 1981 interview with Nancy Bunge, Major asserted that when men came to dominate women, they also controlled language, so in fact what seem to be two separate threads in this book converge into a celebration of the mysterious potency of both women and language. Against this mythic backdrop, the book presents the relationships of various members of the Ingram family of Inlet, Connecticut, a place that has passed a law that grows out of fear of the power of women's blood. The book's main characters decidedly lack a mythic dimension, which may help explain why some of their conversations consist of randomly typed letters, suggesting that what they say to each other doesn't really matter.

Still, the aura of larger forces survives in this book. Certainly the inclusion of twenty-three black-and-white reproductions of Major's haunting paintings push the novel even further beyond the boundaries of realism. When speaking to Alice Scharper in 1990, Major declared this book his least accessible. Perhaps he said this because one cannot render the mythological dimension of reality in readily grasped concepts. Despite *Emergency Exit*'s elusiveness, it pulls in and holds the reader.

MY AMPUTATIONS

My Amputations (1986), like *Emergency Exit* and *Reflex and Bone Structure,* uses expressionistic language in a episodic structure that correlates with the way it looks on the page: when Major first conceived of the book, he decided to write it in panels composed of words. It also includes talk of its own artifice, though not nearly as much as the two novels directly preceding it. But its movement, which W. Lawrence Hogue describes

as jazzlike, has at its base a more traditional narrative structure that presents a story inspired by events from Clarence Major's life.

A parolee who apparently read some of Major's *New Black Poetry* anthology in prison decided he looked enough like Major to collect Major's royalty check from his publisher. Fortunately he demanded Major's money from someone who definitely knew he was not Clarence Major, so the ruse failed. But the incident obviously captured Major's imagination. *My Amputations* presents the story of Mason Ellis, an ex-convict, who read voraciously in prison and concluded that a writer named Clarence McKay had appropriated and profited from Ellis' work. So Ellis gets the papers he needs to represent himself as Clarence McKay and collect the attention and money he considers his due. Ellis shares many characteristics with Clarence Major: he spends his youth in Chicago, joins the air force, reads widely, and knows a great deal about art. But Ellis has nothing but contempt for postmodernism and the notion that the text has no reality beyond itself, a view shared by both Clarence McKay, whom Mason Ellis takes to calling The Imposter, and Clarence Major. When the book eventually includes some of Mason Ellis' work, another distinction between him and McKay/Major becomes apparent: he can't write.

While posing as McKay, Mason Ellis appears at various universities in this country and abroad, but no one, including people who have written about McKay's work, seems to notice the senselessness of the work Mason Ellis reads and the comments he makes. One woman takes him to bed and does note that he has a smaller penis than McKay, whom she also claims to have bedded. The novel suggests that the confusion between literature and celebrity offers one explanation for Ellis' ability to wander the world reading and speaking gibberish without being challenged. Even Mason Ellis describes himself as a comedian, not a literary figure, and one audience member asks McKay to reconcile his small reputation with the supposed excellence of his work.

Since McKay and Ellis are both black, this fact becomes the center of literary discussion. When people ask Ellis if he wrote Ralph Ellison's *Native Son* and Richard Wright's *Invisible Man,* they reveal the extent to which all black authors become homogenized in the minds of white audiences. When they ask if he knows Toni Morrison or James Baldwin, they reveal the assumption that black writers all hang out together. And when they raise questions about whether black critics disapprove of McKay's work because it fails to express enough anger, they reveal the sociological stance toward African American writing that Major has resisted for his entire career. Given this focus on personality, celebrity, and sociology, it makes sense that Mason Ellis' audience fails to note that he can't write well or talk meaningfully.

Like Major, Ellis speaks of inventing himself, and, again like Major, he travels widely in Europe and Africa as part of this search for his true identity. But one important fact distinguishes Ellis' quest from Major's: Ellis attempts to do this while pretending to be someone else and finances his travels by diverting a grant from the Magnan-Rockford Foundation awarded to Clarence McKay. Not surprisingly, his attempt to find his true identity while masquerading as someone else proves futile.

As he travels through Europe and Africa, many lively, even violent events take place, but none of them have much impact on Ellis. Everywhere he goes he tries to connect with people, but since he projects his own dishonest nature on everyone else and trusts no one, he fails at this task. As the book continues, his paranoia and delusions grow. He suspects The Imposter of orchestrating events. He thinks he recognizes people, but when he calls them by what he considers their names and they ignore him, he refuses to reevaluate his conviction. At one point he makes the mistake of signing a document for the Magnan-Rockford Foundation with his own name instead of Clarence McKay's, and as a result, his paranoia escalates. Thus the trips he has undertaken to discover new dimensions of himself and achieve peace instead drive him into a frenzy that grows exponentially as his travels continue. He has an envelope he must deliver to Chief Q. Tee in Monrovia in order to secure the

success of his African trip. He gets the envelope to Q. Tee, but when opened, the note reads "Keep this nigger"—the beginning of the sentence "Keep this nigger-boy running" from Ralph Ellison's *Invisible Man.* The message is clear: Ellis has nowhere left to run and can look forward to spending the rest of his life in alienation.

Although all Major's poetry collections and novels enjoyed critical praise, the chorus grew especially loud for *My Amputations.* The book earned the 1986 Western States Book Award for Fiction, for which Denise Levertov, Robert Haas, Jonathan Galassi, and Sanda Cisneros served as jurors.

Clarence Major wrote this novel while living in Nice on a Fulbright grant. Like Mason Ellis, he traveled a great deal, but his journeys reached a happier conclusion. He enjoyed enormous productivity during this period, explaining later that Paris nourished in him the same artistic energy that it has in so many others. After failing at three marriages, he was now married to his present wife, Pamela Ritter. Major told Alan Katz that he expected his work to stop dealing with issues of identity because, unlike Ellis Mason, he believed that he now had a firm enough sense of himself to risk losing himself in others' lives.

SUCH WAS THE SEASON

Some critics characterize Major's next novel, *Such Was the Season* (1987), as more traditional than his earlier work because it has a clear narrative sequence. But Major argues, persuasively, when talking with Larry McCaffery and Jerzy Kutnik in 1992, that his experimentation simply moved into a new direction. He later admitted to Nancy Bunge that the novel has traditional movement and also pointed out that he wanted it to have a conventional look on the page so that the text itself would not distract the reader from the story and especially from what Major sees as the novel's strength: its voice.

That voice comes from its central character, Annie Eliza, an African American woman in her seventies who lives in Atlanta. The novel presents absolutely everything that passes through her head: meaningless information from television advertisements about deodorants or perfume sprays, distant memories set off by current events, pride at how she looks in her red wig, pain she unconvincingly dismisses, laughter at herself when her teeth fall out, shock at what she considers excessive sexual information, and, most frequently, her thoughts about and reactions to other people. Her honesty can lead to sharp judgments, as when she describes Councilman Cherokee Barnswell's "young floozy with one of them real short dresses hitting bout halfway cross her thighs" who "kept smiling through all that makeup caked on her face. She looked like somebody dressed up for a scare party" (p. 24). But other times, she makes generous, even profound judgments, as when her nephew Juneboy hugs her brother Ballard, who doesn't like being touched. After Ballard responds positively, she reflects on the source of her brother's shyness: "All I could think about was how much everybody had suffered, how much my brothers, my sisters, my momma, my poppa, Juneboy and Lauren, me and Bibb, my sons, everybody, all the others, had suffered, and was scared, like Ballard" (p. 41). Thus Major offers an astonishingly complete rendering of Annie Eliza's complex consciousness.

He does so in a manner that does not confuse the reader with random information so much as it helps the reader understand, appreciate, and even come to love his central character. Major wanted to write a book with a voice so powerful that it alone would hold the reader throughout the novel and continue to haunt after completing the book. He has succeeded in achieving this, primarily because beneath and through all the detail, Annie Eliza's deep decency shines. As the novel proceeds, it reveals that her minister son, Jeremiah, in whom she has always taken enormous pride, may go to jail for illegal dealings. When his problems emerge, Annie Eliza expresses no self-pity even though she must feel deep disappointment and humiliation. Instead, she successfully coaxes her family members into facing reality and making the best of it.

Critics have commented on the authenticity of the speech Major creates for Annie Eliza. That

authenticity definitely enhances the vitality of Annie Eliza's characterization, but more important, everything that passes through her head, whether trivial, mean-spirited or brave, feels true. Major identifies a work's emotional truth, as opposed to its realism, as its most important characteristic.

Major admits that, like Juneboy, the character whose visit to Annie Eliza's home sets the novel in motion, he traveled to Atlanta to visit his aunt and this event inspired the novel. But Major quickly adds that very few of the novel's incidents actually happened during this visit or at any other time. Indeed, Major feels that the fact that the only character with a tie to him plays a relatively peripheral role signals that he has achieved the ability to lose himself in others' perspectives. Juneboy, like Major himself, not only wants to find himself, he talks about it, and Annie Eliza interrupts him because she finds such conversation strange. Major has moved so far beyond a concern with his own identity that he can imagine and convincingly render how peculiar this focus might look to others. Juneboy, like Major, has achieved worldly success; his research on sickle-cell anemia has won him a professorship at Yale. This also fails to impress Annie Eliza. But she deeply appreciates his kindness to her, to her family, and to his white girlfriend and hopes he has acquired a stronger sense of family connection through his trip. Still, she looks forward to his departure so that she can have her house to herself once more.

Major told Nancy Bunge in 1995 that he found this book both compelling and easy to write because he got lost in a familiar voice he had heard all his life: Annie Eliza is based on many of the women around him as he grew up, including his mother. He reports that writing it taught him how well he knew these women, allowed him to understand what a large role they play in his personality, and to own and cultivate the side of his character most strongly tied to them. The cover of *Such Was the Season* features one of Major's paintings, as do the covers of most of the novels and poetry collections to follow.

PAINTED TURTLE: WOMAN WITH GUITAR

Although *Painted Turtle: Woman with Guitar* (1988) appeared in print one year after *Such Was the Season,* Major began the work culminating in this novel years earlier. Indeed, the writing that led to *Painted Turtle* laid the foundation for *Such Was the Season*. Major told Nancy Bunge in 1995 that while attempting a failed book about Dorothy Dandridge, he began learning how to immerse himself in a character, or a person, totally unlike himself. The best parts of the Dandridge book survive in *Painted Turtle*. Whereas *Such Was the Season* came quickly because Major found himself writing in a voice he had known all his life, writing *Painted Turtle* required three years of research about the Zuni culture that produced his central character. His intense interest in and study of Indian cultures, including the Zuni, developed during the years he taught at the University of Colorado, and he often visited reservations in the Southwest.

He also struggled to find the right perspective for telling Painted Turtle's story. At first, he made her the narrator, but then he discovered that he felt more comfortable having her fellow musician and eventual lover Baldwin Saiyataca tell the story. Since "Baldy" does not know Painted Turtle's early life firsthand, he imaginatively reconstructs it from what she has told him. Major has said he is pleased when some readers make the mistake of claiming that Painted Turtle narrates the book because it convinces him that she remains the book's center.

Baldy's version of Painted Turtle's past portrays her as someone not completely comfortable with Zuni ways. Because Zuni men have privileges denied her as a female, she wishes she were a boy. At the age of twelve she learns how great an advantage men have in her culture when a man rapes her and she is encouraged to feel grateful that he is a Zuni, not someone from a different culture. She becomes pregnant and gives birth to twins, which Zuni culture sees as problematic. She attempts to drown her sons, declaring death preferable to the lives they must lead; as a result, she finds herself institutionalized.

Despite the obvious problems with Painted Turtle's situation in Zuni society, her life spins apart when she leaves it. She engages in self-destructive behavior like wandering through random houses and prostituting herself. Just when it seems as though she has completely lost direction, sitting in the squad car after her arrest for prostitution, she consoles herself by recalling how beautiful Segovia's guitar sounded on the radio that morning.

She eventually comes to own and trust her love of music so completely that she puts it at the center of the life she builds for herself. Baldy first meets her when their mutual agent has sent him to convince her to make her music more commercial, but when he sees her reacting to her audience's indifference by teaching herself to play even better, he understands that the purity of her passion for playing well would not only make it impossible for him to convince her to adopt a more commercial approach, he has no desire to try. He simply wants to be with her.

Although she no longer lives among the Zuni, the culture remains part of her. She returns home for funerals, helps her relatives with Zuni rituals, and looks for Spirit Lake, the place where Zuni drink from the Sacred Spring and, as a result, experience rebirth.

Baldy himself has a Navajo father and a Hopi mother and, as a result, shares Painted Turtle's sense of alienation. Like Painted Turtle, making music plays a central role in his life, along with his attachment to her. When he takes her to visit his parents, she discovers that even though his mother and father, like Painted Turtle and Baldy, come from different cultures, they get along well. After their visit, Baldy confesses his selfish treatment of his father; Painted Turtle agrees that his behavior fell short but accepts him all the same. They become a couple that can talk to each other honestly because they both have the capacity to live with the other's flaws. After a lifetime of not fitting in, they feel completely comfortable with each other. They have found the Sacred Lake, they conclude, in their daily life together.

Although a plot summary may make this novel sound sentimental, it evades this potential trap because both Painted Turtle and Baldy speak in indirect and understated ways that force the reader to feel and articulate the novel's themes. Painted Turtle and Baldy differ strikingly from Annie Eliza because they are as restrained as she is open; the book also presents them from a much greater distance. In this novel Major not only continues to engage others' perspectives but also immerses himself in an entirely different voice and point of view than that dominating *Such Was the Season.*

Major has said that in this novel he brought together poetry and prose, because Painted Turtle's songs appear frequently in the text. But even the prose writing crosses the line into poetry, leaving room for the reader's reactions to fill out the book's significance, as when Baldy tries to describe the joy his relationship with Painted Turtle brings him: "I was as joined together as tree and earth. Where before in my spirit bobcats had sung like jays and muledeer acted like mice and black-tailed hares barked like chipmunks, now love turned me into the flesh of a song itself" (p. 152). This reliance on subtlety and metaphor shows how completely Major has rendered an American Indian stance here; little wonder that the *New York Times* named *Painted Turtle* a notable book. Major shows, once again, that although culture certainly matters, the heart of good literature rests deeper than cultural divisions.

Major's involvement with Zuni culture and the various attempts at capturing insights collected in *Painted Turtle* left him with enough poetry to fill a collection, *Some Observations of a Stranger at Zuni in the Later Part of the Century* (1989). The title poem discusses the legendary figure Esteban de Dorantes, a black man who appeared in Zuni society in the sixteenth century and whose story ignited Major's interest in the Zuni. In an introductory note, Major explains that the poems also emerged from his memories of stories his grandparents told him about Indian ancestors in the Southwest. Although he composed the poems in this collection during the same period as *Painted Turtle,* it presents Indian life from different and diverse perspec-

tives, among them an examination of Hollywood's rendition of Indians, "In Hollywood with the Zuni God of War."

The year before *Some Observations of a Stranger at Zuni* appeared, Major released a long poem published as *Surfaces and Masks* (1988). Though the work began as a journal Major kept during a sabbatical year spent in Venice, he realized that his account needed the rhythm of poetry. The poem presents Venice from multiple angles, describing the experiences of Clarence and his wife Pamela, but also alluding to Venice's past as well as the experiences of many other writers who have felt compelled to describe Venice's richness, among them Henry James, Thomas Mann, and William Dean Howells. Major also published a collection of short stories, *Fun and Games* (1990), which won a Los Angeles Times Book Critic Award nomination. Thus the books that appeared between 1987 and 1990 offered evidence that Major had recently passed through a period of intense geographic, cultural, literary, and personal expansion.

ANTHOLOGIES AND DICTIONARY

A few years later, in 1993, Clarence Major began publishing a series of large and important projects focusing on African American literature and language. At the beginning of his career, he had published *The New Black Poetry* (1969) and *The Dark and Feeling: Black American Writers and Their Work* (1974) as well as a *Dictionary of Afro-American Slang* (1970). Through the years, he had kept track of African American slang, so when he was offered a contract to produce *Juba to Jive: A Dictionary of African-American Slang* (1994), he was ready for it. Major not only has a long-standing interest in the vitality of African American speech but also in the reality that language constantly changes, and it makes him proud to know that some writers have told him they keep copies of *Juba to Jive* on their desks to use as they write. He has said, however, that he didn't enjoy the mechanical process of putting it together, except when he had a chance to invent examples of usage.

Much more pleasurable was the research for *Calling the Wind: Twentieth Century African-American Short Stories* (1993) and for *The Garden Thrives: Twentieth Century African-American Poetry* (1996). He relished devouring library books that had not been checked out for decades and discovering wonderful work which he had the privilege of calling to people's attention: "I like people to see that there is a greater breadth and depth to the body of work...than has been represented in anthologies." He told Nancy Bunge that this assignment "was a pleasure because you have to take a break from your own writing and from yourself. It was engergizing and refreshing to read a lot of good work" (*Conversations*, p. 119). The books he created as a result of his expeditions into long-ignored sections of the library stacks have sold thousands of copies and garnered a collection of enthusiastic reviews. *Calling the Wind* was a 1993 *Publishers Weekly* Best Book of the Year selection and a Quality Paperback Book Club selection. During this period he also curated an exhibit of African American painters, which included his own work, titled "Spirit Made Visible," at the Natsoulas Art Gallery in Davis, California, in 1994.

DIRTY BIRD BLUES

Perhaps not surprisingly, considering that Major argues for a strong link between African American literature and music, the novel he published after all this intense engagement with African American literature, language, and painting focuses on an African American blues singer. At the same time, through his characterization of Manfred Banks in *Dirty Bird Blues* (1996), Major stretches himself, for he describes his protagonist to Nancy Bunge in 1995 as a large, jolly, outgoing man so completely different from himself that his affection for Banks astonishes him. That fondness comes through in the book, inviting the reader to join Major in entering the perspective of a joyful man.

The opening establishes Manfred's goodwill. Shot while attempting to break into the home of his wife Cleo's new boyfriend, the music running through his head drowns out his awareness of the wounds. When he runs into an injured woman on

his way into the emergency room, he forgets himself in his concern for her until her child points out the blood on his jacket. Emergency room personnel trying to identify the most seriously injured announce criteria that make him the person in need of immediate attention: this amazes him. Through the whole ordeal, music runs through his head. As the nurse who tended his wound escorts him from the emergency room, "He hummed to himself. He did that. That was him.... He said what he needed to say, talking to himself, keeping himself company, especially when things got bad, humming now the Leadbelly song about hanging crepe on the door like when somebody died" (p. 8). Manfred also uses songs to express joy, as he does when his daughter and wife return to him: "It was like the meaning of his life suddenly revealed itself to him. Ain't gon sing the blues, no mo. My baby girl never seen new shoes. No mo, long time. My wife buys her dresses at the Salvation Army store. No mo, long time" (p. 97).

Although Major sees Manfred as completely different from himself, they both make art out of need, not choice. Also like Major, Manfred has lived in Chicago, Atlanta, and Winder, Georgia, and attempts to work as a crane operator and a welder in Omaha, Nebraska, during the 1950s, just as Major worked as a steelworker who welded and operated cranes in Omaha in 1957 and 1958. The novel's ending suggests that Manfred will find his way to making art full time, just as Major did.

Besides music, Manfred loves his wife, Cleo, and their daughter, Karina. But his wife left him when his drinking got so out of control he could not support his family. He moves from Chicago to Omaha, hoping to turn his life around there. He continues to drink more than he would like, but he does hold down jobs and make a home for his wife and child. When his Chicago friend and fellow musician Solly joins Manfred in Omaha and Manfred loses his job as a welder because his racist boss thinks he has been fraternizing with a white woman, Manfred begins drinking heavily and almost hits his wife. Manfred begins to get angry at the man who fired him but realizes that his own lack of discipline operates much more destructively on his life than anything his boss could do to him. He stops drinking, and although he cannot support himself with his music, his reputation grows and his marriage improves. Meanwhile, his friend Solly, unable to give up womanizing or alcohol, starts a fight with Manfred, which Manfred wins.

Throughout the novel, Manfred has had a series of dreams, many of them joyously anticipating that his musical career will work out for him. In a couple of them, the person who starts off as Cleo turns into Jorena, the woman who hires him to sing in her bar, suggesting that his love for his wife and his love for his music intertwine and nourish each other. The final dream has him sitting with Cleo while a man tells him he will record Manfred; he wakes to happily join his daughter and wife, and the book ends. The novel clearly suggests that Manfred will succeed at building a successful musical career and marriage.

Dirty Bird Blues not only takes the reader inside the head of someone who, like Painted Turtle, has completely given himself over to music, it also realizes the hero's path as set out time and time again in myth. The hero leaves home to face his shadow, or those personal flaws that he has previously ignored. In Manfred's case, he faces the self-destructive tendencies that lead him to drink. The hero's defeat of the dragon is a symbol for defeating the shadow by facing and integrating it. Correspondingly, Manfred defeats his friend Solly, who represents the destructive impulses he wants to transcend. After accepting and integrating the shadow, the hero accepts his anima, or his feminine side, just as Manfred reaches for his wife and daughter at end of the novel.

Dirty Bird Blues is a joy to read. Unpleasant things happen, but in the text, as in Manfred Banks's head, all that music diminishes the pain of the difficult events. Major keeps the novel's plot and characters in motion, despite the word and sound play simultaneously going on in his protagonist's mind. Major has said that he listened to the blues while writing the book, and it shows. His visual gifts also reveal themselves in the novel's vivid imagery. And the deep

humanity of the book reveals itself in the ease with which the reader connects with all these characters and in the reader's passionate hope that Manfred will stop drinking, reconcile with his wife, and throw himself into building a musical career.

The fusion of accepting one's feminine side and making art in *Dirty Bird Blues* in some ways articulates one important dimension of Major's work between the mid-1980s and 2002. In *Such Was the Season,* he becomes one with the perspective and voices of the women he knew growing up; in *Painted Turtle* he becomes one with a woman Zuni musician; and in *Come By Here* he loses himself in his mother's voice. *Inside Diameter: The France Poems* (1985) includes many painterly descriptions of women. Even earlier, *Emergency Exit* (1979) talks about women's power. Women consistently play an important role in Major's work, but while early in his career he tends to render them externally, as he continues to write, he eventually describes women's experiences from the inside, suggesting that his empathy with and understanding of women has deepened.

CONFIGURATIONS: NEW AND SELECTED POEMS, 1958–1998

That *Configurations* collects work from eight of Major's previous poetry collections seems reason enough for making it a finalist for the National Book Award. But it also includes 148 pages of new and previously uncollected poems, many of them about nature, an apparently new subject in Major's oeuvre, although the dates on the poems suggest he has been writing about it since at least 1976. Many of these poems are like intricate, vivid paintings, as though Major believes one can celebrate nature by rendering it accurately. In some he continues his project of entering into other awarenesses, this time inhabiting the inner lives of birds, insects, and flowers. In "At the Zoo in Spain" he guesses that the flamingos dream of their own rebirth while standing patiently on one leg; in "The Apple-Maggot Fly" he imagines himself into the romantic yearnings of his subject; and in "The Jake Flower" he celebrates the flower's persistent cheer. Other poems help readers understand how giving oneself over to noticing one's surroundings enriches one's life, an insight conveyed not didactically but through Major's compelling descriptions of scenes.

Major also moves in a new direction by including poems that engage in social commentary. A number of critics have praised "The Slave Trade: View from the Middle Passage," an epic that combines the perspective of Mfu, a slave who jumped from the ship transporting him across the Atlantic, with a broader historic consideration of slavery in Europe and the Americas. He also includes "Descendant of Solomon and the Queen of Sheba," where Major writes about the difficulty of being black, and in "Waiter in a California Vietnamese Restaurant" he imagines himself into the perspective of a Vietnamese man who escaped being shot only because the boy pointing a rifle at him froze. Ironically, some of Major's very early poems write of death, but the overwhelming majority of his later poems quietly argue for an unfathomable richness in daily life, unless the burden of oppression weighs too heavily on people for them to notice.

Bernard Bell's *Clarence Major and His Art* (2001), a book with Major's self-portrait on the cover, includes color reproductions of sixteen of his paintings, along with poetry, excerpts from his prose, and critical essays about Major. This emphasis on Major's visual work makes sense considering that Major has described painting as his most significant activity. In the early 2000s this aspect of Major's talent received wide recognition. For instance, his paintings appeared in one-person shows at the Schacknow Museum of Fine Arts in Plantation, Florida; at the Hamilton Club Gallery in Paterson, New Jersey; and at the Phoenix Gallery in Sacramento, California. The *Boston Globe* positively reviewed a 2010 exhibit at the Pierre Menard Gallery in Cambridge, Massachusetts. His painting began to play a more central role in his poetry and fiction during this period.

WAITING FOR SWEET BETTY

The first part of Major's next poetry collection, *Waiting for Sweet Betty* (2002), describes natural settings in a way that invites the reader to see them as pictorial works of art. But the section concludes with a few poems that involve human society and describe little beauty, stressing instead that dealing with human structures requires patience and humor. The second section begins with poems alluding to Van Gogh and a painting by Rembrandt, suggesting that these painters connect the poem's speaker intensely to life. But the next poem, "Portrait of the Great White Hunter Foxhunting in the Absence of Big Game," leads the reader into a depressing world, relieved only at the end by the beauty of nature: light, oranges, and apples. Aside from a poem where the speaker loses himself in a painting by Edward Hopper, the remaining poems in this section talk about ambiguous experiences in foreign cultures. The first two parts, then, suggest that nature and art offer welcome relief from society's shortcomings.

The final section begins with a series of visual, imagistic poems that seem like word paintings. The title poem ostensibly talks about waiting for a flower to appear, but the speaker links its blossoming to white people accepting that they are also black and black people catching beautiful windflowers. Then the poem goes off into a Whitmanesque catalog wherein the speaker identifies with various people who, like him, wait. In the end this poem, although ostensibly about looking forward to the appearance of flowers, seems quietly to express impatience with the persistence of racism. The last two poems deal with pictures by Thomas Eakins. In the first, "Thomas Eakins' Delaware River Paintings," nature is beautiful, but the black men in the picture pole boats filled with white hunters. So, despite the attractive natural elements in this painting, its social components offend. And in the final poem, "Thomas Eakins and the Photograph of a Man in Motion," the speaker likes to think the forward motion of the man in the photograph will take him somewhere, but the knowledge that our history has too frequently taken us nowhere new gives him doubts. Overall, *Waiting for Sweet Betty* seems a celebration of the beauty of nature and art that also expresses a quiet annoyance with society's inability to move beyond racism. Tellingly, the speaker in these poems, although aware of social problems, still enjoys many of life's pleasures and remains hopeful and patient.

ONE FLESH

In an interview with Nancy Bunge in 1995 while he worked on *Dirty Bird Blues,* Clarence Major confessed that although his most recent novels had given him a chance to enjoy other perspectives than his own, he hoped to return someday to writing about himself. The novel *One Flesh* (2003) seems both to continue his exploration of others' points of view and to give his readers some entry into Major's perspective. Major has explained that his son's marriage to an Asian American woman provided the immediate inspiration for writing *One Flesh,* which focuses on a relationship between John Canoe, an African American painter with a white mother, and Susie Chang, a Chinese American woman born to parents who cling to Chinese culture even though they live in the United States. Both John and Susie rest uncomfortably between cultures. Moreover, stares and comments from people who find a union between an Asian woman and an African American man jarring remind them that even others perceive them as alienated.

Family issues exacerbate their discomfort. John ostensibly enjoys a good relationship with his mother but frequently feels that she fails to understand him, and for most of his life, relatives on her side of the family ignore his existence. John carries an anger toward his father that he admits his father can never assuage, probably because John feels his father abandoned him and his mother. Susie's parents believe that when she discovered a world other than Chinatown at the University of California at Davis her life began to deteriorate because she came to see herself as American, not Chinese, and, as a result, began to assert her independence. Like John, she makes art: Susie writes poetry. Just before their nontra-

ditional wedding, John tells himself that it makes complete sense that they shape new rituals since they are both iconoclasts.

But rather than simply presenting the triumphant union of two independent artists who managed to find each other in a world populated by righteous conformists, *One Flesh* makes it clear that although John and Susie do not regret their choices, they also yearn for connection. Although the wedding goes beautifully, Susie sobs afterward because no one in her family attended even though she sent them invitations. John notices that only a handful of his teaching colleagues appear for the ceremony even though he had invited many more of them. John has a dream that his father—who, as usual, excuses himself from appearing at the wedding—not only takes part in the ceremony but assures his son that he will tell him precisely what to do: John feels enormous relief. When John joins his new wife and his mother in a post-wedding embrace, he knows this apparently small event will remain precious to him for the rest of his life.

John worries about marriage, fearing that it will impede his individuality, but after the ceremony he discovers a new feeling of safety, presumably because now he has a place where he clearly belongs. Still, terror surfaces in moments when he thinks of difficulties that may lurk in the future, and the novel ends with an image suggesting that he experiences deep fear when Mei Wong, Susie's friend, points out to him that one person will now presumably meet all his needs.

While *One Flesh* ends with an ambivalent view of marriage, Clarence Major reported to Robert Fleming in 2004 that, after three failed marriages, his union with Pamela Ritter is working out just fine, which may help explain why his last three novels have focused on men who have found women they love and with whom they want to spend their lives. Major shares other characteristics with John Canoe. Both grow up in Chicago and then leave to seek out the art scene in New York City; both call home to mothers who live in Evanston; John's mother is white, and Clarence Major's mother looks white; both love Van Gogh and horses; both are vegetarians; both put following their impulses at the center of their art; and since both are accomplished painters, both have the intense visual awareness that repeatedly reveals itself through John's comments on his surroundings. For instance, when John wakes up, he sees the world like this: "Saturday morning was purple and penny rust with silver and gold edges like the frame-line around one of those Italian paintings by, say, Giotto or Fra Angelico, and it was all thanks to the bright sunrise.... Up by the windows, through squinting eyes, John saw the familiar long strips and crossbars of sunlight, egg-yoke yellow, lying side by side on the floor like parts of a deliberate composition" (p. 7). Major's courageous persistence in experimenting, both as a writer and as a painter, suggests that he also shares John Canoe's hopefulness, patience, and compassion. When a man who sees John and Susie walking down the street together insults them, John imagines how much pain the man must feel to speak so cruelly. And after Susie's father tells John he does not approve of his daughter marrying someone African American, John walks away from him, but also understands and sympathizes with his point of view. John's ability to see things from others' perspectives not only helps him defend himself against abuse, it enriches the awareness he brings to his art and to loving Susie.

MYSELF PAINTING

The book jacket description of the poetry collection *Myself Painting* (2008) correctly describes it as work that attempts to render Major's process as an artist. Not surprisingly, many poems offer a wide range of commentary on painting. "In Search of a Motif for Expressive Female Figuration" tumbles through image after image, suggesting the painter's process of considering possibilities; "My Corner" reports that the painter would rather look at objects than himself; and "When the Model Does Not Show" explains how painters respond when their models do not appear. Major dedicates the collection to the memory of the man who first taught him to paint, Gus Nall.

But he also dedicates it to his wife, Pamela Ritter, and the collection includes a number of poems about love between men and women, such as "The Wedding," "By Candlelight," and "Last Light." A few poems also deal with larger themes, like "All of Us" and "Black or White," where Major again attempts to convey the absurdity of racism. But the poem "In Line" gives perhaps the most complete account of Major's frame of mind. In it, the women standing in line with him complain about the pharmacist's slowness. The poem's narrator agrees with them, but he doesn't mean it: as he stands in line he entertains himself with various points of view. He first thinks about Gauguin's paintings of plants, then about Van Gogh's Japanese work, and eventually moves on to Walt Whitman's fascination with the rich possibilities of a blade of grass. He even sees the line itself as educative, for though he understands the frustration of the people complaining about the slow clerk, he also feels compassion for him and believes that these internal experiences teach him important truths that neither he nor anyone else could adequately explain. And he believes that completely realizing what he has learned while standing in this line will require great patience.

This poem articulates themes central to the rich body of work Clarence Major has produced. His love of learning has carried him through one literary genre after another, kept him returning to the easel to paint the insights he cannot reach with words, and inspired him to stop articulating his own views long enough to read, record, and collect the language and literature of others. Throughout all these processes, he happily loses himself in one perspective after another because he finds this an irreplaceable way to learn about the world while simultaneously realizing new dimensions of himself. But the astonishing range of achievement that has resulted from all this exploration leads Major not into self-congratulation but into a compassion and a sense of life's richness so profound that he can even patiently wait for everyone else to understand what he has known since childhood: the tragic absurdity of racism.

Selected Bibliography

WORKS OF CLARENCE MAJOR

NOVELS AND SHORT STORIES

All-Night Visitors. New York: Olympia, 1969. Unexpurgated edition, Boston: Northeastern University Press, 1998.

NO. New York: Emerson Hall, 1973.

Reflex and Bone Structure. New York: Fiction Collective, 1975.

Emergency Exit. New York: Fiction Collective, 1979.

My Amputations. New York: Fiction Collective, 1986. Tuscaloosa: University of Alabama Press, 2008.

Such Was the Season. San Francisco: Mercury House, 1987. Baton Rouge: Louisiana State University Press, 2003.

Painted Turtle: Woman with Guitar. Los Angeles: Sun and Moon Press, 1988.

Fun and Games: Short Fictions. Duluth, Minn.: Holy Cow! Press, 1990.

Dirty Bird Blues. San Francisco: Mercury House, 1996. New York: Berkley Putnam, 1997.

One Flesh. New York: Kensington, 2003.

POETRY

Swallow the Lake. Middletown, Conn.: Wesleyan University Press, 1970.

Private Line. London: Paul Breman, 1971. (Chapbook.)

Symptoms and Madness. New York: Corinth, 1971.

The Cotton Club. Detroit: Broadside, 1972.(Chapbook.)

The Syncopated Cakewalk. New York: Barlenmir House, 1974.

Inside Diameter: The France Poems. London and New York: Permanent Press, 1985.

Surfaces and Masks: A Poem. Minneapolis: Coffee House Press, 1988.

Some Observations of a Stranger at Zuni in the Latter Part of the Century. New American Poetry Series 2. Los Angeles: Sun and Moon Press, 1989.

Parking Lots. Mount Horeb, Wis.: Perishable Press, 1992.

Configurations: New and Selected Poems, 1958–1998. Port Townsend, Wash.: Copper Canyon, 1998.

Waiting for Sweet Betty. Port Townsend, Wash.: Copper Canyon, 2002.

Myself Painting. Baton Rouge: Louisiana State University Press, 2008.

NONFICTION

The Dark and Feeling: Black American Writers and Their Work. New York: Third Press, 1974.

Necessary Distance: Essays and Criticism. Minneapolis: Coffee House Press, 2001.

Come By Here: My Mother's Life. New York: John Wiley, 2002.

DICTIONARIES

Dictionary of Afro-American Slang. New York: International, 1970. Reprinted as *Black Slang: Dictionary of Afro-American Talk.* London: Routledge and Kegan Paul, 1971.

Juba to Jive: A Dictionary of African-American Slang. New York: Viking, 1994.

EDITED ANTHOLOGIES

The New Black Poetry. New York: International, 1969.

Calling the Wind: Twentieth Century African-American Short Stories. New York: HarperCollins, 1993.

The Garden Thrives: Twentieth Century African-American Poetry. New York: HarperCollins, 1996.

PAPERS

Clarence Major's manuscripts and correspondence are held in the Clarence Major Archives in Special Collections at the Elmer L. Andersen Library of the University of Minnesota, Minneapolis.

BIBLIOGRAPHIES

Bell, Bernard. "Selected Bibliography of Clarence Major's Works." In *Clarence Major and His Art: Portraits of an African American Postmodernist.* Edited by Bernard Bell. Chapel Hill and London: University of North Carolina Press, 2001. Pp. 265–271.

Weixlmann, Joe. "Clarence Major: A Checklist of Criticism." *Obsidian: Black Literature in Review* 4, no. 2:101–113 (1978).

Weixlmann, Joe, and Clarence Major. "Toward a Primary Bibliography of Clarence Major." *Black American Literature Forum* 13:70–72 (1979).

Weixlmann, Joe, and Clarence Major. "A Checklist of Books by Clarence Major." *African American Review* 28:139–140 (spring 1994).

CRITICAL AND BIOGRAPHICAL STUDIES

Bell, Bernard W., ed. *Clarence Major and His Art.* Chapel Hill and London: University of North Carolina Press, 2001. (Contains critical essays by Bell, James W. Coleman, Stuart Klawans, Steve Hayward, Jerome Klinkowitz, Nathaniel Mackey, Lisa C. Roney, Linda Furgerson Selzer, Stephen F. Soitos, and Joe Weixlmann.)

Bolling, Doug. "A Reading of Clarence Major's Short Fiction." *Black American Literature Forum* 13, no. 2:51–56 (summer 1979).

Clarence Major Issue. *African American Review* 28, no. 1:95–108 (spring 1994).

Hogue, W. Lawrence. Introduction to *My Amputations.* Tuscaloosa: University of Alabama Press, 2008. Pp. vii–xviii.

McCaffery, Larry, and Sinda Gregory. "Major's *Reflex and Bone Structure* and the Anti-Detective Tradition." *Black American Literature Forum* 13, no. 2:39–45 (summer 1979).

Selzer, Linda F. "Clarence Major and Mark Twain Abroad." In *The Heritage Series of Black Poetry, 1962–1975: A Research Compendium.* Edited by Lauri Ramey and Paul Breman. Burlington, Vt.: Ashgate, 2007. Pp. 71–83.

Weixlmann, Joe. "African American Deconstruction of the Novel in the Work of Ishmael Reed and Clarence Major." *MELUS* 17, no. 4: 57–79 (winter 1991–1992).

INTERVIEWS

Bunge, Nancy L. "Clarence Major." In her *Finding the Words: Conversations with Writers Who Teach.* Athens, Ohio: Swallow/Ohio, 1985. Pp. 53–67. Reprinted in her *Conversations with Clarence Major.* Jackson: University Press of Mississippi, 2002. Pp. 35–47.

____________. "What You Know Gets Expanded." In her *Conversations with Clarence Major.* Jackson: University Press of Mississippi, 2002. Pp. 109–122.

Bunge, Nancy L., ed. *Conversations with Clarence Major.* Jackson: University Press of Mississippi, 2002.

Fleming, Robert. "35 Years as a Literary Maverick." *Black Issues Book Review* 6:54–57 (March–April 2004).

Katz, Alan. "Transition Is Tugging at a Local Avant-Garde Author." *Denver Post,* June 15, 1986. Reprinted in *Conversations with Clarence Major.* Edited by Nancy L. Bunge. Jackson: University Press of Mississippi, 2002. Pp. 51–54.

Klinkowitz, Jerome. "Clarence Major: An Interview with a Post-Contemporary Author." *Black American Literature Forum* 12:32–38 (spring 1978).

McCaffery, Larry, and Jerzy Kutnik. "Beneath a Precipice: An Interview with Clarence Major." *Some Other Frequency.* Edited by Larry McCaffery. Philadelphia: University of Pennsylvania Press, 1996. Reprinted in *Conversations with Clarence Major.* Edited by Nancy L. Bunge. Jackson: University Press of Mississippi, 2002. Pp. 70–92.

Major, Clarence. "A Conversation Between Jacob Lawrence and Clarence Major." *Black Scholar* 9:14–25 (1977).

Miller, E. Ethelbert. "Views on Black Literature: An Interview with Clarence Major." *New Directions* 3:4–7 (October 1976).

Scharper, Alice. "Clarence Major." *Poets & Writers Magazine,* January–February 1991. Reprinted in *Conversations with Clarence Major.* Edited by Nancy L. Bunge Jackson: University Press of Mississippi, 2002. Pp. 63–69.

CAROLINE MILLER

(1903—1992)

Emily Wright

"The Housewife Who Won a Pulitzer Prize: Southern Writer Who Achieved Honor Calls Herself a Cinderella." This was the headline of a 1934 *Baltimore Sun* article about Caroline Pafford Miller, who had just received the Pulitzer Prize for her novel *Lamb in His Bosom.* When she attended the Pulitzer banquet in May 1934 to receive the prize, Miller exclaimed, "Look at my silver slippers. I'm Cinderella" (Bishop, "Ethnographic Study," pp. 56, 36; except where noted, page numbers below refer to this collection).

No doubt Miller did feel like a fairy-tale princess, given her sudden ascent from obscurity to fame. The wife of a school superintendent and mother of three small children, she had only a high school education and hailed from the very heart of what H. L. Mencken famously called the "Sahara of the Bozart." Caroline Miller had spent her entire life in the South; indeed, she had spent her entire life in south Georgia, except for two short trips to Tennessee and Florida—until the day she traveled to New York City for the award of the Pulitzer.

Miller's receipt of the Pulitzer Prize was the high point of her novel's success. After its publication by Harper & Brothers in 1933, *Lamb in His Bosom* received a series of glowing reviews from both the southern and northeastern literary establishments, rose to the best-seller list, was awarded the French Prix Femina–Vie Heureuse Americaine in 1934, went through numerous printings and reprintings, and was translated into several languages.

Caroline Miller's moment in the spotlight was intense, but it was brief. As Cinderella, she enjoyed only one night at the ball. The manuscripts she produced over the remainder of her life either went unpublished or, if published, received no recognition—and even *Lamb in His Bosom* soon faded from memory. As David M. Craig explains in his entry on Miller for the *Dictionary of Literary Biography,* "Since the 1930s ... Miller has received scant critical attention. When she is mentioned, she is referred to as a minor historical or regionalist author" (p. 209).

Miller was indeed a minor historical and regionalist author. The scope of her text is modest and local, devoted to re-creating the lives of nonslaveholding southern pioneers with as much historical accuracy as possible, and while her writing is sometimes powerful and lyrical, it is also sometimes cumbersome and awkward. Nonetheless, *Lamb in His Bosom* is an important document in American literary history. It brings to life a class of Americans whose experience has been marginalized; it provides a valuable transcription of the feminine frontier experience; and its reception reveals important patterns in the discursive relationship between the South and the nation. Any novel that wins the Pulitzer Prize has something interesting to tell us about American culture and American literary history, and *Lamb in His Bosom* is no exception.

The implications of her novel's reception, however, cannot have been on Miller's mind at its inception. When Miller first began work on *Lamb in His Bosom,* she was a young housewife seeking expression for her creativity and finding it in her own backyard, among her own south Georgia kin.

INCEPTION

Caroline Miller was born in Waycross, Georgia, on August 26, 1903, the youngest of seven children born to her schoolteacher father, Elias Pafford, and his wife, Levy Zan Hall. The Paf-

ford and Hall families had arrived in Georgia prior to the Civil War and had played a vital role in the local community as preachers, teachers, and farmers.

Miller spent most of her young years in Waycross. Her father died after she completed the ninth grade, and her mother died when she was a junior in high school, after which time she lived with her two older sisters, Levy Magdalen and Ollie Mae, until she graduated from Waycross High School in 1921. Her older sisters managed to scrape together the money for piano and locution lessons for Caroline, and while in high school she distinguished herself as an actress, performing in such productions as *Little Lord Fauntleroy, Evangeline*, *Enoch Arden*, and *Pygmalian.* She also was the district winner in a University of Georgia–sponsored oral interpretation contest and took second place at the state level.

After graduation she was severely disappointed to learn that the family's finances would not allow for the fulfillment of her dream of attending the University of Georgia, where she had hoped to study drama. Apparently on the rebound from that disappointment, within two months of graduation, in August 1921, she married her high school English teacher, William D. Miller. After her marriage, she attempted to contribute to the family finances by writing short stories, and in 1924 she won the *Sunday American Magazine* short story contest for "The Greatest of These," a slight tale about a thrill-seeking flapper who comes to realize that her best hope for happiness lies not with the nervous and fun-loving Jimmy Tate but with the staid and predictable John Morgan.

Merging her interest in writing with her love of acting, Miller also served as sponsor to the Student Players, a group of high school students who produced plays directed by Miller and a talented high school student named King Bowden. Miller and Bowden wrote several plays together, and in 1928 they won second place out of sixty entries in a contest sponsored by the Town Theatre of Savannah, for *Red Calico*. This play has been lost, but according to the *Savannah Morning News,* "It was a serious little drama of south Georgia swamp and country life, tragic and somber in its moral elements as well as in its plot." Presaging remarks that would later be made about *Lamb in His Bosom,* the Savannah paper noted that "definite as was the locale, there were universal elements ... in the play which lifted it out of the folk drama class and gave it wider appeal" (p. 30). *Red Calico* also won second place in the Little Theater Guild contest in New York.

In 1927 Miller bore her first child, William D. Miller Jr., and the following year the family moved to nearby Baxley, Georgia, where Miller's husband had accepted a position as superintendent of schools. In 1929 Miller gave birth to twin sons, whom she nicknamed Nip and Tuck. According to her husband, Miller became restless after the birth of the twins and began devoting more time to her writing. She worked for some time on a novel called "The Cat of God," about the Cherokee Indians, and "The Judas Tree," about a woman's experience with mental illness. She became very excited when "Judas Tree" was submitted for publication and was dismayed when it was rejected. Meanwhile, she had taken to loading her three small children into the family Model-T Ford, traipsing around the countryside and talking to the elderly people she found living in the piney woods around Baxley. As she later explained to Nell Bates Penland of the Atlanta *Journal,*

> When my twins were 2 years old I thought I would break under the strain of trying to take care of them and do the hundreds of other little things any normal wife and mother is called upon to do. But one day it suddenly occurred to me that I was not half so weighted down with duties as the pioneer women used to be. Even my mother and my grandmother, who had such large families, seemed to get through with much less effort and energy than I was expending. I couldn't help wondering why. They had something, something very real, very tangible, yet almost indefinable, that anchored them and gave them faith and courage, and I needed that something very much. From that day I turned to the examples set by the pioneer women of Georgia. I gathered my material around Baxley and in the surrounding country, and it has been a wonderful help to me.
>
> (p. 48)

According to Miller, then, her primary motivation for conducting her research was a personal

search for inspiration. As she became more involved in her explorations, however, Miller's somewhat aimless collection of family stories and interviews with rural inhabitants took focus as she began orienting her efforts toward the writing of *Lamb in His Bosom,* which is based largely on the lives of Miller's ancestors. Her maternal great-grandfather, who came to Georgia as a "New Light" preacher, is the basis of one of the characters in *Lamb in His Bosom,* and many of the events described in the novel were actual experiences of her ancestors. As reported in the *Savannah Morning News,* Miller wrote to a friend that "almost every incident in *Lamb in His Bosom* actually occurred.... Some of the incidents in the novel I heard from my uncles and aunts and some from my mother. I got most of the 'local color' from hereabouts, but the facts from family history and the history of other families" (p. 37).

For "local color," Miller scoured the countryside, looking for information about the material culture of the antebellum southern pioneer. She learned about the food that was eaten in the early to mid-nineteenth century, the way it was prepared, what household tasks were considered essential, which tools were used to accomplish them, and many other details of frontier life. She is said to have recorded this information in a series of notebooks, where she also kept careful records of the flavorful backwoods speech she heard. Her three children accompanied her as she gathered this information and played at her feet as she wrote her novel, which is dedicated to them.

Upon completion of the manuscript, she sent it to Julia Peterkin, who had recently won the Pulitzer for *Scarlet Sister Mary* (1928), a novel in the local color tradition set among the Gullah of South Carolina. Peterkin responded positively to the novel and gave Miller the name of her agent, who eventually took the manuscript to Harper. To the delight of Caroline and her family, it was accepted for publication.

LAMB IN HIS BOSOM

On the basis of her research, Miller produced a narrative centering on the life of Cean (pronounced "say-un") Carver, from her marriage to her first husband, Lonzo Smith, to her late middle age. Moving into the raw log cabin her husband has built, Cean earnestly assumes her household responsibilities and soon finds herself pregnant with the first of many children. With Lonzo, Cean conceives fourteen children, twelve of whom she brings to live birth, and the narrative attends closely to her emotional responses to her children and to her own reproductive capacity. A few years after Lonzo dies of an ax wound, Cean enjoys a second, middle-aged love affair with Dermid O'Connor, a "New Light" preacher whom she marries and with whom she conceives her last child. In the latter part of the novel, the text's attention to Cean's individual life recedes as the narrative opens out to take in the entire community, becoming a record of the births and deaths of Cean's children and grandchildren and following the fate of a brother who moves to California, where he dies. In this section of the novel, Cean manages her homestead alone while Dermid fights in the Civil War, and the novel ends with his return.

The narrative is replete with close descriptions of material conditions on the Georgia frontier—of implements used in various agricultural tasks; procedures for cooking over an open fire or for skinning animals; the decoration, design, and use patterns of the log cabin in which the Carvers live; and many other such details of daily life on the southern frontier. With remarkable accuracy, she also transcribes the antique dialect found among isolated southern pioneers whose language still retained Elizabethan survivals.

Lamb in His Bosom also re-creates the worldview of its protagonists. Citing verses from popular religious songs and describing backwoods religious revivals, Miller conveys the Calvinist fervor that provided spiritual sustenance to embattled and isolated frontier communities. She also presents an accurate picture of gender relations in the nineteenth century. As Cean is settling into the new home to which her husband has brought her, she thinks that, now that she is married, "she belonged to him, to cook his victuals and to wash his clothes" (p. 3). From

that point on, Cean is everything a frontier "goodwife" was expected to be—industrious, obedient, faithful, loving, and prolific. Finally, the novel presents an accurate picture of political attitudes among nonslaveholding pioneers of the antebellum South.

Whereas novels such as Stark Young's *So Red the Rose* (1934) and Margaret Mitchell's *Gone with the Wind* (1936) focus on the antebellum planter class, in *Lamb in His Bosom* that class exists only in the coastal regions to the east of the Carvers' settlement, and they are referred to as "the Coast planters" or "the Coast bloods." The men who travel to the coast every year for trading purposes carry back to their wives and children glowing descriptions of the fine clothes, horses, and houses and numerous slaves of the Coast planters, who become the objects of envy of the men and women in the backwoods community. In the 1850s, as the movement toward secession gains momentum, Lonzo Carver begins to refer to "the Coast planters" as "the Old Line Whigs" who are agitating for war. On visits to the coast, he listens to their speeches, but although he never speaks out against their rhetoric, "Lonzo hated the Whigs.... They were the hot-heads that itched for a war" (p. 253) that, Lonzo recognizes, will not serve his interests:

> Talk of states' rights was too deep for Lonzo; the sovereign right of a commonwealth to secede was an argument that he could not follow. Talk of Tarheel fire-eaters in Carolina, and Copperheads in the North, who would fight on the side of the South, if it came to that, was interesting, but outside the bounds of his own life. He owned not one black; never would own one; he would be a master-fool to run off up North and fight over a nigger! And as for the sovereign right of a commonwealth to secede, he did not know.
>
> (pp. 236–237)

In this passage and throughout *Lamb in His Bosom,* Caroline Miller speaks for a class whose existence has been overshadowed by the one above it. Materially, spiritually, and politically, *Lamb in His Bosom* re-creates the lives of a group of southerners whom historians call "plain whites," "middle whites," or "middling whites." Furthermore, it does so with remarkable accuracy. As the historian Elizabeth Fox-Genovese points out in her afterword to the 1993 reprint of *Lamb in His Bosom,* antebellum poor whites and yeoman farmers left few records of their experiences, and as a result, their history has been reconstructed from a variety of primary sources such as statistics on population, size of holdings, crop production, church membership, and political participation. Pointing out that Miller's account of the daily lives of this class of whites conforms in remarkable detail to the information gleaned by historians from those statistics, she concludes that *Lamb in His Bosom* is perhaps the most thorough and accurate account available of nonslaveholding white southern pioneers. In a 1970 M.A. thesis, Denver William Sherry describes the book as one of the best existing examples of southern dialect during the Civil War period.

Both southern and northeastern critics expressed appreciation for the historical aspect of *Lamb in His Bosom.* They also praised the poetic quality of its prose. On September 17, 1933, the *Christian Science Monitor* lauded its "beauty of expression," on the same day the *New York Times* hailed its "wonderful freshness" (p. 14), and on September 2, 1933, the *Saturday Review of Literature* enthused over its "many passages of lyrical descriptive prose." On the book jacket of the first edition, Sinclair Lewis said, "There is a fine sense of beauty here."

The *Saturday Review of Literature* described this beauty as "disembodied," but, as the southern reviewer Corra Harris pointed out, the body is unusually central in this text, where "breeding, childbirth—labor, joy, and grief—mark the course true love takes" (p. 19). They also mark the course of the narrative, for Cean's relationship to her body and to the children she bears forms the strand upon which the plot of the novel develops. As Harris noted, though, Cean is not the only prolific agent in this text. "Never has so much life been portrayed in one simple tale," Harris wrote. "Every living creature in it is fertile" (p. 19). Here Harris notes the connection Miller makes between the nature outside of Cean and the nature within her. Beginning with the conception of her first child, Cean experiences her body as implicated in the cycle of birth and rebirth in nature, and throughout the text Miller renders her

descriptions of the Georgia wilderness as objective correlatives for the internal maternal and sexual life of the protagonist. For example, when Cean discovers that she is pregnant with her first child, her "eyes followed the rows of young corn, all of a size, all of a green."

> She was thinking how she had dropped the grains of seed corn: and they had lain in the dark through cool nights and hot days; they had burst the soil, new and different, unrecognizable in poison green, disowning the seed that sought sustenance downward with white roots in black earth, sustenance for bright-green blades growing toward the sun, toward far-off tassels high in the air, and heavy ears of corn that would be other new seed grains.
>
> (p. 18)

Toward the end of the novel, Cean once again turns to nature to understand her position in life:

> Lonzo had brought her a century plant from the Coast, and Cean set it in a far corner of her yard and watered it. She wondered how anybody would ever know if it counted a hundred years right till it was time for it to bloom. She would not be here, nor Lonzo, nor the last youngest child that she might bear.... In a hundred years ... she would be dead and rotten long ago. There would be nothing alive that she had known—not a child, nor a cow, nor a bird.... She and hers would be gone, like prince's feathers and old-maid flowers and bachelor-buttons that die with killing frost, leaving only dried seeds for a careful hand to garner if it will; blazing-star and mulberry geraniums will leave roots to sleep in the earth like a wild thing; Cean would leave no roots to wake again to the sun of another year. Her children, she judged, were her seeds and roots and new life.
>
> (pp. 238–239)

The intense display and interfusion of external and internal nature accomplished in such passages as these seem to be the elements that, for many reviewers, lifted the work out of competence into importance, making it, as the southern reviewer Jane Judge asserted, "far more than regional in its conception and scope" (p. 15). However, at the same time that Miller's attention to internal and external nature lends *Lamb in His Bosom* a universal quality, it is also one of the reasons why the novel was neglected in ensuing years.

RECEPTION: GENDER

The post–World War II era has been described as an especially masculinist one. Women had moved into the workforce in large numbers during the war, and the masculine power structure made both conscious and unconscious efforts to reassert itself in the ensuing decades. During this time "female literature" in general did not find favor with the masculine literary establishment, and hostility toward such literature was exacerbated in the case of *Lamb* by the fact that this novel is an especially feminine text.

Lamb represents the consciousness of a particularly fecund woman whose mind and body are preoccupied well into her middle age by the bearing, birthing, and rearing of her children. This maternal focus seems to have repulsed some critics. W. J. Stuckey, for example, speaks snidely of the way Cean " 'births' her children and then rises up immediately to carry on the household chores" (p. 100). Especially problematic for many male critics has been the narrative shift that occurs toward the end of the novel: as Cean passes her childbearing years, the text's attention to her individual life recedes as the narrative opens out to take in the entire community, and male critics have consistently considered this narrative shift a flaw. In his otherwise favorable review for the *New York Times,* Louis Kronenberger complained that in the latter part of the book, "the sap and poetry go out of it.... The births, the deaths, the marriages are no longer rich chunks out of a unique little world, but mere jottings in a parish register" (p. 14). Echoing Kronenberger, David M. Craig maintains that *Lamb* has "serious flaws as a novel. For all its happenings, it lacks a plot, a coherent sequence of episodes" (p. 209). Particularly unsatisfactory to Craig is the way Miller painstakingly records the births, miscarriages, and deaths of Cean's children. For Craig, "This transcription of the kind one might keep in a family Bible does not work.... It substitutes a profuse biological progression for the discriminating sequence of art" (p. 209). Less generously, Stuckey, in his critical review of the Pulitzer Prize novels, maintains that *Lamb* "hardly deserves to be called a novel. It is a grab bag of incidents ... loosely tied together by a chronologi-

cal thread having to do with the lives of the Smith-Carver clan" (pp. 100–101).

In his preface, Stuckey asserts, "Structurally, a novel should be coherent. Plot, style, characters, and tone should all contribute toward the central effect of the book" (p. ix). For Stuckey, Craig, and Kronenberger, *Lamb* fails to meet these criteria, which reflect the formalist literary theory of their times. However, Elizabeth Fox-Genovese's more sympathetic reading of the novel suggests that it does meet these criteria—that the plot of *Lamb* supports its content in such a way as to achieve its central effect: the authentic realization of Cean's maternal consciousness.

The shift in focus that has troubled male critics occurs as Cean enters her late middle age. At this point, approximately two-thirds of the way through the narrative, Miller presents the long passage previously quoted in which she views her children as "her seeds and roots and new life." It is after this significant passage that Miller's attention shifts away from Cean toward her "seeds and roots"—her children and her children's children. Thus the plot of the novel can be seen as mirroring the mind of its protagonist and in the process reflecting the experience of many women whose participation in the continuance of their communities takes the form of the children to whom they have given life. As Fox-Genovese points out, although *Lamb* is "unlike the novels of self-conscious self-discovery of which Kronenberger presumably approved," its plot can be seen as corroborating its content, for the "absorption of events into a more general, less differential pattern may be seen as a faithful, and highly crafted, representation of the changing consciousness of this one woman—perhaps all women—as she moves through the cycle of her life" (pp. 354–355).

Fox-Genovese's feminist interpretation was unavailable to critics of the 1940s and 1950s, when male hegemony over the theorization and canonization of literature seems to have been at least partly responsible for the omission of *Lamb in His Bosom* from the canon of southern literature—not only in the manner just described but in other ways as well. The sheer popularity and commercial success of the novel antagonized the (male) guardians of high culture, and once *Lamb* won the Pulitzer, it was seen as usurping an award more properly belonging to more deserving (male) writers. During the late 1920s and throughout the 1930s writers such as Sinclair Lewis, Thomas Wolfe, William Faulkner, and Ernest Hemingway were passed over for the Pulitzer in favor of such novels as *Lamb in His Bosom* and *Gone with the Wind*—both of which texts have probably been treated with more condescension by the critical community than they would have been had they not won the Pulitzer.

For all these reasons—the novel's female form and themes, its popularity with the reading public, and its receipt of the Pulitzer Prize—*Lamb*'s neglect can in part be ascribed to male domination of the literary-critical establishment. However, in the later decades of the twentieth century, that domination began to be challenged, and yet Miller continued to be overlooked. In such studies as *Tomorrow Is Another Day: The Woman Writer in the South* (1981), *Southern Women's Writing: Colonial to Contemporary* (1995), *The Female Tradition in Southern Literature* (1993), and *Female Pastoral: Women Writers Re-Visioning the South* (1991), feminist southernists restored many previously neglected texts to the literary-historical record and set about revising the canon so as to include those texts. However, in none of these assessments is *Lamb* so much as mentioned. Even *The History of Southern Women's Literature* (2002) makes only passing reference to *Lamb in His Bosom.*

The continuing neglect of *Lamb in His Bosom* by revisionist scholars points to another explanation for the waning popularity of the novel in the decades after its publication. Close analysis of the kinds of writings recovered by feminist scholars reveals that they are virtually all by and/or about African American women, upper-class white women, and poor white women. From Harriet Jacobs' *Incidents in the Life of a Slave Girl* (1861) to the diaries of antebellum planters' wives and daughters to novels about poor whites by the likes of Elizabeth Madox Roberts, Olive Dargan, and Hariette Arnow, the previously lost, neglected, or underestimated writings that have

been recovered and published in recent decades have represented every class and race of southern womanhood except the class of "middle" whites to which Miller's characters belong. Thus it would appear that gender is not the only reason for the exclusion of *Lamb* from the literary-historical record. Ultimately, it seems, it was the class of Miller's characters that both lifted her novel into the spotlight in the 1930s and relegated it to obscurity thereafter.

RECEPTION REVISITED: CLASS

Throughout American history, the white South has been understood as consisting of a genteel planter class and a debased poor white class. The image of the poor white can be traced back to William Byrd's eighteenth-century histories of the dividing line and from there through George Washington Harris's tales of *Sut Lovingood* (1867) to William Alexander Percy's diatribes against poor whites in *Lanterns on the Levee* (1941) and William Faulkner's unflattering depictions of the Snopeses in the Snopes trilogy (1940–1959). Meanwhile, the images of the courteous, kindly planter and of the plantation as pastoral idyll can be traced from John Pendleton Kennedy's *Swallow Barn* (1832) through the postbellum plantation fiction of Thomas Nelson Page to Stark Young's *So Red the Rose*. Not only have images of the cavalier "aristocrat" and degenerate "poor white trash" been powerfully present throughout southern literary history; they have been the only classes of white southern society to be recognized in discourse about the South. As many scholars of southern literature and culture have lamented, northerners and southerners alike have presented the white antebellum South as consisting only of these two classes

The ideological causes of this two-class myth have been uncovered primarily by scholars investigating literary depictions of poor whites. They point out that the image of the debased and/or comic poor white was created and perpetuated by privileged southerners not only for entertainment purposes but also for political ones: by exaggerating the numbers and low condition of poor whites, defenders of the southern power structure pointed up the superiority of the ruling class. To the same end, the same class of southerners generated the stereotype of the genteel planter, an image that has served the purposes of southern apologists throughout American history.

Nonsouthern readers and writers have participated in perpetuating these images for a different set of reasons that have changed over time. Abolitionist writers featured the most degenerate of "poor white trash" in order to show the evil effects of slavery upon lower-class whites as well as blacks; postbellum readers eagerly consumed local colorists' comic portraits of the type; and in the 1920s and 1930s, economic tensions experienced throughout the nation became focused on the plight of southern mill workers and tenant farmers. Meanwhile, from the mid-nineteenth century through the mid-twentieth, the image of an all-white landed leisure class has offered readers outside the South an imaginative antidote to the increasing commercialism, industrialism, and ethnic diversity of American culture.

For all of these reasons, imaginative discourse about the South has virtually erased from the literary record the class of middle whites that Miller describes. Thus southern commentators on *Lamb in His Bosom* were deeply appreciative of the attention Miller brought to this largest class of southerners. Given that only about a quarter of white southerners owned slaves, most of the white readers of *Lamb in His Bosom* descended from characters much like Miller's, and they felt that their class had been overlooked in discourse about the South. Writing in *Holland's: The Magazine of the South,* Alice Phelan pointed out that "after all, the aristocratic planters who owned large slave-operated plantations had many white neighbors who had nothing but toil and sweat for themselves, and who had to depend upon their own efforts to drag out an existence in the face of hostile Nature" (p. 61). Corra Harris wrote that although Miller's characters were "as close to us as our immediate ancestors," they had "missed the spotlight of history" (p. 20), and other reviewers expressed pleasure that Miller's novel was becoming a part of public discourse about the South. Harry Stillwell Edwards wrote in the *Waycross Journal-Herald* that Miller had

"directed public attention to the once forgotten pioneer people of Southeast Georgia" (p. 22), and H. A. Stallings crowed in the same paper that "[*Lamb in His Bosom*] is the truth of a Georgia frontier whose epic, long forgotten in the rush of noisier though not always more vital events, now has an interpreter to which the wide world listens" (p. 21). Even as recently as 1992, the *Atlanta Journal-Constitution* columnist Celestine Sibley expressed appreciation to Miller for reinstating her ancestors in discourse about the South. In her column of July 15, shortly after Miller's death, Sibley made a distinction between *Lamb in His Bosom* and *Gone with the Wind* that has become quite common. "I think I have loved 'Lamb in His Bosom' most of my life," she wrote, explaining that she

> identified with the South Georgia backwoods characters who lived before and during the Civil War. My ancestors are more Caroline Miller than Margaret Mitchell characters. They, too, settled in Appling County, not a white column or a slave to their name—just ox cart, rough cabin, hard work and hard living interspersed with such fun as they could manage.

From the 1930s through the 1990s, middle-class southerners have expressed appreciation for Miller's effort on behalf of their ancestors, especially because, as Stallings proclaimed, the "wide world" did "listen" to *Lamb in His Bosom.* Given the large readership *Lamb* attracted, readers outside the South were made to understand that most of the settlers of the South were not aristocrats and did not own slaves. However, although this is the message Miller herself wanted to convey and the one that was most frequently commented upon in southern reviews, in the Northeast, *Lamb in His Bosom* appears to have corrected a different impression about the South—the impression that the nonaristocratic classes of the South fell wholesale into the category of "poor white trash." Harry Hansen wrote in the *New York World-Telegram,*

> One of the best uses of the Pulitzer prize is to turn the glare of publicity on little-known books. In this instance it does us all a great service. For the story of the Georgia farmers told by Caroline Miller deserves to be known, in justice to the farmers themselves. Recent books about the south have dealt with almost nothing but abnormality and degradation.
>
> (p. 33)

Time magazine made more explicit the distinction Hansen suggested: in a favorable review of *Lamb in His Bosom* written before the novel won the Pulitzer, the reviewer describes Cean Carver and her family as "Georgia crackers" but goes on to make an important distinction: "by 'civilized' or 'modern' standards, they were poor whites," he explains, "but not trash" (p. 16).

Miller seems to have succeeded, at least briefly and at least in the case of a handful of reviewers outside the South, in gaining a "hearing" for the nonslaveholding white pioneer. Apparently her description of poor but honest, hardworking, proud, devout, literate, property-owning pioneers was sufficient to make it clear to discerning northern reviewers that in addition to the aristocracy of legend and the "abnormal and degraded" poor whites of 1920s journalistic discourse, there was another, larger class of whites in the South that fit in neither category.

Given the prevalence of the "two-class" image of the South, however, it is surprising that Miller's novel became as popular as it did. If northerners and southerners alike have seemed to conspire to omit the antebellum middle white southerner from discourse about the South, why was this very class of character so warmly embraced in the 1930s? The mere mention of 1930s America calls to mind the Great Depression, of course, and indeed, the Great Depression had everything to do with the popularity and acclaim directed toward *Lamb in His Bosom.*

The southern historian C. Vann Woodward argued in his seminal 1958 article "The Search for Southern Identity" that one of the ways in which the South was at one time different from the rest of the nation was that the South had experienced long-standing poverty. This difference was especially notable in the 1920s, when the South lagged behind the national experience of unprecedented prosperity. During this period of especially marked differentiation between the South and the rest of the nation, the South came under heated attack not only for its persistent

poverty but also for the racial and religious bigotry exposed by the rise in the number of lynchings in the South, the anti-Catholic sentiment apparent in Al Smith's campaign for president, and the Scopes trial. But in the 1930s the long-standing economic difference between the region and the rest of the nation receded as economic calamity brought the contemporary national experience closer to the southern historical experience. At this point in time, a nation in the grips of its first experience of wholesale poverty suspended its attack on the South, looking to the South's past for models of endurance and recovery.

During the 1930s, four historical novels set in the South rose to the best-seller lists and were awarded Pulitzer Prizes: T. S. Stribling's *The Store* (1932), Miller's *Lamb in His Bosom,* Mitchell's *Gone with the Wind* (1936), and Marjorie Kinnan Rawlings's *The Yearling* (1938), awarded the Pulitzer in 1933, 1934, 1937, and 1939, respectively. All of these novels describe southerners' struggles to overcome poverty and defeat, and their favorable reception indicates that during the Depression, the southern historical experience offered inspiration to the nation. One reviewer said as much of *Lamb in His Bosom*; reviewing the novel for the *New York Herald Tribune* in 1933, Mary Ross observed, "This year of helplessness and chaos and want in cities and on farms has given an added appeal" to a novel dealing with the "self-sufficing family life of earlier American times" (p. 11). Indeed, throughout the Depression regional tales of an earlier America were especially popular, providing readers with an imaginative escape from the trials of the times through a return to a more bucolic and hopeful past, while also reminding them that their forebears had weathered hard times and emerged triumphant.

Thus it appears to have been the class of Miller's protagonists—the fact that they were "middle" white southerners who had everything in common with American pioneers around the country and little in common with the southern "aristocrats" and "poor white trash" of legend—that at least partly accounts for the popularity and acclaim heaped upon *Lamb in His Bosom.* However, if Miller's novel briefly challenged the long-standing myth of a two-class white South, that myth soon reasserted itself. As the Great Depression began to ease in the late 1930s, the national and southern experiences again began to diverge. In 1938 President Roosevelt labeled the South "The Nation's Economic Problem No. 1," and the problematization of the South regained force toward midcentury because of the region's resistance to integration. At the same time, Miller's humble tale of southern pioneers quickly faded in favor of thirties novels that reinforced the public's two-class perception of the white South, such as *Tobacco Road* (1932) and *Gone with the Wind* (1936).

In an interesting twist of fate, it was the success of *Lamb in His Bosom* that sent the Macmillan editor Harold S. Latham on a tour of the South, seeking other southern writers like Caroline Miller. On this trip he met Margaret Mitchell, and the rest is publishing and moviemaking history. Paradoxically, Mitchell, like Miller, had taken great pains to describe the antebellum white South accurately, and she described it much as Miller did—with a small and decidedly unaristocratic planter class, numerous yeoman farmers, and "plantation plain" houses, which were rambling, comfortable farmhouses just a generation or two away from log cabins. However, readers of the novel tend to forget the early descriptions of *Gone with the Wind* in favor of more epic and dramatic later scenes. Even more commonly, the American public has based its understanding of the novel on David O. Selznick's glamorized and popularized movie version of the novel, which recasts the work according to the Old South legends of popular fiction. When the movie premiered in December 1939, the rolling prologue presented the South as "A Land of Cavaliers and Cotton," and so it has always been understood. Mitchell knew as well as Miller did that there were few southerners who could rightly be called aristocrats in the antebellum South, but despite both writers' efforts to correct that misimpression, the myth persisted that the antebellum South was a land of genteel aristocrats living lives of untold luxury on gracious plantations.

Just as *Gone with the Wind* was adapted to film in such a way as to perpetuate the myth of a southern aristocracy, so Erskine Caldwell's tragicomic portraits of southern "poor white trash" reinforced the public's image of southern poor whites as comically ignorant, perversely sexual, and spontaneously violent. Caldwell's *Tobacco Road* and *God's Little Acre* (1933) and their play and film versions were almost as popular in the late 1930s and early 1940s as *Gone with the Wind.*

Thus the myth of a two-class white South reasserted itself with a vengeance in the years after *Lamb in His Bosom* was published. Although, as Corra Harris noted, Miller had turned the "spotlight of history" on the southern middle white, the moment didn't last. Miller's moment in the spotlight was similarly brief.

LATER LIFE AND WORKS

After traveling to New York to receive the Pulitzer, Miller returned to south Georgia with high hopes for a literary career. Her husband watched their children while she traveled around the country on a book promotion tour and made appearances closer to home as well. In Georgia, she broadened her intellectual circle by striking up a friendship with Frank Daniels, the book reviewer at the Atlanta *Journal,* and James Pope, the Atlanta *Journal* city editor. She worked continuously on her writing, and in the ten years after she received the Pulitzer succeeded in publishing three short stories and a second novel. However, her works were not well received, and her personal life was turbulent and disappointing.

Miller's receipt of the Pulitzer seems to have had an explosive effect on her marriage. Whereas the Millers normally spent their summers in nearby St. Simons Island, Georgia, Caroline's fame made it impossible for them to enjoy any privacy there, so in the summer after she received the Pulitzer, they rented a house in Waynesville, North Carolina, from a florist named Clyde Ray Jr. He introduced the Millers to his literary and artistic friends, who often took Caroline with them to cultural events while Bill, six years older than Caroline, watched their three children. A growing attraction between Caroline Miller and Clyde Ray resulted in Miller filing for divorce from her husband in October 1936. The divorce and subsequent custody hearing were acrimonious, complete with public and private charges of alcoholism, adultery, and violence, as well as arguments over money and bitter disputes over custody of the Millers' oldest child. In the course of these events, public opinion turned against Miller in her hometown of Waycross, and at the turn of the new year of 1937, she felt compelled to leave and did so, with no plan except to go west. After a few days' driving, she located a house on the Gulf, in Biloxi, Mississippi, where she stayed while the divorce was finalized. She married Clyde Ray Jr. in September 1937 and spent the remainder of her life in Waynesville.

Within a year after marrying Ray, she gave birth to her fourth son, Clyde Hosea Ray, and her last child, a daughter, Caroline Patience Ray, was born in 1941. Throughout these years Miller's letters are full of enthusiasm about her children, her husband, and her writing. While Miller often complained of having too many demands on her time to write ("*Who* could write with a youngun on every side?" she protested in a letter dated May 16, 1941), her tone is generally cheerful and positive. However, by the late forties that tone changes. Her letters begin to express more criticism of her second husband, and references to ill health and hospitalizations begin to appear as well. Surely, too, she was disappointed by the lackluster reception of the works she had published since *Lamb in His Bosom.*

In those later works, as in *Lamb in His Bosom,* Miller remained firmly within the tradition of historical realism. Although a number of her unpublished works are set in modern times, only her first manuscript, "The Judas Tree," and her first publication, "The Greatest of These," ventured outside that tradition, addressing modern women in modern-day circumstances. In the rest of her published works, Miller located her modernist sensibility in historical settings. "Loving Wife" (1937), for example, is set in the antebellum era but contains a critique of marriage and a protest against patriarchy. Sary, a

black servant, tells the story of the head of the household, Lucius, who after the death of his first wife marries a younger woman named Elise. Lucius's strictness with his young wife and his insistence on domestic perfection soon begins to stifle the high-spirited Elise. A younger man comes onto the scene and spends some time at the couple's home. The attraction he and Elise feel toward each other is obvious to Lucius, who takes the young man on a duck hunt and kills him, disguising the murder as an accident. From that point forward, Elise transforms into a shadow of her former self, walking through her days like a ghost, defeated, and the story concludes with these lines:

> Just to look at her, you never would have thought that she was less or more than any other woman who gives her life to a good man to hoard or spend, as it may please him. But as old Sary said once, long ago, "Lif' de corner o' de quietes' seemin' life, and you're pretty sure to find heartbreak like green mold on its underside, and little shet-mouthed things will scamper away to hide like white wood-lice when you turn over an old log. Once deep winter shets down, don' no ripples run over froze ponds."
>
> (p. 48)

The eloquence of this concluding paragraph indicates a possible reason for Miller's choice of an African American as her center of consciousness. Just as Miller had done a remarkable job of transcribing the speech of south Georgia whites in *Lamb in His Bosom*, so in this story her best writing occurs when she speaks in the richly colorful, cadenced dialect of the southern African Americans of an older time.

Coexisting with such local color elements as Sary's dialect, however, is also a modernist interest in sexuality. This interest is also located in Sary, who serves not only as a dialect character but also as a sexualized double for Elise. As explained in a couple of paragraphs early in the story, Sary's romantic history closely resembles Elise's. As a young woman Sary had also fallen in love with a young and exciting man, Jules, who had known "how to make Sary remember him, because he had handled her like a sweet fiddle" (p. 44). Just as Elise's beloved is killed by her husband, so Sary's beloved is also killed by her husband, Carmel, who, though he is a "good-hearted man," thinks a woman is "no more than a good firestool hewed out of a block of hickory" (p. 44). Both Elise and Sary are forced by "good-hearted" but domineering men to renounce passion. However, whereas Elise's passion expresses itself through shining eyes and a flushed face, Sary's passion is described in much earthier terms:

> Jules handled a woman the selfsame way he handled a fiddle. And how now does a man handle a fiddle? He lays it up against his shoulder, and leans his face over it, and makes tunes out of its wood.... Any woman will be a soft-tongued fiddle, if her man handles her right. The longer you keep a fiddle, and the wiser your fingers be on its strings, the sweeter it will sing for you....
>
> (p. 15)

Sary's affair with Jules suggests the sexual aspect of the white character's thwarted desire. Published in the midst of Miller's divorce, the story may also have reflected Miller's own feelings about her first and second husbands and her fear that if she stayed with her first husband, as Elise and Sary stay with theirs, she would become a shadow of herself. In a letter dated September 23, 1936, Miller explained to her brother-in-law that to return to her first marriage would be to "just endure, stagnate, and die"—a fate reflected in the deathly demeanor of Elise in "Loving Wife."

In another short story, "Indian Wooing," published a few years earlier, in January 1935, Miller had again combined her fascination with history with her interest in portraying female sexuality. "Indian Wooing" appears to be an excerpt from an unpublished manuscript titled "Cat of God," about the Cherokee Indians. The excerpt focuses on Woly, a young Indian maiden, and the budding attraction between herself and Koe-o, a cocky young brave who, at the story's climax, holds Woly underwater until she passes out, then revives her on the riverbank, orders her to obey him, and performs a kind of communion ceremony when he cuts both their arms and commingles their blood. "Indian Wooing" is an odd story, perhaps partly because it was excerpted from a longer work but also because of the way it combines Christian and Native American

elements. The story, which may owe something to the influence of D. H. Lawrence, whose works Miller was reading around this time, is a woman's coming-of-age narrative, and to convey the element of transformation, Miller draws on two of the most important initiation rituals in the Christian tradition: baptism and communion, both of which are rendered here as erotic. To convey the erotic power of a woman's coming-of-age, however, she once again locates female desire in the racial other. It is an Indian maiden, not a white woman, who is "impatient in the time of the budding year and budding flesh" (p. 34), who is excited by the sight of "his shoulders stronger than the branching trunk of a young acorn tree, his haunches lithe and lean" and of his "lean, gold body" (p. 36).

In these stories, as in *Lamb in His Bosom,* Miller attends closely to the life of the body. In *Lamb,* this attention centers primarily on a white woman's relationship to her maternal body, whereas in these short stories, it centers primarily on the burgeoning sexuality of young women of color. In all of these cases, however, Miller addressed female sexuality with a frankness unusual for the time, especially in south Georgia. In the 1930s other southern women writers, such as Frances Newman and Evelyn Scott, were entering the modernist mainstream and taking some of the risks in content and form associated with modernist literature. Like them, Caroline Miller was aware of, and interested in, the larger intellectual conversation about sexuality that was taking place in the early part of the century, and her fiction clearly reveals the influence of ideas about sexuality disseminated by writers such as Sigmund Freud, Havelock Ellis, and D. H. Lawrence. At the same time, however, her writing remained firmly rooted in the tradition of historical realism, as evidenced by her close attention to historical accuracy in both *Lamb in His Bosom* and *Lebanon,* her second novel, published by Doubleday, Doran in 1944.

Lebanon tells the story of Lebanon Fairgale, a character much like Cean Carver of *Lamb in His Bosom.* In a rather conventional romance plot, she falls in love with a man who is above her in station. Realizing that they cannot be together, she marries the tavernkeeper Fernald d'Aussy, with whom she travels west to the Mississippi frontier. Skilled in the ways of the woods, Lebanon adapts well to her new environment, but her husband does not. Turning to drink, he spends most of his time in town and leaves her to her own devices out in the woods. As a result of her distance from the townsfolk, and the ill will of a jealous neighbor, the townspeople turn against Lebanon, and when her husband and son die in an epidemic, they accuse her of murder. She is eventually rescued by a longtime admirer, the preacher Jairus Mountjoy, who resembles the likable Dermid O'Connor of *Lamb in His Bosom.*

When *Lebanon* was accepted for publication by Doubleday, Doran, Miller was grateful, not only for obvious reasons but also because of the paper shortage experienced during World War II. In a letter of September 16, 1942, she remarks, "With the paper shortage and all, I was very lucky to sell the book." Later, on February 23, 1944, she remarks that her editor "has cut what he thinks would stand cutting." As it turned out, he may have cut more than she realized. According to Miller's niece Joanne Bishop in her portrait of Caroline Miller, the novel was cut to 100,000 words, and Miller was always bitterly disappointed by the cuts, blaming them for the novel's lack of success.

It is likely that Miller's original manuscript was better than the published novel. As published, the novel contains some unexplained shifts and unclear motivations that presumably were explained and clarified in the original manuscript. Miller's original version was likely a more complete narrative of Lebanon Fairgale's consciousness as it develops through her confrontations with harsh nature and an even harsher society—one that prevents her from marrying her true love, treats her with hostility and suspicion because of her sexual attractiveness, and finally brings the long arm of the law down upon her for no good reason. The autobiographical element of *Lebanon* is undeniable. Just as Miller had left south Georgia headed west, so does Lebanon Fairgale; just as Miller had been vilified by her neighbors in Baxley, so is Lebanon vilified by her neighbors in Mississippi; and just as

Miller's name and reputation were dragged through a court of law during her divorce, so Lebanon is brought to court on the basis of false accusations. Perhaps because of these autobiographical elements, Miller describes Lebanon's responses with subtlety and skill. She also exhibits the same painstaking attention to historical detail as in *Lamb in His Bosom,* especially with regard to dialect; as in *Lamb,* the archaic, Elizabethan language of the southern pioneer is captured with remarkable accuracy. However, the novel's plot twists and turns are rather melodramatic, and for that reason, as well as the waning popularity of historical realism, the novel probably would not have done as well as *Lamb* even if it had not been cut.

Miller's last publication was "Cricket," a short story printed by *Ladies' Home Journal* in 1945. "Cricket" consists of an old black man's reminiscences about his childhood before the Civil War. In this story, as in "Loving Wife," Miller renders African American dialect with accuracy and skill, but the story itself is somewhat plotless, being little more than an idle reminiscence of its narrator. This same plotlessness characterizes many of her unpublished short stories, approximately twenty of which are housed in the Emory University library. These stories are undated but were probably written primarily in the 1930s and 1940s, when Miller's letters frequently reference her effort to write and publish stories as a way of supplementing the family income. They may have been written in later decades, however, as Miller is said to have written something every day for the remainder of her life. She maintained a voluminous correspondence with her family, especially her sister Maggie, and wrote not only the unpublished short stories but also several screenplays and four novels. Her last literary effort was a novel titled "Pray, Love, Remember," and she apparently considered it her finest work. She insisted that one of her sons submit it to Harper, which had published *Lamb in His Bosom,* and was devastated when it was declined.

After the mid-1940s, Miller never published again. It was also in the mid-forties that she underwent the first of several lengthy hospitalizations for what appears to have been some combination of mental and physical collapse. While the nature of her health problems remains unclear, she apparently was unwell to some extent throughout the remainder of her life. After Clyde Ray's death in 1976, she lived alone. Her beloved sister and closest confidante, Maggie, died in 1971, but Miller maintained a correspondence with Maggie's daughter, Joanne Bishop. In her declining years, her letters to Bishop are filled with enthusiastic descriptions of the flowers she cultivated, nostalgic reminiscences of her hometown and childhood, and affectionate interest in her niece's and her own children's lives. At the end of her life, according to Bishop in her portrait of Miller,

> She spent eight years in a little mountain home on her farm so remote that visitors had to drive through a cow pasture, taking care to close both gates, to get to it. Immediately guests recognized her home, for there was the familiar border of flowers on both sides of the walk that had always welcomed her friends. She lived quietly there, doors unlocked, surrounded by her books and writing materials. Quilting, embroidery, and knitting projects were close at hand. Some of the children and grandchildren lived close enough to call on her often, and visits from the others always called for feasting and celebrating for the whole clan.
>
> (p. 22)

Throughout her declining years, Miller received periodic recognition, with occasional articles in the *Atlanta Journal-Constitution,* the *Asheville Citizen-Times*, or the *Waycross Journal-Herald* reminding readers about the reclusive author and her Pulitzer Prize–winning novel. Shortly before her death, Miller received one last round of recognition. In 1991 the town of Baxley decided to commemorate the fifty-seventh anniversary of Miller's return to Baxley from New York after her receipt of the Pulitzer. The mayor declared August 24, 1991, to be Caroline Miller Ray Day. The popular *Atlanta Journal-Constitution* columnist Celestine Sibley, a longtime admirer of *Lamb in His Bosom,* spoke at the event and wrote about it in the Atlanta paper. Miller was invited to Baxley for the day but by this time had been moved to a nursing home and could not travel. Her nephew Ward Pafford appeared at the ceremony

and read from a letter she had written in which she expressed affection for the south Georgia places and people of her youth.

Two years later, in 1993, Peachtree Publishers, a small Atlanta publishing company, reprinted *Lamb in His Bosom* with an afterword by the noted historian Elizabeth Fox-Genovese. Although Miller was aware that the reprint was being released and was pleased by this development, she did not live to see it. On July 12, 1992, she died in the Haywood County Hospital. She was buried in Green Hill Cemetery in Waynesville, North Carolina, where a small ceramic statue of a reclining lamb adorns her grave. In the summer of 1996, when the Olympics were held in Atlanta, she was one of nine authors featured in an exhibit mounted by the Atlanta Public Library designed to highlight the diversity of voices in Georgia literature. In 2007 she was inducted into the Georgia Writers Hall of Fame, and in 2009 she became a member of the Georgia Women of Achievement Hall of Fame.

CONCLUSION

Caroline Miller was born Caroline Pafford and died Caroline Ray. In a letter dated June 18, 1943, she told her sister Maggie that she would rather be known as Mrs. Clyde Ray Jr. than as Caroline Miller. Toward the end of her life, her eldest son said she would like to be remembered only as Caroline Pafford. But Caroline Miller is the name under which all of her works were published, and it is the name by which she will always be known. In a way, this is fitting. Although her marriage to William D. Miller was not a successful one, those early years with him seem to have been the high point of her life. Possessed of youth, good health, hope for the future, children whom she loved deeply, talent, and drive, the young Caroline Miller had a bright future that became much more bright when her first novel was published and perhaps too bright when it was awarded the Pulitzer. Although none of her subsequent works lived up to the standard of *Lamb in His Bosom,* in this one work a young south Georgia housewife named Caroline Miller made her claim to fame, and it is by that name she should be remembered.

Selected Bibliography

WORKS OF CAROLINE MILLER

NOVELS

Lamb in His Bosom. New York: Harper & Bros., 1933. Reprint, Atlanta: Peachtree, 1993; reissue, 2011.

Lebanon. New York: Doubleday, Doran, 1944.

SHORT STORIES

"The Greatest of These." *Waycross Journal-Herald,* February 19, 1924, p. 2.

"Indian Wooing." *Pictorial Review,* January 1934, pp. 12–13, 34–37.

"Loving Wife." *Pictorial Review,* January 1937, pp. 14–15, 44–47.

"Cricket." *Ladies' Home Journal,* April 1945, pp. 25, 163–165.

CORRESPONDENCE AND MANUSCRIPTS

Miller's papers are housed at the Manuscript, Archives, and Rare Book Library of Emory University. The Caroline Pafford Miller Collection includes newspaper clippings, letters, copies of Miller's published short stories, and numerous unpublished short stories, novels, and screenplays. All of the letters referenced in the latter part of the essay are housed in these archives, which also include the following:

Bishop, Joanne. "An Ethnographic Study on the 1934 Pulitzer Prize Novel *Lamb in His Bosom* by Caroline Miller." 1987. (A collection of newspaper clippings, with an introduction, written by Caroline Miller's niece for a class she took at the University of Georgia in fall 1987.) Box 10, Folder 12, Caroline Pafford Miller Collection, Manuscript, Archives, and Rare Book Library of Emory University.

CRITICAL AND BIOGRAPHICAL STUDIES

Bishop, Joanne. "Caroline Miller: A Portrait." 2001. (A twenty-four-page biographical document written by Caroline Miller's niece.) Box 12, Folder 3, Caroline Pafford Miller Collection, Manuscript, Archives, and Rare Book Library of Emory University.

Bradbury, John M. *Renaissance in the South: A Critical History of the Literature, 1920–1950.* Chapel Hill: University of North Carolina Press, 1963.

Craig, David M. "Caroline Miller." *Dictionary of Literary Biography.* Vol. 9, *American Novelists, 1910–1945.* Edited by James J. Martine. Detroit: Gale, 1981. Pp. 208–210.

Fox-Genovese, Elizabeth. Afterword to *Lamb in His Bosom.* Atlanta: Peachtree, 1993.

CAROLINE MILLER

Hurst, Robert Latimer. "Georgia's Lamb: Episodes in the Life of Caroline Miller." *Douglas Enterprise* [Douglas, Ga.], May 26, 2004–December 21, 2005. (A biography of Miller published in seventy-nine installments.)

———. "Finding Georgia's Lost Lamb." *Georgia Backroads*, summer 2009, pp. 44–47.

Miller, William D., Sr. "What Price Fame?" 1937. (A six-page typescript written by Caroline Miller's first husband about the dissolution of the marriage.) Box 11, Folder 1, Caroline Pafford Miller Collection, Manuscript, Archives, and Rare Book Library of Emory University.

Sherry, Denver William. "A Dialect Study of Caroline Miller's *Lamb in His Bosom*." M.A. thesis, University of Florida, 1970. Box 1, Folders 10–11, Caroline Pafford Miller Collection, Manuscript, Archives, and Rare Book Library of Emory University.

Stuckey, W. J. *The Pulitzer Prize Novels: A Critical Backward Look.* Norman: University of Oklahoma Press, 1966.

Wright, Emily. "The 'Other South' of Caroline Miller: A Case Study in Regional Stereotypes and Canon Formation." *Southern Quarterly* 40, no. 1:93–108 (fall 2001).

———. "Caroline Miller, 1903–1922." *Southern Quarterly* 42, no. 2:109–114 (winter 2004).

HOWARD FRANK MOSHER

(1942—)

Ann McKinstry Micou

KINGDOM COUNTY, THE fictional world of the regional novelist Howard Frank Mosher, is a wild, mountainous, beautiful place somewhere between the northeast corner of Vermont and Canada. Inspired by the history, lore, and legend of a bygone Yankee and French Canadian culture, Mosher's stories recall William Faulkner and Mark Twain, whom critics reference in their reviews of Mosher's work. His signal achievement is to bring this frontier territory and its memorable inhabitants to life in a manner at once humorous and poignant, tender and ironic, hopeful and elegiac.

Between 1977 and 2010 Mosher published nine well-received novels and a novella accompanied by six short stories, a memoir, a tale illustrating photographs of northeastern Vermont, and introductions to six works of nonfiction. He contributed stories to literary journals such as *Cimarron Review, Colorado Quarterly, Echo Review,* and *Four Quarters,* and travel pieces and book reviews to periodicals such as the *New York Times* and *Boston Globe.*

REVERING THE NORTH COUNTRY

His 1997 memoir, *North Country: A Personal Journey Through the Borderland,* illuminates the autobiographical elements in his fiction. Born in 1942 in the Catskill Mountain village of Tannersville, New York, he grew up in nearby Chichester, New York. At age four he traveled to the Adirondacks with his grandparents and at five caught his first trout. Exhilarated by heading north, he fished each summer in Quebec's Laurentian Mountains with his father, Howard Hudson Mosher, and adopted uncle, Reginald Bennett. Reading about the North Woods in books by Robert W. Service and Jack London and in tales about Paul Bunyan, he felt a profound affinity for the North Country.

Chichester's furniture factory closed when Mosher was ten. He asked his uncle what could be done about the death of the village; the latter replied that sometimes the only way to preserve a place was to write about it. Mosher and his parents moved to his grandfather's farm near Lake Ontario and the Canadian border, where the twenty-six-room farmhouse was filled with family members: storytellers like his grandfather Howard Leroy Mosher, his first North Country individualist; and his great-aunt Jane, the formidable protagonist in *On Kingdom Mountain* (2007).

In 1960 Mosher graduated from Cato-Meridian Central School in Cato, New York, where his father was principal. An English major at Syracuse University, Mosher received a bachelor's degree from the School of Arts and Sciences in 1964. (His grandfather sold his farm to pay for Mosher's education, as does Austen's grandfather in the 1994 novel *Northern Borders.*) During the summers between semesters, he worked for Bernie Silverman, a door-to-door brush salesman who introduced him to the Nick Adams stories from Ernest Hemingway's *In Our Time.* With his wife, Phillis, Mosher moved to Brownington in Vermont's Northeast Kingdom. The superintendent hired them to teach at Orleans High School after the following exchange: "Do you like to fish?" "Only for trout, and only every day" (p. 99). They spent a decade in Brownington, where their children were born: Jake Mosher is a writer in southwest Montana; Annie Mosher is a songwriter and folk-rock singer in Nashville, Tennessee. Howard and Phillis moved to nearby Irasburg, Vermont, and stayed.

Shortly after his arrival in Vermont, Mosher enrolled in a master's program at the University of Vermont, where his papers are now archived. He taught classes and completed a master's thesis on villainy in literature, receiving his degree in 1967. Based on this study of unmitigated wickedness in four villains (Marlowe's Barabas, Shakespeare's Richard III and Aaron of *Titus Andronicus,* and Shelley's Count Cenci), Mosher judged the complete villain to be a flat character morally but a highly valuable character aesthetically. (His own consummate villain is Oconaluftee in his 2010 novel *Walking to Gatlinburg.*)

Mosher enjoyed teaching, and hunting and fishing with his students, but these activities proved too time-consuming for him to write. He hired out on farms, clerked at stores, wrote feature stories for newspapers, and taught basic literacy classes to adults, helping unemployed loggers, truck drivers, waitresses, mill workers, and farmhands write autobiographies. In the 1970s he did social work with young people who had dropped out of school. Phillis worked in a rural sheltered workshop for mentally and emotionally handicapped children and adults. Some of those they helped often stayed with them.

In a single defection from his beloved North Country, Mosher enrolled in 1969 in the MFA creative writing program at the University of California–Irvine, hoping to find "a shortcut" to writing a good novel (p. 158). After two days, he was waiting at a stoplight; a telephone company man, spying Mosher's green license plates, pulled up beside his car: "I'm from Vermont, too. Go back home where you belong while you still can" (p. 159). Back in the Northeast Kingdom, he worked as an apprentice horse logger for Jake Blodgett; he and his longtime partner, Hazel, were models for Noël and Bangor in the 1978 novella "Where the Rivers Flow North." Mosher used Jake's stories of logging, hill farming, and whiskey running in that novella and in his "wild and woolly" (p. 181) novel *Disappearances* (1977). Experiences of other friends from this period, such as Mosher's landlady Verna Fletcher, in "Burl," were raw material for his fiction.

The early writing days were a struggle. Mosher tacked his magazine rejection slips to his disused barn and blasted them with his shotgun. After he published his first story, "Alabama Jones," he hired the New York literary agent Don Congdon, who admired "Where the Rivers Flow North" but counseled that publishers would want a full-length novel first. Intrepidly, Mosher quit his job, sold his house, and wrote *Disappearances* full time. Slowly he found recognition: a Guggenheim Fellowship for fiction in 1979, an American Academy and Institute of Arts and Letters Literature Award in 1981, a National Endowment for the Arts fiction fellowship in 1987, and an honor from Governor Madeleine Kunin as one of thirty Extraordinary Vermonters in 1990. *A Stranger in the Kingdom* (1989) won the ACLU Foundation of Vermont Civil Liberties in the Arts Award in 1991 and, together with *Disappearances,* the New England Book Award the same year. *Hunger Mountain: The Vermont College Journal of Arts and Letters* inaugurated the annual Howard Frank Mosher Short Fiction Prize in 2004; the Vermont Arts Council presented him with the Governor's Award for Excellence in the Arts in 2005. Jay Craven of Kingdom County Productions began making films of his work.

Among his friends and literary mentors were the essayist Edward Hoagland and the lyric poet James Hayford, both Vermonters, and the western novelist Wallace Stegner, who spent summers in nearby Greensboro. Hoagland wrote in Nicholas Delbanco's *Writers and Their Craft* that Mosher is "perhaps my best writing friend, and also an admirable novelist" (p. 147). Hayford encouraged him to stay in the Northeast Kingdom and dedicated his children's novel, *Gridley Firing,* to him for his indispensable help. Stegner strongly supported his work; in a blurb, he called *A Stranger in the Kingdom* "exciting and memorable."

EVOKING A SENSE OF PLACE

Kingdom County is an "out-of-the-way and little-known fragment of a much earlier rural America," Austen Kittredge reminisces in *Northern Borders* (p. 1). The setting embraces the Upper and Lower

Kingdom Rivers that flow north; the High Falls; vast woods, cedar bogs, and swamps; blue clay; Kingdom, Lord, Allen, and Anderson Mountains; and, to the north, Lake Memphremagog, with the nearest hospital. The center is called Kingdom Common, with a rectangular green to accommodate baseball games, the annual fair, and Ethan Allen's statue. Nearby are the courthouse, two churches, the barbershop, the Common Hotel, the commission-sales auction barn and meadow behind, the American Heritage furniture mill, the Kingdom Common Academy, the library, and the train station. Outlying areas include Lost Nation Hollow; Lord Hollow; Hell's Gate; Christian Ridge, where the hill people live; the ethnic enclaves of Irishtown, for workers who brought the railroad to Kingdom County; and Little Quebec, home to French Canadians.

In *Where the Bluebird Sings to the Lemonade Springs,* Wallace Stegner defines "sense of place" as knowing a place through "working in it in all weathers, making a living from it, suffering from its catastrophes, loving its mornings or evenings or hot noons, valuing it for the profound investment of labor and feeling that you, your parents and grandparents, your all-but-unknown ancestors have put into it" (p. 205). Critics who have admired Mosher's palpable sense of place include Sudip Bose, writing in the *Washington Post* on *The Fall of the Year* in 1999 ("deeply felt sense of place"); Steve Amick, reviewing *On Kingdom Mountain* for the *Washington Post* ("wonderfully intriguing sense of place"); and Christopher Lehmann-Haupt of the *New York Times* on *A Stranger in the Kingdom* ("you enjoy its sense of place").

As Mosher continued to develop what he called in his memoir "the geography of my fictional territory" (p. 198), critics began describing him as a regional writer. Reviewing *North Country,* David M. Shribman of the *Boston Globe* called Mosher "so accomplished a regional writer that he doesn't mind being described that way." Mosher told Robin Dougherty of the *Boston Globe* that a regional novel, in one sense, "couldn't be set anywhere else." Wayne Franklin and Michael Steiner, in their introduction to *Mapping American Culture* (1992), identified "the resuscitation of the regional novel" as one of the more interesting developments in American literature in the 1980s. Among the groups of books written by authors "deeply rooted in the locales they deal with," they listed "the 'Northeast Kingdom' books of Vermont writer Howard Frank Mosher" (p. 20). Joseph Coates, discussing American short stories in a 1990 piece for the *Chicago Tribune,* saw "a return to regionalism among our best writers" and cited on his list New England's Howard Frank Mosher.

Various critics have associated Mosher with the regional novelist William Faulkner. The educator and writer Jay Parini, in *One Matchless Time: A Life of William Faulkner* (2004), mentions Faulkner's influence on later generations of writers: "His commitment to a particular place and interlocking circles of characters is reflected in worlds created by such writers as Louise Erdrich and Howard Frank Mosher" (p. 432). Dean Flower, writing in the *Hudson Review* on *Where the Rivers Flow North,* remarked, "Occasionally, through the restraint and humor, we can hear a romanticizing, Faulknerian voice." Joe Sherman, in his *Fast Lane on a Dirt Road,* writes that Mosher's story "High Water" is about "a farm boy determined to get his jalopy to the track in Quebec despite a kind of Faulknerian hurdle—torrential rains that sweep away bridges" (p. 166). In *New England's Gothic Literature,* Faye Ringel calls Mosher's themes "Faulknerian—hunting as initiation, the lawlessness of an isolated region, the weight of the past" (p. 211). Other critics have referred specifically to Faulkner's Yoknapatawpha County, including Matt Schudel, writing in the *Washington Post* on the 2004 novel *Waiting for Teddy Williams* (Mosher "has tilled his own New England Yoknapatawpha County in eight previous works of fiction") and Noel Perrin in *Inquiry*, on *Where the Rivers Flow North* (Kingdom County's "true affinity is with Yoknapatawpha County").

Critics connecting Mosher to Mark Twain, also a regional writer, include Bruce DeSilva of the Associated Press on *Walking to Gatlinburg* ("a superb storyteller who is the closest thing we have to Mark Twain"); Bruce Allen of the *Christian Science Monitor* on *Disappearances*

("outrageous and wonderful tall tales, many of them worthy of Mark Twain"); Thomas Bahr, writing in *Agni 41* on *Northern Borders* ("Like Twain, Mosher writes with a deep longing for a vanished past"); and Ron Franscell of the *Denver Post* on the 2003 novel *The True Account* ("as splendid a liar as Twain himself"). Referring specifically to comparisons with *Huckleberry Finn* are critics such as Chris Goodrich, writing in the *Los Angeles Times* on *Northern Borders* ("you will likely end it thinking of 'Huck Finn' "); Carolyn See in the *Washington Post* on *Walking to Gatlinburg* ("that locale recalls Huck Finn"); Barbara Lloyd McMichael in the *Seattle Times* on *The True Account* ("in terms of style, cross Don Quixote with Huckleberry Finn"); and Thomas LeClair in *Commonweal* on Bill in *Disappearances* ("a Huck Finn boy now a Faulknerian lawyer").

TELLING A STORY

Mosher's characters originate in the earliest settlers of Kingdom County, many of whom came from Canada. He comments in *North Country,* "One of the deepest satisfactions of a rural northern existence is the continuity of life from season to season, year to year, youth to old age, generation to generation" (p. 254). In *Disappearances* he identifies "energy and endurance" as the attributes that "the austere and uncompromised land ... exacted of the men and women who still depended on it for their livelihoods" (p. 16). These men and women are independent-minded and rugged, noble and stoical, eccentric and cantankerous, diligent and proud, solicitous of neighbors while suspicious of strangers. Critics have complimented Mosher's characterizations, including Bruce DeSilva of the Associated Press on *Waiting for Teddy Williams* ("Every character Mosher creates is quirky and memorable"); and Sudip Bose, writing in the *Washington Post* on *Northern Borders* ("his talent for creating lively, living characters ... is Mosher's greatest gift").

Mosher's plots are original, seriocomic, and seamless. Geoffrey Wolff wrote in *New Times* that "Where the Rivers Flow North" is "so tightly constructed that I cannot pick at this or that thread without unweaving the whole thing." Barbara Fisher of the *Boston Globe* called *The Fall of the Year* a "neatly plotted novel." Mosher's prose is lyrical and literate, garnished with vivid representations of the natural world and intricate explanations of outdoor tasks. Mosher is "exactly accurate about a thousand details," wrote Alice Cary in the *Boston Sunday Herald,* quoting part of Edward Hoagland's blurb for *Disappearances.* Reviewing *A Stranger in the Kingdom* in the *New York Times,* Lee Smith noted Mosher's "lucid, straightforward style that's a pleasure to read."

Above all, Mosher is a storyteller, his voice a gift inherited in large part from his grandfather, whose way of spinning a yarn Mosher described in *North Country* as "easy, speculative, spellbinding" (p. 59). Mosher passed on a "slightly speculative, wry resonance" to Father George in *Fall of the Year* (p. 252) and a "speculative and faintly ironic" manner to Henry Coville in *Disappearances* (p. 4). Ron Franscell, writing in the *Denver Post* on *The True Account,* found that "Mosher's voice is pitch-perfect, satirical without being too sardonic."

Jane Kinneson, the protagonist of *On Kingdom Mountain,* considers Charles Dickens a "magnanimous" writer (p. 48), an attribute that pinpoints Mosher's attitude toward his own characters (and toward other authors: Alice Cary emphasized in her *Boston Globe* interview Mosher's tireless generosity in composing blurbs and sending supportive letters to publishers on behalf of other writers). In addition to Dickens, other writers Mosher admires are Jane Austen, Mark Twain, William Shakespeare, Henry David Thoreau, and Robert Frost. Mosher holds Frost in special esteem. In *Marie Blythe* (1983), Frost advises Academy graduates to "go their own way, like a brook that finds its own best course down a mountainside" (p. 369). The poet visits Jane Kinneson in *On Kingdom Mountain* to botanize for alpine plants. At school, Austen in *Northern Borders* memorizes Frost's poem "Nothing Gold Can Stay." In *Disappearances,* Bill recognizes himself in the boy in "Birches" who lives too far from the village to learn baseball.

Rich local color suffuses Mosher's imagery. In *Waiting for Teddy Williams,* E. A.'s perfect curve ball dips "like a swallow skimming over the river dipping to pick a bug off the surface" (p. 150). In *A Stranger in the Kingdom,* Judge Allen's voice is "like river ice breaking up in the spring" (p. 82). "The big maples cracked in the cold like rifle shots" in *Disappearances* (p. 148). In *The Rivers Flow North,* a logger's muscles jump "like log chains snaking through underbrush" (p. 81); partridges fly up low and fast, burring their wings "like a big John Deere starting up" (p. 28). In *Northern Borders,* Austen's grandfather makes a rasping noise in his throat "like his big log saw striking a knot in the buttend of a hemlock log" (p. 82). The bears come down the trees "like great sooty firemen" in *On Kingdom Mountain* (p. 234).

The kinds of genres Mosher employs include "picaresque" (Barbara Lloyd McMichael, *Seattle Times,* on *The True Account*); "mountain lore and magical realism" (Carole Goldberg, the *Hartford Courant,* on *On Kingdom Mountain*); "mythic" (Noel Perrin, *Inquiry,* on "Where the Rivers Flow North"); "Gothic" (Faye Ringel on *A Stranger in the Kingdom* in *New England's Gothic Literature,* p. 210); "comic novel" (Brad Leithauser, the *Boston Globe,* on *Waiting for Teddy Williams*); and "historical" (Don Mitchell on *Where the Rivers Flow North* in his book *Vermont,* p. 312). Finally, the novelist Ernest Hebert has credited Mosher with the invention of the "Eastern," a term Mosher defines in a 1997 *Atlantic Unbound* interview with Katy Bacon as "high-action, picaresque stories ... comparable to Westerns, but set in the East."

On his book tour for *Walking to Gatlinburg* in the spring of 2010, Mosher explained his way of transforming history into fiction. "Above all, I establish the story and the characters, then retrace the history," he told Ben Fulton of the *Salt Lake Tribune.* His approach to the Lewis and Clark expedition in *The True Account* is often irreverent and hilarious, yet he thrice traveled the Lewis and Clark trail to absorb the real story. "I'm an inveterate inventor," he told Nick Zaino of the *Optimistic Curmudgeon.* To serve his plot in *On Kingdom Mountain,* for example, Mosher moved the 1864 Confederate Raid on St. Albans, Vermont, east to Kingdom County.

Mosher's fiction contains three principal, interconnected themes. The first theme evokes the significance of the past, its succeeding generations, and its history and traditions. The second conveys the challenges posed by the passage of time, progress and development, and impermanence and change. The third underscores the importance of connections with earlier generations, relationships within a community, and ties to the land.

First, the past in Mosher's stories represents a vanishing culture that continues to shape the present and the future. The main characters reflect upon the influence of history and heritage upon their lives. In *A Stranger in the Kingdom,* Jim Kinneson observes that in the Kingdom "the past was still part of the present" (p. 420). Similarly, Jane Kinneson proclaims in *On Kingdom Mountain* that "the past lives on as part of the present. Indeed, it *is* the present" (p. 198). Cordelia speaks in *Disappearances* about "time, its cyclical and illusory nature, and the recurrence of themes and events down through the generations" (p. 95). The deaf-mute, itinerant painter known as the "dog-cart man," one of Mosher's array of unusual, recurring minor characters, boldly covers the sides of barns and other surfaces with landscapes and tableaux, mystically mixing "past, present, and even perhaps the future" in *On Kingdom Mountain* (p. 135).

Second, though the land and its history are timeless, the landscape is changing. Mosher wrote in his memoir that "growing up in the North Country had been a process of encountering one inevitable major change after another" (p. 57). These changes are reflected in his stories. In *Northern Borders,* Austen's grandfather sums up: "The farms are all gone. The big woods are gone. The best of the hunting and fishing is gone" (p. 288). Inexorable progress affects Noël Lord's ancestral land, to be flooded by a power dam in "Where the Rivers Flow North," and Jane Kinneson's family mountain, to be bisected by a highway in *On Kingdom Mountain.* Both Noël and Quebec Bill in *Disappearances* leave King-

dom County for years and, "longing for permanence," return (p. 101). In his memoir Mosher wrote, "All my life I have been haunted by disappearances—of towns, farms, big woods, and people" (p. 207). In *Disappearances*, Bill echoes those words: Quebec Bill "was haunted by disappearances and the possibility of disappearances" (p. 159). In *Northern Borders,* Abiah warns Austen that times are not immutable, as does Colonel Allen to E. A. in *Waiting for Teddy Williams.* Private True Teague Kinneson in *The True Account* celebrates change as the only constant in life.

Third, in addition to relationships with ancestors and the past, connections occur in the context of communities and the land. When in need, Austen's grandfather in *Northern Borders* calls on neighbors, "men he'd helped in haying and sugaring time, as they'd helped him" (p. 70). Several stories highlight the tradition of the Underground Railroad. "They lived in a house at the end of the road and were friends to mankind," reads the motto over the Kinneson lintel in *On Kingdom Mountain* (p. 30). A recurrent idea in *Walking to Gatlinburg* is that everything is connected, especially human actions and their consequences. In the story "Kingdom County Come" (*Where the Rivers Flow North*), Henry Coville belongs to the land and chooses when and where to return to it. Mosher wrote in his memoir that fishing is what connects him with "that harsh and lovely remnant of an earlier Vermont" (p. 100). Jane Kinneson in *On Kingdom Mountain* also feels connected through fishing to the river and her beloved mountain, past and present. In her study *In Search of America: The Image of the United States in Travel Writing of the 1980s and 1990s,* Malgorzata Rutkowska found that, for Mosher, continuity of life and personal attachment to the land are the "most important values that the North Country people have managed to preserve" (p. 88).

Some of the ancillary motifs in his fiction relate to optimism, intolerance, the supernatural, and the symbolism of regional pastimes such as fishing and baseball. First, despite obstacles, Mosher's characters retain their optimism. True's epitaph in *The True Account* salutes his "hopefulness" (p. 342). Bill, the narrator of *Disappearances,* describes Quebec Bill as an indefatigable optimist: "His hopefulness was as inexorable as the northern Vermont weather, and much more dependable" (p. 3). In a related vein, Mosher's enthusiasm for hearing and telling stories, his ebullience, radiates through the characters. Charlie in *A Stranger in the Kingdom* is "ebullient" playing ball with Reverend Andrews (p. 52); Rob in *Northern Borders* is "ebullient" watching the sharpshooter (p. 167); Bangor in "Where the Rivers Flow North" fishes, "luckless and ebullient" (p. 79); and Quebec Bill's son says that his father's "ebullience, while authentic, must have been generated in part by desperation" (p. 227). Tellingly, Wallace Stegner's blurb for *Where the Rivers Flow North* describes the book as "full of invention, people, humor, country, energy, lingo, ebullience."

Second, intolerance is alive in Kingdom County. Father George writes in *The Fall of the Year,* "Outsiders ... have often found Kingdom Common, at least at first, to be a hostile place" (p. 108). This motif is related to the theme of change, manifested as fear of those who are perceived as different, and to the theme of connections, suspicion of those who appear not to belong. Racism is blatant in *A Stranger in the Kingdom* and *On Kingdom Mountain.* Prejudice against French Canadians is evinced in *A Stranger in the Kingdom* (Editor Kinneson's parents do not allow him to court a French Canadian girl) and *On Kingdom Mountain* (the parents of Pilgrim Kinneson and Manon Thibeau do not sanction their courtship). Reviewing *A Stranger in the Kingdom,* Jeff Danziger of the *Christian Science Monitor* judged Mosher "the best writer on the French Canadian culture ... in Vermont." In Mosher's story "The Church of the Latter Day Saints," some individuals firebomb a newly built tabernacle and drive out the minister.

Third, many Kingdom County residents believe in supernatural events. In his introduction to Joseph Citro's *Green Mountain Ghosts, Ghouls, and Unsolved Mysteries* (1994), Mosher admits to an initial skepticism about psychic phenomena, but as an apprentice writer he kept

an open mind. In "Thunder from a Cloudless Sky," an essay for the *Washington Post Magazine,* he describes an inexplicable experience of his own. His stories contain suspicions of werewolves, strange disappearances in the cedar bog, and people with second sight. Pliny Templeton's ghost walks on the Fourth of July in *A Stranger in the Kingdom*; two elderly ladies who bake bread for the striking mill workers vanish in *The Fall of the Year*; a statue talks in *Waiting for Teddy Williams,* as does a turtle in *Walking to Gatlinburg*; a dead sea captain is sighted in *Marie Blythe.* While Austen is in a hunting stand in *Northern Borders,* a horned owl on a nearby branch produces "a mystical memory" (p. 191).

Fourth, Mosher's lifelong passion for fishing is reflected in "Where the Rivers Flow North," *Disappearances, A Stranger in the Kingdom, Northern Borders,* and *On Kingdom Mountain.* In his memoir, he refers reverently to Hemingway's "Big Two-Hearted River." Ron Ellis, editor for *Of Woods and Waters: A Kentucky Outdoors Reader*, was inspired by the Hemingway story and searched for other stories exploring similar themes ("nature and hunting and fishing"), and found them in writers such as Howard Frank Mosher (p. xxv). Indeed, Mosher (whose fly rod developed a "transcendent talismanic and autobiographical significance," p. 36) devotes one chapter, "A Fishing Idyll," to the topic: "And once again I felt connected through a fighting trout to a flowing river and the twilit northern country it flowed through" (p. 212). *The New Great American Writers Cookbook, Vol. 2,* published Mosher's recipe for Northern New England Brook Trout. In a *Yankee Magazine* article titled "This New England: Newport, Vermont," Mosher refers to that "most hopeful of pursuits, fishing" (January, 1985, p. 163).

Fifth, Kingdom County shares Mosher's veneration for baseball in general and the Red Sox in particular. In an essay ("Red Sox Nation, North") for *Vermont Life*, Mosher reminisces about town-team baseball in Irasburg, where he played and coached, and the emblematic nature of the Red Sox. Tom Verducci, in "At the End of the Curse, a Blessing" in *Great Baseball Writing,* wryly calls *Waiting for Teddy Williams* a "fanciful tale" (p. 379). Two months after the novel's publication in 2004, the Red Sox won the World Series for the first time since 1918. *Yankee Magazine* published Mosher's sole short story about baseball, "Something Might Be Gaining."

WRITING ABOUT THE PAST TO KEEP IT ALIVE

Mosher's main purpose as a novelist is to tell a good story, at the same time preserving a heritage and culture whose values he treasures. Some of his disparate characters also chronicle the past: Calvin Goodman's journals about Rene Bonhomme's early history in *Disappearances*; Twilight Anderson's religious tracts on the annihilation of Kingdom County in "Where the Rivers Flow North"; Captain Benedict's diaries in *Marie Blythe*; Pliny's ecclesiastical history in *A Stranger in the Kingdom*; Father George's "Short History of Kingdom County" in *The Fall of the Year*; Morgan Kinneson's letters in *On Kingdom Mountain*; and Austen's grandfather's survey and record of the Great Lost Corner in Labrador "before it disappeared" under the flood from the hydro dam in *Northern Borders* (p. 269). Mosher's young narrators, voracious readers, are writers-in-training to record their pasts. Jim Kinneson in *A Stranger in the Kingdom* began as a boy to write little stories; in *The Fall of the Year,* Frank Bennett says, "I'd see and hear something I could write my own story about someday" (p. 53); *Northern Borders* is Austen Kittredge's memoir.

Into his nine novels and one novella Mosher has woven the distinctive genealogies of his featured families. The Bonhommes and Goodmans, Andersons and Lords, Kinnesons, Kittredges, and Allens forged and defended their destinies in the wilderness, founding Kingdom County; logging, trapping, hunting, hauling, running whiskey, and farming; building schools and churches; embracing abolition; fighting in the Civil War; and passing along their freedom-loving, antiauthoritarian ways to generations of descendants.

DISAPPEARANCES *AND* WHERE THE RIVERS FLOW NORTH

In *Disappearances* (1977), Mosher's first published novel, Bill Bonhomme learns from his father about his ancestry. The family's original habitant, René St. Laurent Bonhomme, born in Quebec in 1778, traveled in 1796 to what would be Kingdom County, founded Kingdom Common, established the first tavern, and changed his name to Goodman. Kingdom County, covered with impenetrable forest, was accessible only by water: he became the family's first whiskey runner. He married the blond, blue-eyed daughter of the Scottish settler Calvin Matthews and disappeared in the swamp in the 1850s. His son, Calvin, went to Yale, became a minister, built the Kingdom Common library, and founded the first Universalist Church in northern Vermont. Calvin's son, William Shakespeare Goodman, cast from bronze a life-size statue of Ethan Allen capturing Fort Ticonderoga and built round barns on the surrounding hills. Calvin's daughter, Cordelia, was a scholar at the Academy. Her brother, William, was mortally wounded with the First Vermont Militia at Bull Run. Their father traveled to Virginia to collect his body; the coffin, opened at home, was empty. Calvin's grandson William, left in Cordelia's care, ran away, trapped, smuggled whiskey, had twelve children, and disappeared. His son William changed his name to Quebec Bill Bonhomme and searched for his family for fifteen years. He married the French Canadian Evangeline Coville and had a son, Bill. His wife disappeared with their newborn to a Montreal convent, where Quebec Bill found her and brought her home. (Evangeline's brother, Henry Coville, a fabled whiskey runner, plays a role in "The Church of the Latter Day Saints," "The Peacock," "Kingdom County Come," "Where the Rivers Flow North," *Disappearances,* and *Northern Borders.*)

Bill Bonhomme lives in Lord Hollow in 1932 with his father, mother, and aged great-great-aunt Cordelia. Quebec Bill calls his fourteen-year-old son Wild Bill, hoping he will inherit his father's all-embracing approach to life; Bill is more like his uncle Henry Coville, perceiving life through a screen of irony, "like the layer of hardwood charcoal through which good bourbon is filtered" (p. 273). Quebec Bill tries sugaring and an animal farm; the snow kills his orchard, his "Eden" (p. 150). Having lost everything, he shows "ultimate hopefulness in the face of ultimate futility" (p. 134). Desperate for hay for his wife's cows, he makes a whiskey run on Lake Memphremagog with Bill and Henry. He audaciously grabs Carcajou's whiskey and burns his barn. Carcajou, a terrifying whiskey hijacker with an Indian name meaning "wolverine" and long white hair, pursues them. Despite being shot and harpooned, he is impossible to kill. Carcajou wounds Quebec Bill in the leg. Struggling across the snow carrying his father, Bill collapses. Cordelia materializes with a musket. "William Goodman!" she screams as she shoots Carcajou. He disappears. Bill looks down at his father: he too has disappeared. Bill needs a year to recover from his father's death. By 1976 the bog is inundated by an Army Corps of Engineers dam; gone too are the wild animals, the flowers, and the whitewater river. The rainbow trout have stopped coming up over the falls in the spring. Lake Memphremagog is lined with camps and resorts. Kingdom County has disappeared.

The Book of the Month Club chose *Disappearances* as an alternate selection in 1978. In *Commonweal,* Thomas LeClair stated that Mosher "knows how to mix comedy with moving remembrance, suspense with local lore, the authentic past with the tourist present." In differing views, Frances Taliaferro in *Harper's Magazine* wondered whether the novel was an allegory: "Mosher leaves us uncertain and uncomfortable." In his *New York Times* review Sheldon Frank found "an annoying mixture of genres—a puzzling combination of family saga, tall tale, and nature reverie."

In the title novella of the collection *Where the Rivers Flow North* (1978), which Mosher wrote first but published second, Noël Anderson Lord lives with his Indian housekeeper, Bangor, making cedar oil in a still on the property of his great-great-grandfather, Twilight Anderson. After the 1759 retaliatory raid on St. Francis with Rogers' Rangers, Anderson, the first white man to come down from Canada, built a sawmill in

what would become Kingdom County. He made a fortune selling pine for masts to the navies of King George and General Washington. To atone for the massacre, he returned to St. Francis to marry an Indian woman. In 1810 his son, George, declared the independence of Kingdom Territory from Great Britain and Vermont and was killed by militiamen. George's son, Joseph, reintegrated Kingdom Republic into America and built sawmills and a furniture factory in Kingdom Common, where he erected William Shakespeare Goodman's statue of Ethan Allen. Joseph persuaded the Boston and Montreal Railroad to pass through the village and hired the flamboyant French Canadian logger Gilles Lourdes to build a driving dam on the Upper Kingdom River. Joseph started a merino sheep herd, married, had a daughter, Abigail, enlisted in a Vermont regiment at sixty, and was killed at Bull Run. In 1854 Abigail married Lourdes and moved to his logging camp, where every year he drove a million feet of spruce and fir through the notch to the sawmills. They had a son, Noël Anderson Lord (anglicized from Lourdes), in 1855. At sixteen he was the best man on the river. After an accident in which his hand was severed, he wore an iron cant hook. His father died running the river drunk in a bateau; Noël left Kingdom County for thirty years.

When Noël returns in 1921, he finds "some enduring fragment of the original wilderness" (p. 122). "Everything else in his life had proved transitory" (p. 123), but the one hundred virgin pines remain unchanged. His grandfather had sold his woodland holdings to the Connecticut Valley Lumber Company, which granted Noël a lifetime lease on the driving dam and the camp. Against everyone's objections, the court allows the Northern Vermont Power Company to construct a huge dam, which will "obliterate irrevocably the river and flume and wild bog to the north" (p. 110). Blasting starts at the foot of the notch. The company offers Noël money to shut his driving dam, then more money; it wants to move his camp up to the trees and build a tourist park; finally, it exchanges the trees for closing the gate. Proud, tired, and stubborn, he fells, bucks up, and skids the trees with Bangor. The work rejuvenates him; he shaves every day (as his friend Henry Coville does before he kills himself in "Kingdom County Come.") The trees turn out to be hollow: emblematically, they do not embody the "incorruptibility and permanence" he had attributed to them (p. 134). After months of drought, it begins to rain hard, presaging the Great Flood of 1927. The logging trucks cannot make it up the trace: he must send the logs down the river. Defiant to the end, he extracts his calked boots and pike pole from the pile of possessions that Bangor had packed for their emigration to Oregon, opens the bull wheel and center boom, and leaps onto a free log to send the logs downriver. Losing his balance, he catches his hook on the crosspiece, clinging to it with his good arm; when the crosspiece splits, he falls into the pond and drowns.

Edmund Fuller, writing in the *Wall Street Journal,* called the title novella "brilliantly done"; Geoffrey Wolff, in *New Times,* "at once noble and savagely comic"; and Noel Perrin, in *Inquiry,* "a fine strong piece of work." Don Mitchell, in *Vermont,* called the novella "about the life and death of an early eco-terrorist" his "favorite" (p. 312).

The stories in *Where the Rivers Flow North* are fluent, shapely, and wistful. In "Alabama Jones," William could join the girl he loves in a traveling carnival but chooses to stay in the Kingdom. After the bank threatens to foreclose on Burl's farm in "Burl," she makes and sells moonshine; a revenue agent does not arrest her but later returns to marry her. Walter helps his half-brother Eben in "First Snow" by banking his house against the snow and other neighborly gestures. Fed up with poverty and bad luck, Eben, for the first time in their lives, shuts his door in Walter's face. The dying owner of a missing pet peacock is inconsolable in "The Peacock"; to Henry Coville, the man's eyes seem "as lifeless and unresponding as the window curtains, hanging limp in the heat" (p. 41). Despite his father's scorn in "High Water," Waterman devises a way to cross a roaring river to save the heifers, sacrificing his beloved racing car. In "Kingdom County Come," Henry Coville, once a logger at Noël Lord's camp, had put his mask on a fellow

mule driver during a gas attack in the Great War and lost a lung. Back in the Kingdom, he works as a guide and bootlegger. His other lung is decaying. He travels by canoe to Lord's Bog, where he shelters in a beaver house. With "meticulous concern for detail" (p. 66), he shaves every day. When he cuts his wrists, he reflects that "the cedar water was too dark to stain, and the translation was not unpleasant, less like departing his life than joining the bog" (p. 72).

The stories were praised by Dean Flower in the *Hudson Review* as "scrupulously made, clean of affectation as newly-planed boards, and subtly mortised and tenoned"; by Edmund Fuller in the *Wall Street Journal* as "superior work, rich in texture and character"; and by Don Mitchell in *Vermont* as "haunting and accessible" (p. 312).

Chris Braithwaite of the *Chronicle* (Barton, Vermont), found the novel "readable, absorbing, well and carefully plotted, at times exciting and at times amusing." The *Christian Science Monitor*'s Bruce Allen disagreed, calling it "formula fiction," only of interest "because it's always worth observing what a really first-rate writer is attempting."

MARIE BLYTHE *AND* A STRANGER IN THE KINGDOM

The adversity met by the title character in *Marie Blythe* (1983), Mosher's second novel, reflects Jane Kinneson's maxim in *On Kingdom Mountain*: "Strife [is] the way of the world" (p. 109). Marie's challenges begin in 1899 when she, her French Canadian father, and half-Indian mother are smuggled in a cattle car to Hell's Gate, a mill town (modeled on Chichester) near Kingdom Common run by the paternalistic Captain Benedict. Marie faces intimidating odds, which she confronts with determination and intelligence. Her parents die; Benedict's son seduces her; she suffers a miscarriage. She picks potatoes and drives horses in a pulp camp in the Allagash. (The foreman, her companion, goes through the ice with his team. "He could have jumped clear, but didn't," she proudly reports to the boss, p. 176.) She supports herself as a dancer, spends time in jail, contracts consumption, and becomes a nurse in the state sanatorium. Back at Hell's Gate, she varnishes chairs during the day and learns to read and write at night. In a metaphor for Marie's life, "the trout kept coming, jumping, tailwalking, falling back, gathering strength ... then coming again ... the fish was going to reach the pools above or beat itself to death trying" (pp. 285–286).

"The real key" to his third novel, *A Stranger in the Kingdom*, published in 1989, "was the trout-fishing Kinneson family, which in many ways resembles my own extended family," wrote Mosher in *North Country* (p. 102). Charles MacPhearson Kinneson, born in Scotland in 1730, was a pirate before applying for a New Hampshire Land Grant. He came to northern Vermont in 1781, married Memphremagog (Beautiful Waters), the daughter of Sabattis, an Abenaki trapper and storyteller, and founded the *Kingdom Monitor.* He built potato distilleries to fund the establishment of the First Reformed Presbyterian Church. His brother, True Teague, was with Ethan Allen at Fort Ticonderoga; his son James was involved with a Fenian invasion of Canada; his son Ticonderoga went out west in 1804 with Uncle True. James's son, Charles (Mad Charlie), killed the slave hunter Satan Smithfield and brought the former slave Pliny Templeton to Vermont via the Underground Railroad in 1840. Charles's first wife was Belinda, the daughter of John Brown, with whom Charles set up the eastern-Vermont-to-Montreal leg of the Underground Railroad. Charles's second wife, the gypsy Replacement Mari, was the mother of Elijah, Welcome, and Resolvèd Kinneson. Charles murdered Pliny over the split between the Reformed and United wings of the Presbyterian Church and was put in Waterbury asylum. His son, James, was editor of what was by then called the *Kingdom County Monitor* when Teddy Roosevelt came through Vermont in 1912. James's son, Charles, continues the tradition as editor.

Charles Kinneson's family—his wife and sons, Charlie (a lawyer) and Jim (a teenager)—is engaging, close-knit, and life loving. In 1952 a new preacher, Walter Andrews, an African American former Royal Canadian Air Force of-

ficer, arrives from Canada with his son. (The novel was inspired by the Irasburg Affair, in which a black family moved to Irasburg in 1968, was attacked by night riders with shotguns, and driven out of town.) Some residents make racist remarks about the Andrews family. When the murdered and mutilated body of a young housekeeper hired by Resolvèd Kinneson is found in the quarry, a search turns up Andrews' RCAF service revolver. Arrested and jailed, Andrews hires Charlie to defend him; the Kinnesons are united in believing Andrews innocent. Editor Kinneson deplores "the class differences so insidiously entrenched in any small town" (p. 220). He wonders why there was a "conspiracy of silence" (p. 283) and why so few people defended Andrews. "If it was fear, fear of what, exactly? Of Negroes? Of outsiders, strangers? Of change?" (p. 406).

A Stranger in the Kingdom won the New England Book Award in 1991 as well as the ACLU Foundation of Vermont Civil Liberties in the Arts Award. Lee Smith, writing in the *New York Times,* found the book "that rarity, both a 'good read' and a fine novel." Grace Edwards-Yearwood wrote in the *Los Angeles Times:* "In this fine novel, Mosher ... avoids constructing larger than life heroes and avoids reducing the villains to stereotypical, bumbling bigots." Some critics found fault. In the *New York Times,* Christopher Lehmann-Haupt noted, "Its only real flaw is its occasional obviousness. You sometimes anticipate its next plot turn by as many as a dozen pages." William O'Rourke, in *Signs of the Literary Times,* disliked the "false charm ... that is often more annoying than ingratiating" and the "colorful cartoon characters" (p. 145).

NORTHERN BORDERS *AND* THE FALL OF THE YEAR

In Mosher's fourth novel, *Northern Borders* (1994), Austen reminisces about his Kittredge ancestors, "existing in my memory, and on these pages, and nowhere else" (p. 291). His ancestor Sojourner Kittredge, a Loyalist schoolteacher and part-time sawyer, fled the American Revolution for Canada in 1775. At the headwaters of a river draining north, he thought he had reached Canada. He named the township Lost Nation and established a sawmill and the Atheneum country school. In 1790 he offered ten thousand acres to Vermont for a university. The state built one in Burlington but set aside a scholarship for the Atheneum. His great-grandson, Gleason, had two daughters, Maiden Rose and Liz; he named a foundling Austen Gleason Kittredge, who, raised by Aunt Maiden Rose, worked the farm and sawmill. Austen's wife, Abiah, was an orphan from the British Isles. Austen, their grandson, comes to live in Lost Nation in 1948 to take advantage of the family scholarship.

Austen narrates his coming-of-age in discrete stories about life with his grandparents on the farm. Remaining neutral in their Forty Years' War with each other, he reveals his grandfather's humanity, adopting a circus elephant and helping a French Canadian family in hard times; and his cussedness, raising the level of his millpond and endangering his wife's precious apple orchard. Austen links farming chores with the "harsh yet lovely cycles of the natural world around us" (p. 174). He describes the Kittredge reunion for the ritual cleaning of the ancestral graveyard, "our visible link with the past" (p. 206), and the Shakespeare play mounted each year, "despite all of the hardship and loss and despair on that remote, soon-to-be-abandoned farm in northern Vermont" (p. 228). Austen evokes the sweetness in the crusty old man's behavior toward him, the heartbreak in the revelation that the Indian woman he had loved in Labrador died in childbirth, and the praise in his farewell words: "You're a good fella to go down the river with" (p. 289).

Northern Borders was a *New York Times* Notable Book of the Year (1994); *School Library Journal* best adult book for high school students (1995); one of two hundred book club favorites in *The Readers' Choice* (2000); one of the best novels of the nineties in *A Reader's Guide* (2000); and a book of recognized merit in *Dictionary of American Children's Fiction* (2002). Fannie Flagg wrote in the *New York Times* that Mosher has "a remarkable ability to tell a story and to create

characters with truth and integrity without using gimmicks." Chris Goodrich, in the *Los Angeles Times,* found "Mosher has constructed the book like sedimentary rock, each chapter a stratum in young Austen's life and the layers becoming more dense, more profound, as the novel progresses." Thomas Bahr, in *Agni,* demurred: "The episodic structure of the narrative sometimes feels stitched together rather than organic."

In Mosher's fifth novel, *The Fall of the Year* (1999), Father George Lecoeur writes in his history: "The village of Kingdom Common could be a remarkably tolerant place to live and work and raise a family. Or it could be as cruel as any place on the face of the earth" (p. 7). Born in 1890, Lecoeur flew in the Great War, bought with whiskey-smuggling money Twilight Anderson's Big House, and was "an unorthodox priest and greatest scholar and third baseman in the history of Kingdom County" according to Frank Bennett, the narrator of the novel (p. 3). Through Father George's tutelage, Frank becomes a man. He befriends an idiot savant ill used by the village, draws lessons from Father George's mediating skills with a feuding family, and sympathizes with a Chinese gentleman who is clever, hardworking, and cruelly deported by the town officers as an enemy alien. Frank teaches Father George's citizenship class for immigrants, challenging the town's attempts to sabotage it, and plays guide to an illusionist whom the town tries to cheat out of his fee. In Little Quebec he meets the gypsy clairvoyant Louvia and the young woman Chantal, whose blue eyes are "the color of the morning glories on the railing" (p. 34). Frank works on his whiskey-smuggling novel, reads chapters of Father George's manuscript, and (true to Jane's adage in *On Kingdom Mountain,* "All the best stories are about love," p. 276) discovers first love and the secret concerning Father George and Louvia. (Other hidden lovers in Mosher's fiction are Grandfather Kittredge and Myra in *Northern Borders,* and Morgan Kinneson and Slidell Dinwiddie and Pilgrim Kinneson and Manon Thibeau in *Walking to Gatlinburg.*)

The Fall of the Year was a Book Sense 76 Top Ten Pick in 1999. Sudip Bose in the *Washington Post* called it "an elegy for a disappearing place." Kimberly B. Marlowe, writing in the *New York Times,* found that "each exchange between the two [Frank and Father George] is a small story in itself, in dialogue so right that you feel like you're eavesdropping on a small, special world."

"SECOND SIGHT" AND THE TRUE ACCOUNT

The chapters of Mosher's story "Second Sight" accompany photographs of the Northeast Kingdom in John M. Miller's *Granite & Cedar* (2001). The state plans to build Interstate 91 directly through Kingdom County and the Kingdom Mountain cemetery, where Jane Hubbell's parents are buried. Jane, born in 1887 and reputed to have second sight, has always lived on Kingdom Mountain. She accepts the inevitable (the interstate is as inexorable as the glacier that carved out the Kingdom's hills and valleys a thousand years earlier) but insists upon moving her parents' bodies before the state sets foot on her property. On the way to the cemetery, Jane and her nephew Rob pass the cellar holes and barn foundations of long-abandoned farmsteads. Rob studies a gravestone inscription: "A Canuck Lumberjack. Died Fightin" (p. 56). (In *North Country,* Mosher spies a grave marked "Chas Dewey Age 33 Died Fighten," p. 73). Rob worries about the advent of summer people's houses; Jane thinks second homes are better than no homes.

In Mosher's sixth novel, *The True Account: A Novel of the Lewis & Clark & Kinneson Expeditions* (2003), True Kinneson asserts, "The greatest achievements in the history of the world have all sprung from the imagination" (p. 160). An adventurer, angler, and playwright, he tutors his nephew Ticonderoga (Ti), age seventeen. In 1804 True, hearing that President Jefferson seeks to discover a route by river to the Pacific, applies to lead the expedition. A bemused Jefferson has already chosen Captains Meriwether Lewis and William Clark but gives the Kinnesons twenty gold pieces, a horse, and a mule. Setting out on their two-year trek, True and Ti confer with Lewis and Clark in their winter quarters in St. Louis. The heart of the story is True's chivalry

and sense of fair play: the ensuing race to the Pacific would be meaningless without helping Lewis and Clark with "good old-fashioned Vermont ingenuity" (p. 201). He rescues the Corps of Discovery numerous times through his inventiveness, although the captains are often dismissive of him and Ti and unappreciative of the Indians. True and Ti reach the Pacific and win the competition. Lewis complains of protecting and assisting people "who had been nothing but a thorn in his side since leaving St. Louis" (p. 315). Earlier, in a fight with the Sioux, Ti is horrified at his own "capacity for barbarism," reminiscent of Morgan Kinneson's repugnance at some of his actions in *Walking to Gatlinburg*. Ti marries a Blackfoot, Yellow Sage Flower Who Tells Wise Stories, and becomes the first American painter of Louisiana; True marries and takes Flame Danielle Boone back to Vermont.

The True Account was a Book Sense 76 Top Ten Pick in 2003. Matt Schudel wrote in the *Washington Post* that Mosher's "elaborate conceit in this clever piece of revisionist fiction is to publish what purports to be a 19th-century manuscript telling what really happened on that mythic American odyssey." Michael McGregor, writing in the *Oregon Historical Quarterly,* remarked that "it is Mosher's willingness to unleash his imagination that makes his book succeed." He averred that Mosher's main inspiration was "the western world's first novel, Don Quixote," a connection also made by the *Virginia Quarterly Review* ("some of the most outrageous and endearing characters we have seen since the writings of Cervantes") and Barbara Lloyd McMichael in the *Seattle Times* ("a Yankee Don Quixote").

WAITING FOR TEDDY WILLIAMS *AND* ON KINGDOM MOUNTAIN

In *Waiting for Teddy Williams* (2004), Mosher's seventh novel, Ethan (E. A.) Allen descends from Colonel Ethan Allen, the outlaw-hero in the struggle between the New Hampshire Grants and the Yorkers, who, with his brother, General Ira Allen, built the Canada Post Road to smuggle cattle across the border. His grandson, Emancipator, used it to carry fugitive slaves to Canada and was hanged with John Brown at Harpers Ferry in 1859. His son, Patrick, tried with inebriated friends to annex the province of Quebec and was killed by local farmers. Patrick's son, Gleason, went mad and tried to blow up his family members in their beds (something his own great-great-grandfather endeavored but failed to do, Mosher has said in interviews). Gleason's son, Outlaw, ran whiskey on the Post Road and was shot by federal revenuers. His daughter was the mother of Gypsy Lee Allen.

On one level, this novel is a gratifying baseball story; at its core, it is the classical quest of a son for his father. Eight-year-old E. A. lives with his grandmother and his mother, Gypsy Lee, who supports them by writing and singing songs in neighboring taverns (one of the songs, "Nobody's Child," was written and recorded by Mosher's daughter). E. A. longs to discover the identity of his father; his sole confidant is the statue of Colonel Allen on the green. Sharing Kingdom County's passion for baseball, E. A. and Gypsy build their own Fenway Park on Gran's meadow, where Gypsy tirelessly provides batting practice. A stranger comes to town and starts giving E. A. playing tips. E. A. learns that this "big, laconic, watchful" man, Teddy Williams, is his father, on parole after eight years in prison for killing two high school boys in an automobile accident (p. 89). E. A. and his father gradually form a bond as they work on E. A.'s pitching. Their developing relationship is as moving and significant as the thrilling finale, when an eighteen-year-old E. A. pitches for the Red Sox with one game in the balance. Gypsy, Teddy, and the Outlaws, the town team, are in the Boston stadium to cheer for this son of Kingdom Common.

Waiting for Teddy Williams was the number one Book Sense Pick in September 2004 and a Book Sense Book of the Year finalist for the same year; *Publishers Weekly* gave it a starred review. David Hinckley observed in the *New York Daily News* that Mosher "doesn't hesitate to stack improbable plot devices alongside true-life wisdom about the game of baseball, and he has

the writing skills to make them work together like a well-turned double play." Yvonne Daley, in her *Vermont Writers: A State of Mind,* wrote, "like so many of Mosher's tales, this is a story of hope, of overcoming adversity, of the strength of the human spirit" (p. 38). The *Denver Post*'s Ron Franscell noted that "Mosher's blend of quirky characters, contemporary mythology, and mischievous prose is utterly original and entertaining." However, Barbara Lloyd McMichael of the *Seattle Times* found the plotting "episodic," the outcome "predictable," and the "baseball fantasia to be too feel-good to be true."

In Mosher's eighth novel, *On Kingdom Mountain* (2007), Jane Kinneson, defending her ancestral land against a proposed state highway, asserts that "to a true Kingdom Mountain Kinneson, progress is saving the last of our dwindling wild countryside for future generations so that they may know where they came from and who their ancestors were and, knowing that, have a clearer idea of who they are and who they may yet become" (pp. 197–198). Her great-great-grandfather, Venturing Seth Kinneson, was captured as a boy by Jane's Memphremagog ancestors and witnessed his parents' killing by Indians. Seth walked to Kingdom Mountain from Massachusetts in 1775, pulling his sledge with one of his oxen, the injured one limping behind. He built a one-room log cabin for his wife, Huswife, and his small son, Freethinker, who later barricaded Lake Memphremagog in the War of 1812 and helped fugitive slaves and immigrants cross the border into Canada. His son, Quaker Meeting, had two sons, Pilgrim and Morgan, and adopted an abandoned Abenaki baby called Pharoah's Daughter. After returning from seeking Pilgrim, who vanished during the Battle of Gettysburg, Morgan married his stepsister, Pharoah's Daughter. His daughter, Jane Hubbell Kinneson, is, by her descent through her mother from Chief Joseph Hubert (anglicized to Hubbell), the last of the Memphremagog Abenakis.

In 1930, Jane is beautiful and fearless at fifty. She is adamant in her opposition to the Connector, which her cousin Eben proposes to build through her property to Canada, and fights its construction all the way to the United States Supreme Court. She is obsessed by family secrets, such as her Uncle Pilgrim's disappearance and her father Morgan's silence when he returned. She was deferential to her domineering father when he insisted that she stalk roebucks with him rather than attend the homecoming ball with Ira Allen, now a judge and widower who has thrice asked Jane to marry him. And she is vulnerable, falling in love with Henry Satterfield, a gentlemanly stunt pilot and possible bandit, who desires the gold left by Confederate raiders who robbed the local bank in 1864. Jane believes Kingdom Common is still a "civilized" village (p. 253), but when Henry, who is half Creole, flies over the water tower and sees a painted racial slur, he leaves, with the gold.

On Kingdom Mountain was a Book Sense Pick for August 2007. Joshua Henkin wrote in the *Boston Globe,* "Mosher has written a picaresque caper that is also a paean to a place and time, and he has done so with sentiment but without sentimentality." By contrast, Steve Amick remarked in the *Washington Post,* "Distracted by this sometimes mid-sentence wavering, I found myself struggling to get a handle on exactly whose consciousness I'd drifted into, overly aware of the storyteller pulling the strings." Barbara Lloyd McMichael of the *Seattle Times* wrote that "the plot hangs together by the thinnest of threads and relies on an almost inexcusable amount of coincidence."

WALKING TO GATLINBURG

The backdrop to *Walking to Gatlinburg* (2010), Mosher's ninth novel, is the Civil War: "The madness it had fomented infested the entire land" (p. 6). The household of seventeen-year-old Morgan Kinneson is a way station on the Underground Railroad. His older brother Pilgrim attended Harvard and, a pacifist, joined the Union Army as a medical officer. After Pilgrim vanishes during the Battle of Gettysburg, Morgan pledges to find him. All the Kinnesons are readers; the young Kinnesons are, prophetically, partial to *The Odyssey* and *Pilgrim's Progress.* Morgan's "odyssey" (pp. 4, 30, 300) begins in 1864 when

he escorts an aging fugitive slave, Jesse Moses, to the last station before Canada. Morgan sneaks away to hunt a moose: returning, he finds Jesse, hanged. Guilt-stricken, he shoots Ludi Too, Jesse's murderer and one of four psychopathic convicts who escaped execution at a prison in Elmira. The others are still at large and on his trail. Into Morgan's pocket Jesse had slipped a stone map with runes carved on it, signifying the way stations of the Underground Railroad.

Over the course of a year, Morgan's experiences, making his hazardous and heroic way down the Great Smoky Mountains, transform him. He meets altruistic human beings and individuals of incalculable evil, all of whom are connected. He evolves from a boy running a trapline and milking his father's cows in Vermont to a man who concludes that retaliation is justified when faced with atrocities committed against innocents. As he proceeds south, he serially murders the killers pursuing him. Members of the Underground Railroad are unfailingly helpful. In an exquisitely detailed account, a blacksmith makes a rifle from Morgan's grandfather's old gun. The finished barrels, polished with beeswax, "had a blue-gray sheen, like the big lake at home under a gray November sky" (p. 151). Before he has quitted the abolitionist North, he has witnessed women, children, and old men being bid for on the block and a freed black woman abased for money. "He felt like a man at war, not with an enemy wearing a different-colored uniform, but with his former self" (p. 125). He falls in love with a fugitive slave named Slidell Dinwiddie. As a Christian, she cannot condone his actions, but her comforting words stay with him as he continues his quest: "If there was great and unspeakable evil in the world, was there not also ... great kindness and love?" (p. 299).

Walking to Gatlinburg received a *Kirkus* starred review. Bruce DeSilva of the Associated Press praised the story as "beautifully told in Mosher's charming, homespun style." Carolyn See of the *Washington Post* wrote, "The whole novel ... is a homage, not only to American life of the past but to American literature as well ... a welcome treat." In the *Boston Globe,* Katherine A. Powers noted the effects of the Civil War on Mosher's "ravaged phantasmagorical world."

SEEKING A VANISHING WAY OF LIFE

Mosher's memoir, *North Country: A Personal Journey* (1997), depicts a cross-country trip along America's northernmost frontiers. Having witnessed a way of life "vanished like the dying elms on a thousand New England village greens," he wanted "to identify the qualities that characterized these regions, and to assess what they might look like twenty, fifty, one hundred years from now" (p. 2). On the route, he is curious, a good listener, engaged, appreciative (especially when he exchanges glances with a wolf), and intrepid. Interspersed with stories about the North Country are anecdotes about his life in the Northeast Kingdom. As he travels slowly west, he feels, like Nick Adams, he is witnessing "the end of something" (p. 7).

A fisherman in Lubec, Maine, tells him that he has seen his community transformed from a prosperous port to a dying fishing village. Describing the fragility of the landscape, a Québécois bush pilot urges Mosher to write that once it is gone it will not come back. In Akwesasne Mohawk Territory, Dr. Solomon Cook envisions an active seaport that will one day guarantee jobs and prosperity. At the Timber Wolf Point Resort in Minnesota, the owner considers his job not a business but a way of life worth holding on to. A rancher in Warroad, Minnesota, intends to keep farming and does not care how many part-time jobs it takes. In Montana, John Olson says the residents are careful not to intrude but watch out for each other. At Big Beaver, Saskatchewan, customs agent Rick Gilmore believes writers like A. B. Guthrie, Wallace Stegner, and Norman Maclean have preserved the past in their books. The Blackfoot rancher Rob Powell tells him living in the mountains gives "a special, almost mystical feel for the land and everything that lives and grows on it" (p. 200). In the Yaak Valley of Montana, the hunting guide Jack Pride believes "we know how to handle our wilderness responsibly, and intend to. That way, the Yaak will be the last best place for a long time to come—for everybody" (p. 217).

David M. Shribman, writing in the *Boston Globe,* found that the memoir "has the humanity that permeates his novels, the irony ... , and the sense of mystery." Thomas McNamee remarked in the *New York Times,* "Lost souls, lonely places, and small pleasures alike have their particular dignity when Mr. Mosher shines the light of his sympathy on them." Richard Wolkomir wrote in *Smithsonian,* "What Mosher discovers on his trip is his own borderlands life." Noel Perrin noted in the *Washington Post,* "The good in this book is very good. Mosher is an excellent reporter." Gavin Scott, writing in the *Chicago Tribune,* faulted what he termed Mosher's "literary reach." The title "seems more redolent of Chamber of Commerce boosterism and wistful General Store calendars than political fact."

INTRODUCING THE WORK OF OTHERS

The books bearing Mosher's introductions and forewords concern topics he has cherished throughout his writing career: lyrical writing about the natural world, conservation and preservation, oral histories and legends of a lost way of life, and the wilderness, particularly Labrador.

For *Songs of the North: A Sigurd Olson Reader* (1987), Mosher chose essays that reflect "the serenity and positivism of Sigurd Olson the man, his passionate vision as a preservationist, and his range, power, and lyricism as a nature writer" (p. xi). Olson read broadly from authors dear to Mosher: Henry David Thoreau, Walt Whitman, Ernest Hemingway, the voyageur poet William Henry Drummond, and the nineteenth-century explorers David Thompson and Alexander Mackenzie (whose maps True Kinneson studies in *The True Account*).

In his foreword to *Deer Camp: Last Light in the Northeast Kingdom* (1992), Mosher salutes John M. Miller's photographs, which celebrate "hunters and the wild and remote places where they hunt" and the personal narratives that "record a way of life passed down from generation to generation since the first hunter set foot in Vermont's Green Mountains" (p. xii). Mosher's foreword to Joseph A. Citro's *Green Mountain Ghosts, Ghouls, and Unsolved Mysteries* (1994) hails a "splendid gallery" of "spine-tingling" ghost stories, "horrific" historical events, "outrageous" Vermont characters, and "inexplicable happenings" (p. 12).

In his introduction to James West Davidson and John Rugge's *Great Heart: The History of a Labrador Adventure* (1997), Mosher presents the background to the tale. In 1903 Leonidas Hubbard Jr. set off with Dillon Wallace and George Elson to explore the interior of the Labrador-Ungava peninsula. Hubbard died on the journey while Wallace lived to narrate the story of their odyssey in the popular book *The Lure of the Labrador Wild* (as a child, Mosher read a battered copy in his grandparents' attic). Leonidas' widow publicly disputed his account, with the result that she and Wallace mounted competing expeditions in 1905; both wrote books describing their journeys. The theme of *Great Heart* is that the "great wilderness where its story took place is now shrinking fast, and treasuring the book may well be one of the best ways to preserve what is still left unspoiled of the land itself" (p. xix).

In his foreword to *Notes Left Behind: Last and Selected Poems* (1997) Mosher celebrates James Hayford's "golden legacy," a selection of poems that are "gloriously in touch with the natural world we all once lived in" (p. xi). Mosher's introduction to Reginald Bennett's *The Mountains Look Down: A History of Chichester, a Company Town in the Catskills* (1999) portrays the town where Mosher grew up and the character of the author. The book is "a shining tribute to the truth about a bygone way of life"; Bennett was "a Chichester native with a profound vision of the past and how it shapes the future" (p. 13).

LOOKING BACK—AND FORTH

Mosher's generous, ebullient, nostalgic exploration of Kingdom County and its inhabitants introduces and illuminates a vanished world. The special and engaging features of that world cannot be seen again but endure in his trenchant and accessible fiction.

Selected Bibliography

WORKS OF HOWARD FRANK MOSHER

NOVELS, SHORT STORIES, ESSAYS, AND MEMOIR

Disappearances. New York: Viking, 1977. Jaffrey, N.H.: A Nonpareil Book, David R. Godine, 1984. (Here and below, page citations in the text refer to the latter listed edition.)

Where the Rivers Flow North. Novella and six stories. New York: Viking, 1978. New York: Penguin, 1985.

Marie Blythe. New York: Viking, 1983. New York: Penguin, 1985.

A Stranger in the Kingdom. New York: Doubleday, 1989. New York: Laurel Trade Paperback, Dell, 1989.

Northern Borders. New York: Doubleday Delta, 1994.

North Country: A Personal Journey Through the Borderland. Boston: Houghton Mifflin, 1997. Boston: Mariner Books, 1998.

"Thunder From a Cloudless Sky." Published in *Washington Post Magazine,* July 12, 1998. (Essay.)

The Fall of the Year. Boston: Houghton Mifflin, 1999. Boston: Mariner Books, 2000.

"Second Sight." In *Granite & Cedar: The People and the Land of Vermont's Northeast Kingdom.* Photographs by John M. Miller. North Pomfret, Vt.: Thistle Hill Publications; Middlebury: Vermont Life Center, 2001. Distributed by University Press of New England.

The True Account: A Novel of the Lewis & Clark & Kinneson Expeditions. Boston: Houghton Mifflin, 2003. Boston: Mariner Books, 2003.

Waiting for Teddy Williams. Boston: Houghton Mifflin, 2004.

On Kingdom Mountain. Boston: Houghton Mifflin, 2007.

Walking to Gatlinburg. New York: Shaye Areheart, 2010.

FOREWORDS, INTRODUCTIONS, AND EDITIONS

Introduction to *Songs of the North: A Sigurd Olson Reader.* Edited by Howard Frank Mosher. New York: Penguin, 1987.

Foreword to *Deer Camp: Last Light in the Northeast Kingdom.* Photographs and text by John M. Miller. Edited by Meg Ostrum. Cambridge, Mass.: MIT Press; Middlebury: Vermont Folklife Center, 1992.

Foreword to *Green Mountain Ghosts, Ghouls, and Unsolved Mysteries,* by Joseph A. Citro. Montpelier: Vermont Life; Shelburne, Vt.: Chapters, 1994.

Introduction to *Great Heart: The History of a Labrador Adventure,* by James West Davidson and John Rugge. New York: Kodansha International, 1997.

Foreword to *Notes Left Behind: Last and Selected Poems,* by James Hayford. Burlington, Vt.: Oriole Books, 1997.

Introduction to *The Mountains Look Down: A History of Chichester, a Company Town in the Catskills,* by Reginald Bennett. Fleischmanns, N.Y.: Purple Mountain Press, 1999.

ARCHIVES

The Howard Frank Mosher papers are held at the University Archives of the University of Vermont. The collection contains correspondence, several manuscript drafts (including "The Counterman," a 1988 draft of *A Stranger in the Kingdom*, sections of *Northern Borders*, and an unpublished work titled "The Chief"), reviews, awards, contracts, financial records, and published works.

REVIEWS

Anonymous. *Virginia Quarterly Review* 79 (autumn 2003), p. 130. (Review of *The True Account: A Novel of the Lewis and Clark and Kinneson Expeditions.*)

Allen, Bruce. *Christian Science Monitor,* January 9, 1984, p. 20. (Review of *Marie Blythe.*)

Amick, Steve. "Exploring a Lighthearted Landscape." *Washington Post,* July 12, 2007, p. C9. (Review of *On Kingdom Mountain.*)

Bahr, Thomas. "Howard Frank Mosher's *Northern Borders.*" *Agni* 41:187–188 (1995).

Bose, Sudip. "God's Little Acre." *Washington Post,* October 17, 1999, p. X3. (Review of *The Fall of the Year.*)

Braithwaite, Chris. "Howard Mosher Returns with Success." *Chronicle* (Barton, Vt.), November 9, 1983, pp. 23–24. (Review of *Marie Blythe.*)

Danziger, Jeff. Review of *A Stranger in the Kingdom* . *Christian Science Monitor,* September 20, 1989, p. 13.

DeSilva, Bruce. "Mosher's *Walking to Gatlinburg* Is Epic Tale of Heroism." *Pittsburgh Tribune-Review,* March 7, 2010, p. F4.

Edwards-Yearwood, Grace. "Hidden Hypocrisy in a Vermont Idyll." *Los Angeles Times,* November 12, 1989, p. 12. (Review of *A Stranger in the Kingdom.*)

Flagg, Fannie. "The 40 Years' Domestic War." *New York Times Book Review,* September 4, 1994. (Review of *Northern Borders.*)

Flower, Dean. "Picking Up the Pieces." *Hudson Review* 32, no. 2:293–307 (summer 1979). (Review of *Where the Rivers Flow North.*)

Franscell, Ron. "Northwestward Ho! Pvt. Kinneson's Trailblazing Lightens Up Extensive Coverage of Lewis and Clark." *Denver Post,* June 1, 2003, Pp. EE-01. (Review of *The True Account: A Novel of the Lewis and Clark and Kinneson Expedition.*)

———. "Baseball Gets New Classic: Poignant Tale Strikes Nostalgic Chords." *Denver Post,* August 8, 2004, p. F11. (Review of *Waiting for Teddy Williams.*)

Frank, Sheldon. "A Mix of Tall Tales." *New York Times Book Review,* February 5, 1978. (Review of *Disappearances.*)

Fuller, Edmund. "A Pride of Short Story Collections." *Wall Street Journal,* October 30, 1978, p. 24. (Review of *Where the Rivers Flow North.*)

Goldberg, Carole. "A Singular Sense of Self, A Dogged Defense of Place." *Hartford Courant,* July 8, 2007, p. G3. (Review of *On Kingdom Mountain.*)

Goodrich, Chris. "A Complex, Yet Idyllic, Story of Childhood in Vermont." *Los Angeles Times,* September 27, 1994, p. E5. (Review of *Northern Borders.*)

Henkin, Joshua. "Characters, Story Move 'Mountain.'"" *Boston Globe,* July 24, 2007. (Review of *On Kingdom Mountain.*)

LeClair, Thomas. "Books—Critics Choices for Christmas." *Commonweal,* December 9, 1977, pp. 796–797. (Review of *Disappearances.*)

Lehmann-Haupt, Christopher. "Ugly Racial Feelings and Murder in a Not-So-Idyllic Vermont." *New York Times Book Review,* October 26, 1989, p. C25. (Review of *A Stranger in the Kingdom.*)

Marlowe, Kimberly B. Review of *The Fall of the Year. New York Times Book Review,* November 7, 1999.

McGregor, Michael. Review of *The True Account: A Novel of the Lewis and Clark and Kinneson Expeditions. Oregon Historical Quarterly,* fall, 2004, p. 524.

McMichael, Barbara Lloyd. "A Yankee Don Quixote on The Trail of Lewis and Clark." *Seattle Times,* June 20, 2003, p. H41. (Review of *The True Account: A Novel of the Lewis and Clark and Kinneson Expeditions.*)

———. "Baseball and Boyhood in a Batty Burg." *Seattle Times,* July 30, 2004, p. H39. (Review of *Waiting for Teddy Williams.*)

———. "A Search for Gold Turns Up Romance." *Seattle Times,* July 22, 2007, p. K10. (Review of *On Kingdom Mountain.*)

McNamee, Thomas. "Borderline Cases." *New York Times Book Review,* May 11, 1997, p. 12. (Review of *North Country.*)

Mitchell, Rob. "Sox Fan's Coming-of-Age Tale in a League of Its Own." *Boston Herald,* August 29, 2004, p. 35. (Review of *Waiting for Teddy Williams.*)

Perrin, Noel. "The Myth of Land." *Inquiry* 2, no. 1:20–21 (1978). (Review of *Where the Rivers Flow North.*)

———. "The Road Not Taken." *Washington Post,* May 18, 1997, p. X10. (Review of *North Country.*)

Powers, Katherine A.. "The Distinct Literary Landscape of Weimar Noir." *Boston Globe,* May 2, 2010. (Review of *Walking to Gatlinburg.*)

Schudel, Matt. "Discovery Channels." *Washington Post,* June 8, 2003, p. T7. (Review of *The True Account: A Novel of the Lewis and Clark and Kinneson Expeditions.*)

Scott, Gavin. "In Search of Adventure Along the U.S.–Canadian Border." *Chicago Tribune,* June 29, 1997, p. 7. (Review of *North Country.*)

See, Carolyn. Review of *Walking to Gatlinburg. Washington Post,* March 19, 2010, p. C3.

Shribman, David M. "On the line 'twixt states and provinces." *Boston Globe,* June 15, 1997. (Review of *North Country.*)

Smith, Lee. "The Case of the Hopeless Case." *New York Times Book Review,* October 29, 1989. (Review of *A Stranger in the Kingdom.*)

Taliaferro, Frances. Review of *Disappearances. Harper's Magazine,* January, 1978, p. 86.

Wolff, Geoffrey. "Kingdom County Has Come: Welcome." *New Times* 12, no. 11:85–86 (1978). (Review of *Where the Rivers Flow North.*)

Wolkomir, Richard. Review of *North Country. Smithsonian* 28, no. 6 (September 1997).

INTERVIEWS

Bacon, Katy. "A Disappearing Eden." *Atlantic Unbound,* October 2, 1997 (http://www.theatlantic.com/past/docs/unbound/bookauth/hfmint.htm).

Dougherty, Robin. "Finding One's Way Back into the Past." *Boston Globe,* June 15, 2003, p. H8.

Fulton, Ben. "New England Odyssey." *Salt Lake Tribune,* April 8, 2010 (http://www.sltrib.com/sltrib/lifestyle/49366485-80/mosher-vermont-war-walking.html.csp).

Zaino, Nick. "Howard Frank Mosher: An American Writer." *Optimistic Curmudgeon,* October 26, 2007 (http://optimisticcurmudgeon.blogspot.com/2007_10_01_archive.html).

OTHER SOURCES

Daley, Yvonne. *Vermont Writers: A State of Mind.* Hanover, N.H.: University Press of New England, 2005.

Delbanco, Nicholas, and Laurence Goldstein, eds. *Writers and Their Craft: Short Stories and Essays on the Narrative.* Detroit: Wayne State University Press, 1991.

Ellis, Ron, ed. *Of Woods and Waters: A Kentucky Outdoors Reader.* Lexington: University Press of Kentucky, 2005.

Franklin, Wayne, and Michael Steiner. "Taking Place: Toward the Regrounding of American Studies." In their *Mapping American Culture.* Iowa City: University of Iowa Press, 1995.

Mitchell, Don. "Recommended Reading: Fiction and Poetry." In his *Vermont.* New York and London: Fodor's, 2001. (Photography by Luke Powell.)

O'Rourke, William. *Signs of the Literary Times: Essays, Reviews, Profiles, 1970–1992.* Albany: State University of New York Press, 1993.

Parini, Jay. *One Matchless Time: A Life of William Faulkner.* New York: HarperCollins, 2004.

Ringel, Faye. *New England's Gothic Literature: History and Folklore of the Supernatural from the Seventeenth Through the Twentieth Centuries.* Lewiston, N.Y.: E. Mellen Press, 1995.

Rutkowska, Malgorzata. *In Search of America: The Image of the United States in Travel Writing of the 1980s and 1990s.* Lublin, Poland: UMCS, 2006.

Sherman, Joe. *Fast Lane on a Dirt Road: Vermont Transformed, 1945–1990.* Woodstock Vt.: Countryman Press, 1991.

Stegner, Wallace. "The Sense of Place." In his *Where the Bluebird Sings to the Lemonade Springs: Living and Writing in the West.* New York: Random House, 1992.

Verducci, Tom. "At the End of the Curse, A Blessing." Published in *Sports Illustrated: Great Baseball Writing.* New York: Time Home Entertainment Inc., 2005.

FILMS BASED ON THE WORKS OF HOWARD FRANK MOSHER

High Water. Directed by Jay Craven. Catamount Arts, 1989.

Where the Rivers Flow North. Directed by Jay Craven. Kingdom County Productions, 1994.

Stranger in the Kingdom. Directed by Jay Craven. Kingdom County Productions, 1997.

Disappearances. Directed by Jay Craven. Kingdom County Productions, 2006.

ALICE NOTLEY

(1945—)

Karin Gottshall

"My own lifelong project," Alice Notley writes in the preface to her 2005 collection of essays, *Coming After,* "has been twofold: to be a woman poet taking up as much literary space as any male poet, but most especially through poetry to discover The Truth" (p. vi). This twofold project has found expression in a body of work consisting of some thirty-five books written over four decades, books which have approached "truth" from a wide range of perspectives. In the imagistic, lyrical poems of the 1970s and *The Descent of Alette,* Notley's 1996 feminist epic, as well as in the autobiographical poems of *Mysteries of Small Houses* (1998) and the densely written narrative work of the 2000s, Notley has continuously found new, inventive structures and forms to guide her truth-seeking. As Joel Brouwer wrote in the *New York Times* in 2007, Notley has been "assigned ... any number of identities: native of the American West, Parisian expatriate, feminist, experimentalist, political poet, Language poet ... and member of the New York School's second generation, to name a few. Each of these labels sheds a little light on Notley's work, but it's the fact of their sheer number that's most illuminating: this is a poet who persistently exceeds, or eludes, the sum of her associations" ("A State of Disobedience").

Over and over in Notley's work the quest for truth seems to center on the problem of identity: What constitutes a unique and authentic self within the intimacy of family, and where does the desire to merge into love and the family unit tense against the desire to maintain one's individuality? More broadly, what constitutes a unique self as independent from the cultural and historical forces that impact the individual, and how can the experience of that distinct self be meaningfully expressed to others? Given this concern, it makes sense that among Notley's other subjects, especially in her more recent work, would be the politics of oppression—forces that directly and indirectly shape and stunt the formation and coherence of identity, especially female identity.

"It's disgusting," Notley writes in *Coming After,* "that one's content must be directed by the cruelty of others. But if one's purpose is a poet's traditional one of mediation between the soul ... and the world with its manifold tyrannies, one will include as content the stories of a harassed and rebellious life" (p. 65). Throughout her career Notley has sought this point of mediation, though the politics of identity in her poems have grown increasingly direct. In early poems, such as "Dear Dark Continent," from Notley's 1973 collection *Incidentals in the Day World,* nuances of feminine identity are explored in the context of family life: a subsuming of self—or danger of being subsumed—expressed in passages such as "I'm wife I'm mother I'm / myself and him and I'm myself and him and him" (reprinted in *Grave of Light,* 2006, p. 8). By contrast, in her book-length narrative of 2006, *Alma; or, The Dead Women,* which chronicles the terrorist attacks of September 11, 2001, and the buildup to war in Afghanistan and Iraq, Notley's politics are overt and strident. The book's characters—mythological beings serving as a kind of chorus commenting on the events as they unfold—scream and curse against war, violence, and oppression, try to find ways of existing in a world in which their interests are not represented or advocated for, and attempt to reconcile their desire for peace with feelings of outrage toward those holding the reins of power.

One outward signal of Notley's interest in feminine identity is the fact that seven of her

book titles contain women's names—most notably her own, in *Alice Ordered Me to Be Made* (1976). The practice of including her name is common in Notley's poetics—especially in the work of the 1970s, which has fewer of the fictional and mythological characters populating her later poems and is, rather, populated by Notley herself and her first husband, Ted Berrigan, and other friends and acquaintances. In the early poems, "Alice" draws attention to the poet herself as maker and embeds her as a character within the poem's frame.

Another name that has appeared frequently in Notley's work is that of her first husband, the poet Ted Berrigan. Berrigan, who died in 1983, is referenced in her early work as husband and partner, sometimes as antagonist. As members of what is known as the second generation of New York School poets, the two supported and influenced each other's work. Notley's first book, *165 Meeting House Lane* (1971), takes its title from the house in Southampton, Long Island, where Notley lived with Berrigan and composed the collection. As a series of sonnets, the book resonates with Berrigan's best-known work, *The Sonnets,* published in 1964. Indeed, throughout her career Notley has found inspiration in Berrigan's person and poetics. Sometimes the influence is clearly formal, as in the list poems "The 10 Best Weathers of 1983" and "The Ten Best Issues of Comic Books," contained in Notley's 1988 collection *At Night the States,* which echo poems such as "Things to Do in New York City" and "10 Things I Do Every Day" in Berrigan's collection *Many Happy Returns* (1968). In other poems, the influence is personal. Later poems, such as "I Must Have Called and So He Comes," in *Mysteries of Small Houses* (1998), contain or take the form of addresses to and conversations with Berrigan.

Often, Berrigan appears in dreams, or in dream spaces within the poems, such as "From the Dreams," from *At Night the States* (1987), which begins, "Come live on the floor with me, he / said, & I did that, gladly" (p. 43). Dreaming and dream imagery have always been important in Notley's poems. In her essay "Ron Padgett's Visual Imagination," she writes, "Much more mysterious than words, the figures in dreams are funny, elegant, and changeable. We think with them every night" (*Coming After,* p. 40). Notley often thinks with them in poems, too, mentioning dreams and dreaming as early as her first poem in her first book, and sometimes making poems of them entire—for example, the sequence "3 Dreams" in the 1976 collection *For Frank O'Hara's Birthday*, which recounts three dream situations without analysis or commentary apart from linguistic and formal choices. More recent works drift in and out of dreamscapes, and the surreal imagery and narrative of poems such as *The Descent of Alette* and *Alma; or, The Dead Women* owe much of their power and resonance to their resemblance to the "figures" and logic of dreams.

If identity and individuality are among Notley's fundamental concerns, the exploration of dream narratives and imagery provide a lens through which to catch a glimpse of an authentic self at the very point at which that self intersects with creative expression. In her later work, such as *Reason and Other Women* (2010), Notley explores the brain and neural experience itself, privileging typing errors and other unconscious acts of expression just as she has often privileged the unconscious gestures of dreams.

BIOGRAPHY

Alice Notley was born November 8, 1945, in Bisbee, Arizona, where her father, Albert Notley, worked at Bisbee Auto Supply. Her mother was born Beulah Oliver. In 1947 the family moved to Needles, California, where Notley was raised with three siblings and lived throughout her high school years. Her father was an employee and part-owner of Needles Auto Supply, and her mother was employed as a bookkeeper there.

Notley's parents hoped to give their children a Christian upbringing, though, as Notley writes in her autobiographical book *Tell Me Again* (1982), by the age of seven she "was already beginning to feel that what God was and how to live had to do with stories and poems and how they felt and sounded" (p. 5). At around age

fifteen she stopped attending church altogether. An avid reader, at age sixteen or seventeen she discovered Emily Dickinson and William Blake. "I think that without knowing it," she writes, "I was looking for something with as much resonance as the Bible to 'know by heart'—some words that could seduce me into a place of truth-knowing, but a place that gave a lot more comfort than the Bible ever had" (pp. 15–16).

After high school Notley attended Barnard College in New York City, earning a bachelor's degree in English in 1967. From there she went on to the Writers' Workshop at the University of Iowa. Dissatisfied, she left after one year, traveling to San Francisco, Spain, and Morocco, but returned to Iowa the following February and completed her master of fine arts degree in 1969. It was after her time away that Notley met the New York poet Ted Berrigan, who held a writer-in-residence post at the workshop. They were married in 1972, having by that time spent two years moving together from Iowa to Long Island, New York, Providence, and Bolinas, California. The couple settled for a time in Chicago, where Berrigan had a teaching post at Northeastern Illinois University and Notley edited the mimeographed magazine *CHICAGO*. In Chicago, Anselm Berrigan, their first child, was born.

In 1973 Notley moved with Berrigan and Anselm to England, where Berrigan took on a teaching post at the University of Essex. That year Notley's father died of cirrhosis of the liver. She writes in the *Contemporary Authors Autobiography (CAA)* series, "I ... flew to Needles a week or two before his death, and I had my final conversation with him and helped watch over him in the hospital as he entered a coma" (p. 226).

Notley and Berrigan's second child, Edmund, was born in 1974, and that year the family moved back to Chicago. The following year they moved to New York City. Berrigan by this time had contracted hepatitis, which severely damaged his liver, and would remain in poor health for the remainder of his life.

Living at 101 St. Mark's Place, the couple scraped together a living. Notley writes, "since we were a continuous open salon/workshop, we managed to extract bits of money and teensy loans in exchange for the reading of people's work" (*CAA,* p. 227). Notley also taught workshops at the Poetry Project of St. Mark's Church and received a National Endowment for the Arts grant.

Notley's first book, *165 Meeting House Lane,* was published in 1971, and she has published a book nearly every year since—in some years two. In regard to her poems of the 1970s and 1980s, Notley writes of the influence of other second-generation New York School poets, especially women, claiming they were "part of the first really strong and numerous generation of American women poets. With Anne Waldman and Bernadette Mayer, I was creating a certain female voice" (*CAA,* p. 229).

In July 1983 Berrigan died of cirrhosis of the liver, the same condition that killed Notley's father. She writes of her grief, "I learned that I'd been living on the surface of life and assuming too much the complacencies of my culture, that existence is not mysterious or that its mysteries will always be hidden from us, that the only truth lies in daily life and in the possibility of humane social interaction" (*CAA,* p. 231). After Berrigan's death, Notley lived on survivor's benefits, secretarial work for Allen Ginsberg, and the teaching of workshops.

In 1987 Ted Berrigan's daughter from a previous marriage, Kate, was killed in a traffic accident in New York. Notley had been close to Kate, and it was after this death that she began thinking of writing "something epic in scale, since being devastated by her death, I felt close to large dangerous powers" (*CAA,* p. 172).

Also in 1987, Notley began a romantic relationship with her longtime friend Douglas Oliver. Oliver moved to New York in 1988, and the two were married.

Tragedy struck again in 1988. Notley's brother, Albert, died of a morphine overdose after suffering post-traumatic stress disorder from his time serving in Vietnam. Notley writes that Albert's death "has been one of the most pivotal events of my life, crystallizing so much for me about politics, sexual politics, war, and poetry" (*CAA,* p. 234).

During the early 1990s Notley edited, with Oliver, the magazine *Scarlet,* and continued to teach and give readings. She also taught during the summer at the Naropa Institute in Boulder, Colorado. Anselm and Edmund left home for college; both have since become respected poets.

In 1992 Oliver took a position at the British Institute in Paris. Notley moved there with him, finally giving up the apartment on St. Mark's Place where she had lived since 1976. In Paris, Notley taught workshops and often returned to the United States to give readings and lectures. Of her life there, Notley wrote, "I write, I jog, I workshop people, I write a lot of letters. I dream all night about the geography of Needles" (*CAA,* p. 238).

In 2000 Douglas Oliver died of cancer. Notley has continued to reside in Paris since. In 2001 she told Brian Kim Stefans for the online magazine *Jacket*, "As much as I love New York, I felt a huge removal of pressure when I moved here, though I am very lonely" (December 2001).

Over her long career, Notley has garnered many awards for her poetry. She received a 1981 Poetry Center Book Award for *How Spring Comes,* a 1983 GE Foundation award, a Pulitzer Prize nomination and Los Angeles Times Book Prize in 1998 for *Mysteries of Small Houses,* an award from the American Academy of Arts and Letters and a Shelly Memorial Award from the Poetry Society of America in 2001. In 2007 she won a Lenore Marshall Prize for the Year's Most Outstanding Book of Poetry, selected by the Academy of American Poets, for *Grave of Light.*

WORKS: THE 1970S

In the author's note at the beginning of *Grave of Light: New and Selected Poems, 1970–2005* (2006), Notley writes: "My publishing history is awkward and untidy, though colorful and even beautiful" (p. xi). The Notley completist will discover the truth of this statement. The awkward untidiness is due to the fact that many of Notley's early books were published in long out-of-print, small editions by defunct presses. These can prove difficult and even impossible to find without great luck or deep pockets or both. Many of Notley's first collections, such as *165 Meeting House Lane,* which was published in a limited edition of 250 and features a cover illustration by the poet Philip Whalen, and *Incidentals in the Day World,* are artifacts of the proliferation in the 1970s of small-press mimeographed books published in editions of 250 or 500. Even some of Notley's more recent collections, such as *Iphigenia* (2002) and *From the Beginning* (2004), were published by small presses in such small numbers that they can prove difficult to lay hands on. This makes *Grave of Light* an especially useful volume. While the collection is limited in the space it can afford readily available works such as *Désamère* (1995) and *The Descent of Alette* (1996), it does contain many early poems and the otherwise rare *Iphigenia* in its entirety. Notley's unconventional publishing history, which has remained consistent across her career—even after her adoption by Penguin in the 1990s—can be seen as a metaphor for the maverick spirit that has infused her work and life.

Given Notley's interests in identity and the imagery and logic of dreams, it's fitting that the first poem in her first book, *165 Meeting House Lane*, published in 1971, begins with the lines "I dreamed of a clipper ship / Gold on blue THE CHASEY ALICE" (p. 1). The book contains twenty-four numbered sonnets of varying degrees of adherence to the most rigid demands of the form. Notley has always counted William Carlos Williams and Frank O'Hara among her primary influences, and the importance of both poets can be seen in *Meeting House*. Williams' influence is evident in the poems' spare, imagistic quality and their relaxed, loosely musical lines. Williams is also mentioned by name in sonnet 6, a poem listing things "We like," which also includes some anti-poetic items like "hypos," "moldy creepers," and "Mick / Jagger mouths" (p. 6). O'Hara's influence can be seen in the conversational tone throughout the book despite the poems' formalism, and in the poet's concern with and celebration of city life. An example is sonnet 3, which describes taking "The new way through town, snow still clean, warmer / I walk erect loose arms & red shawl scarf / New antique shops I'll never

enter" (p. 3). Though Notley was living on Long Island when she wrote this book, the tableaux of town and community life in *Meeting House* prefigure the poems she would later write about her life in New York City.

The city has itself been an important influence on Notley; it figures prominently in these early books as the backdrop for love and motherhood and intense engagement with language and, in later books, such as *The Descent of Alette* and *Reason and Other Women* (2010), as a kind of fantastical, metaphorical representation of inner life. In the preface to *Coming After,* Notley writes of the book reviews included: "It is important that all of the poets dealt with at length live or lived in cities.... I am that sort of poet too, and in that way I am always of the New York School and its friends.... I love the city voice and hate what the city has become and how the world has become a city" (p. vii). While the landscape of her childhood home—the desert Southwest—has also played an important role in Notley's poems, it is clear that the city as both setting and idea—especially New York and Paris, where she has spent most of her adult life—has gotten into her blood and imagination.

Notley's next two collections, *Phoebe Light* and *Incidentals in the Day World,* both published in 1973, show greater variety of form. They include free-verse poems, many of which relax across the page in long, staggered lines reminiscent of William Carlos Williams, interspersed with much more compact verses, some only one line long. Notley's more formal impulses are evident here as well. An example is the title poem of *Incidentals in the Day World,* a love poem to husband and baby, which carries a soft, chiming end rhyme, often slant, throughout. It begins:

> You and baby you know me and I am
> my ankles and angles and cavern–
> haired particular whim
>
> a bank of violets devours
> deposits itself again and again
>
> (reprinted in *Grave of Light*, p. 9)

The subtle music of these lines, their rising rhythms, the slant rhyme of am/whim/again, and the lack of punctuation typify the breezy, playful structures of these first books, and its subject of marriage, motherhood, and domestic concerns represents common early themes. It should be noted that *Phoebe Light* also contains a poem that is partially in prose, "The Development of My Mind and Character"—an early example of a form that continues to play an important role in Notley's work.

From Notley's next chapbook-length collection, *For Frank O'Hara's Birthday* (1976), only two poems are included in *Grave of Light:* "But He Says I Misunderstood" and "Your Dailiness." The first is an exploration of the lives of two poets, one male the other—the poem's speaker—female. The male poet teaches, has prestige, money, and "Power," while the female poet "got pregnant" and is "a slave, well mildly, to a baby" (reprinted in *Grave of Light*, p. 25). "Your Dailiness," a poem in epistolary form, is a meditation on death and loss in the context of motherhood and youth. Its descriptions of the deaths of family members, suicides, and dreams of death juxtapose poignantly with an account of the birth of the speaker's son. This poem was written while Notley was living in England, where "layers of death // pervade beautifully the beautiful landscape" (reprinted in *Grave of Light*, p. 24). "Your Dailiness" is a departure in form for Notley at this point: with its long, narrative lines and more conventional syntax and punctuation, the poem does build on earlier concerns with storytelling but more closely resembles physically poems Notley will write in the 1980s and 1990s.

Notley's next book, *Alice Ordered Me to Be Made* (1976), represents a departure in a different direction, one which also has roots in her earlier poems and is developed further in later work. Profoundly lyrical almost to the point of being pure poetry, the poems in *Alice* seem more Cubist or abstract, in the style of Gertrude Stein, than representational. Indeed, as the poet Robert Creeley writes in the blurb he provided for the book's cover, "extraordinary, Gertrude Stein–like realization of words as *feeling*." Context for the book's language-based "feeling" may be provided in Notley's endnote for the book's first poem, "Alice Ordered Me to Be Made": *"Near my father*

dying in hospital, April 1975" (p. 6). Seen as a response to loss, the book is poignant in its enactment of the ineffectuality of conventional syntax to express a very specific sadness. Notley's entirely subjective use of language is exemplified in poems such as "This Crazy Wickedness, Little Nests of Light," which closes with the lines,

Should I worship
Should I warship
This sound echo is always
clear to the ear
I long for my keep light
sail salt same say
raft rag rain
red silver trellis wait
sheltered inside my body shrine

(p. 17)

The wordplay of "worship"/"warship" and the accumulation of connotations and multiple meanings that results, the emotional content conveyed without the use of conventional narrative, is an example of the kind of complexity in this extraordinary and difficult book.

A Diamond Necklace (1977) marks a return to the loose sonnet form and also contains the rhyming ballad "Greensleeves," a romance about a harpist and a singer and the necessity for each of playing or singing his or her own music: "And the hell's that she never sings / To him the songs she loves him for" (p. 20). The book's long poem, "Hurricane Belle," is not included in *Grave of Light,* so presumably it was not deemed interesting enough for the volume by Notley. However, the poem is notable in that, in a book containing a number of poems in regular stanza forms and in rhyme, it is more imagistic and has the appearance of some of the earlier, Williams-inspired poems in the way it makes use of indentations and the full page to create a loose, scattered form reminiscent of Williams' variable foot.

Songs for the Unborn Second Baby (1979) returns to themes of domesticity and motherhood. The language of the book is somewhat abstracted in the manner of *Alice Ordered Me to Be Made,* but *Songs* is more narrative in structure and content, some sections even being divided into passages headed with dates, giving the whole a time line and sense of context. What's more, the theme of the book is more unified and focused, being closely arranged around aspects of pregnancy and motherhood. The book is one long poem in ten sections, and while it too makes use of the page-filling, variously indented style inherited from Williams, and much of it is in breathy, long, free-verse lines, the poem does coalesce at points into brief, short-lined, songlike passages. For example:

My God
is that I've
stolen already
breast and pit
from and for it

(reprinted in *Grave of Light*, p. 4)

Here "it" would seem to be the growing fetus, and this passage explores the complexity of the idea of selfhood in pregnancy and the relationship between mother and unborn child. Sharing a single body, "breast and pit" (of the stomach?) seem "stolen" *from* the child if they are seen by the mother as belonging to herself alone, but she has stolen them from herself and *for* the child if she views these aspects of herself as existing for the child's use. This is a wonderful Notlean paradox, taking on the challenging work of articulating the obscured boundaries of the self in such an intimate relationship.

WORKS: THE 1980S

When I Was Alive (1980) can be seen primarily as a book of love poems—a sometimes troubled love—to Berrigan and to New York City. There is also a sense, as the book's title suggests, of the erasure of the self—perhaps of the self in the humbling context of history. In "Poem," for example, the narrator looks out at night from a third-floor window over St. Mark's Place, "Lonely from the beginning of time until now"—a line which references Ezra Pound's translation of Rihoku's poem "Lament of the Frontier Guard." Notley also draws from the bleakness of the Rihoku poem's imagery, describing an unpopulated cityscape of "bricks and concrete," and closing with the lines "And who will know the desolation of St. Mark's Place /

With Alice Notley's name forgotten and / This night never having been?" (p. 3). Notley suggests that loneliness "from the beginning of time," its emptiness, is the truth of the scene she is looking upon, rather than its usual bustle, given the fleetingness of human life—and aligns herself with that emptiness in an act of self-abdication. Yet, as she does so often, Notley simultaneously asserts herself through the articulation of her own name in the poem.

In the book's title poem the speaker describes walking in the breeze, wearing a thin dress that billows and fills with wind. It's a sensual poem of physical existence, ending with the surprising move of switching to present tense: "my / heart transparent // as I walk towards Marion's ..." (p. 19). Though the language here is simpler and the syntax more conventional than the lines with the tense change in "Expanding Rooms," and here the situation is quotidian rather than dream haunted, this change serves a similar purpose of adding dimensionality to the speaker's perspective on herself. As she is doubled in "Expanding Rooms" through the consciousness of her dreaming self, in "When I Was Alive" she is doubled through the act of the recent—even ongoing—memory of vital and sensual experience.

As can be seen in these two examples from *When I Was Alive,* the language of the book is simpler and more straightforward than that of its immediate predecessors, but the subject matter is no less complex, the states of being explored no less nuanced. It's a playful book that both observes and perhaps winks slyly at the conventions of poetry in pieces addressed to the moon and the goddess Diana and in poems such as "A Roundelay Between Two Shepherdesses," a humorous dialogue in rhymed common meter that updates the pastoral tradition with allusions to city life and contemporary culture.

The year 1981 saw the publication of *How Spring Comes,* a chapbook-length collection organized around two long poems, "The Prophet" and "September's Book." "The Prophet" is a long-lined poem made up of aphoristic, prophetic statements mixed with social commentary and details of quotidian life. The poem is notable for its humor in passages mixing the instructional with the prosaic, such as a passage advising the poor to cut tiny photographs of carpets from catalogs and paste them to the floors, and passages such as this, that seem specific to Notley's life as a wife and mother: "Small sons awaken with bright bird noises, / But oneself awakens differently. The goal of awakening is black coffee" (p. 15).

"September's Book," also several pages long, is a poem exploring relationships between women and men. There are sections of dialogue and sections in the voices of male characters observing women, or explaining their feelings for women. An ambitious and imaginative section of the poem is a modern-day retelling of Shakespeare's *Twelfth Night,* with a young girl in a T-shirt narrating the story as the Viola character. Disguised as a boy she falls in love with an older man who is, in turn, in love with a female painter. The man insists that the narrator attend the painter's parties, "& right now she fancies / women, & I'm become this boyish-woman boy-woman little / girl butch oh it's me she fancies, how funny" (p. 39).

As can be seen from these examples, *Spring* contains poems that are less focused on language's musical qualities than poems in previous books. The long poems, especially, seem more intent on storytelling than lyricism—though some of the shorter poems in the book have a more songlike quality reminiscent of earlier work. The tone employed in *Spring* continues to play a role in Notley's work. While tone is admittedly a hard quality to pin down, it comes through here in denser syntax, the relative lack of poetic embellishment, and the use of Latinate words and abstractions as opposed to the simple nouns of domestic life that are prevalent in previous books. Formally, the poems in *Spring* are also denser—there is very little of the loose, variously indented lineation that's so common in earlier work. These differences are important because, slim as it is, *How Spring Comes* marks a transitional moment in Notley's work, a point at which she begins the shift from a lyrical style to one that is more densely constructed and narrative.

Waltzing Matilda (1981) continues this shift. As we have seen, Notley was conceptual in terms

of book projects even in the earliest stages of her career. More recent books are even more so, consisting of book-length epics and novels in verse, but even in the 1970s Notley's books had their own characters and organizing principals, with form and style varying greatly between books. This is very much true of *Waltzing Matilda* as well, and the book's most fundamental gesture is dialogue. While it includes short lyric poems that hearken back to earlier collections, its centerpiece is a series of poems in the form of conversations.

"The Bouquet of Dark Red Mums" (p. 65) records a surrealistic and paratactic discussion in two acts among nine flowers. "Elephant & Ocean" (p. 65) imagines a tempestuous love affair between the two speakers who, in their differences, mostly speak at cross-purposes without any real understanding. "The Wall of Paintings" (p. 69) is a series of lines spoken by such figures as "LADY IN THE CLOCK" and "LADY WITH BREASTS," and again, although the poem's characters are all talking to each other there seems to be very little listening or true communication between them. These conversational pieces are all the more fitting in the book considering that *Waltzing Matilda*'s penultimate piece is an actual interview between Notley and George Schneeman, a self-taught New York painter who often collaborated on visual art projects with Ted Berrigan and Anne Waldman and other second-generation New York School poets. The interview explores Schneeman's ideas about texture, color, genre scenes, and the painting of figures, and is especially interesting as a record of two artists of different media attempting to pin down general aspects of artistic vision and process. But having been preceded in the book by poetic conversations such as "Elephant & Ocean," in which miscommunication and failure to listen are the rule, the misunderstandings and failures to communicate in the interview with Schneeman are highlighted. Notley has transcribed all of her concerns about the tape deck, as well as bracketing places where speech becomes inaudible. In the context of the book's other failed conversations, the attempt at true communication seems especially tenuous, and the understanding that is arrived at, at the conversation's end, is all the more moving for the fragility of its conveyance in the form of spoken human speech.

Other innovative forms in *Waltzing Matilda* include series of lyrical journal entries, examples being "Day Book" and "Waltzing Matilda," which is notable because it includes an entry written the day after John Lennon's murder and speaks to the sense of collective sadness after that tragedy. Another long poem, "My Bodyguard," is written in the form of collaged lines of overheard dialogue. In the essay titled "Voice" in Notley's book of essays, *Coming After,* Notley writes of this poem and others like it in subsequent books:

> In the late seventies and early eighties I wrote a number of poems containing many voices. I used peoples' voices verbatim, from the room and also from the street and from the media; I thought at the time I was being practical about writing in a crowded apartment, though also I was in a state of fascination with the voices of others. I thought as well I probably didn't have so much to say on my own, in terms of "saying something"; but I knew I had things to make and wonderful materials. Now it seems clear to me that I invariably created a unified work, out of various peoples' voices and words, which reflected my individual self and situation.
>
> (p. 148)

"How does a person happen to become a poet?" Notley begins her brief autobiographical volume *Tell Me Again* (1982). The book features a cover illustration by Notley herself: an abstract desert landscape with a starry sky overhead. The work is entirely focused on Notley's youth, telling of growing up in Needles, California, where she excelled in school and "lived to go to the movies" (p. 8). She writes of being a nonconformist: "As I got older it got clearer to me that it wasn't going to be the same for me as for the other kids I knew. I tried for sameness for a couple of years but I was feeling miserable; it turned out that giving in to being different felt better. Though it didn't feel all that much better" (p. 10). She recalls formative relationships with her high school principal, who loaned her Henry Miller's *Tropic of Cancer,* and of the English teacher she

fell in love with, though he encouraged Notley to become a pianist rather than a writer.

In *Tell Me Again,* Notley also writes of her extended family. She tells of the "first death"—that of her father's sister Dorothy, who died when Notley was six, after a period of time in the Arizona State Mental Hospital. The death was shrouded in mystery—"there was some vague talk of spinal meningitis"—and seems to have been a scarring family tragedy. "My father never got over what happened to Dorothy," Notley writes. It was an "unspoken-of sorrow ... that didn't happen to me, but that made my father be so and so me be so. I don't like secrets, they're hard on the people who don't know them, as well as on the ones who won't or can't tell them. There must be found a way to tell them" (p. 4).

Notley also writes in *Tell Me Again* of her grandparents on her mother's side, who lived in Phoenix and whom the Notleys often visited. Notley writes that her grandmother "bragged about our Indian ancestress, supposedly a Comanche, who had to be guarded all the time because the Indians were always trying to steal her from her husband" (p. 3). Native American history and spirituality and the search for facts about Indian ancestry are themes in Notley's 2006 book *Alma; or, The Dead Women.*

By the time Notley's next book of poems, *Sorrento,* was published in 1984, Berrigan had passed away. The book is especially poignant when read with that in mind, because it picks up the lyrical journal form experimented with in *Waltzing Matilda* to tell the story of a trip taken with Berrigan and their two sons to Notley's hometown of Needles. The entries span a period of two weeks, from the end of August to mid-September 1981, and, sometimes in prose, sometimes in brief, narrative-lineated poems, describe the experience of visiting family and friends, books read, things said by the children, and old trunks gone through in the Notley home. One of the most beautiful passages in the book, from the entry for Sunday, September 6, creates a collage of family identity by listing the items found in such trunks: "Socialist letters from England to Great Uncle; own baby things; clothes too fat for; beautiful fabrics & beautifully sewn clothes; my grandfather's straight-edged razor; my mother's graduation dress, wedding corsage; my father's glasses; flag-like designs my uncle made when he was recuperating from being shot in the head in the war" (p. 13).

Notley has never refrained from contextualizing her work through prefaces, notes, and dates, giving hints about or even straightforward explanations of her poems' content. The final poem in her 1985 collection *Margaret & Dusty,* entitled "Sweetheart," is contextualized through the date printed at the end: "1/18/84." While many of the poems in the book are dated from before or appear to have been written before the death of Ted Berrigan, this final poem introduces the theme of Berrigan's death and the grief over that loss which will recur in Notley's work from this point on. The poem begins, "If I address it to you I have not, have I, / let go of you yet. I'm sorry" (p. 74). It speaks of a kind of disassociation of the self in grief: "I would like not to think, it / makes me foreigner of myself," and "this person who sleeps in my bed / she's slept there forever and yet / there was another." The sense of self-exile is uncomfortable, yet the poem makes a turn in its last lines:

> O Poem really addressed
> to me, it's you are found indulgent
> fit and of comfort, lustre, real light
> I praise you, thank you
> for being what I have tonight
>
> (p. 75)

There is an intentional confusion here, as in these lines the apostrophic address "O Poem" comes within the poem that the speaker began by addressing to someone she had yet to let go of and in the next line says is addressed to herself. The poem's final layering of addressees (and selves) both complicates and resolves the sense of dissociation in the earlier lines, since it ends with comfort, praise, and gratitude for the solace of poetry rather than the unwanted sense of being foreign to oneself. The feeling does not disappear, but is transformed through the act of writing.

Loss runs throughout Notley's 1987 book *At Night the States,* in which "Sweetheart" is reprinted, and there are several other poems of

grief. The book's title poem uses the refrain "At night the states" to begin each stanza, and repeating that double abstraction with its connotations of both darkness and spatial vastness creates a counterpoint to the poem's otherwise intimate and personal grief. It's a long poem, written in short lines, almost all enjambed, and in fragmented language that seems to enact the disjointed, circular thinking of the bereaved:

> Oh being alone I call out my
> name
> and once you did and do still in
> a way
> you do call out your name
> to these states whose way is to walk
> on by that's why I write too much
>
> At night the states
> whoever you love that's who you
> love
>
> (reprinted in *Grave of Light*, p. 161)

As is the case so often in Notley's work, there is a conflation of the self with the "other" in the way both the person calling out and the name being called undergo metamorphosis in the first five lines, as well as a strong assertion of the existence of an independent self in the statement "whoever you love that's who you / love." This tension in Notley's work between dissolving into the other and defining oneself as separate has been seen in the context of love and motherhood, and here is articulated in her poetry of mourning, as well.

The chapbook *From a Work in Progress,* also from 1988, was produced in conjunction with a reading by Notley at the Dia Art Foundation on December 8 of that year. It contains a long poem and a lyric essay titled "Notes on 'The Poetry of Everyday Life,' " which was first presented as a lecture at the Poetry Project at St. Mark's Church in New York City. In the essay, Notley articulates the same kinds of concerns with the mutability and multiplicity of self or selves that she so often approaches in her poems, and she also explores the connection between dream and art:

> Dreamer as artist, shaper, knower, the one who knows about stories, the one who can make several people be one, who combines places & words & feelings into the "truth." That one as the part of you that has no name, no person's name, the one in touch with the gods—for there are two of you ...
>
> (p. 37)

The poem "From a Work in Progress" is a kind of origin story, imagining the possibility of the universe "beginning with a stain" (p. 7). The poem interlaces mythological images of creation with personal scenes of birth and death, asking the question, "How many ones have there ever been? How many people ever? How / many have you known, how many have you been?" (p. 27). This mythmaking impulse, which seems to begin to fully take shape for the first time in "From a Work in Progress," will be developed and explored by Notley through her work of the 1990s and early 2000s, and continues to be a central aspect of her poetry.

WORKS: THE 1990S

Notley's next chapbook, *Homer's Art* (1990), marks another important development: the exploration of the political. The book contains a long poem about the death of Notley's brother, titled "White Phosphorous," two shorter poems, and a mini-essay about the possibility of writing an epic for our times. The essay floats a hypothetical situation: "Say someone you know dies many years after the Vietnam War, as a consequence of it" (p. 6). She then asks how one might satisfy the desire to write an epic poem about that situation, especially as a woman who "has no real access to the story" (p. 6). As Notley writes in her essay "The 'Feminine' Epic" in *Coming After,* her brother Al, who was a sniper in the Vietnam War, had, years after his tour ended, "developed acute post-traumatic stress disorder, become heavily addicted to drugs, was admitted to a succession of hospitals ... finally entered a rehab and underwent a kind of cure." Nevertheless, Al died, "accidentally OD'd a week after leaving that rehab" (p. 172). She closes "Homer's Art" with the statement, "What a service to poetry it might be to steal story away from the novel & give it back to rhythm & sound, give it back to the line. Another service would be

to write a long poem, a story poem, with a female narrator/hero.... Perhaps someone might discover that original mind inside herself right now, in these times. Anyone might" (p. 7).

"White Phosphorus" introduces a technique Notley has become known for, especially because of its use in her epic *The Descent of Alette*. In these poems she breaks her lines into segments contained within quotation marks, as a way, she says in her introduction to *Alette,* "to measure the poem.... The quotation marks make the reader slow down and silently articulate—not slur over mentally—the phrases at the pace, and with the stresses, I intend" (p. v). The poem itself is Notley's most political to this point, and uses the death of the brother in the poem as a way of critiquing power and capitalism:

> "*Everyone's* just like a soldier" "everyone fights, everyone works"
> "For the army of money we guess" "Slave to a faceless" "our country is
> unthinking soldier" "money the" "uniform government texture of air,
> army of money"
>
> (p. 17)

Along with the formal innovation of the quotation marks, Notley introduces, in "White Phosphorus," the figure of the owl. " 'My brother' 'is Owl,' " she writes (p. 23), and the owl will be used often as a figure symbolic of wisdom and power and as a representative of the dead in the books that follow *Homer's Art*.

First published in 1992 in a volume titled *The Scarlet Cabinet,* which also contains work by Douglas Oliver, Notley's epic *The Descent of Alette* was reprinted by Penguin in 1996. A visionary and ambitious work, *Alette* seems to have been a fulfillment of the desire Notley expressed in "Homer's Art" for "a long poem, a story poem, with a female narrator/hero."

Alette tells the story of a heroine living in a dark, dreamlike subterranean world of subway cars and stations, where all the inhabitants are oppressed by a mysterious "tyrant" who prevents them from rising to the surface. The heroine travels through a series of subway cars in which people work at invisible tasks, have animal heads, or burn continuously. At one point the heroine makes the decision to go into an uncharted place; the train dissolves and she floats through a huge eyeball and into series of caves, which a character she meets there describes as " 'something like' 'our middle depths' 'or middle psyche' " (p. 47). Here she has the sensation of becoming a plurality—of being all the people from the subway as well as herself. In one grotto she finds a lapis stone—part of the tyrant's heart—and vows to return it to him. Her ultimate intention is to defeat him.

The heroine then travels down a corridor leading to a dark river she wades across, then into a forest. There she searches for a mother figure, whom she finally finds—though the woman is headless, speaking through her severed neck. The heroine helps her to become whole, and then the mother figure points her on her way. She next meets a talking owl, which the heroine recognizes as her dead father. The owl feeds her part of a mouse and, telling her she must die a "little death" (p. 107), tears her apart with his talons and beak. The heroine loses consciousness. Awakening, she is whole again and is told that she has taken on qualities of the owl, which she will need to defeat the tyrant.

The heroine goes to the tyrant's home and is admitted because she has the heart fragment. The tyrant endeavors to convince the heroine that he embodies all of reality, showing her dioramas in his museum-like house that seem to contain all of the world. Through the house they reenter the subway, where they ride together until they stop at a station where a river of blood flows. The heroine realizes the river is made of the tyrant's blood, and in it she sees a fabric scrap which, using her owl qualities, she flies toward and retrieves. She swallows it and recovers her memories: she remembers that her name is Alette and that her brother died in battle. Notley has said the name "Alette" came about because she was thinking of her brother, Al, when she wrote the poem, and because her own name "is Alice: 'Alette' is more like 'girl-owl.' " The poem, she says, is "dedicated to my father, another Al, because he's the owl in Book Three" (*Coming After,* p. 178).

Alette then follows the river, finding the tyrant's vulnerability—a cave with a plant growing from its floor. She uses her owl talons to uproot the plant, and this kills the tyrant. In the final scene Alette rises up from the subway to the earth above with those who have been trapped below. Despite the joy of seeing blue sky, they face the question of whether, since the tyrant seemed to contain all reality, humanity must " 'continue' 'to live in' 'this corpse of him' " (p. 148).

Susan McCabe writes of *Alette* in the *Antioch Review,* "this long poem, Notley's most ambitious to date, matches its vital experimentalism with an unabashed feminism, an element understated in her earlier work" (p. 274). Part of that experimentalism is the technique of the line fragmented into quotation-mark-enclosed segments. McCabe writes that it "reveals how quotation usually signals citational authority, but here it ruptures the line, unsettling epic voice and legitimacy" (p. 274). Notley writes in the author's note to the Penguin edition that she intended the fragments primarily as units of sound, but writes in her essay "The 'Feminine' Epic," "I don't think you can write a real epic ... without some, even a lot of, regularity of line. I wanted something regular, but also catchy—not some prosy long-line spinoff of the what-had-come-before.... I wanted something all my own" (*Coming After,* p. 173).

Additionally, the fragments in quotations represent the fluidity of self that is part of the book's subject—Alette becomes a plurality as she ventures into the caves, absorbing the people who were in the subway with her. The quotation marks remind the reader that Alette is not just speaking for herself; as a heroine charged with changing the world, her story represents a multitude.

Notley's first *Selected Poems* was published in 1993, containing portions of *Alette* but, more importantly, making available poems from the early, limited-edition books, which were at that point already hard to find. The book seems not to have garnered much critical attention—indeed, up until 1996, when Notley signed on with Penguin for the republication of *Alette* and subsequent books, there were very few reviews or critical evaluations of her work in the mainstream literary press.

The volume *Close to Me & Closer ... (The Language of Heaven) and Désamère,* published in 1995, collects two long poems that, as Notley writes in her preface, "have in common a pervasive use of dialogue and certain preoccupations: the meaning of the word 'human' ... and a search for a mystical ground common to all life" (p. 3). "Close to Me ..." is a dialogue between a daughter and her dead father. Formally the poem uses ellipsis marks between phrases to make the voice of the father, heard across planes of existence, distant and strange. The daughter's voice is represented in verse. "Désamère," written after Notley's move to Paris, is also a dialogue, this time between the dead French poet Robert Desnos and a woman named Amère. Notley writes that Desnos' "voice in my poem is oracular by reason of his known aptitude for dreaming, his life experience (including his death as a result of Nazi internment), and also his insouciance. Insouciance is a freeing quality that can open poetry to truth" (p. 3).

Notley writes of her book *Mysteries of Small Houses,* published in 1998, "I was firstly trying to realize the first person singular as fully and nakedly as possible, saying 'I' in such a way as to make myself really nervous.... Saying I in that way I tried to trace I's path through my past" ("The Poetics of Disobedience").

Seeing the "I" in *Mysteries* as a character moving through the events of Notley's life is an instructive way of looking at the book, which employs self-observation throughout. *Mysteries* moves chronologically through Notley's life and often steps slightly outside the usual parameters of the first person in order to comment on its situations, as in the poem "The Obnoxious Truth," about a piano recital Notley was praised for but felt she botched. It closes "I didn't play it right. / Look at these gold lamé shoes, look at my hair" (p. 16). The book closes with the beautiful poem "Lady Poverty," which offers a kind of summation of the life story told in *Mysteries:* "the shape of a life is impoverishment—what / can that mean / except that loss is both beauty

and knowledge—" (p. 138). These affirming words ring true because the life story has been one of great loss, so their wisdom seems authentic and hard-won. The poem closes, "but now I seem to know that the name of a self is poverty / that the pronoun I means such and that starting so / poorly, I can live" (p. 139).

Byzantine Parables, a chapbook published in 1998, contains two long poems that in many ways anticipate Notley's later work. The poems are delivered in the manner of raw thought and privilege the unconscious through dream imagery as well as through the inclusion of typographical slips, as in this example from "Parable of Christian": "reconsis reconstitute us from this em mes" (p. 1). This poem, which images the mind as an ornate church, prefigures Notley's later collection *Reason and Other Women,* which expands upon the conceit.

WORKS: THE 2000S

Of her 2001 book-length poem, *Disobedience,* Notley writes:

> *Disobedience* didn't exactly set out to be disobedient; it set out actually to try to do the kinds of things I'd previously done in different poems all in the same poem.... But it got more and more pissed off as it confronted the political from an international vantage, dealt with being a woman in France, with turning fifty and being a poet and thus seemingly despised or at least ignored.
>
> ("The Poetics of Disobedience," p. 2)

The poem, written after Notley's move to Paris, is formally composed of one- to four-page sections, each of which is itself broken into segments separated by a solid line. It does tell a story, but perhaps more loosely than the poems Notley refers to. Its damning commentary on contemporary culture and poetics, politics, and the oppression of women is interwoven with fragments of dream life and conversation with a Robert Mitchum–like detective character, whom the poem's speaker refers to as her "will" (p. 32). *Disobedience* is, despite its anger, often irreverently humorous, as when the poem's speaker says, "my rule for this poem / is honesty, my other rule is Fuck You" (p. 158). Fundamentally the poem is concerned with Notley's overarching project: the discovery of truth, in part through an understanding of self. "There is such a thing as absolute definition," the detective tells the speaker; "that's what I've just detected. / *You* are absolute ... / I, myself, I say. / Yes" (p. 134).

The long poem *Iphigenia,* published in chapbook form in 2002 and reprinted in its entirety in *Grave of Light* in 2006, is loosely framed as a Greek tragedy, at times referring to and even addressing its audience. The voice of the poem seems to combine Notley's and that of the heroine Iphigenia, who was sacrificed to Athena by her father, Agamemnon, when the goddess becalmed his fleet. Notley's second husband, Douglas Oliver, died in the spring of 2001, and the poem speaks of and mourns the deaths of both a love and a brother. At times the poem is addressed to the brother, and the brother responds, "Sister, we will protect you, the dead, not the gods" (p. 313). Referring to the story of Iphigenia, the speaker says, "I still don't understand the story I'm caught in / the whim of the wind" (p. 310), and her helplessness and sense of injustice is poignant and raw. "Why are we still in this one / story?" (p. 311), she asks, and at the end addresses the "audience": "Do you know this story?" (p. 316).

Published in 2004, the chapbook *From the Beginning* was written, according to the date at the end of its one long poem, in June and July of 2000. The poem is both elegy and cri de coeur. Combining prose and verse, the poem begins with the image of a man sitting up in bed and a woman's shadow "in the wall" (p. 5). The poem moves, like so much of Notley's work, through dream imagery. Also like much of Notley's work, *From the Beginning* is self-referential, and seems to seek the reconstitution of the dead on the page. "His profile is on this page, looking," she writes, continuing, "There are two planes or worlds one tilted up diagonally towards the other which expands slantwise but less so across the page" (p. 6). The poem is wrenching in its expression of grief, as in the following grief-fragmented excerpt: "it is still terrifying to love a dead I'm afraid to look over my shoulder at who isn't there now. The love will make me fly the certitude I

was insane away from the room to find heal for someone who" (p. 16).

In the preface to her prose collection *Coming After* (2005), Notley describes her approach in these essays: "I wanted to be clear, and not consciously innovative in language" (p. v). The book contains assessments and book reviews of poets such as Frank O'Hara and Anselm Hollo, she also writes of the work of other second-generation New York school poets including Anne Waldman and Ted Berrigan. Of O'Hara, Notley writes: "O'Hara was the first poet I ever read who 'sounded like me.' Obviously he doesn't sound at all like me.... But poetry is intimacy, it's an instantaneous transferral of mind" (p. 5). This definition of poetry seems very true to Notley's own writing, which strives to "transfer" the mind on unconscious and conscious levels and invites the reader into the most intimate experiences of love and grief.

Coming After's second section contains essays on the topics "American Poetic Music at the Moment," "Voice," "Thinking and Poetry," "Women and Poetry," and "The 'Feminine' Epic." "Women and Poetry" is especially interesting in its tone, reminiscent of the anger of *Disobedience,* and ends powerfully:

> Very few people, male or female, seem capable of making a life that doesn't conform to the patterns that so benefit ... tyrants. Finally [women] are allowed to write, hysterically pile up pages in a dead-end world using dead-end forms of articulation written on dead trees. Everything must change and very very soon. Women and poetry, is a joke—Where is the world?
>
> (p. 170)

Returning to the epic mode, Notley published *Alma; or, The Dead Women* in 2006. A volume of nearly 350 pages, *Alma*'s primary form is the prose poem. The narrative, which begins in July 2001 and closes in March 2003, tells the story of the September 11 terrorist attacks and the lead-up to the Iraq War through the voices of several recurring characters. Alma herself is a goddess figure who both observes and dreams the world, injecting heroin into a hole in her forehead. The "dead women" are a group of characters attending her, including a prostitute, a fetus, the personification of light, and a "hippy"—seemingly a projection of Notley as a young woman. Like a Greek chorus, these characters observe, grieve, curse, and attempt to find some meaningful response to world events. In the context of the book, "dead" means a state of nonparticipation in injustice and war, a denial of the life that is complicit, through its very being, with the violence of the governments overseeing it. Eventually most of the characters are transformed into owls, expressing an even further negation in rejecting the human form.

Occasionally Notley's authorial voice comes through, to interject or confer with Alma and the dead women. In one passage she refers to her own earlier book as she rages against the idea of war against Iraq, where the first writing and poems evolved and the first epic, about the heroine Inanna, was told: "i feel that they bomb her when they bomb Iraq, and they bomb my poem *The Descent of Alette*" (p. 123). As difficult as it is imaginative, *Alma* searches for a way to respond to violence and oppression, not politically so much as personally—a way to live in the face of war.

Notley's second selected poems, *Grave of Light,* was also published in 2006. It brought the poet new critical recognition and gathered together poems from some of her more obscure collections, as well as unpublished poems written in 1970 and poems from forthcoming books. *Grave of Light* shows the range and scope of Notley's career, and just how fully this prolific and expressive poet has lived through her work. As Brian Teare wrote in the *Boston Review,* "part of what makes *Grave of Light* so satisfying is that it ultimately exposes the impossibility and even the undesirability of the separation of life and art, of what we call soul and its articulation as voice" (January–February 2007).

In the books that followed, *In the Pines* (2007) and *Reason and Other Women* (2010), Notley continued to explore the expanses and boundaries of the self through art. In the long elegiac title poem of *In the Pines,* she asks, "If I find your soul do you want it? Do you even know? Do you even know what part of you you are?" (p. 55). Notley uses fragmented syntax, la-

ment, and the folksy lyrics of American plainsong to express grief in ways that are fresh and original. However, as Joel Brouwer wrote of *In the Pines* in his *New York Times* review, "The radical freshness of [Notley's] poems stems not from what they talk about, but how they talk, in a stream-of-consciousness style that both describes and dramatizes the movement of the poet's restless mind, leaping associatively from one idea or sound to the next without any irritable reaching after reason or plot."

Reason and Other Women returns to the image Notley first explored in *Byzantine Parables* of the mind as church. Here the book's arc is a metaphorical journey into the mind itself, beginning with the first section, "The Expanding Basilica," and the first poem, "Entering the Building" (which recalls the gesture of the hero or heroine in epic to begin the quest), and traveling into deeper and deeper reaches of consciousness. As the depths are explored, the church, with its religious iconography and mosaics, grows into a city. Abstractions such as Reason and Justice are personified—another means Notley has found to explore and converse with aspects of the self. In the preface to *Reason,* Notley writes that it "had a complicated genesis, in Byzantine art, to a lesser extent in Christine de Pizan's *La Cité des Dames,* and in dreams, intentions, structural maps, and schemes of color symbolism and numbers, all of which shifted about in my mind as I composed on the computer, often forgetting what I was supposed to be doing—the Plan—as I wrote myself into a different state of consciousness" (p. 7).

Over the course of her long career, Alice Notley has, like her heroine Alette, sought relentlessly for the way past the "Tyrant" in all his forms of oppression—political, cultural, and intellectual. She has pursued what she claims is her "lifelong project ... through poetry to discover The Truth" in forms and experiments as numerous as the considerable number of her published books. Her voice and scope of intellect and imagination are utterly singular in contemporary American poetry, as is her ambition. As Brouwer wrote, Notley "seeks to establish or continue no tradition except one that literally can't exist—the celebration of the singular thought sung at a particular instant in a unique voice—and it seems she's getting closer to it all the time."

Selected Bibliography

WORKS OF ALICE NOTLEY

Poetry

165 Meeting House Lane. N.p.: "C" Press, 1971.

Phoebe Light: [poems]. Bolinas, Calif.: Big Sky Books, 1973.

Incidentals in the Day World. With Philip Guston. New York: Angel Hair Books, 1973.

For Frank O'Hara's Birthday. With Frank O'Hara. Cambridge, U.K.: Street Editions, 1976.

Alice Ordered Me to Be Made: Poems 1975. Chicago: Yellow Press, 1976.

A Diamond Necklace. New York: Frontward Books, 1977.

Songs for the Unborn Second Baby. Lenox, Mass.: United Artists, 1979.

When I Was Alive. New York: Vehicle Editions, 1980.

How Spring Comes. West Branch, Iowa: Toothpaste Press, 1981.

Waltzing Matilda. New York: Kulchur Foundation, 1981.

Sorrento. With David Trinidad. Los Angeles: Sherwood Press, 1984.

Margaret & Dusty: Poems. St. Paul, Minn.: Coffee House Press, 1985.

Parts of a Wedding. New York[?]: Unimproved Editions Press, 1986.

At Night the States. With George Schneeman. Chicago: Yellow Press, 1987.

From a Work in Progress. Readings in Contemporary Poetry 10. New York: Dia Art Foundation, 1988.

Homer's Art. Curriculum of the Soul 9. Canton, N.Y: Institute of Further Studies, 1990.

The Scarlet Cabinet: A Compendium of Books. With Douglas Oliver. New York: Scarlet Editions, 1992.

To Say You. Riverdale, Md.: Pyramid Atlantic, 1994.

Selected Poems of Alice Notley. Hoboken, N.J: Talisman House, 1993.

Close to Me & Closer ... (The Language of Heaven) and Désamère. Oakland, Calif.: O Books, 1995.

The Descent of Alette. New York: Penguin, 1996.

Mysteries of Small Houses. New York: Penguin, 1998.

Byzantine Parables. Poetical Histories 45. Cambridge, U.K.: Peter Riley, 1998.

Disobedience. New York: Penguin, 2001.

Iphigenia. Belladonna 36. Brooklyn, N.Y.: Belladona Books, 2002.

From the Beginning. Woodacre, Calif: Owl Press, 2004.

Alma; or, The Dead Women. New York: Granary Books, 2006.

Grave of Light: New and Selected Poems, 1970–2005. Middletown, Conn: Wesleyan University Press, 2006.

In the Pines. New York: Penguin, 2007.

Reason and Other Women. Tucson, Ariz.: Chax Press, 2010.

ESSAYS

Coming After: Essays on Poetry. Poets on Poetry Series. Ann Arbor: University of Michigan Press, 2005.

"The Poetics of Disobedience." Written for a conference on Contemporary American and English Poetics, held at King's College London, Centre for American Studies, February 28, 1998. Available from Electronic Poetry Center (SUNY Buffalo), http://epc.buffalo.edu/authors/notley/disob.html

OTHER WORKS

Tell Me Again. Santa Barbara, Calif.: Am Here Books / Immediate Editions, 1982. (Autobiography.)

Anne's White Glove. Produced in New York, 1985; published in *New American Writing,* 1987, pp. 1–26. (Play.)

Contemporary Authors Autobiography Series. Vol. 27. Detroit: Gale, 1997.

CRITICAL STUDIES AND REVIEWS

"Alice Notley." *Contemporary Authors Online*. Detroit: Gale, 2007.

Brouwer, Joel. "A State of Disobedience." *New York Times Book Review,* October 14, 2007 (http://www.nytimes.com/2007/10/14/books/review/Brouwer-t.html).

McCabe, Susan. "Alice Notley's Epic Entry: 'An Ecstasy of Finding Another Way of Being.' " *Antioch Review* 56, no. 3:273–280 (summer 1998).

Teare, Brian. "Whole New World." *Boston Review,* January–February 2007 (http://bostonreview.net/BR32.1/teare.php).

INTERVIEWS

Baker, David. "Evident Being: A Conversation with Alice Notley." *Kenyon Review*, October 2009 (http://www.kenyonreview.org/kro_full.php?file=notley-interview.php).

Keelan, Claudia. "A Conversation: September 2002–December 2003." *American Poetry Review* 33, no. 3:15 (May–June 2004).

Stephans, Brian Kim. "Brian Kim Stefans Interviews Alice Notley." *Jacket* 15 (http://jacketmagazine.com/15/stef-iv-not.html), December 2001.

ANNE RIVERS SIDDONS

(1936—)

Margaret T. McGehee

WITH FOURTEEN MILLION copies of her books in print as of the year 2000 and book contracts totaling over $16 million by 2006, the southern fiction writer Anne Rivers Siddons has converted herself into national and international literary currency. Sixteen of her twenty books have landed on the *New York Times* best-seller lists, most for multiple weeks. As Laura Miller of the *New York Times* put it in 2004, Siddons is one of a handful of popular women novelists whose sales make them the "Godzillas of the fiction trade."

In her career Siddons has written eighteen novels, a book of essays, and a travel guide to Atlanta. Her first novel, *Heartbreak Hotel* (1976), sold an impressive 10,000 copies in hardback and 600,000 in paperback. But her next two books, *The House Next Door* (1978) and *Fox's Earth* (1981), met with poor reviews and did not sell well. Soon after, her publisher asked her to completely rework a book manuscript that she had spent two years writing. She did not publish again until 1987, in part because of a severe depression that afflicted her from approximately 1983 to 1986. Things began to change for the better in 1988 with the publication of her epic Atlanta novel *Peachtree Road,* a book that cemented her place within the ranks of best-selling popular fiction writers. By 1992 this book had sold 100,000 hardback copies and 800,000 paperbacks. *Outer Banks* (1991) sold over 100,000 hardcover copies as well. Four years after the publication of *Peachtree Road,* Harper-Collins offered Siddons a three-book contract. *Colony* (1992), one of the three works under that contract, sold 150,000 hardback copies and had a $150,000 publicity campaign to back it. Many of her novels have been translated into multiple languages.

Like her good friend Pat Conroy, Siddons has become a southern popular fiction luminary. In 1985 she was named Auburn's Alumna of the Year, and Georgia Author of the Year in 1988. She holds an honorary doctorate in humanities from Oglethorpe University (1991), and in 2007 Siddons was inducted into the Georgia Writers Hall of Fame. Two of her works have been adapted into films: *Heartbreak Hotel* was made into *Heart of Dixie* (MGM) in 1989, and *The House Next Door* was adapted into a Lifetime television movie in 2006.

HarperCollins typically released Siddons' books in the late spring to early fall months of May to October, a marketing strategy that suggests the publisher considered her novels "beach books" or light "summer reading." But Siddons' fiction represents more than entertainment. A glance at some of her titles—*Peachtree Road, Downtown, Colony, Outer Banks, Hill Towns, Islands, Low Country, The House Next Door*—makes obvious that place matters. Closer examination reveals that Siddons' rich development and characterization of place and time do more than establish setting. Specific places and times are central as the means by which Siddons establishes conflicts for characters and reveals her own conflicts and ambivalence concerning her identity as a southern white woman who came of age in the civil-rights-era South.

In interviews and fiction, Siddons' language suggests a conception of "southern" identity as monolithic, static, and white, even as moments in her own life or in the imagined lives of her female protagonists complicate this understanding. Siddons recognizes this identity as oppressive to white women of her class in the South and consistently highlights what she understands as the dramatic repercussions of trying to abandon

it: ostracism and social death. Siddons challenges the norms associated with southern white womanhood through the female protagonists in her work, but she herself has clung to the identity throughout her life.

From biographical details, interviews, and writing about herself, Siddons emerges as a woman writer caught between an appreciation for the older, more conservative, nostalgic understanding of a singular South (and "the way things used to be") and an appreciation for a fresh, critical examination of the social conflicts at the heart of white southern identity. In interviews, Siddons has expressed regret and a sense of guilt for not becoming involved in the civil rights movement. By writing her female characters in *Peachtree Road* and *Downtown* (1994) into the movement, Siddons uses fiction to reimagine her own lack of activism and experience. But there are also limits to the fantasy of confronting racial inequality. Like Siddons, the characters are outsiders whose involvement in the movement remains superficial. Like Siddons, these fictional activists only rarely involve themselves in any sort of racial resistance or struggle; when they do (as in the case of Lucy in *Peachtree Road*), they are ostracized and then punished with death.

BEGINNINGS

Sybil Anne Rivers was born January 9, 1936, in Fairburn, Georgia. Twenty-five miles southwest of Atlanta, the city of Fairburn, where Siddons' family had lived for six generations, numbered just over fifteen hundred people in 1940. Siddons' father, Marvin, according to a biography from Harper Collins, was a "prestigious Atlanta lawyer"; her mother, Katherine, worked as a secretary at Campbell High School. Reared, as she put it, to be "a perfect Southern belle," Siddons was a head cheerleader, a homecoming queen, and the Centennial Queen of Fairburn. She received straight As during high school. But she felt ashamed of her intelligence, Siddons told the Trinidadian author V. S. Naipaul in *A Turn in the South:* "I spent twelve years trying to hide the fact that I was a bright child." In a farming community such as Fairburn, she said, "intellect has had no place" (pp. 39–40).

Siddons left Fairburn in 1954 to attend Alabama's second-largest public university, nearby Auburn Polytechnic University (renamed Auburn University in 1960). She joined Auburn's chapter of the Delta Delta Delta sorority, which had formed on campus the spring before her arrival. During her sophomore year she was selected for membership in Owls, an honorary organization that recognized "scholastic ability and campus leadership" among Auburn women. In May 1956 Siddons was deemed by the Auburn student newspaper, the *Plainsman,* as "Loveliest of the Plains," an honor bestowed weekly to a female undergraduate. Her photograph appeared on the paper's front page. Here, Siddons appears as the quintessential southern belle—demure, carefree, young, and beautiful (with a hat to protect her delicate white skin). Dressed in a one-piece strapless bathing suit and wide-brimmed straw hat, a smiling Anne Rivers poses on the beach; her head is coyly cocked to the side, her eyes averted from the camera. The caption reads: "Basking in the sun on the sands of Lake Chewacla is this week's loveliest, Anne Rivers. A junior in art from Fairburne [*sic*], Ga., Anne recommends this pleasant way to study for finals but doesn't guarantee its results."

As a feature editor and later columnist for the *Plainsman,* Siddons ensured that her name appeared more often than her face and figure in the weekly campus paper. Her "Passing Stream" columns tended to be pedestrian in topic (although the humor and wit that characterize her later "Viewpoint" columns in *Atlanta* magazine are present in these pieces). In some, Siddons offers her opinion on local and campus-related issues—the need for more restaurants in the area around Auburn, the pros and cons of an honor system, her belief in Auburn's need for a ghost, or her disapproval of the lack of female participation in a survey about students' satisfaction with Auburn's dining services. She bemoans the absence on campus of what she terms "thinking students" engaged in "midnight philosophy swapping sessions" and offers humorous critiques of Elvis mania, social teas, and sorority rush. These columns are what one expects to find in a student newspaper—entertaining and charming pieces,

but not threatening, challenging, or radically opinionated in tone and substance.

However, her column appearing in the October 18, 1957, issue of the *Plainsman,* titled "Death of a Columnist," marked a significant break from her typical style, tone, and content. In this piece Siddons gets serious and gets angry, delving into a critique of the immorality of white-on-black violence in the Jim Crow South. This column also suggests a glimmer of growing dissatisfaction with the roles assigned to white southern women like herself. It's hard to know what exactly sparked Siddons' fire. Her 1976 novel *Heartbreak Hotel* tells the story of Maggie Deloach, a coed at a state university in Alabama (meant to resemble Auburn) whose column on integration in the school paper meets with disdain from many of those around her (including the school administration, her sorority sisters, and her boyfriend). The book is admittedly semiautobiographical. Siddons told one interviewer that she wrote it to make sense of her college years, which she had found to be a "strange and awfully unsatisfying time" ("Bookmark: Conversations with Don Noble"). The fictional Maggie witnesses the violent beating of an African American man, which inspires her to speak out against racism, but there is no indication that Siddons had a similar traumatic moment of conversion.

In a 1988 article about the film version of this book, *Heart of Dixie,* Anne Rivers Siddons mentioned she first understood "the idea of equality" when studying slavery in a high school history class. Siddons stated to Eileen M. Drennen of the *Atlanta Journal-Constitution,* "A white light [went] through my brain: This is wrong, why didn't I know this?" She had to ask herself, "Why haven't I seen it? I've been living in the middle of it since I was born!" There is no indication from the biographical details of her life that her parents advocated racial tolerance or openly discussed racial issues in her home. She told Drennen that her racial awakening came in an epiphanic moment she believes other southerners have shared: "It could not be a process of formal education—it almost has to be an epiphany. Nobody was going to tell you." (In her interview with V. S. Naipaul she said that she had once been called a "nigger-lover" in a high school history class after speaking out against a historical event she thought was "not right," though she does not specify the event.)

Siddons put her epiphany into practice, or at least into her writing, in "Death of a Columnist." In this *Plainsman* column Siddons attempts to render invalid the central argument of "states' rights" used by segregationists to protest federally enforced desegregation of public schools. The bottom line for Siddons in this piece is that many white southerners' violent reactions to desegregation are morally wrong. She claims: "The only rights concerned are the rights of free men in a supposedly democratic nation.... free men, who walk and talk and laugh and cry and, strange as it may seem, my friends, think and feel just like we do." The frustration driving this piece seems to derive from the lack of any emotional, fundamentally human response to the events in Arkansas. Siddons writes:

> I'm tired of listening to people gather in little groups and talk in sanctimonious whispers about the latest from Little Rock. I'm tired of the ever-increasing flood of jokes and cartoons and clichés that follow in the wake of all the turmoil like little scraps of garbage dropped when the vultures leave. I'm tired of the blind, ignorant prejudice on one side and the pseudo-intellectual, disinterested wits on the other side. I'm tired of that endless bickering over meaningless points of obsolete laws and the thousand and one stupid technicalities. They're not important. They're a smoke screen we've thrown up so we won't have to face the fact that we're violating a moral law.

For Anne Rivers Siddons, the argument that segregation was a part of an "established way of life" held no water. "Social customs, regional tastes, personal preferences," she writes, "have absolutely nothing to do with this issue of integration at all. What we are advocating when we gather in howling mobs like animals and throw stones and wreck automobiles and beat helpless individuals is wrong, and I don't care from which of the myriad angles you choose to look at it. It's still wrong."

Although she attacks states' rights segregationists, it is important to note that throughout

the column, Siddons uses a collective "we," ratifying the notion of a monolithic white South with which she clearly identifies. This column is the earliest manifestation of her ambivalence toward southern mores. She opposes the system of segregation but is not ready to remove herself from the group of white southerners with whom she disagrees. Siddons launches into a biting attack on the segregationists who use the argument of "state's rights" as a justification for racist beliefs and behavior. That argument, she asserts, offers "a lovely façade to hide issues behind. We're not arguing a state's right to self government. The mess in Little Rock and all the other similar messes don't have a darned thing to do with state's rights." The paradox—of wanting to challenge the status quo of a racially segregated society but not relinquishing her identification with that society—surfaces in most of Siddons' writing. The column represents one moment where she decided to lay her views on the line (or at least on the newspaper page), but she nevertheless clings to the notion of a white southern "we."

She further criticizes white southerners' adherence to a way of life rooted in a belief in white superiority. "*We* aren't worried about having to change *our* own standards, *our* own values," Siddons sarcastically claims (italics added here and below). "*We* like us the way *we* are, even if we're dead wrong. So let's go and fling a few stones and to the devil with worrying about *our* own moral petticoats. Let 'em drag in the mud. It's good old southern mud." Again, the collective "we" suggests that Siddons herself is not beyond reproach and that she does not want to separate herself entirely from the family and friends included in that "we." She contends that "*we're* slobs. Also snobs. Regional snobs," even as she simultaneously claims, "I love the south, *we* all love it." Her jabs at those who defend segregation are evidence of the diversity of white southerners' views toward racial issues.

Thirty years later, her understanding of the South and of white southerners as monolithic appears to have remained relatively unchanged. In attempting to explain to V. S. Naipaul how many white southerners' racist attitudes and anxieties were connected to a colonial identity, she stated (italics again added): "*We* were a conquered and occupied people, the only people in the United States to be like that. And this—*our* attitude to blacks—was the only way *we* could feel or exercise our power at all. *We* were a poor agricultural community, and *we* had bone-deep memories of real conquest and occupation and total humiliation." Completely ignoring Native Americans as a "conquered and occupied people" in this moment, Siddons also ignores the diversity of multiple southerners' experiences, in effect rendering southerners as a unified white "community" and explaining away racism as their form of resistance in the face of alleged colonialism. Through the repetitious use of "we" and "us," Siddons again includes herself within the racial hierarchy described. She continued: "*We* were untraveled people, the bulk of *us* uneducated. The only way *we* had of coping with change was by pretending it wasn't there. When the civil-rights movement was beginning, though it was just there, in Alabama, *we* could pretend it wasn't there. And when change did come it was brought to *us* right to our door by those black hands, which *we* hated and feared more than anything else in the world."

The title "Death of a Columnist" proved apt, for it marked Siddons' final appearance in the *Plainsman*'s pages. Auburn's administration had asked her to pull the column, but she refused. When she wrote a second column (which did not appear in the newspaper), she was fired from the paper's staff, according to her later publisher HarperCollins.

The awakening of her racial consciousness while at Auburn and during her early years working in Atlanta has clearly informed her fiction writing. A little over twenty years after her column appeared in Auburn's paper, Siddons' novels *Heartbreak Hotel, Peachtree Road,* and *Downtown* would each showcase a southern, middle-class white female main character's growing awareness in the 1950s and 1960s of the racial, economic, and gender inequalities of the society in which she was steeped. It is difficult to separate the characters' experiences from Siddons' own; in many instances, art clearly

imitates life. As Siddons herself said to Eileen Drennen, "Every book I have written has veered over to the civil rights movement.... So I know I'm not finished with it. Something isn't settled."

GOLDEN SIDEWALKS: ANNE RIVERS SIDDONS IN AND OF 1960S ATLANTA

It is crucial to examine Siddons' experiences working and living in Atlanta during the 1960s to better understand her fictional constructions of civil-rights-era Atlanta and of southern white female characters more broadly. Out of such an examination comes a portrait of a woman conflicted by her love of the South and Atlanta and by her desire to reject the social taboos placed upon her as a white, educated southern woman in and of that place and time.

In interviews about her first years in Atlanta, Siddons frequently expresses the overwhelming excitement that she felt about coming to work in the city during a time of possibility for young, white professionals. After graduating from Auburn in 1958 with a degree in commercial art, Siddons moved to Atlanta to work in the advertising departments of the Retail Credit Company and then Citizens & Southern (C&S) National Bank. Her attraction to Atlanta had been long in developing. For a young white woman from the rural railroad town of Fairburn and the small college town of Auburn, the urban space of Atlanta in the 1960s seemed vibrant, exciting, and full of potential adventure.

Siddons remained at C&S Bank until her writing came across the radar of the legendary *Atlanta* magazine editor Jim Townsend. First appearing in May 1961, *Atlanta* magazine, the chamber of commerce's glossy monthly publication, was clearly geared toward promoting Atlanta to the business world and attracting businessmen, their interests, and their families to Atlanta. Between June 1962 and December 1964, when her name is listed as "senior editor" for the first time, Siddons' byline appears only occasionally, most often for photo essays in which she wrote short texts and captions to accompany photo layouts.

Caption writing—pithy writing meant to define and describe through words what we see in an image—may have contributed to the development of her writing style and her perceived ability to "capture" an historical moment and place. For example, in a 1964 photo essay showcasing the homes and landscape of Atlanta's wealthy Buckhead district, Siddons' words overlay the stunning, full-page images of grandeur and elite living.

In her writing for this piece, Siddons' opinion of 1960s Buckhead is unclear. At times she expresses a certain reverence for this well-established place, and the focus on oldness and the association of Buckhead to Camelot—doubly referencing King Arthur's domain and President Kennedy's administration—suggest an enchanted quality to the place and to the leaders that inhabit it. She admires Buckhead for its persistence, but the description of "crumbling statuary" definitely characterizes it as aged and weathered. Neither Siddons' brief text nor the accompanying photographs—haunting images of houses lodged on green expanses behind iron fences or dense woods and located at a distance from the roads around them—give any indications of human life, suggesting the fixity, bounded-ness, exclusivity, and wealth of the area of Atlanta that housed many of the city's white power brokers. The whiteness of this place goes unmentioned. Twenty years later she would borrow from herself in this passage when describing that "cloistered wedge of Atlanta" in *Peachtree Road*. Note the similarity between Siddons' article for *Atlanta* and the following passage from her 1988 novel: "residential Buckhead, that cloistered, deep green rectangle of great old trees and winding streets and fine, not-so-old houses set far back on emerald velvet lawns, carved out of deep hardwood forests, cushioned and insulated from the sweat, smells and cacophony of the city proper, to the south, by layers of money" (p. 33).

Much of Siddons' writing for *Atlanta* now seems like practice for her later novels. Siddons' articles celebrate Atlanta's progress and economic growth, and through them, Siddons participates in crafting an image of the city as a white man's town. In a 1965 article titled "The Button-Down Builders," for example, she celebrates as "the vertebrae of civil organizations" what she terms

a "new breed of contractors," a group of white builders who "wear Brooks Brothers suits and belong to the best private clubs"; men whose "wives are Junior Leaguers" and whose "children go to private schools." The "button-down builders" are distinct from the working-class builder, the stereotypically shifty "weather-scarred, leather-faced old-timer in carpenter's overalls" or the "well-fed, red-necked teamster type, hat pulled low over evasive eyes" (p. 58). In other articles, such as "The Man to Know in the Restaurants" and "The Breakaways," Siddons spotlights the "maitres d'hotel" of Atlanta's new restaurants in the business district and Buckhead area and showcases Atlanta businessmen's weekend hobbies—flying sailplanes, skydiving, motorcycle riding, and auto racing. Although Siddons describes in one article the training that women must undergo to become Delta Airlines stewardesses, women rarely appeared in the pages of *Atlanta* magazine in the 1960s, except as the wives of the businessmen to whom the magazine speaks. Instead, downtown Atlanta is figured primarily as a man's playground and, more specifically, as the middle- and upper-class white man's terrain.

The "paeans to progress" written monthly for *Atlanta* included the regular "Young Man on the Go" column, a piece that featured one of the young, successful, and white men involved in Atlanta's moving and shaking. *Atlanta* magazine's staff referred to these fellows as the "YMOGs." This regular feature highlighted, as the scholar Charles Rutheiser writes in *Imagineering Atlanta,* "the new breed of white, male, twenty- to thirty-something go-getters who were cheerleading Atlanta's rise to greatness" (pp. 49–50). As a sometime writer of this column, Siddons participated in the cheerleading of the cheerleaders.

Siddons' participation in civic boosterism is not surprising given that *Atlanta* magazine served as the chamber of commerce's mouthpiece and given what scholars have argued about its historical role. As Rutheiser points out, *Atlanta* magazine "projected an image of the city as bright, alive, vital, striving, and predominately white.... As house organ of the Chamber of Commerce, the magazine's ability to be something other than an extended advertisement for the vision of Atlanta's white power structure was well-nigh impossible" (p. 50). Miriam Greenberg, in her article "Branding Cities," writes that *Atlanta* magazine sought to make the South into a "modern, economically viable part of the union, erasing its burdensome heritage of slavery, segregation, and racism" (pp. 235, 237). Such a magazine allowed for the branding of the city, resulting in the "simultaneous marketing and production of a monolithic, consumer-oriented version of the urban imaginary" (p. 229). Siddons and her *Atlanta* cohort participated in the construction of an urban imaginary by projecting an exclusive Atlanta shepherded by white businessmen.

YOUNG WOMAN ON THE GO

Evaluating this period in her life and career, Siddons does not attempt to distance or remove herself from the YMOGs, their social networks and circles, or their insularity. Despite claiming willful ignorance of Atlantans outside her class position and geographical location at that time, Siddons was not unaware of the violence perpetrated against blacks in many parts of the South. In media coverage, she and other Atlantans "had seen dogs and clubs and hate-contorted faces on the television-sets, over our dinners. We read regularly reports of murders in the sick-sweet black nights of the Mississippi Delta." But Atlanta seemed starkly different from the other southern sites of violence, in part because of what she perceived as its position as the "epicenter" of the Freedom Struggle and Dr. Martin Luther King Jr.'s position as "its great hero and master spirit" ("Removing the Rose-Colored Glasses," p. 138).

In 1966 Anne Rivers married Heyward Siddons—a well-to-do Princeton graduate, advertising executive, and divorcé with four young sons whom she met, according to a *Boston Globe* article, when interviewing him for *Atlanta* magazine. Soon after marrying she returned to advertising, working first at Burke-Dowling Adams (1967–1969) and then at Burton Campbell Advertising (1969–1974). She continued to be listed on *Atlanta*'s masthead as a "contributing

editor" from October 1967 to January 1970; in January 1968, her first-person column "Viewpoint" began to appear regularly in the magazine. The content of "Viewpoint" came primarily from her life, particularly her marriage to Heyward; several of those articles appeared in her first book, *John Chancellor Makes Me Cry* (1975). In 1974 Siddons left advertising to become a full-time writer, setting up shop in a writing studio at her home in the posh Brookhaven neighborhood within Buckhead and each night reading her day's work to her husband over cocktails. A piece she wrote for *Georgia* magazine came to the attention of Larry Ashmead, an editor at Doubleday in New York, and he offered Siddons a two-book contract. When he later left Doubleday for Simon & Schuster and then for Harper & Row, Siddons followed.

Even prior to the summer of 1966, Siddons had been exposed to the stark reality of racism in Atlanta and to her own place within that reality. In 1965 Siddons, accompanied by photographer Vernon Merritt (her frequent collaborator on photo essays for *Atlanta*), attended the dinner held at the old Dinkler Hotel to honor Martin Luther King Jr.'s receipt of the 1964 Nobel Peace Prize. The former mayor Ivan Allen wrote in his autobiography, *Mayor,* that despite initial resentment toward King on the part of the white Atlanta business community, two dozen white business leaders eventually agreed that the city should host a biracial dinner for King. Atlanta's mayor had not expected many white business leaders to show, but most did attend the gathering of fifteen hundred guests, black and white. Following dinner, the crowd stood and sang "We Shall Overcome," proving at least to *Life* magazine in February 1965 that "once more Atlanta earned its reputation as the most progressive city in the South on race relations" (p. 4).

Upon leaving the banquet, however, Siddons and Merritt encountered a group of vociferous, drunk men. As Siddons described it in *Atlanta* decades later,

> They were fearless with bourbon; you could smell them 5 feet away. They were dressed in tailored dark suits and tweed jackets and polished Cordovans; their pink scalps showed through fresh crew cuts, and badges on their lapels said they were members of the International Congress of Communication Facilitators, or something.
>
> "Whole lot of fancy big niggers down there," they slurred, jostling and pushing. And to me, catching me by the shoulder and spinning me around, one of them said, "What are you, a little white nigger lover?"
>
> "Yes," I said, beginning to sob with anger. The young lieutenants moved silently into place around Dr. King, staring down the conventioneers. They might have been watching a picnic on a sunny day.
>
> ("Removing the Rose-Colored Glasses," pp. 138, 140)

After the mob departed, Siddons remarked on the similarities between these men, "prosperous, cleancut, probably pleasant enough on their own home turf," and the YMOGs featured in *Atlanta* magazine. "They're us," she said to her companion Merritt. As a result of that encounter, Siddons states, "never again, after the night I first saw Atlanta plain, did my heart ring like a silver bell simply at the thought of it." "And after that there was no more gold. The sidewalks didn't glitter anymore. It was a long time coming, the moment when I saw us as we were and are" (p. 140).

Here again is Siddons' deep ambivalence. Her use of "us" and "we" suggests an understanding of southern (in this case, Atlantan) whites as a monolithic group, and she locates herself within this group even as her attitudes differentiate her from the white men she describes. Although her initial infatuation with the city faded away, Siddons continued to love Atlanta's "energy and brashness, its sheer YMOGness," even as she understood the racial undercurrents and inequalities that girded the city's identity. Again, Siddons' ambivalence surfaces in her emotional response to that moment. She shows a desire for Atlanta to be the harmonious place it projected through the carefully planned biracial dinner, but she comes to the realization that the harmony was mere illusion.

Siddons' views on race, as revealed in interviews and as suggested within her fiction, are neither straightforwardly conservative nor progressive. Again, she appears stuck in what would perhaps be best described as a state of

white liberal guilt. Much of her writing has involved her attempt to make sense of and to deal with that guilt. As Siddons stated to Naipaul, "I deal with race in some form in every book I've written. It's my great war, I guess. I write to find out where I am now, what I think, to make order and simplicity in my own world. It's an impossible task. You can't simplify that. You can only clarify bits of it" (p. 41). In part, the quest to "clarify" derives from her inability as a white woman of a certain generation to fully comprehend African Americans' historical experience. And perhaps it comes from frustration at realizing too late in life how she could have tried to better understand the experiences of those outside of her insular Buckhead world and those who did not share her set of gender and racial norms. "I didn't march, back when marching would have been passionate and real and spontaneous," she told Naipaul. "I was a young woman newly come to Atlanta and still deeply caught in that web of what is seemly and what is not." Constrained during the 1960s by the gender and racial conventions of Atlanta society, but also holding herself back during that period, Siddons finally attempted, like many white citizens of the South, to understand the race relations of that period.

Even though she indicates that racial incidents may have raised her consciousness about such issues, she still remained true to her rearing as a "perfect Southern belle." Again using a collective "we," this time to refer to southern white women of her generation and class, she told Naipaul, "we all knew ... that the highest we could aspire to was capturing a husband who would then provide for us. And we believed that.... Our mothers and grandmothers believed it was the best they could give us, the protection of a man. I have a theory that Southern madhouses are full of gifted women who were stifled" (p. 42). This aspiration involved playing the part of the "good little girl," a phrase that recurs in numerous interviews and a role she has played throughout most of her life. " 'Be nice,' " she stated on *Good Morning America* in 1991, "hovers like a buzzard"; the message given to women like herself was to play down intellect and "be nice" in order to attract a husband. This meant, as she told Naipaul, that a woman had to suppress her desire to learn or to be different: "We never prized our minds. We never prized our individuality. It was all right to make good grades.... But to be a great thinker, to have a great talent and pursue it, would cut you right out of the herd. And that was the thing we were most afraid of. It could send you walking alone" (p. 42). Siddons stated to Naipaul, "The things that could have enriched us and set us apart were the things that we learned, by omission, were wrong" (p. 43).

Resentment and regret are central themes in Siddons' interviews, emotions her fiction addresses through strong white female characters who defy convention in ways that the "good little girl" Siddons never did. In her opinion, the fear of ostracism from her social networks of family and friends kept Siddons from fully understanding until later in life the gender and racial codes that enveloped her. "What I resent is the power that examination might have liberated earlier. In my writing and my life," she told Naipaul. "I am regretting the years of waste."

CIVIL-RIGHTS-ERA ATLANTA(S) IN PEACHTREE ROAD *AND* DOWNTOWN

Siddons' fiction represents a place where she attempts to reclaim that waste. *Peachtree Road* (1988) is her most acclaimed and most epic work to date. In the foreword to the 1998 reprint of this novel, she states that *Peachtree Road* involved "writing a bittersweet love song to a place that would cease to exist before the book was published. It has always been the nature of Atlanta to change like a chameleon, to be gone somewhere else entirely before the eye and heart could hold it." Told from the point of view of a well-to-do, reclusive Buckhead native named Shep Bondurant, this novel focuses primarily on the escapades and downfall of Shep's cousin Lucy. After her abusive father abandons their family, Lucy, her mother, brother, and sister—perceived as "white trash" by Shep's mother—move into Shep's parents' Buckhead home. Shep and Lucy form an instant connection, a bond that endures until the final pages of the novel. Siddons chronicles their relationship from the mid-

1940s to the 1980s, providing as backdrop the story of Atlanta's growth into an international city during the same period.

From the beginning, Lucy is depicted as a manipulative and reckless girl but one who has been deeply scarred by her father's abandonment. She seeks comfort in the presence of males: Shep; the group of Buckhead boys with whom she and Shep play as kids; and a chain of high school boyfriends, husbands, activists, and strangers. She alienates herself from other women, including her mother, aunt, sister, the group of high school girls known as the Pinks, and any other cohort of females she finds herself among. Unsurprisingly, the white elite of Buckhead do not look favorably on Lucy. As a child, she leads a pack of boys to vandalize an abandoned home in Buckhead known as the Pink Castle. As a teenager, she stays out all night after school dances and comes home disheveled. Eventually Lucy elopes with her high school boyfriend, Red Chastain, but after a severe beating at his hands, she divorces him and returns to the Bondurants in Atlanta. Later she marries a kind and loving activist named Jack Venable and appears to turn things around in her life. But even he and their daughter are not enough to prevent a series of mental breakdowns that culminate in her suicide. Shep observes and narrates their story—and the story of Atlanta's transformation from 1945 to the late 1980s—from his reclusive position inside the Bondurant home, a reclusion brought about by his realization that the Bondurants' money comes from the rent collected from poor African Americans in Atlanta's Pumphouse Hill neighborhood.

The relationship between Shep and Lucy is consistently fraught. At one moment, Shep is Lucy's knight, rescuing her from an abusive husband or a seedy motel room; at other times, he is another sexual conquest, as she drunkenly forces herself upon him more than once in the course of the novel. Shep loves Lucy but equally hates her. Until Lucy's death, his unwavering devotion to her prevents him from being able to commit to Sarah Cameron, his high school and college sweetheart. It is not until the final page of the novel—page 817—that he is able to wrench himself from Lucy's emotional stranglehold.

While *Peachtree Road* stretches from 1945 into the 1980s, *Downtown* (1994) lingers in the two-year period of 1966 to 1968. And while *Peachtree Road* is narrated by an insider viewing upper-class Atlanta society, *Downtown* is narrated by an outsider looking in—this time, Smoky O'Donnell, a young journalist of Irish descent who comes to Atlanta from the dock area of Savannah to work for *Downtown* magazine, the chamber of commerce's monthly publication (meant to resemble *Atlanta* magazine). *Downtown* chronicles twenty-six-year-old Smoky's loss of innocence during a time of significant social change in the United States. Her initial enthrallment with the Buckhead social scene turns to disappointment as she becomes increasingly aware of the racial problems in Atlanta during the late 1960s. Smoky wrestles as well with the conflicts between her Catholic upbringing, the sexual revolution that she witnesses going on before her, and her own sexual desires. Again and again, Smoky comes up against a conflict between what men—her father, her boss, and her Buckhead boyfriend—want for her and what she wants for herself. In this respect, the story is not too far removed from Siddons' experience as a woman working in Atlanta at that same time, even if in the preface to *Downtown* Siddons denies that she is Smoky. She writes there that "the city and the times are as close to my own time Downtown as I could come. No, I'm not Smoky—she's a better woman than I, by far, and very little that happened to her happened to me" (p. viii).

In both of these Atlanta-set novels, Siddons paints a reverential portrait of the white men who transformed Atlanta into a major U.S. city but also takes punches at the southern society in which they were steeped. Such jabs prevent her narratives from fully constructing what the scholar Martyn Bone in his book *The Postsouthern Sense of Place* defines as Siddons' "distinctly idealized vision of the city's historical-geographical development" (p. xiii). Instead, her works suggest that these men, despite transforming Atlanta into an international city and a bas-

tion of capitalist modernization, were just as responsible for keeping African Americans and women in their positions of powerlessness. Furthermore, *Downtown* represents an historical fantasy for Siddons herself—and perhaps for many of her readers—in which she seems to be working through her guilt and ambivalence about that period. Through Smoky, Siddons is able to safely imagine a satisfying resolution to her ambivalence. In this way, the novel is much more than merely a "palimpsest" to *Peachtree Road,* as Bone argues in his analysis of the same texts.

In *Peachtree Road,* Siddons primarily focuses on the period of Atlanta's rapid growth during Ivan Allen's reign as mayor from 1962 to 1970. Shep, the narrator/tour guide in the novel, describes these Buckhead-bred men: "Literally since their births they had known each other, and moved as easily in one another's homes and clubs as they did in their own" (p. 267). The group who remade Atlanta, according to Shep, were "a dwindling handful of men and women, young and old, who had lived within a four-mile radius of each other all their lives" (p. 10). They were men who

> had built family mercantile and service businesses into international concerns, men who had made literally millions from Coca-Cola, either directly or indirectly, men who had dramatically altered the face of the South and in some cases the nation with their monolithic urban and suburban developments; men who had ... brought to the city, in the firestorm decade of the sixties, a major league sports arena, five professional sports teams, a great, dead-white marble arts center and a world-famous conductor to inhabit it, a world-class international airport, a state-of-the-art rapid transit system, a freeway system to boggle the mind, unparalleled convention facilities and the people to fill them—and the peacefully integrated school system that lured in the industry to fuel it all.
>
> (p. 11)

Shep's words are almost identical to those of Mayor Ivan Allen's recollection in his autobiography of his association with and membership in the real-life Buckhead Boy crowd:

> We had gone to the same schools, to the same churches, to the same golf courses, to the same summer camps. We had dated the same girls. We had played within our group, married within our group, partied within our group, and worked within our group.... We were the presidents of five major banks, the heads of the Atlanta-headquartered industries like Coca-Cola, the presidents of the three big utilities, the heads of the three or four top retail establishments, the managers of the leading national-firm branches for the Southeast, the man in charge of the city transit system, the heads of the local businesses ... and the leading realtors.... Nearly ninety percent of us lived inside a half-mile radius of the intersection of Habersham and West Paces Ferry roads.
>
> (pp. 30–31)

In his description of Buckhead's patriarchs, Shep quotes an "intense female journalist" who wrote a feature on these men for *Cityscope* magazine:

> *Insular, careless, totally and imperviously self-assured, chauvinistic in the extreme, naïve and unsophisticated, arrogant, profoundly physical rather than introspective, largely unburdened by intellect and almost laughably White Anglo-Saxon Protestant, they were as cohesive as cousins and as stunningly insensitive as young royalty.... It was a beautiful, bountiful, exuberant, frivolous, snobbish, and silkily secure kingdom, and it was then, as it is still, a very small and strictly delineated world, perhaps no more than four miles square, in a green northern suburb of Atlanta called Buckhead. And yet out of it came the men, and indirectly the women, who ... would change forever the definition of the word "South."*
>
> (p. 15, italics in original)

As with *Downtown* magazine, *Cityscope* imitates *Atlanta.* This fictional article, especially with its references to royalty and kingdom, is reminiscent of Siddons' own article for *Atlanta* (quoted earlier) in which she refers to Buckhead as Camelot.

White leaders courted the black leaders of the day, but both novels suggest that they ignored entirely the plight of Atlanta's poor, black and white. After Shep's father dies, Mayor Ben Cameron (a stand-in for Ivan Allen in both novels) takes him on a driving tour of Atlanta's African American communities, ending up in Pumphouse Hill, near Cabbagetown, an area of dilapidated houses and streets covered in sewage. Shep states, "The tiny houses were all decades older and in far worse repair than in the other neighborhoods, some without whole roofs, most without

one or more windowpanes, all made of unpainted, rotting, green-scummed wood.... The unpaved street was thick with filth and unspeakable things" (p. 540). Unsure why they have come to this miserable place, Shep asks Ben Cameron the reason behind the visit. "I thought you ought to see it firsthand," says Cameron, "Your family owns it" (p. 541). The Bondurant family's money in fact comes from the rent collected on these run-down shacks, but they—specifically, Shep's mother, whose family technically owns them—have done nothing to improve the living conditions within them. Their wealth, in other words, is parasitical, relying on this poverty for its growth and sustenance.

Similarly, in *Downtown,* Smoky's superficially liberal boyfriend Brad Hunt reveals that his family's construction business builds "dangerously substandard low-cost housing for the Negroes in the southeast part of town. Saves the owners a bundle in niceties" (p. 112). Echoing Ben Cameron's words in *Peachtree Road,* Brad claims that "we've got to do better than we have so far, by a long shot" (p. 112), but he never does. Like Shep, his family's money—and the fortune that he will one day inherit—is rooted in the exploitation of the city's poor blacks. Maintaining the Buckhead way of life is also dependent upon African American domestic labor. The Bondurants' black servants, Shem and Martha Cater, live in the garage apartment behind the house; like the other African American servants in the Peachtree Road homes, they cook, clean, and drive for their white patrons, but they remain out of sight. In the moments when racial-spatial connections are revealed through Shep and Smoky, place is not closed off but connected to the people outside of its borders. As much as the Buckhead families and Club members seek to maintain their insularity from the Atlanta beyond their "deep green rectangle," it is against areas such as Pumphouse Hill that they define themselves. And from Siddons' description of that area, we learn that such neighborhoods and their African American denizens are the most disposable in the Buckhead regime's plan for Atlanta's growth.

In *Downtown,* Smoky experiences a moment of racial awakening similar to that of Shep in *Peachtree Road.* Her boss Matt Comfort allows her, with the help of a young documentary photographer named Lucas Geary and a civil rights activist named John Howard, to write the text for a photo essay to complement and promote the efforts of Cameron's Focus commission—that is, a commission of community leaders set up to identify problem areas in the city where they could help. Smoky's first exposé of the day-care situation in the low-income black communities is somewhat reminiscent of Siddons' article on Atlanta's Community Relations Commission in a 1967 issue of *Atlanta.* In the process of investigating the story, Smoky travels to parts of south Atlanta. The description of her drive through the poorer black neighborhoods is almost identical in language to Shep's excursion with Ben Cameron. Smoky narrates that "we ghosted through the black communities to the south of the city's heart: Summerhill, Peoplestown, Joyland. I could not speak.... They were lost, these miniature cities. Lost, and long had been. I saw almost no people" (pp. 196–197). Lucas says to Smoky on their drive, "The city could raise eighteen million dollars to put up a major league stadium ... but they couldn't seem to relocate a single black family whose home they knocked down.... No wonder Stokely Carmichael goes around with his fist in the air" (p. 197). Smoky asks her companion Lucas why he brought her through Atlanta's ghettos: "Because you don't know shit about Atlanta, although you think you do," he says. "Because you think it's all swimming pools in Buckhead and maitre d's knowing your name" (p. 201). Siddons drives home once again the insularity of the Buckhead world that her main character Smoky had thought she desired. In this scene, Siddons shifts the moment of racial awakening from Shep to the semiautobiographical Smoky; from that moment forward, Siddons has Smoky throw herself into involvement in racial justice issues via her writing, rather than becoming a recluse as Shep does.

In both *Peachtree Road* and *Downtown,* race-focused activism becomes a vehicle through which Siddons tries to dismantle the gender

construction of "southern white womanhood." Through Lucy and Smoky, we witness the impact of place—in this case, Buckhead—on the shaping of gender and sexual norms and expectations directly tied at that time in the South more broadly to racial and class expectations as well. In *Peachtree Road,* Lucy threatens her fellow Buckhead inhabitants with her defiance, recklessness, brazenness, and sexual libidinousness. As a result, she is dead by the end of the novel. "The South killed Lucy Bondurant Chastain Venable on the day she was born," Shep tells us early on. "It's what we do best, kill our women. Or maim them. Or make monsters of them, which may be the worst of all" (p. 3). Lucy challenges the conventions of upper-crust Atlanta society by refusing to be the sweet, charming, and chaste belle that she is expected to be. Her sexual romp with Red Chastain, which occurs atop *Gone with the Wind* author Margaret Mitchell's grave, is one example of that rebellion.

Shep states that Lucy came in from high school dances "smeared and crumpled and heavy-eyed and hick-eyed and irrepressible. Her smile grew steadily more brilliant and promissory, and her laugh richer, and her eyes bluer and more intense, and her whole flamelike ethos more glittering. The talk began in earnest in her sophomore year and never ceased" (p. 259). Lucy's defiance, however, is not only sexual but racial. In her teenage years, Lucy is forbidden from hanging out with Glenn Pickens, the son of Ben Cameron's black chauffeur and the future mayor of Atlanta. We find out later that Glenn was not an object of Lucy's affection but rather the subject of her tutoring. Her association with him, however platonic, and her involvement with civil rights issues pose the gravest threat to her social standing. As a student at Agnes Scott College, she writes what her mother Willa describes as "an editorial in the little campus paper she edits about that horrible Martin Luther King and how he's a new American saint" (p. 369). Shep states, "Well, I thought, of course, Lucy and the Negroes again. It was the only thing left that raised Willa's ire, and the only one likely, in these days, to inflame Buckhead society enough to seriously threaten her clawed-out niche in its society" (p. 369).

Lucy's activism gains momentum at the same time that she grows increasingly unstable. After her abusive marriage to Red ends in divorce, Lucy returns to Atlanta and to her childhood home in Buckhead. She becomes involved more directly with civil rights activity and takes a job at a resource center for African Americans, despite protests from her mother and Shep's parents: "Quit that awful business, they had said, and get a decent job somewhere on the Northside—like the society section of the newspaper, or perhaps teaching in a little private academy in Buckhead, or even helping out in the gift shop at Piedmont Hospital [located on Peachtree Road between Downtown and Buckhead] as so many of the [Junior] Leaguers do—or move out of the house" (pp. 449–450). Lucy does move out, leaving the geographical place of Buckhead and the Northside behind, as well as her metaphorical place in it, and becomes further involved in the movement by working for a civil rights publication called *South.*

Lucy does not go unpunished for her transgressions. Having always been mentally unstable, Lucy is in and out of institutions in her adulthood and eventually commits suicide. Those transgressions help define the confining "niche," to use Shep's term, assigned to women within Buckhead society. In many ways, Buckhead stands in for the monolithic white South of Siddons' imagination, and comments made by Siddons outside of her fiction indicate that the gender issues she raises in her writing speak to her problems with that broader southern imaginary. For example, as she stated to George Peterson in a 1987 *Creative Loafing* article:

> I think Southern women are, by and large, sold a bill of goods, and none of it is true. But we don't know that.... Men are never told that if they are good little boys, someone will take care of them. The expectation is that they will learn to care for themselves, and that the world is tough and often not fair. But women are more often told that if they are good little girls, they will be safely kept. And so we women spend our lives trying to placate the gods or trying to be good little girls or be what other people expect us to be. And sometimes it

> works, but I don't think it works very often.... I think there are places that can do numbers on women. That's what I mean by the South wrecking its women.

Similarly, Siddons claims that Lucy represents a generation of women without power who suffered if they tried to challenge the patriarchal values and sexual mores that she sees as constituting "the South." In an interview with the scholar Dana White in the documentary *The Making of Modern Atlanta,* Siddons stated:

> The women of the South have been wounded, circumscribed, kept in a very narrow arena, partly they bought into this ... but the women of Lucy's generation ... in a certain arena and in a certain social class, a very narrow one maybe, if you were different, if you aspired to something different ... you would pay a pretty high price for it. Often madness or, I think, just the loss of selfhood. I can't imagine the loss to the South in sheer woman power and talent and energy and vision that we must have had simply because most of our young women didn't feel that it was possible. You have to think things are possible.... I think of that time as a time when not very much was possible.

Siddons shows this impossibility as applying to gay men as well in her two Atlanta-set novels. In *Peachtree Road,* Mayor Cameron's son kills himself when his love for a younger man goes unrequited. Married and expecting a child with his wife, Julia, Ben Junior decides that his suicide "seemed to be the only way out of the predicament for all of them" (p. 659). In *Downtown,* Smoky's coworker Tom Gordon leaves Atlanta for a job in New Orleans in part because he claims he "just can't stand any more change" in Atlanta and also because he wants to live with his male friend in the French Quarter. Being gay, he tells his colleagues, doesn't matter down there, and at the same time he claims New Orleans to be "one of the few places I've ever been that feels ... timeless" (pp. 407–408). Homosexuality, not to mention hypersexuality, has no place in the white, elite Atlanta imagined here.

Although Siddons briefly touches on male homosexuality, the lack of possibility for the "women of the South"—that is, the *white* women of the South—is really what frames both novels. Buckhead of the 1960s is defined in part by the gender proscriptions of southern ladylike behavior as well as the restrictions placed on middle-class and elite white women of that era who wanted more in their lives than husbands and children and, for those women who worked, wanted more in the workplace in terms of equal treatment with and among their male coworkers. Although initially relegated to compiling the list of cultural events going on in Atlanta, Smoky is eventually allowed by Matt Comfort to write the YMOG, or Young Man on the Go, column that appears in each issue. (The column here obviously has the same name as the real YMOG column in *Atlanta* magazine.) Her interview with YMOG Brad Hunt, her friendship with her coworker and roommate Teddy (a Buckhead daughter), and her position as a writer for the chamber of commerce's mouthpiece of boosterism provide Smoky with an entrée into Buckhead society. Raised in a working-class, staunchly Catholic family, Smoky has a limited and naive understanding of the world beyond Savannah's docks. Smoky must be tutored by Teddy on what to wear and what to expect at Buckhead social gatherings. Living in Colonial Homes, the place "where all the swingers live" and the place to meet "the Buckhead guys—the lawyers and stockbrokers and bankers" (p. 40), Smoky becomes swept up in the pleasures of a Buckhead social life. Yet, as one of "Comfort's People," she also becomes taken with her work life at *Downtown,* and that work is what ultimately leads her to reject the trappings of Buckhead society. As a result of the drive through Summerhill, Smoky becomes increasingly swept up in the effort to effect racial change through her writing, and she ultimately rejects the prospect of a comfortable life in Buckhead as Brad Hunt's wife. Through these acts—rejecting marriage to a Buckhead boy, seeking racial justice, *and* devoting herself to a male-dominated profession—Smoky, much like Lucy, rejects the gender conventions associated with an elite Buckhead life and, in effect, leaves that place and her place in it behind.

Through Smoky's story, Siddons further reimagines Atlanta as more than a capitalist's dreamland and rethinks a white woman's position

during that era. Smoky constantly pushes Matt Comfort to allow her to write more substantial pieces of investigative journalism and, in turn, confronts his chauvinism toward women in the workplace. As she and Brad get closer, he begins to interfere in her work, calling Matt Comfort behind her back to prevent her from going on assignments he deems dangerous. His initially subtle paternalistic qualities—a kiss on the head, the use of the phrase "good girl," his arrangement to get Smoky birth control pills just in case she decides to have premarital sex with him—become increasingly amplified. Finally, perceiving Brad's racist mother behind his progressive facade, Smoky ends things with Brad when he tells her that she doesn't have any boundaries, doesn't "know what the limits are," and that she is acting "so Irish" (p. 319). The breakup was a long time coming because, all along, Smoky had doubts about managing a marriage and a career and doubts about whether she wanted to have children.

The end of her relationship with Brad sends her into the arms of Lucas Geary, with whom she has a temporary but nevertheless liberating and sexually satisfying love affair. The loss of innocence is a general theme in *Downtown,* but Smoky's loss of sexual naïveté in particular becomes a key moment in resolving the character's ambivalence toward the gender and sexual expectations placed upon a southern lady. With Lucas, Smoky embraces her sexual freedom, leaving behind the ideas of her Catholic upbringing. While Lucy's sexual indiscretions in *Peachtree Road* partially constitute her mental unhinging, Smoky's sexual adventures with Lucas are the catalyst to her clarity, revealing to her that the oppressive and repressive moral environment of Buckhead no longer suits her desires. She does not die; she leaves *Atlanta* magazine for *Newsweek* and then leaves the South for New York. Years later, we learn from the book's epilogue, Smoky does marry. What may at first appear to be a return to convention instead turns out to be the final nail in the coffin of southern ladyhood for Smoky: miscegenation. Her spouse is none other than John Howard, the African American activist she had admired from afar during her days in civil-rights-era Atlanta.

The autobiographical element comes into play here, for while Siddons wants Smoky to go farther than she ever did, Siddons only has a limited range of experiences to draw from when writing on race (as opposed to her role at Buckhead social events or at *Atlanta* magazine, which Siddons knew well). While Smoky thoroughly rejects the conventions of southern ladyhood, her challenge of racial mores is less complete. Smoky's work is limited to the printed page, and she never really *does* anything. Rather, she is a mere observer of activism—picket lines downtown, the Black Panthers feeding breakfast to African American children in the poorer parts of town, arguments between Dr. King's Southern Christian Leadership Conference supporters and the more radical Panthers.

Downtown thus appears a safe means for Siddons to come to terms with her own past and her identity—safe in the sense that, at a certain distanced age, she could explore these things without fear of ostracism or social death. In *Tomorrow Is Another Day,* the scholar of southern women's writing Anne Goodwyn Jones makes the argument that fiction allowed white women writers in the South, such as Frances Newman and Margaret Mitchell, a safe space in which they could express their private selves within a safe, public realm. Each writer that she examines "wrestled" in their respective works of fiction "with their own condition and character as southern women, with the expectations implicit in the ideal of the southern lady, and with what was for them the acutely paradoxical nature of writing itself" (p. 50). Siddons was engaged in similar explorations. *Downtown* represents her working through of that awareness. The decade of the sixties, she once stated to Dianne Young of *Southern Living,* is "one of the great unfinished threads of my life" (p. 100). In that respect, *Downtown* comes to represent an attempt by Siddons to deal with her white guilt.

LEAVING ATLANTA, LOOKING TO THE FUTURE

Both of her novels set in civil-rights-era Atlanta function in some ways as the vehicles through

which she could act out a fantasy of racial progressivism and activism and through which she could seek to assuage the shame she feels about not having been more heavily involved. However, it is really through *Downtown,* not *Peachtree Road,* that Siddons finally reaches a sort of closure. For Siddons, the stirring of awareness that Smoky and others experience was also her own even though she—regretfully, in her words—did not participate in movement activities. "I was brought up to be a 'perfect' Southern woman," she writes. "I was also very much in favor of the Civil Rights movement, but I wasn't that brave about it, and I wish I had been. In fact, I wrote *Homeplace* [1987] because I'm very ashamed that I never marched," she told *Creative Loafing*, sentiments she also expressed in her conversation with V. S. Naipaul. A writer's motivation may be beyond proof; however, the parallels between Siddons' and Smoky's experiences in Atlanta suggest an attempt on Siddons' part to reconcile the ambivalence toward the South and her perceptions of southern white womanhood that had somehow limited her (or that she allowed to limit her) during her coming of age in Auburn and Atlanta.

Not surprisingly perhaps, the struggle of southern white female characters to overcome what they perceive as confining aspects of southern society would continue to be the central focus of most of Siddons' novels, even those not set fully in the South (e.g., *Hill Towns* in 1993). In general, her works fall within the category of complicated melodramas centered on southern white female characters caught in complex webs of marital, familial, emotional, psychological, and social problems. And through those works, we get a glimpse, however biased or limiting, of the gender-, race-, and class-specific confines of southern white womanhood during the civil rights era. While many of her earlier works concentrated on Atlanta- or Georgia-rooted families and women, Siddons has shifted her focus in more recent novels to the South Carolina Lowcountry, where she and her husband reside for half of the year (the other half spent in Maine). While her pace of writing seems to have slowed, owing perhaps to rumored health issues or age, she remains a worthy player in the world of best-selling popular fiction, returning to her native state of Georgia in her 2011 novel, *Burnt Mountain.*

Selected Bibliography

WORKS OF ANNE RIVERS SIDDONS

NOVELS

Heartbreak Hotel. New York: Simon & Schuster, 1976.

The House Next Door. New York: Simon & Schuster, 1978.

Fox's Earth. New York: Simon & Schuster, 1981.

Homeplace. New York: Harper & Row, 1987.

Peachtree Road. New York: Harper & Row, 1988.Reprint, New York: HarperPaperback, 1998

King's Oak. New York: Harper & Row, 1990.

Outer Banks. New York: HarperCollins, 1991.

Colony. New York: HarperCollins, 1992.

Hill Towns. New York: HarperCollins, 1993.

Downtown. New York: HarperCollins, 1994.

Fault Lines. New York: HarperCollins, 1995.

Up Island. New York: HarperCollins, 1997.

Low Country. New York: HarperCollins, 1998.

Nora, Nora. New York: HarperCollins, 2000.

Islands. New York: HarperCollins, 2004.

Sweetwater Creek. New York: HarperCollins, 2005.

Off Season. New York: Grand Central Publishing, 2008.

Burnt Mountain. New York: Grand Central Publishing, 2011.

NONFICTION

John Chancellor Makes Me Cry. Garden City, N.Y.: Doubleday, 1975. New York: HarperCollins, 1992.

Go Straight on Peachtree. Garden City, N.Y.: Dolphin Books, 1978.

ARTICLES

"Death of a Columnist." *Auburn Plainsman,* October 18, 1957, p. 4.

"Habersham, West Wesley, Tuxedo, and All That." *Atlanta,* May 1964, pp. 47–52.

"The Button-Down Builders." *Atlanta,* March 1965, pp. 56–59, 104.

"The Man to Know in the New Restaurants." *Atlanta,* April 1965, pp. 70–71.

"The Breakaways." *Atlanta,* September 1966, pp. 43–50.

"The Seeds of Sanity." *Atlanta*, July 1967: 54–57, 104.

"Removing the Rose-Colored Glasses." *Atlanta,* May 2001, pp. 100–102, 138, 140.

PAPERS

Anne Rivers Siddons Papers, Special Collections, Ralph Brown Draughon Library, Auburn University, Auburn, Alabama. Siddons' papers, housed in the Auburn University library, include recorded and print interviews with the author, articles about Siddons, fan mail, book reviews, and hard copies of her published works (domestic and international editions).

CRITICAL AND BIOGRAPHICAL STUDIES

FEATURE ARTICLES AND INTERVIEWS

"Anne Rivers Siddons." HarperCollins Publishers (http://www.harpercollins.com).

"Anne Rivers Siddons." Hachette Book Group USA (http://www.hachettebookgroup.com/features/anneriverssiddons/content/index.asp).

"Bookmark: Conversations with Don Noble." (Publication information unknown—TV program produced by the University of Alabama Center for Public Television and Radio, date unknown.) Anne Rivers Siddons Papers, Special Collections, Ralph Brown Draughon Library, Auburn University, Auburn, Alabama.

Cary, Alice. "Anne Rivers Siddons Preserves Natural Treasures in Low Country." *Bookpage,* July 1998 (http://www.bookpage.com).

Crimmins, Tim, and Dana White. Interview in *The Making of Modern Atlanta.* Eight-part series. Atlanta: WPBA-TV, 1991–1993.

Doten, Patti. "The Woman Behind the Beach Books." *Boston Globe,* August 1, 1996, p. E1.

Drennen, Eileen M. "Anne Rivers Siddons: From Facts to Fiction to Film." *Atlanta Journal-Constitution,* August 20, 1989, p. L1, L10.

Good Morning America, October 29, 1991. Anne Rivers Siddons Papers, Special Collections, Ralph Brown Draughon Library, Auburn University, Auburn, Alabama.

Maryles, Daisy. "Women, Women, Women." *Publishers Weekly,* July 31, 2000, p. 21.

Miller, Laura. "The Last Word: Oh Lad, Poor Lad." *New York Times,* May 23, 2004, p. 29.

Naipaul, V. S. *A Turn in the South.* New York: Vintage International, 1989.

Peterson, George. "Anne Rivers Siddons Tackles Culture Shock." *Creative Loafing,* August 8, 1987, pp. 1B–3B.

Shumate, Richard. "Banking on Her Words," *Atlanta* 32 (August 1992), pp. 41–42, 106–109.

"Splendid Victory for 'The Concerned.' " Editorial. *Life,* February 12, 1965, p. 4.

Tate, Martha. "A Fiction Writer's New Southern Landscape." *Atlanta Homes and Lifestyles,* March–April 1992, pp. 52–55.

A Word on Words. Hosted by John Seigenthaler. Nashville, Tennessee: WDCN, June 10, 1994.

Young, Dianne. "Words of Home." *Southern Living,* September 1994, pp. 100, 102.

OTHER SOURCES

Allen, Ivan, Jr., with Paul Hemphill. *Mayor: Notes on the Sixties.* New York: Simon & Schuster, 1971.

Auburn Plainsman. Ralph Brown Draughon Library, Auburn University, Auburn, Alabama.

Bone, Martyn. *The Postsouthern Sense of Place in Contemporary Fiction.* Baton Rouge: Louisiana State University Press, 2005.

Greenberg, Miriam. "Branding Cities: A Social History of the Urban Lifestyle Magazine." *Urban Affairs Review* 36, no. 2:228–263 (November 2000).

Jones, Anne Goodwyn. *Tomorrow Is Another Day: The Woman Writer in the South, 1859–1936.* Baton Rouge: Louisiana State University Press, 1981.

Rutheiser, Charles. *Imagineering Atlanta: The Politics of Place in the City of Dreams.* London: Verso, 1996.

FILM AND TELEVISION PRODUCTIONS BASED ON THE WORKS OF ANNE RIVERS SIDDONS

Heart of Dixie. (Based on *Heartbreak Hotel.*) Directed by Martin Davidson. MGM, 1989.

The House Next Door. Directed by Jeff Woolnough. Lifetime Movie Network, 2006.

LEE SIEGEL

(1945—)

Stephen J. Burn

Lee Siegel is the author of four ambitious novels that rely on intriguingly complex and artful narrative forms, and as such his novelistic talents have often been overlooked during two decades when the American novel has seemed to be domesticated. Diverted away from the flamboyant excesses and ambitions that flourished in the 1970s—most notably in Thomas Pynchon's *Gravity's Rainbow* (1973)—fashionable forms of American fiction have returned home since the 1990s to reacquaint themselves with traditional notions of realism and to tell tidy stories of familial tensions and Christmases together. In an age when Jonathan Franzen's *Freedom* (2010) has set the standard for the media-friendly contemporary novel—a standard that increasingly resembles the well-made nineteenth-century family saga—Lee Siegel seems out of step with publishing fashions. On one level Siegel's books are involved in what might appear to be an antifictional project—a Möbius-stripping away of the delusions and omissions of contemporary realism, directing attention toward the means and materiality of the literary text—but his work actually engages quite specifically with a literary past that extends deeper than the popular modes of realism that hardened during the nineteenth century.

Siegel's novels, in fact, are preoccupied with ancestors text, with works handed down by a previous generation. Both of Siegel's first two novels make dramatic use of eighteenth-century novelistic and historical materials. In *Love in a Dead Language* (1999), the basketball player Leroy Lovelace shares his surname with the aristocratic libertine from Samuel Richardson's *Clarissa* (1747–1748), while the putative editor who presents the text, Anang Saighal, has written a dissertation on "Love as Game in Laurence Sterne's *Tristram Shandy,*" and draws the reader's attention to the parallels between Sterne's novel and Siegel's. Similarly, in *Love and Other Games of Chance* (2003), one subplot involves a character pretending to be the reincarnation of Warren Hastings, the first governor-general of India (1773–1785). Yet this material from the prehistory of the modern novel is not a sign that Siegel is simply an anachronism. His sense of a living literary past is invariably filtered through a narrative lens that recalls the cutting-edge experiments of later postmodernists. Beyond specific historical allusions, each of Siegel's novels is based around a text drawn from what Ed Park called the "invisible library": a storehouse that "contains books that exist only between the covers of other books—as descriptions, occasionally as brief excerpts, often simply as titles" ("Titles Within a Tale," p. 19). In each of Siegel's novels, the central character's relationship with the narrative's imagined interior text—which is typically inherited from an older man—becomes the platform for a work that synthesizes the traditional rewards of imaginative tale-telling with often dazzling formal and linguistic play.

Each of Siegel's four novels features the word *Love* in the title, and this repetition (alongside the reappearance of characters between books) suggests that the author sees the works as part of a coherent and unified narrative system. The underlying grid that holds these novels together is provided by the four sections (three panels and one coverpiece) of Hieronymus Bosch's famously enigmatic triptych *The Garden of Earthly Delights,* which dates from around the end of the fifteenth century. In his influential study *Hieronymus Bosch* (1966), Charles De Tolnay summarizes the overall purpose of the triptych:

> This is neither a simple didactic sermon nor a positive apotheosis of free love.... it is an encyclopedia of love and at the same time a representation of the sweetness and beauty of mankind's collective dream of an earthly paradise that would bring fulfillment of its deepest unconscious wishes, while at the same time it shows their vanity and fragility ... the paradise contains the germ of its own destruction.
>
> (p. 361)

Similarly nuanced, Siegel's novels also betray an encyclopedic dimension as they explore the many sides of love as his characters move between paradise and destruction.

BACKGROUND AND EARLY WRITING

Lee Siegel was born in Los Angeles in 1945 to Noreen Nash and Lee Siegel Sr. His father ran a successful medical practice and was also medical director at 20th Century Fox, a job that often required world travel to administer to the medical needs of Fox's actors. Siegel's mother was born Norabelle Jean Roth, and her surname's overlap with the novelist Philip Roth and the Sanskrit lexicographer Rudolf Roth is frequently alluded to in Siegel's later fiction. Nash was an actress of some repute during the 1940s and 1950s—starring alongside Elizabeth Taylor, Rock Hudson, James Dean, Clark Gable, Marilyn Monroe, and many others—and she changed her name following the advice of her agent. But Nash withdrew somewhat from acting after a difficult three-month stint in Mexico filming *The Adventures of Casanova* (1948). In an interview for a volume titled *Screen Sirens Scream!* (1999), Nash recalls: "My son was two years old at the time, and by the time he saw me, he hardly remembered who I was. That was the end of location shooting for me.... My family always came first" (p. 179). But while the movie industry was transplanted by family matters in the Siegel household, the influence of his parents' involvement in cinema clearly left its mark on Siegel's later fiction. On a thematic level, a sense of the power of the image, and a vital intimation that "reality" might be fabricated for an audience's pleasure, provide a recurring theme throughout Siegel's novels, while moviemaking is also revisited in the many scenes about early film that make up his second novel, *Love and Other Games of Chance*.

Beyond the specific or thematic fascination with moviemaking, Siegel's parents also provided a cosmopolitan and stimulating cultural environment that nurtured the young man's nascent creativity. During a long and comprehensive interview published in the *Electronic Book Review* in 2006, Siegel recalled of his parent's home that "on Sunday afternoons that house had a salon feeling to it, and there were other people who often came by who also influenced me substantially—lots of writers and movie people." Among those visitors was Henry Miller, who married his fifth wife—Hiroko ("Hoki") Tokuda—at the Siegel home, and who used to play Ping-Pong and share advice with the young man. Siegel recalls:

> Since Henry didn't know how to drive, I'd always pick him up for Sunday ping pong. Those drives from the Pacific Palisades to Beverly Hills and back meant a great deal to me. I loved his voice, the sound of it, as well as everything he said. He was one of my great heroes. I only once showed Henry something I had written. He responded to it by telling me that when Paul Klee was teaching art in Paris, he'd make his right-handed students draw with their left hands. "Try to write with your left hand," Miller advised me. I'm still trying to figure out what that means.
>
> Every time I saw Henry, he'd turn me on to new books, things he loved and wanted other people to love. The first book he gave me was *The Palm Wine Drunkard* by an African novelist. He could, by the way, beat me at ping pong. I could beat Hoki, but she could beat him.
>
> ("Anatomizing")

A second important visitor was Jean Renoir, the son of the impressionist painter Pierre-Auguste Renoir and a major director in his own right. Siegel's father was Renoir's doctor and his mother had appeared in one of his movies; Renoir presented a model to Siegel of the kind of artist he might become—an artist who was profoundly humane and delighted by the world, making art that allowed others to participate in the pleasure that he took in existence. Renoir, in fact, had a hand in one of Siegel's earliest productions. Remarkably, Siegel attempted (and interested publishers in) his first book when he was still in

high school—a volume he titled "Art Appreciation for Grown-ups Under Ten," and Renoir contributed a preface to the manuscript, which is held in the University of California at Los Angeles collection of Renoir's papers.

Having endured rather than enjoyed the literature that he was issued in high school—*The Red Badge of Courage, Evangeline, A Tale of Two Cities*—Siegel's notion of the literary novel was revitalized and amplified by his encounter with Renoir's novel *The Notebooks of Captain George* (1966) and especially Miller's *Tropic of Cancer* (1934). Siegel explained: "Reading the first page of *Tropic of Cancer* changed my life irreparably forever.... There's something about his writing that makes a susceptible young man want to write" ("Anatomizing"). Miller's legacy is clearly important for Siegel's fiction, and Jeff Bursey has argued that the major overlaps between the two writers' works are "the identity of the myth-creating narrator, and the awakening of the central character, often through sexual material but also in sudden lyrical or tender passages" ("A Myth of One's Own").

After completing a B.A. at the University of California at Berkeley—where he majored in comparative literature—in the late 1960s, Siegel moved to New York to pursue an MFA at Columbia University. His decision to go to graduate school emerged partly from an early encounter with William Blake's work. Siegel told the *Electronic Book Review:*

> There are things I read in my teens, things that planted that pernicious seed of wanting to write something important. I remember one night hearing somebody read the *Marriage of Heaven and Hell* on the radio, and thinking it was just amazing and I immediately went out and got it. Blake's work became an early influence on me—his attempt to break down the line between words and images. I studied printmaking in graduate school because of him. But Blake's sensibility was pretty far from my own. It was a sensibility informed by no sense of humor at all.

New York in the 1960s was very different from the city it is today—danger was everywhere, and all the buildings seemed to have bars on their windows. The move to the East Coast was initially challenging, but it allowed Siegel to identify a trinity of intellectual influences, as he explained in an unpublished letter to Henry Miller:

> New York is a terrible city of strangers as far as I am concerned. My only delight here is the opportunity to study with Edward Dahlberg. Do you know him? I have begun to worship him as I worship Jean Renoir and yourself. I am thankful to my parents and now to Columbia University for giving me the opportunity to know this triad of giants.

Dahlberg was very different from the charming Miller and Renoir, who were easy for the young writer to admire. Dahlberg was angry, cantankerous, and anguished, and he presented an alternative model for Siegel: the artist as a kind of martyr to belles lettres.

Living in New York, Siegel wrote with photos of Dostoevsky, Renoir, and Baudelaire above his desk as he explored different creative possibilities. The direct outcome of his encounter with Blake and his studies of printmaking was a volume titled *Vivisections,* which was published by Goliards Press in 1973. *Vivisections* is an unusual mixture of poetry and drawings, and in several ways it looks forward to his more mature literary work. The volume's opening observation, that "all words are borrowed or salvaged from ... strangers" might, in particular, be taken as a kind of key to his later "love" novels. But while Siegel was mixing word and image under the influence of Blake, he was also exploring novelistic opportunities in New York that bore evidence of both his fascination with Russian literature and an emerging interest in the self-referring forms that would become the trademark of much postmodern fiction. The earliest example of this work was a novel titled "The Mirror of Leopold Leopoldovitch Siegelevsky." Even at this early stage of Siegel's career a fascination with the dichotomy between truth and artifice and an obsession with form is much in evidence: "The Mirror of Leopold Leopoldovitch Siegelevsky." is a novel that comes disguised as a Russian manuscript that an editor (named Lee Siegel—the great-grandson of Siegelevsky) claims to have translated. The text is regularly intruded upon by the translator's notes, and so it is a direct ancestor of the mock scholarship that propels his later

novel *Love in a Dead Language*. The manuscript attracted the interest of Don Gold at the William Morris Agency. Gold had also worked with Isaac Bashevis Singer and Chandler Brossard, but although the book was sent to several editors it was never published.

After Columbia, Siegel took a job teaching humanities at Western Washington University in Bellingham, Washington, which he held until 1972. Assigned to teach literature from Gilgamesh to the present, Siegel could select any text he chose, and he used this position to educate himself more fully. Because he enjoyed teaching so much, he decided to pursue a doctorate and (though he would later be hired by a department of religion) it was the literary element in Sanskrit studies that encouraged him to apply to Oxford University. Sanskrit literature is full of elements that later became associated with postmodern fiction—stories within stories, palindromic texts, and so on. In Bhavabhuti's eighth-century *Uttaramacarita,* for example, two characters go to see a play about themselves. A clear line of influence is visible between such works and Siegel's later fiction.

Having been impressed by the mixture of fine writing, erudition, and wit in R. C. Zaehner's books on mysticism, Siegel studied under him at Oxford, where he also fell under the influence of Isaiah Berlin, who was the head of his college. During this period Sanskrit became a profound influence on Siegel's work, and his doctoral thesis (published in 1979 by Oxford University Press) was a study of Gitagovinda's twelfth-century Sanskrit texts. This interest has carried through his career. While the mechanics of translation—analyzing the relationship between words and the concepts and objects they purport to stand for—feeds into his fiction in obvious ways, in 2009 Siegel also published a translation of Jayadeva titled *Gita-govínda: Love Songs of Radha and Krishna* for the Clay Sanskrit Library.

Within a year of completing his D.Phil at Oxford, Siegel was hired by the University of Hawaii, where he is a professor in the Department of Religion. Siegel has had a highly successful academic career, with his scholarly books published by major presses and a string of prestigious awards and fellowships. Siegel's scholarly studies explore love, magic, comedy, and other aspects of Indian culture, but Siegel reached, and in some ways stepped beyond, the threshold of academic writing in his sixth work about India, *City of Dreadful Night* (1995), which began as a scholarly study of horror and the macabre in Indian literature but evolved into a kind of hybrid work that adopts the techniques of narrative fiction to explore an academic subject. The book is a narrative of a research trip to India where Siegel met and followed a wandering storyteller named Brahm Kathuwala. Brahm promises Siegel that "the soul of India is in her stories" (p. 17), and though several members of his audience accuse him of retelling *Dracula* (Brahm retorts that Dracula was reincarnated in Orissa, on the Eastern coast of India), the book becomes a sophisticated study of Indian culture while simultaneously interrogating the theory of tale-telling:

> Stories stitch time and space together and give them structure. All of the stories, each one having limitless versions, each with infinite recensions, are interlocked and interlinked episodes of a greater, amorphous epic.... Every story is embedded in the middle of this great, circular epic. There's no way out of it.
>
> (p. 50)

City of Dreadful Night attracted notice beyond purely academic circles—the book was reviewed in the *Atlantic Monthly*—but this hybrid study is probably most significant because it prepared the ground for Siegel's debut as a novelist, which occurred at the relatively late age of fifty-four. In *City of Dreadful Night,* Siegel used the conventions of fiction in the service of scholarship, but in *Love in a Dead Language* he would use the conventions of scholarship in the service of fiction.

LOVE IN A DEAD LANGUAGE

In a letter to Henry Miller—sent in the late 1960s, during Siegel's New York period—Siegel reflected on his early fiction and noted:

> I am easily influenced by writers and painters. Sometimes I fear this, but I also fear that I shall not be influenced. I want Dostoevsky and Gogol, Ovid and Pindar, Baudelaire and Rimbaud, Aretino, Paracelsus, Brantome, Robert Burton, Stendhal, Flaubert, Casanova, Henry Miller, and many more to help me if I can only emerge with my voice tempered, so that it is stronger, more sonorous, more loud, more beautiful.

Siegel's first novel, *Love in a Dead Language* (1999), represents a mature writer recognizing and negotiating those early influences. Drawing on artistic ideas that had gestated across thirty years—the artistic possibilities that emerge from a collage of text and image, the Chinese box effect of juggling multiple false documents—and fusing them with a wealth of knowledge acquired from the academic study of Indian culture, *Love in a Dead Language* takes as one of its subjects the question of cultural inheritance, whether that inheritance comes from ancestry, geography, or formal training.

As the list in Siegel's letter to Miller suggests, Siegel often finds inspiration in earlier texts, and to that list we might add Denis Diderot, Laurence Sterne, and Miguel de Cervantes. But in blending early cultural influences in *Love in a Dead Language,* two twentieth-century writers stand out as useful touchstones. John Barth, for instance, seems a useful comparison in terms of *The Sot-Weed Factor* (1960), which was created as an elaborate parody of the eighteenth-century novel. In outlining his aesthetic, Barth claimed his "chiefest literary pleasure" was "to take a received melody—an old narrative poem, a classical myth, a shopworn literary convention ... and, improvising like a jazzman within its constraints, reorchestrate it to present purpose" (*The Friday Book,* p. 7). Like Barth, Siegel takes the foundations of *Love in a Dead Language* from improvisations worked upon established texts, and his novel presents itself as a piece of mock Indian scholarship, ostensibly a translation of Vātsyāyana's *Kāmasūtra* by a dissolute professor named Leopold Roth. Woven around this attempted translation is a narrative about Roth that identifies Vladimir Nabokov as the second major ancestor of this text. Despite being a tenured professor of Indian studies, Roth has never made love to an Indian woman, and as he broods on this fact he becomes infatuated with a student of Indian descent named Lalita Gupta, which leads to a story that is part murder mystery and part farcical love story. This retelling of the *Lolita* story was even more evident in the first draft of *Love in a Dead Language,* which included a scene where the central character's father visits a restaurant in Beverly Hills only to discover that Nabokov and Stanley Kubrick are dining there as well. By accident, the father leaves with Nabokov's overcoat, which has notes for a new novel in its pocket.

The melding of these narratives takes place within an unusually polyphonic structure. In *Problems of Dostoevsky's Poetics,* Mikhail Bakhtin summarized the nuanced voice that differentiated the prose novel from other narrative forms: "For the prose artist the world is full of other people's words, among which he must orient himself and whose speech characteristics he must be able to perceive with a very keen ear. He must introduce them into the plane of his own discourse, but in such a way that this plane is not destroyed. He works with a very rich verbal palette" (p. 201). Though disguised as a scholarly text, *Love in a Dead Language* is a model of the novel's rich verbal palette, bringing other voices into play not simply through layered allusions to precursor works but also through the elaborate juggling of different kinds of text. Siegel worked with David Brent at the University of Chicago Press (which had published three of his earlier works), and he helped produce a lush volume that featured pictures, different colored text, and all kinds of other typographical complexities. While the novel explores and exploits the materiality of literary narrative, Siegel also imitates the fragmented forms and branching nonlinear connections of hypertext fictions.

Love in a Dead Language quotes Robert Coover's famous essay on hypertext (which ran in the *New York Times* under the headline "The End of Books"), includes fake Web pages and also several sections that imitate the interactive dimension of hypertext. Yet while many novels influenced by hypertext present, in John Barth's words, only "linear *simulations* of nonlinear ef-

fects" (*Coming Soon!!!* p. 237, emphasis added), what is unusual about Siegel's text is that he moves beyond mere simulation to attempt genuinely interactive nonlinear effects. At one point Siegel presents two pages made up of six fragments that his narrator insists he cannot order, so he encourages "the exacting reader to copy these pages and then cut along their dashed outlines, reconstructing ... a faithful representation of the text" (p. 236). Similarly, he offers elsewhere alternate pages devoted to different chapters, and his narrator informs the reader that "the choice" of which to read first "is yours" (p. 295).

In a set of brilliant and learned reflections, however, Siegel goes even further to analyze the way that a clutch of words can simultaneously reach toward divergent registers. Writing from an academic perspective, Siegel had considered such polyphonic address in *Laughing Matters:*

> The ambiguities in the mythology of Śiva—the apparently simultaneous idealizations of passion and renunciation, eroticism and asceticism, the preservation of the world and a liberation from it—are reiterated by the poet Rāmacandra in the *Rasikarañjana* in a series of duplex stanzas, anagramic charades, in which ... the same letters, in the same order, have two different and incongruous meanings. The ambiguities of the language recapitulate the ambiguities of the god which, in turn, recapitulate unnameable paradoxes inherent in being itself.
>
> (p. 382)

Incorporating this concept into *Love in a Dead Language,* Siegel attempts his own charades by highlighting divergent meanings that emerge according to the spacing between letters. Roth's dissertation, then, is titled *Oflyricheros* (p. xiv), which depending on the way letters are separated reveals either the disappearance of love (O Fly Rich Eros) or a paean to poets (Of Lyric Heros). Similarly, Siegel encourages readers to puzzle over the relationship between the identically lettered question "Am I able to get her?" and the fantasy "Amiable together" (p. xvi).

At the same time, characters' names in the novel suggest deeper meanings. Siegel told Madona Devasahayam, "I am a sucker for Indian languages ... [and] the names in the book had some association. All of them have some reason.... Gupta means 'perfect' and 'hidden.' Anang (in Anang Saighal) means 'bodiless.' " A truly choral text, *Love in a Dead Language* is a fully dialogic novel that destabilizes monologic authority and revels in competing voices, which is perhaps why reviewers such as Paul Di Filippo saw the novel as an attack on Orientalism.

But while Siegel's work is a useful example of both the dialogic novel and of how literary fiction might respond to emerging hypertext technologies, *Love in a Dead Language* also engages in some larger literary debates. Across the last decade of the twentieth century, numerous critics—from Heidi Ziegler to David Foster Wallace—had argued that postmodernism had run its course, and that the reason for its decline could be squarely laid at the door of its cohabitation with metafictional strategies. In stories such as "Westward the Course of Empire Takes its Way," Wallace had attempted to break out of the prison house of metafiction by working metafictional variations upon a metafictional text. Taking Vladimir Nabokov's *Lolita* and *Pale Fire* as a template, Siegel attempts a similar maneuver—arguably with more success than Wallace—that makes his novel a second-order recursion, a kind of meta-metafiction, dominated by a spectacular series of nested stories, language games, and much metafiction that is the source and animus of the text. While Roth, for example, is meant to be translating Vātsyāyana's *Kāmasūtra,* he discovers that "writing about love and sex is not so much writing about love or sex as it is, and cannot escape being, writing about writing" (p. 100n). Yet as Roth's translation and Siegel's text begin to refer to themselves, Siegel embeds the story in a structure that criticizes metafiction. A third of the way through the book, Siegel includes mirrors among a list of "narcissistic themes and images" (p. 117), and he has arranged his text so that mirroring begins to dictate the way the story is related. As Roth, for example, finally makes some progress in his seduction of Lalita, he writes: "It was the happiest moment of my life. That's not really true, but that's how it felt at the time" (p. 190). Then, as the net of repercussions stemming from his affair begins to tighten around him, he writes: "It was the most miserable mo-

ment of my life. That's really true, and that's how it felt at the time" (p. 283). The logic of the narrative's development, then, is dictated by the logic of reflection, so that when Roth begins a section "It could not have turned out better" (p. 211), the reader realizes that this must inevitably be followed by a section that begins "It could not have turned out worse" (p. 213). By structuring his narrative in this way, Siegel manages to dazzle the reader with spirals of recursion, while he simultaneously reveals reading to be a mediated experience *and*—like Wallace—alerts the reader to the costs of metafiction, criticizing (through his novel's heavily mirrored form) the tendency of self-referential fiction to descend into narcissistic mirror-gazing.

Love in a Dead Language received an unexpectedly wide-ranging and positive response from reviewers, critics, and even other novelists—in fact, Siegel's novel elicited a warm letter to the author from the postmodern grandmaster John Barth. Reviewing the novel for the *New York Times Book Review,* Tom LeClair compared the novel to the work of Nabokov and Joyce, before concluding that the book was "a major laughing matter" that "deserves space on the short, high shelf of literary wonders" (p. 14). In the *New York Times,* Richard Bernstein was equally impressed, calling the novel a "hall of fractured mirrors" that recalled Borges and Nabokov, but "whether it is postmodern or not, *Love in a Dead Language* is pulled off with such unhinged élan by Mr. Siegel that is also plain good fun, a clever, literate satire in which almost everything is both travestied and, strangely, loved by its author" (p. E7).

Elsewhere similar notes were being struck—Richard Dyer called the novel "an intellectual extravaganza, but with belly laughs" (p. 5); in the *Washington Post,* Paul Di Filippo called the book an "astonishing ... multimedia work" (p. 5). But of the many excellent reviews the novel received, Steven Moore's essay on the novel for the *American Book Review* is particularly noteworthy because it so thoroughly outlines a tradition for Siegel's novel. Seeing *Love in a Dead Language* as a "defining example of a literary genre that bloomed in the twentieth century: the learned academic novel," Moore maps out affinities to works by David Foster Wallace, Gilbert Sorrentino, Rikki Ducornet, and Carole Maso. Though later work (such as Kasia Boddy's essay) has focused on parallels to Nabokov's work or (as in K. K. Ruthven's monograph) on the novel's approach to forgery, Moore extended his sense of Siegel's literary ancestors in his encyclopedic literary history of experimental fiction, *The Novel: An Alternative History* (2010).

In terms of the overarching structure of Siegel's interconnected fiction, *Love in a Dead Language* corresponds to Bosch's hellscape, the right-hand panel of the *Garden of Earthly Delights*. Presided over by a dead professor—one who recalls a legend about a man who "deserved, for all his debaucheries and infidelities, to suffer in the lowest Hell" (p. 322)—this is the Siegel novel that is most concerned with final judgments and endings, and that emphasizes the torments of sexual love.

LOVE AND OTHER GAMES OF CHANCE

When the manuscript of *Love in a Dead Language* was complete, Siegel returned to his academic interests and set to work on a study of Indian snake charmers. But as the scale of his first novel's success became apparent, Siegel gained the confidence to begin a second novel which was enriched by the research he had undertaken. Snakes and snake charming recur throughout *Love and Other Games of Chance* (2003), and indeed, the central narrative begins with the narrator recalling his early years as Samoo the Snake Boy. Yet while this research provided specific plot elements, it also suggested ideas for the novel's overall architecture. Siegel told the *Electronic Book Review:* "I'd discovered in my research that Snakes and Ladders was an ancient Indian game that the British took over and modulated with a moral dimension, and—although I didn't have the story yet—the decision to write the book flowed from there. The book is a version of the game." Building on this idea, Siegel had conceived of this novel as eventually appearing in a square format, with a

fold-out snakes-and-ladders game attached. But Siegel's new publisher did not view this idea warmly. The unexpected success of Siegel's first novel (the appreciative review in *New York Times* and good sales) attracted agents and trade publishers who lured Siegel away from the University of Chicago Press. Gary Morris of the David Black Agency sold *Love and Other Games of Chance* to Viking Penguin, where Siegel was to work with Salman Rushdie's former editor, Paul Slovak. But while Siegel was pleased and flattered to be working with Slovak, the editor was devoting his promotional energies to the launch of a new book by T. C. Boyle, and Viking balked at the idea of the square-format novel, maintaining that the projected shape of the book would require ordering special boxes when the novel was shipped, which was deemed to be too expensive.

While *Love and Other Games of Chance* emerged from Siegel's research into snake charming, it was also tied to some of his other earlier works. In 1991 Siegel had published a volume titled *Net of Magic: Wonders and Deceptions in India*, which had required unusual research. Siegel recalls spending

> lots of time with itinerant street magicians in India. I studied magic with them and ended up performing with them, first as a stooge and then giving testimonials as to their magic powers. It was quite startling to me that I, a Jew from Beverly Hills with a doctorate from Oxford University, had as my teacher and close friend an itinerant Muslim from a North Indian village who was completely illiterate.
> ("Anatomizing")

Siegel was once a member of the International Brotherhood of Magicians, and much material connected with magic is carried into the central portion of the novel through his comic character Professor Wonderful, while the magician's conceit of pleasurable deception stands, for Siegel, as an analogue for the fiction writer's technique.

At the same time, *Love and Other Games of Chance* also seems to have its roots in Siegel's early ideas for *Love in a Dead Language*. Following the publication of his first novel, Siegel told Michelle Caswell: "I spent a good deal of time trying to imagine reading a book, a book that entertained me enormously, with the idea that, if I could imagine it clearly enough, I might be able to write a version of it down. Once I stopped imagining that the first line was 'Call me Ishmael,' I started writing [*Love in a Dead Language*]." Having completed that novel, Siegel began a 198,000-word story that forms the center of *Love and Other Games of Chance* with the first line "Call me Isaac." The common origins of the two works in this sentence are revealing, because there are multiple connections between these novels about Love. The central conceit of *Love and Other Games of Chance* is embedded in the earlier book, when Roth reflects that "reading, like love, is a game" (p. 8), and both novels include pivotal trips to India, as well as a fictional version of Siegel himself. There is also some overlap in names between the two books: in the earlier novel, Leopold Abraham Roth has a son called Isaac, and in the later work Isaac's father is called Abraham.

The allusion to Melville in the opening line is appropriate for several reasons. First, *Love and Other Games of Chance* marks Siegel's explicit shift toward the mode of the encyclopedic novel, and the Ishmael of Melville's novel who announced that he "swam through libraries" assembling the cetological lore for his text might be taken as the presiding genius of Siegel's book (p. 147). Second, Melville is relevant because—as in all Siegel's novels—the frame story of *Love and Other Games of Chance* is based around the idea of receiving stories from previous generations. The novel begins with Lee Siegel's mother telling him that his father is not the man who has brought him up (Dr. L. E. Siegel, a Beverly Hills physician), but is, in fact, a showman named Isaac Schlossberg. Although his mother believes that Isaac died in 1946, on top of Mount Everest, she gives Lee a Sears & Roebuck carton filled with papers that purport to be Isaac's life story. The box contains one hundred sheets of folded paper covered with writing, a snakes-and-ladders game board, and a single die. The game board has one hundred squares that relate to geographical locations (starting at the lowest place on earth, the Dead Sea, the board runs

through the Wild West and the Mystic East before it arrives at earth's highest point, Mount Everest) and to the folded papers in the box. Each of these papers is numbered and, when read in order, relate the life and loves of Isaac Schlossberg, from his early years appearing in his father's variety act through his various incarnations in India, Britain, Paris, and Russia. The one hundred chapters—each "composed of about two thousand words" (p. 3)—of Isaac's story are embedded within Lee's story and form the bulk of the book, but the two narratives are not isolated. Instead the one hundred chapters are designed to play off the frame tale narrated by Lee Siegel through several similarities, such as the fact that Isaac, like Siegel, has been lied to by his father about his past.

The formal interest of *Love and Other Games of Chance* rests in the way the board's grid relates to the one hundred numbered chapters, which we are encouraged to treat as squares of the board that we can play on, as if they formed a game of snakes and ladders. The game, Siegel explains, is intended

> to be played frivolously ... according to tosses of the die. To play the game, it seems to me, is to become acquainted with the author in the same way we get to know a person in real life. We don't meet people at birth and follow them chronologically, moving through each and every square with them ... we come to know that person better when we hear of their past, when the serpents of their memory reveal what has gone on before.
>
> (p. 5)

This game-board structure has similarities to the work of two writers that Siegel alludes to in the novel. First, references to "Nova Zembla" and "King Humbert" recall Nabokov (pp. 15, 199), and the conceit of a life unfolding according to moves on a board game seems to owe something to Nabokov's chess-suffused novel *The Defense* (1964). In another chess allusion, the last portion of the book is entitled "Endgame," and Isaac's efforts, in the face of a "bleak reality" (p. 50), to convert his life to a board game has affinities with the game of ending that Ham and Clov devise in Samuel Beckett's *Endgame* (1957). But, regardless of literary antecedents, the originality of the board device lies in the way Siegel has carefully interlaced the game's grid of one hundred squares with the text of his story. This is a novel written according to formal constraints, like the "poetic-electronic machine" that Italo Calvino imagines in *The Uses of Literature* (1986), it is an attempt to create a fiction by the governing rules that prescribe a closed form (p. 13). With the novel's narrative particles sealed into two-thousand-word blocks, Siegel has arranged the book so that numerical coincidences frequently occur in incidents from particular chapters, so, for example, in square and chapter 11, Isaac is told about "Finkelman's Industrial Fragrance No. 11" (p. 54). Similarly, as the board is composed of ten rows and ten columns, so Isaac's life is framed by two obsessions that collapse into two tens: performance (notably the ten-in-one shows he takes part in), and love (Isaac falls in love with ten women). At the same time, Siegel cleverly uses the board as an emotional map on which Isaac can locate himself. So when he finds himself isolated in the Soviet Union in chapter 80 (a black square on the left margin of the board), a despairing Isaac can reflect that he is "in a dark square on the edge of the checkered board, repeatedly missing my turn" (p. 327).

It is clear from this kind of careful construction that Siegel is interested in exploring the formal construction of the novel, but what is not clear is how seriously readers are meant to take the conceit of the book as game. The book can be read with great rewards against the conceit, as a linear text from page 1 to page 418. Yet if readers follow the invitation to play the book like a "great aleatory game" (p. 224), letting their encounter with the text be governed by chance, they are apt to think of an argument that Isaac has with his first love, Angel, in square 18. In one of his skittish moods, Isaac tells Angel that snakes and ladders is "a stupid game for little kids.... There's no skill involved. It's all just chance." Angel counters with a defense that paraphrases Siegel's advice about the book, when she claims that "playing it is like living a life. It's nothing more or less than luck" (p. 82). The problem with the dice-driven version of the game is not that Siegel's structure can become "a stupid

game" but rather that if readers' luck is too good then they bypass too many of the local pleasures of Siegel's evolving narrative as they arc toward the empty oblivion of chapter 100.

Contra Angel, such a reading is like living only a shadowy kind of life at best, and the engagement readers may have with the characters will be slim and mysterious. Regardless of any gain in verisimilitude, to proceed through the novel in this way is to risk missing too much of Siegel's linguistic flexibility. Although there are some weaknesses in Siegel's wordplay (he's too skillful and subtle a writer to have to rely on puns like the "Reverend Conwell" or naming a region "Wanktonshire" [pp. 66, 195]), it is his mastery of language as much as the subtlety of the novel's construction that rewards readers of *Love and Other Games of Chance*. Just as Siegel flaunted his talent for wordplay in the "Anagramic Charades" of *Love in a Dead Language,* there is something similar in his second novel when Isaac finds himself playing a game with a man who wants to be paid a penny for every anagram he can make out of Isaac's name. Assuming that he will manage no more than five, Isaac agrees, only to discover (to his horror) that the man's verbal inventiveness produces a long list running from "So crass, I belch gas" to "Gosh, a scribe-class." Isaac ends up paying almost three pounds after only a minute has elapsed (pp. 312–313).

At the same time as he demonstrates his powers of linguistic invention, Siegel offers a parallel exploration of language's limitations. The slippery yet fundamental reality that escapes language's fuzzy net is very much in evidence when Isaac tries to confront his childhood love, Angel, about her new lover:

> "Do you actually sleep with him? And I don't mean 'sleep' in the literal sense. What I mean is, do you actually make love with him? And I don't mean 'make love' in a philosophical sense. What I mean is, does he fuck you? And I don't mean 'fuck' in an expletory sense. What I mean is, do you do *it* with each other?" Angel laughed again, stood up ... tousled my hair, kissed me on the cheek, and said, "I don't know what you mean by *it.*"
>
> (p. 354)

The book is an encyclopedic recapitulation of a life, but it's also a quest to understand love that brings us to the boundaries of language's descriptive power. In this verbally inventive and sophisticated text, Siegel produces postmodern art from classic literary materials, and (given his fondness for allusions to eighteenth-century literature) as he worked on this book's meditation on love he may have had in mind the section from volume 6 of *Tristram Shandy,* where the narrator protests that "I am not *obliged* to set out with a definition of what love is ... so long as I can go on with my story intelligibly" (p. 421). Siegel is as fond of formal innovation as Sterne, but such is his interest in encyclopedic coverage of his subject that he *does* include a definition of love when he introduces the sideshow act, Madame Mnemosyne, who has memorized a dictionary. Her final definition of love is "the affection of one created being to another thence arising" (p. 272), but the book is equally preoccupied with the affection felt for a progenitor. This affection is manifest on several levels, but the network of intertextual relations to the novel's literary ancestors reveal a deep love of both reading and language.

Second novels traditionally receive a sterner examination from reviewers, and critical response to *Love and Other Games of Chance* was somewhat more subdued than the rapturous reception that greeted *Love in a Dead Language*. While Tom LeClair had raved about Siegel's first novel, he criticized his second in *Book* magazine for an excess that destabilized the proportions of the reading experience—the novel, he said, "must have a hundred characters, most with ... little purchase on the reader's affections." Reviewing the novel for the *New York Times,* Eric Weinberger described the novel as being "written in the sustained high pitch of carnal joy, and will, rightly, attract readers for that quality alone," but ultimately he found the book merely funny, lacking "the anger that becomes satire," and he criticized the end for descending into "nervous self-regard." Later the novel's closing lines would be nominated for inclusion in the *American Book Review*'s 2008 collection of the "Best Last Lines," and it's worth noting that several other reviews praised Siegel's novel. Writing in the

Washington Post, Steven Moore drew parallels to the writing of Julio Cortázar and Milorad Pavić, before he "warmly recommended" Siegel's intricate text to readers (p. 5). Daniel Dennett selected *Love and Other Games of Chance* as one of the books of the year for the *Times Literary Supplement* and described it as an "amazing ... intricately crafted cornucopia of magic tricks and side-show lore" (p. 9).

The novel is an encyclopedic text that stresses the fluidity of identity and the central character's movement up and down the game board, so *Love and Other Games of Chance* represents the central panel of Bosch's triptych—the section that offers the most comprehensive views of both creation and sexuality, and which (like a game in motion) is suspended between the two definitive poles of origin and ending that are summarized in the flanking panels of the triptych.

WHO WROTE THE BOOK OF LOVE?

After writing two dense, experimental fictions that showcased his linguistic dexterity and formal invention, Siegel took a momentary retreat from eye-catching formal explorations in his third novel. While his first two books demonstrated his talent for embedding novels in non-novelistic forms, Siegel evidently turned to the more accessible format of the memoir for *Who Wrote the Book of Love?* (2005). Part of the reason for the shift away from the layered puzzles of his early fiction was geographic—much of Siegel's third novel was composed in France, far from his library and research materials. In some ways an offshoot from the rest of his fiction, *Who Wrote the Book of Love?* parallels the comparatively simple cover of Bosch's triptych, with Siegel's emphasis on the emergence of consciousness and the growth of sexual feeling acting as a counterpart to the near-monochrome painting of the creation of the world.

Indeed, Siegel initially conceived of the novel not as an extension of his earlier works but as the first installment of a new pentalogy designed to trace the development of sexual love from the 1950s to the millennium, with each book devoted to a different decade. But while the book is something of an offshoot, in significant ways it also echoes the earlier works. "Though the weaver of tales," Siegel had written in *City of Dreadful Night,* "often stops with *but that's another story,* there are no other stories, no separate, discreet [*sic*] tales. There are no borders. All of the stories are intertwined and overlapping: characters from this one inevitably walk through that one" (p. 50). Staying true to this philosophy, *Who Wrote the Book of Love?* marks the reappearance of Leopold Roth, this time as one of the narrator's fellow pupils, while several of the signal obsessions of *Love and Other Games of Chance* (pomade, Mount Everest) also return.

Who Wrote the Book of Love? is a chronicle of a boy's sexual awakening in Beverly Hills in the 1950s, and it unfolds in ten sections that cover a year each. The narrator of the memoir is an apparently semifictional Lee Siegel, and the memoir begins in 1950, when at the age of four or five he is given a child's guide to sex by his parents. This is a seminal moment for the young Siegel, who will turn out to be obsessed not just with love, but with books and language, too. In this respect the boy has much in common with the book's author, and Siegel subtly stresses this parallel by humorously replaying his own literary strategies through the boy's writing. Just as Siegel attempted to rewrite Nabokov and Melville in his earlier love books, so his young narrator produces a romantic revision of *The Adventures of Tom Sawyer* to prove in a term paper that Tom has sexual intercourse with Becky Thatcher in chapter 31 of the book. But while the adult author gets praised in literary journals, the boy narrator is suspended from school and dropped from the swim team. This is a hard first lesson about literary censorship.

With the book's chronology tied to the narrator's development, transformation becomes the controlling idea behind Siegel's memoir, though his earlier books insist that mutability is embedded in the word "love" itself. Siegel notes near the end of *Love in a Dead Language* that "we cannot comprehend the meaning (either the intent or significance) of our word for *love* ... the meanings of abstract words in a living language

cannot be fixed; by their essential nature they are persistently and insistently changing as the living language changes" (p. 325). Appropriately, *Who Wrote the Book of Love?* builds on this idea, exploring the way the significance attached to the word "love" changes, and develops, as Siegel matures. The narrator views love variously as imaginary, voyeuristic, and deceptive, as he draws nearer to discovering love as a physical fulfillment. But as the concept signified by the word "love" changes for the narrator, so Siegel traces parallel changes in the young Siegel. Some development is inevitable in a memoir, but what is unusual about the metamorphoses of the narrator is the degree of self-consciousness that accompanies his transformations. This becomes clear on the many occasions when the narrator examines himself in the mirror. The first time he does this he is trying out a cowboy outfit:

> I looked at myself in the large mirrors on the closet doors of my mother's dressing room. If the doors were opened at just the right angles to each other, I could see myself from all sides, and, when the mirrors faced each other just so and I squeezed in between them, millions of cowboys lined up behind me, and another million faced me. And all of them were me.
>
> (p. 34)

The narrator's fondness for producing multiple versions of himself in a mirror partly recalls Siegel's observation in *Love and Other Games of Chance* that "the first time we're in love, it's with ourselves" (p. 120), but it also reveals something central to his understanding of selfhood. For the narrator, personal identity is a role that is selected from a number of possible selves in a search to find the form that will be the most successful in love. With this in mind, the narrator positions himself between mirrors to examine the many reflections of his self at key stages in the book, and experiments by adopting different personalities—cowboy, Indian brave, gorilla, and finally poet—to win over the girl of his dreams, and culminate his study of love.

This installment in Siegel's novelistic career is not as overtly flamboyant as his earlier works, but the effects are probably subtler, and there is much authentic narrative and linguistic energy to enjoy in *Who Wrote the Book of Love?* His exuberant humor, his re-creation of midcentury nuclear terror, as well as Siegel's trademark wordplay, should have extended the growing reputation as a writer Siegel established with his first two novels. But a breakthrough to a larger audience proved elusive for Siegel. Prior to the novel's publication, he told *Publishers Weekly* that he had returned to the University of Chicago Press because he did not feel that Penguin had really supported his last novel. This rationale seemed justified because Chicago evidently took great care over the presentation of *Who Wrote the Book of Love?*—indeed, its dust jacket won an award from the Association of American University Presses for its design—but when *Who Wrote the Book of Love?* was released on August 1, 2005, its reception was muted. Apart from a short snippet review in *Booklist*—in which Donna Seaman concluded that "as always, mischievous Siegel revels in the magic of language while offering tart social commentary on everything from Jewish assimilation to racism to the atomic bomb, but never has his humor been sharper or his characters more alluring" (p. 1572)—the novel received only three, albeit universally positive, reviews. The novelist Wilton Barnhardt covered the book for the *Chicago Tribune* and announced that the novel was "hilarious," but added that "Siegel has not just written a royally entertaining comic memoir, but he has given us a time capsule of our one-time national innocence" (p. 1). Stephen Burn in the *American Book Review* noted that the novel was less experimental than Siegel's previous two books, but praised its subtlety and humor before noting that it was a "worthy and more accessible counterpart to his earlier love novels" (p. 19). In England, Tom Payne reviewed the novel for the *Daily Telegraph* and found Siegel's work to be a clever balancing act of literary sophistication and a child's naiveté. It is surely worse, however, to be noticed by lawyers than to be merely ignored by reviewers, and because Siegel's novel took its title from, and worked several variations upon, a 1958 song by the Monotones, ARC records announced their intention to sue Siegel shortly after the book's publication.

Writing more accessible prose had not yielded the kind of breakthrough to a larger audience that Siegel had hoped for, but with the coverpiece of Bosch's triptych behind him it was time to close the loop by moving to the Garden of Eden.

LOVE AND THE INCREDIBLY OLD MAN

The left-hand panel of Bosch's triptych is devoted to the garden of Eden, and as that panel is dominated by the fountain of life, it makes sense that Siegel's fourth novel, *Love and the Incredibly Old Man* (2008), should focus upon Ponce de Leon. Siegel's fascination with Ponce de Leon clearly germinated over a considerable period of time. The fake bibliography at the end of *Love in a Dead Language* includes a book published by the "Ponce de Leon Society" (p. 369). In *Love and Other Games of Chance,* Isaac stars as Ponce de Leon in a Hollywood movie, and in that novel (in a summary that clearly looks forward to *Love and the Incredibly Old Man*) Bugsy Siegel describes the germ for the planned film: "Wouldn't it be something if there really was a Fountain of Youth and this Ponce de Leon actually found it, but didn't tell anybody because he wanted to keep it for himself, and he's still alive today, looking as young as ever" (p. 379). Similarly, the Lee Siegel of *Who Wrote the Book of Love?* attends Ponce de Leon elementary school and stars in "Fountain of Youth!"—a musical comedy that's performed (suggestively) on April 1st in Siegel's school.

From a formal point of view, Siegel's fourth novel, *Love and the Incredibly Old Man* belongs somewhere in the middle of a continuum that runs from the narrative experiments of his first two novels to the more transparent style of *Who Wrote the Book of Love?* but like all of the earlier works its premise is based around a story received from an old man. In this instance, however, the elderly gentleman is extremely elderly—the old man in question claims to be Ponce de Leon who, having lived (as Bugsy Siegel predicted) on the waters of the Fountain of Youth for nearly five hundred years now seeks a ghostwriter to record his story before he dies. Having been impressed by the earlier references to Ponce de Leon in Siegel's fiction, the supposed conquistador hires the novelist to write his life.

The novel sets out, then, with a comic retelling of the Spaniard's life that alternates between chapters in which the old man gives instructions to Siegel about how he should be memorialized, and chapters supposedly written by Siegel to meet his employer's instructions. This structure permits Siegel to stage humorous historical set pieces in one narrative while simultaneously questioning biographical and historical writing in the other, as Ponce tells Siegel, "The important thing is that you write everything I have told you in such a way that readers will forgive me for doing whatever it is that they will imagine I did" (p. 136). Having established this structure, however, the narrative balance begins to shift as Ponce de Leon becomes increasingly impatient. Despite having lived for five centuries, the old man can't tolerate the time it's taking Siegel to finish his book, so the structure fragments as the work goes on, with the Spaniard's voice beginning to drown out the novelist's. Just as Walter Shandy found that life outran his attempt to record it in Sterne's *Tristram Shandy,* so Siegel turns out to be unable to write quickly enough to keep up with Ponce's unreasonable expectations. Pressured by the clock, Siegel begins to cheat. Bosch's panel captures the moment where God introduces Eve to Adam, and so Ponce de Leon turns out to be fascinated by minute descriptions of the beauty of his lovers. But while he's preoccupied with his former lovers, he's rather shaky on literary history, so as the old man begins to berate and pressure the novelist for not writing his story quickly enough, Siegel begins to plagiarize, salvaging memorable first lines from earlier writers:

> "The opening must be seductive," Mr. De Leon had insisted. "First words should make the reader, or the woman want more." In an effort to satisfy my employer, I had drafted opening line after opening line ... nothing seemed to work. I became so desperate that I actually typed "Stately, plump Pedro Menendez came from the stairhead, bearing a bowl of lather on which a mirror and razor lay crossed." Promptly deleting that, and then musing that what was good enough for Kafka ought to be good

> enough for Mr. De Leon, I wrote, "As Ponce de Leon awoke one morning from a troubled dream, he found himself changed in his bed into some monstrous kind of book."
>
> (p. 106)

Much of the reader's fun derives from decoding the deeper resonance of Siegel's exuberant thefts. The chapter that begins "Call me Ponce," for example, imitates *Moby-Dick*'s encyclopedic reach, matching Melville's exhaustive collection of references to whales by constructing an alphabetical list of Ponce's former lovers (p. 162). At the same time as Siegel plays these intertextual games, the novel is driven forward by the interplay between the aloof Spaniard and an increasingly exasperated Siegel, who has to try to explain to Ponce that he can't claim "I loved her more than any other woman ever" in reference to a different woman in every chapter of his memoir (p. 196). Siegel's achievement is to persuade the reader to care about such a self-involved, and possibly delusional, character while staging jokes at his expense and showcasing his own verbal dexterity.

In some ways a more static novel than his earlier works (though that dimension is admittedly offset by the book's remarkable historical range), *Love and the Incredibly Old Man* was, again, mostly overlooked by review editors, though the *Times Literary Supplement* devoted a full-page review to the novel, with Stephen Burns concluding that Siegel's novels offered a rare mix of humor and erudition that deserved a wider audience. Stefan Beck praised the novel as "an audacious and accomplished act of imagination" in the *Barnes & Noble Review*.

While many of Siegel's novels have received relatively little attention from critics and reviewers, ten years into the twenty-first century there are hints that critical taste may be catching up with his work. While the postwar Jewish American novel—as practiced by Philip Roth, Saul Bellow, or E. L. Doctorow—made considerable compromises with the codes of realist fiction, a younger generation of writers has been remaking Jewish American fiction by fusing its heritage with the experimental edge of postmodern fiction. Whether acknowledged or not, Lee Siegel is the authentic ancestor of such ambitious, linguistically extravagant, new works as Joshua Cohen's *Witz* (2010) and Adam Levin's *The Instructions* (2010), and—whatever he writes after the completion of his Bosch triptych—his reputation is likely to grow as critics and writers discover his fiction's complex qualities and many rewards.

Selected Bibliography

WORKS OF LEE SIEGEL

FICTION

Vivisections. Bellingham, Wash.: Goliards, 1973.

Love in a Dead Language. Chicago: University of Chicago Press, 1999.

Love and Other Games of Chance: A Novelty. New York: Viking, 2003; Penguin, 2004.

Who Wrote the Book of Love? Chicago: University of Chicago Press, 2005.

Love and the Incredibly Old Man. Chicago: University of Chicago Press, 2008.

NONFICTION

Sacred and Profane Dimensions of Love in Indian Traditions. Oxford: Oxford University Press, 1979.

Fires of Love/Waters of Peace: Passion and Renunciation in Indian Culture. Honolulu: University of Hawaii Press, 1983.

Laughing Matters: Comic Tradition in India. Chicago: University of Chicago Press, 1987.

Net of Magic: Wonders and Deceptions in India. Chicago: University of Chicago Press, 1991.

City of Dreadful Night: A Tale of Horror and the Macabre in India. Chicago: University of Chicago Press, 1995.

Gitagovínda: Love Songs of Radha and Krishna, by Jayadeva. New York: Clay Sanskrit Library and New York University Press, 2009.(Translator.)

UNCOLLECTED WRITINGS

Letters to Henry Miller. Manuscript, n.d., Young Research Library, Los Angeles.

"Sweet Sensations." *Washington Post Book World,* January 14, 2001, p. 3.

"Passages." *Washington Post Book World,* April 28, 2002, p. 7.

"Hawaii: The Aloha State." In *These United States: Original Essays by Leading Writers on Their State Within the*

Union. Edited by John Leonard. New York: Thunder's Mouth Press, 2003. Pp. 102–111.

CRITICAL AND BIOGRAPHICAL STUDIES

Boddy, Kasia. "Regular Lolitas: The Afterlives of an American Adolescent." In *American Fiction of the 1990s: Reflections of History and Culture*. Edited by Jay Prosser. London: Routledge, 2008. Pp. 164–176.

Burn, Stephen J. "The End of Postmodernism: American Fiction at the Millennium." In *American Fiction of the 1990s: Reflections of History and Culture*. Edited by Jay Prosser. Abingdon, U.K., and New York: Routledge, 2008. Pp. 220–234.

Bursey, Jeff. "A Myth of One's Own: Henry Miller and Lee Siegel." Unpublished manuscript.

McConnachie, James. *The Book of Love: The Story of the Kamasutra*. New York: Metropolitan-Holt, 2008.

Moore, Steven. *The Novel: An Alternative History*. New York: Continuum, 2010.

Moraru, Christian. *Memorious Discourse: Reprise and Representation in Postmodernism*. Madison, N.J.: Fairleigh Dickinson University Press, 2005.

Ruthven, K. K. *Faking Literature*. Cambridge, U.K., and New York: Cambridge University Press, 2001.

REVIEWS

Barnhardt, Wilton. "An Amusing Memoir and Time Capsule of 1950s America." *Chicago Tribune,* July 31, 2005, book section, p. 1.

Beck, Stefan. "*Love and the Incredibly Old Man*." *Barnes & Noble Review,* June 11, 2008 (http://bnreview.barnesandnoble.com/t5/Reviews-Essays/Love-and-the-Incredibly-Old-Man/ba-p/453).

Bernstein, Richard. "Lalita, Post-Modern Object of Desire." *New York Times,* September 8, 1999, p. E7.

Burn, Stephen. "Metamorphosis." *American Book Review* 27, no. 2:19 (2006).

———. "Call Me Ponce." *Times Literary Supplement,* April 18, 2008, p. 19.

Dennett, Daniel C. "Books of the Year." *Times Literary Supplement,* December 5, 2003, p. 9.

Di Filippo, Paul. "Textual Pleasures." *Washington Post Book World,* June 27, 1999, p. 5.

Dyer, Richard. "Intellectual's Sex Life Translates into a Lot of Laughs." *Star-Ledger* (Newark), September 12, 1999, p. 5.

LeClair, Tom. "The Kama Sutra and Then Some." *New York Times Book Review,* May 23, 1999, p. 14.

———. "*Love and Other Games of Chance*." *Book.* March–April 2003.

Moore, Steven. "Indian Love Call." *American Book Review* 21, no. 4:17 (2000).

———. "Magic Acts." *Washington Post Book World,* February 2, 2003, p. 5.

Payne, Tom. "Ice Cream in His Blue Suede Shoes." *Daily Telegraph*, August 13, 2005 (http://www.telegraph.co.uk/culture/books/3646035/Ice-cream-in-his-blue-suede-shoes.html).

Seaman, Donna. "*Who Wrote the Book of Love?*" *Booklist,* May 1, 2005, p. 1572.

Scott, R. C. "Prognostications, Tattoos, and Chance." *Washington Times,* July 13, 2003, p. B6.

Weinberger, Eric. "Ice Ax Envy." *New York Times Book Review,* February 16, 2003 (http://www.nytimes.com/2003/02/16/books/ice-ax-envy.html).

INTERVIEWS

Banker, Ashok. "Conversation in a Dead Language: Reprint of an Interview with Lee Siegel." *Blog Critics,* September 23, 2005.

Burn, Stephen J. "Anatomizing the Language of Love: An Interview with Lee Siegel." *Electronic Book Review*. September 28, 2006 (http://www.electronicbookreview.com/thread/criticalecologies/fabricated).

Caswell, Michelle. "An Interview with Lee Siegel." *Asia Source*. Asia Society, 2003.

Devasahayam, Madona. "The Rediff Interview: Lee Siegel." *Rediff on the Net*, June 2, 1999 (http://www.rediff.com/news/1999/jun/02us2.htm).

Gold, Sarah. "How to Save a Midlist Author." *Publishers Weekly,* June 20, 2005, p. 30.

OTHER SOURCES

Bakhtin, Mikhail. *Problems of Dostoevsky's Poetics.* Edited and translated by Caryl Emerson. Minneapolis: University of Minnesota Press, 1984.

Barth, John. *The Friday Book.* Baltimore: Johns Hopkins University Press, 1997.

———. *Coming Soon!!!* Boston: Houghton Mifflin Harcourt, 2001.

Calvino, Italo. *The Uses of Literature.* Boston: Houghton Mifflin Harcourt, 1986.

Coover, Robert. "The End of Books." *New York Times,* June 21, 1992 (http://www.nytimes.com/books/98/09/27/specials/coover-end.html).

De Tolnay, Charles. *Hieronymus Bosch.* Translated by Michael Bullock and Henry Mins. London: Methuen, 1966.

Park, Ed. "Titles Within a Tale." *New York Times Book Review,* July 26 2009, p. 19.

Parla, Paul, and Charles P. Mitchell. *Screen Sirens Scream! Interviewswith 20 Actresses from Science Fiction, Horror, Film Noir, and Mystery Movies, 1930s to 1960s.* Jefferson, N.C.: McFarland, 2000.

Sterne, Laurence. *The Life and Opinions of Tristram Shandy, Gentleman*. London: Penguin, 2003.

GENEVIEVE TAGGARD

(1894—1948)

Robert Niemi

ONE OF THE most respected and celebrated poets of her day, Genevieve Taggard has fallen into near total obscurity. When she *is* mentioned by latter-day critics, it might be with condescension or scorn. For example, in a 2001 review of Cary Nelson's *Anthology of Modern American Poetry* (2000), no less an authority than Marjorie Perloff dismissed Taggard's 1940 poem "Ode in Time of Crisis" as "just vague rant, as inaccurate and bland as the patriotic sloganeering it opposes" (p. 180). Perloff went on to wonder why Taggard was even included in Nelson's anthology.

Marjorie Perloff's assessment carries a certain intimidating weight. An esteemed doyenne of academic poetry critics, Perloff traffics in the cultural-capital-intensive upper reaches of avant-garde postmodern theory. Yet this may be precisely the problem. From Perloff's vantage point and ideological-aesthetic biases, a poet like Genevieve Taggard offers an easy target. Though she started out as a highly lauded and more or less conventionally romantic lyric poet in the 1920s, during the Great Depression of the 1930s Taggard turned to political verse that protested capitalist inequality and exploitation and dramatized the sufferings and struggles of ordinary working-class people. In other words, Taggard chose to place worldly sociopolitical concerns before lofty aesthetic principles and doomed herself to what elitists regard as pedestrianism—the ultimate sin for Marjorie Perloff and other cultural mandarins for whom social engagement is decidedly passé, even puerile. In short, the eclipse and erasure of Genevieve Taggard has much more to do with deliberate political repression of a perceived outsider (and subversive) than it does with neglect based strictly on meritocratic concerns. But history has vindicated Taggard. As the world capitalist system undergoes ever deeper and more catastrophic cycles of crisis, the life and work of a radical poet like Genevieve Taggard takes on new prescience and relevance—and deserves a second look.

Irene Genevieve "Jed" Taggard was born on November 28, 1894, in Waitsburg, Washington, one of three children of James Nelson Taggard and Alta Gale (Arnold) Taggard, schoolteachers and members of the Disciples of Christ, a mainline Protestant denomination founded in the early nineteenth century. Alta Arnold Taggard, a grandchild of the original Waitsburg settlers, was, in her daughter's words, "a pioneer extrovert, a hard-working, high-handed generous and handsome girl" who always aspired to attend college and "become a Christian gentlewoman." Missouri native James Taggard was principal of the Waitsburg elementary school where Alta Arnold taught first grade. His daughter described him as looking like Abraham Lincoln "but delicate and quixotic." Captivated by Alta's self-possessed bearing and strength of will, James Taggard married her (p. ii).

HAWAII

In 1897, when Genevieve Taggard was two years old, her parents relocated the family to the Hawaiian island of Oahu, where they opened a missionary school at Kalihiwaena, in the hills above Honolulu, that catered to Hawaii's many ethnic groups—Portuguese, Puerto Ricans, Japanese, Chinese, Hawaiian-Chinese, and hapa haoles (white Hawaiians). Though the family lived on the subsistence level, life in the Islands was, in many ways, good. In the preface to *Calling Western Union* (1936) Taggard recalled her childhood and youth there as "happy-go-lucky": "We dressed as children dress now in the sum-

mer, as children did not dress in 1910. And we were accustomed to an immense enjoyment in every day of life. All these things had very little to do with money, because we were poor; but it did not matter very much, in the Islands. This was our Garden of Eden; our newfoundland" (p. iv).

From 1906 to 1910 Taggard studied at Punahou School, Honolulu (where her brother, James Norman, and her sister, Ernestine Kealoha, were also enrolled). In 1907, at the age of thirteen, Taggard began to write poetry. Her first published poem, "Mitchie-Gawa" (about American Indians), appeared in the school magazine, the *Oahuan,* in 1910. A two-year hiatus from Hawaii followed. The Taggards were forced to return to Washington State for a year because of James Taggard's respiratory problems. The other year Genevieve spent teaching on a neighboring island. The Taggard children returned to Punahou School from 1912 to 1914. Thirty-three years later, Taggard invoked this period in the preface to her final verse collection, *Origin: Hawaii* (1947):

> We were living in Pearl Harbor.... I was reading Latin and playing the piano. I did both badly, impressionistically, never accurately, but I touched something I still keep. We had a little Victrola, a light brown oaken one that we carried with us, and a few songs by Schumann in German; our lives were enormously enriched by a friend who took us sailing. Other things stirred me in those days to attempt poems, but what I wrote was sentimental and blurry in imitation of bad models. I am forever indebted, when I remember those years, to the kindness of Mrs. Walter Frear, in whose house we lived on the Peninsula. The German lyrics became a standard of something fine and remote, the bees in our algaroba trees made the same sound that Virgil imitated in the Latin text, and sailing added something new—the masculine pleasure of boats. One's miseries—and there were some which were acute, having to do with my father's illness and the lack of money—became the final push toward writing.
>
> (p. i)

Taggard published verse and short fiction in *Punahou,* the school paper, at regular intervals. In the poem "She Sings" (October 1912), Taggard imagines a perfect fusion with nature, seeing herself as "Näid, the Nymph of the Wave" and "the Old, Old Sea" as her nurturing father. "Song of the Dryads" (April 1913) involves a similar, Whitmanesque conceit. The Dryads—perhaps Taggard and her young companions—"live in the tall, tall trees, / In the limbs, and the trunks and the / leaves / We rustle and shake / We shiver and quake / And lie on their boughs at our ease" (Rauner Special Collections Library, Dartmouth College). Once again, the image drawn is of sublime fusion with the natural world. Taggard's short story "As a Little Child" (June 1913, Rauner Special Collections Library, Dartmouth College) provides a telling contrast to her verse paeans to nature. Probably quasi-autobiographical, "Child" relates a poignant anecdote in the young lives of Paul and Marie, brother and sister in an impoverished, fatherless family that takes in neighbors' washing in order to survive. Marie has already left school "to iron": "It had been a sort of tragedy in her life, but grief was not in her vocabulary and she did not know self-pity. It was only for Paul that she desired." Paul wants to attend school but lacks even a shirt to wear; he is forced to don a despised "ragged brown sack." Marie proposes that Paul pick guavas to sell to the "Lady Teacher" at his school. This simple plan goes awry when Paul accidentally swallows the dime he is paid. He steals a quarter from the teacher and Marie is able to buy and refurbish a shirt for him. After two glorious weeks at school Paul witnesses another student being castigated for stealing a pair of scissors. His conscience stirred, Paul packs his shirt in a "neatly pinned newspaper parcel" and leaves it on his teacher's front steps with a note: "Paul been steal quarter. I been make shirt. To steal is bad. Paul stay home." Already the victim of a social order that renders him destitute, Paul takes to heart a petty righteous morality that prevents him from getting an education—Taggard's wry commentary as to how the moralistic psychology of oppression works on the poor and ignorant to keep them in their place.

WASHINGTON STATE

Genevieve Taggard's tropical sojourn came to a final end in 1914, when the Taggards were forced

to return to the mainland permanently. Impoverished and with few options, they returned to Waitsburg, Washington, where James Taggard's brother, John, owned an apple farm. Though James had lent his brother John $1,500 to buy the farm twenty years earlier, John never paid back the sum. To add grievous insult to injury, John Taggard treated his brother and family as shameful charity cases only fit for a kind of indentured servitude: "The stalwart American who owned us was our uncle who still owed us money. Because long ago we had lent him some money he was soon a jump ahead of his fellow townsmen and then soon possessed several of them. That gave him a taste for the thing—he was a realistic man; he never signed papers unless they were in his favor. We had no papers to show for what he owed to us. When in good time we returned to the wheat country he let us live in the unfinished house he had acquired, and we became his hired help" (*Calling Western Union,* p. xix).

For Genevieve Taggard, the bitter irony of being exploited by a hard-hearted, cheating relative was made far worse by the life she found in Waitsburg. The summers were dusty and bug-ridden and the winters cold, work on the farm was arduous and ill paid, high school was a stultifying "desolate place" and the townsfolk mean-spirited, provincial, and selfish—a far cry from the eternally sunny weather and casual goodness, cheerfulness, and multiracial tolerance of the people she encountered in Hawaii. The contrast between these two worlds was a revelation to Taggard, and its somber lessons would remain with her all her life. In restrained tones she admitted that Waitsburg "seem[ed] to be the active source of many of [my] convictions. It told me what to work against and what to work for" (p. xxv). For the rest of her life she would search for a community that was all-inclusive and just.

BERKELEY, CALIFORNIA

After several abject seasons in Waitsburg, the Taggards relocated to Berkeley, California, where Genevieve and her mother worked as servants in a Berkeley boardinghouse that catered to university students. With borrowed money, Taggard was able to enroll at the University of California at Berkeley as a scholarship student in the fall of 1914, just after World War I had broken out in Europe. There she blossomed intellectually and artistically under the tutelage of the poets Witter Brynner (1881–1968) and Leonard Bacon (1887–1954). Recognized as unusually talented, Taggard joined Chi Omega and the English Club and was appointed editor of the *Occident,* the university's literary magazine; she published her verse therein and began to realistically envision literature and writing as her life's vocation.

During her time at Berkeley, Taggard also came to consider herself a socialist and was confident enough in her political views to sign a petition protesting the red-baiting Espionage Act of 1917. Just before graduating, Taggard fired off a parting shot with "The University's Peril," a controversial editorial in the *Occident* (March 7, 1919) in which she lambasted university officials for discouraging socially engaged discourse on campus: "We are in the stone age of academic possibilities. A professor blushes to speak of temporary events; a pupil goes unanswered when he asks questions about his world instead of dead men's. How well and how beautifully we could exchange our spotless aloof for a little grime, how wisely we might relinquish a false dignity for a real one."

NEW YORK CITY

Soon after graduating from Berkeley in May 1919—the so-called Red Summer, marked by bloody race riots and lynchings in two dozen American cities—Taggard, now in her mid-twenties, moved to New York City to take an apprentice editorial job with the prominent modernist publisher B. W. Huebsch. The timing proved auspicious, as the influenza pandemic of 1918–1919 had begun to loosen its grip on most American cities including New York. Taggard naturally gravitated to Manhattan's Greenwich Village. Rents were cheap, the streets quiet, and a vibrant bohemian scene was beginning to open up. The poets Edna St. Vincent Millay, Marianne

Moore, and Hart Crane lived there at the time, as did the literary-political firebrands John Reed, Max Eastman, Joseph Freeman, and many other artists and writers of note.

In the latter months of 1919 Taggard met a twenty-four-year-old Harvard-educated poet-critic named Robert L. Wolf and the two began a passionate affair, perhaps Taggard's first. Entries from an unpublished journal written by Taggard in January 1920 reveal her tumultuous feelings: "This sudden thing has turned me into a demanding desiring practical *hateful* unpoetic person. Does desire always ruin people? Before I was serene; I made no demands. I was frank. Now I—no." And elsewhere: "O I yearn for him & his yearn-ness. He is to me the essence of life; he is a perfect person; a man Walt Whitman would have loved" (Rauner Special Collections Library, Dartmouth College). After an intense, whirlwind courtship Taggard and Robert L. Wolf married on March 21, 1921—the first day of spring. That same month *Measure: A Journal of Verse,* cofounded by Taggard, Maxwell Anderson, Padraic Colum, and other literary cohorts made its debut. On December 13, 1921—a little less than nine months after her wedding night—and while en route to California, Genevieve and Robert stopped off in Chicago, where Genevieve gave birth to a daughter the couple named Marcia Sarah.

SAN FRANCISCO

In 1922, with Taggard and her family settled in San Francisco, Thomas Seltzer (New York) published *For Eager Lovers,* Taggard's first volume of verse and a book that contains poems primarily about the joys of nature as contrasted with the vicissitudes of romantic love, especially love's tendency to distract the poet from her poetry—and from herself. Indeed, the title, *For Eager Lovers,* connotes more admonition than invitation.

Taggard divided the book into three sections: "The Way Things Go," "Ice Age," and "On the Earth and Under It." "The Way Things Go" further subdivides into four numbered sections with the thirty-two short poems therein forming a rough autobiographical sequence, from youth through marriage to motherhood. In "Just Introduced," Taggard recalls her meeting her future husband, Robert Wolf, as a euphoric, sexually charged encounter: "Only a few hours! / We danced like wind / Thirsty as blown flowers / Heavy lidded, fearful eyed" (p. 10). In "Married," Taggard expresses the heartache of temporary separation from the beloved: "And this dull chant goes through my head, / And this dull moan sinks in my heart: / *Half of my body must be dead. / We are apart"* (p. 14). Yet the next poem, pointedly titled "Leave Me Alone a Little," conveys the opposite sentiment: "Leave me alone a little! / Must I be yours, / When all my heart is pouring with the sea / Out to the moon's impersonal majesty?" (p. 15). More troubling is "Black Laughter," a poem that reveals serious marital discord:

> Our love began
> Between flash and crash,—
> Terror seen and terror heard.
> See what a cripple our love is!
> It is sullen; sometimes it makes walls of black laughter;
> It is fond of words, fond of thick vowels,
> It mimics thunder.
> Between us it limps:
> We wait for it, when we must, faces averted.
>
> (pp. 16–17)

In "The Quiet Woman," Taggard vents her rage, her desire not be possessed and dominated by her husband:

> I will defy you down until my death
> With cold body, indrawn breath;
> ...
> if fond you could see
> All the caged arrogance in me,
> You would not lean so boyishly, so bold,
> To kiss my body, quivering and cold.
>
> (p. 18)

"I Have Moved West" reiterates the woman's implacable desire for complete autonomy: "You cannot hold, you cannot hinder me" (p. 19). With the more measured and poignant "Everyday Alchemy," Taggard offers a protofeminist view

of male-female relationships that detects male weakness beneath the tendency to dominate the women they supposedly love. Disconnected from nature—"no mountain space, no tree with placid leaves"—men must seek their spiritual solace from women: "Men go to women mutely for their peace." Women's fate is to dredge "out of their heart's poverty" peace "for worn men" (p. 46). This decidedly pessimistic assessment of the possibility for an emotionally healthy union of the sexes was a deeply held conviction for Taggard, one she would reiterate in many later poems.

With "Revolution," the final poem in the book, Taggard moves from the politics of interpersonal relationships to politics writ large and provides a preview of the direction Taggard's poetry would take in later years. The poem's central image is that of the seed: a seed of popular discontent that will someday sprout into a "tender green" shoot of rebellion that will "sunder back the dead / Two halves of hemispheres—to pierce the crust / Of ages' rubbish, crowns and cults and dust!" (p. 70).

In a perceptive review for the *Nation* (February 28, 1923), Mark Van Doren noted that Taggard's "passions are those of a lover, but they are also—and this has come to seem inevitable in an American poetess—those of one who likes sometimes to escape from love. The will is sudden and strong with her to live alone with the sea, to penetrate and identify herself with vegetation, wind, and heat, to love that is to say, impersonally and abstractly." Van Doren praised Taggard for her "passion, lucidity, and thorough technical competence" and predicted that she would find "a permanent place" among "the considerable poets of contemporary America."

During this period Taggard taught poetry courses and workshops at 1037 Broadway. As was noted by a biographical piece ("The Gossip Shop," *Bookman,* August 1923), Taggard and her husband made unusual living arrangements: "Within a radius of a few miles she lives, her husband lives, the baby lives; but all under different roofs. This is because they feel (I suppose the baby, though small, is precocious) that they can accomplish more in their different pursuits apart from each other, yet near enough to visit when the spirit moves." Independent living seems to have had the desired, conducive effect on work. Taggard completed *Hawaiian Hilltop,* a chapbook (or "brochure") of seventeen poems about her beloved Hawaii. Published by Wyckoff & Gelber (San Francisco) in November 1923, *Hawaiian Hilltop* celebrates the breathtaking beauty of Hawaii ("Bronze Boy," "Tropic Mother's Melody," "Child Tropics"); its sultry weather ("Kona Storm," "Kona Rain"); the diversity of its indigenous and immigrant peoples ("Native Daphne," "Portygee Love-Song," "To a Brown Face"); and the vibrancy of its ancient myths ("Solar Myth," "Skull Song"). The feeling that permeates this slender volume is one of blazing sunlight, elemental energies, and verdant spaces.

NEW PRESTON, CONNECTICUT

That same year (1923) Taggard and her family moved to a very different kind of world: New Preston, a rural village on Lake Waramaug in western Connecticut, and Taggard's husband, Robert L. Wolf, published his first and only book of verse: *After Disillusion: Poems* (Thomas Seltzer, New York). Over the next several years Taggard tended to her young daughter, coped with an increasingly troubled marriage, wrote poetry, and made fresh forays into editing. At the suggestion of her husband, Taggard put together an anthology of poems originally published in *Masses* and *Liberator* magazines between 1912 and 1924. Published in 1925 by Boni & Liveright, *May Days: An Anthology of Verse from Masses-Liberator* gathers some 175 poems by almost as many poets, male and female, famous and obscure, chosen and edited by Taggard and illustrated with exquisite woodcuts by J. J. Lankes. Max Eastman appears most frequently (twelve poems) but a few other poets also enjoy ample representation: Claude McKay (five poems), Hazel Hall (four poems), Helen Hoyt (four poems), Anne Herendeen (three poems), and Floyd Dell (three poems). Carl Sandburg, John Reed, Will Herford, and many others are afforded a pair of poems. In keeping with the radical tenor of both magazines, many of the poems

in *May Days* are political or of the protest variety. As Taggard notes in her introduction, the Woodrow Wilson era was marked by an awakening of revolutionary consciousness within the intelligentsia that was unprecedented in American history—and deigned not to last too long, once it was perceived as a serious threat to the ruling elites. The crux of the issue proved to be the antiwar stance struck by the *Masses,* which got its editors hauled into court by the government on "conspiracy to obstruct [military] recruiting and enlistment." *Masses* subsequently "faded into the protective coloration of the *Liberator,*" as Taggard wryly puts it, and in the end "the Liberator could not decide whether it wanted to be either a propagandist or an artistic magazine, or both" (p. xii).

Along with poet-colleagues George Sterling and James Rorty, Taggard edited *Continent's End: An Anthology of Contemporary California Poets* (1925). Four of her best poems—"Ice Age," "With Child," "Everyday Alchemy," and "Talking Water"—were included, as was "The Lo! School in Poetry," Taggard's "By Way of Introduction," in which she perceptively discusses the intimidating vastness of California: "a huge, open, varied, unique land, with a freshly made civilization scattered across its surface, but penetrating neither down into its soil, nor abroad, into its recesses.... Man is always afraid of the enormous empty aspects of the earth. They negate him, ignore his outcries, silently and persistently demanding that he reject his mortal consciousness for their immortal, unquestioning agnosticism; constantly insisting that he yield & blot out his frail self in their taciturn cycles. Such towering, overhanging Nature is a rude, ruthless, man-mocking obstacle to any labor of the human spirit" (p. xxvi). Taggard goes on to admit that, nature-loving aspirations to the contrary, she too goes "into the house very hurriedly, of a perfect night. Five minutes of inhuman beauty is all that I can stand" (p. xxvii). In Taggard's view nature's terrifying scale spawns poetry that "too often come[s] from the will, not the emotions, and deliberateness is always a blight" (p. xxviii). She calls for a "new, instinctive poet" with "a simple and unpretentious impulse [that] makes him sing" (p. xxxi): an almost clairvoyant prediction of the emergence many decades later of the ecological, Zen-inspired poetry of William Everson, Gary Snyder, and Lew Welch.

In 1926 Alfred A. Knopf published Taggard's third verse collection, *Words for the Chisel.* The centerpiece of *Words for the Chisel* is "Poppy Juice," a previously unpublished long narrative poem consisting of fifty seven-line stanzas in the rhyme royal (i.e., with the rhyme scheme *a-b-a-b-b-c-c*). The poem is set in Hawaii (though it is not named as such). Lehua, "a hula girl and whore" (p. 18) moves from the interior to a seaside town (not unlike Honolulu) where she meets Eric, "a cold / White angered Swede" (p. 17). The two marry and have a mixed-race son, also called Eric. A native of the Islands, Lehua comes to hate her foreign-born seafaring husband for his prolonged absences and longs only to bring her son to "some far valley shut to sea and ships" (p. 20). The elder Eric dies. And the younger Eric—whose "blood was like a thing at feud" (p. 21) due to his mixed pedigree—disheartens his mother by also taking to the sea, never to return: "He took his father's name, she'd vacantly say, / A father, a father took a son away" (p. 26). Thus "Poppy Juice" reiterates Taggard's already well-developed mythic schema, whereby brown-skinned natives are exploited and abandoned by white interlopers, and women—traditionally associated with nature, nurturance, and a settled sense of place—are forsaken by their men, who pursue an aimless wanderlust.

Many of the shorter poems that bulk out the rest of the volume are too personal and bitter in tone to suggest mere exercises in dramatic versifying; they surely constitute a thinly veiled, blow-by-blow account of the author's increasingly divisive marriage: "One of us will shortly die / And leave the other alone in the end / Stunned, too weary to pretend" ("Elegy in Dialogue," p. 64); "If I must anger and possess you so / And make you turn on me so black an eye / Your anger may not let you out but grow / To be your only being, by and by; / And we will go down clattering at last, / Two empty people, murderously fast" ("Quarrel," p. 68); "Beyond this shock of battle, there will be / No warrior

for our valor, in the grave. / Forbear to wound me utterly, unless / The time has come for that long loneliness" ("Truce," p. 69); "Too late, too late;—for never / Will love be anything / But acrid flesh, forever, / And restlessness, in spring" ("Ballad of Typical Lovers," p. 70). One can only conclude that constant squabbling was the substance of Taggard's married life. At any rate, *Words for the Chisel* met with good reviews. Allen Tate in the *Nation* called Taggard "one of four or five women poets who in the last five years have won a dignified popularity, and she is particularly distinguished in having written consistently better than any of them. She is the best craftsman. Her work is intelligently sustained; it is economical; her material emerges in clean essential outlines" (p. 431).

In New York City in 1926 Hugo Gellert, John F. Sloan, Max Eastman, Michael Gold, Joseph Freeman, Walt Carmon, and James Rorty founded the Marxist journal *New Masses*—replacing *Masses* magazine (1911–1917). Taggard and Robert Wolf became contributing editors. On November 17, 1926, George Sterling, a poet, a close friend of Jack London, and an emotionally generous mentor and friend to Taggard, committed suicide by ingesting cyanide at the age of fifty-six. In a moving tribute to Sterling published in *Overland Monthly and Out West Magazine,* Taggard attempted to "unravel the old problem—Death, Poetry, Indifferent Humanity, and the concrete being of a Person, George Sterling. (I think of your poet's years in terms of pain, because you wanted something you did not achieve.) A poet, under all his masks, wants to be able to give people what they need. And when they neither know what they need, nor find by accident what he has put close to them (hoping they will find it if just made and left to be found), then inevitably the poet dies" (December 1927, p. 368).

NEW YORK STATE

By 1927 Taggard and her family were living in Winterton, New York, a rural hamlet in the Catskills where Taggard edited *The Unspoken and Other Poems* by the San Francisco modernist poet and painter Anne Bremer (1868–1923). Though living in a backwater country town, Taggard was never cut off from the politics of her day. Her name appears as one of many prominent artists and writers who signed an open telegram on August 21, 1927, to President Calvin Coolidge pleading for his intervention to stop the execution of Nicola Sacco and Bartolomeo Vanzetti (all to no avail, as the two Italian anarchists were put to death two days later). Taggard was once more prepared to go public on October 4, 1927, when her friend and former New neighbor, John Herrmann (Josephine Herbst's husband) had three hundred copies of his novel of American high school life, *What Happens* (Contact Editions, Paris), confiscated as "obscene" by U.S. customs officials. The court refused to listen to her testimony—or the proffered testimony of H. L. Mencken, Heywood Broun, Nathan Ash, Harry Hansen, or Taggard's husband, Robert Wolf.

By 1928 Taggard and her family had moved again, to Cornwall-on-Hudson, a few miles north of West Point Military Academy and about equidistant between New Preston, Connecticut, to the east and Winterton, New York, to the west. But skittish geographic cures proved futile. In 1928 Taggard wrote "No More This Home," a poem that clearly mourns the death of her marriage to Robert L. Wolf, done in by unmet needs, emotional Sturm und Drang, and mutual frustrations too volcanic to contain:

No more this home ... nor these doors
To open, to startle, to shut,
Announcing our angers—to cut
The air back and forth like our wills.
Seal the door sills.

(*Collected Poems*, 1938, p. 31)

FRANCE

Separated from Wolf by the summer of 1928, Taggard took her seven-year-old daughter to southern France. She also took an extensive personal collection of books on Emily Dickinson and spent the next year in Provence imbibing the beauty of the countryside and working on two major projects: a compilation of metaphysical

verse from the sixteenth century to the present and the most ambitious undertaking of her life: a meticulously researched and imaginatively written biography of Emily Dickinson, a poet Taggard quite rightly held in the highest regard.

In the autumn of 1928 Alfred A. Knopf published Taggard's fourth verse collection, *Travelling Standing Still: Poems, 1918–1928*, described on the dust jacket as "Miss Taggard's own selection and chronological arrangement of her best poetic work of ten years." Most of the twenty-eight poems in the book had already been reprinted in previous volumes, but the last seven poems, all written in 1927 or 1928, were newly collected. Most notable of these are "B.C." and "Impatient Mary," companion poems about the Blessed Virgin Mary of Christian mythology. In "B.C." [Before Christ], Mary's fate is that of all women; she is a "queer maiden" who has, in effect, been raped and impregnated by God and must sacrifice her own identity to be the vessel of man: "Mary has lost her smile, Mary great / With load of man. There is only / Agony to come, Mary, wait: / Only agony and another loss of your being" (p. 46). "Impatient Mary" counters the notion of woman as sacrificial victim by emphasizing the strength of Mary's maternal instincts: "She could only feel / The chill for him [Jesus], and want to keep / Him safe and cozy in his sleep. / Lie all our mothers, Mary lay / Impatient in the winter hay" (p. 47). The two poems together suggest Taggard's ambivalence about motherhood, ambivalence already eloquently expressed in "With Child," a poem she wrote in the fall of 1921 while pregnant with her daughter, Marcia. Therein Taggard sees the child within her as an alien presence that will supersede her: "Earth's urge, not mine—my little death, not hers; / And the pure beauty yearns and stirs. // It does not heed our ecstasies, it turns / With secrets of its own, its own concerns" (*For Eager Lovers,* p. 51). In a review on December 12, 1928, Edmund Wilson praised Taggard's equanimity, which he found unique and refreshing: "With her eager intellectual appetite, she has devoured our ideas and techniques but she has scarcely been touched by the megrims, the nausea-fits, the moods of sterility that nowadays so often go with them. One looks forward to seeing her take her place as a self-dependent poetic personality, in some ways essentially different from any that we already know" (reprinted in *The Shores of Light: A Literary Chronicle of the Twenties and Thirties*, pp. 345–350).

MASSACHUSETTS

In September 1929—just before the stock market crash—Taggard returned from France to take an appointment teaching English and American literature and poetry courses at Mount Holyoke College in South Hadley, Massachusetts. In one respect the location was ideal for Taggard: only a few miles west of Emily Dickinson's ancestral home in Amherst. In another way the environs were dismal. An isolated all-girls school in a still-puritanical New England, Mount Holyoke was a dreary, repressive institution. Prohibition prevailed, strict curfews applied, smoking and drinking were banned on pain of expulsion, and occasional trips to the nearby city of Holyoke were carefully controlled. But as Helen Flint (class of 1931) would later note, "The amazing fact is that Miss Taggard was able to come into this atmosphere and be herself. The fact that she was able to do this caused her some difficulty and unhappiness on the campus, I believe. It is not surprising that she left after the end of two years of open conflict with the college authorities. Her parting remark to Miss [Mary E.] Wooley [president of the college], according to Miss Taggard's own account, was 'After two years in Mt. Holyoke, I admire the ethics of the business world.'"

Though Taggard clashed with the powers that be, she was a caring, dedicated, and innovative teacher much respected and admired by her students. During this period Taggard met Kenneth Durant, a pro-Soviet journalist and the director (from 1923 to 1944) of the American branch of the Telegraph Agency of the Soviet Union (TASS). Though Durant was married to the literary editor Ernestine Evans, he and Taggard struck up a friendship that would later blossom into a romantic relationship. On the writing front, Taggard completed her biography of Emily Dickinson—which intriguingly posited the Reverend

George Henry Gould (1827–1899), friend of her brother, Austin, as Dickinson's secret lover—an assertion that would stir a good deal of speculation and debate.

Taggard also put the finishing touches on another ambitious and well-executed poetry anthology, *Circumference: Varieties of Metaphysical Verse 1456–1928* (1929). (She derived the title from a favorite Emily Dickinson quote: "My business is circumference.") The depth and range of the selections and Taggard's erudite introduction shows that her knowledge of the history of poetry and poetics was vast. Random House recognized Taggard's growing stature by printing her "Monologue for Mothers" in its series of poetry quartos. But there were setbacks as well. On the afternoon of November 28, 1930—Taggard's thirty-sixth birthday—the small house she shared with her daughter in South Hadley burned down. Helen Flint remembers the fire as a devastating blow to Taggard: "They saved the things. The framework is still there but the spirit's gotten away. Firemen in there, everyone peering in, talking, surmising. After it was all over Miss Taggard went in alone—waded through the water and looked around. The house was so much a part of her and she of it."

In June 1930 Alfred A. Knopf brought out Taggard's *The Life and Mind of Emily Dickinson.* The book garnered mostly excellent reviews. Granville Hicks noted that "Miss Taggard's remarks on specific themes and methods [in Dickinson's poetry] are uncommonly discerning." He called Taggard's biography "by far the best we have on Emily Dickinson" (*Nation,* June 25, 1930, p. 735).

Taggard scored another triumph nine months later on March 30, 1931, when she was awarded a prestigious Guggenheim Fellowship in creative writing. That same year—perhaps not coincidentally—as Taggard's career reached its apogee, her husband's life reached its nadir. Robert L. Wolf was committed to a mental hospital. Much in the same vein as "Everyday Alchemy," Taggard's poem "To the Powers of Darkness" laments the fact that her husband could find no solace in the natural beauty of the world:

My love for whose ruin we have wept
Tears no one weeps for the dead
Hears no more storms as simple as ours are.
He hears rain never. Nature is not his.
The great sane day of light and genial power
Ceases with him and is the Arctic black.
We weep that none may cheer him any more.
No not even the great sun.

(*Not Mine to Finish,* 1934, p. 30)

EUROPE

Tired after years of intense striving and emotionally spent after her ordeal with Robert Wolf, Taggard used her Guggenheim grant money to take her daughter and her sister, Ernestine, to live in Europe from the fall of 1931 until the spring of 1932. The trio spent a few months at each of three exquisite destinations in the Mediterranean: the island of Majorca off the coast of Spain—which proved particularly conducive to writing—then Antibes on the French Riviera, and finally the Italian island of Capri in the Tyrrhenian Sea off Sorrento. Taggard reveled in the beauty of the warm, sunny Mediterranean seas and skies and was reminded often of those idyllic days of her youth in Hawaii. On her thirty-seventh birthday, November 28, 1931, she found herself worlds away from the burnt ruins of her house in South Hadley of exactly one year earlier: a life now renewed and drenched in light and expansive vistas. Inspired to take stock at what she thought would be her life's moment of mid-passage, she wrote "To the Natural World: at 37," a poem that juxtaposes the natural world—"Exquisite ... powerful, joyous, splendid"—with our blundering human lives, "a poor travesty of some greatness." In the poem's final lines Taggard, poised between youth and age, seeks to hold onto a moment of sublime aesthetic contemplation in a protean world:

Weakness with wisdom lie
Ahead with nodding age; error and energy
Behind, dim in regret and chaos where
I left my early self and got the despair
That seizes all who see how folly gone
Is their sweet youth with darkness sudden on.
World deign, for one moment, O deign to culminate

One wave in me; O in me consummate
Your surge with all beholding happy power.
So, overlapping once, here in the midway hour,
Let me watch outward splendor solemnly for
Life's brief in all this bigness, O sun's calm, O
Sea's roar.

(*To the Natural World*, p. 35)

VERMONT

Upon her return to the United States, Taggard secured a job teaching at Bennington College, a small and progressive women's liberal arts college just opened in southern Vermont in the fall of 1932. In the poem "To My Students," which Taggard wrote while teaching at Bennington, she professes modest but distinctly Marxist pedagogical ambitions: "I teach. I expect two percent return. / Sow words, show books; plant thought; burst doors, and point: / See World; see men at work; partake! / Students, I shall be content if you learn / By tiresome emphasis from me: / *'The laws of being are laws of thought.' / 'Thought is conditioned by being, not being by thought,'*" (*Collected Poems,* p. 56). In teaching as in writing, Taggard was always avid to infuse thought, or the written word that provoked or expressed it, with the bracing, shaping realities of worldly experience—the avowed agenda of most intellectuals of her day but sincerely practiced by only a few.

In 1934—some six years after the marriage had actually ended—Taggard was granted a divorce from Robert L. Wolf. In November of that year Harper & Brothers published Taggard's fifth verse collection, *Not Mine to Finish: Poems, 1928–1934,* which gathers forty-five poems she wrote during and after the death of her marriage and her embarkation on a new life. Though typically varied in terms of subject matter, the book features numerous poems of emotional suffering and evil ("No More This Home," "The Trance," "To the Powers of Darkness," "To the Powers of Desolation") countered by poems that describe hope, spiritual resilience, and rebirth ("To the Queen of Heaven," "Changes of the Soul," "Lark," "What to Keep, What to Discard").

Taggard had begun "Evening Love-of-Self," the longest, most ambitious and revealing poem in the book, in New Preston, Connecticut, in 1927. Over the next seven years she reworked and expanded the poem while living in New York City, Cornwall-on-Hudson, Mallorca, and Bennington. For an epigraph, added late in the composition process, Taggard chose a telling quote from "Something to Believe In," an influential philosophical essay by Rebecca Pitts that appeared in *New Masses* (March 13, 1934): "This profound turning away from life and from the world takes place on a large scale only in periods of social stagnation and despair." The poem begins with a life-changing epiphany. A woman (surely Genevieve Taggard) stands outside her country home to watch a "still sunset" in late summer when she suddenly intuits that the sky's fading light is her own spiritual and mortal dissipation: "This evening sky, / Rare, thin, faint, dead. This is myself, myself. Oh / evening wan" (p. 36). Subject to an uncannily vivid glimpse of the void without and within, the woman suffers from insomnia and inner turmoil: "Sleep was a crowded concourse of not wanted / Things, feelings, faces and broken plots" (p. 39). Unmoored from the habituated and familiar, she also recognizes that the conventional notion of a reliably consistent and unified self is a fiction masking nothing more than shifting mood states:

I am tired, so tired of being a person,
—One person and another and another
With spiritual colors in my shifting mind,
With spiritual needs that make me grow like a thistle.

(p. 48)

Desperate to avoid spiritual death through derealization—"I'll come to dust before my date with death"—the poem's speaker determines to "live by rote of my second sight in dreams / And beat the process of tranced decay / By fixing all my might in the zone of things" (p. 4). In other words, salvation (which is self-purification) lies in solitary, deliberate, heightened attention to the concrete particulars of lived experience, especially that of the natural world, a process unfortunately made all but impossible by the constant proximity and stifling influence of the woman's husband: "When he is near I swim against his side / With no wish. Some influence ties us in. / Familiar-strange, he is too, too

familiar" (p. 57). Transformed by her identity-clarifying bout with madness, the woman sees love "that comes too close" as a "great perversion" of love, love turned "monstrous ... / Lost in the object, killed by too perfect nearness / With the remote man" (p. 58). In the end she makes the life-saving decision long attenuated: "I'll not share darkness with him" (p. 58). By "Love-of-Self," Taggard is not referring to some sort of vulgar narcissism but a healthy self-respect that insists on the human right to overcome and survive a suffocating relationship by choosing nature, solitude, and self-cultivation as tools for healing.

NEW YORK AND VERMONT

In the summer of 1934 a small New York press—Arrow Editions Co-operative Association—published *Ten Introductions: A Collection of Modern Verse,* edited by Taggard and her friend and colleague Dudley Fitts. Of the ten poets introduced therein only Robert Fitzgerald (1910–1985) and Lincoln Kirstein (1907–1996) would attain any lasting fame, the former as a respected translator of ancient classics and the latter as a polymath who excelled in ballet, film, literature, theatre, painting, sculpture, and photography.

That fall Taggard began what would prove to be a twelve-year stint teaching creative writing at Sarah Lawrence College, Bronxville, New York. On March 10, 1935, Taggard and Kenneth Durant (who was now divorced from Ernestine Evans) married—and Durant subsequently adopted Taggard's daughter, Marcia. The family took up long-term residence in an 1879 low-rise apartment building at 35 East Thirtieth Street in midtown Manhattan, three blocks south of the Empire State Building. Just before marrying Durant, Taggard spent her last $200 to buy a 1786 farmhouse in East Jamaica, Windham County, Vermont, a few miles south of her grandfather's hometown of Londonderry and abutting the then newly established Green Mountain National Forest. She named her country home "Gilfeather" (after a cold-weather turnip developed in the early 1900s by a local farmer named John Gilfeather). Gilfeather would serve as the summer home for Taggard and her husband for the rest of their lives. Anita Marburg, a Sarah Lawrence colleague who visited Gilfeather in later years, remembers it as "colorful, close to the earth, and to her neighbors.... To find it one walked through the wet ferny wood—sometimes glimpsing a deer—and there it stood silently, in a circle of grass, looking up at the mountains rising above it. When I came to her house, it had become large enough for considerable hospitality: the outside painted white in the old-fashioned style, the inside centering on the kitchen, the colors warm and terra-cotta, a little organ for music and flat irons for book ends." Marburg also recalls that Taggard and her husband "became seasoned Vermonters themselves, proud of their adopted state's history, about which they wrote in prose and poetry. Rich enough to buy machinery, they shared it with local farmers. A Vermont girl was married in their home and spent her honeymoon there. When maple sugar time came, they worked for their neighbor in exchange for winter labor. They liked to go to country dances and to attend Town Meeting Day."

More than just a good neighbor, Taggard became a staunch advocate and defender of working-class Vermonters. When marble workers in the Rutland area went on strike on November 4, 1935, Taggard joined their cause as a member of the United Committee to Aid the Vermont Marble Strikers, organized by the socialist artist Rockwell Kent. She attended meetings and rallies and wrote about their struggle in *Calling Western Union,* her best-known verse collection and the only one exclusively devoted to class issues. Taggard's radicalization was further accelerated, in 1936, by the outbreak of the Spanish Civil War and a visit to the Soviet Union that left her starry-eyed about the redemptive possibilities of state socialism, especially regarding women's status in society. When *Calling Western Union* was published on October 1, 1936, it solidified Taggard's new identity as a proletarian poet and was hailed by Rebecca Pitts, in a review for *New Masses,* as "important revolutionary poetry" (October 1936, p. 22).

Ironically, the best part of *Calling Western Union* may be its prose preface, "Hawaii, Wash-

ington, Vermont: A Frame for the Verse," a perceptive and beautifully written twenty-two page autobiographical essay (originally published in *Scribner's Magazine,* October 1934) in which Taggard traces her family's travails and her own intellectual and moral development from her youth in Hawaii and Washington State to her most recent years as a part-time denizen of rural Vermont. The granddaughter of pioneers, Taggard came to understand that the nineteenth century westward migration across the American continent was largely met with disappointment, backbreaking toil, and a "devil-take-the-hindmost individualism [that] bore a poisonous crop" (p. xii). She notes that her parents, James and Alta Taggard, first left the mainland for Hawaii in 1890 and that "Island life ... changed my parents' minds and their tastes. They had lived with dark people; they had got out of the fatal chain of self-interest; they had seen a life that touched the Orient. At twenty-five they had rejected the small town and all its values; now as middle-aged people they knew how right they had been to reject it. The Island life, for all its faults, offered a liberal and amiable existence" (p. xiv). Forced to return to the mainland for good in 1914, the Taggards found small town life in the Pacific Northwest mean and stultifying—and Taggard came to see that the biting critique of the emotional and intellectual barrenness of American life found in Edgar Lee Masters' *Spoon River Anthology* (1915) or Sherwood Anderson's *Winesburg, Ohio* (1919) or Sinclair Lewis' *Main Street* (1920) was, if anything, on the mild side. Toward the end of the essay, Taggard admits "looking for a good community for many years" (p. xxx)—and even finding it briefly in New York and then in Connecticut. Her first impressions of Vermont was that it was the bucolic community she had been searching for all her life: "At first it looked to me the way it looks to the summer visitor who goes up there to get a rest."

> And then the facts contradicted my hope. I saw canned wood-chuck in the farmers' cellars. I saw slums in Brattleboro and Burlington. I knew children who picked ferns for a few cents a day. I knew a man who worked in a furniture factory for ten cents an hour! I saw his starved wife and children. Slow starvation gives children starry eyes and delicate faces. I saw five men who were a few weeks ago sentenced to jail for their activity in the Vermont Marble Strike. I saw a voucher for two cents one worker got for a week's wages, all that was left after the company deducted for rent and light. I saw a pile of such vouchers. When they eat, the quarry workers eat potatoes and turnips.... In Rutland County the Overseer of the Poor is a Marble Company official.
>
> And so I say I was wrong about Vermont. The poems in this book were written after I began to see why.
>
> (pp. xxxi–xxxii)

Some of the poems in *Calling Western Union* are devoted to satirizing the moral obtuseness of the capitalist class. Particularly effective is "To an American Workman Dying of Starvation":

> Swell guy, you got to die.
> Did you have fun?
> I guess I know you worked.
> I guess I saw you.
> It got you just the same.
> Say it with flowers.
> So long. We got the breaks. But we'll be seeing you.
> There's a little job we got to attend to up here first.
>
> (p. 40)

Suffice to say the capitalist who is addressing the dying worker has no sense of his subaltern as a real human being. "A Middle-Aged, Middle-Class Woman at Midnight" explores a consciousness capable of self-redemption, a consciousness not unlike that of the poet—a woman of relative privilege who tries, for her own sanity, to sequester herself from the class struggles going on all around her:

> Now try to sleep.
> In Vermont near the marble-quarries ... I must not think
> Again, wide awake again. O medicine
> Give blank against that fact, the strike, the cold.
> How cold Vermont can be. It's nerves, I know,
> But I keep thinking how a rat will gnaw
> In an old house. Hunger that has no haste ...
>
> (p. 13)

Ultimately, though, the woman's attempts to disengage from an inexorably political world end in confronting its realities:

I'm sick I tell you. Veronal
Costs money, too. Costs more than I can pay.
And night's long nightmare costs me, costs me much.
I'll not endure this stink of poverty. Sheriffs, cops,
Boss of the town, union enemy, crooks and cousins,
I hope the people win.

(p. 14)

From February 7 to April 15, 1938, Taggard taught "Great Poets," a ten-week course that met on Wednesday evenings at the newly established Writers' School (League of American Writers), Room 516 at 381 Fourth Avenue, in the West Village neighborhood of New York City. Harrison Wood, one of her students, recalls, "Genevieve Taggard was the only truly great teacher I have ever known. If there is such a thing as a genius for teaching she had it in true abundance.... I think Genevieve Taggard could never have conceived of life without poetry; they were integral to each other. It was this inability to see poetry as a separate compartment, dispensable to life, which made her a great teacher."

In December 1938 Harper & Brothers published Taggard's *Collected Poems, 1918–1938,* an impressive summation of the first twenty years of her career as a poet. In the short span of years that immediately followed (1939 to 1942), Taggard continued to write poems but also expended her energies in new roles: as a high profile leftist public intellectual and an experimenter with poetry set to music. On May 7, 1939, Taggard's *Prologue, for Full Chorus of Mixed Voices and Orchestra* was first performed at Carnegie Hall, New York City, and published as a musical score by G. Schirmer, with music by William Schuman. On June 2–4, 1939, Taggard attended the Third American Writers Congress at the New School for Social Research in New York and served as chairman for the Arrangements Committee for the Poetry Craft Session held on Saturday morning, June 3. On May 27, 1940, Taggard was recorded reading her poetry at the City College of New York. On the Fourth of July, 1940, Taggard's *This Is Our Time: Secular Cantata No. 1, Mixed Voice Chorus and Orchestra,* with music by Schuman and Paul Weissleder, was first performed (and subsequently published as a musical score by Boosey & Hawkes). On October 19, 1940, Taggard attended the New York City Conference for Protection of Foreign Born at the Hotel Edison. In 1941 E. C. Schirmer published Taggard's *Lark: Four-Part Chorus for Mixed Voices (A Cappella) with Baritone Solo,* with music by Aaron Copland. In 1942 G. Schirmer published the musical score for Taggard and Schuman's *Holiday Song for Four-Part Chorus of Mixed Voices with Piano Accompaniment.*

In 1942 Harper & Brothers brought out *Long View,* Taggard's seventh book of verse, which collected the poems she published in journals and magazines over the preceding five years. Contained therein are poems of place and natural landscape ("Gilfeather," "Throg's Neck," "In Flame over Vermont"); weather and the seasons ("Hymn to the Sun with Imperative Refrain," "The Coming and Going of Storms," "Vermont and the Northwest Wind," "Primavera," "To Those Who Watch the Skies"); love ("K.D.," to her husband, Kenneth Durant); working-class life ("Autumn Song for Guitar"); politics ("Ode in Time of Crisis," "On the 24th Anniversary of the October Revolution"); the Spanish Civil War ("Noncombatants," "To the Veterans of the Abraham Lincoln Brigade"); and a group of four poems "To the Negro People," one of which—"Proud Day"—celebrates the contralto Marian Anderson's famous concert on the steps of the Lincoln Memorial on Easter Sunday, April 9, 1939, arranged by the Roosevelts after Anderson was barred from Constitution Hall by the Daughters of the American Revolution. Her recital was attended by a biracial audience of seventy-five thousand and heard by millions over the radio. For Taggard, Anderson's triumph signaled not just a victory for African Americans against racism. It also marked an important and deeply moving milestone in the moral growth of the nation: "Never, never forget how the dark people rewarded us / Giving out of their want and their little freedom / This blazing star. This blazing star. / Something spoke in my patriot heart. Proud day" (p. 54). In the collection's title poem, "Long View," Taggard envisions a utopian future time when the struggle for social justice has been won, is now remembered with reverence, and there was "never heard happier laughter" (p. 14).

Also included in *Long View* were six "songs for musical setting" and "Notes on Writing Words for Music," which ends with a long quote from *Illusion and Reality* (1937), a classic work of social critique and historical analysis by the British Marxist theorist and poet Christopher Caudwell (1907–1937), who was killed in action fighting Francisco Franco's Fascist rebels during the Spanish Civil War. The passage that Taggard excerpted—and obviously admired—concerns the revolutionary social function of poetry: "Just because poetry is what it is, it exhibits a reality beyond the reality it brings to birth and nominally portrays a reality, which though secondary, is yet higher and more complex.... Not poetry's abstract statement—its content of facts, but its dynamic role in society—its content of collective emotion, is therefore poetry's *truth*" (pp. 112–113). That Taggard was adhering to Caudwell's notion of poetry's utopian function is evident in remarks she made some years later on the collection's title poem: " 'Long View' was written to break the general pessimism that dominated before we went to war against Hitler. I saw very clearly that we were being weakened for lack of a magnetic picture of our future and I thought it was a poet's business to try to create such pictures" (*California Poetry Folios* 4, April 1947).

Soon after *Long View* came out, Harper & Brothers published *Falcon: Poems on Soviet Themes,* a chapbook of nine poems written between 1936 and 1942 in full-throated praise of the Soviet Union. Oddly, Taggard's ardor for Russian-style communism had not waned—despite the Hitler-Stalin Pact of August 1939, which had disillusioned almost all of her leftist contemporaries. The book was dedicated to Liudmilla Pavlichenko (1916–1974), a female Soviet sniper during World War II credited with 309 Nazi kills.

The tragic death of her younger sister, Ernestine—of a brain tumor in 1943—hit Taggard hard. Though she was only fifty years old, Taggard began to lose much of the stamina and fire that had sustained her through so many struggles in years past. In the five years that remained to her, Taggard spent more time at Gilfeather and wrote about its ample consolations of peace and natural beauty but, on the whole, her work became noticeably more plaintive, elegiac, and world-weary.

In 1945 Taggard self-published *A Part of Vermont,* a slender chapbook of verse collecting eighteen poems with Vermont settings, most of which she had published in other venues over the previous ten years. A few poems, placed near the beginning of the volume—"To Ethan Allen," "The Nursery Rhyme and the Summer Visitor," "Gilfeather Again," "On the Trout Streams"—Taggard wrote especially for *A Part of Vermont.* All the poems contained therein bespeak Taggard's intense love for the natural beauty of rural Vermont in all its seasons, a landscape utterly unlike the Hawaii of her youth but equally cherished.

Toward the end of 1946 Harper & Brothers published *Slow Music,* Taggard's eighth book of verse. The thirty-nine poems contained therein, all written between 1942 and 1945, show Taggard further honing her already terse, sometimes cryptic diction and veering toward ever more somber tones. Two poems eulogize her sister, "The Weed" and "To My Sister—Ernestine Kealoha Taggard, 1900–1943." Other poems deal with the ongoing war ("Report on a War," "Charm for a Young Private," "Salute to the Russian Dead," "Song V") or the immediate landscape ("Gilfeather Again," "A Poem to Explain Everything About a Certain Day in Vermont"). Yet most of the poems in *Slow Music,* though rife with Taggard's usual nature imagery, especially of birds and colors, are somehow more abstract, philosophical, and poignant: "Tragic meaning was my altitude" ("Poet," p. 15); "So much is false in the world; so much is shoddy. / The lonely are many; who has not met them / On the streets of the world, in a stream of everyday faces, / Burdened, gentle, cherished by no one" ("Song III,"p. 22); "The sadness of the old, the veteran old / Purges the crude / Metal" ("The Family," p. 30); "My stupor I obey: / Erupt will I from this sack, / Monster as huge as day / And black as night is black" ("Problem of Evil into Cocoon," p. 42); "In unjust, cyclonic series / In event upon event / This war-world crested them / Over the edge, to death" ("Song V," p. 52).

Clearly these are the utterances of a depressed spirit, stunned by personal loss and by the horrific carnage of a second global war.

In 1947 Taggard was forced to retire from Sarah Lawrence College; even at a relatively progressive college her long-standing Marxist political affiliations had rendered her persona non grata during a period of renewed, rabid anticommunist hysteria. The deep stress of being fired for pursuing her lifelong ideals further damaged Taggard's already tenuous health. Tellingly, Taggard's last book, *Origin: Hawaii,* published in a limited edition in 1947, saw her coming back to her early days: a tacit admission that future days were few. The book contained four new and twenty-four earlier (and previously published) poems about the Islands: a final tribute to the place that had most shaped her sensibilities. In the preface, a passage that begins in reminiscence ends with Taggard restating her socialist political beliefs:

> I have been startled to reflect that "Child Tropics" written in 1921 and "Luau" written in 1946 are on related themes, except that the later poem introduces as counterpoint the reality of racial suffering. In the little church my parents attended in Honolulu I was impressed with the text, "I am come that ye might have life and have it more abundantly." When we sat listening I had only to move my eyes from the minister to see outside the flowering vines and colored trees of abundance. Nevertheless, or perhaps because we lived a rich sensuous life, the text became my own. I have never ceased to think that the text, taken literally, should be the aim of all governments. I scoff at those who tell me solemnly that government must be something else. I am not interested in anything else and come to think of it, neither are you, dear reader.
>
> (p. ix)

In September 1947, Taggard fell ill with hypertension. Though not obese—a primary cause of high blood pressure—Taggard was an intensely driven person and an adult smoker and drinker: traits that likely contributed to the onset of the disease, along with a genetic predisposition, no doubt. A sympathectomy (nerve surgery) brought some relief, but she remained in a frail, debilitated state the rest of her life. Though she occasionally traveled to New York for further treatment, she mostly rusticated at Gilfeather, confined to her bed, slowly dying, but keeping watch out her bedroom window with the natural world she so loved. On November 8, 1948, Genevieve Taggard—spiritually and physically worn out—died in a New York hospital, twenty days short of her fifty-fourth birthday.

Selected Bibliography

WORKS OF GENEVIEVE TAGGARD

Verse Collections

For Eager Lovers. New York: Thomas Seltzer, 1922.

Words for the Chisel. New York: Knopf, 1926.

Travelling Standing Still: Poems, 1918–1928. New York: Knopf, 1928.

Not Mine to Finish: Poems, 1928–1934. New York: Harper, 1934.

Calling Western Union. New York: Harper, 1936.

Collected Poems, 1918–1938. New York: Harper, 1938.

Long View. New York: Harper, 1942.

Falcon: Poems on Soviet Themes. New York: Harper, 1943.

Slow Music. New York: Harper, 1946.

Origin: Hawaii. Honolulu: Donald Angus, 1947.

To the Natural World. Boise, Idaho: Ahsahta Press, 1980.

Chapbooks

Hawaiian Hilltop. San Francisco: Wyckoff & Gelber, 1923.

Monologue for Mothers (Aside). New York: Random House, 1929.

Remembering Vaughan in New England. New York: Arrow Editions, 1933.

A Part of Vermont. East Jamaica, Vt.: River Press, 1945.

Biography

The Life and Mind of Emily Dickinson. New York: Knopf, 1930.

Edited Works

Continent's End: An Anthology of Contemporary California Poets. With George Sterling and James Rorty. San Francisco: Book Club of California, 1925.

May Days: An Anthology of Verse from Masses-Liberator, *1912–1924.* New York: Boni & Liveright, 1925.

Circumference: Varieties of Metaphysical Verse, 1456–1928. New York: Covici Friede, 1929.

Ten Introductions: A Collection of Modern Verse. With Dudley Fitts. New York: Arrow Editions, 1934.

ESSAYS

"A Canticle of Praise Delivered in Greek Theater." *San Francisco Bulletin,* December 2, 1918.

"Mother Papia." *Christian Science Monitor,* November 30, 1920.

"The Monkey-Pod Tree." *Christian Science Monitor,* December 2, 1920.

"The Kiawe Tree in Hawaii." *Christian Science Monitor,* November 27, 1920.

"Banana Ways." *Christian Science Monitor,* November 29, 1920.

"The Escape of the Land-Tanna." *Christian Science Monitor,* December 4, 1920.

"Grandpa Banyan." *Christian Science Monitor,* December 6, 1920.

"A Rocket in Blue Hawaiian Skies." *Christian Science Monitor,* December 8, 1920.

"Mencken and the Poets." *Laughing Horse* 6 (1923).

"The Two-Edged Sword." *Chicago Evening Post,* June 6, 1924.

"A Mechanic for Magnificence." *New Republic,* April 13, 1927.

"Children Really Like Poetry." *New Republic,* November 16, 1927.

"A Note on Elinor Wylie." *American Review,* November–December 1930.

"John Donne: A Link Between the 17th and the 20th Centuries." *Scholastic Magazine,* March 24, 1934.

"Romanticism and Communism." *New Masses,* September 25, 1934.

"The Broadway Theatre—Letter from the U.S." *Za Rubyezhom,* August 5, 1936.

"American Poetry 1912–1916." *Literaturni* [Leningrad], August 23, 1936.

"Through the Eyes of Americans—Observations on Two Flights." *Izvestia,* August 12, 1937.

"Why We Write." *Bulletin of the League of American Writers,* February 1938.

"Growth of Anti-Fascist Feeling Among Intellectuals in the United States." *Izvestia,* November 5, 1938.

"Can We Teach Creative Writing?" *Guardian,* December 1938.

"Literature and the People ... Music and the People U.S.A. 1939." *Literaturnaya Gazeta,* April 5, 1939.

"Americans See the Soviet Pavilion." *Izvestia,* April 6, 1939.

"Mallorcan Memory." *New Masses,* May 16, 1939.

"Can't Divorce Reading or Writing from Life: Both Social Activities." *Book Find News,* December 1943.

"My History Lesson." *Yale Review,* September 1945.

"Children of the Hollow Men." *Christian Register,* November 1946.

BOOK REVIEWS

Fairy Bread, by Laura Binet. *Measure,* June 1922.

Slants, by Clifford Gessler. *Honolulu Star-Bulletin,* January 17, 1925.

A Survey of Modernist Poetry, by Laura Riding and Robert Graves, and *Contemporaries and Snobs,* by Laura Riding. *New York Herald Tribune Books,* January 6, 1929.

Near and Far, by Edmund Blunden. *New York Herald Tribune Books,* August 24, 1930.

Serenata, by T. Randolph Mercein. *New York Herald Tribune Books,* October 19, 1930.

John Deth, A Metaphysical Legend and Other Poems, by Conrad Aiken, and *The Glory of the Nightingales,* by E. A. Robinson. *New York Telegram,* October 10, 1930, October 23, 1930.

Collected Poems, by Robert Frost. *New York Herald Tribune Books,* December 21, 1930.

Letters of Emily Dickinson, edited by Mabel Loomis Todd. *New York Herald Tribune Books,* December 13, 1931.

The Princess Marries the Page, by Edna St. Vincent Millay. *New York Herald Tribune Books,* October 30, 1932.

Emily Dickinson Face to Face, by Martha Dickinson Bianchi. *New York Herald Tribune Books,* December 11, 1932.

A Watch in the Night, by Helen C. White. *New York Herald Tribune Books,* April 23, 1933.

Collected Poems, 1921–1931, by William Carlos Williams. *New Masses,* April 3, 1934.

Keats' Craftsmanship, by M. R. Ridley, and *Autobiography of John Keats,* by Earle V. Weller. *New York Herald Tribune Books,* March 18, 1934, May 20, 1934.

My House of Life, An Autobiography, by Jessie B. Rittenhouse. *New York Herald Tribune Books,* April 22, 1934.

The Lord's Anointed, by Ruth Eleanor McKee. *New York Herald Tribune Books,* April 29, 1934.

Break the Heart's Anger, by Paul Engle. *Partisan Review and Anvil,* May 1936.

The People Yes, by Carl Sandburg. *American Teacher,* January–February 1937.

Over the North Pole, by George Baidukov. Translated by Jessica Smith. *Soviet Russia Today,* February 1938.

Fifth Column, by Ernest Hemingway. *Libiralurnaya Gazeta,* December 20, 1938.

The Knight in the Tiger Skin, by Shotha Rustveli. Translated by Marjory Scott Wardrop. *Soviet Russia Today,* July–August 1939.

Productive Thinking, by Max Wertheimer. *New Republic,* July 29, 1946.

GENEVIEVE TAGGARD

An Introduction to Emily Dickinson, by Henry Wells. *Saturday Review of Literature,* October 4, 1947.

AUTOBIOGRAPHY

Unpublished journal transcript. Papers of Genevieve Taggard, Rauner Special Collections Library, Dartmouth College.

PAPERS

The papers of Genevieve Taggard are divided between the Rauner Special Collections Library, Dartmouth College, Hanover, New Hampshire, and the Manuscripts and Archives Division of the New York Public Library, New York City.

CRITICAL AND BIOGRAPHICAL STUDIES

Allego, Donna M. "Genevieve Taggard's Sentimental Marxism in *Calling Western Union.*" *College Literature* 31, no. 1:27–51 (winter 2004).

Berke, Nancy. "Anything That Burns You: The Social Poetry of Lola Ridge, Genevieve Taggard, and Margaret Walker." *Revista Canaria de Estudios Ingleses* 37:39–53 (November 1998).

———. *Women Poets on the Left: Lola Ridge, Genevieve Taggard, Margaret Walker.* Gainesville: University of Florida Press, 2001.

Cohen, Hyman R. "The Life and Literary Reputation of Genevieve Taggard." Unpublished typescript. Papers of Genevieve Taggard. Rautner Special Collections Library, Dartmouth College.

Flint, Helen. "Memoirs: Genevieve Taggard: Mt. Holyoke 1929–1931." Unpublished typescript. Papers of Genevieve Taggard. Rauner Special Collections Library, Dartmouth College.

Hicks, Granville. "Mystery and Mystification." *Nation,* June 25, 1940, pp. 735–736. (Review of *The Life and Mind of Emily Dickinson.*)

Izzo, David Garrett. "Genevieve Taggard." In *American Women Writers, 1900–1945: A Bio-Bibliographical Critical Sourcebook.* Edited by Laurie Champion. Westport, Conn.: Greenwood Press, 2000. Pp. 338–342.

Marburg, Anita. "Genevieve Taggard As I Knew Her." Unpublished manuscript. Papers of Genevieve Taggard. Rauner Special Collections Library, Dartmouth College.

McCann, Janet. "Genevieve Taggard." In *American* Poets, *1880–1945, First Series.* Edited by Peter Quartermain. Detroit: Gale; 1986. Pp. 375–381.

Perloff, Marjorie, "Janus-Faced Blockbuster." *symploke* 8, nos. 1–2:205–213 (2000). (Review of *Anthology of Modern American Poetry.* Edited by Cary Nelson. New York: Oxford University Press, 2000.)

Porter, Katherine Anne. "A Singing Woman." *New York Herald Tribune,* April 25, 1926.

Tate, Allen. "Careful Artistry." *Nation,* April 28, 1926, pp. 481–482. (Review of *Words for the Chisel.*)

Van Doren, Mark. "Genevieve Taggard and Other Poets." *Nation,* February 28, 1923, p. 246. (Review of *For Eager Lovers.*)

Van Nyhuis, Alison. "Revolution and Modern American Poetry: Genevieve Taggard's *Calling Western Union.*" *Revista Canaria de Estudios Ingleses* 52:129–135 (2006).

Whicher, George F. Review of *The Life and Mind of Emily Dickinson. New York Herald Tribune,* June 22, 1930.

Wilson, Edmund. *The Shores of Light: A Literary Chronicle of the Twenties and Thirties.* New York: Farrar, Straus and Young, 1952. Pp. 345–350.

Wilson, Martha A. "Lola Ridge and Genevieve Taggard: Voices of Resistance." *Arkansas Quarterly* 2, no. 2:124–133 (spring 1993).

Wood, Harrison. "Memoir: Notes on Genevieve Taggard as a Teacher." Unpublished manuscript. Papers of Genevieve Taggard, Rauner Special Collections Library, Dartmouth College.

LAURA INGALLS WILDER

(1867—1957)

Susan Carol Hauser

LAURA INGALLS WILDER is the author of the popular and enduring "Little House" series of young adult novels about pioneer life in late nineteenth-century America. The books are classics in the genre and were among the first such series for young readers. Wilder was also innovative in her approach to her audience: the characters in the stories mature at about the same pace as did her readers. The themes of the books echo American ideals of the time, including hard work, family, community, and freedom. The original eight books were published from 1932 through 1943. A ninth book, discovered after Wilder's death, was published in 1971. A popular television series, *Little House on the Prairie* (1974–1982), was loosely based on Little House stories.

ZIGZAG MIGRATION

Laura Elizabeth Ingalls was born on February 7, 1867, near Pepin, Wisconsin, a developing agricultural region in the Chippewa River valley, a few miles from the Mississippi River and on the edge of what was known locally as the Big Woods. She was the second of five children born to Charles Philip Ingalls (1836–1902) and Caroline Lake Quiner Ingalls (1839–1924). Her sisters Mary, Caroline (Carrie), and Grace lived out full lives. A brother, Charles Frederick, died at nine months of age.

Charles and Caroline Ingalls were married on February 1, 1860, in Concord, Wisconsin. Their extended families had migrated to Wisconsin from the east, the Quiners from Connecticut, the Ingallses from New York. This was common practice at the time, and the families continued to move in consort with each other back and forth across the Midwest, some going ahead, some remaining, some returning and leaving again. This migration pattern, termed the "M-Factor" (movement, migration, and mobility) by the historian George W. Pierson, was at least as common as that of relentless westward migration. M-Factor migration was influenced by unpredictable forces such as weather, natural disasters, social upheaval, and larger economic and migration patterns. Families had little choice but to move somewhere else when subsistence failed in a given area.

Charles and Caroline Ingalls, "Pa and Ma" of the Little House books, participated fully in this zigzag migration. From 1869, when Laura was two years old, through 1879, they moved from Wisconsin to Kansas, with an interim year's stay in Missouri, back to Wisconsin, west to Minnesota, south to Iowa, back to Minnesota, and then to South Dakota. Here, at Caroline's insistence, they took a stand. Their prospects grew with the little railroad town of De Smet, and they remained there the rest of their days. Their daughters Mary, Carrie, and Grace also remained in South Dakota. Only Laura ventured out again.

The two items that always traveled with the Ingalls family were a shepherdess figurine of Caroline's and Charles's fiddle. These objects symbolize two primary forces in the growing-up years of both the fictional and the actual Laura. The shepherdess embodies the hearth, Caroline's domain. She is responsible for the children's emotional well-being, for their education, their appreciation of manners and proper behavior, sensitivity to others, and their participation in the daily family work. This includes cooking, cleaning, and sewing. Through all of these activities and by Caroline's sure and gentle hand, the children know they are needed and loved. These values of work, respect, and love are primary in young Laura's life and in the Little House books.

Charles's fiddle is emblematic of his verve, his passion for life. He is a jack-of-all-trades. He builds their houses, raises crops, takes care of livestock, hunts, runs a business, works as a bookkeeper, storekeeper, and timekeeper. If grasshoppers take out his crop, he walks two hundred miles to work a harvest. He is the family storyteller. It is perhaps his ability to see life as an ongoing narrative that allows him to handle adversity with equanimity. There are few times when he will not pick up his fiddle to entertain or comfort the family. As Hamida Bosmajian puts it, "The fiddle is his image of intimacy.... it swells with melodies and provokes the words that express his desires: carefree attitudes, joy in life, tenderness in love, romance, and the vastness of his yearning." These values of an open heart also infuse young Laura and the Little House books.

In Laura Ingalls' younger life, from birth to age twelve, her family lived most often in the country, either woods or prairie. The children helped with the chores, including shepherding cows, but also had much time for play. They were encouraged in this by their parents, who passed on to their offspring an appreciation of nature as a provider and also as a source of pleasure and joy. This value is also well represented in the Little House books.

When Laura was twelve, in 1879, the family moved to South Dakota near the future site of De Smet, a community that was just beginning to take shape. As was common at the time, towns developed primarily to meet the needs of settlers and migrants for provisions, from building supplies to groceries and clothing. Soon after these way stations formed, however, the inhabitants coalesced into communities that addressed their social, spiritual, and educational needs. Alongside the storefronts and smitheries they built churches, schools, and opera houses. The De Smet opera house served as the community center, a venue not only for traveling shows but for events such as the Fourth of July, adult educational programs, political speeches, talent shows, public meetings, and graduation ceremonies.

In South Dakota the Ingalls family sometimes lived on a claim, a homestead obtained through the Homestead Act of 1862, and sometimes in town, depending on the season, the weather, and other circumstances. Although Laura's preference was for the country, she quickly acclimated to some of the pleasures of town life such as parties and sleigh rides. She also contributed to the family income with various jobs such as claim sitting and sewing. When she was not quite sixteen, in December 1882, and although she had not graduated from high school herself, she taught at the Bouchie school, twelve miles from her home. She boarded with a quarrelsome family on their claim. The unpleasantness of the situation was mitigated by the knowledge that her income would help send her sister Mary, who had been left blind by a childhood illness, to college.

The discomforts of Laura's two-month teaching residency were also mitigated by the attention of a gentleman from town, Almanzo Wilder. Although he was ten years her senior, she knew him from town social activities. Every weekend, regardless of the frequent blizzards and twenty-below temperatures, Almanzo picked her up in his cutter (a light sleigh) on Friday afternoon and took her home to her family. He returned her to Bouchie on Sunday afternoon. In her unpublished autobiography "Pioneer Girl," Wilder insisted that she had no interest in Almanzo: "I was only going with him for the sake of being home over Sunday," she revealed, "and fully intended to stop as soon as my school was out" (quoted in Hill, p. 56). However, after her teaching assignment was over and she was back living at home, she looked out the window one day and saw several cutters with her friends sweeping by on a joyride, Almanzo among them. When he pulled up to her door, she quickly grabbed her coat and hat and joined him in his cutter. As part of their courtship, they gave each other pet names. Almanzo had a sister named Laura and said he had never liked the name; using Laura's middle name, Elizabeth, he dubbed her Bessie. She, in turn, called him Manly, a different diminutive of Almanzo than those used by his family, Mannie and Manzo.

Bessie and Manly became engaged in the summer of 1884 and were married on August 25, 1885. Laura was eighteen years old, Almanzo was twenty-eight.

LESSONS IN FORTITUDE

Wilder transitioned easily to the life of a married adult. She had been taught self-reliance and was used to accepting responsibility for her own actions and for the well-being of her family. She had worked alongside her parents on claims and farms all of her life and had helped support the family by working outside the home in town. She knew what to do and how to do it when she and Almanzo settled into a three-room house on his claim two and a half miles outside of De Smet. Almanzo too was prepared for a married life. He was an experienced farmer and frontiersman. As told in Wilder's *The Long Winter* (1940), when Laura was fourteen years old, he and another young man risked their lives by taking a sled twenty miles into the country to get wheat from a farmer. Supply trains had not been able to get through to De Smet for several months and the townspeople were on the verge of starvation.

The early years of Laura and Almanzo's marriage tested their fortitude. As it had always been, frontier life remained unpredictable and difficult. In their first summer on their claim, in 1886, a hailstorm flattened most of their crop. They moved to a homestead because they could obtain a mortgage on it. Their lives were brightened by the birth of their daughter Rose on December 6, 1886.

However, for the next several years they endured more losses and a tragedy. In 1887 their barn burned down. The following year Laura and Almanzo had diphtheria, and toddler Rose was sent to live for six months with her grandparents while her parents recovered. During recovery, Almanzo suffered a stroke that left him temporarily paralyzed and with permanent damage to his legs. On August 12, 1888, Laura gave birth to a son who lived only twelve days. Less than two weeks after his death, their house burned to the ground. They built a two-room shanty that they lived in through the winter.

Through the disasters, the Wilders and Almanzo's brother Peter maintained and increased a flock of sheep. Sale of this livestock made it possible for the Wilders to make a new start in their life: they decided to move away from South Dakota, resuming the Ingallses' zigzag migration pattern, driven not by wanderlust but by necessity. In 1890 they traveled to Spring Valley, Minnesota, to stay with Almanzo's parents while they made further plans. Following others from the area, they then moved south to Westville, Florida. They hoped that the warm weather would help speed Almanzo's recovery from the stroke. However, they did not adapt well to the climate, the land, or the people. Laura was so uncomfortable and felt so unsafe that she carried a revolver in her pocket. After less than a year, they returned to De Smet.

In De Smet the Wilders rented a house in town, where they both worked for wages, Laura as a seamstress and Almanzo as a carpenter. The times remained difficult for everyone. South Dakota was in drought, and a financial panic in 1893 plunged the country into a depression. In spite of their own financial struggles, they started to save money to buy a farm. Their optimism came not from improved circumstances in South Dakota but from word of the Land of the Big Red Apple, as it was called in advertisements. Friends had traveled to Missouri and come back with stories of successful orchards and farms. In July 1984 the Wilders said goodbye to De Smet and their family and friends and began the six-week wagon ride to Mansfield, Missouri, in the Ozark mountains. With their savings, they bought a farm that they named Rocky Ridge. There they raised Rose, worked the orchards and fields, and raised small livestock, especially chickens, Laura's specialty.

Although they often lived and worked in town, in 1911 they finally built the house at Rocky Ridge that Wilder had dreamed of from the beginning. They used materials from the land itself partly because it was economical to do so but also because they wanted the house to be truly of the land. Wilder had a vision for this. She saw the house as a work of art in itself. It had massive beamed ceilings and a fireplace formed of massive rock slabs. The rooms were small, fitting the physical stature of Manly and Bessie: he was about five feet, four inches tall, she was four feet, eleven inches. She even had a low kitchen counter built so that it would be easy

for her to knead bread. In this house, some twenty years later, the Little House books would be written.

EMERGING WRITER

Although Wilder did not begin the Little House novels until she was in her sixties, her literary life began long before that. Winter evenings in the little houses of Wilder's youth were often spent listening to stories read out loud from Ma Ingalls' books. Prior to her marriage, Caroline had been a schoolteacher and ensured that, even though they often lived in the wilderness, her children would be properly educated. The readings included the Bible and novels such as Henry Ward Beecher's *Norwood* and Mary Jane Holmes's *Millbank* as well as magazines, newspapers, and church publications. Wilder also developed a keen sense of narrative from Pa's unfailing talents as a storyteller and from her own role as narrator of scenery and events for her sister Mary after she became blind.

Wilder was deemed to be the best student scholar in De Smet and would probably have gone to college herself had it not been necessary to send Mary to a college for the blind. At fifteen Laura received her first teaching certificate, a further indication that she was capably educated. Evidence of her writing style appears in her first extant writing, "On the Way Home," a diary she kept of the family's journey from De Smet to Mansfield, Missouri. Published in 1962, it is replete with descriptive details of their journey:

> This is a land of many springs and clear brooks. Some of the earth is yellow and some is red. The road is stony often.
>
> Went through another little town, Lockwood, at 4 o'clock, and camped by a swift-running little creek of the clearest water. It is most delicious water to drink, cold, with a cool, snappy flavor.
>
> Except in towns, we have seen only one schoolhouse so far in Missouri.
>
> We drove in the rain this afternoon, for the first time since we left Dakota. It was a good steady pouring rain, but we kept dry in the wagon and the rain stopped before camping time.
>
> (*A Little House Traveler,* p. 72)

Wilder was twenty-seven years old when the family moved to Missouri. Although she did not engage in significant writing again until she was forty-four, other than letters, she was active in church, lodge, and community affairs. She was well known for her knowledge of and expertise with raising chickens and was sometimes asked to speak on the topic to local farm groups. One such invitation led to a major change in her life: she was unable to attend an event and so wrote out her comments for someone else to read aloud for her. The editor of the *Missouri Ruralist* was in the audience and was so impressed with the speech that he contacted Wilder and asked her to submit something to the bimonthly paper. Her first article, fifteen hundred words, was featured in the issue of February 18, 1911. It praised the virtues of rural life and offered advice for success on a small farm. As with the diary, it contained detailed descriptions. These were coupled with life lessons, as would the stories she would tell twenty years later in the Little House novels.

From 1912 into the 1920s, Wilder served as a columnist and as home editor for the *Missouri Ruralist.* It was the major farm paper in Missouri with a readership of more than 88,000 and is still published today. Her subjects included biographical profiles, beauty advice, articles on foods, and social advice for women, including the value of women's clubs for rural women as well as for those who lived in town. Her articles on rural living included "Haying While the Sun Shines," "Learning to Work Together," and "Keep the Saving Habit," and she occasionally wrote sketches of childhood memories. In general, she espoused conventional values similar to those that would permeate the Little House books: hard work, thrift, self-reliance, honesty, balance, simple pleasures, and the necessity of love. Wilder's byline in the *Ruralist* read, variously, "Mrs. A. J. Wilder," "Laura Ingalls Wilder," and occasionally, "A. J. Wilder," though Almanzo had not written the work.

During this time, as her writing developed,

Wilder also expanded her social and civic activities. A charter member of the Athenians, a women's discussion club, she promoted actions that she recommended in her columns, reaching out to farm women throughout southwestern Missouri by helping them form their own clubs. She helped organize the Mansfield branch of the National Farm Loan Association and served as its secretary-treasurer for ten years, and in 1925 she ran unsuccessfully for a township office.

Wilder also expanded her writing career during this period, in tandem with that of her daughter, Rose Wilder Lane, who had graduated high school in 1904, married in 1909, and was herself embarked on a path that would lead her to become a best-selling novelist. While Lane was working as an editor and writer in San Francisco in 1915, Wilder visited her and also covered the city's Panama-Pacific International Exhibition for the *Missouri Ruralist.* With the help of Lane's publishing connections, Wilder published an article in *McCall's* magazine in June 1919 and another in *Country Gentleman* in January 1925.

"PIONEER GIRL"

Wilder did not set out to write a series of young adult novels about pioneer life in the Midwest. Her first full-length writing on the topic, approximately two hundred pages, was a straightforward autobiography of her earliest memories up to her marriage in 1885. Inspired in part by the vignettes she had published in the *Missouri Ruralist,* Wilder was encouraged in her task by her daughter Rose Wilder Lane. In May 1930 she delivered the handwritten manuscript to Lane, who edited and typed it and then marketed the manuscript through her literary agents, Carl and Zelma Brandt. The response of publishers was varied. Several magazines turned down a proposal to serialize the book, though the *Saturday Evening Post* praised it and lamented that it was not fiction, as that genre was in ascendancy at the time. When Lane switched to a new agent, George T. Bye, he did not think the manuscript was dynamic enough to warrant publication in its current form.

Lane was not deterred by the early rejections of her mother's manuscript, even though she herself did not place much value on publishing for children. She knew that her mother's primary goal was not to make money but rather to make the pioneer heritage known to children and to be recognized for her writing achievements. While "Pioneer Girl" was making the rounds in New York, Lane excerpted early episodes from the manuscript and organized them into text for a proposed children's picture book, "When Grandma Was a Little Girl."

The evolution of Wilder's pioneer stories into young adult fiction began when Lane shared "When Grandma Was a Little Girl" with a writer friend who shared it with Marion Fiery, an editor in Alfred A. Knopf's juvenile literature division. Fiery was enthusiastic about the manuscript. She felt that the writing was lively and compelling, as Rose reported to her mother: "[Fiery] is crazy about your writing; indeed, everyone is who has seen it. She says you make such perfect pictures of everything, and that the characters are all absolutely *real*" (quoted in Miller, 1998, p. 183).

Fiery also liked that the story covered a period of time neglected in children's books and suggested that the appropriate market was not in picture books but in books for eight- to twelve-year-olds. She recommended that the manuscript be expanded to book length and that details about pioneer life be included, such as how things were made, what children did during the day, how they played and worked.

This was the second time it was suggested that Wilder's story be presented as fiction rather than nonfiction, and Lane picked up on the idea. She revealed her picture-book version of "When Grandma Was a Little Girl" to her mother and advised her on how to develop it into a novel. When Wilder had visited Lane in San Francisco, she had received considerable instruction from Lane on writing techniques for her freelance writing.

Lane, who by this point had published novels and short stories, now instructed her mother in writing fiction. She suggested that Wilder start by writing the story in first person if that felt more natural and comfortable for her. Lane could later

change it to third person. Lane also suggested that the picture book text be expanded from one winter to one year. Without knowing she was doing so, she thereby set the format for all of the books in the Little House series.

The "Pioneer Girl" manuscript served as a source book for Wilder through all of the novels and provides an illuminating comparison between the facts of Wilder's life and the content of the Little House books. "Pioneer Girl" is more diary than story and is unshaped in terms of characters and themes. While it appears to be true to the details of Wilder's and the Ingalls family's experiences, it does not seek, as do the Little House books, to present the feeling of Laura's experiences, nor does it seek to edify its readers regarding the Ingalls family values. "Pioneer Girl" also provides details on some of the tribulations of the Ingalls family that are not in the novels, including the birth and death of the boy Charles.

One aspect of the Ingalls life trajectory represented in "Pioneer Girl" that is not included in the novels is the family's zigzag migration pattern. In adapting to writing fiction, Wilder quickly adopted a strong sense of direction both in the writing itself and in the forward movement of the family. As she embarked on the second novel and imagined additional books in a series, she was careful to keep the family moving in a westward direction.

That was the direction of the country at the time. It was the direction of progress and of hope. In the novels, the family does not look back, does not backtrack to Wisconsin or Minnesota, though those episodes are recorded in "Pioneer Girl." *Little House in the Big Woods* (1932), the first book, takes place in Wisconsin, *On the Banks of Plum Creek* (1937) in Minnesota, and *Little House on the Prairie* (1935)in Kansas. *By the Shores of Silver Lake* (1939), *The Long Winter* (1940), and *These Happy Golden Years* (1943) take place in De Smet, South Dakota. Even the story of Almanzo Wilder in *Farmer Boy* (1933), the second book in the series, flows from Almanzo Wilder's childhood home in New York to Minnesota to South Dakota.

TRUE-TO-LIFE STORIES

The Little House books were published as novels, yet readers tended to take their circumstances as fact. The certitude and exactitude of the writing contributed to the myth, as did Rose Wilder Lane's lifelong contention that every word was absolutely true. The easy, genuine tone of the stories made them seem as though they spilled directly from the memory of the author, who, it seemed, spun them effortlessly and in final form from a rocking chair in her Ozark mountain home. It was not until "Pioneer Girl" became available to scholars after Lane's death that fiction came up against fact.

Some readers felt betrayed by the revelation that the novels were fictionalized autobiography. Furthermore, some readers and critics alike found it difficult to believe that an unassuming farm wife in her sixties, as Wilder was when she began writing the Little House books, could suddenly and miraculously achieve such accomplished work. This view fails to give her credit for her nearly twenty years of experience as a writer about agriculture and farm living, or for her intellectual experience such as her participation in women's and social clubs.

There is ample evidence, however, that Wilder knew what she was doing when she intentionally honed her actual experience into coherent stories with clear moral messages. From her lifelong reading, from listening to her father tell stories and from telling them herself, from describing the world to Mary, from her twenty years of experience writing for the *Missouri Ruralist* and from her lessons from Lane, Wilder knew how to spin a good tale. With additional guidance from Lane, she crafted the Little House novels as a compelling read and for best effect in teaching children not only the lessons of history but also the lessons of rectitude and good behavior for both adults and children. The stories suggested that actions thus guided would lead to a contented life, whatever the economic circumstances.

The evidence for Wilder's professional writing skills lies both in her comments on her process and in examples of the process itself. At a Detroit book fair in 1937, she spoke about her

understanding of her novels: "All I have told is true but it is not the whole truth" (quoted in Hill, p. 1). She carefully selected incidents from her life that contributed to her overall intentions for a story, and she omitted incidents that did not. The storyline in *The Long Winter* is primarily one of isolation and survival, with "the Ingalls family and their struggles at the heart of her book and the entire series" (Hill, p. 50). To maintain the power of the situation, Wilder did not include in the book the fact that another family lived with them through that long winter and contributed to the family's survival. When Lane suggested that they or a fictional family be included, Wilder responded, "We can't have anyone living with us.... [It] would spoil the story" (quoted in Hill, p. 50).

Wilder was also willing to make adaptations beyond mere omission. In the first novel in the series, *Little House in the Big Woods,* she states that "as far as a man could go to the north in a day, or a week, or a whole month, there was nothing but woods. There were no houses. There were no roads. There were no people" (p. 1). In fact, the Wilder homestead was not located in the Big Woods. In "Pioneer Girl" she states "It seemed the 'Big Woods' as Pa called them were just north of us a ways." Also, the school she and Mary attended was "only a little way down the road" (quoted in Hill, p. 16), and the Ingallses lived in a strong extended community that included both the Quiners (Ma's family) and the Ingallses.

For effect in the novels, Wilder compresses and adjusts the circumstances of her characters. As Pamela Smith Hill writes, she "transformed these experiences into an almost mythic kind of truth. She deliberately heightened her family's social and physical isolation, a transformation that ultimately strengthened not just her first novel, but the remaining books in the series" (p. 17). An adaptation that perhaps might be more upsetting to faithful readers was the disposition in real life of the family's bulldog, Jack, a faithful companion in three of the novels. In reality, when the Ingallses moved from Wisconsin (*Little House in the Big Woods*) to Kansas (*Little House on the Prairie*), Pa sold Pet and Patty, the family horses, and included Jack in the bargain. Except for the first novel, Jack's presence is fictional, as is his peaceful death from old age in the fifth book, *By the Shores of Silver Lake*.

The personality of the fictional Laura is closely based on Wilder's actual self. She is capable and courageous, as was Wilder in her private life as well as her writing life. Both were unafraid of hard work, and Wilder the writer exhibited that trait in the writing of the books. Many of her early drafts and her communications with her daughter Rose are extant and provide plentiful examples of her consciousness as a writer. As John E. Miller observes, "She had a mature ability to discover significance and meaning in ordinary happenings and convey them to readers in a straightforward—sometimes subtle—style" (1998, p. 126).

Wilder's writing process included extensive editing and polishing of the work through revision. "The only way I can write ... is to wander along with the story, then re-write and re-arrange and change it everywhere" (quoted in Hill, p. 139). She understood the value of precise writing and recognized that the tone of a passage carried as much weight as the information it put forward: "You will hardly believe the difference the use of one word rather than another will make until you begin to hunt for a word with just the right shade of meaning, just the right color for the picture you are painting with words" (p. 140). She wrote all of the manuscripts in pencil on lined school tablets, working from outlines, then revised and recopied them once or twice before turning them over to Lane.

Wilder worked steadfastly to assure that each story evoked the mood she wanted to convey. An early draft of *Little House on the Prairie,* originally called "Indian Country," includes a passage describing the family's journey across the prairie: "It was late afternoon as the white-topped covered wagon moved slowly across the prairie. The two black ponies seemed tired of pulling it, and Mary and Laura were tired of riding in it" (quoted in Hill, pp. 157–158). The draft shows some of the lines crossed out and replaced with "A white-topped covered wagon moved slowly across the prairie, drawn by two black ponies. A man and a woman sat on the

wagon seat in front. The man was driving, his bright blue eyes looking along the wagon trail ahead." Further revisions led to another iteration:

> A white-topped, covered wagon, drawn by two black ponies moved slowly across the prairie in Southern Kansas. A brindle bulldog trotted in the shade underneath.
>
> A man and a woman sat on the spring-seat at the very front of the wagon. The man was driving, his bright blue eyes looking ahead along the wagon trail, his brown beard blowing in the wind.
>
> (quoted in Hill, p. 158)

Wilder made notes for Lane in the margins of most of her manuscripts, beginning with "Pioneer Girl." Lane responded to the marginalia with suggestions and comments; Wilder responded again in kind. This editorial pattern was sustained through the writing of the eight Little House books published during Wilder's lifetime. A ninth book, published as *The First Four Years,* was discovered in Lane's papers after her death. It was apparently a first draft by Wilder and was published without emendation by either Wilder or Lane. Lane, an experienced editor as well as an author, provided the kind of editing that was common by publishing house editors, then as today. In the case of the Wilder-Lane collaboration, this stage in the development of a book took place before the manuscript went to the publisher. Few editorial changes were made once Lane had worked over a manuscript.

Although Lane occasionally inserted sentences, even paragraphs, and sometimes rearranged text, "Wilder's essential voice remains consistent, unique, and appealing" from one draft to the next (Hill, p. 141). Much of Lane's editing was perfunctory. In an early draft of *Little House in the Big Woods,* Wilder wrote,

> But in all the miles and miles and miles of trees there were only a few little log houses scattered far apart just where the Big Woods began. And so far as the little girl could see there was only the one, little gray house she lived with her Father and Mother and her sister Mary and baby sister Carrie. A wagon track ran before the house turning and twisting among the trees of the woods where the wild animals lived.
>
> The little girl was named Laura and she called her father Pa and her mother Ma, not Father and Mother or Papa or Mama as children do now.
>
> (quoted in Hill, p. 140)

Lane's editing changed the flow of the content but not the information or the voice:

> To the east of the little log house, and to the west, there were miles upon miles of trees, and only a few little log houses scattered far apart in the edge of the Big Woods.
>
> So far as the little girl could see, there was only the one little house where she lived with her Father and Mother, her sister Mary and baby sister Carrie. A wagon track ran before the house, turning and twisting out of sight in the woods where the wild animals lived, but the little girl did not know where it went, nor what might be at the end of it.
>
> The little girl was named Laura and she called her father, Pa, and her mother, Ma. In those days and in the place, children did not say Father and Mother, nor Mamma and Papa, as they do now.
>
> (*Little House in the Big Woods,* pp. 2–3)

Through her own efforts and consultation with Lane, Wilder assured that the truth of the fiction was well told. In addition, she assured that the history of the stories as portrayed was accurate. She consulted with experts and with family members, exchanging correspondence with her sisters and aunts regarding details of the Ingalls family saga. She also made three trips to De Smet, in 1931, 1938, and 1939, during which she gathered and verified information. These resources bolstered her memory and allowed her to attend to details such as which flowers bloomed when on the prairie, which songs were sung in church, and the layout of the town of De Smet. Much of the value of the books is attributed to their historic accuracy of the regarding the times: as Miller writes, they "provide keys for unlocking a popular mindset of the 1930s and 1940s as well as the lived history of a significant late-nineteenth-century agricultural frontier" (1994, p. 112).

WRITER-EDITOR, MOTHER-DAUGHTER

The role of Wilder's daughter in the construction and writing of the Little House books did not

become fully known until after Lane's death in 1968 at the age of eighty-one, eleven years after her mother's death at age ninety and more than forty years after the publication of *These Happy Golden Years,* the last of eight books in the Little House series. Lane's estate, including her and her mother's literary papers, passed to Lane's heir, Roger MacBride, the son of a good friend. She had known MacBride most of his life and considered him to be her unofficially adopted grandson. Eventually Lane's papers, including Wilder's manuscript drafts, became available to scholars. It was quickly evident that Lane's editorial influence permeated the manuscripts, though always at an appropriate later stage in the writing.

Lane began her freelance publishing career in 1908; Wilder started writing for the *Missouri Ruralist* in 1911. Lane's accomplishments eventually included the best-selling novel *Let the Hurricane Roar,* published in 1933, based on her mother's childhood stories. A second novel, *Freeland,* was published in 1938. Her other books included biographies of Herbert Hoover and Jack London. She also was a successful ghostwriter. Her articles appeared frequently in national magazines, including the *Saturday Evening Post, Harper's,* and *Country Gentleman.* Several times she lived abroad for extended periods while working as a journalist.

Lane was born in De Smet, South Dakota. Her earliest memories included the period when she lived with her grandparents (Ma and Pa of the Little House books) for several months while her parents were ill with and recovering from diphtheria. She was five when she and her parents moved to Mansfield, Missouri, where she grew up living on Rocky Ridge Farm and in the town of Mansfield. By her own description, she did not fit in. The family was poor for much of her childhood, and when she was in town she felt the disapproval of the town's children. In addition, she was precocious and found the Mansfield school stifling. When she was sixteen, her parents sent her to live with Almanzo's sister Eliza in Crowley, Louisiana, so she could attend a larger high school. After graduating from high school she moved to Kansas City, where she became a telegraph operator. She married Gillette Lane in 1909 and they divorced in 1918. They had one child, a son, who died in infancy.

Rose was close to her parents throughout their lifetimes. She frequently returned to Rocky Ridge to live for long periods, ranging from months to years, and her mother made several extended trips to visit her, most significantly to San Francisco where they worked together on Wilder's writing skills. Both wrote through the Great Depression of the 1930s. *Little House in the Big Woods* was published in 1932. Its success was later attributed in part to its promise of redemption through hard work, perseverance, and beneficent spirit.

During an extended stay at Rocky Ridge beginning in 1928, Lane built a new house for her parents and resided herself in the old house. The houses were just out of sight of each other, and Wilder and Lane walked back and forth with drafts of Little House manuscripts. When Lane was not at Rocky Ridge, they worked by mail. The collaboration was one of editor to author, as Lane said to Wilder early in the relationship, commenting that her editorial recommendations were no more or less than she provided to other authors.

In addition to her editorial astuteness, Lane made other contributions to the collaboration. She connected Wilder with her agents and publishers and helped her understand book contracts. As with the writing, as Wilder came to understand the exigencies of publishing, she also began to articulate her own needs and demands regarding contracts and the books. In 1941, while negotiating with Harper & Brothers for *Little Town on the Prairie,* she renegotiated her royalties from an eight-year-old contract with Harper for *Farmer Boy.*

Both Lane and Wilder encouraged a public perception that Wilder was just a simple granny spinning yarns from her rocking chair. The image was widely accepted and gave credence to the contention that Lane was more than editor for her mother's work. However, Lane's writing style is notably different from Wilder's and provides further evidence that the Little House books were the work of the mother, not the daughter. Although they shared political views in a general

sense—both were conservative—Lane's position tended to be more strident and was clearly articulated in her writing. The voice in her novels is terse and unromantic, unlike Wilder's descriptive voice that evokes images and emotions. The voice of Wilder in the Little House books is clearly present in her earlier writing for the *Missouri Ruralist,* further confirmation that it is her style, not Lane's, that pervades the series.

When Wilder wrote *Little House in the Big Woods,* she expected it to be a one-book project. Neither she nor Lane envisioned the eight-book series that eventually grew from that first effort. It was the public response to *Big Woods* and the next three books, and especially the response of elementary school teachers and students, that inspired the development of a full series. One of the most frequent questions asked was what happened between Laura and Almanzo, and Wilder told her readers that she was planning three more books set in De Smet, ending with Laura and Almanzo's wedding. That would have brought the series to seven. In the end, Wilder realized it would take one more book, bringing the series to eight. The ninth book, *The First Four Years,* is not usually considered to be part of the series. It is addressed to an adult audience and was not published until 1975, eighteen years after Wilder's death.

THE LITTLE HOUSE BOOKS

Some of the success of the Little House novels is attributed to the maturation of the voice and style of the books in concert with the maturation of their readers. In the stories, the fictional Laura is the same age as the narrator. She grows up with each book just as her readers, mostly girls, are also growing up. The first novels are built on the stories that Wilder heard over and over from an early age. Progressing through the series, the novels segue into Wilder's direct memories of her own experiences.

This development was intentional on Wilder's part. Lane also edited the manuscripts for the development, though sometimes she and Wilder disagreed about the level of sophistication that was relevant for each age group. As Wilder became more experienced as a fiction writer, she also gained confidence in her ability to judge the work and relied less often on her daughter's input. Wilder did, however, agree with Lane that identifying a central theme for each novel was essential to a strong storyline. Wilder usually identified the theme after some of the work was complete. She then honed the novel to bring the material in line. The overall series theme of steady migration toward the western horizon also links the novels together.

The Little House books, in addition to having a maturing voice from one book to the next and a defining theme within each book and across the series, bear a consistent moral message that cuts across time and underpins Laura's experiences. These values are expressed in most of her writing, starting with the articles for the *Missouri Ruralist* in 1911. They are generally conventional and traditional and include the virtues of work, family, even-tempered spirit, love, appreciation of nature, and perseverance, especially in the face of misfortune.

Structure, themes, and morals are important elements of the writing, but the power that pulls them together into an artistic rendering is, in the end, Wilder's "powers of perception as a girl, in her detached insight into human nature including her own, and in her ability as a mature woman to sift the memories of her childhood through a dramatic lens that chose what was illuminating and interesting to people and discarded what was dull and uninspiring" (Miller, 1998, p. 240).

The series opens with *Little House in the Big Woods*, published in 1932. Set in Wisconsin, it introduces readers to the Ingalls family and to the fine details of living on the frontier in the late 1880s. Homesteading techniques and skills are fully described, including the making of maple syrup, cheese, and other pantry resources. Readers are also introduced to the cozy, intimate life of a loving family living in solitude and interacting with the forces of nature. The closing words of the book embody the feeling of the overall story:

> But Laura lay awake a little while, listening to Pa's fiddle softly playing and to the lonely sound of the wind in the Big Woods. She looked at Pa sitting on

> the bench by the hearth, the fire-light gleaming on his brown hair and beard and glistening on the honey-brown fiddle. She looked at Ma, gently rocking and knitting.
>
> She thought to herself, "This is now."
>
> She was glad that the house was cozy, and Pa and Ma and the firelight and the music, were now. They could not be forgotten, she thought, because now is now. It can never be a long time ago.
>
> (p. 238)

Farmer Boy, the second book, was published in 1933. Wilder had not yet envisioned the full Little House series, and *Farmer Boy* is not a sequel to *Little House in the Big Woods* but rather a parallel story, the fictionalized biography of Almanzo Wilder. It complies with the overall theme of the series, westward movement, starting with Almanzo's early childhood in New York and continuing with his family's migration to Minnesota and then to South Dakota. Almanzo does not reappear in the series until the fifth book, *By the Shores of Silver Lake,* and is present in the subsequent books.

Before *Farmer Boy* was published, Wilder was already working on a third book, *Little House on the Prairie*. Published in 1935, it picks up the story of the Ingallses and begins their westward migration. It opens with the family leaving their cozy home and journeying by covered wagon to Kansas. The novel ends with the family back in the covered wagon, this time moving to Minnesota. Wilder was by now imagining the longer series, each one covering a single year in young Laura's life.

In October of 1937 Wilder was invited to speak at a Detroit book fair. *On the Banks of Plum Creek,* the fourth book in the series, would be published by the end of the year and would further assure Wilder's growing popularity and success. Schoolchildren and their teachers frequently wrote to her about the books, and she told the Detroit audience that the children's letters, begging for more stories, encouraged her to think further about her childhood and to continue writing about it in novel form. She said that she had come to understand that she had lived through several phases of frontier history and that she wanted children to know about that period of American life. *On the Banks of Plum Creek* interrupts the family's geographic isolation from others. Their homestead is close enough to town that the girls can walk to school and the family plays an active role in the growth of the small community.

At the opening of *By the Shores of Silver Lake,* published in 1939, the Ingallses are still at Plum Creek. However, a grasshopper plague, which has continued into a second year, makes it impossible for their farm to succeed. Adding more misery to their suffering, the family has endured illnesses, including the one that leads to Mary's loss of sight. The family is rescued by an offer of work from Pa's sister and, once again packed into their covered wagon, the family journeys westward, this time to a place in Dakota Territory that would later become De Smet, South Dakota. In this new place, the Ingallses continue to turn to each other for comfort and support.

By the time *Silver Lake* was published in 1939, Wilder was blocking out the remainder of the eight-book series, the last three also taking place in De Smet. Readers recognized that each book stood on its own but that the books were also closely connected. The importance of family values and perseverance continue to inform the characters' actions and feelings.

Little Town on the Prairie, published in 1941, and *These Happy Golden Years,* published in 1943, complete the upbringing of the fictional Laura. As an adolescent and then a teenager, she experiences life away from the hearth: her jobs away from home include working in town, helping to sit a homestead claim, and teaching school. As Wilder promised in her speech at the Detroit book fair, the series has a happy ending, as should all good novels, she said, with the marriage of Laura and Almanzo. The stories took thirteen years in the writing overall.

Wilder's last novel, *The First Four Years,* published in 1971 and written for an adult audience, has sparked controversy among critics. Wilder did not offer it for publication prior to her death, nor did Lane afterward. Reviews of the novel are generally reserved in their judgment of the quality of the book because it does not have

the tight narrative thrust of the Little House series. Perhaps Wilder recognized, after the initial draft, that her gifts as a writer did not extend to novels for adults. Perhaps, after working with the material, she was not interested in remembering that part of her life, which included adult grief and disappointments. Or perhaps she was simply done with writing. She had been working on the novels for thirteen straight years, and she was now seventy-eight years old. Perhaps it was time to rest.

Some critics claim that the book fails because Lane did not edit it, although she certainly had the opportunity to do so. It is just as likely that Lane, like Wilder, did not see the manuscript as viable and decided to not pursue it.

BORDERLANDS

As indicated above, *Little House in the Big Woods* and the books that followed received positive reviews in the *New York Times* and other major publications, which promoted the novels as delightful and lively. These early critiques focused on evaluating the books for their young audiences and for educators and librarians. It was not until several decades after the books were first published that broader critical interpretations were presented on Wilder's work. The variety of approaches taken in such formal criticism include notions of freedom and wildness versus control and domestication; gender and feminist issues; the frontier and notions of space and borders; and cultural issues, including stereotyping of American Indians.

In this criticism, the approaches often conflate. Holly Blackford frames the discussion this way: "Is the prairie empty or full? For what does an American woman look? Is she looking for signs of human touch and connection, or for the raw energy of life rejuvenating itself in nature? For real women and mothers, is the virgin land a muse or the threat of emptiness, loss, and death?" (p. 147). When Laura is younger, she identifies more fully with Pa, whose favorite place to sit is on the threshold of the cabin, between the wild land and the domesticity of home. He is as drawn to the wild as he is to the hearth. Freedom for him is the freedom to move on when he feels like the human world is encroaching too much. For Ma, freedom means freedom from fear, from the wild. The fictional Laura is drawn to both sides: she understands the look in Pa's eyes when he gazes at the horizon, but she adopts Ma's respect for restraint and convention.

Critical studies of the Little House books often address the notion of borders, literal and symbolic. Borders separate but also bring together. Ma and Pa are separated by gender but are joined by their mutual participation in the physical work of the farm and in keeping nature under control, or by collaborating with nature, as some see it. While Pa does most of the farming itself, the planting of crops, for example, Ma contributes as well. She fights a grass fire, feeds the cattle during a blizzard, and participates in daily chores.

There are also borders between Laura and her parents. As a child, she is separated from them by her age, but she is joined with her father in her appreciation of the wildness of nature and joined with her mother in her appreciation of the coziness of the hearth. Much of the pleasure of the books for young readers is the narrator's articulation of these tensions, which feel real and accurate and sometimes carry real threat, as in hailstorms and Mary's illness. Fear is conquered not by altering the situation itself but by bringing to bear the power of oneself in adjusting to adversity. The land may be wild, but a house, actual or symbolic, can be built. The walls provide safety and comfort even though the source of the fear is not removed.

Wilder's descriptions of American Indians also turn on the tension of borders, both geographic and symbolic. As European Americans moved west, Indians were forced to move ahead of them. Pa sees this as the natural order of things. However, he is not fearful of the Indians and in one episode consorts with an Indian chief to deflect a confrontation. His comfort with the Indian peoples can be seen as an extension of his own wildness. For him, the Indians are integral to the wilderness. Perhaps Ma sees them the same way, but from her perspective from inside the

house, that wildness implies danger. In *Little House on the Prairie* she refers to them as "savages" and is unhappy when Laura admires the dark eyes of an Indian baby, confirming Laura's attraction to the wild side of nature.

Because they are novels for young adults, the Little House books also investigate the landscape of growing up and of crossing over borders into adulthood. As Charles Frey writes, Wilder portrays "the margins between family and land, between the inside of the family and its outside, between childhood and maturation."

LEGACY, ACCLAIM, MUSEUMS, ESTATE

Laura Ingalls Wilder died at Rocky Ridge Farm of complications related to diabetes on February 10, 1957, three days after her ninetieth birthday. Almanzo had died eight years earlier, on October 23, 1949, at the age of ninety-two. Rose Wilder Lane died eleven years after Wilder, at age eighty-one, on October 30, 1968, at her Connecticut home. Wilder was born at the end of the Civil War and lived through two world wars. In the course of her life she went from traveling by covered wagon as a child to flying in a jet airplane as an adult to visit her daughter. She also walked a long path in storytelling, from being the recipient of her father's stories, to relating life around her to her blind sister Mary, to farm journalist, to beloved and acclaimed author of the Little House books.

One of Wilder's expressed interests in writing the books was to be recognized as an author. As the series grew, and with it acclaim for the qualities of the novels, Wilder received such acknowledgement on many fronts: hundreds of letters and cards from schoolchildren and their teachers arrived by mail at Rocky Ridge; fans often stopped by the farm to visit; awards accumulated. She was invited to speak at events and did so when her health and energy allowed, usually wearing a red velvet dress. In 1953 Harper & Brothers published a fresh edition of the eight-book series, with new illustrations by Garth Williams.

In her last years she lived contentedly at Rocky Ridge, mostly playing solitaire and reading. She enjoyed westerns, such as those by Luke Short and Zane Grey. She listened to the radio but never owned a television. Friends in her community continued to be important to her, sharing meals with her and helping her with her shopping and other personal chores. Lane lived in Connecticut for more than twenty years, but the two traded visits and remained in touch.

Interest in Wilder and the Little House stories did not end with Wilder's death, and some of her early writings were published posthumously. Two travel journals and a set of letters were published in 2006 in *A Little House Traveler,* with introductions by Lane and MacBride. The Little House stories have been edited for chapter, picture, and board books. A Little House cookbook and a craft book develop foods and activities mentioned in the novels.

Wilder was the recipient of eponymous honors such as a library branch named for her in Detroit, Michigan; a children's reading room in the Pomona, California, public library; and the Mansfield branch of the Wright County Library in Missouri. Laura Ingalls Wilder festivals are held annually at historic sites in the Midwest. Her books have been translated into many languages.

The last five books in the original series (not including *The First Four Years*), *On the Banks of Plum Creek* through *These Happy Golden Years,* published from 1938 through 1943, received American Library Association (ALA) Newbery Honors. In 1954 the ALA established the Laura Ingalls Wilder Award. She was first recipient of the medal, which was designed by the Little House illustrator Garth Williams.

Seven historic sites preserve Wilder's legacy:

- Little House on the Prairie, Independence, Kansas. Site of *Little House on the Prairie*.
- Wilder Homestead, Almanzo Wilder's boyhood home, Malone, New York.
- Laura Ingalls Wilder Museum, Pepin, Wisconsin. Site of *Little House in the Big Woods*.
- Laura Ingalls Wilder Park and Museum, Burr Oak, Iowa. Site of a Wilder homestead that is not included in the Little House books.

- Laura Ingalls Wilder Museum, Walnut Grove, Minnesota. Site of *On the Banks of Plum Creek.*
- Laura Ingalls Wilder Historic Homes and the Laura Ingalls Wilder Memorial Society, De Smet, South Dakota. Site of *The Long Winter, Little Town on the Prairie,* and *These Happy Golden Years.*
- Laura Ingalls Wilder Historic Home and Museum, Rocky Ridge Farm, Mansfield, Missouri. Where the Little House books were written.

These sites are indicative of an enduring interest in Wilder's writings and life. Both young readers and adults continue to learn from and revel in her portrayals of the American pioneer experience. Her expression of pioneer values, her attention to history, and her talent for bringing to life her childhood memories contribute to her ongoing standing as a quintessential American writer.

Selected Bibliography

WORKS OF LAURA INGALLS WILDER

Novels

(Quotations in this essay are from the 1953 Harper & Brothers uniform edition of the Little House series, illustrated by Garth Williams.)

Little House in the Big Woods. New York: Harper, 1932, 1953.

Farmer Boy. New York: Harper, 1933, 1953.

Little House on the Prairie. New York: Harper, 1935, 1953.

On the Banks of Plum Creek. New York: Harper, 1937, 1953.

By the Shores of Silver Lake. New York: Harper, 1939, 1953.

The Long Winter. New York: Harper, 1940, 1953.

Little Town on the Prairie. New York: Harper, 1941, 1953.

These Happy Golden Years. New York: Harper, 1943, 1953.

The First Four Years. New York: Harper & Row, 1971.

A Little House Traveler: Writings from Laura Ingalls Wilder's Journeys Across America. New York: HarperCollins, 2006.

Manuscripts

Wilder's papers are held in several locations. The unpublished autobiography "Pioneer Girl" exists in three iterations. Two are held at the Hoover Presidential Library and Museum in West Branch, Iowa. One is held at the State Historical Society of Missouri. Handwritten drafts of the novels are held in various locations, including the State Historical Society of Missouri; the Laura Ingalls Wilder Memorial Association, Mansfield, Missouri; the Detroit Public Library, Rare Book Room; and the Pomona (California) Public Library.

CRITICAL STUDIES AND REVIEWS

Blackford, Holly. "Civilization and Her Discontents: The Unsettling Nature of Ma in *Little House in the Big Woods.*" *Frontiers: A Journal of Women's Studies* 29, no. 1:147–187 (January 2008).

Bosmajian, Hamida. "Vastness and Contraction of Space in *Little House on the Prairie.*" *Children's Literature* 11:49–63 (1983).

Cameron, Eleanor. "The First Four Years." *New York Times,* March 28, 1971.

Eaton, Anne T. "Farmer Boy." *New York Times,* November 26, 1933.

———. "Little House on the Prairie." *New York Times,* November 3, 1935.

———. "The Long Winter." *New York Times,* January 26, 1941.

———. "These Happy Golden Years." *New York Times,* April 4, 1943.

Frey, Charles. "Laura and Pa: Family and Landscape in *Little House on the Prairie.*" *Children's Literary Association Quarterly* 12, no. 3:125–128 (fall 1987).

Maher, Susan Naramore. "Laura Ingalls Wilder and Caddie Woodlawn: Daughters of a Border Space." *Lion and the Unicorn* 18, no. 2:130–142 (December 1994).

Thurman, Judith. "*Little House on the Prairie*'s Wilder Women." Interview with host Linda Wertheimer. National Public Radio, August 18, 2009 (http://www.npr.org/templates/story/story.php?storyId=111992555).

BIOGRAPHICAL STUDIES

Hill, Pamela Smith. *Laura Ingalls Wilder: A Writer's Life.* Pierre: South Dakota State Historical Society Press, 2007.

Holtz, William. *The Ghost in the Little House: A Life of Rose Wilder.* Colombia: University of Missouri Press, 1993.

Miller, John E. *Laura Ingalls Wilder's Little Town: Where History and Literature Meet.* Lawrence: University Press of Kansas, 1994.

———. *Becoming Laura Ingalls Wilder: The Woman Behind the Legend.* Columbia: University of Missouri Press, 1998.

LAURA INGALLS WILDER

TELEVISION AND STAGE PRODUCTIONS BASED ON THE WORKS OF LAURA INGALLS WILDER

Little House on the Prairie. Television series, NBC, 1974–1982.

Little House: A New Beginning. Television series, NBC, 1982–1983.

Little House on the Prairie: The Musical. Music by Rachel Portman, lyrics by Donna di Novelli, book by Rachel Sheinkin. Premiere: Guthrie Theater, Minneapolis, August 15, 2008.

Cumulative Index

All references include volume numbers in boldface roman numerals followed by page numbers within that volume. Subjects of articles are indicated by boldface type.

"*A*" (Zukofsky), **Supp. III Part 2:** 611, 612, 614, 617, 619, 620, 621, 622, 623, 624, 626, 627, 628, 629, 630, 631; **Supp. IV Part 1:** 154; **Supp. XVI:** 287, *287*
Aal, Katharyn, **Supp. IV Part 1:** 332
Aaron, Daniel, **IV:** 429; **Supp. I Part 2:** 647, 650
Aaron's Rod (Lawrence), **Supp. I Part 1:** 255
Abacus (Karr), **Supp. XI: 240–242,** 248, 254
Abádi-Nagy, Zoltán, **Supp. IV Part 1:** 280, 289, 291
"Abandoned Farmhouse" (Kooser), **Supp. XIX:** 117, 119
"Abandoned House, The" (L. Michaels), **Supp. XVI:** 214
"Abandoned Newborn, The" (Olds), **Supp. X:** 207
"Abandoned Stone Schoolhouse in the Nebraska Sandhills, An" (Kooser), **Supp. XIX:** 124–125
"Abba Jacob" (Nelson), **Supp. XVIII:** 177
Abbey, Edward, **Supp. VIII:** 42; **Supp. X:** 24, 29, 30, 31, 36; **Supp. XIII: 1–18; Supp. XIV:** 179
Abbey's Road (Abbey), **Supp. XIII:** 12
Abbott, Carl, **Supp. XVIII:** 142
Abbott, Edith, **Supp. I Part 1:** 5
Abbott, George, **Supp. IV Part 2:** 585
Abbott, Grace, **Supp. I Part 1:** 5
Abbott, Jack Henry, **Retro. Supp. II:** 210
Abbott, Jacob, **Supp. I Part 1:** 38, 39
Abbott, Lyman, **III:** 293
Abbott, Sean, **Retro. Supp. II:** 213
ABC of Color, An: Selections from Over a Half Century of Writings (Du Bois), **Supp. II Part 1:** 186
ABC of Reading (Pound), **III:** 468, 474–475
"Abdication, An" (Merrill), **Supp. III Part 1:** 326
'Abdu'l-Bahá, **Supp. XX: 117, 122**
Abel, Lionel, **Supp. XIII:** 98
Abel, Sam, **Supp. XIII:** 199
Abelard, Peter, **I:** 14, 22
Abeles, Sigmund, **Supp. VIII:** 272
Abeng (Cliff), **Supp. XXII:** 66, 69–71
Abercrombie, Lascelles, **III:** 471; **Retro. Supp. I:** 127, 128
Abernathy, Milton, **Supp. III Part 2:** 616
Abernon, Edgar Vincent, Viscount d', **Supp. XVI:** 191
Aberration of Starlight (Sorrentino), **Supp. XXI:** 234–235
Abhau, Anna. *See* Mencken, Mrs. August (Anna Abhau)
"Abide with Me" (Hoffman), **Supp. XVIII:** 86
"Ability" (Emerson), **II:** 6
Abingdon, Alexander, **Supp. XVI:** 99
Abish, Walter, **Supp. V:** 44
"Abishag" (Glück), **Supp. V:** 82
"Abnegation, The" (Bronk), **Supp. XXI:** 32
Abney, Lisa, **Supp. XXII:** 9
Abood, Maureen, **Supp. XXII:** 90
"Abortion, The" (Sexton), **Supp. II Part 2:** 682
"Abortions" (Dixon), **Supp. XII:** 153
"About C. D. Wright" (Colburn), **Supp. XV:** 341
"About Effie" (Findley), **Supp. XX: 50**
"About Hospitality" (Jewett), **Retro. Supp. II:** 131
"About Kathryn" (Dubus), **Supp. VII:** 91
"About Language" (Wrigley), **Supp. XVIII:** 300–301
"About Looking Alone at a Place: Arles" (M. F. K. Fisher), **Supp. XVII:** 89, 91
About the House (Auden), **Supp. II Part 1:** 24
About Town: "The New Yorker" and the World It Made (Yagoda), **Supp. VIII:** 151
"Above Pate Valley" (Snyder), **Supp. VIII:** 293
Above the River (Wright), **Supp. III Part 2:** 589, 606
"Abraham" (Schwartz), **Supp. II Part 2:** 663
Abraham, Nelson Algren. *See* Algren, Nelson
Abraham, Pearl, **Supp. XVII:** 49; **Supp. XX: 177**
"Abraham Davenport" (Whittier), **Supp. I Part 2:** 699
"Abraham Lincoln" (Emerson), **II:** 13
Abraham Lincoln: The Prairie Years (Sandburg), **III:** 580, 587–589, 590
Abraham Lincoln: The Prairie Years and the War Years (Sandburg), **III:** 588, 590
Abraham Lincoln: The War Years (Sandburg), **III:** 588, 589–590; **Supp. XVII:** 105
"Abraham Lincoln Walks at Midnight" (Lindsay), **Supp. I Part 2:** 390–391
"Abram Morrison" (Whittier), **Supp. I Part 2:** 699
Abramovich, Alex, **Supp. X:** 302, 309
Abrams, David, **Supp. XXII:** 61
Abrams, M. H., **Supp. XVI:** 19
Abridgment of Universal Geography, An: Together with Sketches of History (Rowson), **Supp. XV:** 243
"Absalom" (Rukeyser), **Supp. VI:** 278–279
Absalom, Absalom! (Faulkner), **II:** 64, 65–67, 72, 223; **IV:** 207; **Retro. Supp. I:** 75, 81, 82, 84, 85, 86, 87, 88, 89, 90, 92, 382; **Supp. V:** 261; **Supp. X:** 51; **Supp. XIV:** 12–13
"Absence of Mercy" (Stone), **Supp. V:** 295
"Absentee, The" (Levertov), **Supp. III Part 1:** 284
Absentee Ownership (Veblen), **Supp. I Part 2:** 642
"Absent-Minded Bartender" (X. J. Kennedy), **Supp. XV:** 159
"Absent Thee from Felicity Awhile" (Wylie), **Supp. I Part 2:** 727, 729
"Absolution" (Fitzgerald), **Retro. Supp. I:** 108
"Absolution" (Sobin), **Supp. XVI:** 289
"Abuelita's Ache" (Mora), **Supp. XIII:** 218
Abysmal Brute, The (London), **II:** 467
Abyssinia and the Imperialists (C. L. R. James), **Supp. XXI:** 166
Abyss of Human Illusion, The (Sorrentino), **Supp. XXI:** 225, 227, 237–238
"Academic Story, An" (Simpson), **Supp. IX:** 279–280
"Academic Zoo, The: Theory—in Practice" (Epstein), **Supp. XIV:** 107–108, 109
"A Capella" (Wrigley), **Supp. XVIII:** 300
"Accident" (Minot), **Supp. VI: 208–209**
"Accident, The" (Southern), **Supp. XI:** 295
"Accident, The" (Strand), **Supp. IV Part 2:** 624
Accident/A Day's News (Wolf), **Supp. IV Part 1:** 310
Accidental Tourist, The (Tyler), **Supp. IV Part 2:** 657, 668–669; **Supp. V:** 227
Accordion Crimes (Proulx), **Supp. VII:** 259–261
"Accountability" (Dunbar), **Supp. II Part 1:** 197, 204
"Account of the Method of Drawing Birds" (Audubon), **Supp. XVI:** 12

"Accusation, The" (Wright), **Supp. III Part 2:** 595
"Accusation of the Inward Man, The" (Taylor), **IV:** 156
"Accusing Message from Dead Father" (Karr), **Supp. XI:** 244
Ace, Goodman, **Supp. IV Part 2:** 574
Achievement in American Poetry (Bogan), **Supp. III Part 1:** 63–64
Acker, Kathy, **Supp. XII:1–20; Supp. XXI:** 236
Ackerley, J. R., **Supp. XX: 237**
Ackerman, Diane, **Supp. XIII:** 154
"Acknowledgment" (Lanier), **Supp. I Part 1:** 364
Ackroyd, Peter, **Supp. V:** 233; **Supp. XVII:** 180
"Acquaintance in the Heavens, An" (Dillard), **Supp. VI:** 34
"Acquainted with the Night" (Frost), **II:** 155; **Retro. Supp. I:** 137; **Supp. XXI:** 26
Across Spoon River (Masters), **Supp. I Part 2:** 455, 457, 459, 460, 466, 474–475, 476
Across the Layers: Poems Old and New (Goldbarth), **Supp. XII:** 181, **187–189**
Across the River and into the Trees (Hemingway), **I:** 491; **II:** 255–256, 261; **Retro. Supp. I:** 172, **184–185; Supp. XIX:** 248
"Actfive" (MacLeish), **III:** 18–19, 22
Actfive and Other Poems (MacLeish), **III:** 3, 17–19, 21
Action (Shepard), **Supp. III Part 2:** 446
Active Anthology (Pound), **Supp. III Part 2:** 617
Active Service (Crane), **I:** 409
"Act of Creation and Its Artifact, The" (Sorrentino), **Supp. XXI:** 229, 235
Act of Love, An (Wolfert), **Supp. XXI:** 270**, 275–277**
Act of Love, An: A Completely Retold Version of the Novel (Wolfert), **Supp. XXI:** 276
Acton, Patricia Nassif, **Supp. X:** 233
Acts and Monuments of These Latter and Perilous Days (Fox), **Supp. XXII:** 36
Acts of Faith (Caputo), **Supp. XIX: 29–30**
"Acts of the Apostles, The" (Bronk), **Supp. XXI:** 28
Actual, The (Bellow), **Retro. Supp. II:** 33
"Actual Experience, Preferred Narratives" (Julier), **Supp. IV Part 1:** 211
Acuff, Roy, **Supp. V:** 335
Ada (Nabokov), **Retro. Supp. I:** 265, 266, 270, 276–277, 278, 279
"Ada" (Stein), **IV:** 43
"Adagia" (Stevens), **IV:** 78, 80, 88, 92
"Adagio" (Hull), **Supp. XXI:** 136–137
"Adam" (Hecht), **Supp. X:** 62
"Adam" (W. C. Williams), **Retro. Supp. I:** 422, 423
"Adam and Eve" (Eugene), **Supp. X:** 204
"Adam and Eve" (Shapiro), **Supp. II Part 2:** 708, 712
"Adamantine Practice of Poetry, The" (Wright), **Supp. XV:** 341–342, 343–344
Adam Bede (G. Eliot), **II:** 181
Adamé, Leonard, **Supp. XIII:** 316
Adam & Eve & the City (W. C. Williams), **Retro. Supp. I:** 423
"Adamic Purity as Double Agent" (Whalen-Bridge), **Retro. Supp. II:** 211–212
"Adam Robinson Acquires Grandparents and a Little Sister" (P. E. Jones), **Supp. XXII:** 151
"Adams" (Saunders), **Supp. XIX:** 232
Adams, Althea. *See* Thurber, Mrs. James (Althea Adams)
Adams, Annie. *See* Fields, Annie Adams
Adams, Brooks, **Supp. I Part 2:** 484
Adams, Charles, **Supp. I Part 2:** 644
Adams, Charles Francis, **I:** 1, 4; **Supp. I Part 2:** 484
Adams, Franklin P., **Supp. I Part 2:** 653; **Supp. IX:** 190; **Supp. XV:** 294, 297
Adams, Henry, **I: 1–24,** 111, 243, 258; **II:** 278, 542; **III:** 396, 504; **IV:** 191, 349; **Retro. Supp. I:** 53, 59; **Retro. Supp. II:** 207; **Supp. I Part 1:** 299–300, 301, 314; **Supp. I Part 2:** 417, 492, 543, 644; **Supp. II Part 1:** 93–94, 105; **Supp. III Part 2:** 613; **Supp. IV Part 1:** 31, 208
Adams, Mrs. Henry (Marian Hooper), **I:** 1, 5, 10, 17–18
Adams, Henry B., **Supp. I Part 1:** 369
Adams, James Truslow, **Supp. I Part 2:** 481, 484, 486
Adams, J. Donald, **IV:** 438
Adams, John, **I:** 1; **II:** 103, 301; **III:** 17, 473; **Supp. I Part 2:** 483, 506, 507, 509, 510, 511, 517, 518, 520, 524
Adams, John Luther, **Supp. XII:** 209
Adams, John Quincy, **I:** 1, 3, 16–17; **Supp. I Part 2:** 685, 686
Adams, Léonie, **Supp. I Part 2:** 707; **Supp. V:** 79; **Supp. IX:** 229; **Supp. XVII:** 75
Adams, Luella, **Supp. I Part 2:** 652
Adams, Noah, **Supp. XVII:** 218
Adams, Phoebe, **Supp. IV Part 1:** 203; **Supp. VIII:** 124
Adams, Samuel, **Supp. I Part 2:** 516, 525
Adams, Timothy Dow, **Supp. XVI:** 67, 69
Ada; or Ardor (Nabokov), **III:** 247
"Ad Castitatem" (Bogan), **Supp. III Part 1:** 50
Adcock, Betty, **Supp. XVIII:** 181–182, 182
Addams, Jane, **Supp. I Part 1: 1–26; Supp. XI:** 200, 202
Addams, John Huy, **Supp. I Part 1:** 2
"Addendum" (Wright), **Supp. V:** 339
Addiego, John, **Supp. XII:** 182
Adding Machine, The (Rice), **I:** 479
Adding Machine, The: Selected Essays (Burroughs), **Supp. III Part 1:** 93, 97
Addison, Joseph, **I:** 8, 105, 106–107, 108, 114, 131, 300, 304; **III:** 430
"Addressed to a Political Shrimp, or, Fly upon the Wheel" (Freneau), **Supp. II Part 1:** 267
"Address to My Soul" (Wylie), **Supp. I Part 2:** 729
"Address to the Deist, An" (Wheatley), **Supp. XX: 287**
"Address to the Devil" (Jarman), **Supp. XVII:** 114
Address to the Government of the United States on the Cession of Louisiana to the French, An (Brown), **Supp. I Part 1:** 146
"Address to the Scholars of New England" (Ransom), **III:** 491
"Address with Exclamation Points, A" (Simic), **Supp. VIII:** 283
Adisa, Opal Palmer, **Supp. XXII:** 66, 74, 78
"Adjutant Bird, The" (Banks), **Supp. V:** 5
Adkins, Nelson F., **II:** 20
Adler, Alfred, **I:** 248
Adler, Betty, **III:** 103
Adler, George J., **III:** 81
Adler, Renata, **Supp. X:** 171
Admiral of the Ocean Sea: A Life of Christopher Columbus (Morison), **Supp. I Part 2:** 486–488
"Admirals" (Chabon), **Supp. XI:** 72
"Admonition, An" (Brodsky), **Supp. VIII:** 33
"Adolescence" (Bidart), **Supp. XV:** 32
"Adolescence" (Dove), **Supp. IV Part 1:** 245
"Adolescence" (Olds), **Supp. X:** 211
"Adolescence II" (Dove), **Supp. IV Part 1:** 242, 244–245
Adolescent's Christmas, An: 1944 (C. Bly), **Supp. XVI:** 31–32
"Adolf Eichmann" (Carruth), **Supp. XVI:** 47
"Adonais" (Shelley), **II:** 516, 540
Adorno, Theodor, **Supp. I Part 2:** 645, 650; **Supp. IV Part 1:** 301
"Adrienne Rich: The Poetics of Change" (Gelpi), **Supp. I Part 2:** 554
"Adultery" (Banks), **Supp. V:** 15
"Adultery" (Dubus), **Supp. VII:** 85
Adultery and Other Choices (Dubus), **Supp. VII:** 83–85
Adulthood Rites (O. Butler), **Supp. XIII:** 63, **64–65**
Adult Life of Toulouse Lautrec by Henri Toulouse Lautrec, The (Acker), **Supp. XII:** 5, 6, **8–9**
Adventure (London), **II:** 466
Adventures in Ancient Egypt (Goldbarth), **Supp. XII:** 191
Adventures in Value (Cummings), **I:** 430
"Adventures of a Book Reviewer" (Cowley), **Supp. II Part 1:** 137, 142
Adventures of Augie March, The (Bellow), **I:** 144, 147, 149, 150, 151, 152–153, 154, 155, 157, 158–159, 164; **Retro. Supp. II:** 19, 20, **22–23,** 24, 30; **Supp. VIII:** 234, 236–237
Adventures of a Young Man (Dos Passos), **I:** 488, 489, 492

Adventures of Captain Bonneville (Irving), **II:** 312
Adventures of Harry Franco, The: A Tale of the Great Panic (Briggs), **Supp. XVIII:** 1, 2, 5–8
Adventures of Harry Richmond, The (Meredith), **Supp. XX: 234**
Adventures of Huckleberry Finn, The (Twain), **I:** 307, 506; **II:** 26, 72, 262, 266–268, 290, 418, 430; **III:** 101, 112–113, 357, 554, 558, 577; **IV:** 198, 201–204, 207; **Retro. Supp. I:** 188; **Retro. Supp. II:** 121; **Supp. I Part 1:** 247; **Supp. IV Part 1:** 247, 257; **Supp. IV Part 2:** 502; **Supp. V:** 131; **Supp. VIII:** 198; **Supp. X:** 230; **Supp. XII:** 16; **Supp. XVI:** 222; **Supp. XX: 171; Supp. XXII:** 81
Adventures of Jimmy (Broughton), **Supp. XV:** 146
Adventures of Roderick Random, The (Smollett), **I:** 134
Adventures of the Letter I (Simpson), **Supp. IX:** 266, **273–274**
Adventures of Tom Sawyer, The (Twain), **II:** 26; **III:** 223, 572, 577; **IV:** 199–200, 203, 204; **Supp. I Part 2:** 456, 470; **Supp. XVI:** 66
Adventures While Preaching the Gospel of Beauty (Lindsay), **Supp. I Part 2:** 374, 376, 381, 382–384, 389, 399
Adventures with Ed (Loeffler), **Supp. XIII:** 1
Advertisements for Myself (Mailer), **III:** 27, 35–38, 41–42, 45, 46; **Retro. Supp. II:** 196, 199, 200, 202, 203, 212; **Supp. IV Part 1:** 90, 284; **Supp. XIV:** 157
"Advertisements for Myself on the Way Out" (Mailer), **III:** 37
"Advice to a Prophet" (Wilbur), **Supp. III Part 2:** 555–557
Advice to a Prophet and Other Poems (Wilbur), **Supp. III Part 2:** 554–558
"Advice to a Raven in Russia" (Barlow), **Supp. II Part 1:** 65, 74, 80, 83
"Advice to Players" (Bidart), **Supp. XV:** 35
Advice to the Lovelorn (film), **Retro. Supp. II:** 328
Advice to the Privileged Orders, Part I (Barlow), **Supp. II Part 1:** 80
Aegerter, Lindsay Pentolfe, **Supp. XXII:** 69
"Aeneas and Dido" (Brodsky), **Supp. VIII:** 24–25
"Aeneas at Washington" (Tate), **IV:** 129
Aeneid (Virgil), **I:** 396; **II:** 542; **III:** 124; **Supp. XV:** 23
Aeneus Tacticus, **I:** 136
Aerial View (Barabtarlo), **Retro. Supp. I:** 278
"Aeria the Evanescent" (Sobin), **Supp. XVI:** 292
Aeschylus, **I:** 274, 433; **III:** 398; **IV:** 358, 368, 370; **Retro. Supp. I:** 65; **Supp. I Part 2:** 458, 494
Aesop, **I:** 387; **II:** 154, 169, 302; **III:** 587
Aesthetic (Croce), **III:** 610
"Aesthetics" (Mumford), **Supp. II Part 2:** 476
"Aesthetics of Silence, The" (Sontag), **Supp. III Part 2:** 459
"Aesthetics of the Shah" (Olds), **Supp. X:** 205
"Affair at Coulter's Notch, The" (Bierce), **I:** 202
Affaire de viol, Une (C. Himes). *See Case of Rape, A* (C. Himes)
"Affair of Outposts, An" (Bierce), **I:** 202
Affliction (Banks), **Supp. V:** 15, 16
Affluent Society, The (Galbraith), **Supp. I Part 2:** 648
Afghanistan Picture Show, An: or, How I Saved the World (Vollmann), **Supp. XVII:** 226, **228–229,** 233
"Aficionados, The" (Carver), **Supp. III Part 1:** 137
"Afloat" (Beattie), **Supp. V:** 29
Afloat and Ashore (Cooper), **I:** 351, 355
"Afoot" (P. N. Warren as Kilina), **Supp. XX: 261–262**
Africa, Its Geography, People, and Products (Du Bois), **Supp. II Part 1:** 179
Africa, Its Place in Modern History (Du Bois), **Supp. II Part 1:** 179
"Africa, to My Mother" (D. Diop), **Supp. IV Part 1:** 16
Africana (H. L. Gates, ed.), **Supp. XX: 99**
African American Century, The : How Black Americans Have Shaped Our Country (H. L. Gates), **Supp. XX: 102**
African American Lives (television production), **Supp. XX: 99**
African American Lives 2 (television production), **Supp. XX: 99**
African American National Biography (H. L. Gates, ed.), **Supp. XX: 99**
African American Writers (Smith, ed.), **Supp. XIII:** 115, 127
"African Book" (Hemingway), **II:** 259
"African Chief, The" (Bryant), **Supp. I Part 1:** 168
"African Fragment" (Brooks), **Supp. III Part 1:** 85
African Queen, The (film), **Supp. XI:** 17
"African Roots of War, The" (Du Bois), **Supp. II Part 1:** 174
African Silences (Matthiessen), **Supp. V:** 203
African Treasury, An (Hughes, ed.), **Supp. I Part 1:** 344
"Afrika Revolution" (Baraka), **Supp. II Part 1:** 53
"AFRO-AMERICAN LYRIC" (Baraka), **Supp. II Part 1:** 59
After (Bukiet), **Supp. XVII:** 43, **44–45**
After All: Last Poems (Matthews), **Supp. IX:** 155, **167–169**
After and Before the Lightning (Ortiz), **Supp. IV Part 2:** 513
"After a Party" (Salinas), **Supp. XIII:** 327
"After Apple-Picking" (Frost), **Retro. Supp. I:** 126, 128
"After Arguing against the Contention That Art Must Come from Discontent" (Stafford), **Supp. XI:** 327
After Confession: Poetry as Autobiography (Harris), **Supp. XIV:** 269
After Confession: Poetry as Autobiography (K. Sontag and D. Graham), **Supp. XV:** 104
"After Cowboy Chicken Came to Town" (Jin), **Supp. XVIII:** 97–98
"After Disappointment" (Jarman), **Supp. XVII:** 118–119
After Disillusion: Poems (Wolf), **Supp. XXII:** 275
After Experience (Snodgrass), **Supp. VI:** 314–316, 317
"After great pain, a formal feeling comes" (Dickinson), **Retro. Supp. I:** 37
"After Hearing a Waltz by Bartók" (Lowell), **II:** 522
After Henry (Didion), **Supp. IV Part 1:** 195, 196, 199, 207, 208, 211
"After Henry" (Didion), **Supp. IV Part 1:** 211
"After Holbein" (Wharton), **IV:** 325; **Retro. Supp. I:** 382
After Ikkyu and Other Poems (Harrison), **Supp. VIII:** 42
"After-Image" (Bierds), **Supp. XVII:** 31–32
"After-Image" (Caldwell), **I:** 309
After-Images: Autobiographical Sketches (Snodgrass), **Supp. VI:** 314, **319–323,** 324, 326–327
After I's (Zukofsky), **Supp. III Part 2:** 628, 629
Afterlife (Monette), **Supp. X:** 153
Afterlife (Updike), **Retro. Supp. I:** 322
Afterlife, The (Levis), **Supp. XI:** 259, **260–264**
"After Magritte" (McClatchy), **Supp. XII:** 264
"After Making Love" (Dunn), **Supp. XI:** 153
Aftermath (Longfellow), **II:** 490
"Aftermath" (Longfellow), **II:** 498
After New Formalism (A. Finch, ed.), **Supp. XVII:** 74
"Afternoon" (Ellison), **Supp. II Part 1:** 238
"Afternoon at MacDowell" (Kenyon), **Supp. VII:** 159
"Afternoon Miracle, An" (O. Henry), **Supp. II Part 1:** 390
Afternoon of a Faun (Hearon), **Supp. VIII: 63–64**
Afternoon of an Author: A Selection of Uncollected Stories and Essays (Fitzgerald), **II:** 94
"Afternoon of a Playwright" (Thurber), **Supp. I Part 2:** 620
Afternoon of the Unreal (Salinas), **Supp. XIII:** 311, **316–318**
"Afternoon with the Old Man, An" (Dubus), **Supp. VII:** 84
"After Punishment Was Done with Me" (Olds), **Supp. X:** 213
"After Reading *Barely and Widely,*" (Zukofsky), **Supp. III Part 2:** 625, 631
"After Reading 'In the Clearing' for the Author, Robert Frost" (Corso), **Supp. XII:** 130

"After Reading *Mickey in the Night Kitchen* for the Third Time before Bed" (Dove), **Supp. IV Part 1:** 249
"After Reading Tu Fu, I Go Outside to the Dwarf Orchard" (Wright), **Supp. V:** 343
"After Reading Wang Wei, I Go Outside to the Full Moon" (Wright), **Supp. V:** 343
After Shocks, Near Escapes (Dobyns), **Supp. XIII: 80–82**
"After Song, An" (W. C. Williams), **Retro. Supp. I:** 413
After Strange Gods (T. S. Eliot), **I:** 588
After Such Knowledge: Memory, History, and the Legacy of the Holocaust (E. Hoffman), **Supp. XVI:** 152–153, **158–161**
"After the Alphabets" (Merwin), **Supp. III Part 1:** 356
"After the Argument" (Dunn), **Supp. XI:** 149
"After the Baptism" (C. Bly), **Supp. XVI:** 40
"After the Burial" (Lowell), **Supp. I Part 2:** 409
"After the Curfew" (Holmes), **Supp. I Part 1:** 308
"After the Death of John Brown" (Thoreau), **IV:** 185
"After the Denim" (Carver), **Supp. III Part 1:** 144
"After the Dentist" (Swenson), **Supp. IV Part 2:** 645
After the Fall (A. Miller), **III:** 148, 149, 156, 161, 162, 163–165, 166
"After the Fire" (Merrill), **Supp. III Part 1:** 328
"After the Flood" (Sanders), **Supp. XVI:** 274–275
After the Fox (film), **Supp. IV Part 2:** 575
After the Genteel Tradition (Cowley), **Supp. II Part 1:** 143
"After the Heart's Interrogation" (Komunyakaa), **Supp. XIII:** 120
After the Lost Generation: A Critical Study of the Writers of Two Wars (Aldridge), **Supp. IV Part 2:** 680; **Supp. XIX:** 250
"After the Night Office—Gethsemani Abbey" (Merton), **Supp. VIII:** 195–196
After the Others (Weigl), **Supp. XIX:** 282, 283–284
"After the Persian" (Bogan), **Supp. III Part 1:** 64
After the Plague (Boyle), **Supp. XX: 20**
"After the Plague" (Boyle), **Supp. XX: 20**
"After the Pleasure Party" (Melville), **III:** 93
"After the Rain" (Halliday), **Supp. XIX:** 91
"After the Resolution" (Dunn), **Supp. XI:** 151
After the Stroke (Sarton), **Supp. VIII:** 264
"After the Surprising Conversions" (Lowell), **I:** 544, 545; **II:** 550; **Retro. Supp. II:** 187
"After 37 Years My Mother Apologizes for My Childhood" (Olds), **Supp. X:** 208
After This (McDermott), **Supp. XVIII:** 155, **166–167**
Afterthoughts (L. P. Smith), **Supp. XIV:** 339, 345
"Afterthoughts on the Rosenbergs" (Fiedler), **Supp. XIII:** 99
"After Twenty Years" (Rich), **Supp. I Part 2:** 559–560
"Afterwake, The" (Rich), **Supp. I Part 2:** 553
"Afterward" (Wharton), **Retro. Supp. I:** 372
"After Working Long" (Kenyon), **Supp. VII:** 170
"After Yitzl" (Goldbarth), **Supp. XII:** 186
"After You, My Dear Alphonse" (Jackson), **Supp. IX:** 119
"After Your Death" (Trethewey), **Supp. XXI:** 255
"After Your Nap" (B. Kelly), **Supp. XVII:** 124
"Again" (Dixon), **Supp. XII:** 157
"Again, Kapowsin" (Hugo), **Supp. VI:** 141
"Again Just Now" (Budbill), **Supp. XIX:** 11
"Against" (Goldbarth), **Supp. XII:** 193
"Against Decoration" (Karr), **Supp. XI:** 248
"Against Epiphanies" (C. Baxter), **Supp. XVII:** 20
Against Interpretation (Sontag), **Supp. III Part 2:** 451, 455; **Supp. XIV:** 15
"Against Interpretation" (Sontag), **Supp. III Part 2:** 456–458, 463
"Against Modernity" (Ozick), **Supp. V:** 272
"Against Nature" (Karr), **Supp. XI:** 243
Against Nature (Updike), **Retro. Supp. I:** 323
Against Our Vanishing: Winter Conversations with Allen Grossman on the Theory and Practice of Poetry (Halliday), **Supp. XIX: 82–84,** 88
"Against Realism" (Halliday), **Supp. XIX:** 93
Against the Cold (Bynner), **Supp. XV:** 51
"Against the Crusades" (Stern), **Supp. IX:** 300
Against the Current: As I Remember F. Scott Fitzgerald (Kroll Ring), **Supp. IX:** 63
Agamben, Giorgio, **Supp. XVI:** 289
Agapida, Fray Antonio (pseudonym). *See* Irving, Washington
"Agassiz" (Lowell), **Supp. I Part 2:** 414, 416
Agassiz, Louis, **II:** 343; **Supp. I Part 1:** 312; **Supp. IX:** 180
Âge cassant, L' (Char; Sobin, trans.), Supp. XVI: 282
"Aged Wino's Counsel to a Young Man on the Brink of Marriage, The" (X. J. Kennedy), **Supp. XV:** 156
Agee, Emma, **I:** 26
Agee, James, **I: 25–47,** 293; **IV:** 215; **Supp. IX:** 109; **Supp. XIV:** 92; **Supp. XV:** 143
"Agent, The" (Wilbur), **Supp. III Part 2:** 557–561
Age of Anxiety, The (Auden), **Supp. II Part 1:** 2, 19, 21
"Age of Conformity, The" (Howe), **Supp. VI:** 117
Age of Grief, The: A Novella and Stories (Smiley), **Supp. VI:** 292, **299–301**
Age of Innocence, The (Wharton), **IV:** 320–322, 327–328; **Retro. Supp. I:** 372, 374, **380–381; Supp. IV Part 1:** 23
Age of Longing, The (Koestler), **I:** 258
Age of Reason, The (Paine), **Supp. I Part 2:** 503, 515–517, 520
"Age of Strolling, The" (Stern), **Supp. IX:** 297
"Ages, The" (Bryant), **Supp. I Part 1:** 152, 155, 166, 167
"Ages of the Women, The" (Gibran), **Supp. XX: 115**
"Aggrandizement, The" (Bronk), **Supp. XXI:** 32
"Aging" (Jarrell), **II:** 388
Aging and Gender in Literature (George), **Supp. IV Part 2:** 450
"Agio Neró" (Mora), **Supp. XIII:** 224
"Agitato ma non Troppo" (Ransom), **III:** 493
"Agnes of Iowa" (Moore), **Supp. X:** 165, 178
Agnes of Sorrento (Stowe), **Supp. I Part 2:** 592, 595–596
Agnon, S. Y., **Supp. V:** 266
"Agosta the Winged Man and Rasha the Black Dove" (Dove), **Supp. IV Part 1:** 246–247
Agrarian Justice (Paine), **Supp. I Part 2:** 517–518
"Agricultural Show, The" (McKay), **Supp. X:** 139
Agrippa: A Book of the Dead (W. Gibson), **Supp. XVI:** 125
Agua de dos ríos/Water from Two Rivers (Espaillat), **Supp. XXI:** 104, 112–113
Agua Fresca: An Anthology of Raza Poetry (Rodríguez, ed.), **Supp. IV Part 2:** 540
Agua Santa/Holy Water (Mora), **Supp. XIII: 222–225**
Agüero Sisters, The (García), **Supp. XI: 185–190**
Aguiar, Marian, **Supp. XXII:** 68
Aguiar, Sarah Appleton, **Supp. XIII:** 30
Ah, Wilderness! (O'Neill), **III:** 400–401; **Supp. IV Part 2:** 587
Ah, Wilderness!: The Frontier in American Literature (Humphrey), **Supp. IX:** 104
Ahearn, Barry, **Retro. Supp. I:** 415
Ahearn, Frederick L., Jr., **Supp. XI:** 184
Ahearn, Kerry, **Supp. IV Part 2:** 604
Ahmed Arabi Pasha, **I:** 453
Ahnebrink, Lars, **III:** 328
Ahrens, Sylvia, **Supp. XX: 162**
Ah Sin (Harte), **Supp. II Part 1:** 354–355

"Ah! Sun-flower" (Blake), **III:** 19
Aida (rock musical), **Supp. XXI:** 148
Aidoo, Ama Ato, **Supp. XXII:** 68
AIDS and Its Metaphors (Sontag), **Supp. III Part 2:** 452, 466–468
Aids to Reflection (Coleridge), **II:** 10
Aiieeeee! An Anthology of Asian-American Writers (The Combined Asian Resources Project), **Supp. X:** 292
Aiken, Conrad, **I: 48–70,** 190, 211, 243; **II:** 55, 530, 542; **III:** 458, 460; **Retro. Supp. I:** 55, 56, 57, 58, 60, 62; **Supp. X:** 50, 115; **Supp. XV:** 144, 297, 298, 302, 306, 309; **Supp. XVII:** 135
"Aimless Love" (Collins), **Supp. XXI:** 61
"Aim Was Song, The" (Frost), **Retro. Supp. I:** 133
Ainger, Arthur Campbell, **Supp. XX: 230**
Ainsworth, Linda, **Supp. IV Part 1:** 274
Ainsworth, William, **III:** 423
Air-Conditioned Nightmare, The (H. Miller), **III:** 186
Airing Dirty Laundry (Reed), **Supp. X:** 241
"Air Is Full of Little Holes, The" (Brockmeier), **Supp. XXII:** 60
"Airmail from Mother" (Kooser), **Supp. XIX:** 120
"Air Plant, The" (Crane), **I:** 401
Air Raid: A Verse Play for Radio (MacLeish), **III:** 21
"Airs above the Ground" (Sarton), **Supp. VIII:** 261
Air Tight: A Novel of Red Russia. See We the Living (Rand)
Air Up There, The (film, Glaser), **Supp. XVII:** 9
"Airwaves" (Mason), **Supp. VIII:** 146
Airways, Inc. (Dos Passos), **I:** 482
"A is for Dining Alone" (M. F. K. Fisher), **Supp. XVII:** 86
Aitken, Robert, **Supp. I Part 2:** 504
Aizenberg, Susan, **Supp. XXI:** 131
Akhmadulina, Bella, **Supp. III Part 1:** 268
Akhmatova, Anna, **Supp. III Part 1:** 268, 269; **Supp. VIII:** 20, 21, 25, 27, 30; **Supp. XXI:** 132
Akhmatova Translations, The (Kenyon), **Supp. VII:** 160
"Akhnilo" (Salter), **Supp. IX:** 260
Akins, Zoë, **Supp. XVI:** 187
Aksenev, Vasily P., **Retro. Supp. I:** 278
"Al Aaraaf" (Poe), **III:** 426–427
Al Aaraaf, Tamerlane, and Minor Poems (Poe), **III:** 410
"Alabama Jones" (Mosher), **Supp. XXII:** 204, 211
"Alain Locke and Cultural Pluralism" (Kallen), **Supp. XIV:** 197
"Alain Locke: Bahá'í Philosopher" (Buck), **Supp. XIV:** 199
Alain Locke: Faith and Philosophy (Buck), **Supp. XIV:** 200
Alarçon, **Supp. XVII:** 74
Alarcón, Justo, **Supp. IV Part 2:** 538, 539, 540
À la Recherche du Temps Perdu (Proust), **IV:** 428
"Alarm" (X. J. Kennedy), **Supp. XV:** 163
"Alastor" (Shelley), **Supp. I Part 2:** 728
"Alatus" (Wilbur), **Supp. III Part 2:** 563
"Alba" (Creeley), **Supp. IV Part 1:** 150
Alba, Richard D., **Supp. XX: 43**
Albee, Edward, **I: 71–96,** 113; **II:** 558, 591; **III:** 281, 387; **IV:** 4, 230; **Retro. Supp. II:** 104; **Supp. VIII:** 331; **Supp. XIII:** 196, 197
Albers, Joseph, **Supp. IV Part 2:** 621
Alberti, Rafael, **Supp. XV:** 75
Albright, Margery, **Supp. I Part 2:** 613
"Album, The" (Morris), **III:** 220
Alcestiad, The (Wilder), **IV:** 357, 374
"Alchemist, The" (Bogan), **Supp. III Part 1:** 50
"Alchemist in the City, The" (Hopkins), **Supp. IV Part 2:** 639
Alchymist's Journal, The (Connell), **Supp. XIV:** 80
"Alcmena" (Winters), **Supp. II Part 2:** 801
Alcott, Abba. *See* Alcott, Mrs. Amos Bronson (Abigail May)
Alcott, Amos Bronson, **II:** 7, 225; **IV:** 172, 173, 184; **Retro. Supp. I:** 217; **Supp. I Part 1:** 28, 29–32, 35, 39, 41, 45; **Supp. II Part 1:** 290; **Supp. XVI:** 84, 89
Alcott, Mrs. Amos Bronson (Abigail May), **IV:** 184; **Supp. I Part 1:** 29, 30, 31, 32, 35
Alcott, Anna. *See* Pratt, Anna
Alcott, Louisa May, **IV:** 172; **Supp. I Part 1: 28–46; Supp. IX:** 128; **Supp. XV:** 338; **Supp. XVI:** 84
Alcott, May, **Supp. I Part 1:** 41
Alcuin: A Dialogue (Brown), **Supp. I Part 1:** 126–127, 133
Alden, Hortense. *See* Farrell, Mrs. James T. (Hortense Alden)
Alden, John, **I:** 471; **II:** 502–503
"Alder Fork, The" (Leopold), **Supp. XIV:** 186
Aldington, Perdita, **Supp. I Part 1:** 258
Aldington, Richard, **II:** 517; **III:** 458, 459, 465, 472; **Retro. Supp. I:** 63, 127; **Supp. I Part 1:** 257–262, 270
Aldington, Mrs. Richard. *See* Doolittle, Hilda
Aldo Leopold: His Life and Work (Meine), **Supp. XIV:** 179
"Aldo Leopold's Intellectual Heritage" (Nash), **Supp. XIV:** 191–192
Aldon, Raymond, **Supp. XV:** 297
Aldrich, Thomas Bailey, **II:** 400; **Supp. II Part 1:** 192; **Supp. XIV:** 45; **Supp. XVIII:** 4
Aldrich, Tom, **Supp. I Part 2:** 415
Aldridge, John W., **Supp. I Part 1:** 196; **Supp. IV Part 1:** 286; **Supp. IV Part 2:** 680, 681; **Supp. VIII:** 189; **Supp. XI:** 228; **Supp. XIX:** 250
Aleck Maury Sportsman (Gordon), **II:** 197, 200, 203–204
Alegría, Claribel, **Supp. IV Part 1:** 208
Aleichem, Sholom, **IV:** 3, 10; **Supp. IV Part 2:** 585
"Alert Lovers, Hidden Sides, and Ice Travelers: Notes on Poetic Form and Energy" (Dunn), **Supp. XI:** 153
"Alesă Debeljak" (Simic), **Supp. VIII:** 279
"Alex" (Oliver), **Supp. VII:** 232
Alexander, Doris, **Supp. XVII:** 99
Alexander, Elizabeth, **Supp. XVIII:** 171, 185, 186; **Supp. XXI:** 246, 257
Alexander, George, **II:** 331
Alexander, Michael, **Retro. Supp. I:** 293
"Alexander Crummell Dead" (Dunbar), **Supp. II Part 1:** 207, 208–209
Alexander's Bridge (Cather), **I:** 313, 314, 316–317, 326; **Retro. Supp. I:** 1, 6, 7, 8
Alexander the Great, **IV:** 322
"Alexandra" (Cather), **Retro. Supp. I:** 7, 9, 17
Alexandrov, V. E., **Retro. Supp. I:** 270
Alexie, Sherman, **Supp. XVIII:** 58
Algonquin Round Table, **Supp. IX:** 190, 191, 197
Algren, Nelson, **I:** 211; **Supp. V:** 4; **Supp. IX: 1–18; Supp. XII:** 126; **Supp. XIII:** 173; **Supp. XIV:** 3; **Supp. XVII:** 161; **Supp. XXI:** 264
Alhambra, The (Irving), **II:** 310–311
Ali, Agha Shahid, **Supp. XVII:** 74
Alias Grace (Atwood), **Supp. XIII:** 20, **31–32**
Alice (film; Allen), **Supp. XV:** 2, 11
"Alice Doane's Appeal" (Hawthorne), **II:** 227
"Alice Drops Her Cigarette on the Floor ... " (Findley), **Supp. XX: 50–51**
Alice in Wonderland (Carroll), **Supp. I Part 2:** 622
Alice Ordered Me to Be Made (Notley), **Supp. XXII:** 224, 227, 228
"Alice Ordered Me to Be Made" (Notley), **Supp. XXII:** 227
Alice's Adventures in Wonderland (Carroll), **Supp. XVI:** 261
"Alicia and I Talking on Edna's Steps" (Cisneros), **Supp. VII:** 64
"Alicia Who Sees Mice" (Cisneros), **Supp. VII:** 60
Alien 3 (screenplay, W. Gibson), **Supp. XVI:** 120, 124
"Ali in Havana" (Talese), **Supp. XVII:** 207, 208
Alison, Archibald, **Supp. I Part 1:** 151, 159
Alison's House (Glaspell), **Supp. III Part 1:** 182, 188, 189
Alive (screenplay, Shanley), **Supp. XIV:** 316
Alive and Writing: Interviews with American Authors of the 1980s (McCaffery and Gregory), **Supp. X:** 260
"Alki Beach" (Hugo), **Supp. VI:** 135
Alla Breve Loving (Wright), **Supp. XV:** 339, 340
"Alla Breve Loving" (Wright), **Supp. XV:** 340
"All Around the Town" (Benét), **Supp. XI:** 48, 58
All at Sea (Lardner), **II:** 427

All Aunt Hagar's Children (E. P. Jones), **Supp. XXII:** 140, 143, **150–153**
"All Aunt Hagar's Children" (P. E. Jones), **Supp. XXII:** 151
"All Boy" (Rawlings), **Supp. X:** 222
Allegiances (Stafford), **Supp. XI: 322–323,** 329
"Allegory of the Cave" (Dunn), **Supp. XI:** 150
"Allegory Unlimited" (Cassill), **Supp. XIX:** 266
Allegro, Johnny (film, Tetzloff), **Supp. XVII:** 62
"Allegro, L' " (Milton), **Supp. XIV:** 8
Allen, Brooke, **Supp. VIII:** 153
Allen, Bruce, **Supp. XXII:** 205, 212
Allen, Dick, **Supp. IX:** 279
Allen, Donald, **Supp. VIII:** 291; **Supp. XIII:** 112
Allen, Frank, **Supp. XI:** 126; **Supp. XII:** 186
Allen, Frederick Lewis, **Supp. I Part 2:** 655
Allen, Gay Wilson, **IV:** 352; **Supp. I Part 2:** 418
Allen, Ivan, **Supp. XXII:** 245
Allen, Paula Gunn. *See* Gunn Allen, Paula
Allen, Robert Moore, **Supp. XX: 164**
Allen, Walter, **I:** 505; **III:** 352; **Supp. IV Part 2:** 685; **Supp. IX:** 231
Allen, Woody, **Supp. I Part 2:** 607, 623; **Supp. IV Part 1:** 205; **Supp. X:** 164; **Supp. XI:** 307; **Supp. XV: 1–18; Supp. XVII:** 48
"Aller et Retour" (Barnes), Supp. III Part 1: 36
Aller Retour New York (H. Miller), **III:** 178, 182, 183
Allerton, Isaac, **Supp. XXII:** 44
Allessandrini, Goffredo, **Supp. IV Part 2:** 520
Alleys of Eden, The (R. O. Butler), **Supp. XII:** 62, **62–64,** 68
All God's Children Need Traveling Shoes (Angelou), **Supp. IV Part 1:** 2, 9–10, 12–13, 17
All God's Chillun Got Wings (O'Neill), **III:** 387, 391, 393–394
All Gone (Dixon), **Supp. XII:** 148, 149
"All Hallows" (Glück), **Supp. V:** 82
"All I Can Remember" (Jackson), **Supp. IX:** 115
"Alligators, The" (Updike), **IV:** 219
Allingham, John Till, **Supp. XV:** 243
All in the Family (Boyce), **Supp. XXI:** 8
"ALL IN THE STREET" (Baraka), **Supp. II Part 1:** 53
Allison, Dorothy, **Supp. XVIII:** 195
"All I Want" (Tapahonso), **Supp. IV Part 2:** 508
"All Little Colored Children Should Play the Harmonica" (Patchett), **Supp. XII:** 309
"All Mountains" (Doolittle), **Supp. I Part 1:** 271
All My Friends Are Going to Be Strangers (McMurtry), **Supp. V:** 224, 228, 229
All My Pretty Ones (Sexton), **Supp. II Part 2:** 678, 679–683
"All My Pretty Ones" (Sexton), **Supp. II Part 2:** 681–682
"All My Sad Captains" (Jewett), **Retro. Supp. II:** 134
All My Sons (A. Miller), **III:** 148, 149, 150, 151–153, 154, 155, 156, 158, 159, 160, 164, 166
All New People (Lamott), **Supp. XX: 135–136**
"All Night, All Night" (Schwartz), **Supp. II Part 2:** 665
All Night Long (Caldwell), **I:** 297
"All-Night Melodies" (Nelson), **Supp. XVIII:** 185
All-Night Visitors (Major), **Supp. XXII: 173–174**
"All of Us" (Major), **Supp. XXII:** 185
All of What We Loved (Bronk), **Supp. XXI:** 32
"All Our Lost Children: Trauma and Testimony in the Performance of Childhood" (Pace), **Supp. XI:** 245
All Our Yesterdays (Parker), **Supp. XIX: 187–188**
"All Out" (Hecht), **Supp. X:** 72
All Over (Albee), **I:** 91–94
"Allowance" (Minot), **Supp. VI:** 206, 207–208
"Alloy" (Rukeyser), **Supp. VI:** 279
"All Parrots Speak" (Bowles), **Supp. IV Part 1:** 89
Allport, Gordon, **II:** 363–364
All Quiet on the Western Front (Remarque), **Supp. IV Part 1:** 380, 381
"ALL REACTION IS DOOMED-!-!-!" (Baraka), **Supp. II Part 1:** 59
"All Revelation" (Frost), **II:** 160–162
All Shot Up (C. Himes), **Supp. XVI:** 143, 144
"All Souls" (Gioia), **Supp. XV:** 117
"All Souls" (Wharton), **IV:** 315–316; **Retro. Supp. I:** 382
"All Souls' Night" (Yeats), **Supp. X:** 69
All Souls' Rising (Bell), **Supp. X:** 12, **13–16,** 17
"All-Star Literary Vaudeville" (Wilson), **IV:** 434–435
Allston, Washington, **II:** 298
All Stories Are True (Wideman), **Supp. X:** 320
"All That Is" (Wilbur), **Supp. III Part 2:** 563
All That Was Possible (Sturgis), **Supp. XX: 227, 232, 235–237**
"All the Bearded Irises of Life: Confessions of a Homospiritual" (Walker), **Supp. III Part 2:** 527
"All the Beautiful Are Blameless" (Wright), **Supp. III Part 2:** 597
ALL: The Collected Poems, 1956–1964 (Zukofsky), **Supp. III Part 2:** 630
ALL: The Collected Short Poems, 1923–1958 (Zukofsky), **Supp. III Part 2:** 629
All the Conspirators (Isherwood), **Supp. XIV:** 156, 159, 160
All the Dark and Beautiful Warriors (Hansberry), **Supp. IV Part 1:** 360, 374
All the Days and Nights: The Collected Stories (Maxwell), **Supp. VIII:** 151, 158, 169
"All the Dead Dears" (Plath), **Retro. Supp. II:** 246; **Supp. I Part 2:** 537
All the Good People I've Left Behind (Oates), **Supp. II Part 2:** 510, 522, 523
"All the Hippos Were Boiled in Their Tanks" (Burroughs and Kerouac), **Supp. III Part 1:** 94
All the King's Men (Warren), **I:** 489; **IV:** 243, 248–249, 252; **Supp. V:** 261; **Supp. VIII:** 126; **Supp. X:** 1; **Supp. XVIII:** 77, 79
All the Little Live Things (Stegner), **Supp. IV Part 2:** 599, 604, 605, 606, 609–610, 611, 613
All the Pretty Horses (film), **Supp. VIII:** 175
All the Pretty Horses (McCarthy), **Supp. VIII:** 175, **182–183,** 188
All the Sad Young Men (Fitzgerald), **II:** 94; **Retro. Supp. I:** 108
"All the Time in the World" (Dubus), **Supp. VII:** 91
"All the Way to Flagstaff, Arizona" (Bausch), **Supp. VII:** 47, 49
"All This and More" (Karr), **Supp. XI:** 243
All Tomorrow's Parties (W. Gibson), **Supp. XVI:** 119, 121, 123, 124, **130**
"All Too Real" (Vendler), **Supp. V:** 189
All Trivia: Triva, More Trivia, Afterthoughts, Last Words (L. P. Smith), **Supp. XIV:** 339
All-True Travels and Adventures of Lidie Newton (Smiley), **Supp. VI:** 292, **305–307**
All We Need of Hell (Crews), **Supp. XI: 114**
Almack, Edward, **Supp. IV Part 2:** 435
al-Maghut, Muhammad, **Supp. XIII:** 278
"Almanac" (Swenson), **Supp. IV Part 2:** 641
Almanac of the Dead (Silko), **Supp. IV Part 2:** 558–559, 560, 561, 570–571
Alma: or, The Dead Women (Notley), **Supp. XXII:** 223, 224, 231, 236
Almon, Bert, **Supp. IX:** 93
"Almost" (Untermeyer), **Supp. XV:** 304
Almost Revolution, The (Priaulx and Ungar), **Supp. XI:** 228
Alnilam (Dickey), **Supp. IV Part 1:** 176, 186, 188–189
"Alone" (Caputo), **Supp. XIX:** 29
"Alone" (Levine), **Supp. V:** 184, 185, 186
"Alone" (Pickering), **Supp. XXI:** 204
"Alone" (Poe), **Retro. Supp. II:** 266
"Alone" (Singer), **IV:** 15
"Alone" (Winters), **Supp. II Part 2:** 786, 811
"Alone and Lonely" (Budbill), **Supp. XIX:** 10
Aloneness (Brooks), **Supp. III Part 1:** 85, 86

Alone with America (Corso), **Supp. XII:** 131
Alone with America (Howard), **Supp. IX:** 326
"Along America's Edges" (Sobin), **Supp. XVI:** 288
"Along the Color Line" (Du Bois), **Supp. II Part 1:** 173
Along the Illinois (Masters), **Supp. I Part 2:** 472
Alouette, L' (Anouilh), Supp. I Part 1: 286–288
"Alphabet" (Nye), **Supp. XIII:** 283
Alphabet, An (Doty), **Supp. XI:** 120
Alphabet for Gourmets, An (M. F. K. Fisher), **Supp. XVII:** 86, 87, 92
Alphabet of Grace, The (Buechner), **Supp. XII:** 52
"Alphabet of My Dead, An" (Pinsky), **Supp. VI:** 235, 250
"Alphabet of Subjects, An" (Zukofsky), **Supp. III Part 2:** 624
"Alpine Christ, The" (Jeffers), **Supp. II Part 2:** 415, 419
Alpine Christ and Other Poems, The (Jeffers), **Supp. II Part 2:** 419
"Alpine Idyll, An" (Hemingway), **II:** 249; **Retro. Supp. I:** 176
Al Que Quiere! (W. C. Williams), **Retro. Supp. I:** 414, 416, **417,** 428
Alraune (Ewers; Endore, trans.), **Supp. XVII:** 54
Alsop, Joseph, **II:** 579
"Altar, The" (Herbert), **Supp. IV Part 2:** 646
"Altar, The" (MacLeish), **III:** 4
"Altar Boy" (Fante), **Supp. XI:** 160, 164
"Altar of the Dead, The" (James), **Retro. Supp. I:** 229
"Altars in the Street, The" (Levertov), **Supp. III Part 1:** 280
Alter, Robert, **Supp. XII:** 167
Altgeld, John Peter, **Supp. I Part 2:** 382, 455
Althea (Masters), **Supp. I Part 2:** 455, 459
Altick, Richard, **Supp. I Part 2:** 423
Altieri, Charles, **Supp. VIII:** 297, 303
Altman, Robert, **Supp. IX:** 143
"Alto" (C. Frost), **Supp. XV:** 101
"Altra Ego" (Brodsky), **Supp. VIII:** 31–32
A Lume Spento (Pound), **Retro. Supp. I:** 283, 285
"Aluminum House" (F. Barthelme), **Supp. XI:** 26
Alvares, Mosseh, **Supp. V:** 11
Alvarez, A., **Supp. I Part 2:** 526, 527; **Supp. II Part 1:** 99; **Supp. IX:** 248
Alvarez, Joseph A., **Supp. XXII:** 13–14
Alvarez, Julia, **Supp. VII: 1–21; Supp. XI:** 177; **Supp. XVII:** 71, 112
"Always a Rose" (L.-Y. Lee), **Supp. XV:** 215, 216
"Always in Good Humor" (Adams), **Supp. XV:** 294
Always Outnumbered, Always Outgunned (Mosley), **Supp. XIII:** 242
"Always the Stories" (Ortiz), **Supp. IV Part 2:** 499, 500, 502, 504, 512
Always the Young Strangers (Sandburg), **III:** 577–578, 579
Always Young and Fair (Richter), **Supp. XVIII: 215–216**
Amadeus (Shaffer), **Supp. XIV:** 330
"Amahl and the Night Visitors: A Guide to the Tenor of Love" (Moore), **Supp. X:** 167
"Am and Am Not" (Olds), **Supp. X:** 212
"Amanita, The" (Francis), **Supp. IX:** 81
Amaranth (Robinson), **III:** 509, 510, 512, 513, 522, 523
"Amateurs, The" (Swados), **Supp. XIX:** 256
Amazing Adele, The (Barillet and Grédy; Loos, trans.), **Supp. XVI:** 194
Amazing Adventures of Kavalier and Clay, The (Chabon), **Supp. XI:** 68, 76, **77–80; Supp. XXII:** 49
Amazing Adventures of the Escapist, The (Chabon, ed.), **Supp. XIX:** 174
Amazing Science Fiction Stories, **Supp. XVI:** 121
Amazons: An Intimate Memoir by the First Woman to Play in the National Hockey League (DeLillo), **Supp. VI:** 2
Ambassador of Peace, An (Abernon), **Supp. XVI:** 191
Ambassadors, The (H. James), **II:** 320, 333–334, 600; **III:** 517; **IV:** 322; **Retro. Supp. I:** 215, 218, 219, 220, 221, **232–233**
Ambelain, Robert, **Supp. I Part 1:** 260, 273, 274
"Ambition Bird, The" (Sexton), **Supp. II Part 2:** 693
Ambition: The Secret Passion (Epstein), **Supp. XIV:** 113–114
Ambler, Eric, **III:** 57
Ambrose Holt and Family (Glaspell), **Supp. III Part 1:** 175, 181, 184, 187, 188
"Ambrose Seyffert" (Masters), **Supp. I Part 2:** 464
"Ambush" (Komunyakaa), **Supp. XIII:** 122
Amen Corner, The (Baldwin), **Retro. Supp. II:** 5, 7; **Supp. I Part 1:** 48, 51, 54, 55, 56
America (Benét), **Supp. XI:** 46, 47, 51
"America" (Ginsberg), **Supp. II Part 1:** 58–59, 317
"America" (song), **IV:** 410
"America, America!" (poem) (Schwartz), **Supp. II Part 2:** 665
"America, Commerce, and Freedom" (Rowson and Reinagle), **Supp. XV:** 240
"America, Seen Through Photographs, Darkly" (Sontag), **Supp. III Part 2:** 464
"America! America!" (story) (Schwartz), **Supp. II Part 2:** 640, 658–659, 660
America and Americans (Steinbeck), **IV:** 52
"America and the Vidal Chronicles" (Pease), **Supp. IV Part 2:** 687
America as a Civilization (Lerner), **III:** 60
America Behind the Color Line (H. L. Gates), **Supp. XX: 102, 105**
America Beyond the Color Line (television program), **Supp. XX: 99**
America Hispana: A Portrait and a Prospect (W. Frank), **Supp. XX: 76**
"America Independent" (Freneau), **Supp. II Part 1:** 261
America Is Worth Saving (Dreiser), **Retro. Supp. II:** 96
American, The (James), **I:** 226; **II:** 326–327, 328, 331, 334; **IV:** 318; **Retro. Supp. I:** 220, **221,** 228, 376, 381
Americana (DeLillo), **Supp. VI:** 2, **3,** 5, 6, 8, 13, 14
American Adam, The (R. W. B. Lewis), **II:** 457–458; **Supp. XIII:** 93
American Almanac (Leeds), **II:** 110
American Anthem (Doctorow and Suares), **Supp. IV Part 1:** 234
"American Apocalypse" (Gunn Allen), **Supp. IV Part 1:** 325
American Aristocracy (film), **Supp. XVI:** 185–186
American Blood, (Nichols), **Supp. XIII:** 268
American Blues (T. Williams), **IV:** 381, 383
American Buffalo (Mamet), **Supp. XIV:** 239, 241, 242, 244–245, 246, 254, 255
American Caravan: A Yearbook of American Literature (Mumford, ed.), **Supp. II Part 2:** 482
American Cause, The (MacLeish), **III:** 3
American Childhood, An (Dillard), **Supp. VI: 19–21,** 23, 24, 25, 26, 30, 31
"American Childhood in the Dominican Republic, An" (Alvarez), **Supp. VII:** 2, 5
American Child Supreme, An: The Education of a Liberation Ecologist (Nichols), **Supp. XIII:** 256, 257, 258, 264, 265, 266, 267, 268, 269
American Civilization (C. L. R. James), **Supp. XXI:** 169
American Claimant, The (Twain), **IV:** 194, 198–199
American Crisis I (Paine), **Supp. I Part 2:** 508
American Crisis II (Paine), **Supp. I Part 2:** 508
American Crisis XIII (Paine), **Supp. I Part 2:** 509
"American Critic, The" (J. Spingarn), **I:** 266
American Culture, Canons, and the Case of Elizabeth Stoddard (Smith and Weinauer), **Supp. XV:** 270
American Daughter, An (Wasserstein), **Supp. XV: 330–332,** 333
American Democrat, The (Cooper), **I:** 343, 346, 347, 353
American Desert (Everett), **Supp. XVIII: 62–63**
American Diary (Webb), **Supp. I Part 1:** 5
American Drama since World War II (Weales), **IV:** 385

American Dream, An (Mailer), **III:** 27, 33–34, 35, 39, 41, 43, 44; **Retro. Supp. II:** 203, **204–205**
American Dream, The (Albee), **I:** 74–76, 77, 89, 94
"American Dreams" (Simpson), **Supp. IX:** 274
American Earth (Caldwell), **I:** 290, 308
"American Emperors" (Poirier), **Supp. IV Part 2:** 690
American Exodus, An (Lange and Taylor), **I:** 293
American Experience, The (Parkes), **Supp. I Part 2:** 617–618
American Express (Corso), **Supp. XII:** 129
"American Express" (Salter), **Supp. IX:** 260–261
"American Fear of Literature, The" (Lewis), **II:** 451
American Female Patriotism (S. Warner as Wetherell), **Supp. XVIII: 260–261,** 262**,** 263
American Fictions (Hardwick), **Supp. X:** 171
American Fictions, 1940–1980 (Karl), **Supp. IV Part 1:** 384; **Supp. XXI:** 234
"American Financier, The" (Dreiser), **II:** 428
American Folkways (book series), **I:** 290
American Guerilla in the Philippines (Wolfert), **Supp. XXI:** 267
"American Heart of Darkness: The Moral Vision of Five Novels of the Vietnam War" (Palm), **Supp. XXII:** 103
American Heroine: The Life and Legend of Jane Addams (A. F. Davis), **Supp. I Part 1:** 1
American Historical Novel, The (Leisy), **Supp. II Part 1:** 125
"American Horse" (Erdrich), **Supp. IV Part 1:** 333
American Humor: A Study of the National Character (Rourke), **IV:** 339, 352; **Supp. XIX:** 147
American Hunger (Wright), **Supp. IV Part 1:** 11
American Indian Anthology, An (Tvedten, ed.), **Supp. IV Part 2:** 505
"American Indian Women: At the Center of Indigenous Resistance in Contemporary North America" (Jaimes and Halsey), **Supp. IV Part 1:** 331
"American in England, An" (Wylie), **Supp. I Part 2:** 707
American Jitters, The: A Year of the Slump (Wilson), **IV:** 427, 428
American Journal (Hayden), **Supp. II Part 1:** 367
American Journey: The Times of Robert F. Kennedy (Plimpton, ed.), **Supp. XVI:** 245
"American Land Ethic, An" (Momaday), **Supp. IV Part 2:** 488
American Landscape, The, **Supp. I Part 1:** 157
American Language, The (Mencken), **II:** 289, 430; **III:** 100, 104, 105, 108, 111, 119–120
American Language, The: Supplement One (Mencken), **III:** 111
American Language, The: Supplement Two (Mencken), **III:** 111
"American Letter" (MacLeish), **III:** 13
"American Liberty" (Freneau), **Supp. II Part 1:** 257
"American Life in Poetry" (column, Kooser), **Supp. XIX:** 116, 127
American Literary History (Harrison), **Supp. VIII:** 37
American Mercury, **Supp. XI:** 163, 164
American Mind, The (Commager), **Supp. I Part 2:** 650
American Moderns: Bohemian New York and the Creation of a New Century (Stansell), **Supp. XVII:** 106
American Moderns: From Rebellion to Conformity (Geismar), **Supp. IX:** 15; **Supp. XI:** 223
"American Names" (Benét), **Supp. XI:** 47
American Nature Writers (Elder, ed.), **Supp. IX:** 25
American Nature Writers (Winter), **Supp. X:** 104
American Negro, The (W. H. Thomas), **Supp. II Part 1:** 168
American Notebooks, The (Hawthorne), **II:** 226
American Novel Since World War II, The (Klein, ed.), **Supp. XI:** 233
Americano, The (film), **Supp. XVI:** 185
"American Original, An: Learning from a Literary Master" (Wilkinson), **Supp. VIII:** 164, 165, 168
American Ornithology (Wilson), **Supp. XVI:** 4, 6
American Pastoral (P. Roth), **Retro. Supp. II:** 279, 289, **292–293; Supp. XI:** 68
American Places (Porter, Stegner and Stegner), **Supp. IV Part 2:** 599
"American Poet" (Shapiro), **Supp. II Part 2:** 701
"American Poetry" (Simpson), **Supp. IX:** 272
American Poetry, 1922: A Miscellany (Untermeyer, ed.), **Supp. XV:** 306
"American Poetry and American Life" (Pinsky), **Supp. VI:** 239–240
American Poetry from the Beginning to Whitman (Untermeyer, ed.), **Supp. XV:** 310
American Poetry since 1900 (Untermeyer, ed.), **Supp. XV:** 306
American Poetry since 1945: A Critical Survey (Stepanchev), **Supp. XI:** 312
American Poetry since 1960 (Mesic), **Supp. IV Part 1:** 175
American Poets since World War II Dictionary of Literary Biography (Gwynn, ed.), **Supp. XV:** 343
American Primer, An (Boorstin), **I:** 253
American Primer, An (Whitman), **IV:** 348
"American Primitive" (W. J. Smith), **Supp. XIII:** 333
American Primitive: Poems (Oliver), **Supp. VII:** 234–237, 238
American Procession, An: The Major American Writers from 1830–1930—the Crucial Century (Kazin), **Supp. VIII: 105–106,** 108
"American Prose Writers" articles (Briggs), **Supp. XVIII:** 11
American Radio Company, The (radio show, Keillor), **Supp. XVI:** 176–177
"American Realist Playwrights, The" (McCarthy), **II:** 562
American Register, or General Repository of History, Politics, and Science, The (Brown, ed.), **Supp. I Part 1:** 146
American Renaissance (Matthiessen), **I:** 259–260; **III:** 310; **Supp. XIII:** 93
"American Rendezvous, An" (Beauvoir), **Supp. IX:** 4
American Scene, The (James), **II:** 336; **III:** 460; **Retro. Supp. I:** 232, 235
American Scenes (Kozlenko, ed.), **IV:** 378
"American Scholar, The" (Emerson), **I:** 239; **II:** 8, 12–13; **Retro. Supp. I:** 62, 74–75, 149, 298; **Retro. Supp. II:** 155; **Supp. I Part 2:** 420; **Supp. IX:** 227, 271; **Supp. XIV:** 104
"American Scholar, The" (Pickering), **Supp. XXI:** 196
Americans in England; or, Lessons for Daughters (Rowson), **Supp. XV:** 240
"American Soldier, The" (Freneau), **Supp. II Part 1:** 269
American Songbag, The (Sandburg), **III:** 583
"American Student in Paris, An" (Farrell), **II:** 45
"American Sublime, The" (Stevens), **IV:** 74
"American Tar, The; or, The Press Gang Defeated" (Rowson and Taylor), **Supp. XV:** 238
"American Temperament, The" (Locke), **Supp. XIV:** 211
American Tragedy, An (Dreiser), **I:** 497, 498, 499, 501, 502, 503, 511–515, 517, 518, 519; **III:** 251; **IV:** 35, 484; **Retro. Supp. II:** 93, 95, **104–108; Supp. XVII:** 155
"American Triptych" (Kenyon), **Supp. VII:** 165
"American Use for German Ideals" (Bourne), **I:** 228
American Village, The (Freneau), **Supp. II Part 1:** 256, 257
"American Village, The" (Freneau), **Supp. II Part 1:** 256
America's Coming-of-Age (Brooks), **I:** 228, 230, 240, 245, 258; **IV:** 427
America's Humor: From Poor Richard to Doonesbury (Blair and Hill), **Retro. Supp. II:** 286
"America's Part in World Peace" (Locke), **Supp. XIV:** 208
America's Rome (Vance), **Supp. IV Part 2:** 684
America: The Story of a Free People (Commager and Nevins), **I:** 253
America Was Promises (MacLeish), **III:** 16, 17
"Amerika" (Snyder), **Supp. VIII:** 301

Ames, Christopher, **Supp. XVIII:** 242–243
Ames, Fisher, **Supp. I Part 2:** 486
Ames, Lois, **Supp. I Part 2:** 541, 547
Ames, William, **IV:** 158
Ames Stewart, Beatrice, **Supp. IX:** 200
Amichai, Yehuda, **Supp. XI:** 267
Amick, Steve, **Supp. XXII:** 205, 216
Amidon, Stephen, **Supp. XI:** 333
Amiel, Henri F., **I:** 241, 243, 250
Amis, Kingsley, **IV:** 430; **Supp. IV Part 2:** 688; **Supp. VIII:** 167; **Supp. XIII:** 93; **Supp. XV:** 117
Amis, Martin, **Retro. Supp. I:** 278
"Amity Hills" (Skloot), **Supp. XX: 204**
Ammons, A. R., **Supp. III Part 2:** 541; **Supp. VII: 23–38; Supp. IX:** 41, 42, 46; **Supp. XII:** 121; **Supp. XV:** 115; **Supp. XVII:** 242; **Supp. XIX:** 83
Ammons, Elizabeth, **Retro. Supp. I:** 364, 369; **Retro. Supp. II:** 140
Amnesia Moon (Lethem), **Supp. XVIII:** 136**, 138–139**
"Among Children" (Levine), **Supp. V:** 192
Among Friends (M. F. K. Fisher), **Supp. XVII:** 89, 90–91, 92
Among My Books (Lowell), **Supp. I Part 2:** 407
"Among School Children" (Yeats), **III:** 249; **Supp. IX:** 52; **Supp. XIV:** 8
"Among the Hills" (Whittier), **Supp. I Part 2:** 703
Among the Isles of Shoals (Thaxter), **Supp. XIII:** 152
"Among Those Present" (Benét), **Supp. XI:** 53
"Amoral Moralist" (White), **Supp. I Part 2:** 648
Amory, Cleveland, **Supp. I Part 1:** 316
Amory, Fred, **Supp. III Part 1:** 2
Amos (biblical book), **II:** 166
Amos and Andy (television program), **Supp. XX: 103**
Amran, David, **Supp. XIV:** 150
"Am Strand von Tanger" (Salter), **Supp. IX:** 257
"AMTRAK" (Baraka), **Supp. II Part 1:** 60
"Amulet, The" (Antin), **Supp. XX: 10**
"Amulets" (Hull), **Supp. XXI:** 139
Amy and Isabelle (Strout), **Supp. X:** 86
"Amy Lowell of Brookline, Mass." (Scott), **II:** 512
Amy Lowell: Portrait of the Poet in Her Time (Gregory), **II:** 512
"Amy Wentworth" (Whittier), **Supp. I Part 2:** 694, 696
Anabase (Perse), **III:** 12
"Anabasis (I)" (Merwin), **Supp. III Part 1:** 342, 346
"Anabasis (II)" (Merwin), **Supp. III Part 1:** 342, 346
Anagrams: A Novel (Moore), **Supp. X:** 163, 164, 167, **169–171,** 172
Analects (Confucius), **Supp. IV Part 1:** 14
Analects, The (Pound, trans.), **III:** 472
Analogy (J. Butler), **II:** 8
"Analysis of a Theme" (Stevens), **IV:** 81
Anarchiad, The, A Poem on the Restoration of Chaos and Substantial Night, in Twenty Four Books (Barlow), **Supp. II Part 1:** 70
Anarchist Woman, An (Hapgood), **Supp. XVII:** 102–103; **Supp. XXI:** 5
Anatomy Lesson, and Other Stories, The (Connell), **Supp. XIV:** 84, 87, 89
"Anatomy Lesson, The" (Connell), **Supp. XIV:** 84, 86, 87
Anatomy Lesson, The (P. Roth), **Retro. Supp. II:** 286, 290; **Supp. III Part 2:** 422–423, 425
"Anatomy Lesson of Dr. Nicholaas Tulp, Amsterdam, 1632, The" (Bierds), **Supp. XVII:** 27–28
Anatomy of Criticism (Frye), **Supp. XIII:** 19; **Supp. XIV:** 15
Anatomy of Melancholy (Burton), **III:** 78; **Supp. XVII:** 229
Anatomy of Nonsense, The (Winters), **Supp. II Part 2:** 811, 812
Anaya, Rudolfo A., **Supp. IV Part 2:** 502; **Supp. XIII:** 213, 220; **Supp. XIX:** 97
"Ancestor" (A. Finch), **Supp. XVII:** 72
Ancestors (Maxwell), **Supp. VIII:** 152, 168
"Ancestors, The" (Tate), **IV:** 128
Ancestral Voice: Conversations with N. Scott Momaday (Woodard), **Supp. IV Part 2:** 484, 485, 486, 489, 493
"Anchorage" (Harjo), **Supp. XII:** 220–221
Ancient Child, The: A Novel (Momaday), **Supp. IV Part 2:** 488, 489–491, 492, 493
"Ancient Egypt/Fannie Goldbarth" (Goldbarth), **Supp. XII:** 191–192
Ancient Evenings (Mailer), **Retro. Supp. II:** 206, 210, 213
Ancient Law, The (Glasgow), **II:** 179–180, 192
Ancient Musics (Goldbarth), **Supp. XII:** 191–192
"Ancient Semitic Rituals for the Dead" (Goldbarth), **Supp. XII:** 191–192
"Ancient World, The" (Doty), **Supp. XI:** 122
& (And) (Cummings), **I:** 429, 431, 432, 437, 445, 446, 448
Andersen, Hans Christian, **I:** 441; **Supp. I Part 2:** 622
Andersen, Hendrik Christian, **Supp. XX: 232**
Anderson, Charles R., **Supp. I Part 1:** 356, 360, 368, 371, 372
Anderson, Frances, **I:** 231
Anderson, Guy, **Supp. X:** 264, 265
Anderson, Henry J., **Supp. I Part 1:** 156
Anderson, Irwin M., **I:** 98–99
Anderson, Mrs. Irwin M., **I:** 98–99
Anderson, Jon, **Supp. V:** 338
Anderson, Judith, **III:** 399
Anderson, Karl, **I:** 99, 103
Anderson, Lorraine, **Supp. XVIII:** 189
Anderson, Margaret, **I:** 103; **III:** 471
Anderson, Margaret Bartlett, **III:** 171
Anderson, Marian, **Supp. XXII:** 283
Anderson, Mary Jane. *See* Lanier, Mrs. Robert Sampson (Mary Jane Anderson)
Anderson, Maxwell, **III:** 159
Anderson, Quentin, **Retro. Supp. I:** 392
Anderson, Robert, **Supp. I Part 1:** 277; **Supp. V:** 108
Anderson, Sally, **Supp. XIII:** 95
Anderson, Sherwood, **I: 97–120,** 211, 374, 375, 384, 405, 423, 445, 480, 487, 495, 506, 518; **II:** 27, 38, 44, 55, 56, 68, 250–251, 263, 271, 289, 451, 456–457; **III:** 220, 224, 382–383, 453, 483, 545, 576, 579; **IV:** 27, 40, 46, 190, 207, 433, 451, 482; **Retro. Supp. I:** 79, 80, 177; **Supp. I Part 2:** 378, 430, 459, 472, 613; **Supp. IV Part 2:** 502; **Supp. V:** 12, 250; **Supp. VIII:** 39, 152; **Supp. IX:** 14, 309; **Supp. XI:** 159, 164; **Supp. XII:** 343; **Supp. XV:** 298; **Supp. XVI:** 17, 20; **Supp. XVII:** 105; **Supp. XX: 69, 75**
Anderson, Mrs. Sherwood (Tennessee Mitchell), **I:** 100; **Supp. I Part 2:** 459, 460
Anderson, T. J., **Supp. XIII:** 132
Anderson, Wendy, **Supp. XXI:** 255
Anderssen, A., **III:** 252
"And Hickman Arrives" (Ellison), **Retro. Supp. II:** 118, 126; **Supp. II Part 1:** 248
And in the Hanging Gardens (Aiken), **I:** 63
"And It Came to Pass" (Wright), **Supp. XV:** 348
And I Worked at the Writer's Trade (Cowley), **Supp. II Part 1:** 137, 139, 141, 143, 147, 148
"...And Ladies of the Club" (J. W. Miller), **Supp. XX: 161**
And Live Apart (Peacock), **Supp. XIX: 196–197**
Andorra (Cameron), **Supp. XII:** 79, 81, **88–91**
"—and Other Poets" (column; Untermeyer), **Supp. XV:** 294
"—and Other Poets" (Untermeyer), Supp. XV: 297
Andral, Gabriel, **Supp. I Part 1:** 302
Andre, Michael, **Supp. XII:** 117–118, 129, 132, 133–134
"Andrea Is Changing Her Name" (Brockmeier), **Supp. XXII:** 61
Andre's Mother (McNally), **Supp. XIII:** 206
Andress, Ursula, **Supp. XI:** 307
"Andrew Jackson" (Masters), **Supp. I Part 2:** 472
Andrews, Bruce, **Supp. IV Part 2:** 426
Andrews, Peter, **Supp. XX: 87**
Andrews, Roy Chapman, **Supp. X:** 172
Andrews, Tom, **Supp. XI:** 317
Andrews, Wayne, **IV:** 310
Andrews, William L., **Supp. IV Part 1:** 13; **Supp. XIX:** 72; **Supp. XX: 105**
Andreyev, Leonid Nikolaevich, **I:** 53; **II:** 425
Andria (Terence), **IV:** 363
"Andromache" (Dubus), **Supp. VII:** 84

"And Summer Will Not Come Again" (Plath), **Retro. Supp. II:** 242
"And That Night Clifford Died" (Levine), **Supp. V:** 195
And the Band Played On (Shilts), **Supp. X:** 145
"And the Moon Be Still as Bright" (Bradbury), **Supp. IV Part 1:** 106
"And the Sea Shall Give up Its Dead" (Wilder), **IV:** 358
And Things That Go Bump in the Night (McNally), **Supp. XIII: 196–197,** 205, 208
And to Think That I Saw It on Mulberry Street (Geisel), **Supp. XVI:** 100, 101, 104
"And *Ut Pictura Poesis* Is Her Name" (Ashbery), **Supp. III Part 1:** 19
And We Are Millions (Ryan), **Supp. XVIII:** 225
"Anecdote and Storyteller" (Howe), **Supp. VI:** 127
"Anecdote of the Jar" (Stevens), **IV:** 83–84
"Anemone" (Rukeyser), **Supp. VI:** 281, 285
"Angel, The" (Buck), **Supp. II Part 1:** 127
"Angel and Unicorn and Butterfly" (Everwine), **Supp. XV:** 76
Angela's Ashes (McCourt), **Supp. XII: 271–279,** 283, 285; **Supp. XXII:** 94
"Angel at the Grave, The" (Wharton), **IV:** 310; **Retro. Supp. I:** 365
"Angel Butcher" (Levine), **Supp. V:** 181
Angel City (Shepard), **Supp. III Part 2:** 432, 445
Angelica (Holding), **Supp. XXII: 120–121**
"Angel Is My Watermark!, The" (H. Miller), **III:** 180
Angell, Carol, **Supp. I Part 2:** 655
Angell, Katharine Sergeant. *See* White, Katharine
Angell, Roger, **Supp. I Part 2:** 655; **Supp. V:** 22; **Supp. VIII:** 139
Angel Landing (Hoffman), **Supp. X: 82–83**
"Angel Levine" (Malamud), **Supp. I Part 2:** 431, 432, 433–434, 437
Angel of Bethesda, The (Mather), **Supp. II Part 2:** 464
"Angel of the Bridge, The" (Cheever), **Supp. I Part 1:** 186–187
"Angel of the Odd, The" (Poe), **III:** 425
Angelo Herndon Jones (Hughes), **Retro. Supp. I:** 203
"Angel on the Porch, An" (Wolfe), **IV:** 451
Angelou, Maya, **Supp. IV Part 1: 1–19; Supp. XI:** 20, 245; **Supp. XIII:** 185; **Supp. XVI:** 259; **Supp. XXI:** 172
"Angel Poem, The" (Stern), **Supp. IX:** 292
Angels and Earthly Creatures (Wylie), **Supp. I Part 2:** 709, 713, 724–730
Angels Flight (Connelly), **Supp. XXI:** 72, **72–73,** 75, 80
Angels in America: A Gay Fantasia on National Themes (Kushner), **Supp. IX:** 131, 134, **141–146**
"Angels of the Love Affair" (Sexton), **Supp. II Part 2:** 692
"Angel Surrounded by Paysans" (Stevens), **IV:** 93
Angel That Troubled the Waters, The (Wilder), **IV:** 356, 357–358
"Anger" (Creeley), **Supp. IV Part 1:** 150–152
Anger (Sarton), **Supp. VIII: 256**
"Anger against Children" (R. Bly), **Supp. IV Part 1:** 73
Angle of Ascent (Hayden), **Supp. II Part 1:** 363, 367, 370
"Angle of Geese" (Momaday), **Supp. IV Part 2:** 485
Angle of Geese and Other Poems (Momaday), **Supp. IV Part 2:** 487, 491
Angle of Repose (Stegner), **Supp. IV Part 2:** 599, 605, 606, 610–611
"*Angle of Repose* and the Writings of Mary Hallock Foote: A Source Study" (Williams-Walsh), **Supp. IV Part 2:** 611
"Anglo-Mongrels and the Rose" (Loy), **Supp. XXII:** 156, 159, 166–167
Anglo-Saxon Century, The (Dos Passos), **I:** 474–475, 483
Angoff, Charles, **III:** 107
"Angola Question Mark" (Hughes), **Supp. I Part 1:** 344
Angry Hills, The (Uris), **Supp. XX: 246, 250**
Angry Wife, The (Sedges), **Supp. II Part 1:** 125
"Angry Women Are Building: Issues and Struggles Facing American Indian Women Today" (Gunn Allen), **Supp. IV Part 1:** 324
"Animal, Vegetable, and Mineral" (Bogan), **Supp. III Part 1:** 66
"Animal Acts" (Simic), **Supp. VIII:** 278
Animal and Vegetable Physiology Considered with Reference to Natural Theology (Roget), **Supp. I Part 1:** 312
"Animal Bodies: Corporeality, Class, and Subject Formation in *The Wide, Wide World*" (Mason), **Supp. XVIII:** 263
Animal Dreams (Kingsolver), **Supp. VII:** 199, 204–207
Animal Magnetism (Prose), **Supp. XVI:** 251, 260
"Animals, The" (Merwin), **Supp. III Part 1:** 348
"Animals Are Passing from Our Lives" (Levine), **Supp. V:** 181, 182
Animals in That Country, The (Atwood), **Supp. XIII:** 20, 33
Animals of the Soul: Sacred Animals of the Oglala Sioux (Brown), **Supp. IV Part 2:** 487
"Animals You Eat, The" (X. J. Kennedy), **Supp. XV:** 169
"Animula" (Eliot), **Retro. Supp. I:** 64
Anita Loos Rediscovered (M. A. Loos), **Supp. XVI:** 196
Ankor Wat (Ginsberg), **Supp. II Part 1:** 323
"Annabelle" (Komunyakaa), **Supp. XIII:** 117
"Annabel Lee" (Poe), **Retro. Supp. I:** 273; **Retro. Supp. II:** 266
Anna Christie (O'Neill), **III:** 386, 389, 390; **Supp. XXII:** 24
"Anna Grasa" (Weigl), **Supp. XIX:** 278
"Anna in Mourning" (Weigl), **Supp. XIX:** 288
Anna Karenina (Tolstoy), **I:** 10; **II:** 290; **Retro. Supp. I:** 225; **Supp. V:** 323
"Anna Karenina" (Trilling), Supp. III Part 2: 508
Annan, Noel, **Supp. XX: 240**
"Anna's Grace" (Weigl), **Supp. XIX:** 282–283
"Anna Who Was Mad" (Sexton), **Supp. II Part 2:** 692
"Ann Burlak" (Rukeyser), **Supp. VI:** 280
"Anne" (Oliver), **Supp. VII:** 232
"Anne" (R. H. Davis), **Supp. XVI:** 91, 92
"Anne at the Symphony" (Shields), **Supp. VII:** 310
"Anne Bradstreet's Poetic Voices" (Requa), **Supp. I Part 1:** 107
Anne of Geierstein: or, The Maiden of the Mist (Scott), **Supp. XX: 234**
Anne Sexton: The Artist and Her Critics (McClatchy), **Supp. XII:** 253
"Ann from the Street" (Dixon), **Supp. XII:** 146–147
"Ann Garner" (Agee), **I:** 27
"Anniad, The" (Brooks), **Supp. III Part 1:** 77, 78
Annie (musical), **Supp. IV Part 2:** 577
Annie Allen (Brooks), **Supp. III Part 1:** 76–79
Annie Dillard Reader, The (Dillard), **Supp. VI:** 23
Annie Hall (film; Allen), **Supp. IV Part 1:** 205; **Supp. XV:** 1, 2, 4, 5, **6–7,** 14
Annie John (Kincaid), **Supp. VII:** 184–186, 193
Annie Kilburn, a Novel (Howells), **II:** 275, 286, 287
"Annihilation" (X. J. Kennedy), **Supp. XV:** 168
"Annihilation of Matter, The" (Bronk), **Supp. XXI:** 30
Anniversary (Shields), **Supp. VII:** 320, 322, 323, 324
"Annunciation" (Nelson), **Supp. XVIII:** 174
"Annunciation, The" (Le Sueur), **Supp. V:** 130
Ann Vickers (Lewis), **II:** 453
"A No-Account Creole, A" (Chopin), **Retro. Supp. II:** 64
"Anodyne" (Komunyakaa), **Supp. XIII:** 130
Another America/Otra America (Kingsolver), **Supp. VII:** 207–209
"Another Animal" (Swenson), **Supp. IV Part 2:** 639
Another Animal: Poems (Swenson), **Supp. IV Part 2:** 639–641, 649

Another Antigone (Gurney), **Supp. V:** 97, 98, 100, 101, 102, 105
"Another August" (Merrill), **Supp. III Part 1:** 326
"Another Beer" (Matthews), **Supp. IX:** 158
Another Country (Baldwin), **Retro. Supp. II: 9–11,** 14; **Supp. I Part 1:** 51, 52, 56–58, 63, 67, 337; **Supp. II Part 1:** 40; **Supp. VIII:** 349
"Another Language" (Jong), **Supp. V:** 131
Another Mother Tongue: Gay Words, Gay Worlds (Grahn), **Supp. IV Part 1:** 330
"Another Night in the Ruins" (Kinnell), **Supp. III Part 1:** 239, 251
"Another Night with Snow" (W. V. Davis), **Supp. XXI:** 90, 91
"Another Old Woman" (W. C. Williams), **Retro. Supp. I:** 423
Another Part of the Forest (Hellman), **Supp. I Part 1:** 282–283, 297
Another Republic: 17 European and South American Writers (Strand, trans.), **Supp. IV Part 2:** 630
Another Roadside Attraction (Robbins), **Supp. X:** 259, 261, 262, 263, 264, 265–266, **267–269,** 274, 275, 277, 284
Another Side of Bob Dylan (album, Dylan), **Supp. XVIII:** 25
"Another Spring Uncovered" (Swenson), **Supp. IV Part 2:** 644
Another Thin Man (film), **Supp. IV Part 1:** 355
Another Time (Auden), **Supp. II Part 1:** 15
Another Turn of the Crank (Berry), **Supp. X:** 25, 35
"Another upon the Same" (Taylor), **IV:** 161
"Another Voice" (Wilbur), **Supp. III Part 2:** 557
"Another Wife" (Anderson), **I:** 114
"Another Winter Night" (Budbill), **Supp. XIX:** 10
Another Woman (film; Allen), **Supp. XV:** 11
Another You (Beattie), **Supp. V:** 29, 31, 33–34
Anouilh, Jean, **Supp. I Part 1:** 286–288, 297
Ansa, Tina McElroy, **Supp. XVIII:** 195
Ansky, S., **IV:** 6
Ansky, Shloime, **Supp. IX:** 131, 138
"Answer, The" (Jeffers), **Supp. III Part 2:** 423
Answered Prayers: The Unfinished Novel (Capote), **Supp. III Part 1:** 113, 125, 131–132; **Supp. XVI:** 245
"Answering the Deer: Genocide and Continuance in the Poetry of American Indian Women" (Gunn Allen), **Supp. IV Part 1:** 322, 325
"Answer of Minerva, The: Pacifism and Resistance in Simone Weil" (Merton), **Supp. VIII:** 204
Antaeus (Wolfe), **IV:** 461
"Ante-Bellum Sermon, An" (Dunbar), **Supp. II Part 1:** 203–204
Antheil, George, **III:** 471, 472; **IV:** 404
Anthem (Rand), **Supp. IV Part 2:** 523
Anthology of Holocaust Literature (Glatstein, Knox, and Margoshes, eds.), **Supp. X:** 70
Anthology of Modern American Poetry (Nelson, ed.), **Supp. XXII:** 271
Anthology of Twentieth-Century Brazilian Poetry, An (Bishop and Brasil, eds.), **Retro. Supp. II:** 50; **Supp. I Part 1:** 94
Anthon, Kate, **I:** 452
Anthony, Andrew, **Supp. XVI:** 235, 245, 246
Anthony, Saint, **III:** 395
Anthony, Susan B., **Supp. XI:** 200
"Anthropologist as Hero, The" (Sontag), **Supp. III Part 2:** 451
"Anthropology of Water, The" (Carson), **Supp. XII: 102–103**
Anthropos: The Future of Art (Cummings), **I:** 430
Antichrist (Nietzsche), **III:** 176
"Anti-Father" (Dove), **Supp. IV Part 1:** 246
"Anti-Feminist Woman, The" (Rich), **Supp. I Part 2:** 550
Antigone (Sophocles), **Supp. I Part 1:** 284; **Supp. X:** 249
Antin, David, **Supp. VIII:** 292; **Supp. XII:** 2, 8
Antin, Mary, **Supp. IX:** 227; **Supp. XVI:** 148, 149; **Supp. XX: 1–16**
Anti-Oedipus: Capitalism and Schizophrenia (Deleuze and Guattari), **Supp. XII:** 4
Antiphon, The (Barnes), **Supp. III Part 1:** 43–44
"Antiquities" (Mather), **Supp. II Part 2:** 452
"Antiquity of Freedom, The" (Bryant), **Supp. I Part 1:** 168
"Antislavery Tocsin, An" (Douglass), **Supp. III Part 1:** 171
Antoine, Andre, **III:** 387
Antonioni, Michelangelo, **Supp. IV Part 1:** 46, 47, 48
Antony and Cleopatra (Shakespeare), **I:** 285
"Antony on Behalf of the Play" (Burke), **I:** 284
"An trentiesme de mon Eage, L'" (MacLeish), **III:** 9
Antrim, Donald, **Supp. XX:** 90
"Ants" (R. Bly), **Supp. IV Part 1:** 71
Anxiety of Influence, The (Bloom), **Supp. XIII:** 46
"Any City" (Untermeyer), **Supp. XV:** 296
"Any Object" (Swenson), **Supp. IV Part 2:** 640
Anyplace but Here (Bontemps and Conroy), **Supp. XXII:** 11
"Any Porch" (Parker), **Supp. IX:** 194
Anything Else (film; Allen), **Supp. XV:** 2, 11
"Anywhere Out of This World" (Baudelaire), **II:** 552
Any Woman Can't (Wasserstein), **Supp. XV:** 322
Any Woman's Blues (Jong), **Supp. V:** 115, 123, 126
Anzaldúa, Gloria, **Supp. IV Part 1:** 330; **Supp. XIII:** 223
"Apache Tears" (Cliff), **Supp. XXII:** 76
"Aphorisms on Futurism" (Loy), **Supp. XXII:** 159
"Aphorisms on Society" (Stevens), **Retro. Supp. I:** 303
"Apiary IX" (C. Frost), **Supp. XV:** 106
"Apisculptures" (Bierds), **Supp. XVII:** 29
Apollinaire, Guillaume, **I:** 432; **II:** 529; **III:** 196; **IV:** 80; **Retro. Supp. II:** 326; **Supp. XV:** 182
Apologies to the Iroquois (Wilson), **IV:** 429
"Apology" (C. Frost), **Supp. XV:** 103
"Apology, An" (Malamud), **Supp. I Part 2:** 435, 437
"Apology for Bad Dreams" (Jeffers), **Supp. II Part 2:** 427, 438; **Supp. XVII:** 112
"Apology for Crudity, An" (Anderson), **I:** 109
Apology for Poetry (Sidney), **Supp. II Part 1:** 105
"Apostle of the Tules, An" (Harte), **Supp. II Part 1:** 356
"Apostrophe to a Dead Friend" (Kumin), **Supp. IV Part 2:** 442, 451, 452
"Apostrophe to a Pram Rider" (White), **Supp. I Part 2:** 678
"Apostrophe to Man (on reflecting that the world is ready to go to war again)" (Millay), **III:** 127
"Apostrophe to Vincentine, The" (Stevens), **IV:** 90
"Apotheosis" (Kingsolver), **Supp. VII:** 208
"Apotheosis of Martin Luther King, The" (Hardwick), **Supp. III Part 1:** 203–204
Appalachia (Wright), **Supp. V:** 333, 345
Appalachia Inside Out (Miller, Higgs, and Manning, eds.), **Supp. XX: 166**
"Appalachian Book of the Dead III" (Wright), **Supp. V:** 345
"Appalachian Education: A Critique and Suggestions for Reform" (J. W. Miller), **Supp. XX: 165**
"Appalachian Literature: At Home in This World" (J. W. Miller), **Supp. XX: 165**
"Appalachian Values/American Values" (J. W. Miller), **Supp. XX: 165**
Appaloosa (Parker), **Supp. XIX:** 187
"Appeal to H. G. Wells" (Sturgis), **Supp. XX: 233, 240**
"Appeal to Progressives, An" (Wilson), **IV:** 429
Appeal to Reason (Paine), **I:** 490
Appeal to the World, An (Du Bois), **Supp. II Part 1:** 184
Appearance and Reality (Bradley), **I:** 572
"Appendix to 'The Anniad' " (Brooks), **Supp. III Part 1:** 77
Apple, Max, **Supp. VIII:** 14; **Supp. XVII: 1–11,** 49–50
Apple, Sam, **Supp. XVII:** 8

"Apple, The" (Kinnell), **Supp. III Part 1:** 250
Applebaum, Anne, **Supp. XVI:** 153
Applebome, Peter, **Supp. XXI:** 38
Applegarth, Mabel, **II:** 465, 478
"Apple-Maggot Fly, The" (Major), **Supp. XXII:** 182
"Apple of Discord, The" (Humphrey), **Supp. IX:** 109
"Apple Peeler" (Francis), **Supp. IX:** 82
"Apple Rind" (C. Frost), **Supp. XV:** 102
"Apples" (Brockmeier), **Supp. XXII:** 51, 53
"Apples, The" (Di Piero), **Supp. XIX:** 46
Appleseed, Johnny (pseudonym). *See* Chapman, John (Johnny Appleseed)
Apple That Astonished Paris, The (Collins), **Supp. XXI:** 53, 57
Appleton, Nathan, **II:** 488
Appleton, Thomas Gold, **Supp. I Part 1:** 306; **Supp. I Part 2:** 415
"Apple Tree, The" (McCarriston), **Supp. XIV:** 263, 268
"Applicant, The" (Plath), **Retro. Supp. II:** 252; **Supp. I Part 2:** 535, 544, 545
"Application, The" (Neugeboren), **Supp. XVI:** 219, 220, 225
"Applications of the Doctrine" (Hass), **Supp. VI: 100–101**
Appointment, The (film), **Supp. IX:** 253
Appointment in Samarra (O'Hara), **III:** 361, 363–364, 365–367, 371, 374, 375, 383
Appreciation of Sarah Orne Jewett (Cary), **Retro. Supp. II:** 132
"Approaches, The" (Merwin), **Supp. III Part 1:** 350
"Approaching Artaud" (Sontag), **Supp. III Part 2:** 470–471
"Approaching Prayer" (Dickey), **Supp. IV Part 1:** 175
Approach to Literature, An: A Collection of Prose and Verse with Analyses and Discussions (Brooks, Warren, and Purser), **Su pp. XIV:**4
"Approach to Thebes, The" (Kunitz), **Supp. III Part 1:** 265–267
Approach to Vedanta, An (Isherwood), **Supp. XIV:** 157, 163, 164
"Appropriation of Cultures, The" (Everett), **Supp. XVIII:** 66
Approximately Paradise (Skloot), **Supp. XX: 196, 202, 203–204**
"Après-midi d'un faune, L' " (Mallarmé), **III:** 8
"April" (Bierds), **Supp. XVII:** 29
"April" (W. C. Williams), **Retro. Supp. I:** 422
"April" (Winters), **Supp. II Part 2:** 788
April, Steve. *See* Lacy, Ed
April Galleons (Ashbery), **Supp. III Part 1:** 26
"April Galleons" (Ashbery), **Supp. III Part 1:** 26
April Hopes (Howells), **II:** 285, 289
"April Lovers" (Ransom), **III:** 489–490
"April Showers" (Wharton), **Retro. Supp. I:** 361
"April Today Main Street" (Olson), **Supp. II Part 2:** 581
April Twilights (Cather), **I:** 313; **Retro. Supp. I:** 5
"Apt Pupil" (King), **Supp. V:** 152
Arabian Nights, **I:** 204; **II:** 8; **Supp. I Part 2:** 584, 599; **Supp. IV Part 1:** 1
"Arabic Coffee" (Nye), **Supp. XIII:** 276
"Araby" (Joyce), **I:** 174; **Supp. VIII:** 15
Aragon, Louis, **I:** 429; **III:** 471; **Retro. Supp. II:** 85, 321
Arana-Ward, Marie, **Supp. VIII:** 84
Ararat (Glück), **Supp. V:** 79, 86–87
Arbre du voyageur, L' (W. J. Smith; Haussmann, trans.), Supp. XIII: 347
Arbus, Diane, **Supp. XII:** 188
Arbuthnott, John (pseudonym). *See* Henry, O.
"Arc, The" (Bidart), **Supp. XV:** 25–26, 27
Archaeologist of Morning (Olson), **Supp. II Part 2:** 557
Archaeology of the Circle: New and Selected Poems (Weigl), **Supp. XIX:** 282
"Archaic Maker, The" (Merwin), **Supp. III Part 1:** 357
"Archaic Torso of Apollo" (Rilke), **Supp. XV:** 148
"Archaischer Torso Apollos" (Rilke), **Supp. XVII:** 244
"Archbishop, The" (Gioia), **Supp. XV:** 126, 127
Archer (television show), **Supp. IV Part 2:** 474
Archer, William, **IV:** 131; **Retro. Supp. I:** 228
Archer at Large (Macdonald), **Supp. IV Part 2:** 473
Archer in Hollywood (Macdonald), **Supp. IV Part 2:** 474
"Archetype and Signature: The Relationship of Poet and Poem" (Fiedler), **Supp. XIII:** 101
"Archibald Higbie" (Masters), **Supp. I Part 2:** 461
"Architect, The" (Bourne), **I:** 223
Architect, The (Briggs and Ranlett), **Supp. XVIII:** 3
Arctic Dreams (Lopez), **Supp. V:** 211
Arctic Refuge: A Circle of Testimony (Haines), **Supp. XII:** 205
"Arcturus" (Connell), **Supp. XIV:** 88
À rebours (Huysmans), **Supp. XX: 239**
Arendt, Hannah, **II:** 544; **Retro. Supp. I:** 87; **Retro. Supp. II:** 28, 117; **Supp. I Part 2:** 570; **Supp. IV Part 1:** 386; **Supp. VIII:** 98, 99, 100, 243; **Supp. XII:** 166–167
Arensberg, Louise, **Supp. XXII:** 162
Arensberg, Walter, **IV:** 408; **Retro. Supp. I:** 416; **Supp. XXII:** 162
Aren't You Happy for Me? (Bausch), **Supp. VII:** 42, 51, 54
Areopagitica (Milton), **Supp. I Part 2:** 422
"Are You a Doctor?" (Carver), **Supp. III Part 1:** 139–141
"Are You Mr. William Stafford? (Stafford), **Supp. XI:** 317
Argall: The True Story of Pocahontas and Captain John Smith (Vollmann), **Supp. XVII:** 225, 226, 231, 232, 233
"Argonauts of 49, California's Golden Age" (Harte), **Supp. II Part 1:** 353, 355
"Arguments of Everlasting" (B. Kelly), **Supp. XVII:** 129
"Arguments with the Gestapo Continued: II" (Wright), **Supp. XV:** 344
"Arguments with the Gestapo Continued: Literary Resistance" (Wright), **Supp. XV:** 344
Ari (musical, Uris), **Supp. XX: 247**
Aria da Capo (Millay), **III:** 137–138
Ariadne's Thread: A Collection of Contemporary Women's Journals (Lifshin, ed.), **Supp. XVI:** 37–38
"Arias, 1971" (Hull), **Supp. XXI:** 135
Ariel (Plath), **Retro. Supp. II: 250–255; Supp. I Part 2:** 526, 539, 541; **Supp. V:** 79; **Supp. XXI:** 58; **Supp. XXII:** 93
"Ariel" (Plath), **Supp. I Part 2:** 542, 546
"Ariel Poems" (Eliot), **I:** 579
Ariosto, Ludovico, **Supp. XV:** 175
"Ariosto: Critical Notice of His Life and Genius" (Hunt), **Supp. XV:** 175
Arise, Arise (Zukofsky), **Supp. III Part 2:** 619, 629
Aristides. *See* Epstein, Joseph
"Aristocracy" (Emerson), **II:** 6
Aristocracy and Justice (More), **I:** 223
Aristocrat, The (Richter), **Supp. XVIII:** 220
Aristophanes, **I:** 436; **II:** 577; **Supp. I Part 2:** 406
Aristotle, **I:** 58, 265, 280, 527; **II:** 9, 12, 198, 536; **III:** 20, 115, 145, 157, 362, 422, 423; **IV:** 10, 18, 74–75, 89; **Supp. I Part 1:** 104, 296; **Supp. I Part 2:** 423; **Supp. IV Part 1:** 391; **Supp. IV Part 2:** 526, 530; **Supp. X:** 78; **Supp. XI:** 249; **Supp. XII:** 106; **Supp. XIV:** 242–243
Aristotle Contemplating the Bust of Homer (Rembrandt), **Supp. IV Part 1:** 390, 391
"Arkansas Traveller" (Wright), **Supp. V:** 334
Arlen, Harold, **Supp. XXII:** 6
"Arm, The" (X. J. Kennedy), **Supp. XV:** 169
"Armadillo, The" (Bishop), **Supp. I Part 1:** 93
Armadillo in the Grass (Hearon), **Supp. VIII: 58–59**
"Armageddon" (Ransom), **III:** 489, 492
Armageddon (Uris), **Supp. XX: 243, 247, 248, 252–253**
Armah, Aiy Kwei, **Supp. IV Part 1:** 373
Armies of the Night, The (Mailer), **III:** 39–40, 41, 42, 44, 45, 46; **Retro. Supp. II:** 205, 206–207, 208; **Supp. IV Part 1:** 207; **Supp. XIV:** 49, 162
"Arm in Arm" (Simpson), **Supp. IX:** 267–268
Arminius, Jacobus, **I:** 557
Armitage, Shelley, **Supp. IV Part 2:** 439

Arm of Flesh, The (Salter), **Supp. IX:** 251
"Armor" (Dickey), **Supp. IV Part 1:** 179
Armored Attack (film), **Supp. I Part 1:** 281
Arms, George W., **Supp. I Part 2:** 416–417
Armstrong, George, **Supp. I Part 2:** 386
Armstrong, Louis, **Retro. Supp. II:** 114
"'Arm the Paper Arm': Kenneth Koch's Postmodern Comedy" (Chinitz), **Supp. XV:** 180, 185
"Army" (Corso), **Supp. XII:** 117, 127
Army Brat (W. J. Smith), **Supp. XIII:** 331, 347
Arna Bontemps Langston Hughes: Letters 1925–1967 (Nichols), **Retro. Supp. I:** 194
"Arna Bontemps Talks About the Renaissance" (Collins), **Supp. XXII:** 7
Arner, Robert D., **Retro. Supp. II:** 62
"Arnie" (Budbill), **Supp. XIX:** 6
Arnold, Edwin T., **Supp. VIII:** 189
Arnold, George W., **Supp. I Part 2:** 411
Arnold, Marilyn, **Supp. IV Part 1:** 220
Arnold, Matthew, **I:** 222, 228, 275; **II:** 20, 110, 338, 541; **III:** 604; **IV:** 349; **Retro. Supp. I:** 56, 325; **Supp. I Part 2:** 416, 417, 419, 529, 552, 602; **Supp. IX:** 298; **Supp. XIV:** 11, 335; **Supp. XIX:** 41; **Supp. XXI:** 90
Arnold, Thurman, **Supp. I Part 2:** 645
Aronson, Steven M. L., **Supp. V:** 4
Around about America (Caldwell), **I:** 290
"Arrangement in Black and White" (Parker), **Supp. IX:** 198
"Arrival at Santos" (Bishop), **Retro. Supp. II:** 46; **Supp. IX:** 45–46
"Arrival of the Bee Box, The" (Plath), **Retro. Supp. II:** 255
Arrivistes, The: Poem 1940–1949 (Simpson), **Supp. IX:** 265, **267–268**
Arrogance (J. Scott), **Supp. XVII: 186–188,** 189, 191, 192, 194
"Arrow" (Dove), **Supp. IV Part 1:** 250
Arrowsmith (Lewis), **I:** 362; **II:** 445–446, 449
"Arsenal at Springfield, The" (Longfellow), **Retro. Supp. II:** 168
"Arson at Midnight" (Nelson), **Supp. XVIII:** 186
"Arson Plus" (Hammett), **Supp. IV Part 1:** 343; **Supp. XXI:** 68
"Ars Poetica" (Dove), **Supp. IV Part 1:** 250
"Ars Poetica" (Dunn), **Supp. XI:** 154
"Ars Poetica" (MacLeish), **III:** 9–10
"Ars Poetica" (X. J. Kennedy), **Supp. XV:** 154
"*Ars Poetica:* A Found Poem" (Kumin), **Supp. IV Part 2:** 455
"Ars Poetica; or, Who Lives in the Ivory Tower" (McGrath), **Supp. X:** 117
"Ars Poetica: Some Recent Criticism" (Wright), **Supp. III Part 2:** 603
"Art" (Emerson), **II:** 13
Art (Reza), **Supp. XXI:** 148
"Art and Neurosis" (Trilling), **Supp. III Part 2:** 502
Art and Technics (Mumford), **Supp. II Part 2:** 483
Art & Ardor: Essays (Ozick), **Supp. V:** 258, 272
Art as Experience (Dewey), **I:** 266
Art by Subtraction (Reid), **IV:** 41
Art de toucher le clavecin, L' (Couperin), III: 464
Artemis to Actaeon and Other Verse (Wharton), **Retro. Supp. I:** 372
Arte of English Poesie (Puttenham), **Supp. I Part 1:** 113
"Art History" (Cliff), **Supp. XXII:** 75–76
Arthur, Anthony, **Supp. IV Part 2:** 606
Arthur Mervyn; or, Memoirs of the Year 1793 (Brown), **Supp. I Part 1:** 137–140, 144
"Article of Faith" (Sobin), **Supp. XVI:** 291
Articles of Light & Elation (Sobin), **Supp. XVI:** 291
Articulation of Sound Forms in Time (Howe), **Supp. IV Part 2:** 419, 431–433
"Artificer" (X. J. Kennedy), **Supp. XV:** 160
"Artificial Nigger, The" (O'Connor), **III:** 343, 351, 356, 358; **Retro. Supp. II:** 229, 232
Artist, The: A Drama without Words (Mencken), **III:** 104
Artist as Revolutionary, The (Buhle), **Supp. XXI:** 172
"Artist of the Beautiful, The" (Hawthorne), **Retro. Supp. I:** 149
Artistry of Grief (Torsney), **Retro. Supp. I:** 224
"Artists' and Models' Ball, The" (Brooks), **Supp. III Part 1:** 72
Art of Detective Fiction, The (Swales), **Supp. XIX:** 183
"Art of Disappearing, The" (Nye), **Supp. XIII:** 287
Art of Drowning, The (Collins), **Supp. XXI:** 54, 60, 64
Art of Eating, The (M. F. K. Fisher), **Supp. XVII:** 87, 90, 91
Art of Fiction, The (Gardner), **Supp. VI:** 73
"Art of Fiction, The" (H. James), **Retro. Supp. I:** 226; **Retro. Supp. II:** 223
Art of Hunger, The (Auster), **Supp. XII:** 22
"Art of Keeping Your Mouth Shut, The" (Heller), **Supp. IV Part 1:** 383
"Art of Literature and Commonsense, The" (Nabokov), **Retro. Supp. I:** 271
Art of Living and Other Stories, The (Gardner), **Supp. VI:** 72
Art of Love, The (Koch), **Supp. XV:** 182
"Art of Love, The" (Koch), **Supp. XV:** 182
Art of Poetry, The (Koch), **Supp. XV:** 175–176, 178, 188
"Art of Poetry, The" (Koch), **Supp. XV:** 182
"Art of Poetry, The" (McClatchy), **Supp. XII:** 262
"Art of Romare Bearden, The" (Ellison), **Retro. Supp. II:** 123
"Art of Storytelling, The" (Simpson), **Supp. IX:** 277
Art of Sylvia Plath, The (Newman), **Supp. I Part 2:** 527
Art of the Moving Picture, The (Lindsay), **Supp. I Part 2:** 376, 391–392, 394; **Supp. XVI:** 185
Art of the Novel (H. James), **Retro. Supp. I:** 227
"Art of Theodore Dreiser, The" (Bourne), **I:** 235
Art of the Personal Essay, The (Lopate, comp.), **Supp. XIII:** 280–281; **Supp. XVI:** 266
Art of the Self, The: Essays a Propos "Steps" (Kosinski), Supp. VII: 222
Art of the Wasted Day, The (Hampl), **Supp. XXII:** 85
Arts and Sciences (Goldbarth), **Supp. XII: 184–186**
Arts and Sciences: A Seventies Seduction (Mallon), **Supp. XIX:** 132, 135
"Art's Bread and Butter" (Benét), **Retro. Supp. I:** 108
Arvin, Newton, **I:** 259; **II:** 508; **Retro. Supp. I:** 19, 137
Asali, Muna, **Supp. XIII:** 121, 126
"As a Little Child" (Taggard), **Supp. XXII:** 272
Asbury, Herbert, **Supp. IV Part 1:** 353
Ascent of F6, The (Auden), **Supp. II Part 1:** 11, 13
Ascent to Truth, The (Merton), **Supp. VIII:** 208
Asch, Nathan, **Supp. XV:** 133, 134
Asch, Sholem, **IV:** 1, 9, 11, 14; **Retro. Supp. II:** 299
Ascherson, Neal, **Supp. XII:** 167
Ascher-Walsh, Rebecca, **Supp. XIX:** 54
"As Close as Breathing" (Jarman), **Supp. XVII:** 120
As David Danced (Bronk), **Supp. XXI:** 24
"As David Danced" (Bronk), **Supp. XXI:** 26
As Does New Hampshire and Other Poems (Sarton), **Supp. VIII:** 259
"As Evening Lays Dying" (Salinas), **Supp. XIII:** 319
"As Flowers Are" (Kunitz), **Supp. III Part 1:** 265
"Ash" (Sobin), **Supp. XVI:** 284–285
Ash, Nathan, **Supp. XXII:** 277
Ashbery, John, **Retro. Supp. I:** 313; **Supp. I Part 1:** 96; **Supp. III Part 1: 1–29; Supp. III Part 2:** 541; **Supp. IV Part 2:** 620; **Supp. VIII:** 272; **Supp. IX:** 52; **Supp. XI:** 139; **Supp. XIII:** 85; **Supp. XV:** 176, 177, 178, 188, 250; **Supp. XIX:** 40, 83; **Supp. XXI:** 227
"Ashes" (Lamott), **Supp. XX: 141**
"Ashes" (Levine), **Supp. V:** 188
"Ashes of the Beacon" (Bierce), **I:** 209
Ashes: Poems Old and New (Levine), **Supp. V:** 178, 188–189
Ashford, Margaret Mary (Daisy), **II:** 426
"Ash Wednesday" (Garrett), **Supp. VII:** 109–110

"Ash Wednesday" (Merton), **Supp. VIII:** 199
Ash Wednesday (T. S. Eliot), **I:** 570, 574–575, 578–579, 580, 582, 584, 585; **Retro. Supp. I:** 64
"Ash Wednesday" (T. S. Eliot), **Supp. IV Part 2:** 436
Asian American Authors (Hsu and Palubinskas, eds.), **Supp. X:** 292
Asian American Heritage: An Anthology of Prose and Poetry (Wand), **Supp. X:** 292
Asian Figures (Mervin), **Supp. III Part 1:** 341
Asian Journal of Thomas Merton, The (Merton), **Supp. VIII:** 196, 206, 208
"Asian Peace Offers Rejected without Publication" (R. Bly), **Supp. IV Part 1:** 61
"Asides on the Oboe" (Stevens), **Retro. Supp. I:** 305
"As I Ebb'd with the Ocean of Life" (Whitman), **IV:** 342, 345–346; **Retro. Supp. I:** 404, 405
As I Lay Dying (Faulkner), **II:** 60–61, 69, 73, 74; **IV:** 100; **Retro. Supp. I:** 75, 82, 84, 85, 86, 88, 89, 91, 92; **Supp. IV Part 1:** 47; **Supp. VIII:** 37, 178; **Supp. IX:** 99, 103, 251; **Supp. XIV:** 24
"As I Lay with My Head in Your Lap, Camerado" (Whitman), **IV:** 347
Asimov, Isaac, **Supp. IV Part 1:** 116; **Supp. XVI:** 122
Asinof, Eliot, **II:** 424
As I Remember It (PBS documentary), **Supp. XVIII:** 277
Asirvatham, Sandy, **Supp. XVI:** 249
"As Is the Daughter, So Is Her Mother" (Patchett), **Supp. XII:** 310
"As It Was in the Beginning" (Benét), **Supp. XI:** 56
"As I Walked Out One Evening" (Auden), **Supp. II Part 1:** 13; **Supp. XV:** 126; **Supp. XX: 138**
"As I Went Down by Havre de Grace" (Wylie), **Supp. I Part 2:** 723
Ask a Policeman (Hinojosa), **Supp. XIX: 110–111**
"Ask Me" (Stafford), **Supp. XI:** 326–327
Ask Me Tomorrow (Cozzens), **I:** 365–367, 379
Ask the Dust (Fante), **Supp. XI:** 159, 160, 166, **167–169,** 172, 173, 174
"Ask the Optimist!" (Saunders), **Supp. XIX:** 235
Ask Your Mama (Hughes), **Supp. I Part 1:** 339, 341–342
Ask Your Mama: 12 Moods for Jazz (Hughes), **Retro. Supp. I:** 210, 211
As Little Children (R. P. Smith), **Supp. XIV:** 333
"As One Put Drunk into the Packet Boat" (Ashbery), **Supp. III Part 1:** 18
"Asparagus" (Nelson), **Supp. XVIII:** 178
"Aspects of Robinson" (Kees), **Supp. XV:** 134
Aspects of the Novel (Forster), **Retro. Supp. I:** 232; **Supp. VIII:** 155; **Supp. XXI:** 233
"Aspen and the Stream, The" (Wilbur), **Supp. III Part 2:** 555, 556
Aspern Papers, The (James), **Supp. V:** 101, 102
"Aspern Papers, The" (James), **Retro. Supp. I:** 219, 227, 228
Asphalt Georgics (Carruth), **Supp. XVI:** 54
Asphalt Jungle (film, Huston), **Supp. XIII:** 174
"Asphodel" (Welty), **IV:** 265, 271
"Asphodel, That Greeny Flower" (W. C. Williams), **Retro. Supp. I:** 429
"Aspic and Buttermilk" (Olds), **Supp. X:** 213
Asquith, Herbert Henry, **Retro. Supp. I:** 59
"Ass" (Cisneros), **Supp. VII:** 67
Assante, Armand, **Supp. VIII:** 74
Assassin, The: A Play in Three Acts (Shaw), **Supp. XIX:** 248
Assassins, The (Oates), **Supp. II Part 2:** 512, 517–519
"Assault" (Millay), **III:** 130–131
"Assemblage of Husbands and Wives, An" (Lewis), **II:** 455–456
Assembly (O'Hara), **III:** 361
As She Climbed Across the Table (Lethem), **Supp. XVIII: 140–141,** 148
Assignment, Wildlife (LaBastille), **Supp. X: 99,** 104
"Assimiliation in Recent American Jewish Autobiographies" (Krupnick), **Supp. XVI:** 153
Assistant, The (Malamud), **Supp. I Part 2:** 427, 428, 429, 431, 435, 441–445, 451; **Supp. XVI:** 220
Assommoir, L' (Zola), II: 291; *III:* 318
Assorted Prose (Updike), **IV:** 215–216, 218; **Retro. Supp. I:** 317, 319, 327
Astaire, Adele, **Supp. XVI:** 187
*As They Were (*M. F. K. Fisher), **Supp. XVII:** 88, 89, 91
Astor, Mary, **Supp. IV Part 1:** 356; **Supp. XII:** 173
Astoria, or, Anecdotes of an Enterprise beyond the Rocky Mountains (Irving), **II:** 312
"Astounding News by Electric Express via Norfolk! The Atlantic Crossed in Three Days Signal Triumph of Mr. Monck's Flying-Machine . . ." (Poe), **III:** 413, 420
Astraea (Holmes), **III:** 82
Astro, Richard, **Supp. I Part 2:** 429, 445
"Astrological Fricassee" (H. Miller), **III:** 187
Astrophil and Stella (Sidney), **Supp. XIV:** 128
"As Weary Pilgrim" (Bradstreet), **Supp. I Part 1:** 103, 109, 122
As We Know (Ashbery), **Supp. III Part 1:** 9, 21–25
"As We Know" (Ashbery), **Supp. III Part 1:** 21–22
Aswell, Edward C., **IV:** 458, 459, 461
"Asylum, The" (Carruth), **Supp. XVI:** 48–49
"As You Like It" (Chopin), **Supp. I Part 1:** 217
As You Like It (Shakespeare), **Supp. I Part 1:** 308
"At a Bar in Charlotte Amalie" (Updike), **IV:** 214
"At a Lecture" (Brodsky), **Supp. VIII:** 33
"At a March against the Vietnam War" (R. Bly), **Supp. IV Part 1:** 61
"At a Reading" (McClatchy), **Supp. XII:** 256–257
"Atavism of John Tom Little Bear, The" (O. Henry), **Supp. II Part 1:** 410
"At Chênière Caminada" (Chopin), **Supp. I Part 1:** 220
"At Chinese Checkers" (Berryman), **I:** 182
Atchity, Kenneth John, **Supp. XI:** 227
"At Death's Window" (Lamott), **Supp. XX: 144**
At Eighty-Two (Sarton), **Supp. VIII:** 264
"At Every Gas Station There Are Mechanics" (Dunn), **Supp. XI:** 144
At Fault (Chopin), **Retro. Supp. II:** 57, 60, **62–63; Supp. I Part 1:** 207, 209–211, 220
"At Fifty" (Bronk), **Supp. XXI:** 31
At Heaven's Gate (Warren), **IV:** 243, 247–248, 251
Atheism Refuted: in a Discourse to Prove the Existence of God (Paine), **Supp. I Part 2:** 517
"Athénaïse" (Chopin), **Retro. Supp. II:** 66, 67; **Supp. I Part 1:** 219–220
Atherton, Gertrude, **I:** 199, 207–208
Athey, Jean L., **Supp. XI:** 184
At Home: Essays, 1982–1988 (Vidal), **Supp. IV Part 2:** 682, 687, 688
"At Home With" (column; Leland), **Supp. XV:** 69
"At Kino Viejo, Mexico" (Ríos), **Supp. IV Part 2:** 541
Atkinson, Brooks, **IV:** 288; **Supp. IV Part 2:** 683; **Supp. XIX:** 244
Atlantis (Doty), **Supp. XI:** 121, **126–129**
"Atlantis" (Doty), **Supp. XI:** 127–128
Atlas, James, **Supp. V:** 233; **Supp. XV:** 25
Atlas, The (Vollmann), **Supp. XVII:** 226, 227
Atlas Shrugged (Rand), **Supp. IV Part 2:** 517, 521, 523, 524–526, 528, 531
At Liberty (T. Williams), **IV:** 378
"At Melville's Tomb" (H. Crane), **I:** 393; **Retro. Supp. II:** 76, 78, 80, 82
"At Mother Teresa's" (Nye), **Supp. XIII:** 276
"At Nightfall" (Kooser), **Supp. XIX:** 122–123
At Night the Salmon Move (Carver), **Supp. III Part 1:** 142
At Night the States (Notley), **Supp. XXII:** 224, 231–232
"At night the states" (Notley), **Supp. XXII:** 232
"At North Farm" (Ashbery), **Supp. III Part 1:** 1–2
At Paradise Gate (Smiley), **Supp. VI:** 292, **293–294**
"At Paso Rojo" (Bowles), **Supp. IV Part 1:** 87

At Play in the Fields of the Lord (Matthiessen), **Supp. V:** 199, 202, 204–206, 212
"At Play in the Paradise of Bombs" (Sanders), **Supp. XVI:** 272–273, 274, 277
"At Pleasure By" (Pinsky), **Supp. VI:** 245
At Risk (Hoffman), **Supp. X:** 87
"At Sea" (Hemingway), **II:** 258
"At Shaft 11" (Dunbar), **Supp. II Part 1:** 212
"At Slim's River" (Haines), **Supp. XII:** 208–209
"At St. Croix" (Dubus), **Supp. VII:** 83, 87
At Sundown (Whittier), **Supp. I Part 2:** 704
"At Sunset" (Simic), **Supp. VIII:** 282
Attaway, William, **Supp. XXI:** 264
Attebery, Brian, **Supp. IV Part 1:** 101
Attendant, The (Bronk), **Supp. XXI:** 24
"Attendant, The" (Bronk), **Supp. XXI:** 26
"At That Time, or The History of a Joke" (Paley), **Supp. VI:** 229–230
At the Back of the North Wind (Macdonald), **Supp. XIII:** 75
"At the Birth of an Age" (Jeffers), **Supp. II Part 2:** 432
"At the Bomb Testing Site" (Stafford), **Supp. XI:** 317–318, 321, 323
At the Bottom of the River (Kincaid), **Supp. VII:** 182–184, 185
"At the 'Cadian Ball" (Chopin), **Retro. Supp. II:** 64, 65, 68
"At the Cancer Clinic" (Kooser), **Supp. XIX:** 127
"At the Chelton-Pulver Game" (Auchincloss), **Supp. IV Part 1:** 27
"At the Drugstore" (Taylor), **Supp. V:** 323
At the Edge of the Body (Jong), **Supp. V:** 115, 130
"At the End of the Curse, a Blessing" (Verducci), **Supp. XXII:** 209
At the End of the Open Road (Simpson), **Supp. IX:** 265, 269, **271–273,** 277
At the End of This Summer: Poems 1948–1954, **Supp. XII:** 211
"At the End of War" (Eberhart), **I:** 522–523
"At the Executed Murderer's Grave" (Wright), **Supp. III Part 2:** 595, 597
"At the Fishhouses" (Bishop), **Retro. Supp. II:** 45; **Supp. I Part 1:** 90, 92
At the Gates of the Animal Kingdom (Hempel), **Supp. XXI:** 115, **122–124**
"At the Grave of My Guardian Angel: St. Louis Cemetery, New Orleans" (Levis), **Supp. XI:** 268–269
"At the Gym" (Doty), **Supp. XI:** 135
"At the Indian Store" (McCarriston), **Supp. XIV:** 271
"At the Lake" (Oliver), **Supp. VII:** 244
"At the Landing" (Welty), **IV:** 265–266; **Retro. Supp. I:** 348
"At the Last" (Bynner), **Supp. XV:** 44
"At the Last Rites for Two Hot Rodders" (X. J. Kennedy), **Supp. XV:** 166
"At the Mountains of Madness" (Lovecraft), **Supp. XXII:** 58
"At the Owl Club, North Gulfport, Mississippi, 1950" (Trethewey), **Supp. XXI:** 249
"At the Premiere" (Keillor), **Supp. XVI:** 167
At the Rendezvous of Victory (C. L. R. James), **Supp. XXI:** 172
At the Root of Stars (Barnes), **Supp. III Part 1:** 34
"At the Slackening of the Tide" (Wright), **Supp. III Part 2:** 597
"At the Tomb of Walt Whitman" (Kunitz), **Supp. III Part 1:** 262
"At the Tourist Centre in Boston" (Atwood), **Supp. XIII:** 33
"At the Town Dump" (Kenyon), **Supp. VII:** 167
"At the Worcester Museum" (Pinsky), **Supp. VI:** 251
"At the Zoo in Spain" (Major), **Supp. XXII:** 182
"Atticus Finch and the Mad Dog: Harper Lee's *To Kill a Mockingbird*" (Jones), **Supp. VIII:** 128
"Atticus Finch—Right and Wrong" (Freedman), **Supp. VIII:** 127–128
"Attic Which Is Desire, The" (W. C. Williams), **Retro. Supp. I:** 422
"At Tikal" (Bronk), **Supp. XXI: 28–29**
"At Times in Flight: A Parable" (H. Roth), **Supp. IX:** 234
Attitudes toward History (Burke), **I:** 274
Atwan, Robert, **Supp. XVI:** 273, 277
At Weddings and Wakes (McDermott), **Supp. XVIII:** 155, **160–162,** 166
"At White River" (Haines), **Supp. XII:** 208–209
Atwood, Margaret, **Supp. IV Part 1:** 252; **Supp. V:** 119; **Supp. XI:** 317; **Supp. XIII: 19–39,** 291, 306; **Supp. XXI:** 39, 42
"Atwood's Gorgon Touch" (Davey), **Supp. XIII:** 33
"Aubade" (McCarriston), **Supp. XIV:** 271
"Aubade: November" (McCarriston), **Supp. XIV:** 261–262
"Aubade of an Early Homo Sapiens" (C. Frost), **Supp. XV:** 97–98
"Aubade: Opal and Silver" (Doty), **Supp. XI:** 129
"Au Bal Musette" (Van Vechten), **Supp. II Part 2:** 735
Auchincloss, Hugh D., **Supp. IV Part 2:** 679
Auchincloss, Louis, **I:** 375; **III:** 66; **Retro. Supp. I:** 370, 373; **Supp. IV Part 1: 21–38**
"Auction" (Simic), **Supp. VIII:** 278
"Auction, The" (Crane), **I:** 411
"Auction Model 1934" (Z. Fitzgerald), **Supp. IX:** 61
Auden, W. H., **I:** 71, 381, 539; **II:** 367, 368, 371, 376, 586; **III:** 17, 134, 269, 271, 292, 476–477, 504, 527, 530, 542, 615; **IV:** 136, 138, 240, 430; **Retro. Supp. I:** 430; **Retro. Supp. II:** 183, 242, 244, 323; **Supp. I Part 1:** 270; **Supp. I Part 2:** 552, 610; **Supp. II Part 1: 1–28; Supp. III Part 1:** 2, 3, 14, 26, 60, 61, 64, 341; **Supp. III Part 2:** 591, 595; **Supp. IV Part 1:** 79, 84, 136, 225, 302, 313; **Supp. IV Part 2:** 440, 465; **Supp. V:** 337; **Supp. VIII:** 19, 21, 22, 23, 30, 32, 155, 190; **Supp. IX:** 94, 287, 288; **Supp. X:** 35, 57, 59, 115–116, 117, 118–119; **Supp. XI:** 243, 244; **Supp. XII:** 253, 264–265, 266, 269–270; **Supp. XIV:** 156, 158, 160, 162, 163; **Supp. XV:** 74, 117–118, 139, 144, 186; **Supp. XIX:** 147, 151; **Supp. XX: 138; Supp. XXI:** 60, 98
"Auden's OED" (McClatchy), **Supp. XII:** 264–265
"Audition" (Alvarez), **Supp. VII:** 10
Audubon, John James, **III:** 210; **IV:** 265; **Supp. IX:** 171; **Supp. XVI: 1–14**
Audubon, John Woodhouse, **Supp. XVI:** 10
Audubon, Maria Rebecca, **Supp. XVI:** 11
Audubon, Victor Gifford, **Supp. XVI:** 10
Audubon and His Journals (M. Audubon, ed.), **Supp. XVI:** 11, 12
Audubon Reader, The: The Best Writings of John James Audubon (Sanders, ed.), **Supp. XVI:** 269
Auer, Jane. *See* Bowles, Jane
Auerbach, Eric, **III:** 453
Auerbach, Nina, **Supp. I Part 1:** 40
"August" (Oliver), **Supp. VII:** 235
"August" (Rich), **Supp. I Part 2:** 564
"August 1968" (Auden), **Supp. II Part 1:** 25
"August Darks, The" (Clampitt), **Supp. IX:** 43, **50–51,** 52
Augustine, Saint, **I:** 279, 290; **II:** 537; **III:** 259, 270, 292, 300; **IV:** 69, 126; **Retro. Supp. I:** 247; **Supp. VIII:** 203; **Supp. XI:** 245; **Supp. XIII:** 89; **Supp. XXI:** 83; **Supp. XXII:** 92–93
August Snow (Price), **Supp. VI:** 264
"Au Jardin" (Pound), **III:** 465–466
Aunt Carmen's Book of Practical Saints (Mora), **Supp. XIII: 227–229**
"Aunt Cynthy Dallett" (Jewett), **II:** 393
"Aunt Gladys" (Karr), **Supp. XI:** 241
"Aunt Granny Lith" (Offutt), **Supp. XIX:** 165, 166
"Aunties, The" (Lamott), **Supp. XX: 141**
"Aunt Imogen" (Robinson), **III:** 521
"Aunt Jemima of the Ocean Waves" (Hayden), **Supp. II Part 1:** 368, 379
"Aunt Jennifer's Tigers" (Rich), **Supp. XV:** 252
Aunt Jo's Scrapbooks (Alcott), **Supp. I Part 1:** 43
"Aunt Mary" (Oliver), **Supp. VII:** 232
"Aunt Mary" (Stowe), **Supp. I Part 2:** 587
"Aunt Moon's Young Man" (Hogan), **Supp. IV Part 1:** 400
"Aunt Rectita's Good Friday" (X. J. Kennedy), **Supp. XV:** 166
"Aunt Sarah" (Lowell), **II:** 554
"Aunt Sue's Stories" (Hughes), **Retro. Supp. I:** 197, 199

"Aunt Violet's Canadian Honeymoon/ 1932" (Shields), **Supp. VII:** 311
"Aunt Violet's Things" (Shields), **Supp. VII:** 311–312
"Aurelia: Moon Jellies" (Mora), **Supp. XIII:** 224
"Aurelio" (Di Piero), **Supp. XIX:** 38
Aurora 7 (Mallon), **Supp. XIX:** 132, **135–136**
Aurora Leigh (E. Browning), **Retro. Supp. I:** 33; **Supp. XI:** 197
Aurora Means Dawn (Sanders), **Supp. XVI:** 268
Auroras of Autumn, The (Stevens), **Retro. Supp. I:** 297, 300, **309–312**
"Auroras of Autumn, The" (Stevens), **Retro. Supp. I:** 311, 312; **Supp. III Part 1:** 12
Auschwitz: the Nazis and the "Final Solution" (television documentary), Supp. XVII: 40
Auslander, Joseph, **Supp. XIV:** 120
"Auspex" (Frost), **Retro. Supp. I:** 122
"Auspex" (Lowell), **Supp. I Part 2:** 424
Austen, Jane, **I:** 130, 339, 375, 378; **II:** 272, 278, 287, 568–569, 577; **IV:** 8; **Retro. Supp. I:** 354; **Supp. I Part 1:** 267; **Supp. I Part 2:** 656, 715; **Supp. IV Part 1:** 300; **Supp. VIII:** 125, 167; **Supp. IX:** 128; **Supp. XII:** 310; **Supp. XV:** 338; **Supp. XX:** **108;** **Supp. XXII:** 206
Auster, Paul, **Supp. XII:** **21–39;** **Supp. XIV:** 292; **Supp. XXI:** 20
Austerities (Simic), **Supp. VIII:** **276–278,** 283
"Austerities" (Simic), **Supp. VIII:** 277
Austin, Mary Hunter, **Retro. Supp. I:** 7; **Supp. IV Part 2:** 503; **Supp. X:** 29; **Supp. XIII:** 154
"Authentic Unconscious, The" (Trilling), **Supp. III Part 2:** 512
Author and Agent: Eudora Welty and Diarmuid Russell (Kreyling), **Retro. Supp. I:** 342, 345, 347, 349–350
"Author at Sixty, The" (Wilson), **IV:** 426
"Author of 'Beltraffio,' The" (James), **Retro. Supp. I:** 227
"Author's Explanation, The" (Larsen), **Supp. XVIII:** 131
"Author's House" (Fitzgerald), **Retro. Supp. I:** 98
"Author's Reflections, An: Willie Loman, Walter Younger, and He Who Must Live" (Hansberry), **Supp. IV Part 1:** 370
"Author to Her Book, The" (Bradstreet), **Supp. I Part 1:** 119; **Supp. V:** 117–118; **Supp. XV:** 125–126
"Autobiographical Note" (H. Miller), **III:** 174–175
"Autobiographical Notes" (Baldwin), **Supp. I Part 1:** 54
"Autobiographical Notes" (Holmes), **Supp. I Part 1:** 301
"Autobiographic Chapter, An" (Bourne), **I:** 236
Autobiography (Franklin), **II:** 102, 103, 108, 121–122, 302
Autobiography (James), **I:** 462
"Autobiography" (MacLeish), **III:** 20
Autobiography (Van Buren), **III:** 473
Autobiography (W. C. Williams), **Supp. I Part 1:** 254
Autobiography (Zukofsky), **Supp. III Part 2:** 627
"Autobiography in the Shape of a Book Review" (Bynner), **Supp. XV:** 40
"Autobiography of a Confluence, The" (Gunn Allen), **Supp. IV Part 1:** 321
Autobiography of Alice B. Toklas, The (Stein), **IV:** 26, 30, 35, 43; **Supp. IV Part 1:** 11, 81
Autobiography of an Ex-Colored Man, The (Johnson), **Supp. II Part 1:** 33, 194; **Supp. XVIII:** 127; **Supp. XXII:** 7
Autobiography of a Schizophrenic Girl (Renée), **Supp. XVI:** 64, 66
Autobiography of a Thief, The (Hapgood), **Supp. XVII:** 96, 101–102
Autobiography of Benjamin Franklin (Franklin), **Supp. IV Part 1:** 5
Autobiography of LeRoi Jones, The (Baraka), **Retro. Supp. I:** 411
Autobiography of Malcolm X (Little), **Supp. I Part 1:** 66; **Supp. X:** 27; **Supp. XIII:** 264; **Supp. XXII:** 95
Autobiography of Mark Twain, The (Twain), **IV:** 209
Autobiography of My Mother, The (Kincaid), **Supp. VII:** 182, 188–190, 191, 192, 193
Autobiography of Red: A Novel in Verse (Carson), **Supp. XII:** 97, **106–110**
Autobiography of Upton Sinclair, The (Sinclair), **Supp. V:** 276, 282
Autobiography of W. E. B. Du Bois, The (Du Bois), **Supp. II Part 1:** 159, 186
Autobiography of William Carlos Williams, The (W. C. Williams), **Retro. Supp. I:** 51, 428
Autocrat of the Breakfast-Table, The (Holmes), **Supp. I Part 1:** 306–307
"Automatic Gate, The" (Southern), **Supp. XI:** 294
"Automotive Passacaglia" (H. Miller), **III:** 186
"Autopsy Room, The" (Carver), **Supp. III Part 1:** 137
"Auto Wreck" (Shapiro), **Supp. II Part 2:** 706
"Autre Temps" (Wharton), **IV:** 320, 324
"Autumn, Mist" (Hull), **Supp. XXI:** 133
"Autumn Afternoon" (Farrell), **II:** 45
"Autumnal" (Eberhart), **I:** 540–541
"Autumn Begins in Martins Ferry, Ohio" (Wright), **Supp. III Part 2:** 599
"Autumn Courtship, An" (Caldwell), **I:** 309
"Autumn Equinox" (Skloot), **Supp. XX:** **202**
Autumn Garden, The (Hellman), **Supp. I Part 1:** 285–286, 290
"Autumn Garden, The: Mechanics and Dialectics" (Felheim), **Supp. I Part 1:** 297
"Autumn Holiday, An" (Jewett), **II:** 391; **Retro. Supp. II:** 140–141
"Autumn Musings" (Harte), **Supp. II Part 1:** 336
Autumn Spring (Pickering), **Supp. XXI:** 204–205, 206
"Autumn Within" (Longfellow), **II:** 499
"Autumn Woods" (Bryant), **Supp. I Part 1:** 164
"Au Vieux Jardin" (Aldington), **Supp. I Part 1:** 257
"Aux Imagistes" (W. C. Williams), **Supp. I Part 1:** 266
Avakian, Aram, **Supp. XI:** 294, 295, 309
"Ave Atque Vale" (Bynner), Supp. XV: 49
Avedon, Richard, **Supp. I Part 1:** 58; **Supp. V:** 194; **Supp. X:** 15
Aveling, Edward, **Supp. XVI:** 85
"Avenue" (Pinsky), **Supp. VI:** 248
Avenue Bearing the Initial of Christ into the New World: Poems 1946–1964 (Kinnell), **Supp. III Part 1:** 235, 239–241
"Avenue of the Americas" (Simic), **Supp. VIII:** 278
"Average Torture" (Karr), **Supp. XI:** 243
Avery, George C., **Supp. XX:** **84**
Avery, John, **Supp. I Part 1:** 153
"Avey" (Toomer), **Supp. IX:** 317
Avon's Harvest (Robinson), **III:** 510
Awake and Sing! (Odets), **Supp. II Part 2:** 530, 531, 536–538, 550; **Supp. IV Part 2:** 587
Awakening, The (Chopin), **Retro. Supp. I:** 10; **Retro. Supp. II:** 57, 59, 60, 67, **68–71,** 73; **Supp. I Part 1:** 200, 201, 202, 211, 220–225; **Supp. V:** 304; **Supp. VIII:** 198; **Supp. XII:** 170
Awakening Land, The (Richter), **Supp. XVIII:** 207, 215
Awful Rowing Toward God, The (Sexton), **Supp. II Part 2:** 694–696
Awiakta, Marilou, **Supp. IV Part 1:** 319, 335
Awkward Age, The (James), **II:** 332; **Retro. Supp. I:** 229, **230–231**
Axe Handles (Snyder), **Supp. VIII:** **303–305**
Axel's Castle: A Study in the Imaginative Literature of 1870 to 1930 (Wilson), **I:** 185; **II:** 577; **IV:** 428, 431, 438, 439, 443; **Supp. VIII:** 101
"Ax-Helve, The" (Frost), **Retro. Supp. I:** 133
Azikewe, Nnamdi, **Supp. IV Part 1:** 361
"Aztec Angel" (Salinas), **Supp. XIII:** 314
Aztec Treasure House, The: New and Selected Essays (Connell), **Supp. XIV:** 80, 97

Babbitt (Lewis), **II:** 442, 443–445, 446, 447, 449; **III:** 63–64, 394; **IV:** 326
Babbitt, Irving, **I:** 247; **II:** 456; **III:** 315, 461, 613; **IV:** 439; **Retro. Supp. I:** 55; **Supp. I Part 2:** 423
Babcock, Elisha, **Supp. II Part 1:** 69
Babel, Isaac, **IV:** 1; **Supp. IX:** 260; **Supp. XII:** 308–309; **Supp. XVII:** 41
Babel, Isaak, **Supp. XIV:** 83, 84
Babel to Byzantium (Dickey), **Supp. IV Part 1:** 177, 185

Babeuf, François, **Supp. I Part 2:** 518
"Babies, The" (Strand), **Supp. IV Part 2:** 625
Babouk (Endore), **Supp. XVII: 56–57,** 61, 64
Baby, Come on Inside (Wagoner), **Supp. IX: 335**
"Baby, The" (Barthelme), **Supp. IV Part 1:** 49
Baby Doll (T. Williams), **IV:** 383, 386, 387, 389, 395
"Baby Face" (Sandburg), **III:** 584
"Babylon Revisited" (Fitzgerald), **II:** 95; **Retro. Supp. I:** 109
"Baby or the Botticelli, The" (Gass), **Supp. VI:** 92
"Baby Pictures of Famous Dictators" (Simic), **Supp. VIII:** 276
"Baby's Breath" (Bambara), **Supp. XI:** 15, 16
"Babysitter, The" (Coover), **Supp. V:** 43–44
"Baby Villon" (Levine), **Supp. V:** 182
Bacall, Lauren, **Supp. IV Part 1:** 130
"Baccalaureate" (MacLeish), **III:** 4
Bacchae, The (Euripides), **Supp. VIII:** 182
Bach, Johann Sebastian, **Supp. I Part 1:** 363; **Supp. III Part 2:** 611, 612, 619
Bachardy, Don, **Supp. XIV:** 166, 170, 172, 173
Bache, Richard, **Supp. I Part 2:** 504
Bachelard, Gaston, **Supp. XIII:** 225; **Supp. XVI:** 292
"Bachelor Girl, The" (Boyce), **Supp. XXI:** 3
Bachelor Girls (Wasserstein), **Supp. XV: 327–328,** 332
Bachman, John, **Supp. XVI:** 10, 11
Bachmann, Ingeborg, **Supp. IV Part 1:** 310; **Supp. VIII:** 272
Bachofen, J. J., **Supp. I Part 2:** 560, 567
Back Bog Beast Bait (Shepard), **Supp. III Part 2:** 437, 438
Backbone (C. Bly), **Supp. XVI: 34–36,** 37, 40, 41
Back Country, The (Snyder), **Supp. VIII: 296–299**
"Back from the Argentine" (Leopold), **Supp. XIV:** 186
"Background with Revolutionaries" (MacLeish), **III:** 14–15
"Back in the Saddle Again" (Swados), **Supp. XIX:** 259
Back in the World (Wolff), **Supp. VII:** 344, 345
Backis, Charles, **Supp. XXI:** 195
"Backlash Blues, The" (Hughes), **Supp. I Part 1:** 343
"Backlash of Kindness, A" (Nye), **Supp. XIII:** 285, 286
"Backslider, The" (R. Fisher), **Supp. XIX:** 70, 71
"Back Street Guy" (Halliday), **Supp. XIX:** 88
Back to China (Fiedler), **Supp. XIII: 102–103**
Back to Methuselah (Shaw), **IV:** 64
"Backwacking: A Plea to the Senator" (Ellison), **Retro. Supp. II:** 126; **Supp. II Part 1:** 248
Backward Glance, A (Wharton), **Retro. Supp. I:** 360, 363, 366, 378, 380, 382; **Supp. XX: 229**
"Backward Glance o'er Travel'd Roads, A" (Whitman), **IV:** 348
Bacon, Francis, **II:** 1, 8, 11, 15–16, 111; **III:** 284; **Retro. Supp. I:** 247; **Supp. I Part 1:** 310; **Supp. I Part 2:** 388; **Supp. IX:** 104; **Supp. XIV:** 22, 210
Bacon, Helen, **Supp. X:** 57
Bacon, Katy, **Supp. XXII:** 207
Bacon, Leonard, **II:** 530; **Supp. XXII:** 273
Bacon, Roger, **IV:** 69
"Bacterial War, The" (Nemerov), **III:** 272
Bad and the Beautiful, The (film), **Supp. XVIII:** 250
Bad Boy Brawly Brown (Mosley), **Supp. XIII:** 237, 239, 240–241
Bad Boys (Cisneros), **Supp. VII:** 58
"Bad Dream" (Taylor), **Supp. V:** 320
Badè, William Frederic, **Supp. IX:** 178
"Bad Fisherman, The" (Wagoner), **Supp. IX:** 328
Bad for Each Other (film), **Supp. XIII:** 174
"Badger" (Clare), **II:** 387
Badger, A. G., **Supp. I Part 1:** 356
Bad Government and Silly Literature (C. Bly), **Supp. XVI:** 37, 38, 40
Badlands (film; Malick), **Supp. XV:** 351
"Bad Lay" (McCarriston), **Supp. XIV:** 267
Badley, Linda, **Supp. V:** 148
Bad Man, A (Elkin), **Supp. VI: 47**
Bad Man Ballad (Sanders), **Supp. XVI:** 268
Bad Man Blues: A Portable George Garrett (Garrett), **Supp. VII:** 111
"Bad Music, The" (Jarrell), **II:** 369
"Bad People" (Halliday), **Supp. XIX:** 90, 91
"Bad Summer on K2, A" (Krakauer and Child), **Supp. XVIII:** 107, 108
"Bad Woman, A" (Fante), **Supp. XI:** 165
Baeck, Leo, **Supp. V:** 260
Baecker, Diann L., **Supp. VIII:** 128
Baer, William, **Supp. XIII:** 112, 118, 129
Baez, Joan, **Supp. IV Part 1:** 200; **Supp. VIII:** 200, 202; **Supp. XVIII:** 24, 25–26, 27
Bag of Bones (King), **Supp. V:** 139, 148, 151
"Bagpipe Music" (MacNeice), **Supp. X:** 117
"Bahá'í Faith: Only Church in World That Does Not Discriminate" (Locke), **Supp. XIV:** 200
Bahá'u'lláh, **Supp. XX: 117, 121, 122**
"Bahá'u'lláh in the Garden of Ridwan" (Hayden), **Supp. II Part 1:** 370, 378
Bahr, David, **Supp. XV:** 66
Bahr, Thomas, **Supp. XXII:** 206, 214
"Bailbondsman, The" (Elkin), **Supp. VI:** 49, **50,** 58
Bailey, Gamaliel, **Supp. I Part 2:** 587, 590
Bailey, Peter, **Supp. XVI:** 69
Bailey, William, **Supp. IV Part 2:** 631, 634
Bailey's Café (Naylor), **Supp. VIII: 226–228**
Bailyn, Bernard, **Supp. I Part 2:** 484, 506
Bair, Deirdre, **Supp. X:** 181, 186, 187, 188, 192, 194, 195, 196, 197
Baird, Linnett, **Supp. XII:** 299
Baird, Peggy, **I:** 385, 401
Bakan, David, **I:** 59
Baker, Carlos, **II:** 259
Baker, Chet, **Supp. XXI:** 131
Baker, David, **Supp. IX:** 298; **Supp. XI:** 121, 142, 153; **Supp. XII:** 175, 191–192; **Supp. XIX:** 115
Baker, George Pierce, **III:** 387; **IV:** 453, 455
Baker, Gladys, **Supp. XIV:** 121
Baker, Houston, **Supp. XXII:** 6
Baker, Houston A., Jr., **Retro. Supp. II:** 121; **Supp. IV Part 1:** 365; **Supp. X:** 324
Baker, Katherine, **Supp. XX: 69**
Baker, Kevin, **Supp. XIV:** 96
Baker, Mabel, **Supp. XVIII:** 259, 263, 266–267, 269
Baker, Nicholson, **Supp. XIII: 41–57**
Baker, Robert, **Supp. XVI:** 288, 290
Bakerman, Jane S., **Supp. IV Part 2:** 468
Bakhtin, Mikhail, **Retro. Supp. II:** 273; **Supp. IV Part 1:** 301; **Supp. X:** 120, 239; **Supp. XXII:** 259
Bakst, Léon, **Supp. IX:** 66
Bakunin, Mikhail Aleksandrovich, **IV:** 429
Balaban, John, **Supp. XIX:** 281
Balakian, Jan, **Supp. XV:** 327
"Balance" (Bierds), **Supp. XVII:** 31
"Balance" (Nelson), **Supp. XVIII:** 174–175
Balbo, Ned, **Supp. XVII:** 120; **Supp. XIX:** 161
Balbuena, Bernado de, **Supp. V:** 11
Balch, Emily Greene, **Supp. I Part 1:** 25
Balcony, The (Genet), **I:** 84
Bald Soprano, The (Ionesco), **I:** 74
Baldwin, David, **Supp. I Part 1:** 47, 48, 49, 50, 51, 54, 65, 66
Baldwin, James, **Retro. Supp. II: 1–17; Supp. I Part 1: 47–71,** 337, 341; **Supp. II Part 1:** 40; **Supp. III Part 1:** 125; **Supp. IV Part 1:** 1, 10, 11, 163, 369; **Supp. V:** 201; **Supp. VIII:** 88, 198, 235, 349; **Supp. X:** 136, 324; **Supp. XI:** 288, 294; **Supp. XIII:** 46, 111, 181, 186, 294; **Supp. XIV:** 54, 71, 73, 306; **Supp. XVI:** 135, 141, 143; **Supp. XVIII:** 25; **Supp. XX: 147; Supp. XXI:** 245
Baldwin, Samuel, **Supp. I Part 1:** 48
Balitas, Vincent D., **Supp. XVI:** 222
Balkian, Nona, **Supp. XI:** 230
Balkun, Mary McAleer, **Supp. XX: 281**
Ball, Gordon, **Supp. XIV:** 148
Ball, John, **Supp. XV:** 202
"Ballad: Between the Box Cars" (Warren), **IV:** 245
"Ballade" (MacLeish), **III:** 4

"Ballade at Thirty-Five" (Parker), **Supp. IX:** 192
"Ballade for the Duke of Orléans" (Wilbur), **Supp. III Part 2:** 556
"Ballade of Broken Flutes, The" (Robinson), **III:** 505
"Ballade of Meaty Inversions" (White), **Supp. I Part 2:** 676
"Ballad of a Thin Man" (song, Dylan), **Supp. XVIII:** 30, 31
"Ballad of Aunt Geneva, The" (Nelson), **Supp. XVIII:** 175
"Ballad of Billie Potts, The" (Warren), **IV:** 241–242, 243, 253
"Ballad of Carmilhan, The" (Longfellow), **II:** 505
"ballad of chocolate Mabbie, the" (Brooks), **Supp. IV Part 1:** 15
"Ballad of Dead Ladies, The" (Villon), **Retro. Supp. I:** 286
Ballad of Dingus Magee, The (Markson), **Supp. XVII:** 139, 141
"Ballad of East and West, The" (Kipling), **Supp. IX:** 246; **Supp. XX: 23**
"Ballad of Jesse Neighbours, The" (Humphrey), **Supp. IX:** 100
"Ballad of Jesus of Nazareth, A" (Masters), **Supp. I Part 2:** 459
"Ballad of John Cable and Three Gentlemen" (Merwin), **Supp. III Part 1:** 342
"Ballad of Larry and Club" (Jarman), **Supp. XVII:** 115
"Ballad of Nat Turner, The" (Hayden), **Supp. II Part 1:** 378
"Ballad of Pearl May Lee, The" (Brooks), **Supp. III Part 1:** 74, 75
Ballad of Remembrance, A (Hayden), **Supp. II Part 1:** 367
"Ballad of Remembrance, A" (Hayden), **Supp. II Part 1:** 368, 372, 373
"Ballad of Ruby, The" (Sarton), **Supp. VIII:** 259–260
"Ballad of San Isidro, The" (Espaillat), **Supp. XXI:** 108
"Ballad of Sue Ellen Westerfield, The" (Hayden), **Supp. II Part 1:** 364
Ballad of the Brown Girl, The (Cullen), **Supp. IV Part 1:** 167, 168, 169–170, 173
"Ballad of the Brown Girl, The" (Cullen), **Supp. IV Part 1:** 168
"Ballad of the Children of the Czar, The" (Schwartz), **Supp. II Part 2:** 649
"Ballad of the Girl Whose Name Is Mud" (Hughes), **Retro. Supp. I:** 205
"Ballad of the Goodly Fere", **III:** 458
"Ballad of the Harp-Weaver" (Millay), **III:** 135
"Ballad of the Sad Cafe, The" (McCullers), **II:** 586, 587, 588, 592, 595, 596–600, 604, 605, 606
"Ballad of the Sixties" (Sarton), **Supp. VIII:** 259
"Ballad of Trees and the Master, A" (Lanier), **Supp. I Part 1:** 370
"Ballad of Typical Lovers" (Taggard), **Supp. XXII:** 277
"Ballad of William Sycamore, The" (Benét), **Supp. XI:** 44, 47
Ballads and Other Poems (Longfellow), **II:** 489; **III:** 412, 422; **Retro. Supp. II:** 157, 168
Ballads for Sale (Lowell), **II:** 527
"Ballads of Lenin" (Hughes), **Supp. I Part 1:** 331
Ballantyne, Sheila, **Supp. V:** 70
Ballard, J. G., **Supp. XVI:** 123, 124; **Supp. XVIII:** 136
Ballard, Josephine. *See* McMurtry, Josephine
"Ballena" (Mora), **Supp. XIII:** 224
"Ballet in Numbers for Mary Ellen, A" (Karr), **Supp. XI:** 241
"Ballet of a Buffoon, The" (Sexton), **Supp. II Part 2:** 693
"Ballet of the Fifth Year, The" (Schwartz), **Supp. II Part 2:** 650
Ball Four (Bouton), **Supp. XX: 274**
"Ball Game, The" (Creeley), **Supp. IV Part 1:** 140
Ballistics (Collins), **Supp. XXI:** 57, 65
"Ballistics" (Collins), **Supp. XXI:** 65
"Balloon Hoax, The" (Poe), **III:** 413, 420
"Balm of Recognition, The: Rectifying Wrongs through Generations" (E. Hoffman, lecture), **Supp. XVI:** 155
Balo (Toomer), **Supp. III Part 2:** 484
Balsan, Consuelo, **IV:** 313–314
Balthus, **Supp. IV Part 2:** 623
Balthus Poems, The (Dobyns), **Supp. XIII:** 87
Baltimore, Lord, **I:** 132
Balzac, Honoré de, **I:** 103, 123, 339, 376, 474, 485, 499, 509, 518; **II:** 307, 322, 324, 328, 336, 337; **III:** 61, 174, 184, 320, 382; **IV:** 192; **Retro. Supp. I:** 91, 217, 218, 235; **Retro. Supp. II:** 93; **Supp. I Part 2:** 647; **Supp. XVI:** 72
Bambara, Toni Cade, **Supp. XI: 1–23**
Banana Bottom (McKay), **Supp. X:** 132, **139–140**
Bananas (film; Allen), **Supp. XV:** 3, 4
Bancal, Jean, **Supp. I Part 2:** 514
Bancroft, George, **I:** 544; **Supp. I Part 2:** 479; **Supp. XXII:** 33
Band, Millen, **Supp. XVIII:** 238
Bandaged Nude, The (Ryan as Finnegan), **Supp. XVIII:** 233, **235–236**
Bandbox (Mallon), **Supp. XIX:** 132, 143
Band of Angels (Warren), **IV:** 245, 254–255
Bandung Files (television series), **Supp. XXI:** 170
Bang the Drum Slowly (Harris), **II:** 424–425
Banjo: A Story without a Plot (McKay), **Supp. X:** 132, **138–139**
"Banjo Song, A" (Dunbar), **Supp. II Part 1:** 197
Bankhead, Tallulah, **IV:** 357; **Supp. IV Part 2:** 574
"Banking Potatoes" (Komunyakaa), **Supp. XIII:** 126
"Bank of England Restriction, The" (Adams), **I:** 4
Banks, Joanne Trautmann, **Supp. XIII:** 297
Banks, Russell, **Supp. V: 1–19,** 227; **Supp. IX:** 153; **Supp. X:** 85; **Supp. XI:** 178; **Supp. XII:** 295, 309, 343; **Supp. XX: 90**
"Banned Poem" (Nye), **Supp. XIII:** 282
Bannon, Barbara, **Supp. XI:** 228
"Banyan" (Swenson), **Supp. IV Part 2:** 651, 652
"Baptism" (Olsen). *See* "O Yes" (Olsen)
"Baptism" (Trethewey), **Supp. XXI:** 246
Baptism, The (Baraka), **Supp. II Part 1:** 40, 41–42, 43
Baptism of Desire (Erdrich), **Supp. IV Part 1:** 259
Barabtarlo, Gennady, **Retro. Supp. I:** 278
Baraka, Imamu Amiri (LeRoi Jones), **Retro. Supp. I:** 411; **Retro. Supp. II:** 280; **Supp. I Part 1:** 63; **Supp. II Part 1: 29–63,** 247, 250; **Supp. III Part 1:** 83; **Supp. IV Part 1:** 169, 244, 369; **Supp. VIII:** 295, 329, 330, 332; **Supp. X:** 324, 328; **Supp. XIII:** 94; **Supp. XIV:** 125, 144; **Supp. XXI:** 172, 227, 228
"Bar at the Andover Inn, The" (Matthews), **Supp. IX:** 168
"Barbados" (Marshall), **Supp. XI:** 281
"Barbara Frietchie" (Whittier), **Supp. I Part 2:** 695–696
Barbarella (film), **Supp. XI:** 293, **307–308**
"Barbarian Status of Women, The" (Veblen), **Supp. I Part 2:** 636–637
Barbarous Coast, The (Macdonald), **Supp. IV Part 2:** 472, 474
Barbary Shore (Mailer), **III:** 27, 28, 30–31, 33, 35, 36, 40, 44; **Retro. Supp. II: 199–200,** 207; **Supp. XIV:** 162
Barber, David, **Supp. IV Part 2:** 550; **Supp. XII:** 188–189
Barber, Rowland, **Supp. IV Part 2:** 581
Barber, Samuel, **Supp. IV Part 1:** 84
"Barber's Unhappiness, The" (Saunders), **Supp. XIX:** 229
"Barclay of Ury" (Whittier), **Supp. I Part 2:** 693
Barcott, Bruce, **Supp. XVII:** 32
Bard of Savagery, The: Thorstein Veblen and Modern Social Theory (Diggins), **Supp. I Part 2:** 650
"Barefoot Boy, The" (Whittier), **Supp. I Part 2:** 691, 699–700
Barefoot in the Park (Simon), **Supp. IV Part 2:** 575, 578–579, 586, 590
Bare Hills, The (Winters), **Supp. II Part 2:** 786, 788
"Bare Hills, The" (Winters), **Supp. II Part 2:** 790
Barely and Widely (Zukofsky), **Supp. III Part 2:** 627, 628, 635
Barenblat, Rachel, **Supp. XIII:** 274
Barfield, Owen, **III:** 274, 279
"Bargain Lost, The" (Poe), **III:** 411
Barillas, William, **Supp. XIV:** 177
Barillet, Pierre, **Supp. XVI:** 194
Barker, Arthur, **Supp. XIII:** 167
Barker, Clive, **Supp. V:** 142
Barking Dog (Budbill), **Supp. XIX:** 1, 5
"Barking Man" (Bell), **Supp. X:** 9

Barking Man and Other Stories (Bell), **Supp. X: 9**
Barksdale, Richard, **Retro. Supp. I:** 202, 205; **Supp. I Part 1:** 341, 346
Barlow, Joel, **Supp. I Part 1:** 124; **Supp. I Part 2:** 511, 515, 521; **Supp. II Part 1: 65–86,** 268
Barlow, Judith, **Supp. XXI:** 6
Barlow, Ruth Baldwin (Mrs. Joel Barlow), **Supp. II Part 1:** 69
"B.A.R. Man, The" (Yates), **Supp. XI:** 341
Barnaby Rudge (Dickens), **III:** 421
Barnard, Frederick, **Supp. I Part 2:** 684
Barnard, Rita, **Retro. Supp. II:** 324
Barn Blind (Smiley), **Supp. VI: 292–293**
"Barn Burning" (Faulkner), **II:** 72, 73; **Supp. IV Part 2:** 682; **Supp. XX: 174**
Barnes, Djuna, **Supp. III Part 1: 31–46; Supp. IV Part 1:** 79, 80; **Supp. XVI:** 282; **Supp. XXII:** 165, 167
Barnes, Kim, **Supp. XVIII:** 293
Barnet, Andrea, **Supp. XXII:** 159, 164
Barnett, Claudia, **Supp. XV:** 323, 330, 334
Barnett, Samuel, **Supp. I Part 1:** 2
Barnhardt, Wilton, **Supp. XXII:** 266
"Barn Owl" (Kooser), **Supp. XIX:** 123
Barnstone, Tony, **Supp. XIII:** 115, 126
Barnstone, Willis, **Supp. I Part 2:** 458
Barnum, P. T., **Supp. I Part 2:** 703
Baroja, Pío, **I:** 478
Baron, Zach, **Supp. XVIII:** 150
"Baroque Comment" (Bogan), **Supp. III Part 1:** 56, 58
"Baroque Sunburst, A" (Clampitt), **Supp. IX:** 49
"Baroque Wall-Fountain in the Villa Sciarra, A" (Wilbur), **Supp. III Part 2:** 553
Barr, Robert, **I:** 409, 424
Barracks Thief, The (Wolff), **Supp. VII:** 344–345
"Barred Owl" (Offutt), **Supp. XIX:** 170
Barren Ground (Glasgow), **II:** 174, 175, 178, 179, 184–185, 186, 187, 188, 189, 191, 192, 193, 194; **Supp. X:** 228
Barrés, Auguste M., **I:** 228
Barresi, Dorothy, **Supp. XV:** 100, 102
Barrett, Amy, **Supp. XVIII:** 136
Barrett, E. B., **Supp. XV:** 309
Barrett, Elizabeth, **Supp. IV Part 2:** 430
Barrett, George, **Supp. IX:** 250
Barrett, Ralph, **Supp. I Part 2:** 462
Barrie, J. M., **Supp. XX: 234**
Barrier, Rober G., **Supp. XXI:** 48–49
Barrier of a Common Language: An American Looks at Contemporary British Poetry (Gioia), **Supp. XV:** 112, **116–117**
"Barroco: An Essay" (Sobin), **Supp. XVI:** 291
Barron, Jonathan, **Supp. IX:** 299
Barrow, John, **II:** 18
Barrus, Clara, **I:** 220
Barry, Iris, **Supp. XIII:** 170
Barry, Philip, **Retro. Supp. I:** 104; **Supp. IV Part 1:** 83; **Supp. V:** 95
Barstow, Elizabeth Drew. *See* Stoddard, Elizabeth
Bartas, Seigneur du, **IV:** 157
Barth, John, **I: 121–143; Supp. I Part 1:** 100; **Supp. III Part 1:** 217; **Supp. IV Part 1:** 48, 379; **Supp. V:** 39, 40; **Supp. IX:** 208; **Supp. X:** 263, 301, 302, 307; **Supp. XI:** 309; **Supp. XII:** 29, 289, 316; **Supp. XIII:** 41, 101, 104; **Supp. XVII:** 183; **Supp. XVIII:** 136, 140, 141; **Supp. XX: 21; Supp. XXII:** 259, 261
Barth, Karl, **III:** 40, 258, 291, 303, 309; **IV:** 225; **Retro. Supp. I:** 325, 326, 327
Barth, Robert C., **Supp. XV:** 169
Barthé, Richmond, **Retro. Supp. II:** 115
Barthelme, Donald, **Supp. IV Part 1: 39–58,** 227; **Supp. V:** 2, 39, 44; **Supp. VIII:** 75, 138; **Supp. X:** 263; **Supp. XI:** 25; **Supp. XII:** 29; **Supp. XIII:** 41, 46; **Supp. XVI:** 206; **Supp. XIX:** 235
Barthelme, Frederick, **Supp. XI: 25–41; Supp. XXI:** 38
Barthelme, Peter, **Supp. XI:** 25
Barthelme, Steven, **Supp. XI:** 25, 27, 37
Barthes, Roland, **Supp. IV Part 1:** 39, 119, 126; **Supp. XIII:** 83; **Supp. XVI:** 285, 294; **Supp. XVII:** 244
Bartholomew and the Oobleck (Geisel), **Supp. XVI:** 104
"Bar Time" (B. Collins), **Supp. XVII:** 245
"Bartleby, the Scrivener; A Story of Wall-Street" (Melville), **III:** 88–89; **Retro. Supp. I:** 255
Bartleby in Manhattan and Other Essays (Hardwick), **Supp. III Part 1:** 204, 210
"Bartleby the Scrivener" (Melville), **Supp. XVIII:** 4
Bartlet, Phebe, **I:** 562
Bartlett, Lee, **Supp. VIII:** 291
Bartlett, Mary Dougherty, **Supp. IV Part 1:** 335
Barton, Bruce, **III:** 14; **Retro. Supp. I:** 179
Barton, Priscilla. *See* Morison, Mrs. Samuel Eliot (Priscilla Barton)
Barton, Ralph, **Supp. XVI:** 195
Barton, Rev. William E., **Retro. Supp. I:** 179
Bartov, Omer, **Supp. XVI:** 153–154
Bartram, John, **Supp. I Part 1:** 244
Bartram, William, **II:** 313; **Supp. IX:** 171; **Supp. X:** 223
Barzun, Jacques, **Supp. XIV:** 54
"Basement" (Bambara), **Supp. XI:** 5
Basement Tapes, The (album, Dylan), **Supp. XVIII:** 27, 30, 32
"Base of All Metaphysics, The" (Whitman), **IV:** 348
"Base Stealer, The" (Francis), **Supp. IX:** 82
Bashevis, Isaac. *See* Singer, Isaac Bashevis
Bashir, Antonious, **Supp. XX: 116, 120**
Basil Stories, The (Fitzgerald), **Retro. Supp. I:** 109
Basin and Range (McPhee), **Supp. III Part 1:** 309
"Basin of Eggs, A" (Swenson), **Supp. IV Part 2:** 645
"Basket, The" (Lowell), **II:** 522
"Basketball and Beefeaters" (McPhee), **Supp. III Part 1:** 296
"Basketball and Poetry: The Two Richies" (Dunn), **Supp. XI:** 140
"Basketball Player" (L. Michaels), **Supp. XVI:** 209
Baskin, Leonard, **Supp. X:** 58, 71; **Supp. XV:** 348
Bass, George, **Supp. XXII:** 6
Bass, Rick, **Supp. XIV:** 227; **Supp. XVI: 15–29; Supp. XXI:** 40, 45
Bassard, Katherine Clay, **Supp. XXII:** 148
Basso, Hamilton, **Retro. Supp. I:** 80
Bastard, The (Caldwell), **I:** 291, 292, 308
"Bastille Day" (Lamott), **Supp. XX: 143**
"Bat, The" (Kenyon), **Supp. VII:** 168
Bataille, Georges, **Supp. VIII:** 4; **Supp. XII:** 1
"Batard" (London), **II:** 468–469
Batchelor, John Calvin, **Supp. XIX:** 142
Bate, W. J., **II:** 531
Bates, Arlo, **Retro. Supp. I:** 35
Bates, Blanche, **Supp. XVI:** 182
Bates, Kathy, **Supp. XIII:** 207
Bates, Lee, **Retro. Supp. II:** 46
Bates, Milton J., **Supp. XII:** 62
Bates, Sylvia Chatfield, **II:** 586
Bateson, Gregory, **Supp. XV:** 146
"Bath, The" (Carver), **Supp. III Part 1:** 144, 145
"Bath, The" (Snyder), **Supp. VIII:** 302
Bathwater Wine (Coleman), **Supp. XI:** 83, 90, **91**
"Batter my heart, three person'd God" (Donne), **Supp. I Part 2:** 726; **Supp. XVII:** 119
"Battle, The" (Simpson), **Supp. IX:** 268–269
Battle Cry (film), **Supp. XX: 246**
Battle Cry (Uris), **Supp. XX: 243, 246, 248–250, 255, 256**
Battlefield Where the Moon Says I Love You, The (Stanford), **Supp. XV:** 345
Battle for the Solomons (Wolfert), **Supp. XXI:** 267
Battle-Ground, The (Glasgow), **II:** 175, 176, 177, 178, 193
"Battle Hymn of the Republic" (Sandburg), **III:** 585
"Battle Hymn of the Republic, The" (Howe), **III:** 505
"Battle Hymn of the Republic, The" (Updike), **Retro. Supp. I:** 324
Battle of Angels (T. Williams), **IV:** 380, 381, 383, 385, 386, 387
"Battle of Lovell's Pond, The" (Longfellow), **II:** 493
Battle of the Atlantic, The (Morison), **Supp. I Part 2:** 490
"Battle of the Baltic, The" (Campbell), **Supp. I Part 1:** 309
"Battle of the Bunker, The" (Snodgrass), **Supp. VI:** 319–320
"***Battle of the Century!!!, The***" (Goldbarth), **Supp. XII:** 193

Battle-Pieces and Aspects of the War (Melville), **II:** 538–539; **III:** 92; **IV:** 350; **Retro. Supp. I:** 257
"Battler, The" (Hemingway), **II:** 248; **Retro. Supp. I:** 175
"Baubles after Bombs" (Peacock), **Supp. XIX:** 200
"Baudelaire" (Schwartz), **Supp. II Part 2:** 663
Baudelaire, Charles, **I:** 58, 63, 384, 389, 420, 569; **II:** 543, 544–545, 552; **III:** 137, 141–142, 143, 409, 417, 418, 421, 428, 448, 466, 474; **IV:** 74, 79, 80, 87, 211, 286; **Retro. Supp. I:** 56, 90; **Retro. Supp. II:** 261, 262, 322, 326; **Supp. I Part 1:** 271; **Supp. III Part 1:** 4, 6, 105; **Supp. XIII:** 77, 284; **Supp. XV:** 165; **Supp. XXI:** 228
Baudrillard, Jean, **Supp. IV Part 1:** 45
Bauer, Dale, **Retro. Supp. I:** 381
Bauer, Douglas, **Supp. XII:** 290
Baum, L. Frank, **Supp. I Part 2:** 621; **Supp. IV Part 1:** 101, 113; **Supp. XII:** 42
Baumann, Walter, **III:** 478
Bausch, Richard, **Supp. VII: 39–56; Supp. XVII:** 21
Bawer, Bruce, **Supp. VIII:** 153; **Supp. IX:** 135; **Supp. X:** 187
Baxter, Charles, **Supp. XII:** 22; **Supp. XIV:** 89, 92; **Supp. XVII: 13–24**
Baxter, John, **Supp. XI:** 302
Baxter, Richard, **III:** 199; **IV:** 151, 153; **Supp. I Part 2:** 683
"Baxter's Procrustes" (Chesnutt), **Supp. XIV:** 76
"Bay City Blues" (Chandler), **Supp. IV Part 1:** 129
Baylies, William, **Supp. I Part 1:** 153
Baym, Nina, **Supp. IV Part 2:** 463; **Supp. X:** 229; **Supp. XVI:** 92; **Supp. XVIII:** 258, 259
"Bayou" (Di Piero), **Supp. XIX:** 37
Bayou Folk (Chopin), **Retro. Supp. II: 64–65,** 73; **Supp. I Part 1:** 200, 216, 218
Baziotes, William, **Supp. XV:** 144
"B.C." (Taggard), **Supp. XXII:** 278
Beach, Anna Hampstead, **Supp. XVII:** 75
Beach, Joseph Warren, **I:** 309, 500; **II:** 27; **III:** 319
Beach, Sylvia, **IV:** 404; **Retro. Supp. I:** 109, 422; **Supp. XXII:** 165
"Beach Women, The" (Pinsky), **Supp. VI:** 241
"Beaded Pear, The" (Simpson), **Supp. IX:** 276
Beagle, Peter, **Supp. X:** 24
Beam, Jeffrey, **Supp. XII:** 98
Beaman, E. O., **Supp. IV Part 2:** 604
Bean, Michael, **Supp. V:** 203
Bean, Robert Bennett, **Supp. II Part 1:** 170
Bean Eaters, The (Brooks), **Supp. III Part 1:** 79–81
Be Angry at the Sun (Jeffers), **Supp. II Part 2:** 434
"Beanstalk Country, The" (T. Williams), **IV:** 383
Bean Trees, The (Kingsolver), **Supp. VII:** 197, 199–201, 202, 207, 209
"Bear" (Hogan), **Supp. IV Part 1:** 412
Bear, The (Faulkner), **Supp. VIII:** 184
"Bear, The" (Faulkner), **II:** 71–72, 73, 228; **IV:** 203; **Supp. IV Part 2:** 434; **Supp. IX:** 95; **Supp. X:** 30; **Supp. XIV:** 32; **Supp. XXI:** 37
"Bear, The" (Kinnell), **Supp. III Part 1:** 244
"Bear, The" (Momaday), **Supp. IV Part 2:** 480, 487
Bear and His Daughter: Stories (Stone), **Supp. V:** 295, 308
Beard, Charles, **I:** 214; **IV:** 429; **Supp. I Part 2:** 481, 490, 492, 632, 640, 643, 647
Beard, James, **I:** 341; **Supp. XVII:** 89, 90
Beard, Mary, **Supp. I Part 2:** 481
"Bearded Oaks" (Warren), **IV:** 240
Bearden, Romare, **Retro. Supp. I:** 209; **Supp. VIII:** 337, 342; **Supp. XXI:** 249
"Beard of Bees, A" (X. J. Kennedy), **Supp. XV:** 171
Beardon, Romare, **Supp. XV:** 144
"Beards, The" (Lethem), **Supp. XVIII:** 148
Beardsley, Aubrey, **II:** 56; **IV:** 77
Beaser, Robert, **Supp. XV:** 259
"Beast" (Swenson), **Supp. IV Part 2:** 639
"Beast & Burden, The: Seven Improvisations" (Komunyakaa), **Supp. XIII:** 120, 121
Beast God Forgot to Invent, The (Harrison), **Supp. VIII:** 37, 46, **51–52**
Beast in Me, The (Thurber), **Supp. I Part 2:** 615
"Beast in the Jungle, The" (James), **I:** 570; **II:** 335; **Retro. Supp. I:** 235; **Supp. V:** 103–104
Beast in View (Rukeyser), **Supp. VI:** 272, 273, 279, 280
Beasts of Bethlehem, The (X. J. Kennedy), **Supp. XV:** 163
"Beat! Beat! Drums!" (Whitman), **III:** 585
Beat Down to Your Soul: What Was the Beat Generation? (Charters, ed.), **Supp. XIV:** 152
"Beatific Effigies" (Bronk), **Supp. XXI:** 31
Beaton, Cecil, **Supp. XVI:** 191
"Beatrice Palmato" (Wharton), **Retro. Supp. I:** 379
Beats, The (Krim, ed.), **Supp. XV:** 338
Beattie, Ann, **Supp. V: 21–37; Supp. XI:** 26; **Supp. XII:** 80, 139, 294; **Supp. XXI:** 118
Beattie, L. Elisabeth, **Supp. XX: 164, 165**
Beatty, General Sam, **I:** 193
Beaty, Jerome, **Supp. IV Part 1:** 331
"Beau Monde of Mrs. Bridge, The" (Connell), **Supp. XIV:** 88, 89
Beaumont, Francis, **Supp. I Part 2:** 422
"Beauties of Santa Cruz, The" (Freneau), **Supp. II Part 1:** 260
Beautiful and Damned, The (Fitzgerald), **II:** 88, 89–91, 93, 263; **Retro. Supp. I: 103–105,** 105, 106, 110; **Supp. IX:** 56, 57
Beautiful Changes, The (Wilbur), **Supp. III Part 2:** 544–550
"Beautiful Changes, The" (Wilbur), **Supp. III Part 2:** 549, 550
"Beautiful Child, A" (Capote), **Supp. III Part 1:** 113, 125
"Beautiful & Cruel" (Cisneros), **Supp. VII:** 63, 67
"Beautiful Wall, Machu Picchu, The" (Bronk), **Supp. XXI:** 31, 32
"Beautiful Woman Who Sings, The" (Gunn Allen), **Supp. IV Part 1:** 326
"Beauty" (Emerson), **II:** 2, 5
"Beauty" (Sanders), **Supp. XVI:** 277
"Beauty" (Wylie), **Supp. I Part 2:** 710
"Beauty and the Beast" (Dove), **Supp. IV Part 1:** 245
"Beauty and the Beast" (fairy tale), **IV:** 266; **Supp. X:** 88
"Beauty and the Shoe Sluts" (Karr), **Supp. XI:** 250
Beauty of the Husband, The: A Fictional Essay in Twenty-Nine Tangos (Carson), **Supp. XII: 113–114**
Beauty Queen, The (P. N. Warren), **Supp. XX: 268–269**
Beauty's Punishment (Rice), **Supp. VII:** 301
Beauty's Release: The Continued Erotic Adventures of Sleeping Beauty (Rice), **Supp. VII:** 301
Beauvoir, Simone de, **IV:** 477; **Supp. I Part 1:** 51; **Supp. III Part 1:** 200–201, 208; **Supp. IV Part 1:** 360; **Supp. IX:** 4
"Be Careful" (Zach; Everwine, trans.), **Supp. XV:** 86
Be Careful How You Live (Lacy), **Supp. XV:** 203–204
"Because I could not stop for Death—" (Dickinson), **Retro. Supp. I: 38–40,** 41, 43, 44
"Because It Happened" (Goldbarth), **Supp. XII:** 192
"Because of Libraries We Can Say These Things" (Nye), **Supp. XIII:** 283
"Because You Mentioned the Spiritual Life" (Dunn), **Supp. XI:** 154
Bech: A Book (Updike), **IV:** 214; **Retro. Supp. I:** 329, 335
Beck, Dave, **I:** 493
Beck, Jack, **Supp. IV Part 2:** 560
Beck, Nicholas, **Supp. XVIII:** 252
Beck, Stefan, **Supp. XXII:** 268
Becker, Carl, **Supp. I Part 2:** 492, 493
Becker, Paula. *See* Modersohn, Mrs. Otto (Paula Becker)
Beckett, Samuel, **I:** 71, 91, 142, 298, 461; **III:** 387; **IV:** 95; **Retro. Supp. I:** 206; **Supp. IV Part 1:** 297, 368–369; **Supp. IV Part 2:** 424; **Supp. V:** 23, 53; **Supp. XI:** 104; **Supp. XII:** 21, 150–151; **Supp. XIII:** 74; **Supp. XIV:** 239; **Supp. XVII:** 185; **Supp. XX: 17; Supp. XXI:** 18; **Supp. XXII:** 263
Beckett, Tom, **Supp. IV Part 2:** 419

Beckford, William, **I:** 204
Beckonings (Brooks), **Supp. III Part 1:** 85
"Becky" (Toomer), **Supp. III Part 2:** 481, 483; **Supp. IX:** 312
Becky and Her Friends (Hinojosa), **Supp. XIX: 108–109**
Becoming a Man: Half a Life Story (Monette), **Supp. X:** 146, 147, 149, 151, 152, **155–157**
"Becoming a Meadow" (Doty), **Supp. XI:** 124–125
"Becoming and Breaking: Poet and Poem" (Ríos), **Supp. IV Part 2:** 539
Becoming Canonical in American Poetry (Morris), **Retro. Supp. I:** 40
Becoming Light: New and Selected Poems (Jong), **Supp. V:** 115
Bécquer, Gustavo Adolfo, **Supp. XIII:** 312
"Bed, The" (Dixon), **Supp. XII:** 154
Beddoes, Thomas Lovell, **III:** 469; **Retro. Supp. I:** 285
Bedichek, Roy, **Supp. V:** 225
Bedient, Calvin, **Supp. IX:** 298; **Supp. XII:** 98
"Bed in the Sky, The" (Snyder), **Supp. VIII:** 300
Bednarik, Joseph, **Supp. VIII:** 39
"Bedrock" (Proulx), **Supp. VII:** 253
"Bee, The" (Lanier), **Supp. I Part 1:** 364
Beecher, Catharine, **Supp. I Part 2:** 581, 582–583, 584, 586, 588, 589, 591, 599; **Supp. X:** 103; **Supp. XI:** 193
Beecher, Charles, **Supp. I Part 2:** 588, 589
Beecher, Edward, **Supp. I Part 2:** 581, 582, 583, 584, 588, 591
Beecher, Harriet. *See* Stowe, Harriet Beecher
Beecher, Henry Ward, **II:** 275; **Supp. I Part 2:** 581; **Supp. XI:** 193; **Supp. XVIII:** 4
Beecher, Lyman, **Supp. I Part 2:** 580–581, 582, 583, 587, 588, 599; **Supp. XI:** 193
Beecher, Mrs. Lyman (Roxanna Foote), **Supp. I Part 2:** 580–581, 582, 588, 599
Beeching, Jack, **Supp. X:** 114, 117, 118, 123, 125, 126
"Beehive" (Toomer), **Supp. IX:** 317
"Bee Hunt, The" (Irving), **II:** 313
"Beekeeper's Daughter, The" (Plath), **Retro. Supp. II:** 246–247
"Bee Meeting, The" (Plath), **Retro. Supp. II:** 254–255
Bee Poems (Plath), **Retro. Supp. II:** 254–255
Beer, John, **Supp. XVII:** 239
Beer, Thomas, **I:** 405
Beerbohm, Max, **III:** 472; **IV:** 436; **Supp. I Part 2:** 714
"Beer Bottle" (Kooser), **Supp. XIX:** 117
"Beer in the Sergeant Major's Hat, or The Sun Also Sneezes" (Chandler), **Supp. IV Part 1:** 121
Beers, Henry A., **Supp. XX: 68**
"Bees Bees Bees" (J. Scott), **Supp. XVII:** 188, 190
Beethoven, Ludwig van, **II:** 536; **III:** 118; **IV:** 274, 358; **Supp. I Part 1:** 363; **Supp. VIII:** 103
Beet Queen, The (Erdrich), **Supp. IV Part 1:** 259, 260, 264–265, 266, 273, 274, 275
Befo' de War: Echoes in Negro Dialect (Gordon), **Supp. II Part 1:** 201
"Before" (Goldbarth), **Supp. XII:** 175
"Before" (Snyder), **Supp. VIII:** 301
Before Adam (London), **II:** 466
Before Breakfast (O'Neill), **Supp. XXII:** 22
Before Disaster (Winters), **Supp. II Part 2:** 786, 800
"Before Disaster" (Winters), **Supp. II Part 2:** 801, 815
"Before I Knocked" (D. Thomas), **III:** 534
Beforelife, The (F. Wright), **Supp. XVII:** 240, 245–246
"Before March" (MacLeish), **III:** 15
Before My Life Began (Neugeboren), **Supp. XVI: 224–225**
"Before the Altar" (Lowell), **II:** 516
"Before the Birth of one of her children" (Bradstreet), **Supp. I Part 1:** 118
"Before the Sky Darkens" (Dunn), **Supp. XI:** 155
"Begat" (Sexton), **Supp. II Part 2: 693**
Beggarman, Thief (Shaw), **Supp. XIX:** 251–252
Beggar on Horseback (Kaufman and Connelly), **III:** 394
"Beggar Said So, The" (Singer), **IV:** 12
Beggars in the House of Plenty (Shanley), **Supp. XIV:** 316, **327–328**
Beggar's Opera, The (Gay), **Supp. I Part 2:** 523
Begiebing, Robert, **Retro. Supp. II:** 210
Begin Again (Paley), **Supp. VI:** 221
"Beginning and the End, The" (Jeffers), **Supp. II Part 2:** 420–421, 424
"Beginning of Decadence, The" (Jeffers), **Supp. II Part 2:** 420
"Beginning of Enthusiasm, The" (Salinas), **Supp. XIII:** 327–328
Beginning of Wisdom, The (Benét), **I:** 358; **Supp. XI:** 44
Be Glad You're Neurotic (Bisch), **Supp. I Part 2:** 608
"Begotten of the Spleen" (Simic), **Supp. VIII:** 277
"Behaving Like a Jew" (Stern), **Supp. IX: 290–291,** 294
"Behavior" (Emerson), **II:** 2, 4
Behavior of Titans, The (Merton), **Supp. VIII:** 201
Behind a Mask (Alcott), **Supp. I Part 1:** 36–37, 43–44
"Behind a Wall" (Lowell), **II:** 516
Behind the Movie Camera (radio show), **Supp. XV:** 147
"Behold the Key" (Malamud), **Supp. I Part 2:** 437
Behrendt, Stephen, **Supp. X:** 204
Behrman, S. N., **Supp. V:** 95
Beidler, Peter G., **Supp. IV Part 2:** 557
Beidler, Philip D., **Supp. XII:** 69
Beige Dolorosa (Harrison), **Supp. VIII:** 40, 51
Beiles, Sinclair, **Supp. XII:** 129
Beiliss, Mendel, **Supp. I Part 2:** 427, 446, 447, 448
"Being a Constellation" (A. Finch), **Supp. XVII:** 72
"Being a Lutheran Boy-God in Minnesota" (R. Bly), **Supp. IV Part 1:** 59, 67
Being and Race (Johnson), **Supp. VI:** 193, 199
Being and Time (Heidegger), **Supp. VIII:** 9
Being Busted (Fiedler), **Supp. XIII:** 95, 102, 104
Being John Malkovich (Kaufman), **Supp. XV:** 16
Being Perfect (Quindlen), **Supp. XVII:** 167, 179
Being There (Kosinski), **Supp. VII:** 215, 216, 222–223
Beiswanger, George, **Retro. Supp. II:** 220
Belasco, David, **Supp. XVI:** 182; **Supp. XXI:** 151
Bel Canto (Patchett), **Supp. XII:** 307, 310, **320–322**
Belchamber (Sturgis), **Supp. XX: 227, 233, 238–240**
"Beleaguered City, The" (Longfellow), **II:** 498
Belfry of Bruges, The, and Other Poems (Longfellow), **II:** 489; **Retro. Supp. II:** 157, 168
"Belief" (Levine), **Supp. V:** 186, 190
"Belief in the Self Abandoned, The" (Bronk), **Supp. XXI:** 30
"Beliefs of Writers, The" (Doctorow), **Supp. IV Part 1:** 235–236
Believeniks! (Lethem and Sorrentino), **Supp. XVIII:** 148–149
Believers (C. Baxter), **Supp. XVII:** 20–21, 22
"Believers" (C. Baxter), **Supp. XVII:** 21
"Believers, The/Los Creyentes" (Kingsolver), **Supp. VII:** 208
Belinda (Rice), **Supp. VII:** 301–302
"Belinda's Petition" (Dove), **Supp. IV Part 1:** 245
"Belita" (Ríos), **Supp. IV Part 2:** 541
Belitt, Ben, **Supp. XII:** 260
Bell, Archibald, **Supp. XX: 284, 285**
Bell, Bernard, **Supp. XXII:** 182
Bell, Clive, **IV:** 87
Bell, Daniel, **Supp. I Part 2:** 648
Bell, George Kennedy Allen, **Retro. Supp. I:** 65
Bell, Madison Smartt, **Supp. X: 1–20; Supp. XVII:** 236; **Supp. XIX:** 58–59, 60–61; **Supp. XXI:** 48
Bell, Marvin, **Supp. V:** 337, 339; **Supp. IX:** 152; **Supp. XI:** 316
Bell, Michael, **Retro. Supp. II:** 139
Bell, Pearl, **Supp. XI:** 233
Bell, Quentin, **Supp. I Part 2:** 636
Bell, Whitfield J., Jr., **II:** 123
Bellafante, Gina, **Supp. VIII:** 85
Bellamy, Edward, **II:** 276; **Supp. I Part 2:** 641; **Supp. XI:** 200, 203

Bellarosa Connection, The (Bellow), **Retro. Supp. II:** 31, 32
"Belle Dollinger" (Masters), **Supp. I Part 2:** 463
Belleforest, François de, **IV:** 370
"Belle Zoraïde, La" (Chopin), **Supp. I Part 1:** 215–216
Bell Jar, The (Plath), **Retro. Supp. II:** 242, **249–250; Supp. I Part 2:** 526, 527, 529, 531–536, 539, 540, 541, 542, 544
Belloc, Hilary, **III:** 176; **IV:** 432
"Bellocq" (Trethewey), **Supp. XXI:** 253
Bellocq, E. J., **Supp. XXI:** 246, 251
Bellocq's Ophelia (Trethewey), **Supp. XXI:** 243, 246**, 251–254**
"Bellocq's Ophelia" (Trethewey), **Supp. XXI:** 254
Bellow, Saul, **I:** 113, 138–139, **144–166,** 375, 517; **II:** 579; **III:** 40; **IV:** 3, 19, 217, 340; **Retro. Supp. II: 19–36,** 118, 279, 307, 324; **Supp. I Part 2:** 428, 451; **Supp. II Part 1:** 109; **Supp. IV Part 1:** 30; **Supp. V:** 258; **Supp. VIII:** 98, 176, 234, 236–237, 245; **Supp. IX:** 212, 227; **Supp. XI:** 64, 233; **Supp. XII:** 159, 165, 170, 310; **Supp. XIII:** 106; **Supp. XV:** 143; **Supp. XVI:** 208; **Supp. XVIII:** 90; **Supp. XIX:** 157, 158, 261; **Supp. XX: 244; Supp. XXII:** 268
Bellows, George, **Supp. XV:** 295
"Bells, The" (Poe), **III:** 593; **Retro. Supp. II:** 266; **Supp. I Part 2:** 388
"Bells, The" (Sexton), **Supp. II Part 2:** 673
"Bells for John Whiteside's Daughter" (Ransom), **III:** 490
"Bells of Lynn, The" (Longfellow), **II:** 498
"Bells of San Blas, The" (Longfellow), **II:** 490–491, 493, 498
"Bell Tower, The" (Melville), **III:** 91
"Belly, The" (Dobyns), **Supp. XIII:** 87
"Belonging" (Pickering), **Supp. XXI:** 202
"Belonging Kind, The" (W. Gibson and J. Shirley), **Supp. XVI:** 123
Beloved (Morrison), **Supp. III Part 1:** 364, 372–379; **Supp. IV Part 1:** 13–14; **Supp. V:** 259; **Supp. VIII:** 343; **Supp. XIII:** 60; **Supp. XXII:** 78, 109
Beloved, The (Gibran), **Supp. XX: 125**
"Beloved, The" (Halliday), **Supp. XIX:** 92
Beloved Lady: A History of Jane Addams' Ideas on Reform and Peace (Farrell), **Supp. I Part 1:** 24
Beloved Stranger, The (Bynner), **Supp. XV:** 44, 50
Bemorse, John, **Supp. XX: 62**
Benchley, Robert, **I:** 48, 482; **II:** 435; **III:** 53; **Supp. IX:** 190, 195, 204
Benda, W. T., **Retro. Supp. I:** 13
Bender, Aimee, **Supp. XXII:** 49
Bending of a Twig, The (Coke), **Supp. XX: 235**
Bend Sinister (Nabokov), **III:** 253–254; **Retro. Supp. I:** 265, 266, 270
"Beneath the Sidewalk" (Dunn), **Supp. XI:** 145
"Beneath the Smooth Skin of America" (Sanders), **Supp. XVI:** 275
Benedict, Elizabeth, **Supp. XVIII:** 289
Benedict, Ruth, **Supp. IX:** 229
Benefactor, The (Sontag), **Supp. III Part 2:** 451, 455, 468, 469
"Benefit Performance" (Malamud), **Supp. I Part 2:** 431
Benét, Laura, **Supp. XI:** 44
Benét, Rosemary, **Supp. XI:** 44, 51
Benét, Stephen Vincent, **I:** 358; **II:** 177; **III:** 22; **IV:** 129; **Supp. XI: 43–61**
Benét, William Rose, **II:** 530; **Retro. Supp. I:** 108; **Supp. I Part 2:** 709; **Supp. XI:** 43, 44; **Supp. XIV:** 119, 122, 129
Ben Franklin's Wit and Wisdom (Franklin), **II:** 111
Ben-Gurion, David, **Supp. XX: 243**
Ben-Hur (film), **Supp. IV Part 2:** 683
Benigna Machiavelli (Gilman), **Supp. XI:** 201, 208
Benitez, R. Michael, **Retro. Supp. II:** 264
Benito Cereno (Lowell), **II:** 546; **Retro. Supp. II:** 181
"Benito Cereno" (Melville), **III:** 91; **Retro. Supp. I:** 255; **Retro. Supp. II:** 188; **Supp. XVII:** 185
Benito's Dream Bottle (Nye), **Supp. XIII:** 278
"Bênitou's Slave, The" (Chopin), **Retro. Supp. II:** 64
Benjamin, Walter, **Supp. IX:** 133; **Supp. XVI:** 290, 291
Benjamin Franklin (Van Doren), **Supp. I Part 2:** 486
"Benjamin Pantier" (Masters), **Supp. I Part 2:** 461
Bennett, Anne Virginia, **II:** 184
Bennett, Arnold, **I:** 103; **II:** 337; **Supp. XVI:** 190
Bennett, Elizabeth, **Supp. VIII:** 58
Bennett, Patrick, **Supp. V:** 225
Bennett, Paula, **Retro. Supp. I:** 29, 33, 42; **Supp. XX: 286**
Bennett, Reginald, **Supp. XXII:** 218
Bennett, William, **Supp. VIII:** 245
Benson, A. C., **Supp. XX: 238**
Benson, Arthur, **Supp. XX: 233**
Benson, E. F., **Supp. XX: 229**
Benson, Heidi, **Supp. XVIII:** 136
Benson, Jackson J., **Supp. IV Part 2:** 613
Benson, Martin, **Supp. XVIII:** 38
Benstock, Shari, **Retro. Supp. I:** 361, 368, 371, 382; **Supp. XX: 240**
Bentham, Jeremy, **I:** 279; **Supp. I Part 2:** 635
Bentley, Anna, **Supp. XXI:** 5
Bentley, Arthur, **Supp. XXI:** 4, 5
Bentley, Eric R., **IV:** 396
Bentley, Nelson, **Supp. IX:** 324
Bentley, Richard, **III:** 79, 86
Benton, Robert, **Supp. IV Part 1:** 236
"Bent Tones" (Wright), **Supp. XV:** 346
Benveniste, Emile, **Supp. XVI:** 292
Benzel, Jan, **Supp. XVI:** 112
Beowulf, **Supp. II Part 1:** 6; **Supp. XVII:** 70, 73
Beran, Carol, **Supp. XIII:** 25
"Berck-Plage" (Plath), **Retro. Supp. II:** 253–254
Bercovitch, Sacvan, **Retro. Supp. I:** 408; **Retro. Supp. II:** 325, 330; **Supp. I Part 1:** 99; **Supp. I Part 2:** 659
Berdyaev, Nikolai, **I:** 494; **III:** 292
"Bereaved Apartments" (Kingsolver), **Supp. VII:** 203
"Bereavement in their death to feel" (Dickinson), **Retro. Supp. I:** 43, 44
"Berenice" (Poe), **III:** 415, 416, 425; **Retro. Supp. II:** 270
Bérénice (Racine), **II:** 573
Berenson, Bernard, **Retro. Supp. I:** 381; **Supp. IV Part 1:** 314; **Supp. XIV:** 335, 336, 337; **Supp. XVII:** 99; **Supp. XXI:** 5
Berenson, Mary Smith, **Supp. XXI:** 4, 5, 6
Berg, James, **Supp. XIV:** 157, 159
Berg, Stephen, **Supp. IV Part 1:** 60
Berger, Alan, **Supp. XVII:** 39
Berger, Charles, **Retro. Supp. I:** 311
Berger, John, **Supp. XVI:** 284
Berger, Roger, **Supp. XIII:** 237
Berger, Thomas, **III:** 258; **Supp. XII:** 171
Bergman, Ingmar, **I:** 291; **Supp. XV:** 7, 8, 12
Bergson, Henri, **I:** 224; **II:** 163, 165, 166, 359; **III:** 8, 9, 488, 619; **IV:** 86, 122, 466, 467; **Retro. Supp. I:** 55, 57, 80; **Supp. IV Part 1:** 42; **Supp. XXII:** 158
Berkeley, Anthony, **Supp. IV Part 1:** 341
Berkeley, George, **II:** 10, 349, 357, 480, 554
Berkman, Leonard, **Supp. XV:** 321
Berkowitz, Gerald, **Supp. IV Part 2:** 590
Berlin, Isaiah, **Supp. XXII:** 258
Berlin Alexanderplatz (Döblin), **Supp. XV:** 137
Berlin Stories (Isherwood), **Supp. IV Part 1:** 82; **Supp. XIV:** 155, 156, 161, 162, 164, 165
Berlioz, Hector, **Supp. XV:** 33
Berlyne, Daniel E., **Supp. I Part 2:** 672
Berman, Alexander, **Supp. XVII:** 103
Berman, Carolyn Vellenga, **Supp. XXII:** 147
Bernard Clare (Farrell), **II:** 38, 39
Bernard of Clairvaux, Saint, **I:** 22; **II:** 538
Bernays, Thekla, **Retro. Supp. II:** 65
Berne, Suzanne, **Supp. XII:** 320
Berne, Victoria (pseudonym). *See* Fisher, M. F. K.
Berneis, Peter, **IV:** 383
Bernhard, Brendan, **Supp. XIV:** 163
Bernhard, Thomas, **Supp. XX: 91**
Bernhardt, Sarah, **I:** 484; **Retro. Supp. I:** 377
Bernice (Glaspell), **Supp. III Part 1:** 179
"Bernice Bobs Her Hair" (Fitzgerald), **II:** 88; **Retro. Supp. I:** 103
Bernstein, Aline, **IV:** 455, 456
Bernstein, Andrea, **Supp. IX:** 146

Bernstein, Charles, **Supp. IV Part 2:** 421, 426
Bernstein, Elizabeth, **Supp. XII:** 318
Bernstein, Leonard, **I:** 28; **Supp. I Part 1:** 288, 289; **Supp. IV Part 1:** 83, 84
Bernstein, Melvin, **Supp. XIV:** 41, 46
Bernstein, Michael André, **Retro. Supp. I:** 427
Bernstein, Richard, **Supp. IX:** 253, 262; **Supp. XII:** 113; **Supp. XIV:** 33; **Supp. XXII:** 261
Berrett, Jesse, **Supp. XIII:** 241, 242
Berrigan, Ted, **Supp. XIV:** 150; **Supp. XXII:** 224, 225, 228, 231
Berroa y Canelo, Quiterio, **Supp. XXI:** 104
"Berry" (Hughes), **Supp. I Part 1:** 329, 330
Berry, Faith, **Retro. Supp. I:** 194, 201
Berry, Walter, **IV:** 313–314, 326
Berry, Wendell, **Supp. VIII:** 304; **Supp. X: 21–39; Supp. XII:** 202; **Supp. XIII:** 1–2; **Supp. XIV:** 179; **Supp. XVI:** 39, 56; **Supp. XVIII:** 192; **Supp. XXI:** 90
"Berry Feast, A" (Snyder), **Supp. VIII:** 289, 297
Berryman, John, **I: 167–189,** 405, 441–442, 521; **II:** 554; **III:** 273; **IV:** 138, 430; **Retro. Supp. I:** 430; **Retro. Supp. II:** 175, 178; **Supp. I Part 2:** 546; **Supp. II Part 1:** 109; **Supp. III Part 2:** 541, 561, 595, 596, 603; **Supp. IV Part 2:** 620, 639; **Supp. V:** 179–180, 337; **Supp. IX:** 152; **Supp. XI:** 240; **Supp. XV:** 93; **Supp. XVII:** 111; **Supp. XXII:** 83
Berryman, Mrs. John, **I:** 168–169
Berryman's Sonnets (Berryman), **I:** 168, 175–178
"Berry Territory" (Snyder), **Supp. VIII:** 304
Berthoff, Warner, **Supp. I Part 1:** 133
Bertolucci, Bernardo, **Supp. IV Part 1:** 94
"Bertrand Hume" (Masters), **Supp. I Part 2:** 463–464
"Best, the Most, The" (Carruth), **Supp. XVI:** 59
Best American Essays 1987, The (G. Talese and R. Atwan, eds.), **Supp. XVI:** 273
Best American Essays 1988, The (Dillard, ed.), **Supp. VIII:** 272
Best American Essays 1989, The (Wolff, ed.), **Supp. XVII:** 208
Best American Essays 1993, The (J. Epstein, ed.), **Supp. XVI:** 275
Best American Essays 1997, The (Frazier, ed.), **Supp. VIII:** 272; **Supp. XVII:** 207
Best American Essays 1999, The (E. Hoagland and R. Atwan, eds.), **Supp. XVI:** 277
Best American Essays for College Students, The (R. Atwan, ed.), **Supp. XVI:** 273
Best American Fantasy, 2010 (Brockmeier, ed.), **Supp. XXII:** 49–50
Best American New Voices 2001 (C. Baxter, ed.), **Supp. XVII:** 22
Best American Poetry, The: 1988 (Ashbery, ed.), **Supp. III Part 1:** 26
Best American Poetry 2000, The (Dove and Lehman, eds.), **Supp. XXI:** 246
Best American Poetry 2006, The (Collins, ed.), **Supp. XXI:** 54
Best American Short Stories, **I:**174; **II:** 587; **III:** 443; **Supp. IV Part 1:** 102, 315; **Supp. IX:** 114; **Supp. X:** 301
Best American Short Stories, 1915–1050, The, **Supp. IX:** 4
Best American Short Stories 1965, The (Foley, ed.), **Supp. XVI:** 225
Best American Short Stories 1982, The (Gardner, ed.), **Supp. XVII:** 16
Best American Short Stories 1983, The (A. Tyler, ed.), **Supp. XVI:** 37
Best American Short Stories 1986, The (Carver, ed.), **Supp. XVII:** 17
Best American Short Stories 1988, The (Helprin, ed.), **Supp. XVI:** 16
Best American Short Stories 1989, The (Atwood, ed.), **Supp. XVII:** 18; **Supp. XXI:** 39, 42
Best American Short Stories 1991, The (Adams and Kenison, eds.), **Supp. XVI:** 256
Best American Short Stories 1997, **Supp. XXII:** 75
Best American Short Stories 2001, The (Kenison and Kingsover, eds.), **Supp. XVI:** 24
Best American Short Stories of 1942, The, **Supp. V:** 316
Best American Short Stories of 1944, The, **Supp. IX:** 119
Best American Short Stories of the Century (Updike, ed.), **Supp. X:** 163
Best American Short Stories of the Eighties, The (Ravenal, ed.), **Supp. IV Part 1:** 93
Best American Sports Writing of the Century, The (Halberstam, ed.), **Supp. XVII:** 204
"Best China Saucer, The" (Jewett), **Retro. Supp. II:** 145–146
Bester, Alfred, **Supp. XVI:** 123
Best Hour of the Night, The (Simpson), **Supp. IX: 277–279**
Bestiaire, Le (Apollinaire), **IV:** 80
Bestiary, A (Wilbur), **Supp. III Part 2:** 552
"Bestiary for the Fingers of My Right Hand" (Simic), **Supp. VIII:** 274, 275
Best Man, The: A Play About Politics (Vidal), **Supp. IV Part 2:** 683
"Best of Everything, The" (Yates), **Supp. XI:** 341
Best of Pickering, The (Pickering), **Supp. XXI:** 192, 198
Best of Plimpton (Plimpton), **Supp. XVI:** 238, 239, 240
Best Short Plays, The (Mayorga), **IV:** 381
Best Short Stories, The (O'Brien, ed.), **I:** 289
Best Short Stories by Negro Writers, The (Hughes, ed.), **Supp. I Part 1:** 345
Best Short Stories of 1926, The (O'Brien, ed.), **Supp. XVIII:** 279
Best Short Stories of 1934 (O'Brien, ed.), **Supp. XVIII:** 227
Best Short Stories of 1938 (O'Brien, ed.), **Supp. XIX:** 256; **Supp. XX: 34**
Best That Ever Did It, The (Lacy), **Supp. XV:** 201–202
Best Times, The: An Informal Memoir (Dos Passos), **I:** 475, 482
Best Words, Best Order: Essays on Poetry (Dobyns), **Supp. XIII:** 74, **76–78,** 87
Best Years of Our Lives, The (film; Wyler), **Supp. XV:** 195
"BETANCOURT" (Baraka), **Supp. II Part 1:** 33, 34
Bête humaine, La (Zola), **III:** 316, 318
"Bethe" (Hellman), **Supp. I Part 1:** 293
Bethea, David, **Supp. VIII:** 27
Bethel Merriday (Lewis), **II:** 455
Bethke, Bruce, **Supp. XVI:** 121
Bethlehem in Broad Daylight (Doty), **Supp. XI:** 121, **122–123**
Bethune, Mary McLeod, **Retro. Supp. I:** 197; **Supp. I Part 1:** 333
Bethurum, Dorothy, **IV:** 121
"Betrayal" (Lanier), **Supp. I Part 1:** 364
"Betrothed" (Bogan), **Supp. III Part 1:** 49–51
Bettelheim, Bruno, **Supp. I Part 2:** 622; **Supp. X:** 77, 84; **Supp. XIV:** 126; **Supp. XVI:** 33
Better Days (Price), **Supp. VI:** 264
Better Sort, The (James), **II:** 335
"Better Things in Life, The" (Loos), **Supp. XVI:** 194
Betty Leicester (Jewett), **II:** 406
Betty Leicester's Christmas (Jewett), **II:** 406; **Retro. Supp. II:** 145
Between Angels (Dunn), **Supp. XI: 149–159**
"Between Angels" (Dunn), **Supp. XI:** 150
Between Fantoine and Agapa (Pinget), **Supp. V:** 39
"Between Memory and History: A Writer's Voice" (Kreisler), **Supp. XVI:** 155
Between Silences: A Voice from China (Jin), **Supp. XVIII:** 91, 92, 93
"Between the Porch and the Altar" (Lowell), **II:** 540–541
"Between the World and Me" (Wright), **Supp. II Part 1:** 228
Between Time and Timbuktu (Vonnegut), **Supp. II Part 2:** 753, 759
Beuka, Robert A., **Supp. XIX:** 263; **Supp. XXI:** 47
"Be Very Afraid—Of Loss of Liberty at Home" (P. N. Warren), **Supp. XX: 272–273**
Bevis, Howard L., **Supp. I Part 2:** 611
Bevis, John, **Supp. I Part 2:** 503
"Bewitched" (Wharton), **IV:** 316
Bewley, Marius, **I:** 336
Beyle, Marie Henri. *See* Stendhal
Beyond (Goldbarth), **Supp. XII:** 192
Beyond a Boundary (C. L. R. James), **Supp. XXI:** 159, 170–171

Beyond Black Bear Lake (LaBastille), **Supp. X:** 95, **99–102,** 108
"Beyond Charles River to the Acheron" (Lowell), **II:** 541
Beyond Criticism (Shapiro), **Supp. II Part 2:** 703, 711
Beyond Culture (Trilling), **Supp. III Part 2:** 508–512
Beyond Desire (Anderson), **I:** 111
Beyond Document: The Art of Nonfiction Film (Warren, ed.), **Supp. IV Part 2:** 434
Beyond Good and Evil (Nietzsche), **Supp. IV Part 2:** 519
"Beyond Harm" (Olds), **Supp. X:** 210
Beyond Katrina: A Meditation on the Mississippi Gulf Coast (Trethewey), **Supp. XXI:** 248
"Beyond My Solitude" (Gibran), **Supp. XX: 119**
"Beyond the Alps" (Lowell), **II:** 547, 550
"Beyond the Bayou" (Chopin), **Supp. I Part 1:** 215
Beyond the Boom: New Voices on American Life, Culture and Politics (Teachout), **Supp. XIX:** 137
Beyond the Horizon (O'Neill), **III:** 389; **Supp. XXI:** 13; **Supp. XXII:** 22
Beyond the Hundredth Meridian: John Wesley Powell and the Second Opening of the West (Stegner), **Supp. IV Part 2:** 599, 603–604, 611
"Beyond the Kittery Bridge" (Hatlen), **Supp. V:** 138
Beyond the Law (film) (Mailer), **Retro. Supp. II:** 205
"Beyond the Sea (at the sanatorium)" (Salinas), **Supp. XIII:** 325
Beyond the Wall: Essays from the Outside (Abbey), **Supp. XIII:** 13
Beyond the Writers' Workshop: New Ways to Write Creative Nonfiction (C. Bly), **Supp. XVI:** 41
Beyond Tragedy (Niebuhr), **III:** 300–303
Bezner, Kevin, **Supp. XII:** 202
B. F.'s Daughter (Marquand), **III:** 59, 65, 68, 69
Bhagavad Gita, **III:** 566; **IV:** 183
"Biafra: A People Betrayed" (Vonnegut), **Supp. II Part 2:** 760
Bianchi, Martha Dickinson, **I:** 470; **Retro. Supp. I:** 35, 37, 38
Bible, **I:** 191, 280, 414, 421, 490, 506; **II:** 6, 12, 15, 17, 108, 231, 237, 238, 252, 267, 302; **III:** 28, 199, 308–309, 341, 343, 350, 356, 402, 492, 519, 565, 577; **IV:** 11, 13, 42, 57, 60, 67, 152, 153, 154, 155, 164, 165, 296, 337, 341, 367, 369, 370, 371, 438; **Retro. Supp. I:** 91; **Supp. I Part 1:** 4, 6, 63, 101, 104, 105, 113, 193, 369; **Supp. I Part 2:** 388, 433, 494, 515, 516, 517, 583, 584, 587, 589, 653, 689, 690, 691; **Supp. IV Part 1:** 284; **Supp. VIII:** 20; **Supp. IX:** 246; **Supp. XIV:** 225. *See also* names of biblical books; New Testament; Old Testament
Biblia Americana (Mather), **Supp. II Part 2:** 442
Biblical Dialogues between a Father and His Family (Rowson), **Supp. XV:** 245–246
"Bibliography of the King's Book, A, or, Eikon Basilike" (Howe), **Supp. IV Part 2:** 435
Bibliography of the King's Book, A; or, Eikon Basilike (Almack), **Supp. IV Part 2:** 435
Bickel, Freddy. *See* March, Fredric
Bidart, Frank, **Retro. Supp. II:** 48, 50, 52, 182, 183, 184; **Supp. XV: 19–37; Supp. XVIII:** 91,92; **Supp. XIX:** 82
Bid Me to Live (Doolittle), **Supp. I Part 1:** 258, 260, 268, 269, 270
"*Bien* Pretty" (Cisneros), **Supp. VII:** 70
"Bienvenidos" (Mora), **Supp. XIII:** 220
Bierce, Albert, **I:** 191, 209
Bierce, Ambrose, **I: 190–213,** 419; **II:** 74, 264, 271; **IV:** 350; **Retro. Supp. II:** 72
Bierce, Mrs. Ambrose, **I:** 194–195, 199
Bierce, Day, **I:** 195, 199
Bierce, Helen, **I:** 210
Bierce, Leigh, **I:** 195, 198, 208
Bierce, General Lucius Verus, **I:** 191
Bierce, Marcus, **I:** 190, 191
Bierce, Mrs. Marcus, **I:** 190, 191
Bierds, Linda, **Supp. XVII: 25–37**
Biffle, Kent, **Supp. V:** 225
"Bi-Focal" (Stafford), **Supp. XI:** 318, 321
Bigamist's Daughter, A (McDermott), **Supp. XVIII:** 155, **156–158,** 160, 166
Big as Life (Doctorow), **Supp. IV Part 1:** 231, 234
Big Bad Love (film, Howard), **Supp. XXI:** 39
Big Bad Love (L. Brown), **Supp. XXI:** 40, 42, **44–45**
"Big Bite" (Mailer), **Retro. Supp. II:** 204
"Big Blonde" (Parker), **Supp. IX:** 189, 192, 193, 195, 196, 203
Big Bozo, The (Glaspell), **Supp. III Part 1:** 182
Bigelow, Gordon, **Supp. X:** 222, 227, 229
Bigelow, Jacob, **Supp. I Part 1:** 302
Bigelow Papers, Second Series, The (Lowell), **Supp. I Part 2:** 406, 415–416
Bigelow Papers, The (Lowell), **Supp. I Part 2:** 406, 407, 408, 410, 411–412, 415, 417, 424
Big Fix, The (Lacy), **Supp. XV:** 204–205
Bigfoot Dreams (Prose), **Supp. XVI:** 253–254
Big Funk, The: A Casual Play (Shanley), **Supp. XIV:** 316, **327**
"Big Game" (Boyle), **Supp. XX: 20**
Big Game, The (film), **Supp. XIX:** 244
Big Gold Dream, The (C. Himes), **Supp. XVI:** 143, 144
"Bight, The" (Bishop), **Retro. Supp. II:** 38, 45
Big Hunger: Stories 1932–1959 (Fante), **Supp. XI:** 160
Big Knife, The (Odets), **Supp. II Part 2:** 546, 547, 548
Big Knockover, The (Hammett), **Supp. I Part 1:** 292; **Supp. IV Part 1:** 344, 345, 356
Big Laugh, The (O'Hara), **III:** 362, 373–375
Big Man (Neugeboren), **Supp. XVI:** 219, **220,** 221, 225
Big Money, The (Dos Passos), **I:** 482, 483, 486–487, 489; **Supp. I Part 2:** 646, 647
Big Picture (Everett), **Supp. XVIII:** 54, 66
"Big Picture" (Everett), **Supp. XVIII:** 66
"Big Picture" (Halliday), **Supp. XIX:** 93
"Big Rock Candy Figgy Pudding Pitfall, The" (Didion), **Supp. IV Part 1:** 195
Big Rock Candy Mountain, The (Stegner), **Supp. IV Part 2:** 596, 597, 598, 599, 600, 603, 604, 605, 606–607, 608, 610–611
Bigsby, C. W. E. (Christopher), **Supp. IX:** 137, 140; **Supp. XV:** 332
Big Sea, The (Hughes), **Retro. Supp. I:** 195, 197, 199, 201, 204; **Supp. I Part 1:** 322, 332, 333; **Supp. II Part 1:** 233–234; **Supp. XIX:** 77; **Supp. XXII:** 3
Big Sky, The (Mora), **Supp. XIII:** 221
Big Sleep, The (Chandler), **Supp. IV Part 1:** 122–125, 127, 128, 134
Big Sleep, The (film), **Supp. IV Part 1:** 130; **Supp. XVIII:** 148
Big Strike, The (Ryan as Quin), **Supp. XVIII:** 226,**232–233**
Big Sur (Kerouac), **Supp. III Part 1:** 230
Big Sur and the Oranges of Hieronymous Bosch (H. Miller), **III:** 189–190
Big Town, The (Lardner), **II:** 426, 429
"Big Two-Hearted River" (Hemingway), **II:** 249; **Retro. Supp. I:** 170–171; **Supp. IX:** 106; **Supp. XIV:** 227, 235
"Big Wind" (Roethke), **III:** 531
"Big Winner Rises Late, The" (Dunn), **Supp. XI:** 146
"Bilingual/*Bilingüe" (essay; Espaillat), Supp. XXI:* 103
"Bilingual/*Bilingüe" (poem; Espaillat), Supp. XXI:* 104
"Bilingual Christmas" (Mora), **Supp. XIII:** 216–217
"Bilingual Sestina" (Alvarez), **Supp. VII:** 10
"Bill" (Winters), **Supp. II Part 2:** 792
"Bill, The" (Malamud), **Supp. I Part 2:** 427, 430, 434
"Bill Collector's Vacation, The" (Hampl), **Supp. XXII:** 83
"Billie Holiday" (Carruth), **Supp. XVI:** 50
Billings, Gladys. *See* Brooks, Mrs. Van Wyck
Billings, Josh, **Supp. XVIII:** 1, 4
Bill of Rites, a Bill of Wrongs, a Bill of Goods, A (Morris), **III:** 237
"Bill's Beans" (Nye), **Supp. XIII:** 283
"Billy" (Gordon), **Supp. IV Part 1:** 306
"Billy" (McCarriston), **Supp. XIV:** 265
Billy Bathgate (Doctorow), **Supp. IV Part 1:** 217, 219, 222, 224, 227, 229–231, 231, 232, 233, 238

Billy Bathgate (film), **Supp. IV Part 1:** 236
Billy Budd, Sailor (Melville), **III:** 40, 93–95; **IV:** 105; **Retro. Supp. I:** 249, **258–260**
Billy Collins Live: A Performance at the Peter Norton Symphony Space April 20, 2005 (CD, Collins), **Supp. XXI:** 51
"Billy Gardner's Ground Out" (Skloot), **Supp. XX: 205, 207**
Billy Phelan's Greatest Game (W. Kennedy), **Supp. VII:** 131, 132, 134, 135, 142–147, 149, 151, 153, 155
Billy Ray's Farm: Essays from a Place Called Tula (L. Brown), **Supp. XXI:** 48, 49
Billy's Boy (P. N. Warren), **Supp. XX: 261, 265–267**
Billy the Kid, **Supp. IV Part 2:** 489, 490, 492
Biloxi Blues (Simon), **Supp. IV Part 2:** 576, 577, 584, 586–587, 590
"Bimini" (Hemingway), **II:** 258
Bingham, Anne, **Supp. XV:** 239
Bingham, Millicent Todd, **I:** 470; **Retro. Supp. I:** 36
Bingham, Remica L., **Supp. XXI:** 256
Bingo Palace, The (Erdrich), **Supp. IV Part 1:** 259, 260, 261, 263–264, 265, 266–267, 268–269, 270, 271–273, 274, 275
"Binsey Poplars" (Hopkins), **Supp. I Part 1:** 94; **Supp. IV Part 2:** 639
Binswanger, Ludwig, **Supp. XV:** 26
Biographia Literaria (Coleridge), **II:** 10; **Retro. Supp. I:** 308
"Biography" (Francis), **Supp. IX:** 77
"Biography" (Pinsky), **Supp. VI:** 235, 236, 239, 241, **243,** 249, 250
Biography and Poetical Remains of the Late Margaret Miller Davidson (Irving), **II:** 314
"Biography in the First Person" (Dunn), **Supp. XI:** 144
"Biography of an Armenian Schoolgirl" (Nye), **Supp. XIII:** 275, 280
"Biography of a Story" (Jackson), **Supp. IX:** 113
Biondi, Joann, **Supp. XI:** 103
"Biopoetics Sketch for *Greenfield Review*" (Harjo), **Supp. XII:** 216
"Birchbrook Mill" (Whittier), **Supp. I Part 2:** 699
"Birches" (Frost), **II:** 154; **Retro. Supp. I:** 132; **Supp. XIII:** 147
Bird, Alan, **Supp. I Part 1:** 260
Bird, Gloria, **Supp. XII:** 216
Bird, Isabella, **Supp. X:** 103
Bird, Robert M., **III:** 423
"Bird, The" (Simpson), **Supp. IX:** 269–270
"Bird, the Bird, the Bird, The" (Creeley), **Supp. IV Part 1:** 149
"Bird Banding with the Biologists" (Ray), **Supp. XVIII:** 194
Bird by Bird: Some Instructions on Writing and Life (Lamott), **Supp. XX: 132, 137–138**
"Bird came down the Walk, A" (Dickinson), **Retro. Supp. I:** 37
"Bird Frau, The" (Dove), **Supp. IV Part 1:** 245
"Bird in Hand" (screen story) (West and Ingster), **Retro. Supp. II:** 330
Bird Kingdom of the Mayas (LaBastille), **Supp. X:** 96
Birds and Beasts (W. J. Smith), **Supp. XIII:** 346
"Birds for Christmas, The" (Richard), **Supp. XIX:** 221
Bird's Nest, The (Jackson), **Supp. IX: 124–125**
Birds of America (McCarthy), **II:** 579–583; **Supp. X:** 177
Birds of America (Moore), **Supp. X:** 163, 165, 167, 168, 171, **177–179**
Birds of America, The (Audubon), **Supp. XVI: 5–6,** 7, 9, 10, 12, 13
"Birds of Killingsworth, The" (Longfellow), **Retro. Supp. II:** 164
Birds of North America (Audubon Society), **Supp. X:** 177
"Birds of Vietnam, The" (Carruth), **Supp. XVI:** 55
"Bird-Witted" (Moore), **III:** 214
Birkelo, Cheryl, **Supp. XX: 220–221**
Birkerts, Sven, **Supp. IV Part 2:** 650; **Supp. V:** 212; **Supp. VIII:** 85; **Supp. X:** 311; **Supp. XX: 92**
Birkhead, L. M., **III:** 116
"Birmingham Sunday" (Hughes), **Supp. I Part 1:** 343
Birnbaum, Henry, **Supp. XII:** 128
Birnbaum, Robert, **Supp. X:** 13; **Supp. XVI:** 75
Birney, James G., **Supp. I Part 2:** 587, 588
Birstein, Ann, **Supp. VIII:** 100
"Birthday, A" (Untermeyer), **Supp. XV:** 296
Birthday Basket for Tía, A (Mora), **Supp. XIII:** 221
"Birthday Cake" (Carruth), **Supp. XVI:** 59
"Birthday Cake for Lionel, A" (Wylie), **Supp. I Part 2:** 721
"Birthday Girl: 1950" (McCarriston), **Supp. XIV:** 261
"Birthday of Mrs. Pineda, The" (Ríos), **Supp. IV Part 2:** 542, 546
"Birthday Poem, A" (Hecht), **Supp. X:** 64
"Birthday Present, A" (Plath), **Supp. I Part 2:** 531
"Birthmark, The" (Ellison), **Retro. Supp. II:** 116; **Supp. II Part 1:** 237–238
"Birth-mark, The" (Hawthorne), **Retro. Supp. I:** 152
Birth-mark, The: Unsettling the Wilderness in American Literary History (Howe), **Supp. IV Part 2:** 422, 431, 434
Birth of a Nation, The (film), **Supp. I Part 1:** 66
Birth of a World: Bolívar in Terms of His Peoples (W. Frank), **Supp. XX: 80**
Birth of the Poet, The (Gordon), **Supp. XII:** 7
Birth of Tragedy, The (Nietzsche), **Supp. IV Part 1:** 105, 110; **Supp. IV Part 2:** 519; **Supp. VIII:** 182
"Birth of Venus, The" (Botticelli), **IV:** 410
"Birth of Venus, The" (Rukeyser), **Supp. VI:** 281
"Birthplace Revisited" (Corso), **Supp. XII:** 123
"Birthright" (McKay), **Supp. X:** 136
Bisch, Louis E., **Supp. I Part 2:** 608
Bisco, John, **Supp. XVIII:** 11
"B is for Bachelors" (M. F. K. Fisher), **Supp. XVII:** 86
Bishop, Elizabeth, **Retro. Supp. I:** 140, 296, 303; **Retro. Supp. II: 37–56,** 175, 178, 189, 233, 234, 235; **Supp. I Part 1: 72–97,** 239, 320, 326; **Supp. III Part 1:** 6, 7, 10, 18, 64, 239, 320, 326; **Supp. III Part 2:** 541, 561; **Supp. IV Part 1:** 249, 257; **Supp. IV Part 2:** 439, 626, 639, 641, 644, 647, 651, 653; **Supp. V:** 337; **Supp. IX:** 40, 41, 45, 47, 48; **Supp. X:** 58; **Supp. XI:** 123, 136; **Supp. XIII:** 115, 348; **Supp. XV:** 20–21, 100, 101, 112, 119, 249, 251; **Supp. XVII:** 36, 76; **Supp. XXI:** 58, 84, 131
Bishop, James, Jr., **Supp. XIII:** 1, 5, 6, 7, 9, 11, 15
Bishop, John Peale, **I:** 432, 440; **II:** 81, 85, 86–87, 91, 209; **IV:** 35, 140, 427; **Retro. Supp. I:** 109; **Supp. I Part 2:** 709
Bishop, John W., **Supp. I Part 1:** 83
Bishop, Judith, **Supp. XVI:** 295
Bishop, Morris, **Supp. I Part 2:** 676
Bishop, William Thomas, **Supp. I Part 1:** 83
"Bishop Orders His Tomb at St. Praxed's Church, The" (R. Browning), **Supp. XV:** 127
"Bishop's Beggar, The" (Benét), **Supp. XI:** 56
"Bismarck" (Chapman), **Supp. XIV:** 52, 53
Bismark, Otto von, **Supp. I Part 2:** 643
"Bistro Styx, The" (Dove), **Supp. IV Part 1:** 250–251
Bitov, Andrei, **Retro. Supp. I:** 278
Bits of Gossip (R. H. Davis), **Supp. XVI:** 82–83, 84, 85, 89
"Bitter Drink, The" (Dos Passos), **Supp. I Part 2:** 647
"Bitter Farce, A" (Schwartz), **Supp. II Part 2:** 640, 657–658
"Bitter Pills for the Dark Ladies" (Jong), **Supp. V:** 118
Bitterroot (Burke), **Supp. XIV:** 34, 35
"Bittersweet Nightshade" (Skloot), **Supp. XX: 202**
Bitter Victory (Hardy; Kinnell, trans.), **Supp. III Part 1:** 235
Bittner, William, **Supp. XX: 74,Supp. XX: 77, 76, 78, 80**
Bitzer, G. W. "Billy", **Supp. XVI:** 183
Bixby, Horace, **IV:** 194
Bjerre, Thomas Aervold, **Supp. XXI:** 41, 47
Bjorkman, Frances Maule, **Supp. V:** 285

Bjorkman, Stig, **Supp. XV:** 6
Björnson, Björnstjerne, **II:** 275
Black, Cheryl, **Supp. XXI:** 6
Black 100, The (Salley), **Supp. XIV:** 195
Blackamerican Literature, 1760-Present (R. Miller), **Supp. X:** 324
Black American Literature Forum, **Supp. XI:** 86, 92, 93
Black and Blue (Quindlen), **Supp. XVII:** 166, **176–178**
"Black and Tan" (Bell), **Supp. X:** 9
Black and White (Sorrentino), **Supp. XXI:** 228
Black Armour (Wylie), **Supp. I Part 2:** 708, 709, 712–714, 729
"Black Art" (Baraka), **Supp. II Part 1:** 49, 50–51, 59, 60
"Black Art, The" (Sexton), **Supp. II Part 2:** 682
"Black Ball, The" (Ellison), **Retro. Supp. II:** 124
Black Bart and the Sacred Hills (Wilson), **Supp. VIII:** 330, 331
Black Beetles in Amber (Bierce), **I:** 204, 209
"Blackberries" (Komunyakaa), **Supp. XIII:** 126
"Blackberry Eating" (Kinnell), **Supp. III Part 1:** 250
"Blackberrying" (D. West), **Supp. XVIII:** 283
Blackberry Winter (Warren), **IV:** 243, 251, 252
Black Betty (Mosley), **Supp. XIII:** 237, **Supp. XIII:** 240, 243
"Black Birch in Winter, A" (Wilbur), **Supp. III Part 2:** 561
Black Boy (Wright), **IV:** 477, 478, 479, 480–482, 488, 489, 494; **Retro. Supp. II:** 117; **Supp. II Part 1:** 235–236; **Supp. IV Part 1:** 11; **Supp. XVIII:** 286
"Black Boys and Native Sons" (Howe), **Retro. Supp. II:** 112
Blackburn, Alex, **Supp. XIII:** 112
Blackburn, Paul, **Supp. XXII:** 164, 169
Blackburn, William, **IV:** 100
"Black Buttercups" (Clampitt), **Supp. IX:** 42
Black Cargo, The (Marquand), **III:** 55, 60
Black Cargoes: A History of the Atlantic Slave Trade (Cowley), **Supp. II Part 1:** 140
"Black Cat, The" (Poe), **III:** 413, 414, 415; **Retro. Supp. II:** 264, 267, 269, 270
Black Cherry Blues (Burke), **Supp. XIV:** 30
"Black Christ, The" (Cullen), **Supp. IV Part 1:** 170, 171–172
Black Christ and Other Poems, The (Cullen), **Supp. IV Part 1:** 166, 170
"Black Clay Fish from Oaxaca, A" (Bronk), **Supp. XXI:** 31
"Black Cottage, The" (Frost), **Retro. Supp. I:** 128
"BLACK DADA NIHILISMUS" (Baraka), **Supp. II Part 1:** 39, 41
"Black Death" (Hurston), **Supp. VI:** 153
Black Dog, Red Dog (Dobyns), **Supp. XIII:** 87, **88–89**
"Black Dog, Red Dog" (Dobyns), **Supp. XIII:** 89
"Black Earth" (Moore), **III:** 197, 212
Black Echo, The (Connelly), **Supp. XXI:** 67, 68, 75, 80
Black Fire (Jones and Neal, eds.), **Supp. X:** 324, 328
Black Fire: An Anthology of Afro American Writing (Baraka, ed.), **Supp. II Part 1:** 53
Black Flame, The (Du Bois), **Supp. II Part 1:** 159, 185–186
Black Folk, Then and Now: An Essay in the History and Sociology of the Negro Race (Du Bois), **Supp. II Part 1:** 159, 178, 183, 185
Blackford, Holly, **Supp. XXII:** 300
"Black Fox, The" (Whittier), **Supp. I Part 2:** 692
Black Freckles (Levis), **Supp. XI:** 257, 271
"Black Gang", **IV:** 406, 407
Black Genius (Mosley, ed.), **Supp. XIII:** 246
"Black Hood, The" (Francis), **Supp. IX:** 83, 91
Black House, The (Theroux), **Supp. VIII:** 319
Black Humor (Johnson), **Supp. VI:** 187, 199
Black Ice, The (Connelly), **Supp. XXI:** **70,** 75
Black Image in the White Mind, The (Fredrickson), **Supp. I Part 2:** 589
"Black Is My Favorite Color" (Malamud), **Supp. I Part 2:** 437
Black Jacobins, The (C. L. R. James), **Supp. XXI:** 159, 166–167
"Black Jewel, The" (Merwin), **Supp. III Part 1:** 355
Black Lamb and Grey Falcon (R. West), **Supp. XVI:** 152
"Black Laughter" (Taggard), **Supp. XXII:** 274
"Blacklegs" (B. Kelly), **Supp. XVII:** 131
Black Light (Kinnell), **Supp. III Part 1:** 235, 243
"Blacklist and the Cold War, The" (Kramer), **Supp. I Part 1:** 295
Black Literature in America (Baker), **Supp. X:** 324
Black Magic, A Pictorial History of the Negro in American Entertainment (Hughes), **Supp. I Part 1:** 345
Black Magic: Collected Poetry 1961–1967 (Baraka), **Supp. II Part 1:** 45, 49–50
"Blackmailers Don't Shoot" (Chandler), **Supp. IV Part 1:** 121–122
Black Manhattan (Johnson), **Supp. IV Part 1:** 169
Black Mass, A (Baraka), **Supp. II Part 1:** 46, 48–49, 56, 57
"Black Mesa, The" (Merrill), **Supp. III Part 1:** 328
Black Metropolis (Cayton and Drake), **IV:** 475, 486, 488
Black Misery (Hughes), **Supp. I Part 1:** 336
Blackmur, Helen Dickson (Mrs. R. P. Blackmur), **Supp. II Part 1:** 90
Blackmur, Richard P., **I:** 50, 63, 67, 280, 282, 386, 455, 472; **II:** 320, 537; **III:** 194, 208, 462, 478, 497; **Supp. II Part 1: 87–112,** 136; **Supp. II Part 2:** 543, 643; **Supp. XII:** 45
Black Music (Baraka), **Supp. II Part 1:** 47, 51
Black Nativity (Hughes), **Retro. Supp. I:** 196
Black No More (Schuyler), **Supp. XVI:** 142; **Supp. XIX:** 73
Black on Black: "Baby Sister" and Selected Writings (C. Himes), **Supp. XVI:** 145
"Black or White" (Major), **Supp. XXII:** 185
"Blackout" (Hay), **Supp. XIV:** 121
"Black Panther" (Hughes), **Retro. Supp. I:** 211
"Black Petal" (L.-Y. Lee), **Supp. XV:** 224–225
Black Power (Wright), **IV:** 478, 488, 494
"Black Rainbow, A: Modern Afro-American Poetry" (Dove and Waniek), **Supp. IV Part 1:** 244
Black Reconstruction (Du Bois), **Supp. II Part 1:** 159, 162, 171, 182
Black Riders and Other Lines, The (Crane), **I:** 406, 419
Black Riviera, The (Jarman), **Supp. XVII:** 109, 110, **115–116**
"Black Rook in Rainy Weather" (Plath), **Supp. I Part 2:** 543, 544
Blacks (Brooks), **Supp. III Part 1:** 69, 72, 86, 87
Blacks, The (Genet), **Supp. IV Part 1:** 8
Black Skin, White Masks (Fanon), **Retro. Supp. II:** 118
Black Sleuth, The (J. Bruce), **Supp. XVI:** 143
Black Spear, The (Hayden), **Supp. II Part 1:** 375
Black Spring (H. Miller), **III:** 170, 175, 178, 180–182, 183, 184; **Supp. X:** 187
"Black Stone Lying on a White Stone" (Vallejo), **Supp. XIII:** 324
Black Sun (Abbey), **Supp. XIII:** 4, **8–9,** 17
"Black Swan" (B. Kelly), **Supp. XVII:** 130–131
"Black Swan, The" (Jarrell), **II:** 382
Black Swan, The (Merrill), **Supp. III Part 1:** 319, 320
"Black Tambourine" (Crane), **I:** 387–388; **II:** 371
Black Thunder (Bontemps), **Supp. XXII:** 4, 9
"Black Tuesday" (Swenson), **Supp. IV Part 2:** 646
Black Virgin Mountain (Heinemann), **Supp. XXII:** 103, **114–116**
Black Voices (Chapman), **IV:** 485
"Blackwater Mountain" (Wright), **Supp. V:** 335, 340
"Black Wedding, The" (Singer), **IV:** 12–13

Blackwell, Alice Stone, **Supp. XI:** 195, 197
Blackwell, Elizabeth, **Retro. Supp. II:** 146
Black Woman, The (Bambara, ed.), **Supp. XI:** 1
"Black Workers" (Hughes), **Retro. Supp. I:** 202
"Black Writer and the Southern Experience, The" (Walker), **Supp. III Part 2:** 521
Black Zodiac (Wright), **Supp. V:** 333, 344, 345
Blade Runner (film), **Supp. XI:** 84
Blades, John, **Supp. XX: 87**
"Blades of Steel" (R. Fisher), **Supp. XIX:** 72
Blaine, Anita McCormick, **Supp. I Part 1:** 5
Blaine, Nell, **Supp. XV:** 179
Blair, Hugh, **II:** 8, 17; **Supp. I Part 2:** 422
Blair, Robert, **Supp. I Part 1:** 150
Blair, Walter, **II:** 20; **Retro. Supp. II:** 286
Blaisdell, Gus, **Supp. XIV:** 87
Blake, Casey Nelson, **Supp. XX: 69, 70, 78**
Blake, William, **I:** 381, 383, 389, 390, 398, 447, 476, 525, 526, 533; **II:** 321; **III:** 5, 19, 22, 195, 196, 197, 205, 485, 528, 540, 544–545, 567, 572; **IV:** 129; **Retro. Supp. II:** 76, 300; **Supp. I Part 1:** 80; **Supp. I Part 2:** 385, 514, 517, 539, 552, 708; **Supp. V:** 208, 257, 258; **Supp. VIII:** 26, 99, 103; **Supp. X:** 120; **Supp. XII:** 45; **Supp. XIV:** 344; **Supp. XVI:** 282; **Supp. XVII:** 119; **Supp. XX: 115, 116; Supp. XXII:** 225, 257
Blakely, Barbara, **Supp. XIII:** 32
Blanc, Marie Thérèse, **Retro. Supp. II:** 135
Blanc-Bentzon, Mme. Thérèse, **II:** 405
Blanchard, Paula, **Retro. Supp. II:** 131, 133–134, 135
Blanche, Jacques-Émile, **Supp. XX: 232**
Blanchot, Maurice, **Supp. XVI:** 288
Blancs, Les (Hansberry), **Supp. IV Part 1:** 359, 364, 365, 369, 372–374
Blancs, Les: The Collected Last Plays of Lorraine Hansberry (Nemiroff, ed.), **Supp. IV Part 1:** 365, 368, 374
"'Blandula, Tenulla, Vagula' " (Pound), **III:** 463; **Supp. V:** 336, 337, 345
Blankenship, Tom, **IV:** 193
"Blank Paper" (Peacock), **Supp. XIX:** 198–199
Blank Wall, The (Holding), **Supp. XXII:** 119, 120, 121, 130**, 131–133,** 134
Blanshard, Rufus A., **I:** 67
Blassingame, John, **Supp. XX: 106**
Blauvelt, William Satake, **Supp. V:** 171, 173
Blavatsky, Elena Petrovna, **III:** 176
"Blazing in Gold and Quenching in Purple" (Dickinson), **Retro. Supp. I:** 30
Bleak House (Dickens), **II:** 291; **Supp. IV Part 1:** 293
Blechman, Burt, **Supp. I Part 1:** 290
"Bleeder" (Dobyns), **Supp. XIII:** 88
"Bleeding" (Swenson), **Supp. IV Part 2:** 646–647
"Blessed Is the Man" (Moore), **III:** 215
"Blessed Man of Boston, My Grandmother's Thimble, and Fanning Island, The" (Updike), **IV:** 219
"Blessing, A" (Wright), **Supp. III Part 2:** 600, 606
Blessing on the Moon, A (Skibell), **Supp. XVII:** 48
Blessings (Quindlen), **Supp. XVII:** 167, **178–179**
"Blessing the Animals" (Komunyakaa), **Supp. XIII:** 129–130
"Blessing the Children" (Hogan), **Supp. IV Part 1:** 401
Bless Me, Ultima (Anya), **Supp. XIII:** 220
Blew, Mary Clearman, **Supp. XIV:** 227
Bligh, S. M., **I:** 226
Blind Alleys (film), **Supp. XXI:** 146
Blind Assassin, The (Atwood), **Supp. XIII:** 20, **32**
Blind Bow-Boy, The (Van Vechten), **Supp. II Part 2:** 737, 740–742
"Blind Date" (Halliday), **Supp. XIX:** 85
Blind Date (Kosinski), **Supp. VII:** 215, 224–225
"Blinded by the Light" (Boyle), **Supp. XX: 20**
Blind Lion, The (Gunn Allen), **Supp. IV Part 1:** 324
"Blind Man's Holiday" (O. Henry), **Supp. II Part 1:** 401
Blind Man with a Pistol (C. Himes), **Supp. XVI:** 143, 144
Blindness and Insight (de Man), **Retro. Supp. I:** 67
"Blind Poet, The: Sidney Lanier" (Warren), **Supp. I Part 1:** 371, 373
"Blindsided" (P. E. Jones), **Supp. XXII:** 151–152
"Blind Tom" (R. H. Davis), **Supp. XVI:** 89, 90
Blithedale Romance, The (Hawthorne), **II:** 225, 231, 239, 241–242, 271, 282, 290; **IV:** 194; **Retro. Supp. I:** 63, 149, 152, 156–157, **162–163; Supp. I Part 2:** 579; **Supp. II Part 1:** 280; **Supp. VIII:** 153, 201
Blitzstein, Marc, **Supp. I Part 1:** 277
Blix (Norris), **III:** 314, 322, 327, 328, 333
Blixen, Karen Denisen Baroness. *See* Dinesen, Isak
"Blizzard in Cambridge" (Lowell), **II:** 554
Blizzard Voices, The (Kooser), **Supp. XIX: 123**
Bloch, Ernest, **Supp. XX: 75**
Block, Lawrence, **Supp. XXI:** 67
Blok, Aleksandr Aleksandrovich, **IV:** 443
"Blond" (Trethewey), **Supp. XXI:** 244
Blonde Bait (Lacy), **Supp. XV:** 204
Blonde on Blonde (album, Dylan), **Supp. XVIII:** 20, 27, 30
Blondin, Antoine, **Supp. XVI:** 230
"Blood" (Hoffman), **Supp. XVIII:** 86
"Blood" (Singer), **IV:** 15, 19
Blood, Tin, Straw (Olds), **Supp. X: 212–215**
Blood and Guile (Hoffman), **Supp. XVIII: 83–84**
Blood and Guts in High School (Acker), **Supp. XII:** 5, 6, **11–12**
"Blood Bay, The" (Proulx), **Supp. VII:** 262–263
"Blood-Burning Moon" (Toomer), **Supp. III Part 2:** 483; **Supp. IX:** 314–315
"Bloodchild" (O. Butler), **Supp. XIII:** 61, **69–70**
Bloodchild and Other Stories (O. Butler), **Supp. XIII:** 69
"Blood Donor" (Hay), **Supp. XIV:** 121
Blood for a Stranger (Jarrell), **II:** 367, 368–369, 370–371, 375, 377
Blood Issue (Crews), **Supp. XI:** 103
Bloodlines (Wright), **Supp. V:** 332, 335, 340
Blood Meridian; or, The Evening Redness in the West (McCarthy), **Supp. VIII:** 175, 177, **180–182,** 188, 190
Blood of My Blood (Gambino), **Supp. XX: 35**
"Blood of the Conquistadores, The" (Alvarez), **Supp. VII:** 7
"Blood of the Lamb, The" (hymn), **Supp. I Part 2:** 385
Blood of the Martyr (Crane), **I:** 422
"Blood of the Martyrs, The" (Benét), **Supp. XI:** 56, 58
Blood of the Prophets, The (Masters), **Supp. I Part 2:** 458, 459, 461
Blood on the Forge (Attaway), **Supp. II Part 1:** 234–235
Blood on the Tracks (album, Dylan), **Supp. XVIII:** 20, 27, 30
"Blood Relatives" (Apple), **Supp. XVII:** 6
"Blood Returns, The" (Kingsolver), **Supp. VII:** 209
"Bloodshed" (C. Ozick), **Supp. XVII:** 43
Bloodshed and Three Novellas (Ozick), **Supp. V:** 259–260, 261, 266–268
"Blood Stains" (Francis), **Supp. IX:** 86
Blood Work (Connelly), **Supp. XXI: 72**
Blood Work (film, Eastwood), **Supp. XXI:** 74
Bloody Crossroads, The: Where Literature and Politics Meet (Podhoretz), **Supp. VIII: 241–242**
Bloom, Alice, **Supp. IV Part 1:** 308
Bloom, Allan, **Retro. Supp. II:** 19, 30, 31, 33–34
Bloom, Claire, **Retro. Supp. II:** 281; **Supp. IX:** 125
Bloom, Harold, **Retro. Supp. I:** 67, 193, 299; **Retro. Supp. II:** 81, 210, 262; **Supp. IV Part 2:** 620, 689; **Supp. V:** 178, 272; **Supp. VIII:** 180; **Supp. IX:** 146, 259; **Supp. XII:** 261; **Supp. XIII:** 46, 47; **Supp. XIV:** 14; **Supp. XV:** 134; **Supp. XVII:** 70, 141
Bloom, Larry, **Supp. XIII:** 133
Bloom, Leopold, **I:** 27, 150; **III:** 10
Bloom, Lynn Z., **Supp. IV Part 1:** 6
Bloomfield, Leonard, **I:** 64

Bloomingdale Papers, The (Carruth), **Supp. XVI:** 48–50
"Blossom and Fruit" (Benét), **Supp. XI:** 52–53
Blotner, Joseph, **Retro. Supp. I:** 88
Blouin, Lenora, **Supp. VIII:** 266
"Blowin' in the Wind" (song, Dylan), **Supp. XVIII:** 24, 25, 26, 29
Blue Angel (Prose), **Supp. XVI:** 249, 259–260
Blue Angel, The (film), **Supp. XVIII:** 243
Blue Arabesque: A Search for the Sublime (Hampl), **Supp. XXII:** 86, 98–99
"Blue Battalions, The" (Crane), **I:** 419–420
"Bluebeard" (Barthelme), **Supp. IV Part 1:** 47
"Bluebeard" (Millay), **III:** 130
"Blueberries" (Frost), **Retro. Supp. I:** 121, 128
Blue Calhoun (Price), **Supp. VI:** 265–266
Blue Caterpillar, The (Pickering), **Supp. XXI:** 202–203
Blue City (Macdonald, as Millar), **Supp. IV Part 2:** 466–467
Blue Devils of Nada, The: A Contemporary American Approach to Aesthetics (Murray), **Supp. XIX: 159–160**
Blue Estuaries, The: Poems, 1923–1968 (Bogan), **Supp. III Part 1:** 48, 57, 66
Blue Hammer, The (Macdonald), **Supp. IV Part 2:** 462
"Blue Hotel, The" (Crane), **I:** 34, 415–416, 423
"Blue Hour, The" (Komunyakaa), **Supp. XIII:** 130
Blue in the Face (Auster), **Supp. XII:** 21
Blue Jay's Dance, The: A Birth Year (Erdrich), **Supp. IV Part 1:** 259–260, 265, 270, 272
"Blue Juniata" (Cowley), **Supp. II Part 1:** 144
Blue Juniata: Collected Poems (Cowley), **Supp. II Part 1:** 140
"Blue Lick" (Offutt), **Supp. XIX:** 164, 165
Blue Light (Mosley), **Supp. XIII: 245–247,** 248, 249
"Blue Light Lounge Sutra for the Performance Poets at Harold Park Hotel" (Komunyakaa), **Supp. XIII:** 125
"Blue Meridian" (Toomer), **Supp. III Part 2:** 476, 487; **Supp. IX:** 320
"Blue Moles" (Plath), **Supp. I Part 2:** 539
Blue Mountain Ballads (music) (Bowles), **Supp. IV Part 1:** 84
Blue Movie (Southern), **Supp. XI:** 309
"Blue Notes" (Matthews), **Supp. IX:** 169
Blue Pastoral (Sorrentino), **Supp. XXI:** 226, 235–236
Blue Pastures (Oliver), **Supp. VII:** 229–230, 245
"Blueprint for Negro Writing" (Wright), **Supp. XVIII:** 282–283
"Blueprints" (Kingsolver), **Supp. VII:** 203
Blue Religion, The (Connelly, ed.), **Supp. XXI:** 74–75, 79
Blue Rhine, Black Forest (Untermeyer), **Supp. XV:** 310
"Blue Ribbon at Amesbury, A" (Frost), **Retro. Supp. I:** 138
"Blues Ain't No Mockin Bird" (Bambara), **Supp. XI:** 3
"Blues and the Fable in the Flesh, The" (lecture, Murray), **Supp. XIX:** 153
"Blues Chant Hoodoo Rival" (Komunyakaa), **Supp. XIII:** 117, 118
Blue Screen (Parker), **Supp. XIX:** 186
"Blues for Another Time" (Dunn), **Supp. XI:** 148
"Blues for Jimmy" (McGrath), **Supp. X:** 116
"Blues for John Coltraine, Dead at 41" (Matthews), **Supp. IX:** 157
Blues for Mister Charlie (Baldwin), **Retro. Supp. II:** 8; **Supp. I Part 1:** 48, 61–62, 63
"Blues for Warren" (McGrath), **Supp. X:** 116
Blue Shoe (Lamott), **Supp. XX: 138–140**
Blues If You Want (Matthews), **Supp. IX:** 155, **163–165**
"Blues I'm Playing, The" (Hughes), **Retro. Supp. I:** 204; **Supp. XIX:** 75
"Blue Sky, The" (Snyder), **Supp. VIII:** 306
"Blues on a Box" (Hughes), **Retro. Supp. I:** 208
"Blues People" (Ellison), **Retro. Supp. II:** 124
Blues People: Negro Music in White America (Baraka), **Retro. Supp. II:** 124; **Supp. II Part 1:** 30, 31, 33–35, 37, 41, 42, 53
"Blue Spruces in Pairs, a Bird Bath Between": (Bronk), **Supp. XXI:** 30
Bluest Eye, The (Morrison), **Supp. III Part 1:** 362, 363–367, 379; **Supp. IV Part 1:** 2, 253; **Supp. VIII:** 213, 214, 227; **Supp. XI:** 4, 91
Bluestone, George, **Supp. IX:** 7, 15
Blue Swallows, The (Nemerov), **III:** 269, 270, 271, 274–275, 278, 284, 286–288
"Blue Tattoo" (Nelson and Espeland), **Supp. XVIII:** 181
Blue Voyage (Aiken), **I:** 53, 56
Blum, Gustav, **Supp. XV:** 194
Blum, Morgan, **I:** 169
Blum, W. C (pseudonym). *See* Watson, James Sibley, Jr.
Blumenthal, Nathaniel. *See* Branden, Nathaniel
Blumenthal, Sidney, **Supp. VIII:** 241
Blunden, Edmund, **Supp. XIX:** 133
Blunt, Wilfrid Scawen, **III:** 459
Bly, Carol, **Supp. XVI: 31–43**
Bly, Robert, **I:** 291; **Supp. III Part 2:** 599; **Supp. IV Part 1: 59–77,** 177; **Supp. IV Part 2:** 623; **Supp. V:** 332; **Supp. VIII:** 279; **Supp. IX:** 152, 155, 265, 271, 290; **Supp. X:** 127; **Supp. XI:** 142; **Supp. XIII:** 284; **Supp. XV:** 74, 176; **Supp. XVI:** 32, 36, 39, 177, 212, 230; **Supp. XVII:** 243, 244; **Supp. XXI:** 83, 84–86, 87, 91, 93, 94, 95; **Supp. XXII:** 83
"B Negative" (X. J. Kennedy), **Supp. XV: 156–157**
"Boarder, The" (Simpson), **Supp. IX:** 269
Boarding House Blues (Farrell), **II:** 30, 43, 45
Boas, Franz, **I:** 214; **Supp. I Part 2:** 641; **Supp. VIII:** 295; **Supp. IX:** 329; **Supp. XIV:** 199, 209, 210
"Boat, The" (Oliver), **Supp. VII:** 247
"Boat, The" (Sexton), **Supp. II Part 2:** 692
Boating Party, The (Renoir), **Supp. XII:** 188
Boat of Quiet Hours, The (Kenyon), **Supp. VII:** 167–169, 171
"Boat of Quiet Hours, The" (Kenyon), **Supp. VII:** 168
"Bob and Spike" (Wolfe), **Supp. III Part 2:** 580
"Bobby Shafter's Gone to Sea" (Swados), **Supp. XIX:** 267
"Bob Dylan's 115th Dream" (song, Dylan), **Supp. XVIII:** 25
Bobrowski, Johannes, **Supp. XV:** 78
Bob the Gambler (F. Barthelme), **Supp. XI:** 30, 31, 32, 34–35, 36–37
Boccaccio, Giovanni, **III:** 283, 411; **IV:** 230
Bocock, Maclin, **Supp. X:** 79
Boddy, Kasia, **Supp. XXII:** 261
Bodelson, Anders, **Supp. XVI:** 33
Bodenheim, Maxwell, **II:** 42, 530; **Retro. Supp. I:** 417; **Supp. I Part 1:** 257
"Bodies" (Oates), **Supp. II Part 2:** 520
"Bodies and Souls: The Haitian Revolution and Madison Smartt Bell's *All Souls' Rising*" (Trouillot), **Supp. X:** 14
Bodies of Water (Cliff), **Supp. XXII:** 66–67, 74–75
Bodies of Work: Essays (Acker), **Supp. XII:** 7
Bodily Harm (Atwood), **Supp. XIII: 25–27**
Bodley Head Jack London (London), **II:** 483
Body (Crews), **Supp. XI: 108–109**
"Body, The" (Heldreth), **Supp. V:** 151
Body and Soul (Conroy), **Supp. XVI:** 63, **72–74,** 77
"Body and Soul: A Meditation" (Kumin), **Supp. IV Part 2:** 442, 452
Body and Soul: Essays on Poetry (Jarman), **Supp. XVII:** 110, **111–112**
"Body and Soul: Parts of a Life" (Jarman), **Supp. XVII:** 112, 113
Body and the Song, The (Bishop), **Retro. Supp. II:** 40
"Body Bright" (Sanders), **Supp. XVI:** 276
Body of Martin Aquilera, The (Everett), **Supp. XVIII:** 57
Body of Poetry, The: Essays on Women, Form, and the Poetic Self (A. Finch), **Supp. XVII:** 69–70, **77–78**
Body of This Death: Poems (Bogan), **Supp. III Part 1:** 47, 49–52, 58
Body of Waking (Rukeyser), **Supp. VI:** 274, 281

"Body of Waking" (Rukeyser), **Supp. VI:** 279
"Body on Fire, the Soul in Flight, The" (Jarman), **Supp. XVII:** 111, 112
Body Rags (Kinnell), **Supp. III Part 1:** 235, 236, 243–245, 250, 253, 254
"Body's Curse, The" (Dobyns), **Supp. XIII:** 87
"Body's Weight" (Espaillat), **Supp. XXI:** 111
"Body's Weight, The" (Dobyns), **Supp. XIII:** 89
Body Traffic (Dobyns), **Supp. XIII:** 87, 89
"'Body with the Lamp Lit Inside, The' " (Mills), **Supp. IV Part 1:** 64
Boehm, David, **Supp. XVII:** 58
Boehme, Jakob, **I:** 10
Bogan, Louise, **I:** 169, 185; **Retro. Supp. I:** 36; **Supp. I Part 2:** 707, 726; **Supp. III Part 1: 47–68; Supp. VIII:** 171, 265; **Supp. IX:** 229; **Supp. X:** 58, 102; **Supp. XIII:** 347; **Supp. XIV:** 129; **Supp. XVII:** 75
Bogan, Major Benjamin Lewis, **IV:** 120
Bogart, Humphrey, **Supp. I Part 2:** 623; **Supp. IV Part 1:** 130, 356
Bogdanovich, Peter, **Supp. V:** 226
Bogey Man, The (Plimpton), **Supp. XVI:** 241
Boggs, Francis W., **Supp. XVI:** 182
"Bogs" (Pickering), **Supp. XXI:** 198
"Bohemian, The" (Hapgood), **Supp. XVII:** 103
"Bohemian, The" (Harte), **Supp. II Part 1:** 339
"Bohemian Girl, The" (Cather), **Retro. Supp. I:** 7
"Bohemian Hymn, The" (Emerson), **II:** 19
"Bohemians" (Saunders), **Supp. XIX:** 234
"Boids and Beasties" (Geisel), **Supp. XVI:** 100
Boissevain, Eugen, **III:** 124
Boissière, Ralph de, **Supp. XXI:** 160
Boit, Edward, **Retro. Supp. I:** 366
Bojorquez, Jennifer, **Supp. XII:** 318
Boker, George, **Supp. XV:** 269
"Bold Words at the Bridge" (Jewett), **II:** 394
Boleslavsky, Richard, **Supp. XIV:** 240, 243
Boleyn, Anne, **Supp. I Part 2:** 461
Bolick, Katie, **Supp. XVI:** 167
Bolivar, Simon, **Supp. I Part 1:** 283, 284, 285
Bolonik, Kera, **Supp. XVIII:** 60
Bolton, Guy, **Supp. I Part 1:** 281
Bolts of Melody: New Poems of Emily Dickinson (Todd and Bingham, eds.), **I:** 470; **Retro. Supp. I:** 36
"Bomb" (Corso), **Supp. XII:** 117, 124, 125–126, 127
Bombeck, Erma, **Supp. XVII:** 168
Bombs Away (Steinbeck), **IV:** 51–52
"Bona and Paul" (Toomer), **Supp. IX:** 307, 318–319
Bonaparte, Marie, **III:** 418; **Retro. Supp. II:** 264, 266
"Bon-Bon" (Poe), **III:** 425
Bond, The (Boyce), **Supp. XXI: 5, 11–12**
Bond, The (N. Boyce), **Supp. XVII:** 99, 100
Bondage (Hwang), **Supp. XXI:** 147
Bondsman, The (Massinger), **Supp. XV:** 238
Bondwoman's Narrative, by Hannah Crafts, a Fugitive Slave, Recently Escaped from North Carolina, The, **Supp. XX: 105**
Bone, Martyn, **Supp. XXII:** 247
Bone, Robert, **Supp. IX:** 318–319; **Supp. XI:** 283; **Supp. XVIII:** 285
Bone by Bone (Matthiessen), **Supp. V:** 199, 212, 213, 214
"Bone Deposit" (Ray), **Supp. XVIII:** 194
Boners (Abingdon). *See Schoolboy Howlers* (Abingdon)
"Bones" (Goldbarth), **Supp. XII: 173–174**
"Bones and Jewels" (Monette), **Supp. X:** 159
"Bones and Shells" (Sanders), **Supp. XVI:** 271–272
"Bones of a House" (Cowley). *See* "Blue Juniata"
Bones on Black Spruce Mountain, The (Budbill), **Supp. XIX: 11–12**
Bonetti, Kay, **Supp. VIII:** 47, 152, 159, 160, 165, 168, 170, 223; **Supp. XII:** 61; **Supp. XIV:** 232, 234; **Supp. XXI:** 36
Bonfire of the Vanities, The (Wolfe), **Supp. III Part 2:** 584–586
Bonheur, Rosa, **Supp. XV:** 276
Bonhoeffer, Dietrich, **Supp. VIII:** 198
Boni, Charles, **Supp. XIV:** 288
Boni and Liveright, **Retro. Supp. I:** 59, 80, 178
Bonicelli, Vittorio, **Supp. XI:** 307
Bonifacius (Mather), **Supp. II Part 2:** 461, 464
Bonnefoy, Yves, **Supp. III Part 1:** 235, 243
Bonner, Robert, **Retro. Supp. I:** 246
Bonneville, Mme. Marguerite, **Supp. I Part 2:** 520, 521
Bonneville, Nicolas de, **Supp. I Part 2:** 511, 518, 519
Bonney, William. *See* Billy the Kid
Bontemps, Arna, **Retro. Supp. I:** 194, 196, 203; **Supp. I Part 1:** 325; **Supp. IV Part 1:** 170; **Supp. IX:** 306, 309; **Supp. XVIII:** 282; **Supp. XXII: 1–16**
Book, A (Barnes), **Supp. III Part 1:** 36, 39, 44
Book about Myself, A (Dreiser), **I:** 515; **Retro. Supp. II:** 104
"Book as a Container of Consciousness, The" (Gass), **Supp. VI:** 92
Booker, Keith, **Supp. XV:** 197
"Bookies, Beware!" (Heller), **Supp. IV Part 1:** 383
"Book Notes and News" (column, Boyce), **Supp. XXI:** 2
Book of American Negro Poetry, The (Johnson), **Supp. IV Part 1:** 165, 166; **Supp. XXII:** 11
Book of Americans, A (Benét), **Supp. XI:** 46, 47, 51
Book of Beb, The (Buechner), **Supp. XII:** 53
Book of Breeething, The (Burroughs), **Supp. III Part 1:** 97, 103
Book of Burlesques, A (Mencken), **III:** 104
Book of Common Prayer, A (Didion), **Supp. IV Part 1:** 196, 198, 203–205, 207, 208
Book of Daniel, The (Doctorow), **Supp. IV Part 1:** 218, 219, 220–222, 227, 231, 237–238, 238; **Supp. V:** 45
Book of Dreams (Kerouac), **Supp. III Part 1:** 225
"Book of Ephraim, The" (Merrill), **Supp. III Part 1:** 330–334
Book of Folly, The (Sexton), **Supp. II Part 2:** 691, 692–694
Book of Gods and Devils, The (Simic), **Supp. VIII: 281**
Book of Guys, The (Keillor), **Supp. XVI:** 177
"Book of Hours of Sister Clotilde, The" (Lowell), **II:** 522
Book of Jamaica, The (Banks), **Supp. V:** 11, 12, 16
"Book of Life" (Bidart), **Supp. XV:** 23
Book of Living Verse, The; English and American Poetry from the Thirteenth Century to the Present Day (Untermeyer, ed.), **Supp. XV:** 310
Book of Love, A (Vildrac; Bynner, trans.), **Supp. XV:** 50
Book of Lyrics (Bynner), **Supp. XV:** 51
Book of Martyrs (Fox). *See Acts and Monuments of These Latter and Perilous Days* (Fox)
Book of Medicines, The (Hogan), **Supp. IV Part 1:** 397, 410, 411–414
"Book of Medicines, The" (Hogan), **Supp. IV Part 1:** 412, 413
"Book of Memory, The" (Auster), **Supp. XII:** 21–22
Book of My Nights (L.-Y. Lee), **Supp. XV:** 215, **223–226**
Book of Negro Folklore, The (Hughes, ed.), **Supp. I Part 1:** 345; **Supp. XXII:** 11–12
Book of Nightmares, The (Kinnell), **Supp. III Part 1:** 235, 236, 243, 244, 246–254
Book of One's Own, A: People and Their Diaries (Mallon), **Supp. XIX:** 134
Book of Prefaces, A (Mencken), **III:** 99–100, 105
Book of Repulsive Women, The (Barnes), **Supp. III Part 1:** 33
Book of Roses, The (Parkman), **Supp. II Part 2:** 597, 598
Book of the Body, The (Bidart), **Supp. XV:** 21, **25–27**
"Book of the Dead, The" (Rukeyser), **Supp. VI:** 272, 278, 279; **Supp. XV:** 349
"Book of the Grotesque, The" (Anderson), **I:** 106
Book of the Homeless, The (Wharton), **Retro. Supp. I:** 377

Book of the Hopi (Waters), **Supp. X:** 124
Book of Tobit (Bible), **Supp. XII:** 54
Book of Verses, A (Masters), **Supp. I Part 2:** 458
Book of Yaak, The (Bass), **Supp. XVI: 18–19**
"Book of Yolek, The" (Hecht), **Supp. X:** 69, **70–71**
"Books" (Collins), **Supp. XXI:** 55
"Books Considered" (Bloom), **Supp. I Part 1:** 96
"Books I Left Behind, The" (Pickering), **Supp. XXI:** 196
Books in My Life, The (H. Miller), **II:** 176, 189
"Books/P,L,E, The" (Goldbarth), **Supp. XII:** 190
Bookviews, **Supp. XI:** 216
"Book World Live", **Supp. XVIII:** 143–144
"Boolean Algebra: X_2=X" (Bronk), **Supp. XXI:** 30
"Boom" (Nemerov), **III:** 278
Boom! (T. Williams), **IV:** 383
Boomer Girls: Poems by Women of the Baby Boom Generation (Gemin and Sergi, eds.), **Supp. XXI:** 246
Boom Town (Wolfe), **IV:** 456
"Boom Town" (Wolfe), **IV:** 469
Boone, Daniel, **II:** 207; **III:** 444; **IV:** 192, 193
Boorstin, Daniel, **I:** 253
Booth, Charles, **Supp. I Part 1:** 13
Booth, John Wilkes, **III:** 588
Booth, Philip, **I:** 522; **Supp. IX:** 269; **Supp. XI:** 141; **Supp. XIII:** 277; **Supp. XV:** 92
Booth, General William, **Supp. I Part 2:** 384, 386
Borah, William, **III:** 475
Borden, Lizzie, **II:** 5
Borderlands/La Frontera: The New Mestiza (Anzaldúa), **Supp. XIII:** 223
Border Matters (Saldívar), **Supp. XIX:** 112–113
Borders (Mora), **Supp. XIII:** 213, **215–217**
Border Trilogy (McCarthy), **Supp. VIII:** 175, 182
"Border View, Hot Springs, Texas" (W. V. Davis), **Supp. XXI:** 95
Borel, Pétrus, **III:** 320
Borges, Jorge Luis, **I:** 123, 135, 138, 140, 142; **Supp. III Part 2:** 560; **Supp. IV Part 2:** 623, 626, 630; **Supp. V:** 238; **Supp. VIII:** 15, 348, 349; **Supp. XII:** 21, 147; **Supp. XV:** 34; **Supp. XVI:** 201, 206; **Supp. XVII:** 47; **Supp. XIX:** 131
"Borges and I" (Bidart), **Supp. XV:** 34, 35
"Borinken Blues" (Komunyakaa), **Supp. XIII:** 117
"Born, The" (Lamott), **Supp. XX: 143–144**
"Born a Square: The Westerner's Dilemma" (Stegner), **Supp. IV Part 2:** 595; **Supp. V:** 224
"Born Bad" (Cisneros), **Supp. VII:** 62
Born on the Fourth of July (Kovic), **Supp. XIX:** 17
"Borough of Cemeteries" (Shaw), **Supp. XIX:** 246
Borrowed Time: An AIDS Memoir (Monette), **Supp. X:** 145, 146, 147, 152, 154, 155
Bose, Sudip, **Supp. XXII:** 205, 206, 214
Bosmajian, Hamida, **Supp. XXII:** 290
"Bosque del Apache Wildlife Refuge" (Mora), **Supp. XIII:** 218
Boss Dog, The: A Story of Provence (M. F. K. Fisher), **Supp. XVII:** 91
Bost, Suzanne, **Supp. XXII:** 66, 70, 75, 78
"Boston" (Hardwick), **Supp. III Part 1:** 201
Boston (Sinclair), **Supp. V:** 282, 288–289
Boston, B. H., **Supp. XIII:** 312
Boston Adventure (Stafford), **Retro. Supp. II:** 177, 178
"Boston Common" (Berryman), **I:** 172
"Boston Hymn" (Emerson), **II:** 13, 19
Bostonians, The (H. James), **I:** 9; **II:** 282; **IV:** 202; **Retro. Supp. I:** 216, 225
Boston Marriage (Mamet), **Supp. XIV:** 247
"Boston Nativity, The" (Lowell), **II:** 538
Boswell, James, **IV:** 431; **Supp. I Part 2:** 656
Boswell: A Modern Comedy (Elkin), **Supp. VI:** 42, **44–45,** 57
Bosworth, Patricia, **Supp. IV Part 2:** 573, 591
"Bothersome Sex and O'Brien, The" (Ryan as Quin), **Supp. XVIII:** 238
Botticelli (McNally), **Supp. XIII:** 197
Botticelli, Sandro, **IV:** 410; **Retro. Supp. I:** 422
"Botticellian Trees, The" (W. C. Williams), **Retro. Supp. I:** 422
"Bottle of Milk for Mother, A" (Algren), **Supp. IX:** 3
"Bottle of Perrier, A" (Wharton), **IV:** 316
"Bottles" (Kenyon), **Supp. VII:** 171
"Bottom Line, The" (Elkin), **Supp. VI:** 52, **53**
Bottom: On Shakespeare (Zukofsky), **Supp. III Part 2:** 622, 624, 625, 626, 627, 629
Boublil, Alain, **Supp. XXI:** 155
Boucher, Anthony, **Supp. IV Part 2:** 473; **Supp. XV:** 203, 205
Boucicault, Dion, **Supp. XXII:** 70
Boughton, Henrietta Breckenridge. *See* Young, Barbara
Boukreev, Anatoli, **Supp. XVIII:** 112
Boulanger, Nadia, **Supp. IV Part 1:** 81
"Boulot and Boulette" (Chopin), **Supp. I Part 1:** 211
Boulton, Agnes, **III:** 403; **Supp. XXII: 17–31**
Bound East for Cardiff (O'Neill), **III:** 388
Bound for Glory (Guthrie), **Supp. XVIII:** 23
"Bounty" (Saunders), **Supp. XIX:** 226, 227
"Bouquet, The" (Stevens), **IV:** 90
"Bouquet of Dark Red Mums, The" (Notley), **Supp. XXII:** 230
"Bouquet of Roses in Sunlight" (Stevens), **IV:** 93
Bourdin, Henri L., **Supp. I Part 1:** 251
Bourgeois, Monique, **Supp. XXII:** 99–100
Bourgeois Poet, The (Shapiro), **Supp. II Part 2:** 701, 703, 704, 713, 714–716
Bourget, James, **IV:** 319
Bourget, Paul, **II:** 325, 338; **IV:** 311, 315; **Retro. Supp. I:** 224, 359, 373; **Supp. XX: 232**
Bourjaily, Vance, **III:** 43; **Supp. IX:** 260
Bourke-White, Margaret, **I:** 290, 293, 295, 297
Bourne, Charles Rogers, **I:** 215
Bourne, Mrs. Charles Rogers, **I:** 215
Bourne, Randolph, **I: 214–238,** 243, 245, 246–247, 251, 259; **Supp. I Part 2:** 524; **Supp. XV:** 141, 298, 301
Boursicot, Bernard, **Supp. XXI:** 152, 153, 154
Bouton, Jim "Bulldog", **Supp. XX: 274**
Bowden, Charles, **Supp. XIII:** 17
Bowditch, Nathaniel, **Supp. I Part 2:** 482
Bowen, Barbara, **Supp. IX:** 311
Bowen, Elizabeth, **Retro. Supp. I:** 351; **Supp. IV Part 1:** 299; **Supp. VIII:** 65, 165, 251, 265; **Supp. IX:** 128
Bowen, Francis, **Supp. I Part 2:** 413
Bowen, Henry, **Supp. XVIII:** 4
Bowen, Louise de Koven, **Supp. I Part 1:** 5
Bowen, Michael, **Supp. VIII:** 73
Bowers, John, **Supp. XI:** 217–218
"Bowlers Anonymous" (Dobyns), **Supp. XIII:** 86
Bowles, Emily, **Supp. XVIII:** 200, 202
Bowles, Jane (Jane Auer), **II:** 586; **Supp. IV Part 1:** 89, 92
Bowles, Paul, **I:** 211; **II:** 586; **Supp. II Part 1:** 17; **Supp. IV Part 1: 79–99**
Bowles, Samuel, **I:** 454, 457; **Retro. Supp. I:** 30, 32, 33
"Bowl of Blood, The" (Jeffers), **Supp. II Part 2:** 434
"Bowls" (Moore), **III:** 196
Bowman, James, **I:** 193
"Bows to Drouth" (Snyder), **Supp. VIII:** 303
Box, Edgar (pseudonym). *See* Vidal, Gore
Box and Quotations from Chairman Mao Tse-tung (Albee), **I:** 89–91, 94
Boxer and the Spy, The (Parker), **Supp. XIX:** 190
Box Garden, The (Shields), **Supp. VII:** 314–315, 320
"Box of Pastels, A" (Kooser), **Supp. XIX:** 128
"Box Seat" (Toomer), **Supp. III Part 2:** 484; **Supp. IX:** 316, 318
Boy, A (Ashbery), **Supp. III Part 1:** 5
"Boy and Dog" (L. Brown), **Supp. XXI:** 38, 42, **43–44**
Boyce, Horace, **II:** 136
Boyce, Neith, **Supp. XVII:** 96, 97, 98–99, 100, 106; **Supp. XXI: 1–16**
Boyd, Brian, **Retro. Supp. I:** 270, 275
Boyd, Janet L., **Supp. X:** 229
Boyd, Nancy (pseudonym). *See* Millay, Edna St. Vincent

Boyd, Thomas, **I:** 99; **IV:** 427
Boyesen, H. H., **II:** 289
"Boyhood" (Collins), **Supp. XXI:** 64
"Boyhood" (Farrell), **II:** 28
"Boy in France, A" (Salinger), **III:** 552–553
Boy in the Water (Dobyns), **Supp. XIII:** 75, **84**
Boyle, Kay, **IV:** 404
Boyle, T. Coraghessan, **Supp. VIII: 1–17; Supp. XX: 17–32; Supp. XXI:** 226; **Supp. XXII:** 262
Boyle, Thomas John. *See* Boyle, T. C.
Boynton, H. W., **Supp. IX:** 7
Boynton, Percy Holmes, **Supp. I Part 2:** 415
Boynton, Robert, **Supp. XVII:** 209; **Supp. XVIII:** 105, 107, 116
"Boy on a Train" (Ellison), **Retro. Supp. II:** 124
"Boy Riding Forward Backward" (Francis), **Supp. IX:** 82
"Boys and Girls" (Cisneros), **Supp. VII:** 59–60
Boy's Froissart, The (Lanier), **Supp. I Part 1:** 361
Boy's King Arthur, The (Lanier), **Supp. I Part 1:** 361
Boy's Mabinogion, The (Lanier), **Supp. I Part 1:** 361
"Boys of '29, The" (Holmes), **Supp. I Part 1:** 308
Boys of '76, The (Coffin), **III:** 577
Boy's Percy, The (Lanier), **Supp. I Part 1:** 361
Boy's Town (Howells), **I:** 418
Boy's Will, A (Frost), **II:** 152, 153, 155–156, 159, 164, 166; **Retro. Supp. I:** 124, 127, 128, 131; **Retro. Supp. II:** 168
"Boy Up a Tree" (Hoffman), **Supp. XVIII:** 86
"Boy Who Wrestled with Angels, The" (Hoffman), **Supp. X:** 90
"Boy with One Shoe, The" (Jewett), **Retro. Supp. II:** 132
"Brace, The" (Bausch), **Supp. VII:** 48
Bracebridge Hall, or, The Humorists (Irving), **I:** 339, 341; **II:** 308–309, 313
Bracher, Frederick, **I:** 378, 380; **Supp. I Part 1:** 185
Brackenridge, Hugh Henry, **Supp. I Part 1:** 124, 127, 145; **Supp. II Part 1:** 65
Brackett, Leigh, **Supp. IV Part 1:** 130
Bradbury, John M., **I:** 288–289; **IV:** 130, 135
Bradbury, Malcolm, **Supp. VIII:** 124; **Supp. XVIII:** 140
Bradbury, Ray, **Supp. I Part 2:** 621–622; **Supp. IV Part 1: 101–118; Supp. XVI:** 122; **Supp. XVII:** 41
"Brad Carrigan, American" (Saunders), **Supp. XIX:** 233
Braddon, Mary E., **Supp. I Part 1:** 35, 36
Bradfield, Scott, **Supp. VIII:** 88
Bradford, Gamaliel, **I:** 248, 250
Bradford, Roark, **Retro. Supp. I:** 80
Bradford, William, **Retro. Supp. II:** 161, 162; **Supp. I Part 1:** 110, 112; **Supp. I Part 2:** 486, 494; **Supp. XXII: 33–47**
Bradlee, Ben, **Supp. V:** 201
Bradley, Bill, **Supp. VIII:** 47
Bradley, F. H., **Retro. Supp. I:** 57, 58
Bradley, Francis Herbert, **I:** 59, 567–568, 572, 573
Bradshaw, Barbara, **Supp. XIII:** 313
Bradstreet, Anne, **I:** 178–179, 180, 181, 182, 184; **III:** 505; **Retro. Supp. I:** 40; **Supp. I Part 1: 98–123,** 300; **Supp. I Part 2:** 484, 485, 496, 546, 705; **Supp. V:** 113, 117–118; **Supp. XIII:** 152; **Supp. XIV:** 128; **Supp. XVIII:** 304; **Supp. XXII:** 46
Bradstreet, Elizabeth, **Supp. I Part 1:** 108, 122
Bradstreet, Simon, **I:** 178; **Supp. I Part 1:** 103, 110, 116
Bradstreet, Mrs. Simon. *See* Bradstreet, Anne
Brady, Alice, **III:** 399
Brady, Matthew, **Supp. XVIII:** 4
Bragdon, Claude, **Supp. XX: 117**
"Bragdowdy and the Busybody, The" (Thurber), **Supp. I Part 2:** 617
Bragg, Rick, **Supp. XVIII:** 195
"Brahma" (Emerson), **II:** 19, 20
Brahms, Johannes, **III:** 118, 448
"Brahms in Delirium" (Skloot), **Supp. XX: 203**
Braided Creek (Kooser and Harrison), **Supp. XIX:** 126
"Braiding" (L.-Y. Lee), **Supp. XV:** 214
"Brain and the Mind, The" (James), **II:** 346
Brainard, Joe, **Supp. XV:** 33
"Brain Damage" (Barthelme), **Supp. IV Part 1:** 44
"Braindead Megaphone, The" (Saunders), **Supp. XIX:** 235
Braindead Megaphone, The: Essays (Saunders), **Supp. XIX: 234–236**
"Brain Scan" (Skloot), **Supp. XX: 200**
"Brain to the Heart, The" (Komunyakaa), **Supp. XIII:** 120
Braithwaite, Chris, **Supp. XXII:** 212
Braithwaite, William Stanley, **Retro. Supp. I:** 131; **Supp. IX:** 309; **Supp. XV:** 296–297, 301–302, 305, 306
Brakhage, Stan, **Supp. XII:** 2
Braly, Malcolm, **Supp. XVIII:** 147
"Bramble, The" (Wrigley), **Supp. XVIII:** 301
Brame, Gloria, **Supp. XV:** 113
Bramer, Monte, **Supp. X:** 152
Branch Will Not Break, The (Wright), **Supp. III Part 2:** 596, 598–601; **Supp. IV Part 1:** 60; **Supp. IX:** 159
Brancusi, Constantin, **III:** 201; **Retro. Supp. I:** 292
Brande, Dorothea, **Supp. I Part 2:** 608
Brandel, Marc, **Supp. XXI:** 276
Branden, Nathaniel, **Supp. IV Part 2:** 526, 528
"Branding Cities" (Greenberg), **Supp. XXII:** 244
"Brand-Name Blues" (Kaufmann), **Supp. XI:** 39
Brand New Life, A (Farrell), **II:** 46, 48
Brando, Marlon, **II:** 588; **Supp. IV Part 2:** 560; **Supp. XVIII:** 251
Brandon, Henry, **Supp. I Part 2:** 604, 612, 618
Brandt, Alice, **Supp. I Part 1:** 92
Brandt, Carl, **Supp. XI:** 45
Brant, Sebastian, **III:** 447, 448
Braque, Georges, **III:** 197; **Supp. IX:** 66
Brashford, Jake, **Supp. X:** 252
Brasil, Emanuel, **Supp. I Part 1:** 94
"Brasília" (Plath), **Supp. I Part 2:** 544, 545
"Brass Buttons" (McCoy), **Supp. XIII:** 161
"Brass Candlestick, The" (Francis), **Supp. IX:** 89
Brass Check, The (Sinclair), **Supp. V:** 276, 281, 282, 284–285
"Brass Ring, The" (Carver), **Supp. III Part 1:** 137
"Brass Spittoons" (Hughes), **Supp. I Part 1:** 326–327
Brass Verdict, The (Connelly), **Supp. XXI: 78–79**
Brats (X. J. Kennedy), **Supp. XV:** 163
Brautigan, Richard, **III:** 174; **Supp. VIII:** 42, 43; **Supp. XII:** 139; **Supp. XVI:** 172; **Supp. XXI:** 53
Brave Cowboy, The (Abbey), **Supp. XIII:** 4–5
Brave Men (Pyle), **Supp. XVII:** 61
Brave New World (Huxley), **II:** 454; **Supp. XIII:** 29; **Supp. XVIII:** 137
"Brave New World" (MacLeish), **III:** 18
Bravery of Earth, A (Eberhart), **I:** 522, 524, 525, 526, 530
"Brave Tailors of Maida, The" (Talese), **Supp. XVII:** 208
"Brave Words for a Startling Occasion" (Ellison), **Retro. Supp. II:** 118
Braving the Elements (Merrill), **Supp. III Part 1:** 320, 323, 325–327, 329
Bravo, The (Cooper), **I:** 345–346, 348
"Bravura" (Francis), **Supp. IX:** 90
Brawley, Benjamin, **Supp. I Part 1:** 327, 332
Brawl in a Tavern, A (Shaw), **Supp. XIX:** 241
Brawne, Fanny, **I:** 284; **II:** 531
Braxton, Joanne, **Supp. IV Part 1:** 12, 15
Brazil (Bishop), **Retro. Supp. II:** 45; **Supp. I Part 1:** 92
"Brazil" (Marshall), **Supp. XI:** 281
Brazil (Updike), **Retro. Supp. I:** 329, 330, 334
"Brazil, January 1, 1502" (Bishop), **Retro. Supp. II:** 47
Braziller, George, **Supp. X:** 24
Brazzi, Rossano, **Supp. IV Part 2:** 520
"Bread" (Dickey), **Supp. IV Part 1:** 182
"Bread" (Olds), **Supp. X:** 206
"Bread Alone" (Wylie), **Supp. I Part 2:** 727
Bread in the Wilderness (Merton), **Supp. VIII:** 197, 208

"Bread of Desire, The" (Nelson), **Supp. XVIII:** 177
Bread of Idleness, The (Masters), **Supp. I Part 2:** 460
"Bread of This World, The" (McGrath), **Supp. X:** 119, 127
Bread of Time, The (Levine), **Supp. V:** 180
Bread without Sugar (Stern), **Supp. IX: 297–298**
"Break, The" (Sexton), **Supp. II Part 2:** 689
"Breakaways, The" (Siddons), **Supp. XXII:** 244
Breakfast at Tiffany's (Capote), **Supp. III Part 1:** 113, 117, 119–121, 124, 126
Breakfast of Champions (Vonnegut), **Supp. II Part 2:** 755, 759, 769, 770, 777–778
Breaking and a Death, A (Kees), **Supp. XV:** 145
Breaking and Entering (X. J. Kennedy), **Supp. XV:** 153, **160–162**
Breaking Hard Ground (D. Hunter), **Supp. XVI:** 38
Breaking Ice (McMillan, ed.), **Supp. XIII:** 182–183
Breaking Open (Rukeyser), **Supp. VI:** 274, 281
"Breaking Open" (Rukeyser), **Supp. VI:** 286
Breaking Ranks: A Political Memoir (Podhoretz), **Supp. VIII: 239–241,** 245
"Breaking the Code of Silence: Ideology and Women's Confessional Poetry" (Harris), **Supp. XIV:** 269
"Breaking Up of the Winships, The" (Thurber), **Supp. I Part 2:** 616
Breast, The (P. Roth), **Retro. Supp. II:** 287–288; **Supp. III Part 2:** 416, 418
"Breast, The" (Sexton), **Supp. II Part 2:** 687
"Breasts" (Simic), **Supp. VIII:** 275
"Breath" (Espaillat), **Supp. XXI:** 109
"Breath" (Levine), **Supp. V:** 185
Breathe No More, My Lady (Lacy), **Supp. XV:** 203
Breathing Lessons (Tyler), **Supp. IV Part 2:** 669–670
Breathing the Water (Levertov), **Supp. III Part 1:** 274, 283, 284
"Breath of Life, The" (C. Baxter), **Supp. XVII:** 23
Breath's Burials (Sobin), **Supp. XVI: 288–289**
Breaux, Zelia, **Retro. Supp. II:** 114
Brecht, Bertolt, **I:** 60, 301; **III:** 161, 162; **IV:** 394; **Supp. I Part 1:** 292; **Supp. II Part 1:** 10, 26, 56; **Supp. IV Part 1:** 359; **Supp. IX:** 131, 133, 140; **Supp. X:** 112; **Supp. XIII:** 206, 286; **Supp. XIV:** 162; **Supp. XVIII:** 33
Breen, Joseph I., **IV:** 390
Breines, Ron, **Supp. XVIII:** 97
Breit, Harvey, **I:** 433; **III:** 575; **Retro. Supp. II:** 230; **Supp. XVIII:** 254; **Supp. XXI:** 277
Breman, Paul, **Supp. XXII:** 8
Bremer, Anne, **Supp. XXII:** 277
Bremer, Fredrika, **Supp. I Part 1:** 407
Brendan: A Novel (Buechner), **Supp. XII:** 53
Brennan, Matthew C., **Supp. XV:** 113, 125; **Supp. XIX:** 121
Brent, David, **Supp. XXII:** 259
Brent, Linda, **Supp. IV Part 1:** 12, 13
Brentano, Franz, **II:** 350; **Supp. XIV:** 198, 199
Brer Rabbit (tales), **Supp. IV Part 1:** 11, 13; **Supp. XIV:** 88
Breslin, James E. B., **Retro. Supp. I:** 430
Breslin, John B., **Supp. IV Part 1:** 308
Breslin, Paul, **Supp. VIII:** 283
Bresson, Robert, **Supp. IV Part 1:** 156
"Bresson's Movies" (Creeley), **Supp. IV Part 1:** 156–157
Breton, André, **III:** 425; **Supp. XIII:** 114; **Supp. XVII:** 244
Brett, George, **II:** 466; **Supp. V:** 286
Brett, Reginald Baliol, **Supp. XX: 230**
Brevoort, Henry, **II:** 298
Brew, Kwesi, **Supp. IV Part 1:** 10, 16
Brewer, Gaylord, **Supp. XV:** 330
"Brewing of Soma, The" (Whittier), **Supp. I Part 2:** 704
Brewsie and Willie (Stein), **IV:** 27
Brewster, Martha, **Supp. I Part 1:** 114
"Brewsterville Croesus, A" (Briggs), **Supp. XVIII:** 16
Brewsterville letters (Briggs), **Supp. XVIII:** 1, 5, **15–16**
"Brian Age 7" (Doty), **Supp. XI:** 136
Briand, Paul, **Supp. XVIII:** 155
"Briar Patch, The" (Warren), **IV:** 237
Briar Rose (Coover), **Supp. V:** 52
"Briar Rose (Sleeping Beauty)" (Sexton), **Supp. II Part 2:** 690
Brice, Fanny, **II:** 427
"Brick, The" (Nye), **Supp. XIII:** 276
"Bricklayer in the Snow" (Fante), **Supp. XI:** 164–165
"Brick Layer's Lunch Hour, The" (Ginsberg), **Supp. II Part 1:** 318
Brickman, Marshall, **Supp. XV:** 5
"Bricks, The" (Hogan), **Supp. IV Part 1:** 413
"Bridal Ballad, The" (Poe), **III:** 428
"Bridal Bed, The" (Gibran), **Supp. XX: 124**
Bridal Dinner, The (Gurney), **Supp. V:** 109, 110
"Bride Comes to Yellow Sky, The" (Crane), **I:** 34, 415, 416, 423
Bridegroom, The (Jin), **Supp. XVIII: 97–98**
"Bridegroom, The" (Jin), **Supp. XVIII:** 98
Bridegroom Cometh, The (W. Frank), **Supp. XX: 77**
"Bride in the 30's, A" (Auden), **Supp. II Part 1:** 9
Bride of Lammermoor (Scott), **II:** 291
Bride of Samoa (film), **Supp. IV Part 1:** 82
"Bride of the Innisfallen, The" (Welty), **IV:** 278–279; **Retro. Supp. I:** 353
Bride of the Innisfallen, The, and Other Stories (Welty), **IV:** 261, 275–279; **Retro. Supp. I:** 352–353, 355
Brides of the South Wind: Poems 1917–1922 (Jeffers), **Supp. II Part 2:** 419
Bridge, Horatio, **II:** 226
"BRIDGE, THE" (Baraka), **Supp. II Part 1:** 32, 36
Bridge, The (H. Crane), **I:** 62, 109, 266, 385, 386, 387, 395–399, 400, 402; **IV:** 123, 341, 418, 419, 420; **Retro. Supp. I:** 427; **Retro. Supp. II:** 76, 77, 81, 83, **84–87; Supp. V:** 342; **Supp. IX:** 306
Bridge, The (Talese), **Supp. XVII:** 202, 203, 208
Bridge at Remagen, The (film), **Supp. XI:** 343
"Bridge Burners, The" (Van Vechten), **Supp. II Part 2:** 733
Bridgehead: The Drama of Israel (W. Frank), **Supp. XX: 80**
Bridge of San Luis Rey, The (Wilder), **I:** 360; **IV:** 356, 357, 360–363, 365, 366
Bridge of Years, The (Sarton), **Supp. VIII:** 253
"Bridges" (Kingsolver), **Supp. VII:** 208
Bridges, Harry, **I:** 493; **Supp. XVIII:** 238; **Supp. XIX:** 264
Bridges, Lloyd, **Supp. XV:** 202
Bridges, Robert, **II:** 537; **III:** 527; **Supp. I Part 2:** 721; **Supp. II Part 1:** 21; **Supp. XIV:** 336, 341, 342, 343
"Bridging" (Apple), **Supp. XVII:** 5
Bridgman, P. W., **I:** 278
"Bridle, The" (Carver), **Supp. III Part 1:** 138
"Brief and Blameless Outline of the Ontogeny of Crow, A" (Wright), **Supp. XV:** 347
Brief and Frightening Reign of Phil, The (Saunders), **Supp. XIX: 230–231,** 233
"Brief Début of Tildy, The" (O. Henry), **Supp. II Part 1:** 408
"Brief Encounters on the Inland Waterway" (Vonnegut), **Supp. II Part 2:** 760
Brief History of the Dead, The (Brockmeier), **Supp. XXII: 57–59,** 61
Briefings (Ammons), **Supp. VII:** 29
Brief Interviews with Hideous Men (Wallace), **Supp. X: 308–310**
"Brief Interviews with Hideous Men" (Wallace), **Supp. X:** 309
"Briefly It Enters, and Briefly Speaks" (Kenyon), **Supp. VII:** 174
"Brief Study of the British, A" (Saunders), **Supp. XIX:** 235
Brier, His Book (J. W. Miller), **Supp. XX: 165, 168, 170**
"Brier Grows Wild, The" (J. W. Miller), **Supp. XX: 170**
"Brier Losing Touch with His Traditions, The" (J. W. Miller), **Supp. XX: 165, 169**
Brier Poems, The (J. W. Miller), **Supp. XX: 168**
"Brier Sermon, The—You Must Be Born Again" (J. W. Miller), **Supp. XX: 165, 169–170**
Briffault, Robert, **Supp. I Part 2:** 560, 567

"Brigade de Cuisine" (McPhee), **Supp. III Part 1:** 307–308
Brigadier and the Golf Widow, The (Cheever), **Supp. I Part 1:** 184–185, 192
Briggs, Charles Frederick, **Supp. I Part 2:** 411; **Supp. XVIII: 1–18**
brigham, besmilr, **Supp. XV:** 349
"Bright and Morning Star" (Wright), **IV:** 488
Bright Book of Life: American Novelists and Storytellers from Hemingway to Mailer (Kazin), **Supp. VIII:** 102, 104
Bright Center of Heaven (Maxwell), **Supp. VIII: 153–155,** 164
"Brightness from the North" (B. Kelly), **Supp. XVII:** 131
Brighton Beach Memoirs (Simon), **Supp. IV Part 2:** 576, 577, 584, 586–587, 590
Bright Procession (Sedges), **Supp. II Part 1:** 125
Bright Room Called Day, A (Kushner), **Supp. IX:** 133, **138–141,** 142
Brillat-Savarin, Jean Anthelme, **Supp. XVII:** 82, 86, 87
"Brilliance" (Doty), **Supp. XI:** 124, 128
"Brilliant Leaves" (Gordon), **II:** 199
"Brilliant Sad Sun" (W. C. Williams), **Retro. Supp. I:** 422
"Bringing Back the Trumpeter Swan" (Kumin), **Supp. IV Part 2:** 454
Bringing It All Back Home (album, Dylan), **Supp. XVIII:** 20, 25, 26, 30
Bringing It All Back Home (McNally), **Supp. XIII:** 197–198
Bringing the Devil to His Knees (C. Baxter), **Supp. XVII:** 22
"Bringing the Strange Home" (Dunn), **Supp. XI:** 141
"Bring the Day!" (Roethke), **III:** 536
Brinkley, Douglas, **Supp. XIII:** 9
Brinkmeyer, Robert H., Jr., **Supp. XI:** 38
Brinnin, John Malcolm, **IV:** 26, 27, 28, 42, 46; **Supp. XV:** 139
Brissot, Jacques Pierre, **Supp. I Part 2:** 511
"Britain's Negro Problem in Sierra Leone" (Du Bois), **Supp. I Part 1:** 176
"British Guiana" (Marshall), **Supp. XI:** 281–282
"British Poets, The" (Holmes), **Supp. I Part 1:** 306
"British Prison Ship, The" (Freneau), **Supp. II Part 1:** 261
Brittan, Gordon G., Jr., **Supp. XIV:** 234
Britten, Benjamin, **II:** 586; **Supp. II Part 1:** 17; **Supp. IV Part 1:** 84
Broadwater, Bowden, **II:** 562
Broadway, Broadway (McNally). *See It's Only a Play* (McNally)
Broadway, J. William, **Supp. V:** 316
Broadway Bound (Simon), **Supp. IV Part 2:** 576, 577, 584, 586–587, 590
Broadway Danny Rose (film; Allen), **Supp. XV:** 9
"Broadway Sights" (Whitman), **IV:** 350
Broccoli, Albert R. "Cubby", **Supp. XI:** 307
Brock
Bröck, Sabine, **Supp. XI:** 275, 277, 278
Brockmeier, Kevin, **Supp. XXII: 49–63**
Brodhead, Richard, **Retro. Supp. II:** 139; **Supp. XIV:** 61
Brodkey, Harold, **Supp. VIII:** 151; **Supp. X:** 160
Brodskii, Iosif Alexsandrovich. *See* Brodsky, Joseph
Brodsky, Joseph, **Supp. VIII: 19–35; Supp. X:** 65, 73; **Supp. XV:** 134, 135, 256
Brody, Alter, **Supp. XV:** 302, 307
Brodyar, Anatole, **Supp. XIV:** 106
Brokeback Mountain (film), **Supp. XX: 273**
"Brokeback Mountain" (Proulx), **Supp. VII:** 264–265
"Broken Balance, The" (Jeffers), **Supp. II Part 2:** 426
"Broken Field Running" (Bambara), **Supp. XI:** 10, 11
Broken Frieze, The (Everwine), **Supp. XV:** 74, 75, 89
Broken Ground, The (Berry), **Supp. X:** 30
"Broken Home, The" (Merrill), **Supp. III Part 1:** 319, 325
"Broken Oar, The" (Longfellow), **Retro. Supp. II:** 169
"Broken Promise" (MacLeish), **III:** 15
Broken Span, The (W. C. Williams), **IV:** 419; **Retro. Supp. I:** 424
"Broken Tower, The" (H. Crane), **I:** 385, 386, 400, 401–402; **Retro. Supp. II:** 89, 90
Broken Vessels (Dubus), **Supp. VII:** 90–91; **Supp. XI:** 347
"Broken Vessels" (Dubus), **Supp. VII:** 90
Broken Wings, The (al-Ajni&hudot;a al-Mutakassirah) (Gibran), **Supp. XX: 115, 124, 125**
"Broker" (H. Roth), **Supp. IX:** 234
Bromfield, Louis, **IV:** 380
"Brompton Cocktail" (Mamet), **Supp. XIV:** 252
Bromwich, David, **Retro. Supp. I:** 305; **Supp. XII:** 162
"Broncho That Would Not Be Broken, The" (Lindsay), **Supp. I Part 2:** 383
Bronk, William, **Supp. XV:** 115; **Supp. XXI: 17–34**
Brontë, Anne, **Supp. IV Part 2:** 430
Brontë, Branwell, **I:** 462
Brontë, Charlotte, **I:** 458; **II:** 175; **Supp. IV Part 2:** 430; **Supp. IX:** 128; **Supp. XII:** 104, 303; **Supp. XV:** 338; **Supp. XVI:** 158; **Supp. XX: 108**
Brontë, Emily, **I:** 458; **Retro. Supp. I:** 43; **Supp. IV Part 2:** 430; **Supp. IX:** 128; **Supp. X:** 78, 89; **Supp. XV:** 338
"Bronze" (Francis), **Supp. IX:** 76
"Bronze" (Merrill), **Supp. III Part 1:** 336
Bronze Booklets on the History, Problems, and Cultural Contributions of the Negro series, **Supp. XIV:** 202
"Bronze Buckaroo, The" (Baraka), **Supp. II Part 1:** 49
"Bronze Horses, The" (Lowell), **II:** 524
"Bronze Tablets" (Lowell), **II:** 523
Bronzeville Boys and Girls (Brooks), **Supp. III Part 1:** 79
"Bronzeville Mother Loiters in Mississippi, A. Meanwhile, a Mississippi Mother Burns Bacon" (Brooks), **Supp. III Part 1:** 80
"Brooch, The" (Singer), **IV:** 20
Brook, Peter, **Retro. Supp. II:** 182
Brooke, Rupert, **II:** 82; **III:** 3
Brook Evans (Glaspell), **Supp. III Part 1:** 182–185
"Brooking Likeness" (Glück), **Supp. V:** 85
"Brooklyn" (Marshall), **Supp. XI:** 281, 282
"Brooklyn" (Shaw), **Supp. XIX:** 239, 240
Brooks, Albert (Al Pew), **Supp. XXI:** 22
Brooks, Cleanth, **I:** 280, 282; **III:** 517; **IV:** 236, 279; **Retro. Supp. I:** 40, 41, 90; **Retro. Supp. II:** 235; **Supp. I Part 2:** 423; **Supp. III Part 2:** 542; **Supp. V:** 316; **Supp. IX:** 153, 155; **Supp. X:** 115, 123; **Supp. XIV: 1–20; Supp. XIX:** 246
Brooks, David, **Supp. IV Part 2:** 623, 626, 630; **Supp. VIII:** 232
Brooks, Gwendolyn, **Retro. Supp. I:** 208; **Supp. III Part 1: 69–90; Supp. IV Part 1:** 2, 15, 244, 251, 257; **Supp. XI:** 1, 278; **Supp. XIII:** 111, 112, 296; **Supp. XIV:** 73; **Supp. XVIII:** 175, 181, 185; **Supp. XXI:** 230
Brooks, Mel, **Supp. IV Part 1:** 390; **Supp. IV Part 2:** 591
Brooks, Paul, **Supp. IX:** 26, 31, 32
Brooks, Phillips, **II:** 542; **Retro. Supp. II:** 134; **Supp. XIII:** 142
Brooks, Van Wyck, **I:** 106, 117, 215, 222, 228, 230, 231, 233, 236, **239–263,** 266, 480; **II:** 30, 271, 285, 309, 337, 482; **III:** 394, 606; **IV:** 171, 312, 427, 433; **Retro. Supp. II:** 46, 137; **Supp. I Part 2:** 423, 424, 650; **Supp. II Part 1:** 137; **Supp. VIII:** 98, 101; **Supp. XIV:** 11; **Supp. XV:** 298, 301; **Supp. XX: 68**
Brooks, Mrs. Van Wyck (Eleanor Kenyon Stimson), **I:** 240, 245, 250, 252
Brooks, Mrs. Van Wyck (Gladys Billings), **I:** 258
Broom of the System, The (Wallace), **Supp. X:** 301, **302–305,** 310
"Brooms" (Simic), **Supp. VIII:** 275
Brosi, George, **Supp. XX: 166**
Brosnan, Jim, **II:** 424–425; **Supp. XX: 195**
Brossard, Chandler, **Supp. XXII:** 258
Brother Carl (Sontag), **Supp. III Part 2:** 452
"Brother Death" (Anderson), **I:** 114
Brother Fire (Di Piero), **Supp. XIX:** 35, 38, 45–47
Brotherhood of the Grape, The (Fante), **Supp. XI:** 160, **171–172**
Brother in Elysium, The: Ideas of Friendship and Society in the United States (Bronk), **Supp. XXI:** 21, 22, 25, 31
"Brothers" (Anderson), **I:** 114

Brothers, The (F. Barthelme), **Supp. XI:** 25, 28, 29, 30, 32–33
Brothers and Keepers (Wideman), **Supp. X:** 320, 321–322, 323, **325–327,** 328, 329–330, 331, 332
Brothers Ashkenazi, The (Singer), **IV:** 2
Brothers Karamazov, The (Dostoevsky), **II:** 60; **III:** 146, 150, 283; **Supp. IX:** 102, 106; **Supp. XI:** 172; **Supp. XII:** 322
Brothers of No Kin (Richter), **Supp. XVIII:** 209
"Brothers of No Kin" (Richter), **Supp. XVIII:** 208
Brother to Dragons: A Tale in Verse and Voices (Warren), **IV:** 243–244, 245, 246, 251, 252, 254, 257
Broughton, James, **Supp. XV:** 146
Broughton, Rhoda, **II:** 174; **IV:** 309, 310; **Supp. XX: 232**
Broun, Heywood, **I:** 478; **II:** 417; **IV:** 432; **Supp. IX:** 190; **Supp. XXII:** 277
Broussais, François, **Supp. I Part 1:** 302
Brouwer, Joel, **Supp. XXII:** 223, 237
Browder, Earl, **I:** 515; **Supp. XX: 76, 77**
Brower, David, **Supp. X:** 29
Brower, Reuben, **Supp. XV:** 20
Brown, Alice, **II:** 523; **Retro. Supp. II:** 136
Brown, Andrew, **Supp. XVI:** 150
Brown, Ashley, **Retro. Supp. II:** 48; **Supp. I Part 1:** 79, 80, 82, 84, 92
Brown, Charles Brockden, **I:** 54, 211, 335; **II:** 74, 267, 298; **III:** 415; **Supp. I Part 1: 124–149; Supp. II Part 1:** 65, 292
Brown, Mrs. Charles Brockden (Elizabeth Linn), **Supp. I Part 1:** 145, 146
Brown, Clifford, **Supp. V:** 195
Brown, Deborah, **Supp. XVII:** 75
Brown, Dee, **Supp. IV Part 2:** 504
Brown, Elijah, **Supp. I Part 1:** 125
Brown, George Douglas, **III:** 473
Brown, Harry, **Supp. IV Part 2:** 560
Brown, Harvey, **Supp. XIV:** 148
Brown, Himan, **Supp. XIX:** 241, 242
Brown, H. Rap, **Supp. XXI:** 171
Brown, John, **II:** 13; **IV:** 125, 126, 172, 237, 249, 254; **Supp. I Part 1:** 345; **Supp. VIII:** 204
Brown, Joseph Epes, **Supp. IV Part 2:** 487
Brown, Larry, **Supp. XVIII:** 195; **Supp. XXI: 35–50**
Brown, Leonard, **Supp. IX:** 117
Brown, Mary Armitt, **Supp. I Part 1:** 125
Brown, Percy, **II:** 20
Brown, Robert E., **Supp. X:** 12
Brown, Scott, **Supp. XI:** 178
Brown, Slater, **IV:** 123; **Retro. Supp. II:** 79
Brown, Solyman, **Supp. I Part 1:** 156
Brown, Sterling, **Retro. Supp. I:** 198; **Supp. IV Part 1:** 169; **Supp. XIV:** 202; **Supp. XXII:** 1, 8, 12
Brown, Tina, **Supp. XVI:** 176–177
Brown, Wesley, **Supp. V:** 6
Brown Decades, The (Mumford), **Supp. II Part 2:** 475, 478, 491–492
Brown Dog (Harrison), **Supp. VIII:** 51
Brown Dog of the Yaak: Essays on Art and Activism (Bass), **Supp. XVI:** 22
"Brown Dwarf of Rügen, The" (Whittier), **Supp. I Part 2:** 696
Browne, Charles Farrar, **II:** 289; **IV:** 193, 196; **Supp. XVIII:** 1, 4
Browne, Roscoe Lee, **Supp. VIII:** 345
Browne, Thomas, **II:** 15–16, 304; **III:** 77, 78, 198, 487; **IV:** 147; **Supp. IX:** 136; **Supp. XII:** 45; **Supp. XVI:** 292
Browne, William, **Supp. I Part 1:** 98
Brownell, W. C., **II:** 14
Brownell, William Crary, **Retro. Supp. I:** 365, 366
Browner, Stephanie P., **Supp. XVIII:** 17
Brown Girl, Brownstones (Marshall), **Supp. XI:** 275, 276, **278–280,** 282
Brownies' Book, The (Hughes), **Supp. I Part 1:** 321
Browning, Elizabeth Barrett, **I:** 458, 459; **Retro. Supp. I:** 33, 43; **Supp. XVIII:** 175–176; **Supp. XX: 108**
Browning, Oscar, **Supp. XX: 231**
Browning, Robert, **I:** 50, 66, 103, 458, 460, 468; **II:** 338, 478, 522; **III:** 5, 8, 467, 469, 484, 511, 521, 524, 606, 609; **IV:** 135, 245, 366, 416; **Retro. Supp. I:** 43, 55, 217; **Retro. Supp. II:** 188, 190; **Supp. I Part 1:** 2, 6, 79, 311; **Supp. I Part 2:** 416, 468, 622; **Supp. III Part 1:** 5, 6; **Supp. IV Part 2:** 430; **Supp. X:** 65; **Supp. XV:** 92, 250, 275
Brownmiller, Susan, **Supp. X:** 252
"Brown River, Smile" (Toomer), **Supp. IV Part 1:** 16
Brownstone Eclogues and Other Poems (Aiken), **I:** 65, 67
Brown: The Last Discovery of America (Rodriguez), **Supp. XIV:** 297, 298, 300, **305–309,** 310, 311–312
Broyard, Anatole, **Supp. IV Part 1:** 39; **Supp. VIII:** 140; **Supp. X:** 186; **Supp. XI:** 348; **Supp. XVI:** 213
Broyles, Yolanda Julia, **Supp. XIX:** 112
Bruccoli, Matthew, **Retro. Supp. I:** 98, 102, 105, 114, 115, 359; **Supp. IV Part 2:** 468, 470
Bruce, John Edward, **Supp. XVI:** 143
Bruce, Lenny, **Supp. VIII:** 198
Bruce, Virginia, **Supp. XII:** 173
Bruce-Novoa, Juan, **Supp. VIII:** 73, 74
Bruchac, Joseph, **Supp. IV Part 1:** 261, 319, 320, 321, 322, 323, 325, 328, 398, 399, 403, 408, 414; **Supp. IV Part 2:** 502, 506
Brueghel, Pieter, **I:** 174; **Supp. I Part 2:** 475
Brueghel, Pieter, the Elder, **Retro. Supp. I:** 430
Bruell, Edwin, **Supp. VIII:** 126
Brugh, Spangler Arlington. *See* Taylor, Robert
"Bruja: Witch" (Mora), **Supp. XIII:** 214, 220, 221, **Supp. XIII:** 222
Brulé, Claude, **Supp. XI:** 307
Brumer, Andy, **Supp. XIII:** 88
Brummels, J. V., **Supp. XIX:** 119
Brunner, Emil, **III:** 291, 303
"Brush Fire" (J. Wright), **Supp. XVII:** 241
Brustein, Robert, **Supp. VIII:** 331
Brutus, **IV:** 373, 374; **Supp. I Part 2:** 471
"Brutus and Antony" (Masters), **Supp. I Part 2:** 472
"Bryan, Bryan, Bryan, Bryan" (Lindsay), **Supp. I Part 2:** 394, 395, 398
Bryan, George, **Retro. Supp. II:** 76
Bryan, Sharon, **Supp. IX:** 154
Bryan, William Jennings, **I:** 483; **IV:** 124; **Supp. I Part 2:** 385, 395–396, 455, 456
Bryant, Austin, **Supp. I Part 1:** 152, 153
Bryant, Frances, **Supp. I Part 1:** 153
Bryant, Louise, **Supp. X:** 136
Bryant, Peter, **Supp. I Part 1:** 150, 151, 152, 153. *See also* George, Peter
Bryant, William Cullen, **I:** 335, 458; **II:** 311; **III:** 81; **IV:** 309; **Retro. Supp. I:** 217; **Retro. Supp. II:** 155; **Supp. I Part 1: 150–173,** 312, 362; **Supp. I Part 2:** 413, 416, 420; **Supp. IV Part 1:** 165; **Supp. XIII:** 145; **Supp. XIX:** 4
Bryant, Mrs. William Cullen (Frances Fairchild), **Supp. I Part 1:** 153, 169
Bryer, Jackson R., **Supp. IV Part 2:** 575, 583, 585, 586, 589, 591; **Supp. XIII:** 200, **Supp. XIII:** 205
Bryher, Jackson R. (pseudonym). *See* Ellerman, Winifred
Brynner, Witter, **Supp. XXII:** 273
Bubber Goes to Heaven (Bontemps), **Supp. XXII:** 4
"Bubbs Creek Haircut" (Snyder), **Supp. VIII:** 306
Buber, Martin, **II:** 228; **III:** 45, 308, 528; **IV:** 11; **Supp. I Part 1:** 83, 88; **Supp. XVI:** 291
Buccaneers, The (Wharton), **IV:** 327; **Retro. Supp. I:** 382
Buchanan Dying (Updike), **Retro. Supp. I:** 331, 335
Buchbinder, David, **Supp. XIII:** 32
Buchwald, Art, **Supp. XII:** 124–125; **Supp. XVI:** 110–111
Buchwald, Emilie, **Supp. XVI:** 35, 36
Buck, Dudley, **Supp. I Part 1:** 362
Buck, Gene, **II:** 427
Buck, Pearl S., **Supp. II Part 1: 113–134; Supp. XIV:** 274
Buckdancer's Choice (Dickey), **Supp. IV Part 1:** 176, 177, 178, 180
"Buckdancer's Choice" (Dickey), **Supp. IV Part 1:** 191
Bucke, Richard Maurice, **Retro. Supp. I:** 407
"Buck Fever" (Humphrey), **Supp. IX:** 109
"Buck in the Snow, The" (Millay), **III:** 135
Buckley, Christopher, **Supp. IX:** 169; **Supp. XI:** 257, 329; **Supp. XV:** 76–77, 86
Buckley, James, Jr., **Supp. XVII:** 220
Buckminster, Joseph, **Supp. II Part 1:** 66–67, 69
Bucknell, Katherine, **Supp. XIV:** 170

Bucolics (Auden), **Supp. II Part 1:** 21, 24
Budbill, David, **Supp. XIX: 1–16**
Budd, Louis J., **IV:** 210
Buddha, **I:** 136; **II:** 1; **III:** 173, 179, 239, 567; **Supp. I Part 1:** 363; **Supp. I Part 2:** 397
"Buddha Boy" (Saunders), **Supp. XIX:** 235
"Buddha's Last Instruction, The" (Oliver), **Supp. VII:** 239
Budding Prospects (Boyle), **Supp. VIII: 8–9; Supp. XX: 27–28**
Buechner, Frederick, **III:** 310; **Supp. XII: 41–59**
Buell, Lawrence, **Supp. V:** 209; **Supp. IX:** 29; **Supp. XV:** 269, 282
"Buffalo" (Peacock), **Supp. XIX:** 198
"Buffalo, The" (Moore), **III:** 215
"Buffalo Bill". *See* Cody, William
Buffalo Girls (screenplay) (McMurtry), **Supp. V:** 232
Buffalo Girls (McMurtry), **Supp. V:** 229
Buffett, Jimmy, **Supp. VIII:** 42
Buffon, Comte de, **II:** 101
Buford, Fanny McConnell, **Retro. Supp. II:** 117
Bugeja, Michael, **Supp. X:** 201
Bugged for Murder (Lacy), **Supp. XV:** 205
"Buglesong" (Stegner), **Supp. IV Part 2:** 606
Buhle, Paul, **Supp. XXI:** 172
"Buick" (Shapiro), **Supp. II Part 2:** 705
"Builders" (Yates), **Supp. XI: 342–343**
Builders, The (Glasgow), **II:** 183–184, 193
"Builders, The" (Hay), **Supp. XIV:** 125
Builders in Sand (W. Frank), **Supp. XX: 68**
Builders of the Bay Colony (Morison), **Supp. I Part 2:** 484–485
"Builders of the Bridge, The" (Mumford), **Supp. II Part 2:** 475
"Building" (Snyder), **Supp. VIII:** 305
"Building, Dwelling, Thinking" (Heidegger), **Retro. Supp. II:** 87
Building a Character (Stanislavsky), **Supp. XIV:** 243
" 'Building' Larry Brown(s) at Algonquin Books of Chapel Hill" (Perry), **Supp. XXI:** 42
"Building of the Ship, The" (Longfellow), **II:** 498; **Retro. Supp. II:** 159, 167, 168
"Build Soil" (Frost), **Retro. Supp. I:** 138, 139
"Build Soil" (Snyder), **Supp. VIII:** 304
Build-Up, The (W. C. Williams), **Retro. Supp. I:** 423
Bukiet, Melvin Jules, **Supp. XVII: 39–51**
Bukowski, Charles, **Supp. III Part 1:** 147; **Supp. XI:** 159, 161, 172, 173; **Supp. XVII:** 245
Bulgakov, Mikhail, **Supp. XIV:** 97
"Bulgarian Poetess, The" (Updike), **IV:** 215, 227; **Retro. Supp. I:** 329
Bull, Ole, **II:** 504
"Bulldozer, The" (Francis), **Supp. IX:** 87
"Bullet in the Brain" (Wolff), **Supp. VII:** 342–343
Bullet Park (Cheever), **Supp. I Part 1:** 185, 187–193, 194, 195
Bullets over Broadway (film; Allen), **Supp. XV:** 12, **12–13**
Bullfight, The (Mailer), **Retro. Supp. II:** 205
Bullins, Ed, **Supp. II Part 1:** 34, 42
Bullock, Sandra, **Supp. X:** 80
"Bull-Roarer, The" (Stern), **Supp. IX:** 297
"Bully, The" (Dubus), **Supp. VII:** 84
"Bulsh" (X. J. Kennedy), **Supp. XV:** 161
Bultmann, Rudolf, **III:** 309
Bulwark, The (Dreiser), **I:** 497, 506, 516–517; **Retro. Supp. II:** 95, 96, 105, 108
Bulwer-Lytton, Edward George, **IV:** 350
"Bums in the Attic" (Cisneros), **Supp. VII:** 62
Bunche, Ralph, **Supp. I Part 1:** 343; **Supp. XIV:** 202; **Supp. XXII:** 12
"Bunchgrass Edge of the World, The" (Proulx), **Supp. VII:** 263
Bunge, Nancy, **Supp. XVII:** 218; **Supp. XXII:** 175, 177, 178, 180, 183
"Bunner Sisters, The" (Wharton), **IV:** 317
Bunting, Basil, **Retro. Supp. I:** 422; **Supp. III Part 2:** 616, 620, 624; **Supp. XIV:** 286
Buñuel, Luis, **III:** 184; **Retro. Supp. II:** 337
Bunyan, John, **I:** 445; **II:** 15, 104, 228; **IV:** 80, 84, 156, 437; **Supp. I Part 1:** 32
Bunyan, Paul, **Supp. XXII:** 203
Burana, Lily, **Supp. XI:** 253
Burbank, Luther, **I:** 483
Burbank, Rex, **IV:** 363
Burch, Michael, **Supp. XXI:** 99
Burchfield, Alice, **Supp. I Part 2:** 652, 660
Burden of Proof, The (Turow), **Supp. XVII: 216–217,** 218
Burden of Southern History, The (Woodward), **Retro. Supp. I:** 75
Burdens of Formality, The (Lea, ed.), **Supp. X:** 58
Burger, Gottfried August, **II:** 306
Burgess, Anthony, **Supp. IV Part 1:** 227; **Supp. IV Part 2:** 685; **Supp. V:** 128
Burgh, James, **Supp. I Part 2:** 522
"Burglar of Babylon, The" (Bishop), **Retro. Supp. II:** 47; **Supp. I Part 1:** 93
Burgum, E. B., **IV:** 469, 470
Burham, Philip, **Supp. XX: 44**
Buried Child (Shepard), **Supp. III Part 2:** 433, 447, 448; **Supp. XIV:** 327
"Buried Lake, The" (Tate), **IV:** 136
Burke, Carolyn, **Supp. XXII:** 156, 158, 162, 165, 167, 168
Burke, Edmund, **I:** 9; **III:** 310; **Supp. I Part 2:** 496, 511, 512, 513, 523; **Supp. II Part 1:** 80; **Supp. XVII:** 236
Burke, James Lee, **Supp. XIV: 21–38; Supp. XXI:** 67, 72, 80
Burke, Kenneth, **I: 264–287,** 291; **III:** 497, 499, 546; **IV:** 123, 408; **Retro. Supp. I:** 297; **Retro. Supp. II:** 117, 120; **Supp. I Part 2:** 630; **Supp. II Part 1:** 136; **Supp. VIII:** 105; **Supp. IX:** 229; **Supp. XIV:** 3; **Supp. XXI:** 89
Burke, William, **Supp. XXI:** 215
"Burl" (Mosher), **Supp. XXII:** 204, 211
Burley, Justin, **Supp. XVI:** 158
"Burly Fading One, The" (Hayden), **Supp. II Part 1:** 366
Burn, Stephen ?/, **Supp. XXII:** 266
"Burned" (Levine), **Supp. V:** 186, 192
"Burned Diary, The" (Olds), **Supp. X:** 215
Burne-Jones, Edward, **Supp. XXII:** 156
Burnett, Allison, **Supp. XVII:** 22
Burnett, David, **Supp. XI:** 299
Burnett, Frances Hodgson, **Supp. I Part 1:** 44
Burnett, Whit, **III:** 551; **Supp. XI:** 294
Burney, Fanny, **Supp. XV:** 232; **Supp. XX: 108**
Burnham, James, **Supp. I Part 2:** 648
Burnham, John Chynoweth, **I:** 59
"Burning, The" (Welty), **IV:** 277–278; **Retro. Supp. I:** 353
Burning Angel (Burke), **Supp. XIV:** 30, 32
Burning Bright (Steinbeck), **IV:** 51, 61–62
Burning Bright: An Anthology of Sacred Poetry (Hampl, ed.), **Supp. XXII:** 87
"Burning Bush" (Cliff), **Supp. XXII:** 75
Burning Bush (Untermeyer), **Supp. XV: 309**
"Burning Bush" (Untermeyer), **Supp. XV:** 309
Burning Bush, The (H. and G. Herczeg), **Supp. XVII:** 62
Burning Chrome (W. Gibson), **Supp. XVI:** 118, 122, **128**
"Burning Chrome" (W. Gibson), **Supp. XVI:** 117, 120, 123, 124, 128
Burning City (Benét), **Supp. XI:** 46, 58
Burning Daylight (London), **II:** 474, 481
Burning Down the House: Essays on Fiction (C. Baxter), **Supp. XVII:** 13, 20, 21
Burning House, The (Beattie), **Supp. V:** 29
"Burning Ladder, The" (Gioia), **Supp. XV:** 118
Burning Mystery of Anna in 1951, The (Koch), **Supp. XV:** 182–183
"Burning of Paper Instead of Children, The" (Rich), **Supp. I Part 2:** 558
"Burning Shit at An Khe" (Weigl), **Supp. XIX:** 279–280
Burning the Days (Salter), **Supp. XIX:** 252
Burning the Days: Recollections (Salter), **Supp. IX:** 245, 246, 248, 260, **261–262**
"Burning the Small Dead" (Snyder), **Supp. VIII:** 298
"Burning Tobacco Beds" (J. W. Miller), **Supp. XX: 167**
Burns, Carol, **Supp. XVIII:** 162
Burns, David, **III:** 165–166
Burns, Ken, **Supp. XIV:** 14
Burns, Michael, **Supp. XV:** 339

Burns, Robert, **II:** 150, 306; **III:** 592; **IV:** 453; **Supp. I Part 1:** 158; **Supp. I Part 2:** 410, 455, 683, 685, 691, 692; **Supp. IX:** 173; **Supp. XII:** 171; **Supp. XIII:** 3; **Supp. XVIII:** 82
Burns, Stephen ?/, **Supp. XXII:** 268
Burns, Stephen J. ?/, **Supp. XX: 85**
Burnshaw, Stanley, **Retro. Supp. I:** 298, 303; **Supp. III Part 2:** 615
"Burn the Cities" (West), **Retro. Supp. II:** 338
Burnt Mountain (Siddons), **Supp. XXII:** 253
Burnt Norton (T. S. Eliot), **I:** 575, 580–581, 582, 584, 585; **III:** 10
"Burnt Norton" (T. S. Eliot), **Retro. Supp. I:** 66; **Supp. XV:** 216
Burnt-Out Case, A (Greene), **Supp. VIII:** 4
"Burnt-out Spa, The" (Plath), **Retro. Supp. II:** 246
Burn Witch Burn (A. Merritt), **Supp. XVII:** 58
Burr, Aaron, **I:** 7, 549, 550; **II:** 300; **IV:** 264; **Supp. I Part 2:** 461, 483
Burr: A Novel (Vidal), **Supp. IV Part 2:** 677, 682, 684, 685, 687, 688, 689, 691
Burr Oaks (Eberhart), **I:** 533, 535
Burroughs, Edgar Rice, **Supp. IV Part 1:** 101
Burroughs, John, **I:** 220, 236, 506; **IV:** 346; **Supp. IX:** 171
Burroughs, William S., **III:** 45, 174, 258; **Supp. II Part 1:** 320, 328; **Supp. III Part 1: 91–110,** 217, 226; **Supp. IV Part 1:** 79, 87, 90; **Supp. XI:** 297, 308; **Supp. XII:** 1, 3, 118, 121, 124, 129, 131, 136; **Supp. XIV:** 137, 140–141, 143–144, 150; **Supp. XVI:** 123, 135; **Supp. XVII:** 225; **Supp. XVIII:** 137
Burrow, Trigant, **Supp. II Part 1:** 6
Burrows, Ken, **Supp. V:** 115
Bursey, Jeff, **Supp. XXII:** 257
Burson, Claudia, **Supp. XV:** 343
Burstein, Janet, **Supp. XVII:** 41, 44, 48
"Bursts of Light" (Bronk), **Supp. XXI:** 33
Burt, Stephen, **Supp. XV:** 341, 342, 345, 347, 351; **Supp. XVII:** 18, 246
Burt, Steve, **Supp. V:** 83
Burtis, Thomson, **Supp. XIII:** 163
Burton, Robert, **II:** 535; **III:** 77, 78; **Supp. I Part 1:** 349
Burton, Sue D., **Supp. XIX:** 90
Burton, William Evans, **III:** 412
"Burying Ground by the Ties" (MacLeish), **III:** 14
Bury My Heart at Wounded Knee (Brown), **Supp. IV Part 2:** 504
Bury the Dead (Shaw), **IV:** 381; **Supp. XIX: 242–244,** 249, 252
"Bus Along St. Clair: December, A" (Atwood), **Supp. XIII:** 33
Busch, Frederick, **Supp. X:** 78; **Supp. XII:** 343; **Supp. XVII:** 175
Bush, Barney, **Supp. XII:** 218, 222
Bush, Douglas, **Supp. I Part 1:** 268; **Supp. XIV:** 10
"Busher Comes Back, The" (Lardner), **II:** 422
"Busher's Letters Home, A" (Lardner), **II:** 418–419, 421
Bushrui, Suheil, **Supp. XX: 113, 117, 120, 122, 126–127**
"Business and Poetry" (Gioia), **Supp. XV:** 113, 115
"Business Deal" (West), **IV:** 287
"Business Man, A" (Jewett), **Retro. Supp. II:** 132
Business of Memory, The: The Art of Remembering in an Age of Forgetting (C. Baxter, ed.), **Supp. XVII:** 21
"Business Trip" (Hoffman), **Supp. XVIII:** 86
Buss, Helen M., **Supp. IV Part 1:** 12
Butcher, Margaret Just, **Supp. XIV:** 203
"Butcher, The" (Southern), **Supp. XI:** 294
"Butcher Shop" (Simic), **Supp. VIII:** 273
But Gentlemen Marry Brunettes (Loos), **Supp. XVI:** 190–191
"But He Says I Misunderstood" (Notley), **Supp. XXII:** 227
Butler, Benjamin, **I:** 457
Butler, Dorothy. *See* Farrell, Mrs. James T. (Dorothy Butler)
Butler, Elizabeth, **Supp. I Part 1:** 260
Butler, Ethel, **Supp. XIV:** 125
Butler, Hugo, **Supp. XVII:** 63
Butler, James D., **Supp. IX:** 175
Butler, Joseph, **II:** 8, 9
Butler, Judith, **Supp. XII:** 6
Butler, Maud. *See* Falkner, Mrs. Murray C. (Maud Butler)
Butler, Nicholas Murray, **I:** 223; **Supp. I Part 1:** 23; **Supp. III Part 2:** 499
Butler, Octavia, **Supp. XIII: 59–72**
Butler, Robert Olen, **Supp. XII: 61–78,** 319
Butler, Samuel, **II:** 82, 86; **IV:** 121, 440; **Supp. VIII:** 171
Butler-Evans, Elliot, **Retro. Supp. II:** 121
"But Only Mine" (Wright), **Supp. III Part 2:** 595
Butscher, Edward, **Supp. I Part 2:** 526
Butter Battle Book, The (Geisel), **Supp. XVI:** 110
"Buttercups" (Lowell), **Retro. Supp. II:** 187
Butterfield, R. W., **I:** 386
Butterfield, Stephen, **Supp. IV Part 1:** 3, 11
Butterfield 8 (O'Hara), **III:** 361
"Butterflies Under Persimmon" (Jarman), **Supp. XVII:** 120
Butterfly (Harvey), **Supp. XIII:** 184
"Butterfly, The" (Brodksy), **Supp. VIII:** 26
"Butterfly and the Traffic Light, The" (Ozick), **Supp. V:** 263, 265
Butterfly Plague, The (Findley), **Supp. XX: 50, 52, 53**
Butterfly Stories (Vollmann), **Supp. XVII:** 226
"Butterfly-toed Shoes" (Komunyakaa), **Supp. XIII:** 126
Butter Hill and Other Poems (Francis), **Supp. IX:** 88, 89
"Button-Down Builders, The" (Siddons), **Supp. XXII:** 243–244
Buttons, Red, **Supp. IV Part 2:** 574
Buttrick, George, **III:** 301; **Supp. XII:** 47–48
"But What Is the Reader to Make of This?" (Ashbery), **Supp. III Part 1:** 25
Butz, Earl, **Supp. X:** 35
"Buz" (Alcott), **Supp. I Part 1:** 43
Buzinski, Jim, **Supp. XX: 273**
Byatt, A. S., **Supp. XXI:** 147
By Avon River (Doolittle), **Supp. I Part 1:** 272
"By Blue Ontario's Shore" (Whitman), **Retro. Supp. I:** 399, 400
"By Candlelight" (Major), **Supp. XXII:** 185
"By Disposition of Angels" (Moore), **III:** 214
"By Earth" (Olds), **Supp. X:** 214
"By Fire" (Olds), **Supp. X:** 214
Bygones (Untermeyer), **Supp. XV:** 304, **308–309,** 312, 313
By Land, By Sea (Hoffman), **Supp. XVIII:** 86
By Land and by Sea (Morison), **Supp. I Part 2:** 492
Byles, Mather, **Supp. XX: 279, 282**
By-Line: Ernest Hemingway (Hemingway), **II:** 257–258
By Love Possessed (Cozens), **I:** 358, 365, 372–374, 375, 376, 377, 378, 379
"By Morning" (Swenson), **Supp. IV Part 2:** 642
"By Night" (Francis), **Supp. IX:** 76
Bynner, Witter, **II:** 513, 527; **Supp. XIII:** 347; **Supp. XV: 39–54**
Byrd, William, **Supp. IV Part 2:** 425; **Supp. XXI:** 35; **Supp. XXII:** 193
Byrne, Donn, **IV:** 67
Byron, George Gordon, Lord, **I:** 343, 568, 577; **II:** 135, 193, 296, 301, 303, 310, 315, 331, 566; **III:** 82, 137, 170, 409, 410, 412, 469; **IV:** 245, 435; **Supp. I Part 1:** 150, 312, 349; **Supp. I Part 2:** 580, 591, 683, 685, 719; **Supp. XIII:** 139; **Supp. XVI:** 188, 203, 206, 210
"Byron's Cain" (L. Michaels), **Supp. XVI:** 203
"Bystanders" (Matthews), **Supp. IX:** 160
By the Bias of Sound (Sobin), **Supp. XVI:** 281
By the North Gate (Oates), **Supp. II Part 2:** 504
"By the People" (Stratton-Porter), **Supp. XX: 221**
By the Shores of Silver Lake (L. I. Wilder), **Supp. XXII:** 294, 295, 299
"By the Waters of Babylon" (Benét), **Supp. XI:** 56, 58
By the Waters of Manhattan (Reznikoff), **Supp. XIV:** 288, 293, 294
By the Waters of Manhattan: An Annual (Reznikoff), **Supp. XIV:** 277, 280, 289

By the Waters of Manhattan: Selected Verse (Reznikoff), **Supp. XIV:** 281, 291
By the Well of Living and Seeing and the Fifth Book of the Maccabees (Reznikoff), **Supp. XIV:** 281
By the Well of Living and Seeing: New and Selected Poems 1918–1973 (Reznikoff), **Supp. XIV:** 281, 287–288, 295
By Way of Orbit (O'Neill), **III:** 405
Byzantine Parables (Notley), **Supp. XXII:** 235, 237

"C 33" (H. Crane), **I:** 384; **Retro. Supp. II:** 76
Cabala, The (Wilder), **IV:** 356, 358–360, 369, 374
Cabaret (film), **Supp. XIV:** 155, 162
Cabaret (play), **Supp. XIV:** 162; **Supp. XVII:** 45
Cabbages and Kings (O. Henry), **Supp. II Part 1:** 394, 409
Cabell, James Branch, **II:** 42; **III:** 394; **IV:** 67, 359, 360; **Retro. Supp. I:** 80; **Supp. I Part 2:** 613, 714, 718, 721; **Supp. X:** 223
"Cabin, The" (Carver), **Supp. III Part 1:** 137, 146
Cabin, The: Reminiscence and Diversions (Mamet), **Supp. XIV:** 240
Cabinet of Dr. Caligari, The (film), **Retro. Supp. I:** 268
Cable, George Washington, **II:** 289; **Retro. Supp. II:** 65; **Supp. I Part 1:** 200; **Supp. II Part 1:** 198; **Supp. XIV:** 63
Cables to the Ace; or, Familiar Liturgies of Misunderstanding (Merton), **Supp. VIII:** 208
Cabot, James, **II:** 14; **IV:** 173
Cabot, John, **Supp. I Part 2:** 496, 497
Cachoeira Tales and Other Poems, The (Nelson), **Supp. XVIII: 178–179**
"Cachoiera Tales, The" (Nelson), **Supp. XVIII:** 179
Cactus Flower (Barillet and Grédy), **Supp. XVI:** 194
"Caddy's Diary, A" (Lardner), **II:** 421–422
"Cadence" (Dubus), **Supp. VII:** 84–85
Cadieux, Isabelle, **Supp. XIII:** 127
"Cadillac Flambé" (Ellison), **Retro. Supp. II:** 119, 126; **Supp. II Part 1:** 248
Cadillac Jack (McMurtry), **Supp. V:** 225
Cadillac Jukebox (Burke), **Supp. XIV:** 32
Cadle, Dean, **Supp. I Part 2:** 429
Cady, Edwin H., **II:** 272
"Caedmon" (Garrett), **Supp. VII:** 96–97
Caesar, Julius, **II:** 12, 502, 561–562; **IV:** 372, 373
Caesar, Sid, **Supp. IV Part 2:** 574, 591
"Cafeteria, The" (Singer), **Retro. Supp. II:** 316
Cage, John, **Supp. IV Part 1:** 84; **Supp. V:** 337, 341
"Cage and the Prairie: Two Notes on Symbolism, The" (Bewley), **Supp. I Part 1:** 251
Cage of Age, The (Bronk), **Supp. XXI:** 32
Cage of Spines, A (Swenson), **Supp. IV Part 2:** 641–642, 647
Cagney, James, **Supp. IV Part 1:** 236; **Supp. XIII:** 174
Cagney, William, **Supp. XIII:** 174
Cahalan, James, **Supp. XIII:** 1, 2, 3, 4, 12
Cahan, Abraham, **Supp. IX:** 227; **Supp. XIII:** 106; **Supp. XXI:** 3, 14
Cahill, Tim, **Supp. XIII:** 13
Cain, James M., **III:** 99; **Supp. IV Part 1:** 130; **Supp. XI:** 160; **Supp. XIII:** 159, 165
Cain, Kathleen Shine, **Supp. XX: 247, 248**
Caird, G. B., **Supp. XXI:** 91–92
Cairns, Huntington, **III:** 103, 108, 114, 119
Cairo! Shanghai! Bombay! (Williams and Shapiro), **IV:** 380
Cake (Bynner), **Supp. XV:** 50
Cakes and Ale (Maugham), **III:** 64
Calabria, Frank, **Supp. XIII:** 164
Calamity Jane (Martha Jane Canary), **Supp. V:** 229–230; **Supp. X:** 103
"Calamus" (Whitman), **IV:** 342–343; **Retro. Supp. I:** 52, 403, 404, 407
Calasso, Roberto, **Supp. IV Part 1:** 301
Calderón, Hector, **Supp. IV Part 2:** 544
Caldwell, Christopher, **Supp. IV Part 1:** 211
Caldwell, Erskine, **I:** 97, 211, **288–311; IV:** 286; **Supp. IV Part 2:** 601; **Supp. XXI:** 35; **Supp. XXII:** 196
Caldwell, Mrs. Erskine (Helen Lannegan), **I:** 289
Caldwell, Mrs. Erskine (Margaret Bourke-White), **I:** 290, 293–295, 297
Caldwell, Mrs. Erskine (Virginia Fletcher), **I:** 290
Caldwell, Reverend Ira Sylvester, **I:** 289, 305
Caldwell, Zoe, **Supp. XIII:** 207
Caleb Williams (Godwin), **III:** 415
"Calendar" (Creeley), **Supp. IV Part 1:** 158
Calendar of Saints for Unbelievers, A (Wescott), **Supp. XIV:** 342
Calendars (A. Finch), **Supp. XVII: 76–77**
Calhoun, John C., **I:** 8; **III:** 309
"Caliban in the Coal Mines" (Untermeyer), **Supp. XV:** 296
"California" (Carruth), **Supp. XVI:** 56
"California" (Didion), **Supp. IV Part 1:** 195
"California, This Is Minnesota Speaking" (Dunn), **Supp. XI:** 146
California and Oregon Trail, The (Parkman), **Supp. I Part 2:** 486
"California Hills in August" (Gioia), **Supp. XV:** 118–119
Californians (Jeffers), **Supp. II Part 2:** 415, 418, 420
"California Oaks, The" (Winters), **Supp. II Part 2:** 798
"California Plush" (Bidart), **Supp. XV:** 23
"California Republic" (Didion), **Supp. IV Part 1:** 205
"California Requiem, A" (Gioia), **Supp. XV:** 126
California Suite (film), **Supp. IV Part 2:** 589
California Suite (Simon), **Supp. IV Part 2:** 581, 582
"Caligula" (Lowell), **II:** 554
Callahan, John F., **Retro. Supp. II:** 119, 126, 127
"Call at Corazón" (Bowles), **Supp. IV Part 1:** 82, 87
Calle, Sophia, **Supp. XII:** 22
"Called Back" (Kazin), **Supp. VIII:** 104
Calley, Captain William, **II:** 579
Calley, John, **Supp. XI:** 305
Callicott, J. Baird, **Supp. XIV:** 184
Calligrammes (Apollinaire), **I:** 432
"Calling Jesus" (Toomer), **Supp. III Part 2:** 484
Calling Myself Home (Hogan), **Supp. IV Part 1:** 397, 399, 400, 401, 413
Calling the Wind: Twentieth Century African-American Short Stories (Major, ed.), **Supp. XXII:** 172
Calling Western Union (Taggard), **Supp. XXII:** 271–272, **281–283**
Call It Experience (Caldwell), **I:** 290–291, 297
"Call It Fear" (Harjo), **Supp. XII:** 220
Call It Sleep (H. Roth), **Supp. VIII:** 233; **Supp. IX:** 227, 228, **229–231; Supp. XIII:** 106
"Call Letters: Mrs. V. B." (Angelou), **Supp. IV Part 1:** 15
Call Me Ishmael (Olson), **Supp. II Part 2:** 556; **Supp. XXI:** 21
Call Me Shakespeare (Endore), **Supp. XVII:** 65
Call of the Gospel, The (Mather), **Supp. II Part 2:** 448
Call of the Wild, The (London), **II:** 466, 470–471, 472, 481
"Call of the Wild, The" (Snyder), **Supp. VIII:** 301
"Calloway's Code" (O. Henry), **Supp. II Part 1:** 404
"Call to Arms" (Mumford), **Supp. II Part 2:** 479
Call to Arms, The (film), **Retro. Supp. I:** 325
Calmer, Ned, **Supp. XI:** 219
Calvert, George H., **Supp. I Part 1:** 361
Calverton, V. F., **Supp. VIII:** 96
Calvin, John, **II:** 342; **IV:** 160, 490
Calvino, Italo, **Supp. IV Part 2:** 623, 678; **Supp. XIX:** 34; **Supp. XXI:** 225; **Supp. XXII:** 263
Cambridge Companion to Native American Literature, The (Porter and Roemer, eds.), **Supp. XX: 270**
Cambridge Edition of the Works of F. Scott Fitzgerald, The (Bruccoli, ed.), **Retro. Supp. I:** 115

Cambridge Film Handbook for *On the Waterfront* (Rapf), **Supp. XVIII:** 251
"Cambridge Thirty Years Ago" (Lowell), **Supp. I Part 2:** 419
Cambridge University Press, **Retro. Supp. I:** 115
"Camellia Sabina" (Moore), **III:** 208, 215
"Cameo" (Trethewey), **Supp. XXI:** 250
"Cameo Appearance" (Simic), **Supp. VIII:** 283
"Camera Notes" (column, Stratton-Porter), **Supp. XX: 217**
Camera Obscura (Nabokov), **III:** 255
Cameron, Angus, **Supp. XXI:** 268, 269, 275, 278
Cameron, Elizabeth, **I:** 10, 17
Cameron, Kenneth W., **II:** 16
Cameron, Peter, **Supp. XII: 79–95**
Cameron, Sharon, **Retro. Supp. I:** 43; **Retro. Supp. II:** 40
Camerson, Don, **I:** 10, 17
Camino, Léon Felipe, **Retro. Supp. II:** 89
Camino Real (T. Williams), **IV:** 382, 385, 386, 387, 388, 391, 392, 395, 398
Camões, Luiz Vaz de, **II:** 133; **Supp. I Part 1:** 94
"Camouflaging the Chimera" (Komunyakaa), **Supp. XIII: 122–123**
Camp, James, **Supp. XV:** 165
Camp, Walter, **II:** 423
Campana, Dino, **Supp. V:** 337
Campbell, Alan, **Supp. IV Part 1:** 353; **Supp. IX:** 196, 198, 201
Campbell, Alexander, **Supp. I Part 2:** 381, 395
Campbell, Donna, **Retro. Supp. II:** 139
Campbell, E. Simms, **Supp. XXII:** 12
Campbell, Helen, **Supp. XI:** 200, 206
Campbell, James, **Supp. XII:** 127
Campbell, James Edwin, **Supp. II Part 1:** 202
Campbell, Joanna (pseudonym). *See* Bly, Carol
Campbell, Joseph, **I:** 135; **IV:** 369, 370; **Supp. IX:** 245
Campbell, Lewis, **III:** 476
Campbell, Thomas, **II:** 8, 303, 314; **III:** 410; **Supp. I Part 1:** 309, 310
Campbell, Virginia, **Supp. XIII:** 114
Campbell, Will D., **Supp. XXI:** 247
Campbell (Hale), Janet, **Supp. IV Part 2:** 503
"Campers Leaving: Summer 1981" (Kenyon), **Supp. VII:** 169
"Camp Evergreen" (Kenyon), **Supp. VII:** 168
"Camping in Madera Canyon" (Swenson), **Supp. IV Part 2:** 649
Campion, Thomas, **I:** 439; **Supp. VIII:** 272
Campo, Rafael, **Supp. XVII:** 112
Camus, Albert, **I:** 53, 61, 292, 294, 494; **II:** 57, 244; **III:** 292, 306, 453; **IV:** 6, 211, 236, 442, 487; **Retro. Supp. I:** 73; **Retro. Supp. II:** 20; **Supp. I Part 2:** 621; **Supp. VIII:** 11, 195, 241; **Supp. XI:** 96; **Supp. XIII:** 74, 165, 233, 247; **Supp. XVII:** 137
Camuto, Christopher, **Supp. V:** 212–213
"Canada" (Di Piero), **Supp. XIX:** 39
Canada Fragrant with Resin, **Supp. XVI:** 149
Canadé, Eugene, **Supp. XXI:** 22, 23
"Canadian Mosaic, The" (Beran), **Supp. XIII:** 25
"Canadians and Pottawatomies" (Sandburg), **III:** 592–593
"Can a Good Wife Be a Good Sport?" (T. Williams), **IV:** 380
"Canal, The: A Poem on the Application of Physical Science to Political Economy" (Barlow), **Supp. II Part 1:** 73
Canary, Martha Jane. *See* Calamity Jane (Martha Jane Canary)
"Canary for One, A" (Hemingway), **Retro. Supp. I:** 170, 189
Canary in a Cat House (Vonnegut), **Supp. II Part 2:** 758
"Canary in Bloom" (Dove), **Supp. IV Part 1:** 248
Canby, Henry Seidel, **IV:** 65, 363
"Cancer" (McClatchy), **Supp. XII:** 266
"Cancer Match, The" (Dickey), **Supp. IV Part 1:** 182
"Cancíon y Glosa" (Merwin), **Supp. III Part 1:** 342
Candide (Hellman), **I:** 28; **Supp. I Part 1:** 288–289, 292
Candide (Voltaire), **Supp. I Part 1:** 288–289; **Supp. XI:** 297; **Supp. XVI:** 189
Candide (Voltaire; Wilbur, trans.), **Supp. III Part 2:** 560
"Candle Hat" (Collins), **Supp. XXI:** 60
Candle in the Cabin, The (Lindsay), **Supp. I Part 2:** 398, 400
"Candles" (Plath), **Retro. Supp. II:** 248, 257
Candles in Babylon (Levertov), **Supp. III Part 1:** 283
Candles in the Sun (T. Williams), **IV:** 381
Candles of Your Eyes, The (Purdy), **Supp. VII:** 278
Candy (Southern), **Supp. XI:** 297, **298–299,** 305
"Candy-Man Beechum" (Caldwell), **I:** 309
Cane (Toomer), **Supp. III Part 2:** 475, 481–486, 488; **Supp. IV Part 1:** 164, 168; **Supp. IX:** 305, 306, 307, **308–320; Supp. XIX:** 73; **Supp. XX: 73**
"Cane in the Corridor, The" (Thurber), **Supp. I Part 2:** 616
Canfield, Cass, **Supp. I Part 2:** 668
Canfield, Dorothy, **Retro. Supp. I:** 4, 11, 14, 18; **Supp. XX: 39**. *See also* Fisher, Dorothy Canfield
Can Grande's Castle (Lowell), **II:** 518, 524
"Canicula di Anna" (Carson), **Supp. XII: 101–102**
"Canis Major" (Frost), **Retro. Supp. I:** 137
"Canned Stuff" (Pickering), **Supp. XXI:** 198
Cannery Row (Steinbeck), **IV:** 50, 51, 64–65, 66, 68
Cannibal Galaxy, The (Ozick), **Supp. V:** 270
Cannibals and Christians (Mailer), **III:** 38–39, 40, 42; **Retro. Supp. II:** 203, 204, 205
Canning, George, **I:** 7, 8
Canning, Richard, **Supp. X:** 147
Cannon, Jimmy, **II:** 424
Cannon, Steve, **Retro. Supp. II:** 111
Cannon between My Knees, A (Gunn Allen), **Supp. IV Part 1:** 324
Canolle, Jean, **Supp. XVI:** 194
"Canonization, The" (Donne), **Supp. XIV:** 8
"Can Poetry Matter?" (Gioia), **Supp. XV:** 113, 114
Can Poetry Matter?: Essays on Poetry and American Culture (Gioia), **Supp. XV:** 112, **113–115**
"Canso" (Merwin), **Supp. III Part 1:** 344
Can Such Things Be? (Bierce), **I:** 203, 204, 205, 209
Canterbury Tales (Chaucer), **II:** 504; **III:** 411; **IV:** 65
Canterbury Tales, The (Chaucer), **Supp. XIX:** 4
"Canticle of Her Coming and Going" (Espaillat), **Supp. XXI:** 106
"Canto Amor" (Berryman), **I:** 173
Canto I (Pound), **III:** 469, 470; **Retro. Supp. I:** 286
Canto II (Pound), **III:** 470
Canto III (Pound), **III:** 470
Canto IV (Pound), **III:** 470
Canto VIII (Pound), **III:** 472
Canto IX (Pound), **III:** 472
Canto X (Pound), **III:** 472
Canto XIII (Pound), **III:** 472
Canto XXXIX (Pound), **III:** 468
Canto LXV (Pound), **Retro. Supp. I:** 292
Canto LXXXI (Pound), **III:** 459; **Retro. Supp. I:** 293
Cantor, Lois, **Supp. IV Part 1:** 285
Cantos (Pound), **I:** 482; **III:** 13–14, 17, 457, 462, 463, 466, 467, 469–470, 472–473, 474, 475, 476, 492; **Retro. Supp. I:** 284, 292, **292–293,** 293, 427; **Supp. I Part 1:** 272; **Supp. II Part 1:** 5; **Supp. II Part 2:** 420, 557, 564, 644; **Supp. IV Part 1:** 153; **Supp. V:** 343, 345; **Supp. VIII:** 305; **Supp. XIV:** 55, 96; **Supp. XV:** 349
"Cantus Planis" (Pound), **III:** 466
Cantwell, Robert, **Retro. Supp. I:** 85; **Supp. VIII:** 96; **Supp. XIII:** 292
"Can You Carry Me" (O'Hara), **III:** 369
Can You See Me Yet? (Findley), **Supp. XX: 52–53**
Canzoneri, Robert, **IV:** 114, 116
Canzoni (Pound), **Retro. Supp. I:** 286, 288, 413
"Cap" (Shaw), **Supp. IV Part 1:** 345
"Cape Breton" (Bishop), **Supp. I Part 1:** 92; **Supp. IX:** 45
Cape Cod (Thoreau), **II:** 540
"Cape Cod, Rome, and Jerusalem" (Chapman), **Supp. XIV:** 55
Capitalism: The Unknown Ideal (Rand), **Supp. IV Part 2:** 518, 527, 531, 532
Caponi, Gena Dagel, **Supp. IV Part 1:** 95

Capote, Truman, **Supp. I Part 1:** 291, 292; **Supp. III Part 1: 111–133; Supp. III Part 2:** 574; **Supp. IV Part 1:** 198, 220; **Supp. VIII:** 105; **Supp. XII:** 43, 249; **Supp. XV:** 146; **Supp. XVI:** 245–246; **Supp. XVII:** 236
Capouya, Emile, **Supp. I Part 1:** 50
Cappetti, Carla, **Supp. IX:** 4, 8
Capra, Frank, **Supp. XVI:** 102
Capra, Fritjof, **Supp. X:** 261
Capron, Marion, **Supp. IX:** 193
"Capsule History of Conservation, A" (Stegner), **Supp. IV Part 2:** 600
"Captain Carpenter" (Ransom), **III:** 491
Captain Craig (Robinson), **III:** 508, 523; **Supp. II Part 1:** 192
"Captain Jim's Friend" (Harte), **Supp. II Part 1:** 337
"Captain Jones's Invitation" (Freneau), **Supp. II Part 1:** 261
"Captain's Son, The" (Taylor), **Supp. V:** 314, 325, 327
"Captain's Wife, The" (Salter), **Supp. IX:** 261
"Capt Christopher Levett (of York)" (Olson), **Supp. II Part 2:** 576, 577
Captive Israel (Reznikoff), **Supp. XIV:** 283
"Captivity and Restoration of Mrs. Mary Rowlandson, The" (Howe), **Supp. IV Part 2:** 419, 431, 434
"Captivity of the Fly" (MacLeish), **III:** 19
"Captured Goddess, The" (Lowell), **II:** 520
Caputi, Jane, **Supp. IV Part 1:** 334, 335
Caputo, Philip, **Supp. XI:** 234; **Supp. XIX: 17–31; Supp. XXII:** 104
Capuzzo, Michael, **Supp. XIII:** 254
Car (Crews), **Supp. XI: 110–111**
Carabi, Angels, **Supp. VIII:** 223; **Supp. XII:** 215
"Caramels" (Zinberg), **Supp. XV:** 195
"Caravaggio: Swirl & Vortex" (Levis), **Supp. XI:** 258, 269
Caravan (Bynner), **Supp. XV:** 50
Carby, Hazel B., **Supp. IV Part 1:** 13; **Supp. XXI:** 171
"Carcassonne" (Faulkner), **Retro. Supp. I:** 81
Card, Antha E., **Supp. I Part 2:** 496
Cárdenas, Lupe, **Supp. IV Part 2:** 538, 539, 540
Cardinale, Anthony, **Supp. XVII:** 239
Cardinale, Ernesto, **Supp. XII:** 225
"Cardinal Ideograms" (Swenson), **Supp. IV Part 2:** 645
"Cards" (Beattie), **Supp. V:** 31
"Career Woman" (Hay), **Supp. XIV:** 131
Carefree (film, Sandrich), **Supp. XVII:** 59
"Careful" (Carver), **Supp. III Part 1:** 138
Careful and Strict Enquiry into the Modern Prevailing Notions of That Freedom of Will, Which Is Supposed to be Essential to Moral Agency, Vertue and Vice, Reward and Punishment, Praise and Blame, A (Edwards), **I:** 549, 557, 558, 562
Carel: A Poem and Pilgrimage in the Holy Land (Melville), **III:** 92–93
Careless Love and Its Apostrophes (Bronk), **Supp. XXI:** 32
"Carentan O Carentan" (Simpson), **Supp. IX:** 267
Carew, Thomas, **IV:** 453
Carey, Gary, **Supp. XVI:** 186
Carey, Mathew, **Supp. XV:** 238
"Car Games" (Conroy), **Supp. XVI:** 72
Cargill, Oscar, **Supp. II Part 1:** 117
Caribbean as Columbus Saw It (Morison and Obregon), **Supp. I Part 2:** 488
"Caribou Kitchen" (A. Finch), **Supp. XVII:** 76–77
Caribou Rising: Defending the Porcupine Herd, Gwich-'in Culture, and the Arctic National Wildlife Refuge (Bass), **Supp. XVI:** 27–28, 28
Carl, K. A., **III:** 475
Carleton, George W., **Supp. XVIII:** 4
Carlin, George, **Supp. XXI:** 51
Carlin, Terry, **Supp. XXI:** 4, 5, 14
Carlisle, Harry, **Supp. XVIII:** 223, 233
Carl Krinken: His Christmas Stocking (S. and A. Warner), **Supp. XVIII:** 264
"Carlos Who Died, and Left Only This, The" (Ríos), **Supp. IV Part 2:** 547
Carlotta (empress of Mexico), **Supp. I Part 2:** 457
Carl Sandburg (Golden), **III:** 579
Carlson, Susan L., **Supp. XV:** 323
Carlyle, Thomas, **I:** 103, 279; **II:** 5, 7, 11, 15–16, 17, 20, 145, 315; **III:** 82, 84, 85, 87; **IV:** 169, 182, 338, 350; **Retro. Supp. I:** 360, 408; **Supp. I Part 1:** 2, 349; **Supp. I Part 2:** 410, 422, 482, 485, 552
"Carma" (Toomer), **Supp. III Part 2:** 481–483; **Supp. IX:** 312–313
"Carmen de Boheme" (Crane), **I:** 384
Carmen Jones (film), **Supp. I Part 1:** 66
Carmina Burana, **Supp. X:** 63
Carmon, Walt, **Supp. XXII:** 277
Carnegie, Andrew, **I:** 483; **IV:** 192; **Supp. I Part 2:** 639, 644; **Supp. V:** 285
Carnegie, Dale, **Supp. I Part 2:** 608
"Carnegie Hall: Rescued" (Moore), **III:** 215
Carne-Ross, D. S., **Supp. I Part 1:** 268, 269
Carnes, Mark C., **Supp. X:** 14
"Carnets" poems (Sobin), **Supp. XVI:** 286–287
Carnovsky, Morris, **III:** 154
"Carol for Carolyn, A" (A. Finch), **Supp. XVII:** 74, 75
Caroling Dusk: An Anthology of Verse by Negro Poets (Cullen), **Supp. IV Part 1:** 166, 169
"Carol of Occupations" (Whitman), **I:** 486
"Carolyn Kizer and the Chain of Women" (A. Finch), **Supp. XVII:** 74–75
Carolyn Kizer: Perspectives on Her Life and Work (A. Finch), **Supp. XVII: 74–75**
"Carpe Diem" (Frost), **Supp. XII:** 303
"Carpe Noctem, if You Can" (Thurber), **Supp. I Part 2:** 620
Carpenter, Dan, **Supp. V:** 250
Carpenter, David, **Supp. VIII:** 297
Carpenter, Edward, **Supp. XX: 230**
Carpenter, Frederic I., **II:** 20
"Carpenter Bee" (Trethewey), **Supp. XXI:** 250
Carpentered Hen and Other Tame Creatures, The (Updike), **IV:** 214; **Retro. Supp. I:** 320
Carpenter's Gothic (Gaddis), **Supp. IV Part 1:** 288, 289–291, 293, 294
Carr, Dennis W., **Supp. IV Part 2:** 560
Carr, Elias, **Supp. XIV:** 57
Carr, Rosemary. *See* Benét, Rosemary
Carrall, Aaron, **Supp. IV Part 2:** 499
Carrel, Alexis, **IV:** 240
"Carrell/Klee/and Cosmos's Groom" (Goldbarth), **Supp. XII:** 183
"Carriage from Sweden, A" (Moore), **III:** 212
Carrie (King), **Supp. V:** 137
Carried Away (Harrison), **Supp. VIII:** 39
Carrier of Ladders (Merwin), **Supp. III Part 1:** 339, 346, 350–352, 356, 357
"Carriers of the Dream Wheel" (Momaday), **Supp. IV Part 2:** 481
Carriers of the Dream Wheel: Contemporary Native American Poetry (Niatum, ed.), **Supp. IV Part 2:** 484, 505
Carrington, Carroll, **I:** 199
"Carrion Spring" (Stegner), **Supp. IV Part 2:** 604
Carroll, Charles, **Supp. I Part 2:** 525
Carroll, Lewis, **I:** 432; **II:** 431; **III:** 181; **Supp. I Part 1:** 44; **Supp. I Part 2:** 622, 656; **Supp. XVI:** 103
"Carrots, Noses, Snow, Rose, Roses" (Gass), **Supp. VI:** 87
Carrouges, Michel, **Supp. IV Part 1:** 104
"Carrousel, The" (Rilke), **III:** 558
Carruth, Hayden, **Supp. IV Part 1:** 66; **Supp. VIII:** 39; **Supp. IX:** 291; **Supp. XIII:** 112; **Supp. XIV:** 273–274; **Supp. XVI: 45–61; Supp. XIX:** 1; **Supp. XXI:** 31
Carruth, Joe-Anne McLaughlin, **Supp. XVI:** 47
"Carry" (Hogan), **Supp. IV Part 1:** 412
"Carrying On" (Dunn), **Supp. XI:** 145
Cars of Cuba (García), **Supp. XI:** 190
Carson, Anne, **Supp. XII: 97–116; Supp. XV:** 252
Carson, Johnny, **Supp. IV Part 2:** 526
Carson, Rachel, **Supp. V:** 202; **Supp. IX: 19–36; Supp. X:** 99; **Supp. XVI:** 36
Carson, Tom, **Supp. XI:** 227
Cart, Michael, **Supp. X:** 12
Carter, Elliott, **Supp. III Part 1:** 21
Carter, Hodding, **Supp. XIV:** 2
Carter, Jared, **Supp. XVII:** 110
Carter, Jimmy, **Supp. I Part 2:** 638; **Supp. XIV:** 107
Carter, Marcia, **Supp. V:** 223
Carter, Mary, **Supp. IV Part 2:** 444
Carter, Paul, **Supp. XX: 77, 78**
Carter, Peter, **Supp. XVIII:** 267
Carter, Stephen, **Supp. XI:** 220
Cartesian Sonata and Other Novellas (Gass), **Supp. VI: 92–93**

Cartier, Jacques, **Supp. I Part 2:** 496, 497
Cartier-Bresson, Henri, **Supp. VIII:** 98
"Cartographies of Silence" (Rich), **Supp. I Part 2:** 571–572
"Cartography" (Espaillat), **Supp. XXI:** 107
Cartwright, Louis, **Supp. XIV:** 147, 149, 151
Carver, Raymond, **Supp. III Part 1: 135–151; Supp. IV Part 1:** 342; **Supp. V:** 22, 23, 220, 326; **Supp. VIII:** 15; **Supp. X:** 85, 167; **Supp. XI:** 26, 65, 116, 153; **Supp. XII:** 79, 139, 289, 294; **Supp. XIX:** 209; **Supp. XXI:** 36, 115, 116, 118, 119
Carver: A Life in Poems (Nelson), **Supp. XVIII:** 171, 172, **181–182,** 183
Cary, Alice, **Retro. Supp. II:** 145; **Supp. XV:** 273; **Supp. XXII:** 206
Cary, Phoebe, **Supp. XV:** 273
Cary, Richard, **Retro. Supp. II:** 132, 137
"Casabianca" (Bishop), **Retro. Supp. II:** 42; **Supp. I Part 1:** 86
Casablanca (film), **Supp. VIII:** 61; **Supp. XV:** 14
Casanova: His Known and Unknown Life (Endore), **Supp. XVII:** 54
"Casa solariega, La" ("The Family Mansion") (Espaillat), **Supp. XXI:** 107
"Case Against Mist, The" (Halliday), **Supp. XIX:** 91
Case for West-Indian Self-Government, The (C. L. R. James), **Supp. XXI:** 159, 161
Case of Rape, A (C. Himes), **Supp. XVI:** 143
Case of the Crushed Petunias, The (T. Williams), **IV:** 381
Case of the Officers of Excise (Paine), **Supp. I Part 2:** 503–504
Casey, John, **Supp. X:** 164
Cash, Arthur, **Supp. IV Part 1:** 299
Cashman, Nellie, **Supp. X:** 103
Casiero, Robert, **Supp. XIV:** 167
Casino Royale (film), **Supp. XI: 306–307**
Caskey, William, **Supp. XIV:** 166
"Cask of Amontillado, The" (Poe), **II:** 475; **III:** 413; **Retro. Supp. II:** 268, 269, 270, 273
Caso, Frank, **Supp. XVIII:** 95
Caspary, Vera, **Supp. XIX:** 78
Casper, Robert N., **Supp. XV:** 339, 347
Casper and His Friends (S. and A. Warner), **Supp. XVIII:** 264
Cassada (Salter), **Supp. IX: 251–252**
Cassady, Carolyn, **Supp. XIV:** 150
Cassady, Neal, **Supp. II Part 1:** 309, 311; **Supp. XIV:** 137, 144
"Cassandra Southwick" (Whittier), **Supp. I Part 2:** 693
Cassell, Verlin, **Supp. XI:** 315
Cassill, Ronald Verlin, **Supp. V:** 323; **Supp. XVIII:** 72; **Supp. XIX:** 266
Cassirer, Ernst, **I:** 265; **IV:** 87, 89
Cass Timberlane (Lewis), **II:** 455–456
Cast a Cold Eye (McCarthy), **II:** 566
Castaway (Cozzens), **I:** 363, 370, 374, 375, 379
"Caste in America" (Du Bois), **Supp. II Part 1:** 169
Castiglione, Baldassare, **I:** 279; **III:** 282
"Castilian" (Wylie), **Supp. I Part 2:** 714
Castillo, Ana, **Supp. XI:** 177
"Castle in Lynn, A" (McCarriston), **Supp. XIV:** 265, 268
"Castles and Distances" (Wilbur), **Supp. III Part 2:** 550
Castle Sinister (Marquand), **III:** 58
Cast of Thousands (Loos), **Supp. XVI:** 192, 193, 195
Castro, Fidel, **II:** 261, 434; **Supp. XX: 80**
Cast the First Stone (C. Himes), **Supp. XVI:** 135, 137–138
"Casual Incident, A" (Hemingway), **II:** 44
"Casualty Report" (Halliday), **Supp. XIX:** 85
Caswell, Michelle, **Supp. XXII:** 262
"Cat, The" (Matthews), **Supp. IX: 157–158**
Cat, You Better Come Home (Keillor), **Supp. XVI:** 177
"Catbird Seat, The" (Thurber), **Supp. I Part 2:** 623
"Catch" (Francis), **Supp. IX:** 82
Catch-22 (Heller), **III:** 558; **Supp. IV Part 1:** 379, 380, 381–382, 383, 384–386, 387, 390, 391, 392, 393, 394; **Supp. V:** 244, 248; **Supp. XII:** 167–168
Catcher in the Rye, The (Salinger), **I:** 493; **III:** 551, 552, 553–558, 567, 571; **Retro. Supp. I:** 102; **Retro. Supp. II:** 222, 249; **Supp. I Part 2:** 535; **Supp. V:** 119; **Supp. VIII:** 242; **Supp. XI:** 65; **Supp. XVII:** 2
"Catching Frogs" (Kenyon), **Supp. VII:** 170
Catching the Mermother (A. Finch), **Supp. XVII:** 72
catechism of d neoamerican hoodoo church (Reed), **Supp. X:** 240, 241
Catered Affair, The (film), **Supp. IV Part 2:** 683
"Cathay" (Goldbarth), **Supp. XII:** 185, 186
Cathay (Pound), **II:** 527; **Retro. Supp. I:** 289
Cathedral (Carver), **Supp. III Part 1:** 144–146; **Supp. XII:** 139
"Cathedral" (Carver), **Supp. III Part 1:** 144–145
Cathedral, The (Lowell), **Supp. I Part 2:** 407, 416–417
Cather, Willa, **I: 312–334,** 405; **II:** 51, 96, 177, 404, 412; **III:** 453; **IV:** 190; **Retro. Supp. I: 1–23,** 355, 382; **Retro. Supp. II:** 71, 136; **Supp. I Part 2:** 609, 719; **Supp. IV Part 1:** 31; **Supp. VIII:** 101, 102, 263; **Supp. X:** 103; **Supp. XIII:** 253; **Supp. XIV:** 112; **Supp. XV:** 40, 51; **Supp. XVI:** 226; **Supp. XVIII:** 207; **Supp. XIX:** 131
Catherine, Saint, **II:** 211
Catherine II, **Supp. I Part 2:** 433
Catholic Art and Culture (Watkin), **Retro. Supp. II:** 187
"Catholic Novelist in the Protestant South, The" (O'Connor), **Retro. Supp. II:** 223, 224
"Cathy Queen of Cats" (Cisneros), **Supp. VII:** 59
Cat Inside, The (Burroughs), **Supp. III Part 1:** 105
Cat in the Hat, The (Geisel), **Supp. XVI:** 106–107, 112
Cat in the Hat Come Back, The (Geisel), **Supp. XVI:** 107
"Cat in the Hat for President, The" (Coover), **Supp. V:** 44, 46–47
Cat in The Hat Songbook, The (Geisel), **Supp. XVI:** 104
Cato, **II:** 114, 117
Cat on a Hot Tin Roof (T. Williams), **II:** 190; **IV:** 380, 382, 383, 386, 387, 389, 390, 391, 394, 395, 397–398
"Cat People: What Dr. Seuss Really Taught Us" (Menand), **Supp. XVI:** 106
Cat's Cradle (Vonnegut), **Supp. II Part 2:** 758, 759, 767–768, 770, 771, 772; **Supp. V:** 1
Cat's Eye (Atwood), **Supp. XIII: 29–30**
Catskill Eagle, A (Parker), **Supp. XIX:** 185
"Cat's Meow, A" (Brodsky), **Supp. VIII:** 31
Cat's Quizzer, The (Geisel), **Supp. XVI:** 111
"Catterskill Falls" (Bryant), **Supp. I Part 1:** 160
"Cattle Car Complex" (T. Rosenbaum), **Supp. XVII:** 48
Catullus, **Supp. XII:** 2, 13, **112; Supp. XV:** 23, 27, 35, 36
Catullus, Gaius Valerius, **I:** 381; **Supp. I Part 1:** 261; **Supp. I Part 2:** 728
Catullus (Gai Catulli Veronensis Liber) (Zukofsky), **Supp. III Part 2:** 625, 627, 628, 629
"Catullus: *Carmina" (Carson), Supp. XII:* **112**
"Catullus: Excrucior" (Bidart), Supp. XV: 32, 35
"Cat Walked Through the Casserole, The" (Nelson and Espeland), **Supp. XVIII: 181**
Cat Walked Through the Casserole and Other Poems for Children (Nelson and Espeland), **Supp. XVIII:** 181
"Cat Who Aspired to Higher Things, The" (X. J. Kennedy), **Supp. XV:** 163
"Caucasian Storms Harlem, The" (R. Fisher), **Supp. XIX:** 78
Caudwell, Christopher, **Supp. X:** 112; **Supp. XXII:** 284
"Caul, The" (Banks), **Supp. V:** 10–11
Cause for Wonder (Morris), **III:** 232–233
"Causerie" (Tate), **IV:** 129
Causes and Consequences (Chapman), **Supp. XIV:** 41, 49, 51
"Causes of American Discontents before 1768, The" (Franklin), **II:** 120
Causley, Charles, **Supp. XV:** 117

Cavafy, Constantine P., **Supp. IX:** 275; **Supp. XI:** 119, 123; **Supp. XXI:** 131
Cavalcade of America, The (radio program), **III:** 146
Cavalcanti (Pound, opera), **Retro. Supp. I:** 287
Cavalcanti, Guido, **I:** 579; **III:** 467; **Supp. III Part 2:** 620, 621, 622, 623
Cavalieri, Grace, **Supp. IV Part 2:** 630, 631
"Cavalry Crossing the Ford" (Whitman), **IV:** 347
"Cave, The" (Bass), **Supp. XVI:** 23
Cave, The (Warren), **IV:** 255–256
Cavell, Stanley, **Retro. Supp. I:** 306–307, 309
Cavender's House (Robinson), **III:** 510
Caver, Christine, **Supp. XXI:** 215
"Caviar" (Boyle), **Supp. XX: 19**
Caviare at the Funeral (Simpson), **Supp. IX:** 266, **276–277**
"Cawdor" (Jeffers), **Supp. II Part 2:** 431
Caxton, William, **III:** 486
Cayton, Horace, **IV:** 475, 488
Cazamian, Louis, **II:** 529
"Ceiling, The" (Brockmeier), **Supp. XXII:** 52–53
Celan, Paul, **Supp. X:** 149; **Supp. XII:** 21, 110–111; **Supp. XVI:** 284–285, 288; **Supp. XVII:** 241
"Celebrated Jumping Frog of Calaveras County, The" (Twain), **IV:** 196
Celebrated Jumping Frog of Calaveras County, The, and Other Sketches (Twain), **IV:** 197
Celebration (Crews), **Supp. XI:** 103, **108**
Celebration (Swados), **Supp. XIX: 269–270**
Celebration at Dark (W. J. Smith), **Supp. XIII:** 332
"Celebration for June 24th" (McGrath), **Supp. X:** 116
Celebration of the Sound Through (Sobin), **Supp. XVI:** 284–285
Celebrations after the Death of John Brennan (X. J. Kennedy), **Supp. XV:** 165
Celebrity (film; Allen), **Supp. XV:** 11
"Celebrity" (Pickering), **Supp. XXI:** 198
"Celery" (Stein), **IV:** 43
"Celestial Games" (Conroy), **Supp. XVI:** 72
"Celestial Globe" (Nemerov), **III:** 288
Celestial Navigation (Tyler), **Supp. IV Part 2:** 662–663, 671
"Celestial Railroad, The" (Hawthorne), **Retro. Supp. I:** 152; **Supp. I Part 1:** 188
Celibate Season, A (Shields), **Supp. VII:** 323, 324
Cellini (Shanley), **Supp. XIV:** 316, **329–330**
"Cemetery at Academy, California" (Levine), **Supp. V:** 182
Cemetery Nights (Dobyns), **Supp. XIII:** 85, 87, 89
"Censors As Critics: *To Kill a Mockingbird* As a Case Study" (May), **Supp. VIII:** 126
"Census-Taker, The" (Frost), **Retro. Supp. I:** 129
"Centaur, The" (Swenson), **Supp. IV Part 2:** 641
Centaur, The (Updike), **IV:** 214, 216, 217, 218, 219–221, 222; **Retro. Supp. I:** 318, 322, 324, 331, 336
"Centennial Meditation of Columbia, The" (Lanier), **Supp. I Part 1:** 362
Centeno, Agusto, **IV:** 375
"Centipede" (Dove), **Supp. IV Part 1:** 246
"Central Man, The" (Bloom), **Supp. IV Part 2:** 689
"Central Park" (Lowell), **II:** 552
Central Park (Wasserstein and Drattel), **Supp. XV:** 333
Central Park West (Allen), **Supp. XV:** 13
Century of Dishonor, A (Jackson), **Retro. Supp. I:** 31
"Cerebral Snapshot, The" (Theroux), **Supp. VIII:** 313
"Ceremonies" (Rukeyser), **Supp. VI:** 279
Ceremony (Silko), **Supp. IV Part 1:** 274, 333; **Supp. IV Part 2:** 557–558, 558–559, 559, 561–566, 570; **Supp. XVIII:** 59
Ceremony (Wilbur), **Supp. III Part 2:** 550–551
"Ceremony, The" (Harjo), **Supp. XII:** 230
"Ceremony, The—Anatomy of a Massacre" (E. Hoffman, play), **Supp. XVI:** 160
Ceremony in Lone Tree (Morris), **III:** 229–230, 232, 238, 558
Ceremony of Brotherhood, A (Anaya and Ortiz, eds.), **Supp. IV Part 2:** 502
Cerf, Bennett, **III:** 405; **IV:** 288; **Retro. Supp. II:** 330; **Supp. XIII:** 172; **Supp. XIX:** 244
"Certain Attention to the World, A" (Haines), **Supp. XII:** 201
"Certain Beasts, Like Cats" (Bronk), **Supp. XXI:** 30
Certain Distance, A (Francis), **Supp. IX:** 85
"Certain Music, A" (Rukeyser), **Supp. VI:** 273
Certain Noble Plays of Japan (Pound), **III:** 458
Certain People (Wharton), **Retro. Supp. I:** 382
"Certain Poets" (MacLeish), **III:** 4
"Certain Testimony" (Bausch), **Supp. VII:** 48
Certificate, The (Singer), **IV:** 1; **Retro. Supp. II: 314–315**
"Cerulean" (Everett), **Supp. XVIII:** 66
Cervantes, Lorna Dee, **Supp. IV Part 2:** 545
Cervantes, Miguel de, **I:** 130, 134; **II:** 8, 272, 273, 276, 289, 302, 310, 315; **III:** 113, 614; **IV:** 367; **Retro. Supp. I:** 91; **Supp. I Part 2:** 406; **Supp. V:** 277; **Supp. XIII:** 17
Césaire, Aimé, **Supp. X:** 132, 139; **Supp. XIII:** 114
"Cesarean" (Kenyon), **Supp. VII:** 173
Cézanne, Paul, **II:** 576; **III:** 210; **IV:** 26, 31, 407; **Supp. V:** 333, 341–342; **Supp. XIX:** 36
Chabon, Michael, **Supp. XI: 63–81; Supp. XVI:** 259; **Supp. XIX:** 135, 138, 174, 223; **Supp. XX: 177; Supp. XXII:** 49
Chaboseau, Jean, **Supp. I Part 1:** 260
Chace, Bill, **Supp. XXI:** 256
Chaikin, Joseph, **Supp. III Part 2:** 433, 436–437
"Chain, The" (Kumin), **Supp. IV Part 2:** 452
Chainbearer, The (Cooper), **I:** 351, 352–353
"Chain of Love, A" (Price), **Supp. VI: 258–259,** 260
Chain Saw Dance, The (Budbill), **Supp. XIX: 5–6**
Chains of Dew (Glaspell), **Supp. III Part 1:** 181
Chalk Face (W. Frank), **Supp. XX: 73–74**
Challacombe, Robert Hamilton, **III:** 176
Challenge (Untermeyer), **Supp. XV:** 296, 303
"Challenge" (Untermeyer), **Supp. XV:** 296
Chalmers, George, **Supp. I Part 2:** 514, 521
"Chambered Nautilus, The" (Holmes), **Supp. I Part 1:** 254, 307, 312–313, 314
Chamberlain, John, **Supp. I Part 2:** 647; **Supp. IV Part 2:** 525
Chamberlain, Neville, **II:** 589; **Supp. I Part 2:** 664
Chamber Music (Joyce), **III:** 16
Chambers, Richard, **Supp. III Part 2:** 610, 611, 612
Chambers, Whittaker, **Supp. III Part 2:** 610; **Supp. IV Part 2:** 526; **Supp. XV:** 143
Chameleon (C. Baxter), **Supp. XVII:** 14–15
"Champ, The" (Zinberg), **Supp. XV:** 193
"Champagne Regions" (Ríos), **Supp. IV Part 2:** 553
"Champion" (Lardner), **II:** 420–421, 428, 430
Champion, Laurie, **Supp. VIII:** 128
Champollion-Figeac, Jean Jacques, **IV:** 426
"Chance" (Doolittle), **Supp. I Part 1:** 271
Chance, Frank, **II:** 418
Chance Acquaintance, A (Howells), **II:** 278
"Chance Encounter, A" (Swados), **Supp. XIX:** 261, 262
"Chanclas" (Cisneros), **Supp. VII:** 61
Chandler, Raymond, **Supp. III Part 1:** 91; **Supp. IV Part 1: 119–138,** 341, 344, 345; **Supp. IV Part 2:** 461, 464, 469, 470, 471, 472, 473; **Supp. XI:** 160, 228; **Supp. XII:** 307; **Supp. XIII:** 159, 233; **Supp. XIV:** 21; **Supp. XV:** 119; **Supp. XVI:** 122; **Supp. XVII:** 137; **Supp. XVIII:** 136,137, 137–138; **Supp. XIX:** 178, 189; **Supp. XXI:** 67; **Supp. XXII:** 119

Chaney, "Professor" W. H., **II:** 463–464
Chang, Leslie C., **Supp. IV Part 1:** 72
"Change, The: Kyoto-Tokyo Express" (Ginsberg), **Supp. II Part 1:** 313, 329
Changed Man, A (Prose), **Supp. XVI:** 261–262
"Changeling" (Espaillat), **Supp. XXI:** 100
Changeling (Middleton), **Retro. Supp. I:** 62
"Changeling, The" (Lowell), **Supp. I Part 2:** 409
"Changeling, The" (Whittier), **Supp. I Part 2:** 697
Change of World, A (Rich), **Supp. I Part 2:** 551, 552
"Changes of Mind" (Baker), **Supp. XIII:** 52
"Changes of the Soul" (Taggard), **Supp. XXII:** 280
"Change the Joke and Slip the Yoke" (Ellison), **Retro. Supp. II:** 118
Changing Light at Sandover, The (Merrill), **Supp. III Part 1:** 318, 319, 323, 327, 332, 335–336; **Supp. XII:** 269–270; **Supp. XV:** 264
"Changing Same, The" (Baraka), **Supp. II Part 1:** 47, 51, 53
Changing the Bully Who Rules the World: Reading and Thinking about Ethics (C. Bly), **Supp. XVI:** 32, **39–40,** 41
Chanler, Mrs. Winthrop, **I:** 22; **IV:** 325
Channing, Carol, **IV:** 357
Channing, Edward, **Supp. I Part 2:** 479–480
Channing, Edward Tyrrel, **Supp. I Part 1:** 155; **Supp. I Part 2:** 422
Channing, William Ellery, **I:** 336; **II:** 224, 495; **IV:** 172, 173, 176, 177; **Retro. Supp. I:** 54; **Supp. I Part 1:** 103; **Supp. I Part 2:** 589
Channing, William Henry, **IV:** 178; **Supp. II Part 1:** 280, 285
Chanson de Roland, La, **I:** 13
"Chanson un Peu Naïve" (Bogan), **Supp. III Part 1:** 50–51
"Chanteuse" (Doty), **Supp. XI:** 119
"Chant for May Day" (Hughes), **Supp. I Part 1:** 331
Chants (Mora), **Supp. XIII: 214–215**
Chaos (Dove), **Supp. IV Part 1:** 243
"Chaperone, The" (Van Vechten), **Supp. II Part 2:** 728
Chaplin, Charles Spencer "Charlie," **I:** 27, 32, 43, 386, 447; **III:** 403; **Supp. I Part 2:** 607; **Supp. IV Part 1:** 146; **Supp. IV Part 2:** 574; **Supp. XX: 75; Supp. XXI:** 170; **Supp. XXII:** 25, 26
"Chaplinesque" (H. Crane), **Retro. Supp. II:** 79
"Chapman" (Rukeyser), **Supp. VI:** 273
Chapman, Abraham, **IV:** 485
Chapman, George, **Supp. I Part 2:** 422
Chapman, John (Johnny Appleseed), **Supp. I Part 2:** 397
Chapman, John Jay, **IV:** 436; **Supp. XIV: 39–56**
Chapman, Stephen, **Supp. XIII:** 12
Chappell, Fred, **Supp. IV Part 1:** 69; **Supp. XI:** 317; **Supp. XVIII:** 87
Chapters in a Mythology: The Poetry of Sylvia Plath (Kroll), **Supp. I Part 2:** 541–543
Chapters on Erie (Adams and Adams), **Supp. I Part 2:** 644
Chapter Two (Simon), **Supp. IV Part 2:** 575, 586
"Chapter VI" (Hemingway), **II:** 252
Char, René, **Supp. XVI:** 282; **Supp. XVII:** 244
"Character" (Emerson), **II:** 6
"Character of Presidents, The" (Doctorow), **Supp. IV Part 1:** 224
"Character of Socrates, The" (Emerson), **II:** 8–9
Character of the Poet, The (Simpson), **Supp. IX:** 273, 275, 278
"Characters in Fiction" (McCarthy), **II:** 562
"Charades" (Moore), **Supp. X:** 178
"Charge It" (Fante), **Supp. XI:** 164–165
Chariot in the Sky: A Story of the Jubilee Singers (Bontemps), **Supp. XXII:** 6, 13
"Charity" (Peacock), **Supp. XIX:** 221–222
Charity (Richard), **Supp. XIX: 220–222**
Charlatan, The (Singer), **IV:** 1
"Charles" (Jackson), **Supp. IX:** 125
Charles, Larry, **Supp. XVIII:** 21
"Charles Baxter, August Kleinzahler, Adrienne Rich: Contemporary Stevensians and the Problem of 'Other Lives' " (S. Burt), **Supp. XVII:** 18–19
Charles Goodnight: Cowman and Plainsman (Haley), **Supp. V:** 226
Charles Simic: Essays on the Poetry (Weigl), **Supp. VIII:** 269
Charles the Bold, Duke of Burgundy, **III:** 487
Charleville, Victoria Verdon, **Supp. I Part 1:** 200–201, 205, 206, 210
Charley's Aunt (B. Thomas), **II:** 138
Charlie Chan Is Dead: An Anthology of Contemporary Asian American Fiction (Hagedorn), **Supp. X:** 292
"Charlie Christian Story, The" (Ellison), **Retro. Supp. II:** 121
"Charlie Howard's Descent" (Doty), **Supp. XI:** 122
Charlotte: A Tale of Truth (Rowson), **Supp. I Part 1:** 128; **Supp. XV: 234–235,** 238. *See also Charlotte Temple* (Rowson)
Charlotte's Daughter; or, The Three Orphans (Rowson), **Supp. XV: 246**
Charlotte's Web (White), **Supp. I Part 2:** 655, 656, 658, 667, 670
Charlotte Temple (Rowson), **Supp. XV:** 229**, 238–239**. *See also Charlotte: A Tale of Truth* (Rowson)
Charm, The (Creeley), **Supp. IV Part 1:** 139, 141, 144, 149–150
Charmed Life, A (McCarthy), **II:** 571–574
Charming Billy (McDermott), **Supp. XVIII:** 155, **162–164,** 166
Charms for the Easy Life (Gibbons), **Supp. X:** 45, **47–48**
Charnel Rose, The (Aiken), **I:** 50, 57, 62
Charon's Cosmology (Simic), **Supp. VIII: 276–278**
Charterhouse, The (Percy), **Supp. III Part 1:** 388
Chart for Rough Water (W. Frank), **Supp. XX: 78**
Charvat, William, **II:** 244
Charyn, Jerome, **Supp. XVII:** 5
Chase, Mary Ellen, **Retro. Supp. II:** 243, 245
Chase, Richard, **IV:** 202, 443; **Retro. Supp. I:** 40, 395
Chase, Salmon P., **Supp. I Part 2:** 584
Chase, Stuart, **Supp. I Part 2:** 609
Chase, The (Foote), **Supp. I Part 1:** 281
Chasing the Dime (Connelly), **Supp. XXI: 74**
"Chaste Land, The" (Tate), **IV:** 122
Château, The (Maxwell), **Supp. VIII:** 152, 160, **165–167,** 168, 169
Chatham, Russell, **Supp. VIII:** 40
"Chattanooga Nights" (L. Brown), **Supp. XXI:** 39
Chatterdon, The Black Death, and Meriwether Lewis (Reznikoff), **Supp. XIV:** 288
Chatterton, Thomas, **Supp. I Part 1:** 349; **Supp. I Part 2:** 410, 716
Chatterton, Wayne, **Supp. IX:** 2, 4, 11–12
Chatwin, Bruce, **Supp. VIII:** 322
Chaucer, Geoffrey, **I:** 131; **II:** 11, 504, 516, 542, 543; **III:** 283, 411, 473, 492, 521; **Retro. Supp. I:** 135, 426; **Supp. I Part 1:** 356, 363; **Supp. I Part 2:** 422, 617; **Supp. V:** 259; **Supp. XII:** 197; **Supp. XVII:** 70; **Supp. XIX:** 4
Chauncy, Charles, **I:** 546–547; **IV:** 147
Chavez, César, **Supp. V:** 199
Chávez, Denise, **Supp. IV Part 2:** 544; **Supp. XI:** 316
Chavez, Lydia, **Supp. VIII:** 75
Chavkin, Allan, **Supp. IV Part 1:** 259
Chavkin, Nancy Feyl, **Supp. IV Part 1:** 259
Chawla, Louise, **Supp. XXI:** 24
Chayefsky, Paddy, **Supp. XI:** 306
Cheang, Shu Lea, **Supp. XI:** 20
"Cheat Takes Over" (Leopold), **Supp. XIV:** 189
"Cheers" (Carver), **Supp. III Part 1:** 138
Cheetham, James, **Supp. I Part 2:** 521
Cheever, Benjamin Hale, **Supp. I Part 1:** 175
Cheever, David W., **Supp. I Part 1:** 304
Cheever, Ezekiel, **Supp. I Part 1:** 174, 193
Cheever, Federico, **Supp. I Part 1:** 175
Cheever, Fred, **Supp. I Part 1:** 174
Cheever, Frederick L., **Supp. I Part 1:** 174
Cheever, John, **Retro. Supp. I:** 116, 333, 335; **Supp. I Part 1: 174–199; Supp. V:** 23, 95; **Supp. VIII:** 151; **Supp. IX:** 114, 208; **Supp. XI:** 65, 66, 99; **Supp. XII:** 140; **Supp. XIV:** 93; **Supp. XV:** 119, 142
Cheever, Mrs. John (Mary Winternitz), **Supp. I Part 1:** 175
Cheever, Mary Liley, **Supp. I Part 1:** 174

Cheever, Susan. *See* Cowley, Susan Cheever (Susan Cheever)
Cheever Evening, A (Gurney), **Supp. V:** 95
Chekhov, Anton, **I:** 52, 90; **II:** 27, 38, 44, 49, 198, 542; **III:** 362, 467; **IV:** 17, 53, 359, 446; **Retro. Supp. I:** 5, 355; **Retro. Supp. II:** 299; **Supp. I Part 1:** 196; **Supp. II Part 1:** 6; **Supp. IV Part 2:** 585; **Supp. V:** 265; **Supp. VIII:** 153, 332; **Supp. IX:** 260, 265, 274; **Supp. XI:** 66; **Supp. XII:** 94, 307; **Supp. XIII:** 79; **Supp. XIV:** 87, 242; **Supp. XV:** 320, 329; **Supp. XVIII:** 102; **Supp. XIX:** 172, 241; **Supp. XXII:** 60
"Chekhov's Sense of Writing as Seen Through His Letters" (Dobyns), **Supp. XIII:** 77–78
"Chemin de Fer" (Bishop), **Retro. Supp. II:** 41; **Supp. I Part 1:** 80, 85, 86
Cheney, Brainard, **Retro. Supp. II:** 229
Cheney, Matthew, **Supp. XXII:** 50
Chenzira, Ayoka, **Supp. XI:** 19
Chéri (Colette; stage adaptation, Loos), **Supp. XVI:** 194
Cherkovski, Neeli, **Supp. XII:** 118, 132, 134
Chernyshevski, Nikolai, **III:** 261, 262, 263; **Retro. Supp. I:** 269
Cherokee Lottery, The: A Sequence of Poems (W. J. Smith), **Supp. XIII: 340–344**
Cherry (Karr), **Supp. XI:** 239, **251–254**
"Cherrylog Road" (Dickey), **Supp. XVIII:** 191
Cherry Orchard, The (Chekhov), **IV:** 359, 426; **Supp. VIII:** 153
Cheslock, Louis, **III:** 99, 118, 119
Chesnutt, Charles Waddell, **Supp. II Part 1:** 174, 193, 211; **Supp. IV Part 1:** 257; **Supp. XIV: 57–78**
"Chess House, The" (Dixon), **Supp. XII:** 139
Chessman, Caryl, **Supp. I Part 2:** 446
Chester, Alfred, **Retro. Supp. II:** 111, 112; **Supp. X:** 192
Chesterfield, Lord, **II:** 36
Chesterton, Gilbert Keith, **I:** 226; **IV:** 432
Cheuse, Alan, **Supp. IV Part 2:** 570
Chevigny, Bell Gale, **Supp. XI:** 283
"Chicago" (Sandburg), **III:** 581, 592, 596; **Supp. III Part 1:** 71
Chicago (Shepard), **Supp. III Part 2:** 439
Chicago: City on the Make (Algren), **Supp. IX:** 1, 3
"*Chicago Defender* Sends a Man to Little Rock, The" (Brooks), **Supp. III Part 1:** 80–81
"Chicago Hamlet, A" (Anderson), **I:** 112
Chicago Loop (Theroux), **Supp. VIII:** 324
"Chicago Picasso, The" (Brooks), **Supp. III Part 1:** 70–71, 84
Chicago Poems (Sandburg), **III:** 579, 581–583, 586
"Chicano/Borderlands Literature and Poetry" (Ríos), **Supp. IV Part 2:** 537, 538, 542, 545
Chick, Nancy, **Supp. IV Part 1:** 1
"Chickamauga" (Bierce), **I:** 201
"Chickamauga" (Wolfe), **IV:** 460
Chickamauga (Wright), **Supp. V:** 333, 343–344
"Chickamauga" (Wright), **Supp. V:** 334
"Chicken Market" (Skloot), **Supp. XX: 198, 200**
"Chiefly about War Matters" (Hawthorne), **II:** 227; **Retro. Supp. I:** 165
"Chiffon" (Hull), **Supp. XXI:** 138
"Child" (Plath), **Supp. I Part 2:** 544
Child, Greg, **Supp. XVIII:** 107
Child, Julia, **Supp. XVII:** 89, 90
Child, Lydia Maria, **Supp. XIII:** 141; **Supp. XVIII:** 11
"Child, The" (Ríos), **Supp. IV Part 2:** 543
"Child by Tiger, The" (Wolfe), **IV:** 451
"Childhood" (Wright), **Supp. V:** 341
Childhood, A: The Biography of a Place (Crews), **Supp. XI:** 102–103, 245
"Childhood, When You Are in It . . ." (Kenyon), **Supp. VII:** 160, 170
"Childhood Sketch" (Wright), **Supp. III Part 2:** 589
"Child Is Born, A" (Benét), **Supp. XI:** 46
"Child Is the Meaning of This Life, The" (Schwartz), **Supp. II Part 2:** 659–660
"Childlessness" (Merrill), **Supp. III Part 1:** 323
"Childless Woman" (Plath), **Supp. I Part 2:** 544
Child-Life (Whittier and Larcom, eds.), **Supp. XIII:** 142
Child-Life in Prose (Whittier and Larcom, eds.), **Supp. XIII:** 142
Childlike Life of the Black Tarantula, The (Acker), **Supp. XII:** 4, 6, **7–8**
"Child Margaret" (Sandburg), **III:** 584
"Child of Courts, The" (Jarrell), **II:** 378, 379, 381
Child of God (McCarthy), **Supp. VIII: 177–178**
Child of My Heart (McDermott), **Supp. XVIII:** 155, **164–166**
"CHILD OF THE THIRTIES" (Baraka), **Supp. II Part 1:** 60
"Child on Top of a Greenhouse" (Roethke), **III:** 531
Children (Gurney), **Supp. V:** 95, 96
"Children" (Stowe), **Supp. I Part 2:** 587
"Children, The" (Jarman), **Supp. XVII:** 116
Children, The (Wharton), **IV:** 321, 326; **Retro. Supp. I:** 381
"Children, the Sandbar, That Summer" (Rukeyser), **Supp. VI:** 274
Children and Others (Cozzens), **I:** 374
Children Is All (Purdy), **Supp. VII:** 277, 278, 282
"Children of Adam" (Whitman), **IV:** 342; **Retro. Supp. I:** 403, 405
Children of Job, The: American Second-Generation Witnesses to the Holocaust (A. Berger), **Supp. XVII:** 39
Children of Light (Stone), **Supp. V:** 304–306
Children of Light and the Children of Darkness, The (Niebuhr), **III:** 292, 306, 310
Children of the Frost (London), **II:** 469, 483
Children of the Holocaust (H. Epstein), **Supp. XVII:** 48; **Supp. XXII:** 95
"Children of the Lord's Supper, The" (Tegnér), **Retro. Supp. II:** 155, 157
Children of the Market Place (Masters), **Supp. I Part 2:** 471
"Children on Their Birthdays" (Capote), **Supp. III Part 1:** 114, 115
"Children Selecting Books in a Library" (Jarrell), **II:** 371
Children's Hour, The (Hellman), **Supp. I Part 1:** 276–277, 281, 286, 297
"Children's Rhymes" (Hughes), **Supp. I Part 1:** 340
Childress, Mark, **Supp. X:** 89
Child's Garden of Verses, A (Stevenson), **Supp. IV Part 1:** 298, 314; **Supp. XIII:** 75
"Child's Nature, A" (Jin), **Supp. XVIII:** 93
"Child's Reminiscence, A" (Whitman), **IV:** 344
Childwold (Oates), **Supp. II Part 2:** 519–520
Chill, The (Macdonald), **Supp. IV Part 2:** 473
Chills and Fever (Ransom), **III:** 490, 491–492, 493
Chilly Scenes of Winter (Beattie), **Supp. V:** 21, 22, 23, 24, 26, 27
Chime of Words, A: The Letters of Logan Pearsall Smith (Tribble, ed.), **Supp. XIV:** 348–349
Chimera (C. Frost), **Supp. XV:** 94, 95, 100
"Chimes for Yahya" (Merrill), **Supp. III Part 1:** 329
Chin, Frank, **Supp. V:** 164, 172
Chin, Mei, **Supp. XVIII:** 95
"China" (Johnson), **Supp. VI: 193–194**
Chinaberry Tree, The (Fauset), **Supp. XIX:** 73
"Chinaman's Hat" (Kingston), **Supp. V:** 169
China Men (Kingston), **Supp. V:** 157, 158, 159, 160, 161, 164–169; **Supp. X:** 292; **Supp. XV:** 220
"China Poet, The" (Sturgis), **Supp. XX: 233, 240**
China Trace (Wright), **Supp. V:** 332, 340, 341, 342
"Chinese Apples" (Di Piero), **Supp. XIX:** 40
Chinese Apples: New and Selected Poems (Di Piero), **Supp. XIX:** 33, 36, 37, 38, 39, 40, 44, 45, 46, 47–48
Chinese Classics (Legge), **III:** 472
Chinese Materia Medica (P. Smith), **III:** 572
"Chinese New Year" (Hull), **Supp. XXI:** 135
"Chinese Nightingale, The" (Lindsay), **Supp. I Part 2:** 392–393, 394
Chinese Nightingale and Other Poems, The (Lindsay), **Supp. I Part 2:** 392

Chinese Siamese Cat, The (Tan), **Supp. X:** 289
Chinese Translations, The (Bynner), **Supp. XV:** 47, 52
Chinitz, David, **Supp. XV:** 180, 185
"Chinoiseries" (Lowell), **II:** 524–525
Chip (Untermeyer), **Supp. XV:** 310
Chirico, Giorgio de, **Supp. III Part 1:** 14
Chirico, Miriam M., **Supp. XV:** 323
"Chiron" (Winters), **Supp. II Part 2:** 801
"Chitlins at the Waldorf" (Crouch), **Supp. XIX:** 158
"Chloroform Jags" (J. Scott), **Supp. XVII:** 189
Chodorov, Jerome, **IV:** 274
"Choice, The" (Karr), **Supp. XI:** 251
"Choice of Accommodations, A" (Lahiri), **Supp. XXI:** 183
"Choice of Profession, A" (Malamud), **Supp. I Part 2:** 437
Choice of Wars, A (Shaw), **Supp. XIX:** 245
Chomei, Kamo No, **IV:** 170, 171, 184
Chomsky, Noam, **Supp. IV Part 2:** 679
Choosing not Choosing (Cameron), **Retro. Supp. I:** 43
Chopin, Felix, **Supp. I Part 1:** 202
Chopin, Frédéric, **Supp. I Part 1:** 363
Chopin, Jean, **Supp. I Part 1:** 206
Chopin, Kate, **II:** 276; **Retro. Supp. I:** 10, 215; **Retro. Supp. II: 57–74; Supp. I Part 1: 200–226; Supp. V:** 304; **Supp. X:** 227; **Supp. XVIII:** 194
"Choral: The Pink Church" (W. C. Williams), **Retro. Supp. I:** 428
"Chord" (Merwin), **Supp. III Part 1:** 356
"Chords and Dischords" (column; Untermeyer), **Supp. XV:** 294
Choruses from Iphigenia in Aulis (Doolittle, trans.), **Supp. I Part 1:** 257, 268, 269
"Chosen Blindness" (Karr), **Supp. XI:** 251
Chosen Country (Dos Passos), **I:** 475, 490–491
Chosen Place, The Timeless People, The (Marshall), **Supp. XI:** 275, 276, **282–284**
Chosön (Lowell), **II:** 513
Choukri, Mohamed, **Supp. IV Part 1:** 92
Chovteau, Mane Thérèse, **Supp. I Part 1:** 205
"ChrisEaster" (Peacock), **Supp. XIX:** 198, 199
Chrisman, Robert, **Supp. IV Part 1:** 1
Christabel (Coleridge), **Supp. IV Part 2:** 465
"Christ for Sale" (Lowell), **II:** 538
Christian, Graham, **Supp. XII:** 193
Christian Dictionary, A (Wilson), **IV:** 153
"Christian in World Crisis, The" (Merton), **Supp. VIII:** 203
Christianity and Power Politics (Niebuhr), **III:** 292, 303
"Christianity and the Survival of Creation" (Berry), **Supp. X:** 30
"Christian Minister, The" (Emerson), **II:** 10
Christian Philosopher, The (Mather), **Supp. II Part 2:** 463–464
Christian Realism and Practical Problems (Niebuhr), **III:** 292, 308
"Christian Roommates, The" (Updike), **IV:** 226–227; **Retro. Supp. I:** 319, 323
Christiansen, Carrie, **I:** 210
Christian's Secret of a Happy Life, The (H. W. Smith), **Supp. XIV:** 333–334
Christie, Agatha, **Supp. IV Part 1:** 341; **Supp. IV Part 2:** 469
Christ in Concrete (di Donato), **Supp. XX: 33, 34–40, 42, 43, 46**
"Christ in Concrete" (di Donato), **Supp. XX: 34**
Christine (King), **Supp. V:** 139, 148
"Christ Light, The" (Chopin), **Retro. Supp. II:** 61
"Christmas" (Saunders), **Supp. XIX:** 232
"Christmas, or the Good Fairy" (Stowe), **Supp. I Part 2:** 586
"Christmas 1944" (Levertov), **Supp. III Part 1:** 274
"Christmas Banquet, The" (Hawthorne), **II:** 227
Christmas Card, A (Theroux), **Supp. VIII:** 322
Christmas Carol, A (Dickens), **Retro. Supp. I:** 196; **Supp. I Part 2:** 409–410; **Supp. X:** 252, 253
"Christmas Eve at Johnson's Drugs N Goods" (Bambara), **Supp. XI:** 11–12
"Christmas Eve in the Time of War: A Capitalist Meditates by a Civil War Monument" (Lowell), **II:** 538
"Christmas Eve under Hooker's Statue" (Lowell), **II:** 539–540
"Christmas Gift" (Warren), **IV:** 252–253
"Christmas Greeting, A" (Wright), **Supp. III Part 2:** 601
"Christmas Hymn, A" (Wilbur), **Supp. III Part 2:** 557
Christmas Memory, A (Capote), **Supp. III Part 1:** 118, 119, 129
"Christmass Poem" (West), **Retro. Supp. II:** 338
Christmas Story (Mencken), **III:** 111
"Christmas to Me" (Lee), **Supp. VIII:** 113
Christographia (Taylor), **IV:** 164–165
Christ on a Clothesline (Loy), **Supp. XXII:** 168
"*Christ on the Cross*/Nuestro Señor Crucificado" (Mora), **Supp. XIII:** 229
Christopher, Mary (pseudonym). *See* West, Dorothy
Christopher and His Kind: 1929–1939 (Isherwood), **Supp. XIV:** 157, 163, 164, 171
"Christopher Cat" (Cullen), **Supp. IV Part 1:** 173
Christopher Columbus, Mariner (Morison), **Supp. I Part 2:** 488
Christopher Isherwood: A Critical Biography (Finney), **Supp. XIV:** 158
Christophersen, Bill, **Supp. IX:** 159, 167; **Supp. XI:** 155; **Supp. XIII:** 87; **Supp. XXI:** 103
"Christ's Passion" (Karr), **Supp. XI:** 251
Christus: A Mystery (Longfellow), **II:** 490, 493, 495, 505–507; **Retro. Supp. II:** 161, 165, 166
Chroma (F. Barthelme), **Supp. XI:** 30, 33, 34
"Chroma" (F. Barthelme), **Supp. XI:** 31
"Chronicle of Race Relations, A" (Du Bois), **Supp. II Part 1:** 182
Chronicle of the Conquest of Granada (Irving), **II:** 310
Chronicles: Volume One (Dylan), **Supp. XVIII:** 20, 21, 23, 24, 28, **32–33**
"Chronologues" (Goldbarth), **Supp. XII:** 183, 184
"Chrysanthemums, The" (Steinbeck), **IV:** 53
"Chrysaor" (Longfellow), **II:** 498
Chu, Louis, **Supp. X:** 291
Chuang, Hua, **Supp. X:** 291
Chuang-Tzu, **Supp. VIII:** 206
"Chunk of Amethyst, A" (R. Bly), **Supp. IV Part 1:** 72
Church, Margaret, **IV:** 466
"Church and the Fiction Writer, The" (O'Connor), **Retro. Supp. II:** 223, 233; **Supp. XVIII:** 161
"Church Going" (Larkin), **Supp. XXI:** 93
"Churchgoing" (Nelson), **Supp. XVIII:** 173
Churchill, Charles, **Supp. XV:** 232
Churchill, Winston, **I:** 9, 490; **Supp. I Part 2:** 491
Church of Dead Girls, The (Dobyns), **Supp. XIII:** 75, **83–84**
"Church of Omnivorous Light, The" (Wrigley), **Supp. XVIII:** 306–307
"Church of the Latter Day Saints, The" (Mosher), **Supp. XXII:** 208
"Church Porch, The" (Herbert), **IV:** 153
Church Psalmody, Selected from Dr. Watts and Other Authors (Mason and Greene, ed.), **I:** 458
Ciannic, Saint, **II:** 215
Ciano, Edda, **IV:** 249
Ciardi, John, **I:** 169, 179, 535; **III:** 268; **Supp. IV Part 1:** 243; **Supp. IV Part 2:** 639; **Supp. IX:** 269, 324; **Supp. XII:** 119
Cicada (Haines), **Supp. XII: 206–207**
"Cicadas" (Wilbur), **Supp. III Part 2:** 549
Cicero, **I:** 279; **II:** 8, 14–15; **III:** 23; **Supp. I Part 2:** 405
Cider House Rules, The (Irving), **Supp. VI:** 164, **173–175**
"Cigales" (Wilbur), **Supp. III Part 2:** 549
"Cigarette" (L. Michaels), **Supp. XVI:** 214
Cimarron, Rose (Burke), **Supp. XIV:** 22, 35
"Cimetière Marin, Le" (Valéry), **IV:** 91–92
Cimino, Michael, **Supp. X:** 126
Cincinnati Kid, The (film), **Supp. XI: 306**
"Cinderella" (Jarrell), **II:** 386
"Cinderella" (Perrault), **IV:** 266, 267
"Cinderella" (Sexton), **Supp. II Part 2:** 691

"Cinema, The" (Salter), **Supp. IX:** 257
Cinema of Tony Richardson, The: Essays and Interviews (Phillips), **Supp. XI:** 306
Cinthio, **IV:** 370
Ciolkowski, Laura, **Supp. XVI:** 24
CIOPW (Cummings), **I:** 429
"Circe" (Welty), **Retro. Supp. I:** 353
Circle Game, The (Atwood), **Supp. XIII:** 20, 33
"Circle in the Fire, A" (O'Connor), **III:** 344–345, 349–350, 351, 353, 354; **Retro. Supp. II:** 229, 232
"Circle of Breath" (Stafford), **Supp. XI:** 318, 322
Circle of Hanh, The (Weigl), **Supp. XIX:** 273, 275, 282, **284–286**
"Circles" (Emerson), **I:** 455, 460
"Circles" (Lowell), **II:** 554
Circumference: Varieties of Metaphysical Verse 1456–1928 (Taggard, ed.), **Supp. XXII:** 279
"Circus, The" (Porter), **III:** 443, 445
"Circus Animals' Desertion" (Yeats), **I:** 389
"Circus in the Attic" (Warren), **IV:** 253
Circus in the Attic, The (Warren), **IV:** 243, 251–253
"Circus in Three Rings" (Plath), **Retro. Supp. II:** 243; **Supp. I Part 2:** 536
Circus of Needs, A (Dunn), **Supp. XI: 147–148**
"Cirque d'Hiver" (Bishop), **Supp. I Part 1:** 85
Cisneros, Sandra, **Supp. IV Part 2:** 544; **Supp. VII: 57–73; Supp. XI:** 177; **Supp. XVII:** 71; **Supp. XXII:** 177
Cities of the Interior (Nin), **Supp. X:** 182
Cities of the Plain (McCarthy), **Supp. VIII:** 175, **186–187**
Cities of the Red Night (Burroughs), **Supp. III Part 1:** 106
"Citizen Cain" (Baraka), **Supp. II Part 1:** 49
Citizen Kane (film), **Retro. Supp. I:** 115; **Supp. V:** 251; **Supp. XI:** 169
"Citizen of the World" (Goldsmith), **II:** 299
Citro, Joseph, **Supp. XXII:** 208, 218
"City" (Francis), **Supp. IX:** 87
City and the Pillar, The (Vidal), **Supp. IV Part 2:** 677, 680–681; **Supp. XIV:** 170
"*City and the Pillar, The,* as Gay Fiction" (Summers), **Supp. IV Part 2:** 680–681
"City Articles" series (Briggs), **Supp. XVIII:** 12
City Block (W. Frank), **Supp. XX: 71, 72, 76**
City Boy (L. Michaels), **Supp. XVI:** 212
"City Boy" (L. Michaels), **Supp. XVI:** 203–204
City Dog (Di Piero), **Supp. XIX:** 33–34, 35, 38, 46, 48
"City Dog" (Di Piero), **Supp. XIX:** 47
City in History, The (Mumford), **Supp. II Part 2:** 495
"City in the Sea, The" (Poe), **III:** 411; **Retro. Supp. II:** 274
City in Which I Love You, The (L.-Y. Lee), **Supp. XV:** 212, **215–220**
"City in Which I Love You, The" (L.-Y. Lee), **Supp. XV:** 215, **217–218**
City Life (Barthelme), **Supp. IV Part 1:** 44, 47
City of Bones (Connelly), **Supp. XXI: 74–75,** 77
"City of Change, A" (Bynner), **Supp. XV:** 45
City of Dreadful Night (Siegel), **Supp. XXII:** 258
City of Glass (Auster), **Supp. XII:** 22, **24–26**
City of God, The (St. Augustine), **IV:** 126
City of Names (Brockmeier), **Supp. XXII:** 55–56, 57
"City of Refuge, The" (R. Fisher), **Supp. XIX:** 65, 66, **67–68**
City of Refuge, The: The Collected Stories of Rudolph Fisher (McCluskey, ed.), **Supp. XIX:** 68–69
City of the Living and Other Stories, The (Stegner), **Supp. IV Part 2:** 599, 609, 613
City of Words: American Fiction 1950-1970 (T. Tanner), **Supp. XVI:** 69
City of Your Final Destination, The (Cameron), **Supp. XII:** 79, 82, **91–94**
"City on a Hill" (Lowell), **II: 552**
"City Person Encountering Nature, A" (Kingston), **Supp. V:** 170
"City Planners, The" (Atwood), **Supp. XIII:** 33
City Without Men (film), **Supp. XVIII:** 247
City Without Walls (Auden), **Supp. II Part 1:** 24
Civil Disobedience (Thoreau), **IV:** 185; **Supp. I Part 2:** 507
Civilization in the United States (Stearns), **I:** 245
"Civil Rights" (Lanier), **Supp. I Part 1:** 357
CivilWarLand in Bad Decline (Saunders), **Supp. XIX: 224–227**
"CivilWarLand in Bad Decline" (Saunders), **Supp. XIX:** 224–225, 227
Civitatis Anthology of African American Slave Narratives, The (H. L. Gates and Andrews, eds.), **Supp. XX: 105**
Cixous, Hélène, **Supp. X:** 102; **Supp. XIII:** 297; **Supp. XV:** 347
Claiborne, Craig, **Supp. XVII:** 89
Claiborne, William, **I:** 132
Claiming an Identity They Taught Me to Despise (Cliff), **Supp. XXII:** 66, 67–68, 70
Claiming of Sleeping Beauty, The (Rice), **Supp. VII:** 301
Clampitt, Amy, **Supp. IX: 37–54; Supp. X:** 120; **Supp. XI:** 249; **Supp. XV:** 251, 256
Clancy's Wake, At (Crane), **I:** 422
"Clandeboye" (Leopold), **Supp. XIV:** 189
Clara Howard; or, The Enthusiasm of Love (Brown), **Supp. I Part 1:** 145
Clara's Ole Man (Bullins), **Supp. II Part 1:** 42
Clare, John, **II:** 387; **III:** 528; **Supp. XVI:** 295
Clarel: A Poem and Pilgrimage in the Holy Land (Melville), **Retro. Supp. I:** 257
Clarence Major and His Art (Bell), **Supp. XXII:** 182
Clarissa (Richardson), **II:** 111; **Supp. I Part 2:** 714; **Supp. V:** 127; **Supp. XV:** 231; **Supp. XX: 236**
Clark, Alex, **Supp. XII:** 307
Clark, Charles, **I:** 470
Clark, Eleanor. *See* Warren, Mrs. Robert Penn (Eleanor Clark)
Clark, Francis Edward, **II:** 9
Clark, Geoffrey, **Supp. XI:** 342
Clark, Harry Hayden, **Supp. I Part 2:** 423
Clark, John Bates, **Supp. I Part 2:** 633
Clark, Kenneth, **Supp. XIV:** 342, 348; **Supp. XIX:** 151
Clark, Lewis Gaylord, **Supp. XVIII:** 4, 7, 8
Clark, Shirley, **Supp. XXI:** 22
Clark, Thomas, **Supp. III Part 2:** 629; **Supp. IV Part 1:** 140, 145, 147
Clark, Walter, **Supp. XI:** 315
Clark, William, **III:** 14; **IV:** 179, 283
Clark, Willis Gaylord, **Supp. I Part 2:** 684
Clarke, James Freeman, **Supp. II Part 1:** 280
Clarke, John, **Supp. IV Part 1:** 8
Clarke, John J., **III:** 356
Clarke, Samuel, **II:** 108
Clark Lectures, **Retro. Supp. I:** 65
Claros varones de Belken (Hinojosa). *See Fair Gentlemen of Belken County* (Hinojosa)
Clash by Night (Odets), **Supp. II Part 2:** 531, 538, 544–546, 550, 551
Classical Tradition, The (Highet), **Supp. I Part 1:** 268
Classic Ballroom Dances (Simic), **Supp. VIII:** 271, **276–278,** 283
Classics and Commercials: A Literary Chronicle of the Forties (Wilson), **IV:** 433
"CLASS STRUGGLE" (Baraka), **Supp. III Part 1:** 55
"Claude Glass, The: 1890" (Bierds), **Supp. XVII:** 27
Claudel, Paul, **I:** 60
Claudelle Inglish (Caldwell), **I:** 304
Clavel, Marcel, **I:** 343
"CLAY" (Baraka), **Supp. II Part 1:** 54
Clay, Henry, **I:** 8; **Supp. I Part 2:** 684, 686
Clay's Ark (O. Butler), **Supp. XIII:** 63
Clayton, John J., **Supp. IV Part 1:** 238
"Clean, Well Lighted Place, A" (Hemingway), **Retro. Supp. I:** 181
"Clear, with Light Variable Winds" (Lowell), **II:** 522
"Clear Days" (White), **Supp. I Part 2:** 664, 665
Clearing (Berry), **Supp. X:** 22
"Clearing, A" (Simpson), **Supp. IX:** 280
"Clearing, The" (Kenyon), **Supp. VII:** 174

"Clearing the Title" (Merrill), **Supp. III Part 1:** 336
"Clearing Up the Question of Stesichoros' Blinding by Helen" (Carson), **Supp. XII:** 107–108
"Clear Morning" (Glück), **Supp. V:** 88
"Clearness" (Wilbur), **Supp. III Part 2:** 544, 550
"Clear Night" (Wright), **Supp. V:** 341
Clear Pictures: First Loves, First Guides (Price), **Supp. VI:** 253, 254, 255, 256, 265
Clear Springs (Mason), **Supp. VIII:** 134–136, 137–138, 139, 147
Cleary, Rebecca Lauck, **Supp. XVIII:** 195
Cleaver, Eldridge, **Retro. Supp. II:** 12; **Supp. IV Part 1:** 206; **Supp. X:** 249
"Cleaving, The" (L.-Y. Lee), **Supp. XV:** 215, **218–220**
Cleland, John, **Supp. V:** 48, 127
Clemenceau, Georges, **I:** 490
"Clemency" (Wrigley), **Supp. XVIII:** 307–308
Clemens, Jane, **I:** 247
Clemens, Orion, **IV:** 193, 195
Clemens, Samuel Langhorne. *See* Twain, Mark
Clemens, Mrs. Samuel Langhorne (Olivia Langdon), **I:** 197, 208, 247; **Supp. I Part 2:** 457
Clemens, Susie, **IV:** 208
Clementine Recognitions (novel), **Supp. IV Part 1:** 280
Clements, Colin Campbell, **Supp. XVI:** 190
Clemons, Walter, **Supp. IV Part 1:** 305, 307
Cleopatra, **III:** 44; **IV:** 373; **Supp. I Part 1:** 114
"Clepsydra" (Ashbery), **Supp. III Part 1:** 10–15
"Clerks, The" (Robinson), **III:** 517–518
"Cleveland" (Halliday), **Supp. XIX:** 90
Cleveland, Carol, **Supp. IX:** 120, 125
Cleveland, Ceil, **Supp. V:** 222
Cleveland, Grover, **II:** 126, 128, 129, 130, 137, 138; **Supp. I Part 2:** 486
"Clever Magician Carrying My Heart, A" (Salinas), **Supp. XIII:** 323
Cliff, Michelle, **Supp. XXII: 65–80**
"Cliff, The" (C. Baxter), **Supp. XVII:** 16–17
Clifford, Craig, **Supp. IX:** 99
Clift, Montgomery, **III:** 161
Clifton, Lucille, **Supp. XVIII:** 177
Climate of Monastic Prayer, The (Merton), **Supp. VIII:** 205, 207
Climb, The (Boukreev), **Supp. XVIII:** 112
"Climber, The" (Mason), **Supp. VIII:** 140–141
Climbing High: A Woman's Account of Surviving the Everest Tragedy (Gammelgaard), **Supp. XVIII:** 112
"Climbing the Tower" (Crews), **Supp. XI:** 102
Clinton, De Witt, **I:** 338
"Clipped Wings" (H. Miller), **III:** 176–177
Clippinger, David, **Supp. XXI:** 24
Clive, Robert, **Supp. I Part 2:** 505
Clock Winder, The (Tyler), **Supp. IV Part 2:** 661–662, 670
Clock Without Hands (McCullers), **II:** 587–588, 604–606
Clockwork Orange, A (Burgess), **Supp. XIII:** 29
Clorindy (Cook), **Supp. II Part 1:** 199
"Close, The" (Jarman), **Supp. XVII:** 113
"Close Calls" (Wolff), **Supp. VII:** 332–333
"Closed Book, A" (Mosley), **Supp. XIII:** 237
Close Quarters (Heinemann), **Supp. XXII:** 103, **104–109,** 111, 115
Close Range: Wyoming Stories (Proulx), **Supp. VII:** 261–265
Closers, The (Connelly), **Supp. XXI: 76–77**
Closest Possible Union, The (J. Scott), **Supp. XVII: 185–186,** 188, 191
Close the Book (Glaspell), **Supp. III Part 1:** 179
"Close the Book" (Lowell), **II:** 554
Close to Me & Closer ... (The Language of Heaven) and Désamère (Notley), **Supp. XXII:** 234
Close to Shore: A True Story of Terror in an Age of Innocence (Capuzzo), **Supp. XIII:** 254
Closet Writing & Gay Reading: The Case of Melville's Pierre (Creech), **Retro. Supp. I:** 254
Closing Circle, The (Commoner), **Supp. XIII:** 264
Closing of the American Mind, The (Bloom), **Retro. Supp. II:** 19, 30, 31
"Closing of the Rodeo, The" (W. J. Smith), **Supp. XIII:** 332
Closing Time (Heller), **Supp. IV Part 1:** 382, 386, 391–394
Closset, Marie, **Supp. VIII:** 251, 265
"Cloud, The" (Shelley), **Supp. I Part 2:** 720
"Cloud and Fame" (Berryman), **I:** 173
Cloud Forest, The: A Chronicle of the South American Wilderness (Matthiessen), **Supp. V:** 202, 204
"Cloud on the Way, The" (Bryant), **Supp. I Part 1:** 171
"Cloud River" (Wright), **Supp. V:** 341
"Clouds" (Levine), **Supp. V:** 184
Cloudsplitter (Banks), **Supp. V:** 16
"Clover" (Lanier), **Supp. I Part 1:** 362–364
Clover and Other Poems (Lanier), **Supp. I Part 1:** 362
"Clown" (Corso), **Supp. XII:** 127
Clown in the Belfry, The: Writings on Faith and Fiction (Buechner), **Supp. XII:** 53
Cluck, Julia, **Supp. I Part 2:** 728
Clum, John M., **Supp. XIII: 200,** 201, 209
Cluny, Hugo, **IV:** 290
Clurman, Harold, **I:** 93; **IV:** 381, 385
Clytus, Radiclani, **Supp. XIII:** 128, **Supp. XIII:** 129, 132
"C.O." (Wrigley), **Supp. XVIII:** 298
"Coal: Beginning and End" (Winters), **Supp. II Part 2:** 791
Coale, Howard, **Supp. XIII:** 15
"Coals" (Hoffman), **Supp. XVIII:** 86
"Coast, The" (column), **Supp. IV Part 1:** 198
"Coast Guard's Cottage, The" (Wylie), **Supp. I Part 2:** 723
Coast of Trees, A (Ammons), **Supp. VII:** 24, 34
"Coast-Range Christ, The" (Jeffers), **Supp. II Part 2:** 414, 419
"Coast-Road, The" (Jeffers), **Supp. II Part 2:** 425
"Coat, The" (Everwine), **Supp. XV:** 80
Coates, Joseph, **Supp. VIII:** 80; **Supp. XXII:** 205
Coates, Robert, **I:** 54; **IV:** 298
"Coatlicue's Rules: Advice from an Aztec Goddess" (Mora), **Supp. XIII:** 223
"Coats" (Kenyon), **Supp. VII:** 172
Cobb, Lee J., **III:** 153
Cobb, Ty, **III:** 227, 229
Cobbett, William, **Supp. I Part 2:** 517; **Supp. XV:** 237
"Cobbler Keezar's Vision" (Whittier), **Supp. I Part 2:** 699
"Cobweb, The" (Carver), **Supp. III Part 1:** 148
Cobwebs From an Empty Skull (Bierce), **I:** 195
Coccimiglio, Vic, **Supp. XIII:** 114
"Cock-a-Doodle-Doo!" (Melville), **III:** 89
"Cockayne" (Emerson), **II:** 6
"Cock-Crow" (Gordon), **II:** 219
Cock Pit (Cozzens), **I:** 359, 378, 379
Cockpit (Kosinski), **Supp. XII:** 21
Cockpit: A Novel (Kosinski), **Supp. VII:** 215, 223–224, 225
"Cock Robin Takes Refuge in the Storm House" (Snodgrass), **Supp. VI:** 319
Cocktail Hour, The (Gurney), **Supp. V:** 95, 96, 100, 101, 103, 105, 108
Cocktail Hour and Two Other Plays: Another Antigone and *The Perfect Party* (Gurney), **Supp. V:** 100
Cocktail Party, The (Eliot), **I:** 571, 582–583; **III:** 21; **Retro. Supp. I:** 65; **Supp. V:** 101, 103
Cocteau, Jean, **III:** 471; **Retro. Supp. I:** 82, 378; **Supp. IV Part 1:** 82; **Supp. XVI:** 135; **Supp. XX: 236**
"Coda: Wilderness Letter" (Stegner), **Supp. IV Part 2:** 595
"Code, The" (Frost), **Retro. Supp. I:** 121, 128
Codman, Florence, **Supp. II Part 1:** 92, 93
Codman, Ogden, Jr., **Retro. Supp. I:** 362, 363
Codrescu, Andrei, **Supp. XXII:** 155
Cody, William ("Buffalo Bill"), **I:** 440; **III:** 584; **Supp. V:** 230
Coffey, Michael, **Supp. V:** 243; **Supp. XV:** 65; **Supp. XX: 88**
Coffey, Warren, **III:** 358
Coffin, Charles, **III:** 577
Cogan, David J., **Supp. IV Part 1:** 362
Cogan, Joshua, **Supp. XXI:** 247

Coghill, Nevill, **Supp. II Part 1:** 4; **Supp. XIV:** 13
Cohan, George M., **II:** 427; **III:** 401
Cohen, Edward M., **Supp. XVI:** 212
Cohen, Esther, **Supp. XV:** 323
Cohen, Hettie, **Supp. II Part 1:** 30
Cohen, Joshua, **Supp. XXII:** 268
Cohen, Marty, **Supp. X:** 112
Cohen, Norman J., **Supp. IX:** 132, 143
Cohen, Rosetta, **Supp. XV:** 257
Cohen, Sarah Blacher, **Supp. V:** 273
Cohen, Victor, **Supp. XVIII:** 235, 236
"Coherent Decentering: Towards a New Model of the Poetic Self" (A. Finch), **Supp. XVII:** 76
"Coin" (Goldbarth), **Supp. XII:** 187
Coindreau, Maurice, **III:** 339
Coiner, Constance, **Supp. XIII:** 297, 302
Coit, Lille Hitchcock, **Supp. X:** 103
"Coitus" (Pound), **III:** 466
Coke, Desmond, **Supp. XX: 235**
Colburn, Nadia Herman, **Supp. XV:** 339, 341, 347
"Cold, The" (Kenyon), **Supp. VII:** 164
"Cold, The" (Winters), **Supp. II Part 2:** 790–791, 809, 811
"Cold-blooded Creatures" (Wylie), **Supp. I Part 2:** 729
Colden, Cadwallader, **Supp. I Part 1:** 250
"Colder the Air, The" (Bishop), **Supp. I Part 1:** 86
Cold Feet (Harrison), **Supp. VIII:** 39
Cold Frame (C. Frost), **Supp. XV:** 93, 96
Cold Ground Was My Bed Last Night (Garrett), **Supp. VII:** 98
"Cold Ground Was My Bed Last Night" (Garrett), **Supp. VII:** 100
"Cold Night, The" (W. C. Williams), **Retro. Supp. I:** 418
"Cold Plunge into Skin Diving, A" (Knowles), **Supp. XII:** 241
Cold Spring, A (Bishop), **Retro. Supp. II:** 45
Cold Springs Harbor (Yates), **Supp. XI:** 348
Cold War American Poetry, **Supp. V:** 182
Cold War and the Income Tax, The (Wilson), **IV:** 430
Cole, Bruce, **Supp. XX: 106**
Cole, Goody, **Supp. I Part 2:** 696–697
Cole, Lester, **Retro. Supp. II:** 329
Cole, Nat King, **Retro. Supp. I:** 334; **Supp. X:** 255
Cole, Thomas, **Supp. I Part 1:** 156, 158, 171
Cole, William, **Supp. XIX:** 120
"Coleman" (Karr), **Supp. XI:** 244
Coleman, Wanda, **Supp. XI: 83–98**
Coleridge, Samuel Taylor, **I:** 283, 284, 447, 522; **II:** 7, 10, 11, 19, 71, 169, 273, 301, 502, 516, 549; **III:** 77, 83–84, 424, 461, 488, 523; **IV:** 74, 173, 250, 349, 453; **Retro. Supp. I:** 65, 308; **Supp. I Part 1:** 31, 311, 349; **Supp. I Part 2:** 376, 393, 422; **Supp. IV Part 2:** 422, 465; **Supp. V:** 258; **Supp. IX:** 38, 50; **Supp. XIII:** 139; **Supp. XIV:** 21–22; **Supp. XV:** 250; **Supp. XXI:** 52, 55
Coles, Katharine, **Supp. IV Part 2:** 630
Colette, Sidonie-Gabrielle, **Supp. VIII:** 40, 171; **Supp. XVI:** 193–194
"Coliseum, The" (Poe), **III:** 411
Collage of Dreams (Spencer), **Supp. X:** 196
"Collapse of Tomorrow, The" (Mumford), **Supp. II Part 2:** 482
"Collected by a Valetudinarian" (E. Stoddard), **Supp. XV:** 286–287
Collected Earlier Poems (Hecht), **Supp. X:** 58, 59
Collected Earlier Poems (W. C. Williams), **Retro. Supp. I:** 414, 428
Collected Earlier Poems 1940–1960 (Levertov), **Supp. III Part 1:** 273, 275
Collected Essays (Tate), **IV:** 133–134
Collected Essays of Ralph Ellison, The (Ellison), **Retro. Supp. II:** 119
Collected Essays of Robert Creeley, The (Creeley), **Supp. IV Part 1:** 153, 154
Collected Later Poems (W. C. Williams), **Retro. Supp. I:** 428
Collected Plays (A. Miller), **III:** 158
Collected Plays, 1974–1983 (Gurney), **Supp. V:** 99
Collected Poems (Aiken), **I:** 50
Collected Poems (Burke), **I:** 269
Collected Poems (Cummings), **I:** 430, 439, 441
Collected Poems (Doolittle), **Supp. I Part 1:** 264–267, 269
Collected Poems (Frost), **Retro. Supp. I:** 136
Collected Poems (Hull), **Supp. XXI:** 141
Collected Poems (Kees; Justice, ed.), **Supp. XV:** 134
Collected Poems (Lindsay), **Supp. I Part 2:** 380, 387, 392, 396–397, 400
Collected Poems (Lowell), **Supp. XV:** 20
Collected Poems (Markson), **Supp. XVII:** 143
Collected Poems (Moore), **III:** 194, 215
Collected Poems (Price), **Supp. VI:** 267
Collected Poems (Simpson), **Supp. IX:** 279
Collected Poems (W. C. Williams), **IV:** 415; **Retro. Supp. I:** 430
Collected Poems (Winters), **Supp. II Part 2:** 791, 810
Collected Poems (Wright), **Supp. III Part 2:** 602
Collected Poems (Yeats), **Supp. XV:** 152
Collected Poems, 1918–1938 (Taggard), **Supp. XXII:** 283
Collected Poems, 1923–1953 (Bogan), **Supp. III Part 1:** 64
Collected Poems, 1936–1976 (Francis), **Supp. IX:** 77, 80, **87**
Collected Poems, The (Stevens), **III:** 273; **IV:** 75, 76, 87, 93; **Retro. Supp. I:** 296, 309
Collected Poems 1909–1935 (Eliot), **I:** 580; **Retro. Supp. I:** 66
Collected Poems 1909–1962 (Eliot), **I:** 583
Collected Poems 1917–1952 (MacLeish), **III:** 3, 4, 19
Collected Poems 1921–1931 (W. C. Williams), **Retro. Supp. I:** 422; **Supp. XIV:** 285
Collected Poems 1930–1960 (Eberhart), **I:** 522, 525–526, 540, 541
Collected Poems: 1939–1989 (W. J. Smith), **Supp. XIII:** 332, 340, 343, 345
Collected Poems: 1940–1978 (Shapiro), **Supp. II Part 2:** 703, 717
Collected Poems: 1951–1971 (Ammons), **Supp. VII:** 24, 26–29, 32, 33
Collected Poems: 1956–1976 (Wagoner), **Supp. IX:** 323, **328–329**
Collected Poems of Amy Clampitt, The (Clampitt), **Supp. IX:** 37, 44, 53
Collected Poems of George Garrett (Garrett), **Supp. VII:** 109
Collected Poems of Hart Crane, The (Crane), **I:** 399–402
Collected Poems of James Agee, The (Fitzgerald, ed.), **I:** 27–28
Collected Poems of James T. Farrell, The (Farrell), **II:** 45
Collected Poems of Langston Hughes, The (Rampersad and Roessel, ed.), **Retro. Supp. I:** 194, 196, 212
Collected Poems of Muriel Rukeyser, The (Rukeyser), **Supp. VI:** 274
Collected Poems of Thomas Merton, The, **Supp. VIII:** 207, 208
Collected Poetry (Auden), **Supp. II Part 1:** 18
Collected Prose (Wright), **Supp. III Part 2:** 596
Collected Prose, The (Bishop), **Retro. Supp. II:** 51
Collected Recordings (W. C. Williams), **Retro. Supp. I:** 431
Collected Shorter Poems, 1946-1991 (Carruth), **Supp. XVI:** 47
Collected Short Stories, The (Wharton), **Retro. Supp. I:** 362, 363, 366
Collected Sonnets (Millay), **III:** 136–137
Collected Stories, 1939–1976 (Bowles), **Supp. IV Part 1:** 92
Collected Stories, The (Paley), **Supp. VI:** 218
Collected Stories, The (Price), **Supp. VI:** 266
Collected Stories, The (Theroux), **Supp. VIII:** 318
Collected Stories, The (Wharton), **Retro. Supp. I:** 361
Collected Stories of Amy Hempel, The (Hempel), **Supp. XXI:** 115, 117
Collected Stories of Eudora Welty, The (Welty), **Retro. Supp. I:** 355
Collected Stories of Isaac Bashevis Singer (Singer), **Retro. Supp. II: 307–308**
Collected Stories of Katherine Anne Porter (Porter), **III:** 454
Collected Stories of Peter Taylor (Taylor), **Supp. V:** 314, 320, 323–324, 325, 326
Collected Stories of Richard Yates, The, **Supp. XI:** 349
Collected Stories of Wallace Stegner (Stegner), **Supp. IV Part 2:** 599, 605

Collected Stories of William Faulkner (Faulkner), **II:** 72; **Retro. Supp. I:** 75
Collected Stories of William Humphrey, The (Humphrey), **Supp. IX:** 106
Collected Works (Bierce), **I:** 204, 208–210
Collected Works of Buck Rogers in the 25th Century, The (Bradbury), **Supp. IV Part 1:** 101
Collected Writings, The (Z. Fitzgerald; Bruccoli, ed.), **Supp. IX:** 65, 68
Collecting the Animals (Everwine), **Supp. XV:** 73, 75, **78–81,** 85, 88
Collection of Epigrams, **II:** 111
Collection of Poems, on American Affairs, and a Variety of Other Subjects . . . (Freneau), **Supp. II Part 1:** 274
Collection of Select Aphorisms and Maxims (Palmer), **II:** 111
"Collectors" (Carver), **Supp. III Part 1:** 141–142
Collette, **Supp. XVII:** 86
Collier, John, **Supp. XXI:** 8
Collier, Lucy Wood, **Supp. XXI:** 8
Collier, Michael, **Supp. XVII:** 23, 110
Collingwood, R. G., **I:** 278
Collins, Billy, **Supp. XI:** 143; **Supp. XIV:** 123; **Supp. XVII:** 245; **Supp. XXI: 51–66**
Collins, Doug, **Supp. V:** 5
Collins, Eddie, **II:** 416
Collins, L. M., **Supp. XXII:** 7
Collins, Richard, **Supp. XI:** 171
Collins, Ronald, **Supp. XXI:** 24
Collins, Wilkie, **Supp. I Part 1:** 35, 36; **Supp. IV Part 1:** 341; **Supp. XX: 236**
Collins, William, **Supp. I Part 2:** 714
Collinson, Peter , **II:** 114
Collinson, Peter (pseudonym). *See* Hammett, Dashiell
Colloff, Pamela, **Supp. XIII:** 281
Colloque Sentimental (ballet), **Supp. IV Part 1:** 83
"Colloquy" (Kees), **Supp. XV:** 133
"Colloquy in Black Rock" (Lowell), **II:** 535; **Retro. Supp. II:** 178
"Colloquy of Monos and Una, The" (Poe), **III:** 412
"Colloquy on a Bed" (Bronk), **Supp. XXI:** 31
Colonel's Dream, The (Chesnutt), **Supp. XIV:** 63, 75–76
Colônia, Regina, **Retro. Supp. II:** 53
Colony (Siddons), **Supp. XXII:** 239
Color (Cullen), **Supp. IV Part 1:** 164, 166, 167, 168
"Colorado" (Beattie), **Supp. V:** 27
Color and Democracy: Colonies and Peace (Du Bois), **Supp. II Part 1:** 184, 185
Color Curtain, The (Wright), **IV:** 478, 488
"Colored Americans" (Dunbar), **Supp. II Part 1:** 197
Colored People (H. L. Gates), **Supp. XX: 101, 103, 104–105, 109, 111**
"Color Line, The" (Douglass), **Supp. III Part 1:** 163–165
Color Line, The (W. B. Smith), **Supp. II Part 1:** 168
Color of a Great City, The (Dreiser), **Retro. Supp. II:** 104
Color of Darkness (Purdy), **Supp. VII:** 271
Color Purple, The (Walker), **Supp. III Part 2:** 517, 518, 520, 525–529, 532–537; **Supp. VIII:** 141; **Supp. X:** 252, 330; **Supp. XX: 107**
Color Schemes (Cheang; film), **Supp. XI:** 20
"Colors of Night, The" (Momaday), **Supp. IV Part 2:** 490
"Colors without Objects" (Swenson), **Supp. IV Part 2:** 645
"Color: The Unfinished Business of Democracy" (Locke), **Supp. XIV:** 202, 207
Colossus, The (Plath), **Retro. Supp. II: 245–247; Supp. I Part 2:** 529, 531, 536, 538, 540; **Supp. V:** 79; **Supp. XI:** 317
"Colossus, The" (Plath), **Retro. Supp. II:** 250
Colossus of Maroussi, The (H. Miller), **III:** 178, 185–186
"Colt, The" (Stegner), **Supp. IV Part 2:** 600
Coltelli, Laura, **Supp. IV Part 1:** 323, 330, 335, 409; **Supp. IV Part 2:** 493, 497, 559
Colter: The True Story of the Best Dog I Ever Had (Bass), **Supp. XVI:** 23
Coltrane, John, **Supp. VIII:** 197; **Supp. XXII:** 172
Colum, Mary, **I:** 246, 252, 256; **Supp. I Part 2:** 708, 709
"Columba" (Cliff), **Supp. XXII:** 74, 76
Columbiad, The (Barlow), **Supp. II Part 1:** 67, 72, 73, 74, 75–77, 79
Columbia History of the American Novel, **Supp. XV:** 270
Columbia Literary History of the United States, **Supp. XV:** 270
"Columbian Ode" (Dunbar), **Supp. II Part 1:** 199
"Columbia U Poesy Reading—1975" (Corso), **Supp. XII:** 134
Columbus, Christopher, **I:** 253; **II:** 6, 310; **III:** 8; **Supp. I Part 2:** 397, 479, 480, 483, 486–488, 491, 495, 497, 498
"Columbus to Ferdinand" (Freneau), **Supp. II Part 1:** 255
Comanche Moon (McMurtry), **Supp. V:** 232
"Come, Break With Time" (Bogan), **Supp. III Part 1:** 52
Come Along with Me (Jackson), **Supp. IX:** 117, 118, 122
Come Back, Charleston Blue (film), **Supp. XVI:** 144
Comeback, The (Gurney), **Supp. V:** 97
"Come Back to the Raft Ag'in, Huck Honey!" (Fiedler), **Supp. XIII:** 93, **96–97,** 101
Come Blow Your Horn (Simon), **Supp. IV Part 2:** 574, 575, 577, 578, 586, 587, 591
Come By Here (Major), **Supp. XXII:** 171, 182
"Come Dance with Me in Ireland" (Jackson), **Supp. IX:** 119
"Comedian as the Letter C, The" (Stevens), **IV:** 84–85, 88; **Retro. Supp. I:** 297, 301, 302
"Comedy Cop" (Farrell), **II:** 45
Comedy of a Country House (J. Sturgis), **Supp. XX: 238**
"Comedy's Greatest Era" (Agee), **I:** 31
"Come In" (Frost), **Retro. Supp. I:** 139
"Come On, Baby" (Zinberg), **Supp. XV:** 195
"Come on Back" (Gardner), **Supp. VI:** 73
"Come Out into the Sun" (Francis), **Supp. IX:** 82
Come Out into the Sun: Poems New and Selected (Francis), **Supp. IX: 82–83**
"Come out the Wilderness" (Baldwin), **Supp. I Part 1:** 63
Comer, Anjanette, **Supp. XI:** 305
Comer, Cornelia, **I:** 214
"Come Rain or Come Shine" (song), **Supp. XXII:** 6
"Come Shining: The Spiritual South" (exhibition; Luster), **Supp. XV:** 350
Come with Me: Poems for a Journey (Nye), **Supp. XIII:** 279
"Comforts of Home, The" (O'Connor), **III:** 349, 351, 355; **Retro. Supp. II:** 237
Comic Artist, The (Glaspell and Matson), **Supp. III Part 1:** 182
"Comic Imagination of the Young Dickens, The" (Wright), **Supp. III Part 2:** 591
"Comic Textures and Female Communities 1937 and 1977: Clare Boothe and Wendy Wasserstein" (Carlson), **Supp. XV:** 323
Comic Tragedies (Alcott), **Supp. I Part 1:** 33
Coming After (Notley), **Supp. XXII:** 223, 227, 230, 232, 236
"Coming Close" (Levine), **Supp. V:** 192
Coming Forth by Day of Osiris Jones, The (Aiken), **I:** 59
"Coming Home" (Gordon), **Supp. IV Part 1:** 309
"Coming Home to Vermont" (McCarriston), **Supp. XIV:** 269
"Coming in From the Cold" (Walker), **Supp. III Part 2:** 526
Coming into Eighty (Sarton), **Supp. VIII:** 262
"Coming into Eighty" (Sarton), **Supp. VIII:** 262
Coming into the Country (McPhee), **Supp. III Part 1:** 298, 301–306, 309, 310
Coming Into Writing (Cixous), **Supp. X:** 102
Coming of Age in Mississippi (Moody), **Supp. IV Part 1:** 11
Comings Back (Goldbarth), **Supp. XII:** 180
"Coming to Canada--Age Twenty Two" (Shields), **Supp. VII:** 311
Coming to Canada: Poems (Shields), **Supp. VII:** 311–312

"Coming to Memoir as a Journalist" (Epstein), **Supp. XXII:** 95
"Coming to the Morning" (Merwin), **Supp. III Part 1:** 356
"Coming to This" (Strand), **Supp. IV Part 2:** 627
Comiskey, Charles, **II:** 422
Commager, Henry Steele, **I:** 253; **Supp. I Part 1:** 372; **Supp. I Part 2:** 484, 647, 650
Command the Morning (Buck), **Supp. II Part 1:** 125
"CommComm" (Saunders), **Supp. XIX:** 234
"Commencement Address, A" (Brodsky), **Supp. VIII:** 31
"Commencement Day Address, The" (Schwartz), **Supp. II Part 2:** 660
Commentaries (Caesar), **II:** 502, 561
"Commentary" (Auden), **Supp. II Part 1:** 13
"Comment on Curb" (Hughes), **Supp. I Part 1:** 340
"Comments/Questions" (Nelson), **Supp. XVIII:** 172
"Commerce" (Nye), **Supp. XIII:** 281
Commins, Saxe, **Retro. Supp. I:** 73; **Retro. Supp. II:** 337
Commodity of Dreams & Other Stories, A (Nemerov), **III:** 268–269, 285
Common Carnage (Dobyns), **Supp. XIII:** 87
"Common Ground, A" (Levertov), **Supp. III Part 1:** 277
"Common Life, The" (Auden), **Supp. IV Part 1:** 302, 313
"Common Meter" (R. Fisher), **Supp. XIX:** 71
Common Room, A: Essays 1954–1987 (Price), **Supp. VI:** 264–265, 267
Commons, John, **Supp. I Part 2:** 645
Common Sense (Paine), **II:** 117; **Supp. I Part 1:** 231; **Supp. I Part 2:** 505, 506–508, 509, 513, 516, 517, 521
Communal Cot (Loy), **Supp. XXII:** 168
"Communication" (Dobyns), **Supp. XIII:** 91
"Communion" (Dubus), **Supp. VII:** 91
Communion (Mora), **Supp. XIII: 217–219**
Communist Manifesto, The (Marx and Engels), **II:** 463; **Supp. XXI:** 162–163
"Community Life" (Moore), **Supp. X:** 178
"Community of Glaciers, The" (Bass), **Supp. XVI:** 23
Comnes, Gregory, **Supp. IV Part 1:** 283, 284, 291
"Companions, The" (Nemerov), **III:** 269, 278, 287
Company of Poets, A (Simpson), **Supp. IX:** 265, 275
Company of Women, The (Gordon), **Supp. IV Part 1:** 302–304, 304, 306, 313
Company She Keeps, The (McCarthy), **II:** 562, 563–566
"Comparisons of Wonder" (Jarman), **Supp. XVII:** 114
Compass Flower, The (Merwin), **Supp. III Part 1:** 353, 357
"Compassionate Friendship" (Doolittle), **Supp. I Part 1:** 257, 258, 259, 260, 271
"Compatibility" (C. Frost), **Supp. XV:** 103
"Compendium" (Dove), **Supp. IV Part 1:** 248
"Complaint" (W. C. Williams), **Retro. Supp. I:** 418
"Complete Birth of the Cool, The" (Wright), **Supp. XV:** 343, 344
Complete Collected Poems of William Carlos Williams, 1906–1938, The (W. C. Williams), **Retro. Supp. I:** 424
"Complete Destruction" (W. C. Williams), **IV:** 413
"Complete Life of John Hopkins, The" (O. Henry), **Supp. II Part 1:** 405
Complete Poems (Frost), **II:** 155, 164
Complete Poems (Reznikoff), **Supp. XIV:** 281
Complete Poems (Sandburg), **III:** 590–592, 594, 596
Complete Poems, The (Bishop), **Retro. Supp. II:** 49; **Supp. I Part 1:** 72, 82, 94
Complete Poems, The (Bradbury), **Supp. IV Part 1:** 105
Complete Poems, The: 1927–1979 (Bishop), **Retro. Supp. II:** 51
Complete Poems of Emily Dickinson, The (Bianchi and Hampson, eds.), **Retro. Supp. I:** 35
Complete Poems of Emily Dickinson, The (Johnson, ed.), **I:** 470
Complete Poems of Frederick Goddard Tuckerman, The (Momaday), **Supp. IV Part 2:** 480
Complete Poems of Hart Crane, **Retro. Supp. II:** 81
Complete Poems to Solve, The (Swenson), **Supp. IV Part 2:** 652
Complete Poetical Works (Hulme), **III:** 464
Complete Poetical Works (Longfellow), **Retro. Supp. II:** 154
Complete Poetical Works (Lowell), **II:** 512, 516–517
Complete Poetical Works of Amy Lowell, The, **Supp. XV:** 295–296
Complete Stories (O'Connor), **Supp. X:** 1
Complete Tragedies, The: Euripedes II, **Supp. XV:** 50
"Complete with Starry Night and Bourbon Shots" (Goldbarth), **Supp. XII:** 192–193
Complete Works of Kate Chopin, The (Seyersted, ed.), **Supp. I Part 1:** 212, 225
Complete Works of the Gawain-Poet (Gardner), **Supp. VI:** 64, 65
"Complex Histories, Contested Memories: Some Reflections on Remembering Difficult Pasts" (E. Hoffman, lecture), **Supp. XVI:** 155
"Complicated Thoughts About a Small Son" (White), **Supp. I Part 2:** 678
"Compliments of the Season" (O. Henry), **Supp. II Part 1:** 392, 399
"Compline" (Auden), **Supp. II Part 1:** 23
"Composing a Life" (Pickering), **Supp. XXI:** 191, 196
Composition as Explanation (Stein), **IV:** 32, 33, 38
"Composition as Explanation" (Stein), **IV:** 27, 28
"Compounding *of* Consciousness" (James), **II:** 358–359
Comprehensive Bibliography (Hanneman), **II:** 259
Compton-Burnett, Ivy, **I:** 93; **II:** 580
"Comrade Laski, C.P.U.S.A. \[M.L.\]" (Didion), **Supp. IV Part 1:** 200
Comstock, Anthony, **Retro. Supp. II:** 95
Comus (Milton), **II:** 12; **Supp. I Part 2:** 622
Conan Doyle, Arthur. *See* Doyle, Arthur Conan
Conceptions of Reality in Modern American Poetry (Dembo), **Supp. I Part 1:** 272
"Concept of Character in Fiction, The" (Gass), **Supp. VI:** 85, **86**
Concept of Dread, The (Kierkegaard), **III:** 305
Concerning Children (Gilman), **Supp. XI:** 206
"Concerning Mold upon the Skin, Etc." (J. Scott), **Supp. XVII:** 188
"Concerning Necessity" (Carruth), **Supp. XVI:** 57
"Concerning Some Recent Criticism of His Work" (Doty), **Supp. XI:** 131
Concerning the End for Which God Created the World (Edwards), **I:** 549, 557, 559
Concerto for Two Pianos, Winds, and Percussion (Bowles), **Supp. IV Part 1:** 83
Conchologist's First Book, The (Poe), **III:** 412
Conclusive Evidence (Nabokov), **III:** 247–250, 252
"Concord Hymn" (Emerson), **II:** 19
Concrete Blonde, The (Connelly), **Supp. XXI: 70–71,** 78, 80
"Concrete Universal, The: Observations on the Understanding of Poetry" (Ransom), **III:** 480
Concurring Beasts (Dobyns), **Supp. XIII:** 76
Condensed Novels and Other Papers (Harte), **Supp. II Part 1:** 342
"Condition, The" (Karmi; Everwine, trans.), **Supp. XV:** 78
Condition of Man, The (Mumford), **Supp. II Part 2:** 483, 484, 486, 495–496, 498
"Condolence" (Parker), **Supp. IX:** 191
"Condominium, The" (Elkin), **Supp. VI:** 49, **50–51,** 55, 56
Condon, Charles R., **Supp. XIII:** 163
Condor and the Cows, The: A South American Travel Diary (Isherwood and Caskey), **Supp. XIV:** 166

"Condor and the Guests, The" (Connell), **Supp. XIV:** 86
Condorcet, Marquis de, **Supp. I Part 2:** 511
Conduct of Life, The (Emerson), **II:** 1–5, 8
Conduct of Life, The (Mumford), **Supp. II Part 2:** 485, 496–497
"Conductor of Nothing, The" (Levine), **Supp. V:** 189
Coney Island of the Mind, A (Ferlinghetti), **Supp. XIX:** 4; **Supp. XXI:** 53
"Conference Male, The" (Mora), **Supp. XIII:** 218
"Confession" (Peacock), **Supp. XIX:** 206
"Confessional" (Bidart), **Supp. XV:** 29–30, 31
"Confessional Poem" (Nelson), **Supp. XVIII:** 174
Confession de Claude, La (Zola), **I:** 411
"Confession of a House-Breaker, The" (Jewett), **Retro. Supp. II:** 146–147
Confession of Jereboam O. Beauchamp, The (pamphlet), **IV:** 253
Confessions (Augustine), **I:** 279; **Supp. XVI:** 288; **Supp. XXII:** 93
Confessions (Rousseau), **I:** 226
Confessions of a Barbarian: Selections from the Journals of Edward Abbey, 1951–1989 (Abbey; Petersen, ed.), **Supp. XIII:** 2, 4
"Confessions of a Latina Author" (Mora), **Supp. XIII:** 221
"Confessions of a Wannabe Negro" (McKnight), **Supp. XX: 152–153, 158**
Confessions of Nat Turner, The (Styron), **IV:** 98, 99, 105, 113–117; **Supp. X:** 16, 250
Confetti (Mora), **Supp. XIII:** 221
Confidence (James), **II:** 327, 328
Confidence-Man, The (Melville), **III:** 91; **Retro. Supp. I:** 255–256, 257; **Retro. Supp. II:** 121; **Supp. XIV:** 49
Confidence Man, The (Van Vechten), **Supp. II Part 2:** 737
Confidential Clerk, The (Eliot), **I:** 570, 571–572, 583, 584; **Retro. Supp. I:** 65
Confident Years, 1885–1915, The (Brooks), **I:** 257, 259; **Supp. I Part 2:** 650
"Configurations" (Ammons), **Supp. VII:** 28
Configurations: New and Selected Poems, 1958–1998 (Major), **Supp. XXII: 182**
Confronting the Horror: The Novels of Nelson Algren (Giles), **Supp. IX:** 11, 15
Confucius, **II:** 1; **III:** 456, 475; **Supp. IV Part 1:** 14
Confusion (Cozzens), **I:** 358, 359, 377, 378
"Confusion of Planes We Must Wander in Sleep, The" (Weigl), **Supp. XIX:** 283
Congdon, Don, **Supp. XXII:** 204
Congo (film), **Supp. IV Part 1:** 83
Congo (screenplay, Shanley), **Supp. XIV:** 316
"Congo, The" (Lindsay), **Supp. I Part 2:** 388–389, 392, 395
Congo and Other Poems, The (Lindsay), **Supp. I Part 2:** 379, 382, 389, 390, 391
"Congregation" (Trethewey), **Supp. XXI:** 245, 247
"Congress of the Insomniacs, The" (Simic), **Supp. VIII:** 281–282
Congreve, William, **III:** 195; **Supp. V:** 101; **Supp. XVIII:** 12
Coningsby (Disraeli), **II:** 127
"Conjectural Reading" (Bronk), **Supp. XXI:** 31
Conjectures of a Guilty Bystander (Merton), **Supp. VIII:** 197, 206, 207
Conjugal Bliss: A Comedy of Marital Arts (Nichols), **Supp. XIII:** 269
"Conjugation of the Paramecium, The" (Rukeyser), **Supp. VI:** 271
Conjugations and Reiterations (Murray), **Supp. XIX:** 161
"Conjuration" (Wilbur), **Supp. III Part 2:** 551
Conjure (recording), **Supp. X:** 241
Conjure (Reed), **Supp. X:** 240, 242
Conjure-Man Dies, The: A Mystery Tale of Dark Harlem (R. Fisher), **Supp. XVI:** 143; **Supp. XIX:** 65, 71, **77–78**
Conjure Woman, The (Chesnutt), **Supp. II Part 1:** 193; **Supp. XIV:** 57, **58–61,** 62, 63
Conklin, Grof, **Supp. I Part 2:** 672
Conklin, Peggy, **Supp. XXII:** 27
Conkling, Hilda, **II:** 530
Conkling, Roscoe, **III:** 506
Conley, Robert J., **Supp. V:** 232
Conley, Susan, **Supp. XIII:** 111, 112
Connaroe, Joel, **Supp. IV Part 2:** 690
"Connecticut Lad, A" (White), **Supp. I Part 2:** 677
"Connecticut Valley" (Cowley), **Supp. II Part 1:** 141–142
Connecticut Yankee in King Arthur's Court, A (Twain), **I:** 209; **II:** 276; **IV:** 205
Connell, Evan S., **Supp. XIV: 79–100**
Connell, Norreys (pseudonym). *See* O'Riordan, Conal Holmes O'Connell
Connelly, Marc, **III:** 394; **Supp. I Part 2:** 679; **Supp. IX:** 190
Connelly, Michael, **Supp. XXI: 67–82**
Connery, Thomas B., **Supp. XVII:** 106
Connoisseur, The (Connell), **Supp. XIV:** 87
"Connoisseur of Chaos" (Stevens), **IV:** 89; **Retro. Supp. I:** 306
Connolly, Cyril, **Supp. XIV:** 158, 343, 348
Connors, Elizabeth. *See* Lindsay, Mrs. Vachel (Elizabeth Connors)
Conover, Roger, **Supp. I Part 1:** 95
Conover, Roger L., **Supp. XXII:** 155, 162
Conquering Horse (Manfred), **Supp. X:** 126
"Conqueror Worm, The" (Poe), **Retro. Supp. II:** 261
Conquest of Canaan (Dwight), **Supp. I Part 1:** 124
Conquistador (MacLeish), **III:** 2, 3, 13–14, 15
Conrad, Alfred, **Retro. Supp. II:** 245
Conrad, Alfred H., **Supp. I Part 2:** 552
Conrad, C. A., **Supp. XXII:** 155
Conrad, David, **Supp. I Part 2:** 552
Conrad, Jacob, **Supp. I Part 2:** 552
Conrad, Joseph, **I:** 123, 343, 394, 405, 409, 415, 421, 485, 506, 575–576, 578; **II:** 58, 73, 74, 91, 92, 144, 263, 320, 338, 595; **III:** 28, 102, 106, 328, 464, 467, 491, 512; **IV:** 476; **Retro. Supp. I:** 80, 91, 106, 108, 231, 274, 377; **Retro. Supp. II:** 222; **Supp. I Part 1:** 292; **Supp. I Part 2:** 621, 622; **Supp. IV Part 1:** 197, 341; **Supp. IV Part 2:** 680; **Supp. V:** 249, 251, 262, 298, 307, 311; **Supp. VIII:** 4, 310; **Supp. XIV:** 112; **Supp. XVI:** 158, 212; **Supp. XVIII:** 98, 102; **Supp. XIX:** 27; **Supp. XX: 195**
Conrad, Paul, **Supp. I Part 2:** 552
Conrad, Peter, **Supp. IV Part 2:** 688
"Conrad Aiken: From Savannah to Emerson" (Cowley), **Supp. II Part 1:** 43
Conrad Richter's Ohio Trilogy (Edwards), **Supp. XVIII:** 220
Conroy, Frank, **Supp. VIII:** 145; **Supp. XI:** 245; **Supp. XVI: 63–78; Supp. XXII:** 50
Conroy, Jack, **Supp. XXII:** 1, 5, 10
Conroy, Pat, **Supp. XVIII:** 193; **Supp. XXII:** 239
Cons, Scams, and Grifts (Gores), **Supp. XXI:** 70
Conscience with the Power and Cases thereof (Ames), **IV:** 158
"Conscientious Objector, The" (Shapiro), **Supp. II Part 2:** 710
"Consciousness and Dining" (Harrison), **Supp. VIII:** 46
"Conscription Camp" (Shapiro), **Supp. II Part 2:** 705
"Consejos de Nuestra Señora de Guadalupe: Counsel from the Brown Virgin" (Mora), **Supp. XIII:** 224
"Conservation Esthetic" (Leopold), **Supp. XIV:** 179, 181, 186, 189–190
"Conserving Natural and Cultural Diversity: The Prose and Poetry of Pat Mora" (Murphy), **Supp. XIII:** 214
Considerable Town, A (M. F. K. Fisher), **Supp. XVII:** 90
"Considerations by the Way" (Emerson), **II:** 2, 5
Consider the Oyster (M. F. K. Fisher), **Supp. XVII:** 84, 87
Considine, Bob, **II:** 424
"Consolation" (Bausch), **Supp. VII:** 48
"Consolations" (Stafford), **Supp. XI:** 329
"Conspiracy of History, The: E. L. Doctorow's *The Book of Daniel*" (Levine), **Supp. IV Part 1:** 221
Conspiracy of Kings, The (Barlow), **Supp. II Part 1:** 80
Conspiracy of Pontiac, The (Parkman), **Supp. II Part 2:** 590, 595, 596, 599–600
Constab Ballads (McKay), **Supp. X:** 131, 133

Constance (Kenyon), **Supp. VII:** 170–172
Constancy (Boyce), **Supp. XVII:** 100; **Supp. XXI:** 6, 7, 12
"Constellation Orion, The" (Kooser), **Supp. XIX:** 120
Construction of Boston, The (Koch), **Supp. XV:** 187
"Constructive Work" (Du Bois), **Supp. II Part 1:** 172
"Consumer's Report" (X. J. Kennedy), **Supp. XV:** 161–162
"Consumption" (Bryant), **Supp. I Part 1:** 169–170
Contact Collection of Contemporary Writers (McAlmon), **Supp. XXII:** 166
"Contagiousness of Puerperal Fever, The" (Holmes), **Supp. I Part 1:** 303–304
"Contemplation in a World of Action" (Merton), **Supp. VIII:** 204
"Contemplation of Poussin" (Sarton), **Supp. VIII:** 261
"Contemplations" (Bradstreet), **Supp. I Part 1:** 112, 113, 119–122
Contemporaries (Kazin), **Supp. VIII:** 102, **103–104**
Contemporary American Playwrights (Bigsby), **Supp. XV:** 332
Contemporary American Poetry (Poulin, ed.), **Supp. IX:** 272; **Supp. XI:** 259
Contemporary Authors Autobiography, **Supp. XXII:** 225
Contending Forces (Hopkins), **Supp. XVIII:** 284
"Contentment" (Holmes), **Supp. I Part 1:** 307
"Contents" (Halliday), **Supp. XIX:** 92
"Contest, The" (Paley), **Supp. VI:** 223, 230, 231
"Contest for Aaron Gold, The" (P. Roth), **Supp. III Part 2:** 403
Continental Drift (Banks), **Supp. V:** 13–14, 16, 227
Continental Op, The (Hammett), **Supp. IV Part 1:** 344
Continent's End: An Anthology of Contemporary California Poets (Taggard, Sterling, and Rorty, eds.), **Supp. XXII:** 276
Continuing Education, A (Pickering), **Supp. XXI:** 194, 195–196
Continuity of American Poetry, The (Pearce), **Supp. I Part 1:** 111; **Supp. I Part 2:** 475
Continuous Harmony, A: Essays Cultural and Agricultural (Berry), **Supp. X:** 33
Continuous Life, The (Strand), **Supp. IV Part 2:** 630, 631–633
Contoski, Victor, **Supp. XII:** 181
"Contract" (Lardner), **II:** 432
"Contraption, The" (Swenson), **Supp. IV Part 2:** 643
"Contrariness of the Mad Farmer, The" (Berry), **Supp. X:** 35
"Contrition" (Dubus), **Supp. VII:** 84
"Control Burn" (Snyder), **Supp. VIII:** 301
"Control Is the Mainspring" (Komunyakaa), **Supp. XIII:** 122, 124
"Controlling the 'Sloppiness of Things' in Frank Conroy's *Stop-Time*" (Strychacz), **Supp. XVI:** 69–70
Control of Nature, The (McPhee), **Supp. III Part 1:** 310–313
"Conventional Wisdom, The" (Elkin), **Supp. VI: 52–53**
"Convergence" (Ammons), **Supp. VII:** 28
"Convergence of the Twain, The" (Hardy), **Supp. VIII:** 31, 32
Conversation (Aiken), **I:** 54
Conversation at Midnight (Millay), **III:** 138
"Conversation of Eiros and Charmion, The" (Poe), **III:** 412
"Conversation on Conversation" (Stowe), **Supp. I Part 2:** 587
"Conversations in Moscow" (Levertov), **Supp. III Part 1:** 282
Conversations on Some of the Old Poets (Lowell), **Supp. I Part 2:** 405
Conversations with Albert Murray (Maguire, ed.), **Supp. XIX:** 160–161
Conversations with Byron (Blessington), **Retro. Supp. II:** 58
Conversations with Eudora Welty (Prenshaw, ed.), **Retro. Supp. I:** 339, 340, 341, 342, 343, 352, 354
"Conversations with Helmholtz" (Allen), **Supp. XV:** 15
Conversations with Ishmael Reed (Dick and Singh, eds.), **Supp. X:** 244
Conversations with James Baldwin (Standley and Pratt, eds.), **Retro. Supp. II:** 6
Conversations with Richard Wilbur (Wilbur), **Supp. III Part 2:** 542–543
"Conversation with My Father, A" (Paley), **Supp. VI:** 220
"Conversion of the Jews, The" (P. Roth), **Retro. Supp. II:** 281; **Supp. III Part 2:** 404, 406
Convict, The: Stories (Burke), **Supp. XIV:** 25
"Convicta et Combusta" (J. Scott), **Supp. XVII:** 189
"Convoy" (Weigl), **Supp. XIX:** 278
Conway, Jill, **Supp. I Part 1:** 19
Coode, John, **I:** 132
Cook, Bruce, **Supp. XII:** 130, 131, 133–134
Cook, Captain James, **I:** 2
Cook, Eleanor, **Retro. Supp. I:** 311
Cook, Elisha, **Supp. IV Part 1:** 356
Cook, Elizabeth Christine, **II:** 106
Cook, George Cram "Jig", **Supp. XXI:** 5, 6
Cook, Mercer, **Supp. IV Part 1:** 368
Cook, Richard, **Supp. XXII:** 158
Cooke, Alistair, **III:** 113, 119, 120
Cooke, Delmar G., **II:** 271
Cooke, Grace MacGowan, **Supp. V:** 285
Cooke, Philip Pendleton, **III:** 420
Cooke, Rose Terry, **II:** 401; **Retro. Supp. II:** 51, 136, 138; **Supp. XIII:** 152
"Cookie" (Taylor), **Supp. V:** 320
"Cookies, The" (Nye), **Supp. XIII:** 281
Cooking of Provincial France, The (M. F. K. Fisher), **Supp. XVII:** 89
Cook-Lynn, Elizabeth, **Supp. IV Part 1:** 325
Coolbrith, Ina, **I:** 193, 196
"Coole Park" (Yeats), **Supp. VIII:** 155, 159
"Coole Park and Ballylee" (Yeats), **Supp. VIII:** 156
Cooler by the Lake (Heinemann), **Supp. XXII:** 103, **114**
Cooley, John, **Supp. V:** 214
Cooley, Peter, **Supp. XIII:** 76
Coolidge, Calvin, **I:** 498; **II:** 95; **Supp. I Part 2:** 647
Cooling Time: An American Poetry Vigil (Wright), **Supp. XV:** 353
"Cool Million, A" (screen story) (West and Ingster), **Retro. Supp. II:** 330
Cool Million, A (West), **III:** 425; **IV:** 287, 288, 297–299, 300; **Retro. Supp. II:** 321, 322–323, 328, **335–337**
"Cool Tombs" (Sandburg), **III:** 554
Coon, Ross, **IV:** 196
Cooney, Seamus, **Supp. XIV:** 289
"Coon Hunt" (White), **Supp. I Part 2:** 669
Co-op (Sinclair), **Supp. V:** 290
Cooper, Bernard, **Supp. XI:** 129
Cooper, Frederic Taber, **Supp. XX: 219–220**
Cooper, Gary, **Supp. IV Part 2:** 524
Cooper, James Fenimore, **I:** 211, 257, **335–357; II:** 74, 277, 295–296, 302, 306, 309, 313, 314; **III:** 51; **IV:** 205, 333; **Retro. Supp. I:** 246; **Retro. Supp. II:** 160; **Supp. I Part 1:** 141, 155, 156, 158, 171, 372; **Supp. I Part 2:** 413, 495, 579, 585, 652, 660; **Supp. IV Part 1:** 80; **Supp. IV Part 2:** 463, 469; **Supp. V:** 209–210; **Supp. VIII:** 189; **Supp. XIV:** 227; **Supp. XVIII:** 4
Cooper, Mrs. James Fenimore (Susan A. De Lancey), **I:** 338, 351, 354
Cooper, Jane, **Supp. XV:** 259
Cooper, Rand Richards, **Supp. XVI:** 74
Cooper, Susan Fenimore, **I:** 337, 354
Cooper, William, **I:** 337–338, 351
Cooper, Mrs. William, **I:** 337
Coover, Robert, **Supp. IV Part 1:** 388; **Supp. V: 39–55; Supp. XII:** 152; **Supp. XIV:** 96; **Supp. XVII:** 6; **Supp. XXI:** 236; **Supp. XXII:** 259
Copacetic (Komunyakaa), **Supp. XIII: 116–118,** 126
Cope, Wendy, **Supp. XV:** 117
Copland, Aaron, **II:** 586; **Supp. I Part 1:** 281; **Supp. III Part 2:** 619; **Supp. IV Part 1:** 79, 80–81, 84; **Supp. XXII:** 283
Coplas de Don Jorge Manrique (Longfellow, trans.), **II:** 488, 492
Coppée, François Edouard Joachim, **II:** 325
Copperhead, The (Frederic), **II:** 134–135
Copperhead Cane (J. W. Miller), **Supp. XX: 163, 164, 166–167**
Copper Sun (Cullen), **Supp. IV Part 1:** 167, 168
Coppola, Francis Ford, **Supp. XI:** 171, 172; **Supp. XII:** 75

Coprolites (Goldbarth), **Supp. XII: 177–178,** 180, 183
Coral and Captive Israel (Reznikoff), **Supp. XIV:** 288
"Coral Ring, The" (Stowe), **Supp. I Part 2:** 586
"Cora Unashamed" (Hughes), **Supp. I Part 1:** 329, 330
"Corazón del Corrido" (Mora), **Supp. XIII:** 225
Corban Ephphata (Li Lin Lee), **Supp. XV:** 225
Corbett, Gentlemen Jim, **II:** 416
Corbett, William, **Supp. XI:** 248; **Supp. XVI:** 286, 295
Corbière, Jean Antoine, **II:** 354–355, 528
Cordiall Water, A: A garland of Odd & Old Receipts to Assuage the Ills of Man and Beast (M. F. K. Fisher), **Supp. XVII:** 88, 90
Cording, Robert, **Supp. IX:** 328; **Supp. XII:** 184
Core, George, **Supp. XVIII:** 86; **Supp. XXI:** 193
Corelli, Marie, **III:** 579
Corey, Lewis, **Supp. I Part 2:** 645
"Corinna's Going a-Maying" (Herrick), **Supp. XIV:** 8, 9
"Coriolan" (Eliot), **I:** 580
"Coriolanus and His Mother" (Schwartz), **Supp. II Part 2:** 643, 644–645
"Corkscrew" (Hammett), **Supp. IV Part 1:** 345, 347
Corkum, Gerald, **I:** 37
Corky's Brother (Neugeboren), **Supp. XVI:** 225
"Corky's Brother" (Neugeboren), **Supp. XVI:** 225
Corliss, Richard, **Supp. VIII:** 73
Corman, Cid, **Supp. III Part 2:** 624, 625, 626, 627, 628; **Supp. IV Part 1:** 144; **Supp. VIII:** 292; **Supp. XV:** 74, 153; **Supp. XXI:** 23, 27
"Corn" (Lanier), **Supp. I Part 1:** 352, 353, 354, 356–361, 364, 366
Corn, Alfred, **Supp. IX:** 156; **Supp. XV:** 250
Corneille, Pierre, **Supp. I Part 2:** 716; **Supp. IX:** 131
Cornell, Esther, **I:** 231
Cornell, Joseph, **Supp. XXI:** 131; **Supp. XXII:** 167, 168
Cornell, Katherine, **IV:** 356
Cornell, Valerie, **Supp. XX: 94–95**
"Corners" (Dunn), **Supp. XI:** 148
Cornhuskers (Sandburg), **III:** 583–585
"Corn-Planting, The" (Anderson), **I:** 114
Cornucopia: New and Selected Poems, 1975–2002 (Peacock), **Supp. XIX: 203–204**
"Coroner's Report" (Wrigley), **Supp. XVIII:** 295
"Corporal of Artillery" (Dubus), **Supp. VII:** 84, 85
"Corpse Plant, The" (Rich), **Supp. I Part 2:** 555
Corpus Christi (McNally), **Supp. XIII: 205–206,** 209
Corradi, Juan, **Supp. IV Part 1:** 208
Corrections, The (Franzen), **Supp. XIX:** 54; **Supp. XX: 83, 84, 85, 90, 91, 91–93, 95**
"Correspondences" (Baudelaire), **I:** 63
"Corrido de Gregorio Cortez" (Mora), **Supp. XIII:** 225
"Corrigenda" (Komunyakaa), **Supp. XIII:** 115, 116
Corrosive Sublimate (Sorrentino), **Supp. XXI:** 226, 228
Corruption City (McCoy), **Supp. XIII:** 175
Corso, Gregory, **Supp. II Part 1:** 30; **Supp. IV Part 1:** 90; **Supp. XII: 117–138; Supp. XIV:** 150; **Supp. XVI:** 135; **Supp. XXI:** 53
Corsons Inlet (Ammons), **Supp. VII:** 25–26, 28–29, 36
"Corsons Inlet" (Ammons), **Supp. VII:** 25–26
Cortázar, Julio, **Retro. Supp. I:** 278; **Supp. XXII:** 265
"Cortège for Rosenbloom" (Stevens), **IV:** 81
Cortez, Hernando, **III:** 2
" 'Coruscating Glamour': Lynda Hull and the Movies" (Goldstein), **Supp. XXI:** 134
Cory, William Johnson, **Supp. XX: 230, 231**
Coser, Lewis, **Supp. I Part 2:** 650
Cosgrave, Patrick, **Retro. Supp. II:** 185
Cosmic Optimism: A Study of the Interpretation of Evolution by American Poets from Emerson to Robinson (Conner), **Supp. I Part 1:** 73
Cosmological Eye, The (H. Miller), **III:** 174, 184
"Cosmological Eye, The" (H. Miller), **III:** 183
"Cosmos" (Beattie), **Supp. V:** 35
"Cost, The" (Hecht), **Supp. X:** 62–63
Costello, Bonnie, **Retro. Supp. II:** 40
Costner, Kevin, **Supp. VIII:** 45
"Cost of Living, The" (Malamud), **Supp. I Part 2:** 429, 437
"Costume as Metaphor" (Bronk), **Supp. XXI:** 26
Cott, Jonathan, **Supp. XVI:** 104, 106
"Cottagers' Corner" column (D. West), **Supp. XVIII:** 286
"Cottage Street, 1953" (Wilbur), **Supp. III Part 2:** 543, 561
"Cottagette, The" (Gilman), **Supp. XI:** 207
Cotten, Joseph, **Supp. IV Part 2:** 524
Cotter, James Finn, **Supp. X:** 202
Cotton, John, **Supp. I Part 1:** 98, 101, 110, 111, 116
Cotton, Joseph, **Supp. XII:** 160
Cotton, Seaborn, **Supp. I Part 1:** 101
Cotton Club, The (Major), **Supp. XXII:** 174
"Cotton Club Classics" (Halliday), **Supp. XIX:** 92, 93
Cotton Comes to Harlem (C. Himes), **Supp. XVI:** 143, 144
Cotton Comes to Harlem (film, O. Davis), **Supp. XVI:** 144
"Cotton Song" (Toomer), **Supp. IX:** 312
Couch, W. T., **Supp. X:** 46
Coughlin, Ruth Pollack, **Supp. VIII:** 45
Coulette, Henri, **Supp. V:** 180; **Supp. XIII:** 312; **Supp. XV:** 74, 75
Coultrap-McQuin, Susan, **Supp. XVI:** 85, 92
"Council of State, A" (Dunbar), **Supp. II Part 1:** 211, 213
"Count Dracula" (Allen), **Supp. XV:** 15
"Countee Cullen at 'The Heights' " (Tuttleton), **Supp. IV Part 1:** 166
Counterfeiters, The (Gide), **Supp. IV Part 1:** 80; **Supp. IV Part 2:** 681
"Countering" (Ammons), **Supp. VII:** 28
Counterlife, The (P. Roth), **Retro. Supp. II:** 279, 280, 291; **Supp. III Part 2:** 424–426
Counter-Statement (Burke), **I:** 270–272; **IV:** 431
"Countess, The" (Whittier), **Supp. I Part 2:** 691, 694
Count Frontenac and New France Under Louis XIV (Parkman), **Supp. II Part 2:** 607, 609–610
"Counting Small-Boned Bodies" (R. Bly), **Supp. IV Part 1:** 62
"Counting the Children" (Gioia), **Supp. XV: 122–123**
"Counting the Mad" (Justice), **Supp. VII:** 117
Count of Monte Cristo, The (Dumas), **III:** 386, 396; **Supp. XVII:** 64, 216
"Countries We Live In, The" (Zach; Everwine, trans.), **Supp. XV:** 87
"Country Boy in Boston, The" (Howells), **II:** 255
Country By-Ways (Jewett), **II:** 402
Country Doctor, A (Jewett), **II:** 391, 392, 396, 404–405; **Retro. Supp. II:** 131, 141, 146
"Country Full of Swedes" (Caldwell), **I:** 297, 309
Country Girl, The (Odets), **Supp. II Part 2:** 546, 547, 548–549
"Country House" (Kumin), **Supp. IV Part 2:** 446
"Country Husband, The" (Cheever), **Supp. I Part 1:** 184, 189
"Country Life" (Pickering), **Supp. XXI:** 197
"Country Marriage" (C. Frost), **Supp. XV:** 99
Countrymen of Bones (R. O. Butler), **Supp. XII:** 62, **65–66**
"Country Mouse, The" (Bishop), **Retro. Supp. II:** 37, 38, 51
Country Music: Selected Early Poems (Wright), **Supp. V:** 332, 335, 338, 342
Country of a Thousand Years of Peace, The (Merrill), **Supp. III Part 1:** 321, 322, 331
"Country of Elusion, The" (O. Henry), **Supp. II Part 1:** 407
Country Of Language, The (Sanders), **Supp. XVI:** 277
Country of Marriage, The (Berry), **Supp. X:** 33
Country of Strangers, A (Richter), **Supp. XVIII:** 217

Country of Survivors (Di Piero), **Supp. XIX:** 36
Country of the Pointed Firs, The (Jewett), **II:** 392, 399, 405, 409–411; **Retro. Supp. I:** 6; **Retro. Supp. II:** 134, 136, 139, 140, 141, 145, 146, 147; **Supp. VIII:** 126; **Supp. XIII:** 152
"Country Printer, The" (Freneau), **Supp. II Part 1:** 269
"Country Wife, The" (Gioia), **Supp. XV:** 120
Count Your Bullets (film), **Supp. XVII:** 141
Count Zero (W. Gibson), **Supp. XVI:** 19, **126–127,** 129
Coup, The (Updike), **Retro. Supp. I:** 331, 334, 335
"Coup de Grâce, The" (Bierce), **I:** 202
Couperin, François, **III:** 464
"Couple, The" (Olds), **Supp. X:** 206
"Couple of Hamburgers, A" (Thurber), **Supp. I Part 2:** 616
"Couple of Nuts, A" (Z. Fitzgerald), **Supp. IX:** 58, 71, 72
"Couples" (Halliday), **Supp. XIX:** 89
Couples (Updike), **IV:** 214, 215, 216, 217, 227, 229–230; **Retro. Supp. I:** 320, 327, 330; **Supp. XII:** 296
Cournos, John, **III:** 465; **Supp. I Part 1:** 258
"Course in Creative Writing, A" (Stafford), **Supp. XI:** 327
"Course of a Particular, The" (Stevens), **Retro. Supp. I:** 312
"Coursier de Jeanne d'Arc, Le" (McCarriston), **Supp. XIV:** 267–268
Courtier, The (Castiglione), **III:** 282
" 'Courtin,' The" (Lowell), **Supp. I Part 2:** 415
"Courting of Sister Wisby, The" (Jewett), **Retro. Supp. II:** 134, 135, 146
"Courting the Famous Figures at the Grotto of Improbable Thought" (B. Kelly), **Supp. XVII:** 127–128
"Courtship" (Dove), **Supp. IV Part 1:** 248
"Courtship, Diligence" (Dove), **Supp. IV Part 1:** 248
Courtship of Miles Standish, The (Longfellow), **II:** 489, 502–503; **Retro. Supp. II:** 155, **161–162,** 163, 166, 168
"Cousin Aubrey" (Taylor), **Supp. V:** 328
Cousine Bette (Balzac), **Retro. Supp. II:** 98
Couturier, Maurice, **Supp. IV Part 1:** 44
Covarrubias, Miguel, **Supp. XVI:** 187
"Covered Bridges" (Kingsolver), **Supp. VII:** 203
"Cover Photograph" (Nelson), **Supp. XVIII:** 173
"Cover Stories" (Skloot), **Supp. XX: 195, 207**
"Cover Versions" (Halliday), **Supp. XIX:** 84
Cowan, Lester, **III:** 148
Cowan, Louise, **IV:** 120, 125
Coward, Noel, **Retro. Supp. I:** 65; **Supp. I Part 1:** 332; **Supp. V:** 101; **Supp. XV:** 329
"Cowardice" (Theroux), **Supp. VIII:** 313
Cowboy Mouth (Shepard), **Supp. III Part 2:** 441–442
"Cowboys" (Salter). *See* "Dirt" (Salter)
Cowboys (Shepard), **Supp. III Part 2:** 432
Cowboys #2 (Shepard), **Supp. III Part 2:** 437, 438
Cowell, Henry, **Supp. IV Part 1:** 80, 82
Cowen, Philip, **Supp. XX: 2**
Cowen, Wilson Walker, **Supp. IV Part 2:** 435
Cowie, Alexander, **IV:** 70
"Cow in Apple Time, The" (Frost), **II:** 154; **Retro. Supp. I:** 131
Cowl, Jane, **IV:** 357
Cowley, Abraham, **III:** 508; **IV:** 158; **Supp. I Part 1:** 357
Cowley, Malcolm, **I:** 246, 253, 254, 255, 256, 257, 283, 385; **II:** 26, 57, 94, 456; **III:** 606; **IV:** 123; **Retro. Supp. I:** 73, 91, 97; **Retro. Supp. II:** 77, 83, 89, 221, 330; **Supp. I Part 1:** 174; **Supp. I Part 2:** 609, 610, 620, 647, 654, 678; **Supp. II Part 1:** 103, **135–156; Supp. VIII:** 96; **Supp. XV:** 142; **Supp. XX: 76**
Cowley, Marguerite Frances Baird (Mrs. Malcolm Cowley), **Supp. I Part 2:** 615; **Supp. II Part 1:** 138, 139
Cowley, Muriel Maurer (Mrs. Malcolm Cowley), **Supp. II Part 1:** 139
Cowley, Susan Cheever (Susan Cheever), **Supp. I Part 1:** 175; **Supp. IX:** 133
Cowper, William, **II:** 17, 304; **III:** 508, 511; **Supp. I Part 1:** 150, 151, 152; **Supp. I Part 2:** 539
"Cow Wandering in the Bare Field, The" (Jarrell), **II:** 371, 388
Cox, Martha Heasley, **Supp. IX:** 2, 4, 11–12
Cox, Sidney, **Retro. Supp. I:** 131; **Supp. XXI:** 19, 21
Cox, Stephen, **Supp. IV Part 2:** 523, 524
Cox, Steve, **Supp. XIX:** 116, 128
Coxey, Jacob, **II:** 464
"Coxon Fund, The" (James), **Retro. Supp. I:** 228
"Coy Mistress" (A. Finch), **Supp. XVII:** 72
Coyne, Patricia, **Supp. V:** 123
"Coyote Ortiz: *Canis latrans latrans* in the Poetry of Simon Ortiz" (P. C. Smith), **Supp. IV Part 2:** 509
Coyote's Daylight Trip (Gunn Allen), **Supp. IV Part 1:** 320, 324
Coyote Was Here (Ortiz), **Supp. IV Part 2:** 499
Cozzens, James Gould, **I: 358–380; II:** 459
Crabbe, George, **II:** 304; **III:** 469, 508, 511, 521
"Crab-Boil" (Dove), **Supp. IV Part 1:** 249
"Cracked Looking-Glass, The" (Porter), **III:** 434, 435, 446
"Cracker Chidlings" (Rawlings), **Supp. X:** 224, 228
Cracks (Purdy), **Supp. VII:** 277–278
Crack-Up, The (Fitzgerald), **II:** 80; **III:** 35, 45; **Retro. Supp. I:** 113, 115; **Supp. V:** 276; **Supp. IX:** 61
"Crack-Up, The" (Fitzgerald), **I:** 509; **Retro. Supp. I:** 113, 114
"Crack-up of American Optimism, The: Vachel Lindsay, the Dante of the Fundamentalists" (Viereck), **Supp. I Part 2:** 403
Cradle Will Rock, The (Blitzstein), **Supp. I Part 1:** 277, 278
Craft of Fiction, The (Lubbock), **I:** 504; **Supp. VIII:** 165
Craft of Peter Taylor, The (McAlexander, ed.), **Supp. V:** 314
Craig, David M., **Supp. XXII:** 187, 191, 192
Craig, Gordon, **III:** 394; **Supp. XXI:** 6
Crain, Jane Larkin, **Supp. V:** 123; **Supp. XII:** 167, 168
Crais, Robert, **Supp. XXI:** 70
Cram, Ralph Adams, **I:** 19
Cramer, Steven, **Supp. XI:** 139; **Supp. XV:** 26
Crandall, Reuben, **Supp. I Part 2:** 686
Crane, Agnes, **I:** 406
Crane, Edmund, **I:** 407
Crane, Hart, **I:** 61, 62, 97, 109, 116, 266, **381–404; II:** 133, 215, 306, 368, 371, 536, 542; **III:** 260, 276, 453, 485, 521; **IV:** 122, 123–124, 127, 128, 129, 135, 139, 140, 141, 341, 380, 418, 419; **Retro. Supp. I:** 427; **Retro. Supp. II: 75–91; Supp. I Part 1:** 86; **Supp. II Part 1:** 89, 152; **Supp. III Part 1:** 20, 63, 350; **Supp. V:** 342; **Supp. VIII:** 39; **Supp. IX:** 38, 229, 320; **Supp. X:** 115, 116, 120; **Supp. XI:** 123, 131; **Supp. XII:** 198; **Supp. XV:** 138; **Supp. XIX:** 35; **Supp. XX: 80; Supp. XXI:** 131, 132, 136, 230; **Supp. XXII:** 274
Crane, Jonathan, Jr., **I:** 407
Crane, Jonathan Townley, **I:** 406
Crane, Mrs. Jonathan Townley, **I:** 406
Crane, Luther, **I:** 406
Crane, Milton, **Supp. XV:** 144
Crane, Nellie, **I:** 407
Crane, R. S., **Supp. I Part 2:** 423
Crane, Stephen, **I:** 34, 169–170, 201, 207, 211, **405–427,** 477, 506, 519; **II:** 58, 144, 198, 262, 263, 264, 276, 289, 290, 291; **III:** 314, 317, 334, 335, 454, 505, 585; **IV:** 207, 208, 256, 350, 475; **Retro. Supp. I:** 231, 325; **Retro. Supp. II:** 97, 123; **Supp. I Part 1:** 314; **Supp. III Part 2:** 412; **Supp. IV Part 1:** 350, 380; **Supp. IV Part 2:** 680, 689, 692; **Supp. VIII:** 98, 105; **Supp. IX:** 1, 14; **Supp. X:** 223; **Supp. XI:** 95; **Supp. XII:** 50; **Supp. XIV:** 21, 50, 51, 227; **Supp. XVII:** 71, 228; **Supp. XVIII:** 74, 75
Crane, William, **I:** 407
Cranford (Gaskell), **Supp. IX:** 79
Crashaw, William, **IV:** 145, 150, 151, 165
"Crash Report" (McGrath), **Supp. X:** 116
Crater, The (Cooper), **I:** 354, 355
Cratylus (Plato), **II:** 10
Cravan, Arthur, **Supp. XXII:** 164, 169

"Craven Street Gazette" (Franklin), **II:** 119
"Crawdad, The" (F. Wright), **Supp. XVII:** 244
Crawdad Creek (Sanders), **Supp. XVI:** 269
Crawford, Brad, **Supp. XI:** 133
Crawford, Eva, **I:** 199
Crawford, F. Marion, **III:** 320
Crawford, Joan, **Supp. I Part 1:** 67
Crawford, Kathleen, **I:** 289
"Crayon House" (Rukeyser), **Supp. VI:** 273
Crayon Miscellany, The (Irving), **II:** 312–313
Crazed, The (Jin), **Supp. XVIII: 99–100**
"Crazy about her Shrimp" (Simic), **Supp. VIII:** 282
"Crazy Cock" (H. Miller), **III:** 177
Crazy Gypsy (Salinas), **Supp. XIII:** 311, **313–315,** 316
"Crazy Gypsy" (Salinas), **Supp. XIII:** 313–314
Crazy Horse, **Supp. IV Part 2:** 488, 489
Crazy Horse (McMurtry), **Supp. V:** 233
Crazy Horse in Stillness (Heyen), **Supp. XIII:** 344
"Crazy in the Stir" (C. Himes), **Supp. XVI:** 137
Crazy Kill, The (C. Himes), **Supp. XVI:** 143
Creating a Role (Stanislavsky), **Supp. XIV:** 243
"Creation, According to Coyote, The" (Ortiz), **Supp. IV Part 2:** 505
Creation: A Novel (Vidal), **Supp. IV Part 2:** 677, 685, 688
"Creation of Anguish" (Nemerov), **III:** 269
"Creation Story" (Gunn Allen), **Supp. IV Part 1:** 325
"Creative and Cultural Lag" (Ellison), **Retro. Supp. II:** 116; **Supp. II Part 1:** 229; **Supp. XVIII:** 283
Creative Criticism (Spingarn), **I:** 266
"Creative Democracy" (Locke), **Supp. XIV:** 208
Creative Present, The (Balkian and Simmons, eds.), **Supp. XI:** 230
Creatures in an Alphabet (illus. Barnes), **Supp. III Part 1:** 43
"Credences of Summer" (Stevens), **IV:** 93–94
"Credentials" (Halliday), **Supp. XIX:** 90
"Credo" (Bynner), **Supp. XV:** 50
"Credo" (Du Bois), **Supp. II Part 1:** 169
"Credo" (Jeffers), **Supp. II Part 2:** 424
"Credos and Curios" (Thurber), **Supp. I Part 2:** 606, 613
Creech, James, **Retro. Supp. I:** 254
"Creed for Americans, A" (Benét), **Supp. XI:** 52
"Creed of a Beggar, The" (Lindsay), **Supp. I Part 2:** 379
Creegan, Andy, **Supp. XIX:** 205
Creekmore, Hubert, **II:** 586
Creeley, Robert, **Retro. Supp. I:** 411; **Supp. II Part 1:** 30; **Supp. III Part 1:** 2; **Supp. III Part 2:** 622, 626, 629; **Supp. IV Part 1: 139–161,** 322, 325; **Supp. XI:** 317; **Supp. XIII:** 104, 112; **Supp. XIV:** 150; **Supp. XVI:** 283; **Supp. XXI:** 23, 27, 227, 230; **Supp. XXII:** 227
Creelman, James Ashmore, **Supp. XVI:** 186–187
"Cremona Violin, The" (Lowell), **II:** 523
"Crêpe de Chine" (Doty), **Supp. XI:** 128
"Cressy" (Harte), **Supp. II Part 1:** 354, 356
"Cretan Woman, The" (Jeffers), **Supp. II Part 2:** 435
Crèvecoeur, Michel-Guillaume Jean de, **I:** 229; **Supp. I Part 1: 227–252**
Crèvecoeur's Eighteenth-Century Travels in Pennsylvania and New York (Adams), **Supp. I Part 1:** 251
Crevel, René, **Supp. XIV:** 343
Crewe-Jones, Florence, **Supp. XVII:** 58
Crewe Train (Macaulay), **Supp. XII:** 88
Crews, Harry, **Supp. X:** 11, 12; **Supp. XI: 99–117,** 245; **Supp. XVIII:** 195; **Supp. XXI:** 35, 38, 40, 44
Crichton, Michael, **Supp. XIV:** 316
Crick, Philip, **Supp. XVI:** 289
Cricket (C. L. R. James; Grimshaw, ed.), **Supp. XXI:** 172
"Cricket" (C. Miller), **Supp. XXII:** 199
"Crickets" (R. O. Butler), **Supp. XII:** 71
Criers and Kibitzers, Kibitzers and Criers (Elkin), **Supp. VI: 45–46,** 57
Crime and Punishment (Dostoevsky), **II:** 60, 130; **IV:** 484; **Supp. IV Part 2:** 525; **Supp. VIII:** 282; **Supp. XII:** 281; **Supp. XVII:** 155; **Supp. XVIII:** 278; **Supp. XIX:** 276
Crime at Scottsboro, The (Endore), **Supp. XVII:** 59
Crime Beat (Connelly), **Supp. XXI:** 67, 79
Crimes and Misdemeanors (film; Allen), **Supp. XV:** 1, 2, **11,** 12
Crisis papers (Paine), **Supp. I Part 2:** 508–509, 510
"Criteria of Negro Art" (Du Bois), **Supp. II Part 1:** 181; **Supp. XIX:** 66–67
"Critiad, The" (Winters), **Supp. II Part 2:** 794, 799
Critical Anthology A (Untermeyer), **Supp. XV:** 310
Critical Essays on Charlotte Perkins Gilman (Karpinski, ed.), **Supp. XI:** 201
Critical Essays on Peter Taylor (McAlexander), **Supp. V:** 319, 320, 323–324
Critical Essays on Robert Bly (W. V. Davis), **Supp. IV Part 1:** 64, 69
Critical Essays on Wallace Stegner (Arthur), **Supp. IV Part 2:** 606
Critical Fable, A (Lowell), **II:** 511–512, 527, 529–530
Critical Guide to Leaves of Grass, A (J. Miller), **IV:** 352
Critical Response to Joan Didion, The (Felton), **Supp. IV Part 1:** 210
Critical Temper of Alain Locke, The: A Selection of His Essays on Art and Culture (Stewart, ed.), **Supp. XIV:** 196, **210–211,** 213
"Critic as Artist, The" (Wilde), **Supp. X:** 189
Criticism and Fiction (Howells), **II:** 288
Criticism and Ideology (Eagleton), **Retro. Supp. I:** 67
Criticism in the Borderlands (Calderón and Saldívar, eds.), **Supp. IV Part 2:** 544
"Critics, The" (Jong), **Supp. V:** 119
"Critics and Connoisseurs" (Moore), **III:** 209
Critic's Notebook, A (Howe), **Supp. VI:** 126–128
"Critic's Task, The" (Kazin), **Supp. VIII:** 103
"Critic Who Does Not Exist, The" (Wilson), **IV:** 431
"Critique de la Vie Quotidienne" (Barthelme), **Supp. IV Part 1:** 50
Critique of Pure Reason (Kant), **Supp. XVI:** 184
Croce, Benedetto, **I:** 58, 255, 265, 273, 281; **III:** 610
Crockett, Davy, **II:** 307; **III:** 227; **IV:** 266; **Supp. I Part 2:** 411
"Crocodilopolis" (Cliff), **Supp. XXII:** 76
Crofter and the Laird, The (McPhee), **Supp. III Part 1:** 301–302, 307
Croly, Herbert, **I:** 229, 231, 235; **IV:** 436
Cromwell, Oliver, **IV:** 145, 146, 156; **Supp. I Part 1:** 111
Cronenberg, David, **Supp. XXI:** 152, 154
Cronin, A. J., **Supp. XVII:** 59
Cronin, Dr. Archibald, **III:** 578
Cronin, Justin, **Supp. X:** 10
Crooke, Dr. Helkiah, **Supp. I Part 1:** 98, 104
Crooked Little Heart (Lamott), **Supp. XX: 138**
Crooks, Alan, **Supp. V:** 226
Crooks, Robert, **Supp. XIII:** 237
"Crop, The" (O'Connor), **Retro. Supp. II:** 223–225
Crosby, Caresse, **I:** 385; **III:** 473; **Retro. Supp. II:** 85; **Supp. XII:** 198
Crosby, Harry, **I:** 385; **Retro. Supp. II:** 85
"Cross" (Hughes), **Supp. I Part 1:** 325; **Supp. XVIII:** 124
Crossan, John Dominic, **Supp. V:** 251
"Cross Country Snow" (Hemingway), **II:** 249
Cross Creek (Rawlings), **Supp. X:** 223, 226, 228, **231–232,** 233, 234, 235
Cross Creek Cookery (Rawlings), **Supp. X:** 233
Crossing, The (McCarthy), **Supp. VIII:** 175, **184–186**
"Crossing, The" (Swenson), **Supp. IV Part 2:** 644
"Crossing Brooklyn Ferry" (Whitman), **IV:** 333, 340, 341; **Retro. Supp. I:** 389, 396, 397, 400–401
"Crossing into Poland" (Babel), **Supp. XIV:** 84
Crossings (Chuang), **Supp. X:** 291
"Crossings" (Hogan), **Supp. IV Part 1:** 412
Crossing the Water (Plath), **Retro. Supp. II:** 248; **Supp. I Part 2:** 526, 538

Crossing to Safety (Stegner), **Supp. IV Part 2:** 599, 606, 612, 613–614
"Cross of Snow, The" (Longfellow), **II:** 490; **Retro. Supp. II:** 169–170
"Crossover" (O. Butler), **Supp. XIII:** 61
"Cross-Roads, The" (Lowell), **II:** 523
"Crossroads of the World Etc." (Merwin), **Supp. III Part 1:** 347, 348
Cross-Section (Seaver), **IV:** 485
Cross the Border, Close the Gap (Fiedler), **Supp. XIII:** 104
Cross Ties (X. J. Kennedy), **Supp. XV:** 165, **166–167**
"Cross Ties" (X. J. Kennedy), **Supp. XV:** 158
Crouch, Stanley, **Supp. XIX:** 158
"Croup" (Karr), **Supp. XI:** 243
Crouse, Russel, **III:** 284
"Crow" (Hogan), **Supp. IV Part 1:** 405
Crow (Hughes), **Supp. XV:** 347, 348
"Crow, The" (Creeley), **Supp. IV Part 1:** 148–149
Crow and the Heart,The (Carruth), **Supp. XVI:** 47–48
"Crowded Street, The" (Bryant), **Supp. I Part 1:** 168
Crowder, A. B., **Supp. XI:** 107
"Crow Jane" (Baraka), **Supp. II Part 1:** 38
Crowninshield, Frank, **III:** 123; **Supp. IX:** 201
Crown of Columbus (Erdrich and Dorris), **Supp. IV Part 1:** 260
"Crows, The" (Bogan), **Supp. III Part 1:** 50, 51
Crucial Instances (Wharton), **Retro. Supp. I:** 365, 367
Crucible, The (A. Miller), **III:** 147, 148, 155, 156–158, 159, 166; **Supp. XIII:** 206
"Crucified" (Gibran), **Supp. XX: 119**
"Crucifix in the Filing Cabinet" (Shapiro), **Supp. II Part 2:** 712
"Crude Foyer" (Stevens), **Retro. Supp. I:** 310
"Cruel and Barbarous Treatment" (McCarthy), **II:** 562, 563
"Cruel Mother, The" (B. Kelly), **Supp. XVII:** 126
Cruise of the Dazzler, The (London), **II:** 465
Cruise of the Snark, The (London), **II:** 476–477
"Cruising with the Beach Boys" (Gioia), **Supp. XV:** 118
" 'Crumbling Idols' by Hamlin Garland" (Chopin), **Supp. I Part 1:** 217
"Crusade of the Excelsior, The" (Harte), **Supp. II Part 1:** 336, 354
"Crusoe in England" (Bishop), **Retro. Supp. II:** 50; **Supp. I Part 1:** 93, 95, 96; **Supp. III Part 1:** 10, 18
Cruz-Hacker, Alba, **Supp. XXI:** 107
Cry, the Beloved Country (Paton), **Supp. VIII:** 126
Cryer, Dan, **Supp. VIII:** 86, 88; **Supp. XII:** 164
Crying of Lot 49, The (Pynchon), **Supp. II Part 2:** 618, 619, 621, 630–633
"Crying Sisters, The" (Rand), **Supp. IV Part 2:** 524
"Crying Wolf" (C. Frost), **Supp. XV:** 101
"Cry of the Graves, The" (Gibran), **Supp. XX: 124**
Cryptogram, The (Mamet), **Supp. XIV:** 240, 247, 255
"Crystal, The" (Aiken), **I:** 60
"Crystal, The" (Lanier), **Supp. I Part 1:** 364, 370
"Crystal Cage, The" (Kunitz), **Supp. III Part 1:** 258
Crystal Vision (Sorrentino), **Supp. XXI:** 235, 236
"Crytal" (Sobin), **Supp. XVI:** 283
Cry to Heaven (Rice), **Supp. VII:** 300–301
"Cuba" (Hemingway), **II:** 258
"Cuba Libre" (Baraka), **Supp. II Part 1:** 33
Cuba: Prophetic Island (W. Frank), **Supp. XX: 80, 81**
"Cubism, Barcelona" (Hull), **Supp. XXI:** 137
Cudjoe, Selwyn, **Supp. IV Part 1:** 6
"Cudjo's Own Story of the Last American Slaver" (Hurston), **Supp. VI:** 153
Cudlipp, Thelma, **I:** 501
Cudworth, Ralph, **II:** 9, 10
"Cuentista" (Mora), **Supp. XIII:** 224
"Cuento de agua santa, Un" (Mora), **Supp. XIII:** 224
Cujo (King), **Supp. V:** 138–139, 143, 149, 152
Cukor, George, **Supp. XVI:** 192
Cullen, Countee, **Retro. Supp. I:** 207; **Retro. Supp. II:** 114; **Supp. I Part 1:** 49, 325; **Supp. III Part 1:** 73, 75, 76; **Supp. IV Part 1: 163–174; Supp. IX:** 306, 309; **Supp. X:** 136, 140; **Supp. XIII:** 186; **Supp. XVIII:** 122,131, 185, 279, 280, 282, 284; **Supp. XIX:** 78; **Supp. XXII:** 3, 6, 7, 8
"Cultivation of Christmas Trees, The" (Eliot), **I:** 579
"Cult of Personality in American Letters, The" (Swados), **Supp. XIX:** 265
"Cult of the Best, The" (Arnold), **I:** 223
"Cultural Exchange" (Hughes), **Supp. I Part 1:** 341
"Cultural Pluralism: A New Americanism" (Locke), **Supp. XIV:** 195
"Cultural Relativism and Ideological Peace" (Locke), **Supp. XIV:** 202, 212
"Culture" (Emerson), **III:** 2, 4
"Culture, Self, and Style" (Gass), **Supp. VI:** 88
"Culture and Religion" (Olds), **Supp. X:** 214
Culture of Cities, The (Mumford), **Supp. II Part 2:** 492, 494–495
Cummings, E. E., **I:** 44, 48, 64, 105, 176, **428–450,** 475, 477, 482, 526; **III:** 20, 196, 476; **IV:** 384, 402, 415, 427, 433; **Retro. Supp. II:** 178, 328; **Supp. I Part 2:** 622, 678; **Supp. III Part 1:** 73; **Supp. IV Part 2:** 637, 641; **Supp. IX:** 20; **Supp. XV:** 312, 338
Cummings, Robert, **Supp. IV Part 2:** 524
Cummins, James, **Supp. XVII:** 74
Cunard, Lady, **III:** 459
Cunningham, J. V., **Supp. XV:** 169
Cunningham, Merce, **Supp. IV Part 1:** 83; **Supp. XV:** 187
Cunningham, Michael, **Supp. XII:** 80; **Supp. XV: 55–71**
Cup of Gold (Steinbeck), **IV:** 51, 53, 61–64, 67
"Cupola, The" (Bogan), **Supp. III Part 1:** 53
"Curandera" (Mora), **Supp. XIII:** 214, 222
Curé de Tours, Le (Balzac), **I:** 509
Cure for Dreams, A: A Novel (Gibbons), **Supp. X: 45–47,** 48, 50
Curie, Marie, **IV:** 420, 421; **Supp. I Part 2:** 569
Curie, Pierre, **IV:** 420
Curiosa Americana (Mather), **Supp. II Part 2:** 463
Curiosities (Matthews), **Supp. IX:** 151, 152
"Curious Case of Sidd Finch, The" (Plimpton), **Supp. XVI:** 244
"Curious Shifts of the Poor" (Dreiser), **Retro. Supp. II:** 97
"Current" (Espaillat), **Supp. XXI:** 106
"Currents and Counter-Currents in Medical Science" (Holmes), **Supp. I Part 1:** 305
"Curried Cow" (Bierce), **I:** 200
Curry, Professor W. C., **IV:** 122
Curse of the Jade Scorpion, The (film; Allen), **Supp. XV:** 11
Curse of the Starving Class (Shepard), **Supp. III Part 2:** 433, 447–448
Curse of the Werewolf, The (film), **Supp. XVII:** 56
"Curse on a Thief, A" (X. J. Kennedy), **Supp. XV:** 171
"Curtain, The" (Chandler), **Supp. IV Part 1:** 122
Curtain Calls: British and American Women and the Theater, 1660–1820 (Saar), **Supp. XV:** 237
Curtain of Green, A (Welty), **IV:** 261–264, 268, 283
"Curtain of Green, A" (Welty), **IV:** 263–264
Curtain of Green and Other Stories, A (Welty), **Retro. Supp. I:** 343, 344, 345, 346, 347, 355
Curtain of Trees (opera), **Supp. IV Part 2:** 552
"Curtain Raiser, A" (Stein), **IV:** 43, 44
"Curtains" (Cisneros), **Supp. VII:** 66
Curtin, John, **Supp. IX:** 184
Curtis, George William, **Supp. I Part 1:** 307; **Supp. XVIII:** 3, 14
Curve (Goldbarth), **Supp. XII:** 181
Curve of Binding Energy, The (McPhee), **Supp. III Part 1:** 301
Curzon, Mary, **III:** 52
Cushing, Caleb, **Supp. I Part 2:** 684, 686
Cushman, Howard, **Supp. I Part 2:** 652
Cushman, Stephen, **Retro. Supp. I:** 430
"Custard Heart, The" (Parker), **Supp. IX:** 201
Custer, General George, **I:** 489, 491

Custer Died for Your Sins (Deloria), **Supp. IV Part 1:** 323; **Supp. IV Part 2:** 504
"Custom House, The" (Hawthorne), **II:** 223; **Retro. Supp. I:** 147–148, 157; **Supp. XXI:** 181
Custom of the Country, The (Wharton), **IV:** 318; **Retro. Supp. I:** 374, **375–376**
"Cut" (Plath), **Retro. Supp. II:** 253
"Cut-Glass Bowl, The" (Fitzgerald), **II:** 88
Cutting, Bronson, **III:** 600
Cutting Lisa (Everett), **Supp. XVIII: 56**
"Cuttings, *later*" (Roethke), **III:** 532
"Cyberpunk" (Bethke), **Supp. XVI:** 121
Cyberspace trilogy (W. Gibson). *See* Sprawl trilogy (W. Gibson)
"Cycles, The" (Pinsky), **Supp. VI:** 250–252
Cynic's Word Book, The (Bierce), **I:** 197, 205, 208, 209, 210
Cynthia Ozick (Lowin), **Supp. V:** 273
Cynthia Ozick's Comic Art (Cohen), **Supp. V:** 273
Cynthia Ozick's Fiction (Kauvar), **Supp. V:** 273
"Czeslaw Milosz and Memory" (Hampl), **Supp. XXII:** 92

Da Capo: Best Music Writing 2002 (Lethem, ed.), **Supp. XVIII:** 148
Dacey, Philip, **Supp. IV Part 1:** 70
Dacier, André, **II:** 10
"Dad" (Cullen), **Supp. IV Part 1:** 167
"Daddy" (Plath), **Retro. Supp. II:** 250–251; **Supp. I Part 2:** 529, 542, 545, 546; **Supp. II Part 2:** 688; **Supp. XXII:** 30
Daddy's Little Boy (Collins), **Supp. XXI:** 54
"Daemon, The" (Bogan), **Supp. III Part 1:** 58, 61
"Daemon Lover, The" (Jackson), **Supp. IX:** 116–117
"Daffodils" (Nelson and Espeland), **Supp. XVIII:** 181
"Daffodils" (Wordsworth), **Supp. XIII:** 284
"Daffy Duck in Hollywood" (Ashbery), **Supp. III Part 1:** 18
D'Agata, John, **Supp. XII:** 97, 98
Dago Red (Fante), **Supp. XI:** 160, 169
Dahl, Roald, **Supp. IX:** 114
Dahlberg, Edward, **I:** 231; **Retro. Supp. I:** 426; **Supp. III Part 2:** 624; **Supp. XIV:** 148; **Supp. XVIII:** 148; **Supp. XXII:** 257
Dahlberg, R'lene, **Supp. XIV:** 148
Daiches, David, **Retro. Supp. II:** 243; **Supp. I Part 2:** 536
Daily Horoscope (Gioia), **Supp. XV:** 112, **118–121,** 126
"Daily Horoscope" (Gioia), **Supp. XV:** 119
Daily Modernism (Podnieks), **Supp. X:** 189
Dain Curse, The (Hammett), **Supp. IV Part 1:** 348
"Daisies" (Glück), **Supp. V:** 88
"Daisy" (Oates), **Supp. II Part 2:** 523
Daisy (S. and A. Warner), **Supp. XVIII:** 268
Daisy-Head Mayzie (Geisel), **Supp. XVI:** 112
Daisy Miller (H. James), **Retro. Supp. I:** 216, 220, 222, 223, 228, 231; **Supp. XVIII:** 165
"Daisy Miller" (H. James), **II:** 325, 326, 327, 329; **IV:** 316
Dale, Charlie, **Supp. IV Part 2:** 584
Daley, Yvonne, **Supp. XXII:** 216
Dali, Salvador, **II:** 586; **Supp. IV Part 1:** 83; **Supp. XIII:** 317
Dalibard, Thomas-François, **II:** 117
"Dallas-Fort Worth: Redband and Mistletoe" (Clampitt), **Supp. IX:** 45
"Dalliance of Eagles, The" (Whitman), **IV:** 348
Dalva (Harrison), **Supp. VIII:** 37, 45, 46, **48–49**
Daly, Carroll John, **Supp. IV Part 1:** 343, 345
Daly, John, **II:** 25, 26
Daly, Julia Brown, **II:** 25, 26
"Dalyrimple Goes Wrong" (Fitzgerald), **II:** 88
"Dam, The" (Rukeyser), **Supp. VI:** 283
Damas, Leon, **Supp. X:** 139
Damascus Gate (Stone), **Supp. V:** 308–311
Damballah (Wideman), **Supp. X:** 319, 320, 321, 322, 323, 326, 327, 331, 333–334
Dameshek, Brandon, **Supp. XIX:** 273, 277, 287
Damnation of Theron Ware, The (Frederic), **II:** 140–143, 144, 146, 147; **Retro. Supp. I:** 325
Damned If I Do (Everett), **Supp. XVIII:** 66
"Damned Thing, The" (Bierce), **I:** 206
Damon, Matt, **Supp. VIII:** 175
Damon, S. Foster, **I:** 26; **II:** 512, 514, 515
"Damon and Vandalia" (Dove), **Supp. IV Part 1:** 252
Dana, H. W. L., **I:** 225
Dana, Richard Henry, **I:** 339, 351; **Supp. I Part 1:** 103, 154, 155; **Supp. I Part 2:** 414, 420
Dana, Richard Henry, Jr., **III:** 81; **Supp. XX: 227**
Dana, Robert, **Supp. V:** 178, 180
"Dana Gioia and Fine Press Printing" (Peich), **Supp. XV:** 117
"Dance, The" (Crane), **I:** 109
"Dance, The" (Roethke), **III:** 541
"Dance, The" (W. C. Williams), **Supp. XVII:** 113
Dance and the Railroad, The (Hwang), **Supp. XXI:** 145, 146
Dance of Death, The (Auden), **Supp. II Part 1:** 10
Dance of Death, The (Bierce and Harcourt), **I:** 196
Dance of Life, The (Ellis), **Supp. XX: 117**
Dance of the Sleepwalkers (Calabria), **Supp. XIII:** 164
"Dance of the Solids, The" (Updike), **Retro. Supp. I:** 323
"Dancer" (Hoffman), **Supp. XVIII:** 86
"Dancer, The" (Swados), **Supp. XIX:** 261, 263–264
"Dancers Work by Forgetting" (Espaillat), **Supp. XXI:** 102
Dances with Wolves (film), **Supp. X:** 124
Dance to the Music of Time, A (Powell), **Supp. XVIII:** 146
Dancing After Hours (Dubus), **Supp. VII:** 91
Dancing Bears, The (Merwin), **Supp. III Part 1:** 343–344
Dancing on the Stones (Nichols), **Supp. XIII:** 256, 257, 259, 267, 269
"Dancing the Jig" (Sexton), **Supp. II Part 2:** 692
Dandelion Wine (Bradbury), **Supp. IV Part 1:** 101, 109–110
Dandurand, Karen, **Retro. Supp. I:** 30
"Dandy Frightening the Squatters, The" (Twain), **IV:** 193–194
Dangel, Mary Jo, **Supp. XVIII:** 156
Dangerous Crossroads (film), **Supp. XIII:** 163
Dangerous Moonlight (Purdy), **Supp. VII:** 278
"Dangerous Road Before Martin Luther King" (Baldwin), **Supp. I Part 1:** 52
"Dangerous Summer, The" (Hemingway), **II:** 261
Dangerous Thoughts (Ryan as Quin), **Supp. XVIII:** 226
"Dangers of Authorship, The" (Blackmur), **Supp. II Part 1:** 147
Dangling Man (Bellow), **I:** 144, 145, 147, 148, 150–151, 153–154, 158, 160, 161, 162, 163; **Retro. Supp. II:** 19, 20–21, 22, 23; **Supp. VIII:** 234; **Supp. XIX:** 157
"Dang Little Squirt" (Bontemps), **Supp. XXII:** 4
Daniel (biblical book), **Supp. I Part 1:** 105
Daniel (film), **Supp. IV Part 1:** 236
Daniel, Arnaut, **III:** 467
Daniel, Robert W., **III:** 76
Daniel, Samuel, **Supp. I Part 1:** 369
Daniel Deronda (G. Eliot), **I:** 458
Daniels, Frank, **Supp. XXII:** 196
Daniels, Kate, **Supp. XVII:** 112
Danielson, Linda, **Supp. IV Part 2:** 569
D'Annunzio, Gabriele, **II:** 515
Danny and the Deep Blue Sea: An Apache Dance (Shanley), **Supp. XIV:** 315, **318–319,** 320, 321, 323, 324
Danny O'Neill pentalogy (Farrell), **II:** 35–41
Danse Macabre (King), **Supp. IV Part 1:** 102; **Supp. V:** 144
"Danse Russe" (W. C. Williams), **IV:** 412–413
"Dans le Restaurant" (Eliot), **I:** 554, 578
Dans l'ombre des cathédrales (Ambelain), **Supp. I Part 1:** 273
Dante Alighieri, **I:** 103, 136, 138, 250, 384, 433, 445; **II:** 8, 274, 278, 289,

490, 492, 493, 494, 495, 504, 508, 524, 552; **III:** 13, 77, 124, 182, 259, 278, 448, 453, 467, 533, 607, 609, 610–612, 613; **IV:** 50, 134, 137, 138, 139, 247, 437, 438; **Retro. Supp. I:** 62, 63, 64, 66, 360; **Retro. Supp. II:** 330; **Supp. I Part 1:** 256, 363; **Supp. I Part 2:** 422, 454; **Supp. III Part 2:** 611, 618, 621; **Supp. IV Part 2:** 634; **Supp. V:** 277, 283, 331, 338, 345; **Supp. VIII:** 27, 219–221; **Supp. X:** 120, 121, 125; **Supp. XII:** 98; **Supp. XV:** 254; **Supp. XVII:** 227, 241

Danvis Tales: Selected Stories (Robinson; Budbill, ed.), **Supp. XIX:** 6

Danziger, Adolphe, **I:** 199–200

Danziger, Jeff, **Supp. XXII:** 208

Dar (Nabokov), **III:** 246, 255

D'Arcy, Randall, **Supp. XVII:** 76

Dardis, Tom, **Supp. XVIII:** 249

"Dare's Gift" (Glasgow), **II:** 190

Dark and Feeling, The: Black American Writers and Their Work (Major), **Supp. XXII:** 180

Dark Angel, The (Bolton), **Supp. I Part 1:** 281

"Dark Angel Travels With Us to Canada and Blesses Our Vacation, The" (Dunn), **Supp. XI:** 146

Dark Carnival (Bradbury), **Supp. IV Part 1:** 102

Darker (Strand), **Supp. IV Part 2:** 619, 626–628

Darker Face of the Earth, The (Dove), **Supp. IV Part 1:** 255–257

Dark Green, Bright Red (Vidal), **Supp. IV Part 2:** 677

Dark Half, The (King), **Supp. V:** 141

Dark Harbor: A Poem (Strand), **Supp. IV Part 2:** 633–634

"Dark Hills, The" (Robinson), **III:** 523

Dark Horses (X. J. Kennedy), **Supp. XV: 167–170**

Dark Hours, The (W. V. Davis), **Supp. XXI: 91–92,** 93

Dark Laughter (Anderson), **I:** 111, 116; **II:** 250–251

"Darkling Alphabet, A" (Snodgrass), **Supp. VI:** 323

Darkling Child (Merwin and Milroy), **Supp. III Part 1:** 346

"Darkling Summer, Ominous Dusk, Rumorous Rain" (Schwartz), **Supp. II Part 2:** 661

"Darkling Thrush" (Hardy), **Supp. IX:** 40

"Dark Men, The" (Dubus), **Supp. VII:** 86

Dark Mirrors (Sobin), **Supp. XVI:** 295

Dark Mother, The (W. Frank), **Supp. XX: 70–71**

Dark Mountains, The (Hoffman), **Supp. XVIII: 76–77**

Darkness and the Light, The (Hecht), **Supp. X:** 58

Darkness More Than Night, A (Connelly), **Supp. XXI: 73–74,** 80

"Darkness on the Edge of Town" (O'Brien), **Supp. V:** 246

Darkness Surrounding Us, The (Sorrentino), **Supp. XXI:** 227, 228

Darkness under the Trees/Walking behind the Spanish (Salinas), **Supp. XIII:** 311, **319–324**

"Dark Night" (St. John of the Cross), **Supp. XV:** 30

Dark Night of the Soul, The (St. John of the Cross), **I:** 1, 585

"Dark Ones" (Dickey), **Supp. IV Part 1:** 182

Dark Power (Holding), **Supp. XXII: 122–123,** 124

Dark Princess: A Romance (Du Bois), **Supp. II Part 1:** 179, 181–182

Dark Room, The (T. Williams), **IV:** 381

Dark Sacred Night (CD), **Supp. XXI:** 75

Dark Shadows (television show), **Supp. XIX:** 57

"Dark Summer" (Bogan), **Supp. III Part 1:** 51, 53

Dark Summer: Poems (Bogan), **Supp. III Part 1:** 52–53, 57

"Dark Tower, The" (column), **Supp. IV Part 1:** 168, 170

Dark Tower, The: The Gunslinger (King), **Supp. V:** 152

Dark Tower IV, The: Wizard and Glass (King), **Supp. V:** 139

Dark Tunnel, The (Macdonald as Millar), **Supp. IV Part 2:** 465, 466

"Dark TV Screen" (Simic), **Supp. VIII:** 282

"Dark Voyage, The" (McLay), **Supp. XIII:** 21

"Dark Walk, The" (Taylor), **Supp. V:** 320–321, 322, 326

Darkwater: Voices from Within the Veil (Du Bois), **Supp. II Part 1:** 178, 180, 183

Dark Waves and Light Matter (Goldbarth), **Supp. XII:** 176, 193

Dark World (Carruth), **Supp. XVI:** 55

"Darling" (Nye), **Supp. XIII:** 283–284

"Darling, The" (Chekhov), **Supp. IX:** 202

Darling-Darling (Barillet and Grédy; Loos, trans.), **Supp. XVI:** 194

Darnell, Linda, **Supp. XII:** 173

Darragh, Tina, **Supp. IV Part 2:** 427

Darreu, Robert Donaldson, **Supp. II Part 1:** 89, 98, 102

Darrow, Clarence, **Supp. I Part 1:** 5; **Supp. I Part 2:** 455

Dartmouth, Earl of, **Supp. XX: 284**

Darwin, Charles, **I:** 457; **II:** 323, 462, 481; **III:** 226, 231; **IV:** 69, 304; **Retro. Supp. I:** 254; **Retro. Supp. II:** 60, 65; **Supp. I Part 1:** 368; **Supp. IX:** 180; **Supp. XI:** 203; **Supp. XVI:** 13; **Supp. XX: 18**

"Darwin in 1881" (Schnackenberg), **Supp. XV:** 253, 254, 258

Daryush, Elizabeth, **Supp. V:** 180

Dasburg, Andrew, **Supp. XXI:** 6

Dash, Julie, **Supp. XI:** 17, 18, 20

Dashell, Alfred, **Supp. X:** 224

"DAS KAPITAL" (Baraka), **Supp. II Part 1:** 55

Datlow, Ellen, **Supp. XVI:** 123

"Datum Centurio" (Wallace), **Supp. X:** 309

Daudet, Alphonse, **II:** 325, 338

"Daughter" (Caldwell), **I:** 309

"Daughter in the House" (X. J. Kennedy), **Supp. XV:** 160

Daughter of Earth (Smedly), **Supp. XIII:** 295

Daughter of the Land, A (Stratton-Porter), **Supp. XX: 222**

Daughter of the Snows, A (London), **II:** 465, 469–470

"Daughters" (Anderson), **I:** 114

Daughters (Marshall), **Supp. XI:** 275, 276, 277, **286–288,** 289, 290

"Daughters, 1900" (Nelson), **Supp. XVIII:** 175

Daughters, I Love You (Hogan), **Supp. IV Part 1:** 397, 399, 401

"Daughters of Invention" (Alvarez), **Supp. VII:** 9

Daughters of the Dust (Dash; film), **Supp. XI:** 17, 18; **Supp. XX: 154**

Daumier, Honoré, **IV:** 412

Dave, R. A., **Supp. VIII:** 126

Davenport, Abraham, **Supp. I Part 2:** 699

Davenport, Gary, **Supp. IX:** 98

Davenport, Guy, **Supp. XIV:** 96; **Supp. XXI:** 235

Davenport, Herbert J., **Supp. I Part 2:** 642

Davenport, James, **I:** 546

Daves, E. G., **Supp. I Part 1:** 369

Davey, Frank, **Supp. XIII:** 33

"David" (Garrett), **Supp. VII:** 109–110

"David" (Gordon), **Supp. IV Part 1:** 298–299

David, Gray, **Supp. XX: 260**

"David and Agnes, a Romance" (Keillor), **Supp. XVI:** 175

David Blaize (Benson), **Supp. XX: 234**

David Copperfield (Dickens), **I:** 458; **II:** 290; **Retro. Supp. I:** 33; **Supp. XVI:** 65, 72; **Supp. XX: 234**

"David Crockett's Other Life" (Nye), **Supp. XIII:** 282

Davideis (Cowley), **IV:** 158

David Harum (Westcott), **I:** 216

"David Lynch Keeps His Head" (Wallace), **Supp. X:** 314

David Show, The (Gurney), **Supp. V:** 97

Davidson, Cathy, **Supp. XV:** 238

Davidson, Donald, **I:** 294; **III:** 495, 496; **IV:** 121, 122, 124, 125, 236; **Supp. II Part 1:** 139; **Supp. XIV:** 2; **Supp. XX: 164**

Davidson, James West, **Supp. XXII:** 218

Davidson, Jo, **Supp. XXI:** 7

Davidson, John, **Retro. Supp. I:** 55

Davidson, Michael, **Supp. VIII:** 290, 293, 294, 302–303

Davidson, Sara, **Supp. IV Part 1:** 196, 198, 203

Davidson, Sue, **Supp. XIX:** 260

Davidsz de Heem, Jan, **Supp. XI:** 133

Davie, Donald, **III:** 478; **Supp. IV Part 2:** 474; **Supp. V:** 331; **Supp. X:** 55, 59; **Supp. XVII:** 111, 112, 121

Davies, Arthur, **III:** 273

Davies, Sir John, **III:** 541
Davies, Marion, **Supp. XVI:** 186
Da Vinci, Leonardo, **I:** 274; **II:** 536; **III:** 210
Davis, Allen F., **Supp. I Part 1:** 1, 7
Davis, Allison, **Supp. I Part 1:** 327
Davis, Angela, **Supp. I Part 1:** 66; **Supp. X:** 249
Davis, Arthur B., **Supp. XVIII:** 119
Davis, Bette, **I:** 78; **Supp. I Part 1:** 67
Davis, Bill, **Supp. XIII:** 267
Davis, Christina, **Supp. XV:** 264
Davis, Cynthia, **Supp. XVIII:** 281, 286
Davis, Donald, **Supp. XIII:** 93
Davis, Elizabeth Gould, **Supp. I Part 2:** 567
Davis, George, **II:** 586
Davis, Glover, **Supp. V:** 180, 182, 186
Davis, Jefferson, **II:** 206; **IV:** 122, 125, 126
Davis, Jordan, **Supp. XV:** 178, 181, 186, 188
Davis, Katie, **Supp. VIII:** 83
Davis, L. J., **Supp. XI:** 234
Davis, Lydia, **Supp. XII:** 24; **Supp. XVII:** 21
Davis, Marcia, **Supp. XVIII:** 91, 100
Davis, Mary H., **Supp. XVIII:** 77
Davis, Miles, **Supp. XV:** 346; **Supp. XXII:** 172
Davis, Ossie, Jr., **Supp. IV Part 1:** 362; **Supp. XVI:** 144
Davis, Rebecca Harding, **Supp. I Part 1:** 45; **Supp. XIII:** 292, 295, 305; **Supp. XVI: 79–96**
Davis, Richard Harding, **III:** 328; **Supp. II Part 1:** 393; **Supp. XVI:** 85
Davis, Robert Gorham, **II:** 51; **IV:** 108
Davis, Stuart, **IV:** 409; **Supp. XV:** 295; **Supp. XXI:** 6
Davis, Thadious, **Supp. XVIII:** 120, 121, 123, 127, 129
Davis, Thulani, **Supp. XI:** 179; **Supp. XIII:** 233, 234, 239
Davis, William Virgil, **Supp. IV Part 1:** 63, 64, 68, 69, 70; **Supp. XXI: 83–96**
Davison, Peter, **Supp. XXI:** 91
Davy's Lake (M. Finch), **Supp. XVII:** 69
Dawn (Dreiser), **I:** 498, 499, 503, 509, 515, 519
Dawn (O. Butler), **Supp. XIII:** 63, **64**
"Dawnbreaker" (Hayden), **Supp. II Part 1:** 370
Dawn in Russia (W. Frank), **Supp. XX: 76**
Dawn Patrol, The (film), **Supp. XIV:** 81
"Dawn Patrol: A Review of the Literature of the Negro for 1948" (Locke), **Supp. XIV:** 211
Dawson, Edward, **IV:** 151
Dawson, Emma, **I:** 199
Dawson, Ruth, **Supp. XI:** 120
Day, Dorothy, **II:** 215; **Supp. I Part 2:** 524; **Supp. X:** 142
Day, Fred Holland, **Supp. XX: 114, 115**
Day, Georgiana, **Supp. I Part 2:** 585
Day, Richard, **Supp. XVIII:** 251
Dayan, Joan, **Retro. Supp. II:** 270
"Day Book" (Notley), **Supp. XXII:** 230
Day Book, A (Creeley), **Supp. IV Part 1:** 155
"Daybreak" (Kinnell), **Supp. III Part 1:** 250
"Daybreak Blues" (Kees), **Supp. XV:** 133
"Day-Breakers, The" (Bontemps), **Supp. XXII:** 8
"Daybreak in Alabama" (Hughes), **Retro. Supp. I:** 211; **Supp. I Part 1:** 344
Day by Day (Lowell), **Retro. Supp. II:** 184, 186, 191
"Day-Care Field Trip: Aquarium" (Karr), **Supp. XI:** 243
"Day-Dream, A" (Bryant), **Supp. I Part 1:** 160
"Day-Dream of a Grocer, The" (Twain), **Supp. XVIII:** 9
"Day for Poetry and Song, A" (Douglass), **Supp. III Part 1:** 172
"Day in the Life of Half of Rumpelstiltskin, A" (Brockmeier), **Supp. XXII:** 50, 52, 53
"Day Lady Died, The" (O'Hara), **Supp. XIX:** 85
Day Late and a Dollar Short, A (McMillan), **Supp. XIII:** 184, **Supp. XIII:** 185, **191–192**
"Day longs for the evening, The" (Levertov), **Supp. III Part 1:** 274
Daynard, Jodi, **Supp. XVIII:** 97
Day of a Stranger (Merton), **Supp. VIII:** 203
"Day of Days, A" (James), **II:** 322
Day of Doom (Wigglesworth), **IV:** 147, 155, 156
Day of the Body (C. Frost), **Supp. XV:** 93, **98–100,** 106
Day of the Locust, The (West), **I:** 298; **IV:** 288, 299–306; **Retro. Supp. II:** 321, 323, 324, 329, **337–338; Supp. II Part 2:** 626; **Supp. XI:** 296; **Supp. XII:** 173; **Supp. XIII:** 170; **Supp. XIV:** 328; **Supp. XVIII:** 246
"Day on the Big Branch, A" (Nemerov), **III:** 275–276
"Day on the Connecticut River, A" (Merrill), **Supp. III Part 1:** 336
Day Room, The (DeLillo), **Supp. VI:** 4
"Days" (Emerson), **II:** 19, 20
"Days and Nights" (Koch), **Supp. XV:** 179, 180
"Days and Nights: A Journal" (Price), **Supp. VI:** 265
Days Before, The (Porter), **III:** 433, 453
Days in the Yellow Leaf (Hoffman), **Supp. XVIII:** 75
"Days of 1935" (Merrill), **Supp. III Part 1:** 325, 328
"Days of 1941 and '44" (Merrill), **Supp. III Part 1:** 336
"Days of 1964" (Merrill), **Supp. III Part 1:** 328, 352
"Days of 1971" (Merrill), **Supp. III Part 1:** 328
"Days of 1981" (Doty), **Supp. XI:** 123
"Days of Awe: The Birth of Lucy Jane" (Wasserstein), **Supp. XV:** 332
"Days of Edward Hopper" (Haines), **Supp. XII:** 210
"Days of Heaven" (Bass), **Supp. XVI:** 20
Days of Obligation: An Argument with My Mexican Father (Rodriguez), **Supp. XIV:** 298, 300, **302–305,** 307, 310
Days of Our Lives (soap opera), **Supp. XI:** 83
Days of Our Lives Lie in Fragments: New and Old Poems (Garrett), **Supp. VII:** 109–110, 111
Days of the Phoenix (Brooks), **I:** 266
Days of Wine and Roses (J. P. Miller), **Supp. XIII:** 262
Days: Tangier Journal, 1987–1989 (Bowles), **Supp. IV Part 1:** 94
Days to Come (Hellman), **Supp. I Part 1:** 276, 277–278
Days without End (O'Neill), **III:** 385, 391, 397
"Day's Work, A" (Capote), **Supp. III Part 1:** 120
"Day's Work, A" (Porter), **III:** 443, 446
"Day the Presidential Candidate Came to Ciudad Tamaulipas, The" (Caldwell), **I:** 309
"Day the Singer Fell, The" (Swados), **Supp. XIX:** 258
Day the World ended, The (Coover), **Supp. V:** 1
"Day with Conrad Green, A" (Lardner), **II:** 428–429, 430
"Deacon's Masterpiece, The" (Holmes), **Supp. I Part 1:** 302, 307
"Dead, The" (Collins), **Supp. XXI:** 64
"Dead, The" (Joyce), **I:** 285; **III:** 343
Dead and the Living, The (Olds), **Supp. X:** 201, **204–206,** 207
"Dead Body, The" (Olds), **Supp. X:** 210
"Dead by the Side of the Road, The" (Snyder), **Supp. VIII:** 301
"Dead Doe" (B. Kelly), **Supp. XVII:** 128–129
Dead End (Kingsley), **Supp. I Part 1:** 277, 281
Dead Father, The (Barthelme), **Supp. IV Part 1:** 43, 47, 50–51
"Dead Fiddler, The" (Singer), **IV:** 20
Dead Fingers Talk (Burroughs), **Supp. III Part 1:** 103
"Dead Hand" series (Sinclair), **Supp. V:** 276, 277, 281
"Dead Languages, The" (Humphrey), **Supp. IX:** 109
Dead Lecturer, The (Baraka), **Supp. II Part 1:** 31, 33, 35–37, 49
Deadline at Dawn (Odets), **Supp. II Part 2:** 546
"Dead-Lock and Its Key, A" (E. Stoddard), **Supp. XV:** 286
"Dead Loon, The" (Bynner), **Supp. XV: 44–45**
Deadly Affair, A (Lacy), **Supp. XV:** 205–206
Deadly is the Female (film), **Supp. XVII:** 62
Dead Man's Walk (McMurtry), **Supp. V:** 231, 232
Dead Man's Walk (screenplay; McMurtry and Ossana), **Supp. V:** 231

Dead Man Walking (opera libretto, McNally), **Supp. XIII:** 207
Dead Poets Society (film), **Supp. XXI:** 192, 193, 194, 199
"Dead Reckoning" (Jarman), **Supp. XVII:** 113
"Dead Soldier's Talk, The" (Jin), **Supp. XVIII:** 92
Dead Souls (Gogol), **I:** 296
"Dead Souls on Campus" (Kosinski), **Supp. VII:** 222
"Dead Wingman, The" (Jarrell), **II:** 374
"Dead Yellow Women" (Hammett), **Supp. IV Part 1:** 345
Dead Zone, The (King), **Supp. V:** 139, 143, 144, 148, 152
Dean, James, **I:** 493
Dean, Man Mountain, **II:** 589
Deane, Silas, **Supp. I Part 2:** 509, 524
"Dean of Men" (Taylor), **Supp. V:** 314, 323
Dean's December, The (Bellow), **Retro. Supp. II:** 30–31
"Dear Adolph" (Benét), **Supp. XI:** 46
"Dear America" (Ortiz), **Supp. IV Part 2:** 503
"Dear Dark Continent" (Notley), **Supp. XXII:** 223
"Dearest M—" (Carruth), **Supp. XVI:** 59
"Dear Judas" (Jeffers), **Supp. II Part 2:** 431–432, 433
Dear Juliette (Sarton), **Supp. VIII:** 265
Dear Lovely Death (Hughes), **Retro. Supp. I:** 203; **Supp. I Part 1:** 328
Dear Rafe (Hinojosa), **Supp. XIX:** 98, **105–106**
"Dear Villon" (Corso), **Supp. XII:** 135
"Dear World" (Gunn Allen), **Supp. IV Part 1:** 321
Deasy, Philip, **Supp. XX: 42**
Death (Allen), **Supp. XV:** 3
"Death" (Corso), **Supp. XII:** 127
"Death" (Lowell), **II:** 536
"Death" (Mailer), **III:** 38
"Death" (W. C. Williams), **Retro. Supp. I:** 422
"Death" (West), **IV:** 286
"Death and Absence" (Glück), **Supp. V:** 82
Death and Birth of David Markand, The (W. Frank), **Supp. XX: 76–77**
Death and Taxes (Parker), **Supp. IX:** 192
"Death and the Child" (Crane), **I:** 414
"Death as a Society Lady" (Hecht), **Supp. X:** 71–72
Death before Bedtime (Vidal as Box), **Supp. IV Part 2:** 682
"Death Be Not Proud" (Donne), **Supp. XVI:** 158
"Death by Water" (Eliot), **I:** 395, 578
Death Comes for the Archbishop (Cather), **I:** 314, 327, 328–330; **Retro. Supp. I:** 16–18, 21; **Supp. XIII:** 253
Death in Paradise (Parker), **Supp. XIX:** 186
Death in the Afternoon (Hemingway), **II:** 253; **IV:** 35; **Retro. Supp. I:** 182; **Supp. VIII:** 182; **Supp. XVI:** 205; **Supp. XIX:** 246; **Supp. XX: 76**
"Death in the Country, A" (Benét), **Supp. XI:** 53–54
Death in the Family, A (Agee), **I:** 25, 29, 42, 45
Death in the Fifth Position (Vidal as Box), **Supp. IV Part 2:** 682
"Death in the Woods" (Anderson), **I:** 114, 115
Death in the Woods and Other Stories (Anderson), **I:** 112, 114, 115
Death in Venice (Mann), **III:** 231; **Supp. IV Part 1:** 392; **Supp. V:** 51
"Death in Viet Nam" (Salinas), **Supp. XIII:** 315
"Death in Winter" (C. Frost), **Supp. XV:** 98
Death Is a Lonely Business (Bradbury), **Supp. IV Part 1:** 102, 103, 111–112, 115
"Death Is Not the End" (Wallace), **Supp. X:** 309
Death Is the Place (Bronk), **Supp. XXI:** 32
Death Kit (Sontag), **Supp. III Part 2:** 451, 468–469
Death Likes It Hot (Vidal as Box), **Supp. IV Part 2:** 682
"*Death*/Muerta" (Mora), **Supp. XIII:** 228
Death Notebooks, The (Sexton), **Supp. II Part 2:** 691, 694, 695
"Death of a Columnist" (Siddons), **Supp. XXII:** 241–242
Death of Adam, The: Essays on Modern Thought (Robinson), **Supp. XXI:** 212
"Death of a Jazz Musician" (W. J. Smith), **Supp. XIII:** 334
Death of a Kinsman, The (Taylor), **Supp. V:** 324, 326
"Death of an Old Seaman" (Hughes), **Retro. Supp. I:** 199
"Death of a Pig" (White), **Supp. I Part 2:** 665–668
Death of a Salesman (A. Miller), **I:** 81; **III:** 148, 149, 150, 153–154, 156, 157, 158, 159, 160, 163, 164, 166; **IV:** 389; **Supp. IV Part 1:** 359; **Supp. XIV:** 102, 239, 254, 255; **Supp. XV:** 205; **Supp. XX: 27**
"Death of a Soldier, The" (Stevens), **Retro. Supp. I:** 299, 312. *see also* "Lettres d'un Soldat" (Stevens)
"Death of a Soldier, The" (Wilson), **IV:** 427, 445
"Death of a Toad" (Wilbur), **Supp. III Part 2:** 550
"Death of a Traveling Salesman" (Welty), **IV:** 261; **Retro. Supp. I:** 344
"Death of a Young Son by Drowning" (Atwood), **Supp. XIII:** 33
Death of Bessie Smith, The (Albee), **I:** 76–77, 92
Death of Billy the Kid, The (Vidal), **Supp. IV Part 2:** 683
Death of Cock Robin, The (Snodgrass), **Supp. VI:** 315, **317–319,** 324
Death of Dreams, A (Hoffman), **Supp. XVIII:** 79
"Death of General Wolfe, The" (Paine), **Supp. I Part 2:** 504
"Death of Halpin Frayser, The" (Bierce), **I:** 205
"Death of Justina, The" (Cheever), **Supp. I Part 1:** 184–185
Death of Life, The (Barnes), **Supp. III Part 1:** 34
Death of Malcolm X, The (Baraka), **Supp. II Part 1:** 47
"Death of Marilyn Monroe, The" (Olds), **Supp. X:** 205
"Death of Me, The" (Malamud), **Supp. I Part 2:** 437
"Death of Slavery, The" (Bryant), **Supp. I Part 1:** 168–169
"Death of St. Narcissus, The" (Eliot), **Retro. Supp. I:** 291
"Death of the Ball Turret Gunner, The" (Jarrell), **II:** 369–370, 372, 374, 375, 376, 378
"Death of the Fathers, The" (Sexton), **Supp. II Part 2:** 692
"Death of the Flowers, The" (Bryant), **Supp. I Part 1:** 170
Death of the Fox (Garrett), **Supp. VII:** 99, 101–104, 108
"Death of the Hat, The" (Collins), **Supp. XXI:** 59
"Death of the Hired Man, The" (Frost), **III:** 523; **Retro. Supp. I:** 121, 128; **Supp. IX:** 261
Death of the Kapowsin Tavern (Hugo), **Supp. VI:** 133–135
"Death of the Kapowsin Tavern" (Hugo), **Supp. VI:** 137, 141
"Death of the Lyric, The: The Achievement of Louis Simpson" (Jarman and McDowell), **Supp. IX:** 266, 270, 276
"Death of Venus, The" (Creeley), **Supp. IV Part 1:** 143, 144–145
"Death on All Fronts" (Ginsberg), **Supp. II Part 1:** 326
"Deaths" (Dunn), **Supp. XI:** 147
"Death Sauntering About" (Hecht), **Supp. X:** 72
Deaths for the Ladies (and Other Disasters) (Mailer), **Retro. Supp. II:** 203
Death's Jest-Book (Beddoes), **Retro. Supp. I:** 285
Death Song (McGrath), **Supp. X:** 127
"Death the Carnival Barker" (Hecht), **Supp. X:** 72
"Death the Film Director" (Hecht), **Supp. X:** 72
"Death the Judge" (Hecht), **Supp. X:** 72
"Death the Mexican Revolutionary" (Hecht), **Supp. X:** 72
"Death the Oxford Don" (Hecht), **Supp. X:** 72
"Death the Painter" (Hecht), **Supp. X:** 72
Death the Proud Brother (Wolfe), **IV:** 456
"Death to Van Gogh's Ear!" (Ginsberg), **Supp. II Part 1:** 320, 322, 323
"Death Warmed Over!" (Bradbury), **Supp. IV Part 1:** 104–105, 112
Death Wish, The (Holding), **Supp. XXII:** 120, **123,** 134, 135
Débâcle, La (Zola), **III:** 316
"Debate with the Rabbi" (Nemerov), **III:** 272

Debeljak, Alesă, **Supp. VIII:** 272
De Bellis, Jack, **Supp. I Part 1:** 366, 368, 372
Debo, Annette, **Supp. XXI:** 254
DeBoer-Langworthy, Carol, **Supp. XVII:** 98, 99, 100
De Bosis, Lauro, **IV:** 372
"Debriefing" (Sontag), **Supp. III Part 2:** 468–470
Debs, Eugene, **I:** 483, 493; **III:** 580, 581; **Supp. I Part 2:** 524; **Supp. IX:** 1, 15
Debt to Pleasure, The (Lanchester), **Retro. Supp. I:** 278
Debussy, Claude, **Retro. Supp. II:** 266; **Supp. XIII:** 44
"Decades" (Sorrentino), **Supp. XXI:** 229
Decameron (Boccaccio), **III:** 283, 411; **Supp. IX:** 215
"Deceased" (Hughes), **Retro. Supp. I:** 208
"December" (Oliver), **Supp. VII:** 245
"December 1, 1994" (Stern), **Supp. IX:** 299
December 7 (film, Ford), **Supp. XVIII:** 247
"December 24" (Di Piero), **Supp. XIX:** 39
"December 28: Returning to Chicago" (Di Piero), **Supp. XIX:** 39
"December Dawn" (Skloot), **Supp. XX:** **202**
"December Eclogue" (Winters), **Supp. II Part 2:** 794
"Decent Woman, A" (Boulton), **Supp. XXII:** 22–23
De Cenzo, Giorgia, **Supp. XXI:** 256
Deception (P. Roth), **Retro. Supp. II:** 291; **Supp. III Part 2:** 426–427
"Deceptions" (Dobyns), **Supp. XIII:** 77
De Chiara, Ann. *See* Malamud, Mrs. Bernard (Ann de Chiara)
De Chirico, Giorgio, **Supp. XIII:** 317
"Decided Loss, A" (Poe), **II:** 411
"Decisions to Disappear" (Dunn), **Supp. XI:** 144
"Decisive Moment, The" (Auster), **Supp. XIV:** 292
Decker, James A., **Supp. III Part 2:** 621
Declaration of Gentlemen and Merchants and Inhabitants of Boston, and the Country Adjacent, A (Mather), **Supp. II Part 2:** 450
"Declaration of Paris, The" (Adams), **I:** 4
Declaration of the Rights of Man and the Citizen, **Supp. I Part 2:** 513, 519
Declaration of Universal Peace and Liberty (Paine), **Supp. I Part 2:** 512
Declension in the Village of Chung Luong (Weigl), **Supp. XIX:** 287, 288
Decline and Fall (Waugh), **Supp. I Part 2:** 607; **Supp. XV:** 142
Decline and Fall of the English System of Finance, The (Paine), **Supp. I Part 2:** 518
Decline and Fall of the Roman Empire, The (Gibbons), **Supp. III Part 2:** 629
"Decline of Book Reviewing, The" (Hardwick), **Supp. III Part 1:** 201–202
Decline of the West, The (Spengler), **I:** 270; **IV:** 125
"Decolonizing the Tongue: Reading Speech and Aphasia in the Work of Michelle Cliff" (Aguiar), **Supp. XXII:** 68
Deconstructing Harry (film; Allen), **Supp. XV:** 12, **13**
"Décor" (X. J. Kennedy), **Supp. XV:** 171
"Decoration Day" (Jewett), **II:** 412; **Retro. Supp. II:** 138
Decoration of Houses, The (Wharton and Codman), **IV:** 308; **Retro. Supp. I:** 362, 363–364, 366
"Decoy" (Ashbery), **Supp. III Part 1:** 13–14
Decter, Midge, **Supp. XX:** **248**
Dedalus, Stephen, **Supp. XIX:** 47
"De Daumier-Smith's Blue Period" (Salinger), **III:** 560–561
"Dedication" (Nelson), **Supp. XVIII:** 173, 180
"Dedication and Household Map" (Erdrich), **Supp. IV Part 1:** 272
"Dedication Day" (Agee), **I:** 34
"Dedication for a Book" (Hay), **Supp. XIV:** 125
"Dedication for a Book of Criticism" (Winters), **Supp. II Part 2:** 801
"Dedication in Postscript, A" (Winters), **Supp. II Part 2:** 801
Dedications and Other Darkhorses (Komunyakaa), **Supp. XIII:** 112, **113–114**
"Dedication to Hunger" (Glück), **Supp. V:** 83
"Dedication to My Wife, A" (Eliot), **I:** 583
Dee, Ruby, **Supp. IV Part 1:** 362
Deeds of Utmost Kindness (Gander), **Supp. XV:** 340
"Deep Breath at Dawn, A" (Hecht), **Supp. X:** 58
Deep End, The (film), **Supp. XXII:** 120, 131, 133
Deeper into Movies: The Essential Kael Collection from '69 to '72 (Kael), **Supp. IX:** 253
"Deeper Wisdom, The" (Hay), **Supp. XIV:** 129
Deep Green Sea (R. O. Butler), **Supp. XII:** 62, **74**
Deephaven (Jewett), **II:** 398–399, 400, 401, 410, 411; **Retro. Supp. II:** 133, 134, 135, 136, 137, 138, 140, 141, 143, 144
"Deep Sight and Rescue Missions" (Bambara), **Supp. XI:** 18–19
Deep Sightings and Rescue Missions: Fiction, Essays, and Conversations (Bambara), **Supp. XI:** 1, 3, **14–20**
Deep Sleep, The (Morris), **III:** 224–225
Deep South (Caldwell), **I:** 305, 309, 310
Deepstep Come Shining (Wright), **Supp. XV:** 337, 341, 344, **349–350,** 351, 353
"Deep Water" (Marquand), **III:** 56
"Deep Woods" (Nemerov), **III:** 272–273, 275
"Deer at Providencia, The" (Dillard), **Supp. VI:** 28, 32
Deer Camp: Last Light in the Northeast Kingdom (Ostrum, ed.), **Supp. XXII:** 218
"Deer Dancer" (Harjo), **Supp. XII:** 224–225
"Deer Ghost" (Harjo), **Supp. XII:** 225
Deer Park, The (Mailer), **I:** 292; **III:** 27, 31–33, 35–36, 37, 39, 40, 42, 43, 44; **Retro. Supp. II: 200–202,** 205, 207, 211
Deer Park, The: A Play (Mailer), **Retro. Supp. II:** 205
Deer Pasture, The (Bass), **Supp. XVI:** 15, 16, 23
Deerslayer, The (Cooper), **I:** 341, 349, 350, 355; **Supp. I Part 1:** 251
Defence, The (Nabokov), **Supp. XXII:** 263
"Defence of Poesie, The" (Bronk), **Supp. XXI:** 32
"Defence of Poesy, The" (Sidney), **Supp. V:** 250
"Defence of Poetry" (Longfellow), **II:** 493–494
"Defender of the Faith" (P. Roth), **Retro. Supp. II:** 281; **Supp. III Part 2:** 404, 407, 420
"Defending *The Searchers* (Scenes in the Life of an Obsession)*" (Lethem), Supp. XVIII:* 136,141
"Defenestration in Prague" (Matthews), **Supp. IX:** 168
Defenestration of Prague (Howe), **Supp. IV Part 2:** 419, 426, 429–430
Defense, The (Nabokov), **III:** 251–252; **Retro. Supp. I:** 266, 268, **270–272**
"Defense of Poetry" (Francis), **Supp. IX:** 83–84
Defiant Ones, The (film), **Supp. I Part 1:** 67
"Defining the Age" (W. V. Davis), **Supp. IV Part 1:** 64
"Definition" (Ammons), **Supp. VII:** 28
Defoe, Daniel, **I:** 204; **II:** 104, 105, 159, 304–305; **III:** 113, 423; **IV:** 180; **Supp. I Part 2:** 523; **Supp. V:** 127
De Forest, John William, **II:** 275, 280, 288, 289; **IV:** 350
DeFrees, Madeline, **Supp. XVIII:** 293
Degas, Brian, **Supp. XI:** 307
Degler, Carl, **Supp. I Part 2:** 496
"Degrees of Fidelity" (Dunn), **Supp. XI:** 148, 156
Deguy, Michel, **Supp. XV:** 178
De Haven, Tom, **Supp. XI:** 39; **Supp. XII:** 338–339
Deitch, Joseph, **Supp. VIII:** 125
"Dejection" (Coleridge), **II:** 97
DeJong, Constance, **Supp. XII:** 4
DeJong, David Cornel, **I:** 35
Dekker,Thomas, **Supp. XVII:** 232
de Kooning, Willem, **Supp. XII:** 198; **Supp. XV:** 177, 178
Delacroix, Henri, **I:** 227
De La Mare, Walter, **III:** 429; **Supp. II Part 1:** 4; **Supp. XVII:** 69
Delamotte, Eugenia C., **Supp. XI:** 279
De Lancey, James, **I:** 338
De Lancey, Mrs. James (Anne Heathcote), **I:** 338

De Lancey, Susan A. *See* Cooper, Mrs. James Fenimore

De Lancey, William Heathcote, **I:** 338, 353

Delano, Amasa, **III:** 90

Delattre, Roland A., **I:** 558

De Laurentiis, Dino, **Supp. XI:** 170, 307

De la Valdéne, Guy, **Supp. VIII:** 40, 42

Delbanco, Nicholas, **Supp. XXII:** 204

Del Cabral, Manuel, **Supp. XXI:** 104

DelCorso's Gallery (Caputo), **Supp. XIX:** 22–23

Delectorskaya, Lydia, **Supp. XXII:** 99

De l'éducation d'un homme sauvage (Itard), **Supp. I Part 2:** 564

"Delft" (Goldbarth), **Supp. XII:** 189

Delft: An Essay-Poem (Goldbarth), **Supp. XII:** 187

Delicate Balance, A (Albee), **I:** 86–89, 91, 93, 94

Delicate Balance, The (Hay), **Supp. XIV:** 121, 122, 124, 129, 133–134

"Delicate Balance, The" (Hay), **Supp. XIV:** 122

"Delicate Prey, The" (Bowles), **Supp. IV Part 1:** 86

Delicate Prey and Other Stories, The (Bowles), **Supp. IV Part 1:** 86–87

Délie (Scève), **Supp. III Part 1:** 11

Delights & Shadows (Kooser), **Supp. XIX:** 115, 116, 117, 121, **127–128**

DeLillo, Don, **Retro. Supp. I:** 278; **Retro. Supp. II:** 279; **Supp. VI: 1–18; Supp. IX:** 212; **Supp. XI:** 68; **Supp. XII:** 21, 152; **Supp. XVII:** 183; **Supp. XVIII:** 136, 140; **Supp. XIX:** 54; **Supp. XX: 83, 87, 91**

De Lint, Charles, **Supp. XXII:** 59

DeLisle, Anne, **Supp. VIII:** 175

Deliverance (Dickey), **Supp. IV Part 1:** 176, 186–188, 190; **Supp. X:** 30; **Supp. XX: 173–174**

Deliverance, The (Glasgow), **II:** 175, 176, 177–178, 181

"Delivering" (Dubus), **Supp. VII:** 87

Dell, Floyd, **I:** 103, 105; **Supp. I Part 2:** 379; **Supp. XV:** 295; **Supp. XVII:** 96; **Supp. XXI:** 6; **Supp. XXII:** 275

Della Francesca, Piero, **Supp. XV:** 262

"Della Primavera Trasportata al Morale" (W. C. Williams), **Retro. Supp. I:** 419, 422

DeLoria, Philip J., **Supp. XIV:** 306

Deloria, Vine, Jr., **Supp. IV Part 1:** 323; **Supp. IV Part 2:** 504

"Delta Autumn" (Faulkner), **II:** 71

"Delta Factor, The" (Percy), **Supp. III Part 1:** 386

Delta of Venus: Erotica (Nin), **Supp. X:** 192, 195

Delta Wedding (Welty), **IV:** 261, 268–271, 273, 281; **Retro. Supp. I:** 349–350, 351

Delusions (Berryman), **I:** 170

De Man, Paul, **Retro. Supp. I:** 67; **Supp. XVII:** 70

DeMarinis, Rick, **Supp. XIV:** 22

DeMars, James, **Supp. IV Part 2:** 552

Dembo, L. S., **I:** 386, 391, 396, 397, 398, 402; **III:** 478; **Supp. I Part 1:** 272; **Supp. XIV:** 277, 282, 288, 290

"Dementia Translucida" (Bierds), **Supp. XVII:** 33

Demetrakopoulous, Stephanie A., **Supp. IV Part 1:** 12

DeMille, Cecil B., **Supp. IV Part 2:** 520; **Supp. XV:** 42

Demme, Jonathan, **Supp. V:** 14

Democracy (Adams), **I:** 9–10, 20; **Supp. IV Part 1:** 208; **Supp. XIX:** 139

Democracy (Didion), **Supp. IV Part 1:** 198, 208–210

"Democracy" (Lowell), **Supp. I Part 2:** 419

Democracy and Education (Dewey), **I:** 232

Democracy and Other Addresses (Lowell), **Supp. I Part 2:** 407

Democracy and Social Ethics (Addams), **Supp. I Part 1:** 8–11

Democracy in America (Tocqueville), **Retro. Supp. I:** 235; **Supp. XIV:** 306

Democratic Vistas (Whitman), **IV:** 333, 336, 348–349, 351, 469; **Retro. Supp. I:** 408; **Supp. I Part 2:** 456

Democritus, **I:** 480–481; **II:** 157; **III:** 606; **Retro. Supp. I:** 247

"Demon Lover, The" (Rich), **Supp. I Part 2:** 556

"Demonstrators, The" (Welty), **IV:** 280; **Retro. Supp. I:** 355

DeMott, Benjamin, **Supp. IV Part 1:** 35; **Supp. V:** 123; **Supp. XIII:** 95; **Supp. XIV: 106**

DeMott, Robert, **Supp. VIII:** 40, 41

Demuth, Charles, **IV:** 404; **Retro. Supp. I:** 412, 430; **Supp. XXI:** 6

"Demystified Zone" (Paley), **Supp. VI:** 227

Denmark Vesey (opera) (Bowles), **Supp. IV Part 1:** 83

Dennett, Daniel, **Supp. XXII:** 265

Denney, Joseph Villiers, **Supp. I Part 2:** 605

Denney, Reuel, **Supp. XII:** 121; **Supp. XXI:** 19

Dennie, Joseph, **II:** 298; **Supp. I Part 1:** 125

Denniston, Dorothy Hamer, **Supp. XI:** 276, 277

"Den of Lions" (Plath), **Retro. Supp. II:** 242

"Dental Assistant, The" (Simpson), **Supp. IX:** 280

Den Uyl, Douglas, **Supp. IV Part 2:** 528, 530

"Deodand, The" (Hecht), **Supp. X:** 65

"Departing" (Cameron), **Supp. XII:** 81

"Departure" (Glück), **Supp. V:** 89

"Departure" (Plath), **Supp. I Part 2:** 537

"Departure, The" (Freneau), **Supp. II Part 1:** 264

"Departure from Hydra, The" (Koch), **Supp. XV:** 180–181

Departures (Justice), **Supp. VII:** 124–127

Departures and Arrivals (Shields), **Supp. VII:** 320, 322

"Depressed by a Book of Bad Poetry, I Walk Toward an Unused Pasture and Invite the Insects to Join Me" (Wright), **Supp. III Part 2:** 600

"Depressed Person, The" (Wallace), **Supp. X:** 309

"Depression Days" (Mora), **Supp. XIII:** 224–225

"Deprived of Unhappiness" (Pickering), **Supp. XXI:** 203

De Puy, John, **Supp. XIII:** 12

D'Erasmo, Stacey, **Supp. IX:** 121

Derby, J. C., **Supp. XVIII:** 4

De Reilhe, Catherine, **Supp. I Part 1:** 202

De Rerum Natura (Lucretius), **II:** 162

"De Rerum Virtute" (Jeffers), **Supp. II Part 2:** 424

De Rioja, Francisco, **Supp. I Part 1:** 166

"Derivative Sport in Tornado Alley" (Wallace), **Supp. X:** 314

Derleth, August, **Supp. I Part 2:** 465, 472

Deronda, Daniel, **II:** 179

Derricotte, Toi, **Supp. XVIII:** 177

Derrida, Jacques, **Supp. IV Part 1:** 45; **Supp. XV:** 215, 224; **Supp. XVI:** 285, 288

Deruddere, Dominique, **Supp. XI:** 173

Der Wilde Jäger (Bürger), **II:** 306

Derzhavin, Gavrila Romanovich, **Supp. VIII:** 27

Desai, Anita, **Supp. XVI:** 156, 157, 158

Désamère (Notley), **Supp. XXII:** 226

De Santis, Christopher, **Retro. Supp. I:** 194

Descartes, René, **I:** 255; **III:** 618–619; **IV:** 133

"Descendant of Solomon and the Queen of Sheba" (Major), **Supp. XXII:** 182

Descendents, The (Glasgow), **II:** 173, 174–175, 176

Descending Figure (Glück), **Supp. V:** 83–84

"Descending Theology: Christ Human" (Karr), **Supp. XI:** 251

"Descending Theology: The Garden" (Karr), **Supp. XI:** 251

"Descent, The" (W. C. Williams), **Retro. Supp. I:** 428, 429

"Descent from the Cross" (Eliot), **Retro. Supp. I:** 57, 58

"Descent in the Maelström, A" (Poe), **Retro. Supp. II:** 274

"Descent into Proselito" (Knowles), **Supp. XII:** 237

"Descent into the Maelström, A" (Poe), **III:** 411, 414, 416, 424

Descent of Alette, The (Notley), **Supp. XXII:** 223, 224, 226, 227, 233–234

Descent of Man (Boyle), **Supp. VIII:** 1, 12–13; **Supp. XX: 17, 18, 20**

"Descent of Man" (Boyle), **Supp. VIII:** 14; **Supp. XX: 18**

Descent of Man, The (Darwin), **Supp. XIV:** 192

Descent of Man, The (Wharton), **IV:** 311; **Retro. Supp. I:** 367

Descent of Man and Other Stories, The (Wharton), **Retro. Supp. I:** 367

Descent of Winter, The (W. C. Williams), **Retro. Supp. I:** 419, 428
De Schloezer, Doris, **III:** 474
"Describers" (Halliday), **Supp. XIX:** 85
"Description" (Doty), **Supp. XI:** 126
"Description of the great Bones dug up at Clavarack on the Banks of Hudsons River A.D. 1705, The" (Taylor), **IV:** 163, 164
"Description without Place" (Stevens), **Retro. Supp. I:** 422
"Desert" (Hughes), **Retro. Supp. I:** 207
"Deserted Cabin" (Haines), **Supp. XII:** 203
Deserted Village, The (Goldsmith), **II:** 304
Desert Is My Mother, The/El desierto es mi madre (Mora), **Supp. XIII:** 214, 221
Desert Music, The (W. C. Williams), **IV:** 422; **Retro. Supp. I:** 428, 429
"Desert Music, The" (W. C. Williams), **Retro. Supp. I:** 428, 429
"Desert Places" (Frost), **II:** 159; **Retro. Supp. I:** 121, 123, 129, 138, 299; **Supp. XIV:** 229
Desert Rose, The (McMurtry), **Supp. V:** 225, 231
Desert Solitaire (Abbey), **Supp. X:** 30; **Supp. XIII: 7–8,** 12; **Supp. XIV:** 177, 179
"Design" (Frost), **II:** 158, 163; **Retro. Supp. I:** 121, 126, 138, 139; **Supp. IX:** 81; **Supp. XVII:** 132; **Supp. XVIII:** 298
"Designated National Park, A" (Ortiz), **Supp. IV Part 2:** 509
"Designs on a Point of View" (Everwine), **Supp. XV:** 76
DeSilva, Bruce, **Supp. XXII:** 205, 206, 217
Des Imagistes (Pound), **II:** 513; **Supp. I Part 1:** 257, 261, 262
Desire (album, Dylan), **Supp. XVIII:** 28
"Desire" (Beattie), **Supp. V:** 29
Desire (Bidart), **Supp. XV: 32–34,** 35
"Desire" (Everwine), **Supp. XV:** 85
"Desire and Denial" (Bronk), **Supp. XXI:** 26
"Désirée's Baby" (Chopin), **Retro. Supp. II:** 64, 65; **Supp. I Part 1:** 213–215
Desire under the Elms (O'Neill), **III:** 387, 390
"Desolate Field, The" (W. C. Williams), **Retro. Supp. I:** 418
"Desolation, A" (Ginsberg), **Supp. II Part 1:** 313
Desolation Angels (Kerouac), **Supp. III Part 1:** 218, 225, 230
"Desolation Is a Delicate Thing" (Wylie), Supp. I Part 2: 729
"Desolation Row" (song, Dylan), **Supp. XVIII:** 30
Despair (Nabokov), **Retro. Supp. I:** 270, 274
Desperate Characters (Fox), **Supp. XX: 91**
"Despisals" (Rukeyser), **Supp. VI:** 282
Des Pres, Terrence, **Supp. X:** 113, 120, 124
"Destiny and the Lieutenant" (McCoy), **Supp. XIII:** 171
"Destruction of Kreshev, The" (Singer), **IV:** 13; **Retro. Supp. II:** 307
Destruction of the European Jews, The (Hilberg), **Supp. V:** 267
"Destruction of the Goetheanum, The" (Salter), **Supp. IX:** 257
"Destruction of the Long Branch, The" (Pinsky), **Supp. VI:** 239, 240, 243–244, 245, 247, 250
Destructive Element, The (Spender), **Retro. Supp. I:** 216
"Detail & Parody for the poem 'Paterson' " (W. C. Williams), **Retro. Supp. I:** 424
Detmold, John, **Supp. I Part 2:** 670
De Tolnay, Charles, **Supp. XXII:** 255
Detour at Night (Endore), **Supp. XVII:** 64
Deuce, The (R. O. Butler), **Supp. XII:** 62, **69–70,** 72
Deus Lo Volt! (Connell), **Supp. XIV:** 80, 81, 95
Deuteronomy (biblical book), **II:** 166
Deutsch, Andre, **Supp. XI:** 297, 301
Deutsch, Babette, **Supp. I Part 1:** 328, 341; **Supp. XV:** 305
Deutsch, Michel, **Supp. IV Part 1:** 104
"Devaluation Blues: Ruminations on Black Families in Crisis" (Coleman), **Supp. XI:** 87
Devane, William, **Supp. XI:** 234
Devasahayam, Madona, **Supp. XXII:** 260
"Development of My Mind and Character, The" (Notley), **Supp. XXII:** 227
"Development of the Literary West" (Chopin), **Retro. Supp. II:** 72
"Development of the Modern English Novel, The" (Lanier), **Supp. I Part 1:** 370–371
DeVeriante (Herbert of Cherbury), **II:** 108
"Devil and Daniel Webster, The" (Benét), **III:** 22; **Supp. XI:** 45–46, 47, 50–51, 52
Devil and Daniel Webster and Other Writings, The (Benét), **Supp. XI:** 48
"Devil and Tom Walker, The" (Irving), **II:** 309–310
Devil At Large, The: Erica Jong on Henry Miller (Jong), **Supp. V:** 115, 131
Devil-Doll, The (film, Browning), **Supp. XVII:** 58–59
Devil Finds Work, The (Baldwin), **Retro. Supp. II:** 14; **Supp. I Part 1:** 48, 52, 66–67
Devil in a Blue Dress (Mosley), **Supp. XIII:** 237, 239
"Devil in Manuscript, The" (Hawthorne), **II:** 226; **Retro. Supp. I:** 150–151
Devil in Paradise, A (H. Miller), **III:** 190
"Devil in the Belfry, The" (Poe), **III:** 425; **Retro. Supp. II:** 273
"Devil Is a Busy Man, The" (Wallace), **Supp. X:** 309
Devil's Dictionary, The (Bierce), **I:** 196, 197, 205, 208, 209, 210
Devil's Stocking, The (Algren), **Supp. IX:** 5, 16
"Devil's Thumb, The" (Krakauer), **Supp. XVIII:** 107
Devil's Tour, The (Karr), **Supp. XI:** 240, **242–244**
Devil Tree, The (Kosinski), **Supp. VII:** 215, 222, 223
"Devising" (Ammons), **Supp. VII:** 28
Devlin, Paul, **Supp. XIX:** 159
De Voto, Bernard, **I:** 247, 248; **II:** 446; **Supp. IV Part 2:** 599, 601
"Devout Meditation in Memory of Adolph Eichmann, A" (Merton), **Supp. VIII:** 198, 203
De Vries, Peter, **Supp. I Part 2:** 604
Dewberry, Elizabeth, **Supp. XII:** 62, 72
Dewey, John, **I:** 214, 224, 228, 232, 233, 266, 267; **II:** 20, 27, 34, 229, 361; **III:** 112, 294–295, 296, 303, 309–310, 599, 605; **IV:** 27, 429; **Supp. I Part 1:** 3, 5, 7, 10, 11, 12, 24; **Supp. I Part 2:** 493, 641, 647, 677; **Supp. V:** 290; **Supp. IX:** 179; **Supp. XIV:** 3; **Supp. XV:** 41
Dewey, Joseph, **Supp. IX:** 210
Dewey, Thomas, **IV:** 161
Dewey Defeats Truman (Mallon), **Supp. XIX:** 132, 137, **138**
Dexter, Peter, **Supp. XIV:** 221
De Young, Charles, **I:** 194
Dhairyam, Sagari, **Supp. IV Part 1:** 329, 330
Dharma Bums, The (Kerouac), **Supp. III Part 1:** 230, 231; **Supp. VIII:** 289, 305
"D. H. Lawrence" (Bynner), **Supp. XV:** 46
D. H. Lawrence: An Unprofessional Study (Nin), **Supp. X:** 182–183
D. H. Lawrence: The World of the Major Novels (Sanders), **Supp. XVI:** 267
D'Houdetot, Madame, **Supp. I Part 1:** 250
"Diabetes" (Dickey), **Supp. IV Part 1:** 182
Diaghilev, Sergei, **Supp. I Part 1:** 257
Dial (publication), **I:** 58, 109, 115, 116, 215, 231, 233, 245, 261, 384, 429; **II:** 8, 430; **III:** 194, 470, 471, 485; **IV:** 122, 171, 427; **Retro. Supp. I:** 58; **Retro. Supp. II:** 78; **Supp. I Part 2:** 642, 643, 647; **Supp. II Part 1:** 168, 279, 291; **Supp. II Part 2:** 474; **Supp. III Part 2:** 611
"Dialectical Materialism" (Weigl), **Supp. XIX:** 281
Dialectical Materialism and the Fate of Humanity (C. L. R. James), **Supp. XXI:** 169
"Dialectics of Love, The" (McGrath), **Supp. X:** 116
"Dialogue" (Rich), **Supp. I Part 2:** 560
Dialogue, A (Baldwin and Giovanni), **Supp. I Part 1:** 66
"Dialogue Between Franklin and the Gout" (Franklin), **II:** 121
"Dialogue Between General Wolfe and General Gage in a Wood near Boston, A" (Paine), **Supp. I Part 2:** 504

"Dialogue between Old England and New" (Bradstreet), **Supp. I Part 1:** 105–106, 110–111, 116

"Dialogue between the Writer and a Maypole Dresser, A" (Taylor), **IV:** 155

Dialogues (Bush, ed.), **III:** 4

Dialogues in Limbo (Santayana), **III:** 606

"Dialogue: William Harvey; Joan of Arc" (Goldbarth), **Supp. XII:** 178

Dialogue with a Dead Man (J. W. Miller), **Supp. XX: 163, 164, 167**

"Diamond as Big as the Ritz, The" (Fitzgerald), **II:** 88–89

Diamond Cutters and Other Poems, The (Rich), **Supp. I Part 2:** 551, 552, 553

"Diamond Guitar, A" (Capote), **Supp. III Part 1:** 124

Diamond Necklace, A (Notley), **Supp. XXII:** 228

"Diana and Persis" (Alcott), **Supp. I Part 1:** 32, 41

"Diaper Brigade, The" (Ryan as Quin), **Supp. XVIII:** 230

Diaries of Charlotte Perkins Gilman (Knight, ed.), **Supp. XI:** 201

"Diary–1903" (Boyce), **Supp. XXI:** 8

Diary of a Chambermaid, The (film; Renoir), **Supp. XVI:** 193

Diary of Anaïs Nin, The (1931–1974), **Supp. X:** 181, 185–189, 191, 192, 193, 195

Diary of Anne Frank, The, **Supp. XXI:** 245

Diary of a Rapist, The: A Novel (Connell), **Supp. XIV:** 80, 82, 94

Diary of a Yuppie (Auchincloss), **Supp. IV Part 1:** 31, 32–33

Diary of "Helena Morley", The (Bishop, trans.), **Retro. Supp. II:** 45, 51; **Supp. I Part 1:** 92

Dias, Robert Vas, **Supp. XXII:** 164, 169

Díaz del Castillo, Bernál, **III:** 13, 14

Dick, Philip K., **Supp. XVI:** 123; **Supp. XVIII:** 136, 137, 138, 139, 142; **Supp. XXII:** 49

Dickens, Charles, **I:** 152, 198, 505; **II:** 98, 179, 186, 192, 271, 273–274, 288, 290, 297, 301, 307, 316, 322, 559, 561, 563, 577, 582; **III:** 146, 247, 325, 368, 411, 421, 426, 572, 577, 613–614, 616; **IV:** 21, 192, 194, 211, 429; **Retro. Supp. I:** 33, 91, 218; **Retro. Supp. II:** 204; **Supp. I Part 1:** 13, 34, 35, 36, 41, 49; **Supp. I Part 2:** 409, 523, 579, 590, 622, 675; **Supp. IV Part 1:** 293, 300, 341; **Supp. IV Part 2:** 464; **Supp. VIII:** 180; **Supp. IX:** 246; **Supp. XI:** 277; **Supp. XII:** 335, 337; **Supp. XIII:** 233; **Supp. XV:** 62; **Supp. XVI:** 63, 65–66, 72–73, 202; **Supp. XVIII:** 7, 136, 146; **Supp. XX: 21, 87, 195; Supp. XXII:** 206

Dickey, James, **I:** 29, 535; **III:** 268; **Retro. Supp. II:** 233; **Supp. III Part 1:** 354; **Supp. III Part 2:** 541, 597; **Supp. IV Part 1: 175–194; Supp. V:** 333; **Supp. X:** 30; **Supp. XI:** 312, 317; **Supp. XV:** 115, 348; **Supp. XVIII:** 191, 299; **Supp. XIX:** 282; **Supp. XXI:** 35

Dick Gibson Show, The (Elkin), **Supp. VI:** 42, **48–49**

Dickie, Margaret, **Retro. Supp. II:** 53, 84

Dickinson, Donald, **Retro. Supp. I:** 206, 212

Dickinson, Edward, **I:** 451–452, 453

Dickinson, Mrs. Edward, **I:** 451, 453

Dickinson, Emily, **I:** 384, 419, 433, **451–473; II:** 272, 276, 277, 530; **III:** 19, 194, 196, 214, 493, 505, 508, 556, 572, 576; **IV:** 134, 135, 331, 444; **Retro. Supp. I: 25–50; Retro. Supp. II:** 39, 40, 43, 45, 50, 76, 134, 155, 170; **Supp. I Part 1:** 29, 79, 188, 372; **Supp. I Part 2:** 375, 546, 609, 682, 691; **Supp. II Part 1:** 4; **Supp. III Part 1:** 63; **Supp. III Part 2:** 600, 622; **Supp. IV Part 1:** 31, 257; **Supp. IV Part 2:** 434, 637, 641, 643; **Supp. V:** 79, 140, 332, 335; **Supp. VIII:** 95, 104, 106, 108, 198, 205, 272; **Supp. IX:** 37, 38, 53, 87, 90; **Supp. XII:** 226; **Supp. XIII:** 153, 339; **Supp. XIV:** 45, 127–128, 133, 261, 284; **Supp. XV:** 287, 303, 309; **Supp. XVI:** 288; **Supp. XVII:** 71, 73, 74, 75, 132; **Supp. XVIII:** 301; **Supp. XIX:** 86; **Supp. XX: 106, 108; Supp. XXI:** 52, 61, 64, 132, 214; **Supp. XXII:** 81, 82, 225, 277–278

Dickinson, Gilbert, **I:** 469

Dickinson, Goldsworthy Lowes, **Supp. XIV:** 336

Dickinson, Lavinia Norcross, **I:** 451, 453, 462, 470

Dickinson, Mrs. William A. (Susan Gilbert), **I:** 452, 453, 456, 469, 470

Dickinson, William Austin, **I:** 451, 453, 469

Dickinson and the Strategies of Reticence (Dobson), **Retro. Supp. I:** 29, 42

Dickson, Helen. *See* Blackmur, Helen Dickson

Dickstein, Morris, **Supp. XIII:** 106

"Dick Whittington and His Cat", **Supp. I Part 2:** 656

"DICTATORSHIP OF THE PROLETARIAT, THE" (Baraka), **Supp. II Part 1:** 54

Dictionary of Afro-American Slang (Major), **Supp. XXII:** 172, 174, 180

Dictionary of Literary Biography (Barron and Meyer, eds.), **Supp. XVIII:** 173; **Supp. XIX:** 195

Dictionary of Literary Biography (Gwynn, ed.), **Supp. XVIII:** 173; **Supp. XIX:** 121

Dictionary of Literary Biography (Kibler, ed.), **Supp. IX:** 94, 109; **Supp. XI:** 297

Dictionary of Literary Biography (Knight, ed.), **Supp. XIV:** 144

Dictionary of Literary Biography (Martine, ed.), **Supp. XXII:** 187

Dictionary of Literary Biography (Sicher, ed.), **Supp. XVII:** 41

Dictionary of Modern English Usage, A (Fowler), **Supp. I Part 2:** 660

"Dictum: For a Masque of Deluge" (Merwin), **Supp. III Part 1:** 342–343

"Didactic Poem" (Levertov), **Supp. III Part 1:** 280

Diderot, Denis, **II:** 535; **IV:** 440; **Supp. XVI:** 293; **Supp. XVII:** 145

Did I Ever Tell You How Lucky You Are? (Geisel), **Supp. XVI:** 109

Didion, Joan, **Retro. Supp. I:** 116; **Retro. Supp. II:** 209; **Supp. I Part 1:** 196, 197; **Supp. III Part 1:** 302; **Supp. IV Part 1: 195–216; Supp. XI:** 221; **Supp. XII:** 307

Dido, **I:** 81

Di Donato, Peter, **Supp. XX: 34**

Di Donato, Pietro, **Supp. XX: 33–47**

"Did 'Paco's Story' Deserve Its Award" (Kakutani), **Supp. XXII:** 109

"Did You Ever Dream Lucky?" (Ellison), **Supp. II Part 1:** 246

"Die-Hard, The" (Benét), **Supp. XI:** 54–55, 56

Diehl, Digby, **Supp. IV Part 1:** 204

Dien Cai Dau (Komunyakaa), **Supp. XIII:** 121, **122–124,** 125, 131, 132

Dies, Martin, **Supp. XVIII:** 229

"Dies Irae" (Lowell), **II:** 553

Die Zeit Ohne Beispiel, (Goebbels), **III:** 560

Difference Engine, The (W. Gibson and B. Sterling), **Supp. XVI:** 121, 124, **128–129**

Different Drummer, A (Larkin; film), **Supp. XI:** 20

Different Fleshes (Goldbarth), **Supp. XII:** 181–182, 188

Different Hours (Dunn), **Supp. XI:** 139, 142, 143, 155

Different Seasons (King), **Supp. V:** 148, 152

Different Ways to Pray (Nye), **Supp. XIII:** 274, 275, 277, 285, 287

"Different Ways to Pray" (Nye), **Supp. XIII:** 275

"Difficulties of a Statesman" (Eliot), **I:** 580

"Difficulties of Modernism and the Modernism of Difficulty" (Poirier), **Supp. II Part 1:** 136

Diff'rent (O'Neill), **III:** 389; **Supp. XXII:** 22

Di Filippo, Paul, **Supp. XXII:** 260, 261

DiGaetani, John L., **Supp. XIII:** 200

"Digging" (Sanders), **Supp. XVI:** 272

"Digging in the Garden of Age I Uncover a Live Root" (Swenson), **Supp. IV Part 2:** 649

Diggins, John P., **Supp. I Part 2:** 650

"Dignity of Life, The" (C. Bly), **Supp. XVI:** 34, 36–37

Digregorio, Charles, **Supp. XI:** 326

"Dilemma" (Budbill), **Supp. XIX:** 2

"Dilemma of Determinism, The" (James), **II:** 347–348, 352

"Dilemma of the Negro Writer, The" (speech, C. Himes), **Supp. XVI:** 140

"Dilettante, The" (Wharton), **IV:** 311, 313

"Dilettante, The: A Modern Type" (Dunbar), **Supp. II Part 1:** 199

Dillard, Annie, **Supp. VI: 19–39; Supp. VIII:** 272; **Supp. X:** 31; **Supp. XIII:** 154
Dillard, R. H. W., **Supp. XII:** 16
Dillman, Bradford, **III:** 403; **Supp. XII:** 241
Dillon, Brian, **Supp. X:** 209
Dillon, George, **III:** 141; **Supp. III Part 2:** 621
Dillon, Millicent, **Supp. IV Part 1:** 95
Dilsaver, Paul, **Supp. XIII:** 112
Dilthey, Wilhelm, **I:** 58
Dime-Store Alchemy: The Art of Joseph Cornell, **Supp. VIII:** 272
"Diminuendo" (Dunn), **Supp. XI:** 152–153
"Dimout in Harlem" (Hughes), **Supp. I Part 1:** 333
"Dinah's Lament" (Nelson), **Supp. XVIII:** 183
Dinesen, Isak, **IV:** 279; **Supp. VIII:** 171; **Supp. XVI:** 250
Dining Room, The (Gurney), **Supp. V:** 105–106
"Dinner at ------, A" (O. Henry), **Supp. II Part 1:** 402
"Dinner at Sir Nigel's" (Bowles), **Supp. IV Part 1:** 94
Dinner at the Homesick Restaurant (Tyler), **Supp. IV Part 2:** 657, 667–668
"Dinner at Uncle Borris's" (Simic), **Supp. VIII:** 272
Dinner Bridge (Lardner), **II:** 435
Dinosaur Tales (Bradbury), **Supp. IV Part 1:** 103
"Diogenes Invents a Game" (Karr), **Supp. XI:** 240–241
"Diogenes Tries to Forget" (Karr), **Supp. XI:** 241
Diomede, Matthew, **Supp. XX: 46**
Dionysis in Doubt (Robinson), **III:** 510
Diop, Birago, **Supp. IV Part 1:** 16
Diop, David, **Supp. IV Part 1:** 16
Di Piero, W. S., **Supp. XVII:** 241; **Supp. XIX: 33–48**
Di Prima, Diane, **Supp. III Part 1:** 30; **Supp. XIV:** 125, 144, 148, 150
Dirda, Michael, **Supp. XXI:** 233
Direction of Poetry, The: An Anthology of Rhymed and Metered Verse Written in the English Language since 1975 (Richman, ed.), **Supp. XV:** 250, 251
Direction of Poetry, The: Rhymed and Metered Verse Written in the English Language since 1975 (Richman), **Supp. XI:** 249
"Directive" (Bishop), **Retro. Supp. II:** 42
"Directive" (Frost), **III:** 287; **Retro. Supp. I:** 140; **Supp. VIII:** 32, 33
"Dire Cure" (Matthews), **Supp. IX:** 168
"Dirge" (Dunbar), **Supp. II Part 1:** 199
"Dirge without Music" (Millay), **III:** 126
"Dirt" (Salter), **Supp. IX:** 257, 260, 261
"Dirt and Desire: Essay on the Phenomenology of Female Pollution in Antiquity" (Carson), **Supp. XII: 111**
Dirty Bird Blues (Major), **Supp. XXII: 180–181**
Dirty Dingus Magee (film), **Supp. XVII:** 139
"Dirty English Potatoes" (X. J. Kennedy), **Supp. XV:** 165
"Dirty Memories" (Olds), **Supp. X:** 211
Dirty Story (Shanley), **Supp. XIV:** 316, 331
"Dirty Word, The" (Shapiro), **Supp. II Part 2:** 710
Dirty Work (L. Brown), **Supp. XXI:** 37, 39, 40, 42, **45**
Disappearance of the Jews, The (Mamet), **Supp. XIV:** 249–250, 250–251, 252, 254
Disappearances (Auster), **Supp. XII:** 23
"Disappearances" (Hogan), **Supp. IV Part 1:** 401
Disappearances (Mosher), **Supp. XXII:** 204, 205, 206, 207, 208, 209, **210**
"Disappeared, The " (C. Baxter), **Supp. XVII:** 19
Disappearing Acts (McMillan), **Supp. XIII:** 182, 183, **188–189,** 192
Disappearing Ink: Poetry at the End of Print Culture (Gioia), **Supp. XV:** 112
"Disappointment, The" (Creeley), **Supp. IV Part 1:** 143
"Disappointment and Desire" (R. Bly), **Supp. IV Part 1:** 71
Disappointment Artist, The (Lethem), **Supp. XVIII:** 135, 141, **148**
"Discards" (Baker), **Supp. XIII:** 53, 55–56
Discerning the Signs of the Times (Niebuhr), **III:** 300–301, 307–308
Disch, Thomas M., **Supp. XIX:** 1
"Disciple of Bacon, The" (Epstein), **Supp. XII:** 163–164
"Discipline" (L. Brown), **Supp. XXI:** 44
Discomfort, Zone, The: A Personal History (Franzen), **Supp. XX: 83, 84, 95**
"Discordants" (Aiken), **I:** 65
Discourse on Method (Descartes), **I:** 255
"Discourtesies" (Kirsch), **Supp. XV:** 341
"Discovering Theme and Structure in the Novel" (Schuster), **Supp. VIII:** 126
"Discovery" (Freneau), **Supp. II Part 1:** 258
"Discovery of the Madeiras, The" (Frost), **Retro. Supp. I:** 139
"Discovery of What It Means to Be an American, The" (Baldwin), **Supp. I Part 1:** 54–55
Discovery! The Search for Arabian Oil (Stegner), **Supp. IV Part 2:** 599
"Discrete Series" (Zukofsky), **Supp. III Part 2:** 616
"Discretions of Alcibiades" (Pinsky), **Supp. VI:** 241
"Disease, The" (Rukeyser), **Supp. VI:** 279
Disenchanted, The (play, Schulberg and Breit), **Supp. XVIII:** 254
Disenchanted, The (Schulberg), **II:** 98; **Retro. Supp. I:** 113; **Supp. XVIII: 247–250,** 253
Disenchantments: An Anthology of Modern Fairy Tale Poetry (Mieder), **Supp. XIV:** 126
"Dish of Green Pears, A" (Ríos), **Supp. IV Part 2:** 552
"Disillusion and Dogma" (Untermeyer), **Supp. XV:** 306
Dismantling the Silence (Simic), **Supp. VIII: 273–274,** 275, 276
Disney, Walt, **III:** 275, 426
"Disney of My Mind" (Chabon), **Supp. XI:** 63
Disobedience (Notley), **Supp. XXII:** 235, 236
Dispatches (Herr), **Supp. XI:** 245; **Supp. XIX:** 17
"Displaced Person, The" (O'Connor), **III:** 343–344, 350, 352, 356; **Retro. Supp. II:** 229, 232, 236
"Disposal" (Snodgrass), **Supp. VI:** 314
Dispossessed, The (Berryman), **I:** 170, 172, 173, 174, 175, 176, 178
"Disquieting Muses, The" (Plath), **Supp. I Part 2:** 538
Disraeli, Benjamin, **II:** 127
Dissent (Didion), **Supp. IV Part 1:** 208
"Dissent in Ashcroft's America" (P. N. Warren), **Supp. XX: 273**
"Dissenting Opinion on Kafka, A" (Wilson), **IV:** 437–438
Dissent in Three American Wars (Morison, Merk, and Freidel), **Supp. I Part 2:** 495
Dissertation on Liberty and Necessity, Pleasure and Pain, A (Franklin), **II:** 108
Dissertations on Government; the Affairs of the Bank: and Paper Money (Paine), **Supp. I Part 2:** 510
"Distance" (Carver), **Supp. III Part 1:** 146
"Distance" (Everwine), **Supp. XV:** 85
"Distance" (Paley), **Supp. VI:** 222
"Distance, The" (Karr), **Supp. XI:** 241
"Distance from the Sea, A" (Kees), **Supp. XV:** 147
"Distance Nowhere" (Hughes), **Retro. Supp. I:** 207
"Distance Up Close, The" (Peacock), **Supp. XIX:** 196–197, 198
"Distant Episode, A" (Bowles), **Supp. IV Part 1:** 84–85, 86, 90
Distant Episode, A: The Selected Stories (Bowles), **Supp. IV Part 1:** 79
Distinguished Guest, The (Miller), **Supp. XII: 299–301**
Distortions (Beattie), **Supp. V:** 21, 23, 24, 25, 27
"Distrest Shepherdess, The" (Freneau), **Supp. II Part 1:** 258
District of Columbia (Dos Passos), **I:** 478, 489–490, 492
Disturber of the Peace (Manchester), **III:** 103
Disturbing the Peace (Yates), **Supp. XI:** 345, 346
"Diver, The" (Hayden), **Supp. II Part 1:** 368, 372, 373
"Divided Life of Jean Toomer, The" (Toomer), **Supp. III Part 2:** 488
Divided Self, The (Laing), **Supp. XX: 95**
Divina Commedia (Longfellow, trans.), **II:** 490, 492, 493

"Divina Pastora, La" (C. L. R. James), **Supp. XXI:** 160
"Divine, The" (Di Piero), **Supp. XIX:** 41
"Divine Collaborator" (Simic), **Supp. VIII:** 282
Divine Comedies (Merrill), **Supp. III Part 1:** 324, 329–332
Divine Comedy (Dante), **I:** 137, 265, 400, 446; **II:** 215, 335, 490, 492, 493; **III:** 13, 448, 453; **Supp. V:** 283, 331, 338, 345; **Supp. X:** 253; **Supp. XIV:** 6; **Supp. XIX:** 36, 39
"Divine Image, The" (Blake), **Supp. V:** 257
Divine Pilgrim, The (Aiken), **I:** 50, 55
Divine Tragedy, The (Longfellow), **II:** 490, 500, 505, 506, 507; **Retro. Supp. II:** 165, 166
Divine Weekes and Workes (Sylvester, trans.), **Supp. I Part 1:** 104
Divine Weeks (Du Bartas), **IV:** 157–158
Diving into the Wreck: Poems 1971–1972 (Rich), **Supp. I Part 2:** 550, 559–565, 569; **Supp. XV:** 252
"Diving Past African Violets" (A. Finch), **Supp. XVII:** 72
Diving Rock on the Hudson, A (H. Roth), **Supp. IX:** 236, **237–238**
"Divinity in Its Fraying Fact, A" (Levis), **Supp. XI:** 271
"Divinity School Address" (Emerson), **II:** 12–13
"Divisions upon a Ground" (Hecht), **Supp. X:** 58
"Divorce" (Karr), **Supp. XI:** 244
"Divorced Fathers and Pizza Crusts" (Halliday), **Supp. XIX:** 93
Divorced in America: Marriage in an Age of Possibility (Epstein), **Supp. XIV:** 113
"Divorce Dream" (Halliday), **Supp. XIX:** 90
Dix, Douglas Shields, **Supp. XII:** 14
Dixie City Jam (Burke), **Supp. XIV:** 32
Dixon, Ivan, **Supp. IV Part 1:** 362
Dixon, Stephen, **Supp. XII: 139–158**
Dixon, Terrell F., **Supp. XVI:** 21
Dixon, Thomas, Jr., **Supp. II Part 1:** 169, 171, 177
Djinn (Robbe-Grillet), **Supp. V:** 48
D'Lugoff, Burt, **Supp. IV Part 1:** 362, 370
Dmytryk, Edward, **Supp. XX: 41**
Do, Lord, Remember Me (Garrett), **Supp. VII:** 98–100, 110
"Doaksology, The" (Wolfe), **IV:** 459
Do Androids Dream of Electric Sheep? (Dick), **Supp. XVIII:** 137
Dobie, J. Frank, **Supp. V:** 225; **Supp. XIII:** 227
Döblin, Alfred, **Supp. XV:** 137
Dobriansky, Lev, **Supp. I Part 2:** 648, 650
Dobrin, Sidney I., **Supp. XVIII:** 192, 195
Dobson, Joanne, **Retro. Supp. I:** 29, 31, 42; **Supp. XVIII:** 259
Dobyns, Stephen, **Supp. XIII: 73–92**
"Docking at Palermo" (Hugo), **Supp. VI:** 137–138
"Dock Rats" (Moore), **III:** 213
"Dock-Witch, The" (Ozick), **Supp. V:** 262, 264
"Doc Mellhorn and the Pearly Gates" (Benét), **Supp. XI:** 55
"Doctor, The" (Dubus), **Supp. VII:** 80–81
"Doctor and the Doctor's Wife, The" (Hemingway), **II:** 248; **Retro. Supp. I:** 174, 175
Doctor Breen's Practice, a Novel (Howells), **I:** 282
Doctor Faustus (Mann), **III:** 283
Doctor Jazz (Carruth), **Supp. XVI:** 47, 59
"Doctor Jekyll" (Sontag), **Supp. III Part 2:** 469
"Doctor Leavis and the Moral Tradition" (Trilling), **Supp. III Part 2:** 512–513
Doctor Martino and Other Stories (Faulkner), **II:** 72; **Retro. Supp. I:** 84
"Doctor of the Heart, The" (Sexton), **Supp. II Part 2:** 692
Doctorow, E. L., **Retro. Supp. I:** 97; **Supp. III Part 2:** 590, 591; **Supp. IV Part 1: 217–240; Supp. V:** 45; **Supp. XVI:** 73; **Supp. XVII:** 183; **Supp. XX: 84, 90; Supp. XXI:** 18–19; **Supp. XXII:** 268
Doctor Sax (Kerouac), **Supp. III Part 1:** 220–222, 224–227
Doctor Sleep (Bell), **Supp. X: 9–11**
"Doctors' Row" (Aiken), **I:** 67
Doctor's Son and Other Stories, The (O'Hara), **III:** 361
Doctor Stories, The (W. C. Williams), **Retro. Supp. I:** 424
"Doctor's Wife, The" (Ozick), **Supp. V:** 262, 265
Doctor Zhivago (Pasternak), **IV:** 434, 438, 443
"Documentary" (Simic), **Supp. VIII:** 282
Dodd, Elizabeth, **Supp. V:** 77
Dodd, Wayne, **Supp. IV Part 2:** 625
Dodge, Mabel, **Supp. XX: 69; Supp. XXI:** 5, 6, 8, 12; **Supp. XXII:** 158, 161. *See also* Luhan, Mabel Dodge
Dodson, Owen, **Supp. I Part 1:** 54
Dodsworth (Lewis), **II:** 442, 449–450, 453, 456
Doenitz, Karl, **Supp. I Part 2:** 491
Does Civilization Need Religion? (Niebuhr), **III:** 293–294
"Does 'Consciousness' Exist?" (James), **II:** 356
"Does Education Pay?" (Du Bois), **Supp. II Part 1:** 159
"Dog" (B. Kelly), **Supp. XVII:** 126
Dog (Shepard), **Supp. III Part 2:** 434
"Dog Act, The" (Komunyakaa), **Supp. XIII:** 114–115
"Dog and the Playlet, The" (O. Henry), **Supp. II Part 1:** 399
Dog Beneath the Skin, The (Auden), **Supp. II Part 1:** 10
"Dog Creek Mainline" (Wright), **Supp. V:** 340
"Dogfight" (W. Gibson and Swanwick), **Supp. XVI:** 128
Dog in the Manger, The (Vega; Merwin, trans.), **Supp. III Part 1:** 341, 347
Dog of the Marriage, The (Hempel), **Supp. XXI:** 115, 116, 117, 118, **126–127**
Dogs Bark, but the Caravan Rolls On (Conroy), **Supp. XVI:** 63, 70, 74, **75–76**
Dogs Bark, The: Public People and Private Places (Capote), **Supp. III Part 1:** 120, 132
"Dog's Eye" (J. W. Miller), **Supp. XX: 167**
Dog Soldiers (Stone), **Supp. V:** 298, 299–301
Dog Star, The (Di Piero), **Supp. XIX:** 38, **40–41,** 43
"Dog Stories" (Prose), **Supp. XVI:** 256
Dog & the Fever, The (Quevedo), **Retro. Supp. I:** 423
"Dogtown Letters, The" (Jarman and R. McDowell), **Supp. XVII:** 111
"Dogwood, The" (Levertov), **Supp. III Part 1:** 276
"Dogwood Tree, The: A Boyhood" (Updike), **IV:** 218; **Retro. Supp. I:** 318, 319
Doig, Ivan, **Supp. XIV:** 227
"Doing Battle with the Wolf" (Coleman), **Supp. XI:** 87–88
Doing Literary Business: American Women Writers in the Nineteenth Century (Coultrap-McQuin), **Supp. XVI:** 85
Doings and Undoings (Podhoretz), **Supp. VIII: 236–237**
"Do-It-Yourself" (C. Baxter), **Supp. XVII:** 14–15
Dolan, Jill, **Supp. XV:** 327
Dolben, Digby Mackworth, **Supp. XX: 230**
"Dolce Far' Niente" (Humphrey), **Supp. IX:** 106
Dolci, Carlo, **III:** 474–475
Dollars and Cents (A. Warner), **Supp. XVIII:** 264
"Dollhouse, The" (Haines), **Supp. XII:** 204
Dollmaker's Ghost, The (Levis), **Supp. XI:** 259, 260, **264–268**
Doll's House, A (Ibsen), **III:** 523; **IV:** 357; **Supp. XVI:** 182
Dolmetsch, Arnold, **III:** 464
Dolores Claiborne (King), **Supp. V:** 138, 141, 147, 148, 149–150, 152
"Dolph Heyliger" (Irving), **II:** 309
Dolphin, The (Lowell), **Retro. Supp. II:** 183, 186, 188, **190–191; Supp. XII:** 253–254
"Dolphins" (Francis), **Supp. IX:** 83
Dome of Many-Coloured Class, A (Lowell), **II:** 515, 516–517
Domesday Book (Masters), **Supp. I Part 2:** 465, 466–469, 471, 473, 476
"Domestic Economy" (Gilman), **Supp. XI:** 206
"Domestic Manners" (Hardwick), **Supp. III Part 1:** 211
Domestic Work (Trethewey), **Supp. XXI:** 243, 244, **248–251,** 254
"Domestic Work, 1937" (Trethewey), **Supp. XXI:** 248

"Dominant White, The" (McKay), **Supp. X:** 134
Dominguez, Robert, **Supp. VIII:** 83
Domini, John, **Supp. XIX:** 45; **Supp. XXI:** 235
Dominique, Jean. *See* Closset, Marie
Donahoe, Edward, **Supp. XVIII:** 132
Donahue, Phil, **Supp. IV Part 2:** 526; **Supp. X:** 311
Donaldson, Susan, **Supp. XXII:** 148
Doña Perfecta (Galdós), **II:** 290
Dong, Stella, **Supp. XVI:** 222
Don Juan (Byron), **Supp. XV:** 259
"DON JUAN IN HELL" (Baraka), **Supp. II Part 1:** 33
Donkey of God, The (Untermeyer), **Supp. XV:** 310
"Donna mi Prega" (Cavalcanti), **Supp. III Part 2:** 620, 621, 622
Donn-Byrne, Brian Oswald. *See* Byrne, Donn
Donne, John, **I:** 358–359, 384, 389, 522, 586; **II:** 254; **III:** 493; **IV:** 83, 88, 135, 141, 144, 145, 151, 156, 165, 331, 333; **Retro. Supp. II:** 76; **Supp. I Part 1:** 80, 364, 367; **Supp. I Part 2:** 421, 424, 467, 725, 726; **Supp. III Part 2:** 614, 619; **Supp. VIII:** 26, 33, 164; **Supp. IX:** 44; **Supp. XII:** 45, 159; **Supp. XIII:** 94, 130; **Supp. XIV:** 122; **Supp. XV:** 92, 251; **Supp. XVI:** 158, 204; **Supp. XVIII:** 35, 39, 50–51, 307
Donne's Sermons: Selected Passages (L. P. Smith, ed.), **Supp. XIV:** 342
Donoghue, Denis, **I:** 537; **Supp. IV Part 1:** 39; **Supp. VIII:** 105, 189
Donohue, H. E. F., **Supp. IX:** 2, 3, 15, 16
"Do Not Weep Maiden, For War Is Kind" (Crane), **Supp. XVIII:** 75
Donovan, Josephine, **Retro. Supp. II:** 138, 139, 147
Don Quixote (Cervantes), **I:** 134; **II:** 291, 434; **III:** 113, 614; **Supp. I Part 2:** 422; **Supp. IX:** 94
Don Quixote: Which Was a Dream (Acker), **Supp. XII:** 5, **12–14**
Don't Ask (Levine), **Supp. V:** 178
Don't Ask Questions (Marquand), **III:** 58
Don't Bet on the Prince: Contemporary Feminist Fairy Tales in North America and England (Zipes), **Supp. XIV:** 126
Don't Drink the Water (Allen), **Supp. XV:** 3, **14**
Don't Look Back (film, Pennebaker), **Supp. XVIII:** 19
"Don't Shoot the Warthog" (Corso), **Supp. XII:** 123
"Don't Tell Mother" (Wasserstein), **Supp. XV:** 319
"Don't Think Twice, It's All Right" (song, Dylan), **Supp. XVIII:** 24
Don't Worry About the Kids (Neugeboren), **Supp. XVI:** 226
"Don't Worry About the Kids" (Neugeboren), **Supp. XVI:** 226
Don't You Want to Be Free? (Hughes), **Retro. Supp. I:** 203; **Supp. I Part 1:** 339
"Doodler, The" (Merrill), **Supp. III Part 1:** 321
Doolan, Moira, **Retro. Supp. II:** 247
Doolittle, Hilda (H. D.), **II:** 517, 520–521; **III:** 194, 195–196, 457, 465; **IV:** 404, 406; **Retro. Supp. I:** 288, 412, 413, 414, 415, 417; **Supp. I Part 1: 253–275; Supp. I Part 2:** 707; **Supp. III Part 1:** 48; **Supp. III Part 2:** 610; **Supp. IV Part 1:** 257; **Supp. V:** 79; **Supp. XV:** 43, 249, 301, 302; **Supp. XVII:** 77; **Supp. XXII:** 88
Doolittle, Thomas, **IV:** 150
"Doomed by Our Blood to Care" (Orfalea), **Supp. XIII:** 278
"Doomsday" (Plath), **Retro. Supp. II:** 242
Doomsters, The (Macdonald), **Supp. IV Part 2:** 462, 463, 472, 473
"Door, The" (Creeley), **Supp. IV Part 1:** 145, 146, 156–157
"Door, The" (White), **Supp. I Part 2:** 651, 675–676
"Door in the Dark, The" (Frost), **II:** 156
Door in the Hive, A (Levertov), **Supp. III Part 1:** 283, 284
"Door of the Trap, The" (Anderson), **I:** 112
Doors (Hoffman), **Supp. XVIII:** 86–87
"Doors" (Hoffman), **Supp. XVIII:** 86–87
"Doors, Doors, Doors" (Sexton), **Supp. II Part 2:** 681
Doors, The, **Supp. X:** 186
"Doorways into the Depths" (Sanders), **Supp. XVI:** 272
Doreski, William, **Retro. Supp. II:** 185
Dorfman, Ariel, **Supp. IX:** 131, 138
Dorfman, Joseph, **Supp. I Part 2:** 631, 647, 650
Dorman, Jen, **Supp. XI:** 240
Dorn, Edward, **Supp. IV Part 1:** 154
Dorn, Sarah, **Supp. XXI:** 243
"Dorothea Dix, Samaritan" (J. Scott), **Supp. XVII:** 189
Dorr, Julia, **Supp. XV:** 286
Dorris, Michael, **Supp. IV Part 1:** 260, 272
Dos Passos, John, **I:** 99, 288, 374, 379, **474–496,** 517, 519; **II:** 74, 77, 89, 98; **III:** 2, 28, 29, 70, 172, 382–383; **IV:** 340, 427, 433; **Retro. Supp. I:** 105, 113, 187; **Retro. Supp. II:** 95, 196; **Supp. I Part 2:** 646; **Supp. III Part 1:** 104, 105; **Supp. V:** 277; **Supp. VIII:** 101, 105; **Supp. XIV:** 24; **Supp. XV:** 135, 137, 182; **Supp. XVII:** 105, 107; **Supp. XXI:** 8
"Dos Passos: Poet Against the World" (Cowley), **Supp. II Part 1:** 143, 145
Dostoevsky, Fyodor, **I:** 53, 103, 211, 468; **II:** 60, 130, 275, 320, 587; **III:** 37, 61, 155, 174, 176, 188, 189, 267, 272, 283, 286, 354, 357, 358, 359, 467, 571, 572; **IV:** 1, 7, 8, 17, 21, 50, 59, 106, 110, 128, 134, 285, 289, 476, 485, 491; **Retro. Supp. II:** 20, 204, 299; **Supp. I Part 1:** 49; **Supp. I Part 2:** 445, 466; **Supp. IV Part 2:** 519, 525; **Supp. VIII:** 175; **Supp. X:** 4–5; **Supp. XI:** 161; **Supp. XII:** 322; **Supp. XVI:** 63; **Supp. XVII:** 225; **Supp. XVIII:** 278, 280; **Supp. XX: 45**
Doty, Mark, **Supp. IX:** 42, 300; **Supp. XI: 119–138; Supp. XXI:** 129, 130, 131, 139, 141
Doty, M. R. *See* Dawson, Ruth; Doty, Mark
Double, The (Dostoevsky), **Supp. IX:** 105
"Double, The" (Levis), **Supp. XI:** 260, **261–263**
Double, The (Rank), **Supp. IX:** 105
Double Agent, The (Blackmur), **Supp. II Part 1:** 90, 108, 146
Double Axe, The (Jeffers), **Supp. II Part 2:** 416, 434
"Double Blind" (Skloot), **Supp. XX: 194, 208**
Doubleday, Frank, **I:** 500, 502, 515, 517; **III:** 327
Doubleday, Mrs. Frank, **I:** 500
Double Deuce (Parker), **Supp. XIX:** 183
Double Down (F. and S. Barthelme), **Supp. XI:** 27, 34, 35, 36–38
Double Dream of Spring, The (Ashbery), **Supp. III Part 1:** 11–13
Double Fold: Libraries and the Assault on Paper (Baker), **Supp. XIII:** 52, 56
Double Game (Calle), **Supp. XII:** 22
"Double Gap, The" (Auchincloss), **Supp. IV Part 1:** 33
"Double-Headed Snake of Newbury, The" (Whittier), **Supp. I Part 2:** 698
Double Honeymoon (Connell), **Supp. XIV:** 80, 87
Double Image, The (Levertov), **Supp. III Part 1:** 274, 276
"Double Image, The" (Sexton), **Supp. II Part 2:** 671, 677–678
Double Indemnity (film), **Supp. IV Part 1:** 130
"Double Limbo" (Komunyakaa), **Supp. XIII:** 132
Double Man, The (Auden), **Supp. III Part 1:** 16; **Supp. X:** 118
"Double Ode" (Rukeyser), **Supp. VI:** 282–283, 286
Double Persephone (Atwood), **Supp. XIII:** 19
Double Play (Parker), **Supp. XIX: 189–190**
Doubles in Literary Psychology (Tymms), **Supp. IX:** 105
Double Vision: American Thoughts Abroad (Knowles), **Supp. XII:** 249
"Doubt on the Great Divide" (Stafford), **Supp. XI:** 322
Dougherty, Robin, **Supp. XXII:** 205
Dougherty, Steve, **Supp. X:** 262
Douglas, Aaron, **Supp. I Part 1:** 326
Douglas, Alfred, **Supp. X:** 151
Douglas, Ann, **Supp. XII:** 136; **Supp. XVIII:** 258; **Supp. XX: 69**
Douglas, Claire, **III:** 552
Douglas, Ellen, **Supp. XXI:** 38
Douglas, George (pseudonym). *See* Brown, George Douglas
Douglas, Kirk, **Supp. XIII:** 5–6
Douglas, Lloyd, **IV:** 434

Douglas, Marjory Stoneman, **Supp. XVIII:** 195
Douglas, Melvyn, **Supp. V:** 223
Douglas, Michael, **Supp. XI:** 67
Douglas, Paul, **III:** 294
Douglas, Stephen A., **III:** 577, 588–589; **Supp. I Part 2:** 456, 471
Douglas, William O., **III:** 581
Douglass, Frederick, **Supp. I Part 1:** 51, 345; **Supp. I Part 2:** 591; **Supp. II Part 1:** 157, 195, 196, 292, 378; **Supp. III Part 1: 153–174; Supp. IV Part 1:** 1, 2, 13, 15, 256; **Supp. VIII:** 202; **Supp. XVIII:** 16; **Supp. XX: 109, 281**
Douglass Pilot, The (Baldwin, ed.), **Supp. I Part 1:** 49
Dove, Belle, **I:** 451
Dove, Rita, **Supp. IV Part 1: 241–258; Supp. XVII:** 71, 110; **Supp. XVIII:** 172, 174; **Supp. XXI:** 243, 246, 247, 249, 251
"Dover Beach" (Arnold), **Retro. Supp. I:** 325; **Supp. XIX:** 41
Dow, Lorenzo, **IV:** 265
Dowd, Douglas, **Supp. I Part 2:** 645, 650
"Do We Understand Each Other?" (Ginsberg), **Supp. II Part 1:** 311
Dowie, William, **Supp. V:** 199
Do with Me What You Will (Oates), **Supp. II Part 2:** 506, 515–517
Dowling, Eddie, **IV:** 394
Down and Out (Shanley), **Supp. XIV:** 317
"Down at City Hall" (Didion), **Supp. IV Part 1:** 211
"Down at the Cross" (Baldwin), **Retro. Supp. II:** 1, 2, 7, 12, 13, 15; **Supp. I Part 1:** 60, 61
"Down at the Dinghy" (Salinger), **III:** 559, 563
"Down by the Station, Early in the Morning" (Ashbery), **Supp. III Part 1:** 25
Downey, Sharon D., **Supp. XX: 244**
Downhill Racer (film), **Supp. IX:** 253
"Down Home" (J. W. Miller), **Supp. XX: 169**
"Down in Alabam" (Bierce), **I:** 193
Downing, Ben, **Supp. XII:** 175, 189, 190–191
Downing, Major Jack (pseudonym). *See* Smith, Seba
Down in My Heart (Stafford), **Supp. XI:** 313, 315
Down Mailer's Way (Solotaroff), **Retro. Supp. II:** 203
"Down the Highway" (song, Dylan), **Supp. XVIII:** 24
Down the Rabbit Hole: Adventures and Misadventures in the Realm of Children's Literature (Lanes), **Supp. XVI:** 104
Down There on a Visit (Isherwood), **Supp. XIV:** 159, 161, 164, **168–169,** 170, 171
Down the River (Abbey), **Supp. XIII:** 12–13
"Down the River with Henry Thoreau" (Abbey), **Supp. XIII:** 12–13
Down These Mean Streets (P. Thomas), **Supp. XIII:** 264
Down the Starry River (Purdy), **Supp. VII:** 278
Down to the River: Portraits of Iowa Musicians (Dyas), **Supp. XIX:** 174
Downtown (Siddons), **Supp. XXII:** 239, 240, 242, **247–249, 251–252,** 253
"Downtrodden Mary's Failed Campaign of Terror" (Saunders), **Supp. XIX:** 226
"Downward Path to Wisdom, The" (Porter), **III:** 442, 443, 446
"Down Where I Am" (Hughes), **Supp. I Part 1:** 344
Down with Starvation Wages in Southeast Missouri (C. L. R. James), **Supp. XXI:** 169
"Dowsing for Joy" (Skloot), **Supp. XX: 203**
Dowson, Ernest C., **I:** 384
Doyle, Arthur Conan, **Retro. Supp. I:** 270; **Supp. IV Part 1:** 128, 341; **Supp. IV Part 2:** 464, 469; **Supp. XI:** 63
Doyle, C. W., **I:** 199
"Draba" (Leopold), **Supp. XIV:** 186
Drabble, Margaret, **Supp. IV Part 1:** 297, 299, 305
Drabelle, Dennis, **Supp. XIII:** 13
Drach, Ivan, **Supp. III Part 1:** 268
Dracula (film), **Supp. IV Part 1:** 104; **Supp. XVII:** 57
"Draft Horse, The" (Frost), **Retro. Supp. I:** 141
"Draft Lyrics for *Candide*" (Agee), **I:** 28
Draft of XVI Cantos, A (Pound), **III:** 472; **Retro. Supp. I:** 292
Draft of XXX Cantos, A (Pound), **III:** 196; **Retro. Supp. I:** 292
Drafts &Fragments (Pound), **Retro. Supp. I:** 293
Dragon Country (T. Williams), **IV:** 383
Dragon Seed (Buck), **Supp. II Part 1:** 124
Dragon's Teeth (Sinclair), **Supp. V:** 290
Drake, Benjamin, **Supp. I Part 2:** 584
Drake, Daniel, **Supp. I Part 2:** 584
Drake, Sir Francis, **Supp. I Part 2:** 497
Drake, Robert, **Supp. XX: 274**
Drake, St. Clair, **IV:** 475
Drake, Sylvia, **Supp. XXI:** 155
Drake, William, **Supp. XV:** 295
Dramatic Duologues (Masters), **Supp. I Part 2:** 461
"Drapery Factory, Gulfport. Mississippi, 1956" (Trethewey), **Supp. XXI:** 246
Drattel, Deborah, **Supp. XV:** 333
Drat These Brats (X. J. Kennedy), **Supp. XV:** 163
"Draught" (Cowley), **Supp. II Part 1:** 141, 142
Drayton, Michael, **IV:** 135; **Retro. Supp. II:** 76
"Dr. Bergen's Belief" (Schwartz), **Supp. II Part 2:** 650
Dr. Bloodmoney (Dick), **Supp. XVIII:** 138
"Dreadful Has Already Happened, The" (Strand), **Supp. IV Part 2:** 627
"Dream, A" (Ginsberg), **Supp. II Part 1:** 312
"Dream, A" (Tate), **IV:** 129
"Dream, The" (Hayden), **Supp. II Part 1:** 368, 377
Dream at the End of the World, The: Paul Bowles and the Literary Renegades in Tangier (Green), **Supp. IV Part 1:** 95
"Dream Avenue" (Simic), **Supp. VIII:** 282
"Dream Boogie" (Hughes), **Retro. Supp. I:** 208; **Supp. I Part 1:** 339–340
"Dreambook Bestiary" (Komunyakaa), **Supp. XIII:** 120
Dreamer (Johnson), **Supp. VI:** 186, **196–199**
dreamer examines his pillow, the (Shanley), **Supp. XIV:** 315, **327**
"Dreamer in a Dead Language" (Paley), **Supp. VI:** 217
Dreaming in Cuban (García), **Supp. XI:** 178, **179–185,** 190
"Dreaming of Hair" (L.-Y. Lee), **Supp. XV:** 214
"Dreaming the Breasts" (Sexton), **Supp. II Part 2:** 692
"Dreaming Water" (Espaillat), **Supp. XXI:** 102
"Dream Interpreted, The" (Paine), **Supp. I Part 2:** 505
Dream Jumbo (Longo), **Supp. XVI:** 124
Dream Keeper, The (Hughes), **Supp. I Part 1:** 328, 332, 333, 334
Dream Keeper and Other Poems, The (Hughes), **Retro. Supp. I:** 201, 202
Dreamland (Baker), **Supp. XIV:** 96
"Dream-Land" (Poe), **Retro. Supp. II:** 274
Dream Life of Balso Snell, The (West), **IV:** 286, 287, 288–290, 291, 297; **Retro. Supp. II:** 321, 322, 327, 328, **330–332**
Dream of a Common Language, The: Poems, 1974–1977 (Rich), **Supp. I Part 2:** 551, 554, 569–576
Dream of Arcadia: American Writers and Artists in Italy (Brooks), **I:** 254
Dream of Governors, A (Simpson), **Supp. IX:** 265, **269–270**
"Dream of Italy, A" (Masters), **Supp. I Part 2:** 458
"Dream of Mourning, The" (Glück), **Supp. V:** 84
"Dream of the Blacksmith's Room, A" (R. Bly), **Supp. IV Part 1:** 73
"Dream of the Cardboard Lover" (Haines), **Supp. XII:** 204
Dream of the Golden Mountains, The (Cowley), **Supp. II Part 1:** 139, 141, 142, 144
"Dream Pang, A" (Frost), **II:** 153
"Dreams About Clothes" (Merrill), **Supp. III Part 1:** 328–329
Dreams from Bunker Hill (Fante), **Supp. XI:** 160, 166, **172–173**
"Dreams of Adulthood" (Ashbery), **Supp. III Part 1:** 26
"Dreams of Glory on the Mound" (Plimpton), **Supp. XVI:** 238–239
"Dreams of Math" (Kenyon), **Supp. VII:** 160–161

"Dreams of the Animals" (Atwood), **Supp. XIII:** 33
"Dream Variations" (Hughes), **Retro. Supp. I:** 198; **Supp. I Part 1:** 323
"Dream Vision" (Olsen), **Supp. XIII:** 295–296
Dream Work (Oliver), **Supp. VII:** 234–235, 236–238, 240
Dred: A Tale of the Great Dismal Swamp (Stowe), **Supp. I Part 2:** 592
Dreiser, Theodore, **I:** 59, 97, 109, 116, 355, 374, 375, 475, 482, **497–520; II:** 26, 27, 29, 34, 38, 44, 74, 89, 93, 180, 276, 283, 428, 444, 451, 456–457, 467–468; **III:** 40, 103, 106, 251, 314, 319, 327, 335, 453, 576, 582; **IV:** 29, 35, 40, 135, 208, 237, 475, 482, 484; **Retro. Supp. I:** 325, 376; **Retro. Supp. II: 93–110,** 114, 322; **Supp. I Part 1:** 320; **Supp. I Part 2:** 461, 468; **Supp. III Part 2:** 412; **Supp. IV Part 1:** 31, 236, 350; **Supp. IV Part 2:** 689; **Supp. V:** 113, 120; **Supp. VIII:** 98, 101, 102; **Supp. IX:** 1, 14, 15, 308; **Supp. XI:** 207; **Supp. XIV:** 111; **Supp. XVII:** 95, 96–97, 105, 155; **Supp. XVIII:** 1, 6, 76, 226; **Supp. XXI:** 275
"Drenched in Light" (Hurston), **Supp. VI:** 150–151
Drennen, Eileen M., **Supp. XXII:** 241, 243
Dresser, Paul, **Retro. Supp. II:** 94, 103
Dress Gray (teleplay), **Supp. IV Part 2:** 683
Dress Gray (Truscott), **Supp. IV Part 2:** 683
"Dressing for Dinner" (Ríos), **Supp. IV Part 2:** 548
Dressing Up for the Carnival (Shields), **Supp. VII:** 328
"Dress Rehearsal" (Skloot), **Supp. XX: 204**
Drew, Bettina, **Supp. IX:** 2, 4
Drew, Elizabeth, **Retro. Supp. II:** 242, 243
Drexler, Eric, **Supp. XVI:** 121
Dreyfus, Alfred, **Supp. I Part 2:** 446
"Dr. Hanray's Second Chance" (Richter), **Supp. XVIII:** 218
Drift and Mastery (Lippmann), **I:** 222–223
"Driftwood" (C. Frost), **Supp. XV:** 106–107
"Drinker, The" (Lowell), **II:** 535, 550
"Drinking Cold Water" (Everwine), **Supp. XV:** 80–81
"Drinking from a Helmet" (Dickey), **Supp. IV Part 1:** 180
Drinking Gourd, The (Hansberry), **Supp. IV Part 1:** 359, 365–367, 374
Drinks before Dinner (Doctorow), **Supp. IV Part 1:** 231, 234–235
Driscoll, David, **Supp. XIX:** 241, 242
Drive, He Said (Larner), **Supp. XVI:** 220
"Drive Home, The" (Banks), **Supp. V:** 7
"Driver" (Merrill), **Supp. III Part 1:** 331
"Driving Alone in Winter" (W. V. Davis), **Supp. XXI:** 89, 90, 94
"Driving Through Minnesota During the Hanoi Bombings" (R. Bly), **Supp. IV Part 1:** 61; **Supp. XVII:** 243
"Driving through Oregon" (Haines), **Supp. XII:** 207
"Driving toward the Lac Qui Parle River" (R. Bly), **Supp. IV Part 1:** 61
"Dr. Jack-o'-Lantern" (Yates), **Supp. XI:** 340–341
Dr. Jekyll and Mr. Hyde (film), **Supp. XVII:** 57
"Drone" (Coleman), **Supp. XI:** 85–86
Drop City (Boyle), **Supp. XX: 30–31**
"Drowned Man, The: Death between Two Rivers" (McGrath), **Supp. X:** 116
"Drowning" (Boyle), **Supp. XX: 18**
"Drowning 1954" (Keillor), **Supp. XVI:** 172
Drowning Pool, The (film), **Supp. IV Part 2:** 474
Drowning Pool, The (Macdonald), **Supp. IV Part 2:** 470, 471
Drowning Season, The (Hoffman), **Supp. X: 82**
Drowning with Others (Dickey), **Supp. IV Part 1:** 176, 178, 179
"Drowsy Day, A" (Dunbar), **Supp. II Part 1:** 198
Dr. Seuss. *See* Geisel, Theodor Seuss (Dr. Seuss)
Dr. Seuss and Mr. Geisel (J. and N. Morgan), **Supp. XVI:** 103
Dr. Seuss Goes to War: The World War II Editorial Cartoons of Theodor Seuss Geisel (Minear), **Supp. XVI:** 101
Dr. Seuss's ABC (Geisel), **Supp. XVI:** 99
Dr. Strangelove; or, How I Learned to Stop Worrying and Love the Bomb (film), **Supp. XI:** 293, **301–305**
Drugiye Berega (Nabokov), **III:** 247–250, 252
"Drug Shop, The, or Endymion in Edmonstoun" (Benét), **Supp. XI:** 43
"Drug Store" (Shapiro), **Supp. II Part 2:** 705
"Drugstore in Winter, A" (Ozick), **Supp. V:** 272
Drukman, Steven, **Supp. XIII:** 195, 197, 202
"Drum" (Hogan), **Supp. IV Part 1:** 413
"Drum, The" (Alvarez), **Supp. VII:** 7
"Drumlin Woodchuck, A" (Frost), **II:** 159–160; **Retro. Supp. I:** 138
Drummond, William, **Supp. I Part 1:** 369
Drummond de Andrade, Carlos, **Supp. IV Part 2:** 626, 629, 630
Drums at Dusk (Bontemps), **Supp. XXII:** 5, 9–10
Drum-Taps (Whitman), **IV:** 346, 347, 444; **Retro. Supp. I:** 406
"Drunken Fisherman, The" (Lowell), **II:** 534, 550
"Drunken Sisters, The" (Wilder), **IV:** 374
Drunk in the Furnace, The (Merwin), **Supp. III Part 1:** 345–346
"Drunk in the Furnace, The" (Merwin), **Supp. III Part 1:** 346
Druten, John van, **Supp. XIV:** 162
"Dr. Williams' Position" (Pound), **Supp. XVII:** 226–227
Dryden, John, **II:** 111, 542, 556; **III:** 15; **IV:** 145; **Retro. Supp. I:** 56; **Supp. I Part 1:** 150; **Supp. I Part 2:** 422; **Supp. IX:** 68; **Supp. XIV:** 5; **Supp. XV:** 258; **Supp. XX: 280**
Drye, Captain Frank, **Retro. Supp. II:** 115
Dry Salvages, The (Eliot), **I:** 581
"Dry Salvages, The" (Eliot), **Retro. Supp. I:** 66
"Dry September" (Faulkner), **II:** 72, 73
Dry Sun, Dry Wind (Wagoner), **Supp. IX:** 323, 324
D'Souza, Dinesh, **Supp. X:** 255
"Dual" (Goldbarth), **Supp. XII:** 188
"Dual Curriculum" (Ozick), **Supp. V:** 270
"Dualism" (Reed), **Supp. X:** 242
Duane's Depressed (McMurtry), **Supp. V:** 233
Du Bartas, Guillaume, **Supp. I Part 1:** 98, 104, 111, 118, 119
Duberman, Martin, **Supp. I Part 2:** 408, 409
"Dubin's Lives" (Malamud), **Supp. I Part 2:** 451
Dubious Honors (M. F. K. Fisher), **Supp. XVII:** 91
"Dubliners" (J. Joyce), **Supp. XVI:** 41
Dubliners (Joyce), **I:** 130, 480; **III:** 471; **Supp. VIII:** 146
Dublin's Lives (Malamud), **Supp. XIX:** 142
Du Bois, Nina Gomer (Mrs. W. E. B. Du Bois), **Supp. II P art 1:** 158; **Supp. XIV:** 200
Du Bois, Shirley Graham, **Supp. II Part 1:** 186; **Supp. XXI:** 171. *See also* Graham, Shirley
Du Bois, W. E. B., **I:** 260; **Supp. I Part 1:** 5, 345; **Supp. II Part 1:** 33, 56, 61, **157–189,** 195; **Supp. IV Part 1:** 9, 164, 170, 362; **Supp. X:** 133, 134, 137, 139, 242; **Supp. XIII:** 185, **Supp. XIII:** 186, 233, 238, 243, 244, 247; **Supp. XIV:** 54, 69, 72, 201, 202; **Supp. XVI:** 135; **Supp. XVIII:** 119, 122, 126, 130; **Supp. XIX:** 67, 69, 77; **Supp. XX: 102, 105, 106; Supp. XXI:** 166, 277; **Supp. XXII:** 3
Dubreuil, Jean, **Supp. IV Part 2:** 425
Dubus, Andre, **Supp. VII: 75–93; Supp. XI:** 347,**Supp. XI:** 349; **Supp. XIV:** 21
Duchamp, Marcel, **IV:** 408; **Retro. Supp. I:** 416, 417, 418, 430; **Supp. IV Part 2:** 423, 424; **Supp. XII:** 124; **Supp. XV:** 157; **Supp. XXII:** 162, 163, 168
"Duchess at Prayer, The" (Wharton), **Retro. Supp. I:** 365
Duchess of Malfi, The (Webster), **IV:** 131
Duck Soup (film), **Supp. IV Part 1:** 384
Duck Variations, The (Mamet), **Supp. XIV:** 239, 240, 249
Ducornet, Rikki, **Supp. XXII:** 261
Dudley, Anne. *See* Bradstreet, Anne
Dudley, Joseph, **III:** 52
Dudley, Thomas, **III:** 52; **Supp. I Part 1:** 98, 99, 110, 116

"Duet, With Muffled Brake Drums" (Updike), **Retro. Supp. I:** 319
Duet for Cannibals (Sontag), **Supp. III Part 2:** 452, 456
Duffey, Bernard, **Supp. I Part 2:** 458, 471
Duffield, Pitts, **Supp. XXI:** 3
Duffus, R. L., **Supp. I Part 2:** 650
Duffy, Martha, **Supp. IV Part 1:** 207; **Supp. XX: 244**
Duffy, William, **Supp. XVI:** 32
Du Fu (Tu Fu), **Supp. XV:** 217
Dufy, Raoul, **I:** 115; **IV:** 80
Dugan, Alan, **Supp. XIII:** 76
Dugan, James, **Supp. XV:** 197
Duhamel, Marcel, **Supp. XVI:** 135, 143
Dujardin, Edouard, **I:** 53
"Duke de l'Omelette, The" (Poe), **III:** 411, 425
"Duke in His Domain, The" (Capote), **Supp. III Part 1:** 113, 126
Duke of Deception, The (G. Wolff), **Supp. II Part 1:** 97; **Supp. XI:** 246
"Duke's Child, The" (Maxwell), **Supp. VIII:** 172
"Dulce et Decorum Est" (Owen), **Supp. XVIII:** 92
"Dulham Ladies, The" (Jewett), **II:** 407, 408; **Retro. Supp. II:** 143
Duluth (Vidal), **Supp. IV Part 2:** 677, 685, 689, 691–692
Dumas, Alexandre, **III:** 386; **Supp. XVII:** 64
"Dumb Oax, The" (Lewis), **Retro. Supp. I:** 170
"Dummy, The" (Sontag), **Supp. III Part 2:** 469
"Dump Ground, The" (Stegner), **Supp. IV Part 2:** 601
Dunant, Sarah, **Supp. XIX:** 186
Dunayevskaya, Raya, **Supp. XXI:** 169
Dunbar, Alice Moore (Mrs. Paul Laurence Dunbar), **Supp. II Part 1:** 195, 200, 217
Dunbar, Paul Laurence, **Supp. I Part 1:** 320; **Supp. II Part 1:** 174, **191–219; Supp. III Part 1:** 73; **Supp. IV Part 1:** 15, 165, 170; **Supp. X:** 136; **Supp. XI:** 277; **Supp. XIII:** 111; **Supp. XXII:** 11
Duncan, Harry, **Supp. XV:** 75
Duncan, Isadora, **I:** 483; **Supp. XV:** 42, 50
Duncan, Robert, **Retro. Supp. II:** 49; **Supp. III Part 2:** 625, 626, 630, 631; **Supp. VIII:** 304; **Supp. XVI:** 282–283
Dunciad, The (Pope), **I:** 204
Dunford, Judith, **Supp. VIII:** 107
Dunlap, William, **Supp. I Part 1:** 126, 130, 137, 141, 145
Dunn, Stephen, **Supp. XI: 139–158; Supp. XIX:** 85
Dunne, Finley Peter, **II:** 432
Dunne, John Gregory, **Supp. IV Part 1:** 197, 198, 201, 203, 207
"Dunnet Shepherdess, A" (Jewett), **II:** 392–393; **Retro. Supp. II:** 139
Dunning, Stephen, **Supp. XIV:** 126
Dunning, William Archibald, **Supp. II Part 1:** 170; **Supp. XIV:** 48
Dunnock, Mildred, **III:** 153
Dunster, Henry, **Supp. I Part 2:** 485
"Duo Tried Killing Man with Bacon" (Goldbarth), **Supp. XII:** 176
Dupee, F. W., **I:** 254; **II:** 548; **Supp. VIII:** 231; **Supp. IX:** 93, 96
DuPlessis, Rachel Blau, **Supp. IV Part 2:** 421, 426, 432; **Supp. XVI:** 284
Duplicate Keys (Smiley), **Supp. VI:** 292, **294–296**
Duplications, The (Koch), **Supp. XV:** 181, 183, 186
Durable Fire, A (Sarton), **Supp. VIII:** 260
Durand, Asher, B., **Supp. I Part 1:** 156, 157
Durand, Régis, **Supp. IV Part 1:** 44
"Durango Suite" (Gunn Allen), **Supp. IV Part 1:** 326
Durant, Kenneth, **Supp. XXII:** 278, 281
"Durations" (Matthews), **Supp. IX:** 152–153, 154
Dürer, Albrecht, **III:** 212; **Supp. XII:** 44
Durham, David Anthony, **Supp. XVIII:** 100
"During Fever" (Lowell), **II:** 547
Durkheim, Émile, **I:** 227; **Retro. Supp. I:** 55, 57; **Supp. I Part 2:** 637, 638
Durrell, Lawrence, **III:** 184, 190; **IV:** 430; **Supp. X:** 108, 187; **Supp. XVI:** 294
Dürrenmatt, Friedrich, **Supp. IV Part 2:** 683
Duse, Eleonora, **II:** 515, 528
Dusk and Other Stories (Salter), **Supp. IX: 260–261**
Dusk of Dawn: An Essay Toward an Autobiography of a Race Concept (Du Bois), **Supp. II Part 1:** 159, 183, 186
"Dust" (R. Fisher), **Supp. XIX:** 71
"Dusting" (Alvarez), **Supp. VII:** 4
"Dusting" (Dove), **Supp. IV Part 1:** 247, 248
"Dusting" (Schnackenberg), **Supp. XV:** 256
"Dust of Snow" (Frost), **II:** 154
Dust Tracks on a Road (Hurston), **Supp. IV Part 1:** 5, 11; **Supp. VI:** 149, 151, 158–159
"Dusty Braces" (Snyder), **Supp. VIII:** 302
Dutchman (Baraka), **Supp. II Part 1:** 38, 40, 42–44, 54, 55
"Dutch Nick Massacre, The" (Twain), **IV:** 195
"Dutch Picture, A" (Longfellow), **Retro. Supp. II:** 171
Dutton, Charles S., **Supp. VIII:** 332, 342
Dutton, Clarence Earl, **Supp. IV Part 2:** 598
Duvall, Robert, **Supp. V:** 227
"Duwamish" (Hugo), **Supp. VI:** 136
"Duwamish, Skagit, Hoh" (Hugo), **Supp. VI:** 136–137
"Duwamish No. 2" (Hugo), **Supp. VI:** 137
Duyckinck, Evert, **III:** 77, 81, 83, 85; **Retro. Supp. I:** 155, 247, 248; **Supp. I Part 1:** 122, 317
Duyckinck, George, **Supp. I Part 1:** 122
"Dvonya" (Simpson), **Supp. IX:** 274
Dwellings: A Spiritual History of the Living World (Hogan), **Supp. IV Part 1:** 397, 410, 415–416, 417
Dwight, Sereno E., **I:** 547
Dwight, Timothy, **Supp. I Part 1:** 124; **Supp. I Part 2:** 516, 580; **Supp. II Part 1:** 65, 69
Dworkin, Andrea, **Supp. XII:** 6
Dwyer, Jim, **Supp. XVI:** 16, 19
Dyas, Sandra, **Supp. XIX:** 174
Dybbuk, A, or Between Two Worlds: Dramatic Legend in Four Acts (Kushner), **Supp. IX:** 138
Dybbuk, The (Ansky), **IV:** 6
Dyer, Geoff, **Supp. X:** 169
Dyer, Joyce, **Supp. XX: 166**
Dyer, R. C. ?/, **Supp. XIII:** 162
Dyer, Richard ?/, **Supp. XXII:** 261
Dying Animal, The (P. Roth), **Retro. Supp. II:** 288
"Dying Elm, The" (Freneau), **Supp. II Part 1:** 258
"Dying Indian, The" (Freneau), **Supp. II Part 1:** 262
"Dying Man, The" (Roethke), **III:** 540, 542, 543–545
Dykeman, Wilma, **Supp. XX: 163**
Dylan, Bob, **Supp. VIII:** 202; **Supp. XIII:** 114, 119; **Supp. XV:** 349, 350; **Supp. XVIII: 19–34; Supp. XXII:** 83
Dylan's Visions of Sin (Ricks), **Supp. XVIII:** 20
"Dynamics of Heroic Action, The" (lecture, Murray), **Supp. XIX:** 153
Dynamo (O'Neill), **III:** 396
"Dynasties" (Gibran), **Supp. XX: 118**
"Dysfunctional Narratives: Or, 'Mistakes Were Made' " (C. Baxter), **Supp. XVII:** 20
"Dysfunctional Nation" (Karr), **Supp. XI:** 245
Dyson, A. E., **Retro. Supp. II:** 247
Dyson, Freeman, **Supp. XVII:** 42

"Each and All" (Emerson), **II:** 19
Each in His Season (Snodgrass), **Supp. VI:** 324, 327
"Each Like a Leaf" (Swenson), **Supp. IV Part 2:** 644
Eads, Martha Greene, **Supp. XVIII:** 49
Eady, Cornelius, **Supp. XXI:** 246
Eager, Allen, **Supp. XI:** 294
"Eagle, The" (Tate), **IV:** 128
"Eagle and the Mole, The" (Wylie), **Supp. I Part 2:** 710, 711, 713, 714, 729
"Eagle and the Skylark, The" (Gibran), **Supp. XX: 124**
Eagle as Wide as the World, The (X. J. Kennedy), **Supp. XV:** 162, 164
"Eagle Poem" (Harjo), **Supp. XII:** 224, 226
"Eagles" (Dickey), **Supp. IV Part 1:** 186

Eagle's Mile, The (Dickey), **Supp. IV Part 1:** 178, 185–186
"Eagle That Is Forgotten, The" (Lindsay), **Supp. I Part 2:** 382, 387
Eagleton, Terry, **Retro. Supp. I:** 67
Eakin, Paul John, **Supp. VIII:** 167, 168; **Supp. XIII:** 225; **Supp. XVI:** 70
Eakins, Thomas, **Supp. XIV:** 338; **Supp. XXII:** 18–19
Eames, Emma, **Supp. XX: 232, 240**
Eames, Roscoe, **II:** 476
"Earl: My Life with a Louse" (Keillor), **Supp. XVI:** 176
"Earl Painter" (Banks), **Supp. V:** 14–15
"Early Adventures of Ralph Ringwood, The" (Irving), **II:** 314
Early Americana (Richter), **Supp. XVIII:** 208, 210, 211, 220
Early Autumn (Parker), **Supp. XIX:** 184–185
Early Ayn Rand, The: A Selection of Her Unpublished Fiction (Rand), **Supp. IV Part 2:** 520
Early Dark (Price), **Supp. VI:** 262
Early Diary of Anaïs Nin, The, **Supp. X:** 184, 192
Early Elkin (Elkin), **Supp. VI: 42–43,** 45
"Early Evenin' Blues" (Hughes), **Retro. Supp. I:** 205
"Early Evening, Frankfort, Kentucky" (Trethewey), **Supp. XXI:** 243, 250
"Early History of a Seamstress" (Reznikoff), **Supp. XIV:** 277, 289
Early History of a Sewing-Machine Operator (Reznikoff), **Supp. XIV:** 289
"Early History of a Sewing-Machine Operator" (Reznikoff), **Supp. XIV:** 277
"Early History of a Writer" (Reznikoff), **Supp. XIV:** 278, 290
"Early in the Morning" (L.-Y. Lee), **Supp. XV:** 214
Early Lectures of Ralph Waldo Emerson, The (Emerson), **II:** 11
Early Light (Di Piero), **Supp. XIX:** 38, **38–40**
Early Lives of Melville, The (Sealts), **Retro. Supp. I:** 257
"Early Marriage" (Richter), **Supp. XVIII:** 209
Early Martyr and Other Poems, An (W. C. Williams), **Retro. Supp. I:** 423
"Early Morning: Cape Cod" (Swenson), **Supp. IV Part 2:** 641
"Early Spring between Madison and Bellingham" (R. Bly), **Supp. IV Part 1:** 71
Earnhardt, Dale, **Supp. XII:** 310
Earnshaw, Doris, **Supp. IV Part 1:** 310
"Earth" (Bryant), **Supp. I Part 1:** 157, 164, 167
"Earth, The" (Sexton), **Supp. II Part 2:** 696
Earth Abides (Stewart), **Supp. XVIII:** 138
"Earth and Fire" (Berry), **Supp. X:** 27
Earth as Air, The: An Ars Poetica (Sobin), **Supp. XVI: 285–286**
"Earth Being" (Toomer), **Supp. IX:** 320
Earth Goat (online), **Supp. XXII:** 61
Earth Gods, The (Gibran), **Supp. XX: 116, 123**
"Earthly Care a Heavenly Discipline" (Stowe), **Supp. I Part 2:** 586
"Earthly City of the Jews, The" (Kazin), **Retro. Supp. II:** 286
Earthly Meditations (Wrigley), **Supp. XVIII:** 304–305
"Earthly Meditations" (Wrigley), **Supp. XVIII:** 304–306
Earthly Possessions (Tyler), **Supp. IV Part 2:** 665–666, 671
Earth Power Coming (Ortiz, ed.), **Supp. IV Part 2:** 502
"Earth's Holocaust" (Hawthorne), **II:** 226, 231, 232, 242; **III:** 82; **Retro. Supp. I:** 152
Earth Without You, The (F. Wright), **Supp. XVII:** 243
East Coker (Eliot), **I:** 580, 581, 582, 585, 587
"East Coker" (Eliot), **Retro. Supp. I:** 66; **Supp. VIII:** 195, 196
"Easter" (Toomer), **Supp. III Part 2:** 486
"Easter, an Ode" (Lowell), **II:** 536
"Easter 1916" (Yeats), **Supp. XXI:** 61
"Easter Morning" (Ammons), **Supp. VII:** 34
"Easter Morning" (Clampitt), **Supp. IX:** 45
"Easter Ode, An" (Dunbar), **Supp. II Part 1:** 196
Easter Parade, The (Yates), **Supp. XI:** 346, 349
"Easter Sermon, 1866" (Nelson), **Supp. XVIII:** 177
"Easter Service" (Di Piero), **Supp. XIX:** 39–40
"Easter Sunday: Recollection" (Gunn Allen), **Supp. IV Part 1:** 322
"Easter Wings" (Herbert), **Supp. IV Part 2:** 646
"East European Cooking" (Simic), **Supp. VIII:** 277
East Is East (Boyle), **Supp. VIII:** 1–3; **Supp. XX: 23–24, 25, 28**
Eastlake, William, **Supp. XIII:** 12
East Lynne (Wood), **Supp. I Part 1:** 35, 36; **Supp. I Part 2:** 459, 462; **Supp. XVI:** 182
Eastman, Elaine Goodale, **Supp. X:** 103
Eastman, Max, **Supp. III Part 2:** 620; **Supp. X:** 131, 134, 135, 137; **Supp. XV:** 295; **Supp. XVI:** 185; **Supp. XVII:** 96; **Supp. XXI:** 6; **Supp. XXII:** 274, 275, 277
East of Eden (Steinbeck), **IV:** 51, 56–57, 59
"East of the Sun and West of the Moon" (Merwin), **Supp. III Part 1:** 344
Easton, Alison, **Retro. Supp. II:** 143, 144, 145
Easton, Bret Ellis, **Supp. XI:** 65
Easton, Nina J., **Supp. XIX:** 137
Easton, Robert, **Supp. IV Part 2:** 461, 474
East Wind (Lowell), **II:** 527
East Wind: West Wind (Buck), **Supp. II Part 1:** 114–115
Easy Rawlins mysteries, **Supp. XIII:** 236, **237–241,** 242
Easy Rider (film), **Supp. XI:** 293, **308,** 309
Eat a Bowl of Tea (Chu), **Supp. X:** 291
"Eating " (Bass), **Supp. XVI:** 23–24
"Eating Alone" (L.-Y. Lee), **Supp. XV:** 214
Eating Naked (Dobyns), **Supp. XIII: 78–79**
"Eating Out" (L. Michaels), **Supp. XVI:** 209
"Eating Poetry" (Strand), **Supp. IV Part 2:** 626
"Eating the Whole" (C. Frost), **Supp. XV:** 101
"Eating Together" (L.-Y. Lee), **Supp. XV:** 214
"Eating with My Fingers" (C. Frost), **Supp. XV:** 97
Eaton, Edith, **Supp. X:** 291
Eaton, Peggy, **Supp. I Part 2:** 461
Eaton, Winnifred, **Supp. X:** 291
"Eatonville Anthology, The" (Hurston), **Supp. VI:** 152
Eat Pray Love (Gilbert), **Supp. XXII:** 83, 90
Eat the Document (film, Pennebaker), **Supp. XVIII:** 19, 26, 27, 28
"Ebb and Flow, The" (Taylor), **IV:** 161
"Ebenezer Marsh, 1725" (Schnackenberg), **Supp. XV:** 256
Eben Holden (Bacheller), **I:** 216
Eberhardt, Isabelle, **Supp. IV Part 1:** 92
Eberhart, Mrs., **I:** 521–522, 530
Eberhart, Richard, **I: 521–543; II:** 535–536; **III:** 527; **IV:** 416; **Retro. Supp. II:** 176, 178; **Supp. I Part 1:** 83; **Supp. XII:** 119
Eble, Kenneth E., **Supp. I Part 1:** 201
"Ecce Homo" (Cliff), **Supp. XXII:** 76
Eccentricities of a Nightingale (T. Williams), **IV:** 382, 385, 397, 398
Ecclesiastica Historia Integram Ecclesiae (Taylor), **IV:** 163
"Echart" (Sobin), **Supp. XVI:** 289
"Echo, The" (Bowles), **Supp. IV Part 1:** 84, 86, 87
Echoes inside the Labyrinth (McGrath), **Supp. X:** 127
Echo Park (Connelly), **Supp. XXI: 77–78**
Eckehart, Meister, **Supp. XV:** 225
Eckhart, Maria, **Supp. V:** 212
Eclipse (Hogan), **Supp. IV Part 1:** 397, 400, 402
Eclipse, a Nightmare (Montalembert), **Supp. XV:** 349
Eclogues (Virgil), **Supp. VIII:** 31
"Ecologue" (Ginsberg), **Supp. II Part 1:** 326
"Ecologues of These States 1969–1971" (Ginsberg), **Supp. II Part 1:** 325
Ecology of a Cracker Childhood (Ray), **Supp. XVIII:** 189, 191, 192, 193, **195–199,** 201, 202, 204
"Economics of Negro Emancipation in the United States, The" (Du Bois), **Supp. II Part 1:** 174

"Economics of the Cracker Landscape: Poverty as an Environmental Issue in Larry Brown's *Joe" (Watson), Supp. XXI:* 46
"Economic Theory of Women's Dress, The" (Veblen), **Supp. I Part 2:** 636
Economy of the Unlost: Reading Simonides of Keos with Paul Celan (Carson), **Supp. XII:** 110–111
Ecotactics: The Sierra Club Handbook for Environmental Activists (Mitchell and Stallings, eds.), **Supp. IV Part 2:** 488
"Ecstasy" (Bierds), **Supp. XVII:** 34
"Ecstasy" (Olds), **Supp. X:** 206
"Ecstasy of Influence, The" (Lethem), **Supp. XVIII:** 150
"Ecstatic" (Komunyakaa), **Supp. XIII:** 131
Edda, **Supp. X:** 114
Eddy, Mary Baker, **I:** 583; **III:** 506
Edel, Leon, **I:** 20; **II:** 338–339; **Retro. Supp. I:** 218, 224, 231
Edelberg, Cynthia, **Supp. IV Part 1:** 155
"Eden and My Generation" (Levis), **Supp. XI:** 270
Edenbaum, Robert, **Supp. IV Part 1:** 352
Eden Tree (Bynner), **Supp. XV:** 42, 51
Edenville Owls (Parker), **Supp. XIX:** 190
Eder, Richard, **Supp. XII:** 189; **Supp. XV:** 62, 187, 259, 261
Edgar Huntly; or, Memoirs of a Sleep-Walker (Brown), **Supp. I Part 1:** 140–144, 145
"Edge" (Plath), **Retro. Supp. II:** 256; **Supp. I Part 2:** 527, 547
Edge, Mary E., **II:** 316
"Edge of Possibility, The: Susan Warner and the World of Sunday School Fiction" (S. Gates), **Supp. XVIII:** 267
"Edge of the Great Rift, The" (Theroux), **Supp. VIII:** 325
Edge of the Sea, The (Carson), **Supp. IX:** 19, **25–31,** 32
Edgers, Geoff, **Supp. XV:** 113
Edgeworth, Maria, **II:** 8; **Supp. XV:** 231; **Supp. XX: 108**
Edible Woman, The (Atwood), **Supp. XIII:** 19, 20, **20–21**
"Edict by the King of Prussia, An" (Franklin), **II:** 120
Edie: An American Biography (Stein), **Supp. XVI:** 245
Edinburgh Days: or, Doing What I Want to Do (Pickering), **Supp. XXI:** 200–201
Edison, Thomas A., **I:** 483; **Supp. I Part 2:** 392
Edith Wharton (Joslin), **Retro. Supp. I:** 376
Edith Wharton: A Biography (Lewis), **Retro. Supp. I:** 362
Edith Wharton: A Woman in Her Time (Auchincloss), **Retro. Supp. I:** 370
Edith Wharton: Matters of Mind and Spirit (Singley), **Retro. Supp. I:** 373
Edith Wharton's Argument with America (Ammons), **Retro. Supp. I:** 364
Edith Wharton's Brave New Politics (Bauer), **Retro. Supp. I:** 381
Edith Wharton's Letters from the Underworld (Waid), **Retro. Supp. I:** 360
Edith Wharton: Traveller in the Land of Letters (Goodwyn), **Retro. Supp. I:** 370
"Editing and Glosses" (Reznikoff), **Supp. XIV:** 283
Editing of Emily Dickinson, The (Franklin), **Retro. Supp. I:** 41
"Editor and the Schoolma'am, The" (Frederic), **II:** 130
"Editor's Easy Chair" (Howells), **II:** 276
"Editor's Study, The" (Howells), **II:** 275, 276, 285
"Editor Whedon" (Masters), **Supp. I Part 2:** 463
Edlin, Mari, **Supp. X:** 266
Edman, Irwin, **III:** 605
Edmond (Mamet), **Supp. XIV:** 241, 248, 249, 250
Edmondson, Belinda, **Supp. XXII:** 70
Edmundson, Mark, **Retro. Supp. II:** 262
Edsel (Shapiro), **Supp. II Part 2:** 703, 704, 717–719
Edson, Margaret, **Supp. XVIII: 35–52**
Edson, Russell, **Supp. VIII:** 279
"Educated American Woman, An" (Cheever), **Supp. I Part 1:** 194
"Education, An" (Ozick), **Supp. V:** 267
Education and Living (Bourne), **I:** 252
"Education by Poetry" (Frost), **Supp. XV:** 215
"Education of a Storyteller, The" (Bambara), **Supp. XI:** 20
Education of Black People, The (Du Bois), **Supp. II Part 1:** 186
Education of Harriet Hatfield, The (Sarton), **Supp. VIII: 257–258**
Education of Henry Adams, The (Adams), **I:** 1, 5, 6, 11, 14, 15–18, 19, 20–21, 111; **II:** 276; **III:** 504; **Retro. Supp. I:** 53, 59; **Supp. IX:** 19; **Supp. XIV:** 299
*Education of H*y*m*a*n K*a*p*l*a*n, The* (Rosten), **Supp. XVII:** 9
"Education of Mingo, The" (Johnson), **Supp. VI:** 193, 194
"Education of Norman Podhoretz, The" (Goldberg), **Supp. VIII:** 238
Education of Oscar Fairfax, The (Auchincloss), **Supp. IV Part 1:** 25, 36
"Education of the Poet" (Glück), **Supp. V:** 78, 80
Education sentimentale (Flaubert), **III:** 315
"Education the Imagination" (Koch), **Supp. XV:** 175–176, 177
Edwards, Clifford, **Supp. XVIII:** 220
Edwards, Eli. *See* McKay, Claude
Edwards, Esther, **I:** 545
Edwards, Harry Stillwell, **Supp. XXII:** 193
Edwards, John, **I:** 478
Edwards, Jonathan, **I: 544–566; II:** 432; **Retro. Supp. II:** 187; **Supp. I Part 1:** 301, 302; **Supp. I Part 2:** 552, 594, 700; **Supp. IV Part 2:** 430; **Supp. VIII:** 205
Edwards, Sarah, **I:** 545
Edwards, Thomas, **Supp. XV:** 20
Edwards, Thomas R., **Supp. XVI:** 207
Edwards, Timothy, **I:** 545
Edwards-Yearwood, Grace, **Supp. VIII:** 81; **Supp. XXII:** 213
"Edwin Arlington Robinson" (Cowley), **Supp. II Part 1:** 144
Edwin Arlington Robinson (Winters), **Supp. II Part 2:** 812
Edwin Booth (play), **Supp. IV Part 1:** 89
E. E. Cummings (Marks), **I:** 438
E. E. Cummings: A Miscellany (Cummings), **I:** 429, 441
E. E. Cummings: A Miscellany, Revised (Cummings), **I:** 429
"Effects of Analogy" (Stevens), **Retro. Supp. I:** 297
Effluences from the Sacred Caves; More Selected Essays and Reviews (Carruth), **Supp. XVI:** 46
"Effort at Speech between Two People" (Rukeyser), **Supp. VI:** 276, 284
"Efforts of Affection" (Moore), **III:** 214
"Efforts of Affection: A Memoir of Marianne Moore" (Bishop), **Retro. Supp. II:** 52
Egan, Jennifer, **Supp. XIX: 49–63**
Egan, Leona, **Supp. XXI:** 6
"Egg, The" (Anderson), **I:** 113, 114
"Egg, The" (Snyder), **Supp. VIII:** 302
Eggleston, George Cary, **Supp. XVIII:** 15
"Eggplant Epithalamion, The" (Jong), **Supp. V:** 119
"Eggs" (Olds), **Supp. X:** 206
"Eggshell" (Stern), **Supp. IX:** 299
Egoist, The (Meredith), **II:** 186
Egorova, Lubov, **Supp. IX:** 58
"Egotism, or the Bosom Sergent" (Hawthorne), **II:** 227, 239
"Egyptian Pulled Glass Bottle in the Shape of a Fish, An" (Moore), **III:** 195, 213
Ehrenfels, Christian von, **Supp. XIV:** 198
Ehrenpreis, Irvin, **Supp. XII:** 128
Ehrenreich, Barbara, **Supp. XVII:** 210
Ehrhart, W. D., **Supp. XIX:** 281
Ehrlich, Gretel, **Supp. XIV:** 227; **Supp. XVIII:** 189
Eichmann, Adolf, **Supp. XII:** 166
Eichmann in Jerusalem (Arendt), **Retro. Supp. II:** 28; **Supp. VIII:** 243; **Supp. XII:** 166
"Eichmann in New York: The New York Intellectuals and the Hannah Arendt Controversy" (Rabinbach), **Supp. XII:** 166
"Eidolon" (Warren), **IV:** 239
"Eiger Dreams" (Krakauer), **Supp. XVIII:** 107
Eiger Dreams: Ventures Among Men and Mountains (Krakauer), **Supp. XVIII:** 105, 106, 107
Eight Cousins (Alcott), **Supp. I Part 1:** 29, 38, 42, 43
18 Poems from the Quechua (Strand, trans.), **Supp. IV Part 2:** 630
"18 West 11th Street" (Merrill), **Supp. III Part 1:** 323, 328

1876: A Novel (Vidal), **Supp. IV Part 2:** 677, 684, 688, 689, 691, 692; **Supp. XIX:** 141
"18,000 CDs" (Halliday), **Supp. XIX:** 92
"Eighth Air Force" (Jarrell), **II:** 373–374, 377
Eight Harvard Poets, **I:** 429, 475
"Eighth Avenue Incident" (Halliday), **Supp. XIX:** 89–90
"Eighth Day, The" (Apple), **Supp. XVII:** 6, 50
"Eighth Ditch, The" (Baraka), **Supp. II Part 1:** 40
"'80s Pastoral: Frederick Barthelme's *Moon Deluxe* Ten Years On" (Peters), **Supp. XI:** 39
Eight Men (Wright), **IV:** 478, 488, 494
80 Flowers (Zukofsky), **Supp. III Part 2:** 631
Eikon Basilike, The, **Supp. IV Part 2:** 435
Eileen (Masters), **Supp. I Part 2:** 460
Eimi (Cummings), **I:** 429, 433, 434, 439–440
"Einstein" (MacLeish), **III:** 5, 8, 10–11, 18–19
Einstein, Albert, **I:** 493; **III:** 8, 10, 21, 161; **IV:** 69, 375, 410, 411, 421; **Retro. Supp. I:** 63; **Supp. I Part 2:** 609, 643; **Supp. III Part 2:** 621; **Supp. V:** 290; **Supp. XII:** 45
Eiseley, Loren, **III:** 227–228
Eisenhower, Dwight D., **I:** 136, 376; **II:** 548; **III:** 215; **IV:** 75; **Supp. I Part 1:** 291; **Supp. III Part 2:** 624; **Supp. V:** 45
Eisenstadt, Jill, **Supp. XVIII:** 135
Eisenstein, Sergei, **I:** 481; **Supp. XXI:** 170
Eisinger, Chester E., **I:** 302; **II:** 604; **Supp. IX:** 15
Eisner, Douglas, **Supp. X:** 155
Elam, Angela, **Supp. XI:** 290
El Bernardo (Balbuena), **Supp. V:** 11
Elbert, Sarah, **Supp. I Part 1:** 34, 41
Elder, Donald, **II:** 417, 426, 435, 437; **Supp. XV:** 137
Elder, John, **Supp. IX:** 25
Elder, Lonne, III, **Supp. IV Part 1:** 362
Elder, Richard, **Supp. XII:** 172
"Elder Sister, The" (Olds), **Supp. X:** 205–206
Elder Statesman, The (Eliot), **I:** 572, 573, 583; **Retro. Supp. I:** 53, 65
E. L. Doctorow (Harter and Thompson), **Supp. IV Part 1:** 217
Eldredge, Kay, **Supp. IX:** 254, 259
Eldridge, Florence, **III:** 154, 403; **IV:** 357
Eleanor of Aquitaine, **III:** 470
Eleanor of Guienne, **I:** 14
"Elect, The" (Taylor), **Supp. V:** 323
"Elections, Nicaragua, 1984" (Kingsolver), **Supp. VII:** 208
Elective Affinities (Goethe; Bogan and Mayer, trans.), **Supp. III Part 1:** 63
Electra (Euripides), **III:** 398
Electra (Sophocles), **III:** 398; **IV:** 370; **Supp. IX:** 102
"Electra on Azalea Path" (Plath), **Supp. I Part 2:** 538
"Electrical Storm" (Bishop), **Supp. I Part 1:** 93
"Electrical Storm" (Hayden), **Supp. II Part 1:** 370
"Electric Arrows" (Proulx), **Supp. VII:** 256
"Electricity Saviour" (Olds), **Supp. X:** 215
Electric Kool-Aid Acid Test, The (Wolfe), **Supp. III Part 2:** 575–577, 582–584; **Supp. XI:** 239
Electric Lady, The (film), **Supp. XI:** 309
Electronic Book Review, **Supp. XXII:** 256, 257, 261
Elegant Extracts (Knox), **II:** 8
"Elegant Tom Dillar" (Briggs), **Supp. XVIII:** 17
Elegiac Feelings American (Corso), **Supp. XII: 131–134**
"Elegiac Fragments" (Everwine), **Supp. XV:** 89
Elegies (Rukeyser), **Supp. VI:** 273
"Elegies" (Rukeyser), **Supp. VI:** 272
"Elegies for Paradise Valley" (Hayden), **Supp. II Part 1:** 363
"Elegy" (Bidart), **Supp. XV:** 25, 29
Elegy (Levis), **Supp. XI:** 257, 259, 261, **271–272**
"Elegy" (Merwin), **Supp. III Part 1:** 351
"Elegy" (Stafford), **Supp. XI:** 322
"Elegy" (Tate), **IV:** 128
"Elegy, for the U.S.N. Dirigible, Macon, An" (Winters), **Supp. II Part 2:** 810
"Elegy Ending in the Sound of a Skipping Rope" (Levis), **Supp. XI:** 271–272
"Elegy for 41 Whales Beached in Florence, Oregon, June 1979" (Bierds), **Supp. XVII:** 27
"Elegy for D. H. Lawrence, An" (W. C. Williams), **Retro. Supp. I:** 421
"Elegy for My Father" (Strand), **Supp. IV Part 2:** 628
"Elegy for My Mother" (Wagoner), **Supp. IX:** 330
"Elegy for Redondo Beach" (Jarman), **Supp. XVII:** 112, 113
Elegy for September, An (Nichols), **Supp. XIII:** 268
"Elegy for Thelonious" (Komunyakaa), **Supp. XIII:** 118
"Elegy for the Native Guards" (Trethewey), **Supp. XXI:** 255
"Elegy for the U.S.N. Dirigible, Macon, A" (Winters), **Supp. II Part 2:** 810
"Elegy in Dialogue" (Taggard), **Supp. XXII:** 276
"Elegy of Last Resort" (Nemerov), **III:** 271
"Elegy with a Thimbleful of Water in the Cage" (Levis), **Supp. XI:** 272
Elegy Written in a Country Churchyard (Gray), **I:** 68
"Elegy Written in a Country Churchyard" (Gray), **Supp. XIV:** 8
"Elementary Scene, The" (Jarrell), **II:** 387, 388, 389
"Elements" (M. Frank), **Supp. X:** 213
Elements of Style, The (Strunk), **Supp. I Part 2:** 670
"Elenita, Cards, Palm, Water" (Cisneros), **Supp. VII:** 64
"Eleonora" (Poe), **III:** 412
Eleothriambos (Lee), **IV:** 158
"Elephant & Ocean" (Notley), **Supp. XXII:** 230
"Elephants" (Moore), **III:** 203
"Elephant's Dance, The" (D. West), **Supp. XVIII:** 281
"Elevator, The" (Dixon), **Supp. XII:** 154
"Elevator Boy" (Hughes), **Retro. Supp. I:** 200; **Supp. I Part 1:** 326
"Eleven" (Cisneros), **Supp. VII:** 69
Eleven Essays in the European Novel (Blackmur), **Supp. II Part 1:** 91, 111
Eleven Kinds of Loneliness (Yates), **Supp. XI: 340–343,** 349
Eleven Poems on the Same Theme (Warren), **IV:** 239–241
"Eleven Times a Poem" (Corso), **Supp. XII:** 132, 133
El Greco (Doménikos Theotokópoulos), **I:** 387; **III:** 212
El-Hage, George N., **Supp. XX: 116**
"El-Hajj Malik El-Shabazz" (Hayden), **Supp. II Part 1:** 379
"Eli, the Fanatic" (P. Roth), **Supp. III Part 2:** 407–408
Elia, Nada, **Supp. XXII:** 73
Eliade, Mircea, **Supp. XVI:** 292
Elie, Paul, **Supp. XXII:** 91–92
Eliot, Charles William, **I:** 5; **II:** 345; **Retro. Supp. I:** 55; **Supp. I Part 2:** 479; **Supp. IX:** 94
Eliot, George, **I:** 375, 458, 459, 461, 467; **II:** 179, 181, 191–192, 275, 319, 324, 338, 577; **IV:** 311, 322; **Retro. Supp. I:** 218, 220, 225; **Supp. I Part 1:** 370; **Supp. I Part 2:** 559, 579; **Supp. IV Part 1:** 31, 297; **Supp. IV Part 2:** 677; **Supp. V:** 258; **Supp. IX:** 38, 43, 51; **Supp. XI:** 68; **Supp. XII:** 335; **Supp. XIV:** 344; **Supp. XX: 108**
Eliot, T. S., **I:** 48, 49, 52, 59, 60, 64, 66, 68, 105, 107, 215–216, 236, 243, 256, 259, 261, 266, 384, 386, 395, 396, 399, 403, 430, 433, 441, 446, 475, 478, 479, 482, 521, 522, 527, **567–591; II:** 65, 96, 158, 168, 316, 371, 376, 386, 529, 530, 532, 537, 542, 545; **III:** 1, 4, 5, 6, 7–8, 9, 10, 11, 14, 17, 20, 21, 23, 26, 34, 174, 194, 195–196, 205–206, 220, 236, 239, 269, 270–271, 277–278, 301, 409, 428, 435, 436, 453, 456–457, 459–460, 461–462, 464, 466, 471, 476, 478, 485, 488, 492, 493, 498, 504, 509, 511, 517, 524, 527, 539, 572, 575, 586, 591, 594, 600, 613; **IV:** 27, 74, 82, 83, 95, 122, 123, 127, 129, 134, 138, 140, 141, 191, 201, 237, 331, 379, 402, 403, 418, 419, 420, 430, 431, 439, 442, 491; **Retro. Supp. I: 51–71,** 74, 80, 89, 91, 171, 198, 210, 283, 289, 290, 292, 296, 298, 299, 311, 324, 359, 411, 413, 414, 416, 417, 420, 428; **Retro. Supp. II:** 79, 178, 189, 262, 326; **Supp. I Part 1:** 257, 264, 268, 270, 274, 299; **Supp. I Part 2:** 387, 423, 455, 536, 554, 624,

659, 721; **Supp. II Part 1:** 1, 4, 8, 20, 30, 91, 98, 103, 136, 314; **Supp. III Part 1:** 9, 10, 26, 31, 37, 41, 43, 44, 48, 62–64, 73, 91, 99–100, 105–106, 273; **Supp. III Part 2:** 541, 611, 612, 617, 624; **Supp. IV Part 1:** 40, 47, 284, 380, 404; **Supp. IV Part 2:** 436; **Supp. V:** 79, 97, 101, 338, 343, 344; **Supp. VIII:** 19, 21, 93, 102, 105, 182, 195, 205, 290, 292; **Supp. IX:** 158–159, 229; **Supp. X:** 59, 115, 119, 124, 187, 324; **Supp. XI:** 242; **Supp. XII:** 45, 159, 198, 308; **Supp. XIII:** 77, 104, 115, 332, 341–342, 344, 346; **Supp. XIV:** 5, 13, 107, 287, 290, 306, 347; **Supp. XV:** 20, 51, 139, 177, 181, 186, 216, 218, 250, 251, 258, 298, 302, 303, 306, 307; **Supp. XVI:** 158–159, 204, 207, 282; **Supp. XVII:** 36, 71, 75, 111, 240; **Supp. XVIII:** 136; **Supp. XIX:** 12; **Supp. XX:** **86, 108, 199**

Eliot's Early Years (Gordon), **Retro. Supp. I:** 55

"Elizabeth" (Longfellow), **I:** 502

"Elizabeth, 1905" (Schnackenberg), **Supp. XV:** 253, 256

Elizabeth Appleton (O'Hara), **III:** 362, 364, 375–377

"Elizabeth Bishop (1911–1979)" (Merrill), **Retro. Supp. II:** 53

"Elizabeth Bishop in Brazil" (Brown), **Supp. I Part 1:** 96

"Elizabeth Bishop's *North & South" (Lowell), Retro. Supp. II:* 40–41

"Elizabeth Gone" (Sexton), **Supp. II Part 2:** 674, 681

Elizabeth Rex (Findley), **Supp. XX:** **62–63**

Elizabeth Stoddard and the Boundaries of Bourgeois Culture (Mahoney), **Supp. XV:** 270

Elk Heads on the Wall (Ríos), **Supp. IV Part 2:** 540

Elkin, Stanley, **Supp. VI: 41–59**

"Elk Song" (Hogan), **Supp. IV Part 1:** 406

Ella in Bloom (Hearon), **Supp. VIII:** **70–71**

Elledge, Jim, **Supp. XIII:** 88

Ellen Foster: A Novel (Gibbons), **Supp. X:** 41, **42–44,** 46, 47, 49, 50

Ellen Montgomery's Bookshelf (S. and A. Warner), **Supp. XVIII:** 264

Ellen Rogers (Farrell), **II:** 42–43

"Ellen's Dream" (Gioia), **Supp. XV:** 128

"Ellen West" (Bidart), **Supp. XV: 26–27**

Eller, Ernest, **Supp. I Part 2:** 497

Ellerman, Winifred, **Supp. I Part 1:** 258–259. *See also* McAlmon, Mrs. Robert (Winifred Ellerman)

"El libro de la sexualidad" (Simic), Supp. VIII: 283

Ellington, Duke, **Retro. Supp. II:** 115; **Supp. IV Part 1:** 360; **Supp. IX:** 164

Elliot, Charles, **Supp. V:** 161

Elliot, George P., **Supp. XV:** 92

Elliott, George B., **III:** 478

Ellipse, The: Selected Poems of Leonardo Sinisgalli (Di Piero, trans.), **Supp. XIX:** 34

"Ellipsis" (C. Frost), **Supp. XV:** 107

Ellis, Albert, **Supp. IV Part 2:** 527

Ellis, Anne, **Supp. XVI:** 38

Ellis, Bret Easton, **Supp. XII:** 81; **Supp. XVIII:** 135

Ellis, Brett Easton, **Supp. X:** 7

Ellis, Charles, **Supp. I Part 1:** 99

Ellis, Havelock, **II:** 276; **Supp. XX: 117, 235; Supp. XXII:** 198

Ellis, John Harvard, **Supp. I Part 1:** 103

Ellis, Katherine, **IV:** 114

Ellis, Kelly, **Supp. XXI:** 249

Ellis, Ron, **Supp. XXII:** 209

Ellis, Thomas Sayers, **Supp. XXI:** 246

Ellison, Harlan, **Supp. XIII:** 61

Ellison, Ralph, **IV:** 250, 493; **Retro. Supp. II:** 3, **111–130; Supp. II Part 1:** 33, **221–252; Supp. IV, Part 1:** 374; **Supp. VIII:** 105, 245; **Supp. IX:** 114, 316; **Supp. X:** 324; **Supp. XI:** 18, 92, 275; **Supp. XIII:** 186, 233, 305; **Supp. XIV:** 306; **Supp. XV:** 194; **Supp. XVI:** 135, 139; **Supp. XVIII:** 59, 61, 62, 277, 283; **Supp. XIX:** 148, 149, 155

Ellmann, Maud, **Supp. IV Part 1:** 302

Ellmann, Richard, **Supp. VIII:** 105; **Supp. XV:** 74

Ellroy, James, **Supp. XIV:** 26; **Supp. XXI:** 71

Elman, Richard, **Supp. V:** 40

"Elmer" (Faulkner), **Retro. Supp. I:** 79, 80

Elmer Gantry (Lewis), **I:** 26, 364; **II:** 447–449, 450, 455

Elmer the Great (Lardner), **II:** 427

"Elms" (Glück), **Supp. V:** 85

"Elms Dying, The—And My Friend, Lew Stillwell, Dead" (Bronk), **Supp. XXI:** 31

Eloges (Perse), **Supp. XIII:** 344

"Eloquence of Grief, An" (Crane), **I:** 411

"El Río Grande" (Mora), **Supp. XIII:** 224

"*El* Round up" (Alvarez), **Supp. VII:** 11

"El Salvador: Requiem and Invocation" (Levertov), **Supp. III Part 1:** 284

Elsasser, Henry, **I:** 226

"Elsa Wertman" (Masters), **Supp. I Part 2:** 462–463

Elsie John and Joey Martinez: Two Stories (Huncke), **Supp. XIV:** 148

Elsie Venner (Holmes), **Supp. I Part 1:** 243, 315–316

Elton, Charles, **Supp. XIV:** 192

Éluard, Paul, **III:** 528; **Supp. IV Part 1:** 80; **Supp. XVII:** 244

Elvins, Kells, **Supp. III Part 1:** 93, 101

Ely, Richard T., **Supp. I Part 1:** 5; **Supp. I Part 2:** 640, 645

"Emancipation. A Life Fable" (Chopin), **Retro. Supp. II:** 59; **Supp. I Part 1:** 207–208

"Emancipation in the British West Indies" (Emerson), **II:** 13

"Emancipation Proclamation, The" (Emerson), **II:** 13

Emanuel, James, **Supp. I Part 1:** 346

Embargo, The (Bryant), **Supp. I Part 1:** 152–153

Embarrassments (James), **Retro. Supp. I:** 229

Embezzler, The (Auchincloss), **Supp. IV Part 1:** 24, 30–31

"Embroidery, The" (C. Frost), **Supp. XV:** 97

"Emerald" (Doty), **Supp. XI:** 131

"Emerald, The" (Merrill), **Supp. III Part 1:** 328

Emerald City (Egan), **Supp. XIX:** 49, **52–53**

"Emerald City" (Egan), **Supp. XIX:** 52

"Emergence of Flight from Aristotle's Mud, The" (Goldbarth), **Supp. XII:** 190

Emergency Exit (Major), **Supp. XXII:** 174, **175,** 182

"Emergency Haying" (Carruth), **Supp. XVI:** 55

"Emergency Room" (Mora), **Supp. XIII:** 218

"Emerging Voices: The Teaching of Writing" (Mora), **Supp. XIII:** 220

Emerson, and Other Essays (Chapman), **Supp. XIV:** 41–44

Emerson, Ellen, **Supp. I Part 1:** 33

Emerson, John, **Supp. XVI:** 185, 186, 190, 192

Emerson, Ralph Waldo, **I:** 98, 217, 220, 222, 224, 228, 239, 246, 251, 252, 253, 257, 260, 261, 283, 386, 397, 402, 424, 433, 444, 447, 455, 458, 460–461, 463, 464, 485, 561; **II: 1–24,** 49, 92, 127–128, 169, 170, 226, 233, 237, 273–274, 275, 278, 289, 295, 301, 313, 315, 336, 338, 344, 402, 491, 503; **III:** 53, 82, 171, 174, 260, 277, 409, 424, 428, 453, 454, 507, 576–577, 606, 614; **IV:** 60, 167, 169, 170, 171, 172, 173–174, 176, 178, 183, 186, 187, 192, 201, 202, 211, 335, 338, 340, 342, 350; **Retro. Supp. I:** 34, 53, 54, 57, 62, 74–75, 76, 125, 148–149, 152–153, 159, 217, 250, 298, 392, 400, 403; **Retro. Supp. II:** 96, 113, 135, 142, 155, 207, 262; **Supp. I Part 1:** 2, 28–29, 31, 33, 188, 299, 308–309, 317, 358, 365, 366, 368; **Supp. I Part 2:** 374, 383, 393, 407, 413, 416, 420, 422, 474, 482, 580, 582, 602, 659, 679; **Supp. II Part 1:** 280, 288; **Supp. III Part 1:** 387; **Supp. IV Part 2:** 439, 597, 619; **Supp. V:** 118; **Supp. VIII:** 42, 105, 106, 108, 198, 201, 204, 205, 292; **Supp. IX:** 38, 90, 175, 176, 181; **Supp. X:** 42, 45, 121, 223; **Supp. XI:** 203; **Supp. XIII:** 141, 145, 233, 246, **Supp. XIII:** 247; **Supp. XIV:** 41–44, 46, 54, 104, 177; **Supp. XV:** 219, 224; **Supp. XVI:** 84; **Supp. XVII:** 42, 236; **Supp. XX: 115, 116; Supp. XXI:** 217

"Emerson and the Essay" (Gass), **Supp. VI:** 88

"Emerson the Lecturer" (Lowell), **Supp. I Part 2:** 420, 422

Emerson-Thoreau Award, **Retro. Supp. I:** 67
Emery, Clark, **III:** 478
Emery, Mary Lou, **Supp. XXII:** 73
E. M. Forster (Trilling), **Supp. III Part 2:** 496, 501, 504
"Emigre in Autumn, An" (Gioia), **Supp. XV:** 120
"Emily Dickinson and Class" (Erkkila), **Retro. Supp. I:** 42–43
Emily Dickinson Editorial Collective, **Retro. Supp. I:** 47
Emily Dickinson in Southern California (X. J. Kennedy), **Supp. XV: 164–165**
"Emily Dickinson's Defunct" (Nelson), **Supp. XVIII:** 173
Emily Dickinson: Woman Poet (Bennett), **Retro. Supp. I:** 42
Eminent Victorians (Strachey), **Supp. I Part 2:** 485
Emma (Austen), **Supp. XVIII:** 149
"Emma and Eginhard" (Longfellow), **III:** 505
"Emma Enters a Sentence of Elizabeth Bishop's" (Gass), **Supp. VI:** 93
Emmanuel Appodocca: or, A Blighted Life (Philip), **Supp. XXI:** 160
"Emmaus" (Di Piero), **Supp. XIX:** 42, 43
Emperor Jones, The (O'Neill), **II:** 278; **III:** 391, 392
Emperor of Haiti (Hughes), **Supp. I Part 1:** 339
"Emperor of Ice Cream, The" (Stevens), **IV:** 76, 80–81
"Emperors" (Dunn), **Supp. XI:** 155
"Emperor's New Clothes, The" (Anderson), **I:** 441
"Empire" (Ford), **Supp. V:** 69
Empire: A Novel (Vidal), **Supp. IV Part 2:** 677, 684, 686, 690; **Supp. XIX:** 132
"Empire Builders" (MacLeish), **III:** 14
Empire Falls (Russo), **Supp. XII: 339–343**
Empire of Summer, The (Doty), **Supp. XI:** 120
Empire of the Senseless (Acker), **Supp. XII:** 5, **6, 14–16**
"Empires" (Simic), **Supp. VIII:** 282
"Emporium" (Shapiro), **Supp. II Part 2:** 705
Empress of the Splendid Season (Hijuelos), **Supp. VIII: 86–89**
Empson, William, **I:** 522, 533; **II:** 536; **III:** 286, 497, 498, 499; **IV:** 136, 431; **Retro. Supp. I:** 263; **Retro. Supp. II:** 253; **Supp. XVI:** 190
Empty Hands, The (Bronk), **Supp. XXI:** 31
"Empty Hills, The" (Winters), **Supp. II Part 2:** 792, 793, 796
Empty Mirror, Early Poems (Ginsberg), **Supp. II Part 1:** 308, 311, 313–314, 319, 329
"Empty Room" (Hughes), **Supp. I Part 1:** 337
"Empty Threat, An" (Frost), **II:** 159
Emshwiller, Ed, **Supp. XVIII:** 145
"Encantadas, The" (Melville), **III:** 89; **Supp. XVIII:** 4
Enchanter, The (Nabokov), **Retro. Supp. I:** 266
"Enclosed Dreams, Highways and Labyrinths: Jonathan Lethem's *Amnesia Moon" (Rossi), Supp. XVIII:* 139
"Encomium Twenty Years Later" (Tate), **I:** 381
"Encounter" (Espaillat), **Supp. XXI:** 107
"Encounter, The" (Pound), **III:** 466
Encounter in April (Sarton), **Supp. VIII:** 259
"Encounter in April" (Sarton), **Supp. VIII:** 259
"Encountering the Sublime" (McClatchy), **Supp. XII:** 261
"Encounter on the Seine: Black Meets Brown" (Baldwin), **Retro. Supp. II:** 2
Encounters with Chinese Writers (Dillard), **Supp. VI:** 19, 23, 31
Encounters with the Archdruid (McPhee), **Supp. III Part 1:** 292–294, 301; **Supp. X:** 30
Encyclopedia of Arkansas History and Culture, The (online), **Supp. XXII:** 50
Encyclopedia of Scotland, The (A. Finch), **Supp. XVII: 70–71**
Encyclopedia of World Biography, The, **Supp. XXI:** 74
"End, The" (Olds), **Supp. X:** 205
"Endangered Species" (Mora), **Supp. XIII:** 219–220
Endecott and the Red Cross (Lowell), **II:** 545
Endgame (Beckett), **Supp. XIII:** 196; **Supp. XXII:** 263
"Endgame" (Tan), **Supp. X:** 290
"Endicott and the Red Cross" (Hawthorne), **Retro. Supp. II:** 181, 187–188
"End of Books, The" (Coover), **Supp. V:** 53
End of Books, The" (Coover), **Supp. XXII:** 259
End of Dreams, The (Skloot), **Supp. XX: 196, 202–203**
End of Education, The (Postman), **Supp. XI:** 275
"End of FIRPO in the World, The" (Saunders), **Supp. XIX:** 229
"End of Season" (Warren), **IV:** 239–240
"End of Something, The" (Hemingway), **II:** 248
End of the Affair, The (Greene), **Supp. XI:** 99
End of the Age of Innocence, The (Price), **Retro. Supp. I:** 377
"End of the Line, The" (Jarrell), **III:** 527
"End of the Rainbow, The" (Jarrell), **II:** 386
End of the Road (film), **Supp. XI:** 309
End of the Road, The (Barth), **I:** 121, 122, 126–131; **Supp. XI:** 309; **Supp. XVIII:** 140, 141
"End of the World, The" (Gioia), **Supp. XV:** 126
"End of the World, The" (MacLeish), **III:** 8
Endor (Nemerov), **III:** 269, 270, 279
Endore, Guy, **Supp. XVII: 53–67**
"Ends" (Dixon), **Supp. XII:** 153
End to Innocence, An: Essays on Culture and Politics (Fiedler), **Supp. XIII: 98–99**
Endure: The Diaries of Charles Walter Stetson (Stetson), **Supp. XI:** 196
"Enduring Chill, The" (O'Connor), **III:** 349, 351, 357; **Retro. Supp. II:** 236
Enduring Vision of Norman Mailer, The (Leeds), **Retro. Supp. II:** 204
Endymion (Keats), **IV:** 405; **Retro. Supp. I:** 412
End Zone (DeLillo), **Supp. VI:** 2, 3, 4, 10, 11, 12
Enemies (Boyce and Hapgood), **Supp. XVII:** 100; **Supp. XXI:** 7, 13
Enemies: A Love Story (Singer), **IV:** 1; **Retro. Supp. II: 310–311**
Enemy, The: Time (T. Williams), **IV:** 391
Enemy of the People, An (adapt. Miller), **III:** 154–156
"Energy Vampire" (Ginsberg), **Supp. II Part 1:** 326
"Enforcement of the Slave Trade Laws, The" (Du Bois), **Supp. II Part 1:** 161
"Engaging the Past" (Bell), **Supp. X:** 17
Engel, Bernard F., **I:** 532
Engels, Friedrich, **IV:** 429, 443–444; **Supp. I Part 1:** 13; **Supp. XXI:** 162
Engineer of Beasts, The (Sanders), **Supp. XVI:** 270
Engineer of Moonlight (DeLillo), **Supp. VI:** 4
Engineers and the Price System, The (Veblen), **I:** 475–476; **Supp. I Part 2:** 638, 642, 648
Engines of Creation: the Coming Era of Nanotechnology (Drexler), **Supp. XVI:** 121
"England" (Moore), **III:** 203, 207, 214
Englander, Nathan, **Supp. XX: 177, 179**
Engle, Paul, **III:** 542; **Retro. Supp. II:** 220, 221; **Supp. V:** 337; **Supp. XI:** 315; **Supp. XIII:** 76; **Supp. XVIII:** 72
English, Zoë, **Supp. XVI:** 293
English Elegy, The: Studies in the Genre from Spenser to Yeats (Sacks), **Supp. IV Part 2:** 450
English Hours (James), **II:** 337; **Retro. Supp. I:** 235
English Language, The (L. P. Smith), **Supp. XIV:** 341
English-Latin Gradus or Verse Dictionary, An (Ainger), **Supp. XX: 230**
Englishmen of Letters (James), **II:** 327
English Notebooks, The (Hawthorne), **II:** 226, 227–228
English Novel, The (Lanier), **Supp. I Part 1:** 371
English Poets, The: Lessing, Rousseau (Lowell), **Supp. I Part 2:** 407
English Prosody and Modern Poetry (Shapiro), **Supp. II Part 2:** 710
English Traits (Emerson), **II:** 1, 5, 6–7, 8
"English Writers on America" (Irving), **II:** 308
Engstrand, Stuart, **Supp. I Part 1:** 51

"Enigma Variations" (Nelson), **Supp. XVIII:** 177
"Enoch and the Gorilla" (O'Connor), **Retro. Supp. II:** 225
Enormous Changes at the Last Minute (Paley), **Supp. VI:** 218
"Enormous Changes at the Last Minute" (Paley), **Supp. VI:** 226, 232
"Enormous Radio, The" (Cheever), **Supp. I Part 1:** 175–177, 195
Enormous Radio and Other Stories, The (Cheever), **Supp. I Part 1:** 175–177
Enormous Room, The (Cummings), **I:** 429, 434, 440, 445, 477; **Supp. XXI:** 277
"Enough for a Lifetime" (Buck), **Supp. II Part 1:** 127
Enough Rope (Parker), **Supp. IX:** 189, 192
Enquiry Concerning Political Justice (Godwin), **Supp. I Part 1:** 126, 146
"En Route" (Boulton), **Supp. XXII:** 25
Entered From the Sun (Garrett), **Supp. VII:** 105–106, 107–109
"Entering the Building" (Notley), **Supp. XXII:** 237
"Entering the Kingdom" (Oliver), **Supp. VII:** 234
Entertaining Strangers (Gurney), **Supp. V:** 98, 99
Enter without Desire (Lacy), **Supp. XV:** 201
Entrance: Four Chicano Poets, **Supp. XIII:** 316
Entrance to Porlock, The (Buechner), **Supp. XII:** 52
Entries (Berry), **Supp. X:** 23
"Entropy" (Pynchon), **Supp. II Part 2:** 619, 621
Entry in an Unknown Hand (F. Wright), **Supp. XVII:** 240, 244, 245
Environmental Imagination, The (Buell), **Supp. V:** 209; **Supp. IX:** 29
"Envoy" (Collins), **Supp. XXI:** 57
"Envoys, The" (Merrill), **Supp. III Part 1:** 326
"Envy; or, Yiddish in America" (Ozick), **Supp. V:** 263, 265–266
"Eolian Harp, The" (Coleridge), **I:** 284
"Eototo" (Sobin), **Supp. XVI:** 283–284
"Ephemera, The" (Franklin), **II:** 121
Ephesians (biblical book), **Supp. I Part 1:** 117
Epictetus, **III:** 566
"Epicurean, The" (Auchincloss), **Supp. IV Part 1:** 25
Epicurus, **I:** 59
Epidemic of Genius, An (Wolfert), **Supp. XXI:** 278
"Epigram" (Lowell), **II:** 550
"Epilogue" (Lowell), **Retro. Supp. II:** 191
"Epimanes" (Poe), **III:** 411
"Epimetheus" (Longfellow), **II:** 494
"Epiphany" (X. J. Kennedy), **Supp. XV:** 166, 167
"Epipsychidion" (Shelley), **Supp. I Part 2:** 718
Episode in Palmetto (Caldwell), **I:** 297, 307
"Epistle" (L.-Y. Lee), **Supp. XV:** 212
Epistle to a Godson (Auden), **Supp. II Part 1:** 24
"Epistle to Be Left in the Earth" (MacLeish), **III:** 13
"Epistle to George William Curtis" (Lowell), **Supp. I Part 2:** 416
"Epistle to Léon-Paul Fargue" (MacLeish), **III:** 15
"Epitaph Ending in And, The" (Stafford), **Supp. XI:** 321–322
Epitaph for a Dead Beat (Markson), **Supp. XVII: 136–138,** 141; 139
Epitaph for a Desert Anarchist (Bishop), **Supp. XIII:** 1
Epitaph for a Tramp (Markson), **Supp. XVII:** 136, 137, 139 142
"Epitaph for Fire and Flower" (Plath), **Supp. I Part 2:** 537
"Epitaph for the Race of Man" (Millay), **III:** 127–128
"Epithalamium" (Auden), **Supp. II Part 1:** 15
"Epstein" (P. Roth), **Retro. Supp. II:** 281; **Supp. III Part 2:** 404, 406–407, 412, 422
Epstein, Barbara, **Supp. XIX:** 268
Epstein, Helen, **Supp. XVII:** 47; **Supp. XXII:** 95
Epstein, Jason, **Supp. VIII:** 233
Epstein, Joseph, **Supp. IV Part 2:** 692; **Supp. VIII:** 236, 238; **Supp. XIV: 101–117; Supp. XVI:** 230, 275
Epstein, Leslie, **Supp. XII: 159–174; Supp. XVIII:** 92, 99
Epstein, Philip, **Supp. XII:** 159
"Equal in Paris" (Baldwin), **Retro. Supp. II:** 3; **Supp. I Part 1:** 52
"Equals" (Untermeyer), **Supp. XV:** 304
Equation for Evil (Caputo), **Supp. XIX:** 25–26
"Equations of the Light" (Gioia), **Supp. XV:** 125
"Equilibrists, The" (Ransom), **III:** 490, 494
"Equipment for Pennies" (H. Roth), **Supp. IX:** 233
Erasmus, Desiderius, **Supp. XV:** 258
Erasure (Everett), **Supp. XVIII:** 54, 60, **61–62**
"Erat Hora" (Pound), **III:** 463; **Retro. Supp. I:** 413
Erdrich, Louise, **Supp. IV Part 1: 259–278,** 333, 404; **Supp. X:** 290; **Supp. XVIII:** 189
"Erectus" (Karr), **Supp. XI:** 243
"Ere Sleep Comes Down to Soothe the Weary Eyes" (Dunbar), **Supp. II Part 1:** 199, 207–208
"Ergo Non Sum. Est." (Bronk), **Supp. XXI:** 31
Erikson, Erik, **I:** 58, 214, 218
Erisman, Fred, **Supp. VIII:** 126
Erkkila, Betsy, **Retro. Supp. I:** 42; **Supp. XX: 281, 287, 287–288**
Ernest, John, **Supp. XXI:** 24
"Ernest: or Parent for a Day" (Bourne), **I:** 232
Ernst, Max, **Retro. Supp. II:** 321
"Eros" (Komunyakaa), **Supp. XIII:** 130
"Eros and Anteros" (E. Stoddard), **Supp. XV:** 283
Eros and Civilization (Marcuse), **Supp. XII:** 2
"Eros at Temple Stream" (Levertov), **Supp. III Part 1:** 278–279
Eros the Bittersweet (Carson), **Supp. XII:** 97, **98–99**
"Eros Turannos" (Robinson), **III:** 510, 512, 513–516, 517, 518
"Eroticism in Women" (Nin), **Supp. X:** 195
"Errand" (Carver), **Supp. III Part 1:** 149
Erskine, Albert, **IV:** 261; **Retro. Supp. II:** 117
Erskine, John, **I:** 223; **Supp. X:** 183; **Supp. XIV:** 120
Erstein, Hap, **Supp. IV Part 2:** 589, 590
"Escape" (MacLeish), **III:** 4
Escape Artist, The (Wagoner), **Supp. IX:** 324, **334–335**
Escher, M. C., **Supp. XII:** 26; **Supp. XVI:** 102
"Escudilla" (Leopold), **Supp. XIV:** 188
Eshleman, Clayton, **Supp. XVI:** 284
"Eskimo Love" (Apple), **Supp. XVII:** 5
Espaillat, Rhina P., **Supp. XXI: 97–114**
Espeland, Pamela, **Supp. XVIII:** 180, 181
Espen, Hal, **Supp. X:** 15
Espey, John, **III:** 463, 468, 478
Esposito, Michael, **Supp. XX: 34, 40**
Esposito, Scott, **Supp. XVII:** 234
Essais (Renouvier), **II:** 344–345
Essay Concerning Human Understanding, An (Locke), **I:** 554; **II:** 8, 348–349
Essay on American Poetry (Brown), **Supp. I Part 1:** 156
"Essay on Aristocracy" (Paine), **Supp. I Part 2:** 515
"Essay on Friendship, An" (McClatchy), **Supp. XII:** 258–259
"Essay on Love" (Carruth), **Supp. XVI:** 56
Essay on Man (Pope), **II:** 111; **Supp. I Part 2:** 516
"Essay on Marriage" (Carruth), **Supp. XVI:** 48
Essay on Our Changing Order (Veblen), **Supp. I Part 2:** 629, 642
"Essay on Poetics" (Ammons), **Supp. VII:** 29–31
Essay on Projects (Defoe), **II:** 104
"Essay on Psychiatrists" (Pinsky), **Supp. VI:** 237, 238, 241, 242, 249, 250
Essay on Rime (Shapiro), **I:** 430; **Supp. II Part 2:** 702, 703, 708–711
"Essay on Sanity" (Dunn), **Supp. XI:** 147
"Essay on the Character of Robespierre" (Paine), **Supp. I Part 2:** 515
Essay on the Chinese Written Character (Fenollosa), **III:** 474
"Essay on What I Think About Most" (Carson), **Supp. XII: 111–112**
Essays (Emerson), **II:** 1, 7, 8, 12–13, 15, 21
Essays, Speeches, and Public Letters by William Faulkner (Meriweather, ed.), **Retro. Supp. I:** 77

Essays in Anglo-Saxon Law (Adams), **I:** 5
Essays in London (James), **II:** 336
Essays in Radical Empiricism (James), **II:** 355, 356–357
Essays on Norman Mailer (Lucid), **Retro. Supp. II:** 195
Essays on the Nature and Principles of Taste (Alison), **Supp. I Part 1:** 151
Essays to Do Good (Mather), **II:** 104; **Supp. II Part 2:** 461, 467
"Essay: The Love of Old Houses" (Doty), **Supp. XI:** 136
"Essay Toward a Point of View, An" (Brooks), **I:** 244
"Essence, Absence, and Sobin's *Venus Blue*" (English), **Supp. XVI:** 293
Essential Haiku, The (Hass), **Supp. VI:** 102
Essential Keats (Levine, ed.), **Supp. V:** 179
"Essential Oils—are wrung" (Dickinson), **I:** 471; **Retro. Supp. I:** 43, 46
"Essentials" (Toomer), **Supp. III Part 2:** 486
Essentials: A Philosophy of Life in Three Hundred Definitions and Aphorisms (Toomer), **Supp. III Part 2:** 486
Essentials: Definitions and Aphorisms (Toomer), **Supp. IX:** 320
"Essentials of Spontaneous Prose" (Kerouac), **Supp. III Part 1:** 227–228
Estampas del valle y otras obras (Hinojosa). *See Valley, The* (Hinojosa)
"Estate Sale" (Nye), **Supp. XIII:** 283
Estess, Sybil, **Supp. IV Part 2:** 449, 452
Esther (Adams), **I:** 9–10, 20
"Esther" (Toomer), **Supp. IX:** 313–314
"Esther Kahn" (Symons), **Supp. XX: 239**
"Esthétique du Mal" (Stevens), **IV:** 79; **Retro. Supp. I:** 300, 311, 312
"Estoy-eh-muut and the Kunideeyahs (Arrowboy and the Destroyers)" (film), **Supp. IV Part 2:** 560
Estrada, Genaro, **Retro. Supp. II:** 89
Estray, The (Longfellow, ed.), **Retro. Supp. II:** 155
Esty, William, **III:** 358
"Etching, An" (Masters), **Supp. I Part 2:** 458
"Eternal Goodness, The" (Whittier), **Supp. I Part 2:** 704
Eternal Spring, The (Boyce), **Supp. XVII:** 100; **Supp. XXI:** 4, 5, 11
"Eternity, An" (W. C. Williams), **Retro. Supp. I:** 423
"Eternity Is Now" (Roethke), **III:** 544–545
"Ethan Brand" (Hawthorne), **II:** 227
Ethan Frome (Wharton), **IV:** 316–317, 327; **Retro. Supp. I:** 372–373; **Supp. IX:** 108; **Supp. XVIII:** 216
"Ethical Turn in Postcolonial Theory and Narrative, The: Michelle Cliff's *No Telephone to Heaven*" (Moynagh), **Supp. XXII:** 73
Ethics (Spinoza), **IV:** 12; **Retro. Supp. II:** 300
"Ethics of Culture, The" (Locke), **Supp. XIV:** 211
"Ethnics of Frank Costello, The" (Talese), **Supp. XVII:** 202
"Etude" (Kooser), **Supp. XIX:** 115
Etulain, Richard, **Supp. IV Part 2:** 597, 601, 604, 606, 607, 608, 610, 611
"Etymology" (Nelson), **Supp. XVIII:** 185
Euclid, **III:** 6, 620
"Euclid Alone Has Looked on Beauty Bare" (Millay), **III:** 133
"Euclidean Spaces: Linear Time" (Bronk), **Supp. XXI:** 31
Eugene, Frank, **Supp. X:** 204
Eugene Onegin (Pushkin), **III:** 246, 263
Eugene Onegin (Pushkin; Nabokov, trans.), **Retro. Supp. I:** 266, 267, 272
Eugenides, Jeffrey, **Supp. XIX:** 138; **Supp. XXI:** 229
Eugénie, Empress, **IV:** 309
Eugénie Grandet (Balzac), **II:** 328
"Eugénie Grandet" (Barthelme), **Supp. IV Part 1:** 47
"Eulogy for Richard Hugo (1923–1982)" (Wagoner), **Supp. IX:** 330–331
"Eulogy on the Flapper" (Z. Fitzgerald), **Supp. IX:** 71
Eumenides (Aeschylus), **Retro. Supp. I:** 65
"E Unibus Pluram: Television and U.S. Fiction" (Wallace), **Supp. X:** 315–316
"Euphemisms" (Matthews), **Supp. IX: 167–168**
Eureka (Poe), **III:** 409, 424, 428–429
Eurekas (Goldbarth), **Supp. XII:** 181
Euripides, **I:** 325; **II:** 8, 282, 543; **III:** 22, 145, 398; **IV:** 370; **Supp. I Part 1:** 268, 269, 270; **Supp. I Part 2:** 482; **Supp. V:** 277
"Euripides and Professor Murray" (Eliot), **Supp. I Part 1:** 268
"Euripides—A Playwright" (West), **IV:** 286; **Retro. Supp. II:** 326
"Europe" (Ashbery), **Supp. III Part 1:** 7–10, 13, 18
European Discovery of America, The: The Northern Voyages (Morison), **Supp. I Part 2:** 496–497
Europeans, The (H. James), **I:** 452; **II:** 327, 328; **Retro. Supp. I:** 216, 220
Europe Central (Vollmann), **Supp. XVII:** 225, 226, 227, 229, 231, **233–235,** 236
"Europe! Europe!" (Ginsberg), **Supp. II Part 1:** 320, 322
Europe of Trusts, The: Selected Poems (Howe), **Supp. IV Part 2:** 420, 422, 426
Europe without Baedeker (Wilson), **IV:** 429
Eurydice in the Underworld (Acker), **Supp. XII:** 7
Eustace, Saint, **II:** 215
Eustace Chisholm and the Works (Purdy), **Supp. VII:** 273–274, 279–280
"Euthanasia" (Tate), **IV:** 122
"Evaluation" (Bronk), **Supp. XXI:** 32
Eva-Mary (McCarriston), **Supp. XIV:** 259, 260, **263–268**
"Evangeline" (Dixon), **Supp. XII:** 153
Evangeline (Longfellow), **II:** 489, 501–502; **Retro. Supp. II:** 155, **156–159,** 162, 164; **Supp. I Part 2:** 586
Evanier, David, **Supp. XVI:** 212
Evans, Alice, **Supp. XVII:** 71, 72
Evans, Mary Ann. *See* Eliot, George
Evans, Oliver, **Supp. IV Part 1:** 85, 91
Evans, Sandy, **Supp. XIII:** 129
Evans, Walker, **I:** 36, 38, 293; **Retro. Supp. II:** 85
Eve (A. Finch), **Supp. XVII: 72–74**
"Eve" (W. C. Williams), **Retro. Supp. I:** 423
Even Cowgirls Get the Blues (Robbins), **Supp. X:** 259, 260, 261, 262–263, 264, 266, **269–271,** 272, 274, 277, 284; **Supp. XIII:** 11
"Evening" (Carver), **Supp. III Part 1:** 148
Evening (Minot), **Supp. VI:** 204–205, 208, **213–215**
"Evening at a Country Inn" (Kenyon), **Supp. VII:** 167
"Evening in Advent, An" (W. V. Davis), **Supp. XXI:** 92
"Evening in a Sugar Orchard" (Frost), **Retro. Supp. I:** 133
"Evening in Nuevo Leon, An" (Caldwell), **I:** 309
"Evening in the Sanitarium" (Bogan), **Supp. III Part 1:** 61
Evening Light, The (Skloot), **Supp. XX: 196, 201–202**
"Evening Love-of-Self" (Taggard), **Supp. XXII:** 280–281
"Evening of the 4th of July, The" (Kees), **Supp. XV:** 140, 142
"Evening on the Cote d'Azur" (Yates), **Supp. XI:** 349
Evening Performance, An: New and Selected Short Stories (Garrett), **Supp. VII:** 109
"Evenings at Home" (Hardwick), **Supp. III Part 1:** 195–196
"Evening's at Seven, The" (Thurber), **Supp. I Part 2:** 616
"Evening Star" (Bogan), **Supp. III Part 1:** 56
Evening Star, The (McMurtry), **Supp. V:** 230
Evening Star, The (screenplay, McMurtry), **Supp. V:** 232
"Evening Sun" (Kenyon), **Supp. VII:** 168
Evening Sun Turned Crimson, The (Huncke), **Supp. XIV:** 140, 149–150
"Evening Sun Turned Crimson, The" (Huncke), **Supp. XIV:** 137–138, 139
"Evening Wind, The" (Bryant), **Supp. I Part 1:** 164
"Evening without Angels" (Stevens), **Retro. Supp. I:** 302
Evening with Richard Nixon, An (Vidal), **Supp. IV Part 2:** 683
"Even Sea, The" (Swenson), **Supp. IV Part 2:** 641
Even Stephen (Perelman and West), **Retro. Supp. II:** 328
"Event, An" (Wilbur), **Supp. III Part 2:** 547, 554

"Event, The" (Dove), **Supp. IV Part 1:** 242, 247–248
"Eventide" (Brooks), **Supp. III Part 1:** 73
"Eventide" (Purdy), **Supp. VII:** 270
"Event Itself, The" (Carruth), **Supp. XVI:** 47
Eve of Saint Agnes, The (Keats), **II:** 82, 531
"Eve of St. Agnes, The" (Clampitt), **Supp. IX:** 40
"Ever a Bridegroom: Reflections on the Failure of Texas Literature" (McMurtry), **Supp. V:** 225
Everett, Alexander Hill, **Supp. I Part 1:** 152
Everett, Percival, **Supp. XVIII: 53–67**
Everlasting Story of Nory, The (Baker), **Supp. XIII:** 52, **Supp. XIII: 53–55**
"Everly Brothers, The" (Skloot), **Supp. XX: 199**
Ever-Present Past, The (Hamilton), **Supp. XVI:** 196
Evers, Medgar, **IV:** 280; **Retro. Supp. II:** 13; **Supp. I Part 1:** 52, 65
Everson, William, **Supp. XXII:** 276
Everwine, Peter, **Supp. V:** 180; **Supp. XIII:** 312; **Supp. XV: 73–90**
"Everybody's Protest Novel" (Baldwin), **Retro. Supp. II:** 4; **Supp. I Part 1:** 50, 51
"Everybody's Reading Li Po' Silk-screened on a Purple T-Shirt" (Komunyakaa), **Supp. XIII:** 120
Everybody's Story: Writing by Older Minnesotans (C. Bly, ed.), **Supp. XVI:** 38
"Everybody Was Very Nice" (Benét), **Supp. XI:** 53
"Everyday Alchemy" (Taggard), **Supp. XXII:** 274–275, 276, 279
"Every-Day Girl, A" (Jewett), **Retro. Supp. II:** 132
"Everyday Use" (Walker), **Supp. III Part 2:** 534
"Every-Day Work" (Jewett), **Retro. Supp. II:** 132
Everyone Says I Love You (film; Allen), **Supp. XV:** 11
Every Pleasure (Goldbarth), **Supp. XII:** 181
Every Soul Is a Circus (Lindsay), **Supp. I Part 2:** 384, 394, 399
"Everything Is a Human Being" (Walker), **Supp. III Part 2:** 527
Everything Is Illuminated (Foer), **Supp. XII:** 169
Everything Is Now (Cliff), **Supp. XXII:** 67, 74, 76
"Everything Stuck to Him" (Carver), **Supp. III Part 1:** 143
Everything That Moves (Schulberg), **Supp. XVIII:** 254
Everything That Rises Must Converge (O'Connor), **III:** 339, 348–349, 350–351; **Retro. Supp. II:** 235, **236–237**
"Everything That Rises Must Converge" (O'Connor), **III:** 349, 352, 357; **Retro. Supp. II:** 236
Everything You Always Wanted to Know about Sex (film; Allen), **Supp. XV:** 4–5, 13
Eve's Diary (Twain), **IV:** 208–209
"Eve Speaks" (Untermeyer), **Supp. XV:** 300
"Eve the Fox" (Gunn Allen), **Supp. IV Part 1:** 331
"Evidence" (Harjo), **Supp. XII:** 219
"Evidence-cum-Witness: Subaltern History, Violence, and the (De)formation of a Nation in Michelle Cliff's *No Telephone to Heaven*" (Sethuraman), **Supp. XXII:** 73
Evidence of the Senses, The (Kelley), **Supp. IV Part 2:** 529
Evidence of Things Not Seen, The (Baldwin), **Retro. Supp. II:** 15
"Evil Seekers, The" (Sexton), **Supp. II Part 2:** 696
"Evolution" (Swenson), **Supp. IV Part 2:** 639
Evolving the Idol: The Poetry of Gustaf Sobin (Crick), **Supp. XVI:** 289
Ewing, Jon, **Supp. X:** 253
Ewings, The (O'Hara), **III:** 383
"Examination at the Womb Door" (Hughes), **Supp. XV:** 347
"Examination of the Hero in a Time of War" (Stevens), **Retro. Supp. I:** 305–306, 308
"Excavation of Troy" (MacLeish), **III:** 18
Excellent Becomes the Permanent, The (Addams), **Supp. I Part 1:** 25
"Excelsior" (Longfellow), **Retro. Supp. II:** 169
"Excerpts from Swan Lake" (Cameron), **Supp. XII:** 80, **84**
"Excerpts from the Epistemology Workshops" (Rand), **Supp. IV Part 2:** 529
"Excess of Charity" (Wylie), **Supp. I Part 2:** 720
"Exchange, The" (Swenson), **Supp. IV Part 2:** 644
"Excitement, The " (Jarman), **Supp. XVII:** 120–121
"Exclusive" (Olds), **Supp. X:** 206
"Excrement Poem, The" (Kumin), **Supp. IV Part 2:** 448
"Excursion" (Garrett), **Supp. VII:** 100
Excursions (Thoreau), **IV:** 188
"Excursion to Canada, An" (Thoreau), **Supp. XVIII:** 4
"Excursus of Reassurance in Begonia Time, An" (Carruth), **Supp. XVI:** 58
Executioner (Weigl), **Supp. XIX:** 277
Executioner's Song, The (Mailer), **Retro. Supp. II:** 108, 209
Exekiel, **Supp. XXI:** 91
"Exercise and Abstinence" (Swados), **Supp. XIX:** 265
Exercises in History, Chronology, and Biography, in Question and Answer (Rowson), **Supp. XV:** 245
Ex-Friends: Falling Out with Allen Ginsberg, Lionel and Diana Trilling, Lillian Hellman, Hannah Arendt, and Norman Mailer (Podhoretz), **Supp. VIII:** 239, **242–244**
"Exhausted Bug, The" (R. Bly), **Supp. IV Part 1:** 73
"Exhortation" (Bogan), **Supp. III Part 1:** 58
"Exhortation" (McKay), **Supp. X:** 135
"Exile" (Gass), **Supp. VI:** 92
"Exile" (Oates), **Supp. II Part 2:** 523
Exile, The (Buck), **Supp. II Part 1:** 119, 131
"Exiles, The" (Bradbury), **Supp. IV Part 1:** 113
"Exiles, The" (Whittier), **Supp. I Part 2:** 692–693
Exiles and Fabrications (Scott), **II:** 512
Exile's Daughter, The (Spencer), **Supp. II Part 1:** 121
"Exile's Departure, The" (Whittier), **Supp. I Part 2:** 683
Exiles from Paradise: Zelda and Scott Fitzgerald (Mayfield), **Supp. IX:** 65
"Exile's Letter" (Karr), **Supp. XI:** 241
Exile's Return (Cowley), **Supp. III Part 1:** 136, 138, 140, 141, 144, 147, 148
"Exile's Return, The" (Lowell), **II:** 539; **Retro. Supp. II:** 187
Exiles: Three Short Novels (Caputo), **Supp. XIX:** 25, **26–27**
"Existences" (Stafford), **Supp. XI:** 324
Existentialism from Dostoevsky to Sartre (W. Kaufmann), **Supp. XVII:** 137
Exit into History (Hoffman), **Supp. XVI:** 148, 150, **151–153**
Exit to Eden (Rampling), **Supp. VII:** 301–302
Exley, Frederick, **Supp. XVII:** 135
Exley, Frederick, **Supp. XVI:** 69
Exodus (biblical book), **IV:** 300
Exodus (film), **Supp. XX: 246**
Exodus (Uris), **Supp. IV Part 1:** 379; **Supp. XX: 243–244, 244, 245, 247, 248, 250–251, 257**
Exodus Revisited (Uris), **Supp. XX: 247**
"Exorcism" (Snodgrass), **Supp. VI:** 314
"Exorcism, An" (Malamud), **Supp. I Part 2:** 435
Exorcist, The (film), **Supp. I Part 1:** 66
"Expanded Composition, The" (Major), **Supp. XXII:** 174
"Expanding Rooms" (Notley), **Supp. XXII:** 229
"Expanses" (Dickey), **Supp. IV Part 1:** 186
"Ex Parte" (Lardner), **II:** 432
"Expatiation on the Combining of Weathers at Thirty-seventh and Indiana Where the Southern More or Less Crosses th e Dog, The" (Carruth), **Supp. XVI:**51–52
"Expectant Father Compares His Wife to a Rabbit, An" (White), **Supp. I Part 2:** 678
"Expedition to the Pole, An" (Dillard), **Supp. VI:** 32, 34
"Expelled" (Cheever), **Supp. I Part 1:** 174, 186
Expense of Greatness, The (Blackmur), **Supp. II Part 1:** 90, 107
Expense of Vision, The (Holland), **Retro. Supp. I:** 216

"Expensive Gifts" (Miller), **Supp. XII:** 294
"Expensive Moment, The" (Paley), **Supp. VI:** 222, **227–228,** 230
Expensive People (Oates), **Supp. II Part 2:** 509, 510–511
"Experience" (Emerson), **Supp. XIV:** 42
"Experience and Fiction" (Jackson), **Supp. IX:** 121
"Experience and the Objects of Knowledge in the Philosophy of F. H. Bradley" (Eliot), **I:** 572; **Retro. Supp. I:** 59
Experience of Literature, The (Trilling), **Supp. III Part 2:** 493
"Experiences and Principles of an Historian" (Morison), **Supp. I Part 2:** 492
Experimental Death Unit # 1 (Baraka), **Supp. II Part 1:** 46
"Experimental Life, The" (Bourne), **I:** 217, 220
"Experiment in Misery, An" (S. Crane), **I:** 411; **Retro. Supp. II:** 97
Experiments and Observations on Electricity (Franklin), **II:** 102, 114–115
"Expiation" (Hoffman), **Supp. XVIII:** 86
"Expiation" (Wharton), **Retro. Supp. I:** 367
"Explaining Evil" (Gordon), **Supp. IV Part 1:** 310
"Explaining Ted Kooser" (Gioia), **Supp. XIX:** 121
"Explanation" (Stevens), **IV:** 79
Explanation of America, An (Pinsky), **Supp. VI:** 237, **241–243**
Exploding Gravy (X. J. Kennedy), **Supp. XV:** 163
"Exploit" (Wharton), **IV:** 324
"Exploration in the Great Tuolumne Cañon" (Muir), **Supp. IX:** 181
"Explorer, The" (Brooks), **Supp. III Part 1:** 79–80
"Exploring the Magalloway" (Parkman), **Supp. II Part 2:** 591
Expositor's Bible, The (G. A. Smith), **III:** 199
Expressions of Sea Level (Ammons), **Supp. VII:** 24, 28, 36
Extract from Captain Stormfeld's Visit to Heaven (Twain), **IV:** 209–210
Extracts from Adam's Diary (Twain), **IV:** 208–209
"Exulting, The" (Roethke), **III:** 544
"Eye, The" (Bowles), **Supp. IV Part 1:** 93
Eye, The (Nabokov), **III:** 251
Eye-Beaters, Blood, Victory, Madness, Buckhead and Mercy, The (Dickey), **Supp. IV Part 1:** 178, 182–183
"Eye for an Eye, An" (Humphrey), **Supp. IX:** 108
"Eye in the Rock, The" (Haines), **Supp. XII:** 208, 209
Eye in the Sky (Dick), **Supp. XVIII:** 138
"Eye-Mote, The" (Plath), **Retro. Supp. II:** 246, 247
"Eye of Paris, The" (H. Miller), **III:** 183–184
Eye of the Poet, The: Six Views of the Art and Craft of Poetry (Citino, ed.), **Supp. XIII:** 115; **Supp. XXI:** 54
"Eye of the Rock, The" (Haines), **Supp. XII:** 208
"Eye of the Story, The" (Porter), **IV:** 279
Eye of the Story, The: Selected Essays and Reviews (Welty), **Retro. Supp. I:** 339, 342, 344, 345, 346, 351, 354, 355, 356
"Eyes, The" (Wharton), **IV:** 315
"Eyes like They Say the Devil Has" (Ríos), **Supp. IV Part 2:** 543, 544
Eyes of the Dragon, The (King), **Supp. V:** 139, 152
Eyes of the Heart: A Memoir of the Lost and Found (Buechner), **Supp. XII:** 53
"Eyes of Zapata" (Cisneros), **Supp. VII:** 70
"Eyes to See" (Cozzens), **I:** 374
Eye-to-Eye (Nye), **Supp. XIII:** 274
Eysturoy, Annie O., **Supp. IV Part 1:** 321, 322, 323, 328
Ezekiel (biblical book), **II:** 541
"Ezekiel" (R. Fisher), **Supp. XIX:** 71
Ezekiel, Mordecai, **Supp. I Part 2:** 645
"Ezekiel Learns" (R. Fisher), **Supp. XIX:** 71
"Ezra Pound" (Bynner), **Supp. XV:** 49
"Ezra Pound: His Cantos" (Zukofsky), **Supp. III Part 2:** 612, 619, 622
Ezra Pound's Mauberley (Espey), **III:** 463
"Ezra Pound's Very Useful Labors" (Schwartz), **Supp. II Part 2:** 644

Faas, Ekbert, **Supp. VIII:** 292
"Fabbri Tape, The" (Auchincloss), **Supp. IV Part 1:** 21–22
Faber, Geoffrey, **Retro. Supp. I:** 63
Faber Book of Movie Verse, The (French and Wlaschin, eds.), **Supp. XVI:** 294
"Fable" (Merwin), **Supp. III Part 1:** 343
"Fable" (Wylie), **Supp. I Part 2:** 714
Fable, A (Faulkner), **II:** 55, 73; **Retro. Supp. I:** 74
"Fable, A" (Glück), **Supp. V:** 86
"Fable, The" (Winters), **Supp. II Part 2:** 792, 793, 796
"Fable Containing a Reflection the Size of a Match Head in Its Pupil, A" (Brockmeier), **Supp. XXII:** 59
"Fable Ending in the Sound of a Thousand Parakeets, A" (Brockmeier), **Supp. XXII:** 59
Fable for Critics, A (Lowell), **Supp. I Part 2:** 406, 407–408, 409, 412–413, 416, 420, 422
"Fable for Critics, A" (Lowell), **Supp. XVIII:** 3, 8
"Fable of the War, A" (Nemerov), **III:** 272
Fables (Gay), **II:** 111
Fables and Distances: New and Selected Essays (Haines), **Supp. XII:** 197, 199, 207–208, 211
Fables for Our Time (Thurber), **Supp. I Part 2:** 610
Fables of Identity: Studies in Poetic Mythology (Frye), **Supp. X:** 80
Fables of La Fontaine, The (Moore), **III:** 194, 215
"Fables of Representation: Poetry of the New York School" (Hoover), **Supp. XV:** 179
"Fables of the Fallen Guy" (Rosaldo), **Supp. IV Part 2:** 544
"Fables of the Moscow Subway" (Nemerov), **III:** 271
"Fable with a Photograph of a Glass Mobile on the Wall, A" (Brockmeier), **Supp. XXII:** 59
"Fable with Slips of White Paper Spilling from the Pockets, A" (Brockmeier), **Supp. XXII:** 59
Fabulators, The (Scholes), **Supp. V:** 40
Fabulous Small Jews (Epstein), **Supp. XIV:** 112
Face against the Glass, The (Francis), **Supp. IX: 80–81**
Face in the Crowd, A (film, Kazan), **Supp. XVIII:** 252–253
Face of Time, The (Farrell), **II:** 28, 34, 35, 39
Faces of Jesus, The (Buechner), **Supp. XII:** 53
Face to the Wind (film), **Supp. XVII:** 141
Face Value (Hwang), **Supp. XXI:** 148, 154, 155
Fachinger, Petra, **Supp. XVI:** 153
"Facing It" (Komunyakaa), **Supp. XIII:** 117, 124, 125
Facing Shadows (Jin), **Supp. XVIII:** 92, **93**
Facing the Music (L. Brown), **Supp. XXI:** 39, 42, **42–44**
"Facing the Music" (L. Brown), **Supp. XXI: 38–39,** 41, 42, 43
"*Facing the Music:* What's Wrong with All Those Happy Endings" (Neal), **Supp. XXI:** 41
"Facing West from California's Shores" (Jeffers), **Supp. II Part 2:** 437–438
Fact, Fiction, and Representation: Four Novels by Gilbert Sorrentino (Mackey), **Supp. XXI:** 236
"Fact in Fiction, The" (McCarthy), **II:** 562
"Fact of Blackness, The" (Fanon), **Supp. XX: 152**
"Facts" (Franzen), **Supp. XX: 85**
"Facts" (Levine), **Supp. V:** 193
"Facts" (Oliver), **Supp. VII:** 231–232
"Facts" (Snyder), **Supp. VIII:** 301
"Facts, The" (Lardner), **II:** 431
Facts, The: A Novelist's Autobiography (P. Roth), **Retro. Supp. II:** 280, 291; **Supp. III Part 2:** 401, 405, 417, 426
"Facts and Traditions Respecting the Existence of Indigenous Intermittent Fever in New England" (Holmes), **Supp. I Part 1:** 303
"Facts in the Case of M. Valdemar, The" (Poe), **III:** 416
Faderman, Lillian, **Retro. Supp. II:** 135; **Supp. XIII:** 313

Fadiman, Clifton, **II:** 430, 431, 443, 591–592; **Supp. IX:** 8; **Supp. XVI:** 100, 106; **Supp. XVII:** 87, 90
Fading, My Parmacheene Belle (J. Scott), **Supp. XVII: 184–185,** 188
"Fado" (McClatchy), **Supp. XII:** 265–266
Faerie Queene, The (Spenser), **III:** 487; **IV:** 253; **Supp. XIV:** 6; **Supp. XV:** 181
Faery, Rebecca Blevins, **Retro. Supp. I:** 374
Fagan, Kathy, **Supp. V:** 180; **Supp. XV:** 73
Fagan, Louise, **Supp. XIX:** 204, 205
Fahrenheit 451 (Bradbury), **Supp. IV Part 1:** 101, 102, 104, 107–109, 110, 113; **Supp. XIII:** 29
"Failure" (Gioia), **Supp. XV:** 125
"Failure" (Zach; Everwine, trans.), **Supp. XV:** 86
"Failure of David Barry, The" (Jewett), **Retro. Supp. II:** 132
Fainlight, Ruth, **Supp. XV:** 261, 264
Faint Perfume (Gale), **Supp. I Part 2:** 613
Fair, Bryan K., **Supp. VIII:** 128
Fairbanks, Douglas, **Supp. XVI:** 185, 186
Fairchild, Frances. *See* Bryant, Mrs. William Cullen (Frances Fairchild)
Fairchild, Hoxie, **Supp. XIV:** 120
Fairfield, Flora (pseudonym). *See* Alcott, Louisa May
Fair Gentlemen of Belken County (Hinojosa), **Supp. XIX: 105**
Fairly Conventional Woman, A (Shields), **Supp. VII:** 312, 316, 318
"Fairly Sad Tale, A" (Parker), **Supp. IX:** 192
Fair Warning (R. O. Butler), **Supp. XII:** 62, **75–76**
Faith (Goldbarth), **Supp. XII:** 181, **182–183**
Faith and History (Niebuhr), **III:** 308
Faith and the Good Thing (Johnson), **Supp. VI:** 187, **188–190,** 191, 193, 194, 196
Faith for Living (Mumford), **Supp. II Part 2:** 479–480
Faithful Narrative of the Surprising Works of God in the Conversion of Many Hundred Souls in Northampton, and the Neighboring Towns and Villages of New-Hampshire in New-England, A (Edwards), **I:** 545, 562
"Faith Healer" (Komunyakaa), **Supp. XIII:** 117
"Faith in a Tree" (Paley), **Supp. VI:** 217–218, 224, 230
"Faith in Search of Understanding" (Updike), **Retro. Supp. I:** 327
"Faith of an Historian" (Morison), **Supp. I Part 2:** 492
"Faith of Fishermen, The" (J. W. Miller), **Supp. XX: 170**
Faker's Dozen, A (Bukiet), **Supp. XVII:** 47
Falcoff, Mark, **Supp. VIII:** 88
Falcon (Hammett), **Supp. IV Part 1:** 351
Falconer (Cheever), **Supp. I Part 1:** 176, 193–195, 196
Falconer, A. F., **Supp. XIV:** 2
"Falcon of Ser Federigo, The" (Longfellow), **II:** 505
Falcon: Poems on Soviet Themes (Taggard), **Supp. XXII:** 284
Falk, Peter, **Supp. XI:** 174
Falkner, Dean, **II:** 55
Falkner, John, **II:** 55
Falkner, Murray, **II:** 55
Falkner, Murray C., **II:** 55
Falkner, Mrs. Murray C. (Maud Butler), **II:** 55
Falkner, William C., **II:** 55
"Fall" (Francis), **Supp. IX:** 76
"Fall, The" (Bass), **Supp. XVI:** 25
"Fall 1961" (Lowell), **II:** 550
"Fallen Western Star: The Decline of San Francisco as a Literary Region" (Gioia), **Supp. XV:** 112, **115–116**
"Fallen Western Star" Wars, The: A Debate about Literary California (Foley, ed.), **Supp. XV:** 112, 116
"Fall in Corrales" (Wilbur), **Supp. III Part 2:** 556
Falling (Dickey), **Supp. IV Part 1:** 178, 181–182
"Falling" (Dickey), **Supp. IV Part 1:** 182
"Falling Asleep over the Aeneid" (Lowell), **II:** 542; **Retro. Supp. II:** 188
Falling in Place (Beattie), **Supp. V:** 28–29
"Falling into Holes in Our Sentences" (R. Bly), **Supp. IV Part 1:** 71
"Fall Journey" (Stafford), **Supp. XI:** 322
Fall of America, The: 1965–1971 (Ginsberg), **Supp. II Part 1:** 323, 325, 327; **Supp. XV:** 264
Fall of Eve, The (Loos), **Supp. XVI:** 187
Fall of the City, The: A Verse Play for Radio (MacLeish), **III:** 20
"Fall of the House of Usher, The" (Poe), **III:** 412, 414, 415, 419; **Retro. Supp. II:** 270
Fall of the Magicians, The (Kees), **Supp. XV:** 144
Fall of the Year, The (Mosher), **Supp. XXII:** 205, 206, 208, 209**, 214**
Fallows, James, **Supp. VIII:** 241
Fall Quarter (Kees), **Supp. XV:** 141
Fall & Rise (Dixon), **Supp. XII:** 147–148, 148, 153, 157
Falls, Robert, **Supp. XXI:** 148
"Falls, The" (Olds), **Supp. X:** 215
"Falls, The" (Saunders), **Supp. XIX:** 229
"Falls Fight, The" (Howe), **Supp. IV Part 2:** 431–432
Falon, Janet Ruth, **Supp. IV Part 2:** 422
False Coin (Swados), **Supp. XIX: 260–261,** 263
"False Dawn" (Wharton), **Retro. Supp. I:** 381
"False Documents" (Doctorow), **Supp. IV Part 1:** 220, 236
"False Leads" (Komunyakaa), **Supp. XIII:** 116
Falwell, Jerry, **Supp. XX: 273**
Fame and Obscurity: Portraits by Gay Talese (Talese), **Supp. XVII:** 202, 203, 204
Fame & Folly: Essays (Ozick), **Supp. V:** 272
"Familiar Epistle to a Friend, A" (Lowell), **Supp. I Part 2:** 416
Familiar Territory: Observations on American Life (Epstein), **Supp. XIV: 106**
"Familiar Things" (Pickering), **Supp. XXI:** 204
"Family" (Sanders), **Supp. XVI:** 276
"Family" (Wilson), **IV:** 426
Family, Kinship, and Sympanthy in Nineteenth-Century America (Weinstein), **Supp. XVIII:** 261
"Family, The" (Taggard), **Supp. XXII:** 284
"Family Affair, A" (Chopin), **Retro. Supp. II:** 71
"Family and Socialism, The" (Ryan as Quin), **Supp. XVIII:** 238
Family Arsenal, The (Theroux), **Supp. VIII:** 322
Family Chronicle: An Odyssey from Russia to America (Reznikoff), **Supp. XIV:** 277, 288, 289
Family Devotions (Hwang), **Supp. XXI:** 145, 146
"Family History" (Mora), **Supp. XIII:** 217
"Family History, A" (R. H. Davis), **Supp. XVI:** 82
Family Honor (Parker), **Supp. XIX:** 186
Family Life (Banks), **Supp. V:** 7
"Family Matters" (Alvarez), **Supp. VII:** 10
Family Moskat, The (Singer), **IV:** 1, 17, 20, 46; **Retro. Supp. II:** 304
"Family of Little Feet, The" (Cisneros), **Supp. VII:** 61
Family Party, A (O'Hara), **III:** 362
Family Pictures (Brooks), **Supp. III Part 1:** 69, 85, 86
Family Pictures (Miller), **Supp. XII:** 291, **295–297,** 299
"Family Portrait" (Trethewey), **Supp. XXI:** 250
"Family Reunion" (J. W. Miller), **Supp. XX: 167**
"Family Reunion" (X. J. Kennedy), **Supp. XV:** 169
Family Reunion, The (Eliot), **I:** 570–571, 572, 581, 584, 588; **Retro. Supp. I:** 62, 65
"Family Secrets" (Kingsolver), **Supp. VII:** 208
"Family Sideshow, The" (Karr), **Supp. XI:** 245
"Family Story, The" (Skloot), **Supp. XX: 195**
"Family Ties" (Mora), **Supp. XIII:** 215
"Family Tree" (Komunyakaa), **Supp. XIII:** 117–118, 126
"Family Wasserstein, The" (Hoban), **Supp. XV:** 319, 325
Famous American Negroes (Hughes), **Supp. I Part 1:** 345

"Famous Gilson Bequest, The" (Bierce), **I:** 204
Famous Last Words (Findley), **Supp. XX: 49, 55–56**
Famous Negro Athletes (Bontemps), **Supp. XXII:** 6
Famous Negro Music Makers (Hughes), **Supp. I Part 1:** 345
"Famous New York Trials" (Ellison), **Supp. II Part 1:** 230
Fanatics, The (Dunbar), **Supp. II Part 1:** 213–214
Fancher, Edwin, **Retro. Supp. II:** 202
Fancher, Lou, **Supp. XVI:** 177
"Fancy and Imagination" (Poe), **III:** 421
Fancy Dancer, The (P. N. Warren), **Supp. XX: 267–268**
"Fancy Flights" (Beattie), **Supp. V:** 25
"Fancy's Show Box" (Hawthorne), **II:** 238
"Fancy Woman, The" (Taylor), **Supp. V:** 316–317, 319, 323
"Fang" (Goldbarth), **Supp. XII:** 190
Fanny: Being the True History of the Adventures of Fanny Hackabout-Jones (Jong), **Supp. V:** 115, 127
Fanny Hill (Cleland), **Supp. V:** 48, 127
Fan of Swords, The (al-Maghut), **Supp. XIII:** 278
Fanon, Frantz, **Retro. Supp. II:** 118; **Supp. X:** 131, 141; **Supp. XX: 152**
Fanshawe (Hawthorne), **II:** 223–224; **Retro. Supp. I:** 149, 151
Fan's Notes, A (Exley), **Supp. XVI:** 69
"Fantasia on 'The Nut-Brown Maid' " (Ashbery), **Supp. III Part 1:** 19
"Fantasia on the Relations between Poetry and Photography" (Strand), **Supp. IV Part 2:** 631
"Fantastic Fables" (Bierce), **I:** 209
Fante, John, **Supp. XI: 159–176**
Faraday, Michael, **I:** 480–481
Far and Away (Jarman), **Supp. XVII:** 110, 115
"Far and Away" (Jarman), **Supp. XVII:** 115
"Farewell" (Emerson), **II:** 13
"Farewell" (Ryan as Quin), **Supp. XVIII:** 229
Farewell, My Lovely (Chandler), **Supp. IV Part 1:** 122, 125–126, 127, 128, 130
"Farewell, My Lovely!" (White), **Supp. I Part 2:** 661–663, 665
Farewell, The (Gibran), **Supp. XX: 121**
"Farewell Performance" (Merrill), **Supp. III Part 1:** 336–337
Farewell-Sermon Preached at the First Precinct in Northampton, after the People's Publick Rejection of their Minister, A (Edwards), **I:** 548, 562
"Farewell Sweet Dust" (Wylie), **Supp. I Part 2:** 727–728
"Farewell to America, A" (Wheatley), **Supp. XX: 283**
Farewell to Arms, A (Hemingway), **I:** 212, 421, 476, 477; **II:** 68–69, 248–249, 252–253, 254, 255, 262, 265; **Retro. Supp. I:** 171, 178, **180–182,** 187, 189; **Retro. Supp. II:** 108; **Supp. IV Part 1:** 380–381, 381; **Supp. VIII:** 179; **Supp. XII:** 241–242; **Supp. XXI:** 277
"Farewell to Miles" (Berryman), **I:** 173
"Farewell to My Union Brothers" (Ryan as Quin), **Supp. XVIII:** 238
Farewell to Reform (Chamberlain), **Supp. I Part 2:** 647
Farewell to Sport (Gallico), **Supp. XVI:** 238
"Farewell to the Middle Class" (Updike), **Retro. Supp. I:** 321
Far Field, The (Roethke), **III:** 528, 529, 539, 545, 547–548
"Far Field, The" (Roethke), **III:** 537, 540
Far-Flung (Cameron), **Supp. XII:** 81
Far from the Madding Crowd (Hardy), **II:** 291
Faríd, 'Umar ibn al-, **Supp. XX: 117**
Faris, Athénaíse Charleville, **Supp. I Part 1:** 204
Farley, Abbie, **I:** 458
Farley, Harriet, **Supp. XIII:** 140
"Farm, The" (Creeley), **Supp. IV Part 1:** 155
Farmer (Harrison), **Supp. VIII:** 39, **44–45**
Farmer, Frances, **Supp. XV:** 196–197
Farmer, Richard, **Supp. XIV:** 2
"Farmer and the Fox, The" (Leopold), **Supp. XIV:** 188
Farmer Boy (L. I. Wilder), **Supp. XXII:** 294, 297, 299
"Farmers' Daughters, The" (W. C. Williams), **Retro. Supp. I:** 423
Farmers Hotel, The (O'Hara), **III:** 361
"Farmer's Sorrow, A" (Jewett), **Retro. Supp. II:** 132
"Farmer's Wife, The" (Sexton), **Supp. II Part 2:** 676
"Farm Garden" (Nelson), **Supp. XVIII:** 186
"Farm Implements and Rutabagas in a Landscape" (Ashbery), **Supp. III Part 1:** 13
Farming: A Hand Book (Berry), **Supp. X:** 31, 35
"Farmlights in Iowa" (Kooser), **Supp. XIX:** 120
"Farm on the Great Plains, The" (Stafford), **Supp. XI:** 322
Farnol, Jeffrey, **Supp. I Part 2:** 653
Far North (Shepard), **Supp. III Part 2:** 433, 435
"Far Northern Birch, The" (Francis), **Supp. IX:** 90
Farnsworth, Elizabeth, **Supp. XI:** 139
"Farrago" (Kees), **Supp. XV:** 145
Farrand, Max, **II:** 122
Farrar, Geraldine, **Retro. Supp. I:** 10
Farrar, John, **II:** 191; **Supp. XI:** 47
Farrell, Barry, **Supp. XIV:** 142
Farrell, James Francis, **II:** 25, 26
Farrell, James T., **I:** 97, 288, 475, 508, 517, 519; **II: 25–53,** 416, 424; **III:** 28, 114, 116, 118, 119, 317, 382; **IV:** 211, 286; **Retro. Supp. II:** 196, 327; **Supp. I Part 2:** 679; **Supp. VIII:** 96, 97; **Supp. XIV:** 3; **Supp. XV:** 141
Farrell, Mrs. James T. (Dorothy Butler), **II:** 26
Farrell, Mrs. James T. (Hortense Alden), **II:** 26, 27, 45, 48
Farrell, John, **II:** 26
Farrell, John C., **Supp. I Part 1:** 24
Farrell, Kate, **Supp. XV:** 187–188,**Supp. XV:** 190
Farrell, Kevin, **II:** 26
Farrell, Mary, **II:** 25
"Far Rockaway" (Schwartz), **Supp. II Part 2:** 649
Farrow, Mia, **Supp. XV:** 8, 10
Far Side of the Dollar, The (Macdonald), **Supp. IV Part 2:** 473
Farther Off from Heaven (Humphrey), **Supp. IX:** 93, 96, 101, **103–104,** 105, 109
Far Tortuga (Matthiessen), **Supp. V:** 201, 206–207
"Fascinating Fascism" (Sontag), **Supp. III Part 2:** 465
"Fascination of Cities, The" (Hughes), **Supp. I Part 1:** 325
Fashion, Power, Guilt and the Charity of Families (Shields), **Supp. VII:** 323
Fasman, Jonathan, **Supp. V:** 253
Fast, Howard, **Supp. I Part 1:** 295; **Supp. XXI:** 277
Fast, Jonathan, **Supp. V:** 115
Fast and Loose (Wharton), **Retro. Supp. I:** 361
"Faster than Light" (Nelson), **Supp. XVIII:** 178–179
"Fastest Runner on Sixty-first Street, The" (Farrell), **II:** 45
Fast Lane on a Dirt Road (Sherman), **Supp. XXII:** 205
Fast Sooner Hound, The (Bontemps and Conroy), **Supp. XXII:** 5, 10–11
"Fat" (Carver), **Supp. III Part 1:** 141
Fatal Interview (Millay), **III:** 128–129, 130
"Fatality" (Bausch), **Supp. VII:** 54
Fatal Lady (film), **Supp. XIII:** 166
"Fate" (Emerson), **II:** 2–3, 4, 16; **Supp. XIV:** 42
"Fate" (Koch), **Supp. XV:** 183
"Fate" (Mailer), **Retro. Supp. II:** 207
"Fate of Pleasure, The" (Trilling), **Supp. III Part 2:** 510
Fate of the Jury, The (Masters), **Supp. I Part 2:** 466, 468, 469
"Fat Girl, The" (Dubus), **Supp. VII:** 84, 85
"Father" (Kooser), **Supp. XIX:** 117, 127
"Father" (Levine), **Supp. V:** 188
"Father" (Sanders), **Supp. XVI:** 277
"Father" (Trethewey), **Supp. XXI:** 253
"Father" (Walker), **Supp. III Part 2:** 522
"Father, The" (Carver), **Supp. III Part 1:** 137, 140
Father, The (Olds), **Supp. X: 209–211**
"Father Abraham" (Faulkner), **Retro. Supp. I:** 81, 82
Fatheralong: A Meditation on Fathers and Sons, Race and Society (Wideman), **Supp. X:** 320, 332–333, 334, 335
"Father and Daughter" (Eberhart), **I:** 539

Father and Glorious Descendant (Lowe), **Supp. X:** 291
"Father and Son" (Eberhart), **I:** 539
Father and Son (Farrell), **II:** 34, 35, 290, 291
Father and Son (Gosse), **Supp. VIII:** 157
"Father and Son" (Hughes), **Retro. Supp. I:** 204; **Supp. I Part 1:** 329, 339
"Father and Son" (Kunitz), **Supp. III Part 1:** 262
Father and Son (L. Brown), **Supp. XXI:** 36, 40, 41, **46–47**
"Father and Son" (Schwartz), **Supp. II Part 2:** 650
Father Bombo's Pilgrimage to Mecca (Freneau), **Supp. II Part 1:** 254
"Father Fitzgerald" (Nelson and Espeland), **Supp. XVIII:** 181
"Father Guzman" (Stern), **Supp. IX: 293,** 296
"Father John Melby and the Ghost of Amy Elizabeth" (Brockmeier), **Supp. XXII:** 60
Father of the Blues (Bontemps as Handy), **Supp. XXII:** 5
"Father out Walking on the Lawn, A" (Dove), **Supp. IV Part 1:** 246
"Fathers" (Creeley), **Supp. IV Part 1:** 157–158
Fathers, The (Tate), **IV:** 120, 127, 130, 131–133, 134, 141; **Supp. X:** 52
Fathers and Crows (Vollmann), **Supp. XVII:** 226, 231–232
"Fathers and Sons" (Hemingway), **II:** 249, 265–266; **Retro. Supp. I:** 175
"Father's Body, The" (Dickey), **Supp. IV Part 1:** 176
"Father's Day" (Connelly), **Supp. XXI:** 79–80
"Father's Story, A" (Dubus), **Supp. VII:** 88
"Father's Voice" (Stafford), **Supp. XI:** 322
"Fat Lady, The" (Carruth), **Supp. XVI:** 48
"Fat Man, Floating" (Dunn), **Supp. XI:** 144
Faulkner, Barry, **Supp. XV:** 41
Faulkner, William, **I:** 54, 97, 99, 105, 106, 115, 117, 118, 123, 190, 204–205, 211, 288, 289, 291, 292, 297, 305, 324, 374, 378, 423, 480, 517; **II:** 28, 51, **54–76,** 131, 174, 194, 217, 223, 228, 230, 259, 301, 306, 431, 458–459, 542, 594, 606; **III:** 45, 70, 108, 164, 218, 220, 222, 236–237, 244, 292, 334, 350, 382, 418, 453, 454, 482, 483; **IV:** 2, 4, 33, 49, 97, 98, 100, 101, 120, 131, 203, 207, 211, 217, 237, 257, 260, 261, 279, 280, 352, 461, 463; **Retro. Supp. I: 73–95,** 215, 339, 347, 356, 379, 382; **Retro. Supp. II:** 19, 221, 326; **Supp. I Part 1:** 196, 197, 242, 372; **Supp. I Part 2:** 450, 621; **Supp. III Part 1:** 384–385, 396; **Supp. IV Part 1:** 47, 130, 257, 342; **Supp. IV Part 2:** 434, 463, 468, 502, 677, 682; **Supp. V:** 58, 59, 138, 210, 226, 237, 261, 262, 334–336; **Supp. VIII:** 37, 39, 40, 104, 105, 108, 175, 176, 180, 181, 183, 184, 188, 189, 215; **Supp. IX:** 20, 95; **Supp. X:** 44, 228; **Supp. XI:** 92, 247; **Supp. XII:** 16, 289, 310, 313; **Supp. XIII:** 100, 169; **Supp. XIV:** 1, 12–13, 21, 24, 93, 306; **Supp. XV:** 92, 135, 338; **Supp. XVI:** 148, 189; **Supp. XVII:** 225; **Supp. XVIII:** 76, 84, 90, 148, 249; **Supp. XIX:** 97, 154, 166; **Supp. XX: 137, 162, 185, 195; Supp. XXI:** 36, 38, 256; **Supp. XXII:** 193, 203, 205
Faulkner: A Collection of Critical Essays (Warren), **Retro. Supp. I:** 73
Faulkner at Nagano (Jelliffe, ed.), **I:** 289; **II:** 63, 65
Faulkner-Cowley File, The: Letters and Memories 1944–1962 (Cowley, ed.), **Retro. Supp. I:** 73, 92; **Supp. II Part 1:** 140, 141
"Faun" (Plath), **Supp. I Part 2:** 537
"Fauna" (Jeffers), **Supp. II Part 2:** 415
Fauset, Arthur Huff, **Supp. XVIII:** 126
Fauset, Jessie, **Supp. I Part 1:** 321, 325; **Supp. IV Part 1:** 164
Fauset, Jessie Redmon, **Supp. XVIII:** 122,127; **Supp. XIX:** 69, 78
Faust (Goethe), **I:** 396; **II:** 489; **III:** 395; **Supp. II Part 1:** 16; **Supp. IX:** 141
Faust, Beatrix Hapgood, **Supp. XXI:** 8
Faust, Clarence H., **II:** 20
Faute de l'Abbé Mouret, La (Zola), **III:** 322
Favor Island (Merwin), **Supp. III Part 1:** 346, 347
"Favor of Love, A" (Peacock), **Supp. XIX:** 203
"Favrile" (Doty), **Supp. XI:** 131
"Fawn, with a Bit of Green" (Swados), **Supp. XIX:** 258
Fay (L. Brown), **Supp. XXI:** 40, 41, 47
Fay, Bernard, **IV:** 41
"Fear, The" (Frost), **Retro. Supp. I:** 128
Fear and Trembling (Kierkegaard), **Supp. XX: 132**
"Fear & Fame" (Levine), **Supp. V:** 192
Fearful Child, The (C. Frost), **Supp. XV:** 96, 97, 106
"Fearful Child, The" (C. Frost), **Supp. XV:** 96
Fearing, Kenneth, **Supp. XV:** 138
"Fearless" (Mosley), **Supp. XIII:** 241
Fearless Jones (Mosley), **Supp. XIII: 241–242**
"Fear of Concrete" (Halliday), **Supp. XIX:** 91
Fear of Fifty: A Midlife Memoir (Jong), **Supp. V:** 114, 115, 116, 131
Fear of Flying (Jong), **Supp. V:** 113, 115, 116, 119–123, 124, 129
"Feast, The" (Kinnell), **Supp. III Part 1:** 239, 250
Feast of All Saints, The (Rice), **Supp. VII:** 299–301
Feast of Love, The (C. Baxter), **Supp. XVII:** 13, 21–22
Feast of Love, The (film, R. Benton), **Supp. XVII:** 22
Feast of Snakes, A (Crews), **Supp. XI:** 102, **107–108; Supp. XXI:** 40
"Feast of Stephen, The" (Hecht), **Supp. X:** 63–64
"Featherbed for Critics, A" (Blackmur), **Supp. II Part 1:** 93, 151
Feather Crowns (Mason), **Supp. VIII: 146–147**
"Feathers" (Carver), **Supp. III Part 1:** 145
Feathers (Van Vechten), **Supp. II Part 2:** 736, 749
"Feathers, The" (Hogan), **Supp. IV Part 1:** 416
"February" (Ellison), **Supp. II Part 1:** 229
"February 14th" (Levine), **Supp. V:** 194
February in Sydney (Komunyakaa), **Supp. XIII: 124–125,** 129
"February in Sydney" (Komunyakaa), **Supp. XIII:** 125
"February: Thinking of Flowers" (Kenyon), **Supp. VII:** 171
"Feces" (McClatchy), **Supp. XII:** 266, 267–268
Fechner, Gustav, **II:** 344, 355, 358, 359, 363
Feder, Lillian, **IV:** 136; **Supp. XVI:** 49, 50
Federal Arts Project, **Supp. III Part 2:** 618
Federigo, or, The Power of Love (Nemerov), **III:** 268, 276, 282, 283–284, 285
"Fedge, The" (Halliday), **Supp. XIX:** 93
"Fedora" (Chopin), **Supp. I Part 1:** 220
Fedorko, Kathy A., **Retro. Supp. I:** 361, 374
"Feeling and Precision" (Moore), **III:** 206
Feeling Italian: The Art of Ethnicity in America (Ferraro), **Supp. XX: 43**
"Feeling of Effort, The" (James), **II:** 349
Feeling Very Strange: The Slipstream Anthology (Kelly and Kessel, eds.), **Supp. XIX:** 231
"Feel Like a Bird" (Swenson), **Supp. IV Part 2:** 639
"Feel Me" (Swenson), **Supp. IV Part 2:** 647
Feeney, Mary, **Supp. IX:** 152, 154
Feinsilver, Pamela, **Supp. XX: 135**
Feinstein, Herbert, **Supp. XIX:** 260
Feinstein, Sascha, **Supp. XIII:** 125
Feldman, Charles K., **Supp. XI:** 307
Fellini, Federico, **Supp. XII:** 172; **Supp. XV:** 8
"Fellini the Cat" (Peacock), **Supp. XIX:** 206
"Fellow Citizens" (Sandburg), **III:** 553
Fellows, John, **Supp. I Part 2:** 520
Fellow Travelers (Mallon), **Supp. XIX:** 132, **143–144**
"Felo de Se" (Wylie), **Supp. I Part 2:** 727, 729
Felton, Sharon, **Supp. IV Part 1:** 210
"Female Author" (Plath), **Retro. Supp. II:** 243
"Female Frailty" (Freneau), **Supp. II Part 1:** 258
"Female Laughter and Comic Possibilities: *Uncommon Women and Others*" (Chirico), **Supp. XV:** 323

Female Patriot, The; or, Nature's Rights (Rowson), **Supp. XV:** 237–238
Female Prose Writers of America (Hart), **Supp. XVIII:** 257, 264
"Female Voice in *To Kill a Mockingbird,* The: Narrative Strategies in Film and Novel" (Shakelford), **Supp. VIII:** 129
" 'Feminine' Epic, The" (Notley), **Supp. XXII:** 232, 234, 236
"Feminine Landscape of Leslie Marmon Silko's *Ceremony,* The" (Gunn Allen), **Supp. IV Part 1:** 324
Feminism and the Politics of Literary Reputation: The Example of Erica Jong (Templin), **Supp. V:** 116
"Feminismo" (Robbins), **Supp. X:** 272
"Feminist Criticism in the Wilderness" (Showalter), **Supp. X:** 97
"Feminist Manifesto" (Loy), **Supp. XXII:** 160
Feminization of American Culture, The (Douglas), **Supp. XVIII:** 258
"Fence, The" (Oliver), **Supp. VII:** 232
"Fence Posts" (Snyder), **Supp. VIII:** 304
Fences (Wilson), **Supp. VIII:** 329, 330, 331, **334–337,** 350
Fenick, Elizabeth, **Retro. Supp. II:** 221
"Fenimore Cooper's Literary Offenses" (Twain), **IV:** 204–205
Fennell, Frank L., **Supp. XVII:** 177–178
Fenollosa, Ernest, **III:** 458, 465, 466, 474, 475, 477; **Retro. Supp. I:** 289; **Supp. IV Part 1:** 154
Fenollosa, Mrs. Ernest, **III:** 458
"Fenstad's Mother" (C. Baxter), **Supp. XVII:** 18
Fenton, Charles, **Supp. XI:** 43
Fenton, James, **Supp. XV:** 117
Ferdinand: Including "It Was" (Zukofsky), Supp. III Part 2: 630
"Fergus" (Bourne), **I:** 229
Ferguson, James, **Supp. I Part 2:** 503
Ferguson, Otis, **Supp. IX:** 7
Ferguson, William, **Supp. XII:** 189
Ferguson Affair, The (Macdonald), **Supp. IV Part 2:** 473
Fergusson, Francis, **I:** 265, 440; **Supp. XV:** 20
Ferlinghetti, Lawrence, **Supp. IV Part 1:** 90; **Supp. VIII:** 290, 292; **Supp. XII:** 121, 125; **Supp. XIII:** 275; **Supp. XIX:** 4; **Supp. XXI:** 53
Fermata, The (Baker), **Supp. XIII: 49–52,** 54
"Fern" (Toomer), **Supp. III Part 2:** 481; **Supp. IX:** 313
Fern, Fanny, **Retro. Supp. I:** 246; **Supp. V:** 122
Fernández, Enrique, **Supp. VIII:** 73
Fernandez, Ramon, **Retro. Supp. I:** 302, 303; **Supp. XVI:** 214
"Fern-Beds in Hampshire Country" (Wilbur), **Supp. III Part 2:** 558
"Fern Hill" (D. Thomas), **IV:** 93; **Supp. XX: 204**
"Fern-Life" (Larcom), **Supp. XIII:** 143
Ferragammo, Salvatore, **Supp. XVI:** 192
Ferraro, Thomas J., **Supp. XX: 34, 43**
Ferreo, Guglielmo, **Supp. I Part 2:** 481
Ferris, Anthony, **Supp. XX: 124**
"Ferry, The" (Cliff), **Supp. XXII:** 74
Fessenden, Thomas Green, **II:** 300
Fessier, Michael, **Supp. XIII:** 164
"Festival Aspect, The" (Olson), **Supp. II Part 2:** 585
"Festival of Regrets, The" (Wasserstein), **Supp. XV:** 333
Fetching the Dead (Sanders), **Supp. XVI:** 269
Fêtes galantes (Verlaine), **IV:** 79
"Fetish" (McClatchy), **Supp. XII:** 256
Fetterley, Judith, **Retro. Supp. II:** 139
"Feud" (Zinberg), **Supp. XV:** 195
"Fever" (Carver), **Supp. III Part 1:** 145
"Fever 103°" (Plath), **Supp. I Part 2:** 541
Fever Pitch (Hornby), **Supp. XII:** 286
Fever: Twelve Stories (Wideman), **Supp. X:** 320
"Few Don'ts by an Imagiste, A" (Pound), **III:** 465; **Retro. Supp. I:** 288; **Supp. I Part 1:** 261–262
"Few Stray Comments on the Cultivation of the Lyric, A" (Sobin), **Supp. XVI:** 285
"Few Words of Introduction, A" (McNally), **Supp. XIII:** 198–199
Fiamengo, Janice, **Supp. XIII:** 35
Fiber (Bass), **Supp. XVI:** 22
"*Fiber:* A Post-Pastoral Georgic" (Gifford), **Supp. XVI:** 22
Ficke, Arthur Davison, **Supp. XIII:** 347; **Supp. XV:** 40, 42, 43, 46, 48, 49
"Fiction" (Stafford), **Supp. XI:** 327
"Fiction: A Lens on Life" (Stegner), **Supp. IV Part 2:** 595, 596, 600
Fictional World of William Hoffman, The (Frank, ed.), **Supp. XVIII:** 74, 79, 80, 87
Fiction and the Figures of Life (Gass), **Supp. VI:** 85
Fiction of Joseph Heller, The (Seed), **Supp. IV Part 1:** 391
Fiction of Paule Marshall, The (Denniston), **Supp. XI:** 276
Fiction of the Forties (Eisinger), **I:** 302; **II:** 604
Fictions in Autobiography: Studies in the Art of Self-Invention (Eakin), **Supp. XVI:** 70
"Fiction Writer and His Country, The" (O'Connor), **III:** 342; **Retro. Supp. II:** 223, 225; **Supp. II Part 1:** 148
Fiddler's Trance, The (Skloot), **Supp. XX: 196, 202**
Fidelity (Glaspell), **Supp. III Part 1:** 177
Fiedler, Leslie A., **II:** 27; **III:** 218; **Retro. Supp. II:** 280, 324; **Supp. II Part 1:** 87; **Supp. IV Part 1:** 42, 86; **Supp. IX:** 3, 227; **Supp. X:** 80; **Supp. XIII: 93–110; Supp. XIV:** 11; **Supp. XVIII:** 146; **Supp. XIX:** 251
Fiedler on the Roof: Essays on Literature and Jewish Identity (Fiedler), **Supp. XIII:** 106–107
"Fie! Fie! Fi-Fi!" (Fitzgerald), **Retro. Supp. I:** 100
Field, Eugene, **Supp. II Part 1:** 197
Field, John, **IV:** 179
"Field Events" (Bass), **Supp. XVI:** 19
"Field Full of Black Cats, A" (C. Frost), **Supp. XV:** 101
Field Guide, (Hass), **Supp. VI:** 97–98, **99–101,** 102, 103, 106
Field Guide to Contemporary Poetry and Poetics (Friebert and Young, eds.), **Supp. XI:** 270
"Field Guide to the Western Birds" (Stegner), **Supp. IV Part 2:** 609
Fielding, Henry, **I:** 134; **II:** 302, 304–305; **III:** 61; **Supp. I Part 2:** 421, 422, 656; **Supp. IV Part 2:** 688; **Supp. V:** 127; **Supp. IX:** 128; **Supp. XI:** 277; **Supp. XVIII:** 2, 7
Fielding, Richard, **Supp. XV:** 232
"Field-larks and Blackbirds" (Lanier), **Supp. I Part 1:** 355
Field of Honor (Hay), **Supp. XIV:** 120–121, 125, 130
"Field of Honor" (Hay), **Supp. XIV:** 120–121, 129–130
Field of Vision, The (Morris), **III:** 226–228, 229, 232, 233, 238
"Field Report" (Corso), **Supp. XII:** 124, **136**
"Fields" (Wright), **Supp. XV:** 342
Fields, Annie Adams, **II:** 401, 402, 403–404, 406, 412; **IV:** 177; **Retro. Supp. II:** 134, 135, 142; **Supp. I Part 1:** 317; **Supp. XVI:** 84, 88
Fields, James T., **II:** 274, 279, 402–403; **Retro. Supp. II:** 135; **Supp. I Part 1:** 317; **Supp. XIII:** 150; **Supp. XVI:** 84, 88
Fields, Mrs. James T., **Supp. XIV:** 44, 46. *See* Fields, Annie Adams
Fields, Joseph, **IV:** 274
Fields, The (Richter), **Supp. XVIII: 213–214,** 220
Fields, W. C., **II:** 427; **IV:** 335
"Fields at Dusk, The" (Salter), **Supp. IX:** 260
Fields of Fire (Webb), **Supp. XXII:** 115
Fields of Praise, The (Nelson), **Supp. XVIII:** 171, 173, **177–178**
Fields of Wonder (Hughes), **Retro. Supp. I:** 206, 207; **Supp. I Part 1:** 333–334
Fierce Invalids Home from Hot Climates (Robbins), **Supp. X:** 267, 276–277, **282–285**
Fiery, Marion, **Supp. XXII:** 293
Fiery Chariot, The (Hurston), **Supp. VI:** 155–156
15 Poems (Banks), **Supp. V:** 5
"Fifteenth Farewell" (Bogan), **Supp. III Part 1:** 51, 58
"Fifth Avenue, Uptown" (Baldwin), **Supp. I Part 1:** 52
"Fifth Avenue—Spring Afternoon" (Untermeyer), **Supp. XV:** 296
Fifth Book of Peace, The (Kingston), **Supp. V:** 173
Fifth Chinese Daughter (Wong), **Supp. X:** 291
Fifth Column, The (Hemingway), **II:** 254, 258; **Retro. Supp. I:** 184
"Fifth Column of the Fencerow" (Leopold), **Supp. XIV:** 185
Fifth Decad of Cantos, The (Pound), **Retro. Supp. I:** 292

"Fifth Movement: *Autobiography*" (Zukofsky), **Supp. III Part 2:** 611
Fifth Sunday (Dove), **Supp. IV Part 1:** 251, 252–253
"Fifth Sunday" (Dove), **Supp. IV Part 1:** 252
50 Poems (Cummings), **I:** 430, 440, 442–443, 444–445, 446
Fifty Best American Short Stories (O'Brien), **III:** 56
"Fifty Dollars" (Elkin), **Supp. VI: 43–44**
"55 Miles to the Gas Pump" (Proulx), **Supp. VII:** 264
55 Poems (Zukofsky), **Supp. III Part 2:** 611, 621
"Fifty Grand" (Hemingway), **II:** 250, 424; **Retro. Supp. I:** 177
"Fifty Suggestions" (Poe), **Retro. Supp. II:** 266
"52 Oswald Street" (Kinnell), **Supp. III Part 1:** 251
Fifty Years Among Authors, Editors, and Publishers (Derby), **Supp. XVIII:** 4
"Fifty Years Among the Black Folk" (Du Bois), **Supp. II Part 1:** 169
"Fifty Years of American Poetry" (Jarrell), **Retro. Supp. I:** 52
Fig Connection, The (Franzen and Siebert), **Supp. XX: 84**
Fight, The (Mailer), **Retro. Supp. II:** 207, 208
Fight Back: For the Sake of the People, For the Sake of the Land (Ortiz), **Supp. IV Part 2:** 497, 498, 499, 503, 510–512, 514
"Fighters, The" (Zinberg), **Supp. XV:** 193
Fight for Freedom (Hughes), **Supp. I Part 1:** 345
Fighting Angel (Buck), **Supp. II Part 1:** 119, 131
Fighting France; From Dunkerque to Belfort (Wharton), **Retro. Supp. I:** 377, 378
Fightin': New and Collected Stories (Ortiz), **Supp. IV Part 2:** 513
"Figlia che Piange, La" (Eliot), **I:** 570, 584; **III:** 9
Figliola, Samantha, **Supp. V:** 143
"Figure a Poem Makes, The" (Frost), **Retro. Supp. I:** 139
"Figured Wheel, The" (Pinsky), **Supp. VI:** 243, 244, 245, 246
Figured Wheel, The: New and Collected Poems (Pinsky), **Supp. VI:** 247–248
"Figure in the Carpet, The" (James), **Retro. Supp. I:** 228, 229
"Figure in the Doorway, The" (Frost), **Retro. Supp. I:** 138
Figure of Fulfillment, The (Lerperger; Miller, trans.), **Supp. XX: 165, 167–168**
Figures from the Double World (McGrath), **Supp. X: 118–119**
Figures in Black: Words, Signs, and the "Racial" Self (H. L. Gates), **Supp. XX: 99, 100, 106, 107**
"Figures in the Clock, The" (McCarthy), **II:** 561–562
Figures Made Visible in the Sadness of Time (Everwine), **Supp. XV:** 75, 88
Figures of Time (Hayden), **Supp. II Part 1:** 367
"Filling Out a Blank" (Wagoner), **Supp. IX:** 324
Fillmore, Millard, **III:** 101
Film Flam: Essays on Hollywood (McMurtry), **Supp. V:** 228
Films of Ayn Rand, The (Cox), **Supp. IV Part 2:** 524
Filo, John, **Supp. XII:** 211
Filreis, Alan, **Supp. XXI:** 262, 267, 268, 269, 271, 273, 275, 277, 278
Filson, John, **Retro. Supp. I:** 421
Final Beast, The (Buechner), **Supp. XII: 49–51**
"Finale" (Longfellow), **II:** 505, 506–507
"Final Fear" (Hughes), **Supp. I Part 1:** 338
Final Harvest: Emily Dickinson's Poems (Johnson, ed.), **I:** 470, 471
"Finally Harriet" (Wolfert), **Supp. XXI: 265–267**
Final Payments (Gordon), **Supp. IV Part 1:** 297, 299, 300–302, 304, 306, 314
"Final Report, A" (Maxwell), **Supp. VIII:** 169
"Final Soliloquy of the Interior Paramour" (Stevens), **Retro. Supp. I:** 312
Final Solution, The (Reitlinger), **Supp. XII:** 161
Financier, The (Dreiser), **I:** 497, 501, 507, 509; **Retro. Supp. II:** 94, 101–102, 105; **Supp. XVIII:** 246
Finch, Annie, **Supp. XVII: 69–79**
Finch, Henry Leroy, **Supp. XVII:** 69
Finch, Margaret Rockwell, **Supp. XVII:** 69
Finch, Robert, **Supp. XIV:** 186–187
Find a Victim (Macdonald), **Supp. IV Part 2:** 467, 472, 473
Fin de Chéri, La (Colette; stage adaptation, Loos), **Supp. XVI:** 194
Finder, Henry, **Supp. XX: 90**
"Fin de Saison Palm Beach" (White), **Supp. I Part 2:** 673
"Finding a Bible in an Abandoned Cabin" (Wrigley), **Supp. XVIII: 293–294, 296, 297, 300, 301, 303**
Finding a Form (Gass), **Supp. VI:** 91–92, 93
Finding a Girl in America (Dubus), **Supp. VII:** 85–88
"Finding a Girl in America" (Dubus), **Supp. VII:** 87
"Finding Beads" (Hogan), **Supp. IV Part 1:** 400
Finding Losses (Bronk), **Supp. XXI:** 31, 32
"Finding of Zach, The" (Dunbar), **Supp. II Part 1:** 212
Findings and Keepings: Analects for an Autobiography (Mumford), **Supp. II Part 2:** 483
Finding the Center: Narrative Poetry of the Zuni Indians (Tedlock), **Supp. IV Part 2:** 509
Finding the Islands (Merwin), **Supp. III Part 1:** 353, 357
"Finding the Place: A Migrant Childhood" (Stegner), **Supp. IV Part 2:** 597
Findley, Timothy, **Supp. XX: 49–65**
"Find the Woman" (Macdonald, as Millar), **Supp. IV Part 2:** 466
Fine, David, **Supp. XI:** 160
Fine, Richard, **Supp. XVIII:** 248
Fine Clothes to the Jew (Hughes), **Retro. Supp. I:** 200, 201, 203, 205; **Supp. I Part 1:** 326–328
"Fine Old Firm, A" (Jackson), **Supp. IX:** 120
Fine Preserving (Plagemann), **Supp. XVII:** 91
Fine Preserving: M. F. K. Fisher's Annotated Edition of Catherine Plagemann's Cookbook (Plagemann; M. F. K. Fisher, ed.), **Supp. XVII:** 91
Finer Grain, The (James), **II:** 335
Fine Writing (L. P. Smith), **Supp. XIV:** 347
"Finis" (X. J. Kennedy), **Supp. XV:** 169
"Finished Basement" (Di Piero), **Supp. XIX:** 47
Finished Man, The (Garrett), **Supp. VII:** 96, 97–98
Fink, Jonathan, **Supp. XXI:** 244, 245, 248, 255, 256
Fink, Mike, **IV:** 266
Finkelstein, Norman, **Supp. XXI:** 24, 33
Finkle, David, **Supp. XXI:** 47
Finley, John H., **II:** 418
Finn, David, **Supp. VIII:** 106–107
Finnegan, Robert (pseudonym). *See* Ryan, Paul William
Finnegans Wake (Joyce), **III:** 7, 12, 14, 261; **IV:** 182, 369–370, 418, 421; **Supp. I Part 2:** 620; **Supp. II Part 1:** 2; **Supp. XIII:** 191; **Supp. XVIII:** 32
Finney, Brian, **Supp. XIV:** 158, 160, 161, 165, 166, 167, 169
"Finnish Rhapsody" (Ashbery), **Supp. III Part 1:** 26
Finster, Howard, **Supp. XV:** 349
Firbank, Ronald, **IV:** 77, 436
"Fire" (Hughes), **Supp. I Part 1:** 327
"Fire and Cloud" (Wright), **IV:** 488
"Fire and Ice" (Frost), **II:** 154; **Retro. Supp. I:** 133; **Supp. XIX:** 122
Fire and Ice (Stegner), **Supp. IV Part 2:** 598, 607–608
"Fire and the Cloud, The" (Hurston), **Supp. VI:** 158
"Fire and the Hearth, The" (Faulkner), **II:** 71
Firebird (Doty), **Supp. XI:** 119–120, 121, **132–133,** 134
"Firebombing, The" (Dickey), **Supp. IV Part 1:** 180–181, 187, 189–190
"Fireborn Are at Home in Fire, The" (Sandburg), **III:** 591
"Fire by Night" (R. Fisher), **Supp. XIX:** 70–71
"Fire Chaconne" (Francis), **Supp. IX:** 87
Firecrackers (Van Vechten), **Supp. II Part 2:** 740, 742–744, 749

Fire: From "A Journal of Love," the Unexpurgated Diary of Anaïs Nin, 1934–1937, **Supp. X:** 184, 185, 189, 194, 195
"Fireman, The " (Bass), **Supp. XVI:** 24
Fireman's Wife and Other Stories, The (Bausch), **Supp. VII:** 48, 54
Fire Next Time, The (Baldwin), **Retro. Supp. II:** 5, 8, 9; **Supp. I Part 1:** 48, 49, 52, 60–61
"Fire Next Time, The" (Baldwin). *See* "Down at the Cross" (Baldwin)
"Fire of Driftwood, The" (Longfellow), **II:** 499; **Retro. Supp. II:** 159, 168
"Fire of Life" (McCullers), **II:** 585
Fire on the Mountain (Abbey), **Supp. XIII:** 6
"Fire Poem" (Merrill), **Supp. III Part 1:** 321
"Fires" (Bass), **Supp. XVI:** 20
"Fires" (Carver), **Supp. III Part 1:** 136–139, 147
Fire Screen, The (Merrill), **Supp. III Part 1:** 319, 325–329
"Fire Season" (Didion), **Supp. IV Part 1:** 199
"Fire Sequence" (Winters), **Supp. II Part 2:** 791, 796, 800
Fire Sermon (Morris), **III:** 238–239
"Fire Sermon, The" (Eliot), **Retro. Supp. I:** 60–61
Fires: Essays, Poems, Stories (Carver), **Supp. III Part 1:** 136, 140, 142, 146–147
Fireside Travels (Lowell), **Supp. I Part 2:** 407, 419–420
Firestarter (King), **Supp. V:** 140, 141, 144; **Supp. IX:** 114
"fire the bastards" (Green), **Supp. IV Part 1:** 285
"Fire-Truck, A" (Wilbur), **Supp. III Part 2:** 556
"Fireweed" (Clampitt), **Supp. IX: 44–45**
"Firewood" (Banks), **Supp. V:** 15
"Fireworks" (Ford), **Supp. V:** 69
"Fireworks" (Shapiro), **Supp. II Part 2:** 707
Fireworks: A History and Celebration (Plimpton), **Supp. XVI:** 245
Fir-Flower Tablets (Lowell), **II:** 512, 526–527
Firger, Jessica, **Supp. XIX:** 51, 58, 59, 62
Firkins, Oscar W., **II:** 271; **Supp. XV:** 297, 309
"Firmament, The" (Bryant), **Supp. I Part 1:** 162
Firmat, Gustavo Pérez, **Supp. VIII:** 76, 77, 79; **Supp. XI:** 184
"First American, The" (Toomer), **Supp. III Part 2:** 480, 487
"First Birth" (Olds), **Supp. X:** 212
First Book of Africa, The (Hughes), **Supp. I Part 1:** 344–345
First Book of Jazz, The (Hughes), **Supp. I Part 1:** 345
First Book of Negroes, The (Hughes), **Supp. I Part 1:** 345
First Book of Rhythms, The (Hughes), **Supp. I Part 1:** 345
First Book of the West Indies, The (Hughes), **Supp. I Part 1:** 345
Firstborn (Glück), **Supp. V:** 80, 81, 82, 84
"Firstborn" (Wright), **Supp. V:** 340
"First Chaldaic Oracle" (Carson), **Supp. XII: 111**
"First Communion" (Fante), **Supp. XI:** 160
"First Confession" (X. J. Kennedy), **Supp. XV: 154–155**
"First Day of School, The" (Gibbons), **Supp. X:** 41, 42
"First Death in Nova Scotia" (Bishop), **Supp. I Part 1:** 73
"First Formal" (Olds), **Supp. X:** 212
First Four Books of Poems, The (Glück), **Supp. V:** 81, 83
First Four Years, The (L. I. Wilder), **Supp. XXII:** 296, 298, 299–300
"First Grade" (Stafford), **Supp. XI:** 328
First Hand (Bierds), **Supp. XVII:** 32, 34–36
"First Hawaiian Bank" (Nye), **Supp. XIII:** 278
"First Heat" (Taylor), **Supp. V:** 323
First Hour, The (Di Piero), **Supp. XIX:** 36–37, 40
"First Hour of the Night, The" (Bidart), **Supp. XV: 30–32**
"First Hunters and the Last, The" (Sobin), **Supp. XVI:** 292
"First Job, The" (Cisneros), **Supp. VII:** 62
"1st Letter on Georges" (Olson), **Supp. II Part 2:** 578
First Light (C. Baxter), **Supp. XVII:** 15, **17–18,** 19, 22
First Light (Preston), **Supp. XVII:** 18
First Light (Wagoner), **Supp. IX:** 330
"First Love" (Welty), **IV:** 264; **Retro. Supp. I:** 347
First Love: A Lyric Sequence (Untermeyer), **Supp. XV:** 295
First Man, The (O'Neill), **III:** 390
First Manifesto (McGrath), **Supp. X:** 115
"First Meditation" (Roethke), **III:** 545–546
"First Noni Daylight, The" (Harjo), **Supp. XII:** 219
"First Passover" (Longfellow), **II:** 500–501
"First Person Female" (Harrison), **Supp. VIII:** 40, 41, 48
"First Place, The" (Wagoner), **Supp. IX:** 328
First Poems (Buechner), **Supp. XII:** 45
First Poems (Merrill), **Supp. III Part 1:** 318–321, 323
First Poems 1946–1954 (Kinnell), **Supp. III Part 1:** 235, 238–239
"First Praise" (W. C. Williams), **Retro. Supp. I:** 413
First Principles (Spencer), **Supp. I Part 1:** 368
"First Reader" (Collins), **Supp. XXI:** 55–56
"First Ride and First Walk" (Goldbarth), **Supp. XII:** 182–183
"First Seven Years, The" (Malamud), **Supp. I Part 2:** 431
"First Sex" (Olds), **Supp. X:** 208
"First Snow" (Mosher), **Supp. XXII:** 211
"First Snow in Alsace" (Wilbur), **Supp. III Part 2:** 545, 546, 559
"First Song" (Kinnell), **Supp. III Part 1:** 239
"First Spade in the West, The" (Fiedler), **Supp. XIII:** 103
"First Steps" (McClatchy), **Supp. XII:** 256
First There Is the Need (Reznikoff), **Supp. XIV:** 291
"First Things First" (Auden), **Supp. II Part 1:** 13
"First Thought, Best Thought" (Ginsberg), **Supp. II Part 1:** 327
"First Time I Saw Paris, The" (Fante), **Supp. XI:** 174
"First Travels of Max" (Ransom), **III:** 490–491
"First Tycoon of Teen, The" (Wolfe), **Supp. III Part 2:** 572
"First Views of the Enemy" (Oates), **Supp. II Part 2:** 508
"First Wife, The" (Buck), **Supp. II Part 1:** 127
First Words before Spring (Untermeyer), **Supp. XV:** 310
"First World War" (White), **Supp. I Part 2:** 665
"Fish" (F. Barthelme), **Supp. XI:** 26
"Fish" (Levis), **Supp. XI:** 259–260
Fish, Stanley, **Supp. IV Part 1:** 48; **Supp. XIV:** 14, 15
"Fish, The" (Bishop), **Supp. XV:** 100, 102
"Fish, The" (Moore), **III:** 195, 197, 209, 211, 213–214; **Supp. XXI:** 26
"Fish, The" (Oliver), **Supp. VII:** 236
"Fish, The/Lago Chapala" (Everwine), **Supp. XV:** 82–83
"Fish and Shadow" (Pound), **III:** 466
"Fishboy" (Richard), **Supp. XIX:** 212–213
Fishboy: A Ghost's Story (Richard), **Supp. XIX:** 209, **213–220,** 221
Fishburne, Laurence, **Supp. VIII:** 345
"Fish Cannery" (Fante), **Supp. XI:** 167
Fisher, Alexander Metcalf, **Supp. I Part 2:** 582
Fisher, Alfred, **Retro. Supp. II:** 243
Fisher, Barbara, **Supp. XXII:** 206
Fisher, Craig, **Supp. V:** 125
Fisher, Dorothy Canfield, **Retro. Supp. I:** 21, 133; **Supp. II Part 1:** 117. *See also* Canfield, Dorothy
Fisher, Mary, **Supp. I Part 2:** 455
Fisher, M. F. K., **Supp. XVII: 81–93**
Fisher, Phillip, **Retro. Supp. I:** 39
Fisher, Rudolph, **Retro. Supp. I:** 200; **Supp. I Part 1:** 325; **Supp. X:** 139; **Supp. XVI:** 143; **Supp. XIX: 65–80**
Fisher, Vardis, **Supp. IV Part 2:** 598
Fisher King, The (Marshall), **Supp. XI:** 275–276, **288–290**
"Fisherman, The" (Merwin), **Supp. II Part 1:** 346

"Fisherman and His Wife, The" (Welty), **IV:** 266
"Fisherman from Chihuahua, The" (Connell), **Supp. XIV:** 86
"Fishing" (Harjo), **Supp. XII:** 227–228
"Fishing Idyll, A" (Mosher), **Supp. XXII:** 209
"Fish in the Stone, The" (Dove), **Supp. IV Part 1:** 245, 257
"Fish in the unruffled lakes" (Auden), **Supp. II Part 1:** 8–9
"Fish R Us" (Doty), **Supp. XI:** 135
Fisk, James, **I:** 4, 474
Fiske, John, **Supp. I Part 1:** 314; **Supp. I Part 2:** 493
"Fit Against the Country, A" (Wright), **Supp. III Part 2:** 591–592, 601
Fitch, Clyde, **Supp. IV Part 2:** 573
Fitch, Elizabeth. *See* Taylor, Mrs. Edward (Elizabeth Fitch)
Fitch, James, **IV:** 147
Fitch, Noël Riley, **Supp. X:** 186, 187
"Fitting, The" (Hull), **Supp. XXI:** 134, 135
Fitts, Dudley, **I:** 169, 173; **Supp. I Part 1:** 342, 345; **Supp. XIII:** 346; **Supp. XXII:** 281
FitzGerald, Edward, **Supp. I Part 2:** 416; **Supp. III Part 2:** 610
Fitzgerald, Ella, **Supp. XIII:** 132
Fitzgerald, F. Scott, **I:** 107, 117, 118, 123, 188, 221, 288, 289, 358, 367, 374–375, 382, 423, 476, 482, 487, 495, 509, 511; **II: 77–100,** 257, 263, 272, 283, 415, 416, 417–418, 420, 425, 427, 430, 431, 432, 433, 434, 436, 437, 450, 458–459, 482, 560; **III:** 2, 26, 35, 36, 37, 40, 44, 45, 69, 106, 244, 284, 334, 350–351, 453, 454, 471, 551, 552, 572; **IV:** 27, 49, 97, 101, 126, 140, 191, 222, 223, 287, 297, 427, 471; **Retro. Supp. I:** 1, 74, **97–120,** 178, 180, 186, 215, 359, 381; **Retro. Supp. II:** 257, 321, 326, 328; **Supp. I Part 1:** 196, 197; **Supp. I Part 2:** 622; **Supp. III Part 2:** 409, 411, 585; **Supp. IV Part 1:** 123, 197, 200, 203, 341; **Supp. IV Part 2:** 463, 468, 607, 689; **Supp. V:** 23, 95, 226, 251, 262, 276, 313; **Supp. VIII:** 101, 103, 106, 137; **Supp. IX:** 15, 20, 55, 57–63, 199; **Supp. X:** 225; **Supp. XI:** 65, 221, 334; **Supp. XII:** 42, 173, 295; **Supp. XIII:** 170, 263; **Supp. XV:** 135; **Supp. XVI:** 64, 75, 191, 192, 294; **Supp. XVIII:** 148, 246, 248, 251, 254; **Supp. XX: 74; Supp. XXI:** 262; **Supp. XXII:** 82, 92
Fitzgerald, Robert, **I:** 27–28; **III:** 338, 348; **Retro. Supp. II:** 179, 221, 222, 223, 228, 229; **Supp. IV Part 2:** 631; **Supp. XV:** 112, 249; **Supp. XXII:** 281
Fitzgerald, Zelda (Zelda Sayre), **I:** 482; **II:** 77, 79, 82–85, 88, 90–91, 93, 95; **Supp. IV Part 1:** 310; **Supp. IX: 55–73; Supp. X:** 172. *See also* Sayre, Zelda
"Fitzgerald's Tragic Sense" (Schorer), **Retro. Supp. I:** 115
"Fitzgerald: The Romance of Money" (Cowley), **Supp. II Part 1:** 143
5 Detroits (Levine), **Supp. V:** 178
Five Came Back (West), **IV:** 287
Five Corners (screenplay, Shanley), **Supp. XIV:** 316
"Five-Dollar Bill, The" (D. West as Mary Christopher), **Supp. XVIII:** 282
"Five Dollar Guy, The" (W. C. Williams), **Retro. Supp. I:** 423
Five Easy Pieces (film), **Supp. V:** 26
"Five Elephants" (Dove), **Supp. IV Part 1:** 244–245
"Five Fucks" (Lethem), **Supp. XVIII:** 139
Five Groups of Verse (Reznikoff), **Supp. XIV:** 279, 282
Five Hundred Hats of Bartholomew Cubbins, The (Geisel), **Supp. XVI:** 100
Five Hundred Scorpions (Hearon), **Supp. VIII:** 57, 65, **66**
Five Indiscretions (Ríos), **Supp. IV Part 2:** 545–547
Five Men and Pompey (Benét), **Supp. XI:** 43, 44
Five Plays (Hughes), **Retro. Supp. I:** 197, 209
"Five Psalms" (Jarman), **Supp. XVII:** 120
Five Temperaments (Kalstone), **Retro. Supp. II:** 40
5,000 Fingers of Dr. T, The (film), **Supp. XVI:** 103
Five Young American Poets, **I:** 170; **II:** 367
Fixer, The (Malamud), **Supp. I Part 2:** 428, 435, 445, 446–448, 450, 451
"Fixin' Road" (Boulton), **Supp. XXII:** 23
Fjellestad, Danuta Zadworna, **Supp. XVI:** 150
Flaccus, Kimball, **Retro. Supp. I:** 136
Flacius, Matthias, **IV:** 163
"Flagellant's Song" (X. J. Kennedy), **Supp. XV:** 165
Flag for Sunrise, A (Stone), **Supp. V:** 301–304
Flagg, Fannie, **Supp. XXII:** 213–214
Flag of Childhood, The: Poems from the Middle East (Nye, ed.), **Supp. XIII:** 280
"Flag of Summer" (Swenson), **Supp. IV Part 2:** 645
Flagons and Apples (Jeffers), **Supp. II Part 2:** 413, 414, 417–418
Flags in the Dust (Faulkner), **Retro. Supp. I:** 81, 82, 83, 86, 88
Flamel, Nicolas, **Supp. XII:** 178
Flaming Corsage, The (W. Kennedy), **Supp. VII:** 133, 153–156
Flammarion, Camille, **Supp. I Part 1:** 260
Flanagan, John T., **Supp. I Part 2:** 464, 465, 468
Flanner, Janet, **Supp. XVI:** 195
"Flannery O'Connor: Poet to the Outcast" (Sister Rose Alice), **III:** 348
Flappers and Philosophers (Fitzgerald), **II:** 88; **Retro. Supp. I:** 103; **Supp. IX:** 56
Flash and Filigree (Southern), **Supp. XI:** 295, **296–297**
"Flashcards" (Dove), **Supp. IV Part 1:** 250
Flash Fiction: Seventy-two Very Short Stories (J. Thomas, ed.), **Supp. XVI:** 268
"Flash in the Pan" (Shaw), **Supp. XIX:** 245
Flatt, Lester, **Supp. V:** 335
Flaubert, Gustave, **I:** 66, 123, 130, 272, 312, 314, 315, 477, 504, 506, 513, 514; **II:** 182, 185, 194, 198–199, 205, 209, 230, 289, 311, 316, 319, 325, 337, 392, 401, 577, 594; **III:** 196, 207, 251, 315, 461, 467, 511, 564; **IV:** 4, 29, 31, 37, 40, 134, 285, 428; **Retro. Supp. I:** 5, 215, 218, 222, 225, 235, 287; **Supp. III Part 2:** 411, 412; **Supp. XI:** 334; **Supp. XIV:** 87, 336
"Flavia and Her Artists" (Cather), **Retro. Supp. I:** 5
Flavoring of New England, The (Brooks), **I:** 253, 256
Flavor of Man, The (Toomer), **Supp. III Part 2:** 487
"Flaw, The" (Peacock), **Supp. XIX:** 206
Flaxman, Josiah, **Supp. I Part 2:** 716
"Flea, The" (Donne), **Supp. XVIII:** 307
"Flèche d'Or" (Merrill), **Supp. III Part 1:** 328
Flecker, James Elroy, **Supp. I Part 1:** 257
"Flee on Your Donkey" (Sexton), **Supp. II Part 2:** 683, 685
Fleming, Ian, **Supp. XI:** 307; **Supp. XX: 195**
Fleming, Rene, **Supp. XII:** 321
Fleming, Robert ?/, **Supp. XXII:** 184
Fleming, Robert E. ?/, **Supp. XVII:** 155
Flesch, Rudolf, **Supp. XVI:** 105, 106
Flesh and Blood (Cunningham), **Supp. XV: 63–65**
Flesh and Blood (play; Cunnigham and Gaitens), **Supp. XV:** 65
"Fleshbody" (Ammons), **Supp. VII:** 27
Fletcher, H. D., **II:** 517, 529
Fletcher, John, **Supp. IV Part 2:** 621
Fletcher, John Gould, **I:** 243; **II:** 517, 529; **III:** 458; **Supp. I Part 1:** 263; **Supp. I Part 2:** 422; **Supp. XV:** 298, 302, 306, 307, 308
Fletcher, Phineas, **Supp. I Part 1:** 369
Fletcher, Virginia. *See* Caldwell, Mrs. Erskine (Virginia Fletcher)
Fleurs du mal, Les (Beaudelaire; Millay and Dillon, trans.), **III:** 141–142
"Flight" (Bierds), **Supp. XVII:** 36
"Flight" (Updike), **IV:** 218, 222, 224; **Retro. Supp. I:** 318
Flight (White), **Supp. XVIII:** 127
"Flight, The" (Haines), **Supp. XII:** 204–205
"Flight, The" (Roethke), **III:** 537–538
Flight among the Tombs (Hecht), **Supp. X:** 58, **71–74**
"Flight for Freedom" (McCoy), **Supp. XIII:** 170
"Flight from Byzantium" (Brodsky), **Supp. VIII:** 30–31

"Flight of Besey Lane, The" (Jewett), **Retro. Supp. II:** 139
Flight of the Rocket, The (Fitzgerald), **II:** 89
Flights of the Harvest-Mare (Bierds), **Supp. XVII:** 26–27
Flight to Canada (Reed), **Supp. X:** 240, **249–252**
Flinn, Mary, **Supp. XVII:** 110
Flint, F. S., **II:** 517; **III:** 459, 464, 465; **Retro. Supp. I:** 127; **Supp. I Part 1:** 261, 262
Flint, Helen, **Supp. XXII:** 278
Flint, R. W., **Supp. XVI:** 47, 49, 57
"Flitting Flies" (X. J. Kennedy), **Supp. XV:** 166, **167**
Flivver King, The (Sinclair), **Supp. V:** 290
Floating House, The (Sanders), **Supp. XVI:** 269
Floating Light Bulb, The (Allen), **Supp. XV:** 2, 3, 13
Floating Opera, The (Barth), **I:** 121, 122–126, 127, 129, 130, 131
"Floating Poem, Unnumbered, The" (Rich), **Supp. I Part 2:** 572–573
"Floating Trees" (Wright), **Supp. XV:** 348
Flood (Matthews), **Supp. IX:** 154, **160–161**
Flood (Warren), **IV:** 252, 256–257
"Flood of Years, The" (Bryant), **Supp. I Part 1:** 159, 170, 171; **Supp. I Part 2:** 416
"Floor and the Ceiling, The" (W. J. Smith), **Supp. XIII:** 345, 346
"Floor Plans" (Komunyakaa), **Supp. XIII:** 114
"Floral Conversation" (Peacock), **Supp. XIX:** 200
"Floral Decorations for Bananas" (Stevens), **IV:** 8
Florida (Acker), **Supp. XII:** 5
"Florida" (Bishop), **Retro. Supp. II:** 43
"Florida Road Workers" (Hughes), **Retro. Supp. I:** 203
"Florida Sunday, A" (Lanier), **Supp. I Part 1:** 364, 366
Florist's Daughter, The (Hampl), **Supp. XXII:** 84, 85, 94, **95–98**
"Flossie Cabanis" (Masters), **Supp. I Part 2:** 461–462
"Flounder" (Trethewey), **Supp. XXI:** 244, 245, 246, 251
Flow Chart (Ashbery), **Supp. VIII:** 275
"Flowchart" (Ashbery), **Supp. III Part 1:** 26
Flower, Dean, **Supp. XXII:** 205, 212
Flower, Fruit, and Thorn Pieces (Richter), **Supp. XVI:** 182
Flower-de-Luce (Longfellow), **II:** 490
Flower Drum Song (Rodgers and Hammerstein), **Supp. XXI:** 148
Flower Drum Song, The (Lee), **Supp. XXI:** 148
Flower Fables (Alcott), **Supp. I Part 1:** 33
"Flower-Fed Buffaloes, The" (Lindsay), **Supp. I Part 2:** 398
"Flower Garden" (Jackson), **Supp. IX:** 119
"Flower-gathering" (Frost), **II:** 153
Flower Herding on Mount Monadnock (Kinnell), **Supp. III Part 1:** 235, 239, 241–244
"Flower Herding on Mount Monadnock" (Kinnell), **Supp. III Part 1:** 242
"Flowering Death" (Ashbery), **Supp. III Part 1:** 22
"Flowering Dream, The" (McCullers), **II:** 591
"Flowering Judas" (Porter), **III:** 434, 435–436, 438, 441, 445, 446, 450–451
Flowering Judas and Other Stories (Porter), **III:** 433, 434
Flowering of New England, The (Brooks), **IV:** 171–172; **Supp. VIII:** 101
Flowering of the Rod (Doolittle), **Supp. I Part 1:** 272
Flowering Peach, The (Odets), **Supp. II Part 2:** 533, 547, 549–550
"Flowering Plum" (Glück), **Supp. V:** 82
"Flowers for Marjorie" (Welty), **IV:** 262
"Flowers of the Fallow" (Larcom), **Supp. XIII:** 143, 145–146
"Flowers Well if anybody" (Dickinson), **Retro. Supp. I:** 30
"Fluff and Mr. Ripley" (D. West), **Supp. XVIII:** 284
"Fly, The" (Kinnell), **Supp. III Part 1:** 249
"Fly, The" (Shapiro), **Supp. II Part 2:** 705
"Fly, The" (Simic), **Supp. VIII:** 278
Flye, Father James Harold, **I:** 25, 26, 35–36, 37, 42, 46; **IV:** 215
"Fly in Buttermilk, A" (Baldwin), **Retro. Supp. II:** 8
Flying at Night: Poems 1965–1985 (Kooser), **Supp. XIX:** 128
"Flying High" (Levertov), **Supp. III Part 1:** 284
"Flying Home" (Ellison), **Retro. Supp. II:** 117, **125–126; Supp. II Part 1:** 235, 238–239
"Flying Home" (Kinnell), **Supp. III Part 1:** 250
"Flying Home" and Other Stories (Ellison), **Retro. Supp. II:** 119, 124
"Flying Home from Utah" (Swenson), **Supp. IV Part 2:** 645
"Flying over Clouds" (Gioia), **Supp. XV:** 118
"Flying to Hanoi" (Rukeyser), **Supp. VI:** 279
Flynn, Elizabeth Gurley, **Supp. XVIII:** 225
Flynn, Richard, **Supp. XVII:** 115; **Supp. XVIII:** 183
Fly-Truffler, The (Sobin), **Supp. XVI: 294–295,** 296
Foata, Anne, **Supp. XI:** 104
FOB (Hwang), **Supp. XXI:** 143, 144, 145, 146, **148–150**
Focillon, Henri, **IV:** 90
Focus (A. Miller), **III:** 150–151, 156
Foer, Jonathan Safran, **Supp. XII:** 169; **Supp. XX: 177**
Foerster, Norman, **I:** 222; **Supp. I Part 2:** 423, 424; **Supp. IV Part 2:** 598
"Fog" (Sandburg), **III:** 586
"Fog Galleon" (Komunyakaa), **Supp. XIII:** 127
"Foggy and dripping" (Kooser), **Supp. XIX:** 125
"Foggy Lane, The" (Simpson), **Supp. IX:** 274
"Fog Man, The" (Boyle), **Supp. XX: 20**
Folded Leaf, The (Maxwell), **Supp. III Part 1:** 62; **Supp. VIII: 159–162**
Folding Star, The (Hollinghurst), **Supp. XIII:** 52
Foley, Jack, **Supp. X:** 125; **Supp. XV:** 112, 116; **Supp. XVII:** 77
Foley, Martha, **II:** 587; **Supp. XVI:** 225
Folk-Lore in the Old Testament (Frazer), **Supp. XX: 116–117**
Folks from Dixie (Dunbar), **Supp. II Part 1:** 211–212
Folkways (Sumner), **III:** 102
Follain, Jean, **Supp. IX:** 152, 154
Follett, Wilson, **I:** 405; **Supp. XIII:** 173
Follower of Dusk (Salinas), **Supp. XIII:** 326
"Following the Bones" (W. V. Davis), **Supp. XXI:** 96
Following the Equator (Twain), **II:** 434; **IV:** 208
Follow Me Home (Hoffman), **Supp. XVIII:** 86
Folly (Minot), **Supp. VI:** 205, 208, **210–213**
Folly of Others, The (Boyce), **Supp. XVII:** 100; **Supp. XXI:** 10
Folsom, Charles, **Supp. I Part 1:** 156
Folsom, Ed, **Retro. Supp. I:** 392
Folson, Marcia McClintock, **Retro. Supp. II:** 139
Fonda, Henry, **Supp. I Part 1:** 67; **Supp. IV Part 1:** 236
Fonda, Jane, **III:** 284; **Supp. XI:** 307
Fonda, Peter, **Supp. VIII:** 42; **Supp. XI:** 293, 308
"Fondled Memories" (Molesworth), **Supp. XIX:** 121–122
"Fond Memories of a Black Childhood" (D. West), **Supp. XVIII:** 289
Foner, Eric, **Supp. I Part 2:** 523
Fong and the Indians (Theroux), **Supp. VIII:** 314, 315, **316–317**
Fontanne, Lynn, **III:** 397
Food and Drink (Untermeyer), **Supp. XV:** 310
Fool for Love (Shepard), **Supp. III Part 2:** 433, 447, 448
"Foolishness" (Pickering), **Supp. XXI:** 197
Fools (Simon), **Supp. IV Part 2:** 584–585
Fool's Progress, The: An Honest Novel (Abbey), **Supp. XIII:** 4, **13–15**
Foot Book, The (Geisel), **Supp. XVI:** 108
Foote, Horton, **Supp. I Part 1:** 281; **Supp. VIII:** 128, 129
Foote, Mary Hallock, **Retro. Supp. II:** 72; **Supp. IV Part 2:** 611
Foote, Roxanna. *See* Beecher, Mrs. Lyman (Roxanna Foote)

Foote, Samuel, **Supp. I Part 2:** 584
Foote, Stephanie, **Retro. Supp. II:** 139
"Foot Fault" (pseudonym). *See* Thurber, James
Footing on This Earth, A (Hay), **Supp. XIV:** 125, 126, 130
"Footing up a Total" (Lowell), **II:** 528
"Footnote to Howl" (Ginsberg), **Supp. II Part 1:** 316–317
"Footnote to Weather Forecasts, A" (Brodsky), **Supp. VIII:** 32
Footprints (Hearon), **Supp. VIII: 69–70**
Footprints (Levertov), **Supp. III Part 1:** 272, 281
"Footsteps of Angels" (Longfellow), **II:** 496
"For A, at Fourteen" (Weigl), **Supp. XIX:** 287
For a Bitter Season: New and Selected Poems (Garrett), **Supp. VII:** 99–100
"For a Dead Kitten" (Hay), **Supp. XIV:** 119–120
"For a Dead Lady" (Robinson), **III:** 508, 513, 517
"For a Ghost Who Once Placed Bets in the Park" (Levis), **Supp. XI:** 265
"For a Lamb" (Eberhart), **I:** 523, 530, 531
"For All" (Snyder), **Supp. VIII:** 304
"For All Tuesday Travelers" (Cisneros), **Supp. VII:** 67–68
"For a Lost Child" (Stafford), **Supp. XI:** 329
"For a Marriage" (Bogan), **Supp. III Part 1:** 52
"For an Emigrant" (Jarrell), **II:** 371
"For Anna Akmatova" (Lowell), **II:** 544
"For Anna Mae Pictou Aquash, Whose Spirit Is Present Here and in the Dappled Stars" (Harjo), **Supp. XII:** 225
"For Anne, at a Little Distance" (Haines), **Supp. XII:** 207
"For Annie" (Poe), **III:** 427; **Retro. Supp. II:** 263
"For an Old Friend Encountered Unexpectedly" (Espaillat), **Supp. XXI:** 111–112
"For a Southern Man" (Cisneros), **Supp. VII:** 67
"For Bailey" (Angelou), **Supp. IV Part 1:** 15
Forbes, Malcolm, **Supp. IV Part 1:** 94
"Forbidden, The" (Glück), **Supp. XIV:** 269
"For Bill Nestrick (1940–96)" (Bidart), **Supp. XV:** 35
For Bread Alone (Choukri), **Supp. IV Part 1:** 92
"Force" (Di Piero), **Supp. XIX:** 35–36, 42, 44
Force of Desire, The (Bronk), **Supp. XXI:** 31, 32
Force of Evil (film, Polonsky), **Supp. XXI:** 261, 272, 275
Force of Spirit, The (Sanders), **Supp. XVI:** 277–278
Forché, Carolyn, **Supp. IV Part 1:** 208; **Supp. XIX:** 193
Ford, Arthur, **Supp. IV Part 1:** 140
Ford, Ford Madox, **I:** 288, 405, 409, 417, 421, 423; **II:** 58, 144, 198, 257, 263, 265, 517, 536; **III:** 458, 464–465, 470–471, 472, 476; **IV:** 27, 126, 261; **Retro. Supp. I:** 127, 177, 178, 186, 231, 286–287, 418; **Supp. II Part 1:** 107; **Supp. III Part 2:** 617; **Supp. VIII:** 107; **Supp. XIV:** 3
Ford, Harrison, **Supp. VIII:** 323
Ford, Harry, **Supp. V:** 179; **Supp. XIII:** 76
Ford, Henry, **I:** 295, 480–481; **III:** 292, 293; **Supp. I Part 1:** 21; **Supp. I Part 2:** 644; **Supp. III Part 2:** 612, 613; **Supp. IV Part 1:** 223; **Supp. V:** 290
Ford, John, **Supp. I Part 2:** 422; **Supp. III Part 2:** 619; **Supp. XVIII:** 247
Ford, Mary K., **Supp. XX: 239**
Ford, Richard, **Supp. IV Part 1:** 342; **Supp. V:** 22, **57–75**
Ford, Webster (pseudonym). *See* Masters, Edgar Lee
"Fording and Dread" (Harrison), **Supp. VIII:** 41
"Ford Madox Ford" (Lowell), **II:** 547; **Retro. Supp. II:** 188
"For Dudley" (Wilbur), **Supp. III Part 2:** 558
Fordyce, David, **II:** 113
For Eager Lovers (Taggard), **Supp. XXII: 274–275**
Foregone Conclusion, A (Howells), **II:** 278–279, 282
"Foreign Affairs" (Kunitz), **Supp. III Part 1:** 265
"Foreigner, A" (Bynner), **Supp. XV:** 46
"Foreigner, The" (Jewett), **II:** 409–410; **Retro. Supp. II:** 133, 142
"Foreigners" (Jarman), **Supp. XVII:** 113
"Foreign Language, The" (Franzen), **Supp. XX: 84**
"Foreign Shores" (Salter), **Supp. IX:** 260
Forensic and the Navigators (Shepard), **Supp. III Part 2:** 439
Forerunner, The (Boyce), **Supp. XXI:** 2, 4, **10–11**
Forerunner, The: His Parables and Poems (Gibran), **Supp. XX: 115, 118–119, 119**
Foreseeable Future, The (Price), **Supp. VI:** 265
Foreseeable Futures (Matthews), **Supp. IX:** 155, **163,** 169
"For Esmé with Love and Squalor" (Salinger), **III:** 560
"Forest" (Simic), **Supp. VIII:** 273
Forest, Jean-Claude, **Supp. XI:** 307
Forester's Letters (Paine), **Supp. I Part 2:** 508
"Forest Hymn, A" (Bryant), **Supp. I Part 1:** 156, 162, 163, 164, 165, 170
"Forest in the Seeds, The" (Kingsolver), **Supp. VII:** 203
Forest of the South, The (Gordon), **II:** 197
"Forest of the South, The" (Gordon), **II:** 199, 201
Forest without Leaves (Adams and Haines), **Supp. XII:** 209
"Forever, Said the Duck" (Lethem), **Supp. XVIII:** 139
"Forever and the Earth" (Bradbury), **Supp. IV Part 1:** 102
"Forever in That Year" (Carruth), **Supp. XVI:** 51
"Forever Young" (Jarman and R. McDowell), **Supp. XVII:** 111
"For Fathers of Girls" (Dunn), **Supp. XI:** 146
For Frank O'Hara's Birthday (Notley), **Supp. XXII:** 224, 227
"For/From Lew" (Snyder), **Supp. VIII:** 303
"For Garrison Keillor, Fantasy Is a Lot More Fun then Reality" (Letofsky), **Supp. XVI:** 167
"For George Santayana" (Lowell), **II:** 547
"Forgetfulness" (Collins), **Supp. XXI:** 58
"Forgiveness" (Peacock), **Supp. XIX:** 200
Forgotten Helper, The: A Story for Children (Moore), **Supp. X:** 175
"Forgotten in an Old Notebook" (F. Wright), **Supp. XVII:** 244
Forgotten Village, The (Steinbeck), **IV:** 51
"For Grizzel McNaught (1709–1792)" (A. Finch), **Supp. XVII:** 72
Forgue, Guy J., **III:** 118, 119
For Her Dark Skin (Everett), **Supp. XVIII:** 56, 60
"FOR HETTIE" (Baraka), **Supp. II Part 1:** 32
"FOR HETTIE IN HER FIFTH MONTH" (Baraka), **Supp. II Part 1:** 32, 38
"For Homer" (Corso), **Supp. XII:** 135
"For I'm the Boy" (Barthelme), **Supp. IV Part 1:** 47
"For Jeff" (Kooser), **Supp. XIX:** 125
"For Jessica, My Daughter" (Strand), **Supp. IV Part 2:** 629
"For John, Who Begs Me not to Enquire Further" (Sexton), **Supp. II Part 2:** 676
"For Johnny Pole on the Forgotten Beach" (Sexton), **Supp. II Part 2:** 675
"For Joy to Leave Upon" (Ortiz), **Supp. IV Part 2:** 508
"Fork" (Simic), **Supp. VIII:** 275
"For Karl Shapiro, Having Gone Back to the Sonnet" (Kooser), **Supp. XIX:** 118
For Lancelot Andrewes (Eliot), **Retro. Supp. I:** 64
For Lizzie and Harriet (Lowell), **Retro. Supp. II:** 183, 186, 190
"Forlorn Hope of Sidney Lanier, The" (Leary), **Supp. I Part 1:** 373
For Love (Creeley), **Supp. IV Part 1:** 139, 140, 142–145, 147–149, 150, 154
"For Love" (Creeley), **Supp. IV Part 1:** 145
For Love (Miller), **Supp. XII: 297–299,** 299
For Love of Imabelle (C. Himes), **Supp. XVI:** 135, 143, 144
"Formal Elegy" (Berryman), **I:** 170
Formal Feeling Comes, A (A. Finch, ed.), **Supp. XVII: 71–72**

"Formalist Criticism: Its Principles and Limits" (Burke), **I:** 282
Forman, Milos, **Supp. IV Part 1:** 236
"Form and Function of the Novel, The" (Goldbarth), **Supp. XII:** 183
"For Marse Chouchoute" (Chopin), **Retro. Supp. II:** 60
"For Mary Ann Youngren" (Bidart), **Supp. XV:** 29
"Format and Form" (A. Rich), **Supp. XVII:** 74
"Formation of a Separatist, I" (Howe), **Supp. IV Part 2:** 427
"Form Is Emptiness" (Baraka), **Supp. II Part 1:** 51
"For Mr. Death Who Stands with His Door Open" (Sexton), **Supp. II Part 2:** 695
Forms of Discovery (Winters), **Supp. II Part 2:** 812, 813
Forms of Fiction, The (Gardner and Dunlap), **Supp. VI:** 64
"For My Children" (Karr), **Supp. XI:** 254
"For My Daughter" (Kees), **Supp. XV:** 141, 147
"For My Daughter" (Olds), **Supp. X:** 206
"For My Former Wife, Watching TV, in the Past" (Kooser), **Supp. XIX:** 120
"For My Lover, Returning to His Wife" (Sexton), **Supp. II Part 2:** 688
Fornés, Maria Irene, **Supp. XXI:** 144
"For Night to Come" (Stern), **Supp. IX:** 292
"For Once, Then, Something" (Frost), **II:** 156–157; **Retro. Supp. I:** 126, 133, 134
"For Peg: A Remnant of Song Still Distantly Sounding" (Carruth), **Supp. XVI:** 54
"For Pot-Boiling" (Hay), **Supp. XIV:** 128
"For Radicals" (Bourne), **I:** 221
"For Rainer Gerhardt" (Creeley), **Supp. IV Part 1:** 142–143, 147
Forrestal, James, **I:** 491; **Supp. I Part 2:** 489
Forrester, Fanny, **Supp. XVIII:** 13
"For Richard After All" (Kingsolver), **Supp. VII:** 208
"For Sacco and Vanzetti" (Kingsolver), **Supp. VII:** 208
"Forsaken Merman" (Arnold), **Supp. I Part 2:** 529
"For S.F.S. 1875–1962" (J. W. Miller), **Supp. XX: 166**
For Spacious Skies (Buck), **Supp. II Part 1:** 131
Forster, E. M., **I:** 292; **IV:** 201; **Retro. Supp. I:** 59, 232; **Supp. III Part 2:** 503; **Supp. V:** 258; **Supp. VIII:** 155, 171; **Supp. IX:** 128; **Supp. XII:** 79, 81; **Supp. XIV:** 159, 160, 163; **Supp. XV:** 62; **Supp. XVI:** 236; **Supp. XVIII:** 143; **Supp. XX: 229, 235, 239, 240; Supp. XXI:** 233
Forster, John, **II:** 315
Fort, Paul, **II:** 518, 528, 529; **Retro. Supp. I:** 55
"For the Ahkoond" (Bierce), **I:** 209
For the Body (Nelson), **Supp. XVIII:** 173
For the Century's End: Poems 1990–1999 (Haines), **Supp. XII: 211–213**
"For the Dedication of the New City Library, Boston" (Holmes), **Supp. I Part 1:** 308
"For the Fallen" (Levine), **Supp. V:** 188
For the Health of the Land: Previously Unpublished Essays and Other Writings (Leopold), **Supp. XIV:** 183
"For the Lady in the Black Raincoat Who Slept Through an Entire Poetry Reading" (Espaillat), **Supp. XXI:** 108
"For the Last Wolverine" (Dickey), **Supp. IV Part 1:** 182
"For the Lovers of the Absolute" (Simic), **Supp. VIII:** 278–279
"For the Man Cutting the Grass" (Oliver), **Supp. VII:** 235
"For the Marriage of Faustus and Helen" (H. Crane), **I:** 395–396, 399, 402; **Retro. Supp. II:** 78–79, 82
"For the Meeting of the National Sanitary Association, 1860" (Holmes), **Supp. I Part 1:** 307
For the New Intellectual (Rand), **Supp. IV Part 2:** 521, 526–527, 527, 532
"For the New Railway Station in Rome" (Wilbur), **Supp. III Part 2:** 554
"For the Night" (Kenyon), **Supp. VII:** 163
"For Theodore Roethke: 1908–1963" (Lowell), **II:** 554
"For the Poem *Patterson*" (W. C. Williams), **Retro. Supp. I:** 424
"For the Poets of Chile" (Levine), **Supp. V:** 188
"FOR THE REVOLUTIONARY OUTBURST BY BLACK PEOPLE" (Baraka), **Supp. II Part 1:** 55
"For the Sleepless" (Dunn), **Supp. XI:** 145
For the Time Being (Auden), **Supp. II Part 1:** 2, 17, 18
For the Time Being (Dillard), **Supp. VI:** 23, 27, 29, 32, **34–35**
"For the Twentieth Century" (Bidart), **Supp. XV:** 35
For the Union Dead (Lowell), **II:** 543, 550–551, 554, 555; **Retro. Supp. II:** 181, 182, 186, 189; **Supp. X:** 53
"For the Union Dead" (Lowell), **II:** 551; **Retro. Supp. II:** 189
"For the Walking Dead" (Komunyakaa), **Supp. XIII:** 121
"For the West" (Snyder), **Supp. VIII:** 299
"For the Word Is Flesh" (Kunitz), **Supp. III Part 1:** 262–264
"Fortress, The" (Glück), **Supp. V:** 82
"Fortress, The" (Sexton), **Supp. II Part 2:** 682
Fortress of Solitude, The (Lethem), **Supp. XVIII:** 135, 136, **145–148,** 150
"Fort Robinson" (Kooser), **Supp. XIX:** 120
"Fortunate Traveler" (Hull), **Supp. XXI:** 140
Fortune, T. Thomas, **Supp. II Part 1:** 159
Fortune's Bones: The Manumission Requiem (Nelson), **Supp. XVIII:** 171, 172–173, 182–183
Fortune's Daughter (Hoffman), **Supp. X:** 77, 85
"Fortune Spill, The" (Nelson), **Supp. XVIII:** 175
45 Mercy Street (Sexton), **Supp. II Part 2:** 694, 695, 697
Forty Poems Touching on Recent American History (Bly, ed.), **Supp. IV Part 1:** 61
42nd Parallel, The (Dos Passos), **I:** 482, 484–485
Forty Stories (Barthelme), **Supp. IV Part 1:** 47, 49, 53, 54
For Whom the Bell Tolls (Hemingway), **II:** 249, 254–255, 261; **III:** 18, 363; **Retro. Supp. I:** 115, 176–177, 178, **184,** 187; **Supp. XVII:** 229
Foscolo, Ugo, **II:** 543
Foss, Sam Walter, **Supp. II Part 1:** 197
"Fossils, The" (Kinnell), **Supp. III Part 1:** 244
Foster, Edward, **Supp. IV Part 2:** 431, 434; **Supp. XVI:** 281, 293; **Supp. XXI:** 33
Foster, Edward Halsey, **Supp. XII:** 120, 129, 130, 135; **Supp. XVIII:** 265, 268
Foster, Emily, **II:** 309
Foster, Frances Smith, **Supp. XX: 287**
Foster, Hannah, **Supp. XV:** 234
Foster, John Wilson, **Supp. XIII:** 32–33
Foster, Phil, **Supp. IV Part 2:** 574
Foster, Richard, **Supp. XV:** 269
Foster, Stephen, **Supp. I Part 1:** 100–101; **Supp. I Part 2:** 699
Foucault, Michel, **Supp. VIII:** 5; **Supp. XII:** 98; **Supp. XV:** 344; **Supp. XVI:** 285
"Founder, The" (Stern), **Supp. IX:** 297
Founding of Harvard College, The (Morison), **Supp. I Part 2:** 485
"Fountain, The" (Bryant), **Supp. I Part 1:** 157, 165, 166, 168
Fountain, The (O'Neill), **III:** 391
Fountain and Other Poems, The (Bryant), **Supp. I Part 1:** 157
Fountainhead, The (film), **Supp. IV Part 2:** 524
Fountainhead, The (Rand), **Supp. IV Part 2:** 517, 521–523, 525, 531
Fountainhead, The: A Fiftieth Anniversary Celebration (Cox), **Supp. IV Part 2:** 523
"Fountain Piece" (Swenson), **Supp. IV Part 2:** 641
4-H Club (Shepard), **Supp. III Part 2:** 439
"Four Ages of Man, The" (Bradstreet), **Supp. I Part 1:** 111, 115
Four American Indian Literary Masters (Velie), **Supp. IV Part 2:** 486
"Four Beasts in One; the Homo Cameleopard" (Poe), **III:** 425
Four Black Revolutionary Plays (Baraka), **Supp. II Part 1:** 45; **Supp. VIII:** 330
"Four Brothers" (Di Piero), **Supp. XIX:** 37
"Four Brothers, The" (Sandburg), **III:** 585

Four Dogs and a Bone and the Wild Goose (Shanley), **Supp. XIV:** 316, **328–329**
"Four Evangelists, The" (Komunyakaa), **Supp. XIII:** 131
"Four for Sir John Davies" (Roethke), **III:** 540, 541
"Four Girls, The" (Alvarez), **Supp. VII:** 7
"Four Horse Songs" (Harjo), **Supp. XII:** 220
"400-Meter Free Style" (Kumin), **Supp. IV Part 2:** 442
"400-Pound CEO, The" (Saunders), **Supp. XIX:** 225
Fourier, Charles, **II:** 342
"Four in a Family" (Rukeyser), **Supp. VI:** 272
Four in Hand: A Quartet of Novels (Warner), **Supp. VIII:** 164
"Four Lakes' Days" (Eberhart), **I:** 525
"Four Mad Studies" (Di Piero), **Supp. XIX:** 37
"Four Meetings" (James), **II:** 327
Four Million, The (O. Henry), **Supp. II Part 1:** 394, 408
"Four Monarchyes" (Bradstreet), **Supp. I Part 1:** 105, 106, 116
"Four Mountain Wolves" (Silko), **Supp. IV Part 2:** 561
Four of a Kind (Marquand), **III:** 54, 55
"Four of the Horsemen (Hypertense and Stroke, Coronary Occlusion and Cerebral Insult)" (Karr), **Supp. XI:** 250
"Four Poems" (Bishop), **Supp. I Part 1:** 92
"Four Preludes on Playthings of the Wind" (Sandburg), **III:** 586
Four Quartets (T. S. Eliot), **I:** 570, 576, 580–582, 585, 587; **II:** 537; **III:** 539; **Retro. Supp. I:** 66, 67; **Supp. II Part 1:** 1; **Supp. IV Part 1:** 284; **Supp. V:** 343, 344; **Supp. VIII:** 182, 195; **Supp. XIII:** 344; **Supp. XIV:** 167; **Supp. XV:** 216, 260, 266
Four Saints in Three Acts (Stein), **IV:** 30, 31, 33, 43, 44–45
"Four Seasons" (Bradstreet), **Supp. I Part 1:** 112–113
Four Seasons of Success, The (Schulberg), **Supp. XVIII:** 254
"Four Sides of One Story" (Updike), **Retro. Supp. I:** 328
"Four Skinny Trees" (Cisneros), **Supp. VII:** 64
"14: In A Dark Wood: Wood Thrushes" (Oliver), **Supp. VII:** 244
"14 Men Stage Head Winter 1624/ 25" (Olson), **Supp. II Part 2:** 574
14 Stories (Dixon), **Supp. XII:** 141, **145–147**
Fourteen Hundred Thousand (Shepard), **Supp. III Part 2:** 439
Fourteen Sisters of Emilio Montez O'Brien, The (Hijuelos), **Supp. VIII: 82–85**
Fourteen Stories (Buck), **Supp. II Part 1:** 126
"Fourteenth Ward, The" (H. Miller), **III:** 175
Fourth Book of Peace, The (Kingston), **Supp. V:** 173
"Fourth Down" (Marquand), **III:** 56
Fourth Group of Verse, A (Reznikoff), **Supp. XIV:** 282, 284
"Fourth of July in Maine" (Lowell), **II:** 535, 552–553
Fourth Wall, The (Gurney), **Supp. V:** 109–110
Fowler, Douglas, **Supp. IV Part 1:** 226, 227
Fowler, Gene, **Supp. VIII:** 290
Fowler, Henry Watson, **Supp. I Part 2:** 660
Fowler, Karen Joy, **Supp. XXII:** 49
Fowler, Singrid, **Supp. VIII:** 249, 258
Fowler, Virginia C., **Supp. VIII:** 224
Fox, Alan, **Supp. XIII:** 120
Fox, Dixon Ryan, **I:** 337
Fox, Joe, **Supp. IX:** 259, 261
Fox, John, **Supp. XIII:** 166; **Supp. XXII:** 36
Fox, Linda C., **Supp. XIII:** 217–218
Fox, Paula, **Supp. XX: 91**
Fox, Ruth, **Supp. I Part 2:** 619
"Fox, The" (Levine), **Supp. V:** 181, 189
Fox-Genovese, Elizabeth, **Supp. IV Part 1:** 286; **Supp. XXII:** 190, 192, 200
Fox in Socks (Geisel), **Supp. XVI:** 108, 112
"Fox Night" (Jarman), **Supp. XVII:** 120
Fox of Peapack, The (White), **Supp. I Part 2:** 676, 677–678
"Fox of Peapack, The" (White), **Supp. I Part 2:** 677
"Fox Point Health Clinic, 1974" (Halliday), **Supp. XIX:** 89, 93
Fox's Earth (Siddons), **Supp. XXII:** 239
Foye, Raymond, **Supp. XIV:** 150
Fradkin, Lori, **Supp. XIX:** 52
Fraenkel, Michael, **III:** 178, 183
"Fragging" (Komunyakaa), **Supp. XIII:** 123
Fragile Beauty, A: John Nichols' Milagro Country: Text and Photographs from His Life and Work (Nichols), **Supp. XIII:** 268
"Fragility" (Shields), **Supp. VII:** 318
"Fragment" (Ashbery), **Supp. III Part 1:** 11, 13, 14, 19, 20
"Fragment" (Lowell), **II:** 516
"Fragment" (Ortiz), **Supp. IV Part 2:** 507
"Fragment of a Meditation" (Tate), **IV:** 129
"Fragment of an Agon" (Eliot), **I:** 579–580
"Fragment of a Prologue" (Eliot), **I:** 579–580
"Fragment of New York, 1929" (Eberhart), **I:** 536–537
"Fragments" (Emerson), **II:** 19
"Fragments for Fall" (Salinas), **Supp. XIII:** 320–321
"Fragments of a Hologram Rose" (W. Gibson), **Supp. XVI:** 122, 123, 128
"Fragments of a Liquidation" (Howe), **Supp. IV Part 2:** 426
Fragonard, Jean Honoré, **III:** 275; **IV:** 79
Fraiman, Susan, **Supp. IV Part 1:** 324
"Frame for Poetry, A" (W. J. Smith), **Supp. XIII:** 333
France, Anatole, **IV:** 444; **Supp. I Part 2:** 631; **Supp. XIV:** 79
France and England in North America (Parkman), **Supp. II Part 2:** 596, 600–605, 607, 613–614
Franchere, Hoyt C., **II:** 131
Franchiser, The (Elkin), **Supp. VI: 51–52,** 58
Franciosi, Robert, **Supp. XIV:** 283
Francis, Lee, **Supp. IV Part 2:** 499
Francis, Richard, **Supp. XV:** 121
Francis, Robert, **Supp. IX: 75–92**
Francis of Assisi, Saint, **III:** 543; **IV:** 69, 375, 410; **Supp. I Part 2:** 394, 397, 441, 442, 443
Franco, Francisco, **II:** 261
Franco, Harry (pseudonym). *See* Briggs, Charles Frederick
Franconia (Fraser), **Retro. Supp. I:** 136
"Franconia" tales (Abbott), **Supp. I Part 1:** 38
Frank, Anne, **Supp. X:** 149; **Supp. XVII:** 39
Frank, Frederick S., **Retro. Supp. II:** 273
Frank, James M., **Supp. XIV:** 1
Frank, Jerome, **Supp. I Part 2:** 645
Frank, Joseph, **II:** 587
Frank, Mary, **Supp. X:** 213
Frank, Robert, **Supp. XI:** 295; **Supp. XII:** 127; **Supp. XIV:** 150
Frank, Sheldon, **Supp. XXII:** 210
Frank, Waldo, **I:** 106, 109, 117, 229, 236, 245, 259, 400; **Retro. Supp. II:** 77, 79, 83; **Supp. IX:** 308, 309, 311, 320; **Supp. XV:** 298; **Supp. XX: 67–82**
Frank, W. L., Jr., **Supp. XVIII:** 77
Frankel, Charles, **III:** 291
Frankel, Haskel, **Supp. I Part 2:** 448
Frankenberg, Lloyd, **I:** 436, 437, 445, 446; **III:** 194
Frankenheimer, John, **Supp. XI:** 343
Frankenstein (film), **Supp. IV Part 1:** 104; **Supp. XVII:** 57
Frankenstein (Gardner), **Supp. VI:** 72
Frankenstein (Shelley), **Supp. XII:** 79
Frankfurter, Felix, **I:** 489
"Frankie" (Keillor), **Supp. XVI:** 167
Frankie and Johnny (film), **Supp. XIII:** 206
Frankie and Johnny in the Clair de Lune (McNally), **Supp. XIII: 200,** 201
Franklin, Benjamin, **II:** 6, 8, 92, **101–125,** 127, 295, 296, 302, 306; **III:** 74, 90; **IV:** 73, 193; **Supp. I Part 1:** 306; **Supp. I Part 2:** 411, 503, 504, 506, 507, 510, 516, 518, 522, 524, 579, 639; **Supp. VIII:** 202, 205; **Supp. XIII:** 150; **Supp. XIV:** 306; **Supp. XVIII:** 12; **Supp. XX: 284**
Franklin, Cynthia, **Supp. IV Part 1:** 332
Franklin, Ruth, **Supp. XVI:** 160
Franklin, R. W., **Retro. Supp. I:** 29, 41, 43, 47
Franklin, Sarah, **II:** 122
Franklin, Temple, **II:** 122
Franklin, Wayne, **Supp. XXII:** 205
Franklin, William, **II:** 122; **Supp. I Part 2:** 504

Franklin Evans (Whitman), **Retro. Supp. I:** 393
"Frank O'Connor and *The New Yorker*" (Maxwell), **Supp. VIII:** 172
Franks, Lucinda, **Supp. XIII:** 12
"Frank Sinatra Has a Cold" (Talese), **Supp. XVII:** 203
"Frank Stanford of the Mulberry Family: An Arkansas Epilogue" (Wright), **Supp. XV:** 339–340
"Franny" (Salinger), **III:** 564, 565–566
Franny and Zooey (Salinger), **III:** 552, 564–567; **IV:** 216; **Supp. XIII:** 263
Franscell, Ron, **Supp. XXII:** 206, 216
Franzen, Jonathan, **Retro. Supp. II:** 279; **Supp. XIX:** 54; **Supp. XX: 83–97; Supp. XXII:** 255
Fraser, G. S., **Supp. XII:** 128; **Supp. XIV:** 162
Fraser, Joe, **III:** 46
Fraser, Marjorie Frost, **Retro. Supp. I:** 136
Frayn, Michael, **Supp. IV Part 2:** 582
Frazee, E. S., **Supp. I Part 2:** 381
Frazee, Esther Catherine. *See* Lindsay, Mrs. Vachel Thomas (Esther Catherine Frazee)
Frazer, Sir James G., **I:** 135; **II:** 204; **III:** 6–7; **IV:** 70; **Retro. Supp. I:** 80; **Supp. I Part 1:** 18; **Supp. I Part 2:** 541; **Supp. XX: 117**
Frazier, Ian, **Supp. VIII:** 272
Frazier, Kathleen, **Supp. XXI:** 22
"Freak Show, The" (Sexton), **Supp. II Part 2:** 695
Freaks: Myths and Images of the Secret Self (Fiedler), **Supp. XIII:** 106, 107
Freckles (film), **Supp. XX: 223**
Freckles (Stratton-Porter), **Supp. XX: 211, 218, 218–219, 222**
Freddy's Book (Gardner), **Supp. VI: 72**
Frederic, Harold, **I:** 409; **II: 126–149,** 175, 276, 289; **Retro. Supp. I:** 325
"Frederick Douglass" (Dunbar), **Supp. II Part 1:** 197, 199
"Frederick Douglass" (Hayden), **Supp. II Part 1:** 363
Frederick Douglass: Slave, Fighter, Freeman (Bontemps), **Supp. XXII:** 13
Frederick the Great, **II:** 103; **Supp. I Part 2:** 433
Fredrickson, George M., **Supp. I Part 2:** 589
"Free" (O'Hara), **III:** 369
Free, and Other Stories (Dreiser), **Retro. Supp. II:** 104
Free Agents (Apple), **Supp. XVII: 5–6**
Free Air (Lewis), **II:** 441
Freedman, Monroe H., **Supp. VIII:** 127
Freedman, Richard, **Supp. V:** 244
Freedom (Franzen), **Supp. XXII:** 255
"Freedom" (Larsen), **Supp. XVIII:** 124
"Freedom" (White), **Supp. I Part 2:** 659
"Freedom, New Hampshire" (Kinnell), **Supp. III Part 1:** 238, 239, 251
"Freedom and Discipline" (Carruth), **Supp. XVI:** 50
Freedom Business, The (Nelson), **Supp. XVIII: 186**
Freedom Is the Right to Choose: An Inquiry into the Battle for the American Future (MacLeish), **III:** 3
"Freedom's a Hard-Bought Thing" (Benét), **Supp. XI:** 47, 48
"Freedom's Plow" (Hughes), **Supp. I Part 1:** 346
Free Enterprise (Cliff), **Supp. XXII:** 66–67, **77–78**
"Free Fantasia: Tiger Flowers" (Hayden), **Supp. II Part 1:** 363, 366
Freeing of the Dust, The (Levertov), **Supp. III Part 1:** 281–282
"Free Lance, The" (Mencken), **III:** 104, 105
Free-Lance Pallbearers, The (Reed), **Supp. X:** 240, **242–243,** 244
Freeland (Lane), **Supp. XXII:** 297
Free Life, A (Jin), **Supp. XVIII: 101–102**
Freeloaders, The (Lacy), **Supp. XV:** 204
"Free Man" (Hughes), **Supp. I Part 1:** 333
Freeman, Chris, **Supp. XIV:** 157, 159
Freeman, Douglas Southall, **Supp. I Part 2:** 486, 493
Freeman, John, **Supp. XVIII:** 90
Freeman, Joseph, **II:** 26; **Supp. I Part 2:** 610; **Supp. XXII:** 274, 277
Freeman, Mary E. Wilkins, **II:** 401; **Retro. Supp. II:** 51, 136, 138; **Supp. IX:** 79
Freeman, Morgan, **Supp. XII:** 317
Freeman, Suzanne, **Supp. X:** 83
Free Man, The (Richter), **Supp. XVIII:** 215
"Free Man's Worship, A" (Russell), **Supp. I Part 2:** 522
Freewheelin' Bob Dylan, The (album, Dylan), **Supp. XVIII:** 20, 24, 29
Freilicher, Jane, **Supp. XV:** 178
Freinman, Dorothy, **Supp. IX:** 94
Frémont, John Charles, **Supp. I Part 2:** 486
Fremont-Smith, Eliot, **Supp. XIII:** 263
Fremstad, Olive, **I:** 319; **Retro. Supp. I:** 10
French, Warren, **Supp. XII:** 118–119
French Chef, The (television program), **Supp. XVII:** 89
French Connection, The (film), **Supp. V:** 226
French Leave (X. J. Kennedy), **Supp. XV:** 165
French Poets and Novelists (James), **II:** 336; **Retro. Supp. I:** 220
"French Scarecrow, The" (Maxwell), **Supp. VIII:** 169, 170
French Ways and Their Meaning (Wharton), **IV:** 319; **Retro. Supp. I:** 378
Freneau, Eleanor Forman (Mrs. Philip Freneau), **Supp. II Part 1:** 266
Freneau, Philip M., **I:** 335; **II:** 295; **Supp. I Part 1:** 124, 125, 127, 145; **Supp. II Part 1:** 65, **253–277**
Frenzy (Everett), **Supp. XVIII: 59–60**
Frescoes for Mr. Rockefeller's City (MacLeish), **III:** 14–15
"Fresh Air" (Koch), **Supp. XV:** 181, 185
Fresh Air Fiend: Travel Writings, 1985–2000 (Theroux), **Supp. VIII:** 325
Fresh Brats (X. J. Kennedy), **Supp. XV:** 163
"Freshman" (Sanders), **Supp. XVI:** 277
Freud, Sigmund, **I:** 55, 58, 59, 66, 67, 135, 241, 242, 244, 247, 248, 283; **II:** 27, 370, 546–547; **III:** 134, 390, 400, 418, 488; **IV:** 7, 70, 138, 295; **Retro. Supp. I:** 80, 176, 253; **Retro. Supp. II:** 104; **Supp. I Part 1:** 13, 43, 253, 254, 259, 260, 265, 270, 315; **Supp. I Part 2:** 493, 527, 616, 643, 647, 649; **Supp. IV Part 2:** 450; **Supp. VIII:** 103, 196; **Supp. IX:** 102, 155, 161, 308; **Supp. X:** 193, 194; **Supp. XII:** 14–15; **Supp. XIII:** 75; **Supp. XIV:** 83; **Supp. XV:** 219; **Supp. XVI:** 157–158, 161, 292; **Supp. XXII:** 165, 198
"Freud and Literature" (Trilling), **Supp. III Part 2:** 502–503
Freudian Psychology and Veblen's Social Theory, The (Schneider), **Supp. I Part 2:** 650
Freudian Wish and Its Place in Ethics, The (Holt), **I:** 59
"Freud's Room" (Ozick), **Supp. V:** 268
Freud: The Mind of the Moralist (Sontag and Rieff), **Supp. III Part 2:** 455
"Freud: Within and Beyond Culture" (Trilling), **Supp. III Part 2:** 508
Frey, Charles, **Supp. XXII:** 301
Frey, Hillary, **Supp. XIX:** 55; **Supp. XXII:** 53
Frey, James, **Supp. XXII:** 95
"Friday Morning Trial of Mrs. Solano, The" (Ríos), **Supp. IV Part 2:** 538, 548
Friebert, Stuart, **Supp. XIX:** 276
Frieburger, William, **Supp. XIII:** 239
Friede, Donald, **Supp. XVII:** 85, 86, 87, 90
Friedenberg, Edgar Z., **Supp. VIII:** 240
Friedman, Bruce Jay, **I:** 161; **Supp. IV Part 1:** 379
Friedman, Lawrence S., **Supp. V:** 273
Friedman, Milton, **Supp. I Part 2:** 648
Friedman, Norman, **I:** 431–432, 435, 439
Friedman, Stan, **Supp. XII:** 186
Friedmann, Georges, **Supp. I Part 2:** 645
"Fried Sausage" (Simic), **Supp. VIII:** 270
Friend, Julius, **Retro. Supp. I:** 80
Friend, The (Coleridge), **II:** 10
"Friend Husband's Latest" (Sayre), **Retro. Supp. I:** 104
"Friendly Debate between a Conformist and a Non-Conformist, A" (Wild), **IV:** 155
"Friendly Neighbor" (Keillor), **Supp. XVI:** 172
Friend of the Earth, A (Boyle), **Supp. VIII:** 12, 16; **Supp. XX: 29–30**
"Friend of the Fourth Decade, The" (Merrill), **Supp. III Part 1:** 327
"Friends" (Beattie), **Supp. V:** 23, 27
"Friends" (Paley), **Supp. VI:** 219, 226
"Friends" (Sexton), **Supp. II Part 2:** 693
Friend's Delight, The (Bierce), **I:** 195

"Friends from Philadelphia" (Updike), **Retro. Supp. I:** 319
"Friendship" (Emerson), **Supp. II Part 1:** 290
Friends: More Will and Magna Stories (Dixon), **Supp. XII:** 148, 149
"Friends of Heraclitus, The" (Simic), **Supp. VIII:** 284
"Friends of Kafka, The" (Singer), **Retro. Supp. II:** 308
"Friends of the Family, The" (McCarthy), **II:** 566
"Friend to Alexander, A" (Thurber), **Supp. I Part 2:** 616
"Frigate Pelican, The" (Moore), **III:** 208, 210–211, 215
"Frill, The" (Buck), **Supp. XIV:** 274
"Fringe, The" (Bass), **Supp. XVI:** 19
Frobenius, Leo, **III:** 475; **Supp. III Part 2:** 620
Froebel, Friedrich, **Supp. XIV:** 52–53
Frog (Dixon), **Supp. XII:** 151
"Frog Dances" (Dixon), **Supp. XII:** 151
"Frog Pond, The" (Kinnell), **Supp. III Part 1:** 254
"Frogs" (Nelson), **Supp. XVIII:** 176
"Frog Takes a Swim" (Dixon), **Supp. XII:** 152
Frohock, W. M., **I:** 34, 42
Frolic of His Own, A (Gaddis), **Supp. IV Part 1:** 279, 291, 292–294; **Supp. XX: 91**
"From a Mournful Village" (Jewett), **Retro. Supp. II:** 146
"From an Alabama Farm" (Nelson), **Supp. XVIII:** 182
"From an Old House in America" (Rich), **Supp. I Part 2:** 551, 565–567
From Another World (Untermeyer), **Supp. XV:** 293, 303, 310–311, 313
"From a Roadside Motel" (F. Wright), **Supp. XVII:** 245
"From a Survivor" (Rich), **Supp. I Part 2:** 563
From A to Z (musical review; Allen), **Supp. XV:** 3, 13
From a Work in Progress (Notley), **Supp. XXII:** 232
"From a Work in Progress" (Notley), **Supp. XXII:** 232
From a Writer's Notebook (Brooks), **I:** 254
From Bauhaus to Our House (Wolfe), **Supp. III Part 2:** 580, 581, 584
From Bondage (H. Roth), **Supp. IX:** 236, **238–240**
"From *Chants* to *Borders* to *Communion" (Fox), Supp. XIII:* 217, 217–218
"From Chicago" (Anderson), **I:** 108–109
From Death to Morning (Wolfe), **IV:** 450, 456, 458
"From Dick to Lethem: The Dickian Legacy, Postmodernism, and Avant-Pop in Jonathan Lethem's *Amnesia Moon" (Rossi), Supp. XVIII:* 137, 138–139
"From Discord, a Wife Makes a Nice New Life—Too Nice" (Linfield), **Supp. XVII:** 177
From Down to the Village (Budbill), **Supp. XIX: 6–7**
"From Feathers to Iron" (Kunitz), **Supp. III Part 1:** 261
"From Fifth Avenue Up" (Barnes), **Supp. III Part 1:** 33, 44
"From Gorbunov and Gorchakov" (Brodsky), **Supp. VIII:** 26
"From Grand Canyon to Burbank" (H. Miller), **III:** 186
"From Hell to Breakfast", **Supp. IX:** 326–327
From Here to Eternity (film), **Supp. XI:** 221
From Here to Eternity (J. Jones), **I:** 477; **Supp. XI:** 215, 216, 217, 218, **219–221,** 223, 224, 226, 229, 230, 231, 232, 234; **Supp. XIX:** 248; **Supp. XX: 248; Supp. XXII:** 140
From Here to Eternity (miniseries), **Supp. XI:** 234
From Jordan's Delight (Blackmur), **Supp. II Part 1:** 91
"From Lumaghi Mine" (Wrigley), **Supp. XVIII:** 295
Fromm, Erich, **I:** 58; **Supp. VIII:** 196
From Morn to Midnight (Kaiser), **I:** 479
"From Native Son to Invisible Man" (Locke), **Supp. IX:** 306
"From Pico, the Women: A Life" (Creeley), **Supp. IV Part 1:** 149
From Plotzk to Boston (Antin), **Supp. XX: 2**
From Ritual to Romance (Weston), **II:** 540; **III:** 12; **Supp. I Part 2:** 439
From Room to Room (Kenyon), **Supp. VII:** 163–165, 166, 167
"From Room to Room" (Kenyon), **Supp. VII:** 159, 163–165
From Sand Creek: Rising in this Heart Which Is Our America (Ortiz), **Supp. IV Part 2:** 512–513
"From Sea Cliff, March" (Swenson), **Supp. IV Part 2:** 649
From Stone Orchard: A Collection of Memories (Findley), **Supp. XX: 57**
"From the Antigone" (Yeats), **III:** 459
From the Ashes: Voices of Watts (Schulberg, ed.), **Supp. XVIII:** 254
From the Barrio: A Chicano Anthology (Salinas and Faderman, eds.), **Supp. XIII:** 313
From the Beginning (Notley), **Supp. XXII:** 226, 235–236
From the Briarpatch File: On Context, Procedure, and American Identity (Murray), **Supp. XIX:** 161
"From the Childhood of Jesus" (Pinsky), **Supp. VI:** 244–245, 247
"From the Corpse Woodpiles, From the Ashes" (Hayden), **Supp. II Part 1:** 370
"From the Country to the City" (Bishop), **Supp. I Part 1:** 85, 86
"From the Cupola" (Merrill), **Supp. III Part 1:** 324–325, 331
"From the Dark Side of the Earth" (Oates), **Supp. II Part 2:** 510
"From the Diary of a New York Lady" (Parker), **Supp. IX:** 201
"From the Diary of One Not Born" (Singer), **IV:** 9
"From the Dreams" (Notley), **Supp. XXII:** 224
"From the East, Light" (Carver), **Supp. III Part 1:** 138
From the First Nine: Poems 1946–1976 (Merrill), **Supp. III Part 1:** 336
"From the Flats" (Lanier), **Supp. I Part 1:** 364
From the Flower Courtyard (Everwine), **Supp. XV:** 75
From the Heart of Europe (Matthiessen), **III:** 310
From the Meadow: Selected and New Poems (Everwine), **Supp. XV: 75, 88–89**
"From the Memoirs of a Private Detective" (Hammett), **Supp. IV Part 1:** 343
"From the Nursery" (Kenyon), **Supp. VII:** 171
"From the Poets in the Kitchen" (Marshall), **Supp. XI:** 277
From the Terrace (O'Hara), **III:** 362
"From the Thirties: Tillie Olsen and the Radical Tradition" (Rosenfelt), **Supp. XIII:** 296, 304
"From Trollope's Journal" (Bishop), **Retro. Supp. II:** 47
"Front, A" (Jarrell), **II:** 374
Front, The (film), **Supp. I Part 1:** 295
"Front and the Back Parts of the House, The" (Maxwell), **Supp. VIII:** 169
Frontier Eden (Bigelow), **Supp. X:** 227
"Frontiers of Culture" (Locke), **Supp. XIV:** 213
"Front Lines" (Snyder), **Supp. VIII:** 301
Front Runner, The (P. N. Warren), **Supp. XX: 259, 262–264**
Frost, A. B., **Retro. Supp. II:** 72
Frost, Carol, **Supp. XV: 91–109**
Frost, Isabelle Moodie, **II:** 150, 151
Frost, Jeanie, **II:** 151
Frost, Richard, **Supp. XV:** 92
Frost, Robert, **I:** 26, 27, 60, 63, 64, 171, 229, 303, 326, 418; **II:** 55, 58, **150–172,** 276, 289, 388, 391, 471, 523, 527, 529, 535; **III:** 5, 23, 67, 269, 271, 272, 275, 287, 453, 510, 523, 536, 575, 581, 591; **IV:** 140, 190, 415; **Retro. Supp. I:** 67, **121–144,** 276, 287, 292, 298, 299, 311, 413; **Retro. Supp. II:** 40, 47, 50, 146, 178, 181; **Supp. I Part 1:** 80, 242, 263, 264; **Supp. I Part 2:** 387, 461, 699; **Supp. II Part 1:** 4, 19, 26, 103; **Supp. III Part 1:** 63, 74–75, 239, 253; **Supp. III Part 2:** 546, 592, 593; **Supp. IV Part 1:** 15; **Supp. IV Part 2:** 439, 445, 447, 448, 599, 601; **Supp. VIII:** 20, 30, 32, 98, 100, 104, 259, 292; **Supp. IX:** 41, 42, 75, 76, 80, 87, 90, 266, 308; **Supp. X:** 64, 65, 66, 74, 120, 172; **Supp. XI:** 43, 123, 150, 153, 312; **Supp. XII:** 130, 241, 303, 307; **Supp. XIII:** 143, 147, 334–335; **Supp. XIV:** 42, 122, 222, 229; **Supp. XV:** 21, 51, 65, 96, 212, 215, 250, 256, 293, 296, 299, 301, 302, 306,

348; **Supp. XVII:** 36, 110, 115–116; **Supp. XVIII:** 298, 300; **Supp. XIX:** 1, 123; **Supp. XX: 69, 199; Supp. XXI:** 19, 28, 51, 99, 104, 107, 205; **Supp. XXII:** 206
Frost, William Prescott, **II:** 150–151
"Frost: A Dissenting Opinion" (Cowley), **Supp. II Part 1:** 143
Frost: A Time to Talk (Francis), **Supp. IX:** 76, **85–86**
"Frost at Midnight" (Coleridge), **Supp. X:** 71
"Frost Flowers" (Kenyon), **Supp. VII:** 168
"Frost: He Is Sometimes a Poet and Sometimes a Stump-Speaker" (News-Week), **Retro. Supp. I:** 137
Frothingham, Nathaniel, **I:** 3
Frothingham, Octavius B., **IV:** 173
"Frozen City, The" (Nemerov), **III:** 270
"Frozen Fields, The" (Bowles), **Supp. IV Part 1:** 80
"Fruit Garden Path, The" (Lowell), **II:** 516
"Fruit of the Flower" (Cullen), **Supp. IV Part 1:** 167
Fruit of the Tree, The (Wharton), **IV:** 314–315; **Retro. Supp. I:** 367, **370–371,** 373
"Fruit of Travel Long Ago" (Melville), **III:** 93
Fruits and Vegetables (Jong), **Supp. V:** 113, 115, 117, 118, 119
"Fruits of the Sea, The" (Di Piero), **Supp. XIX:** 47
Frumkes, Lewis Burke, **Supp. XII:** 335–336
Fry, Christopher, **Supp. I Part 1:** 270
Fry, Roger, **Supp. XIV:** 336
Fry, Stephen M., **Supp. XIX:** 159
Frye, Joanne, **Supp. XIII:** 292, 296, 298, 302
Frye, Northrop, **Supp. I Part 2:** 530; **Supp. II Part 1:** 101; **Supp. X:** 80; **Supp. XIII:** 19; **Supp. XIV:** 11, 15; **Supp. XVI:** 149, 156; **Supp. XX: 50**
Fryer, Judith, **Retro. Supp. I:** 379
F. Scott Fitzgerald: A Critical Portrait (Piper), **Supp. IX:** 65
"F. S. F., 1896–1996, R.I.P." (Doctorow), **Retro. Supp. I:** 97
Fuchs, Daniel, **Supp. XIII:** 106
Fuchs, Miriam, **Supp. IV Part 1:** 284
Fuehrer Bunker, The (Snodgrass), **Supp. VI:** 314, 315–317, 319–321
Fuel (Nye), **Supp. XIII:** 277, **282–284**
"Fuel" (Nye), **Supp. XIII:** 283
Fuertes, Gloria, **Supp. V:** 178
Fugard, Athol, **Supp. VIII:** 330; **Supp. XIII:** 205
Fugitive Group, The (Cowan), **IV:** 120
Fugitive Kind, The (T. Williams), **IV:** 381, 383
Fugitives, The (group), **IV:** 122, 124, 125, 131, 237, 238
Fugitives, The: A Critical Account (Bradbury), **IV:** 130
"Fugitive Slave Law, The" (Emerson), **II:** 13
Fugitive's Return (Glaspell), **Supp. III Part 1:** 182–184
Fuller, B. A. G., **III:** 605
Fuller, Edmund, **Supp. XXII:** 211, 212
Fuller, Hiram, **Supp. XVIII:** 12,14
Fuller, Jesse "Lonecat", **Supp. XV:** 147
Fuller, Margaret, **I:** 261; **II:** 7, 276; **IV:** 172; **Retro. Supp. I:** 155–156, 163; **Retro. Supp. II:** 46; **Supp. I Part 2:** 524; **Supp. II Part 1: 279–306; Supp. IX:** 37; **Supp. XVIII:** 3, 11, 12, 16
Fuller, Thomas, **II:** 111, 112
Fullerton, Morton, **Supp. XX: 231**
Fullerton Street (Wilson), **Supp. VIII:** 331
"Full Fathom Five" (Plath), **Supp. I Part 2:** 538
Full Measure: Modern Short Stories on Aging (D. Sennett, ed.), **Supp. XVI:** 37
Full Monty, The (musical, McNally), **Supp. XIII:** 207
"Full Moon" (Hayden), **Supp. II Part 1:** 370
Full Moon and Other Plays (Price), **Supp. VI:** 266
"Full Moon and You're Not Here" (Cisneros), **Supp. VII:** 71–72
"Full Moon: New Guinea" (Shapiro), **Supp. II Part 2:** 707
"Fullness of Life, The" (Wharton), **Retro. Supp. I:** 363
Full of Life (Fante), **Supp. XI:** 160
Full of Life (film), **Supp. XI:** 170
Full of Lust and Good Usage (Dunn), **Supp. XI: 145–147**
"Full Summer" (Olds), **Supp. X:** 212
Fulton, Ben, **Supp. XXII:** 207
Fulton, Robert, **Supp. I Part 2:** 519; **Supp. II Part 1:** 73
Fun and Games (Major), **Supp. XXII:** 180
"Functional Poem" (Halliday), **Supp. XIX:** 85
Function of Criticism, The (Winters), **Supp. II Part 2:** 812, 813
"Fundamentalism" (Tate), **IV:** 125
"Fundamental Project of Technology, The" (Kinnell), **Supp. III Part 1:** 253
"Funeral of Bobò, The" (Brodsky), **Supp. VIII:** 27, 28
"Funnel" (Sexton), **Supp. II Part 2:** 675
"Furious Seasons, The" (Carver), **Supp. III Part 1:** 137
Furious Seasons and Other Stories (Carver), **Supp. III Part 1:** 142, 143, 146
"Furious Versions" (L.-Y. Lee), **Supp. XV: 215–217,** 218**,** 220
"Furnished Room, The" (Hayden), **Supp. II Part 1:** 386–387, 394, 397, 399, 406, 408
"Furor Scribendi" (O. Butler), **Supp. XIII:** 70
Furors Die (Hoffman), **Supp. XVIII: 80–81**
Fur Person, The (Sarton), **Supp. VIII: 264–265**
Further Adventures with You (Wright), **Supp. XV:** 339, 342, **343–345**
Further Fables for Our Time (Thurber), **Supp. I Part 2:** 612
"Further in Summer than the Birds" (Dickinson), **I:** 471
Further Poems of Emily Dickinson (Bianchi and Hampson, ed.), **Retro. Supp. I:** 35
Further Range, A (Frost), **II:** 155; **Retro. Supp. I:** 132, 136, 137, 138, 139
"Fury, The (Skloot), **Supp. XX: 197**
"Fury of Aerial Bombardment, The" (Eberhart), **I:** 535–536
"Fury of Flowers and Worms, The" (Sexton), **Supp. II Part 2:** 694
"Fury of Rain Storms, The" (Sexton), **Supp. II Part 2:** 695
Fury of the Jungle (film), **Supp. XIII:** 163
Fussell, Paul, **Supp. V:** 241
"Future, if Any, of Comedy, The" (Thurber), **Supp. I Part 2:** 620
Future in the Present, The (C. L. R. James), **Supp. XXI:** 172
Future is Ours, Comrade, The: Conversations with the Russians (Kosinski), **Supp. VII:** 215
Futureland: Nine Stories of an Imminent World (Mosley), **Supp. XIII: 247–249**
"Future Life, The" (Bryant), **Supp. I Part 1:** 170
Future of Southern Letters, The (J. W. Miller), **Supp. XX: 161**
Future of the Race, The (H. L. Gates), **Supp. XX: 101, 104, 111**
Future Punishment of the Wicked, The (Edwards), **I:** 546

"Gabriel" (Rich), **Supp. I Part 2:** 557
Gabriel, Ralph H., **Supp. I Part 1:** 251
Gabriel, Trip, **Supp. V:** 212
Gabriel Conroy (Harte), **Supp. II Part 1:** 354
"Gabriel's Truth" (Kenyon), **Supp. VII:** 166
Gaddis, William, **Supp. IV Part 1: 279–296; Supp. IV Part 2:** 484; **Supp. V:** 52; **Supp. IX:** 208; **Supp. X:** 301, 302; **Supp. XX: 83, 91; Supp. XXI:** 226
Gadiot, Pud, **Supp. XI:** 295
Gain (Powers), **Supp. IX:** 212, **220–221**
Gaines, Ernest J., **Supp. X:** 24, 250
Gaines, James R., **Supp. IX:** 190
Gainor, J. Ellen, **Supp. XXI:** 6
Gaitens, Peter, **Supp. XV:** 65
Galamain, Ivan, **Supp. III Part 2:** 624
Galassi, Jonathan, **Supp. XVIII:** 92; **Supp. XIX:** 34; **Supp. XXII:** 177
Galatea 2.2 (Powers), **Supp. IX:** 212, **219–220**
"Galatea Encore" (Brodsky), **Supp. VIII:** 31
Galbraith, John Kenneth, **Supp. I Part 2:** 645, 650
Galdós, Benito Pérez. *See* Pérez Galdós, Benito
Gale, Zona, **Supp. I Part 2:** 613; **Supp. VIII:** 155
Galehouse, Maggie, **Supp. XXI:** 215

"Gale in April" (Jeffers), **Supp. II Part 2:** 423
Galignani, Giovanni Antonio, **II:** 315
Galileo Galilei, **I:** 480–481; **Supp. XII:** 180; **Supp. XIII:** 75
Gallagher, Tess, **Supp. XVI:** 36; **Supp. XVII:** 110; **Supp. XXI:** 246
Gallant, Mavis, **Supp. VIII:** 151
Gallatin, Albert, **I:** 5
"Gallery" (Goldbarth), **Supp. XII:** 188
"Gallery of Real Creatures, A" (Thurber), **Supp. I Part 2:** 619
Gallico, Paul, **Supp. XVI:** 238
Gallows Songs (Snodgrass), **Supp. VI:** 317
Gallup, Donald, **III:** 404, 478
Galsworthy, John, **III:** 70, 153, 382
Galton Case, The (Macdonald), **Supp. IV Part 2:** 463, 473, 474
Galvin, Frances, **Supp. XXI:** 5
"Gal Young 'Un" (Rawlings), **Supp. X:** 228
Gambino, Richard, **Supp. XX: 35**
"Gambler, the Nun, and the Radio, The" (Hemingway), **II:** 250
"Gambler's Wife, The" (Dunbar), **Supp. II Part 1:** 196
Gambone, Philip, **Supp. XII:** 81
"Gambrel Roof, A" (Larcom), **Supp. XIII:** 144
"Game at Salzburg, A" (Jarrell), **II:** 384, 389
Game Management (Leopold), **Supp. XIV:** 182
"Game of Catch, A" (Wilbur), **Supp. III Part 2:** 552
Game Players of Titan, The (Dick), **Supp. XVIII:** 138
"Games in Frank Conroy's *Stop-Time*" (T. Adams), **Supp. XVI:** 67
"Games Two" (Wilbur), **Supp. III Part 2:** 550
Gammelgaard, Lene, **Supp. XVIII:** 112
"Gamut, The" (Angelou), **Supp. IV Part 1:** 15
Gander, Forrest, **Supp. XV:** 339, 340, 342
Gandhi, Indira, **Supp. X:** 108
Gandhi, Mahatma, **III:** 179, 296–297; **IV:** 170, 185, 367; **Supp. VIII:** 203, 204; **Supp. X:** 27
Gandhi on Non-Violence (Merton, ed.), **Supp. VIII:** 204–205
Gang of Five: Leaders at the Center of the Conservative Crusade (Easton), **Supp. XIX:** 137
"Gang of Mirrors, The" (Simic), **Supp. VIII:** 283
Gansevoort, Guert, **III:** 94
Gansevoort, Peter, **III:** 92
"Gap" (Bierds), **Supp. XVII:** 35–36
Garabedian, Michael, **Supp. XIII:** 115
Garbage (Ammons), **Supp. VII:** 24, 35–36
Garbage (Dixon), **Supp. XII:** 147, 148
Garbage Man, The (Dos Passos), **I:** 478, 479, 481, 493
Garber, Frederick, **Supp. IX:** 294–295
Garbo, Greta, **Supp. I Part 2:** 616
García, Cristina, **Supp. VIII:** 74; **Supp. XI: 177–192**
García Lorca, Federico. *See* Lorca, Federico García
"García Lorca: A Photograph of the Granada Cemetery, 1966" (Levis), **Supp. XI:** 264
García Márquez, Gabriel, **Supp. V:** 244; **Supp. VIII:** 81, 82, 84, 85; **Supp. XII:** 147, 310, 316, 322; **Supp. XIII:** 226; **Supp. XVII:** 45
Gardaphe, Fred, **Supp. XX: 38, 41**
"Garden" (Marvell), **IV:** 161; **Supp. XVI:** 204
"Garden, The" (Glück), **Supp. V:** 83
"Garden, The" (Strand), **Supp. IV Part 2:** 629
"Garden Among Tombs" (B. Kelly), **Supp. XVII:** 126
"Garden by Moonlight, The" (Lowell), **II:** 524
"Gardener Delivers a Fawn, The" (C. Frost), **Supp. XV:** 99
Gardener's Son, The (McCarthy), **Supp. VIII:** 187
Garden God, The: A Tale of Two Boys (Reid), **Supp. XX: 235**
"Gardenias" (Doty), **Supp. XI:** 122
"Gardenias" (Monette), **Supp. X:** 159
"Garden Lodge, The" (Cather), **I:** 316, 317
Garden of Adonis, The (Gordon), **II:** 196, 204–205, 209
Garden of Earthly Delights, A (Oates), **Supp. II Part 2:** 504, 507–509
Garden of Earthly Delights, The (Bosch), **Supp. XXII:** 255, 261
"Garden of Eden" (Hemingway), **II:** 259
Garden of Eden, The (Hemingway), **Retro. Supp. I:** 186, **187–188**
"Garden of Flesh, Garden of Stone" (B. Kelly), **Supp. XVII:** 128
"Garden of the Moon, The" (Doty), **Supp. XI:** 122
Garden of the Prophet, The (Gibran), **Supp. XX: 119, 122**
"Garden of the Trumpet Tree, The" (B. Kelly), **Supp. XVII:** 131
"Gardens, The" (Oliver), **Supp. VII:** 236
"Gardens of Mont-Saint-Michel, The" (Maxwell), **Supp. VIII:** 169
"Gardens of the Villa D'Este, The" (Hecht), **Supp. X:** 59
"Gardens of Zuñi, The" (Merwin), **Supp. III Part 1:** 351
Garden Thieves, The: Twentieth Century African-American Poetry (Major, ed.), **Supp. XXII:** 172
Gardiner, Judith Kegan, **Supp. IV Part 1:** 205
Gardner, Erle Stanley, **Supp. IV Part 1:** 121, 345
Gardner, Isabella, **IV:** 127
Gardner, John, **Supp. I Part 1:** 193, 195, 196; **Supp. III Part 1:** 136, 142, 146; **Supp. VI: 61–76**
Gardner, Thomas, **Supp. XXI:** 214
Gardons, S. S. *See* Snodgrass, W. D.
"Gare de Lyon" (M. F. K. Fisher), **Supp. XVII:** 91
Garfield, John, **Supp. XII:** 160
Garibaldi, Giuseppe, **I:** 4; **II:** 284
Garibay, Angel M., **Supp. XV:** 77
Garland, Hamlin, **I:** 407; **II:** 276, 289; **III:** 576; **Retro. Supp. I:** 133; **Retro. Supp. II:** 72; **Supp. I Part 1:** 217; **Supp. IV Part 2:** 502; **Supp. XVIII:** 6
Garland Companion, The (Zverev), **Retro. Supp. I:** 278
"Garments" (Gibran), **Supp. XX: 124**
Garments the Living Wear (Purdy), **Supp. VII:** 278–279, 280–281
Garner, Dwight, **Supp. X:** 202; **Supp. XVIII:** 89
Garnett, Edward, **I:** 405, 409, 417; **III:** 27
Garrett, George P., **Supp. I Part 1:** 196; **Supp. VII: 95–113; Supp. X:** 3, 7; **Supp. XI:** 218; **Supp. XVIII:** 74, 75
Garrigue, Jean, **Supp. XII:** 260
Garrison, Deborah, **Supp. IX:** 299
Garrison, Fielding, **III:** 105
Garrison, William Lloyd, **Supp. I Part 2:** 524, 588, 683, 685, 686, 687; **Supp. XIV:** 54
"Garrison of Cape Ann, The" (Whittier), **Supp. I Part 2:** 691, 694
Garry Moore Show (television show), **Supp. IV Part 2:** 575
"Garter Motif" (White), **Supp. I Part 2:** 673
Gartner, Zsuzsi, **Supp. X:** 276
Garvey, Marcus, **Supp. III Part 1:** 175, 180; **Supp. IV Part 1:** 168; **Supp. X:** 135, 136; **Supp. XXI:** 166, 168; **Supp. XXII:** 7
Gas (Kaiser), **I:** 479
Gas-House McGinty (Farrell), **II:** 41–42
Gaskell, Elizabeth, A., **Supp. I Part 2:** 580
Gasoline (Corso), **Supp. XII:** 118, **121–123,** 134
Gass, William H., **Supp. V:** 44, 52, 238; **Supp. VI: 77–96; Supp. IX:** 208; **Supp. XII:** 152; **Supp. XIV:** 305; **Supp. XVII:** 183
Gassner, John, **IV:** 381; **Supp. I Part 1:** 284, 292
"Gas Stations" (Apple), **Supp. XVII:** 4
Gastronomical Me, The (M. F. K. Fisher), **Supp. XVII:** 84, 85, 87, 91, 92
Gates, David, **Supp. V:** 24; **Supp. XIII:** 93; **Supp. XVI:** 73, 74; **Supp. XX: 92**
Gates, Elmer, **I:** 515–516
Gates, Henry Louis, Jr., **Retro. Supp. I:** 194, 195, 203; **Supp. X:** 242, 243, 245, 247; **Supp. XVIII:** 287; **Supp. XIX:** 147, 149; **Supp. XX: 99–112, 279, 286**
Gates, Lewis E., **III:** 315, 330
Gates, Sondra Smith, **Supp. XVIII:** 267, 269
Gates, The (Rukeyser), **Supp. VI:** 271, 274, 281
"Gates, The" (Rukeyser), **Supp. VI:** 286
Gates, Tudor, **Supp. XI:** 307
Gates of Ivory, the Gates of Horn, The (McGrath), **Supp. X:** 118
Gates of Wrath, The; Rhymed Poems (Ginsberg), **Supp. II Part 1:** 311, 319

"Gathering" (Trethewey), **Supp. XXI:** 249
Gathering Forces, The (C. L. R. James), **Supp. XXI:** 171
"Gathering of Dissidents, A" (Applebaum), **Supp. XVI:** 153
Gathering of Fugitives, A (Trilling), **Supp. III Part 2:** 506, 512
Gathering of Zion, The: The Story of the Mormon Trail (Stegner), **Supp. IV Part 2:** 599, 602–603
Gather Together in My Name (Angelou), **Supp. IV Part 1:** 2, 3, 4–6, 11
Gathorne-Hardy, Robert, **Supp. XIV:** 344, 347, 348, 349
Gaudier-Brzeska, Henri, **III:** 459, 464, 465, 477
Gaughran, Richard, **Supp. XXI:** 47–48
Gauguin, Paul, **I:** 34; **IV:** 290; **Supp. IV Part 1:** 81; **Supp. XII:** 128
"Gauguin in Oregon" (Skloot), **Supp. XX: 203**
"Gauley Bridge" (Rukeyser), **Supp. VI:** 278
Gauss, Christian, **II:** 82; **IV:** 427, 439–440, 444
Gauthier, Jacquie, **Supp. XIX:** 204
Gautier, Théophile, **II:** 543; **III:** 466, 467; **Supp. I Part 1:** 277
Gay, John, **II:** 111; **Supp. I Part 2:** 523; **Supp. XIV:** 337
Gay, Peter, **I:** 560
Gay, Sydney Howard, **Supp. I Part 1:** 158; **Supp. XVIII:** 3
Gay, Walter, **IV:** 317
Gayatri Prayer, The, **III:** 572
Gay Canon, The (Drake), **Supp. XX: 274**
"Gay Chaps at the Bar" (Brooks), **Supp. III Part 1:** 74, 75
" 'Gay Culture': Still of the Wild Frontier" (P. N. Warren), **Supp. XX: 272**
Gaylord, Winfield R., **III:** 579–580
Gay Talese Reader, The: Portraits & Encounters (Talese), **Supp. XVII:** 202, 208
"Gazebo" (Carver), **Supp. III Part 1:** 138, 144, 145
Gazer's Spirit, The (Hollander), **Supp. XIX:** 121
Gazer Within, The, and Other Essays by Larry Levis, **Supp. XI:** 270
Gazzara, Ben, **Supp. VIII:** 319
Gazzo, Michael V., **III:** 155
"Geese Gone Beyond" (Snyder), **Supp. VIII:** 304
Geffen, David, **Supp. XXI:** 154
"Gegenwart" (Goethe), **Supp. II Part 1:** 26
Geisel, Theodor Seuss (Dr. Seuss), **Supp. X:** 56; **Supp. XVI: 97–115**
Geismar, Maxwell, **II:** 178, 431; **III:** 71; **Supp. IX:** 15; **Supp. XI:** 223
Gelb, Arthur, **IV:** 380; **Supp. XXI:** 12
Gelb, Barbara, **Supp. XXI:** 12
Gelbart, Larry, **Supp. IV Part 2:** 591
Gelder, Robert Van, **Supp. XIII:** 166
Gelfant, Blanche H., **II:** 27, 41; **Supp. XVII:** 161
Gelfman, Jean, **Supp. X:** 3
Gellert, Hugo, **Supp. XXII:** 277
Gellhorn, Martha. *See* Hemingway, Mrs. Ernest (Martha Gellhorn)
Gelpi, Albert, **Supp. I Part 2:** 552, 554, 560
Gelpi, Barbara, **Supp. I Part 2:** 560
Gemin, Pamela, **Supp. XXI:** 246
Gemini: an extended autobiographical statement on my first twenty-five years of being a black poet (Giovanni), **Supp. IV Part 1:** 11
"Gen" (Snyder), **Supp. VIII:** 302
"Gender Norms" (Radinovsky), **Supp. XV:** 285
"Gender of Sound, The" (Carson), **Supp. XII: 106**
"Genealogy" (Komunyakaa), **Supp. XIII:** 129
"General Aims and Theories" (Crane), **I:** 389
General Died at Dawn, The (Odets), **Supp. II Part 2:** 546
"General Gage's Confession" (Freneau), **Supp. II Part 1:** 257
"General Gage's Soliloquy" (Freneau), **Supp. II Part 1:** 257
General History of the Robberies and Murders of the Most Notorious Pyrates from Their First Rise and Settlement in the Island of New Providence to the Present Year, A (Johnson), **Supp. V:** 128
"General William Booth Enters into Heaven" (Lindsay), **Supp. I Part 2:** 374, 382, 384, 385–388, 389, 392, 399
General William Booth Enters into Heaven and Other Poems (Lindsay), **Supp. I Part 2:** 379, 381, 382, 387–388, 391
"Generation of the Dispossessed" (P. N. Warren), **Supp. XX: 272**
"Generations of Men, The" (Frost), **Retro. Supp. I:** 128; **Supp. XIII:** 147
Generous Man, A (Price), **Supp. VI:** 259, 260, 261
Genesis (biblical book), **I:** 279; **II:** 540; **Retro. Supp. I:** 250, 256; **Supp. XII:** 54
"Genesis" (Stegner), **Supp. IV Part 2:** 604
Genesis: Book One (Schwartz), **Supp. II Part 2:** 640, 651–655
Gene Stratton-Porter (Richards), **Supp. XX: 217–218**
Gene Stratton-Porter, Naturalist and Novelist (Long), **Supp. XX: 212**
"Gene Stratton-Porter: Women's Advocate" (Obuchowski), **Supp. XX: 222**
Genet, Jean, **I:** 71, 82, 83, 84; **Supp. IV Part 1:** 8; **Supp. XI:** 308; **Supp. XII:** 1; **Supp. XIII:** 74; **Supp. XVII:** 95
"Genetic Coding" (Sorrentino), **Supp. XXI:** 227
"Genetic Expedition" (Dove), **Supp. IV Part 1:** 249, 257
"Genetics of Justice" (Alvarez), **Supp. VII:** 19
"Genial Host, The" (McCarthy), **II:** 564
"Genie in the Bottle, The" (Wilbur), **Supp. III Part 2:** 542
"Genius, The" (MacLeish), **III:** 19
Genius and Lust: A Journey through the Major Writings of Henry Miller (Mailer), **Retro. Supp. II:** 208
"Genius Child" (Hughes), **Retro. Supp. I:** 203
"Genius of Bob Dylan, The" (Lethem), **Supp. XVIII:** 146
"Genius," The (Dreiser), **I:** 497, 501, 509–511, 519; **Retro. Supp. II:** 94–95, **102–103,** 104, 105
"Genteel Tradition in American Philosophy, The" (Santayana), **I:** 222
"Gentle Communion" (Mora), **Supp. XIII:** 218–219
Gentle Crafter, The (O. Henry), **Supp. II Part 1:** 410
"Gentle Lena, The" (Stein), **IV:** 37, 40
Gentleman Caller, The (T. Williams), **IV:** 383
"Gentleman from Cracow, The" (Singer), **IV:** 9
"Gentleman of Bayou Têche, A" (Chopin), **Supp. I Part 1:** 211–212
"Gentleman of Shalott, The" (Bishop), **Supp. I Part 1:** 85, 86
Gentleman's Agreement (Hobson), **III:** 151
"Gentleman's Agreement" (Richard), **Supp. XIX:** 220–221
Gentlemen Prefer Blondes (Loos; musical adaptation), **Supp. XVI:** 193
Gentlemen Prefer Blondes: The Illuminating Diary of a Professional Lady (Loos), **Supp. XVI:** 181, 183, 186, **188–189**
Gentlemen Prefer "Books" (J. Yeats), Supp. XVI: 190
Gentle People, The: A Brooklyn Fable (Shaw), **Supp. XIX:** 244–245, 249
Gentry, Marshall Bruce, **Supp. IV Part 1:** 236
"Genuine Man, The" (Emerson), **II:** 10
"Genus Narcissus" (Trethewey), **Supp. XXI:** 256
Geo-Bestiary (Harrison), **Supp. VIII:** 53
"Geode" (Frost), **II:** 161
Geographical History of America, The (Stein), **IV:** 31, 45; **Supp. XVIII:** 148
Geography and Plays (Stein), **IV:** 29–30, 32, 43, 44
Geography III (Bishop), **Retro. Supp. II:** 50; **Supp. I Part 1:** 72, 73, 76, 82, 93, 94, 95
Geography of a Horse Dreamer (Shepard), **Supp. III Part 2:** 432
Geography of Home, The: California's Poetry of Place (Bluckey and Young, eds.), **Supp. XIII:** 313
Geography of Lograire, The (Merton), **Supp. VIII:** 208
Geography of the Heart (Johnson), **Supp. XI:** 129
"Geometric Poem, The" (Corso), **Supp. XII:** 132, 133–134
George, Diana Hume, **Supp. IV Part 2:** 447, 449, 450
George, Henry, **II:** 276; **Supp. I Part 2:** 518
George, Jan, **Supp. IV Part 1:** 268

George, Lynell, **Supp. XIII:** 234–235, 237, 249
George, Peter, **Supp. XI:** 302, 303, 304
George and the Dragon (Shanley), **Supp. XIV:** 315
George Bernard Shaw: His Plays (Mencken), **III:** 102
George Mills (Elkin), **Supp. VI: 53–54**
George Palmer Putnam: Representative American Publisher (Greenspan), **Supp. XVIII:** 257
"George Robinson: Blues" (Rukeyser), **Supp. VI:** 279
George's Mother (Crane), **I:** 408
"George Thurston" (Bierce), **I:** 202
George Washington Crossing the Delaware (Koch), **Supp. XV:** 186
Georgia Boy (Caldwell), **I:** 288, 305–306, 308, 309, 310
"Georgia Dusk" (Toomer), **Supp. IX:** 309
"Georgia: Invisible Empire State" (Du Bois), **Supp. II Part 1:** 179
"Georgia Night" (Toomer), **Supp. III Part 2:** 481
Georgia Scenes (Longstreet), **II:** 70, 313; **Supp. I Part 1:** 352
Georgics (Virgil), **Retro. Supp. I:** 135; **Supp. XVI:** 22
Georgoudaki, Ekaterini, **Supp. IV Part 1:** 12
Gerald McBoing-Boing (film), **Supp. XVI:** 102
"Geraldo No Last Name" (Cisneros), **Supp. VII:** 60–61
Gerald's Game (King), **Supp. V:** 141, 148–150, 151, 152
Gerald's Party (Coover), **Supp. V:** 49–50, 51, 52
Gérando, Joseph Marie de, **II:** 10
"Geranium" (O'Connor), **Retro. Supp. II:** 221, 236
Gerard, Jeremy, **Supp. XXI:** 147
Gerber, Dan, **Supp. VIII:** 39
Gerhardt, Rainer, **Supp. IV Part 1:** 142
"German Girls! The German Girls!, The" (MacLeish), **III:** 16
"German Refugee, The" (Malamud), **Supp. I Part 2:** 436, 437
"Germany's Reichswehr" (Agee), **I:** 35
Germinal (Zola), **III:** 318, 322
Gernsback, Hugo, **Supp. IV Part 1:** 101
"Gernsback Continuum, The" (W. Gibson), **Supp. XVI:** 123, 128
"Gerontion" (Eliot), **I:** 569, 574, 577, 578, 585, 588; **III:** 9, 435, 436; **Retro. Supp. I:** 290; **Supp. XV:** 341; **Supp. XVI:** 158–159
Gerry, Elbridge, **Supp. I Part 2:** 486
"Gerry's Jazz" (Komunyakaa), **Supp. XIII:** 125
Gershwin, Ira, **Supp. I Part 1:** 281
"Gert" (Monette), **Supp. X:** 158
Gertrude of Stony Island Avenue (Purdy), **Supp. VII:** 281–282
Gertrude Stein (Sprigge), **IV:** 31
Gertrude Stein: A Biography of Her Work (Sutherland), **IV:** 38
"Gertrude Stein and the Geography of the Sentence" (Gass), **Supp. VI:** 87
Gesell, Silvio, **III:** 473
"Gestalt at Sixty" (Sarton), **Supp. VIII:** 260
"Gesture of a Woman-in-Process" (Trethewey), **Supp. XXI:** 249–250
"Gesture toward an Unfound Renaissance, A" (Stafford), **Supp. XI:** 323
"Get It Again" (Halliday), **Supp. XIX:** 85
Getlin, Josh, **Supp. V:** 22; **Supp. VIII:** 75, 76, 78, 79
"Getting Along" (Larcom), **Supp. XIII:** 144
"Getting Along with Nature" (Berry), **Supp. X:** 31–32
"Getting Away from Already Pretty Much Being Away from It All" (Wallace), **Supp. X:** 314–315
"Getting Born" (Shields), **Supp. VII:** 311
Getting Even (Allen), **Supp. XV:** 3, 14, 15
"Getting Lucky" (L. Michaels), **Supp. XVI:** 205, 209
"Getting Out of Jail on Monday" (Wagoner), **Supp. IX:** 327
"Getting There" (Plath), **Supp. I Part 2:** 539, 542
"Getting to the Poem" (Corso), **Supp. XII:** 135
Getty, J. Paul, **Supp. X:** 108
Getty, Norris, **Supp. XV:** 136–137, 138, 139, 142, 143, 145, 146
Gettysburg, Manila, Acoma (Masters), **Supp. I Part 2:** 471
"Gettysburg: July 1, 1863" (Kenyon), **Supp. VII:** 172
Gevers, Nick, **Supp. XXII:** 59
Ghachem, Malick, **Supp. X:** 17
Ghazálí, al-, **Supp. XX: 117**
"Ghazals: Homage to Ghalib" (Rich), **Supp. I Part 2:** 557
Ghost, The (Crane), **I:** 409, 421
"Ghost, The" (Peacock), **Supp. XIX:** 199
"Ghost Cat" (Peacock), **Supp. XIX:** 206
"Ghost Chant, et alii" (Komunyakaa), **Supp. XIII:** 114
Ghost in the Music, A (Nichols), **Supp. XIII:** 267
"Ghostlier Demarcations, Keener Sounds" (Vendler), **Supp. I Part 2:** 565
"Ghostly Father, I Confess" (McCarthy), **II:** 565–566
Ghostly Lover, The (Hardwick), **Supp. III Part 1:** 194–196, 208, 209
Ghost Money (Hull), **Supp. XXI:** 129, **132–135,** 136
Ghost of Meter, The (A. Finch), **Supp. XVII:** 71, 73
"Ghost of the Buffaloes, The" (Lindsay), **Supp. I Part 2:** 393
Ghost of Tradition, The (Walzer), **Supp. XVIII:** 174
Ghosts (Auster), **Supp. XII:** 22, **24, 26–27**
Ghosts (Ibsen), **III:** 152
Ghosts (Wharton), **IV:** 316, 327
Ghosts of Tsavo: Stalking the Mystery Lions of East Africa (Caputo), **Supp. XIX:** 28
Ghost Town (Coover), **Supp. V:** 52–53
Ghost Trio, The (Bierds), **Supp. XVII:** 29, **30**
Ghost Writer, The (P. Roth), **Retro. Supp. II:** 22, 290, 291; **Supp. III Part 2:** 420–421; **Supp. XVII:** 43
Giachetti, Fosco, **Supp. IV Part 2:** 520
"Giacometti" (Wilbur), **Supp. III Part 2:** 551
Giacometti, Alberto, **Supp. VIII:** 168, 169
Giacomo, Padre, **II:** 278–279
Giant's House, The: A Romance (McCracken), **Supp. X:** 86
"Giant Snail" (Bishop), **Retro. Supp. II:** 49
Giant Weapon, The (Winters), **Supp. II Part 2:** 810
"Giant Woman, The" (Oates), **Supp. II Part 2:** 523
Gibbon, Edward, **I:** 4, 378; **IV:** 126; **Supp. I Part 2:** 503; **Supp. III Part 2:** 629; **Supp. XIII:** 75; **Supp. XIV:** 97
Gibbons, James, **Supp. XVII:** 228
Gibbons, Kaye, **Supp. X: 41–54; Supp. XII:** 311
Gibbons, Reginald, **Supp. X:** 113, 124, 127; **Supp. XV:** 105; **Supp. XIX:** 40, 41–42, 281
Gibbons, Richard, **Supp. I Part 1:** 107
"Gibbs" (Rukeyser), **Supp. VI:** 273
Gibbs, Barbara, **Supp. IV Part 2:** 644
Gibbs, Wolcott, **Supp. I Part 2:** 604, 618; **Supp. VIII:** 151
Gibran, Kahlil, **Supp. XX: 69, 113–129**
"GIBSON" (Baraka), **Supp. II Part 1:** 54
Gibson, Charles Dana, **Supp. X:** 184
Gibson, Graeme, **Supp. XIII:** 20
Gibson, Wilfrid W., **Retro. Supp. I:** 128
Gibson, William, **Supp. XVI: 117–133; Supp. XXII:** 49
Giddins, Gary, **Supp. XIII:** 245
Gide, André, **I:** 271, 290; **II:** 581; **III:** 210; **IV:** 53, 289; **Supp. I Part 1:** 51; **Supp. IV Part 1:** 80, 284, 347; **Supp. IV Part 2:** 681, 682; **Supp. VIII:** 40; **Supp. X:** 187; **Supp. XIV:** 24, 348; **Supp. XVII:** 242
Gideon Planish (Lewis), **II:** 455
Gielgud, John, **I:** 82; **Supp. XI:** 305
Gierow, Dr. Karl Ragnar, **III:** 404
Gifford, Bill, **Supp. XI:** 38
Gifford, Terry, **Supp. XVI:** 22
"Gift, The" (Creeley), **Supp. IV Part 1:** 153
"Gift, The" (Doolittle), **Supp. I Part 1:** 267
Gift, The (Hyde), **Supp. XVIII:** 150
"Gift, The" (Jarman), **Supp. XVII:** 116
"Gift, The" (L.-Y. Lee), **Supp. XV:** 213, 214
Gift, The (Nabokov), **III:** 246, 255, 261–263; **Retro. Supp. I:** 264, 266, **268–270,** 273, 274–275, 278
"Gift from the City, A" (Updike), **Retro. Supp. I:** 320
"Gift of God, The" (Robinson), **III:** 512, 517, 518–521, 524

Gift of the Black Folk, The: The Negroes in the Making of America (Du Bois), **Supp. II Part 1:** 179
"Gift of the Magi, The" (O. Henry), Supp. II Part 1: 394, 406, 408
"Gift of the *Osuo,* The" (Johnson), **Supp. VI:** 194
"Gift of the Prodigal, The" (Taylor), **Supp. V:** 314, 326
"Gift Outright, The" (Frost), **II:** 152; **Supp. IV Part 1:** 15
Gigi (Colette; stage adaptation, Loos), **Supp. XVI:** 193
"Gigolo" (Plath), **Retro. Supp. II:** 257
"G.I. Graves in Tuscany" (Hugo), **Supp. VI:** 138
"Gila Bend" (Dickey), **Supp. IV Part 1:** 185–186
Gilbert, Elizabeth, **Supp. XXII:** 83, 90
Gilbert, Jack, **Supp. IX:** 287
Gilbert, Peter, **Supp. IX:** 291, 300
Gilbert, Roger, **Supp. XI:** 124
Gilbert, Sandra M., **Retro. Supp. I:** 42; **Retro. Supp. II:** 324; **Supp. IX:** 66; **Supp. XV:** 270
Gilbert, Susan. *See* Dickinson, Mrs. William A.
Gilbert and Sullivan, **Supp. IV Part 1:** 389
"Gilbert Stuart Portrait of Washington, The" (Kooser), **Supp. XIX:** 124
Gil Blas (Le Sage), **II:** 290
Gilded Age, The (Twain), **III:** 504; **IV:** 198
Gilded Lapse of Time, A (Schnackenberg), **Supp. XV:** 258, **260–263**
"Gilded Lapse of Time, A" (Schnackenberg), **Supp. XV:** 257
"Gilded Six-Bits, The" (Hurston), **Supp. VI:** 154–155
Gilder, R. W., **Retro. Supp. II:** 66; **Supp. I Part 2:** 418
Gildersleeve, Basil, **Supp. I Part 1:** 369
Gilead (Robinson), **Supp. XXI:** 212, **216–220,** 223
Giles, H. A., **Retro. Supp. I:** 289
Giles, James R., **Supp. IX:** 11, 15; **Supp. XI:** 219, 223–224, 228, 234
"Giles Corey of the Salem Farms" (Longfellow), **II:** 505, 506; **Retro. Supp. II:** 166, 167
Giles Goat-Boy (Barth), **I:** 121, 122–123, 129, 130, 134, 135–138; **Supp. V:** 39
Gill, Brendan, **Supp. I Part 2:** 659, 660
Gillespie, Nick, **Supp. XIV:** 298, 311
Gillette, Chester, **I:** 512
Gilligan, Carol, **Supp. XIII:** 216; **Supp. XXII:** 18
Gillis, Jim, **IV:** 196
Gillis, Steve, **IV:** 195
Gilman, Charlotte Perkins, **Supp. I Part 2:** 637; **Supp. V:** 121, 284, 285; **Supp. XI: 193–211; Supp. XIII:** 295, 306; **Supp. XVI:** 84
Gilman, Daniel Coit, **Supp. I Part 1:** 361, 368, 370
Gilman, Richard, **IV:** 115; **Supp. IV Part 2:** 577; **Supp. XIII:** 100; **Supp. XIX:** 251
Gilmore, Eddy, **Supp. I Part 2:** 618
Gilmore, Lyman, **Supp. XXI:** 20, 22, 24
Gilmore, Mikal, **Supp. XVI:** 123, 124
Gilpin, Charles, **III:** 392
Gilpin, Dewitt, **Supp. XV:** 197
Gilpin, Laura, **Retro. Supp. I:** 7
Gilpin, Sam, **Supp. V:** 213
Gilpin, William, **Supp. IV Part 2:** 603
"Gil's Furniture Bought & Sold" (Cisneros), **Supp. VII:** 61–62, 64
Gilyard, Keith, **Supp. XXI:** 246
"Gimcrackery" articles (Briggs), **Supp. XVIII:** 8–9
"Gimpel the Fool" (Singer), **IV:** 14; **Retro. Supp. II:** 22, 307
Gimpel the Fool and Other Stories (Singer), **IV:** 1, 7–9, 10, 12
"Gin" (Levine), **Supp. V:** 193
"Gingerbread House, The" (Coover), **Supp. V:** 42–43
Gingerbread Lady, The (Simon), **Supp. IV Part 2:** 580, 583–584, 588
Gingerich, Willard, **Supp. IV Part 2:** 510
Gingertown (McKay), **Supp. X:** 132, 139
Gingold, Hermione, **Supp. XV:** 13
Gingrich, Arnold, **Retro. Supp. I:** 113; **Supp. XVII:** 88; **Supp. XX: 34**
Ginna, Robert, **Supp. IX:** 259
Ginsberg, Allen, **I:** 183; **Retro. Supp. I:** 411, 426, 427; **Retro. Supp. II:** 280; **Supp. II Part 1:** 30, 32, 58, **307–333; Supp. III Part 1:** 2, 91, 96, 98, 100, 222, 226; **Supp. III Part 2:** 541, 627; **Supp. IV Part 1:** 79, 90, 322; **Supp. IV Part 2:** 502; **Supp. V:** 168, 336; **Supp. VIII:** 239, 242–243, 289; **Supp. IX:** 299; **Supp. X:** 120, 204; **Supp. XI:** 135, 297; **Supp. XII:** 118–119, 121–122, 124, 126, 130–131, 136, 182; **Supp. XIV:** 15, 53, 54, 125, 137, 141, 142, 143–144, 148, 150, 269, 280, 283; **Supp. XV:** 134, 177, 263; **Supp. XVI:** 123, 135; **Supp. XVII:** 138, 243; **Supp. XVIII:** 20, 27, 29, 30; **Supp. XXI:** 53; **Supp. XXII:** 172, 225
Gioia, Dana, **Supp. IX:** 279; **Supp. XII:** 209; **Supp. XIII:** 337; **Supp. XV: 111–131,** 251; **Supp. XVII:** 69, 72, 112; **Supp. XIX:** 117, 144; **Supp. XXI:** 99
Giono, Jean, **Supp. XVI:** 135
Giotto di Bondone, **Supp. I Part 2:** 438; **Supp. XI:** 126
Giovani, Regula, **Supp. XV:** 270
Giovanni, Nikki, **Supp. I Part 1:** 66; **Supp. II Part 1:** 54; **Supp. IV Part 1:** 11; **Supp. VIII:** 214; **Supp. XXII:** 11
Giovanni's Room (Baldwin), **Retro. Supp. II:** 5, 6, **6–7,** 8, 10; **Supp. I Part 1:** 51, 52, 55–56, 57, 60, 63, 67; **Supp. III Part 1:** 125
Giovannitti, Arturo, **I:** 476; **Supp. XV:** 299, 301, 302, 307
"Giraffe" (Swenson), **Supp. IV Part 2:** 651
Giraldi, Giovanni Battista. *See* Cinthio
"Girl" (Kincaid), **Supp. VII:** 182–183
"Girl, The" (Olds), **Supp. X:** 207
"Girl Friend Poems" (Wright), **Supp. XV:** 349
"Girl from Lynn Bathes Horse!!" (McCarriston), **Supp. XIV:** 266
"Girl from Red Lion, P.A., A" (Mencken), **III:** 111
Girl in Glass, The: Love Poems (W. J. Smith), **Supp. XIII:** 335
Girl in Landscape (Lethem), **Supp. XVIII:** 136, **141–143**
"Girl in the Grave, The" (McCoy), **Supp. XIII:** 170
Girl Like I, A (Loos), **Supp. XVI:** 181, 183, 184, 187, 194, 196
"Girl of the Golden West" (Didion), **Supp. IV Part 1:** 195, 208, 211
Girl of the Golden West, The (Puccini), **III:** 139
Girl of the Limberlost (film), **Supp. XX: 223**
Girl of the Limberlost (Stratton-Porter), **Supp. XX: 211, 221–222**
"Girl on a Scaffold" (C. Frost), **Supp. XV:** 98
"Girl on the Baggage Truck, The" (O'Hara), **III:** 371–372
Girls at Play (Theroux), **Supp. VIII:** 314, 315, 316, **317**
"Girls at the Sphinx, The" (Farrell), **II:** 45
"Girls in Their Summer Dresses, The" (Shaw), **Supp. XIX:** 246
Girl Sleuth, The: A Feminist Guide (Mason), **Supp. VIII:** 133, 135, **139,** 142
"Girl's Story, A" (Bambara), **Supp. XI:** 10–11
"Girl the Prince Liked, The" (Z. Fitzgerald), **Supp. IX:** 71
Girl Who Had to Die, The (Holding), **Supp. XXII: 126–127**
Girl Who Loved Tom Gordon, The (King), **Supp. V:** 138, 152
"Girl Who Raised Pigeons, The" (P. E. Jones), **Supp. XXII:** 143
Girl with Curious Hair (Wallace), **Supp. X:** 301, **305–308**
"Girl with Curious Hair" (Wallace), **Supp. X:** 306
"Girl with Silver Eyes, The" (Hammett), **Supp. IV Part 1:** 344, 345
"Girl with Talent, The" (Z. Fitzgerald), **Supp. IX:** 71
Girodias, Maurice, **III:** 171; **Supp. XI:** 297
Giroux, Robert, **Retro. Supp. II:** 177, 229, 235; **Supp. IV Part 1:** 280; **Supp. VIII:** 195; **Supp. XV:** 146
Gish, Dorothy, **Retro. Supp. I:** 103
Gish, Lillian, **Supp. XVI:** 184
Gissing, George, **II:** 138, 144
Gitagovinda, **Supp. XXII:** 258
Gita-govínda: Love Songs of Radha and Krishna (Jayadeva; Siegel, trans.), **Supp. XXII:** 258
Gittings, Robert, **II:** 531
"Given" (C. Frost), **Supp. XV:** 96
"Give Us Back Our Country" (Masters), **Supp. I Part 2:** 472

Give Us This Day (film, Dmytryk), **Supp. XX: 40–41**
"Give Way, Ye Gates" (Roethke), **III:** 536
"Give Your Heart to the Hawks" (Jeffers), **Supp. II Part 2:** 433
"Giving Blood" (Updike), **IV:** 226; **Retro. Supp. I:** 332
Giving Good Weight (McPhee), **Supp. III Part 1:** 307
"Giving in to You" (X. J. Kennedy), **Supp. XV:** 160
"Giving Myself Up" (Strand), **Supp. IV Part 2:** 627
G. K. the DJ (Keillor), **Supp. XVI:** 171
Glackens, William, **Retro. Supp. II:** 103
Gladden, Washington, **III:** 293; **Supp. I Part 1:** 5
Gladstone, William Ewart, **Supp. I Part 2:** 419
"Gladys Poem, The" (Alvarez), **Supp. VII:** 10
"Glance at German 'Kultur,' A" (Bourne), **I:** 228
Glance Away, A (Wideman), **Supp. X:** 320
"Glance from the Bridge, A" (Wilbur), **Supp. III Part 2:** 551
"Glance in the Mirror, A" (Swados), **Supp. XIX:** 261–262
Glance toward Shakespeare, A (Chapman), **Supp. XIV:** 44
Glancy, Diane, **Supp. XXI:** 246
Glanville-Hicks, Peggy, **Supp. IV Part 1:** 84
Glare (Ammons), **Supp. VII:** 35–36
Glasgow, Cary, **II:** 173, 182
Glasgow, Ellen, **II: 173–195; IV:** 328; **Supp. X:** 228, 234
Glasmon, Kubec, **Supp. XIII:** 166
Glaspell, Susan, **Supp. III Part 1: 175–191; Supp. X:** 46; **Supp. XVII:** 99; **Supp. XXI:** 5
"Glass" (Francis), **Supp. IX:** 80
Glass, Irony, and God (Carson), **Supp. XII:** 97, **104–106**
Glass, Philip, **Supp. XXI:** 146, 147
"Glass Ark, The" (Komunyakaa), **Supp. XIII:** 129
Glass Bees, The (Jünger; Bogan and Mayer, trans.), **Supp. III Part 1:** 63
"Glass Blower of Venice" (Malamud), **Supp. I Part 2:** 450
"Glass Essay, The" (Carson), **Supp. XII: 104–105**
"Glass Face in the Rain, A: New Poems" (Stafford), **Supp. XI: 327–328**
Glass Key, The (Hammett), **Supp. IV Part 1:** 351–353
"Glass Meadows" (Bausch), **Supp. VII:** 53–54
Glass Menagerie, The (T. Williams), **I:** 81; **IV:** 378, 379, 380, 382, 383, 385, 386, 387, 388, 389, 390, 391, 392, 393–394, 395, 398; **Supp. IV Part 1:** 84
"Glass Mountain, The" (Barthelme), **Supp. IV Part 1:** 47
"Glass Tent, The" (Everwine), **Supp. XV:** 76
Glatstein, Jacob, **Supp. X:** 70
Glazer, Nathan, **Supp. VIII:** 93, 243
"Gleaners, The" (Merwin), **Supp. III Part 1:** 346
Gleanings in Europe (Cooper), **I:** 346
Gleason, Ralph J., **Supp. IX:** 16
Glenday, Michael, **Retro. Supp. II:** 210
Glengarry Glen Ross (film), **Supp. XIV:** 242
Glengarry Glen Ross (Mamet), **Supp. XIV:** 239, 240, 242, 245, 246, 250, 254, 255
Glimcher, Arne, **Supp. VIII:** 73
"Glimpses" (Jones), **Supp. XI:** 218
Glimpses of the Moon, The (Wharton), **II:** 189–190; **IV:** 322–323; **Retro. Supp. I:** 381
"Glimpses of Vietnamese Life" (Levertov), **Supp. III Part 1:** 282
Glisson, J. T., **Supp. X:** 234
Gloria Mundi (Frederic), **II:** 144–145
Gloria Naylor (Fowler), **Supp. VIII:** 224
"Glorious Fourth, The" (Ryan as Quin), **Supp. XVIII:** 229
Glorious Ones, The (Prose), **Supp. XVI:** 251
Glory of Hera, The (Gordon), **II:** 196–197, 198, 199, 217–220
Glory of the Conquered, The (Glaspell), **Supp. III Part 1:** 176
Glossary of Literary Terms (Abrams), **Supp. XVI:** 19
Glotfelty, Cheryll, **Supp. IX:** 25
Glover, Joyce Lee, **Supp. XIX:** 112
Glow, The (Wrigley), **Supp. XVIII:** 295
"Glow, The" (Wrigley), **Supp. XVIII:** 296–297, 307
Gluck, Christoph Willibald, **II:** 210, 211
Glück, Louise, **Supp. V: 77–94; Supp. VIII:** 272; **Supp. X:** 209; **Supp. XIV:** 269; **Supp. XV:** 19, 252; **Supp. XVII:** 241
"Glutton, The" (Shapiro), **Supp. II Part 2:** 705
"Glutton for Punishment, A" (Yates), **Supp. XI:** 341
Glyph (Everett), **Supp. XVIII: 60–61**
Gnädiges Fräulein, The (T. Williams), **IV:** 382, 395, 398
Gnomes and Occasions (Nemerov), **III:** 269
Gnomologia (Fuller), **II:** 111
"Gnothis Seauton" (Emerson), **II:** 11, 18–19
Go (Holmes), **Supp. XIV:** 144
"Go Ahead; Goodbye; Good Luck; and Watch Out" (Bronk), **Supp. XXI:** 31
"Goal of Intellectual Men, The" (Eberhart), **I:** 529–530
Go-Between, The (Hartley), **Supp. I Part 1:** 293
Gobineau, Joseph Arthur de, **Supp. XIV:** 209
God (Allen), **Supp. XV:** 3
God and the American Writer (Kazin), **Supp. VIII: 108–109**
Godard, Jean-Luc, **Supp. I Part 2:** 558
Godbey (Masters), **Supp. I Part 2:** 472
God Bless You, Mr. Rosewater (Vonnegut), **Supp. II Part 2:** 758, 767, 768–769, 771, 772
Goddess Abides, The (Buck), **Supp. II Part 1:** 129, 131–132
Gödel, Kurt, **Supp. IV Part 1:** 43
Godfather (Puzo), **Supp. IV Part 1:** 390
Godfires (Hoffman), **Supp. XVIII: 81–82**
God in Ruins, A (Uris), **Supp. XX: 247, 256**
"God in the Doorway" (Dillard), **Supp. VI:** 28
"God is a distant-stately Lover" (Dickinson), **I:** 471
Godkin, E. L., **II:** 274
God Knows (Heller), **Supp. IV Part 1:** 386, 388–389
God Made Alaska for the Indians (Reed), **Supp. X:** 241
God of His Fathers, The (London), **II:** 469
God of Vengeance (Asch), **IV:** 11
Go Down, Moses (Faulkner), **Retro. Supp. I:** 75, 82, 85, 86, 88, 89, 90, 92; **Supp. XVIII:** 203
"Go Down, Moses" (Faulkner), **II:** 71–72
Go Down, Moses (Hayden), **Supp. II Part 1:** 365
Go Down, Moses and Other Stories (Faulkner), **II:** 71; **Supp. X:** 52
"Go Down Death A Funeral Sermon" (Johnson), **Supp. IV Part 1:** 7
"God Rest Ye Merry, Gentlemen" (Hemingway), **IV:** 122
Godric (Buechner), **Supp. XII:** 53
Gods, The (Goldbarth), **Supp. XII:** 189, 190
Gods Arrive, The (Wharton), **IV:** 326–327; **Retro. Supp. I:** 382
God Save the Child (Parker), **Supp. XIX:** 183–184
"God Save the Rights of Man" (Freneau), **Supp. II Part 1:** 268
"God|Children" (Swenson), **Supp. IV Part 2:** 645
"God's Christ Theory" (Carson), **Supp. XII: 106**
God's Country (Everett), **Supp. XVIII: 57–58,** 64, 65
God's Country and My People (Morris), **III:** 238
Gods Determinations touching his Elect: and the Elects Combat in their Conversion, and Coming up to God in Christ together with the Comfortable Effects thereof (Taylor), **IV:** 155–160, 165
God-Seeker, The (Lewis), **II:** 456
God Sends Sunday (Bontemps), **Supp. XXII:** 2, 3, 9
God's Favorite (Simon), **Supp. IV Part 2:** 575, 586, 588, 590
"God's Fool" (Gibran), **Supp. XX: 118**
God's Little Acre (Caldwell), **I:** 288, 289, 290, 297, 298–302, 305–306, 309, 310; **Supp. XXII:** 196
God's Man: A Novel in Wood Cuts (Ward), **I:** 31
Gods of Winter, The (Gioia), **Supp. XV:** 112, **121–125**
"Gods of Winter, The" (Gioia), **Supp. XV:** 117

"God's Peace in November" (Jeffers), **Supp. II Part 2:** 420
God's Silence (F. Wright), **Supp. XVII:** 240, 246–247
"God Stiff" (Carson), **Supp. XII: 106**
God's Trombones (Johnson), **Supp. II Part 1:** 201
"God's Youth" (Untermeyer), **Supp. XV:** 296
"God the Father and the Empty House" (McCarriston), **Supp. XIV:** 273
Godwin, William, **II:** 304; **III:** 415; **Supp. I Part 1:** 126, 146; **Supp. I Part 2:** 512, 513–514, 522, 709, 719
God without Thunder (Ransom), **III:** 495–496, 499
Godwulf Manuscript, The (Parker), **Supp. XIX: 178–182**
Goebbels, Josef, **III:** 560
Goebel, Irma, **Supp. X:** 95
Goen, C. C., **I:** 560
Goethe, Johann Wolfgang von, **I:** 181, 396, 587–588; **II:** 5, 6, 320, 344, 488, 489, 492, 502, 556; **III:** 395, 453, 607, 612, 616; **IV:** 50, 64, 173, 326; **Retro. Supp. I:** 360; **Retro. Supp. II:** 94; **Supp. I Part 2:** 423, 457; **Supp. II Part 1:** 26; **Supp. III Part 1:** 63; **Supp. IX:** 131, 308; **Supp. X:** 60; **Supp. XI:** 169; **Supp. XVIII:** 278; **Supp. XX: 84**
Go for the Body (Lacy), **Supp. XV:** 201, 204
Gogan, Robert, **Supp. XXI:** 24
Gogol, Nikolai, **I:** 296; **IV:** 1, 4; **Retro. Supp. I:** 266, 269; **Supp. VIII:** 14; **Supp. XVII:** 45; **Supp. XVIII:** 102; **Supp. XXII:** 59
Goia, Dana, **Supp. XIX:** 121
"Going, Going, Gone" (Skloot), **Supp. XX: 207**
Going, William T., **Supp. VIII:** 126
Going After Cacciato (O'Brien), **Supp. V:** 237, 238, 239, 244–246, 248, 249
Going All the Way (Wakefield), **Supp. VIII:** 43
"Going Critical" (Bambara), **Supp. XI:** 14
Going Down (Markson), **Supp. XVII:** 136, 138, **139–140,** 141, 142–143, 144, 145
Going for the Rain (Ortiz), **Supp. IV Part 2:** 499, 505–508, 509, 514
"Going Home by Last Night" (Kinnell), **Supp. III Part 1:** 244
"Going Home in America" (Hardwick), **Supp. III Part 1:** 205
"Going North" (Salinas), **Supp. XIII:** 316
Going Places (L. Michaels), **Supp. XVI:** 201, **203–206**
"Going Places" (L. Michaels), **Supp. XVI:** 203
"Going South" (J. W. Miller), **Supp. XX: 169**
Going South (Lardner and Buck), **II:** 427
Going To and Fro and Walking Up and Down (Reznikoff), **Supp. XIV:** 280, 282, 284, 285
Going to Meet the Man (Baldwin), **Supp. I Part 1:** 60, 62–63; **Supp. XX: 147**
"Going to Meet the Man" (Baldwin), **Retro. Supp. II:** 8, 9; **Supp. I Part 1:** 62–63
"Going to Naples" (Welty), **IV:** 278; **Retro. Supp. I:** 352, 353
"Going to Shrewsbury" (Jewett), **II:** 393
"Going to the Bakery" (Bishop), **Supp. I Part 1:** 93
Going-to-the-Stars (Lindsay), **Supp. I Part 2:** 398
Going-to-the-Sun (Lindsay), **Supp. I Part 2:** 397–398
Going to the Territory (Ellison), **Retro. Supp. II:** 119, 123–124
"Going towards Pojoaque, A December Full Moon/72" (Harjo), **Supp. XII:** 218
"Going Under" (Dubus), **Supp. VII:** 83
"Gold" (Francis), **Supp. IX:** 82
Gold (O'Neill), **III:** 391
Gold, Don, **Supp. XXII:** 258
Gold, Michael, **II:** 26; **IV:** 363, 364, 365; **Retro. Supp. II:** 323; **Supp. I Part 1:** 331; **Supp. I Part 2:** 609; **Supp. XIV:** 288; **Supp. XXII:** 277
Goldbarth, Albert, **Supp. XII: 175–195**
Goldbarth's Book of Occult Phenomena (Goldbarth), **Supp. XII:** 181
Goldberg, Carole, **Supp. XXII:** 207
Goldberg, S. L., **Supp. VIII:** 238
"Gold Bug, The" (Poe), **III:** 410, 413, 419, 420
Gold Bug Variations, The (Powers), **Supp. IX:** 210, 212, **216–217,** 219
Gold Cell, The (Olds), **Supp. X: 206–209**
Gold Diggers, The (Monette), **Supp. X:** 153
Golde, Miss (Mencken's Secretary), **III:** 104, 107
Golden, Harry, **III:** 579, 581; **Supp. VIII:** 244
Golden, Mike, **Supp. XI:** 294, 295, 297, 299, 303
Golden Age, The (Gurney), **Supp. V:** 101–103
Golden Apples (Rawlings), **Supp. X: 228–229,** 230, 234
Golden Apples, The (Welty), **IV:** 261, 271–274, 281, 293; **Retro. Supp. I:** 341, 342, 343, **350–351,** 352, 355
Golden Apples of the Sun, The (Bradbury), **Supp. IV Part 1:** 102, 103
Golden Book of Springfield, The (Lindsay), **Supp. I Part 2:** 376, 379, 395, 396
Golden Bough, The (Frazer), **II:** 204, 549; **III:** 6–7; **Supp. I Part 1:** 18; **Supp. IX:** 123; **Supp. X:** 124
Golden Bowl, The (James), **II:** 320, 333, 335; **Retro. Supp. I:** 215, 216, 218–219, 232, **234–235,** 374
Golden Boy (Odets), **Supp. II Part 2:** 538, 539, 540–541, 546, 551
Golden Calves, The (Auchincloss), **Supp. IV Part 1:** 35
Golden Child (Hwang), **Supp. XXI:** 147–148
Golden Day, The (Mumford), **Supp. II Part 2:** 471, 475, 477, 483, 484, 488–489, 493
Golden Fleece, The (Gurney), **Supp. V:** 97
Golden Gate (film, Madden), **Supp. XXI:** 147
Golden Gate, The (Seth), **Supp. XVII:** 117
Golden Grove, The: Selected Passages from the Sermons and Writings of Jeremy Taylor (L. P. Smith), **Supp. XIV:** 345
"Golden Heifer, The" (Wylie), **Supp. I Part 2:** 707
"Golden Honeymoon, The" (Lardner), **II:** 429–430, 431
Golden Journey, The (W. J. Smith and Bogan, comps.), **Supp. XIII:** 347
Golden Ladder series (S. and A. Warner), **Supp. XVIII:** 267
"Golden Lads" (Marquand), **III:** 56
Golden Legend, The (Longfellow), **II:** 489, 490, 495, 505, 506, 507; **Retro. Supp. II:** 159, 165, 166
Golden Mean and Other Poems, The (Tate and Wills), **IV:** 122
"Golden Retrievals" (Doty), **Supp. XI:** 132
Golden Shakespeare, The: An Anthology (L. P. Smith), **Supp. XIV:** 349
Golden Slippers: An Anthology of Negro Poetry for Young Readers (Bontemps, ed.), **Supp. XXII:** 5, 11
Goldensohn, Lorrie, **Retro. Supp. II:** 51
Golden State (Bidart), **Supp. XV:** 21, **23–25**
"Golden State" (Bidart), **Supp. XV:** 23, 24, 25
Golden States (Cunningham), **Supp. XV:** 55, **56–59,** 63
Golden Treasury of Best Songs and Lyrical Poems in the English Language (Palgrave), **Retro. Supp. I:** 124
Golden Treasury of the Best Songs and Lyrical Poems in the English Language (Palgrave), **Supp. XIV:** 340
Golden Whales of California and Other Rhymes in the American Language, The (Lindsay), **Supp. I Part 2:** 394–395, 396
"Goldfish Bowl, The" (Francis), **Supp. IX:** 78
Gold Fools (Sorrentino), **Supp. XXI:** 237
Goldin Boys, The (Epstein), **Supp. XIV:** 112
Golding, Arthur, **III:** 467, 468
Golding, William, **Supp. IV Part 1:** 297
Goldini, Carlo, **II:** 274
Goldkorn Tales (Epstein), **Supp. XII: 163–164**
Goldman, Albert, **Supp. XI:** 299
Goldman, Arnold, **Supp. XXI:** 13
Goldman, Emma, **III:** 176, 177; **Supp. I Part 2:** 524; **Supp. XVII:** 96, 103, 104
Goldman, William, **Supp. IV Part 2:** 474

"Gold Mountain Stories" project (Kingston), **Supp. V:** 164
Gold of Chickaree, The (S. and A. Warner), **Supp. XVIII:** 267, 268, 269
Goldring, Douglas, **III:** 458
Goldsmith, Oliver, **II:** 273, 282, 299, 304, 308, 314, 315, 514; **Retro. Supp. I:** 335; **Supp. I Part 1:** 310; **Supp. I Part 2:** 503, 714, 716; **Supp. XVIII:** 12
Gold Standard and the Logic of Naturalism, The (W. B. Michaels), **Retro. Supp. I:** 369
Goldstein, Laurence, **Supp. XXI:** 134
Goldstein, Rebecca, **Supp. XVII:** 44
Goldwater, Barry, **I:** 376; **III:** 38
Goldwyn, Samuel, **Retro. Supp. II:** 199; **Supp. I Part 1:** 281
Golem, The (Leivick), **IV:** 6
"Golgotha Is a Mountain" (Bontemps), **Supp. XXII:** 3, 8
"Goliardic Song" (Hecht), **Supp. X:** 63
"Go Like This" (Moore), **Supp. X:** 165
Goll, Ivan, **Supp. III Part 1:** 235, 243–244; **Supp. III Part 2:** 621
Gomes, Albert, **Supp. XXI:** 160
Goncharova, Natalya, **Supp. IX:** 66
Goncourt, Edmond de, **II:** 325, 328; **III:** 315, 317–318, 321; **Retro. Supp. I:** 226
Goncourt, Jules de, **II:** 328; **III:** 315, 317–318, 321
Gone Fishin' (Mosley), Supp. XIII: **235–236,** 240
"Gone to War" (E. Stoddard), **Supp. XV:** 282
"Gone West" (Rodriguez), **Supp. XIV:** 308
Gone with the Wind (film), **Retro. Supp. I:** 113
Gone with the Wind (Mitchell), **II:** 177; **Retro. Supp. I:** 340; **Supp. XX: 243; Supp. XXII:** 190, 195
Gongora y Argote, Luis de, **II:** 552
Gonzalez, David, **Supp. VIII:** 85
González, Jovita, **Supp. XIX:** 99
Gooch, Brad, **Supp. XII:** 121
Good, George, **Supp. XI:** 306
"Good, the Plaid, and the Ugly, The" (Wasserstein), **Supp. XV:** 327
"Good and Not So Good, The" (Dunn), **Supp. XI:** 141
"Good Anna, The" (Stein), **IV:** 37, 40, 43
Good As Gold (Heller), **Supp. IV Part 1:** 386, 388, 394
Good as I Been to You (album, Dylan), **Supp. XVIII:** 28
Good Boys and Dead Girls and Other Essays (Gordon), **Supp. IV Part 1:** 309–310
Good Brother, The (Offutt), **Supp. XIX:** 163**, 168–169**
"Good-by and Keep Cold" (Frost), **Retro. Supp. I:** 135
"Good-bye" (Emerson), **II:** 19
"Goodbye, Christ" (Hughes), **Retro. Supp. I:** 202, 203
Goodbye, Columbus (P. Roth), **Retro. Supp. II:** 280, 281, 290; **Supp. III Part 2:** 403–406; **Supp. XIV:** 112; **Supp. XX: 177**
"Goodbye, Columbus" (P. Roth), **Supp. III Part 2:** 401, 404, 408–409, 411
Goodbye, Columbus and Five Short Stories (P. Roth), **Retro. Supp. II:** 279
"Goodbye, Goldeneye" (Swenson), **Supp. IV Part 2:** 651
"Goodbye, Mr. Chipstein" (Epstein), **Supp. XIV:** 103, 108
"Goodbye, My Brother" (Cheever), **Supp. I Part 1:** 175, 177, 193
"Goodbye and Good Luck" (Paley), **Supp. VI:** 219, 223
Goodbye Girl, The (film), **Supp. IV Part 2:** 589
Goodbye Girl, The (musical), **Supp. IV Part 2:** 576, 588
Goodbye Girl, The (Simon), **Supp. IV Part 2:** 575
Goodbye Look, The (Macdonald), **Supp. IV Part 2:** 473, 474
"Good-Bye My Fancy" (Whitman), **IV:** 348
"Goodbye to All That" (Didion), **Supp. IV Part 1:** 197
Goodbye to All That (Graves), **I:** 477
Goodbye to Berlin (Isherwood), **Supp. XIV:** 159, 161, 162, 169
"Good-Bye to the Mezzogiorno" (Auden), **Supp. II Part 1:** 19
"Goodbye to the Poetry of Calcium" (Wright), **Supp. III Part 2:** 599
"Good Company" (Matthews), **Supp. IX:** 160
"Good Country People" (O'Connor), **III:** 343, 350, 351, 352, 358; **Retro. Supp. II:** 229, 232
Good Day to Die, A (Harrison), **Supp. VIII: 42–44,** 45, 47
Good Doctor, The (Simon), **Supp. IV Part 2:** 575, 585
Good Earth, The (Buck), **Supp. I Part 1:** 49; **Supp. II Part 1:** 115–175, 118, 125, 132
Good European, The (Blackmur), **Supp. II Part 1:** 91
Good Evening Mr. & Mrs. America, and All the Ships at Sea (Bausch), **Supp. VII:** 41, 47, 52
"Good Friday" (Jarman), **Supp. XVII:** 116
"Good Girl" (Peacock), **Supp. XIX:** 199
Good Gray Poet, The (O'Connor), **Retro. Supp. I:** 407
Good Health and How We Won It (Sinclair), **Supp. V:** 285–286
Good Hearts (Price), **Supp. VI:** 259, 265
"Good Job Gone, A" (Hughes), **Retro. Supp. I:** 204
Good Journey, A (Ortiz), **Supp. IV Part 2:** 497, 499, 503, 505, 509–510, 514
Good Luck in Cracked Italian (Hugo), **Supp. VI:** 133, 137–138
Goodman, Allegra, **Supp. XII:** 159; **Supp. XVI:** 205; **Supp. XX: 177**
Goodman, Ellen, **Supp. XVI:** 103
Goodman, Jack, **Supp. XXI:** 277
Goodman, Jenny, **Supp. XV:** 343, 344
Goodman, Paul, **I:** 218, 261; **III:** 39; **Supp. I Part 2:** 524; **Supp. VIII:** 239–240
Goodman, Philip, **III:** 105, 108
Goodman, Walter, **Supp. IV Part 2:** 532
Good Man Is Hard to Find, A (O'Connor), **III:** 339, 343–345
"Good Man Is Hard to Find, A" (O'Connor), **III:** 339, 344, 353; **Retro. Supp. II:** 230–231
Good Man Is Hard to Find and Other Stories, A (O'Connor), **Retro. Supp. II:** 229, **230–232**
Good Morning, America (Sandburg), **III:** 592–593
"Good Morning, Major" (Marquand), **III:** 56
Good Morning, Midnight (Rhys), **Supp. III Part 1:** 43
"Good Morning, Revolution" (Hughes), **Retro. Supp. I:** 201, 203
Good Morning Blues: The Autobiography of Count Basie (Murray), **Supp. XIX:** 159
Good Morning Revolution: Uncollected Writings of Social Protest (Hughes), **Retro. Supp. I:** 194, 201, 202, 209
Good Mother, The (Miller), **Supp. XII:** 289, **290–294,** 299, 301
Good News (Abbey), **Supp. XIII: 11–12**
"Good News from New-England" (Johnson), **Supp. I Part 1:** 115
Good News of Death and Other Poems (Simpson), **Supp. IX:** 265, **268–269**
"Goodnight, Saigon" (lecture, Caputo), **Supp. XIX:** 17, 30
Good Night, Willie Lee, I'll See You in the Morning (Walker), **Supp. III Part 2:** 520, 531
"Good Oak" (Leopold), **Supp. XIV:** 185, 187, 191
"Good Old Times, The: New York Fifty Years Ago" (Briggs), **Supp. XVIII:** 15
"Good Pine, A" (Offutt), **Supp. XIX:** 174
Goodrich, Chris, **Supp. XXII:** 206, 214
Goodrich, Samuel G., **Supp. I Part 1:** 38
Good Scent from a Strange Mountain, A (R. O. Butler), **Supp. XII:** 62, **70–72**
Good School, A (Yates), **Supp. XI:** 334, **346–347,** 348, 349
"*Good Shepherdess, The*/La Buena Pastora" (Mora), **Supp. XIII:** 228–229
Good Will (Smiley), **Supp. VI:** 292, **299–300**
Goodwin, K. L., **III:** 478
Goodwin, Stephen, **Supp. V:** 314, 316, 322, 323, 325
"Good Word for Winter, A" (Lowell), **Supp. I Part 2:** 420
Goodwyn, Janet, **Retro. Supp. I:** 370
Goody, Alex, **Supp. XXII:** 160
"Goophered Grapevine, The" (Chesnutt), **Supp. XIV:** 57, **58–61**
"Goose Fish, The" (Nemerov), **III:** 272, 284
"Goose Pond" (Kunitz), **Supp. III Part 1:** 262
Goose-Step, The (Sinclair), **Supp. V:** 276

Gordimer, Nadine, **Supp. XV:** 251
Gordon, Ambrose, **Supp. XV:** 144
Gordon, A. R., **III:** 199
Gordon, Caroline, **II: 196–222,** 536, 537; **III:** 454, 482; **IV:** 123, 126–127, 139, 282; **Retro. Supp. II:** 177, 222, 229, 233, 235; **Supp. II Part 1:** 139
Gordon, Charles G., **I:** 454
Gordon, Don, **Supp. X:** 119
Gordon, Eugene, **Supp. II Part 1:** 170; **Supp. XVIII:** 280
Gordon, Fran, **Supp. XIII:** 111
Gordon, James Morris, **II:** 197
Gordon, Lois, **Supp. IV Part 1:** 48; **Supp. V:** 46
Gordon, Lyndall, **Retro. Supp. I:** 55
Gordon, Mary, **Supp. IV Part 1: 297–317**
Gordon, Neil, **Supp. XVI:** 156
Gordon, Peter, **Supp. XII:** 3–4, 4–5, 8
Gordon, Ruth, **IV:** 357; **Supp. XX: 50**
Gore, Thomas Pryor, **Supp. IV Part 2:** 679
Gores, Joe, **Supp. XXI:** 70
Gorey, Edward, **IV:** 430, 436
Gorilla, My Love (Bambara), **Supp. XI:** 1, **2–7**
"Gorilla, My Love" (Bambara), **Supp. XI:** 2, 3–4
Gorki, Maxim, **I:** 478; **II:** 49; **III:** 402; **IV:** 299; **Supp. I Part 1:** 5, 51; **Supp. XIX:** 241
Gorney, Cynthia, **Supp. XVI:** 112
Gorra, Michael, **Supp. V:** 71
Goslings, The (Sinclair), **Supp. V:** 276, 281
Go South to Sorrow (Rowan), **Supp. XIV:** 306
Gospel According to Joe, The (Gurney), **Supp. V:** 99
"Gospel According to Saint Mark, The" (Gordon), **Supp. IV Part 1:** 310
Gospel according to the Son (Mailer), **Retro. Supp. II:** 213
"Gospel for the Twentieth Century, The" (Locke), **Supp. XIV:** 206
"Gospel of Beauty, The" (Lindsay), **Supp. I Part 2:** 380, 382, 384, 385, 391, 396
Gospels, The (di Donato), **Supp. XX: 45–46**
Gospel Singer, The (Crews), **Supp. XI:** 102, **109**
Gosse, Edmund, **II:** 538; **IV:** 350; **Supp. VIII:** 157
"Gossip" (Conroy), **Supp. XVI:** 71–72
Gossips, Gorgons, and Crones: The Fates of the Earth (Caputi), **Supp. IV Part 1:** 335
Go Tell It on the Mountain (Baldwin), **Retro. Supp. II:** 1, 2, 3, **4–5,** 7, 14; **Supp. I Part 1:** 48, 49, 50, 51, 52, 53–54, 55, 56, 57, 59, 61, 63, 64, 67; **Supp. II Part 1:** 170
Gotera, Vince, **Supp. XIII:** 115, 116, 119, 121, 127
Gothic Revival, The: An Essay on the History of Taste (Clark), **Supp. XIV:** 348
Gothic Writers (Thomson, Voller, and Frank, eds.), **Retro. Supp. II:** 273
"Go to the Devil and Shake Yourself" (song), **Supp. I Part 2:** 580
"Go to the Shine That's on a Tree" (Eberhart), **I:** 523
Go to the Widow-Maker (Jones), **Supp. XI:** 214, **225–226,** 227, 229, 233
"Gots Is What You Got" (Di Piero), **Supp. XIX:** 35, 36, 38, 41, 42, 45–46
Gottfried, Alex, **Supp. XIX:** 260
Gottfried, Martin, **Supp. IV Part 2:** 584
Gotthelf, Allan, **Supp. IV Part 2:** 528
Gottlieb, Adolph, **Supp. XV:** 144
Gottlieb, Edward, **Supp. XX: 250**
Gottlieb, Morton, **Supp. XVI:** 196
Gottlieb, Robert, **Supp. IV Part 2:** 474
Gottschalk and the Grande Tarantelle (Brooks), **Supp. III Part 1:** 86
"Gottschalk and the Grande Tarantelle" (Brooks), **Supp. III Part 1:** 86–87
Gould (Dixon), **Supp. XII:** 152, **153**
Gould, Edward Sherman, **I:** 346
Gould, Janice, **Supp. IV Part 1:** 322, 327; **Supp. XII:** 229
Gould, Jay, **I:** 4
Gould, Joe, **Supp. XV:** 143
Gourd Dancer, The (Momaday), **Supp. IV Part 2:** 481, 487, 491, 493
Gourmont, Remy de, **I:** 270, 272; **II:** 528, 529; **III:** 457, 467–468, 477; **Retro. Supp. I:** 55
Gouverneurs de la Rosée (Roumain), **Supp. IV Part 1:** 360, 367
Government Girl (film, Nichols), **Supp. XVIII:** 247
"Governors of Wyoming, The" (Proulx), **Supp. VII:** 264
Goyen, William, **Supp. V:** 220
Grabhorn, Janet, **Supp. XV:** 142
"Grace" (Budbill), **Supp. XIX:** 2
"Grace" (Dubus), **Supp. VII:** 91
"Grace" (Harjo), **Supp. XII:** 224
Grace Notes (Dove), **Supp. IV Part 1:** 248–250, 252
Grace (Eventually): Thoughts on Faith (Lamott), **Supp. XX: 143–145**
Grade, Chaim, **Supp. XVII:** 41
"Graduation" (Dubus), **Supp. VII:** 84
Grady, Henry W., **Supp. I Part 1:** 370
Graeber, Laurel, **Supp. V:** 15
Graham, Billy, **I:** 308
Graham, David, **Supp. XV:** 104; **Supp. XIX:** 81
Graham, Don, **Supp. XI:** 252, 254
Graham, Jorie, **Supp. IX:** 38, 52; **Supp. X:** 73; **Supp. XII:** 209; **Supp. XIII:** 85; **Supp. XVII:** 110, 111, 133, 240, 241, 242
Graham, Martha, **Supp. XI:** 152
Graham, Maryemma, **Retro. Supp. I:** 201, 204
Graham, Nan, **Supp. XII:** 272
Graham, Sheilah, **II:** 94; **Retro. Supp. I:** 97, 113–114, 115; **Supp. IX:** 63
Graham, Shirley, **Supp. I Part 1:** 51; **Supp. XXI:** 277. *See also* Du Bois, Shirley Graham
Graham, Stephen, **Supp. I Part 2:** 397
Graham, Tom (pseudonym). *See* Lewis, Sinclair
Grahn, Judy, **Supp. IV Part 1:** 325, 330
"Grain Field" (Crapsey), **Supp. XVII:** 77
Grainger, Percy, **Supp. I Part 2:** 386
Grain of Mustard Seed, A (Sarton), **Supp. VIII: 259–260,** 263
Gramar (Lowth), **II:** 8
Grammar of Motives, A (Burke), **I:** 272, 275, 276–278, 283, 284
Gramsci, Antonio, **Supp. XX: 35–36**
Granados, Gabriel Bernal, **Supp. XV:** 350
Granath, Jack, **Supp. XVIII:** 93
Granberry, Edwin, **I:** 288
Grand Canyon, Inc. (Everett), **Supp. XVIII:** 66
Grand Design, The (Dos Passos), **I:** 489–490
"Grande Malade, The" (Barnes), **Supp. III Part 1:** 36
"Grandfather" (Dunn), **Supp. XI:** 147
"Grandfather and Grandson" (Singer), **Retro. Supp. II:** 307
Grandfathers, The (Richter), **Supp. XVIII: 219–220**
"Grandfather's Blessing" (Alvarez), **Supp. VII:** 2
"Grand Forks" (Bierds), **Supp. XVII:** 34
"Grand Forks" (Simpson), **Supp. IX:** 280–281
"Grand Inquisitor" (Dostoevsky), **IV:** 106
Grandissimes (Cable), **II:** 291
"Grand-Master Nabokov" (Updike), **Retro. Supp. I:** 317
"Grand Miracle, The" (Karr), **Supp. XI:** 251
"Grandmother" (Gunn Allen), **Supp. IV Part 1:** 320, 325
"Grandmother in Heaven" (Levine), **Supp. V:** 186
"Grandmother of the Sun: Ritual Gynocracy in Native America" (Gunn Allen), **Supp. IV Part 1:** 328
Grandmothers of the Light: A Medicine Woman's Sourcebook (Gunn Allen, ed.), **Supp. IV Part 1:** 332, 333–334
"Grandmother Songs, The" (Hogan), **Supp. IV Part 1:** 413
"Grandpa and the Statue" (A. Miller), **III:** 147
"Grandparents" (Lowell), **II:** 550
"Grandsire Bells, The" (Bierds), **Supp. XVII:** 28–29
"Grandstand Complex, The" (McCoy), **Supp. XIII:** 166
Grange, Red, **II:** 416
Granger's Index to Poetry (anthology), **Retro. Supp. I:** 37, 39
Granite & Cedar (Miller), **Supp. XXII:** 214
Grant, Gavin, **Supp. XIX:** 175
Grant, Lee, **Supp. XIII:** 295
Grant, Madison, **Supp. II Part 1:** 170
Grant, Richard, **Supp. X:** 282
Grant, Ulysses S., **I:** 4, 15; **II:** 542; **III:** 506, 584; **IV:** 348, 446; **Supp. I Part 2:** 418
Grantwood, **Retro. Supp. I:** 416, 417
"Grapes, The" (Hecht), **Supp. X:** 65–66
"Grape Sherbet" (Dove), **Supp. IV Part 1:** 246
Grapes of Wrath, The (Steinbeck), **I:** 301; **III:** 589; **IV:** 51, 53–55, 59, 63, 65,

67, 68, 69; **Supp. V:** 290; **Supp. XI:** 169; **Supp. XIV:** 181; **Supp. XV:** 351; **Supp. XX: 28**
"Grapevine, The" (Ashbery), **Supp. III Part 1:** 4
"Grass" (Sandburg), **III:** 584
Grass, Günter, **Supp. VIII:** 40
Grass County (Kooser), **Supp. XIX:** 119
"Grasse: The Olive Trees" (Wilbur), **Supp. III Part 2:** 550
Grass Harp, The (Capote), **Supp. III Part 1:** 114–117, 123
Grass Still Grows, The (A. Miller), **III:** 146
Gratitude to Old Teachers (R. Bly), **Supp. IV Part 1:** 73
Graupner, Gottlieb, **Supp. XV:** 240, 244
"Grave, A" (Moore), **III:** 195, 202, 208, 213
Grave, The (Blair), **Supp. I Part 1:** 150
"Grave, The" (Porter), **III:** 433, 443, 445–446
"Grave, The" (Winters), **Supp. II Part 2:** 795, 796
"Graven Image" (O'Hara), **III:** 320
Grave of Light: New and Selected Poems, 1970–2005 (Notley), **Supp. XXII:** 226, 235, 236
Grave of the Right Hand, The (Wright), **Supp. V:** 332, 338, 339
"Grave Piece" (Eberhart), **I:** 533
Graves, Billy, **Supp. I Part 2:** 607
Graves, John, **Supp. V:** 220
Graves, Morris, **Supp. X:** 264
Graves, Peter, **Supp. IV Part 2:** 474
Graves, Rean, **Supp. I Part 1:** 326
Graves, Robert, **I:** 437, 477, 523; **Supp. I Part 2:** 541; **Supp. IV Part 1:** 280, 348; **Supp. IV Part 2:** 685
"Graveyard Blues" (Trethewey), **Supp. XXI:** 245, 255, 256
Graveyard for Lunatics, A (Bradbury), **Supp. IV Part 1:** 102, 114–116
Gravity's Rainbow (Pynchon), **Supp. II Part 2:** 617, 618–619, 621–625, 627, 630, 633–636; **Supp. IV Part 1:** 279; **Supp. V:** 44; **Supp. XIV:** 49; **Supp. XVII:** 236; **Supp. XXII:** 255
Gray, Cecil, **Supp. I Part 1:** 258
Gray, Francine Du Plessix, **Supp. V:** 169
Gray, James, **III:** 207; **Supp. I Part 2:** 410
Gray, Jeffrey, **Supp. XV:** 27
Gray, Paul, **Supp. IV Part 1:** 305; **Supp. IV Part 2:** 639; **Supp. XVI:** 74; **Supp. XVIII:** 94
Gray, Thomas, **I:** 68; **Supp. I Part 1:** 150; **Supp. I Part 2:** 422, 716
Gray, Thomas A., **Supp. I Part 2:** 710
"Gray Heron, The" (Kinnell), **Supp. III Part 1:** 250
"Gray Mills of Farley, The" (Jewett), **Retro. Supp. II:** 132, 144
"Gray Poem" (Everwine), **Supp. XV:** 81
Grayson, Charles, **Supp. XIII:** 171
"Gray Squirrel" (Francis), **Supp. IX:** 90
"Gray Wolf's H 'ant, The" (Chesnutt), **Supp. XIV:** 60
Grealy, Lucy, **Supp. XII:** 310
Greasy Lake (Boyle), **Supp. VIII: 14–15**
"Greasy Lake" (Boyle), **Supp. VIII:** 15; **Supp. XX: 18–19**
Greasy Lake & Other Stories (Boyle), **Supp. XX: 17, 18–19**
"Great Adventure of Max Breuck, The" (Lowell), **II:** 522
Great American Novel, The (P. Roth), **Retro. Supp. II:** 283, 288–289; **Supp. III Part 2:** 414–416
Great American Short Novels (Phillips, ed.), **Supp. VIII:** 156
Great Battles of the World (Crane), **I:** 415
"Great Carousel, The" (Untermeyer), **Supp. XV:** 296
Great Christian Doctrine of Original Sin Defended, The . . . (Edwards), **I:** 549, 557, 559
Great Circle (Aiken), **I:** 53, 55, 57
"Great Class-Reunion Bazaar, The" (Theroux), **Supp. VIII:** 312
Great Day, The (Hurston), **Supp. VI:** 154
Great Days (Barthelme), **Supp. IV Part 1:** 39
Great Days, The (Dos Passos), **I:** 491
Great Digest (Pound, trans.), **III:** 472
"Great Divider, The" (Saunders), **Supp. XIX:** 235
"Great Elegy for John Donne" (Brodsky), **Supp. VIII:** 21, 23
"Greater Good, A" (Di Piero), **Supp. XIX:** 39
Greater Inclination, The (Wharton), **Retro. Supp. I:** 363, **364–365,** 366
Greater Sea, The (Gibran), **Supp. XX: 118**
"Greater Self, The" (Gibran), **Supp. XX: 118**
"Greater Torment, The" (Blackmur), **Supp. II Part 1:** 92
Greatest Hits 1969–1996 (Salinas), **Supp. XIII:** 311
"Greatest of These, The" (C. Miller), **Supp. XXII:** 188, 196
"Greatest Thing in the World, The" (Mailer), **Retro. Supp. II:** 196
Great Expectations (Acker), **Supp. XII:** 5, **9–11**
Great Expectations (Dickens), **III:** 247; **Supp. I Part 1:** 35; **Supp. XVI:** 73; **Supp. XVIII:** 146
"Great Expectations, No Satisfaction" (D. Gates), **Supp. XVI:** 73
"Great Figure, The" (W. C. Williams), **IV:** 414
"Great Fillmore Street Buffalo Drive, The" (Momaday), **Supp. IV Part 2:** 493
Great Gatsby, The (Fitzgerald) (Modern Library), **Retro. Supp. I:** 113
Great Gatsby, The (Fitzgerald), **I:** 107, 375, 514; **II:** 77, 79, 83, 84, 85, 87, 91–93, 94, 96, 98; **III:** 244, 260, 372, 572; **IV:** 124, 297; **Retro. Supp. I:** 98, 105, **105–108,** 110, 114, 115, 335, 359; **Retro. Supp. II:** 107, 201; **Supp. II Part 2:** 626; **Supp. III Part 2:** 585; **Supp. IV Part 2:** 468, 475; **Supp. IX:** 57, 58; **Supp. X:** 175; **Supp. XI:** 65, 69, 334; **Supp. XVI:** 64, 75; **Supp. XVIII:** 76, 148, 165; **Supp. XX: 59, 60, 61, 72; Supp. XXII:** 81, 82, 88
Great God Brown, The (O'Neill), **III:** 165, 391, 394–395
Great Goodness of Life: A Coon Show (Baraka), **Supp. II Part 1:** 47
Great Heart: The History of a Labrador Adventure (Davidson and Rugge), **Supp. XXII:** 218
Great Inclination, The (Wharton), **IV:** 310
"Great Infirmities" (Simic), **Supp. VIII:** 277
Great Jones Street (DeLillo), **Supp. VI:** 2, 3, 8–9, 11, 12
"Great Lawsuit, The: Man *versus* Men: Woman *versus* Women" (Fuller), **Retro. Supp. I:** 156; **Supp. II Part 1:** 292
"Great Men and Their Environment" (James), **II:** 347
"Great Mississippi Bubble, The" (Irving), **II:** 314
Great Railway Bazaar, The: By Train through Asia (Theroux), **Supp. VIII:** 318, 319, **320–321,** 322
"Great Scott" (Conroy), **Supp. XVI:** 75, 77
"Great Sleigh-Ride of Brewsterville, The" (Briggs), **Supp. XVIII:** 16
Great Stories of Suspense (Millar, ed.), **Supp. IV Part 2:** 474
Great Topics of the World (Goldbarth), **Supp. XII:** 187, 189, 191
Great Valley, The (Masters), **Supp. I Part 2:** 465
Great World and Timothy Colt, The (Auchincloss), **Supp. IV Part 1:** 25, 31, 32
Grédy, Jean-Pierre, **Supp. XVI:** 194
"Greek Boy, The" (Bryant), **Supp. I Part 1:** 168
Greek Mind/Jewish Soul: The Conflicted Art of Cynthia Ozick (Strandberg), **Supp. V:** 273
"Greek Partisan, The" (Bryant), **Supp. I Part 1:** 168
"Greeks, The" (McCarriston), **Supp. XIV:** 271
"Greeks, the Chines, or Say the Mayans, The" (Bronk), **Supp. XXI:** 31
Greeley, Horace, **II:** 7; **IV:** 197, 286–287
Green, Ashbel, **Supp. IV Part 2:** 474
Green, Henry, **IV:** 279; **Retro. Supp. I:** 354; **Supp. III Part 1:** 3; **Supp. XI:** 294–295, 296, 297; **Supp. XII:** 315
Green, Jack, **Supp. IV Part 1:** 284–285
Green, Martin, **Supp. I Part 1:** 299
Green, Michelle, **Supp. IV Part 1:** 95
Green, Rose Basile, **Supp. XX: 33, 41**
"Green Automobile, The" (Ginsberg), **Supp. II Part 1:** 322
Greenberg, Clement, **Supp. XV:** 141, 143, 144, 145
Greenberg, Eliezer, **Supp. I Part 2:** 432
Greenberg, Jonathan, **Supp. XII:** 285
Greenberg, Miriam, **Supp. XXII:** 244
Greenberg, Samuel, **I:** 393

Green Bough, A (Faulkner), **Retro. Supp. I:** 84
"Green Canoe" (Halliday), **Supp. XIX:** 88
Green Centuries (Gordon), **II:** 196, 197–207, 209
"Green Crab's Shell, A" (Doty), **Supp. XI:** 126
"Green Door, The" (O. Henry), **Supp. II Part 1:** 395
Greene, A. C., **Supp. V:** 223, 225
Greene, Graham, **I:** 480; **II:** 62, 320; **III:** 57, 556; **Retro. Supp. I:** 215; **Supp. I Part 1:** 280; **Supp. IV Part 1:** 341; **Supp. V:** 298; **Supp. IX:** 261; **Supp. XI:** 99,**Supp. XI:** 104; **Supp. XIII:** 233; **Supp. XVIII:** 79; **Supp. XIX:** 29–30
Greene, Helga, **Supp. IV Part 1:** 134, 135
Greene, J. Lee, **Retro. Supp. II:** 121
Greene, Nathanael, **Supp. I Part 2:** 508
Greene, Richard Tobias, **III:** 76
Greene, Robert, **Supp. XVII:** 232
Green Eggs and Ham (Geisel), **Supp. XVI:** 108, 109
"Greene-ing of the Portables, The" (Cowley), **Supp. II Part 1:** 140
"Greenest Continent, The" (Stevens), **Retro. Supp. I:** 304
Greenfeld, Josh, **III:** 364
Greenfield, Josh, **Supp. XIX:** 269
"Green Hell" (Boyle), **Supp. XX: 18**
Green Hills of Africa (Hemingway), **II:** 253; **Retro. Supp. I:** 182, 186
Greening of America, The (C. Reich), **Supp. XVII:** 3
"Green Lagoons, The" (Leopold), **Supp. XIV:** 188
"Green Lampshade" (Simic), **Supp. VIII:** 283
Greenlanders, The (Smiley), **Supp. VI:** 292, **296–298,** 299, 305, 307
Greenlaw, Edwin A., **IV:** 453
"Greenleaf" (O'Connor), **III:** 350, 351; **Retro. Supp. II:** 233, 237
Greenman, Walter F., **I:** 217, 222
Green Memories (Mumford), **Supp. II Part 2:** 474, 475, 479, 480–481
Green Mountain Ghosts, Ghouls, and Unsolved Mysteries (Citro), **Supp. XXII:** 208, 218
"Green Pasture, The" (Leopold), **Supp. XIV:** 184
Green Pastures, The (Connelly), **Supp. II Part 1:** 223
"Green Red Brown and White" (Swenson), **Supp. IV Part 2:** 639
"Green River" (Bryant), **Supp. I Part 1:** 155, 164
Green Shadows, White Whale (Bradbury), **Supp. IV Part 1:** 102, 103, 116
"Green Shirt, The" (Olds), **Supp. X:** 209
"Greensleeves" (Jarman), **Supp. XVII:** 113
"Greensleeves" (Notley), **Supp. XXII:** 228
Greenslet, Ferris, **I:** 19; **Retro. Supp. I:** 9, 10, 11, 13; **Retro. Supp. II:** 41
Greenspan, Alan, **Supp. IV Part 2:** 526
Greenspan, Ezra, **Supp. XVIII:** 257
Greenstreet, Sydney, **Supp. IV Part 1:** 356
"Green Thought, A" (L. Michaels), **Supp. XVI:** 204
"Green-Thumb Boy" (Nelson), **Supp. XVIII:** 182
Greenwald, Ted, **Supp. IV Part 2:** 423
Green Wall, The (Wright), **Supp. III Part 2:** 591, 593, 595
Green Wave, The (Rukeyser), **Supp. VI:** 273, 280
"Green Ways" (Kunitz), **Supp. III Part 1:** 265
Green with Beasts (Merwin), **Supp. III Part 1:** 340, 344–346
Greenwood, Grace, **Supp. XIII:** 141
"Greeting Card Verse" (Peacock), **Supp. XIX:** 200
Gregerson, Linda, **Supp. IV Part 2:** 651; **Supp. X:** 204–205; **Supp. XI:** 142
"Gregorio Valdes" (Bishop), **Retro. Supp. II:** 51
Gregory, Alyse, **I:** 221, 226, 227, 231
Gregory, Horace, **II:** 512; **Supp. III Part 2:** 614, 615; **Supp. IX:** 229; **Supp. XV:** 143
Gregory, Lady Isabella Augusta, **III:** 458
Gregory, Sinda, **Supp. X:** 260, 268
Grendel (Gardner), **Supp. VI:** 63, **67,** 68, 74
Grenstone Poems (Bynner), **Supp. XV:** 44
"Gretel in Darkness" (Glück), **Supp. V:** 82
Gretta (Caldwell), **I:** 301, 302
Greuze, Jean Baptiste, **Supp. I Part 2:** 714
Grey, Zane, **Supp. XIII:** 5
Gridley Firing (Hayford), **Supp. XXII:** 204
"Grief Has Stamped" (Pedersen; Nelson, trans.), **Supp. XVIII:** 180
Grieg, Michael, **Supp. XV:** 133, 148
Griffin, Bartholomew, **Supp. I Part 1:** 369
Griffin, John Howard, **Supp. VIII:** 208; **Supp. XXI:** 74
Griffin, Merv, **Supp. IV Part 2:** 526
Griffith, Albert J., **Supp. V:** 325
Griffith, D. W., **I:** 31, 481–482; **Retro. Supp. I:** 103, 325; **Supp. XI:** 45; **Supp. XVI:** 183, 184; **Supp. XXI:** 170
Griffith, Paul, **Supp. XVIII:** 173, 175
Griffiths, Clyde, **I:** 511
Grile, Dod (pseudonym). *See* Bierce, Ambrose
Grimm, Herman, **II:** 17
Grimm brothers, **II:** 378; **III:** 101, 491, 492; **IV:** 266; **Supp. I Part 2:** 596, 622; **Supp. X:** 78, 84, 86
Grimshaw, Anna, **Supp. XXI:** 172
Grinnell, George Bird, **Supp. XVI:** 13
Gris, Juan, **I:** 442; **Retro. Supp. I:** 430
Griswold, Rufus Wilmot, **III:** 409, 429; **Retro. Supp. II:** 261, 262; **Supp. XV:** 277, 278; **Supp. XVI:** 8, 10–11
Grogg, Sam, Jr., **Supp. IV Part 2:** 468, 471
Gromer, Crystal, **Supp. XII:** 297
Gronlund, Laurence, **II:** 276
Grooms, Red, **Supp. XV:** 178
Grooves: A Kind of Mystery (Brockmeier), **Supp. XXII:** 55, 56, 59
"Groping for Trouts" (Gass), **Supp. VI:** 87
Grosholz, Emily, **Supp. XII:** 185; **Supp. XIX:** 37–38, 278
Gross, Robert A., **Supp. XIX:** 151
Gross, Terry, **Supp. XVI:** 167; **Supp. XXI:** 247, 255
"Grosse Fuge" (Doty), Supp. XI: 126–127
Grossman, Allen, **Retro. Supp. II:** 83; **Supp. XVIII:** 91; **Supp. XIX:** 82, 86, 94
Grosz, George, **III:** 172; **IV:** 438; **Retro. Supp. II:** 321; **Supp. X:** 137
"Grotesque in Modern Fiction, The" (E. Hoffman, Ph.D. dissertation), **Supp. XVI:** 147
"Groundhog, The" (Eberhart), **I:** 523, 530–532, 533
"Ground on Which I Stand, The" (Wilson), **Supp. VIII:** 331
"Ground Swell" (Jarman), **Supp. XVII:** 118
Group, The (McCarthy), **II:** 570, 574–578
"Group of Two, A" (Jarrell), **II:** 368
Group Therapy (Hearon), **Supp. VIII: 64–65**
"Grove" (Goldbarth), **Supp. XII:** 176
Groves of Academe, The (McCarthy), **II:** 568–571
Growing into Love (X. J. Kennedy), **Supp. XV:** 153, **158–160**
Growing Pains (J. S. Untermeyer), **Supp. XV:** 303
"Growing Season, The" (Caldwell), **I:** 309
Growing Up Gay: A Literary Anthology (Singer, ed.), **Supp. IV Part 1:** 330
"Growing Up Good in Maycomb" (Shaffer), **Supp. VIII:** 128
"Grown-Up" (Jewett), **Retro. Supp. II:** 134
"Growth" (Lowell), **II:** 554
"Growth and Decay in Recent Verse" (Untermeyer), **Supp. XV:** 299
Growth of the American Republic, The (Morison and Commager), **Supp. I Part 2:** 484
"Growtown Buggle, The" (Jewett), **Retro. Supp. II:** 132
Gruenberg, Louis, **III:** 392
Grumbach, Doris, **II:** 560
"Gryphon" (C. Baxter), **Supp. XVII:** 14, 17
"Guacamaja" (Leopold), **Supp. XIV:** 188–189
Guardian Angel, The (Holmes), **Supp. I Part 1:** 315–316
"Guardian of the Law" (R. Fisher), **Supp. XIX:** 71
Guard of Honor (Cozzens), **I:** 370–372, 375, 376–377, 378, 379
Guardsman, The (Molnar), **Supp. XVI:** 187

Guare, John, **Supp. XIII:** 196, 207
Gubar, Susan, **Retro. Supp. I:** 42; **Retro. Supp. II:** 324; **Supp. IX:** 66; **Supp. XV:** 270
Guerard, Albert, Jr., **Supp. X:** 79; **Supp. XIII:** 172
Guérin, Maurice de, **I:** 241
"Guerrilla Handbook, A" (Baraka), **Supp. II Part 1:** 36
Guess and Spell Coloring Book, The (Swenson), **Supp. IV Part 2:** 648
Guess Who's Coming to Dinner (film), **Supp. I Part 1:** 67
Guest, Judith, **Supp. XVI:** 36
Guest, Val, **Supp. XI:** 307
Guest Book (Bynner), **Supp. XV:** 51
"Guests of Mrs. Timms, The" (Jewett), **II:** 408; **Retro. Supp. II:** 135
Guevara, Martha, **Supp. VIII:** 74
Guevara, Fray Miguel de, **Supp. XXI:** 104
"Guevara . . .Guevara" (Salinas), **Supp. XIII:** 312–313, 315
Guggenheim, Peggy, **Supp. XXII:** 165
Guided Tours of Hell (Prose), **Supp. XVI:** 257, 261
"Guided Tours of Hell" (Prose), **Supp. XVI:** 257
Guide for the Perplexed (Maimonides), **Supp. XVII:** 46
Guide in the Wilderness, A (Cooper), **I:** 337
"Guidelines" (Espaillat), **Supp. XXI:** 99
"Guide to Dungeness Spit, A" (Wagoner), **Supp. IX:** 325–326, 329
Guide to Ezra Pound's Selected Cantos' (Kearns), Retro. Supp. I: 292
Guide to Kulchur (Pound), **III:** 475
Guide to the Ruins (Nemerov), **III:** 269, 270–271, 272
Guillén, Nicolás, **Retro. Supp. I:** 202; **Supp. I Part 1:** 345
Guillevic, Eugene, **Supp. III Part 1:** 283
"Guilt, The" (Peacock), **Supp. XIX:** 200
"Guilty Man, The" (Kunitz), **Supp. II Part 1:** 263
Guilty of Everything: The Autobiography of Herbert Huncke (Huncke), **Supp. XIV:** 138, 140, 141, 150
Guilty Pleasures (Barthelme), **Supp. IV Part 1:** 44, 45, 53
Guimond, James, **Supp. XXI:** 228
Guinness, Alec, **Retro. Supp. I:** 65; **Supp. XX: 50**
Gulag Archipelago, The (Solzhenitsyn), **Supp. XVII:** 229
"Gulf, The" (Dunn), **Supp. XI:** 149
Gulistan (Saadi), **II:** 19
Gullible's Travels (Lardner), **II:** 426, 427
Gulliver, Adelaide Cromwell, **Supp. XVIII:** 286
"Gulliver Found" (Bronk), **Supp. XXI:** 33
Gulliver's Travels (Swift), **I:** 209, 348, 366; **II:** 301; **Supp. I Part 2:** 656; **Supp. XI:** 209; **Supp. XVI:** 110
"Gulls" (Hayden), **Supp. II Part 1:** 367
"Gulls, The" (Nemerov), **III:** 272
"Gulls on Dumps" (Di Piero), **Supp. XIX:** 41
"Gun, The" (Dobyns), **Supp. XIII:** 88
Gun, with Occasional Music (Lethem), **Supp. XVIII: 137–138**
Günderode: A Translation from the German (Fuller), **Supp. II Part 1:** 293
Gundy, Jeff, **Supp. XI:** 315; **Supp. XVI:** 46, 265, 275
Gunfight at the O.K. Corral (film), **Supp. XX: 246**
Gunman's Rhapsody (Parker), **Supp. XIX:** 187
Gunn, Robin Wright, **Supp. XXI:** 243, 244
Gunn, Thom, **Supp. IX:** 269
Gunn, Thomas, **Supp. V:** 178
Gunn Allen, Paula, **Supp. IV Part 1: 319–340,** 404; **Supp. IV Part 2:** 499, 502, 557, 568; **Supp. XII:** 218
"Gunnar's Sword" (C. Bly), **Supp. XVI:** 34, 35, 37, 42
"Guns as Keys; and the Great Gate Swings" (Lowell), **II:** 524
Gurdjieff, Georges, **Supp. V:** 199; **Supp. IX:** 320
Gurganus, Allan, **Supp. XII:** 308–309, 310
Gurko, Leo, **III:** 62
Gurney, A. R., **Supp. V: 95–112; Supp. IX:** 261
Gurney, Mary (Molly) Goodyear, **Supp. V:** 95
Gussow, Mel, **Supp. IX:** 93; **Supp. XII:** 325, 328, 341
Gustavus Vassa, the African (Vassa), **Supp. IV Part 1:** 11
Gusto, Thy Name Was Mrs. Hopkins: A Prose Rhapsody (Francis), **Supp. IX:** 89
Gute Mensch von Sezuan, Der (Brecht), **Supp. IX:** 138
Gutenberg, Johann, **Supp. I Part 2:** 392
Guthrie, A. B., **Supp. X:** 103
Guthrie, Woody, **Supp. XVIII:** 23
Gutman, Herbert, **Supp. I Part 1:** 47
Guttenplan, D. D., **Supp. XI:** 38
"Gutting of Couffignal, The" (Hammett), **Supp. IV Part 1:** 345
Guy Domville (James), **II:** 331; **Retro. Supp. I:** 228
"Gwendolyn" (Bishop), **Retro. Supp. II:** 51
Gwynn, R. S., **Supp. XVIII:** 184
Gypsy Ballads (Hughes, trans.), **Supp. I Part 1:** 345
Gypsy's Curse, The (Crews), **Supp. XI: 110**
"Gyroscope, The" (Rukeyser), **Supp. VI:** 271
Gysin, Brion, **Supp. XII:** 129

Haardt, Sara. *See* Mencken, Mrs. H. L. (Sara Haardt)
Haas, Robert, **Supp. XXII:** 177
Habakkuk (biblical book), **III:** 200, 347
Habibi (Nye), **Supp. XIII:** 273, **279**
"Habit" (James), **II:** 351
Habitations of the Word (Gass), **Supp. VI:** 88
"Hack, The" (Swados), **Supp. XIX:** 267
Hacker, Marilyn, **Supp. XV:** 250; **Supp. XVII:** 71, 76, 112; **Supp. XVIII:** 177, 178
Hackett, David, **Supp. XII:** 236
Hadda, Janet, **Retro. Supp. II:** 317
Haddád, 'Abd al-Masíh, **Supp. XX: 116**
Haeckel, Ernst Heinrich, **II:** 480
Haegert, John, **Supp. XVI:** 69
Hafif, Marcia, **Supp. IV Part 2:** 423
Hagar's Daughter (P. Hopkins), **Supp. XVI:** 143
Hagedorn, Jessica, **Supp. X:** 292
Hagen, Beulah, **Supp. I Part 2:** 679
Hager, Kelly, **Supp. XVIII:** 183
Haggard, Rider, **III:** 189
Hagoromo (play), **III:** 466
Hagstrum, Jean, **Supp. XV:** 74
"Hail Mary" (Fante), **Supp. XI:** 160, 164
Haines, George, IV, **I:** 444
Haines, John, **Supp. XII: 197–214**
"Hair" (Corso), **Supp. XII:** 117, 126, 127
"Hair, The" (Carver), **Supp. III Part 1:** 137
"Haircut" (Lardner), **II:** 430, 436
"Hair Dressing" (Untermeyer), **Supp. XV:** 304, 305
Hairpiece: A Film for Nappy-Headed People (Chenzira; film), **Supp. XI:** 19–20
"Hairs" (Cisneros), **Supp. VII:** 59
Hairs/Pelitos (Cisneros), **Supp. VII:** 58
Hairy Ape, The (O'Neill), **III:** 391, 392, 393
"Haïta the Shepherd" (Bierce), **I:** 203
Haj, The (Uris), **Supp. XX: 244, 245, 247, 255–256**
Haldeman, Anna, **Supp. I Part 1:** 2
Hale, Edward Everett, **Supp. I Part 2:** 584; **Supp. XI:** 193, 200
Hale, John Parker, **Supp. I Part 2:** 685
Hale, Nancy, **Supp. VIII:** 151, 171
Haley, Alex, **Supp. I Part 1:** 47, 66
Haley, J. Evetts, **Supp. V:** 226
"Half a Century Gone" (Lowell), **II:** 554
Half-a-Hundred: Tales by Great American Writers (Grayson, ed.), **Supp. XIII:** 171
Half Asleep in Frog Pajamas (Robbins), **Supp. X:** 259, **279–282**
Half Breed, The (film), **Supp. XVI:** 185
Half-Century of Conflict, A (Parkman), **Supp. II Part 2:** 600, 607, 610
"Half Deity" (Moore), **III:** 210, 214, 215
"Half Hour of August" (Ríos), **Supp. IV Part 2:** 552
Half-Lives (Jong), **Supp. V:** 115, 119
Half Moon Street: Two Short Novels (Theroux), **Supp. VIII:** 322, 323
Half of Paradise (Burke), **Supp. XIV:** 22, 24
Half-Past Nation Time (Johnson), **Supp. VI:** 187
"Half-Skinned Steer, The" (Proulx), **Supp. VII:** 261–262
"Half Sonnets" (Jarman), **Supp. XVII:** 115
Half Sun Half Sleep (Swenson), **Supp. IV Part 2:** 645–646
Halfway (Kumin), **Supp. IV Part 2:** 441–442

"Halfway" (Rich), **Supp. I Part 2:** 553
Halfway Home (Monette), **Supp. X:** 154
Halfway to Silence (Sarton), **Supp. VIII:** 261
Half You Don't Know, The: Selected Stories (Cameron), **Supp. XII:** 79, 80, 81
Haliburton, Thomas Chandler, **II:** 301; **IV:** 193; **Supp. I Part 2:** 411
Halifax, Lord, **II:** 111
Hall, Daniel, **Supp. XII:** 258
Hall, Donald, **I:** 567; **III:** 194; **Supp. IV Part 1:** 63, 72; **Supp. IV Part 2:** 621; **Supp. IX:** 269; **Supp. XIV:** 82, 126; **Supp. XV:** 21, 153, 176; **Supp. XVI:** 39, 230, 235; **Supp. XX: 194; Supp. XXI:** 86
Hall, Hazel, **Supp. XXII:** 275
Hall, James, **II:** 313; **Supp. I Part 2:** 584, 585
Hall, James Baker, **Supp. X:** 24
Hall, Timothy L., **Supp. VIII:** 127, 128
Halleck, Fitz-Greene, **Supp. I Part 1:** 156, 158
"Hallelujah: A Sestina" (Francis), **Supp. IX:** 82
"Hallelujah on the Bum" (Abbey), **Supp. XIII:** 2
"Haller's Second Home" (Maxwell), **Supp. VIII:** 169
Halliday, Mark, **Supp. XV:** 19, 20, 21, 23, 25, 27, 30; **Supp. XIX: 81–95**
Hallock, Rev. Moses, **Supp. I Part 1:** 153
Hall of Mirrors, A (Stone), **Supp. V:** 295, 296–299, 300, 301
"Hallowe'en" (Huncke), **Supp. XIV:** 145
"Halloween Party, The" (Chabon), **Supp. XI:** 72
Halloween Tree, The (Bradbury), **Supp. IV Part 1:** 102, 112–113
"Halls, The" (Halliday), **Supp. XIX:** 90
Hallwas, John E., **Supp. I Part 2:** 454
Halpern, Daniel, **Supp. IV Part 1:** 94–95, 95
Halsey, Theresa, **Supp. IV Part 1:** 330, 331
"Halt in the Desert, A" (Brodsky), **Supp. VIII:** 24
"Halves" (Dunn), **Supp. XI:** 149
Hamburg, Victoria, **Supp. XVI:** 126
Hamerik, Asger, **Supp. I Part 1:** 356
Hamill, Pete, **Supp. XX: 244, 255**
Hamill, Sam, **Supp. X:** 112, 125, 126, 127
Hamilton, Alexander, **I:** 485; **Supp. I Part 2:** 456, 483, 509
Hamilton, Alice, **Supp. I Part 1:** 5
Hamilton, David, **Supp. IX:** 296
Hamilton, Edith, **Supp. XVI:** 196
Hamilton, Lady Emma, **II:** 524
Hamilton, Hamish, **Supp. I Part 2:** 617
Hamilton, Walton, **Supp. I Part 2:** 632
Hamilton Stark (Banks), **Supp. V:** 8, 9–10, 11
"Hamlen Brook" (Wilbur), **Supp. III Part 2:** 564
"Hamlet" (Laforgue), **I:** 573; **III:** 11
Hamlet (Miller and Fraenkel), **III:** 178, 183
Hamlet (Shakespeare), **I:** 53, 183, 205, 377, 586–587; **II:** 158, 531; **III:** 7, 11, 12, 183; **IV:** 116, 131, 227; **Supp. I Part 1:** 369; **Supp. I Part 2:** 422, 457, 471; **Supp. IV Part 2:** 612; **Supp. IX:** 14
Hamlet, The (Faulkner), **II:** 69–71, 73, 74; **IV:** 131; **Retro. Supp. I:** 82, 91, 92; **Supp. VIII:** 178; **Supp. IX:** 103; **Supp. XI:** 247
"Hamlet and His Problems" (Eliot), **I:** 586–587
Hamlet of A. MacLeish, The (MacLeish), **III:** 11–12, 14, 15, 18
Hamlin, Eva, **Retro. Supp. II:** 115
"Hammer" (Bidart), **Supp. XV:** 35
Hammer, Adam, **Supp. XIII:** 112
Hammer, Langdon, **Retro. Supp. II:** 45, 53; **Supp. X:** 65
"Hammer Man, The" (Bambara), **Supp. XI:** 4–5
Hammett, Dashiell, **IV:** 286; **Retro. Supp. II:** 327; **Supp. I Part 1:** 286, 289, 291, 292, 293, 294, 295; **Supp. III Part 1:** 91; **Supp. IV Part 1:** 120, 121, **341–357; Supp. IV Part 2:** 461, 464, 468, 469, 472, 473; **Supp. IX:** 200; **Supp. XI:** 228; **Supp. XIII:** 159; **Supp. XIV:** 21; **Supp. XVII:** 137; **Supp. XIX:** 178; **Supp. XXI:** 68
Hammon, Jupiter, **Supp. XXII:** 11
Hammond, John, **Supp. XVIII:** 24
Hammond, Karla, **Supp. IV Part 2:** 439, 442, 448, 637, 640, 644, 648
Hampl, Patricia, **Supp. IX:** 291; **Supp. XI:** 126; **Supp. XVII:** 21; **Supp. XXII: 81–101**
Hampson, Alfred Leete, **Retro. Supp. I:** 35–36, 38
"Hamrick's Polar Bear" (Caldwell), **I:** 309–310
Hamsun, Knut, **Supp. VIII:** 40; **Supp. XI:** 161, 167; **Supp. XII:** 21, 128
Hancock, John, **Supp. I Part 2:** 524; **Supp. XX: 282**
Hancock, Wade, **Supp. XVI:** 34
Handbook of North American Indians (Sando), **Supp. IV Part 2:** 510
Handcarved Coffins: A Nonfiction Account of an American Crime (Capote), **Supp. III Part 1:** 131
Handel, Georg Friedrich, **III:** 210; **IV:** 369
"Handfasting" (Wright), **Supp. XV:** 343
"Handfuls" (Sandburg), **III:** 584
"Handle with Care" (Fitzgerald), **Retro. Supp. I:** 114
Handley, William R., **Supp. XVIII:** 58
Handmaid's Tale, The (Atwood), **Supp. XIII:** 19, 20, **27–29**
"Hand of Casino, 1954, A" (Skloot), **Supp. XX: 194, 202**
"Hand of Emmagene, The" (Taylor), **Supp. V:** 314, 325–326
Hand of the Potter, The: A Tragedy in Four Acts (Dreiser), **Retro. Supp. II:** 104; **Supp. XVII:** 96
"Hands" (Anderson), **I:** 106, 107
"Hands" (Mora), **Supp. XIII:** 215
Hands of Orlac, The (M. Renard; Crewe-Jones, trans.), **Supp. XVII:** 58
Hand to Mouth (Auster), **Supp. XII:** 21
"Hand to Mouth" (Auster), **Supp. XII:** 31
Handy, Lowney, **Supp. XI:** 217, 220, 221, 225
Handy, W. C., **Supp. VIII:** 337
Handy Guide for Beggars, A (Lindsay), **Supp. I Part 2:** 376–378, 380, 382, 399
Haney, David, **Supp. XXI:** 253
"Hanged Man, A" (Cliff), **Supp. XXII:** 74
"Hanging Burley" (J. W. Miller), **Supp. XX: 167**
Hanging Garden, The (Wagoner), **Supp. IX: 338–339**
"Hanging Gardens of Tyburn, The" (Hecht), **Supp. X:** 58
"Hanging of the Crane, The" (Longfellow), **Retro. Supp. II:** 169, 171
Hanging On (Conroy), **Supp. XVI:** 69
"Hanging Pictures in Nanny's Room" (Kenyon), **Supp. VII:** 164
"Hanging the Wash" (Alvarez), **Supp. VII:** 4
"Hangman, The" (Sexton), **Supp. II Part 2:** 680, 691
Hangover Mass (X. J. Kennedy), **Supp. XV:** 165
Hangsaman (Jackson), **Supp. IX:** 116, 123, **124**
Hanh, Thich Nhat, **Supp. V:** 199
Hanks, Lucy, **III:** 587
Hanks, Nancy. *See* Lincoln, Mrs. Thomas (Nancy Hanks)
Hanley, Lynne T., **Supp. IV Part 1:** 208
"Hanlon Mountain in Mist" (J. W. Miller), **Supp. XX: 164, 166–167**
Hanna, Mark, **Supp. I Part 2:** 395
Hannah, Barry, **Supp. X:** 285; **Supp. XIX:** 209; **Supp. XXI:** 38, 118
Hannah and Her Sisters (film; Allen), **Supp. XV:** 9, **10–11**
"Hannah Armstrong" (Masters), **Supp. I Part 2:** 461
"Hannah Binding Shoes" (Larcom), **Supp. XIII:** 141, 143
"Hannah Byde" (D. West), **Supp. XVIII:** 280
Hannah's House (Hearon), **Supp. VIII:** 58, **60–61**
Hanneman, Audre, **II:** 259
Hannibal Lecter, My Father (Acker), **Supp. XII:** 6
Hanoi (McCarthy), **II:** 579
"Hanoi Drifting, January 2003" (Weigl), **Supp. XIX:** 288
Hansberry, Lorraine, **Supp. IV Part 1: 359–377; Supp. VIII:** 329
Hanscom, Leslie, **Supp. XI:** 229
"Hansel and Gretel" (Prose), **Supp. XVI:** 256, 258
Hansen, Erik, **Supp. V:** 241
Hansen, Harry, **IV:** 366; **Supp. XXII:** 194, 277
Han-shan, **Supp. VIII:** 292
Hanson, Curtis, **Supp. XI:** 67

Han Suyin, **Supp. X:** 291
Hanzlicek, C. G., **Supp. XV:** 73
Hapgood, Charles H., II, **Supp. XXI:** 6
Hapgood, Hutchins, **Supp. XVII: 95–108; Supp. XXI:** 1, 3, 9, 10
Hapgood, Norman, **Supp. XXI:** 2
Hapgoods, The: Three Earnest Brothers (Marcaccio), **Supp. XVII:** 106
"Happenings: An Art of Radical Juxtaposition" (Sontag), **Supp. III Part 2:** 456
"Happenstance" (Komunyakaa), **Supp. XIII:** 130
Happenstance (Shields), **Supp. VII:** 315–318, 320, 323, 324, 326
Happersberger, Lucien, **Supp. I Part 1:** 51
"Happiest I've Been, The" (Updike), **IV:** 219
Happily Ever After (Quindlen), **Supp. XVII:** 167
"Happiness" (Oliver), **Supp. VII:** 236
"Happiness" (Sandburg), **III:** 582–583
Happiness of Getting It Down Right, The (Steinman, ed.), **Supp. VIII:** 172
"Happiness of the Garden Variety" (Richard), **Supp. XIX:** 212
"Happy Birthday" (Bambara), **Supp. XI:** 4
Happy Birthday (Loos), **Supp. XVI:** 193
Happy Birthday, Wanda June (Vonnegut), **Supp. II Part 2:** 759, 776–777
Happy Birthday of Death, The (Corso), **Supp. XII: 127–129**
Happy Childhood, A (Matthews), **Supp. IX:** 155, 160, **161–163**
Happy Days (Beckett), **Retro. Supp. I:** 206
Happy Days, 1880–1892 (Mencken), **III:** 100, 111, 120
"Happy End" (Simic), **Supp. VIII:** 276–277
"Happy Failure, The" (Melville), **III:** 90
Happy Families Are All Alike (Taylor), **Supp. V:** 322–323, 325
Happy Isles of Oceania, The: Paddling the Pacific (Theroux), **Supp. VIII:** 324
"Happy Journey to Trenton and Camden, The" (Wilder), **IV:** 366
"Happy Man, The" (Lethem), **Supp. XVIII:** 139
"Happy Marriage, The" (MacLeish), **III:** 15–16
Happy Marriage and Other Poems, The (MacLeish), **III:** 4
Happy to Be Here (Keillor), **Supp. XVI:** 165, 171
"Happy To Be Here" (Keillor), **Supp. XVI:** 168
"Hapworth 16, 1924" (Salinger), **III:** 552, 571–572
"Harbor Dawn, The" (H. Crane), **Supp. XXI:** 132, 136
"Harbor Lights" (Doty), **Supp. XI:** 122
Harcourt, Alfred, **II:** 191, 451–452; **III:** 587; **Retro. Supp. I:** 131; **Supp. XV:** 308
Harcourt, Lewis, **Supp. XX: 232–233**
Harcourt, T. A., **I:** 196
Hard Candy, a Book of Stories (T. Williams), **IV:** 383
"Hardcastle Crags" (Plath), **Supp. I Part 2:** 537
"Hard Daddy" (Hughes), **Retro. Supp. I:** 200
"Hardened Criminals, The" (Lethem), **Supp. XVIII:** 139
Harder They Fall, The (Schulberg), **Supp. XV:** 194, 201
Hard Facts (Baraka), **Supp. II Part 1:** 54, 55, 58
Hard Freight (Wright), **Supp. V:** 332, 339–340
Hard Hours, The (Hecht), **Supp. X:** 57, **59–62,** 63, 64
Hardie, Kier, **Supp. I Part 1:** 5
Harding, Walter, **IV:** 177, 178
Harding, Warren G., **I:** 486; **II:** 253, 433; **Supp. I Part 1:** 24
"Hard Kind of Courage, The" (Baldwin), **Supp. I Part 1:** 52
Hard Laughter (Lamott), **Supp. XX: 132–133**
Hard Maple (S. and A. Warner), **Supp. XVIII:** 264
"Hard Rain's A-Gonna Fall, A" (song, Dylan), **Supp. XVIII:** 26, 29
"Hard Time Keeping Up, A" (Ellison), **Retro. Supp. II:** 124
Hard Times (Dickens), **Supp. I Part 2:** 675
"Hard Times in Elfland, The" (Lanier), **Supp. I Part 1:** 365
"Hard Traveling: *Fay*'s Deep South Landscape of Violence" (Beuka), **Supp. XXI:** 47
Hardwick, Elizabeth, **II:** 543, 554, 566; **Retro. Supp. II:** 179, 180, 183, 184, 190, 221, 228–229, 245; **Supp. I Part 1:** 196; **Supp. III Part 1: 193–215; Supp. IV Part 1:** 299; **Supp. V,** 319; **Supp. X,** 171; **Supp. XII:** 209; **Supp. XIV:** 89
"Hard Work 1956" (Dunn), **Supp. XI:** 147
Hardy, Barbara, **Supp. I Part 2:** 527
Hardy, Oliver, **Supp. I Part 2:** 607; **Supp. IV Part 2:** 574
Hardy, René, **Supp. III Part 1:** 235
Hardy, Thomas, **I:** 59, 103, 292, 317, 377; **II:** 181, 184–185, 186, 191–192, 271, 275, 372, 523, 542; **III:** 32, 453, 485, 508, 524; **IV:** 83, 135, 136; **Retro. Supp. I:** 141, 377–378; **Supp. I Part 1:** 217; **Supp. I Part 2:** 429, 512; **Supp. II Part 1:** 4, 26; **Supp. VIII:** 32; **Supp. IX:** 40, 78, 85, 108, 211; **Supp. X:** 228; **Supp. XI:** 311; **Supp. XIII:** 294, **Supp. XIII:** 130; **Supp. XIV:** 24; **Supp. XV:** 170; **Supp. XVIII:** 74; **Supp. XIX:** 86, 87; **Supp. XX: 195; Supp. XXI:** 109
Hardy and the Poetry of Truth-Seeking (Halliday), **Supp. XIX:** 82
Harjo, Joy, **Supp. IV Part 1:** 325, 404; **Supp. IV Part 2:** 499, 507; **Supp. XII: 215–234; Supp. XVIII:** 189
Harlan's Race (P. N. Warren), **Supp. XX: 264–265**
"Harlem" (Hughes), **Retro. Supp. I:** 194, 204; **Supp. I Part 1:** 340; **Supp. VIII:** 213
Harlem, Mecca of the New Negro (Locke), **Supp. XIV:** 201
"Harlem Dancer, The" (McKay), **Supp. X:** 134
Harlem Gallery (Tolson), **Retro. Supp. I:** 208, 209, 210
Harlem Glory: A Fragment of Aframerican Life (McKay), **Supp. X:** 132, **141–142**
Harlem: Negro Metropolis (McKay), **Supp. X:** 132, 141, 142
Harlem Renaissance Remembered, The (Bontemps, ed.), **Supp. XXII:** 7
"Harlem Runs Wild" (McKay), **Supp. X:** 140
Harlem Shadows (McKay), **Supp. X:** 131–132, 136
Harlem Underground (Lacy), **Supp. XV:** 206
"Harlequin of Dreams, The" (Lanier), **Supp. I Part 1:** 365
Harlot's Ghost (Mailer), **Retro. Supp. II:** 211–212
Harlow, Jean, **IV:** 256; **Retro. Supp. I:** 110
"Harm" (C. Frost), **Supp. XV:** 101
Harmon, William, **Retro. Supp. I:** 37; **Supp. XI:** 248
"Harmonic" (F. Barthelme), **Supp. XI:** 26
Harmonium (Stevens), **III:** 196; **IV:** 76, 77, 78, 82, 87, 89, 92; **Retro. Supp. I:** 296, 297, 299, **300–302,** 301, 302
"Harmony of the Gospels" (Taylor), **IV:** 149
Harmony of the World (C. Baxter), **Supp. XVII:** 16–17
"Harmony of the World" (C. Baxter), **Supp. XVII:** 16
Harnett, Vincent, **Supp. XV:** 198
"Harp, The" (Weigl), **Supp. XIX:** 278
Harper (film), **Supp. IV Part 2:** 473
Harper, Donna, **Retro. Supp. I:** 194, 195, 209
Harper, Frances E. Watkins, **Supp. II Part 1:** 201–202; **Supp. XVIII:** 284; **Supp. XXII:** 11
Harper, Gordon Lloyd, **Retro. Supp. II:** 23
Harper, Michael, **Supp. XV:** 74
Harper, Michael S., **Retro. Supp. II:** 116, 123
Harper, William Rainey, **Supp. I Part 2:** 631
Harper's Anthology of 20th Century Native American Poetry (Niatum, ed.), **Supp. IV Part 1:** 331
"Harriet" (Lowell), **II:** 554
Harrigan, Edward, **II:** 276; **III:** 14
Harrington, Michael, **I:** 306
Harrington, Ollie, **Supp. XVI:** 142–143
Harris, Celia, **Retro. Supp. I:** 9
Harris, Corra, **Supp. XXII:** 190, 193, 196
Harris, George ?/, **II:** 70
Harris, George Washington ?/, **Supp. XXII:** 193

Harris, Joel Chandler, **III:** 338; **Supp. I Part 1:** 352; **Supp. II Part 1:** 192, 201; **Supp. XIV:** 61; **Supp. XX: 103**
Harris, Judith, **Supp. XIV:** 269
Harris, Julie, **II:** 587, 601; **Supp. IX:** 125
Harris, Leonard, **Supp. XIV:** 196, 211–212
Harris, MacDonald, **Supp. XI:** 65
Harris, Marie, **Supp. IX:** 153
Harris, Peter, **Supp. X:** 206, 207
Harris, Susan K., **Supp. XV:** 269
Harris, Thomas, **Supp. XIV:** 26; **Supp. XXI:** 67, 78
Harris, Victoria Frenkel, **Supp. IV Part 1:** 68, 69
Harris, Violet J., **Supp. XXII:** 10, 13
Harris, Wilson, **Supp. XXI:** 170
Harrison, Colin, **Supp. XIV:** 26
Harrison, Hazel, **Retro. Supp. II:** 115
Harrison, Jim, **Supp. VIII: 37–56; Supp. XIX:** 125, 126
Harrison, Kathryn, **Supp. X:** 191
Harrison, Ken, **Supp. IX:** 101
Harrison, Oliver (pseudonym). *See* Smith, Harrison
Harry: A Portrait (Boyce), **Supp. XVII:** 104; **Supp. XXI:** 7, **13–14**
Harryhausen, Ray, **Supp. IV Part 1:** 115
Harryman, Carla, **Supp. XV:** 344
"Harry of Nothingham" (Hugo), **Supp. VI:** 146–147
"Harry's Death" (Carver), **Supp. III Part 1:** 146
"Harsh Judgment, The" (Kunitz), **Supp. III Part 1:** 264
Hart, Albert Bushnell, **Supp. I Part 2:** 479, 480, 481
Hart, Bernard, **I:** 241, 242, 248–250, 256
Hart, Henry, **Retro. Supp. II:** 187; **Supp. XIV:** 97
Hart, James D., **Supp. XVIII:** 257
Hart, John Seely, **Supp. XVIII:** 257, 258, 264
Hart, Lorenz, **III:** 361
Hart, Moss, **Supp. IV Part 2:** 574; **Supp. XV:** 329
Hart, Pearl, **Supp. X:** 103
"Hart Crane" (Tate), **I:** 381
"Hart Crane and Poetry: A Consideration of Crane's Intense Poetics with Reference to 'The Return' " (Grossman), **Retro. Supp. II:** 83
Harte, Anna Griswold, **Supp. II Part 1:** 341
Harte, Bret, **I:** 193, 195, 203; **II:** 289; **IV:** 196; **Retro. Supp. II:** 72; **Supp. II Part 1: 335–359,** 399; **Supp. XV:** 115
Harte, Walter Blackburn, **I:** 199
Harter, Carol C., **Supp. IV Part 1:** 217
Hartley, David, **III:** 77
Hartley, Lois, **Supp. I Part 2:** 459, 464–465
Hartley, L. P., **Supp. I Part 1:** 293
Hartley, Marsden, **IV:** 409, 413; **Retro. Supp. I:** 430; **Supp. X:** 137; **Supp. XV:** 298
Hartman, Geoffrey, **Supp. IV Part 1:** 119; **Supp. XII:** 130, 253
Hartman, Saidiya, **Supp. XX: 154**
Harum, David, **II:** 102
"Harvard" (Lowell), **II:** 554
Harvard College in the Seventeenth Century (Morison), **Supp. I Part 2:** 485
"Harvest" (E. P. Jones), **Supp. XXII:** 141
"Harvest, The" (Hempel), **Supp. XXI:** 115, **122–123**
Harvester, The (Stratton-Porter), **Supp. XX: 211, 212, 218, 221**
"*Harvester, The:* The Natural Bounty of Gene Stratton-Porter" (Birkelo), **Supp. XX: 220–221**
"Harvesters of Night and Water" (Hogan), **Supp. IV Part 1:** 412
"Harvest Song" (Toomer), **Supp. III Part 2:** 483
Harvill Book of 20th Century Poetry in English, **Supp. X:** 55
"Harv Is Plowing Now" (Updike), **Retro. Supp. I:** 318
Haselden, Elizabeth Lee, **Supp. VIII:** 125
Haskell, Mary, **Supp. XX: 115, 117**
Hass, Robert, **Supp. VI: 97–111; Supp. VIII:** 24, 28; **Supp. XI:** 142, 270; **Supp. XIV:** 83, 84; **Supp. XXI:** 60
Hassam, Childe, **Retro. Supp. II:** 136
Hassan, Ihab, **IV:** 99–100, 115; **Supp. XI:** 221
Hasse, Henry, **Supp. IV Part 1:** 102
Hasty-Pudding, The (Barlow), **Supp. II Part 1:** 74, 77–80
"Hater of Mediocrity, The" (Boulton), **Supp. XXII:** 23
Hate That Hate Produced, The (CBS documentary), **Supp. XX: 102**
Hatful of Rain, A (Gazzo), **III:** 155
Hatlen, Burton, **Supp. V:** 138, 139–140; **Supp. XXI:** 24
"Hattie Bloom" (Oliver), **Supp. VII:** 232
Haunch, Paunch, and Jowl (Ornitz), **Supp. IX:** 227
"Haunted Landscape" (Ashbery), **Supp. III Part 1:** 22
Haunted Merchant, The (Briggs), **Supp. XVIII:** 2, 8
"Haunted Mind" (Simic), **Supp. VIII:** 282
"Haunted Mind, The" (Hawthorne), **II:** 230–231
"Haunted Oak, The" (Dunbar), **Supp. II Part 1:** 207, 208
"Haunted Palace, The" (Poe), **III:** 421
"Haunted Valley, The" (Bierce), **I:** 200
Haunting, The (film), **Supp. IX:** 125
Haunting of Hill House, The (Jackson), **Supp. IX:** 117, 121, 126
Hauptmann, Gerhart, **III:** 472
Haussmann, Sonja, **Supp. XIII:** 331, **Supp. XIII:** 347
"Havanna vanities come to dust in Miami" (Didion), **Supp. IV Part 1:** 210
Havel, Hippolyte, **Supp. XXI:** 4, 6
Haven, Cynthia, **Supp. XV:** 252, 264
Haven's End (Marquand), **III:** 55, 56, 63, 68
"Have You Ever Faked an Orgasm" (Peacock), **Supp. XIX:** 199
"Have You Ever Tried to Enter the Long Black Branches" (Oliver), **Supp. VII:** 247
"Having Been Interstellar" (Ammons), **Supp. VII:** 25
"Having It Out With Melancholy" (Kenyon), **Supp. VII:** 171
"Having Lost My Sons, I Confront the Wreckage of the Moon: Christmas, 1960" (Wright), **Supp. III Part 2:** 600
"Having Snow" (Schwartz), **Supp. II Part 2:** 652
"Hawaii, Washington, Vermont: A Frame for the Verse" (Taggard), **Supp. XXII:** 281–282
Hawaiian Hilltop (Taggard), **Supp. XXII:** 275
Hawai'i One Summer (Kingston), **Supp. V:** 157, 160, 166, 169–170
Haweis, Stephen, **Supp. XXII:** 157, 158, 159, 161, 163, 165
"Hawk, The" (Francis), **Supp. IX:** 81
Hawke, David Freeman, **Supp. I Part 2:** 511, 516
Hawkes, John, **I:** 113; **Retro. Supp. II:** 234; **Supp. III Part 1:** 2; **Supp. V:** 40; **Supp. IX:** 212; **Supp. XVII:** 183; **Supp. XXI:** 210
Hawkins, Gary, **Supp. XXI:** 35, 39
Hawkins, William, **II:** 587
Hawk in the Rain, The (Hughes), **Retro. Supp. II:** 244; **Supp. I Part 2:** 537, 540
Hawk Is Dying, The (Crews), **Supp. XI: 111**
Hawk Moon (Shepard), **Supp. III Part 2:** 445
Hawks, Howard, **Supp. IV Part 1:** 130; **Supp. XVIII:** 148
"Hawk's Cry in Autumn, The" (Brodsky), **Supp. VIII:** 29
"Hawk's Shadow" (Glück), **Supp. V:** 85
Hawk's Well, The (Yeats), **III:** 459–460
Hawley, Adelaide, **Supp. XIV:** 207
Hawley, Joseph, **I:** 546
Hawthorne (James), **II:** 372–378; **Retro. Supp. I:** 220, **223–224**
"Hawthorne" (Longfellow), **Retro. Supp. II:** 169
"Hawthorne" (Lowell), **II:** 550
Hawthorne, Julian, **II:** 225; **Supp. I Part 1:** 38; **Supp. XV:** 274
Hawthorne, Nathaniel, **I:** 106, 204, 211, 340, 355, 363, 384, 413, 458, 561–562; **II:** 7, 8, 40, 60, 63, 74, 89, 127–128, 138, 142, 198, **223–246,** 255, 259, 264, 267, 272, 274, 277, 281, 282, 295, 307, 309, 311, 313, 322, 324, 326, 402, 408, 446, 501, 545; **III:** 51, 81–82, 83, 84, 85, 87, 88, 91, 92, 113, 316, 359, 412, 415, 421, 438, 453, 454, 507, 565, 572; **IV:** 2, 4, 167, 172, 179, 194, 333, 345, 453; **Retro. Supp. I:** 1, 53, 59, 62, 63, 91, **145–167,** 215, 218, 220, 223, 248–249, 252, 257, 258, 330, 331, 365; **Retro. Supp. II:** 136, 142, 153, 156–157, 158, 159, 187, 221; **Supp. I Part 1:** 38, 188, 197, 317, 372; **Supp. I Part 2:** 420, 421, 545, 579, 580, 582, 587,

595, 596; **Supp. III Part 2:** 501; **Supp. IV Part 1:** 80, 127, 297; **Supp. IV Part 2:** 463, 596; **Supp. V:** 152; **Supp. VIII:** 103, 105, 108, 153, 201; **Supp. IX:** 114; **Supp. X:** 78; **Supp. XI:** 51, 78; **Supp. XII:** 26; **Supp. XIII:** 102; **Supp. XIV:** 48; **Supp. XV:** 269, 272, 282; **Supp. XVI:** 83, 84, 157; **Supp. XVII:** 42; **Supp. XVIII:** 258, 260; **Supp. XXI:** 201

Hawthorne, Mrs. Nathaniel (Sophia Peabody), **II:** 224, 244; **III:** 75, 86

Hawthorne, Rose, **II:** 225

Hawthorne, Una, **II:** 225

"Hawthorne and His Mosses" (Melville), **Retro. Supp. I:** 254; **Supp. XIV:** 48

"Hawthorne Aspect [of Henry James], The" (Eliot), **Retro. Supp. I:** 63

"Hawthorne in Solitude" (Cowley), **Supp. II Part 1:** 143

Hay, John, **I:** 1, 10, 12, 14–15; **Supp. I Part 1:** 352

Hay, Mrs. John, **I:** 14

Hay, Sara Henderson, **Supp. XIV: 119–135**

Hayakawa, S. I., **I:** 448; **Supp. I Part 1:** 315; **Supp. XV:** 176

Hayden, Robert, **Supp. II Part 1: 361–383; Supp. IV Part 1:** 169; **Supp. XIII:** 115, 127; **Supp. XIV:** 119, 123

Hayden, Sterling, **Supp. XI:** 304

Haydn, Hiram, **IV:** 100, 358

Hayduke Lives! (Abbey), **Supp. XIII: 16**

Hayek, Friedrich A. von, **Supp. IV Part 2:** 524

Hayes, Helen, **Supp. XVI:** 193, 195

Hayes, Ira, **Supp. IV Part 1:** 326

Hayes, Richard, **Supp. V:** 320

Hayes, Rutherford B., **Supp. I Part 2:** 419

Hayford, James, **Supp. XXII:** 204, 218

Haygood, Wil, **Supp. VIII:** 79

"Haying While the Sun Shines" (L. I. Wilder), **Supp. XXII:** 290

Hayne, Paul Hamilton, **Supp. I Part 1:** 352, 354, 355, 360, 372

Haynes, Todd, **Supp. XVIII:** 23

Haynes-Smith, William, **Supp. XX: 231, 232, 233**

Hayward, Florence, **Retro. Supp. II:** 65

Hayward, John, **Retro. Supp. I:** 67

Hayward, Leland, **Supp. XIX:** 250

Haywood, "Big" Bill, **I:** 483; **Supp. V:** 286

Hazard, Grace, **II:** 530

Hazard of Fortunes, A (Howells), **Retro. Supp. II:** 288

Hazard of New Fortunes, A (Howells), **II:** 275, 276, 286–297, 290

Hazel, Robert, **Supp. VIII:** 137, 138

Hazen, General W. B., **I:** 192, 193

Hazlitt, Henry, **Supp. IV Part 2:** 524

Hazlitt, William, **I:** 58, 378; **II:** 315; **Supp. XXI:** 205

Hazmat (McClatchy), **Supp. XII: 265–270**

Hazo, Samuel, **I:** 386; **Supp. XIV:** 123, 124

Hazzard, Shirley, **Supp. VIII:** 151

H.D. *See* Doolittle, Hilda

"He" (Porter), **III:** 434, 435

"Head and Shoulders" (Fitzgerald), **Retro. Supp. I:** 101

Headhunter (Findley), **Supp. XX: 57–59, 60, 61**

"Head-Hunter, The" (O. Henry), **Supp. II Part 1:** 403

"Headless Hawk, The" (Capote), **Supp. III Part 1:** 124

Headlines (T. Williams), **IV:** 381

Headlong Hall (Peacock), **Supp. I Part 1:** 307

Headmaster, The (McPhee), **Supp. III Part 1:** 291, 294, 298

"Head of Joaquín Murrieta, The" (Rodriguez), **Supp. XIV:** 303

Headsman, The (Cooper), **I:** 345–346

Heads of Grain (al-Sanábil) (Gibran), **Supp. XX: 124**

"Headwaters" (Momaday), **Supp. IV Part 2:** 486

"Head Wound" (Halliday), **Supp. XIX:** 92

Healy, Eloise Klein, **Supp. XI:** 121, 124, 126, 127, 129, 137

Healy, Tim, **II:** 129, 137

Heaney, Sally, **Supp. XVII:** 241

Heaney, Seamus, **Retro. Supp. II:** 245; **Supp. IX:** 41, 42; **Supp. X:** 67, 122; **Supp. XI:** 249; **Supp. XV:** 256; **Supp. XXI:** 54, 243

"Heard through the Walls of the Race-track Glen Motel" (X. J. Kennedy), **Supp. XV:** 170

Hearn, Lafcadio, **I:** 211; **II:** 311

Hearon, Shelby, **Supp. VIII: 57–72**

Hearst, Patty, **Supp. IV Part 1:** 195

Hearst, William Randolph, **I:** 198, 207, 208; **IV:** 298

Heart and Perimeter (Bierds), **Supp. XVII: 28–29**

"Heart and the Lyre, The" (Bogan), **Supp. III Part 1:** 65

"Heartbeat" (Harjo), **Supp. XII:** 221–222

Heartbreak Hotel (Siddons), **Supp. XXII:** 239, 241, 242

Heartbreak Kid, The (film), **Supp. IV Part 2:** 575, 589

Heart for the Gods of Mexico, A (Aiken), **I:** 54

"Hear the Nightingale Sing" (Gordon), **II:** 200

Hear the Wind Blow (Sanders), **Supp. XVI:** 268

Heart is a Lonely Hunter, The (McCullers), **II:** 586, 588–593, 604, 605

Heart of a Woman, The (Angelou), **Supp. IV Part 1:** 2, 5, 7–9, 9, 14, 17

Heart of Darkness (Conrad), **Retro. Supp. II:** 292; **Supp. V:** 249, 311; **Supp. VIII:** 4, 316; **Supp. XIX:** 28; **Supp. XX: 18, 57–58**

"Heart of Darkness" (Conrad), **I:** 575, 578; **II:** 595; **Supp. XVI:** 212

Heart of Darkness (Didion), **Supp. IV Part 1:** 207

Heart of Dixie (film), **Supp. XXII:** 239, 241

Heart of Happy Hollow, The (Dunbar), **Supp. II Part 1:** 214

Heart of Knowledge, The: American Indians on the Bomb (Gunn Allen and Caputi, eds.), **Supp. IV Part 1:** 334–335

"Heart of Knowledge, The: Nuclear Themes in Native American Thought and Literature" (Caputi), **Supp. IV Part 1:** 335

"Heart of the Park, The " (O'Connor), **Retro. Supp. II:** 225

Heart of the West (O. Henry), **Supp. II Part 1:** 410

"Hearts, The" (Pinsky), **Supp. VI:** 245–247, 248

"'Hearts and Flowers' " (MacLeish), **III:** 8

"Hearts and Heads" (Ransom), **Supp. I Part 1:** 373

"Heart's Graveyard Shift, The" (Komunyakaa), **Supp. XIII:** 120

Heart-Shape in the Dust (Hayden), **Supp. II Part 1:** 365, 366

Heart's Needle (Snodgrass), **I:** 400

"Heart's Needle" (Snodgrass), **Supp. VI: 311–313,** 320

"Hearts of Oak" (Rowson), **Supp. XV:** 243

"Heart Songs" (Proulx), **Supp. VII:** 254

Heart Songs and Other Stories (Proulx), **Supp. VII:** 252–256, 261

Heart to Artemis, The (Bryher), **Supp. I Part 1:** 259

Heartwood (Burke), **Supp. XIV:** 35

Heath, Shirley, **Supp. XX: 90**

Heath Anthology of American Literature, The, **Supp. IX:** 4; **Supp. XV:** 270, 313

Heathcote, Anne. *See* De Lancey, Mrs. James

"Heathen Chinee, The" (Harte), **Supp. II Part 1:** 350–351, 352

Heathen Days, 1890–1936 (Mencken), **III:** 100, 111

Heath-Stubbs, John, **Supp. XV:** 153

Heat's On, The (C. Himes), **Supp. XVI:** 143, 144

"Heaven" (Dunn), **Supp. XI:** 154

"Heaven" (Levine), **Supp. V:** 182

"Heaven" (Patchett), **Supp. XII:** 309

Heaven and Earth: A Cosmology (Goldbarth), **Supp. XII: 187**

"Heaven and Earth in Jest" (Dillard), **Supp. VI:** 24, 28

"Heaven as Anus" (Kumin), **Supp. IV Part 2:** 448

Heavenly Conversation, The (Mather), **Supp. II Part 2:** 460

"Heavenly Feast, The" (Schnackenberg), **Supp. XV:** 257, 259

Heavens (Untermeyer), **Supp. XV:** 306

Heavens and Earth (Benét), **Supp. XI:** 44

Heaven's Coast (Doty), **Supp. XI:** 119, 121, **129–130,** 134

Heaven's Prisoners (Burke), **Supp. XIV:** 23, 29

"Heavy Angel, The" (Everwine), **Supp. XV:** 80

"Heavy Bear Who Goes with Me, The" (Schwartz), **Supp. II Part 2:** 646
"Heavy Trash" (Halliday), **Supp. XIX:** 92, 93
Hebert, Ernest, **Supp. XXII:** 207
"He Came Also Still" (Zukofsky), **Supp. III Part 2:** 612
Hecht, Anthony, **IV:** 138; **Supp. III Part 2:** 541, 561; **Supp. X: 55–75; Supp. XII:** 269–270; **Supp. XV:** 251, 256
Hecht, Ben, **I:** 103; **II:** 42; **Supp. I Part 2:** 646; **Supp. XI:** 307; **Supp. XIII:** 106
Hecht, S. Theodore, **Supp. III Part 2:** 614
Heckewelder, John, **II:** 503
"Hedge Island" (Lowell), **II:** 524
Hedges, William I., **II:** 311–312
"He 'Digesteth Harde Yron' " (Moore), **Supp. IV Part 2:** 454
Hedin, Robert, **Supp. XII:** 200, 202
Hedylus (Doolittle), **Supp. I Part 1:** 259, 270
"Heel & Toe To the End" (W. C. Williams), **Retro. Supp. I:** 430
Heffernan, Michael, **Supp. XII:** 177
"HEGEL" (Baraka), **Supp. II Part 1:** 53
Hegel, Georg Wilhelm Friedrich, **I:** 265; **II:** 358; **III:** 262, 308–309, 480, 481, 487, 607; **IV:** 86, 333, 453; **Supp. I Part 2:** 633, 635, 640, 645; **Supp. XVI:** 289
"Hegemony of Race, The" (Du Bois), **Supp. II Part 1:** 181
Hegger, Grace Livingston. *See* Lewis, Mrs. Sinclair (Grace Livingston Hegger)
"He Had Spent His Youth Dreaming" (Dobyns), **Supp. XIII:** 90
Heidegger, Martin, **II:** 362, 363; **III:** 292; **IV:** 491; **Retro. Supp. II:** 87; **Supp. V:** 267; **Supp. VIII:** 9; **Supp. XVI:** 283, 288
Heidenmauer, The (Cooper), **I:** 345–346
Heidi Chronicles, The (Wasserstein), **Supp. IV Part 1:** 309; **Supp. XV:** 319, **325–327**
"Height of the Ridiculous, The" (Holmes), **Supp. I Part 1:** 302
Heilbroner, Robert, **Supp. I Part 2:** 644, 648, 650
Heilbrun, Carolyn G., **Supp. IX:** 66; **Supp. XI:** 208; **Supp. XIV:** 161, 163; **Supp. XX: 108**
Heilman, Robert Bechtold, **Supp. XIV:** 11, 12
Heilpern, John, **Supp. XIV:** 242
Heim, Michael, **Supp. V:** 209
Heine, Heinrich, **II:** 272, 273, 277, 281, 282, 387, 544; **IV:** 5; **Supp. XV:** 293, 299; **Supp. XVI:** 188
Heineman, Frank, **Supp. III Part 2:** 619
Heinemann, Larry, **Supp. XXII: 103–117**
Heinlein, Robert, **Supp. IV Part 1:** 102; **Supp. XVI:** 122; **Supp. XVIII:** 149
Heinz, Helen. *See* Tate, Mrs. Allen (Helen Heinz)
Heiress, The (film), **Retro. Supp. I:** 222
"Heirs" (Nye), **Supp. XIII:** 284
"He Is Not Worth the Trouble" (Rowson), **Supp. XV:** 240
"He Knew" (C. Himes), **Supp. XVI:** 137
"Helas" (Creeley), **Supp. IV Part 1:** 150, 158
Helburn, Theresa, **IV:** 381
Heldreth, Leonard, **Supp. V:** 151
"Helen" (Lowell), **II:** 544
"Helen, Thy Beauty Is to Me" (Fante), **Supp. XI:** 169
"Helen: A Courtship" (Faulkner), **Retro. Supp. I:** 81
"Helen I Love You" (Farrell), **II:** 28, 45
Helen in Egypt (Doolittle), **Supp. I Part 1:** 260, 272, 273, 274; **Supp. XV:** 264
Helen Keller: Sketch for a Portrait (Brooks), **I:** 254
"Helen of Tyre" (Longfellow), **II:** 496
Heliodora (Doolittle), **Supp. I Part 1:** 266
"He Lives On the Landing" (Espaillat), **Supp. XXI:** 108
"Helix" (Sobin), **Supp. XVI:** 283
Hellbox (O'Hara), **III:** 361
Heller, Joseph, **III:** 2, 258; **IV:** 98; **Retro. Supp. II:** 324; **Supp. I Part 1:** 196; **Supp. IV Part 1: 379–396; Supp. V:** 244; **Supp. VIII:** 245; **Supp. XI:** 307; **Supp. XII:** 167–168; **Supp. XV:** 322; **Supp. XVII:** 139
"Hell-Heaven" (Lahiri), **Supp. XXI: 181–183,** 183, 184–186, 188
Hellman, Lillian, **I:** 28; **III:** 28; **Supp. I Part 1: 276–298; Supp. IV Part 1:** 1, 12, 83, 353, 355, 356; **Supp. VIII:** 243; **Supp. IX:** 196, 198, 200–201, 204
Hellmann, Lillian, **Retro. Supp. II:** 327
Hello (Creeley), **Supp. IV Part 1:** 155, 157
"Hello, Hello Henry" (Kumin), **Supp. IV Part 2:** 446
"Hello, Stranger" (Capote), **Supp. III Part 1:** 120
Hello Dolly! (musical play), **IV:** 357
Hellyer, John, **Supp. I Part 2:** 468
Helm, Bob, **Supp. XV:** 147
Helm, Levon, **Supp. XVIII:** 26
Helmets (Dickey), **Supp. IV Part 1:** 175, 178, 180
"Helmsman, The" (Doolittle), **Supp. I Part 1:** 266
"Help" (Barth), **I:** 139
"Help Her to Believe" (Olsen). *See* "I Stand There Ironing" (Olsen)
Helprin, Mark, **Supp. XIX:** 142
"Helsinki Window" (Creeley), **Supp. IV Part 1:** 158
"Hema and Kaushik" (Lahiri), **Supp. XXI:** 183, 188
Hemenway, Robert E., **Supp. IV Part 1:** 6
Hemingway, Dr. Clarence Edwards, **II:** 248, 259
Hemingway, Ernest, **I:** 28, 64, 97, 99, 105, 107, 117, 150, 162, 190, 211, 221, 288, 289, 295, 367, 374, 378, 421, 423, 445, 476, 477, 478, 482, 484–485, 487, 488, 489, 491, 495, 504, 517; **II:** 27, 44, 51, 58, 68–69, 78, 90, 97, 127, 206, **247–270,** 289, 424, 431, 456, 457, 458–459, 482, 560, 600; **III:** 2, 18, 20, 35, 36, 37, 40, 61, 108, 220, 334, 363, 364, 382, 453, 454, 471–472, 476, 551, 575, 576, 584; **IV:** 27, 28, 33, 34, 35, 42, 49, 97, 108, 122, 126, 138, 190, 191, 201, 216, 217, 257, 297, 363, 404, 427, 433, 451; **Retro. Supp. I:** 74, 98, 108, 111, 112, 113, 115, **169–191,** 215, 292, 359, 418; **Retro. Supp. II:** 19, 24, 30, 68, 115, 123; **Supp. I Part 2:** 621, 658, 678; **Supp. II Part 1:** 221; **Supp. III Part 1:** 146; **Supp. III Part 2:** 617; **Supp. IV Part 1:** 48, 102, 123, 197, 236, 342, 343, 344, 348, 350, 352, 380–381, 383; **Supp. IV Part 2:** 463, 468, 502, 607, 679, 680, 681, 689, 692; **Supp. V:** 237, 240, 244, 250, 336; **Supp. VIII:** 40, 101, 105, 179, 182, 183, 188, 189, 196; **Supp. IX:** 16, 57, 58, 94, 106, 260, 262; **Supp. X:** 137, 167, 223, 225; **Supp. XI:** 214, 221; **Supp. XIII:** 96, 255, 270; **Supp. XIV:** 24, 83; **Supp. XV:** 69, 135; **Supp. XVI:** 203, 205–206, 208, 210, 233, 236–237, 281–282; **Supp. XVII:** 4, 105, 107, 137, 228, 229; **Supp. XVIII:** 74, 90, 102; **Supp. XIX:** 131, 154, 157, 246; **Supp. XX: 45, 74, 76; Supp. XXI:** 7, 8, 36, 262
Hemingway, Mrs. Ernest (Hadley Richardson), **II:** 257, 260, 263
Hemingway, Mrs. Ernest (Martha Gellhorn), **II:** 260
Hemingway, Mrs. Ernest (Mary Welsh), **II:** 257, 260
Hemingway, Mrs. Ernest (Pauline Pfeiffer), **II:** 260
"Hemingway in Paris" (Cowley), **Supp. II Part 1:** 144
"Hemingway Story, A" (Dubus), **Supp. VII:** 91
"Hemingway: The Old Lion" (Cowley), **Supp. II Part 1:** 143
"Hemp, The" (Benét), **Supp. XI:** 44
Hempel, Amy, **Supp. XIX:** 209; **Supp. XXI: 115–128**
"Henchman, The" (Whittier), **Supp. I Part 2:** 696
Henderson, Alice Corbin, **Supp. I Part 2:** 387; **Supp. XV:** 302–303
Henderson, Darwin L., **Supp. XIII:** 213, 221–222
Henderson, Jane, **Supp. VIII:** 87; **Supp. XX: 84**
Henderson, Katherine, **Supp. IV Part 1:** 203, 207
Henderson, Linda. *See* Hogan, Linda
Henderson, Robert W., **Supp. VIII:** 124
Henderson, Stephen, **Supp. IV Part 1:** 365
Henderson, the Rain King (Bellow), **I:** 144, 147, 148, 152, 153, 154, 155, 158, 160, 161, 162–163; **Retro. Supp. II:** 19, **24–25,** 30
"Hen Flower, The" (Kinnell), **Supp. III Part 1:** 247–248
Henie, Sonja, **Supp. XII:** 165

Henkin, Joshua, **Supp. XXII:** 216
Henle, James, **II:** 26, 30, 38, 41; **Supp. IX:** 2
Henley, Beth, **Supp. XXI:** 145
Hennesy, Dale, **Supp. XV:** 5
Henninger, Katherine, **Supp. XXI:** 253
Henri, Robert, **IV:** 411; **Supp. I Part 2:** 376
Henry, Arthur, **I:** 515; **Retro. Supp. II:** 97
Henry, DeWitt, **Supp. XI:** 342
Henry, O., **I:** 201; **III:** 5; **Supp. I Part 2:** 390, 462; **Supp. II Part 1: 385–412; Supp. XV:** 40
Henry, Robert, **Retro. Supp. II:** 103
Henry, William A., III, **Supp. IV Part 2:** 574
Henry and Clara (Mallon), **Supp. XIX:** 132, **136–137,** 139, 141
Henry and June (film), **Supp. X:** 186
Henry and June: From the Unexpurgated Diary of Anaïs Nin, **Supp. X:** 184, 185, 187, 194
Henry Holt and Company, **Retro. Supp. I:** 121, 131, 133, 136
Henry IV (Shakespeare), **III:** 166; **Supp. VIII:** 164
"Henry James, Jr." (Howells), **II:** 289; **Retro. Supp. I:** 220
"Henry James and the Art of Teaching" (Rowe), **Retro. Supp. I:** 216
"Henry Manley, Living Alone, Keeps Time" (Kumin), **Supp. IV Part 2:** 451
"Henry Manley Looks Back" (Kumin), **Supp. IV Part 2:** 451
"Henry Manley" poems (Kumin), **Supp. IV Part 2:** 446
Henry Miller Reader, The (Durrell, ed.), **III:** 175, 190
"Henry's Confession" (Berryman), **I:** 186
Henry VIII (Shakespeare), **Supp. IX:** 235
Henslee, **Supp. IV Part 1:** 217
Henson, Josiah, **Supp. I Part 2:** 589
Hentoff, Margot, **Supp. IV Part 1:** 205
Hentz, Caroline Lee, **Supp. I Part 2:** 584
Henze, Hans Werner, **Supp. II Part 1:** 24
"He of the Assembly" (Bowles), **Supp. IV Part 1:** 90
Hepburn, Katharine, **Supp. IX:** 189; **Supp. XI:** 17
Heraclitus, **II:** 1, 163; **IV:** 86
Herakles: A Play in Verse (MacLeish), **III:** 21, 22
Herald of the Autochthonic Spirit (Corso), **Supp. XII:** 134–136
He Ran All the Way (film), **Supp. XVII:** 63
Herberg, Will, **III:** 291
Herbert, Edward, **II:** 11
Herbert, Francis (pseudonym). *See* Bryant, William Cullen
Herbert, George, **II:** 12; **IV:** 141, 145, 146, 151, 153, 156, 165; **Retro. Supp. II:** 40; **Supp. I Part 1:** 80, 107, 108, 122; **Supp. IV Part 2:** 646; **Supp. XV:** 92, 212, 251; **Supp. XXI:** 109
Herbert, Zbigniew, **Supp. VIII:** 20
Herbert Huncke Reader, The (Schafer, ed.), **Supp. XIV:** 137, 138, 139, 140, 145, 147, 150, 151–152
Herbert of Cherbury, Lord, **II:** 108
"Herbert White" (Bidart), **Supp. XV:** 24, 27
Herbst, Josephine, **Retro. Supp. II:** 325, 328; **Supp. XIII:** 295
"Her Choice" (Larcom), **Supp. XIII:** 144
"Her Dead Brother" (Lowell), **Retro. Supp. II:** 188
"Her Dream Is of the Sea" (Ríos), **Supp. IV Part 2:** 546
"Here" (Kenyon), **Supp. VII:** 164
Here and Beyond (Wharton), **Retro. Supp. I:** 382
Here and Now (Levertov), **Supp. III Part 1:** 275, 276
"Here and There" (Wallace), **Supp. X:** 305–306
Here Comes the Mystery Man (Sanders), **Supp. XVI:** 269
Heredia, Juanita, **Supp. XI:** 185, 190
Heredity and Variation (Lock), **Retro. Supp. I:** 375
Heredity: A Psychological Study of Its Phenomena, Laws, Causes, and Consequences (Ribot), **Supp. XX: 238**
"Here Inside My Forehead" (Rasmussen; Nelson and Espeland, trans.), **Supp. XVIII:** 180
Here is Your War (Pyle), **Supp. XVII:** 61
Here Let Us Feast (M. F. K. Fisher), **Supp. XVII:** 86, 87
Here Lies (Parker), **Supp. IX:** 192
Herendeen, Anne, **Supp. XXII:** 275
Here on Earth (Hoffman), **Supp. X:** 77, 89
Heresy and the Ideal: On Contemporary Poetry (Baker), **Supp. XI:** 142
"Here to Learn" (Bowles), **Supp. IV Part 1:** 93
"Here to Yonder" (Hughes), **Retro. Supp. I:** 205
"Her Father's Letters" (Milburn), **Supp. XI:** 242
"Her Favorite Story" (Richard), **Supp. XIX:** 211, 212
Herford, Reverend Brooke, **I:** 471
Herford, Will, **Supp. XXII:** 275
"Her Game" (Skloot), **Supp. XX: 196, 202**
Hergesheimer, Joseph, **Supp. I Part 2:** 620; **Supp. XVI:** 187
"Heritage" (Cullen), **Supp. IV Part 1:** 164–165, 168, 170, 171
"Heritage" (Hogan), **Supp. IV Part 1:** 413
"Her Kind" (Sexton), **Supp. II Part 2:** 687
Herland (Gilman), **Supp. XI:** 208–209
Herman, Florence. *See* Williams, Mrs. William Carlos (Florence Herman)
Herman, Jan, **Supp. XIV:** 150–151
Herman, William (pseudonym). *See* Bierce, Ambrose
"Her Management" (Swenson), **Supp. IV Part 2:** 642
"Herman Melville" (Auden), **Supp. II Part 1:** 14
Herman Melville (Mumford), **Supp. II Part 2:** 471, 476, 489–491
"Hermes of the Ways" (Doolittle), **Supp. I Part 1:** 266
"Hermes: Port Authority: His Song" (Di Piero), **Supp. XIX:** 47
Hermetic Definition (Doolittle), **Supp. I Part 1:** 271, 272, 273, 274
"Hermitage, The" (Haines), **Supp. XII:** 205–206
Hermit and the Wild Woman, The (Wharton), **IV:** 315; **Retro. Supp. I:** 371
"Hermit and the Wild Woman, The" (Wharton), **Retro. Supp. I:** 372
"Hermit Meets the Skunk, The" (Kumin), **Supp. IV Part 2:** 447
Hermit of 69th Street, The: The Working Papers or Norbert Kosky (Kosinski), **Supp. VII:** 215, 216, 223, 226–227
"Hermit of Saba, The" (Freneau), **Supp. II Part 1:** 259
"Hermit Picks Berries, The" (Kumin), **Supp. IV Part 2:** 447
Hermit's Story, The (Bass), **Supp. XVI:** 23–24
"Hermit Thrush, A" (Clampitt), **Supp. IX:** 40
Hernández, Miguel, **Supp. V:** 194; **Supp. XIII:** 315, 323; **Supp. XXI:** 104
Herne, James A., **II:** 276; **Supp. II Part 1:** 198
Hernton, Calvin, **Supp. X:** 240
"Hero, The" (Moore), **III:** 200, 211, 212
Hero, The: A Study in Tradition, Myth, and Drama (Raglan), **I:** 135; **Supp. XIX:** 147
Hero and the Blues, The (Murray), **Supp. XIX:** 153, 154
Hérodiade (Mallarmé), **I:** 66
Herodotus, **Supp. I Part 2:** 405
Heroes, The (Ashbery), **Supp. III Part 1:** 3
Hero in America, The (Van Doren), **II:** 103
"Heroines of Nature: Four Women Respond to the American Landscape" (Norwood), **Supp. IX:** 24
"Heron, The" (Roethke), **III:** 540–541
"Her One Bad Eye" (Karr), **Supp. XI:** 244
"Her Own People" (Warren), **IV:** 253
Her Place in These Designs (Espaillat), **Supp. XXI:** 99, 104
"Her Quaint Honour" (Gordon), **II:** 196, 199, 200
Herr, Michael, **Supp. XI:** 245; **Supp. XIX:** 17
Herreshoff, David, **Supp. XIX:** 265
Herrick, Robert, **II:** 11, 18, 444; **III:** 463, 592; **IV:** 453; **Retro. Supp. I:** 319; **Retro. Supp. II:** 101; **Supp. I Part 2:** 646; **Supp. XIII:** 334; **Supp. XIV:** 8, 9; **Supp. XV:** 155; **Supp. XXI:** 14
Herrmann, John, **Retro. Supp. II:** 328; **Supp. XXII:** 277
Herron, George, **Supp. I Part 1:** 7
"Hers" (column, Prose), **Supp. XVI:** 254
Herschdorfer, Helen, **Supp. XXI:** 262
Herschel, Sir John, **Supp. I Part 1:** 314

"Her Sense of Timing" (Elkin), **Supp. VI:** 56, 58

Hersey, John, **IV:** 4; **Supp. I Part 1:** 196; **Supp. XVI:** 105–106; **Supp. XX: 251**

"Her Sweet turn to leave the Homestead" (Dickinson), **Retro. Supp. I:** 44

Herzog (Bellow), **I:** 144, 147, 149, 150, 152, 153, 154, 155, 156, 157, 158, 159–160; **Retro. Supp. II:** 19, **26–27; Supp. IV Part 1:** 30; **Supp. XIX:** 157

Herzog, Tobey C., **Supp. XXII:** 116

Heschel, Abraham, **Supp. XXI:** 110, 112

Hesford, Walter A., **Supp. XV:** 215, 217, 218

"He/She" (Dunn), **Supp. XI:** 149

"Hesitation Blues" (Hughes), **Retro. Supp. I:** 211

He Sleeps (McKnight), **Supp. XX: 151, 152–155, 158**

"He Sleeps" (McKnight), **Supp. XX: 152, 155**

Hesse, Hermann, **Supp. V:** 208

Hester, Carolyn, **Supp. XVIII:** 24

"Hetch Hetchy Valley" (Muir), **Supp. IX:** 185

He Who Gets Slapped (Andreyev), **II:** 425

"He Who Spits at the Sky" (Stegner), **Supp. IV Part 2:** 605

"He Will Not Leave a Note" (Ríos), **Supp. IV Part 2:** 548

Hewitt, James, **Supp. XV:** 240

Hewlett, Maurice, **I:** 359

Heyen, William, **Supp. XIII:** 285, 344; **Supp. XV:** 212

"Hey! Hey!" (Hughes), **Supp. I Part 1:** 327–328

Hey Rub-a-Dub-Dub (Dreiser), **I:** 515; **II:** 26; **Retro. Supp. II:** 104, 105, 108

"Hey Sailor, What Ship?" (Olsen), **Supp. XIII:** 293, 294, 298, **299**

Heyward, DuBose, **Supp. XVIII:** 281; **Supp. XIX:** 78

Hiawatha (Longfellow), **Supp. I Part 1:** 79; **Supp. III Part 2:** 609, 610; **Supp. XXI:** 53

"Hibernaculum" (Ammons), **Supp. VII:** 26–27

Hichborn, Philip, **Supp. I Part 2:** 707, 708

Hichborn, Mrs. Philip. *See* Wylie, Elinor

"Hic Jacet" (W. C. Williams), **Retro. Supp. I:** 414

Hickok, Guy, **Supp. XXI:** 7

Hickok, James Butler ("Wild Bill"), **Supp. V:** 229, 230

Hicks, Granville, **I:** 254, 259, 374; **II:** 26; **III:** 342, 355, 452; **Supp. I Part 1:** 361; **Supp. I Part 2:** 609; **Supp. IV Part 1:** 22; **Supp. IV Part 2:** 526; **Supp. VIII:** 96, 124; **Supp. XII:** 250; **Supp. XIII:** 263; **Supp. XXI:** 276; **Supp. XXII:** 279

Hicks, Sally, **Supp. XXI:** 255

Hicok, Bethany, **Retro. Supp. II:** 39

"Hidden" (Nye), **Supp. XIII:** 283

"Hidden Gardens" (Capote), **Supp. III Part 1:** 125

Hidden Law, The (Hecht), **Supp. X:** 58

"Hidden Name and Complex Fate" (Ellison), **Supp. II Part 1:** 245

Hidden Wound, The (Berry), **Supp. X:** 23, 25, 26–27, 29, 34, 35

"Hide-and-Seek" (Francis), **Supp. IX:** 81

"Hiding" (Minot), **Supp. VI:** 203, 206

Hiding Place (Wideman), **Supp. X:** 320, 321, 327, 329, 331–332, 333

"Hidin' Out in Honky Heaven: On Race Relations in Vermont" (Budbill), **Supp. XIX:** 5

Hienger, Jorg, **Supp. IV Part 1:** 106

Hieronymus Bosch (De Tolnay), **Supp. XXII:** 255

Higgins, George, **Supp. IV Part 1:** 356

Higginson, Thomas Wentworth, **I:** 451–452, 453, 454, 456, 458, 459, 463, 464, 465, 470; **Retro. Supp. I:** 26, 31, 33, 35, 39, 40; **Supp. I Part 1:** 307, 371; **Supp. IV Part 2:** 430

Higgs, Robert, **Supp. XX: 166**

"High Bridge above the Tagus River at Toledo, The" (W. C. Williams), **Retro. Supp. I:** 429

"High Dive: A Variant" (Kumin), **Supp. IV Part 2:** 442

"High Diver" (Francis), **Supp. IX:** 82

"Higher Keys, The" (Merrill), **Supp. III Part 1:** 335–336

Higher Learning in America, The (Veblen), **Supp. I Part 2:** 630, 631, 641, 642

Highet, Gilbert, **Supp. I Part 1:** 268

High Noon (film), **Supp. V:** 46

"High on Sadness" (Komunyakaa), **Supp. XIII:** 114

"High School Senior" (Olds), **Supp. X:** 212

Highsmith, Patricia, **Supp. IV Part 1:** 79, 94, 132; **Supp. XXII:** 136

"High Tide" (Marquand), **III:** 56

High Tide in Tucson: Essays from Now or Never (Kingsolver), **Supp. VII:** 198, 201, 209

"High-Toned Old Christian Woman, A" (Stevens), **Retro. Supp. I:** 301

"High Water" (Mosher), **Supp. XXII:** 205, 211

"Highway, The" (Merwin), **Supp. III Part 1:** 346

Highway 61 Revisited (album, Dylan), **Supp. XVIII:** 20, 27, 30, 32

"Highway 61 Revisited" (song, Dylan), **Supp. XVIII:** 30

"Highway 99E from Chico" (Carver), **Supp. III Part 1:** 136

"Highway Apple Trees" (Espaillat), **Supp. XXI: 100–102**

High Window, The (Chandler), **Supp. IV Part 1:** 127–129, 130, 131

"High Yaller" (R. Fisher), **Supp. XIX:** 72

Hijuelos, Oscar, **Supp. IV Part 1:** 54; **Supp. VIII: 73–91**

Hike and the Aeroplane (Lewis), **II:** 440–441

Hilberg, Raul, **Supp. V:** 267

Hildebrand, Al, **III:** 118

Hiler, Hilaire, **Retro. Supp. II:** 327; **Supp. III Part 2:** 617

"Hill, A" (Hecht), **Supp. X:** 59–60, 63

Hill, Abram, **Supp. XV:** 194

Hill, Anita, **Supp. XX: 110**

Hill, Hamlin, **Retro. Supp. II:** 286

Hill, James J., **Supp. I Part 2:** 644

Hill, Joe, **I:** 493; **Supp. XVIII:** 224

Hill, Lee, **Supp. XI:** 293, 294, 297, 299, 301, 305, 307

Hill, Pamela Smith, **Supp. XXII:** 295

Hill, Patti, **I:** 289

Hill, Peggy, **Supp. XIII:** 163

"Hill, The" (Strand), **Supp. IV Part 2:** 627

"Hill, The" (Toomer), **Supp. III Part 2:** 486

Hill, Vernon, **Supp. I Part 2:** 397

"Hillcrest" (Robinson), **III:** 504

Hill-Lubin, Mildred A., **Supp. IV Part 1:** 13

Hillman, Sidney, **Supp. I Part 1:** 5

Hillringhouse, Mark, **Supp. IX:** 286, 288, 299

Hills Beyond, The (Wolfe), **IV:** 450, 451, 460, 461

"Hills Beyond, The" (Wolfe), **IV:** 460

Hillside and Seaside in Poetry (Larcom, ed.), **Supp. XIII:** 142

"Hillside Thaw, A" (Frost), **Retro. Supp. I:** 133

"Hills Like White Elephants" (Hemingway), **Retro. Supp. I:** 170

Hills of the Shatemuc, The (S. Warner), **Supp. XVIII:** 266

"Hill-Top View, A" (Jeffers), **Supp. II Part 2:** 417

Hill Towns (Siddons), **Supp. XXII:** 239, 253

"Hill Wife, The" (Frost), **II:** 154; **Retro. Supp. I:** 131

Hillyer, Catherine, **Supp. XV:** 244

Hillyer, Robert, **I:** 475; **Supp. IX:** 75; **Supp. XIV:** 11

Hilton, James, **Supp. XIII:** 166

"Hiltons' Holiday, The" (Jewett), **II:** 391; **Retro. Supp. II:** 134

Him (Cummings), **I:** 429, 434–435

Himes, Chester Bomar, **Retro. Supp. II:** 117; **Supp. I Part 1:** 51, 325; **Supp. XIII:** 233; **Supp. XVI: 135–146**

Himes, Norman, **Supp. V:** 128

"Him on a Bicycle" (Weigl), **Supp. XIX:** 276

"Him with His Foot in His Mouth" (Bellow), **Retro. Supp. II:** 34

Him with His Foot in His Mouth and Other Stories (Bellow), **Retro. Supp. II:** 31

Hinchman, Sandra K., **Supp. IV Part 1:** 210

Hinckley, David, **Supp. XXII:** 215

Hindemith, Paul, **IV:** 357; **Supp. IV Part 1:** 81

Hindsell, Oliver, **Supp. XIII:** 162

Hindus, Milton, **Supp. XIV:** 288, 291, 292, 293

Hines, Suzanne, **Supp. XIV:** 151

Hinge Picture (Howe), **Supp. IV Part 2:** 423–424

Hinojosa, Rolando, **Supp. XIX: 97–114**

"Hinterlands" (W. Gibson), **Supp. XVI:** 123, 128
"Hippies: Slouching towards Bethlehem" (Didion), **Supp. IV Part 1:** 200
Hippolytus (Euripides), **II:** 543; **Supp. I Part 1:** 270
Hippolytus Temporizes (Doolittle), **Supp. I Part 1:** 270
"Hips" (Cisneros), **Supp. VII:** 61, 62
"Hipster's Hipster" (Ginsberg), **Supp. XIV:** 141
Hirsch, Edward D., **Supp. V:** 177; **Supp. IX:** 262; **Supp. XIV:** 15; **Supp. XV:** 78, 225; **Supp. XVII:** 23; **Supp. XIX:** 202
Hirsch, Sidney, **Supp. XIV:** 1. *See* Mttron-Hirsch, Sidney
Hirschfeld, Jane, **Supp. XVII:** 241
Hirschorn, Clive, **Supp. IV Part 2:** 577, 579
Hirson, Roger, **Supp. XI:** 343
"His Bride of the Tomb" (Dunbar), **Supp. II Part 1:** 196
"His Chest of Drawers" (Anderson), **I:** 113, 114
"His Father's Whistle" (Wrigley), **Supp. XVIII:** 299
His First, Best Country (J. W. Miller), **Supp. XX: 163, 166, 172–175**
"His Last Day" (C. Himes), **Supp. XVI:** 137
"His Lover" (Dubus), **Supp. VII:** 86
"His Music" (Dunn), **Supp. XI:** 149
"His Own Key" (Ríos), **Supp. IV Part 2:** 543
His Picture in the Papers (film; Emerson), **Supp. XVI:** 185
His Religion and Hers (Gilman), **Supp. XI:** 209
Hiss, Alger, **Supp. XV:** 143
"Hiss, Chambers, and the Age of Innocence" (Fiedler), **Supp. XIII:** 99
"His Shield" (Moore), **III:** 211
"His Story" (Cisneros), **Supp. VII:** 67
His Thought Made Pockets & the Plane Buckt (Berryman), **I:** 170
"His Three Women" (Gioia), **Supp. XV:** 119–120
Histoire comparée des systèmes de philosophie (Gérando), **II:** 10
Historical and Moral View of the Origin and Progress of the French Revolution (Wollstonecraft), **Supp. I Part 1:** 126
"Historical Conceptualization" (Huizinga), **I:** 255
Historical Evidence and the Reading of Seventeenth-Century Poetry (Brooks), **Supp. XIV:** 11
"Historical Interpretation of Literature, The" (Wilson), **IV:** 431, 433, 445
Historical Jesus, The: The Life of a Mediterranean Jewish Peasant (Crossan), **Supp. V:** 251
"Historical Value of Crèvecoeur's *Voyage . . .," (Adams), Supp. I Part 1:* 251
"History" (Emerson), **II:** 13, 15
"History" (Hughes), **Supp. I Part 1:** 344
History (Lowell), **Retro. Supp. II:** 183, 190
"History" (Simic), **Supp. VIII:** 279
"History, Myth, and the Western Writer" (Stegner), **Supp. IV Part 2:** 596, 601
"History among the Rocks" (Warren), **IV:** 252
History as a Literary Art (Morison), **Supp. I Part 2:** 493
"History as Fate in E. L. Doctorow's Tale of a Western Town" (Arnold), **Supp. IV Part 1:** 220
"History Is the Memory of Time" (Olson), **Supp. II Part 2:** 574
"History Lesson" (Trethewey), **Supp. XXI:** 248, 249
"History Lessons" (Komunyakaa), **Supp. XIII:** 126
History Man, The (Bradbury), **Supp. XVIII:** 140
"History of a Literary Movement" (Nemerov), **III:** 270
"History of a Literary Radical, The" (Bourne), **I:** 215, 235, 236
History of a Radical: Essays by Randolph Bourne (Brooks), **I:** 245
"History of Buttons, The" (Goldbarth), **Supp. XII:** 187
History of English Literature (Taine), **III:** 323
History of English Prosody (Saintsbury), **Supp. XV:** 181
History of Fortus, The (Emerson), **II:** 8
History of Henry Esmond, The (Thackeray), **II:** 91, 130
History of Modern Poetry, A (Perkins), **Supp. I Part 2:** 475; **Supp. XV:** 185
History of My Heart (Pinsky), **Supp. VI:** 243, 244, 245
History of New York, from the Beginning of the World to the End of the Dutch Dynasty, A (Irving), **II:** 300–303, 304, 310
History of Pendennis, The (Thackeray), **II:** 291
"History of Red, The" (Hogan), **Supp. IV Part 1:** 411
"History of Rodney, The" (Bass), **Supp. XVI:** 20
History of Roxbury Town (Ellis), **Supp. I Part 1:** 99
History of Southern Literature, The (Rubin), **Supp. XX: 161**
History of the African-American People (Proposed) by Strom Thurmond, The (Everett and Kincaid), **Supp. XVIII:** 62, **63–64**
History of the Conquest of Mexico (Prescott), **Retro. Supp. I:** 123
History of the Conquest of Peru (Morison, ed.), **Supp. I Part 2:** 494
History of the Dividing Line betwixt Virginia and North Carolina (Byrd), **Supp. IV Part 2:** 425
History of the Life and Voyages of Christopher Columbus, A (Irving), **II:** 310, 314
History of the Navy of the United States of America (Cooper), **I:** 347
History of the Rise and Fall of the Slavepower in America (Wilson), **Supp. XIV:** 48, 49
History of the Russian Revolution, A (Trotsky), **Supp. XXI:** 161
History of the United States (Bancroft), **Supp. XXII:** 33
History of the United States of America during the Administrations of Thomas Jefferson and James Madison (Adams), **I:** 6–9, 10, 20, 21
History of the Work of Redemption, A (Edwards), **I:** 560
History of United States Naval Operations in World War II (Morison), **Supp. I Part 2:** 490–492
History of Womankind in Western Europe, The, **Supp. XI:** 197
"History Teacher, The" (Collins), **Supp. XXI:** 57
"History Through a Beard" (Morison), **Supp. I Part 2:** 490
His Toy, His Dream, His Rest (Berryman), **I:** 169, 170, 183, 184–186
"His Words" (Roethke), **III:** 544
Hitchcock, Ada. *See* MacLeish, Mrs. Archibald (Ada Hitchcock)
Hitchcock, Alfred, **IV:** 357; **Supp. IV Part 1:** 132; **Supp. VIII:** 177; **Supp. XX: 253; Supp. XXII:** 119
Hitchcock, George, **Supp. X:** 127; **Supp. XVII:** 110
"Hitch Haiku" (Snyder), **Supp. VIII:** 297
"Hitch-Hikers, The" (Welty), **IV:** 262
"Hitchhiking Is Illegal in Nevada" (Lethem), **Supp. XVIII:** 136
Hitchins, Christopher, **Supp. VIII:** 241
Hitler, Adolf, **I:** 261, 290, 492; **II:** 146, 454, 561, 565, 592; **III:** 2, 3, 110, 115, 140, 156, 246, 298, 446; **IV:** 5, 17, 18, 298, 372; **Supp. I Part 2:** 431, 436, 446, 664; **Supp. V:** 290
Hitler, Wendy, **III:** 404
Hitler Lives ? (film), **Supp. XVI:** 102
Hix, H. L., **Supp. XV:** 114
H. L. Mencken, a Portrait from Memory (Angoff), **III:** 107
"H. L. Mencken Meets a Poet in the West Side Y.M.C.A." (White), **Supp. I Part 2:** 677
H. L. Mencken: The American Scene (Cairns), **III:** 119
H. M. Pulham, Esquire (Marquand), **II:** 482–483; **III:** 58, 59, 65, 68–69
Hnizdovsky, Jacques, **Supp. XIII:** 346
"Hoadley's Test Case in Indiana" (Neugeboren), **Supp. XVI:** 219
Hoagland, Edward, **Supp. XIV:** 80; **Supp. XVI:** 277; **Supp. XXII:** 204, 206
Hoagland, Tony, **Supp. XIX:** 81, 89
"Hoarder, The" (Sexton), **Supp. II Part 2:** 692
"Hoarfrost" (C. Baxter), **Supp. XVII:** 15
Hoban, Phoebe, **Supp. XV:** 319, 325
Hobb, Gormley, **I:** 203
Hobbes, Thomas, **I:** 277; **II:** 9, 10, 540; **III:** 306; **IV:** 88; **Supp. XII:** 33; **Supp. XIV:** 5, 7
Hobson, Geary, **Supp. IV Part 1:** 321; **Supp. IV Part 2:** 502
Hobson, J. A., **I:** 232
Hobson, John A., **Supp. I Part 2:** 650

Hobson, Laura Z., **III:** 151
Hocking, Agnes, **Supp. VIII:** 251
Hocking, William Ernest, **III:** 303
Hodges, Campbell B., **Supp. XIV:** 8
Hodgson, Captain Joseph, **III:** 328
Hoffa, Jimmy, **I:** 493
Hoffenberg, Mason, **Supp. XI:** 294, 297, 299, 305
Hoffer, Eric, **Supp. VIII:** 188; **Supp. XIX:** 264
Hoffman, Abbie, **Supp. XIV:** 150
Hoffman, Alice, **Supp. X: 77–94; Supp. XIII:** 13
Hoffman, Allen, **Supp. XVII:** 42, 44
Hoffman, Daniel, **Retro. Supp. II:** 265
Hoffman, Daniel G., **I:** 405; **II:** 307; **Supp. XI:** 152
Hoffman, Dustin, **Supp. IV Part 1:** 236
Hoffman, E. T. A., **Supp. XVI:** 157
Hoffman, Eva, **Supp. XVI: 147–164**
Hoffman, Frederick J., **I:** 60, 67; **II:** 443; **IV:** 113
Hoffman, Josiah Ogden, **II:** 297, 300
Hoffman, Matilda, **II:** 300, 314
Hoffman, Paul, **Supp. XV:** 141–142
Hoffman, Roy, **Supp. XX: 177**
Hoffman, Todd, **Supp. XVIII:** 101
Hoffman, William, **Supp. XVIII: 69–88**
Hoffman, William M., **Supp. X:** 153
Hoffmann, E. T. A., **III:** 415
Hofmann, Hans, **Supp. XV:** 144
Hofmeister, Tim, **Supp. XIX:** 115
Ho for a Hat (W. J. Smith), **Supp. XIII:** 346
Hofstadter, Richard, **Supp. VIII:** 98, 99, 108
Hogan, Linda, **Supp. IV Part 1:** 324, 325, **397–418; Supp. XVIII:** 189
Hogan, Randolph, **Supp. XVI:** 252–253
Hogan, Ron, **Supp. XVIII:** 138, 139
Hogarth, William, **Supp. XII:** 44
Hogg, James, **I:** 53; **Supp. I Part 1:** 349; **Supp. IX:** 275
Hoggart, Richard, **Supp. XIV:** 299
"Hog-Nosed Snake, The" (Kooser), **Supp. XIX:** 128
Hogue, W. Lawrence, **Supp. XXII:** 175–176
Hohne, Karen, **Supp. V:** 147
Hojoki (Chomei), **IV:** 170
Holbrook, David, **Supp. I Part 2:** 526–527, 546
Holcroft, Thomas, **Supp. I Part 2:** 514
Holden, Jonathan, **Supp. XI:** 143
Holden, Raymond, **Supp. XIV:** 121–122
Holden, William, **Supp. XI:** 307
Hölderlin, Friedrich, **Supp. XVI:** 48
Holding, Elisabeth Sanxay, **Supp. XXII: 119–137**
"Holding On" (Levine), **Supp. V:** 184
Holding the Line: Women in the Great Arizona Mine Strike of 1983 (Kingsolver), **Supp. VII:** 197, 201–202, 204
"Holding the Mirror Up to Nature" (Nemerov), **III:** 275, 276
"Hold Me" (Levine), **Supp. V:** 186
Hold the Press (film), **Supp. XIII:** 163
Hold with the Hares (Zinberg), **Supp. XV:** 197–198,**Supp. XV:** 203
"Hole in the Floor, A" (Wilbur), **Supp. III Part 2:** 556–557
Holiday (Barry), **Retro. Supp. I:** 104
"Holiday" (Porter), **III:** 454
Holiday (W. Frank), **Supp. XX: 72–73**
Holiday, Billie, **Supp. I Part 1:** 80; **Supp. IV Part 1:** 2, 7; **Supp. XIX:** 147
Holiday Song for Four-Part Chorus of Mixed Voices with Piano Accompaniment (Taggard and Schuman), **Supp. XXII:** 283
Holinshed, Raphael, **IV:** 370
Holladay, Polly, **Supp. XXI:** 6
Holland, Josiah, **Supp. I Part 2:** 420
Holland, Laurence Bedwell, **Retro. Supp. I:** 216
Holland, Theodore, **I:** 453
Holland, Mrs. Theodore, **I:** 453, 455, 465
Holland, William, **IV:** 381
Hollander, John, **Supp. III Part 2:** 541; **Supp. IV Part 2:** 642; **Supp. IX:** 50, 153, 155; **Supp. XII:** 254, 255, 260; **Supp. XV:** 256; **Supp. XVII:** 112; **Supp. XIX:** 121
Holley, Marietta, **Supp. XIII:** 152
Holliday, Billie, **Supp. XXI:** 131
Hollinghurst, Alan, **Supp. XIII:** 52
Hollins Critic (Nelson), **Supp. XIX:** 3
Hollis, Thomas Brand, **Supp. I Part 2:** 514
Hollow Men, The (T. S. Eliot), **I:** 574, 575, 578–579, 580, 585; **III:** 586; **Retro. Supp. I:** 63, 64
"Hollow Tree, A" (R. Bly), **Supp. IV Part 1:** 64, 66
Hollyberrys at the Shore, The, **Supp. X:** 42
"Hollywood!" (Vidal), **Supp. IV Part 2:** 688
Hollywood: American Movie-City (Rand, unauthorized), **Supp. IV Part 2:** 519
Hollywood: A Novel of America in the 1920s (Vidal), **Supp. IV Part 2:** 677, 684, 686, 688, 690, 691
Hollywood Ending (film; Allen), **Supp. XV:** 11
Hollywood on Trial (film), **Supp. I Part 1:** 295
Holmes, Abiel, **Supp. I Part 1:** 300, 301, 302, 310
Holmes, Mrs. Abiel (Sarah Wendell), **Supp. I Part 1:** 300
Holmes, John, **I:** 169; **Supp. II Part 1:** 87; **Supp. IV Part 2:** 440–441; **Supp. XIV:** 119
Holmes, John Clellon, **Supp. XII:** 118; **Supp. XIV:** 144, 150
Holmes, Martha Stoddard, **Supp. XX: 205, 207**
Holmes, Oliver Wendell, **I:** 487; **II:** 225, 273–274, 402, 403; **III:** 81–82, 590, 591–592; **IV:** 429, 436; **Retro. Supp. II:** 155; **Supp. I Part 1:** 103, 243, 254, **299–319; Supp. I Part 2:** 405, 414, 415, 420, 593, 704, 705; **Supp. XI:** 194
Holmes, Oliver Wendell, Jr., **I:** 3, 19; **Supp. IV Part 2:** 422
Holmes, Mrs. Oliver Wendell (Amelia Jackson), **Supp. I Part 1:** 303
Holmes, Steven J., **Supp. IX:** 172, 177
Holmes, Ted, **Supp. V:** 180
Holmes, William Henry, **Supp. IV Part 2:** 603–604
Holocaust (Reznikoff), **Supp. XIV:** 281, **291–293**
Holocaust in American Life, The (Novick), **Supp. XVI:** 154
Holt, Edwin E., **I:** 59
Holt, Felix, **II:** 179
Holt, Henry, **II:** 348; **III:** 587
Holt, Patricia, **Supp. XIV:** 89
Holtby, Winifred, **Supp. I Part 2:** 720
Holy Ghostly, The (Shepard), **Supp. III Part 2:** 437–438, 447
"Holy Innocents, The" (Lowell), **II:** 539
Holy Sonnets (Donne), **IV:** 145; **Supp. I Part 1:** 367; **Supp. III Part 2:** 619; **Supp. XIII:** 130–131; **Supp. XVIII:** 50–51
"Holy Terror, A" (Bierce), **I:** 203
"Holy Terror, The" (Maxwell), **Supp. VIII:** 169
Holy the Firm (Dillard), **Supp. VI:** 23, **29,** 30, 31, 32
Holy War, The (Bunyan), **IV:** 156
"Homage to Arthur Rimbaud" (Wright), **Supp. V:** 339
Homage to Baudelaire (Duncan, ed.), **Supp. XV:** 75
Homage to Catalonia (Orwell), **Supp. XVII:** 229
"Homage to Che Guevara" (Banks), **Supp. V:** 5
Homage to Clio (Auden), **Supp. II Part 1:** 24
"Homage to Elizabeth Bishop" (Ivask, ed.), **Supp. I Part 1:** 96
"Homage to Ezra Pound" (Wright), **Supp. V:** 339
Homage to Frank O'Hara (Ashbery), **Supp. III Part 1:** 2–3
"Homage to Franz Joseph Haydn" (Hecht), **Supp. X:** 69
"Homage to Hemingway" (Bishop), **IV:** 35
Homage to Mistress Bradstreet (Berryman), **I:** 168, 169, 170–171, 172, 174, 175, 178–183, 184, 186
"Homage to Paul Cézanne" (Wright), **Supp. V:** 341–342
Homage to Sextus Propertius (Pound), **Retro. Supp. I:** 290
"Homage to Sextus Propertius" (Pound), **III:** 462, 476; **Supp. III Part 2:** 622
"Homage to Shakespeare" (Cheever), **Supp. I Part 1:** 180
"Homage to the Empress of the Blues" (Hayden), **Supp. II Part 1:** 379
"Homage to the Memory of Wallace Stevens" (Justice), **Supp. VII:** 126
Homage to Theodore Dreiser (Warren), **I:** 517
Homans, Margaret, **Supp. X:** 229
"Home" (Hughes), **Supp. I Part 1:** 329, 330
"Home" (Mora), **Supp. XIII:** 217
Home (Robinson), **Supp. XXI:** 212, **220–223**
Home (Updike), **Retro. Supp. I:** 320

"Home" (Weigl), **Supp. XIX:** 287
"Home, Home on the Strange" (J. D. Reed), **Supp. XVI:** 174
"Home, Sweet Home" (Fante), **Supp. XI:** 164, 165
Home, The (Gilman), **Supp. XI: 206–207**
"Home, The" (Jarman), **Supp. XVII:** 116
"Home Address" (Bronk), **Supp. XXI:** 27
"Home after Three Months Away" (Lowell), **II:** 547
Home and Colonial Library (Murray), **Retro. Supp. I:** 246
"Home and the Open Road: The Nonfiction of Larry Brown" (Barrier), **Supp. XXI:** 48–49
Home as Found (Cooper), **I:** 348, 349, 350, 351
Home at the End of the World, A (Cunningham), **Supp. XV: 59–62,** 63
"Home Away from Home, A" (Humphrey), **Supp. IX:** 101
Home Book of Shakespeare Quotations (Stevenson), **Supp. XIV:** 120
"Home Burial" (Frost), **Retro. Supp. I:** 124, 125, 128, **129–130; Supp. VIII:** 31; **Supp. XV:** 159; **Supp. XIX:** 9
Homecoming (Alvarez), **Supp. VII:** 1, 3–5, 9
"Homecoming" (Carruth), **Supp. XVI:** 55
"Homecoming" (McGrath), **Supp. X:** 116
"Homecoming, The" (Gioia), **Supp. XV:** 123, 124
Homecoming, The (Wilson), **Supp. VIII:** 330
Homecoming Game, The (Nemerov), **III:** 268, 282, 284–285
"Home during a Tropical Snowstorm I Feed My Father Lunch" (Karr), **Supp. XI:** 241–242, 248
Home Economics (Berry), **Supp. X:** 28, 31–32, 35, 36, 37
"Home Economics for Halfbacks" (Skloot), **Supp. XX: 195, 207**
Home from the Hill (film), **Supp. IX:** 95
Home from the Hill (Humphrey), **Supp. IX:** 93, 95, **96–98,** 104, 106, 109
"Home Grown" (Vital), **Supp. XVI:** 160
"Homeland" (Merwin), **Supp. III Part 1:** 351
Homeland and Other Stories (Kingsolver), **Supp. VII:** 199, 202–204, 207
Home on the Range (Baraka), **Supp. II Part 1:** 47
Homeplace (Siddons), **Supp. XXII:** 253
Home Place, The (Morris), **III:** 221, 222, 232
Homeplace, The (Nelson), **Supp. XVIII: 174–175**
Homer, **I:** 312, 433; **II:** 6, 8, 133, 302, 543, 544, 552; **III:** 14, 21, 278, 453, 457, 473, 567; **IV:** 54, 371; **Retro. Supp. I:** 59; **Supp. I Part 1:** 158, 283; **Supp. I Part 2:** 494; **Supp. X:** 36, 120, 122; **Supp. XIV:** 21; **Supp. XVII:** 70, 227
Homer, Louise, **Retro. Supp. I:** 10
Homer, Winslow, **Supp. XXI:** 243
"Home Range" (Leopold), **Supp. XIV:** 184, 185
"Home Repairs" (Skloot), **Supp. XX: 204**
Homer's Art (Notley), **Supp. XXII:** 232
"Homer's Art" (Notley), **Supp. XXII:** 232–233
"Homesick Blues" (Hughes), **Supp. I Part 1:** 327
Home: Social Essays (Baraka), **Supp. II Part 1:** 45, 61
"Homesteading on the Extraterrestrial Frontier" (Abbott), **Supp. XVIII:** 142
Home to Harlem (McKay), **Supp. X:** 132, 137–138, **138–139; Supp. XVIII:** 127
"Home Videos" (Brockmeier), **Supp. XXII:** 60
Homeward Bound (Cooper), **I:** 348
"Homeward Star, The" (Palmer), **Supp. XV:** 81–82
Homewood trilogy (Wideman), **Supp. X:** 319
"Homework" (Cameron), **Supp. XII:** 80, **83,** 84
"Homily" (Tate), **IV:** 121–122
Homing with the Birds (Stratton-Porter), **Supp. XX: 212, 216, 222**
"Homme Moyen Sensuel, L' " (Pound), **III:** 462
Homme révolté, L' (Camus), III: 306
"Homoeopathy and Its Kindred Delusions" (Holmes), **Supp. I Part 1:** 303–304, 305
Homo Ludens (Huizinga), **II:** 416–417, 425
"Homosexual Villain, The" (Mailer), **III:** 36
"Homo Will Not Inherit" (Doty), **Supp. XI:** 128
"Homunculus, The: A Novel in One Chapter" (McKnight), **Supp. XX: 152**
Hone and Strong Diaries of Old Manhattan, The (Auchincloss, ed.), **Supp. IV Part 1:** 23
"Honey" (Beattie), **Supp. V:** 33
"Honey" (Wright), **Supp. III Part 2:** 589
"Honey, We'll Be Brave" (Farrell), **II:** 45
Honey and Salt (Sandburg), **III:** 594–596
"Honey and Salt" (Sandburg), **III:** 594
"Honey Babe" (Hughes), **Supp. I Part 1:** 334
"Honey Tree, The" (Oliver), **Supp. VII:** 236
Hong, Maxine. *See* Kingston, Maxine Hong
Hongo, Garrett, **Supp. X:** 292; **Supp. XIII:** 114; **Supp. XVII:** 112
"Honkytonk" (Shapiro), **Supp. II Part 2:** 705
"Honky Tonk in Cleveland, Ohio" (Sandburg), **III:** 585
Honorable Men (Auchincloss), **Supp. IV Part 1:** 23
Honor Thy Father (Talese), **Supp. XVII:** 204–205, 210
Hood, Tom, **I:** 195
"Hoodoo in America" (Hurston), **Supp. VI:** 153–154
"Hook" (Wright), **Supp. III Part 2:** 604
Hook, Sidney, **I:** 265; **Supp. IV Part 2:** 527; **Supp. VIII:** 96, 100; **Supp. XIV:** 3
Hooker, Adelaide. *See* Marquand, Mrs. John P. (Adelaide Hooker)
Hooker, Isabella Beecher, **Supp. XI:** 193
Hooker, Samuel, **IV:** 162, 165
Hooker, Thomas, **II:** 15–16; **IV:** 162
Hooper, Marian. *See* Adams, Mrs. Henry (Marian Hooper)
Hoosier Holiday, A (Dreiser), **Retro. Supp. II:** 104
Hoover, Herbert, **Supp. I Part 2:** 638
Hoover, J. Edgar, **Supp. XIII:** 170
Hoover, Paul, **Supp. XV:** 179
"Hope" (Bontemps), **Supp. XXII:** 2
"Hope" (Jarrell), **II:** 389
"Hope" (Matthews), **Supp. IX:** 163
Hope, A. D., **Supp. XIII:** 347
Hope, Lynn, **Supp. II Part 1:** 38
"Hope Atherton's Wanderings" (Howe), **Supp. IV Part 2:** 432
Hope of Heaven (O'Hara), **III:** 361
"Hopes Rise" (Boyle), **Supp. XX: 20**
"Hop-Frog" (Poe), **Retro. Supp. II:** 264, 268, 269
Hopkin, Pauline, **Supp. XVI:** 143
Hopkins, Anne Yale, **Supp. I Part 1:** 100, 102, 113
Hopkins, Gerard Manley, **I:** 171, 179, 397, 401, 522, 525, 533; **II:** 537; **III:** 197, 209, 523; **IV:** 129, 135, 141, 421; **Retro. Supp. II:** 40; **Supp. I Part 1:** 79, 81, 94; **Supp. III Part 2:** 551; **Supp. IV Part 1:** 178; **Supp. IV Part 2:** 637, 638, 639, 641, 643; **Supp. V:** 337; **Supp. IX:** 39, 42; **Supp. X:** 61, 115; **Supp. XIII:** 294; **Supp. XIV:** 83; **Supp. XV:** 250, 347; **Supp. XVI:** 282; **Supp. XVII:** 241; **Supp. XVIII:** 78, 79; **Supp. XX: 230**
Hopkins, Gerard Walter Sturgis, **Supp. XX: 229, 233, 240**
Hopkins, L. A., **I:** 502
Hopkins, Lemuel, **Supp. II Part 1:** 70
Hopkins, Miriam, **IV:** 381; **Supp. I Part 1:** 281
Hopkins, Pauline, **Supp. XVIII:** 284
Hopkins, Samuel, **I:** 547, 549
Hopkins, Vivian, **II:** 20
Hopkinson, Francis, **Supp. I Part 2:** 504
Hopper (Strand), **Supp. IV Part 2:** 632
Hopper, Dennis, **Supp. XI:** 293, 308
Hopper, Edward, **IV:** 411, 413; **Supp. IV Part 2:** 619, 623, 631, 634; **Supp. XIX:** 117
Hopwood, Avery, **Supp. IV Part 2:** 573
Horace, **II:** 8, 154, 169, 543, 552, 568; **III:** 15; **IV:** 89; **Supp. I Part 2:** 423; **Supp. IX:** 152; **Supp. X:** 65; **Supp. XII:** 258, 260, 262
Horae Canonicae (Auden), **Supp. II Part 1:** 21
"Horatian Ode" (Marvell), **IV:** 135
"Horatian Ode upon Cromwell's Return from Ireland" (Marvell), **Supp. XIV:** 10
Horgan, Paul, **Supp. XV:** 46, 49, 52
Horkheimer, Max, **Supp. I Part 2:** 645; **Supp. IV Part 1:** 301

Horn, Dara, **Supp. XVII:** 50; **Supp. XX: 177**
Horn, Mother, **Supp. I Part 1:** 49, 54
Hornby, Nick, **Supp. XII:** 286
Horn of Africa (Caputo), **Supp. XIX:** 21–23
"Horn of Plenty" (Hughes), **Retro. Supp. I:** 210; **Supp. I Part 1:** 342
Horovitz, Israel, **Supp. XV:** 321
Horowitz, James. *See* Salter, James
Horowitz, Mark, **Supp. V:** 219, 231
"Horrible" (Halliday), **Supp. XIX:** 91
"Horse, The" (Levine), **Supp. V:** 182
"Horse, The" (Wright), **Supp. III Part 2:** 592, 601
Horse Eats Hay (play), **Supp. IV Part 1:** 82
Horse Feathers (film), **Supp. IV Part 1:** 384
"Horseflies" (Wrigley), **Supp. XVIII:** 307
Horse Has Six Legs, The (Simic), **Supp. VIII:** 272
"Horselaugh on Dibber Lannon" (Fante), **Supp. XI:** 164
Horseman, Pass By (McMurtry), **Supp. V:** 220–221, 224
"Horses" (Doty), **Supp. XI:** 122
Horses and Men (Anderson), **I:** 112–113, 114
"Horses and Men in Rain" (Sandburg), **III:** 584
"Horse Show, The" (W. C. Williams), **Retro. Supp. I:** 423
Horses Make a Landscape More Beautiful (Walker), **Supp. III Part 2:** 521, 533
"Horse Thief" (Caldwell), **I:** 310
"Horseweed" (Offutt), **Supp. XIX:** 166, 167
Horse With a Green Vinyl Mane (P. N. Warren), **Supp. XX: 261**
"Horsie" (Parker), **Supp. IX:** 193
Horton, George Moses, **Supp. XXII:** 11
Horton, Philip, **I:** 383, 386, 387, 393, 441; **Supp. XV:** 138
Horton Hatches the Egg (Geisel), **Supp. XVI:** 100, 112
Horton Hears a Who! (Geisel), **Supp. XVI:** 102
Horwitz, Tony, **Supp. XVIII:** 195–196
Hosea (biblical book), **II:** 166
Hospers, John, **Supp. IV Part 2:** 528
"Hospice" (Hull), **Supp. XXI:** 138
Hospital, Janette Turner, **Supp. IV Part 1:** 311–302
Hospital Sketches (Alcott), **Supp. I Part 1:** 34, 35
Hostages to Fortune (Humphrey), **Supp. IX:** 96, **104–106,** 109
Hostess to Murder (Holding), **Supp. XXII:** 126, **127**
"Hot Combs" (Trethewey), **Supp. XXI:** 249
"Hot Cross Bum" (Loy), **Supp. XXII:** 168
"Hot Dog" (Stern), **Supp. IX: 298–299**
"Hotel Bar" (McClatchy), **Supp. XII:** 269
Hotel Dwellers, The (Lacy), **Supp. XV:** 205
Hotel Insomnia (Simic), **Supp. VIII:** 280, **281–282**
Hotel Lambosa and Other Stories (Koch), **Supp. XV:** 186
Hotel New Hampshire, The (Irving), **Supp. VI:** 163, 164, **172–173,** 177, 179; **Supp. XIX:** 164
"Hot-Foot Hannibal" (Chesnutt), **Supp. XIV:** 60
"Hot Night on Water Street" (Simpson), **Supp. IX:** 269, 270
"Hot Time, A" (Gunn Allen), **Supp. IV Part 1:** 333
Houdini, Harry, **IV:** 437
"Hound of Heaven" (Thompson), **Retro. Supp. I:** 55
"Hourglass, The" (Kees), **Supp. XV:** 147
"Hour in Chartres, An" (Bourne), **I:** 228
Hours, The (Cunningham), **Supp. XII:** 80; **Supp. XV: 65–68**
"Hours before Eternity" (Caldwell), **I:** 291
House, Bridge, Fountain, Gate (Kumin), **Supp. IV Part 2:** 448, 449, 451, 454
House, Edward, **Supp. I Part 2:** 643
"House, The" (Merrill), **Supp. III Part 1:** 323
House at Pooh Corner, The (Milne), **Supp. IX:** 189
"House at the End of the World, The" (Brockmeier), **Supp. XXII:** 52, 53
House Behind the Cedars, The (Chesnutt), **Supp. XIV: 69–71**
Houseboat Days (Ashbery), **Supp. III Part 1:** 18–20
Housebreaker of Shady Hill and Other Stories, The (Cheever), **Supp. I Part 1:** 184
"House by the Sea, The" (E. Stoddard), **Supp. XV:** 277
House by the Sea, The (Sarton), **Supp. VIII:** 264
House Divided, A (Buck), **Supp. II Part 1:** 118
"House Divided, The/La Casa Divida" (Kingsolver), **Supp. VII:** 207
"House Guest" (Bishop), **Retro. Supp. II:** 49; **Supp. I Part 1:** 93
Household Saints (film), **Supp. XVI:** 256
Household Saints (Prose), **Supp. XVI:** 252–253, 254, 261
"House in Athens, The" (Merrill), **Supp. III Part 1:** 323
House in the Uplands, A (Caldwell), **I:** 297, 301, 306
"House in Turk Street, The" (Hammett), **Supp. IV Part 1:** 344
"House in Winter, The" (Sarton), **Supp. VIII:** 259
"Housekeeping" (Alvarez), **Supp. VII:** 3–5, 10
Housekeeping (Robinson), **Supp. XXI:** 210–211, **212–216,** 218, 223
"Housekeeping" (Trethewey), **Supp. XXI:** 249
"Housekeeping for Men" (Bourne), **I:** 231
House Made of Dawn (Momaday), **Supp. IV Part 1:** 274, 323, 326; **Supp. IV Part 2:** 479, 480, 481–484, 485, 486, 504, 562
Houseman, John, **Supp. IV Part 1:** 173
House Next Door, The (Siddons), **Supp. XXII:** 239
House Next Door, The (television movie), **Supp. XXII:** 239
House of Dust, The: A Symphony (Aiken), **I:** 50
House of Earth trilogy (Buck), **Supp. II Part 1:** 118, 123
House of Five Talents, The (Auchincloss), **Supp. IV Part 1:** 21, 25–27
"House of Flowers" (Capote), **Supp. III Part 1:** 123
House of Games (Mamet), **Supp. XIV:** 243
House of Houses (Mora), **Supp. XIII:** 213, 215, 218, 219, 223–224, **225–227,** 228, 229
House of Incest (Nin), **Supp. III Part 1:** 43; **Supp. X:** 187, 190, 193
House of Life, The: Rachel Carson at Work (Brooks), **Supp. IX:** 26
House of Light (Oliver), **Supp. VII:** 238–240
House of Mirth, The (Wharton), **II:** 180, 193; **IV:** 311–313, 314, 316, 318, 323, 327; **Retro. Supp. I:** 360, 366, 367, **367–370,** 373, 380; **Supp. XX: 239, 240**
"House of Mist, The" (Rand), **Supp. IV Part 2:** 524
"House of My Own, A" (Cisneros), **Supp. VII:** 64
"House of Night, The" (Freneau), **Supp. II Part 1:** 259, 260
"House of Representatives and Me, The" (Conroy), **Supp. XVI:** 75
House of Sleeping Beauties, The (Hwang), **Supp. XXI:** 146
House of the Far and Lost, The (Wolfe), **IV:** 456
"House of the Injured, The" (Haines), **Supp. XII:** 203
"House of the One Father" (Antin), **Supp. XX: 3, 13**
House of the Prophet, The (Auchincloss), **Supp. IV Part 1:** 31
House of the Seven Gables (Hawthorne), **I:** 106; **II:** 60, 224, 225, 231, 237, 239, 240–241, 243, 244; **Retro. Supp. I:** 63, 149, **160–162,** 163, 164; **Supp. I Part 2:** 579
House of the Solitary Maggot, The (Purdy), **Supp. VII:** 274–275
"House on 15th S.W., The" (Hugo), **Supp. VI:** 140
"House on Main Street, The" (B. Kelly), **Supp. XVII:** 127
House on Mango Street, The (Cisneros), **Supp. VII:** 58, 59–64, 65, 66, 67, 68, 72
"House on Mango Street, The" (Cisneros), **Supp. VII:** 59
House on Marshland, The (Glück), **Supp. V:** 81–83, 84

"House on Moscow Street, The" (Nelson), **Supp. XVIII:** 174
"House on the Heights, A" (Capote), **Supp. III Part 1:** 120
"House on the Hill, The" (Robinson), **III:** 505, 524
"House Raising" (Offutt), **Supp. XIX:** 166
"Houses" (Hogan), **Supp. IV Part 1:** 402
"Houses, The" (Merwin), **Supp. III Part 1:** 354
"Houses of the Spirit" (Karr), **Supp. XI:** 250
"House Sparrows" (Hecht), **Supp. X: 68**
"House That Doesn't House, The" (Bronk), **Supp. XXI:** 34
House That Tai Maing Built, The (Lee), **Supp. X:** 291
"House Unroofed by the Gale" (Tu Fu), **II:** 526
"House Where Mark Twain Was Born, The" (Masters), **Supp. I Part 2:** 472
"Housewife" (Hempel), **Supp. XXI:** 124
"Housewife" (Sexton), **Supp. II Part 2:** 682
Housman, A. E., **III:** 15, 136, 606; **Supp. II Part 1:** 4; **Supp. IV Part 1:** 165; **Supp. XV:** 40–41
Houston Trilogy (McMurtry), **Supp. V:** 223–225
How" (Ginsberg), **Supp. XIV:** 142, 143
"How" (Moore), **Supp. X:** 167
"How About This?" (Carver), **Supp. III Part 1:** 141
"How America Came to the Mountains" (J. W. Miller), **Supp. XX: 169**
"How Annandale Went Out" (Robinson), **III:** 513
Howard, Arliss, **Supp. XXI:** 39
Howard, Ben, **Supp. XVI:** 54
Howard, Gerald, **Supp. XII:** 21
Howard, Jane, **Retro. Supp. I:** 334
Howard, June, **Retro. Supp. II:** 139
Howard, Leon, **Supp. I Part 2:** 408, 422, 423
Howard, Maureen, **Supp. XII:** 285; **Supp. XVII:** 183
Howard, Richard, **Retro. Supp. II:** 43; **Supp. IV Part 2:** 624, 626, 640; **Supp. VIII:** 273; **Supp. IX:** 324, 326; **Supp. X:** 152; **Supp. XI:** 317; **Supp. XII:** 254; **Supp. XIII:** 76; **Supp. XV:** 23, 24
Howard, Vilma, **Retro. Supp. II:** 111, 112
Howards, J. Z., **Supp. VIII:** 178
Howards End (Forster), **Supp. XII:** 87
Howarth, Cora, **I:** 408, 409
Howbah Indians (Ortiz), **Supp. IV Part 2:** 513
"How Black Sees Green and Red" (McKay), **Supp. X:** 136
How Britain Rules Africa (Padmore), **Supp. XXI:** 166
"How David Did Not Care" (R. Bly), **Supp. IV Part 1:** 73
"How Did I Love Him?" (Nelson), **Supp. XVIII:** 176
"How Do I Love Thee?" (Browning), **Supp. XVIII:** 176
Howe, Darcus, **Supp. XXI:** 170
Howe, E.W., **I:** 106
Howe, Florence, **Supp. XIII:** 295, 306
Howe, Harriet, **Supp. XI:** 200, 201
Howe, Irving, **IV:** 10; **Retro. Supp. I:** 369; **Retro. Supp. II:** 112, 286; **Supp. I Part 2:** 432; **Supp. II Part 1:** 99; **Supp. VI: 113–129; Supp. VIII:** 93, 232; **Supp. IX:** 227; **Supp. X:** 203, 245; **Supp. XII:** 160; **Supp. XIII:** 98; **Supp. XIV:** 103–104, 104; **Supp. XVII:** 50; **Supp. XIX:** 257, 265
Howe, James Wong, **Supp. I Part 1:** 281; **Supp. V:** 223
Howe, Julia Ward, **III:** 505; **Retro. Supp. II:** 135
Howe, M. A. DeWolfe, **I:** 258; **II:** 406; **Supp. XIV:** 54
Howe, Mary Manning, **Supp. IV Part 2:** 422
Howe, Samuel, **Supp. I Part 1:** 153
Howe, Susan, **Retro. Supp. I:** 33, 43; **Supp. IV Part 2: 419–438; Supp. XVI:** 284
Howell, Chris, **Supp. XIII:** 112
Howell, James, **II:** 111
Howells, Margaret, **II:** 271
Howells, William C., **II:** 273
Howells, William Dean, **I:** 109, 192, 204, 210, 211, 254, 355, 407, 411, 418, 459, 469; **II:** 127–128, 130, 131, 136, 137, 138, 140, **271–294,** 322, 331–332, 338, 397–398, 400, 415, 444, 451, 556; **III:** 51, 118, 314, 327–328, 461, 576, 607; **IV:** 192, 202, 342, 349; **Retro. Supp. I:** 220, 334, 362, 378; **Retro. Supp. II:** 93, 101, 135, 288; **Supp. I Part 1:** 306, 318, 357, 360, 368; **Supp. I Part 2:** 414, 420, 645–646; **Supp. II Part 1:** 198, 352; **Supp. IV Part 2:** 678; **Supp. VIII:** 98, 101, 102; **Supp. XI:** 198, 200; **Supp. XIV:** 45–46; **Supp. XV:** 269, 274, 285, 287; **Supp. XVIII:** 6
Howells, Mrs. William Dean (Elinor Mead), **II:** 273
Howells, Winifred, **II:** 271
"Howells as Anti-Novelist" (Updike), **Retro. Supp. I:** 334
Howells: His Life and World (Brooks), **I:** 254
Hower, Edward, **Supp. XII:** 330, 343
Howes, Barbara, **Supp. XIII:** 331
How Good Is David Mamet, Anyway? (Heilpern), **Supp. XIV:** 242
"How I Became a Shadow" (Purdy), **Supp. VII:** 269
"How I Came to Vedanta" (Isherwood), **Supp. XIV:** 164
"How I Come to You" (Peacock), **Supp. XIX:** 198
"How I Learned to Sweep" (Alvarez), **Supp. VII:** 4
"How I Spent My Forties" (Wasserstein), **Supp. XV:** 325, 330, 332
"How It Began" (Stafford), **Supp. XI:** 327
"How It Feels to Be Colored Me" (Hurston), **Supp. VI:** 152
"How It Is" (Budbill), **Supp. XIX:** 10
"How It Is" (Everwine), **Supp. XV:** 79, 86
"How I Told My Child About Race" (Brooks), **Supp. III Part 1:** 78
"How I Went to the Mines" (Harte), **Supp. II Part 1:** 336
"How I Write" (Franzen), **Supp. XX: 84**
"How I Write" (Welty), **IV:** 279, 280
"How I Wrote *The Promised Land*" (Antin), **Supp. XX: 3**
"How Jonah Did Not Care" (R. Bly), **Supp. IV Part 1:** 73
Howl (Ginsberg), **Retro. Supp. I:** 426; **Supp. III Part 1:** 92; **Supp. IV Part 1:** 90; **Supp. V:** 336; **Supp. VIII:** 290; **Supp. XIV:** 15, 126, 157; **Supp. XVIII:** 20, 29
"How Laddie and the Princess Spelled Down at the Christmas Bee" (Stratton-Porter), **Supp. XX: 216**
Howl and Other Poems (Ginsberg), **Supp. II Part 1:** 308, 317–318, 319; **Supp. X:** 123
Howlett, William, **Retro. Supp. I:** 17
Howl: Original Draft Facsimile, Transcript and Variant Versions (Gimsberg), **Supp. XIV:** 142
"How Many Midnights" (Bowles), **Supp. IV Part 1:** 86–87
"How Many Nights" (Kinnell), **Supp. III Part 1:** 245–246
How Much? (Blechman), **Supp. I Part 1:** 290
"How Much Are You Worth" (Salinas), **Supp. XIII:** 325–326
"How Much Earth" (Levine), **Supp. V:** 184
How Much Earth: The Fresno Poets (Buckley, Oliveira, and Williams, eds.), **Supp. XIII:** 313
"How Not to Forget" (Bartov), **Supp. XVI:** 153–154
"How Poetry Comes to Me" (Corso), **Supp. XII:** 122
"How Poetry Comes to Me" (Snyder), **Supp. VIII:** 305
How Reading Changed My Life (Quindlen), **Supp. XVII:** 167, 179–180
"How She Came By Her Name: An Interview with Louis Massiah" (Bambara), **Supp. XI:** 20
"How Soon Hath Time" (Ransom), **IV:** 123
How Spring Comes (Notley), **Supp. XXII:** 226, 229
How Stella Got Her Groove Back (McMillan), **Supp. XIII:** 185, **190–191**
How the Alligator Missed Breakfast (Kinney), **Supp. III Part 1:** 235, 253
"How the Devil Came Down Division Street" (Algren), **Supp. IX:** 3
How the García Girls Lost Their Accents (Alvarez), **Supp. VII:** 3, 5–9, 11, 15, 17, 18
How the Grinch Stole Christmas! (Geisel), **Supp. XVI:** 102
How the Other Half Lives (Riis), **I:** 293

"How the Saint Did Not Care" (R. Bly), **Supp. IV Part 1:** 73
"How the Women Went from Dover" (Whittier), **Supp. I Part 2:** 694, 696, 697
"How To" (Carruth), **Supp. XVI:** 51
How To Be Alone: Essays (Franzen), **Supp. XX: 83, 90, 93–94**
"How to Be an Other Woman" (Moore), **Supp. X:** 165, 167, 168
"How to Become a Writer" (Moore), **Supp. X:** 167, 168
"How to Be Happy: Another Memo to Myself" (Dunn), **Supp. XI:** 145
How To Cook a Wolf (M. F. K. Fisher), **Supp. XVII:** 84–85, 87
How to Develop Your Personality (Shellow), **Supp. I Part 2:** 608
How to Know God: The Yoga Aphorisms of Patanjali (Isherwood and Prabhavananda)), **Supp. XIV:** 164
"How To Like It" (Dobyns), **Supp. XIII: 85–86**
"How to Live on $36,000 a Year" (Fitzgerald), **Retro. Supp. I:** 105
"How to Live. What to Do" (Stevens), **Retro. Supp. I:** 302
"How Tom is Doin' " (Kees), **Supp. XV:** 143
How to Read (Pound), **Supp. VIII:** 291
How to Read a Novel (Gordon), **II:** 198
How to Read a Poem and Fall in Love with Poetry (Hirsch), **Supp. XIX:** 202
How to Read a Poem . . . and Start a Poetry Circle (Peacock), **Supp. XIX:** 194, 202–203, 205
How to Save Your Own Life (Jong), **Supp. V:** 115, 123–125, 130
"How to Study Poetry" (Pound), **III:** 474
"How to Talk to Your Mother" (Moore), **Supp. X:** 167, 172
How to Win Friends and Influence People (Carnegie), **Supp. I Part 2:** 608
How to Worry Successfully (Seabury), **Supp. I Part 2:** 608
How to Write (Stein), **IV:** 32, 34, 35
"How to Write a Blackwood Article" (Poe), **III:** 425; **Retro. Supp. II:** 273
"How to Write a Memoir Like This" (Oates), **Supp. III Part 2:** 509
"How to Write Like Somebody Else" (Roethke), **III:** 540
How to Write Short Stories (Lardner), **II:** 430, 431
"How Vincentine Did Not Care" (R. Bly), **Supp. IV Part 1:** 73
How We Became Human: New and Selected Poems (Harjo), **Supp. XII: 230–232**
"How We Danced" (Sexton), **Supp. II Part 2:** 692
How We Got Insipid (Lethem), **Supp. XVIII:** 149
"How We Got in Town and Out Again" (Lethem), **Supp. XVIII:** 149
"How You Sound??" (Baraka), **Supp. II Part 1:** 30
Hoy, Philip, **Supp. X:** 56, 58
Hoyer, Linda Grace (pseudonym). *See* Updike, Mrs. Wesley
Hoyt, Constance, **Supp. I Part 2:** 707
Hoyt, Elinor Morton. *See* Wylie, Elinor
Hoyt, Helen, **Supp. XXII:** 275
Hoyt, Henry (father), **Supp. I Part 2:** 707
Hoyt, Henry (son), **Supp. I Part 2:** 708
Hoyt, Henry Martyn, **Supp. I Part 2:** 707
Hsu, Kai-yu, **Supp. X:** 292
Hsu, Ruth Y., **Supp. XV:** 212
Hubba City (Reed), **Supp. X:** 241
Hubbard, Elbert, **I:** 98, 383
Hubbell, Jay B., **Supp. I Part 1:** 372
"Hubbub, The" (Ammons), **Supp. VII:** 35
Huber, François, **II:** 6
Huckins, Olga, **Supp. IX:** 32
Huckleberry Finn (Twain). *See Adventures of Huckleberry Finn, The* (Twain)
Hud (film), **Supp. V:** 223, 226
Hudgins, Andrew, **Supp. X:** 206; **Supp. XVII:** 111, 112; **Supp. XVIII:** 176
Hudson, Henry, **I:** 230
"Hudsonian Curlew, The" (Snyder), **Supp. VIII:** 302
Hudson River Bracketed (Wharton), **IV:** 326–327; **Retro. Supp. I:** 382
Huebsch, B. W., **III:** 110
Hueffer, Ford Madox, **Supp. I Part 1:** 257, 262. *See also* Ford, Ford Madox
Huene-Greenberg, Dorothee von, **Supp. XX: 46**
Huff (television series), **Supp. XIX:** 222
Hug Dancing (Hearon), **Supp. VIII: 67–68**
Huge Season, The (Morris), **III:** 225–226, 227, 230, 232, 233, 238
Hugging the Jukebox (Nye), **Supp. XIII: 275–276,** 277
"Hugging the Jukebox" (Nye), **Supp. XIII:** 276
Hughes, Brigid, **Supp. XVI:** 247
Hughes, Carolyn, **Supp. XII:** 272, 285
Hughes, Frieda, **Supp. I Part 2:** 540, 541
Hughes, Glenn, **Supp. I Part 1:** 255
Hughes, H. Stuart, **Supp. VIII:** 240
Hughes, James Nathaniel, **Supp. I Part 1:** 321, 332
Hughes, Ken, **Supp. XI:** 307
Hughes, Langston, **Retro. Supp. I: 193–214; Retro. Supp. II:** 114, 115, 117, 120; **Supp. I Part 1: 320–348; Supp. II Part 1:** 31, 33, 61, 170, 173, 181, 227, 228, 233, 361; **Supp. III Part 1:** 72–77; **Supp. IV Part 1:** 15, 16, 164, 168, 169, 173, 243, 368; **Supp. VIII:** 213; **Supp. IX:** 306, 316; **Supp. X:** 131, 136, 139, 324; **Supp. XI:** 1; **Supp. XIII:** 75, 111, 132, 233; **Supp. XVI:** 135, 138; **Supp. XVIII:** 90, 277, 279, 280, 281, 282; **Supp. XIX:** 72, 75, 77; **Supp. XXI:** 243; **Supp. XXII:** 3, 4, 5, 6, 8, 13–14
Hughes, Nicholas, **Supp. I Part 2:** 541
Hughes, Robert, **Supp. X:** 73
Hughes, Ted, **IV:** 3; **Retro. Supp. II:** 244, 245, 247, 257; **Supp. I Part 2:** 536, 537, 538, 539, 540, 541; **Supp. XV:** 117, 347, 348; **Supp. XXII:** 30
Hughes, Thomas, **Supp. I Part 2:** 406
"Hugh Harper" (Bowles), **Supp. IV Part 1:** 94
Hughie (O'Neill), **III:** 385, 401, 405
Hugh Selwyn Mauberley (Pound), **I:** 66, 476; **III:** 9, 462–463, 465, 468; **Retro. Supp. I: 289–290,** 291, 299; **Supp. XIV:** 272
Hugo, Richard, **Supp. VI: 131–148; Supp. IX:** 296, 323, 324, 330; **Supp. XI:** 315, 317; **Supp. XII:** 178; **Supp. XIII:** 112, 113, 133; **Supp. XVIII:** 293, 299; **Supp. XXI:** 243
Hugo, Victor, **II:** 290, 490, 543; **Supp. IV Part 2:** 518; **Supp. IX:** 308
Hui-neng, **III:** 567
Huis Clos (Sartre), **Supp. IV Part 1:** 84
Huizinga, Johan, **I:** 225; **II:** 416–417, 418, 425
Hulbert, Ann, **Supp. XI:** 38–39
Hull, Lynda, **Supp. XI:** 131; **Supp. XXI: 129–142**
Hulme, Thomas E., **I:** 68, 69, 475; **III:** 196, 209, 463–464, 465; **IV:** 122; **Supp. I Part 1:** 261, 262; **Supp. XV:** 43
Human, All Too Human (Nietzsche), **Supp. X:** 48
"Human Culture" (Emerson), **II:** 11–12
Human Factor, The (Greene), **Supp. V:** 298
"Human Figures" (Doty), **Supp. XI:** 123–124
"Human Fly, The" (Boyle), **Supp. XX: 19**
"Human Geography" (Jarman), **Supp. XVII:** 116
"Human Immortality" (James), **II:** 353–354
"Human Life" (Emerson), **II:** 11–12
"Human Pig" (Jin), **Supp. XVIII:** 99
Human Rights, Human Wrongs: The Oxford Amnesty Lectures, 2001, **Supp. XVI:** 155
"Human Soul as a Rube Goldberg Device, The: A Choose-Your-Own-Adventure-Story" (Brockmeier), **Supp. XXII:** 60–61
Human Stain, The (P. Roth), **Retro. Supp. II:** 279, 289, 294–295
"Human Things" (Nemerov), **III:** 279
Human Universe (Olson), **Supp. II Part 2:** 571
"Human Universe" (Olson), **Supp. II Part 2:** 565, 567
Human Vibration (Richter), **Supp. XVIII:** 209
Human Wishes (Hass), **Supp. VI:** 105–106, 107
Human Work (Gilman), **Supp. XI:** 206
Humbert, Humbert, **Supp. X:** 283
Humble Inquiry into the Rules of the Word of God, An, Concerning the Qualifications Requisite to a Complete Standing and Full Communion in the Visible Christian Church (Edwards), **I:** 548
Humboldt, Alexander von, **III:** 428
Humboldt's Gift (Bellow), **Retro. Supp. II:** 19, 28–29, 34; **Supp. XIII:** 320

Hume, David, **I:** 125; **II:** 349, 357, 480; **III:** 618
Humes, Harold, **Supp. V:** 201; **Supp. XIV:** 82
Humes, Harry, **Supp. XIX:** 281
Humes, H. L. "Doc", **Supp. XI:** 294
"Humility" (Hoffman), **Supp. XVIII:** 86
Hummer, T. R., **Supp. XIX:** 278; **Supp. XXI:** 91
"Hummingbirds, The" (Welty), **IV:** 273
Humphrey, William, **Supp. IX: 93–112; Supp. XV:** 353
Humphreys, Christmas, **Supp. V:** 267
Humphreys, David, **Supp. II Part 1:** 65, 69, 70, 268
Humphreys, Josephine, **Supp. XII:** 311
Humphries, Rolfe, **III:** 124; **Retro. Supp. I:** 137
Hunchback of Notre Dame, The (film), **Supp. IV Part 1:** 101
Hunches in Bunches (Geisel), **Supp. XVI:** 111
Huncke, Herbert, **Supp. XII:** 118; **Supp. XIV: 137–153**
Huncke's Journal (Huncke), **Supp. XIV:** 139, 144, 145, 146
Hundred Camels in the Courtyard, A (Bowles), **Supp. IV Part 1:** 90
"Hundred Collars, A" (Frost), **Retro. Supp. I:** 128; **Supp. XIII:** 147
Hundred Secret Senses, The (Tan), **Supp. X:** 289, 293, 295, 297, 298, 299
Hundreds of Hens and Other Poems for Children by Halfdan Rasmussen (Nelson and Espeland, trans.), **Supp. XVIII:** 180
Hundred White Daffodils, A: Essays, Interviews, Newspaper Columns, and One Poem (Kenyon), **Supp. VII:** 160–162, 165, 166, 167, 174
Huneker, James, **III:** 102
Hunger (Hamsun), **Supp. XI:** 167
"Hunger" (Hogan), **Supp. IV Part 1:** 411
"Hunger . . ." (Rich), **Supp. I Part 2:** 571
"Hungerfield" (Jeffers), **Supp. II Part 2:** 416–417, 436
Hungerfield and Other Poems (Jeffers), **Supp. II Part 2:** 422
Hunger of Memory: The Education of Richard Rodriguez (Rodriguez), **Supp. XIV:** 297, 298, **298–302**, 310
Hungry Ghosts, The (Oates), **Supp. II Part 2:** 504, 510
Hungry Hearts (Prose), **Supp. XVI:** 253
Hunnewell, Susannah, **Supp. VIII:** 83
Hunt, Harriot K., **Retro. Supp. II:** 146
Hunt, Leigh, **II:** 515–516; **Supp. XV:** 175
Hunt, Richard Morris, **IV:** 312
Hunt, Robert, **Supp. XV:** 42, 49, 52
Hunt, William, **II:** 343
"Hunter" (Bierds), **Supp. XVII:** 30
Hunter, Dianna, **Supp. XVI:** 38
Hunter, Dr. Joseph, **II:** 217
Hunter, J. Paul, **Supp. IV Part 1:** 332
Hunter, Kim, **Supp. I Part 1:** 286
"Hunter of Doves" (Herbst), **Retro. Supp. II:** 325
"Hunter of the West, The" (Bryant), **Supp. I Part 1:** 155
Hunters, The (film), **Supp. IX:** 250
Hunters, The (Salter), **Supp. IX:** 246, **249–250**
Hunters and Gatherers (Prose), **Supp. XVI:** 257
"Hunters in the Snow" (Brueghel), **I:** 174; **Retro. Supp. I:** 430
"Hunters in the Snow" (Wolff), **Supp. VII:** 339–340
"Hunter's Moon—Eating the Bear" (Oliver), **Supp. VII:** 234
"Hunter's Vision, The" (Bryant), **Supp. I Part 1:** 160
Hunting for Hope: A Father's Journey (Sanders), **Supp. XVI:** 276–277, 278
"Hunting Is Not Those Heads on the Wall" (Baraka), **Supp. II Part 1:** 45
Huntington, Collis P., **I:** 198, 207
"Hunt in the Black Forest, The" (Jarrell), **II:** 379–380
Huntley, Jobe, **Supp. I Part 1:** 339
"Hurrah, Hurrah" (Nelson), **Supp. XVIII:** 175
Hurray Home (Wideman), **Supp. X:** 320
Hurricane (radio play, Boyce), **Supp. XXI:** 13
"Hurricane, The" (Crane), **I:** 401
"Hurricane, The" (Freneau), **Supp. II Part 1:** 262
"Hurricane Belle" (Notley), **Supp. XXII:** 228
"Hurry Kane" (Lardner), **II:** 425, 426, 427
"Hurry up Please It's Time" (Sexton), **Supp. II Part 2:** 694, 695
Hurst, Fannie, **Supp. XVIII:** 278, 279
Hurston, Zora Neale, **Retro. Supp. I:** 194, 198, 200, 201, 203; **Supp. I Part 1:** 325, 326, 332; **Supp. II Part 1:** 33; **Supp. IV Part 1:** 5, 11, 12, 164, 257; **Supp. VI: 149–161; Supp. VIII:** 214; **Supp. X:** 131, 139, 232, 242; **Supp. XI:** 85; **Supp. XIII:** 185, 233, 236, 295, 306; **Supp. XVIII:** 122, 279, 280, 282; **Supp. XIX:** 72, 75; **Supp. XX: 107; Supp. XXII:** 12
Hurt, John, **Supp. XIII:** 132
Husbands and Wives (film; Allen), **Supp. XV: 12**
"Husband's Song, The" (Di Piero), **Supp. XIX:** 39
Husband's Story, The (Shields), **Supp. VII:** 316. *See also* "Happenstance" (Shields)
Husserl, Edmund, **II:** 362, 363; **IV:** 491; **Supp. IV Part 1:** 42, 43
Hussey, Jo Ella, **Supp. XII:** 201
Hustler, The (film), **Supp. XI:** 306
Huston, John, **I:** 30, 31, 33, 35; **II:** 588; **III:** 161; **Supp. IV Part 1:** 102, 116, 355; **Supp. XI:** 307; **Supp. XIII:** 174
"Huswifery" (Taylor), **IV:** 161; **Supp. I Part 2:** 386
"Hut, The" (Sobin), **Supp. XVI:** 284–285
Hutchens, John K., **Supp. IX:** 276
Hutcheson, Francis, **I:** 559
Hutchins, Patricia, **III:** 478
Hutchinson, Abigail, **I:** 562
Hutchinson, Anne, **Supp. I Part 1:** 100, 101, 113; **Supp. IV Part 2:** 434; **Supp. VIII:** 202, 205
Hutchinson, George, **Supp. XVIII:** 119–120, 121, 132
Hutchinson, Thomas, **Supp. XX: 282**
Hutton, James, **Supp. IX:** 180
Huwayyik, Yusuf, **Supp. XX: 115**
Huxley, Aldous, **II:** 454; **III:** 281, 428, 429–430; **IV:** 77, 435; **Supp. I Part 2:** 714; **Supp. XIV:** 3, 164; **Supp. XVI:** 189, 192; **Supp. XVIII:** 137
Huxley, Julian, **Supp. VIII:** 251; **Supp. X:** 108
Huxley, Juliette, **Supp. VIII:** 251, 265
Huxley, Thomas, **III:** 102, 108, 113, 281; **Retro. Supp. II:** 60, 65, 93
Huxley, Thomas Henry, **Supp. I Part 1:** 368
Huysmans, Joris Karl (Charles Marie Georges), **I:** 66; **III:** 315; **IV:** 286; **Retro. Supp. II:** 326; **Supp. XX: 239**
"*Hwame, Koshkalaka,* and the Rest: Lesbians in American Indian Cultures" (Gunn Allen), **Supp. IV Part 1:** 330
Hwang, David Henry, **Supp. X:** 292; **Supp. XXI: 143–157**
"Hyacinth Drift" (Rawlings), **Supp. X: 226–227**
Hyde, Lewis, **Supp. XVIII:** 150
"Hydrangeas" (C. Frost), **Supp. XV:** 106
"Hydras, The" (Merwin), **Supp. III Part 1:** 349
Hydriotaphia, The; or, Death of Dr. Browne: An Epic Farce about Death and Primitive Capital Accumulation (Kushner), **Supp. IX:** 133, **136–138**
"Hydriotaphia; or, Urne-Buriall" (Browne), **Supp. IX:** 136–137
Hyman, Stanley Edgar, **I:** 129, 264, 363, 377, 379; **Retro. Supp. II:** 118; **Supp. IX:** 113, 114, 117, 118, 121, 122, 128
Hymen (Doolittle), **Supp. I Part 1:** 266
"Hymie's Bull" (Ellison), **Retro. Supp. II:** 124; **Supp. II Part 1:** 229
"Hymn Books" (Emerson), **II:** 10
"HYMN FOR LANIE POO" (Baraka), **Supp. II Part 1:** 31, 37
"Hymn from a Watermelon Pavilion" (Stevens), **IV:** 81
"Hymn of the Sea, A" (Bryant), **Supp. I Part 1:** 157, 163, 165
"Hymns of the Marshes" (Lanier), **Supp. I Part 1:** 364
"Hymn to Death" (Bryant), **Supp. I Part 1:** 169, 170
"Hymn to Earth" (Wylie), **Supp. I Part 2:** 727–729
"Hymn to the Night" (Longfellow), **Supp. I Part 2:** 409
Hynes, Jennifer, **Supp. XV:** 207
Hynes, Samuel, **Supp. XIV:** 159
Hyperion (Longfellow), **II:** 488, 489, 491–492, 496; **Retro. Supp. II:** 58, 155–156
"Hypocrite Auteur" (MacLeish), **III:** 19
"Hypocrite Swift" (Bogan), **Supp. III Part 1:** 55
"Hysteria" (Eliot), **I:** 570

I (Dixon), **Supp. XII:** 141, 155, **156–157**
I, etcetera (Sontag), **Supp. III Part 2:** 451–452, 469
I, Governor of California and How I Ended Poverty (Sinclair), **Supp. V:** 289
I, the Jury (Spillane), **Supp. XVIII:** 236
"I, Too" (Hughes), **Retro. Supp. I:** 193, 199; **Supp. I Part 1:** 320
I Accuse! (film), **Supp. IV Part 2:** 683
"I Almost Remember" (Angelou), **Supp. IV Part 1:** 15
"'I Always Wanted You to Admire My Fasting'; or, Looking at Kafka"(P. Roth), **Retro. Supp. II:** 282
I am a Camera (Druten), **Supp. XIV:** 162
"I am a cowboy in the boat of Ra" (Reed), **Supp. X:** 242
"I Am a Dangerous Woman" (Harjo), **Supp. XII:** 216, 219
"I Am Alive" (Momaday), **Supp. IV Part 2:** 489
I Am a Sonnet (Goldbarth), **Supp. XII:** 181
"I Am a Writer of Truth" (Fante), **Supp. XI:** 167
"'I Am Cherry Alive,' the Little Girl Sang" (Schwartz), **Supp. II Part 2:** 663
"I Am Dying, Meester?" (Burroughs), **Supp. III Part 1:** 98
I Am Elijah Thrush (Purdy), **Supp. VII:** 274
"I Am in Love" (Stern), **Supp. IX:** 295
"I Am Not Flattered" (Francis), **Supp. IX:** 78
I Am! Says the Lamb (Roethke), **III:** 545
"I Am You Again" (Nelson), **Supp. XVIII:** 173
"I and My Chimney" (Melville), **III:** 91
I and Thou (Buber), **III:** 308
"I Apologize" (Komunyakaa), **Supp. XIII:** 120, **Supp. XIII:** 121
I Apologize for the Eyes in My Head (Komunyakaa), **Supp. XIII: 119–121,** 126
"I Believe I Shall Die an Impenetrable Secret": The Writings of Elizabeth Barstow Stoddard (Giovani), **Supp. XV:** 270
Ibn Rushd (Averroes), **Supp. XX: 117**
Ibn Síná (Avicenna), **Supp. XX: 117**
Ibsen, Henrik, **II:** 27, 276, 280, 291–292; **III:** 118, 145, 148, 149, 150, 151, 152, 154–155, 156, 161, 162, 165, 511, 523; **IV:** 397; **Retro. Supp. I:** 228; **Retro. Supp. II:** 94; **Supp. IV Part 2:** 522; **Supp. XIV:** 89; **Supp. XVII:** 100; **Supp. XIX:** 241
"I Came Out of the Mother Naked" (R. Bly), **Supp. IV Part 1:** 62–63, 68
I Can Lick 30 Tigers Today! and Other Stories (Geisel), **Supp. XVI:** 108
"I Cannot Forget with What Fervid Devotion" (Bryant), **Supp. I Part 1:** 154
I Can Read with My Eyes Shut! (Geisel), **Supp. XVI:** 111
"I Can Speak!$_{tm}$" (Saunders), **Supp. XIX:** 231
"I Can't Stand Your Books: A Writer Goes Home" (Gordon), **Supp. IV Part 1:** 314
"Icarium Mare" (Wilbur), **Supp. III Part 2:** 563
"Icarus in Winter" (C. Frost), **Supp. XV:** 94
Icarus's Mother (Shepard), **Supp. III Part 2:** 446
"Ice" (Bambara), **Supp. XI:** 16
"Ice Age" (Taggard), **Supp. XXII:** 276
Ice at the Bottom of the World, The (Richard), **Supp. XIX:** 209, **210–213,** 218, 220
"Iceberg, The" (Merwin), **Supp. III Part 1:** 345
Ice-Cream Headache, The, and Other Stories (Jones), **Supp. XI:** 215, 227
Ice Fire Water: A Leib Goldkorn Cocktail (Epstein), **Supp. XII: 164–166**
"Ice Fisherman, The" (C. Baxter), **Supp. XVII:** 15
"Ice House, The" (Gordon), **II:** 201
"Ice Man, The" (Di Piero), **Supp. XIX:** 40
Iceman Cometh, The (O'Neill), **I:** 81; **III:** 151, 385, 386, 401, 402–403; **Supp. VIII:** 345; **Supp. XVI:** 193; **Supp. XVII:** 103; **Supp. XXII:** 28
"Ice Palace, The" (Fitzgerald), **II:** 83, 88; **Retro. Supp. I:** 103
Ice-Shirt, The (Vollmann), **Supp. XVII:** 226, 231, 232, 233
"Ice Storm, The" (Ashbery), **Supp. III Part 1:** 26
"Ice-Storm, The" (Pinsky), **Supp. VI:** 247–248
"Ichabod" (Whittier), **Supp. I Part 2:** 687, 689–690; **Supp. XI:** 50
"I Chop Some Parsley While Listening to Art Blakey's Version of 'Three Blind Mice' " (Collins), **Supp. XXI:** 60
"Icicles" (Francis), **Supp. IX:** 83
"Icicles" (Gass), **Supp. VI:** 83
Ickes, Harold, **Supp. I Part 1:** 5
Iconographs (Swenson), **Supp. IV Part 2:** 638, 646–648, 651
"Icosaphere, The" (Moore), **III:** 213
"I Could Believe" (Levine), **Supp. V:** 189
"I Could Take" (Carruth), **Supp. XVI:** 56
I Could Tell You Stories: Sojourns in the Land of Memory (Hampl), **Supp. XXII:** 84, **92–94**
"I Cry, Love! Love!" (Roethke), **III:** 539–540
Ida (Stein), **IV:** 43, 45
"Idea, The" (Carver), **Supp. III Part 1:** 143
"Idea, The" (Strand), **Supp. IV Part 2:** 631
Ideal Husband (Wilde), **II:** 515
Idea of Florida in the American Literary Imagination, The (Rowe), **Supp. X:** 223
"Idea of Form at Spruce Creek, The" (Weigl), **Supp. XIX:** 283–284
"Idea of Ice, The" (C. Baxter), **Supp. XVII:** 15
"Idea of Order, An" (Wiman), **Supp. XVIII:** 173
"Idea of Order at Key West, The" (Stevens), **IV:** 89–90; **Retro. Supp. I:** 302, 303, 313
Ideas of Order (Stevens), **Retro. Supp. I:** 296, 298, **302–303,** 303, 305
"Identity Theft: True Memory, False Memory, and the Holocaust" (R. Franklin), **Supp. XVI:** 160
Ideograms in China (Michaux; Sobin, trans.), **Supp. XVI:** 288
"Ideographs" (Olds), **Supp. X:** 205
Ides of March, The (Wilder), **IV:** 357, 372
"I Did Not Learn Their Names" (Ellison), **Retro. Supp. II:** 124
"I Died with the First Blow & Was Reborn Wrong" (Coleman), **Supp. XI:** 91
"Idiom of a Self, The" (Pinsky), **Supp. VI:** 240
"Idiot, The" (Crane), **I:** 401
Idiot, The (Dostoevsky), **I:** 468
"Idiots First" (Malamud), **Supp. I Part 2:** 434–435, 437, 440–441
"Idiot Wind" (song, Dylan), **Supp. XVIII:** 30
I Don't Need You Any More (A. Miller), **III:** 165
Idoru (W. Gibson), **Supp. XVI:** 119, 124, **129–130**
"I Dream I'm the Death of Orpheus" (Rich), **Supp. I Part 2:** 557–558
I Dreamt I Became a Nymphomaniac! Imagining (Acker), **Supp. XII:** 4, 6, **8,** 11
"I Dreamt You Young" (Espaillat), **Supp. XXI:** 107
"Idyll" (Shaw), **Supp. XIX:** 241
Idylls of the King (Tennyson), **III:** 487; **Supp. I Part 2:** 410; **Supp. XIII:** 146
Idyl of Work, An (Larcom), **Supp. XIII:** 139, 142, 146–147, 150
"If" (Creeley), **Supp. IV Part 1:** 158
If Beale Street Could Talk (Baldwin), **Retro. Supp. II:** 13–14; **Supp. I Part 1:** 48, 59–60, 67
"If Biblical Law Ruled Modern Society . . . " (P. N. Warren), **Supp. XX: 272**
If Blessing Comes (Bambara), **Supp. XI:** 1
I Feel a Little Jumpy around You (Nye and Janeczko, eds.), **Supp. XIII:** 280
"I felt a Funeral, in my Brain" (Dickinson), **Retro. Supp. I:** 38
"If Grown-Ups Were Smart" (Nelson and Espeland), **Supp. XVIII:** 181
If He Hollers Let Him Go (C. Himes), **Supp. XVI:** 135, 138–139, 142
"If I Could Be Like Wallace Stevens" (Stafford), **Supp. XI:** 327
"If I Could Do Whatever I Wanted" (Nelson and Espeland), **Supp. XVIII:** 181
"If I Could Only Live at the Pitch That Is Near Madness" (Eberhart), **I:** 523, 526–527
If I Could Write This in Fire (Cliff), **Supp. XXII:** 67, 69

"If I Could Write This in Fire, I Would Write This in Fire" (Cliff), **Supp. XXII:** 65–66, 68–69
If I Die in a Combat Zone (O'Brien), **Supp. V:** 238, 239, 240, 245
"If I Had My Way" (Creeley), **Supp. IV Part 1:** 157
"If I Might Be" (Chopin), Retro. Supp. II: 61
"I Find the Real American Tragedy" (Dreiser), **Retro. Supp. II:** 105
If I Ran the Circus (Geisel), **Supp. XVI:** 105
If I Ran the Zoo (Geisel), **Supp. XVI:** 104–105
If It Die (Gide), **I:** 290
"If It Were Not for You" (Carruth), **Supp. XVI:** 57
"If I Were a Man" (Gilman), **Supp. XI:** 207
"If I Were the Wind" (Leopold), **Supp. XIV:** 184
If Morning Ever Comes (Tyler), **Supp. IV Part 2:** 658–659
If Mountains Die: A New Mexico Memoir (Nichols), **Supp. XIII:** 255, 257, 267
I Forgot to Go to Spain (Harrison), **Supp. VIII:** 39, **52–53**
If the River Was Whiskey (Boyle), **Supp. VIII: 15–16; Supp. XX: 17, 19**
"If They Knew Yvonne" (Dubus), **Supp. VII:** 81
"If We Had Bacon" (H. Roth), **Supp. IX:** 232, 234
"If We Had Known" (Francis), **Supp. IX:** 78
"If We Must Die" (McKay), **Supp. IV Part 1:** 3; **Supp. X:** 132, 134
"If We Take All Gold" (Bogan), **Supp. III Part 1:** 52
If You Call This a Cry Song (Carruth), **Supp. XVI:** 56
If You Want to Write (Ueland), **Supp. XVII:** 13
I Gaspiri (Lardner), **II:** 435
"I Gather the Limbs of Osiris" (Pound), **Retro. Supp. I:** 287
I Get on the Bus (McKnight), **Supp. XX: 148–150, 152**
"I Give You Back" (Harjo), **Supp. XII:** 223
Ignatius of Loyola, **IV:** 151; **Supp. XI:** 162
Ignatow, David, **Supp. XIII:** 275
"Ignis Fatuus" (Tate), **IV:** 128
"Ignorant Lust after Knowledge, The" (Bronk), **Supp. XXI:** 31
"I Go Back to May 1937" (Olds), **Supp. X:** 207
I Go Dreaming Serenades (Salinas), **Supp. XIII:** 316
I Got the Blues (Odets), **Supp. II Part 2:** 530
Iguana Killer, The (Ríos), **Supp. IV Part 2:** 542–544
"I Had Eight Birds Hatcht in One Nest" (Bradstreet), **Supp. I Part 1:** 102, 115, 117, 119
"I had no time to Hate" (Dickinson), **Retro. Supp. I:** 44–45, 46
I Had Trouble in Getting to Solla Sollew (Geisel), **Supp. XVI:** 108, 109
"I Have a Rendezvous with Life" (Cullen), **Supp. IV Part 1:** 168
"I Have Increased Power" (Ginsberg), **Supp. II Part 1:** 313
"I Have Moved West" (Taggard), **Supp. XXII:** 274
"I Have Seen Black Hands" (Wright), **Supp. II Part 1:** 228
"I Hear an Army" (Joyce), **Supp. I Part 1:** 262
"I heard a Fly buzz when I died" (Dickinson), **Retro. Supp. I:** 38
"I Heard Immanuel Singing" (Lindsay), **Supp. I Part 2:** 379
I Heard It Through the Grapevine (Turner), **Supp. XX: 110**
"I Hear It Was Charged against Me" (Whitman), **IV:** 343
"I Held a Shelley Manuscript" (Corso), **Supp. XII:** 128
"I Held His Name" (Ríos), **Supp. IV Part 2:** 547
"Ike and Nina" (Boyle), **Supp. XX: 19**
I Knew a Phoenix (Sarton), **Supp. VIII:** 249, 251–252
"I Know a Man" (Creeley), **Supp. IV Part 1:** 147–148, 149
I Know Some Things: Stories about Childhood by Contemporary Writers (Moore, ed.), **Supp. X:** 175
"I Know Why the Caged Bird Cannot Read" (Prose), **Supp. XVI:** 259
I Know Why the Caged Bird Sings (Angelou), **Supp. IV Part 1:** 2–4, 5, 7, 11, 12, 13, 14, 15, 17; **Supp. XVI:** 259
"Ikon: The Harrowing of Hell" (Levertov), **Supp. III Part 1:** 284
Ile (O'Neill), **III:** 388
"I Led Three Lives" (television program), **Supp. XX: 195**
"I Let Him Take Me" (Cisneros), **Supp. VII:** 71
Iliad (Bryant, trans.), **Supp. I Part 1:** 158
Iliad (Homer), **II:** 470; **Supp. IV Part 2:** 631; **Supp. IX:** 211; **Supp. X:** 114; **Supp. XVII:** 117; **Supp. XXI:** 36
Iliad (Pope, trans.), **Supp. I Part 1:** 152
"I like to see it lap the Miles" (Dickinson), **Retro. Supp. I:** 37
"I Live Up Here" (Merwin), **Supp. III Part 1:** 349
"I'll Be Doing More of Same" (Franzen), **Supp. XX: 89**
"Illegal Alien" (Mora), **Supp. XIII:** 215
"Illegal Days, The" (Paley), **Supp. VI:** 222
"Illegibility" (F. Wright), **Supp. XVII:** 244
Illig, Joyce, **Retro. Supp. II:** 20
"Illinois" (Masters), **Supp. I Part 2:** 458
"Illinois Bus Ride" (Leopold), **Supp. XIV:** 189
Illinois Poems (Masters), **Supp. I Part 2:** 472
"Illinois Village, The" (Lindsay), **Supp. I Part 2:** 381
"Ill-Lit" (F. Wright), **Supp. XVII:** 245
Ill-Lit: Selected & New Poems (F. Wright), **Supp. XVII:** 245
Illness as Metaphor (Sontag), **Supp. III Part 2:** 452, 461, 466
I'll Take My Stand ("Twelve Southerners"), **II:** 196; **III:** 496; **IV:** 125, 237; **Supp. X:** 25, 52–53; **Supp. XIV:** 3
"I'll Take You to Tennessee" (Connell), **Supp. XIV:** 82
Illumination (Frederic), **II:** 141
Illumination, The (Brockmeier), **Supp. XXII:** 61
Illumination Night (Hoffman), **Supp. X:** 85, **86,** 88, 89
Illuminations (Rimbaud), **Supp. XXI:** 233
Illusion and Reality (Caudwell), **Supp. XXII:** 284
Illusion comique, L' (Corneille), **Supp. IX:** 138
"Illusion of Eternity, The" (Eberhart), **I:** 541
"Illusion of Fiction in Frank Conroy's *Stop-Time,* The" (R. Ramsey), **Supp. XVI:** 69
Illusions (Dash; film), **Supp. XI:** 20
"Illusions" (Emerson), **II:** 2, 5, 14, 16
Illustrated Man, The (Bradbury), **Supp. IV Part 1:** 102, 103, 113
Illustrations of China and Its People (Thompson), **Supp. XXI:** 151
Illustrations of Political Economy (Martineau), **Supp. II Part 1:** 288
"I Look at My Hand" (Swenson), **Supp. IV Part 2:** 638, 647
I Love Gootie: My Grandmother's Story (Apple), **Supp. XVII: 9–10**
I Love Myself When I Am Laughing . . . : A Zora Neale Hurston Reader (Walker), **Supp. III Part 2:** 531, 532
"I'm a Fool" (Anderson), **I:** 113, 114, 116; **Supp. I Part 2:** 430
Image and Idea (Rahv), **Supp. II Part 1:** 146
Image and the Law, The (Nemerov), **III:** 268, 269–271, 272
"Image in the Mirror, The" (Swados), **Supp. XIX:** 265
"Images" (Hass), **Supp. VI:** 103
"Images and 'Images' " (Simic), **Supp. VIII:** 274
"Images for Godard" (Rich), **Supp. I Part 2:** 558
"Images of Walt Whitman" (Fiedler), **IV:** 352
"Imaginary Dialogue, An" (Espaillat), **Supp. XXI:** 103
"Imaginary Friendships of Tom McGrath, The" (Cohen), **Supp. X:** 112
"Imaginary Iceberg, The" (Bishop), **Retro. Supp. II:** 42; **Supp. I Part 1:** 86, 88
"Imaginary Jew, The" (Berryman), **I:** 174–175
Imaginary Letters (Pound), **III:** 473–474
Imaginary Paintings (C. Baxter), **Supp. XVII:** 18–19

"Imaginary Prisons" (Schnackenberg), **Supp. XV:** 257, 258
Imagination and Fancy; or, Selections from the English Poets, illustrative of those first requisites of their art; with markings of the best passages, critical notices of the writers, and an essay in answer to the question'What is Poetry?' (Hunt), II: 515–516
"Imagination as Value" (Stevens), **Retro. Supp. I:** 298
"Imagination of Disaster, The" (Gordon), **Supp. IV Part 1:** 306
Imaginative Qualities of Actual Things (Sorrentino), **Supp. XXI:** 226, 230, 231–232, 234
"Imagine a Day at the End of Your Life" (Beattie), **Supp. V:** 33
Imagined London: A Tour of the World's Greatest Fictional City (Quindlen), **Supp. XVII:** 167, 180
Imagineering Atlanta (Rutheiser), **Supp. XXII:** 244
"Imagine Kissing Pete" (O'Hara), **III:** 372; **Supp. VIII:** 156
Imaging Robert: My Brother, Madness, and Survival (Neugeboren), **Supp. XVI:** 225, **226–229**
"Imagining How It Would Be to Be Dead" (Eberhart), **I:** 533
Imagining Los Angeles: A City in Fiction (Fine), **Supp. XI:** 160
"Imagining Their Own Hymns" (B. Kelly), **Supp. XVII:** 126–127
"Imagining the Midwest" (Sanders), **Supp. XVI:** 275–276
Imagining the Worst: Stephen King and the Representations of Women (Lant and Thompson), **Supp. V:** 141
"Imagisme" (Pound), **Retro. Supp. I:** 288
Imagistes, Des: An Anthology of the Imagists (Pound, ed.), **III:** 465, 471; **Retro. Supp. I:** 288
Imago (O. Butler), **Supp. XIII:** 63, **65–66**
"Imago" (Stevens), **IV:** 74, 89
Imagoes (Coleman), **Supp. XI:** 89–90
I Married a Communist (P. Roth), **Retro. Supp. II:** 289, 293–294
I Married an Angel (film), **Supp. XVI:** 193
"I May, I Might, I Must" (Moore), **III:** 215
"I'm Crazy" (Salinger), **III:** 553
"I'm Here" (Roethke), **III:** 547
Imitations (Lowell), **II:** 543, 544–545, 550, 555; **Retro. Supp. II:** 181, 187
"Imitations of Drowning" (Sexton), **Supp. II Part 2:** 684, 686
"Immaculate Man" (Gordon), **Supp. IV Part 1:** 311
"Immanence of Dostoevsky, The" (Bourne), **I:** 235
"Immigrants" (Mora), **Supp. XIII:** 216
Immigrant Saint: The Life of Mother Cabrini (di Donato), **Supp. XX: 44**
"Immigrant Story, The" (Paley), **Supp. VI:** 230
Immobile Wind, The (Winters), **Supp. II Part 2:** 786
"Immobile Wind, The" (Winters), **Supp. II Part 2:** 788, 811
"Immolatus" (Komunyakaa), **Supp. XIII:** 126
"Immoral Proposition, The" (Creeley), **Supp. IV Part 1:** 144
"Immortal Autumn" (MacLeish), **III:** 13
"Immortality Ode" (Nemerov), **III:** 87
Immortality Ode (Wordsworth), **II:** 17; **Supp. I Part 2:** 673
"Immortal Woman, The" (Tate), **IV:** 130, 131, 137
"I'm Not Ready to Die Yet" (Harjo), **Supp. XII:** 231
I'm Not There (film, Haynes), **Supp. XVIII:** 23
"I'm on My Way" (Salinas), **Supp. XIII:** 320
"Impasse" (Hughes), **Supp. I Part 1:** 343
"Impatient Mary" (Taggard), **Supp. XXII:** 278
Imperative Duty, An, a Novel (Howells), **II:** 286
Imperial Eyes: Travel Writing and Transculturation (Pratt), **Retro. Supp. II:** 48
Imperial Germany and the Industrial Revolution (Veblen), **Supp. I Part 2:** 642, 643
Imperial Way, The: By Rail from Peshawar to Chittagong (Theroux), **Supp. VIII:** 323
"Implosions" (Rich), **Supp. I Part 2:** 556
"Imp of the Perverse, The" (Poe), **III:** 414–415; **Retro. Supp. II:** 267
Impolite Interviews, **Supp. XI:** 293
"Importance of Artists' Biographies, The" (Goldbarth), **Supp. XII:** 183, 184, 191
Importance of Being Earnest, The (Wilde), **Supp. XIV:** 324, 339
"Important Houses, The" (Gordon), **Supp. IV Part 1:** 315
"Impossible Indispensability of the Ars Poetica, The" (Carruth), **Supp. XVI:** 57
"Impossible to Tell" (Pinsky), **Supp. VI:** 247, 248
"Imposter, The" (West), **Retro. Supp. II:** 322, 327
"Impressionism and Symbolism in *Heart of Darkness*" (Watt), **Supp. VIII:** 4
"Impressions of a European Tour" (Bourne), **I:** 225
"Impressions of a Plumber" (H. Roth), **Supp. IX:** 228, 234
"Impressions of Europe, 1913–1914" (Bourne), **I:** 225
"I Must Have Called and So He Comes" (Notley), **Supp. XXII:** 224
"I'm Walking behind the Spanish" (Salinas), **Supp. XIII:** 323–324
"I/Myself" (Shields), **Supp. VII:** 311
"In Absence" (Lanier), **Supp. I Part 1:** 364
"In Absentia" (Bowles), **Supp. IV Part 1:** 94
"In a Cab" (Untermeyer), **Supp. XV:** 296
"In a Country Cemetery" (Kooser), **Supp. XIX:** 120
Inada, Lawson Fusao, **Supp. V:** 180
"In a Dark Room, Furniture" (Nye), **Supp. XIII:** 274
"In a Dark Time" (Roethke), **III:** 539, 547, 548
In a Different Voice (Gilligan), **Supp. XXII:** 18
"In a Disused Graveyard" (Frost), **Retro. Supp. I:** 126, 133
In a Dusty Light (Haines), **Supp. XII:** 207
"In a Garden" (Lowell), **II:** 513
"In a Hard Intellectual Light" (Eberhart), **I:** 523
"In a Hollow of the Hills" (Harte), **Supp. II Part 1:** 354
In America (Sontag), **Supp. XIV:** 95–96
"In Amicitia" (Ransom), **IV:** 141
In a Narrow Grave: Essays on Texas (McMurtry), **Supp. V:** 220, 223
"Inanna" (A. Finch), **Supp. XVII:** 72
"In Another Country" (Hemingway), **I:** 484–485; **II:** 249
In April Once (Percy), **Retro. Supp. I:** 341
"In a Prominent Bar in Secaucus One Day" (X. J. Kennedy), **Supp. XV:** 154, 155–156
In A Shallow Grave (Purdy), **Supp. VII:** 272
"In a Station of the Metro" (Pound), **Retro. Supp. I:** 288; **Supp. I Part 1:** 265; **Supp. XIV:** 284–285
"In a Strange Town" (Anderson), **I:** 114, 115
"In Athens Once" (Rodriguez), **Supp. XIV:** 303
"In a Tub" (Hempel), **Supp. XXI:** 119
In Battle for Peace: The Story of My 83rd Birthday (Du Bois), **Supp. II Part 1:** 185
In Bed One Night & Other Brief Encounters (Coover), **Supp. V:** 49, 50
"In Bertram's Garden" (Justice), **Supp. VII:** 117
"In Blackwater Woods" (Oliver), **Supp. VII:** 244, 246
In Black & Whitey (Lacy), **Supp. XV:** 206–207
"In Broad Daylight" (Jin), **Supp. XVIII:** 94
In Broken Country (Wagoner), **Supp. IX:** 330
"In California" (Simpson), **Supp. IX:** 271
"In Camp" (Stafford), **Supp. XI:** 329
"Incant against Suicide" (Karr), **Supp. XI:** 249
"In Celebration of My Uterus" (Sexton), **Supp. II Part 2:** 689
"Incendiary, The" (Rowson), **Supp. XV:** 234
"In Certain Places and Certain Times There Can Be More of You" (Dunn), **Supp. XI:** 144
Incest: From "A Journal of Love," the Unexpurgated Diary of Anaïs Nin, 1932–1934 (Nin), **Supp. X:** 182, 184, 185, 187, 191
"In Chandler Country" (Gioia), **Supp. XV:** 119
Inchbald, Elizabeth, **II:** 8

"In Cheever Country" (Gioia), **Supp. XV:** 119
Inchiquin, the Jesuit's Letters (Ingersoll), **I:** 344
"Incident" (Cullen), **Supp. IV Part 1:** 165, 166
Incidental Numbers (Wylie), **Supp. I Part 2:** 708
Incidentals (Sandburg), **III:** 579
Incidentals in the Day World (Notley), **Supp. XXII:** 223, 226, 227
Incident at Vichy (A. Miller), **III:** 165, 166
Incidents in the Life of a Slave Girl (Brent), **Supp. IV Part 1:** 13
Incidents in the Life of a Slavegirl (Jacobs), **Supp. XVI:** 85
"Incipience" (Rich), **Supp. I Part 2:** 559
"In Clare" (McCarriston), **Supp. XIV:** 270–271
Including Horace (Untermeyer), **Supp. XV:** 301, 303–304
In Cold Blood: A True Account of a Multiple Murder and Its Consequences (Capote), **Retro. Supp. II:** 107–108; **Supp. I Part 1:** 292; **Supp. III Part 1:** 111, 117, 119, 122, 123, 125–131; **Supp. III Part 2:** 574; **Supp. IV Part 1:** 220; **Supp. XIV:** 162
In Cold Hell, in Thicket (Olson), **Supp. II Part 2:** 571
"In Cold Hell, in Thicket" (Olson), **Supp. II Part 2:** 558, 563–564, 566, 572, 580
"Incomparable Light, The" (Eberhart), **I:** 541
Incorporative Consciousness of Robert Bly, The (Harris), **Supp. IV Part 1:** 68
In Country (Mason), **Supp. VIII:** 133, **142–143,** 146
"In Country of Conscience" (J. W. Miller), **Supp. XX: 165**
"Incredible Survival of Coyote, The" (Snyder), **Supp. VIII:** 297
"Increment" (Ammons), **Supp. VII:** 28
In Defense of Ignorance (Shapiro), **Supp. II Part 2:** 703, 704, 713–714
In Defense of Reason (Winters), **Supp. I Part 1:** 268
In Defense of Women (Mencken), **III:** 109
Independence Day (film), **Supp. X:** 80
Independence Day (Ford), **Supp. V:** 57, 62–63, 67–68
"Independent Candidate, The, a Story of Today" (Howells), **II:** 277
"Indestructible Mr. Gore, The" (Vidal), **Supp. IV Part 2:** 679
Index of American Design, **Supp. III Part 2:** 618
"India" (Rodriguez), **Supp. XIV:** 302
"Indian at the Burial-Place of His Fathers, An" (Bryant), **Supp. I Part 1:** 155–156, 167–168
"Indian Burying Ground, The" (Freneau), **Supp. II Part 1:** 264, 266
"Indian Camp" (Hemingway), **II:** 247–248, 263; **Retro. Supp. I:** 174–175, 176, 177, 181; **Supp. XVI:** 208
Indian Country (Caputo), **Supp. XIX:** 22–25
Indian Country (Matthiessen), **Supp. V:** 211
"Indian Country" (McCarriston), **Supp. XIV:** 271
"Indian Country" (Simpson), **Supp. IX:** 274
Indian Earth (Bynner), **Supp. XV:** 46
"Indian Girls" (McCarriston), **Supp. XIV:** 272–273
"Indian Manifesto" (Deloria), **Supp. IV Part 1:** 323
"Indian Names" (Sigourney), **Retro. Supp. II:** 47
"Indian Student, The" (Freneau), **Supp. II Part 1:** 264
"Indian Student, The" (Simpson), **Supp. IX:** 280
Indian Summer (Howells), **II:** 275, 279–281, 282
Indian Summer (Knowles), **Supp. XII:** 249, 250
Indian Summer: Musings on the Gift of Life (Pickering), **Supp. XXI:** 204
"Indian Uprising, The" (Barthelme), **Supp. IV Part 1:** 44
"Indian Wooing" (C. Miller), **Supp. XXII:** 197–198
Indifferent Children, The (Auchincloss), **Supp. IV Part 1:** 25
Indirections (Cox), **Supp. XXI:** 21
Indiscretions (Pound), **Retro. Supp. I:** 284
"Indispensability of the Eyes, The" (Olds), **Supp. X:** 202
"In Distrust of Merits" (Moore), **III:** 201, 214
"Individual and the State, The" (Emerson), **II:** 10
Individualism, Old and New (Dewey), **Supp. I Part 2:** 677
"Indolence" (Pickering), **Supp. XXI:** 203
In Dreams Begin Responsibilities (Schwartz), **Supp. II Part 2:** 642, 645–650
"In Dreams Begin Responsibilities" (Schwartz), **Supp. II Part 2:** 641, 649, 654
In Dubious Battle (Steinbeck), **IV:** 51, 55–56, 59, 63
"In Durance" (Pound), **Retro. Supp. I:** 285
"Industry of Hard Kissing, The" (Ríos), **Supp. IV Part 2:** 547
"In Duty Bound" (Gilman), **Supp. XI:** 196–197
"I Need, I Need" (Roethke), **III:** 535–536
"I Need Help" (Stern), **Supp. IX:** 290
"Ineffectual Marriage" (Loy), **Supp. XXII:** 165
"Inés in the Kitchen" (García), **Supp. XI:** 190
"I never saw a Moor" (Dickinson), **Retro. Supp. I:** 37
I Never Told Anybody: Teaching Poetry Writing in a Nursing Home (Koch), **Supp. XV:** 190
"I Never Will Be Married, I'd Rather Be Excus'd" (Rowson), **Supp. XV:** 240
Inevitable Exiles (Kielsky), **Supp. V:** 273
"Inevitable Trial, The" (Holmes), **Supp. I Part 1:** 318
"Inexhaustible Hat, The" (Wagoner), **Supp. IX:** 327
"In Extremis" (Berry), **Supp. X:** 23
"Infancy" (Wilder), **IV:** 375
"Infant Boy at Midcentury" (Warren), **IV:** 244–245, 252
Infante, Guillermo Cabrera, **Retro. Supp. I:** 278
"Infant Sea Turtles" (F. Wright), **Supp. XVII:** 245
Infants of the Spring (Thurman), **Supp. XVIII:** 281; **Supp. XIX:** 73
Inferno (Dante), **IV:** 139; **Supp. V:** 338; **Supp. VIII:** 219–221
Inferno of Dante, The (Pinsky), **Supp. VI:** 235, 248
"Infidelity" (Komunyakaa), **Supp. XIII:** 130
Infidels (album, Dylan), **Supp. XVIII:** 28
"Infiltration of the Universe" (MacLeish), **III:** 19
Infinite Jest: A Novel (Wallace), **Supp. X:** 301, **310–314; Supp. XX: 91**
"Infinite Reason, The" (MacLeish), **III:** 19
"Infirmity" (Lowell), **II:** 554
"Infirmity" (Roethke), **III:** 548
In Five Years Time (Haines), **Supp. XII:** 206
"In Flower" (Snodgrass), **Supp. VI:** 325
"Influence of Landscape upon the Poet, The" (Eliot), **Retro. Supp. I:** 67
"In Football Season" (Updike), **IV:** 219
Informer, The (film), **Supp. III Part 2:** 619
Ingersoll, Charles J., **I:** 344
Ingersoll, Robert Green, **Supp. II Part 1:** 198
Ingraham, Lloyd, **Supp. XVI:** 184
Ingster, Boris, **Retro. Supp. II:** 330
Inhabitants, The (Morris), **III:** 221–222
"Inheritance and Invention in Li-Young Lee's Poetry" (Xiaojing), **Supp. XV:** 214
"Inheritance of Tools, The" (Sanders), **Supp. XVI:** 273
Inheritors (Glaspell), **Supp. III Part 1:** 175, 179–181, 186, 189
"In Hollywood with the Zuni God of War" (Major), **Supp. XXII:** 180
"In Honor of David Anderson Brooks, My Father" (Brooks), **Supp. III Part 1:** 79
"Inhumanist, The" (Jeffers), **Supp. II Part 2:** 423, 426
"In Illo Tempore" (Karr), **Supp. XI:** 242
"In Interims: Outlyer" (Harrison), **Supp. VIII:** 38
"Initial" (F. Wright), **Supp. XVII:** 243
"Injudicious Gardening" (Moore), **III:** 198
"Injustice" (Paley), **Supp. VI:** 220
Injustice Collectors, The (Auchincloss), **Supp. IV Part 1:** 25

Ink, Blood, Semen (Goldbarth), **Supp. XII:** 181, 183
Ink Truck, The (W. Kennedy), **Supp. VII:** 132, 133–138, 140, 141, 149, 152
In Life Sentences: Literary Essays (Epstein), **Supp. XIV:** 112
"In Limbo" (Wilbur), **Supp. III Part 2:** 544, 561
In Limestone Country (Sanders), **Supp. XVI:** 272
"In Line" (Major), **Supp. XXII:** 185
In Love and Trouble: Stories of Black Women (Walker), **Supp. III Part 2:** 520, 521, 530, 531, 532
In Mad Love and War (Harjo), **Supp. XII: 224–226**
"In Memoriam" (Emerson), **II:** 13
"In Memoriam" (Hay), **Supp. XIV:** 122, 127
"In Memoriam" (Tennyson), **Retro. Supp. I:** 325; **Supp. I Part 2:** 416
In Memoriam: 1933 (Reznikoff), **Supp. XIV:** 280, 285
In Memoriam to Identity (Acker), **Supp. XII:** 5, **16–18**
"In Memory of Arthur Winslow" (Lowell), **II:** 541, 547, 550; **Retro. Supp. II:** 187
"In Memory of Congresswoman Barbara Jordan" (Pinsky), **Supp. VI:** 250
"In Memory of Joe Brainard" (Bidart), **Supp. XV:** 33
"In Memory of My Feelings" (O'Hara), **Supp. XV:** 215–216
"In Memory of W. B. Yeats" (Auden), **Supp. VIII:** 19, 30; **Supp. XI:** 243, 244; **Supp. XIX:** 85
"In Memory of W. H. Auden" (Stern), **Supp. IX:** 288
"In Mercy on Broadway" (Doty), **Supp. XI:** 132
In Morocco (Wharton), **Retro. Supp. I:** 380; **Supp. IV Part 1:** 81
Inmost Leaf, The: A Selection of Essays (Kazin), **Supp. VIII:** 102, 103
In Motley (Bierce), **I:** 209
In My Father's Court (Singer), **IV:** 16–17; **Retro. Supp. II: 301–302**
"In My Life" (Dubus), **Supp. VII:** 81
"In Navaho Country" (Bronk), **Supp. XXI:** 30
Inner Circle, The (Boyle), **Supp. XX: 24, 26**
Inner Landscape (Sarton), **Supp. VIII:** 259
Inner Room, The (Merrill), **Supp. III Part 1:** 336
"In Nine Sleep Valley" (Merrill), **Supp. III Part 1:** 328
Innocent Mrs. Duff, The (Holding), **Supp. XXII:** 119, 120, 123, **130–131**, 135, 136
Innocents, The: A Story for Lovers (Lewis), **II:** 441
Innocents Abroad, The; or, The New Pilgrim's Progress (Twain), **II:** 275, 434; **IV:** 191, 196, 197–198
Innocents at Cedro, The: A Memoir of Thorstein Veblen and Some Others (Duffus), **Supp. I Part 2:** 650
"In Off the Cliffs of Moher" (McCarriston), **Supp. XIV:** 270
In Old Plantation Days (Dunbar), **Supp. II Part 1:** 214
In Ole Virginia (Page), **Supp. II Part 1:** 201
In Orbit (Morris), **III:** 236
In Other Words (Swenson), **Supp. IV Part 2:** 650–652
In Other Words: Literature by Latinas of the United States (Fernandez, ed.), **Supp. XXI:** 104
In Our Terribleness (Some elements and meaning in black style) (Baraka), **Supp. II Part 1:** 52, 53
In Our Time (Hemingway), **I:** 117; **II:** 68, 247, 252, 263; **IV:** 42; **Retro. Supp. I:** 170, 173, 174, 178, 180; **Supp. IX:** 106
"In Our Time" (Wolfe), **Supp. III Part 2:** 584
"Inpatient" (Kenyon), **Supp. VII:** 169
In Persuasion Nation (Saunders), **Supp. XIX: 231–234**
"In Persuasion Nation" (Saunders), **Supp. XIX:** 233–234
In Pharaoh's Army: Memories of the Lost War (Wolff), **Supp. VII:** 331–334, 335, 338
"In Plaster" (Plath), **Supp. I Part 2:** 540
"In Prague, in Montmartre" (Bierds), **Supp. XVII:** 27
"In Praise of Johnny Appleseed" (Lindsay), **Supp. I Part 2:** 397
"In Praise of Limestone" (Auden), **Supp. II Part 1:** 20–21; **Supp. VIII:** 23
In Pursuit of a Vanishing Star (Sobin), **Supp. XVI: 294**
In Quest of the Ordinary (Cavell), **Retro. Supp. I:** 307
Inquiry into the Moral and Religious Character of the American Government, An (H. Warner), **Supp. XVIII:** 259
Inquiry into the Nature of Peace, An (Veblen), **Supp. I Part 2:** 642
Inquisitor, The (Rowson), **Supp. XV: 232,** 238
In Radical Pursuit (Snodgrass), **Supp. VI:** 312, 316, 318
In Reckless Ecstasy (Sandburg), **III:** 579
In Recognition of William Gaddis (Kuehl and Moore), **Supp. IV Part 1:** 279
"In Retirement" (Malamud), **Supp. I Part 2:** 437
"In Retrospect" (Angelou), **Supp. IV Part 1:** 15
"In Right" (Wolfert), **Supp. XXI:** 263, 264, 272
"Inroads of Time, The" (D. West), **Supp. XVIII:** 286–287
In Russia (A. Miller), **III:** 165
"In Sabine" (Chopin), **Supp. I Part 1:** 213
"In School-Days" (Whittier), **Supp. I Part 2:** 699–700
"Inscription for the Entrance to a Wood" (Bryant), **Supp. I Part 1:** 154, 155, 161–162
Inscriptions, 1944–1956 (Reznikoff), **Supp. XIV:** 281
In Search of America: The Image of the United States in Travel Writing of the 1980s and 1990s (Rutkowska), **Supp. XXII:** 208
"In Search of a Motif for Expressive Female Figuration" (Major), **Supp. XXII:** 184
In Search of Bisco (Caldwell), **I:** 296
In Search of Nella Larsen: A Biography of the Color Line (Hutchinson), **Supp. XVIII:** 120
"In Search of Our Mothers' Gardens" (Walker), **Supp. III Part 2:** 520–532, 524, 525, 527, 529, 532–533, 535, 536; **Supp. IX:** 306; **Supp. XVIII:** 200, 283
"In Search of Thomas Merton" (Griffin), **Supp. VIII:** 208
"In Search of Yage" (Burroughs), **Supp. III Part 1:** 98
"Insect Life in Florida" (Hull), **Supp. XXI:** 133
Insel (Loy), **Supp. XXII:** 167
"Insertion of Self into a Space of Borderless Possibilities, The" (Fjellestad), **Supp. XVI:** 150
"In Shadow" (Crane), **I:** 386
"In Sickness and in Health" (Auden), **Supp. II Part 1:** 15
"In Sickness and in Health" (Humphrey), **Supp. IX:** 94
Inside Diameter: The France Poems (Major), **Supp. XXII:** 182
Inside His Mind (A. Miller), **III:** 154
Inside Memory (Findley), **Supp. XX: 51, 63**
"Inside Norman Mailer" (Apple), **Supp. XVII:** 3, 4
"Insider Baseball" (Didion), **Supp. IV Part 1:** 211
Inside Sports magazine, **Supp. V:** 58, 61
"Insipid Profession of Jonathan Horneboom, The" (Lethem), **Supp. XVIII:** 149
"In So Many Dark Rooms" (Hogan), **Supp. IV Part 1:** 400
"Insomnia" (Bishop), **Supp. I Part 1:** 92
"Insomniac" (Plath), **Supp. I Part 2:** 539
"In Spain, Throwing Carnations" (P. N. Warren), **Supp. XX: 272**
"Inspiration for Greatness" (Caldwell), **I:** 291
"Instability of Race Types, The" (Boas), **Supp. XIV:** 209
"Installation #6" (Beattie), **Supp. V:** 33
Instinct of Workmanship and the State of the Industrial Arts, The (Veblen), **Supp. I Part 2:** 642
Instincts of the Herd in Peace and War, The (Trotter), **I:** 249
Institute (Calvin), **IV:** 158, 160
"Instruction Manual, The" (Ashbery), **Supp. III Part 1:** 6–7, 10, 12
Instructions, The (Levin), **Supp. XXII:** 268
"Instructions for the Afternoon" (Gioia), **Supp. XV:** 120

"Instruction to Myself" (Brooks), **Supp. III Part 1:** 87
Instrument, The (O'Hara), **III:** 362, 364
"In Such Times, Ties Must Bind" (Nye), **Supp. XIII:** 286
"Insurance and Social Change" (Stevens), **Retro. Supp. I:** 297
Insurgent Mexico (Reed), **I:** 476
In Suspect Terrain (McPhee), **Supp. III Part 1:** 309, 310
"In Tall Grass" (Sandburg), **III:** 585
"Integer Vitae" (Horace), **Supp. XV:** 304
Intellectual History, An (Senghor), **Supp. X:** 139
"Intellectual Pre-Eminence of Jews in Modern Europe, The" (Veblen), **Supp. I Part 2:** 643–644
Intellectual Things (Kunitz), **Supp. III Part 1:** 260, 262–264
Intellectual versus the City, The (White), **I:** 258
"In Temporary Pain" (Bynner), **Supp. XV:** 41–42
Intentions (Wilde), **Retro. Supp. I:** 56
"Interest in Life, An" (Paley), **Supp. VI:** 222, 224–225
Interest of Great Britain Considered, with Regard to Her Colonies and the Acquisition of Canada and Guadeloupe, The (Franklin), **II:** 119
Interior Landscapes (Vizenor), **Supp. IV Part 1:** 262
Interiors (film; Allen), **Supp. IV Part 1:** 205; **Supp. XV: 1, 7,** 10
Interlocking Lives (Koch), **Supp. XV:** 185
"Interlude" (A. Lowell), **Retro. Supp. II:** 46
Interlunar (Atwood), **Supp. XIII:** 35
"Intermezzo" (Schnackenberg), **Supp. XV:** 254
"In Terms of the Toenail: Fiction and the Figures of Life" (Gass), **Supp. VI:** 85
"International Episode, An" (James), **II:** 327
International Workers Order, **Retro. Supp. I:** 202
Interpretation of Christian Ethics, An (Niebuhr), **III:** 298–300, 301, 302
"Interpretation of Dreams, The" (Matthews), **Supp. IX:** 162–163
Interpretation of Music of the XVIIth and XVIIIth Centuries, The (Dolmetsch), **III:** 464
Interpretations and Forecasts: 1922–1972 (Mumford), **Supp. II Part 2:** 481
Interpretations of Poetry and Religion (Santayana), **III:** 611
Interpreter of Maladies (Lahiri), **Supp. XXI:** 175–176, **177–180,** 183
"Interpreter of Maladies" (Lahiri), **Supp. XXI:** 183, 184
Interpreters and Interpretations (Van Vechten), **Supp. II Part 2:** 729, 733–734
"Interrogate the Stones" (MacLeish), **III:** 9
Interrogations at Noon (Gioia), **Supp. XV:** 112, **125–127,** 128, 129
"Interrupted Conversation, An" (Van Vechten), **Supp. II Part 2:** 735
"Interrupted Elegy" (Peacock), **Supp. XIX:** 200
Intersect: Poems (Shields), **Supp. VII:** 310–311
Intersexes, The (Prime-Stevenson as Mayne), **Supp. XX: 235**
Interstate (Dixon), **Supp. XII:** 140, 152–153, 153, 156
"Interview" (Hay), **Supp. XIV:** 132
"Interview, The" (Thurber), **Supp. I Part 2:** 616
"Interview With a Lemming" (Thurber), **Supp. I Part 2:** 603
"Interview with Peter Everwine, An" (Veinberg and Buckley), **Supp. XV:** 76–77
"Interview with the Crab" (Lethem), **Supp. XVIII:** 148
Interview with the Vampire (Rice), **Supp. VII:** 287, 288–291, 297–298, 303
"Interview with the Vampire" (Rice), **Supp. VII:** 288
Interzone (Burroughs), **Supp. IV Part 1:** 90
"In the Absence of Bliss" (Kumin), **Supp. IV Part 2:** 453
"In the Afternoon" (Dunn), **Supp. XI:** 146
"In the Alley" (Elkin), **Supp. VI: 46–47**
In the American Grain (W. C. Williams), **Retro. Supp. I:** 420–421
In the American Jungle (W. Frank), **Supp. XX: 76**
In the American Tree (Silliman), **Supp. IV Part 2:** 426
In the Bank of Beautiful Sins (Wrigley), **Supp. XVIII: 300–302**
In the Bar of a Tokyo Hotel (T. Williams), **IV:** 382, 386, 387, 391, 393
In the Beauty of the Lilies (Updike), **Retro. Supp. I:** 322, 325, 326, 327, 333
"In the Beeyard" (Bierds), **Supp. XVII:** 29
"In the Beginning" (Quindlen), **Supp. XVII:** 166
"In the Beginning . . ." (Simic), **Supp. VIII:** 270, 271
In the Belly of the Beast: Letters from Prison (Abbott), **Retro. Supp. II:** 210
"In the Black Morning" (Wolfert), **Supp. XXI:** 265
"In the Black Museum" (Nemerov), **III:** 275
"In the Blink of God's Eye" (P. E. Jones), **Supp. XXII:** 150
"In the Bodies of Words" (Swenson), **Supp. IV Part 2:** 651
"In the Cage" (Gass), **Supp. VI:** 85
In the Cage (James), **Retro. Supp. I:** 229
"In the Cage" (James), **II:** 332; **Retro. Supp. I:** 231
"In the Cage" (Lowell), **Retro. Supp. II:** 187
"In the Cave at Lone Tree Meadow" (Haines), **Supp. XII:** 212
"In the Cemetery Where Al Jolson Is Buried" (Hempel), **Supp. XXI:** 115, **121–122**
"In the City Ringed with Giants" (Kingsolver), **Supp. VII:** 209
"In the Clearing" (Brodsky), **Supp. VIII:** 32
In the Clearing (Frost), **II:** 153, 155, 164; **Retro. Supp. I:** 121, 122, 141
"In the Closet of the Soul" (Walker), **Supp. III Part 2:** 526
"In the Cold Air Register" (W. V. Davis), **Supp. XXI:** 94
"In the Confidence of a Story-Writer" (Chopin), **Retro. Supp. II:** 66–67; **Supp. I Part 1:** 217
In the Country of Last Things (Auster), **Supp. XII:** 23, **29–30,** 31, 32
"In the Courtyard of the Isleta Missions" (R. Bly), **Supp. IV Part 1:** 71
"In the Dark" (Levine), **Supp. V:** 194
"In the Dark New England Days" (Jewett), **Retro. Supp. II:** 139
"In the Days of Prismatic Colour" (Moore), **III:** 205, 213
In the Days of the Comet (Wells), **Supp. XX: 233, 240**
In the Electric Mist with Confederate Dead (Burke), **Supp. XIV:** 30, 31–32
"In the Field" (Wilbur), **Supp. III Part 2:** 558
"In the First Stanza" (C. Kizer), **Supp. XVII:** 75
"In the Fleeting Hand of Time" (Corso), **Supp. XII:** 122–123
"In the Footsteps of Gutenberg" (Mencken), **III:** 101
"In the Forest" (Simpson), **Supp. IX:** 270
"In the Forest of the Laughing Elephant" (Caputo), **Supp. XIX:** 27
"In the Forties" (Lowell), **II:** 554
In the Garden of the North American Martyrs (Wolff), **Supp. VII:** 341–342
In the Garret (Van Vechten), **Supp. II Part 2:** 735
"In the Grove: The Poet at Ten" (Kenyon), **Supp. VII:** 160
"In the Hall of Mirrors" (Merrill), **Supp. III Part 1:** 322
In the Harbor (Longfellow), **II:** 491
In the Heart of the Heart of the Country (Gass), **Supp. VI: 82–83,** 84, 85, 93
In the Heat of the Night (Ball), **Supp. XV:** 202
In the Heat of the Night (film), **Supp. I Part 1:** 67
In the Hollow of His Hand (Purdy), **Supp. VII:** 278–280
In the House of Light (Everwine, trans.), **Supp. XV:** 73, 75, **76–78,** 82
In the Lake of the Woods (O'Brien), **Supp. V:** 240, 243, 250–252
In the Land of the White Death: A Epic Story of Survival in the Siberian Arctic (Albanov), **Supp. XVIII:** 114
"In the Last Days" (Everwine), **Supp. XV:** 88, 89
In the Loyal Mountains (Bass), **Supp. XVI: 19–20**

"In the Loyal Mountains" (Bass), **Supp. XVI:** 20
In the Mecca (Brooks), **Supp. III Part 1:** 74
"In the Mecca" (Brooks), **Supp. III Part 1:** 70, 83–84
In the Midst of Life (Bierce), **I:** 200–203, 204, 206, 208, 212
"In the Miro District" (Taylor), **Supp. V:** 323
In the Miro District and Other Stories (Taylor), **Supp. V:** 325–326
In the Money (W. C. Williams), **Retro. Supp. I:** 423
"In the Motel" (X. J. Kennedy), **Supp. XV:** 163
"In the Naked Bed, in Plato's Cave" (Schwartz), **Supp. II Part 2:** 646–649
In the Name of the Neither (Sobin), **Supp. XVI:** 291
"In the Night" (Kincaid), **Supp. VII:** 183
In the Night Season: A Novel (Bausch), **Supp. VII:** 52–53
"In the Old Neighborhood" (Dove), **Supp. IV Part 1:** 241, 257
"In the Old World" (Oates), **Supp. II Part 2:** 503, 504
"In the Park" (Huncke), **Supp. XIV:** 139
In the Pines (Notley), **Supp. XXII:** 236–237
"In the Pit" (Proulx), **Supp. VII:** 255, 261
In the Pond (Jin), **Supp. XVIII: 95–96**
In the Presence of the Sun (Momaday), **Supp. IV Part 2:** 489, 490, 491–493, 493
"In the Quiet Night" (Li Po), **Supp. XV:** 47
"In the Realm of the Fisher King" (Didion), **Supp. IV Part 1:** 211
"In the Red Room" (Bowles), **Supp. IV Part 1:** 93
"In the Region of Ice" (Oates), **Supp. II Part 2:** 520
In the Room We Share (Simpson), **Supp. IX:** 279
"In These Dissenting Times" (Walker), **Supp. III Part 2:** 522
"In the Shadow of Gabriel, A.D.1550" (Frederic), **II:** 139
In the Shadow of Memory (Skloot), **Supp. XX: 193, 196, 205, 205–206**
"In the Shadow of Memory" (Skloot), **Supp. XX: 206**
In the Shadow of the Morning: Essays on Wild Lands, Wild Waters, and a Few Untamed People (Caputo), **Supp. XIX:** 28–29
In the Spirit of Crazy Horse (Matthiessen), **Supp. V:** 211
"In the Subway" (Untermeyer), **Supp. XV:** 296
In the Summer House (Jane Bowles), **Supp. IV Part 1:** 83, 89
In the Tennessee Country (Taylor), **Supp. V:** 328
"In the Thick of Darkness" (Salinas), **Supp. XIII:** 325
"In the Time of the Blossoms" (Mervin), **Supp. III Part 1:** 352
In the Time of the Butterflies (Alvarez), **Supp. VII:** 1, 12–15, 18
"In the Tube" (Jarman), **Supp. XVII:** 121
"In the Tunnel Bone of Cambridge" (Corso), **Supp. XII:** 120–121
"In the Upper Pastures" (Kumin), **Supp. IV Part 2:** 453
In the Valley (Frederic), **II:** 133–134, 136, 137
"In the Village" (Bishop), **Retro. Supp. II:** 38; **Supp. I Part 1:** 73, 74–75, 76, 77, 78, 88
"In the Waiting Room" (Bishop), **Retro. Supp. II:** 50; **Supp. I Part 1:** 81, 94, 95; **Supp. IV Part 1:** 249
"In the Ward: The Sacred Wood" (Jarrell), **II:** 376, 377
In the Western Night: Collected Poems 1965–90 (Bidart), **Supp. XV:** 19, **30–32**
"In the White Night" (Beattie), **Supp. V:** 30–31
"In the Wind My Rescue Is" (Ammons), **Supp. VII:** 25
"In the Winter Dark" (Peacock), **Supp. XIX:** 206
In the Winter of Cities (T. Williams), **IV:** 383
"In the X-Ray of the Sarcophagus of Tapero" (Goldbarth), **Supp. XII:** 191
"In the Yard" (Swenson), **Supp. IV Part 2:** 647
In the Zone (O'Neill), **III:** 388
In This, Our Life (film), **Supp. I Part 1:** 67
"In This Country, but in Another Language, My Aunt Refuses to Marry the Men Everyone Wants Her To" (Paley), **Supp. VI:** 225
"In This Dream" (J. W. Miller), **Supp. XX: 170**
In This Hung-up Age (Corso), **Supp. XII: 119–120,** 129
In This Our Life (Glasgow), **II:** 175, 178, 189
In This Our World (Gilman), **Supp. XI:** 196, 200, 202
"In Those Days" (Jarrell), **II:** 387–388
"Intimately Connected to the Zeitgeist" (Franzen), **Supp. XX: 94**
"In Time of War" (Auden), **Supp. II Part 1:** 8, 13
"Into Egypt" (Benét), **Supp. XI:** 56, 57–58
Intolerance (film; Griffith), **Supp. XVI:** 184
"Into My Own" (Frost), **II:** 153; **Retro. Supp. I:** 127
"Into Night" (McKnight), **Supp. XX: 151–152**
Into the Interior (Cliff), **Supp. XXII:** 67, 78–79
"Into the Night Life . . ." (H. Miller), **III:** 180, 184
"Into the Nowhere" (Rawlings), **Supp. X:** 220
Into the Stone (Dickey), **Supp. IV Part 1:** 178
"Into the Stone" (Dickey), **Supp. IV Part 1:** 179
Into the Stone and Other Poems (Dickey), **Supp. IV Part 1:** 176
Into the Wild (Krakauer), **Supp. XVIII:** 106, **107–108,** 116, 117
Into Thin Air: A Personal Account of the Mount Everest Disaster (Krakauer), **Supp. XVII:** 210; **Supp. XVIII:** 105, **109–113,** 117
In Touch: The Letters of Paul Bowles (J. Miller, ed.), **Supp. IV Part 1:** 95
"Intoxicated, The" (Jackson), **Supp. IX:** 116
"Intrigue" (Crane), **I:** 419
"Introducing the Fathers" (Kumin), **Supp. IV Part 2:** 452
Introductio ad Prudentiam (Fuller), **II:** 111
"Introduction to a Haggadah" (Paley), **Supp. VI:** 219
Introduction to Objectivist Epistemology (Rand), **Supp. IV Part 2:** 527, 528–529
Introduction to Objectivist Epistemology 2nd ed. (Rand), **Supp. IV Part 2:** 529
"Introduction to Poetry" (Collins), **Supp. XXI:** 57
Introduction to Poetry, An (Gioia and X. J. Kennedy), **Supp. XV:** 113, 153
"Introduction to Some Poems, An" (Stafford), **Supp. XI:** 311, 324
Introduction to the Geography of Iowa, The (Doty), **Supp. XI:** 120
"Introduction to the Hoh" (Hugo), **Supp. VI:** 136–137
"Introduction to *The New Writing in the USA*" (Creeley), **Supp. IV Part 1:** 153–154
"Introduction to William Blake, An" (Kazin), **Supp. VIII:** 103
Introitus (Longfellow), **II:** 505, 506–507
"Intruder, The" (Dubus), **Supp. VII:** 76–78, 91
Intruder, The (Maeterlinck), **I:** 91
Intruder in the Dust (Faulkner), **II:** 71, 72; **Supp. XVI:** 148
"Invaders, The" (Haines), **Supp. XII:** 205
Invaders, The (W. Frank), **Supp. XX: 79–80**
Invasion of Privacy: The Cross Creek Trial of Marjorie Kinnan Rawlings (Acton), **Supp. X:** 233
Inventing Memory: A Novel of Mothers and Daughters (Jong), **Supp. V:** 115, 129
Inventing the Abbotts (Miller), **Supp. XII: 294–295**
"Invention of Autobiography. The" (Hampl), **Supp. XXII:** 93–94
"Invention of God in a Mouthful of Milk, The" (Karr), **Supp. XI:** 250
Invention of Solitude, The (Auster), **Supp. XII:** 21–22
Inventions of the March Hare (Eliot), **Retro. Supp. I:** 55–56, 58
"Inventions of the March Hare" (Eliot), **Retro. Supp. I:** 55
"Inventory" (Parker), **Supp. IX:** 192
"Inverted Forest, The" (Salinger), **III:** 552, 572

"Investigation" (Ryan as Quin), **Supp. XVIII:** 227–228
"Investigations of a Dog" (Kafka), **IV:** 438
"Investiture, The" (Banks), **Supp. V:** 7
"Investiture at Cecconi's" (Merrill), **Supp. III Part 1:** 336
"Invisible" (Pickering), **Supp. XXI:** 201
Invisible Circus, The (Egan), **Supp. XIX:** 49, **50–52**
Invisible Company, The (Sanders), **Supp. XVI:** 270–271
Invisible Man (Ellison), **IV:** 493; **Retro. Supp. II:** 3, 12, 111, 112, 113, 117, 119, **120–123,** 125; **Supp. II Part 1:** 40, 170, 221, 224, 226, 227, 230, 231–232, 235, 236, 241–245; **Supp. IX:** 306; **Supp. X:** 242; **Supp. XI:** 18, 92; **Supp. XVIII:** 59; **Supp. XIX:** 154, 155
Invisible: Poems (Nye), **Supp. XIII:** 277
Invisible Spectator, An (Sawyer-Lauçanno), **Supp. IV Part 1:** 95
Invisible Swords (Farrell), **II:** 27, 46, 48–49
Invisible Worm, The (Millar), **Supp. IV Part 2:** 465
Invitation to a Beheading (Nabokov), **III:** 252–253, 254, 257–258; **Retro. Supp. I:** 265, 270, 273
"Invitation to the Country, An" (Bryant), **Supp. I Part 1:** 160
"Invocation" (McKay), **Supp. X:** 134
"Invocation" (Untermeyer), **Supp. XV:** 296
"Invocation to Kali" (Sarton), **Supp. VIII:** 260
"Invocation to the Social Muse" (MacLeish), **III:** 15
"In Weather" (Hass), **Supp. VI: 102–103**
"In Your Fugitive Dream" (Hugo), **Supp. VI:** 143
"In Your Good Dream" (Hugo), **Supp. VI:** 143–144
"Iola, Kansas" (Clampitt), **Supp. IX: 45–46**
Iola Leroy (Harper), **Supp. XVIII:** 284
Ion (Doolittle, trans.), **Supp. I Part 1:** 269, 274
Ion (Plato), **I:** 523
"Ione" (Dunbar), **Supp. II Part 1:** 199
Ionesco, Eugène, **I:** 71, 74, 75, 84, 295; **II:** 435; **Supp. VIII:** 201; **Supp. XIX:** 131
Ionica (Cory), **Supp. XX: 230**
Ionica II (Cory), **Supp. XX: 230**
"I Only Am Escaped Alone to Tell Thee" (Nemerov), **III:** 272, 273–274
"I Opened All the Portals Wide" (Chopin), **Retro. Supp. II:** 71
I Ought to Be in Pictures (Simon), **Supp. IV Part 2:** 584
Iphigenia (Notley), **Supp. XXII:** 226, 235
Iphigenia in Tauris (Euripedes), **Supp. XV:** 42, 50
I Promessi Sposi (Manzoni), **II:** 291
"I Put My Hand on My Son's Head" (Kooser), **Supp. XIX:** 120
Iram, Dhát al-'Imád (Gibran), **Supp. XX: 116**
"Iraq Drifting, July 2003" (Weigl), **Supp. XIX:** 288
"Irascibles, The" (Kees), **Supp. XV:** 145–146
Ireland: A Terrible Beauty (Uris), **Supp. XX: 244, 245–246, 246, 254**
"I Remember" (Sexton), **Supp. II Part 2:** 680
"Irenicon" (Shapiro), **Supp. II Part 2:** 704
Irigaray, Luce, **Supp. XII:** 6
Iris (Jarman), **Supp. XVII:** 110, **116–117**
"Iris by Night" (Frost), **Retro. Supp. I:** 132
"Irises" (L.-Y. Lee), **Supp. XV:** 214–215
Irish in America, The (Coffey, ed.), **Supp. XIX:** 133
Irish Stories of Sarah Orne Jewett, The (Jewett), **Retro. Supp. II:** 142
Irish Triangle, An (Barnes), **Supp. III Part 1:** 34
"Iron Characters, The" (Nemerov), **III:** 279, 282
"Iron Hans" (Sexton), **Supp. II Part 2:** 691
Iron Heel, The (London), **II:** 466, 480
Iron John: A Book about Men (R. Bly), **Supp. IV Part 1:** 59, 67; **Supp. XVI:** 177
"Iron Table, The" (Jane Bowles), **Supp. IV Part 1:** 82–83
"Iron Throat, The" (Olsen), **Supp. XIII:** 292, 297, 299
Ironweed (W. Kennedy), **Supp. VII:** 132, 133, 134, 135, 142, 144, 145–147, 148, 150, 153
"Irony as Art: The Short Fiction of William Humphrey" (Tebeaux), **Supp. IX:** 109
"Irony Is Not Enough: Essay on My Life as Catherine Deneuve" (Carson), **Supp. XII: 112–113**
Irony of American History, The (Niebuhr), **III:** 292, 306–307, 308
"Irrational Element in Poetry, The" (Stevens), **Retro. Supp. I:** 298, 301
"Irrevocable Diameter, An" (Paley), **Supp. VI:** 231–232
Irvine, Lorna, **Supp. XIII:** 26
Irving, Ebenezer, **II:** 296
Irving, Sir Henry, **IV:** 350
Irving, John, **Supp. VI: 163–183; Supp. X:** 77, 85
Irving, John Treat, **II:** 296
Irving, Peter, **II:** 296, 297, 298, 299, 300, 303
Irving, Washington, **I:** 211, 335, 336, 339, 343; **II: 295–318,** 488, 495; **III:** 113; **IV:** 309; **Retro. Supp. I:** 246; **Supp. I Part 1:** 155, 157, 158, 317; **Supp. I Part 2:** 377, 487, 585; **Supp. II Part 1:** 335; **Supp. IV Part 1:** 380; **Supp. XVIII:** 12
Irving, William, **II:** 296
Irving, William, Jr., **II:** 296, 297, 298, 299, 303
Irwin, Mark, **Supp. XII:** 21, 22, 24, 29
Irwin, Robert, **Supp. XX: 120**
Irwin, William Henry, **Supp. II Part 1:** 192
Is 5 (Cummings), **I:** 429, 430, 434, 435, 440, 445, 446, 447
"Isaac and Abraham" (Brodsky), **Supp. VIII:** 21
"Isaac and Archibald" (Robinson), **III:** 511, 521, 523
Isaacs, Neil D., **Supp. XIX:** 255
"Isabelle" (Saunders), **Supp. XIX:** 225
"Isabel Sparrow" (Oliver), **Supp. VII:** 232
Isaiah (biblical book), **Supp. I Part 1:** 236; **Supp. I Part 2:** 516; **Supp. XXI:** 107
"Isaiah Beethoven" (Masters), **Supp. I Part 2:** 461
"I Saw in Louisiana a Live-Oak Growing" (Whitman), **I:** 220
"I Shall Be Released" (Dylan), **Supp. XV:** 349
I Shall Spit on Your Graves (film), **Supp. I Part 1:** 67
Isháq, Adib, **Supp. XX: 117**
Isherwood, Christopher, **II:** 586; **Supp. II Part 1:** 10, 11, 13; **Supp. IV Part 1:** 79, 82, 102; **Supp. XI:** 305; **Supp. XIV: 155–175; Supp. XVI:** 194
Isherwood Century, The (Berg and Freeman), **Supp. XIV:** 157, 159
Isherwood's Fiction (Schwerdt), **Supp. XIV:** 155
Ishiguro, Kazuo, **Supp. VIII:** 15
Ishi Means Man (Merton), **Supp. VIII:** 208
"Ishmael's Dream" (Stern), **Supp. IX:** 287
I Should Have Stayed Home (McCoy), **Supp. XIII:** 167, **168–170,** 171
"I Should Worry" (Kees), **Supp. XV:** 140
"I Sigh in the Afternoon" (Salinas), **Supp. XIII:** 318
"I Sing the Body Electric" (Whitman), **Retro. Supp. I:** 394, 395
"Isis: Dorothy Eady, 1924" (Doty), **Supp. XI:** 122
"Is It O.K. to Be a Luddite?" (Pynchon), **Supp. XVI:** 128
"Is It True?" (Hughes), **Supp. I Part 1:** 342
I: Six Nonlectures (Cummings), **I:** 430, 433, 434
"Island" (Hughes), **Supp. I Part 1:** 340
Island Garden, An (Thaxter), **Retro. Supp. II:** 136; **Supp. XIII:** 152
Island Holiday, An (Henry), **I:** 515
Island in the Atlantic (W. Frank), **Supp. XX: 79**
"Island of the Fay, The" (Poe), **III:** 412, 417
Islands (Siddons), **Supp. XXII:** 239
"Islands, The" (Hayden), **Supp. II Part 1:** 373
"Island Sheaf, An" (Doty), **Supp. XI:** 136
Islands in the Stream (Hemingway), **II:** 258; **Retro. Supp. I:** 186
Isn't It Romantic (Wasserstein), **Supp. XV: 323–325,** 327
Is Objectivism a Religion? (Ellis), **Supp. IV Part 2:** 527

"Isolation of Modern Poetry, The" (Schwartz), **Supp. II Part 2:** 644
"Israel" (Reznikoff), **Supp. XIV:** 283
Israel Potter, or Fifty Years of Exile (Melville), **III:** 90; **Supp. XVIII:** 4
"Israfel" (Poe), **III:** 411
Is Sex Necessary? (Thurber and White), **Supp. I Part 2:** 607, 612, 614, 653
"Issues, The" (Olds), **Supp. X:** 205
"Istanbul" (Collins), **Supp. XXI:** 60
"I Stand Here Ironing" (Olsen), **Supp. XIII:** 292, 294, 296, 298, 300, 305
I Stole a Million (West), **IV:** 287
"Is Verse a Dying Technique?" (Wilson), **IV:** 431
It (Creeley), **Supp. IV Part 1:** 157, 158
IT (King), **Supp. V:** 139, 140, 141, 146–147, 151, 152
"It" (Olds), **Supp. X:** 208
Italian American Reconciliation: A Folktale (Shanley), **Supp. XIV:** 315, **324–326,** 328, 330
Italian Backgrounds (Wharton), **Retro. Supp. I:** 370
Italian Hours (James), **I:** 12; **II:** 337; **Retro. Supp. I:** 235
Italian Journeys (Howells), **II:** 274
"Italian Morning" (Bogan), **Supp. III Part 1:** 58
Italian Villas and Their Gardens (Wharton), **IV:** 308; **Retro. Supp. I:** 361, 367
Italie, Hillel, **Supp. XV:** 128
It All Adds Up: From the Dim Past to the Uncertain Future (Bellow), **Retro. Supp. II:** 32
"It Always Breaks Out" (Ellison), **Retro. Supp. II:** 126; **Supp. II Part 1:** 248
Itard, Jean-Marc Gaspard, **Supp. I Part 2:** 564
"I taste a liquor never brewed" (Dickinson), **Retro. Supp. I:** 30, 37
It Came from Outer Space (film), **Supp. IV Part 1:** 102
It Can't Happen Here (Lewis), **II:** 454
"It Don't Mean a Thing If It Ain't Got That Swing" (Matthews), **Supp. IX: 164–165**
I Tell You Now (Ortiz), **Supp. IV Part 2:** 500
"Ithaca" (Glück), **Supp. V:** 89
It Happened One Night (Capra), **Supp. XV:** 197
It Has Come to Pass (Farrell), **II:** 26
"I think to live May be a Bliss" (Dickinson), **Retro. Supp. I:** 44
"I Thought It Was Harry" (Bronk), **Supp. XXI:** 31
I Thought of Daisy (Wilson), **IV:** 428, 434, 435
"Itinerary of an Obsession" (Kumin), **Supp. IV Part 2:** 450
"It Is a Strange Country" (Ellison), **Supp. II Part 1:** 238
"It Is Dangerous to Read Newspapers" (Atwood), **Supp. XIII:** 33
"It Must Be Abstract" (Stevens), **IV:** 95; **Retro. Supp. I:** 307
"It Must Change" (Stevens), **Retro. Supp. I:** 300, 307, 308
"It Must Give Pleasure" (Stevens), **Retro. Supp. I:** 307, 308, 309
"'It Out-Herods Herod. Pray You, Avoid It' " (Hecht), **Supp. X:** 62, 64
"It's All Over Now, Baby Blue" (song, Dylan), **Supp. XVIII:** 30
It's Loaded, Mr. Bauer (Marquand), **III:** 59
It's Nation Time (Baraka), **Supp. II Part 1:** 52, 53
"It's Nation Time" (Baraka), **Supp. II Part 1:** 53
It's Only a Play (McNally), **Supp. XIII:** 198
It Was (Zukofsky), **Supp. III Part 2:** 630
It Was the Nightingale (Ford), **III:** 470–471
"It Was When" (Snyder), **Supp. VIII:** 300
Ivanhoe (Scott), **I:** 216; **Supp. I Part 2:** 410
Ivens, Bryna, **Supp. XV:** 311, 312
Ivens, Joris, **I:** 488; **Retro. Supp. I:** 184
"Iverson Boy, The" (Simpson), **Supp. IX:** 280
"Ives" (Rukeyser), **Supp. VI:** 273, 283
Ives, George H., **Supp. I Part 1:** 153
Ivory Grin, The (Macdonald), **Supp. IV Part 2:** 471, 472
"Ivory Novel, The" (Halliday), **Supp. XIX:** 90
Ivory Tower, The (James), **II:** 337–338
"Ivory Tower, The: Louis Untermeyer as Critic" (Aiken), **Supp. XV:** 298
Ivry, Sara, **Supp. XX: 179**
"Ivy Winding" (Ammons), **Supp. VII:** 33
Iwamatsu, Mako, **Supp. XXI:** 150
"I Wandered Lonely as a Cloud" (Wordsworth), **Retro. Supp. I:** 121–122; **Supp. X:** 73; **Supp. XIV:** 184
"I want, I want" (Plath), **Retro. Supp. II:** 246
"I Wanted to Be There When My Father Died" (Olds), **Supp. X:** 210
"I Want to Be a Father Like the Men" (Cisneros), **Supp. VII:** 71
"I Want to Be Miss America" (Alvarez), **Supp. VII:** 18
"I Want to Know Why" (Anderson), **I:** 114, 115, 116; **II:** 263
"I Want You Women Up North To Know" (Olsen), **Supp. XIII:** 292, 297
"I Was Born in Lucerne" (Levine), **Supp. V:** 181, 189
"I Was Really Very Hungry" (M. F. K. Fisher), **Supp. XVII:** 91
"I Went into the Maverick Bar" (Snyder), **Supp. VIII:** 301
"I Will Lie Down" (Swenson), **Supp. IV Part 2:** 640
I Will Say Beauty (C. Frost), **Supp. XV:** 96, **105–107**
I Wonder As I Wander (Hughes), **Retro. Supp. I:** 196, 203; **Supp. I Part 1:** 329, 332–333
I Would Have Saved Them If I Could (L. Michaels), **Supp. XVI:** 203, 205, **206–210**
"Iyani: It goes this Way" (Gunn Allen), **Supp. IV Part 1:** 321
"I years had been from home" (Dickinson), **I:** 471
Iyer, Pico, **Supp. V:** 215
Izzo, David Garrett, **Supp. XIV:** 155, 156, 159, 160, 161, 163, 169, 171

Jab (Halliday), **Supp. XIX: 91–94**
"Jachid and Jechidah" (Singer), **IV:** 15
Jack and Jill (Alcott), **Supp. I Part 1:** 42
"Jack and the Beanstalk" (Hay), **Supp. XIV:** 124
"Jack in the Pot" (D. West), **Supp. XVIII:** 283
Jack Kelso (Masters), **Supp. I Part 2:** 456, 471–472
Jacklight (Erdrich), **Supp. IV Part 1:** 259, 270
Jack London, Hemingway, and the Constitution (Doctorow), **Supp. IV Part 1:** 220, 222, 224, 232, 235
Jackman, Harold, **Supp. XVIII:** 131
Jackpot (Caldwell), **I:** 304
"Jack Schmidt, Arts Administrator" (Keillor), **Supp. XVI:** 171
"Jack Schmidt on the Burning Sands" (Keillor), **Supp. XVI:** 171
Jackson, Amelia. *See* Holmes, Mrs. Oliver Wendell (Amelia Jackson)
Jackson, Andrew, **I:** 7, 20; **III:** 473; **IV:** 192, 248, 298, 334, 348; **Supp. I Part 2:** 456, 461, 473, 474, 493, 695
Jackson, Blyden, **Supp. I Part 1:** 337
Jackson, Charles, **Supp. I Part 1:** 303
Jackson, George, **Supp. I Part 1:** 66
Jackson, Helen Hunt, **I:** 459, 470; **Retro. Supp. I:** 26, 27, 30–31, 32, 33
Jackson, James, **Supp. I Part 1:** 302, 303
Jackson, J. O., **III:** 213
Jackson, Joe, **Supp. I Part 2:** 441
Jackson, Katherine Gauss, **Supp. VIII:** 124
Jackson, Lawrence ?/, **Retro. Supp. II:** 113, 115
Jackson, Lawrence P. ?/, **Supp. XXII:** 140
Jackson, Melanie, **Supp. X:** 166
Jackson, Michael, **Supp. VIII:** 146
Jackson, Richard, **II:** 119; **Supp. IX:** 165
Jackson, Shelley, **Supp. XVIII:** 136
Jackson, Shirley, **Supp. IX: 113–130**
Jackson, Thomas J. ("Stonewall"), **IV:** 125, 126
"Jackson Hotel" (Hull), **Supp. XXI:** 134, 135
"Jackson Square" (Levertov), **Supp. III Part 1:** 276
Jackstraws (Simic), **Supp. VIII:** 280, 282–283
"Jackstraws" (Simic), **Supp. VIII: 283**
Jack Tier (Cooper), **I:** 354, 355
"Jacob" (Garrett), **Supp. VII:** 109–110
"Jacob" (Schwartz), **Supp. II Part 2:** 663
Jacob, Max, **Supp. XV:** 178, 182
"Jacob and the Indians" (Benét), **Supp. XI:** 47–48

Jacobs, Catherine Haydon, **Supp. XXI:** 98
Jacobs, Harriet, **Supp. XVI:** 85
Jacobs, Jill Suzanne, **Supp. XX: 178, 186**
Jacobs, Rita D., **Supp. XII:** 339
Jacobsen, Josephine, **Supp. XIII:** 346; **Supp. XIV:** 260
"Jacob's Ladder" (Rawlings), **Supp. X:** 224, 228
Jacob's Ladder, The (Levertov), **Supp. III Part 1:** 272, 276–278, 281
"Jacob's Ladder, The" (Levertov), **Supp. III Part 1:** 278
Jacobson, Dale, **Supp. X:** 112
Jacobson, Kristin, **Supp. XVIII:** 113
Jacobson, Leslie, **Supp. XV:** 323
Jacoby, Russell, **Supp. IV Part 2:** 692
"Jacquerie, The" (Lanier), **Supp. I Part 1:** 355, 356, 360, 364, 370
Jacques le fataliste (D. Diderot), **Supp. XVII:** 145
Jade Mountain, The: A Chinese Anthology, Being Three Hundred Poems of the T'ang Dynasty (Bynner, trans.), **II:** 527; **Supp. XV:** 46, 47, 48
Jafsie and John Henry: Essays on Hollywood, Bad Boys, and Six Hours of Perfect Poker (Mamet), **Supp. XIV:** 252
Jaguar Totem (LaBastille), **Supp. X:** 99, 106, **107–109**
Jailbird (Vonnegut), **Supp. II Part 2:** 760, 779–780
Jaimes, M. Annette, **Supp. IV Part 1:** 330, 331
Jain, Manju, **Retro. Supp. I:** 53, 58
"Jake Flower, The" (Major), **Supp. XXII:** 182
Jake's Women (Simon), **Supp. IV Part 2:** 576, 588
"Jakie's Mother" (Fante), **Supp. XI:** 164
Jakobson, Roman, **Supp. IV Part 1:** 155
"Jamaica Kincaid's New York" (Kincaid), **Supp. VII:** 181
James, Alice, **I:** 454; **Retro. Supp. I:** 228, 235
James, A. Lloyd, **Supp. XIV:** 343
James, Caryn, **Supp. X:** 302, 303
James, C. L. R. (Cyril Lionel Robert), **Supp. XXI: 159–173**
James, Etta, **Supp. X:** 242
James, Henry, **I:** 4, 5, 9, 10, 12, 15, 16, 20, 52, 93, 109, 211, 226, 228, 244, 246, 251, 255, 258, 259, 336, 363, 374, 375, 379, 384, 409, 429, 436, 439, 452, 454, 459, 461–462, 463, 464, 485, 500, 504, 513, 514, 517–518, 571; **II:** 38, 58, 60, 73, 74, 95, 138, 140, 144, 147, 196, 198, 199, 228, 230, 234, 243, 259, 267, 271, 272, 275, 276, 278, 281, 282, 283, 284, 285, 286, 287, 288, 290, 306, 309, 316, **319–341,** 398, 404, 410, 415, 427, 444, 542, 544, 547–548, 556, 600; **III:** 44, 51, 136, 194–195, 199, 206, 208, 218, 228–229, 237, 281, 319, 325, 326, 334, 409, 453, 454, 457, 460, 461, 464, 511, 522, 576, 607; **IV:** 8, 27, 34, 37, 40, 53, 58, 73, 74, 134, 168, 172, 182, 198, 202, 285, 308, 309, 310, 311, 314, 316, 317, 318, 319, 321, 322, 323, 324, 328, 347, 352, 359, 433, 439, 476; **Retro. Supp. I:** 1, 8, 53, 56, 59, 108, 112, **215–242,** 272, 283, 284, 362, 366, 367, 368, 371, 373, 374, 375, 376, 377, 378, 379; **Retro. Supp. II:** 93, 135, 136, 203, 223; **Supp. I Part 1:** 35, 38, 43; **Supp. I Part 2:** 414, 454, 608, 609, 612–613, 618, 620, 646; **Supp. II Part 1:** 94–95; **Supp. III Part 1:** 14, 200; **Supp. III Part 2:** 410, 412; **Supp. IV Part 1:** 31, 35, 80, 127, 197, 349, 353; **Supp. IV Part 2:** 613, 677, 678, 682, 689, 693; **Supp. V:** 97, 101, 103, 258, 261, 263, 313; **Supp. VIII:** 98, 102, 156, 166, 168; **Supp. IX:** 121; **Supp. XI:** 153; **Supp. XIII:** 102; **Supp. XIV:** 40, 110, 112, 335, 336, 348, 349; **Supp. XV:** 41; **Supp. XVII:** 5, 47; **Supp. XVIII:** 160, 258; **Supp. XX: 227, 228, 232, 233, 238, 240; Supp. XXI:** 225; **Supp. XXII:** 89
James, Henry (father), **II:** 7, 275, 321, 337, 342–344, 364; **IV:** 174; **Supp. I Part 1:** 300
James, Henry (nephew), **II:** 360
James, Horace, **Supp. XIV:** 57
James, P. D., **Supp. XIX:** 131
James, William, **I:** 104, 220, 224, 227, 228, 255, 454; **II:** 20, 27, 165, 166, 276, 321, 337, **342–366,** 411; **III:** 303, 309, 509, 599, 600, 605, 606, 612; **IV:** 26, 27, 28–29, 31, 32, 34, 36, 37, 43, 46, 291, 486; **Retro. Supp. I:** 57, 216, 227, 228, 235, 295, 300, 306; **Supp. I Part 1:** 3, 7, 11, 20; **Supp. XIV:** 40, 50, 197, 199, 212, 335; **Supp. XVII:** 97
James, William (grandfather), **II:** 342
James Baldwin: The Legacy (Troupe, ed.), **Retro. Supp. II:** 15
James Baldwin—The Price of the Ticket (film), **Retro. Supp. II:** 2
James Dickey and the Politics of Canon (Suarez), **Supp. IV Part 1:** 175
"James Dickey on Yeats: An Interview" (Dickey), **Supp. IV Part 1:** 177
James Hogg: A Critical Study (Simpson), **Supp. IX:** 269, 276
"James Is a Girl" (Egan), **Supp. XIX:** 61
James Jones: A Friendship (Morris), **Supp. XI:** 234
James Jones: An American Literary Orientalist Master (Carter), **Supp. XI:** 220
"James Jones and Jack Kerouac: Novelists of Disjunction" (Stevenson), **Supp. XI:** 230
James Jones: Reveille to Taps (television documentary), **Supp. XI:** 234
Jameson, F. R., **Supp. IV Part 1:** 119
Jameson, Sir Leander Starr, **III:** 327
James Shore's Daughter (Benét), **Supp. XI:** 48
"James Thurber" (Pollard), **Supp. I Part 2:** 468
"James Whitcomb Riley (From a Westerner's Point of View)" (Dunbar), **Supp. II Part 1:** 198
Jammes, Francis, **II:** 528; **Retro. Supp. I:** 55
"Jan, the Son of Thomas" (Sandburg), **III:** 593–594
Jan. 31 (Goldbarth), **Supp. XII:** 177, **178–179,** 180
Janeczko, Paul, **Supp. XIII:** 280
Jane Eyre (Brontë), **Supp. XVI:** 158; **Supp. XXII:** 120
Janet, Pierre, **I:** 248, 249, 252; **Retro. Supp. I:** 55, 57
Jane Talbot: A Novel (Brown), **Supp. I Part 1:** 145–146
"Janet Waking" (Ransom), **III:** 490, 491
"Janice" (Jackson), **Supp. IX:** 117
Janowitz, Tama, **Supp. X:** 7
Jantz, Harold S., **Supp. I Part 1:** 112
"January" (Barthelme), **Supp. IV Part 1:** 54
"January" (W. V. Davis), **Supp. XXI:** 89, 90
January Man, The (screenplay, Shanley), **Supp. XIV:** 316
"January Thaw" (Leopold), **Supp. XIV:** 183–184
"Janus" (Beattie), **Supp. V:** 31
Janzen, Jean, **Supp. V:** 180
"Japan" (Collins), **Supp. XXI:** 56
Japanese Americans: The Formation and Transformations of an Ethnic Group (Spickard), **Supp. XXI:** 149
"Japanese Beetles" (X. J. Kennedy), **Supp. XV:** 161, 165
Japanese by Spring (Reed), **Supp. X:** 241, **253–255**
Japanese Cooking: A Simple Art (Tsuji), **Supp. XVII:** 90
"Japan's Young Dreams" (Geisel), **Supp. XVI:** 102
Jara, Victor, **Supp. IV Part 2:** 549
Jarman, Mark, **Supp. IV Part 1:** 68; **Supp. IX:** 266, 270, 276; **Supp. XII:** 209; **Supp. XV:** 251; **Supp. XVIII:** 178
Jarmon, Mark, **Supp. XVII: 109–122**
Jarrell, Randall, **I:** 167, 169, 173, 180; **II: 367–390,** 539–540; **III:** 134, 194, 213, 268, 527; **IV:** 352, 411, 422; **Retro. Supp. I:** 52, 121, 135, 140; **Retro. Supp. II:** 44, 177, 178, 182; **Supp. I Part 1:** 89; **Supp. I Part 2:** 552; **Supp. II Part 1:** 109, 135; **Supp. III Part 1:** 64; **Supp. III Part 2:** 541, 550; **Supp. IV Part 2:** 440; **Supp. V:** 315, 318, 323; **Supp. VIII:** 31, 100, 271; **Supp. IX:** 94, 268; **Supp. XI:** 311, 315; **Supp. XII:** 121, 260, 297; **Supp. XV:** 93, 153; **Supp. XVII:** 111
Jarrell, Mrs. Randall (Mary von Schrader), **II:** 368, 385
Jarry, Alfred, **Retro. Supp. II:** 326; **Supp. XV:** 177–178, 182, 188
Jarvis, John Wesley, **Supp. I Part 2:** 501, 520
Jaskoski, Helen, **Supp. IV Part 1:** 325; **Supp. XXII:** 166

"Jasmine" (Komunyakaa), **Supp. XIII:** 132
"Jason" (Hecht), **Supp. X:** 62
"Jason" (MacLeish), **III:** 4
Jason and Medeia (Gardner), **Supp. VI:** 63, **68–69**
Jaspers, Karl, **III:** 292; **IV:** 491
Jauss, David, **Supp. XXI:** 129, 132, 133, 134, 139
Jay, William, **I:** 338
Jayber Crow (Berry), **Supp. X:** 28, 34
"Jaz Fantasia" (Sandburg), **III:** 585
"Jazz Age Clerk, A" (Farrell), **II:** 45
Jazz Country: Ralph Ellison in America (Porter), **Retro. Supp. II:** 127
"Jazzonia" (Hughes), **Supp. I Part 1:** 324
Jazz Poetry Anthology, The (Komunyakaa and Feinstein, eds.), **Supp. XIII:** 125
"Jazztet Muted" (Hughes), **Supp. I Part 1:** 342
J. B.: A Play in Verse (MacLeish), **II:** 163, 228; **III:** 3, 21–22, 23; **Supp. IV Part 2:** 586
"Jealous" (Ford), **Supp. V:** 71
Jealousies, The: A Faery Tale, by Lucy Vaughan Lloyd of China Walk, Lambeth (Keats), **Supp. XII:** 113
Jean-Christophe (Rolland), **Supp. XX: 70**
"Jean Harlow's Wedding Night" (Wasserstein), **Supp. XV:** 328
Jean Huguenot (Benét), **Supp. XI:** 44
"Jeff Briggs's Love Story" (Harte), **Supp. II Part 1:** 355
Jeffers, Robinson, **I:** 66; **III:** 134; **Retro. Supp. I:** 202; **Supp. II Part 2: 413–440; Supp. VIII:** 33, 292; **Supp. IX:** 77; **Supp. X:** 112; **Supp. XI:** 312; **Supp. XV:** 113, 114, 115; **Supp. XVII:** 111, 112, 117; **Supp. XXI:** 87
Jeffers, Una Call Kuster (Mrs. Robinson Jeffers), **Supp. II Part 2:** 414
Jefferson, Blind Lemon, **Supp. VIII:** 349
Jefferson, Margo, **Supp. XX: 87**
Jefferson, Thomas, **I:** 1, 2, 5, 6–8, 14, 485; **II:** 5, 6, 34, 217, 300, 301, 437; **III:** 3, 17, 18, 294–295, 306, 310, 473, 608; **IV:** 133, 243, 249, 334, 348; **Supp. I Part 1:** 146, 152, 153, 229, 230, 234, 235; **Supp. I Part 2:** 389, 399, 456, 474, 475, 482, 507, 509, 510, 511, 516, 518–519, 520, 522; **Supp. X:** 26; **Supp. XIV:** 191; **Supp. XX: 285**
Jefferson and/or Mussolini (Pound), **Retro. Supp. I:** 292
"Jefferson Davis as a Representative American" (Du Bois), **Supp. II Part 1:** 161
J-E-L-L-O (Baraka), **Supp. II Part 1:** 47
"Jelly-Bean, The" (Fitzgerald), **II:** 88
"Jellyfish, A" (Moore), **III:** 215
Jemie, Onwuchekwa, **Supp. I Part 1:** 343
Jenkins, J. L., **I:** 456
Jenkins, Joe, **Supp. XX: 117, 120, 122**
Jenkins, Kathleen, **III:** 403
Jenkins, Susan, **IV:** 123
Jenks, Deneen, **Supp. IV Part 2:** 550, 554
Jenks, Tom, **Supp. XIX:** 51
Jennie Gerhardt (Dreiser), **I:** 497, 499, 500, 501, 504–505, 506, 507, 519; **Retro. Supp. II:** 94, **99–101**
"Jennie M'Grew" (Masters), **Supp. I Part 2:** 468
Jennifer Lorn (Wylie), **Supp. I Part 2:** 709, 714–717, 718, 721, 724
Jennison, Peter S., **Supp. XIX:** 268
"Jenny Garrow's Lover" (Jewett), **II:** 397
"Jerboa, The" (Moore), **III:** 203, 207, 209, 211–212
Jeremiah, **Supp. X:** 35
Jeremy's Version (Purdy), **Supp. VII:** 274
"Jericho" (Lowell), **II:** 536
"Jerry's Garage" (Budbill), **Supp. XIX:** 7
"Jersey City Gendarmerie, Je T'aime" (Lardner), **II:** 433
Jersey Rain (Pinsky), **Supp. VI:** 235, **247–250**
"Jerusalem" (Nye), **Supp. XIII:** 287
Jerusalem: Song of Songs (Uris), **Supp. XX: 244–245, 246, 255**
Jerusalem the Golden (Reznikoff), **Supp. XIV:** 280, 285, 286
Jessup, Richard, **Supp. XI:** 306
"Je Suis Perdu" (Taylor), Supp. V: 314, 321–322
Jesuits in North America in the Seventeenth Century, The (Parkman), **Supp. II Part 2:** 597, 603–605
Jesus, **I:** 27, 34, 68, 89, 136, 552, 560; **II:** 1, 16, 197, 198, 214, 215, 216, 218, 219, 239, 373, 377, 379, 537, 538, 539, 549, 569, 585, 591, 592; **III:** 39, 173, 179, 270, 291, 296–297, 300, 303, 305, 307, 311, 339, 340, 341, 342, 344, 345, 346, 347, 348, 352, 353, 354, 355, 436, 451, 489, 534, 564, 566, 567, 582; **IV:** 51, 69, 86, 107, 109, 117, 137, 138, 141, 144, 147, 149, 150, 151, 152, 155, 156, 157, 158, 159, 163, 164, 232, 241, 289, 293, 294, 296, 331, 364, 392, 396, 418, 430; **Supp. I Part 1:** 2, 54, 104, 107, 108, 109, 121, 267, 371; **Supp. I Part 2:** 379, 386, 458, 515, 580, 582, 583, 587, 588, 683; **Supp. V:** 280
Jesus, the Son of Man (Gibran), **Supp. XX: 115–116, 117, 122–123**
"Jesus Asleep" (Sexton), **Supp. II Part 2:** 693
"Jesus of Nazareth, Then and Now" (Price), **Supp. VI:** 268
"Jesus Papers, The" (Sexton), **Supp. II Part 2:** 693
"Jesus Raises Up the Harlot" (Sexton), **Supp. II Part 2:** 693
"Jesus Stories, The" (Brockmeier), **Supp. XXII:** 52
Jetée, La (film), **Supp. IV Part 2:** 436
"Jeune Parque, La" (Valéry), **IV:** 92
"Jew as Writer/The Writer as Jew, The: Reflections on Literature and Identity" (Apple), **Supp. XVII:** 1, 9
"Jewbird, The" (Malamud), **Supp. I Part 2:** 435
"Jewboy, The" (P. Roth), **Supp. III Part 2:** 412
Jewett, Caroline, **II:** 396
Jewett, Katharine, **Retro. Supp. II:** 46
Jewett, Mary, **II:** 396, 403
Jewett, Rutger, **Retro. Supp. I:** 381
Jewett, Sarah Orne, **I:** 313; **II: 391–414; Retro. Supp. I:** 6, 7, 19; **Retro. Supp. II:** 51, 52, **131–151,** 156; **Supp. I Part 2:** 495; **Supp. VIII:** 126; **Supp. IX:** 79; **Supp. XIII:** 153
Jewett, Theodore Furber, **II:** 395
Jewett, Dr. Theodore Herman, **II:** 396–397, 402
"Jew for Export, The" (Mamet), **Supp. XIV:** 251–252
Jew in Our Day, The (W. Frank), **Supp. XX: 79**
Jew in the American Novel, The (Fiedler), **Supp. XIII:** 106
"Jewish Graveyards, Italy" (Levine), **Supp. V:** 190
"Jewish Hunter, The" (Moore), **Supp. X:** 163, 165, **174**
Jewison, Norman, **Supp. XI:** 306; **Supp. XIV:** 316
Jews of Shklov (Schneour), **IV:** 11
Jews without Money (Gold), **Supp. XIV:** 288–289
JFK (film), **Supp. XIV:** 48
Jig of Forslin, The: A Symphony (Aiken), **I:** 50, 51, 57, 62, 66
"Jig Tune: Not for Love" (McGrath), **Supp. X:** 116
"Jihad" (McClatchy), **Supp. XII:** 266
"Jilting of Granny Weatherall, The" (Porter), **III:** 434, 435, 438
Jim Crow's Last Stand (Hughes), **Retro. Supp. I:** 205
Jiménez, Juan Ramón, **Supp. XIII:** 315, 323
Jimmie Higgins (Sinclair), **Supp. V:** 288
"Jimmy Harlow" (X. J. Kennedy), **Supp. XV:** 170
Jimmy's Blues (Baldwin), **Retro. Supp. II:** 8, 9, 15
Jim's Book: A Collection of Poems and Short Stories (Merrill), **Supp. III Part 1:** 319
Jin, Ha, **Supp. XVIII: 89–104**
Jitney (Wilson), **Supp. VIII:** 330, 331, 351
Jitterbug Perfume (Robbins), **Supp. X:** 273, **274–276,** 279
Joachim, Harold, **Retro. Supp. I:** 58
Joan, Pope, **IV:** 165
Joanna and Ulysses (Sarton), **Supp. VIII: 254–255**
Joan of Arc, **IV:** 241; **Supp. I Part 1:** 286–288; **Supp. I Part 2:** 469
Joans, Ted, **Supp. IV Part 1:** 169
Job (biblical book), **II:** 165, 166–167, 168; **III:** 21, 199, 512; **IV:** 13, 158; **Supp. I Part 1:** 125
Job, The (Burroughs and Odier), **Supp. III Part 1:** 97, 103
Job, The: An American Novel (Lewis), **II:** 441
"Job History" (Proulx), **Supp. VII:** 262
Jobim, Antonio Carlos, **Supp. IV Part 2:** 549
Jobim, Antônio Carlos, **Supp. XXI:** 100

"Job of the Plains, A" (Humphrey), **Supp. IX:** 101
"Jody Rolled the Bones" (Yates), **Supp. XI:** 335, 341
"Joe" (Alvarez), **Supp. VII:** 7–8
Joe (Brown), **Supp. XVIII:** 195
Joe (L. Brown), **Supp. XXI:** 41, **45–46,** 47
"Joe, the Vanishing American" (Swados), **Supp. XIX:** 258–259
Joe Hill: A Biographical Novel (Stegner), **Supp. IV Part 2:** 599
Joe Jones (Lamott), **Supp. XX: 134–135**
"Joe Louis: The King as a Middle-Aged Man" (Talese), **Supp. XVII:** 202
"Joe's Jitters" (Bronk), **Supp. XXI:** 27
Joe Turner's Come and Gone (Wilson), **Supp. VIII:** 334, **337–342,** 345
Joe versus the Volcano (screenplay, Shanley), **Supp. XIV:** 316
"Joey Martiney" (Huncke), **Supp. XIV:** 149
Johannes in Eremo (Mather), **Supp. II Part 2:** 453
John XXIII, Pope, **Supp. I Part 2:** 492
John (biblical book), **I:** 68; **Supp. XV:** 222, 224
"John" (Shields), **Supp. VII:** 310–311
John, Augustus, **Supp. XXII:** 157
John, Elton, **Supp. XXI:** 148
"John, John Chinaman" (Buck), **Supp. II Part 1:** 128
John Addington Symonds: A Biographical Study (Brooks), **I:** 240, 241
John-a Dreams: A Tale (J. Sturgis), **Supp. XX: 233**
"John Archer's Nose" (R. Fisher), **Supp. XIX:** 71–72, 78
John Barleycorn (London), **II:** 467, 481
John Brown (Du Bois), **Supp. II Part 1:** 171–172
"John Brown" (Emerson), **II:** 13
"John Brown" (Lindsay), **Supp. I Part 2:** 393
John Brown's Body (Benét), **II:** 177; **Supp. XI:** 45, 46, 47, **56–57**
John Brown: The Making of a Martyr (Warren), **IV:** 236
John Bull in America; or, The New Munchausen (Paulding), **I:** 344
"John Burke" (Olson), **Supp. II Part 2:** 579, 580
"John Burns of Gettysburg" (Harte), **Supp. II Part 1:** 343
"John Carter" (Agee), **I:** 27
John Chancellor Makes Me Cry (Siddons), **Supp. XXII:** 245
"John Coltrane: Where Does Art Come From?" (Baraka), **Supp. II Part 1:** 60
John Deth: A Metaphysical Legend and Other Poems (Aiken), **I:** 61
"John Endicott" (Longfellow), **II:** 505, 506; **Retro. Supp. II:** 165–166, 167
"John Evereldown" (Robinson), **III:** 524
John Fante Reader, The (Cooper, ed.), **Supp. XI:** 174
John Fante: Selected Letters, 1932–1981 (Cooney, ed.), **Supp. XI:** 170
"John Gardner: The Writer As Teacher" (Carver), **Supp. III Part 1:** 136, 146–147
John Gaunt (R. H. Davis), **Supp. XVI:** 89
John Jay Chapman and His Letters (Howe), **Supp. XIV:** 54
John Keats (Lowell), **II:** 530–531
"John Kinsella's Lament for Mrs. Mary Moore" (Yeats), **Supp. XVII:** 144
"John Lamar" (R. H. Davis), **Supp. XVI:** 89–90
John Lane, **Retro. Supp. I:** 59
"John L. Sullivan" (Lindsay), **Supp. I Part 2:** 394, 395
"John Marr" (Melville), **III:** 93
John Marr and Other Sailors (Melville), **III:** 93; **Retro. Supp. I:** 257
John Muir: A Reading Bibliography (Kimes and Kimes), **Supp. IX:** 178
Johnny Appleseed and Other Poems (Lindsay), **Supp. I Part 2:** 397
"Johnny Bear" (Steinbeck), **IV:** 67
Johnny Got His Gun (Trumbo), **Supp. XXI:** 45
"Johnny Mnemonic" (W. Gibson), **Supp. XVI:** 122, 123–125, 128, 131
"Johnny Panic and the Bible of Dreams" (Plath), **Retro. Supp. II:** 245
"Johnny Ray" (Ríos), **Supp. IV Part 2:** 543
Johnny Tremain (Forbes), **Supp. XIX:** 235
John of the Cross (Saint), **I:** 585; **Supp. IV Part 1:** 284; **Supp. XV:** 223; **Supp. XVII:** 112
John Paul Jones: A Sailor's Biography (Morison), **Supp. I Part 2:** 494–495
"John Redding Goes to Sea" (Hurston), **Supp. VI:** 150
Johns, George Sibley, **Retro. Supp. II:** 65
Johns, Orrick, **Retro. Supp. II:** 71
John Sloan: A Painter's Life (Brooks), **I:** 254
"John Smith Liberator" (Bierce), **I:** 209
Johnson, Alexandra, **Supp. X:** 86
Johnson, Alvin, **I:** 236; **Supp. XV:** 304
Johnson, Ben, **Retro. Supp. I:** 56
Johnson, Buffie, **Supp. IV Part 1:** 94
Johnson, Charles, **Supp. I Part 1:** 325; **Supp. V:** 128; **Supp. VI: 185–201; Supp. X:** 239; **Supp. XIII:** 182; **Supp. XIX:** 160
Johnson, Charles S., **Supp. IX:** 309; **Supp. XXII:** 6, 7
Johnson, Claudia Durst, **Supp. VIII:** 126–127
Johnson, Clifton, **Supp. XXI:** 248, 250
Johnson, Denis, **Supp. XXI:** 118, 131
Johnson, Dennis, **Supp. XIX:** 209
Johnson, Diane, **Supp. XIII:** 127
Johnson, Dianne, **Retro. Supp. I:** 196
Johnson, Eastman, **IV:** 321
Johnson, Edward, **IV:** 157; **Supp. I Part 1:** 110, 115
Johnson, Fenton, **Supp. XI:** 129
Johnson, Georgia Douglas, **Supp. IV Part 1:** 164
Johnson, Helene, **Supp. XVIII:** 282
Johnson, James Weldon, **Retro. Supp. II:** 114; **Supp. I Part 1:** 324, 325; **Supp. II Part 1:** 33, 194, 200, 202–203, 206–207; **Supp. III Part 1:** 73; **Supp. IV Part 1:** 7, 11, 15, 16, 164, 165, 166, 169; **Supp. X:** 42, 136, **246; Supp. XVIII:** 122, 127, 282; **Supp. XIX:** 73
Johnson, Joyce, **Supp. XIV:** 150
Johnson, Kent, **Supp. XV:** 347
Johnson, Lady Bird, **Supp. IV Part 1:** 22
Johnson, Lyndon B., **I:** 254; **II:** 553, 582; **Retro. Supp. II:** 27
Johnson, Marguerite. *See* Angelou, Maya
Johnson, Maurice, **Supp. XV:** 136, 137, 138
Johnson, Michael K., **Supp. XVIII:** 59, 64
Johnson, Mordecai, **Supp. XIV:** 202
Johnson, Nunnally, **Supp. IV Part 1:** 355
Johnson, Pamela Hansford, **IV:** 469
Johnson, Rafer, **Supp. I Part 1:** 271
Johnson, Reed, **Supp. IV Part 2:** 589
Johnson, Richard, **Supp. XIII:** 132
Johnson, Robert, **Supp. IV Part 1:** 146; **Supp. VIII:** 15, 134
Johnson, Robert K., **Supp. IV Part 2:** 573, 584
Johnson, Robert Underwood, **Supp. IX:** 182, 184, 185
Johnson, Samuel, **II:** 295; **III:** 491, 503; **IV:** 452; **Retro. Supp. I:** 56, 65; **Supp. I Part 1:** 33; **Supp. I Part 2:** 422, 498, 503, 523, 656; **Supp. IV Part 1:** 34, 124; **Supp. XI:** 209; **Supp. XII:** 159; **Supp. XIII:** 55, 347; **Supp. XVI:** 204; **Supp. XVII:** 1
Johnson, Sarah Anne, **Supp. XVIII:** 145; **Supp. XIX:** 49, 50, 52, 54, 55, 56, 58, 59, 60, 61
Johnson, Steve, **Supp. XVI:** 177
Johnson, Thomas H., **I:** 470–471; **IV:** 144, 158; **Retro. Supp. I:** 26, 28, 36, 39, 40, 41, 43
Johnson, Walter, **II:** 422
Johnson, Willard "Spud", **Supp. XV:** 42, 46
"Johnson Girls, The" (Bambara), **Supp. XI:** 7
Johnsrud, Harold, **II:** 562
Johnston, Basil, **Supp. IV Part 1:** 269
Johnston, Mary, **II:** 194
Johnston, Robert M., **Supp. I Part 1:** 369
"John Sutter" (Winters), **Supp. II Part 2:** 810
John's Wife (Coover), **Supp. V:** 51–52
John the Baptist, **I:** 389; **II:** 537, 591
John Wesley Harding (album, Dylan), **Supp. XVIII:** 27
Jolas, Eugène, **Retro. Supp. II:** 85, 328; **Supp. IV Part 1:** 80
Jolie Blon's Bounce (Burke), **Supp. XIV:** 26, 33–34
Jolly (Mamet), **Supp. XIV:** 240, 254
"Jolly Corner, The" (James), **I:** 571; **Retro. Supp. I:** 235
"Jon" (Saunders), **Supp. XIX:** 232, 234
"Jonah" (Lowell), **II:** 536
Jonah's Gourd Vine (Hurston), **Supp. VI:** 149, 155

"Jonathan Edwards" (Holmes), **Supp. I Part 1:** 302, 315
"Jonathan Edwards in Western Massachusetts" (Lowell), **II:** 550
Jonathan Franzen at the End of Postmodernism (Burns), **Supp. XX: 85**
Jonathan Troy (Abbey), **Supp. XIII:** 4, 13
Jones, Anne ?/, **Supp. X:** 8
Jones, Anne Goodwyn ?/, **Supp. XXII:** 252
Jones, Carolyn M., **Supp. VIII:** 128; **Supp. XIX:** 160
Jones, Chuck, **Supp. XVI:** 102
Jones, David, **Supp. XVII:** 241
Jones, Derek Anson, **Supp. XVIII:** 38, 39
Jones, Edith Newbold. *See* Wharton, Edith
Jones, Edward P., **Supp. XXI:** 247; **Supp. XXII: 139–153**
Jones, E. Stanley, **III:** 297
Jones, Everett LeRoi. *See* Baraka, Imamu Amiri
Jones, George Frederic, **IV:** 309
Jones, Grover, **Supp. XIII:** 166
Jones, Harry, **Supp. I Part 1:** 337
Jones, Howard Mumford, **I:** 353; **Supp. IV Part 2:** 606; **Supp. XIV:** 11
Jones, James, **III:** 40; **IV:** 98; **Supp. XI: 213–237; Supp. XIX:** 248, 252; **Supp. XX: 248**
Jones, James Earl, **Supp. VIII:** 334; **Supp. XI:** 309
Jones, Jennifer, **Supp. IV Part 2:** 524
Jones, John Paul, **II:** 405–406; **Supp. I Part 2:** 479, 480, 494–495
Jones, Kirkland ?/, **Supp. XXII:** 9
Jones, Kirkland C. ?/, **Supp. XVIII:** 173, 174, 175
Jones, LeRoi. *See* Baraka, Imamu Amiri
Jones, Louis B., **Supp. XVI:** 41
Jones, Loyal, **Supp. XX: 170**
Jones, Lucretia Stevens Rhinelander, **IV:** 309
Jones, Madison, **Retro. Supp. II:** 235; **Supp. X:** 1
Jones, Major (pseudonym). *See* Thompson, William T.
Jones, Malcolm, **Supp. V:** 219; **Supp. XX: 93, 138**
Jones, Mildred, **Supp. XVIII:** 281
Jones, Robert Edmond, **III:** 387, 391, 394, 399; **Supp. XXI:** 6, 12
Jones, Sharon L., **Supp. XVIII:** 280, 285, 286
Jones, Tommy Lee, **Supp. V:** 227
"Jones's Private Argyment" (Lanier), **Supp. I Part 1:** 352
"Jones's *The Thin Red Line:* The End of Innocence" (Michel-Michot), **Supp. XI:** 224–225
Jong, Allan, **Supp. V:** 115
Jong, Erica, **Supp. V: 113–135**
Jong-Fast, Molly Miranda, **Supp. V:** 115
Jonson, Ben, **I:** 58, 358; **II:** 11, 16, 17, 18, 436, 556; **III:** 3, 463, 575–576; **IV:** 395, 453; **Retro. Supp. II:** 76; **Supp. I Part 2:** 423; **Supp. IV Part 2:** 585; **Supp. XX: 197**
Jonsson, Thorsten, **Retro. Supp. I:** 73
Joplin, Janis, **Supp. IV Part 1:** 206; **Supp. XI:** 239
Joplin, Scott, **Supp. IV Part 1:** 223
Jordan, A. Van, **Supp. XVIII:** 172
Jordan, Barbara, **Supp. VIII:** 63; **Supp. XI:** 249
Jordan, David, **Supp. XIX:** 141
Jordan, June, **Supp. XII:** 217; **Supp. XXII:** 172
Jordan, Marie, **Supp. XV:** 224
Jo's Boys (Alcott), **Supp. I Part 1:** 32, 35, 40–41, 42
Joseph Heller (Ruderman), **Supp. IV Part 1:** 380
"Josephine Has Her Day" (Thurber), **Supp. I Part 2:** 606
Josephine Stories, The (Fitzgerald), **Retro. Supp. I:** 109
"Joseph Martinez" (Huncke), **Supp. XIV:** 149
"Joseph Pockets" (Stern), **Supp. IX:** 292
Josephson, Matthew, **I:** 259
"José's Country" (Winters), **Supp. II Part 2:** 789, 790
Joshua (biblical book), **Supp. I Part 2:** 515
Joslin, Katherine, **Retro. Supp. I:** 376
Journal (Emerson), **Supp. I Part 1:** 309
"Journal" (L. Michaels), **Supp. XVI:** 213
Journal (Thoreau), **IV:** 175
Journal (Woolman), **Supp. VIII:** 202
"Journal for My Daughter" (Kunitz), **Supp. III Part 1:** 268
"Journal of an Airman" (Auden), **Supp. XIX:** 151
Journal of Arthur Stirling, The (Sinclair), **Supp. V:** 280
"Journal of a Solitary Man, The" (Hawthorne), **II:** 226
Journal of a Solitude (Sarton), **Supp. VIII:** 256, 262–263
Journal of My Other Self (Rilke), **Retro. Supp. II:** 20
Journal of the Fictive Life (Nemerov), **III:** 267, 268, 269, 272, 273, 274, 280–281, 284–285, 286, 287
Journal of the Plague Year, A (Defoe), **III:** 423
"Journal of the Year of the Ox, A" (Wright), **Supp. V:** 343
Journals (Thoreau), **Supp. I Part 1:** 299
Journals and Other Documents on the Life and Voyages of Christopher Columbus (Morison, ed.), **Supp. I Part 2:** 494
Journals of Ralph Waldo Emerson, The (Emerson), **II:** 8, 17, 21
Journals of Susanna Moodie, The: Poems (Atwood), **Supp. XIII:** 33
"Journey, A" (Wharton), **Retro. Supp. I:** 364
"Journey, The" (Winters), **Supp. II Part 2:** 795
"Journey, The" (Wright), **Supp. III Part 2:** 605–606
"Journey, the Arrival and the Dream, The" (Gioia), **Supp. XV:** 120
"Journey, The: For Jane at Thirteen" (Kumin), **Supp. IV Part 2:** 442
Journey and Other Poems, The (Winters), **Supp. II Part 2:** 786, 794, 795, 796, 799, 800, 801
Journey Around My Room: The Autobiography of Louise Bogan—A Mosaic (Bogan), **Supp. III Part 1:** 47, 48, 52, 53
Journey Down, The (Bernstein), **IV:** 455
Journey Home, The (Abbey), **Supp. XIII:** 2, 12
"Journey into Speech, A" (Cliff), **Supp. XXII:** 69
Journeyman (Caldwell), **I:** 297, 302–304, 307, 309
Journeyman: Travels of a Writer (Findley), **Supp. XX: 50**
Journey of Tai-me, The (Momaday), **Supp. IV Part 2:** 485
"Journey of the Magi" (Eliot), **Retro. Supp. I:** 64
Journey to a War (Auden and Isherwood), **Supp. II Part 1:** 13; **Supp. XIV:** 156, 158, 162
Journey to Love (W. C. Williams), **IV:** 422; **Retro. Supp. I:** 429
Journey to My Father; Isaac Bashevis Singer (Zamir), **Retro. Supp. II:** 317
"Journey to Nine Miles" (Walker), **Supp. III Part 2:** 527
"Journey to the Interior" (W. J. Smith), **Supp. XIII:** 339, 340
Journey with Genius: Recollections and Reflections Concerning the D. H. Lawrences (Bynner), **Supp. XV:** 46
Jowett, Benjamin, **Supp. XIV:** 335
"Joy" (Moore), **Supp. X:** 174
"Joy" (Singer), **IV:** 9; **Retro. Supp. II:** 307
Joyce, Cynthia, **Supp. X:** 194, 195, 196
Joyce, James, **I:** 53, 105, 108, 130, 174, 256, 285, 377, 395, 475–476, 478, 480, 483, 576; **II:** 27, 42, 58, 73, 74, 198, 209, 264, 320, 569; **III:** 7, 16, 26–27, 45, 174, 181, 184, 261, 273, 277, 343, 396, 398, 465, 471, 474; **IV:** 32, 73, 85, 95, 103, 171, 182, 211, 286, 370, 412, 418, 419, 428, 434, 456; **Retro. Supp. I:** 59, 63, 75, 80, 89, 91, 108, 109, 127, 287, 290, 292, 334, 335, 420; **Retro. Supp. II:** 221, 326; **Supp. I Part 1:** 257, 262, 270; **Supp. I Part 2:** 437, 546, 613, 620; **Supp. II Part 1:** 136; **Supp. III Part 1:** 35, 36, 65, 225, 229; **Supp. III Part 2:** 611, 617, 618; **Supp. IV Part 1:** 40, 47, 80, 227, 300, 310; **Supp. IV Part 2:** 424, 677; **Supp. V:** 261, 331; **Supp. VIII:** 14, 40, 103; **Supp. IX:** 211, 229, 235, 308; **Supp. X:** 115, 137, 194, 324; **Supp. XI:** 66; **Supp. XII:** 139, 151, 165, 191, 289; **Supp. XIV:** 83; **Supp. XVI:** 41, 189, 282; **Supp. XVII:** 44; **Supp. XIX:** 151, 172; **Supp. XXI:** 7; **Supp. XXII:** 141, 143–144
Joy Comes in the Morning (J. Rosen), **Supp. XVII:** 50
Joy Luck Club, The (Tan), **Supp. X:** 289, 291, 293, 294, 296, 297, 298, 299

"Joy of Sales Resistance, The" (Berry), **Supp. X:** 36

J R (Gaddis), **Supp. IV Part 1:** 279, 280, 285–289, 291, 294; **Supp. IV Part 2:** 484; **Supp. XXI:** 226

Juana Inés de la Cruz, Sor, **Supp. XXI:** 94, 104

Juan de la Cruz (John of the Cross), **Supp. XXI:** 99, 104

"Juan's Song" (Bogan), **Supp. III Part 1:** 50

Juba to Jive: A Dictionary of African-American Slang (Major), **Supp. XXII:** 172, 180

Jubilate Agno (Smart), **Supp. IV Part 2:** 626

Judah, Hettie, **Supp. XIII:** 246

Judah the Pious (Prose), **Supp. XVI:** 249, 250, 262

"Judas Maccabaeus" (Longfellow), **II:** 506; **Retro. Supp. II:** 165, 167

Judd, Sylvester, **II:** 290; **Supp. I Part 2:** 420

Judd Rankin's Daughter (Glaspell), **Supp. III Part 1:** 186–188

Jude the Obscure (Hardy), **Supp. I Part 1:** 217

Judevine (Budbill), **Supp. XIX:** 4, **8–9,** 12

Judevine: A Play in Three Acts/Two Acts (Budbill), **Supp. XIX: 12–13**

Judge, Jane, **Supp. XXII:** 191

"Judgement Day" (O'Connor), **III:** 349, 350; **Retro. Supp. II:** 236

Judgment Day (Farrell), **II:** 29, 31, 32, 34, 39

"Judgment of Paris, The" (Merwin), **Supp. III Part 1:** 350

Judgment of Paris, The (Vidal), **Supp. IV Part 2:** 680, 682

"Judgment of the Sage, The" (Crane), **I:** 420

Judith (Farrell), **II:** 46, 48

"Judith" (Garrett), **Supp. VII:** 109–110

"Juggernaut" (Bass), **Supp. XVI:** 16–17

"Jug of Sirup, A" (Bierce), **I:** 206

"Jugurtha" (Longfellow), **II:** 499

"Juice or Gravy" (P. Roth), **Retro. Supp. II:** 279

"Juke Box Love Song" (Hughes), **Retro. Supp. I:** 209

"Julia" (Hellman), **Supp. I Part 1:** 280, 293

"Julia Miller" (Masters), **Supp. I Part 2:** 461

Julian (Vidal), **Supp. IV Part 2:** 677, 684–685, 685, 689

Julian the Apostate, **Retro. Supp. I:** 247

"Julian Vreden" (Bowles), **Supp. IV Part 1:** 94

Julie and Romeo (Ray), **Supp. XII:** 308, 310

Julien, Isaac, **Supp. XI:** 19

Julie; ou, La nouvelle Héloïse (Rousseau), **Supp. XVI:** 184

Julier, Laura, **Supp. IV Part 1:** 211

Julip (Harrison), **Supp. VIII: 51**

Julius Caesar (Shakespeare), **I:** 284

"July Midnight" (Lowell), **II:** 521

Jumel, Madame, **Supp. I Part 2:** 461

Jumping Out of Bed (R. Bly), **Supp. IV Part 1:** 71

"Jump-Up Day" (Kingsolver), **Supp. VII:** 203

"Junctions" (Lamott), **Supp. XX: 143**

"June 1940" (Kees), **Supp. XV:** 141

"June Light" (Wilbur), **Supp. III Part 2:** 545

June Moon (Lardner and Kaufman), **II:** 427

"June Recital" (Welty), **IV:** 272–273

Juneteenth (Ellison), **Retro. Supp. II:** 119, 124, **126–128**

"Juneteenth" (Ellison), **Retro. Supp. II:** 119, 126; **Supp. II Part 1:** 248

"June the Third" (Gander), **Supp. XV:** 340

Jung, Carl, **I:** 58, 135, 241, 248, 252, 402; **III:** 400, 534, 543; **Supp. I Part 2:** 439; **Supp. IV Part 1:** 68, 69; **Supp. VIII:** 45; **Supp. X:** 193; **Supp. XV:** 214; **Supp. XX: 63, 117**

Junger, Ernst, **Supp. III Part 1:** 63

Jungle, The (Sinclair), **III:** 580; **Supp. V:** 281–284, 285, 289

Jungle Lovers (Theroux), **Supp. VIII:** 314, 315, 316, **317**

"Junior Addict" (Hughes), **Supp. I Part 1:** 343

"Juniper" (Francis), **Supp. IX:** 79

"Junk" (Wilbur), **Supp. III Part 2:** 556

Junker, Howard, **Supp. XV:** 116

Junkie: Confessions of an Unredeemed Drug Addict (Burroughs), **Supp. III Part 1:** 92, 94–96, 101

Junky (Burroughs), **Supp. XIV:** 143

Juno and the Paycock (O'Casey), **Supp. IV Part 1:** 361

"Jupiter Doke, Brigadier General" (Bierce), **I:** 204

Jupiter Laughs (A. Cronin), **Supp. XVII:** 59

Jurgen (Cabell), **III:** 394; **IV:** 286; **Retro. Supp. I:** 80; **Supp. I Part 2:** 718

Jury of Her Peers, A: American Women Writers from Anne Bradstreet to Annie Proulx (Showalter), **Supp. XX: 274**

Jusserand, Jules, **II:** 338

Just above My Head (Baldwin), **Retro. Supp. II:** 14–15

"Just a Little One" (Parker), **Supp. IX:** 191

Just and the Unjust, The (Cozzens), **I:** 367–370, 372, 375, 377, 378, 379

Just an Ordinary Day (Jackson), **Supp. IX:** 120

Just Before Dark: Collected Nonfiction (Harrison), **Supp. VIII:** 41, 45, 46, 53

"Just Before the War with the Eskimos" (Salinger), **III:** 559

"Just Boys" (Farrell), **II:** 45

"Just for the Thrill: An Essay on the Difference Between Women and Men" (Carson), **Supp. XII: 103–104**

"Justice" (Hughes), **Supp. I Part 1:** 331

"Justice, A" (Faulkner), **Retro. Supp. I:** 83

Justice, Donald, **Retro. Supp. I:** 313; **Supp. III Part 2:** 541; **Supp. V:** 180, 337, 338, 341; **Supp. VII: 115–130; Supp. XI:** 141, 315; **Supp. XIII:** 76, 312; **Supp. XV:** 74, 93, 118, 119, 134; **Supp. XVII:** 110, 120, 246; **Supp. XX: 199**

Justice and Expediency (Whitter), **Supp. I Part 2:** 686

"Justice Denied in Massachusetts" (Millay), **III:** 140

Justice for Salcido (Endore), **Supp. XVII:** 63

Justice of Gold in the Damnation of Sinners, The (Edwards), **I:** 559

"Justice to Feminism" (Ozick), **Supp. V:** 272

"Just Introduced" (Taggard), **Supp. XXII:** 274

Just Kids (Smith), **Supp. XXII:** 94

"Just Like a Woman" (Dylan), **Supp. XV:** 350

"Just Like Job" (Angelou), **Supp. IV Part 1:** 15

"Just One of the Boys" (Swados), **Supp. XIX:** 259

Just Whistle: A Valentine (Wright), **Supp. XV: 346–348**

Just Wild About Harry (H. Miller), **III:** 190

Juvenal, **II:** 8, 169, 552

"K, The" (Olson), **Supp. II Part 2:** 558, 563, 569

Kabir, **Supp. IV Part 1:** 74

"Kabnis" (Toomer), **Supp. III Part 2:** 481, 484; **Supp. IX:** 309, 310, **319–320**

Kachel, Elsie. *See* Stevens, Mrs. Wallace (Elsie Kachel)

"Kaddish" (Ginsberg), **Supp. II Part 1:** 319, 327

Kaddish and Other Poems, 1958–1960 (Ginsberg), **Supp. II Part 1:** 309, 319–320; **Supp. XIV:** 269

Kael, Pauline, **Supp. IX:** 253; **Supp. XV:** 147, 148

Kafka, Franz, **II:** 244, 565, 569; **III:** 51, 253, 418, 566, 572; **IV:** 2, 113, 218, 437–439, 442; **Retro. Supp. II:** 20, 221, 282; **Supp. I Part 1:** 197; **Supp. III Part 1:** 105; **Supp. III Part 2:** 413; **Supp. IV Part 1:** 379; **Supp. IV Part 2:** 623; **Supp. VIII:** 14, 15, 103; **Supp. XII:** 21, 37, 98, 168; **Supp. XIII:** 305; **Supp. XVI:** 17, 201, 206, 209; **Supp. XVII:** 244; **Supp. XX: 18, 21, 85, 87; Supp. XXII:** 89, 90, 94

Kafka Americana (Lethem and Scholtz), **Supp. XVIII:** 144–145

Kaganoff, Penny, **Supp. XI:** 122

Kagan's Superfecta (A. Hoffman), **Supp. XVII:** 42

Kahane, Jack, **III:** 171, 178

Kahn, Otto, **I:** 385; **IV:** 123; **Retro. Supp. II:** 81, 84, 85; **Supp. XX: 75**

Kahn, R. T., **Supp. XI:** 216

"Kai, Today" (Snyder), **Supp. VIII:** 300

Kaiser, Georg, **I:** 479

Kaiser, Henry, **Supp. I Part 2:** 644

Kakutani, Michiko, **Supp. IV Part 1:** 196, 201, 205, 211, 212; **Supp. V:** 63;

Supp. VIII: 81, 84, 86, 88, 141; **Supp. X:** 171, 301, 302, 310, 314; **Supp. XI:** 38, 179; **Supp. XII:** 165, 171, 172, 299; **Supp. XVI:** 71; **Supp. XVII:** 6; **Supp. XIX:** 142; **Supp. XX:** **92, 94;** **Supp. XXII:** 109
Kalem, T. E., **Supp. IV Part 2:** 585
Kalevala (Finnish epic), **II:** 503, 504; **Retro. Supp. II:** 155
Kalevala (Lönnrot), **Retro. Supp. II:** 159, 160
Kalfus, Ken, **Supp. XVII:** 50
Kalki: A Novel (Vidal), **Supp. IV Part 2:** 677, 682, 685, 691, 692
Kallan, Richard A., **Supp. XX: 244**
Kallen, Horace, **I:** 229; **Supp. I Part 2:** 643; **Supp. XIV:** 195, 197, 198
Kallman, Chester, **II:** 586; **Supp. II Part 1:** 15, 17, 24, 26
"Kallundborg Church" (Whittier), **Supp. I Part 2:** 696
Kalstone, David, **Retro. Supp. II:** 40
Kamel, Rose, **Supp. XIII:** 306
Kamenev, Lev, **Supp. XXI:** 167
Kamera Obskura (Nabokov), **III:** 255
Kamhi, Michelle Moarder, **Supp. IV Part 2:** 529, 530
Kaminsky, Wally, **Supp. XVIII:** 72
Kamp, David, **Supp. XVIII:** 150
Kandy-Kolored Tangerine-Flake Streamline Baby, The (Wolfe), **Supp. III Part 2:** 569, 573–576, 580, 581
Kane, Julie, **Supp. XVII:** 78
Kane, Lesley, **Supp. XIV:** 250
Kanellos, Nicolás, **Supp. VIII:** 82; **Supp. XIII:** 213
Kanin, Garson, **Supp. IV Part 2:** 574
"Kansas City Coyote" (Harjo), **Supp. XII:** 219, 222
"Kansas Emigrants, The" (Whittier), **Supp. I Part 2:** 687
Kant, Immanuel, **I:** 61, 277, 278; **II:** 10–11, 362, 480, 580–581, 582, 583; **III:** 300, 480, 481, 488, 612; **IV:** 90; **Supp. I Part 2:** 640; **Supp. IV Part 2:** 527; **Supp. XIV:** 198, 199; **Supp. XVI:** 184
Kanter, Hal, **IV:** 383
Kapital, Das (Marx), **III:** 580; **Supp. XXI:** 161, 162, 163
Kaplan, Abraham, **I:** 277
Kaplan, Justin, **I:** 247–248; **Retro. Supp. I:** 392
Kaplan, Mary Jo, **Supp. XIX:** 266
Kaplan, Steven, **Supp. V:** 238, 241, 243, 248
Karate Is a Thing of the Spirit (Crews), **Supp. XI: 112–113**
Karbo, Karen, **Supp. X:** 259, 262
"Karintha" (Toomer), **Supp. IX:** 311
Karl, Frederick R., **Supp. IV Part 1:** 384; **Supp. XXI:** 234
"Karloff and the Rock" (Di Piero), **Supp. XIX:** 44
Karl Shapiro's America (film), **Supp. II Part 2:** 703
Karmi, T., **Supp. XV:** 78, 88
Karr, Mary, **Supp. XI: 239–256; Supp. XIII:** 285; **Supp. XV:** 223; **Supp. XVI:** 63, 70, 77; **Supp. XVII:** 242
Kasabian, Linda, **Supp. IV Part 1:** 206
Kasper, Catherine, **Supp. XVI:** 294–295
Kate Chopin (Toth), **Retro. Supp. II:** 71
Kate Chopin: A Critical Biography (Seyersted), **Retro. Supp. II:** 65; **Supp. I Part 1:** 225
Kate Chopin and Edith Wharton: An Annotated Bibliographical Guide to Secondary Sources (Springer), **Supp. I Part 1:** 225
Kate Chopin and Her Creole Stories (Rankin), **Retro. Supp. II:** 57; **Supp. I Part 1:** 200, 225
"Kate Chopin's *The Awakening* in the Perspective of Her Literary Career" (Arms), **Supp. I Part 1:** 225
Kate Vaiden (Price), **Supp. VI:** 264, 265
"Käthe Kollwitz" (Rukeyser), **Supp. VI:** 283, 284
Katherine and Jean (Rice), **Supp. VII:** 288
"Kathleen" (Whittier), **Supp. I Part 2:** 693
Kathleen and Frank: The Autobiography of a Family (Isherwood), **Supp. XIV:** 158, 171
Kathy Goes to Haiti (Acker), **Supp. XII:** 5
Katz, Alan, **Supp. XXII:** 177
Katz, Alex, **Supp. XV:** 185
Katz, Jonathan, **Supp. XII:** 179
Katz, Steve, **Supp. V:** 44
Katz, Steven T., **Supp. XVI:** 154
Katzenberg, Jffrey, **Supp. XXI:** 154
Kauffman, Carol, **Supp. XI:** 295
Kauffmann, Stanley, **III:** 452; **Supp. I Part 2:** 391; **Supp. XVI:** 74
Kaufman, Boris, **Supp. XVIII:** 251
Kaufman, Charlie, **Supp. XV:** 16
Kaufman, George S., **II:** 427, 435, 437; **III:** 62, 71–72, 394; **Retro. Supp. II:** 327; **Supp. IV Part 2:** 574; **Supp. IX:** 190; **Supp. XV:** 329
Kaufmann, James, **Supp. XI:** 39
Kaufmann, Walter, **Supp. XVII:** 137
Kauvar, Elaine M., **Supp. V:** 273
Kavanaugh (Longfellow), **I:** 458; **II:** 489, 491; **Retro. Supp. II:** 156; **Supp. I Part 2:** 420
Kaveney, Roz, **Supp. XI:** 39
Kawabata, Yasunari, **Supp. XV:** 186; **Supp. XXI:** 146
Kaye-Smith, Sheila, **Supp. XVIII:** 130–131
Kazan, Elia, **III:** 153, 163; **IV:** 383; **Supp. I Part 1:** 66, 295; **Supp. XVI:** 193; **Supp. XVIII:** 250–251, 252
Kazin, Alfred, **I:** 248, 417, 419, 517; **II:** 177, 459; **IV:** 236; **Retro. Supp. II:** 206, 243, 246, 286; **Supp. I Part 1:** 195, 196, 294, 295, 296; **Supp. I Part 2:** 536, 631, 647, 650, 678, 679, 719; **Supp. II Part 1:** 143; **Supp. IV Part 1:** 200, 382; **Supp. V:** 122; **Supp. VIII: 93–111; Supp. IX:** 3, 227; **Supp. XIII:** 98, 106; **Supp. XIV:** 11; **Supp. XV:** 142
Keach, Stacey, **Supp. XI:** 309
Kean, Danuta, **Supp. XXI:** 80
Keane, Sarah, **Supp. I Part 1:** 100
Kearns, Cleo McNelly, **Retro. Supp. I:** 57
Kearns, George, **Retro. Supp. I:** 292
Keating, AnnLouise, **Supp. IV Part 1:** 330
Keaton, Buster, **I:** 31; **Supp. I Part 2:** 607; **Supp. IV Part 2:** 574
Keaton, Diane, **Supp. XV:** 5
Keats, John, **I:** 34, 103, 284, 314, 317–318, 385, 401, 448; **II:** 82, 88, 97, 214, 368, 512, 516, 530–531, 540, 593; **III:** 4, 10, 45, 122, 133–134, 179, 214, 237, 272, 275, 469, 485, 523; **IV:** 360, 405, 416; **Retro. Supp. I:** 91, 301, 313, 360, 395, 412; **Supp. I Part 1:** 82, 183, 266, 267, 312, 349, 362, 363, 365; **Supp. I Part 2:** 410, 422, 424, 539, 552, 675, 719, 720; **Supp. III Part 1:** 73; **Supp. IV Part 1:** 123, 168, 325; **Supp. IV Part 2:** 455; **Supp. VIII:** 41, 273; **Supp. IX:** 38, 39, 45; **Supp. XI:** 43, 320; **Supp. XII:** 9, 113, 255; **Supp. XIII:** 131, 281; **Supp. XIV:** 274; **Supp. XV:** 92; **Supp. XVII:** 76, 112; **Supp. XIX:** 33, 276; **Supp. XX: 115, 116; Supp. XXI:** 131
Keats, John (other), **Supp. IX:** 190, 195, 200
"Keela, the Outcast Indian Maiden" (Welty), **IV:** 263
Keeley, Mary Paxton, **Supp. XV:** 136
"Keen Scalpel on Racial Ills" (Bruell), **Supp. VIII:** 126
Keep, The (Egan), **Supp. XIX:** 49, **56–61**
"Keep A-Inchin' Along" (Van Vechten), Supp. III Part 2: 744
Keeping (Goldbarth), **Supp. XII:** 179–180, 180
"Keeping Informed in D.C." (Nemerov), **III:** 287
Keeping Slug Woman Alive: A Holistic Approach to American Indian Texts (Sarris), **Supp. IV Part 1:** 329
"'Keeping Their World Large' " (Moore), **III:** 201–202
Keeping the Night (Everwine), **Supp. XV:** 75, **81–85**, 86
"Keeping Things Whole" (Strand), **Supp. IV Part 2:** 624
Keep It Simple: A Defense of the Earth (Nichols), **Supp. XIII:** 268
"Keep the Saving Habit" (L. I. Wilder), **Supp. XXII:** 290
Kees, Weldon, **Supp. X:** 118; **Supp. XII:** 198; **Supp. XV:** 113, 114, 115, **133–149**
Keillor, Garrison, **Supp. XII:** 343; **Supp. XIII:** 274; **Supp. XVI: 165–179; Supp. XXI:** 53, 62; **Supp. XXII:** 83
Keillor, Gary Edward. *See* Keiller, Garrison
Keith, Brian, **Supp. IV Part 2:** 474
Keith, Minor C., **I:** 483
Kelleghan, Fiona, **Supp. XVIII:** 136, 139, 140
Keller, A. G., **III:** 108
Keller, Christopher J., **Supp. XVIII:** 192, 195
Keller, Helen, **I:** 254, 258

Keller, Lynn, **Supp. IV Part 2:** 423; **Supp. V:** 78, 80
Kelley, David, **Supp. IV Part 2:** 528, 529
Kelley, Florence, **Supp. I Part 1:** 5, 7
Kelley, Mary, **Supp. XVIII:** 257, 260
Kelley, Robin, **Supp. XVIII:** 231
Kellogg, Reverend Edwin H., **III:** 200
Kellogg, Paul U., **Supp. I Part 1:** 5, 7, 12
Kelly, **II:** 464
Kelly, Brigit Pegeen, **Supp. XVII: 123–134**
Kelly, Emmett, **Supp. XI:** 99, 106
Kelly, Gene, **Supp. XXI:** 148
Kelly, James Patrick, **Supp. XVIII:** 145; **Supp. XIX:** 231
Kelly, Walt, **Supp. XI:** 105
Kelly, William, **Supp. XV:** 75, 88
Kelsh, Nick, **Supp. XVII:** 167, 179
Kemble, Fanny, **Retro. Supp. I:** 228
Kemble, Gouverneur, **II:** 298
Kemble, Peter, **II:** 298
Kempton, Murray, **Supp. VIII:** 104
Kempton-Wace Letters, The (London and Strunsky), **II:** 465
Kennan, George F., **Supp. VIII:** 241
Kennedy, Albert J., **Supp. I Part 1:** 19
Kennedy, Arthur, **III:** 153
Kennedy, Burt, **Supp. IV Part 1:** 236
Kennedy, Jeffery, **Supp. XXI:** 6
Kennedy, J. Gerald, **Retro. Supp. II:** 271
Kennedy, John F., **I:** 136, 170; **II:** 49, 152–153; **III:** 38, 41, 42, 234, 411, 415, 581; **IV:** 229; **Supp. I Part 1:** 291; **Supp. I Part 2:** 496; **Supp. VIII:** 98, 104, 203; **Supp. XII:** 132
Kennedy, Mrs. John F., **I:** 136
Kennedy, John Pendleton, **II:** 313; **Supp. XXII:** 193
Kennedy, Robert, **Supp. V:** 291
Kennedy, Robert F., **I:** 294; **Supp. I Part 1:** 52; **Supp. XI:** 343
Kennedy, Sarah, **Supp. XVIII:** 293, 299, 301
Kennedy, William, **Supp. VII: 131–157; Supp. XVII:** 135; **Supp. XIX:** 141; **Supp. XX: 90**
Kennedy, X. J., **Supp. V:** 178, 182; **Supp. XV:** 113, **151–173**
Kenner, Hugh, **III:** 475, 478; **IV:** 412; **Supp. I Part 1:** 255; **Supp. IV Part 2:** 474; **Supp. XV:** 147; **Supp. XXI:** 235
"Kenneth Koch's 'Serious Moment' " (Spurr), **Supp. XV:** 183
Kenneth Millar/Ross Macdonald: A Checklist (Bruccoli), **Supp. IV Part 2:** 464, 469, 471
Kenney, Michael, **Supp. XIX:** 51, 52–53
Kenney, Susan, **Supp. XVIII:** 288, 289
Kenny, Maurice, **Supp. IV Part 2:** 502
Kent, George, **Supp. IV Part 1:** 11
Kent, Rockwell, **Supp. XV:** 41; **Supp. XXII:** 281
Kenton, Edna, **Supp. XXI:** 6
Kenton, Maxwell. *See* Burnett, David; Hoffenberg, Mason; Southern, Terry
"Kent State, May 1970" (Haines), **Supp. XII:** 211
Kentucky Straight (Offutt), **Supp. XIX: 163–167,** 171, 172
Kenya, the Land of Conflict (Kenyatta), **Supp. XXI:** 166
Kenyatta, Jomo, **Supp. X:** 135; **Supp. XXI:** 166
Kenyon, Jane, **Supp. VII: 159–177; Supp. VIII:** 272
Keogh, Tom, **Supp. XVI:** 230
Kepler, Johannes, **III:** 484; **IV:** 18
Keplinger, David, **Supp. XIX:** 273
Keppel, Frederick P., **I:** 214
"Kéramos" (Longfellow), **II:** 494; **Retro. Supp. II:** 167, 169
Kéramos and Other Poems (Longfellow), **II:** 490
Kercheval, Jesse Lee, **Supp. XIX:** 51
Kerim, Ussin, **Supp. IX:** 152
Kermode, Frank, **IV:** 133; **Retro. Supp. I:** 301
Kern, Jerome, **II:** 427
Kerouac, Jack, **III:** 174; **Retro. Supp. I:** 102; **Supp. II Part 1:** 31, 307, 309, 318, 328; **Supp. III Part 1:** 91–94, 96, 100, **217–234; Supp. IV Part 1:** 90, 146; **Supp. V:** 336; **Supp. VIII:** 42, 138, 289, 305; **Supp. IX:** 246; **Supp. XII:** 118, 121, 122, 123, 126, 131, 132; **Supp. XIII:** 275, 284; **Supp. XIV:** 137, 138, 141, 142, 143–144; **Supp. XV:** 134, 221; **Supp. XVI:** 123; **Supp. XVII:** 135, 138; **Supp. XX: 17**
Kerr, Deborah, **Supp. XI:** 307
Kerr, Orpheus C. (pseudonym). *See* Newell, Henry
Kerr, Walter, **Supp. IV Part 2:** 575, 579
Kerridge, Richard, **Supp. XVI:** 26
Kesey, Ken, **III:** 558; **Supp. III Part 1:** 217; **Supp. V:** 220, 295; **Supp. X:** 24, 265; **Supp. XI:** 104
Kessel, John, **Supp. XVIII:** 145; **Supp. XIX:** 231
Kessler, Milton, **Supp. XIX:** 195
Kesten, Stephen, **Supp. XI:** 309
Ketchum, Liza, **Supp. XIX:** 266
Ketchup (Shanley), **Supp. XIV:** 315
Kevane, Bridget, **Supp. XI:** 185, 190
"Key, The" (Welty), **IV:** 262
"Keys" (Nye), **Supp. XIII:** 281
"Key to the Highway" (Halliday), **Supp. XIX:** 84
Key to Uncle Tom's Cabin, A (Stowe), **Supp. I Part 2:** 580
Key West (H. Crane), **Retro. Supp. II:** 84
"Key West" (H. Crane), **I:** 400
Key West: An Island Sheaf (Crane), **I:** 385, 399–402
"Khalil the Heretic" (Gibran), **Supp. XX: 124**
Khrushchev, Nikita, **I:** 136
Kiang Kang-hu, **Supp. XV:** 45, 47
Kick for a Bite, A (Cobbett), **Supp. XV:** 237
"Kicking the Candles Out" (Jarman), **Supp. XVII:** 113
Kid, The (Aiken), **I:** 61
Kid, The (Chaplin), **I:** 386
Kidder, Tracy, **Supp. III Part 1:** 302; **Supp. XVIII:** 106, 114
Kidman, Nicole, **Supp. X:** 80
"Kidnapping in the Family, A" (Fante), **Supp. XI:** 164
"Kid's Guide to Divorce, The" (Moore), **Supp. X:** 167, 172
Kidwell, Clara Sue, **Supp. IV Part 1:** 333
Kielsky, Vera Emuma, **Supp. V:** 273
Kiely, Brendan, **Supp. XVII:** 75
Kieran, John, **II:** 417
Kierkegaard, Søren Aabye, **II:** 229; **III:** 292, 305, 309, 572; **IV:** 438, 491; **Retro. Supp. I:** 326; **Retro. Supp. II:** 222; **Supp. V:** 9; **Supp. VIII:** 7–8; **Supp. XX: 132**
Kiernan, Robert F., **Supp. IV Part 2:** 684
Kieseritsky, L., **III:** 252
Kilgo, Jim, **Supp. XVIII:** 192
"Kilim" (McClatchy), **Supp. XII:** 258
Kilina, Patricia (pseudonym). *See* Warren, Patricia Nell
"Killed at Resaca" (Bierce), **I:** 202
"Killed at the Ford" (Longfellow), **Retro. Supp. II:** 170–171
Killens, John Oliver, **Supp. IV Part 1:** 8, 369
"Killer in the Rain" (Chandler), **Supp. IV Part 1:** 122
"Killers, The" (Hemingway), **II:** 249; **Retro. Supp. I:** 188, 189
Killing Mister Watson (Matthiessen), **Supp. V:** 212, 214
"Killing of a State Cop, The" (Ortiz), **Supp. IV Part 2:** 499
Killing of Sister George, The (Marcus), **Supp. I Part 1:** 277
"Killings" (Dubus), **Supp. VII:** 85–86
"Killing the Ghost of Ripton" (Carruth), **Supp. XIX:** 1
"Killing the Plants" (Kenyon), **Supp. VII:** 167, 168
Kilmer, Joyce, **Supp. I Part 2:** 387; **Supp. XV:** 294
Kilpatrick, James K., **Supp. X:** 145
Kilvert, Francis, **Supp. VIII:** 172
Kim (Kipling), **Supp. X:** 230
Kim, Alfred, **Supp. XI:** 140
Kim, Sharon, **Supp. XVIII:** 267
Kimball, Frederic, **Supp. XXI:** 146
Kimball, J. Golden, **Supp. IV Part 2:** 602
Kimbrough, Mary Craig. *See* Sinclair, Mary Craig (Mary Craig Kimbrough)
Kimes, Maymie B., **Supp. IX:** 178
Kimes, William F., **Supp. IX:** 178
Kimmelman, Bert, **Supp. XXI:** 24
"Kin" (Welty), **IV:** 277; **Retro. Supp. I:** 353
Kinard, Agnes Dodds, **Supp. XIV:** 122, 123, 127
Kincaid, Jamaica, **Supp. VII: 179–196**
Kincaid, James, **Supp. XVIII:** 62, 63
"Kindness" (Dunn), **Supp. XI:** 149, 150
"Kindness" (Nye), **Supp. XIII:** 285
"Kindness" (Plath), **Retro. Supp. II:** 256
Kind of Light that Shines on Texas, The (McKnight), **Supp. XX: 151–152**
"Kind of Light that Shines on Texas, The" (McKnight), **Supp. XX: 151**

Kind of Order, A Kind of Folly, A: Essays and Conversations (Kunitz), **Supp. III Part 1:** 262, 268
Kindred (O. Butler), **Supp. XIII: 59–60,** 69
"Kind Sir: These Woods" (Sexton), **Supp. II Part 2:** 673
Kinds of Love (Sarton), **Supp. VIII: 253–254,** 256
Kinfolk (Buck), **Supp. II Part 1:** 126
King, Alexander, **IV:** 287
King, Carole, **Supp. XII:** 308
King, Clarence, **I:** 1
King, Ernest, **Supp. I Part 2:** 491
King, Fisher, **II:** 425
King, Francis, **Supp. XIV:** 155, 156, 166, 169
King, Grace, **Retro. Supp. II:** 136
King, Martin Luther, Jr., **Retro. Supp. II:** 12, 13; **Supp. XVIII:** 24; **Supp. XX: 281**
King, Michael, **Supp. XII:** 182
King, Queen, Knave (Nabokov), **III:** 251; **Retro. Supp. I:** 270
King, Starr, **Supp. II Part 1:** 341, 342
King, Stephen, **Supp. IV Part 1:** 102, 104; **Supp. IV Part 2:** 467; **Supp. V: 137–155; Supp. IX:** 114; **Supp. XIII:** 53
King, Tabitha (Mrs. Stephen King), **Supp. V:** 137
King, The (Barthelme), **Supp. IV Part 1:** 47, 52
"King, The" (Gibran), **Supp. XX: 123–124**
King Coffin (Aiken), **I:** 53–54, 57
"King David" (Benét), **Supp. XI:** 44
"King David" (Reznikoff), **Supp. XIV:** 283
Kingdom and the Power, The (Talese), **Supp. XVII:** 202, 203, 204, 210
Kingdom by the Sea, The: A Journey around Great Britain (Theroux), **Supp. VIII:** 323
"Kingdom County Come" (Mosher), **Supp. XXII:** 211–212
Kingdom of Earth (T. Williams), **IV:** 382, 386, 387, 388, 391, 393, 398
"Kingdom of Earth, The" (T. Williams), **IV:** 384
Kingfisher, The (Clampitt), **Supp. IX:** 38
"Kingfishers, The" (Olson), **Supp. II Part 2:** 557, 558–563, 582
King Jasper (Robinson), **III:** 523
King Kong (film), **Supp. IV Part 1:** 104; **Supp. XVII:** 58
King Lear (Shakespeare), **I:** 538; **II:** 540, 551; **Retro. Supp. I:** 248; **Supp. IV Part 1:** 31, 36; **Supp. IX:** 14; **Supp. XI:** 172; **Supp. XV:** 349
King Leopold's Soliloquy (Twain), **IV:** 208
King My Father's Wreck, The (Simpson), **Supp. IX:** 266, 267, 270, 275, 276
King of Babylon Shall Not Come Against You, The (Garrett), **Supp. VII:** 110–111; **Supp. X:** 3
"King of Beasts" (P. N. Warren), **Supp. XX: 272**
"King of Folly Island, The" (Jewett), **II:** 394; **Retro. Supp. II:** 132, 133
King of Kings (film), **Supp. IV Part 2:** 520
King of Paris (Endore), **Supp. XVII:** 64
"King of the Bingo Game" (Ellison), **Retro. Supp. II:** 117, 125; **Supp. II Part 1:** 235, 238, 240–241
"King of the Cats, The" (Benét), **Supp. XI:** 49–50
"King of the Clock Tower" (Yeats), **III:** 473
"King of the Desert, The" (O'Hara), **III:** 369
King of the Fields, The (Singer), **Retro. Supp. II:** 317
King of the Jews (Epstein), **Supp. XII:** 161, **166–170,** 172
King of the Mountain (Garrett), **Supp. VII:** 96, 97
"King of the River" (Kunitz), **Supp. III Part 1:** 263, 267–268
"King of the Sea" (Marquand), **III:** 60
"King over the Water" (Blackmur), **Supp. II Part 1:** 107
"King Pandar" (Blackmur), **Supp. II Part 1:** 92, 102
"King Pest" (Poe), **Retro. Supp. II:** 273
Kingsblood Royal (Lewis), **II:** 456
Kingsbury, John, **Supp. I Part 1:** 8
"King's Daughters, Home for Unwed Mothers, 1948" (Stanford), **Supp. XV:** 345
King's Henchman, The (Millay), **III:** 138–139
Kingsley, Sidney, **Supp. I Part 1:** 277, 281
King's Mare, The (Canolle; Loos, trans.), **Supp. XVI:** 194
"King's Missive, The" (Whittier), **Supp. I Part 2:** 694
Kingsolver, Barbara, **Supp. VII: 197–214; Supp. XIII:** 16; **Supp. XVIII:** 189
King's Stilts, The (Geisel), **Supp. XVI:** 100, 104
Kingston, Earll, **Supp. V:** 160
Kingston, Maxine Hong, **Supp. IV Part 1:** 1, 12; **Supp. V: 157–175,** 250; **Supp. X:** 291–292; **Supp. XI:** 18, 245; **Supp. XV:** 220, 223
"King Volmer and Elsie" (Whittier), **Supp. I Part 2:** 696
Kinkaid, Jamaica, **Supp. XXII:** 65
Kinmont, Alexander, **Supp. I Part 2:** 588–589
Kinnaird, John, **Retro. Supp. I:** 399
Kinnell, Galway, **Supp. III Part 1: 235–256; Supp. III Part 2:** 541; **Supp. IV Part 2:** 623; **Supp. V:** 332; **Supp. VIII:** 39; **Supp. XI:** 139; **Supp. XII:** 241; **Supp. XV:** 212; **Supp. XVI:** 53; **Supp. XXII:** 83
Kinsella, Thomas, **Supp. XX: 195–196, 197, 207**
Kinsey, Alfred, **IV:** 230; **Supp. XIV:** 140
Kinzie, Mary, **Supp. XII:** 181
"Kipling" (Trilling), **Supp. III Part 2:** 495
Kipling, Rudyard, **I:** 421, 587–588; **II:** 271, 338, 404, 439; **III:** 55, 328, 508, 511, 521, 524, 579; **IV:** 429; **Supp. IV Part 2:** 603; **Supp. X:** 255; **Supp. XX: 23**
Kirby, David, **Supp. XIII:** 89; **Supp. XIX:** 81
Kirkland, Caroline, **Supp. XVIII:** 258
Kirkland, David, **Supp. XVI:** 186
Kirkland, Jack, **I:** 297
Kirkpatrick, Jeane, **Supp. VIII:** 241
Kirkus, Virginia, **Supp. XV:** 198
Kirkwood, Cynthia A., **Supp. XI:** 177, 178, 179
Kirp, David L., **Supp. XI:** 129
Kirsch, Adam, **Supp. XV:** 251, 260, 264, 266, 341, 347, 350–351
Kirstein, Lincoln, **Supp. II Part 1:** 90, 97; **Supp. IV Part 1:** 82, 83; **Supp. XXII:** 281
"Kiss, The" (Di Piero), **Supp. XIX:** 45, 47
Kiss, The (Harrison), **Supp. X:** 191
"Kiss, The" (Sexton), **Supp. II Part 2:** 687
"Kiss Away" (C. Baxter), **Supp. XVII:** 20
Kissel, Howard, **Supp. IV Part 2:** 580
Kiss Hollywood Good-by (Loos), **Supp. XVI:** 190, 195
Kissinger, Henry, **Supp. IV Part 1:** 388; **Supp. XII:** 9, 14
Kiss of the Spider Woman, the Musical (McNally), **Supp. XIII:** 207, **Supp. XIII:** 208
Kiss Tomorrow Good-bye (McCoy), **Supp. XIII:** 170, **172–173,** 174
"Kit and Caboodle" (Komunyakaa), **Supp. XIII:** 115
Kit Brandon: A Portrait (Anderson), **I:** 111
Kitchen, Judith, **Supp. IV Part 1:** 242, 245, 252; **Supp. IX:** 163; **Supp. XI:** 312, 313, 315, 317, 319, 320, 326, 329; **Supp. XV:** 215, 219
"Kitchenette" (Brooks), **Retro. Supp. I:** 208
Kitchen God's Wife, The (Tan), **Supp. X:** 289, 292, 293, 294–295, 296–297, 298–299
"Kitchen Terrarium: 1983" (McCarriston), **Supp. XIV:** 270
Kit O'Brien (Masters), **Supp. I Part 2:** 471
Kittel, Frederick August. *See* Wilson, August
Kittredge, Charmian. *See* London, Mrs. Jack (Charmian Kittredge)
Kittredge, William, **Supp. VIII:** 39; **Supp. XI:** 316; **Supp. XII:** 209; **Supp. XIII:** 16
"Kitty Hawk" (Frost), **II:** 164; **Retro. Supp. I:** 124, 141
Kizer, Carolyn, **Supp. XVII:** 71, 72, 73, 74
Klaidman, Stephen, **Supp. XIX:** 269
Klail City (Hinojosa), **Supp. XIX:** 97, **101–103**
Klail City Death Trip (Hinojosa). *See Ask a Policeman* (Hinojosa); *Becky and*

Her Friends (Hinojosa); *Dear Rafe* (Hinojosa); *Fair Gentlemen of Belken County* (Hinojosa); *Klail City* (Hinojosa); *Korean Love Songs from Klail City Death Trip* (Hinojosa); *Partners in Crime: A Rafe Buenrostro Mystery* (Hinojosa); *Rites and Witnesses: A Comedy* (Hinojosa); *Useless Servants, The* (Hinojosa); *Valley, The* (Hinojosa)
Klein, Joe, **Supp. XII:** 67–68
Klein, Marcus, **Supp. I Part 2:** 432; **Supp. XI:** 233
Kleist, Heinrich von, **Supp. IV Part 1:** 224
Kline, Franz, **Supp. XII:** 198
Kline, George, **Supp. VIII:** 22, 28
Klinghoffer, David, **Supp. XVI:** 74
Klinkowitz, Jerome, **Supp. IV Part 1:** 40; **Supp. X:** 263; **Supp. XI:** 347; **Supp. XXI:** 233
Klise, James, **Supp. XXII:** 53
Kloefkorn, Bill, **Supp. XIX:** 119
Knapp, Adeline, **Supp. XI:** 200
Knapp, Friedrich, **III:** 100
Knapp, Samuel, **I:** 336
Knapp, Samuel Lorenzo, **Supp. XV:** 246
"Kneeling Down to Look into a Culvert" (R. Bly), **Supp. XXI:** 88
Kneel to the Rising Sun (Caldwell), **I:** 304, 309
"Knees/Dura-Europos" (Goldbarth), **Supp. XII:** 185
"Knife" (Simic), **Supp. VIII:** 275
Knight, Arthur, **Supp. XIV:** 144
Knight, Etheridge, **Supp. XI:** 239
"Knight in Disguise, The" (Lindsay), **Supp. I Part 2:** 390
Knightly Quest, The (T. Williams), **IV:** 383
Knight's Gambit (Faulkner), **II:** 72
Knish, Anne. *See* Ficke, Arthur Davison
"Knit One, Purl Two" (K. Snodgrass), **Supp. XVI:** 42
"Knock" (Dickey), **Supp. IV Part 1:** 182
Knocked Out Loaded (album, Dylan), **Supp. XVIII:** 28
"Knocking Around" (Ashbery), **Supp. III Part 1:** 22
"Knocking on Heaven's Door" (Lamott), **Supp. XX: 140–141**
"Knocking on Three, Winston" (Epstein), **Supp. XIV:** 109
Knock on Any Door (film, Ray), **Supp. XVII:** 150
Knock on Any Door (W. Motley), **Supp. XVII: 150–155,** 159, 160; 158
Knockout Artist, The (Crews), **Supp. XI: 113–114**
Knoll, Robert E., **Supp. XV:** 118
Knopf, Alfred A., **III:** 99, 105, 106, 107; **Retro. Supp. I:** 13, 19, 317; **Supp. I Part 1:** 324, 325, 327; **Supp. IV Part 1:** 125, 354; **Supp. XIII:** 172
Knopf, Blanche, **Supp. I Part 1:** 324, 325, 327, 328, 332, 341; **Supp. IV Part 1:** 128, 346, 348; **Supp. XIII:** 169
"Knot, The" (Rich), **Supp. I Part 2:** 555
Knotts, Kristina, **Supp. XIII:** 238
"Knowing, The" (Olds), **Supp. X:** 215
"Knowledge Forwards and Backwards" (Stern), **Supp. IX:** 296
"Knowledge of Plates" (Bronk), **Supp. XXI:** 33
Knowles, John, **Supp. IV Part 2:** 679; **Supp. XII: 235–250; Supp. XX: 84**
Known World, The (E. P. Jones), **Supp. XXII:** 139, 140, 142, **146–150,** 150
Knox, Frank, **Supp. I Part 2:** 488, 489
Knox, Israel, **Supp. X:** 70
Knox, Vicesimus, **II:** 8
Knoxville: Summer of 1915 (Agee), **I:** 42–46
Knudson, R. Rozanne, **Supp. IV Part 2:** 648
Kober, Arthur, **Supp. I Part 1:** 292
Koch, Frederick, **IV:** 453
Koch, John, **Supp. VIII:** 88
Koch, Kenneth, **Supp. XV: 175–192; Supp. XIX:** 81
Koch, Vivienne, **III:** 194; **IV:** 136, 140; **Retro. Supp. I:** 428, 430
"Kochinnenako in Academe: Three Approaches to Interpreting a Keres Indian Tale" (Gunn Allen), **Supp. IV Part 1:** 329
"Kodachromes of the Island" (Hayden), **Supp. II Part 1:** 367, 380
Koestler, Arthur, **I:** 258; **Supp. I Part 2:** 671
Kokkinen, Eila, **Supp. XIV:** 146, 148
Kolba, Ellen D., **Supp. XVIII:** 257
Kolbenheyer, Dr. Frederick, **Supp. I Part 1:** 207
Kolodny, Annette, **Supp. X:** 97, 103, 229
"Komodo" (C. Frost), **Supp. XV:** 95
Komunyakaa, Yusef, **Supp. XIII: 111–136; Supp. XXI:** 129, 139
Konigsberg, Allan Stewart. *See* Allen, Woody
Kon-Tiki (Heyerdahl), **II:** 477
Koopman, Harry Lyman, **Retro. Supp. I:** 40
Ko; or, A Season on Earth (Koch), **Supp. XV:** 175, 180, 181, 183, 186
Kooser, Ted, **Supp. XV:** 113, 115; **Supp. XIX: 115–130; Supp. XXI:** 243
Kootz, Samuel, **Supp. XV:** 144
Kora and Ka (Doolittle), **Supp. I Part 1:** 270
Kora in Hell (W. C. Williams), **Retro. Supp. I:** 416, **417–418,** 419, 430, 431; **Supp. XXI:** 232
Korb, Rena, **Supp. XI:** 2
Korczak, Janosz, **Supp. X:** 70
Korean Love Songs from Klail City Death Trip (Hinojosa), **Supp. XIX:** 98, **103–104**
Kornblatt, Joyce Reiser, **Supp. XV:** 62
Kornfield, Jack, **Supp. XX: 142**
Korrektur (Bernhard), **Supp. XX: 91**
Kort, Amy, **Supp. XIII:** 148
Korwin, Yala, **Supp. XXI:** 99
Kosinski, Jerzy, **Supp. VII: 215–228; Supp. XII:** 21
"Kostas Tympakianakis" (Merrill), **Supp. III Part 1:** 326
Koteliansky, S. S., **Supp. VIII:** 251, 265
Kouidis, Virginia M., **Supp. XXII:** 161, 162, 166, 167, 169
Kovic, Ron, **Supp. XIX:** 17; **Supp. XXII:** 104
Kowloon Tong (Theroux), **Supp. VIII:** 325
Kozlenko, William, **IV:** 378, 381
Krabbenhoft, Ken, **Supp. XVII:** 112
Kraft, James, **Supp. XV:** 40, 41, 42, 43, 52
Krakauer, Jon, **Supp. XVII:** 210; **Supp. XVIII: 105–118**
Kramer, Dale, **Supp. I Part 2:** 669
Kramer, Hilton, **III:** 537; **Supp. I Part 1:** 295, 296; **Supp. VIII:** 239; **Supp. XV:** 113; **Supp. XIX:** 269
Kramer, Lawrence, **Supp. IV Part 1:** 61, 65, 66; **Supp. IX:** 291
Kramer, Peter D., **Supp. XVI:** 229
Kramer, Stanley, **II:** 421, 587
Krapp's Last Tape (Beckett), **I:** 71; **III:** 387; **Retro. Supp. I:** 206
Krassner, Paul, **Supp. IV Part 1:** 385; **Supp. XI:** 293
Kraus, Karl, **Supp. XX: 84**
Krauth, Leland, **Supp. XVIII:** 58
Kreisler, Harry, **Supp. XVI:** 155
Kreitman, Esther, **IV:** 2
"Kremlin of Smoke" (Schnackenberg), **Supp. XV:** 257–258
Kreymborg, Alfred, **II:** 530; **III:** 465; **IV:** 76; **Retro. Supp. I:** 417; **Supp. XV:** 301, 306; **Supp. XXII:** 161–162
Krim, Seymour, **Supp. XV:** 338; **Supp. XVI:** 217; **Supp. XVIII:** 285
Krisak, Len, **Supp. XXI:** 99, 104
Kristeva, Julia, **Supp. XII:** 6
Kristofferson, Kris, **Supp. XIII:** 119
Kristol, Irving, **Supp. VIII:** 93, 244; **Supp. XIII:** 98
Krivak, Andrew, **Supp. XVII:** 242
Kroll, Jack, **Supp. IV Part 2:** 590
Kroll, Judith, **Supp. I Part 2:** 541–543, 544, 546
Kroll Ring, Frances. *See* Ring, Frances Kroll
Krondorfer, Björn, **Supp. XVI:** 160
Kronenberger, Louis, **Supp. XXII:** 191, 192
Krook, Dorothea, **Retro. Supp. II:** 243
Kropotkin, Peter, **I:** 493; **Supp. I Part 1:** 5; **Supp. IV Part 2:** 521
Kruif, Paul de, **II:** 446
Krupat, Arnold, **Supp. IV Part 2:** 500
Krupnick, Mark, **Supp. XVI:** 153
Krutch, Joseph Wood, **II:** 459; **III:** 425; **IV:** 70, 175
Kublai Khan, **III:** 395
"Kubla Khan" (Coleridge), **Supp. XIII:** 131, 283
Kubrick, Stanley, **Supp. IV Part 1:** 392; **Supp. XI:** 293,**Supp. XI:** 301, 302–303
"Kubuku Rides (This Is It) " (L. Brown), **Supp. XXI:** 39, 42–43
Kuehl, John, **Supp. IV Part 1:** 279, 284, 285, 287
Kuehl, Linda, **Supp. IV Part 1:** 199
"Kugelmass Episode, The" (Allen), **Supp. XV:** 15, 16

Kukachin, Princess, **III:** 395
"Ku Klux" (Hughes), **Retro. Supp. I:** 205
Kulshrestha, Chirantan, **Retro. Supp. II:** 21
Kumin, Maxine, **Supp. IV Part 2: 439–457; Supp. XIII:** 294; **Supp. XVII:** 71, 75–76; **Supp. XX: 164**
Kundera, Milan, **Supp. VIII:** 241
Kunerth, Jeff, **Supp. XXI:** 47
Kunitz, Stanley, **I:** 179, 180, 181, 182, 521; **II:** 545; **Supp. III Part 1: 257–270; Supp. V:** 79; **Supp. XI:** 259; **Supp. XIII:** 341
Kuo, Helena, **Supp. X:** 291
Kuropatkin, General Aleksei Nikolaevich, **III:** 247–248
Kurth, Peter, **Supp. XVIII:** 145
Kurzy of the Sea (Barnes), **Supp. III Part 1:** 34
Kushner, Tony, **Supp. IX: 131–149; Supp. XX: 177; Supp. XXI:** 145
Kussy, Bella, **IV:** 468
Kutnik, Jerzy, **Supp. XXII:** 177
Kuttner, Henry, **Supp. IV Part 1:** 102
Kuzma, Greg, **Supp. XV:** 118

LaBastille, Anne, **Supp. X: 95–110**
"Labor's Cultural Degradation" (Swados), **Supp. XIX:** 264–265
"Labours of Hercules, The" (Moore), **III:** 201
La Bruyère, Jean de, **I:** 58
La Bufera e Altro (Montale), **Supp. V:** 337
LaBute, Neil, **Supp. XXI:** 147
Labyrinth of Love (Untermeyer), **Supp. XV:** 312
Labyrinth of Solitude, The (Paz), **Supp. XIII:** 223
Lacan, Jacques, **Supp. IV Part 1:** 45; **Supp. VIII:** 5; **Supp. XII:** 98
La Casa en Mango Street (Cisneros), **Supp. VII:** 58–59
Lachaise, Gaston, **I:** 434
"Lackawanna" (Merwin), **Supp. III Part 1:** 350
Lackawanna Elegy (Goll; Kinnell, trans.), **Supp. III Part 1:** 235, 243–244
Laclède, Pierre, **Supp. I Part 1:** 205
"Lacquer Prints" (Lowell), **II:** 524–525
Lacy, Ed, **Supp. XV: 193–210**
Ladder, The (Rasmussen; Nelson, trans.), **Supp. XVIII:** 180–181
Ladder of Years (Tyler), **Supp. IV Part 2:** 657, 671–672
Ladders to Fire (Nin), **Supp. X:** 185
Laddie (Stratton-Porter), **Supp. XX: 211, 213**
"Laddie, the Princess and the Pie" (Stratton-Porter), **Supp. XX: 216**
"Ladies" (Coleman), **Supp. XI:** 93
Ladies Almanack (Barnes), **Supp. III Part 1:** 37–39, 42; **Supp. XXII:** 167
Ladies Auxiliary, The (Mirvis), **Supp. XX: 177, 179–185**
"Ladies in Spring" (Welty), **IV:** 276–277; **Retro. Supp. I:** 353
Lady, The (Richter), **Supp. XVIII: 211–212,** 220
Lady Audley's Secret (Braddon), **Supp. I Part 1:** 35, 36
"Lady Barberina" (James), **Retro. Supp. I:** 227
"Lady Bates" (Jarrell), **II:** 380–381
Lady Chatterley's Lover (Lawrence), **III:** 170; **IV:** 434; **Supp. XVI:** 267
Lady from Louisiana (film, Vorhaus), **Supp. XVII:** 59
"Lady from Redhorse, A" (Bierce), **I:** 203
Lady in Kicking Horse Reservoir, The (Hugo), **Supp. VI:** 134, **138–139**
Lady in the Lake, The (Chandler), **Supp. IV Part 1:** 127, 129–130
"Lady in the Lake, The" (Chandler), **Supp. IV Part 1:** 129
Lady in the Lake, The (film), **Supp. IV Part 1:** 130
"Lady in the Pink Mustang, The" (Erdrich), **Supp. IV Part 1:** 270
"Lady Is Civilized, The" (Taylor), **Supp. V:** 315
Lady Is Cold, The (White), **Supp. I Part 2:** 653
Lady Killer (Holding), **Supp. XXII:** 126, **127,** 130
"Lady Lazarus" (Plath), **Retro. Supp. II:** 250, 251, 255; **Supp. I Part 2:** 529, 535, 542, 545
Lady of Aroostook, The (Howells), **II:** 280
"Lady of Bayou St. John, A" (Chopin), **Retro. Supp. II:** 58
"Lady of the Lake, The" (Malamud), **Supp. I Part 2:** 437
Lady Oracle (Atwood), **Supp. XIII:** 21, **23–24**
"Lady Poverty" (Notley), **Supp. XXII:** 234–235
Lady Sings the Blues (film), **Supp. I Part 1:** 67
"Lady's Maid's Bell, The" (Wharton), **IV:** 316
"Lady Wentworth" (Longfellow), **II:** 505
"Lady with a Lamp" (Parker), **Supp. IX:** 193
"Lady with the Heron, The" (Merwin), **Supp. III Part 1:** 343
"Lady with the Pet Dog, The" (Chekov), **Supp. XXII:** 60
"Lady with the Pet Tribble, The" (Brockmeier), **Supp. XXII:** 60
La Farge, John, **I:** 1, 2, 20; **II:** 322, 338; **Retro. Supp. I:** 217
La Farge, Oliver, **Supp. IV Part 2:** 503
Lafayette, Marquis de, **I:** 344, 345; **II:** 405–406; **Supp. I Part 2:** 510, 511, 683
"La Figlia che Piange" (Eliot), **Retro. Supp. I:** 63
La Follette, Robert, **I:** 483, 485, 492; **III:** 580
La Fontaine, Jean de, **II:** 154; **III:** 194; **IV:** 80
Laforgue, Jules, **I:** 386, 569, 570, 572–573, 575, 576; **II:** 528; **III:** 8, 11, 466; **IV:** 37, 79, 80, 122; **Retro. Supp. I:** 55, 56; **Supp. XIII:** 332, 335, 346; **Supp. XV:** 165
La Gallienne, Eva, **Supp. VIII:** 251
"Lager Beer" (Dunbar), **Supp. II Part 1:** 193
"La Gringuita: On Losing a Native Language" (Alvarez), **Supp. VII:** 18
Laguna Woman (Silko), **Supp. IV Part 2:** 557, 560–561
Lahiri, Jhumpa, **Supp. XXI: 175–189**
Lahr, John, **Supp. XXI:** 18
Laing, R. D., **Supp. I Part 2:** 527; **Supp. XX: 94**
La kabbale pratique (Ambelain), **Supp. I Part 1:** 273
"Lake, The" (Bradbury), **Supp. IV Part 1:** 101
Lake, The (play), **Supp. IX:** 189
Lakeboat (Mamet), **Supp. XIV:** 240–241
"Lake Chelan" (Stafford), **Supp. XI:** 321
Lake Effect Country (Ammons), **Supp. VII:** 34, 35
"Lake Isle of Innisfree, The" (Yeats), **Retro. Supp. I:** 413; **Supp. XIX:** 92
"Lake Return" (Wright), **Supp. XV:** 345
Lake Wobegon Days (Keillor), **Supp. XVI:** 165, 166, **173–174**
Lake Wobegon Summer 1956 (Keillor), **Supp. XVI:** 178
Lalic, Ivan V., **Supp. VIII:** 272
Lamantia, Philip, **Supp. VIII:** 289
Lamb, Brian, **Supp. XIX:** 156; **Supp. XX: 101**
Lamb, Charles, **III:** 111, 207; **Supp. VIII:** 125
Lamb, Wendy, **Supp. IV Part 2:** 658
Lambardi, Marilyn May, **Retro. Supp. II:** 45–46
Lamb in His Bosom (C. Miller), **Supp. XXII:** 187, **189–191,** 193–194, 195, 197, 198, 199, 200
"Lame Feet of Salvation, The" (W. V. Davis), **Supp. XXI:** 87–88
"Lament" (Wilbur), **Supp. III Part 2:** 550
"Lamentations" (Glück), **Supp. V:** 83, 84
"Lament for Dark Peoples" (Hughes), **Retro. Supp. I:** 199
"Lament for Saul and Jonathan" (Bradstreet), **Supp. I Part 1:** 111
"Lament-Heaven" (Doty), **Supp. XI:** 125
"Lament of a New England Mother, The" (Eberhart), **I:** 539
Laments for the Living (Parker), **Supp. IX:** 192
"Lame Shall Enter First, The" (O'Connor), **III:** 348, 351, 352, 355, 356–357, 358; **Retro. Supp. II:** 237
Lamia (Keats), **II:** 512; **III:** 523
Lamming, George, **Supp. XXI:** 170
Lamott, Anne, **Supp. XX: 131–146**
La Motte-Fouqué, Friedrich Heinrich Karl, **III:** 77, 78
L'Amour, Louis, **Supp. XIII:** 5
Lamp for Nightfall, A (Caldwell), **I:** 297
Lamplit Answer, The (Schnackenberg), **Supp. XV:** 251, 254, **256–260**
"Lance" (Nabokov), **Retro. Supp. I:** 266

Lancelot (Percy), **Supp. III Part 1:** 384, 395–396
Lancelot (Robinson), **III:** 513, 522
Lanchester, John, **Retro. Supp. I:** 278
"Land" (Emerson), **II:** 6
"Land Aesthetic, The" (Callicott), **Supp. XIV:** 184
"Land and Language" (J. W. Miller), **Supp. XX: 170**
Landau, Deborah, **Supp. XI:** 122, 123
"Land beyond the Blow, The" (Bierce), **I:** 209
"Land Ethic, The" (Leopold), **Supp. XIV:** 179, 180, 183, 191, 192
Landfall (Wagoner), **Supp. IX:** 330
"Landing in Luck" (Faulkner), **Retro. Supp. I:** 85
"Landing on the Moon" (Swenson), **Supp. IV Part 2:** 643
"Landings" (Hoffman), **Supp. XVIII:** 86
"Landing Under Water, I See Roots" (A. Finch), **Supp. XVII:** 76
Landlord at Lion's Head, The (Howells), **II:** 276, 287–288
Landmarks of Healing: A Study of House Made of Dawn (Scarberry-García), **Supp. IV Part 2:** 486
Land of Little Rain, The (Dillard), **Supp. VI: 27–28**
Land of Look Behind, The (Cliff), **Supp. XXII:** 65–66, 68–69
Land of the Free U.S.A. (MacLeish), **I:** 293; **III:** 16–17
Land of Unlikeness (Lowell), **II:** 537–538, 539, 547; **Retro. Supp. II:** 177, 178, **184–185**
Landor, Walter Savage, **III:** 15, 469; **Supp. I Part 2:** 422
"Landscape" (Sarton), **Supp. VIII:** 259
"Landscape #11" (Halliday), **Supp. XIX:** 93
Landscape and Journey (W. V. Davis), **Supp. XXI:** 83, 88, 90, **92–93,** 95
"Landscape as a Nude" (MacLeish), **III:** 14
Landscape at the End of the Century (Dunn), **Supp. XI:** 139, 143, **150–151**
"Landscape Chamber, The" (Jewett), **II:** 408–409
"Landscape for the Disappeared" (Komunyakaa), **Supp. XIII:** 120, 126
Landscape in American Poetry (Larcom), **Supp. XIII:** 142
"Landscape Painter, A" (James), **II:** 322; **Retro. Supp. I:** 219
"Landscape Symbolism in Kate Chopin's *At Fault*" (Arner), **Retro. Supp. II:** 62
"Landscape: The Eastern Shore" (Barth), **I:** 122
"Landscape with Boat" (Stevens), **Retro. Supp. I:** 306
"Landscape with the Fall of Icarus" (Brueghel), **Retro. Supp. I:** 430
Land's End: A Walk through Provincetown (Cunningham), **Supp. XV:** 69
Land That Drank the Rain, The (Hoffman), **Supp. XVIII:** 76, 80, 81, 82
"Land Where There Is No Death, The" (Benét), **Supp. XI:** 56
Lane, Ann, **Supp. XI:** 195, 208
Lane, Cornelia. *See* Anderson, Mrs. Sherwood
Lane, Homer, **Supp. II Part 1:** 6; **Supp. XIV:** 160
Lane, Nathan, **Supp. XIII:** 207
Lane, Rose Wilder, **Supp. IV Part 2:** 524; **Supp. XXII:** 293–294, 295, 296, 297, 301
Lanes, Selma G., **Supp. XVI:** 104, 107
Lang, Andrew, **Retro. Supp. I:** 127
Lang, Violet, **Supp. XII:** 119
Langdon, Olivia. *See* Clemens, Mrs. Samuel Langhorne (Olivia Langdon)
Lange, Carl Georg, **II:** 350
Lange, Dorothea, **I:** 293; **Supp. XIV:** 181
Langland, Joseph, **III:** 542
Langston Hughes, American Poet (Walker), **Supp. III Part 2:** 530–531
Langston Hughes and the "Chicago Defender": Essays on Race, Politics, and Culture (De Santis, ed.), **Retro. Supp. I:** 194
Langston Hughes: Modern Critical Views (Bloom, ed.), **Retro. Supp. I:** 193
Langston Hughes Reader, The (Hughes), **Retro. Supp. I:** 202; **Supp. I Part 1:** 345
Langston Hughes: The Poet and His Critics (Barksdale), **Retro. Supp. I:** 202
"Language, Visualization and the Inner Library" (Shepard), **Supp. III Part 2:** 436, 438, 449
Language and Imagery of the Bible, The (Caird), **Supp. XXI:** 91–92
"Language and the Writer" (Bambara), **Supp. XI:** 18
Language As Gesture (Blackmur), **Supp. II Part 1:** 108
Language as Symbolic Action (Burke), **I:** 275, 282, 285
Language Book, The (Andrews and Bernstein), **Supp. IV Part 2:** 426
Language in Thought and Action (Hayakawa), **I:** 448
"Language of Being and Dying, The" (Gass), **Supp. VI:** 91
"Language of Home, The" (Wideman), **Supp. X:** 320, 323–324
Language of Life, The (Moyers, television series), **Supp. XIII:** 274, 276
Language of the American South, The (Brooks), **Supp. XIV:** 14
"Language of the Brag, The" (Olds), **Supp. X:** 204
"Language We Know, The" (Ortiz), **Supp. IV Part 2:** 500
Lanier, Clifford, **Supp. I Part 1:** 349, 350, 353, 355, 356, 371
Lanier, James F. D., **Supp. I Part 1:** 350
Lanier, Lyle H., **Supp. X:** 25
Lanier, Robert Sampson, **Supp. I Part 1:** 349, 351, 355, 356, 361
Lanier, Mrs. Robert Sampson (Mary Jane Anderson), **Supp. I Part 1:** 349
Lanier, Sidney, **IV:** 444; **Supp. I Part 1: 349–373; Supp. I Part 2:** 416; **Supp. IV Part 1:** 165
Lanier, Mrs. Sidney (Mary Day), **Supp. I Part 1:** 351, 355, 357, 361, 362, 364, 370, 371
"Lanier as Poet" (Parks), **Supp. I Part 1:** 373
"Lanier's Reading" (P. Graham), **Supp. I Part 1:** 373
"Lanier's Use of Science for Poetic Imagery" (Beaver), **Supp. I Part 1:** 373
Lankes, J. J., **Supp. XXII:** 275
Lannegan, Helen. *See* Caldwell, Mrs. Erskine
Lannin, Paul, **II:** 427
Lanny Budd novels (Sinclair), **Supp. V:** 290
Lant, Kathleen Margaret, **Supp. V:** 141
Lanterns on the Levee (Percy), **Supp. XXII:** 193
Lanthenas, François, **Supp. I Part 2:** 515
"Lanyard, The" (Collins), **Supp. XXI:** 56, **62–64**
Laotzu, **III:** 173, 189, 567; **Supp. XV:** 39, 46, 48
Lapine, James, **Supp. XXI:** 147–148
"Lapis Lazuli" (Yeats), **I:** 532; **III:** 40
Laplace, Pierre Simon de, **III:** 428
Lapouge, M. G., **Supp. I Part 2:** 633
Lappa, Katherine, **Supp. XV:** 176
Lapsing to Grace (Espaillat), **Supp. XXI:** 99, 100
Lapsley, Gaillard, **Supp. XX: 231**
Laqueur, Thomas, **Supp. XVI:** 154
Larbaud, Valery, **IV:** 404; **Supp. XIII:** 332; **Supp. XIV:** 338
Larcom, Lucy, **Retro. Supp. II:** 145; **Supp. XIII: 137–157**
Larcom's Poetical Works (Larcom), **Supp. XIII:** 142
Lardner, John, **II:** 437
Lardner, Ring, **I:** 487; **II:** 44, 91, 259, 263, **415–438; III:** 566, 572; **IV:** 433; **Retro. Supp. I:** 105; **Retro. Supp. II:** 222; **Supp. I Part 2:** 609; **Supp. IX:** 200; **Supp. XVI:** 189
Lardner, Ring, Jr., **Supp. XI:** 306
"Lardner, Shakespeare and Chekhov" (Matthews), **II:** 430
"Large Bad Picture" (Bishop), **Retro. Supp. II:** 43; **Supp. I Part 1:** 73, 80–82, 85, 86, 89, 90
"Large Coffee" (Lardner), **II:** 437
Large Glass, or The Bride Stripped Bare by Her Bachelors, Even (Duchamp), **Supp. IV Part 2:** 423, 424
Largo (Handel), **IV:** 369
"Lark" (Taggard), **Supp. XXII:** 280
Lark, The (Hellman), **Supp. I Part 1:** 286–288, 297
Lark: Four-Part Chorus for Mixed Voices (A Capella) with Baritone Solo (Taggard and Copland), **Supp. XXII:** 283
Larkin, Philip, **Supp. I Part 2:** 536; **Supp. XI:** 243, 249; **Supp. XIII:** 76, 85; **Supp. XV:** 117, 251; **Supp. XVII:** 110; **Supp. XVIII:** 173; **Supp. XX: 199; Supp. XXI:** 84, 93
Larkin, Sharon Alile, **Supp. XI:** 20
Larmore, Phoebe, **Supp. X:** 266

Larner, Jeremy, **Supp. XVI:** 220
La Rochefoucauld, François de, **I:** 279; **II:** 111; **Supp. XIV:** 130
"La Rose des Vents" (Wilbur), **Supp. III Part 2:** 550
"Larry Brown's *Dirty Work:* A Study of Man's Responsibility for Suffering" (Prevost), **Supp. XXI:** 45
Larry's Party (Shields), **Supp. VII:** 324, 326–327
Larsen, Nella, **Supp. I Part 1:** 325, 326; **Supp. IV Part 1:** 164; **Supp. XVIII: 119–134**
Larson, Charles, **Supp. IV Part 1:** 331
Larson, Clinton, **Supp. XI:** 328
Larson, Kelli, **Supp. XVIII:** 131
LaRue, Dorie, **Supp. XXI:** 43
"Larval Stage of a Bookworm" (Mencken), **III:** 101
La Salle and the Discovery of the Great West (Parkman), **Supp. II Part 2:** 595, 598, 605–607; **Supp. XVIII:** 114
Lasch, Christopher, **I:** 259
Lasher (Rice), **Supp. VII:** 299–300
Lask, Thomas, **III:** 576; **Supp. XVI:** 250
Laski, Harold, **Supp. I Part 2:** 632, 643
Lassalle, Ferdinand, **IV:** 429
Lasser, Louise, **Supp. XV:** 4
"Last Acts" (Olds), **Supp. X:** 210
Last Adam, The (Cozzens), **I:** 362–363, 364, 368, 375, 377, 378, 379
Last Analysis, The (Bellow), **I:** 152, 160, 161; **Retro. Supp. II:** 26
Last and Lost Poems of Delmore Schwartz (Phillips, ed.), **Supp. II Part 2:** 661, 665
Last Avant-Garde, The: The Making of the New York School of Poets (Lehman), **Supp. XV:** 178–179, 187
Last Beautiful Days of Autumn, The (Nichols), **Supp. XIII:** 254, 255, 267, 269
Last Blue (Stern), **Supp. IX: 299–300**
Last Book, The (Pickering), **Supp. XXI:** 203–204
Last Carousel, The (Algren), **Supp. IX:** 16
Last Centennial, The (P. N. Warren as Kilina), **Supp. XX: 261–262**
"Last Child" (X. J. Kennedy), **Supp. XV:** 162, 165
Last Coyote, The (Connelly), **Supp. XXI: 71**
"Last Day in the Field, The" (Gordon), **II:** 200
"Last Day of the Last Furlough" (Salinger), **III:** 552–553
"Last Days of Alice" (Tate), **IV:** 129
"Last Days of August, The" (Nye), **Supp. XIII:** 284
"Last Days of John Brown, The" (Thoreau), **IV:** 185
Last Days of Louisiana Red, The (Reed), **Supp. X:** 240, **248–249**
Last Decade, The (Trilling), **Supp. III Part 2:** 493, 499
"Last Demon, The" (Singer), **IV:** 15, 21
Last Detective, The (Crais), **Supp. XXI:** 70
Last Exit to Brooklyn (Selby), **Supp. III Part 1:** 125; **Supp. XXI:** 227, 231
Last Flower, The (Thurber), **Supp. I Part 2:** 610
"Last Frontier" (McCarriston), **Supp. XIV:** 272
Last Gentleman, The (Percy), **Supp. III Part 1:** 383–388, 392–393
"Last Good Country, The" (Hemingway), **II:** 258–259
Last Good Time, The (Bausch), **Supp. VII:** 45–46
"Last Hiding Places of Snow, The" (Kinnell), **Supp. III Part 1:** 252
"Last Hours, The" (Dunn), **Supp. XI:** 141
Last House: Reflections, Dreams, and Observations, 1943–1991 (M. F. K. Fisher), **Supp. XVII:** 92
Last Husband and Other Stories, The (Humphrey), **Supp. IX:** 94
Last Jew in America, The (Fiedler), **Supp. XIII:** 103
"Last Jew in America, The" (Fiedler), **Supp. XIII:** 103
Last Laugh, Mr. Moto (Marquand), **III:** 57
"Last Leaf, The" (Holmes), **Supp. I Part 1:** 302, 309
"Last Leaf, The" (Porter), **III:** 444
"Last Lie, The" (Weigl), **Supp. XIX:** 279
"Last Light" (Major), **Supp. XXII:** 185
"Last Look at the Lilacs" (Stevens), **IV:** 74
Last Man, The (Kees), **Supp. XV:** 142, 143, 145
"Last May" (Dixon), **Supp. XII: 143**
"Last Mermother, The" (A. Finch), **Supp. XVII:** 72
"Last Mohican, The" (Malamud), **Supp. I Part 2:** 437–438, 450, 451
"Lastness" (Kinnell), **Supp. III Part 1:** 248–249
"Last Night" (Olds), **Supp. X:** 212
"Last Night at Tía's" (Alvarez), **Supp. VII:** 5
Last Night of Summer, The (Caldwell), **I:** 292–293
Last of Mr. Norris, The (Isherwood), **Supp. XIV:** 161
"Last of the Brooding Miserables, The" (Karr), **Supp. XI:** 250
"Last of the Caddoes, The" (Humphrey), **Supp. IX:** 101
Last of the Crazy People, The (Findley), **Supp. XX: 51–52**
"Last of the Gold Star Mothers, The" (C. Bly), **Supp. XVI:** 34, 35, 36
"Last of the Legions, The" (Benét), **Supp. XI:** 56, 57
Last of the Mohicans, The (Cooper), **I:** 341, 342, 349
Last of the Red Hot Lovers (Simon), **Supp. IV Part 2:** 575, 583, 589
"Last of the Valerii, The" (James), **II:** 327; **Retro. Supp. I:** 218
"Last One, The" (Merwin), **Supp. III Part 1:** 355
Last Picture Show, The (film), **Supp. V:** 223, 226
Last Picture Show, The (McMurtry), **Supp. V:** 220, 222–223, 233
Last Place on Earth, The: Scott and Amundsen's Race to the South Pole (Huntford), **Supp. XVIII:** 114
Last Puritan, The (Santayana), **III:** 64, 600, 604, 607, 612, 615–617
"Last Ride Together, The" (Browning), **I:** 468
"Last River, The" (Kinnell), **Supp. III Part 1:** 236
Last Song, The (Harjo), **Supp. XII:** 218
"Last Song for the Mend-It Shop" (Nye), **Supp. XIII:** 283
"Last Tango in Fresno" (Salinas), **Supp. XIII:** 318
Last Tycoon, The: An Unfinished Novel (Fitzgerald), **II:** 84, 98; **Retro. Supp. I:** 109, 114, **114–115; Retro. Supp. II:** 337; **Supp. IV Part 1:** 203; **Supp. IX:** 63; **Supp. XII:** 173; **Supp. XIII:** 170; **Supp. XVIII:** 248, 250
"Last WASP in the World, The" (Fiedler), **Supp. XIII:** 103
"Last Watch, The" (Gibran), **Supp. XX: 119**
Last Watch of the Night: Essays Too Personal and Otherwise (Monette), **Supp. X:** 147, 148, 153, **157–159**
"Last Word, The" (column, Quindlen), **Supp. XVII:** 165, 167, 170
Last Word, The: Letters between Marcia Nardi and William Carlos Williams (O'Neil, ed.), **Retro. Supp. I:** 427
"Last Words" (Levine), **Supp. V:** 190
"Last Words" (Olds), **Supp. X:** 210
Last Worthless Evening, The (Dubus), **Supp. VII:** 87–88
"Las Vegas (What?) Las Vegas (Can't Hear You! Too Noisy) Las Vegas! ! ! !" (Wolfe), **Supp. III Part 2:** 572
"Late" (Bogan), **Supp. III Part 1:** 53
"Late Air" (Bishop), **Supp. I Part 1:** 89
"Late Autumn" (Sarton), **Supp. VIII:** 261
"Late Bronze, Early Iron: A Journey Book" (Sobin), **Supp. XVI:** 290
Late Child, The (McMurtry), **Supp. V:** 231
"Late Conversation" (Doty), **Supp. XI:** 122
"Late Elegy for John Berryman, A" (W. V. Davis), **Supp. XXI:** 91
"Late Encounter with the Enemy, A" (O'Connor), **III:** 345; **Retro. Supp. II:** 232
Late Fire, Late Snow (Francis), **Supp. IX: 89–90**
Late George Apley, The (Marquand), **II:** 482–483; **III:** 50, 51, 52, 56–57, 58, 62–64, 65, 66
Late George Apley, The (Marquand and Kaufman), **III:** 62
"Late Hour" (Everwine), **Supp. XV:** 85
Late Hour, The (Strand), **Supp. IV Part 2:** 620, 629–630
"Lately, at Night" (Kumin), **Supp. IV Part 2:** 442
"Late Moon" (Levine), **Supp. V:** 186
"Late Night Ode" (McClatchy), **Supp. XII:** 262–263

Later (Creeley), **Supp. IV Part 1:** 153, 156, 157
Later Life (Gurney), **Supp. V:** 103, 105
La Terre (Zola), **III:** 316, 322
Later the Same Day (Paley), **Supp. VI:** 218
"Late September in Nebraska" (Kooser), **Supp. XIX:** 120
Late Settings (Merrill), **Supp. III Part 1:** 336
"Late Sidney Lanier, The" (Stedman), **Supp. I Part 1:** 373
"Late Snow & Lumber Strike of the Summer of Fifty-Four, The" (Snyder), **Supp. VIII:** 294
"Late Start, A" (L. Brown), **Supp. XXI:** 40–41
"Latest Freed Man, The" (Stevens), **Retro. Supp. I:** 306
"Latest Injury, The" (Olds), **Supp. X:** 209
Latest Literary Essays and Addresses (Lowell), **Supp. I Part 2:** 407
"Late Subterfuge" (Warren), **IV:** 257
"Late Summer Lilies" (Weigl), **Supp. XIX:** 288
"Late Supper, A" (Jewett), **Retro. Supp. II:** 137
"Late Victorians" (Rodriguez), **Supp. XIV:** 303–304
"Late Walk, A" (Frost), **II:** 153; **Retro. Supp. I:** 127
Latham, Edyth, **I:** 289
Lathrop, George Parsons, **Supp. I Part 1:** 365
Lathrop, H. B., **Supp. III Part 2:** 612
Lathrop, Julia, **Supp. I Part 1:** 5
Latière de Trianon, La (Wekerlin), **II:** 515
"La Tigresse" (Van Vechten), **Supp. II Part 2:** 735, 738
Latimer, Hugh, **II:** 15
Latimer, Margery, **Supp. IX:** 320
La Traviata (Verdi), **III:** 139
"Latter-Day Warnings" (Holmes), **Supp. I Part 1:** 307
La Turista (Shepard), **Supp. III Part 2:** 440
Lauber, John, **Supp. XIII:** 21
Laud, Archbishop, **II:** 158
"Lauds" (Auden), **Supp. II Part 1:** 23
"Laughing Man, The" (Salinger), **III:** 559
Laughing Matters (Siegel), **Supp. XXII:** 260
Laughing to Keep From Crying (Hughes), **Supp. I Part 1:** 329–330
"Laughing with One Eye" (Schnackenberg), **Supp. XV:** 253
Laughlin, James, **III:** 171; **Retro. Supp. I:** 423, 424, 428, 430, 431; **Supp. VIII:** 195; **Supp. XV:** 140; **Supp. XVI:** 284; **Supp. XXI:** 29
Laughlin, Jay, **Supp. II Part 1:** 94
Laughlin, J. Laurence, **Supp. I Part 2:** 641
Laughter in the Dark (Nabokov), **III:** 255–258; **Retro. Supp. I:** 270
Laughter on the 23rd Floor (Simon), **Supp. IV Part 2:** 575, 576, 588, 591–592
"Launcelot" (Lewis), **II:** 439–440
"Laura Dailey's Story" (Bogan), **Supp. III Part 1:** 52
Laurel, Stan, **Supp. I Part 2:** 607; **Supp. IV Part 2:** 574
Laurel and Hardy Go to Heaven (Auster), **Supp. XII:** 21
Laurence, Alexander, **Supp. XVIII:** 138
Laurence, Dan H., **II:** 338–339
Laurens, John, **Supp. I Part 2:** 509
Lauter, Paul, **Supp. XV:** 313
Lautréamont, Comte de, **III:** 174
Lavender Locker Room, The (P. N. Warren), **Supp. XX: 261, 273–274**
Law, John, **Supp. XI:** 307
Law and Order (television), **Supp. XVII:** 153
Law and the Testimony, The (S. and A. Warner), **Supp. XVIII:** 264
Lawd Today (Wright), **IV:** 478, 492
Law for the Lion, A (Auchincloss), **Supp. IV Part 1:** 25
"Law Lane" (Jewett), **II:** 407
"Lawns of June, The" (Peacock), **Supp. XIX:** 196
"Law of Nature and the Dream of Man, The: Ruminations of the Art of Fiction" (Stegner), **Supp. IV Part 2:** 604
Lawrence, D. H., **I:** 291, 336, 377, 522, 523; **II:** 78, 84, 98, 102, 264, 517, 523, 532, 594, 595; **III:** 27, 33, 40, 44, 46, 172, 173, 174, 178, 184, 229, 261, 423, 429, 458, 546–547; **IV:** 138, 339, 342, 351, 380; **Retro. Supp. I:** 7, 18, 203, 204, 421; **Retro. Supp. II:** 68; **Supp. I Part 1:** 227, 230, 243, 255, 257, 258, 263, 329; **Supp. I Part 2:** 546, 613, 728; **Supp. II Part 1:** 1, 9, 20, 89; **Supp. IV Part 1:** 81; **Supp. VIII:** 237; **Supp. X:** 137, 193, 194; **Supp. XII:** 172; **Supp. XIV:** 310; **Supp. XV:** 45, 46, 158, 254; **Supp. XVI:** 267; **Supp. XX: 69; Supp. XXII:** 198
Lawrence, Frieda, **Supp. XV:** 46
Lawrence, Rhoda, **Supp. I Part 1:** 45
Lawrence, Seymour, **Supp. IX:** 107; **Supp. XI:** 335, 346, 348
Lawrence, T. E., **Supp. XIV:** 159
Lawrence of Arabia (Aldington), **Supp. I Part 1:** 259
Lawrence of Arabia (film), **Supp. I Part 1:** 67
Laws (Plato), **Supp. IV Part 1:** 391
Laws of Ice, The (Price), **Supp. VI:** 264
Laws of Our Fathers, The (Turow), **Supp. XVII: 218–219**
Lawson, John Howard, **I:** 479, 482
Lawton Girl, The (Frederic), **II:** 132–133, 144
Layachi, Larbi (Driss ben Hamed Charhadi), **Supp. IV Part 1:** 92, 93
Layard, John, **Supp. XIV:** 160
Lay Down My Sword and Shield (Burke), **Supp. XIV:** 22, 25, 34
"Layers, The" (Kunitz), **Supp. III Part 1:** 260, 266–267
"Layers, The: Some Notes on 'The Abduction' " (Kunitz), **Supp. III Part 1:** 266
"Lay-mans Lamentation, The" (Taylor), **IV:** 162–163
Lay of the Land, The: Metaphor as Experience and History in American Life and Letters (Kolodny), **Supp. X:** 97
"Layover" (Hass), **Supp. VI:** 109
"Lay Preacher" (Dennie), **Supp. I Part 1:** 125
Layton, Irving, **Supp. XII:** 121
Lazar, Irving "Swifty", **Supp. XIX:** 250
Lazarillo de Tormes (Mendoza), **III:** 182
Lazar Malkin Enters Heaven (S. Stern), **Supp. XVII:** 42; **Supp. XX: 178**
Lazarus Laughed (O'Neill), **III:** 391, 395–396
Lazer, Hank, **Supp. IX:** 265
Lea, Luke, **IV:** 248
Leachman, Cloris, **Supp. XXI:** 146
Leacock, Stephen, **Supp. IV Part 2:** 464
"LEADBELLY GIVES AN AUTOGRAPH" (Baraka), **Supp. II Part 1:** 49
Leaflets: Poems, 1965–1968 (Rich), **Supp. I Part 2:** 551, 556–557
"League of American Writers, The: Communist Organizational Activity among American Writers 1929–1942" (Wolfe), **Supp. III Part 2:** 568
League of Brightened Philistines and Other Papers, The (Farrell), **II:** 49
Leahy, Anna, **Supp. XXI:** 246
"Leakage" (Skloot), **Supp. XX: 202**
Leal, Luis, **Supp. XIX:** 98, 112
"Leaning" (Webb), **Supp. XX: 56**
Leaning Forward (Paley), **Supp. VI:** 221
"Leaning Tower, The" (Porter), **III:** 442, 443, 446–447
Leaning Tower and Other Stories, The (Porter), **III:** 433, 442, 443–447
"Leap, The" (Dickey), **Supp. IV Part 1:** 182
"Leaping Up into Political Poetry" (R. Bly), **Supp. IV Part 1:** 61, 63
Leap Year (Cameron), **Supp. XII:** 79–80, 81, **85–86,** 88
Lear, Edward, **III:** 428, 536; **Supp. XVI:** 103
Lear, Linda, **Supp. IX:** 19, 22, 25, 26
Learned Ladies, The (Molière; Wilbur, trans.), **Supp. III Part 2:** 560
"Learning a Dead Language" (Merwin), **Supp. III Part 1:** 345
Learning a Trade: A Craftsman's Notebooks, 1955–1997 (Price), **Supp. VI:** 254, 255, 267
"Learning Bones" (Espaillat), **Supp. XXI:** 107
Learning to Love: Exploring Solitude and Freedom (Merton), **Supp. VIII:** 200
"Learning to Read" (Harper), **Supp. II Part 1:** 201–202
"Learning to Speak" (Everwine), **Supp. XV:** 79
"Learning to Work Together" (L. I. Wilder), **Supp. XXII:** 290
Learning Tree, The (Park), **Supp. XIX:** 154
Leary, Lewis, **III:** 478
Leary, Paris, **Supp. IV Part 1:** 176

Leary, Timothy, **Supp. X:** 265; **Supp. XIV:** 150
Lease, Joseph, **Supp. XXI:** 246
Least Heat Moon, William, **Supp. V:** 169
Leather-Stocking Tales, The (Cooper), **I:** 335
Leatherwood God, The (Howells), **II:** 276, 277, 288
Leave It to Beaver (television show), **Supp. XX: 103**
"Leave Me Alone a Little" (Taggard), **Supp. XXII:** 274
"Leaves" (Updike), **Retro. Supp. I:** 323, 329, 335
Leaves and Ashes (Haines), **Supp. XII:** 206
Leaves from the Notebook of a Tamed Cynic (Niebuhr), **III:** 293
Leaves of Grass (1856) (Whitman), **Retro. Supp. I:** 399–402
Leaves of Grass (1860) (Whitman), **Retro. Supp. I:** 402–405
Leaves of Grass (Whitman), **II:** 8; **IV:** 331, 332, 333, 334, 335, 336, 340, 341–342, 348, 350, 405, 464; **Retro. Supp. I:** 387, 388, 389, 390, **392–395,** 406, 407, 408; **Retro. Supp. II:** 93; **Supp. I Part 1:** 365; **Supp. I Part 2:** 416, 579; **Supp. III Part 1:** 156; **Supp. V:** 170; **Supp. VIII:** 275; **Supp. IX:** 265; **Supp. X:** 120; **Supp. XIV:** 334; **Supp. XV:** 218; **Supp. XVIII:** 4; **Supp. XIX:** 276; **Supp. XXI:** 205; **Supp. XXII:** 92
"Leaves of Grass" (Whitman), **IV:** 463
Leaves of the Tree, The (Masters), **Supp. I Part 2:** 460
"Leaving" (Hogan), **Supp. IV Part 1:** 400
"Leaving" (Wilbur), **Supp. III Part 2:** 563
"Leaving, The" (B. Kelly), **Supp. XVII:** 127, 132
Leaving a Doll's House: A Memoir (C. Bloom), **Retro. Supp. II:** 281
Leaving Another Kingdom: Selected Poems (Stern), **Supp. IX:** 296
"Leaving Bartram's Garden in Southwest Philadelphia" (Di Piero), **Supp. XIX:** 46
"Leaving Brooklyn" (Neugeboren), **Supp. XVI:** 226
Leaving Cheyenne (McMurtry), **Supp. V:** 220, 221–222, 224, 229
Leaving Home (Keillor), **Supp. XVI:** 175
"Leaving One, The" (Offutt), **Supp. XIX:** 165–166
"Leaving the Island" (Olds), **Supp. X:** 214
"Leaving the Yellow House" (Bellow), **Retro. Supp. II:** 27, 32
"Leaving Town" (Kenyon), **Supp. VII:** 163
Leavis, F. R., **I:** 522; **III:** 462–463, 475, 478; **Retro. Supp. I:** 67; **Retro. Supp. II:** 243; **Supp. I Part 2:** 536; **Supp. VIII:** 234, 236, 245
Leavis, Queenie, **Supp. XX: 232**
"Leavis-Snow Controversy, The" (Trilling), **Supp. III Part 2:** 512
Leavitt, Caroline, **Supp. XX: 186**
Leavitt, David, **Supp. VIII:** 88
Lebanon (C. Miller), **Supp. XXII:** 198–199
Le Braz, Anatole, **Supp. XIII:** 253
Le Carre, John, **Supp. XX: 195**
Lecker, Robert, **Supp. XIII:** 21
LeClair, Thomas (Tom), **Supp. IV Part 1:** 286; **Supp. V:** 53; **Supp. XII:** 152; **Supp. XX: 93; Supp. XXII:** 206, 210, 261, 264
Le Conte, Joseph, **II:** 479; **III:** 227–228
"Lecture, The" (Singer), **IV:** 21
"LECTURE PAST DEAD CATS" (Baraka), **Supp. II Part 1:** 52
Lectures in America (Stein), **IV:** 27, 32, 33, 35, 36, 41, 42
"Lectures on Poetry" (Bryant), **Supp. I Part 1:** 159, 161
Lectures on Rhetoric (Blair), **II:** 8
"Leda and the Swan" (Yeats), **III:** 347; **Supp. IX:** 52
Ledger (Fitzgerald), **Retro. Supp. I:** 109, 110
Lee (Masters), **Supp. I Part 2:** 471
Lee, Baayork, **Supp. XXI:** 148
Lee, C. Y., **Supp. XXI:** 148
Lee, Don, **Supp. XII:** 295; **Supp. XVII:** 13, 14, 15, 16
Lee, Don L. *See* Madhubuti, Haki R.
Lee, Gypsy Rose, **II:** 586; **III:** 161; **Supp. IV Part 1:** 84
Lee, Harper, **Supp. VIII: 113–131**
Lee, Harriett, **Supp. XV:** 230
Lee, James Kyun-Jin, **Supp. XV:** 213
Lee, James W., **Supp. IX:** 94, 97, 109
Lee, James Ward, **Supp. VIII:** 57
Lee, Li Lin, **Supp. XV:** 211, 212
Lee, Li-Young, **Supp. XV: 211–228; Supp. XVII:** 241
Lee, Richard E., **Supp. XIX:** 226, 227
Lee, Robert E., **II:** 150, 206; **IV:** 126; **Supp. I Part 2:** 471, 486
Lee, Samuel, **IV:** 158
Lee, Spike, **Retro. Supp. II:** 12; **Supp. XI:** 19; **Supp. XIII:** 179, 186; **Supp. XVI:** 144; **Supp. XX: 110**
Lee, Virginia Chin-lan, **Supp. X:** 291
Leeds, Barry, **Retro. Supp. II:** 204
Leeds, Daniel, **II:** 110
Leeds, Titan, **II:** 110, 111
Leeming, David, **Retro. Supp. II:** 4, 10
"Lees of Happiness, The" (Fitzgerald), **II:** 88
"Le Filme" (Weigl), **Supp. XIX:** 288
Left Out in the Rain: New Poems 1947–1985 (Snyder), **Supp. VIII:** 305
"Legacy" (Dunn), **Supp. XI:** 148
"Legacy" (Komunyakaa), **Supp. XIII:** 132
"Legacy" (W. V. Davis), **Supp. XXI:** 93–94
"Legacy of Aldo Leopold, The" (Stegner), **Supp. XIV:** 193
Legacy of Fear, A (Farrell), **II:** 39
"Legacy of the Ancestral Arts, The" (Locke), **Supp. XIV:** 201
Legacy of the Civil War, The: Meditations on the Centennial (Warren), **IV:** 236
"Legal Alien" (Mora), **Supp. XIII:** 215
"Legal Tender Act, The" (Adams), **I:** 5
Légende de la mort, La (Le Braz), **Supp. XIII:** 253
"Legend of Duluoz, The" (Kerouac), **Supp. III Part 1:** 218, 226, 227, 229
"Legend of Lillian Hellman, The" (Kazin), **Supp. I Part 1:** 297
"Legend of Monte del Diablo, The" (Harte), **Supp. II Part 1:** 339
"Legend of Paper Plates, The" (Haines), **Supp. XII:** 204
"Legend of Sammtstadt, A" (Harte), **Supp. II Part 1:** 355
"Legend of Sleepy Hollow, The" (Irving), **II:** 306–308
Legends (Lowell), **II:** 525–526
Legends and Dreams (P. N. Warren), **Supp. XX: 261**
Legends of New England (Whittier), **Supp. I Part 2:** 684, 692
Legends of the Fall (Harrison), **Supp. VIII:** 38, 39, **45–46,** 48
Legends of the West (Hall), **II:** 313
Léger, Fernand, **Retro. Supp. I:** 292
Legge, James, **III:** 472
Leggett, William, **Supp. I Part 1:** 157
"Legion, The" (Karr), **Supp. XI:** 243
"Legs" (Halliday), **Supp. XIX:** 90
Legs (W. Kennedy), **Supp. VII:** 133, 134, 138–142, 143, 151
Le Guin, Ursula K., **Supp. IV Part 1:** 333; **Supp. XXII:** 49
Lehan, Richard, **Retro. Supp. II:** 104
Lehman, David, **Supp. IX:** 161; **Supp. XIII:** 130; **Supp. XV:** 178–179, 180, 187, 190; **Supp. XXI:** 246
Lehmann, John, **Retro. Supp. II:** 243; **Supp. XIV:** 158, 159
Lehmann, Paul, **III:** 311
Lehmann-Haupt, Christopher, **Retro. Supp. II:** 291; **Supp. IV Part 1:** 205, 209, 306; **Supp. IX:** 95, 103; **Supp. XVI:** 73, 210, 294, 295; **Supp. XXII:** 205, 213
Lehrer, Jim, **Supp. XVIII:** 39
Leiber, Fritz, **Supp. XVI:** 123
Leibling, A. J., **Supp. XIV:** 112
Leibniz, Gottfried Wilhelm von, **II:** 103; **III:** 428
Leibowitz, Herbert A., **I:** 386; **Supp. XV:** 78
Leich, Roland, **Supp. XIV:** 123
Leichum, Laura, **Supp. XIX:** 197
Leighton, Betty, **Supp. XXI:** 42
Leithauser, Brad, **Retro. Supp. I:** 133; **Supp. XV:** 250; **Supp. XVII:** 112; **Supp. XXII:** 207
Leitz, Robert, **Supp. XIV:** 62
Leivick, H., **IV:** 6
Lekachman, Robert, **Supp. I Part 2:** 648
Leland, Charles, **Supp. II Part 1:** 193
Leland, Charles Godfrey, **I:** 257
Leland, John, **Supp. XV:** 69; **Supp. XIX:** 157
Lem, Stanislaw, **Supp. IV Part 1:** 103
"Le marais du cygne" (Whittier), **Supp. I Part 2:** 687
Lemay, Harding, **Supp. VIII:** 125; **Supp. IX:** 98
Lemercier, Eugène, **Retro. Supp. I:** 299

"Lemorne *versus* Huell" (E. Stoddard), **Supp. XV:** 270, 273, 283
Le Morte D'Arthur Notes (Gardner), **Supp. VI:** 65, 66
Lenin, V. I., **I:** 366, 439, 440; **III:** 14–15, 262, 475; **IV:** 429, 436, 443–444; **Supp. I Part 2:** 647; **Supp. XXI:** 164
"Lenore" (Poe), **III:** 411
"Lenox Avenue: Midnight" (Hughes), **Retro. Supp. I:** 198
"Lens of Poetry, The" (Bronk). *See Attendant, The* (Bronk)
Leonard, Elmore, **Supp. IV Part 1:** 356; **Supp. X:** 5; **Supp. XIV:** 26
Leonard, John, **Supp. IV Part 1:** 24; **Supp. IV Part 2:** 474; **Supp. V:** 164, 223–224; **Supp. XI:** 13; **Supp. XVIII:** 147, 148; **Supp. XIX:** 269; **Supp. XXI:** 233, 239
Leonardo da Vinci, **Supp. XII:** 44; **Supp. XXII:** 171
León-Portilla, Miguel, **Supp. XV:** 77
Leontiev, Constantine, **Supp. XIV:** 98
Leopard, The (Lampedusa), **Supp. XII:** 13–14
Leopardi, Giacomo, **II:** 543; **Supp. XIX:** 33, 43
"Leopard Man's Story, The" (London), **II:** 475
Leopard's Mouth Is Dry and Cold Inside, The (Levis), **Supp. XI:** 258
Leopold, Aldo, **Supp. V:** 202; **Supp. X:** 108; **Supp. XIV: 177–194; Supp. XXI:** 203
"Leper's Bell, the" (Komunyakaa), **Supp. XIII:** 118
Lerman, Leo, **Supp. X:** 188; **Supp. XVI:** 194
Lerner, Max, **III:** 60; **Supp. I Part 2:** 629, 630, 631, 647, 650, 654
Lerperger, Emil, **Supp. XX: 165, 167**
"Lesbos" (Plath), **Retro. Supp. II:** 254
Lesesne, Teri, **Supp. XIII:** 277
LeSieg, Theo (pseudonym). *See* Geisel, Theodor Seuss (Dr. Seuss)
Leskov, Nikolai, **IV:** 299
Leslie, Alfred, **Supp. XII:** 127
"Less and Less Human, O Savage Spirit" (W. Stevens), **Supp. XVI:** 64
Lesser, Wendy, **Supp. IV Part 2:** 453; **Supp. XII:** 297; **Supp. XVI:** 201
Lessing, Gotthold, **Supp. I Part 2:** 422
"Lesson, The" (Bambara), **Supp. XI:** 5–6
"Lesson, The" (Dunbar), **Supp. II Part 1:** 199
"Lesson, The" (Olsen), **Supp. XIII:** 297
"Lesson for the Ill Clothed and Ill Fed, A" (Ryan as Quin), **Supp. XVIII:** 230–231
Lesson of the Master, The (James), **Supp. XVIII:** 248
"Lesson of the Master, The" (James), **Retro. Supp. I:** 227
Lesson of the Masters: An Anthology of the Novel from Cervantes to Hemingway (Cowley-Hugo, ed.), **Supp. II Part 1:** 140
"Lesson on Concealment, A" (Brown), **Supp. I Part 1:** 133
"Lessons" (Epstein), **Supp. XII:** 163
"Lessons of the Body" (Simpson), **Supp. IX:** 267
Less than One (Brodsky), **Supp. VIII:** 22, 29–31
Lester, Jerry, **Supp. IV Part 2:** 574
Lester, Ketty, **Supp. XV:** 133, 147
Le Style Apollinaire (Zukofsky), **Supp. III Part 2:** 616
Le Sueur, Meridel, **Supp. V:** 113, 130; **Supp. XII:** 217
"Let America Be America Again" (Hughes), **Retro. Supp. I:** 202; **Supp. I Part 1:** 331
Let Evening Come (Kenyon), **Supp. VII:** 160, 169–171
Lethem, Jonathan, **Supp. IX:** 122; **Supp. XVIII: 135–153; Supp. XXII:** 49
Let It Come Down (Bowles), **Supp. IV Part 1:** 87
Let It Ride (Pickering), **Supp. XXI:** 198–199
"Let Me Be" (Levine), **Supp. V:** 181, 189
"Let Me Begin Again" (Levine), **Supp. V:** 181, 189
"Let No Charitable Hope" (Wylie), **Supp. I Part 2:** 713–714, 729
Let No Man Write My Epitaph (film, Leacock), **Supp. XVII:** 150, 158
Let No Man Write My Epitaph (W. Motley), **Supp. XVII:** 150, **158–160**
Let Noon Be Fair (W. Motley), **Supp. XVII: 161**
Letofsky, Irv, **Supp. XVI:** 167
"Let one Eye his watches keep/While the Other Eye doth sleep" (Fletcher), **Supp. IV Part 2:** 621
Let's Balance the Books (radio show; Untermeyer), **Supp. XV:** 311
"Letter . . ." (Whittier), **Supp. I Part 2:** 687
"Letter, A" (Bogan), **Supp. III Part 1:** 54
"Letter, May 2, 1959" (Olson), **Supp. II Part 2:** 579, 580
"Letter, Much Too Late" (Stegner), **Supp. IV Part 2:** 613
"Letter, The" (Boulton), **Supp. XXII:** 22
"Letter, The" (Gioia), **Supp. XV:** 120
"Letter, The" (Malamud), **Supp. I Part 2:** 435–436
"Letter about Money, Love, or Other Comfort, If Any, The" (Warren), **IV:** 245
Letter Addressed to the People of Piedmont, on the Advantages of the French Revolution, and the Necessity of Adopting Its Principles in Italy, A (Barlow), **Supp. II Part 1:** 80, 81
"Letter for Marion, A" (McGrath), **Supp. X:** 116
"Letter from Aldermaston" (Merwin), **Supp. III Part 1:** 347
"Letter from a London Attic" (Pickering), **Supp. XXI:** 194
"Letter from a Region in My Mind" (Baldwin). *See* "Down at the Cross"
"Letter from Aunt Belle, A" (Kooser), **Supp. XIX:** 117
Letter from Li Po, A (Aiken), **I:** 68
"Letter from 'Manhattan' " (Didion), **Supp. IV Part 1:** 205
"Letter from the Country" (column, C. Bly), **Supp. XVI:** 33
Letter from the End of the Twentieth Century (Harjo), **Supp. XII:** 223
"Letter from the End of the Twentieth Century" (Harjo), **Supp. XII:** 227
"Letter Home" (Trethewey), **Supp. XXI:** 254
"Letter on Céline" (Kerouac), **Supp. III Part 1:** 232
Letters (Cato), **II:** 114
Letters (Landor), **Supp. I Part 2:** 422
Letters (White), **Supp. I Part 2:** 651, 653, 675, 680
Letters (Wolfe), **IV:** 462
"Letters, The" (Swados), **Supp. XIX:** 261, 262
Letters and Leadership (Brooks), **I:** 228, 240, 245, 246
"Letters for the Dead" (Levine), **Supp. V:** 186
Letters from an American Farmer (Crèvecoeur), **Supp. I Part 1:** 227–251
Letters from Maine (Sarton), **Supp. VIII: 261**
"Letters from Maine" (Sarton), **Supp. VIII:** 261
"Letters from My Father" (R. O. Butler), **Supp. XII:** 71
Letters from the Country (C. Bly), **Supp. XVI: 33–34,** 35, 37
Letters from the Earth (Twain), **IV:** 209
Letters from the East (Bryant), **Supp. I Part 1:** 158
"Letters from the Ming Dynasty" (Brodsky), **Supp. VIII:** 28
Letters of a Traveller (Bryant), **Supp. I Part 1:** 158
Letters of a Traveller, Second Series (Bryant), **Supp. I Part 1:** 158
Letters of Emily Dickinson, The (Johnson and Ward, eds.), **I:** 470; **Retro. Supp. I:** 28
Letters of William James (Henry James, ed.), **II:** 362
Letters on Various Interesting and Important Subjects . . . (Freneau), **Supp. II Part 1:** 272
Letters to a Niece (Adams), **I:** 22
Letters to a Teacher (Pickering), **Supp. XXI:** 195, 201–202
Letters to a Young Poet (Rilke), **Supp. XIII:** 74; **Supp. XV:** 93
"Letters to Dead Imagists" (Sandburg), **I:** 421
"Letters Written on a Ferry While Crossing Long Island Sound" (Sexton), **Supp. II Part 2:** 683
"Letter to Abbé Raynal" (Paine), **Supp. I Part 2:** 510
Letter to a Man in the Fire: Does God Exist or Does He Care? (Price), **Supp. VI:** 267–268
"Letter to American Teachers of History, A" (Adams), **I:** 19
Letter to an Imaginary Friend (McGrath), **Supp. X:** 111, 112–113, 116, **119–125**

"Letter to a Reader" (Sanders), **Supp. XVI:** 266, 267, 268, 269, 275
"Letter to a Young Author" (P. N. Warren), **Supp. XX: 272**
"Letter to a Young Contributor" (Higginson), **Retro. Supp. I:** 31
"Letter to a Young Writer" (Price), **Supp. VI:** 267
"Letter to Bell from Missoula" (Hugo), **Supp. VI:** 142–143
"Letter to E. Franklin Frazier" (Baraka), **Supp. II Part 1:** 49
"Letter to Elaine Feinstein" (Olson), **Supp. II Part 2:** 561
"Letter to Freddy" (music) (Bowles), **Supp. IV Part 1:** 82
"Letter to Garber from Skye" (Hugo), **Supp. VI:** 146
"Letter to George Washington" (Paine), **Supp. I Part 2:** 517
"Letter to His Brother" (Berryman), **I:** 172, 173
Letter to His Countrymen, A (Cooper), **I:** 346, 347, 349
"Letter to Kizer from Seattle" (Hugo), **Supp. VI:** 142
Letter to Lord Byron (Auden), **Supp. II Part 1:** 11
"Letter to Lord Byron" (Mumford), **Supp. II Part 2:** 494
"Letter to Matthews from Barton Street Flats" (Hugo), **Supp. VI:** 133
"Letter to Minnesota" (Dunn), **Supp. XI:** 146
"Letter to Mr." (Poe), **III:** 411
"Letter Too Late to Vallejo" (Salinas), **Supp. XIII:** 313, 324
"Letter to Sister Madeline from Iowa City" (Hugo), **Supp. VI:** 142–143
"Letter to Soto" (Salinas), **Supp. XIII:** 325
"Letter to the Lady of the House" (Bausch), **Supp. VII:** 48
"Letter to the Rising Generation, A" (Comer), **I:** 214
"Letter to Walt Whitman" (Doty), **Supp. XI:** 135–136
"Letter to Wendell Berry, A" (Stegner), **Supp. IV Part 2:** 600
"Letter Writer, The" (Singer), **IV:** 20–21
"Let the Air Circulate" (Clampitt), **Supp. IX:** 45
Let the Hurricane Roar (Lane), **Supp. XXII:** 297
"Letting Down of the Hair, The" (Sexton), **Supp. II Part 2:** 692
Letting Go (P. Roth), **Retro. Supp. II:** 282, 283; **Supp. III Part 2:** 403, 404, 409–412
"Letting the Puma Go" (Dunn), **Supp. XI:** 149
"Lettres d'un Soldat" (Stevens), **Retro. Supp. I:** 299
Let Us Go into the Starry Night (Shanley), **Supp. XIV:** 317
Let Us Highly Resolve (Stratton-Porter), **Supp. XX: 223**
Let Us Now Praise Famous Men (Agee and Evans), **I:** 25, 27, 35, 36–39, 42, 45, 293
Let Your Mind Alone! (Thurber), **Supp. I Part 2:** 608
Leutze, Emanuel, **Supp. X:** 307
Levels of the Game (McPhee), **Supp. III Part 1:** 292, 294, 301
Levertov, Denise, **Retro. Supp. I:** 411; **Supp. III Part 1: 271–287; Supp. III Part 2:** 541; **Supp. IV Part 1:** 325; **Supp. VIII:** 38, 39; **Supp. XVI:** 39, 40; **Supp. XIX:** 282; **Supp. XXI:** 228; **Supp. XXII:** 83, 168, 177
Levi, Primo, **Supp. X:** 149; **Supp. XVII:** 48
Leviathan (Auster), **Supp. XII:** 27, **33–34**
"Leviathan" (Lowell), **II:** 537, 538
"Leviathan" (Merwin), **Supp. III Part 1:** 345
Levin, Adam, **Supp. XXII:** 268
Levin, Harry, **Supp. I Part 2:** 647
Levin, Jennifer, **Supp. X:** 305
Levin, Meyer, **Supp. XX: 34**
Lévinas, Emmanuel, **Supp. XVI:** 290, 291
Levine, Ellen, **Supp. V:** 4; **Supp. XI:** 178
Levine, Paul, **Supp. IV Part 1:** 221, 224
Levine, Philip, **Supp. III Part 2:** 541; **Supp. V: 177–197,** 337; **Supp. IX:** 293; **Supp. XI:** 123, 257, 259, 267, 271, 315; **Supp. XIII:** 312; **Supp. XV:** 73, 74, 212; **Supp. XIX:** 45
Levine, Rosalind, **Supp. XII:** 123
Levine, Sherry, **Supp. XII:** 4
Levis, Larry, **Supp. V:** 180; **Supp. IX:** 299; **Supp. XI: 257–274; Supp. XIII:** 312; **Supp. XV:** 73; **Supp. XVII:** 110
Lévi-Strauss, Claude, **Supp. I Part 2:** 636; **Supp. IV Part 1:** 45; **Supp. IV Part 2:** 490; **Supp. XVIII:** 190
Levitation: Five Fictions (Ozick), **Supp. V:** 268–270
"Levitation with Baby" (Nelson), **Supp. XVIII:** 173
Levitt, Saul, **Supp. XV:** 197
Levy, Alan, **Supp. IV Part 2:** 574, 589
Levy, G. Rachel, **Supp. I Part 2:** 567
Levy, Julien, **Supp. XXII:** 167, 168
Lévy-Bruhl, Lucien, **Retro. Supp. I:** 57
Levy Mayer and the New Industrial Era (Masters), **Supp. I Part 2:** 473
Lewes, George Henry, **II:** 569
Lewin, Albert, **Supp. XIV:** 279, 293
Lewis, C. Day, **III:** 527
Lewis, Dr. Claude, **II:** 442
Lewis, David Levering, **Supp. XVIII:** 127; **Supp. XIX:** 74, 75; **Supp. XXII:** 13
Lewis, Edith, **I:** 313; **Retro. Supp. I:** 19, 21, 22
Lewis, Edwin, J., **II:** 439, 442
Lewis, Jerry, **Supp. IV Part 2:** 575; **Supp. X:** 172
Lewis, John L., **I:** 493
Lewis, Lilburn, **IV:** 243
Lewis, Lorene, **Supp. IV Part 2:** 596, 597
Lewis, Lucy, **IV:** 243
Lewis, Maggie, **Supp. V:** 23
Lewis, Meriwether, **II:** 217; **III:** 14; **IV:** 179, 243, 283
Lewis, Merrill, **Supp. IV Part 2:** 596, 597
Lewis, Michael, **II:** 451, 452; **Supp. XVII:** 210
Lewis, Robert Q., **Supp. IV Part 2:** 574
Lewis, R. W. B., **I:** 386, 561; **II:** 457–458; **Retro. Supp. I:** 362, 367; **Supp. I Part 1:** 233; **Supp. XIII:** 93
Lewis, Sinclair, **I:** 116, 212, 348, 355, 362, 374, 378, 487, 495; **II:** 27, 34, 74, 79, 271, 277, 306, **439–461,** 474; **III:** 28, 40, 51, 60, 61, 63–64, 66, 70, 71, 106, 394, 462, 572, 606; **IV:** 53, 326, 366, 455, 468, 475, 482; **Retro. Supp. I:** 332; **Retro. Supp. II:** 95, 108, 197, 322; **Supp. I Part 2:** 378, 613, 709; **Supp. IV Part 2:** 678; **Supp. V:** 278; **Supp. IX:** 308; **Supp. X:** 137; **Supp. XVII:** 41; **Supp. XVIII:** 278; **Supp. XXII:** 190
Lewis, Mrs. Sinclair (Dorothy Thompson), **II:** 449–450, 451, 453
Lewis, Mrs. Sinclair (Grace Livingston Hegger), **II:** 441
Lewis, Wyndham, **III:** 458, 462, 465, 470; **Retro. Supp. I:** 59, 170, 292; **Supp. III Part 2:** 617
Lexicon Tetraglotton (Howell), **II:** 111
"Lexington Avenue Musedog" (Peacock), **Supp. XIX:** 204
"Leyenda" (Mora), **Supp. XIII:** 214
Leyner, Mark, **Supp. XIX:** 223
Leyte (Morison), **Supp. I Part 2:** 491
"Liar, The" (Baraka), **Supp. II Part 1:** 36
"Liars, The" (Sandburg), **III:** 586
Liars' Club, The: A Memoir (Karr), **Supp. XI:** 239, 240, 241, 242, **244–248,** 252, 254; **Supp. XVI:** 70
Liar's Dice (C. Frost), **Supp. XV:** 93, 96
"Liar's Dice" (C. Frost), **Supp. XV:** 94, 107
Liars in Love (Yates), **Supp. XI:** 348, 349
Libation Bearers, The (Aeschylus), **III:** 398; **Supp. IX:** 103
Li Bay. *See* Li Po
Libby, Anthony, **Supp. XIII:** 87
Libera, Padre, **II:** 278
Liberal Imagination, The (Trilling), **III:** 308; **Retro. Supp. I:** 97, 216; **Supp. II Part 1:** 146; **Supp. III Part 2:** 495, 498, 501–504
Liberation (J. Scott), **Supp. XVII:** 192, **194–196**
"Liberation" (Winters), **Supp. II Part 2:** 791
Liber Brunenesis (yearbook), **IV:** 286
Liberties, The (Howe), **Supp. IV Part 2:** 426–428, 430, 432
Liberties of America, The (H. Warner), **Supp. XVIII:** 259
Liberty Jones (play), **Supp. IV Part 1:** 83
"Liberty Tree" (Paine), **Supp. I Part 2:** 505
Libra (DeLillo), **Supp. VI:** 2, **4, 5,** 6, **7,** 9, 10, 12, 13, 14, 16
Library for Juana, A (Mora), **Supp. XIII:** 218

Library of America, **Retro. Supp. I:** 2
"Library of Babel, The" (J. Borges), **Supp. XVII:** 47
"Library of Law, A" (MacLeish), **III:** 4
"Library of Moloch, The" (Bukiet), **Supp. XVII:** 47, 49
"Librettos for Eros" (Gander), **Supp. XV:** 340
Lice, The (Merwin), **Supp. III Part 1:** 339, 341–342, 346, 348, 349, 355
Lichtenberg, Georg Christoph, **Supp. XIV:** 339
Lichtenstein, Roy, **Supp. I Part 2:** 665; **Supp. XV:** 186
"Liddy's Orange" (Olds), **Supp. X:** 209
"Lie, The" (Antin), **Supp. XX: 7, 9–10**
Lieberman, Laurence, **Supp. XI:** 323–324
Liebestod (Wagner), **I:** 284, 395
Liebling, A. J., **IV:** 290; **Supp. VIII:** 151; **Supp. XVI:** 167
Lie Down in Darkness (Styron), **IV:** 98, 99, 100–104, 105, 111; **Supp. XI:** 343
Lie of the Mind, A (Shepard), **Supp. III Part 2:** 433, 435, 441, 447–449
"Lies" (Haines), **Supp. XII:** 204
Lies (Hoffman), **Supp. XVIII: 78–79**
"Lies and Consequences" (Pickering), **Supp. XXI:** 204
Lies Like Truth (Clurman), **IV:** 385
Lieutenant, The (Dubus), **Supp. VII:** 78
"Life" (Wharton), **Retro. Supp. I:** 372
Life along the Passaic River (W. C. Williams), **Retro. Supp. I:** 423
Life Among the Savages (Jackson), **Supp. IX:** 115, **125**
"Life and Death Kisses, The" (Grossman), **Supp. XIX:** 87
Life and Gabriella (Glasgow), **II:** 175, 176, 182–183, 184, 189
"Life and I" (Wharton), **Retro. Supp. I:** 360, 361, 362
"Life and Letters" (Epstein), **Supp. XIV:** 104–105
Life and Letters of Harrison Gray Otis, Federalist, 1765–1848, The (Morison), **Supp. I Part 2:** 480–481
Life and Letters of Sir Henry Wotton (L. P. Smith), **Supp. XIV:** 340–341
Life and Mind of Emily Dickinson, The (Taggard), **Supp. XXII:** 279
Life and Times of Frederick Douglass, Written by Himself, The (Douglass), **Supp. III Part 1:** 155, 159–163
Life and Writings of Horace McCoy, The (Wolfson), **Supp. XIII:** 172, 174
"Life as a Visionary Spirit" (Eberhart), **I:** 540, 541
"Life at Angelo's, A" (Benét), **Supp. XI:** 53
Life at Happy Knoll (Marquand), **III:** 50, 61
Life Before Man (Atwood), **Supp. XIII: 24–25**
"Life Cycle of Common Man" (Nemerov), **III:** 278
"Lifecycle Stairmaster" (Karr), **Supp. XI:** 250
Life Estates (Hearon), **Supp. VIII: 68–69**
Life for Life's Sake (Aldington), **Supp. I Part 1:** 256
Life Full of Holes, A (Layachi), **Supp. IV Part 1:** 92
"Lifeguard" (Updike), **IV:** 226; **Retro. Supp. I:** 325
"Lifeguard, The" (Dickey), **Supp. IV Part 1:** 179–180
"Life in the 30s" (column, Quindlen), **Supp. XVII:** 165, 167–169
Life in the Clearings (Shields), **Supp. VII:** 313
"Life in the Country: A City Friend Asks, 'Is It Boring?' " (Paley), **Supp. VI:** 231
Life in the Forest (Levertov), **Supp. III Part 1:** 282–283
Life in the Iron Mills (R. H. Davis), **Supp. XIII:** 292, 295, 299, 305; **Supp. XVI:** 79–82, **85–88,** 91
Life in the Iron Mills and Other Stories (T. Olson, ed.), **Supp. XVI:** 83
Life in the Theatre, A (Mamet), **Supp. XIV:** 241, 255
Life Is a Miracle: An Essay Against Modern Superstition (Berry), **Supp. X:** 35
"Life Is Fine" (Hughes), **Supp. I Part 1:** 334, 338
"Life Is Motion" (Stevens), **IV:** 74
Life & Letters of Gene Stratton-Porter (Meehan), **Supp. XX: 213**
Life of Albert Gallatin, The (Adams), **I:** 6, 14
Life of an Ordinary Woman, The: Anne Ellis (A. Ellis), **Supp. XVI:** 38
Life of Captain Cipriani, The: An Account of British Government in the West Indies (C. L. R. James), **Supp. XXI:** 161
Life of Dryden (Johnson), **Retro. Supp. II:** 223
Life of Emily Dickinson, The (Sewall), **Retro. Supp. I:** 25
Life of Forms, The (Focillon), **IV:** 90
Life of Franklin Pierce (Hawthorne), **Retro. Supp. I:** 163
Life of George Cabot Lodge, The (Adams), **I:** 21
Life of George Washington (Irving), **II:** 314, 315–316
Life of Henry James (Edel), **Retro. Supp. I:** 224
"Life of Irony, The" (Bourne), **I:** 219
Life of Jesus (Renan), **Supp. XX: 122**
"Life of Lincoln West, The" (Brooks), **Supp. III Part 1:** 86
Life of Mary, The (Rilke; F. Wright, trans.), **Supp. XVII:** 244
Life of Michelangelo (Grimm), **II:** 17
"Life of Nancy, The" (Jewett), **Retro. Supp. II:** 133, 144
Life of Oliver Goldsmith, The, with Selections from His Writings (Irving), **II:** 315
Life of Phips (Mather), **Supp. II Part 2:** 451, 452, 459
Life of Poetry, The (Rukeyser), **Supp. VI:** 271, 273, 275–276, 282, 283, 286
Life of Samuel Johnson (Boswell), **Supp. I Part 2:** 656
Life of Savage (Johnson), **Supp. I Part 2:** 523
Life of the Drama, The (Bentley), **IV:** 396
"Life of the Mind, The" (Kees), **Supp. XV:** 140
Life of the Right Reverend Joseph P. Machebeuf, The (Howlett), **Retro. Supp. I:** 17
Life of Thomas Paine, author of Rights of Men, With a Defence of his Writings (Chalmers), **Supp. I Part 2:** 514
Life of Thomas Paine, The (Cobbett), **Supp. I Part 2:** 517
"Life of Towne, The" (Carson), **Supp. XII: 102**
"Life on Beekman Place, A" (Naylor), **Supp. VIII:** 214
"Life on the Black List" (Endore), **Supp. XVII:** 63
Life on the Hyphen: The Cuban-American Way (Firmat), **Supp. VIII:** 76; **Supp. XI:** 184
Life on the Mississippi (Twain), **I:** 209; **IV:** 198, 199; **Supp. I Part 2:** 440
"Life on the Rocks: The Galápagos" (Dillard), **Supp. VI:** 32
"Life Stories, East and West" (E. Hoffman), **Supp. XVI:** 157
Life Story (Baker), **II:** 259
Life Studies (Lowell), **I:** 400; **II:** 384, 386, 543, 546–550, 551, 555; **Retro. Supp. II:** 180, 185, 186, 188, 189, 191; **Supp. I Part 2:** 543; **Supp. XI:** 240, 244, 250, 317; **Supp. XII:** 255; **Supp. XIV:** 15; **Supp. XV:** 252
"Life Studies" (Lowell), **Retro. Supp. II:** 188
"Life Styles in the Golden Land" (Didion), **Supp. IV Part 1:** 200
Life Supports: New and Collected Poems (Bronk), **Supp. XXI:** 19, 31, 32
"Life That Is, The" (Bryant), **Supp. I Part 1:** 169
"Life Work" (Stafford), **Supp. XI:** 329–330
"Life You Save May Be Your Own, The" (O'Connor), **III:** 344, 350, 354; **Retro. Supp. II:** 229, 230, 233
Lifshin, Lyn, **Supp. XVI:** 37
"Lifting, The" (Olds), **Supp. X:** 210
"Ligeia" (Poe), **III:** 412, 414; **Retro. Supp. II:** 261, 270, 271, 275
Liggett, Walter W., **Supp. XIII:** 168
Light, James F., **IV:** 290; **Retro. Supp. II:** 325
Light, Kate, **Supp. XVII:** 109
Light and Dark (Bronk), **Supp. XXI: 27–29,** 31
"Light and the Sufferer" (Lethem), **Supp. XVIII:** 139–140
Light around the Body, The (R. Bly), **Supp. IV Part 1:** 61–62, 62; **Supp. XVII:** 243; **Supp. XXI:** 84–85
"Light Comes Brighter, The" (Roethke), **III:** 529–530
"Light from Above" (Eberhart), **I:** 541
Light in August (Faulkner), **II:** 63–64, 65, 74; **IV:** 207; **Retro. Supp. I:** 82, 84, 85, 86, 89, 92; **Supp. XIV:** 12

Light in the Forest, The (Richter), **Supp. XVIII: 216–217**
Light in the Morning (Baker), **Supp. XVIII:** 263, 269
"Light Man, A" (James), **II:** 322; **Retro. Supp. I:** 219
"Lightning" (Barthelme), **Supp. IV Part 1:** 53
"Lightning" (Bynner), **Supp. XV:** 44
"Lightning" (Oliver), **Supp. VII:** 235
"Lightning, The" (Swenson), **Supp. IV Part 2:** 645
"Lightning Flash, The" (Gibran), **Supp. XX: 123**
"Lightning Rod Man, The" (Melville), **III:** 90; **Supp. XVIII:** 4
"Light of the World, The" (Hemingway), **II:** 249
"Lights in the Windows" (Nye), **Supp. XIII:** 280
"Light Through the Window, The" (Brockmeier), **Supp. XXII:** 52, 59
Light Verse and Satires (Bynner), **Supp. XV:** 52
Light Years (Salter), **Supp. IX: 257–259**
"LIKE, THIS IS WHAT I MEANT!" (Baraka), **Supp. II Part 1:** 59
"Like All the Other Nations" (Paley), **Supp. VI:** 220
"Like a Rolling Stone" (song, Dylan), **Supp. XVIII:** 20, 30
"Like Decorations in a Nigger Cemetery" (Stevens), **IV:** 74, 79; **Retro. Supp. I:** 305
Like Ghosts of Eagles (Francis), **Supp. IX:** 86
"Like Life" (Moore), **Supp. X:** 163, 165, **172–173**
Like Life: Stories (Moore), **Supp. X:** 163, **171–175,** 177, 178
"Like Talk" (Mills), **Supp. XI:** 311
"Like the New Moon I Will Live My Life" (R. Bly), **Supp. IV Part 1:** 71
Li'l Abner (Capp), **IV:** 198
"Lilacs" (Lowell), **II:** 527
"Lilacs, The" (Wilbur), **Supp. III Part 2:** 557–558
"Lilacs for Ginsberg" (Stern), **Supp. IX:** 299
Liliom (Molnar), **Supp. XVI:** 187
Lilith's Brood (O. Butler), **Supp. XIII:** 63
Lillabulero Press, **Supp. V:** 4, 5
Lillian Hellman (Adler), **Supp. I Part 1:** 297
Lillian Hellman (Falk), **Supp. I Part 1:** 297
Lillian Hellman: Playwright (Moody), **Supp. I Part 1:** 280
Lillo, George, **II:** 111, 112
"Lily Daw and the Three Ladies" (Welty), **IV:** 262
Lima, Agnes de, **I:** 231, 232
Lima, Maria Helena, **Supp. XXII:** 73
Lima Beans (Kreymborg), **Supp. XXII:** 163
"Limbo: Altered States" (Karr), **Supp. XI:** 249–250
"Limen" (Trethewey), **Supp. XXI:** 250
Lime Orchard Woman, The (Ríos), **Supp. IV Part 2:** 538, 547–550, 553
"Lime Orchard Woman, The" (Ríos), **Supp. IV Part 2:** 548
Limitations (Turow), **Supp. XVII: 222–223**
"Limits" (Emerson), **II:** 19
Lincoln, Abraham, **I:** 1, 4, 30; **II:** 8, 13, 135, 273, 555, 576; **III:** 576, 577, 580, 584, 587–590, 591; **IV:** 192, 195, 298, 347, 350, 444; **Supp. I Part 1:** 2, 8, 26, 309, 321; **Supp. I Part 2:** 379, 380, 382, 385, 390, 397, 399, 418, 424, 454, 456, 471, 472, 473, 474, 483, 579, 687; **Supp. VIII:** 108; **Supp. IX:** 15; **Supp. XIV:** 73
Lincoln, Kenneth, **Supp. IV Part 1:** 329; **Supp. IV Part 2:** 507
Lincoln, Thomas, **III:** 587
Lincoln, Mrs. Thomas (Nancy Hanks), **III:** 587
Lincoln: A Novel (Vidal), **Supp. IV Part 2:** 677, 684, 685, 688, 689–690, 691, 692
Lincoln Lawyer, The (Connelly), **Supp. XXI: 77,** 78
Lincoln on Race and Slavery (H. L. Gates), **Supp. XX: 108–109**
"Lincoln Relics, The" (Kunitz), **Supp. III Part 1:** 269
Lincoln: The Man (Masters), **Supp. I Part 2:** 471, 473–474
Lindbergh, Charles A., **I:** 482
"Linden Branch, The" (MacLeish), **III:** 19, 20
Linden Hills (Naylor), **Supp. VIII:** 214, 218, **219–223**
Linderman, Lawrence, **Supp. IV Part 2:** 579, 583, 585, 589
Lindner, April, **Supp. XV:** 111, 119
Lindsay, Howard, **III:** 284
Lindsay, John, **Supp. I Part 2:** 374
Lindsay, Olive, **Supp. I Part 2:** 374, 375, 392
Lindsay, Vachel, **I:** 384; **II:** 263, 276, 530; **III:** 5, 505; **Retro. Supp. I:** 133; **Supp. I Part 1:** 324; **Supp. I Part 2: 374–403,** 454, 473, 474; **Supp. III Part 1:** 63, 71; **Supp. XV:** 293, 297, 299, 301, 306; **Supp. XVI:** 184–185
Lindsay, Mrs. Vachel (Elizabeth Connors), **Supp. I Part 2:** 398, 399, 473
Lindsay, Vachel Thomas, **Supp. I Part 2:** 374, 375
Lindsay, Mrs. Vachel Thomas (Esther Catherine Frazee), **Supp. I Part 2:** 374, 375, 384–385, 398
Lindsey, David, **Supp. XIV:** 26
"Line, The" (Olds), **Supp. X:** 206
Lineage of Ragpickers, Songpluckers, Elegiasts, and Jewelers, A (Goldbarth), **Supp. XII:** 191
"Line of Least Resistance, The" (Wharton), **Retro. Supp. I:** 366
Line Out for a Walk, A: Familiar Essays (Epstein), **Supp. XIV: 107**
"Liner Notes for the Poetically Unhep" (Hughes), **Retro. Supp. I:** 210
"Lines After Rereading T. S. Eliot" (Wright), **Supp. V:** 343
"Lines Composed a Few Miles Above Tintern Abbey" (Wordsworth), **Supp. III Part 1:** 12
"Lines Composed Over Three Thousand Miles from Tintern Abbey" (Collins), **Supp. XXI:** 57–58
"Lines for an Interment" (MacLeish), **III:** 15
"Lines for My Father" (Cullen), **Supp. IV Part 1:** 167
"Lines from Israel" (Lowell), **II:** 554
"Lines from Pietro Longhi" (Sobin), **Supp. XVI:** 289
"Lines on Revisiting the Country" (Bryant), **Supp. I Part 1:** 164
"Lines Suggested by a Tennessee Song" (Agee), **I:** 28
"Line-Storm Song, A" (Frost), **Retro. Supp. I:** 127
"Lines Written at Port Royal" (Freneau), **Supp. II Part 1:** 264
"Lines Written in an Asylum" (Carruth), **Supp. XVI:** 48
"Lines Written in Manassas", **Supp. XV:** 99–100
Lineup, The (Connelly), **Supp. XXI:** 67, 68–69
"Line Written in the Dark Illegible Next Day" (F. Wright), **Supp. XVII:** 242
Linfield, Susie, **Supp. XVII:** 169, 177
Lingeman, Richard, **Supp. X:** 82; **Supp. XXII:** 104
Linn, Elizabeth. *See* Brown, Mrs. Charles Brockden (Elizabeth Linn)
Linn, John Blair, **Supp. I Part 1:** 145
Linnaeus, Carolus, **II:** 6; **Supp. I Part 1:** 245
"Linnets" (Levis), **Supp. XI:** 260, 261
"Linoleum Roses" (Cisneros), **Supp. VII:** 63, 66
Linotte: 1914–1920 (Nin), **Supp. X:** 193, 196, 197
Linschoten, Hans, **II:** 362, 363, 364
"Lion" (B. Kelly), **Supp. XVII:** 133
"Lion and Honeycomb" (Nemerov), **III:** 275, 278, 280
Lion and the Archer, The (Hayden), **Supp. II Part 1:** 366, 367
Lion and the Honeycomb, The (Blackmur), **Supp. II Part 1:** 91
Lion Country (Buechner), **Supp. XII:** 52, 53
Lionel Lincoln (Cooper), **I:** 339, 342
"Lion for Real, The" (Ginsberg), **Supp. II Part 1:** 320
Lionhearted, The: A Story about the Jews of Medieval England (Reznikoff), **Supp. XIV:** 280, 289
Lion in the Garden (Meriweather and Millgate), **Retro. Supp. I:** 91
"Lionizing" (Poe), **III:** 411, 425
"Lions, Harts, and Leaping Does" (Powers), **III:** 356
Lions and Shadows: An Education in the Twenties (Isherwood), **Supp. XIV:** 158, 159, 160, 162
"Lions in Sweden" (Stevens), **IV:** 79–80
Lipman, William R., **Supp. XIII:** 170

Li Po, **Supp. XI:** 241; **Supp. XII:** 218; **Supp. XV:** 47, 217
Lippmann, Walter, **I:** 48, 222–223, 225; **III:** 291, 600; **IV:** 429; **Supp. I Part 2:** 609, 643; **Supp. VIII:** 104
Lips Together, Teeth Apart (McNally), **Supp. XIII: 201–202,** 208, 209
Lipsyte, Robert, **Supp. XVI:** 220
Lipton, James, **Supp. IV Part 2:** 576, 577, 579, 583, 586, 588
Lipton, Lawrence, **Supp. IX:** 3
Lisbon Traviata, The (McNally), **Supp. XIII:** 198, **199–200,** 201, 204, 208
Lish, Gordon, **Supp. XIX:** 209; **Supp. XXI:** 115, 121
Lisicky,Paul, **Supp. XI:** 120, 131, 135
Lisk, Thomas, **Supp. XXI:** 24
"Lisp, The" (Olds), **Supp. X:** 211
Listen, Ruben Fontanez (Neugeboren), **Supp. XVI: 220–221**
"Listeners, The" (de la Mare), **Supp. XVII:** 69
"Listeners and Readers: The Unforgetting of Vachel Lindsay" (Trombly), **Supp. I Part 2:** 403
"Listening" (J. W. Miller), **Supp. XX: 167**
"Listening" (Paley), **Supp. VI:** 218, 231, 232
"Listening" (Stafford), **Supp. XI:** 321, 322
Listening to Prozac (P. Kramer), **Supp. XVI:** 229
"Listening to the Desert" (Henderson), **Supp. XIII:** 221–222
"Listening to the Mockingbird" (Woodard), **Supp. VIII:** 128
Listening to Your Life: Daily Meditations with Frederick Buechner (Buechner), **Supp. XII:** 53
Listen to the Desert/Oye al desierto (Mora), **Supp. XIII:** 221
"Listen to the People" (Benét), **Supp. XI:** 51–52
Liston, Sonny, **III:** 38, 42
Li T'ai-po, **II:** 526
"Litany" (Ashbery), **Supp. III Part 1:** 21–22, 25, 26
"Litany" (Collins), **Supp. XXI:** 56–57
"Litany" (Sandburg), **III:** 593
"Litany, The" (Gioia), **Supp. XV:** 125, 126
"Litany for Dictatorships" (Benét), **Supp. XI:** 46, 58
"Litany for Survival, A" (Lorde), **Supp. XII:** 220
"Litany of the Dark People, The" (Cullen), **Supp. IV Part 1:** 170, 171
"Litany of the Heroes" (Lindsay), **Supp. I Part 2:** 397
"Litany of Washington Street, The" (Lindsay), **Supp. I Part 2:** 376, 398–399
Literary Anthropology (Trumpener and Nyce), **Retro. Supp. I:** 380
Literary Art and Activism of Rick Bass, The (Weltzien), **Supp. XVI:** 20–21
"Literary Blacks and Jews" (Ozick), **Supp. V:** 272
"Literary Career of Elizabeth Barstow Stoddard, The" (Matlack), **Supp. XV:** 269
Literary Criticism: A Short History (Brooks and Wimsatt), **Supp. XIV:** 12
"Literary Criticism of Georg Lukács, The" (Sontag), **Supp. III Part 2:** 453
Literary Disruptions (Klinkowitz), **Supp. XXI:** 233
Literary Essays of Thomas Merton, The, **Supp. VIII:** 207
"Literary Folk As They Came and Went with Ourselves" (E. Stoddard), **Supp. XV:** 274
Literary Friends and Acquaintance (Howells), **Supp. I Part 1:** 318; **Supp. XV:** 287
"Literary Heritage of Tennyson, The" (Locke), **Supp. XIV:** 197
Literary History of the United States (Spiller et al., ed.), **Supp. I Part 1:** 104; **Supp. II Part 1:** 95
"Literary Importation" (Freneau), **Supp. II Part 1:** 264
"Literary Life of America, The" (Brooks), **I:** 245
Literary Outlaw: The Life and Times of William S. Burroughs (Morgan), **Supp. XIV:** 141
Literary Situation, The (Cowley), **Supp. II Part 1:** 135, 140, 144, 146, 147, 148
"Literary Worker's Polonius, The" (Wilson), **IV:** 431, 432
"Literature" (Emerson), **II:** 6
Literature (X. J. Kennedy), **Supp. XV:** 153
Literature and American Life (Boynton), **Supp. I Part 2:** 415
Literature and Life (Howells), **Supp. XIV:** 45–46
Literature and Morality (Farrell), **II:** 49
"Literature and Place: Varieties of Regional Experience" (Erisman), **Supp. VIII:** 126
"Literature as a Symptom" (Warren), **IV:** 237
"Literature in Low Life" (Hapgood), **Supp. XVII:** 103
"Literature of Exhaustion, The" (Barth), **Supp. IV Part 1:** 48
"Lithuanian Nocturne" (Brodsky), **Supp. VIII:** 29
"Lit Instructor" (Stafford), **Supp. XI:** 321
Littauer, Kenneth, **Retro. Supp. I:** 114
Little Acts of Kindness (Budbill), **Supp. XIX:** 3, **14–15**
"Little Bernhardt" (Shaw), **Supp. XIX:** 246
Little Big Man (Berger), **Supp. XII:** 171
Little Big Man (film), **Supp. X:** 124
Littlebird, Harold, **Supp. IV Part 2:** 499
Littlebird, Larry, **Supp. IV Part 2:** 499, 505
Little Birds: Erotica (Nin), **Supp. X:** 192, 195
"Little Brown Baby" (Dunbar), **Supp. II Part 1:** 206
"Little Brown Jug" (Baraka), **Supp. II Part 1:** 51
Little Casino (Sorrentino), **Supp. XXI:** 237, 238
"Little Clown, My Heart" (Cisneros), **Supp. VII:** 71
"Little Cosmic Dust Poem" (Haines), **Supp. XII:** 209–210
"Little Country Girl, A" (Chopin), **Retro. Supp. II:** 71
"Little Curtis" (Parker), **Supp. IX:** 193
Little Disturbances of Man, The (Paley), **Supp. VI:** 218
"Little Dog" (Hughes), **Supp. I Part 1:** 329
Little Dorrit (Dickens), **Supp. I Part 1:** 35
"Little Edward" (Stowe), **Supp. I Part 2:** 587
"Little Elegy" (X. J. Kennedy), **Supp. XV:** 155
Little Essays Drawn from the Writings of George Santayana (L. P. Smith), **Supp. XIV:** 342
"Little Expressionless Animals" (Wallace), **Supp. X:** 305
"Little Fable" (Hay), **Supp. XIV:** 131
Littlefield, Catherine, **Supp. IX:** 58
Little Fling, A (Pickering), **Supp. XXI:** 203
Little Foxes, The (Hellman), **Supp. I Part 1:** 276, 278–279, 281, 283, 297
"Little Fred, the Canal Boy" (Stowe), **Supp. I Part 2:** 587
"Little French Mary" (Jewett), **II:** 400
Little Friend, Little Friend (Jarrell), **II:** 367, 372, 375–376
"Little Gidding" (Eliot), **I:** 582, 588; **II:** 539; **Retro. Supp. I:** 66
"Little Girl, My Stringbean, My Lovely Woman" (Sexton), **Supp. II Part 2:** 686
"Little Girl, The" (Paley), **Supp. VI:** 222, **228–229**
"Little Girl Tells a Story to a Lady, A" (Barnes), **Supp. III Part 1:** 36
"Little Goose Girl, The" (Grimm), **IV:** 266
Little Ham (Hughes), **Retro. Supp. I:** 203; **Supp. I Part 1:** 328, 339
Little House in the Big Woods (L. I. Wilder), **Supp. XXII:** 294, 295, 296, 297, 298–299, 300
Little House on the Prairie (L. I. Wilder), **Supp. XXII:** 294, 295–296, 297, 299, 301
Little House on the Prairie (television series), **Supp. XXII:** 289
"Little House" series (L. A. Wilder), **Supp. XXII:** 289
Little House Traveler, A (L. I. Wilder), **Supp. XXII:** 301
Little King, The (Bynner), **Supp. XV:** 42, 50
Little Lady of the Big House, The (London), **II:** 481–482
Little Liar, The (film; Ingraham), **Supp. XVI:** 184–185
"Little Lion Face" (Swenson), **Supp. IV Part 2:** 651
"Little Lobelia's Song" (Bogan), **Supp. III Part 1:** 66

"Little Local Color, A" (Henry), **Supp. II Part 1:** 399

Little Lord Fauntleroy (Burnett), **Retro. Supp. I:** 188; **Supp. XVI:** 182

"Little Lyric" (Hughes), **Supp. I Part 1:** 334

Little Man, Little Man (Baldwin), **Supp. I Part 1:** 67

"Little Man at Chehaw Station, The" (Ellison), **Retro. Supp. II:** 123

Little Me (musical), **Supp. IV Part 2:** 575

Little Men (Alcott), **Supp. I Part 1:** 32, 39, 40

"Little Morning Music, A" (Schwartz), **Supp. II Part 2:** 662–663

Little Ocean (Shepard), **Supp. III Part 2:** 447

"Little Old Girl, A" (Larcom), **Supp. XIII:** 144

"Little Old Spy" (Hughes), **Supp. I Part 1:** 329

Little Orphan Annie (film), **Supp. XVIII:** 244

"Little Owl Who Lives in the Orchard" (Oliver), **Supp. VII:** 239

"Little Peasant, The" (Sexton), **Supp. II Part 2:** 690

"Little Rapids, The" (Swenson), **Supp. IV Part 2:** 645

Little Red Song Book (Hill), **Supp. XVIII:** 224

Little Regiment and Other Episodes of the American Civil War, The (Crane), **I:** 408

Little River: New and Selected Poems (McCarriston), **Supp. XIV: 269–272**

"Little Road not made of Man , A" (Dickinson), **Retro. Supp. I:** 44

Little Sister, The (Chandler), **Supp. IV Part 1:** 122, 130, 131–132

"Little Sleep's-Head Sprouting Hair in the Moonlight" (Kinnell), **Supp. III Part 1:** 247

"Little Snow White" (Grimm), **IV:** 266

Little Star (Halliday), **Supp. XIX:** 82, **84–85,** 87

"Little Star" (Halliday), **Supp. XIX:** 83, 84, 93

"Little Testament of Bernard Martin, Aet. 30" (Mumford), **Supp. II Part 2:** 472, 473, 474

"Little Things" (Olds), **Supp. X:** 208

Little Tour in France (James), **II:** 337

Little Women (Alcott), **Supp. I Part 1:** 28, 29, 32, 35, 37, 38, 39–40, 41, 43, 44; **Supp. IX:** 128

Little Yellow Dog, A (Mosley), **Supp. XIII:** 237, 241

"Liturgy and Spiritual Personalism" (Merton), **Supp. VIII:** 199

Litz, A. Walton, **Retro. Supp. I:** 306

"Liu Ch'e" (Pound), **III:** 466

"Live" (Sexton), **Supp. II Part 2:** 684, 686

Live from Baghdad (screenplay, Shanley), **Supp. XIV:** 316

Live from Golgotha (Vidal), **Supp. IV Part 2:** 677, 682, 691, 692

Live Now and Pay Later (Garrett), **Supp. VII:** 111

"Live-Oak with Moss" (Whitman), **Retro. Supp. I:** 403

Live or Die (Sexton), **Supp. II Part 2:** 670, 683–687

Liveright, Horace, **Retro. Supp. I:** 80, 81, 83; **Supp. I Part 2:** 464; **Supp. XX: 71, 75; Supp. XXII:** 25

Livermore, Elizabeth, **Supp. XXII:** 70

Lives (Plutarch), **II:** 5, 104

Lives of a Cell, The (L. Thomas), **Retro. Supp. I:** 322, 323

Lives of Distinguished American Naval Officers (Cooper), **I:** 347

"Lives of Gulls and Children, The" (Nemerov), **III:** 271, 272

Lives of the Animals (Wrigley), **Supp. XVIII: 306–308**

Lives of the Artists (Vasari), **Supp. I Part 2:** 450

"Lives of the Bohemians" (Lethem), **Supp. XVIII:** 135

Lives of the Muses, The: Nine Women and the Artists They Inspired (Prose), **Supp. XVI:** 250, 260

"Lives of the Philosophers, The" (Brockmeier), **Supp. XXII:** 59, 61

Lives of the Poets (Doctorow), **Supp. IV Part 1:** 234

"Lives of the Poets" (Doctorow), **Supp. IV Part 1:** 234

"Lives of the—Wha'?, The" (Goldbarth), **Supp. XII:** 191

"Living" (Wright), **Supp. XV:** 345

Living, The (Dillard), **Supp. VI:** 23

"Living at Home" (Gordon), **Supp. IV Part 1:** 311

Living by Fiction (Dillard), **Supp. VI:** 23, 31, **32,** 33

Living by the Word (Walker), **Supp. III Part 2:** 521, 522, 526, 527, 535

Living End, The (Elkin), **Supp. VI: 54,** 58

Living Instead (Bronk), **Supp. XXI:** 32

"Living in the Flatlands" (Carruth), **Supp. XVI:** 54

Living Is Easy, The (D. West), **Supp. XVIII:** 277, 280, **284–286,** 287

"Living Like Weasels" (Dillard), **Supp. VI:** 26, 33

Living Novel, The (Hicks), **III:** 342

Living of Charlotte Perkins Gilman, The (Gilman), **Supp. XI:** 193, 209

Living off the Country: Essays on Poetry and Place (Haines), **Supp. XII:** 199, 203, 207

"Living on a Giant" (X. J. Kennedy), **Supp. XV:** 163

Living Out Loud (Quindlen), **Supp. XVII:** 166, **167–169**

Living Reed, The (Buck), **Supp. II Part 1:** 129–130

Livingston, Myra Cohn, **Supp. XV:** 153, 162

Living Theater, **Retro. Supp. I:** 424

"Living There" (Dickey), **Supp. IV Part 1:** 182–183

Living the Spirit: A Gay American Indian Anthology (Roscoe, ed.), **Supp. IV Part 1:** 330

Living to Prowl (Pickering), **Supp. XXI:** 203

"Living with a Peacock" (O'Connor), **III:** 350

"Livvie" (Welty), **IV:** 265; **Retro. Supp. I:** 348–349

"Livvie Is Back" (Welty), **Retro. Supp. I:** 351

Livy, **II:** 8

Lizzie (film), **Supp. IX:** 125

"Llantos de La Llorona: Warnings from the Wailer" (Mora), **Supp. XIII:** 217, 224

"L'Lapse" (Barthelme), **Supp. IV Part 1:** 45–47, 48

Llosa, Mario Vargas, **Supp. XIX:** 131

Lloyd, Fabien. *See* Cravan, Arthur

Lloyd, Henry Demarest, **Supp. I Part 1:** 5

Lloyd George, Harold, **I:** 490

"LMFBR" (Snyder), **Supp. VIII:** 302

"Loaded Inflections" (Halliday), **Supp. XIX:** 90, 91

"Loam" (Sandburg), **III:** 584–585

"Loan, The" (Malamud), **Supp. I Part 2:** 427, 428, 431, 437

Loberer, Eric, **Supp. XV:** 339

"Local" (McCarriston), **Supp. XIV:** 270

Local Color (Capote), **Supp. III Part 1:** 120

"Local Color" (London), **II:** 475

"Local Family Keeps Son Happy" (Keillor), **Supp. XVI:** 168, 169

Local Girls (Hoffman), **Supp. X:** 77, **90–91,** 92

"Local Girls" (Hoffman), **Supp. X:** 90

Local Habitation & A Name, A (Kooser), **Supp. XIX:** 116, 118, **119–120**

Local Men (Whitehead), **Supp. XV:** 339

Local Time (Dunn), **Supp. XI:** 143, **148–149**

Local Wonders: Seasons in the Bohemian Alps (Kooser), **Supp. XIX:** 115, **126**

"Location" (Halliday), **Supp. XIX:** 87

Lock, Helen, **Supp. XIII:** 233, 237–238

Lock, Robert H., **IV:** 319; **Retro. Supp. I:** 375

Locke, Alain, **Retro. Supp. II:** 115; **Supp. I Part 1:** 323, 325, 341; **Supp. II Part 1:** 53, 176, 182, 228, 247; **Supp. IV Part 1:** 170; **Supp. IX:** 306, 309; **Supp. X:** 134, 137, 139; **Supp. XIV: 195–219; Supp. XVIII:** 122; **Supp. XIX:** 69, 75; **Supp. XXII:** 7, 13

Locke, Duane, **Supp. IX:** 273

Locke, John, **I:** 554–555, 557; **II:** 15–16, 113–114, 348–349, 480; **III:** 294–295; **IV:** 149; **Supp. I Part 1:** 130, 229, 230; **Supp. I Part 2:** 523

Locke, Sondra, **II:** 588

"Locked House, A" (Snodgrass), **Supp. VI:** 323

Locked Room, The (Auster), **Supp. XII:** 22, 24, **27–28**

Locket, The (Masters), **Supp. I Part 2:** 460

Lockridge, Ross, Jr., **Supp. XIX:** 263
"Locksley Hall" (Tennyson), **Supp. IX:** 19
Lockwood Concern, The (O'Hara), **III:** 362, 364, 377–382
"Locus" (Ammons), **Supp. VII:** 28
"Locus" (Hayden), **Supp. II Part 1:** 361–362, 381
"Locusts, the Plaza, the Room, The" (Kees), **Supp. XV:** 141
Loden, Barbara, **III:** 163
Lodge, Henry Cabot, **I:** 11–12, 21
Lodge, Mrs. Henry Cabot, **I:** 11–12, 19
Lodge, Thomas, **IV:** 370
Loeb, Gerald, **Supp. IV Part 2:** 523
Loeb, Jacques, **I:** 513; **Retro. Supp. II:** 104; **Supp. I Part 2:** 641
Loeffler, Jack, **Supp. XIII:** 1, 3, 12, 14, 16
Loftus, Mary J., **Supp. XXI:** 245
Lofty Dogmas (A. Finch, M. Kumin and D. Brown, eds.), **Supp. XVII:** 75–76
"Log" (Merrlll), **Supp. III Part 1:** 328
Logan, Rayford W., **Supp. II Part 1:** 171, 194; **Supp. XIV:** 73
Logan, William, **Supp. X:** 201, 213; **Supp. XI:** 131, 132; **Supp. XII:** 98, 107, 113, 184; **Supp. XV:** 212, 226, 251, 257, 260–261, 262,**Supp. XV:** 263, 266
Log Book of "The Loved One," The, **Supp. XI:** 306
Logenbach, James, **Supp. XVII:** 183
"Logging and Pimping and 'Your Pal, Jim' " (Maclean), **Supp. XIV:** 229
Logue, Christopher, **Supp. XIV:** 82
Lohengrin (Wagner), **I:** 216
Lohrfinck, Rosalind, **III:** 107, 117
Lolita (Nabokov), **III:** 246, 247, 255, 258–261; **Retro. Supp. I:** 263, 264, 265, 266, 269, 270, **272–274,** 275; **Supp. V:** 127, 252; **Supp. VIII:** 133; **Supp. XVI:** 294; **Supp. XXII:** 260
"Lolita" (Parker), **Supp. IX:** 193
Lolly Dinks' Doings (E. Stoddard), **Supp. XV:** 273,**Supp. XV:** 286
Lombardi, Marilyn May, **Retro. Supp. II:** 40
London, Eliza, **II:** 465
London, Jack, **I:** 209; **II:** 264, 440, 444, 451, **462–485; III:** 314, 580; **Supp. IV Part 1:** 236; **Supp. V:** 281; **Supp. IX:** 1, 14; **Supp. XIII:** 312; **Supp. XIV:** 227; **Supp. XV:** 115; **Supp. XVI:** 181; **Supp. XVIII:** 90; **Supp. XXII:** 203
London, Mrs. Jack (Bessie Maddern), **II:** 465, 466, 473, 478
London, Mrs. Jack (Charmian Kittredge), **II:** 466, 468, 473, 476, 478, 481
London, John, **II:** 464, 465
London, Scott, **Supp. XIV:** 301, 307, 311
London Embassy, The (Theroux), **Supp. VIII:** 323
London Fields (Amis), **Retro. Supp. I:** 278
"London Letter" (column; Eliot), **Supp. XV:** 306
London Magazine (Plath), **Supp. I Part 2:** 541
London Snow: A Christmas Story (Theroux), **Supp. VIII:** 322
London Suite (Simon), **Supp. IV Part 2:** 576, 581, 582, 588
London: The Biography (Ackroyd), **Supp. XVII:** 180
Loneliness of the Long Distance Runner, The (Sillitoe), **Supp. XX: 195**
Lonely Are the Brave (film), **Supp. XIII:** 6
"Lonely Coast, A" (Proulx), **Supp. VII:** 264
Lonely Crusade (C. Himes), **Supp. XVI:** 135, 139–140
Lonely for the Future (Farrell), **II:** 46, 47
"Lonely Gay Teen Seeking Same" (Egan), **Supp. XIX:** 61
Lonely Impulse of Delight, A (Shanley), **Supp. XIV:** 317–318
"Lonely Street, The" (W. C. Williams), **IV:** 413
"Lonely Worker, A" (Jewett), **Retro. Supp. II:** 132
Lonergan, Wayne, **Supp. I Part 1:** 51
Lonesome Boy (Bontemps), **Supp. XXII:** 6, 13–14
Lonesome Dove (McMurtry), **Supp. V:** 226–228, 231, 232, 233
Lonesome Traveler (Kerouac), **Supp. III Part 1:** 219, 225
"Lonesome Whistle Blowing" (Skow), **Supp. XVI:** 174
"Lone Striker, A" (Frost), **Retro. Supp. I:** 136, 137
Long, Ada, **Supp. V:** 178
Long, Haniel, **Supp. XV:** 46, 49
Long, Huey, **I:** 489; **II:** 454; **IV:** 249; **Supp. IV Part 2:** 679; **Supp. XIV:** 14
Long, John Luther, **Supp. XXI:** 150
Long, Judith Reick, **Supp. XX: 212, 215, 217, 223**
Long, Ray, **II:** 430; **III:** 54
Long after Midnight (Bradbury), **Supp. IV Part 1:** 102
Long Ago in France: The Years in Dijon (M. F. K. Fisher), **Supp. XVII:** 91
Long and Happy Life, A (Price), **Supp. VI:** 258, **259–260,** 262, 264, 265
Long Approach, The (Kumin), **Supp. IV Part 2:** 452–453, 453
Longbottom, Robert, **Supp. XXI:** 148
Long Christmas Dinner, The (Wilder), **IV:** 357, 365; **Supp. V:** 105
Long Christmas Dinner and Other Plays (Wilder), **IV:** 365–366
Long Day's Dying, A (Buechner), **Supp. XII: 45–47**
Long Day's Journey into Night (O'Neill), **III:** 385, 401, 403–404; **Supp. IV Part 1:** 359; **Supp. XIV:** 327; **Supp. XXI:** 13; **Supp. XXII:** 27, 29, 30
Long Desire, A (Connell), **Supp. XIV:** 79, 80, 97
"Long Distance" (Stafford), **Supp. XI:** 329
"Long-Distance Runner, The" (Paley), **Supp. VI:** 221–222, 228, 230
Long Dream, The (Wright), **IV:** 478, 488, 494
"Long Embrace, The" (Levine), **Supp. V:** 187
"Long Enough" (Rukeyser), **Supp. VI:** 274
"Longest Night of My Life, The " (Nichols), **Supp. XIII:** 269
Longfellow, Henry Wadsworth, **I:** 458, 471; **II:** 274, 277, 295–296, 310, 313, 402, **486–510; III:** 269, 412, 421, 422, 577; **IV:** 309, 371; **Retro. Supp. I:** 54, 123, 150, 155, 362; **Retro. Supp. II: 153–174; Supp. I Part 1:** 158, 299, 306, 317, 362, 368; **Supp. I Part 2:** 405, 406, 408, 409, 414, 416, 420, 586, 587, 602, 699, 704; **Supp. II Part 1:** 291, 353; **Supp. III Part 2:** 609; **Supp. IV Part 1:** 165; **Supp. IV Part 2:** 503; **Supp. XII:** 260; **Supp. XIII:** 141; **Supp. XIV:** 120; **Supp. XVIII:** 4; **Supp. XXI:** 51
"Long Feud" (Untermeyer), **Supp. XV:** 309
Long Feud: Selected Poems (Untermeyer), **Supp. XV:** 312
"Long Fourth, A" (Taylor), **Supp. V:** 313
Long Fourth and Other Stories, A (Taylor), **Supp. V:** 318–319
Long Gay Book, A (Stein), **IV:** 42
Long Goodbye, The (Chandler), **Supp. IV Part 1:** 120, 122, 132–134, 135
Long Goodbye, The (T. Williams), **IV:** 381
"Long Hair" (Snyder), **Supp. VIII:** 300
Longing for Home, The: Recollections and Reflections (Buechner), **Supp. XII:** 53
Longinus, Dionysius Cassius, **I:** 279
"Long-Legged House, The" (Berry), **Supp. X:** 21, 24–25, 27, 31
Long Live Man (Corso), **Supp. XII:** 129–130, 132
Long Love, The (Sedges), **Supp. II Part 1:** 125
Long Made Short (Dixon), **Supp. XII:** 152
Long March, The (Styron), **IV:** 97, 99, 104–107, 111, 113, 117
"Long Night, The" (Bambara), **Supp. XI:** 9
"Long Novel, A" (Ashbery), **Supp. III Part 1:** 6
Longo, Robert, **Supp. XVI:** 124
Long Patrol, The (Mailer), **III:** 46
"Long Point Light" (Doty), **Supp. XI:** 127
Long Road of Woman's Memory, The (Addams), **Supp. I Part 1:** 17–18
"Long Run, The" (Wharton), **IV:** 314
Long Season, The (Brosnan), **II:** 424, 425; **Supp. XX: 195**
"Long Shadow of Lincoln, The: A Litany" (Sandburg), **III:** 591, 593
Longshot O'Leary (McGrath), **Supp. X:** 117
"Long Shower, The" (Francis), **Supp. IX:** 90
"Long Stemmed Roses" (Jarman), **Supp. XVII:** 115

Longstreet, Augustus B., **II:** 70, 313; **Supp. I Part 1:** 352; **Supp. V:** 44; **Supp. X:** 227
"Long Summer" (Lowell), **II:** 553–554
"Long Term" (Dunn), **Supp. XI:** 149
Longtime Companion (film), **Supp. X:** 146, 152
Long Valley, The (Steinbeck), **IV:** 51
Long View (Taggard), **Supp. XXII: 283–284**
Long Voyage Home, The (O'Neill), **III:** 388
"Long Wail, A" (Crews), **Supp. XI:** 101
"Long Walk, The" (Bogan), **Supp. III Part 1:** 61
Long Walks and Intimate Talks (Paley), **Supp. VI:** 221
Long Way from Home, A (McKay), **Supp. X:** 132, 140
Long Winter, The (L. I. Wilder), **Supp. XXII:** 291, 294, 295
Lönnrot, Elias, **Retro. Supp. II:** 159
Looby, Christopher, **Supp. XIII:** 96
Look, Stranger! (Auden), **Supp. II Part 1:** 11
"Look, The" (Olds), **Supp. X:** 210
Look at Me (Egan), **Supp. XIX:** 49, **53–56,** 60, 61
Look at the Harlequins (Nabokov), **Retro. Supp. I:** 266, 270
"Look for My White Self" (Ammons), **Supp. VII:** 25
Look Homeward, Angel (Wolfe), **II:** 457; **IV:** 450, 452, 453, 454, 455–456, 461, 462, 463, 464, 468, 471; **Supp. XI:** 216
"Looking" (Sanders), **Supp. XVI:** 277
"Looking a Mad Dog Dead in the Eyes" (Komunyakaa), **Supp. XIII:** 114
"Looking at Each Other" (Rukeyser), **Supp. VI:** 280, 285–286
"Looking at Kafka" (P. Roth), **Supp. III Part 2:** 402
"Looking at Women" (Sanders), **Supp. XVI:** 274
"Looking Back" (Harjo), **Supp. XII:** 218
"Looking Back" (Merwin), **Supp. III Part 1:** 352
"Looking Back at Girlhood" (Jewett), **Retro. Supp. II:** 131, 133
Looking Backward (Bellamy), **II:** 276; **Supp. I Part 2:** 641; **Supp. XI:** 200
"Looking for a Ship" (McPhee), **Supp. III Part 1:** 312–313
"Looking for Dragon Smoke" (R. Bly), **Supp. IV Part 1:** 60
Looking for Holes in the Ceiling (Dunn), **Supp. XI:** 139, **143–145**
Looking for Langston (Julien; film), **Supp. XI:** 19, 20
Looking for Lincoln (television production), **Supp. XX: 99**
Looking for Luck (Kumin), **Supp. IV Part 2:** 453, 454–455
"Looking for Mr. Green" (Bellow), **Retro. Supp. II:** 27
"Looking for the Buckhead Boys" (Dickey), **Supp. IV Part 1:** 182, 183
"Looking Forward to Age" (Harrison), **Supp. VIII:** 49
"Looking from Inside My Body" (R. Bly), **Supp. IV Part 1:** 71
"Looking Glass, The" (Wharton), **Retro. Supp. I:** 382
"Lookout's Journal" (Snyder), **Supp. VIII:** 291
"Looks Like They'll Never Learn" (McCoy), **Supp. XIII:** 166
"Look to the Woods" (P. N. Warren), **Supp. XX: 272**
"Look to Thy Heart . . ." (Hay), **Supp. XIV:** 130
Loon, Hendrik Willem van, **Supp. XVI:** 185
Loon Lake (Doctorow), **Supp. IV Part 1:** 219, 222, 224–227, 230, 231, 232, 233
"Loon Point" (O'Brien), **Supp. V:** 237
Loos, Adolf, **Supp. XVI:** 187
Loos, Anita, **Supp. XVI: 181–199**
Loos, Mary Anita, **Supp. XVI:** 196
Loose Canons (H. L. Gates), **Supp. XX: 101, 108, 109–110, 111**
Loosestrife (Dunn), **Supp. XI: 152–154**
"Loosestrife" (Dunn), **Supp. XI:** 154
"Loose Woman" (X. J. Kennedy), **Supp. XV:** 159
Loose Woman: Poems (Cisneros), **Supp. VII:** 58, 71–72
Lopate, Edward, **Supp. XVI:** 266
Lopate, Philip, **Supp. XII:** 184; **Supp. XIII:** 280–281; **Supp. XVI:** 230
Lopatnikoff, Nikolai, **Supp. XIV:** 123
Lopez, Barry, **Supp. IV Part 1:** 416; **Supp. V:** 211; **Supp. X:** 29, 31; **Supp. XIII:** 16; **Supp. XIV:** 227
Lopez, Rafael, **Supp. IV Part 2:** 602
Lorax, The (Geisel), **Supp. XVI:** 109–110
Lorca, Federico García, **IV:** 380; **Supp. I Part 1:** 345; **Supp. IV Part 1:** 83; **Supp. VIII:** 38, 39; **Supp. XIII:** 315, 323, 324; **Supp. XV:** 186; **Supp. XXI:** 100
Lord, Judge Otis P., **I:** 454, 457, 458, 470
Lorde, Audre, **Supp. I Part 2:** 550, 571; **Supp. IV Part 1:** 325; **Supp. XI:** 20; **Supp. XII:** 217, 220; **Supp. XIII:** 295; **Supp. XVII:** 71
Lord Jim (Conrad), **I:** 422; **II:** 26; **Retro. Supp. II:** 292; **Supp. I Part 2:** 623; **Supp. IV Part 2:** 680; **Supp. V:** 251
"Lord of Hosts" (Pinsky), **Supp. VI:** 244
Lord of the Flies (W. Golding), **Supp. XVI:** 65
Lord of the Rings (Tolkien), **Supp. V:** 140
Lords of Misrule, The (X. J. Kennedy), **Supp. XV:** 154, **170–171**
Lords of the Housetops (Van Vechten), **Supp. II Part 2:** 736
Lord's Prayer, **I:** 579
Lord Timothy Dexter of Newburyport, Mass. (Marquand), **III:** 55
Lord Weary's Castle (Lowell), **II:** 538, 542–551; **Retro. Supp. II:** 178, **186–187,** 188; **Supp. XV:** 252
"Lorelei" (Plath), **Retro. Supp. II:** 246; **Supp. I Part 2:** 538
"Lorenzo" (Bynner), **Supp. XV:** 46, 50
Lorimer, George Horace, **II:** 430; **Retro. Supp. I:** 101, 113
Lorre, Peter, **Supp. IV Part 1:** 356
"Los Alamos" (Momaday), **Supp. IV Part 2:** 482
Los Amigos de Becky (Hinojosa). *See Becky and Her Friends* (Hinojosa)
"Los Angeles, 1980" (Gunn Allen), **Supp. IV Part 1:** 325
"Los Angeles Days" (Didion), **Supp. IV Part 1:** 211
"Lo! School in Poetry, The" (Taggard), **Supp. XXII:** 276
"Loser, The" (Talese), **Supp. XVII:** 202, 208
Loser and Still Champion: Muhammad Ali (Schulberg), **Supp. XVIII:** 254
Losey, Joseph, **IV:** 383
Lose Your Mother: A Journey Along the Atlantic Slave Route (Hartman), **Supp. XX: 154**
"Losing a Language" (Merwin), **Supp. III Part 1:** 356
Losing Battles (Welty), **IV:** 261, 281–282; **Retro. Supp. I:** 341, 352, **353–354**
"Losing the Marbles" (Merrill), **Supp. III Part 1:** 337
"Losing Track of Language" (Clampitt), **Supp. IX:** 38, 40
Losses (Jarrell), **II:** 367, 372, 373–375, 376, 377, 380–381
"Losses" (Jarrell), **II:** 375–376
Lossky, N. O., **Supp. IV Part 2:** 519
"Loss of Breath" (Poe), **III:** 425–426
"Loss of My Arms and Legs, The" (Kingsolver), **Supp. VII:** 208
"Loss of the Creature, The" (Percy), **Supp. III Part 1:** 387
"Lost" (Wagoner), **Supp. IX:** 328
"Lost, The/Los Perdidos" (Kingsolver), **Supp. VII:** 208
"Lost and Found" (Levine), **Supp. V:** 188
"Lost and Found" (Nelson), **Supp. XVIII:** 176
"Lost Bodies" (Wright), **Supp. V:** 342
"Lost Boy, The" (Wolfe), **IV:** 451, 460, 466–467
"Lost Decade, The" (Fitzgerald), **II:** 98
"Lost Fugue for Chet" (Hull), **Supp. XXI:** 137–138, 141
Lost Galleon and Other Tales, The (Harte), **Supp. II Part 1:** 344
Lost Get-Back Boogie, The (Burke), **Supp. XIV:** 22, 25
"Lost Girls, The" (Hogan), **Supp. IV Part 1:** 406–407
Lost Grizzlies, The: A Search for Survivors in the Wilderness of Colorado (Bass), **Supp. XVI:** 25, 26
Lost Highway (film), **Supp. X:** 314
Lost Illusions (Balzac), **I:** 500
"Lost in Nostalgia: The Autobiographies of Eva Hoffman and Richard Rodriguez" (Fachinger), **Supp. XVI:** 153
Lost in the Bonewheel Factory (Komunyakaa), **Supp. XIII: 114–115,** 116
Lost in the City (E. P. Jones), **Supp. XXII:** 140, 142, **143–146,** 148, 149
Lost in the Cosmos: The Last Self-Help Book (Percy), **Supp. III Part 1:** 397

Lost in the Funhouse (Barth), **I:** 122, 135, 139; **Supp. X:** 307
"Lost in the Whichy Thicket" (Wolfe), **Supp. III Part 2:** 573, 574
Lost in Translation (E. Hoffman), **Supp. XVI:** 147, **148–151,** 153, 154, 159
"Lost in Translation" (Hass), **Supp. VIII:** 28
"Lost in Translation" (Merrill), **Supp. III Part 1:** 324, 329–330
Lost in Yonkers (film), **Supp. IV Part 2:** 588
Lost in Yonkers (Simon), **Supp. IV Part 2:** 576, 577, 584, 587–588, 590–591
"Lost Jerusalem" (Untermeyer), **Supp. XV:** 307
Lost Lady, A (Cather), **I:** 323–325, 327; **Retro. Supp. I: 15–16,** 20, 21, 382
Lost Light (Connelly), **Supp. XXI:** 72, **75–76**
"Lost Lives" (Sorrentino), **Supp. XXI:** 226
"Lost Lover, A" (Jewett), **II:** 400–401, 402; **Retro. Supp. II:** 137
"Lost Loves" (Kinnell), **Supp. III Part 1:** 237, 245
Lost Man's River (Matthiessen), **Supp. V:** 212, 213, 214, 215
"Lost on September Trail, 1967" (Ríos), **Supp. IV Part 2:** 540
Lost Puritan (Mariani), **Retro. Supp. II:** 189
Lost Roads Project, The: A Walk-In Book of Arkansas (exhibition; Wright and Luster), **Supp. XV:** 337, 348
"Lost Sailor, The" (Freneau), **Supp. II Part 1:** 264
Lost Son, The (Roethke), **III:** 529, 530–532, 533
"Lost Son, The" (Roethke), **III:** 536, 537–539, 542
"Lost Sons" (Salter), **Supp. IX:** 260
Lost Souls (Singer). *See* Meshugah (Singer)
Lost Weekend, The (Jackson), **Supp. XIII:** 262
"Lost World, A" (Ashbery), **Supp. III Part 1:** 9
"Lost World, The" (Chabon), **Supp. XI:** 72–73
Lost World, The (Jarrell), **II:** 367, 368, 371, 379–380, 386, 387
"Lost World, The" cycle (Chabon), **Supp. XI: 71–73**
"Lost World of Richard Yates, The: How the Great Writer of the Age of Anxiety Disappeared from Print" (O'Nan), **Supp. XI:** 348
"Lost Young Intellectual, The" (Howe), **Supp. VI:** 113, **115–116**
Lost Zoo, The: (A Rhyme for the Young, But Not Too Young) (Cullen), **Supp. IV Part 1:** 173
Loti, Pierre, **II:** 311, 325; **Supp. IV Part 1:** 81
"Lot of People Bathing in a Stream, A" (Stevens), **IV:** 93
Lotringer, Sylvère, **Supp. XII:** 4
"Lot's Wife" (Nemerov), **III:** 270
"Lottery, The" (Jackson), **Supp. IX:** 113, 114, 118, 120, **122–123**
Lottery, The; or, The Adventures of James Harris (Jackson), **Supp. IX:** 113, 115, 116, 124, 125
Lotze, Hermann, **III:** 600
Loud and Clear (Quindlen), **Supp. XVII:** 167, **170–172**
Louganis, Greg, **Supp. XX: 264**
"Louie, His Cousin & His Other Cousin" (Cisneros), **Supp. VII:** 60
Louis, Joe, **II:** 589; **Supp. IV Part 1:** 360
Louis, Pierre Charles Alexandre, **Supp. I Part 1:** 302, 303
"Louisa, Please Come Home" (Jackson), **Supp. IX:** 122
Louis Lambert (Balzac), **I:** 499
"Louis Simpson and Walt Whitman: Destroying the Teacher" (Lazer), **Supp. IX:** 265
"Louis Zukofsky: *All: The Collected Short Poems, 1923–1958*" (Creeley), **Supp. IV Part 1:** 154
"Lounge" (Francis), **Supp. IX:** 83
Lounsberry, Barbara, **Supp. XVII:** 208
Lounsbury, Thomas R., **I:** 335
Louter, Jan, **Supp. XI:** 173
"Love" (Collins), **Supp. XXI:** 61
"Love," (Gibran), **Supp. XX: 119**
"Love" (Olson), **Supp. II Part 2:** 571
"Love" (Paley), **Supp. VI:** 219, 222, 230
Love, Deborah, **Supp. V:** 208, 210
Love Alone: 18 Elegies for Rog (Monette), **Supp. X:** 146, 154
Love Always (Beattie), **Supp. V:** 29, 30, 35
Love among the Cannibals (Morris), **III:** 228, 230–231
"Love Among the Ruins" (Mosley), **Supp. XIII:** 247
Love and Death (film; Allen), **Supp. XV:** 2, **5–6,** 7, 11
Love and Death in the American Novel (Fiedler), **Supp. XIII:** 93, 96, **99–101,** 104
Love and Exile (Singer), **Retro. Supp. II: 302–304,** 315
Love and Fame (Berryman), **I:** 170
Love and Friendship (Bloom), **Retro. Supp. II:** 31, 33–34
Love and Glory (Parker), **Supp. XIX:** 189
"Love and How to Cure It" (Wilder), **IV:** 365
Love and Other Games of Chance (Siegel), **Supp. XXII:** 255, 256, **261–265,** 266, 267
Love and Scorn: New and Selected Poems (C. Frost), **Supp. XV:** 95, 96, 100, 103–105, 106
Love and Theft (album, Dylan), **Supp. XVIII:** 28, 31
"Love and the Hate, The" (Jeffers), **Supp. II Part 2:** 434–435
Love and the Incredibly Old Man (Siegel), **Supp. XXII: 267–268**
Love and Will (Dixon), **Supp. XII:** 148, 149
Love and Work (Price), **Supp. VI:** 261
"Love as a Great Power" (Bronk), **Supp. XXI:** 31
"Love Calls Us to the Things of This World" (Wilbur), **Supp. III Part 2:** 544, 552–553
Love Course, The (Gurney), **Supp. V:** 98
Lovecraft, H. P., **Supp. XXII:** 49
Loved One, The (film), **Supp. XI: 305–306,** 307
Loved One, The (Waugh), **Supp. XI:** 305
Love Expert, The (film; Kirkland), **Supp. XVI:** 186
Love Feast (Buechner), **Supp. XII:** 52
Love for Love (Congreve), **Supp. XVIII:** 12
"Love Fossil" (Olds), **Supp. X:** 203
Love in a Dead Language (Siegel), **Supp. XXII:** 255, **258–261,** 265–266, 267
Love in Buffalo (Gurney), **Supp. V:** 96
"Love—In Other Words" (Lee), **Supp. VIII:** 113
"Love in the Air" (Jin), **Supp. XVIII:** 93–94
"Love in the Morning" (Dubus), **Supp. VII:** 91
Love in the Ruins: The Adventures of a Bad Catholic at a Time near the End of the World (Percy), **Supp. III Part 1:** 385, 387, 393–394, 397–398
Love in the Western World (de Rougemont), **Retro. Supp. I:** 328
"Love Is a Deep and a Dark and a Lonely" (Sandburg), **III:** 595
Lovejoy, Elijah P., **Supp. I Part 2:** 588
Lovejoy, Owen R., **Supp. I Part 1:** 8
Lovejoy, Thomas, **Supp. X:** 108
Lovelace, Richard, **II:** 590
"Love Letter (Schnackenberg), **Supp. XV:** 258–259
Love Letters (film), **Supp. IV Part 2:** 524
Love Letters (Gurney), **Supp. V:** 105, 108–109
Love Letters, The (Massie), **Supp. IV Part 2:** 524
Love Letters and Two Other Plays: The Golden Age and *What I Did Last Summer* (Gurney), **Supp. V:** 100
"Love Lies Sleeping" (Bishop), **Retro. Supp. II:** 42
Love Life (Mason), **Supp. VIII:** 145–146
"Love Life" (Mason), **Supp. VIII: 145–146**
Lovell, Julia, **Supp. XVIII:** 101
Lovely Bones, The (Sebold), **Supp. XXII:** 55
Lovely Lady, The (Lawrence), **Retro. Supp. I:** 203
"Lovely Lady, The" (Lawrence), **Supp. I Part 1:** 329
Love Me (Keillor), **Supp. XVI:** 178
Love Medicine (expanded version) (Erdrich), **Supp. IV Part 1:** 263, 273, 274, 275
Love Medicine (Erdrich), **Supp. IV Part 1:** 259, 260, 261, 263, 265, 266, 267–268, 270, 271, 274–275; **Supp. X:** 290
"Love Minus Zero/No Limit" (song, Dylan), **Supp. XVIII:** 31
"Love Nest, The" (Lardner), **II:** 427, 429

Love Nest, The, and Other Stories (Lardner), **II:** 430–431, 436
Lovenheim, Barbara, **Supp. X:** 169
"Love of Annunziata, The" (di Donato), **Supp. XX: 40**
"Love of Elsie Barton: A Chronicle, The" (Warren), **IV:** 253
Love of Landry, The (Dunbar), **Supp. II Part 1:** 212
"Love of Morning, The" (Levertov), **Supp. III Part 1:** 284
Love of the Last Tycoon, The: A Western. *See Last Tycoon, The*
"Love on the Bon Dieu" (Chopin), **Supp. I Part 1:** 213
Love Poems (Sexton), **Supp. II Part 2:** 687–689
Love Poems of May Swenson, The (Swenson), **Supp. IV Part 2:** 652, 653
"Love Poet" (Agee), **I:** 28
"Lover" (Hoffman), **Supp. XVIII:** 87
"Love Ritual" (Mora), **Supp. XIII:** 215
Loveroot (Jong), **Supp. V:** 115, 130
"Lovers, The" (Berryman), **I:** 174
"Lovers, The" (Buck), **Supp. II Part 1:** 128
"Lover's Garden, A" (Ginsberg), **Supp. II Part 1:** 311
"Lovers of the Poor, The" (Brooks), **Supp. III Part 1:** 81, 85
Lovers Should Marry (Martin), **Supp. IV Part 1:** 351
"Lover's Song" (Yeats), **Supp. I Part 1:** 80
"Love Rushes By" (Salinas), **Supp. XIII:** 326–327
"Love's Ghost" (Nelson), **Supp. XVIII:** 176
Lovesick (Stern), **Supp. IX: 295–296**
Love's Labour's Lost (Shakespeare), **III:** 263
Love's Old Sweet Song (Saroyan), **Supp. IV Part 1:** 83
"Love Song During Riot with Many Voices" (Hull), **Supp. XXI:** 136
"Love Song of J. Alfred Prufrock, The" (T. S. Eliot), **I:** 52, 66, 569–570; **III:** 460; **Retro. Supp. I:** 55, 56, 57, 60; **Supp. II Part 1:** 5; **Supp. XIII:** 346; **Supp. XVI:** 150
"Love Song of St. Sebastian" (Eliot), **Retro. Supp. I:** 57
"Love Songs" (Loy), **Supp. XXII:** 161
"Love Songs to Joannes" (Loy), **Supp. XXII:** 161, 163
Love's Pilgrimage (Sinclair), **Supp. V:** 286
"Love the Wild Swan" (Jeffers), **Supp. VIII:** 33
Love to Mamá: A Tribute to Mothers (Mora, ed.), **Supp. XIII:** 221
Lovett, Robert Morss, **II:** 43
"Love-Unknown" (Herbert), **Supp. I Part 1:** 80
Love! Valor! Compassion! (film), **Supp. XIII:** 206
Love! Valour! Compassion! (McNally), **Supp. XIII:** 199, **203–204,** 208, 209
"Love *versus* Law" (Stowe), **Supp. I Part 2:** 585–586
"Love Wall" (Peacock), **Supp. XIX:** 200
Love with a Few Hairs (Mrabet), **Supp. IV Part 1:** 92
Loving a Woman in Two Worlds (R. Bly), **Supp. IV Part 1:** 66, 67, 68–69, 71, 72
"Loving on Borrowed Time" (J. W. Miller), **Supp. XX: 164**
"Loving Shepherdess, The" (Jeffers), **Supp. II Part 2:** 432
"Loving the Killer" (Sexton), **Supp. II Part 2:** 688
"Loving Wife" (C. Miller), **Supp. XXII:** 196–197, 199
Lovin' Molly (film), **Supp. V:** 223, 226
Low Country (Siddons), **Supp. XXII:** 239
Lowe, John, **Supp. XIII:** 238
Lowe, Pardee, **Supp. X:** 291
Lowell, Abbott Lawrence, **I:** 487; **II:** 513; **Supp. I Part 2:** 483
Lowell, Amy, **I:** 231, 384, 405, 475, 487; **II:** 174, **511–533,** 534; **III:** 465, 581, 586; **Retro. Supp. I:** 131, 133, 288; **Retro. Supp. II:** 46, 175; **Supp. I Part 1:** 257–259, 261–263, 265, 266; **Supp. I Part 2:** 465, 466, 707, 714, 729; **Supp. XIV:** 128; **Supp. XV:** 43, 293, 295, 297, 298, 299, 300, 301, 303, 306; **Supp. XX: 69; Supp. XXII:** 161
Lowell, Blanche, **Supp. I Part 2:** 409
Lowell, Harriet, **II:** 553, 554
Lowell, James Russell, **I:** 216, 458; **II:** 273, 274, 289, 302, 320, 402, 529, 530, 532, 534, 551; **III:** 409; **IV:** 129, 171, 175, 180, 182–183, 186; **Retro. Supp. I:** 228; **Retro. Supp. II:** 155, 175, 326; **Supp. I Part 1:** 168, 299, 300, 303, 306, 311, 312, 317, 318, 362; **Supp. I Part 2: 404–426; Supp. II Part 1:** 197, 291, 352; **Supp. XV:** 278, 279; **Supp. XVI:** 84; **Supp. XVIII:** 2–3, 4, 8, 12
Lowell, Mrs. James Russell (Maria White), **Supp. I Part 2:** 405, 406, 414, 424
Lowell, Percival, **II:** 513, 525, 534
Lowell, Robert, **I:** 172, 381, 382, 400, 442, 521, 544–545, 550; **II:** 371, 376, 377, 384, 386–387, 532, **534–557; III:** 39, 44, 142, 508, 527, 528–529, 606; **IV:** 120, 138, 402, 430; **Retro. Supp. I:** 67, 140, 411; **Retro. Supp. II:** 27, 40, 44, 46, 48, 50, **175–193,** 221, 228–229, 235, 245; **Supp. I Part 1:** 89; **Supp. I Part 2:** 538, 543, 554; **Supp. III Part 1:** 6, 64, 84, 138, 147, 193, 194, 197–202, 205–208; **Supp. III Part 2:** 541, 543, 555, 561, 599; **Supp. IV Part 2:** 439, 620, 637; **Supp. V:** 81, 179, 180, 315–316, 337, 344; **Supp. VIII:** 27, 100, 271; **Supp. IX:** 325; **Supp. X:** 53, 58; **Supp. XI:** 146, 240, 244, 250, 317; **Supp. XII:** 253–254, 255; **Supp. XIII:** 76; **Supp. XIV:** 15, 126, 269; **Supp. XV:** 20, 22, 93, 184, 249, 251, 253, 340; **Supp. XVII:** 239; **Supp. XIX:** 197; **Supp. XX: 199, 203; Supp. XXI:** 131
Lowell, Rose, **Supp. I Part 2:** 409
"Lowell in the Classrom" (Vendler), **Retro. Supp. II:** 191
Lowenthal, Michael, **Supp. XII:** 82
Lower Depths, The (Gorki), **III:** 402
"Lower the Standard" (Shapiro), **Supp. II Part 2:** 715
Lowes, John Livingston, **II:** 512, 516, 532; **IV:** 453, 455
Lowin, Joseph, **Supp. V:** 273
"Low-Lands" (Pynchon), **Supp. II Part 2:** 620, 624
Lowle, Percival, **Supp. I Part 2:** 404
Lownsbrough, John, **Supp. IV Part 1:** 209, 211
Lowry, Beverly, **Supp. XXI:** 48
Lowry, Malcolm, **Supp. XVII:** 135, 136
Lowth, Richard, **II:** 8
Loy, Mina, **III:** 194; **Supp. XXII: 155–170**
Loy, Myrna, **Supp. IV Part 1:** 355
"Loyal Woman's No, A" (Larcom), **Supp. XIII:** 142, 143–144
"Luani of the Jungle" (Hughes), **Supp. I Part 1:** 328
Lubbock, Percy, **I:** 504; **II:** 337; **IV:** 308, 314, 319, 322; **Retro. Supp. I:** 366, 367, 373; **Supp. VIII:** 165; **Supp. XX: 231**
Lubin, Isidor, **Supp. I Part 2:** 632
Lubow, Arthur, **Supp. VIII:** 310
Lucas, Victoria (pseudonym). *See* Plath, Sylvia
Luce, Dianne C., **Supp. VIII:** 189
Lucid, Robert F., **Retro. Supp. II:** 195, 204
"Lucid Eye in Silver Town, The" (Updike), **IV:** 218
"Lucid Walking" (A. Finch), **Supp. XVII:** 72
"Lucinda Matlock" (Masters), **Supp. I Part 2:** 461, 465
"Luck" (Dunn), **Supp. XI:** 149
Luck of Barry Lyndon, The (Thackeray), **II:** 290
"Luck of Roaring Camp, The" (Harte), **Supp. II Part 1:** 335, 344, 345–347
"Luck of the Bogans, The" (Jewett), **Retro. Supp. II:** 142
Lucky Life (Stern), **Supp. IX: 290–291**
"Lucky Lucy's Daily Dream Book" (Di Piero), **Supp. XIX:** 38–39
Lucretius, **I:** 59; **II:** 162, 163; **III:** 600, 610–611, 612; **Supp. I Part 1:** 363
Lucy (Kincaid), **Supp. VII:** 180, 185, 186, 187–188, 194
Lucy, Saint, **II:** 211
Lucy Crown (Shaw), **Supp. XIX:** 251
Lucy Gayheart (Cather), **I:** 331; **Retro. Supp. I:** 19
"Lucy Tavish's Journey" (E. Stoddard), **Supp. XV:** 286
Lucy Temple (Rowson). *See Charlotte's Daughter; or, The Three Orphans*
Ludlow, Andrea, **Supp. XVIII:** 90
Ludvigson, Susan, **Supp. IV Part 2:** 442, 446, 447, 448, 451
Lueders, Edward, **Supp. XVI:** 265
"Luggage" (Bidart), **Supp. XV:** 35

Luhan, Mabel Dodge, **Retro. Supp. I:** 7; **Supp. XV:** 46, 50. *See also* Dodge, Mabel
Lu Ji, **Supp. VIII:** 303
Luke (biblical book), **III:** 606
"Luke Havergal" (E. A. Robinson), **Supp. XVII:** 69
"Luke Havergal" (Robinson), **III:** 524
Lukeman, Gary, **Supp. XV:** 221
Luks, George, **IV:** 411; **Retro. Supp. II:** 103
"Lullaby" (Auden), **Supp. II Part 1:** 9
"Lullaby" (Bishop), **Supp. I Part 1:** 85
"Lullaby" (Everwine), **Supp. XV:** 89
"Lullaby" (Silko), **Supp. IV Part 2:** 560, 568–569
"Lullaby for Amy" (Jarmaṇ), **Supp. XVII:** 113, 121
"Lullaby of Cape Cod" (Brodsky), **Supp. VIII:** 27–28
Lullaby Raft (Nye), **Supp. XIII:** 278
Lullaby Raft (Nye, album), **Supp. XIII:** 274
Lullaby: The Comforting of Cock Robin (Snodgrass), **Supp. VI:** 324
"Lulls" (Walker), **Supp. III Part 2:** 525
"Lulu" (Wedekind), **Supp. XII:** 14
Lulu on the Bridge (film), **Supp. XII:** 21
Lulu's Library (Alcott), **Supp. I Part 1:** 43
"Lumber" (Baker), **Supp. XIII:** 55, 56
"Lumens, The" (Olds), **Supp. X:** 209
Lume Spento, A (Pound), **III:** 470
Lumet, Sidney, **Supp. IV Part 1:** 236; **Supp. IX:** 253
Luminous Debris: Reflecting on Vestige in Provence and Languedoc (Sobin), **Supp. XVI: 291–293,** 293–294
"Lumumba's Grave" (Hughes), **Supp. I Part 1:** 344
"Luna, Luna" (Mora), **Supp. XIII:** 217
Lunar Baedecker (Loy), **Supp. XXII:** 165,**Supp. XXII:** 167, 166, 168
Lunar Baedecker and Time-Tables (Loy), **Supp. XXII:** 168
Lunar Follies (Sorrentino), **Supp. XXI:** 226, 237, 238–239
Lunsford, Bascom Lamar, **Supp. XX: 163**
Lupercal (Hughes), **Retro. Supp. II:** 245; **Supp. I Part 2:** 540
Lupton, Mary Jane, **Supp. IV Part 1:** 7
Lure of the Labrador Wild, The (Wallace), **Supp. XXII:** 218
Luria, Isaac, **IV:** 7
Lurie, Alison, **Supp. X:** 166; **Supp. XVI:** 103, 111–112
Lust and Other Stories (Minot), **Supp. VI:** 205
Luster, Deborah, **Supp. XV:** 337,**Supp. XV:** 353, 348, 349, 350
Lustgarten, Edith, **III:** 107
Lustra (Pound), **Retro. Supp. I:** 289, 290
Luther, Martin, **II:** 11–12, 506; **III:** 306, 607; **IV:** 490
"Luther on Sweet Auburn" (Bambara), **Supp. XI:** 16–17
Lux, Thomas, **Supp. XI:** 270; **Supp. XIX:** 276
Luxury Girl, The (McCoy), **Supp. XIII:** 163
Lyall, Sarah, **Supp. XIII:** 247
Lycidas (Milton), **II:** 540; **IV:** 347; **Retro. Supp. I:** 60; **Retro. Supp. II:** 186; **Supp. I Part 1:** 370; **Supp. IX:** 41
Lycographia (Paullini), **Supp. XVII:** 55
"Lydia and Marian" (Rowson), **Supp. XV:** 234
Lydon, Susan, **Supp. XII:** 170
Lyell, Charles, **Supp. IX:** 180
Lyell, Frank H., **Supp. VIII:** 125
Lyford, Harry, **Supp. I Part 2:** 679
"Lying" (Wilbur), **Supp. III Part 2:** 547, 562
"Lying and Looking" (Swenson), **Supp. IV Part 2:** 652
"Lying in a Hammock at William Duffy's Farm in Pine Island, Minnesota" (Wright), **Supp. III Part 2:** 589, 599, 600
"Lying in the Pollen and Water" (C. Frost), **Supp. XV:** 96
Lying Ladies, The (Ryan as Finnegan), **Supp. XVIII: 233–235,** 237
Lyles, Lois F., **Supp. XI:** 7, 8
Lyly, John, **III:** 536; **Supp. I Part 1:** 369
Lynch, Anne, **Supp. XV:** 273
Lynch, Doris, **Supp. XVI:** 294
Lynchburg (Gander), **Supp. XV:** 340
"Lynched Man, The" (Karr), **Supp. XI:** 241
Lynchers, The (Wideman), **Supp. X:** 320
"Lynching, The" (McKay), **Supp. I Part 1:** 63
"Lynching of Jube Benson, The" (Dunbar), **Supp. II Part 1:** 214
"Lynching Song" (Hughes), **Supp. I Part 1:** 331
Lynd, Staughton, **Supp. VIII:** 240
Lynda Hull: Collected Poems (Hull), **Supp. XXI:** 129
Lynn, Kenneth, **Supp. XIII:** 96–97
Lynn, Kenneth S., **Supp. XIV:** 103
Lynn, Vera, **Supp. XI:** 304
Lyon, George Ella, **Supp. XX: 161–162**
Lyon, Kate, **I:** 409; **II:** 138, 143, 144
Lyon, Thomas, **Supp. IX:** 175
"Lyonnesse" (Plath), **Supp. I Part 2:** 541
Lyons, Bonnie, **Supp. V:** 58; **Supp. VIII:** 138
Lyotard, Jean-François, **Supp. IV Part 1:** 54
Lyrical Ballads (Wordsworth), **III:** 583; **IV:** 120; **Supp. IX:** 274; **Supp. XI:** 243; **Supp. XV:** 21; **Supp. XIX:** 1
Lyrics of Love and Laughter (Dunbar), **Supp. II Part 1:** 207
Lyrics of Lowly Life (Dunbar), **Supp. II Part 1:** 197, 199, 200, 207
Lyrics of the Hearthside (Dunbar), **Supp. II Part 1:** 206
Lytal, Tammy, **Supp. XI:** 102
Lytle, Andrew, **IV:** 125; **Retro. Supp. II:** 220, 221, 235; **Supp. II Part 1:** 139; **Supp. X:** 1, 25; **Supp. XI:** 101
Lyttelton, Alfred, **Supp. XX: 230**
Lytton of Knebworth. *See* Bulwer-Lytton, Edward George

Mabie, Hamilton W., **Supp. XVIII:** 257
MCabe, Susan, **Supp. XXII:** 234
McAlexander, Hubert H., **Supp. V:** 314, 319, 320, 323
McAlmon, Robert, **IV:** 404; **Retro. Supp. I:** 418, 419, 420; **Retro. Supp. II:** 328; **Supp. I Part 1:** 259; **Supp. III Part 2:** 614; **Supp. XXII:** 166, 215
McAlmon, Mrs. Robert (Winifred Ellerman), **III:** 194. *See also* Ellerman, Winifred
McAninch, Jerry, **Supp. XI:** 297, 298
Macaulay, Catherine, **Supp. I Part 2:** 522
Macaulay, Rose, **Supp. XII:** 88; **Supp. XIV:** 348
Macaulay, Thomas, **II:** 15–16; **III:** 113, 591–592
Macauley, Robie, **Retro. Supp. II:** 228; **Supp. X:** 56
Macbeth (Shakespeare), **I:** 271; **IV:** 227; **Retro. Supp. I:** 131; **Supp. I Part 1:** 67; **Supp. I Part 2:** 457; **Supp. IV Part 1:** 87; **Supp. XIV:** 8
Macbeth (silent film), **Supp. XVI:** 184
MacBeth, George, **Retro. Supp. II:** 250
MacBride, Roger, **Supp. XXII:** 297, 301
McCafferty, Larry, **Supp. XVII:** 227
McCaffery, Larry, **Supp. IV Part 1:** 217, 227, 234; **Supp. V:** 53, 238; **Supp. VIII:** 13, 14; **Supp. X:** 260, 268, 301, 303, 307; **Supp. XVI:** 117; **Supp. XXII:** 177
McCann, Jannet, **Supp. XXI:** 92
McCarriston, Linda, **Supp. X:** 204; **Supp. XIV: 259–275**
McCarthy, Charles Joseph, Jr. *See* McCarthy, Cormac
McCarthy, Cormac, **Supp. VIII: 175–192; Supp. XII:** 310; **Supp. XVII:** 185; **Supp. XXI:** 38, 40; **Supp. XXII:** 49
McCarthy, Eugene, **Retro. Supp. II:** 182
McCarthy, Joseph, **I:** 31, 492; **II:** 562, 568; **Supp. I Part 1:** 294, 295; **Supp. I Part 2:** 444, 611, 612, 620; **Supp. XV:** 198, 311–312
McCarthy, Mary, **II: 558–584; Supp. I Part 1:** 84; **Supp. IV Part 1:** 209, 297, 310; **Supp. VIII:** 96, 99, 100; **Supp. X:** 177; **Supp. XI:** 246; **Supp. XIV:** 3; **Supp. XV:** 142; **Supp. XVI:** 64, 70; **Supp. XVII:** 43
McCay, Maura, **Supp. XII:** 271, 276
McClanahan, Ed, **Supp. X:** 24
McClanahan, Thomas, **Supp. XII:** 125–126
McClatchy, J. D., **Supp. XII: 253–270; Supp. XV:** 185, 257, 258
McClellan, John L., **I:** 493
McClung, Isabelle, **Retro. Supp. I:** 5
McClure, John, **Retro. Supp. I:** 80
McClure, Michael, **Supp. II Part 1:** 32; **Supp. VIII:** 289; **Supp. XVI:** 283
McClure, S. S., **I:** 313; **II:** 465; **III:** 327; **Retro. Supp. I:** 5, 6, 9; **Supp. XV:** 40
McCluskey, John, Jr., **Supp. XIX:** 65, 68, 71, 72, 78
McCombs, Judith, **Supp. XIII:** 33
McConagha, Alan, **Supp. XVI:** 166
McConnell, Frank, **Supp. X:** 260, 274

McCorkle, Jill, **Supp. X:** 6; **Supp. XVIII:** 195
McCourt, Frank, **Supp. XII: 271–287**
McCoy, Horace, **Supp. XIII: 159–177**
McCracken, Elizabeth, **Supp. X:** 86; **Supp. XII:** 310, 315–316, 321
McCrae, Fiona, **Supp. XVIII:** 60, 62
McCullers, Carson, **I:** 113, 190, 211; **II: 585–608; IV:** 282, 384, 385, 386; **Retro. Supp. II:** 324; **Supp. II Part 1:** 17; **Supp. IV Part 1:** 31, 84; **Supp. IV Part 2:** 502; **Supp. VIII:** 124; **Supp. XII:** 309; **Supp. XIV:** 120; **Supp. XV:** 338
McCullers, Reeves, **III:** 585, 586, 587
McDavid, Raven I., **III:** 120; **Supp. XIV:** 14
McDermott, Alice, **Supp. XII:** 311; **Supp. XVIII: 155–169**
McDermott, John J., **II:** 364
MacDiarmid, Hugh, **Supp. X:** 112
Macdonald, C. G., **Supp. XVII:** 73–74
Macdonald, Dwight, **I:** 233, 372, 379; **III:** 39; **Supp. V:** 265; **Supp. XIV:** 340; **Supp. XV:** 140
McDonald, E. J., **Supp. I Part 2:** 670
Macdonald, George, **Supp. XIII:** 75
MacDonald, Jeanette, **II:** 589
Macdonald, Ross, **Supp. IV Part 1:** 116, 136; **Supp. IV Part 2: 459–477; Supp. XIII:** 233; **Supp. XVIII:** 137,136; **Supp. XXI:** 67
MacDonald, Ruth K., **Supp. XVI:** 102
McDonnell, Thomas P., **Supp. XX: 45**
MacDougall, Ruth Doan, **Supp. XV:** 58; **Supp. XVI:** 174
MacDowell, Edward, **I:** 228; **III:** 504, 508, 524
McDowell, Frederick P. W., **II:** 194
McDowell, Mary, **Supp. I Part 1:** 5
McDowell, Robert, **Supp. IX:** 266, 270, 276, 279
MacDowell, Robert, **Supp. XI:** 249
McDowell, Robert, **Supp. XVII:** 109, 110, 111
McDowell. Deborah, **Supp. XVIII:** 125, 129
McElderry, Margaret K., **Supp. XV:** 162
McElligot's Pool (Geisel), **Supp. XVI:** 104
McElrath, Joseph, **Supp. XIV:** 62
McElroy, Joseph, **Supp. IV Part 1:** 279, 285
McEuen, Kathryn, **II:** 20
McEwen, Arthur, **I:** 206
McFarland, Ron, **Supp. IX:** 323, 327, 328, 333
McGann, Jerome, **Retro. Supp. I:** 47
McGill, Meredith, **Supp. XVIII:** 17
McGillis, Ian, **Supp. XVIII:** 150
MacGillivray, William, **Supp. XVI:** 8
McGinity, Keren, **Supp. XX: 9**
McGovern, Edythe M., **Supp. IV Part 2:** 573, 582, 585
McGovern, George, **III:** 46
MacGowan, Christopher, **Retro. Supp. I:** 430
MacGowan, Kenneth, **III:** 387, 391
McGrath, Douglas, **Supp. XV:** 12
McGrath, Joseph, **Supp. XI:** 307, 309
McGrath, Patrick, **Supp. IX:** 113; **Supp. XXII:** 58
McGrath, Thomas, **Supp. X: 111–130**
"McGrath on McGrath" (McGrath), **Supp. X:** 119, 120
McGuane, Thomas, **Supp. V:** 53, 220; **Supp. VIII:** 39, 40, 42, 43
MacGuffin, The (Elkin), **Supp. VI: 55–56**
McGuiness, Daniel, **Supp. XV:** 261
Machado y Ruiz, Antonio, **Supp. XIII:** 315, 323
Machan, Tibor, **Supp. IV Part 2:** 528
McHaney, Pearl, **Supp. XXI:** 244, 255, 256, 257
McHaney, Thomas, **Supp. XVIII:** 199,203
Machen, Arthur, **IV:** 286
Machiavelli, Niccolò, **I:** 485; **Supp. XIX:** 34
"Machine-Gun, The" (Jarrell), **II:** 371
"Machine Song" (Anderson), **I:** 114
McHugh, Heather, **Supp. XIX:** 84
McHugh, Vincent, **Supp. XV:** 147
McInerney, Jay, **Supp. X:** 7, 166; **Supp. XI:** 65; **Supp. XII:** 81; **Supp. XVIII:** 148
"Mac in Love" (Dixon), **Supp. XII: 142**
McIntire, Holly, **Supp. V:** 338
McIntosh, Maria, **Retro. Supp. I:** 246
Mack, Maynard, **Supp. XIV:** 12
Mackail, John William, **Supp. I Part 1:** 268; **Supp. I Part 2:** 461
McKay, Claude, **Supp. I Part 1:** 63; **Supp. III Part 1:** 75, 76; **Supp. IV Part 1:** 3, 79, 164; **Supp. IX:** 306; **Supp. X: 131–144; Supp. XI:** 91; **Supp. XVII:** 74; **Supp. XVIII:** 122, 127, 280, 282; **Supp. XIX:** 73; **Supp. XX: 69; Supp. XXII:** 275
McKay, Donald, **Supp. I Part 2:** 482
McKay, Nellie Y., **Supp. XX: 105**
McKee, Elizabeth, **Retro. Supp. II:** 221, 222
McKee, Ellen, **Retro. Supp. II:** 67
McKenney, Eileen, **IV:** 288; **Retro. Supp. II:** 321, 330
McKenney, Ruth, **IV:** 288; **Retro. Supp. II:** 321; **Supp. XVIII:** 238
MacKenzie, Agnes, **I:** 199
Mackenzie, Captain Alexander, **III:** 94
Mackenzie, Compton, **II:** 82; **Retro. Supp. I:** 100, 102
McKenzie, Geraldine, **Supp. XII:** 107
MacKenzie, Margaret, **I:** 199
Mackey, Louis, **Supp. XXI:** 236, 237
McKibben, Bill, **Supp. XVIII:** 192
McKinley, William, **I:** 474; **III:** 506; **Supp. I Part 2:** 395–396, 707
MacKinnon, Catharine, **Supp. XII:** 6
McKnight, Reginald, **Supp. XX: 147–159**
MacLachlan, Suzanne L., **Supp. XII:** 300,**Supp. XII:** 299
McLaverty, Michael, **Supp. X:** 67
McLay, Catherine, **Supp. XIII:** 21
Maclean, Alasdair, **Supp. V:** 244
McLean, Carolyn (pseudonym). *See* Bly, Carol
Maclean, Norman, **Supp. XIV: 221–237; Supp. XVI:** 98
MacLeish, Archibald, **I:** 283, 293, 429; **II:** 165, 228; **III: 1–25,** 427; **Supp. I Part 1:** 261; **Supp. I Part 2:** 654; **Supp. IV Part 1:** 359; **Supp. IV Part 2:** 586; **Supp. X:** 120; **Supp. XIV:** 11
MacLeish, Mrs. Archibald (Ada Hitchcock), **III:** 1
MacLeish, Kenneth, **III:** 1
McLennan, Gordon Lawson, **Supp. IX:** 89
McLeod, A. W., **Supp. I Part 1:** 257
McLuhan, Marshall, **Supp. IV Part 2:** 474
McLure, Michael, **Supp. XIV:** 150
Macmahon, Arthur, **I:** 226
McMahon, Helen, **Supp. IV Part 2:** 579
McMichael, Barbara Lloyd, **Supp. XXII:** 206, 207, 215, 216
McMichael, George, **Supp. VIII:** 124
McMichael, Morton, **Supp. I Part 2:** 707
McMichaels, James, **Supp. XIII:** 114
McMillan, James B., **Supp. VIII:** 124
McMillan, Terry, **Supp. XIII: 179–193**
McMullan, Jim, **Supp. XIV:** 124
McMurtry, Josephine, **Supp. V:** 220
McMurtry, Larry, **Supp. V: 219–235; Supp. X:** 24; **Supp. XI:** 172
McNally, Terrence, **Supp. XIII: 195–211**
McNally, T. M., **Supp. XX: 92**
McNamee, Thomas, **Supp. XXII:** 218
McNamer, Deirdre, **Supp. XI:** 190
McNeese, Gretchen, **Supp. V:** 123
MacNeice, Louis, **II:** 586; **III:** 527; **Supp. II Part 1:** 17, 24; **Supp. IV Part 2:** 440; **Supp. X:** 116; **Supp. XIII:** 347
McNeil, Claudia, **Supp. IV Part 1:** 360, 362
M-a-c-n-o-l-i-a (Jordan), **Supp. XVIII:** 172
McPhee, John, **Supp. III Part 1: 289–316; Supp. X:** 29, 30; **Supp. XVIII:** 106–107, 114
MacPherson, Aimee Semple, **Supp. V:** 278
McPherson, Dolly, **Supp. IV Part 1:** 2, 3, 4, 6, 8, 11, 12
McPherson, James Alan, **Supp. XXII:** 141
McPherson, James Allen, **Retro. Supp. II:** 126
Macpherson, Jay, **Supp. XIII:** 19
MacPherson, Kenneth, **Supp. I Part 1:** 259
McPhillips, Robert, **Supp. XV:** 119, 250, 251, 252, 264, 266
McQuade, Molly, **Supp. VIII:** 277, 281; **Supp. IX:** 151, 163; **Supp. XX: 90**
McQueen, Steve, **Supp. XI:** 306
Macrae, John, **I:** 252–253
McRobbie, Angela, **Supp. IV Part 2:** 691
MacShane, Frank, **Supp. IV Part 2:** 557; **Supp. XI:** 214, 216
"MacSwiggen" (Freneau), **Supp. II Part 1:** 259
McTaggart, John, **I:** 59
McTeague (Norris), **III:** 314, 315, 316–320, 322, 325, 327–328, 330, 331, 333, 335; **Retro. Supp. II:** 96; **Supp. IX:** 332

McWilliams, Carey, **Supp. XI:** 169
Madama Butterfly (opera, Puccini), **III:** 139; **Supp. XXI:** 150, 155
"Madam and the Minister" (Hughes), **Supp. I Part 1:** 335
"Madam and the Wrong Visitor" (Hughes), **Supp. I Part 1:** 335
"Madame and Ahmad" (Bowles), **Supp. IV Part 1:** 93
"Madame Bai and the Taking of Stone Mountain" (Bambara), **Supp. XI:** 14–15
Madame Bovary (Flaubert), **II:** 185; **Retro. Supp. I:** 225; **Retro. Supp. II:** 70; **Supp. XI:** 334; **Supp. XX: 58**
"Madame Célestin's Divorce" (Chopin), **Supp. I Part 1:** 213
Madame Curie (film), **Retro. Supp. I:** 113
"Madame de Mauves" (James), **II:** 327; **Retro. Supp. I:** 218, 220
Madame de Treymes (Wharton), **IV:** 314, 323; **Retro. Supp. I:** 376
"Madame Rose Hanie" (Gibran), **Supp. XX: 124**
"Madam's Calling Cards" (Hughes), **Retro. Supp. I:** 206
Madden, David, **Supp. IV Part 1:** 285
Maddern, Bessie. *See* London, Mrs. Jack (Bessie Maddern)
Mad Dog Black Lady (Coleman), **Supp. XI: 85–89,** 90
Mad Dog Blues (Shepard), **Supp. III Part 2:** 437, 438, 441
Maddox, Lucy, **Supp. IV Part 1:** 323, 325
Mad Ducks and Bears: Football Revisited (Plimpton), **Supp. XVI:** 243
Mademoiselle Coeur-Brisé (Sibon, trans.), **IV:** 288
Mademoiselle de Maupin (Gautier), **Supp. I Part 1:** 277
"Mad Farmer, Flying the Flag of Rough Branch, Secedes from the Union, The" (Berry), **Supp. X:** 35
"Mad Farmer Manifesto, The: The First Amendment" (Berry), **Supp. X:** 35
"Mad Farmer's Love Song, The" (Berry), **Supp. X:** 35
Madheart (Baraka), **Supp. II Part 1:** 47
Madhouse, The (Farrell), **II:** 41
Madhubuti, Haki R. (Don L. Lee), **Supp. II Part 1:** 34, 247; **Supp. IV Part 1:** 244
Madison, Dolley, **II:** 303
Madison, James, **I:** 1, 2, 6–9; **II:** 301; **Supp. I Part 2:** 509, 524
"Madison Smartt Bell: *The Year of Silence*" (Garrett), **Supp. X:** 7
Mad Love (film, Freund), **Supp. XVII:** 58
"Madman, A" (Updike), **Retro. Supp. I:** 320
Madman, The: His Parables and Poems (Gibran), **Supp. XX: 115, 118, 125**
"Madman's Song" (Wylie), **Supp. I Part 2:** 711, 729
Madonick, Michael, **Supp. XVII:** 123
"Madonna" (Lowell), **II:** 535–536
"Madonna of the Evening Flowers" (Lowell), **II:** 524
"Madonna of the Future, The" (James), **Retro. Supp. I:** 219
"Mad Song" (Gioia), **Supp. XV:** 128
Madwoman in the Attic, The (Gilbert and Gubar), **Retro. Supp. I:** 42; **Supp. IX:** 66
"Maelzel's Chess-Player" (Poe), **III:** 419, 420
"Maestria" (Nemerov), **III:** 275, 278–279
Maeterlinck, Maurice, **I:** 91, 220; **Supp. XX: 115, 116**
"Magazine-Writing Peter Snook" (Poe), **III:** 421
Magdeburg Centuries (Flacius), **IV:** 163
Magellan, Ferdinand, **Supp. I Part 2:** 497
Maggie: A Girl of the Streets (S. Crane), **I:** 407, 408, 410–411, 416; **IV:** 208; **Retro. Supp. II:** 97, 107; **Supp. XVII:** 228
Maggie Cassidy (Kerouac), **Supp. III Part 1:** 220–221, 225, 227, 229, 232
"Maggie of the Green Bottles" (Bambara), **Supp. XI:** 2–3
"Maggie's Farm" (song, Dylan), **Supp. XVIII:** 25, 26
"Magi" (Plath), **Supp. I Part 2:** 544–545
"Magi, The" (Garrett), **Supp. VII:** 97
"Magic" (Pickering), **Supp. XXI:** 202
"Magic" (Porter), **III:** 434, 435
"Magical Thinking" (Hull), **Supp. XXI:** 137, 139
Magic Barrel, The (Malamud), **Supp. I Part 2:** 427, 428, 430–434
"Magic Barrel, The" (Malamud), **Supp. I Part 2:** 427, 428, 431, 432–433
Magic Christian, The (film), **Supp. XI:** 309
Magic Christian, The (Southern), **Supp. XI:** 297, **299–301,** 309
Magic City (Komunyakaa), **Supp. XIII: 125–127,** 128, 131
"Magic Flute, The" (Epstein), **Supp. XII:** 165
Magic Flute, The (Mozart), **III:** 164
Magician of Lublin, The (Singer), **IV:** 6, 9–10; **Retro. Supp. II: 308–309**
Magician's Assistant, The (Patchett), **Supp. XII:** 307, 310, **317–320,** 322
"Magician's Wife, The" (Gordon), **Supp. IV Part 1:** 306
Magic Journey, The (Nichols), **Supp. XIII:** 266–267
Magic Keys, The (Murray), **Supp. XIX: 157–158**
Magic Kingdom, The (Elkin), **Supp. VI:** 42, **54–55,** 56, 58
"Magic Mirror, The: A Study of the Double in Two of Doestoevsky's Novels" (Plath), **Supp. I Part 2:** 536
Magic Mountain, The (Mann), **III:** 281–282; **Supp. IV Part 2:** 522; **Supp. XII:** 321; **Supp. XVII:** 137
Magic Tower, The (Willams), **IV:** 380
Magnaghi, Ambrogio, **Supp. XVI:** 286
Magnalia Christi Americana (Mather), **II:** 302; **Supp. I Part 1:** 102; **Supp. I Part 2:** 584; **Supp. II Part 2:** 441, 442, 452–455, 460, 467, 468; **Supp. IV Part 2:** 434
Magnificat (Nelson), **Supp. XVIII: 176–177**
"Magnificent Little Gift" (Salinas), **Supp. XIII:** 318
"Magnifying Mirror" (Karr), **Supp. XI:** 240
Magpie, The (Baldwin, ed.), **Supp. I Part 1:** 49
Magpie's Shadow, The (Winters), **Supp. II Part 2:** 786, 788
"Magpie's Song" (Snyder), **Supp. VIII:** 302
Magritte, René, **Supp. IV Part 2:** 623
Maguire, Roberta S., **Supp. XIX:** 160–161
Magus, The (Fowles), **Supp. XIX:** 58
Mahan, Albert Thayer, **Supp. I Part 2:** 491
Mahan, David C., **Supp. XXI:** 86
"Mahatma Joe" (Bass), **Supp. XVI:** 19
"Mahogany Tree, The" (M. F. K. Fisher), **Supp. XVII:** 88
Mahomet and His Successors (Irving), **II:** 314
Mahoney, Jeremiah, **IV:** 285
Mahoney, Lynn, **Supp. XV:** 270
"Maiden in a Tower" (Stegner), **Supp. IV Part 2:** 613
"Maiden Without Hands" (Sexton), **Supp. II Part 2:** 691
"Maid of St. Philippe, The" (Chopin), **Retro. Supp. II:** 63
"Maid's Shoes, The" (Malamud), **Supp. I Part 2:** 437
Mailer, Fanny, **III:** 28
Mailer, Isaac, **III:** 28
Mailer, Norman, **I:** 261, 292, 477; **III: 26–49,** 174; **IV:** 98, 216; **Retro. Supp. II:** 182, **195–217,** 279; **Supp. I Part 1:** 291, 294; **Supp. III Part 1:** 302; **Supp. IV Part 1:** 90, 198, 207, 236, 284, 381; **Supp. IV Part 2:** 689; **Supp. VIII:** 236; **Supp. XI:** 104, 218, 222, 229; **Supp. XIV:** 49, 53, 54, 111, 162; **Supp. XVII:** 225, 228, 236; **Supp. XVIII:** 19–20; **Supp. XX: 90**
"Maimed Man, The" (Tate), **IV:** 136
Maimonides, Moses, **Supp. XVII:** 46–47
Main Currents in American Thought: The Colonial Mind, 1625–1800 (Parrington), **I:** 517; **Supp. I Part 2:** 484
"Maine Roustabout, A" (Eberhart), **I:** 539
"Maine Speech" (White), **Supp. I Part 2:** 669–670
Maine Woods, The (Thoreau), **IV:** 188
Mains d'Orlac, Les (M. Renard), **Supp. XVII:** 58
Main Street (Lewis), **I:** 362; **II:** 271, 440, 441–442, 447, 449, 453; **III:** 394; **Supp. XIX:** 142; **Supp. XXII:** 282
"Maintenance" (Pickering), **Supp. XXI:** 204
Maitland, Margaret Todd, **Supp. XVI:** 292
Majdoubeh, Ahmad, **Supp. XX: 116**
Major, Clarence, **Supp. XXII: 171–186**

"Majorat, Das" (Hoffman), **III:** 415
Major Barbara (Shaw), **III:** 69
"Major Chord, The" (Bourne), **I:** 221
Majors and Minors (Dunbar), **Supp. II Part 1:** 197, 198
"Major's Tale, The" (Bierce), **I:** 205
Make Believe (J. Scott), **Supp. XVII: 191–192,** 193, 194, 195
Make-Believe Town: Essays and Remembrances (Mamet), **Supp. XIV:** 240, 251
Make It New (Pound), **III:** 470
Makers and Finders (Brooks), **I:** 253, 254, 255, 257, 258
Makers of the Modern World (Untermeyer), **Supp. XV:** 312
"Making a Change" (Gilman), **Supp. XI:** 207
"Making a Living" (Sexton), **Supp. II Part 2:** 695
"Making Changes" (L. Michaels), **Supp. XVI:** 204
"Making Do" (Hogan), **Supp. IV Part 1:** 406
Making Face, Making Soul: Haciendo Caras, Creative and Critical Perspectives by Feminists of Color (Anzaldúa, ed.), **Supp. IV Part 1:** 330
Making It (Podhoretz), **Supp. VIII:** 231, 232, 233, **237–238,** 239, 244
"Making Light of Auntie" (X. J. Kennedy), **Supp. XV:** 163
"Making of a Marginal Farm, The" (Berry), **Supp. X:** 22
Making of Americans, The (Stein), **IV:** 35, 37, 40–42, 45, 46; **Supp. III Part 1:** 37
"Making of Ashenden, The" (Elkin), **Supp. VI:** 49, 50
"Making of a Soldier USA, The" (Simpson), **Supp. IX:** 270
"Making of Garrison Keillor, The" (McConagha), **Supp. XVI:** 166"
Making of Modern Atlanta, The (documentary), **Supp. XXII:** 251
"Making of Paths, The" (Stegner), **Supp. IV Part 2:** 614
"Making of Poems, The" (W. J. Smith), **Supp. XIII:** 348
Making of the Modern Mind (Randall), **III:** 605
Making the Light Come: The Poetry of Gerald Stern (Somerville), **Supp. IX:** 296–297
"Making Up Stories" (Didion), **Supp. IV Part 1:** 196, 203, 205
Making Your Own Days: The Pleasures of Reading and Writing Poetry (Koch), **Supp. XV:** 188
Maladies de la volonté, Les (Ribot), **Supp. XX: 238**
Malady of the Ideal, The: Oberman, Maurice de Guérin, and Amiel (Brooks), **I:** 240, 241, 242
Malamud, Bernard, **I:** 144, 375; **II:** 424, 425; **III:** 40, 272; **IV:** 216; **Retro. Supp. II:** 22, 279, 281; **Supp. I Part 2: 427–453; Supp. IV Part 1:** 297, 382; **Supp. V:** 257, 266; **Supp. IX:** 114, 227; **Supp. XIII:** 106, 264, 265, 294; **Supp. XVI:** 220
Malamud, Mrs. Bernard (Ann de Chiara), **Supp. I Part 2:** 451
Malanga, Gerard, **Supp. III Part 2:** 629
Malaquais, Jean, **Retro. Supp. II:** 199
Malatesta, Sigismondo de, **III:** 472, 473
Malcolm (Purdy), **Supp. VII:** 270–273, 277
"Malcolm Cowley and the American Writer" (Simpson), **Supp. II Part 1:** 147
Malcolm Lowry's "Volcano": Myth Symbol Meaning (Markson), **Supp. XVII:** 142, 144
"MALCOLM REMEMBERED (FEB. 77)" (Baraka), **Supp. II Part 1:** 60
Malcolm X, **Retro. Supp. II:** 12, 13; **Supp. I Part 1:** 52, 63, 65, 66; **Supp. IV Part 1:** 2, 10; **Supp. VIII:** 330, 345; **Supp. X:** 240; **Supp. XIV:** 306
Malcolm X (film), **Retro. Supp. II:** 12
"Maldrove" (Jeffers), **Supp. II Part 2:** 418
Male, Roy, **II:** 239
Male Animal, The (Thurber), **Supp. I Part 2:** 605, 606, 610–611
"Malediction upon Myself" (Wylie), **Supp. I Part 2:** 722
Malefactors, The (Gordon), **II:** 186, 199, 213–216; **IV:** 139
"Malest Cornifici Tuo Catullo" (Ginsberg), **Supp. II Part 1:** 315
Malick, Terrence, **Supp. XI:** 234; **Supp. XV:** 351
Malin, Irving, **I:** 147; **Supp. XVI:** 71–72
"Malinche's Tips: Pique from Mexico's Mother" (Mora), **Supp. XIII:** 223
"Malinke's Atonement" (Antin), **Supp. XX: 10**
"Mallard" (C. Frost), **Supp. XV:** 98, 99
Mallarmé, Stéphane, **I:** 66, 569; **II:** 529, 543; **III:** 8, 409, 428; **IV:** 80, 86; **Retro. Supp. I:** 56; **Supp. I Part 1:** 261; **Supp. II Part 1:** 1; **Supp. III Part 1:** 319–320; **Supp. III Part 2:** 630; **Supp. XIII:** 114; **Supp. XV:** 158; **Supp. XVI:** 282, 285
Mallia, Joseph, **Supp. XII:** 26, 29, 37
Mallon, Anne-Marie, **Supp. XXI:** 215
Mallon, Thomas, **Supp. IV Part 1:** 200, 209; **Supp. XIX: 131–145**
Maloff, Saul, **Supp. VIII:** 238
Malory, Thomas, **II:** 302; **III:** 486; **IV:** 50, 61; **Supp. IV Part 1:** 47
"Mal Paso Bridge" (Jeffers), **Supp. II Part 2:** 415, 420
Malraux, André, **I:** 33–34, 127, 509; **II:** 57, 376; **III:** 35, 310; **IV:** 236, 247, 434; **Retro. Supp. I:** 73; **Retro. Supp. II:** 115–116, 119; **Supp. II Part 1:** 221, 232; **Supp. XIX:** 157
Maltese Falcon, The (film), **Supp. IV Part 1:** 342, 353, 355
Maltese Falcon, The (Hammett), **IV:** 286; **Supp. IV Part 1:** 345, 348–351
Mama (McMillan), **Supp. XIII:** 182, **187–188**
"Mama and Daughter" (Hughes), **Supp. I Part 1:** 334
Mama Day (Naylor), **Supp. VIII: 223–226,** 230
"Mama I Remember" (Nelson), **Supp. XVIII:** 173
Mama Poc: An Ecologist's Account of the Extinction of a Species (LaBastille), **Supp. X:** 99, **104–105,** 106
Mama's Bank Account (K. Forbes), **Supp. XVII:** 9
Mama's Promises (Nelson), **Supp. XVIII: 173–174**
"Mama Still Loves You" (Naylor), **Supp. VIII:** 214
Mambo Hips and Make Believe (Coleman), **Supp. XI: 94–96**
Mambo Kings, The (film), **Supp. VIII:** 73, 74
Mambo Kings Play Songs of Love, The (Hijuelos), **Supp. VIII:** 73–74, **79–82**
"Ma'me Pélagie" (Chopin), **Retro. Supp. II:** 64
Mamet, David, **Supp. XIV: 239–258,** 315
"Mamie" (Sandburg), **III:** 582
Mammedaty, Novarro Scott. *See* Momaday, N. Scott
"Mammon and the Archer" (O. Henry), **Supp. II Part 1:** 394, 408
Mammonart (Sinclair), **Supp. V:** 276–277
"Mammy" (D. West), **Supp. XVIII:** 283
"Mamouche" (Chopin), **Retro. Supp. II:** 66
Mamoulian, Rouben, **Supp. XVIII:** 281
"Man" (Corso), **Supp. XII:** 130
"Man" (Herbert), **II:** 12
"Man Against the Sky, The" (Robinson), **III:** 509, 523
"Man and a Woman Sit Near Each Other, A" (R. Bly), **Supp. IV Part 1:** 71
Man and Boy (Morris), **III:** 223, 224, 225
"Man and the Snake, The" (Bierce), **I:** 203
"Man and Woman" (Caldwell), **I:** 310
Manassas (Sinclair), **Supp. V:** 280, 281, 285
"Man Bring This Up Road" (T. Williams), **IV:** 383–384
"Man Carrying Thing" (Stevens), **IV:** 90
Manchester, William, **III:** 103
"Man Child, The" (Baldwin), **Supp. I Part 1:** 63
Man Could Stand Up, A (Ford), **I:** 423
"Mandarin's Jade" (Chandler), **Supp. IV Part 1:** 125
Mandel, Charlotte, **Supp. XVI:** 57
Mandelbaum, Maurice, **I:** 61
Mandelstam, Osip, **Retro. Supp. I:** 278; **Supp. III Part 1:** 268; **Supp. VIII:** 21, 22, 23, 27; **Supp. XIII:** 77; **Supp. XV:** 254, 261, 263
"Mandelstam: The Poem as Event" (Dobyns), **Supp. XIII:** 78
"Mandolin" (Dove), **Supp. IV Part 1:** 247
"Mandoline" (Verlaine), **IV:** 79
"Man Eating" (Kenyon), **Supp. VII:** 173
"Manet in Late Summer" (Skloot), **Supp. XX: 201**

"Man Feeding Pigeons" (Clampitt), **Supp. IX: 49–50,** 52
Manfred, Frederick, **Supp. X:** 126
Man From Limbo, The (Endore), **Supp. XVII:** 55
"Mango Says Goodbye Sometimes" (Cisneros), **Supp. VII:** 64
Manhattan (film; Allen), **Supp. IV Part 1:** 205; **Supp. XV:** 5, **7–8,** 13
"Manhattan Dawn" (Justice), **Supp. VII:** 117
"Manhattan: Luminism" (Doty), **Supp. XI:** 135
Manhattan Murder Mystery (film; Allen), **Supp. XV:** 5, 11
Manhattan Transfer (Dos Passos), **I:** 26, 475, 478, 479, 480, 481, 482–484, 487; **II:** 286; **Supp. I Part 1:** 57
"Mania" (Lowell), **II:** 554
"Manic in the Moon, The" (Thurber), **Supp. I Part 2:** 620
Manifest; and Furthermore (Bronk), **Supp. XXI:** 32
"Manifesto: A Press Release from PRKA" (Saunders), **Supp. XIX:** 235
Manikin, The (J. Scott), **Supp. XVII: 189–191,** 192, 194
"Man in Black" (Plath), **Supp. I Part 2:** 538
Man in Prehistory (Chard), **Supp. XII:** 177–178
Man in the Black Coat Turns, The (R. Bly), **Supp. IV Part 1:** 66–68, 71, 73
"Man in the Brooks Brothers Shirt, The" (McCarthy), **II:** 563–564
"Man in the Drawer, The" (Malamud), **Supp. I Part 2:** 437
Man in the Flying Lawn Chair and Other Excursions and Observations, The (Plimpton), **Supp. XVI:** 234
Man in the Gray Flannel Suit, The (Wilson), **Supp. IV Part 1:** 387
Man in the High Castle, The (Dick), **Supp. XVIII:** 138
Man in the Middle, The (Wagoner), **Supp. IX:** 324, **332–333**
"Man in the Rain, The" (Ryan as Quin), **Supp. XVIII:** 226
"Man in the Toolhouse, The" (Swados), **Supp. XIX:** 263
Mankiewicz, Herman, **Supp. XVI:** 189
Mankiewicz, Joseph, **Retro. Supp. I:** 113
Mankowitz, Wolf, **Supp. XI:** 307
"Man Made of Words, The" (Momaday), **Supp. IV Part 2:** 481, 484–485, 486, 487, 488
Man-Made World, The (Gilman), **Supp. XI:** 207
"Man-Moth, The" (Bishop), **Retro. Supp. II:** 42; **Supp. I Part 1:** 85–87, 88
Mann, Charles, **Retro. Supp. II:** 40
Mann, Erika, **Supp. II Part 1:** 11
Mann, Seymour (Samuel Weisman), **Supp. V:** 113
Mann, Thomas, **I:** 271, 490; **II:** 42, 539; **III:** 231, 281–282, 283; **IV:** 70, 73, 85; **Supp. IV Part 1:** 392; **Supp. IV Part 2:** 522; **Supp. V:** 51; **Supp. IX:** 21; **Supp. XI:** 275; **Supp. XII:** 173, 310, 321; **Supp. XIV:** 87; **Supp. XVII:** 137; **Supp. XIX:** 147, 151, 157; **Supp. XX: 85**
Mannequins' Demise: A Play in Eight Scenes (Budbill), **Supp. XIX: 12**
Mannerhouse (Wolfe), **IV:** 460
Manner Music, The (Reznikoff), **Supp. XIV: 293–295**
"Manners" (Bishop), **Supp. I Part 1:** 73
"Manners" (Emerson), **II:** 4, 6
"Manners, Morals, and the Novel" (Trilling), **Supp. III Part 2:** 502, 503
Mannheim, Karl, **I:** 279; **Supp. I Part 2:** 644
Manning, Ambrose, **Supp. XX: 166**
Manning, Frederic, **III:** 459
Manning, Robert, **Supp. IX:** 236
Mannix, Daniel P., **Supp. II Part 1:** 140
Man Nobody Knows, The (B. Barton), **Retro. Supp. I:** 179
Mano, D. Keith, **Supp. XVI:** 250
Mano, Guy Levis, **Supp. XVI:** 282
"Man of Indeterminate Age on a Subway Grate, A" (DI Piero), **Supp. XIX:** 47
"Man of Letters" (Pickering), **Supp. XXI:** 192, 195–196
"Man of Letters as a Man of Business, The" (Howells), **Supp. XIV:** 45–46
"Man of No Account, The" (Harte), **Supp. II Part 1:** 339
"Man of the Crowd, The" (Poe), **III:** 412, 417; **Retro. Supp. I:** 154
Man on Spikes (Asinof), **II:** 424
Man on Stage (Dixon), **Supp. XII:** 141, **154–155**
"Man on the Dump, The" (Stevens), **IV:** 74; **Retro. Supp. I:** 306
"Man on the Train, The" (Percy), **Supp. III Part 1:** 387
Manor, The (Singer), **IV:** 6, 17–19
Manrique, Jorge, **Retro. Supp. II:** 154
Mansart Builds a School (Du Bois), **Supp. II Part 1:** 185–186
Man's Fate (Malraux), **I:** 127; **Retro. Supp. II:** 121
"Man's Fate A Film Treatment of the Malraux Novel" (Agee), **I:** 33–34
Mansfield, June, **Supp. X:** 183, 194
Mansfield, Katherine, **III:** 362, 453
Mansfield, Stephanie, **Supp. IV Part 1:** 227
Man's Hope (Malraux), **IV:** 247
Mansion, The (Faulkner), **II:** 73; **Retro. Supp. I:** 74, 82
Man's Nature and His Communities (Niebuhr), **III:** 308
Manson, Charles, **Supp. IV Part 1:** 205
"Man Splitting Wood in the Daybreak, The" (Kinnell), **Supp. III Part 1:** 254
"Man's Pride" (Jeffers), **Supp. II Part 2:** 417
"Man's Story, The" (Anderson), **I:** 114
Man's Woman, A (Norris), **III:** 314, 322, 328, 329, 330, 332, 333
Man That Corrupted Hadleyburg, The (Twain), **I:** 204; **IV:** 208
"Man That Was Used Up, The" (Poe), **III:** 412, 425
"Mantis" (Zukofsky), **Supp. III Part 2:** 617
"'Mantis': An Interpretation" (Zukofsky), **Supp. III Part 2:** 617–618
"Man to Know in the Restaurants, The" (Siddons), **Supp. XXII:** 244
Man to Send Rain Clouds, The (Rosen, ed.), **Supp. IV Part 2:** 499, 505, 513
"Man to Send Rain Clouds, The" (Silko), **Supp. IV Part 2:** 559
Mantrap (Lewis), **II:** 447
Manuductio Ad Ministerium (Mather), **Supp. II Part 2:** 465–467
"Manuelzinho" (Bishop), **Retro. Supp. II:** 47–48
Manuscript Books of Emily Dickinson, The (Franklin, ed.), **Retro. Supp. I:** 29, 41
"Man Waiting for It to Stop, A" (Dunn), **Supp. XI:** 144
"Man Who Became a Woman, The" (Anderson), **I:** 114
"Man Who Carries the Desert Around Inside Himself, The: For Wally" (Komunyakaa), **Supp. XIII:** 125
"Man Who Closed Shop, The" (Dunn), **Supp. XI:** 149
Man Who Gave Up His Name, The (Harrison), **Supp. VIII:** 45, 52
Man Who Had All the Luck, The (A. Miller), **III:** 148, 149, 164, 166
"Man Who Knew Belle Star, The" (Bausch), **Supp. VII:** 46
"Man Who Knew Coolidge, The" (Lewis), **II:** 449
Man Who Knew Coolidge, The: Being the Soul of Lowell Schmaltz, Constructive and Nordic Citizen (Lewis), **II:** 450
Man Who Lived Underground, The (Wright), **Supp. II Part 1:** 40
"Man Who Lived Underground, The" (Wright), **IV:** 479, 485–487, 492; **Retro. Supp. II:** 121
"Man Who Made Me Love Him, The" (Weigl), **Supp. XIX:** 278
"Man Who Makes Brooms, The" (Nye), **Supp. XIII:** 276
"Man Who Studied Yoga, The" (Mailer), **III:** 35–36; **Retro. Supp. II:** 200
"Man Who Wanted to Win, The" (McCoy), **Supp. XIII:** 161
Man Who Was There, The (Morris), **III:** 220–221
"Man Who Writes Ants, The" (Merwin), **Supp. III Part 1:** 348
"Man with a Family" (Humphrey), **Supp. IX:** 94
Man without a Country, The (Hale), **I:** 488
"Man with the Blue Guitar, The" (Stevens), **I:** 266; **IV:** 85–87; **Retro. Supp. I: 303–305,** 306, 307, 309
Man with the Blue Guitar and Other Poems, The (Stevens), **IV:** 76; **Retro. Supp. I:** 303, 422
Man with the Golden Arm, The (Algren), **Supp. V:** 4; **Supp. IX:** 1, 3, **9–11,** 14, 15
Man with the Golden Arm, The (film), **Supp. IX:** 3
"Man with the Golden Beef, The" (Podhoretz), **Supp. IX:** 3

"Man with the Hoe, The" (Markham), **Supp. XV:** 115
Many a Monster (Ryan as Finnegan), **Supp. XVIII:** 233, **236–238**
Manyan Letters (Olson), **Supp. II Part 2:** 571
Many Circles (Goldbarth), **Supp. XII:** 193
"Many Handles" (Sandburg), **III:** 594
"Many Happy Returns" (Auden), **Supp. II Part 1:** 15
Many Happy Returns (Berrigan), **Supp. XXII:** 224
Many Loves (W. C. Williams), **Retro. Supp. I:** 424
"Many Mansions" (H. Roth), **Supp. IX:** 233, 234
Many Marriages (Anderson), **I:** 104, 111, 113
"Many of Our Waters: Variations on a Poem by a Black Child" (Wright), **Supp. III Part 2:** 602
"Many Swans" (Lowell), **II:** 526
"Many Thousands Gone" (Baldwin), **Retro. Supp. II:** 4; **Supp. I Part 1:** 51
"Many Wagons Ago" (Ashbery), **Supp. III Part 1:** 22
Many-Windowed House, A (Cowley), **Supp. II Part 1:** 141, 143
"Many-Windowed House, A" (Cowley), **Supp. II Part 1:** 137
Mao II (DeLillo), **Supp. VI:** 2, 4, **5**, 6, **7**, 8, 9, 14, 16
"Map, The" (Bishop), **Retro. Supp. II:** 41; **Supp. I Part 1:** 72, 82, 85–88, 93
"Map, The" (Strand), **Supp. IV Part 2:** 623–624
"Maple Leaf, The" (Joplin), **Supp. IV Part 1:** 223
"Maple Tree, The" (D. West), **Supp. XVIII:** 284
Map of Another Town: A Memoir of Provence (M. F. K. Fisher), **Supp. XVII:** 88, 89, 92
"Map of Montana in Italy, A" (Hugo), **Supp. VI:** 139
Mapp and Lucia (Benson), **Supp. XX: 229**
Mapping American Culture (Franklin and Steiner), **Supp. XXII:** 205
"Maps" (Hass), **Supp. VI:** 103–104
Mapson, Jo-Ann, **Supp. IV Part 2:** 440, 454
Map to the Next World, A: Poems and Tales (Harjo), **Supp. XII: 228–230**
"Maquillage" (Hull), **Supp. XXI:** 133
"Mara" (Jeffers), **Supp. II Part 2:** 434
Ma Rainey's Black Bottom (Wilson), **Supp. VIII:** 331, **332–334,** 346, 349, 350
Marat, Jean Paul, **IV:** 117; **Supp. I Part 2:** 514, 515, 521
"Marathon" (Glück), **Supp. V:** 85
Marble Faun, The (Faulkner), **II:** 55, 56; **Retro. Supp. I:** 79
Marble Faun, The; or, The Romance of Monte Beni (Hawthorne), **II:** 225, 239, 242–243, 290, 324; **IV:** 167; **Retro. Supp. I:** 63, 149, 163, **164–165; Supp. I Part 1:** 38; **Supp. I Part 2:** 421, 596; **Supp. XIII:** 102
Marbles (Brodsky), **Supp. VIII:** 26–27
Marburg, Anita, **Supp. XXII:** 281
Marcaccio, Michael, **Supp. XVII:** 97, 106
"March" (W. C. Williams), **Retro. Supp. I:** 418
March, Alan, **Supp. XVI:** 242
March, Fredric, **III:** 154, 403; **IV:** 357; **Supp. X:** 220
"March, March on Down the Field" (Shaw), **Supp. XIX:** 246
Marchalonis, Shirley, **Supp. XIII:** 138, 140, 141, 143, 147–148
"Marché aux Oiseaux" (Wilbur), **Supp. III Part 2:** 550
"Märchen, The" (Jarrell), **II:** 378–379
March Hares (Frederic), **II:** 143–144
Marching Men (Anderson), **I:** 99, 101, 103–105, 111
"Marching Music" (Simic), **Supp. VIII:** 281
"Marcia" (R. H. Davis), **Supp. XVI:** 91–92
Marcks, Greg, **Supp. XVIII:** 150
Marco Millions (O'Neill), **III:** 391, 395
Marcosson, Isaac, **III:** 322
Marcus, Greil, **Supp. XVIII:** 30, 53
Marcus, Steven, **Retro. Supp. II:** 196, 200
Marcus Aurelius, **II:** 1; **III:** 566; **Supp. XVIII:** 304
Marcuse, Herbert, **Supp. I Part 2:** 645; **Supp. VIII:** 196; **Supp. XII:** 2
Mardi and a Voyage Thither (Melville), **I:** 384; **II:** 281; **III:** 77–79, 84, 87, 89; **Retro. Supp. I:** 247, 254, 256
Margaret (Judd), **II:** 290
Margaret & Dusty (Notley), **Supp. XXII:** 231
"Margaret Fuller, 1847" (Clampitt), **Supp. IX:** 43
"Marginalia" (Wilbur), **Supp. III Part 2:** 544
Margin of Hope, A: An Intellectual Autobiography (Howe), **Supp. VI:** 113–114, 117, 125, 128
"Margins of Maycomb, The: A Rereading of *To Kill a Mockingbird*" (Phelps), **Supp. VIII:** 128
Margoshes, Samuel, **Supp. X:** 70
"Margrave" (Jeffers), **Supp. II Part 2:** 426
Margret Howth (R. H. Davis), **Supp. XVI:** 81, 83, 84, **88–89**
Margret Howth: A Story of Today (J. Yellin, ed.), **Supp. XVI:** 88
Margulies, Donald, **Supp. XXI:** 145
"Maria Concepción" (Porter), **III:** 434–435, 451
Mariani, Paul L., **Retro. Supp. I:** 412, 419; **Retro. Supp. II:** 189
Marianne Moore Reader, (Moore), **III:** 199
Marie Antoinette (film), **Retro. Supp. I:** 113
Marie Blythe (Mosher), **Supp. XXII:** 206, 209, **212**
Marie Laveau (Prose), **Supp. XVI:** 251
Mariella Gable, Sister, **III:** 339, 355
"Marijuana and a Pistol" (C. Himes), **Supp. XVI:** 137
"Marijuana Notation" (Ginsberg), **Supp. II Part 1:** 313
Maril, Herman, **Supp. XXI:** 22, 23
Marilyn: A Biography (Mailer), **Retro. Supp. II:** 208
"Marin" (Cisneros), **Supp. VII:** 60, 61
Marin, Jay, **Retro. Supp. II:** 325
"Marina" (Eliot), **I:** 584, 585; **Retro. Supp. I:** 64
Mariners, Renegades, and Castaways (C. L. R. James), **Supp. XXI:** 159, 169–170
"Marine Surface, Low Overcast" (Clampitt), **Supp. IX: 47–48**
Marinetti, F. T., **Supp. XXII:** 159, 160, 161, 163
Marinetti, Tommaso, **Retro. Supp. I:** 59
Marionettes, The (Faulkner), **Retro. Supp. I:** 79
Maritain, Jacques, **I:** 402
Maritime Compact (Paine), **Supp. I Part 2:** 519
Maritime History of Massachusetts, 1783–1860, The (Morison), **Supp. I Part 2:** 481–483
Marjolin, Jean-Nicolas, **Supp. I Part 1:** 302
Marjorie Kinnan Rawlings: Sojourner at Cross Creek (Silverthorne), **Supp. X:** 220, 234
"Mark, The" (Bogan), **Supp. III Part 1:** 52
Marker, Chris, **Supp. IV Part 2:** 434, 436
"Market" (Hayden), **Supp. II Part 1:** 368, 369
Marketplace, The (Frederic), **II:** 145–146
Markham, Edwin, **I:** 199, 207; **Supp. XV:** 115
Markings (Hammarskjold), **Supp. II Part 1:** 26
Mark of the Vampire (film, Browning), **Supp. XVII:** 58
Markopoulos, Gregory, **Supp. XII:** 2
Markowick-Olczakova, Hanna, **Supp. X:** 70
Marks, Alison, **Supp. I Part 2:** 660
Marks, Barry A., **I:** 435, 438, 442, 446
Markson, David, **Supp. XVII: 135–147**
Mark Twain in Eruption (Twain), **IV:** 209
Mark Twain's America (De Voto), **I:** 248
Mark Twain's Autobiography (Twain), **IV:** 209
Marley, Bob, **Supp. IX:** 152
Marlowe, Christopher, **I:** 68, 368, 384; **II:** 590; **III:** 259, 491; **Retro. Supp. I:** 127; **Retro. Supp. II:** 76; **Supp. I Part 2:** 422; **Supp. XXI:** 227
Marlowe, Kimberly B., **Supp. XXII:** 214
"Marlowe Takes on the Syndicate" (Chandler), **Supp. IV Part 1:** 135
Marne, The (Wharton), **IV:** 319, 320; **Retro. Supp. I:** 378
Marquand, John, **Supp. XI:** 301
Marquand, Mrs. John P. (Adelaide Hooker), **III:** 57, 61

Marquand, Mrs. John P. (Christina Sedgwick), **III:** 54, 57
Marquand, J. P., **I:** 362, 375; **II:** 459, 482–483; **III: 50–73,** 383; **Supp. I Part 1:** 196; **Supp. IV Part 1:** 31; **Supp. V:** 95
Marquand, Philip, **III:** 52
Marquis, Don, **Supp. I Part 2:** 668
Marrásh, Francis al-, **Supp. XX: 117**
"Marriage" (Corso), **Supp. XII:** 117, 124, **127–128**
Marriage (Moore), **III:** 194
"Marriage" (Moore), **III:** 198–199, 213
"Marriage, A" (Untermeyer), **Supp. XV:** 305
Marriage A-la-Mode (Dryden), **Supp. IX:** 68
Marriage and Other Science Fiction (Goldbarth), **Supp. XII:** 189, 190
"Marriage in the Sixties, A" (Rich), **Supp. I Part 2:** 554
Marriage of Heaven and Hell (Blake), **Supp. XXII:** 257
"Marriage of Heaven and Hell, The" (Blake), **III:** 544–545; **Supp. VIII:** 99
"Marriage of Phaedra, The" (Cather), **Retro. Supp. I:** 5
Married (Strindberg), **Supp. XXII:** 23
"Married" (Taggard), **Supp. XXII:** 274
Married Men (Wolfert), **Supp. XXI:** 277
Marrow of Tradition, The (Chesnutt), **Supp. XIV:** 63, **71–75,** 76
Marryat, Captain Frederick, **III:** 423
"Marrying Absurd" (Didion), **Supp. IV Part 1:** 200
"Marrying Iseult?" (Updike), **Retro. Supp. I:** 329
Marrying Man (Simon), **Supp. IV Part 2:** 588
"Marrying the Hangman" (Atwood), **Supp. XIII:** 34
Marry Me: A Romance (Updike), **Retro. Supp. I:** 329, 330, 332
"Mars and Hymen" (Freneau), **Supp. II Part 1:** 258
Marsden, Dora, **III:** 471; **Retro. Supp. I:** 416
Marsena (Frederic), **II:** 135, 136–137
Marsh, Edward, **Supp. I Part 1:** 257, 263
Marsh, Frederick T., **Supp. XX: 39, 46**
Marsh, Fred T., **Supp. IX:** 232
Marsh, John R., **Supp. XIX:** 187
Marsh, Mae, **Supp. I Part 2:** 391
Marshall, George, **III:** 3
Marshall, John, **Supp. I Part 2:** 455; **Supp. XVI:** 117; **Supp. XIX:** 62
Marshall, Paule, **Supp. IV Part 1:** 8, 14, 369; **Supp. XI:** 18, **275–292; Supp. XIII:** 295; **Supp. XX: 154**
Marshall, Tod, **Supp. XV:** 224; **Supp. XVII:** 25, 26, 29, 32
"Marshall Carpenter" (Masters), **Supp. I Part 2:** 463
"Marshes of Glynn, The" (Lanier), **Supp. I Part 1:** 364, 365–368, 370, 373
"'Marshes of Glynn, The': A Study in Symbolic Obscurity" (Ross), **Supp. I Part 1:** 373
Marsh Island, A (Jewett), **II:** 405; **Retro. Supp. II:** 134
"Marshland Elegy" (Leopold), **Supp. XIV:** 187, 189
"Mars Is Heaven!" (Bradbury), **Supp. IV Part 1:** 103, 106
Mars-Jones, Adam, **Supp. XXI:** 116
Marsman, Henrik, **Supp. IV Part 1:** 183
Marston, Ed, **Supp. IV Part 2:** 492
Marta y Maria (Valdes), **II:** 290
"Martha's Lady" (Jewett), **Retro. Supp. II:** 140, 143
Marthe, Saint, **II:** 213
Martial, **II:** 1, 169; **Supp. IX:** 152
Martian Chronicles, The (Bradbury), **Supp. IV Part 1:** 102, 103, 106–107
Martian Time-Slip (Dick), **Supp. XVIII:** 142
Martin, Benjamin, **Supp. I Part 2:** 503
Martin, Charles, **Supp. XVII:** 112
Martin, Dick, **Supp. XII:** 44
Martin, Jay, **I:** 55, 58, 60, 61, 67; **III:** 307; **Retro. Supp. II:** 326, 327, 329; **Supp. XI:** 162
Martin, John, **Supp. XI:** 172
Martin, Judith, **Supp. V:** 128
Martin, Nell, **Supp. IV Part 1:** 351, 353
Martin, Reginald, **Supp. X:** 247, 249
Martin, Robert, **Supp. XX: 165**
Martin, Stephen-Paul, **Supp. IV Part 2:** 430
Martin, Tom, **Supp. X:** 79
Martin du Gard, Roger, **Supp. I Part 1:** 51
Martineau, Harriet, **Supp. II Part 1:** 282, 288, 294; **Supp. XVIII:** 7
Martin Eden (London), **II:** 466, 477–481
Martinelli, Sheri, **Supp. IV Part 1:** 280
Martínez, Guillermo, **Supp. XIII:** 313
Martini, Adrienne, **Supp. XVIII:** 35
Mart'nez, Rafael, **Retro. Supp. I:** 423
Martone, John, **Supp. V:** 179
Marty (Chayefsky), **Supp. XV:** 205
"Martyr, The" (Porter), **III:** 454
Martz, Louis L., **IV:** 151, 156, 165; **Supp. I Part 1:** 107; **Supp. XIV:** 12; **Supp. XXI:** 85
Marvell, Andrew, **IV:** 135, 151, 156, 161, 253; **Retro. Supp. I:** 62, 127; **Retro. Supp. II:** 186, 189; **Supp. I Part 1:** 80; **Supp. XII:** 159; **Supp. XIV:** 10; **Supp. XVI:** 204; **Supp. XXI:** 227
"Marvella, for Borrowing" (Ríos), **Supp. IV Part 2:** 551
"Marvelous Sauce, The", **Supp. XVII:** 189
Marvels and Masterpieces (al-Badá'i' wa'l-Tará'if) (Gibran), **Supp. XX: 116, 124**
Marx, Eleanor, **Supp. XVI:** 85
Marx, Karl, **I:** 60, 267, 279, 283, 588; **II:** 376, 462, 463, 483, 577; **IV:** 429, 436, 443–444, 469; **Retro. Supp. I:** 254; **Supp. I Part 2:** 518, 628, 632, 633, 634, 635, 639, 643, 645, 646; **Supp. III Part 2:** 619; **Supp. IV Part 1:** 355; **Supp. VIII:** 196; **Supp. IX:** 133; **Supp. X:** 119, 134; **Supp. XIII:** 75; **Supp. XXI:** 162, 263
Marx, Leo, **Supp. I Part 1:** 233
"Marxism and Monastic Perpectives" (Merton), **Supp. VIII:** 196
Mary (Nabokov), **Retro. Supp. I: 267–268,** 270, 277
"Mary" (Trethewey), **Supp. XXI:** 246
"Mary Karr, Mary Karr, Mary Karr, Mary Karr" (Harmon), **Supp. XI:** 248
Maryles, Daisy, **Supp. XII:** 271
Mary Magdalene, **I:** 303
Mary; or, The Test of Honour (Rowson), **Supp. XV: 233,** 236
"Mary O'Reilly" (Anderson), **II:** 44
"Mary Osaka , I Love You" (Fante), **Supp. XI:** 169
"Mary Snorak the Cook, Skermo the Gardener, and Jack the Parts Man Provide Dinner for a Wandering Stranger" (Grossman), **Supp. XIX:** 87
"Mary's Song" (Plath), **Supp. I Part 2:** 541
"Mary Winslow" (Lowell), **Retro. Supp. II:** 187
Marzynski, Marian, **Supp. XVI:** 153
Masefield, John, **II:** 552; **III:** 523
Masked and Anonymous (film, Dylan and Charles), **Supp. XVIII:** 21, 28
Mask for Janus, A (Merwin), **Supp. III Part 1:** 339, 341, 342
Maslin, Janet, **Supp. XVI:** 213; **Supp. XXI:** 79
Maslow, Abraham, **Supp. I Part 2:** 540
Maso, Carole, **Supp. XXII:** 261
Mason, Bobbie Ann, **Supp. VIII: 133–149; Supp. XI:** 26; **Supp. XII:** 294, 298, 311; **Supp. XX: 162**
Mason, Charlotte, **Supp. XIV:** 201
Mason, David, **Supp. V:** 344; **Supp. XV:** 116, 251; **Supp. XVII:** 109, 110, 112, 121; **Supp. XVIII:** 182, 183
Mason, Jennifer, **Supp. XVIII:** 263
Mason, Lowell, **I:** 458
Mason, Marsha, **Supp. IV Part 2:** 575, 586
Mason, Otis Tufton, **Supp. I Part 1:** 18
Mason, Walt, **Supp. XV:** 298
Mason & Dixon (Pynchon), **Supp. XVII:** 232
"Mason Jars by the Window" (Ríos), **Supp. IV Part 2:** 548
Masque of Mercy, A (Frost), **II:** 155, 165, 167–168; **Retro. Supp. I:** 131, 140
"Masque of Mummers, The" (MacLeish), **III:** 18
"Masque of Pandora, The" (Longfellow), **Retro. Supp. II:** 167
Masque of Pandora, The, and Other Poems (Longfellow), **II:** 490, 494, 506; **Retro. Supp. II:** 169
Masque of Poets, A (Lathrop, ed.), **Retro. Supp. I:** 31; **Supp. I Part 1:** 365, 368
Masque of Reason, A (Frost), **II:** 155, 162, 165–167; **Retro. Supp. I:** 131, 140; **Retro. Supp. II:** 42
"Masque of the Red Death, The" (Poe), **III:** 412, 419, 424; **Retro. Supp. II:** 262, 268–269
"Masquerade" (Banks), **Supp. V:** 7
Massachusetts, Its Historians and Its History (Adams), **Supp. I Part 2:** 484
"Massachusetts 1932" (Bowles), **Supp. IV Part 1:** 94

"Massachusetts to Virginia" (Whittier), **Supp. I Part 2:** 688–689
"Massacre and the Mastermind, The" (Bausch), **Supp. VII:** 49
"Massacre at Scio, The" (Bryant), **Supp. I Part 1:** 168
"Massacre of the Innocents, The" (Simic), **Supp. VIII:** 282
Masses and Man (Toller), **I:** 479
"Masseur de Ma Soeur, Le" (Hecht), **Supp. X:** 58
Massey, Raymond, **Supp. IV Part 2:** 524
"Mass Eye and Ear: The Ward" (Karr), **Supp. XI:** 244
"Mass for the Day of St. Thomas Didymus" (Levertov), **Supp. III Part 1:** 283
Massie, Chris, **Supp. IV Part 2:** 524
Massing, Michael, **Supp. IV Part 1:** 208
Massinger, Philip, **Supp. I Part 2:** 422; **Supp. XV:** 238
Master Builder, The (Ibsen), **Supp. IV Part 2:** 522
Master Class (McNally), **Supp. XIII: 204–205,** 208
"Masterful" (Matthews), **Supp. IX: 161–162**
Mastering the Art of French Cooking (Child), **Supp. XVII:** 89
"Master Misery" (Capote), **Supp. III Part 1:** 117
Master of Dreams: A Memoir of Isaac Bashevis Singer (Telushkin), **Retro. Supp. II:** 317
"Master of Secret Revenges, The" (Gass), **Supp. VI:** 93
Master of the Crossroads (Bell), **Supp. X: 16–17**
"'Masterpiece of Filth, A': Portrait of Knoxville Forgets to Be Fair" (Howards), **Supp. VIII:** 178
Masterpieces of American Fiction, **Supp. XI:** 198
"Master Player, The" (Dunbar), **Supp. II Part 1:** 200
Masters, Edgar Lee, **I:** 106, 384, 475, 480, 518; **II:** 276, 529; **III:** 505, 576, 579; **IV:** 352; **Retro. Supp. I:** 131; **Supp. I Part 2:** 378, 386, 387, **454–478; Supp. III Part 1:** 63, 71, 73, 75; **Supp. IV Part 2:** 502; **Supp. IX:** 308; **Supp. XIV:** 282–283; **Supp. XV:** 256, 293, 297, 301, 306
Masters, Hardin W., **Supp. I Part 2:** 468
Masters, Hilary, **Supp. IX:** 96
Masters of Sociological Thought (Coser), **Supp. I Part 2:** 650
Masters of the Dew (Roumain), **Supp. IV Part 1:** 367
"Masters of War" (song, Dylan), **Supp. XVIII:** 24
"Master's Pieces, The" (H. L. Gates), **Supp. XX: 109**
Matchmaker, The (Wilder), **IV:** 357, 369, 370, 374; **Supp. XX: 50**
Mate of the Daylight, The, and Friends Ashore (Jewett), **II:** 404; **Retro. Supp. II:** 146–147
Materassi, Mario, **Supp. IX:** 233
Mather, Cotton, **II:** 10, 104, 302, 506, 536; **III:** 442; **IV:** 144, 152–153, 157; **Supp. I Part 1:** 102, 117, 174, 271; **Supp. I Part 2:** 584, 599, 698; **Supp. II Part 2: 441–470; Supp. IV Part 2:** 430, 434
Mather, Increase, **II:** 10; **IV:** 147, 157; **Supp. I Part 1:** 100
Mathews, Cornelius, **III:** 81; **Supp. I Part 1:** 317
Mathews, Shailer, **III:** 293
"Matinees" (Merrill), **Supp. III Part 1:** 319, 327
"Matins" (C. Frost), **Supp. XV:** 105
"Matins" (Glück), **Supp. V:** 88
"Matins" (Nelson), **Supp. XVIII:** 177
Matisse, Henri, **III:** 180; **IV:** 90, 407; **Supp. I Part 2:** 619; **Supp. VIII:** 168; **Supp. IX:** 66; **Supp. X:** 73, 74; **Supp. XXII:** 98, 99
"Matisse: Blue Interior with Two Girls–1947" (Hecht), **Supp. X: 73–74**
"Matisse: The Red Studio" (Snodgrass), **Supp. VI:** 316–317
Matlack, James, **Supp. XV:** 269, 271, 286
Matlock, Lucinda, **Supp. I Part 2:** 462
Matos, Juan, **Supp. XXI:** 104
Matrimaniac, The (film), **Supp. XVI:** 185, 186
Matrix Trilogy, The (film), **Supp. XVI:** 271
Matson, Harold, **Supp. XIII:** 164, 166, 167, 169, 172
Matson, Peter, **Supp. IV Part 1:** 299
Matson, Suzanne, **Supp. VIII:** 281
Matters of Fact and Fiction: Essays 1973–1976 (Vidal), **Supp. IV Part 2:** 687
Matthew (biblical book), **IV:** 164; **Supp. XV:** 222
Matthew Arnold (Trilling), **Supp. III Part 2:** 500–501
Matthews, Jackson, **Supp. XVI:** 282
Matthews, T. S., **II:** 430; **Supp. XV:** 142
Matthews, William, **Supp. V:** 4, 5; **Supp. IX: 151–170; Supp. XIII:** 112; **Supp. XXI:** 87
Matthiessen, F. O., **I:** 254, 259–260, 517; **II:** 41, 554; **III:** 310, 453; **IV:** 181; **Retro. Supp. I:** 40, 217; **Retro. Supp. II:** 137; **Supp. IV Part 2:** 422; **Supp. XIII:** 93; **Supp. XIV:** 3; **Supp. XXI:** 277
Matthiessen, Peter, **Supp. V: 199–217,** 332; **Supp. XI:** 231, 294; **Supp. XIV:** 82; **Supp. XVI:** 230; **Supp. XIX:** 268
Mattingly, Garrett, **Supp. IV Part 2:** 601
Mattu, Ravi, **Supp. XVI:** 124
"Maud Island" (Caldwell), **I:** 310
Maud Martha (Brooks), **Supp. III Part 1:** 74, 78–79, 87; **Supp. XI:** 278
"Maud Muller" (Whittier), **Supp. I Part 2:** 698
Maugham, W. Somerset, **III:** 57, 64; **Supp. IV Part 1:** 209; **Supp. X:** 58; **Supp. XIV:** 161
Maule's Curse: Seven Studies in the History of American Obscurantism (Winters), **Supp. II Part 2:** 807–808, 812
"Mau-mauing the Flak Catchers" (Wolfe), **Supp. III Part 2:** 577
Maupassant, Guy de, **I:** 309, 421; **II:** 191–192, 291, 325, 591; **IV:** 17; **Retro. Supp. II:** 65, 66, 67, 299; **Supp. I Part 1:** 207, 217, 223, 320; **Supp. XIV:** 336
"Maurice Barrès and the Youth of France" (Bourne), **I:** 228
Maurier, George du, **II:** 338
Maurras, Charles, **Retro. Supp. I:** 55
Maus II: And Here My Troubles Began (A. Speigelman), **Supp. XVII:** 48
Mauve Gloves & Madmen, Clutter & Vine (Wolfe), **Supp. III Part 2:** 581
Maverick, Augustus, **Supp. XVIII:** 4
Maverick in Mauve (Auchincloss), **Supp. IV Part 1:** 26
"Mavericks, The" (play) (Auchincloss), **Supp. IV Part 1:** 34
"Mavericks, The" (story) (Auchincloss), **Supp. IV Part 1:** 32
"Max" (H. Miller), **III:** 183
Max, D. T., **Supp. XXI:** 117
Max and the White Phagocytes (H. Miller), **III:** 178, 183–184
Maximilian (emperor of Mexico), **Supp. I Part 2:** 457–458
Maximilian: A Play in Five Acts (Masters), **Supp. I Part 2:** 456, 457–458
"Maximus, to Gloucester" (Olson), **Supp. II Part 2:** 574
"Maximus, to himself" (Olson), **Supp. II Part 2:** 565, 566, 567, 569, 570, 572
Maximus Poems, The (Olson), **Retro. Supp. I:** 209; **Supp. II Part 2:** 555, 556, 563, 564–580, 584; **Supp. VIII:** 305; **Supp. XV:** 170, 264, 349; **Supp. XVI:** 287
Maximus Poems 1–10, The (Olson), **Supp. II Part 2:** 571
Maximus Poems IV, V, VI (Olson), **Supp. II Part 2:** 555, 580, 582–584
Maximus Poems Volume Three, The (Olson), **Supp. II Part 2:** 555, 582, 584–585
"Maximus to Gloucester, Letter 19 (A Pastoral Letter)" (Olson), **Supp. II Part 2:** 567
"Maximus to Gloucester, Sunday July 19" (Olson), **Supp. II Part 2:** 580
"Maximus to himself June 1964" (Olson), **Supp. II Part 2:** 584
Maxwell, Glyn, **Supp. XV:** 252, 253, 260, 261, 263, 264
Maxwell, William, **Supp. I Part 1:** 175; **Supp. III Part 1:** 62; **Supp. VIII: 151–174; Supp. XVII:** 23
May, Abigail (Abba). *See* Alcott, Mrs. Amos Bronson (Abigail May)
May, Elaine Tyler, **Supp. XXII:** 81, 95
May, Jill, **Supp. VIII:** 126
"May 24, 1980" (Brodsky), **Supp. VIII:** 28
"May 1968" (Olds), **Supp. X:** 211–212
"Mayan Glyphs Unread, The" (Bronk), **Supp. XXI:** 31
"Mayan Warning" (Mora), **Supp. XIII:** 214

Maybe (Hellman), **Supp. IV Part 1:** 12
"Maybe" (Oliver), **Supp. VII:** 239
"Maybe, Someday" (Ritsos), **Supp. XIII:** 78
May Blossom (Belasco), **Supp. XVI:** 182
"Mayday" (Faulkner), **Retro. Supp. I:** 80
"May Day" (Fitzgerald), **II:** 88–89; **Retro. Supp. I:** 103
"May Day Dancing, The" (Nemerov), **III:** 275
May Days (Pickering), **Supp. XXI:** 197–198
May Days: An Anthology of Verse from Masses-Liberator (Taggard, ed.), **Supp. XXII:** 275–276
"May Day Sermon to the Women of Gilmer County, Georgia, by a Woman Preacher Leaving the Baptist Church" (Dickey), **Supp. IV Part 1:** 182
Mayer, Elizabeth, **Supp. II Part 1:** 16; **Supp. III Part 1:** 63
Mayer, John, **Retro. Supp. I:** 58
Mayer, Louis B., **Supp. XII:** 160; **Supp. XVIII:** 250
Mayes, Wendell, **Supp. IX:** 250
Mayfield, Sara, **Supp. IX:** 65
Mayflower, The (Stowe), **Supp. I Part 2:** 585, 586
Mayle, Peter, **Supp. XVI:** 295
Maynard, Joyce, **Supp. V:** 23
Maynard, Tony, **Supp. I Part 1:** 65
Mayne, Xavier. *See* Prime-Stevenson, Edward Irenaeus
Mayo, Robert, **III:** 478
Mayor (Allen), **Supp. XXII:** 245
Mayorga, Margaret, **IV:** 381
"May-Pole of Merry Mount, The" (Hawthorne), **Supp. XXII:** 44
"Maypole of Merrymount, The" (Hawthorne), **II:** 229
"May Queen" (Di Piero), **Supp. XIX:** 41
May Sarton: Selected Letters 1916–1954, **Supp. VIII:** 265
"May Sun Sheds an Amber Light, The" (Bryant), **Supp. I Part 1:** 170
"May Swenson: The Art of Perceiving" (Stanford), **Supp. IV Part 2:** 637
"Maze" (Eberhart), **I:** 523, 525–526, 527
Mazel (R. Goldstein), **Supp. XVII:** 44
Mazur, Gail, **Supp. XVIII:** 92
Mazurkiewicz, Margaret, **Supp. XI:** 2
Mazzini, Giuseppe, **Supp. I Part 1:** 2, 8; **Supp. II Part 1:** 299
M. Butterfly (Hwang), **Supp. X:** 292; **Supp. XXI:** 143, 147**, 150–154**
Mc. Names starting with Mc are alphabetized as if spelled Mac.
"M. Degas Teaches Art & Science at Durfee Intermediate School, Detroit, 1942" (Levine), **Supp. V:** 181, 193
"Me, Boy Scout" (Lardner), **II:** 433
Me, Vashya! (T. Williams), **IV:** 381
Mead, Elinor. *See* Howells, Mrs. William Dean (Elinor Mead)
Mead, George Herbert, **II:** 27, 34; **Supp. I Part 1:** 5; **Supp. I Part 2:** 641
Mead, Margaret, **Supp. I Part 1:** 49, 52, 66; **Supp. IX:** 229
Mead, Taylor, **Supp. XV:** 187
Meade, Frank, **Retro. Supp. II:** 114
Meade, Marion, **Supp. IX:** 191, 193, 194, 195
Meadow, Lynne, **Supp. XIII:** 198
"Meadow House" (Carruth), **Supp. XVI:** 48
Meadowlands (Glück), **Supp. V:** 88–90
"Mean, Mrs." (Gass), **Supp. VI:** 83
"Me and the Mule" (Hughes), **Supp. I Part 1:** 334
"Meaningless Institution, A" (Ginsberg), **Supp. II Part 1:** 313
"Meaning of a Literary Idea, The" (Trilling), **Supp. III Part 2:** 498
"Meaning of Birds, The" (C. Smith), **Supp. X:** 177
"Meaning of Death, The, An After Dinner Speech" (Tate), **IV:** 128, 129
"Meaning of Life, The" (Tate), **IV:** 137
"Meaning of Simplicity, The" (Ritsos), **Supp. XIII:** 78
Means of Escape (Caputo), **Supp. XIX:** 18, 21, 25
Mean Spirit (Hogan), **Supp. IV Part 1:** 397, 404, 407–410, 415, 416–417
Meantime, The (Bronk), **Supp. XXI:** 31
Mearns, Hughes, **III:** 220
"Measure" (Hass), **Supp. VI: 99–100,** 101
"Measuring My Blood" (Vizenor), **Supp. IV Part 1:** 262
Meatyard, Gene, **Supp. X:** 30
Me: By Jimmy (Big Boy) Valente (Keillor), **Supp. XVI:** 177
Mechan, Dennis B., **Supp. XVI:** 267–268
Mechanic, The (Bynner and DeMille), **Supp. XV:** 42, 50
"Mechanism" (Ammons), **Supp. VII:** 28
"Mechanism in Thought and Morals" (Holmes), **Supp. I Part 1:** 314
Mecom, Mrs. Jane, **II:** 122
"Meddlesome Jack" (Caldwell), **I:** 309
Medea (Jeffers), **Supp. II Part 2:** 435
Medea and Some Poems, The (Cullen), **Supp. IV Part 1:** 169, 173
"Me Decade and the Third Great Awakening, The" (Wolfe), **Supp. III Part 2:** 581
"Médecin Malgré Lui, Le" (W. C. Williams), **IV:** 407–408
"Medfield" (Bryant), **Supp. I Part 1:** 157
Medical History of Contraception, A (Himes), **Supp. V:** 128
"Medicine Song" (Gunn Allen), **Supp. IV Part 1:** 326
Médicis, Marie de, **II:** 548
Medina (McCarthy), **II:** 579
"Meditation, A" (Eberhart), **I:** 533–535
"Meditation 1.6" (Taylor), **IV:** 165
"Meditation 1.20" (Taylor), **IV:** 165
"Meditation 2.68A" (Taylor), **IV:** 165
"Meditation 2.102" (Taylor), **IV:** 150
"Meditation 2.112" (Taylor), **IV:** 165
"Meditation 20" (Taylor), **IV:** 154–155
"Meditation 40" (Second Series) (Taylor), **IV:** 147
"Meditation at Lagunitas" (Hass), **Supp. VI:** 104–105; **Supp. XXI:** 60
"Meditation at Oyster River" (Roethke), **III:** 537, 549
Meditations (Descartes), **III:** 618
Meditations (Marcus Aurelius), **Supp. XVIII:** 304
"Meditations for a Savage Child" (Rich), **Supp. I Part 2:** 564–565
Meditations from a Movable Chair (Dubus), **Supp. VII:** 91
"Meditations in a Swine Yard" (Komunyakaa), **Supp. XIII:** 131
"Meditations of an Old Woman" (Roethke), **III:** 529, 540, 542, 543, 545–547, 548
Meditations on the Insatiable Soul (R. Bly), **Supp. IV Part 1:** 72–73
Meditative Poems, The (Martz), **IV:** 151
"Mediterranean, The" (Tate), **IV:** 129
"Medium of Fiction, The" (Gass), **Supp. VI:** 85–86
"Medley" (Bambara), **Supp. XI:** 9
"Medusa" (Bogan), **Supp. III Part 1:** 50, 51
Meehan, Jeannette Porter, **Supp. XX: 213, 214, 217, 220, 224**
Meehan, Thomas, **Supp. IV Part 2:** 577–578, 586, 590
Meek, Martha, **Supp. IV Part 2:** 439, 440, 441, 442, 445, 447, 448
Meeker, Richard K., **II:** 190
Meese, Elizabeth, **Supp. XIII:** 297
"Meeting" (J. W. Miller), **Supp. XX: 167**
"Meeting, The" (F. Wright), **Supp. XVII:** 245
"Meeting and Greeting Area, The" (Cameron), **Supp. XII: 84–85**
Meeting by the River, A (Isherwood), **Supp. XIV:** 164, **170–171,** 172
"Meeting-House Hill" (Lowell), **II:** 522, 527
"Meeting in the Kitchen, The" (Schnackenberg), **Supp. XV:** 256
"Meeting South, A" (Anderson), **I:** 115
"Meeting the Mountains" (Snyder), **Supp. VIII:** 300
Meeting Trees (Sanders), **Supp. XVI:** 269
Meet Me at the Morgue (Macdonald), **Supp. IV Part 2:** 472
Mehta, Sonny, **Supp. XI:** 178
Mehta, Ved, **Supp. XX: 87**
Meine, Curt, **Supp. XIV:** 179
Meiners, R. K., **IV:** 136, 137, 138, 140
Meinong, Alexius, **Supp. XIV:** 198, 199
Meisner, Sanford, **Supp. XIV:** 240, 242
Meister, Charles W., **II:** 112
Mejia, Jaime, **Supp. XIX:** 97
"Melancholia" (Dunbar), **Supp. II Part 1:** 194
Melancholy Baby (Parker), **Supp. XIX:** 186
"Melanctha" (Stein), **IV:** 30, 34, 35, 37, 38–40, 45
"Melancthon" (Moore), **III:** 212, 215
Melbourne House (S. and A. Warner), **Supp. XVIII:** 268
Meliboeus Hipponax (Lowell). *See Biglow Papers, The* (Lowell)
Melinda and Melinda (Allen), **Supp. XV:** 16
Mellaart, James, **Supp. I Part 2:** 567
Mellard, James, **Supp. IV Part 1:** 387
Mellon, Andrew, **III:** 14

Mellor, W. M., **Supp. XX: 56**
Melnick, Jeffrey, **Supp. X:** 252
Melnyczuk, Askold, **Supp. IV Part 1:** 70
Melodrama Play (Shepard), **Supp. III Part 2:** 440–441, 443, 445
Melodramatists, The (Nemerov), **III:** 268, 281–283, 284
Melopoeia (Espaillat and Tavano), **Supp. XXI:** 99–100
Melting-Pot, The (Zangwill), **I:** 229
"Melungeons" (Offutt), **Supp. XIX:** 171
Melville, Allan, **III:** 74, 77
Melville, Gansevoort, **III:** 76
Melville, Herman, **I:** 104, 106, 211, 288, 340, 343, 348, 354, 355, 561–562; **II:** 27, 74, 224–225, 228, 230, 232, 236, 255, 259, 271, 272, 277, 281, 295, 307, 311, 319, 320, 321, 418, 477, 497, 539–540, 545; **III:** 29, 45, 70, **74–98,** 359, 438, 453, 454, 507, 562–563, 572, 576; **IV:** 57, 105, 194, 199, 202, 250, 309, 333, 345, 350, 380, 444, 453; **Retro. Supp. I:** 54, 91, 160, 215, 220, **243–262; Retro. Supp. II:** 76; **Supp. I Part 1:** 147, 238, 242, 249, 309, 317, 372; **Supp. I Part 2:** 383, 495, 579, 580, 582, 602; **Supp. IV Part 2:** 463, 613; **Supp. V:** 279, 281, 298, 308; **Supp. VIII:** 48, 103, 104, 105, 106, 108, 156, 175, 181, 188; **Supp. XI:** 83; **Supp. XII:** 282; **Supp. XIII:** 294, 305; **Supp. XIV:** 48, 227; **Supp. XV:** 287; **Supp. XVII:** 42, 185; **Supp. XVIII:** 1, 4, 6, 7, 9; **Supp. XXI:** 169; **Supp. XXII:** 174, 262
Melville, Mrs. Herman (Elizabeth Shaw), **III:** 77, 91, 92
Melville, Maria Gansevoort, **III:** 74, 77, 85
Melville, Thomas, **III:** 77, 79, 92; **Supp. I Part 1:** 309
Melville, Whyte, **IV:** 309
Melville Goodwin, USA (Marquand), **III:** 60, 65–66
Melville's Marginalia (Cowen), **Supp. IV Part 2:** 435
"Melville's Marginalia" (Howe), **Supp. IV Part 2:** 435
Member of the Wedding, The (McCullers), **II:** 587, 592, 600–604, 605, 606; **Supp. VIII:** 124
"Meme Ortiz" (Cisneros), **Supp. VII:** 60
Memmon (song cycle) (Bowles), **Supp. IV Part 1:** 82
Memnoch the Devil (Rice), **Supp. VII:** 289, 290, 294, 296–299
"Memoir" (Hempel), **Supp. XXI:** 118
"Memoir" (Untermeyer), **II:** 516–517
"Memoir, A" (Koch), **Supp. XV:** 184
"Memoirist's Apology, A" (Karr), **Supp. XI:** 245, 246
Memoir of Mary Ann, A (O'Connor), **III:** 357
Memoir of Thomas McGrath, A (Beeching), **Supp. X:** 114, 118
Memoirs (W. Frank), **Supp. XX: 67, 69, 70, 81**
Memoirs of Arii Taimai (Adams), **I:** 2–3
"Memoirs of Carwin, the Biloquist" (Brown), **Supp. I Part 1:** 132
Memoirs of Hecate County (Wilson), **IV:** 429
Memoirs of Margaret Fuller Ossoli (Fuller), **Supp. II Part 1:** 280, 283, 285
"Memoirs of Stephen Calvert" (Brown), **Supp. I Part 1:** 133, 144
Memorabilia (Xenophon), **II:** 105
Memorable Providences (Mather), **Supp. II Part 2:** 458
Memorial, The: Portrait of a Family (Isherwood), **Supp. XIV:** 156, 159, 160–161
"Memorial Day" (Cameron), **Supp. XII:** 80, **82–83**
"Memorial for the City" (Auden), **Supp. II Part 1:** 20
"Memorial Rain" (MacLeish), **III:** 15
"Memorial to Ed Bland" (Brooks), **Supp. III Part 1:** 77
"Memorial Tribute" (Wilbur), **Supp. IV Part 2:** 642
"Memories" (Whittier), **Supp. I Part 2:** 699
Memories of a Catholic Girlhood (McCarthy), **II:** 560–561, 566; **Supp. XI:** 246; **Supp. XVI:** 64, 70
"Memories of East Texas" (Karr), **Supp. XI:** 239
"Memories of Uncle Neddy" (Bishop), **Retro. Supp. II:** 38; **Supp. I Part 1:** 73, 93
"Memories of West Street and Lepke" (Lowell), **II:** 550
"Memory" (Epstein), **Supp. XII:** 163
"Memory" (Everwine), **Supp. XV:** 82
"Memory, A" (Welty), **IV:** 261–262; **Retro. Supp. I:** 344–345
"Memory, Narrative, and the Discourses of Identity in *Abeng* and *No Telephone to Heaven*" (Smith), **Supp. XXII:** 70
"Memory, The" (Gioia), **Supp. XV:** 119
Memory and Enthusiasm: Essays, 1975–1985 (Di Piero), **Supp. XIX:** 34, 41, 42
"Memory and Imagination" (Hampl), **Supp. XXII:** 94
Memory Gardens (Creeley), **Supp. IV Part 1:** 141, 157
"Memory Harbor" (Skloot), **Supp. XX: 201**
Memory of Murder, A (Bradbury), **Supp. IV Part 1:** 103
Memory of Old Jack, The (Berry), **Supp. X:** 34
Memory of Two Mondays, A (A. Miller), **III:** 153, 156, 158–159, 160, 166
"Memo to Non-White Peoples" (Hughes), **Retro. Supp. I:** 209
Men, Women and Ghosts (Lowell), **II:** 523–524
Menaker, Charlotte, **Supp. XIX:** 266
Menaker, Daniel, **Supp. VIII:** 151
Menand, Louis, **Supp. XIV:** 40, 197; **Supp. XVI:** 106, 107
Men and Angels (Gordon), **Supp. IV Part 1:** 304–305, 306, 308
Men and Brethen (Cozzens), **I:** 363–365, 368, 375, 378, 379
Men and Cartoons (Lethem), **Supp. XVIII:** 145, **148**
"Men and Women" (R. Bly), **Supp. IV Part 1:** 72
"Men at Forty" (Justice), **Supp. VII:** 126–127
Mencius (Meng-tzu), **IV:** 183
Mencken, August, **III:** 100, 108
Mencken, August, Jr., **III:** 99, 109, 118–119
Mencken, Mrs. August (Anna Abhau), **III:** 100, 109
Mencken, Burkhardt, **III:** 100, 108
Mencken, Charles, **III:** 99
Mencken, Gertrude, **III:** 99
Mencken, H. L., **I:** 199, 210, 212, 235, 245, 261, 405, 514, 515, 517; **II:** 25, 27, 42, 89, 90, 91, 271, 289, 430, 443, 449; **III: 99–121,** 394, 482; **IV:** 76, 432, 440, 475, 482; **Retro. Supp. I:** 1, 101; **Retro. Supp. II:** 97, 98, 102, 265; **Supp. I Part 2:** 484, 629–630, 631, 647, 651, 653, 659, 673; **Supp. II Part 1:** 136; **Supp. IV Part 1:** 201, 314, 343; **Supp. IV Part 2:** 521, 692, 693; **Supp. XI:** 163–164, 166; **Supp. XIII:** 161; **Supp. XIV:** 111; **Supp. XV:** 297, 301, 303; **Supp. XVI:** 187–188, 189; **Supp. XVII:** 106; **Supp. XXII:** 23, 187, 277
Mencken, Mrs. H. L. (Sara Haardt), **III:** 109, 111
"Men Deified Because of Their Cruelty" (Simic), **Supp. VIII:** 282
Mendelbaum, Paul, **Supp. V:** 159
Mendele, **IV:** 3, 10
Mendelief, Dmitri Ivanovich, **IV:** 421
Mendelsohn, Daniel, **Supp. X:** 153, 154; **Supp. XV:** 257, 258, 261, 266
Mendes, Alfred, **Supp. XXI:** 160
"Mending Wall" (Frost), **II:** 153–154; **Retro. Supp. I:** 128, 130; **Supp. X:** 64
Men from the Boys, The (Lacy), **Supp. XV:** 202, 205
Men in the Off Hours (Carson), **Supp. XII: 111–113**
"Men in the Storm, The" (Crane), **I:** 411
"Men Loved Wholly Beyond Wisdom" (Bogan), **Supp. III Part 1:** 50
"Men Made Out of Words" (Stevens), **IV:** 88
Men Must Act (Mumford), **Supp. II Part 2:** 479
Mennes, John, **II:** 111
Mennoti, Gian Carlo, **Supp. IV Part 1:** 84
Men of Brewster Place, The (Naylor), **Supp. VIII:** 213, **228–230**
"Men of Color, to Arms!" (Douglass), **Supp. III Part 1:** 171
Men of Good Hope: A Story of American Progressives (Aaron), **Supp. I Part 2:** 650
Mens' Club, The (film), **Supp. XVI:** 212–213
Men's Club, The (L. Michaels), **Supp. XVI:** 206, **210–212**
"Menstruation at Forty" (Sexton), **Supp. II Part 2:** 686

"Mental Hospital Garden, The" (W. C. Williams), **Retro. Supp. I:** 428
Mental Radio (Sinclair), **Supp. V:** 289
Mentoria; or, The Young Lady's Friend (Rowson), **Supp. XV: 233–234,** 238
"Men We Carry in Our Minds, The" (Sanders), **Supp. XVI:** 273
Men Who Made the Nation, The (Dos Passos), **I:** 485
Men Without Women (Hemingway), **II:** 249; **Retro. Supp. I:** 170, 176; **Supp. IX:** 202
"Merced" (Rich), **Supp. I Part 2:** 563
"Mercedes" (E. Stoddard), **Supp. XV:** 278
"Mercedes Hospital" (Bishop), **Retro. Supp. II:** 51
"Mercenary, A" (Ozick), **Supp. V:** 267
Mercer, Johnny, **Supp. XXII:** 6
Merchandising (Hwang), **Supp. XXI:** 147
Merchant of Venice, The (Shakespeare), **IV:** 227; **Supp. XIV:** 325
Mercury Theatre, **Retro. Supp. I:** 65
Mercy, Pity, Peace, and Love (Ozick), **Supp. V:** 257, 258
Mercy, The (Levine), **Supp. V:** 194–195
Mercy of a Rude Stream (H. Roth), **Supp. IX:** 231, 234, **235–242**
Mercy Philbrick's Choice (Jackson), **Retro. Supp. I:** 26, 27, 33
Mercy Street (Sexton), **Supp. II Part 2:** 683, 689
Meredith, George, **II:** 175, 186; **Supp. IV Part 1:** 300
Meredith, Mary. *See* Webb, Mary
Meredith, William, **II:** 545; **Retro. Supp. II:** 181
"Merely by Wilderness" (Peacock), **Supp. XIX:** 199
"Merely to Know" (Rich), **Supp. I Part 2:** 554
"Mère Pochette" (Jewett), **II:** 400
"Merger II, The" (Auchincloss), **Supp. IV Part 1:** 34
"Mericans" (Cisneros), **Supp. VII:** 69
"Merida, 1969" (Matthews), **Supp. IX:** 151
"Meridian" (Clampitt), **Supp. IX: 48–49**
Meridian (Walker), **Supp. III Part 2:** 520, 524, 527, 528, 531–537
Mérimée, Prosper, **II:** 322
Meriwether, James B., **Retro Supp. I:** 77, 91
"Meriwether Connection, The" (Cowley), **Supp. II Part 1:** 142
Merker, Kim K., **Supp. XI:** 261; **Supp. XV:** 75, 77
"Merlin" (Emerson), **II:** 19, 20
Merlin (Robinson), **III:** 522
"Merlin Enthralled" (Wilbur), **Supp. III Part 2:** 544, 554
"Mermother" (A. Finch), **Supp. XVII:** 72
Merril, Judith, **Supp. XVI:** 123
Merrill, Christopher, **Supp. XI:** 329
Merrill, James, **Retro. Supp. I:** 296; **Retro. Supp. II:** 53; **Supp. III Part 1: 317–338; Supp. III Part 2:** 541, 561; **Supp. IX:** 40, 42, 48, 52; **Supp. X:** 73; **Supp. XI:** 123, 131, 249; **Supp. XII:** 44, 254, 255, 256, 261–262, 269–270; **Supp. XIII:** 76, 85; **Supp. XV:** 249, 250, 253; **Supp. XVII:** 123
Merrill, Mark (pseudonym). *See* Markson, David
Merrill, Robert, **Retro. Supp. II:** 201
Merrill, Ronald, **Supp. IV Part 2:** 521
Merritt, Abraham, **Supp. XVII:** 58
Merritt, Theresa, **Supp. VIII:** 332
Merritt, Vernon, **Supp. XXII:** 245
"Merry-Go-Round" (Hughes), **Retro. Supp. I:** 194, 205; **Supp. I Part 1:** 333
Merry-Go-Round, The (Van Vechten), **Supp. II Part 2:** 734, 735
Merry Month of May, The (Jones), **Supp. XI: 227–228**
Merry Widow, The (Lehar), **III:** 183
Merton, Thomas, **III:** 357; **Supp. VIII: 193–212; Supp. XXII:** 83, 90
Merwin, W. S., **Supp. III Part 1: 339–360; Supp. III Part 2:** 541; **Supp. IV Part 2:** 620, 623, 626; **Supp. V:** 332; **Supp. IX:** 152, 155, 290; **Supp. XIII:** 274, 277; **Supp. XV:** 222, 342; **Supp. XIX:** 82; **Supp. XXI:** 95
Meryman, Richard, **Supp. IV Part 2:** 579, 583
Meshugah (Singer), **Retro. Supp. II: 315–316**
Mesic, Michael, **Supp. IV Part 1:** 175
Mesic, Penelope, **Supp. X:** 15
Message in the Bottle, The (Percy), **Supp. III Part 1:** 387–388, 393, 397
"Message in the Bottle, The" (Percy), **Supp. III Part 1:** 388
"Message of Flowers and Fire and Flowers, The" (Brooks), **Supp. III Part 1:** 69
Messengers Will Come No More, The (Fiedler), **Supp. XIII:** 103
Messerli, Douglas, **Supp. XVI:** 293
Messiah (Vidal), **Supp. IV Part 2:** 677, 680, 681–682, 685, 691, 692
"Messiah, The" (Wasserstein), **Supp. XV:** 328
Messiah of Stockholm, The (Ozick), **Supp. V:** 270–271; **Supp. XVII:** 42
Messud, Claire, **Supp. XVIII:** 98
Metamorphic Tradition in Modern Poetry (Quinn), **IV:** 421
Metamorphoses (Ovid), **II:** 542–543; **III:** 467, 468; **Supp. XV:** 33; **Supp. XVI:** 20; **Supp. XX: 280**
Metamorphoses (Pound, trans.), **III:** 468–469
Metamorphosis (Kafka), **Supp. XXI:** 89
Metamorphosis, The (Kafka), **IV:** 438; **Retro. Supp. II:** 287–288; **Supp. VIII:** 3
"Metamorphosis and Survival" (Woodcock), **Supp. XIII:** 33
"Metaphor as Mistake" (Percy), **Supp. III Part 1:** 387–388
Metaphor & Memory: Essays (Ozick), **Supp. V:** 272
Metaphor of Trees and Last Poems (Bronk), **Supp. XXI:** 32
"Metaphors of a Magnifico" (Stevens), **IV:** 92
Metaphysical Club, The (Menand), **Supp. XIV:** 40, 197
"Metaphysical Poets, The" (Eliot), **I:** 527, 586
"Metaphysics" (Ginsberg), **Supp. II Part 1:** 313
Metcalf, Paul, **Supp. XIV:** 96
"Meteor, The" (Bradbury), **Supp. IV Part 1:** 102
Methinks the Lady...(Endore), **Supp. XVII:** 61–62
"Metonymy as an Approach to the Real World" (Bronk), **Supp. XXI:** 30
Metress, Christopher P., **Supp. V:** 314
Metrical History of Christianity, The (Taylor), **IV:** 163
Metropolis, The (Sinclair), **Supp. V:** 285
"Metterling Lists, The" (Allen), **Supp. XV:** 15
"Metzengerstein" (Poe), **III:** 411, 417
Mew, Charlotte, **Retro. Supp. II:** 247
Mewshaw, Michael, **Supp. V:** 57; **Supp. X:** 82
"Mexican Hands" (Ryan as Quin), **Supp. XVIII:** 227
"Mexico" (Lowell), **II:** 553, 554
"Mexico, Age Four" (Salinas), **Supp. XIII:** 315
Mexico City Blues (Kerouac), **Supp. III Part 1:** 225, 229
"Mexico Is a Foreign Country: Five Studies in Naturalism" (Warren), **IV:** 241, 252
"Mexico's Children" (Rodriguez), **Supp. XIV:** 302
Meyer, Carolyn, **Supp. XIX:** 194–195, 197
Meyer, Donald B., **III:** 298
Meyer, Ellen Hope, **Supp. V:** 123
Meyer, Robert, **Supp. XXI:** 23
Meyers, Jeffrey, **Retro. Supp. I:** 124, 138; **Retro. Supp. II:** 191
Meynell, Alice, **Supp. I Part 1:** 220
Mezey, Robert, **Supp. IV Part 1:** 60; **Supp. V:** 180; **Supp. XIII:** 312; **Supp. XV:** 74
Mezzanine, The (Baker), **Supp. XIII: 41–43,** 44, 45, 48, 55
"Mezzo Cammin" (Longfellow), **II:** 490
"Mi Abuelo" (Ríos), **Supp. IV Part 2:** 541
Miami (Didion), **Supp. IV Part 1:** 199, 210
Miami and the Siege of Chicago (Mailer), **Retro. Supp. II:** 206
Miasma (Holding), **Supp. XXII: 121–122**
"Michael" (Wordsworth), **III:** 523
Michael, Magali Cornier, **Supp. XIII:** 32
"Michael Angelo: A Fragment" (Longfellow), **II:** 490, 494, 495, 506; **Retro. Supp. II:** 167
"Michael Egerton" (Price), **Supp. VI:** 257–258, 260
Michael Kohlhaas (Kleist), **Supp. IV Part 1:** 224
Michael O'Halloran (Stratton-Porter), **Supp. XX: 222**

Michaels, Leonard, **Supp. XVI: 201–215**
Michaels, Walter Benn, **Retro. Supp. I:** 115, 369, 379
Michael Scarlett (Cozens), **I:** 358–359, 378
"Michael's Veterans Remember" (Espaillat), **Supp. XXI:** 110
Michaux, Henri, **Supp. XVI:** 288
Michelangelo, **I:** 18; **II:** 11–12; **III:** 124; **Supp. I Part 1:** 363; **Supp. XVII:** 112
Michel-Michot, Paulette, **Supp. XI:** 224–225
Michelson, Albert, **IV:** 27
Mickelsson's Ghosts (Gardner), **Supp. VI:** 63, **73–74**
Mickiewicz, Adam, **Supp. II Part 1:** 299
"Microscope" (Trethewey), **Supp. XXI:** 251
Midair (Conroy), **Supp. XVI:** 63, **71–72**
"Mid-Air" (Conroy), **Supp. XVI:** 69, 71
Mid-American Chants (Anderson), **I:** 109, 114
"Midas" (Winters), **Supp. II Part 2:** 801
"Mid-August at Sourdough Mountain Lookout" (Snyder), **Supp. VIII:** 292–293
Midcentury (Dos Passos), **I:** 474, 475, 478, 490, 492–494; **Supp. I Part 2:** 646
Mid-Century American Poets, **III:** 532
"Mid-Day" (Doolittle), **Supp. I Part 1:** 266–267
"Middle Age" (Lowell), **II:** 550
"Middle-Aged, Middle-Class Woman at Midnight, A" (Taggard), **Supp. XXII:** 282–283
"Middleaged Man, The" (Simpson), **Supp. IX:** 274–275
Middle Ages, The (Gurney), **Supp. V:** 96, 105, 108
Middlebrook, Diane Wood, **Supp. IV Part 2:** 444, 451
"Middle Daughter, The" (Kingsolver), **Supp. VII:** 209
Middlemarch (G. Eliot), **I:** 457, 459; **II:** 290, 291; **Retro. Supp. I:** 225; **Supp. I Part 1:** 174; **Supp. IX:** 43; **Supp. XI:** 68; **Supp. XII:** 335
Middle of My Tether, The: Familiar Essays (Epstein), **Supp. XIV: 106–107**
"Middle of Nowhere, The" (Wagoner), **Supp. IX:** 327–328
Middle of the Journey, The (Trilling), **Supp. III Part 2:** 495, 504–506
"Middle of the Way" (Kinnell), **Supp. III Part 1:** 242
"Middle Passage" (Hayden), **Supp. II Part 1:** 363, 375–376
Middle Passage (Johnson), **Supp. VI: 194–196,** 198, 199; **Supp. XIII:** 182
"Middle Toe of the Right Foot, The" (Bierce), **I:** 203
Middleton, Thomas, **Retro. Supp. I:** 62
Middle Years, The (James), **II:** 337–338; **Retro. Supp. I:** 235
"Middle Years, The" (James), **Retro. Supp. I:** 228, 272
"Midnight" (Dunn), **Supp. XI:** 147
"Midnight Consultations, The" (Freneau), **Supp. II Part 1:** 257
Midnight Cry, A (Mather), **Supp. II Part 2:** 460
"Midnight Gladness" (Levertov), **Supp. III Part 1:** 284–285
"Midnight Magic" (Mason), **Supp. VIII:** 146
Midnight Magic: Selected Stories of Bobbie Ann Mason (Mason), **Supp. VIII:** 148
Midnight Mass (Bowles), **Supp. IV Part 1:** 93
"Midnight Postscript" (F. Wright), **Supp. XVII:** 245, 246
"Midnight Show" (Shapiro), **Supp. II Part 2:** 705
"Midpoint" (Updike), **Retro. Supp. I:** 321, 323, 327, 330, 335
Midpoint and Other Poems (Updike), **IV:** 214
"Midrash on Happiness" (Paley), **Supp. VI:** 217
"Midsummer" (Bronk), **Supp. XXI:** 30
"Midsummer in the Blueberry Barrens" (Clampitt), **Supp. IX:** 40–41
"Midsummer Letter" (Carruth), **Supp. XVI:** 47
Midsummer Night's Dream, A (Shakespeare), **Supp. I Part 1:** 369–370; **Supp. X:** 69
Midsummer Night's Sex Comedy, A (film; Allen), **Supp. XV:** 8
"Midwest" (Stafford), **Supp. XI:** 317
"Midwest Poetics" (C. Baxter), **Supp. XVII:** 18
Mieder, Wolfgang, **Supp. XIV:** 126
Mies van der Rohe, Ludwig, **Supp. IV Part 1:** 40
Mighty Aphrodite (film; Allen), **Supp. XV:** 11
"Mighty Fortress, A" (Leopold), **Supp. XIV:** 185
"Mighty Lord, The (Rowson), **Supp. XV:** 243
"Migration, The" (Tate), **IV:** 130
Mihailovitch, Bata, **Supp. VIII:** 272
Mikado, The (Gilbert and Sullivan), **Supp. XXI:** 151
Miklitsch, Robert, **Supp. IV Part 2:** 628, 629
Mila 18 (Uris), **Supp. IV Part 1:** 379; **Supp. XX: 244, 247, 248, 251–252, 253**
Milagro Beanfield War, The (film), **Supp. XIII:** 267
Milagro Beanfield War, The (Nichols), **Supp. XIII:** 253, **265–266**
Milburn, Michael, **Supp. XI:** 239, 242
Milch, David, **Supp. XI:** 348
Mild Day, The (Bronk), **Supp. XXI:** 32
Miles, Barry, **Supp. XII:** 123
Miles, Jack, **Supp. VIII:** 86
Miles, Josephine, **Supp. XIII:** 275
Miles, Julie, **I:** 199
Miles, Kitty, **I:** 199
"Miles of Night, The" (Halliday), **Supp. XIX:** 91
Milestone, Lewis, **Supp. I Part 1:** 281
Miles Wallingford (Cooper). *See Afloat and Ashore* (Cooper)
Milford, Kate, **Supp. XVIII:** 150
Milford, Nancy, **II:** 83; **Supp. IX:** 60
Milhaud, Darius, **Supp. IV Part 1:** 81
Miligate, Michael, **IV:** 123, 130, 132
"Militant Nudes" (Hardwick), **Supp. III Part 1:** 210–211
Milk (film), **Supp. XX: 269**
"Milk Bottles" (Anderson), **I:** 114
"Milk Prose" (Weigl), **Supp. XIX:** 278
Milk Train Doesn't Stop Here Anymore, The (T. Williams), **IV:** 382, 383, 384, 386, 390, 391, 392, 393, 394, 395, 398
Mill, James, **II:** 357
Mill, John Stuart, **III:** 294–295; **Supp. XI:** 196; **Supp. XIV:** 22
Millar, Kenneth. *See* Macdonald, Ross
Millar, Margaret (Margaret Sturm), **Supp. IV Part 2:** 464, 465
Millay, Cora, **III:** 123, 133–134, 135–136
Millay, Edna St. Vincent, **I:** 482; **II:** 530; **III: 122–144; IV:** 433, 436; **Retro. Supp. II:** 48; **Supp. I Part 2:** 707, 714, 726; **Supp. IV Part 1:** 168; **Supp. IV Part 2:** 607; **Supp. V:** 113; **Supp. IX:** 20; **Supp. XIV:** 120, 121, 122, 127; **Supp. XV:** 42, 46, 51, 250, 293, 307; **Supp. XVII:** 69, 75, 96; **Supp. XXII:** 273
Millennium Approaches (Kushner), **Supp. IX:** 141, 142, 145
Miller, Arthur, **I:** 81, 94; **III: 145–169; Supp. IV Part 1:** 359; **Supp. IV Part 2:** 574; **Supp. VIII:** 334; **Supp. XIII:** 127; **Supp. XIV:** 102, 239; **Supp. XVI:** 194
Miller, Mrs. Arthur (Ingeborg Morath), **III:** 162–163
Miller, Mrs. Arthur (Marilyn Monroe), **III:** 161, 162–163
Miller, Mrs. Arthur (Mary Grace Slattery), **III:** 146, 161
Miller, Brown, **Supp. IV Part 1:** 67
Miller, Carol, **Supp. IV Part 1:** 400, 405, 409, 410, 411
Miller, Caroline, **Supp. XXII: 187–201**
Miller, Henry, **I:** 97, 157; **III:** 40, **170–192; IV:** 138; **Retro. Supp. II:** 327; **Supp. I Part 2:** 546; **Supp. V:** 119, 131; **Supp. X:** 183, 185, 187, 194, 195; **Supp. XIII:** 1, 17; **Supp. XXII:** 88, 256, 257, 258
Miller, Henry (actor), **Supp. XVI:** 182
Miller, Herman, **Supp. I Part 2:** 614, 617
Miller, James E., Jr., **IV:** 352
Miller, Jean Baker, **Supp. XXII:** 18
Miller, Jeffrey, **Supp. IV Part 1:** 95
Miller, J. Hillis, **Supp. IV Part 1:** 387
Miller, Jim Wayne, **Supp. XX: 161–176**
Miller, Joaquin, **I:** 193, 195, 459; **Supp. II Part 1:** 351
Miller, John Duncan, **Supp. I Part 2:** 604
Miller, John E., **Supp. XXII:** 295
Miller, John M., **Supp. XXII:** 214, 218
Miller, Jonathan, **Retro. Supp. II:** 181
Miller, Laura, **Supp. XIII:** 48; **Supp. XIX:** 53, 54, 56; **Supp. XXII:** 239
Miller, Marilyn, **Supp. XVI:** 187
Miller, Matt, **Supp. XV:** 211
Miller, Matthew, **Supp. XVI:** 47, 51
Miller, Orilla, **Supp. I Part 1:** 48

Miller, Perry, **I:** 546, 547, 549, 550, 560; **IV:** 186; **Supp. I Part 1:** 31, 104; **Supp. I Part 2:** 484; **Supp. IV Part 2:** 422; **Supp. VIII:** 101
Miller, R. Baxter, **Retro. Supp. I:** 195, 207
Miller, Robert Ellis, **II:** 588
Miller, Ruth, **Supp. X:** 324
Miller, Stuart, **Supp. XVI:** 242
Miller, Sue, **Supp. X:** 77, 85; **Supp. XI:** 190; **Supp. XII: 289–305**
Miller of Old Church, The (Glasgow), **II:** 175, 181
"Miller's Tale" (Chaucer), **III:** 283
Miller Williams and the Poetry of the Particular (Burns), **Supp. XV:** 339
Millett, Kate, **Supp. X:** 193, 196
Millgate, Michael, **Retro. Supp. I:** 91
Mill Hand's Lunch Bucket (Bearden), **Supp. VIII:** 337
Millhauser, Steven, **Supp. XXII:** 49
Millier, Brett C., **Retro. Supp. II:** 39
Milligan, Bryce, **Supp. XIII:** 274, 275, 277
Million Little Pieces, A (Frey), **Supp. XXII:** 95
Millions of Strange Shadows (Hecht), **Supp. X:** 57, **62–65**
"Million Young Workmen, 1915, A" (Sandburg), **III:** 585
Millroy the Magician (Theroux), **Supp. VIII:** 325
Mills, Alice, **Supp. XIII:** 233
Mills, Benjamin Fay, **III:** 176
Mills, C. Wright, **Supp. I Part 2:** 648, 650
Mills, Florence, **Supp. I Part 1:** 322
Mills, Ralph J., Jr., **III:** 530; **Supp. IV Part 1:** 64; **Supp. XI:** 311
Mills, Tedi López, **Supp. XVI:** 281
Mills of the Kavanaughs, The (Lowell), **II:** 542–543, 546, 550; **III:** 508; **Retro. Supp. II:** 178, 179, 188
"Mills of the Kavanaughs, The" (Lowell), **II:** 542–543
Milne, A. A., **Supp. IX:** 189
Milne, A. J. M., **I:** 278
Milosz, Czeslaw, **Supp. III Part 2:** 630; **Supp. VIII:** 20, 22; **Supp. XI:** 267, 312; **Supp. XVII:** 241; **Supp. XX: 165; Supp. XXI:** 132; **Supp. XXII:** 92
Miltner, Robert, **Supp. XI:** 142
Milton, Edith, **Supp. VIII:** 79; **Supp. X:** 82
Milton, John, **I:** 6, 138, 273, 587–588; **II:** 11, 15, 113, 130, 411, 540, 542; **III:** 40, 124, 201, 225, 274, 468, 471, 486, 487, 503, 511; **IV:** 50, 82, 126, 137, 155, 157, 241, 279, 347, 422, 461, 494; **Retro. Supp. I:** 60, 67, 127, 360; **Retro. Supp. II:** 161, 295; **Supp. I Part 1:** 124, 150, 370; **Supp. I Part 2:** 412, 422, 491, 501, 522, 622, 722, 724; **Supp. IV Part 2:** 430, 634; **Supp. VIII:** 294; **Supp. X:** 22, 23, 36; **Supp. XII:** 180; **Supp. XIV:** 5, 7; **Supp. XX: 108**
Milton, John R., **Supp. IV Part 2:** 503
Milton and His Modern Critics (L. P. Smith), **Supp. XIV:** 347
"Milton by Firelight" (Snyder), **Supp. II Part 1:** 314; **Supp. VIII:** 294
"Miltonic Sonnet, A" (Wilbur), **Supp. III Part 2:** 558
Mimesis (Auerbach), **III:** 453
"Mimnermos and the Motions of Hedonism" (Carson), **Supp. XII: 99–100**
"Mimnermos Interviews, The" (Carson), **Supp. XII: 100–101**
Mims, Edwin, **Supp. I Part 1:** 362, 364, 365, 371
"Mind" (Wilbur), **Supp. III Part 2:** 554
"Mind, The" (Kinnell), **Supp. III Part 1:** 245
Mind Breaths: Poems 1972–1977 (Ginsberg), **Supp. II Part 1:** 326
Mindfield: New and Selected Poems (Corso), **Supp. XII: 136**
"Mind in the Modern World" (Trilling), **Supp. III Part 2:** 512
"Mind Is Shapely, Art Is Shapely" (Ginsberg), **Supp. II Part 1:** 327
Mindlin, Henrique, **Supp. I Part 1:** 92
Mind of My Mind (O. Butler), **Supp. XIII:** 62, 63
Mind of Primitive Man, The (Boas), **Supp. XIV:** 209
Mind-Reader, The (Wilbur), **Supp. III Part 2:** 560–562
"Mind-Reader, The" (Wilbur), **Supp. III Part 2:** 561–562
"Mind's Landscape on an Early Winter Day, The" (Bronk), **Supp. XXI:** 28
Mindwheel (Pinsky), **Supp. VI:** 235
Minear, Richard H., **Supp. XVI:** 101, 102
"Mined Country" (Wilbur), **Supp. III Part 2:** 546–548
"Minefields" (Espaillat), **Supp. XXI:** 106
"Mine Own John Berryman" (Levine), **Supp. V:** 179–180
Miner, Bob, **Supp. V:** 23
Miner, Earl, **III:** 466, 479
Miner, Madonne, **Supp. XIII:** 29
"Minerva Writes Poems" (Cisneros), **Supp. VII:** 63–64, 66
Mingus, Charles, **Supp. IX:** 152
"Mingus in Diaspora" (Matthews), **Supp. IX:** 166
"Mingus in Shadow" (Matthews), **Supp. IX:** 168–169
Ming Yellow (Marquand), **III:** 56
"Minimal, The" (Roethke), **III:** 531–532
Minimus Poems, The (X. J. Kennedy), **Supp. XV:** 169–170
"Mini-novela: *Rosa y sus espinas" (Mora), Supp. XIII:* 218
"Minions of Midas, The" (London), **II:** 474–475
Minister's Charge, The, or The Apprenticeship of Lemuel Barber (Howells), **II:** 285–286, 287
Minister's Wooing, The (Stowe), **II:** 541
"Minister's Wooing, The" (Stowe), **Supp. I Part 2:** 592–595
"Ministration of Our Departed Friends, The" (Stowe), **Supp. I Part 2:** 586–587
"Minneapolis Poem, The" (Wright), **Supp. III Part 2:** 601–602
Minnesota Grain Show, The (radio, Keillor), **Supp. XVI:** 170
"Minnesota Transcendentalist" (Peseroff), **Supp. IV Part 1:** 71
Minnie, Temple, **II:** 344
Minority Report: H. L. Mencken's Notebooks (Mencken), **III:** 112
Minor Pleasures of Life, The (Macaulay), **Supp. XIV:** 348
"Minor Poems" (Eliot), **I:** 579
"Minor Poet" (Hay), **Supp. XIV:** 127
"Minor Topics" (Howells), **II:** 274
Minot, Susan, **Supp. VI: 203–215**
"Minotaur Loves His Labyrinth, The" (Simic), **Supp. VIII:** 270, 279, 281
"Minstrel Man" (Hughes), **Supp. I Part 1:** 325
Mint (Nye), **Supp. XIII:** 277
"Minting Time" (Sarton), **Supp. VIII:** 259
Mint Snowball (Nye), **Supp. XIII:** 277–278, **284–285**
"Mint Snowball" (Nye), **Supp. XIII:** 278, 284
"Mint Snowball II" (Nye), **Supp. XIII:** 284, 285
Minty Alley (C. L. R. James), **Supp. XXI:** 159, 161
Mintzlaff, Dorothy, **Supp. XV:** 153
Minus, Marian, **Supp. XVIII:** 282
Minutes to Go (Corso, Gysin, Beiles and Burroughs), **Supp. XII:** 129
Mi querido Rafa (Hinojosa). *See Dear Rafe* (Hinojosa)
Mirabell: Books of Number (Merrill), **Supp. III Part 1:** 332–334
"Miracle" (Carver), **Supp. III Part 1:** 139–140
Miracle at Verdun (Chlumberg), **Supp. XIX:** 242
"Miracle for Breakfast, A" (Bishop), **Retro. Supp. II:** 43
Miracle of Catfish, A (L. Brown), **Supp. XXI:** 39–40, 47, **48**
"Miracle of Lava Canyon, The" (Henry), **Supp. II Part 1:** 389, 390
Miracle of Mindfulness, The: A Manual on Meditation (Thich Nhat Hanh), **Supp. V:** 199–200
Mirage (Masters), **Supp. I Part 2:** 459, 470, 471
"Mirages, The" (Hayden), **Supp. II Part 1:** 373
"Miranda" (Buck), **Supp. II Part 1:** 128
Miranda, Carmen, **Supp. XII:** 165
Miranda, Francisco de, **Supp. I Part 2:** 522
"Miranda Over the Valley" (Dubus), **Supp. VII:** 81–83
"Miriam" (Capote), **Supp. III Part 1:** 117, 120, 122
"Miriam" (Whittier), **Supp. I Part 2:** 691, 703
"Miriam Tazewell" (Ransom), **Supp. X:** 58
"Mirror" (Merrill), **Supp. III Part 1:** 322
"Mirror" (Plath), **Retro. Supp. II:** 248–249, 257

"Mirror, The" (Glück), **Supp. V:** 83
"Mirroring Evil: Nazi Images/Recent Art" (Epstein), **Supp. XII:** 166
"Mirror of Leopold Leopoldovitch Siegelevsky, The" (Siegel), **Supp. XXII:** 257–258
Mirrors (Creeley), **Supp. IV Part 1:** 156
Mirrors and Windows (Nemerov), **III:** 269, 275–277
"Mirrors of Chartres Street" (Faulkner), **II:** 56
Mirsky, Norman, **Supp. XX: 244**
Mirvis, Tova, **Supp. XX: 177–191**
Misanthrope, The (Molière; Wilbur, trans.), **Supp. III Part 2:** 552, 560
Miscellaneous Poems (Rowson), **Supp. XV:** 243
Miscellaneous Works of Mr. Philip Freneau, Containing His Essays and Additional Poems (Freneau), **Supp. II Part 1:** 263, 264, 266
Miscellany of American Poetry, A (Untermeyer, ed.), **Supp. XV:** 305, 310
Misérables, Les (Hugo), **II:** 179; **Supp. I Part 1:** 280
Misery (King), **Supp. V:** 140, 141, 142, 147–148, 151, 152
Mises, Ludwig von, **Supp. IV Part 2:** 524
Misfits, The (A. Miller), **III:** 147, 149, 156, 161–162, 163
"Misogamist, The" (Dubus), **Supp. VII:** 86–87
Misread City, The: New Literary Los Angeles (Gioia and Timberg, eds.), **Supp. XV:** 116
Misrepresentations Corrected, and Truth Vindicated, in a Reply to the Rev. Mr. Solomon Williams's Book (Edwards), **I:** 549
Miss Crandall's School for Young Ladies & Little Misses of Color (Nelson and Alexander), **Supp. XVIII:** 171, 175, 181, **185–186**
"Miss Cynthie" (R. Fisher), **Supp. XIX:** 65, 69
Miss Doll, Go Home (Markson), **Supp. XVII:** 138
"Miss Ella" (Z. Fitzgerald), **Supp. IX:** 57, 59, **71–72**
"Miss Emily and the Bibliographer" (Tate), **Supp. II Part 1:** 103
"Miss Furr and Miss Skeene" (Stein), **IV:** 29–30
"Missing Child" (Simic), **Supp. VIII:** 282
"Missing in Action" (Komunyakaa), **Supp. XIII:** 123, 124
Missing/Kissing: Missing Marisa, Kissing Christine (Shanley), **Supp. XIV:** 316
Missing Link (X. J. Kennedy), **Supp. XV:** 165
"Missing Poem, The" (Halliday), **Supp. XIX:** 93–94
"Mission of Jane, The" (Wharton), **Retro. Supp. I:** 367
"Missions, The" (Rodriguez), **Supp. XIV:** 303
Mission to Moscow (film), **Supp. I Part 1:** 281
"Mississippi" (Bass), **Supp. XVI:** 17
"Mississippi" (Faulkner), **Retro. Supp. I:** 77
"Mississippi" (Simpson), **Supp. IX:** 271
"Miss Kate in H-1" (Twain), **IV:** 193
Miss Kelly (Holding), **Supp. XXII: 133–134**
Miss Leonora When Last Seen (Taylor), **Supp. V:** 323
Miss Lonelyhearts (West), **I:** 107; **II:** 436; **III:** 357; **IV:** 287, 288, 290–297, 300, 301, 305, 306; **Retro. Supp. II:** 321, 322, 325, 328, **332–335**
Miss Mamma Aimee (Caldwell), **I:** 308, 309, 310
"Miss Mary Pask" (Wharton), **IV:** 316; **Retro. Supp. I:** 382
"Miss McEnders" (Chopin), **Retro. Supp. II:** 67
"Missoula Softball Tournament" (Hugo), **Supp. VI:** 132
Miss Ravenel's Conversion from Secession to Loyalty (De Forest), **IV:** 350
Miss Saigon (musical), **Supp. XXI:** 155
"Miss Tempy's Watchers" (Jewett), **II:** 401; **Retro. Supp. II:** 139
"Miss Terriberry to Wed in Suburbs" (Updike), **Retro. Supp. I:** 335
"Miss Urquhart's Tiara" (Jarman), **Supp. XVII:** 116
"Mist, The" (King), **Supp. V:** 144
"Mistaken Charity, A" (Freeman), **Retro. Supp. II:** 138
"Mister Brother" (Cunningham), **Supp. XV:** 68
Misterioso (Sorrentino), **Supp. XXI:** 236, 237
"Mister Toussan" (Ellison), **Retro. Supp. II:** 124–125; **Supp. II Part 1:** 238
"Mistress of Sydenham Plantation, The" (Jewett), **Retro. Supp. II:** 141
Mitcham, Matthew, **Supp. XX: 264**
Mitchell, Burroughs, **Supp. XI:** 218, 222, 227
Mitchell, Don, **Supp. XXII:** 207, 211, 212
Mitchell, Margaret, **II:** 177; **Supp. XX: 243; Supp. XXII:** 195
Mitchell, Roger, **Supp. IV Part 1:** 70; **Supp. XV:** 213, 215
Mitchell, Dr. S. Weir, **IV:** 310
Mitchell, Tennessee. *See* Anderson, Mrs. Sherwood (Tennessee Mitchell)
Mitchell, Verner, **Supp. XVIII:** 281, 286
Mitchell, Wesley C., **Supp. I Part 2:** 632, 643
"Mitchie-Gawa" (Taggard), **Supp. XXII:** 272
Mitch Miller (Masters), **Supp. I Part 2:** 456, 466, 469–471, 474, 475, 476
Mitchum, Robert, **Supp. IX:** 95, 250
Mitgang, Herbert, **Supp. IV Part 1:** 220, 226, 307; **Supp. VIII:** 124; **Supp. XIX:** 251; **Supp. XX: 243**
Mitla Pass (Uris), **Supp. XX: 244, 247, 248, 256**
Mixed Company: Collected Short Stories (Shaw), **Supp. XIX:** 251
"Mixed Sequence" (Roethke), **III:** 547
Miyazawa Kenji, **Supp. VIII:** 292
Mizener, Arthur, **II:** 77, 81, 84, 94; **IV:** 132; **Supp. XVIII:** 249
Mizner, Addison, **Supp. XVI:** 191
Mizner, Wilson, **Supp. XVI:** 191, 195
Mladenoff, Nancy, **Supp. X:** 176
"M'liss: An Idyl of Red Mountain" (Harte), **Supp. II Part 1:** 339
"Mnemonic Devices" (Goldbarth), **Supp. XII:** 183
"Mobile in Back of the Smithsonian, The" (Swenson), **Supp. IV Part 2:** 646
Mobilio, Albert, **Supp. VIII:** 3; **Supp. XVIII:** 144; **Supp. XIX:** 45
Moby Dick (film), **Supp. IV Part 1:** 102, 116
Moby-Dick (Melville), **Supp. XXII:** 81, 268
Moby Dick; or, The Whale (Melville), **I:** 106, 354; **II:** 33, 224–225, 236, 539–540; **III:** 28–29, 74, 75, 77, 81, 82, 83–86, 87, 89, 90, 91, 93, 94, 95, 359, 453, 556; **IV:** 57, 199, 201, 202; **Retro. Supp. I:** 160, 220, 243, 244, 248, **249–253,** 254, 256, 257, 335; **Retro. Supp. II:** 121, 186, 275; **Supp. I Part 1:** 249; **Supp. I Part 2:** 579; **Supp. IV Part 2:** 613; **Supp. V:** 281; **Supp. VIII:** 106, 188, 198; **Supp. XXI:** 159
Mock, John, **Supp. XIII:** 174
"Mocking-Bird, The" (Bierce), **I:** 202
"Mock Orange" (Glück), **Supp. V:** 84–85
Modarressi, Mitra, **Supp. IV Part 2:** 657
Models of Misrepresentation: On the Fiction of E. L. Doctorow (Morris), **Supp. IV Part 1:** 231
Model World and Other Stories, A (Chabon), **Supp. XI:** 66
Modern American and British Poetry (Untermeyer, ed.), **Supp. XV:** 306
Modern American Poetry (Untermeyer, ed.), **Supp. XV:** 293, 303, 306, 312
Modern American Verse (Untermeyer, ed.), **Supp. XV:** 301
Modern Brazilian Architecture (Bishop, trans.), **Supp. I Part 1:** 92
Modern British Poetry (Untermeyer, ed.), **Supp. XV:** 305, 308, 312
Modern Fiction Studies, **Supp. V:** 238
*Modern Fiction Studies (*Haegert), **Supp. XVI:** 69
Modern Instance a Novel, A (Howells), **II:** 275, 279, 282–283, 285
Modern Library, The, **Retro. Supp. I:** 112, 113
Modern Mephistopheles, A (Alcott), **Supp. I Part 1:** 37–38
Modern Poetic Sequence, The (Rosenthal), **Supp. V:** 333
"Modern Poetry" (Crane), **I:** 390
Modern Poetry and the Tradition (Brooks), **Supp. XIV: 5–7**
"Modern Race Creeds and Their Fallacies" (Locke), **Supp. XIV:** 210
Modern Rhetoric, with Readings (Brooks and Warren), **Supp. XIV:** 11

"Modern Sorcery" (Simic), **Supp. VIII:** 283
Modern Times (album, Dylan), **Supp. XVIII:** 28, 31, 33
"Modern Times" (Zukofsky), **Supp. III Part 2:** 624
Modern Writer, The (Anderson), **I:** 117
Modersohn, Otto, **Supp. I Part 2:** 573
Modersohn, Mrs. Otto (Paula Becker), **Supp. I Part 2:** 573–574
"Modes of Being" (Levertov), **Supp. III Part 1:** 282
Modest Enquiry into the Nature and Necessity of a Paper-Currency, A (Franklin), **II:** 108–109
"Modest Proposal, A" (Swift), **I:** 295; **Retro. Supp. II:** 287
"Modest Proposal with Feline Feeling, A" (Neugeboren), **Supp. XVI:** 219
"Modest Self-Tribute, A" (Wilson), **IV:** 431, 432
Moeller, Philip, **III:** 398, 399
"Moench von Berchtesgaden, Der" (Voss), **I:** 199–200
Moers, Ellen, **Retro. Supp. II:** 99
Moe's Villa and Other Stories (Purdy), **Supp. VII:** 270, 280
Moffat, Juan, **Supp. XX: 52**
Mogen, David, **Supp. IV Part 1:** 106
Mohammed, **I:** 480; **II:** 1
Mohawk (Russo), **Supp. XII: 326–328**
Moir, William Wilmerding, **Supp. V:** 279
Moldaw, Carol, **Supp. XV:** 264; **Supp. XVII:** 127, 130
"Moles" (Oliver), **Supp. VII:** 235
Molesworth, Charles, **Supp. IV Part 1:** 39; **Supp. VIII:** 292, 306; **Supp. XIX:** 121–122
Molière (Jean-Baptiste Poquelin), **III:** 113; **Supp. I Part 2:** 406; **Supp. III Part 2:** 552, 560; **Supp. IV Part 2:** 585; **Supp. V:** 101
"Molino Rojo, El" (Ríos), **Supp. IV Part 2:** 544
Moll Flanders (Defoe), **Supp. V:** 127; **Supp. XIII:** 43
"Molloch in State Street" (Whittier), **Supp. I Part 2:** 687
"Moll Pitcher" (Whittier), **Supp. I Part 2:** 684
"Molly Brant, Iroquois Matron" (Gunn Allen), **Supp. IV Part 1:** 331
Molnar, Ferenc, **Supp. XVI:** 187
"Moloch" (H. Miller), **III:** 177
Momaday, N. Scott, **Supp. IV Part 1:** 274, 323, 324, 404; **Supp. IV Part 2: 479–496,** 504, 557, 562; **Supp. XII:** 209; **Supp. XVIII:** 58
" 'Momentary Stay against Confusion,' A: Frank Conroy's *Stop-Time*" (T. Adams), **Supp. XVI:** 69
Moment of Untruth (Lacy), **Supp. XV:** 206, 207
Moments of the Italian Summer (Wright), **Supp. III Part 2:** 602
Moment to Moment: Poems of a Mountain Recluse (Budbill), **Supp. XIX:** 2, 7, **9–10**
"Momus" (Robinson), **III:** 508
Monaghan, Charles, **Supp. XIX:** 155
Monaghan, Pat, **Supp. XI:** 121
Monaghan, Patricia, **Supp. XVII:** 76, 123, 127, 129
Mona Lisa Overdrive (W. Gibson), **Supp. XVI:** 119, 120, **127–128**
"Mon Ami" (Bourne), **I:** 227
Monet, Claude, **Retro. Supp. I:** 378
"Monet's 'Waterlilies' " (Hayden), **Supp. II Part 1:** 361–362
Monette, Paul, **Supp. X: 145–161**
Money (Amis), **Retro. Supp. I:** 278
"Money" (Matthews), **Supp. IX:** 166
"Money" (Nemerov), **III:** 287
Money, Money, Money (Wagoner), **Supp. IX:** 324, **333–334**
Moneyball: The Art of Winning an Unfair Game (M. Lewis), **Supp. XVII:** 210
Moneychangers, The (Sinclair), **Supp. V:** 285
Money Writes! (Sinclair), **Supp. V:** 277
Monica, Saint, **IV:** 140
Monikins, The (Cooper), **I:** 348, 354
Monk, Thelonious, **Supp. XVIII:** 62
Monk and the Hangman's Daughter, The (Bierce), **I:** 199–200, 209
"Monkey" (Weigl), **Supp. XIX:** 278
"Monkey Garden, The" (Cisneros), **Supp. VII:** 63
"Monkey Puzzle, The" (Moore), **III:** 194, 207, 211
Monkeys (Minot), **Supp. VI:** 203–205, **206–210**
"Monkeys, The" (Moore), **III:** 201, 202
Monkey Wars, The (Weigl), **Supp. XIX:** 276, 278–280
Monkey Wrench Gang, The (Abbey), **Supp. VIII:** 42; **Supp. XIII: 9–11,** 16
"Monk of Casal-Maggiore, The" (Longfellow), **II:** 505
"Monocle de Mon Oncle, Le" (Stevens), **IV:** 78, 84; **Retro. Supp. I:** 301; **Supp. III Part 1:** 20; **Supp. X:** 58
"Monolog from a Mattress" (Untermeyer), **Supp. XV:** 307
"Monologue for Mothers" (Taggard), **Supp. XXII:** 279
Monro, Harold, **III:** 465; **Retro. Supp. I:** 127; **Supp. XV:** 296
Monroe, Harriet, **I:** 235, 384, 390, 393; **III:** 458, 581, 586; **IV:** 74; **Retro. Supp. I:** 58, 131; **Retro. Supp. II:** 82, 83; **Supp. I Part 1:** 256, 257, 258, 262, 263, 267; **Supp. I Part 2:** 374, 387, 388, 464, 610, 611, 613, 614, 615, 616; **Supp. XIV:** 286; **Supp. XV:** 43, 299, 302
Monroe, James, **Supp. I Part 2:** 515, 517
Monroe, Lucy, **Retro. Supp. II:** 70
Monroe, Marilyn, **III:** 161, 162–163
Monroe's Embassy; or, the Conduct of the Government in Relation to Our Claims to the Navigation of the Mississippi (Brown), **Supp. I Part 1:** 146
"Monsoon Season" (Komunyakaa), **Supp. XIII:** 122
Monsour, Leslie, **Supp. XV:** 125
"Monster, The" (Crane), **I:** 418
Monster, The, and Other Stories (Crane), **I:** 409
Montage of a Dream Deferred (Hughes), **Retro. Supp. I:** 194, **208–209; Supp. I Part 1:** 333, 339–341
Montagu, Ashley, **Supp. I Part 1:** 314
"Montaigne" (Emerson), **II:** 6
Montaigne, Michel de, **II:** 1, 5, 6, 8, 14–15, 16, 535; **III:** 600; **Retro. Supp. I:** 247; **Supp. XIV:** 105; **Supp. XXI:** 111, 205
Montale, Eugenio, **Supp. III Part 1:** 320; **Supp. V:** 337–338; **Supp. VIII:** 30; **Supp. XV:** 112
Montalembert, Hughes de, **Supp. XV:** 349
"Montana Memory" (Maclean), **Supp. XIV:** 221
"Montana; or the End of Jean-Jacques Rousseau" (Fiedler), **Supp. XIII: 97–98**
"Montana Ranch Abandoned" (Hugo), **Supp. VI:** 139
"Mont Blanc" (Shelley), **Supp. IX:** 52
Montcalm, Louis Joseph de, **Supp. I Part 2:** 498
Montcalm and Wolfe (Parkman), **Supp. II Part 2:** 596, 609, 610, 611–613
Montemarano, Nicholas, **Supp. XVI:** 227
Montgomery, Benilde, **Supp. XIII:** 202
Montgomery, Robert, **Supp. I Part 2:** 611; **Supp. IV Part 1:** 130
Month of Sundays, A (Updike), **Retro. Supp. I:** 325, 327, 329, 330, 331, 333, 335
Monti, Luigi, **II:** 504
Montoya, José, **Supp. IV Part 2:** 545
"Montrachet-le-Jardin" (Stevens), **IV:** 82
Mont-Saint-Michel and Chartres (Adams), **I:** 1, 9, 12–14, 18, 19, 21; **Supp. I Part 2:** 417
Montserrat (Hellman), **Supp. I Part 1:** 283–285
Montserrat (Robles), **Supp. I Part 1:** 283–285
"Monument, The" (Bishop), **Supp. I Part 1:** 89
Monument, The (Strand), **Supp. IV Part 2:** 629, 630
"Monument in Utopia, A" (Schnackenberg), **Supp. XV:** 261, 263
"Monument Mountain" (Bryant), **Supp. I Part 1:** 156, 162
"Monument to After-Thought Unveiled, A" (Frost), **Retro. Supp. I:** 124
Moo (Smiley), **Supp. VI:** 292, **303–305**
Moods (Alcott), **Supp. I Part 1:** 33, 34–35, 43
Moody, Anne, **Supp. IV Part 1:** 11
Moody, Richard, **Supp. I Part 1:** 280
Moody, Rick, **Supp. XXI:** 117
Moody, Ron, **Supp. XXII:** 49
Moody, William Vaughn, **III:** 507; **IV:** 26
Moody, Mrs. William Vaughn, **I:** 384; **Supp. I Part 2:** 394
"Moon" (A. Finch), **Supp. XVII:** 77
Moon, Henry Lee, **Supp. XVIII:** 281, 285
"Moon and the Night and the Men, The" (Berryman), **I:** 172

"Moon Deluxe" (F. Barthelme), **Supp. XI:** 26, 27, 33, 36
Mooney, Tom, **I:** 505
"Moon-Face" (London), **II:** 475
Moon-Face and Other Stories (London), **II:** 483
"Moon Flock" (Dickey), **Supp. IV Part 1:** 186
Moon for the Misbegotten, A (O'Neill), **III:** 385, 401, 403, 404
Moon in a Mason Jar (Wrigley), **Supp. XVIII: 295–298**
Moon in Its Flight, The (Sorrentino), **Supp. XXI:** 226
"Moon in Its Flight, The" (Sorrentino), **Supp. XXI:** 229
Moon Is a Gong, The (Dos Passos). *See Garbage Man, The* (Dos Passos)
Moon Is Down, The (Steinbeck), **IV:** 51
Moon Lady, The (Tan), **Supp. X:** 289
"Moonlight Alert" (Winters), **Supp. II Part 2:** 801, 811, 815
"Moonlight: Chickens on a Road" (Wrigley), **Supp. XVIII:** 295–296, 297
"Moonlit Night" (Reznikoff), **Supp. XIV:** 285–286
Moon of the Caribbees, The (O'Neill), **III:** 388
Moon Palace (Auster), **Supp. XII:** 22, 27, **30–32**
"Moonshine" (Komunyakaa), **Supp. XIII:** 127, 128
"Moon Solo" (Laforgue), **Supp. XIII:** 346
Moonstone, The (Collins), **Supp. XX: 236**
Moonstruck (screenplay, Shanley), **Supp. XIV:** 315, 316, **321–324**
"Moon upon her fluent Route, The" (Dickinson), **I:** 471
Moony's Kid Don't Cry (T. Williams), **IV:** 381
Moore, Arthur, **Supp. I Part 1:** 49
Moore, Deborah Dash, **Supp. XX: 246**
Moore, George, **I:** 103
Moore, Hannah, **Supp. XV:** 231
Moore, John Milton, **III:** 193
Moore, Lorrie, **Supp. VIII:** 145; **Supp. X: 163–180**
Moore, Marianne, **I:** 58, 285, 401, 428; **III: 193–217,** 514, 592–593; **IV:** 74, 75, 76, 91, 402; **Retro. Supp. I:** 416, 417; **Retro. Supp. II:** 39, 44, 48, 50, 82, 178, 179, 243, 244; **Supp. I Part 1:** 84, 89, 255, 257; **Supp. I Part 2:** 707; **Supp. II Part 1:** 21; **Supp. III Part 1:** 58, 60, 63; **Supp. III Part 2:** 612, 626, 627; **Supp. IV Part 1:** 242, 246, 257; **Supp. IV Part 2:** 454, 640, 641; **Supp. XIV:** 124, 130; **Supp. XV:** 306, 307; **Supp. XVII:** 131; **Supp. XXI:** 98; **Supp. XXII:** 273–274
Moore, Marie Lorena. *See* Moore, Lorrie
Moore, Mary Tyler, **Supp. V:** 107
Moore, Mary Warner, **III:** 193
Moore, Dr. Merrill, **III:** 506
Moore, Steven, **Supp. IV Part 1:** 279, 283, 284, 285, 287; **Supp. XII:** 151; **Supp. XVII:** 230, 231, 232; **Supp. XXII:** 261, 265
Moore, Sturge, **III:** 459
Moore, Thomas, **II:** 296, 299, 303; **Supp. IX:** 104; **Supp. X:** 114
Moore, Virginia, **Supp. XV:** 308
Moorehead, Caroline, **Supp. XIV:** 337
Moorepack, Howard, **Supp. XV:** 199
"Moorings" (Hoffman), **Supp. XVIII:** 87
Moos, Malcolm, **III:** 116, 119
"Moose, The" (Bishop), **Retro. Supp. II:** 50; **Supp. I Part 1:** 73, 93, 94, 95; **Supp. IX:** 45, 46
"Moose Wallow, The" (Hayden), **Supp. II Part 1:** 367
"Moquihuitzin's Answer" (Everwine), **Supp. XV:** 78
Mora, Pat, **Supp. XIII: 213–232**
"Moral Bully, The" (Holmes), **Supp. I Part 1:** 302
"Moral Character, the Practice of Law, and Legal Education" (Hall), **Supp. VIII:** 127
"Moral Equivalent for Military Service, A" (Bourne), **I:** 230
"Moral Equivalent of War, The" (James), **II:** 361; **Supp. I Part 1:** 20
"Moral Imperatives for World Order" (Locke), **Supp. XIV:** 207, 213
Moralités Légendaires (Laforgue), **I:** 573
"Morality and Mercy in Vienna" (Pynchon), **Supp. II Part 2:** 620, 624
"Morality of Indian Hating, The" (Momaday), **Supp. IV Part 2:** 484
"Morality of Poetry, The" (Wright), **Supp. III Part 2:** 596–597, 599
Moral Man and Immoral Society (Niebuhr), **III:** 292, 295–297
"Morals Is Her Middle Name" (Hughes), **Supp. I Part 1:** 338
"Morals of Chess, The" (Franklin), **II:** 121
"Moral Substitute for War, A" (Addams), **Supp. I Part 1:** 20
"Moral Theology of Atticus Finch, The" (Shaffer), **Supp. VIII:** 127
"Moral Thought, A" (Freneau), **Supp. II Part 1:** 262
Moran, Thomas, **Supp. IV Part 2:** 603–604
Moran of the Lady Letty (Norris), **II:** 264; **III:** 314, 322, 327, 328, 329, 330, 331, 332, 333
Morath, Ingeborg. *See* Miller, Mrs. Arthur (Ingeborg Morath)
Moravec, Paul, **Supp. XIX:** 123
Moravia, Alberto, **I:** 301
Moré, Gonzalo, **Supp. X:** 185
More, Henry, **I:** 132
More, Paul Elmer, **I:** 223–224, 247; **Supp. I Part 2:** 423
Moreau, Gustave, **I:** 66
"More Blues and the Abstract Truth" (Wright), **Supp. XV:** 345
More Boners (Abingdon), **Supp. XVI:** 99
More Conversations with Eudora Welty (Prenshaw, ed.), **Retro. Supp. I:** 340, 341, 342, 343, 344, 352, 353, 354
More Dangerous Thoughts (Ryan as Quin), **Supp. XVIII:** 226, **229–230,** 231, 238
More Die of Heartbreak (Bellow), **Retro. Supp. II:** 31, 33, 34
"More Girl Than Boy" (Komunyakaa), **Supp. XIII:** 117
"More Light! More Light! (Hecht), **Supp. X:** 60
"Morella" (Poe), **III:** 412; **Retro. Supp. II:** 270
"More Love in the Western World" (Updike), **Retro. Supp. I:** 327–328, 329
"Morels" (W. J. Smith), **Supp. XIII: 336–339**
Moreno, Gary, **Supp. XV:** 5
"More Observations Now" (Conroy), **Supp. XVI:** 75
"More of a Corpse Than a Woman" (Rukeyser), **Supp. VI:** 280
"More Pleasant Adventures" (Ashbery), **Supp. III Part 1:** 1
More Poems to Solve (Swenson), **Supp. IV Part 2:** 640, 642, 648
More Stately Mansions (O'Neill), **III:** 385, 401, 404–405
"More Than Human" (Chabon), **Supp. XI:** 71–72
More Things Change The More They Stay the Same, The (J. W. Miller), **Supp. XX: 164**
More Triva (L. P. Smith), **Supp. XIV:** 339
Morgan, Edmund S., **IV:** 149; **Supp. I Part 1:** 101, 102; **Supp. I Part 2:** 484
Morgan, Edwin, **Supp. IV Part 2:** 688
Morgan, Emanuel. *See* Bynner, Witter
Morgan, Henry, **II:** 432; **IV:** 63
Morgan, Jack, **Retro. Supp. II:** 142
Morgan, J. P., **I:** 494; **III:** 14, 15
Morgan, Judith, **Supp. XVI:** 103
Morgan, Neil, **Supp. XVI:** 103
Morgan, Robert, **Supp. V:** 5; **Supp. XX: 161, 162**
Morgan, Robin, **Supp. I Part 2:** 569
Morgan, Ted, **Supp. XIV:** 141
Morgan's Passing (Tyler), **Supp. IV Part 2:** 666–667, 668, 669
Morgenstern, Dan, **Supp. XIX:** 159
Morgenthau, Hans, **III:** 291, 309
Morgesons, The (E. Stoddard), **Supp. XV:** 270, 273, 274, 278, **279–282,** 283
Morgesons and Other Writings, Published and Unpublished, The (Buell and Zagarell), **Supp. XV:** 269
Moricand, Conrad, **III:** 190
Morison, Samuel Eliot, **Supp. I Part 2: 479–500; Supp. XXII:** 35
Morison, Mrs. Samuel Eliot (Elizabeth Shaw Greene), **Supp. I Part 2:** 483
Morison, Mrs. Samuel Eliot (Priscilla Barton), **Supp. I Part 2:** 493, 496, 497
Morita, Pat, **Supp. XXI:** 146
"Morituri Salutamus" (Longfellow), **II:** 499, 500; **Retro. Supp. II:** 169; **Supp. I Part 2:** 416
"Moriturus" (Millay), **III:** 126, 131–132
Morley, Christopher, **III:** 481, 483, 484; **Supp. I Part 2:** 653; **Supp. IX:** 124
Morley, Edward, **IV:** 27
Morley, Lord John, **I:** 7

Mormon Country (Stegner), **Supp. IV Part 2:** 598, 601–602
"Morning, The" (Updike), **Retro. Supp. I:** 329
"Morning after My Death, The" (Levis), **Supp. XI:** 260, 263–264
"Morning Arrives" (F. Wright), **Supp. XVII:** 244
Morning Face (Stratton-Porter), **Supp. XX: 223**
Morning for Flamingos, A (Burke), **Supp. XIV:** 30, 31, 32
"Morning Glory" (Merrill), **Supp. III Part 1:** 337
Morning Glory, The (R. Bly), **Supp. IV Part 1:** 63–65, 66, 71
"Morning Imagination of Russia, A" (W. C. Williams), **Retro. Supp. I:** 428
Morning in Antibes (Knowles), **Supp. XII:** 249
Morning in the Burned House (Atwood), **Supp. XIII:** 20, 35
Morning Is Near Us, The (Glaspell), **Supp. III Part 1:** 184–185
Morning Noon and Night (Cozzens), **I:** 374, 375, 376, 377, 379, 380
"Morning of the Day They Did It, The" (White), **Supp. I Part 2:** 663
"Morning Prayers" (Harjo), **Supp. XII:** 231
"Morning Roll Call" (Anderson), **I:** 116
"Morning Roudup" (Sorrentino), **Supp. XXI:** 228
"Morning Shadows" (Skloot), **Supp. XX: 199**
"Mornings in a New House" (Merrill), **Supp. III Part 1:** 327
Mornings Like This (Dillard), **Supp. VI:** 23, 34
"Morning Song" (Plath), **Retro. Supp. II:** 252
Morning Watch, The (Agee), **I:** 25, 39–42
"Morning with Broken Window" (Hogan), **Supp. IV Part 1:** 405
Morrell, Ottoline, **Retro. Supp. I:** 60
Morris, Bernard E., **Supp. XV:** 154, 169
Morris, Christopher D., **Supp. IV Part 1:** 231, 236
Morris, Gary, **Supp. XXII:** 262
Morris, George Sylvester, **Supp. I Part 2:** 640
Morris, Gouverneur, **Supp. I Part 2:** 512, 517, 518
Morris, Lloyd, **III:** 458
Morris, Robert, **Supp. I Part 2:** 510
Morris, Timothy, **Retro. Supp. I:** 40
Morris, William, **II:** 323, 338, 523; **IV:** 349; **Supp. I Part 1:** 260, 356; **Supp. XI:** 202
Morris, Willie, **Supp. XI:** 216, 231, 234; **Supp. XIX:** 151, 252
Morris, Wright, **I:** 305; **III: 218–243,** 558, 572; **IV:** 211
Morrison, Charles Clayton, **III:** 297
Morrison, Jim, **Supp. IV Part 1:** 206
Morrison, Toni, **Retro. Supp. II:** 15, 118; **Supp. III Part 1: 361–381; Supp. IV Part 1:** 2, 13, 14, 250, 253, 257; **Supp. V:** 169, 259; **Supp. VIII:** 213, 214; **Supp. X:** 85, 239, 250, 325; **Supp. XI:** 4, 14, 20, 91; **Supp. XII:** 289, 310; **Supp. XIII:** 60, 185; **Supp. XVI:** 143; **Supp. XVII:** 183; **Supp. XX: 108; Supp. XXI:** 172, 243; **Supp. XXII:** 65, 78
"Morro Bay" (Jeffers), **Supp. II Part 2:** 422
Morrow, W. C., **I:** 199
Morse, Jedidiah, **Supp. XV:** 243
Morse, Robert, **Supp. XI:** 305
Morse, Samuel F. B., **Supp. I Part 1:** 156
Morse, Samuel French, **Supp. XXI:** 17, 19, 23, 27
Mortal Acts, Mortal Words (Kinnell), **Supp. III Part 1:** 235, 236, 237, 249–254
Mortal Antipathy, A (Holmes), **Supp. I Part 1:** 315–316
"Mortal Enemies" (Humphrey), **Supp. IX:** 109
"Mortal Eternal" (Olds), **Supp. X:** 214
Mortal No, The (Hoffman), **IV:** 113
Mortal Stakes (Parker), **Supp. XIX:** 183–184
Morte D'Arthur, Le (Malory), **Supp. IV Part 1:** 47
Mortmere Stories, The (Isherwood and Upward), **Supp. XIV:** 159
Morton, David, **Supp. IX:** 76
Morton, Jelly Roll, **Supp. X:** 242
Morton, Thomas, **Supp. XXII:** 44, 45, 46
"Mosaic of the Nativity: Serbia, Winter 1993" (Kenyon), **Supp. VII:** 173
Mosby's Memoirs and Other Stories (Bellow), **Retro. Supp. II:** 27
"Moscow, Idaho" (Offutt), **Supp. XIX:** 170
Moscow under Fire (Caldwell), **I:** 296
Moser, Barry, **Supp. XIV:** 223
Moses (Untermeyer), **Supp. XV: 309**
Moses, Man of the Mountain (Hurston), **Supp. VI:** 149, 158, 160
"Moses on Sinai" (Untermeyer), **Supp. XV:** 300
Mosher, Howard Frank, **Supp. XXII: 203–221**
Moskowitz, Alfred, **Supp. XXI:** 98, 106
Mosle, Sara, **Supp. XI:** 254
Mosley, Walter, **Supp. XIII: 233–252; Supp. XVI:** 143
Mosquito Coast, The (film), **Supp. VIII:** 323
Mosquito Coast, The (Theroux), **Supp. VIII:** 321, **322–323**
Mosquitos (Faulkner), **II:** 56; **Retro. Supp. I:** 79, 81
Moss, Howard, **III:** 452; **Supp. IV Part 2:** 642; **Supp. IX:** 39; **Supp. XIII:** 114; **Supp. XV:** 143, 152
Moss, Stanley, **Supp. XI:** 321
Moss, Thylias, **Supp. XI:** 248
Mosses from an Old Manse (Hawthorne), **I:** 562; **II:** 224; **III:** 82, 83; **Retro. Supp. I:** 157, 248
"Moss of His Skin" (Sexton), **Supp. II Part 2:** 676
Most, Doug, **Supp. XVIII:** 101
"Most Extraordinary Case, A" (James), **II:** 322; **Retro. Supp. I:** 218
"Most Girl Part of You, The" (Hempel), **Supp. XXI:** 116
Most Likely to Succeed (Dos Passos), **I:** 491
"Most of It, The" (Frost), **Retro. Supp. I:** 121, 125, 129, 139; **Supp. XVIII:** 300
"Most Popular Novels in America, The" (Mabie), **Supp. XVIII:** 257
Motel Chronicles (Shepard), **Supp. III Part 2:** 445
"Mother" (Kooser), **Supp. XIX:** 117, 126, 127
"Mother" (Paley), **Supp. VI: 222–223**
"Mother" (Snyder), **Supp. VIII:** 298
Mother (Whistler), **IV:** 369
Mother, The (Buck), **Supp. II Part 1:** 118–119
"Mother and Jack and the Rain" (Sexton), **Supp. II Part 2:** 686
"Mother and Son" (Tate), **IV:** 128, 137–138
Mother Country: Britain, the Welfare State and Nuclear Pollution (Robinson), **Supp. XXI:** 211
Mother Courage and Her Children (Brecht), **III:** 160; **Supp. IX:** 140; **Supp. XII:** 249
"Mother Earth: Her Whales" (Snyder), **Supp. VIII:** 302
"Motherhood" (Swenson), **Supp. IV Part 2:** 645
Mother Hubbard (Reed), **Supp. X:** 241
Motherless Brooklyn (Lethem), **Supp. XXII:** 49
Motherless in Brooklyn (Lethem), **Supp. XVIII:** 135, **143–144**
Mother Love (Dove), **Supp. IV Part 1:** 250–251, 254
"Mother Marie Therese" (Lowell), **Retro. Supp. II:** 188
Mother Night (Vonnegut), **Supp. II Part 2:** 757, 758, 767, 770, 771
"Mother Rosarine" (Kumin), **Supp. IV Part 2:** 442
"Mothers and Daughters in the Fiction of the New Republic" (Davidson), **Supp. XV:** 238
Mother's Recompense, The (Wharton), **IV:** 321, 324; **Retro. Supp. I:** 382
"Mother's Tale, A" (Agee), **I:** 29–30
"Mother's Things" (Creeley), **Supp. IV Part 1:** 141
"Mother's Voice" (Creeley), **Supp. IV Part 1:** 156
Mother to Daughter, Daughter to Mother (Olsen, ed.), **Supp. XIII:** 295
"Mother Tongue" (Simic), **Supp. VIII:** 283
"Mother to Son" (Hughes), **Retro. Supp. I:** 199, 203; **Supp. I Part 1:** 321–322, 323
Motherwell, Robert, **Supp. XV:** 145; **Supp. XXI:** 125
"Mother Writes to the Murderer, The: A Letter" (Nye), **Supp. XIII:** 276
Moths of the Limberlost (Stratton-Porter), **Supp. XX: 218**

"Motion, The" (Olson), **Supp. II Part 2:** 571
Motion of History, The (Baraka), **Supp. II Part 1:** 55, 56
"Motive for Metaphor, The" (Stevens), **IV:** 89; **Retro. Supp. I:** 310
Motiveless Malignity (Auchincloss), **Supp. IV Part 1:** 31
Motley, John Lothrop, **Supp. I Part 1:** 299; **Supp. I Part 2:** 479; **Supp. XX: 228, 231**
Motley, Willard, **Supp. XVII: 149–163**
"Motor Car, The" (White), **Supp. I Part 2:** 661
Motor-Flight Through France (Wharton), **I:** 12; **Retro. Supp. I:** 372
Mott, Michael, **Supp. VIII:** 204, 208
Mottetti: Poems of Love: The Motets of Eugenio Montale (Montale; Gioia, trans.), **Supp. XV:** 112, **127–128**
Mouawad, Nelly, **Supp. XX: 126**
"Mountain, The" (Frost), **Retro. Supp. I:** 121
"Mountain Hermitage, The: Pages from a Japanese Notebook" (Passin), **Supp. XIII:** 337
Mountain Interval (Frost), **II:** 154; **Retro. Supp. I:** 131, 132, 133
"Mountain Lion" (Hogan), **Supp. IV Part 1:** 412
"Mountain Music" essays (Sanders), **Supp. XVI:** 276–277
Mountain on the Desert, The (Richter), **Supp. XVIII:** 216, 219
Mountainous Journey, A (Tuqan), **Supp. XIII:** 278
Mountains, The (Wolfe), **IV:** 461
Mountains and Rivers without End (Snyder), **Supp. VIII:** 295, **305–306**
"Mountains grow unnoticed, The" (Dickinson), **Retro. Supp. I:** 46
Mountains Have Come Closer, The (J. W. Miller), **Supp. XX: 165, 168, 169–170**
Mountains Look Down, The: A History of Chichester, a Company Town in the Catskills (Bennett), **Supp. XXII:** 218
Mountains of California, The (Muir), **Supp. IX:** 183
"Mountain Whippoorwill, The" (Benét), **Supp. XI:** 44–45, 46, 47
"Mount-Joy: or Some Passages Out of the Life of a Castle-Builder" (Irving), **II:** 314
"Mount Venus" (Wright), **Supp. XV:** 346
"Mourners" (Kooser), **Supp. XIX:** 127
"Mourners, The" (Malamud), **Supp. I Part 2:** 431, 435, 436–437
Mourners Below (Purdy), **Supp. VII:** 274, 280
"Mourning and Melancholia" (Freud), **Supp. IV Part 2:** 450; **Supp. XVI:** 161
Mourning Becomes Electra (O'Neill), **III:** 391, 394, 398–400
"Mourning Doves" (Pedersen; Nelson, trans.), **Supp. XVIII:** 180
"Mourning Poem for the Queen of Sunday" (Hayden), **Supp. II Part 1:** 379–380
"Mouse Elegy" (Olds), **Supp. X:** 209
Mouse Is Born, A (Loos), **Supp. XVI:** 193
"Mouse Roulette Wheel, The" (C. Bly), **Supp. XVI:** 34
Moustapha's Eclipse (McKnight), **Supp. XX: 147, 150**
"Mouth of Brass" (Humphrey), **Supp. IX:** 101
Moveable Feast, A (Hemingway), **II:** 257; **Retro. Supp. I:** 108, 171, **186–187**
Movement, The: Documentary of a Struggle for Equality (Student Nonviolent Coordinating Committee), **Supp. IV Part 1:** 369
"Move over Macho, Here Comes Feminismo" (Robbins), **Supp. X:** 272
Movers and Shakers (Sochen), **Supp. XXI:** 1
"Move to California, The" (Stafford), **Supp. XI:** 318, 321
"Movie" (Shapiro), **Supp. II Part 2:** 707
Movie at the End of the World, The (McGrath), **Supp. X:** 127
Moviegoer, The (Percy), **Supp. III Part 1:** 383–385, 387, 389–392, 394, 397
"Movie Magazine, The: A Low 'Slick' " (Percy), **Supp. III Part 1:** 385
Movies (Dixon), **Supp. XII:** 147
Movies About the Movies (Ames), **Supp. XVIII:** 242–243
"Moving Around" (Matthews), **Supp. IX:** 155
"Moving Finger, The" (Wharton), **Retro. Supp. I:** 365
"Moving Inward at Last" (Bly), **Supp. XXI:** 84–85
Moving On (McMurtry), **Supp. V:** 223–224
"Moving On" (Pickering), **Supp. XXI:** 197
Moving Pictures: Memoirs of a Hollywood Prince (Schulberg), **Supp. XVIII:** 242, 243, 254
Moving Target, The (Macdonald), **Supp. IV Part 2:** 462, 463, 467, 470, 471, 473, 474
Moving Target, The (Merwin), **Supp. III Part 1:** 346, 347–348, 352, 357
"Mowbray Family, The" (Farrell and Alden), **II:** 45
"Mowing" (Frost), **II:** 169–170; **Retro. Supp. I:** 127, 128
"Moxan's Master" (Bierce), **I:** 206
Moxley, Jennifer, **Supp. XVII:** 70
Moyers, Bill, **Supp. IV Part 1:** 267; **Supp. VIII:** 331; **Supp. XI:** 126, 132; **Supp. XII:** 217; **Supp. XIII:** 274, 276; **Supp. XV:** 212
Moynagh, Maureen, **Supp. XXII:** 73
Moynihan, Daniel Patrick, **Retro. Supp. II:** 123; **Supp. VIII:** 241; **Supp. XIX:** 150–151
"Mozart" (C. Frost), **Supp. XV:** 94
Mozart, Wolfgang Amadeus, **I:** 479, 588; **IV:** 74, 358; **Supp. IV Part 1:** 284
"Mozart and the Gray Steward" (Wilder), **IV:** 358
Mrabet, Mohammed, **Supp. IV Part 1:** 92, 93
Mr. and Mrs. Baby and Other Stories (Strand), **Supp. IV Part 2:** 631
"Mr. and Mrs. Fix-It" (Lardner), **II:** 431
Mr. Arcularis (Aiken), **I:** 54, 56
"Mr. Big" (Allen), **Supp. XV:** 15
Mr. Bridge (Connell), **Supp. XIV:** 80, 82, 93
Mr. Brown Can Moo! Can You? (Geisel), **Supp. XVI:** 104
"Mr. Bruce" (Jewett), **II:** 397; **Retro. Supp. II:** 134, 143
"Mr. Burnshaw and the Statue" (Stevens), **Retro. Supp. I:** 298, 303
"Mr. Carson Death on His Nights Out" (McGrath), **Supp. X:** 118
Mr. Clemens and Mark Twain (Kaplan), **I:** 247–248
"Mr. Coffee and Mr. Fixit" (Carver), **Supp. III Part 1:** 145
"Mr. Cornelius Johnson, Office-Seeker" (Dunbar), **Supp. II Part 1:** 211, 213
"Mr. Costyve Duditch" (Toomer), **Supp. III Part 2:** 486
"Mr. Dajani, Calling from Jericho" (Nye), **Supp. XIII:** 286–287
"Mr. Edwards and the Spider" (Lowell), **I:** 544; **II:** 550; **Retro. Supp. II:** 187
Mr. Field's Daughter (Bausch), **Supp. VII:** 47–48, 51–52
"Mr. Flood's Party" (Robinson), **III:** 512
"Mr. Forster's Pageant" (Maxwell), **Supp. VIII:** 172
"Mr. Frost's Chickens" (Oliver), **Supp. VII:** 232–233
Mr. Hodge and Mr. Hazard (Wylie), **Supp. I Part 2:** 708, 709, 714, 721–724
"Mr. Hueffer and the Prose Tradition" (Pound), **III:** 465
Mr. Ives' Christmas (Hijuelos), **Supp. VIII: 85–86**
Mr. Kelso's Lion (Bontemps), **Supp. XXII:** 7
"Mr. Longfellow and His Boy" (Sandburg), **III:** 591
"Mr. Luna and History" (Ríos), **Supp. IV Part 2:** 551
"Mr. Mitochondria" (Stollman), **Supp. XVII:** 50
Mr. Moto Is So Sorry (Marquand), **III:** 57, 58
Mr. Norris Changes Trains (Isherwood), **Supp. XIV:** 161
"Mr. Preble Gets Rid of His Wife" (Thurber), **Supp. I Part 2:** 615
"Mr. Rolfe" (Wilson), **IV:** 436
Mr. Rutherford's Children (S. and A. Warner), **Supp. XVIII:** 264
"Mrs. Adis" (Kaye-Smith), **Supp. XVIII:** 130–131
Mrs. Albert Grundy: Observations in Philistia (Frederic), **II:** 138–139
Mr. Sammler's Planet (Bellow), **I:** 144, 147, 150, 151, 152, 158; **Retro. Supp. II:** 19, 28, 30
"Mrs. Bilingsby's Wine" (Taylor), **Supp. V:** 323

Mrs. Bridge: A Novel (Connell), **Supp. XIV:** 79, 80, 81, 82, **89–94,** 95
"Mrs. Cassidy's Last Year" (Gordon), **Supp. IV Part 1:** 306
Mrs. Dalloway (Woolf), **Supp. IV Part 1:** 299; **Supp. VIII:** 5; **Supp. XV:** 55, 65–66
"Mr. Shelley Speaking" (Wylie), **Supp. I Part 2:** 719
"Mrs. Jellison" (Hay), **Supp. XIV:** 123
"Mrs. Krikorian" (Olds), **Supp. X:** 211
"Mrs. Maecenas" (Burke), **I:** 271
"Mrs. Mandrill" (Nemerov), **III:** 278
"Mrs. Manstey's View" (Wharton), **Retro. Supp. I:** 362, 363
"Mrs. Mobry's Reason" (Chopin), **Retro. Supp. II:** 61
Mr. Spaceman (R. O. Butler), **Supp. XII:** 62, **74–75**
Mrs. Reynolds (Stein), **IV:** 43
"Mrs. Sen's" (Lahiri), **Supp. XXI: 177–178,** 180–181
Mrs. Stevens Hears the Mermaids Singing (Sarton), **Supp. VIII:** 252–253, **256–257**
Mrs. Ted Bliss (Elkin), **Supp. VI: 56,** 58
"Mrs. Turner Cutting the Grass" (Shields), **Supp. VII:** 319–320
"Mrs. Walpurga" (Rukeyser), **Supp. VI:** 273
"Mr. Thompson's Prodigal" (Harte), **Supp. II Part 1:** 354
Mr. Vertigo (Auster), **Supp. XII: 34–35,** 36
"Mr. Vonnegut in Sumatra" (Saunders), **Supp. XIX:** 235
"Mr. Whittier" (Scott), **Supp. I Part 2:** 705
Mr. Wilson's War (Dos Passos), **I:** 485
"MS. Found in a Bottle" (Poe), **III:** 411, 416; **Retro. Supp. II:** 274
"Ms. Lot" (Rukeyser), **Supp. VI:** 281
Ms. Magazine, **Supp. V:** 259
Mttron-Hirsch, Sidney, **III:** 484–485
"Muchas Gracias Por Todo" (Nye), **Supp. XIII:** 282–283
"Much Madness is divinest Sense" (Dickinson), **Retro. Supp. I:** 37–38
"Muck-A-Muck" (Harte), **Supp. II Part 1:** 342
"Mud Below, The" (Proulx), **Supp. VII:** 262
Mudge, Alden, **Supp. XIV:** 35
Mudrick, Marvin, **Retro. Supp. II:** 289
"Mud Season" (Kenyon), **Supp. VII:** 167–168
Mueller, Lisel, **Supp. I Part 1:** 83, 88; **Supp. XIV:** 268
Muggli, Mark, **Supp. IV Part 1:** 207
Muhammad, Elijah, **Supp. I Part 1:** 60
Muir, Edwin, **I:** 527; **II:** 368; **III:** 20; **Supp. XXII:** 166
Muir, John, **Supp. VIII:** 296; **Supp. IX:** 33, **171–188; Supp. X:** 29; **Supp. XIV:** 177, 178, 181
Muirhead, Deborah, **Supp. XVIII:** 186
Mujica, Barbara, **Supp. VIII:** 89
Mulas, Franco, **Supp. XX: 38**
Mulatto (Hughes), **Retro. Supp. I:** 197, 203; **Supp. I Part 1:** 328, 339
Mulching of America, The (Crews), **Supp. XI:** 107
Muldoon, William, **I:** 500–501
Mule Bone (Hughes and Hurston), **Retro. Supp. I:** 194, 203; **Supp. VI:** 154
Mules and Men (Hurston), **Supp. VI:** 149, 153, 154, 160
Mulford, Prentice, **I:** 193
Mulligan, Robert, **Supp. VIII:** 128, 129
Mulligan Stew (Sorrentino), **Supp. XII:** 139; **Supp. XXI:** 233
Mullins, Eustace, **III:** 479
Mullins, Priscilla, **II:** 502–503
"Multiplication of Wool, The" (Sanders), **Supp. XVI:** 268
Multitudes, Multitudes (Clampitt), **Supp. IX:** 39
Mumbo Jumbo (Reed), **Supp. X:** 240, 242, **245–248,** 251
Mumford, Lewis, **I:** 245, 250, 251, 252, 259, 261; **II:** 271, 473–474; **Supp. I Part 2:** 632, 638; **Supp. II Part 2: 471–501**
Mumford, Sophia Wittenberg (Mrs. Lewis Mumford), **Supp. II Part 2:** 474, 475
"Mummers, The" (Di Piero), **Supp. XIX:** 44
Mummy, The (film), **Supp. IV Part 1:** 104; **Supp. XVII:** 57
Mundo y Palabra (Espaillat), **Supp. XXI:** 104
"Mundus et Infans" (Auden), **Supp. II Part 1:** 15
"Munich, 1938" (Lowell), **II:** 554
"Munich Mannequins, The" (Plath), **Retro. Supp. II:** 256
"Municipal Report, A" (Henry), **Supp. II Part 1:** 406–407
Munro, Alice, **Supp. IX:** 212; **Supp. X:** 290; **Supp. XII:** 289–290, 310
Munsey, Frank, **I:** 501
Munson, Gorham, **I:** 252, 388, 432; **Retro. Supp. II:** 77, 78, 79, 82, 83; **Supp. I Part 2:** 454; **Supp. XX: 70, 74**
Münsterberg, Hugo, **Supp. XIV:** 197
Murakami, Haruki, **Supp. XVI:** 124
"Murano" (Doty), **Supp. XI:** 131
Murasaki, Lady, **II:** 577
Muratori, Fred, **Supp. XVI:** 281
Muray, Nicholas, **Supp. I Part 2:** 708
Murder, My Sweet (film), **Supp. IV Part 1:** 130
"Murderer Guest, The" (Gordon), **Supp. IV Part 1:** 306
"Murderers" (L. Michaels), **Supp. XVI:** 207–208
Murder in Mount Holly (Theroux), **Supp. VIII:** 315–316
Murder in the Cathedral (T. S. Eliot), **I:** 571, 573, 580, 581; **II:** 20; **Retro. Supp. I:** 65; **Retro. Supp. II:** 222
Murder of Lidice, The (Millay), **III:** 140
"Murders in the Rue Morgue, The" (Poe), **III:** 412, 416, 419–420; **Retro. Supp. II:** 271, 272; **Supp. XIX:** 77
Murdoch, Iris, **Supp. VIII:** 167; **Supp. XVIII:** 136,149
Murnau, F. W., **Supp. XV:** 128
Murphy, Brenda, **Supp. XXI:** 6
Murphy, Jacqueline Shea, **Retro. Supp. II:** 143
Murphy, Patrick, **Supp. XIII:** 214
Murphy, Richard, **Retro. Supp. II:** 250
Murray, Albert, **Retro. Supp. II:** 119, 120; **Supp. XIX: 147–162**
Murray, Bill, **Supp. XXI:** 51
Murray, Edward, **I:** 229
Murray, G. E., **Supp. X:** 201; **Supp. XI:** 143, 155
Murray, Gilbert, **III:** 468–469
Murray, Jan, **Supp. IV Part 2:** 574
Murray, John, **II:** 304; **III:** 76, 79; **Retro. Supp. I:** 246
Murray, Judith Sargent, **Supp. XV:** 236–237
Murray, Les, **Supp. XIX:** 131
Murray, Margaret A., **Supp. V:** 128
Murrell, John A., **IV:** 265
Mursell, James L., **Supp. I Part 2:** 608
"Muse" (Ammons), **Supp. VII:** 29
"Muse, Postmodern and Homeless, The" (Ozick), **Supp. V:** 272
"Musée des Beaux Arts" (Auden), **Retro. Supp. I:** 430; **Supp. II Part 1:** 14
"Musée des Beaux Arts Revisited" (Collins), **Supp. XXI:** 60
"Muse of Aboutness, The" (Baker), **Supp. XVI:** 288
Muses Are Heard, The (Capote), **Supp. III Part 1:** 126
"Muses of Terrence McNally, The" (Zinman), **Supp. XIII:** 207–208
"Muse's Tragedy, The" (Wharton), **Retro. Supp. I:** 364
Museum (Dove), **Supp. IV Part 1:** 245–247, 248
"Museum" (Hass), **Supp. VI:** 107
Museums and Women (Updike), **Retro. Supp. I:** 321
"Museum Vase" (Francis), **Supp. IX:** 83
"Mushrooms" (Plath), **Retro. Supp. II:** 246; **Supp. I Part 2:** 539
"Music" (Oliver), **Supp. VII:** 236
Music (al-Músíqá) (Gibran), **Supp. XX: 115, 124**
Music After the Great War (Van Vechten), **Supp. II Part 2:** 732
Music and Bad Manners (Van Vechten), **Supp. II Part 2:** 733
Music Appreciation (Skloot), **Supp. XX: 196, 197–201**
"Music for a Farce" (Bowles), **Supp. IV Part 1:** 83
Music for Chameleons (Capote), **Supp. III Part 1:** 120, 125–127, 131, 132
"Music for Museums?" (Van Vechten), **Supp. II Part 2:** 732
"Music for the Movies" (Van Vechten), **Supp. II Part 2:** 733
"Music from Spain" (Welty), **IV:** 272
Music Like Dirt (Bidart), **Supp. XV:** 35
"Music Like Dirt" (Bidart), **Supp. XV:** 35
Music of Chance, The (Auster), **Supp. XII:** 21, 23, **32–33**
"Music of My Own Kind Too, The" (Budbill), **Supp. XIX:** 10
"Music of Prose, The" (Gass), **Supp. VI:** 92

Music of Spain, The (Van Vechten), **Supp. II Part 2:** 734, 735
"Music of the Spheres" (Epstein), **Supp. XII:** 165
"Music School" (B. Kelly), **Supp. XVII:** 124
Music School, The (Updike), **IV:** 214, 215, 219, 226, 227; **Retro. Supp. I:** 320, 328, 329, 330
"Music School, The" (Updike), **Retro. Supp. I:** 326, 329, 335
"Music Swims Back to Me" (Sexton), **Supp. II Part 2:** 673
Muske, Carol, **Supp. IV Part 2:** 453–454
"Mussel Hunter at Rock Harbor" (Plath), **Supp. I Part 2:** 529, 537
Musset, Alfred de, **I:** 474; **II:** 543
Mussolini, Benito, **III:** 115, 473, 608; **IV:** 372, 373; **Supp. I Part 1:** 281, 282; **Supp. I Part 2:** 618; **Supp. V:** 290; **Supp. XVI:** 191
"Mustafa Ferrari" (X. J. Kennedy), **Supp. XV:** 170–171
Mustich, James, **Supp. XXI:** 52
"Must the Novelist Crusade?" (Welty), **IV:** 280
"Mutability of Literature, The" (Irving), **II:** 308
"Mutation of the Spirit" (Corso), **Supp. XII:** 132, 133
Mute, The (McCullers), **II:** 586
Mutilated, The (T. Williams), **IV:** 382, 386, 393
Mutiny of the Elsinore, The (London), **II:** 467
"Muttsy" (Hurston), **Supp. XVIII:** 279
Muyumba, Walton, **Supp. XIX:** 158
"My Adventures as a Social Poet" (Hughes), **Retro. Supp. I:** 194, 207
"My Alba" (Ginsberg), **Supp. II Part 1:** 320, 321
My Alexandria (Doty), **Supp. XI:** 119, 120, 121, **123–125,** 130
"My Amendment" (Saunders), **Supp. XIX:** 232
My Amputations (Major), **Supp. XXII:** 174**, 175–176**
My Ántonia (Cather), **I:** 321–322; **Retro. Supp. I:** 1, 3, 4, **11–13,** 14, 17, 18, 22; **Supp. IV Part 2:** 608; **Supp. XVI:** 226
"My Appearance" (Wallace), **Supp. X:** 306–307
My Argument with the Gestapo: A Macaronic Journal (Merton), **Supp. VIII:** 207; **Supp. XV:** 344
"My Arkansas" (Angelou), **Supp. IV Part 1:** 15
"My Aunt" (Holmes), **Supp. I Part 1:** 302, 310
"My Beginnings" (Simpson), **Supp. IX:** 273
"My Bird Problem" (Franzen), **Supp. XX: 94**
"My Bodyguard" (Notley), **Supp. XXII:** 230
My Bondage and My Freedom (Douglass), **Supp. III Part 1:** 155, 173
My Brother (Kincaid), **Supp. VII:** 191–193
"My Brother Paul" (Dreiser), **Retro. Supp. II:** 94
"My Brothers the Silent" (Merwin), **Supp. III Part 1:** 349–350
"My Brother's Work" (Dunn), **Supp. XI:** 147
"My Brother Takes a Hammer to the Mirror" (F. Wright), **Supp. XVII:** 244
"My Butterfly" (Frost), **II:** 151; **Retro. Supp. I:** 124
"My Children, and a Prayer for Us" (Ortiz), **Supp. IV Part 2:** 507
"My College Sex Group" (Peacock), **Supp. XIX:** 199
"My Coney Island Uncle" (Swados), **Supp. XIX:** 267–268
"My Confession" (McCarthy), **II:** 562
"My Confessional Sestina" (Gioia), **Supp. XV:** 123
"My Corner" (Major), **Supp. XXII:** 184
My Country and My People (Yutang), **Supp. X:** 291
"My Country 'Tis of Thee" (Reznikoff), **Supp. III Part 2:** 616
"My Daughter Considers Her Body" (Skloot), **Supp. XX: 197–198, 200**
My Days of Anger (Farrell), **II:** 34, 35–36, 43
"My Dear Niece" (Boyce), **Supp. XXI:** 10
"My Dear Republican Mother" (C. Bly), **Supp. XVI:** 31–32
My Death My Life by Pier Paolo Pasolini (Acker), **Supp. XII:** 7
My Dog Stupid (Fante), **Supp. XI:** 160, **170–171**
My Dog Tulip (Ackerley), **Supp. XX: 237**
My Emily Dickinson (Howe), **Retro. Supp. I:** 33, 43; **Supp. IV Part 2:** 430–431
"My English" (Alvarez), **Supp. VII:** 2
Myers, Linda A., **Supp. IV Part 1:** 10
"My Extended Family" (Theroux), **Supp. VIII:** 311
"My Father" (Budbill), **Supp. XIX:** 5
"My Father" (L. Michaels), **Supp. XVI:** 214
"My Father" (Sterne), **IV:** 466
"My Father at Eighty-Five" (R. Bly), **Supp. IV Part 1:** 73
"My Father Is a Simple Man" (Salinas), **Supp. XIII:** 324
"My Father Is with Me" (Budbill), **Supp. XIX:** 15
"My Father: October 1942" (Stafford), **Supp. XI:** 323
My Father Photographed with Friends (Bronk), **Supp. XXI:** 26–27,**Supp. XXI:** 31
"My Father Photographed with Friends" (Bronk), **Supp. XXI:** 23, 27
"My Fathers Came From Kentucky" (Lindsay), **Supp. I Part 2:** 395
"My Father's Friends" (Maxwell), **Supp. VIII:** 171
"My Father's Ghost" (Wagoner), **Supp. IX:** 330
"My Father's God" (Fante), **Supp. XI:** 160, 174
"My Father's House" (L.-Y. Lee), **Supp. XV:** 225
"My Father's Love Letters" (Komunyakaa), **Supp. XIII:** 127
"My Father Speaks to me from the Dead" (Olds), **Supp. X:** 210
"My Father's Telescope" (Dove), **Supp. IV Part 1:** 246, 248
"My Father with Cigarette Twelve Years Before the Nazis Could Break His Heart" (Levine), **Supp. V:** 194
"My Favorite Murder" (Bierce), **I:** 205
My Favorite Plant: Writers and Gardeners on the Plants They Love (Kincaid), **Supp. VII:** 193–194
My Favorites in Suspense (Hitchcock, ed.), **Supp. XXII:** 119
"My Fifty-Plus Years Celebrate Spring" (Salinas), **Supp. XIII:** 327
"My First Book" (Harte), **Supp. II Part 1:** 343
My First Summer in the Sierra (Muir), **Supp. IX:** 172, 173, **178–181,** 183, 185; **Supp. XIV:** 177
"My Flamboyant Grandson" (Saunders), **Supp. XIX:** 231–232
"My Fountain Pen" (McClatchy), **Supp. XII:** 254, 260
My Friend, Henry Miller (Perlès), **III:** 189
My Friend, Julia Lathrop (Addams), **Supp. I Part 1:** 25
"My Friend, Walt Whitman" (Oliver), **Supp. VII:** 245
"My Garden Acquaintance" (Lowell), **Supp. I Part 2:** 420
My Garden \[Book\]: (Kincaid), **Supp. VII:** 193–194
"My Good-bye" (Weigl), **Supp. XIX:** 288
"My Grandfather" (Lowell), **II:** 554
"My Grandmother's Love Letters" (H. Crane), **Retro. Supp. II:** 78
"My Grandson, Home at Last" (Angelou), **Supp. IV Part 1:** 13
My Green Hills of Jamaica (McKay), **Supp. X:** 132, 142
My Guru and His Disciple (Isherwood), **Supp. XIV:** 157, 164, 172
"My Heart" (Collins), **Supp. XXI:** 58
My Heart's in the Highlands (Saroyan), **Supp. IV Part 1:** 83
"My High School Reunion" (Kingston), **Supp. V:** 169
"My House New-Painted" (Bronk), **Supp. XXI:** 30
"My Ideal Home" (Stratton-Porter), **Supp. XX: 222**
"My Indigo" (L.-Y. Lee), **Supp. XV:** 214
"My Kinsman, Major Molineux" (Hawthorne), **II:** 228, 229, 237–239, 243; **Retro. Supp. I:** 153–154, 158, 160, 161; **Retro. Supp. II:** 181, 187; **Supp. XVI:** 157
My Kinsman, Major Molineux (Lowell), **II:** 545–546

"My Last Afternoon with Uncle Devereux Winslow" (Lowell), **II:** 547–548; **Retro. Supp. II:** 189
"My Last Drive" (Hardy), **Supp. VIII:** 32
"My Last Duchess" (Browning), **Supp. XV:** 121
"My Life" (Strand), **Supp. IV Part 2:** 627
My Life, Starring Dara Falcon (Beattie), **Supp. V:** 31, 34–35
My Life a Loaded Gun: Dickinson, Plath, Rich, and Female Creativity (Bennett), **Retro. Supp. I:** 29
My Life and Hard Times (Thurber), **Supp. I Part 2:** 607, 609
My Life as a Man (P. Roth), **Retro. Supp. II:** 281, 286, 289; **Supp. III Part 2:** 401, 404, 405, 417–418
"My Life as a P.I.G., or the True Adventures of Smokey the Cop" (Abbey), **Supp. XIII:** 3
"My life closed twice before its close" (Dickinson), **Retro. Supp. I:** 38
"My Life had stood a Loaded Gun" (Dickinson), **Retro. Supp. I:** 42, 43, 45, 46; **Supp. IV Part 2:** 430
My Life of Absurdity (C. Himes), **Supp. XVI:** 145
"My Life with Medicine" (Nye), **Supp. XIII:** 282
"My Life with *Playboy*" (Plimpton), **Supp. XVI:** 246
"My Life with R. H. Macy" (Jackson), **Supp. IX:** 118
"My Little Utopia" (Simic), **Supp. VIII:** 283
My Lives and How I Lost Them (Cullen), **Supp. IV Part 1:** 173
"My Lord Bag of Rice" (C. Bly), **Supp. XVI:** 40
My Lord Bag of Rice: New and Selected Stories (C. Bly), **Supp. XVI:** 41
"My Lost City" (Fitzgerald), **Retro. Supp. I:** 102
"My Lost Youth" (Longfellow), **II:** 487, 499; **Retro. Supp. II:** 168
My Love Affair with America: The Cautionary Tale of a Cheerful Conservative (Podhoretz), **Supp. VIII:** 232, 233, 237, **244–246**
"My Lover Has Dirty Fingernails" (Updike), **Retro. Supp. I:** 332, 333
"My Lucy Friend Who Smells Like Corn" (Cisneros), **Supp. VII:** 68–69
"My Mammogram" (McClatchy), **Supp. XII:** 263–264
"My Man Bovanne" (Bambara), **Supp. XI:** 2
"My Mariner" (Larcom), **Supp. XIII:** 147
My Mark Twain (Howells), **II:** 276
"My Metamorphosis" (Harte), **Supp. II Part 1:** 339
"My Moby Dick" (Humphrey), **Supp. IX:** 95
"My Monkey" (Nelson), **Supp. XVIII:** 178
"My Moral Life" (Halliday), **Supp. XIX:** 89
My Mortal Enemy (Cather), **I:** 327–328; **Retro. Supp. I:** 16–17; **Supp. I Part 2:** 719
My Mother, My Father and Me (Hellman), **Supp. I Part 1:** 290–291
"My Mother and My Sisters" (Ortiz), **Supp. IV Part 2:** 499
My Mother: Demonology (Acker), **Supp. XII:** 6
"My Mother Is Speaking from the Desert" (Gordon), **Supp. IV Part 1:** 309, 314
"My Mother's Goofy Song" (Fante), **Supp. XI:** 164
"My Mother's Memoirs, My Father's Lie, and Other True Stories" (Banks), **Supp. V:** 15
"My Mother's Nipples" (Hass), **Supp. VI:** 109
"My Mother's Story" (Kunitz), **Supp. III Part 1:** 259
"My Mother Then and Now" (Wasserstein), **Supp. XV:** 327
"My Mother with Purse the Summer They Murdered the Spanish Poet" (Levine), **Supp. V:** 194
My Movie Business: A Memoir (Irving), **Supp. VI:** 164
"My Name" (Cisneros), **Supp. VII:** 60
"My Negro Problem—And Ours" (Podhoretz), **Supp. VIII: 234–236**
"My New Diet" (Karr), **Supp. XI:** 241
"My Number" (Collins), **Supp. XXI:** 64
"My Old Man" (Hemingway), **II:** 263
My Other Life (Theroux), **Supp. VIII:** 310, 324
"My Own Story" (E. Stoddard), **Supp. XV:** 273, 279, 283
My Own True Name: New and Selected Poems for Young Adults, 1984–1999 (Mora), **Supp. XIII:** 222
"My Parents Have Come Home Laughing" (Jarman), **Supp. XVII:** 113
"My Passion for Ferries" (Whitman), **IV:** 350
"My People" (Hughes), **Retro. Supp. I:** 197; **Supp. I Part 1:** 321–322, 323
"My Philosophy" (Allen), **Supp. XV:** 15
"My Playmate" (Whittier), **Supp. I Part 2:** 699–700
"My Priests" (Monette), **Supp. X:** 159
Myra Breckinridge (Vidal), **Supp. IV Part 2:** 677, 685–686, 689, 691
"My Raptor" (A. Finch), **Supp. XVII:** 72
"My Recollections of S. B. Fairchild" (Jackson), **Supp. IX:** 118–119
"My Religion" (Carson), **Supp. XII: 105–106**
"My Road to Hell Was Paved" (Patchett), **Supp. XII:** 310–311
Myron (Vidal), **Supp. IV Part 2:** 677, 685, 686, 691
"My Roomy" (Lardner), **II:** 420, 421, 428, 430
"My Sad Self" (Ginsberg), **Supp. II Part 1:** 320
My Secret History (Theroux), **Supp. VIII:** 310, 324
"Myself" (Audubon), **Supp. XVI:** 1–2, 5, 12
Myself Painting (Major), **Supp. XXII: 184–185**
"My Shoes" (Simic), **Supp. VIII:** 275
"My Side of the Matter" (Capote), **Supp. III Part 1:** 114, 115
My Silk Purse and Yours: The Publishing Scene and American Literary Art (Garrett), **Supp. VII:** 111; **Supp. X:** 7
My Sister Eileen (McKenney), **IV:** 288; **Retro. Supp. II:** 321
My Sister's Hand in Mine: The Collected Works of Jane Bowles, **Supp. IV Part 1:** 82–83
"My Son" (Strand), **Supp. IV Part 2:** 629
My Son, John (film), **Supp. I Part 1:** 67
"My Son, the Murderer" (Malamud), **Supp. I Part 2:** 437
"My Son the Man" (Olds), **Supp. X:** 212
"My Speech to the Graduates" (Allen), **Supp. XV:** 16
"Mysteries of Caesar, The" (Hecht), **Supp. X:** 73
"Mysteries of Eleusis, The" (Hardwick), **Supp. III Part 1:** 195
Mysteries of Pittsburgh, The (Chabon), **Supp. XI:** 65, 68, **69–71; Supp. XIX:** 135
Mysteries of Small Houses (Notley), **Supp. XXII:** 223, 224, 226, 234–235
"Mysterious Case of R, The" (Conroy), **Supp. XVI:** 72
Mysterious Stranger, The (Twain), **IV:** 190–191, 210
Mystery, A (Shields). *See Swann* (Shields)
"Mystery, The" (Dunbar), **Supp. II Part 1:** 199, 210
"Mystery, The" (Glück), **Supp. V:** 91
Mystery and Manners (O'Connor), **Retro. Supp. II:** 230
"'Mystery Boy' Looks for Kin in Nashville" (Hayden), **Supp. II Part 1:** 366, 372
"Mystery of Coincidence, The" (Conroy), **Supp. XVI:** 74
"Mystery of Heroism, A" (Crane), **I:** 414
"Mystery of Marie Rogêt, The" (Poe), **III:** 413, 419; **Retro. Supp. II:** 271
"Mystic" (Plath), **Retro. Supp. II:** 257; **Supp. I Part 2:** 539, 541
"Mystical Poet, A" (Bogan), **Retro. Supp. I:** 36
"Mystic of Sex, The—A First Look at D. H. Lawrence" (Nin), **Supp. X:** 188
"Mystic Vision in 'The Marshes of Glynn' " (Warfel), **Supp. I Part 1:** 366, 373
"Mystification" (Poe), **III:** 425
"My Strange New Poetry" (Halliday), **Supp. XIX:** 88, 94
My Study Windows (Lowell), **Supp. I Part 2:** 407
"My Teacher" (Conroy), **Supp. XVI:** 75
"Myth" (Rukeyser), **Supp. VI:** 281–282
"Myth" (Trethewey), **Supp. XXI:** 245, 255, 256
"Mythmaker" (Trethewey), **Supp. XXI:** 243
Myth of Sisyphus, The (Camus), **I:** 294; **Supp. XIII:** 165

"Myth of the Happy Worker, The" (Swados), **Supp. XIX:** 265
"Myth of the Isolated Artist, The" (Oates), **Supp. II Part 2:** 520
Myth of the Machine, The (Mumford), **Supp. II Part 2:** 476, 478, 482, 483, 493, 497
"Myth of the Powerful Worker, The" (Swados), **Supp. XIX:** 265
Mythology and the Romantic Tradition in English Poetry (Bush), **Supp. I Part 1:** 268
Myths and Texts (Snyder), **Supp. VIII: 295–296**
"Myths of Bears, The" (Bass), **Supp. XVI:** 19, 20
"My *Tocaya*" (Cisneros), **Supp. VII:** 69
My Uncle Dudley (Morris), **I:** 305; **III:** 219–220
"My Uncle's Favorite Coffee Shop" (Nye), **Supp. XIII:** 283
"My Weariness of Epic Proportions" (Simic), **Supp. VIII:** 276
My Wicked Wicked Ways (Cisneros), **Supp. VII:** 58, 64–68, 71
"My Wicked Wicked Ways" (Cisneros), **Supp. VII:** 58, 64–66
"My Word-house" (Mora), **Supp. XIII:** 219, 225
My Works and Days (Mumford), **Supp. II Part 2:** 475, 477, 481
"My World and My Critics" (Stratton-Porter), **Supp. XX: 220**
My World and Welcome to It (Thurber), **Supp. I Part 2:** 610

Nabokov, Peter, **Supp. IV Part 2:** 490
Nabokov, Véra, **Retro. Supp. I:** 266, 270
Nabokov, Vladimir, **I:** 135; **III: 244–266,** 283, 286; **Retro. Supp. I: 263–281,** 317, 335; **Supp. I Part 1:** 196; **Supp. II Part 1:** 2; **Supp. IV Part 1:** 135; **Supp. V:** 127, 237, 251, 252, 253; **Supp. VIII:** 105, 133, 138; **Supp. IX:** 152, 212, 261; **Supp. X:** 283; **Supp. XI:** 66; **Supp. XII:** 310; **Supp. XIII:** 46, 52; **Supp. XVI:** 148, 294; **Supp. XVIII:** 98, 102; **Supp. XXII:** 263
Nabokov's Dozen (Nabokov), **Retro. Supp. I:** 266
Nabokov's Garden: A Guide to Ada (Mason), **Supp. VIII:** 138
Naca, Kristin, **Supp. XIII:** 133
Nadeau, Robert, **Supp. X:** 261, 270
Nadel, Alan, **Supp. IV Part 1:** 209
Naimy, Mikhail, **Supp. XX: 116, 119, 120**
Naipaul, V. S., **Supp. IV Part 1:** 297; **Supp. VIII:** 314; **Supp. X:** 131; **Supp. XIV:** 111; **Supp. XX: 87;** **Supp. XXI:** 170; **Supp. XXII:** 240, 241, 242, 246, 253
Naison, Mark, **Supp. XVIII:** 231
Naked and the Dead, The (Mailer), **I:** 477; **III:** 26, 27, 28–30, 31, 33, 35, 36, 44; **Retro. Supp. II: 197–199;** **Supp. IV Part 1:** 381; **Supp. XI:** 218; **Supp. XIX:** 248; **Supp. XX: 248;** **Supp. XXI:** 277
Naked Author (di Donato), **Supp. XX: 45**
Naked Babies (Quindlen and Kelsh), **Supp. XVII:** 167, 179
Naked in Garden Hills (Crews), **Supp. XI:** 102, **110**
Naked Lunch (Burroughs), **Supp. III Part 1:** 92–95, 97–105; **Supp. IV Part 1:** 90
"Naked Nude" (Malamud), **Supp. I Part 2:** 450
Naked Poetry (Berg and Mezey, eds.), **Supp. IV Part 1:** 60
Naked Poetry (Levine), **Supp. V:** 180
Naked Revenge (film), **Supp. XVII:** 141
Nall, Gus, **Supp. XXII:** 172, 184
Namedropping: Mostly Literary Memoirs (Coover), **Supp. V:** 40
"Name in the Papers" (Hughes), **Supp. I Part 1:** 330
Name Is Archer, The (Macdonald, under Millar), **Supp. IV Part 2:** 466
"Name Is Burroughs, The" (Burroughs), **Supp. III Part 1:** 93
Name Is Fogarty, The: Private Papers on Public Matters (Farrell), **II:** 49
"Names" (Carruth), **Supp. XVI:** 54, 56
"Names, The" (Collins), **Supp. XXI:** 54, 61–62
Names, The (DeLillo), **Supp. VI:** 3, 10, 13, 14
Names, The (Momaday), **Supp. IV Part 2:** 479, 480, 483, 486, 487, 488, 489
Namesake, The (Lahiri), **Supp. XXI:** 176, 184, **186–188**
Names and Faces of Heroes, The (Price), **Supp. VI:** 258, 260
Names of the Lost, The (Levine), **Supp. V:** 177–178, 179, 187–188
"Naming for Love" (Carruth), **Supp. XVI:** 48
"Naming Myself" (Kingsolver), **Supp. VII:** 208
"Naming of Names, The" (Sanders), **Supp. XVI:** 268
Naming of the Beasts, The (Stern). *See Rejoicings: Selected Poems, 1966–1972* (Stern)
Naming the Unseen (Ray), **Supp. XVIII:** 192, **193–195**
"Naming the Unseen" (Ray), **Supp. XVIII:** 203
Nana (Zola), **III:** 321
"Nancy Culpepper" (Mason), **Supp. VIII:** 141
Nancy Drew stories, **Supp. VIII:** 133, 135, 137, 142
"Nancy Knapp" (Masters), **Supp. I Part 2:** 461
"Naola Beauty Academy, New Orleans, 1943" (Trethewey), **Supp. XXI:** 246
"Naomi Shihab Nye: U.S. Mideast-History a Harbinger of 9-11?" (Nye), **Supp. XIII:** 286
"Naomi Trimmer" (X. J. Kennedy), **Supp. XV:** 170
"Nap, The" (Banks), **Supp. V:** 7
"Napoleon" (Emerson), **II:** 6
Napoleon I, **I:** 6, 7, 8, 474; **II:** 5, 309, 315, 321, 523; **Supp. I Part 1:** 153; **Supp. I Part 2:** 518, 519
Napolitano, Louise, **Supp. XX: 35, 45, 46–47**
Narcissa and Other Fables (Auchincloss), **Supp. IV Part 1:** 21, 34
"Narcissus as Narcissus" (Tate), **IV:** 124
"Narcissus Leaves the Pool" (Epstein), **Supp. XIV:** 110
Narcissus Leaves the Pool: Familiar Essays (Epstein), **Supp. XIV:** 110
Nardal, Paulette, **Supp. X:** 139
Nardi, Marcia, **Retro. Supp. I:** 426, 427
"Narragansett Boulevard" (Halliday), **Supp. XIX:** 91
Narration (Stein), **IV:** 27, 30, 32, 33, 36
Narrative of a Four Months' Residence among the Natives of a Valley of the Marquesas Islands (Melville), **III:** 76
Narrative of Arthur Gordon Pym, The (Poe), **III:** 412, 416; **Retro. Supp. II:** 265, **273–275;** **Supp. XI:** 293
"Narrative of Arthur Gordon Pym, The" (Poe), **Supp. XXII:** 58
Narrative of the Life of Frederick Douglass, an American Slave, Written by Himself (Douglass), **Supp. III Part 1:** 154–159, 162, 165; **Supp. IV Part 1:** 13; **Supp. VIII:** 202
"Narrativity Scenes" (Wright), **Supp. XV:** 345
Narrenschiff, Das (Brant), **III:** 447
"Narrow Fellow in the Grass, A" (Dickinson), **Retro. Supp. I:** 30, 37
Narrow Heart, A: Portrait of a Woman (Gordon), **II:** 197, 217
Narrow Rooms (Purdy), **Supp. VII:** 274
Narrows, The (Connelly), **Supp. XXI:** 71, **76**
Nasby, Petroleum, **Supp. XVIII:** 1
Nash, Noreen, **Supp. XXII:** 256
Nash, Ogden, **Supp. XXI:** 51
Nash, Roderick, **Supp. IX:** 185; **Supp. XIV:** 191–192
Nash, Susan Smith, **Supp. XVI:** 274
Nash, Thomas, **Supp. III Part 1:** 387–388
Nashe, Thomas, **I:** 358; **Supp. XVII:** 232
Nashville (film), **Supp. IX:** 143
"Nashville Gone to Ashes" (Hempel), **Supp. XXI:** 115, 118, **120–121**
Nashville Skyline (album, Dylan), **Supp. XVIII:** 27
Nason, Elias, **Supp. XV:** 242
Nasser, Gamal Abdel, **IV:** 490
Natalie Mann (Toomer), **Supp. III Part 2:** 484–486
Nathan, George Jean, **II:** 91; **III:** 103, 104, 106, 107; **IV:** 432; **Supp. IV Part 1:** 343; **Supp. IX:** 56–57; **Supp. XIII:** 161; **Supp. XXII:** 23
"Nathanael West" (Herbst), **Retro. Supp. II:** 325
Nathanael West: The Art of His Life (Martin), **Retro. Supp. II:** 325
Nathan Coulter (Berry), **Supp. X:** 24, 33
National Dream, The: Building the Impossible Railway (Findley and Whitehead), **Supp. XX: 51**
"Nationalist, The" (Anderson), **I:** 115
"Nation Is Like Ourselves, The" (Baraka), **Supp. II Part 1:** 53

"Native, The" (Olds), **Supp. X:** 215
"Native American Attitudes to the Environment" (Momaday), **Supp. IV Part 2:** 481, 491
Native American Renaissance (Lincoln), **Supp. IV Part 2:** 507
Native American Testimony (Nabokov, ed.), **Supp. IV Part 2:** 490
"Native Blessing" (Ray), **Supp. XVIII:** 202
Native Guard (Trethewey), **Supp. XXI:** 243, 244, 247, **254–257**
"Native Guard" (Trethewey), **Supp. XXI:** 256
"Native Hill, A" (Berry), **Supp. X:** 21
Native in a Strange Land: Trials & Tremors (Coleman), **Supp. XI: 84–85,** 87
Native of Winby and Other Tales, A (Jewett), **II:** 396; **Retro. Supp. II:** 138
Native Son (Wright), **IV:** 476, 477, 478, 479, 481, 482–484, 485, 487, 488, 491, 495; **Retro. Supp. II:** 107, 116; **Supp. I Part 1:** 51, 64, 67, 337; **Supp. II Part 1:** 170, 235–236; **Supp. IX:** 306; **Supp. XIV:** 73; **Supp. XVII:** 155; **Supp. XVIII:** 283, 286; **Supp. XXI:** 169
"Native Trees" (Merwin), **Supp. III Part 1:** 355
Natorp, Paul, **Supp. XIV:** 198
Natural, The (Malamud), **II:** 424, 425; **Retro. Supp. II:** 288; **Supp. I Part 2:** 438–441, 443
"*Natural, The:* Malamud's World Ceres" (Wasserman), **Supp. I Part 2:** 439
"Natural History" (Olds), **Supp. X:** 210
"Natural History Note" (Hay), **Supp. XIV:** 124, 130
"Natural History of Some Poems, A" (Harrison), **Supp. VIII:** 53
"Natural History of the Dead" (Hemingway), **II:** 206; **Retro. Supp. I:** 176
"Naturally Superior School, A" (Knowles), **Supp. XII:** 235, 240–241
"Natural Method of Mental Philosophy" (Emerson), **II:** 14
"Natural Resources" (Rich), **Supp. I Part 2:** 575
Natural Selection (F. Barthelme), **Supp. XI:** 2, 28, 32, 33
Nature (Emerson), **I:** 463; **II:** 1, 8, 12, 16; **IV:** 171, 172–173
"Nature" (Emerson), **Retro. Supp. I:** 250; **Supp. I Part 2:** 383; **Supp. III Part 1:** 387; **Supp. IX:** 178
"Nature, Inc." (Lewis), **II:** 441
Nature and Destiny of Man, The (Niebuhr), **III:** 292, 303–306, 310
"Nature and Life" (Emerson), **II:** 19
"Nature and Nurture: When It Comes to Twins, Sometimes It's Hard to Tell the Two Apart" (Bausch), **Supp. VII:** 40
"Nature-Metaphors" (Lanier), **Supp. I Part 1:** 352
Nature Morte (Brodsky), **Supp. VIII:** 25
Nature of Evil, The (James), **II:** 343
Nature of Peace, The (Veblen), **Supp. I Part 2:** 642
Nature of Things, The (television show), **Supp. XX: 51**
Nature of True Virtue, The (Edwards), **I:** 549, 557–558, 559
Nature: Poems Old and New (Swenson), **Supp. IV Part 2:** 652
Nature's Economy: A History of Ecological Ideas (Worster), **Supp. IX:** 19
Naumburg, Margaret, **Supp. XX: 68, 74–75**
Nausea (Sartre), **Supp. VIII:** 7
"Navajo Blanket, A" (Swenson), **Supp. IV Part 2:** 649
Navarette, Don Martín de, **II:** 310
Navarro, Ramon, **Supp. IV Part 1:** 206
Navigator, The (film), **I:** 31
Navratilova, Martina, **Supp. XX: 264**
Naylor, Gloria, **Supp. VIII: 213–230; Supp. XX: 108**
Naylor, Paul Kenneth, **Supp. IV Part 2:** 420
Nazimova, **III:** 399
Neal, Darlin', **Supp. XXI:** 41
Neal, Larry, **Retro. Supp. II:** 112, 128; **Supp. X:** 324, 328
Neal, Lawrence P., **Supp. II Part 1:** 53
Neal, Patricia, **Supp. I Part 1:** 286; **Supp. IV Part 2:** 524; **Supp. V:** 223
Neale, Walter, **I:** 192, 208
"Near Damascus" (Di Piero), **Supp. XIX:** 43
Nearer the Moon: From "A Journal of Love," the Unexpurgated Diary of Anaïs Nin, 1937–1939, **Supp. X:** 184, 185
Near-Johannesburg Boy and Other Poems, The (Brooks), **Supp. III Part 1:** 86
Near Klamath (Carver), **Supp. III Part 1:** 137
"Near Perigord" (Pound), **Retro. Supp. I:** 289, 290
"Near Spring" (Pickering), **Supp. XXI:** 198
Near the Ocean (Lowell), **II:** 543, 550, 551–553, 554, 555; **Retro. Supp. II:** 182, 186, 189–190
"Near View of the High Sierra, A" (Muir), **Supp. IX:** 183
Nebeker, Helen, **Supp. IX:** 122
"Nebraska Blizzard" (F. Wright), **Supp. XVII:** 247
Necessary Angel, The (Stevens), **IV:** 76, 79, 89, 90
Necessities of Life: Poems, 1962–1965 (Rich), **Supp. I Part 2:** 553, 555
Nechayev, Sergey, **Supp. XXI:** 164
"Necrological" (Ransom), **III:** 486–489, 490, 492
Ned Christie's War (Conley), **Supp. V:** 232
"Need for a Cultural Base to Civil Rites & Bpower Mooments, The" (Baraka), **Supp. II Part 1:** 48
"Need for Christian Preaching, The" (Buechner), **Supp. XII:** 49
Needful Things (King), **Supp. V:** 139, 146
"Needle" (Simic), **Supp. VIII:** 275
"Needle Trade" (Reznikoff), **Supp. XIV:** 277, 289
"Need of Being Versed in Country Things, The" (Frost), **II:** 154; **Retro. Supp. I:** 133, 135
"Need to Say It, The" (Hampl), **Supp. XXII:** 94
Neel, Philippe, **Supp. XIV:** 338
Neelakantappa, Tara, **Supp. XV:** 104–105
Neeley, Barbara, **Supp. XVI:** 143
"Negative Capability" (Komunyakaa), **Supp. XIII:** 131
Negligible Tales (Bierce), **I:** 209
"Negotiating the Darkness, Fortified by Poets' Strength" (Karr), **Supp. XI:** 254; **Supp. XIII:** 285
Negotiating with the Dead (Atwood), **Supp. XIII:** 20, 35
Negritude movement, **Supp. X:** 131, 139
"Negro" (Hughes), **Supp. I Part 1:** 321–322
Negro, The (Du Bois), **Supp. II Part 1:** 178, 179, 185
Negro, The: The Southerner's Problem (Page), **Supp. II Part 1:** 168
Negro and His Music, The (Locke), **Supp. XIV:** 202
"Negro Artisan, The" (Du Bois), **Supp. II Part 1:** 166
"Negro Artist and the Racial Mountain, The" (Hughes), **Retro. Supp. I:** 200, 207; **Supp. I Part 1:** 323, 325; **Supp. IV Part 1:** 169
Negro Art: Past and Present (Locke), **Supp. XIV:** 202
"Negro Assays the Negro Mood, A" (Baldwin), **Supp. I Part 1:** 52
"Negro Citizen, The" (Du Bois), **Supp. II Part 1:** 179
"Negro Dancers" (Hughes), **Retro. Supp. I:** 199; **Supp. I Part 1:** 324
Negroes in America, The (McKay), **Supp. X:** 132, 136
"Negroes of Farmville, Virginia, The: A Social Study" (Du Bois), **Supp. II Part 1:** 166
Negro Family, The: The Case for National Action (Moynihan), **Retro. Supp. II:** 123
"Negro Farmer, The" (Du Bois), **Supp. II Part 1:** 167
"Negro Fight, The" (column, C. L. R. James), **Supp. XXI:** 169
"Negro Ghetto" (Hughes), **Supp. I Part 1:** 331
Negro in America, The (Locke), **Supp. XIV:** 208
Negro in American Civilization, The (Du Bois), **Supp. II Part 1:** 179
Negro in American Culture, The (Locke and Butcher), **Supp. XIV:** 202–203
Negro in Art, The: A Pictorial Record of the Negro Artist and of the Negro Theme in Art (Locke), **Supp. XIV:** 202
"Negro in Large Cities, The" (Du Bois), **Supp. II Part 1:** 169
"Negro in Literature and Art, The" (Du Bois), **Supp. II Part 1:** 174

Negro in New York, The (Ellison), **Supp. II Part 1:** 230
"Negro in the Black Belt, The: Some Social Sketches" (Du Bois), **Supp. II Part 1:** 166
Negro in the Caribbean, The (Williams), **Supp. XXI:** 166
"Negro in the Three Americas, The" (Locke), **Supp. XIV:** 211
"Negro in the Well, The" (Caldwell), **I:** 309
"Negro Love Song, A" (Dunbar), **Supp. II Part 1:** 204
"Negro Martyrs Are Needed" (C. Himes), **Supp. XVI:** 138
Negro Mother, The (Hughes), **Supp. I Part 1:** 328
Negro Mother and Other Dramatic Recitations, The (Hughes), **Retro. Supp. I:** 203
Negro Novel in America, The (Bone), **Supp. IX:** 318–319; **Supp. XVIII:** 285
Negro Publication Society of America, **Retro. Supp. I:** 205
"Negro Renaissance, The: Jean Toomer and the Harlem of the 1920s" (Bontemps), **Supp. IX:** 306
"Negro Schoolmaster in the New South, A" (Du Bois), **Supp. II Part 1:** 168
"Negro's Contribution to American Culture, The" (Locke), **Supp. XIV:** 210, 211
"Negro Sermon, A: Simon Legree" (Lindsay), **Supp. I Part 2:** 393
"Negro Sings of Rivers, The" (Hughes), **Supp. IV Part 1:** 16
"Negro Speaks of Rivers, The" (Hughes), **Retro. Supp. I:** 199; **Supp. I Part 1:** 321
"Negro Spirituals, The (Locke), **Supp. XIV:** 201
"Negro Takes Stock, The" (Du Bois), **Supp. II Part 1:** 180
"Negro Theatre, The" (Van Vechten), **Supp. II Part 2:** 735
"Negro Voter Sizes Up Taft, A" (Hurston), **Supp. VI:** 160
"Negro Writer and His Roots, The: Toward a New Romanticism" (Hansberry), **Supp. IV Part 1:** 364
"Negro Youth Speaks" (Locke), **Supp. XIV:** 201
"Nehemias Americanus" (Mather), **Supp. II Part 2:** 453
Nehru, Jawaharlal, **IV:** 490
"Neighbor" (Hugo), **Supp. VI:** 135–136
"Neighbors" (Carver), **Supp. III Part 1:** 135, 139, 141; **Supp. XI:** 153
"Neighbors" (Hogan), **Supp. IV Part 1:** 405
"Neighbors, The" (Hay), **Supp. XIV:** 126
"Neighbour Rosicky" (Cather), **I:** 331–332
Neil Simon (Johnson), **Supp. IV Part 2:** 573
"Neil Simon's Jewish-Style Comedies" (Walden), **Supp. IV Part 2:** 584, 591
"Neil Simon: Toward Act III?" (Walden), **Supp. IV Part 2:** 591
Neilson, Heather, **Supp. IV Part 2:** 681
Neiman, Gilbert, **Supp. XV:** 140
"Neither Out Far Nor In Deep" (Frost), **I:** 303; **Retro. Supp. I:** 121, 138
"Nellie Clark" (Masters), **Supp. I Part 2:** 461
Nelson, Alice Dunbar, **Supp. XVII:** 75
Nelson, Cary, **Supp. XVIII:** 226, 227, 230, 231; **Supp. XXII:** 271
Nelson, Ernest, **I:** 388
Nelson, Howard, **Supp. IV Part 1:** 66, 68; **Supp. XIX:** 3; **Supp. XXI:** 95
Nelson, Lord Horatio, **II:** 524
Nelson, Lynn (pseudonym). *See* Nelson, Marilyn
Nelson, Marilyn, **Supp. XVII:** 74, 112; **Supp. XVIII: 171–188**
Nelson, Shirley, **Supp. XII:** 293
Nelson, Steve, **Supp. XVIII:** 226
Nelson Algren (Cox and Chatterton), **Supp. IX:** 11–12
Nelson Algren: A Life on the Wild Side (Drew), **Supp. IX:** 2
Nemerov, David, **II:** 268
Nemerov, Howard, **III: 267–289; IV:** 137, 140; **Supp. III Part 2:** 541; **Supp. IV Part 2:** 455, 650; **Supp. IX:** 114
Nemiroff, Robert Barron, **Supp. IV Part 1:** 360, 361, 365, 369, 370, 374
Neoconservative Criticism: Norman Podhoretz, Kenneth S. Lynn, and Joseph Epstein (Winchell), **Supp. VIII:** 241; **Supp. XIV:** 103
"Neo-Formalism: A Dangerous Nostalgia" (Sadoff), **Supp. XXI:** 100
"Neo-Hoodoo Manifesto, The" (Reed), **Supp. X:** 242
Neon Rain, The (Burke), **Supp. XIV:** 22, 24, 26–27, 28–29, 30
Neon Vernacular (Komunyakaa), **Supp. XIII:** 121, **127–128,** 131
Neon Wilderness, The (Algren), **Supp. IX:** 3, 4
Neo-Slave Narratives (Rushdy), **Supp. X:** 250
Nepantla: Essays from the Land in the Middle (Mora), **Supp. XIII:** 213, **219–221,** 227
Nephew, The (Purdy), **Supp. VII:** 271, 273, 282
"Nereids of Seriphos, The" (Clampitt), **Supp. IX:** 41
Nericcio, William, **Supp. XIV:** 304–305
Neruda, Pablo, **Supp. I Part 1:** 89; **Supp. IV Part 2:** 537; **Supp. V:** 332; **Supp. VIII:** 272, 274; **Supp. IX:** 157, 271; **Supp. X:** 112; **Supp. XI:** 191; **Supp. XII:** 217; **Supp. XIII:** 114, 315, 323; **Supp. XXI:** 61, 100
Nesbit, Edith, **Supp. VIII:** 171
Nesbitt, Robin, **Supp. VIII:** 89
Nessmuk (George Washington Sears), **Supp. XIX:** 10
Nesting Ground, The (Wagoner), **Supp. IX:** 324, **325–326**
Nest of Ninnies, A (Ashbery and Schuyler), **Supp. III Part 1:** 3; **Supp. XV:** 178
Net of Cobwebs (Holding), **Supp. XXII:** 126, **129–130,** 134
Net of Magic: Wonders and Deceptions in India (Siegel), **Supp. XXII:** 262
Nets to Catch the Wind (Wylie), **Supp. I Part 2:** 709, 710–712, 714
Nettleton, Asahel, **I:** 458
"Net to Snare the Moonlight, A" (Lindsay), **Supp. I Part 2:** 387
Neubauer, Carol E., **Supp. IV Part 1:** 9
Neugeboren, Jacob Mordecai. *See* Neugeboren, Jay
Neugeboren, Jay, **Supp. XVI: 217–231**
Neugroschel, Joachim, **Supp. IX:** 138
Neuhaus, Richard John, **Supp. VIII:** 245; **Supp. XIX:** 144
Neumann, Erich, **Supp. I Part 2:** 567; **Supp. IV Part 1:** 68, 69
Neuromancer (W. Gibson), **Supp. XII:** 15; **Supp. XVI:** 117, 119–120, 122, 124, **125–126,** 127, 129, 131
Neurotica: Jewish Writers on Sex (Bukiet, ed.), **Supp. XVII:** 48
"Neurotic America and the Sex Impulse" (Dreiser), **Retro. Supp. II:** 105
Neutra, Richard, **Supp. XVI:** 192
"Never Bet the Devil Your Head" (Poe), **III:** 425; **Retro. Supp. II:** 273
Never Come Morning (Algren), **Supp. IX:** 3, **7–9**
Never in a Hurry: Essays on People and Places (Nye), **Supp. XIII:** 273, **280–282,** 286
"Never Marry a Mexican" (Cisneros), **Supp. VII:** 70
"Never Room with a Couple" (Hughes), **Supp. I Part 1:** 330
"Nevertheless" (Moore), **III:** 214
Nevins, Allan, **I:** 253; **Supp. I Part 2:** 486, 493
"Nevsky Prospekt" (Olds), **Supp. X:** 205
New Adam, The (Untermeyer), **Supp. XV:** 304, 305
New Addresses (Koch), **Supp. XV:** 177, 184
"New Age of the Rhetoricians, The" (Cowley), **Supp. II Part 1:** 135
New American Cyclopedia, **Supp. XVIII:** 4
New American Literature, The (Pattee), **II:** 456
New American Novel of Manners, The (Klinkowitz), **Supp. XI:** 347
"New American Ode, The" (Wright), **Supp. XV:** 346
New American Poetry, 1945–1960 (Allen, ed.), **Supp. XIII:** 112
New American Poetry, The (Allen, ed.), **Supp. VIII:** 291, 292
"New American Writer, A" (W. C. Williams), **Retro. Supp. II:** 335
New and Collected Poems (Reed), **Supp. X:** 241
New and Collected Poems (Wilbur), **Supp. III Part 2:** 562–564
New and Selected Poems (Nemerov), **III:** 269, 275, 277–279
New and Selected Poems (Oliver), **Supp. VII:** 240–241, 245

New and Selected Poems (W. J. Smith), **Supp. XIII:** 332
New and Selected Poems (Wagoner), **Supp. IX: 326–327**
New and Selected Poems, 1958–1998 (Sorrentino), **Supp. XXI:** 229
New and Selected Poems: 1974–1994 (Dunn), **Supp. XI: 151–152**
New and Selected Things Taking Place (Swenson), **Supp. IV Part 2:** 648–650, 651
"New Art Gallery Society, The" (Wolfe), **Supp. III Part 2:** 580
Newberger, Julee, **Supp. XVIII:** 168
New Black Poetry, The (Major, ed.), **Supp. XXII:** 172, 174, 176, 180
"New Capitalist Tool, The" (Wasserstein), **Supp. XV:** 328
Newcomb, Ralph, **Supp. XIII:** 12
Newcomb, Robert, **II:** 111
New Conscience and an Ancient Evil, A (Addams), **Supp. I Part 1:** 14–15, 16
"New Conservatism in American Poetry, The" (Wakoski), **Supp. XVII:** 112
"New Conservatives, The: Intellectuals in Retreat" (Epstein), **Supp. XIV:** 103
New Criticism, The (Ransom), **III:** 497–498, 499, 501
"New Day, A" (Levine), **Supp. V:** 182
Newdick, Robert Spangler, **Retro. Supp. I:** 138
Newdick's Season of Frost (Newdick), **Retro. Supp. I:** 138
New Dictionary of Quotations, A (Mencken), **III:** 111
New Directions Anthology in Prose and Poetry (Laughlin, ed.), **Supp. XVI:** 284
"New Directions in Poetry" (D. Locke), **Supp. IX:** 273
"New Dog, The: Variations on a Text by Jules Laforgue" (C. Frost), **Supp. XV:** 98
Newell, Henry, **IV:** 193
"New England" (Lowell), **II:** 536
"New England" (Robinson), **III:** 510, 524
"New England Bachelor, A" (Eberhart), **I:** 539
"New Englander, The" (Anderson), **I:** 114
New England Girlhood, A (Larcom), **Supp. XIII:** 137, 142, 143, 144, **147–154**
New England Gothic Literature (Ringel), **Supp. XXII:** 205
New England: Indian Summer (Brooks), **I:** 253, 256
New England Local Color Literature (Donovan), **Retro. Supp. II:** 138
"New England Sabbath-Day Chace, The" (Freneau), **Supp. II Part 1:** 273
New-England Tale, A (Sedgwick), **I:** 341
New England Tragedies, The (Longfellow), **II:** 490, 505, 506; **Retro. Supp. II:** 165, 167
New English Canaan (Morton), **Supp. XXII:** 45
New Era in American Poetry, The (Untermeyer, ed.), **Supp. XV:** 301, 303, 306
Newer Ideals of Peace (Addams), **Supp. I Part 1:** 11–12, 15, 16–17, 19, 20–21
"New Experience in Millinery, A" (Stratton-Porter), **Supp. XX: 216**
New Feminist Criticism, The: Essays on Women, Literature, and Theory (Showalter), **Supp. X:** 97
"New Folsom Prison" (Matthews), **Supp. IX:** 165
New Formalism, The: A Critical Introduction (McPhillips), **Supp. XV:** 250, 251, 252, 264
Newfound (J. W. Miller), **Supp. XX: 163, 166, 170–172**
New Found Land: Fourteen Poems (MacLeish), **III:** 12–13
"New Hampshire, February" (Eberhart), **I:** 536
New Hampshire: A Poem with Notes and Grace Notes (Frost), **II:** 154–155; **Retro. Supp. I:** 132, 133, 135
New Hard-Boiled Writers (Panek), **Supp. XIV:** 27
"New Home" (Richter), **Supp. XVIII:** 209
New Industrial State, The (Galbraith), **Supp. I Part 2:** 648
"New Journalism, The" (Wolfe), **Supp. III Part 2:** 571
New Journalism, The (Wolfe and Johnson, eds.), **Supp. III Part 2:** 570, 579–581, 583, 586
New Left, The: The Anti-Industrial Revolution (Rand), **Supp. IV Part 2:** 527
"New Letters from Thomas Jefferson" (Stafford), **Supp. XI:** 324
New Letters on the Air: Contemporary Writers on Radio, **Supp. X:** 165, 169, 173
"New Life" (Glück), **Supp. V:** 90
New Life, A (Malamud), **Supp. I Part 2:** 429–466
"New Life, The" (Bynner), **Supp. XV:** 44
"New Life at Kyerefaso" (Sutherland), **Supp. IV Part 1:** 9
"New Light on Veblen" (Dorfman), **Supp. I Part 2:** 650
"New Man, A" (P. E. Jones), **Supp. XXII:** 144
Newman, Charles, **Supp. I Part 2:** 527, 546–548
Newman, Edwin, **Supp. IV Part 2:** 526
Newman, Frances, **Supp. XXII:** 198
Newman, Judie, **Supp. IV Part 1:** 304, 305
Newman, Paul, **Supp. IV Part 2:** 473, 474
New Man, The (Merton), **Supp. VIII:** 208
"New Mecca, The" (Saunders), **Supp. XIX:** 235, 236
"New Medea, The" (Howells), **II:** 282
New Mexico trilogy (Nichols), **Supp. XIII:** 269
New Morning (album, Dylan), **Supp. XVIII:** 27, 33
"New Mother" (Olds), **Supp. X:** 206
"New Mothers, The" (Shields), **Supp. VII:** 310
New Music (Price), **Supp. VI:** 264, 265
"New Mutants, The" (Fiedler), **Supp. XIII:** 104
"New Name for Some Old Ways of Thinking, A" (James), **II:** 353
New Native American Novel, The: Works in Progress (Bartlett), **Supp. IV Part 1:** 335
"New Natural History, A" (Thurber), **Supp. I Part 2:** 619
New Negro, The (Locke), **Supp. XIX:** 69
"New Negro, The" (Locke), **Supp. XIV:** 201
New Negro, The (Locke, ed.), **Supp. II Part 1:** 176; **Supp. IX:** 309; **Supp. X:** 137; **Supp. XXII:** 8
New Negro, The: An Interpretation (Locke, ed.), **Retro. Supp. I:** 199; **Supp. IV Part 1:** 170; **Supp. XIV:** 195, 201–202
New Negro for a New Century, A (Washington, Wood, and Williams), **Supp. XIV:** 201
New New Journalism, The (R. Boynton), **Supp. XVII:** 209
"New Nomads, The" (E. Hoffman), **Supp. XVI:** 161
"New Orleans" (Carruth), **Supp. XVI:** 50
New Orleans Sketches (Faulkner), **Retro. Supp. I:** 80
New Path to the Waterfall, A (Carver), **Supp. III Part 1:** 138–140, 147, 149
"New Poem, The" (Wright), **Supp. V:** 339, 340
"New Poems" (MacLeish), **III:** 19
"New Poems" (Oliver), **Supp. VII:** 240
New Poems 1960 (Bynner), **Supp. XV:** 51
New Poems: 1980–88 (Haines), **Supp. XII: 209–210**
New Poetry, The (Monroe and Henderson, eds.), **Supp. I Part 2:** 387
"New Poetry Handbook, The" (Strand), **Supp. IV Part 2:** 626
New Poetry of Mexico (Strand, trans.), **Supp. IV Part 2:** 630
New Poets of England and America (Hall, Pack, and Simpson, eds.), **Supp. IV Part 2:** 621
"Newport of Anchuria" (Henry), **Supp. II Part 1:** 409
New Princeton Encyclopedia of Poetry and Poetics (Preminger and Brogan, eds.), **Supp. XV:** 250
"*New Republic* Moves Uptown, The" (Cowley), **Supp. II Part 1:** 142
"New Rose Hotel" (W. Gibson), **Supp. XVI:** 120, 122, 124
"News, The" (McClatchy), **Supp. XII:** 269
"New Season" (Levine), **Supp. V:** 188
New Seeds of Contemplation (Merton), **Supp. VIII:** 200, 208
News from the Glacier: Selected Poems 1960–1980 (Haines), **Supp. XII:** 207, 208–209
"News Item" (Parker), **Supp. IX:** 190
New Song, A (Hughes), **Retro. Supp. I:** 202; **Supp. I Part 1:** 328, 331–332
"New South, The" (Lanier), **Supp. I Part 1:** 352, 354, 370

New Southern Girl, The: Female Adolescence in the Works of 12 Women Authors (Town), **Supp. XVIII:** 195
Newspaper Days, 1899–1906 (Mencken), **III:** 100, 102, 120
"New Spirit, The" (Ashbery), **Supp. III Part 1:** 14, 15
New Spoon River, The (Masters), **Supp. I Part 2:** 461–465, 473
New Star Chamber and Other Essays, The (Masters), **Supp. I Part 2:** 455–456, 459
New Tales of the Vampires (Rice), **Supp. VII:** 290
New Testament, **I:** 303, 457, 458; **II:** 167; **III:** 305; **IV:** 114, 134, 152; **Retro. Supp. I:** 58, 140, 360; **Supp. I Part 1:** 104, 106; **Supp. I Part 2:** 516; **Supp. XVII:** 155. *See also* names of New Testament books
New Testament, A (Anderson), **I:** 101, 114
"New Theory of Thorstein Veblen, A" (Galbraith), **Supp. I Part 2:** 650
Newton, Benjamin Franklin, **I:** 454
Newton, Huey P., **Supp. I Part 1:** 66; **Supp. IV Part 1:** 206
Newton, Isaac, **I:** 132, 557; **II:** 6, 103, 348–349; **III:** 428; **IV:** 18, 149
Newton, Sarah Emily, **Supp. XV:** 234
"New-Wave Format, A" (Mason), **Supp. VIII:** 141, 143, 147
New West of Edward Abbey, The (Ronald), **Supp. XIII:** 4
"New Wife" (Halliday), **Supp. XIX:** 89
New Wolves, The: The Return of the Mexican Wolf to the American Southwest (Bass), **Supp. XVI:** 26–27
New Woman's Survival Sourcebook, The (Rennie and Grimstead, eds.), **Supp. I Part 2:** 569
New World, The (Bronk), **Supp. XXI:** 25–26, 31
New World, The (Bynner), **Supp. XV:** 41, 42
New World, The: Tales (Banks), **Supp. V:** 8, 9, 10
New World Naked, A (Mariani), **Retro. Supp. I:** 419
New Worlds of Literature (Beaty and Hunter, eds.), **Supp. IV Part 1:** 331
New World Writing (Updike), **IV:** 217
New Year Letter (Auden), **Supp. II Part 1:** 14, 16
"New Year's Day" (Wharton), **Retro. Supp. I:** 381
"New Year's Eve" (Schwartz), **Supp. II Part 2:** 640, 656–657
New Year's Eve/1929 (Farrell), **II:** 43
"New Year's Eve 1968" (Lowell), **II:** 554
New Year's Eve: A Play (W. Frank), **Supp. XX: 75**
"New Year's Gift, The" (Stowe), **Supp. I Part 2:** 587
"New Year Two Thousand, The" (Weigl), **Supp. XIX:** 287–288
"New York" (Capote), **Supp. III Part 1:** 122
"New York" (Moore), **III:** 196, 198, 202, 206
"New York 1965" (Bowles), **Supp. IV Part 1:** 94
New York: A Serendipiter's Journey (Talese), **Supp. XVII:** 202, 203
"New York Breeze" (Halliday), **Supp. XIX:** 85
New York City Arts Project, **Supp. III Part 2:** 618
"New York City in 1979"(Acker), **Supp. XII:** 5
New York Edition, **Retro. Supp. I:** 235
"New York Edition" (James), **II:** 336, 337
"New York Gold Conspiracy, The" (Adams), **I:** 4
New York Hat, The (film; Griffith), **Supp. XVI:** 183
New York Intellectuals, **Supp. VIII:** 93
"New York Intellectuals, The" (Howe), **Supp. VI:** 120
"New York Is a City of Things Unnoticed" (Talese), **Supp. XVII:** 202, 209
New York Jew (Kazin), **Supp. VIII:** 95, **97–100**
"New York Theater: Isn't It Romantic" (Wasserstein), **Supp. XV:** 320
New York Trilogy, The (Auster), **Supp. XII:** 21, **24–28**
Next (McNally), **Supp. XIII:** 197
"Next in Line, The" (Bradbury), **Supp. IV Part 1:** 102
Next Room of the Dream, The (Nemerov), **III:** 269, 275, 278, 279–280, 284
"Next Time I Crossed the Line into Oklahoma, The" (Wright), **Supp. XV:** 345
Next-to-Last Things: New Poems and Essays (Kunitz), **Supp. III Part 1:** 257–259, 261, 262, 265, 266, 268
"'Next to Reading Matter' " (Henry), **Supp. II Part 1:** 399
Nexus (H. Miller), **III:** 170, 187, 188, 189
Niatum, Duane, **Supp. IV Part 1:** 331; **Supp. IV Part 2:** 505
Nice and Noir (Schwartz), **Supp. XIV:** 23
"Nice Girl" (Nelson), **Supp. XVIII:** 178
Nice Jewish Boy, The (P. Roth), **Supp. III Part 2:** 412
Nicholas II, Tsar, **Supp. I Part 2:** 447
"Nicholas in the Park" (Halliday), **Supp. XIX:** 88
Nicholls, Peter, **Supp. XIX:** 232
Nichols, Charles, **Retro. Supp. I:** 194
Nichols, Dudley, **Supp. XVIII:** 247
Nichols, John Treadwell, **Supp. XIII: 253–272**
Nichols, Luther, **Supp. X:** 265
Nichols, Mike, **Supp. IV Part 1:** 234; **Supp. IV Part 2:** 577
Nicholson, Colin, **Supp. VIII:** 129
Nicholson, Harold, **Supp. XIV:** 163
Nicholson, Jack, **Supp. V:** 26; **Supp. VIII:** 45; **Supp. XI:** 308
Nicholson, John, **Supp. XVI:** 293
Nick Adams Stories, The (Hemingway), **II:** 258; **Retro. Supp. I:** 174
"Nick and the Candlestick" (Plath), **Supp. I Part 2:** 544
Nickel and Dimed: On (Not) Getting By in America (Ehrenreich), **Supp. XVII:** 210
Nickel Mountain: A Pastoral Novel (Gardner), **Supp. VI:** 63, 64, 68, **69**
"Nicodemus" (Keillor), **Supp. XVI:** 167
Nicoll, Allardyce, **III:** 400
Nicoloff, Philip, **II:** 7
Niebuhr, Gustav, **III:** 292
Niebuhr, H. Richard, **I:** 494
Niebuhr, Lydia, **III:** 292
Niebuhr, Reinhold, **III: 290–313; Supp. I Part 2:** 654; **Supp. XX: 79**
Niedecker, Lorine, **Supp. III Part 2:** 616, 623; **Supp. XIV:** 287
Nielsen, Ed, **Supp. IX:** 254
Nielson, Dorothy, **Supp. I Part 2:** 659
Nietzsche, Friedrich Wilhelm, **I:** 227, 283, 383, 389, 396, 397, 402, 509; **II:** 7, 20, 27, 42, 90, 145, 262, 462, 463, 577, 583, 585; **III:** 102–103, 113, 156, 176; **IV:** 286, 491; **Supp. I Part 1:** 254, 299, 320; **Supp. I Part 2:** 646; **Supp. IV Part 1:** 104, 105–106, 107, 110, 284; **Supp. IV Part 2:** 519; **Supp. V:** 277, 280; **Supp. VIII:** 11, 181, 189; **Supp. X:** 48; **Supp. XII:** 98; **Supp. XIV:** 339; **Supp. XX: 117**
Nieves, Felipe, **Supp. XVIII:** 90
Niflis, N. Michael, **Supp. IV Part 1:** 175
Nigger Heaven (Van Vechten), **Supp. II Part 2:** 739, 744–746; **Supp. XVIII:** 123, 127; **Supp. XIX:** 76
"Nigger Jeff" (Dreiser), **Retro. Supp. II:** 97
Nigger of the "Narcissus," The (Conrad), **II:** 91; **Retro. Supp. I:** 106; **Supp. XVIII:** 224
"NIGGY THE HO" (Baraka), **Supp. II Part 1:** 54
"Night, Death, Mississippi" (Hayden), **Supp. II Part 1:** 369
'Night, Mother (Norman), **Supp. VIII:** 141
"Night above the Avenue" (Merwin), **Supp. III Part 1:** 355
"Night among the Horses, A" (Barnes), **Supp. III Part 1:** 33–34, 39, 44
"Night and the Madman" (Gibran), **Supp. XX: 118**
Night at the Movies, A, or, You Must Remember This: Fictions (Coover), **Supp. V:** 50–51
"Night at the Opera, A" (Matthews), **Supp. IX:** 167
"Night before the Sentence Is Carried Out, The" (Wright), **Supp. XV:** 341
"Nightbird" (Komunyakaa), **Supp. XIII:** 132
Night-Blooming Cereus, The (Hayden), **Supp. II Part 1:** 367, 373
"Night-Blooming Cereus, The" (Hayden), **Supp. II Part 1:** 367
Night-Born, The (London), **II:** 467
"Nightbreak" (Rich), **Supp. I Part 2:** 556
"Nightclub" (Collins), **Supp. XXI:** 60
Night Dance (Price), **Supp. VI:** 264
"Night Dances, The" (Plath), **Supp. I Part 2:** 544
"Night Dream, The" (MacLeish), **III:** 15

"Night Ferry" (Doty), **Supp. XI:** 124
"Nightfishing" (Schnackenberg), **Supp. XV:** 254
"Night I Met Little Floyd, The" (Wright), **Supp. XV:** 345–346
Night in Acadie, A (Chopin), **Retro. Supp. II: 66–67,** 73; **Supp. I Part 1:** 200, 219, 220, 224
"Night in Acadie, A" (Chopin), **Retro. Supp. II:** 66
"Night in June, A" (W. C. Williams), **Retro. Supp. I:** 424
"Night in New Arabia, A" (Henry), **Supp. II Part 1:** 402
Night in Question, The: Stories (Wolff), **Supp. VII:** 342–344
"Night Journey" (Roethke), **Supp. III Part 1:** 260
"Night Letter to the Reader" (Collins), **Supp. XXI:** 55
Night Light (Justice), **Supp. VII:** 126–127
"Nightmare" (Kumin), **Supp. IV Part 2:** 442
Nightmare Factory, The (Kumin), **Supp. IV Part 2:** 444–447, 451
"Nightmare Factory, The" (Kumin), **Supp. IV Part 2:** 445, 453
Nightmare on Main Street (Poe), **Retro. Supp. II:** 262
"Nightmare" poems (Benét), **Supp. XI:** 46, 58
"Night Mirror" (L.-Y. Lee), **Supp. XV:** 225
Night Music (Odets), **Supp. II Part 2:** 541, 543, 544
"Night of First Snow" (R. Bly), **Supp. IV Part 1:** 71
Night of January 16th (Rand), **Supp. IV Part 2:** 527
Night of the Iguana, The (T. Williams), **IV:** 382, 383, 384, 385, 386, 387, 388, 391, 392, 393, 394, 395, 397, 398
"Night of the Iguana, The" (T. Williams), **IV:** 384
"Night of the Living Beanfield: How an Unsuccessful Cult Novel Became an Unsuccessful Cult Film in Only Fourteen Years, Eleven Nervous Breakdowns, and $20 Million" (Nichols), **Supp. XIII:** 267
Night Passage (Parker), **Supp. XIX:** 185–186
Night Rider (Warren), **IV:** 243, 246–247
Nights (Doolittle), **Supp. I Part 1:** 270, 271
Nights and Days (Merrill), **Supp. III Part 1:** 319, 320, 322–325
"Nights and Days" (Rich), **Supp. I Part 2:** 574
"Night's for Cryin,' The" (C. Himes), **Supp. XVI:** 137
"Night Shift" (Plath), **Supp. I Part 2:** 538
Night-Side (Oates), **Supp. II Part 2:** 522
"Night-Side" (Oates), **Supp. II Part 2:** 523
Night-Side, The (Skloot), **Supp. XX: 193, 196, 205, 208**
Nights in the Gardens of Brooklyn (Swados), **Supp. XIX: 261–264**
"Nights in the Gardens of Brooklyn" (Swados), **Supp. XIX:** 261
"Night Sketches: Beneath an Umbrella" (Hawthorne), **II:** 235–237, 238, 239, 242; **Supp. XXI:** 201
"Night Sport" (Hoffman), **Supp. XVIII:** 86, 87
"Night-Sweat" (Lowell), **II:** 554
"Night-Talk" (Ellison), **Retro. Supp. II:** 126; **Supp. II Part 1:** 248
Night Thoughts (Young), **III:** 415
Night Traveler, The (Oliver), **Supp. VII:** 233
"Night Watch" (Gioia), **Supp. XV:** 117
"Night Watch, The" (Wright), **Supp. V:** 339
"Night We All Had Grippe, The" (Jackson), **Supp. IX:** 118
Nightwood (Barnes), **Supp. III Part 1:** 31, 32, 35–37, 39–43
Night World and the Word Night, The (F. Wright), **Supp. XVII:** 240, 244–245
"Nihilist as Hero, The" (Lowell), **II:** 554; **Retro. Supp. II:** 190
Nijinsky, Vaslav, **Supp. XV:** 28–29
Nikolai Gogol (Nabokov), **Retro. Supp. I:** 266
Niles, Thomas, **Retro. Supp. I:** 35
Niles, Thomas, Jr., **Supp. I Part 1:** 39
Nilsson, Christine, **Supp. I Part 1:** 355
Nilsson, Harry, **Supp. XI:** 309
Nilsson, Jenny Lind, **Supp. XVI:** 177
Nimitz, Chester, **Supp. I Part 2:** 491
"Nimram" (Gardner), **Supp. VI:** 73
Nims, John Frederick, **III:** 527; **Supp. XVII:** 112
Nin, Anaïs, **III:** 182, 184, 190; **Supp. III Part 1:** 43; **Supp. IV Part 2:** 680; **Supp. X: 181–200; Supp. XIX:** 134
"9" (Oliver), **Supp. VII:** 244
"9 Failures of the Imagination" (Lethem), **Supp. XVIII:** 148
"Nine-Ball" (Offutt), **Supp. XIX:** 166, 167
Nine Dragons (Connelly), **Supp. XXI:** 74, **79–80**
"Nine from Eight" (Lanier), **Supp. I Part 1:** 352–354
Nine Headed Dragon River: Zen Journals 1969–1982 (Matthiessen), **Supp. V:** 199
Nine Horses (Collins), **Supp. XXI:** 55, 60, 61, 62, 65
"Nine Horses" (Collins), **Supp. XXI:** 61
Ninemile Wolves,The (Bass), **Supp. XVI:** 24–25, 26
"Nine Nectarines" (Moore), **III:** 203, 209, 215
Nine Plays (Reznikoff), **Supp. XIV:** 288
"Nine Poems for the Unborn Child" (Rukeyser), **Supp. VI:** 280–281, 284
Nine Stories (Nabokov), **Retro. Supp. I:** 266
Nine Stories (Salinger), **III:** 552, 558–564
"19 Hadley Street" (Schnackenberg), **Supp. XV:** 253
19 Necromancers from Now (Reed), **Supp. X:** 240
19 Varieties of Gazelle (Nye), **Supp. XIII:** 275, **286–288**
"19 Varieties of Gazelle" (Nye), **Supp. XIII:** 286
1984 (Orwell), **Supp. XIII:** 29; **Supp. XVIII:** 137, 138
"1940" (Stafford), **Supp. XI:** 328–329
"1945–1985: Poem for the Anniversary" (Oliver), **Supp. VII:** 237
1919 (Dos Passos), **I:** 482, 485–486, 487, 489, 490, 492
"1975" (Wright), **Supp. V:** 341
"1910" (Mora), **Supp. XIII:** 215
"1938" (Komunyakaa), **Supp. XIII:** 114
"1939" (Taylor), **Supp. V:** 316
1933 (Levine), **Supp. V:** 185–187
"1933" (Levine), **Supp. V:** 188
"Nineteenth New York, The" (Doctorow), **Supp. IV Part 1:** 232
"1929" (Auden), **Supp. II Part 1:** 6
"1926" (Kees), **Supp. XV:** 135
"93990" (Saunders), **Supp. XIX:** 233
"90 North" (Jarrell), **II:** 370, 371
90 Trees (Zukofsky), **Supp. III Part 2:** 631
95 Poems (Cummings), **I:** 430, 433, 435, 439, 446, 447
"91 Revere Street" (Lowell), **II:** 547; **Retro. Supp. II:** 188; **Supp. XI:** 240
Ninety Percent of Everything (Lethem, Kelly and Kessel), **Supp. XVIII:** 145
"92 Days" (L. Brown), **Supp. XXI:** 44–45
"Nine Years Later" (Brodsky), **Supp. VIII:** 32
"Nirvana" (Lanier), **Supp. I Part 1:** 352
Nirvana Blues, The (Nichols), **Supp. XIII:** 266, 267
Nishikigi (play), **III:** 466
Niven, David, **Supp. XI:** 307
Nixon (film), **Supp. XIV:** 48
Nixon, Richard M., **I:** 376; **III:** 38, 46; **Supp. I Part 1:** 294, 295; **Supp. V:** 45, 46, 51; **Supp. XII:** 14; **Supp. XIV:** 306
"NJ Transit" (Komunyakaa), **Supp. XIII:** 132
Nketia, J. H., **Supp. IV Part 1:** 10
Nketsia, Nana, **Supp. IV Part 1:** 2, 10
Nkize, Julius, **Supp. IV Part 1:** 361
Nkrumah, Kwame, **I:** 490, 494; **Supp. IV Part 1:** 361; **Supp. X:** 135
Nkrumah and the Ghana Revolution (C. L. R. James), **Supp. XXI:** 159, 171–172
NO (Major), **Supp. XXII:** 174
Noailles, Anna de, **IV:** 328
Noa Noa (Gauguin), **I:** 34
Nobel Lecture (Singer), **Retro. Supp. II:** 300
"No Better Than a 'Withered Daffodil' " (Moore), **III:** 216
Noble, David W., **Supp. I Part 2:** 650
Noble, Marianne, **Supp. XVIII:** 267
"Noble Rider and the Sound of Words, The" (Stevens), **Retro. Supp. I:** 299
Noble Savage, The (Coover), **Supp. V:** 40

"No Bobolink reverse His Singing" (Dickinson), **Retro. Supp. I:** 45
Nobodaddy (MacLeish), **III:** 5–6, 8, 10, 11, 18, 19, 20
"Nobodaddy" (W. Blake), **Supp. XVII:** 245
"Nobody in Hollywood" (Bausch), **Supp. VII:** 54
Nobody Knows My Name (Baldwin), **Supp. XIII:** 111
"Nobody Knows My Name" (Baldwin), **Retro. Supp. II:** 8; **Supp. I Part 1:** 52
Nobody Knows My Name: More Notes of a Native Son (Baldwin), **Retro. Supp. II:** 6, 8; **Supp. I Part 1:** 47, 52, 55
"Nobody knows this little Rose" (Dickinson), **Retro. Supp. I:** 30
"Nobody Said Anything" (Carver), **Supp. III Part 1:** 141
"Nobody's Business" (Lahiri), **Supp. XXI:** 183
Nobody's Fool (Russo), **Supp. XII:** 326, **331–335,** 340
"No Change of Place" (Auden), **Supp. II Part 1:** 5
"Noche Triste, La" (Frost), **Retro. Supp. I:** 123
Nock, Albert Jay, **I:** 245; **Supp. IV Part 2:** 521, 524
"No Coward Soul Is Mine" (Brontë), **I:** 458
"No Crime in the Mountains" (Chandler), **Supp. IV Part 1:** 129
"Nocturne" (Komunyakaa), **Supp. XIII:** 126
"Nocturne" (MacLeish), **III:** 8
"Nocturne at Bethesda" (Bontemps), **Supp. XXII:** 3, 8
"Nocturne in a Deserted Brickyard" (Sandburg), **III:** 586
Nocturne of Remembered Spring (Aiken), **I:** 50
No Direction Home (documentary film, Scorsese), **Supp. XVIII:** 22, 23, 29
No Direction Home (Shelton), **Supp. XVIII:** 21
No Door (Wolfe), **IV:** 451–452, 456
"No Door" (Wolfe), **IV:** 456
"No Epitaph" (Carson), **Supp. XII: 111**
No Exit (Sartre), **I:** 82, 130; **Supp. XIV:** 320
No Exit (Sartre; Bowles, trans.), **Supp. IV Part 1:** 84
No Gifts from Chance (Benstock), **Retro. Supp. I:** 361
"No-Good Blues" (Komunyakaa), **Supp. XIII:** 130
No Hero (Marquand), **III:** 57
No Heroes: A Memoir of Coming Home (Offutt), **Supp. XIX:** 163, **172–174,** 175
No! In Thunder (Fiedler), **Supp. XIII:** 101
"Noiseless Patient Spider" (Whitman), **III:** 555; **IV:** 348; **Supp. IV Part 1:** 325
Noises Off (Frayn), **Supp. IV Part 2:** 582
Noi vivi. See We the Living (film)
"No Jury Would Convict" (Shaw), **Supp. XIX:** 245
"No Lamp Has Ever Shown Us Where to Look" (MacLeish), **III:** 9
Nolan, Sidney, **Retro. Supp. II:** 189
No Laughing Matter (Heller and Vogel), **Supp. IV Part 1:** 384, 389
No Love Lost, a Romance of Travel (Howells), **II:** 277
No Man Is an Island (Merton), **Supp. VIII:** 207
"No More This Home" (Taggard), **Supp. XXII:** 277, 280
No Mother to Guide Her (Loos), **Supp. XVI:** 194
No Name in the Street (Baldwin), **Retro. Supp. II:** 13, 14; **Supp. I Part 1:** 47, 48, 52, 65–66, 67
No Nature: New and Selected Poems (Snyder), **Supp. VIII: 305**
Nonconformist's Memorial, The (Howe), **Supp. IV Part 2:** 434, 435–436
Nonconformity (Algren), **Supp. IX:** 15
None but the Lonely Heart (film), **Supp. II Part 2:** 546
Nones (Auden), **Supp. II Part 1:** 21
"Nones" (Auden), **Supp. II Part 1:** 22–23
None Shall Look Back (Gordon), **II:** 205–207, 208
"No No, Bad Daddy" (Nelson), **Supp. XVIII:** 177, 178
"Non-Tenured" (Halliday), **Supp. XIX:** 90, 91
Nonverbal Communication: Notes on the Visual Perception of Human Relations (Kees and Ruesch), **Supp. XV:** 147
"Noon" (Bryant), **Supp. I Part 1:** 157
"No One Remembers" (Levine), **Supp. V:** 187
"Noon Walk on the Asylum Lawn" (Sexton), **Supp. II Part 2:** 673
"Noon Wine" (Porter), **III:** 436, 437–438, 442, 446
"No Pain Whatsoever" (Yates), **Supp. XI:** 341
"No Place for You, My Love" (Welty), **IV:** 278, 279; **Retro. Supp. I:** 353
No Plays of Japan, The (Waley), **III:** 466
No Pockets in a Shroud (McCoy), **Supp. XIII: 166–168,** 171, 172, 173, 174
"No Poem So Fine" (Francis), **Supp. IX:** 83
Norcross, Frances, **I:** 456, 462
Norcross, Louise, **I:** 456, 462
Nordfeldt, B. J. O., **Supp. XXI:** 6
Nordfeldt, Margaret, **Supp. XXI:** 6
Nordyke, Lewis, **Supp. XIII:** 5
No Relief (Dixon), **Supp. XII:** 139, **142–143**
No Resting Place (Humphrey), **Supp. IX:** 94, **106–108**
Norfolk Poems, The (Carruth), **Supp. XVI:** 47, 48
Norma (Bellini), **IV:** 309
Norma Ashe (Glaspell), **Supp. III Part 1:** 175, 186–187
"Normal Motor Adjustments" (Stein and Solomons), **IV:** 26
Norman, Charles, **III:** 479
Norman, Gurney, **Supp. X:** 24
Norman, Jessye, **Supp. XX: 110**
Norman, Marsha, **Supp. VIII:** 141; **Supp. XXI:** 145
Norman Mailer (Poirier), **Retro. Supp. II:** 207–208
Norman Mailer: Modern Critical Views (Bloom), **Retro. Supp. II:** 205
Norman Mailer Revisited (Merrill), **Retro. Supp. II:** 201
Norna; or, The Witch's Curse (Alcott), **Supp. I Part 1:** 33
Norris, Charles, **III:** 320; **Retro. Supp. I:** 100; **Supp. XVIII:** 226
Norris, Frank, **I:** 211, 355, 500, 506, 517, 518, 519; **II:** 89, 264, 276, 289, 307; **III:** 227, **314–336,** 596; **IV:** 29; **Retro. Supp. I:** 100, 325; **Retro. Supp. II:** 96, 101; **Supp. III Part 2:** 412; **Supp. VIII:** 101, 102; **Supp. IX:** 14, 15; **Supp. XV:** 115
"North" (Budbill), **Supp. XIX:** 7–8
"North" (Hugo), **Supp. VI:** 135
North, Milou (pseudonym), **Supp. IV Part 1:** 260. *See also* Dorris, Michael; Erdrich, Louise
North, Sir Thomas, **IV:** 370
"North American Sequence" (Roethke), **I:** 171–172, 183; **III:** 529, 545, 547, 548
"North Beach" (Snyder), **Supp. VIII:** 289
North Country: A Personal Journey Through the Borderland (Mosher), **Supp. XXII: 203–204,** 206, 212, **217–218**
"North Country Sketches" (McClatchy), **Supp. XII:** 256
"Northeast Playground" (Paley), **Supp. VI:** 226–227, 229
Northern Borders (Mosher), **Supp. XXII:** 203, 204, 206, 207, 208, 209, **213–214**
Northern Lights (O'Brien), **Supp. V:** 237, 239, 241–244, 250
"Northern Motive" (Levine), **Supp. V:** 195
Northfield Poems (Ammons), **Supp. VII:** 29
"Northhanger Ridge" (Wright), **Supp. V:** 335, 340
"North Haven" (Bishop), **Retro. Supp. II:** 50
"North Labrador" (Crane), **I:** 386
North of Boston (Frost), **II:** 152, 153–154, 527; **Retro. Supp. I:** 121, 125, 127, **128–130,** 131; **Supp. I Part 1:** 263; **Supp. XIII:** 146
North of Jamaica (Simpson), **Supp. IV Part 2:** 448; **Supp. IX:** 275, 276
North of the Danube (Caldwell), **I:** 288, 290, 293, 294, 309, 310
Northrup, Cyrus, **Supp. I Part 1:** 350
North Sea (Jarman), **Supp. XVII:** 110, 113
"North Sea Undertaker's Complaint, The" (Lowell), **II:** 550
North & South (Bishop), **Retro. Supp. II: 41–43; Supp. I Part 1:** 72, 84, 85, 89

North Star, The (Hellman), **Supp. I Part 1:** 281
Northup, Solomon, **Supp. XIV:** 32
"North Winter" (Carruth), **Supp. XVI:** 53
Norton, Charles Eliot, **I:** 223, 568; **II:** 279, 322–323, 338; **Retro. Supp. I:** 371; **Retro. Supp. II:** 135; **Supp. I Part 1:** 103; **Supp. I Part 2:** 406, 479
Norton, Jody, **Supp. VIII:** 297
Norton, John, **Supp. I Part 1:** 99, 110, 112, 114
Norton Anthology of African American Literature, The, **Supp. X:** 325
Norton Anthology of African American Literature, The (H. L. Gates and McKay, eds.), **Supp. XX: 105**
Norton Anthology of American Literature, **Supp. X:** 325; **Supp. XV:** 270
Norton Anthology of Literature by Women (Gilbert and Gubar, eds.), **Supp. XV:** 270
Norton Anthology of Modern Poetry, The, **Supp. XI:** 259; **Supp. XV:** 258
Norton Anthology of Poetry, The, **Supp. XVIII:** 20
Norton Anthology of Short Fiction, The, **Supp. IX:** 4
Norton Book of Personal Essays, The, **Supp. XIV:** 105
Norton Lectures, **Retro. Supp. I:** 65
Norwood, Vera, **Supp. IX:** 24
No Safe Harbour (Porter), **III:** 447
Nosferatu: An Opera Libretto (Gioia), **Supp. XV:** 112, **128**
"Nosferatu's Serenade" (Gioia), **Supp. XV:** 128
No Siege Is Absolute (Char; version of F. Wright), **Supp. XVII:** 244
"No Snake" (A. Finch), **Supp. XVII:** 72
"No Speak English" (Cisneros), **Supp. VII:** 63
"Nostalgia" (Collins), **Supp. XXI:** 57
"Nostalgia" (Saunders), **Supp. XIX:** 235
Nostalgia for 70 (J. W. Miller), **Supp. XX: 165**
"Nostalgia of the Lakefronts" (Justice), **Supp. VII:** 118, 119, 120
"Nostalgic Mood" (Farrell), **II:** 45
No Star Is Lost (Farrell), **II:** 34, 35, 44
Nostrandt, Jeanne, **Supp. XVIII:** 80–81
Nostromo (Conrad), **II:** 600; **IV:** 245
"Nosty Fright, A" (Swenson), **Supp. IV Part 2:** 651
Not about Nightingales (T. Williams), **IV:** 381
"Not a Womb in the House" (Quindlen), **Supp. XVII:** 166, 171
Not Coming to Be Barked At (Kooser), **Supp. XIX:** 116, **120**
Not Dancing (Dunn), **Supp. XI:** 143, **148**
"Note about *Iconographs,* A" (Swenson), **Supp. IV Part 2:** 646
Notebook (Lowell), **Retro. Supp. II:** 186, 190; **Supp. V:** 343
Notebook 1967–68 (Lowell), **II:** 553–555; **Retro. Supp. II:** 182, 186, 190
Notebook of Malte Laurids Brigge, The (Rilke), **III:** 571
Notebooks (Fitzgerald), **Retro. Supp. I:** 110
Notebooks of Captain George, The (Renoir), **Supp. XXII:** 257
No Telephone to Heaven (Cliff), **Supp. XXII:** 66, 69, 71–72
"Note on Abraham Lincoln" (Vidal), **Supp. IV Part 2:** 688
"Note on Commercial Theatre" (Hughes), **Retro. Supp. I:** 207
"Note on Ezra Pound, A" (Eliot), **Retro. Supp. I:** 290
"Note on Lanier's Music, A" (P. Graham), **Supp. I Part 1:** 373
Note on Literary Criticism, A (Farrell), **II:** 26, 49
"Note on Poetry, A" (Doolittle), **Supp. I Part 1:** 254, 267–268
"Note on Realism, A" (Anderson), **I:** 110
"Note on the Limits of 'History' and the Limits of 'Criticism,' A" (Brooks), **Supp. XIV:** 11
"Note on the Poetry of Love, A" (Untermeyer), **Supp. XV:** 304
"Note on the Truth of the Tales, A" (Vollmann), **Supp. XVII:** 230
"Notes" (Dove), **Supp. IV Part 1:** 246
"Notes for a Moving Picture: The House" (Agee), **I:** 33, 34
"Notes for an Autobiography" (Van Vechten), **Supp. II Part 2:** 749
"Notes for a Novel About the End of the World" (Percy), **Supp. III Part 1:** 393
"Notes for a Preface" (Sandburg), **III:** 591, 596–597
"NOTES FOR A SPEECH" (Baraka), **Supp. II Part 1:** 33
Notes for the Green Box (Duchamp), **Supp. IV Part 2:** 423
Notes from a Bottle Found on the Beach at Carmel (Connell), **Supp. XIV:** 80, 87, 96, 97
Notes from a Sea Diary: Hemingway All the Way (Algren), **Supp. IX:** 16
"Notes from the Childhood and Girlhood" (Brooks), **Supp. III Part 1:** 77
"Notes from the River" (Stern), **Supp. IX:** 285, 287, 294, 295
Notes from Underground (Dostoevsky), **III:** 571; **IV:** 485; **Retro. Supp. II:** 121
Notes Left Behind: Last and Selected Poems (Hayford), **Supp. XXII:** 218
"Notes of a Faculty Wife" (Jackson), **Supp. IX:** 126
"Notes of a Native Daughter" (Didion), **Supp. IV Part 1:** 196, 197, 200, 201
Notes of a Native Son (Baldwin), **Retro. Supp. II:** 1, 2, 3, 5, 6; **Supp. I Part 1:** 50, 52, 54; **Supp. IV Part 1:** 163
"Notes of a Native Son" (Baldwin), **Supp. I Part 1:** 50, 54
Notes of a Son and Brother (James), **II:** 337; **Retro. Supp. I:** 235
"Notes on a Departure" (Trilling), **Supp. III Part 2:** 498
"Notes on Babbitt and More" (Wilson), **IV:** 435
"Notes on 'Camp' " (Sontag), **Supp. III Part 2:** 455–456
"Notes on Camp" (Sontag), **Supp. XIV:** 167
Notes on Democracy (Mencken), **III:** 104, 107–108, 109, 116, 119
Notes on Dialectics (C. L. R. James), **Supp. XXI:** 169
"Notes on Free Verse" (Dobyns), **Supp. XIII:** 77
"Notes on 'Layover' " (Hass), **Supp. VI:** 109
"Notes on Memory and Enthusiasm" (Di Piero), **Supp. XIX:** 42
Notes on Novelists (James), **II:** 336, 337; **Retro. Supp. I:** 235
"Notes on Nukes, Nookie, and Neo-Romanticism" (Robbins), **Supp. X:** 272
"Notes on Poetry" (Eberhart), **I:** 524, 527–528, 529
"Notes on the Craft of Poetry" (Strand), **Supp. IV Part 2:** 626
"Notes on the Decline of Outrage" (Dickey), **Supp. IV Part 1:** 181
"Notes on the New Formalism" (Gioia), **Supp. XV:** 113, 114–115
"Notes on the Novel-as-Autobiography" (P. Bailey), **Supp. XVI:** 69
"Notes on 'The Poetry of Everday Life' " (Notley), **Supp. XXII:** 232
Notes on the State of Virginia (1781–1782) (Jefferson), **Supp. XIV:** 191
"Notes to Be Left in a Cornerstone" (Benét), **Supp. XI:** 46, 58
"Notes toward a Supreme Fiction" (Stevens), **IV:** 87–89; **Retro. Supp. I:** 300, 306, **306–309,** 311; **Supp. I Part 1:** 80
"Notes towards a Poem That Can Never Be Written" (Atwood), **Supp. XIII:** 34–35
"Not Exactly for Talia" (Halliday), **Supp. XIX:** 94
No Thanks (Cummings), **I:** 430, 431, 432, 436, 437, 441, 443, 446
Not Heaven: A Novel in the Form of Prelude, Variations, and Theme (W. Frank), **Supp. XX: 80**
"Nothing" (C. Frost), **Supp. XV:** 94
"Nothing Big" (Komunyakaa), **Supp. XIII:** 121
Nothing for Tigers (Carruth), **Supp. XVI:** 47, 48, 50
"Nothing Gold Can Stay" (Frost), **Retro. Supp. I:** 133
"Nothing in Heaven Functions as It Ought" (X. J. Kennedy), **Supp. XV:** 158–159
Nothing Makes You Free: Writings by Descendants of Jewish Holocaust Survivors (Bukiet, ed.), **Supp. XVII: 39–40,** 48–49
"Nothing Missing" (O'Hara), **III:** 369
Nothing Personal (Baldwin), **Supp. I Part 1:** 58, 60
Nothing Sacred (film), **Supp. XVIII:** 243
"Nothing Song, The" (Snodgrass), **Supp. VI:** 326
"Nothing Stays Put" (Clampitt), **Supp. IX:** 42
"Nothing Will Yield" (Nemerov), **III:** 279

No Third Path (Kosinski), **Supp. VII:** 215
"Not Ideas About the Thing but the Thing Itself" (Stevens), **IV:** 87
"No Time" (Collins), **Supp. XXI:** 61
Notions of the Americans: Picked up by a Travelling Bachelor (Cooper), **I:** 343–345, 346
"Not-Knowing" (Barthelme), **Supp. IV Part 1:** 48
"Not Leaving the House" (Snyder), **Supp. VIII:** 300
Notley, Alice, **Supp. XXII: 223–238**
"'Not Marble nor the Gilded Monument' " (MacLeish), **III:** 12
Not Mine to Finish: Poems, 1928–1934 (Taggard), **Supp. XXII:** 280
"Not My Bones" (Nelson), **Supp. XVIII:** 183
Not Now But Now (M. F. K. Fisher), **Supp. XVII:** 86, 90
"Not Quite Social" (Frost), **II:** 156
"Not Sappho, Sacco" (Rukeyser), **Supp. VI:** 277
"Not Sixteen" (Anderson), **I:** 114
"Not Slightly" (Stein), **IV:** 44
Not So Deep as a Well (Parker), **Supp. IX:** 192
"Not Somewhere Else, but Here" (Rich), **Supp. I Part 2:** 552, 573
Not-So-Simple Neil Simon (McGovern), **Supp. IV Part 2:** 573
Not So Simple: The "Simple" Stories by Langston Hughes (Harper), **Retro. Supp. I:** 194, 209
"Not the Point" (Cameron), **Supp. XII: 83**
"Not They Who Soar" (Dunbar), **Supp. II Part 1:** 199
Not This Pig (Levine), **Supp. V:** 178, 181, 182–183
"Not to Be Satan nor to Deal with Him" (Bronk), **Supp. XXI:** 32
Not to Eat; Not for Love (Weller), **III:** 322
Not Wanted on the Voyage (Findley), **Supp. XX: 50, 56–57, 59**
Not Without Laughter (Hughes), **Retro. Supp. I:** 197, 198, 201; **Supp. I Part 1:** 328, 332; **Supp. XIX:** 73, 154
Nouvelle Héloïse, La (Rousseau), **Supp. XV:** 232
Nova Express (Burroughs), **Supp. III Part 1:** 93, 103, 104; **Supp. XVIII:** 137
Novel, The (Bulwer), **Retro. Supp. II:** 58
Novel, The: An Alternative History (Moore), **Supp. XXII:** 261
"Novel as a Function of American Democracy, The" (Ellison), **Retro. Supp. II:** 124
"Novel Démeublé, The" (Cather), **Retro. Supp. I:** 15
Novel History: Historians and Novelists Confront America's Past (and Each Other) (Carnes), **Supp. X:** 14
"Novelists of 2007" (Halliday), **Supp. XIX:** 90
Novella (Goethe; Bogan and Mayer, trans.), **Supp. III Part 1:** 63
Novellas and Other Writings (Wharton), **Retro. Supp. I:** 360
"Novel of the Thirties, A" (Trilling), **Supp. III Part 2:** 499
Novels and Other Writings (Bercovitch), **Retro. Supp. II:** 325
Novels and Tales of Henry James, The (James), **Retro. Supp. I:** 232
"Novel-Writing and Novel-Reading" (Howells), **II:** 276, 290
"November" (Larcom), **Supp. XIII:** 143
"November Cotton Flower" (Toomer), **Supp. IX:** 312
November Twenty Six Nineteen Sixty Three (Berry), **Supp. X:** 24
"Novices" (Moore), **III:** 200–201, 202, 213
Novick, Peter, **Supp. XVI:** 154–155
"Novogodnee" ("New Year's Greetings") (Tsvetayeva), **Supp. VIII:** 30
"Novotny's Pain" (P. Roth), **Supp. III Part 2:** 403
"No Voyage" (Oliver), **Supp. VII:** 231
No Voyage and Other Poems (Oliver), **Supp. VII:** 230–231, 232
Now and Another Time (Hearon), **Supp. VIII:** 58, **61–62**
Now and Then (Buechner), **Supp. XII:** 49, 53
"Now and Then, America" (Mora), **Supp. XIII:** 217
"Nowhere" (J. Scott), **Supp. XVII:** 189
Nowhere Is a Place: Travels in Patagonia (Theroux and Chatwin), **Supp. VIII:** 322
"Now I Am Married" (Gordon), **Supp. IV Part 1:** 299
"Now I Lay Me" (Hemingway), **II:** 249; **Retro. Supp. I:** 175
"Now I Lay Me" (Olds), **Supp. X:** 208
"Now Is the Air Made of Chiming Balls" (Eberhart), **I:** 523
"No Word" (Kunitz), **Supp. III Part 1:** 263
"No Worst" (Nelson), **Supp. XVIII:** 177, 178
Now Sheba Sings the Song (Angelou), **Supp. IV Part 1:** 16
"Now That We Live" (Kenyon), **Supp. VII:** 165
"Now the Servant's Name Was Malchus" (Wilder), **IV:** 358
"Now We Know" (O'Hara), **III:** 368–369
NOW with Bill Moyers (television), **Supp. XIII:** 286
Noyes, Alfred, **IV:** 434
Nuamah, Grace, **Supp. IV Part 1:** 10
"Nuances of a Theme by Williams" (Stevens), **Retro. Supp. I:** 422
Nuclear Age, The (O'Brien), **Supp. V:** 238, 243, 244, 246–248, 249, 251
"Nuclear Arms and Morality" (Sanders), **Supp. XVI:** 266
"Nude at a Dressing Table" (Peacock), **Supp. XIX:** 204
Nude Croquet (Fiedler), **Supp. XIII:** 103
"Nude Descendig a Staircase" (X. J. Kennedy), **Supp. XV:** 168
Nude Descending a Staircase (Duchamp), **IV:** 408; **Retro. Supp. I:** 416; **Supp. XXII:** 162
Nude Descending a Staircase (X. J. Kennedy), **Supp. XV:** 153, **154–157**
Nugent, Bruce, **Retro. Supp. I:** 200
Nugent, Elliot, **Supp. I Part 2:** 606, 611, 613
Nuggets and Dust (Bierce), **I:** 195
"Nullipara" (Olds), **Supp. X:** 209
Number One (Dos Passos), **I:** 489
"Numbers" (Skloot), **Supp. XX: 196, 207**
"Numbers, Letters" (Baraka), **Supp. II Part 1:** 50
Nunc Dimittis (Brodsky), **Supp. VIII:** 25–26, 28
"Nun No More, A" (Fante), **Supp. XI:** 160
"Nun's Priest's Tale" (Chaucer), **III:** 492
Nunzio, Nanzia, **IV:** 89
Nuptial Flight, The (Masters), **Supp. I Part 2:** 460, 471
"Nuptials" (Tate), **IV:** 122
"Nurse Whitman" (Olds), **Supp. X:** 203
Nurture (Kumin), **Supp. IV Part 2:** 453–454, 455
Nussbaum, Emily, **Supp. XI:** 143
Nussbaum, Felicity A., **Supp. X:** 189
Nutcracker, The (Tchaikovsky), **Retro. Supp. I:** 196
"Nux Postcoenatica" (Holmes), **Supp. I Part 1:** 303
Nyce, James M., **Retro. Supp. I:** 380
Nye, Naomi Shihab, **Supp. XI:** 316; **Supp. XIII: 273–290**
Nyerere, Julius, **Supp. X:** 135
"Nympholepsy" (Faulkner), **Retro. Supp. I:** 81
Nymphs of the Valley ('Ará'is al-Murúj) (Gibran), **Supp. XX: 115, 124, 125**

"Ö" (Dove), **Supp. IV Part 1:** 245
Oak and Ivy (Dunbar), **Supp. II Part 1:** 98
"Oak Bluffs" column (D. West), **Supp. XVIII:** 286
Oak Openings, The (Cooper), **I:** 354, 355
Oandasan, Bill, **Supp. IV Part 2:** 499
Oasis, The (McCarthy), **II:** 566–568
Oates, Joyce Carol, **Supp. II Part 2: 503–527; Supp. IV Part 1:** 205; **Supp. IV Part 2:** 447, 689; **Supp. V:** 323; **Supp. XI:** 239; **Supp. XII:** 343; **Supp. XIII:** 306; **Supp. XIV:** 26, 109
"Oath, The" (Tate), **IV:** 127
Obbligati (Hecht), **Supp. X:** 57
Ober, Harold, **Retro. Supp. I:** 101, 103, 105, 110, 113
Oberndorf, Clarence P., **Supp. I Part 1:** 315
Obey, André, **IV:** 356, 375
"Obit" (Lowell), **II:** 554
"Obituaries" (Collins), **Supp. XXI:** 65
"Objective Value of a Social Settlement, The" (Addams), **Supp. I Part 1:** 4
"Objective Woman, The" (Jong), **Supp. V:** 119
Objectivist Anthology, An, **Supp. XIV:** 287

"Objectivist Ethics, The" (Rand), **Supp. IV Part 2:** 530–532
"Objectivists" Anthology, An (Zukofsky), **Supp. III Part 2:** 613, 615
Object Lessons (Quindlen), **Supp. XVII: 173–174**
"Objects" (Wilbur), **Supp. III Part 2:** 545–547
Oblique Prayers (Levertov), **Supp. III Part 1:** 283
"Oblivion" (Justice), **Supp. VII:** 121
Oblivion Seekers, The (Eberhardt), **Supp. IV Part 1:** 92
"Oblong Box, The" (Poe), **III:** 416
"Obnoxious Truth, The" (Notley), **Supp. XXII:** 234
Obregon, Maurice, **Supp. I Part 2:** 488
O'Briant, Don, **Supp. X:** 8
O'Brien, Edward, **Supp. XV:** 140
O'Brien, Edward J., **I:** 289; **III:** 56; **Supp. XVIII:** 227; **Supp. XIX:** 256; **Supp. XX: 34**
O'Brien, Edwin, **Supp. XVIII:** 208
O'Brien, Fitzjames, **I:** 211
O'Brien, Geoffrey, **Supp. IV Part 2:** 471, 473
O'Brien, Joe, **Supp. XXI:** 5, 6
O'Brien, John, **Supp. V:** 48, 49; **Supp. X:** 239, 244; **Supp. XXI:** 228, 229, 233
O'Brien, Tim, **Supp. V: 237–255; Supp. XI:** 234; **Supp. XVII:** 14; **Supp. XXI:** 122
"Obscene Poem, An" (Creeley), **Supp. IV Part 1:** 150
Obscure Destinies (Cather), **I:** 331–332; **Retro. Supp. I:** 19
"Observation Relative to the Intentions of the Original Founders of the Academy in Philadelphia" (Franklin), **II:** 114
"Observations" (Dillard), **Supp. VI:** 34
Observations (Moore), **III:** 194, 195–196, 197, 199, 203, 205, 215
"Observations Now" (Conroy), **Supp. XVI:** 75
Observations: Photographs by Richard Avedon: Comments by Truman Capote, **Supp. III Part 1:** 125–126
Obuchowski, Mary DeJong, **Supp. XX: 222**
O Canada: An American's Notes on Canadian Culture (Wilson), **IV:** 429–430
"O Carib Isle!" (Crane), **I:** 400–401
O'Casey, Sean, **III:** 145; **Supp. IV Part 1:** 359, 361, 364
"Occidentals" (Ford), **Supp. V:** 71–72
Occom, Samuel, **Supp. XX: 288**
"Occultation of Orion, The" (Longfellow), **Retro. Supp. II:** 168
"Occurrence at Owl Creek Bridge, An" (Bierce), **I:** 200–201; **II:** 264
"Ocean 1212-W" (Plath), **Supp. I Part 2:** 528
"Ocean of Words" (Jin), **Supp. XVIII:** 94
Ocean of Words: Army Stories (Jin), **Supp. XVIII:** 89, 92, **93–94**
O'Connell, Nicholas, **Supp. IX:** 323, 325, 334
O'Connell, Shaun, **Supp. XXI:** 231
O'Connor, Edward F., Jr., **III:** 337
O'Connor, Flannery, **I:** 113, 190, 211, 298; **II:** 606; **III: 337–360; IV:** 4, 217, 282; **Retro. Supp. II:** 179, **219–239,** 272, 324; **Supp. I Part 1:** 290; **Supp. III Part 1:** 146; **Supp. V:** 59, 337; **Supp. VIII:** 13, 14, 158; **Supp. X:** 1, 26, 69, 228, 290; **Supp. XI:** 104; **Supp. XIII:** 294; **Supp. XIV:** 93; **Supp. XV:** 338; **Supp. XVI:** 219; **Supp. XVII:** 43, 114; **Supp. XVIII:** 156, 161, 194; **Supp. XIX:** 166, 209, 223; **Supp. XXI:** 197
O'Connor, Frank, **III:** 158; **Retro. Supp. II:** 242; **Supp. I Part 2:** 531; **Supp. VIII:** 151, 157, 165, 167, 171; **Supp. XV:** 74
O'Connor, Richard, **II:** 467
O'Connor, T. P., **II:** 129
O'Connor, William, **IV:** 346; **Retro. Supp. I:** 392, 407
O'Connor, William Van, **III:** 479; **Supp. I Part 1:** 195
"Octascope" (Beattie), **Supp. V:** 27, 28
"Octaves" (Robinson), **Supp. III Part 2:** 593
"Octet" (Wallace), **Supp. X:** 309
October (Isherwood), **Supp. XIV:** 157, 164
"October" (Oliver), **Supp. VII:** 241
"October" (Swenson), **Supp. IV Part 2:** 649
"October, 1866" (Bryant), **Supp. I Part 1:** 169
"October 1913" (McCarriston), **Supp. XIV:** 266
"October and November" (Lowell), **II:** 554
"October in the Railroad Earth" (Kerouac), **Supp. III Part 1:** 225, 227, 229
October Light (Gardner), **Supp. VI:** 63, **69–71,** 72
"October Maples, Portland" (Wilbur), **Supp. III Part 2:** 556
"October: With Rain" (W. V. Davis), **Supp. XXI:** 94
"Octopus, An" (Moore), **III:** 202, 207–208, 214
"Octopus, The" (Merrill), **Supp. III Part 1:** 321
Octopus, The (Norris), **I:** 518; **III:** 314, 316, 322–326, 327, 331–333, 334, 335
"O Daedalus, Fly Away Home" (Hayden), **Supp. II Part 1:** 377–378
"OD and Hepatitis Railroad or Bust, The" (Boyle), **Supp. VIII:** 1
Odd Couple, The (1985 version, Simon), **Supp. IV Part 2:** 580
Odd Couple, The (film), **Supp. IV Part 2:** 589
Odd Couple, The (Simon), **Supp. IV Part 2:** 575, 579–580, 585, 586; **Supp. XVII:** 8
Odd Jobs (Updike), **Retro. Supp. I:** 334
Odd Mercy (Stern), **Supp. IX: 298–299**
Odd Number (Sorrentino), **Supp. XXI:** 236
"Odds, The" (Hecht), **Supp. X:** 64–65
"Odds, The" (Salinas), **Supp. XIII:** 321
"Ode" (Emerson), **II:** 13
"Ode" (Sobin), **Supp. XVI:** 284–285
"Ode" (X. J. Kennedy), **Supp. XV:** 160
"Ode (Intimations of Immortality)" (Matthews), **Supp. IX:** 162
"Ode for Memorial Day" (Dunbar), **Supp. II Part 1:** 199
"Ode for the American Dead in Asia" (McGrath), **Supp. X:** 119
"Ode: For the Budding of Islands" (Sobin), **Supp. XVI:** 287
"Ode Inscribed to W. H. Channing" (Emerson), **Supp. XIV:** 46
"Ode: Intimations of Immortality" (Wordsworth), **Supp. I Part 2:** 729; **Supp. III Part 1:** 12; **Supp. XIV:** 8
"Ode in Time of Crisis" (Taggard), **Supp. XXII:** 271
Odell, Margeretta Matilda, **Supp. XX: 278, 284, 288**
"Ode: My 24th Year" (Ginsberg), **Supp. II Part 1:** 312
"Ode on a Grecian Urn" (Keats), **I:** 284; **III:** 472; **Supp. XII:** 113; **Supp. XIV:** 8, 9–10; **Supp. XV:** 100; **Supp. XXI:** 64
"Ode on Human Destinies" (Jeffers), **Supp. II Part 2:** 419
"Ode on Indolence" (Keats), **Supp. XII:** 113
"Ode on Melancholy" (Keats), **Retro. Supp. I:** 301
Ode Recited at the Harvard Commemoration (Lowell), **Supp. I Part 2:** 416–418, 424
"Ode Recited at the Harvard Commemoration" (Lowell), **II:** 551
"Ode Secrète" (Valéry), **III:** 609
"Odes of Estrangement" (Sobin), **Supp. XVI:** 289
"Odes to Natural Processes" (Updike), **Retro. Supp. I:** 323
"Ode: The Capris" (Halliday), **Supp. XIX:** 88
"Ode to a Nightingale" (Keats), **II:** 368; **Retro. Supp. II:** 261; **Supp. IX:** 52
"Ode to Autumn" (Masters), **Supp. I Part 2:** 458
"Ode to Cervantes" (Salinas), **Supp. XIII:** 324
"Ode to Coit Tower" (Corso), **Supp. XII:** 122
"Ode to Ethiopia" (Dunbar), **Supp. II Part 1:** 199, 207, 208, 209
"Ode to Fear" (Tate), **IV:** 128
Ode to Harvard and Other Poems, An (Bynner), **Supp. XV:** 41, 44
"Ode to Meaning" (Pinsky), **Supp. VI: 249–250,** 251
"Ode to Night" (Masters), **Supp. I Part 2:** 458
"Ode to Our Young Pro-Consuls of the Air" (Tate), **IV:** 135
"Ode to the Austrian Socialists" (Benét), **Supp. XI:** 46, 58
"Ode to the Confederate Dead" (Tate), **II:** 551; **IV:** 124, 133, 137; **Supp. X:** 52

"Ode to the Johns Hopkins University" (Lanier), **Supp. I Part 1:** 370
"Ode to the Maggot" (Komunyakaa), **Supp. XIII:** 130
"Ode to the Mexican Experience" (Salinas), **Supp. XIII:** 316–317
"Ode to the Virginian Voyage" (Drayton), **IV:** 135
"Ode to the West Wind" (Shelley), **Retro. Supp. I:** 308; **Supp. I Part 2:** 728; **Supp. IX:** 52; **Supp. XII:** 117; **Supp. XIV:** 271–272; **Supp. XV:** 221
"Ode to Walt Whitman" (Benét), **Supp. XI:** 52
Odets, Clifford, **Supp. I Part 1:** 277, 295; **Supp. I Part 2:** 679; **Supp. II Part 2: 529–554; Supp. IV Part 2:** 587; **Supp. V:** 109; **Supp. VIII:** 96; **Supp. XVIII:** 238; **Supp. XX: 34**
Odier, Daniel, **Supp. III Part 1:** 97
"Odi et Amo" (Catullus), **Supp. XV:** 27, 32, 35
O'Donnell, George Marion, **II:** 67
O'Donnell, Mary King, **Supp. XVIII:** 232
O'Donnell, Thomas F., **II:** 131
"Odor of Verbena" (Faulkner), **II:** 66
O'Doul, Lefty, **II:** 425
"Odysseus to Telemachus" (Brodsky), **Supp. VIII:** 25
Odyssey (Bryant, trans.), **Supp. I Part 1:** 158
Odyssey (Homer), **III:** 14, 470; **Retro. Supp. I:** 286, 290; **Retro. Supp. II:** 121; **Supp. I Part 1:** 185; **Supp. IV Part 2:** 631; **Supp. IX:** 211; **Supp. X:** 114; **Supp. XIV:** 191; **Supp. XVII:** 117; **Supp. XXI:** 36
"Odyssey of a Wop, The" (Fante), **Supp. XI:** 164, 165
Oedipus Rex (Sophocles), **I:** 137; **III:** 145, 151, 152, 332; **Supp. I Part 2:** 428
Oedipus Tyrannus (Sophocles), **II:** 203; **Supp. XV:** 265
Oehlschlaeger, Fritz, **Supp. IX:** 123
Oelze, Richard, **Supp. XXII:** 167
"Of Alexander Crummell" (Du Bois), **Supp. II Part 1:** 170
O'Faoláin, Seán, **Supp. II Part 1:** 101
Of a World That Is No More (Singer), **IV:** 16
"Of Booker T. Washington and Others" (Du Bois), **Supp. II Part 1:** 168
"Of Bright & Blue Birds & the Gala Sun" (Stevens), **IV:** 93
"Of Christian Heroism" (Ozick), **Supp. V:** 272
"Of Dying Beauty" (Zukofsky), **Supp. III Part 2:** 610
"Of Epiphanies and Poets" (Phillips), **Supp. XX: 221**
"Of 'Father and Son' " (Kunitz), **Supp. III Part 1:** 262
Offenbach, Jacques, **II:** 427
"Offering for Mr. Bluehart, An" (Wright), **Supp. III Part 2:** 596, 601
"Offerings" (Mason), **Supp. VIII:** 141
"Offertory" (Hempel), **Supp. XXI: 126–127**
Official Entry Blank (Kooser), **Supp. XIX:** 116, **117–118**
"Official Entry Form" (Kooser), **Supp. XIX:** 117
"Official Piety" (Whittier), **Supp. I Part 2:** 687
"Offloading for Mrs. Schwartz" (Saunders), **Supp. XIX:** 225–226
"Of Freemasons, Kings, and Constitutions" (P. N. Warren), **Supp. XX: 273**
"Off-Shore Pirates, The" (Fitzgerald), **II:** 88
Off the Beaten Path (Proulx), **Supp. VII:** 261
Off the Beaten Path: Stories of Place, **Supp. XVI:** 22
"Off the Cuff" (Simpson), **Supp. IX:** 278
"Off the Highway" (Wolfert), **Supp. XXI:** 265
Off the Map (Levine), **Supp. V:** 178
Offut, Chris, **Supp. XIX: 163–176**
O'Flaherty, George, **Supp. I Part 1:** 202, 205–206
O'Flaherty, Kate. *See* Chopin, Kate
O'Flaherty, Thomas, **Supp. I Part 1:** 202, 203–204, 205
O'Flaherty, Thomas, Jr., **Supp. I Part 1:** 202
"Of Maids and Other Muses" (Alvarez), **Supp. VII:** 11
"Of Margaret" (Ransom), **III:** 491
Of Mice and Men (Steinbeck), **IV:** 51, 57–58
"Of Modern Poetry" (Stevens), **IV:** 92
Of Plymouth Plantation (Bradford), **Retro. Supp. II:** 161, 162; **Supp. XXII:** 33, **35–47**
Of Plymouth Plantation (Morison, ed.), **Supp. I Part 2:** 494
"Ofrenda for Lobo" (Mora), **Supp. XIII:** 224
"Often" (Kenyon), **Supp. VII:** 171
"Often, in Dreams, He Moved through a City" (Dobyns), **Supp. XIII:** 90
"Of the Coming of John" (Du Bois), **Supp. II Part 1:** 170
"Of the Culture of White Folk" (Du Bois), **Supp. II Part 1:** 175
Of the Farm (Updike), **IV:** 214, 217, 223–225, 233; **Retro. Supp. I:** 318, 329, 332
"Of the Four-Winged Cherubim as Signature" (Sobin), **Supp. XVI:** 287
"Of 'The Frill' " (McCarriston), **Supp. XIV:** 274
"Of the Passing of the First-Born" (Du Bois), **Supp. II Part 1:** 170
"Of the Sorrow Songs" (Du Bois), **Supp. II Part 1:** 170
"Of the Wings of Atlanta" (Du Bois), **Supp. II Part 1:** 170
Of This Time, Of This Place (Trilling), **Supp. III Part 2:** 498, 504
Of Time and the River (Wolfe), **IV:** 450, 451, 452, 455, 456, 457, 458, 459, 462, 464–465, 467, 468, 469
Of Woman Born: Motherhood as Experience and Institution (Rich), **Supp. I Part 2:** 554, 567–569
Of Women and Their Elegance (Mailer), **Retro. Supp. II:** 209
Ogden, Archie, **Supp. XIII:** 174
Ogden, Henry, **II:** 298
Ogden, Uzal, **Supp. I Part 2:** 516
"Oh, Atonement" (Weigl), **Supp. XIX:** 287
"Oh, Fairest of the Rural Maids" (Bryant), **Supp. I Part 1:** 169
"Oh, Immobility, Death's Vast Associate" (Dobyns), **Supp. XIII:** 89
"Oh, Joseph, I'm So Tired" (Yates), **Supp. XI:** 348
Oh, the Places You'll Go! (Geisel), **Supp. XVI:** 111
Oh, the Thinks You can Think! (Geisel), **Supp. XVI:** 111
"O'Halloran's Luck" (Benét), **Supp. XI:** 47
O'Hara, Frank, **Supp. XII:** 121; **Supp. XV:** 93, 176, 177, 178, 179–180, 182, 186, 187, 215–216; **Supp. XIX:** 81, 85; **Supp. XXII:** 226, 236
O'Hara, J. D., **Supp. IV Part 1:** 43; **Supp. V:** 22; **Supp. XVI:** 221; **Supp. XXI:** 228
O'Hara, John, **I:** 375, 495; **II:** 444, 459; **III:** 66, **361–384; IV:** 59; **Retro. Supp. I:** 99, 112; **Supp. I Part 1:** 196; **Supp. II Part 1:** 109; **Supp. IV Part 1:** 31, 383; **Supp. IV Part 2:** 678; **Supp. V:** 95; **Supp. VIII:** 151, 156; **Supp. IX:** 208; **Supp. XIX:** 209
O'Hara's Choice (Uris), **Supp. XX: 247, 256–257**
O'Hehir, Andrew, **Supp. XII:** 280
O. Henry Biography (C. A. Smith), **Supp. II Part 1:** 395
"Ohio Pagan, An" (Anderson), **I:** 112, 113
Ohio trilogy (Richter), **Supp. XVIII:** 212–215
Oh Mercy (album, Dylan), **Supp. XVIII:** 28, 33
Oh Say Can You Say? (Geisel), **Supp. XVI:** 111
Oil! (Sinclair), **Supp. V:** 276, 277–279, 282, 288, 289
Oil Notes (Bass), **Supp. XVI:** 17
"Oil Painting of the Artist as the Artist" (MacLeish), **III:** 14
O'Keeffe, Georgia, **Supp. IX:** 62, 66; **Supp. XX: 75**
"Oklahoma" (Levis), **Supp. XI:** 267
Oktenberg, Adrian, **Supp. XVII:** 76; **Supp. XXI:** 253
"Old, Old, Old, Old Andrew Jackson" (Lindsay), **Supp. I Part 2:** 398
"Old Amusement Park, An" (Moore), **III:** 216
"Old Angel Midnight" (Kerouac), **Supp. III Part 1:** 229–230
"Old Apple Dealer, The" (Hawthorne), **II:** 227, 233–235, 237, 238
"Old Apple-Tree, The" (Dunbar), **Supp. II Part 1:** 198
"Old Army Game, The" (Garrett), **Supp. VII:** 100–101
"Old Aunt Peggy" (Chopin), **Retro. Supp. II:** 64

"Old Barn at the Bottom of the Fogs, The" (Frost), **Retro. Supp. I:** 138
Old Battle-Ax, The (Holding), **Supp. XXII: 128–129**
Old Beauty and Others, The (Cather), **I:** 331
"Old Boys, Old Girls" (P. E. Jones), **Supp. XXII:** 151
Old Bruin: Commodore Matthew C. Perry, 1794–1858 (Morison), **Supp. I Part 2:** 494–495
"Old Cracked Tune, An" (Kunitz), **Supp. III Part 1:** 264
Old Curiosity Shop, The (Dickens), **I:** 458; **Supp. I Part 2:** 409
Oldest Killed Lake in North America, The (Carruth), **Supp. XVI:** 51
"Oldest Man, The" (M. F. K. Fisher), **Supp. XVII:** 91
"Old Farmer, The" (Jeffers), **Supp. II Part 2:** 418
Old-Fashioned Girl, An (Alcott), **Supp. I Part 1:** 29, 41, 42
"Old Father Morris" (Stowe), **Supp. I Part 2:** 586
"Old Flame, The" (Lowell), **II:** 550
"Old Florist" (Roethke), **III:** 531
"Old Folsom Prison" (Matthews), **Supp. IX:** 165
Old Forest, The (Taylor), **Supp. V:** 320, 321, 326, 327
"Old Forest, The" (Taylor), **Supp. V:** 313, 321, 323, 326
Old Forest and Other Stories (Taylor), **Supp. V:** 326
Old Friends and New (Jewett), **II:** 402; **Retro. Supp. II:** 137, 140
Old Glory, The (Lowell), **II:** 543, 545–546, 555; **Retro. Supp. II:** 188
Old Helmet, The (S. and A. Warner), **Supp. XVIII:** 267
"Old Homestead, The" (Dunbar), **Supp. II Part 1:** 198
"Old House" (Espaillat), **Supp. XXI:** 112, 113
"Old Iron" (Nye), **Supp. XIII:** 276
"Old Ironsides" (Holmes), **Supp. I Part 1:** 302
"Old Lady We Saw, An" (Shields), **Supp. VII:** 310–311
"Old Love" (Singer), **Retro. Supp. II:** 307
"Old McGrath Place, The" (McGrath), **Supp. X:** 114
"Old Maid, The" (Wharton), **Retro. Supp. I:** 381, 382
"Old Man" (Faulkner), **II:** 68, 69
Old Man and the Sea, The (Hemingway), **II:** 250, 256–257, 258, 265; **III:** 40; **Retro. Supp. I:** 180, **185,** 186
"Old Man Drunk" (Wright), **Supp. III Part 2:** 595
"Old Man Feeding Hens" (Francis), **Supp. IX:** 78
"Old Man on the Hospital Porch" (Ríos), **Supp. IV Part 2:** 546–547
Old Man Rubbing His Eyes (R. Bly), **Supp. IV Part 1:** 65
"Old Manse, The" (Hawthorne), **II:** 224
"Old Man's Winter Night, An" (Frost), **Retro. Supp. I:** 126, 131
Old Man Who Love Cheese, The (Keillor), **Supp. XVI:** 177
"Old Man with a Dog" (Wright), **Supp. XV:** 346
Old Marriage and New (Kooser), **Supp. XIX: 120–121**
"Old Meeting House, The" (Stowe), **Supp. I Part 2:** 586
"Old Memory, An" (Dunbar), **Supp. II Part 1:** 198
"Old Men, Old Horses" (P. N. Warren as Kilina), **Supp. XX: 262**
"Old Men, The" (McCarthy), **II:** 566
"Old Men Pitching Horseshoes" (X. J. Kennedy), **Supp. XV:** 166
Old Money (Wasserstein), **Supp. XV: 333–334**
"Old Morgue, The" (Prose), **Supp. XVI:** 250
Old Morning Program, The (radio show, Keillor). *See Prairie Home Companion, A* (radio show, Keillor)
"Old Mortality" (Porter), **III:** 436, 438–441, 442, 445, 446
"Old Mrs. Harris" (Cather), **I:** 332; **Retro. Supp. I:** 19
Old Neighborhood, The (Mamet), **Supp. XIV:** 240, 241, 242, 249–250, 251, 252, 254
Old New York (Wharton), **IV:** 322; **Retro. Supp. I:** 381
"Ol' Doc Hyar" (Campbell), **Supp. II Part 1:** 202
"Old of the Moon" (Offutt), **Supp. XIX:** 165, 166
Old One-Two, The (Gurney), **Supp. V:** 98
"Old Order, The" (Porter), **III:** 443, 444–445, 451
"Old Osawatomie" (Sandburg), **III:** 584
Old Patagonia Express, The: By Train through the Americas (Theroux), **Supp. VIII:** 322
"Old People, The" (Faulkner), **II:** 71–72
"Old Photograph, An" (Kooser), **Supp. XIX:** 121
"Old Poet Moves to a New Apartment 14 Times, The" (Zukofsky), **Supp. III Part 2:** 628
Old Possum's Book of Practical Cats (T. S. Eliot), **Supp. XIII:** 228, 344
"Old Red" (Gordon), **II:** 199, 200, 203
Old Red and Other Stories (Gordon), **II:** 157
Old Régime in Canada, The (Parkman), **Supp. II Part 2:** 600, 607, 608–609, 612
Old Religion, The (Mamet), **Supp. XIV:** 253
Olds, Sharon, **Supp. X: 201–217; Supp. XI:** 139, 142, 244; **Supp. XII:** 229; **Supp. XIV:** 265; **Supp. XVII:** 114, 240; **Supp. XXI:** 249
"Old Saws" (Garrett), **Supp. VII:** 96–97
Old South, The: "A Summer Tragedy" and Other Stories (Bontemps), **Supp. XXII:** 7
"Old Stories" (Skloot), **Supp. XX: 200**
Old Testament, **I:** 109, 181, 300, 328, 401, 410, 419, 431, 457, 458; **II:** 166, 167, 219; **III:** 270, 272, 348, 390, 396; **IV:** 41, 114, 152, 309; **Retro. Supp. I:** 122, 140, 249, 311, 360; **Retro. Supp. II:** 299; **Supp. I Part 1:** 60, 104, 106, 151; **Supp. I Part 2:** 427, 515, 516; **Supp. IX:** 14. *See also* names of Old Testament books
"Old Things, The" (James), **Retro. Supp. I:** 229
"Old Times on the Mississippi" (Twain), **IV:** 199
Oldtown Folks (Stowe), **Supp. I Part 2:** 587, 596–598
"Old Town of Berwick, The" (Jewett), **Retro. Supp. II:** 132
"Old Trails" (Robinson), **III:** 513, 517
"Old Tyrannies" (Bourne), **I:** 233
"Old West" (Bausch), **Supp. VII:** 48
"Old Whorehouse, An" (Oliver), **Supp. VII:** 235
"Old Woman" (Pinsky), **Supp. VI:** 238
"Old Woman of Beare, The" (X. J. Kennedy), **Supp. XV:** 156
"Old Word, The" (Simic), **Supp. VIII:** 282
"Old-World Landowners" (Gogol), **Supp. XV:** 262
Oldys, Francis. *See* Chalmers, George
Oleanna (Mamet), **Supp. XIV:** 239, 241, 245, 248, 250
Olendorf, Donna, **Supp. IV Part 1:** 196
"Olga Poems, The" (Levertov), **Supp. III Part 1:** 279–281
"Olive Groves of Thasos, The" (Clampitt), **Supp. IX: 51–52**
Oliver, Bill, **Supp. VIII:** 138
Oliver, Douglas, **Supp. XXII:** 225, 226, 233, 235
Oliver, Mary, **Supp. VII: 229–248; Supp. X:** 31; **Supp. XVI:** 39; **Supp. XVII:** 111, 240
Oliver, Sydney, **I:** 409
Oliver Goldsmith: A Biography (Irving), **II:** 315
Oliver Twist (Dickens), **I:** 354; **Supp. IV Part 2:** 464
"Olivia" (Salinas), **Supp. XIII:** 316
"Olivier Bergmann" (Halliday), **Supp. XIX:** 93–94
Olivieri, David (pseudonym), **Retro. Supp. I:** 361. *See also* Wharton, Edith
Ollive, Samuel, **Supp. I Part 2:** 503
Olmsted, Frederick Law, **Supp. I Part 1:** 355
Olor de la memoria, El/The Scent of Memory (Espaillat), **Supp. XXI:** 104
Olsen, Lance, **Supp. IV Part 1:** 54; **Supp. IV Part 2:** 623
Olsen, Tillie, **Supp. V:** 114, 220; **Supp. XIII: 291–309; Supp. XVI:** 83, 90
Olshan, Joseph, **Supp. XIX:** 52
Olson, Charles, **Retro. Supp. I:** 209; **Supp. II Part 1:** 30, 328; **Supp. II Part 2: 555–587; Supp. III Part 1:** 9, 271; **Supp. III Part 2:** 542, 624; **Supp. IV Part 1:** 139, 144, 146, 153, 154, 322; **Supp. IV Part 2:** 420, 421, 423, 426; **Supp. VIII:** 290, 291; **Supp.**

XII: 2, 198; **Supp. XIII:** 104; **Supp. XIV:** 96; **Supp. XV:** 177; **Supp. XXI:** 19, 21, 23
Olson, Clarence, **Supp. XX: 84, 85, 86**
Olson, Ray, **Supp. XVII:** 111, 112, 119
"Ol' Tunes, The" (Dunbar), **Supp. II Part 1:** 197
"O Lull Me, Lull Me" (Roethke), **III:** 536–537
O'Malley, Anne, **Supp. XXII:** 56
Omar Khayyam, **Supp. I Part 1:** 363
O'Meally, Robert, **Retro. Supp. II:** 112
Omega the Unknown (comic book series), **Supp. XVIII:** 149
"Omen" (Komunyakaa), **Supp. XIII:** 126, 127
Omensetter's Luck (Gass), **Supp. VI: 80–82,** 87
Omeros (Walcott), **Supp. XV:** 264
"Ominous Baby, An" (Crane), **I:** 411
Ommateum, with Doxology (Ammons), **Supp. VII:** 24–26, 27, 28, 36
Omni-Americans, The: New Perspectives on Black Experience and American Culture (Murray), **Supp. XIX:** 147, **149–151,** 154
"Omnibus Jaunts and Drivers" (Whitman), **IV:** 350
Omoo: A Narrative of Adventures in the South Seas (Melville), **III:** 76–77, 79, 84; **Retro. Supp. I:** 247
O My Land, My Friends (H. Crane), **Retro. Supp. II:** 76
"On Abrigador Hill" (Nelson), **Supp. XVIII:** 183
"On a Certain Condescension in Foreigners" (Lowell), **Supp. I Part 2:** 419
"On a Certain Engagement South of Seoul" (Carruth), **Supp. XVI:** 47
"On a Child Who Lived One Minute" (X. J. Kennedy), **Supp. XV:** 152, 155
"On Acquiring Riches" (Banks), **Supp. V:** 5
On a Darkling Plain (Stegner), **Supp. IV Part 2:** 598, 607
On a Fire on the Moon (Mailer), **Retro. Supp. II:** 206
"On a Hill Far Away" (Dillard), **Supp. VI:** 28
"On a Honey Bee, Drinking from a Glass and Drowned Therein" (Freneau), **Supp. II Part 1:** 273
"On a Monument to a Pigeon" (Leopold), **Supp. XIV:** 187–188
"On a Mountainside" (Wagoner), **Supp. IX:** 332
O'Nan, Stewart, **Supp. XI:** 348
"On an Old Photograph of My Son" (Carver), **Supp. III Part 1:** 140
"Onan's Soliloquy" (X. J. Kennedy), **Supp. XV:** 165
"On a Proposed Trip South" (W. C. Williams), **Retro. Supp. I:** 413
Onassis, Jacqueline Kennedy, **Supp. XVIII:** 287
"On a Tree Fallen across the Road" (Frost), **Retro. Supp. I:** 134
"On a View of Pasadena from the Hills" (Winters), **Supp. II Part 2:** 795, 796–799, 814
"On a Visit to a Halfway House after a Long Absence" (Salinas), **Supp. XIII:** 325
"On a Windy Night" (Dixon), **Supp. XII:** 155
On Becoming a Novelist (Gardner), **Supp. VI:** 64
"On Being an American" (Toomer), **Supp. III Part 2:** 479
"On Being Asked to Write a Poem against the War in Vietnam" (Carruth), **Supp. XVI:** 55–56
"On Being a Woman" (Parker), **Supp. IX:** 201
On Being Blue (Gass), **Supp. VI:** 77, 78, 86, 94; **Supp. XIV:** 305
"On Being Brought from Africa to America" (Wheatley), **Supp. XX: 280–281, 286–287**
"On Being Too Inhibited" (Hay), **Supp. XIV:** 130
"On Being Unable to Read" (Cornell), **Supp. XX: 94–95**
On Beyond Zebra! (Geisel), **Supp. XVI:** 105
"On Burroughs' Work" (Ginsberg), **Supp. II Part 1:** 320
Once (Walker), **Supp. III Part 2:** 519, 522, 530
Once at Antietam (Gaddis), **Supp. IV Part 1:** 285
"Once by the Pacific" (Frost), **II:** 155; **Retro. Supp. I:** 122, 137
"Once More, the Round" (Roethke), **III:** 529
Once More around the Block: Familiar Essays (Epstein), **Supp. XIV: 107**
"Once More to the Lake" (White), **Supp. I Part 2:** 658, 668, 673–675
"On Certain Political Measures Proposed to Their Consideration" (Barlow), **Supp. II Part 1:** 82
"Once There Was Light" (Kenyon), **Supp. VII:** 171–172
"On *Credo Ut Intelligam*" (Bronk), **Supp. XXI:** 31
Ondaatje, Michael, **Supp. IV Part 1:** 252
"On Dining Alone" (M. F. K. Fisher), **Supp. XVII:** 83
On Distant Ground (R. O. Butler), **Supp. XII:** 62, **66–68,** 69, 74
"On Divers Geometries" (Bronk), **Supp. XXI:** 31
"One, The" (Weigl), **Supp. XIX:** 282–283
"1 January 1965" (Brodsky), **Supp. VIII:** 23–24
O'Neale, Sondra, **Supp. IV Part 1:** 2
"One A.M. with Voices" (X. J. Kennedy), **Supp. XV:** 157
"One Arm" (T. Williams), **IV:** 383
One Arm, and Other Stories (T. Williams), **IV:** 383
"One Art" (Bell), **Supp. X:** 2
One Art (Bishop), **Retro. Supp. II:** 51
"One Art" (Bishop), **Retro. Supp. II:** 50; **Supp. I Part 1:** 72, 73, 82, 93, 94–95, 96; **Supp. XV:** 126; **Supp. XXI:** 58
"One Art: The Poetry of Elizabeth Bishop, 1971–1976" (Schwartz), **Supp. I Part 1:** 81
One Big Self: Prisoners of Louisiana (Wright and Luster), **Supp. XV:** 337, 344, 350, **351–353**
"One Blessing had I than the rest" (Dickinson), **Retro. Supp. I:** 45
"One Body" (Hass), **Supp. VI:** 106
One Boy's Boston, 1887–1901 (Morison), **Supp. I Part 2:** 494
"One Coat of Paint" (Ashbery), **Supp. III Part 1:** 26
"One Dash-Horses" (Crane), **I:** 416
One Day (Morris), **III:** 233–236
One Day, When I Was Lost (Baldwin), **Retro. Supp. II:** 13; **Supp. I Part 1:** 48, 66, 67
"One Dead Friend" (Kumin), **Supp. IV Part 2:** 441
One Fish Two Fish Red Fish Blue Fish (Geisel), **Supp. XVI:** 108
One Flesh (Major), **Supp. XXII: 183–184**
One Flew Over the Cuckoo's Nest (Kesey), **III:** 558
"One for the Road" (Swados), **Supp. XIX:** 259
One for the Rose (Levine), **Supp. V:** 178, 179, 181, 187, 189–191
"One for the Rose" (Levine), **Supp. V:** 181, 190
"One Friday Morning" (Hughes), **Supp. I Part 1:** 330
"One Holy Night" (Cisneros), **Supp. VII:** 69–70
"One Home" (Stafford), **Supp. XI:** 321
100 Faces of Death, The, Part IV (Boyle), **Supp. VIII:** 16
100 Great Poets of the English Language (Gioia, ed.), **Supp. XXI:** 99
100 Years of Negro Freedom (Bontemps), **Supp. XXII:** 6
$106,000 Blood Money (Hammett), **Supp. IV Part 1:** 345
"$106,000 Blood Money" (Hammett), **Supp. IV Part 1:** 345, 346
One Hundred Days in Europe (Holmes), **Supp. I Part 1:** 317
180 More: Extraordinary Poems for Every Day (Collins, ed.), **Supp. XXI:** 54
158-Pound Marriage, The (Irving), **Supp. VI:** 163, 164, **167–170**
O'Neil, Elizabeth Murrie, **Retro. Supp. I:** 427
O'Neill, Brendan, **Supp. XII:** 286
O'Neill, Eugene, **I:** 66, 71, 81, 94, 393, 445; **II:** 278, 391, 427, 585; **III:** 151, 165, **385–408; IV:** 61, 383; **Retro. Supp. II:** 82, 104; **Supp. III Part 1:** 177–180, 189; **Supp. IV Part 1:** 359; **Supp. IV Part 2:** 587, 607; **Supp. V:** 277; **Supp. VIII:** 332, 334; **Supp. XIV:** 239, 320, 328; **Supp. XVI:** 193; **Supp. XVII:** 96, 99–100, 103, 105, 107; **Supp. XX: 69; Supp. XXI:** 6, 13; **Supp. XXII:** 17, 18, 22, 28
O'Neill, Oona, **Supp. XXII:** 25, 26

"One Is a Wanderer" (Thurber), **Supp. I Part 2:** 616
One Is the Sun (P. N. Warren), **Supp. XX: 269–270**
One L (Turow), **Supp. XVII: 214,** 215, 217
"One Last Look at the Adige: Verona in the Rain" (Wright), **Supp. III Part 2:** 603
One Life (Rukeyser), **Supp. VI:** 273, 281, 283
One Life at a Time, Please (Abbey), **Supp. XIII:** 13
One Man in His Time (Glasgow), **II:** 178, 184
"One Man's Fortunes" (Dunbar), **Supp. II Part 1:** 211, 212–213
One Man's Initiation (Dos Passos), **I:** 476–477, 479, 488
One Man's Meat (White), **Supp. I Part 2:** 654, 669, 676
"One Man's Meat" (White), **Supp. I Part 2:** 655
One Matchless Time: A Life of William Faulkner (Parini), **Supp. XXII:** 205
"One Moment on Top of the Earth" (Nye), **Supp. XIII:** 282
One More July: A Football Dialogue with Bill Curry (Plimpton), **Supp. XVI:** 243
"One More Song" (Lindsay), **Supp. I Part 2:** 400–401
"One More Thing" (Carver), **Supp. III Part 1:** 138, 144
"One More Time" (Gordon), **II:** 200
One Nation (Stegner), **Supp. IV Part 2:** 599, 608
"One-Night Homecoming" (X. J. Kennedy), **Supp. XV:** 167
"ONE NIGHT STAND" (Baraka), **Supp. II Part 1:** 32
"One of Our Conquerors" (Bourne), **I:** 223
One of Ours (Cather), **I:** 322–323; **Retro. Supp. I:** 1, 3, **13–15,** 20
"One of the Missing" (Bierce), **I:** 201–202
"One of the Rooming Houses of Heaven" (Doty), **Supp. XI:** 131
"One of the Smallest" (Stern), **Supp. IX:** 299–300
"One of Us" (Fante), **Supp. XI:** 165
"One Out of Twelve: Writers Who Are Women in Our Century" (Olsen), **Supp. XIII:** 294
"One Part Humor, 2 Parts Whining" (Kakutani), **Supp. XI:** 38
"One Person" (Wylie), **Supp. I Part 2:** 709, 724–727
"One Sister have I in our house" (Dickinson), **Retro. Supp. I:** 34
165 Meeting House Lane (Notley), **Supp. XXII:** 224, 225, 226
"One Song, The" (Strand), **Supp. IV Part 2:** 619
"One Summer in Spain" (Coover), **Supp. V:** 40
One That Got Away, The (Everett), **Supp. XVIII:** 54
1000 Airplanes on the Roof (Glass, Hwang, and Sirlin), **Supp. XXI:** 147
One Thousand Avant-Garde Plays (Koch), **Supp. XV:** 187
"One Thousandth, The" (Weigl), **Supp. XIX:** 288
One Time, One Place: Mississippi in the Depression, a Snapshot Album (Welty), **Retro. Supp. I:** 339, 343, 344
1 x 1 (One Times One) (Cummings), **I:** 430, 436, 438–439, 441, 446, 447, 448
"One Touch of Nature" (McCarthy), **II:** 580
One Train (Koch), **Supp. XV:** 177, 184
"One Trip Abroad" (Fitzgerald), **II:** 95
One True Thing (film), **Supp. XVII:** 176
One True Thing (Quindlen), **Supp. XVII:** 166, **174–176**
"One Way" (Creeley), **Supp. IV Part 1:** 150–151
One Way or Another (Cameron), **Supp. XII:** 81
One-Way Ticket (Hughes), **Retro. Supp. I:** 206, 207, 208; **Supp. I Part 1:** 333–334
One Way to Heaven (Cullen), **Supp. IV Part 1:** 170, 172
One Way to Reconstruct the Scene (W. V. Davis), **Supp. XXI:** 83, **88–91**
"One Way to Reconstruct the Scene" (W. V. Davis), **Supp. XXI: 88–89,** 90, **91,** 92, 93
One Way to Spell Man (Stegner), **Supp. IV Part 2:** 595, 598, 601, 609
"One Way to Spell Man" (Stegner), **Supp. IV Part 2:** 601
One Whose Eyes Open When You Close Your Eyes, The (F. Wright), **Supp. XVII:** 240, 243
"One Who Skins Cats, The" (Gunn Allen), **Supp. IV Part 1:** 331
"One Who Went Forth to Feel Fear" (Grimms), **Supp. X:** 86
"One Winter I Devise a Plan of My Own" (Ríos), **Supp. IV Part 2:** 549
One Winter Night in August (X. J. Kennedy), **Supp. XV:** 154, 162
One World at a Time (Kooser), **Supp. XIX:** 116, **122–123**
One Writer's Beginnings (Welty), **Retro. Supp. I:** 339, 340, 341, 343, 344, 355–356
"One Year" (Olds), **Supp. X:** 210
On Fire (L. Brown), **Supp. XXI:** 41, **48–49**
"On First Looking Into Chapman's Homer" (Keats), **Supp. XXI:** 64
"On First Looking Out through Juan de la Cosa's Eyes" (Olson), **Supp. II Part 2:** 565, 566, 570, 579
"On First Opening *The Lyric Year*" (W. C. Williams), **Retro. Supp. I:** 414
"On Freedom's Ground" (Wilbur), **Supp. III Part 2:** 562
On Glory's Course (Purdy), **Supp. VII:** 275–276, 279, 280
On Grief and Reason (Brodsky), **Supp. VIII: 31–32**
"On Hearing a Symphony of Beethoven" (Millay), **III:** 132–133
"On Hearing the Airlines Will Use a Psychological Profile to Catch Potential Skyjackers" (Dunn), **Supp. XI:** 144–145
On Human Finery (Bell), **Supp. I Part 2:** 636
"On *Imagerie:* Esther Williams, 1944" (Sobin), **Supp. XVI:** 294
"On Imagination" (Wheatley), **Supp. XX: 281**
"On Imminence: An Essay" (Sobin), **Supp. XVI:** 291
On Kingdom Mountain (Mosher), **Supp. XXII:** 203, 205, 206, 207, 208, 209, 212, 214, **216**
On Liberty (Mill), **Supp. XI:** 196
"On Looking Alone at a Place" (M. F. K. Fisher), **Supp. XVII:** 91
"On Looking at a Copy of Alice Meynell's Poems, Given Me, Years Ago, by a Friend" (Lowell), **II:** 527–528
"On Lookout Mountain" (Hayden), **Supp. II Part 1:** 380
Only a Few of Us Left (Marquand), **III:** 55
"Only Animal, The" (F. Wright), **Supp. XVII:** 245
"Only a Pawn in Their Game" (song, Dylan), **Supp. XVIII:** 24
"Only Bar in Dixon, The" (Hugo), **Supp. VI:** 140, 141
Only Dangerous Thing, The (Di Piero), **Supp. XIX: 37–38**
Only Dark Spot in the Sky, The (Dove), **Supp. IV Part 1:** 244
"Only Good Indian, The" (Humphrey), **Supp. IX:** 101
"Only Goodness" (Lahiri), **Supp. XXI:** 186, 188
Only in America (Golden), **Supp. VIII:** 244
"Only in the Dream" (Eberhart), **I:** 523
"Only Path to Tomorrow, The" (Rand), **Supp. IV Part 2:** 524
"Only Rose, The" (Jewett), **II:** 408
"Only Son of the Doctor, The" (Gordon), **Supp. IV Part 1:** 305, 306
"Only the Cat Escapes", **Supp. XII:** 150–151
"Only the Dead Know Brooklyn" (Wolfe), **IV:** 451
Only When I Laugh (Simon), **Supp. IV Part 2:** 575
Only World, The (Hull), **Supp. XXI:** 129, **138–141**
"On Messrs. Hussey and Coffin" (Wheatley), **Supp. XX: 280**
On Moral Fiction (Gardner), **Supp. VI:** 61, **71,** 72, 73
"On Morality" (Didion), **Supp. IV Part 1:** 196
"On Mt. Philo in November" (Di Piero), **Supp. XIX:** 37, 39
"On My Own" (Levine), **Supp. V:** 181, 189–190
"On My Own Work" (Wilbur), **Supp. III Part 2:** 541–542

On Native Grounds: An Interpretation of Modern American Prose Literature (Kazin), **I:** 517; **Supp. I Part 2:** 650; **Supp. VIII:** 93, 96–97, 98, **100–102**
"On Not Being a Dove" (Updike), **Retro. Supp. I:** 323
"On Open Form" (Merwin), **Supp. III Part 1:** 347–348, 353
On Photography (Sontag), **Supp. III Part 2:** 451, 458, 462–465
"On Political Poetry" (R. Bly), **Supp. IV Part 1:** 61
On Politics: A Carnival of Buncombe (Moos, ed.), **III:** 116
"On Pretentiousness" (Kushner), **Supp. IX:** 131–132
"On Quitting a Little College" (Stafford), **Supp. XI:** 321
"On Reading Eckerman's Conversations with Goethe" (Masters), **Supp. I Part 2:** 458
On Reading Shakespeare (L. P. Smith), **Supp. XIV:** 345–346
"On Reading to Oneself" (Gass), **Supp. VI:** 88, 89
"On Recollection" (Wheatley), **Supp. XX: 287**
On Revolution (Arendt), **Retro. Supp. I:** 87
"On Seeing Larry Rivers' *Washington Crossing the Delaware* at the Museum of Modern Art" (O'Hara), **Supp. XV:** 186
"On Seeing Red" (Walker), **Supp. III Part 2:** 527
"On Social Plays" (A. Miller), **III:** 147, 148, 159
"On Steinbeck's Story 'Flight' " (Stegner), **Supp. IV Part 2:** 596
"On Style" (Sontag), **Supp. III Part 2:** 456–459, 465–466
"On Suicide" (Hay), **Supp. XIV:** 130, 132
"On Teaching the Young Laurel to Shoot" (Bynner), **Supp. XV:** 50
"On the Antler" (Proulx), **Supp. VII:** 252–253
"On the Avenue" (Espaillat), **Supp. XXI:** 112
On the Banks of Plum Creek (L. I. Wilder), **Supp. XXII:** 294, 299
"On the Banks of the Wabash" (Paul Dresser), **Retro. Supp. II:** 94
"On the Beach, at Night" (Whitman), **IV:** 348
"On the Bosom of This Grave and Wasted Land I Will Lay My Head" (Ray), **Supp. XVIII:** 189
On the Boundary (Tillich), **Retro. Supp. I:** 326
"On the Building of Springfield" (Lindsay), **Supp. I Part 2:** 381
"On the Coast of Maine" (Hayden), **Supp. II Part 1:** 381
On the Contrary: Articles of Belief (McCarthy), **II:** 559, 562
"On the Death of a Friend's Child" (Lowell), **Supp. I Part 2:** 409
"On the Death of Cardinal Tisserant" (Bronk), **Supp. XXI:** 32
"On the Death of General Wooster" (Wheatley), **Supp. XX: 287**
"On the Death of Rev. Mr. George Whitefield—1770" (Wheatley), **Supp. XX: 280,Supp. XX: 282–283**
"On the Death of Senator Thomas J. Walsh" (Winters), **Supp. II Part 2:** 802, 806
"On the Death of Yeats" (Bogan), **Supp. III Part 1:** 59
"On the Death of Zhukov" (Brodsky), **Supp. VIII:** 27
"On the Disadvantages of Central Heating" (Clampitt), **Supp. IX:** 41, 47, 52
On the Drumhead: A Selection from the Writing of Mike Quin (Carlisle, ed.), **Supp. XVIII:** 223, 226
"On the Edge" (Levine), **Supp. V:** 181–182
On the Edge and Over (Levine), **Supp. V:** 178, 180–182, 186
On the Edge of the Great Rift: Three Novels of Africa (Theroux), **Supp. VIII:** 316
"On the Eve of the Feast of the Immaculate Conception, 1942" (Lowell), **II:** 538; **Retro. Supp. II:** 185
"On the Eyes of an SS Officer" (Wilbur), **Supp. III Part 2:** 548
"On the Failure of Meaning in the Absence of Objective Analogs" (Bronk), **Supp. XXI:** 31
"On the Fall of General Earl Cornwallis" (Freneau), **Supp. II Part 1:** 261
"On the Folly of Writing Poetry" (Freneau), **Supp. II Part 1:** 263
On the Frontier (Auden and Isherwood), **Supp. II Part 1:** 13; **Supp. XIV:** 163
On the Great Atlantic Rainway: Selected Poems, 1950–1988 (Koch), **Supp. XV:** 177
"On the History of Poetry" (Halliday), **Supp. XIX:** 88, 89
"On the Hysterical Playground" (Watman), **Supp. XX: 93**
"On the Island" (Stern), **Supp. IX:** 290
"On the Late Eclipse" (Bryant), **Supp. I Part 1:** 152
On the Laws of the Poetic Art (Hecht), **Supp. X:** 58
On the Line (Swados), **Supp. XIX: 258–260**
"On the Line" (Swados), **Supp. XIX:** 259
"On the Marginal Way" (Wilbur), **Supp. III Part 2:** 558, 559
On the Mesa (Nichols), **Supp. XIII:** 268
"On the Moon and Matriarchal Consciousness" (Neumann), **Supp. IV Part 1:** 68
"On the Morning after the Sixties" (Didion), **Supp. IV Part 1:** 205, 206
On the Motion and Immobility of Douve (Bonnefoy; Kinnell, trans.), **Supp. III Part 1:** 235
"On the Murder of Lieutenant José del Castillo by the Falangist Bravo Martinez, July 12, 1936" (Levine), **Supp. V:** 187
"On the Night of a Friend's Wedding" (Robinson), **III:** 524
"On the Occasion of a Poem: Richard Hugo" (Wright), **Supp. III Part 2:** 596
On the Occasion of My Last Afternoon (Gibbons), **Supp. X:** 46, **50–53**
On the Origin of Species (Darwin), **Supp. XIV:** 192
"On the Parapet" (Tanner), **Retro. Supp. II:** 205
"On the Platform" (Nemerov), **III:** 287
On the Poetry of Philip Levine: Stranger to Nothing (Levis), **Supp. XI:** 257
"On the Pottlecombe Cornice" (Sturgis), **Supp. XX: 233, 240**
"On the Powers of the Human Understanding" (Freneau), **Supp. II Part 1:** 274
On the Prejudices, Predilections, and Firm Beliefs of William Faulkner (Brooks), **Supp. XIV:** 13
"On the Pulse of Morning" (Angelou), **Supp. IV Part 1:** 15–17
"On the Railway Platform" (Jarrell), **II:** 370
"On the Rainy River" (O'Brien), **Supp. V:** 250
On the Rebound: A Story and Nine Poems (Purdy), **Supp. VII:** 276–277
"On the Religion of Nature" (Freneau), **Supp. II Part 1:** 275
"On the River" (Dunbar), **Supp. II Part 1:** 193
"On the River" (Levine), **Supp. V:** 193
On the River Styx and Other Stories (Matthiessen), **Supp. V:** 212
On the Road (Kerouac), **Retro. Supp. I:** 102; **Supp. III Part 1:** 92, 218, 222–224, 226, 230–231; **Supp. V:** 336; **Supp. X:** 269; **Supp. XIII:** 275; **Supp. XIV:** 138, 150; **Supp. XV:** 221; **Supp. XVIII:** 20, 138; **Supp. XXI:** 53
"On the Road Home" (Stevens), **Retro. Supp. I:** 306
On the Road with the Archangel (Buechner), **Supp. XII:** 54
"On the Rope" (Richard), **Supp. XIX:** 211–212
On These I Stand: An Anthology of the Best Poems of Countee Cullen (Cullen), **Supp. IV Part 1:** 173
"On the Skeleton of a Hound" (Wright), **Supp. III Part 2:** 593
"On the Street" (Peacock), **Supp. XIX:** 199
"On the Street: Monument" (Gunn Allen), **Supp. IV Part 1:** 326
"On the Subway" (Olds), **Supp. X:** 207
"On the System of Policy Hitherto Pursued by Their Government" (Barlow), **Supp. II Part 1:** 82
"On the Teaching of Modern Literature" (Trilling), **Supp. III Part 2:** 509–510
"On the Uniformity and Perfection of Nature" (Freneau), **Supp. II Part 1:** 275
"On the Universality and Other Attributes of the God of Nature" (Freneau), **Supp. II Part 1:** 275
"On the Use of Trisyllabic Feet in Iambic Verse" (Bryant), **Supp. I Part 1:** 156

On the Verge: Emerging Poets (Ellis and Lease, eds.), **Supp. XXI:** 246
On the Waterfront (film, Kazan), **Supp. XVIII: 250–251,** 252, 253
"On the Way Home" (L. I. Wilder), **Supp. XXII:** 292
On the Way toward a Phenomenological Psychology: The Psychology of William James (Linschoten), **II:** 362
"On the Way to Work" (Dunn), **Supp. XI:** 149–150
"On the Wide Heath" (Millay), **III:** 130
"On the Writing of Novels" (Buck), **Supp. II Part 1:** 121
On the Yard (Braly), **Supp. XVIII:** 147
On This Island (Auden), **Supp. II Part 1:** 11
"On Time" (O'Hara), **III:** 369–370
"Ontological Episode of the Asylum" (Carruth), **Supp. XVI:** 48, 50
"Ontology of the Sentence, The" (Gass), **Supp. VI:** 77
"On Top" (Leopold), **Supp. XIV:** 188
"On Top" (Snyder), **Supp. VIII:** 304
"On Translating Akhmatova" (Kunitz), **Supp. III Part 1:** 268
"On Turning Ten" (Collins), **Supp. XXI:** 64
"On Waking to Old Debts" (Keillor), **Supp. XVI:** 167
On William Stafford: The Worth of Local Things (Andrews, ed.), **Supp. XI:** 311, 312, 317, 321, 324, 326
"On Writing" (Carver), **Supp. III Part 1:** 142–143
"On Writing" (Nin), **Supp. X:** 182
Opatoshu, Joseph, **IV:** 9
"Open Boat, The" (Crane), **I:** 408, 415, 416–417, 423; **Retro. Supp. I:** 325; **Supp. XIV:** 51
Open Boat and Other Stories (Crane), **I:** 408
Open Door, The (Skloot), **Supp. XX: 194, 196, 208**
Open Heart: A Patient's Story of Life-Saving Medicine and Life-Giving Friendship (Neugeboren), **Supp. XVI:** 217, **229–230**
Open House (Roethke), **III:** 529–530, 540
"Open House" (Roethke), **III:** 529
"Opening, An" (Swenson), **Supp. IV Part 2:** 639
Opening of the Field, The (Duncan), **Supp. III Part 2:** 625
Opening the Hand (Merwin), **Supp. III Part 1:** 341, 353, 355
"Open Letter" (Roethke), **III:** 532, 534
"Open Letter to Surrealists Everywhere, An" (H. Miller), **III:** 184
Open Meeting, The (Gurney), **Supp. V:** 98
Open Net (Plimpton), **Supp. XVI:** 241
"Open Road, The" (Dreiser), **II:** 44
Open Sea, The (Masters), **Supp. I Part 2:** 471
Open Season: Sporting Adventures (Humphrey), **Supp. IX:** 95
"Open Secret" (Nelson), **Supp. XVIII:** 185
"Open the Gates" (Kunitz), **Supp. III Part 1:** 264–265, 267
"Opera Company, The" (Merrill), **Supp. III Part 1:** 326
Operating Instructions: A Journal of My Son's First Year (Lamott), **Supp. XX: 136–137, 142**
"Operation, The" (Sanders), **Supp. XVI:** 266
"Operation, The" (Sexton), **Supp. II Part 2:** 675, 679
Operation Shylock: A Confession (P. Roth), **Retro. Supp. II:** 279, 280, 291
Operation Sidewinder (Shepard), **Supp. III Part 2:** 434–435, 439, 446–447
Operations in North African Waters (Morison), **Supp. I Part 2:** 490
Operation Wandering Soul (Powers), **Supp. IX:** 212, **217–219**
Opffer, Emil, **Retro. Supp. II:** 80
"Opinion" (Du Bois), **Supp. II Part 1:** 173
Opinionator, The (Bierce), **I:** 209
Opinions of Oliver Allston (Brooks), **I:** 254, 255, 256
O Pioneers! (Cather), **I:** 314, 317–319, 320; **Retro. Supp. I:** 1, 5, 6, **7–9,** 10, 13, 20; **Retro. Supp. II:** 136
Oppen, George, **IV:** 415; **Supp. III Part 2:** 614, 615, 616, 626, 628; **Supp. XIV:** 285, 286, 287; **Supp. XVI:** 282, 283; **Supp. XVII:** 243; **Supp. XXI:** 19,**Supp. XXI:** 29, 23
Oppenheim, James, **I:** 106, 109, 239, 245; **Supp. XV:** 294, 296, 298, 299, 301, 302, 307, 313; **Supp. XX: 68**
Oppenheimer, J. Robert, **I:** 137, 492
Oppenheimer, Judy, **Supp. IX:** 115, 116, 118, 120, 126
"Opportunity for American Fiction, An" (Howells), **Supp. I Part 2:** 645–646
Opposing Self, The (Trilling), **Supp. III Part 2:** 506–507
"Opposition" (Lanier), **Supp. I Part 1:** 368, 373
Oprah's Roots: An African American Lives Special (television production), **Supp. XX: 99**
Opticks: A Poem in Seven Sections (Goldbarth), **Supp. XII:** 177, **178**
Optimist's Daughter, The (Welty), **IV:** 261, 280; **Retro. Supp. I:** 339, 355
"Optimist's Daughter, The" (Welty), **IV:** 280–281
Options (O. Henry), **Supp. II Part 1:** 410
Opus Posthumous (Stevens), **IV:** 76, 78
Opus Posthumous (W. Stevens), **Supp. XVII:** 241
Oracle at Stoneleigh Court, The (Taylor), **Supp. V:** 328
Orage, Alfred, **III:** 473
Orange, Max (pseudonym). *See* Heller, Joseph
Orange Fish, The (Shields), **Supp. VII:** 318, 320, 323, 328
Orangery, The (Sorrentino), **Supp. XXI:** 228
Oranges (McPhee), **Supp. III Part 1:** 298–299, 301, 309
"Oranging of America, The" (Apple), **Supp. XVII:** 3–4, 6
Oranging of America and Other Short Stories, The (Apple), **Supp. XVII:** 1–2, **3–4,** 7, 8
Oration Delivered at Washington, July Fourth, 1809 (Barlow), **Supp. II Part 1:** 80, 83
Orations and Addresses (Bryant), **Supp. I Part 1:** 158
Orators, The (Auden), **Supp. II Part 1:** 6, 7, 11, 18–19
Orb Weaver, The (Francis), **Supp. IX: 81–82**
"Orchard" (Doolittle), **Supp. I Part 1:** 263–264, 265, 266
"Orchard" (Eberhart), **I:** 539
Orchard, The (B. Kelly), **Supp. XVII:** 123, 127, **130–133**
"Orchard, The" (B. Kelly), **Supp. XVII:** 133
Orchard Keeper, The (McCarthy), **Supp. VIII: 175–176**
Orchestra (Davies), **III:** 541
"Orchids" (Roethke), **III:** 530–531
"Or Consider Prometheus" (Clampitt), **Supp. IX:** 44
Ordeal of Mansart, The (Du Bois), **Supp. II Part 1:** 185–186
Ordeal of Mark Twain, The (Brooks), **I:** 240, 247, 248; **II:** 482
Ordering the Façade: Photography and Contemporary Southern Women's Writing (Henninger), **Supp. XXI:** 253
"Order of Insects" (Gass), **Supp. VI:** 83
Order Out of Chaos (McPherson), **Supp. IV Part 1:** 2, 12
"Ordinary Afternoon in Charlottesville, An" (Wright), **Supp. V:** 344
"Ordinary Days" (Dunn), **Supp. XI:** 151
"Ordinary Evening in New Haven, An" (Stevens), **IV:** 91–92; **Retro. Supp. I:** 297, 300, 311, 312
Ordinary Heroes (Turow), **Supp. XVII: 221–222,** 223
Ordinary Love (Smiley), **Supp. VI:** 292, **299–300**
Ordinary Love; and Good Will: Two Novellas (Smiley), **Supp. VI:** 292, **299–300**
Ordinary Miracles (Jong), **Supp. V:** 115, 130–131
"Ordinary Time: Virginia Woolf and Thucydides on War" (Carson), **Supp. XII: 111**
"Ordinary Women, The" (Stevens), **IV:** 81
Ordways, The (Humphrey), **Supp. IX:** 95, **98–100,** 109; **Supp. XV:** 353
"Oread" (Doolittle), **II:** 520–521; **Supp. I Part 1:** 265–266
Oregon Message, An (Stafford), **Supp. XI: 328–329**
Oregon Trail, The (Parkman), **II:** 312; **Supp. II Part 2:** 592, 595–596, 598, 606
Oresteia (Aeschylus), **Supp. IX:** 103
"Orestes at Tauris" (Jarrell), **II:** 376, 377
Orfalea, Gregory, **Supp. XIII:** 278
Orfeo ed Euridice (Gluck), **II:** 210, 211

Orff, Carl, **Supp. X:** 63
"Organizer's Wife, The" (Bambara), **Supp. XI:** 8–9
"Organmeister: Hasse After Marienkirche" (Bierds), **Supp. XVII:** 34
"Orgy" (Rukeyser), **Supp. VI:** 280
Orgy, The (Rukeyser), **Supp. VI:** 274, 283
"Orgy of Southerness, An" (Pickering), **Supp. XXI:** 203
"Orientation of Hope, The" (Locke), **Supp. XIV:** 212–213
Orient Express (Dos Passos), **I:** 480
"Orient Express, The" (Jarrell), **II:** 382, 383–384
Origen, Adamantius, **IV:** 153
"Origin" (Harjo), **Supp. XII:** 219
Original Child Bomb: Points for Meditation to Be Scratched on the Walls of a Cave (Merton), **Supp. VIII:** 203
Original Essays on the Poetry of Anne Sexton (George), **Supp. IV Part 2:** 450
"Original Follies Girl, The" (Z. Fitzgerald), **Supp. IX:** 71
Original Light (Goldbarth), **Supp. XII:** 181, **183–184,** 188
Original Love (Peacock), **Supp. XIX:** **199–201,** 206
Original of Laura, The (Nabokov), **Retro. Supp. I:** 266
"Original Sin" (Jeffers), **Supp. II Part 2:** 426
"Original Sin" (Warren), **IV:** 245
Origin: Hawaii (Taggard), **Supp. XXII:** 272, 284
"Origin of Extermination in the Imagination, The" (Gass), **Supp. VI:** 89
Origin of Species, The (Darwin), **II:** 173, 462; **Supp. XVI:** 13
Origin of the Brunists, The (Coover), **Supp. V:** 39, 41, 52
"Origins and History of Consciousness" (Rich), **Supp. I Part 2:** 570
"Origins of a Nonfiction Writer" (Talese), **Supp. XVII:** 208
"Origins of a Poem" (Levertov), **Supp. III Part 1:** 273
"Origins of the Beat Generation, The" (Kerouac), **Supp. III Part 1:** 231
Origo, Iris, **IV:** 328
"O'Riley's Late-Bloomed Little Son" (X. J. Kennedy), **Supp. XV:** 159
"Orion" (Rich), **Supp. I Part 2:** 557
O'Riordan, Conal Holmes O'Connell, **III:** 465
Orlacs Hände (film, Weine), **Supp. XVII:** 58
Orlando (V. Woolf), **Supp. XVII:** 86
Orlando (Woolf), **Supp. I Part 2:** 718; **Supp. VIII:** 263; **Supp. XII:** 9
Orlando Furioso (Ariosto), **Supp. XV:** 175
Orlovsky, Peter, **Supp. XII:** 121, 126; **Supp. XIV:** 150; **Supp. XVIII:** 27
Ormonde, Czenzi, **Supp. IV Part 1:** 132
Ormond; or, The Secret Witness (Brown), **Supp. I Part 1:** 133–137
Ornament and Crime (Loos), **Supp. XVI:** 187
Orne, Sarah. *See* Jewett, Sarah Orne
Ornithological Biography; or, An Account of the Habits of the Birds of the United States of America, and Interspersed with Delin eations of American Scenery and Manners (Audubon), **Supp. XVI:**13
Ornithological Biography; or, An Account of the Habits of the Birds of the United States of America, and Interspersed with Delineations of American Scenery and Manners (Audubon), **7–10**
"Ornithology" (Hull), **Supp. XXI:** 138–139
Ornitz, Samuel, **Supp. IX:** 227; **Supp. XIII:** 166
Ornstein, Leo, **Supp. XX: 75**
O'Rourke, William, **Supp. XXII:** 213
Orphan Angel, The (Wylie), **Supp. I Part 2:** 707, 709, 714, 717, 719–721, 722, 724
Orphan's Tale, An (Neugeboren), **Supp. XVI:** 222, 223
Orpheus (Rukeyser), **Supp. VI:** 273
"Orpheus" (Winters), **Supp. II Part 2:** 801
"Orpheus, Eurydice, Hermes" (Rilke), **Supp. VIII:** 31, 32
"Orpheus (1)" (Atwood), **Supp. XIII:** 35
"Orpheus (2)" (Atwood), **Supp. XIII:** 35
"Orpheus Alone" (Strand), **Supp. IV Part 2:** 632
Orpheus Descending (T. Williams), **IV:** 380, 381, 382, 385, 386, 387, 389, 391–392, 395, 396, 398
Orr, David, **Supp. XXI:** 62
Orr, Peter, **Supp. I Part 2:** 538, 540, 543
Orse, Brian, **Supp. XX: 264**
Ortega y Gasset, José, **I:** 218, 222; **Supp. IV Part 2:** 521
Ortiz, Simon J., **Supp. IV Part 1:** 319, 404; **Supp. IV Part 2: 497–515,** 557; **Supp. XII:** 217, 218
"Ortlieb's Uptown Taproom" (Di Piero), **Supp. XIX:** 46, 47
O'Ruddy, The (Crane), **I:** 409, 424
Orwell, George, **I:** 489; **II:** 454, 580; **Supp. I Part 2:** 523, 620; **Supp. II Part 1:** 143; **Supp. IV Part 1:** 236; **Supp. V:** 250; **Supp. VIII:** 241; **Supp. XIV:** 112, 158; **Supp. XVII:** 228, 229; **Supp. XVIII:** 137, 138; **Supp. XX: 86**
Osborn, Dwight, **III:** 218–219, 223
"Osborn Look, The" (Morris), **III:** 221
Osgood, Frances, **Supp. XVII:** 75
Osgood, J. R., **II:** 283
O'Shea, Kitty, **II:** 137
O'Shea, Milo, **Supp. XI:** 308
"Oshkikwe's Baby" (traditional Chippewa story), **Supp. IV Part 1:** 333
Oshogay, Delia, **Supp. IV Part 1:** 333
Ossana, Diana, **Supp. V:** 230–231, 232
Ossian, **Supp. I Part 2:** 491
Ossip, Kathleen, **Supp. X:** 201
"Osso Bucco" (Collins), **Supp. XXI:** 60
Ostanovka v Pustyne (A halt in the wilderness) (Brodsky), **Supp. VIII:** 21
Oster, Judith, **Supp. XVI:** 151
Ostriker, Alicia, **Supp. I Part 2:** 540; **Supp. IV Part 2:** 439, 447, 449; **Supp. X:** 207, 208; **Supp. XI:** 143; **Supp. XV:** 251
Ostrom, Hans, **Retro. Supp. I:** 195
Oswald, Lee Harvey, **III:** 234, 235
Oswald II (DeLillo), **Supp. VI:** 16
Oswald's Tale (Mailer), **Retro. Supp. II:** 212–213
O Taste and See (Levertov), **Supp. III Part 1:** 278–279, 281
Othello (Shakespeare), **I:** 284–285
"Other, The" (Sexton), **Supp. II Part 2:** 692
Other America, The (Harrington), **I:** 306
"Other American Renaissance, The" (Tompkins), **Supp. XVIII:** 258
Other Destinies: Understanding the American Indian Novel (Owens), **Supp. IV Part 1:** 404
"Other Frost, The" (Jarrell), **Retro. Supp. I:** 121
Other Gods: An American Legend (Buck), **Supp. II Part 1:** 123, 130–131
Other House, The (James), **Retro. Supp. I:** 229
"Other League of Nations, The" (Ríos), **Supp. IV Part 2:** 552
"Other Margaret, The" (Trilling), **Supp. III Part 2:** 504–505
"Other Miller, The" (Wolff), **Supp. VII:** 343–344
"Other Mothers" (Paley), **Supp. VI:** 225
"Other Night at Columbia, The" (Trilling), **Supp. XII:** 126
"Other People's Secrets" (Hampl), **Supp. XXII:** 94
"Other Robert Frost, The" (Jarrell), **Retro. Supp. I:** 135
Others (Shields), **Supp. VII:** 310
Other Side, The (Gordon), **Supp. IV Part 1:** 299, 306, 307–309, 310–311
Other Side, The/El Otro Lado (Alvarez), **Supp. VII:** 9–12
Other Side of the River, The (Wright), **Supp. V:** 332–333, 342
"Other Side of the River, The" (Wright), **Supp. V:** 335
"Other Tradition, The" (Ashbery), **Supp. III Part 1:** 15, 18
"Other Two, The" (Wharton), **Retro. Supp. I:** 367
Other Voices, Other Rooms (Capote), **Supp. III Part 1:** 113–118, 121, 123–124
"Other Wanderer, The" (Gibran), **Supp. XX: 124**
"Other War, The" (Cowley), **Supp. II Part 1:** 144
"Otherwise" (Kenyon), **Supp. VII:** 172, 174
Otherwise: New and Selected Poems (Kenyon), **Supp. VII:** 167, 172–174
Otherwise Than Being; or, Beyond Essence (Lévinas), **Supp. XVI:** 290, 291
"Other Woman, The" (Anderson), **I:** 114
"Other World, The" (Wrigley), **Supp. XVIII:** 307
Otho the Great: A Tragedy in Five Acts (Keats), **Supp. XII:** 113

Otis, Harrison Gray, **Supp. I Part 2:** 479–481, 483, 486, 488
Otis, James, **III:** 577; **Supp. I Part 2:** 486; **Supp. XV:** 229
O to Be a Dragon (Moore), **III:** 215
Otto, Rudolf, **Supp. XVII:** 243
"Ouija" (McClatchy), **Supp. XII:** 269–270
Oupensky, Peter, **Supp. XIV:** 188
Our America (Michaels), **Retro. Supp. I:** 379
Our America (W. Frank), **I:** 229; **Supp. IX:** 308; **Supp. XX: 69–70, 75**
"Our Assistant's Column" (Twain), **IV:** 193
"Our Bourgeois Literature" (Sinclair), **Supp. V:** 281
Our Brains and What Ails Them (Gilman), **Supp. XI:** 207
Our Century (Wilder), **IV:** 374
"Our Christmas Party" (E. Stoddard), **Supp. XV:** 273, 278
Our Country (Strong), **Supp. XIV:** 64
"Our Countrymen in Chains!" (Whittier), **Supp. I Part 2:** 688
"Our Cultural Humility" (Bourne), **I:** 223, 228
Our Depleted Society (Seymour), **Supp. XIII:** 264
"Our Dust" (Wright), **Supp. XV:** 345, 346
"Our Father Who Drowns the Birds" (Kingsolver), **Supp. VII:** 208–209
"Our First House" (Kingston), **Supp. V:** 169
Our Gang (P. Roth), **Retro. Supp. II:** 287; **Supp. III Part 2:** 414; **Supp. IV Part 1:** 388
"Our Good Day" (Cisneros), **Supp. VII:** 60
Our Ground Time Here Will Be Brief (Kumin), **Supp. IV Part 2:** 450–452
Our House in the Last World (Hijuelos), **Supp. VIII:** 73, **76–79,** 87, 88
"Our Lady" (A. Finch), **Supp. XVII:** 77
"*Our Lady of the Annunciation*/Nuestra Señora de Anunciación" (Mora), **Supp. XIII:** 217, 224, 228
"Our Lady of Troy" (MacLeish), **III:** 3, 20
"Our Limitations" (Holmes), **Supp. I Part 1:** 314
"Our Martyred Soldiers" (Dunbar), **Supp. II Part 1:** 193
"Our Master" (Whittier), **Supp. I Part 2:** 704
"Our Mother Pocahontas" (Lindsay), **Supp. I Part 2:** 393
Our Mr. Wrenn: The Romantic Adventures of a Gentle Man (Lewis), **II:** 441
Our National Parks (Muir), **Supp. IX:** 181, 184
Our New York: A Personal Vision in Words and Photographs (Kazin), **Supp. VIII: 106–107**
Our Nig (Wilson), **Supp. XX: 105**
"Our Old Aunt Who Is Now in a Retirement Home" (Shields), **Supp. VII:** 310
Our Old Home: A Series of English Sketches (Hawthorne), **II:** 225; **Retro. Supp. I:** 163
"Our Own Movie Queen" (Z. Fitzgerald), **Supp. IX:** 71
"Our River Now" (L.-Y. Lee), **Supp. XV:** 224, 225
Our Selves (Bronk), **Supp. XXI:** 32
Ourselves to Know (O'Hara), **III:** 362, 365
Our Sister Killjoy: or, Reflections from a Black-Eyed Squint (Aidoo), **Supp. XXII:** 68
"Our Story Begins" (Wolff), **Supp. VII:** 345
"Our Sweating Selves" (Di Piero), **Supp. XIX:** 36
Our Town (Wilder), **IV:** 357, 364, 365, 366, 368–369
"Our Unplanned Cities" (Bourne), **I:** 229, 230
Our Wonder World, **Retro. Supp. I:** 341
Ouspensky, P. D., **I:** 383; **Supp. XX: 116**
"Out" (Harjo), **Supp. XII:** 219
"'Out, Out' " (Frost), **Retro. Supp. I:** 131
"Outcast" (McKay), **Supp. X:** 135
"Outcasts of Poker Flats, The" (Harte), **Supp. II Part 1:** 345, 347–348
Outcroppings (Harte), **Supp. II Part 1:** 343
Out Cry (T. Williams), **IV:** 383, 393
Outcry, The (James), **Retro. Supp. I:** 235
"Outdoor Shower" (Olds), **Supp. X:** 214
Outer Banks (Siddons), **Supp. XXII:** 239
Outerbridge Reach (Stone), **Supp. V:** 306–308
Outer Dark (McCarthy), **Supp. VIII: 176–177**
Outermost Dream, The: Essays and Reviews (Maxwell), **Supp. VIII: 171–172**
"Outing, The" (Baldwin), **Supp. I Part 1:** 63
"Out Like a Lamb" (Dubus), **Supp. VII:** 91
"Outline of an Autobiography" (Toomer), **Supp. III Part 2:** 478
Outlyer and Ghazals (Harrison), **Supp. VIII:** 41
"Out of Business" (Mora), **Supp. XIII:** 217
Out of Eden: Essays on Modern Art (Di Piero), **Supp. XIX:** 41, 42
"Out of My Deeper Heart" (Gibran), **Supp. XX: 118**
Out of My League (Plimpton), **Supp. XVI:** 233, 239
"Out of Nowhere into Nothing" (Anderson), **I:** 113
"Out of Season" (Hemingway), **II:** 263
"Out of the Cradle Endlessly Rocking" (Whitman), **IV:** 342, 343–345, 346, 351; **Retro. Supp. I:** 404, 406
"Out of the Deeps" (E. Stoddard), **Supp. XV:** 286
"Out of the Hospital and Under the Bar" (Ellison), **Retro. Supp. II:** 118–119; **Supp. II Part 1:** 246
"Out of the Rainbow End" (Sandburg), **III:** 594–595
"Out of the Sea, Early" (Swenson), **Supp. IV Part 2:** 645
"Out of the Snow" (Dubus), **Supp. VII:** 91
Out of the Stars (Purdy), **Supp. VII:** 281–282
"Out of the Woods" (Offutt), **Supp. XIX:** 169–170
Out of the Woods: Stories (Offutt), **Supp. XIX:** 163, 167, **169–172,** 175
"Outrageous" (Pickering), **Supp. XXI:** 202
Outre-Mer: A Pilgrimage beyond the Sea (Longfellow), **II:** 313, 491; **Retro. Supp. II:** 155, 165
"Outside" (Stafford), **Supp. XI:** 318
Outside, The (Glaspell), **Supp. III Part 1:** 179, 187
"Outside In" (Pickering), **Supp. XXI:** 197
Outsider, The (Wright), **IV:** 478, 481, 488, 491–494, 495
Outside World, The (Mirvis), **Supp. XX: 177, 178, 185–190**
Out Went the Candle (Swados), **Supp. XIX: 257**
Out West (Shanley), **Supp. XIV:** 317
"Out with the Old" (Yates), **Supp. XI:** 342
"Ouzo for Robin" (Merrill), **Supp. III Part 1:** 326
"Oval Portrait, The" (Poe), **III:** 412, 415; **Retro. Supp. II:** 270
"Oven Bird, The" (Frost), **Retro. Supp. I:** 131; **Supp. XI:** 153; **Supp. XIX:** 15
"Over 2,000 Illustrations and a Complete Concordance" (Bishop), **Retro. Supp. II:** 45; **Supp. I Part 1:** 90–91
"Over by the River" (Maxwell), **Supp. VIII:** 169, 170
"Overcoat, The" (Gogol), **Supp. XXII:** 59
"Overgrown Pasture, The" (Lowell), **II:** 523
"Overheard through the Walls of the Invisible City" (Bidart), **Supp. XV:** 32
"Over Kansas" (Ginsberg), **Supp. II Part 1:** 320
Overland to the Islands (Levertov), **Supp. III Part 1:** 275, 276
Overlook, The (Connelly), **Supp. XXI: 78**
"Overlooking Lake Champlain" (Di Piero), **Supp. XIX:** 47
"Overnight Pass" (X. J. Kennedy), **Supp. XV:** 168
Overreachers, The (Talese), **Supp. XVII:** 202
"Over-Soul, The" (Emerson), **II:** 7
Over the Blue Mountain (Richter), **Supp. XVIII:** 220
"Over the Hill" (Dubus), **Supp. VII:** 76, 79–80
Overtime (Gurney), **Supp. V:** 104
"Overwhelming Question, An" (Taylor), **Supp. V:** 323

Ovid, **I:** 62; **II:** 542–543; **III:** 457, 467, 468, 470; **Retro. Supp. I:** 63; **Supp. IV Part 2:** 634; **Supp. XII:** 264
"Ovid in Exile" (Di Piero), **Supp. XIX:** 44
"Ovid's Farewell" (McClatchy), **Supp. XII:** 257–258
Owen, David, **II:** 34
Owen, Maureen, **Supp. IV Part 2:** 423
Owen, Wilfred, **II:** 367, 372; **III:** 524; **Supp. X:** 146; **Supp. XVII:** 245; **Supp. XVIII:** 92; **Supp. XIX:** 17
Owens, Hamilton, **III:** 99, 109
Owens, Louis, **Supp. IV Part 1:** 404
"O Where Are You Going?" (Auden), **Supp. X:** 116
"Owl, The" (Wrigley), **Supp. XVIII:** 297–298, 301
Owl in the Attic, The (Thurber), **Supp. I Part 2:** 614
Owl in the Mask of the Dreamer, The: Collected Poems (Haines), **Supp. XII:** 211
"Owl in the Sarcophagus, The" (Stevens), **Retro. Supp. I:** 300
Owl's Clover (Stevens), **Retro. Supp. I:** 298, **303–304**
"Owl's Clover" (Stevens), **IV:** 75
Owl's Insomnia, Poems by Rafael Alberti, The (Strand, trans.), **Supp. IV Part 2:** 630
Owlstone Crown, The (X. J. Kennedy), **Supp. XV:** 162, **164**
"Owl Who Was God, The" (Thurber), **Supp. I Part 2:** 610
Owning Jolene (Hearon), **Supp. VIII: 66–67**
"Owning the Masters" (Nelson), **Supp. XVIII:** 171
Oxford Anthology of American Literature, The, **III:** 197; **Supp. I Part 1:** 254
Oxford Book of American Verse (Matthiessen, ed.), **Retro. Supp. I:** 40
Oxford Book of Children's Verse in America, The (Hall, ed.), **Supp. XIV:** 126
Oxford Companion to Twentieth-Century Poetry (Hamilton, ed.), **Supp. XVII:** 243
Oxford History of the American People, The (Morison), **Supp. I Part 2:** 495–496
Oxford History of the United States, 1783–1917, The (Morison), **Supp. I Part 2:** 483–484
"Oxford Town" (song, Dylan), **Supp. XVIII:** 24
Oxherding Tale (Johnson), **Supp. VI: 190–192,** 193, 194, 196
Oxley, William, **Supp. XV:** 125
"O Yes" (Olsen), **Supp. XIII:** 294, 298, **299–300,** 301
"O Youth and Beauty!" (Cheever), **Retro. Supp. I:** 335
"Oysters" (Sexton), **Supp. II Part 2:** 692
"Ozark Odes" (Wright), **Supp. XV:** 346
Ozick, Cynthia, **Supp. V: 257–274; Supp. VIII:** 141; **Supp. X:** 192; **Supp. XVII:** 42, 43, 49, 50
O-Zone (Theroux), **Supp. VIII:** 323–324

Pace, Patricia, **Supp. XI:** 245
Pacernik, Gary, **Supp. IX:** 287, 291
"Pacific Distances" (Didion), **Supp. IV Part 1:** 211
"Pacific Village" (M. F. K. Fisher), **Supp. XVII:** 83
Pack, Robert, **Supp. IV Part 2:** 621
"Packed Dirt, Churchgoing, a Dying Cat, a Traded Cat" (Updike), **IV:** 219
"Packing Mother's Things" (C. Frost), **Supp. XV:** 97
Pack of Lies (Sorrentino), **Supp. XXI:** 236, 237
Paco's Story (Heinemann), **Supp. XXII:** 103, **109–114,** 115
Paddock, Joe, **Supp. XVI:** 36
Paddock, Nancy, **Supp. XVI:** 36
Padel, Ruth, **Supp. XII:** 107
Padgett, Ron, **Supp. XV:** 190
Padmore, Dorothy, **Supp. XXI:** 166
Padmore, George, **Supp. XXI:** 166
"Paesano with a Trowel" *(Time),* **Supp. XX: 46**
Pafko at the Wall (DeLillo), **Supp. VI:** 4
"Paganini and the Powers of Darkness" (Skloot), **Supp. XX: 201**
"Pagan Prayer" (Cullen), **Supp. IV Part 1:** 170
"Pagan Rabbi, The" (Ozick), **Supp. V:** 262, 264, 265; **Supp. XVII:** 43
Pagan Rabbi and Other Stories, The (Ozick), **Supp. V:** 260, 261, 263–265
Pagan Spain (Wright), **IV:** 478, 488, 495
Page, Geraldine, **Supp. XV:** 7
Page, Kirby, **III:** 297
Page, Thomas Nelson, **II:** 174, 176, 194; **Supp. XIV:** 61; **Supp. XXII:** 193
Page, Walter Hines, **II:** 174, 175; **Supp. I Part 1:** 370
Page, William, **Supp. XVIII:** 2, 11
"Pages from Cold Point" (Bowles), **Supp. IV Part 1:** 85, 86, 87
Paid on Both Sides: A Charade (Auden), **Supp. II Part 1:** 6, 18–19
Paige, Satchel, **Supp. I Part 1:** 234
Paige, T. D. D., **III:** 475
"Pail, The" (R. Bly), **Supp. XXI:** 85
Pain, Joseph, **Supp. I Part 2:** 502
Paine, Albert Bigelow, **I:** 249
Paine, Thomas, **I:** 490; **II:** 117, 302; **III:** 17, 148, 219; **Retro. Supp. I:** 390; **Supp. I Part 1:** 231; **Supp. I Part 2: 501–525; Supp. XI:** 55
"Pain has an Element of Blank" (Dickinson), **Retro. Supp. I:** 44
"Painstaking Historian, The" (Skloot), **Supp. XX: 205–206**
"Paint and Powder" (Z. Fitzgerald), **Supp. IX:** 71
Painted Bird, The (Kosinski), **Supp. VII:** 215–217, 219–221, 222, 227
Painted Desert (F. Barthelme), **Supp. XI:** 28–29, 32
Painted Dresses (Hearon), **Supp. VIII: 63**
"Painted Head" (Ransom), **III:** 491, 494; **Supp. II Part 1:** 103, 314
Painted Turtle: Woman with Guitar (Major), **Supp. XXII: 178–180,** 182
Painted Word, The (Wolfe), **Supp. III Part 2:** 580–581, 584; **Supp. XV:** 143
"Painter, The" (Ashbery), **Supp. III Part 1:** 5–6, 13
Painter Dreaming in the Scholar's House, The (Nemerov), **III:** 269
"Painters" (Rukeyser), **Supp. VI:** 281
"Painting a Mountain Stream" (Nemerov), **III:** 275
"Pair a Spurs" (Proulx), **Supp. VII:** 263–264
"Pair of Bright Blue Eyes, A" (Taylor), **Supp. V:** 321
"Pajamas" (Olds), **Supp. X:** 206
Pakula, Alan, **Supp. XIII:** 264
Palace at 4 A.M. (Giacometti), **Supp. VIII:** 169
Palahniuk, Chuck, **Supp. XXI:** 116
"Palantine, The" (Whittier), **Supp. I Part 2:** 694, 696
Palatella, John, **Retro. Supp. II:** 48
Pale Fire (Nabokov), **III:** 244, 246, 252, 263–265; **Retro. Supp. I:** 264, 265, 266, 270, 271, 272, 276, 278, 335; **Supp. V:** 251, 253; **Supp. XXII:** 260
"Pale Horse, Pale Rider" (Porter), **III:** 436, 437, 441–442, 445, 446, 449
Pale Horse, Pale Rider: Three Short Novels (Porter), **III:** 433, 436–442; **Supp. VIII:** 157
"Pale Pink Roast, The" (Paley), **Supp. VI:** 217
"Pale Rider" (B. Kelly), **Supp. XVII:** 132–133
Paley, Grace, **Supp. VI: 217–233; Supp. IX:** 212; **Supp. X:** 79, 164; **Supp. XII:** 309; **Supp. XXI:** 118; **Supp. XXII:** 172
Paley, William, **II:** 9
Palgrave, Francis Turner, **Retro. Supp. I:** 124; **Supp. XIV:** 340
Palgrave's Golden Treasury (Palgrave), **IV:** 405
Palimpsest (Doolittle), **Supp. I Part 1:** 259, 268, 269, 270–271
Palimpsest (Vidal), **Supp. X:** 186
"Palingenesis" (Longfellow), **II:** 498
Pal Joey (O'Hara), **III:** 361, 367–368
"Pal Joey" stories (O'Hara), **III:** 361
Pallbearers Envying the One Who Rides (Dobyns), **Supp. XIII:** 89
Palm, Edward Frederick, **Supp. XXII:** 103
"Palm, The" (Merwin), **Supp. III Part 1:** 355
Palmer, Charles, **II:** 111
Palmer, Elihu, **Supp. I Part 2:** 520
Palmer, George Herbert, **Supp. XIV:** 197
Palmer, Michael, **Supp. IV Part 2:** 421; **Supp. XVI:** 284; **Supp. XVII:** 240
Palmer, Samuel, **Supp. XV:** 81
Palmerston, Lord, **I:** 15
Palm-of-the-Hand-Stories (Kawabata), **Supp. XV:** 186
"Palm Wine" (McKnight), **Supp. XX: 155**
"Palo Alto: The Marshes" (Hass), **Supp. VI:** 100

Palpable God, A: Thirty Stories Translated from the Bible with an Essay on the Origins and Life of Narrative (Price), **Supp. VI:** 262, 267
Palubinskas, Helen, **Supp. X:** 292
Pamela (Richardson), **Supp. V:** 127; **Supp. XX: 236; Supp. XXII:** 120
Pamela's First Musical (Wasserstein), **Supp. XV:** 333
Panache de bouquets (Komunyakaa; Cadieux, trans.), **Supp. XIII:** 127
Pan-African movement, **Supp. II Part 1:** 172, 175
Pandaemonium (Epstein), **Supp. XII:** 161, **172–173**
"Pandora" (Adams), **I:** 5
Pandora: New Tales of Vampires (Rice), **Supp. VII:** 295
Panek, LeRoy, **Supp. XIV:** 27
"Pangolin, The" (Moore), **III:** 210
Panic: A Play in Verse (MacLeish), **III:** 2, 20
Panic in Needle Park (film), **Supp. IV Part 1:** 198
Pankey, Eric, **Supp. XIX:** 44
Pantagruel (Rabelais), **II:** 112
"Pantaloon in Black" (Faulkner), **II:** 71
Panther and the Lash, The (Hughes), **Retro. Supp. I:** 204, 211; **Supp. I Part 1:** 342–344, 345–346
"Panthers, The" (Southern), **Supp. XI:** 295
"Panties and the Buddha" (Peacock), **Supp. XIX:** 199
"Pan *versus* Moses" (Ozick), **Supp. V:** 262
"Paolo Castelnuovo" (Everwine), **Supp. XV:** 83–84
"Papa and Mama Dance, The" (Sexton), **Supp. II Part 2:** 688
"Papa Who Wakes Up Tired in the Dark" (Cisneros), **Supp. VII:** 62
Pape, Greg, **Supp. V:** 180; **Supp. XIII:** 312; **Supp. XV:** 73
Paper Doll (Parker), **Supp. XIX:** 184
"Paper Dolls Cut Out of a Newspaper" (Simic), **Supp. VIII:** 282
"Paper House, The" (Mailer), **III:** 42–43
Paper Lion (film, March), **Supp. XVI:** 242
Paper Lion: Confessions of a Last-String Quarterback (Plimpton), **Supp. XVI: 242–243**
Papernick, Jon, **Supp. XVII:** 50
Papers on Literature and Art (Fuller), **Supp. II Part 1:** 292, 299
Papini, Giovanni, **Supp. XVI:** 195; **Supp. XXII:** 159, 161, 163
Papp, Joseph, **Supp. IV Part 1:** 234; **Supp. XXI:** 145
"Paprika Johnson" (Barnes), **Supp. III Part 1:** 33
"Par" (Bausch), **Supp. VII:** 54
"Parable from a Christian" (Notley), **Supp. XXII:** 235
"Parable in the Later Novels of Henry James" (Ozick), **Supp. V:** 257
"Parable of the Gift" (Glück), **Supp. V:** 89
"Parable of the Hostages" (Glück), **Supp. V:** 89
"Parable of the King" (Glück), **Supp. V:** 89
Parable of the Sower (O. Butler), **Supp. XIII: 66–67,** 69
Parable of the Talents (O. Butler), **Supp. XIII:** 61,**Supp. XIII:** 66, **67–69**
"Parable of the Trellis" (Glück), **Supp. V:** 89
Parachutes & Kisses (Jong), **Supp. V:** 115, 123, 125–126, 129
"Paradelle for Susan" (Collins), **Supp. XXI:** 58
"Parade of Painters" (Swenson), **Supp. IV Part 2:** 645
"Paradigm, The" (Tate), **IV:** 128
Paradise (Barthelme), **Supp. IV Part 1:** 52
"Paradise" (Caputo), **Supp. XIX:** 26–27
"Paradise" (Doty), **Supp. XI:** 123
Paradise, Piece by Piece (Peacock), **Supp. XIX:** 193, 194–195, 195–196, **201–202**
Paradise Lost (Milton), **I:** 137; **II:** 168, 549; **IV:** 126; **Supp. XII:** 173, 297; **Supp. XV:** 181; **Supp. XX: 280**
Paradise Lost (Odets), **Supp. II Part 2:** 530, 531, 538–539, 550
"Paradise of Bachelors and the Tartarus of Maids, The" (Melville), **III:** 91
Paradise of Bombs, The (Sanders), **Supp. XVI:** 265, 272–273
Paradise Poems (Stern), **Supp. IX: 293–294,** 295
Paradiso (Dante), **Supp. IX:** 50
"Paradoxes and Oxymorons" (Ashbery), **Supp. III Part 1:** 23–24
Paradox of Progressive Thought, The (Noble), **Supp. I Part 2:** 650
Paragon, The (Knowles), **Supp. XII:** 249
"Paragraphs" (Carruth), **Supp. XVI:** 52–53
"Parameters" (Dunn), **Supp. XI:** 154
"Para Mi Tataranieto El Astropionero" (Espaillat), **Supp. XXI:** 104
"Paraphrase" (Crane), **I:** 391–392, 393
"Pardon, The" (Wilbur), **Supp. III Part 2:** 544, 550
Paredes, Américo, **Supp. XIII:** 225; **Supp. XIX:** 97, 98, 100
Paredes, Raymund A., **Supp. XIII:** 320, 321
"Parentage" (Stafford), **Supp. XI:** 321, 322
Parentheses: An Autobiographical Journey (Neugeboren), **Supp. XVI:** 217, 218, 219, 221, 226
"Parents" (F. Barthelme), **Supp. XI:** 34
"Parents Taking Shape" (Karr), **Supp. XI:** 243
"Parents' Weekend: Camp Kenwood" (Kenyon), **Supp. VII:** 169
Pareto, Vilfredo, **II:** 577
Paretsky, Sara, **Supp. IV Part 2:** 462; **Supp. XIV:** 26
Parini, Jay, **Supp. X:** 17; **Supp. XIX:** 120, 129; **Supp. XX: 243; Supp. XXI:** 192; **Supp. XXII:** 205
"Paris" (Collins), **Supp. XXI:** 60
"Paris" (Stern), **Supp. IX:** 300
"Paris, 7 A.M." (Bishop), **Retro. Supp. II:** 41, 42; **Supp. I Part 1:** 85, 89
Paris, Bob, **Supp. XX: 264**
Paris, Paris (Shaw), **Supp. XIX:** 240
Paris France (Stein), **IV:** 45
Park, Ed, **Supp. XXII:** 255
Park, Robert, **IV:** 475
"Park Bench" (Hughes), **Supp. I Part 1:** 331–332
Park City (Beattie), **Supp. V:** 24, 35–36
"Park City" (Beattie), **Supp. V:** 35
Parker, Charlie, **Supp. I Part 1:** 59; **Supp. X:** 240, 242, 246; **Supp. XIII:** 129
Parker, Dorothy, **Retro. Supp. II:** 327; **Supp. IV Part 1:** 353; **Supp. IX:** 62, 114, **189–206; Supp. X:** 164; **Supp. XI:** 28; **Supp. XVIII:** 242, 246, 252
Parker, Emily, **Supp. XVIII:** 102
Parker, Idella, **Supp. X:** 232, 234–235
Parker, Joan, **Supp. XIX:** 187
Parker, Muriel, **Supp. IX:** 232
Parker, Patricia, **Supp. XV:** 242
Parker, Robert B., **Supp. IV Part 1:** 135, 136; **Supp. XIX: 177–192**
Parker, Theodore, **Supp. I Part 1:** 38; **Supp. I Part 2:** 518
Parker, Thomas, **Supp. I Part 1:** 102
"Parker's Back" (O'Connor), **III:** 348, 352, 358
"Parkersburg" (Halliday), **Supp. XIX:** 92
Parkes, Henry Bamford, **Supp. I Part 2:** 617
Park-Fuller, Linda, **Supp. XIII:** 297
Parkman, Francis, **II:** 278, 310, 312; **IV:** 179, 309; **Supp. I Part 2:** 420, 479, 481–482, 486, 487, 493, 498; **Supp. II Part 2: 589–616**
Parkman Reader, The (Morison, ed.), **Supp. I Part 2:** 494
Parks, Gordon, Sr., **Supp. XI:** 17
Parks, Larry, **Supp. I Part 1:** 295
Parks, Rosa, **Supp. I Part 1:** 342
"Park Street Cemetery, The" (Lowell), **II:** 537, 538
Par le Détroit (cantata) (Bowles), **Supp. IV Part 1:** 82
Parliament of Fowls, The (Chaucer), **III:** 492
Parmenides (Plato), **II:** 10
Parnassus (Emerson), **II:** 8, 18
Parnell, Charles Stewart, **II:** 129, 137
Parole (film), **Supp. XIII:** 166
Parole Fixer (film), **Supp. XIII:** 170
Parrington, Vernon Louis, **I:** 254, 517, 561; **III:** 335, 606; **IV:** 173; **Supp. I Part 2:** 484, 640
Parrish, Dillwyn, **Supp. XVII:** 83–84, 90
Parrish, Robert, **Supp. XI:** 307
"Parrot, The" (Merrill), **Supp. III Part 1:** 320
"Parsley" (Dove), **Supp. IV Part 1:** 245, 246
Parson, Annie, **Supp. I Part 2:** 655
Parsons, Elsie Clews, **I:** 231, 235
Parsons, Ian, **Supp. IX:** 95
Parsons, Louella, **Supp. XII:** 173
Parsons, Talcott, **Supp. I Part 2:** 648

Parsons, Theophilus, **II:** 396, 504; **Retro. Supp. II:** 134; **Supp. I Part 1:** 155
"Parthian Shot, The" (Hammett), **Supp. IV Part 1:** 343
Partial Glossary, A (Bronk), **Supp. XXI:** 26
Partial Payments: Essays on Writers and Their Lives (Epstein), **Supp. XIV:** 111
Partial Portraits (James), **II:** 336
"Partial Relief" (Halliday), **Supp. XIX:** 91
Partial Truth (Nelson), **Supp. XVIII: 175–176,** 178
"Particulars" (Pickering), **Supp. XXI:** 197
Parties (Van Vechten), **Supp. II Part 2:** 739, 747–749
"Parting" (Kunitz), **Supp. III Part 1:** 263
"Parting Gift" (Wylie), **Supp. I Part 2:** 714
"Parting Glass, The" (Freneau), **Supp. II Part 1:** 273
"Partings" (Hogan), **Supp. IV Part 1:** 413
Partington, Blanche, **I:** 199
Partisans (Matthiessen), **Supp. V:** 201
"Partner, The" (Roethke), **III:** 541–542
Partners, The (Auchincloss), **Supp. IV Part 1:** 31, 34
Partners in Crime: A Rafe Buenrostro Mystery (Hinojosa), **Supp. XIX: 107–108**
"Part of a Letter" (Wilbur), **Supp. III Part 2:** 551
Part of a Long Story: Eugene O'Neill as a Young Man in Love (Boulton), **Supp. XXII:** 18, 21, 27–30
Part of Speech, A (Brodsky), **Supp. VIII:** 22
"Part of the Bee's Body Embedded in the Flesh, The" (C. Frost), **Supp. XV:** 105, 107
"Part of the Story" (Dobyns), **Supp. XIII:** 79
Part of Vermont, A (Taggard), **Supp. XXII:** 284
Parton, Sara, **Retro. Supp. I:** 246
Partridge, Jeffrey F., **Supp. XV:** 219
Partridge, John, **II:** 110, 111
"Parts of a Journal" (Gordon), **Supp. IV Part 1:** 310
Parts of a World (Stevens), **Retro. Supp. I: 305–306,** 307, 309, 313
"Parturition" (Loy), **Supp. XXII:** 159, 160–161
"Party, The" (Dunbar), **Supp. II Part 1:** 198, 205–206
"Party, The" (Taylor), **Supp. V:** 315
Party at Jack's, The (Wolfe), **IV:** 451–452, 469
"Party Down at the Square, A" (Ellison), **Retro. Supp. II:** 124
Party of Five (television series), **Supp. XIX:** 222
Pascal, Blaise, **II:** 8, 159; **III:** 292, 301, 304, 428; **Retro. Supp. I:** 326, 330
"Paskudnyak" (Pilcer), **Supp. XVII:** 50
"Pass, The" (Neugeboren), **Supp. XVI:** 225
"Passage" (Crane), **I:** 391
"Passage in the Life of Mr. John Oakhurst, A" (Harte), **Supp. II Part 1:** 353–354
"Passages" (Duncan), **Supp. XVI:** 287
"Passages from a Relinquished Work" (Hawthorne), **Retro. Supp. I:** 150
Passages toward the Dark (McGrath), **Supp. X:** 126, 127
"Passage to India" (Whitman), **IV:** 348
Passage to India, A (Forster), **II:** 600; **Supp. XVIII:** 143
Passaro, Vince, **Supp. X:** 167, 302, 309, 310
"Passenger, The" (Brockmeier), **Supp. XXII:** 52
"Passenger Pigeons" (Jeffers), **Supp. II Part 2:** 437
Passin, Herbert, **Supp. XIII:** 337
Passing (Larsen), **Supp. XVIII:** 119, 123, **127–130**
"Passing Beauty" (C. Frost), **Supp. XV:** 97
"Passing of Grandison, The" (Chesnutt), **Supp. XIV:** 62, **66–69**
"Passing of Sister Barsett, The" (Jewett), **Retro. Supp. II:** 138–139, 143
"Passing Show, The" (Bierce), **I:** 208
"Passing Through" (Kunitz), **Supp. III Part 1:** 265
"Passion, The" (Barnes), **Supp. III Part 1:** 36
"Passion, The" (Merwin), **Supp. III Part 1:** 343
Passionate, Accurate Story, The: Making Your Heart's Truth into Literature (C. Bly), **Supp. XVI: 41–42**
Passionate Pilgrim, A (James), **II:** 324; **Retro. Supp. I:** 219
"Passionate Pilgrim, A" (James), **II:** 322, 323–324; **Retro. Supp. I:** 218
Passion Play (Kosinski), **Supp. VII:** 215, 225–226
Passions of Uxport, The (Kumin), **Supp. IV Part 2:** 444
"Passive Resistance" (McKay), **Supp. X:** 133
Passport to the War (Kunitz), **Supp. III Part 1:** 261–264
Passwords (Stafford), **Supp. XI: 329–330**
"Past, The" (Bryant), **Supp. I Part 1:** 157, 170
Past, The (Kinnell), **Supp. III Part 1:** 235, 253–254
"Past, The" (Kinnell), **Supp. III Part 1:** 254
Past and Present (Carlyle), **Supp. I Part 2:** 410
Pasternak, Boris, **II:** 544
"Pastiches et Pistaches" (Van Vechten), **Supp. II Part 2:** 732
"Past Is the Present, The" (Moore), **III:** 199–200
"Pastoral" (Carver), **Supp. III Part 1:** 137, 146
"Pastoral" (Dove), **Supp. IV Part 1:** 249
"Pastoral" (Trethewey), **Supp. XXI:** 257
"Pastoral Hat, A" (Stevens), **IV:** 91
Pastoralia (Saunders), **Supp. XIX: 227–229**
"Pastoralia" (Saunders), **Supp. XIX:** 227, 229
"Pastor Dowe at Tacaté" (Bowles), **Supp. IV Part 1:** 87
Pastorela (ballet) (Kirstein), **Supp. IV Part 1:** 83
Pastorius, Francis Daniel, **Supp. I Part 2:** 700
"Pasture Poems" (Kumin), **Supp. IV Part 2:** 446
Pastures of Heaven, The (Steinbeck), **IV:** 51
Patch, Jerry, **Supp. XVIII:** 38
Patchen, Kenneth, **Supp. III Part 2:** 625
Patchett, Ann, **Supp. XII: 307–324**
Patchwork Planet (Lethem), **Supp. XVIII:** 150
Pater, Walter, **I:** 51, 272, 476; **II:** 27, 338; **III:** 604; **IV:** 74; **Retro. Supp. I:** 56, 79; **Retro. Supp. II:** 326; **Supp. I Part 2:** 552; **Supp. IX:** 66
Paterna (Mather), **Supp. II Part 2:** 451
"Paterson" (Ginsberg), **Supp. II Part 1:** 314–315, 321, 329
Paterson (W. C. Williams), **I:** 62, 446; **IV:** 418–423; **Retro. Supp. I:** 209, 284, 413, 419, 421, **424–428,** 428, 429, 430; **Retro. Supp. II:** 321, 328; **Supp. II Part 2:** 557, 564, 625; **Supp. VIII:** 275, 305; **Supp. XIV:** 96; **Supp. XV:** 264, 349
Paterson, Book Five (W. C. Williams), **IV:** 422–423
Paterson, Book One (W. C. Williams), **IV:** 421–422
Paterson, Isabel, **Supp. IV Part 2:** 524
Paterson, Part Three (W. C. Williams), **IV:** 420–421
Pat Garrett and Billy the Kid (film, Peckinpah), **Supp. XVIII:** 27
"Path, The" (Bryant), **Supp. I Part 1:** 169
Pathfinder, The (Cooper), **I:** 349, 350, 355
Pat Hobby Stories, The (Fitzgerald), **Retro. Supp. I:** 114
"Pathos of Low Life, The" (Hapgood), **Supp. XVII:** 103
"Patience of a Saint, The" (Humphrey), **Supp. IX:** 106
Patient 002 (Skloot), **Supp. XX: 194, 208**
Patinkin, Mandy, **Supp. IV Part 1:** 236
Paton, Alan, **Supp. VIII:** 126
Patria Mia (Pound), **III:** 460–461; **Retro. Supp. I:** 284
"Patria Mia" (Pound), **Retro. Supp. I:** 284
"Patriarch, The" (Alvares), **Supp. V:** 11
"Patrick Kavanagh at First Light" (Skloot), **Supp. XX: 204**
Patrimony: A True Story (P. Roth), **Retro. Supp. II:** 279, 280, 291; **Supp. III Part 2:** 427
Patriot, The (Buck), **Supp. II Part 1:** 122–123
Patriot, The (Connell), **Supp. XIV:** 94–95

Patriotic Gore: Studies in the Literature of the American Civil War (Wilson), **III:** 588; **IV:** 430, 438, 443, 445–445, 446; **Supp. VIII:** 100
"Patriotic Thing, The" (Ryan as Quin), **Supp. XVIII:** 229
"Patriots, The/Los Patriotas" (Kingsolver), **Supp. VII:** 209
Patron Saint of Liars, The (Patchett), **Supp. XII:** 307, 310, **311–314,** 317
Pattee, Fred L., **II:** 456
Patten, Gilbert, **II:** 423
Patten, Simon, **Supp. I Part 2:** 640
Patternmaster (O. Butler), **Supp. XIII:** 61, 62, 63
Patternmaster Series (O. Butler), **Supp. XIII: 62–63**
Pattern Recognition (W. Gibson), **Supp. XVI:** 124, **130–131**
"Patterns" (Lowell), **II:** 524
Patterson, Floyd, **III:** 38
Patterson, Margot, **Supp. XXII:** 85
Patterson, William M., **Supp. I Part 1:** 265
Patton, General George, **III:** 575; **Supp. I Part 2:** 664
"Patty-Cake, Patty-Cake...A Memoir" (Apple), **Supp. XVII:** 7
Paul, Saint, **I:** 365; **II:** 15, 494; **IV:** 122, 154, 164, 335; **Retro. Supp. I:** 247; **Supp. I Part 1:** 188
Paul, Sherman, **I:** 244; **IV:** 179
"Paula Becker to Clara Westhoff" (Rich), **Supp. I Part 2:** 573–574
"Paula Gunn Allen" (Ruppert), **Supp. IV Part 1:** 321
Paul Bowles: Romantic Savage (Caponi), **Supp. IV Part 1:** 95
Paulding, James Kirke, **I:** 344; **II:** 298, 299, 303; **Supp. I Part 1:** 157
Pauley, Jane, **Supp. XXI:** 39
Paul Jones (Hapgood), **Supp. XVII:** 100–101
Paul Marchand, F.M.C. (Chesnutt), **Supp. XIV:** 76
"Paul Monette: The Brink of Summer's End" (film), **Supp. X:** 152
"Paul Revere" (Longfellow), **II:** 489, 501
"Paul Revere's Ride" (Longfellow), **Retro. Supp. II:** 163
"Paul's Case" (Cather), **I:** 314–315; **Retro. Supp. I:** 3, 5
Paulsen, Friedrich, **III:** 600
"Pauper Witch of Grafton, The" (Frost), **Retro. Supp. II:** 42
"Pause by the Water, A" (Merwin), **Supp. III Part 1:** 354
"Pavane for the Nursery, A" (W. J. Smith), **Supp. XIII:** 335
"Pavement, The" (Olson), **Supp. II Part 2:** 571
Pavese, Cesare, **Supp. XXI:** 132
Pavic, Milorad, **Supp. XXII:** 265
Pavilion of Women (Buck), **Supp. II Part 1:** 125–126
"Pawnbroker, The" (Kumin), **Supp. IV Part 2:** 442, 443–444, 451
Pawnbroker, The (Wallant), **Supp. XVI:** 220
"Paying Dues" (Bass), **Supp. XVI:** 16
Payne, Daniel, **Supp. V:** 202
Payne, John Howard, **II:** 309
Payne Tom, **Supp. XXII:** 266
Paz, Octavio, **Supp. III Part 2:** 630; **Supp. VIII:** 272; **Supp. XI:** 191; **Supp. XIII:** 223
P. D. Kimerakov (Epstein), **Supp. XII:** 160, **162**
Peabody, Elizabeth, **Retro. Supp. I:** 155–156, 225
Peabody, Francis G., **III:** 293; **Supp. I Part 1:** 5
Peabody, Josephine Preston, **III:** 507; **Supp. XX: 115**
Peaceable Kingdom, The (Prose), **Supp. XVI:** 256–257
Peace and Bread in Time of War (Addams), **Supp. I Part 1:** 21, 22–23
"Peace Between Black and White in the United States" (Locke), **Supp. XIV:** 205
Peace Breaks Out (Knowles), **Supp. XII:** 249
"Peace March, The" (Simpson), **Supp. IX:** 279
"Peace of Cities, The" (Wilbur), **Supp. III Part 2:** 545
"Peace of Mind" (Boyle), **Supp. XX: 19**
"Peaches—Six in a Tin Box, Sarajevo" (Cisneros), **Supp. VII:** 67
Peachtree Road (Siddons), **Supp. XXII:** 239, 240, 242, **246–247, 248–251,** 252
Peacock, Doug, **Supp. VIII:** 38; **Supp. XIII:** 12
Peacock, Gibson, **Supp. I Part 1:** 360
Peacock, Molly, **Supp. XVII:** 74; **Supp. XIX: 193–207**
"Peacock, The" (Merrill), **Supp. III Part 1:** 320
"Peacock, The" (Mosher), **Supp. XXII:** 211
Peacock, Thomas Love, **Supp. I Part 1:** 307; **Supp. VIII:** 125
"Peacock Room, The" (Hayden), **Supp. II Part 1:** 374–375
"Peacocks of Avignon, The" (Swados), **Supp. XIX:** 263
Pearce, Richard, **Supp. IX:** 254
Pearce, Roy Harvey, **II:** 244; **Supp. I Part 1:** 111, 114; **Supp. I Part 2:** 475
"Pearl" (Kooser), **Supp. XIX:** 127–128
Pearl, The (Steinbeck), **IV:** 51, 62–63
Pearlman, Daniel, **III:** 479
Pearlman, Mickey, **Supp. XIII:** 293, 306
Pearl of Orr's Island, The (Stowe), **Supp. I Part 2:** 592–593, 595
"Pearls" (A. Finch), **Supp. XVII:** 72
Pears, Peter, **II:** 586; **Supp. IV Part 1:** 84
Pearson, Drew, **Supp. XIV:** 126
Pearson, Norman Holmes, **Supp. I Part 1:** 259, 260, 273
"Pear Tree" (C. Frost), **Supp. XV:** 105
"Peasants' Way O' Thinkin' " (McKay), **Supp. X:** 133
Pease, Donald E., **Supp. IV Part 2:** 687
Peck, Gregory, **Supp. VIII:** 128, 129; **Supp. XII:** 160, 173
Peckinpah, Sam, **Supp. XI:** 306; **Supp. XVIII:** 27
"Peck of Gold, A" (Frost), **II:** 155
Peculiar Treasures: A Biblical Who's Who (Buechner), **Supp. XII:** 53
"Pedal Point" (Francis), **Supp. IX:** 87
Pedersen, Inge, **Supp. XVIII:** 179
"Pedersen Kid, The" (Gass), **Supp. VI:** 83
"Pedigree, The" (Creeley), **Supp. IV Part 1:** 150
Peebles, Melvin Van, **Supp. XI:** 17; **Supp. XVI:** 144
"Peed Onk" (Moore). *See* "People Like That Are the Only People Here: Canonical Babbling in Peed Onk" (Moore)
"Peeler, The" (O'Connor), **Retro. Supp. II:** 225
Peich, Michael, **Supp. XV:** 113, 117
Peikoff, Leonard, **Supp. IV Part 2:** 520, 526, 529
Peirce, Charles Sanders, **II:** 20, 352–353; **III:** 599; **Supp. I Part 2:** 640; **Supp. III Part 2:** 626
Pelagius, **III:** 295
"Pelican, The" (Merrill), **Supp. III Part 1:** 320
"Pelican, The" (Wharton), **IV:** 310; **Retro. Supp. I:** 364
Pellacchia, Michael, **Supp. XIII:** 16
Pelley, Denise, **Supp. XIX:** 205
Peltier, Leonard, **Supp. V:** 212
"Pen and Paper and a Breath of Air" (Oliver), **Supp. VII:** 245
Pence, Amy, **Supp. XV:** 211, 223
"Pencil, The" (Chandler), **Supp. IV Part 1:** 135
Pencillings by the Way (Willis), **II:** 313; **Supp. XVIII:** 12
"Pencils" (Sandburg), **III:** 592
Pendleton, Devon, **Supp. XVIII:** 151
"Pendulum" (Bradbury and Hasse), **Supp. IV Part 1:** 102
"Penelope's Song" (Glück), **Supp. V:** 89
Penhally (Gordon), **II:** 197, 199, 201–203, 204
"Penis" (McClatchy), **Supp. XII:** 266–267
Penitent, The (di Donato), **Supp. XX: 44, 45**
Penitent, The (Singer), **Retro. Supp. II: 309–310,** 313
Penland, Nell Bates, **Supp. XXII:** 188
Penn, Robert, **I:** 489
Penn, Sean, **Supp. XI:** 107
Penn, Thomas, **II:** 118
Penn, William, **Supp. I Part 2:** 683
Penna, Sandro, **Supp. XIX:** 34
Pennebaker, D. A., **Supp. XVIII:** 19, 26
"Pennsylvania Pilgrim, The" (Whittier), **Supp. I Part 2:** 700
"Pennsylvania Planter, The" (Freneau), **Supp. II Part 1:** 268
Penny, Rob, **Supp. VIII:** 330
"Penny, The" (D. West), **Supp. XVIII:** 283–284
Penrod (Tarkington), **III:** 223
"Penseroso, Il" (Milton), **Supp. XIV:** 8
Pensieri (Leopardi; Di Piero, trans.), **Supp. XIX:** 34

Pentagon of Power, The (Mumford), **Supp. II Part 2:** 498
Pentimento (Hellman), **Supp. I Part 1:** 280, 292–294, 296; **Supp. IV Part 1:** 12; **Supp. VIII:** 243
"Peonies at Dusk" (Kenyon), **Supp. VII:** 171
People, The (Glaspell), **Supp. III Part 1:** 179
People, Yes, The (Sandburg), **III:** 575, 589, 590, 591
"PEOPLE BURNING, THE" (Baraka), **Supp. II Part 1:** 49
"People in Hell Just Want a Drink of Water" (Proulx), **Supp. VII:** 263
"People Like That Are the Only People Here: Canonical Babbling in Peed Onk" (Moore), **Supp. X:** 168, **178–179**
People Live Here: Selected Poems 1949–1983 (Simpson), **Supp. IX:** 269, 277
"People Next Door, The" (Simpson), **Supp. IX:** 279
People of the Abyss, The (London), **II:** 465–466
"People on the Roller Coaster, The" (Hardwick), **Supp. III Part 1:** 196
People Shall Continue, The (Ortiz), **Supp. IV Part 2:** 510
"People's Surroundings" (Moore), **III:** 201, 202, 203
"People *v.* Abe Lathan, Colored, The" (Caldwell), **I:** 309
"Peppermint Lounge Revisited, The" (Wolfe), **Supp. III Part 2:** 571
Peppis, Paul, **Supp. XXII:** 160
Pepys, Samuel, **Supp. I Part 2:** 653
"Perchance to Dream" (Franzen), **Supp. XX: 90, 93**
Perchance to Dream: Robert B. Parker's Sequel to Raymond Chandler's "Big Sleep" (Parker), Supp. XIX: 189
"Perch'io non spero di tornar giammai" (Cavalcanti), **Supp. III Part 2:** 623
Percy, Thomas, **Supp. XIV:** 2
Percy, Walker, **Supp. III Part 1: 383–400; Supp. IV Part 1:** 297; **Supp. V:** 334; **Supp. X:** 42; **Supp. XIV:** 21; **Supp. XIX:** 209
Percy, William, **Supp. V:** 334
Percy, William Alexander, **Retro. Supp. I:** 341; **Supp. XXII:** 193
Peregrin, Tony, **Supp. XV:** 69
"Peregrine" (Wylie), **Supp. I Part 2:** 712–713, 714
Perelman, Bob, **Supp. XII:** 23
Perelman, S. J., **IV:** 286; **Retro. Supp. I:** 342; **Retro. Supp. II:** 321, 322, 325, 326, 327, 336; **Supp. IV Part 1:** 353; **Supp. XI:** 66
Perestroika (Kushner), **Supp. IX:** 141, 142, 145
Péret, Benjamin, **Supp. VIII:** 272
Peretz, Isaac Loeb, **IV:** 1, 3; **Retro. Supp. II:** 299
Pérez Galdós, Benito, **II:** 275
Perfect Analysis Given by a Parrot, A (T. Williams), **IV:** 395
"Perfect Couple, The" (Nelson), **Supp. XVIII:** 173
"Perfect Day for Bananafish, A" (Salinger), **III:** 563–564, 571
Perfect Fiction, The (Sorrentino), **Supp. XXI:** 228
Perfect Ganesh, A (McNally), **Supp. XIII: 202–203,** 208, 209
"Perfect Gerbil, The: Reading Barthelme's 'The School' " (Saunders), **Supp. XIX:** 235
"Perfect Knight, The" (Chandler), **Supp. IV Part 1:** 120
Perfect Party, The (Gurney), **Supp. V:** 100, 105, 106–107
"Perfect Things" (F. Barthelme), **Supp. XI:** 30, 33–34
"Performance, The" (Dickey), **Supp. IV Part 1:** 178–179, 181
"Perfume" (Mora), **Supp. XIII:** 218
"Perhaps the World Ends Here" (Harjo), **Supp. XII:** 228, 231
Perhaps Women (Anderson), **I:** 114
Pericles (Shakespeare), **I:** 585; **Supp. III Part 2:** 624, 627, 629
"Period Metaphor" (Bronk), **Supp. XXI:** 33
Period of Adjustment (T. Williams), **IV:** 382, 386, 387, 388, 389, 390, 392, 393, 394, 397
"Period Pieces from the Mid-Thirties" (Agee), **I:** 28
"Periphery" (Ammons), **Supp. VII:** 28
Perkins, David, **Supp. I Part 2:** 459, 475; **Supp. XV:** 185
Perkins, Maxwell, **I:** 252, 289, 290; **II:** 87, 93, 95, 252; **IV:** 452, 455, 457, 458, 461, 462, 463, 469; **Retro. Supp. I:** 101, 105, 108, 109, 110, 113, 114, 178; **Supp. IX:** 57, 58, 60, 232; **Supp. X:** 219, 224, 225, 229, 230, 233; **Supp. XI:** 218, 227
Perlès, Alfred, **III:** 177, 183, 187, 189
Perloff, Marjorie, **Supp. I Part 2:** 539, 542; **Supp. IV Part 1:** 68; **Supp. IV Part 2:** 420, 424, 432; **Supp. XXII:** 161, 271
Permanence and Change (Burke), **I:** 274
Permanent Errors (Price), **Supp. VI:** 261
"Permanent Traits of the English National Genius" (Emerson), **II:** 18
Permit Me Voyage (Agee), **I:** 25, 27
"Perosa Canavese" (Everwine), **Supp. XV:** 84
Perrault, Charles, **IV:** 266; **Supp. I Part 2:** 622
Perrin, Noel, **Supp. XVI:** 34; **Supp. XXII:** 205, 207, 211, 218
Perrins, Carol. *See* Frost, Carol
Perry, Anne, **Supp. V:** 335
Perry, Bliss, **I:** 243
Perry, Donna, **Supp. IV Part 1:** 322, 327, 335
Perry, Edgar A., **III:** 410
Perry, Keith Ronald, **Supp. XXI:** 42
Perry, Lincoln, **Supp. V:** 24, 33
Perry, Matthew C., **Supp. I Part 2:** 494–495
Perry, Patsy Brewington, **Supp. I Part 1:** 66
Perry, Phyllis Alesia, **Supp. XVIII:** 96
Perry, Ralph Barton, **I:** 224; **II:** 356, 362, 364; **Supp. XIV:** 197
Perry, Dr. William, **II:** 395, 396
Perse, St.-John, **III:** 12, 13, 14, 17; **Supp. III Part 1:** 14; **Supp. IV Part 1:** 82; **Supp. XIII:** 344; **Supp. XV:** 178
"Persephone in Hell" (Dove), **Supp. IV Part 1:** 250, 251
"Persimmons" (L.-Y. Lee), **Supp. XV:** 211, 213
"Persistence of Desire, The" (Updike), **IV:** 222–223, 228
"Persistence of Poetry, The" (Bynner), **Supp. XV:** 49
"Persistences" (Hecht), **Supp. X: 68–69**
Person, Place, and Thing (Shapiro), **Supp. II Part 2:** 702, 705
Personae of Ezra Pound (Pound), **III:** 458
Personae: The Collected Poems (Pound), **Retro. Supp. I:** 285, 286; **Supp. I Part 1:** 255; **Supp. XVII:** 32
"Personal" (Stern), **Supp. IX:** 299
"Personal and Occasional Pieces" (Welty), **Retro. Supp. I:** 355
"Personal and the Individual, The" (L. Michaels), **Supp. XVI:** 201
Personal Injuries (Turow), **Supp. XVII: 219–220,** 221, 223
"Personalities" (column, Briggs), **Supp. XVIII:** 15
Personal Narrative (Edwards), **I:** 545, 552, 553, 561, 562; **Supp. I Part 2:** 700
Personal Recollection of Joan of Arc (Twain), **IV:** 208
Personals (Bontemps), **Supp. XXII:** 7, 8
"Personals" (Didion), **Supp. IV Part 1:** 200
"Personism" (O'Hara), **Supp. XV:** 181
Persons and Places (Santayana), **III:** 615
Persons in Hiding (film), **Supp. XIII:** 170
Persons in Hiding (Hoover), **Supp. XIII:** 170
Person Sitting in Darkness, A (Twain), **IV:** 208
"Perspective" (Francis), **Supp. IX:** 78
"Perspective: Anniversary D-Day" (Karr), **Supp. XI:** 241
Perspectives by Incongruity (Burke), **I:** 284–285
"Perspectives: Is It Out of Control?" (Gleason), **Supp. IX:** 16
Perspectives on Cormac McCarthy (Arnold and Luce, eds.), **Supp. VIII:** 189
Persse, Dudley Jocelyn, **Supp. XX: 232**
Pertes et Fracas (McCoy), **Supp. XIII:** 175
"Peruvian Child" (Mora), **Supp. XIII:** 218
Peseroff, Joyce, **Supp. IV Part 1:** 71
"Pestilence" (Nelson), **Supp. XVIII:** 186
"Peter" (Cather), **Retro. Supp. I:** 4
"Peter" (Moore), **III:** 210, 212
Peter, Saint, **III:** 341, 346; **IV:** 86, 294
Peterkin, Julia, **Supp. I Part 1:** 328; **Supp. XXII:** 12, 189
"Peter Klaus" (German tale), **II:** 306

Peter Pan (Barrie), **Supp. XV:** 319
"Peter Parley" works (Goodrich), **Supp. I Part 1:** 38
"Peter Pendulum" (Poe), **III:** 425
"Peter Quince at the Clavier" (Stevens), **IV:** 81, 82
Peter Rabbit tales, **Retro. Supp. I:** 335
Peters, Cora, **Supp. I Part 2:** 468
Peters, Jacqueline, **Supp. XII:** 225
Peters, Margot, **Supp. VIII:** 252
Peters, Robert, **Supp. XIII:** 114
Peters, S. H. (pseudonym). *See* Henry, O.
Peters, Timothy, **Supp. XI:** 39
"Peter's Avocado" (Rodriguez), **Supp. XIV:** 308–309
Petersen, David, **Supp. XIII:** 2
Petersen, Donald, **Supp. V:** 180; **Supp. XV:** 74, 92
Peterson, Dorothy, **Supp. XVIII:** 131, 132
Peterson, George, **Supp. XXII:** 250
Peterson, Houston, **I:** 60
Peterson, Roger Tory, **Supp. V:** 202
Peterson, Virgilia, **Supp. IV Part 1:** 30
Peter Whiffle: His Life and Works (Van Vechten), **Supp. II Part 2:** 728–729, 731, 735, 738–741, 749
"Petey and Yotsee and Mario" (H. Roth), **Supp. IX:** 234
"Petition, A" (Winters), **Supp. II Part 2:** 785
"'Pet Negro' System, The" (Hurston), **Supp. VI:** 159
"Petra and Its Surroundings" (Frost), **Retro. Supp. I:** 124
Petrarch, **I:** 176; **II:** 590; **III:** 4
"Petrarch, Shakespeare, and the Blues" (C. Frost), **Supp. XV:** 92, 104, 105
"Petrified Man" (Welty), **IV:** 262; **Retro. Supp. I:** 345, 351
"Petrified Man, The" (Twain), **IV:** 195
"Petrified Woman, The" (Gordon), **II:** 199
Petronius, **III:** 174, 179
Petry, Ann, **Supp. VIII:** 214; **Supp. XI:** 6, 85; **Supp. XVIII:** 286
Pet Sematary (King), **Supp. V:** 138, 143, 152
Pettengill, Richard, **Supp. VIII:** 341, 345, 348
Pettingell, Phoebe, **Supp. XV:** 251, 256–257, 262
Pettis, Joyce, **Supp. XI:** 276, 277, 278, 281
Petty, Jill, **Supp. XXI:** 244, 248, 249, 250
Pfaelzer, Jean, **Supp. XVI:** 88, 90
Pfaff, Timothy, **Supp. V:** 166
Pfeil, Fred, **Supp. XIV:** 36
Pfister, Karin, **IV:** 467, 475
Phaedo (Plato), **II:** 10
Phaedra (Lowell and Barzun, trans.), **II:** 543–544
"Phantasia for Elvira Shatayev" (Rich), **Supp. I Part 2:** 570
Phantasms of War (Lowell), **II:** 512
"Phantom of the Movie Palace, The" (Coover), **Supp. V:** 50–51
Phantom Ship, The (Marryat), **Supp. XVII:** 55
"Pharaoh, The" (Kenyon), **Supp. VII:** 172
Pharr, Mary, **Supp. V:** 147
"Phases" (E. Stoddard), **Supp. XV:** 273
"Phases" (Stevens), **Retro. Supp. I:** 299
Phases of an Inferior Planet (Glasgow), **II:** 174–175
"Pheasant, The" (Carver), **Supp. III Part 1:** 146
Phelan, Alice, **Supp. XXII:** 193
Pheloung, Grant, **Supp. XI:** 39
Phelps, Elizabeth Stuart, **Retro. Supp. II:** 146; **Supp. XIII:** 141; **Supp. XVI:** 80
Phelps, Teresa Godwin, **Supp. VIII:** 128
Phelps, William Lyon "Billy", **Supp. XX: 68, 75, 220**
"Phenomena and Laws of Race Contacts, The" (Locke), **Supp. XIV:** 210
"Phenomenology of Anger, The" (Rich), **Supp. I Part 2:** 562–563, 571
Phenomenology of Moral Experience, The (Mandelbaum), **I:** 61
"Phenomenology of *On Moral Fiction*" (Johnson), **Supp. VI:** 188
Phidias, **Supp. I Part 2:** 482
Philadelphia Fire (Wideman), **Supp. X:** 320, 334
Philadelphia Negro, The (Du Bois), **Supp. II Part 1:** 158, 163–164, 166
Philbrick, Thomas, **I:** 343
"Phil in the Marketplace" (Lethem), **Supp. XVIII:** 148
Philip, Jim, **Supp. XII:** 136
Philip, Maxwell, **Supp. XXI:** 160
Philip, Prince, **Supp. X:** 108
"Philip of Pokanoket" (Irving), **II:** 303
Philippians (biblical book), **IV:** 154
"Philippine Conquest, The" (Masters), **Supp. I Part 2:** 456
"Philip Roth Reconsidered" (Howe), **Retro. Supp. II:** 286
"Philistinism and the Negro Writer" (Baraka), **Supp. II Part 1:** 39, 44
Phillips, Adam, **Supp. XII:** 97–98
Phillips, Anne K., **Supp. XX: 221**
Phillips, Carl, **Supp. XXI:** 246
Phillips, David Graham, **II:** 444; **Retro. Supp. II:** 101
Phillips, Gene D., **Supp. XI:** 306
Phillips, Jayne Anne, **Supp. XIV:** 21
Phillips, J. O. C., **Supp. I Part 1:** 19
Phillips, Robert, **Supp. XIII:** 335, 344
Phillips, Wendell, **Supp. I Part 1:** 103; **Supp. I Part 2:** 524
Phillips, Willard, **Supp. I Part 1:** 154, 155
Phillips, William, **Supp. VIII:** 156
Phillips, William L., **I:** 106
"Philly Babylon" (Di Piero), **Supp. XIX:** 46
"Philosopher, The" (Farrell), **II:** 45
Philosopher of the Forest (pseudonym). *See* Freneau, Philip
Philosophes classiques, Les (Taine), **III:** 323
"Philosophical Cobbler, The" (Sanders), **Supp. XVI:** 268
"Philosophical Concepts and Practical Results" (James), **II:** 352
"Philosophical Investigation of Metaphor, A" (Gass), **Supp. VI:** 79
Philosophical Transactions (Watson), **II:** 114
"Philosophy, Or Something Like That" (P. Roth), **Supp. III Part 2:** 403
"Philosophy and Its Critics" (James), **II:** 360
"Philosophy and the Form of Fiction" (Gass), **Supp. VI:** 85
"Philosophy for People" (Emerson), **II:** 14
"Philosophy in Warm Weather" (Kenyon), **Supp. VII:** 168
"Philosophy Lesson" (Levine), **Supp. V:** 195
Philosophy of Alain Locke, The: Harlem Renaissance and Beyond (Harris, ed.), **Supp. XIV:** 196, 211–212
"Philosophy of Composition, The" (Poe), **III:** 416, 421; **Retro. Supp. II:** 266, 267, 271
Philosophy of Friedrich Nietzsche, The (Mencken), **III:** 102–103
"Philosophy of Handicap, A" (Bourne), **I:** 216, 218
"Philosophy of History" (Emerson), **II:** 11–12
Philosophy of Literary Form, The (Burke), **I:** 275, 281, 283, 291
Philosophy of the Human Mind, The (Stewart), **II:** 8
Philosophy: Who Needs It (Rand), **Supp. IV Part 2:** 517, 518, 527, 533
Philoxenes, **Supp. VIII:** 201
"Phineas" (Knowles), **Supp. XII:** 238–240
Phineas: Six Stories (Knowles), **Supp. XII:** 249
"Phocion" (Lowell), **II:** 536
Phoebe Light (Notley), **Supp. XXII:** 227
Phoenix and the Turtle, The (Shakespeare), **I:** 284
"Phoenix Lyrics" (Schwartz), **Supp. II Part 2:** 665
"Phone Booths, The" (Jarman), **Supp. XVII:** 112–113
"Phony War Films" (Jones), **Supp. XI:** 217, 232
"Photograph: Migrant Worker, Parlier, California, 1967" (Levis), **Supp. XI:** 272
"Photograph of a Bawd Drinking Raleigh Rye" (Trethewey), **Supp. XXI:** 254
"Photograph of a Child on a Vermont Hillside" (Kenyon), **Supp. VII:** 168
"Photograph of My Mother as a Young Girl" (Gioia), **Supp. XV:** 119
"Photograph of the Girl" (Olds), **Supp. X:** 205
"Photograph of the Unmade Bed" (Rich), **Supp. I Part 2:** 558
Photographs (Welty), **Retro. Supp. I:** 343
"Photographs, The" (Barthelme), **Supp. IV Part 1:** 53
"Photography" (Levine), **Supp. V:** 194
Phyrrho, **Retro. Supp. I:** 247
"Physical Universe" (Simpson), **Supp. IX:** 278

"Physicist We Know, A" (Shields), **Supp. VII:** 310
"Physics and Cosmology in the Fiction of Tom Robbins" (Nadeau), **Supp. X:** 270
Physiologie du goût (Brillat-Savarin), **Supp. XVII:** 82, 86
Physiology of Taste, The; or, Meditations on Transcendent Gastronomy (Brillat-Savarin; M. F. K. Fisher, trans.), **Supp. XVII:** 86, 87, 91
"Physiology of Versification, The: Harmonies of Organic and Animal Life" (Holmes), **Supp. I Part 1:** 311
Physique de l'Amour (Gourmont), **III:** 467–468
Piaf, Edith, **Supp. IV Part 2:** 549
Piaget, Jean, **Supp. XIII:** 75
"Piano" (Lawrence), **Supp. XV:** 254
"Piano Fingers" (Mason), **Supp. VIII:** 146
Piano Lesson, The (Bearden), **Supp. VIII:** 342
Piano Lesson, The (Wilson), **Supp. VIII: 342–345**
Piano Man's Daughter, The (Findley), **Supp. XX: 59–61**
Piatt, James, **Supp. I Part 2:** 420
Piatt, John J., **II:** 273
Piazza, Ben, **Supp. XIII:** 163
Piazza, Paul, **Supp. XIV:** 157, 160, 171
"Piazza de Spagna, Early Morning" (Wilbur), **Supp. III Part 2:** 553
Piazza Tales (Melville), **III:** 91
Picabia, Francis, **Retro. Supp. I:** 416; **Retro. Supp. II:** 331; **Supp. XXII:** 162
Picasso (Stein), **IV:** 28, 32, 45
Picasso, Pablo, **I:** 429, 432, 440, 442, 445; **II:** 602; **III:** 197, 201, 470; **IV:** 26, 31, 32, 46, 87, 407, 436; **Retro. Supp. I:** 55, 63; **Supp. IV Part 1:** 81; **Supp. IX:** 66
Piccione, Anthony, **Supp. XV:** 212
"Piccola Comedia" (Wilbur), **Supp. III Part 2:** 561
Pickard, Samuel T., **Supp. I Part 2:** 682
Picked-Up Pieces (Updike), **Retro. Supp. I:** 320, 322, 323, 335
Picker, Lauren, **Supp. VIII:** 78, 83
Picker, Tobias, **Supp. XII:** 253
Pickering, Sam, **Supp. XXI: 191–207**
Pickford, Mary, **Retro. Supp. I:** 325; **Supp. I Part 2:** 391
"Picking and Choosing" (Moore), **III:** 205
"Picnic" (Peacock), **Supp. XIX:** 206
Picnic, Lightning (Collins), **Supp. XXI:** 54, 60
"Picnic, Lightning" (Collins), **Supp. XXI:** 64–65
Picnic Cantata (music) (Bowles), **Supp. IV Part 1:** 89
"Picnic Remembered" (Warren), **IV:** 240
Pictorial History of the Negro in America, A (Hughes), **Supp. I Part 1:** 345
"Picture, The" (Olson), **Supp. II Part 2:** 574
Picture Bride (Son), **Supp. X:** 292
"Picture I Want, The" (Olds), **Supp. X:** 209
Picture of Dorian Gray, The (Wilde), **Supp. IX:** 105
"Picture of Little J. A. in a Prospect of Flowers, A" (Ashbery), **Supp. III Part 1:** 3
Picture Palace (Theroux), **Supp. VIII:** 322
"Pictures" (Pickering), **Supp. XXI:** 197
"Pictures at an Extermination" (Epstein), **Supp. XII:** 161
"Pictures from an Expedition" (Duffy), **Supp. IV Part 1:** 207
Pictures from an Institution (Jarrell), **II:** 367, 385
Pictures from Brueghel (W. C. Williams), **Retro. Supp. I:** 429–431
"Pictures from Brueghel" (W. C. Williams), **Retro. Supp. I:** 419
"Pictures of Columbus, the Genoese, The" (Freneau), **Supp. II Part 1:** 258
Pictures of Fidelman: An Exhibition (Malamud), **Supp. I Part 2:** 450–451
"Pictures of the Artist" (Malamud), **Supp. I Part 2:** 450
Pictures of the Floating World (Lowell), **II:** 521, 524–525
Pictures of Travel (Heine), **II:** 281
Picturesque America; or, the Land We Live In (Bryant, ed.), **Supp. I Part 1:** 158
"Picturesque Ghetto, The" (Hapgood), **Supp. XVII:** 101
"Picturesque: San Cristóbal de las Casas" (Mora), **Supp. XIII:** 218
Picture This (Heller), **Supp. IV Part 1:** 386, 388, 390–391
Picturing Will (Beattie), **Supp. V:** 29, 31–32, 34
"Pie" (X. J. Kennedy), **Supp. XV:** 170
"Piece, A" (Creeley), **Supp. IV Part 1:** 155, 156
"Piece of Moon, A" (Hogan), **Supp. IV Part 1:** 407
Piece of My Heart, A (Ford), **Supp. V:** 57, 58–61, 62
Piece of My Mind, A: Reflections at Sixty (Wilson), **IV:** 426, 430, 438, 441
"Piece of News, A" (Welty), **IV:** 263; **Retro. Supp. I:** 345, 346
Pieces (Creeley), **Supp. IV Part 1:** 155
Pieces and Pontifications (Mailer), **Retro. Supp. II:** 209–210
Pieces of the Frame (McPhee), **Supp. III Part 1:** 293
Pierce, Franklin, **II:** 225, 226, 227; **III:** 88; **Retro. Supp. I:** 150, 163, 164, 165
Pierce, Frederick, **Retro. Supp. I:** 136
Piercy, Josephine K., **Supp. I Part 1:** 103
"Pierian Handsprings" (column, Untermeyer), **Supp. XV:** 294
Pierpont, Claudia Roth, **Supp. X:** 192, 193, 196
Pierre et Jean (Maupassant), **I:** 421
Pierre: or The Ambiguities (Melville), **III:** 86–88, 89; **IV:** 194; **Retro. Supp. I:** 249, 253–254, 256; **Supp. I Part 2:** 579
Pierrepont, Sarah. *See* Edwards, Sarah
Pierrot qui pleure et Pierrot qui rit (Rostand), **II:** 515
Pierson, George W, **Supp. XXII:** 289
Pig Cookies (Ríos), **Supp. IV Part 2:** 537, 550, 552–554
Pigeon Feathers (Updike), **IV:** 214, 218, 219, 221–223, 226
"Pigeon Feathers" (Updike), **Retro. Supp. I:** 318, 322, 323
"Pigeons" (Rilke), **II:** 544
"Pigeons, The" (Espaillat), **Supp. XXI:** 98
"Pigeon Woman" (Swenson), **Supp. IV Part 2:** 644
Pigs in Heaven (Kingsolver), **Supp. VII:** 197, 199, 209–210
Pike County Ballads, The (Hay), **Supp. I Part 1:** 352
Piket, Vincent, **Supp. IV Part 1:** 24
Pilar San-Mallafre, Maria del, **Supp. V:** 40
Pilcer, Sonya, **Supp. XVII:** 50
Pilgrim (Findley), **Supp. XX: 61–62**
"Pilgrim" (Freneau), **Supp. I Part 1:** 125
"Pilgrimage" (Ray), **Supp. XVIII:** 193
"Pilgrimage" (Sontag), **Supp. III Part 2:** 454–455
"Pilgrimage" (Trethewey), **Supp. XXI:** 255
"Pilgrimage, The" (Maxwell), **Supp. VIII:** 169, 171
Pilgrimage of Festus, The (Aiken), **I:** 50, 55, 57
Pilgrimage of Henry James, The (Brooks), **I:** 240, 248, 250; **IV:** 433
Pilgrim at Tinker Creek (Dillard), **Supp. VI:** 22, **23–26,** 28, 29, **30–31,** 34; **Supp. XVIII:** 189
"Pilgrim Makers" (Lowell), **II:** 541
Pilgrim's Harbor (Skloot), **Supp. XX: 196, 207**
Pilgrim's Progress (Bunyan), **I:** 92; **II:** 15, 168, 572; **Supp. I Part 1:** 32, 38; **Supp. I Part 2:** 599
Pili's Wall (Levine), **Supp. V:** 178, 183–184
"Pillar of Fire" (Bradbury), **Supp. IV Part 1:** 113–114
Pillars of Hercules, The: A Grand Tour of the Mediterranean (Theroux), **Supp. VIII:** 325
"Pillow" (L.-Y. Lee), **Supp. XV:** 224
Pilot, The (Cooper), **I:** 335, 337, 339, 342–343, 350
"Pilot from the Carrier, A" (Jarrell), **II:** 374
"Pilots, Man Your Planes" (Jarrell), **II:** 374–375
"Pilots, The" (Levertov), **Supp. III Part 1:** 282
"Pimp's Revenge, A" (Malamud), **Supp. I Part 2:** 435, 450, 451
Pinball (Kosinski), **Supp. VII:** 215, 226
Pinchot, Gifford, **Supp. IX:** 184; **Supp. XIV:** 178
Pindar, **I:** 381; **II:** 543; **III:** 610
"Pine" (Dickey), **Supp. IV Part 1:** 183
Pine Barrens, The (McPhee), **Supp. III Part 1:** 298–301, 309

"Pineys, The" (Stern), **Supp. IX:** 288, 296
Pinget, Robert, **Supp. V:** 39
Pinhook: Finding Wholeness in a Fragmented Land (Ray), **Supp. XVIII:** 189, 192, 202–204
"Pink Dog" (Bishop), **Retro. Supp. II:** 48
"Pink Dress, The" (Boulton), **Supp. XXII:** 19
Pinker, James B., **I:** 409; **Retro. Supp. I:** 231
Pinkerton, Jan, **Supp. V:** 323–324
"Pink Moon—The Pond" (Oliver), **Supp. VII:** 234
Pinktoes (C. Himes), **Supp. XVI: 142**
Pinocchio in Venice (Coover), **Supp. V:** 40, 51
Pinsker, Sanford, **Retro. Supp. II:** 23; **Supp. V:** 272; **Supp. IX:** 293, 327; **Supp. XI:** 251, 254, 317
Pinsky, Robert, **Retro. Supp. II:** 50; **Supp. VI: 235–251; Supp. IX:** 155, 158; **Supp. XIII:** 277, 285; **Supp. XXI:** 243
Pinter, Harold, **I:** 71; **Supp. XIII:** 20, 196; **Supp. XIV:** 239; **Supp. XVI:** 207
Pinto, Ferdinand Mendes (pseudonym). *See* Briggs, Charles Frederick
Pinto and Sons (Epstein), **Supp. XII:** 170, **171–172**
Pinto letters (Briggs), **Supp. XVIII:** 3, **12–13**
"Pinup" (Collins), **Supp. XXI:** 59
"Pioneer Girl" (L. I. Wilder), **Supp. XXII:** 290, 293, 294, 295
Pioneers, The (Cooper), **I:** 336, 337, 339, 340–341, 342, 348; **II:** 313
Pioneers of France in the New World (Parkman), **Supp. III Part 2:** 599, 602
"Pioneers! O Pioneers!" (Whitman), **Retro. Supp. I:** 8
"Pioneer's Vision, The" (Larcom), **Supp. XIII:** 140
Pious and Secular America (Niebuhr), **III:** 308
Pipe Night (O'Hara), **III:** 361, 368
Piper, Dan, **Supp. IX:** 65
Pipers at the Gates of Dawn: The Wisdom of Children's Literature (Cott), **Supp. XVI:** 104
"Piper's Rocks" (Olson), **Supp. IV Part 1:** 153
"Pipistrelles" (B. Kelly), **Supp. XVII:** 129–130
Pipkin, Charles W., **Supp. XIV:** 3
Pippa Passes (Browning), **IV:** 128
Piquion, René, **Supp. I Part 1:** 346
Pirandello, Luigi, **Supp. IV Part 2:** 576, 588
Piranesi, Giovanni Battista, **Supp. XV:** 258
Pirate, The (Robbins), **Supp. XII:** 6
Pirate, The (Scott), **I:** 339
Pirates of Penzance, The (Gilbert and Sullivan), **IV:** 386
Pisan Cantos, The (Pound), **III:** 476; **Retro. Supp. I:** 140, 283, 285, 293; **Supp. III Part 1:** 63; **Supp. V:** 331, 337; **Supp. XIV:** 11; **Supp. XV:** 351
Pisarev, Dimitri, **Supp. XXI:** 164
Piscator, Erwin, **IV:** 394
Pissarro, Camille, **I:** 478
"Pissing off the Back of the Boat into the Nevernais Canal" (Matthews), **Supp. IX:** 160–161
Pistol, The (Jones), **Supp. XI:** 219, **223–224,** 227, 234
Pit, The (Norris), **III:** 314, 322, 326–327, 333, 334
"Pit, The" (Roethke), **III:** 538
"Pit and the Pendulum, The" (Poe), **III:** 413, 416; **Retro. Supp. II:** 264, 269–270, 273
"Pitcher" (Francis), **Supp. IX:** 82
"Pitcher, The" (Dubus), **Supp. VII:** 87
Pitchford, Nicola, **Supp. XII:** 13
"Pits, The" (D. Graham), **Supp. XI:** 252, 254
Pitt, William, **Supp. I Part 2:** 510, 518
Pitts, Rebecca, **Supp. XXII:** 280, 281
"Pittsburgh" (Carruth), **Supp. XVI:** 58
"Pity Me" (Wylie), **Supp. I Part 2:** 729
Pity the Monsters (Williamson), **Retro. Supp. II:** 185
Pius II, Pope, **III:** 472
Pius IX, Pope, **II:** 79
"Piute Creek" (Snyder), **Supp. VIII:** 293
Pixley, Frank, **I:** 196
Pizer, Donald, **III:** 321; **Retro. Supp. II:** 100, 199
"Place" (Hoffman), **Supp. XVIII:** 86
"Place at the Outskirts" (Simic), **Supp. VIII:** 282
Place Called Estherville, A (Caldwell), **I:** 297, 307
Place Called Freedom, A (Sanders), **Supp. XVI:** 269
Place for My Head, A (Hoffman), **Supp. XVIII:** 76
"Place in Fiction" (Welty), **IV:** 260, 279
Place of Dead Roads, The (Burroughs), **Supp. III Part 1:** 196
Place of Love, The (Shapiro), **Supp. II Part 2:** 702, 706
"Place of Poetry, The" (Stevens), **Retro. Supp. I:** 304
Place of Science in Modern Civilization and Other Essays, The (Veblen), **Supp. I Part 2:** 629, 642
"Place of Trumpets, The" (B. Kelly), **Supp. XVII:** 127
Place on Earth, A (Berry), **Supp. X:** 33–34, 36
Places Left Unfinished at the Time of Creation (Santos), **Supp. XIII:** 274
"Places to Look for Your Mind" (Moore), **Supp. X:** 174–175
"Place They'd Never Seen, A: The Theater" (Wasserstein), **Supp. XV:** 332
"Place to Live, A" (Levertov), **Supp. III Part 1:** 281
"Place to Stand, A" (Price), **Supp. VI:** 258
Place to Stand, A (Wagoner), **Supp. IX:** 324
"Place (Any Place) to Transcend All Places, A" (W. C. Williams), **Retro. Supp. I:** 422
Placi, Carlo, **IV:** 328
Plagemann, Catherine, **Supp. XVII:** 91
"Plagiarist, The" (Singer), **IV:** 19
Plague of Dreamers, A (Stern), **Supp. XX: 178**
Plainest Narrative, The (Bronk), **Supp. XXI:** 31
"Plain Language from Truthful James" (Harte). *See* "Heathen Chinee, The"
"Plain Sense of Things, The" (Stevens), **Retro. Supp. I:** 298, 299, 307, 312
"Plain Song" (Carruth), **Supp. XVI:** 54
Plain Song (Harrison), **Supp. VIII: 38–39**
"Plain Song" (Kooser), **Supp. XIX:** 120
"Plain Song for Comadre, A" (Wilbur), **Supp. III Part 2:** 554
"Plain Talk". *See Common Sense* (Paine)
Plaint of a Rose, The (Sandburg), **III:** 579
Plain Truth: Or, Serious Considerations on the Present State of the City of Philadelphia, and Province of Pennsylvania (Franklin), **II:** 117–119
Plainwater: Essays and Poetry (Carson), **Supp. XII:** 97, **99–104**
Plan B (C. Himes), **Supp. XVI:** 143, 144
Plan B: Further Thoughts on Faith (Lamott), **Supp. XX: 142–143**
"Planchette" (London), **II:** 475–476
"Planetarium" (Rich), **Supp. I Part 2:** 557
Planet News: 1961–1967 (Ginsberg), **Supp. II Part 1:** 321
Planet Waves (album, Dylan), **Supp. XVIII:** 27
"Plantation a beginning, a" (Olson), **Supp. II Part 2:** 573
Plant Dreaming Deep (Sarton), **Supp. VIII:** 250, 263
Plante, David, **Supp. IV Part 1:** 310
Planting a Sequoia (Gioia), **Supp. XV:** 117
"Planting a Sequoia" (Gioia), **Supp. XV:** 111, 112, 117, **121–122**
"Plants Fed On By Fawns" (B. Kelly), **Supp. XVII:** 133
Plarr, Victor, **III:** 459, 477
Plath, James, **Retro. Supp. I:** 334
Plath, Sylvia, **Retro. Supp. II:** 181, **241–260; Supp. I Part 2: 526–549,** 554, 571; **Supp. III Part 2:** 543, 561; **Supp. IV Part 2:** 439; **Supp. V:** 79, 81, 113, 117, 118, 119, 344; **Supp. X:** 201, 202, **203,** 215; **Supp. XI:** 146, 240, 241, 317; **Supp. XII:** 217, 308; **Supp. XIII:** 35, 76, 312; **Supp. XIV:** 269; **Supp. XV:** 123, 148, 184, 252, 253, 340; **Supp. XVII:** 239; **Supp. XXI:** 58; **Supp. XXII:** 30, 92, 93
Plath, Warren, **Supp. I Part 2:** 528
Plato, **I:** 224, 279, 383, 389, 485, 523; **II:** 5, 8, 10, 15, 233, 346, 391–392, 591; **III:** 115, 480, 600, 606, 609, 619–620; **IV:** 74, 140, 333, 363, 364; **Retro. Supp. I:** 247; **Retro. Supp. II:**

31; **Supp. I Part 2:** 595, 631; **Supp. IV Part 1:** 391; **Supp. IV Part 2:** 526; **Supp. X:** 78
"Plato" (Emerson), **II:** 6
"Platonic Relationship, A" (Beattie), **Supp. V:** 22
Platonic Scripts (Justice), **Supp. VII:** 115
Platonov, Dmitri, **Supp. VIII:** 30
Platt, Anthony M., **Supp. I Part 1:** 13–14
Platte River (Bass), **Supp. XVI:** 19
"Platte River" (Bass), **Supp. XVI:** 20
Plausible Prejudices: Essays on American Writing (Epstein), **Supp. XIV:** 111
Plautus, Titus Maccius, **IV:** 155; **Supp. III Part 2:** 630
Play and Other Stories, The (Dixon), **Supp. XII:** 148, 149
Playback (script) (Chandler), **Supp. IV Part 1:** 131
Playback (Chandler), **Supp. IV Part 1:** 134–135; **Supp. XVIII:** 138
"Play Ball!" (Francis), **Supp. IX:** 89
Playboy of the Western World, The (Synge), **Supp. III Part 1:** 34
Play Days (Jewett), **Retro. Supp. II:** 135
Play Days: A Book of Stories for Children (Jewett), **II:** 401–402
Player Piano (Vonnegut), **Supp. II Part 2:** 756, 757, 760–765
Players (DeLillo), **Supp. VI:** 3, 6, 8, 14
"Players, The" (W. J. Smith), **Supp. XIII:** 340, 343
"Playground, The" (Bradbury), **Supp. IV Part 1:** 104
Playing at Stillness (Espaillat), **Supp. XXI:** 112
Playing in the Dark (Morrison), **Retro. Supp. II:** 118; **Supp. XIII:** 185–186
"Playing the Bawd at Twenty" (Skloot), **Supp. XX: 204–205**
Play in Poetry (Untermeyer), **Supp. XV:** 310
"Playin with Punjab" (Bambara), **Supp. XI:** 6
Play It Again Sam (Allen), **Supp. XV:** 2, 3, 14
Play It as It Lays (Didion), **Supp. IV Part 1:** 198, 201–203, 203, 211
Play It as It Lays (film), **Supp. IV Part 1:** 198
"Plays and Operas Too" (Whitman), **IV:** 350
Plays of Negro Life: A Source-Book of Native American Drama (Locke and Gregory), **Supp. XIV:** 202
Plays: Winesburg and Others (Anderson), **I:** 113
"Playthings" (Komunyakaa), **Supp. XIII:** 126
"Playtime: Danish Fun" (Larsen), **Supp. XVIII:** 120, 122–123
"Playtime: Three Scandinavian Stories" (Larsen), **Supp. XVIII:** 122–123
Playwright's Voice, The (Savran), **Supp. XIII:** 209; **Supp. XV:** 321
Plaza Suite (Simon), **Supp. IV Part 2:** 575, 581–582, 583, 589
Pleading Guilty (Turow), **Supp. XVII: 218,** 219
"Plea for Captain Brown, A" (Thoreau), **IV:** 185
"Please" (Komunyakaa), **Supp. XIII:** 122
"Please Don't Kill Anything" (A. Miller), **III:** 161
"Please Don't Take My Sunshine Away" (Conroy), **Supp. XVI:** 69
Pleasure Dome (Frankenberg), **I:** 436
Pleasure Dome (Komunyakaa), **Supp. XIII:** 113, 121, **131–133**
Pleasure of Hope, The (Emerson), **II:** 8
"Pleasure of Ruins, The" (McClatchy), **Supp. XII:** 256
"Pleasures of Formal Poetry, The" (Bogan), **Supp. III Part 1:** 51
"Pleasures of Peace, The" (Koch), **Supp. XV:** 180
"Plea to the Protestant Churches, A" (Brooks), **Supp. XIV:** 4
Plimpton, George, **Supp. IV Part 1:** 386; **Supp. V:** 201; **Supp. VIII:** 82, 157; **Supp. IX:** 256; **Supp. XI:** 294; **Supp. XIV:** 82; **Supp. XVI: 233–248**
Pliny the Elder, **Supp. XVI:** 292
Pliny the Younger, **II:** 113
"Ploesti Isn't Long Island" (Zinberg), **Supp. XV:** 195
"Plot against the Giant, The" (Stevens), **IV:** 81
Plotinus, **Supp. XV:** 33; **Supp. XVI:** 291
Plough and the Stars, The (O'Casey), **III:** 159
"Ploughing on Sunday" (Stevens), **IV:** 74
Plowing the Dark (Powers), **Supp. IX:** 212–213, **221–224**
Plum Bun (Fauset), **Supp. XVIII:** 127; **Supp. XIX:** 73
Plumed Serpent, The (Lawrence), **Supp. XV:** 46
"Plumet Basilisk, The" (Moore), **III:** 203, 208, 215
Plumly, Stanley, **Supp. IV Part 2:** 625
Plummer, Amanda, **Supp. IV Part 1:** 236
Plunder (serial movie), **Supp. IV Part 2:** 464
Plunket, Robert, **Supp. XV:** 68
"Plunkville Patriot" (O'Henry), **Supp. II Part 1:** 389
"Pluralism and Ideological Peace" (Locke), **Supp. XIV:** 202, 212
"Pluralism and Intellectual Democracy" (Locke), **Supp. XIV:** 202, 208, 212
Pluralistic Universe, A (James), **II:** 342, 348, 357–358
Plutarch, **II:** 5, 8, 16, 555; **Retro. Supp. I:** 360; **Supp. XVI:** 292
Plymell, Charles, **Supp. XIV:** 149
Plymell, Pam, **Supp. XIV:** 149
Pnin (Nabokov), **III:** 246; **Retro. Supp. I:** 263, 265, 266, 275, 335
"Po' Boy Blues" (Hughes), **Supp. I Part 1:** 327
Pocahontas, **I:** 4; **II:** 296; **III:** 584
"Pocahontas to Her English Husband, John Rolfe" (Gunn Allen), **Supp. IV Part 1:** 331
"Pocketbook and Sauerkraut" (Di Piero), **Supp. XIX:** 35, 36, 41, 42, 45
"Pocket Poem" (Kooser), **Supp. XIX:** 128
Podhoretz, Norman, **IV:** 441; **Retro. Supp. II:** 323; **Supp. IV Part 1:** 382; **Supp. VIII:** 93, **231–247; Supp. IX:** 3; **Supp. XIV:** 103
Podnieks, Elizabeth, **Supp. X:** 189, 190, 191, 192
"Pod of the Milkweed" (Frost), **Retro. Supp. I:** 141
Poe, Edgar Allan, **I:** 48, 53, 103, 190, 194, 200, 210, 211, 261, 340, 459; **II:** 74, 77, 194, 255, 273, 295, 308, 311, 313, 421, 475, 482, 530, 595; **III:** 259, **409–432,** 485, 507, 593; **IV:** 123, 129, 133, 141, 187, 261, 345, 350, 432, 438, 439, 453; **Retro. Supp. I:** 41, 273, 365, 421; **Retro. Supp. II:** 102, 104, 160, 164, 220, **261–277,** 322; **Supp. I Part 1:** 36, 309; **Supp. I Part 2:** 376, 384, 385, 388, 393, 405, 413, 421, 474, 682; **Supp. II Part 1:** 385, 410; **Supp. III Part 2:** 544, 549–550; **Supp. IV Part 1:** 80, 81, 101, 128, 341, 349; **Supp. IV Part 2:** 464, 469; **Supp. VIII:** 105; **Supp. IX:** 115; **Supp. X:** 42, 78; **Supp. XI:** 85, 293; **Supp. XIII:** 100, 111; **Supp. XVI:** 294; **Supp. XVIII:** 3, 11; **Supp. XX: 74**
Poe, Edgar Allen, **Supp. XV:** 275; **Supp. XXI:** 51
Poe Abroad: Influence, Reputation, Affinities (Vines), **Retro. Supp. II:** 261
"Poem" (Bishop), **Retro. Supp. II:** 40; **Supp. I Part 1:** 73, 76–79, 82, 95
"Poem" (Harrison), **Supp. VIII:** 38
"Poem" (Justice), **Supp. VII:** 125
"Poem" (Kunitz), **Supp. III Part 1:** 263
"Poem" (Notley), **Supp. XXII:** 228–229
"Poem" (O'Hara), **Supp. XIX:** 85
"Poem" (Wright), **Supp. III Part 2:** 590
"Poem About George Doty in the Death House, A" (Wright), **Supp. III Part 2:** 594–595, 597–598
"Poem about People" (Pinsky), **Supp. VI: 240–241,** 244, 248
"Poem as Mask, The" (Rukeyser), **Supp. VI:** 281, 285
"Poem Beginning 'The' " (Zukofsky), **Supp. III Part 2:** 610, 611, 614
"Poem Catching Up with an Idea" (Carruth), **Supp. XVI:** 56
"Poem for a Birthday" (Plath), **Supp. I Part 2:** 539
"POEM FOR ANNA RUSS AND FANNY JONES, A" (Baraka), **Supp. II Part 1:** 58
"Poem for Black Hearts, A" (Baraka), **Supp. II Part 1:** 50
"POEM FOR DEEP THINKERS, A" (Baraka), **Supp. II Part 1:** 55
"Poem for D. H. Lawrence" (Creeley), **Supp. IV Part 1:** 141
"Poem for Dorothy, A" (Merwin), **Supp. III Part 1:** 342
"Poem for Hemingway and W. C. Williams" (Carver), **Supp. III Part 1:** 147
"Poem for my Son" (Kumin), **Supp. IV Part 2:** 442

"Poem for People Who Are Understandably Too Busy to Read Poetry" (Dunn), **Supp. XI:** 147
"Poem for Someone Killed in Spain, A" (Jarrell), **II:** 371
"Poem for the Blue Heron, A" (Oliver), **Supp. VII:** 235–236
"Poem for Two Voices" (Everwine), **Supp. XV:** 89
"Poem For Willie Best, A" (Baraka), **Supp. II Part 1:** 36
"Poem in Prose" (Bogan), **Supp. III Part 1:** 58
"Poem in Which I Refuse Contemplation" (Dove), **Supp. IV Part 1:** 249
"Poem Is a Walk, A" (Ammons), **Supp. VII:** 36
"Poem Like a Grenade, A" (Haines), **Supp. XII:** 204
"Poem of Flight, The" (Levine), **Supp. V:** 189
"Poem of Liberation, The" (Stern), **Supp. IX:** 292
Poem of the Cid (Merwin, trans.), **Supp. III Part 1:** 347
"Poem of the Forgotten" (Haines), **Supp. XII:** 202–203
"Poem on the Memorable Victory Obtained by the Gallant Captain Paul Jones" (Freneau), **Supp. II Part 1:** 261
"Poem out of Childhood" (Rukeyser), **Supp. VI:** 272, 277
"Poem Read at the Dinner Given to the Author by the Medical Profession" (Holmes), **Supp. I Part 1:** 310–311
Poems (Auden), **Supp. II Part 1:** 6
Poems (Berryman), **I:** 170
Poems (Bryant), **II:** 311; **Supp. I Part 1:** 155, 157
Poems (Cummings), **I:** 430, 447
Poems (E. Stoddard), **Supp. XV:** 274
Poems (Eliot), **I:** 580, 588; **IV:** 122; **Retro. Supp. I:** 59, 291
Poems (Emerson), **II:** 7, 8, 12–13, 17
Poems (Holmes), **Supp. I Part 1:** 303
Poems (Koch), **Supp. XV:** 179
Poems (Lowell), **Supp. I Part 2:** 405
Poems (Moore), **III:** 194, 205, 215
Poems (Poe), **III:** 411
Poems (Reznikoff), **Supp. XIV:** 282, 283, 284, 285
Poems (Tate), **IV:** 121
Poems (W. C. Williams), **Retro. Supp. I:** 412–413, 416, 424
Poems (W. J. Smith), **Supp. XIII:** 332
Poems (Winters), **Supp. II Part 2:** 809, 810
Poems (Wordsworth), **I:** 468
Poems, 1909–1925 (Eliot), **Retro. Supp. I:** 64
Poems, 1924–1933 (MacLeish), **III:** 7, 15
Poems, 1943–1956 (Wilbur), **Supp. III Part 2:** 554
Poems, The (Freneau), **Supp. II Part 1:** 263
Poems 1918–1975 : The Complete Poems of Charles Reznikoff (Cooney, ed.), **Supp. XIV:** 289
Poems 1940–1953 (Shapiro), **Supp. II Part 2:** 703, 711
Poems 1947–1954 (Kees), **Supp. XV:** 147
Poems: 1947–1957 (W. J. Smith), **Supp. XIII:** 333
Poems 1957–1967 (Dickey), **Supp. IV Part 1:** 178, 181
Poems about God (Ransom), **III:** 484, 486, 491; **IV:** 121
"Poems about Painting" (Snodgrass), **Supp. VI:** 316
Poems and Essays (Ransom), **III:** 486, 490, 492
Poems and New Poems (Bogan), **Supp. III Part 1:** 60–62
"Poems and Places" (Haines), **Supp. XII:** 203
Poems and Poetry of Europe, The (Longfellow, ed.), **Retro. Supp. II:** 155
Poems by Emily Dickinson (Todd and Higginson, eds.), **I:** 469, 470; **Retro. Supp. I:** 35, 39
Poems by Emily Dickinson, Second Series (Todd and Higginson, eds.), **I:** 454; **Retro. Supp. I:** 35
Poems by Emily Dickinson, The (Bianchi and Hampson, eds.), **Retro. Supp. I:** 35
Poems by Emily Dickinson, Third Series (Todd, ed.), **Retro. Supp. I:** 35
Poems by James Russell Lowell, Second Series (Lowell), **Supp. I Part 2:** 406, 409
Poems by Sidney Lanier, (Lanier), **Supp. I Part 1:** 364
Poems from Black Africa (Hughes, ed.), **Supp. I Part 1:** 344
"Poems I Have Lost, The" (Ortiz), **Supp. IV Part 2:** 507
Poems: North & South–A Cold Spring, (Bishop), **Supp. I Part 1:** 83, 89
Poems of a Jew (Shapiro), **Supp. II Part 2:** 703, 712–713
"Poems of a Mountain Recluse" (Budbill), **Supp. XIX:** 9, 10
Poems of Anna Akhmatova, The (Kunitz and Hayward, trans.), **Supp. III Part 1:** 269
Poems of Emily Dickinson, The (Bianchi and Hampson, eds.), **Retro. Supp. I:** 35
Poems of Emily Dickinson, The (Johnson, ed.), **I:** 470
Poems of François Villon (Kinnell, trans.), **Supp. III Part 1:** 235, 243, 249
"Poems of Our Climate, The" (Stevens), **Retro. Supp. I:** 313
Poems of Philip Freneau, Written Chiefly during the Late War (Freneau), **Supp. II Part 1:** 261
Poems of Places (Longfellow, ed.), **II:** 490; **Retro. Supp. II:** 155; **Supp. I Part 1:** 368
Poems of Stanley Kunitz, The (Kunitz), **Supp. III Part 1:** 258, 263, 264, 266, 268
"Poems of These States" (Ginsberg), **Supp. II Part 1:** 323, 325
Poems of Two Friends (Howells and Piatt), **II:** 273, 277
"POEM SOME PEOPLE WILL HAVE TO UNDERSTAND, A" (Baraka), **Supp. II Part 1:** 49
Poems on Slavery (Longfellow), **II:** 489; **Retro. Supp. II:** 157, 168; **Supp. I Part 2:** 406
Poems on Various Subjects (Rowson), **Supp. XV:** 232
Poems on Various Subjects, Religious and Moral (Wheatley), **Supp. XX: 277, 282, 284, 285, 289**
Poem Spoken at the Public Commencement at Yale College, in New Haven; September 1, 1781, A (Barlow), **Supp. II Part 1:** 67–68, 74, 75
Poems to Solve (Swenson), **Supp. IV Part 2:** 642
Poems Written and Published during the American Revolutionary War (Freneau), **Supp. II Part 1:** 273, 274
Poems Written between the Years 1768 and 1794 (Freneau), **Supp. II Part 1:** 269
"Poem That Took the Place of a Mountain" (Olson), **Supp. II Part 2:** 582
"Poem to My First Lover" (Olds), **Supp. X:** 206
"Poem to the Reader" (Olds), **Supp. X:** 213
"Poem with No Ending, A" (Levine), **Supp. V:** 186, 190
"Poem You Asked For, The" (Levis), **Supp. XI:** 259–260
Poe Poe Poe Poe Poe Poe Poe (Hoffman), **Retro. Supp. II:** 265
Poesía Náhuatl, **Supp. XV:** 77
Poésies 1917–1920 (Cocteau), **Retro. Supp. I:** 82
"Poesis: A Conceit" (Sobin), **Supp. XVI:** 288
"Poet" (Taggard), **Supp. XXII:** 284
Poet, The (Connelly), **Supp. XXI: 71,** 78
"Poet, The" (Dunbar), **Supp. II Part 1:** 207, 209–210
"Poet, The" (Emerson), **II:** 13, 19, 20, 170
"Poet, The" (Ortiz), **Supp. IV Part 2:** 505
"Poet and His Book, The" (Millay), **III:** 126, 138
"Poet and His Public, The" (Jarrell), **Supp. I Part 1:** 96
"Poet and His Song, The" (Dunbar), **Supp. II Part 1:** 199
"Poet and the Person, The" (Kinard), **Supp. XIV:** 127
"Poet and the Queen, The" (Shaw), **Supp. XIX:** 241
"Poet and the World, The" (Cowley), **Supp. II Part 1:** 145
"Poet as Anti-Specialist, The" (Swenson), **Supp. IV Part 2:** 638, 643
"Poet as *Curandera*" (Mora), **Supp. XIII:** 214, 220
"Poet as Hero, The: Keats in His Letters" (Trilling), **Supp. III Part 2:** 506–507

"Poet as Religious Moralist, The" (Larson), **Supp. XI:** 328
"Poet at Seven, The" (Rimbaud), **II:** 545
Poet at the Breakfast-Table, The (Holmes), **Supp. I Part 1:** 313–314
"Poète contumace, Le" (Corbiere), **II:** 384–385
"Poet for President, A" (Mora), **Supp. XIII:** 220–221
Poetic Achievement of Ezra Pound, The (Alexander), **Retro. Supp. I:** 293
Poetic Diction: A Study in Meaning (Barfield), **III:** 274, 279
"Poetic Principle, The" (Poe), **III:** 421, 426; **Retro. Supp. II:** 266
"Poetics" (Ammons), **Supp. VII:** 29–30
Poetics (Aristotle), **III:** 422; **Supp. XI:** 249; **Supp. XIII:** 75; **Supp. XIV:** 243; **Supp. XV:** 265
Poetics of Space, The (Bachelard), **Supp. XIII:** 225; **Supp. XVI:** 292
"Poetics of the Periphery: Literary Experimentalism in Kathy Acker's *In Memoriam to Identity" (Acker), Supp. XII:* 17
"Poetics of the Physical World, The" (Kinnell), **Supp. III Part 1:** 239
"Poetics of Tourette Syndrome, The: Language, Neurobiology, and Poetry" (Schleifer), **Supp. XVIII:** 144
Poet in the World, The (Levertov), **Supp. III Part 1:** 271, 273, 278, 282
"Poet or the Growth of a Lit'ry Figure" (White), **Supp. I Part 2:** 676
Poetry (Barber), **Supp. IV Part 2:** 550
"Poetry" (Moore), **III:** 204–205, 215
"Poetry" (Nye), **Supp. XIII:** 282
"Poetry" (Wrigley), **Supp. XVIII:** 301–302
"Poetry, Community and Climax" (Snyder), **Supp. VIII:** 290
"Poetry, Pleasure, and the Hedonist Reader" (Collins), **Supp. XXI:** 54
"Poetry: A Metrical Essay" (Holmes), **Supp. I Part 1:** 310
"Poetry and Belief in Thomas Hardy" (Schwartz), **Supp. II Part 2:** 666
Poetry and Criticism (Nemerov, ed.), **III:** 269
"Poetry and Drama" (Eliot), **I:** 588
Poetry and Fiction: Essays (Nemerov), **III:** 269, 281
"Poetry and Place" (Berry), **Supp. X:** 22, 28, 31, 32
Poetry and Poets (Lowell), **II:** 512
"Poetry and Religion" (Jarman), **Supp. XVII:** 111
Poetry and the Age (Jarrell), **IV:** 352; **Retro. Supp. I:** 121; **Supp. II Part 1:** 135
"Poetry and the Primitive: Notes on Poetry as an Ecological Survival Technique" (Snyder), **Supp. VIII:** 291, 292, 299, 300
"Poetry and the Public World" (MacLeish), **III:** 11
Poetry and the World (Pinsky), **Supp. VI:** 236, 239, 244, 247
Poetry and Truth (Olson), **Supp. II Part 2:** 583
"Poetry As a Way of Life" (Bishop interview), **Retro. Supp. II:** 53
"Poetry as Survival" (Harrison), **Supp. VIII:** 45
"Poetry Failure" (Halliday), **Supp. XIX:** 92
Poetry for Students (Taibl), **Supp. XV:** 255
"Poetry for the Advanced" (Baraka), **Supp. II Part 1:** 58
"Poetry Friendship on Earth" (Halliday), **Supp. XIX:** 90, 91
Poetry Handbook, A (Oliver), **Supp. VII:** 229, 245
Poetry Home Repair Manual, The (Kooser), **Supp. XIX:** 116, 128
Poetry in Motion: 100 Poems from the Subways and Buses (Peacock, ed.), **Supp. XIX:** 195
"Poetry of Barbarism, The" (Santayana), **IV:** 353
Poetry of Chaucer, The (Gardner), **Supp. VI: 63**
Poetry of Meditation, The (Martz), **IV:** 151; **Supp. I Part 1:** 107
Poetry of Mourning: The Modern Elegy from Hardy to Heaney (Ramazani), **Supp. IV Part 2:** 450
Poetry of Stephen Crane, The (Hoffman), **I:** 405
Poetry of the Negro, 1746–1949, The (Hughes and Bontemps), **Supp. I Part 1:** 345; **Supp. XXII:** 11
Poetry 180: A Turning Back to Poetry (Collins, ed.), **Supp. XXI:** 54
Poetry Reading against the Vietnam War, A (Bly and Ray, eds.), **Supp. IV Part 1:** 61, 63
"Poetry Workshop, The" (column, Kumin), **Supp. XX: 164**
"Poetry Wreck, The" (Shapiro), **Supp. II Part 2:** 717
Poetry Wreck, The: Selected Essays (Shapiro), **Supp. II Part 2:** 703, 704, 717
"Poets" (X. J. Kennedy), **Supp. XV:** 158
Poet's Alphabet, A: Reflections on the Literary Art and Vocation (Bogan), **Supp. III Part 1:** 55, 64
Poets and Poetry of America (Griswold), **Supp. XV:** 277
Poet's Choice (Engle and Langland, eds.), **III:** 277, 542
"Poet's Husband Engages in Gourmet Cooking, The" (Espaillat), **Supp. XXI:** 99
Poets of the Old Testament, The (Gordon), **III:** 199
Poets of Today (Wheelock, ed.), **Supp. IV Part 2:** 639
Poets on Poetry (Nemerov, ed.), **III:** 269
"Poet's Tact, and a Necessary Tactlessness, The" (C. Frost), **Supp. XV:** 94–95
"Poet's View, A" (Levertov), **Supp. III Part 1:** 284
"Poet's Voice, The" (Oliver), **Supp. VII:** 245
"Poet Turns on Himself, The" (Dickey), **Supp. IV Part 1:** 177, 181, 185
Poganuc People (Stowe), **Supp. I Part 2:** 581, 596, 599–600
Pogo (comic strip), **Supp. XI:** 105
Pohrt, Tom, **Supp. XIX:** 123
Poincaré, Raymond, **IV:** 320
"Point, The" (Hayden), **Supp. II Part 1:** 373
"Point at Issue!, A" (Chopin), **Retro. Supp. II:** 61; **Supp. I Part 1:** 208
"Point of Age, A" (Berryman), **I:** 173
Point of No Return (Marquand), **III:** 56, 59–60, 65, 67, 69
Point Reyes Poems (R. Bly), **Supp. IV Part 1:** 71
"Points" (Hoffman), **Supp. XVIII:** 86
Points for a Compass Rose (Connell), **Supp. XIV:** 79, 80, 96
"Point Shirley" (Plath), **Supp. I Part 2:** 529, 538
Points in Time (Bowles), **Supp. IV Part 1:** 93
"Points West" (column), **Supp. IV Part 1:** 198
Poirier, Richard, **I:** 136, 239; **III:** 34; **Retro. Supp. I:** 134; **Retro. Supp. II:** 207–208; **Supp. I Part 2:** 660, 665; **Supp. IV Part 2:** 690
Poison Pen (Garrett), **Supp. VII:** 111
Poisonwood Bible, The (Kingsolver), **Supp. VII:** 197–198, 202, 210–213
Poitier, Sidney, **Supp. IV Part 1:** 360, 362
Pokerface (Collins), **Supp. XXI:** 53
"Polack Reverie" (Halliday), **Supp. XIX:** 88
Polanco, Richard, **Supp. XX: 260**
"Polar Bear" (Heller), **Supp. IV Part 1:** 383
"Polar Seas and Sir John Franklin, The" (Briggs), **Supp. XVIII:** 14
Pole, Rupert, **Supp. X:** 185
"Pole Star" (MacLeish), **III:** 16
Po Li, **Supp. I Part 1:** 262
Police (Baraka), **Supp. II Part 1:** 47
"Police" (Corso), **Supp. XII:** 117, 127
"Police Court Saturday Morning" (X. J. Kennedy), **Supp. XV:** 170
"Police Dreams" (Bausch), **Supp. VII:** 47
Politian (Poe), **III:** 412
"Political and Practical Conceptions of Race, The" (Locke), **Supp. XIV:** 209–210
Political Essays (Lowell), **Supp. I Part 2:** 407
Political Fable, A (Coover), **Supp. V:** 44, 46, 47, 49, 51
"Political Fables" (Mather), **Supp. II Part 2:** 450
"Political Interests" (Stevens), **Retro. Supp. I:** 295
"Political Litany, A" (Freneau), **Supp. II Part 1:** 257
"Political Migrations: A Family Story" (Mallon), **Supp. XIX:** 141–142
"Political Pastoral" (Frost), **Retro. Supp. I:** 139
"Political Poem" (Baraka), **Supp. II Part 1:** 36
Politics (Acker), **Supp. XII:** 3, 4

Politics (Macdonald), **I:** 233–234
"Politics" (Paley), **Supp. VI:** 217
"Politics, Structure, and Poetic Development" (McCombs), **Supp. XIII:** 33
"Politics and the English Language" (Orwell), **Retro. Supp. II:** 287; **Supp. I Part 2:** 620
Politics and the Novel (Howe), **Supp. VI:** 113
"Politics and the Personal Lyric in the Poetry of Joy Harjo and C. D. Wright" (Goodman), **Supp. XV:** 344
"Politics of Ethnic Authorship, The: Li-Young Lee, Emerson, and Whitman at the Banquet Table" (Partridge), **Supp. XV:** 219
"Politics of Silence, The" (Monette), **Supp. X:** 148
Polito, Robert, **Supp. XVIII:** 33
Politt, Katha, **Supp. XII:** 159
Polk, James, **Supp. XIII:** 20
Polk, James K., **I:** 17; **II:** 433–434
Pollack, Sydney, **Supp. XIII:** 159
"Pollen" (Nye), **Supp. XIII:** 284
Pollitt, Katha, **Supp. X:** 186, 191, 193; **Supp. XVI:** 39
Pollock, Jackson, **IV:** 411, 420; **Supp. XV:** 145, 177, 178; **Supp. XIX:** 33
"Polly" (Chopin), **Retro. Supp. II:** 72
Polo, Marco, **III:** 395
Polonsky, Abraham, **Supp. XXI:** 261, 275
Polybius, **Supp. I Part 2:** 491
"Polydore" (Chopin), **Retro. Supp. II:** 66
"Pomegranate" (Glück), **Supp. V:** 82
"Pomegranate Seed" (Wharton), **IV:** 316; **Retro. Supp. I:** 382
Ponce de Leon, Luis, **III:** 391
"Pond, The" (Nemerov), **III:** 272
"Pond at Dusk, The" (Kenyon), **Supp. VII:** 168
Ponder Heart, The (Welty), **IV:** 261, 274–275, 281; **Retro. Supp. I:** 351–352
"Ponderosa Pine" (Huncke), **Supp. XIV:** 146
Ponsot, Margaret, **Supp. XVII:** 241
"Pony" (Sanders), **Supp. XVI:** 277
Poodle Springs (Parker and Chandler), **Supp. IV Part 1:** 135; **Supp. XIX:** 189
Poodle Springs Story, The (Chandler), **Supp. IV Part 1:** 135
"Pool, The" (Doolittle), **Supp. I Part 1:** 264–265
Poole, Ernest, **II:** 444
"Pool Lights" (F. Barthelme), **Supp. XI:** 25, 26–27, 36
"Pool Room in the Lions Club" (Merwin), **Supp. III Part 1:** 346
"Poolside" (Skloot), **Supp. XX: 202–203**
"Poor Black Fellow" (Hughes), **Retro. Supp. I:** 204
"Poor Bustard, The" (Corso), **Supp. XII:** 134
"Poor but Happy" (Mamet), **Supp. XIV:** 252, 253
Poore, Charles, **III:** 364; **Supp. XIX:** 257, 264; **Supp. XX: 38**
Poor Fool (Caldwell), **I:** 291, 292, 308
Poorhouse Fair, The (Updike), **IV:** 214, 228–229, 232; **Retro. Supp. I:** 317, 320
"Poor Joanna" (Jewett), **II:** 394
"Poor Man's Pudding and Rich Man's Crumbs" (Melville), **III:** 89–90
"Poor Richard" (James), **II:** 322
Poor Richard's Almanac (undated) (Franklin), **II:** 112
Poor Richard's Almanac for 1733 (Franklin), **II:** 108, 110
Poor Richard's Almanac for 1739 (Franklin), **II:** 112
Poor Richard's Almanac for 1758 (Franklin), **II:** 101
Poor White (Anderson), **I:** 110–111
"Poor Working Girl" (Z. Fitzgerald), **Supp. IX:** 71
Popa, Vasko, **Supp. VIII:** 272
Pope, Alexander, **I:** 198, 204; **II:** 17, 114; **III:** 263, 267, 288, 517; **IV:** 145; **Retro. Supp. I:** 335; **Supp. I Part 1:** 150, 152, 310; **Supp. I Part 2:** 407, 422, 516, 714; **Supp. II Part 1:** 70, 71; **Supp. X:** 32, 36; **Supp. XII:** 260; **Supp. XV:** 258; **Supp. XX: 280**
Pope, James, **Supp. XXII:** 196
Pope-Hennessy, James, **Supp. XIV:** 348
"Pope's Penis, The" (Olds), **Supp. X:** 207
"Poplar, Sycamore" (Wilbur), **Supp. III Part 2:** 549
Popo and Fifina: Children of Haiti (Hughes and Bontemps), **Retro. Supp. I:** 203; **Supp. XXII:** 4, 10, 12
"Poppies" (Oliver), **Supp. VII:** 240
"Poppies in July" (Plath), **Supp. I Part 2:** 544
"Poppies in October" (Plath), **Supp. I Part 2:** 544
"Poppycock" (Francis), **Supp. IX:** 87
"Poppy Juice" (Taggard), **Supp. XXII:** 276
"Poppy Seed" (Lowell), **II:** 523
"Popular Art and the Cultural Tradition" (C. L. R. James), **Supp. XXI:** 170
Popular Book, The: A History of America's Literary Taste (Hart), **Supp. XVIII:** 257, 258
Popular Culture (Goldbarth), **Supp. XII: 186**
Popular History of the United States (Gay), **Supp. I Part 1:** 158
"Popular Songs" (Ashbery), **Supp. III Part 1:** 6
"Populist Manifesto" (Ferlinghetti), **Supp. VIII:** 290
"Porcelain Bowl" (Glück), **Supp. V:** 83
Porcher, Frances, **Retro. Supp. II:** 71
Porco, Mike, **Supp. XVIII:** 24
"Porcupine, The" (Kinnell), **Supp. III Part 1:** 244
Porcupine's Kiss, The (Dobyns), **Supp. XIII: 89–90**
"Por esas coases que pasan" (Hinojosa), **Supp. XIX:** 101
Porgy and Bess (film), **Supp. I Part 1:** 66
Porgy and Bess (play), **Supp. IV Part 1:** 6
"Porn Bought my Football" (Offutt), **Supp. XIX:** 163
"Porphyria's Lover" (Browning), **II:** 522
Portable Beat Reader, The (Charters, ed.), **Supp. XIV:** 152
Portable Blake, The (Kazin, ed.), **Supp. VIII:** 103
Portable Faulkner, The (Cowley, ed.), **II:** 57, 59; **Retro. Supp. I:** 73
Portable Paul and Jane Bowles, The (Dillon), **Supp. IV Part 1:** 95
Portable Veblen, The (Veblen), **Supp. I Part 2:** 630, 650
"Porte-Cochere" (Taylor), **Supp. V:** 320
"Porter" (Hughes), **Supp. I Part 1:** 327
"Porter" (Nelson), **Supp. XVIII:** 175
Porter, Bern, **III:** 171
Porter, Cole, **Supp. IX:** 189
Porter, Eliot, **Supp. IV Part 2:** 599
Porter, Fairfield, **Supp. XV:** 178
Porter, Herman W., **Supp. I Part 1:** 49
Porter, Horace, **Retro. Supp. II:** 4, 127
Porter, Jacob, **Supp. I Part 1:** 153
Porter, Katherine Anne, **I:** 97, 385; **II:** 194, 606; **III: 433–455,** 482; **IV:** 26, 138, 246, 261, 279, 280, 282; **Retro. Supp. I:** 354; **Retro. Supp. II:** 233, 235; **Supp. IV Part 1:** 31, 310; **Supp. V:** 225; **Supp. VIII:** 156, 157; **Supp. IX:** 93, 94, 95, 98, 128; **Supp. X:** 50; **Supp. XIII:** 294; **Supp. XIV:** 3; **Supp. XV:** 338
Porter, Noah, **Supp. I Part 2:** 640
Porter, William Sydney. *See* Henry, O.
Porteus, Beilby, **Supp. I Part 1:** 150
"Portland Going Out, The" (Merwin), **Supp. III Part 1:** 345
Portnoy's Complaint (P. Roth), **Retro. Supp. II: 282–286,** 291; **Supp. III Part 2:** 401, 404, 405, 407, 412–414, 426; **Supp. V:** 119, 122; **Supp. XI:** 140; **Supp. XVII:** 8, 43; **Supp. XX: 177**
Port of Saints (Burroughs), **Supp. III Part 1:** 106
"Portrait" (Dixon), **Supp. XII:** 154
"Portrait, A" (Parker), **Supp. IX:** 192–193
"Portrait, The" (Kunitz), **Supp. III Part 1:** 263
"Portrait, The" (Wharton), **Retro. Supp. I:** 364
"Portrait d'une Femme" (Pound), **Retro. Supp. I:** 288
Portrait in Brownstone (Auchincloss), **Supp. IV Part 1:** 21, 23, 27, 31
"Portrait in Georgia" (Toomer), **Supp. IX:** 314
"Portrait in Greys, A" (W. C. Williams), **Retro. Supp. I:** 416
"Portrait of a Girl in Glass" (T. Williams), **IV:** 383
"Portrait of a Jewelry Drummer" (Untermeyer), **Supp. XV:** 299–300
"Portrait of a Lady" (Eliot), **I:** 569, 570, 571, 584; **III:** 4; **Retro. Supp. I:** 55, 56, 62
Portrait of a Lady, The (James), **I:** 10, 258, 461–462, 464; **II:** 323, 325, 327,

328–329, 334; **Retro. Supp. I:** 215, 216, 217, 219, 220, 223, **224–225,** 232, 233, 381
"Portrait of an Artist" (P. Roth), **Supp. III Part 2:** 412
Portrait of an Eye: Three Novels (Acker), **Supp. XII:** 6, **7–9**
"Portrait of an Invisible Man" (Auster), **Supp. XII:** 21
"Portrait of a Supreme Court Judge" (Untermeyer), **Supp. XV:** 299
Portrait of Bascom Hawkes, A (Wolfe), **IV:** 451–452, 456
Portrait of Edith Wharton (Lubbock), **Retro. Supp. I:** 366
Portrait of Logan Pearsall Smith, Drawn from His Letters and Diaries, A (Russell, ed.), **Supp. XIV:** 349
Portrait of Picasso as a Young Man (Mailer), **Retro. Supp. II:** 213
"Portrait of the Artist as an Old Man, A" (Humphrey), **Supp. IX:** 109
Portrait of the Artist as a Young Man, A (Joyce), **I:** 475–476; **III:** 471, 561; **Retro. Supp. I:** 127; **Retro. Supp. II:** 4, 331; **Supp. IX:** 236; **Supp. XIII:** 53, 95
"Portrait of the Artist with Hart Crane" (Wright), **Supp. V:** 342
"Portrait of the Great White Hunter Foxhunting in the Absence of Big Game" (Major), **Supp. XXII:** 183
"Portrait of the Intellectual as a Yale Man" (McCarthy), **II:** 563, 564–565
"Portrait of the Reader with a Bowl of Cereal, A" (Collins), **Supp. XXI:** 55
"Portrait of the Self . . . , A" (Sobin), **Supp. XVI:** 288
Portraits and Elegies (Schnackenberg), **Supp. XV:** 249, **253–256**
"Portraits of Grief" *(New York Times)*, **Supp. XIX:** 142
"Port Town" (Hughes), **Retro. Supp. I:** 199
Portuguese Voyages to America in the Fifteenth Century (Morison), **Supp. I Part 2:** 488
"Po' Sandy" (Chesnutt), **Supp. XIV:** 60
Poseidon Adventure, The (film), **Supp. XII:** 321
Poseidon Adventure, The (Gallico), **Supp. XVI:** 238
"Poseidon and Company" (Carver), **Supp. III Part 1:** 137
"Positive Obsession" (O. Butler), **Supp. XIII:** 70
Poss, Stanley, **Supp. XIV:** 166
Possession (Byatt), **Supp. XXI:** 147
"Possessions" (H. Crane), **I:** 392–393; **Retro. Supp. II:** 78
Possible World, A (Koch), **Supp. XV:** 184
Postal Inspector (film), **Supp. XIII:** 166
Postcards (Proulx), **Supp. VII:** 249, 256–258, 262
"Postcard to Send to Sumer, A" (Bronk), **Supp. XXI:** 31
"Postcolonialism and Autobiography" (Skinner and Waller), **Supp. XXII:** 78
"Postcolonial Tale, A" (Harjo), **Supp. XII:** 227
"Posthumous Letter to Gilbert White" (Auden), **Supp. II Part 1:** 26
"Post-Larkin Triste" (Karr), **Supp. XI:** 242–243
Postlethwaite, Diana, **Supp. XII:** 317–318; **Supp. XVI:** 176
"Postlude" (W. C. Williams), **Retro. Supp. I:** 415
Postman, Neil, **Supp. XI:** 275
Postman Always Rings Twice, The (Cain), **Supp. XIII:** 165–166
Postman Always Rings Twice, The (film), **Supp. XIV:** 241
"Postmaster and the Clerk, The" (Budbill), **Supp. XIX:** 9
"Postmortem Guide, A" (Dunn), **Supp. XI:** 155
Postrel, Virginia, **Supp. XIV:** 298, 311
"Postscript" (Du Bois), **Supp. II Part 1:** 173
"Postscript" (Nye), **Supp. XIII:** 287
Postsouthern Sense of Place, The (Bone), **Supp. XXII:** 247
"Potato" (Wilbur), **Supp. III Part 2:** 545
"Potatoes' Dance, The" (Lindsay), **Supp. I Part 2:** 394
Pot of Earth, The (MacLeish), **III:** 5, 6–8, 10, 12, 18
"Pot Roast" (Strand), **Supp. IV Part 2:** 629
Potshot (Parker), **Supp. XIX:** 185
Pot Shots at Poetry (Francis), **Supp. IX: 83–84**
Potter, Beatrix, **Supp. I Part 2:** 656; **Supp. XVI:** 100
Potter, Stephen, **IV:** 430
Potter's House, The (Stegner), **Supp. IV Part 2:** 598, 606
Poulenc, Francis, **Supp. IV Part 1:** 81
Poulin, Al, Jr., **Supp. IX:** 272; **Supp. XI:** 259
Pound, Ezra, **I:** 49, 58, 60, 66, 68, 69, 105, 236, 243, 256, 384, 403, 428, 429, 475, 476, 482, 487, 521, 578; **II:** 26, 55, 168, 263, 316, 371, 376, 513, 517, 520, 526, 528, 529, 530; **III:** 2, 5, 8, 9, 13–14, 17, 174, 194, 196, 278, 430, 453, **456–479,** 492, 504, 511, 523, 524, 527, 575–576, 586, 590; **IV:** 27, 28, 407, 415, 416, 433, 446; **Retro. Supp. I:** 51, 52, 55, 58, 59, 63, 82, 89, 127, 140, 171, 177, 178, 198, 216, **283–294,** 298, 299, 359, 411, 412, 413, 414, 417, 418, 419, 420, 423, 426, 427, 430, 431; **Retro. Supp. II:** 178, 183, 189, 326; **Supp. I Part 1:** 253, 255–258, 261–268, 272, 274; **Supp. I Part 2:** 387, 721; **Supp. II Part 1:** 1, 8, 20, 30, 91, 136; **Supp. III Part 1:** 48, 63, 64, 73, 105, 146, 225, 271; **Supp. III Part 2:** 542, **609–617,** 619, 620, 622, 625, 626, 628, 631; **Supp. IV Part 1:** 153, 314; **Supp. V:** 331, 338, 340, 343, 345; **Supp. VIII:** 39, 105, 195, 205, 271, 290, 291, 292, 303; **Supp. IX:** 291; **Supp. X:** 24, 36, 112, 120, 122; **Supp. XII:** 97; **Supp. XIV:** 11, 55, 83, 272, 284, 286, 287, 347; **Supp. XV:** 20, 42, 43, 51, 93, 161, 181, 297, 298, 299, 301, 302, 306; **Supp. XVI:** 47, 282; **Supp. XVII:** 111, 226–227; **Supp. XIX:** 42; **Supp. XXI:** 33; **Supp. XXII:** 165
Pound, Louise, **Retro. Supp. I:** 4; **Supp. XV:** 137
Pound, T. S., **I:** 428
"Pound Reweighed" (Cowley), **Supp. II Part 1:** 143
Powell, Anthony, **Supp. XVIII:** 136, 146; **Supp. XIX:** 131
Powell, Betty, **Retro. Supp. II:** 140
Powell, Dawn, **Supp. IV Part 2:** 678, 682; **Supp. XIX:** 143
Powell, Dick, **Supp. IX:** 250
Powell, John Wesley, **Supp. IV Part 2:** 598, 604, 611
Powell, Lawrence Clark, **III:** 189
Powell, William, **Supp. IV Part 1:** 355
"Power" (Corso), **Supp. XII:** 117, 126, 127, **128**
"Power" (Emerson), **II:** 2, 3
"Power" (Rich), **Supp. I Part 2:** 569
"Power and Light" (Dickey), **Supp. IV Part 1:** 182
Power and the Glory, The (Greene), **III:** 556
"Powerhouse" (Welty), **Retro. Supp. I:** 343, 346
"Power Never Dominion" (Rukeyser), **Supp. VI:** 281
"Power of Fancy, The" (Freneau), **Supp. II Part 1:** 255
Power of Myth, The (Campbell), **Supp. IX:** 245
"Power of Prayer, The" (Lanier), **Supp. I Part 1:** 357
"Power of Stories, The" (Sanders), **Supp. XVI:** 278
"Power of Suggestion" (Auchincloss), **Supp. IV Part 1:** 33
Power of Sympathy, The (Brown), **Supp. II Part 1:** 74
Power Politics (Atwood), **Supp. XIII:** 20, 33–34, 35
Powers, Catherine A., **Supp. XXII:** 217
Powers, J. F., **Supp. V:** 319; **Supp. XVII:** 43
Powers, Kim, **Supp. VIII:** 329, 340
Powers, Richard, **Supp. IX: 207–225; Supp. XVII:** 183; **Supp. XX: 93; Supp. XXII:** 49
Powers of Attorney (Auchincloss), **Supp. IV Part 1:** 31, 32, 33
"Powers of Darkness" (Wharton), **Retro. Supp. I:** 379
Powys, John Cowper, **Supp. I Part 2:** 454, 476; **Supp. IX:** 135
Poynton, Jerome, **Supp. XIV:** 147, 150
Pozorski, Aimee L., **Supp. XXII:** 160, 166
Practical Agitation (Chapman), **Supp. XIV:** 41
Practical Criticism: A Study of Literary Judgment (Richards), **Supp. XIV:** 3, 16
Practical Magic (film), **Supp. X:** 80
Practical Magic (Hoffman), **Supp. X:** 78, 82, **88–89**

"Practical Methods of Meditation, The" (Dawson), **IV:** 151
Practical Navigator, The (Bowditch), **Supp. I Part 2:** 482
Practice of Perspective, The (Dubreuil), **Supp. IV Part 2:** 425
Practice of Reading, The (Donoghue), **Supp. VIII:** 189
Pragmatism: A New Name for Some Old Ways of Thinking (James), **II:** 352
"Pragmatism's Conception of Truth" (James), **Supp. XIV:** 40
Prague Orgy, The (P. Roth), **Retro. Supp. II:** 280
"Praire, The" (Clampitt), **Supp. IX:** 42
"Prairie" (Sandburg), **III:** 583, 584
Prairie, The (Cooper), **I:** 339, 342
"Prairie Birthday" (Leopold), **Supp. XIV:** 185
Prairie Home Companion, A (Keillor, radio program), **Supp. XIII:** 274; **Supp. XVI:** 169–171, 173–178
Prairie Home Morning Show, A (Keillor, radio program), **Supp. XVI:** 171
"Prairie Life, A Citizen Speaks" (Dunn), **Supp. XI:** 145
"Prairies, The" (Bryant), **Supp. I Part 1:** 157, 162, 163, 166
Praise (Hass), **Supp. VI:** 104–105, 106
"Praise for an Urn" (Crane), **I:** 388
"Praise for Sick Women" (Snyder), **Supp. VIII:** 294
"Praise in Summer" (Wilbur), **Supp. III Part 2:** 546–548, 560, 562
"Praise of a Palmtree" (Levertov), **Supp. III Part 1:** 284
"Praise of the Committee" (Rukeyser), **Supp. VI:** 278
"Praises, The" (Goldbarth), **Supp. XII:** 185
"Praises, The" (Olson), **Supp. II Part 2:** 558, 560, 563, 564
Praises and Dispraises (Des Pres), **Supp. X:** 120
Praisesong for the Widow (Marshall), **Supp. IV Part 1:** 14; **Supp. XI:** 18, 276, 278, **284–286,** 287; **Supp. XX: 154**
"Praise to the End!" (Roethke), **III:** 529, 532, 539
Prajadhipok, King of Siam, **I:** 522
Prater Violet (Isherwood), **Supp. XIV: 164–166,** 169–170, 171
Pratt, Anna (Anna Alcott), **Supp. I Part 1:** 33
Pratt, Louis H., **Retro. Supp. II:** 6
Pratt, Mary Louise, **Retro. Supp. II:** 48
Pratt, Parley, **Supp. IV Part 2:** 603
"Prattler" (newspaper column), **I:** 207
"Prattler, The" (Bierce), **I:** 196
"Prayer" (Gioia), **Supp. XV:** 117
"Prayer" (Olds), **Supp. X:** 204
"Prayer" (Peacock), **Supp. XIX:** 198, 199, 200
"Prayer" (Toomer), **Supp. IX:** 318
"Prayer, A" (Kushner), **Supp. IX: 134**
"Prayer for Columbus" (Whitman), **IV:** 348
"Prayer for My Daughter" (Yeats), **II:** 598
"Prayer for My Grandfather to Our Lady, A" (Lowell), **II:** 541–542
"Prayer for my Son" (C. Frost), **Supp. XV:** 98–99
"Prayer for Our Daughters" (Jarman), **Supp. XVII:** 120
Prayer for Owen Meany, A (Irving), **Supp. VI:** 164, 165, 166, **175–176**
"PRAYER FOR SAVING" (Baraka), **Supp. II Part 1:** 52–53
"Prayer in Spring, A" (Frost), **II:** 153, 164
"Prayer Meeting" (Di Piero), **Supp. XIX:** 46, 47
"Prayer on All Saint's Day" (Cowley), **Supp. II Part 1:** 138, 153
Prayers for Dark People (Du Bois), **Supp. II Part 1:** 186
"Prayer to Hermes" (Creeley), **Supp. IV Part 1:** 156, 157
"Prayer to Masks" (Senghor), **Supp. IV Part 1:** 16
"Prayer to the Child of Prague" (Salinas), **Supp. XIII:** 327
"Prayer to the Good Poet" (Wright), **Supp. III Part 2:** 603
"Prayer to the Pacific" (Silko), **Supp. IV Part 2:** 560
"Pray without Ceasing" (Emerson), **II:** 9–10
Praz, Mario, **IV:** 430
"Preacher, The" (Whittier), **Supp. I Part 2:** 698–699
Preacher and the Slave, The (Stegner), **Supp. IV Part 2:** 599, 608, 609
Precaution (Cooper), **I:** 337, 339
"Preconceptions of Economic Science, The" (Veblen), **Supp. I Part 2:** 634
Predecessors, Et Cetera (Clampitt), **Supp. IX:** 37
"Predicament, A" (Poe), **Retro. Supp. II:** 273
Predilections (Moore), **III:** 194
Prefaces and Prejudices (Mencken), **III:** 99, 104, 106, 119
Preface to a Twenty Volume Suicide Note. . . . (Baraka), **Supp. II Part 1:** 31, 33–34, 51, 61
"Preference" (Wylie), **Supp. I Part 2:** 713
"Prejudice against the Past, The" (Moore), **IV:** 91
Prejudices (Mencken), **Supp. I Part 2:** 630
Prejudices: A Selection (Farrell, ed.), **III:** 116
Prejudices: First Series (Mencken), **III:** 105
"Preliminary Remarks on the Poetry in the First Person" (Wright), **Supp. XV:** 339
Prelude, A: Landscapes, Characters and Conversations from the Earlier Years of My Life (Wilson), **IV:** 426, 427, 430, 434, 445
Prelude, The (Wordsworth), **III:** 528; **IV:** 331, 343; **Supp. I Part 2:** 416, 676; **Supp. XI:** 248
Prelude and Liebestod (McNally), **Supp. XIII:** 201
"Preludes" (Eliot), **I:** 573, 576, 577; **Retro. Supp. I:** 55; **Supp. IV Part 2:** 436
Preludes for Memnon (Aiken), **I:** 59, 65
Preludes from Memnon (Aiken), **Supp. X:** 50
"Prelude to an Evening" (Ransom), **III:** 491, 492–493
Prelude to Darkness (Salinas), **Supp. XIII:** 311, **318–319,** 320
"Prelude to the Present" (Mumford), **Supp. II Part 2:** 471
"Premature Burial, The" (Poe), **III:** 415, 416, 418; **Retro. Supp. II:** 270
Preminger, Otto, **Supp. IX:** 3, 9; **Supp. XX: 246–247**
"Premonition" (Hay), **Supp. XIV:** 122
"Premonitions of the Bread Line" (Komunyakaa), **Supp. XIII:** 114, 115
Prenshaw, Peggy Whitman, **Supp. X:** 229
"Preparations" (Silko), **Supp. IV Part 2:** 560
Preparatory Meditations (Taylor), **IV:** 145, 148, 149, 150, 152, 153, 154–155, 164, 165
"Prepare" (Carruth), **Supp. XVI:** 59
Prepositions: The Collected Critical Essays of Louis Zukofsky (Zukofsky), **Supp. III Part 2:** 630
Prescott, Anne, **Supp. IV Part 1:** 299
Prescott, Orville, **Supp. IV Part 2:** 680; **Supp. XI:** 340
Prescott, Peter, **Supp. X:** 83
Prescott, Peter S., **Supp. XVI:** 212
Prescott, William, **Retro. Supp. I:** 123
Prescott, William Hickling, **II:** 9, 310, 313–314; **IV:** 309; **Supp. I Part 2:** 414, 479, 493, 494
"Prescription of Painful Ends" (Jeffers), **Supp. II Part 2:** 424
"Presence, The" (Gordon), **II:** 199, 200
"Presence, The" (Kumin), **Supp. IV Part 2:** 445, 455
Presence and Desire: Essays on Gender, Sexuality, Performance (Dolan), **Supp. XV:** 327
"Presence of Others, The" (Kenyon), **Supp. VII:** 164
Presences (Taylor), **Supp. V:** 325
"Present Age, The" (Emerson), **II:** 11–12
Present Danger, The: Do We Have the Will to Reverse the Decline of American Power? (Podhoretz), **Supp. VIII:** 241
"Present for the Boy, A" (Swados), **Supp. XIX:** 259
Present for Young Ladies, A (Rowson), **Supp. XV:** 245
"Present Hour" (Sandburg), **III:** 593–594
Present Philosophical Tendencies (Perry), **I:** 224
"Present State of Ethical Philosophy, The" (Emerson), **II:** 9
"Present State of Poetry, The" (Schwartz), **Supp. II Part 2:** 666
"Preservation of Innocence" (Baldwin), **Supp. I Part 1:** 51
"Preserving Wildness" (Berry), **Supp. X:** 28, 29, 32

"President and Other Intellectuals, The" (Kazin), **Supp. VIII:** 104
Presidential Papers, The (Mailer), **III:** 35, 37–38, 42, 45; **Retro. Supp. II:** 203, 204, 206
"Presidents" (Merwin), **Supp. III Part 1:** 351
Presnell, Robert, Sr., **Supp. XIII:** 166
Pressley, Nelson, **Supp. XVIII:** 37–38
"PRES SPOKE IN A LANGUAGE" (Baraka), **Supp. II Part 1:** 60
Presumed Innocent (Turow), **Supp. XVII:** 214–216, 223; 217
"Pretext, The" (Wharton), **Retro. Supp. I:** 371
Pretty Baby (film), **Supp. XXI:** 252
Pretty Boy Floyd (McMurtry), **Supp. V:** 231
"Pretty Girl, The" (Dubus), **Supp. VII:** 87–88
"Pretty Mouth and Green My Eyes" (Salinger), **III:** 560
"Previous Condition" (Baldwin), **Supp. I Part 1:** 51, 55, 63
"Previous Tenant, The" (Simpson), **Supp. IX:** 278–279
Prevost, Verbie Lovorn, **Supp. XXI:** 45
Priaulx, Allan, **Supp. XI:** 228
Price, Alan, **Retro. Supp. I:** 377
Price, Reynolds, **Supp. VI: 253–270; Supp. IX:** 256, 257
Price, Richard, **II:** 9; **Supp. I Part 2:** 522; **Supp. XX: 85**
Price, The (A. Miller), **III:** 165–166
"Price Is Right, The" (Skloot), **Supp. XX: 198–199**
"Price of the Harness, The" (Crane), **I:** 414
Pricksongs & Descants; Fictions (Coover), **Supp. V:** 39, 42, 43, 49, 50
"Pride" (Hughes), **Supp. I Part 1:** 331
Pride and Prejudice (Austen), **II:** 290
Prideaux, Tom, **Supp. IV Part 2:** 574, 590
"Priesthood, The" (Winters), **Supp. II Part 2:** 786
Priestly, Joseph, **Supp. I Part 2:** 522
Primary Colors, The (A. Theroux), **Supp. VIII:** 312
"Primary Ground, A" (Rich), **Supp. I Part 2:** 563
"Prime" (Auden), **Supp. II Part 1:** 22
"Primer Class" (Bishop), **Retro. Supp. II:** 38, 51
Primer for Blacks (Brooks), **Supp. III Part 1:** 85
"Primer for the Nuclear Age" (Dove), **Supp. IV Part 1:** 246
Primer mensaje a la América Hispana (W. Frank), **Supp. XX: 76**
Primer of Ignorance, A (Blackmur), **Supp. II Part 1:** 91
Prime-Stevenson, Edward Irenaeus, **Supp. XX: 235**
Primitive, The (C. Himes), **Supp. XVI:** 139, **141–142**
"Primitive Black Man, The" (Du Bois), **Supp. II Part 1:** 176
"Primitive Like an Orb, A" (Stevens), **IV:** 89; **Retro. Supp. I:** 309
Primitive People (Prose), **Supp. XVI:** 255, 256, 257
"Primitive Singing" (Lindsay), **Supp. I Part 2:** 389–390
Primitivism and Decadence (Winters), **Supp. II Part 2:** 786, 803–807, 812
Primrose, Archibald Philip, **Supp. XX: 230**
Prince, Richard, **Supp. XII:** 4
"Prince, The" (Jarrell), **II:** 379
"Prince, The" (Winters), **Supp. II Part 2:** 802
Prince and the Pauper, The (Twain), **IV:** 200–201, 206
Prince Hagen (Sinclair), **Supp. V:** 280
Prince of a Fellow, A (Hearon), **Supp. VIII:** 58, **62–63**
Princess, The (Tennyson), **Supp. I Part 2:** 410
Princess and the Goblins, The (Macdonald), **Supp. XIII:** 75
Princess Casamassima, The (James), **II:** 276, 291; **IV:** 202; **Retro. Supp. I:** 216, 221, 222, 225, **226–227**
"Princess Casamassima, The" (Trilling), **Supp. III Part 2:** 502, 503
Princess of Arcady, A (Henry), **Retro. Supp. II:** 97
"Principles" (Du Bois), **Supp. II Part 1:** 172
Principles of Literary Criticism (Richards), **I:** 274; **Supp. I Part 1:** 264; **Supp. XIV:** 3
Principles of Psychology, The (James), **II:** 321, 350–352, 353, 354, 357, 362, 363–364; **IV:** 28, 29, 32, 37
Principles of Psychology, The (W. James), **Supp. XVII:** 97
Principles of Zoölogy (Agassiz), **Supp. I Part 1:** 312
Prior, Sir James, **II:** 315
Prior, Matthew, **II:** 111; **III:** 521
"Prison, The" (Malamud), **Supp. I Part 2:** 431, 437
"Prisoned Love" (Boyce), **Supp. XXI:** 9
"Prisoner of Ours, The" (Weigl), **Supp. XIX:** 288
Prisoner of Second Avenue, The (Simon), **Supp. IV Part 2:** 583, 584
Prisoner of Sex, The (Mailer), **III:** 46; **Retro. Supp. II:** 206
Prisoner of Zenda, The (film), **Supp. I Part 2:** 615
Prisoner's Dilemma (Powers), **Supp. IX:** 212, **214–216,** 221
Prison Memoirs of an Anarchist (A. Berkman), **Supp. XVII:** 103–104
Pritchard, William, **Supp. XVI:** 71
Pritchard, William H., **Retro. Supp. I:** 131, 141; **Supp. IV Part 1:** 285; **Supp. IV Part 2:** 642; **Supp. XI:** 326
Pritchett, V. S., **II:** 587; **Supp. II Part 1:** 143; **Supp. VIII:** 171; **Supp. XIII:** 168
"Privatation and Publication" (Cowley), **Supp. II Part 1:** 149
Private Contentment (Price), **Supp. VI:** 263
"Private History of a Campaign That Failed" (Twain), **IV:** 195
Private I, The: Privacy in a Public World (Peacock, ed.), **Supp. XIX:** 193, 203
Private Life of Axie Reed, The (Knowles), **Supp. XII:** 249
Private Line (Major), **Supp. XXII:** 174
"Private Man Confronts His Vulgarities at Dawn, A" (Dunn), **Supp. XI:** 146
Private Memoirs and Confessions of a Justified Sinner, The (Hogg), **Supp. IX:** 276
"Private Property and the Common Wealth" (Berry), **Supp. X:** 25
Private Snafu series (Geisel), **Supp. XVI:** 102
"Private Theatricals" (Howells), **II:** 280
Private Women, Public Stage: Literary Domesticity in Nineteenth-Century America (Kelley), **Supp. XVIII:** 257
Privilege, The (Kumin), **Supp. IV Part 2:** 442–444, 451
Prize Stories 1918 : The O. Henry Awards, **Supp. XVI:** 16
"Probe" (Ryan as Quin), **Supp. XVIII:** 229
"Probing the Dark" (Komunyakaa), **Supp. XIII:** 131
"Problem from Milton, A" (Wilbur), **Supp. III Part 2:** 550
"Problem of Anxiety, The" (Koch), **Supp. XV:** 183
"Problem of Being, The" (James), **II:** 360
Problem of Classification in the Theory of Value, The (Locke), **Supp. XIV:** 199
"Problem of Evil into Cocoon" (Taggard), **Supp. XXII:** 284
"Problem of Housing the Negro, The" (Du Bois), **Supp. II Part 1:** 168
"Problem of the Religious Novel, The" (Isherwood), **Supp. XIV:** 172
Problems and Other Stories (Updike), **Retro. Supp. I:** 322, 329
Problems of Dostoevsky's Poetics (Bakhtin), **Supp. XXII:** 259
"Problem Solving" (Goldbarth), **Supp. XII:** 185
Procedures for Underground (Atwood), **Supp. XIII:** 33
"Procedures for Underground" (Atwood), **Supp. XIII:** 33
Procession, The (al-Mawákib) (Gibran), **Supp. XX: 116, 124**
Processional (Lawson), **I:** 479
"Procession at Candlemas, A" (Clampitt), **Supp. IX:** 41
"Proclamation" (Saunders), **Supp. XIX:** 235
Proclus, **Retro. Supp. I:** 247
"Prodigal" (Ammons), **Supp. VII:** 29
"Prodigal" (Hoffman), **Supp. XVIII:** 86
"Prodigal, The" (Bishop), **Supp. I Part 1:** 90, 92
Prodigal Parents, The (Lewis), **II:** 454–455
"Prodigy" (Simic), **Supp. VIII:** 278
Producers, The (film, M. Brooks), **Supp. XVII:** 45
"Proem" (Crane), **I:** 397
"Proem, The: By the Carpenter" (O. Henry), **Supp. II Part 1:** 409

"Professions for Women" (Woolf), **Supp. XIII:** 305
"Professor" (Hughes), **Supp. I Part 1:** 330
"Professor, The" (Bourne), **I:** 223
Professor at the Breakfast Table, The (Holmes), **Supp. I Part 1:** 313, 316
"Professor Clark's Economics" (Veblen), **Supp. I Part 2:** 634
Professor of Desire, The (P. Roth), **Retro. Supp. II:** 288; **Supp. III Part 2:** 403, 418–420
Professor's House, The (Cather), **I:** 325–336; **Retro. Supp. I:** 16
"Professor Veblen" (Mencken), **Supp. I Part 2:** 630
Proffer, Carl R., **Supp. VIII:** 22
Profile Makers, The (Bierds), **Supp. XVII:** 29, **30–32,** 33
"Profile of the Tenderloin Street Prostitute, A" (Vollmann), **Supp. XVII:** 230
Profits of Religion, The (Sinclair), **Supp. V:** 276
"Prognosis" (Warren), **IV:** 245
"Progress" (F. Wright), **Supp. XVII:** 247
"Progress Report" (Simic), **Supp. VIII:** 278
"Project for a Trip to China" (Sontag), **Supp. II Part 2:** 454, 469
"Project for *The Ambassadors*" (James), **Retro. Supp. I:** 229
"Projection" (Nemerov), **III:** 275
"Projective Verse" (Olson), **Supp. III Part 1:** 30; **Supp. III Part 2:** 555, 556, 557, 624; **Supp. IV Part 1:** 139, 153; **Supp. VIII:** 290
"Projector, The" (Baker), **Supp. XIII:** 53, 55
Prokofiev, Sergey Sergeyevich, **Supp. IV Part 1:** 81
"Prolegomena, Section 1" (Pound), **Supp. III Part 2:** 615–616
"Prolegomena, Section 2" (Pound), **Supp. III Part 2:** 616
"Prolegomenon to a Biography of Mailer" (Lucid), **Retro. Supp. II:** 195
Proletarian Literature in the United States (Hicks), **Supp. I Part 2: 609–610**
"Prologue" (MacLeish), **III:** 8, 14
Prologue, for Full Chorus of Mixed Voices and Orchestra (Taggard and Schuman), **Supp. XXII:** 283
"Prologue to a Life" (D. West), **Supp. XVIII:** 280
"Prologue to Our Time" (Mumford), **Supp. III Part 2:** 473
"Prometheus" (Longfellow), **II:** 494
Prometheus Bound (Lowell), **II:** 543, 544, 545, 555
Promise, The (Buck), **Supp. II Part 1:** 124
"Promise, The" (Olds), **Supp. X:** 213
"Promise and Fulfillment" (D. West), **Supp. XVIII:** 278
Promised Land (Parker), **Supp. XIX:** 183, 184, 190
Promised Land, The (M. Antin), **Supp. IX:** 227; **Supp. XVI:** 148, 149; **Supp. XX:** 1, 2, 3, **4–9,** 11
Promised Land, The (Porter), **III:** 447
"Promised Land, The" (R. Fisher), **Supp. XIX:** 72
Promised Lands (Sontag), **Supp. III Part 2:** 452
Promise of American Life, The (Croly), **I:** 229
"Promise of Blue Horses, The" (Harjo), **Supp. XII:** 228
Promise of Rest, The (Price), **Supp. VI:** 262, 266
Promises (Warren), **Supp. XIV:** 15
Promises, Promises (musical), **Supp. IV Part 2:** 575
Promises: Poems 1954–1956 (Warren), **IV:** 244–245, 249, 252
"Promise This When You Be Dying" (Dickinson), **Retro. Supp. I:** 44, 46
Proof, The (Winters), **Supp. II Part 2:** 786, 791, 792–794
Proofs and Theories: Essays on Poetry (Glück), **Supp. V:** 77, 79, 92; **Supp. XIV:** 269
"Propaganda of History, The" (Du Bois), **Supp. II Part 1:** 182
Propertius, Sextus, **III:** 467; **Retro. Supp. II:** 187; **Supp. XII:** 2
Property Of: A Novel (Hoffman), **Supp. X:** 77, 79, **80–82**
"Property of Loss" (W. V. Davis), **Supp. XXI:** 95
"Prophecy of Samuel Sewall, The" (Whittier), **Supp. I Part 2:** 699
Prophet, The (Gibran), **Supp. XX: 113, 115, 119–121, 126**
"Prophet, The" (Notley), **Supp. XXII:** 229
"Prophet and the Child, The" (Gibran), **Supp. XX: 123**
Propheteers, The (Apple), **Supp. XVII: 6–7**
"Prophetic Pictures, The" (Hawthorne), **II:** 227
"Proportion" (Lowell), **II:** 525
"Proposal" (Carver), **Supp. III Part 1:** 149
Proposals Relating to the Education of Youth in Pensilvania (Franklin), **II:** 113
"Proposed New Version of the Bible" (Franklin), **II:** 110
Prose, Francine, **Supp. XII:** 333; **Supp. XVI: 249–264; Supp. XIX:** 209
"Prose for Departure" (Merrill), **Supp. III Part 1:** 336
Prose Pieces (Bynner), **Supp. XV:** 52
"Prose Poem as an Evolving Form, The" (R. Bly), **Supp. IV Part 1:** 64
"Proserpina and the Devil" (Wilder), **IV:** 358
"Prosody" (Espaillat), **Supp. XXI:** 102
"Prosody" (Shapiro), **Supp. II Part 2:** 710
Prospect before Us, The (Dos Passos), **I:** 491
"Prospective Immigrants Please Note" (Rich), **Supp. I Part 2:** 555
Prospect of Peace, The (Barlow), **Supp. II Part 1:** 67, 68, 75
Prospects of Literature, The (L. P. Smith), **Supp. XIV:** 343
Prospects on the Rubicon (Paine), **Supp. I Part 2:** 510–511
Prospectus of a National Institution, to Be Established in the United States (Barlow), **Supp. II Part 1:** 80, 82
Prospice (Browning), **IV:** 366
"Protestant Easter" (Sexton), **Supp. II Part 2:** 684
"Prothalamion" (Schwartz), **Supp. II Part 2:** 649, 652
"Prothalamion" (Spenser), **Retro. Supp. I:** 62
Proud, Robert, **Supp. I Part 1:** 125
"Proud Farmer, The" (Lindsay), **Supp. I Part 2:** 381
Proud Flesh (Humphrey), **Supp. IX:** 94, 95, 96, **102–103,** 104, 105, 109
"Proud Flesh" (Warren), **IV:** 243
Proud Lady (Boyce), **Supp. XXI:** 7, 12
"Proud Lady" (Wylie), **Supp. I Part 2:** 711–712
Proulx, Annie, **Supp. VII: 249–267**
Proust, Marcel, **I:** 89, 319, 327, 377, 461; **II:** 377, 514, 606; **III:** 174, 181, 184, 244–245, 259, 471; **IV:** 32, 201, 237, 301, 312, 328, 359, 428, 431, 434, 439, 443, 466, 467; **Retro. Supp. I:** 75, 89, 169, 335; **Supp. III Part 1:** 10, 12, 14, 15; **Supp. IV Part 2:** 600; **Supp. VIII:** 103; **Supp. IX:** 211; **Supp. X:** 193, 194; **Supp. XII:** 289; **Supp. XIV:** 24, 83, 95; **Supp. XVI:** 295; **Supp. XXI:** 231
Proverbs, **Supp. X:** 45
"Proverbs" (Jarman), **Supp. XVII:** 118
"Providence" (Komunyakaa), **Supp. XIII:** 132
"Provident Woman, A" (Boyce), **Supp. XXI:** 10
"Provincetown Postcards" (F. Wright), **Supp. XVII:** 244
"Provincia deserta" (Pound), **Retro. Supp. I:** 289
"Provisional Remarks on Being / A Poet / of Arkansas" (Wright), **Supp. XV:** 337
Pruette, Lorine, **Supp. IV Part 2:** 522
Prufrock and Other Observations (Eliot), **I:** 569–570, 571, 573, 574, 576–577, 583, 584, 585; **Retro. Supp. I:** 59, 62
"Prufrock's Perivigilium" (T. S. Eliot), **Retro. Supp. I:** 57
Pryor, Richard, **Supp. XIII:** 343
Pryse, Marjorie, **Retro. Supp. II:** 139, 146
"Psalm" (Ginsberg), **Supp. II Part 1:** 312
"Psalm" (Simic), **Supp. VIII:** 282
"Psalm and Lament" (Justice), **Supp. VII:** 116, 117–118, 120–122, 124
"Psalm for Pinhook" (Ray), **Supp. XVIII:** 202
"Psalm of Life, A" (Longfellow), **II:** 489, 496; **Retro. Supp. II:** 164, 168, 169; **Supp. I Part 2:** 409
"Psalm of the West" (Lanier), **Supp. I Part 1:** 362, 364
"Psalm: Our Fathers" (Merwin), **Supp. III Part 1:** 350

Psalms (biblical book), **I:** 83; **II:** 168, 232; **Retro. Supp. I:** 62; **Supp. I Part 1:** 125
Psalms, Hymns, and Spiritual Songs of the Rev. Isaac Watts, The (Worcester, ed.), **I:** 458
Psychiatric Novels of Oliver Wendell Holmes, The (Oberndorf), **Supp. I Part 1:** 315
"Psychology and Form" (Burke), **I:** 270
Psychology: Briefer Course (James), **II:** 351–352
Psychology of Art (Malraux), **IV:** 434
Psychology of Insanity, The (Hart), **I:** 241–242, 248–250
Psychopathia Sexualis (Shanley), **Supp. XIV:** 316, **329**
Psychophysiks (Fechner), **II:** 358
"Pu-239" (Kalfus), **Supp. XVII:** 50
"Publication is the Auction" (Dickinson), **Retro. Supp. I:** 31
"Public Bath, The" (Snyder), **Supp. VIII:** 298
Public Burning, The (Coover), **Supp. IV Part 1:** 388; **Supp. V:** 44, 45, 46–47, 48, 51, 52; **Supp. XVII:** 6
"Public Burning of Julius and Ethel Rosenberg, The: An Historical Romance" (Coover), **Supp. V:** 44
"Public Figure" (Hay), **Supp. XIV:** 124
"Public Garden, The" (Lowell), **II:** 550
Public Good (Paine), **Supp. I Part 2:** 509–510
Public Poetry of Robert Lowell, The (Cosgrave), **Retro. Supp. II:** 185
"Public & Private" (column, Quindlen), **Supp. XVII:** 165, 167, 169–170
Public Speech: Poems (MacLeish), **III:** 15–16
Public Spirit (Savage), **II:** 111
"Public Woman, A" (Cliff), **Supp. XXII:** 76
Puccini, Giacomo, **Supp. XXI:** 150, 151
"Puck" (Monette), **Supp. X:** 157–158
Pudd'nhead Wilson (Twain), **I:** 197
"Pudd'nhead Wilson's Calendar" (Twain), **I:** 197
"Pueblo Revolt, The" (Sando), **Supp. IV Part 2:** 510
Puella (Dickey), **Supp. IV Part 1:** 178, 185
Pulitzer, Alfred, **Retro. Supp. I:** 257
Pull Down Vanity (Fiedler), **Supp. XIII:** 103
Pullman, George, **Supp. I Part 1:** 9
"Pullman Car Hiawatha" (Wilder), **IV:** 365–366
Pull My Daisy (film), **Supp. XII:** 126–127
"Pulp Cutters' Nativity, A" (Budbill), **Supp. XIX:** 9
"Pulpit and the Pew, The" (Holmes), **Supp. I Part 1:** 302
"Pulse-Beats and Pen-Strokes" (Sandburg), **III:** 579
"Pump, The" (Humphrey), **Supp. IX:** 101
Pump House Gang, The (Wolfe), **Supp. III Part 2:** 575, 578, 580, 581
Punch, Brothers, Punch and Other Sketches (Twain), **IV:** 200
Punch: The Immortal Liar, Documents in His History (Aiken), **I:** 57, 61
Punishment Without Vengeance (Vega; Merwin, trans.), **Supp. III Part 1:** 341, 347
"Pupil" (F. Barthelme), **Supp. XI:** 26
"Pupil, The" (H. James), **Supp. XX: 233**
"Pupil, The" (James), **II:** 331; **Retro. Supp. I:** 217, 219, 228
"Purchase" (Banks), **Supp. V:** 6
"Purchase of Some Golf Clubs, A" (O'Hara), **III:** 369
"Purdah" (Plath), **Supp. I Part 2:** 602
Purdy, Charles, **Supp. VIII:** 330
Purdy, James, **Supp. VII: 269–285**
Purdy, Theodore, **Supp. VIII:** 153
Pure (C. Frost), **Supp. XV:** 93, **101–102,** 104, 106
"Pure" (C. Frost), **Supp. XV:** 101–102
"Pure and the Good, The: On Baseball and Backpaking" (Maclean), **Supp. XIV:** 222
"Pure Good of Theory, The" (Stevens), **Retro. Supp. I:** 310
Purgatorio (Dante), **III:** 182
"Purim Parade" (Espaillat), **Supp. XXI:** 108
Puritan Family (Morgan), **Supp. I Part 1:** 101
"Puritanical Pleasures" (Hardwick), **Supp. III Part 1:** 213–214
Puritan Origins of the American Self, The (Bercovitch), **Supp. I Part 1:** 99
Puritan Pronaos, The: Studies in the Intellectual Life of New England in the Seventeenth Century (Morison), **Supp. I Part 2:** 485
"Puritan Realism: *The Wide, Wide World* and *Robinson Crusoe*" (Kim), **Supp. XVIII:** 267
Puritans, The (P. Miller), **Supp. VIII:** 101
"Puritan's Ballad, The" (Wylie), **Supp. I Part 2:** 723
"Purloined Letter, The" (Poe), **Retro. Supp. II:** 271, 272
Purple Cane Road (Burke), **Supp. XIV:** 32, 33
Purple Decades, The (Wolfe), **Supp. III Part 2:** 584
"Purple Hat, The" (Welty), **IV:** 264
Purple Rose of Cairo, The (film; Allen), **Supp. XV:** 1, **9–10,** 12, 14
Purser, John T., **Supp. XIV:** 4
"Pursuit of Happiness" (Simpson), **Supp. IX:** 279
"Pursuit of Happiness, The" (Ashbery), **Supp. III Part 1:** 23
Pursuit of the Prodigal, The (Auchincloss), **Supp. IV Part 1:** 25
Pushcart at the Curb, A (Dos Passos), **I:** 478, 479
"Pushcart Man" (Hughes), **Supp. I Part 1:** 330
Pushcart Prize, XIII, The (Ford), **Supp. V:** 58
Pushcart Prize VII, The (Hendeson, ed.), **Supp. XVII:** 16
Pushcart Prize XIV, The (Henderson, ed.), **Supp. XVII:** 18
Pushcart Prize XX, The (Henderson, ed.), **Supp. XVII:** 20
"Pushing 100" (Mora), **Supp. XIII:** 215
Pushkin, Aleksander, **III:** 246, 261, 262; **Retro. Supp. I:** 266, 269; **Supp. XVI:** 188
Pussy, King of the Pirates (Acker), **Supp. XII:** 6–7
"Pussycat and the Expert Plumber Who Was a Man, The" (A. Miller), **III:** 146–147
Pussycat Fever (Acker), **Supp. XII:** 6
Putnam, George Haven, **Supp. XVIII:** 257, 260
Putnam, George P., **II:** 314; **Supp. XVIII:** 3–4, 14, 260
Putnam, Phelps, **I:** 288
Putnam, Samuel, **II:** 26; **III:** 479; **Supp. III Part 2:** 615
"Put Off the Wedding Five Times and Nobody Comes to It" (Sandburg), **III:** 586–587
Puttenham, George, **Supp. I Part 1:** 113
Puttermesser Papers, The (Ozick), **Supp. V:** 269
"Putting a Burden Down" (Peacock), **Supp. XIX:** 199
"Putting on *Visit to a Small Planet*" (Vidal), **Supp. IV Part 2:** 683
Put Yourself in My Shoes (Carver), **Supp. III Part 1:** 139
"Put Yourself in My Shoes" (Carver), **Supp. III Part 1:** 139, 141
Putzi, Jennifer, **Supp. XV:** 284
Puzo, Mario, **Supp. IV Part 1:** 390
"Puzzle of Modern Society, The" (Kazin), **Supp. VIII:** 103
Pygmalion (Shaw), **Supp. XII:** 14
Pyle, Ernie, **III:** 148; **Supp. V:** 240; **Supp. XVII:** 61
Pylon (Faulkner), **II:** 64–65, 73; **Retro. Supp. I:** 84, 85
Pynchon, Thomas, **III:** 258; **Retro. Supp. I:** 278; **Retro. Supp. II:** 279, 324; **Supp. II Part 2:** 557, **617–638; Supp. III Part 1:** 217; **Supp. IV Part 1:** 53, 279; **Supp. IV Part 2:** 570; **Supp. V:** 40, 44, 52; **Supp. VIII:** 14; **Supp. IX:** 207, 208, 212; **Supp. X:** 260, 301, 302; **Supp. XI:** 103; **Supp. XII:** 289; **Supp. XIV:** 49, 53, 54, 96; **Supp. XVI:** 123, 128; **Supp. XVII:** 183, 225, 232, 236; **Supp. XIX:** 223; **Supp. XX: 21, 83, 87**
Pyne, John, **Supp. XXI:** 7
Pyne, Mary, **Supp. XXI:** 7
Pyrah, Gill, **Supp. V:** 126
"Pyramid Club, The" (Doctorow), **Supp. IV Part 1:** 234
"Pyrography" (Ashbery), **Supp. III Part 1:** 18
Pythagoras, **I:** 332
Pythagorean Silence (Howe), **Supp. IV Part 2:** 426, 428–429

QBVII (television movie), **Supp. XX: 247**
QBVII (Uris), **Supp. XX: 244, 247, 248, 251, 253–254**

"Qebehseneuf" (Goldbarth), **Supp. XII:** 186
"Quadroons, The" (Child), **Supp. XVIII:** 124
"Quai d'Orléans" (Bishop), **Supp. I Part 1:** 89
"Quail for Mr. Forester" (Humphrey), **Supp. IX:** 94
"Quail in Autumn" (W. J. Smith), **Supp. XIII:** 334–335, 339
"Quaker Graveyard in Nantucket, The" (Lowell), **II:** 54, 550; **Retro. Supp. II:** 178, 186–187
"Quake Theory" (Olds), **Supp. X:** 203
Qualey, Carlton C., **Supp. I Part 2:** 650
Quality of Hurt, The (C. Himes), **Supp. XVI:** 137, 145
"Quality of Wine" (Carruth), **Supp. XVI:** 59
"Quality Time" (Kingsolver), **Supp. VII:** 203
"Quandary" (F. Wright), **Supp. XVII:** 244
Quang-Ngau-chè, **III:** 473
Quarles, Francis, **I:** 178, 179
"Quarrel" (Taggard), **Supp. XXII:** 276
Quarry, The (Chesnutt), **Supp. XIV:** 76
"Quarry, The" (Nemerov), **III:** 272
Quarry, The: New Poems (Eberhart), **I:** 532, 539
Quartermain, Peter, **Supp. IV Part 2:** 423, 434
Quatermain, Peter, **Supp. XXII:** 163
"Quaternions, The" (Bradstreet), **Supp. I Part 1:** 104–106, 114, 122
"Quatrains for Ishi" (Komunyakaa), **Supp. XIII:** 129
Queechy (S. Warner as Wetherell), **Supp. XVIII:** 257, **264–266**
"Queen Elizabeth and the Blind Girl or Music for the Dead Children" (B. Kelly), **Supp. XVII:** 124, 125
"Queen of the Blues" (Brooks), **Supp. III Part 1:** 75
Queen of the Damned, The (Rice), **Supp. VII:** 290, 292–293, 297, 299
Queen of the Mob (film), **Supp. XIII:** 170
"Queens of France" (Wilder), **IV:** 365
"Queen's Twin, The" (Jewett), **Retro. Supp. II:** 138
Queen's Twin, The, and Other Stories (Jewett), **Retro. Supp. II:** 140
Queen Victoria (Strachey), **Supp. I Part 2:** 485, 494; **Supp. XIV:** 342
Queer (Burroughs), **Supp. III Part 1:** 93–102
"Queer Beer" (Hansberry), **Supp. IV Part 1:** 374
"Quelques considérations sur la méthode subjective" (James), **II:** 345–346
"Quest, The" (Gibran), **Supp. XX: 124**
"Question" (Swenson), **Supp. IV Part 2:** 640
"Question and Answer" (Hughes), **Retro. Supp. I:** 211
"Questioning Faces" (Frost), **Retro. Supp. I:** 141
"Question Mark in the Circle, The" (Stegner), **Supp. IV Part 2:** 597
"Questionnaire, The" (Snodgrass), **Supp. VI:** 318
"Question of Fidelity, A" (Beauvoir), **Supp. IX:** 4
"Question of Loneliness, A" (Swados), **Supp. XIX:** 262
"Question of Our Speech, The" (Ozick), **Supp. V:** 272
"Question of Simone de Beauvoir, The" (Algren), **Supp. IX:** 4
Questions About Angels (Collins), **Supp. XXI:** 54, 58, 59, 60, 64
Questions for Ecclesiastes (Jarman), **Supp. XVII:** 109, 110, **118–119**
"Questions of Geography" (Hollander), **Supp. I Part 1:** 96
Questions of Travel (Bishop), **Retro. Supp. II: 46–48; Supp. I Part 1:** 72, 83, 92, 94
"Questions of Travel" (Bishop), **Retro. Supp. II:** 47
"Questions to Tourists Stopped by a Pineapple Field" (Merwin), **Supp. III Part 1:** 355
"Questions without Answers" (T. Williams), **IV:** 384
"Quest of the Purple-Fringed, The" (Frost), **Retro. Supp. I:** 139
Quest of the Silver Fleece, The (Du Bois), **Supp. II Part 1:** 176–178
Quevedo y Villegas, Francisco Gómez, **Retro. Supp. I:** 423
Quickly: A Column for Slow Readers (Mailer), **Retro. Supp. II:** 202
Quicksand (Larsen), **Supp. XVIII:** 119, 121, 122, **124–127**
Quicksand and Passing (Larsen; McDowell, ed.), **Supp. XVIII:** 125
"Quies," (Pound), **Retro. Supp. I:** 413
Quiet American, The (Greene), **Supp. XIX:** 29
"Quiet and clear" (Kooser), **Supp. XIX:** 125
Quiet City (Shaw), **Supp. XIX:** 244
Quiet Days in Clichy (H. Miller), **III:** 170, 178, 183–184, 187
"Quiet Desperation" (Simpson), **Supp. IX:** 277–278
"Quiet Light, A" (Skloot), **Supp. XX: 203**
"Quiet of the Mind" (Nye), **Supp. XIII:** 284
"Quiet Woman, The" (Taggard), **Supp. XXII:** 274
"QUILLA" (Trethewey), **Supp. XXI:** 246
"Quilting" (D. West), **Supp. XVIII:** 283
Quin, Mike (pseudonym). *See* Ryan, Paul William
Quincy, Edmund, **Supp. XVIII:** 4
Quindlen, Anna, **Supp. XVI:** 108; **Supp. XVII: 165–181**
Quinlan, Kathleen, **Supp. X:** 80
Quinn, Anthony, **Supp. XXI:** 46
Quinn, John, **III:** 471
Quinn, Paul, **Supp. V:** 71
Quinn, Sister M. Bernetta, **III:** 479; **IV:** 421
Quinn, Vincent, **I:** 386, 401, 402; **Supp. I Part 1:** 270
"Quinnapoxet" (Kunitz), **Supp. III Part 1:** 263
Quinn's Book (W. Kennedy), **Supp. VII:** 133, 148–150, 153
Quintero, José, **III:** 403
Quintilian, **IV:** 123
Quinzaine for This Yule, A (Pound), **Retro. Supp. I:** 285
Quite Contrary: The Mary and Newt Story (Dixon), **Supp. XII: 144,** 153
Quod Erat Demonstrandum (Stein), **IV:** 34
Quo Vadis? (Sienkiewicz), **Supp. IV Part 2:** 518; **Supp. XVI:** 182

Raab, Max, **Supp. XI:** 309
"Rabbi, The" (Hayden), **Supp. II Part 1:** 363, 369
Rabbit, Run (Updike), **IV:** 214, 223, 230–234; **Retro. Supp. I:** 320, 325, 326, 327, 331, 333, 335; **Supp. XI:** 140; **Supp. XII:** 298; **Supp. XVI:** 220
"Rabbit, The" (Barnes), **Supp. III Part 1:** 34
Rabbit at Rest (Updike), **Retro. Supp. I:** 334
Rabbit Factory, The (L. Brown), **Supp. XXI:** 40, **47–48**
"*Rabbit Factory, The:* Escaping the Isolation of the Cage" (Gaughran), **Supp. XXI:** 47–48
Rabbit Is Rich (Updike), **Retro. Supp. I:** 334
Rabbit novels (Updike), **Supp. V:** 269
Rabbit Redux (Updike), **IV:** 214; **Retro. Supp. I:** 332, 333
Rabbit's Umbrella, The (Plimpton), **Supp. XVI:** 244
"Rabbits Who Caused All the Trouble, The" (Thurber), **Supp. I Part 2:** 610
Rabelais, and His World (Bakhtin), **Retro. Supp. II:** 273
Rabelais, François, **I:** 130; **II:** 111, 112, 302, 535; **III:** 77, 78, 174, 182; **IV:** 68; **Supp. I Part 2:** 461
Rabelais and His World (Bakhtin), **Supp. X:** 120
Rabinbach, Anson, **Supp. XII:** 166
Rabinowitz, Paula, **Supp. V:** 161
"Race" (Emerson), **II:** 6
"Race, Privilege, and the Politics of (Re)Writing History: An Analysis of the Novels of Michelle Cliff" (Edmondson), **Supp. XXII:** 70
"Race Contacts and Inter-Racial Relations" (Locke), **Supp. XIV:** 211
"Race Contacts and Inter-Racial Relations: A Study in the Theory and Practice of Race" (lectures, Locke), **Supp. XIV:** 199, 209
Race Contacts and Interracial Relations: Lectures on the Theory and Practice of Race (Locke, Stewart, ed.), **Supp. XIV:** 196, **209–210**
"'RACE LINE' IS A PRODUCT OF CAPITALISM, THE" (Baraka), **Supp. II Part 1:** 61
"Race of Life, The" (Thurber), **Supp. I Part 2:** 614
"Race Problems and Modern Society" (Toomer), **Supp. III Part 2:** 486

Race Questions, Provincialism, and Other American Problems (Royce), **Supp. XIV:** 199
"Race Riot, Tulsa, 1921" (Olds), **Supp. X:** 205
Race Rock (Matthiessen), **Supp. V:** 201
"Races, The" (Lowell), **II:** 554
"Rachel" (D. West), **Supp. XVIII:** 289
Rachel Carson: Witness for Nature (Lear), **Supp. IX:** 19
Rachel River (film, Smolan), **Supp. XVI:** 36
"Racial Progress and Race Adjustment" (Locke), **Supp. XIV:** 210
Racine, Jean Baptiste, **II:** 543, 573; **III:** 145, 151, 152, 160; **IV:** 317, 368, 370; **Supp. I Part 2:** 716
Radcliffe, Ann, **Supp. XX: 108**
"Radical" (Moore), **III:** 211
"Radical Chic" (Wolfe), **Supp. III Part 2:** 577–578, 584, 585
Radical Chic & Mau-mauing the Flak Catchers (Wolfe), **Supp. III Part 2:** 577–578
Radical Empiricism of William James, The (Wild), **II:** 362, 363–364
Radicalism in America, The (Lasch), **I:** 259
"Radical Jewish Humanism: The Vision of E. L. Doctorow" (Clayton), **Supp. IV Part 1:** 238
"Radically Condensed History of Postindustrial Life, A" (Wallace), **Supp. X:** 309
Radical's America, A (Swados), **Supp. XIX: 264–265**
Radinovsky, Lisa, **Supp. XV:** 284, 285
"Radio" (O'Hara), **III:** 369
Radio Days (film; Allen), **Supp. XV:** 9
"Radio Pope" (Goldbarth), **Supp. XII:** 188, 192
Raditzer (Matthiessen), **Supp. V:** 201
Radkin, Paul, **Supp. I Part 2:** 539
"Rafaela Who Drinks Coconut & Papaya Juice on Tuesdays" (Cisneros), **Supp. VII:** 63
Rafelson, Bob, **Supp. XIV:** 241
Raffalovich, Marc-André, **Supp. XIV:** 335
Rafferty, Terence, **Supp. XX: 87, 92**
"Raft, The" (Lindsay), **Supp. I Part 2:** 393
Rag and Bone Shop of the Heart, The: Poems for Men (Bly, Hillman, and Meade, eds.), **Supp. IV Part 1:** 67
Rage in Harlem (C. Himes). *See For Love of Imabelle* (C. Himes)
Rage to Live, A (O'Hara), **III:** 361
Raglan, Lord, **I:** 135
Rago, Henry, **Supp. III Part 2:** 624, 628, 629
Ragtime (Doctorow), **Retro. Supp. II:** 108; **Supp. IV Part 1:** 217, 222–224, 231, 232, 233, 234, 237, 238; **Supp. V:** 45
"Ragtime" (Doctorow), **Supp. IV Part 1:** 234
Ragtime (film), **Supp. IV Part 1:** 236
Ragtime (musical, McNally), **Supp. XIII:** 207
Rahab (W. Frank), **Supp. XX: 71–72, 76**
Rahaim, Liz, **Supp. XVII:** 2
Rahv, Philip, **Retro. Supp. I:** 112; **Supp. II Part 1:** 136; **Supp. VIII:** 96; **Supp. IX:** 8; **Supp. XIV:** 3; **Supp. XV:** 140
"Raid" (Hughes), **Retro. Supp. I:** 208
Raids on the Unspeakable (Merton), **Supp. VIII:** 201, 208
Raikin, Judith, **Supp. XXII:** 66
Rail, DeWayne, **Supp. XIII:** 312
"Rain and the Rhinoceros" (Merton), **Supp. VIII:** 201
Rainbow, The (Lawrence), **III:** 27
"Rainbows" (Marquand), **III:** 56
Rainbow Stories, The (Vollmann), **Supp. XVII:** 226, 227, 230, 231, 233
Rainbow Tulip, The (Mora), **Supp. XIII:** 221
"Rain Country" (Haines), **Supp. XII:** 210
"Rain-Dream, A" (Bryant), **Supp. I Part 1:** 164
Raine, Kathleen, **I:** 522, 527
"Rain Falling Now, The" (Dunn), **Supp. XI:** 147
"Rain in the Heart" (Taylor), **Supp. V:** 317, 319
Rain in the Trees, The (Merwin), **Supp. III Part 1:** 340, 342, 345, 349, 354–356
"Rainmaker, The" (Humphrey), **Supp. IX:** 101
Raintree County (Lockridge), **Supp. XIX:** 263
Rainwater, Catherine, **Supp. V:** 272
"Rainy Day" (Longfellow), **II:** 498
"Rainy Day, The" (Buck), **Supp. II Part 1:** 127
"Rainy Mountain Cemetery" (Momaday), **Supp. IV Part 2:** 486
Rainy Mountain Christmas Doll (painting) (Momaday), **Supp. IV Part 2:** 493
"Rainy Season: Sub-Tropics" (Bishop), **Supp. I Part 1:** 93
"Rainy Sunday" (Espaillat), **Supp. XXI:** 106
"Raise High the Roof Beam, Carpenters" (Salinger), **III:** 567–569, 571
Raise High the Roof Beam, Carpenters; and Seymour: An Introduction (Salinger), **III:** 552, 567–571, 572
Raise Race Rays Raze: Essays Since 1965 (Baraka), **Supp. II Part 1:** 47, 52, 55
Raisin (musical), **Supp. IV Part 1:** 374
Raising Demons (Jackson), **Supp. IX: 125–126**
Raisin in the Sun, A (unproduced screenplay) (Hansberry), **Supp. IV Part 1:** 360
Raisin in the Sun, A (film: Columbia Pictures), **Supp. IV Part 1:** 360, 367
Raisin in the Sun, A (Hansberry), **Supp. IV Part 1:** 359, 360, 361, 362–364; **Supp. VIII:** 343
Raisin in the Sun, A (television film: American Playhouse), **Supp. IV Part 1:** 367, 374
Rajan, R., **I:** 390
"Rake, The" (Mamet), **Supp. XIV:** 240
Rake's Progress, The (opera), **Supp. II Part 1:** 24
Rakosi, Carl, **Supp. III Part 2:** 614, 615, 616, 617, 618, 621, 629; **Supp. XIV:** 286, 287
Ralegh, Sir Walter, **Supp. I Part 1:** 98
Raleigh, John Henry, **IV:** 366
Ralph, Brett, **Supp. XVII:** 245
Ramakrishna, Sri, **III:** 567
Ramakrishna and His Disciples (Isherwood), **Supp. XIV:** 164
Ramazani, Jahan, **Supp. IV Part 2:** 450
"Ramble of Aphasia, A" (O. Henry), **Supp. II Part 1:** 410
Ramey, Phillip, **Supp. IV Part 1:** 94
Rampersad, Arnold, **Retro. Supp. I:** 196, 200, 201, 204; **Supp. IV Part 1:** 244, 250
Rampling, Anne, **Supp. VII:** 201. *See also* Rice, Anne
Rampling, Charlotte, **Supp. IX:** 253
Ramsey, Priscilla R., **Supp. IV Part 1:** 15
Ramsey, Roger, **Supp. XVI:** 69
Ramsey, William, **Supp. XVIII:** 66
Ramus, Petrus, **Supp. I Part 1:** 104
Rand, Ayn, **Supp. I Part 1:** 294; **Supp. IV Part 2: 517–535**
Randall, Jarrell, 1914–1965 (Lowell, Taylor, and Warren, eds.), **II:** 368, 385
Randall, John H., **III:** 605
Randolph, John, **I:** 5–6
"Range-Finding" (Frost), **Retro. Supp. I:** 131
Range of the Possible (T. Marshall), **Supp. XVII:** 36
Rangoon (F. Barthelme), **Supp. XI:** 25
Rangus, Eric, **Supp. XXI:** 244, 254
Rank, Otto, **I:** 135; **Supp. IX:** 105; **Supp. X:** 183, 185, 193
Ranke, Leopold von, **Supp. I Part 2:** 492
Rankin, Daniel, **Retro. Supp. II:** 57, 72; **Supp. I Part 1:** 200, 203, 225
Rankin, Tom, **Supp. XXI:** 36
Rankine, Annette, **Supp. XX: 69**
Ranlett, William H., **Supp. XVIII:** 3
Ransohoff, Martin, **Supp. XI:** 305, 306
Ransom, John Crowe, **I:** 265, 301; **II:** 34, 367, 385, 389, 536–537, 542; **III:** 454, **480–502,** 549; **IV:** 121, 122, 123, 124, 125, 127, 134, 140, 141, 236, 237, 433; **Retro. Supp. I:** 90; **Retro. Supp. II:** 176, 177, 178, 183, 220, 228, 246; **Supp. I Part 1:** 80, 361; **Supp. I Part 2:** 423; **Supp. II Part 1:** 90, 91, 136, 137, 139, 318; **Supp. II Part 2:** 639; **Supp. III Part 1:** 318; **Supp. III Part 2:** 542, 591; **Supp. IV Part 1:** 217; **Supp. V:** 315, 331, 337; **Supp. X:** 25, 56, 58; **Supp. XIV:** 1; **Supp. XIX:** 123
"Rape" (Coleman), **Supp. XI:** 89–90
"Rape, The" (Baraka), **Supp. II Part 1:** 40
Rape of Bunny Stuntz, The (Gurney), **Supp. V:** 109
"Rape of Philomel, The" (Shapiro), **Supp. II Part 2:** 720
"Rape of the Lock, The" (Pope), **Supp. XIV:** 8

Rapf, Joanna, **Supp. XVIII:** 251
Raphael, **I:** 15; **III:** 505, 521, 524; **Supp. I Part 1:** 363
"Rapist" (Dunn), **Supp. XI:** 144
Rap on Race, A (Baldwin and Mead), **Supp. I Part 1:** 66
"Rappaccini's Daughter" (Hawthorne), **II:** 229
"Rapture of the Deep" (Hempel), **Supp. XXI: 123**
"Rapunzel" (Sexton), **Supp. II Part 2:** 691
Rare & Endangered Species: A Novella & Short Stories (Bausch), **Supp. VII:** 51, 54
"Raree Show" (MacLeish), **III:** 9
Rascoe, Burton, **III:** 106, 115
Raskin, Jonah, **Supp. XV:** 116
"Raskolnikov" (Simic), **Supp. VIII:** 282
Rasmussen, Douglas, **Supp. IV Part 2:** 528, 530
Rasmussen, Halfdan, **Supp. XVIII:** 180
Rasselas (Johnson), **Supp. XI:** 209
Rathmann, Andrew, **Supp. XV:** 34
"Rat in the Engine" (Espaillat), **Supp. XXI:** 106
"Ration" (Baraka), **Supp. II Part 1:** 50
"Rationale of Verse, The" (Poe), **III:** 427–428; **Retro. Supp. II:** 266
Ratner, Rochelle, **Supp. XV:** 105
Ratner's Star (DeLillo), **Supp. VI:** 1, 2, 3, 4, 10, 12, 14; **Supp. XVIII:** 140
"Rat of Faith, The" (Levine), **Supp. V:** 192
Rattigan, Terence, **III:** 152
Raugh, Joseph, **Supp. I Part 1:** 286
Rauh, Ida, **Supp. XXI:** 6
Rauschenberg, Robert, **Supp. XV:** 187
Rauschenbusch, Walter, **III:** 293; **Supp. I Part 1:** 7
Ravelstein (Bellow), **Retro. Supp. II:** 19, **33–34**
Raven, Simon, **Supp. XII:** 241
Raven, The (film, Friedlander), **Supp. XVII:** 58
"Raven, The" (Poe), **III:** 413, 421–422, 426; **Retro. Supp. II:** 265, 266–267; **Supp. XVII:** 58
Raven, The, and Other Poems (Poe), **III:** 413
Ravenal, Shannon, **Supp. IV Part 1:** 93
"Raven Days, The" (Lanier), **Supp. I Part 1:** 351
Ravenel, Shannon, **Supp. XXI:** 39
Ravenna, Michael. *See* Welty, Eudora
"Ravens at Deer Creek" (Wrigley), **Supp. XVIII:** 299–300, 306
Raven's Road (Gunn Allen), **Supp. IV Part 1:** 330, 335
Raver, Anne, **Supp. XVIII:** 191
"Ravine, The" (Carruth), **Supp. XVI:** 53
Ravits, Martha, **Supp. XXI:** 215
Raw Heaven (Peacock), **Supp. XIX: 196–197**
Rawlings, Marjorie Kinnan, **Supp. X: 219–237; Supp. XVIII:** 194–195
Rawlins, C. L., **Supp. XVII:** 72, 73
Ray, David, **Supp. IV Part 1:** 61
Ray, Janisse, **Supp. XVIII: 189–206**
Ray, Jeanne Wilkinson, **Supp. XII:** 308, 310
Ray, John, **II:** 111, 112
Ray, Man, **IV:** 404; **Retro. Supp. I:** 416; **Supp. XII:** 124
Ray, Nicholas, **Supp. XVIII:** 253
Ray Bradbury Theatre, The (television show), **Supp. IV Part 1:** 103
Raymond, Henry J., **Supp. XVIII:** 4
"Raymond and Ann" (Budbill), **Supp. XIX:** 9
"Razor's Edge, The" (Wasserstein), **Supp. XV:** 328
Reactionary Essays on Poetry and Ideas (Tate), **Supp. II Part 1:** 106, 146
Read, Deborah, **II:** 122
Read, Forrest, **III:** 478
Read, Herbert, **I:** 523; **II:** 372–373, 377–378; **Retro. Supp. I:** 54; **Supp. III Part 1:** 273; **Supp. III Part 2:** 624, 626
Read, William A., **Supp. XIV:** 4
Reade, Charles, **Supp. I Part 2:** 580
Reader, Constant. *See* Parker, Dorothy
Reader, Dennis J., **Supp. I Part 2:** 454
"Reader, The" (F. Wright), **Supp. XVII:** 246
Reader's Block (Markson), **Supp. XVII: 143–145,** 146
Reader's Encyclopedia, The: An Encyclopedia of World Literature and the Arts (W. Benét), **Supp. XI:** 44
Reader's Guide to William Gaddis's The Recognitions, A (Moore), **Supp. IV Part 1:** 283
Reader's Map of Arkansas (Wright), **Supp. XV:** 348
"Reader's Tale, A" (Doty), **Supp. XI:** 119, 120, 128, 129
"Reading" (Auden), **Supp. VIII:** 155
"Reading, The" (Di Piero), **Supp. XIX:** 41
"Reading, Writing, Region" (J. W. Miller), **Supp. XX: 165**
"Reading an Anthology of Chinese Poems of the Sung Dynasty, I Pause to Admire the Length and Clarity of Their Titles" (Collins), **Supp. XXI:** 56
"Reading at Forty" (Pickering), **Supp. XXI:** 196
"Reading Group Guide", **Supp. XI:** 244–245
"Reading Lao Tzu Again in the New Year" (Wright), **Supp. V:** 343
"Reading Late of the Death of Keats" (Kenyon), **Supp. VII:** 169
"Reading Myself" (Lowell), **II:** 555
Reading Myself and Others (P. Roth), **Retro. Supp. II:** 282; **Supp. V:** 45
"Reading *Ode to the West Wind* 25 Years Later" (McCarriston), **Supp. XIV:** 271–272
"Reading of the Psalm, The" (Francis), **Supp. IX:** 79
"Reading Ovid" (Di Piero), **Supp. XIX:** 44
"Reading Philosophy at Night" (Simic), **Supp. VIII:** 272
Reading Rilke: Reflections on the Problems of Translation (Gass), **Supp. VI:** 92, **93–94**
"Reading Rorty and Paul Celan One Morning in Early June" (Wright), **Supp. V:** 343
"Reading Sarcophagi: An Essay" (Sobin), **Supp. XVI:** 290
"Readings of History" (Rich), **Supp. I Part 2:** 554
"Reading the Signs, Empowering the Eye" (Bambara), **Supp. XI:** 17–18
Reading the Spirit (Eberhart), **I:** 525, 527, 530
Ready, Richard M., **Supp. XIX:** 154
"Ready Or Not" (Baraka), **Supp. II Part 1:** 50
Reagan, Ronald, **Supp. IV Part 1:** 224–225
"Real Bowery, The" (Hapgood), **Supp. XVII:** 103
"Real Class" (Vidal), **Supp. IV Part 1:** 35
Real Cool Killers, The (C. Himes), **Supp. XVI:** 143
Real Dope, The (Lardner), **II:** 422–423
"Real Estate" (Moore), **Supp. X:** 178
"Real Gone Guy, A" (McGrath), **Supp. X:** 117
"Real Horatio Alger Story, The" (Cowley), **Supp. II Part 1:** 143
"Realities" (MacLeish), **III:** 4
"Reality in America" (Trilling), **Supp. III Part 2:** 495, 502
"Reality! Reality! What Is It?" (Eberhart), **I:** 536
Reality Sandwiches, 1953–60 (Ginsberg), **Supp. II Part 1:** 315, 320
"Reality U.S.A." (Halliday), **Supp. XIX:** 89
Real Life of Sebastian Knight, The (Nabokov), **III:** 246; **Retro. Supp. I:** 266, 269, 270, 274
"Really Good Jazz Piano, A" (Yates), **Supp. XI:** 342
"Real Movie, with Stars, The" (Hull), **Supp. XXI:** 136
Real Presence: A Novel (Bausch), **Supp. VII:** 42–43, 50
"Real Revolution Is Love, The" (Harjo), **Supp. XII:** 224, 225–226
"Real Surrounding, The: On Canaletto's Venice" (Bronk), **Supp. XXI:** 32
"Real Thing, The" (H. James), **Retro. Supp. I:** 228; **Retro. Supp. II:** 223
"Real Two-Party System" (Vidal), **Supp. IV Part 2:** 679
Real West Marginal Way, The (Hugo), **Supp. VI:** 132, 134; **Supp. XVIII:** 299
"Real World around Us, The" (Carson), **Supp. IX:** 21
Reaper Essays, The (Jarman and McDowell), **Supp. IX:** 270; **Supp. XVII:** 110–111
"*Reaper* Interviews Jean Doh and Sean Dough, *The*" (Jarman and McDowell), **Supp. XVII:** 110
"Reapers" (Toomer), **Supp. III Part 2:** 481; **Supp. IX:** 312

Reason and Other Women (Notley), **Supp. XXII:** 224, 227, 235, 236, 237
"Reason and Race: A Review of the Literature of the Negro for 1946" (Locke), **Supp. XIV:** 206
"Reason for Moving, A" (Strand), **Supp. IV Part 2:** 624
"Reason for Stories, The: Toward a Moral Fiction" (Stone), **Supp. V:** 298, 300
Reasons for Moving (Strand), **Supp. IV Part 2:** 624–626, 626
"Reasons for Music" (MacLeish), **III:** 19
"Reasons of the Body" (Sanders), **Supp. XVI:** 274
Reasons to Live (Hempel), **Supp. XXI:** 115, 117, 118, **119–122**
Rebecca (du Maurier), **Supp. XIX:** 57–58; **Supp. XXII:** 120
Rebecca, or, The Fille de Chambre (Rowson), **Supp. XV:** 229, **235–236,** 238
Rebecca Harding Davis Reader, A (Pfaelzer, ed.), **Supp. XVI:** 88, 90
Rebel Angels: Twenty-five Poets of the New Formalism (Jarman and Mason, eds.), **Supp. XV:** 251; **Supp. XVII:** 109, 110, 112, 121
"Rebellion" (Lowell), **Retro. Supp. II:** 187
Rebel Powers (Bausch), **Supp. VII:** 41, 45–46, 49–51
Rebel without a Cause (film), **Supp. XII:** 9
"Rebirth" (McKnight), **Supp. XX: 147, 157**
"Rebirth of God and the Death of Man, The " (Fiedler), **Supp. XIII:** 108
Rebolledo, Tey Diana, **Supp. XIII:** 214
Recapitulation (Stegner), **Supp. IV Part 2:** 598, 600, 612–613
"Recapitulation, The" (Eberhart), **I:** 522
"Recapitulations" (Shapiro), **Supp. II Part 2:** 701, 702, 708, 710–711
"Receding Horizons" (Lethem and Scholtz), **Supp. XVIII:** 145
"Recencies in Poetry" (Zukofsky), **Supp. III Part 2:** 615
Recent Killing, A (Baraka), **Supp. II Part 1:** 55
"Recent Negro Fiction" (Ellison), **Supp. II Part 1:** 233, 235
"Recessional" (A. Finch), **Supp. XVII:** 70–71
"Recital, The" (Ashbery), **Supp. III Part 1:** 14
"Recitative" (H. Crane), **I:** 390; **Retro. Supp. II:** 78
Reckless Eyeballing (Reed), **Supp. X:** 241
Reckless Moment, The (film), **Supp. XXII:** 120, 131, 132
Recognitions, The (Gaddis), **Supp. IV Part 1:** 279, 280–285, 286, 287, 288, 289, 291, 292, 294; **Supp. XX: 91**
"Recollection and Perhaps a Tribute, A" (Espaillat), **Supp. XXI:** 103–104
Recollections (R. H. Stoddard), **Supp. XV:** 271
Recollections of Logan Pearsall Smith: The Story of a Friendship (Gathorne-Hardy), **Supp. XIV:** 344
"Reconciliation" (Whitman), **IV:** 347
"Reconstructed but Unregenerate" (Ransom), **III:** 496
"Reconstruction and Its Benefits" (Du Bois), **Supp. II Part 1:** 171
Recovering (Sarton), **Supp. VIII:** 264
Recovering the U.S. Hispanic Literary Heritage (Paredes), **Supp. XIII:** 320
"Recovery" (Dove), **Supp. IV Part 1:** 248
Rector of Justin, The (Auchincloss), **Supp. IV Part 1:** 21, 23, 27–30, 36
"Recurrent Dream" (Nelson), **Supp. XVIII:** 176
"RED AUTUMN" (Baraka), **Supp. II Part 1:** 55
Red Badge of Courage, The (S. Crane), **I:** 201, 207, 212, 405, 406, 407, 408, 412–416, 419, 421, 422, 423, 477, 506; **II:** 264; **III:** 317; **IV:** 350; **Retro. Supp. II:** 108; **Supp. IV Part 1:** 380; **Supp. XIV:** 51; **Supp. XVII:** 228; **Supp. XVIII:** 75; **Supp. XXI:** 277
"Redbirds" (C. Frost), **Supp. XV:** 99
"Red Bow, The" (Saunders), **Supp. XIX:** 232–233, 234
"Redbreast in Tampa" (Lanier), **Supp. I Part 1:** 364
"Red Brocade" (Nye), **Supp. XIII:** 288
Redburn: His First Voyage (Melville), **III:** 79–80, 84; **Retro. Supp. I:** 245, 247–248, 249; **Supp. XVIII:** 6
Red Calico (Miller and Bowden), **Supp. XXII:** 188
"Red Carpet for Shelley, A" (Wylie), **Supp. I Part 2:** 724
Red Channels (Harnett), **Supp. XV:** 198
"Red Clowns" (Cisneros), **Supp. VII:** 63
Red Coal, The (Stern), **Supp. IX: 291–292**
Red Coat, The (Shanley), **Supp. XIV:** 316–317
"Red Cords" (Lamott), **Supp. XX: 142**
"Red Cross" (Hughes), **Retro. Supp. I:** 205
Red Cross (Shepard), **Supp. III Part 2:** 440, 446
Red Death, A (Mosley), **Supp. XIII:** 237, 239, 240
"Red Deer" (C. Frost), **Supp. XV:** 101
Redding, Josephine, **Supp. XXI:** 2
Redding, Saunders, **Supp. I Part 1:** 332, 333
Reddings, J. Saunders, **Supp. IV Part 1:** 164
Red Dust (Levine), **Supp. V:** 178, 183–184, 188
"Red Dust" (Levine), **Supp. V:** 184
"Redemption" (Gardner), **Supp. VI:** 72
Redemption (Uris), **Supp. XX: 244, 246, 247, 248, 254, 255**
"Redeployment" (Nemerov), **III:** 267, 272
Redfield, Robert, **IV:** 475
Redford, Robert, **Supp. IX:** 253, 259; **Supp. XIII:** 267; **Supp. XIV:** 223
Redgrave, Lynn, **Supp. V:** 107
Red Harvest (Hammett), **Supp. IV Part 1:** 346–348, 348; **Supp. IV Part 2:** 468; **Supp. XXI:** 272
Red-Headed Woman (film), **Retro. Supp. I:** 110; **Supp. XVI:** 191
"Red Horse Wind over Albuquerque" (Harjo), **Supp. XII:** 219
Red Hot Vacuum, The (Solotaroff), **Retro. Supp. II:** 281
Rediscovery of America, The (W. Frank), **Supp. XX: 75**
Rediscovery of Man, The (W. Frank), **Supp. XX: 67–68, 80**
"Red Leaves" (Faulkner), **II:** 72
"Red Meat: What Difference Did Stesichoros Make?" (Carson), **Supp. XII:** 107
"Red Pawn" (Rand), **Supp. IV Part 2:** 520
Red Pony, The (Steinbeck), **IV:** 50, 51, 58, 70
Redrawing the Boundaries (Fisher), **Retro. Supp. I:** 39
Red Robins, The (Koch), **Supp. XV:** 185–186, 187
Red Roses for Bronze (Doolittle), **Supp. I Part 1:** 253, 268, 271
Red Rover, The (Cooper), **I:** 342–343, 355
"Red Silk Stockings" (Hughes), **Retro. Supp. I:** 200
Redskins, The (Cooper), **I:** 351, 353
"Red Sox Nation, North" (Mosher), **Supp. XXII:** 209
"Red Star, Winter Orbit" (W. Gibson and B. Sterling), **Supp. XVI:** 123
Red Suitcase (Nye), **Supp. XIII:** 277, 278, 287
Red the Fiend (Sorrentino), **Supp. XXI:** 227, 231, 237
Red Wallflower, A (S. Warner), **Supp. XVIII:** 260
"Red Wheelbarrow, The" (W. C. Williams), **IV:** 411–412; **Retro. Supp. I:** 419, 430
"Red Wind" (Chandler), **Supp. IV Part 1:** 122
"Red Wing Church, The" (Kooser), **Supp. XIX:** 119
"Redwings" (Wright), **Supp. III Part 2:** 603
Reed, Edward Bliss, **Supp. XV:** 297, 298, 300
Reed, Ishmael, **Retro. Supp. II:** 111, 324–325; **Supp. II Part 1:** 34; **Supp. X: 239–257,** 331; **Supp. XIII:** 181, 182; **Supp. XVI:** 143; **Supp. XX: 107; Supp. XXII:** 172
Reed, J. D., **Supp. XVI:** 174
Reed, John, **I:** 48, 476, 483; **Supp. X:** 136; **Supp. XV:** 295, 299; **Supp. XVII:** 96, 99, 100; **Supp. XVIII:** 225; **Supp. XXI:** 6, 12; **Supp. XXII:** 274, 275
Reed, Lou, **Retro. Supp. II:** 266
"Reedbeds of the Hackensack, The" (Clampitt), **Supp. IX:** 41
"Reed of Pan, A" (McCullers), **II:** 585
Reedy, Billy, **Retro. Supp. II:** 65, 67, 71, 73

Reedy, William Marion, **Supp. I Part 2:** 456, 461, 465
Reef, The (Wharton), **IV:** 317–318, 322; **Retro. Supp. I:** 372, **373–374**
Reena and Other Stories (Marshall), **Supp. XI:** 275, 277, 278
"Reese in Evening Shadow" (Skloot), **Supp. XX: 204**
Reeve, F. D., **Supp. XV:** 344, 349
Reeve's Tale (Chaucer), **I:** 131
"Refiguring the Postcolonial Imagination: Tropes of Visuality in Writing by Rhys, Kincaid, and Cliff" (Emery), **Supp. XXII:** 73
"Reflection from Anita Loos" (Empson), **Supp. XVI:** 190
"Reflections" (Carruth), **Supp. XVI:** 54
"Reflections" (Komunyakaa), **Supp. XIII:** 117
Reflections at Fifty and Other Essays (Farrell), **II:** 49
"Reflections by a Fire" (Sarton), **Supp. VIII:** 259
Reflections in a Golden Eye (McCullers), **II:** 586, 588, 593–596, 604; **IV:** 384, 396
Reflections of a Jacobite (Auchincloss), **Supp. IV Part 1:** 31
Reflections on a Gift of Watermelon Pickle (Dunning), **Supp. XIV:** 126
Reflections on Poetry and Poetics (Nemerov), **III:** 269
"Reflections on the Constitution of Nature" (Freneau), **Supp. II Part 1:** 274
"Reflections on the Death of the Reader" (Morris), **III:** 237
Reflections on the End of an Era (Niebuhr), **III:** 297–298
"Reflections on the Life and Death of Lord Clive" (Paine), **Supp. I Part 2:** 505
Reflections on the Revolution in France (Burke), **Supp. I Part 2:** 511, 512
Reflections: Thinking Part I (Arendt), **Supp. I Part 2:** 570
"Reflex Action and Theism" (James), **II:** 345, 363
Reflex and Bone Structure (Major), **Supp. XXII: 174–175**
"Refrains/Remains/Reminders" (Goldbarth), **Supp. XII:** 180–181, 181
"Refuge" (Kingsolver), **Supp. VII:** 208
"Refuge, A" (Goldbarth), **Supp. XII:** 190
Refugee Children: Theory, Research, and Services (Ahearn and Athey, eds.), **Supp. XI:** 184
"Refugees, The" (Jarrell), **II:** 371
"Refusal" (C. Frost), **Supp. XV:** 102
"Refusal to Publish Fifth Book" (Halliday), **Supp. XIX:** 94
Regarding Wave (Snyder), **Supp. VIII: 299–300**
Regina (Epstein), **Supp. XII: 170–171**
"Regional Literature of the South" (Rawlings), **Supp. X:** 228
"Regional Writer, The" (O'Connor), **Retro. Supp. II:** 223, 225
Régnier, Henri de, **II:** 528–529
Regulators, The (King), **Supp. V:** 141
Rehder, Robert, **Supp. IV Part 1:** 69
Rehearsing Absence (Espaillat), **Supp. XXI:** 99
Reich, Tova, **Supp. XVI:** 158
Reichel, Hans, **III:** 183
Reichl, Ruth, **Supp. X:** 79, 85
Reid, B. L., **II:** 41, 47
Reid, Forrest, **Supp. XX: 235**
Reid, Thomas, **II:** 9; **Supp. I Part 1:** 151
Reign of Snakes (Wrigley), **Supp. XVIII:** 293, **302–306**
"Reign of Snakes" (Wrigley), **Supp. XVIII:** 302–304
Reign of Wonder, The (Tanner), **I:** 260
Rein, Yevgeny, **Supp. VIII:** 22
Reinagle, Alexander, **Supp. XV:** 238, 240
"Reincarnation" (Dickey), **Supp. IV Part 1:** 181–182
Reine des pommes, La (C. Himes). *See For Love of Imabelle* (C. Himes)
Reiner, Carl, **Supp. IV Part 2:** 591
Reinfeld, Linda, **Supp. IV Part 2:** 421
Reinhardt, Max, **Supp. XV:** 307
Reinventing the Enemy's Language: Contemporary Native Women's Writing of North America (Bird and Harjo, eds.), **Supp. XII:** 216, 217
Reisman, Jerry, **Supp. III Part 2:** 618
Reiter, Amy, **Supp. XIX:** 54, 56
Reitlinger, Gerald, **Supp. XII:** 161
Reivers, The: A Reminiscence (Faulkner), **I:** 305; **II:** 57, 73; **Retro. Supp. I:** 74, 82, 91
"Rejoicings" (Stern), **Supp. IX:** 289–290
Rejoicings: Selected Poems, 1966–1972 (Stern), **Supp. IX: 289–290**
Relation of My Imprisonment, The (Banks), **Supp. V:** 8, 12–13
"Relations between Poetry and Painting, The" (Stevens), **Retro. Supp. I:** 312
Relations of the Alabama-Georgia Dialect to the Provincial Dialects of Great Britain, The (Brooks), **Supp. XIV:** 3
Relative Stranger, A (C. Baxter), **Supp. XVII:** 19, 22
"Relativity of Beauty, The" (Rawlings), **Supp. X:** 226
Relearning the Alphabet (Levertov), **Supp. III Part 1:** 280, 281
"Release" (C. Baxter), **Supp. XVII:** 15
"Release, The" (MacLeish), **III:** 16
Reles, Abe ("Kid Twist"), **Supp. IV Part 1:** 382
"Relevance of an Impossible Ethical Ideal, The" (Niebuhr), **III:** 298
"Religion" (Dunbar), **Supp. II Part 1:** 199
"Religion" (Emerson), **II:** 6
Religion of Nature Delineated, The (Wollaston), **II:** 108
"Religious Instruction" (Peacock), **Supp. XIX:** 200, 201
Religious Rebel, A: The Letters of "H. W. S." (Mrs. Pearsall Smith) (L. P. Smith), **Supp. XIV:** 349
"Reluctance" (Frost), **II:** 153
Reluctantly: Autobiographical Essays (Carruth), **Supp. XVI:** 45–46, 50
Remains (Snodgrass), **Supp. VI:** 311, **313–314**
"Remains, The" (Strand), **Supp. IV Part 2:** 627
"Remarks on Color" (Wright), **Supp. XV:** 346
"Remarks on Spencer's *Definition of Mind as Correspondence" (James), II:* 345
Remarque, Erich Maria, **Retro. Supp. I:** 113; **Supp. IV Part 1:** 380
Rembrandt, **II:** 536; **IV:** 310; **Supp. IV Part 1:** 390, 391
"Rembrandt, The" (Wharton), **IV:** 310
"Rembrandt's Hat" (Malamud), **Supp. I Part 2:** 435, 437
Rembrandt Takes a Walk (Strand), **Supp. IV Part 2:** 631
"Rembrandt to Rembrandt" (Robinson), **III:** 521–522
Remembered Earth, The: An Anthology of Contemporary Native American Literature (Hobson, ed.), **Supp. IV Part 1:** 321
Remembered Yesterdays (Johnson), **Supp. IX:** 184
"Remembering" (Angelou), **Supp. IV Part 1:** 15
"Remembering Allen Tate" (Cowley), **Supp. II Part 1:** 153
"Remembering Barthes" (Sontag), **Supp. III Part 2:** 451, 471
"Remembering Guston" (Kunitz), **Supp. III Part 1:** 257
"Remembering James Laughlin" (Karr), **Supp. XI:** 242
Remembering Laughter (Stegner), **Supp. IV Part 2:** 598, 606, 607, 608, 611, 614
"Remembering Lobo" (Mora), **Supp. XIII:** 220, 227
"Remembering My Father" (Berry), **Supp. X:** 23
"Remembering My Parents Remembering the Books They Read" (Espaillat), **Supp. XXI:** 107
"Remembering that Island" (McGrath), **Supp. X:** 116
"Remembering the Children of Auschwitz" (McGrath), **Supp. X:** 127
"Remembering the Lost World" (Jarrell), **II:** 388
"Remembering the Sixties" (Simpson), **Supp. IX:** 279
Remember Me to Tom (T. Williams), **IV:** 379–380
"Remember the Moon Survives" (Kingsolver), **Supp. VII:** 209
Remember to Remember (H. Miller), **III:** 186
"Remembrance, A" (Gioia), **Supp. XV:** 112
Remembrance of Things Past (Proust), **Supp. IV Part 2:** 600; **Supp. XII:** 9; **Supp. XIII:** 44
Remembrance Rock (Sandburg), **III:** 590
Reminiscence, A (Ashbery), **Supp. III Part 1:** 2
Remnick, David, **Supp. XVI:** 246
"Remora" (Merrill), **Supp. III Part 1:** 326

"Removal" (White), **Supp. I Part 2:** 664–665
"Removal, The" (Merwin), **Supp. III Part 1:** 350, 351
"Removal Service Request" (Halliday), **Supp. XIX:** 90
Removed from Time (Matthews and Feeney), **Supp. IX:** 154
Remsen, Ira, **Supp. I Part 1:** 369
"Rémy de Gourmont, A Distinction" (Pound), **III:** 467
"Renaissance" (Carruth), **Supp. XVI:** 56
Renaissance in the South (Bradbury), **I:** 288–289
Renaldo and Clara (film, Dylan and Shepard), **Supp. XVIII:** 21, 28, 31
"Renaming the Kings" (Levine), **Supp. V:** 184
Renan, Ernest, **Supp. XX: 122**
Renan, Joseph Ernest, **II:** 86; **IV:** 440, 444
Renard, Jules, **IV:** 79
"Renascence" (Millay), **III:** 123, 125–126, 128; **Supp. XV:** 42
Renault, Mary, **Supp. IV Part 2:** 685
"Rendezvous, The" (Kumin), **Supp. IV Part 2:** 455
René, Norman, **Supp. X:** 146, 152
Renée (anonymous author), **Supp. XVI:** 64, 66
"Renegade, The" (Jackson), **Supp. IX:** 120
Renewal of Life series (Mumford), **Supp. II Part 2:** 476, 479, 481, 482, 485, 495, 497
Renoir, Jean, **Supp. XII:** 259; **Supp. XXII:** 256
Renouvrier, Charles, **II:** 344–345, 346
"Renunciation" (Banks), **Supp. V:** 10
Renza, Louis A., **Retro. Supp. II:** 142
"Repair" (Peacock), **Supp. XIX:** 204
"Repeating Dream" (Gander), **Supp. XV:** 340
Repent in Haste (Marquand), **III:** 59
Reperusals and Re-Collections (L. P. Smith), **Supp. XIV:** 346–347
"Repetitive Heart, The: Eleven Poems in Imitation of the Fugue Form" (Schwartz), **Supp. II Part 2:** 645–646
"Replacing Regionalism" (Murphy), **Retro. Supp. II:** 143
Replansky, Naomi, **Supp. X:** 119
"Reply to Mr. Wordsworth" (MacLeish), **III:** 19
"Report, A" (Jin), **Supp. XVIII:** 93
"Report from a Forest Logged by the Weyhaeuser Company" (Wagoner), **Supp. IX:** 328
"Report from North Vietnam" (Paley), **Supp. VI:** 227
Report from Part One (Brooks), **Supp. III Part 1:** 70, 72, 80, 82–85
Report from Part Two (Brooks), **Supp. III Part 1:** 87
Report on a Game Survey of the North Central States (Leopold), **Supp. XIV:** 182
"Report on the Barnhouse Effect" (Vonnegut), **Supp. II Part 2:** 756
"Report to an Academy, A" (Kafka), **Supp. XX: 18**
"Report to Crazy Horse" (Stafford), **Supp. XI: 324–325**
"Repose of Rivers" (H. Crane), **I:** 393; **Retro. Supp. II:** 78, 81
"Repossession of a Heritage, The" (Zagarell), **Supp. XV:** 270, 281
"Representation and the War for Reality" (Gass), **Supp. VI:** 88
Representative Men (Emerson), **II:** 1, 5–6, 8
"Representing Far Places" (Stafford), **Supp. XI:** 321
Repression and Recovery (Nelson), **Supp. XVIII:** 226
"REPRISE OF ONE OF A. G.'S BEST POEMS" (Baraka), **Supp. II Part 1:** 59
"Reproducing Ourselves Is All Very Well" (E. Hoffman), **Supp. XVI:** 155
Republic (Plato), **I:** 485
"Republican Manifesto, A" (Paine), **Supp. I Part 2:** 511
Republic of Love, The (Shields), **Supp. VII:** 323–324, 326, 327
"Requa" (Olsen), **Supp. XIII:** 294, **302–303,** 304
Requa, Kenneth A., **Supp. I Part 1:** 107
"Requa I" (Olsen). *See* "Requa" (Olsen)
"Request for Offering" (Eberhart), **I:** 526
"Requiem" (Akhmatova), **Supp. VIII:** 20
"Requiem" (LaBastille), **Supp. X:** 105
Requiem for a Nun (Faulkner), **II:** 57, 72–73
Requiem for Harlem (H. Roth), **Supp. IX:** 235, 236, **240–242**
"Rescue, The" (Updike), **IV:** 214
Rescued Year, The (Stafford), **Supp. XI: 321–322**
"Rescued Year, The" (Stafford), **Supp. XI:** 322, 323
"Rescue with Yul Brynner" (Moore), **III:** 215
"Resemblance" (Bishop), **Supp. I Part 1:** 86
"Resemblance between a Violin Case and a Coffin, A" (T. Williams), **IV:** 378–379
"Reservations" (Taylor), **Supp. V:** 323
"Reserved Memorials" (Mather), **Supp. II Part 2:** 446, 449
"Resignación" (Espaillat), **Supp. XXI:** 104
"Resistance to Civil Government" (Thoreau), **Supp. X:** 27, 28
Resist Much, Obey Little (Berry), **Supp. XIII:** 2
Resolution (Parker), **Supp. XIX:** 187
"Resolution and Independence" (Wordsworth), **Supp. XV:** 346
"Resort" (Hampl), **Supp. XXII:** 86–87
Resort and Other Poems (Hampl), **Supp. XXII:** 83, 86–87
Resources of Hope (R. Williams), **Supp. IX:** 146
"Respectable Place, A" (O'Hara), **III:** 369
"Respectable Woman, A" (Chopin), **Retro. Supp. II:** 66
"Respite" (Pedersen; Nelson, trans.), **Supp. XVIII:** 180
Responses (Wilbur), **Supp. III Part 2:** 541
"Response to a Rumor that the Oldest Whorehouse in Wheeling, West Virginia, Has Been Condemned" (Wright), **Supp. III Part 2:** 602
Restif de La Bretonne, Nicolas, **III:** 175
"Rest of Life, The" (Gordon), **Supp. IV Part 1:** 311
Rest of Life, The: Three Novellas (Gordon), **Supp. IV Part 1:** 310–312
Rest of the Way, The (McClatchy), **Supp. XII:** 255, **258–259**
Restoration comedy, **Supp. I Part 2:** 617
Restorers, The (Di Piero), **Supp. XIX:** 42–43, 44
"Restorers, The" (Di Piero), **Supp. XIX:** 43
"Restraint" (F. Barthelme), **Supp. XI:** 26
"Result" (Emerson), **II:** 6
"Résumé" (Parker), **Supp. IX:** 189
"Resurrecting Methuselah" (P. E. Jones), **Supp. XXII:** 151
Resurrection (Della Francesca), **Supp. XV:** 262
"Resurrection" (Harjo), **Supp. XII:** 224
"Resurrection" (Jin), **Supp. XVIII:** 94–95
Resurrection, The (Gardner), **Supp. VI:** 61, 63, **64–65,** 68, 69, 73, 74
"Retort" (Hay), **Supp. XIV:** 133
Retour amont (Char; Sobin, trans.), **Supp. XVI:** 282
Retrieval System, The (Kumin), **Supp. IV Part 2:** 449, 451, 452
"Retrievers in Translation" (Doty), **Supp. XI:** 132
"Retroduction to American History" (Tate), **IV:** 129
"Retrospects and Prospects" (Lanier), **Supp. I Part 1:** 352
"Return" (Corso), **Supp. XII:** 135
"Return" (Creeley), **Supp. IV Part 1:** 141, 145
"Return" (MacLeish), **III:** 12
"Return, The" (Bidart), **Supp. XV:** 32–33
"Return, The" (Bontemps), **Supp. XXII:** 3, 8
"Return, The" (Pound), **Retro. Supp. I:** 288
"Return, The" (Ray), **Supp. XVIII:** 194
"Return, The" (Roethke), **III:** 533
"Return, The: Orihuela, 1965" (Levine), **Supp. V:** 194
"Return: An Elegy, The" (Warren), **IV:** 239
"Return: Buffalo" (Hogan), **Supp. IV Part 1:** 411
"Returning" (Komunyakaa), **Supp. XIII:** 122
"Returning a Lost Child" (Glück), **Supp. V:** 81
"Returning from the Enemy" (Harjo), **Supp. XII:** 229–230
"Returning the Borrowed Road" (Komunyakaa), **Supp. XIII:** 113, 133
"Return of Alcibiade, The" (Chopin), **Retro. Supp. II:** 58, 64

Return of Ansel Gibbs, The (Buechner), **III:** 310; **Supp. XII: 48**
"Return of Eros to Academe, The" (Bukiet), **Supp. XVII:** 47
"Return of Spring" (Winters), **Supp. II Part 2:** 791
Return of the Native, The (Hardy), **II:** 184–185, 186
Return of the Vanishing American, The (Fiedler), **Supp. XIII:** 103
Return to a Place Lit by a Glass of Milk (Simic), **Supp. VIII:** 274, 276, 283
"Return to Lavinia" (Caldwell), **I:** 310
"Return to Thin Air: The Everest Disaster Ten Years Later" *(Outside),* **Supp. XVIII:** 113
Reuben (Wideman), **Supp. X:** 320
Reuben and Rachel; or, Tales of Old Times (Rowson), **Supp. XV: 240–241**
Reunion (Mamet), **Supp. XIV:** 240, 247, 254
"Reunion in Brooklyn" (H. Miller), **III:** 175, 184
Reuther brothers, **I:** 493
"Reveille" (Kingsolver), **Supp. VII:** 208
"Reveille" (Untermeyer), **Supp. XV:** 300
"Reveille, The" (Harte), **Supp. II Part 1:** 342–343
Revelation (biblical book), **II:** 541; **IV:** 104, 153, 154; **Supp. I Part 1:** 105, 273
"Revelation" (O'Connor), **III:** 349, 353–354; **Retro. Supp. II:** 237
"Revelation" (Warren), **III:** 490
Revenge (Harrison), **Supp. VIII:** 39, 45
"Revenge of Hamish, The" (Lanier), **Supp. I Part 1:** 365
"Revenge of Hannah Kemhuff, The" (Walker), **Supp. III Part 2:** 521
"Revenge of Rain-in-the-Face, The" (Longfellow), **Retro. Supp. II:** 170
Reverberator, The (James), **Retro. Supp. I:** 227
"Reverdure" (Berry), **Supp. X:** 22
Reverdy, Pierre, **Supp. XV:** 178, 182
"Reverend Father Gilhooley" (Farrell), **II:** 45
Reverse Transcription (Kushner), **Supp. IX:** 138
Reversible Errors (Turow), **Supp. XVII: 220–221**
"Rev. Freemont Deadman" (Masters), **Supp. I Part 2:** 463
Reviewer's ABC, A (Aiken), **I:** 58
Review of Contemporary Fiction, 1990 (Tabbi, ed.), **Supp. XVII:** 143
"Revolt, against the Crepuscular Spirit in Modern Poetry" (Pound), **Retro. Supp. I:** 286
"Revolution" (C. L. R. James), **Supp. XXI:** 160
"Revolution" (Taggard), **Supp. XXII:** 275
"Revolutionary Answer to the Negro Problem in the USA, The" (statement, C. L. R. James), **Supp. XXI:** 169
Revolutionary Petunias (Walker), **Supp. III Part 2:** 520, 522, 530
Revolutionary Road (Yates), **Supp. XI:** 334, **335–340**
"Revolutionary Symbolism in America" (Burke), **I:** 272
"Revolutionary Theatre, The" (Baraka), **Supp. II Part 1:** 42
Revolution in Taste, A: Studies of Dylan Thomas, Allen Ginsberg, Sylvia Plath, and Robert Lowell (Simpson), **Supp. IX:** 276
"Revolution in the Revolution in the Revolution" (Snyder), **Supp. VIII:** 300
Revon, Marcel, **II:** 525
"Rewaking, The" (W. C. Williams), **Retro. Supp. I:** 430
"Rewrite" (Dunn), **Supp. XI:** 147
Rexroth, Kenneth, **II:** 526; **Supp. II Part 1:** 307; **Supp. II Part 2:** 436; **Supp. III Part 2:** 625, 626; **Supp. IV Part 1:** 145–146; **Supp. VIII:** 289; **Supp. XIII:** 75; **Supp. XIV:** 287; **Supp. XV:** 140, 141, 146; **Supp. XXII:** 168
Reynolds, Ann (pseudonym). *See* Bly, Carol
Reynolds, Clay, **Supp. XI:** 254
Reynolds, David, **Supp. XV:** 269
Reynolds, Sir Joshua, **Supp. I Part 2:** 716
Reynolds, Quentin, **IV:** 286
Reza, Yasmina, **Supp. XXI:** 148
Reznikoff, Charles, **IV:** 415; **Retro. Supp. I:** 422; **Supp. III Part 2:** 615, 616, 617, 628; **Supp. XIV: 277–296**
"Rhapsodist, The" (Brown), **Supp. I Part 1:** 125–126
"Rhapsody on a Windy Night" (Eliot), **Retro. Supp. I:** 55
Rhetoric of Motives, A (Burke), **I:** 272, 275, 278, 279
Rhetoric of Religion, The (Burke), **I:** 275, 279
"Rhobert" (Toomer), **Supp. IX:** 316–317
"Rhode Show" (Mallon), **Supp. XIX:** 137–138
"Rhododendrons" (Levis), **Supp. XI:** 260, 263
Rhubarb Show, The (radio, Keillor), **Supp. XVI:** 178
"Rhyme of Sir Christopher, The" (Longfellow), **II:** 501
Rhymes to Be Traded for Bread (Lindsay), **Supp. I Part 2:** 380, 381–382
Rhys, Ernest, **III:** 458
Rhys, Jean, **Supp. III Part 1:** 42, 43; **Supp. XVIII:** 131
"Rhythm & Blues" (Baraka), **Supp. II Part 1:** 37–38
Rhythms (Reznikoff), **Supp. XIV:** 279, 282, 283
Rhythms II (Reznikoff), **Supp. XIV:** 282, 283, 284
Ribalow, Harold, **Supp. IX:** 236
Ribbentrop, Joachim von, **IV:** 249
Ribicoff, Abraham, **Supp. IX:** 33
Ribot, Théodule Armand, **Supp. XX: 238**
Ricardo, David, **Supp. I Part 2:** 628, 634
Rice, Allen Thorndike, **Retro. Supp. I:** 362
Rice, Anne, **Supp. VII: 287–306**
Rice, Elmer, **I:** 479; **III:** 145, 160–161
Rice, Mrs. Grantland, **II:** 435
Rice, Philip Blair, **IV:** 141
Rice, Stan, **Supp. XII:** 2
Rice, Tim, **Supp. XXI:** 148
Rice, Tom, **Supp. XIV:** 125
Rich, Adrienne, **Retro. Supp. I:** 8, 36, 42, 47, 404; **Retro. Supp. II:** 43, 191, 245; **Supp. I Part 2:** 546–547, **550–578; Supp. III Part 1:** 84, 354; **Supp. III Part 2:** 541, 599; **Supp. IV Part 1:** 257, 325; **Supp. V:** 82; **Supp. VIII:** 272; **Supp. XII:** 217, 229, 255; **Supp. XIII:** 294; **Supp. XIV:** 126, 129; **Supp. XV:** 176, 252; **Supp. XVII:** 32, 74; **Supp. XIX:** 83, 193; **Supp. XXII:** 65, 66
Rich, Arnold, **Supp. I Part 2:** 552
Rich, Frank, **Supp. IV Part 2:** 585, 586; **Supp. V:** 106; **Supp. XXI:** 146
Richard, Mark, **Supp. XIX: 209–222**
Richard Cory (Gurney), **Supp. V:** 99–100, 105
"Richard Hunt's 'Arachne' " (Hayden), **Supp. II Part 1:** 374
Richard II (Shakespeare), **Supp. XVII:** 244
Richard III (Shakespeare), **Supp. I Part 2:** 422
Richards, Bertrand F., **Supp. XX: 217–218**
Richards, Constance S., **Supp. XXII:** 73
Richards, David, **Supp. IV Part 2:** 576
Richards, Grant, **I:** 515
Richards, I. A., **I:** 26, 273–274, 279, 522; **III:** 498; **IV:** 92; **Supp. I Part 1:** 264, 265; **Supp. I Part 2:** 647
Richards, Ivor Armonstrong, **Supp. XIV:** 2–3, 16
Richards, Laura E., **II:** 396; **III:** 505–506, 507
Richards, Leonard, **Supp. XIV:** 48
Richards, Lloyd, **Supp. IV Part 1:** 362; **Supp. VIII:** 331
Richards, Rosalind, **III:** 506
Richards, Tad, **Supp. XVII:** 77
Richardson, Alan, **III:** 295
Richardson, Charles, **Supp. XVIII:** 14, 15
Richardson, Dorothy, **I:** 53; **II:** 320; **Supp. III Part 1:** 65
Richardson, Helen Patges, **Retro. Supp. II:** 95
Richardson, Henry Hobson, **I:** 3, 10
Richardson, Maurice, **Supp. XII:** 241
Richardson, Samuel, **I:** 134; **II:** 104, 111, 322; **Supp. V:** 127; **Supp. IX:** 128; **Supp. XV:** 232; **Supp. XX: 236**
Richardson, Tony, **Supp. XI:** 305, 306
"Richard Wright and Recent Negro Fiction" (Ellison), **Retro. Supp. II:** 116
"Richard Wright's Blues" (Ellison), **Retro. Supp. II:** 117, 124
"Richard Yates: A Requiem" (Lawrence), **Supp. XI:** 335
"Rich Boy, The" (Fitzgerald), **II:** 94; **Retro. Supp. I:** 98, 108
Richer, the Poorer, The: Sketches and Reminiscences (D. West), **Supp. XVIII:** 277, 289
"Riches" (Bausch), **Supp. VII:** 54
Richler, Mordecai, **Supp. XI:** 294, 297

Rich Man, Poor Man (miniseries), **Supp. XIX:** 252
Rich Man, Poor Man (Shaw), **Supp. XIX:** 251–252
Richman, Robert, **Supp. XI:** 249; **Supp. XV:** 120–121, 251
Richmond (Masters), **Supp. I Part 2:** 471
Richmond, M. A., **Supp. XX: 277, 279, 282, 286, 289, 290**
Rich Relations (Hwang), **Supp. XXI:** 146–147
Richter, Conrad, **Supp. X:** 103; **Supp. XVIII: 207–222**
Richter, Jean Paul, **II:** 489, 492; **Supp. XVI:** 182
Rick Bass (Weltzien), **Supp. XVI:** 20
Rickman, Clio, **Supp. I Part 2:** 519
Ricks, Christopher, **Retro. Supp. I:** 56; **Supp. XVIII:** 20, 30, 32
Riddel, Joseph N., **IV:** 95
"Riddle, The" (Hay), **Supp. XIV:** 130
"Ride in an Omnibus, A" (Briggs), **Supp. XVIII:** 9, 16
"Riders to the Blood-Red Wrath" (Brooks), **Supp. III Part 1:** 82–83
Riders to the Sea (Synge), **III:** 157
Ridge, Lola, **Supp. IX:** 308; **Supp. XV:** 307
Riding, Alan, **Supp. XVI:** 294
Riding, Laura, **I:** 437
"Riding Out at Evening" (McCarriston), **Supp. XIV:** 262–263
Riding the Iron Rooster: By Train through China (Theroux), **Supp. VIII:** 324
Riesenberg, Felix, **I:** 360, 361
Riesman, David, **Supp. I Part 2:** 649, 650
"Rif, to Music, The" (Bowles), **Supp. IV Part 1:** 89
Riffs & Reciprocities (Dunn), **Supp. XI: 154–155**
Rifles, The (Vollmann), **Supp. XVII:** 226, 233
Riggs, Marlon, **Supp. XI:** 19
Right Distance, The (Pickering), **Supp. XXI:** 196–197
Right Madness on Skye, The (Hugo), **Supp. VI:** 145–147
Rights of Man (Paine), **Supp. I Part 2:** 508, 511, 512–514, 516, 519, 523
"Rights of Woman" (Rowson), **Supp. XV:** 243
"Rights of Women, The" (Brown). *See Alcuin: A Dialogue* (Brown)
Right Stuff, The (Wolfe), **Supp. III Part 2:** 581–584
Right Thoughts in Sad Hours (Mather), **IV:** 144
Rigney, Barbara Hill, **Supp. VIII:** 215
"Rigorists" (Moore), **III:** 198
Rihani, Ameen, **Supp. XX: 115**
Rihoku, **Supp. XXII:** 228
Riis, Jacob A., **I:** 293; **Supp. I Part 1:** 13; **Supp. XVII:** 101, 106
Riley, James Whitcomb, **I:** 205; **Supp. II Part 1:** 192, 193, 196, 197
Rilke, Rainer Maria, **I:** 445, 523; **II:** 367, 381, 382–383, 389, 543, 544; **III:** 552, 558, 563, 571, 572; **IV:** 380, 443; **Retro. Supp. II:** 20, 187; **Supp. I Part 1:** 264; **Supp. I Part 2:** 573; **Supp. III Part 1:** 239, 242, 246, 283, 319–320; **Supp. IV Part 1:** 284; **Supp. V:** 208, 343; **Supp. VIII:** 30, 40; **Supp. X:** 164; **Supp. XI:** 126; **Supp. XIII:** 74, 88; **Supp. XV:** 93, 212, 222,**Supp. XV:** 223, 225; **Supp. XVI:** 292; **Supp. XVII:** 244; **Supp. XXII:** 89, 90, 94
Rilke on Love and Other Difficulties (Rilke), **Supp. X:** 164
"Rilke's Growth as a Poet" (Dobyns), **Supp. XIII:** 77
"Rimbaud" (Kerouac), **Supp. III Part 1:** 232
Rimbaud, Arthur, **I:** 381, 383, 389, 391, 526; **II:** 528, 543, 545; **III:** 23, 174, 189; **IV:** 286, 380, 443; **Retro. Supp. I:** 56; **Retro. Supp. II:** 187, 326; **Supp. III Part 1:** 14, 195; **Supp. IV Part 2:** 624; **Supp. VIII:** 39, 40; **Supp. XII:** 1, 16, 128, 255; **Supp. XIII:** 284; **Supp. XIV:** 338; **Supp. XVIII:** 23, 33; **Supp. XXI:** 225, 233
Rindge, Debora, **Supp. XXI:** 246
Rinehart, Stanley, **III:** 36
Ring, Frances Kroll, **Supp. IX:** 63, 64
Ring and the Book, The (Browning), **Supp. I Part 2:** 416, 468
Ring cycle (Wagner), **Supp. IV Part 1:** 392
Ringe, Donald, **I:** 339, 343; **Retro. Supp. II:** 270
Ringel, Faye, **Supp. XXII:** 205, 207
"Ringing" (Bierds), **Supp. XVII:** 28
"Ringing the Bells" (Sexton), **Supp. II Part 2:** 672, 687
Ringle, Ken, **Supp. X:** 15
Ring of Heaven: Poems (Hongo), **Supp. X:** 292
Rink, The (musical, McNally), **Supp. XIII:** 207
Rio Lobo (film), **Supp. XVI:** 246
Ríos, Alberto Alvaro, **Supp. IV Part 2: 537–556**
"Riot" (Brooks), **Supp. III Part 1:** 71, 84–85
Ripley, Ezra, **II:** 8; **IV:** 172
Rip-off Red, Girl Detective (Acker), **Supp. XII:** 3–4
Ripostes (Pound), **Retro. Supp. I:** 287–288, 413
Ripostes of Ezra Pound, The, Whereunto Are Appended the Complete Poetical Works of T. E. Hulme, with Prefatory Note (Pound), **III:** 458, 464, 465
Riprap (Snyder), **Supp. VIII: 292–294,** 295
"Riprap" (Snyder), **Supp. VIII:** 293–294
"Rip Van Winkle" (Irving), **II:** 304–306; **Supp. I Part 1:** 185
Rischin, Moses, **Supp. XVII:** 101, 103, 106
Risco-Lozado, Eliezar, **Supp. XIII:** 313
Rise and Shine (Quindlen), **Supp. XVII:** 179
Rise of David Levinsky, The (Cahan), **Supp. IX:** 227; **Supp. XIII:** 106
Rise of Silas Lapham, The (Howells), **II:** 275, 279, 283–285; **IV:** 202; **Retro. Supp. II:** 93, 101
"Rise of the Middle Class" (Banks), **Supp. V:** 10
Rising and Falling (Matthews), **Supp. IX:** 154, **160**
"Rising Daughter, The" (Olds), **Supp. X:** 204
Rising from the Plains (McPhee), **Supp. III Part 1:** 309–310
Rising Glory of America, The (Brackenridge and Freneau), **Supp. I Part 1:** 124; **Supp. II Part 1:** 67, 253, 256, 263
"Rising of the Storm, The" (Dunbar), **Supp. II Part 1:** 199
Rising Sun in the Pacific, The (Morison), **Supp. I Part 2:** 490
Rising Up and Rising Down (Vollmann), **Supp. XVII:** 225, 226, **229–230,** 232, 233, 235–236
Risk Pool, The (Russo), **Supp. XII: 328–331**
Ristovic, Aleksandar, **Supp. VIII:** 272
"Rita Dove: Identity Markers" (Vendler), **Supp. IV Part 1:** 247, 257
Ritchey, John, **Supp. XIV:** 122
Ritchie, Anne Thackeray, **Supp. XX: 231, 233**
"Rite of Passage" (Olds), **Supp. X:** 206
"Rites and Ceremonies" (Hecht), **Supp. X:** 61
Rites and Witnesses: A Comedy (Hinojosa), **Supp. XIX: 106–107**
"Rites of Spring, The" (Morris), **III:** 223
Ritivoi, Andreea Deciu, **Supp. XVI:** 148
Ritschl, Albrecht, **III:** 309, 604
Ritsos, Yannis, **Supp. X:** 112
"Ritsos and the Metaphysical Moment" (Dobyns), **Supp. XIII:** 78
Rittenhouse, David, **Supp. I Part 2:** 507
Rittenhouse, Jessie, **Supp. XV:** 295
"Ritual, The" (Jarman), **Supp. XVII:** 114
"Ritual and Renewal: Keres Traditions in the Short Fiction of Leslie Silko" (Ruoff), **Supp. IV Part 2:** 559
Ritz, The (film), **Supp. XIII:** 206
Ritz, The (McNally), **Supp. XIII:** 198
"Rival, The" (Plath), **Retro. Supp. II:** 254
Riven Rock (Boyle), **Supp. VIII:** 5–6; **Supp. XX: 25–26**
"River" (Ammons), **Supp. VII:** 28
"River, The" (O'Connor), **III:** 344, 352, 353, 354, 356; **Retro. Supp. II:** 229, 231–232
Rivera, Tomás, **Supp. XIII:** 216, 221; **Supp. XIX:** 97, 102
Riverbed (Wagoner), **Supp. IX: 327–328**
"River Driftwood" (Jewett), **Retro. Supp. II:** 132, 133, 147
"River Jordan, The" (DeLillo), **Supp. VI:** 3, 4
River King, The (Hoffman), **Supp. X:** 78, 85, 90, **91–92**
"River Merchant's Wife: A Letter, The" (Pound), **III:** 463
"River Now, The" (Hugo), **Supp. VI:** 144

"River of Rivers in Connecticut, The" (Stevens), **Retro. Supp. I:** 313
River of the Mother of God and Other Essays by Aldo Leopold, The (Leopold), **Supp. XIV:** 180
"River Profile" (Auden), **Supp. II Part 1:** 26
"River Road" (Kunitz), **Supp. III Part 1:** 260
"River Runs Through It, A" (Maclean), **Supp. XIV:** 222–223, **223–229,** 233, 234, 235; **Supp. XVI:** 98
River Runs Through It and Other Stories, A (Maclean), **Supp. XIV:** 221, 223
Rivers, Larry, **Supp. III Part 1:** 3; **Supp. XV:** 177, 178, 186
Rivers and Mountains (Ashbery), **Supp. III Part 1:** 10, 26
Riverside Drive (Simpson), **Supp. IX: 275–276**
Riverside Poetry (Auden, Moore, and Shapiro, eds.), **Supp. XXI:** 98
Rivers to the Sea (Teasdale), **Supp. XV:** 295
River Styx, Ohio, and Other Poems, The (Oliver), **Supp. VII:** 231, 232
"River That Is East, The" (Kinnell), **Supp. III Part 1:** 241–242
"River Towns" (Masters), **Supp. I Part 2:** 473
Rives, Amélie, **II:** 194
Rivière, Jacques, **Retro. Supp. I:** 63
"Rivington's Last Will and Testament" (Freneau), **Supp. II Part 1:** 261
"Rivulet, The" (Bryant), **Supp. I Part 1:** 155, 162
Rix, Alice, **I:** 199
RL's Dream (Mosley), **Supp. XIII:** 234, **244–245,** 249
Roach, Max, **Supp. X:** 239
"Road, Roadsides, and the Disparate Frames of a Sequence" (Sobin), **Supp. XVI:** 288
Road, The (McCarthy), **Supp. XXII:** 49
Road Between, The (Farrell), **II:** 29, 38, 39–40
"Road Between Here and There, The" (Kinnell), **Supp. III Part 1:** 254
"Road Home, The" (Hammett), **Supp. IV Part 1:** 343
Road Home, The (Harrison), **Supp. VIII:** 37, 45, 48, **49–50,** 53
Road Is Before Us, The (Boulton), **Supp. XXII:** 17, 25–26
Roadless Yaak, The: Reflections and Observations about One of Our Last Great Wild Places (Bass, ed.), **Supp. XVI:** 23
"Road Not Taken, The" (R. Frost), **II:** 154; **Retro. Supp. I:** 131; **Supp. XI:** 150; **Supp. XV:** 127
"Roadside Flowers" (Collins), **Supp. XXI:** 61
Roadside Poems for Summer Travellers (Larcom, ed.), **Supp. XIII:** 142
"Roadside Resurrection, A" (L. Brown), **Supp. XXI:** 40, 42
Roads of Destiny (O. Henry), **Supp. II Part 1:** 410
Road through the Wall, The (Jackson), **Supp. IX:** 115, 118, 120, 123–124
"Road to Avignon, The" (Lowell), **II:** 516
"Road to Hell, The" (Fante), **Supp. XI:** 160
Road to Los Angeles, The (Fante), **Supp. XI:** 160, 166, 167, **168,** 172
Road to Many a Wonder, The (Wagoner), **Supp. IX:** 327, **336**
Road to the Temple, The (Glaspell), **Supp. III Part 1:** 175, 182, 186; **Supp. XXI:** 6
Road to Wellville, The (Boyle), **Supp. VIII:** 6–8; **Supp. XX: 24–25, 26, 28**
Road to Xanadu, The (Lowes), **IV:** 453
"Road Warrior" (Pickering), **Supp. XXI:** 204
"Roan Stallion" (Jeffers), **Supp. II Part 2:** 428–429
"Roast-beef" (Stein), **IV:** 43
Roast Leviatham (Untermeyer), **Supp. XV:** 307
"Roast Possum" (Dove), **Supp. IV Part 1:** 247, 248
Robards, Jason, Jr., **III:** 163, 403
Robb, Christina, **Supp. XV:** 251
Robbe-Grillet, Alain, **I:** 123; **IV:** 95; **Supp. IV Part 1:** 42; **Supp. V:** 47, 48
Robber Bride, The (Atwood), **Supp. XIII: 30–31**
Robber Bridegroom, The (Welty), **IV:** 261, 266–268, 271, 274; **Retro. Supp. I:** 347
Robbins, Harold, **Supp. XII:** 6
Robbins, Henry, **Supp. IV Part 1:** 198, 201, 210, 211
Robbins, Katherine Robinson, **Supp. X:** 264
Robbins, Thomas, **Supp. XV:** 271
Robbins, Tom, **Supp. IV Part 1:** 227; **Supp. VIII:** 14; **Supp. X: 259–288; Supp. XIII:** 11
"Robe, The" (Douglas), **IV:** 434
Robert Bly (Sugg), **Supp. IV Part 1:** 68
"Robert Bly" (W. V. Davis), **Supp. IV Part 1:** 70
"Robert Bly and the Trouble with America" (Mitchell), **Supp. IV Part 1:** 70
Robert Bly: An Introduction to the Poetry (Nelson), **Supp. IV Part 1:** 66
Robert Bly: The Poet and His Critics (W. V. Davis), **Supp. IV Part 1:** 63; **Supp. XXI:** 84, **85–86,** 87, 95
Robert Coover: The Universal Fiction-making Process (Gordon), **Supp. V:** 46
Robert Creeley (Ford), **Supp. IV Part 1:** 140
Robert Creeley and the Genius of the American Common Place (Clark), **Supp. IV Part 1:** 140
Robert Creeley's Poetry: A Critical Introduction (Edelberg), **Supp. IV Part 1:** 155
Robert Frost (Meyers), **Retro. Supp. I:** 138
Robert Lowell (Meyers), **Retro. Supp. II:** 191
Robert Lowell and the Sublime (Hart), **Retro. Supp. II:** 187
Robert Lowell's Shifting Colors (Doreski), **Retro. Supp. II:** 185
Robert Lowell: The First Twenty years (Staples), **Retro. Supp. II:** 187
Roberts, Carol, **Supp. XX: 53**
Roberts, David, **Supp. XVIII:** 106
Roberts, Diane, **Supp. X:** 15
Roberts, J. M., **IV:** 454
Roberts, Leo, **II:** 449
Roberts, Margaret, **II:** 449; **IV:** 453, 454
Roberts, Matthew, **Retro. Supp. II:** 324
Roberts, Meade, **IV:** 383
Roberts, Michael, **I:** 527, 536
Roberts, Richard, **III:** 297
Roberts, Victoria, **Supp. XIX:** 205
Roberts, Wally, **Supp. XI:** 119, 120, 126
Roberts, William, **Supp. XI:** 343
Roberts Brothers, **Retro. Supp. I:** 31, 35
Robertson, David, **Supp. VIII:** 305
Robertson, D. B., **III:** 311
Robertson, Lisa, **Supp. XXII:** 155
Robertson, Nan, **Supp. IV Part 1:** 300
Robertson, William, **II:** 8
Robert the Devil (Merwin, trans.), **Supp. III Part 1:** 341, 346
Robeson, Paul, **III:** 392; **Supp. IV Part 1:** 360, 361; **Supp. X:** 137; **Supp. XIX:** 66; **Supp. XXI:** 167
Robeson, Susan L., **Supp. XVIII:** 268
Robespierre, Maximilien, **Supp. I Part 2:** 514, 515, 517
"Robinson" (Kees), **Supp. XV:** 143–144
Robinson, Christopher L., **Supp. XII:** 13, 14
Robinson, Dean, **III:** 506
Robinson, Edward, **III:** 505
Robinson, Edward G., **Supp. XI:** 306
Robinson, Edwin Arlington, **I:** 480; **II:** 388, 391, 529, 542; **III:** 5, **503–526,** 576; **Supp. I Part 2:** 699; **Supp. II Part 1:** 191; **Supp. III Part 1:** 63, 75; **Supp. III Part 2:** 592, 593; **Supp. IX:** 77, 266, 276, 308; **Supp. XV:** 256, 299, 300, 301, 306; **Supp. XVII:** 69; **Supp. XIX:** 123
Robinson, Forrest G., **Supp. IV Part 2:** 597, 601, 604
Robinson, Herman, **III:** 506–507
Robinson, H. M., **IV:** 369, 370
Robinson, Jackie, **Supp. I Part 1:** 338
Robinson, James Harvey, **I:** 214; **Supp. I Part 2:** 492
Robinson, James K., **Supp. IX:** 328
Robinson, Margaret G., **Supp. IV Part 2:** 597, 601, 604
Robinson, Marilynne, **Supp. XXI: 209–224; Supp. XXII:** 50
Robinson, Mary, **Supp. XI:** 26
Robinson, Rowland E., **Supp. XIX:** 6
Robinson, Sugar Ray, **Supp. IV Part 1:** 167
Robinson, Ted, **Supp. XIII:** 166
Robinson Crusoe (Defoe), **II:** 159; **III:** 113, 423; **IV:** 369; **Retro. Supp. II:** 274; **Supp. I Part 2:** 714; **Supp. IV Part 2:** 502
Robison, Mary, **Supp. V:** 22; **Supp. XXI:** 115, 116, 118

Roblès, Emmanuel, **Supp. I Part 1:** 283
"Robstown" (Salinas), **Supp. XIII:** 315
Rochefort, Christina, **Supp. XVI:** 143
Rochefoucauld, Louis Alexandre, **Supp. I Part 2:** 510
"Rock" (Nye), **Supp. XIII:** 287
Rock (Wagoner), **Supp. IX:** 324, **334,** 335
Rock, Catherine, **Supp. XII:** 17
Rock, The (Eliot), **Retro. Supp. I:** 65
Rock, The (Stevens), **Retro. Supp. I:** 309, 312
"Rock, The" (Stevens), **Retro. Supp. I:** 312
Rockaway (Shanley), **Supp. XIV:** 315
"Rock Climbers, The" (Francis), **Supp. IX:** 82
Rock-Drill (Pound), **Retro. Supp. I:** 293
Rockefeller, John D., **I:** 273; **III:** 580; **Supp. I Part 2:** 486; **Supp. V:** 286
Rockefeller, Nelson, **III:** 14, 15
Rockets and Rodeos and Other American Spectacles (Mallon), **Supp. XIX:** 137
Rocket to the Moon (Odets), **Supp. II Part 2:** 541–543, 544
Rock Garden, The (Shepard), **Supp. III Part 2:** 432, 447
"Rocking Horse Winner, The" (Lawrence), **Supp. I Part 1:** 329
Rocking the Boat (Vidal), **Supp. IV Part 2:** 683
"Rockpile, The" (Baldwin), **Supp. I Part 1:** 63
Rock Springs (Ford), **Supp. V:** 57, 58–59, 68–69
Rocky Mountains, The: or, Scenes, Incidents, and Adventures in the Far West; Digested from the Journal of Captain E. L. E Bonneville, of the Army of the United States, and Illustrated from Various Other Sources (Irving), **II:** 312
Rodden, John, **Supp. XVI:** 63, 69, 72
Roddenberry, Gene, **Supp. XXII:** 60
Roderick, David, **Supp. XV:** 223
Roderick Hudson (James), **II:** 284, 290, 324, 326, 328; **Retro. Supp. I:** 219, **220–221,** 221, 226; **Supp. IX:** 142
Rodgers, Richard, **III:** 361
Rodgers, Ronald, **Supp. IV Part 2:** 503
Rodker, John, **III:** 470
Rodman, Selden, **Supp. I Part 1:** 83; **Supp. X:** 115
Rodney, Walter, **Supp. XXI:** 171
"Rodrigo Returns to the Land and Linen Celebrates" (Cisneros), **Supp. VII:** 68
Rodriguez, Randy A., **Supp. XIV:** 312
Rodriguez, Richard, **Supp. XIV: 297–313**
Roethke, Charles, **III:** 531
Roethke, Theodore, **I:** 167, 171–172, 183, 254, 285, 521; **III:** 273, **527–550; IV:** 138, 402; **Retro. Supp. II:** 178, 181, 246; **Supp. I Part 2:** 539; **Supp. III Part 1:** 47, 54, 56, 239, 253, 260–261, 350; **Supp. IV Part 2:** 626; **Supp. IX:** 323; **Supp. XV:** 140, 145, 212; **Supp. XVIII:** 90; **Supp. XX: 199**
"Roger Malvin's Burial" (Hawthorne), **II:** 243; **Retro. Supp. I:** 153
Rogers, Michael, **Supp. X:** 265, 266
Rogers, Pattiann, **Supp. XVIII:** 189
Rogers, Samuel, **II:** 303; **Supp. I Part 1:** 157
Rogers, Will, **I:** 261; **IV:** 388
Roger's Version (Updike), **Retro. Supp. I:** 325, 327, 330
Roget, Peter Mark, **Supp. I Part 1:** 312
"Rogue River Jet-Board Trip, Gold Beach, Oregon, July 4, 1977" (Carver), **Supp. III Part 1:** 140
"Rogue's Gallery" (McCarthy), **II:** 563
Rohr, Richard, **Supp. XX: 143**
Roland de La Platière, Jean Marie, **II:** 554
Rolando Hinojosa and the American Dream (Glover), **Supp. XIX:** 112
Rolando Hinojosa: A Reader's Guide (Zilles), **Supp. XIX:** 112
Rolando Hinojosa Reader, The (Saldívar, ed.), **Supp. XIX:** 112
Rôle du Nègre dans la culture des Amériques, La (Locke), **Supp. XIV:** 202
"Role of a Lifetime, The" (Skloot), **Supp. XX: 203**
"Role of Society in the Artist, The" (Ammons), **Supp. VII:** 34
Rolfe, Alfred, **IV:** 427
Rolfe, Frederick, **Supp. XX: 235**
"Roll, Jordan, Roll" (spiritual), **Supp. IV Part 1:** 16
Rolland, Romain, **Supp. XX: 70**
"Roll Call" (Hoffman), **Supp. XVIII:** 86
"Roll Call" (Komunyakaa), **Supp. XIII:** 123
Rolle, Esther, **Supp. IV Part 1:** 367
Rollin, Charles, **II:** 113
Rolling Stones (O. Henry), **Supp. II Part 1:** 410
Rolling Thunder Logbook (Shepard), **Supp. III Part 2:** 433
Rolling Thunder Logbook, The (Shepard), **Supp. XVIII:** 31
"Rolling Up" (Simpson), **Supp. IX:** 265, 274, 280
Rollins, Howard E., Jr., **Supp. IV Part 1:** 236
Rollins, Hyder E., **Supp. IV Part 1:** 168
Rollins, Sonny, **Supp. V:** 195
"Rollo" tales (Abbott), **Supp. I Part 1:** 38
"Roma I" (Wright), **Supp. V:** 338
"Roma II" (Wright), **Supp. V:** 338
Romains, Jules, **I:** 227
Román, David, **Supp. XIII:** 208
Romance, A (Weigl), **Supp. XIX: 277–278**
"Romance, A" (Weigl), **Supp. XIX:** 278
"Romance and a Reading List" (Fitzgerald), **Retro. Supp. I:** 101
Romance of a Plain Man, The (Glasgow), **II:** 175, 180–181
"Romance of Certain Old Clothes, The" (James), **II:** 322; **Retro. Supp. I:** 218
"Roman Elegies" (Brodsky), **Supp. VIII:** 29
"Roman Fever" (Wharton), **Retro. Supp. I:** 382
"Roman Fountain" (Bogan), **Supp. III Part 1:** 56
"*Romanitas* of Gore Vidal, The" (Tatum), **Supp. IV Part 2:** 684
Romaniuk, Zbigniew, **Supp. XVI:** 154
Romano, John, **Supp. XV:** 253
"Roman Sarcophagus, A" (Lowell), **II:** 544
Roman Spring of Mrs. Stone, The (T. Williams), **IV:** 383, 385
"Romantic, The" (Bogan), **Supp. III Part 1:** 50
Romantic Comedians, The (Glasgow), **II:** 175, 186, 190, 194
Romantic Education, A (Hampl), **Supp. XXII:** 82, 83, **87–90,** 91
Romantic Egoists, The (Auchincloss), **Supp. IV Part 1:** 25
Romantic Egotist, The (Fitzgerald), **II:** 82
"Romantic Egotist, The" (Fitzgerald), **Retro. Supp. I:** 100
"Romanticism and Classicism" (Hulme), **III:** 196
"Romanticism Comes Home" (Shapiro), **Supp. II Part 2:** 713
Romantic Manifesto, The: A Philosophy of Literature (Rand), **Supp. IV Part 2:** 521, 523, 527, 529–530
"Romantic Regionalism of Harper Lee, The" (Erisman), **Supp. VIII:** 126
"Rome" (W. C. Williams), **Retro. Supp. I:** 420
Rome Brothers, **Retro. Supp. I:** 393
Romeo and Juliet (Shakespeare), **Supp. V:** 252; **Supp. VIII:** 223
Romola (G. Eliot), **II:** 291; **IV:** 311
Romulus: A New Comedy (Vidal), **Supp. IV Part 2:** 683
Romulus der Grosse (Dürrenmatt), **Supp. IV Part 2:** 683
Ronald, Ann, **Supp. XIII:** 4, 5, 6, 7, 9, 11
"Rondel for a September Day" (White), **Supp. I Part 2:** 676
"Ron Narrative Reconstructions, The" (Coleman), **Supp. XI:** 83
"Ron Padgett's Visual Imagination" (Notley), **Supp. XXII:** 224
Ronsard, Pierre de, **Supp. X:** 65; **Supp. XV:** 165
Rood, John, **IV:** 261
"Roof, the Steeple, and the People, The" (Ellison), **Retro. Supp. II:** 118, 126; **Supp. II Part 1:** 248
"Room" (Levertov), **Supp. III Part 1:** 282
Roomates (film, P. Yates), **Supp. XVII:** 8, 9
Roomates: My Grandfather's Story (Apple), **Supp. XVII:** 2, **7–9**
"Room at the Heart of Things, A" (Merrill), **Supp. III Part 1:** 337
Room Called Remember, A: Uncollected Pieces (Buechner), **Supp. XII:** 53
"Roomful of Hovings, A" (McPhee), **Supp. III Part 1:** 291, 294
Room of One's Own, A (Woolf), **Supp. V:** 127; **Supp. IX:** 19; **Supp. XIII:** 305
Room Rented by a Single Woman (Wright), **Supp. XV:** 340–341
"Rooms" (Collins), **Supp. XXI:** 61

Room Temperature (Baker), **Supp. XIII:** 41, **43–45,** 48, 50
Room to Swing (Lacy), **Supp. XV:** 202, 203, 205, 207
"Room Upstairs, The" (Gioia), **Supp. XV:** 120–121, 124
Roosevelt, Eleanor, **IV:** 371; **Supp. IV Part 2:** 679
Roosevelt, Franklin, **Supp. V:** 290
Roosevelt, Franklin Delano, **I:** 482, 485, 490; **II:** 553, 575; **III:** 2, 18, 69, 110, 297, 321, 376, 476, 580, 581; **Supp. I Part 2:** 488, 489, 490, 491, 645, 654, 655
Roosevelt, Kermit, **III:** 508
Roosevelt, Theodore, **I:** 14, 62; **II:** 130; **III:** 508; **IV:** 321; **Retro. Supp. I:** 377; **Supp. I Part 1:** 1, 21; **Supp. I Part 2:** 455, 456, 502, 707; **Supp. V:** 280, 282; **Supp. IX:** 184; **Supp. XIX:** 29; **Supp. XX: 221**
Roosevelt After Inauguration And Other Atrocities (Burroughs), **Supp. III Part 1:** 98
"Roosevelt Chair, The" (Skloot), **Supp. XX: 205**
"Roosters" (Bishop), **Retro. Supp. II:** 39, 43, 250; **Supp. I Part 1:** 89
Root, Abiah, **I:** 456
Root, Elihu, **Supp. IV Part 1:** 33
Root, Simeon, **I:** 548
Root, Timothy, **I:** 548
Rootabaga Stories (Sandburg), **III:** 583, 587
"Rootedness: The Ancestor as Foundation" (Morrison), **Supp. III Part 1:** 361
"Roots" (Halliday), **Supp. XIX:** 88
Roots in the Soil (film), **Supp. IV Part 1:** 83
"Rope" (Porter), **III:** 451
Rope, The (O'Neill), **III:** 388
Ropemakers of Plymouth, The (Morison), **Supp. I Part 2:** 494
"Ropes" (Nye), **Supp. XIII:** 276
"Rope's End, The" (Nemerov), **III:** 282
Roquelaure, A. N., **Supp. VII:** 301. *See also* Rice, Anne
Rorem, Ned, **Supp. IV Part 1:** 79, 84
Rorschach Test (F. Wright), **Supp. XVII:** 240, 245
Rorty, James, **Supp. XXII:** 276, 277
"Rosa" (Ozick), **Supp. V:** 271
Rosa, Rodrigo Rey, **Supp. IV Part 1:** 92
Rosaldo, Renato, **Supp. IV Part 2:** 544
"Rosalia" (Simic), **Supp. VIII:** 278
Roscoe, Will, **Supp. IV Part 1:** 330
"Roscoe in Hell" (McKnight), **Supp. XX: 151**
"Rose" (Dubus), **Supp. VII:** 88
Rose (L.-Y. Lee), **Supp. XV:** 211, **212–215,** 218
Rose, Alice, Sister, **III:** 348
Rose, Charlie, **Supp. XIX:** 26, 30
Rose, Mickey, **Supp. XV:** 3
Rose, Philip, **Supp. IV Part 1:** 362
"Rose, The" (Roethke), **III:** 537
"Rose, The" (W. C. Williams), **Retro. Supp. I:** 419
Rose, Where Did You Get That Red?: Teaching Great Poetry to Children (Koch), **Supp. XV:** 189
"Rose for Emily, A" (Faulkner), **II:** 72; **Supp. IX:** 96; **Supp. XX: 179**
Rose-Hued Cities (P. N. Warren), **Supp. XX: 261**
Rose in Bloom (Alcott), **Supp. I Part 1:** 42
"Rose-Johnny" (Kingsolver), **Supp. VII:** 203
Rose Madder (King), **Supp. V:** 141, 148, 150, 152
"Rose-Morals" (Lanier), **Supp. I Part 1:** 364
Rosen, Jonathan, **Supp. XVII:** 50; **Supp. XX: 179**
Rosen, Kenneth, **Supp. IV Part 2:** 499, 505, 513
Rosen, Norma, **Supp. XVII:** 49, 50
Rosenbaum, Alissa Zinovievna. *See* Rand, Ayn
Rosenbaum, Thane, **Supp. XVII:** 48
Rosenberg, Bernard, **Supp. I Part 2:** 650
Rosenberg, Harold, **Supp. XV:** 143; **Supp. XIX:** 159
Rosenberg, Julia, **Supp. XVIII:** 136
Rosenberg, Julius and Ethel, **Supp. I Part 1:** 295; **Supp. I Part 2:** 532; **Supp. V:** 45
Rosenberg, Liz, **Supp. XV:** 251
Rosenbloom, Joel, **Supp. IV Part 2:** 527
Rosenfeld, Alvin H., **Supp. I Part 1:** 120
Rosenfeld, Isaac, **Supp. XII:** 160
Rosenfeld, Paul, **I:** 116, 117, 231, 245
Rosenfelt, Deborah, **Supp. XIII:** 296, 304
Rosenfield, Isaac, **IV:** 3
Rosengarten, Theodore, **Supp. XVIII:** 183
Rosenthal, Ira, **Supp. XIV:** 146–147
Rosenthal, Lois, **Supp. VIII:** 258
Rosenthal, M. L., **II:** 550; **III:** 276, 479; **Supp. V:** 333
Rosenthal, Peggy, **Supp. XVII:** 119
"Rose Pogonias" (Frost), **Retro. Supp. I:** 127
"Rose Red and Snow White" (Grimms), **Supp. X:** 82
"Rose Room" (Sorrentino), **Supp. XXI:** 228
"Roses" (Conroy), **Supp. XVI:** 72
"Roses" (Dove), **Supp. IV Part 1:** 246
"Roses and Skulls" (Goldbarth), **Supp. XII:** 192
"Roses for Lubbock" (Nye), **Supp. XIII:** 281
"Roses Only" (Moore), **III:** 195, 198, 200, 202, 215
Rose Tattoo, The (T. Williams), **IV:** 382, 383, 387, 388, 389, 392–393, 394, 397, 398
Rose Theatre (Sorrentino), **Supp. XXI:** 236
"Rosewood, Ohio" (Matthews), **Supp. IX:** 160
Rosie (Lamott), **Supp. XX: 133–134**
Rosinante to the Road Again (Dos Passos), **I:** 478
Roskies, David, **Supp. XVII:** 39, 44, 49–50
Roskolenko, Harry, **Supp. XV:** 179
Rosmersholm (Ibsen), **III:** 152
Rosmond, Babette, **II:** 432
Ross, Eleanor. *See* Taylor, Eleanor Ross
Ross, Harold, **Supp. I Part 1:** 174; **Supp. I Part 2:** 607, 617, 653, 654, 655, 660; **Supp. VIII:** 151, 170; **Supp. IX:** 190
Ross, Herbert, **Supp. XV:** 2
Ross, Jean, **Supp. XXI:** 144, 146
Ross, John F., **II:** 110
Ross, Lillilan, **Retro. Supp. II:** 198
Ross, Mary, **Supp. XXII:** 195
Ross, Mitchell S., **Supp. IV Part 2:** 692; **Supp. X:** 260
Rossen, Robert, **Supp. XI:** 306
Rosset, Barney, **III:** 171
Rossetti, Christina, **Supp. XIV:** 128
Rossetti, Dante Gabriel, **I:** 433; **II:** 323; **Retro. Supp. I:** 128, 286; **Supp. I Part 2:** 552; **Supp. XXII:** 156
Rossetti, William Michael, **Retro. Supp. I:** 407
Rossi, Umberto, **Supp. XVIII:** 137, 138–139
Rossini, Clare, **Supp. XVII:** 111
Rosskam, Edwin, **IV:** 477
Ross Macdonald (Bruccoli), **Supp. IV Part 2:** 468, 470
Rostand, Edmond, **II:** 515; **Supp. IV Part 2:** 518
Rosten, Leo, **Supp. XVII:** 9
Rosy Crucifixion, The (H. Miller), **III:** 170, 187, 188–189, 190
Rote Walker, The (Jarman), **Supp. XVII:** 110, **113–115**
Roth, Henry, **Supp. IV Part 1:** 314; **Supp. VIII:** 233; **Supp. IX: 227–243; Supp. XIII:** 106
Roth, Philip, **I:** 144, 161; **II:** 591; **Retro. Supp. II:** 22, **279–297; Supp. I Part 1:** 186, 192; **Supp. I Part 2:** 431, 441, 443; **Supp. II Part 1:** 99; **Supp. III Part 2: 401–429; Supp. IV Part 1:** 236, 379, 388; **Supp. V:** 45, 119, 122, 257, 258; **Supp. VIII:** 88, 236, 245; **Supp. IX:** 227; **Supp. XI:** 64, 68, 99, 140; **Supp. XII:** 190, 310; **Supp. XIV:** 79, 93, 111, 112; **Supp. XVI:** 206; **Supp. XVII:** 43, 48, 183; **Supp. XVIII:** 89; **Supp. XXI:** 234; **Supp. XXII:** 268
Roth, Rita, **Supp. XVI:** 112
Roth, William, **Supp. XV:** 142
Rothenberg, Jerome, **Supp. VIII:** 292; **Supp. XII:** 3
Rothermere, Lady Mary, **Retro. Supp. I:** 63
Rothko, Mark, **Supp. XV:** 144
Rothstein, Mervyn, **Supp. VIII:** 142
"Rouge High" (Hughes), **Supp. I Part 1:** 330
Rougemont, Denis de, **II:** 586; **IV:** 216; **Retro. Supp. I:** 328, 329, 330, 331
Rough Edges (Skloot), **Supp. XX: 196**
Roughing It (Twain), **II:** 312; **IV:** 195, 197, 198

Roughing It in the Bush (Shields), **Supp. VII:** 313
"Rough Outline" (Simic), **Supp. VIII:** 276
Rough South of Larry Brown, The (film, Hawkins), **Supp. XXI:** 39
Rougon-Macquart, Les (Zola), **II:** 175–176
Roumain, Jacques, **Retro. Supp. I:** 202; **Supp. IV Part 1:** 360, 367
"Round, The" (Kunitz), **Supp. III Part 1:** 268
"Roundelay Between Two Shepherdesses, A" (Notley), **Supp. XXII:** 229
"Round Trip" (Dunn), **Supp. XI:** 148–149
Round Up (Lardner), **II:** 426, 430, 431
Rourke, Constance, **I:** 258; **IV:** 339, 352
Rourke, Milton, **Retro. Supp. II:** 89
Rousseau, Jean-Jacques, **I:** 226; **II:** 8, 343; **III:** 170, 178, 259; **IV:** 80, 173, 440; **Supp. I Part 1:** 126; **Supp. I Part 2:** 637, 659; **Supp. IV Part 1:** 171; **Supp. XI:** 245; **Supp. XVI:** 292; **Supp. XXI:** 83
Roussel, Raymond, **Supp. III Part 1:** 6, 7, 10, 15, 16, 21; **Supp. XV:** 182
"Route 302" (Halliday), **Supp. XIX:** 93
"Routes" (Everwine), **Supp. XV:** 82
"Route Six" (Kunitz), **Supp. III Part 1:** 258
Route Two (Erdrich and Dorris), **Supp. IV Part 1:** 260
"Routine Things Around the House, The" (Dunn), **Supp. XI:** 148
Rover Boys (Winfield), **III:** 146
Rovit, Earl, **IV:** 102
Rowan, Carl T., **Supp. XIV:** 306
Rowe, Anne E., **Supp. X:** 223
Rowe, John Carlos, **Retro. Supp. I:** 216
Rowell, Charles, **Supp. XXI:** 250, 254, 255
"Rowing" (Sexton), **Supp. II Part 2:** 696
"Rowing Endeth, The" (Sexton), **Supp. II Part 2:** 696
Rowlandson, Mary, **Supp. IV Part 2:** 430, 431
"Rows of Cold Trees, The" (Winters), **Supp. II Part 2:** 790–791, 800
Rowson, Susanna, **Supp. I Part 1:** 128; **Supp. XV: 229–248**
Roxanna Slade (Price), **Supp. VI:** 267
Roxie Hart (Watkins), **Supp. XVI:** 188
Royal Family, The (Vollmann), **Supp. XVII:** 226, 230, 233
"Royal Palm" (Crane), **I:** 401
Royce, Josiah, **I:** 443; **III:** 303, 600; **IV:** 26; **Retro. Supp. I:** 57; **Supp. XIV:** 197, 199; **Supp. XVII:** 97
"Roy McInnes" (Budbill), **Supp. XIX:** 6–7
Royster, Sarah Elmira, **III:** 410, 429
Royte, Elizabeth, **Supp. XV:** 59
Rózewicz, Tadeusz, **Supp. X:** 60
R. S. Thomas: Poetry and Theology (W. V. Davis), **Supp. XXI: 86–87**
Ruas, Charles, **Supp. IV Part 1:** 383
Rubáiyát (Khayyám), **I:** 568
Rubáiyát of Omar Khayyam (Fitzgerald), **Supp. I Part 2:** 416; **Supp. III Part 2:** 610; **Supp. XV:** 156
"Rubber Life" (Prose), **Supp. XVI:** 256
Rub from Snub, A (Swanwick), **Supp. XV:** 237
"Rubicon" (Cliff), **Supp. XXII:** 76
Rubin, Louis, **Supp. I Part 2:** 672, 673, 679; **Supp. X:** 42
Rubin, Louis D., Jr., **IV:** 116, 462–463
Rubin, Stan, **Supp. XIV:** 307, 310
Rubin, Stan Sanvel, **Supp. IV Part 1:** 242, 245, 252
Rubins, Josh, **Supp. XX: 89**
"Ruby Brown" (Hughes), **Supp. I Part 1:** 327
"Ruby Daggett" (Eberhart), **I:** 539
Rucker, Rudy, **Supp. X:** 302
Rudd, Hughes, **Supp. XII:** 141
"Rude Awakening, A" (Chopin), **Retro. Supp. II:** 64
Rudens (Plautus), **Supp. III Part 2:** 630
Ruderman, Judith, **Supp. IV Part 1:** 380
Rudge, Olga, **Supp. V:** 338
Rudikoff, Sonya, **Supp. XIV:** 113
Rueckert, William, **I:** 264
Ruesch, Jurgen, **Supp. XV:** 147
Rugby Chapel (Arnold), **Supp. I Part 2:** 416
"Rugby Road" (Garrett), **Supp. VII:** 100
Rugge, John, **Supp. XXII:** 218
Ruining the New Road (Matthews), **Supp. IX:** 154, **155–157**
"Ruins of Italica, The" (Bryant, trans.), **Supp. I Part 1:** 166
Rukeyser, Muriel, **Retro. Supp. II:** 48; **Supp. VI: 271–289; Supp. XV:** 349; **Supp. XVII:** 74
"Rule of Phase Applied to History, The" (Adams), **I:** 19
Rule of the Bone (Banks), **Supp. V:** 16
"Rules by Which a Great Empire May Be Reduced to a Small One" (Franklin), **II:** 120
Rules For the Dance: A Handbook for Reading and Writing Metrical Verse (Oliver), **Supp. VII:** 229, 247
Rules of the Game, The (film), **Supp. XII:** 259
Rulfo, Juan, **Supp. IV Part 2:** 549
Rumba (film, Gering), **Supp. XVII:** 57
Rumbaut, Rubén, **Supp. XI:** 184
Rümelin-Oesterlen, Natalie, **Supp. XX: 235**
Rumens, Carol, **Supp. XI:** 14; **Supp. XVI:** 212
Rumi, **Supp. XX: 117**
"Rumination of Rivers, The" (Bronk), **Supp. XXI:** 32
Rumkowski, Chaim, **Supp. XII:** 168
Rummel, Mary Kay, **Supp. XIII:** 280
"Rumor and a Ladder" (Bowles), **Supp. IV Part 1:** 93
Rumor of War, A (Caputo), **Supp. XIX: 17–21,** 25, 30
Rumors (Simon), **Supp. IV Part 2:** 582–583, 591
Rumpelstiltskin (Gardner), **Supp. VI:** 72
"Rumpelstiltskin" (Grimm), **IV:** 266
"Rumpelstiltskin" (Sexton), **Supp. II Part 2:** 690
"Runagate Runagate" (Hayden), **Supp. II Part 1:** 377
"Runes" (Nemerov), **III:** 267, 277–278
Run Man Run (C. Himes), **Supp. XVI:** 142, 143
"Runner, The" (Grossman), **Supp. XIX:** 83
"Running" (Wilbur), **Supp. III Part 2:** 558–559
Running Dog (DeLillo), **Supp. VI:** 3, 6, 8, 14
"Running in Church" (A. Finch), **Supp. XVII:** 72
"Running the Table" Conroy), **Supp. XVI:** 75
"Run of Bad Luck, A" (Proulx), **Supp. VII:** 253–254
Run of Jacks, A (Hugo), **Supp. VI:** 131, 133, 134, 135, 136
Run River (Didion), **Supp. IV Part 1:** 197, 199–200, 201
Ruoff, A. LaVonne Brown, **Supp. IV Part 1:** 324, 327; **Supp. IV Part 2:** 559
Rupert, Jim, **Supp. XII:** 215
Ruppert, James, **Supp. IV Part 1:** 321
Rural Hours (Cooper), **Supp. XIII:** 152
"Rural Route" (Wright), **Supp. V:** 340
"Rural South, The" (Du Bois), **Supp. II Part 1:** 174
Rush, Benjamin, **Supp. I Part 2:** 505, 507
Rushdie, Salman, **Supp. IV Part 1:** 234, 297
Rushdy, Ashraf, **Supp. X:** 250
Rushing, Jimmy, **Retro. Supp. II:** 113
Rusk, Dean, **II:** 579
Ruskin, John, **II:** 323, 338; **IV:** 349; **Retro. Supp. I:** 56, 360; **Supp. I Part 1:** 2, 10, 87, 349; **Supp. I Part 2:** 410
Rusnak, Karl, **Supp. XVIII:** 149
Russell, Ada Dwyer, **II:** 513, 527
Russell, Bertrand, **II:** 27; **III:** 605, 606; **Retro. Supp. I:** 57, 58, 59, 60; **Supp. I Part 2:** 522; **Supp. V:** 290; **Supp. XII:** 45; **Supp. XIV:** 337
Russell, Diarmuid, **Retro. Supp. I:** 342, 345, 346–347, 349–350
Russell, George, **Retro. Supp. I:** 342
Russell, Herb, **Supp. I Part 2:** 465–466
Russell, John, **Supp. XIV:** 344, 347, 348
Russell, Peter, **III:** 479
Russell, Richard, **Supp. XI:** 102
Russell, Robert, **Supp. XX: 195**
Russell, Sue, **Supp. IV Part 2:** 653
Russert, Margaret, **Supp. XVIII:** 62
Russert, Tim, **Supp. XII:** 272
Russia at War (Caldwell), **I:** 296
Russian Journal, A (Steinbeck), **IV:** 52, 63
Russo, Richard, **Supp. XI:** 349; **Supp. XII: 325–344**
"Rusty Autumn" (Swenson), **Supp. IV Part 2:** 640
Rutabaga-Roo: I've Got a Song and It's for You (Nye, album), **Supp. XIII:** 274
Ruth (biblical book), **Supp. I Part 2:** 516

Ruth, George Herman ("Babe"), **II:** 423; **Supp. I Part 2:** 438, 440
Rutheiser, Charles, **Supp. XXII:** 244
Ruth Hall (Fern), **Supp. V:** 122
Ruthven, K. K., **Supp. XXII:** 261
Rutkowska, Malgorzata, **Supp. XXII:** 208
Rutledge, Ann, **III:** 588; **Supp. I Part 2:** 471
Ruwe, Donelle R., **Supp. XII:** 215
Ryan, Katy, **Supp. XXI:** 215
Ryan, Kay, **Supp. XXI:** 20
Ryan, Maureen, **Supp. XXI:** 215
Ryan, Paul William, **Supp. XVIII: 223–239**
Ryan, Paul William (Mike Quin), **Supp. XXI:** 264–265
Ryder (Barnes), **Supp. III Part 1:** 31, 36–38, 42, 43
"Ryder" (Rukeyser), **Supp. VI:** 273, 283
Ryle, Herbert Edward, **Supp. XX: 230**
Rymer, Thomas, **IV:** 122
"Ryōkan Says" (Budbill), **Supp. XIX:** 11

S. (Updike), **Retro. Supp. I:** 330, 331, 332, 333
S-1 (Baraka), **Supp. II Part 1:** 55, 57
Saadi, **II:** 19
Saar, Doreen Alvarez, **Supp. XV:** 237
"Sabbath, The" (Stowe), **Supp. I Part 2:** 587
"Sabbath Mom" (White), **Supp. I Part 2:** 671–672
Sabbaths (Berry), **Supp. X:** 31
Sabbath's Theater (P. Roth), **Retro. Supp. II:** 279, 288
"Sabbioneta to Parma" (Di Piero), **Supp. XIX:** 36–37
Sabines, Jaime, **Supp. V:** 178
"Sabotage" (Baraka), **Supp. II Part 1:** 49, 53
"Saboteur" (Jin), **Supp. XVIII:** 97
Sacco, Nicola, **I:** 482, 486, 490, 494; **II:** 38–39, 426; **III:** 139–140; **Supp. I Part 2:** 446; **Supp. V:** 288–289; **Supp. IX:** 199; **Supp. XXII:** 277
Sachs, Hanns, **Supp. I Part 1:** 259; **Supp. X:** 186
Sack Full of Old Quarrels, A (Weigl), **Supp. XIX:** 277
"Sacks" (Carver), **Supp. III Part 1:** 143–144
Sacks, Oliver, **Supp. XVIII:** 143
Sacks, Peter, **Supp. IV Part 2:** 450
Sackville-West, Vita, **Supp. VIII:** 263
"Sacrament of Divorce, The" (Patchett), **Supp. XII:** 309
"Sacrament of Self: Catholic Roots of Contemporary Memoir" (lecture, Hampl), **Supp. XXII:** 81
"Sacraments" (Dubus), **Supp. VII:** 91
Sacred and Profane Memories (Van Vechten), **Supp. II Part 2:** 735, 749
"Sacred Chant for the Return of Black Spirit and Power" (Baraka), **Supp. II Part 1:** 51
"Sacred Factory, The" (Toomer), **Supp. IX:** 320
Sacred Fount, The (James), **II:** 332–333; **Retro. Supp. I:** 219, 228, 232
"Sacred Heart" (Egan), **Supp. XIX:** 52
"Sacred Hoop, The: A Contemporary Perspective" (Gunn Allen), **Supp. IV Part 1:** 324
Sacred Hoop, The: Recovering the Feminine in American Indian Traditions (Gunn Allen), **Supp. IV Part 1:** 319, 320, 322, 324, 325, 328–330, 331, 333, 334
Sacred Journey, The (Buechner), **Supp. XII:** 42, 53
"Sacred Thing, The" (Ryan as Quin), **Supp. XVIII:** 227
Sacred Wood, The (Eliot), **IV:** 431; **Retro. Supp. I:** 59, 60; **Supp. I Part 1:** 268; **Supp. II Part 1:** 136, 146
Sacrifice, The (Bidart), **Supp. XV:** 22, **27–30,** 35
"Sacrifice, The" (Bidart), **Supp. XV:** 29
"Sacrifice, The" (Oates), **Supp. II Part 2:** 523
Sacrilege of Alan Kent, The (Caldwell), **I:** 291–292
"Sad Brazil" (Hardwick), **Supp. III Part 1:** 210
"Sad Dust Glories" (Ginsberg), **Supp. II Part 1:** 376
Sad Dust Glories: Poems Written Work Summer in Sierra Woods (Ginsberg), **Supp. II Part 1:** 326
Sade, Marquis de, **III:** 259; **IV:** 437, 442; **Supp. XII:** 1, 14–15
Sad-Faced Boy (Bontemps), **Supp. XXII:** 5, 12
Sad Flower in the Sand, A (film), **Supp. XI:** 173
Sad Heart at the Supermarket, A (Jarrell), **II:** 386
"Sadie" (Matthiessen), **Supp. V:** 201
"Sadie and Maud" (Brooks), **Supp. XVIII:** 175
Sadness and Happiness (Pinsky), **Supp. VI:** 235, **237–241**
"Sadness of Brothers, The" (Kinnell), **Supp. III Part 1:** 237, 251
"Sadness of Days, The" (Salinas), **Supp. XIII:** 325
Sadness of Days, The: Selected and New Poems (Salinas), **Supp. XIII:** 311, **324–326**
"Sadness of Lemons, The" (Levine), **Supp. V:** 184
Sadoff, Ira, **Supp. XVII:** 241; **Supp. XXI:** 100
"Sad Rite" (Karr), **Supp. XI:** 243
"Sad Strains of a Gay Waltz" (Stevens), **Retro. Supp. I:** 302
"Safe" (Gordon), **Supp. IV Part 1:** 299, 306
"Safe in their Alabaster Chambers" (Dickinson), **Retro. Supp. I:** 30
Safer, Morley, **Supp. XIX:** 25
"Safe Subjects" (Komunyakaa), **Supp. XIII:** 118
"Safeway" (F. Barthelme), **Supp. XI:** 26, 27, 36
Saffin, John, **Supp. I Part 1:** 115
Saffy, Edna, **Supp. X:** 227
"Saga of an American Ranch" (P. N. Warren), **Supp. XX: 261**
"Saga of Arturo Bandini" (Fante), **Supp. XI:** 159, **166–169**
"Saga of King Olaf, The" (Longfellow), **II:** 489, 505; **Retro. Supp. II:** 154, 155, 164
"Sage of Stupidity and Wonder, The" (Goldbarth), **Supp. XII:** 191
Sahl, Mort, **II:** 435–436
"Said" (Dixon), **Supp. XII:** 149–150
Said, Edward, **Supp. XXI:** 153
"Sailing after Lunch" (Stevens), **IV:** 73
Sailing Alone Around the Room: New and Selected Poems (Collins), **Supp. XXI:** 54, 56, 62
"Sailing Home from Rapallo" (Lowell), **Retro. Supp. II:** 189
Sailing through China (Theroux), **Supp. VIII:** 323
"Sailing to Byzantium" (Yeats), **III:** 263; **Supp. VIII:** 30; **Supp. X:** 74; **Supp. XI:** 281
"Sail Made of Rags, The" (Nye), **Supp. XIII:** 277
"Sailor off the Bremen" (Shaw), **Supp. XIX:** 247
"Sailors Lost at Sea" (Shields), **Supp. VII:** 318
"*St Anne*/Santa Ana" (Mora), **Supp. XIII:** 229
"*Saint Anthony of Padua*/San Antonio de Padua" (Mora), **Supp. XIII:** 228
"St. Augustine and the Bullfights" (Porter), **III:** 454
Sainte-Beuve, Charles Augustin, **IV:** 432
St. Elmo (Wilson), **Retro. Supp. I:** 351–352
"Saint Emmanuel the Good, Martyr" (Unamuno; Everwine, trans.), **Supp. XV:** 79
Sainte Vierge, La (Picabia), **Retro. Supp. II:** 331
Saint-Exupéry, Antoine de, **Supp. IX:** 247
"St. Francis Einstein of the Daffodils" (W. C. Williams), **IV:** 409–411
Saint-Gaudens, Augustus, **I:** 18, 228; **II:** 551
Saint-Gaudens, Homer, **Supp. XV:** 41
"St. George, the Dragon, and the Virgin" (R. Bly), **Supp. IV Part 1:** 73
St. George and the Godfather (Mailer), **III:** 46; **Retro. Supp. II:** 206, 208
Saint Jack (Theroux), **Supp. VIII:** 319
St. John, David, **Supp. V:** 180; **Supp. XI:** 270, 272; **Supp. XIII:** 312
St. John, Edward B., **Supp. IV Part 2:** 490
St. John, James Hector. *See* Crèvecoeur, Michel-Guillaume Jean de
"Saint John and the Back-Ache" (Stevens), **Retro. Supp. I:** 310
Saint Judas (Wright), **Supp. III Part 2: 595–599**
"Saint Judas" (Wright), **Supp. III Part 2:** 598–599
St. Louis Woman (Bontemps and Cullen), **Supp. IV Part 1:** 170
St. Mawr (Lawrence), **II:** 595

Saint Maybe (Tyler), **Supp. IV Part 2:** 670–671
"Saint Nicholas" (Moore), **III:** 215
St. Petersburg (Biely), **Supp. XII:** 13
Saint-Phalle, Niki de, **Supp. XV:** 187
"St. Roach" (Rukeyser), **Supp. VI:** 286
"Saint Robert" (Dacey), **Supp. IV Part 1:** 70
Saintsbury, George, **IV:** 440; **Supp. XV:** 181
Saints' Everlasting Rest, The (Baxter), **III:** 199; **IV:** 151, 153
Saint-Simon, Claude Henri, **Supp. I Part 2:** 648
"St. Thomas Aquinas" (Simic), **Supp. VIII:** 281
Saks, Gene, **Supp. IV Part 2:** 577, 588
Salamun, Tomaz, **Supp. VIII:** 272
Salazar, Dixie, **Supp. V:** 180; **Supp. XV:** 73
Saldívar, José David, **Supp. IV Part 2:** 544, 545; **Supp. XIX:** 110, 112–113
Sale, Richard, **Supp. IV Part 1:** 379
Sale, Roger, **Supp. V:** 244
Saleh, Dennis, **Supp. V:** 182, 186
"Salem" (Lowell), **II:** 550
Salemi, Joseph, **Supp. IV Part 1:** 284
Salem's Lot (King), **Supp. V:** 139, 144, 146, 151
"Sale of the Hessians, The" (Franklin), **II: 120**
Salinas, Luis Omar, **Supp. IV Part 2:** 545; **Supp. V:** 180; **Supp. XIII: 311–330; Supp. XV:** 73
"Salinas Is on His Way" (Salinas), **Supp. XIII:** 317
"Salinas Sends Messengers to the Stars" (Salinas), **Supp. XIII:** 317
"Salinas Summering at the Caspian and Thinking of Hamlet" (Salinas), **Supp. XIII:** 320
"Salinas Wakes Early and Goes to the Park to Lecture Sparrows" (Salinas), **Supp. XIII:** 320
Salinger, Doris, **III:** 551
Salinger, J. D., **II:** 255; **III: 551–574; IV:** 190, 216, 217; **Retro. Supp. I:** 102, 116, 335; **Supp. IV Part 2:** 502; **Supp. V:** 23, 119; **Supp. VIII:** 151; **Supp. XI:** 2, 66; **Supp. XIV:** 93
Salisbury, Harrison, **Supp. I Part 2:** 664
Salle, David, **Supp. XII:** 4
Salley, Columbus, **Supp. XIV:** 195
"Sally" (Cisneros), **Supp. VII:** 63
"Sally's Choice" (E. Stoddard), **Supp. XV:** 282
Salmagundi; or, The Whim-Whams and Opinions of Launcelot Langstaff Esq., and Others (Irving), **II:** 299, 300, 304
Salmon, Edward G., **Supp. XVIII:** 258
Salome (Strauss), **IV:** 316
Salon (online magazine), **Supp. VIII:** 310; **Supp. X:** 202
Salt Eaters, The (Bambara), **Supp. XI:** 1, **12–14**
Salt Ecstasies, The (White), **Supp. XI:** 123
Salter, James, **Supp. IX: 245–263; Supp. XVI:** 237, 247; **Supp. XIX:** 252
Salter, Mary Jo, **Supp. IV Part 2:** 653; **Supp. IX:** 37, 292; **Supp. XV:** 251, 253; **Supp. XVII:** 112
Salt Garden, The (Nemerov), **III:** 269, 272–275, 277
"Salt Garden, The" (Nemerov), **III:** 267–268
Salting the Ocean (Nye, ed.), **Supp. XIII:** 280
Salt Lesson, The (C. Frost), **Supp. XV:** 92, 96
"Salt Lesson, The" (C. Frost), **Supp. XV:** 99
"Salts and Oils" (Levine), **Supp. V:** 190
Salt to the Devil (film, Dmytryk), **Supp. XX: 41**
Saltzman, Arthur, **Supp. XIII:** 48
Saltzman, Harry, **Supp. XI:** 307
"Salut au Monde!" (Whitman), **Retro. Supp. I:** 387, 396, 400
"Salute" (MacLeish), **III:** 13
Salute (Shaw), **Supp. XIX:** 244
"Salute to Mister Yates, A" (Dubus), **Supp. XI:** 347, 349
Salvador (Didion), **Supp. IV Part 1:** 198, 207–208, 210
"Salvage" (Clampitt), **Supp. IX:** 41
Salvos: An Informal Book About Books and Plays (W. Frank), **Supp. XX: 75**
Samain, Albert, **II:** 528
Same Door, The (Updike), **IV:** 214, 219, 226; **Retro. Supp. I:** 320
"Same in Blues" (Hughes), **Retro. Supp. I:** 208
Same River Twice, The (Offutt), **Supp. XIX:** 163, 164, **167–168,** 175
"Samhain" (A. Finch), **Supp. XVII:** 72
Sam Lawson's Oldtown Fireside Stories (Stowe), **Supp. I Part 2:** 587, 596, 598–599
Sam Patch, the High, Wide & Handsome Jumper (Bontemps and Conroy), **Supp. XXII:** 5, 11
"Sa'm Pèdi" (Bell), **Supp. X:** 17
"Sampler, A" (MacLeish), **III:** 4
Sampoli, Maria, **Supp. V:** 338
Sampson, Edward, **Supp. I Part 2:** 664, 673
Sampson, Martin, **Supp. I Part 2:** 652
"Sam's Dad" (Lamott), **Supp. XX: 142–143**
Sam's Legacy (Neugeboren), **Supp. XVI:** 221, 222
Samson Agonistes (Milton), **III:** 274
"Samson and Delilah" (Masters), **Supp. I Part 2:** 459
Samuel de Champlain: Father of New France (Morison), **Supp. I Part 2:** 496–497
Samuels, Charles Thomas, **Retro. Supp. I:** 334
"Samuel Sewall" (Hecht), **Supp. X:** 58
"Samwheel" (Lamott), **Supp. XX: 144–145**
Sanborn, Franklin B., **IV:** 171, 172, 178
Sanborn, Kate, **Supp. XIII:** 152
Sanborn, Sara, **Supp. XIV:** 113
Sanchez, Carol Anne, **Supp. IV Part 1:** 335
Sanchez, Carol Lee, **Supp. IV Part 2:** 499, 557
Sanchez, Sonia, **Supp. II Part 1:** 34
Sánchez Beras, César, **Supp. XXI:** 100, 104
Sanctified Church, The (Hurston), **Supp. VI:** 150
"Sanction of the Victims, The" (Rand), **Supp. IV Part 2:** 528
Sanctuary (Faulkner), **II:** 57, 61–63, 72, 73, 74, 174; **Retro. Supp. I:** 73, 84, 86–87, 87; **Supp. I Part 2:** 614; **Supp. XII:** 16
"Sanctuary" (Larsen), **Supp. XVIII:** 119, 130–131
Sanctuary (Wharton), **IV:** 311
"Sanctuary" (Wylie), **Supp. I Part 2:** 711
"Sanctuary, The" (Nemerov), **III:** 272, 274
Sanctuary V (Schulberg), **Supp. XVIII:** 254
"Sanctus" (Nelson), **Supp. XVIII:** 183
Sand, George, **II:** 322; **Retro. Supp. I:** 235, 372; **Supp. XV:** 275
"Sandalphon" (Longfellow), **II:** 498
Sand and Foam: A Book of Aphorisms (Gibran), **Supp. XX: 115, 121–122**
Sandbox, The (Albee), **I:** 74–75, 89
Sandburg, Carl, **I:** 103, 109, 384, 421; **II:** 529; **III:** 3, 20, **575–598; Retro. Supp. I:** 133, 194; **Supp. I Part 1:** 257, 320; **Supp. I Part 2:** 387, 389, 454, 461, 653; **Supp. III Part 1:** 63, 71, 73, 75; **Supp. IV Part 1:** 169; **Supp. IV Part 2:** 502; **Supp. IX:** 1, 15, 308; **Supp. XIII:** 274, 277; **Supp. XV:** 293, 299, 300, 301, 302, 306; **Supp. XXII:** 275
Sandburg, Mrs. Carl (Lillian Steichen), **III:** 580
Sandburg, Helga, **III:** 583
Sandburg, Janet, **III:** 583, 584
Sandburg, Margaret, **III:** 583, 584
Sand County Almanac and Sketches Here and There, A (Leopold), **Supp. XIV:** 177, 178, **182–192**
"Sand Dabs" (Oliver), **Supp. VII:** 245
"Sand Dunes" (Frost), **Retro. Supp. I:** 137; **Retro. Supp. II:** 41
Sander, August, **Supp. IX:** 211
Sanders, Mark, **Supp. XIX:** 119, 121
Sanders, Scott Russell, **Supp. XVI: 265–280**
Sandlin, Tim, **Supp. XXII:** 114
"Sandman, The" (Barthelme), **Supp. IV Part 1:** 47
Sandman's Dust (Bukiet), **Supp. XVII:** 40, 41
Sando, Joe S., **Supp. IV Part 2:** 510
Sandoe, James, **Supp. IV Part 1:** 131; **Supp. IV Part 2:** 470
Sandoz, Mari, **Supp. XV:** 141
Sandperl, Ira, **Supp. VIII:** 200
"Sand-Quarry and Moving Figures" (Rukeyser), **Supp. VI:** 271, 278
Sand Rivers (Matthiessen), **Supp. V:** 203
"Sand Roses, The" (Hogan), **Supp. IV Part 1:** 401
Sands, Diana, **Supp. IV Part 1:** 362
Sands, Robert, **Supp. I Part 1:** 156, 157

"Sands at Seventy" (Whitman), **IV:** 348
"Sandstone Farmhouse, A" (Updike), **Retro. Supp. I:** 318
Sandy Bottom Orchestra,The (Keillor and Nilsson), **Supp. XVI:** 177
Sanford, John, **IV:** 286, 287
San Francisco (film), **Supp. XVI:** 181, 192
"San Francisco" (Hempel), **Supp. XXI:** 118
"San Francisco Blues" (Kerouac), **Supp. III Part 1:** 225
Sangamon County Peace Advocate, The (Lindsay), **Supp. I Part 2:** 379
Sanger, Margaret, **Supp. I Part 1:** 19; **Supp. XXI:** 6
Sankofa (film), **Supp. XX: 154**
Sansom, William, **IV:** 279
Sans Soleil (film), **Supp. IV Part 2:** 436
"Santa" (Sexton), **Supp. II Part 2:** 693
Santa Claus: A Morality (Cummings), **I:** 430, 441
"Santa Fé Trail, The" (Lindsay), **Supp. I Part 2:** 389
"Santa Lucia" (Hass), **Supp. VI:** 105–106
"Santa Lucia II" (Hass), **Supp. VI:** 105–106
Santayana, George, **I:** 222, 224, 236, 243, 253, 460; **II:** 20, 542; **III:** 64, **599–622; IV:** 26, 339, 351, 353, 441; **Retro. Supp. I:** 55, 57, 67, 295; **Retro. Supp. II:** 179; **Supp. I Part 2:** 428; **Supp. II Part 1:** 107; **Supp. X:** 58; **Supp. XIV:** 199, 335, 340, 342; **Supp. XVI:** 189; **Supp. XVII:** 97, 106; **Supp. XX: 228, 229, 231**
Santiago, Esmeralda, **Supp. XI:** 177
"Santorini: Stopping the Leak" (Merrill), **Supp. III Part 1:** 336
Santos, John Phillip, **Supp. XIII:** 274
Santos, Sherod, **Supp. VIII:** 270
Sapir, Edward, **Supp. VIII:** 295; **Supp. XVI:** 283
"Sapphics for Patience" (A. Finch), **Supp. XVII:** 72
Sapphira and the Slave Girl (Cather), **I:** 331; **Retro. Supp. I:** 2, **19–20**
Sappho, **II:** 544; **III:** 142; **Supp. I Part 1:** 261, 269; **Supp. I Part 2:** 458; **Supp. XII:** 98, 99; **Supp. XVII:** 74
"Sappho" (Wright), **Supp. III Part 2:** 595, 604
"Sara" (song, Dylan), **Supp. XVIII:** 28
"Sarah" (Schwartz), **Supp. II Part 2:** 663
Sarah; or, The Exemplary Wife (Rowson), **Supp. XV:** 242
"Saratoga" mysteries (Dobyns), **Supp. XIII:** 79–80
Sargent, John Singer, **II:** 337, 338; **Supp. XX: 231**
Sarlós, Robert K., **Supp. XXI:** 7, 12, 13
Saroyan, Aram, **Supp. XV:** 182
Saroyan, William, **III:** 146–147; **IV:** 393; **Supp. I Part 2:** 679; **Supp. IV Part 1:** 83; **Supp. IV Part 2:** 502; **Supp. XIII:** 280
Sarris, Greg, **Supp. IV Part 1:** 329, 330
Sarton, George, **Supp. VIII:** 249
Sarton, May, **Supp. III Part 1:** 62, 63; **Supp. VIII: 249–268; Supp. XIII:** 296; **Supp. XVII:** 71
Sartoris (Faulkner), **II:** 55, 56–57, 58, 62; **Retro. Supp. I:** 77, 81, 82, 83, 88
Sartor Resartus (Carlyle), **II:** 26; **III:** 82
Sartre, Jean-Paul, **I:** 82, 494; **II:** 57, 244; **III:** 51, 204, 292, 453, 619; **IV:** 6, 223, 236, 477, 487, 493; **Retro. Supp. I:** 73; **Supp. I Part 1:** 51; **Supp. IV Part 1:** 42, 84; **Supp. VIII:** 11; **Supp. IX:** 4; **Supp. XIII:** 74, 171; **Supp. XIV:** 24; **Supp. XVII:** 137
Sassone, Ralph, **Supp. X:** 171
Sassoon, Siegfried, **II:** 367; **Supp. XV:** 308; **Supp. XIX:** 18
Satan in Goray (Singer), **IV:** 1, 6–7, 12; **Retro. Supp. II:** 303, **304–305**
Satan Says (Olds), **Supp. X:** 201, 202, **202–204,** 215
"Satan Says" (Olds), **Supp. X:** 202; **Supp. XVII:** 114
Satanstoe (Cooper), **I:** 351–352, 355
"Sather Gate Illumination" (Ginsberg), **Supp. II Part 1:** 329
"Satire as a Way of Seeing" (Dos Passos), **III:** 172
Satires of Persius, The (Merwin, trans.), **Supp. III Part 1:** 347
Satirical Rogue on Poetry, The (Francis). *See Pot Shots at Poetry* (Francis)
Satori in Paris (Kerouac), **Supp. III Part 1:** 231
"Saturday" (Salinas), **Supp. XIII:** 315
"Saturday Matinee" (Trethewey), **Supp. XXI:** 251
Saturday Night at the War (Shanley), **Supp. XIV:** 315
"Saturday Rain" (Kees), **Supp. XV:** 136
"Saturday Route, The" (Wolfe), **Supp. III Part 2:** 580
Satyagraha (Gandhi), **IV:** 185
"Satyr's Heart, The" (B. Kelly), **Supp. XVII:** 132
Saul and Patsy (C. Baxter), **Supp. XVII:** 22–23
"Saul and Patsy" (C. Baxter), **Supp. XVII:** 17
"Saul and Patsy Are Getting Comfortable in Michigan" (C. Baxter), **Supp. XVII:** 22
"Saul and Patsy Are in Labor" (C. Baxter), **Supp. XVII:** 20, 22
"Saul and Patsy Are Pregnant" (C. Baxter), **Supp. XVII:** 22
Saunders, George, **Supp. XIX: 223–237; Supp. XXII:** 49
Saunders, Richard, **II:** 110
Savage, Augusta, **Retro. Supp. II:** 115
Savage, James, **II:** 111
Savage Holiday (Wright), **IV:** 478, 488
Savage in Limbo: A Concert Play (Shanley), **Supp. XIV:** 315, **319–321,** 323, 324
Savage Love (Shepard and Chaikin), **Supp. III Part 2:** 433
Savage Place, A (Parker), **Supp. XIX:** 185
Savage Wilds (Reed), **Supp. X:** 241
Save Me, Joe Louis (Bell), **Supp. X:** 7, 10, **11–12**
Save Me the Waltz (Z. Fitzgerald), **II:** 95; **Retro. Supp. I:** 110; **Supp. IX:** 58, 59, 65, **66–68**
Savers, Michael, **Supp. XI:** 307
Saving Lives (Goldbarth), **Supp. XII:** 192
Saving Private Ryan (film), **Supp. V:** 249; **Supp. XI:** 234
Savings (Hogan), **Supp. IV Part 1:** 397, 404, 405, 406, 410
Savo, Jimmy, **I:** 440
Savran, David, **Supp. IX:** 145; **Supp. XIII:** 209; **Supp. XV:** 321
"Sawdust" (Offutt), **Supp. XIX:** 164
Sawyer-Lauçanno, Christopher, **Supp. IV Part 1:** 95
Saxon, Lyle, **Retro. Supp. I:** 80
"Saxophone" (Di Piero), **Supp. XIX:** 38
"Sax's and Selves" (Halliday), **Supp. XIX:** 88
"Say All" (Ray), **Supp. XVIII:** 193
Say and Seal (S. and A. Warner), **Supp. XVIII:** 258, 266
Saye and Sele, Lord, **Supp. I Part 1:** 98
Sayer, Mandy, **Supp. XIII:** 118
Sayers, Dorothy, **Supp. IV Part 1:** 341; **Supp. IV Part 2:** 464
Sayers, Valerie, **Supp. XI:** 253; **Supp. XVIII:** 99
"Say Good-bye" (Weigl), **Supp. XIX:** 288
"Sayings/For Luck" (Goldbarth), **Supp. XII:** 176
"Saying What Needs To Be Said" (Skloot), **Supp. XX: 201**
Say! Is This the U.S.A.? (Caldwell), **I:** 293, 294–295, 304, 309, 310
Saylor, Bruce, **Supp. XII:** 253
Sayre, Joel, **Supp. XIII:** 166
Sayre, Nora, **Supp. XII:** 119
Sayre, Zelda, **Retro. Supp. I:** 101, 102–103, 104, 105, 108, 109, 110, 113, 114. *See also* Fitzgerald, Zelda (Zelda Sayre)
"Say Yes" (Wolff), **Supp. VII:** 344
"Say You Love Me" (Peacock), **Supp. XIX:** 198
"Scale" (Halliday), **Supp. XIX:** 92
"Scales of the Eyes, The" (Nemerov), **III:** 272, 273, 277
Scalpel (McCoy), **Supp. XIII: 174–175**
Scalpel (screen treatment, McCoy), **Supp. XIII:** 174
Scandalabra (Zelda Fitzgerald), **Supp. IX:** 60, 61, 65, 67, **68–70**
"Scandal Detectives, The" (Fitzgerald), **II:** 80–81; **Retro. Supp. I:** 99
Scarberry-García, Susan, **Supp. IV Part 2:** 486
Scarborough, Dorothy, **Supp. XVIII:** 279–280
Scarecrow, The (Connelly), **Supp. XXI:** 71, 74, 78, **79**
"Scarecrow, The" (Farrell), **II:** 45
"Scarf, A" (Shields), **Supp. VII:** 328
Scarlet Cabinet, The (Notley), **Supp. XXII:** 233
Scarlet Letter, The (Hawthorne), **II:** 63, 223, 224, 231, 233, 239–240, 241,

243, 244, 255, 264, 286, 290, 291, 550; **Retro. Supp. I:** 63, 145, 147, 152, **157–159,** 160, 163, 165, 220, 248, 330, 335; **Retro. Supp. II:** 100; **Supp. I Part 1:** 38; **Supp. II Part 1:** 386; **Supp. VIII:** 108, 198; **Supp. XII:** 11; **Supp. XVII:** 143; **Supp. XX: 178, 183; Supp. XXII:** 147
"Scarlet Letter Aleph, The" (Mirvis), **Supp. XX: 183**
Scarlet Plague, The (London), **II:** 467
Scarlet Sister Mary (Peterkin), **Supp. XXII:** 189
Scar Lover (Crews), **Supp. XI:** 103, 107, **114–115**
"Scarred Girl, The" (Dickey), **Supp. IV Part 1:** 180
Scates, Maxine, **Supp. XIV:** 264, 265, 274
"Scenario" (H. Miller), **III:** 184
"Scene" (Howells), **II:** 274
"Scene in Jerusalem, A" (Stowe), **Supp. I Part 2:** 587
"Scenes" (Shields), **Supp. VII:** 318
Scènes d'Anabase (chamber music) (Bowles), **Supp. IV Part 1:** 82
"Scenes from a Documentary History of Mississippi" (Trethewey), **Supp. XXI:** 255–256
Scenes from American Life (Gurney), **Supp. V:** 95, 96, 105, 108
Scenes from Another Life (McClatchy), **Supp. XII: 255–256**
"Scenes from Childhood" (W. V. Davis), **Supp. XXI:** 95
"Scenes of Childhood" (Merrill), **Supp. III Part 1:** 322, 323, 327
"Scented Herbage of My Breast" (Whitman), **IV:** 342–343
"Scent of a Woman's Ink" (Prose), **Supp. XVI:** 259
"Scent of Unbought Flowers, The" (Ríos), **Supp. IV Part 2:** 547
Scepticisms (Aiken), **I:** 58
Scève, Maurice, **Supp. III Part 1:** 11
Schad, Christian, **Supp. IV Part 1:** 247
Schafer, Benjamin G., **Supp. XIV:** 144
Schafer, William, **Supp. XIX:** 164, 172
Schaller, George, **Supp. V:** 208, 210–211
Schapiro, Meyer, **II:** 30
Scharmann, Hermann Balthazar, **Supp. XII:** 41
Scharper, Alice, **Supp. XXII:** 175
Schary, Dore, **Supp. IV Part 1:** 365; **Supp. XIII:** 163
Schatz, Tom, **Supp. XVIII:** 242
Schaum, Melita, **Supp. XXII:** 166
Schaumbergh, Count de, **II:** 120
Scheele, Roy, **Supp. XVI:** 54; **Supp. XXI:** 103
Scheeman, George, **Supp. XXII:** 230
Scheffauer, G. H., **I:** 199
"Scheherazade" (Ashbery), **Supp. III Part 1:** 18
Scheick, William, **Supp. V:** 272
Schelberg, Budd, **Supp. XVIII: 241–256**
Scheler, Max, **I:** 58
Schelling, Friedrich, **Supp. I Part 2:** 422
Schenck, Joseph, **Supp. XVI:** 186
Schenk, Margaret, **I:** 199
Scheponik, Peter, **Supp. X:** 210
Scherer, Loline, **Supp. XIII:** 161
Schevill, James, **I:** 116
Schickel, Richard, **Supp. XV:** 1
Schilder, Paul, **Supp. I Part 2:** 622
Schiller, Andrew, **II:** 20
Schiller, Frederick, **Supp. V:** 290
Schiller, Johann Christoph Friedrich von, **I:** 224; **Supp. IV Part 2:** 519; **Supp. XVI:** 292
Schiller, Lawrence, **Retro. Supp. II:** 208, 212, 214
Schimmel, Harold, **Supp. V:** 336
"Schizoid Nature of the Implied Author in Twentieth-Century American Ethnic Novels, The" (Nelson), **Supp. XVIII:** 172
Schlegel, Augustus Wilhelm, **III:** 422, 424
Schlegell, David von, **Supp. IV Part 2:** 423
Schleiermacher, Friedrich, **III:** 290–291, 309
Schleifer, Ronald, **Supp. XVIII:** 144
Schlepping Through the Alps (S. Apple), **Supp. XVII:** 8
Schlesinger, Arthur, Jr., **III:** 291, 297–298, 309
Schmidt, Jon Zlotnik, **Supp. IV Part 1:** 2
Schmidt, Kaspar. *See* Stirner, Max
Schmidt, Michael, **Supp. X:** 55
Schmitt, Carl, **I:** 386–387
Schmitz, Neil, **Supp. X:** 243
Schnackenberg, Gjertrud, **Supp. XV: 249–268**
Schneider, Alan, **I:** 87
Schneider, Louis, **Supp. I Part 2:** 650
Schneider, Romy, **Supp. IV Part 2:** 549
Schneider, Steven, **Supp. IX:** 271, 274
Schnellock, Emil, **III:** 177
Schneour, Zalman, **IV:** 11
"Schnetzer Day" (Halliday), **Supp. XIX:** 93
Schnitzler, Arthur, **Supp. XV:** 307; **Supp. XVI:** 187
Schoerke, Meg, **Supp. XVII:** 110
"Scholar Gypsy, The" (Arnold), **II:** 541
"Scholastic and Bedside Teaching" (Holmes), **Supp. I Part 1:** 305
Schöler, Bo, **Supp. IV Part 1:** 399, 400, 403, 407, 409; **Supp. IV Part 2:** 499
Scholes, Robert, **Supp. V:** 40, 42
Scholtz, Carter, **Supp. XVIII:** 144
Schomburg, Arthur, **Supp. X:** 134; **Supp. XXII:** 6
Schomburg Library of Nineteenth-Century Black Women Writers (H. L. Gates, ed.), **Supp. XX: 105**
Schönberg, Claude-Michel, **Supp. XXI:** 155
Schoolboy Howlers (Abingdon), **Supp. XVI:** 99
Schoolcraft, Henry Rowe, **II:** 503; **Retro. Supp. II:** 160
"School Daze" (Bambara), **Supp. XI:** 19
School Daze (film), **Supp. XI:** 19, 20
"Schoolhouse" (Levis), **Supp. XI:** 258
"School of Giorgione, The" (Pater), **I:** 51
"School Play, The" (Merrill), **Supp. III Part 1:** 336
"Schooner Fairchild's Class" (Benét), **Supp. XI:** 55
Schopenhauer, Arthur, **III:** 600, 604; **IV:** 7; **Retro. Supp. I:** 256; **Retro. Supp. II:** 94; **Supp. I Part 1:** 320; **Supp. I Part 2:** 457; **Supp. X:** 187; **Supp. XVI:** 184
Schorer, Mark, **II:** 28; **III:** 71; **Retro. Supp. I:** 115; **Supp. IV Part 1:** 197, 203, 211; **Supp. XVI:** 206
Schott, Webster, **Supp. IX:** 257
Schotts, Jeffrey, **Supp. XII:** 193
Schrader, Mary von. *See* Jarrell, Mrs. Randall (Mary von Schrader)
Schreiber, Jan, **Supp. XXI:** 105, 111
Schreiner, Olive, **I:** 419; **Supp. XI:** 203
Schroeder, Eric James, **Supp. V:** 238, 244
Schubert, Bernard L., **Supp. XVII:** 58
Schubert, Franz Peter, **Supp. I Part 1:** 363
Schubnell, Matthias, **Supp. IV Part 2:** 486
Schudel, Matt, **Supp. XXII:** 205, 214
Schulberg, Budd, **II:** 98; **Retro. Supp. I:** 113; **Supp. XIII:** 170; **Supp. XV:** 194
Schulberg, Stuart, **Supp. XVIII:** 254
Schulman, Tom, **Supp. XXI:** 193, 194
Schulz, Bruno, **Supp. IV Part 2:** 623; **Supp. XVII:** 41
Schuman, William, **Supp. XII:** 253; **Supp. XXII:** 283
Schumann, Dr. Alanson Tucker, **III:** 505
Schuster, Edgar H., **Supp. VIII:** 126
Schuyler, George S., **III:** 110; **Supp. XVI:** 142; **Supp. XIX:** 78
Schuyler, James, **Supp. XV:** 177, 178
Schuyler, William, **Supp. I Part 1:** 211
"Schuylkill, The" (Halliday), **Supp. XIX:** 92
Schwartz, Delmore, **I:** 67, 168, 188, 288; **IV:** 128, 129, 437; **Retro. Supp. II:** 29, 178; **Supp. II Part 1:** 102, 109; **Supp. II Part 2: 639–668; Supp. VIII:** 98; **Supp. IX:** 299; **Supp. XIII:** 320; **Supp. XIV:** 3; **Supp. XV:** 184; **Supp. XIX:** 257
Schwartz, Leonard, **Supp. XVI:** 289
Schwartz, Lloyd, **Supp. I Part 1:** 81
Schwartz, Marilyn, **Supp. XII:** 126, 128, 130, 132
Schwartz, Meryl F., **Supp. XXII:** 65, 66
Schwartz, Richard B., **Supp. XIV:** 23, 27
Schwarz, A. B. Christa, **Supp. XIX:** 77, 79
Schwed, Peter, **Supp. XXII:** 119
Schweitzer, Albert, **Supp. IV Part 1:** 373
Schweitzer, Harold, **Supp. X:** 210
Schwerdt, Lisa M., **Supp. XIV:** 155, 171
Schwitters, Kurt, **III:** 197; **Retro. Supp. II:** 322, 331, 336; **Supp. IV Part 1:** 79
"Science" (Jeffers), **Supp. II Part 2:** 426
Science and Health with Key to the Scriptures (Eddy), **I:** 383
"Science Favorable to Virtue" (Freneau), **Supp. II Part 1:** 274
Science of English Verse, The (Lanier), **Supp. I Part 1:** 368, 369

"Science of the Night, The" (Kunitz), **Supp. III Part 1:** 258, 265
"Sci-Fi Floater Genius" (Halliday), **Supp. XIX:** 91
Sciolino, Martina, **Supp. XII:** 9
"Scissors" (C. Baxter), **Supp. XVII:** 19
Scofield, Sandra, **Supp. XXI:** 119
Scooter tetralogy (Murray). *See Magic Keys, The* (Murray); *Seven League Boots, The* (Murray); *Spyglass Tree, The* (Murray); *Train Whistle Guitar* (Murray)
Scopes, John T., **III:** 105, 495
"Scorched Face, The" (Hammett), **Supp. IV Part 1:** 344
"Scorn" (C. Frost), **Supp. XV:** 105
"Scorpion, The" (Bowles), **Supp. IV Part 1:** 84, 86
Scorsese, Martin, **Supp. IV Part 1:** 356; **Supp. XVIII:** 22
Scott, Anne Firor, **Supp. I Part 1:** 19
Scott, A. O., **Supp. X:** 301, 302; **Supp. XII:** 343
Scott, Evelyn, **Retro. Supp. I:** 73; **Supp. XXII:** 198
Scott, Gavin, **Supp. XXII:** 218
Scott, George C., **III:** 165–166; **Supp. XI:** 304
Scott, George Lewis, **Supp. I Part 2:** 503, 504
Scott, Hazel, **Supp. XXII:** 12
Scott, Herbert, **Supp. V:** 180
Scott, Howard, **Supp. I Part 2:** 645
Scott, Joanna, **Supp. XVII: 183–197**
Scott, Lizabeth, **Supp. IV Part 2:** 524
Scott, Lynn Orilla, **Retro. Supp. II:** 12
Scott, Mark, **Retro. Supp. I:** 127
Scott, Nathan A., Jr., **II:** 27
Scott, Paul, **Supp. IV Part 2:** 690
Scott, Ridley, **Supp. XIII:** 268
Scott, Walter, **Supp. XVI:** 7, 13
Scott, Sir Walter, **I:** 204, 339, 341, 343, 354; **II:** 8, 17, 18, 217, 296, 301, 303, 304, 308; **III:** 415, 482; **IV:** 204, 453; **Retro. Supp. I:** 99; **Supp. I Part 2:** 579, 580, 685, 692; **Supp. IV Part 2:** 690; **Supp. IX:** 175; **Supp. X:** 51, 114
Scott, Winfield Townley, **II:** 512; **Supp. I Part 2:** 705; **Supp. XV:** 51
Scottsboro boys, **I:** 505; **Supp. I Part 1:** 330
Scottsboro Limited (Hughes), **Retro. Supp. I:** 203; **Supp. I Part 1:** 328, 330–331, 332
Scoundrel Time (Hellman), **Supp. I Part 1:** 294–297; **Supp. IV Part 1:** 12; **Supp. VIII:** 243
Scrambled Eggs Super! (Geisel), **Supp. XVI:** 105
Scrambled Eggs & Whiskey: Poems, 1991–1995 (Carruth), **Supp. XVI:** 47
Scratch (MacLeish), **III:** 22–23
"Scratch Music" (Wright), **Supp. XV:** 343
"Scream, The" (Lowell), **II:** 550
"Screamer, The" (Coleman), **Supp. XI: 92–93**
"Screamers, The" (Baraka), **Supp. II Part 1:** 38
"Screen Guide for Americans" (Rand), **Supp. IV Part 2:** 524
"Screen Memory" (Cliff), **Supp. XXII:** 75
"Screeno" (Schwartz), **Supp. II Part 2:** 660
Screens, The (Genet), **Supp. XII:** 12
Screen Sirens Scream! (Parla and Mitchell), **Supp. XXII:** 256
Scribblers on the Roof: Contemporary American Jewish Fiction (Bukiet and Roskies, eds.), **Supp. XVII:** 39, 49–50
Scripts for the Pageant (Merrill), **Supp. III Part 1:** 332, 333, 335
Scrolls from the Dead Sea, The (Wilson), **IV:** 429
Scruggs, Earl, **Supp. V:** 335
Scudder, Horace Elisha, **II:** 400, 401; **Retro. Supp. II:** 67; **Supp. I Part 1:** 220; **Supp. I Part 2:** 410, 414
Scully, James, **Supp. XII:** 131
"Sculpting the Whistle" (Ríos), **Supp. IV Part 2:** 549
"Sculptor" (Plath), **Supp. I Part 2:** 538
"Sculptor's Funeral, The" (Cather), **I:** 315–316; **Retro. Supp. I:** 5, 6; **Supp. XV:** 40
Scum (Singer), **Retro. Supp. II:** 316–317
Scupoli, Lorenzo, **IV:** 156
"Scythe Song" (Lang), **Retro. Supp. I:** 128
Sea and the Mirror, The: A Commentary on Shakespeare's "The Tempest" (Auden), Supp. II Part 1: 2, 18
Sea around Us, The (Carson), **Supp. IX:** 19, **23–25**
Sea around Us, The (film), **Supp. IX:** 25
Sea Birds Are Still Alive, The (Bambara), **Supp. XI:** 1, 4, **7–12**
"Sea Birds Are Still Alive, The" (Bambara), **Supp. XI:** 8
"Sea-Blue and Blood-Red" (Lowell), **II:** 524
Seabrook, John, **Supp. VIII:** 157
"Sea Burial from the Cruiser Reve" (Eberhart), **I:** 532–533
Seabury, David, **Supp. I Part 2:** 608
"Sea Calm" (Hughes), **Retro. Supp. I:** 199
"Sea Chanty" (Corso), **Supp. XII:** 118
"Sea Dream, A" (Whitter), **Supp. I Part 2:** 699
"Seafarer, The" (Pound, trans.), **Retro. Supp. I:** 287
Seagall, Harry, **Supp. XIII:** 166
Sea Garden (Doolittle), **Supp. I Part 1:** 257, 259, 266, 269, 272
Seager, Allan, **IV:** 305
"Seagulls and Children" (C. Frost), **Supp. XV:** 95
Sea Lady, The (Boyce), **Supp. XXI:** 8, 13
"Sea Lily" (Doolittle), **Supp. I Part 1:** 266
Sea Lions, The (Cooper), **I:** 354, 355
Sealts, Merton M., Jr., **Retro. Supp. I:** 257
Seaman, Donna, **Supp. VIII:** 86; **Supp. X:** 1, 4, 12, 16, 213; **Supp. XV:** 65; **Supp. XVIII:** 102; **Supp. XIX:** 53, 55, 57, 58, 59, 60, 61; **Supp. XXI:** 236; **Supp. XXII:** 266
"Séance, The" (Singer), **IV:** 20
Séance and Other Stories, The (Singer), **IV:** 19–21
"Sea Oak" (Saunders), **Supp. XIX:** 228, 229, 231
Sea of Cortez (Steinbeck), **IV:** 52, 54, 62, 69
Sea of Grass, The (film), **Supp. XVIII:** 211
Sea of Grass, The (Richter), **Supp. XVIII: 210–211,** 215–216, 217, 220
"Sea Pieces" (Melville), **III:** 93
Searchers, The (film, Ford), **Supp. XVIII:** 57, 58, 135–136, 141
Searches and Seizures (Elkin), **Supp. VI: 49**
"Search for Southern Identity, The" (Woodward), **Retro. Supp. I:** 75; **Supp. XXII:** 194
Search for the King, A: A Twelfth-Century Legend (Vidal), **Supp. IV Part 2:** 681
Searching for Caleb (Tyler), **Supp. IV Part 2:** 663–665, 671
"Searching for Poetry: Real *vs.* Fake" (B. Miller), **Supp. IV Part 1:** 67
Searching for Survivors (Banks), **Supp. V:** 7
"Searching for Survivors (I)" (Banks), **Supp. V:** 8
"Searching for Survivors (II)" (Banks), **Supp. V:** 7, 8
Searching for the Ox (Simpson), **Supp. IX:** 266, **274–275**
"Searching for the Ox" (Simpson), **Supp. IX:** 275, 280
"Searching in the Britannia Tavern" (Wagoner), **Supp. IX:** 327
Searching Wing, The, (Hellman), **Supp. I Part 1:** 277, 278, 281–282, 283, 292, 297
Search-Light. *See* Frank, Waldo
"Search Party, The" (Matthews), **Supp. IX: 156**
Searle, Ronald, **Supp. I Part 2:** 604, 605
Sea Road to the Indies (Hart), **Supp. XIV:** 97
"Seascape" (Bishop), **Retro. Supp. II:** 42–43
"Sea's Green Sameness, The" (Updike), **IV:** 217
Seaside and the Fireside, The (Longfellow), **II:** 489; **Retro. Supp. II:** 159, 168
Season in Hell, A (Rimbaud), **III:** 189
Seasons, The (Thomson), **II:** 304; **Supp. I Part 1:** 151
Seasons' Difference, The (Buechner), **Supp. XII: 47**
Seasons of Celebration (Merton), **Supp. VIII:** 199, 208
Seasons of the Heart: In Quest of Faith (Kinard, comp.), **Supp. XIV:** 127
"Seasons of the Soul" (Tate), **IV:** 136–140
Seasons on Earth (Koch), **Supp. XV: 183–184**

"Sea Surface Full of Clouds" (Stevens), **IV:** 82
"Sea Tides" (Hoffman), **Supp. XVIII:** 87
"Sea Treader" (Hoffman), **Supp. XVIII:** 87
"Sea Unicorns and Land Unicorns" (Moore), **III:** 202–203
Seaver, Richard, **Supp. XI:** 301
"Seaweed" (Longfellow), **II:** 498
Sea-Wolf, The (London), **II:** 264, 466, 472–473
Sebald, W. G., **Supp. XIV:** 96; **Supp. XXI:** 92
Sebold, Alice, **Supp. XXII:** 55
Seckler, David, **Supp. I Part 2:** 650
"2nd Air Force" (Jarrell), **II:** 375
Second American Revolution and Other Essays (1976–1982), The (Vidal), **Supp. IV Part 2:** 679, 687, 688
Secondary Colors, The (A. Theroux), **Supp. VIII:** 312
Second Blush, The (Peacock), **Supp. XIX:** 197, **205–206**
Second Chance (Auchincloss), **Supp. IV Part 1:** 33
"Second Chances" (Hugo), **Supp. VI:** 144, 145
Second Coming, The (Percy), **Supp. III Part 1:** 383, 384, 387, 388, 396–397
"Second Coming, The" (Yeats), **III:** 294; **Retro. Supp. I:** 290, 311; **Supp. VIII:** 24; **Supp. XVI:** 159; **Supp. XIX:** 85
Second Decade, The. See Stephen King, The Second Decade: "Danse Macabre" to "The Dark Half" (Magistrale)
Second Dune, The (Hearon), **Supp. VIII:** 58, **59–60**
Second Flowering, A: Works and Days of the Lost Generation (Cowley), **Retro. Supp. II:** 77; **Supp. II Part 1:** 135, 141, 143, 144, 147, 149
Second Growth (Stegner), **Supp. IV Part 2:** 599, 608
"Second Hour of the Night, The" (Bidart), **Supp. XV:** 32, **33–34**
Second Marriage (F. Barthelme), **Supp. XI:** 32, 33
"Second Marriage" (McCarriston), **Supp. XIV:** 262
"Second Mortgage" (Shaw), **Supp. XIX:** 245–246
Second Nature (Hoffman), **Supp. X:** 88, 89
Seconds, The (Bierds), **Supp. XVII: 33–34**
Second Set, The (Komunyakaa and Feinstein, eds.), **Supp. XIII:** 125
Second Sex, The (Beauvoir), **Supp. IV Part 1:** 360
"Second Sight" (Mosher), **Supp. XXII:** 214
Second Stone, The (Fiedler), **Supp. XIII:** 102
"Second Swimming, The" (Boyle), **Supp. VIII:** 13, 14
Second Tree from the Corner (White), **Supp. I Part 2:** 654
"Second Tree from the Corner" (White), **Supp. I Part 2:** 651
Second Twenty Years at Hull-House, The: September 1909 to September 1929, with a Record of a Growing World Consciousness (Addams), **Supp. I Part 1:** 24–25
Second Voyage of Columbus, The (Morison), **Supp. I Part 2:** 488
Second Words, (Atwood), **Supp. XIII:** 35
Second World, The (Blackmur), **Supp. II Part 1:** 91
Secret, The (E. Hoffman), **Supp. XVI:** 151, **155–158,** 161
"Secret, The" (Levine), **Supp. V:** 195
Secret Agent, The (Conrad), **Supp. IV Part 1:** 341
Secret Agent X-9 (Hammett), **Supp. IV Part 1:** 355
"Secret Courts of Men's Hearts, The: Code and Law in Harper Lee's *To Kill a Mockingbird*" (Johnson), **Supp. VIII:** 126
"Secret Dog, The" (Cameron), **Supp. XII: 83–84**
Secret Garden, The (Burnett), **Supp. I Part 1:** 44
"Secret Garden, The" (Hoffman), **Supp. XVIII:** 86
"Secret Gladness, A" (C. Frost), **Supp. XV:** 91
Secret Historie (J. Smith), **I:** 131
Secret History of the Dividing Line (Howe), **Supp. IV Part 2:** 424, 425–426
"Secret Integration, The" (Pynchon), **Supp. II Part 2:** 624
"Secret Life of Musical Instruments, The" (Wright), **Supp. XV:** 343
"Secret Life of Walter Mitty, The" (Thurber), **Supp. I Part 2:** 623; **Supp. XVI:** 233
"Secret Lion, The" (Ríos), **Supp. IV Part 2:** 543, 544
"Secret Ocean, The" (Jarman), **Supp. XVII:** 120
Secret of Poetry, The: Essays (Jarman), **Supp. XVII:** 110, 111, 120
"Secret of the Russian Ballet, The" (Van Vechten), **Supp. II Part 2:** 732
"Secret Prune" (Ríos), **Supp. IV Part 2:** 549
Secret River, The (Rawlings), **Supp. X:** 233
Secrets and Surprises (Beattie), **Supp. V:** 23, 27, 29
Secrets from the Center of the World (Harjo), **Supp. XII: 223–224**
"Secret Sharer, The" (Conrad), **Supp. IX:** 105
"Secret Sharer, The" (J. Conrad), **Supp. XVI:** 158
"Secret Society, A" (Nemerov), **III:** 282
Secrets of the Heart (Gibran), **Supp. XX: 116**
Secrets of the Universe: Scenes from the Journey Home (Sanders), **Supp. XVI:** 273–274
"Secular" (Trethewey), **Supp. XXI:** 249
Secular Journal of Thomas Merton, The, **Supp. VIII:** 206
"Security" (Stafford), **Supp. XI:** 329
Sedges, John (pseudonym). *See* Buck, Pearl S.
Sedgwick, Catherine Maria, **I:** 341; **Supp. I Part 1:** 155, 157
Sedgwick, Christina. *See* Marquand, Mrs. John P. (Christina Sedgwick)
Sedgwick, Ellery, **I:** 217, 229, 231; **III:** 54–55
Sedgwick, Eve, **Supp. XX: 267**
Sedgwick, Henry, **Supp. I Part 1:** 156
Sedgwick, Robert, **Supp. I Part 1:** 156
Sedore, Timothy, **Supp. XIV:** 312
"Seduction and Betrayal" (Hardwick), **Supp. III Part 1:** 207
Seduction and Betrayal: Women and Literature (Hardwick), **Supp. III Part 1:** 194, 204, 206–208, 212, 213; **Supp. XIV:** 89
See, Carolyn, **Supp. XXII:** 206, 217
Seed, David, **Supp. IV Part 1:** 391
"Seed Eaters, The" (Francis), **Supp. IX:** 82
"Seed Leaves" (Wilbur), **Supp. III Part 2:** 558
"Seeds" (Anderson), **I:** 106, 114
Seeds of Contemplation (Merton), **Supp. VIII:** 199, 200, 207, 208
Seeds of Destruction (Merton), **Supp. VIII:** 202, 203, 204, 208
"Seeing Red" (column, Ryan as Quin), **Supp. XVIII:** 226
"See(k)ing the Self: Mirrors and Mirroring in Bicultural Texts" (Oster), **Supp. XVI:** 151
Seeing through the Sun (Hogan), **Supp. IV Part 1:** 397, 400, 401–402, 402, 413
"See in the Midst of Fair Leaves" (Moore), **III:** 215
"Seekers, The" (McGrath), **Supp. X:** 117
"Seeking a Vision of Truth, Guided by a Higher Power" (Burke), **Supp. XIV:** 21, 23
"Seele im Raum" (Jarrell), **II:** 382–383
"Seele im Raum" (Rilke), **II:** 382–383
"See Naples and Die" (Hecht), **Supp. X:** 69, 70
"Seen from the 'L' " (Barnes), **Supp. III Part 1:** 33
"See the Moon?" (Barthelme), **Supp. IV Part 1:** 42, 49–50, 50
Segal, D. (pseudonym). *See* Singer, Isaac Bashevis
Segal, George, **Supp. XI:** 343
Segal, Lore, **Supp. XVI:** 203
Segregation: The Inner Conflict in the South (Warren), **IV:** 237, 238, 246, 252
"*Se:* Hegel's Absolute and Heidegger's *Ereignis*" (Agamben), **Supp. XVI:** 289
Seidel, Frederick, **I:** 185
Seidman, Hugh, **Supp. XXI:** 228
Seize the Day (Bellow), **I:** 144, 147, 148, 150, 151, 152, 153, 155, 158, 162; **Retro. Supp. II:** 19, **23–24,** 27, 32, 34; **Supp. I Part 2:** 428
Selby, Hubert, **Supp. III Part 1:** 125
Selby, Hubert, Jr., **Supp. XXI:** 227
Selby, John, **Retro. Supp. II:** 221, 222

Selden, John, **Supp. XIV:** 344
Seldes, Gilbert, **II:** 437, 445; **Retro. Supp. I:** 108
Selected Criticism: Prose, Poetry (Bogan), **Supp. III Part 1:** 64
Selected Essays (Eliot), **I:** 572
Selected Essays and Reviews (Carruth), **Supp. XVI:** 46
Selected Journals and Other Writings (Audubon), **Supp. XVI:** 10, 12, 13
Selected Letters (Bynner), **Supp. XV:** 52
Selected Letters (W. C. Williams), **Retro. Supp. I:** 430
Selected Letters, 1940–1956 (Kerouac), **Supp. XIV:** 137, 144
Selected Letters of Robert Frost (Thompson, ed.), **Retro. Supp. I:** 125
Selected Levis, The (Levis), **Supp. XI:** 257, 272
Selected Poems (Aiken), **I:** 69
Selected Poems (Ashbery), **Supp. III Part 1:** 25–26
Selected Poems (Brodsky), **Supp. VIII:** 22
Selected Poems (Brooks), **Supp. III Part 1:** 82–83
Selected Poems (Bynner), **Supp. XV:** 51, 52
Selected Poems (Corso), **Supp. XII:** 129
Selected Poems (Dove), **Supp. IV Part 1:** 241, 243, 250
Selected Poems (Frost), **Retro. Supp. I:** 133, 136
Selected Poems (Guillevic; Levertov, trans.), **Supp. III Part 1:** 283
Selected Poems (Hayden), **Supp. II Part 1:** 363, 364, 367
Selected Poems (Hughes), **Retro. Supp. I:** 202; **Supp. I Part 1:** 341, 345, 346
Selected Poems (Hugo), **Supp. VI:** 143
Selected Poems (Jarrell), **II:** 367, 370, 371, 374, 377, 379, 380, 381, 382, 384
Selected Poems (Justice), **Supp. VII:** 115
Selected Poems (Kinnell), **Supp. III Part 1:** 235, 253
Selected Poems (Levine, 1984), **Supp. V:** 178, 179
Selected Poems (Lowell), **II:** 512, 516; **Retro. Supp. II:** 184, 186, 188, 190
Selected Poems (Merton), **Supp. VIII:** 207, 208
Selected Poems (Moore), **III:** 193, 194, 205–206, 208, 215
Selected Poems (Notley), **Supp. XXII:** 234
Selected Poems (Pound), **Retro. Supp. I:** 289, 291
Selected Poems (R. Bly), **Supp. IV Part 1:** 60, 62, 65, 66, 68, 69–71
Selected Poems (Ransom), **III:** 490, 492
Selected Poems (Reznikoff), **Supp. XIV:** 288
Selected Poems (Rukeyser), **Supp. VI:** 274
Selected Poems (Sexton), **Supp. IV Part 2:** 449
Selected Poems (Sorrentino), **Supp. XXI:** 226
Selected Poems (Strand), **Supp. IV Part 2:** 630
Selected Poems, 1923–1943 (Warren), **IV:** 241–242, 243
Selected Poems, 1928–1958 (Kunitz), **Supp. III Part 1:** 261, 263–265
Selected Poems, 1938–1988 (McGrath), **Supp. X:** 127
Selected Poems, 1958–1980 (Sorrentino), **Supp. XXI:** 228
Selected Poems, 1963–1983 (Simic), **Supp. VIII:** 275
Selected Poems 1936–1965 (Eberhart), **I:** 541
Selected Poems: 1957–1987 (Snodgrass), **Supp. VI:** 314–315, 323, 324
Selected Poems 1965–1975 (Atwood), **Supp. XIII: 32–34**
Selected Poems: 1975–2005 (Skloot), **Supp. XX: 196**
Selected Poems II: Poems Selected and New, 1976–1986 (Atwood), **Supp. XIII:** 20, **34–35**
Selected Poems of Ezra Pound (Pound), **Supp. V:** 336
Selected Poems of Gabriela Mistral (Hughes, trans.), **Supp. I Part 1:** 345
Selected Poetry of Amiri Baraka/LeRoi Jones (Baraka), **Supp. II Part 1:** 58
Selected Poetry of Hayden Carruth, The (Carruth), **Supp. XVI:** 53
Selected Stories (Dubus), **Supp. VII:** 88–89
Selected Stories of Richard Bausch, The (Bausch), **Supp. VII:** 42
Selected Translations (Snodgrass), **Supp. VI:** 318, 324, **325–326**
Selected Verse of Margaret Haskins Durber, The (Keillor), **Supp. XVI:** 171
Selected Witter Bynner, The, **Supp. XV:** 52
Selected Works of Djuna Barnes, The (Barnes), **Supp. III Part 1:** 44
Selected Writings 1950–1990 (Howe), **Supp. VI:** 116–117, 118, 120
Selected Writings of John Jay Chapman, The (Barzun), **Supp. XIV:** 54
Select Epigrams from the Greek Anthology (Mackail), **Supp. I Part 2:** 461
"Selecting a Reader" (Kooser), **Supp. XIX:** 119–120
"Selene Afterwards" (MacLeish), **III:** 8
"Self" (James), **II:** 351
Self, William, **Supp. XXII:** 172
Self and the Dramas of History, The (Niebuhr), **III:** 308
Self-Consciousness (Updike), **Retro. Supp. I:** 318, 319, 320, 322, 323, 324
"Self-Exposed, The" (X. J. Kennedy), **Supp. XV:** 159
Self-Help: Stories (Moore), **Supp. X:** 163, 166, **167–169,** 174, 175
"Self-Importance" (Halliday), **Supp. XIX:** 90
Self-Interviews (Dickey), **Supp. IV Part 1:** 179
"Self-Made Man, A" (Crane), **I:** 420
"Self Pity" (C. Frost), **Supp. XV:** 93, 94, 101, 102, 104
Self Portrait (album, Dylan), **Supp. XVIII:** 27
"Self-Portrait" (Creeley), **Supp. IV Part 1:** 156
"Self-Portrait" (Mumford), **Supp. II Part 2:** 471
"(Self) Portrait" (Trethewey), **Supp. XXI:** 253
"Self-Portrait" (Wylie), **Supp. I Part 2:** 729
"Self Portrait at Fifty-three" (Weigl), **Supp. XIX:** 288
Self-Portrait: Ceaselessly into the Past (Millar, ed. Sipper), **Supp. IV Part 2:** 464, 469, 472, 475
"Self-Portrait in a Convex Mirror" (Ashbery), **Supp. III Part 1:** 5, 7, 9, 16–19, 22, 24, 26
"Self-Portrait with 1911 NY Yankees Cap" (Skloot), **Supp. XX: 202**
"Self-Reliance" (Emerson), **II:** 7, 15, 17; **Retro. Supp. I:** 159; **Retro. Supp. II:** 155; **Supp. X:** 42, 45
Selfwolf (Halliday), **Supp. XIX:** 81, **89–91,** 93
Sélincourt, Ernest de, **Supp. I Part 2:** 676
Selinger, Eric, **Supp. XVI:** 47
Selinger, Eric Murphy, **Supp. XI:** 248
Sell, Henry, **Supp. XVI:** 188
Sellers, Isaiah, **IV:** 194–195
Sellers, Peter, **Supp. XI:** 301, 304, 306, 307, 309
Sellers, William, **IV:** 208
Seltzer, Mark, **Retro. Supp. I:** 227
Selznick, David O., **Retro. Supp. I:** 105, 113; **Supp. IV Part 1:** 353; **Supp. XVIII:** 242; **Supp. XXII:** 195
Semi, Allen (pseudonym). *See* Larsen, Nella
"Semi-Lunatics of Kilmuir, The" (Hugo), **Supp. VI:** 145
"Semiotics/The Doctor's Doll" (Goldbarth), **Supp. XII:** 183–184
Semmelweiss, Ignaz, **Supp. I Part 1:** 304
Senancour, Étienne Divert de, **I:** 241
Sendak, Maurice, **Supp. IX:** 207, 208, 213, 214; **Supp. XVI:** 110
Seneca, **II:** 14–15; **III:** 77
Senghor, Leopold Sédar, **Supp. IV Part 1:** 16; **Supp. X:** 132, 139
Senier, Siobhan, **Supp. IV Part 1:** 330
"Senility" (Anderson), **I:** 114
"Senior Partner's Ethics, The" (Auchincloss), **Supp. IV Part 1:** 33
Senlin: A Biography (Aiken), **I:** 48, 49, 50, 52, 56, 57, 64
Sennett, Dorothy, **Supp. XVI:** 43
Sennett, Mack, **III:** 442
"Señora X No More" (Mora), **Supp. XIII:** 218
"Señor Ong and Señor Ha" (Bowles), **Supp. IV Part 1:** 87
Sensational Designs: The Cultural Work of American Fiction, 1790–1860 (Tompkins), **Supp. XVIII:** 258–259
Sense of Beauty, The (Santayana), **III:** 600
Sense of Life in the Modern Novel, The (Mizener), **IV:** 132
"Sense of Shelter, A" (Updike), **Retro. Supp. I:** 318

"Sense of the Meeting, The" (Conroy), **Supp. XVI:** 72
Sense of the Past, The (James), **II:** 337–338
"Sense of the Past, The" (Trilling), **Supp. III Part 2:** 503
"Sense of the Present, The" (Hardwick), **Supp. III Part 1:** 210
"Sense of the Sleight-of-Hand Man, The" (Stevens), **IV:** 93
"Sense of Where You Are, A" (McPhee), **Supp. III Part 1:** 291, 296–298
"Sensibility! O La!" (Roethke), **III:** 536
"Sensible Emptiness, A" (Kramer), **Supp. IV Part 1:** 61, 66
"Sensuality Plunging Barefoot Into Thorns" (Cisneros), **Supp. VII:** 68
"Sentence" (Barthelme), **Supp. IV Part 1:** 47
Sent for You Yesterday (Wideman), **Supp. X:** 320, 321
"Sentimental Education, A" (Banks), **Supp. V:** 10
"Sentimental Journey" (Oates), **Supp. II Part 2:** 522, 523
"Sentimental Journey, A" (Anderson), **I:** 114
Sentimental Journey, A (Sterne), **Supp. I Part 2:** 714
"Sentimental Journeys" (Didion), **Supp. IV Part 1:** 211
Sentimental Journey through France and Italy, A (Sterne), **Supp. XV:** 232
"Sentiment of Rationality, The" (James), **II:** 346–347
"Separated Father" (Halliday), **Supp. XIX:** 92, 93
Separate Flights (Dubus), **Supp. VII:** 78–83
"Separate Flights" (Dubus), **Supp. VII:** 83
Separate Peace, A (Knowles), **Supp. IV Part 2:** 679; **Supp. XII: 241–249**
Separate Way (Reznikoff), **Supp. XIV:** 280
"Separating" (Updike), **Retro. Supp. I:** 321
"Separation, The" (Kunitz), **Supp. III Part 1:** 263
"Sepia High Stepper" (Hayden), **Supp. II Part 1:** 379
September (film; Allen), **Supp. XV:** 11
"September" (Komunyakaa), **Supp. XIII:** 130
"September" (Pickering), **Supp. XXI:** 198
"September 1, 1939" (Auden), **Supp. II Part 1:** 13; **Supp. IV Part 1:** 225; **Supp. VIII:** 30, 32; **Supp. XV:** 117–118
September 11, 2001: American Writers Respond (Heyen), **Supp. XIII:** 285
"September's Book" (Notley), **Supp. XXII:** 229
September Song (Humphrey), **Supp. IX:** 101, 102, **108–109**
"September Twelfth, 2001" (X. J. Kennedy), **Supp. XV:** 171
"Sept Vieillards, Les" (Millay, trans.), **III:** 142
Sequel to Drum-Taps (Whitman), **Retro. Supp. I:** 406
"Sequence, Sometimes Metaphysical" (Roethke), **III:** 547, 548
Sequence of Seven Plays with a Drawing by Ron Slaughter, A (Nemerov), **III:** 269
Sequoya, Jana, **Supp. IV Part 1:** 334
Seraglio, The (Merrill), **Supp. III Part 1:** 331
Seraphita (Balzac), **I:** 499
Seraph on the Suwanee (Hurston), **Supp. VI:** 149, 159–160
Serenissima: A Novel of Venice (Jong). *See Shylock's Daughter: A Novel of Love in Venice (Serenissima)* (Jong)
Sergeant, Elizabeth Shepley, **I:** 231, 236, 312, 319, 323, 328
Sergeant Bilko (television show), **Supp. IV Part 2:** 575
Sergi, Paula, **Supp. XXI:** 246
"Serious Talk, A" (Carver), **Supp. III Part 1:** 138, 144
Serly, Tibor, **Supp. III Part 2:** 617, 619
"Sermon by Doctor Pep" (Bellow), **I:** 151
Sermones (Horace), **II:** 154
"Sermon for Our Maturity" (Baraka), **Supp. II Part 1:** 53
"Sermon in the Cotton Field" (Nelson), **Supp. XVIII:** 177
Sermons and Soda Water (O'Hara), **III:** 362, 364, 371–373, 382
"Sermons on the Warpland" (Brooks), **Supp. III Part 1:** 84
"Serpent in the Wilderness, The" (Masters), **Supp. I Part 2:** 458
Servant of the Bones (Rice), **Supp. VII:** 298, 302
"Servant to Servants, A" (Frost), **Retro. Supp. I:** 125, 128; **Supp. X:** 66
Serve It Forth (M. F. K. Fisher), **Supp. XVII:** 83, 86, 87, 89, 92
Service, Robert ?/, **Supp. XXI:** 51
Service, Robert W. ?/, **Supp. XXII:** 203
Seshachari, Neila, **Supp. V:** 22
"Session, The" (Adams), **I:** 5
"Sestina" (Bishop), **Supp. I Part 1:** 73, 88
Set-angya, **Supp. IV Part 2:** 493
Seth, Vikram, **Supp. XVII:** 117
Seth's Brother's Wife (Frederic), **II:** 131–132, 137, 144
Sethuraman, Ramchandran, **Supp. XXII:** 73
Set This House on Fire (Styron), **IV:** 98, 99, 105, 107–113, 114, 115, 117
Setting Free the Bears (Irving), **Supp. VI:** 163, **166–167,** 169–170
Setting the Tone (Rorem), **Supp. IV Part 1:** 79
Settle, Mary Lee, **Supp. IX:** 96
Settlement Horizon, The: A National Estimate (Woods and Kennedy), **Supp. I Part 1:** 19
"Settling the Colonel's Hash" (McCarthy), **II:** 559, 562
Setzer, Helen, **Supp. IV Part 1:** 217
"Seurat's Sunday Afternoon along the Seine" (Schwartz), **Supp. II Part 2:** 663–665
7 Years from Somehwere (Levine), **Supp. V:** 178, 181, 188–189
Seven against Thebes (Aeschylus; Bacon and Hecht, trans.), **Supp. X:** 57
Seven Ages of Man, The (Wilder), **IV:** 357, 374–375
Seven Deadly Sins, The (Wilder), **IV:** 357, 374–375
Seven Descents of Myrtle, The (T. Williams), **IV:** 382
"Seven Fat Brides, The" (P. Abraham), **Supp. XVII:** 50
Seven Guitars (Wilson), **Supp. VIII:** 331, **348–351**
Seven Lady Godivas, The (Geisel), **Supp. XVI:** 100, 103
Seven League Boots, The (Murray), **Supp. XIX: 156–157**
Seven-League Crutches, The (Jarrell), **II:** 367, 372, 381, 382, 383–384, 389
Seven Mountains of Thomas Merton, The (Mott), **Supp. VIII:** 208
Seven-Ounce Man, The (Harrison), **Supp. VIII:** 51
"Seven Places of the Mind" (Didion), **Supp. IV Part 1:** 200, 210
Seven Plays (Shepard), **Supp. III Part 2:** 434
"Seven Selves, The" (Gibran), **Supp. XX: 118**
"Seven Stanzas at Easter" (Updike), **IV:** 215
Seven Storey Mountain, The (Merton), **Supp. VIII:** 193, 195, 198, 200, 207, 208
Seventh Heaven (Hoffman), **Supp. X:** 87, 89
"Seventh of March" (Webster), **Supp. I Part 2:** 687
"7000 Romaine, Los Angeles 38" (Didion), **Supp. IV Part 1:** 200
"Seventh Street" (Toomer), **Supp. IX:** 316
Seven Types of Ambiguity (Empson), **II:** 536; **IV:** 431
77 Dream Songs (Berryman), **I:** 168, 169, 170, 171, 174, 175, 183–188
73 Poems (Cummings), **I:** 430, 431, 446, 447, 448
Seven Valleys and the Four Valleys, The (Bahá'u'lláh), **Supp. XX: 121**
Sevier, Jack, **IV:** 378
Sévigné, Madame de, **IV:** 361
Sewall, Richard, **Retro. Supp. I:** 25
Sewall, Samuel, **IV:** 145, 146, 147, 149, 154, 164; **Supp. I Part 1:** 100, 110
Sewell, Elizabeth, **Supp. XIII:** 344
"Sex" (Carruth), **Supp. XVI:** 58
Sex, Economy, Freedom and Community (Berry), **Supp. X:** 30, 36
"Sex Camp" (Mamet), **Supp. XIV:** 240
Sex Castle, The (Lacy), **Supp. XV:** 206
Sex & Character (Weininger), **Retro. Supp. I:** 416
"Sext" (Auden), **Supp. II Part 1:** 22
Sexton, Anne, **Retro. Supp. II:** 245; **Supp. I Part 2:** 538, 543, 546; **Supp. II Part 2: 669–700; Supp. III Part 2:** 599; **Supp. IV Part 1:** 245; **Supp. IV Part 2:** 439, 440–441, 442, 444,

447, 449, 451, 620; **Supp. V:** 113, 118, 124; **Supp. X:** 201, 202, 213; **Supp. XI:** 146, 240, 317; **Supp. XII:** 217, 253, 254, 256, 260, 261; **Supp. XIII:** 35, 76, 294, 312; **Supp. XIV:** 125, 126, 132, 269; **Supp. XV:** 123, 252, 340; **Supp. XVII:** 239; **Supp. XIX:** 82, 203; **Supp. XX: 199**
Sexual Behavior in the American Male (Kinsey), **Supp. XIII:** 96–97
Sexual Perversity in Chicago (Mamet), **Supp. XIV:** 239, 240, 246–247, 249
"Sexual Revolution, The" (Dunn), **Supp. XI:** 142
Sexus (H. Miller), **III:** 170, 171, 184, 187, 188
"Sex Without Love" (Olds), **Supp. X:** 206
"Sexy" (Lahiri), **Supp. XXI:** 183–184
Seyersted, Per E., **Retro. Supp. II:** 65; **Supp. I Part 1:** 201, 204, 211, 216, 225; **Supp. IV Part 2:** 558
Seyfried, Robin, **Supp. IX:** 324
Seymour, Miranda, **Supp. VIII:** 167
"Seymour: An Introduction" (Salinger), **III:** 569–571, 572
"Shack" (L. Brown), **Supp. XXI:** 49
Shacochis, Bob, **Supp. VIII:** 80
"Shadow" (Creeley), **Supp. IV Part 1:** 158
"Shadow, The" (Lowell), **II:** 522
Shadow and Act (Ellison), **Retro. Supp. II:** 119; **Supp. II Part 1:** 245–246
"Shadow and Shade" (Tate), **IV:** 128
"Shadow and the Flesh, The" (London), **II:** 475
"Shadow A Parable" (Poe), **III:** 417–418
Shadow Country (Gunn Allen), **Supp. IV Part 1:** 322, 324, 325–326
Shadow Man, The (Gordon), **Supp. IV Part 1:** 297, 298, 299, 312–314, 315
Shadow of a Dream, The, a Story (Howells), **II:** 285, 286, 290
"Shadow of the Crime, The: A Word from the Author" (Mailer), **Retro. Supp. II:** 214
Shadow on the Dial, The (Bierce), **I:** 208, 209
"Shadow Passing" (Merwin), **Supp. III Part 1:** 355
Shadowplay (C. Baxter), **Supp. XVII:** 15, 19–20
Shadows (Gardner), **Supp. VI:** 74
Shadows and Fog (film; Allen), **Supp. XV:** 11
Shadows Burning (Di Piero), **Supp. XIX:** 42, 43–44
Shadows by the Hudson (Singer), **IV:** 1
Shadows of Africa (Matthiessen), **Supp. V:** 203
Shadows on the Hudson (Singer), **Retro. Supp. II: 311–313**
Shadows on the Rock (Cather), **I:** 314, 330–331, 332; **Retro. Supp. I:** 18
Shadow Train (Ashbery), **Supp. III Part 1:** 23–24, 26
"Shad-Time" (Wilbur), **Supp. III Part 2:** 563
Shaffer, Thomas L., **Supp. VIII:** 127, 128
Shaft (Parks; film), **Supp. XI:** 17
Shaftesbury, Earl of, **I:** 559
Shahid, Irfan, **Supp. XX: 113, 127**
Shahn, Ben, **Supp. X:** 24
Shakedown for Murder (Lacy), **Supp. XV:** 203
Shakelford, Dean, **Supp. VIII:** 129
Shaker, Why Don't You Sing? (Angelou), **Supp. IV Part 1:** 16
Shakespear, Mrs. Olivia, **III:** 457; **Supp. I Part 1:** 257
"Shakespeare" (Emerson), **II:** 6
Shakespeare, William, **I:** 103, 271, 272, 284–285, 358, 378, 433, 441, 458, 461, 573, 585, 586; **II:** 5, 8, 11, 18, 72, 273, 297, 302, 309, 320, 411, 494, 577, 590; **III:** 3, 11, 12, 82, 83, 91, 124, 130, 134, 145, 153, 159, 183, 210, 263, 286, 468, 473, 492, 503, 511, 567, 575–576, 577, 610, 612, 613, 615; **IV:** 11, 50, 66, 127, 132, 156, 309, 313, 362, 368, 370, 373, 453; **Retro. Supp. I:** 43, 64, 91, 248; **Retro. Supp. II:** 114, 299; **Supp. I Part 1:** 79, 150, 262, 310, 356, 363, 365, 368, 369, 370; **Supp. I Part 2:** 397, 421, 422, 470, 494, 622, 716, 720; **Supp. II Part 2:** 624, 626; **Supp. IV Part 1:** 31, 83, 87, 243; **Supp. IV Part 2:** 430, 463, 519, 688; **Supp. V:** 252, 280, 303; **Supp. VIII:** 160, 164; **Supp. IX:** 14, 133; **Supp. X:** 42, 62, 65, 78; **Supp. XII:** 54–57, 277, 281; **Supp. XIII:** 111, 115, 233; **Supp. XIV:** 97, 120, 225, 245, 306; **Supp. XV:** 92; **Supp. XVIII:** 278; **Supp. XXII:** 206
Shakespeare and His Forerunners (Lanier), **Supp. I Part 1:** 369
Shakespeare in Harlem (Hughes), **Retro. Supp. I:** 194, 202, 205, 206, 207, 208; **Supp. I Part 1:** 333, 334, 345
Shalit, Gene, **Supp. VIII:** 73
Shalit, Wendy, **Supp. XX: 179, 182, 186**
Shall We Gather at the River (Wright), **Supp. III Part 2:** 601–602; **Supp. XVII:** 241
"Shame" (Oates), **Supp. II Part 2:** 520
"Shame" (Wilbur), **Supp. III Part 2:** 556
"Shame and Forgetting in the Information Age" (C. Baxter), **Supp. XVII:** 21
"Shameful Affair, A" (Chopin), **Retro. Supp. II:** 61
Shamela (Fielding), **Supp. V:** 127
"Shampoo, The" (Bishop), **Retro. Supp. II:** 46; **Supp. I Part 1:** 92
Shange, Ntozake, **Supp. VIII:** 214; **Supp. XVII:** 70; **Supp. XVIII:** 172; **Supp. XXI:** 172
Shank, Randy, **Supp. X:** 252
Shankaracharya, **III:** 567
Shanley, John Patrick, **Supp. XIV: 315–332**
Shannon, Sandra, **Supp. VIII:** 333, 348
"Shape of Flesh and Bone, The" (MacLeish), **III:** 18–19
Shape of Me and Other Stuff, The (Geisel), **Supp. XVI:** 111
Shape of the Journey, The (Harrison), **Supp. VIII:** 53
Shapes of Clay (Bierce), **I:** 208, 209
Shaping Joy, A: Studies in the Writer's Craft (Brooks), **Supp. XIV:** 13
Shapiro, Charles, **Supp. XIX:** 257, 259–260
Shapiro, David, **Supp. XII:** 175, 185
Shapiro, Dorothy, **IV:** 380
Shapiro, Karl, **I:** 430, 521; **II:** 350; **III:** 527; **Supp. II Part 2: 701–724; Supp. III Part 2:** 623; **Supp. IV Part 2:** 645; **Supp. X:** 116; **Supp. XI:** 315; **Supp. XIX:** 117, 118, 119; **Supp. XXI:** 98
Shapiro, Laura, **Supp. IX:** 120; **Supp. XX: 87, 89**
Sharif, Omar, **Supp. IX:** 253
"Shark Meat" (Snyder), **Supp. VIII:** 300
Shatayev, Elvira, **Supp. I Part 2:** 570
Shaviro, Steven, **Supp. VIII:** 189
Shaw, Colonel Robert Gould, **II:** 551
Shaw, Elizabeth. *See* Melville, Mrs. Herman (Elizabeth Shaw)
Shaw, George Bernard, **I:** 226; **II:** 82, 271, 276, 581; **III:** 69, 102, 113, 145, 155, 161, 162, 163, 373, 409; **IV:** 27, 64, 397, 432, 440; **Retro. Supp. I:** 100, 228; **Supp. IV Part 1:** 36; **Supp. IV Part 2:** 585, 683; **Supp. V:** 243–244, 290; **Supp. IX:** 68, 308; **Supp. XI:** 202; **Supp. XII:** 94; **Supp. XIV:** 343; **Supp. XVII:** 100
Shaw, Irwin, **IV:** 381; **Supp. IV Part 1:** 383; **Supp. IX:** 251; **Supp. XI:** 221, 229, 231; **Supp. XIX: 239–254**
Shaw, Joseph Thompson ("Cap"), **Supp. IV Part 1:** 121, 345, 351; **Supp. XIII:** 161
Shaw, Judge Lemuel, **III:** 77, 88, 91
Shaw, Peter, **Supp. XVI:** 70
Shaw, Sarah Bryant, **Supp. I Part 1:** 169
Shaw, Wilbur, Jr., **Supp. XIII:** 162
Shawl, The (Mamet), **Supp. XIV:** 245
Shawl, The (Ozick), **Supp. V:** 257, 260, 271
"Shawl, The" (Ozick), **Supp. V:** 271–272
Shawl and Prarie du Chien, The: Two Plays (Mamet), **Supp. XIV:** 243–244
Shawn, William, **Supp. VIII:** 151, 170
"Shawshank Redemption, The" (King), **Supp. V:** 148
She (Haggard), **III:** 189
Sheaffer, Louis, **Supp. XXI:** 6
Shearer, Flora, **I:** 199
"Sheaves, The" (Robinson), **III:** 510, 524
"She Came and Went" (Lowell), **Supp. I Part 2:** 409
"She-Devil" (Nelson), **Supp. XVIII:** 178
She-Devil Circus (Nelson), **Supp. XVIII:** 176, **178**
Sheed, Wilfrid, **IV:** 230; **Supp. XI:** 233; **Supp. XXI:** 233
Sheeler, Charles, **IV:** 409; **Retro. Supp. I:** 430
"Sheep Child" (B. Kelly), **Supp. XVII:** 131–132
"Sheep Child, The" (Dickey), **Supp. XVII:** 131–132
Sheeper (Rosenthal), **Supp. XIV:** 147
Sheffer, Jonathan, **Supp. IV Part 1:** 95

She Had Some Horses (Harjo), **Supp. XII: 220–223,** 231
"She Had Some Horses" (Harjo), **Supp. XII:** 215, 222
"Shell, The" (Humphrey), **Supp. IX:** 94
Shelley, Mary, **Supp. XX: 108**
Shelley, Percy Bysshe, **I:** 18, 68, 381, 476, 522, 577; **II:** 331, 516, 535, 540; **III:** 412, 426, 469; **IV:** 139; **Retro. Supp. I:** 308, 360; **Supp. I Part 1:** 79, 311, 349; **Supp. I Part 2:** 709, 718, 719, 720, 721, 722, 724, 728; **Supp. IV Part 1:** 235; **Supp. V:** 258, 280; **Supp. IX:** 51; **Supp. XII:** 117, 132, 136–137, 263; **Supp. XIV:** 271–272; **Supp. XV:** 92, 175, 182; **Supp. XX: 115; Supp. XXI:** 131
Shellow, Sadie Myers, **Supp. I Part 2:** 608
"Shelter" (C. Baxter), **Supp. XVII:** 19
"Shelter" (Doty), **Supp. XI:** 132
Sheltered Life, The (Glasgow), **II:** 174, 175, 179, 186, 187–188
Sheltering Sky, The (Bowles), **Supp. IV Part 1:** 82, 84, 85–86, 87
Sheltering Sky, The (film), **Supp. IV Part 1:** 94, 95
Shelton, Frank, **Supp. IV Part 2:** 658
Shelton, Richard, **Supp. XI:** 133; **Supp. XIII:** 7
Shelton, Robert, **Supp. XVIII:** 20, 21, 22, 23, 24, 25, 26
Shelton, Mrs. Sarah. *See* Royster, Sarah Elmira
Shenandoah (Schwartz), **Supp. II Part 2:** 640, 651–652
"Shenandoah" (Shapiro), **Supp. II Part 2:** 704
Shepard, Alice, **IV:** 287
Shepard, Gregory, **Supp. XXII:** 119
Shepard, Harvey, **Supp. XVII:** 240
Shepard, Jim, **Supp. XXI:** 115
Shepard, Odell, **II:** 508; **Supp. I Part 2:** 418
Shepard, Sam, **Supp. III Part 2: 431–450; Supp. XVIII:** 21, 28, 31; **Supp. XXI:** 144, 145
Shepard, Thomas, **I:** 554; **IV:** 158
"Shepherd of Resumed Desire, The" (Wright), **Supp. XV:** 349
Sheppard Lee (Bird), **III:** 423
"She Remembers the Future" (Harjo), **Supp. XII:** 222
Sheridan, Richard Brinsley, **Retro. Supp. I:** 127
Sherlock, William, **IV:** 152
Sherman, Joe, **Supp. XXII:** 205
Sherman, Sarah Way, **Retro. Supp. II:** 145
Sherman, Stuart Pratt, **I:** 222, 246–247; **Supp. I Part 2:** 423
Sherman, Susan, **Supp. VIII:** 265
Sherman, Tom, **IV:** 446
Sherman, William T., **IV:** 445, 446
Sherry, Denver William, **Supp. XXII:** 190
Sherwood, Robert, **II:** 435; **Supp. IX:** 190
Sherwood Anderson & Other Famous Creoles (Faulkner), **I:** 117; **II:** 56
Sherwood Anderson Reader, The (Anderson), **I:** 114, 116
Sherwood Anderson's Memoirs (Anderson), **I:** 98, 101, 102, 103, 108, 112, 116
Sherwood Anderson's Notebook (Anderson), **I:** 108, 115, 117
"She Sings" (Taggard), **Supp. XXII:** 272
She Stoops to Conquer (Goldsmith), **II:** 514
Shestov, Lev, **Supp. VIII:** 20, 24
Shetley, Vernon, **Supp. IX:** 292; **Supp. XI:** 123
"She Wept, She Railed" (Kunitz), **Supp. III Part 1:** 265
"Shiddah and Kuziba" (Singer), **IV:** 13, 15
Shidyak, Paris al-, **Supp. XX: 117**
Shield of Achilles, The (Auden), **Supp. II Part 1:** 21
"Shield of Achilles, The" (Auden), **Supp. II Part 1:** 21, 25
Shields, Carol, **Supp. VII: 307–330**
Shields, John C., **Supp. XX: 279, 280, 281, 286**
Shifting Landscape: A Composite, 1925–1987 (H. Roth), **Supp. IX: 233–235**
Shifts of Being (Eberhart), **I:** 525
Shigematsu, Soiko, **Supp. III Part 1:** 353
Shihab, Aziz, **Supp. XIII:** 273
Shih-hsiang Chen, **Supp. VIII:** 303
Shiksa Goddess; or, How I Spent My Forties (Wasserstein), **Supp. XV:** 319, 320, 325, 332, 333
"Shiloh" (Mason), **Supp. VIII:** 140
Shiloh and Other Stories (Mason), **Supp. VIII:** 133, **139–141,** 143, 145
Shilts, Randy, **Supp. X:** 145
Shimmering Verge, The (one-woman show, Peacock), **Supp. XIX:** 194, **204–205**
Shining, The (King), **Supp. V:** 139, 140, 141, 143–144, 146, 149, 151, 152
"Shining Ones, The" (P. N. Warren), **Supp. XX: 272**
Shining Victory (film, Rapper), **Supp. XVII:** 60
Shinn, Everett, **Retro. Supp. II:** 103
Shi Pei Pu, **Supp. XXI:** 152, 153, 154
"Ship of Death" (Lawrence), **Supp. I Part 2:** 728
Ship of Fools (Porter), **III:** 433, 447, 453, 454; **IV:** 138
Shipping News, The (Proulx), **Supp. VII:** 249, 258–259
"Ships" (O. Henry), **Supp. II Part 1:** 409
Ships Going into the Blue: Essays and Notes on Poetry (Simpson), **Supp. IX:** 275
Ship to America, A (Singer), **IV:** 1
"Shipwreck, The" (Merwin), **Supp. III Part 1:** 346
Shirley, John, **Supp. XVI:** 123, 128
"Shirt" (Pinsky), **Supp. VI: 236–237,** 239, 240, 241, 245, 247
"Shirt Poem, The" (Stern), **Supp. IX:** 292
"Shirts of a Single Color" (Ryan), **Supp. XVIII:** 227
"Shiva and Parvati Hiding in the Rain" (Pinsky), **Supp. VI:** 244
Shively, Charley, **Retro. Supp. I:** 391; **Supp. XII:** 181, 182
Shnayerson, Michael, **Supp. XIX:** 248
Shock of Recognition, The (Wilson), **II:** 530
Shock of the New, The (Hughes), **Supp. X:** 73
Shoe Bird, The (Welty), **IV:** 261; **Retro. Supp. I:** 353
Shoemaker of Dreams (Ferragammo), **Supp. XVI:** 192
"Shoes" (O. Henry), **Supp. II Part 1:** 409
"Shoes of Wandering, The" (Kinnell), **Supp. III Part 1:** 248
Sholl, Betsy, **Supp. XXI:** 129, 131
"Shooters, Inc." (Didion), **Supp. IV Part 1:** 207, 211
"Shooting, The" (Dubus), **Supp. VII:** 84, 85
"Shooting Niagara; and After?" (Carlyle), **Retro. Supp. I:** 408
"Shooting Script" (Rich), **Supp. I Part 2:** 558; **Supp. IV Part 1:** 257
Shooting Star, A (Stegner), **Supp. IV Part 2:** 599, 608–609
"Shooting the Works" (Di Piero), **Supp. XIX:** 41–42
Shooting the Works: On Poetry and Pictures (Di Piero), **Supp. XIX: 41–42**
"Shooting Whales" (Strand), **Supp. IV Part 2:** 630
"Shopgirls" (F. Barthelme), **Supp. XI:** 26, 27, 33, 36
"Shopping with Bob Berwick" (Halliday), **Supp. XIX:** 88
Shop Talk (P. Roth), **Retro. Supp. II:** 282
Shoptaw, John, **Supp. IV Part 1:** 247
Shore Acres (Herne), **Supp. II Part 1:** 198
Shorebirds of North America, The (Matthiessen), **Supp. V:** 204
"Shore House, The" (Jewett), **II:** 397
Shore Leave (Wakeman), **Supp. IX:** 247
"Shoreline Horses" (Ríos), **Supp. IV Part 2:** 553
"Shoreline Life" (Skloot), **Supp. XX: 201**
Shores of Light, The: A Literary Chronicle of the Twenties and Thirties (Wilson), **IV:** 432, 433
Shorey, Paul, **III:** 606
Short Cuts (film), **Supp. IX:** 143
"Short End, The" (Hecht), **Supp. X:** 65
"Shorter View, The" (X. J. Kennedy), **Supp. XV:** 160, 168
Short Fiction of Norman Mailer, The (Mailer), **Retro. Supp. II:** 205
Short Friday and Other Stories (Singer), **IV:** 14–16
Short Guide to a Happy Life, A (Quindlen), **Supp. XVII:** 167, 179
"Short Happy Life of Francis Macomber, The" (Hemingway), **II:** 250, 263–264; **Retro. Supp. I:** 182; **Supp. IV Part 1:** 48; **Supp. IX:** 106
Short Night, The (Turner), **Supp. XV:** 201
Short Novels of Thomas Wolfe, The (Wolfe), **IV:** 456
Short Poems (Berryman), **I:** 170

"SHORT SPEECH TO MY FRIENDS" (Baraka), **Supp. II Part 1:** 35
Short Stories (Rawlings), **Supp. X:** 224
Short Stories: Five Decades (Shaw), **Supp. XIX:** 252–253
"Short Story, The" (Welty), **IV:** 279
Short Story Masterpieces, **Supp. IX:** 4
Short Studies of American Authors (Higginson), **I:** 455
"Short-timer's Calendar" (Komunyakaa), **Supp. XIII:** 125
Shosha (Singer), **Retro. Supp. II: 313–314**
Shostakovich, Dimitri, **IV:** 75; **Supp. VIII:** 21
Shot of Love (album, Dylan), **Supp. XVIII:** 28
"Shots" (Ozick), **Supp. V:** 268
Shotts, Jeffrey, **Supp. XV:** 103, 104
"Should Wizard Hit Mommy?" (Updike), **IV:** 221, 222, 224; **Retro. Supp. I:** 335
Shoup, Barbara, **Supp. XV:** 55, 59, 62, 69
"Shoveling Snow with Buddha" (Collins), **Supp. XXI:** 60
"Shovel Man, The" (Sandburg), **III:** 553
Showalter, Elaine, **Retro. Supp. I:** 368; **Supp. IV Part 2:** 440, 441, 444; **Supp. X:** 97; **Supp. XVI:** 80, 92; **Supp. XX: 274**
"Shower of Gold" (Welty), **IV:** 271–272
Shribman, David M., **Supp. XXII:** 205, 218
"Shrike and the Chipmunks, The" (Thurber), **Supp. I Part 2:** 617
Shrimp Girl (Hogarth), **Supp. XII:** 44
"Shrine and the Burning Wheel, The" (Jarman), **Supp. XVII:** 116
"Shrine with Flowers" (Di Piero), **Supp. XIX:** 43, 44
"Shriveled Meditation" (X. J. Kennedy), **Supp. XV:** 170
Shropshire Lad, A (Housman), **Supp. XV:** 41
"Shrouded Stranger, The" (Ginsberg), **Supp. II Part 1:** 312
"Shroud of Color, The" (Cullen), **Supp. IV Part 1:** 166, 168, 170, 171
Shtetl (film; Marzynski), **Supp. XVI:** 153
Shtetl: The Life and Death of a Small Town and the World of Polish Jews (E. Hoffman), **Supp. XVI:** 152, **153–155**
Shuffle (L. Michaels), **Supp. XVI:** 202, 203, 213
Shuffle Along (musical), **Supp. I Part 1:** 322; **Supp. X:** 136
Shultz, George, **Supp. IV Part 1:** 234
Shurr, William, **Retro. Supp. I:** 43
Shuster, Joel, **Supp. XI:** 67
Shusterman, Richard, **Retro. Supp. I:** 53
"Shut a Final Door" (Capote), **Supp. III Part 1:** 117, 120, 124
Shut Up, He Explained (Lardner), **II:** 432
Shylock's Daughter: A Novel of Love in Venice (Serenissima) (Jong), **Supp. V:** 115, 127, 128–129
"Siasconset: How It Arose and What It Is" (Briggs), **Supp. XVIII:** 9
Siberian Village, The (Dove), **Supp. IV Part 1:** 255, 256
Sibley, Celestine, **Supp. XXII:** 194, 199
Sibley, Mulford Q., **Supp. I Part 2:** 524
"Sibling Mysteries" (Rich), **Supp. I Part 2:** 574
Siblings (Quindlen and Kelsh), **Supp. XVII:** 167, 179
Sibon, Marcelle, **IV:** 288
"Sicilian Emigrant's Song" (W. C. Williams), **Retro. Supp. I:** 413
Sicilian Miniatures (Sobin), **Supp. XVI:** 288
"Sick Wife, The" (Kenyon), **Supp. VII:** 173, 174
"'Sic transit gloria mundi' " (Dickinson), **Retro. Supp. I:** 30
Sid Caesar Show (television show), **Supp. IV Part 2:** 575
Siddons, Anne Rivers, **Supp. XXII: 239–254**
Siddons, Sarah, **II:** 298
Side Effects (Allen), **Supp. XV:** 3, 14, **15–16**
Side of Paradise, This (Fitgerald), **Supp. IX:** 56
Sidnee Poet Heroical, The (Baraka), **Supp. II Part 1:** 55
Sidney, Algernon, **II:** 114
Sidney, Mary, **Supp. I Part 1:** 98
Sidney, Philip, **II:** 470; **Supp. I Part 1:** 98, 111, 117–118, 122; **Supp. I Part 2:** 658; **Supp. II Part 1:** 104–105; **Supp. V:** 250; **Supp. XII:** 264; **Supp. XIV:** 128
Sidney, Sylvia, **Supp. I Part 1:** 67
Sidney Lanier: A Bibliographical and Critical Study (Starke), **Supp. I Part 1:** 371
Sidney Lanier: A Biographical and Critical Study (Starke), **Supp. I Part 1:** 371
Siebert, Kathy, **Supp. XX: 84**
Siege (Shaw), **Supp. XIX:** 244
Siegel, Barry, **Supp. XIV:** 82
Siegel, Catherine, **Supp. XII:** 126
Siegel, Jerry, **Supp. XI:** 67
Siegel, Lee, **Supp. XXII: 255–269**
"Siege of London, The" (James), **Retro. Supp. I:** 227
Siegle, Robert, **Supp. XII:** 8
Sienkiewicz, Henryk, **Supp. IV Part 2:** 518; **Supp. XVI:** 182
"Sierra Kid" (Levine), **Supp. V:** 180–181
Sigal, Clancy, **Supp. XXI:** 44
Sigg, Eric, **Retro. Supp. I:** 53
"Sight" (Merwin), **Supp. III Part 1:** 356
Sighted Singer, The (Halliday), **Supp. XIX:** 82, **86–87**
"Sight in Camp in the Daybreak Gray and Dim, A" (Whitman), **II:** 373
Sights and Spectacles (McCarthy), **II:** 562
"Sights from a Steeple" (Hawthorne), **Retro. Supp. I:** 62; **Supp. XXI:** 201
Sights Unseen (Gibbons), **Supp. X: 49–50**
"Signals" (Carver), **Supp. III Part 1:** 143
"Signature for Tempo" (MacLeish), **III:** 8–9
"Signed Confession of Crimes against the State" (Merton), **Supp. VIII:** 201
Signifying Monkey, The (H. L. Gates), **Supp. X:** 243
Signifying Monkey, The (Hughes), **Retro. Supp. I:** 195
Signifying Monkey, The: A Theory of Afro-American Literary Criticism (H. L. Gates), **Supp. XX: 99, 106–107**
"Signing, The (Dixon), **Supp. XII: 146**
Sign in Sidney Brustein's Window, The (Hansberry), **Supp. IV Part 1:** 359, 365, 369, 370–372
Sign of Jonas, The (Merton), **Supp. VIII:** 194–195, 195, 197, 200, 206, 207
"Sign of Saturn, The" (Olds), **Supp. X:** 206
"Signs, Oakvale, Mississippi, 1941" (Trethewey), **Supp. XXI:** 248–249
Signs and Wonders (Bukiet), **Supp. XVII: 45–46**
Sigourney, Lydia, **Supp. I Part 2:** 684
Sikora, Malgorzata, **Retro. Supp. II:** 324
Silas Marner (G. Eliot), **II:** 26
Silberg, Richard, **Supp. XV:** 116
"Silence" (Moore), **III:** 212
"Silence" (Poe), **III:** 416
"Silence" (Sanders), **Supp. XVI:** 278
"Silence, A" (Clampitt), **Supp. IX:** 53
"Silence—A Fable" (Poe), **III:** 416
Silence and Metaphor (Bronk), **Supp. XXI:** 31, 32
"Silence Before Harvest, The" (Merwin), **Supp. III Part 1:** 352
Silence Dogood Papers, The (Franklin), **II:** 106–107
Silence in the Snowy Fields (R. Bly), **Supp. IV Part 1:** 60–61, 62, 63, 65, 66, 72; **Supp. XXI:** 84, 85
Silence of History, The (Farrell), **II:** 46–47
Silence of the Lambs, The (T. Harris), **Supp. XXI:** 78
Silence Opens, A (Clampitt), **Supp. IX: 53**
Silences (Olsen), **Supp. XIII:** 293, 294, 295, 296, **304–306**
"Silences: When Writers Don't Write" (Olsen), **Supp. XIII:** 294
Silencing the Past: Power and the Production of History (Trouillot), **Supp. X:** 14
"Silent in America" (Levine), **Supp. V:** 183
Silent Life, The (Merton), **Supp. VIII:** 208
Silent Partner, The (Odets), **Supp. II Part 2:** 539
"Silent Poem" (Francis), **Supp. IX:** 86
"Silent Season of a Hero, The" (Talese), **Supp. XVII:** 203–204
"Silent Slain, The" (MacLeish), **III:** 9
"Silent Snow, Secret Snow" (Aiken), **I:** 52
Silent Spring (Carson), **Supp. V:** 202; **Supp. IX:** 19, 24, **31–34; Supp. XIV:** 177; **Supp. XVI:** 36; **Supp. XVIII:** 189
Silhouettes of American Life (R. H. Davis), **Supp. XVI:** 85

"Silken Tent, The" (Frost), **Retro. Supp. I:** 138–139; **Supp. IV Part 2:** 448
Silko, Leslie Marmon, **Supp. IV Part 1:** 274, 319, 325, 333–334, 335, 404; **Supp. IV Part 2:** 499, 505, **557–572; Supp. V:** 169; **Supp. XI:** 18; **Supp. XII:** 217; **Supp. XVIII:** 58
Silliman, Ron, **Supp. IV Part 2:** 426; **Supp. XV:** 344; **Supp. XVII:** 70, 77
Silliman's Blog (R. Silliman), **Supp. XVII:** 70
Silman, Roberta, **Supp. X:** 6
Silverblatt, Michael, **Supp. XV:** 224
"Silver Crown, The" (Malamud), **Supp. I Part 2:** 434–435, 437; **Supp. V:** 266
"Silver Dish, The" (Bellow), **Retro. Supp. II:** 30
"Silver Filigree" (Wylie), **Supp. I Part 2:** 707
"Silver Lake" (B. Kelly), **Supp. XVII:** 130
Silvers, Phil, **Supp. IV Part 2:** 574
Silverthorne, Elizabeth, **Supp. X:** 220, 221, 222, 226, 234
"Silver To Have and to Hurl" (Didion), **Supp. IV Part 1:** 197
Simic, Charles, **Supp. V:** 5, 332; **Supp. VIII:** 39, **269–287; Supp. XI:** 317; **Supp. XV:** 179, 185; **Supp. XIX:** 277, 282
"Similar Cases" (Gilman), **Supp. XI:** 200, 202
Similitudes, from the Ocean and Prairie (Larcom), **Supp. XIII:** 141
Simmel, Georg, **Supp. I Part 2:** 644; **Supp. XVII:** 98
Simmons, Charles, **Supp. XI:** 230
Simmons, Maggie, **Retro. Supp. II:** 21
Simms, Michael, **Supp. XII:** 184
Simms, William Gilmore, **I:** 211
Simon, John, **Supp. IV Part 2:** 691
Simon, Neil, **Supp. IV Part 2: 573–594; Supp. XVII:** 8
Simone, Nina, **Supp. XXI:** 243
"Simon Gerty" (Wylie), **Supp. I Part 2:** 713
Simonides, **Supp. XII:** 110–111
"Simon Ortiz" (Gingerich), **Supp. IV Part 2:** 510
Simon Ortiz (Wiget), **Supp. IV Part 2:** 509
Simonson, Lee, **III:** 396; **Supp. XXI:** 6
"Simple" (Peacock), **Supp. XIX:** 200
"Simple Art of Murder, The" (Chandler), **Supp. IV Part 1:** 121, 341
"Simple Autumnal" (Bogan), **Supp. III Part 1:** 52–53
Simple Heart (Flaubert), **I:** 504
Simple Honorable Man, A (Richter), **Supp. XVIII:** 208, 218, **219,** 220
"Simple Purchase, A" (Peacock), **Supp. XIX:** 199
Simple Speaks his Mind (Hughes), **Retro. Supp. I:** 209; **Supp. I Part 1:** 337
Simple Stakes a Claim (Hughes), **Retro. Supp. I:** 209; **Supp. I Part 1:** 337
Simple's Uncle Sam (Hughes), **Retro. Supp. I:** 209; **Supp. I Part 1:** 337
Simple Takes a Wife (Hughes), **Retro. Supp. I:** 209; **Supp. I Part 1:** 337
Simple Truth, The (Hardwick), **Supp. III Part 1:** 199, 200, 208
Simple Truth, The (Levine), **Supp. V:** 178, 179, 193–194
"Simple Widsom, The" (Skloot), **Supp. XX: 207**
"Simplicity" (Sanders), **Supp. XVI:** 276
Simply Heavenly (Hughes), **Retro. Supp. I:** 209; **Supp. I Part 1:** 338, 339
Simpson, Louis, **Supp. III Part 2:** 541; **Supp. IV Part 2:** 448, 621; **Supp. VIII:** 39, 279; **Supp. IX: 265–283,** 290; **Supp. XI:** 317; **Supp. XII:** 130; **Supp. XIII:** 337
Simpson, Mona, **Supp. XVI:** 206
"Sin" (C. Frost), **Supp. XV:** 96
Sinatra, Frank, **Supp. IX:** 3; **Supp. X:** 119; **Supp. XI:** 213
Sincere Convert, The (Shepard), **IV:** 158
Sincerely, Willis Wayde (Marquand), **III:** 61, 63, 66, 67–68, 69
Sincerity (Rowson), **Supp. XV:** 242
Sincerity and Authenticity (Trilling), **Supp. III Part 2:** 510–512
"Sincerity and Objectification: With Special Reference to the Work of Charles Reznikoff" (Zukofsky), **Supp. XIV:** 286
Sinclair, Mary Craig (Mary Craig Kimbrough), **Supp. V:** 275, 286, 287
Sinclair, Upton, **II:** 34, 440, 444, 451; **III:** 580; **Retro. Supp. II:** 95; **Supp. V: 275–293; Supp. VIII:** 11
Sinclair Lewis: An American Life (Schorer), **II:** 459
"Singapore" (Oliver), **Supp. VII:** 239, 240
Singer, Bennett L., **Supp. IV Part 1:** 330
Singer, Beth, **Supp. XIV:** 203
Singer, Isaac Bashevis, **I:** 144; **IV: 1–24; Retro. Supp. II:** 22, **299–320; Supp. IX:** 114; **Supp. XVIII:** 215, 220; **Supp. XXI:** 106; **Supp. XXII:** 258
Singer, Israel Joshua, **IV:** 2, 16, 17; **Retro. Supp. II:** 302; **Supp. XVII:** 41
Singer, Joshua, **IV:** 4
Singer, Rabbi Pinchos Menachem, **IV:** 16
Singin' and Swingin' and Gettin' Merry Like Christmas (Angelou), **Supp. IV Part 1:** 2, 5, 6–7, 9, 13, 14
"Singing & Doubling Together" (Ammons), **Supp. VII:** 34–35
Singing Jailbirds (Sinclair), **Supp. V:** 277
"Singing the Black Mother" (Lupton), **Supp. IV Part 1:** 7
Single Hound, The (Sarton), **Supp. VIII:** 251, 265
Single Hound, The: Poems of a Lifetime (Dickinson; Bianchi, ed.), **Retro. Supp. I:** 35
Single Man, A (Isherwood), **Supp. XIV:** 157, 164, **169–170,** 171
"Single Sonnet" (Bogan), **Supp. III Part 1:** 56–58
Singley, Carol, **Retro. Supp. I:** 373
Singular Family, A: Rosacoke and Her Kin (Price), **Supp. VI: 258–259,** 260
"Singular First Person, The" (Sanders), **Supp. XVI:** 274
Singularities (Howe), **Supp. IV Part 2:** 431
Sin in Their Blood (Lacy), **Supp. XV:** 200
"Sinister Adolescents, The" (Dos Passos), **I:** 493
Sinister Street (Mackenzie), **II:** 82
Sinking of Clay City, The (Wrigley), **Supp. XVIII: 294–295**
Sinners in the Hands of an Angry God (Edwards), **I:** 546, 552–553, 559, 562
Sinning with Annie, and Other Stories (Theroux), **Supp. VIII:** 318
"Sins of Kalamazoo, The" (Sandburg), **III:** 586
Sintram and His Companions (La Motte-Fouqué), **III:** 78
"Siope" (Poe), **III:** 411
"Sipapu: A Cultural Perspective" (Gunn Allen), **Supp. IV Part 1:** 323
Sipchen, Bob, **Supp. X:** 145
Sipper, Ralph B., **Supp. IV Part 2:** 475
"Sire" (Cisneros), **Supp. VII:** 62–63, 64
"Siren and Signal" (Zukofsky), **Supp. III Part 2:** 611, 612
Sirens of Titan, The (Vonnegut), **Supp. II Part 2:** 757, 758, 760, 765–767
"Sir Galahad" (Tennyson), **Supp. I Part 2:** 410
Sirin, V. (pseudonym), **Retro. Supp. I:** 266. *See also* Nabokov, Vladimir
Sirlin, Jerome, **Supp. XXI:** 147
Sir Vadia's Shadow: A Friendship across Five Continents (Theroux), **Supp. VIII:** 309, 314, 321, 325
"Sis" (F. Barthelme), **Supp. XI:** 26
"S is for Sad" (M. F. K. Fisher), **Supp. XVII:** 86
Sisley, Alfred, **I:** 478
Sissman, L. E., **Supp. X:** 69
"Sister" (Hughes), **Retro. Supp. I:** 208
"Sister" (Lamott), **Supp. XX: 142**
Sister Age (M. F. K. Fisher), **Supp. XVII:** 88, 91
Sister Carrie (Dreiser), **I:** 482, 497, 499, 500, 501–502, 503–504, 505, 506, 515, 519; **III:** 327; **IV:** 208; **Retro. Supp. I:** 376; **Retro. Supp. II:** 93, **96–99; Supp. XVIII:** 76, 243
"Sister of the Minotaur" (Stevens), **IV:** 89; **Supp. IX:** 332
"Sisters" (Boulton), **Supp. XXII:** 20
"Sisters" (Nelson), **Supp. XVIII:** 176
"Sisters, The" (Whittier), **Supp. I Part 2:** 696
Sister's Choice (Showalter), **Retro. Supp. I:** 368
Sisters of the Earth: Women's Prose and Poetry About Nature (Anderson, ed.), **Supp. XVIII:** 189
Sisters Rosensweig, The (Wasserstein), **Supp. XV:** 320, **328–330**
"Sisyphus" (Kumin), **Supp. IV Part 2:** 443, 444, 451
"Sitalkas" (Doolittle), **Supp. I Part 1:** 266
"Sites of Memory" (Cliff), **Supp. XXII:** 69, 74
Sitney, P. Adams, **Supp. XII:** 2
Sitting Bull, **Supp. IV Part 2:** 492

"Sitting in a Rocking Chair Going Blind" (Komunyakaa), **Supp. XIII:** 114
Sitting In: Selected Writings on Jazz, Blues, and Related Topics (Carruth), **Supp. XVI:** 46
"Sitting Up Late with My Father, 1977" (F. Wright), **Supp. XVII:** 247
Sitti's Secrets (Nye), **Supp. XIII:** 278
Situation Normal (A. Miller), **III:** 148, 149, 156, 164
Situation of Poetry, The: Contemporary Poetry and Its Traditions (Pinsky), **Supp. VI: 237–238,** 239, 241, 242
Sitwell, Edith, **IV:** 77; **Supp. I Part 1:** 271
"Six Brothers" (Cisneros), **Supp. VII:** 67
Six Characters in Search of an Author (Pirandello), **Supp. IV Part 2:** 576
"Six Days: Some Rememberings" (Paley), **Supp. VI:** 226
"65290" (Leopold), **Supp. XIV:** 184–185
Six French Poets (Lowell), **II:** 528–529
"Six in All" (Bierds), **Supp. XVII:** 31
"Six Persons" (Baraka), **Supp. II Part 1:** 53
Six Sections from Mountains and Rivers without End (Snyder), **Supp. VIII:** 305
"Sixteen Months" (Sandburg), **III:** 584
1601, or Conversation as It Was by the Fireside in the Time of the Tudors (Twain), **IV:** 201
"Sixth-Month Song in the Foothills" (Snyder), **Supp. VIII:** 297
Sixties, The (magazine) (R. Bly), **Supp. IV Part 1:** 60; **Supp. IX:** 271
"Sixty" (Dunn), **Supp. XI:** 155
"Sixty Acres" (Carver), **Supp. III Part 1:** 141
"64 Elmgrove" (Halliday), **Supp. XIX:** 88
"69 Hidebound Opinions, Propositions, and Several Asides from a Manila Folder concerning the Stuff of Poetry" (Wright), **Supp. XV:** 344–345
Sixty Stories (Barthelme), **Supp. IV Part 1:** 41, 42, 44, 47, 49, 50
63: Dream Palace (Purdy), **Supp. VII:** 270–271
"Six Variations" (Levertov), **Supp. III Part 1:** 277–278
"Six-Year-Old Boy" (Olds), **Supp. X:** 206
"Six Years Later" (Brodsky), **Supp. VIII:** 26, 28
"Size and Sheer Will" (Olds), **Supp. X:** 206
Size of Thoughts, The: Essays and Other Lumber (Baker), **Supp. XIII: 52–53,** 55, 56
Sizwe Bansi Is Dead (Fugard), **Supp. VIII:** 330
Sjöwall, Maj, **Supp. XX: 87**
"Skagway" (Haines), **Supp. XII:** 206
"Skaters, The" (Ashbery), **Supp. III Part 1:** 10, 12, 13, 18, 25
"Skaters, The" (Jarrell), **II:** 368–369
Skau, Michael, **Supp. XII:** 129, 130, 132, 134
Skeeters Kirby (Masters), **Supp. I Part 2:** 459, 470, 471
Skeleton Crew (King), **Supp. V:** 144
"Skeleton in Armor, The" (Longfellow), **Retro. Supp. II:** 168
"Skeleton's Cave, The" (Bryant), **Supp. I Part 1:** 157
Skelton, John, **III:** 521
Skepticisms (Aiken), **Supp. XV:** 298, 302
Sketch Book of Geoffrey Crayon, Gent., The (Irving), **II:** 295, 303, 304–308, 309, 311, 491; **Supp. I Part 1:** 155
Sketches of Art (Jameson), **Retro. Supp. II:** 58
Sketches of Eighteenth Century America (Crèvecoeur), **Supp. I Part 1:** 233, 240–241, 250, 251
"Sketches of Female Biography" (Rowson), **Supp. XV:** 245
Sketches of Switzerland (Cooper), **I:** 346
Sketches Old and New (Twain), **IV:** 198
"Sketch for a Job-Application Blank" (Harrison), **Supp. VIII:** 38
Sketch of Old England, by a New England Man (Paulding), **I:** 344
Skibell, Joseph, **Supp. XVII:** 48
"Skier and the Mountain, The" (Eberhart), **I:** 528–529
"Skin-Boats: 1830, The" (Bierds), **Supp. XVII:** 28
Skinker, Mary Scott, **Supp. IX:** 20
Skinner, Ewart, **Supp. XXII:** 78
Skinny Island (Auchincloss), **Supp. IV Part 1:** 33
Skinny Legs and All (Robbins), **Supp. X:** 267, 273, **276–279**
Skin of Our Teeth, The (Wilder), **IV:** 357, 358, 369–372; **Supp. IV Part 2:** 586; **Supp. XX: 50**
"Skins" (Wright), **Supp. V:** 340
Skins and Bones: Poems 1979–1987 (Gunn Allen), **Supp. IV Part 1:** 321, 331
"Skipper Ireson's Ride" (Whittier), **Supp. I Part 2:** 691, 693–694
"Skirmish at Sartoris" (Faulkner), **II:** 67
"Skirt" (Halliday), **Supp. XIX:** 90
Skirts and Slacks (Di Piero), **Supp. XIX:** 35, 36, 38, 45–47
Skloot, Floyd, **Supp. XX: 193–209**
Skotheim, Robert Allen, **Supp. XVII:** 104
Skow, John, **Supp. V:** 213; **Supp. XVI:** 174
Skube, Michael, **Supp. XVIII:** 96
"Skunk Cabbage" (Bronk), **Supp. XXI:** 31
"Skunk Cabbage" (Oliver), **Supp. VII:** 235, 236
"Skunk Hour" (Lowell), **II:** 548–550; **Retro. Supp. II:** 188, 189; **Supp. XIV:** 269; **Supp. XX: 203**
Sky, The Stars, The Wilderness, The (Bass), **Supp. XVI:** 19, 20
Sky Changes, The (Sorrentino), **Supp. XXI:** 228, 230, 231
"Sky Dance" (Leopold), **Supp. XIV:** 186
"Sky Line" (Taylor), **Supp. V:** 316
"Sky Line, The" (Mumford), **Supp. II Part 2:** 475
"Skyscraper" (Sandburg), **III:** 581–582
Sky's the Limit, The: A Defense of the Earth (Nichols), **Supp. XIII:** 268
"Sky Valley Rider" (Wright), **Supp. V:** 335, 340
Sky-Walk; or the Man Unknown to Himself (Brown), **Supp. I Part 1:** 127–128
"Slang in America" (Whitman), **IV:** 348
Slappy Hooper, the Wonderful Sign Painter (Bontemps and Conroy), **Supp. XXII:** 5, 11
Slapstick (Vonnegut), **Supp. II Part 2:** 753, 754, 778
Slapstick Tragedy (T. Williams), **IV:** 382, 393
Slate, Lane, **Supp. IX:** 251, 253
Slattery, Mary Grace. *See* Miller, Mrs. Arthur (Mary Grace Slattery)
"Slaughterer, The" (Singer), **IV:** 19
Slaughterhouse-Five (Vonnegut), **Supp. II Part 2:** 755, 758–759, 760, 770, 772–776; **Supp. V:** 41, 244; **Supp. XIX:** 235
Slaughter Rule, The (film; Alex and Andrew Smith), **Supp. XIX:** 174
Slave, The (Baraka), **Supp. II Part 1:** 42, 44, 56
Slave, The: A Novel (Singer), **IV:** 13; **Retro. Supp. II: 305–307**
"Slave Canal" (Ray), **Supp. XVIII:** 193
"Slave Coffle" (Angelou), **Supp. IV Part 1:** 16
"Slave of the Sky" (P. N. Warren), **Supp. XX: 261**
"Slave on the Block" (Hughes), **Supp. I Part 1:** 329
Slave Power, The: The Free North and Southern Domination, 1780–1860 (Richards), **Supp. XIV:** 48
"Slave Quarters" (Dickey), **Supp. IV Part 1:** 181
"Slave's Dream, The" (Longfellow), **Supp. I Part 2:** 409
Slave Ship: A Historical Pageant (Baraka), **Supp. II Part 1:** 47–49, 53, 56–57
"Slave-Ships, The" (Whittier), **Supp. I Part 2:** 687–688
Slaves in Algiers; or, A Struggle for Freedom (Rowson), **Supp. XV: 236–237**
"Slave Trade, The: View from the Middle Passage" (Major), **Supp. XXII:** 182
Slavs! Thinking about the Longstanding Problems of Virtue and Happiness (Kushner), **Supp. IX: 146**
Sledge, Eugene, **Supp. V:** 250
Sleek for the Long Flight (Matthews), **Supp. IX:** 154, 155, **157–158**
Sleep (Dixon), **Supp. XII:** 154
"Sleep, The" (Strand), **Supp. IV Part 2:** 627
Sleeper (film; Allen), **Supp. XV:** 5
"Sleeper, The" (Poe), **III:** 411
"Sleeper 1, The" (Hay), **Supp. XIV:** 132–133
"Sleeper 2, The" (Hay), **Supp. XIV:** 132–133
"Sleepers, The" (Whitman), **IV:** 336

"Sleepers in Jaipur" (Kenyon), **Supp. VII:** 172
Sleepers in Moon-Crowned Valleys (Purdy), **Supp. VII:** 274, 275
Sleepers Joining Hands (R. Bly), **Supp. XXI:** 85
"Sleepers Joining Hands" (R. Bly), **Supp. IV Part 1:** 63, 73
Sleeping Beauty (Macdonald), **Supp. IV Part 2:** 474, 475
Sleeping Beauty, The (Carruth), **Supp. XVI:** 53, 57–58
"Sleeping Beauty Syndrome, The: The New Agony of Single Men" (Wasserstein), **Supp. XV:** 328
"Sleeping Fury, The" (Bogan), **Supp. III Part 1:** 58
Sleeping Fury, The: Poems (Bogan), **Supp. III Part 1:** 55–58
Sleeping Gypsy and Other Poems, The (Garrett), **Supp. VII:** 96–98
Sleeping in the Forest (Oliver), **Supp. VII:** 233
"Sleeping in the Forest" (Oliver), **Supp. VII:** 233–234
Sleeping in the Woods (Wagoner), **Supp. IX: 328**
Sleeping on Fists (Ríos), **Supp. IV Part 2:** 540
Sleeping on the Wing: An Anthology of Modern Poetry (Koch and Farrell, eds.), **Supp. XV:** 187–188
"Sleeping Standing Up" (Bishop), **Supp. I Part 1:** 85, 89, 93
"Sleeping with Animals" (Kumin), **Supp. IV Part 2:** 454
Sleeping with One Eye Open (Strand), **Supp. IV Part 2:** 621–624, 623, 628
Sleep in Thunder (Lacy), **Supp. XV:** 206
"Sleepless, The" (L.-Y. Lee), **Supp. XV:** 224
"Sleepless at Crown Point" (Wilbur), **Supp. III Part 2:** 561
Sleepless Nights (Hardwick), **Supp. III Part 1:** 193, 208–211
"Sleepless Nights" (Nelson), **Supp. XVIII:** 174
"Sleep-Walkers, The" (Gibran), **Supp. XX: 118**
Sleepy Lagoon Mystery, The (Endore), **Supp. XVII:** 60
"Sleepy People" (Lethem), **Supp. XVIII:** 140
Sleigh, Tom, **Supp. XIX:** 38, 40
Sleight, Ken, **Supp. XIII:** 12
Slick, Sam (pseudonym). *See* Haliburton, Thomas Chandler
"Slick Gonna Learn" (Ellison), **Retro. Supp. II:** 116; **Supp. II Part 1:** 237–238
"Slight Rebellion off Madison" (Salinger), **III:** 553
"Slight Sound at Evening, A" (White), **Supp. I Part 2:** 672
"Slim Graves Show, The" (Keillor), **Supp. XVI:** 172
"Slim Greer" series (Hayden), **Supp. II Part 1:** 369
"Slim in Hell" (Hayden), **Supp. II Part 1:** 369
"Slim Man Canyon" (Silko), **Supp. IV Part 2:** 560
"Slip, Shift, and Speed Up: The Influence of Robinson Jeffers's Narrative Syntax" (Jarman), **Supp. XVII:** 111, 112
"Slippery Fingers" (Hammett), **Supp. IV Part 1:** 343
Slipping-Down Life, A (Tyler), **Supp. IV Part 2:** 660–661
Sloan, Jacob, **IV:** 3, 6
Sloan, John ?/, **I:** 254; **IV:** 411; **Retro. Supp. II:** 103
Sloan, John F. ?/, **Supp. XXII:** 277
Sloane, John, **Supp. XV:** 295
"Slob" (Farrell), **II:** 25, 28, 31
Slocum, Joshua, **Supp. I Part 2:** 497
Slonim, Véra. *See* Nabokov, Véra
Slopen, Beverly, **Supp. XX: 59**
Slouching towards Bethlehem (Didion), **Supp. IV Part 1:** 196, 197, 200–201, 202, 206, 210
Slovic, Scott, **Supp. XVI:** 277
"Slow Child with a Book of Birds" (Levis), **Supp. XI:** 268
"Slow Down for Poetry" (Strand), **Supp. IV Part 2:** 620
Slow Music (Taggard), **Supp. XXII:** 284
"Slow Pacific Swell, The" (Winters), **Supp. II Part 2:** 790, 793, 795, 796, 799
Slow Parade (Kees), **Supp. XV:** 137
Slow Train Coming (album, Dylan), **Supp. XVIII:** 28
"Slum Church" (Espaillat), **Supp. XXI:** 110–111
"Slumgullions" (Olsen), **Supp. IV Part 1:** 54
Slumgullion Stew: An Edward Abbey Reader (Abbey), **Supp. XIII:** 4
Slung, Michelle, **Supp. XX: 87**
"S & M" (Komunyakaa), **Supp. XIII:** 114
"Small" (C. Frost), **Supp. XV:** 102
Small, Albion, **Supp. I Part 1:** 5
"Small, Good Thing, A" (Carver), **Supp. III Part 1:** 145, 147
Small, Miriam Rossiter, **Supp. I Part 1:** 319
Small Boy and Others, A (James), **II:** 337, 547; **Retro. Supp. I:** 235
"Small but Urgent Request to the Unknowable" (Karr), **Supp. XI:** 243
Small Ceremonies (Shields), **Supp. VII:** 312–315, 320
Small Craft Warnings (T. Williams), **IV:** 382, 383, 384, 385, 386, 387, 392, 393, 396, 398
"Small Degrees" (Brockmeier), **Supp. XXII:** 52, 59
"Small Fry" (Peacock), **Supp. XIX:** 206
Small Place, A (Kincaid), **Supp. VII:** 186–187, 188, 191
"Small Rain, The" (Pynchon), **Supp. II Part 2:** 620
Small Room, The (Sarton), **Supp. VIII:** 252, **255–256**
Smalls, Bob, **II:** 128
"Small Song for Andrew" (Weigl), **Supp. XIX:** 280
Small Time Crooks (film; Allen), **Supp. XV:** 11
Small Town, A (Hearon), **Supp. VIII: 65–66**
"Small Vases from Hebron, The" (Nye), **Supp. XIII:** 283
"Small Vision, The" (Goldbarth), **Supp. XII:** 180
"Small Voice from the Wings" (Everwine), **Supp. XV:** 76
"Small Wire" (Sexton), **Supp. II Part 2:** 696
Small Worlds (A. Hoffman), **Supp. XVII:** 44
Smardz, Zofia, **Supp. XVI:** 155
Smart, Christopher, **III:** 534; **Supp. I Part 2:** 539; **Supp. IV Part 2:** 626
Smart, Joyce H., **Supp. XI:** 169
"Smart Cookie, A" (Cisneros), **Supp. VII:** 64
"Smashup" (Thurber), **Supp. I Part 2:** 616
Smedly, Agnes, **Supp. XIII:** 295
"Smell of a God, The" (Peacock), **Supp. XIX:** 199
"Smelt Fishing" (Hayden), **Supp. II Part 1:** 367
"Smile of the Bathers, The" (Kees), **Supp. XV:** 145
"Smile on the Face of a Kouros, The" (Bronk), **Supp. XXI:** 31
"Smiles" (Dunn), **Supp. XI:** 151
Smiles, Samuel, **Supp. X:** 167
Smiley, Jane, **Supp. VI: 291–309; Supp. XII:** 73, 297; **Supp. XIII:** 127; **Supp. XIX:** 54
Smith, Adam, **II:** 9; **Supp. I Part 2:** 633, 634, 639; **Supp. XVII:** 235
Smith, Annick, **Supp. XIV:** 223
Smith, Benjamin, **IV:** 148
Smith, Bernard, **I:** 260
Smith, Bessie, **Retro. Supp. I:** 343; **Supp. VIII:** 330; **Supp. XIX:** 147
Smith, Charlie, **Supp. X:** 177
Smith, Dale, **Supp. XV:** 136, 138, 139
Smith, Dave, **Supp. V:** 333; **Supp. XI:** 152; **Supp. XII:** 178, 198; **Supp. XIX:** 277, 282
Smith, David, **Supp. XIII:** 246, 247
Smith, David Nichol, **Supp. XIV:** 2
Smith, Dinitia, **Supp. VIII:** 74, 82, 83; **Supp. XVIII:** 162
Smith, Elihu Hubbard, **Supp. I Part 1:** 126, 127, 130
Smith, George Adam, **III:** 199
Smith, Hannah Whitall, **Supp. XIV:** 333, 334, 338
Smith, Harrison, **II:** 61
Smith, Henry Nash, **IV:** 210; **Supp. I Part 1:** 233
Smith, Herbert F., **Supp. I Part 2:** 423
Smith, Iain Crichton, **Supp. XVIII:** 196
Smith, James, **II:** 111
Smith, Jedediah Strong, **Supp. IV Part 2:** 602
Smith, Jerome, **Supp. IV Part 1:** 369
Smith, Joe, **Supp. IV Part 2:** 584
Smith, John, **I:** 4, 131; **II:** 296
Smith, John Allyn, **I:** 168

Smith, Johnston (pseudonym). *See* Crane, Stephen
Smith, Katherine Capshaw, **Supp. XXII:** 10, 13, 13–14
Smith, Kellogg, **Supp. I Part 2:** 660
Smith, Lamar, **II:** 585
Smith, Mrs. Lamar (Marguerite Walters), **II:** 585, 587
Smith, Lane, **Supp. XIX:** 231
Smith, Larry David, **Supp. XVIII:** 22
Smith, Lee, **Supp. XII:** 311; **Supp. XVIII:** 195; **Supp. XXII:** 206, 213
Smith, Lillian, **Supp. XXII:** 67
Smith, Logan Pearsall, **Supp. XIV: 333–351**
Smith, Lula Carson. *See* McCullers, Carson
Smith, Mark, **Supp. XVIII:** 155
Smith, Martha Nell, **Retro. Supp. I:** 33, 43, 46, 47
Smith, Mary Rozet, **Supp. I Part 1:** 5, 22
Smith, Oliver, **II:** 586
Smith, Patricia Clark, **Supp. IV Part 1:** 397, 398, 402, 406, 408, 410; **Supp. IV Part 2:** 509; **Supp. XII:** 218
Smith, Patrick, **Supp. VIII:** 40, 41
Smith, Patti, **Supp. XII:** 136; **Supp. XIV:** 151
Smith, Porter, **III:** 572
Smith, Red, **II:** 417, 424
Smith, Robert McClure, **Supp. XV:** 270
Smith, Robert Pearsall, **Supp. XIV:** 333
Smith, Sarah A., **Supp. XVIII:** 99
Smith, Seba, **Supp. I Part 2:** 411
Smith, Sidonie ?/, **Supp. XXII:** 70
Smith, Sidonie Ann ?/, **Supp. IV Part 1:** 11
Smith, Stevie, **Supp. V:** 84
Smith, Sydney, **II:** 295; **Supp. XIV:** 112
Smith, Thorne, **Supp. IX:** 194
Smith, Valerie, **Supp. XXII:** 146
Smith, Wendy, **Supp. XII:** 330, 335; **Supp. XVIII:** 89, 92
Smith, Wilford Bascom "Pitchfork", **Supp. XIII:** 168
Smith, William, **II:** 114
Smith, William Gardner, **Supp. XVI:** 142–143
Smith, William Jay, **Supp. XIII: 331–350**
"Smoke" (Di Piero), **Supp. XIX:** 38
Smoke (film), **Supp. XII:** 21
Smoke and Steel (Sandburg), **III:** 585–587, 592
"Smokehouse" (Offutt), **Supp. XIX:** 166, 167
"Smokers" (Wolff), **Supp. VII:** 340–341
Smokey Bites the Dust (film, C. Griffith), **Supp. XVII:** 9
"Smoking My Prayers" (Ortiz), **Supp. IV Part 2:** 503
"Smoking Room, The" (Jackson), **Supp. IX:** 116
"Smoky Gold" (Leopold), **Supp. XIV:** 186
Smolan, Sandy, **Supp. XVI:** 36
Smollett, Tobias G., **I:** 134, 339, 343; **II:** 304–305; **III:** 61; **Supp. XVIII:** 7
Smuggler's Bible, A (McElroy), **Supp. IV Part 1:** 285
Smuggler's Handbook, The (Goldbarth), **Supp. XII:** 181, 183
Smugglers of Lost Soul's Rock, The (Gardner), **Supp. VI: 70**
Smyth, Albert Henry, **II:** 123
Smyth, Jacqui, **Supp. XXI:** 215
"Snack Firm Maps New Chip Push" (Keillor), **Supp. XVI:** 168, 169
"Snail, The" (Hay), **Supp. XIV:** 124
"Snake, The" (Berry), **Supp. X:** 31
"Snake, The" (Crane), **I:** 420
"Snakecharmer" (Plath), **Supp. I Part 2:** 538
"Snakes, Mongooses" (Moore), **III:** 207
"Snakeskin" (Kooser), **Supp. XIX:** 123
"Snakes of September, The" (Kunitz), **Supp. III Part 1:** 258
"Snapshot of 15th S.W., A" (Hugo), **Supp. VI:** 141
"Snapshot Rediscovered, A" (X. J. Kennedy), **Supp. XV:** 170
"Snapshots in an Album" (Espaillat), **Supp. XXI:** 111
"Snapshots of a Daughter-in-Law" (Rich), **Supp. I Part 2:** 553–554
Snapshots of a Daughter-in-Law: Poems, 1954–1962 (Rich), **Supp. I Part 2:** 550–551, 553–554; **Supp. XII:** 255
Snaring the Flightless Birds (Bierds), **Supp. XVII:** 26
Sneetches and Other Stories, The (Geisel), **Supp. XVI:** 109
"Sneeze, The" (Chekhov), **Supp. IV Part 2:** 585
Snell, Ebenezer, **Supp. I Part 1:** 151
Snell, Thomas, **Supp. I Part 1:** 153
"Snob, The" (Boulton), **Supp. XXII:** 23
"Snob, The" (Shapiro), **Supp. II Part 2:** 705
Snobbery: The America Version (Epstein), **Supp. XIV:** 102, 114–115
Snodgrass, Kathleen, **Supp. XVI:** 42
Snodgrass, W. D., **I:** 400; **Retro. Supp. II:** 179; **Supp. III Part 2:** 541; **Supp. V:** 337; **Supp. VI: 311–328; Supp. XI:** 141, 315; **Supp. XIII:** 312; **Supp. XV:** 92, 153; **Supp. XVII:** 239
"Snow" (C. Baxter), **Supp. XVII:** 19
"Snow" (Frost), **Retro. Supp. I:** 133
"Snow" (Haines), **Supp. XII:** 212
"Snow" (Sexton), **Supp. II Part 2:** 696
"Snow" (W. V. Davis), **Supp. XXI:** 89, 90, 93
Snow, C. P., **Supp. I Part 2:** 536
Snow, Hank, **Supp. V:** 335
Snow Ball, The (Gurney), **Supp. V:** 99
"Snow-Bound" (Whittier), **Supp. I Part 2:** 700–703
"Snow Bound at Eagle's" (Harte), **Supp. II Part 1:** 356
"Snowflakes" (Longfellow), **II:** 498
"Snow Goose, The" (Gallico), **Supp. XVI:** 238
Snow-Image and Other Twice Told Tales, The (Hawthorne), **II:** 237; **Retro. Supp. I:** 160
"Snowing in Greenwich Village" (Updike), **IV:** 226; **Retro. Supp. I:** 321
"Snow in New York" (Swenson), **Supp. IV Part 2:** 644
Snow Leopard, The (Matthiessen), **Supp. V:** 199, 207–211
"Snow Man, The" (Stevens), **IV:** 82–83; **Retro. Supp. I:** 299, 300, 302, 306, 307, 312; **Supp. XXI:** 60
"Snowmass Cycle, The" (Dunn), **Supp. XI:** 152
Snow: Meditations of a Cautious Man in Winter (Banks), **Supp. V:** 6
Snow Poems, The (Ammons), **Supp. VII:** 32–34
Snowshoe Trek to Otter River (Budbill), **Supp. XIX:** 11
Snow's Music, The (Skloot), **Supp. XX: 196, 204–205**
"Snows of Kilimanjaro, The" (Hemingway), **II:** 78, 257, 263, 264; **Retro. Supp. I:** 98, 182; **Supp. XII:** 249
"Snows of Studiofiftyfour, The" (Plimpton), **Supp. XVI:** 245
"Snow Songs" (Snodgrass), **Supp. VI:** 324
"Snowstorm, The" (Oates), **Supp. II Part 2:** 523
"Snowstorm as It Affects the American Farmer, A" (Crèvecoeur), **Supp. I Part 1:** 251
Snow White (Barthelme), **Supp. IV Part 1:** 40, 47, 48–49, 50, 52; **Supp. V:** 39
"Snowy Egret" (Weigl), **Supp. XIX:** 280–281
"Snowy Mountain Song, A" (Ortiz), **Supp. IV Part 2:** 506
Snyder, Gary, **Supp. III Part 1:** 350; **Supp. IV Part 2:** 502; **Supp. V:** 168–169; **Supp. VIII:** 39, **289–307; Supp. XVI:** 283; **Supp. XXII:** 276
Snyder, Mike, **Supp. XIV:** 36
"So-and-So Reclining on Her Couch" (Stevens), **IV:** 90
"Soapland" (Thurber), **Supp. I Part 2:** 619
Soares, Lota de Macedo, **Retro. Supp. II:** 44; **Supp. I Part 1:** 89, 94
"Sobbin' Women, The" (Benét), **Supp. XI:** 47
Sobin, Gustaf, **Supp. XVI: 281–298**
Sochen, June, **Supp. XXI:** 1
Social Ethics (Gilman), **Supp. XI:** 207
"Social Function of the Story Teller, The" (lecture, Murray), **Supp. XIX:** 153
"Socialism and the Negro" (McKay), **Supp. X:** 135
"Socialism of the Skin, A (Liberation, Honey!)" (Kushner), **Supp. IX:** 135
Social Thought in America: The Revolt against Formalism (White), **Supp. I Part 2:** 648, 650
"Society, Morality, and the Novel" (Ellison), **Retro. Supp. II:** 118, 123–124
"Sociological Habit Patterns in Linguistic Transmogrification" (Cowley), **Supp. II Part 1:** 143

"Sociological Poet, A" (Bourne), **I:** 228
Socrates, **I:** 136, 265; **II:** 8–9, 105, 106; **III:** 281, 419, 606; **Supp. I Part 2:** 458; **Supp. XII:** 98
Socrates Fortlow stories (Mosley), **Supp. XIII: 242–243**
So Forth (Brodsky), **Supp. VIII:** 32–33
"So Forth" (Brodsky), **Supp. VIII:** 33
"Soft Flame" (Skloot), **Supp. XX: 203**
Soft Machine, The (Burroughs), **Supp. III Part 1:** 93, 103, 104
"Soft Mask" (Karr), **Supp. XI:** 243
Soft Side, The (James), **II:** 335; **Retro. Supp. I:** 229
"Soft Spring Night in Shillington, A" (Updike), **Retro. Supp. I:** 318, 319
"Soft Wood" (Lowell), **II:** 550–551
"So Help Me" (Algren), **Supp. IX:** 2
Soil and Survival: Land Stewardship and the Future of American Agriculture (C. Bly, J. Paddock and N. Paddock), **Supp. XVI:** 36–37
"Soirée in Hollywood" (H. Miller), **III:** 186
Sojourner, The (Rawlings), **Supp. X:** 233–234
"Sojourn in a Whale" (Moore), **III:** 211, 213
"Sojourns" (Didion), **Supp. IV Part 1:** 205
Sokolow, Jayme, **Supp. XIX:** 134
Solanus, Jane, **Supp. XVI:** 293
Solar Lottery (Dick), **Supp. XVIII:** 138
Solar Storms (Hogan), **Supp. IV Part 1:** 397, 410, 414–415
"Soldier, The" (Frost), **II:** 155
"Soldier Asleep at the Tomb" (Schnackenberg), **Supp. XV:** 262–263
Soldier Blue (film), **Supp. X:** 124
"Soldier of Fortune" (Wright), **Supp. XV:** 341
"Soldier's Home" (Hemingway), **Retro. Supp. I:** 189
Soldier's Joy (Bell), **Supp. X:** 7, **7–8,** 10, 11
Soldiers of the Storm (film), **Supp. XIII:** 163
Soldiers' Pay (Faulkner), **I:** 117; **II:** 56, 68; **Retro. Supp. I:** 80, 81
"Soldier's Testament, The" (Mumford), **Supp. II Part 2:** 473
"Soliloquy: Man Talking to a Mirror" (Komunyakaa), **Supp. XIII:** 116–117
"Solitary Confinement" (X. J. Kennedy), **Supp. XV:** 157
"Solitary Pond, The" (Updike), **Retro. Supp. I:** 323
So Little Time (Marquand), **III:** 55, 59, 65, 67, 69
"Solitude" (Maupassant), **Supp. I Part 1:** 223
Solo Faces (Salter), **Supp. IX: 259–260**
Solomon, Andy, **Supp. X:** 11
Solomon, Carl, **Supp. XIV:** 143, 150
Solomon, Charles, **Supp. VIII:** 82
Solomon, Deborah, **Supp. XXI:** 245
Solomon, Henry, Jr., **Supp. I Part 2:** 490
Solomons, Leon, **IV:** 26
So Long, See You Tomorrow (Maxwell), **Supp. VIII:** 156, 160, 162, **167–169; Supp. XVII:** 23
"So Long Ago" (Bausch), **Supp. VII:** 41–42
Solotaroff, Robert, **Retro. Supp. II:** 203
Solotaroff, Theodore, **III:** 452–453; **Retro. Supp. II:** 281; **Supp. I Part 2:** 440, 445; **Supp. X:** 79; **Supp. XI:** 340; **Supp. XII:** 291; **Supp. XIX:** 268
Solstice (Di Piero), **Supp. XIX:** 36
"Solstice" (Jeffers), **Supp. II Part 2:** 433, 435
"Solstice, The" (Merwin), **Supp. III Part 1:** 356
"Solus Rex" (Nabokov), **Retro. Supp. I:** 274
"Solutions" (McCarthy), **II:** 578
"Solving the Puzzle" (Dunn), **Supp. XI:** 152
Solzhenitsyn, Alexandr, **Retro. Supp. I:** 278; **Supp. VIII:** 241
"Some Afternoon" (Creeley), **Supp. IV Part 1:** 150–151
Some American People (Caldwell), **I:** 292, 294, 295, 296, 304, 309
"Some Ashes Drifting above Piedra, California" (Levis), **Supp. XI:** 264–265
"Some Aspects of the Grotesque in Southern Fiction" (O'Connor), **Retro. Supp. II:** 223, 224
"Some Birds on a Dun Field" (Bronk), **Supp. XXI:** 27
"Somebody Always Grabs the Purple" (H. Roth), **Supp. IX:** 234
Somebody in Boots (Algren), **Supp. IX:** 3, **5–7,** 12
Somebody's Darling (McMurtry), **Supp. V:** 225
Some Came Running (film), **Supp. XI:** 213
Some Came Running (Jones), **Supp. XI:** 214, 215, 220, **222–223,** 226, 227, 232
Some Can Whistle (McMurtry), **Supp. V:** 229
"Some Children of the Goddess" (Mailer), **Retro. Supp. II:** 204
Someday, Maybe (Stafford), **Supp. XI: 323–325; Supp. XIII:** 281
"Some Dreamers of the Golden Dream" (Didion), **Supp. IV Part 1:** 200
Some Faces in the Crowd (Schulberg), **Supp. XVIII:** 252
"Some Foreign Letters" (Sexton), **Supp. II Part 2:** 674
"Some General Instructions" (Koch), **Supp. XV:** 182
"Some Good News" (Olson), **Supp. II Part 2:** 575, 576, 577
"Some Grass along a Ditch Bank" (Levis), **Supp. XI:** 266
"Some Greek Writings" (Corso), **Supp. XII:** 130
Some Honorable Men: Political Conventions, 1960–1972 (Mailer), **Retro. Supp. II:** 208
Some Imagist Poets (Lowell), **III:** 511, 518, 520; **Supp. I Part 1:** 257, 261
"Some keep the Sabbath going to Church" (Dickinson), **Retro. Supp. I:** 30; **Supp. XVIII:** 301
"Some Laughed" (L. Michaels), **Supp. XVI:** 207
"Some Like Indians Endure" (Gunn Allen), **Supp. IV Part 1:** 330
"Some Like Them Cold" (Lardner), **II:** 427–428, 430, 431; **Supp. IX:** 202
"Some Lines from Whitman" (Jarrell), **IV:** 352
"Some Matters Concerning the Occupant" (Keillor), **Supp. XVI:** 167
"Some Musicians Play Chamber Music for Us" (Bronk), **Supp. XXI:** 27–28
"Some Negatives: X. at the Chateau" (Merrill), **Supp. III Part 1:** 322
"Some Neglected Points in the Theory of Socialism" (Veblen), **Supp. I Part 2:** 635
"Some Notes for an Autobiographical Lecture" (Trilling), **Supp. III Part 2:** 493, 497, 500
"Some Notes on French Poetry" (R. Bly), **Supp. IV Part 1:** 61
"Some Notes on Miss L." (West), **IV:** 290–291, 295; **Retro. Supp. II:** 322
"Some Notes on Organic Form" (Levertov), **Supp. III Part 1:** 272, 279
"Some Notes on Teaching: Probably Spoken" (Paley), **Supp. VI:** 225
"Some Notes on the Gazer Within" (Levis), **Supp. XI:** 270
"Some Notes on Violence" (West), **IV:** 304; **Retro. Supp. II:** 322, 323
"Some Observations Now" (Conroy), **Supp. XVI:** 75
Some Observations of a Stranger at Zuni in the Later Part of the Century (Major), **Supp. XXII:** 179–180
"Some Observations of a Stranger at Zuni in the Later Part of the Century" (Major), **Supp. XXII:** 179
Some of the Dharma (Kerouac), **Supp. III Part 1:** 225
"Someone Is Buried" (Salinas), **Supp. XIII:** 324
"Someone Puts a Pineapple Together" (Stevens), **IV:** 90–91
"Someone's Blood" (Dove), **Supp. IV Part 1:** 245
"Someone Talking" (Harjo), **Supp. XII:** 219–220
"Someone Talking to Himself" (Wilbur), **Supp. III Part 2:** 557
"Someone to Watch Over Me" (Stern), **Supp. IX:** 300
Someone to Watch Over Me: Stories (Bausch), **Supp. VII:** 53
Some People, Places, & Things That Will Not Appear in My Next Novel (Cheever), **Supp. I Part 1:** 184–185
"Some Poets' Criticism and the Age" (Yenser), **Supp. XV:** 113–114
Some Problems of Philosophy: A Beginning of an Introduction to Philosophy (James), **II:** 360–361
"Some Questions You Might Ask" (Oliver), **Supp. VII:** 238–239

"Some Remarks on Humor" (White), **Supp. I Part 2:** 672
"Some Remarks on Rhythm" (Roethke), **III:** 548–549
Somers, Fred, **I:** 196
Somerville, Jane, **Supp. IX:** 289, 296–297
"Some Secrets" (Stern), **Supp. IX:** 286, 287, 288, 289, 295
Some Sort of Epic Grandeur (Bruccoli), **Retro. Supp. I:** 115, 359
"Something" (Oliver), **Supp. VII:** 236
Something Happened (Heller), **Supp. IV Part 1:** 383, 386–388, 389, 392
"*Something Happened:* The Imaginary, the Symbolic, and the Discourse of the Family" (Mellard), **Supp. IV Part 1:** 387
Something in Common (Hughes), **Supp. I Part 1:** 329–330
Something Inside: Conversations with Gay Fiction Writers (Gambone), **Supp. XII:** 81
"Something Matters but We Don't " (Bronk), **Supp. XXI:** 32
"Something Might Be Gaining" (Mosher), **Supp. XXII:** 209
"Something New" (Stern), **Supp. IX:** 290
Something Said (Sorrentino), **Supp. XXI:** 226, 227, 229, 235
"Something's Going to Happen" (Zinberg), **Supp. XV:** 196
"Something Spurious from the Mindinao Deep" (Stegner), **Supp. IV Part 2:** 605
"Something to Believe In" (Pitts), **Supp. XXII:** 280
Something to Declare (Alvarez), **Supp. VII:** 1, 2, 11, 17–19
Something to Remember Me By (Bellow), **Retro. Supp. II:** 32
"Something to Remember Me By" (Bellow), **Retro. Supp. II:** 32
Something Wicked This Way Comes (Bradbury), **Supp. IV Part 1:** 101, 110–111
"Something Wild . . ." (T. Williams), **IV:** 381
"Some Thoughts" (McNally), **Supp. XIII:** 207
"Some Thoughts on the Line" (Oliver), **Supp. VII:** 238
"Sometimes, Reading" (Stafford), **Supp. XI:** 314
"Sometimes It Just Happens That Way, That's All" (Hinojosa), **Supp. XIX:** 101
"Sometimes I Wonder" (Hughes), **Supp. I Part 1:** 337
Sometimes Mysteriously (Salinas), **Supp. XIII:** 311, **326–328**
"Sometimes Mysteriously" (Salinas), **Supp. XIII:** 328
Some Trees (Ashbery), **Supp. III Part 1:** 3–7, 12
"Some Trees" (Ashbery), **Supp. III Part 1:** 2
"Some Views on the Reading and Writing of Short Stories" (Welty), **Retro. Supp. I:** 351
"Somewhere" (Nemerov), **III:** 279–280
"Somewhere Else" (Paley), **Supp. VI:** 227
"Somewhere in Africa" (Sexton), **Supp. II Part 2:** 684–685
"Somewhere Is Such a Kingdom" (Ransom), **III:** 492
"Somewhere near Phu Bai: (Komunyakaa), **Supp. XIII:** 123–124
Some Words (Bronk), **Supp. XXI:** 32
"Some Words with a Mummy" (Poe), **III:** 425
"Some Yips and Barks in the Dark" (Snyder), **Supp. VIII:** 291
Sommers, Michael, **Supp. IV Part 2:** 581
Sommers, William, **I:** 387, 388
"Somnambulisma" (Stevens), **Retro. Supp. I:** 310
"So Much Summer" (Dickinson), **Retro. Supp. I:** 26, 44, 45
"So Much the Worse for Boston" (Lindsay), **Supp. I Part 2:** 398
"So Much Water So Close to Home" (Carver), **Supp. III Part 1:** 143, 146
Son, Cathy, **Supp. X:** 292
"Son, The" (Dove), **Supp. IV Part 1:** 245
"Son and Father" (Pickering), **Supp. XXI:** 197
"Sonata" (Schnackenberg), **Supp. XV:** 259
"Sonata for the Invisible" (Harjo), **Supp. XII:** 228
Sonata for Two Pianos (Bowles), **Supp. IV Part 1:** 83
Son at the Front, A (Wharton), **II:** 183; **IV:** 320; **Retro. Supp. I:** 378
Sondheim, Stephen, **Supp. XII:** 260; **Supp. XVI:** 194
Son Excellence Eugène Rougon (Zola), **III:** 322
Song (B. Kelly), **Supp. XVII:** 123, **127–130**
"Song" (B. Kelly), **Supp. XVII:** 127
"Song" (Bogan), **Supp. III Part 1:** 57
"Song" (Bryant). *See* "Hunter of the West, The"
"Song" (Dunbar), **Supp. II Part 1:** 199
"Song" (Espaillat), **Supp. XXI:** 106–107
"Song" (Ginsberg), **Supp. II Part 1:** 317
"Song" (Kenyon), **Supp. VII:** 169
"Song" (Rich), **Supp. I Part 2:** 560
"Song" (Wylie), **Supp. I Part 2:** 729
"Song, A" (Creeley), **Supp. IV Part 1:** 145
"Song, The" (Gioia), **Supp. XV:** 117
Song and Idea (Eberhart), **I:** 526, 529, 533, 539
"Song: Enlightenment" (X. J. Kennedy), **Supp. XV:** 169
Song for My Father, A: A Play in Two Acts (Budbill), **Supp. XIX:** 3, **15–16**
"Song for Myself and the Deer to Return On" (Harjo), **Supp. XII:** 225
"Song for My Sixtieth Year" (Carruth), **Supp. XVI:** 54
"Song for Occupations, A" (Whitman), **Retro. Supp. I:** 394
"Song for Simeon, A" (Eliot), **Retro. Supp. I:** 64
"Song for the Coming of Smallpox" (Wagoner), **Supp. IX:** 329, 330
"Song for the End of Time" (Gioia), **Supp. XV:** 126–127
"Song for the First People" (Wagoner), **Supp. IX:** 328
"Song for the Last Act" (Bogan), **Supp. III Part 1:** 64
"Song for the Middle of the Night, A" (Wright), **Supp. III Part 2:** 594
"Song for the Rainy Season" (Bishop), **Supp. I Part 1:** 93–94, 96
"Song for the Romeos, A" (Stern), **Supp. IX:** 296
"Song for Woody" (song, Dylan), **Supp. XVIII:** 24
"Song from a Courtyard Window" (Gioia), **Supp. XV:** 119
"Song III" (Taggard), **Supp. XXII:** 284
"Song in the Front Yard, A" (Brooks), **Supp. XVIII:** 181
"Songline of Dawn" (Harjo), **Supp. XII:** 229
"Song: Love in Whose Rich Honor" (Rukeyser), **Supp. VI:** 285
"Song: Now That She Is Here" (Carruth), **Supp. XVI:** 59
"Song of Advent, A" (Winters), **Supp. II Part 2:** 789
"Song of a Man Who Rushed at the Enemy" (Wagoner), **Supp. IX:** 329, 330
"Song of Courage, A" (Masters), **Supp. I Part 2:** 458
Song of God, The: Bhagavad-Gita (Isherwood and Prabhavananda, trans.), **Supp. XIV:** 156, 157, 164
Song of Hiawatha, The (Longfellow), **II:** 501, 503–504; **Retro. Supp. II:** 155, **159–161,** 162, 163
"Song of Innocence, A" (Ellison), **Retro. Supp. II:** 126; **Supp. II Part 1:** 248
"Song of My Fiftieth Birthday, The" (Lindsay), **Supp. I Part 2:** 399
"Song of Myself" (Whitman), **II:** 544; **III:** 572, 584, 595; **IV:** 333, 334, 337–339, 340, 341, 342, 344, 348, 349, 351, 405; **Retro. Supp. I:** 388, 389, 395–399, 400; **Supp. V:** 122; **Supp. IX:** 131, 136, 143, 328, 331; **Supp. XIV:** 139; **Supp. XVIII:** 194, 304; **Supp. XXII:** 81
Song of Napalm (Weigl), **Supp. XIX:** 278–282
"Song of Napalm" (Weigl), **Supp. XIX:** 276–277
Song of Russia (film), **Supp. I Part 1:** 281, 294; **Supp. XVII:** 60–61
"Song of Self" (Huncke), **Supp. XIV:** 138–139, 145
Song of Solomon (biblical book), **III:** 118; **IV:** 150
Song of Solomon (Morrison), **Supp. III Part 1:** 364, 368, 369, 372, 379; **Supp. XVIII:** 55
Song of Songs (biblical book), **II:** 538; **IV:** 153–154; **Supp. XV:** 221
"Song of the Answerer" (Whitman), **Retro. Supp. I:** 393, 399

Song of the Cardinal, The (Stratton-Porter), **Supp. XX: 217, 218, 219**
"Song of the Chattahoochee, The" (Lanier), **Supp. I Part 1:** 365, 368
"Song of the Degrees, A" (Pound), **III:** 466
"Song of the Dryads" (Taggard), **Supp. XXII:** 272
"Song of the Exposition" (Whitman), **IV:** 332
"Song of the Gavilan" (Leopold), **Supp. XIV:** 189
"Song of the Gourd" (Wright), **Supp. XV:** 348–349
"Song of the Greek Amazon" (Bryant), **Supp. I Part 1:** 168
Song of the Lark, The (Cather), **I:** 312, 319–321, 323; **Retro. Supp. I:** 1, 3, 7, **9–11,** 13, 19, 20
"Song of the Open Road" (McGrath), **Supp. X:** 127
"Song of the Open Road" (Whitman), **IV:** 340–341; **Retro. Supp. I:** 400; **Supp. IX:** 265
"Song of the Redwood Tree" (Whitman), **IV:** 348
"Song of the Scullery" (McCarriston), **Supp. XIV:** 272
"Song of the Sky Loom" (traditional Tewa poem), **Supp. IV Part 1:** 325
"Song of the Son" (Toomer), **Supp. III Part 2:** 482–483; **Supp. IX:** 313
"Song of the Sower, The" (Bryant), **Supp. I Part 1:** 169
"Song of the Stars" (Bryant), **Supp. I Part 1:** 163
"Song of the Swamp-Robin, The" (Frederic), **II:** 138
"Song of the Vermonters, The" (Whittier), **Supp. I Part 2:** 692
"Song of Three Smiles" (Merwin), **Supp. III Part 1:** 344
"Song of Wandering Aengus, The" (Yeats), **IV:** 271; **Retro. Supp. I:** 342, 350
"Song of Welcome" (Brodsky), **Supp. VIII:** 32
"Song on Captain Barney's Victory" (Freneau), **Supp. II Part 1:** 261
"Song/Poetry and Language-Expression and Perception" (Ortiz), **Supp. IV Part 2:** 500, 508
"Song: 'Rough Winds Do Shake the Darling Buds of May' " (Simpson), **Supp. IX:** 268
Songs (Boyce), **Supp. XXI:** 9
Songs and Satires (Masters), **Supp. I Part 2:** 465–466
Songs and Sonnets (L. P. Smith), **Supp. XIV:** 341
Songs and Sonnets (Masters), **Supp. I Part 2:** 455, 459, 461, 466
"Songs for a Colored Singer" (Bishop), **Supp. I Part 1:** 80, 85
Songs for a Summer's Day (A Sonnet Cycle) (MacLeish), **III:** 3
Songs for Eve (MacLeish), **III:** 3, 19
"Songs for Eve" (MacLeish), **III:** 19
"Songs for My Father" (Komunyakaa), **Supp. XIII:** 128
Songs for the Unborn Second Baby (Notley), **Supp. XXII:** 228
"Songs for Two Seasons" (C. Frost), **Supp. XV:** 95–96
Songs from This Earth on Turtle's Back: Contemporary American Indian Poetry (Bruchac, ed.), **Supp. IV Part 1:** 320, 328
"Songs of a Housewife" (Rawlings), **Supp. X:** 221–222
"Songs of Billy Bathgate, The" (Doctorow), **Supp. IV Part 1:** 230
Songs of Innocence (Blake), **Supp. I Part 2:** 708
Songs of Jamaica (McKay), **Supp. X:** 131, 133
"Songs of Maximus, The" (Olson), **Supp. II Part 2:** 567
"Songs of Parting" (Whitman), **IV:** 348
Songs of the North: A Sigurd Olson Reader (Mosher, ed.), **Supp. XXII:** 218
Songs of the Sierras (J. Miller), **I:** 459
Songs of Three Centuries (Whittier and Larcom, eds.), **Supp. XIII:** 142
"Song to David" (Smart), **III:** 534
"Song to No Music, A" (Brodsky), **Supp. VIII:** 26
"Song V" (Taggard), **Supp. XXII:** 284
Soniat, Katherine, **Supp. XXI:** 245
Sonneschein, Rosa, **Retro. Supp. II:** 65
"Sonnet" (Rukeyser), **Supp. VI:** 284
"Sonnet Crown for Two Voices" (Bierds), **Supp. XVII:** 35
"Sonnets" (Carruth), **Supp. XVI:** 56
Sonnets, The (Berrigan), **Supp. XXII:** 224
"Sonnets at Christmas" (Tate), **IV:** 135
Sonnets to Orpheus (Rilke), **Supp. XV:** 222
"Sonnet-To Zante" (Poe), **III:** 421
"Sonny's Blues" (Baldwin), **Retro. Supp. II:** 7, 8, 10, 14; **Supp. I Part 1:** 58–59, 63, 67; **Supp. XI:** 288
Son of Laughter, The: A Novel (Buechner), **Supp. XII:** 54
Son of Perdition, The (Cozzens), **I:** 359–360, 377, 378, 379
Son of the Circus, A (Irving), **Supp. VI:** 165, 166, **176–179**
"Son of the Gods, A" (Bierce), **I:** 202
Son of the Morning (Oates), **Supp. II Part 2:** 518, 519, 520–522
Son of the Morning Star: Custer and the Little Bighorn (Connell), **Supp. XIV:** 80, 82, 97
"Son of the Romanovs, A" (Simpson), **Supp. IX:** 273–274
Son of the Wolf, The (London), **II:** 465, 469
"Son of the Wolfman" (Chabon), **Supp. XI:** 76
"Sonrisas" (Mora), **Supp. XIII:** 216, 219
Sons (Buck), **Supp. II Part 1:** 117–118
Sons and Lovers (Lawrence), **III:** 27
Sontag, Kate, **Supp. XV:** 104
Sontag, Susan, **IV:** 13, 14; **Retro. Supp. II:** 279; **Supp. I Part 2:** 423; **Supp. III Part 2: 451–473; Supp. VIII:** 75; **Supp. XIV:** 14, 15, 95–96, 167; **Supp. XVI:** 201, 204, 206; **Supp. XX: 205; Supp. XXI:** 243
"Soonest Mended" (Ashbery), **Supp. III Part 1:** 1, 13
"Sootfall and Fallout" (White), **Supp. I Part 2:** 671
Sophocles, **I:** 274; **II:** 291, 385, 577; **III:** 145, 151, 152, 153, 159, 398, 476, 478, 609, 613; **IV:** 291, 363, 368, 370; **Supp. I Part 1:** 153, 284; **Supp. I Part 2:** 491; **Supp. V:** 97; **Supp. VIII:** 332; **Supp. XV:** 265, 266
"Sophronsiba" (Bourne), **I:** 221
Sorayam, Aram, **Supp. XXII:** 25
Sorcerer's Apprentice, The: Tales and Conjurations (Johnson), **Supp. VI: 192–193,** 194
"Sorcerer's Eye, The" (Nemerov), **III:** 283
Sordello (Browning), **III:** 467, 469, 470
"Sordid? Good God!" (Williams), **Retro. Supp. II:** 334
So Red the Rose (Young), **Supp. XXII:** 190, 193
"Sorghum" (Mason), **Supp. VIII:** 146
Sorokin, Pitirim, **Supp. I Part 2:** 679
Sorrentino, Christopher, **Supp. XVIII:** 148
Sorrentino, Gilbert, **Retro. Supp. I:** 426; **Supp. IV Part 1:** 286; **Supp. XII:** 139; **Supp. XXI: 225–241; Supp. XXII:** 261
Sorrento (Notley), **Supp. XXII:** 231
"Sorrow" (Komunyakaa), **Supp. XIII:** 119
Sorrow Dance, The (Levertov), **Supp. III Part 1:** 279–280, 283
"Sorrowful Guest, A" (Jewett), **Retro. Supp. II:** 137
Sorrows of Fat City, The: A Selection of Literary Essays and Reviews (Garrett), **Supp. VII:** 111
Sorrows of Young Werther, The (Goethe), **Supp. XI:** 169; **Supp. XX: 234, 236**
Sorrows of Young Werther, The (Goethe; Bogan and Mayer, trans.), **Supp. III Part 1:** 63
"Sorry Fugu" (Boyle), **Supp. XX: 19**
"Sorting Facts; or, Nineteen Ways of Looking at Marker" (Howe), **Supp. IV Part 2:** 434, 436
"Sort of Song, A" (W. C. Williams), **Supp. XVII:** 243
"S O S" (Baraka), **Supp. II Part 1:** 50
"So Sassafras" (Olson), **Supp. II Part 2:** 574
"So There" (Creeley), **Supp. IV Part 1:** 157
"So This Is Nebraska" (Kooser), **Supp. XIX:** 120
Sotirov, Vasil, **Supp. IX:** 152
Soto, Gary, **Supp. IV Part 2:** 545; **Supp. V:** 180; **Supp. XI:** 270; **Supp. XIII:** 313, 315, 316, 320, 323; **Supp. XV:** 73
"Soto Thinking of the Ocean" (Salinas), **Supp. XIII:** 321
"Sotto Voce" (Kunitz), **Supp. III Part 1:** 265

Sot-Weed Factor, The (Barth), **I:** 122, 123, 125, 129, 130, 131–134, 135; **Supp. XXII:** 259
Soul, The (Brooks), **I:** 244
Soul and Body of John Brown, The (Rukeyser), **Supp. VI:** 273
Soul Clap Hands and Sing (Marshall), **Supp. XI:** 276, 278, **280–282**
Soul Expeditions (Singer). *See* Shosha (Singer)
Soul Gone Home (Hughes), **Retro. Supp. I:** 203; **Supp. I Part 1:** 328
"Soul inside the Sentence, The" (Gass), **Supp. VI:** 88
Soul Is Here for Its Own Joy, The (Bly, ed.), **Supp. IV Part 1:** 74
Soul of Man under Socialism, The (Wilde), **Supp. IX:** 134–135
"Soul of Spain, The \[In the manner of Gertrude Stein\]" (Hemingway), **Supp. XX: 74**
Soul of the Far East, The (Lowell), **II:** 513
"Soul on Bench" (Halliday), **Supp. XIX:** 91
Soul on Ice (Cleaver), **Retro. Supp. II:** 12, 13
"Souls Belated" (Wharton), **Retro. Supp. I:** 364
"Soul selects her own Society, The" (Dickinson), **Retro. Supp. I:** 37
Souls of Black Folk, The (Du Bois), **Supp. II Part 1:** 33, 40, 160, 168–170, 176, 183; **Supp. IV Part 1:** 164; **Supp. IX:** 305, 306; **Supp. X:** 133; **Supp. XIII:** 185, 238, 243
Souls of Black Folk. The (Du Bois), **Supp. XX: 102**
"Sound, The" (Olds), **Supp. X:** 214
Sound and Beauty (Hwang), **Supp. XXI:** 146
"Sound and Fury" (O. Henry), **Supp. II Part 1:** 402
Sound and the Fury, The (Faulkner), **I:** 480; **II:** 55, 57, 58–60, 73; **III:** 237; **IV:** 100, 101, 104; **Retro. Supp. I:** 73, 75, 77, 82, **83–84,** 86, 88, 89, 90, 91, 92; **Supp. VIII:** 215; **Supp. IX:** 103; **Supp. X:** 44; **Supp. XII:** 33; **Supp. XIV:** 12; **Supp. XVII:** 138; **Supp. XVIII:** 84
"Sound Bites" (Alvarez), **Supp. VII:** 11
Sound I Listened For, The (Francis), **Supp. IX: 78–79,** 87
"Soundless Trumpet, The" (Antin), **Supp. XX: 12**
"Sound Mind, Sound Body" (Lowell), **II:** 554
Sound of a Voice, The (Hwang), **Supp. XXI:** 146
"Sound of Distant Thunder, A" (Elkin), **Supp. VI: 42–43,** 44
"Sound of Light, The" (Merwin), **Supp. III Part 1:** 356
Sound of Mountain Water, The (Stegner), **Supp. IV Part 2:** 595, 596, 598, 600, 608
"Sound of Talking" (Purdy), **Supp. VII:** 270
Sounds of Poetry, The (Pinsky), **Supp. VI:** 236, 247, 248
Soupault, Philippe, **IV:** 288, 404; **Retro. Supp. II:** 85, 321, 324
Source (Doty), **Supp. XI:** 121, **134–137**
"Source" (Doty), **Supp. XI:** 136
"Source, The" (Olds), **Supp. X:** 211
"Source, The" (Porter), **III:** 443
Source of Light, The (Price), **Supp. VI: 262,** 266
"Sources of Soviet Conduct, The" (Kennan), **Supp. VIII:** 241
Sour Grapes (W. C. Williams), **Retro. Supp. I:** 418
"Sourwood Nocturne" (Skloot), **Supp. XX: 202**
"South" (Levis), **Supp. XI:** 266
"South" (Trethewey), **Supp. XXI:** 247, 256
"South, The" (Hughes), **Supp. I Part 1:** 321
South American Journey (W. Frank), **Supp. XX: 79**
"Southbound on the Freeway" (Swenson), **Supp. IV Part 2:** 643
South Dakota Guidebook, The (C. Baxter), **Supp. XVII:** 15
Southern, Terry, **Supp. IV Part 1:** 379; **Supp. V:** 40, 201; **Supp. XI: 293–310; Supp. XVI:** 230
Southern Cross, The (Wright), **Supp. V:** 332, 342
"Southern Cross, The" (Wright), **Supp. V:** 338
"Southerner's Problem, The" (Du Bois), **Supp. II Part 1:** 168
"Southern Girl" (Zelda Fitzgerald), **Supp. IX:** 71
"Southern Gothic" (Trethewey), **Supp. XXI:** 256
"Southern History" (Trethewey), **Supp. XXI:** 256, 257
"Southern Mode of the Imagination, A" (Tate), **IV:** 120
"Southern Romantic, A" (Tate), **Supp. I Part 1:** 373
"Southern Sojourn, A" (Hoffman), **Supp. XVIII:** 87
Southern Terry, **Supp. XIV:** 82
Southey, Robert, **II:** 304, 502; **Supp. I Part 1:** 154
"South Lingers On, The" (R. Fisher), **Supp. XIX:** 69–70
South Moon Under (Rawlings), **Supp. X: 225–226,** 229, 233
South Pacific Affair (Lacy), **Supp. XV:** 206
Southpaw, The (Harris), **II:** 424–425
"South Sangamon" (Cisneros), **Supp. VII:** 66
South to a Very Old Place (Murray), **Supp. XIX: 151–153**
Southwell, Robert, **IV:** 151
Southwick, Marcia, **Supp. XI:** 259
Southworth, E. D. E. N, **Retro. Supp. I:** 246
Souvenir of the Ancient World, Selected Poems of Carlos Drummond de Andrade (Strand, trans.), **Supp. IV Part 2:** 630
"Sow" (Plath), **Supp. I Part 2:** 537
"Sowing and Reaping in *Furors Die*" (Nostrandt), **Supp. XVIII:** 80–81
Soyinka, Wole, **Supp. XX: 100**
"Space" (Brockmeier), **Supp. XXII:** 51
Space between Our Footsteps, The: Poems and Paintings from the Middle East (Nye, ed.), **Supp. XIII:** 280
"Space Quale, The" (James), **II:** 349
"Spaces Between, The" (Kingsolver), **Supp. VII:** 209
"Space Where Sex Should Be, The: Toward a Definition of the Black Literary Tradition" (Nelson), **Supp. XVIII:** 172
Spackman, Peter, **Supp. XVI:** 221
Spacks, Patricia, **Supp. XVI:** 251
"Spain" (Auden), **Supp. II Part 1:** 12–13, 14
"Spain in Fifty-Ninth Street" (White), **Supp. I Part 2:** 677
"Spanish-American War Play" (Crane), **I:** 422
Spanish Ballads (Merwin, trans.), **Supp. III Part 1:** 347
Spanish Bayonet (Benét), **Supp. XI:** 45, 47
Spanish Earth, The (film), **Retro. Supp. I:** 184
Spanish Papers and Other Miscellanies (Irving), **II:** 314
"Spanish Revolution, The" (Bryant), **Supp. I Part 1:** 153, 168
Spanish Student, The (Longfellow), **II:** 489, 506; **Retro. Supp. II:** 165
"Spanish Winter" (Egan), **Supp. XIX:** 52
Spanking the Maid (Coover), **Supp. V:** 47, 48, 49, 52
Spare Change (Parker), **Supp. XIX:** 186–187
Spargo, John, **Supp. I Part 1:** 13
"Spark, The" (Wharton), **Retro. Supp. I:** 381
"Sparkles from the Wheel" (Whitman), **IV:** 348
Sparks, Debra, **Supp. X:** 177
Sparks, Jared, **Supp. I Part 1:** 156
"Sparrow" (Berry), **Supp. X:** 31
Sparrow, Henry, **III:** 587
Sparrow, Mrs. Henry, **III:** 587
"Sparrow's Gate, The" (B. Kelly), **Supp. XVII:** 133
Spaulding, William, **Supp. XVI:** 106
"Spawning Run, The" (Humphrey), **Supp. IX:** 95
"Speak, Gay Memory" (Kirp), **Supp. XI:** 129
"Speak, Hoyt-Schermerhorn" (Lethem), **Supp. XVIII:** 148
Speak, Memory (Nabokov), **III:** 247–250, 252; **Retro. Supp. I:** 264, 265, 266, 267, 268, 277; **Supp. XVI:** 148
Speak, Memory (V. Nabokov), **Supp. XVII:** 47
Speaking and Language (Shapiro), **Supp. II Part 2:** 721
Speaking for Nature: How Literary Naturalists from Henry Thoreau to Rachel Carson Have Shaped America (Brooks), **Supp. IX:** 31

Speaking for Ourselves: American Ethnic Writing (Faderman and Bradshaw, eds.), **Supp. XIII:** 313
Speaking of Accidents (Everwine), **Supp. XV:** 75, 88
"Speaking of Accidents" (Everwine), **Supp. XV:** 88–89
"Speaking of Counterweights" (White), **Supp. I Part 2:** 669
Speaking of Literature and Society (Trilling), **Supp. III Part 2:** 494, 496, 499
"Speaking of Love" (Gioia), **Supp. XV:** 124–125
Speaking of Race, Speaking of Sex: Hate Speech, Civil Rights, and Civil Liberties (H. L. Gates, Griffin, Lively, and Strossen), **Supp. XX: 111**
Speaking on Stage (Kolin and Kullman, eds.), **Supp. IX:** 145
Speaking on Stage: Interviews with Contemporary American Playwrights (Balakian), **Supp. XV:** 327
"Speaking Passions" (Kitchen), **Supp. XV:** 215
Speak of the Devil (Holding), **Supp. XXII: 127**
Speak What We Feel (Not What We Ought to Say): Reflections on Literature and Faith (Buechner), **Supp. XII:** 57
Spear, Roberta, **Supp. V:** 180; **Supp. XV:** 73
"Special Kind of Fantasy, A: James Dickey on the Razor's Edge" (Niflis), **Supp. IV Part 1:** 175
"Special Pleading" (Lanier), **Supp. I Part 1:** 364
"Special Problems in Teaching Leslie Marmon Silko's *Ceremony*" (Gunn Allen), **Supp. IV Part 1:** 333
Special Providence, A (Yates), **Supp. XI:** 342, **344–345**
"Special Time, a Special School, A" (Knowles), **Supp. XII:** 236
Special View of History, The (Olson), **Supp. II Part 2:** 566, 569, 572
Specimen Days (Whitman), **IV:** 338, 347, 348, 350; **Retro. Supp. I:** 408
Specimens of the American Poets, **Supp. I Part 1:** 155
"Spectacles, The" (Poe), **III:** 425
Spectator Bird, The (Stegner), **Supp. IV Part 2:** 599, 604, 606, 611–612
Spector, Robert, **Supp. XIII:** 87
Spectra: A Book of Poetic Experiments (Bynner and Ficke), **Supp. XV:** 43
"Spectre Bridegroom, The" (Irving), **II:** 304
"Spectre Pig, The" (Holmes), **Supp. I Part 1:** 302
"Speculating Woman" (X. J. Kennedy), **Supp. XV:** 168
"Speech Sounds" (O. Butler), **Supp. XIII:** 61, **70**
"Speech to a Crowd" (MacLeish), **III:** 16
"Speech to the Detractors" (MacLeish), **III:** 16
"Speech to the Young" (Brooks), **Supp. III Part 1:** 79, 86
"Speech to Those Who Say Comrade" (MacLeish), **III:** 16
Speedboat (Adler), **Supp. X:** 171
Speed of Darkness, The (Rukeyser), **Supp. VI:** 274, 281
Speed-the-Plow (Mamet), **Supp. XIV:** 241, 246, 249, 250, 251
"Speedy Gonzales Was the Fastest Mouse in Mexico" (P. N. Warren as Kilina), **Supp. XX: 262**
Speilberg, Steven, **Supp. XI:** 234
Speirs, Logan, **Supp. XIX:** 282
"Spell" (Francis), **Supp. IX:** 87
"Spell, The" (Peacock), **Supp. XIX:** 198, 200
"Spell for the Manufacture & Use of a Magic Carpet" (Hull), **Supp. XXI:** 132–133, 139, 141
Spelling Dictionary, A (Rowson), **Supp. XV:** 244
Spence, Thomas, **Supp. I Part 2:** 518
Spence + Lila (Mason), **Supp. VIII:** 133, **143–145**
Spencer, Edward, **Supp. I Part 1:** 357, 360
Spencer, Herbert, **I:** 515; **II:** 345, 462–463, 480, 483, 536; **III:** 102, 315; **IV:** 135; **Retro. Supp. II:** 60, 65, 93, 98; **Supp. I Part 1:** 368; **Supp. I Part 2:** 635
Spencer, Sharon, **Supp. X:** 185, 186, 195, 196
Spencer, Theodore, **I:** 433; **Supp. III Part 1:** 2
Spender, Natasha, **Supp. IV Part 1:** 119, 127, 134
Spender, Stephen, **II:** 371; **III:** 504, 527; **Retro. Supp. I:** 216; **Retro. Supp. II:** 243, 244; **Supp. I Part 2:** 536; **Supp. II Part 1:** 11; **Supp. IV Part 1:** 82, 134; **Supp. IV Part 2:** 440; **Supp. X:** 116
Spengler, Oswald, **I:** 255, 270; **II:** 7, 577; **III:** 172, 176; **Retro. Supp. II:** 324; **Supp. I Part 2:** 647
Spens, Sir Patrick, **Supp. I Part 2:** 404
Spenser, Edmund, **I:** 62; **III:** 77, 78, 89; **IV:** 155, 453; **Retro. Supp. I:** 62; **Supp. I Part 1:** 98, 152, 369; **Supp. I Part 2:** 422, 719
"Spenser's Ireland" (Moore), **III:** 211, 212
Sperry, Margaret, **Supp. IV Part 1:** 169
Spheres of Existence (C. L. R. James), **Supp. XXI:** 172
Sphere: The Form of a Motion (Ammons), **Supp. VII:** 24, 32, 33, 35, 36
"Sphinx" (Hayden), **Supp. II Part 1:** 373
"Spiced Plums" (Ríos), **Supp. IV Part 2:** 553
Spickard, Paul, **Supp. XXI:** 149
"Spider and the Ghost of the Fly, The" (Lindsay), **Supp. I Part 2:** 375
Spider Bay (Van Vechten), **Supp. II Part 2:** 746
"Spider Heart, The" (Peacock), **Supp. XIX:** 200
"Spiders" (Schwartz), **Supp. II Part 2:** 665
Spider's House, The (Bowles), **Supp. IV Part 1:** 87–89, 90, 91
Spider Woman's Granddaughters: Traditional Tales and Contemporary Writing by Native American Women (Gunn Allen, ed.), **Supp. IV Part 1:** 320, 326, 332–333; **Supp. IV Part 2:** 567
Spiegel, Sam, **Supp. XVIII:** 251, 252
Spiegelman, Art, **Supp. XVII:** 48
Spiegelman, Willard, **Supp. XI:** 126
Spielberg, Steven, **Supp. XXI:** 154
Spillane, Mickey, **Supp. IV Part 2:** 469, 472; **Supp. XV:** 200; **Supp. XVIII:** 236, 237
Spiller, Robert E., **I:** 241; **Supp. I Part 1:** 104
Spillers, Hortense, **Supp. XX: 109**
"Spillikins: Gregor Mendel at the Table" (Bierds), **Supp. XVII:** 34–35
Spillville (Hampl), **Supp. XXII:** 98
Spillway (Barnes), **Supp. III Part 1:** 44
Spingarn, Amy, **Supp. I Part 1:** 325, 326
Spingarn, Joel, **I:** 266; **Supp. I Part 1:** 325
Spinoza, Baruch, **I:** 493; **II:** 590, 593; **III:** 600; **IV:** 5, 7, 11, 12, 17; **Retro. Supp. II:** 300; **Supp. I Part 1:** 274; **Supp. I Part 2:** 643; **Supp. XVI:** 184
"Spinoza of Market Street, The" (Singer), **IV:** 12–13; **Retro. Supp. II:** 307
"Spinster" (Plath), **Supp. I Part 2:** 536
"Spinster's Tale, A" (Taylor), **Supp. V:** 314–315, 316–317, 319, 323
Spiral of Memory, The: Interviews (Coltelli, ed.), **Supp. XII:** 215
Spires, Elizabeth, **Supp. X:** 8
"Spire Song" (Bowles), **Supp. IV Part 1:** 80
Spirit and Flame: An Anthology of African American Poetry (Gilyard, ed.), **Supp. XXI:** 246
Spirit and the Flesh, The: Sexual Diversity in American Indian Culture (W. L. Williams), **Supp. IV Part 1:** 330
"Spirit Birth" (Cullen), **Supp. IV Part 1:** 168
Spirit Brides (Gibran). *See Nymphs in the Valley*
Spirit in Man, The (Jung), **Supp. IV Part 1:** 68
"Spirit in Me, The" (Hoffman), **Supp. XVIII:** 87
"Spirit Made Visible" (art exhibit), **Supp. XXII:** 180
Spirit of Culver (West), **IV:** 287
Spirit of Labor, The (Hapgood), **Supp. XVII:** 96, 99, 101–102; **Supp. XXI:** 4
Spirit of Romance, The (Pound), **III:** 470; **Retro. Supp. I:** 286
Spirit of the Ghetto, The: Studies of the Jewish Quarter of New York (Hapgood), **Supp. XVII:** 96, 101, 103, 106
Spirit of Youth and the City Streets, The (Addams), **Supp. I Part 1:** 6–7, 12–13, 16, 17, 19
"Spirits" (Bausch), **Supp. VII:** 46–47
Spirits, and Other Stories (Bausch), **Supp. VII:** 46–47, 54

"Spirit Says, You Are Nothing, The" (Levis), **Supp. XI:** 265–266
Spirits Rebellious (al-Arwá&hudot; al-Mutamarrida) (Gibran), **Supp. XX: 115, 124, 125**
Spiritual Adventures (Symons), **Supp. XX: 239**
Spiritual Conflict, The (Scupoli), **IV:** 156
Spiritual Exercises, The (Loyola), **IV:** 151; **Supp. XI:** 162
"Spiritual Manifestation, A" (Whittier), **Supp. I Part 2:** 699
"Spirituals and Neo-Spirituals" (Hurston), **Supp. VI:** 152–153
Spits, Ellen Handler, **Supp. XII:** 166
"Spitzbergen Tales" (Crane), **I:** 409, 415, 423
Spitzer, Philip, **Supp. XIV:** 21
"Spleen" (Eliot), **I:** 569, 573–574
Spleen de Paris, Le (Baudelaire), **Supp. XIV:** 337
Splendid Drunken Twenties, The (Van Vechten), **Supp. II Part 2:** 739–744
Splendide-Hôtel (Sorrentino), **Supp. XXI:** 233
"Splinters" (Bukiet), **Supp. XVII:** 47
"Split Infinitive" (Pickering), **Supp. XXI:** 204
"Splitting an Order" (Kooser), **Supp. XIX:** 128–129
"Splittings" (Rich), **Supp. I Part 2:** 570–571
"Splitting Wood at Six Above" (Kumin), **Supp. IV Part 2:** 449
Spofford, Harriet Prescott, **Supp. XIII:** 143
Spoils of Poynton, The (James), **I:** 463; **Retro. Supp. I:** 229–230
Spoken Page, The (Nye), **Supp. XIII:** 274
"Spokes" (Auster), **Supp. XII:** 23
Spokesmen (Whipple), **II:** 456
Spook Sonata, The (Strindberg), **III:** 387, 392
Spooky Art, The: A Book about Writing (Mailer), **Retro. Supp. II:** 214
"Spoon, The" (Simic), **Supp. VIII:** 275
Spoon River Anthology (Masters), **I:** 106; **III:** 579; **Supp. I Part 2:** 454, 455, 456, 460–465, 466, 467, 471, 472, 473, 476; **Supp. IX:** 306; **Supp. XIV:** 282–283; **Supp. XIX:** 121; **Supp. XXII:** 282
Sport and a Pastime, A (Salter), **Supp. IX: 254–257; Supp. XVI:** 237
Sporting Club, The (McGuane), **Supp. VIII:** 43
Sport of the Gods, The (Dunbar), **Supp. II Part 1:** 193, 200, 207, 214–217
Sports Illustrated Training with Weights (Parker and Marsh), **Supp. XIX:** 187
"Sportsman Born and Bred, A" (Plimpton), **Supp. XVI:** 241
Sportsman's Sketches, A (Turgenev), **I:** 106; **IV:** 277
Sportswriter, The (Ford), **Supp. V:** 57, 58, 62–67
"Spotted Horses" (Faulkner), **IV:** 260
Sprague, Morteza, **Retro. Supp. II:** 115
Spratling, William, **II:** 56; **Retro. Supp. I:** 80
Sprawl trilogy (W. Gibson), **Supp. XVI:** 117, 122, 124
"Spray, The" (Lethem), **Supp. XVIII:** 148
"Spray Paint King, The" (Dove), **Supp. IV Part 1:** 252–253
Spreading Fires (Knowles), **Supp. XII:** 249
Sprigge, Elizabeth, **IV:** 31
"Spring" (Kooser), **Supp. XIX:** 126
"Spring" (Millay), **III:** 126
"Spring" (Mora), **Supp. XIII:** 217
"Spring 1967" (Carruth), **Supp. XVI:** 55
Spring and All (W. C. Williams), **Retro. Supp. I:** 412, 418, **418–420,** 427, 430, 431
"Spring and All" (W. C. Williams), **Retro. Supp. I:** 419
Spring Awakening (Wedeking, trans. Franzen), **Supp. XX: 85**
"Spring Break-Up" (Carruth), **Supp. XVI:** 56
"Spring Bulletin" (Allen), **Supp. XV:** 15
Springer's Progress (Markson), **Supp. XVII: 141–142,** 143, 146
"Spring Evening" (Farrell), **II:** 45
"Spring Evening" (Kenyon), **Supp. VII:** 173
"Springfield Magical" (Lindsay), **Supp. I Part 2:** 379
Spring in New Hampshire and Other Poems (McKay), **Supp. X:** 131, 135
"Spring Notes from Robin Hill" (Carruth), **Supp. XVI:** 48
"Spring Pastoral" (Wylie), **Supp. I Part 2:** 707
"Spring Pools" (Frost), **II:** 155; **Retro. Supp. I:** 137
"Spring Snow" (Matthews), **Supp. IX:** 160
"SPRING SONG" (Baraka), **Supp. II Part 1:** 60
Springsteen, Bruce, **Supp. VIII:** 143
"Spring Strains" (W. C. Williams), **Retro. Supp. I:** 416
Spring Tides (Morison), **Supp. I Part 2:** 494
Springtime and Harvest (Sinclair), **Supp. V:** 280
"Springtime for You" (Halliday), **Supp. XIX:** 87
Spruance, Raymond, **Supp. I Part 2:** 479, 491
"Spruce Has No Taproot, The" (Clampitt), **Supp. IX:** 41–42
"Spunk" (Hurston), **Supp. VI:** 150, 151–152
Spunk: The Selected Stories (Hurston), **Supp. VI:** 150
Spurr, David, **Supp. XV:** 183
Spy, The (Cooper), **I:** 335, 336, 337, 339, 340; **Supp. I Part 1:** 155
"Spy, The" (Francis), **Supp. IX:** 81
Spy, The (Freneau), **Supp. II Part 1:** 260
Spyglass Tree, The (Murray), **Supp. XIX: 155–156**
Spy in the House of Love, A (Nin), **Supp. X:** 186
Squanto, **Supp. I Part 2:** 486
"Square Business" (Baraka), **Supp. II Part 1:** 49
Square Root of Wonderful, The (McCullers), **II:** 587–588
"Squash in Blossom" (Francis), **Supp. IX:** 81
"Squatter on Company Land, The" (Hugo), **Supp. VI:** 133
"Squatter's Children" (Bishop), **Retro. Supp. II:** 47
"Squeak, Memory" (Bukiet), **Supp. XVII:** 47
Squeeze Play (Auster), **Supp. XII:** 21
Squires, Radcliffe, **IV:** 127; **Supp. XV:** 118
Squirrels (Mamet), **Supp. XIV:** 240
S.S. Gliencairn (O'Neill), **III:** 387, 388, 405
S.S. San Pedro (Cozzens), **I:** 360–362, 370, 378, 379
"Ssshh" (Olds), **Supp. X:** 215
"Stacking the Straw" (Clampitt), **Supp. IX:** 41
Stade, George, **Supp. IV Part 1:** 286
Staël, Madame de, **II:** 298
"Staff of Life, The" (H. Miller), **III:** 187
Stafford, Jean, **II:** 537; **Retro. Supp. II:** 177; **Supp. V:** 316
Stafford, William, **Supp. IV Part 1:** 72; **Supp. IV Part 2:** 642; **Supp. IX:** 273; **Supp. XI: 311–332; Supp. XIII:** 76, 274, 276, 277, 281, 283; **Supp. XIV:** 119, 123; **Supp. XX: 161; Supp. XXI:** 246
"Stage All Blood, The" (MacLeish), **III:** 18
"Staggerlee Wonders" (Baldwin), **Retro. Supp. II:** 15
Stained White Radiance, A (Burke), **Supp. XIV:** 28, 31
Stalin, Joseph, **I:** 261, 490; **II:** 39, 40, 49, 564; **III:** 30, 298; **IV:** 372; **Supp. V:** 290; **Supp. XXI:** 164, 165, 167
"Stalking" (J. W. Miller), **Supp. XX: 167**
"Stalking the Billion-Footed Beast: A Literary Manifesto for the New Social Novel" (Wolfe), **Supp. III Part 2:** 586
Stallings, H. A., **Supp. XXII:** 194
Stallman, R. W., **I:** 405
Stamberg, Susan, **Supp. IV Part 1:** 201; **Supp. XII:** 193
Stamford, Anne Marie, **Supp. XII:** 162
Stanard, Mrs. Jane, **III:** 410, 413
Stand, The (King), **Supp. V:** 139, 140–141, 144–146, 148, 152
"Standard of Liberty, The" (Rowson), **Supp. XV:** 243
"Standard of Living, The" (Parker), **Supp. IX: 198–199**
Stander, Lionel, **Supp. I Part 1:** 289
"Standing and the Waiting, The" (M. F. K. Fisher), **Supp. XVII:** 83
Standing by Words (Berry), **Supp. X:** 22, 27, 28, 31, 32, 33, 35
Standing Fast (Swados), **Supp. XIX: 268–269**
"Standing Halfway Home" (Wagoner), **Supp. IX:** 324
"Standing In" (Caputo), **Supp. XIX:** 26

Stand in the Mountains, A (Taylor), **Supp. V:** 324
Standish, Burt L. (pseudonym). *See* Patten, Gilbert
Standish, Miles, **I:** 471; **II:** 502–503
Standley, Fred L., **Retro. Supp. II:** 6
Stand Still Like the Hummingbird (H. Miller), **III:** 184
"Stand Up" (Salinas), **Supp. XIII:** 315
Stand with Me Here (Francis), **Supp. IX:** 76
Stanford, Ann, **Retro. Supp. I:** 41; **Supp. I Part 1:** 99, 100, 102, 103, 106, 108, 109, 113, 117; **Supp. IV Part 2:** 637
Stanford, Charles Villiers, **Supp. XX: 228**
Stanford, Donald E., **II:** 217
Stanford, Frank, **Supp. XV:** 338, 339, 341, 342–343, 343, 345, 348, 350
Stanford, Ginny (Crouch), **Supp. XV:** 339
Stanford, Leland, **I:** 196, 198
Stanislavsky, Konstantin, **Supp. XIV:** 240, 243
Stanley, Jodee, **Supp. XIX:** 52
"Stanley Kunitz" (Oliver), **Supp. VII:** 237
Stansell, Christine, **Supp. XVII:** 106; **Supp. XXI:** 4
Stanton, Frank L., **Supp. II Part 1:** 192
Stanton, Robert J., **Supp. IV Part 2:** 681
"Stanzas from the Grande Chartreuse" (Arnold), **Supp. I Part 2:** 417
Stanzas in Meditation (Stein), **Supp. III Part 1:** 13
Staples, Hugh, **Retro. Supp. II:** 187
Star, Alexander, **Supp. X:** 310
Starbuck, George, **Retro. Supp. II:** 53, 245; **Supp. I Part 2:** 538; **Supp. IV Part 2:** 440; **Supp. XIII:** 76
Star Child (Gunn Allen), **Supp. IV Part 1:** 324
"Star Dust" (Wrigley), **Supp. XVIII:** 296
Stardust Memories (film; Allen), **Supp. XV:** 1, 4, **8,** 9, 13
"Stare, The" (Updike), **Retro. Supp. I:** 329
"Starfish, The" (R. Bly), **Supp. IV Part 1:** 72
"Staring at the Sea on the Day of the Death of Another" (Swenson), **Supp. IV Part 2:** 652
Star Is Born, A (film), **Supp. IV Part 1:** 198; **Supp. IX:** 198; **Supp. XVIII:** 242, 243
Stark, David, **Supp. XII:** 202
"Stark Boughs on the Family Tree" (Oliver), **Supp. VII:** 232
Starke, Aubrey Harrison, **Supp. I Part 1:** 350, 352, 356, 360, 362, 365, 370, 371
Starkey, David, **Supp. XII:** 180, 181
Star Ledger (Hull), **Supp. XXI:** 129, **136–138**
"Star Ledger" (Hull), **Supp. XXI:** 136
"Starlight" (Levine), **Supp. V:** 188
"Starlight Scope Myopia" (Komunyakaa), **Supp. XIII:** 123, 124
Starnino, Carmine, **Supp. XVII:** 74
"Star of the Nativity" (Brodsky), **Supp. VIII:** 33
Starr, Ellen Gates, **Supp. I Part 1:** 4, 5, 11
Starr, Jean. *See* Untermeyer, Jean Starr
Starr, Ringo, **Supp. XI:** 309
Star Rover, The (London), **II:** 467
"Starry Night, The" (Sexton), **Supp. II Part 2:** 681
"Stars" (Frost), **II:** 153
Stars, the Snow, the Fire, The: Twenty-five Years in the Northern Wilderness (Haines), **Supp. XII: 199–201,** 206, 209
Star Shines over Mt. Morris Park, A (H. Roth), **Supp. IX:** 227, 236, **236–237**
"Stars of the Summer Night" (Longfellow), **II:** 493
"Stars over Harlem" (Hughes), **Retro. Supp. I:** 207
"Star-Spangled" (García), **Supp. XI:** 177, 178
Star-Spangled Girl, The (Simon), **Supp. IV Part 2:** 579
"Star-Splitter, The" (Frost), **Retro. Supp. I:** 123, 133
Stars Principal (McClatchy), **Supp. XII: 256–258**
"Star That Would Not Shine, The" (C. L. R. James), **Supp. XXI:** 160
"Starting from Paumanok" (Whitman), **IV:** 333
Starting Out in the Thirties (Kazin), **Supp. VIII: 95–97**
Star Trek television series, **Supp. XXII:** 60
"Starved Lovers" (MacLeish), **III:** 19
Starved Rock (Masters), **Supp. I Part 2:** 465
"Starving Again" (Moore), **Supp. X:** 163, 172, 175
"State, The" (Bourne), **I:** 233
State and Main (Mamet), **Supp. XIV:** 241
"Statement of Principles" (Ransom), **III:** 496
"Statement: Phillipa Allen" (Rukeyser), **Supp. VI:** 283–284
"Statements on Poetics" (Snyder), **Supp. VIII:** 291, 292
"Statement with Rhymes" (Kees), **Supp. XV:** 139
"State of the Art, The" (Elkin), **Supp. VI:** 52
"State of the Arts, The" (Wasserstein), **Supp. XV:** 332
State of the Nation (Dos Passos), **I:** 489
"State of the Union" (Vidal), **Supp. IV Part 2:** 678
Static Element, The: Selected Poems of Natan Zach (Everwine, trans.), **Supp. XV:** 73, 75, **85–88**
"Statue, The" (Berryman), **I:** 173
"Statue and Birds" (Bogan), **Supp. III Part 1:** 50
"Statue of an Unkown Soldier, The" (Kooser), **Supp. XIX:** 124
"Statues, The" (Schwartz), **Supp. II Part 2:** 654, 659
"Status Rerum" (Pound), **Supp. I Part 1:** 257
Stavans, Ilan, **Supp. XI:** 190
"Stave Church" (W. V. Davis), **Supp. XXI:** 93, 94
"Staying Alive" (Levertov), **Supp. III Part 1:** 281
Staying Alive (Wagoner), **Supp. IX:** 324, **326**
"Staying at Ed's Place" (Swenson), **Supp. IV Part 2:** 648
Staying Put : Making a Home in a Restless World (Sanders), **Supp. XVI:** 274–275
Stay Me, Oh Comfort Me: Journals and Stories, 1933–1941 (M. F. K. Fisher), **Supp. XVII:** 92
Stayton, Richard, **Supp. IX:** 133
Steadman, Goodman, **IV:** 147
"Steak" (Snyder), **Supp. VIII:** 301
Steal Away: Selected and New Poems (Wright), **Supp. XV:** 337, 340, 348, 350–351
Stealing Beauty (Minot), **Supp. VI:** 205
Stealing Glimpses (McQuade), **Supp. IX:** 151
Stealing the Language: The Emergence of Women's Poetry in America (Ostriker), **Supp. XV:** 251
"Stealing the Thunder: Future Visions for American Indian Women, Tribes, and Literary Studies" (Gunn Allen), **Supp. IV Part 1:** 331
"Steam Shovel Cut" (Masters), **Supp. I Part 2:** 468
Stearns, Harold, **I:** 245; **Supp. XVII:** 106
Stedman, Edmund Clarence, **Supp. I Part 1:** 372; **Supp. II Part 1:** 192; **Supp. XV:** 115, 269, 273, 274, 282, 286
Steel, Sharon, **Supp. XIX:** 61
Steele, Margaret, **Supp. XXI:** 5
Steele, Max, **Supp. XIV:** 82
Steele, Sir Richard, **I:** 378; **II:** 105, 107, 300; **III:** 430
Steele, Timothy, **Supp. XV:** 251; **Supp. XVII:** 112
Steele, Wilbur Daniel, **Supp. XXI:** 5
Steelwork (Sorrentino), **Supp. XXI:** 227, 230, 231, 232
Steenburgen, Mary, **Supp. IV Part 1:** 236
Steeple Bush (Frost), **II:** 155; **Retro. Supp. I:** 140; **Retro. Supp. II:** 42
"Steeple-Jack, The" (Moore), **III:** 212, 213, 215
"Steerage" (Goldbarth), **Supp. XII:** 187
Steers, Nina, **Retro. Supp. II:** 25
Stefans, Brian Kim, **Supp. XXII:** 226
Steffens, Lincoln, **II:** 577; **III:** 580; **Retro. Supp. I:** 202; **Retro. Supp. II:** 101; **Supp. I Part 1:** 7; **Supp. XVII:** 98, 101, 106–107; **Supp. XXI:** 2, 3, 5, 7, 10
Stegner, Page, **IV:** 114, 116; **Supp. IV Part 2:** 599
Stegner, Wallace, **Supp. IV Part 2: 595–618; Supp. V:** 220, 224, 296; **Supp. X:** 23, 24; **Supp. XIV:** 82, 193, 230, 233; **Supp. XVIII:** 192; **Supp. XXII:** 204, 205, 208
"Stegner's Short Fiction" (Ahearn), **Supp. IV Part 2:** 604
Steichen, Edward, **III:** 580, 594–595

Steichen, Lillian. *See* Sandburg, Mrs. Carl (Lillian Steichen)
Steier, Rod ?/, **Supp. VIII:** 269
Steiger, Rod ?/, **Supp. XI:** 305
Stein, Edith, **Supp. XXII:** 92–93, 167
Stein, Gertrude, **I:** 103, 105, 476; **II:** 56, 251, 252, 257, 260, 262–263, 264, 289; **III:** 71, 454, 471–472, 600; **IV:** **24–48,** 368, 375, 404, 415, 443, 477; **Retro. Supp. I:** 108, 170, 176, 177, 186, 418, 422; **Retro. Supp. II:** 85, 207, 326, 331; **Supp. I Part 1:** 292; **Supp. III Part 1:** 13, 37, 225, 226; **Supp. III Part 2:** 626; **Supp. IV Part 1:** 11, 79, 80, 81, 322; **Supp. IV Part 2:** 468; **Supp. V:** 53; **Supp. IX:** 55, 57, 62, 66; **Supp. XII:** 1, 139; **Supp. XIV:** 336; **Supp. XVI:** 187; **Supp. XVII:** 98, 105, 107; **Supp. XVIII:** 148; **Supp. XXI:** 7, 33; **Supp. XXII:** 158, 159
Stein, Jean, **Supp. XVI:** 245
Stein, Karen F., **Supp. XIII:** 29, 30
Stein, Leo, **IV:** 26; **Supp. XIV:** 336; **Supp. XV:** 298
Stein, Lorin, **Supp. XII:** 254; **Supp. XVIII:** 137, 139
Steinbeck, John, **I:** 107, 288, 301, 378, 495, 519; **II:** 272; **III:** 382, 453, 454, 589; **IV: 49–72; Retro. Supp. II:** 19, 196; **Supp. IV Part 1:** 102, 225; **Supp. IV Part 2:** 502; **Supp. V:** 290, 291; **Supp. VIII:** 10; **Supp. IX:** 33, 171; **Supp. XI:** 169; **Supp. XIII:** 1, 17; **Supp. XIV:** 21, 181; **Supp. XVII:** 228; **Supp. XVIII:** 90, 102, 254; **Supp. XIX:** 3
Steinbeck, Olive Hamilton, **IV:** 51
Steinberg, Saul, **Supp. VIII:** 272
Steinberg, Sybil, **Supp. XVII:** 165, 166
Steinem, Gloria, **Supp. IV Part 1:** 203
Steiner, George, **Retro. Supp. I:** 327; **Supp. IV Part 1:** 286; **Supp. XVI:** 230
Steiner, Michael, **Supp. XXII:** 205
Steiner, Nancy, **Supp. I Part 2:** 529
Steiner, Stan, **Supp. IV Part 2:** 505
Steinfels, Margaret, **Supp. XVII:** 170
Steinhoff, Eirik, **Supp. XVI:** 290
Steinman, Michael, **Supp. VIII:** 172
Steinmetz, Charles Proteus, **I:** 483
Steinway Quintet Plus Four, The (Epstein), **Supp. XII:** 159, **162–166**
Stekel, Wilhelm, **III:** 554
Stella (Goethe), **Supp. IX:** 133, 138
Stella (Kushner), **Supp. IX:** 133
Stella, Joseph, **I:** 387
"Stellaria" (Francis), **Supp. IX:** 83
Stelligery and Other Essays (Wendell), **Supp. I Part 2:** 414
St. Elmo (Evans), **Supp. XXII:** 120
Stendhal, **I:** 316; **III:** 465, 467; **Supp. I Part 1:** 293; **Supp. I Part 2:** 445
Stepanchev, Stephen, **Supp. XI:** 312
Stephen, Leslie, **IV:** 440
Stephen, Sir Leslie, **IV:** 440; **Supp. I Part 1:** 306
Stephen, Saint, **II:** 539; **IV:** 228
Stephen Crane (Berryman), **I:** 169–170, 405
Stephen King, The Second Decade: "Danse Macabre" to "The Dark Half" (Magistrale), Supp. V: 138, 146, 151
Stephen King: The Art of Darkness (Winter), **Supp. V:** 144
Stephens, Jack, **Supp. X:** 11, 14, 15, 17
Stephens, James, **Supp. XIX:** 204
Stephenson, Gregory, **Supp. XII:** 120, 123
Stephenson, Neal, **Supp. XXII:** 49
"Stepping Out" (Dunn), **Supp. XI:** 140, 141
Steps (Kosinski), **Supp. VII:** 215, 221–222, 225
"Steps" (Nye), **Supp. XIII:** 288
Steps to the Temple (Crashaw), **IV:** 145
"Steps Toward Poverty and Death" (R. Bly), **Supp. IV Part 1:** 60
Stepto, Robert B., **Retro. Supp. II:** 116, 120, 123
Sterile Cuckoo, The (Nichols), **Supp. XIII:** 258, **259–263,** 264
Sterling, Bruce, **Supp. XVI:** 118, 121, 123, 124, 128–129
Sterling, George, **I:** 199, 207, 208, 209; **II:** 440; **Supp. V:** 286; **Supp. XXII:** 276, 277
Stern, Bernhard J., **Supp. XIV:** 202, 213
Stern, Daniel, **Supp. VIII:** 238
Stern, Frederick C., **Supp. X:** 114, 115, 117
Stern, Gerald, **Supp. IX: 285–303; Supp. XI:** 139, 267; **Supp. XV:** 211, 212
Stern, Madeleine B., **Supp. I Part 1:** 35
Stern, Maurice, **IV:** 285
Stern, Philip Van Doren, **Supp. XIII:** 164
Stern, Richard, **Retro. Supp. II:** 291
Stern, Richard G., **Retro. Supp. II:** 204
Stern, Steven, **Supp. XVII:** 42, 48, 49; **Supp. XX: 178**
"Sterne" (Schwartz), **Supp. II Part 2:** 663
Sterne, Laurence, **II:** 302, 304–305, 308; **III:** 454; **IV:** 68, 211, 465; **Supp. I Part 2:** 714; **Supp. IV Part 1:** 299; **Supp. V:** 127; **Supp. X:** 324; **Supp. XV:** 232
Sterritt, David, **Supp. IV Part 2:** 574
Stetson, Caleb, **IV:** 178
Stetson, Charles Walter, **Supp. XI:** 195, 196, 197, 202, 204, 209
Steve Nelson, American Radical (Nelson), **Supp. XVIII:** 226
Stevens, Frances Simpson, **Supp. XXII:** 159, 162
Stevens, Wallace, **I:** 60, 61, 266, 273, 462, 521, 528, 540–541; **II:** 56, 57, 530, 552, 556; **III:** 19, 23, 194, 216, 270–271, 272, 278, 279, 281, 453, 463, 493, 509, 521, 523, 600, 605, 613, 614; **IV: 73–96,** 140, 141, 332, 402, 415; **Retro. Supp. I:** 67, 89, 193, 284, 288, **295–315,** 335, 403, 411, 416, 417, 422; **Retro. Supp. II:** 40, 44, 326; **Supp. I Part 1:** 80, 82, 257; **Supp. II Part 1:** 9, 18; **Supp. III Part 1:** 2, 3, 12, 20, 48, 239, 318, 319, 344; **Supp. III Part 2:** 611; **Supp. IV Part 1:** 72, 393; **Supp. IV Part 2:** 619, 620, 621, 634; **Supp. V:** 337; **Supp. VIII:** 21, 102, 195, 271, 292; **Supp. IX:** 41; **Supp. X:** 58; **Supp. XI:** 123, 191, 312; **Supp. XIII:** 44, 45; **Supp. XV:** 39, 41, 92, 115, 250, 261, 298, 302, 306, 307; **Supp. XVI:** 64, 158, 202, 210, 288; **Supp. XVII:** 36, 42, 110, 129, 130, 240, 241; **Supp. XIX:** 7, 40, 86, 87; **Supp. XXI:** 19, 28, 60, 133; **Supp. XXII:** 162
Stevens, Mrs. Wallace (Elsie Kachel), **IV:** 75
"Stevens and the Idea of the Hero" (Bromwich), **Retro. Supp. I:** 305
Stevens and the Interpersonal (Halliday), **Supp. XIX: 85–86**
Stevenson, Adlai, **II:** 49; **III:** 581
Stevenson, Anne, **Supp. XV:** 121; **Supp. XVII:** 74
Stevenson, Burton E., **Supp. XIV:** 120
Stevenson, David, **Supp. XI:** 230
Stevenson, Robert Louis, **I:** 2, 53; **II:** 283, 290, 311, 338; **III:** 328; **IV:** 183–184, 186, 187; **Retro. Supp. I:** 224, 228; **Supp. I Part 1:** 49; **Supp. II Part 1:** 404–405; **Supp. IV Part 1:** 298, 314; **Supp. VIII:** 125; **Supp. XIII:** 75; **Supp. XIV:** 40; **Supp. XVII:** 69; **Supp. XXI:** 204
Stevick, Robert D., **III:** 509
Stewart, Dugald, **II:** 8, 9; **Supp. I Part 1:** 151, 159; **Supp. I Part 2:** 422
Stewart, George, **Supp. XVIII:** 138
Stewart, Jeffrey C., **Supp. XIV:** 196, 209, 210
Stewart, Randall, **II:** 244; **Supp. XX: 164**
Stewart, Robert E., **Supp. XI:** 216
"St. Francis of Assisi" (Di Piero), **Supp. XIX:** 43
Stickeen (Muir), **Supp. IX:** 182
"Sticks and Stones" (L. Michaels), **Supp. XVI:** 205
Sticks and Stones (Mumford), **Supp. II Part 2:** 475, 483, 487–488
Sticks & Stones (Matthews), **Supp. IX:** 154, 155, 157, 158
Stieglitz, Alfred, **Retro. Supp. I:** 416; **Retro. Supp. II:** 103; **Supp. VIII:** 98; **Supp. XVII:** 96; **Supp. XX: 74, 75**
"Stigmata" (Oates), **Supp. II Part 2:** 520
Stiles, Ezra, **II:** 108, 122; **IV:** 144, 146, 148
Still, James, **Supp. XX: 163**
Still, William Grant, **Retro. Supp. I:** 203
"Stillborn" (Plath), **Supp. I Part 2:** 544
"Still Here" (Hughes), **Retro. Supp. I:** 211
"Still Just Writing" (Tyler), **Supp. IV Part 2:** 658
"Still Life" (Hecht), **Supp. X:** 68
"Still Life" (Malamud), **Supp. I Part 2:** 450
Still Life (Pickering), **Supp. XXI:** 198
"Still Life" (Pickering), **Supp. XXI:** 198
"Still Life" (Sandburg), **III:** 584
"Still Life: Moonlight Striking up on a Chess-Board" (Lowell), **II:** 528
"Still Life Or" (Creeley), **Supp. IV Part 1:** 141, 150, 158
Still Life with Oysters and Lemon (Doty), **Supp. XI:** 119, 121, **133–134**

Still Life with Woodpecker (Robbins), **Supp. X:** 260, **271–274,** 282
"Still Moment, A" (Welty), **IV:** 265; **Retro. Supp. I:** 347
Stillness (Gardner), **Supp. VI:** 74
"Stillness in the Air" (Dickinson), **Supp. XV:** 261
Stillness of Dancing, The (Bierds), **Supp. XVII: 27–28**
"Still Small Voices, The" (Fante), **Supp. XI:** 164
Still Such (Salter), **Supp. IX:** 246
"Still the Place Where Creation Does Some Work on Itself" (W. V. Davis), **Supp. IV Part 1:** 68
Stimpson, Catharine R., **Supp. IV Part 2:** 686
Stimson, Eleanor Kenyon. *See* Brooks, Mrs. Van Wyck
"Stimulants, Poultices, Goads" (Wright), **Supp. XV:** 349
"Stings" (Plath), **Retro. Supp. II:** 255; **Supp. I Part 2:** 541
"Stirling Street September" (Baraka), **Supp. II Part 1:** 51
Stirner, Max, **II:** 27
"Stirrup-Cup, The" (Lanier), **Supp. I Part 1:** 364
Stitt, Peter, **Supp. IV Part 1:** 68; **Supp. IV Part 2:** 628; **Supp. IX:** 152, 163, 291, 299; **Supp. XI:** 311, 317; **Supp. XIII:** 87; **Supp. XV:** 98, 99; **Supp. XIX:** 121
Stivers, Valerie, **Supp. X:** 311
St. John, David, **Supp. XV:** 73, 253
St. Louis Woman (Bontemps and Cullen), **Supp. XXII:** 6
St. Mark, Tyler, **Supp. XX: 260**
Stock, Noel, **III:** 479
Stockton, Frank R., **I:** 201
Stoddard, Charles Warren, **I:** 193, 195, 196; **Supp. II Part 1:** 192, 341, 351
Stoddard, Elizabeth, **II:** 275; **Supp. XV: 269–291**
Stoddard, Richard, **Supp. I Part 1:** 372
Stoddard, Richard Henry, **Supp. XV:** 269, 271, 272, 273, 274, 278, 279, 286
Stoddard, Solomon, **I:** 545, 548; **IV:** 145, 148
Stoffman, Judy, **Supp. XVIII:** 97
Stoic, The (Dreiser), **I:** 497, 502, 508, 516; **Retro. Supp. II:** 95, 96, 101, 108
Stokes, Geoffrey, **Supp. XV:** 256
Stokes, Olivia Egleston Phelps, **Supp. XVIII:** 261
"Stolen Calf, The" (Dunbar), **Supp. II Part 1:** 196
Stolen Jew, The (Neugeboren), **Supp. XVI: 222–224,** 225
Stolen Past, A (Knowles), **Supp. XII:** 249
Stolen Words: Forays into the Origins and Ravages of Plagiarism (Mallon), **Supp. XIX: 134–135**
Stollman, Aryeh Lev, **Supp. XVII:** 49
Stolmar, Thomas, **Supp. XVIII:** 138
Stomping the Blues (Murray), **Supp. XIX: 158–159**
"Stone" (Ozick), **Supp. XVII:** 50
Stone, Edward, **III:** 479
Stone, Herbert S., **Supp. XXI:** 2
Stone, I. F., **Supp. XIV:** 3
Stone, Irving, **II:** 463, 466, 467
Stone, Oliver, **Supp. XIV:** 48, 316
Stone, Phil, **II:** 55
Stone, Richard, **Supp. XIV:** 54
Stone, Robert, **Supp. V: 295–312; Supp. X:** 1; **Supp. XIX:** 54
Stone, Rosetta (pseudonym). *See* Geisel, Theodor Seuss (Dr. Seuss)
Stone, Wilmer, **Supp. I Part 1:** 49
Stone and the Shell, The (Hay), **Supp. XIV:** 122, 123, 127, 130
"Stone Bear, The" (Haines), **Supp. XII:** 206–207, 212
"Stone City" (Proulx), **Supp. VII:** 251–253
Stone Country (Sanders), **Supp. XVI:** 271–272
Stone Diaries, The (Shields), **Supp. VII:** 307, 315, 324–326, 327
"Stone Dreams" (Kingsolver), **Supp. VII:** 203
Stone Harp, The (Haines), **Supp. XII: 204,** 205, 206, 207
Stonemason, The (McCarthy), **Supp. VIII:** 175, 187
"Stones" (Hoffman), **Supp. XVIII:** 86
"Stones" (Kumin), **Supp. IV Part 2:** 447
"Stones, The" (Plath), **Supp. I Part 2:** 535, 539
"Stones in My Passway, Hellhounds on My Trail" (Boyle), **Supp. VIII:** 15
Stones of Florence, The (McCarthy), **II:** 562
"Stone Walls" (Sarton), **Supp. VIII:** 259
"Stop" (Wilbur), **Supp. III Part 2:** 556
Stop-Loss (screenplay, Richard), **Supp. XIX:** 222
"Stop Me If You've Heard This One" (Lardner), **II:** 433
Stopover: Tokyo (Marquand), **III:** 53, 57, 61, 70
Stoppard, Tom, **Retro. Supp. I:** 189
"Stopping by Woods" (Frost), **II:** 154
"Stopping by Woods on a Snowy Evening" (Frost), **Retro. Supp. I:** 129, 133, 134, 135, 139
Stopping Westward (Richards), **II:** 396
"Stop Player. Joke No. 4" (Gaddis), **Supp. IV Part 1:** 280
Stop-Time (Conroy), **Supp. XVI: 63–71,** 72, 75, 76–77
"Store, The" (P. E. Jones), **Supp. XXII:** 144–145
Store, The (Stribling), **Supp. VIII:** 126; **Supp. XXII:** 195
"*Store* and *Mockingbird:* Two Pulitzer Novels about Alabama" (Going), **Supp. VIII:** 126
Store of a Million Items, The (Cliff), **Supp. XXII:** 67, 74, 75
"Store of a Million Items, The" (Cliff), **Supp. XXII:** 75
Storer, Edward, **Supp. I Part 1:** 261, 262
Stories, Fables and Other Diversions (Nemerov), **III:** 268–269, 285
Stories: Elizabeth Stoddard, **Supp. XV:** 270
"Stories for Sale" (Kolba), **Supp. XVIII:** 257
Stories for the Sixties (Yates, ed.), **Supp. XI:** 343
Stories from Our Living Past (Prose), **Supp. XVI:** 251
Stories from the Italian Poets (Hunt), **Supp. XV:** 175
Stories from the Old Testament Retold (L. P. Smith), **Supp. XIV:** 342
Stories from World Literature, **Supp. IX:** 4
"Stories in the Snow" (Leopold), **Supp. XIV:** 183
Stories of an Imaginary Childhood (Bukiet), **Supp. XVII: 41–44,** 45
Stories of F. Scott Fitzgerald, The (Cowley, ed.), **Retro. Supp. I:** 115
Stories of F. Scott Fitzgerald, The (Fitzgerald), **II:** 94
Stories of Modern America, **Supp. IX:** 4
Stories of Stephen Dixon, The (Dixon), **Supp. XII:** 152
Stories of the Spanish Civil War (Hemingway), **II:** 258
Stories Revived (James), **II:** 322
Stories that Could Be True (Stafford), **Supp. XI: 325–327**
Stories Toto Told Me (Rolfe), **Supp. XX: 235**
Storm, The (Buechner), **Supp. XII: 54–57**
"Storm, The" (Chopin), **Retro. Supp. II:** 60, 68; **Supp. I Part 1:** 218, 224
Storm, The (al-'Awásif) (Gibran), **Supp. XX: 116, 124, 125**
"Storm Fear" (Frost), **II:** 153; **Retro. Supp. I:** 127
"Storm Ship, The" (Irving), **II:** 309
"Storm Warnings" (Kingsolver), **Supp. VII:** 207–208
"Stormy Weather" (Ellison), **Supp. II Part 1:** 233
"Story" (Everwine), **Supp. XV:** 89
"Story, A" (Jarrell), **II:** 371
Story, Julian, **Supp. XX: 232**
Story, Richard David, **Supp. IV Part 2:** 575, 588
Story, William Wetmore, **Supp. XX: 228**
"Story about Chicken Soup, A" (Simpson), **Supp. IX: 272–273**
"Story about the Anteater, The" (Benét), **Supp. XI:** 53
"Story About the Body, A" (Hass), **Supp. VI: 107–108**
"Story for Teddy, A" (Swados), **Supp. XIX:** 266–267
Story for Teddy, A—and Others (Swados), **Supp. XIX: 266–268**
"Story Hearer, The" (Paley), **Supp. VI:** 230, 231
"Story Hour" (Hay), **Supp. XIV:** 124
"Story Hour" (Jarman), **Supp. XVII:** 116
Story Hour: A Second Look at Cinderella, Bluebeard, and Company (Hay), **Supp. XIV:** 119, 124, 125, 132, 133
Story of a Country Town, The (Howe), **I:** 106
Story of a Lover, The (Hapgood), **Supp. XVII:** 99, 100, 104; **Supp. XXI:** 3, 5, 7

Story of an American Family, The: Letters of the Hapgood Family, 1648–1917 (Boyce), **Supp. XVII:** 97; **Supp. XXI:** 9, 14
"Story of an Hour, The" (Chopin), **Retro. Supp. II:** 72; **Supp. I Part 1:** 212–213, 216
Story of a Novel, The (Wolfe), **IV:** 456, 458
"Story of a Proverb, The" (Lanier), **Supp. I Part 1:** 365
"Story of a Proverb, The: A Fairy Tale for Grown People" (Lanier), **Supp. I Part 1:** 365
Story of a Story and Other Stories, The: A Novel (Dixon), **Supp. XII:** 155
Story of a Wonder Man, The (Lardner), **II:** 433–434
"Story of a Year, The" (James), **Retro. Supp. I:** 218
Story of George Washington Carver, The (Bontemps), **Supp. XXII:** 13
Story of G.I. Joe, The (film, Wellman), **Supp. XVII:** 61, 62
"Story of Gus, The" (A. Miller), **III:** 147–148
"Story of How a Wall Stands, A" (Ortiz), **Supp. IV Part 2:** 499, 507
Story of Mount Desert Island, Maine, The (Morison), **Supp. I Part 2:** 494
Story of My Boyhood and Youth, The (Muir), **Supp. IX: 172–174,** 176
Story of My Father, The: A Memoir (Miller), **Supp. XII:** 301
Story of O, The (Réage), **Supp. XII:** 9, 10
Story of Our Lives, The (Strand), **Supp. IV Part 2:** 620, 628–629, 629
"Story of Poppy Van Buster, The" (Briggs), **Supp. XVIII:** 8
Story of the Negro (Bontemps), **Supp. XXII:** 6, 12–13
Story of the Normans, The, Told Chiefly in Relation to Their Conquest of England (Jewett), **II:** 406
Story of the Telegraph, The (Briggs, and Maverick), **Supp. XVIII:** 4
"Story of Toby, The" (Melville), **III:** 76
"Story of To-day, A" (Davis). *See also Margret Howth*
"Story of To-day, A" (R. H. Davis), **Supp. XVI:** 88, 89
Story of Utopias, The (Mumford), **Supp. II Part 2:** 475, 483–486, 495
Story of Wine in California, The (M. F. K. Fisher), **Supp. XVII:** 88
Story on Page One, The (Odets), **Supp. II Part 2:** 546
Storyteller (Silko), **Supp. IV Part 2:** 558, 559, 560, 561, **566–570**
"Storyteller" (Silko), **Supp. IV Part 2:** 569
"*Storyteller:* Grandmother Spider's Web" (Danielson), **Supp. IV Part 2:** 569
"Storyteller's Notebook, A" (Carver), **Supp. III Part 1:** 142–143
Story Teller's Story, A: The Tale of an American Writer's Journey through His Own Imaginative World and through the World of Facts . . . (Anderson), **I:** 98, 101, 114, 117
"Story That Could Be True, A" (Stafford), **Supp. XI:** 326
"Stout Gentleman, The" (Irving), **II:** 309
Stover at Yale (Johnson), **III:** 321
Stowe, Calvin, **IV:** 445; **Supp. I Part 2:** 587, 588, 590, 596, 597
Stowe, Charles, **Supp. I Part 2:** 581, 582
Stowe, Eliza, **Supp. I Part 2:** 587
Stowe, Harriet Beecher, **II:** 274, 399, 403, 541; **Retro. Supp. I:** 34, 246; **Retro. Supp. II:** 4, 138, 156; **Supp. I Part 1:** 30, 206, 301; **Supp. I Part 2: 579–601; Supp. III Part 1:** 154, 168, 171; **Supp. IX:** 33; **Supp. X:** 223, 246, 249, 250; **Supp. XI:** 193; **Supp. XIII:** 141, 295; **Supp. XV:** 278; **Supp. XVI:** 82, 85
Stowe, Samuel Charles, **Supp. I Part 2:** 587
Stowe, William, **Supp. IV Part 1:** 129
Strachey, Lytton, **I:** 5; **IV:** 436; **Retro. Supp. I:** 59; **Supp. I Part 2:** 485, 494; **Supp. XIV:** 342; **Supp. XVI:** 191
"Stradivari" (Bierds), **Supp. XVII:** 28
Straight Cut (Bell), **Supp. X:** 5, **6–7,** 10
Straight Man (Russo), **Supp. XII: 335–339,** 340
Straits: Poems (Koch), **Supp. XV:** 184
Strand, Mark, **Supp. IV Part 2: 619–636; Supp. V:** 92, 332, 337, 338, 343; **Supp. IX:** 155; **Supp. XI:** 139, 145; **Supp. XII:** 254; **Supp. XIII:** 76; **Supp. XV:** 74
Strand, Paul, **Supp. VIII:** 272
Strandberg, Victor, **Supp. V:** 273
Strange, Sharan, **Supp. XXI:** 246
"Strange Beautiful Woman, A" (Nelson), **Supp. XVIII:** 173
Strange Bedfellows (Woods), **Supp. XXI:** 70
Strange Case of Dr. Jekyll and Mr. Hyde, The (Stevenson), **II:** 290
Strange Children, The (Gordon), **II:** 196, 197, 199, 211–213
Strange Commonplace, A (Sorrentino), **Supp. XXI:** 232, 237, 238
Strange Crime in Bermuda, The (Holding), **Supp. XXII: 124–125,** 127, 129
Strange Fire (Bukiet), **Supp. XVII: 46**
"Strange Fruit" (Harjo), **Supp. XII:** 224, 225
"Strange Fruit" (song), **Supp. I Part 1:** 80; **Supp. XVIII:** 228
Strange Interlude (O'Neill), **III:** 391, 397–398; **IV:** 61; **Supp. XXII:** 24
Stranger, The (Camus), **I:** 53, 292; **Supp. VIII:** 11; **Supp. XV:** 352
"Stranger, The" (Rich), **Supp. I Part 2:** 555, 560
"Stranger, The" (Salinger), **III:** 552–553
"Stranger in My Own Life, A: Alienation in American Indian Poetry and Prose" (Gunn Allen), **Supp. IV Part 1:** 322
Stranger in the Kingdom, A (Mosher), **Supp. XXII:** 204, 205, 206, 207, 208, 209, **212–213**
"Stranger in the Village" (Baldwin), **Retro. Supp. II:** 3; **Supp. I Part 1:** 54; **Supp. IV Part 1:** 10
"Stranger in Town" (Hughes), **Supp. I Part 1:** 334
"Strangers" (Howe), **Supp. VI:** 120
Strangers and Wayfarers (Jewett), **Retro. Supp. II:** 138
"Strangers from the Horizon" (Merwin), **Supp. III Part 1:** 356
Strangers on a Train (Highsmith), **Supp. IV Part 1:** 132
"Strange Story, A" (Taylor), **Supp. V:** 323
"Strange Story, A" (Wylie), **Supp. I Part 2:** 723
Strange Things (Atwood), **Supp. XIII:** 35
"Strato in Plaster" (Merrill), **Supp. III Part 1:** 328
Stratton-Porter, Gene, **Supp. XX: 211–225**
Straus, Ralph, **Supp. XIII:** 168
Straus, Roger, **Supp. VIII:** 82; **Supp. XV:** 59
Strauss, Harold, **Supp. XV:** 137
Strauss, Johann, **I:** 66
Strauss, Richard, **IV:** 316
Strauss, Robert, **Supp. XI:** 141, 142
Stravinsky (De Schloezer), **III:** 474
Stravinsky, Igor, **Retro. Supp. I:** 378; **Supp. IV Part 1:** 81; **Supp. XI:** 133; **Supp. XV:** 265
"Stravinsky's Three Pieces 'Grotesques,' for String Quartet" (Lowell), **II:** 523
Straw, The (O'Neill), **III:** 390
"Strawberry Milkshake" (Halliday), **Supp. XIX:** 92, 94
"Stray Document, A" (Pound), **II:** 517
"Strays" (Richard), **Supp. XIX:** 210–211, 220
Streaks of the Tulip, The: Selected Criticism (W. J. Smith), **Supp. XIII:** 333, 334, 344, **347–348**
Streamline Your Mind (Mursell), **Supp. I Part 2:** 608
Strecker, Trey, **Supp. XXI:** 238
"Street, Cloud" (Ríos), **Supp. IV Part 2:** 549
Street, The (Petry), **Supp. XVIII:** 286
Streetcar Named Desire, A (T. Williams), **IV:** 382, 383, 385, 386, 387, 389–390, 395, 398; **Supp. IV Part 1:** 359
Street in Bronzeville, A (Brooks), **Retro. Supp. I:** 208; **Supp. III Part 1:** 74–78
"Street Moths" (X. J. Kennedy), **Supp. XV:** 170
"Street Musicians" (Ashbery), **Supp. III Part 1:** 18
"Street of Crocodiles" (Hull), **Supp. XXI:** 130
"Street off Sunset, A" (Jarrell), **II:** 387
"Streets" (Dixon), **Supp. XII: 145–146**
Streets in the Moon (MacLeish), **III:** 5, 8–11, 15, 19
"Streets of Laredo" (screenplay) (McMurtry and Ossana), **Supp. V:** 226, 230
Streets of Laredo (McMurtry), **Supp. V:** 230

Streets of Night (Dos Passos), **I:** 478, 479–480, 481, 488
Streitfield, David, **Supp. XIII:** 234; **Supp. XVI:** 63
Strength of Fields, The (Dickey), **Supp. IV Part 1:** 178
"Strength of Fields, The" (Dickey), **Supp. IV Part 1:** 176, 184–185
"Strength of Gideon, The" (Dunbar), **Supp. II Part 1:** 212
Strength of Gideon and Other Stories, The (Dunbar), **Supp. II Part 1:** 211, 212
"Strenuous Artistry" (Zagarell), **Supp. XV:** 281
Strether, Lambert, **II:** 313
Stribling, T. S., **Supp. VIII:** 126
Strickland, Barbara, **Supp. XIX:** 102
Strickland, Joe (pseudonym). *See* Arnold, George W.
"Strictly Bucolic" (Simic), **Supp. VIII:** 278
Strictly Business (O. Henry), **Supp. II Part 1:** 410
"Strike, The" (Olsen), **Supp. XIII:** 292, 297
Strike at Shane's, The (Skloot), **Supp. XX: 216**
"Strikers" (Untermeyer), **Supp. XV:** 296
Strindberg, August, **I:** 78; **III:** 145, 165, 387, 390, 391, 392, 393; **IV:** 17; **Supp. XVII:** 100; **Supp. XXII:** 23
"String, The" (Dickey), **Supp. IV Part 1:** 179
String Light (Wright), **Supp. XV: 345–346**
"String Quartet, The" (Weigl), **Supp. XIX:** 278
"Strivings of the Negro People" (Du Bois), **Supp. II Part 1:** 167
Stroby, W. C., **Supp. XIV:** 26
Strohbach, Hermann, **Supp. XI:** 242
"Stroke of Good Fortune, A" (O'Connor), **III:** 344; **Retro. Supp. II:** 229, 232
Strom, Stephen, **Supp. XII:** 223
Strong, Anna Louise, **Supp. XVIII:** 238
Strong, George Templeton, **IV:** 321
Strong, Josiah, **Supp. XIV:** 64
"Strong Draughts of Their Refreshing Minds" (Dickinson), **Retro. Supp. I:** 46
Strong Motion (Franzen), **Supp. XX: 85, 88–89, 92, 95**
Strong Opinions (Nabokov), **Retro. Supp. I:** 263, 266, 270, 276
"Strong Room of the House, The" (Bronk), **Supp. XXI:** 32
"Strong Women" (Dorman), **Supp. XI:** 240
Strout, Elizabeth, **Supp. X:** 86
Structure of Nations and Empires, The (Niebuhr), **III:** 292, 308
"Structure of Rime, The" (Duncan), **Supp. XVI:** 287
Structuring the Void (Klinkowitz), **Supp. XXI:** 233
Struggle, The (film; Griffith), **Supp. XVI:** 191
"Strumpet Song" (Plath), **Retro. Supp. II:** 246; **Supp. I Part 2:** 536
Strunk, William, **Supp. I Part 2:** 652, 662, 670, 671, 672
Strunsky, Anna, **II:** 465
"Strut for Roethke, A" (Berryman), **I:** 188
Strychacz, Thomas F., **Supp. XVI:** 69–70
Stuart, Dabney, **Supp. XVIII:** 79
Stuart, Gilbert, **I:** 16
Stuart, J. E. B., **III:** 56
Stuart, Jesse, **Supp. XX: 162–163, 165**
Stuart, Michael, **Supp. XV:** 140
Stuart Little (White), **Supp. I Part 2:** 655–658
Stuckey, W. J., **Supp. XXII:** 191–192
"Student, The" (Moore), **III:** 212, 215
"Student of Clouds" (Collins), **Supp. XXI:** 60
"Student of Salmanaca, The" (Irving), **II:** 309
"Student's Wife, The" (Carver), **Supp. III Part 1:** 141
Studies in American Indian Literature: Critical Essays and Course Designs (Gunn Allen), **Supp. IV Part 1:** 324, 333
Studies in Classic American Literature (Lawrence), **II:** 102; **III:** 33; **IV:** 333; **Retro. Supp. I:** 421
Studies in Short Fiction (Malin), **Supp. XVI:** 71
Studies in the Psychology of Sex (Ellis), **Supp. XX: 235**
"Studs" (Farrell), **II:** 25, 28, 31
Studs Lonigan: A Trilogy (Farrell), **II:** 25, 26, 27, 31–34, 37, 38, 41–42
"Study in Orange and White" (Collins), **Supp. XXI:** 60
"Study of Images" (Stevens), **IV:** 79
"Study of Lanier's Poems, A" (Kent), **Supp. I Part 1:** 373
Study of Milton's Prosody (Bridges), **II:** 537
"Study of the Negro Problems, The" (Du Bois), **Supp. II Part 1:** 165
Stuewe, Paul, **Supp. IV Part 1:** 68
Stuhlmann, Gunther, **Supp. X:** 182, 184, 185, 187
Stultifera Navis (Brant), **III:** 447
Sturak, John Thomas, **Supp. XIII:** 162, 163, 165, 168
Sturgeon, Theodore, **Supp. XVIII:** 145
Sturgis, George, **III:** 600
Sturgis, Howard, **IV:** 319; **Retro. Supp. I:** 367, 373
Sturgis, Howard Overing, **Supp. XX: 227–242**
Sturgis, Julian Russell, **Supp. XX: 228, 233, 238**
Sturgis, Susan, **III:** 600
Sturm, Margaret. *See* Millar, Margaret
Stuttaford, Genevieve, **Supp. IX:** 279
Stuyvesant, Peter, **II:** 301
"Style" (Nemerov), **III:** 275
Styles of Radical Will (Sontag), **Supp. III Part 2:** 451, 459, 460–463
"Stylist, The" (Egan), **Supp. XIX:** 51, 52
Styne, Jule, **Supp. XVI:** 193
Styron, William, **III:** 40; **IV:** 4, **97–119,** 216; **Supp. V:** 201; **Supp. IX:** 208; **Supp. X:** 15–16, 250; **Supp. XI:** 229, 231, 343; **Supp. XIV:** 82; **Supp. XVI:** 235–236
Suares, J. C., **Supp. IV Part 1:** 234
Suarez, Ernest, **Supp. IV Part 1:** 175; **Supp. V:** 180
Suarez, Ray, **Supp. XXI:** 243
"Sub, The" (Dixon), **Supp. XII:** 146
Subjection of Women, The (Mill), **Supp. XI:** 196, 203
"Subjective Necessity for Social Settlements" (Addams), **Supp. I Part 1:** 4
"Subject of Childhood, A" (Paley), **Supp. VI:** 221; **Supp. XXI:** 118
"Submarginalia" (Howe), **Supp. IV Part 2:** 422
Substance and Shadow (James), **II:** 344
"Subterranean Homesick Blues" (song, Dylan), **Supp. XVIII:** 25
Subterraneans, The (Kerouac), **Supp. III Part 1:** 225, 227–231
"Subtitle" (Kees), **Supp. XV:** 139
Subtreasury of American Humor, A (White and White), **Supp. I Part 2:** 668
"Suburban Culture, Imaginative Wonder: The Fiction of Frederick Barthelme" (Brinkmeyer), **Supp. XI:** 38
Suburban Sketches (Howells), **II:** 274, 277
"Subversive Element, The" (Ryan as Quin), **Supp. XVIII:** 230
"Subverted Flower, The" (Frost), **Retro. Supp. I:** 139
"Subway, The" (Tate), **IV:** 128
"Subway Singer, The" (Clampitt), **Supp. IX:** 45
"Success" (Mora), **Supp. XIII:** 217
Successful Love and Other Stories (Schwartz), **Supp. II Part 2:** 661, 665
Succession, The: A Novel of Elizabeth and James (Garrett), **Supp. VII:** 104–107, 108
"Success is counted sweetest" (Dickinson), **Retro. Supp. I:** 30, 31–32, 38; **Supp. XV:** 126
Success Stories (Banks), **Supp. V:** 14–15
"Success Story" (Banks), **Supp. V:** 15
"Such Counsels You Gave to Me" (Jeffers), **Supp. II Part 2:** 433
Such Silence (Milburn), **Supp. XI:** 242
"Such Things Happen Only in Books" (Wilder), **IV:** 365
Such Was the Season (Major), **Supp. XXII: 177–178,** 179, 182
Suddenly, Last Summer (film) (Vidal), **Supp. IV Part 2:** 683
Suddenly Last Summer (T. Williams), **I:** 73; **IV:** 382, 383, 385, 386, 387, 389, 390, 391, 392, 395–396, 397, 398
Suder (Everett), **Supp. XVIII: 54–55**
Sudermann, Hermann, **I:** 66
Sugg, Richard P., **Supp. IV Part 1:** 68

"Suggestion from a Friend" (Kenyon), **Supp. VII:** 171
"Suicide" (Barnes), **Supp. III Part 1:** 33
"Suicide off Egg Rock" (Plath), **Supp. I Part 2:** 529, 538
Suicides and Jazzers (Carruth), **Supp. XVI:** 46
"Suicide's Note" (Hughes), **Retro. Supp. I:** 199
"Suitable Surroundings, The" (Bierce), **I:** 203
"Suitcase, The" (Ozick), **Supp. V:** 262, 264
"Suite for Augustus, A" (Dove), **Supp. IV Part 1:** 245
"Suite for Emily" (Hull), **Supp. XXI:** 139–140
"Suite for Lord Timothy Dexter" (Rukeyser), **Supp. VI:** 283, 285
"Suite from the Firebird" (Stravinsky), **Supp. XI:** 133
"Suitor, The" (Kenyon), **Supp. VII:** 164–165
Sukarno, **IV:** 490
Sukenick, Ronald, **Supp. V:** 39, 44, 46; **Supp. XII:** 139
Sula (Morrison), **Supp. III Part 1:** 362, 364, 367, 368, 379; **Supp. VIII:** 219
Sullivan, Andrew, **Supp. IX:** 135
Sullivan, Arthur, **Supp. XX: 228**
Sullivan, Frank, **Supp. IX:** 201
Sullivan, Harry Stack, **I:** 59
Sullivan, Jack, **Supp. X:** 86; **Supp. XII:** 331
Sullivan, Noel, **Retro. Supp. I:** 202; **Supp. I Part 1:** 329, 333
Sullivan, Richard, **Supp. VIII:** 124
Sullivan, Walter, **Supp. VIII:** 168
"Sullivan County Sketches" (Crane), **I:** 407, 421
"Sumach and Goldenrod: An American Idyll" (Mumford), **Supp. II Part 2:** 475
Suma Genji (Play), **III:** 466
Sumerian Vistas (Ammons), **Supp. VII:** 34, 35
"Summa Lyrica" (Grossman), **Supp. XIX:** 86
"Summer" (Emerson), **II:** 10
Summer (Gioia), **Supp. XV:** 117
"Summer" (Lowell), **II:** 554
Summer (Wharton), **IV:** 317; **Retro. Supp. I:** 360, 367, 374, **378–379,** 382
Summer, Bob, **Supp. X:** 1, 5, 6, 42
Summer and Smoke (T. Williams), **IV:** 382, 384, 385, 386, 387, 395, 397, 398; **Supp. IV Part 1:** 84
Summer Anniversaries, The (Justice), **Supp. VII:** 115, 117
Summer Blue (Skloot), **Supp. XX: 196, 207–208**
"Summer Commentary, A" (Winters), **Supp. II Part 2:** 808
"Summer Day" (O'Hara), **III:** 369
"Summer Days, The" (Oliver), **Supp. VII:** 239
Summer Never Ends (W. Frank), **Supp. XX: 78**
"Summer Night" (Hughes), **Supp. I Part 1:** 325
"Summer Night, A" (Auden), **Supp. II Part 1:** 8
"Summer Night—Broadway" (Untermeyer), **Supp. XV:** 296
"Summer Noon: 1941" (Winters), **Supp. II Part 2:** 811
"Summer of '82" (Merwin), **Supp. III Part 1:** 355–356
Summer on the Lakes in 1843 (Fuller), **Supp. II Part 1:** 279, 295–296
"Summer People" (Hemingway), **II:** 258–259
"Summer People, The" (Jackson), **Supp. IX:** 120
"Summer People, The" (Merrill), **Supp. III Part 1:** 325–326
"Summer Perdu" (Halliday), **Supp. XIX:** 89
"Summer Planning" (Halliday), **Supp. XIX:** 92
"Summer Ramble, A" (Bryant), **Supp. I Part 1:** 162, 164
Summers, Claude J., **Supp. IV Part 2:** 680–681; **Supp. XIV:** 161, 169
Summers, Robert, **Supp. IX:** 289
"Summer Solstice, New York City" (Olds), **Supp. X:** 207
"Summer's Reading, A" (Malamud), **Supp. I Part 2:** 430–431, 442
"Summer Storm" (Gioia), **Supp. XV:** 127
"Summer Storm" (Simpson), **Supp. IX:** 268
"'Summertime and the Living . . .' " (Hayden), **Supp. II Part 1:** 363, 366
Summertime Island (Caldwell), **I:** 307–308
"Summer Tragedy" (Bontemps), **Supp. XXII:** 9
"Summer: West Side" (Updike), **Retro. Supp. I:** 320
"Summer with Tu Fu, A" (Carruth), **Supp. XVI:** 55, 58
"Summit Beach, 1921" (Dove), **Supp. IV Part 1:** 249
Summoning of Stones, A (Hecht), **Supp. X:** 57, 58, **58–59**
"Summons" (Untermeyer), **Supp. XV:** 296
Summons to Memphis, A (Taylor), **Supp. V:** 313, 314, 327
Summons to the Free, A (Benét), **Supp. XI:** 47
Sumner, Charles, **I:** 3, 15; **Supp. I Part 2:** 685, 687
Sumner, John, **Retro. Supp. II:** 95
Sumner, John B., **I:** 511
Sumner, William Graham, **III:** 102, 108; **Supp. I Part 2:** 640
"Sumptuous Destination" (Wilbur), **Supp. III Part 2:** 553
"Sun" (Moore), **III:** 215
"Sun" (Swenson), **Supp. IV Part 2:** 640
"Sun, Sea, and Sand" (Marquand), **III:** 60
Sun Also Rises, The (Hemingway), **I:** 107; **II:** 68, 90, 249, 251–252, 260, 600; **III:** 36; **IV:** 35, 297; **Retro. Supp. I:** 171, **177–180,** 181, 189; **Supp. I Part 2:** 614; **Supp. XIII:** 263; **Supp. XVIII:** 74
"Sun and Moon" (Kenyon), **Supp. VII:** 168
"Sun and the Still-born Stars, The" (Southern), **Supp. XI:** 295
Sun at Midnight (Soseki; Merwin and Shigematsu, trans.), **Supp. III Part 1:** 353
"Sun Crosses Heaven from West to East Bringing Samson Back to the Womb, The" (R. Bly), **Supp. IV Part 1:** 73
"Sun Dance Shield" (Momaday), **Supp. IV Part 2:** 491
Sunday, Billy, **II:** 449
"Sunday Afternoons" (Komunyakaa), **Supp. XIII:** 127
Sunday after the War (H. Miller), **III:** 184
"Sunday at Home" (Hawthorne), **II:** 231–232
"Sunday Following Mother's Day, The" (P. E. Jones), **Supp. XXII:** 145
"Sunday Morning" (Stevens), **II:** 552; **III:** 278, 463, 509; **IV:** 92–93; **Retro. Supp. I:** 296, 300, 301, 304, 307, 313; **Supp. XV:** 120; **Supp. XVI:** 210; **Supp. XVII:** 42; **Supp. XIX:** 40; **Supp. XXI:** 28, 133
"Sunday Morning Apples" (Crane), **I:** 387
"Sunday Morning Prophecy" (Hughes), **Supp. I Part 1:** 334
"Sunday Morning with the Sensational Nightingales" (Collins), **Supp. XXI:** 60
"Sundays" (B. Kelly), **Supp. XVII:** 124–125
"Sundays" (Salter), **Supp. IX:** 257
"Sundays, They Sleep Late" (Rukeyser), **Supp. VI:** 278
"Sundays of Satin-Legs Smith, The" (Brooks), **Supp. III Part 1:** 74, 75
"Sundays Visiting" (Ríos), **Supp. IV Part 2:** 541
Sundial, The (Jackson), **Supp. IX: 126–127**
Sundog (Harrison), **Supp. VIII: 46–48**
Sun Dogs (R. O. Butler), **Supp. XII: 64–65**
Sun Do Move, The (Hughes), **Supp. I Part 1:** 339
Sundquist, Eric, **Supp. XIV:** 66, 71
"Sunfish" (C. Frost), **Supp. XV:** 100–101, 102
"Sunflower Sutra" (Ginsberg), **Supp. II Part 1:** 317, 321; **Supp. XV:** 215
Sunlight Dialogues, The (Gardner), **Supp. VI:** 63, **68,** 69, 70
"Sunlight Is Imagination" (Wilbur), **Supp. III Part 2:** 549
"Sunny Ridge, The" (Halliday), **Supp. XIX:** 92
Sun Out: Selected Poems, 1952–1954 (Koch), **Supp. XV:** 179
"Sunrise" (Lanier), **Supp. I Part 1:** 370
"Sunrise and the Bomb" (Halliday), **Supp. XIX:** 84, 85, 92
"Sunrise runs for Both, The" (Dickinson), **Retro. Supp. I:** 45

Sunrise with Seamonsters: Travels and Discoveries, 1964–1984 (Theroux), **Supp. VIII:** 311, 313, 323, 325
"Sun Rising" (Donne), **Supp. VIII:** 164
"Sunset" (Ransom), **III:** 484
"Sunset from Omaha Hotel Window" (Sandburg), **III:** 584
Sunset Gun (Parker), **Supp. IX:** 192
Sunset Limited (Burke), **Supp. XIV:** 32, 33
Sunset Limited (Harrison), **Supp. VIII:** 51
"Sunset Maker, The" (Justice), **Supp. VII:** 123
Sunset Maker, The: Poems, Stories, a Memoir (Justice), **Supp. VII:** 116, 118, 119, 123–124
Sunshine Boys, The (film), **Supp. IV Part 2:** 589
Sunshine Boys, The (Simon), **Supp. IV Part 2:** 575, 584–585
"Sunthin' in the Pastoral Line" (Lowell), **Supp. I Part 2:** 415–416
Sun to Sun (Hurston), **Supp. VI:** 154
Sun Tracks (Ortiz), **Supp. IV Part 2:** 499, 500
Sun Under Wood (Hass), **Supp. VI:** 103, 108–109
"Superb Lily, The" (Pinsky), **Supp. VI:** 250
"Super Goat Man" (Lethem), **Supp. XVIII:** 148
"Superman Comes to the Supermarket" (Mailer), **Retro. Supp. II:** 204
"Supermarket in California, A" (Ginsberg), **Supp. XI:** 135
"Supernatural Love" (Schnackenberg), **Supp. XV:** 257, 259–260
Supernatural Love: Poems 1976–1992 (Schnackenberg), **Supp. XV:** 253, 256, 260, 263
Suplee, Curt, **Supp. XVI:** 202
"Supper After the Last, The" (Kinnell), **Supp. III Part 1:** 239
"Supposedly Fun Thing I'll Never Do Again, A" (Wallace), **Supp. X:** 315
Supposedly Fun Thing I'll Never Do Again, A: Essays and Arguments (Wallace), **Supp. X: 314–316**
Suppressed Desires (Glaspell and Cook), **Supp. III Part 1:** 178; **Supp. XXI:** 6
Suppression of the African Slave Trade to the United States of America, 1638–1870 (Du Bois), **Supp. II Part 1:** 157, 162
Supreme Fiction, The (Stevens), **Supp. XVI:** 158
"Supremes, The" (Jarman), **Supp. XVII:** 115
Sure Hand of God, The (Caldwell), **I:** 297, 302
Sure Signs: New and Selected Poems (Kooser), **Supp. XIX:** 116, 117, **121–122**
"Surety and Fidelity Claims" (Stevens), **Retro. Supp. I:** 296, 309
Surface of Earth, The (Price), **Supp. VI:** 261–262
"Surfaces" (Ammons), **Supp. VII:** 36
Surfaces and Masks (Major), **Supp. XXII:** 180
Surfacing (Atwood), **Supp. XIII:** 20, 21, **22–23,** 24, 33, 35
"Surgeon at 2 A.M." (Plath), **Supp. I Part 2:** 545
Surmmer Knowledge (Schwartz), **Supp. II Part 2:** 662, 665
"Surprise" (Kenyon), **Supp. VII:** 173
Surprised by Sin: The Reader in Paradise Lost (Fish), **Supp. XIV:** 15
"Surround, The Imagining Herself as the Environment,/She Speaks to James Wright at Sundow" (Dickey), **Supp. IV Part 1:** 185
"Survey of Literature" (Ransom), **III:** 480
"Survey of the Literature, A" (Saunders), **Supp. XIX:** 235
"Surveyor, The" (H. Roth), **Supp. IX:** 233, 234
Survival (Atwood), **Supp. XIII:** 20, 22, 35
"Survival as Tao, Beginning at 5:00 A.M." (Carruth), **Supp. XVI:** 56
Survival of the Bark Canoe, The (McPhee), **Supp. III Part 1:** 301, 302, 308, 313
Survival This Way: Interviews with American Indian Poets (Bruchac), **Supp. IV Part 2:** 506
"Surviving Love" (Berryman), **I:** 173
Survivor (O. Butler), **Supp. XIII:** 62, 63
Susan and Anna Warner (Foster), **Supp. XVIII:** 265
Susan and God (film; Cukor), **Supp. XVI:** 192
Susanna Moodie: Voice and Vision (Shields), **Supp. VII:** 313
Susan Warner ("Elizabeth Wetherell") (A. Warner), **Supp. XVIII:** 259, 260
Suspect in Poetry, The (Dickey), **Supp. IV Part 1:** 177
"Sustained by Fiction" (Hoffman), **Supp. X:** 90, 92
"Susto" (Ríos), **Supp. IV Part 2:** 553
Sutherland, Donald, **IV:** 38, 44; **Supp. IX:** 254
Sutherland, Efua, **Supp. IV Part 1:** 9, 16
Sutherland-Smith, James, **Supp. X:** 211, 212
Sut Lovingood (Harris) ?/, **Supp. XXII:** 193
Sut Lovingood's Yarns (Harris) ?/, **II:** 70
Sutton, Roger, **Supp. X:** 266
Sutton, Walter, **III:** 479
Suttree (McCarthy), **Supp. VIII: 178–180,** 189
Suvero, Mark di, **Supp. IX:** 251
Svevo, Italo, **Supp. XIV:** 112
Swados, Harvey, **Supp. XI:** 222; **Supp. XIX: 255–271**
Swales, Martin, **Supp. XIX:** 183
Swallow, Alan, **Supp. X:** 112, 115, 116, 120, 123
Swallow Barn (J. P. Kennedy), **II:** 313
Swallow Barn (Kennedy), **Supp. XXII:** 193
Swallow the Lake (Major), **Supp. XXII:** 174
"Swamp Boy" (Bass), **Supp. XVI:** 20
Swan, Barbara, **Supp. IV Part 2:** 447
Swan, Jon, **Supp. IV Part 1:** 176
Swan Lake (Tchaikovsky), **Supp. IX:** 51
"Swan Legs" (Stern), **Supp. IX:** 299
Swann (Shields), **Supp. VII:** 315, 318–323, 326
Swann, Brian, **Supp. IV Part 2:** 500
Swanson, Gloria, **II:** 429
Swanson, Stevenson, **Supp. XIV:** 111
Swanton, John Reed, **Supp. VIII:** 295
Swan Watch (Schulberg), **Supp. XVIII:** 254
Swanwick, John, **Supp. XV:** 237
Swanwick, Michael, **Supp. XVI:** 128
"Swarm, The" (Plath), **Retro. Supp. II:** 255
"Sway" (Simpson), **Supp. IX:** 276
Sweat (Hurston), **Supp. VI:** 152
Swedenborg, Emanuel, **II:** 5, 10, 321, 342, 343–344, 396
Sweeney Agonistes (Eliot), **I:** 580; **Retro. Supp. I:** 64, 65; **Retro. Supp. II:** 247
"Sweeney Among the Nightingales" (Eliot), **III:** 4
"Sweeper, The" (Kooser), **Supp. XIX:** 125
Sweet, Blanche, **Supp. I Part 2:** 391
Sweet, Timothy, **Supp. IV Part 1:** 330
Sweet and Lowdown (film; Allen), **Supp. XV:** 11
Sweet and Sour (O'Hara), **III:** 361
"Sweet Armageddon" (Hoffman), **Supp. XVIII:** 85, 86
Sweet Bird of Youth (T. Williams), **IV:** 382, 383, 385, 386, 387, 388, 389, 390, 391, 392, 395, 396, 398; **Supp. IV Part 1:** 84, 89
Sweet Charity (musical), **Supp. IV Part 2:** 575
Sweet Flypaper of Life, The (Hughes), **Supp. I Part 1:** 335–336
"Sweetheart" (Notley), **Supp. XXII:** 231
"Sweetheart of the Song Tra Bong, The" (O'Brien), **Supp. V:** 243, 249
"Sweethearts" (Ford), **Supp. V:** 69
Sweet Hereafter, The (Banks), **Supp. V:** 15–16
Sweet Lorain (Weigl), **Supp. XIX:** 282
Sweet Machine (Doty), **Supp. XI:** 121, **131–132,** 135
Sweet Sue (Gurney), **Supp. V:** 105, 107–108
Sweet Sweetback's Baadasss Song (Peebles; film), **Supp. XI:** 17
Sweet Thursday (Steinbeck), **IV:** 50, 52, 64–65
Sweet Will (Levine), **Supp. V:** 178, 187, 189, 190
"Sweet Will" (Levine), **Supp. V:** 190
"Sweet Words on Race" (Hughes), **Retro. Supp. I:** 211
Sweezy, Paul, **Supp. I Part 2:** 645
"Swell-Looking Girl, A" (Caldwell), **I:** 310
Swenson, May, **Retro. Supp. II:** 44; **Supp. IV Part 2: 637–655; Supp. XIX:** 123
Swetman, Glenn R., **Supp. XXI:** 91
"Swift" (Schwartz), **Supp. II Part 2:** 663

Swift, Jonathan, **I:** 125, 194, 209, 441; **II:** 110, 302, 304–305, 577; **III:** 113; **IV:** 68; **Retro. Supp. I:** 66; **Supp. I Part 2:** 406, 523, 603, 656, 665, 708, 714; **Supp. IV Part 1:** 51; **Supp. IV Part 2:** 692; **Supp. XI:** 105, 209; **Supp. XII:** 276; **Supp. XV:** 258; **Supp. XVI:** 110; **Supp. XVIII:** 2, 12
"Swimmer" (Francis), **Supp. IX:** 82
"Swimmer" (Skloot), **Supp. XX: 199, 200**
"Swimmer, The" (Cheever), **Supp. I Part 1:** 185, 187
"Swimmer, The" (Glück), **Supp. V:** 82
"Swimmers" (Untermeyer), **Supp. XV:** 300
"Swimmers, The" (Fitzgerald), **Retro. Supp. I:** 110, 111
"Swimmers, The" (Tate), **IV:** 136
"Swimming" (Harjo), **Supp. XII:** 218
Swinburne, Algernon C., **I:** 50, 384, 568; **II:** 3, 4, 129, 400, 524; **IV:** 135; **Retro. Supp. I:** 100; **Supp. I Part 1:** 79; **Supp. I Part 2:** 422, 552; **Supp. XIV:** 120, 344
"Swinburne as Poet" (Eliot), **I:** 576
Swinger of Birches, A: A Portrait of Robert Frost (Cox), **Retro. Supp. I:** 132
"Swinging an Arc Before Him As He Goes" (Espaillat), **Supp. XXI:** 108
"Swinging on a Birch-Tree" (Larcom), **Supp. XIII:** 147
Swiss, Tom, **Supp. XIX:** 40
Switch, The (Dixon), **Supp. XII:** 141
Swope, D. B., **Supp. IX:** 95
Sword Blades and Poppy Seed (Lowell), **II:** 518, 520, 522, 532
Sword of God, The: Jeanne D'Arc (Endore), **Supp. XVII:** 55
Sybil (Auchincloss), **Supp. IV Part 1:** 25
Sybil and Chryssa (S. and A. Warner), **Supp. XVIII:** 264
"Sycamore" (Stern), **Supp. IX:** 294
"Sycamore, The" (Moore), **III:** 216
"Sycamores, The" (Whittier), **Supp. I Part 2:** 699
Sylvester, Johnny, **Supp. I Part 2:** 438
Sylvester, Joshua, **I:** 178, 179; **II:** 18; **III:** 157; **Supp. I Part 1:** 98, 104, 114, 116
Sylvia (Gurney), **Supp. V:** 105
"Sylvia" (L. Michaels), **Supp. XVI:** 202, 213
"Sylvia" (Larcom), **Supp. XIII:** 144
"Sylvia" (Stern), **Supp. IX:** 297
Sylvia: A Fictional Memoir (L. Michaels), **Supp. XVI:** 202, 213
Sylvia Plath: Method and Madness (Butscher), **Supp. I Part 2:** 526
Sylvia Plath: Poetry and Existence (Holbrook), **Supp. I Part 2:** 526–527
"Sylvia's Death" (Sexton), **Supp. II Part 2:** 671, 684, 685
"Symbol and Image in the Shorter Poems of Herman Melville" (Dickey), **Supp. IV Part 1:** 176
Symbolist Movement in Literature, The (Symons), **I:** 50, 569; **Retro. Supp. I:** 55
Symonds, John Addington, **I:** 241, 242, 251, 259; **IV:** 334; **Supp. XIV:** 329, 335; **Supp. XX: 230**
Symons, Arthur, **I:** 50, 569; **Retro. Supp. I:** 55; **Supp. XX: 239**
Symons, Julian, **Supp. IV Part 1:** 343, 351
"Sympathy" (Dunbar), **Supp. IV Part 1:** 15
Sympathy of Souls, A (Goldbarth), **Supp. XII:** 175, 176, **186–187**
"Symphony, The" (Lanier), **Supp. I Part 1:** 352, 360–361, 364; **Supp. I Part 2:** 416
Symposium (Plato), **Retro. Supp. II:** 31; **Supp. IV Part 1:** 391
Symposium: To Kill a Mockingbird (Alabama Law Review), **Supp. VIII:** 127, 128
Symptoms and Madness (Major), **Supp. XXII:** 174
Symptoms of Being 35 (Lardner), **II:** 434
Synanon (Endore), **Supp. XVII:** 65
Synanon (film, Quine), **Supp. XVII:** 65
Synanon City (Endore), **Supp. XVII:** 65
Syncopated Cakewalk, The (Major), **Supp. XXII:** 174
Synge, John Millington, **I:** 434; **III:** 591–592; **Supp. III Part 1:** 34; **Supp. VIII:** 155
Synthetic Philosophy (Spencer), **II:** 462–463
"Syringa" (Ashbery), **Supp. III Part 1:** 19–21, 25
"Syrinx" (Clampitt), **Supp. IX:** 53
"Syrinx" (Merrill), **Supp. III Part 1:** 328
Syrkin, Marie, **Supp. XIV:** 279, 288, 291
"System, The" (Ashbery), **Supp. III Part 1:** 14, 15, 18, 21–22
System of Dante's Hell, The (Baraka), **Supp. II Part 1:** 39–41, 55
"System of Dante's Inferno, The" (Baraka), **Supp. II Part 1:** 40
"System of Doctor Tarr and Professor Fether, The" (Poe), **III:** 419, 425
System of General Geography, A (Brown), **Supp. I Part 1:** 146
Szaylay, Michael, **Supp. XXI:** 267
Sze, Mai-mai, **Supp. X:** 291
Szentgyorgyi, Tom, **Supp. IX:** 135, 136, 140, 141–142
Szulc, Tad, **Supp. XVI:** 154
Szymborka, Wislawa, **Supp. XI:** 267
Szymborska, Wislawa, **Supp. XVIII:** 29

"T-2 Tanker Blues" (Snyder), **Supp. VIII:** 294
Tabios, Eileen, **Supp. XV:** 214, 225, 226
"Table of Delectable Contents, The" (Simic), **Supp. VIII:** 276
Tabloid Dreams (R. O. Butler), **Supp. XII: 70–72,** 74
Tacey Cromwell (Richter), **Supp. XVIII: 211,** 215, 217
Tacitus, Cornelius, **I:** 485; **II:** 113
Tadic, Novica, **Supp. VIII:** 272
Taft (Patchett), **Supp. XII:** 307, 312, **314–317**
"Tag" (Hughes), **Supp. I Part 1:** 341
Taggard, Genevieve, **IV:** 436; **Supp. XXII: 271–287**
Taggart, John, **Supp. IV Part 2:** 421
Tagore, Rabindranath, **I:** 383; **Supp. XX: 117**
"Taibele and Her Demon" (Singer), **Retro. Supp. II:** 307
Taibl, Erika, **Supp. XV:** 255
"Tailor Shop, The" (H. Miller), **III:** 175
"Tails" (Dixon), **Supp. XII:** 154
Taine, Hippolyte, **I:** 503; **II:** 271; **III:** 323; **IV:** 440, 444
"Tain't So" (Hughes), **Supp. I Part 1:** 330
"Taipei Tangle" (Halliday), **Supp. XIX:** 91
Takasago (play), **III:** 466
Take Away the Darkness (Bynner), **Supp. XV:** 51
Take Heart (Peacock), **Supp. XIX: 197–199,** 206
Take Me Back: A Novel (Bausch), **Supp. VII:** 41, 43–45, 46, 49
"Take My Saddle from the Wall: A Valediction" (McMurtry), **Supp. V:** 219
"'Take No for an Answer' " (Didion), **Supp. IV Part 1:** 203
"Take Pity" (Malamud), **Supp. I Part 2:** 427, 428, 435, 436, 437
"Takers, The" (Olds), **Supp. X:** 205
"Take the I Out" (Olds), **Supp. X:** 213
Take the Money and Run (film; Allen), **Supp. XV: 3–4,** 6
"Taking Away the Name of a Nephew" (Ríos), **Supp. IV Part 2:** 545–546
Taking Care of Mrs. Carroll (Monette), **Supp. X:** 153
"Taking of Captain Ball, The" (Jewett), **Retro. Supp. II:** 134
"Taking Off Emily Dickinson's Clothes" (Collins), **Supp. XXI:** 59, 60
"Taking Out the Lawn Chairs" (Karr), **Supp. XI:** 241
"Taking the Bypass" (J. Epstein), **Supp. XIV:** 110; **Supp. XVI:** 230
"Taking the Forest" (Howe), **Supp. IV Part 2:** 433
"Taking the Lambs to Market" (Kumin), **Supp. IV Part 2:** 455
Talbot, Daniel, **Supp. XIX:** 264
"Tale, A" (Bogan), **Supp. III Part 1:** 50, 51
Taleb-Khyar, Mohamed, **Supp. IV Part 1:** 242, 243, 244, 247, 257
Talented Mr. Ripley, The (Highsmith), **Supp. XXII:** 119
"Tale of Jerusalem, A" (Poe), **III:** 411
Tale of Possessors Self-Dispossessed, A (O'Neill), **III:** 404
Tale of the Body Thief, The (Rice), **Supp. VII:** 290, 293–294, 297
Tale of Two Cities, A (film), **Supp. I Part 1:** 67
"Tale of Two Liars, A" (Singer), **IV:** 12
Tales (Baraka), **Supp. II Part 1:** 39, 55
Tales (Poe), **III:** 413
Tales and Stories for Black Folks (Bambara, ed.), **Supp. XI:** 1
Tales before Midnight (Benét), **Supp. XI:** 46, 53, 57

Talese, Gay, **Supp. XVI:** 273; **Supp. XVII: 199–211**
Tales of a Traveller (Irving), **II:** 309–310
Tales of a Wayside Inn (Longfellow), **II:** 489, 490, 501, 502, 504–505; **Retro. Supp. II:** 154, **162–165**
Tales of Glauber-Spa (Bryant, ed.), **Supp. I Part 1:** 157
Tales of Manhattan (Auchincloss), **Supp. IV Part 1:** 23
Tales of Men and Ghosts (Wharton), **IV:** 315; **Retro. Supp. I:** 372
Tales of Rhoda, The (Rice), **Supp. VII:** 288
Tales of Soldiers and Civilians (Bierce), **I:** 200–203, 204, 206, 208, 212
Tales of the Argonauts (Harte), **Supp. II Part 1:** 337, 348, 351
Tales of the Fish Patrol (London), **II:** 465
Tales of the Grotesque and Arabesque (Poe), **II:** 273; **III:** 412, 415; **Retro. Supp. II:** 270
Tales of the Jazz Age (Fitzgerald), **II:** 88; **Retro. Supp. I:** 105; **Supp. IX:** 57
Tales You Won't Believe (Stratton-Porter), **Supp. XX: 217**
Taliaferro, Frances, **Supp. XXII:** 210
"Talisman, A" (Moore), **III:** 195–196
Talisman, The (King), **Supp. V:** 140, 144, 152
"Talkin Bout Sonny" (Bambara), **Supp. XI:** 6–7
"Talking" (Merwin), **Supp. III Part 1:** 354
Talking All Morning (R. Bly), **Supp. IV Part 1:** 59, 60, 61, 62, 64, 65
Talking Dirty to the Gods (Komunyakaa), **Supp. XIII: 130–131**
Talking History (television program), **Supp. XXI:** 172
"Talking Horse" (Malamud), **Supp. I Part 2:** 435
Talking Soft Dutch (McCarriston), **Supp. XIV: 260–263,** 266, 270, 271
"Talking to Barr Creek" (Wagoner), **Supp. IX:** 328
"Talking to Sheep" (Sexton), **Supp. II Part 2:** 695
Talking to the Sun: An Illustrated Anthology of Poems for Young People (Koch and Farrell, eds.), **Supp. XV:** 188
"Talking Water" (Taggard), **Supp. XXII:** 276
"Talk of Heroes" (C. Bly), **Supp. XVI:** 34
"Talk of the Town" (*The New Yorker* column), **IV:** 215; **Supp. IV Part 1:** 53, 54
"Talk on Guadalcanal" (Wolfert), **Supp. XXI:** 264
Talk Talk (Boyle), **Supp. XX: 24**
"Talk with the Yellow Kid, A" (Bellow), **I:** 151
Tallent, Elizabeth, **Supp. IV Part 2:** 570
Tallman, Warren, **Supp. IV Part 1:** 154
TallMountain, Mary, **Supp. IV Part 1:** 324–325
Talma, Louise, **IV:** 357
Talmadge, Constance, **Supp. XVI:** 186, 187, 196
Talmadge, Norma, **Supp. XVI:** 186, 187, 196
Talmadge Girls, The (Loos), **Supp. XVI:** 186, 196
Talmey, Allene, **Supp. IV Part 1:** 197; **Supp. XIII:** 172
Talmud, **IV:** 8, 17
Taltos: Lives of the Mayfair Witches (Rice), **Supp. VII:** 299–300
"Tamar" (Jeffers), **Supp. II Part 2:** 427–428, 436
Tamar and Other Poems (Jeffers), **Supp. II Part 2:** 416, 419
Tambourines to Glory (Hughes), **Supp. I Part 1:** 338–339
"Tame Indians" (Jewett), **Retro. Supp. II:** 141
"Tamerlane" (Poe), **III:** 426
Tamerlane and Other Poems (Poe), **III:** 410
"Tammany Man, The" (Hapgood), **Supp. XVII:** 103
"Tam O'Shanter" (Burns), **II:** 306
Tamsen Donner: A Woman's Journey (Whitman), **Supp. XXI:** 246
Tan, Amy, **Supp. X: 289–300**
Tangential Views (Bierce), **I:** 209
"Tangier 1975" (Bowles), **Supp. IV Part 1:** 94
"Tankas" (McClatchy), **Supp. XII:** 266
Tanner, Laura E., **Supp. X:** 209; **Supp. XXI:** 217
Tanner, Obour, **Supp. XX: 281, 288**
Tanner, Tony, **I:** 260, 261; **Retro. Supp. II:** 205; **Supp. IV Part 1:** 285; **Supp. XVI:** 65, 69
Tannhäuser (Wagner), **I:** 315
"Tan Ta Ra, Cries Mars...," (Wagoner), **Supp. IX:** 325
Tao of Physics, The (Capra), **Supp. X:** 261
Tao Teh Ching (Bynner, trans.), **Supp. XV:** 46, 47
Tapahonso, Luci, **Supp. IV Part 1:** 404; **Supp. IV Part 2:** 499, 508
Tape for the Turn of the Year (Ammons), **Supp. VII:** 31–33, 35
"Tapestry" (Ashbery), **Supp. III Part 1:** 22–23
"Tapestry" (P. E. Jones), **Supp. XXII:** 152
"Tapiama" (Bowles), **Supp. IV Part 1:** 89–90
"Tapiola" (W. C. Williams), **Retro. Supp. I:** 429
Tappan, Arthur, **Supp. I Part 2:** 588
Tapping the White Cane of Solitude (F. Wright), **Supp. XVII:** 243
Taps at Reveille (Fitzgerald), **II:** 94, 96; **Retro. Supp. I:** 113
Tar: A Midwest Childhood (Anderson), **I:** 98, 115; **II:** 27
Tarantino, Quentin, **Supp. IV Part 1:** 356
Tarantula (Dylan), **Supp. XVIII:** 21, 29, **31–32**
Tar Baby (Morrison), **Supp. III Part 1:** 364, 369–372, 379; **Supp. IV Part 1:** 13
Tarbell, Ida, **III:** 322, 580; **Retro. Supp. II:** 101
"Target Practice" (Offutt), **Supp. XIX:** 171
"Target Study" (Baraka), **Supp. II Part 1:** 49–50, 54
Tarkington, Booth, **II:** 444; **III:** 70; **Retro. Supp. I:** 100; **Supp. XV:** 41
Tarnawsky, Yuriy (George) Orest, **Supp. XX: 259**
Tarpon (film), **Supp. VIII:** 42
Tarr, Rodger L., **Supp. X:** 222, 224, 226
Tárrega, Francisco, **Supp. XXI:** 100
Tartt, Donna, **Supp. XVIII:** 135
Tartuffe (Molière; Wilbur, trans.), **Supp. III Part 2:** 560
Tarumba, Selected Poems of Jaime Sabines (Levine and Trejo, trans.), **Supp. V:** 178
Tarzan Finds a Son (film, Weismuller), **Supp. XX: 18**
"Tarzan Is an Expatriate" (Theroux), **Supp. VIII:** 313
Tasis, Juan de, **Supp. XXI:** 104
Task, The (Cowper), **II:** 304
Tasker Street (Halliday), **Supp. XIX:** 82, **87–89**
Tasso, Torquato, **I:** 276
Taste of Palestine, A: Menus and Memories (Shihab), **Supp. XIII:** 273
Tate, Alan, **Supp. XV:** 141
Tate, Allen, **I:** 48, 49, 50, 67, 69, 381, 382, 386, 390, 396, 397, 399, 402, 441, 468; **II:** 197–198, 367, 536, 537, 542, 551, 554; **III:** 424, 428, 454, 482, 483, 485, 493, 495, 496, 497, 499, 500, 517; **IV: 120–143,** 236, 237, 433; **Retro. Supp. I:** 37, 41, 90; **Retro. Supp. II:** 77, 79, 82, 83, 89, 176, 178, 179; **Supp. I Part 1:** 364, 371; **Supp. I Part 2:** 423; **Supp. II Part 1:** 90–91, 96, 98, 103–104, 136, 139, 144, 150, 151, 318; **Supp. II Part 2:** 643; **Supp. III Part 2:** 542; **Supp. V:** 315, 331; **Supp. X:** 1, 52; **Supp. XIV:** 2; **Supp. XXI:** 256; **Supp. XXII:** 277
Tate, Mrs. Allen (Caroline Gordon). *See* Gordon, Caroline
Tate, Mrs. Allen (Helen Heinz), **IV:** 127
Tate, Mrs. Allen (Isabella Gardner), **IV:** 127
Tate, Benjamin Lewis Bogan, **IV:** 127
Tate, Greg, **Supp. XIII:** 233, 237
Tate, James, **Supp. V:** 92, 338; **Supp. VIII:** 39, 279; **Supp. XV:** 250; **Supp. XVII:** 242
Tate, John Allen, **IV:** 127
Tate, Michael Paul, **IV:** 127
Tate, Nancy, **II:** 197
Tattooed Countess, The (Van Vechten), **I:** 295; **Supp. II Part 2:** 726–728, 738, 742
Tattooed Feet (Nye), **Supp. XIII:** 274
"Tattoos" (McClatchy), **Supp. XII:** 266–267, 268
"Tattoos" (Wright), **Supp. V:** 335, 340
Tatum, Anna, **I:** 516
Tatum, James, **Supp. IV Part 2:** 684
Taupin, René, **II:** 528, 529; **Supp. III Part 2:** 614, 615, 617, 621
Tavano, John, **Supp. XXI:** 99

Tawney, Richard Henry, **Supp. I Part 2:** 481
Taylor, Bayard, **II:** 275; **Supp. I Part 1:** 350, 361, 362, 365, 366, 372; **Supp. XV:** 269
Taylor, Cora. *See* Howarth, Cora
Taylor, Deems, **III:** 138
Taylor, Edward, **III:** 493; **IV: 144–166; Supp. I Part 1:** 98; **Supp. I Part 2:** 375, 386, 546
Taylor, Mrs. Edward (Elizabeth Fitch), **IV:** 147, 165
Taylor, Mrs. Edward (Ruth Wyllys), **IV:** 148
Taylor, Eleanor Ross, **Supp. V:** 317, 318
Taylor, Elizabeth, **II:** 588
Taylor, Frank, **III:** 81
Taylor, Frederick Winslow, **Supp. I Part 2:** 644
Taylor, Graham, **Supp. I Part 1:** 5
Taylor, Henry, **Retro. Supp. I:** 212; **Supp. XI:** 317; **Supp. XIII:** 333
Taylor, Henry W., **IV:** 144
Taylor, Jeremy, **II:** 11; **III:** 487; **Supp. I Part 1:** 349; **Supp. XII:** 45; **Supp. XIV:** 344, 345
Taylor, John, **IV:** 149
Taylor, Katherine, **Supp. VIII:** 251
Taylor, Kezia, **IV:** 148
Taylor, Nathaniel W., **Supp. I Part 2:** 580
Taylor, Paul, **I:** 293
Taylor, Peter, **Retro. Supp. II:** 179; **Supp. V: 313–329; Supp. XIV:** 3
Taylor, Raynor, **Supp. XV:** 238
Taylor, Richard, **IV:** 146
Taylor, Robert, **Supp. I Part 1:** 294; **Supp. XV:** 135, 138; **Supp. XVI:** 277
Taylor, Samuel A., **Supp. XX: 253**
Taylor, Stephan, **Supp. XVI:** 203
Taylor, Thomas, **II:** 10
Taylor, William, **IV:** 145–146
Taylor, Zachary, **I:** 3; **II:** 433–434
Tchelitchew, Peter, **II:** 586
Tea and Sympathy (Anderson), **Supp. I Part 1:** 277; **Supp. V:** 108
"Tea at the Palaz of Hoon" (Stevens), **Retro. Supp. I:** 300, 302, 306
"Teacher's Pet" (Thurber), **Supp. I Part 2:** 605–606
"Teaching and Story Telling" (Maclean), **Supp. XIV:** 234
Teaching a Stone to Talk: Expeditions and Encounters (Dillard), **Supp. VI:** 23, 26, 28, 32, 33, 34–35
"Teaching Hanh the Blues" (Weigl), **Supp. XIX:** 287
Teachings of Don B., The (Barthelme), **Supp. IV Part 1:** 53
Teachout, Terry, **Supp. XIX:** 137
Teale, Edwin Way, **Supp. XIII:** 7
Teall, Dorothy, **I:** 221
Team Team Team (film), **Supp. IX:** 251
"Tea on the Mountain" (Bowles), **Supp. IV Part 1:** 90
"Tea Party, The" (MacLeish), **III:** 11
Tear and a Smile, A (Dam'a wa Ibtisáma) (Gibran), **Supp. XX: 116, 118, 124**
Teare, Brian, **Supp. XXII:** 236
"Tears, Idle Tears" (Lord Tennyson), **Supp. XIV:** 8
"Tears of the Pilgrims, The" (McClatchy), **Supp. XII:** 256
Teasdale, Sara, **Retro. Supp. I:** 133; **Supp. I Part 2:** 393, 707; **Supp. XIV:** 127; **Supp. XV:** 295, 297, 301, 305, 307, 308; **Supp. XVII:** 69, 75
"Tease" (Swados), **Supp. XIX:** 267
Tebeaux, Elizabeth, **Supp. IX:** 109
"Technical Manifesto of Futurist Literature" (Marinetti), **Supp. XXII:** 161
Technics and Civilization (Mumford), **Supp. I Part 2:** 638; **Supp. II Part 2:** 479, 493, 497
Technics and Human Development (Mumford), **Supp. I Part 2:** 638; **Supp. II Part 2:** 497
"Technology, The" (Egan), **Supp. XIX:** 61
"Teddy" (Salinger), **III:** 561–563, 571
"Te Deum" (Reznikoff), **Supp. XIV:** 281
Tedlock, Dennis, **Supp. IV Part 2:** 509
"Teeth Mother Naked at Last, The" (R. Bly), **Supp. IV Part 1:** 63, 68, 73
Teggart, Richard, **Supp. I Part 2:** 650
Tegnér, Esaias, **Retro. Supp. II:** 155
Teilhard de Chardin, Pierre, **Supp. I Part 1:** 314
Telephone, The (film), **Supp. XI:** 309
"Telephone Call, A" (Parker), **Supp. IX: 202–203**
"Telephone Number of the Muse, The" (Justice), **Supp. VII:** 124–125
Telephone Poles and Other Poems (Updike), **IV:** 214, 215
"Television" (Beattie), **Supp. V:** 33
Teller, Edward, **I:** 137
"Telling" (Ortiz), **Supp. IV Part 2:** 509
"Telling It in Black and White: The Importance of the Africanist Presence in *To Kill a Mockingbird*" (Baecker), **Supp. VIII:** 128
Telling Secrets (Buechner), **Supp. XII:** 53–54
Telling Stories (Didion), **Supp. IV Part 1:** 197
"Telling Stories" (Didion), **Supp. IV Part 1:** 197
"Telling the Bees" (Whittier), **Supp. I Part 2:** 694–695
Telling the Little Secrets (J. Burstein), **Supp. XVII:** 44
Telling the Truth: The Gospel as Tragedy, Comedy, and Fairy Tale (Buechner), **Supp. XII:** 53
"Tell Me" (Hughes), **Supp. VIII:** 213
"Tell Me, Sir, ... What Is 'Black' Literature?" (H. L. Gates), **Supp. XX: 108**
Tell Me, Tell Me (Moore), **III:** 215
Tell Me Again (Notley), **Supp. XXII:** 224, 230–231
Tell Me Again How the White Heron Rises and Flies across the Nacreous River at Twilight toward the Distant Islands (Carruth), **Supp. XVI:**56
Tell Me a Riddle (film), **Supp. XIII:** 295
Tell Me a Riddle (Olsen), **Supp. XIII:** 294, 296, **298–302,** 303, 305
"Tell Me a Riddle" (Olsen), **Supp. XIII:** 294, 297, 298, **300–302,** 305
"Tell Me a Story" (McDermott), **Supp. XVIII:** 177
Tell Me How Long the Train's Been Gone (Baldwin), **Retro. Supp. II:** 9, **11–12,** 14; **Supp. I Part 1:** 48, 52, 63–65, 67
"Tell Me My Fortune" (Epstein), **Supp. XII:** 163
Tell Me True: Memoir, History, and Writing a Life (Hampl and May, eds.), **Supp. XXII:** 81–82, 84, **94–95**
Tell Me Your Answer True (Sexton), **Supp. II Part 2:** 683
Tell My Horse (Hurston), **Supp. VI:** 149, 156, 158
"Tell-Tale Heart, The" (Poe), **III:** 413, 414–415, 416; **Retro. Supp. II:** 267, 269, 270
"Tell the Women We're Going" (Carver), **Supp. III Part 1:** 138, 144
"Telluride Blues—A Hatchet Job" (Abbey), **Supp. XIII:** 10
Telushkin, Dvorah, **Retro. Supp. II:** 317
Temblor (Howe), **Supp. IV Part 2:** 431
Tempering of Eugene O'Neill, The (D. Alexander), **Supp. XVII:** 99
"Temper of Steel, The" (Jones), **Supp. XI:** 218
Tempers, The (W. C. Williams), **Retro. Supp. I: 413–414,** 415, 416, 424
Tempest, The (Shakespeare), **I:** 394; **II:** 12; **III:** 40, 61, 263; **Retro. Supp. I:** 61; **Supp. IV Part 2:** 463; **Supp. V:** 302–303; **Supp. XII:** 54–57; **Supp. XV:** 255, 256
Temple, Minnie, **II:** 323
Temple, The (Herbert), **IV:** 145, 153
Temple, William, **III:** 303
Temple House (E. Stoddard), **Supp. XV:** 273, **284–286**
Temple of My Familiar, The (Walker), **Supp. III Part 2:** 521, 527, 529, 535, 537; **Supp. IV Part 1:** 14
"Temple of the Holy Ghost, A" (O'Connor), **III:** 344, 352; **Retro. Supp. II:** 232
Templin, Charlotte, **Supp. V:** 116
Temporary Shelter (Gordon), **Supp. IV Part 1:** 299, 305–307
"Temporary Shelter" (Gordon), **Supp. IV Part 1:** 306
Temptation Game, The (Gardner), **Supp. VI:** 72
"Temptation of St. Anthony, The" (Barthelme), **Supp. IV Part 1:** 47
Temptations, The, **Supp. X:** 242
"10 Best Weathers of 1983, The" (Notley), **Supp. XXII:** 224
"10 Things I Do Every Day" (Berrigan), **Supp. XXII:** 224
"Tenancy, A" (Merrill), **Supp. III Part 1:** 322, 323
"Tenant" (Hoffman), **Supp. XVIII:** 86
Tenants, The (Malamud), **Supp. I Part 2:** 448–450
"Ten Best Issues of Comic Books, The" (Notley), **Supp. XXII:** 224
Ten Commandments (McClatchy), **Supp. XII: 262–265**

Ten Days That Shook the World (Reed), **II:** 577; **Supp. X:** 136; **Supp. XVIII:** 225
Tendencies in Modern American Poetry (Lowell), **II:** 529
"Tender, Hilarious Reminiscences of Life in Mythical Lake Wobegon" (MacDougall), **Supp. XVI:** 174
Tender Buttons (G. Stein), **I:** 103, 105; **IV:** 27, 42–43; **Retro. Supp. II:** 331; **Supp. XV:** 347
"Tenderfoot" (Haines), **Supp. XII:** 209
Tender Is the Night (Fitzgerald), **I:** 375; **II:** 79, 84, 91, 95–96, 97, 98, 420; **Retro. Supp. I:** 105, 108, 109, **110–112,** 114; **Supp. IX:** 59, 60, 61; **Supp. XV:** 197; **Supp. XXI:** 11
"Tenderloin" (Crane), **I:** 408
"Tenderly" (Dobyns), **Supp. XIII:** 86–87
'Tender Man, A" (Bambara), **Supp. XI:** 9–10
"Tenderness" (Dunn), **Supp. XI:** 149, 150
"Tender Offer, The" (Auchincloss), **Supp. IV Part 1:** 34
"Tender Organizations, The" (C. Bly), **Supp. XVI:** 40, 42
"Tenebrae" (Komunyakaa), **Supp. XIII:** 132
Tenenbaum, Joseph, **Supp. XX: 253**
"Ten Forty-Four" (Kingsolver), **Supp. VII:** 208
Ten Indians (Bell), **Supp. X:** 7, **12**
Ten Introductions: A Collection of Modern Verse (Taggard and Fitts, ed.), **Supp. XXII:** 281
Tennant, Agnieszka, **Supp. XX: 140**
"Ten Neglected American Writers Who Deserve to Be Better Known" (Cantor), **Supp. IV Part 1:** 285
Tennent, Gilbert, **I:** 546
Tennessee Day in St. Louis (Taylor), **Supp. V:** 324
"Tennessee's Partner" (Harte), **Supp. II Part 1:** 345, 348–350
"Tennis" (Pinsky), **Supp. VI:** 241, 242
Tennis Court Oath, The (Ashbery), **Supp. III Part 1:** 7, 9, 12, 14, 26
Ten North Frederick (O'Hara), **III:** 361
Tennyson, Alfred, Lord, **I:** 587–588; **II:** 18, 82, 273, 338, 404, 439, 604; **III:** 5, 409, 469, 485, 511, 521, 523; **Retro. Supp. I:** 100, 325; **Retro. Supp. II:** 135; **Supp. I Part 1:** 349, 356; **Supp. I Part 2:** 410, 416, 552; **Supp. IX:** 19; **Supp. X:** 157; **Supp. XIII:** 111; **Supp. XIV:** 40, 120; **Supp. XV:** 275; **Supp. XVIII:** 78
"Tenochtitlan" (Bronk), **Supp. XXI:** 31
"Ten O'Clock News" (Ortiz), **Supp. IV Part 2:** 503–504
Ten Poems (Dove), **Supp. IV Part 1:** 244
Ten Poems of Francis Ponge Translated by Robert Bly and Ten Poems of Robert Bly Inspired by the Poems by Francis Ponge (R. Bly), **Supp. IV Part 1:** 71
"Tension in Poetry" (Tate), **IV:** 128, 129, 135
Tenth Muse, The (Bradstreet), **Supp. I Part 1:** 102, 103, 114
10,000 Days of Thunder: A History of the Vietnam War (Caputo), **Supp. XIX:** 29
"Tent on the Beach, The" (Whittier), **Supp. I Part 2:** 703
"Teodoro Luna Confesses after Years to His Brother, Anselmo the Priest, Who Is Required to Understand, But Who Understands Anyway, More Than People Think" (Ríos), **Supp. IV Part 2:** 552
Teodoro Luna's Two Kisses (Ríos), **Supp. IV Part 2:** 550–552, 553
"Tepeyac" (Cisneros), **Supp. VII:** 69
"Terce" (Auden), **Supp. II Part 1:** 22
Terence, **IV:** 155, 363; **Supp. I Part 2:** 405
Terkel, Studs, **Supp. IV Part 1:** 364
"Term" (Merwin), **Supp. III Part 1:** 356–357
"Terminal Days at Beverly Farms" (Lowell), **Retro. Supp. II:** 189
Terminating, or Sonnet LXXV, or "Lass Meine Schmerzen nicht verloren sein, or Ambivalence" (Kushner), Supp. IX: 132
Terminations (James), **Retro. Supp. I:** 229
"Terminus" (Emerson), **II:** 13, 19
"Terminus" (Wharton), **Retro. Supp. I:** 371
"Terms in Which I Think of Reality, The" (Ginsberg), **Supp. II Part 1:** 311
Terms of Endearment (film), **Supp. V:** 226
Terms of Endearment (McMurtry), **Supp. V:** 224–225
"Terrace, The" (Wilbur), **Supp. III Part 2:** 550
Terrarium (Sanders), **Supp. XVI:** 270
"Terrence McNally" (Bryer), **Supp. XIII:** 200
"Terrence McNally" (Di Gaetani), **Supp. XIII:** 200
Terrence McNally: A Casebook (Zinman), **Supp. XIII:** 209
"Terrible Peacock, The" (Barnes), **Supp. III Part 1:** 33
Terrible Threes, The (Reed), **Supp. X:** 241, 253
Terrible Twos, The (Reed), **Supp. X:** 241, **252–253**
"Terrific Mother" (Moore), **Supp. X:** 178
Territory Ahead, The (Morris), **III:** 228–229, 236
Terrorism (Wright), **Supp. XV:** 341, 342
"Terrorism" (Wright), **Supp. XV:** 341
Terry, Edward A., **II:** 128, 129
Terry, Rose, **Supp. I Part 2:** 420
Tertium Organum (Ouspensky), **I:** 383; **Supp. XX: 116**
Tess of the d'Ubervilles (Hardy), **II:** 181; **Retro. Supp. II:** 100
"Testament" (Berry), **Supp. X:** 36
"Testament" (Carruth), **Supp. XVI:** 59
"Testament (Or, Homage to Walt Whitman)" (Jong), **Supp. V:** 130
"Testament of Flood" (Warren), **IV:** 253
Testament of François Villon, The (Pound, opera), **Retro. Supp. I:** 287
"Testament: Vermeer in December" (Bierds), **Supp. XVII:** 33
"Testimonia on the Question of Stesichoros' Blinding by Helen" (Carson), **Supp. XII:** 107
"Testimonies of a Roasted Chicken" (Jarman), **Supp. XVII:** 120
"Testimony" (Komunyakaa), **Supp. XIII:** 129
"Testimony of James Apthorp, The" (Kees), **Supp. XV:** 146
Testimony: The United States (1885–1890): Recitative (Reznikoff), **Supp. XIV:** 279, 280, 281, 285, **289–291**
Testimony: The United States (1891–1900): Recitative (Reznikoff), **Supp. XIV:** 291
Testing-Tree, The (Kunitz), **Supp. III Part 1:** 260, 263, 264, 267, 268
"Testing-Tree, The" (Kunitz), **Supp. III Part 1:** 269
Test of Poetry, A (Zukofsky), **Supp. III Part 2:** 618, 622
"Teutonic Scholar" (X. J. Kennedy), **Supp. XV:** 161
"Texas Moon, and Elsewhere, The" (McMurtry), **Supp. V:** 225
Texas Poets in Concert: A Quartet (Gwynn, ed.), **Supp. XIII:** 277
Texas Summer (Southern), **Supp. XI:** 309
Texasville (McMurtry), **Supp. V:** 228, 233
Thacher, Molly Day, **IV:** 381
Thackeray, William Makepeace, **I:** 194, 354; **II:** 182, 271, 282, 288, 316, 321, 322; **III:** 64, 70; **IV:** 326; **Retro. Supp. I:** 218; **Supp. I Part 1:** 307; **Supp. I Part 2:** 421, 495, 579; **Supp. IV Part 1:** 297; **Supp. IX:** 200; **Supp. XI:** 277; **Supp. XIV:** 306; **Supp. XX: 228**
Thaddeus, Janice Farrar, **Supp. IV Part 1:** 299
"Thailand" (Barthelme), **Supp. IV Part 1:** 41
Thalberg, Irving, **Retro. Supp. I:** 109, 110, 114; **Supp. XVI:** 191, 192
Thales, **I:** 480–481
Thalia Trilogy (McMurtry), **Supp. V:** 220–223, 234
Tham, Claire, **Supp. VIII:** 79
"Thanatopsis" (Bryant), **Supp. I Part 1:** 150, 154, 155, 170
Thanatos Syndrome, The (Percy), **Supp. III Part 1:** 385, 397–399
"Thanks Can Be Named to Death" (Peacock), **Supp. XIX:** 199
"Thanksgiving" (Glück), **Supp. V:** 83
"Thanksgiving, A" (Auden), **Supp. II Part 1:** 26
"Thanksgiving for a Habitat" (Auden), **Supp. II Part 1:** 24
Thanksgivings (Traherne), **Supp. XVI:** 288
"Thanksgiving Spirit" (Farrell), **II:** 45
Thanksgiving Visitor, The (Capote), **Supp. III Part 1:** 116, 118, 119

"Thank You, Esther Forbes" (Saunders), **Supp. XIX:** 235
Thank You, Fog (Auden), **Supp. II Part 1:** 24
"Thank You, Lord" (Angelou), **Supp. IV Part 1:** 15
Thank You, Mr. Moto (Marquand), **III:** 57, 58
Thank You and Other Poems (Koch), **Supp. XV:** 180–181
"Thank You in Arabic" (Nye), **Supp. XIII:** 273, 281
"Thar's More in the Man Than Thar Is in the Land" (Lanier), **Supp. I Part 1:** 352–353, 359–360
"That Evening Sun" (Faulkner), **II:** 72; **Retro. Supp. I:** 75, 83
That Horse (Hogan), **Supp. IV Part 1:** 397, 404, 405
"That House, This Room" (W. V. Davis), **Supp. XXI:** 90
"That I Had the Wings" (Ellison), **Supp. II Part 1:** 238
That Night (McDermott), **Supp. XVIII:** 155, **158–160,** 162, 163, 166
"That's the Place Indians Talk About" (Ortiz), **Supp. IV Part 2:** 511
That Tantalus (Bronk), **Supp. XXI:** 31
"That the Soul May Wax Plump" (Swenson), **Supp. IV Part 2:** 650
"That the Universe Is Chrysalid" (Sobin), **Supp. XVI:** 284
"That Tree" (Porter), **III:** 434–435, 446, 451
That Was the Week That Was (television program), **Supp. XIV:** 125
"That Year" (Olds), **Supp. X:** 203
"Thaw" (C. Frost), **Supp. XV:** 93, 104, 105
Thaxter, Celia, **Retro. Supp. II:** 136, 147; **Supp. XIII:** 143, 153
Thayer, Abbott, **I:** 231
Thayer, Scofield, **I:** 231; **Retro. Supp. I:** 58
Thayer and Eldridge, **Retro. Supp. I:** 403
"Theater" (Toomer), **Supp. IX:** 309, 317–318
"Theater Chronicle" (McCarthy), **II:** 562
"Theater Problems? Call Dr. Chekhov" (Wasserstein), **Supp. XV:** 320
Theatricals (James), **Retro. Supp. I:** 228
The Blacker the Berry: A Novel of Negro Life (Thurman), **Supp. XVIII:** 281; **Supp. XIX:** 73
"Theft" (Porter), **III:** 434, 435
Theft, A (Bellow), **Retro. Supp. II:** 31–32, 34
The Harder They Fall (Schulberg), **Supp. XVIII: 247,** 253
The Harder They Fall: Celebrities Tell Their Real-Life Stories of Addiction and Recovery (F. Wright), **Supp. XVII:** 240
Their Eyes Were Watching God (Hurston), **Supp. VI:** 149, 152, 156–157; **Supp. XX: 107**
Their Heads Are Green and Their Hands Are Blue: Scenes from the Non-Christian World (Bowles), **Supp. IV Part 1:** 89
"Their Losses" (Taylor), **Supp. V:** 320
"Their Sleep" (W. V. Davis), **Supp. XXI:** 93
Their Wedding Journey (Howells), **II:** 277–278; **Retro. Supp. I:** 334
them (Oates), **Supp. II Part 2:** 503, 511–514
Theme Is Freedom, The (Dos Passos), **I:** 488–489, 492, 494
Theme Time Radio Hour (radio show, Dylan), **Supp. XVIII:** 28
"Theme with Variations" (Agee), **I:** 27
"Then" (Barthelme), **Supp. IV Part 1:** 48
"Then as Now" (Cliff), **Supp. XXII:** 76
"The Night Rhonda Ferguson Was Killed" (P. E. Jones), **Supp. XXII:** 144
"Then It All Came Down" (Capote), **Supp. III Part 1:** 125, 131
Theocritus, **II:** 169; **Retro. Supp. I:** 286
"Theodore the Poet" (Masters), **Supp. I Part 2:** 461
Theological Position, A (Coover), **Supp. V:** 44
Theophrastus, **I:** 58
"Theoretical and Scientific Conceptions of Race, The" (Locke), **Supp. XIV:** 209
"Theories of Time and Space" (Trethewey), **Supp. XXI:** 255
Theory and Practice of Rivers and Other Poems, The (Harrison), **Supp. VIII:** 47, 49
Theory of Business Enterprise, The (Veblen), **Supp. I Part 2:** 638, 641, 644
Theory of Flight (Rukeyser), **Supp. VI:** 272, 275, **277–278,** 284
"Theory of Flight" (Rukeyser), **Supp. VI:** 277–278
Theory of Moral Sentiments, The (A. Smith), **Supp. I Part 2:** 634
Theory of the Leisure Class, The (Veblen), **I:** 475–476; **Supp. I Part 2:** 629, 633, 641, 645; **Supp. IV Part 1:** 22
"There" (Taylor), **Supp. V:** 323
"There Are No Such Trees in Alpine California" (Haines), **Supp. XII:** 207
"There Goes (Varoom! Varoom!) That Kandy-Kolored Tangerine-Flake Streamline Baby" (Wolfe), **Supp. III Part 2:** 569–571
"There Have Been Changes" (Pickering), **Supp. XXI:** 202–203
"There Is a Lesson" (Olsen), **Supp. XIII:** 292, 297
"There is a Man" (Espaillat), **Supp. XXI:** 108–109
"There Is Only One of Everything" (Atwood), **Supp. XIII:** 34
There Is Something Out There (McNally). *See And Things That Go Bump in the Night* (McNally)
"There Must Be" (Peacock), **Supp. XIX:** 199
"There's a certain Slant of light" (Dickinson), **Retro. Supp. I:** 38
There's a Wocket in My Pocket! (Geisel), **Supp. XVI:** 111
Thérèse de Lisieux, Saint, **Supp. VIII:** 195
"There She Is She Is Taking Her Bath" (Anderson), **I:** 113, 114
"There Was a Child Went Forth" (Whitman), **IV:** 348
"There Was a Man, There Was a Woman" (Cisneros), **Supp. VII:** 70
"There Was an Old Woman She Had So Many Children She Didn't Know What to Do" (Cisneros), **Supp. VII:** 60
"There Was a Youth Whose Name Was Thomas Granger" (Olson), **Supp. II Part 2:** 558, 560, 563
There Were Giants in the Land (Benét), **Supp. XI:** 50
There You Are (Simpson), **Supp. IX: 279–280**
"There You Are" (Simpson), **Supp. IX:** 279
"Thermopylae" (Clampitt), **Supp. IX:** 43
Theroux, Alexander, **Supp. VIII:** 312
Theroux, Marcel, **Supp. VIII:** 325
Theroux, Paul, **Supp. V:** 122; **Supp. VIII: 309–327**
"These Are My People" (Hayden), **Supp. II Part 1:** 365
"These are the days when Birds come back" (Dickinson), **Retro. Supp. I:** 30
"These Days" (Olds), **Supp. X:** 215
"These Flames and Generosities of the Heart: Emily Dickinson and the Illogic of Sumptuary Values" (Howe), **Supp. IV Part 2:** 431
"These Hands" (Brockmeier), **Supp. XXII:** 51, 52, 53
These Happy Golden Years (L. I. Wilder), **Supp. XXII:** 294, 297, 299
These Low Grounds (Turpin), **Supp. XVIII:** 283
"These saw Visions" (Dickinson), **Retro. Supp. I:** 46
These Thirteen (Faulkner), **II:** 72
These Three (film), **Supp. I Part 1:** 281
These Times (Untermeyer), **Supp. XV: 299–300,** 303
"These Times" (Untermeyer), **Supp. XV:** 300
"Thessalonica: A Roman Story" (Brown), **Supp. I Part 1:** 133
Thévenaz, Paul, **Supp. XV:** 42
Thew, Harvey, **Supp. XIII:** 166
"They Ain't the Men They Used To Be" (Farrell), **II:** 45
"They Burned the Books" (Benét), **Supp. XI:** 46
They Came Like Swallows (Maxwell), **Supp. VIII: 155–159,** 168, 169
"They Can't Turn Back" (Baldwin), **Supp. I Part 1:** 52
They Do Not: The Letters of a Non-Professional Lady Arranged for Public Consumption (Clements), **Supp. XVI:** 190
They Feed They Lion (Levine), **Supp. V:** 178, 179, 181, 184–185, 186
"They Feed They Lion" (Levine), **Supp. V:** 188

"They Lion Grow" (Levine), **Supp. V:** 184–185
"They're Not Your Husband" (Carver), **Supp. III Part 1:** 141, 143
They're Playing Our Song (musical), **Supp. IV Part 2:** 589
They Seek a City (Bontemps and Conroy), **Supp. XXII:** 5, 11
They Shall Inherit the Laughter (Jones), **Supp. XI:** 217, 218, 232
"They Shall Not Die" (Ryan as Quin), **Supp. XVIII:** 228–229
They Shoot Horses (film), **Supp. XIII:** 159
They Shoot Horses, Don't They? (McCoy), **Supp. XIII:** 159, **164–166,** 168, 171, 172, 174
"They Sing, They Sing" (Roethke), **III:** 544
They Stooped to Folly (Glasgow), **II:** 175, 186–187
They Were Expendable (film), **Supp. XVIII:** 247
They Whisper (R. O. Butler), **Supp. XII: 72–73**
They Who Knock at Our Gates: A Complete Gospel of Immigration (Antin), **Supp. XX: 2–3, 10–11, 12**
Thidwick the Big-Hearted Moose (Geisel), **Supp. XVI:** 104
"Thief's Philosophy of Life, The" (Hapgood), **Supp. XVII:** 103
"Thief's Wife, The" (B. Kelly), **Supp. XVII:** 125–126
"Thieves" (Yates), **Supp. XI:** 349
Thieves of Paradise (Komunyakaa), **Supp. XIII:** 113, **128–130,** 132
"Thimble, The" (Kenyon), **Supp. VII:** 164
"Thing and Its Relations, The" (James), **II:** 357
"Things" (Haines), **Supp. XII:** 207
"Things" (Kenyon), **Supp. VII:** 169
"Things, The" (Kinnell), **Supp. III Part 1:** 246
Things As They Are (Stein), **IV:** 34, 37, 40
"Things Can Be Named to Death" (Peacock), **Supp. XIX:** 199
"Things Don't Stop" (Nye), **Supp. XIII:** 287
Things Gone and Things Still Here (Bowles), **Supp. IV Part 1:** 91
"Things of August" (Stevens), **Retro. Supp. I:** 309
Things of This World (Wilbur), **Supp. III Part 2:** 552–555
Things That Fall from the Sky (Brockmeier), **Supp. XXII: 50–53**
"Things That Fall from the Sky" (Brockmeier), **Supp. XXII:** 51, 53
Things Themselves: Essays and Scenes (Price), **Supp. VI:** 261
Things They Carried, The (T. O'Brien), **Supp. V:** 238, 239, 240, 243, 248–250; **Supp. XVII:** 14; **Supp. XXI:** 122
"Things to Do in New York City" (Berrigan), **Supp. XXII:** 224
"Thing That Killed My Father Off, The" (Carver), **Supp. III Part 1:** 143
Thingy World!: or, How We Got to Where We Are: A Satire in One Act (Budbill), **Supp. XIX: 13–14**
"Think about It" (Conroy), **Supp. XVI:** 75
Think Back on Us . . . (Cowley), **Supp. II Part 1:** 139, 140, 142
Think Fast, Mr. Moto (Marquand), **III:** 57, 58
"Thinking about Barbara Deming" (Paley), **Supp. VI:** 227
"Thinking about Being Called Simple by a Critic" (Stafford), **Supp. XI:** 328
Thinking about the Longstanding Problems of Virtue and Happiness: Essays, a Play, Two Poems, and a Prayer (Kushner), **Supp. IX:** 131, 134, 135
"Thinking about the Past" (Justice), **Supp. VII:** 123–124
"Thinking about Western Thinking" (Didion), **Supp. IV Part 1:** 204, 206
"'Thinking against Oneself': Reflections on Cioran" (Sontag), **Supp. III Part 2:** 459–460
"Thinking Back Through Our Mothers: Traditions in Canadian Women's Writing" (Shields), **Supp. VII:** 307–308
"Thinking for Berky" (Stafford), **Supp. XI:** 320
"Thinking like a Mountain" (Leopold), **Supp. XIV:** 188, 189
"Thinking of the Lost World" (Jarrell), **II:** 338–389
Thinking Out Loud (Quindlen), **Supp. XVII:** 167, **169–170**
Thin Man, The (film), **Supp. IV Part 1:** 342, 355
Thin Man, The (Hammett), **Supp. IV Part 1:** 354–355
"Thinnest Shadow, The" (Ashbery), **Supp. III Part 1:** 5
"Thin People, The" (Plath), **Supp. I Part 2:** 538, 547
Thin Red Line, The (film; Malick), **Supp. V:** 249; **Supp. XV:** 351
Thin Red Line, The (Jones), **Supp. XI:** 219, **224–225,** 229, 231, 232, 233, 234
"Thin Strips" (Sandburg), **III:** 587
"Third and Final Continent, The" (Lahiri), **Supp. XXI: 178–180**
"Third Avenue in Sunlight" (Hecht), **Supp. X:** 61
"Third Body, A" (R. Bly), **Supp. IV Part 1:** 71
Third Circle, The (Norris), **III:** 327
"Third Expedition, The" (Bradbury), **Supp. IV Part 1:** 103, 106
Third Generation, The (C. Himes), **Supp. XVI:** 135, **140–141**
Third Life of Grange Copeland, The (Walker), **Supp. III Part 2:** 520, 527–536
Third Mind, The (Burroughs), **Supp. XII:** 3
Third Rose, The (Brinnin), **IV:** 26
"Third Sermon on the Warpland, The" (Brooks), **Supp. III Part 1:** 85
"Third Thing That Killed My Father Off, The" (Carver), **Supp. III Part 1:** 144
Third Violet, The (Crane), **I:** 408, 417–418
Thirlwall, John C., **Retro. Supp. I:** 430
"Thirst: Introduction to Kinds of Water" (Carson), **Supp. XII: 103**
"13, 1977, 21" (Lethem), **Supp. XVIII:** 148
13 by Shanley (Shanley), **Supp. XIV:** 316
13 Seconds: A Look Back at the Kent State Shootings (Caputo), **Supp. XIX:** 29
Thirteen Hands: A Play in Two Acts (Shields), **Supp. VII:** 322–323
Thirteen O'Clock (Benét), **Supp. XI:** 46
Thirteen Other Stories (Purdy), **Supp. VII:** 278
Thirteen Stories and Thirteen Epitaphs (Vollmann), **Supp. XVII:** 226
"Thirteenth and Pennsylvania" (Stafford), **Supp. XI:** 324
Thirteenth Month, The (Pedersen; Nelson, trans.), **Supp. XVIII:** 179–180
"Thirteen Ways of Looking at a Blackbird" (Stevens), **IV:** 94; **Supp. IX:** 47; **Supp. XVII:** 130
"Thirteen Ways of Looking at a Blackbird" (W. Stevens), **Supp. XX: 110**
Thirteen Ways of Looking at a Black Man (H. L. Gates), **Supp. XX: 102, 110**
30/6 (poetry chapbook), **Supp. V:** 5, 6
"30. Meditation. 2. Cor. 5.17. He Is a New Creature" (Taylor), **IV:** 144
30: Pieces of a Novel (Dixon), **Supp. XII:** 152, **153–154**
"Thirty Bob a Week" (Davidson), **Retro. Supp. I:** 55
"Thirty Delft Tiles" (Doty), **Supp. XI:** 131
"35/10" (Olds), **Supp. X:** 206
"35,000 Feet—The Lanterns" (Goldbarth), **Supp. XII:** 182
31 Letters and 13 Dreams (Hugo), **Supp. VI:** 141–144
Thirty Poems (Bryant), **Supp. I Part 1:** 157, 158
Thirty-Six Poems (Warren), **IV:** 236, 239, 240
"33" (Alvarez), **Supp. VII:** 4
"3275" (Monette), **Supp. X:** 148, 159
Thirty Years (Marquand), **III:** 56, 60–61
Thirty Years of Treason (Bentley), **Supp. I Part 1:** 297
This, My Letter (Hay), **Supp. XIV:** 121, 122, 129, 131
"This, That & the Other" (Nemerov), **III:** 269
This Body Is Made of Camphor and Gopherwood (R. Bly), **Supp. IV Part 1:** 63–65, 66, 71; **Supp. XXI:** 85
This Boy's Life: A Memoir (T. Wolff), **Supp. VII:** 334–339, 340, 343; **Supp. XI:** 246, 247
"This Bright Dream" (Benét), **Supp. XI:** 55
This Coffin Has No Handles (McGrath), **Supp. X:** 117
"This Configuration" (Ashbery), **Supp. III Part 1:** 22

"This Corruptible" (Wylie), **Supp. I Part 2:** 727, 729
"This Crazy Wickedness, Little Nests of Light" (Notley), **Supp. XXII:** 228
"This Crutch That I Love" (Nye), **Supp. XIII:** 288
"This Gentile World" (H. Miller), **III:** 177
"This Hand" (Wylie), **Supp. I Part 2:** 713
"This Hour" (Olds), **Supp. X:** 212
"This House I Cannot Leave" (Kingsolver), **Supp. VII:** 208
This Hunger (Nin), **Supp. X:** 185
"This Is a Photograph of Me" (Atwood), **Supp. XIII:** 33
"This Is a Poem, Good Afternoon" (Keillor), **Supp. XVI:** 167
"This Is It" (Stern), **Supp. IX:** 290
"This Is Just to Say" (W. C. Williams), **Supp. XI:** 328
"This Is My Heart" (Harjo), **Supp. XII:** 230
This Is Not a Novel (Markson), **Supp. XVII:** 145–146
"This Is Not Who We Are" (Nye), **Supp. XIII:** 285, 286
This Is Our Time: Secular Cantata No. 1, Mixed Voice Chorus and Orchestra (Taggard, Schuman and Weissleder), **Supp. XXII:** 283
"This Is Us, Excellent" (Richard), **Supp. XIX:** 212
"This Is What I Said" (Salinas), **Supp. XIII:** 322
This Journey (Wright), **Supp. III Part 2:** 605–606
"This Lime-Tree Bower My Prison" (Coleridge), **Supp. XXI:** 52, 55
This Man and This Woman (Farrell), **II:** 42
"This Monkey, My Back" (Boyle), **Supp. XX: 17**
"This Morning" (Kenyon), **Supp. VII:** 164
"This Morning, This Evening, So Soon" (Baldwin), **Supp. I Part 1:** 63
"This Morning Again It Was in the Dusty Pines" (Oliver), **Supp. VII:** 240
This Music Crept by Me upon the Waters (MacLeish), **III:** 21
"This New England: Newport, Vermont" (Mosher), **Supp. XXII:** 209
This People Israel: The Meaning of Jewish Existence (Baeck), **Supp. V:** 260
"This Personal Maze Is Not the Prize" (Selinger), **Supp. XI:** 248
"This Place in the Ways" (Rukeyser), **Supp. VI:** 273–274
This Property Is Condemned (T. Williams), **IV:** 378
This Proud Heart (Buck), **Supp. II Part 1:** 119–120
This Same Sky: A Collection of Poems from around the World (Nye, ed.), **Supp. XIII:** 280
"This Sandwich Has No Mayonnaise" (Salinger), **III:** 552–553
This Shape We're In (Lethem), **Supp. XVIII:** 145
"This Shape We're In" (Lethem), **Supp. XVIII:** 148
This Side of Paradise (Fitzgerald), **I:** 358; **II:** 77, 80, 81, 82–83, 84, 85–87, 88; **Retro. Supp. I:** 99–100, **101–102,** 103, 105, 106, 110, 111; **Supp. XVIII:** 248
This Singing World: An Anthology of Modern Poetry for Young People (Untermeyer, ed.), **Supp. XV:** 306
This Strange Joy: Selected Poems of Sandro Penna (Di Perio, trans.), **Supp. XIX:** 34
This Stubborn Self: Texas Autobiographies (Almon), **Supp. XIII:** 288
This Thing Don't Lead to Heaven (Crews), **Supp. XI: 112**
This Time: New and Selected Poems (Stern), **Supp. IX:** 290–291, **299**
"Thistle Seed in the Wind" (Francis), **Supp. IX:** 81
"Thistles in Sweden, The" (Maxwell), **Supp. VIII:** 169
"This Tokyo" (Snyder), **Supp. VIII:** 298
This Tree Will Be Here for a Thousand Years (revised edition) (R. Bly), **Supp. IV Part 1:** 66
This Tree Will Be Here for a Thousand Years (R. Bly), **Supp. IV Part 1:** 65–66, 71, 72
This Very Earth (Caldwell), **I:** 297, 302
This Wheel's on Fire: Levon Helm and the Story of the Band (Helm), **Supp. XVIII:** 26
This Woman (di Donato), **Supp. XX: 33, 41–42, 46**
Thoens, Karen, **Supp. V:** 147
Thomas, Brandon, **II:** 138
Thomas, Debra, **Supp. XIII:** 114
Thomas, D. M., **Supp. VIII:** 5
Thomas, Dylan, **I:** 49, 64, 382, 432, 526, 533; **III:** 21, 521, 528, 532, 534; **IV:** 89, 93, 136; **Supp. I Part 1:** 263; **Supp. III Part 1:** 42, 47; **Supp. V:** 344; **Supp. VIII:** 21; **Supp. IX:** 114; **Supp. X:** 115; **Supp. XV:** 74; **Supp. XVII:** 135; **Supp. XX: 199, 204**
Thomas, Edna Lewis, **Supp. XVIII:** 281
Thomas, Edward, **II:** 154; **Retro. Supp. I:** 127, 131, 132; **Supp. I Part 1:** 263; **Supp. II Part 1:** 4
Thomas, James, **Supp. XVI:** 268
Thomas, Joseph, **Supp. XVIII:** 183
Thomas, J. Parnell, **Supp. I Part 1:** 286; **Supp. XV:** 198
Thomas, Lewis, **Retro. Supp. I:** 323
Thomas, Rob, **Supp. XVIII:** 100, 101
Thomas, R. S., **Supp. XXI:** 83, 86–87, 93, 95, 96
Thomas, William I., **Supp. I Part 2:** 641
Thomas-a-Kempis, **Retro. Supp. I:** 247
Thomas and Beulah (Dove), **Supp. IV Part 1:** 242, 247–248, 249; **Supp. XVIII:** 174; **Supp. XXI:** 249
Thomas Aquinas (Saint), **I:** 13, 14, 265, 267; **III:** 270; **Retro. Supp. II:** 222; **Supp. IV Part 2:** 526
"Thomas at the Wheel" (Dove), **Supp. IV Part 1:** 248
"Thomas Eakins and the Photograph of a Man in Motion" (Major), **Supp. XXII:** 183
"Thomas Eakins' Delaware River Paintings" (Major), **Supp. XXII:** 183
"Thomas McGrath: Words for a Vanished Age" (Vinz), **Supp. X:** 117
Thomas Merton on Peace, **Supp. VIII:** 208
Thomas Merton Studies Center, The, **Supp. VIII:** 208
Thompson, Barbara, **Supp. V:** 322
Thompson, Cy, **I:** 538
Thompson, Dorothy, **II:** 449–450, 451, 453; **Supp. XV:** 307
Thompson, Edward, **Supp. XXI:** 172
Thompson, E. P., **Supp. X:** 112, 117
Thompson, Francis, **Retro. Supp. I:** 55
Thompson, Frank, **II:** 20
Thompson, George, **Supp. I Part 2:** 686
Thompson, Hunter S., **Supp. VIII:** 42; **Supp. XI:** 105; **Supp. XIII:** 1, 17; **Supp. XVII:** 95, 102, 228
Thompson, James R., **Supp. IV Part 1:** 217
Thompson, John, **Supp. V:** 323; **Supp. XXI:** 151
Thompson, Juliet, **Supp. XX: 117**
Thompson, Lawrance, **II:** 508
Thompson, Lawrance Roger, **Retro. Supp. I:** 138, 141
Thompson, Morton, **Supp. XIII:** 170
Thompson, Theresa, **Supp. V:** 141
Thompson, William T., **Supp. I Part 2:** 411
Thomson, James, **II:** 304; **Supp. I Part 1:** 150, 151
Thomson, Virgil, **IV:** 45; **Supp. IV Part 1:** 81, 83, 84, 173; **Supp. XVI:** 195
"Thoreau" (Lowell), **Supp. I Part 2:** 420, 422
Thoreau, Henry David, **I:** 98, 104, 228, 236, 257, 258, 261, 305, 433; **II:** 7, 8, 13, 17, 101, 159, 224, 273–274, 295, 312–313, 321, 457–458, 540, 546–547; **III:** 171, 174, 186–187, 189, 208, 214–215, 453, 454, 507, 577; **IV: 167–189,** 191, 341; **Retro. Supp. I:** 51, 62, 122; **Retro. Supp. II:** 13, 96, 142, 158; **Supp. I Part 1:** 29, 34, 116, 188, 299, 358; **Supp. I Part 2:** 383, 400, 420, 421, 507, 540, 579, 580, 655, 659, 660, 664, 678; **Supp. III Part 1:** 340, 353; **Supp. IV Part 1:** 236, 392, 416; **Supp. IV Part 2:** 420, 430, 433, 439, 447; **Supp. V:** 200, 208; **Supp. VIII:** 40, 42, 103, 105, 198, 201, 204, 205, 292, 303; **Supp. IX:** 25, 90, 171; **Supp. X:** 21, 27, 28–29, 101, 102; **Supp. XI:** 155; **Supp. XIII:** 1, 17; **Supp. XIV:** 40, 54, 106, 177, 181; **Supp. XVIII:** 4; **Supp. XX: 116, 221; Supp. XXI:** 203, 217; **Supp. XXII:** 206
Thoreau, John, **IV:** 171, 182
Thoreau, Mrs. John, **IV:** 172
"Thorn, The" (Gordon), **Supp. IV Part 1:** 314
Thorne, Francis, **Supp. XII:** 253

"Thorn Merchant, The" (Komunyakaa), **Supp. XIII:** 119–120
Thornton, Billy Bob, **Supp. VIII:** 175
Thornton, Lionel, **III:** 291
"Thorofare" (Minot), **Supp. VI: 209–210**
"Thorow" (Howe), **Supp. IV Part 2:** 419, 420, 421, 431, 433–434
Thorp, Willard, **Supp. XIII:** 101
Thorslev, Peter L., Jr., **I:** 524
Thorstein Veblen (Dowd), **Supp. I Part 2:** 650
Thorstein Veblen (Qualey, ed.), **Supp. I Part 2:** 650
Thorstein Veblen: A Chapter in American Economic Thought (Teggart), **Supp. I Part 2:** 650
Thorstein Veblen: A Critical Interpretation (Riesman), **Supp. I Part 2:** 649, 650
Thorstein Veblen: A Critical Reappraisal (Dowd, ed.), **Supp. I Part 2:** 650
Thorstein Veblen and His America (Dorfman), **Supp. I Part 2:** 631, 650
Thorstein Veblen and the Institutionalists: A Study in the Social Philosophy of Economics (Seckler), **Supp. I Part 2:** 650
"Those before Us" (Lowell), **II:** 550
"Those Being Eaten by America" (R. Bly), **Supp. IV Part 1:** 62
Those Bones Are Not My Child (Bambara), **Supp. XI:** 1, 14, **20–22**
Those Extraordinary Twins (Twain), **IV:** 205–206
"Those Graves in Rome" (Levis), **Supp. XI:** 266
"Those of Us Who Think We Know" (Dunn), **Supp. XI:** 146
Those That Be in Bondage (Webber), **Supp. XXI:** 160
"Those Times . . ." (Sexton), **Supp. II Part 2:** 670, 684
"Those Various Scalpels" (Moore), **III:** 202
"Those Were the Days" (Levine), **Supp. V:** 190
"Those Who Don't" (Cisneros), **Supp. VII:** 60
"Those Who Thunder" (Hogan), **Supp. IV Part 1:** 406
"Thought, A" (Sarton), **Supp. VIII:** 262
Thought and Character of William James (Perry), **II:** 362
Thoughtbook of Francis Scott Key Fitzgerald (Fitzgerald), **Retro. Supp. I:** 99
"Thought Experiment" (Saunders), **Supp. XIX:** 235
"Thoughtful Roisterer Declines the Gambit, The" (Hecht), **Supp. X:** 63
"Thought of Heaven, The" (Stern), **Supp. IX:** 297
"Thoughts after Lambeth" (Eliot), **I:** 587; **Retro. Supp. I:** 324
Thoughts and Reflections (Lord Halifax), **II:** 111
Thoughts in Solitude (Merton), **Supp. VIII:** 207
"Thoughts on Being Bibliographed" (Wilson), **IV:** 435
"Thoughts on the Establishment of a Mint in the United States" (Paine), **Supp. I Part 2:** 512
"Thoughts on the Gifts of Art" (Kenyon), **Supp. VII:** 167
Thousand Acres, A (Smiley), **Supp. VI:** 292, **301–303**
"Thousand and Second Night, The" (Merrill), **Supp. III Part 1:** 324
"Thousand Dollar Vagrant, The" (Olsen), **Supp. XIII:** 292, 297
"Thousand Faces of Danny Torrance, The" (Figliola), **Supp. V:** 143
"Thousand Genuflections, A" (McCarriston), **Supp. XIV:** 266
Thousand-Mile Walk to the Gulf, A (Muir), **Supp. IX: 177–178**
"Thou Shalt Not Steal" (McClatchy), **Supp. XII:** 264
"Thread, The" (Merwin), **Supp. III Part 1:** 351
Three (film), **Supp. IX:** 253
3-3-8 (Marquand), **III:** 58
"Three Academic Pieces" (Stevens), **IV:** 90
"Three Agee Wards, The" (Morris), **III:** 220–221
"Three American Singers" (Cather), **Retro. Supp. I:** 10
"Three Around the Old Gentleman" (Berryman), **I:** 188
"Three Avilas, The" (Jeffers), **Supp. II Part 2:** 418
"Three Black Women Writers" (C. L. R. James), **Supp. XXI:** 172
Three Books of Song (Longfellow), **II:** 490
"Three Bushes" (Yeats), **Supp. I Part 1:** 80
Three Cantos (Pound), **Retro. Supp. I:** 290
Three Centuries of Harvard (Morison), **Supp. I Part 2:** 485
Three Circles of Light (di Donato), **Supp. XX: 33, 42–43, 44, 46**
Three Comrades (Remarque), **Retro. Supp. I:** 113
"Three Corollaries of Cultural Relativism" (Locke), **Supp. XIV:** 202
"Three-Day Blow, The" (Hemingway), **II:** 248
Three Essays on America (Brooks), **I:** 246
Three Farmers on Their Way to a Dance (Powers), **Supp. IX:** 211–212, **213–214,** 222
"Three Fates, The" (Benét), **Supp. XI:** 48–49, 50
"Three Generations of Secrets" (A. Finch), **Supp. XVII:** 73
"Three Gifts, The" (Gibran), **Supp. XX: 124**
Three Gospels (Price), **Supp. VI:** 267
"Three Kings, The: Hemingway, Faulkner, and Fitzgerald" (Ford), **Supp. V:** 59
Three Lives (Auchincloss), **Supp. IV Part 1:** 25
Three Lives (Stein), **I:** 103; **IV:** 26, 27, 31, 35, 37–41, 42, 45, 46; **Supp. IX:** 306
"THREE MOVEMENTS AND A CODA" (Baraka), **Supp. II Part 1:** 50
Three One Act Plays (Riverside Drive, Old Saybrook, and *Central Park West)* (Allen), **Supp. XV:** 3
Three on the Tower: The Lives and Works of Ezra Pound, T. S. Eliot, and William Carlos Williams (Simpson), **Supp. IX:** 276
Three Papers on Fiction (Welty), **IV:** 261
Three-Penny Opera (Brecht), **I:** 301; **Supp. XIV:** 162
"Three Percent Own All the Wealth" (Ryan as Quin), **Supp. XVIII:** 231–232
Three Philosophical Poets (Santayana), **III:** 610–612
"Three Pigs in Five Days" (Prose), **Supp. XVI:** 257, 258
"Three Players of a Summer Game" (T. Williams), **IV:** 383
Three Poems (Ashbery), **Supp. III Part 1:** 2, 3, 14, 15, 18, 24–26
"Three Poems for my Daughter" (Di Piero), **Supp. XIX:** 40
"Three Pokes of a Thistle" (Nye), **Supp. XIII:** 281
Three Roads, The (Macdonald, under Millar), **Supp. IV Part 2:** 466, 467
"Three Silences of Molinos, The" (Longfellow), **Retro. Supp. II:** 169
Three Sisters, The (Chekhov), **Supp. XV:** 323
"Three Sisters, The" (Cisneros), **Supp. VII:** 64
Three Soldiers (Dos Passos), **I:** 477–478, 480, 482, 488, 493–494; **Supp. XXI:** 277
"Three Songs at the End of Summer" (Kenyon), **Supp. VII:** 169–170
"Three Steps to the Graveyard" (Wright), **Supp. III Part 2:** 593, 596
Three Stories and Ten Poems (Hemingway), **II:** 68, 263; **Supp. XVII:** 105
Three Taverns, The (Robinson), **III:** 510
"Three Taverns, The" (Robinson), **III:** 521, 522
Three Tenant Families (Agee), **I:** 37–38
Three Tenors, One Vehicle: A Book of Songs (X. J. Kennedy, Camp, and Waldrop), **Supp. XV:** 165
"Three Types of Poetry" (Tate), **IV:** 131
"Three Vagabonds of Trinidad" (Harte), **Supp. II Part 1:** 338
"Three Waterfalls, The" (Lanier), **Supp. I Part 1:** 350
"Three-Way Mirror" (Brooks), **Supp. III Part 1:** 69–70
Three Weeks in Spring (Parker and Parker), **Supp. XIX:** 187
"Three Women" (Plath), **Supp. I Part 2:** 539, 541, 544, 545, 546
Three Young Poets (Swallow, ed.), **Supp. X:** 116
Threnody (Emerson), **Supp. I Part 2:** 416
"Threnody" (Emerson), **II:** 7

"Threnody for a Brown Girl" (Cullen), **Supp. IV Part 1:** 166
"Threshing-Floor, The" (Baldwin), **Supp. I Part 1:** 50
Threshold (film), **Supp. IX:** 254
"Threshold" (Goldbarth), **Supp. XII:** 175
Threshold (Jackson), **Supp. IX:** 117
"Throat" (Goldbarth), **Supp. XII:** 177–178
Throne of Labdacus, The (Schnackenberg), **Supp. XV:** 260, **263–266**
Thrones (Pound), **Retro. Supp. I:** 293
Through Dooms of Love (Kumin), **Supp. IV Part 2:** 444
"Through the Black Curtain" (Kingston), **Supp. V:** 169
Through the Forest: New and Selected Poems, 1977–1987 (Wagoner), **Supp. IX: 330–331**
"Through the Hills of Spain" (Salinas), **Supp. XIII:** 315
"Through the Hole in the Mundane Millstone" (West), **Retro. Supp. II:** 321, 322
Through the Ivory Gate (Dove), **Supp. IV Part 1:** 242, 243, 251, 252, 253–254, 254
"Through the Kitchen Window, Chiapas" (Nye), **Supp. XIII:** 277
Through the Safety Net (C. Baxter), **Supp. XVII:** 17, 22
"Through the Smoke Hole" (Snyder), **Supp. VIII:** 299
"Thrush Relinquished, The" (Grossman), **Supp. XIX:** 83
Thucydides, **II:** 418; **IV:** 50; **Supp. I Part 2:** 488, 489, 492; **Supp. IV Part 1:** 391; **Supp. XIII:** 233
Thunderbolt and Lightfoot (film), **Supp. X:** 126
"Thunder from a Cloudless Sky" (Mosher), **Supp. XXII:** 209
"Thunderhead" (MacLeish), **III:** 19
Thurber, James, **I:** 487; **II:** 432; **IV:** 396; **Supp. I Part 2: 602–627,** 653, 654, 668, 672, 673, 679; **Supp. II Part 1:** 143; **Supp. IV Part 1:** 349; **Supp. IX:** 118; **Supp. XIV:** 104; **Supp. XVI:** 167; **Supp. XVII:** 4
Thurber, Mrs. James (Althea Adams), **Supp. I Part 2:** 613, 615, 617
Thurber, Mrs. James (Helen Muriel Wismer), **Supp. I Part 2:** 613, 617, 618
Thurber, Robert, **Supp. I Part 2:** 613, 617
Thurber, Rosemary, **Supp. I Part 2:** 616
Thurber, William, **Supp. I Part 2:** 602
Thurber Album, The (Thurber), **Supp. I Part 2:** 611, 619
Thurber Carnival, The (Thurber), **Supp. I Part 2:** 620; **Supp. XIV:** 104
Thurman, Judith, **Supp. IV Part 1:** 309
Thurman, Wallace, **Retro. Supp. I:** 200; **Supp. I Part 1:** 325, 326, 328, 332; **Supp. IV Part 1:** 164; **Supp. X:** 136, 139; **Supp. XVI:** 135; **Supp. XVIII:** 279, 281; **Supp. XIX:** 78; **Supp. XXII:** 2
"Thursday" (Millay), **III:** 129
"Thurso's Landing" (Jeffers), **Supp. II Part 2:** 433
"Thus Do I Refute Gioia" (Junker), **Supp. XV:** 116
"Thus Far by Faith" (Nelson), **Supp. XVIII:** 177
Thus Spake Zarathustra (Nietzsche), **II:** 463; **Supp. IV Part 1:** 110; **Supp. IV Part 2:** 519
Thwaite, Lady Alicia. *See* Rawlings, Marjorie Kinnan
Thy Neighbor's Wife (Talese), **Supp. XVII:** 204, 205–206, 207, 208, 210
"Tiara" (Doty), **Supp. XI:** 122
"Tibetan Time" (Prose), **Supp. XVI:** 255
Ticket for a Seamstitch, A (Harris), **II:** 424–425
Tickets for a Prayer Wheel (Dillard), **Supp. VI:** 22, 34
Ticket That Exploded, The (Burroughs), **Supp. III Part 1:** 93, 103, 104
Tickless Time (Glaspell), **Supp. III Part 1:** 179
Ticknor, George, **II:** 488; **Supp. I Part 1:** 313
Ticknor, William, **Supp. XVIII:** 258
"Ti Démon" (Chopin), **Supp. I Part 1:** 225
Tide of Time, The (Masters), **Supp. I Part 2:** 471
"Tide of Voices" (Hull), **Supp. XXI:** 132, 133–134, 136
"Tide Rises, the Tide Falls, The" (Longfellow), **I:** 498
"Tides" (Hoffman), **Supp. XVIII:** 86
Tidewater Blood (Hoffman), **Supp. XVIII: 82–83**
Tidyman, Ernest, **Supp. V:** 226
Tietjens, Eunice, **Supp. XV:** 47, 297
"Tiger" (Blake), **Supp. I Part 1:** 80; **Supp. VIII:** 26
Tiger (Bynner), **Supp. XV:** 42, 50
"Tiger, The" (Buechner), **Supp. XII:** 48
Tiger in the House, The (Van Vechten), **Supp. II Part 2:** 736
Tiger Joy (Benét), **Supp. XI:** 45
Tiger-Lilies (Lanier), **Supp. I Part 1:** 350–351, 357, 360, 371
Tiger Who Wore White Gloves, The: or, What You Are, You Are (Brooks), **Supp. III Part 1:** 86
Till, Emmett, **Supp. I Part 1:** 61
Tillich, Paul, **II:** 244; **III:** 291, 292, 303, 309; **IV:** 226; **Retro. Supp. I:** 325, 326, 327; **Supp. V:** 267; **Supp. XIII:** 74, 91
Tillie Olsen: A Study of the Short Fiction (Frye), **Supp. XIII:** 292, 296, 298, 299, 302
Tillman, Lynne, **Supp. XII:** 4
Tillotson, John, **II:** 114
Tillotson, Kristen, **Supp. XVII:** 23
Tillstrom, Burr, **Supp. XIV:** 125
Till the Day I Die (Odets), **Supp. II Part 2:** 530, 533–536, 552
Tilton, Eleanor, **Supp. I Part 1:** 317
Tilton, Theodore, **Supp. XVIII:** 4
Timaeus (Plato), **II:** 10; **III:** 609
Tim: A Story of School Life (Sturgis), **Supp. XX: 227, 230, 232, 233–235**
Timber (Jonson), **II:** 16
Timberg, Scott, **Supp. XV:** 116
"Timberwolf" (Halliday), **Supp. XIX:** 91
Timbuktu (Auster), **Supp. XII:** 34, **35–36**
"Time" (Matthews), **Supp. IX: 165–166**
"Time" (Merrill), **Supp. III Part 1:** 325
"Time and Again" (Sanders), **Supp. XVI:** 269
Time and a Place, A (Humphrey), **Supp. IX:** 95, 98, **100–102**
"Time and the Garden" (Winters), **Supp. II Part 2:** 801, 809
"Time and the Liturgy" (Merton), **Supp. VIII:** 199
Time and Tide: A Walk through Nantucket (Conroy), **Supp. XVI:** 63, 71, **76–77**
"Time Exposure" (C. Baxter), **Supp. XVII:** 20–21
Time Exposures, by Search-Light (W. Frank), **Supp. XX: 75**
Time in the Rock (Aiken), **I:** 65
Time Is Noon, The (Buck), **Supp. II Part 1:** 129, 130–131
Time & Money (Matthews), **Supp. IX:** 155, **165–167**
"Time of Friendship, The" (Bowles), **Supp. IV Part 1:** 90–91
"Time of Her Time, The" (Mailer), **III:** 37, 45; **Retro. Supp. II:** 200
Time of Our Time, The (Mailer), **Retro. Supp. II:** 213–214
Time of the Assassins, The: A Study of Rimbaud (H. Miller), **III:** 189
Time Out of Mind (album, Dylan), **Supp. XVIII:** 28
"Time Past" (Morris), **III:** 232
"Time Present" (Morris), **III:** 232
"Times" (Beattie), **Supp. V:** 31
"Times, The" (Emerson), **II:** 11–12
Times Are Never So Bad, The (Dubus), **Supp. VII:** 87–88
Time's Arrow (Amis), **Retro. Supp. I:** 278
"Time Shall Not Die" (Chandler), **Supp. IV Part 1:** 120
Times of Melville and Whitman, The (Brooks), **I:** 257
Times They Are A-Changin', The (album, Dylan), **Supp. XVIII:** 20, 25
"Times They Are A-Changin,' The" (song, Dylan), **Supp. XVIII:** 30
"Timesweep" (Sandburg), **III:** 595–596
Time to Act, A (MacLeish), **III:** 3
Time to Be Born, A (Powell), **Supp. XIX:** 143
Time to Go (Dixon), **Supp. XII:** 147
Time to Kill (film), **Supp. IV Part 1:** 130
Time to Speak, A (MacLeish), **III:** 3
Time Will Darken It (Maxwell), **Supp. VIII:** 159, **162–164,** 169
"Timing of Sin, The" (Dubus), **Supp. VII:** 91
Tim O'Brien (Herzog), **Supp. V:** 239
Timoleon (Melville), **III:** 93; **Retro. Supp. I:** 257
Timothy Dexter Revisited (Marquand), **III:** 55, 62, 63

Timothy Findley: Stories from a Life (Roberts), **Supp. XX: 53**
Timrod, Henry, **Supp. XVIII:** 31, 33
Tin Can, The (W. J. Smith), **Supp. XIII:** 334, **Supp. XIII:** 336, 337
"Tin Can, The" (W. J. Smith), **Supp. XIII: 337–339**
Tin Can Tree, The (Tyler), **Supp. IV Part 2:** 659–660
Tinguely, Jean, **Supp. XV:** 187
Tinker, Chauncey Brewster, **Supp. XIV:** 12
Tintern Abbey (Wordsworth), **Supp. I Part 2:** 673, 675
Tiny Alice (Albee), **I:** 81–86, 87, 88, 94
"Tiny Mummies! The True Story of the Ruler of 43rd Street's Land of the Walking Dead" (Wolfe), **Supp. III Part 2:** 573, 574
Tip on a Dead Jockey and Other Stories (Shaw), **Supp. XIX:** 251
"Tip-Top Club, The" (Keillor), **Supp. XVI:** 172
"Tired" (Hughes), **Supp. I Part 1:** 331
"Tired and Unhappy, You Think of Houses" (Schwartz), **Supp. II Part 2:** 649
"Tiresias" (Garrett), **Supp. VII:** 96–97
'Tis (McCourt), **Supp. XII:** 271, **279–286**
Tisch (Dixon), **Supp. XII:** 141, **155–156**
Titan, The (Dreiser), **I:** 497, 501, 507–508, 509, 510; **Retro. Supp. II:** 94, 101, 102
Titian, **Supp. I Part 2:** 397, 714
"Tito's Goodbye" (García), **Supp. XI:** 190
To a Blossoming Pear Tree (Wright), **Supp. III Part 2:** 602–605
"To a Blossoming Pear Tree" (Wright), **Supp. III Part 2:** 604
"To Abolish Children" (Shapiro), **Supp. II Part 2:** 717
To Abolish Children and Other Essays (Shapiro), **Supp. II Part 2:** 703
"To a Caty-Did, the Precursor of Winter" (Freneau), **Supp. II Part 1:** 274–275
"To a Chameleon" (Moore), **III:** 195, 196, 215
"To a Conscript of 1940" (Read), **II:** 372–373, 377–378
"To a Contemporary Bunk Shooter" (Sandburg), **III:** 582
"To a Cough in the Street at Midnight" (Wylie), **Supp. I Part 2:** 727, 729–730
"To a Defeated Savior" (Wright), **Supp. III Part 2:** 593–594, 596
"To a Face in the Crowd" (Warren), **IV:** 239
"To a Fish Head Found on the Beach near Malaga" (Levine), **Supp. V:** 185
"To a Friend" (Nemerov), **III:** 272
"To a Friend Whose Work Has Come to Triumph" (Sexton), **Supp. II Part 2:** 683
To a God Unknown (Steinbeck), **I:** 107; **IV:** 51, 59–60, 67
"To a Greek Marble" (Aldington), **Supp. I Part 1:** 257
"To a Locomotive in Winter" (Whitman), **IV:** 348
"To a Military Rifle" (Winters), **Supp. II Part 2:** 810, 811, 815
"To a Mouse" (Burns), **Supp. IX:** 173
"To an American Workman Dying of Starvation" (Taggard), **Supp. XXII:** 282
"To an Athlete Dying Young" (Houseman), **Supp. XVII:** 121
"To a Negro Jazz Band in a Parisian Cabaret" (Hughes), **Supp. I Part 1:** 325
"To an Old Philosopher in Rome" (Stevens), **III:** 605; **Retro. Supp. I:** 312
"To an Old Poet in Peru" (Ginsberg), **Supp. II Part 1:** 322
"To a Now-Type Poet" (X. J. Kennedy), **Supp. XV:** 161
"To Answer Your Question" (Jarman), **Supp. XVII:** 114–115
"To Any Would-Be Terrorists" (Nye), **Supp. XIII:** 285, 286
"To a Poet" (Rich), **Supp. I Part 2:** 571; **Supp. XIX:** 83
"To a Prize Bird" (Moore), **III:** 215
"To a Republican, with Mr. Paine's Rights of Man" (Freneau), **Supp. II Part 1:** 267
"To a Shade" (Yeats), **III:** 18
"To a Skylark" (Shelley), **Supp. I Part 2:** 720; **Supp. X:** 31
"Toast to Harlem, A" (Hughes), **Supp. I Part 1:** 338
"To Aunt Rose" (Ginsberg), **Supp. II Part 1:** 320
"To Autumn" (Keats), **Supp. IX:** 50
"To a Waterfowl" (Bryant), **Supp. I Part 1:** 154, 155, 162, 171
"To a Young Poet" (X. J. Kennedy), **Supp. XV:** 161
"To a Young Writer" (Stegner), **Supp. X:** 24
Tobacco Road (Caldwell), **I:** 288, 289, 290, 295–296, 297, 298, 302, 307, 309, 310; **IV:** 198; **Supp. XXII:** 196
"To Be a Monstrous Clever Fellow" (Fante), **Supp. XI:** 167
"To Become Music or Break" (Jauss), **Supp. XXI:** 133
To Bedlam and Part Way Back (Sexton), **Retro. Supp. II:** 245; **Supp. II Part 2:** 672–678; **Supp. IV Part 2:** 441; **Supp. XI:** 317
"To Beethoven" (Lanier), **Supp. I Part 1:** 364
To Begin Again: Stories and Memoirs, 1908–1929 (M. F. K. Fisher), **Supp. XVII:** 92
Tobey, Mark, **Supp. X:** 264
To Be Young, Gifted, and Black: Lorraine Hansberry in Her Own Words (Nemiroff), **Supp. IV Part 1:** 372, 374
"To Big Mary from an Ex-Catholic" (Mora), **Supp. XIII:** 217, 224, 228
"Tobin's Palm" (O. Henry), **Supp. II Part 1:** 408; **Supp. XV:** 40
Tobit (apocryphal book), **I:** 89
"To Build a Fire" (London), **II:** 468
Toby Tyler: or, Ten Weeks with a Circus (Otis), **III:** 577
"To Change in a Good Way" (Ortiz), **Supp. IV Part 2:** 511
"To Charlotte Cushman" (Lanier), **Supp. I Part 1:** 364
"To Cole, the Painter, Departing for Europe" (Bryant), **Supp. I Part 1:** 157, 161
Tocqueville, Alexis de, **III:** 261; **IV:** 349; **Retro. Supp. I:** 235; **Supp. I Part 1:** 137; **Supp. I Part 2:** 659, 660; **Supp. II Part 1:** 281, 282, 284; **Supp. XIV:** 306, 312
"To Crispin O'Conner" (Freneau), **Supp. II Part 1:** 268
"To Da-Duh, In Memoriam" (Marshall), **Supp. XI:** 276
"TODAY" (Baraka), **Supp. II Part 1:** 55
"Today" (Ginsberg), **Supp. II Part 1:** 328
"Today Is a Good Day To Die" (Bell), **Supp. X:** 7
"Today Will Be a Quiet Day" (Hempel), **Supp. XXI:** 117,**Supp. XXI:** 118
Todd, Mabel Loomis, **I:** 454, 470; **Retro. Supp. I:** 33, 34, 35, 39, 47
"To Death" (Levertov), **Supp. III Part 1:** 274
"To Delmore Schwartz" (Lowell), **II:** 547; **Retro. Supp. II:** 188
"to disembark" (Brooks), **Supp. III Part 1:** 86
"To Dorothy on Her Exclusion from The Guinness Book of Records" (X. J. Kennedy), **Supp. XV:** 166
"To Dr. Thomas Shearer" (Lanier), **Supp. I Part 1:** 370
"To Earthward" (Frost), **II:** 154
"To Edwin V. McKenzie" (Winters), **Supp. II Part 2:** 801
"To Eleonora Duse" (Lowell), **II:** 528
"To Elizabeth Ward Perkins" (Lowell), **II:** 516
"To Elsie" (W. C. Williams), **Retro. Supp. I:** 419
"To Emily Dickinson" (H. Crane), **Retro. Supp. II:** 76
"To E. T." (Frost), **Retro. Supp. I:** 132
To Feel These Things (L. Michaels), **Supp. XVI:** 205, **213–214**
"To Feel These Things" (L. Michaels), **Supp. XVI:** 214
Toffler, Alvin, **Supp. IV Part 2:** 517
"To Fill" (Moore), **Supp. X:** 168, 169
"To Gabriela, a Young Writer" (Mora), **Supp. XIII:** 220
To Have and Have Not (film), **Supp. XV:** 347
To Have and Have Not (Hemingway), **I:** 31; **II:** 253–254, 264; **Retro. Supp. I:** 182, **183,** 187
"To Helen" (Poe), **III:** 410, 411, 427; **Retro. Supp. II:** 102
"To Hell With Dying" (Walker), **Supp. III Part 2:** 523
"To His Excellency General Washington" (Wheatley), **Supp. XX: 289**
"To His Father" (Jeffers), **Supp. II Part 2:** 415

Toilet, The (Baraka), **Supp. II Part 1:** 37, 40–42
"To James Russell Lowell" (Holmes), **Supp. I Part 1:** 311
To Jerusalem and Back (Bellow), **Retro. Supp. II:** 29
"To Jesus on His Birthday" (Millay), **III:** 136–137
"To John Keats" (Lowell), **II:** 516
"To Judge Faolain, Dead Long Enough: A Summons" (McCarriston), **Supp. XIV:** 264–265
"To Justify My Singing" (Wright), **Supp. III Part 2:** 590
"To Kill a Deer" (C. Frost), **Supp. XV:** 102
To Kill a Mockingbird (film), **Supp. VIII:** 128–129
To Kill a Mockingbird (Lee), **Supp. VIII: 113–129; Supp. XVI:** 259; **Supp. XIX:** 142
"*To Kill a Mockingbird:* Harper Lee's Tragic Vision" (Dave), **Supp. VIII:** 126
To Kill a Mockingbird: Threatening Boundaries (Johnson), **Supp. VIII:** 126
Toklas, Alice B., **IV:** 27; **Supp. IV Part 1:** 81, 91; **Supp. XVI:** 187
"Tokyo Story" (Wasserstein), **Supp. XV:** 328
"To Light" (Hogan), **Supp. IV Part 1:** 402
"To Live and Diet" (Wasserstein), **Supp. XV:** 328
Tolkien, J. R. R., **Supp. V:** 140
Tolkin, Michael, **Supp. XI:** 160
Toller, Ernst, **I:** 479
"To Lose the Earth" (Sexton), **Supp. II Part 2:** 684, 685
Tolson, Melvin, **Retro. Supp. I:** 208, 209, 210
Tolstoy, Leo, **I:** 6, 7, 58, 103, 312, 376; **II:** 191–192, 205, 271, 272, 275, 276, 281, 285, 286, 320, 407, 542, 559, 570, 579, 606; **III:** 37, 45, 61, 323, 467, 572; **IV:** 17, 21, 170, 285; **Retro. Supp. I:** 91, 225; **Retro. Supp. II:** 299; **Supp. I Part 1:** 2, 3, 6, 20; **Supp. IV Part 1:** 392; **Supp. V:** 277, 323; **Supp. IX:** 246; **Supp. XI:** 68; **Supp. XII:** 310, 322; **Supp. XIV:** 87, 97, 98; **Supp. XIX:** 241
"To Lu Chi" (Nemerov), **III:** 275
Tom (Cummings), **I:** 430
"Tom" (Oliver), **Supp. VII:** 232
"Tom, Tom, the Piper's Son" (Ransom), **Supp. X:** 58
"To M, with a Rose" (Lanier), **Supp. I Part 1:** 364
To Make a Prairie (Kumin), **Supp. IV Part 2:** 440, 441
"To Make Words Disappear" (Simpson), **Supp. IX:** 265–266
Tomás and the Library Lady (Mora), **Supp. XIII:** 216, 221
"Tomatoes" (Francis), **Supp. IX:** 82
"Tom Ball's Barn" (Kooser), **Supp. XIX:** 119
"Tom Brown at Fisk" (Du Bois), **Supp. II Part 1:** 160
Tom Brown's School Days (Hughes), **Supp. I Part 2:** 406
"Tomb Stone" (Dickey), **Supp. IV Part 1:** 185
"Tombstone Blues" (song, Dylan), **Supp. XVIII:** 30
Tomcat in Love (O'Brien), **Supp. V:** 238, 240, 243, 252–254
"Tomcat's Wife, The" (C. Bly), **Supp. XVI:** 40
Tomcat's Wife and Other Stories, The (C. Bly), **Supp. XVI:** 40–41
"Tom Fool at Jamaica" (Moore), **III:** 215
To Mix with Time (Swenson), **Supp. IV Part 2:** 637, 643–645, 645
Tom Jones (Fielding), **I:** 131; **Supp. V:** 127
Tomlinson, Charles, **Supp. XVI:** 284
Tommy Gallagher's Crusade (Farrell), **II:** 44
Tommyknockers, The (King), **Supp. V:** 139, 144
"Tommy's Burglar" (Henry), **Supp. II Part 1:** 399, 401
"Tommy Stames" (Budbill), **Supp. XIX:** 8
Tomo Cheeki (pseudonym). *See* Freneau, Philip
Tomorrow Is Another Day (E. P. Jones), **Supp. XXII:** 252
Tomorrow is Another Day (film, Feist), **Supp. XVII:** 62
"Tomorrow the Moon" (Dos Passos), **I:** 493
"Tom Outland's Story" (Cather), **I:** 325–326
Tompkins, Jane, **Supp. XVI:** 89; **Supp. XVIII:** 258, 259, 263
Tompson, Benjamin, **Supp. I Part 1:** 110, 111
"Tom-Rock Through Eels" (Hempel), **Supp. XXI:** 116, 118, **123–124**
Tom Sawyer (musical) (Gurney), **Supp. V:** 96
Tom Sawyer (Twain). *See Adventures of Tom Sawyer, The* (Twain)
Tom Sawyer Abroad (Twain), **II:** 482; **IV:** 19, 204
Tom Sawyer Detective (Twain), **IV:** 204
"Tom's Husband" (Jewett), **Retro. Supp. II:** 132, 141
Tom Swift (Stratemeyer), **III:** 146
"Tom Wolfe's Guide to Etiquette" (Wolfe), **Supp. III Part 2:** 578
"To My Brother Killed: Haumont Wood: October, 1918" (Bogan), **Supp. III Part 1:** 58
"To My Class, on Certain Fruits and Flowers Sent Me in Sickness" (Lanier), **Supp. I Part 1:** 370
"To My Father's Ghost" (Everwine), **Supp. XV:** 76
"To My Ghost Reflected in the Auxvasse River" (Levis), **Supp. XI:** 265
"To My Greek" (Merrill), **Supp. III Part 1:** 326
"To My Mother" (Berry), **Supp. X:** 23
"To My Sister—Ernestine Kealoha Taggard, 1900–1943" (Taggard), **Supp. XXII:** 284
"To My Small Son, at the Photographer's" (Hay), **Supp. XIV:** 121
"To My Small Son, on Certain Occasions" (Hay), **Supp. XIV:** 121
"To My Students" (Taggard), **Supp. XXII:** 280
"To Name is to Possess" (Kincaid), **Supp. VII:** 194
Tone, Aileen, **I:** 21–22
"Tongue Is, The" (Komunyakaa), **Supp. XIII:** 113
"Tongue of the Jews" (Bukiet), **Supp. XVII:** 47
Tongues (Shepard and Chaikin), **Supp. III Part 2:** 433
Tongues of Angels, The (Price), **Supp. VI:** 265
Tongues Untied (Riggs; film), **Supp. XI:** 19, 20
"Tonight" (Lowell), **II:** 538
Tonight Is the Night of the Prom (Jarman), **Supp. XVII:** 110, **112–113**
"Tonight Is the Night of the Prom" (Jarman), **Supp. XVII:** 113
Tony Kushner in Conversation (Vorlicky, ed.), **Supp. IX:** 132
"Too Anxious for Rivers" (Frost), **II:** 162
"Too Blue" (Hughes), **Retro. Supp. I:** 207
"Too Damn Close: Thresholds and Their Maintenance in Rick Bass's Work" (Kerridge), **Supp. XVI:** 26
"Too Early" (Leopold), **Supp. XIV:** 186
"Too Early Spring" (Benét), **Supp. XI:** 53
"Too Far from Home" (Bowles), **Supp. IV Part 1:** 94–95
Too Far from Home: Selected Writings of Paul Bowles (Halpern, ed.), **Supp. IV Part 1:** 94, 95
Too Far to Go: The Maples Stories (Updike), **Retro. Supp. I:** 321
"Too Good To Be True": The Life and Art of Leslie Fiedler (Winchell), **Supp. XIII:** 94, 98, 99, 101
Toohey, John Peter, **Supp. IX:** 190
Toolan, David, **Supp. IV Part 1:** 308
Too Late (Dixon), **Supp. XII: 143–144**
"Too Late" (Pickering), **Supp. XXI:** 197
"Too-Late Born, The" (Hemingway), **III:** 9
Toole, John Kennedy, **Supp. XIV:** 21
"Toolless" (Pickering), **Supp. XXI:** 204
Too Many Bottles (Holding), **Supp. XXII:** 126, **134–135**
Toomer, Jean, **Retro. Supp. II:** 79; **Supp. I Part 1:** 325, 332; **Supp. III Part 2: 475–491; Supp. IV Part 1:** 16, 164, 168; **Supp. IX: 305–322; Supp. XIII:** 305; **Supp. XVIII:** 122; **Supp. XX: 73; Supp. XXII:** 6
Toomer, Nathan Eugene Pinchback. *See* Toomer, Jean
Too Much Johnson (film), **Supp. IV Part 1:** 83
"To One Who Said Me Nay" (Cullen), **Supp. IV Part 1:** 166

"Tooth, The" (Jackson), **Supp. IX:** 122
Tooth and Claw (Boyle), **Supp. XX: 20**
Tooth of Crime, The (Shepard), **Supp. III Part 2:** 432, 441–445, 447
"Too Young" (O'Hara), **III:** 369
Topaz (film), **Supp. XX: 253**
Topaz (Uris), **Supp. XX: 247, 248, 253**
"Top Israeli Official Hints at 'Shared' Jerusalem" (Nye), **Supp. XIII:** 287
"To P. L., 1916–1937" (Levine), **Supp. V:** 185
"To Please a Shadow" (Brodsky), **Supp. VIII:** 30
"Top of the Food Chain" (Boyle), **Supp. XX: 20**
"Top of the Hill" (Jewett), **II:** 406
"Topography" (Olds), **Supp. X:** 208
Topper (T. Smith), **Supp. IX:** 194
To Praise the Music (Bronk), **Supp. XXI:** 31, 32
Torah, **IV:** 19
"Torch Songs" (Wrigley), **Supp. XVIII:** 296
Torday, Daniel, **Supp. XXII:** 151
Torpedo 8: The Story of Swede Larsen's Bomber Squadron (Wolfert), **Supp. XXI:** 267
"Torquemada" (Bukiet), **Supp. XVII:** 44
"Torquemada" (Longfellow), **II:** 505; **Retro. Supp. II:** 164
Torrence, Ridgely, **III:** 507
Torrent and the Night Before, The (Robinson), **III:** 504
Torrents of Spring, The (Hemingway), **I:** 117; **II:** 250–251
Torres, Héctor A., **Supp. XIII:** 225
Torres, Louis, **Supp. IV Part 2:** 529, 530
Torres-Saillant, Silvio, **Supp. XXI:** 104, 105, 108, 109
Torsney, Cheryl, **Retro. Supp. I:** 224
Tortilla Curtain, The (Boyle), **Supp. VIII: 9–10; Supp. XX: 28–29**
Tortilla Flat (Steinbeck), **IV:** 50, 51, 61, 64
Tortilla Flats (Steinbeck), **Supp. XX: 28**
Tory Lover, The (Jewett), **II:** 406; **Retro. Supp. II:** 144–145
"Toscana" (Dixon), **Supp. XII:** 154
"To Sir Toby" (Freneau), **Supp. II Part 1:** 269
"To Sophy, Expectant" (Mumford), **Supp. II Part 2:** 475
"To Speak of Woe That Is in Marriage" (Lowell), **II:** 550
"To Statecraft Embalmed" (Moore), **III:** 197
To Stay Alive (Levertov), **Supp. III Part 1:** 280–282
"Total Eclipse" (Dillard), **Supp. VI:** 28
Toth, Emily, **Retro. Supp. II:** 71
Toth, Susan Allan, **Retro. Supp. II:** 138
"To the Americans of the United States" (Freneau), **Supp. II Part 1:** 271
"To the Apennines" (Bryant), **Supp. I Part 1:** 157, 164
"To the Bleeding Hearts Association of American Novelists" (Nemerov), **III:** 281
"To the Botequim & Back" (Bishop), **Retro. Supp. II:** 51
To the Bright and Shining Sun (Burke), **Supp. XIV:** 22, 25
"To the Citizens of the United States" (Paine), **Supp. I Part 2:** 519–520
"To the Dandelion" (Lowell), **Supp. I Part 2:** 424
"To the End" (Haines), **Supp. XII:** 212–213
To the Ends of the Earth: The Selected Travels of Paul Theroux, **Supp. VIII:** 324
To the Finland Station: A Study in the Writing and Acting of History (Wilson), **IV:** 429, 436, 443–444, 446
"To the Governor & Legislature of Massachusetts" (Nemerov), **III:** 287
To the Green Man (Jarman), **Supp. XVII:** 110, 120–121
To the Holy Spirit (Winters), **Supp. II Part 2:** 810
"To the Keeper of the King's Water Works" (Freneau), **Supp. II Part 1:** 269
"To the Lacedemonians" (Tate), **IV:** 134
"To the Laodiceans" (Jarrell), **Retro. Supp. I:** 121, 140
To the Lighthouse (Woolf), **I:** 309; **II:** 600; **Retro. Supp. II:** 337; **Supp. VIII:** 155
"To the Man on Trail" (London), **II:** 466
"To the Memory of the Brave Americans Under General Greene" (Freneau), **Supp. II Part 1:** 262, 274
"To the Muse" (Wright), **Supp. III Part 2:** 601
"To the Natural World: at 37" (Taggard), **Supp. XXII:** 279–280
"To the Nazi Leaders" (Hay), **Supp. XIV:** 121
"To the New World" (Jarrell), **II:** 371
"To the One of Fictive Music" (Stevens), **IV:** 89; **Retro. Supp. I:** 297, 300
"To the One Upstairs" (Simic), **Supp. VIII:** 283
"To the Peoples of the World" (Du Bois), **Supp. II Part 1:** 172
To the Place of Trumpets (B. Kelly), **Supp. XVII: 123–127;** 132
"To the Pliocene Skull" (Harte), **Supp. II Part 1:** 343–344
"To the Powers of Darkness" (Taggard), **Supp. XXII:** 279, 280
"To the Powers of Desolation" (Taggard), **Supp. XXII:** 280
"To the Queen of Heaven" (Taggard), **Supp. XXII:** 280
"To the Reader" (Baudelaire), **II:** 544–545
"To The Reader" (Jarman), **Supp. XVII:** 115
"To the Reader" (Levertov), **Supp. III Part 1:** 277
"To the Right Honourable William, Earl of Dartmouth" (Wheatley), **Supp. XX: 278, 284, 287–288**
"To the River Arve" (Bryant), **Supp. I Part 1:** 163
"To the Snake" (Levertov), **Supp. III Part 1:** 277
"To the Stone-Cutters" (Jeffers), **Supp. II Part 2:** 420
"To the Unseeable Animal" (Berry), **Supp. X:** 31
"To the Western World" (Simpson), **Supp. IX:** 269, 270
To the White Sea (Dickey), **Supp. IV Part 1:** 186, 190–191
"To the Young Who Want to Die" (Brooks), **Supp. III Part 1:** 85–86
"To Tlaoc of the Rain" (Everwine), **Supp. XV:** 77
"To Train a Writer" (Bierce), **I:** 199
"Touch, The" (Sexton), **Supp. II Part 2:** 687
Touch and Go (M. F. K. Fisher and D. Parrish), **Supp. XVII:** 84
"Touching the Tree" (Merwin), **Supp. III Part 1:** 355
Touching the World (Eakin), **Supp. VIII:** 167
Touch of Danger, A (Jones), **Supp. XI:** 226, **228–229**
Touch of the Poet, A (O'Neill), **III:** 385, 401, 404
Touchstone, The (Wharton), **Retro. Supp. I:** 365
"Touch-up Man" (Komunyakaa), **Supp. XIII:** 119
Tough Guys Don't Dance (Mailer), **Retro. Supp. II:** 211
"Tough People" (Offutt), **Supp. XIX:** 170–171
Toulet, Paul Jean, **IV:** 79
Tour (McNally), **Supp. XIII:** 197
"Tour 5" (Hayden), **Supp. II Part 1:** 381
To Urania (Brodsky), **Supp. VIII:** 22, 28–29
Tourgée, Albion W., **Supp. XIV:** 63
"Tour Guide" (Komunyakaa), **Supp. XIII:** 114
"Tourist Death" (MacLeish), **III:** 12
Tourmaline (J. Scott), **Supp. XVII: 192–194,** 195
Tour of Duty (Dos Passos), **I:** 489
Touron the Prairies, A (Irving), **II:** 312–313
Toussaint L'Ouverture, **Supp. XXI:** 166
Toussaint L'Ouverture (C. L. R. James), **Supp. XXI:** 167
Tovey, Donald Francis, **Supp. XIV:** 336
To Walk a Crooked Mile (McGrath), **Supp. X:** 117
Toward a New Synthesis (Begiebing), **Retro. Supp. II:** 210
"Toward Nightfall" (Simic), **Supp. VIII:** 277
Towards a Better Life (Burke), **I:** 270
"Towards a Chicano Poetics: The Making of the Chicano Subject, 1969–1982" (Saldívar), **Supp. IV Part 2:** 544
Towards an Enduring Peace (Bourne), **I:** 232
"Towards Morning" (Pedersen; Nelson, trans.), **Supp. XVIII:** 180
Toward the Blanched Alphabets (Sobin), **Supp. XVI:** 290
Toward the Gulf (Masters), **Supp. I Part 2:** 465–466

"Toward the Solstice" (Rich), **Supp. I Part 2:** 575–576
Toward Wholeness in Paule Marshall's Fiction (Pettis), **Supp. XI:** 276
"Tower" (Merwin), **Supp. III Part 1:** 343
"Tower Beyond Tragedy, The" (Jeffers), **Supp. II Part 2:** 429–430
Tower of Ivory (MacLeish), **III:** 3–4
Towers, Robert, **Supp. IX:** 259; **Supp. XVI:** 211
"To What Red Hell" (C. Himes), **Supp. XVI:** 137
"To Whistler, American" (Pound), **III:** 465–466
"To Wine" (Bogan), **Supp. III Part 1:** 57, 58
Town, Caren J., **Supp. XVIII:** 195, 199
Town, The (Faulkner), **II:** 57, 73; **Retro. Supp. I:** 74, 82
Town, The (Richter), **Supp. XVIII:** 207, **214–215,** 217
Town and the City, The (Kerouac), **Supp. III Part 1:** 222–224; **Supp. XIV:** 143
"Town Crier" (Bierce), **I:** 193, 194, 195, 196
"Town Crier Exclusive, Confessions of a Princess Manqué: 'How Royals Found Me "Unsuitable" to Marry Their Larry' " (Elkin), **Supp. VI:** 56
Town Down the River, The (Robinson), **III:** 508
"Town Dump, The" (Nemerov), **III:** 272, 275, 281
Towne, Robert, **Supp. XI:** 159, 172, 174
"Townhouse Interior with Cat" (Clampitt), **Supp. IX:** 40
"Townies" (Dubus), **Supp. VII:** 86
Town in the Forest, The: Life Story of Richmond, New Hampshire (Boyce; Faust, ed.), **Supp. XXI:** 8
"Town of the Sound of a Twig Breaking" (Carson), **Supp. XII: 102**
"Town Poor, The" (Jewett), **Retro. Supp. II:** 138, 139, 143
Townsend, Alison, **Supp. XIII:** 222
Townsend, Ann, **Supp. V:** 77
Townsend, Jim, **Supp. XXII:** 243
"Towns in Colour" (Lowell), **II:** 523–524
Townsman, The (Sedges), **Supp. II Part 1:** 124–125
"To World War Two" (Koch), **Supp. XV:** 184
Toys in a Field (Komunyakaa), **Supp. XIII: 121–122**
"Toys in a Field" (Komunyakaa), **Supp. XIII:** 122
Toys in the Attic (Hellman), **Supp. I Part 1:** 289–290
Tracer (F. Barthelme), **Supp. XI:** 31–32, 33
Traces of Thomas Hariot, The (Rukeyser), **Supp. VI:** 273, 274, 283
"Tracing Life with a Finger" (Caldwell), **I:** 291
Tracker (Wagoner), **Supp. IX:** 329, **336–337**
"Tracking" (Wagoner), **Supp. IX:** 329
"Track Meet, The" (Schwartz), **Supp. II Part 2:** 665
Tracks (Erdrich), **Supp. IV Part 1:** 259, 262–263, 269, 272, 273–274, 274, 275
"Tract" (W. C. Williams), **Retro. Supp. I:** 414
"Tract against Communism, A" (Twelve Southerners), **IV:** 125, 237
Tractatus (Wittgenstein), **Supp. XVII:** 143
Tracy, Benjamin, **Supp. XVIII:** 4
Tracy, D. H., **Supp. XVIII:** 178
Tracy, Lee, **IV:** 287, 288
Tracy, Steven, **Retro. Supp. I:** 195
"Trade, The" (Levine), **Supp. V:** 193
Trading Twelves (Callahan and Murray, eds.), **Retro. Supp. II:** 119
Trading Twelves: The Selected Letters of Ralph Ellison and Albert Murray (Murray and Callahan, eds.), **Supp. XIX:** 148, 158
" 'Traditional' Marriage: A Secular Affair" (P. N. Warren), **Supp. XX: 273**
"Tradition and Industrialization" (Wright), **IV:** 489–490
"Tradition and Mythology: Signatures of Landscape in Chicana Poetry" (Rebolledo), **Supp. XIII:** 214
"Tradition and the Individual Talent" (Eliot), **I:** 441, 574, 585; **Retro. Supp. I:** 59, 286
Tragedies, Life and Letters of James Gates Percival (Swinburne), **Supp. I Part 2:** 422
Tragedy of Bees, A (P. N. Warren), **Supp. XX: 261**
"Tragedy of Bees, A" (P. N. Warren), **Supp. XX: 272**
Tragedy of Don Ippolito, The (Howells), **II:** 279
"Tragedy of Error, A" (James), **II:** 322; **Retro. Supp. I:** 218
Tragedy of Pudd'nhead Wilson, The (Twain), **IV:** 206–207
Tragic America (Dreiser), **Retro. Supp. II:** 95
"Tragic Dialogue" (Wylie), **Supp. I Part 2:** 724
Tragic Ground (Caldwell), **I:** 297, 306
Tragic Muse, The (James), **Retro. Supp. I:** 227
Traherne, Thomas, **IV:** 151; **Supp. III Part 1:** 14; **Supp. V:** 208; **Supp. XV:** 212; **Supp. XVI:** 282, 288, 295
"Trail, The" (W. J. Smith), **Supp. XIII:** 342
Trailerpark (Banks), **Supp. V:** 12
"Trailing Arbutus, The" (Whittier), **Supp. I Part 2:** 691
Trail of the Lonesome Pine, The (Fox), **Supp. XIII:** 166
"Train, The" (O'Connor), **Retro. Supp. II:** 225
"Train Rising Out of the Sea" (Ashbery), **Supp. III Part 1:** 22
"Trains" (Banks), **Supp. V:** 8
"Train Tune" (Bogan), **Supp. III Part 1:** 64
Train Whistle Guitar (Murray), **Supp. XIX: 153–155,** 157
"Traits of Indian Character" (Irving), **II:** 303
Trakl, Georg, **Supp. XVII:** 241
Tramp Abroad, A (Twain), **IV:** 200
Tramping With a Poet in the Rockies (S. Graham), **Supp. I Part 2:** 397
Tramp's Excuse, The (Lindsay), **Supp. I Part 2:** 379, 380, 382
"Trance, The" (Taggard), **Supp. XXII:** 280
"Transaction" (Cliff), **Supp. XXII:** 75
"Transatlantic" (Toomer), **Supp. III Part 2:** 486
Transatlantic Sketches (James), **II:** 324; **Retro. Supp. I:** 219
"Transcendental Etude" (Rich), **Supp. I Part 2:** 576
"Transcontinental Highway" (Cowley), **Supp. II Part 1:** 141
"Transducer" (Ammons), **Supp. VII:** 28
"Transfiguration" (Jarman), **Supp. XVII:** 118, 119
"Transfigured Bird" (Merrill), **Supp. III Part 1:** 320–321
"Transformations" (Harjo), **Supp. XII:** 226
Transformations (Sexton), **Supp. II Part 2:** 689–691; **Supp. IV Part 2:** 447; **Supp. XIV:** 125
Transforming Madness: New Lives for People Living with Mental Illness (Neugeboren), **Supp. XVI:** 229
"Transit" (Conroy), **Supp. XVI:** 72
Transit to Narcissus, A (Mailer), **Retro. Supp. II:** 196
"Translation" (Espaillat), **Supp. XXI:** 107
"Translation and Transposition" (Carne-Ross), **Supp. I Part 1:** 268–269
"Translation of a Fragment of Simonides" (Bryant), **Supp. I Part 1:** 153, 155
"Translations" (Rich), **Supp. I Part 2:** 563
Translations of Ezra Pound, The (Kenner, ed.), **III:** 463
Translations of the Gospel Back into Tongues (Wright), **Supp. XV: 342–343,** 346
"Trans-National America" (Bourne), **I:** 229, 230
"Transparency" (X. J. Kennedy), **Supp. XV:** 159–160
"Transparent Itineraries: 1983" (Sobin), **Supp. XVI:** 287
"Transparent Itineraries: 1984" (Sobin), **Supp. XVI:** 287
"Transparent Itineraries: 1992" (Sobin), **Supp. XVI:** 289
"Transparent Itineraries" poems (Sobin), **Supp. XVI:** 290
Transparent Man, The (Hecht), **Supp. X:** 57, **69–71**
"Transparent Man, The" (Hecht), **Supp. X: 69–70**
Transparent Things (Nabokov), **Retro. Supp. I:** 266, 270, 277
"Transport" (Simic), **Supp. VIII:** 282
Transport to Summer (Stevens), **IV:** 76, 93; **Retro. Supp. I:** 309–312
Tranströmer, Thomas, **Supp. IV Part 2:** 648
"Traps for the Unwary" (Bourne), **I:** 235

Trash Trilogy (McMurtry), **Supp. V:** 225–226, 231
Traubel, Horace, **IV:** 350
"Travel: After a Death" (Kenyon), **Supp. VII:** 169
Travel Alarm (Nye), **Supp. XIII:** 277
"Traveled World, The" (Pickering), **Supp. XXI:** 203
"Traveler, The" (Haines), **Supp. XII:** 203–204, 210
"Traveler, The" (Stegner), **Supp. IV Part 2:** 605
Traveler at Forty, A (Dreiser), **I:** 515
Traveler from Altruria, a Romance A, (Howells), **II:** 285, 287
Traveler's Tree, The: New and Selected Poems (W. J. Smith), **Supp. XIII:** 332, 347
"Traveling" (Paley), **Supp. VI:** 230
"Traveling Light" (Wagoner), **Supp. IX:** 329
Traveling Mercies: Some Thoughts on Faith (Lamott), **Supp. XX: 132, 140–142**
"Traveling Onion, The" (Nye), **Supp. XIII:** 276
Traveling through the Dark (Stafford), **Supp. XI:** 311, 316, **318–321**
"Traveling through the Dark" (Stafford), **Supp. XI:** 318–320, 321, 323, 329
Travelling in Amherst: A Poet's Journal, 1931–1954, **Supp. IX: 88–89**
Travelling Standing Still: Poems, 1918–1928 (Taggard), **Supp. XXII:** 278
Travels in Alaska (Muir), **Supp. IX:** 182, 185–186
"Travels in Georgia" (McPhee), **Supp. III Part 1:** 293–294
"Travels in North America" (Kees), **Supp. XV:** 133–134
Travels in the Congo (Gide), **III:** 210
"Travels in the South" (Ortiz), **Supp. IV Part 2:** 506
Travels with Charley (Steinbeck), **IV:** 52
"Travel Writing: Why I Bother" (Theroux), **Supp. VIII:** 310
Travis, Merle, **Supp. V:** 335
Travisano, Thomas, **Retro. Supp. II:** 40
Treasure Hunt (Buechner), **Supp. XII:** 52
Treasure Island (Stevenson), **Supp. X:** 230
Treasure of the Humble, The (Maeterlinck), **Supp. XX: 116**
"Treasure of the Redwoods, A" (Harte), **Supp. II Part 1:** 337
Treasury of Art Masterpieces, A: From the Renaissance to the Present Day (Craven), **Supp. XII:** 44
Treasury of English Aphorisms, A (L. P. Smith), **Supp. XIV:** 344
Treasury of English Prose, A (L. P. Smith, ed.), **Supp. XIV:** 341
Treasury of the Theatre, A (Gassner), **Supp. I Part 1:** 292
Treasury of Yiddish Stories, A (Howe and Greenberg, eds.), **Supp. I Part 2:** 432
Treat 'Em Rough (Lardner), **II:** 422–423
Treatise Concerning Religious Affections (Edwards), **I:** 547, 552, 554, 555, 557, 558, 560, 562
Treatise Concerning the Lord's Supper (Doolittle), **IV:** 150
"Treatise on Poetry" (Milosz), **Supp. VIII:** 20
Treatise on Right and Wrong, A (Mencken), **III:** 110, 119
"Treatise on Tales of Horror, A" (Wilson), **IV:** 438
Treatise on the Gods, A (Mencken), **III:** 108–109, 119
"Treatment" (Wright), **Supp. XV:** 343
Trece poetas del mundo azteca (León-Portilla), **Supp. XV:** 77
Tre Croce (Tozzi), **Supp. III Part 2:** 616
"Tree, a Rock, a Cloud, A" (McCullers), **II:** 587
"Tree, The" (Pound), **Retro. Supp. I:** 286; **Supp. I Part 1:** 255
"Tree, the Bird, The" (Roethke), **III:** 548
"Tree at My Window" (Frost), **II:** 155
Tree Grows in Brooklyn, A (B. Smith), **Supp. XVII:** 9
Tree Grows in Brooklyn, A (film; Kazan), **Supp. XVI:** 193
"Tree House at Night, The" (Dickey), **Supp. IV Part 1:** 179
Tree Is Older Than You Are, The (Nye, ed.), **Supp. XIII:** 280
"Tree of Laughing Bells, The" (Lindsay), **Supp. I Part 2:** 376
"Tree of Life, The" (Swados), **Supp. XIX:** 268
"Tree of Night, A" (Capote), **Supp. III Part 1:** 114, 120
Tree of Night and Other Stories, A (Capote), **Supp. III Part 1:** 114
"Trees, The" (Rich), **Supp. I Part 2:** 555
Trees, The (Richter), **Supp. XVIII: 212–213,** 220
"Trees Listening to Bach" (Merrill), **Supp. III Part 1:** 336
Tree That Came to Stay, The (Quindlen), **Supp. XVII:** 167
Tree Where Man Was Born, The (Matthiessen), **Supp. V:** 199, 203, 204
Trejo, Ernesto, **Supp. V:** 178, 180; **Supp. XIII:** 313, 316; **Supp. XV:** 73
Trelawny, Edward John, **Supp. I Part 2:** 721
"Trellis for R., A" (Swenson), **Supp. IV Part 2:** 647
Tremblay, Bill, **Supp. XIII:** 112
Tremble (Wright), **Supp. XV: 348–349**
"Trespass" (Frost), **Retro. Supp. I:** 139
Trespassing (Pickering), **Supp. XXI:** 202
"Trespassing" (Pickering), **Supp. XXI:** 202
Trethewey, Eric, **Supp. XXI:** 243, 244
Trethewey, Natasha, **Supp. XXI: 243–259**
"Tretitoli, Where the Bomb Group Was" (Hugo), **Supp. VI:** 138
Trevelyan, Robert C., **Supp. XIV:** 334
Trevor-Roper, Hugh, **Supp. XIV:** 348
Trial, The (Kafka), **IV:** 113; **Retro. Supp. II:** 20
"Trial, The" (Rukeyser), **Supp. VI:** 278
"Trial by Existence, The" (Frost), **II:** 166
Trial of a Poet, The (Shapiro), **Supp. II Part 2:** 710
Trial of the Hawk, The: A Comedy of the Seriousness of Life (Lewis), **II:** 441
Trials of the Human Heart (Rowson), **Supp. XV:** 237, 239
Tribal Secrets: Recovering American Indian Intellectual Traditions (Warrior), **Supp. IV Part 1:** 329
"Tribute" (A. Finch), **Supp. XVII:** 72, 73–74
"Tribute, A" (Easton), **Supp. IV Part 2:** 461
"Tribute, The" (Doolittle), **Supp. I Part 1:** 267
"Tribute (To My Mother)" (Cullen), **Supp. IV Part 1:** 166
Tribute to Freud (Doolittle), **Supp. I Part 1:** 253, 254, 258, 259, 260, 268
Tribute to the Angels (Doolittle), **Supp. I Part 1:** 272
"Trick on the World, A" (Ríos), **Supp. IV Part 2:** 553
"Tricks" (Olds), **Supp. X:** 203–204
"Trick Scenery" (F. Barthelme), **Supp. XI:** 26
Trifler, The (Masters), **Supp. I Part 2:** 459–460
Trifles (Glaspell), **Supp. III Part 1:** 175, 178, 179, 182, 186, 187; **Supp. X:** 46; **Supp. XXI:** 12
Trifonov, Iurii V., **Retro. Supp. I:** 278
Triggering Town, The: Lectures and Essays on Poetry and Writing (Hugo), **Supp. VI:** 133, 140
Trilling, Diana, **II:** 587, 600; **Supp. I Part 1:** 297; **Supp. XII:** 126; **Supp. XXI:** 271, 275
Trilling, Lionel, **I:** 48; **II:** 579; **III:** 308, 310, 319, 327; **IV:** 201, 211; **Retro. Supp. I:** 19, 97, 121, 216, 227; **Supp. III Part 2: 493–515; Supp. V:** 259; **Supp. VIII:** 93, 98, 190, 231, 236, 243; **Supp. IX:** 266, 287; **Supp. XIII:** 100–101; **Supp. XIV:** 280, 288–289; **Supp. XV:** 20, 140, 152
Trilogy (Doolittle), **Supp. I Part 1:** 271, 272
Trilogy of Desire (Dreiser), **I:** 497, 508; **Retro. Supp. II:** 94, 96, **101–102**
Trimberger, Ellen Kay, **Supp. XVII:** 96, 106; **Supp. XXI:** 12
Trimmed Lamp, The (O. Henry), **Supp. II Part 1:** 410
"Trinc" (McGrath), **Supp. X:** 127
Trinity (Uris), **Supp. XX: 243, 244, 245, 246, 247, 248, 253, 254–255**
Trio (Baker), **Supp. I Part 1:** 277
Trio (Saroyan), **Supp. XXII:** 25
"Triolets for Triolet" (Nelson), **Supp. XVIII:** 179
"Trip" (F. Barthelme), Supp. XI: 26
Triple Thinkers, The: Ten Essays on Literature (Wilson), **IV:** 428, 431; **Supp. II Part 1:** 146
"Triplex" (Doolittle), **Supp. I Part 1:** 271
Tripmaster Monkey: His Fake Book (Kingston), **Supp. V:** 157, 158, 169, 170–173

Trippings in Authorland (Forrester), **Supp. XVIII:** 13
Trippings of Tom Pepper, The (Briggs), **Supp. XVIII:** 3, **13–14**
"Trip to Hanoi" (Sontag), **Supp. III Part 2:** 460–462
Trip to Parnassus, A; or, The Judgement of Apollo on Dramatic Authors and Performers (Rowson), **Supp. XV: 232–233**
"Triptych" (Eberhart), **I:** 522, 539
Tristam Shandy (Sterne), **Supp. XXII:** 267
Tristan and Iseult, **Retro. Supp. I:** 328, 329, 330, 331
Tristessa (Kerouac), **Supp. III Part 1:** 225, 227, 229
Tristram (Robinson), **III:** 521, 522, 523
Tristram Shandy (Sterne), **I:** 299; **IV:** 465–466; **Supp. V:** 127; **Supp. XVIII:** 60
"Triumph" (C. L. R. James), **Supp. XXI:** 160
"Triumphal March" (Eliot), **I:** 580; **III:** 17; **Retro. Supp. I:** 64
Triumph of Achilles, The (Glück), **Supp. V:** 79, 84–86, 92
"Triumph of a Modern, The, or, Send for the Lawyer" (Anderson), **I:** 113, 114
"Triumph of the Egg, The" (Anderson), **I:** 113
Triumph of the Egg, The: A Book of Impressions from American Life in Tales and Poems (Anderson), **I:** 112, 114
Triumph of the Spider Monkey, The (Oates), **Supp. II Part 2:** 522
Triumphs of the Reformed Religion in America (Mather), **Supp. II Part 2:** 453
Trivial Breath (Wylie), **Supp. I Part 2:** 709, 722–724
Trivia; or, the Art of Walking the Streets of London (Gay), **Supp. XIV:** 337
Trivia: Printed from the Papers of Anthony Woodhouse, Esq. (L. P. Smith), **Supp. XIV:** 336, **337–340**
"Trivia Tea" (Skloot), **Supp. XX: 205**
Trocchi, Alexander, **Supp. XI:** 294, 295, 301
Troilus and Criseyde (Chaucer), **Retro. Supp. I:** 426
Trois contes (Flaubert), **IV:** 31, 37
Trojan Horse, The: A Play (MacLeish), **III:** 21
"Trojan Women, The" (Maxwell), **Supp. VIII:** 169
Troll Garden, The (Cather), **I:** 313, 314–316, 322; **Retro. Supp. I:** 5, 6, 8, 14
"Trolling for Blues" (Wilbur), **Supp. III Part 2:** 563–564
Trollope, Anthony, **I:** 10, 375; **II:** 192, 237; **III:** 51, 70, 281, 382; **Retro. Supp. I:** 361
Trombly, Albert Edmund, **Supp. I Part 2:** 403
Trombold, John, **Supp. XVIII:** 111
"Trompe L'Oeil" (Collins), **Supp. XXI:** 60
"Troop Train" (Shapiro), **Supp. II Part 2:** 707
"Tropes of the Text" (Gass), **Supp. VI:** 88
Tropic of Cancer (H. Miller), **III:** 170, 171, 174, 177, 178–180, 181, 182, 183, 187, 190; **Supp. V:** 119; **Supp. X:** 187; **Supp. XXII:** 230, 257
Tropic of Capricorn (H. Miller), **III:** 170, 176–177, 178, 182, 183, 184, 187, 188–189, 190
"Tropic of Cuba" (di Donato), **Supp. XX: 45**
Trotsky, Leon, **I:** 366; **II:** 562, 564; **IV:** 429; **Supp. XXI:** 161, 164, 165, 167, 168
Trotter, W., **I:** 249
Troubled Air, The (Shaw), **Supp. XIX: 249–250**
Troubled Island (opera; Hughes and Still), **Retro. Supp. I:** 203
Troubled Lovers in History (Goldbarth), **Supp. XII:** 176, **192–193**
Trouble Follows Me (Macdonald, under Millar), **Supp. IV Part 2:** 466
Trouble in July (Caldwell), **I:** 297, 304–305, 306, 309
Trouble Island (Hughes), **Supp. I Part 1:** 328
"Trouble of Marcie Flint, The" (Cheever), **Supp. I Part 1:** 186
Trouble with Francis, The: An Autobiography (Francis), **Supp. IX:** 76, 77, 82, **84–85**
Trouble with God, The (Francis), **Supp. IX:** 88
"Trouble with Poetry, The" (Collins), **Supp. XXI:** 57
Trouble with Poetry and Other Poems, The (Collins), **Supp. XXI:** 55, 57, 62
"Trouble with the Stars and Stripes" (Nye), **Supp. XIII:** 277
Trouillot, Michel-Rolphe, **Supp. X:** 14–15
Troupe, Quincy, **Retro. Supp. II:** 15, 111; **Supp. X:** 242
"Trout" (Hugo), **Supp. VI:** 135
Trout Fishing in America (Brautigan), **Supp. VIII:** 43
"Trouvée" (Bishop), **Retro. Supp. II:** 49
Troy (film), **Supp. XX: 273**
"Truce" (Taggard), **Supp. XXII:** 276–277
"Truce of the Bishop, The" (Frederic), **II:** 139–140
"Truck Stop: Minnesota" (Dunn), **Supp. XI:** 145–146
True Account, The: A Novel of the Lewis & Clark & Kinneson Expeditions (Mosher), **Supp. XXII:** 206, 207, 208, **214–215**
True and False: Heresy and Common Sense for the Actor (Mamet), **Supp. XIV:** 241, 243
True Blood (television series), **Supp. XIX:** 174
Trueblood, Valerie, **Supp. XIII:** 306
True Confessions (Dunne), **Supp. IV Part 1:** 198
True Confessions (film), **Supp. IV Part 1:** 198
Trueheart, Charles, **Supp. XXI:** 238
True History of the Conquest of New Spain, The (Castillo), **III:** 13
True Intellectual System of the Universe, The (Cuddleworth), **II:** 10
"True Love" (Olds), **Supp. X:** 212
Trueman, Matthew (pseudonym). *See* Lowell, James Russell
"True Morality" (Bell), **Supp. X:** 13
"True Romance" (Everett), **Supp. XVIII:** 65
Truesdale, C. W., **Supp. XXI:** 246
True Stories (Atwood), **Supp. XIII:** 34–35
"True Stories" (Atwood), **Supp. XIII:** 34
"True Stories of Bitches" (Mamet), **Supp. XIV:** 246, 252
"Truest Sport, The: Jousting with Sam and Charlie" (Wolfe), **Supp. III Part 2:** 581–582
"True Vine" (Wylie), **Supp. I Part 2:** 723
True West (Shepard), **Supp. III Part 2:** 433, 441, 445, 447, 448
Truman, Harry, **III:** 3
Truman Capote: In Which Various Friends, Enemies, Acquaintances, and Detractors Recall His Turbulent Career (Plimpton), **Supp. XVI:**245
Truman Show, The (film), **Supp. XVI:** 271
Trumbo, Dalton, **Supp. I Part 1:** 295; **Supp. XIII:** 6; **Supp. XVII:** 63; **Supp. XX: 246; Supp. XXI:** 45
Trumbull, John, **Supp. II Part 1:** 65, 69, 70, 268
Trump, Donald, **Supp. IV Part 1:** 393
Trumpener, Katie, **Retro. Supp. I:** 380
"Trumpet Player" (Hughes), **Supp. I Part 1:** 333
"Trumpet Player, 1963" (Halliday), **Supp. XIX:** 92
Trumpet Shall Sound, The (Wilder), **IV:** 356
Trumpet Unblown, The (Hoffman), **Supp. XVIII:** 71, **74–75**
Trunk Music (Connelly), **Supp. XXI: 72,** 75
"Truro Bear, The" (Oliver), **Supp. VII:** 234
Truscott, Lucian K., **Supp. IV Part 2:** 683
Trust (Ozick), **Supp. V:** 257–258, 259, 260–263, 270, 272
Trust Me (Updike), **Retro. Supp. I:** 322
"Trust Yourself" (Emerson), **II:** 10
"Truth" (Emerson), **II:** 6
"Truth, The" (Halliday), **Supp. XIX:** 87, 88, 94
"Truth, The" (Jarrell), **II:** 381–382
Truth About Celia, The (Brockmeier), **Supp. XXII: 53–55**
"Truth about God, The" (Carson), **Supp. XII: 105–106**
"Truth be told" (Trethewey), **Supp. XXI:** 255, 256
"Truthful James" (Harte), **IV:** 196
"Truth Is, The" (Hogan), **Supp. IV Part 1:** 401–402

"Truth Is Forced, The" (Swenson), **Supp. IV Part 2:** 652
"Truth of the Matter, The" (Nemerov), **III:** 270
Truth Serum (Cooper), **Supp. XI:** 129
"Truth the Dead Know, The" (Sexton), **Supp. II Part 2:** 681
"Trying to Evangelize a Cut Flower" (Peacock), **Supp. XIX:** 199
Trying to Find Chinatown (Hwang), **Supp. XXI:** 147
Trying to Save Piggy Sneed (Irving), **Supp. VI: 19–165**
"Trying to Talk with a Man" (Rich), **Supp. I Part 2:** 559
"Tryptich I" (Bell), **Supp. X:** 7
"Tryst, The" (Wharton), **Retro. Supp. I:** 378
"Try the Girl" (Chandler), **Supp. IV Part 1:** 125
"Ts'ai Chih" (Pound), **III:** 466
T. S. Eliot and American Philosophy (Jain), **Retro. Supp. I:** 58
T. S. Eliot's Silent Voices (Mayer), **Retro. Supp. I:** 58
Tsuji, Shizuo, **Supp. XVII:** 90
Tsvetayeva, Marina, **Supp. VIII:** 30
"Tuberoses" (E. Stoddard), **Supp. XV:** 282
Tucker, Benjamin R., **Supp. XXI:** 9
Tuckerman, Frederick Goddard, **IV:** 144
Tucker's People (Wolfert), **Supp. XXI:** 261, 262, 263, 267, **267–275,** 278
"Tuesday, November 5th, 1940" (Benét), **Supp. XI:** 46, 52
"Tuesday April 25th 1966" (Olson), **Supp. II Part 2:** 585
"Tuesday Night at the Savoy Ballroom" (Komunyakaa), **Supp. XIII:** 132
Tuffield, Aviva, **Supp. XVI:** 147, 148
"Tuft of Flowers, The" (Frost), **II:** 153; **Retro. Supp. I:** 126, 127
Tufts, James Hayden, **Supp. I Part 2:** 632
Tu Fu, **II:** 526; **Supp. XV:** 47
Tu Fu (Ayscough), **II:** 527
Tugwell, Rexford Guy, **Supp. I Part 2:** 645
"Tulip" (Hammett), **Supp. IV Part 1:** 356
"Tulip Man, The" (McCarriston), **Supp. XIV:** 261
"Tulips" (Nye), **Supp. XIII:** 281
"Tulips" (Plath), **Retro. Supp. II:** 252–253; **Supp. I Part 2:** 540, 542, 544
"Tulips" (Snodgrass), **Supp. VI:** 325
Tulips and Chimneys (Cummings), **I:** 436, 437, 440, 445, 447
Tully, Jim, **III:** 103, 109
Tumble Home (Hempel), **Supp. XXI:** 115, **124–125**
"Tumble Home" (Hempel), **Supp. XXI:** 115, 116, **124–125,** 126
Tumble Tower (Modarressi and Tyler), **Supp. IV Part 2:** 657
"Tuned in Late One Night" (Stafford), **Supp. XI:** 327–328
Tunnel, The (Gass), **Supp. V:** 44; **Supp. VI: 89–91,** 94
"Tunnel, The" (Strand), **Supp. IV Part 2:** 622
"Tunnels" (Komunyakaa), **Supp. XIII:** 123
Tuqan, Fadwa, **Supp. XIII:** 278
Tura, Cosimo, **III:** 474–475
Turandot and Other Poems (Ashbery), **Supp. III Part 1:** 3
Turco, Lewis, **Supp. XV:** 118
Turgenev, Ivan Sergeevich, **I:** 106; **II:** 263, 271, 275, 280, 281, 288, 319, 320, 324–325, 338, 407; **III:** 461; **IV:** 17, 277; **Retro. Supp. I:** 215, 222; **Supp. VIII:** 167
Turgot, Anne Robert Jacques, **II:** 103; **Supp. I Part 1:** 250
"Turkey and Bones and Eating and We Liked It" (Stein), **IV:** 44
Turman, Glynn, **Supp. IV Part 1:** 362
Turnbull, Dr. George, **II:** 113
Turnbull, Lawrence, **Supp. I Part 1:** 352
"Turned" (Gilman), **Supp. XI:** 207
Turner, Addie, **IV:** 123
Turner, Darwin, **Supp. I Part 1:** 339; **Supp. IV Part 1:** 165
Turner, Frederick Jackson, **Supp. I Part 2:** 480, 481, 632, 640; **Supp. IV Part 2:** 596
Turner, Nat, **IV:** 113–114, 115, 116, 117
Turner, Patricia A., **Supp. XIII:** 237; **Supp. XX: 110**
Turner, Russell. *See* Lacy, Ed
Turner, Victor, **Supp. IV Part 1:** 304
"Turning Away Variations on Estrangement" (Dickey), **Supp. IV Part 1:** 183
Turning Point, The (McCoy), **Supp. XIII:** 175
"Turning Thirty, I Contemplate Students Bicycling Home" (Dove), **Supp. IV Part 1:** 250
Turning Wind, A (Rukeyser), **Supp. VI:** 272–273, 279–280
Turn in the South, A (Naipaul), **Supp. XXII:** 240
Turn of the Screw, The (H. James), **Retro. Supp. I:** 219, 231; **Supp. IV Part 2:** 682
"Turn of the Screw, The" (H. James), **II:** 331–332; **Retro. Supp. I:** 228, 229, 231, 232; **Supp. XVII:** 143
Turns and Movies and Other Tales in Verse (Aiken), **I:** 65
"Turn with the Sun, A" (Knowles), **Supp. XII:** 237–238
"Turn Your Radio On" (J. W. Miller), **Supp. XX: 169**
Turow, Scott, **Supp. V:** 220; **Supp. XVII: 213–224**
Turpin, E. Walters, **Supp. XVIII:** 283
Turrinus, Lucius Mamilius, **IV:** 373
"Turtle" (Hogan), **Supp. IV Part 1:** 401
Turtle, Swan (Doty), **Supp. XI: 121–122**
"Turtle, Swan" (Doty), **Supp. XI:** 121–122
Turtle Island (Snyder), **Supp. VIII: 300–303**
Turtle Moon (Hoffman), **Supp. X:** 77, **87–88,** 89
"Turtle Shrine near Chittagong, The" (Nye), **Supp. XIII:** 277
Turturro, John, **Supp. XI:** 174
Tuscan Cities (Howells), **II:** 280
Tuskegee movement, **Supp. II Part 1:** 169, 172
Tuten, Frederic, **Supp. VIII:** 75, 76; **Supp. XIII:** 237, 249
Tuten, James, **Supp. XVIII:** 195
Tuthill, Louisa Cavolne, **Supp. I Part 2:** 684
"Tutored Child, The" (Kunitz), **Supp. III Part 1:** 264
Tuttleton, James W., **Supp. IV Part 1:** 166, 168
"T.V.A." (Agee), **I:** 35
Tvedten, Brother Benet, **Supp. IV Part 2:** 505
"TV Men" (Carson), **Supp. XII: 105, 112**
Twain, Mark, **I:** 57, 103, 107, 109, 190, 192, 193, 195, 197, 203, 209, 245, 246, 247–250, 255, 256, 257, 260, 261, 292, 342, 418, 469, 485; **II:** 70, 140, 259, 262, 266–268, 271, 272, 274–275, 276, 277, 280, 285–286, 287, 288, 289, 301, 304, 306, 307, 312, 415, 432, 434, 436, 446, 457, 467, 475, 476, 482; **III:** 65, 101, 102, 112–113, 114, 220, 347, 357, 409, 453, 454, 504, 507, 554, 558, 572, 575, 576; **IV: 190–213,** 333, 349, 451; **Retro. Supp. I:** 169, 194, 195; **Retro. Supp. II:** 123; **Supp. I Part 1:** 37, 39, 44, 247, 251, 313, 317; **Supp. I Part 2:** 377, 385, 393, 410, 455, 456, 457, 473, 475, 579, 602, 604, 618, 629, 651, 660; **Supp. II Part 1:** 193, 344, 354, 385; **Supp. IV Part 1:** 386, 388; **Supp. IV Part 2:** 463, 468, 603, 607, 693; **Supp. V:** 44, 113, 131; **Supp. VIII:** 40, 189; **Supp. IX:** 14, 171; **Supp. X:** 51, 227; **Supp. XII:** 343; **Supp. XIII:** 1, 17; **Supp. XV:** 41; **Supp. XVI:** 66, 208; **Supp. XVIII:** 1, 9, 13; **Supp. XXI:** 205; **Supp. XXII:** 89, 203, 205, 206
"Twa Sisters, The" (ballad), **Supp. I Part 2:** 696
Twelfth Night (Shakespeare), **Supp. IV Part 1:** 83; **Supp. IX:** 14; **Supp. XXII:** 229
"12 O'Clock News" (Bishop), **Retro. Supp. II:** 48
Twelve Men (Dreiser), **Retro. Supp. II:** 94, 104
Twelve Moons (Oliver), **Supp. VII:** 231, 233–236, 238, 240
Twelve Southerners, **IV:** 125; **Supp. X:** 25
Twelve Years a Slave (Northup), **Supp. XIV:** 32
Twentieth Century Authors, **I:** 376, 527
"Twentieth Century Fiction and the Black Mask of Humanity" (Ellison), **Retro. Supp. II:** 118
Twentieth Century Pleasures (Hass), **Supp. VI:** 103, 106, 109
Twenty Drawings (Gibran), **Supp. XX: 116**
"28" (Levine), **Supp. V:** 187, 191
"Twenty-Four Poems" (Schwartz), **Supp. II Part 2:** 646, 649

"2433 Agnes, First Home, Last House in Missoula" (Hugo), **Supp. VI:** 139–140
"Twenty Hill Hollow" (Muir), **Supp. IX:** 178
"Twenty Minutes" (Salter), **Supp. IX:** 260
"Twenty-One Love Poems" (Rich), **Supp. I Part 2:** 572–573
"Twenty-One Poems" (MacLeish), **III:** 19
Twenty Poems (Haines), **Supp. XII:** 204, **205–206**
Twenty Poems of Anna Akhmatova (Kenyon), **Supp. VII:** 165–166
Twenty Questions: (Posed by Poems) (McClatchy), **Supp. XII:** 254, **259–262**
27 Wagons Full of Cotton and Other One-Act Plays (T. Williams), **IV:** 381, 383
Twenty-seventh City, The (Franzen), **Supp. XX: 83–84, 84, 85, 86–88, 88, 89, 91, 92, 95**
Twenty Thousand Leagues under the Sea (Verne), **I:** 480; **Supp. XI:** 63
"Twenty Years Ago" (Lindsay), **Supp. I Part 2:** 384, 399
Twenty Years at Hull-House (Addams), **Supp. I Part 1:** 3, 4, 11, 16
Twersky, David, **Supp. XX: 244**
Twice over Lightly: New York Ten and Now (Hayes and Loos), **Supp. XVI:** 195
Twice-Told Tales (Hawthorne), **I:** 354; **II:** 224; **III:** 412, 421; **Retro. Supp. I:** 154–155, 160
Twichell, Chase, **Supp. V:** 16; **Supp. XVII:** 110, 112
Twilight (Frost), **II:** 151
"Twilight's Last Gleaming" (Burroughs and Elvins), **Supp. III Part 1:** 93, 94, 101
Twilight Sleep (Wharton), **IV:** 320–322, 324–325, 327, 328; **Retro. Supp. I:** 381
"Twin, The" (Olds), **Supp. X:** 207
"Twin Beds in Rome" (Updike), **Retro. Supp. I:** 332
"Twins of Table Mountain, The" (Harte), **Supp. II Part 1:** 355
"Twist, The" (Olson), **Supp. II Part 2:** 570
Twitch and Shout (film), **Supp. XVIII:** 143
Twitchell-Waas, Jeffrey ?/, **Supp. XXII:** 163
Twitchel-Waas, Jeffrey ?/, **Supp. XVIII:** 99
Two Admirals, The (Cooper), **I:** 350
Two against One (F. Barthelme), **Supp. XI:** 32, 33, 36
"Two Boys" (Moore), **Supp. X:** 173
"Two Brothers, The" (Jewett), **Retro. Supp. II:** 132
Two-Character Play, The (T. Williams), **IV:** 382, 386, 393, 398
Two Citizens (Wright), **Supp. III Part 2:** 602–604
"Two Deer" (Bass), **Supp. XVI:** 24
"Two Domains, The" (Goldbarth), **Supp. XII:** 192
"Two-Eleven All Around" (Offutt), **Supp. XIX:** 170
"Two Environments, The" (Trilling), **Supp. III Part 2:** 510
"Two-Fisted Self Pity" (Broyard), **Supp. XI:** 348
Two for Texas (Burke), **Supp. XIV:** 25, 34
"Two Friends" (Cather), **I:** 332
"Two Gardens in Linndale" (Robinson), **III:** 508
Two Gentlemen in Bonds (Ransom), **III:** 491–492
Two: Gertrude Stein and Her Brother (Stein), **IV:** 43
"Two Ghosts" (Francis), **Supp. IX:** 87
"Two Hangovers" (Wright), **Supp. III Part 2:** 596
Two-Headed Poems (Atwood), **Supp. XIII:** 34
Two Hot to Handle (Lacy), **Supp. XV:** 206
Two Hours to Doom (Bryant), **Supp. XI:** 302
"Two Hundred Years in an Hour" (Boyce), **Supp. XXI:** 8
"Two Kitchens in Provence" (M. F. K. Fisher), **Supp. XVII:** 88, 91
"Two Ladies in Retirement" (Taylor), **Supp. V:** 320
Two Letters to the Citizens of the United States, and One to General Washington (Barlow), **Supp. II Part 1:** 80
"Two Lives, The" (Hogan), **Supp. IV Part 1:** 400, 402, 403, 406, 411
Two Long Poems (Stern), **Supp. IX:** 296
"Two Look at Two" (Frost), **Supp. XXI:** 26
"Two Lovers and a Beachcomber by the Real Sea" (Plath), **Supp. I Part 2:** 536
"Two Men" (McClatchy)", **Supp. XII:** 269
Two Men (E. Stoddard), **Supp. XV:** 272, 273, **283–284**
Two Men of Sandy Bar (Harte), **Supp. II Part 1:** 354
Twomey, Jay, **Supp. XVII:** 111
"Two Moods of Love" (Cullen), **Supp. IV Part 1:** 166
Two Moons (Mallon), **Supp. XIX:** 132, **138–141**
"Two Morning Monologues" (Bellow), **I:** 150; **Retro. Supp. II:** 20
"Two Nations of Black America, The" *(Frontline),* **Supp. XX: 99**
Two-Ocean War, The (Morison), **Supp. I Part 2:** 491
"Two of Hearts" (Hogan), **Supp. IV Part 1:** 410
"Two on a Party" (T. Williams), **IV:** 388
"Two or Three Things I Dunno About John Cassavetes" (Lethem), **Supp. XVIII:** 148
"Two Pendants: For the Ears" (W. C. Williams), **Retro. Supp. I:** 423
"Two Poems of Going Home" (Dickey), **Supp. IV Part 1:** 182–183
"Two Portraits" (Chopin), **Supp. I Part 1:** 218
"Two Presences, The" (R. Bly), **Supp. IV Part 1:** 65
"Two Rivers" (Stegner), **Supp. IV Part 2:** 605
Tworkov, Jack, **Supp. XII:** 198
"Two Scenes" (Ashbery), **Supp. III Part 1:** 4
Two Serious Ladies (Jane Bowles), **Supp. IV Part 1:** 82
"Two Silences" (Carruth), **Supp. XVI:** 55
"Two Sisters" (Farrell), **II:** 45
Two Sisters: A Memoir in the Form of a Novel (Vidal), **Supp. IV Part 2:** 679
"Two Sisters of Persephone" (Plath), **Retro. Supp. II:** 246
"Two Songs on the Economy of Abundance" (Agee), **I:** 28
Two Sons, The (Boyce), **Supp. XXI:** 7, 13
"Two Tales of Clumsy" (Schnackenberg), **Supp. XV:** 258
"Two Temples, The" (Melville), **III:** 89–90
Two Thousand Seasons (Armah), **Supp. IV Part 1:** 373
Two Towns in Provence (M. F. K. Fisher), **Supp. XVII:** 91
Two Trains Running (Wilson), **Supp. VIII: 345–348**
"Two Tramps in Mudtime" (Frost), **II:** 164; **Retro. Supp. I:** 137; **Supp. IX:** 261
"Two Views of a Cadaver Room" (Plath), **Supp. I Part 2:** 538
"Two Villages" (Paley), **Supp. VI:** 227
"Two Voices in a Meadow" (Wilbur), **Supp. III Part 2:** 555
Two Weeks in Another Town (Shaw), **Supp. XIX:** 251
"Two Witches" (Frost), **Retro. Supp. I:** 135
"Two Words" (Francis), **Supp. IX:** 81
Two Worlds Walking: A Mixed-Blood Anthology (Glancy and Truesdale, eds.), **Supp. XXI:** 246
Two Years before the Mast (Dana), **I:** 351
"Tyger, The" (Blake), **Supp. XVII:** 128
Tyler, Anne, **Supp. IV Part 2: 657–675; Supp. V:** 227, 326; **Supp. VIII:** 141; **Supp. X:** 1, 77, 83, 85; **Supp. XII:** 307; **Supp. XVI:** 37; **Supp. XVIII:** 157, 195
Tyler, Royall, **I:** 344; **Retro. Supp. I:** 377
Tymms, Ralph, **Supp. IX:** 105
Tyndale, William, **II:** 15
Tyndall, John, **Retro. Supp. II:** 93
Typee: A Peep at Polynesian Life (Melville), **III:** 75–77, 79, 84; **Retro. Supp. I:** 245–246, 249, 252, 256
Types From City Streets (Hapgood), **Supp. XVII:** 103
"Typewriter, The" (D. West), **Supp. XVIII:** 279
Typewriter Town (W. J. Smith), **Supp. XIII:** 332
"Typhus" (Simpson), **Supp. IX:** 277
Tyranny of the Normal (Fiedler), **Supp. XIII: 107–108**

"Tyranny of the Normal" (Fiedler), **Supp. XIII:** 107–108
"Tyrant of Syracuse" (MacLeish), **III:** 20
"Tyrian Businesses" (Olson), **Supp. II Part 2:** 567, 568, 569
Tytell, John, **Supp. XIV:** 140
Tzara, Tristan, **Supp. III Part 1:** 104, 105

U and I (Baker), **Supp. XIII: 45–47,** 48, 52, 55
Überdie Seelenfrage (Fechner), **II:** 358
Ubik (Dick), **Supp. XVIII:** 136
Ubu Roi (Jarry), **Supp. XV:** 178, 186
Ueland, Brenda, **Supp. XVII:** 13
Uhry, Alfred, **Supp. XX: 177**
Ukrainian Dumy (P. N. Warren as Kilina and Tarnawsky, trans.), **Supp. XX: 261**
"Ulalume" (Poe), **III:** 427; **Retro. Supp. II:** 264, 266
Ulin, David, **Supp. XIII:** 244; **Supp. XVI:** 74
Ullman, Leslie, **Supp. IV Part 2:** 550; **Supp. XVIII:** 175
Ultimate Good Luck, The (Ford), **Supp. V:** 57, 61–62
Ultimate Punishment: A Lawyer's Reflections on Dealing with the Death Penalty (Turow), **Supp. XVII:** 220–221
Ultima Thule (Longfellow), **II:** 490; **Retro. Supp. II:** 169
"Ultima Thule" (Nabokov), **Retro. Supp. I:** 274
Ultramarine (Carver), **Supp. III Part 1:** 137, 138, 147, 148
Ulysses (Joyce), **I:** 395, 475–476, 478, 479, 481; **II:** 42, 264, 542; **III:** 170, 398; **IV:** 103, 418, 428, 455; **Retro. Supp. I:** 59, 63, 290, 291; **Retro. Supp. II:** 121; **Supp. I Part 1:** 57; **Supp. III Part 2:** 618, 619; **Supp. IV Part 1:** 285; **Supp. IV Part 2:** 424; **Supp. V:** 261; **Supp. IX:** 102; **Supp. X:** 114; **Supp. XIII:** 43, 191; **Supp. XV:** 305; **Supp. XVII:** 140, 227
"*Ulysses,* Order and Myth" (Eliot), **Retro. Supp. I:** 63
"Umbrella, The" (Peacock), **Supp. XIX:** 203–204
Unaccountable Worth of the World, The (Price), **Supp. VI:** 267
Unaccustomed Earth (Lahiri), **Supp. XXI:** 176, **181–183,** 183, 188
"Unaccustomed Earth" (Lahiri), **Supp. XXI:** 186
Unamuno y Jugo, Miguel de, **III:** 310; **Supp. XV:** 79
"Unattached Smile, The" (Crews), **Supp. XI:** 101
"Unbelievable Thing Usually Goes to the Heart of the Story, The: Magic Realism in the Fiction of Rick Bass" (Dwyer), **Supp. XVI:** 16
"Unbeliever, The" (Bishop), **Retro. Supp. II:** 43
"Unborn Song" (Rukeyser), **Supp. VI:** 274
Unbought Spirit: A John Jay Chapman Reader (Stone, ed.), **Supp. XIV:** 54
Uncalled, The (Dunbar), **Supp. II Part 1:** 200, 211, 212
Uncentering the Earth: Copernicus and The Revolutions of the Heavenly Spheres (Vollmann), **Supp. XVII:** 226
Uncertain Certainty, The: Interviews, Essays, and Notes on Poetry (Simic), **Supp. VIII:** 270, 273, 274
Uncertainty and Plenitude: Five Contemporary Poets (Stitt), **Supp. IX:** 299
"Uncle" (Levine), **Supp. V:** 186
"Uncle Adler" (Kooser), **Supp. XIX:** 120
"Uncle Christmas" (Ríos), **Supp. IV Part 2:** 552
"Uncle Jim's Baptist Revival Hymn" (Lanier and Lanier), **Supp. I Part 1:** 353
"Uncle Lot" (Stowe), **Supp. I Part 2:** 585–586
"Uncle Moustapha's Eclipse" (McKnight), **Supp. XX: 148**
Uncle Remus Tales (Harris), **Supp. II Part 1:** 201
"Uncle Tomitudes" (Briggs), **Supp. XVIII:** 14
Uncle Tom's Cabin (Stowe), **II:** 291; **Supp. I Part 1:** 49; **Supp. I Part 2:** 410, 579, 582, 589–592; **Supp. II Part 1:** 170; **Supp. III Part 1:** 154, 171; **Supp. IX:** 19; **Supp. X:** 246, 249, 250; **Supp. XIII:** 95; **Supp. XVI:** 82, 85, 88; **Supp. XVIII:** 14
Uncle Tom's Children (Wright), **IV:** 476, 478, 488; **Supp. II Part 1:** 228, 235; **Supp. XVIII:** 283
"Uncle Wiggily in Connecticut" (Salinger), **III:** 559–560, 563
"Unclouded Day, The" (Proulx), **Supp. VII:** 254–255
"Uncommon Visage" (Brodsky), **Supp. VIII:** 31
"Uncommon Woman: An Interview with Wendy Wasserstein" (Cohen), **Supp. XV:** 323
Uncommon Women and Others (Wasserstein), **Supp. XV:** 320–321, **322–323**
Uncompromising Fictions of Cynthia Ozick (Pinsker), **Supp. V:** 272
"Unconscious Came a Beauty" (Swenson), **Supp. IV Part 2:** 646
"Uncreation, The" (Pinsky), **Supp. VI:** 245
"Undead, The" (Wilbur), **Supp. III Part 2:** 556
"Undefeated, The" (Hemingway), **II:** 250; **Retro. Supp. I:** 180
Under a Glass Bell (Nin), **Supp. X:** 186
"Under Ben Bulben" (Yeats), **Supp. V:** 220
Undercliff: Poems 1946–1953 (Eberhart), **I:** 528, 536–537
Under Cover (Goldbarth), **Supp. XII:** 177, 180, 193
Undercover Doctor (film), **Supp. XIII:** 170
"Under Cygnus" (Wilbur), **Supp. III Part 2:** 558
"Under Forty" (Trilling), **Supp. III Part 2:** 494
Underground, The Story of a People (Tenenbaum), **Supp. XX: 253**
Underground Man, The (film), **Supp. IV Part 2:** 474
Underground Man, The (Macdonald), **Supp. IV Part 2:** 474, 475
"Under Libra: Weights and Measures" (Merrill), **Supp. III Part 1:** 328
Under Milk Wood (D. Thomas), **III:** 21
"Undersea" (Carson), **Supp. IX:** 21
Understanding Cynthia Ozick (Friedman), **Supp. V:** 273
Understanding Drama (Brooks and Heilman), **Supp. XIV:** 12
Understanding E. L. Doctorow (Fowler), **Supp. IV Part 1:** 226
Understanding Fiction (Brooks and Warren), **IV:** 279; **Supp. XIV:** 11
Understanding Fiction (Brooks and Warren, eds.), **Supp. XIX:** 246
Understanding Flannery O'Connor (Whitt), **Retro. Supp. II:** 226
Understanding Nicholson Baker (Saltzman), **Supp. XIII:** 48
Understanding Poetry: An Anthology for College Students (Brooks and Warren), **IV:** 236; **Retro. Supp. I:** 40, 41; **Supp. XIV:** 4–5
Understanding Robert Bly (W. V. Davis), **Supp. XXI: 84–85,** 88
Understanding Tim O'Brien (Kaplan), **Supp. V:** 241
Understanding To Kill a Mockingbird: A Student Casebook to Issues, Sources, and Documents (Johnson), **Supp. VIII:** 127
Undertaker's Garland, The (Wilson and Bishop), **IV:** 427
Under the Banner of Heaven: A Story of Violent Faith (Krakauer), **Supp. XVIII:** 105, **114–116,** 117
"Under the Cedarcroft Chestnut" (Lanier), **Supp. I Part 1:** 364
"Under the Harbour Bridge" (Komunyakaa), **Supp. XIII:** 125
"Under the Influence" (Sanders), **Supp. XVI:** 274, 277
Under the Lilacs (Alcott), **Supp. I Part 1:** 42–43, 44
"Under the Maud Moon" (Kinnell), **Supp. III Part 1:** 246–247
Under the Mountain Wall: A Chronicle of Two Seasons in the Stone Age (Matthiessen), **Supp. V:** 202
Under the Red Flag (Jin), **Supp. XVIII:** 89, **94–95**
"Under the Rose" (Pynchon), **Supp. II Part 2:** 620
Under the Sea-Wind: A Naturalist's Picture of Ocean Life (Carson), **Supp. IX:** 19, **22–23**
Under the Shadow (Sorrentino), **Supp. XXI:** 236–237
Under the Sign of Saturn (Sontag), **Supp. III Part 2:** 451, 452, 458, 470–471
"Under the Sign of Saturn" (Sontag), **Supp. III Part 2:** 470

"Under the Sky" (Bowles), **Supp. IV Part 1:** 87

" 'Under the Umbrella of Black Civilization': A Conversation with Reginald McKnight" (Ashe), **Supp. XX: 154**

Under the Volcano (M. Lowry), **Supp. XVII:** 135, 139, 140

"Under the Willows" (Lowell), **Supp. I Part 2:** 416

Under the Willows and Other Poems (Lowell), **Supp. I Part 2:** 424

"Undertow" (Boyce), **Supp. XXI:** 10

Underwood, Wilbur, **Retro. Supp. II:** 79

Underworld (DeLillo), **Supp. VI:** 2, 4–5, 6–7, 8, 9, 10, 11, **13–15; Supp. XI:** 68; **Supp. XX: 91**

Underworld, The (Wolfert). *See Tucker's World* (Wolfert)

Undine (La Motte-Fouqué), **II:** 212; **III:** 78

Undiscovered Country, The (Howells), **II:** 282

"Undressing, The" (C. Frost), **Supp. XV:** 98

Uneasy Chair, The (Stegner), **Supp. IV Part 2:** 599

"Unemployed, Disabled, and Insane, The" (Haines), **Supp. XII:** 211–212

Unending Blues (Simic), **Supp. VIII: 278–279**

"Unexpected Freedom" (Peacock), **Supp. XIX:** 199

"Unexpressed" (Dunbar), **Supp. II Part 1:** 199

"Unfinished Bronx, The" (Paley), **Supp. VI:** 228

Unfinished Crime, The (Holding), **Supp. XXII:** 120, **123–124,** 135, 136

"Unfinished Poems" (Eliot), **I:** 579

"Unfinished Song" (C. Frost), **Supp. XV:** 97

Unfinished Woman, An (Hellman), **Supp. I Part 1:** 292, 293, 294; **Supp. IV Part 1:** 12, 353–354; **Supp. IX:** 196, 200–201

Unforeseen Wilderness, The: An Essay on Kentucky's Red River Gorge (Berry), **Supp. X:** 28, 29, 30, 36

Unforgotten Years (L. P. Smith), **Supp. XIV:** 333, 334, 335, 336, 347

"Unfortunate Coincidence" (Parker), **Supp. IX:** 190

Unframed Originals (Merwin), **Supp. III Part 1:** 341

Ungar, Sanford, **Supp. XI:** 228

Ungaretti, Giuseppe, **Supp. V:** 337

Unguided Tour (Sontag), **Supp. III Part 2:** 452

"Unheimliche, Das" (The Uncanny) (Freud), **Supp. XVI:** 157–158

Unholy Sonnets (Jarman), **Supp. XVII:** 109, 110, **119–120; Supp. XVIII:** 178

"Unholy Sonnets" (Jarman), **Supp. XVII:** 118, 119–120

"Unidentified Flying Object" (Hayden), **Supp. II Part 1:** 368

"Unifying Principle, The" (Ammons), **Supp. VII:** 28

"Unimportant Man, An" (D. West), **Supp. XVIII:** 280

"Union" (Hughes), **Supp. I Part 1:** 331

"Union Street: San Francisco, Summer 1975" (Carver), **Supp. III Part 1:** 138

United States Army in World War II (Morison), **Supp. I Part 2:** 490

United States Constitution, **I:** 6, 283

United States Essays, 1951–1991 (Vidal), **Supp. IV Part 2:** 678, 687

"United States of Huck, The: Introduction to *Adventures of Huckleberry Finn" (Saunders), Supp. XIX:* 235

United States of Poetry, The (television series), **Supp. XIII:** 274

"Unity through Diversity" (Locke), **Supp. XIV:** 212, 213

Universal Baseball Asociation, Inc., J. Henry Waugh, Prop., The (Coover), **Supp. V:** 39, 41–42, 44, 46

Universal Passion (Young), **III:** 111

"Universe of Death, The" (H. Miller), **III:** 184

Universe of Time, A (Anderson), **II:** 27, 28, 45, 46, 48, 49

"Universities" (Emerson), **II:** 6

"Universities: A Mirage? " (Mora), **Supp. XIII:** 219

"University" (Shapiro), **Supp. II Part 2:** 704–705, 717

"University Avenue" (Mora), **Supp. XIII:** 216

"University Days" (Thurber), **Supp. I Part 2:** 605

"University Hospital, Boston" (Oliver), **Supp. VII:** 235

"University's Peril, The" (Taggard), **Supp. XXII:** 273

"Unknowable, The" (Levine), **Supp. V:** 195

"Unknown Girl in the Maternity Ward" (Sexton), **Supp. II Part 2:** 676

"Unknown Love, The" (Chandler), **Supp. IV Part 1:** 120

Unknown Rilke, The (Rilke; F. Wright, trans.), **Supp. XVII:** 244

"Unknown War, The" (Sandburg), **III:** 594

Unkown Constellations, The (Swados), **Supp. XIX:** 256

Unleashed (anthology), **Supp. XI:** 132

Unleashed: Poems by Writers' Dogs (Hempel and Shepard, eds.), **Supp. XXI:** 115

"Unlighted Lamps" (Anderson), **I:** 112

Unlit Lamp, The (Holding), **Supp. XXII: 121,** 130

Unloved Wife, The (Alcott), **Supp. I Part 1:** 33

Unmarried Woman, An (film), **Supp. IV Part 1:** 303

"Unnatural Mother, The" (Gilman), **Supp. XI:** 207

"Unnatural State of the Unicorn" (Komunyakaa), **Supp. XIII:** 119

"Unparalleled Adventure of One Hans Pfaall, The" (Poe), **III:** 424

"Unpleasant Profession of Jonathan Hoag, The" (Heinlein), **Supp. XVIII:** 149

Unprecedented Era, The (Goebbels), **III:** 560

"Unprofitable Servant, The" (O. Henry), **Supp. II Part 1:** 403

Unpublished Poems of Emily Dickinson (Bianchi and Hampson, ed.), **Retro. Supp. I:** 35

Unpunished (Gilman), **Supp. XI:** 208

Unraveling Strangeness, The (Weigl), **Supp. XIX: 287–288**

"Unreal City" (Eliot), **Supp. XV:** 218

"Unreasoning Heart" (Untermeyer), **Supp. XV:** 309

"Unsaid (Gioia), **Supp. XV:** 129

"Unseen, The" (Pinsky), **Supp. VI:** 243–244

"Unseen, The" (Singer), **Retro. Supp. II:** 307

Unseen Hand, The (Shepard), **Supp. III Part 2:** 439, 445–446

Unselected Poems (Levine), **Supp. V:** 179

Unsettling of America, The: Culture and Agriculture (Berry), **Supp. X:** 22, 26, 29, 32, 33, 35; **Supp. XIV:** 177, 179

Unspeakable Gentleman, The (Marquand), **III:** 53–54, 60, 63

Unspeakable Practices, Unnatural Acts (Barthelme), **Supp. IV Part 1:** 39

"Unspeakable Things Unspoken: The Afro-American Presence in American Literature" (Morrison), **Supp. III Part 1:** 375, 377–379

Unspoken and Other Poems, The (Bremer), **Supp. XXII:** 277

"Untelling, The" (Strand), **Supp. IV Part 2:** 629

Unterecker, John, **I:** 386

Untermeyer, Jean Starr, **II:** 530; **Supp. XV:** 294, 295, 303, 307, 308, 310

Untermeyer, Louis, **II:** 516–517, 530, 532; **III:** 268; **Retro. Supp. I:** 124, 133, 136; **Supp. III Part 1:** 2; **Supp. IX:** 76; **Supp. XIV:** 119, 123; **Supp. XV: 293–318; Supp. XXI:** 277

Untimely Papers (Bourne), **I:** 218, 233

"Untitled" (C. Frost), **Supp. XV:** 103

"Untitled Blues" (Komunyakaa), **Supp. XIII:** 117

Unto the Sons (Talese), **Supp. XVII:** 199–200, **206–207,** 208, 209, 210

"Untrustworthy Speaker, The" (Glück), **Supp. V:** 86

"Unused" (Anderson), **I:** 112, 113

Unvanquished, The (Faulkner), **II:** 55, 67–68, 71; **Retro. Supp. I:** 84; **Supp. I Part 2:** 450

"Unvexed Isles, The" (Warren), **IV:** 253

"Unwedded" (Larcom), **Supp. XIII:** 144

"Unweepables, The" (Karr), **Supp. XI:** 243

"Unwelcome Guest, An" (Papernick), **Supp. XVII:** 50

Unwelcome Man, The (W. Frank), **Supp. XX: 70, 76**

Unwelcome Words (Bowles), **Supp. IV Part 1:** 93, 94

"Unwelcome Words" (Bowles), **Supp. IV Part 1:** 94, 95

Unwin, T. Fisher, **Supp. XI:** 202

"Unwithered Garland, The" (Kunitz), **Supp. III Part 1:** 265
Unwobbling Pivot, The (Pound, trans.), **III:** 472
"Unwritten, The" (Merwin), **Supp. III Part 1:** 352
"Unwritten Law" (Glück), **Supp. V:** 91
Up (Sukenick), **Supp. V:** 39
Up Above the World (Bowles), **Supp. IV Part 1:** 82, 91, 92
"Up and Down" (Merrill), **Supp. III Part 1:** 328
Upanishads, **IV:** 183
Up Country: Poems of New England (Kumin), **Supp. IV Part 2:** 446, 447–448, 453
"Update" (Dunn), **Supp. XI:** 150–151
Updike, John, **I:** 54; **III:** 572; **IV: 214–235; Retro. Supp. I:** 116, **317–338; Retro. Supp. II:** 213, 279, 280; **Supp. I Part 1:** 186, 196; **Supp. IV Part 2:** 657; **Supp. V:** 23, 43, 95, 119; **Supp. VIII:** 151, 167, 236; **Supp. IX:** 208; **Supp. XI:** 65, 66, 99, 140; **Supp. XII:** 140, 296, 298, 310; **Supp. XIII:** 45–46, 47, 52; **Supp. XIV:** 79, 93, 111; **Supp. XVI:** 205, 207, 220; **Supp. XX: 17; Supp. XXI:** 116, 226
Updike, Mrs. Wesley, **IV:** 218, 220
Up from Slavery (Washington), **Supp. II Part 1:** 169; **Supp. IX:** 19
Upham, Thomas Goggswell, **II:** 487
"Upholsterers, The" (Lardner), **II:** 435
"Up in Michigan" (Hemingway), **II:** 263; **Supp. XIX:** 241
Upjohn, Richard, **IV:** 312
"Upon a Spider Catching a Fly" (Taylor), **IV:** 161
"Upon a Wasp Child with Cold" (Taylor), **IV:** 161
"Upon Meeting Don L. Lee, in a Dream" (Dove), **Supp. IV Part 1:** 244
"Upon My Dear and Loving Husband His Going into England, Jan. 16, 1661" (Bradstreet), **Supp. I Part 1:** 110
"Upon Returning to the Country Road" (Lindsay), **Supp. I Part 2:** 382
"Upon the Burning of Our House, July 10th, 1666" (Bradstreet), **Supp. I Part 1:** 107–108, 122
"Upon the Sweeping Flood" (Taylor), **IV:** 161
"Upon Wedlock, and Death of Children" (Taylor), **IV:** 144, 147, 161
"Upset, An" (Merrill), **Supp. III Part 1:** 336
Upstairs and Downstairs (Vonnegut), **Supp. II Part 2:** 757
Upstate (Wilson), **IV:** 447
Upton, Lee, **Supp. X:** 209
"Upturned Face" (Crane), **I:** 423
Upward, Allen, **Supp. I Part 1:** 262
Upward, Edward, **Supp. XIV:** 159, 160
"Upward Moon and the Downward Moon, The" (R. Bly), **Supp. IV Part 1:** 71
Urania: A Rhymed Lesson (Holmes), **Supp. I Part 1:** 300
"Urban Convalescence, An" (Merrill), **Supp. III Part 1:** 322–324
"Urban Renewal" (Komunyakaa), **Supp. XIII:** 113
Urdang, Constance, **Supp. XV:** 74
"Urganda and Fatima" (Rowson), **Supp. XV:** 234
Urial Accosta: A Play (Reznikoff), **Supp. XIV:** 282, 288
Urich, Robert, **Supp. V:** 228
"Uriel" (Emerson), **II:** 19
Uris, Leon, **Supp. IV Part 1:** 285, 379; **Supp. XX: 243–258**
Uroff, Margaret D., **Supp. I Part 2:** 542
"Us" (Sexton), **Supp. II Part 2:** 687
U.S. 1 (Rukeyser), **Supp. VI:** 272, 278, 283, 285
U.S.A. (Dos Passos), **I:** 379, 475, 478, 482–488, 489, 490, 491, 492, 493, 494, 495; **Retro. Supp. II:** 197; **Supp. I Part 2:** 646; **Supp. III Part 1:** 104, 105; **Supp. XIV:** 24
"U.S.A. School of Writing, The" (Bishop), **Retro. Supp. II:** 43
"U.S. Commercial Orchid, The" (Agee), **I:** 35
"Used-Boy Raisers, The" (Paley), **Supp. VI:** 218, 228
"Used Cars on Oahu" (Nye), **Supp. XIII:** 282
"Used Side of the Sofa, The" (Ríos), **Supp. IV Part 2:** 551
Useless Servants, The (Hinojosa), **Supp. XIX:** 98, 103, 104, **109–110**
Use of Fire, The (Price), **Supp. VI:** 265
"Use of Force, The" (W. C. Williams), **Retro. Supp. I:** 424
Use of Poetry and the Use of Criticism, The (Eliot), **Retro. Supp. I:** 65
Uses of Enchantment, The: The Meaning and Importance of Fairy Tales (Bettelheim), **Supp. XIV:** 126
Uses of Enchantment, The: The Meaning and Importance of Fairy Tales (Bettleheim), **Supp. X:** 77
"Uses of Hell, The" (E. Hoffman), **Supp. XVI:** 154
"Uses of Hell, The: An Exchange"(Novick, Katz, and Szulc), **Supp. XVI:** 154
Uses of Literacy, The (Hoggart), **Supp. XIV:** 299
Uses of Literature, The (Calvino), **Supp. XXII:** 263
"Uses of Poetry, The" (W. C. Williams), **Retro. Supp. I:** 412
"Uses of the Blues, The" (Baldwin), **Retro. Supp. II:** 8
"Use-Unuse of Us, The" (Bronk), **Supp. XXI:** 32
"USFS 1919: The Ranger, the Cook, and a Hole in the Sky" (Maclean), **Supp. XIV:** 230, 234
Ushant: An Essay (Aiken), **I:** 49, 54, 55, 56, 57
"Usher 11" (Bradbury), **Supp. I Part 2:** 622
"Using Parrots to Kill Mockingbirds: Yet Another Racial Prosecution and Wrongful Conviction in Maycomb" (Fair), **Supp. VIII:** 128
Ustedes y Nosotros: Nuevo Mensaje a Ibero-América (W. Frank), **Supp. XX: 79**
Usual Star, The (Doolittle), **Supp. I Part 1:** 270
"Usurpation (Other People's Stories)" (Ozick), **Supp. V:** 268, 271
Utopia 14 (Vonnegut), **Supp. II Part 2:** 757
V. (Pynchon), **Supp. II Part 2:** 618, 620–622, 627–630; **Supp. IV Part 1:** 279
"Vacation" (Stafford), **Supp. XI:** 321, 322
"Vacation Trip" (Stafford), **Supp. XI:** 322
Vachel Lindsay: A Poet in America (Masters), **Supp. I Part 2:** 473, 474
"Vachel Lindsay: The Midwest as Utopia" (Whitney), **Supp. I Part 2:** 403
"Vachel Lindsay Writes to Floyd Dell" (Tanselle), **Supp. I Part 2:** 403
"Vacillation" (Yeats), **Supp. XV:** 253
Vadim, Roger, **Supp. XI:** 293, 307
"Vag" (Dos Passos), **I:** 487–488
Vagina Monologues, The (Ensler), **Supp. XIX:** 204–205
Valediction (Parker), **Supp. XIX:** 185
Valentine, Jean, **Supp. V:** 92
Valentine, Saint, **IV:** 396
Valentines (Kooser), **Supp. XIX:** 116, 123, **128–129**
Valentino, Rudolph, **I:** 483
Valéry, Paul, **II:** 543, 544; **III:** 279, 409, 428, 609; **IV:** 79, 91, 92, 428, 443; **Retro. Supp. II:** 187
"Valhalla" (Francis), **Supp. IX:** 77
Valhalla and Other Poems (Francis), **Supp. IX:** 76
Validity in Interpretation (Hirsch), **Supp. XIV:** 15
Valitsky, Ken, **Supp. XII:** 7
Vallejo, César, **Supp. V:** 332; **Supp. IX:** 271; **Supp. XIII:** 114, 315, 323; **Supp. XXI:** 132
"Valley, The" (Bass), **Supp. XVI:** 20, 22
Valley, The (Hinojosa), **Supp. XIX:** 97, 99, **100–101**
"Valley Between, The" (Marshall), **Supp. XI:** 278
Valley of Decision, The (Wharton), **IV:** 311, 315; **Retro. Supp. I:** 365–367
"Valley of the Monsters, The" (Peacock), **Supp. XIX:** 198
Valley of the Moon, The (London), **II:** 467, 481
"Valley of Unrest, The" (Poe), **III:** 411
Valli, Alida, **Supp. IV Part 2:** 520
"Valor" (Bausch), **Supp. VII:** 54
Valparaiso (DeLillo), **Supp. VI:** 4, 12
"Value of a Place, The" (Bass), **Supp. XVI:** 18
"Values and Fictions" (Toomer), **Supp. III Part 2:** 485–486
"Values and Imperatives" (Locke), **Supp. XIV:** 199, 202, 212
Values of Veblen, The: A Critical Appraisal (Rosenberg), **Supp. I Part 2:** 650

"Vampire" (Karr), **Supp. XI:** 241
Vampire Armand, The (Rice), **Supp. VII:** 290, 294–295
Vampire Chronicles, The (Rice), **Supp. VII:** 290
Vampire Lestat, The (Rice), **Supp. VII:** 290–292, 298, 299
Van Aalst, Mariska, **Supp. XIX:** 50, 51
Van Buren, Martin, **II:** 134, 312; **III:** 473
Vande Kieft, Ruth M., **IV:** 260
Vanderbilt, Cornelius, **III:** 14
Van Dine, S. S., **Supp. IV Part 1:** 341
Van Doren, Carl, **I:** 252–253, 423; **II:** 103, 111, 112; **Supp. I Part 2:** 474, 486, 707, 709, 717, 718, 727; **Supp. II Part 1:** 395; **Supp. VIII:** 96–97
Van Doren, Mark, **I:** 168; **III:** 4, 23, 589; **Supp. I Part 2:** 604; **Supp. III Part 2:** 626; **Supp. VIII:** 231; **Supp. IX:** 266, 268; **Supp. XV:** 152, 305, 307; **Supp. XXII:** 275
Vandover and the Brute (Norris), **III:** 314, 315, 316, 320–322, 328, 333, 334
Van Duyn, Mona, **Supp. IX:** 269
Van Dyke, Annette, **Supp. IV Part 1:** 327
Van Dyke, Henry, **I:** 223; **II:** 456
Van Gogh, Vincent, **I:** 27; **IV:** 290; **Supp. I Part 2:** 451; **Supp. IV Part 1:** 284; **Supp. XXII:** 171–172
Van Gogh's Room at Arles (Elkin), **Supp. VI: 56**
"Vanilla Dunk" (Lethem), **Supp. XVIII:** 139
"Vanisher, The" (Whittier), **Supp. I Part 2:** 691
Vanishing Point (Markson), **Supp. XVII:** 135, 137, 138, 145–146
"Vanishing Red, The" (Frost), **Retro. Supp. II:** 47
"Vanity" (B. Diop), **Supp. IV Part 1:** 16
Vanity Fair (Thackeray), **I:** 354; **II:** 91; **III:** 70; **Supp. IX:** 200
"Vanity of All Wordly Things, The" (Bradstreet), **Supp. I Part 1:** 102, 119
Vanity of Duluoz (Kerouac), **Supp. III Part 1:** 221, 222
"Vanity of Existence, The" (Freneau), **Supp. II Part 1:** 262
Van Matre, Lynn, **Supp. V:** 126
Vann, Barbara, **Supp. XV:** 187
Vanquished, The (Faulkner), **I:** 205
Van Rensselaer, Stephen, **I:** 351
Van Vechten, Carl, **I:** 295; **IV:** 76; **Supp. I Part 1:** 324, 327, 332; **Supp. I Part 2:** 715; **Supp. II Part 2: 725–751; Supp. X:** 247; **Supp. XVI:** 135; **Supp. XVII:** 96, 97, 101, 104; **Supp. XVIII:** 123, 131, 132, 279, 280; **Supp. XIX:** 76; **Supp. XX: 69; Supp. XXI:** 5, 8; **Supp. XXII:** 5, 158, 160
Vanzetti, Bartolomeo, **I:** 482, 486, 490, 494; **II:** 38–39, 426; **III:** 139–140; **Supp. I Part 2:** 446, 610, 611; **Supp. V:** 288–289; **Supp. IX:** 199; **Supp. XXII:** 277
"Vapor Trail Reflected in the Frog Pond" (Kinnell), **Supp. III Part 1:** 242–243
"Vapor Trails" (Snyder), **Supp. VIII:** 298
"Variation: Ode to Fear" (Warren), **IV:** 241
"Variation on a Sentence" (Bogan), **Supp. III Part 1:** 60
"Variation on Gaining a Son" (Dove), **Supp. IV Part 1:** 248
"Variation on Pain" (Dove), **Supp. IV Part 1:** 248
"Variations: The air is sweetest that a thistle guards" (Merrill), **Supp. III Part 1:** 321
"Variations: White Stag, Black Bear" (Merrill), **Supp. III Part 1:** 321
"Varick Street" (Bishop), **Supp. I Part 1:** 90, 92
Varieties of Metaphysical Poetry, The (Eliot), **Retro. Supp. I:** 65
Varieties of Religious Experience, The (William James), **II:** 344, 353, 354, 359–360, 362; **IV:** 28, 291; **Supp. IX:** 19
Variety (film), **Supp. XII:** 7
Variorum (Whitman), **Retro. Supp. I:** 406
Various Antidotes (J. Scott), **Supp. XVII: 188–189**
Various Miracles (Shields), **Supp. VII:** 318–320, 323, 324
"Various Miracles" (Shields), **Supp. VII:** 318–319, 324
Various Poems (Zach), **Supp. XV:** 86
"Various Tourists" (Connell), **Supp. XIV:** 79
"Varmint Question, The" (Leopold), **Supp. XIV:** 180–181
Varno, David, **Supp. XIX:** 205
Vasari, Giorgio, **Supp. I Part 2:** 450; **Supp. III Part 1:** 5
Vasquez, Robert, **Supp. V:** 180
Vassall Morton (Parkman), **Supp. II Part 2:** 595, 597–598
Vasse, W. W., **III:** 478
Vaudeville for a Princess (Schwartz), **Supp. II Part 2:** 661–662
Vaughan, Henry, **IV:** 151; **Supp. XV:** 251
Vaughn, Robert, **Supp. XI:** 343
"Vaunting Oak" (Ransom), **III:** 490
Vazirani, Reetika, **Supp. XIII:** 133
Veblen (Hobson), **Supp. I Part 2:** 650
Veblen, Andrew, **Supp. I Part 2:** 640
Veblen, Oswald, **Supp. I Part 2:** 640
Veblen, Thorstein, **I:** 104, 283, 475–476, 483, 498, 511; **II:** 27, 272, 276, 287; **Supp. I Part 2: 628–650; Supp. IV Part 1:** 22
Veblen, Mrs. Thorstein (Ellen Rolfe), **Supp. I Part 2:** 641
Veblenism: A New Critique (Dobriansky), **Supp. I Part 2:** 648, 650
"Veblen's Attack on Culture" (Adorno), **Supp. I Part 2:** 650
Vechten, Carl Van, **Retro. Supp. I:** 199
Vectors and Smoothable Curves (Bronk), **Supp. XXI: 24–26,** 32
Vedanta for Modern Man (Isherwood, ed.), **Supp. XIV:** 164
Vedanta for the Western World (Isherwood, ed.), **Supp. XIV:** 164
Vedas, **IV:** 183
Vega, Janine Pommy, **Supp. XIV:** 148
Vega, Lope de, **Retro. Supp. I:** 285; **Supp. III Part 1:** 341, 347
Vegetable, The (Fitzgerald), **Retro. Supp. I:** 105; **Supp. IX:** 57
Vegetable, The, or From President to Postman (Fitzgerald), **II:** 91
"Vegetable Love" (Apple), **Supp. XVII:** 4
"Vegetable Wisdom" (Halliday), **Supp. XIX:** 88
Veinberg, Jon, **Supp. V:** 180; **Supp. XIII:** 313; **Supp. XV:** 76–77, 86
Vein of Iron (Glasgow), **II:** 175, 186, 188–189, 191, 192, 194
Vein of Riches, A (Knowles), **Supp. XII:** 249
Vein of Words (J. W. Miller), **Supp. XX: 165**
Velie, Alan R., **Supp. IV Part 2:** 486
Velocities: New and Selected Poems, 1966–1992 (Dobyns), **Supp. XIII:** 86–87, 87, 88
"Velocity" (Collins), **Supp. XXI:** 61
"Velorio" (Cisneros), **Supp. VII:** 66
"Velvet Gentleman, The (Skloot), **Supp. XX: 201**
"Velvet Shoes" (Wylie), **Supp. I Part 2:** 711, 714
Venant, Elizabeth, **Supp. XI:** 343
Vencloca, Thomas, **Supp. VIII:** 29
Vendler, Helen H., **Retro. Supp. I:** 297; **Retro. Supp. II:** 184, 191; **Supp. I Part 1:** 77, 78, 92, 95; **Supp. I Part 2:** 565; **Supp. IV Part 1:** 245, 247, 249, 254, 257; **Supp. IV Part 2:** 448; **Supp. V:** 78, 82, 189, 343; **Supp. XII:** 187, 189; **Supp. XV:** 20, 184
"Venetian Blind, The" (Jarrell), **II:** 382–383
Venetian Glass Nephew, The (Wylie), **Supp. I Part 2:** 707, 709, 714, 717–719, 721, 724
Venetian Life (Howells), **II:** 274, 277, 279
Venetian Vespers, The (Hecht), **Supp. X:** 57, **65–69**
"Venetian Vespers, The" (Hecht), **Supp. X:** 65, **66–67**
Venice Observed (McCarthy), **II:** 562
Ventadorn, Bernard de, **Supp. IV Part 1:** 146
"Ventriloquists' Conversations" (Gentry), **Supp. IV Part 1:** 236
"Venus, Cupid, Folly and Time" (Taylor), **Supp. V:** 322–323
Venus and Adonis (film), **Supp. IV Part 1:** 82
Venus and Don Juan (C. Frost), **Supp. XV:** 93, **102–103,** 104, 107
"Venus and Don Juan" (C. Frost), **Supp. XV:** 103
Venus Blue (Sobin), **Supp. XVI: 293–294,** 294
Venus in Sparta (Auchincloss), **Supp. IV Part 1:** 25
"Venus Pandemos" (Halliday), **Supp. XIX:** 85, 89, 90, 93
"Venus's-flytraps" (Komunyakaa), **Supp. XIII:** 126, 127
"Veracruz" (Hayden), **Supp. II Part 1:** 371, 373
Verducci, Tom, **Supp. XXII:** 209
Verga, Giovanni, **II:** 271, 275

Verghese, Abraham, **Supp. X:** 160
Verhaeren, Emile, **I:** 476; **II:** 528, 529
Verlaine, Paul, **II:** 529, 543; **III:** 466; **IV:** 79, 80, 86, 286; **Retro. Supp. I:** 56, 62; **Retro. Supp. II:** 326
"Vermeer" (Nemerov), **III:** 275, 278, 280
Vermeer, Jan, **Retro. Supp. I:** 335
"Vermont" (Carruth), **Supp. XVI:** 54
Vermont Notebook, The (Ashbery), **Supp. III Part 1:** 1
Vermont Writers: A State of Mind (Daley), **Supp. XXII:** 216
"Vernal Ague, The" (Freneau), **Supp. II Part 1:** 258
Verne, Jules, **I:** 480; **Retro. Supp. I:** 270; **Supp. XI:** 63
Vernon, John, **Supp. X:** 15
Verplanck, Gulian C., **Supp. I Part 1:** 155, 156, 157, 158
Verrazano, Giovanni da, **Supp. I Part 2:** 496, 497
Verse (Zawacki), **Supp. VIII:** 272
"Verse for Urania" (Merrill), **Supp. III Part 1:** 329, 330
Verses (Wharton), **Retro. Supp. I:** 362
Verses, Printed for Her Friends (Jewett), **II:** 406
"Verses for Children" (Lowell), **II:** 516
"Verses Made at Sea in a Heavy Gale" (Freneau), **Supp. II Part 1:** 262
"Verses on the Death of T. S. Eliot" (Brodsky), **Supp. VIII:** 19
"Version of a Fragment of Simonides" (Bryant), **Supp. I Part 1:** 153, 155
Verulam, Baron. *See* Bacon, Francis
Very, Jones, **III:** 507
"Very Hot Sun in Bermuda, The" (Jackson), **Supp. IX:** 126
Very Old Bones (W. Kennedy), **Supp. VII:** 133, 148, 150–153
Very Persistent Gappers of Frip, The (Saunders), **Supp. XIX: 229–230**
"Very Proper Gander, The" (Thurber), **Supp. I Part 2:** 610
"Very Short Story, A" (Hemingway), **II:** 252; **Retro. Supp. I:** 173
"Vesalius in Zante" (Wharton), **Retro. Supp. I:** 372
Vesey, Denmark, **Supp. I Part 2:** 592
Vesey, Desmond, **Supp. XIV:** 162
"Vespers" (Auden), **Supp. II Part 1:** 23
"Vespers" (Glück), **Supp. V:** 88
Vestal Lady on Brattle, The (Corso), **Supp. XII:** 119, **120–121**, 134
Vested Interests and the Common Man, The (Veblen), **Supp. I Part 2:** 642
"Vesuvius at Home" (Rich), **Retro. Supp. I:** 42
"Veteran, The" (Crane), **I:** 413
"Veterans' Cemetery" (Gioia), **Supp. XV:** 117
"Veteran Sirens" (Robinson), **III:** 512, 524
"Veterinarian" (X. J. Kennedy), **Supp. XV:** 168
"Vetiver" (Ashbery), **Supp. III Part 1:** 26
Vetter, Lara, **Supp. XXII:** 166
"Via Dieppe-Newhaven" (H. Miller), **III:** 183
"Via Negativa" (Salter), **Supp. IX:** 257
Vicar of Wakefeld, The (Goldsmith), **I:** 216
Vicious Circle, The (film, Wilder), **Supp. XVII:** 62
"Vicissitudes of the Avant-Garde, The" (Gass), **Supp. VI:** 91
Vico, Giambattista, **Supp. XX: 38**
Victim, The (Bellow), **I:** 144, 145, 147, 149, 150, 151, 152, 153, 155, 156, 158, 159, 164; **IV:** 19; **Retro. Supp. II:** 21, 22, 34
"Victor" (Mumford), **Supp. II Part 2:** 476
Victoria (Rowson), **Supp. XV:** 231
Victorian in the Modern World, A (Hapgood), **Supp. XVII:** 95, 97, 100, 101, 103, 105, 106; **Supp. XXI:** 8
"Victoria's Secret" (Collins), **Supp. XXI:** 58–59
"Victories" (Untermeyer), **Supp. XV:** 300
"Victory at Sea" (television series), **Supp. I Part 2:** 490
"Victory comes late" (Dickinson), **Retro. Supp. I:** 45
"Victory of the Moon, The" (Crane), **I:** 420
Vida, Vendela, **Supp. XIX:** 49, 50, 53, 57, 58, 59, 61, 62
Vidal, Gore, **II:** 587; **IV:** 383; **Supp. IV Part 1:** 22, 35, 92, 95, 198; **Supp. IV Part 2: 677–696; Supp. IX:** 96; **Supp. X:** 186, 195; **Supp. XIV:** 156, 170, 338; **Supp. XIX:** 131, 132
Video Poems (Collins), **Supp. XXI:** 53
Viebahn, Fred, **Supp. IV Part 1:** 248
Viera, Joseph M., **Supp. XI:** 178, 186
Viereck, Peter, **Supp. I Part 2:** 403
Viertel, Berthold, **Supp. XIV:** 165
Viertel, Salka, **Supp. XVI:** 192
Viet Journal (Jones), **Supp. XI: 230–231**
Vietnam (McCarthy), **II:** 578–579
"Vietnam in Me, The" (O'Brien), **Supp. V:** 241, 252
Vie unanime, La (Romains), **I:** 227
"View, The" (Roussel), **Supp. III Part 1:** 15, 16, 21
View from 80, The (Cowley), **Supp. II Part 1:** 141, 144, 153
"View from an Institution" (F. Wright), **Supp. XVII:** 244
"View from the Backyard" (W. V. Davis), **Supp. XXI:** 96
View from the Bridge, A (A. Miller), **III:** 147, 148, 156, 158, 159–160
View from the Seventh Layer, The (Brockmeier), **Supp. XXII: 59–61**
"View from the Seventh Layer, The" (Brockmeier), **Supp. XXII:** 61
View of My Own, A: Essays in Literature and Society (Hardwick), **Supp. III Part 1:** 194, 200
"View of the Capital from the Library of Congress" (Bishop), **Retro. Supp. II:** 45
View of the Soil and Climate of the United States, A (Brown, trans.), **Supp. I Part 1:** 146
"View of the Woods, A" (O'Connor), **III:** 349, 351, 358; **Retro. Supp. II:** 237
"Viewpoint" (column, Siddons), **Supp. XXII:** 240, 245
"Views of the Mysterious Hill: The Appearance of Parnassus in American Poetry" (Strand), **Supp. IV Part 2:** 631
"Vigil" (Karr), **Supp. XI:** 241
"Vigil, The" (Dante), **III:** 542
"Vigil at Heiligenkreuz" (W. V. Davis), **Supp. XXI:** 93
"Vignette" (Trethewey), **Supp. XXI:** 253, 254
Vigny, Alfred Victor de, **II:** 543
Vildrac, Charles, **Supp. XV:** 50
Vile Bodies (Waugh), **Supp. I Part 2:** 607
Villa, Pancho, **I:** 210; **III:** 584
"Village Blacksmith, The" (Longfellow), **Retro. Supp. II:** 167, 168; **Supp. I Part 2:** 409
Village Hymns, a Supplement to Dr. Watts's Psalms and Hymns (Nettleton), **I:** 458
"Village Improvement Parade, The" (Lindsay), **Supp. I Part 2:** 388, 389
Village Magazine, The (Lindsay), **Supp. I Part 2:** 379–380, 382
Village Virus, The (Lewis), **II:** 440
"Villanelle at Sundown" (Justice), **Supp. VII:** 119, 122–123
"Villanelle of Change" (Robinson), **III:** 524
Villard, Oswald, **Supp. I Part 1:** 332
"Villa Selene" (Simpson), **Supp. IX:** 279
Villon, François, **II:** 544; **III:** 9, 174, 592; **Retro. Supp. I:** 286; **Supp. I Part 1:** 261; **Supp. III Part 1:** 235, 243, 249, 253; **Supp. III Part 2:** 560; **Supp. IX:** 116
"Villonaud for This Yule" (Pound), **Retro. Supp. I:** 286
"Vincenzo Tailor" (Di Piero), **Supp. XIX:** 38
Vindication of the Rights of Woman (Wollstonecraft), **Supp. I Part 1:** 126; **Supp. XI:** 203
Vines, Lois Davis, **Retro. Supp. II:** 261
Vintage Book of Amnesia, The (Lethem, ed.), **Supp. XVIII:** 138
"Vintage Thunderbird, A" (Beattie), **Supp. V:** 27
Vinz, Mark, **Supp. X:** 117
Viol de Lucrèce, Le (Obey), **IV:** 356
Violence (Bausch), **Supp. VII:** 48–49, 54
Violent Bear It Away, The (O'Connor), **III:** 339, 345–348, 350, 351, 354, 355, 356, 357; **Retro. Supp. II:** 233, **234–236**
Violent Hero, Wilderness Heritage and Urban Reality, The: A Study of the Private Eye in the Novels of Dashiell Hammett, Raymond Chandler and Ross Macdonald (Parker), **Supp. XIX:** 177
"Violent Vet, The" (O'Brien), **Supp. V:** 238
Violin (Rice), **Supp. VII:** 302
Viorst, Judith, **Supp. X:** 153
Viper Run (Karr), **Supp. XI: 248–251**

Virgil, **I:** 312, 322, 587; **II:** 133, 542; **IV:** 137, 359; **Retro. Supp. I:** 135; **Supp. I Part 1:** 153; **Supp. I Part 2:** 494; **Supp. IV Part 2:** 631
"Virgin and Child with Music and Numbers" (Bronk), **Supp. XXI:** 30
"Virgin and the Dynamo" (Adams), **III:** 396
"Virgin Carrying a Lantern, The" (Stevens), **IV:** 80
Virgin Huntress, The (Holding), **Supp. XXII:** 119, 124, **135–136**
Virginia (Glasgow), **II:** 175, 178, 181–182, 193, 194
"Virginia" (Lindsay), **Supp. I Part 2:** 398
"Virginia Britannia" (Moore), **III:** 198, 208–209
"Virginians Are Coming Again, The" (Lindsay), **Supp. I Part 2:** 399
Virginia Reels (Hoffman), **Supp. XVIII:** 79, 86
Virgin Spain (W. Frank), **Supp. XX: 76**
"Virgins Plus Curtains Minus Dots" (Loy), **Supp. XXII:** 161
Virgin Time: In Search of the Contemplative Life (Hampl), **Supp. XXII:** 82, 83–84, **90–92**
"Virgin Violeta" (Porter), **III:** 454
"Virility" (Ozick), **Supp. V:** 262, 265
Virtual Light (W. Gibson), **Supp. XVI:** 124, **129,** 130
Virtue of Selfishness, The: A New Concept of Egoism (Rand), **Supp. IV Part 2:** 527, 530–532
"Virtuoso" (Francis), **Supp. IX:** 82
Virtuous Woman, A (Gibbons), **Supp. X: 44–45,** 46, 50
Visconti, Luchino, **Supp. V:** 51
Viscusi, Robert, **Supp. XX: 46**
Visible Saints: The History of a Puritan Idea (Morgan), **IV:** 149
"Vision, A" (Olds), **Supp. X:** 214
"Vision, A" (Winters), **Supp. II Part 2:** 785, 795
"Vision and Prayer" (D. Thomas), **I:** 432
"Visionary, The" (Poe), **III:** 411
Visionary Farms, The (Eberhart), **I:** 537–539
Visioning, The (Glaspell), **Supp. III Part 1:** 175–177, 180, 187, 188
Vision in Spring (Faulkner), **Retro. Supp. I:** 79
Vision of Columbus (Barlow), **Supp. I Part 1:** 124; **Supp. II Part 1:** 67, 68, 70–75, 77, 79
Vision of Sir Launfal, The (Lowell), **Supp. I Part 1:** 311; **Supp. I Part 2:** 406, 409, 410
"Vision of the World, A" (Cheever), **Supp. I Part 1:** 182, 192
Visions of Cody (Kerouac), **Supp. III Part 1:** 225–227
Visions of Gerard (Kerouac), **Supp. III Part 1:** 219–222, 225, 227, 229
"Visions of the Daughters of Albion" (Blake), **III:** 540
"Visit" (Ammons), **Supp. VII:** 28–29
"Visit, The" (Kenyon), **Supp. VII:** 169
"Visitant, The" (Dunn), **Supp. XI:** 147
"*Visitation, The*/La Visitación" (Mora), **Supp. XIII:** 217, 224, 228
"Visit Home, A" (Stafford), **Supp. XI:** 318
Visit in 2001, The (musical, McNally), **Supp. XIII:** 207
"Visiting My Own House in Iowa City" (Stern), **Supp. IX:** 300
"Visit of Charity, A" (Welty), **IV:** 262
"Visitors" (J. W. Miller), **Supp. XX: 167**
"Visitors" (Salinas), **Supp. XIII:** 318
"Visitors, The/Los Visitantes" (Kingsolver), **Supp. VII:** 208
"Visits to St. Elizabeths" (Bishop), **Retro. Supp. II:** 47
"Visit to a Small Planet" (teleplay) (Vidal), **Supp. IV Part 2:** 682
Visit to a Small Planet: A Comedy Akin to Vaudeville (Vidal), **Supp. IV Part 2:** 682–683
"Visit to Avoyelles, A" (Chopin), **Supp. I Part 1:** 213
"Visit to Manafon, A" (W. V. Davis), **Supp. XXI:** 96
"Vissi d'Arte" (Moore), **Supp. X: 173–174**
Vistas of History (Morison), **Supp. I Part 2:** 492
"Vita" (Stafford), **Supp. XI:** 330
"Vita Brevis" (Hull), **Supp. XXI:** 138
Vital, David, **Supp. XVI:** 160
Vital Provisions (Price), **Supp. VI:** 262–263
"Vitamins" (Carver), **Supp. III Part 1:** 138
Vita Nova (Glück), **Supp. V:** 90–92
Vitruvius, **Supp. XVI:** 292
Vittorio, the Vampire (Rice), **Supp. VII:** 295–296
Viudas (Dorfman), **Supp. IX:** 138
"Viva Vargas!" (Allen), **Supp. XV:** 15
Viviparous Quadrupeds of North America, The (Audubon and Bachman), **Supp. XVI:** 10
Vivisections (Siegel), **Supp. XXII:** 257
Vizenor, Gerald, **Supp. IV Part 1:** 260, 262, 329, 404; **Supp. IV Part 2:** 502
Vladimir Nabokov: The American Years (Nabokov), **Retro. Supp. I:** 275
Vlag, Piet, **Supp. XV:** 295
"Vlemk, the Box Painter" (Gardner), **Supp. VI:** 73
"V-Letter" (Shapiro), **Supp. II Part 2:** 707
V-Letter and Other Poems (Shapiro), **Supp. II Part 2:** 702, 706
"Vocabulary of Dearness" (Nye), **Supp. XIII:** 284
"Vocation" (Stafford), **Supp. XI:** 312, 321
Vocation and a Voice, A (Chopin), **Retro. Supp. II:** 67, 72
"Vocation and a Voice, A" (Chopin), **Retro. Supp. II:** 72; **Supp. I Part 1:** 200, 220, 224, 225
Vogel, David, **Supp. XV:** 88
Vogel, Speed, **Supp. IV Part 1:** 390
"Vogue Vista" (Peacock), **Supp. XIX:** 200
"Voice" (F. Wright), **Supp. XVII:** 245
"Voice" (Notley), **Supp. XXII:** 230
"Voice, The" (Dunn), **Supp. XI:** 152
Voiced Connections of James Dickey, The (Dickey), **Supp. IV Part 1:** 177
"Voice from the Wilderness" (Ray), **Supp. XVIII:** 202
"Voice from the Woods, A" (Humphrey), **Supp. IX:** 101
"Voice from Under the Table, A" (Wilbur), **Supp. III Part 2:** 553, 554
Voice of Reason, The: Essays in Objectivist Thought (Rand), **Supp. IV Part 2:** 527, 528, 532
"Voice of Rock, The" (Ginsberg), **Supp. II Part 1:** 313
Voice of the Butterfly, The (Nichols), **Supp. XIII:** 270
Voice of the City, The (O. Henry), **Supp. II Part 1:** 410
"Voice of the Mountain, The" (Crane), **I:** 420
Voice of the Negro (Barber), **Supp. II Part 1:** 168
"Voice of the Past, The" (Skloot), **Supp. XX: 207**
Voice of the People, The (Glasgow), **II:** 175, 176
Voice of the Turtle: American Indian Literature 1900–1970 (Gunn Allen, ed.), **Supp. IV Part 1:** 332, 334
Voices from the Moon (Dubus), **Supp. VII:** 88–89
"Voices from the Other World" (Merrill), **Supp. III Part 1:** 331
Voices in the House (Sedges), **Supp. II Part 1:** 125
Voices of a Summer Day (Shaw), **Supp. XIX:** 251
Voices of the Night (Longfellow), **II:** 489, 493; **Retro. Supp. II:** 154, 157, 168
"Voices of Village Square, The" (Wolfe), **Supp. III Part 2:** 571–572
Voice That Is Great within Us, The (Caruth, ed.), **Supp. XIII:** 112
Void Moon (Connelly), **Supp. XXI: 73,** 74
Voigt, Ellen Bryan, **Supp. XIII:** 76
Voix humaine, La (Cocteau), **Supp. XX: 236**
Volkening, Henry, **Retro. Supp. II:** 117; **Supp. XV:** 142
Vollmann, William T., **Supp. XIV:** 96; **Supp. XVII: 225–237; Supp. XX: 93**
Volney, Constantin François de Chasseboeuf, **Supp. I Part 1:** 146
Voltaire, **I:** 194; **II:** 86, 103, 449; **III:** 420; **IV:** 18; **Retro. Supp. II:** 94; **Supp. I Part 1:** 288–289; **Supp. I Part 2:** 669, 717; **Supp. XV:** 258; **Supp. XX: 285**
Voltaire! Voltaire! (Endore), **Supp. XVII:** 65
Volunteers, The (Rowson and Reinagle), **Supp. XV:** 238
Vonnegut, Kurt, **Retro. Supp. I:** 170; **Supp. II Part 2:** 557, 689, **753–784; Supp. IV Part 1:** 227, 392; **Supp. V:**

40, 42, 237, 244, 296; **Supp. X:** 260; **Supp. XI:** 104; **Supp. XII:** 139, 141; **Supp. XVIII:** 242, 252; **Supp. XXI:** 226
Vonnegut, Kurt, Jr., **Supp. XVII:** 41, 135; **Supp. XIX:** 223
"Voracities and Verities" (Moore), **III:** 214
Vore, Nellie, **I:** 199
Vorlicky, Robert, **Supp. IX:** 132, 135, 136, 141, 144, 147
Vorse, Mary Heaton, **Supp. XVII:** 99; **Supp. XX: 76; Supp. XXI:** 5, 6, 9, 13
"Vorticism" (Pound), **Retro. Supp. I:** 288
Vosjoli, Philippe de, **Supp. XX: 253**
Voss, Richard, **I:** 199–200
"Vow, The" (Hecht), **Supp. X:** 64
"Vowels 2" (Baraka), **Supp. II Part 1:** 51
Vow of Conversation, A: Journal, 1964–1965 (Merton), **Supp. VIII:** 206
Vox (Baker), **Supp. XIII: 47–49,** 50, 52, 53
"Voyage" (MacLeish), **III:** 15
Voyage, The (Caputo), **Supp. XIX:** 25, 27–28
"Voyage, The" (Irving), **II:** 304
Voyage, The, and Other Versions of Poems by Baudelaire (Lowell), **Retro. Supp. II:** 187
Voyage dans la Haute Pennsylvanie et dans l'état de New-York (Crèvecoeur), **Supp. I Part 1:** 250–251
Voyage of the Beagle (Darwin), **Supp. IX:** 211
Voyage Out, The (Woolf), **Supp. XV:** 65
"Voyager, The" (Everwine), **Supp. XV:** 75
"Voyages" (H. Crane), **I:** 393–395; **Retro. Supp. II:** 78, 80, 81
"Voyages" (Levine), **Supp. V:** 190
Voyages and Discoveries of the Companions of Columbus (Irving), **II:** 310
Voyage to Pagany, A (W. C. Williams), **IV:** 404; **Retro. Supp. I:** 418–419, **420–421,** 423
Voyaging Portraits (Sobin), **Supp. XVI:** 282, 287
"Voyeur, The" (Gioia), **Supp. XV:** 125
"Voz de America" (column, W. Frank), **Supp. XX: 80**
Voznesensky, Andrei, **II:** 553; **Supp. III Part 1:** 268; **Supp. III Part 2:** 560
Vrbovska, Anca, **Supp. IV Part 2:** 639
V. S. Naipaul: An Introduction to His Work (Theroux), **Supp. VIII:** 314, 318
"V. S. Pritchett's Apprenticeship" (Maxwell), **Supp. VIII:** 172
"Vulgarity in Literature" (Huxley), **III:** 429–430
"Vultures" (Oliver), **Supp. VII:** 235
"V. V." (Alcott), **Supp. I Part 1:** 37

W (Viva) (Cummings), **I:** 429, 433, 434, 436, 443, 444, 447
Wabash (R. O. Butler), **Supp. XII:** 61, **68–69**
Wade, Grace, **I:** 216
"Wading at Wellfleet" (Bishop), **Retro. Supp. II:** 42, 43; **Supp. I Part 1:** 80, 85, 86
Wadsworth, Charles, **I:** 454, 470; **Retro. Supp. I:** 32, 33
Wagenknecht, Edward, **II:** 508; **Supp. I Part 2:** 408, 584; **Supp. IV Part 2:** 681
"Wages of Poetry, The" (Wright), **Supp. XV:** 337
Wagner, Erica, **Supp. XXI:** 117
Wagner, Jean, **Supp. I Part 1:** 341, 346; **Supp. IV Part 1:** 165, 167, 171
Wagner, Richard, **I:** 284, 395; **II:** 425; **III:** 396, 507; **Supp. IV Part 1:** 392
Wagner, Robert, **Supp. IX:** 250
"Wagnerians, The" (Auchincloss), **Supp. IV Part 1:** 23
"Wagner Matinee, A" (Cather), **I:** 315–316; **Retro. Supp. I:** 5, 8
Wagoner, David, **Supp. IX: 323–340; Supp. XII:** 178; **Supp. XX: 200**
Wahlöö, Per, **Supp. XX: 87**
Waid, Candace, **Retro. Supp. I:** 360, 372, 373
Waif, The (Longfellow, ed.), **Retro. Supp. II:** 155
"Waif of the Plains, A" (Harte), **Supp. II Part 1:** 354
Wain, John, **Supp. XIV:** 166
"Wait" (Kinnell), **Supp. III Part 1:** 250
"Waiter in a California Vietnamese Restaurant" (Major), **Supp. XXII:** 182
"Waiting" (Dubus), **Supp. VII:** 87
Waiting (Jin), **Supp. XVIII:** 89, **96–97,** 99
"Waiting" (W. C. Williams), **Retro. Supp. I:** 418
"Waiting, The" (L.-Y. Lee), **Supp. XV:** 218
"Waiting, The" (Olds), **Supp. X:** 209
"Waiting between the Trees" (Tan), **Supp. X:** 290
"Waiting by the Gate" (Bryant), **Supp. I Part 1:** 171
Waiting for God (Weil), **I:** 298
Waiting for Godot (Beckett), **I:** 78, 91, 298; **Supp. IV Part 1:** 368–369
Waiting for Lefty (Odets), **Supp. I Part 1:** 277; **Supp. II Part 2:** 529, 530–533, 540; **Supp. V:** 109; **Supp. XIX:** 242
Waiting for Sweet Betty (Major), **Supp. XXII: 183**
Waiting for Teddy Williams (Mosher), **Supp. XXII:** 205, 206, 207, 208, 209, **215–216**
Waiting for the End of the World (Bell), **Supp. X: 4–5,** 11
"Waiting for the Ladies" (L. Brown), **Supp. XXI:** 44
Waiting for the Verdict (R. H. Davis), **Supp. XVI:** 85, 89, 90
"Waiting in a Rain Forest" (Wagoner), **Supp. IX:** 329
Waiting Room, The (Kees), **Supp. XV:** 133, 148
Waiting to Exhale (McMillan), **Supp. XIII:** 184, 185, **189–190,** 191
"Waiting to Freeze" (Banks), **Supp. V:** 5, 6
Waiting to Freeze: Poems (Banks), **Supp. V:** 6, 8
Waits, Tom, **Supp. VIII:** 12
Wait until Spring, Bandini (Fante), **Supp. XI:** 160, 161, 164, 165, **166–167**
Wait until Spring, Bandini (film), **Supp. XI:** 173
"Wake, The" (Dove), **Supp. IV Part 1:** 250
"Wakefield" (Hawthorne), **Retro. Supp. I:** 154, 159
Wakefield, Dan, **Supp. VIII:** 43; **Supp. XVI:** 220; **Supp. XIX:** 257, 258
Wakefield, Richard, **Supp. IX:** 323
"Wake Island" (Rukeyser), **Supp. VI:** 273
Wakeman, Frederic, **Supp. IX:** 247
Wake Up and Live! (Brande), **Supp. I Part 2:** 608
"Waking" (C. Frost), **Supp. XV:** 93
Waking, The (Roethke), **III:** 541
"Waking Early Sunday Morning" (Lowell), **II:** 552; **Retro. Supp. II:** 190
"Waking in the Blue" (Lowell), **II:** 547; **Retro. Supp. II:** 180
"Waking in the Dark" (Rich), **Supp. I Part 2:** 559
"Waking Up the Rake" (Hogan), **Supp. IV Part 1:** 415–416, 416
Wakoski, Diane, **Supp. V:** 79; **Supp. XII:** 184; **Supp. XV:** 252; **Supp. XVII:** 112
Walbridge, John, **Supp. XX: 125**
Walcott, Charles C., **II:** 49
Walcott, Derek, **Supp. VIII:** 28; **Supp. X:** 122, 131; **Supp. XV:** 256
Walcott, Jersey Joe, **Supp. V:** 182
Wald, Alan, **Supp. XV:** 202; **Supp. XVIII:** 223; **Supp. XXI:** 261, 262, 271, 275–276, 277, 278
Wald, Lillian, **Supp. I Part 1:** 12
Walden (Thoreau), **Supp. XIV:** 177, 227; **Supp. XV:** 275; **Supp. XVIII:** 14, 80, 189
Walden, Daniel, **Supp. IV Part 2:** 584, 591; **Supp. V:** 272
Walden; or, Life in the Woods (Thoreau), **I:** 219, 305; **II:** 8, 142, 159, 312–313, 458; **IV:** 168, 169, 170, 176, 177–178, 179–182, 183, 187; **Retro. Supp. I:** 62; **Supp. I Part 2:** 579, 655, 664, 672; **Supp. VIII:** 296; **Supp. X:** 27, 101; **Supp. XIII:** 152
Waldman, Anne, **Supp. XIV:** 150
Waldmeir, Joseph, **III:** 45
Waldmeir, Joseph J., **Supp. I Part 2:** 476
Waldo (Theroux), **Supp. VIII:** 313, 314, **314–315**
Waldo Frank: A Study (Munson), **Supp. XX: 74**
Waldron, Jeremy, **Supp. XVII:** 235
Waldrop, Keith, **Supp. XV:** 153, 165
Waley, Arthur, **II:** 526; **III:** 466; **Supp. V:** 340
"Walk, A" (Snyder), **Supp. VIII:** 297

Walkabout Year: Twelve Months in Australia (Pickering), **Supp. XXI:** 199, 200
"Walk at Sunset, A" (Bryant), **Supp. I Part 1:** 155
"Walk before Mass, A" (Agee), **I:** 28–29
Walker, Alice, **Retro. Supp. I:** 215; **Supp. I Part 2:** 550; **Supp. III Part 2:** 488, **517–540; Supp. IV Part 1:** 14; **Supp. VIII:** 141, 214; **Supp. IX:** 306, 311; **Supp. X:** 85, 228, 252, 325, 330; **Supp. XIII:** 179, 185, 291, 295; **Supp. XVI:** 39; **Supp. XVIII:** 200, 283; **Supp. XX: 84, 107, 108; Supp. XXI:** 172; **Supp. XXII:** 172
Walker, Cheryl, **Supp. XI:** 145
Walker, David, **Supp. V:** 189; **Supp. XVII:** 246
Walker, Franklin D., **III:** 321
Walker, Gue, **Supp. XII:** 207
Walker, Margaret, **Supp. XVIII:** 282; **Supp. XX: 106**
Walker, Marianne, **Supp. VIII:** 139
Walker, Obadiah, **II:** 113
Walker, Scott, **Supp. XV:** 92
Walker in the City, A (Kazin), **Supp. VIII: 93–95,** 99
Walk Hard (Blum and Hill), **Supp. XV:** 194
Walk Hard-Talk Loud (Zinberg), **Supp. XV:** 194, 202
"Walking" (Hogan), **Supp. IV Part 1:** 416
"Walking" (Thoreau), **Supp. IV Part 1:** 416; **Supp. IX:** 178
"Walking Along in Winter" (Kenyon), **Supp. VII:** 167
"Walking around the Block with a Three-Year-Old" (Wagoner), **Supp. IX:** 331–332
"Walking at Noon Near the Burlington Depot in Lincoln, Nebraska" (Kooser), **Supp. XIX:** 122
"Walking Backwards into the Future" (R. Williams), **Supp. IX:** 146
Walking Down the Stairs: Selections from Interviews (Kinnell), **Supp. III Part 1:** 235, 249
"Walking Home" (Schnackenberg). *See* "Laughing with One Eye" (Schnackenberg)
"Walking Home at Night" (Ginsberg), **Supp. II Part 1:** 313
"Walking Is Almost Falling" (Peacock), **Supp. XIX:** 196, 197
Walking Light (Dunn), **Supp. XI:** 140, 141, 153
"Walking Man of Rodin, The" (Sandburg), **III:** 583
"Walking Sticks and Paperweights and Water Marks" (Moore), **III:** 215
Walking Tall (Dunn), **Supp. XI:** 140
Walking the Black Cat (Simic), **Supp. VIII:** 280, **282–284**
Walking to Gatlinburg (Mosher), **Supp. XXII:** 204, 205, 206, 207, 208, 209, 215, **216–217**
Walking to Martha's Vineyard (F. Wright), **Supp. XVII:** 240, 241, 245, 246
Walking to Sleep (Wilbur), **Supp. III Part 2:** 557–560
"Walking to Sleep" (Wilbur), **Supp. III Part 2:** 544, 557, 559, 561, 562
"Walking Wounded" (Shaw), **Supp. XIX:** 248
Walkin' the Dog (Mosley), **Supp. XIII:** 242
"Walk in the Moonlight, A" (Anderson), **I:** 114
Walk Me to the Distance (Everett), **Supp. XVIII: 55–56,** 57
Walk on the Wild Side, A (Algren), **Supp. V:** 4; **Supp. IX:** 3, **12–13,** 14
"Walks in Rome" (Merrill), **Supp. III Part 1:** 337
Walk to the River, A (Hoffman), **Supp. XVIII: 77–78**
Walk with Tom Jefferson, A (Levine), **Supp. V:** 179, 187, 190–191
"Wall, The" (Bronk), **Supp. XXI:** 31
"Wall, The" (Brooks), **Supp. III Part 1:** 70, 71, 84
Wall, The (Hersey), **IV:** 4; **Supp. XX: 251**
"Wall, The" (Roethke), **III:** 544
"Wall, The" (Sexton), **Supp. II Part 2:** 696
Wallace, Daniel, **Supp. XXII:** 49
Wallace, David, **Supp. XXI:** 277
Wallace, David Foster, **Retro. Supp. II:** 279; **Supp. X: 301–318; Supp. XVII:** 226; **Supp. XIX:** 223; **Supp. XX: 91, 93; Supp. XXII:** 260, 261
Wallace, Henry, **I:** 489; **III:** 111, 475; **Supp. I Part 1:** 286; **Supp. I Part 2:** 645
Wallace, Jim, **Supp. XX: 143**
Wallace, Mike, **Supp. IV Part 1:** 364; **Supp. IV Part 2:** 526; **Supp. XX: 102**
Wallace, Richard, **Supp. XVIII:** 101–102
Wallace Stevens (Kermode), **Retro. Supp. I:** 301
Wallace Stevens: The Poems of our Climate (Bloom), **Retro. Supp. I:** 299
Wallace Stevens: Words Chosen out of Desire (Stevens), **Retro. Supp. I:** 297
Wallach, Eli, **III:** 161
Wallant, Edward Lewis, **Supp. XVI:** 220
Wallas, Graham, **Supp. I Part 2:** 643
"Walled City" (Oates), **Supp. II Part 2:** 524
Wallenstein, Anna. *See* Weinstein, Mrs. Max (Anna Wallenstein)
Waller, Edmund, **III:** 463
Waller, Fats, **IV:** 263
Waller, Nicole, **Supp. XXII:** 78
Walling, William English, **Supp. I Part 2:** 645; **Supp. XV:** 295
"Wall of Paintings, The" (Notley), **Supp. XXII:** 230
Wall of the Sky, the Wall of the Eye, The (Lethem), **Supp. XVIII:** 139
Walls Do Not Fall, The (Doolittle), **Supp. I Part 1:** 271, 272
Walls of Jericho, The (R. Fisher), **Supp. XIX:** 65, 67, 70, **72–77,** 78
"Wall Songs" (Hogan), **Supp. IV Part 1:** 413
Wall Writing (Auster), **Supp. XII:** 23–24
Walpole, Horace, **I:** 203; **Supp. I Part 2:** 410, 714
Walpole, Hugh, **Retro. Supp. I:** 231; **Supp. XX: 232**
Walpole, Robert, **IV:** 145
Walsh, David M., **Supp. XV:** 5
Walsh, Ed, **II:** 424
Walsh, George, **Supp. IV Part 2:** 528
Walsh, Raoul, **Supp. XIII:** 174
Walsh, Richard J., **Supp. II Part 1:** 119, 130
Walsh, William, **Supp. IV Part 1:** 242, 243, 246, 248, 252, 254, 257
"Walt, the Wounded" (Di Piero), **Supp. XIX:** 37
"Walt and Will" (Apple), **Supp. XVII:** 6
Walter, Eugene, **Supp. XVI:** 230
Walter, Joyce, **Supp. XV:** 121
Walter Benjamin at the Dairy Queen: Reflections at Sixty and Beyond (McMurtry), **Supp. V:** 232
Walters, Barbara, **Supp. XIV:** 125
Walters, Marguerite. *See* Smith, Mrs. Lamar (Marguerite Walters)
"Walter T. Carriman" (O'Hara), **III:** 368
Walton, Izaak, **Supp. I Part 2:** 422
"Walt Whitman" (Kooser), **Supp. XIX:** 118
"Walt Whitman" (Masters), **Supp. I Part 2:** 458
"Walt Whitman at Bear Mountain" (Simpson), **Supp. IX:** 265
Walt Whitman Bathing (Wagoner), **Supp. IX: 331–332**
Walt Whitman Handbook (Allen), **IV:** 352
Walt Whitman Reconsidered (Chase), **IV:** 352
"Waltz, The" (Parker), **Supp. IX:** 204
"Waltzer in the House, The" (Kunitz), **Supp. III Part 1:** 258
Waltzing Matilda (Notley), **Supp. XXII:** 229–230
"Waltzing Matilda" (Notley), **Supp. XXII:** 230
Waltzing the Magpies: A Year in Australia (Pickering), **Supp. XXI:** 199, 200
Walzer, Kevin, **Supp. XII:** 202; **Supp. XV:** 118; **Supp. XVIII:** 174
Wambaugh, Joseph, **Supp. X:** 5; **Supp. XXI:** 67
Wampeters, Foma, & Granfalloons (Vonnegut), **Supp. II Part 2:** 758, 759–760, 776, 779
Wand, David Hsin-fu, **Supp. X:** 292
"Wanderer, The" (W. C. Williams), **Retro. Supp. I:** 414, 421
Wanderer, The: His Parables and His Sayings (Gibran), **Supp. XX: 116, 123–124**
"Wanderers, The" (Welty), **IV:** 273–274
"Wandering Jew, The" (Robinson), **III:** 505, 516–517
Wanderings of Oisin (Yeats), **Supp. I Part 1:** 79
Wang, Dorothy, **Supp. X:** 289
Wang Wei, **Supp. XV:** 47
Waniek, Marilyn Nelson, **Supp. IV Part 1:** 244. *See also* Nelson, Marilyn
"Wan Lee, the Pagan" (Harte), **Supp. II Part 1:** 351

"Want, The" (Olds), **Supp. X:** 210
Want Bone, The (Pinsky), **Supp. VI:** 236–237, 244–245, 247
"Wanted: An Ontological Critic" (Ransom), **III:** 498
"Wanting to Die" (Sexton), **Supp. II Part 2:** 684, 686; **Supp. XIV:** 132
"Wants" (Paley), **Supp. VI:** 219
Waples, Dorothy, **I:** 348
Wapshot Chronicle, The (Cheever), **Supp. I Part 1:** 174, 177–180, 181, 196
Wapshot Scandal, The (Cheever), **Supp. I Part 1:** 180–184, 187, 191, 196
"War" (Findley), **Supp. XX: 49**
"War" (Jin), **Supp. XVIII:** 93
"War" (Kingston), **Supp. V:** 169
"War" (Simic), **Supp. VIII:** 282
"War, Response, and Contradiction" (Burke), **I:** 283
"War and Peace" (Sanders), **Supp. XVI:** 277
War and Peace (Tolstoy), **I:** 6, 7; **II:** 191, 205, 291; **IV:** 446; **Supp. V:** 277; **Supp. XI:** 68; **Supp. XIV:** 97
War and Remembrance (Wouk), **Supp. XX: 243**
"War and the Small Nations" (Gibran), **Supp. XX: 127**
War and War (F. Barthelme), **Supp. XI:** 25
"War Between Men and Women, The" (Thurber), **Supp. I Part 2:** 615
War Bulletins (Lindsay), **Supp. I Part 2:** 378–379
Ward, Aileen, **II:** 531
Ward, Artemus (pseudonym). *See* Browne, Charles Farrar
Ward, Douglas Turner, **Supp. IV Part 1:** 362
Ward, Henry, **Supp. I Part 2:** 588
Ward, Mrs. Humphry, **II:** 338
Ward, Leo R., **Supp. VIII:** 124
Ward, Lester F., **Supp. I Part 2:** 640; **Supp. XI:** 202, 203
Ward, Lynn, **I:** 31
Ward, Nathaniel, **Supp. I Part 1:** 99, 102, 111, 116
Ward, Theodora, **I:** 470; **Retro. Supp. I:** 28
Ward, William Hayes, **Supp. I Part 1:** 371
"War Debt, A" (Jewett), **Retro. Supp. II:** 138, 141
"War Diary" (Boyce), **Supp. XVII:** 104; **Supp. XXI:** 6
"War Diary, A" (Bourne), **I:** 229
War Dispatches of Stephen Crane, The (Crane), **I:** 422
"Ward Line, The" (Morris), **III:** 220
Warfel, Harry R., **Supp. I Part 1:** 366
War Games (Morris), **III:** 238
War in Heaven, The (Shepard and Chaikin), **Supp. III Part 2:** 433
War Is Kind (Crane), **I:** 409; **III:** 585
"War Is Kind" (Crane), **I:** 419
Warlock (Harrison), **Supp. VIII:** 45, **46**
Warm as Wool (Sanders), **Supp. XVI:** 269
"Warming" (Trethewey), **Supp. XXI:** 245
Warner, Anna, **Supp. XVIII:** 258–275
Warner, Charles Dudley, **II:** 405; **IV:** 198
Warner, Jack, **Supp. XII:** 160–161; **Supp. XVIII:** 249
Warner, John R., **III:** 193
Warner, Oliver, **I:** 548
Warner, Susan, **Retro. Supp. I:** 246; **Supp. XV:** 275; **Supp. XVIII: 257–275**
Warner, Sylvia Townsend, **Supp. VIII:** 151, 155, 164, 171
Warner, W. Lloyd, **III:** 60
Warner Family and the Warner Books, The (Baker), **Supp. XVIII:** 259, 267
"Warning" (Hughes), **Supp. I Part 1:** 343
"Warning" (Pound), **III:** 474
"Warning, The" (Creeley), **Supp. IV Part 1:** 150
"Warning, The" (Longfellow), **II:** 498
Warning Hill (Marquand), **III:** 55–56, 60, 68
"War of Eyes, A" (Coleman), **Supp. XI:** 93–94
War of Eyes and Other Stories, A (Coleman), **Supp. XI: 91–92**
War of the Classes (London), **II:** 466
"War of the Wall, The" (Bambara), **Supp. XI:** 15–16
"War of Vaslav Nijinsky, The" (Bidart), **Supp. XV:** 21–22, **27–29**
"War Poems" (Sandburg), **III:** 581
Warren, Austin, **I:** 265, 268, 271; **Supp. I Part 2:** 423
Warren, Earl, **III:** 581
Warren, Gabriel, **IV:** 244
Warren, Mercy Otis, **Supp. XV:** 230
Warren, Patricia Nell, **Supp. XX: 259–276**
Warren, Robert Penn, **I:** 190, 211, 517; **II:** 57, 217, 228, 253; **III:** 134, 310, 382–383, 454, 482, 485, 490, 496, 497; **IV:** 121, 122, 123, 125, 126, **236–259,** 261, 262, 279, 340–341, 458; **Retro. Supp. I:** 40, 41, 73, 90; **Retro. Supp. II:** 220, 235; **Supp. I Part 1:** 359, 371; **Supp. I Part 2:** 386, 423; **Supp. II Part 1:** 139; **Supp. III Part 2:** 542; **Supp. V:** 261, 316, 318, 319, 333; **Supp. VIII:** 126, 176; **Supp. IX:** 257; **Supp. X:** 1, 25, 26; **Supp. XI:** 315; **Supp. XII:** 254, 255; **Supp. XIV:** 1, 2, 3, 4, 11, 14, 15; **Supp. XVIII:** 77, 78–79; **Supp. XIX:** 246; **Supp. XXI:** 256
Warren, Mrs. Robert Penn (Eleanor Clark), **IV:** 244
Warren, Rosanna, **IV:** 244; **Supp. XV:** 251, 261, 262, 263; **Supp. XIX:** 34
Warrington Poems, The (Ríos), **Supp. IV Part 2:** 540
Warrior, Robert Allen, **Supp. IV Part 1:** 329
"Warrior, The" (Gunn Allen), **Supp. IV Part 1:** 326
"Warrior: 5th Grade" (Olds), **Supp. X:** 214
"Warrior Road" (Harjo), **Supp. XII:** 217
Wars, The (Findley), **Supp. XX: 53–54**
Warshavsky, Isaac (pseudonym). *See* Singer, Isaac Bashevis
Warshow, Robert, **Supp. I Part 1:** 51
Wars I Have Seen (Stein), **IV:** 27, 36, 477
Wartime (Fussell), **Supp. V:** 241
War Trash (Jin), **Supp. XVIII:** 89, **100–101**
"War Widow, The" (Frederic), **II:** 135–136
"Was" (Creeley), **Supp. IV Part 1:** 155
"Was" (Faulkner), **II:** 71
"Wash" (Faulkner), **II:** 72
Wash, Richard, **Supp. XII:** 14
"Washboard Wizard" (Nelson), **Supp. XVIII:** 182
"Washed in the Rain" (Fante), **Supp. XI:** 165
"Washing of Hands, A" (Kooser), **Supp. XIX:** 115
Washington, Booker T., **Supp. I Part 2:** 393; **Supp. II Part 1:** 157, 160, 167, 168, 171, 225; **Supp. XIV:** 198, 199, 201; **Supp. XVIII:** 121–122
Washington, D.C. (Vidal), **Supp. IV Part 2:** 677, 684, 686–687, 690
Washington, George, **I:** 453; **II:** 313–314; **Supp. I Part 2:** 399, 485, 508, 509, 511, 513, 517, 518, 520, 599
Washington, Mary Helen, **Supp. XVIII:** 119, 284
Washington Crossing the Delaware (Rivers), **Supp. XV:** 186
Washington Post Book World (Lesser), **Supp. IV Part 2:** 453; **Supp. VIII:** 80, 84, 241; **Supp. X:** 282
Washington Square (James), **II:** 327, 328; **Retro. Supp. I:** 215, 220, **222–223**
"Washington Square, 1946" (Ozick), **Supp. V:** 272
Washington Square Ensemble, The (Bell), **Supp. X:** 1, **3–4**
"Was Lowell an Historical Critic?" (Altick), **Supp. I Part 2:** 423
Wasserman, Earl R., **Supp. I Part 2:** 439, 440
Wasserman, Jakob, **Supp. I Part 2:** 669
Wasserstein, Wendy, **Supp. IV Part 1:** 309; **Supp. XV: 319–336**
Wasson, Ben, **Retro. Supp. I:** 79, 83
"Waste Carpet, The" (Matthews), **Supp. IX: 158–159**
Waste Land, The (T. S. Eliot), **I:** 107, 266, 298, 395, 396, 482, 570–571, 572, 574–575, 577–578, 580, 581, 584, 585, 586, 587; **III:** 6–8, 12, 196, 277–278, 453, 471, 492, 586; **IV:** 122, 123, 124, 140, 418, 419, 420; **Retro. Supp. I:** 51, 60, **60–62,** 63, 64, 66, 210, 290, 291, 299, 311, 420, 427; **Retro. Supp. II:** 85, 121, 190; **Supp. I Part 1:** 272; **Supp. I Part 2:** 439, 455, 614; **Supp. II Part 1:** 4, 5, 11, 96; **Supp. III Part 1:** 9, 10, 41, 63, 105; **Supp. IV Part 1:** 47, 284; **Supp. V:** 338; **Supp. IX:** 158, 305; **Supp. X:** 125; **Supp. XIII:** 341–342, 344, 346; **Supp. XIV:** 6, 284; **Supp. XV:** 21, 181, 261, 306; **Supp. XVI:** 204; **Supp. XVII:** 140–141, 144, 227; **Supp. XVIII:** 78, 79–80; **Supp. XIX:** 288

"Waste Land, The": A Facsimile and Transcript of the Original Drafts Including the Annotations of Ezra Pound (Eliot, ed.), **Retro. Supp. I:** 58
Waste Land and Other Poems, The (T. S. Eliot), **Supp. XV:** 305
Wat, Alexander, **Supp. XVI:** 155, 161
Watch, The (Bass), **Supp. XVI: 16–17**
"Watch, The, —" (Bass), **Supp. XVI:** 17
Watch and Ward (James), **II:** 323; **Retro. Supp. I:** 218, **219,** 220
"Watcher" (Trethewey), **Supp. XXI:** 247
"Watcher, The" (R. Bly), **Supp. IV Part 1:** 71
"Watcher by the Dead, A" (Bierce), **I:** 203
Watchfires (Auchincloss), **Supp. IV Part 1:** 23
"Watching Crow, Looking toward the Manzano Mountains" (Harjo), **Supp. XII:** 219
"Watching the Oregon Whale" (A. Finch), **Supp. XVII:** 77
"Watching the Sunset" (Coleman), **Supp. XI:** 92
Watch on the Rhine (Hellman), **Supp. I Part 1:** 276, 278, 279–281, 283–284; **Supp. IV Part 1:** 83
"Water" (Emerson), **II:** 19
"Water" (Komunyakaa), **Supp. XIII:** 132
"Water" (Lowell), **II:** 550
"Waterbird" (Swenson), **Supp. IV Part 2:** 651
"Water Borders" (Dillard), **Supp. VI:** 27
"Water Buffalo" (Komunyakaa), **Supp. XIII:** 122
"Watercolor of Grantchester Meadows" (Plath), **Supp. I Part 2:** 537
Water Cure, The (Everett), **Supp. XVIII: 64–66**
"Waterfall, The" (Clampitt), **Supp. IX:** 44
Waterfront (Schulberg), **Supp. XVIII: 251–252**
"Water Hose Is on Fire, The" (Simic), **Supp. XV:** 185
Waterhouse, Keith, **Supp. VIII:** 124
"Waterlily Fire" (Rukeyser), **Supp. VI:** 285, 286
Waterlily Fire: Poems 1935–1962 (Rukeyser), **Supp. VI:** 274, 283, 285
Watermark (Brodsky), **Supp. VIII:** 29
Water-Method Man, The (Irving), **Supp. VI:** 163, **167–179,** 180
Water Music (Boyle), **Supp. VIII:** 1, 3–5, 8, 14; **Supp. XX: 20–22**
"Water Music for the Progress of Love in a Life-Raft Down the Sammamish Slough" (Wagoner), **Supp. IX:** 326
"Water People" (Burke), **Supp. XIV:** 21
"Water Picture" (Swenson), **Supp. IV Part 2:** 641
"Water Rising" (Hogan), **Supp. IV Part 1:** 400
Waters, Ethel, **II:** 587
Waters, Frank, **Supp. X:** 124
Waters, Muddy, **Supp. VIII:** 345
Watershed (Everett), **Supp. XVIII: 58–59,** 64
"Watershed" (Kingsolver), **Supp. VII:** 208
"Watershed" (Warren), **IV:** 239
"Watershed, The" (Auden), **Supp. II Part 1:** 5
Waters of Kronos, The (Richter), **Supp. XVIII:** 207, 208, **218–219,** 220
Waters of Siloe, The (Merton), **Supp. VIII:** 196, 208
Waterston, Sam, **Supp. IX:** 253
Water Street (Merrill), **Supp. III Part 1:** 321–323
"Water Walker" (Wilbur), **Supp. III Part 2:** 548, 560
Water-Witch, The (Cooper), **I:** 342–343
Waterworks, The (Doctorow), **Supp. IV Part 1:** 218, 222, 223, 231–233, 234
"Water Works, The" (Doctorow), **Supp. IV Part 1:** 234
Watkin, E. I., **Retro. Supp. II:** 187
Watkins, Floyd C., **IV:** 452
Watkins, James T., **I:** 193, 194
Watkins, Maureen, **Supp. XVI:** 188
Watkins, Mel, **Supp. X:** 330; **Supp. XIII:** 246
Watman, Max, **Supp. XX: 92**
Watrous, Peter, **Supp. VIII:** 79
Watson, Brook, **Supp. XX: 284**
Watson, Burton, **Supp. XV:** 47
Watson, James Sibley, Jr., **I:** 261
Watson, Jay, **Supp. XVIII:** 195; **Supp. XXI:** 46
Watson, J. B., **II:** 361
Watson, Richard, **Supp. I Part 2:** 516, 517
Watson, William, **II:** 114
Watt, Ian, **Supp. VIII:** 4
Watteau, Jean Antoine, **III:** 275; **IV:** 79
Watts, Emily Stipes, **Supp. I Part 1:** 115
Waugh, Evelyn, **I:** 480; **III:** 281; **Supp. I Part 2:** 607; **Supp. IV Part 2:** 688; **Supp. XI:** 305, 306; **Supp. XIX:** 131
"Wave" (Snyder), **Supp. VIII:** 299
Wave, A (Ashbery), **Supp. III Part 1:** 1, 4, 24–26
"Wave, A" (Ashbery), **Supp. III Part 1:** 9, 19, 24–25
"Wave, The" (MacLeish), **III:** 19
"Wave, The" (Untermeyer), **Supp. XV:** 300
"Wavemaker Falters, The" (Saunders), **Supp. XIX:** 225
"Waxwings" (Francis), **Supp. IX:** 82
Way, The (Steiner and Witt, eds.), **Supp. IV Part 2:** 505
"Way Down, The" (Kunitz), **Supp. III Part 1:** 263
"Way It Is, The" (Ellison), **Supp. II Part 1:** 245
"Way It Is, The" (Jones), **Supp. XI:** 229
Way It Is, The (Stafford), **Supp. XIII:** 274
"Way It Is, The" (Strand), **Supp. IV Part 2:** 627
"Wayland" (Sanders), **Supp. XVI:** 275
Wayne, John, **Supp. IV Part 1:** 200
Way of Chuang-Tzu, The (Merton), **Supp. VIII:** 208
"Way of Exchange in James Dickey's Poetry, The" (Weatherby), **Supp. IV Part 1:** 175
Way of Life According to Laotzu, The (Bynner), **Supp. XV:** 46, 48
Way Out, A (Frost), **Retro. Supp. I:** 133
Wayside Motor Inn, The (Gurney), **Supp. V:** 96, 105, 109
"Ways of Breaking: Lynda Hull's 'Ornithology' " (Jauss), **Supp. XXI:** 139
"Ways of Talking" (Jin), **Supp. XVIII:** 93
Ways of the Hour, The (Cooper), **I:** 354
Ways of White Folks, The (Hughes), **Retro. Supp. I:** 203, 204; **Supp. I Part 1:** 329, 330, 332
Way Some People Die, The (Macdonald), **Supp. IV Part 2:** 470, 471, 472, 474
Way Some People Live, The (Cheever), **Supp. I Part 1:** 175
"Way the Cards Fall, The" (Komunyakaa), **Supp. XIII:** 117
"Way the Luck Runs, The" (Wolfert), **Supp. XXI:** 265
"Way Things Are, The" (Turow, unpub.), **Supp. XVII:** 215, 218
Way to Rainy Mountain, The (Momaday), **Supp. IV Part 2:** 485–486, 487–489, 491, 493
Way to Wealth, The (Franklin), **II:** 101–102, 110; **Supp. XX: 27**
Wayward and the Seeking, The: A Collection of Writings by Jean Toomer (Toomer), **Supp. III Part 2:** 478–481, 484, 487
Wayward Bus, The (Steinbeck), **IV:** 51, 64–65
"Way We Live Now, The" (Sontag), **Supp. III Part 2:** 467–468
"Way You'll Never Be, A" (Hemingway), **II:** 249
"W. D. Sees Himself Animated" (Snodgrass), **Supp. VI:** 327
"W. D. Sits in Kafka's Chair and Is Interrogated Concerning the Assumed Death of Cock Robin" (Snodgrass), **Supp. VI:** 319
"W. D. Tries to Warn Cock Robin" (Snodgrass), **Supp. VI:** 319
"We" (Alexander), **Supp. XVIII:** 185
Weaks, Mary Louise, **Supp. X:** 5
Weales, Gerald, **II:** 602
"Wealth," from *Conduct of Life, The* (Emerson), **II:** 2, 3–4
"Wealth," from *English Traits* (Emerson), **II:** 6
Wealth of Nations, The (A. Smith), **II:** 109
"We Are Looking at You, Agnes" (Caldwell), **I:** 309
We Are Still Married: Stories and Letters (Keillor), **Supp. XVI:** 176, 177
"We Are the Crazy Lady and Other Feisty Feminist Fables" (Ozick), **Supp. V:** 259
Weary Blues, The (Hughes), **Retro. Supp. I:** 195, 197, 198, 199, 200, 203, 205; **Supp. I Part 1:** 325

"Weary Blues, The" (Hughes), **Retro. Supp. I:** 198, 199; **Supp. I Part 1:** 324, 325
"Weary Kingdom" (Irving), **Supp. VI:** 163
Weasels and Wisemen: Ethics and Ethnicity in the Work of David Mamet (Kane), **Supp. XIV:** 250
Weather and the Women Treat Me Fair, The (Everett), **Supp. XVIII:** 66
Weatherby, H. L., **Supp. IV Part 1:** 175
Weather Central (Kooser), **Supp. XIX:** 116, **123–125**
"Weathering Out" (Dove), **Supp. IV Part 1:** 248
"Weather Within, The" (M. F. K. Fisher), **Supp. XVII:** 88, 91
Weaver, Harriet, **III:** 471
Weaver, James, **Supp. XVIII:** 72
Weaver, Michael, **Supp. XVIII:** 176, 177
Weaver, Mike, **Retro. Supp. I:** 430
Weaver, Will, **Supp. XVI:** 39
"Weaving" (Larcom), **Supp. XIII:** 142, **Supp. XIII:** 144–145, 150, 151
"Web" (Oliver), **Supp. VII:** 236
Web and the Rock, The (Wolfe), **IV:** 451, 455, 457, 459–460, 462, 464, 467, 468
Webb, Beatrice, **Supp. I Part 1:** 5
Webb, Mary, **I:** 226
Webb, Phyllis, **Supp. XX: 56**
Webb, Sidney, **Supp. I Part 1:** 5
Webb, W. P., **Supp. V:** 225
Webber, A. R. F., **Supp. XXI:** 160
Weber, Brom, **I:** 383, 386
Weber, Carl, **Supp. IX:** 133, 138, 141
Weber, Max, **I:** 498; **Supp. I Part 2:** 637, 648
Weber, Sarah, **Supp. I Part 1:** 2
Weberman, A. J., **Supp. XVIII:** 27
Web of Earth, The (Wolfe), **IV:** 451–452, 456, 458, 464, 465
"Web of Life, The" (Nemerov), **III:** 282
Webster, Brenda, **Supp. XVI:** 157, 161
Webster, Daniel, **II:** 5, 9; **Supp. I Part 2:** 659, 687, 689, 690
Webster, John, **I:** 384; **Supp. I Part 2:** 422
Webster, Noah, **Supp. I Part 2:** 660; **Supp. II Part 1:** 77
Wector, Dixon, **II:** 103
Wedding, The (D. West), **Supp. XVIII:** 277, **287–289**
"Wedding, The" (Everwine), **Supp. XV:** 83
"Wedding, The" (Major), **Supp. XXII:** 185
Wedding, The (television miniseries), **Supp. XVIII:** 277, 289
"Wedding Cake" (Nye), **Supp. XIII:** 283
"Wedding Dance, The" (Di Piero), **Supp. XIX:** 47
"Wedding in Brownsville, A" (Singer), **IV:** 15
Wedding in Hell, A (Simic), **Supp. VIII:** 280, **282**
"Wedding of the Rose and Lotus, The" (Lindsay), **Supp. I Part 2:** 387
"Wedding Supper, The" (Rowson), **Supp. XV:** 243
"Wedding Toast, A" (Wilbur), **Supp. III Part 2:** 561
Wedekind, Frank, **III:** 398; **Supp. XX: 85; Supp. XXII:** 23
Wedge, The (W. C. Williams), **Retro. Supp. I:** 424
"Wednesday at the Waldorf" (Swenson), **Supp. IV Part 2:** 647
"We Don't Live Here Anymore" (Dubus), **Supp. VII:** 78–79, 85
"Weed" (McCarriston), **Supp. XIV:** 259, 273
"Weed, The" (Bishop), **Supp. I Part 1:** 80, 88–89
"Weed, The" (Taggard), **Supp. XXII:** 284
"Weeds, The" (McCarthy), **II:** 566
"Weekend" (Beattie), **Supp. V:** 27
"Weekend" (Hempel), **Supp. XXI:** 124
Weekend, The (Cameron), **Supp. XII:** 80, 81, **86–88**
"Weekend at Ellerslie, A" (Wilson), **IV:** 431
Weekend Edition (National Public Radio), **Supp. IX:** 299; **Supp. XVII:** 240, 242
"Week in the Word, A" (Hampl), **Supp. XXII:** 85
Week on the Concord and Merrimack Rivers, A (Thoreau), **IV:** 168, 169, 177, 182–183; **Supp. I Part 2:** 420; **Supp. XIV:** 227
Weeks, Edward, **III:** 64
Weeks, Jerome, **Supp. VIII:** 76
"Weeping Burgher" (Stevens), **IV:** 77
"Weeping Women" (Levertov), **Supp. III Part 1:** 282
We Fished All Night (W. Motley), **Supp. XVII: 155–158,** 159, 160
We Fly Away (Francis), **Supp. IX: 79–80,** 84
We Happy Few (Hinojosa), **Supp. XIX:** 99, **111–112**
We Have Always Lived in the Castle (Jackson), **Supp. IX:** 121, 126, **127–128**
"We Have Our Arts So We Won't Die of Truth" (Bradbury), **Supp. IV Part 1:** 105
We Have Tomorrow (Bontemps), **Supp. XXII:** 6, 12
Weich, Dave, **Supp. XII:** 321; **Supp. XVIII:** 91
"Weighing In" (Espaillat), **Supp. XXI:** 111
"Weight" (Wideman), **Supp. X:** 321
"Weights" (C. Baxter), **Supp. XVII:** 16
Weigl, Bruce, **Supp. VIII:** 269, 274; **Supp. XV:** 342; **Supp. XIX: 273–290**
Weil, Dorothy, **Supp. XV:** 231
Weil, James L., **Supp. XXI:** 23, 31
Weil, Robert, **Supp. IX:** 236
Weil, Simone, **I:** 298; **Supp. XV:** 259; **Supp. XXII:** 93
Weiland (C. B. Brown), **Supp. XIII:** 100
Weinauer, Ellen, **Supp. XV:** 270, 284
Weinberger, Eliot, **Supp. IV Part 1:** 66; **Supp. VIII:** 290, 292; **Supp. XVI:** 284
Weinberger, Eric, **Supp. XXII:** 264
Weinfield, Henry, **Supp. XXI:** 24, 28, 33
Weininger, Otto, **Retro. Supp. I:** 416
Weinraub, Judith, **Supp. XXI:** 39
Weinreb, Mindy, **Supp. X:** 24
Weinreich, Regina, **Supp. XIV:** 22
Weinstein, Cindy, **Supp. XVIII:** 261
Weinstein, Hinda, **IV:** 285
Weinstein, Max, **IV:** 285
Weinstein, Mrs. Max (Anna Wallenstein), **IV:** 285, 287
Weinstein, Nathan. *See* West, Nathanael
Weinstein, Selma, **Supp. XXI:** 170
Weisheit, Rabbi, **IV:** 76
Weismuller, Johnny, **Supp. X:** 264; **Supp. XX: 18**
Weiss, David, **Supp. XVI:** 55
Weiss, Jane, **Supp. XVIII:** 267, 269
Weiss, Peter, **IV:** 117
Weiss, Theodore, **Supp. IV Part 2:** 440; **Supp. IX:** 96
Weissleder, Paul, **Supp. XXII:** 283
Weist, Dianne, **Supp. X:** 80
Weithas, Art, **Supp. XI:** 231
Welch, Dave, **Supp. XXI:** 118
Welch, Don, **Supp. XIX:** 119
Welch, James, **Supp. IV Part 1:** 404; **Supp. IV Part 2:** 503, 513, 557, 562
Welch, Lew, **Supp. V:** 170; **Supp. VIII:** 303; **Supp. XXII:** 276
"Welcome from War" (Rukeyser), **Supp. VI:** 286
"Welcome Morning" (Sexton), **Supp. II Part 2:** 696
"Welcome the Wrath" (Kunitz), **Supp. III Part 1:** 261
Welcome to Hard Times (Doctorow), **Supp. IV Part 1:** 218, 219–220, 222, 224, 230, 238
Welcome to Hard Times (film), **Supp. IV Part 1:** 236
"Welcome to New Dork" (Leonard), **Supp. XVIII:** 148
Welcome to Our City (Wolfe), **IV:** 461
Welcome to the Monkey House (Vonnegut), **Supp. II Part 2:** 758
Welcome to the Moon (Shanley), **Supp. XIV:** 318
Welcome to the Moon and Other Plays (Shanley), **Supp. XIV:** 315, **316–319**
Weld, Theodore, **Supp. I Part 2:** 587, 588
Weld, Tuesday, **Supp. XI:** 306
Welded (O'Neill), **III:** 390; **Supp. XXII:** 24
"Welfare Worker, Disenchanted, Contemplates Friday Afternoon, The" (Trethewey), **Supp. XXI:** 246
"Well, The" (Momaday), **Supp. IV Part 2:** 483
"Well Dressed Man with a Beard, The" (Stevens), **Retro. Supp. I:** 297
Wellek, René, **I:** 253, 261, 282; **II:** 320; **Supp. XIV:** 12, 14
Weller, George, **III:** 322
Welles, Gideon, **Supp. I Part 2:** 484
Welles, Orson, **IV:** 476; **Supp. I Part 1:** 67; **Supp. IV Part 1:** 82, 83; **Supp. V:** 251; **Supp. VIII:** 46; **Supp. XI:** 169, 307
"Wellfleet Whale, The" (Kunitz), **Supp. III Part 1:** 263, 269

Wellfleet Whale and Companion Poems, The (Kunitz), **Supp. III Part 1:** 263
Wellink, Yvonne, **Supp. XVIII:** 257
Wellman, Flora, **II:** 463–464, 465
"Well Rising, The" (Stafford), **Supp. XI:** 318
Wells, H. G., **I:** 103, 226, 241, 243, 253, 405, 409, 415; **II:** 82, 144, 276, 337, 338, 458; **III:** 456; **IV:** 340, 455; **Retro. Supp. I:** 100, 228, 231; **Supp. XVI:** 190; **Supp. XXI:** 8
Wellspring, The (Olds), **Supp. X: 211–212**
Well Wrought Urn, The: Studies in the Structure of Poetry (Brooks), **Supp. XIV:** 1, **8–9,** 14, 15, 16
Welsh, Mary, **Supp. XIX:** 248. *See also* Hemingway, Mrs. Ernest (Mary Welsh)
Welty, Eudora, **II:** 194, 217, 606; **IV: 260–284; Retro. Supp. I:** 339–358; **Retro. Supp. II:** 235; **Supp. IV Part 2:** 474; **Supp. V:** 59, 315, 336; **Supp. VIII:** 94, 151, 171; **Supp. X:** 42, 290; **Supp. XII:** 310, 322; **Supp. XIV:** 3; **Supp. XV:** 338
Welty, Eurora, **Supp. XIX:** 151
Weltzien, O. Alan, **Supp. XVI:** 20–21, 28
"We miss Her, not because We see—" (Dickinson), **Retro. Supp. I:** 46
We Must Dance My Darlings (Trilling), **Supp. I Part 1:** 297
Wendell, Barrett, **III:** 507; **Supp. I Part 2:** 414; **Supp. XIV:** 197
Wendell, Sarah. *See* Holmes, Mrs. Abiel (Sarah Wendell)
Wendy Wasserstein: A Casebook (Barnett), **Supp. XV:** 323, 330
"Wendy Wasserstein's Three Sisters: Squandered Privilege" (Brewer), **Supp. XV:** 330
Wept of Wish-ton-Wish, The (Cooper), **I:** 339, 342, 350
Werbe, Peter, **Supp. XIII:** 236
"We Real Cool" (Brooks), **Supp. III Part 1:** 80
We're Back! A Dinosaur's Story (screenplay, Shanley), **Supp. XIV:** 316
"We're Friends Again" (O'Hara), **III:** 372–373
"Were the Whole Realm of Nature Mine" (Watts), **I:** 458
Werewolf (M. Sommers), **Supp. XVII:** 55
Were-Wolf, The (C. Housman), **Supp. XVII:** 55
Werewolf of Paris, The (Endore), **Supp. XVII:** 55–56
Werewolves in Their Youth (Chabon), **Supp. XI:** 66, **76–77**
Werlock, Abby, **Supp. XIII:** 293
Werthman, Michael, **Supp. V:** 115
"Wer-Trout, The" (Proulx), **Supp. VII:** 255–256
Wescott, Glenway, **I:** 288; **II:** 85; **III:** 448, 454; **Supp. VIII:** 156; **Supp. XIV:** 342; **Supp. XVI:** 195
"We Shall All Be Born Again But We Shall Not All Be Saved" (Matthews), **Supp. IX:** 162
West, Anthony, **Supp. IV Part 1:** 284
West, Benjamin, **Supp. I Part 2:** 511
West, Dorothy, **Supp. XIII:** 295; **Supp. XVIII: 277–291; Supp. XIX:** 72
West, James, **II:** 562
West, Nathanael, **I:** 97, 107, 190, 211, 298; **II:** 436; **III:** 357, 425; **IV: 285–307; Retro. Supp. II: 321–341; Supp. IV Part 1:** 203; **Supp. VIII:** 97; **Supp. XI:** 85, 105, 159, 296; **Supp. XII:** 173, 310; **Supp. XIII:** 106, 170; **Supp. XVIII:** 251, 253, 254
West, Nathaniel, **Supp. XIX:** 223
West, Ray, **Supp. XV:** 142
West, Rebecca, **II:** 412, 445; **Supp. XVI:** 152, 153
Westall, Julia Elizabeth. *See* Wolfe, Mrs. William Oliver (Julia Elizabeth Westall)
"We Stand United" (Benét), **Supp. XI:** 46
"West Authentic, The: Willa Cather" (Stegner), **Supp. IV Part 2:** 608
"West Coast, The: Region with a View" (Stegner), **Supp. IV Part 2:** 608–609
"West Coast Waterfront: End of an Era" (Swados), **Supp. XIX:** 264
Westcott, Edward N., **II:** 102
"Western Association of Writers" (Chopin), **Supp. I Part 1:** 217
"Western Ballad, A" (Ginsberg), **Supp. II Part 1:** 311
Western Borders, The (Howe), **Supp. IV Part 2:** 424–425
Western Canon: The Books and Schools of the Ages (Bloom), **Supp. IX:** 146
Western Lands, The (Burroughs), **Supp. III Part 1:** 106
"Western North Carolina" (Halliday), **Supp. XIX:** 85
Western Star (Benét), **Supp. XI:** 46, 47, 57
"Westland" (C. Baxter), **Supp. XVII:** 18, 19
"West Marginal Way" (Hugo), **Supp. VI:** 131, 135
West of Eden: Writers in Hollywood, 1928–1940 (Fine), **Supp. XVIII:** 248
West of Yesterday, East of Summer: New and Selected Poems, 1973–1993 (Monette), **Supp. X:** 159
West of Your City (Stafford), **Supp. XI:** 316, **317–318,** 321, 322
Weston, Jessie L., **II:** 540; **III:** 12; **Supp. I Part 2:** 438
"West Real" (Ríos), **Supp. IV Part 2:** 539, 540
West-running Brook (Frost), **II:** 155; **Retro. Supp. I:** 136, 137
"West-running Brook" (Frost), **II:** 150, 162–164
"West Wall" (Merwin), **Supp. III Part 1:** 355
"Westward Beach, A" (Jeffers), **Supp. II Part 2:** 418
Westward Ho (Harrison), **Supp. VIII:** 51, **52**
Westward the Course of Empire (Leutze), **Supp. X:** 307
"Westward the Course of Empire Takes Its Way" (Wallace), **Supp. X: 307–308; Supp. XXII:** 260
"West Wind" (Oliver), **Supp. VII:** 246
"West Wind, The" (Bryant), **Supp. I Part 1:** 155
West Wind: Poems and Prose Poems (Oliver), **Supp. VII:** 243, 246–248
"Wet Casements" (Ashbery), **Supp. III Part 1:** 18–20
We the Living (film), **Supp. IV Part 2:** 520
We the Living (Rand), **Supp. IV Part 2:** 520–521
Wetherell, Elizabeth (pseudonym). *See* Warner, Susan
Wet Parade (Sinclair), **Supp. V:** 289
Wetzsteon, Ross, **Supp. XXI:** 12
"We've Adjusted Too Well" (O'Brien), **Supp. V:** 247
Wevill, David, **Retro. Supp. II:** 247, 249
"We Wear the Mask" (Dunbar), **Supp. II Part 1:** 199, 207, 209–210
Weybright, Victor, **Supp. XIII:** 172
Weyden, Rogier van der, **Supp. IV Part 1:** 284
Whalen, Marcella, **Supp. I Part 1:** 49
Whalen, Philip, **Supp. VIII:** 289; **Supp. XXII:** 226
Whalen-Bridge, John, **Retro. Supp. II:** 211–212
"Whales off Wales, The" (X. J. Kennedy), **Supp. XV:** 163
"Whales Weep" (Boyle), **Supp. XX: 19**
"Whales Weep Not!" (D. H. Lawrence), **Supp. XVII:** 77
Wharton, Edith, **I:** 12, 375; **II:** 96, 180, 183, 186, 189–190, 193, 283, 338, 444, 451; **III:** 69, 175, 576; **IV:** 8, 53, 58, **308–330; Retro. Supp. I:** 108, 232, **359–385; Supp. IV Part 1:** 23, 31, 35, 36, 80, 81, 310; **Supp. IX:** 57; **Supp. XII:** 308; **Supp. XIV:** 337, 347; **Supp. XVI:** 189; **Supp. XVIII:** 278; **Supp. XX: 227, 229, 232, 239, 240**
Wharton, Edward Robbins, **IV:** 310, 313–314, 319
"What" (Dunn), **Supp. XI:** 144
What a Kingdom It Was (Kinnell), **Supp. III Part 1:** 235, 238, 239
"What America Would Be Like without Blacks" (Ellison), **Retro. Supp. II:** 123
What Are Masterpieces (Stein), **IV:** 30–31
What Are Years (Moore), **III:** 208–209, 210, 215
"What Are Years?" (Moore), **III:** 211, 213
What a Way to Go (Morris), **III:** 230–232
"What a Wonder among the Instruments Is the Walloping Trombone!" (Carruth), **Supp. XVI:** 51
"What Became of the Flappers?" (Zelda Fitzgerald), **Supp. IX:** 71
"What Can I Tell My Bones?" (Roethke), **III:** 546, 549

"What Child Is This?" (Jarman), **Supp. XVII:** 113–114, 115
"What Do We Have Here" (Carson), **Supp. XII: 101**
"What Do We See" (Rukeyser), **Supp. VI:** 282
What Do Women Want? Bread Roses Sex Power (Jong), **Supp. V:** 115, 117, 129, 130
"What Do You Do in San Francisco?" (Carver), **Supp. III Part 1:** 143
What D'Ya Know for Sure (Zinberg), **Supp. XV:** 196
Whatever Happened to Gloomy Gus of the Chicago Bears? (Coover), **Supp. V:** 51, 52
Whatever Happened to Jacy Farrow? (Cleveland), **Supp. V:** 222
"What Every Boy Should Know" (Maxwell), **Supp. VIII:** 169
"What Feels Like the World" (Bausch), **Supp. VII:** 46
"What Fort Sumter Did for Me" (E. Stoddard), **Supp. XV:** 282
"What Girls Read" (Salmon), **Supp. XVIII:** 258
"What God Is Like to Him I Serve" (Bradstreet), **Supp. I Part 1:** 106–107
"What Happened Here Before" (Snyder), **Supp. VIII:** 302
"What Happened to Georgia" (Ray), **Supp. XVIII:** 194
What Happens (Herrmann), **Supp. XXII:** 277
What Have I Ever Lost by Dying? (R. Bly), **Supp. IV Part 1:** 71–72
What Have You Lost? (Nye, ed.), **Supp. XIII:** 280
"What I Believe" (Mumford), **Supp. II Part 2:** 479
"What I Call What They Call Onanism" (Goldbarth), **Supp. XII:** 175
What I Did Last Summer (Gurney), **Supp. V:** 96, 100, 107, 108
"What if God" (Olds), **Supp. X:** 208
What I Have Done with Birds: Character Studies of Native American Birds (Stratton-Porter), **Supp. XX: 218**
"What I Have to Defend, What I Can't Bear Losing" (Stern), **Supp. IX:** 286, 287, 288, 298
"What I Knew" (Nelson), **Supp. XVIII:** 178
"What I Know about Being a Playwright" (McNally), **Supp. XIII:** 195, 207
"What I Mean" (Ortiz), **Supp. IV Part 2:** 497
"What Is an Emotion" (James), **II:** 350
What Is Art? (Tolstoy), **I:** 58
"What Is Civilization? Africa's Answer" (Du Bois), **Supp. II Part 1:** 176
"What Is College For?" (Bourne), **I:** 216
"What Is Exploitation?" (Bourne), **I:** 216
What Is Found There: Notebooks on Poetry and Politics (A. Rich), **Supp. XVII:** 74
"What Is It?" (Carver), **Supp. III Part 1:** 139
What Is Man? (Twain), **II:** 434; **IV:** 209
"What Is Poetry" (Ashbery), **Supp. III Part 1:** 19
"What Is Seized" (Moore), **Supp. X:** 164, 168, 169, 172, 175
"What Is the Earth?" (Olds), **Supp. X:** 213
"What Is This Poet" (Stern), **Supp. IX:** 295
What Is To Be Done? (Lenin), **Supp. XXI:** 164
"What I Think" (Hogan), **Supp. IV Part 1:** 406
What Maisie Knew (H. James), **II:** 332; **Retro. Supp. I:** 229, **230; Supp. XVIII:** 160
What Makes Sammy Run? (NBC broadcast, Schulberg and Schulberg), **Supp. XVIII:** 254
What Makes Sammy Run? (Schulberg), **Supp. XIII:** 170; **Supp. XVIII:** 241, **244–247,** 248, 249, 253
"What Makes Sammy Run?" (Schulberg), **Supp. XVIII:** 241
What Moon Drove Me to This? (Harjo), **Supp. XII: 218–220**
"What Must" (MacLeish), **III:** 18
What My Father Believed (Wrigley), **Supp. XVIII:** 298–300
"What My Father Believed" (Wrigley), **Supp. XVIII: 298–299**
What Price Hollywood? (film), **Supp. XVIII:** 243
"What Sally Said" (Cisneros), **Supp. VII:** 63
What Saves Us (Weigl), **Supp. XIX:** 282
"What's Happening in America" (Sontag), **Supp. III Part 2:** 460–461
"What She Couldn't Tell" (Hampl), **Supp. XXII:** 92
"What's in Alaska?" (Carver), **Supp. III Part 1:** 141, 143
"What's in a Name" (H. L. Gates), **Supp. XX: 101**
What's New, Pussycat? (film; Allen), **Supp. XI:** 307; **Supp. XV:** 1, 2, 14
"What's New in American and Canadian Poetry" (R. Bly), **Supp. IV Part 1:** 67
What's O'Clock (Lowell), **II:** 511, 527, 528
What's Up, Tiger Lily? (film; Allen), **Supp. XV:** 2, **3**
"What the Arts Need Now" (Baraka), **Supp. II Part 1:** 47
"What the Body Can Say" (Trethewey), **Supp. XXI:** 255
"What the Brand New Freeway Won't Go By" (Hugo), **Supp. VI:** 132–133
"What the Gypsies Told My Grandmother While She Was Still a Young Girl" (Simic), **Supp. VIII:** 283
"What the Prose Poem Carries with It" (R. Bly), **Supp. IV Part 1:** 64
"What They Wanted" (Dunn), **Supp. XI:** 151
What Thou Lovest Well (Hugo), **Supp. VI:** 140, 141
"What Thou Lovest Well Remains American" (Hugo), **Supp. VI:** 140, 141
What Time Collects (Farrell), **II:** 46, 47–48
What to Do? (Chernyshevsky), **Retro. Supp. I:** 269
"What to Keep, What to Discard" (Taggard), **Supp. XXII:** 280
What Use Are Flowers? (Hansberry), **Supp. IV Part 1:** 359, 368–369, 374
What Was Literature? (Fiedler), **Supp. XIII:** 96–97, **105–106**
What Was Mine (Beattie), **Supp. V:** 33, 35
What Was the Relationship of the Lone Ranger to the Means of Production? (Baraka), **Supp. II Part 1:** 58
"What We Came Through" (Goldbarth), **Supp. XII:** 179–180
"What Were the White Things?" (Hempel), **Supp. XXI:** 126
What We Talk About When We Talk About Love (Carver), **Supp. III Part 1:** 142–146; **Supp. XII:** 139
"What Why When How Who" (Pinsky), **Supp. VI:** 244
What Will Suffice: Contemporary American Poets on the Art of Poetry (Buckley and Young, eds.), **Supp. XIII:** 313
What Work Is (Levine), **Supp. V:** 181, 187, 192–193
"What You Hear from Em" (Taylor), **Supp. V:** 314, 320, 324
"What You Want" (O. Henry), **Supp. II Part 1:** 402
"What You Would Do" (Weigl), **Supp. XIX:** 288
Wheatley, Phillis, **Supp. XIII:** 111; **Supp. XVII:** 74–75; **Supp. XX: 106, 277–291**
Whedon, Tony, **Supp. XXI:** 131, 132
Wheeler, David, **Supp. XVI:** 277
Wheeler, John, **II:** 433
Wheeler, Monroe, **Supp. XV:** 295
Wheelock, John Hall, **IV:** 461; **Supp. IX:** 268; **Supp. XIV:** 120; **Supp. XV:** 301
Wheel of Life, The (Glasgow), **II:** 176, 178, 179, 183
Wheelwright, Philip, **Supp. XV:** 20
"When" (Olds), **Supp. X:** 207
When Boyhood Dreams Come True (Farrell), **II:** 45
"When Death Came April Twelve 1945" (Sandburg), **III:** 591, 593
"When Death Comes" (Oliver), **Supp. VII:** 241
"When De Co'n Pone's Hot" (Dunbar), **Supp. II Part 1:** 202–203
"When God First Said" (Zach; Everwine trans.), **Supp. XV:** 87
"When Grandma Died—1942" (Shields), **Supp. VII:** 311
"When Howitzers Began" (Carruth), **Supp. XVI:** 55
"When I Buy Pictures" (Moore), **III:** 205
"When I Came from Colchis" (Merwin), **Supp. III Part 1:** 343
"When I Have Fears I May Cease to Be" (Keats), **Supp. XIX:** 92
"When I Left Business for Literature" (Anderson), **I:** 101
"When I Love You" (Peacock), **Supp. XIX:** 199

"When in Rome—Apologia" (Komunyakaa), **Supp. XIII:** 120
"When It Comes" (Olds), **Supp. X:** 213
"When It's Clear and Hot" (Trethewey), **Supp. XXI:** 246
When I Was Alive (Notley), **Supp. XXII:** 228
"When I Was Alive" (Notley), **Supp. XXII:** 229
"When I Was Seventeen" (Kincaid), **Supp. VII:** 181
"When I Was Twenty-five" (Talese), **Supp. XVII:** 202
When Knighthood Was in Flower (Major), **III:** 320
"[When] Let by rain" (Taylor), **IV:** 160–161
"When Lilacs Last in the Dooryard Bloom'd" (Whitman), **IV:** 347–348, 351; **Retro. Supp. I:** 406; **Supp. IV Part 1:** 16; **Supp. XV:** 215
"When Malindy Sings" (Dunbar), **Supp. II Part 1:** 200, 204–205
When Peoples Meet: A Study of Race and Culture (Locke and Stern), **Supp. XIV:** 202, 213
When She Was Good (P. Roth), **Retro. Supp. II:** 282, 283, 284; **Supp. III Part 2:** 403, 405, 410–413
"When Sue Wears Red" (Hughes), **Retro. Supp. I:** 195, 204
"When the Dead Ask My Father about Me" (Olds), **Supp. X:** 210
"When the Frost Is on the Punkin" (Riley), **Supp. II Part 1:** 202
When the Jack Hollers (Hughes), **Retro. Supp. I:** 203; **Supp. I Part 1:** 328
"When the Last Riders" (Zach; Everwine, trans.), **Supp. XV:** 75, 86
"When the Light Gets Green" (Warren), **IV:** 252
"When the Model Does Not Show" (Major), **Supp. XXII:** 184
"When the Peace Corps Was Young" (Theroux), **Supp. VIII:** 314
When the Sun Tries to Go On (Koch), **Supp. XV:** 185
"When the Sun Tries to Go On" (Koch), **Supp. XV:** 179, 180
"When the World Ended as We Knew It" (Harjo), **Supp. XII:** 231
When Time Was Born (Farrell), **II:** 46, 47
"When We Dead Awaken: Writing as Re-Vision" (Rich), **Supp. I Part 2:** 552–553, 560
"When We Gonna Rise" (Baraka), **Supp. II Part 1:** 48
"When We Have To" (Salinas), **Supp. XIII:** 322–323
"WHEN WE'LL WORSHIP JESUS" (Baraka), **Supp. II Part 1:** 54
"When We Sold the Tent" (Espaillat), **Supp. XXI:** 102
"When we speak of God, is it God we speak of?" (J. Logan), **Supp. XVII:** 113
"When Women Throw Down Bundles: Strong Women Make Strong Nations" (Gunn Allen), **Supp. IV Part 1:** 328
"'When You Finally See Them': The Unconquered Eye in *To Kill a Mockingbird*" (Champion), **Supp. VIII:** 128
"When You Lie Down, the Sea Stands Up" (Swenson), **Supp. IV Part 2:** 643
"Where Blue Is Blue" (Richard), **Supp. XIX:** 221
Where Does One Go When There's No Place Left to Go? (Crews), **Supp. XI:** 103
"Where Go the Boats" (R. Stevenson), **Supp. XVII:** 69
Where Horizons Go (Espaillat), **Supp. XXI:** 99, 103, 104
"Where I Come from Is Like This" (Gunn Allen), **Supp. IV Part 1:** 319
"Where I'm Calling From" (Carver), **Supp. III Part 1:** 145
Where I'm Calling From: New and Selected Stories (Carver), **Supp. III Part 1:** 138, 148
"Where I Ought to Be" (Erdrich), **Supp. IV Part 1:** 265
Where Is My Wandering Boy Tonight? (Wagoner), **Supp. IX: 335–336**
"Where Is the Island?" (Francis), **Supp. IX:** 78
"Where Is the Voice Coming From?" (Welty), **IV:** 280; **Retro. Supp. I:** 355
Where Joy Resides (Isherwood), **Supp. XIV:** 156
"Where Knock Is Open Wide" (Roethke), **III:** 533–535
"Where My Sympathy Lies" (H. Roth), **Supp. IX:** 234
Where's My Money? (Shanley), **Supp. XIV:** 316, 328, **330–331**
Where the Bluebird Sings to the Lemonade Springs (Stegner), **Supp. IV Part 2:** 596, 597, 598, 600, 604, 606, 613; **Supp. XXII:** 205
"Where the Bones Move" (W. V. Davis), **Supp. XXI:** 92
Where the Cross Is Made (O'Neill), **III:** 388, 391
Where the Rivers Flow North (Mosher), **Supp. XXII:** 205, 207, 208, **210–212**
"Where the Rivers Flow North" (Mosher), **Supp. XXII:** 204, 206, 207, 208, 209, **210–211**
Where the Sea Used to Be (Bass), **Supp. XVI:** 21
"Where the Sea Used to Be" (Bass), **Supp. XVI:** 20, 21
"*Where the Sea Used to Be:* Rick Bass and the Novel of Ecological Education" (Dixon), **Supp. XVI:** 21
"Where the Soft Air Lives" (Nye), **Supp. XIII:** 275
Where the Twilight Never Ends (Haines), **Supp. XII:** 211
Where the Wild Grape Grows: Selected Writings, 1930–1950 (D. West; Mitchell and Davis, eds.), **Supp. XVIII:** 283, 286
Where the Wild Things Are (Sendak), **Supp. IX:** 207
"Wherever Home Is" (Wright), **Supp. III Part 2:** 605, 606
Where Water Comes Together With Other Water (Carver), **Supp. III Part 1:** 147, 148
"Where We Crashed" (Hugo), **Supp. VI:** 138
"Where We Must Look for Help" (R. Bly), **Supp. XXI:** 84
"Where You Are" (Doty), **Supp. XI:** 131
Where You'll Find Me, and Other Stories (Beattie), **Supp. V:** 30–31
Whicher, Stephen, **II:** 20
"Which Is More Than I Can Say for Some People" (Moore), **Supp. X:** 177, 178
Which Ones Are the Enemy? (Garrett), **Supp. VII:** 98
"Which Theatre Is the Absurd One?" (Albee), **I:** 71
"Which Way to the Future?" (Rehder), **Supp. IV Part 1:** 69
While I Was Gone (Miller), **Supp. XII:** 290, **301–303**
"While Seated in a Plane" (Swenson), **Supp. IV Part 2:** 645
While the Messiah Tarries (Bukiet), **Supp. XVII:** 43, **46–47**
While We've Still Got Feet (Budbill), **Supp. XIX:** 5, 7, **10–11,** 15
Whilomville Stories (Crane), **I:** 414
"Whip, The" (Robinson), **III:** 513
Whipple, Thomas K., **II:** 456, 458; **IV:** 427
"Whippoorwill, The" (Francis), **Supp. IX:** 90
"Whip-poor-will, The" (Thurber), **Supp. I Part 2:** 616
Whirlpool (film, Preminger), **Supp. XVII:** 62
"Whispering Gallery, The" (Komunyakaa), **Supp. XIII:** 132
"Whispering Leaves" (Glasgow), **II:** 190
Whispering to Fool the Wind (Ríos), **Supp. IV Part 2:** 540–541, 544, 545
"Whispers in the Next Room" (Simic), **Supp. VIII:** 278
"Whispers of Heavenly Death" (Whitman), **IV:** 348
"Whispers of Immortality" (Eliot), **Supp. XI:** 242
Whistle (Jones), **Supp. XI:** 219, 224, **231–234**
"Whistle, The" (Franklin), **II:** 121
"Whistle, The" (Komunyakaa), **Supp. XIII:** 111, 126
"Whistle, The" (Welty), **IV:** 262
Whistler, James, **I:** 484; **III:** 461, 465, 466; **IV:** 77, 369
Whistler, James Abbott McNeill, **Supp. XIV:** 335–336
"Whistling Dick's Christmas Stocking" (O. Henry), **Supp. II Part 1:** 390, 392
Whistling in the Dark (Garrett), **Supp. VII:** 111
Whistling in the Dark: True Stories and Other Fables (Garrett), **Supp. VII:** 95
Whitcher, Frances Miriam Berry, **Supp. XIII:** 152
"White" (Simic), **Supp. VIII: 275–276**
White, Barbara, **Retro. Supp. I:** 379
White, Dana, **Supp. XXII:** 251

White, E. B., **Retro. Supp. I:** 335; **Supp. I Part 2:** 602, 607, 608, 612, 619, 620, **651–681; Supp. II Part 1:** 143; **Supp. VIII:** 171; **Supp. IX:** 20, 32; **Supp. XVI:** 167

White, Elizabeth Wade, **Supp. I Part 1:** 100, 103, 111

White, Henry Kirke, **Supp. I Part 1:** 150

White, James L., **Supp. XI:** 123

White, Joel, **Supp. I Part 2:** 654, 678

White, Katharine. (Katharine Sergeant Angell), **Supp. I Part 2:** 610, 653, 655, 656, 669; **Supp. VIII:** 151, 171

White, Lillian, **Supp. I Part 2:** 651

White, Lucia, **I:** 258

White, Maria. *See* Lowell, Mrs. James Russell (Maria White)

White, Morton, **I:** 258; **Supp. I Part 2:** 647, 648, 650

White, Roberta, **Supp. XII:** 293

White, Stanford, **Supp. IV Part 1:** 223

White, Stanley, **Supp. I Part 2:** 651, 655

White, T. H., **III:** 522

White, T. W., **III:** 411, 415

White, Walter, **Supp. I Part 1:** 345; **Supp. XVIII:** 123, 127; **Supp. XIX:** 73

White, William, **Retro. Supp. II:** 326

White, William A., **I:** 252

White Album, The (Didion), **Supp. IV Part 1:** 198, 202, 205–207, 210

"White Album, The" (Didion), **Supp. IV Part 1:** 205, 206

"White Angel" (Cunningham), **Supp. XV:** 59

"White Apache" (Markson), **Supp. XVII:** 136

White Boys (McKnight), **Supp. XX: 155–157**

"White Boys, The" (McKnight), **Supp. XX: 155–157**

White Buildings (H. Crane), **I:** 385, 386, 390–395, 400; **Retro. Supp. II:** 77–78, **80–81,** 82, 83, 85

White Butterfly (Mosley), **Supp. XIII:** 237, 238, 240

White Center (Hugo), **Supp. VI:** 144–145

"White Center" (Hugo), **Supp. VI:** 144, 146

Whited, Stephen, **Supp. XI:** 135

White Deer, The (Thurber), **Supp. I Part 2:** 606

White Doves at Morning (Burke), **Supp. XIV:** 22–23, 32, 35–36

"White Eagle, The" (Chopin), **Retro. Supp. II:** 72

White Fang (London), **II:** 471–472, 481

Whitefield, George, **I:** 546; **Supp. XX: 280**

White-Footed Deer and Other Poems (Bryant), **Supp. I Part 1:** 157

White Goddess, The (Graves), **Supp. IV Part 1:** 280

White-Haired Lover (Shapiro), **Supp. II Part 2:** 703, 717

Whitehead, Alfred North, **III:** 605, 619, 620; **IV:** 88; **Supp. I Part 2:** 554, 647

Whitehead, Mrs. Catherine, **IV:** 116

Whitehead, Colson, **Supp. XIII:** 233, 241

Whitehead, James, **Supp. XV:** 339

Whitehead, Margaret, **IV:** 114, 115, 116

Whitehead, William, **Supp. XX: 50–51, 53**

White Heat (Walsh), **Supp. XIII:** 174

"White Heron, A" (Jewett), **II:** 409; **Retro. Supp. II:** 17

White Heron and Other Stories, A (Jewett), **II:** 396

White Horses (Hoffman), **Supp. X: 83–85,** 90, 92

White House Diary, A (Lady Bird Johnson), **Supp. IV Part 1:** 22

White-Jacket; or, The World in a Man-of-War (Melville), **III:** 80, 81, 84, 94; **Retro Supp. I:** 248, 249, 254; **Supp. XVIII:** 7, 9

White Lantern, The (Connell), **Supp. XIV:** 97

"White Lies" (Trethewey), **Supp. XXI:** 244, 246, 251

"White Lights, The" (Robinson), **III:** 524

"White Lilies, The" (Glück), **Supp. V:** 88

White Man, Listen! (Wright), **IV:** 478, 488, 489, 494

"White Mulberry Tree, The" (Cather), **I:** 319; **Retro. Supp. I:** 7, 9, 17

White Mule (W. C. Williams), **Retro. Supp. I:** 423

"White Negro, The" (Mailer), **III:** 36–37; **Retro. Supp. II:** 202

"Whiteness of the Whale, The" (Melville), **III:** 84, 86

"White Night" (Oliver), **Supp. VII:** 236

"White Nights" (Auster), **Supp. XII:** 23–24

White Noise (DeLillo), **Supp. VI:** 1, 3–4, 5–7, 10, 11–12, 16; **Supp. XVIII:** 140; **Supp. XX: 91**

White Oxen and Other Stories, The (Burke), **I:** 269, 271

White Paper on Contemporary American Poetry (McClatchy), **Supp. XII:** 253, **259–260**

"White Phosphorous" (Notley), **Supp. XXII:** 232, 233

"White Pine" (Oliver), **Supp. VII:** 244

White Pine: Poems and Prose Poems (Oliver), **Supp. VII:** 243–246

White Sail (Sorrentino), **Supp. XXI:** 228

"White Silence, The" (London), **II:** 468

"White Silk" (Nye), **Supp. XIII:** 275

"White Snake, The" (Sexton), **Supp. II Part 2:** 691

"White Spot" (Anderson), **I:** 116

"White-Tailed Hornet, The" (Frost), **Retro. Supp. I:** 138

"White Trash Cowboys of *Father and Son,* The" (Bjerre), **Supp. XXI:** 41

Whitfield, Raoul, **Supp. IV Part 1:** 345

Whitfield, Stephen J., **Supp. XX: 243, 244**

Whitlock, Brand, **II:** 276

Whitman (Masters), **Supp. I Part 2:** 473, 475, 476

Whitman, George, **IV:** 346, 350

Whitman, Ruth, **Supp. XXI:** 246

Whitman, Sarah Wyman, **Retro. Supp. II:** 136

Whitman, Walt, **I:** 61, 68, 98, 103, 104, 109, 219, 220, 227, 228, 242, 246, 250, 251, 260, 261, 285, 381, 384, 386, 396, 397, 398, 402, 419, 430, 459, 460, 483, 485, 486, 577; **II:** 7, 8, 18, 127, 140, 273–274, 275, 289, 295, 301, 320, 321, 373, 445, 446, 451, 457, 494, 529, 530, 552; **III:** 171, 175, 177, 181–182, 189, 203, 234, 260, 426, 430, 453, 454, 461, 505, 507–508, 511, 528, 548, 552, 555, 559, 567, 572, 576, 577, 579, 584, 585, 595, 606, 609; **IV:** 74, 169, 191, 192, 202, **331–354,** 405, 409, 416, 444, 450–451, 457, 463, 464, 469, 470, 471; **Retro. Supp. I:** 8, 52, 194, 254, 283, 284, 333, **387–410,** 412, 417, 427; **Retro. Supp. II:** 40, 76, 93, 99, 155, 156, 158, 170, 262; **Supp. I Part 1:** 6, 79, 167, 311, 314, 325, 365, 368, 372; **Supp. I Part 2:** 374, 384, 385, 387, 389, 391, 393, 399, 416, 436, 455, 456, 458, 473, 474, 475, 525, 540, 579, 580, 582, 682, 691; **Supp. III Part 1:** 6, 20, 156, 239–241, 253, 340; **Supp. III Part 2:** 596; **Supp. IV Part 1:** 16, 169, 325; **Supp. IV Part 2:** 597, 625; **Supp. V:** 113, 118, 122, 130, 170, 178, 183, 277, 279, 332; **Supp. VIII:** 42, 95, 105, 126, 198, 202, 269; **Supp. IX:** 8, 9, 15, 38, 41, 44, 48, 53, 131, 292, 298, 299, 308, 320; **Supp. X:** 36, 112, 203, 204; **Supp. XI:** 83, 123, 132, 135, 203, 321; **Supp. XII:** 132, 185, 190, 256; **Supp. XIII:** 1, 77, 115, 153, 221, 304, 335; **Supp. XIV:** 89, 312, 334, 335, 338; **Supp. XV:** 41, 93, 181, 183, 212, 213, 218, 250, 275, 301, 302, 303, 309, 352; **Supp. XVI:** 209; **Supp. XVII:** 42, 71, 112, 133; **Supp. XVIII:** 4, 194, 196, 304; **Supp. XIX:** 118, 276; **Supp. XX: 69, 115, 116, 221; Supp. XXI:** 169, 217, 227, 256; **Supp. XXII:** 81, 82, 86, 92

"Whitman Pinch Hits, 1861" (Skloot), **Supp. XX: 203**

"Whitman: The Poet and the Mask" (Cowley), **Supp. II Part 1:** 143

Whitmarsh, Jason, **Supp. VIII:** 283

Whitmer, Peter, **Supp. X:** 264, 265

Whitney, Blair, **Supp. I Part 2:** 403

Whitney, Josiah, **Supp. IX:** 180, 181

Whitt, Margaret Earley, **Retro. Supp. II:** 226

Whittemore, Reed, **III:** 268; **Supp. XI:** 315

Whittier, Elizabeth, **Supp. I Part 2:** 700, 701, 703; **Supp. XIII:** 141, 142

Whittier, John Greenleaf, **I:** 216; **II:** 275; **III:** 52; **Retro. Supp. I:** 54; **Retro. Supp. II:** 155, 163, 169; **Supp. I Part 1:** 168, 299, 313, 317, 372; **Supp. I Part 2:** 420, 602, **682–707; Supp. VIII:** 202, 204; **Supp. XI:** 50; **Supp. XIII:** 140, 145; **Supp. XV:** 246

Whittier, Mary, **Supp. I Part 2:** 683

"Whittier Birthday Speech" (Twain), **Supp. I Part 1:** 313

"Who" (Kenyon), **Supp. VII:** 174

"Who" (Sobin), **Supp. XVI:** 284–285
"Who Am I—Who I Am" (Corso), **Supp. XII:** 134
"Who Be Kind To" (Ginsberg), **Supp. II Part 1:** 323
"Whoever Was Using This Bed" (Carver), **Supp. III Part 1:** 148
"Whoever You Are Holding Me Now in Hand" (Whitman), **IV:** 342; **Retro. Supp. I:** 52
Who Gathered and Whispered behind Me (Goldbarth), **Supp. XII:** 181, 182
"Who in One Lifetime" (Rukeyser), **Supp. VI:** 276, 279
Who Is Witter Bynner? (Kraft), **Supp. XV:** 40, 52
"Who Is Your Mother? Red Roots of White Feminism" (Gunn Allen), **Supp. IV Part 1:** 329
Whole Hog (Wagoner), **Supp. IX: 337–338**
"Whole Mess...Almost, The" (Corso), **Supp. XII:** 135
"Whole Moisty Night, The" (R. Bly), **Supp. IV Part 1:** 69
Whole New Life, A (Price), **Supp. VI:** 265, **266,** 267
"Whole Self, The" (Nye), **Supp. XIII:** 275
"Whole Soul, The" (Levine), **Supp. V:** 192
"Whole Story, The" (Strand), **Supp. IV Part 2:** 622
Whole Town's Talking, The (Loos), **Supp. XVI:** 187
"Whole World Knows, The" (Welty), **IV:** 272; **Retro. Supp. I:** 343
Who'll Stop the Rain (film), **Supp. V:** 301
Who Lost an American? (Algren), **Supp. IX: 15–16**
Who Owns America? (symposium), **Supp. XIV:** 4
"Who Puts Together" (Hogan), **Supp. IV Part 1:** 403, 405, 412–413
"Whore of Mensa, The" (Allen), **Supp. XV:** 15
Whores for Gloria (Vollmann), **Supp. XVII:** 226, 230
Whorf, Benjamin Lee, **Supp. XVI:** 283
Who's Afraid? (Holding), **Supp. XXII:** 120**, 125–126**
Who's Afraid of Virginia Woolf? (Albee), **I:** 71, 77–81, 83, 85, 86, 87, 94; **IV:** 230
Who Shall Be the Sun? Poems Based on the Lore, Legends, and Myths of the Northwest Coast and Plateau Indians (Wagoner), **Supp. IX:** 328, **329–330,** 337
"Whosis Kid, The" (Hammett), **Supp. IV Part 1:** 344
"Who Sit Watch in Daylight" (Wright), **Supp. XV:** 342
"Who's Passing for Who?" (Hughes), **Supp. I Part 1:** 330
"Who Speak on the Page?" (Sanders), **Supp. XVI:** 278
Who Will Run the Frog Hospital?: A Novel (Moore), **Supp. X:** 163, 165, 169, **175–177**
Who Wrote the Book of Love? (Siegel), **Supp. XXII: 265–267,** 267
Why Are We in Vietnam? (Mailer), **III:** 27, 29, 30, 33, 34–35, 39, 42, 44; **Retro. Supp. II:** 205–206
"Why Bother?" (Franzen). *See* "Perchance to Dream" (Franzen)
"Why China?" (Egan), **Supp. XIX:** 51, 52
"Why Did the Balinese Chicken Cross the Road?" (Walker), **Supp. III Part 2:** 527
"Why Do the Heathens Rage?" (O'Connor), **III:** 351
"Why Do You Write About Russia?" (Simpson), **Supp. IX:** 277
"Why I Am a Danger to the Public" (Kingsolver), **Supp. VII:** 204
Why I Am Not a Christian (Russell), **Supp. I Part 2:** 522
Why I Came to Judevine (Budbill), **Supp. XIX:** 2, **7–8,** 15
"Why I Entered the Gurdjieff Work" (Toomer), **Supp. III Part 2:** 481
"Why I Like Laurel" (Patchett), **Supp. XII:** 309
"Why I Live at the P.O." (Welty), **IV:** 262; **Retro. Supp. I:** 345
"Why I Make Sam Go to Church" (Lamott), **Supp. XX: 141**
"Why Is Economics Not an Evolutionary Science?" (Veblen), **Supp. I Part 2:** 634
"Why I Write" (Didion), **Supp. IV Part 1:** 201, 203
"Why I Wrote *Phil:* An Exclusive Essay for Amazon.com" (Saunders), **Supp. XIX:** 230–231
Why Johnny Can't Read: And What You Can Do About It (Flesch), **Supp. XVI:** 105
"Why Negro Women Leave Home" (Brooks), **Supp. III Part 1:** 75
Why Poetry Matters (Parini), **Supp. XIX:** 120, 129
"Why Resign from the Human Race?" (Swados), **Supp. XIX:** 265
"Why the Little Frenchman Wears His Hand in a Sling" (Poe), **III:** 425
"Why We Are Forgiven" (Weigl), **Supp. XIX:** 282–283
Why We Behave Like Microbe Hunters (Thurber), **Supp. I Part 2:** 606
Why We Were in Vietnam (Podhoretz), **Supp. VIII:** 241
"Why Write?" (Updike), **Retro. Supp. I:** 317
"Wichita Vortex Sutra" (Ginsberg), **Supp. II Part 1:** 319, 321, 323–325, 327
Wickes, George, **Supp. XIV:** 165
Wickford Point (Marquand), **III:** 50, 58, 64–65, 69
Wicks, Robert Russell, **Supp. XII:** 49
Wide, Wide World, The (S. Warner as Wetherell), **Supp. XV:** 275; **Supp. XVIII:** 257, 260**, 262–264,** 265
"Wide Empty Landscape with a Death in the Foreground" (Momaday), **Supp. IV Part 2:** 492
Wideman, John Edgar, **Retro. Supp. II:** 123; **Supp. X:** 239, 250, **319–336; Supp. XI:** 245; **Supp. XIII:** 247; **Supp. XVIII:** 89; **Supp. XXI:** 246
Widener, Jeff, **Supp. XVIII:** 91
"Wideness" (Pickering), **Supp. XXI:** 203
"Wide Net, The" (Welty), **IV:** 266
Wide Net and Other Stories, The (Welty), **IV:** 261, 264–266, 271; **Retro. Supp. I: 347–349,** 352, 355
Widening Spell of the Leaves, The (Levis), **Supp. XI:** 258, 259, 261, **268–269,** 271
"Wide Prospect, The" (Jarrell), **II:** 376–377
Wide Sargasso Sea (Rhys), **Supp. XVIII:** 131
"Widow" (Peacock), **Supp. XIX:** 206
"Widower" (Robison), **Supp. XXI:** 118
Widow for One Year, A (Irving), **Supp. VI:** 165, **179–181**
Widow's Mite (Holding), **Supp. XXII: 136**
Widows of Thornton, The (Taylor), **Supp. V:** 320, 321
"Widow's Wish, The" (Briggs), **Supp. XVIII:** 15
Wieland; or, The Transformation. An American Tale (Brown), **Supp. I Part 1:** 128–132, 133, 137, 140
Wiene, Robert, **Retro. Supp. I:** 268
Wiener, John, **Supp. IV Part 1:** 153
Wieners, John, **Supp. II Part 1:** 32
Wiesel, Elie, **Supp. XVII:** 47, 48, 49
Wiest, Dianne, **Supp. XV:** 12
"Wife, Forty-five, Remembers Love, A" (Shields), **Supp. VII:** 310
"Wifebeater, The" (Sexton), **Supp. II Part 2:** 693
"Wife for Dino Rossi, A" (Fante), **Supp. XI:** 165
"Wife of His Youth, The" (Chesnutt), **Supp. XIV: 63–66**
Wife of His Youth and Other Stories of the Color Line, The (Chesnutt), **Supp. XIV:** 62, 63
"Wife of Jesus Speaks, The" (Karr), **Supp. XI:** 250–251
"Wife of Nashville, A" (Taylor), **Supp. V:** 320
"Wife's Story, The" (R. H. Davis), **Supp. XVI:** 85, 91, 92–93
Wife's Story, The (Shields), **Supp. VII:** 316. *See also* Happenstance
"Wife-Wooing" (Updike), **IV:** 226
Wigan, Gareth, **Supp. XI:** 306
Wiget, Andrew, **Supp. IV Part 2:** 509
Wigglesworth, Michael, **IV:** 147, 156; **Supp. I Part 1:** 110, 111
Wilbur, Richard, **III:** 527; **Retro. Supp. II:** 50; **Supp. III Part 1:** 64; **Supp. III Part 2: 541–565; Supp. IV Part 2:** 626, 634, 642; **Supp. V:** 337; **Supp. VIII:** 28; **Supp. X:** 58, 120; **Supp. XII:** 258; **Supp. XIII:** 76, 336; **Supp. XV:** 51, 251, 256; **Supp. XVII:** 26; **Supp. XVIII:** 178; **Supp. XX: 199; Supp. XXI:** 247
Wilcocks, Alexander, **Supp. I Part 1:** 125

Wilcox, Ella Wheeler, **Supp. II Part 1:** 197
Wilcox, Kirstin, **Supp. XX: 283, 284, 285**
Wild, John, **II:** 362, 363–364
Wild, Peter, **Supp. V:** 5
Wild, Robert, **IV:** 155
"Wild, The" (Berry), **Supp. X:** 30
Wild 90 (film) (Mailer), **Retro. Supp. II:** 205
Wild and Woolly (film), **Supp. XVI:** 185
Wild Boy of Aveyron, The (Itard). *See* De l'éducation d'un homme sauvage
Wild Boys, The: A Book of the Dead (Burroughs), **Supp. III Part 1:** 106–107
Wild Card Quilt: Taking A chance on Home (Ray), **Supp. XVIII:** 189, 192, 193, 196, 198, **200–202,** 204
Wilde, Oscar, **I:** 50, 66, 381, 384; **II:** 515; **IV:** 77, 350; **Retro. Supp. I:** 56, 102, 227; **Retro. Supp. II:** 76, 326; **Supp. IV Part 2:** 578, 679, 683; **Supp. V:** 106, 283; **Supp. IX:** 65, 66, 68, 189, 192; **Supp. X:** 148, 151, 188–189; **Supp. XIV:** 324, 334; **Supp. XV:** 350
Wilder, Amos Parker, **IV:** 356
Wilder, Mrs. Amos Parker (Isabella Thornton Niven), **IV:** 356
Wilder, Billy, **Supp. IV Part 1:** 130; **Supp. XI:** 307
Wilder, Ingalls /Laura?/, **Supp. XXI:** 2
Wilder, Isabel, **IV:** 357, 366, 375
Wilder, Laura Ingalls, **Supp. XXII: 289–303**
Wilder, Thornton, **I:** 360, 482; **IV: 355–377,** 431; **Retro. Supp. I:** 109, 359; **Supp. I Part 2:** 609; **Supp. IV Part 2:** 586; **Supp. V:** 105; **Supp. IX:** 140; **Supp. XII:** 236–237; **Supp. XX: 50**
"Wilderness" (Leopold), **Supp. XIV:** 190
Wilderness (Parker), **Supp. XIX:** 177, **188–189**
"Wilderness" (Sandburg), **III:** 584, 595
Wilderness (Warren), **IV:** 256
"Wilderness, The" (Merwin), **Supp. III Part 1:** 340, 345
"Wilderness, The" (Robinson), **III:** 524
Wilderness of Vision, The: On the Poetry of John Haines (Bezner and Walzer, eds.), **Supp. XII:** 202
Wilderness Plots: Tales about the Settlement of the American Land (Sanders), **Supp. XVI:** 267–268, 269
Wilderness World of Anne LaBastille, The (LaBastille), **Supp. X: 105,** 106
Wild Flag, The (White), **Supp. I Part 2:** 654
"Wildflower, The" (W. C. Williams), **Retro. Supp. I:** 420
"Wild Flowers" (Caldwell), **I:** 310
"Wildflowers" (Minot), **Supp. VI:** 208
"Wild Geese" (Oliver), **Supp. VII:** 237
"Wild Honey Suckle, The" (Freneau), **Supp. II Part 1:** 253, 264, 266
Wild in the Country (Odets), **Supp. II Part 2:** 546
"Wild in the Woods" (Skloot), **Supp. XX: 206**
Wild Iris, The (Glück), **Supp. V:** 79, 87–89, 91
Wildlife (Ford), **Supp. V:** 57, 69–71
Wildlife in America (Matthiessen), **Supp. V:** 199, 201, 204
"Wildlife in American Culture" (Leopold), **Supp. XIV:** 190, 191
"Wild Light" (Skloot), **Supp. XX: 200**
Wild Man, The (P. N. Warren), **Supp. XX: 260, 270–272**
"Wildness" (Sanders), **Supp. XVI:** 276
Wild Old Wicked Man, The (MacLeish), **III:** 3, 20
Wild Palms, The (Faulkner), **II:** 68–69; **Retro. Supp. I:** 85
"Wild Palms, The" (Faulkner), **II:** 68
"Wild Peaches" (Wylie), **Supp. I Part 2:** 707, 712
Wild Roses of Cape Ann and Other Poems (Larcom), **Supp. XIII:** 142, 147
Wild Seed (O. Butler), **Supp. XIII:** 62, 63
"Wild Swans at Coole, The " (W. B. Yeats), **Supp. XVI:** 48
"Wild Swans at Norfolk, The" (Carruth), **Supp. XVI:** 48
"Wild Thing" (L. Brown), **Supp. XXI:** 44
Wild Thorn (Hoffman), **Supp. XVIII: 84–85**
Wild to the Heart (Bass), **Supp. XVI:** 16
"Wild Turkeys: Dignity of the Damned" (B. Kelly), **Supp. XVII:** 129
"Wildwest" (MacLeish), **III:** 14
Wiley, Craig, **Supp. VIII:** 313
Wilhelm Meister (Goethe), **II:** 291
Wilkes, John, **Supp. I Part 2:** 503, 519, 522
Wilkie, Curtis, **Supp. V:** 11
Wilkins, Roy, **Supp. I Part 1:** 345
Wilkinson, Alec, **Supp. VIII:** 164, 168, 171
Wilkinson, Max, **Supp. IX:** 251
Will, The (Swados), **Supp. XIX: 265–266**
Willard, Nancy, **Supp. XIX:** 138
Willard, Samuel, **IV:** 150
Willard Gibbs (Rukeyser), **Supp. VI:** 273, 283, 284
Willcutts, Tim, **Supp. XVII:** 239, 241, 246
Willett, Ralph, **Supp. XIV:** 27
Willey, Basil, **Retro. Supp. II:** 243
"William Butler Yeats Among the Ghosts" (Skloot), **Supp. XX: 204–205**
William Carlos Williams (Koch), **Retro. Supp. I:** 428
William Carlos Williams: An American Artist (Breslin), **Retro. Supp. I:** 430
William Carlos Williams and Alterity (Ahearn), **Retro. Supp. I:** 415
William Carlos Williams and the Meanings of Measure (Cushman), **Retro. Supp. I:** 430
William Carlos Williams: The American Background (Weaver), **Retro. Supp. I:** 430
William Faulkner: A Critical Study (Howe), **Supp. VI:** 119–120, 125
William Faulkner: Early Prose and Poetry (Faulkner), **Retro. Supp. I:** 80
William Faulkner: First Encounters (Brooks), **Supp. XIV:** 13
"William Faulkner's Legend of the South" (Cowley), **Supp. II Part 1:** 143
"William Faulkner: The Stillness of *Light in August" (Kazin), Supp. VIII:* 104
William Faulkner: The Yoknapatawpha Country (Brooks), **Supp. XIV: 12–13,** 16
William Faulkner: Toward Yoknapatawpha and Beyond (Brooks), **Supp. XIV:** 13
"William Humphrey, 73, Writer of Novels about Rural Texas" (Gussow), **Supp. IX:** 93
William Humphrey, Destroyer of Myths (Almon), **Supp. IX:** 93
William Humphrey. Boise State University Western Writers Series (Winchell), **Supp. IX:** 109
"William Humphrey Remembered" (Masters), **Supp. IX:** 96
William Humphrey. Southwestern Series (Lee), **Supp. IX:** 109
"William Ireland's Confession" (A. Miller), **III:** 147–148
William James and Phenomenology: A Study of the "Principles of Psychology" (Wilshire), II: 362
William Lloyd Garrison (Chapman), **Supp. XIV:** 46–51, 52, 53, 55
William Maxwell Portrait, A: Memories and Appreciations (C. Baxter, Collier, and Hirsch, eds.), **Supp. XVII:** 23
Williams, Annie Laurie, **Supp. IX:** 93
Williams, Blanch Colton, **Supp. XVIII:** 279
Williams, Cecil, **II:** 508
Williams, Charles, **Supp. II Part 1:** 15, 16
Williams, C. K., **Supp. XIII:** 114; **Supp. XVII:** 112
Williams, Cratis, **Supp. XX: 163**
Williams, Dakin, **IV:** 379
Williams, David Reichard, **Supp. XIII:** 162
Williams, Edward, **IV:** 404
Williams, Edwina Dakin, **IV:** 379
Williams, Eric, **Supp. XXI:** 166, 170, 171
Williams, Esther, **Supp. XII:** 165
Williams, Fannie Barrier, **Supp. XIV:** 201
Williams, Garth, **Supp. XXII:** 301
Williams, George, **Supp. V:** 220
Williams, Henry Sylvester, **Supp. XXI:** 166
Williams, Horace, **IV:** 453
Williams, Joan, **Supp. IX:** 95
Williams, John A., **Supp. XVI:** 143
Williams, John Sharp, **IV:** 378
Williams, Jonathan, **Supp. XXII:** 168
Williams, Kenny J., **Supp. XX: 281, 286**
Williams, Lyle, **Supp. XIV:** 22
Williams, Michael, **Supp. V:** 286
Williams, Miller, **Supp. XIV:** 126; **Supp. XV:** 339; **Supp. XVIII:** 177
Williams, Paul, **IV:** 404
Williams, Raymond, **Supp. IX:** 146

Williams, Roger, **Supp. I Part 2:** 699
Williams, Rose, **IV:** 379
Williams, Sherley Anne, **Supp. V:** 180
Williams, Solomon, **I:** 549
Williams, Stanley T., **II:** 301, 316; **Supp. I Part 1:** 251
Williams, Stephen, **IV:** 148
Williams, Ted, **IV:** 216; **Supp. IX:** 162
Williams, Tennessee, **I:** 73, 81, 113, 211; **II:** 190, 194; **III:** 145, 147; **IV:** 4, **378–401; Supp. I Part 1:** 290, 291; **Supp. IV Part 1:** 79, 83, 84, 359; **Supp. IV Part 2:** 574, 682; **Supp. IX:** 133; **Supp. XI:** 103; **Supp. XIII:** 331; **Supp. XIV:** 250, 315; **Supp. XVI:** 194
Williams, Terry Tempest, **Supp. XIII:** 16; **Supp. XVIII:** 189
Williams, Walter L., **Supp. IV Part 1:** 330, 331
Williams, William, **IV:** 404, 405
Williams, William Carlos, **I:** 61, 62, 229, 255, 256, 261, 285, 428, 438, 446, 539; **II:** 133, 536, 542, 543, 544, 545; **III:** 194, 196, 198, 214, 269, 409, 453, 457, 458, 464, 465, 591; **IV:** 30, 74, 75, 76, 94, 95, 286, 287, **402–425; Retro. Supp. I:** 51, 52, 62, 209, 284, 285, 288, 296, 298, **411–433; Retro. Supp. II:** 178, 181, 189, 250, 321, 322, 326, 327, 328, 334, 335; **Supp. I Part 1:** 254, 255, 259, 266; **Supp. II Part 1:** 9, 30, 308, 318; **Supp. II Part 2:** 421, 443; **Supp. III Part 1:** 9, 147, 239, 271, 275, 276, 278, 350; **Supp. III Part 2:** 542, 610, 613, 614, 615, 616, 617, 621, 622, 626, 628; **Supp. IV Part 1:** 151, 153, 246, 325; **Supp. V:** 180, 337; **Supp. VIII:** 195, 269, 272, 277, 292; **Supp. IX:** 38, 268, 291; **Supp. X:** 112, 120, 204; **Supp. XI:** 311, 328; **Supp. XII:** 198; **Supp. XIII:** 77, 90, 335; **Supp. XIV:** 280, 284, 285, 293; **Supp. XV:** 42, 51, 182, 250, 306, 307; **Supp. XVI:** 48, 282; **Supp. XVII:** 36, 113, 227, 243; **Supp. XIX:** 1, 42, 117, 119, 121; **Supp. XXI:** 226, 227, 230, 233; **Supp. XXII:** 162, 165, 168, 226, 227, 228
Williams, Mrs. William Carlos (Florence Herman), **IV:** 404
Williams, Wirt, **Supp. XIV:** 24
Williamson, Alan, **Retro. Supp. II:** 185; **Supp. XIX:** 91
Williamson, J. W., **Supp. XX: 164**
William Styron's Nat Turner: Ten Black Writers Respond (Clarke, ed.), **IV:** 115
Williams-Walsh, Mary Ellen, **Supp. IV Part 2:** 611
William the Conqueror, **Supp. I Part 2:** 507
William Wetmore Story and His Friends (James), **Retro. Supp. I:** 235; **Supp. XX: 228**
William Wilson (Gardner), **Supp. VI:** 72
"William Wilson" (Poe), **II:** 475; **III:** 410, 412; **Retro. Supp. II:** 269; **Supp. IX:** 105
"Willie" (Angelou), **Supp. IV Part 1:** 15
Willie Masters' Lonesome Wife (Gass), **Supp. VI:** 77, **84–85, 86–87**
"Willing" (Moore), **Supp. X:** 178
Willis, Bruce, **Supp. IV Part 1:** 236
Willis, Gordon, **Supp. XV:** 7
Willis, Mary Hard, **Supp. V:** 290–291
Willis, Nathaniel Parker, **II:** 313; **Supp. I Part 2:** 405; **Supp. XVIII:** 12
Williwaw (Vidal), **Supp. IV Part 2:** 677, 680, 681
"Willow Woman" (Francis), **Supp. IX:** 78
Wills, Garry, **Supp. I Part 1:** 294; **Supp. IV Part 1:** 355
Wills, Ridley, **IV:** 122
Wills, Ross B., **Supp. XI:** 169
"Will to Believe, The" (James), **II:** 352; **Supp. XIV:** 50
Will to Believe, The, and Other Essays in Popular Philosophy (James), **II:** 356; **IV:** 28
Will to Change, The: Poems, 1968–1970 (Rich), **Supp. I Part 2:** 551, 557–559
"Will We Plug Chips into Our Brains?" (W. Gibson), **Supp. XVI:** 117–118
Will You Please Be Quiet, Please? (Carver), **Supp. III Part 1:** 138, 140, 144
"Will You Please Be Quiet, Please?" (Carver), **Supp. III Part 1:** 137, 141
"Will You Tell Me?" (Barthelme), **Supp. IV Part 1:** 42, 47
Wilsdorf, Anne, **Supp. XVI:** 177
Wilshire, Bruce, **II:** 362, 364
Wilshire, Gaylord, **Supp. V:** 280
Wilson, Adrian, **Supp. XV:** 147
Wilson, Alexander, **Supp. XVI:** 4, 6
Wilson, Angus, **IV:** 430, 435
Wilson, August, **Supp. VIII: 329–353; Supp. XIX:** 132
Wilson, Augusta Jane Evans, **Retro. Supp. I:** 351
Wilson, Earl, **Supp. X:** 264
Wilson, Edmund, **I:** 67, 185, 236, 247, 260, 434, 482; **II:** 79, 80, 81, 86, 87, 91, 97, 98, 146, 276, 430, 530, 562, 587; **III:** 588; **IV:** 308, 310, **426–449; Retro. Supp. I:** 1, 97, 100, 101, 103, 104, 105, 115, 274; **Retro. Supp. II:** 321, 327, 329; **Supp. I Part 1:** 372; **Supp. I Part 2:** 407, 646, 678, 709; **Supp. II Part 1:** 19, 90, 106, 136, 137, 143; **Supp. III Part 2:** 612; **Supp. IV Part 2:** 693; **Supp. VIII:** 93, 95, 96, 97, 98–99, 100, 101, 103, 105, 162; **Supp. IX:** 55, 65, 190; **Supp. X:** 186; **Supp. XI:** 160; **Supp. XIII:** 170; **Supp. XIV:** 338; **Supp. XV:** 142, 308; **Supp. XVI:** 194; **Supp. XX: 76, 81; Supp. XXII:** 278
Wilson, Edmund (father), **IV:** 441
Wilson, E. O., **Supp. X:** 35
Wilson, Harriet, **Supp. XX: 105**
Wilson, Henry, **Supp. XIV:** 48
Wilson, Reuel, **II:** 562
Wilson, Robert, **Supp. XI:** 144
Wilson, Sloan, **Supp. IV Part 1:** 387
Wilson, Thomas, **IV:** 153
Wilson, Tracy, **Supp. XVIII:** 101
Wilson, Victoria, **Supp. X:** 166
Wilson, Woodrow, **I:** 245, 246, 490; **II:** 183, 253; **III:** 105, 581; **Supp. I Part 1:** 21; **Supp. I Part 2:** 474, 643; **Supp. V:** 288
Wilton, David, **IV:** 147
Wiman, Christian, **Supp. XV:** 251, 253, 264; **Supp. XVII:** 74; **Supp. XVIII:** 173, 174
Wimberly, Lowry, **Supp. XV:** 136, 137
Wimsatt, William K., **Supp. XIV:** 12
Winchell, Mark, **Supp. VIII:** 176, 189
Winchell, Mark Royden, **Supp. VIII:** 241; **Supp. IX:** 97, 98, 109; **Supp. XIII:** 94, 98, 99, 101; **Supp. XIV:** 103, 106, 111
Winckelmann, Johann Joachim, **Supp. XII:** 178
Wind, Sand, and Stars (Saint-Exupéry), **Supp. IX:** 247
Wind Across the Everglades (film, Ray), **Supp. XVIII:** 253
Wind Chrysalid's Rattle (Sobin), **Supp. XVI:** 283
"Windfall" (B. Kelly), **Supp. XVII:** 132
Windflower Home Almanac of Poetry, The (Kooser, ed.), **Supp. XIX:** 119
Windham, Donald, **IV:** 382
"Windhover" (Hopkins), **I:** 397; **II:** 539; **Supp. IX:** 43
Winding Stair and Other Poems, The (Yeats), **Supp. XV:** 253
"Winding Street, The" (Petry), **Supp. XI:** 6
"Window" (Pinsky), **Supp. VI:** 237, 247
"Window, The" (Hull), **Supp. XXI:** 140–141
Windows (Creeley), **Supp. IV Part 1:** 157, 158
"Windows" (Jarrell), **II:** 388, 389
"Window Seat, A" (Goldbarth), **Supp. XII:** 185
Wind Remains, The (opera) (Bowles), **Supp. IV Part 1:** 83
"Winds, The" (Welty), **IV:** 265; **Retro. Supp. I:** 348, 350
"Winds and Clouds over a Funeral" (Jin), **Supp. XVIII:** 94
Winds of War (Wouk), **Supp. XX: 243**
"Wind up Sushi" (Goldbarth), **Supp. XII:** 186–187
"Windy Day at the Reservoir, A" (Beattie), **Supp. V:** 33
Windy McPherson's Son (Anderson), **I:** 101, 102–103, 105, 111
"Wine" (Carver), **Supp. III Part 1:** 138
"Wine Menagerie, The" (H. Crane), **I:** 389, 391; **Retro. Supp. II:** 82
Wine of the Puritans, The: A Study of Present-Day America (Brooks), **I:** 240
"Wine of Wizardry, A" (Sterling), **I:** 208
Winer, Linda, **Supp. IV Part 2:** 580; **Supp. XV:** 332
Winesburg, Ohio: A Group of Tales of Ohio Small Town Life (Anderson), **I:** 97, 102, 103, 104, 105–108; **III:** 112, 113, 114, 116, 224, 579; **Supp. V:** 12; **Supp. IX:** 306, 308; **Supp. XI:** 164; **Supp. XVI:** 17; **Supp. XXII:** 282
Winfrey, Oprah, **Supp. XIX:** 194, 204; **Supp. XX: 83, 93**

Wing-and-Wing, The (Cooper), **I:** 350, 355
Winged Seed, The: A Remembrance (L.-Y. Lee), **Supp. XV:** 211, **220–223**
Winged Words: American Indian Writers Speak (Coltelli), **Supp. IV Part 2:** 493, 497
"Wingfield" (Wolff), **Supp. VII:** 341–342
"Wings, The" (Doty), **Supp. XI:** 124
Wings of the Dove, The (James), **I:** 436; **II:** 320, 323, 333, 334–335; **Retro. Supp. I:** 215, 216, 217, 232, **233–234; Supp. II Part 1:** 94–95; **Supp. IV Part 1:** 349
"Wink of the Zenith, The" (Skloot), **Supp. XX: 207**
Wink of the Zenith, The: The Shaping of a Writer's Life (Skloot), **Supp. XX: 195, 196, 207**
"Winky" (Saunders), **Supp. XIX:** 228–229, 229
Winner Names the Age, The: A Collection of Works by Lillian Smith (Cliff, ed.), **Supp. XXII:** 67
Winner Take Nothing (Hemingway), **II:** 249; **Retro. Supp. I:** 170, 175, 176, 181
"Winnie" (Brooks), **Supp. III Part 1:** 86
Winokur, Maxine. *See* Kumin, Maxine
Winslow, Art, **Supp. XVIII:** 102
Winslow, Devereux, **II:** 547
Winslow, Harriet, **II:** 552–553
Winslow, Ola Elizabeth, **I:** 547
Winslow, Warren, **II:** 540
Winston, Andrew, **Supp. XII:** 189
Winston, Michael R., **Supp. XIV:** 197
Winter, Douglas, **Supp. V:** 144
Winter, Johnny and Edgar, **Supp. V:** 334
Winter, Kate, **Supp. X:** 104
"Winter Branch, A" (Irving), **Supp. VI:** 163
"Winter Burial, A" (Clampitt), **Supp. IX:** 48
Winter Carnival (film), **Retro. Supp. I:** 113
"Winter Daybreak at Vence, A" (Wright), **Supp. III Part 1:** 249–250
Winter Diary, A (Van Doren), **I:** 168
"Winter Dreams" (Fitzgerald), **II:** 80, 94; **Retro. Supp. I:** 108
"Winter Drive, A" (Jewett), **Retro. Supp. II:** 147
"Winter Eden, A" (Frost), **Retro. Supp. I:** 137
"Winter Father, The" (Dubus), **Supp. VII:** 83, 87
Winter Hours: Prose, Prose Poems, and Poems (Oliver), **Supp. VII:** 230, 247
"Winter in Dunbarton" (Lowell), **II:** 547; **Retro. Supp. II:** 187
"Wintering" (Plath), **Retro. Supp. II:** 255
Winter Insomnia (Carver), **Supp. III Part 1:** 138
Winter in the Blood (Welch), **Supp. IV Part 2:** 562
"Winter Landscape" (Berryman), **I:** 174; **Retro. Supp. I:** 430
Winter Light (W. V. Davis), **Supp. XXI: 92,** 93
"Winter Light" (W. V. Davis), **Supp. XXI:** 90, 92
Winter Lightning (Nemerov), **III:** 269
Winter Morning Walks: One Hundred Postcards to Jim Harrison (Kooser), **Supp. XIX:** 116, **125–126**
Winter News (Haines), **Supp. XII:** 199, **201–204,** 207–208, 208
Winternitz, Mary. *See* Cheever, Mrs. John (Mary Winternitz)
Winter: Notes from Montana (Bass), **Supp. XVI:** 17–18
Winter of Our Discontent, The (Steinbeck), **IV:** 52, 65–66, 68
"Winter on Earth" (Toomer), **Supp. III Part 2:** 486
"Winter Piece, A" (Bryant), **Supp. I Part 1:** 150, 155
"Winter Rains, Cataluña" (Levine), **Supp. V:** 182
"Winter Remembered" (Ransom), **III:** 492–493
"Winter Roses" (W. V. Davis), **Supp. XXI:** 94
Winterrowd, Prudence, **I:** 217, 224
Winters, Jonathan, **Supp. XI:** 305
Winters, Yvor, **I:** 59, 63, 386, 393, 397, 398, 402, 471; **III:** 194, 498; **IV:** 153; **Retro. Supp. II:** 76, 77, 78, 82, 83, 85, 89; **Supp. I Part 1:** 268; **Supp. II Part 2:** 416, 666, **785–816; Supp. IV Part 2:** 480; **Supp. V:** 180, 191–192; **Supp. XIV:** 287; **Supp. XV:** 74, 341
"Winter Sacrament" (Bronk), **Supp. XXI:** 33
"Winter Scenes" (Bryant). *See* "Winter Piece, A"
Winterset (Anderson), **III:** 159
"Winter Shrub, A" (Bronk), **Supp. XXI:** 28
"Winter Skyline Late" (F. Wright), **Supp. XVII:** 245
"Winter Sleep" (Wylie), **Supp. I Part 2:** 711, 729
Winter's Night (Boyce), **Supp. XXI:** 7, **12–13**
Winter's Tale, The (Shakespeare), **Supp. XIII:** 219
Winter Stars (Levis), **Supp. XI:** 259, **266–268**
"Winter Stars" (Levis), **Supp. XI:** 267–268
Winter Stop-Over (Everwine), **Supp. XV:** 74, 76
"Winter Stop-Over" (Everwine), **Supp. XV:** 76
"Winter Swan" (Bogan), **Supp. III Part 1:** 52
Winter Thunder (X. J. Kennedy), **Supp. XV:** 167
"Winter Thunder" (X. J. Kennedy), **Supp. XV:** 169
"Winter Trees" (Pedersen; Nelson, trans.), **Supp. XVIII:** 180
Winter Trees (Plath), **Retro. Supp. II:** 257; **Supp. I Part 2:** 526, 539, 541
"Winter Walk" (W. V. Davis), **Supp. XXI:** 92
"Winter Weather Advisory" (Ashbery), **Supp. III Part 1:** 26
"Winter Wheat" (Hoffman), **Supp. XVIII:** 86, 87
"Winter without Snow, The" (C. Frost), **Supp. XV:** 96, 105–106
"Winter Words" (Levine), **Supp. V:** 192
Winthrop, John, **Supp. I Part 1:** 99, 100, 101, 102, 105; **Supp. I Part 2:** 484, 485
Winthrop Covenant, The (Auchincloss), **Supp. IV Part 1:** 23
"Wires of the Night, The" (Collins), **Supp. XXI:** 64
Wirt, William, **I:** 232
Wirth, Louis, **IV:** 475
Wisconsin Death Trip (Levy), **Supp. XIX:** 102
"Wisdom Cometh with the Years" (Cullen), **Supp. IV Part 1:** 166
Wisdom of the African World (McKnight, ed.), **Supp. XX: 157–158**
Wisdom of the Desert, The: Sayings from the Desert Fathers of the Fourth Century (Merton), **Supp. VIII:** 201
Wisdom of the Heart, The (H. Miller), **III:** 178, 184
Wise Blood (O'Connor), **III:** 337, 338, 339–343, 344, 345, 346, 350, 354, 356, 357; **Retro. Supp. II:** 219, 221, 222, 223, **225–228**
Wise Men, The (Price), **Supp. VI:** 254
"Wiser Than a God" (Chopin), **Retro. Supp. II:** 61; **Supp. I Part 1:** 208
Wishes, Lies, and Dreams: Teaching Children to Write Poetry (Koch), **Supp. XV:** 176, 189
"Wish for a Young Wife" (Roethke), **III:** 548
Wishful Thinking: A Theological ABC (Buechner), **Supp. XII:** 53
Wishing Tree, The: Christopher Isherwood on Mystical Religion (Adjemian, ed.), **Supp. XIV:** 164, 173
Wismer, Helen Muriel. *See* Thurber, Mrs. James (Helen Muriel Wismer)
Wisse, Ruth, **Supp. XII:** 167, 168
Wister, Owen, **I:** 62; **Retro. Supp. II:** 72; **Supp. XIV:** 39
Wit (Edson), **Supp. XVIII:** 35–36, 37, **38–51**
"Witchbird" (Bambara), **Supp. XI:** 11
"Witch Burning" (Plath), **Supp. I Part 2:** 539
Witchcraft of Salem Village, The (Jackson), **Supp. IX:** 121
"Witch Doctor" (Hayden), **Supp. II Part 1:** 368, 380
Witches of Eastwick, The (Updike), **Retro. Supp. I:** 330, 331
Witching Hour, The (Rice), **Supp. VII:** 299–300
"Witch of Coös, The" (Frost), **II:** 154–155; **Retro. Supp. I:** 135; **Retro. Supp. II:** 42
"Witch of Owl Mountain Springs, The: An Account of Her Remarkable Powers" (Taylor), **Supp. V:** 328
"Witch of Wenham, The" (Whittier), **Supp. I Part 2:** 694, 696
Witek, Terri, **Supp. XVII:** 117

"With a Little Help from My Friends" (Kushner), **Supp. IX:** 131
With Bold Knife and Fork (M. F. K. Fisher), **Supp. XVII:** 89, 91
"With Che at Kitty Hawk" (Banks), **Supp. V:** 6
"With Che at the Plaza" (Banks), **Supp. V:** 7
"With Che in New Hampshire" (Banks), **Supp. V:** 6
"With Child" (Taggard), **Supp. XXII:** 276, 278
"Withdrawal Symptoms" (Mora), **Supp. XIII:** 216
"Withered Skins of Berries" (Toomer), **Supp. III Part 2:** 485; **Supp. IX:** 320
Withers, Harry Clay, **Supp. XIII:** 161
Witherspoon, John, **Supp. I Part 2:** 504
With Eyes at the Back of Our Heads (Levertov), **Supp. III Part 1:** 276–277
With Her in Ourland (Gilman), **Supp. XI:** 208–209
With His Pistol in His Hand (Paredes), **Supp. XIII:** 225; **Supp. XIX:** 98
"Within the Words: An Apprenticeship" (Haines), **Supp. XII:** 197
"With Kit, Age 7, at the Beach" (Stafford), **Supp. XI:** 323
"With Mercy for the Greedy" (Sexton), **Supp. II Part 2:** 680
With My Trousers Rolled (Epstein), **Supp. XIV:** 101, 105
Without a Hero (Boyle), **Supp. VIII:** 16; **Supp. XX: 20**
Without Feathers (Allen), **Supp. XV:** 3, 14, 15
Without Stopping (Bowles), **Supp. IV Part 1:** 79, 81, 85, 90, 91, 92
"Without Tradition and within Reason: Judge Horton and Atticus Finch in Court" (Johnson), **Supp. VIII:** 127
With Shuddering Fall (Oates), **Supp. II Part 2:** 504–506
"With the Dog at Sunrise" (Kenyon), **Supp. VII:** 170
With the Empress Dowager of China (Carl), **III:** 475
"With the Horse in the Winter Pasture" (McCarriston), **Supp. XIV:** 262
With the Old Breed: At Peleliu and Okinawa (Sledge), **Supp. V:** 249–250
"With the Violin" (Chopin), **Retro. Supp. II:** 61
"Witness" (Clampitt), **Supp. IX:** 42–43, 45, 46
"Witness" (Dubus), **Supp. VII:** 89
"Witness" (Harjo), **Supp. XII:** 227–228
Witness (McNally), **Supp. XIII:** 197
"Witness" (Nelson), **Supp. XVIII:** 186
"Witness, The" (Porter), **III:** 443–444
"Witness for Poetry, A" (Stafford), **Supp. XI:** 324
"Witness for the Defense" (Hay), **Supp. XIV:** 124
"Witnessing My Father's Will" (Karr), **Supp. XI:** 241
"Witnessing to a Shared World" (Sanders), **Supp. XVI:** 278
Witness to the Times! (McGrath), **Supp. X:** 118
Witness Tree, A (Frost), **II:** 155; **Retro. Supp. I:** 122, 137, 139
Wit's End: Days and Nights of the Algonquin Round Table (Gaines), **Supp. IX:** 190
Wits Recreations (Mennes and Smith), **II:** 111
Witt, Shirley Hill, **Supp. IV Part 2:** 505
Witte, John, **Supp. XX: 200**
Wittels, Anne F., **Supp. XV:** 59
Wittenberg, Judith Bryant, **Retro. Supp. II:** 146
Wittgenstein, Ludwig, **Retro. Supp. I:** 53; **Supp. III Part 2:** 626–627; **Supp. X:** 304; **Supp. XII:** 21; **Supp. XV:** 344, 346
Wittgensteins' Mistress (Markson), **Supp. XVII:** 135, 142, 143, 145
Wittliff, William, **Supp. V:** 227
"Witty War, A" (Simpson), **Supp. IX:** 268
Witz (Cohen), **Supp. XXII:** 268
"Wives and Mistresses" (Hardwick), **Supp. III Part 1:** 211–212
Wizard of Loneliness, The (Nichols), **Supp. XIII:** 259, 263, 264
Wizard of Oz, The (Baum), **Supp. IV Part 1:** 113
Wizard of Oz, The (film), **Supp. X:** 172, 214
Wizard's Tide, The: A Story (Buechner), **Supp. XII:** 54
"WLT (The Edgar Era)" (Keillor), **Supp. XVI:** 172
WLT: A Radio Romance (Keillor), **Supp. XVI:** 176
Wobegon Boy (Keillor), **Supp. XVI:** 177
Wodehouse, P. G., **Supp. IX:** 195; **Supp. XXI:** 204–205
Woiwode, Larry, **Supp. VIII:** 151; **Supp. XVI:** 206
Wojahn, David, **Supp. IX:** 161, 292, 293; **Supp. XXI:** 130, 131, 132, 138, 139, 141
Wolcott, James, **Supp. IX:** 259
Wolf, Christa, **Supp. IV Part 1:** 310, 314
Wolf, Daniel, **Retro. Supp. II:** 202
Wolf, Robert L., **Supp. XXII:** 274, 277, 279, 280
Wolf: A False Memoir (Harrison), **Supp. VIII:** 40, **41–42,** 45
Wolfe, Ben, **IV:** 454
Wolfe, Gregory, **Supp. XIV:** 307
Wolfe, James, **Supp. I Part 2:** 498
Wolfe, Linnie, **Supp. IX:** 176
Wolfe, Mabel, **IV:** 454
Wolfe, Thomas, **I:** 288, 289, 374, 478, 495; **II:** 457; **III:** 40, 108, 278, 334, 482; **IV:** 52, 97, 357, **450–473; Retro. Supp. I:** 382; **Supp. I Part 1:** 29; **Supp. IV Part 1:** 101; **Supp. IX:** 229; **Supp. X:** 225; **Supp. XI:** 213, 216, 217, 218; **Supp. XIII:** 17; **Supp. XIV:** 122; **Supp. XVIII:** 78; **Supp. XX: 163**
Wolfe, Tom, **Supp. III Part 2: 567–588; Supp. IV Part 1:** 35, 198; **Supp. V:** 296; **Supp. X:** 264; **Supp. XI:** 239; **Supp. XV:** 143; **Supp. XVII:** 202; **Supp. XVIII:** 72, 117
Wolfe, William Oliver, **IV:** 454
Wolfe, Mrs. William Oliver (Julia Elizabeth Westall), **IV:** 454
"Wolfe Homo Scribens" (Cowley), **Supp. II Part 1:** 144
Wolfert, Ira, **Supp. XXI: 261–279**
Wolfert's Roost (Irving), **II:** 314
Wolff, Cynthia Griffin, **Retro. Supp. I:** 379; **Supp. IV Part 1:** 203
Wolff, Donald, **Supp. XIII:** 316, 317, 326
Wolff, Geoffrey, **Supp. II Part 1:** 97; **Supp. XI:** 239, 245, 246; **Supp. XXII:** 206, 211
Wolff, Tobias, **Retro. Supp. I:** 190; **Supp. V:** 22; **Supp. VII: 331–346; Supp. X:** 1; **Supp. XI:** 26, 239, 245, 246, 247; **Supp. XV:** 223; **Supp. XVI:** 39, 41, 63, 70, 77
Wolfreys, Julian, **Supp. XVIII:** 61
Wolfson, P. J., **Supp. XIII:** 172
"Wolf Town" (Carson), **Supp. XII: 102**
Wolf Willow: A History, a Story, and a Memory of the Last Plains Frontier (Stegner), **Supp. IV Part 2:** 595, 596, 597, 598, 599, 600, 601, 604, 606, 611, 613, 614
Wolitzer, Hilma, **Supp. XV:** 55
Wolitzer, Meg, **Supp. XV:** 65
Wolkomir, Richard, **Supp. XXII:** 218
Wollaston, William, **II:** 108
Wollstonecraft, Mary, **Supp. I Part 1:** 126; **Supp. I Part 2:** 512, 554
"Woman" (Bogan), **Supp. X:** 102
"Woman, I Got the Blues" (Komunyakaa), **Supp. XIII:** 117
"Woman, Why Are You Weeping?" (Kenyon), **Supp. VII:** 174–175
"Woman, Young and Old, A" (Paley), **Supp. VI:** 222, 225
Woman Aroused, The (Lacy), **Supp. XV:** 199–200
Woman at the Washington Zoo, The (Jarrell), **II:** 367, 386, 387, 389
Woman Before an Aquarium (Hampl), **Supp. XXII:** 83, 86, 98
"Woman Before an Aquarium" (Hampl), **Supp. XXII:** 85, 98
"Womand and the Woman's Movement" (Briggs), **Supp. XVIII:** 14
"Woman Dead in Her Forties, A" (Rich), **Supp. I Part 2:** 574–575
"Woman Hanging from the Thirteenth Floor Window, The" (Harjo), **Supp. XII:** 216, 221
"Woman Hollering Creek" (Cisneros), **Supp. VII:** 70
Woman Hollering Creek and Other Stories (Cisneros), **Supp. VII:** 58, 68–70
"Womanhood" (Brooks), **Supp. III Part 1:** 77
"Woman in Rain" (X. J. Kennedy), **Supp. XV:** 168
Woman in the Dark (Hammett), **Supp. IV Part 1:** 343
"Woman in the House, A" (Caldwell), **I:** 310

Woman in the Nineteenth Century (Fuller), **Retro. Supp. I:** 156; **Supp. II Part 1:** 279, 292, 294–296; **Supp. XI:** 197, 203; **Supp. XVIII:** 3, 11
"Woman in the Shoe, The" (Ryan as Quin), **Supp. XVIII:** 231
Woman in White, The (Collins), **Supp. I Part 1:** 35, 36
"Womanizer, The" (Ford), **Supp. V:** 71, 72
"Woman Like Yourself, A" (C. Frost), **Supp. XV:** 107
Woman Lit by Fireflies, The (Harrison), **Supp. VIII: 50–51**
"Woman Loses Cookie Bake-Off, Sets Self on Fire" (R. O. Butler), **Supp. XII:** 72
Woman of Andros, The (Wilder), **IV:** 356, 363–364, 367, 368, 374
Woman of Means, A (Taylor), **Supp. V:** 319–320
Woman on the Edge of Time (Piercy), **Supp. XIII:** 29
Woman on the Porch, The (Gordon), **II:** 199, 209–211
"Woman on the Stair, The" (MacLeish), **III:** 15–16
"Woman's Dream, A" (E. Stoddard), **Supp. XV:** 278
Woman's Fiction: A Guide to Novels By and About Women in America, 1820–1870 (Baym), **Supp. XVIII:** 258
"Woman's Heartlessness" (Thaxter), **Retro. Supp. II:** 147
Woman's Honor (Glaspell), **Supp. III Part 1:** 179
"Woman Singing" (Ortiz), **Supp. IV Part 2:** 513
Woman's Place, A (C. L. R. James and Weinstein), **Supp. XXI:** 170
Woman's Share in Primitive Culture (Mason), **Supp. I Part 1:** 18
"Woman Struck by Car Turns into Nymphomaniac" (R. O. Butler), **Supp. XII:** 72
"Woman's Work" (Alvarez), **Supp. VII:** 4
"Woman Uses Glass Eye to Spy on Philandering Husband" (R. O. Butler), **Supp. XII:** 70, 72
Woman Warrior (Kingston), **Supp. IV Part 1:** 12; **Supp. V:** 157, 158, 159, 160–164, 166, 169; **Supp. X:** 291–292; **Supp. XIV:** 162
Woman Warrior, The (Kingston), **Supp. XV:** 220
Woman Who Fell from the Sky, The (Harjo), **Supp. XII: 226–228**
"Woman Who Fell From the Sky, The" (Iroquois creation story), **Supp. IV Part 1:** 327
Woman Who Owned the Shadows, The (Gunn Allen), **Supp. IV Part 1:** 320, 322, 326, 327–328
"Woman Who Plays Trumpet Is Deported, A" (Cliff), **Supp. XXII:** 74
Woman Within, The (Glasgow), **II:** 183, 190–191
"Womanwork" (Gunn Allen), **Supp. IV Part 1:** 326
Women (Bukowski), **Supp. XI:** 172
"Women" (Didion), **Supp. IV Part 1:** 205
"Women" (Swenson), **Supp. IV Part 2:** 647
Women, The (Boyle), **Supp. XX: 24, 26–27**
Women, The (film), **Retro. Supp. I:** 113
Women, The (film; Cukor), **Supp. XVI:** 181, 192
"Women and Children First" (Prose), **Supp. XVI:** 254
Women and Children First: Stories (Prose), **Supp. XVI:** 254
Women and Economics (Gilman), **Supp. I Part 2:** 637; **Supp. V:** 284; **Supp. XI:** 200, **203–204,** 206
"Women and Poetry" (Notley), **Supp. XXII:** 236
Women and Thomas Harrow (Marquand), **III:** 50, 61, 62, 66, 68, 69–70, 71
Women and Vodka (Markson as Merrill, ed.), **Supp. XVII:** 136
Women and Wilderness (LaBastille), **Supp. X:** 97, **102–104**
"Women as They Are" (Rowson), **Supp. XV:** 243
Women at Point Sur, The (Jeffers), **Supp. II Part 2:** 430–431
Women in Love (Lawrence), **III:** 27, 34
Women of Brewster Place, The: A Novel in Seven Stories (Naylor), **Supp. VIII:** 213, **214–218**
Women of Manhattan: An Upper West Side Story (Shanley), **Supp. XIV:** 315, **326–327**
"Women of My Color" (Coleman), **Supp. XI:** 88–89
Women of Trachis (Pound, trans.), **III:** 476
Women on the Wall, The (Stegner), **Supp. IV Part 2:** 599, 605, 606
Women Poets in English (Stanford, ed.), **Retro. Supp. I:** 41
"Women Reformers and American Culture, 1870–1930" (Conway), **Supp. I Part 1:** 19
"Women's Movement, The" (Didion), **Supp. IV Part 1:** 206
"Women Waiting" (Shields), **Supp. VII:** 320
"Women We Love Whom We Never See Again" (R. Bly), **Supp. IV Part 1:** 66
"Women We Never See Again" (R. Bly), **Supp. IV Part 1:** 66
Women with Men (Ford), **Supp. V:** 57, 71–72
"Wonder" (Olds), **Supp. X:** 210
Wonder Boys (Chabon), **Supp. XI:** 67, **73–75,Supp. XI:** 78; **Supp. XVI:** 259
Wonder Boys (film), **Supp. XI:** 67
Wonderful O, The (Thurber), **Supp. I Part 2:** 612
"Wonderful Old Gentleman, The" (Parker), **Supp. IX:** 197
"Wonderful Pen, The" (Swenson), **Supp. IV Part 2:** 650
Wonderful Words, Silent Truth: Essays on Poetry and a Memoir (Simic), **Supp. VIII:** 270
Wonderland (Oates), **Supp. II Part 2:** 511, 512, 514–515
Wonders Hidden (Sanders), **Supp. XVI:** 269
Wonders of the African World (television series), **Supp. XX: 99**
Wonders of the Invisible World, The (Mather), **Supp. II Part 2:** 456–459, 460, 467
Wonder-Working Providence (Johnson), **IV:** 157
Wong, Hertha, **Supp. IV Part 1:** 275
Wong, Jade Snow, **Supp. X:** 291
Wong, Nellie, **Supp. XVII:** 72
Wong, Shawn, **Supp. XV:** 221
Wong, Timothy, **Supp. XVIII:** 94
"Wood" (Nye), **Supp. XIII:** 276
Wood, Audrey, **IV:** 381
Wood, Charles Erskine Scott, **Supp. XV:** 301
Wood, Clement, **Supp. XV:** 298
Wood, Clement Biddle, **Supp. XI:** 307
Wood, Harrison, **Supp. XXII:** 283
Wood, Mrs. Henry, **Supp. I Part 1:** 35
Wood, James, **Supp. XIV:** 95–96; **Supp. XIX:** 138
Wood, Mabel, **I:** 199
Wood, Michael, **Supp. IV Part 2:** 691
Wood, Norman Barton, **Supp. XIV:** 201
Wood, Susan, **Supp. XVI:** 123
Woodard, Calvin, **Supp. VIII:** 128
Woodard, Charles L., **Supp. IV Part 2:** 484, 493
Woodard, Deborah, **Supp. XIII:** 114
Woodberry, George Edward, **III:** 508
Woodbridge, Frederick, **I:** 217, 224
Woodbridge, John, **Supp. I Part 1:** 101, 102, 114
"Wood-Choppers, The" (Chopin), **Retro. Supp. II:** 72
Woodcock, George, **Supp. XIII:** 33
Woodcome, Beth, **Supp. XVII:** 240
"Wood Dove at Sandy Spring, The" (MacLeish), **III:** 19
"Wooden Spring" (Rukeyser), **Supp. VI:** 285
"Wooden Umbrella, The" (Porter), **IV:** 26
Woodhull, Victoria, **Supp. XVIII:** 4
"Woodnotes" (Emerson), **II:** 7, 19
"Wood-Pile, The" (Frost), **Retro. Supp. I:** 128; **Supp. IV Part 2:** 445
Woodrow, James, **Supp. I Part 1:** 349, 366
"Woods, Books, and Truant Officers, The" (Maclean), **Supp. XIV:** 221, 225
"Woods, New York, The" (Bronk), **Supp. XXI:** 27
Woods, Paula L., **Supp. XXI:** 70
Woods, Robert A., **Supp. I Part 1:** 19
Woods, The (Mamet), **Supp. XIV:** 241, 254–255
Woodswoman (LaBastille), **Supp. X:** 95, **96–99,** 108
Woodswoman III: Book Three of the Woodswoman's Adventures (LaBastille), **Supp. X:** 95, **106–107**
"Wood Thrush" (Kenyon), **Supp. VII:** 172

Woodward, C. Vann, **IV:** 114, 470–471; **Retro. Supp. I:** 75, 76; **Supp. XIX:** 152; **Supp. XXII:** 194
"Woof: A Plea of Sorts" (Saunders), **Supp. XIX:** 235
"Wooing the Inanimate" (Brodsky), **Supp. VIII:** 32
Woolcott, Alexander, **Supp. IX:** 197
Wooley, Bryan, **Supp. V:** 225
Woolf, Leonard, **Supp. IX:** 95
Woolf, Virginia, **I:** 53, 79, 112, 309; **II:** 320, 415; **IV:** 59; **Retro. Supp. I:** 59, 75, 170, 215, 291, 359; **Supp. I Part 2:** 553, 714, 718; **Supp. IV Part 1:** 299; **Supp. V:** 127; **Supp. VIII:** 5, 155, 251, 252, 263, 265; **Supp. IX:** 66, 109; **Supp. XI:** 134, 193; **Supp. XII:** 81, 98, 289; **Supp. XIII:** 305; **Supp. XIV:** 341–342, 342, 343, 346, 348; **Supp. XV:** 55, 65; **Supp. XIX:** 134
Woollcott, Alexander, **IV:** 432; **Retro. Supp. II:** 327; **Supp. I Part 2:** 664; **Supp. IX:** 190, 194
Woollstonecraft, Mary, **Supp. XVI:** 184
"Woolly Mammoth" (X. J. Kennedy), **Supp. XV:** 163–164
Woolman, John, **Supp. VIII:** 202, 204, 205
Woolson, Constance Fenimore, **Retro. Supp. I:** 224, 228
Woolverton, Linda, **Supp. XXI:** 148
Wooster, David, **Supp. XX: 288**
Worcester, Samuel, **I:** 458
Word and Idioms: Studies in the English Language (L. P. Smith), **Supp. XIV:** 343
"Word by Word" (column, Lamott), **Supp. XX: 140**
Word of God and the Word of Man, The (Barth), **Retro. Supp. I:** 327
"Word out of the Sea, A" (Whitman), **IV:** 344
Words (Creeley), **Supp. IV Part 1:** 139, 150–153, 154, 155, 158
"Words" (Creeley), **Supp. IV Part 1:** 152
"Words" (Gioia), **Supp. XV:** 125
"Words" (Merwin), **Supp. III Part 1:** 352
"Words" (Plath), **Supp. I Part 2:** 547
"Words" (Shields), **Supp. VII:** 323
"Words, The" (Wagoner), **Supp. IX:** 326
"Words above a Narrow Entrance" (Wagoner), **Supp. IX:** 325
"Words for a Bike-Racing, Osprey-Chasing Wine-Drunk Squaw Man" (Gunn Allen), **Supp. IV Part 1:** 325
Words for Dr. Y (Sexton), **Supp. II Part 2:** 698
"Words for Hart Crane" (Lowell), **I:** 381; **II:** 547; **Retro. Supp. II:** 188
"Words for Maria" (Merrill), **Supp. III Part 1:** 327
Words for the Chisel (Taggard), **Supp. XXII: 276–277**
"Words for the Unknown Makers" (Kunitz), **Supp. III Part 1:** 264
Words for the Wind (Roethke), **III:** 529, 533, 541, 543, 545
"Words for the Wind" (Roethke), **III:** 542–543
Words in the Mourning Time (Hayden), **Supp. II Part 1:** 361, 366, 367
"Words in the Mourning Time" (Hayden), **Supp. II Part 1:** 370–371
"Words into Fiction" (Welty), **IV:** 279
"Words into Worlds Won't Go" (Major), **Supp. XXII:** 174
"Words Like Freedom" (Hughes), **Retro. Supp. I:** 207
"Words of a Young Girl" (Lowell), **II:** 554
Words under the Words: Selected Poems (Nye), **Supp. XIII:** 277
Wordsworth, Dorothy, **Supp. IX:** 38
Wordsworth, William, **I:** 283, 522, 524, 525, 588; **II:** 7, 11, 17, 18, 97, 169, 273, 303, 304, 532, 549, 552; **III:** 219, 263, 277, 278, 511, 521, 523, 528, 583; **IV:** 120, 331, 343, 453, 465; **Retro. Supp. I:** 121, 196; **Supp. I Part 1:** 150, 151, 154, 161, 163, 312, 313, 349, 365; **Supp. I Part 2:** 375, 409, 416, 422, 607, 621, 622, 673, 674, 675, 676, 677, 710–711, 729; **Supp. II Part 1:** 4; **Supp. III Part 1:** 12, 15, 73, 279; **Supp. IV Part 2:** 597, 601; **Supp. V:** 258; **Supp. VIII:** 273; **Supp. IX:** 38, 41, 265, 274; **Supp. X:** 22, 23, 65, 120; **Supp. XI:** 248, 251, 312; **Supp. XIII:** 214; **Supp. XIV:** 184; **Supp. XV:** 93, 250; **Supp. XIX:** 1; **Supp. XX: 108, 116; Supp. XXI:** 131
" 'Word Which Made All Clear, The': The Silent Close of *The House of Mirth" (Benstock), Supp. XX: 240*
Work (Alcott), **Supp. I Part 1:** 32–33, 42
Work (Dixon), **Supp. XII:** 141, **143**
"Work" (Halliday), **Supp. XIX:** 85
"Work" (Oliver), **Supp. VII:** 243
Work and Love (Dunn), **Supp. XI: 147–148**
"Worker" (Coleman), **Supp. XI:** 89
Working a Passage; or, Life on a Liner (Briggs), **Supp. XVIII:** 2, **9–10**
Working Class Movement in America, The (E. Marx and E. Aveling), **Supp. XVI:** 85
Working Papers: Selected Essays and Reviews (Carruth), **Supp. XVI:** 46
"Working Roots: A Collection of Poetry and Prose" (Trethewey), **Supp. XXI:** 245
"Working the Landscape" (Dunn), **Supp. XI:** 151
Workin' on the Chain Gang: Shaking Off the Dead Hand of History (Mosley), **Supp. XIII:** 247, 248
"Work Notes '66" (Baraka), **Supp. II Part 1:** 47
Work of Art (Lewis), **II:** 453–454
"Work of Shading, The" (Simic), **Supp. VIII:** 277–278
Work of Stephen Crane, The (Follett, ed.), **I:** 405
"Work on Red Mountain, The" (Harte), **Supp. II Part 1:** 339
"Workshop" (Espaillat), **Supp. XXI:** 105
Works of Love, The (Morris), **III:** 223–224, 225, 233
Works of Witter Bynner, The (Kraft, ed.), **Supp. XV:** 52
"World, The" (Bronk), **Supp. XXI:** 32
"World, The" (Simic), **Supp. VIII:** 282
World, the Worldless, The (Bronk), **Supp. XXI: 29–31**
World According to Garp, The (Irving), **Supp. VI:** 163, 164, **170–173,** 181
World and Africa, The: An Inquiry into the Part Which Africa Has Played in World History (Du Bois), **Supp. II Part 1:** 184–185
"World and All Its Teeth, The" (Nye), **Supp. XIII:** 282
"World and the Door, The" (O. Henry), **Supp. II Part 1:** 402
"World and the Jug, The" (Ellison), **Retro. Supp. II:** 112, 119, 123
"World as We Know It, The" (Barresi), **Supp. XV:** 100
World Authors 1950–1970, **Supp. XIII:** 102
World Below, The (Miller), **Supp. XII: 303–304**
World Below the Window, The: Poems 1937–1997 (W. J. Smith), **Supp. XIII:** 332, 340, 345
World Doesn't End, The (Simic), **Supp. VIII:** 272, **279–280**
World Elsewhere, A: The Place of Style in American Literature (Poirier), **I:** 239
"World Ends Here, The" (Harjo), **Supp. XII:** 227–228
World Enough and Time (Warren), **IV:** 243, 253–254
World Gone Wrong (album, Dylan), **Supp. XVIII:** 28
"World I Live In, The" (T. Williams), **IV:** 388
World I Never Made, A (Farrell), **II:** 34, 35, 424
World in the Attic, The (Morris), **III:** 222–223, 224
World in the Evening, The (Isherwood), **Supp. XIV:** 157, 164, 165, **166–167,** 170
World Is a Wedding, The (Schwartz), **Supp. II Part 2:** 643, 654–660
"World Is a Wedding, The" (Schwartz), **Supp. II Part 2:** 655–656, 657
"World Is Too Much with Us, The" (Wordsworth), **Supp. I Part 1:** 312
Worldly Hopes (Ammons), **Supp. VII:** 34
Worldly Philosophers, The (Heilbroner), **Supp. I Part 2:** 644, 650
World of Apples, The (Cheever), **Supp. I Part 1:** 191, 193
World of David Wagoner, The (McFarland), **Supp. IX:** 323
"World of Easy Rawlins, The" (Mosley), **Supp. XIII:** 234, 236
World of Gwendolyn Brooks, The (Brooks), **Supp. III Part 1:** 83, 84
World of H. G. Wells, The (Brooks), **I:** 240, 241, 242

World of Light, A (Skloot), **Supp. XX: 196, 205, 206–207**
"World of Light, A" (Skloot), **Supp. XX: 194, 207**
World of Light, A: Portraits and Celebrations (Sarton), **Supp. III Part 1:** 62; **Supp. VIII:** 249, 253, 262
World of Our Fathers: The Journey of the Eastern European Jews to America and the Life They Found and Made (Howe), **Sup p. XIV:**104; **Supp. VI:** 113, 114, 116, 118, 119, **120–125**
"World of Pure Experience, A" (James), **II:** 356–357
World of Raymond Chandler, The (Spender), **Supp. IV Part 1:** 119
World of Sex, The (H. Miller), **III:** 170, 178, 187
"World of the Perfect Tear, The" (McGrath), **Supp. X:** 116, 118
World of the Ten Thousand Things, The: Selected Poems (Wright), **Supp. V:** 333
"World of Tomorrow, The" (White), **Supp. I Part 2:** 663
World of Washington Irving, The (Brooks), **I:** 256–257
World Over, The (Wharton), **Retro. Supp. I:** 382
World Revolution (C. L. R. James), **Supp. XXI:** 167
"Worlds" (Goldbarth), **Supp. XII:** 183, 189
World's Body, The (Ransom), **III:** 497, 499; **Supp. II Part 1:** 146
World's End (Boyle), **Supp. VIII: 11–12; Supp. XX: 22–23**
World's End and Other Stories (Theroux), **Supp. VIII:** 322
"World's Fair" (Berryman), **I:** 173
World's Fair (Doctorow), **Supp. IV Part 1:** 217, 224, 227–229, 234, 236–237
World's Fair, The (Fitzgerald), **II:** 93
Worlds of Color (Du Bois), **Supp. II Part 1:** 185–186
"Worlds of Color" (Du Bois), **Supp. II Part 1:** 175
World So Wide (Lewis), **II:** 456
"World's Worst Boyfriends, The" (Wasserstein), **Supp. XV:** 328
"World-Telegram" (Berryman), **I:** 173
World to Come, The (D. Horn), **Supp. XVII:** 50
World View on Race and Democracy: A Study Guide in Human Group Relations (Locke), **Supp. XIV:** 205, 206
World within the Word, The (Gass), **Supp. VI:** 77
"World Without Objects Is a Sensible Place, A" (Wilbur), **Supp. III Part 2:** 550
"World Without Rodrigo, The" (Cisneros), **Supp. VII:** 68
"Worm Moon" (Oliver), **Supp. VII:** 234
"Worn Path, A" (Welty), **IV:** 262; **Retro. Supp. I:** 345–346
"Worsening Situation" (Ashbery), **Supp. III Part 1:** 17–18
"Worship" (Emerson), **II:** 2, 4–5
"Worship and Church Bells" (Paine), **Supp. I Part 2:** 521
Worster, Donald, **Supp. IX:** 19
Worthington, Marjorie, **Supp. XII:** 13
Wouk, Herman, **Supp. XX: 243**
Wouldn't Take Nothing for My Journey Now (Angelou), **Supp. IV Part 1:** 10, 12, 14, 15, 16
"Wound" (Pedersen; Nelson, trans.), **Supp. XVIII:** 180
Wound and the Bow, The: Seven Studies in Literature (Wilson), **IV:** 429
Wounded (Everett), **Supp. XVIII:** 54, **64,** 65
Wounds in the Rain (Crane), **I:** 409, 414, 423
Woven Stone (Ortiz), **Supp. IV Part 2:** 501, 514
Woven Stories (Ortiz), **Supp. IV Part 2:** 503
"Wraith, The" (Roethke), **III:** 542
"Wrath of God, The" (Fante), **Supp. XI:** 160, 164
"Wreath for a Bridal" (Plath), **Supp. I Part 2:** 537
"Wreath for Emmet Till, A" (Nelson), **Supp. XVIII:** 177
Wreath for Emmett Till, A (Nelson), **Supp. XVIII:** 171, 173, 175, 181, **183–185**
Wreath for Garibaldi and Other Stories, A (Garrett), **Supp. VII:** 99–101
"Wreath of Women" (Rukeyser), **Supp. VI:** 280
Wreckage (Jin), **Supp. XVIII: 98–99**
Wreckage of Agathon, The (Gardner), **Supp. VI:** 63, **65–66**
Wrecking Crew (Levis), **Supp. XI: 259–260**
"Wreck of Rivermouth, The" (Whittier), **Supp. I Part 2:** 694, 696–697
"Wreck of the Deutschland" (Hopkins), **Supp. X:** 61
"Wreck of the Hesperus, The" (Longfellow), **Retro. Supp. II:** 168, 169
Wrestler's Cruel Study, The (Dobyns), **Supp. XIII: 82–83**
"Wrestler with Sharks, A" (Yates), **Supp. XI:** 341
Wright, Bernie, **I:** 191, 193
Wright, C. D. (Carolyn Doris), **Supp. XV: 337–355**
Wright, Charles, **Supp. V:** 92, **331–346; Supp. VIII:** 272; **Supp. XIII:** 114; **Supp. XVII:** 71; **Supp. XXI:** 95, 255
Wright, Chauncey, **II:** 344
Wright, Frank Lloyd, **I:** 104, 483
Wright, Franz, **Supp. XVII: 239–249**
Wright, George, **III:** 479
Wright, Harold Bell, **II:** 467–468
Wright, Holly, **Supp. VIII:** 272
Wright, James, **I:** 291; **Supp. III Part 1:** 249; **Supp. III Part 2:** 541, **589–607; Supp. IV Part 1:** 60, 72; **Supp. IV Part 2:** 557, 558, 561, 566, 571, 623; **Supp. V:** 332; **Supp. IX:** 152, 155, 159, 265, 271, 290, 293, 296; **Supp. X:** 69, 127; **Supp. XI:** 150; **Supp. XII:** 217; **Supp. XIII:** 76; **Supp. XV:** 79, 93, 212; **Supp. XVII:** 239, 241, 243, 244; **Supp. XIX:** 122, 273
Wright, Nathalia, **IV:** 155
Wright, Philip Green, **III:** 578, 579, 580
Wright, Richard, **II:** 586; **IV:** 40, **474–497; Retro. Supp. II:** 4, 111, 116, 120; **Supp. I Part 1:** 51, 52, 64, 332, 337; **Supp. II Part 1:** 17, 40, 221, 228, 235, 250; **Supp. IV Part 1:** 1, 11, 84, 374; **Supp. VIII:** 88; **Supp. IX:** 316; **Supp. X:** 131, 245, 254; **Supp. XI:** 85; **Supp. XII:** 316; **Supp. XIII:** 46, 233; **Supp. XIV:** 73; **Supp. XVI:** 135, 139, 141, 143; **Supp. XVIII:** 277, 282, 286; **Supp. XXI:** 169
Wright, Mrs. Richard (Ellen Poplar), **IV:** 476
Wright, Sarah, **Supp. IV Part 1:** 8; **Supp. XIII:** 295
Wright, William, **Retro. Supp. II:** 76, 77
Wrigley, Robert, **Supp. XVIII: 293–308**
"Writer" (Sanders), **Supp. XVI:** 277
"Writer, The" (Wilbur), **Supp. III Part 2:** 561, 562
"Writer as Alaskan, The" (Haines), **Supp. XII:** 199
Writer in America, The (Brooks), **I:** 253, 254, 257
Writer in America, The (Stegner), **Supp. IV Part 2:** 597, 599, 607
"Writers" (Lowell), **II:** 554
Writer's Almanac, The (Keillor, radio program), **Supp. XIII:** 274; **Supp. XVI:** 178
Writer's America, A: Landscape in Literature (Kazin), **Supp. VIII:** 106
Writers and Their Craft (Delbanco, ed.), **Supp. XXII:** 204
"Writer's Bed, A" (Mirvis), **Supp. XX: 179**
Writer's Capital, A (Auchincloss), **Supp. IV Part 1:** 21, 23, 24, 31
"Writer's Credo, A" (Abbey), **Supp. XIII:** 1, 17
Writer's Eye, A: Collected Book Reviews (Welty), **Retro. Supp. I:** 339, 354, 356
Writers in America (Schulberg), **Supp. XVIII:** 242, 243, 250, 254
Writers in Revolt (Southern, Seaver, and Trocchi, eds.), **Supp. XI:** 301
Writer's Life, A (Talese), **Supp. XVII:** 208–209, 210
Writer's Notebook, A (Maugham), **Supp. X:** 58
Writers on America (U.S. Department of State, ed.), **Supp. XIII:** 288
Writers on the Left (Aaron), **IV:** 429; **Supp. II Part 1:** 137
Writers on Writing (Prose), **Supp. XVI:** 259
"Writer's Prologue to a Play in Verse" (W. C. Williams), **Retro. Supp. I:** 424
"Writer's Quest for a Parnassus, A" (T. Williams), **IV:** 392
Writers' Workshop (University of Iowa), **Supp. V:** 42
"Writers Workshop, The" (Conroy), **Supp. XVI:** 76

"Writing" (Nemerov), **III:** 275
"Writing About the Universe" (Mosley), **Supp. XIII:** 247
"Writing American Fiction" (P. Roth), **Retro. Supp. II:** 279; **Supp. I Part 1:** 192; **Supp. I Part 2:** 431; **Supp. III Part 2:** 414, 420, 421; **Supp. V:** 45
"Writing and a Life Lived Well" (Patchett), **Supp. XII:** 308
"Writing and Writers: *Disjecta Membra" (Sorrentino), Supp. XXI:* 235
Writing a Woman's Life (Heilbrun), **Supp. IX:** 66
"Writing Between Worlds" (Mirvis), **Supp. XX: 177, 178, 179**
Writing Brave and Free: Encouraging Words for People Who Want to Start Writing (Kooser and Cox), **Supp. XIX:** 116, 128
Writing Chicago: Modernism, Ethnography, and the Novel (Cappetti), **Supp. IX:** 4, 8
Writing Creative Nonfiction: The Literature of Reality (Talese and Lounsberry, eds.), **Supp. XVII:** 208
Writing Dylan: The Songs of a Lonesome Traveler (Smith), **Supp. XVIII:** 22
Writing from the Center (Sanders), **Supp. XVI:** 266, 275–276
"Writing from the Inside Out: Style Is Not the Frosting; It's the Cake" (Robbins), **Supp. X:** 266
"Writing here last autumn of my hopes of seeing a hoopoe" (Updike), **Retro. Supp. I:** 335
Writing in Restaurants (Mamet), **Supp. XIV:** 246
"Writing Lesson, The" (Gordon), **Supp. IV Part 1:** 306
Writing Life, The (Dillard), **Supp. VI:** 23, 31
"Writing of Apollinaire, The" (Zukofsky), **Supp. III Part 2:** 616, 617
"Writing of *Fearless Jones,* The" (Mosley), **Supp. XIII:** 242
Writing on the Wall, The, and Literary Essays (McCarthy), **II:** 579
Writings to an Unfinished Accompaniment (Merwin), **Supp. III Part 1:** 352
"Writing the Universe-Mind" (Tabios), **Supp. XV:** 225
Writing the World (Stafford), **Supp. XI:** 314
"Writing to Save Our Lives" (Milligan), **Supp. XIII:** 274
Writing Vietnam, Writing Life: Caputo, Heinemann, O'Brien, Butler (Herzog), **Supp. XXII:** 116
Writin' Is Fightin' (Reed), Supp. X: 241
"Writ on the Eve of My 32nd Birthday" (Corso), **Supp. XII:** 129–130
"Written History as an Act of Faith" (Beard), **Supp. I Part 2:** 492
"Written on the Land" (J. W. Miller), **Supp. XX: 170**
"Wrong Man, The" (Larsen), **Supp. XVIII:** 124
"Wrong Notes" (S. Kauffmann), **Supp. XVI:** 74
"Wrought Figure" (McCarriston), **Supp. XIV:** 272
"Wunderkind" (McCullers), **II:** 585
Wunderlich, Mark, **Supp. XI:** 119, 132
Wundt, Wilhelm, **II:** 345
Wurster, William Wilson, **Supp. IV Part 1:** 197
WUSA (film), **Supp. V:** 301
Wuthering Heights (E. Brontë), **Supp. V:** 305; **Supp. X:** 89
WWII (Jones), **Supp. XI:** 219, 231
Wyandotté (Cooper), **I:** 350, 355
Wyatt, Robert B., **Supp. V:** 14
Wyatt, Thomas, **Supp. I Part 1:** 369
Wycherly Woman, The (Macdonald), **Supp. IV Part 2:** 473
Wych Hazel (S. and A. Warner), **Supp. XVIII:** 267, **268–269**
Wydra, Ewa. *See* Hoffman, Eva
Wyeth, Andrew, **Supp. XIX:** 117
Wyler, William, **Supp. XV:** 195
Wylie, Elinor, **IV:** 436; **Supp. I Part 2: 707–730; Supp. III Part 1:** 2, 63, 318–319; **Supp. XI:** 44; **Supp. XIV:** 127; **Supp. XV:** 307
Wylie, Horace, **Supp. I Part 2:** 708, 709
Wylie, Philip, **III:** 223
Wyllys, Ruth. *See* Taylor, Mrs. Edward (Ruth Wyllys)
"Wyoming Valley Tales" (Crane), **I:** 409
Wyzewa, Théodore de, **Supp. XIV:** 336

Xaipe (Cummings), **I:** 430, 432–433, 447
Xenogenesis trilogy (O. Butler), **Supp. XIII: 63–66,** 69
Xenophon, **II:** 105
X Factor, The: A Quest for Excellence" (Plimpton), Supp. XVI: 241
X Files (television series), **Supp. XVI:** 125
Xiaojing, Zhou, **Supp. XV:** 214
Xingu and Other Stories (Wharton), **IV:** 314, 320; **Retro. Supp. I:** 378
Xionia (Wright), **Supp. V:** 333
XLI Poems (Cummings), **I:** 429, 432, 440, 443

Yabroff, Jennie, **Supp. XIX:** 50, 58, 61
Yacoubi, Ahmed, **Supp. IV Part 1:** 88, 92, 93
Yage Letters, The (Burroughs), **Supp. III Part 1:** 94, 98, 100
Yagoda, Ben, **Supp. VIII:** 151
Yamamoto, Isoroku, **Supp. I Part 2:** 491
Yancey's War (Hoffman), **Supp. XVIII:** 71, **75–76**
Yankee City (Warner), **III:** 60
Yankee Clipper (ballet) (Kirstein), **Supp. IV Part 1:** 82
Yankee in Canada, A (Thoreau), **IV:** 188
Yankey in London (Tyler), **I:** 344
"Yánnina" (Merrill), **Supp. III Part 1:** 329
"Yanosz Korczak's Last Walk" (Markowick-Olczakova), **Supp. X:** 70
Yarboro, Chelsea Quinn, **Supp. V:** 147
Yardley, Jonathan, **Supp. V:** 326; **Supp. XI:** 67
"Yard Sale" (Kenyon), **Supp. VII:** 169
Yates, Richard, **Supp. XI: 333–350**
"Year, The" (Sandburg), **III:** 584
Year at the Races, A (Parker and Parker), **Supp. XIX:** 187
"Year Between, The" (Neugeboren), **Supp. XVI:** 226
Year in Provence, A (Mayle), **Supp. XV:** 295
Yearling, The (Rawlings), **Supp. X:** 219, **230–231,** 233, 234; **Supp. XXII:** 195
"Year of Grace" (Swados), **Supp. XIX:** 262–263
Year of Happy, A (Goldbarth), **Supp. XII:** 180
"Year of Mourning, The" (Jeffers), **Supp. II Part 2:** 415
Year of Silence, The (Bell), **Supp. X:** 1, **5–6,** 7
"Year of Silence, The" (Brockmeier), **Supp. XXII:** 59
"Year of the Double Spring, The" (Swenson), **Supp. IV Part 2:** 647
Year's Best Fantasy and Horror, 2004, **Supp. XXII:** 55
Year's Best Science Fiction, The (Merril, ed.), **Supp. XVI:** 123
Year's Life, A (Lowell), **Supp. I Part 2:** 405
"Years of Birth" (Cowley), **Supp. II Part 1:** 149
Years of Conscience: The Muckrakers: An Anthology of Reform Journalism (Swados, ed.), **Supp. XIX:** 264
Years of My Youth (Howells), **II:** 276
"Years of Wonder" (White), **Supp. I Part 2:** 652, 653
"Years Without Understanding, The" (Weigl), **Supp. XIX:** 282–283
Years With Ross, The (Thurber), **Supp. I Part 2:** 619
Yeats, Jack, **Supp. XVI:** 190
Yeats, Jack B., **Supp. XX: 201**
Yeats, John Butler, **III:** 458; **Supp. XX: 69**
Yeats, William Butler, **I:** 69, 172, 384, 389, 403, 434, 478, 494, 532; **II:** 168–169, 566, 598; **III:** 4, 5, 8, 18, 19, 20, 23, 29, 40, 205, 249, 269, 270–271, 272, 278, 279, 294, 347, 409, 457, 458–460, 472, 473, 476–477, 521, 523, 524, 527, 528, 533, 540, 541, 542, 543–544, 591–592; **IV:** 89, 93, 121, 126, 136, 140, 271, 394, 404; **Retro. Supp. I:** 59, 66, 127, 141, 270, 283, 285, 286, 288, 290, 311, 342, 350, 378, 413; **Retro. Supp. II:** 185, 331; **Supp. I Part 1:** 79, 80, 254, 257, 262; **Supp. I Part 2:** 388, 389; **Supp. II Part 1:** 1, 4, 9, 20, 26, 361; **Supp. III Part 1:** 59, 63, 236, 238, 253; **Supp. IV Part 1:** 81; **Supp. IV Part 2:** 634; **Supp. V:** 220; **Supp. VIII:** 19, 21, 30, 155, 156, 190, 239, 262, 292; **Supp. IX:** 43, 119; **Supp. X:** 35, 58, 119, 120; **Supp. XI:** 140; **Supp. XII:** 132, 198, 217, 266; **Supp. XIII:** 77, **Supp. XIII:** 87; **Supp. XIV:** 7;

Supp. XV: 36, 41, 181, 186; **Supp. XVI:** 47–48, 159; **Supp. XVII:** 36; **Supp. XXI:** 61
Yee, Amy, **Supp. XVIII:** 93, 94
Yellin, Jean Fagan, **Supp. XVI:** 88, 89
Yellow Back Radio Broke-Down (Reed), **Supp. X:** 240, 242, **243–245**
"Yellow Dog Café" (Komunyakaa), **Supp. XIII:** 126
Yellow Face (Hwang), **Supp. XXI:** 143, 148, **154–156**
"Yellow Girl" (Caldwell), **I:** 310
Yellow Glove (Nye), **Supp. XIII:** 275, **276–277**
"Yellow Glove" (Nye), **Supp. XIII:** 276
"Yellow Gown, The" (Anderson), **I:** 114
Yellow House on the Corner, The (Dove), **Supp. IV Part 1:** 244, 245, 246, 254
"Yellow Raft, The" (Connell), **Supp. XIV: 85–86**
"Yellow River" (Tate), **IV:** 141
"Yellow Violet, The" (Bryant), **Supp. I Part 1:** 154, 155
"Yellow Wallpaper, The" (Gilman), **Supp. XI: 198–199,** 207; **Supp. XVI:** 84
"Yellow Woman" (Keres stories), **Supp. IV Part 1:** 327
"Yellow Woman" (Silko), **Supp. IV Part 2:** 567–568
Yelverton, Theresa, **Supp. IX:** 181
Yenser, Stephen, **Supp. X:** 207, 208; **Supp. XV:** 113–114
"Yentl the Yeshiva Boy" (Singer), **IV:** 15, 20
Yerkes, Charles E., **I:** 507, 512
Yerma (opera) (Bowles), **Supp. IV Part 1:** 89
Yertle the Turtle and Other Stories (Geisel), **Supp. XVI:** 109
"Yes" (Stafford), **Supp. XI:** 329
Yes, Mrs. Williams (W. C. Williams), **Retro. Supp. I:** 423
Yes, Yes, No, No (Kushner), **Supp. IX:** 133
"Yes and It's Hopeless" (Ginsberg), **Supp. II Part 1:** 326
Yesenin, Sergey, **Supp. VIII:** 40
"Yes: I Mean So OK–Love" (Bronk), **Supp. XXI:** 31
"Yes! No!" (Oliver), **Supp. VII:** 243–244
Yesterday and Today: A Comparative Anthology of Poetry (Untermeyer, ed.), **Supp. XV:** 309
Yesterday's Self: Nostalgia and the Immigrant Identity (Ritivoi), **Supp. XVI:** 148
Yesterday Will Make You Cry (C. Himes), **Supp. XVI:** 137
"Yet Another Example of the Porousness of Certain Borders" (Wallace), **Supp. X:** 309
"Yet Do I Marvel" (Cullen), **Supp. IV Part 1:** 165, 169
Yet Other Waters (Farrell), **II:** 29, 38, 39, 40
"Yevtushenko" (Kooser), **Supp. XIX:** 124
Yevtushenko, Yevgeny, **Supp. III Part 1:** 268
Yezzi, David, **Supp. XII:** 193
Yiddish Policemen's Union, The (Chabon), **Supp. XXII:** 49
Yizkor Book, **Supp. XVI:** 154
...y no se lo tragó la tierra (Rivera), **Supp. XIX:** 99, 101
Y no se lo trago la tierra (And the Earth Did Not Cover Him) (Rivera), **Supp. XIII:** 216
¡Yo! (Alvarez), **Supp. VII:** 1, 15–17
"Yogurt of Vasirin Kefirovsky, The" (Apple), **Supp. XVII:** 3, 4
Yohannan, J. D., **II:** 20
"Yoke, The" (Bidart), **Supp. XV:** 33
Yonge, Charlotte, **II:** 174
"Yonnondio" (Whitman), **Supp. XIII:** 304
Yonnondio: From the Thirties (Olsen), **Supp. XIII:** 295, 295, **Supp. XIII:** 292, 296, **303–304,** 305
"Yore" (Nemerov), **III:** 283
York, Jake Adam, **Supp. XXI:** 257
York, Lorraine, **Supp. XX: 51**
"York Beach" (Toomer), **Supp. III Part 2:** 486
Yorke, Dorothy, **Supp. I Part 1:** 258
Yorke, Henry Vincent. *See* Green, Henry
"York Garrison, 1640" (Jewett), **Retro. Supp. II:** 141
Yosemite, The (Muir), **Supp. IX:** 185
"Yosemite Glaciers: Ice Streams of the Great Valley" (Muir), **Supp. IX:** 181
Yoshe Kalb (Singer), **IV:** 2
"You, Andrew Marvell" (MacLeish), **III:** 12–13
"You, Dr. Martin" (Sexton), **Supp. II Part 2:** 673
You, Emperors, and Others: Poems 1957–1960 (Warren), **IV:** 245
"You, Genoese Mariner" (Merwin), **Supp. III Part 1:** 343
"You, Reader" (Collins), **Supp. XXI:** 55
"You All Know the Story of the Other Woman" (Sexton), **Supp. II Part 2:** 688
You Are Happy (Atwood), **Supp. XIII:** 34
"You Are Happy" (Atwood), **Supp. XIII:** 34
"You Are in Bear Country" (Kumin), **Supp. IV Part 2:** 453, 455
"You Are Not I" (Bowles), **Supp. IV Part 1:** 87
"You Begin" (Atwood), **Supp. XIII:** 34
You Bright and Risen Angels (Vollmann), **Supp. XVII:** 225, 226
"You Bring Out the Mexican in Me" (Cisneros), **Supp. VII:** 71
You Came Along (film), **Supp. IV Part 2:** 524
"You *Can* Go Home Again" (TallMountain), **Supp. IV Part 1:** 324–325
"You Can Have It" (Levine), **Supp. V:** 188–189
You Can't Go Home Again (Wolfe), **IV:** 450, 451, 454, 456, 460, 462, 468, 469, 470
You Can't Keep a Good Woman Down (Walker), **Supp. III Part 2:** 520, 525, 531
You Can't Pet a Possom (Bontemps), **Supp. XXII:** 4, 12
You Can't Take It with You (Kaufman and Hart), **Supp. XIV:** 327
"You Can't Tell a Man by the Song He Sings" (P. Roth), **Supp. III Part 2:** 406
"You Don't Know What Love Is" (Carver), **Supp. III Part 1:** 147
You Don't Love Me Yet (Lethem), **Supp. XVIII: 149–150**
"You Have Left Your Lotus Pods on the Bus" (Bowles), **Supp. IV Part 1:** 91
You Have Seen Their Faces (Caldwell), **I:** 290, 293–294, 295, 304, 309
You Know Me, Al: A Busher's Letters (Lardner), **Supp. XVI:** 189
You Know Me Al (comic strip), **II:** 423
You Know Me Al (Lardner), **II:** 26, 415, 419, 422, 431
"You Know What" (Beattie), **Supp. V:** 33
"You Know Who You Are" (Nye), **Supp. XIII:** 275
You Might As Well Live: The Life and Times of Dorothy Parker (Keats), **Supp. IX:** 190
"You Must Relax!" (J. Scott), **Supp. XVII:** 189
You Must Revise Your Life (Stafford), **Supp. XI:** 312–313, 313–314, 315
"Young" (Sexton), **Supp. II Part 2:** 680
Young, Al, **Supp. X:** 240
Young, Art, **IV:** 436
Young, Barbara, **Supp. XX: 119, 123**
Young, Brigham, **Supp. IV Part 2:** 603
Young, Courtland, **Supp. XXII:** 21
Young, David, **Supp. XIX:** 276
Young, Dianne, **Supp. XXII:** 252
Young, Edward, **II:** 111; **III:** 415, 503
Young, Gary, **Supp. XV:** 88
Young, Mary, **Supp. XIII:** 236, 238, 239, 240
Young, Philip, **II:** 306; **Retro. Supp. I:** 172
Young, Stark, **Supp. XXII:** 193
Young Adventure (Benét), **Supp. XI:** 44
"Young America" (Brooks), **Supp. XV:** 298
"Young Child and His Pregnant Mother, A" (Schwartz), **Supp. II Part 2:** 650
Young Christian, The (Abbott), **Supp. I Part 1:** 38
"Young Dr. Gosse" (Chopin), **Supp. I Part 1:** 211, 216
Younger Choir, The (anthology), **Supp. XV:** 294
Younger Quire, The (Untermeyer), **Supp. XV:** 294, 297
"Young Folks, The" (Salinger), **III:** 551
Young Folk's Cyclopaedia of Persons and Places (Champlin), **III:** 577
"Young Girl's Lament, A" (Jin), **Supp. XVIII:** 99
"Young Goodman Brown" (Hawthorne), **II:** 229; **Retro. Supp. I:** 151–152, 153, 154; **Supp. XI:** 51; **Supp. XIV:** 48, 50
Young Harvard: First Poems of Witter Bynner (Bynner), **Supp. XV:** 41

Young Hearts Crying (Yates), **Supp. XI:** 348
"Young Housewife, The" (W. C. Williams), **Retro. Supp. I:** 415
Young Immigrants, The (Lardner), **II:** 426
"Young Lady's Friend, The: Verses, Addressed to a Young Lady, on Her Leaving School" (Rowson), **Supp. XV:** 234
"Young Lions" (P. E. Jones), **Supp. XXII:** 145
Young Lions, The (Shaw), **Supp. XIX: 248–249**
Young Lonigan: A Boyhood in Chicago Streets (Farrell), **II:** 31, 41
Young Manhood of Studs Lonigan, The (Farrell), **II:** 31, 34
"Young Man on the Go" (column, Siddons), **Supp. XXII:** 244
Young Men and Fire (Maclean), **Supp. XIV:** 221, **231–233**
Young People's Pride (Benét), **Supp. XI:** 44
Young Poet's Primer (Brooks), **Supp. III Part 1:** 86
Youngren, J. Alan, **Supp. XVI:** 174
"Young Sammy's First Wild Oats" (Santayana), **III:** 607, 615
"Young Sor Juana, The" (Mora), **Supp. XIII:** 218
"Your Arkansas Traveler" (Schulberg), **Supp. XVIII:** 252
"Your Dailiness" (Notley), **Supp. XXII:** 227
"Your Death" (Dove), **Supp. IV Part 1:** 250
"You're History" (Hampl), **Supp. XXII:** 84, 95
You're Only Old Once! (Geisel), **Supp. XVI:** 111
"You're Ugly, Too" (Moore), **Supp. X:** 171
"Your Face on the Dog's Neck" (Sexton), **Supp. II Part 2:** 686
"Your Hand, Your Hand" (Hoffman), **Supp. XVIII:** 79
Your Job in Germany (film, Capra), **Supp. XVI:** 102
Your Job in Japan (film, Capra), **Supp. XVI:** 102
"Your Life" (Stafford), **Supp. XI:** 329
"Your Mother's Eyes" (Kingsolver), **Supp. VII:** 209
"You Take a Train through a Foreign Country" (Dobyns), **Supp. XIII:** 90
"Youth" (Hughes), **Supp. I Part 1:** 321; **Supp. XXII:** 12
"Youth" (Huncke), **Supp. XIV:** 145
Youth and Life (Bourne), **I:** 217–222, 232
Youth and the Bright Medusa (Cather), **I:** 322; **Retro. Supp. I:** 14
"Youthful Religious Experiences" (Corso), **Supp. XII:** 117
Youth of Parnassus, and Other Stories, The (L. P. Smith), **Supp. XIV:** 336
Youth's First Steps in Geography (Rowson), **Supp. XV:** 243
You Touched Me! (Williams and Windham), **IV:** 382, 385, 387, 390, 392–393
"You Touch Me" (X. J. Kennedy), **Supp. XV:** 166
You Went Away (Findley), **Supp. XX: 49**
"You Who Sleep Soundly Through Our Bleakest Hour" (Espaillat), **Supp. XXI:** 110
Yurchenco, Henrietta, **Supp. XVIII:** 20
Yurka, Blanche, **Supp. I Part 1:** 67
Yutang, Adet, **Supp. X:** 291
Yutang, Anor, **Supp. X:** 291
Yutang, Lin, **Supp. X:** 291; **Supp. XVI:** 190
Yutang, Mei-mei, **Supp. X:** 291
Yvernelle: A Legend of Feudal France (Norris), **III:** 314
Y & X (Olson), **Supp. II Part 2:** 556

Zabel, Morton Dauwen, **II:** 431; **III:** 194, 215; **Supp. I Part 2:** 721
Zach, Natan, **Supp. XV:** 75, 82, 85
Zaehner, R. C., **Supp. XXII:** 258
Zagajewski, Adam, **Supp. XVII:** 241
Zagarell, Sandra, **Supp. XV:** 269, 270, 278, 281, 282
Zagarell, Sandra A., **Retro. Supp. II:** 140, 143
"Zagrowsky Tells" (Paley), **Supp. VI:** 229
Zaino, Nick, **Supp. XXII:** 207
Zakrzewska, Marie, **Retro. Supp. II:** 146
Zaleski, Jeff, **Supp. XI:** 143; **Supp. XIX:** 54
Zall, Paul, **Supp. XIV:** 156
Zaltzberg, Charlotte, **Supp. IV Part 1:** 374
"Zambesi and Ranee" (Swenson), **Supp. IV Part 2:** 647
Zamir, Israel, **Retro. Supp. II:** 303, 317
Zamora, Bernice, **Supp. IV Part 2:** 545
Zamoyski, Adam, **Supp. XV:** 257
Zangwill, Israel, **I:** 229; **Supp. XX: 2**
Zanita: A Tale of the Yosemite (Yelverton), **Supp. IX:** 181
Zanuck, Darryl F., **Supp. XI:** 170; **Supp. XII:** 165
Zapata, Emiliano, **Supp. XIII:** 324
"Zapatos" (Boyle), **Supp. VIII:** 15
Zapruder, Matthew, **Supp. XVI:** 55
Zarathustra, **III:** 602
Zawacki, Andrew, **Supp. VIII:** 272
"Zaydee" (Levine), **Supp. V:** 186
Zebra-Striped Hearse, The (Macdonald), **Supp. IV Part 2:** 473
Zechariah (biblical book), **IV:** 152
Zeidner, Lisa, **Supp. IV Part 2:** 453
"Zeitl and Rickel" (Singer), **IV:** 20
Zeke and Ned (McMurtry and Ossana), **Supp. V:** 232
Zeke Proctor, Cherokee Outlaw (Conley), **Supp. V:** 232
Zelazo, Suzanne, **Supp. XXII:** 158, 167
Zelda: A Biography (Milford), **Supp. IX:** 60
"Zelda and Scott: The Beautiful and Damned" (National Portrait Gallery exhibit), **Supp. IX:** 65
Zelig (film; Allen), **Supp. XV:** 4, **6, 8–9**
Zen and the Birds of Appetite (Merton), **Supp. VIII:** 205–206, 208
Zend-Avesta (Fechner), **II:** 358
Zeno, **Retro. Supp. I:** 247
Zero db and Other Stories (Bell), **Supp. X:** 1, 5, 6
"Zeus over Redeye" (Hayden), **Supp. II Part 1:** 380
Zevi, Sabbatai, **IV:** 6
Ziegfeld, Florenz, **II:** 427–428
Ziegler, Cyd, **Supp. XX: 273**
Ziegler, Heidi, **Supp. XXII:** 260
Zigrosser, Carl, **I:** 226, 228, 231
Zilles, Klaus, **Supp. XIX:** 112
Zimmerman, Paul D., **Supp. IV Part 2:** 583, 589, 590
Zimmerman, Robert. *See* Dylan, Bob
Zimmerman, Robert Allen. *See* Dylan, Bob
Zinberg, Leonard S. *See* Lacy, Ed
Zinman, Toby Silverman, **Supp. XIII:** 207–208, 209
Zinn, Howard, **Supp. V:** 289
Zinovyev, Grigory, **Supp. XXI:** 167
Zinsser, Hans, **I:** 251, 385
Zip: A Novel of the Left and Right (Apple), **Supp. XVII: 4–5**
Zipes, Jack, **Supp. XIV:** 126
"Zipper, The" (L. Michaels), **Supp. XVI:** 214
"Zizi's Lament" (Corso), **Supp. XII:** 123
Zodiac, The (Dickey), **Supp. IV Part 1:** 178, 183–184, 185
Zola, Émile, **I:** 211, 411, 474, 500, 502, 518; **II:** 174, 175–176, 182, 194, 275, 276, 281, 282, 319, 325, 337, 338; **III:** 315, 316, 317–318, 319–320, 321, 322, 323, 393, 511, 583; **IV:** 326; **Retro. Supp. I:** 226, 235; **Retro. Supp. II:** 93; **Supp. I Part 1:** 207; **Supp. II Part 1:** 117
Zolotow, Maurice, **III:** 161
"Zone" (Bogan), **Supp. III Part 1:** 60–61
Zone Journals (Wright), **Supp. V:** 332–333, 342–343
"Zooey" (Salinger), **III:** 564–565, 566, 567, 569, 572
"Zoo Revisited" (White), **Supp. I Part 2:** 654
Zoo Story, The (Albee), **I:** 71, 72–74, 75, 77, 84, 93, 94; **III:** 281
Zorach, William, **I:** 260
Zuccotti, Susan, **Supp. XVI:** 154
Zuckerman Bound: A Trilogy and Epilogue (P. Roth), **Supp. III Part 2:** 423
Zuckerman Unbound (P. Roth), **Retro. Supp. II:** 283; **Supp. III Part 2:** 421–422
Zueblin, Charles, **Supp. I Part 1:** 5
Zuger, Abigail, **Supp. X:** 160
Zukofsky, Celia (Mrs. Louis), **Supp. III Part 2:** 619–621, 623, 625, 626–629, 631
Zukofsky, Louis, **IV:** 415; **Retro. Supp. I:** 422; **Supp. III Part 2: 619–636; Supp. IV Part 1:** 154; **Supp. XIV:** 279, 282, 285, 286–287
Zukofsky, Paul, **Supp. III Part 2:** 622, 623–626, 627, 628
Zuleika Dobson (Beerbohm), **Supp. I Part 2:** 714
Zulus (Everett), **Supp. XVIII:** 54, **56–57**